DICTIONARY OF CANADIAN BIOGRAPHY

DICTIONARY OF CANADIAN BIOGRAPHY

DICTIONNAIRE BIOGRAPHIQUE DU CANADA

FRANCESS G. HALPENNY GENERAL EDITOR

JEAN HAMELIN DIRECTEUR GÉNÉRAL ADJOINT

VOLUME XI

TORONTO

HENRI PILON supervisory editor

ROBERT J. BURNS, PAULETTE CHIASSON
CHARLES DOUGALL, RONALD EDWARDS, CHRISTOPHER F. HEADON
VICTOR L. RUSSELL, CATHERINE A. WAITE
manuscript editors

PHYLLIS CREIGHTON translations editor
JOAN MITCHELL bibliographies editor
DEBORAH MARSHALL editorial assistant

QUEBEC

HUGUETTE FILTEAU, MICHEL PAQUIN codirecteurs de la rédaction
GÉRARD GOYER rédacteur-historien principal

LUCIE BOUFFARD, FRANCE GALARNEAU, THÉRÈSE P. LEMAY
MICHEL DE LORIMIER, JEAN PROVENCHER, JACQUELINE ROY
ALAN STILLAR, ROBERT TREMBLAY
rédacteurs-historiens

JEAN-PIERRE ASSELIN réviseur-historien

TRANSLATOR JOHN S. WOOD

UNIVERSITY OF TORONTO PRESS

LES PRESSES DE L'UNIVERSITÉ LAVAL

DICTIONARY OF CANADIAN BIOGRAPHY

VOLUME XI

1881 TO 1890

UNIVERSITY OF TORONTO PRESS
Toronto Buffalo London

ISBN 0-8020-3367-9 (regular edition)

Canadian Cataloguing in Publication Data
Main entry under title:

Dictionary of Canadian biography.

Added t.p. in English and French.
Issued also in French.
Contents: v.1. 1000–1700. – v.2. 1701–1740. – v.3. 1741–1770. – v.4. 1771–1800. – v.9. 1861–1870. – v.10. 1871–1880. – v.11. 1881–1890.
Includes bibliographies and indexes.
ISBN 0-8020-3142-0 (v.1) ISBN 0-8020-3240-0 (v.2)
ISBN 0-8020-3314-8 (v.3) ISBN 0-8020-3351-2 (v.4)
ISBN 0-8020-3319-9 (v.9) ISBN 0-8020-3287-7 (v.10)
ISBN 0-8020-3367-9 (v.11)
1. Canada – Biography – Dictionaries.
FC25.D52 920'.071 C66-3190-9
F1005.D49

Contents

Introduction

VOLUME XI is the seventh volume of the *Dictionary of Canadian biography/Dictionnaire biographique du Canada* to be published. The programme of publication began in 1966 with volume I, devoted to persons of Canadian interest who died between the years 1000 and 1700. Volume II (published in 1969) examined the lives of persons who died or who were last known to be living in the years 1701–40; volume III (published in 1974) the years 1741–70; volume IV (published in 1979) the years 1771–1800. The 17th and 18th centuries have thus been covered in published volumes, and an *Index, volumes I to IV* was published in 1981. At the same time, the DCB/DBC has been preparing and publishing volumes for the 19th century: volume IX (published in 1976) covered death and floruit dates 1861–70, and volume X (published in 1972) covered 1871–80. Volume XI, presenting persons who died or were last known to be living between 1881 and 1890, continues this sequence. For the next several years the DCB/DBC will be devoting its efforts to completing volumes for the years 1801 to 1860 (volumes V–VIII) and 1891 to 1900 (volume XII).

The Introduction to volume I contains an account of the founding of the DCB by means of the generous bequest of James Nicholson (1861–1952), and of the establishment of the DBC with the support of the Université Laval. The DCB/DBC, while continuing to develop the collaboration on which its immense bicultural and bilingual project depends, has maintained the principles and standards of operation and selection set out in the preliminary pages of its first volumes. Acknowledgements of volume XI record the gratitude of the DCB/DBC for the assistance of the Social Sciences and Humanities Research Council of Canada which, through its Negotiated Grants Division, has supported our work generously and sympathetically. They have enabled us to carry the project forward in the spirit and manner of its founders, and with the great benefit for contributors and editors of working simultaneously in related periods.

Volume XI, like volumes IX and X, covers only one decade. Yet the rapidly growing population of Canada and the scale and complexity of its activities in the second half of the 19th century have made volume XI our longest to date. Like volume IX, it does not contain an introductory essay: in the Introduction to volume IX we explained that the circumstances of the volumes for the later 19th century are not conducive to the kind of essays included in volumes I to IV. The shorter time-span of each volume and the transcontinental setting make it impossible to describe a general background or to isolate themes.

We are, however, providing guides to the contents of volume XI of a different sort, in the form of two special indexes. An Index of Identifications directs readers to biographies by the occupations of their subjects, and thus makes it easy for them to identify specific examples of such groups as businessmen, government officials, clergymen, and military officers. A Geographical Index arranges subjects according to their places of activity, so that the important and lesser known persons who affected the development of particular areas can be quickly found. In addition, the subjects of the biographies in volume XI are listed at the beginning of the volume for quick reference. We hope that these finding aids, as well as the cross-references included in the biographies (for an explanation on how to use them, see the Editorial Notes), will enable readers to pursue their interests by a variety of routes through the volume. The *Index, volumes I to IV* contains similar finding aids for those volumes as a group and as volumes I–IV, IX, and X of the DCB/DBC are reprinted individually the finding aids will be added to them. We should like to point out to our readers that these additions respond to their suggestions, for which we are grateful.

The 382 contributors to volume XI, writing in either English or French, have provided 586 biographies ranging in length from fewer than 600 words to some 10,000 words. They were invited to contribute because of their special knowledge of the period and of the persons who figured in it, and all have been asked to write in accordance with the DCB/DBC's *Directives to contributors*. It sets out a general aim to authors for articles:

> Biographers should endeavour to provide a readable and stimulating treatment of their subject. Factual information should come from primary sources if possible. Biographies should not be mere catalogues of events nor should they be compilations of previous studies of the subject. The achievements of the subjects should be seen against the background of the period in which they lived and the events in which they participated. Relevant anecdote and/or quotation of the subject's own words should be used discreetly to illuminate character or personality.

In the biographies of volume XI the regions of present-day Canada are represented at various stages in their history. In the far west, Vancouver Island and British Columbia experience the hectic years of the gold rush, cease to be separate colonies, enter confederation with a strong concern for the transcontinental railway whose fortunes are an important topic of the volume, and begin the development of new communities and resource industries. The story is told in biographies such as Sir Anthony Musgrave, governor, Richard Clement Moody, royal engineer, Robert Dunsmuir, colliery owner, and Samuel H. Myers, labour organizer in the mines. The prairie west continues to support the far-flung operations of the fur trade but the expansion of settlement and other types of commerce are changing the patterns of life and work; John Palliser's expedition in 1857–60 and the establishment in 1873 of the North-West Mounted Police are symbols of change. Perhaps the most potent factor in the history of the prairie west from 1869 to 1885 was Louis Riel. The events at Red River in 1869–70 and in the northwest in 1885 bring into focus all the factors of change and development in that part of the continent. Volume XI has, in addition to Riel, biographies of persons associated with the fur trade, such as Andrew McDermot; of those identified with the efforts of the churches, such as David Anderson and John Black; of policemen and treaty-makers such as Éphrem-A. Brisebois and Alexander Morris; of early political leaders of Manitoba such as Andrew Graham Ballenden Bannatyne and John Norquay; and of the native peoples whose existence was cast into turmoil by the coming of white civilization – Isapo-muxika (Crowfoot), Mistahimaskwa (Big Bear), and Pītikwahanapiwīyin (Poundmaker).

For Ontario and Quebec the volume presents a society that is growing rapidly in numbers and communities but which also reveals the signs of maturity. Biographies for these two provinces show the elaboration of existing governmental and administrative institutions as well as the establishment of new ones, notably with the coming of confederation; the expansion of religious, educational, agricultural, literary and artistic, charitable, and scientific endeavours; and the advance of commercial, financial, and industrial activities. The political history of the Province of Canada and then of the provinces of Ontario and Quebec can be followed with such major figures as Sir Matthew Crooks Cameron, Joseph-Édouard Cauchon, Pierre-Joseph-Olivier Chauveau, Sir Francis Hincks, Joseph-Alfred Mousseau, and Louis-Victor Sicotte (and, for that matter, with figures less significant but no less interesting such as Frederick Chase Capreol and Schuyler Shibley). Business has a strong representation, with, to mention only a few, Sir Hugh Allan, Isaac Buchanan, Guillaume-Eugène Chinic, William Gooderham, Sr and Jr, and Louis-Adélard Senécal; the presence of William McMaster and Sir John Rose testifies to the increasing importance of massive movements of capital, while Mathew Hamilton Gault and Robert Hay illustrate the new importance of large-scale manufacturing, and Charles John Brydges and Francis Shanly the powerful influence of the railway. In education there is Chauveau and Egerton Ryerson; in religion, Ignace Bourget and John Joseph Lynch; in the arts and letters, Isabella Valancy Crawford, John Charles Dent, James D. Duncan, Antoine Gérin-Lajoie, and Susanna Strickland Moodie; in social services, Marie Fisbach; in science and medicine, Joseph-Alexandre Crevier, Sir John Henry Lefroy, and Alexander Murray.

In the four Atlantic provinces the introduction of responsible government, the pro-confederate and anti-confederate campaigns (as well as that for repeal after 1867 in Nova Scotia), and the relations between church and state were hotly debated issues in the period covered by volume XI. The biographies of John Hamilton Gray and Sir Albert James Smith for New Brunswick, William Annand, William Alexander Henry, Archibald Woodbury McLelan, and Sir William Young for Nova Scotia, Edward Palmer and James Colledge Pope for Prince Edward Island, and Sir Edward Mortimer Archibald, Charles James Fox Bennett, and Robert John Parsons for Newfoundland provide means for entering into these debates. Because persons engaged in political activity could not be far removed from the economic and social concerns of the day, these biographies also illustrate other preoccupations of the various communities, preoccupations which are evident as well in such biographies as those of Hibbert Binney, Charles R. Bowring, John Mockett Cramp, and William Brydone Jack.

The DCB/DBC, in the midst of a large and complex programme for the 19th century, is conscious of the many special contributions which have been made to its work. Volume XI is a long one, and it reflects in its length and multiplicity of story and theme an increasing variety in the development of Canada. It has imposed a heavy task of new research and interpretation upon our many contributors, and we are grateful for this further example of a great collaborative endeavour in Canadian scholarship.

During the several stages in the editorial preparation of volume XI, a number of persons were involved, some of whom were members of the staff in either Toronto or Quebec when the work began or was in its early years, and some of whom had longer and more continuous contact with our contributors and one another in a variety of tasks from preliminary research to editing to translation to proof as the volume assumed its final shape. We wish to pay tribute to the experience, determination, and skill of the many members of our staff who have worked diligently to produce volume XI in the tradition of the DCB/DBC.

FRANCESS G. HALPENNY

JEAN HAMELIN

Acknowledgements

THE *Dictionary of Canadian biography/Dictionnaire biographique du Canada* receives assistance, advice, and encouragement from many institutions and individuals. They cannot all be named nor can their kindness and support be adequately acknowledged.

The DCB/DBC, which owes its founding to the generosity of the late James Nicholson, has been sustained over the years by its parent institutions, the University of Toronto and the University of Toronto Press and the Université Laval and Les Presses de l'université Laval. Beginning in 1973 the Canada Council provided generous grants to the two university presses which made possible the continuation and acceleration of the DCB/DBC's publication programme, and this assistance has been generously maintained and amplified by the Social Sciences and Humanities Research Council of Canada created in 1978. We should like to give special thanks to the SSHRCC not only for its financial support but also for the encouragement it has given us as we strive to complete our volumes, and in particular to Jean G. Lengellé, who was Director of the Negotiated Grants Division through much of the time volume XI was in preparation. We also acknowledge with gratitude the assistance provided by the Ministry of Culture and Recreation of the Province of Ontario through its Wintario programme and also the assistance of the ministries of Education and Intergovernmental Affairs of the Province of Quebec in 1977–78.

Of the numerous individuals who assisted in the preparation of volume XI, we owe particular thanks to our contributors who made this work truly a community effort. We also have had the benefit of special consultation with a number of persons, some of them also contributors. We should like to thank: Frederick H. Armstrong, Phyllis R. Blakeley, Denis Bousquet, Hartwell Bowsfield, Lovell C. Clark, Gilbert-Louis Comeault, Stanley Cuthand, Hugh A. Dempsey, Andrée Désilets, R. B. Donovan, C.S.B., I. M. Drummond, Raymond Dumais, Jean Fleury, Micheline Fortin, Goldwin S. French, Armand Gagné, Serge Gagnon, Agathe Garon, Robert Garon, Frances Gundry, Marcel Hamelin, René Hardy, David M. Hayne, H. T. Holman, Barry E. Hyman, Basil Johnson, David Keane, Jean-Marie LeBlanc, Marion MacRae, Monique Mailloux, André Martineau, Marianne Mithun, Shirley Morriss, G. D. O'Gorman, C.S.B., Margaret A. Ormsby, Gladys Barbara Pollack, D. S. Richardson, Ian Ross Robertson, Shirlee Anne Smith, Stephen A. Speisman, Ian M. Stewart, G. M. Story, David A. Sutherland, Philippe Sylvain, Nive Voisine, Ann Yandle, and Brian J. Young. We should like to mention the assistance of the late A. S. Abel.

Throughout the preparation of volume XI we have enjoyed willing cooperation from libraries and archives in Canada and elsewhere. We are particularly grateful to the administrators and staffs of those institutions to which we have most frequently appealed. In addition to the Public Archives of Canada in Ottawa and the provincial archives in all the provinces, they are: in Ontario, the University of Toronto Library, the Metropolitan Toronto Library, and the United Church Archives; in Québec, the *archives civiles* and *judiciaires*, the Archives de l'archidiocèse de Québec, the Bibliothèque and the Archives du séminaire de Québec, the Bibliothèque générale de l'université Laval, and the Bibliothèque de l'Assemblée nationale. In addition, essential help was given by the Maritime History Group Archives at St John's, the New Brunswick Museum at Saint John, the Hudson's Bay Company Archives in Winnipeg, and the Glenbow-Alberta Institute in Calgary. We should also like to thank the staffs of the *archives départementales* and *municipales* of France and of the various record offices in Great Britain who answered our numerous requests for information so kindly. We are grateful for the generous assistance provided by the Baker Library at Harvard University.

The editors of volume XI were assisted in the preparation of the volume by colleagues in both offices. In addition to Mary McD. Maude, Executive Editor at the Toronto office until 1978, and Gaston Tisdel, *directeur des recherches* at the Quebec office until 1977, editorial and research assistance has been given in Toronto by Mary P. Bentley, Wendy Cameron, Curtis Fahey, Jane E. Graham, Susan Lynch, David Roberts, and Stuart R. J. Sutherland, and in Quebec by Michèle Brassard, Céline Cyr, Christiane Demers, Marcelle Duquet, Hélène Filteau, Claudette Jones, John Keyes, and Diane Verret. Paula Reynolds and Danielle Comarmond were administrative assistants and Deborah Marshall headed the secretarial staff in Toronto. Pierrette Desrosiers was in charge of the secretariat in the Quebec office, assisted by Monique Baron, Fabienne Lizotte, Hélène Lizotte, and Suzanne East. We have benefited from the advice of Jacques Chouinard and Roch-André Rompré of the editorial department of Les Presses de l'université Laval, and of the staffs of the Office de la langue française of Quebec and of the Translation Bureau of the Secretary of State.

We should like to recognize the guidance and encouragement we have received from the two presses with which the DCB/DBC is associated, and in particular from Harald Bohne, H. C. Van Iersel, John Parsons, and Pauline Johnston at the University of Toronto Press and Claude Frémont, J.-Arthur Bédard, and Jacques Beaulieu at Les Presses de l'université Laval.

DICTIONNAIRE BIOGRAPHIQUE DU CANADA   DICTIONARY OF CANADIAN BIOGRAPHY

Subjects of Biographies

ACHINTRE, Auguste (1834–86)
Akwirente, Joseph. *See* Onasakenrat, Joseph
Alexander, Robert (1822–84)
Allan, Sir Hugh (1810–82)
Alleyn, Charles Joseph (1817–90)
Anderson, Alexander Caulfield (1814–84)
Anderson, David (1814–85)
Anderson, Samuel (1839–81)
Annand, William (1808–87)
Archambeault, Louis (1814–90)
Archibald, Sir Edward Mortimer (1810–84)
Archibald, Thomas Dickson (1813–90)
Armstrong, George (1821–88)
Armstrong, James Sherrard (1821–88)
Ash, John (d. 1886)
Aubert, Pierre (1814–90)
Aubin, Napoléon (1812–90)
Auclair, Joseph (1813–87)

BABBITT, John (1845–89)
Babineau, François-Xavier (1825–90)
Badgley, William (1801–88)
Baile, Joseph-Alexandre (1801–88)
Baillie Hamilton, Ker (1804–89)
Bannatyne, Andrew Graham Ballenden (1829–89)
Barker, Edward John (1799–1884)
Barlow, Robert (1813–83)
Barnard, Francis Jones (1829–89)
Barnston, George (d. 1883)
Barrett, Michael (1816–87)
Bayfield, Henry Wolsey (1795–1885)
Beardy. *See* Kamīyistowesit
Beaubien, Pierre (1796–1881)
Beauchemin, Charles-Odilon (1822–87)
Beaudry, Jean-Louis (1809–86)
Becher, Henry Corry Rowley (1817–85)
Beddome, Henry Septimus (d. 1881)
Bélanger, François-Xavier (1833–82)
Bennett, Charles James Fox (1793–1883)
Benson, William Thomas (1824–85)
Bibaud, François-Maximilien (1823–87)
Big Bear. *See* Mistahimaskwa
Bigsby, John Jeremiah (1792–1881)
Binney, Hibbert (1819–87)
Birchall, Reginald (1866–90)
Black, James (1797–1886)
Black, John (1818–82)
Blackburn, Josiah (1823–90)
Blain de Saint-Aubin, Emmanuel-Marie (1833–83)
Blanchet, Augustin-Magloire (1797–1887)
Blanchet, Joseph-Godric (1829–90)
Bois, Louis-Édouard (1813–89)
Bonami, *dit* Lespérance, Alexis (1796–1890)
Boomer, Michael (1810–88)
Botsford, Bliss (1813–90)
Bourgeau, Victor (1809–88)
Bourget, Ignace (1799–1885)
Bourinot, John (1814–84)
Bourne, Adolphus (1795–1886)
Bowles, George John (1837–87)
Bowring, Charles R. (1840–90)
Braun, Antoine-Nicolas (1815–85)
Brennan, Margaret, named Sister Teresa (1831–87)
Brisebois, Éphrem-A. (1850–90)
Bronson, Henry Franklin (1817–89)
Brouse, William Henry (1824–81)
Brousseau, Léger (1826–90)
Brown, Michael Septimus (1818–86)
Brown, Thomas Storrow (1803–88)
Browne, George (1811–85)
Brunel, Alfred (1818–87)
Brush, George (1793–1883)
Brydges, Charles John (1827–89)
Buchanan, Isaac (1810–83)
Buck, Walter M. (1826–81)
Buckland, George (1804–85)
Burpee, Isaac (1825–85)
Burtis, William Richard Mulharen (1818–82)
Butcher, Mark (1814–83)

CADDY, John Herbert (1801–83)
Caldwell, William Bletterman (d. 1882)
Calvin, Dileno Dexter (1798–1884)
Cameron, George Frederick (1854–85)
Cameron, John (1820–88)
Cameron, Sir Matthew Crooks (1822–87)
Campbell, Colin (1822–81)
Campbell, Duncan (1818–86)
Campbell, George William (1810–82)
Campbell, Stewart (1812–85)
Capreol, Frederick Chase (1803–86)
Carey, Daniel (1829–90)
Carrier, Charles William (1839–87)
Carroll, John Saltkill (1809–84)
Cary, Lucius Bentinck, 10th Viscount Falkland (1803–84)

GAGNON, Ferdinand (1849–86)
Gamble, William (1805–81)
Gatty, Juliana Horatia (Ewing) (1841–85)
Gaudet, Joseph (1818–82)
Gault, Mathew Hamilton (1822–87)
Gauvreau, Pierre (1813–84)
Geezhigo-w-ininih. *See* Kezhegowinninne
Gendron, Pierre-Samuel (d. 1889)
Gérin, Elzéar (1843–87)
Gérin-Lajoie, Antoine (1824–82)
Gervais, Gualbert (1844–88)
Giard, Louis (1809–87)
Gibbs, Thomas Nicholson (1821–83)
Gidney, Angus Morrison (1803–82)
Gilmour, Allan (1805–84)
Girouard, Gilbert-Anselme (1846–85)
Girroir, Hubert (1825–84)
Glackmeyer, Louis-Édouard (1793–1881)
Glen, Thomas (1796–1887)
Glenn, John (1833–86)
Glover, Sir John Hawley (1829–85)
Good, James (d. 1889)
Gooderham, William (1790–1881)
Gooderham, William (1824–89)
Gordon, John (1828–82)
Gosse, Philip Henry (1810–88)
Gossip, William (1809–89)
Gould, Joseph (1808–86)
Gow, Peter (1818–86)
Grasett, Henry James (1808–82)
Gray, John Hamilton (1811–87)
Gray, John Hamilton (1814–89)
Grieve, Walter (d. 1887)
Gros Ours. *See* Mistahimaskwa
Gurney, Edward (1817–84)

HAMILTON, John (1802–82)
Hamilton, John (1827–88)
Hannan, Michael (1821–82)
Hans Hendrik (d. 1889)
Hardisty, Richard Charles (d. 1889)
Hardisty, William Lucas (d. 1881)
Harris, James Stanley (1803–88)
Harris, John (1841–87)
Harris, Joseph Hemington (1800–81)
Hart, Theodore (1816–87)
Harvey, Alexander (1827–86)
Hay, Robert (1808–90)
Hay, William (1818–88)
Hayes, Isaac Israel (1832–81)
Haynes, John Carmichael (1831–88)
Hébert, Nicolas-Tolentin (1810–88)
Henderson, Alexander (1824–87)
Hendrik. *See* Hans Hendrik
Henry, William Alexander (1816–88)
Henson, Josiah (1789–1883)
Herbomez, Louis-Joseph d' (1822–90)
Hibbard, Ashley (1827–86)
Higginson, Sir James Macaulay (1805–85)
Hill, Henry George (d. 1882)
Hincks, Sir Francis (1807–85)
Hind, William George Richardson (1833–89)
Hogg, Simon Jackson (1845–87)
Holman, Sarah (Dalton) (d. 1888)
Honeyman, David (1817–89)
Hooper, Edmund John Glyn (1818–89)
Hope, Adam (1813–82)
Houde, Frédéric (1847–84)
Howard, Henry (1815–87)
Howard, John George (1803–90)
Howard, Robert Palmer (1823–89)
Howley, Thomas (d. 1889)
Howorth, William (d. 1881)
Hoyles, Sir Hugh William (1814–88)
Hume, Catherine Honoria (Blake) (d. 1886)
Humphreys, Thomas Basil (1840–90)
Hunter, James (1817–82)
Huntington, Lucius Seth (1827–86)
Hyman, William (1807–82)

IRUMBERRY DE SALABERRY, Charles-René-Léonidas d' (1820–82)
Isapo-muxika (d. 1890)
Isbister, Alexander Kennedy (1822–83)

JACK, William Brydone (1817–86)
Jacobs, Peter. *See* Pahtahsega
Jacques, John (1804–86)
Jamot, Jean-François (1828–86)
Johnson, George Henry Martin (1816–84)
Johnson, John (1792–1886)
Johnston, William (1848–85)
Joseph, Abraham (1815–86)
Juchereau Duchesnay, Henri-Jules (1845–87)
Juneau, Félix-Emmanuel (1816–86)

KACHENOOTING, George. *See* Steinhauer, Henry Bird
Kah-pah-yak-as-to-cum. *See* Kāpeyakwāskonam
Kamīyistowesit (d. 1889)
Kapapamahchakwew (d. 1885)
Kāpeyakwāskonam (d. 1886)
Katzmann, Mary Jane (Lawson) (1828–90)
Ka-we-zauce. *See* Kiwisānce
Keefer, Samuel (1811–90)
Kelly, Michael John (d. 1890)
Kelly, William Moore (1827–88)
Kemp, Alexander Ferrie (1822–84)
Kennedy, Sir Arthur Edward (1809–83)
Kennedy, William (1814–90)
Kennedy, William Nassau (1839–85)
Kezhegowinninne (d. 1889)
Kingston, George Templeman (1816–86)
Kishigowininy. *See* Kezhegowinninne

Kittson, Norman Wolfred (1814–88)
Kiwisãnce (d. probably 1886)
Kukatosi-poka (d. 1889)

LAFRAMBOISE, Maurice (1821–82)
Laidlaw, George (1828–89)
Landry, Jean-Étienne (1815–84)
Lang, George (d. 1881)
Langevin, Edmond (1824–89)
Lareau, Edmond (1848–90)
Larochelle, Louis-Napoléon (1834–90)
La Rocque, Joseph (1808–87)
La Rue, François-Alexandre-Hubert (1833–81)
Lauder, Abram William (1834–84)
Laurin, Joseph (1811–88)
Lavigne, Azarie (1841–90)
Lavigueur, Célestin (1831–85)
Lawrason, Lawrence (1803–82)
Lawrence, William Dawson (1817–86)
Leach, William Turnbull (1805–86)
Leahey, Richard Henry (d. 1889)
Leblanc, Augustin (1799–1882)
Leclerc, Nazaire (1820–83)
Le Cygne. *See* Onasakenrat, Joseph
Lefroy, Sir John Henry (1817–90)
Legge, Charles (1829–81)
LePage, John (1812–86)
Leroy, Pierre-Auguste (b. 1846, d. after 1886)
Lespérance, Pierre (1819–82)
Lesslie, James (1802–85)
Letellier de Saint-Just, Luc (1820–81)
Little, James (1803–83)
Little Child. *See* Kiwisãnce
Little Pine. *See* Minahikosis
Lobley, Joseph Albert (1840–89)
Lockerby, Elizabeth Newell (Bacon) (1831–84)
Longley, Avard (1823–84)
Longworth, Francis (1807–83)
Longworth, John (1814–85)
Loranger, Thomas-Jean-Jacques (1823–85)
Lord, William Warren (1798–1890)
Lunn, William (1796–1886)
Lyall, William (1811–90)
Lynch, John (1798–1884)
Lynch, John Joseph (1816–88)

McARTHUR, Alexander (1843–87)
McBeath, Robert (1805–86)
McCaul, John (1807–87)
McCord, Andrew Taylor (1805–81)
McCormick, Robert (1800–90)
McCurdy, James MacGregor (1830–86)
McDermot, Andrew (1790–1881)
McDonald, Angus (d. 1887)
McDonald, Angus (1830–89)
Macdonald, Edward C. (d. 1889)
Macdonald, John (1824–90)
Macdonell, Allan (1808–88)
MacDonnell, Sir Richard Graves (1814–81)
MacDougall, Dugald Lorn (1811–85)
Macgeorge, Robert Jackson (1808–84)
Mack, Theophilus (1820–81)
Mackay, Joseph (1810–81)
McKay, Smith (1817–89)
McKeand, Alfred (1849–87)
McKenney, Henry (d. 1886)
McKiernan, Charles, known as Joe Beef (d. 1889)
Mackieson, John (1795–1885)
MacKintosh, John (1790–1881)
McLean, Allan (1855–81)
McLean, John (b. 1798 or 1800, d. 1890)
McLean, John (1828–86)
McLelan, Archibald Woodbury (1824–90)
McMaster, William (1811–87)
McMillan, John (1816–86)
McMillan, Joseph C. (1836–89)
McMurray, Thomas (b. 1831, d. in or after 1884)
McMurrich, John (1804–83)
McQuesten, Calvin (1801–85)
McVicar, Kate (d. 1886)
Marchand, Louis (1800–81)
Marling, Alexander (1832–90)
Martin, Félix (1804–86)
Mee-may. *See* Mīmīy
Merrill, Horace (1809–83)
Metcalf, William George (1847–85)
Michel, Sir John (1804–86)
Miller, James Andrews (1839–86)
Miller, John Classon (1836–84)
Millier, Hilaire (1823–89)
Mīmīy (d. 1884)
Minahikosis (d. 1885)
Mistahimaskwa (d. 1888)
Montgomery, Donald (1848–90)
Moody, Richard Clement (1813–87)
Moore, Dennis (1817–87)
Morris, Alexander (1826–89)
Morris, Edward (1813–87)
Morrison, Angus (1822–82)
Morrison, Joseph Curran (1816–85)
Morrison, Thomas Fletcher (1808–86)
Morton, Silvanus (1805–87)
Moss, Thomas (1836–81)
Mousseau, Joseph-Alfred (1838–86)
Muir, John (1799–1883)
Mulvany, Charles Pelham (1835–85)
Munro, Hector (1807–88)
Munson, Mrs Letitia (fl. 1882)
Murray, Alexander (1810–84)
Murray, George (1825–88)
Musgrave, Sir Anthony (1828–88)
Myers, Samuel H. (1838–87)

Editorial Notes

PROPER NAMES

Persons have been entered under family name rather than title, pseudonym, popular name, nickname, or name in religion. Where possible the form of the surname is based on the signature, although contemporary usage is taken into account. Common variant spellings are included in parentheses.

In the case of French names, "La," "Le," "Du," and "Des" (but not "de") are considered part of the name and are capitalized; when both parts of the name are capitalized in the signature, French style treats the family name as two words: François-Alexandre-Hubert LA RUE. Some compound names occur in this period: Luc LETELLIER de Saint-Just; cross-references are made in the text from the compounds to the main entry under the family name: from Saint-Just to Letellier.

Married women and *religieuses* have been entered under their maiden names, with cross-references to the entry from their husbands' names or their names in religion: Eliza Lanesford FOSTER (Cushing); Marie FISBACH, named Marie du Sacré-Cœur (Roy).

Indian names have presented a particular problem, since an Indian might be known by his own name (written in a variety of ways by French and English unfamiliar with Indian languages) and by a French, English, or other European nickname or baptismal name; moreover, by the late 18th century some Indian families, such as the Johnsons, were using family surnames in the European style. Because it is impossible to establish an original spelling for an Indian name, the form chosen is the one found in standard sources or the one linguists now regard as correct. An effort has been made to include major variants of the original name, as well as European names, with appropriate cross-references: KAPAPAMAHCHAKWEW (Papamahchakwayo, Wandering Spirit, sometimes known in French as Esprit Errant).

CROSS-REFERENCES WITHIN VOLUME XI

The first time the name of a person who has a biography in volume XI appears in another biography his family name is printed in capitals and level small capitals: Egerton RYERSON; Alexis BONAMI, *dit* Lespérance.

CROSS-REFERENCES TO OTHER VOLUMES

An asterisk following a name indicates either that the person has a biography in a volume already published – James William Johnston*; Louis-Joseph Papineau* – or that he will receive a biography in a volume to be published – Robert Baldwin*; Honoré Mercier*. Birth and death (or floruit) dates for such persons are given in the index as an indication of the volume in which the biography will be found.

PLACE-NAMES

Place-names are generally given in the form used at the time of reference with the modern name included in parentheses. Many sources have been used as guides to establish 19th-century place-names: G. P. V. Akrigg and H. B. Akrigg, *1001 British Columbia place names* (2nd ed., Vancouver, 1970); E. J. Holmgren and P. M. Holmgren, *Over 2000 place names of Alberta* (3rd ed., Saskatoon, Sask., 1976); *Lovell's gazetteer of British North America . . .*, ed. P. A. Crossby (Montreal, 1881); Hormidas Magnan, *Dictionnaire historique et géographique des paroisses, missions et municipalités de la province de Québec* (Arthabaska, Qué., 1925); *Manitoba historical atlas . . .*, ed. John Warkentin and R. I. Ruggles (HSSM pub., Winnipeg, 1970); Nick and Helma Mika, *Places in Ontario: their name origins and history* (1v. to date., Belleville, Ont., 1977–); *Municipalités et paroisses dans la province de Québec*, C.-E. Deschamps, compil. (Québec, 1896); *Place names of N.S.*; Alan Rayburn, *Geographical names of New Brunswick* (Ottawa, 1975), and *Geographical names of Prince Edward Island* (Ottawa, 1973); *The Riel rebellions: a cartographic history*, comp. W. A. Oppen (n.p., 1979); W. H. Smith, *Smith's Canadian gazetteer comprising statistical and general information respecting all parts of the upper province, or Canada West* (Toronto, 1846; repr. 1970); Walbran, *B.C. coast names*. For complete information about titles given in shortened form the reader is referred to the General Bibliography.

Modern Canadian names are based whenever possible on the Gazetteer of Canada series issued by the Canadian Permanent Committee on Geographical Names, Ottawa, on the *Canada gazetteer atlas* (n.p., 1980), and on the *Répertoire géographique du Québec* ([Québec]), 1969), published by the Ministère des terres et forêts du Québec. For places outside Canada, the *National geographic atlas of the world*, ed. M. B. Grosvenor *et al.* (4th ed., Washington, 1975) has been a major source of reference. Place-names outside Canada are identified by administrative division if they are not to be found in *The new Canadian Oxford atlas* (Toronto, 1977) or the *Atlas Larousse canadien*, Benoît Brouillette et Maurice Saint-Yves, édit. (Québec et Montréal, 1971).

In the period of the union, from 10 Feb. 1841 to 1 July 1867, the former provinces of Lower and Upper Canada are generally referred to in English as Canada East and West, respectively.

EDITORIAL NOTES

QUOTATIONS

Quotations have been translated when the language of the original passage is different from that of the text of the biography. All passages quoted from government documents and works published in both French and English are given in the accepted translations of these works. The wording, spelling, punctuation, and capitalization of original quotations are not altered unless necessary for meaning, in which case the changes are made within square brackets. A name appearing within square brackets has been added or substituted for the original in order to provide a cross-reference to a biography within the volume or in another volume.

BIBLIOGRAPHIES

Each biography is followed by a bibliography. Sources frequently used by authors and editors are cited in shortened form in individual bibliographies; the General Bibliography (pp. 955–85) gives these sources in full. Many abbreviations are used in the individual bibliographies, especially for archival sources; a list of these can be found on p.2 and p.954.

The individual bibliographies are generally arranged alphabetically according to the five sections of the General Bibliography: archival sources, printed primary sources (including a section on contemporary newspapers), reference works, studies and theses, and journals. Wherever possible, references to manuscript material give the location of the original documents, rather than of copies. In general the items in individual bibliographies are the sources listed by the contributors, but these items have often been supplemented by bibliographic investigation in the DCB/DBC offices. Any special bibliographical comments by contributors appear within square brackets.

BIOGRAPHIES

List of Abbreviations

AAQ	Archives de l'archidiocèse de Québec
AASB	Archives de l'archevêché de Saint-Boniface
AC	Archives civiles
ACAM	Archives de la chancellerie de l'archevêché de Montréal
ADB	*Australian dictionary of biography*
ANQ	Archives nationales du Québec
ANQ-M	Archives nationales du Québec, centre régional de Montréal
ANQ-MBF	Archives nationales du Québec, centre régional de la Mauricie/Bois-Francs
ANQ-Q	Archives nationales du Québec, centre d'archives de la Capitale
ANQ-SLSJ	Archives nationales du Québec, centre régional du Saguenay/Lac-Saint-Jean
AO	Archives of Ontario
AP	Archives paroissiales
ASN	Archives du séminaire de Nicolet
ASQ	Archives du séminaire de Québec
ASSM	Archives du séminaire de Saint-Sulpice, Montréal
AUM	Archives de l'université de Montréal
AVM	Archives de la ville de Montréal
AVQ	Archives de la ville de Québec
BCHQ	*British Columbia Historical Quarterly*
BE	Bureau d'enregistrement
BNQ	Bibliothèque nationale du Québec
BRH	*Le Bulletin des recherches historiques*
CCHA	Canadian Catholic Historical Association
CHA	Canadian Historical Association
CHR	*Canadian Historical Review*
CMS	Church Missionary Society
CPC	*Canadian parliamentary companion*
CTA	City of Toronto Archives
DAB	*Dictionary of American biography*
DCB	*Dictionary of Canadian biography*
DNB	*Dictionary of national biography*
DOLQ	*Dictionnaire des œuvres littéraires du Québec*
HBC	Hudson's Bay Company
HBCA	Hudson's Bay Company Archives
HBRS	Hudson's Bay Record Society
HPL	Hamilton Public Library
HSSM	Historical and Scientific Society of Manitoba
IBC	Inventaire des biens culturels
JIP	*Journal de l'Instruction publique*
MTL	Metropolitan Toronto Library
NWMP	North-West Mounted Police
OH	*Ontario History*
PABC	Provincial Archives of British Columbia
PAC	Public Archives of Canada
PAM	Provincial Archives of Manitoba
PANB	Provincial Archives of New Brunswick
PANL	Provincial Archives of Newfoundland and Labrador
PANS	Public Archives of Nova Scotia
PAPEI	Public Archives of Prince Edward Island
PRO	Public Record Office
QUA	Queen's University Archives
RHAF	*Revue d'histoire de l'Amérique française*
RPQ	*Répertoire des parlementaires québécois*
RSC	Royal Society of Canada
SCHÉC	Société canadienne d'histoire de l'Église catholique
SH	*Social History*
UCA	United Church Archives
UNBL	University of New Brunswick Library
USPG	United Society for the Propagation of the Gospel
UTA	University of Toronto Archives
UWO	University of Western Ontario Library

BIOGRAPHIES

A

ACHINTRE, AUGUSTE (baptized **Joseph-Frédéric-Auguste**), journalist and essayist; b. 19 March 1834 at Besançon, France, son of Guillaume-Auguste Achintre, a pharmacist, and Anne-Marie Duprey; d. 25 June 1886 in Montreal, Que.

Before coming to Canada, Auguste Achintre led an eventful life. After his father's death, he was brought up at Aix-en-Provence by his uncle Joseph Achintre, a professor of humanities at the university, who had a decisive influence on him. After trying a military career Achintre returned to literature and studied in Paris with the great masters of the time. He also took courses at the Conservatoire Royal de Musique et de Déclamation in Paris in order "to lose his southern accent." Going to the West Indies for a few weeks, he remained on the island of Haiti for five years; there he launched newspapers, published a few books, and dabbled in politics before being imprisoned and condemned to death. When a republic was restored in Haiti by Fabre-Nicolas Geffrard in 1859, Achintre was pardoned and appointed Haitian ambassador to Washington. But by the time he reached New York, after a shipwreck had taken him to Bermuda, the new régime had been temporarily overthrown and he was no longer an ambassador. He then joined a French theatrical company which was touring America. It brought him to Montreal around 1861. He then decided to make a career in journalism in Canada, where he finally settled in 1866.

For nearly 20 years Achintre contributed to such papers as *L'Événement* of Quebec City and to *La Minerve*, *La Presse*, and especially *Le Pays* of Montreal; according to his contemporary Gustave-Adolphe Drolet*, he even "edited" *Le Pays* for a while. He was also editor of *L'Opinion publique* of Montreal in 1875, moving thus from polemical journals to a publication which, in his own words, aimed at being "artistic and literary" and catered to all readers irrespective of their political allegiance. But Achintre eventually wearied his readers, and George-Édouard Desbarats*, one of the founders of the journal, had to resume direction of the paper in 1876 to give it "a character more in keeping with the taste, intelligence and customs of Canadian families." Achintre then decided to return to France. In a letter to his protector, Hector-Louis Langevin*, he expressed both his disillusionment and his hopes: "An abrupt departure; decided upon all at once. . . . I am going to attempt in France, on a stage better prepared for me, what I was unable to accomplish here. I hope and believe I shall find there, in literary work, a livelihood that it is impossible to earn in Canada in this kind of occupation." But Achintre was apparently no more successful in his native country, since he was back in Montreal as a journalist in the 1880s.

If Achintre has a place in Canadian letters, it is not as a journalist but as an author. In 1871 he published, at Montreal, *Manuel électoral: portraits et dossiers parlementaires du premier parlement de Québec*. With its colourful portraits and careful documentation, the *Manuel* was a great success when it appeared, and it is still widely consulted by historians. In 1876, Achintre and Joseph-Alexandre CREVIER published a study entitled *L'Île Ste. Hélène: passé, présent et avenir; géologie, paléontologie, flore et faune*. He also wrote the libretti of two operas, and he published in Paris *La dame verte; bluette*, and in Canada several studies commissioned by the Canadian government on natural resources, canals, and the future of the country.

In addition to these works, which made their mark on contemporary Canadian literature, then still in its infancy, the following minor texts, signed by Achintre, should also be mentioned: *Cantate; la Confédération* (1868), celebrating a federated Canada, put to music by Jean-Baptiste Labelle* and performed at the Montreal City Hall on 7 Jan. 1868; the series of "Croquis à la plume" published in *La Presse* (21 March–23 May 1885); and short stories and essays in the *Nouvelles soirées canadiennes*, including "La salutation des morts" (1883), "Une promenade aux environs de San-Francisco" (1882), and "L'hiver en Canada" (1883).

ANDRÉE DÉSILETS

[In addition to *Manuel électoral*, Auguste Achintre was the author, with Joseph-Alexandre Crevier, of *L'Île Ste. Hélène: passé, présent et avenir; géologie, paléontologie, flore et faune* (Montréal, 1876). Useful in the preparation of the biography were the newspapers to which Achintre contributed: *L'Événement* (Québec), as well as *La Minerve*, *L'Opinion publique*, *Le Pays* (Montréal), and *La Presse*. A.D.]

Le Canadien, 28 juin 1886. *La Patrie*, 26 juin 1886. Beaulieu et J. Hamelin, *Journaux du Québec*. *DOLQ*, I. *Dominion annual register*, 1886. Le Jeune, *Dictionnaire*. Wallace, *Macmillan dict.* G.-A. Drolet, *Zouaviana: étape de trente ans, 1868–1898* . . . (2e éd., Montréal, 1898). "Biographies canadiennes," *BRH*, 20 (1914): 189–90. "Les disparus," *BRH*, 34 (1928): 76.

AKWIRENTE, JOSEPH. *See* ONASAKENRAT

ALEXANDER, ROBERT, merchant and politician; b. 1822 in Bonavista, Nfld, and baptized 27 Jan. 1823, son of William Alexander and Elizabeth Newell; d. 26 or 27 Jan. 1884 at Liverpool, England.

Robert Alexander's father, a Scottish-born merchant at Bonavista, died when Robert was six years old. Along with two brothers and a sister, Robert was raised, apparently at Bonavista, by his mother who remarried in 1842. He probably apprenticed as a clerk in a mercantile business at St John's, most likely in the firm of J. and W. Stewart and Company, based in Greenock, Scotland, which had had close connections with his father's business and of which Robert became the managing partner in Newfoundland on 3 June 1861.

J. and W. Stewart had operated in Newfoundland since the early 19th century, exporting fish and seal products and importing provisions from the United States and Canada and manufactured goods from Britain. After the deaths of the two Stewart brothers, James and William, in the 1830s, the business had been controlled by its British shareholders and managed by a succession of agents in St John's. When Alexander assumed control in 1861, J. and W. Stewart was one of the largest firms in the city. In 1866 it was shipping 38,142 quintals of cod, mainly to Portugal, Spain, and Brazil, and 28,364 seal skins valued at $21,273 to Greenock, representing about ten per cent of the total exports of these two products from St John's in that year. It had been the first Newfoundland firm to export fish to Brazil. During the 1870s J. and W. Stewart supplied three steamers for the annual seal hunt and in 1875 one of them, the *Proteus*, established a local record for the most seals brought in by a steamer in one year: 44,377 seals taken in two voyages.

As a prominent leader of the small group of Water Street merchants who controlled the Newfoundland economy, Alexander was from 1864 to 1876 a member of the St John's Chamber of Commerce and from 1863 to 1876 a director of the Union Bank of Newfoundland, the more successful of Newfoundland's two locally owned banks in the 1870s. Besides being the agent for the Imperial Fire and Life Insurance Company of London, he was a director of several local companies, including the St John's Marine Insurance Company, the Floating Dry Dock Company, and the Newfoundland Boot and Shoe Manufacturing Company. Alexander also had shares in 23 vessels newly registered in Newfoundland between the years 1861 and 1875.

In politics Alexander was a Conservative. During the 1869 general election, in which confederation with Canada was the central issue, he used the considerable influence of J. and W. Stewart through its branches in the Bonavista district to help elect the anti-confederate candidates, James L. Noonan, Francis Winton, and William M. Barnes. Alexander's only foray into active politics was in 1874 when, as a supporter of Frederic Bowker Terrington Carter*'s party, he was elected in the strongly Protestant district of Fortune Bay. This victory was made possible through the direct intervention of the district's dominant mercantile firm, Newman and Company. Alexander not only held political views in common with those of Newman and Company, but also had close business connections with the firm; since the 1850s J. and W. Stewart had leased the Newman premises in St John's and in the 1870s acted as their agent in that city. Business commitments and ill health apparently restricted Alexander's activities in the legislature and he did not seek re-election in 1878. By that date also he appears to have withdrawn from any direct involvement in the management of J. and W. Stewart.

Alexander died at Liverpool in 1884 while on a visit to improve his health. His estate, worth over £17,000, was divided among relatives, close friends, and local charities. Among the donations were £500 each for the St John's Church of England Orphanage and the Colonial and Continental Church Society, £1,000 each for the erection of a sailor's home at St John's and for the fund to complete the Cathedral of St John the Baptist, and £2,000 for the establishment of an Alexander Charity Fund to be used for the maintenance of poor widows and orphans at Bonavista. His benevolence was lauded in St John's since the bequests were, according to the *Evening Mercury*, "the first left by any of the merchants who have made money here." His memory was perpetuated further by the name given to Alexander Bay in Bonavista Bay.

MELVIN BAKER

Anglican Church (Bonavista, Nfld.), Birth registers, 1786–1845; Marriage registers, 1786–1891 (copies at PANL). Maritime Hist. Group Arch., Alexander name file; Board of Trade ser.107-8 (entries for Robert Alexander and J. and W. Stewart and Company); Derek Bussey, "St. John's Mercantile Trade, 1880" (typescript, 1973); Owen Hewitt, "Shipping St. John's Harbour 1866" (typescript, 1973). St Andrew's Presbyterian Church (St John's), Parish registers, 1842–91 (copies at PANL). Supreme Court of Newfoundland (St John's), Registry, will of Robert Alexander, probated 12 Feb. 1884.

Nfld., House of Assembly, *Journal*, 1846–89. *Evening Mercury*, 28 Jan., 1 Feb. 1884. *Royal Gazette* (St John's),

1829–81. *Business and general directory of Nfld.*, 1877. *Chafe's sealing book* (1905). *The Newfoundland almanack . . .*, comp. Philip Tocque (St John's), 1863. Devine, *Ye olde St. John's* (1936). W. D. MacWhirter, "A political history of Newfoundland, 1865–1874" (MA thesis, Memorial Univ. of Newfoundland, St John's, 1963). Paul O'Neill, *The story of St. John's, Newfoundland* (2v., Erin, Ont., 1975–76), II.

ALLAN, Sir HUGH, shipping magnate, railway promoter, financier, and capitalist; b. 29 Sept. 1810 at Saltcoats (Strathclyde), Scotland, second of five sons of Alexander Allan and Jean Crawford; m. 13 Sept. 1844 Matilda Caroline Smith, and they had nine daughters and four sons; d. 9 Dec. 1882 at Edinburgh, Scotland, and was buried 27 December in Montreal, Que.

Hugh Allan was born into an Ayrshire family with large shipping interests. From the early 1800s his father and older brother, James, operated vessels on the North Atlantic between Glasgow and the St Lawrence. After a parish-school education in Saltcoats, Hugh at age 13 began working in the family's Greenock counting-house of Allan, Kerr and Company. He immigrated to Montreal in 1826 and clerked with grain merchant William Kerr until 1830, when he embarked on a "grand tour" that included Upper Canada, New York, a return to his native Scotland, and his first visit to London. In April 1831 Hugh returned to Canada and after meeting James Millar*, a fellow Ayrshireman who may have acted as Alexander Allan's Montreal agent, became commission agent in Millar's general merchandising firm of Millar, Parlane and Company, one of Montreal's leading importers. Participating in several areas of the firm's operations (including shipping, shipbuilding, and purchasing grain from local merchants), Allan advanced rapidly in the company and, as was so often the case in the Montreal merchant community, the primary catalysts in his success were family connections, social bonds, and access to capital. In 1835 the company was reconstituted as Millar, Edmonstone and Company; Hugh was named a partner and with his father's assistance quickly helped expand the firm's shipping operations. The next year the company acquired the 214-ton barque *Thistle*, the first vessel in what was to become one of the largest merchant fleets on the North Atlantic. Several other vessels, built by Montreal master shipwright E. D. Merritt, were added over the next two years, including the *Alliance*, a 434-ton steamer for the Montreal–Quebec City run, which probably also towed the firm's sailing ships through the difficult Sainte-Marie current to the Montreal harbour. A large portion of the capital required for this expansion was supplied by mortgages held on these ships by Allan's father and brothers in Scotland.

Most of the early ships, such as the *Gypsy, Blonde,* and *Brunette*, were ocean-going but Allan, recognizing the advantages of uniting river and ocean transportation, began building small schooners for use on the St Lawrence: with this dual capacity and the general improvement in the St Lawrence valley economy the company's business expanded rapidly. By the mid 1840s the firm controlled 5 to 12 per cent of the total ocean-going trade of Montreal, bringing trade items such as pig-iron and soap from Glasgow and carrying Canadian wheat to British markets. The addition of the *Albion, Caledonia, Montreal, Amy Anne, Toronto, Canada,* and *Favourite* to the fleet for both river and overseas traffic gave Edmonstone, Allan and Company (as the firm was renamed in 1839) the largest shipping capacity of any Montreal-based firm. In 1848 it had a capital of £30–40,000 and two years later was described by a credit-rating service as an "old safe & [respectable] House." Its business increased by 25 per cent in 1851 and it maintained a network of agents as far west as Brantford and London in Canada West into the 1850s. By 1859 Edmonstone, Allan and Company, "one of the Wealthiest concerns in the Province," was known for its responsible management, its links to trading houses in London, Liverpool, and Glasgow, and the spreading of its owners' influence into allied shipping, railway, and banking concerns: it was "as good as a Bank," and run by "active, pushing" men. The firm continued as one segment of the intricate shipping interests of the Allan family and in April 1863 became H. and A. Allan.

Even by the early 1850s Allan's shipping ambitions had been outstripping those of William Edmonstone, his older partner. As president of the Montreal Board of Trade (1851–54), Allan advocated the establishment of a government-subsidized, regular steamship line between Montreal and British ports. Such an enterprise, he argued, would not only provide regular mail service but would also benefit Canada by increasing the number of immigrants and by protecting her exports and imports which many contemporaries believed were threatened by the American Drawback Laws of 1845–46. The deepening of the St Lawrence ship channel through Lac Saint-Pierre to 16 feet in 1853 made possible the inauguration of this service. But, though Allan took the initiative as official head of the Montreal business community and personally as an entrepreneur, there was keen competition. Samuel Cunard* expressed interest, as did a consortium formed in 1852 (including Thomas RYAN, Luther Hamilton Holton*, and James Blackwood Greenshields of Montreal along with the Liverpool firm of McKean, McLarty and Lamont). At the same time, expecting to secure the contract, Allan raised capital from his family (including his younger brother Andrew*) and Canadian investors such as George Burns Symes*, William Edmonstone, Sir George Simpson*, William Dow*, John Gordon McKenzie,

Robert Anderson, and John Watkins, and formed a rival syndicate. Despite its Canadian investors, the syndicate was an international enterprise based on careful family management on both sides of the Atlantic: Andrew had immigrated to Montreal in 1839 to join Hugh while two other brothers, James and Bryce, handled business in Greenock and Liverpool. Despite Allan's lobbying and his powerful position in the Montreal commercial élite, the rival consortium, incorporated as the Canadian Steam Navigation Company in 1853, was awarded the first government subsidy of £24,000 for the Montreal-Liverpool run, which began that year. The shortcomings of this firm were obvious almost immediately, however, and Allan decided to utilize new technology (steam, screw propellors, and iron hulls) in his continuing attempt to capture the contract. Instead of building ships in Canada as Edmonstone, Allan and Company had done in the 1840s, Allan's syndicate commissioned two fast and powerful steamers, the *Canadian* and the *Indian*, from Clyde shipbuilders late in 1853. On 18 Dec. 1854 the syndicate was incorporated as the Montreal Ocean Steamship Company and in 1856, with the help of Conservative politicians such as John ROSE, George-Étienne Cartier*, and Lewis Thomas DRUMMOND, it finally secured the contract, and the £24,000 subsidy, to provide regular fortnightly steamship service between Montreal and Liverpool during the summer season and between Portland, Maine, and Liverpool from November to May. By 1859 service was on a weekly basis and Allan reported his capital investment in the company at £3,500,000.

Since much of his profit depended on improved navigation facilities, direct subsidies, and troop-carrying, as well as mail and other government contracts, Allan was assiduous in pampering Canadian and British officials. For example, a former troop-carrier, the *Sarmatian*, was refitted to carry the Marquess of Lorne [Campbell*] and Princess Louise to Canada in 1878. With 25 servants and a special piano, the royal party of 14 was lodged in staterooms decorated with blue silk, the royal arms, and self-adjusting mahogany beds in which seasickness was "rendered impossible, the bed adjusting itself to every motion of the vessel, so that its pitch and roll cannot be felt."

Royalty was of course only the cream of Allan's business; his ships also carried immigrants, troops, the mail, wheat, and general cargo. Like most shippers to Britain, Allan profited from that country's wars in Africa and the Crimea. In 1862 the British secretary for war, Sir George Cornewall Lewis, brought suit against Allan for "exorbitant" and "enormous" charges in conveying military baggage at rates at least five times those of other carriers. Allan responded in a "rough" and "overbearing" manner, seizing the baggage until the case was settled. The transport of immigrants was a company specialty. In the 1850s for a fare of £3 10*s*. passengers travelled in steerage and provided their own food, although like most companies Allan's carried "a good supply of biscuits." By the 1870s the Montreal Ocean Steamship Company (popularly known as the Allan Line) had a government contract for the conveyance of "assisted passengers." The firm's promotional literature noted that indigent passengers would receive free Grand Trunk rail passes from the government and assured immigrants that "Canada is a cheap place to live in" where even the poorest could have "the confident hope" of becoming a landowner. The captains guaranteed a "religious, sober but cheerful atmosphere" on their ships, and female steerage passengers were provided with stewardesses and assured of the strict separation of the sexes. Less reassuring were the company's six-shilling "steerage passenger kit," which included "a patent life-preserving pillow," and the fact that death regularly occurred among passengers.

As Allan's transatlantic trade in immigrants, manufactured goods, and natural resources expanded he was forced to look to North American railways: an ambitious steamship-fleet owner preferred not to leave major supply routes to the vagaries of competition. Although by the early 1870s Allan had become Canada's most flamboyant railway entrepreneur, he had moved slowly into railways. He had stock in the Champlain and St Lawrence Railroad in 1851 and lost heavily in Detroit and Milwaukee Railway stock, but he was not an important promoter until the significance of the Grand Trunk Railway's monopoly became apparent.

In 1859, when the Victoria Bridge opened in Montreal for through traffic from Canada West to Portland, Allan and the Grand Trunk made a ten-year traffic arrangement. His steamers were soon dependent upon Grand Trunk deliveries: 1,304 of 1,885 freight-car loads shipped by Allan from Portland in 1873 came from the American Midwest via the Grand Trunk. Allan was frustrated by this dependence. He wanted the Grand Trunk to triple its winter deliveries to Portland to 35,000 tons and to coordinate freight arrivals with the departures of his steamers. He also felt threatened by the railway's arrangements with competing New York and Boston shippers and by rumours that it planned to establish its own steamship line. Worried about access to his western hinterland, Allan in 1873 expressed "a desire to protect ourselves."

Coinciding with Allan's disenchantment with the Grand Trunk was the Canadian government's commitment to build a railway to British Columbia. By 1870 his lieutenants had appeared on railway boards with charters to build west. Constructing its line west from Ottawa, the Canada Central Railway had Allan's lawyer, John Joseph Caldwell Abbott*, as its vice-president in 1870. Another of Allan's agents, Louis Beaubien*, was the major promoter of the Montreal

Northern Colonization Railway of which Allan became president in 1871; purportedly a local railway to transport firewood from the Laurentians to Montreal the road had a flexible charter permitting connections to the Canada Central Railway. Capitalizing on the French Canadian colonization movement and support from priests such as François-Xavier-Antoine Labelle*, Allan's railway benefited from generous laws and financial guarantees from the provincial government, municipal subsidies from most communities along the route, and a $1,000,000 subscription from the city of Montreal. For a short period three of Allan's associates (John HAMILTON, Abbott, and Beaubien) were directors of the North Shore Railway which was to join Quebec City with Montreal. Allan also owned half the stock in the proposed Ontario and Quebec Railway which would link Toronto and Peterborough to the Ottawa valley line. These railways would funnel trade to the port of Montreal and could be integrated into a major trunk system to the Pacific. He was also on the incorporating boards of two railways in the Maritimes: the Eastern Railway (1870) and the Northern and Western Railway (1871–72). His experience with government contracts, his connections with prominent Conservatives such as Sir John A. Macdonald*, and his reputation as a leading employer and model citizen in Montreal made Hugh Allan, probably Canada's most important capitalist by the 1870s, a logical contender for the Pacific contract.

It was the minister of finance, Francis HINCKS, who in August 1871 told Allan that Northern Pacific Railroad backers in the United States led by George William McMullen and Charles Mather Smith were also interested in the Pacific contract. In December Allan signed an agreement with the Americans and began enticing prominent Canadians to support the syndicate he was forming. As usual, his approach was through the pocketbook. He predicted that Charles John BRYDGES of the Grand Trunk would join for $200,000 worth of stock and David Lewis Macpherson* for $250,000. Neither, however, did join and Macpherson, hostile to American involvement, soon established a rival, Toronto-based syndicate. In June 1872 Macpherson's group was incorporated as the Interoceanic Railway Company of Canada and Allan's as the Canada Pacific Railway Company.

With a federal election called for August 1872 Allan had more luck with the politicians. After trying unsuccessfully to unite the Ontario syndicate with Allan's group, Macdonald left Montreal matters in the hands of Cartier and Hincks. Although anti-American and employed as the lawyer for the Grand Trunk, Cartier, in failing health, was forced to accept Allan's terms. Using the influence of his clerical friends, stressing French Canadian nationalism, and alluding to the economic impact of his Montreal Northern Colonization Railway which would have its terminus in Cartier's riding (Montreal East), Allan brought Macdonald's Quebec lieutenant into line. Thomas WHITE, editor of the Montreal *Gazette*, met with Cartier for a three-hour discussion of railway policy, and two city aldermen and four city councillors called on him at home. Five prominent Montrealers including Joseph-Adolphe Chapleau*, a rising young Conservative, and Charles-André Leblanc*, an old school friend, visited Cartier in Ottawa and urged him to award the Pacific contract to Allan. By 1 July 1872 Allan felt he had won over 27 of Cartier's 45 French Canadian MPS. On 30 July the politician signed an agreement drawn up by Allan and Abbott which acceded to the former's wishes concerning the railway. Nevertheless, despite massive last-minute contributions from Allan, Cartier was defeated in Montreal East.

Although the Conservatives were returned to power, Allan's plans to build the Pacific railway came apart in the months after the election. Macdonald finally forced him to make a clean break with his American backers but the Americans, incensed at being dropped, threatened the prime minister with a public disclosure of their involvement, not only in the railway but also in the Conservative election campaign. Allan was apparently able to mollify them before he embarked for England late in February 1873 in an attempt to raise capital. The crisis seemed over. However, his lack of success with the powerful London financial houses was soon overshadowed by the disaster which was now taking shape at home. The vague yet persistent rumours of scandal that had permeated Montreal for months were about to take concrete form in Ottawa. On 2 April Lucius Seth HUNTINGTON rose in the House of Commons to charge that Allan, financed partially by Americans, had purchased control of the western railway by contributing huge sums to the Conservatives. The Pacific Scandal had broken. Allan's damning correspondence with his American backers as well as his financial manipulation of the Conservatives eventually became public knowledge and led to the collapse of the Macdonald government on 5 November. Allan himself had returned from England to testify before the royal commission on the Pacific railway.

The scandal and the subsequent trimming of the project by the government of Alexander Mackenzie* ended Allan's involvement in the western road but his interest in other railways continued. Still active as president of the now bankrupt Montreal Northern Colonization Railway, he engineered its takeover by the Quebec government in 1875. He was active in the St Lawrence International Bridge Company and his bank, the Merchants' Bank of Canada, continued to lend money to railways such as the Kingston and Pembroke, the Grand Junction, and the Cobourg, Peterborough and Marmora Railway and Mining

Company. Just before his death he participated in three different syndicates, each organized to buy the Quebec, Montreal, Ottawa and Occidental Railway from the Quebec government.

Allan had used some of the same tactics in trying to gain a monopoly of the shipping trade on the St Lawrence. Although himself a shareholder in the Richelieu Company, formed a generation earlier by Montreal and Richelieu valley professional men and merchants [*see* Jacques-Félix Sincennes*], Allan challenged it by establishing the Canadian Navigation Company to operate on the upper St Lawrence and in 1869 by buying two steamers which he threatened to use on the Quebec City–Saguenay run. In return for his promise to divert the steamers elsewhere the Richelieu Company offered him an annual "indemnity" of $4,000 for five years and free wharfage for his vessels at their Quebec City docks. He soon pressured the company on another route by selling a Canadian Navigation Company steamer to the Union Navigation Company (apparently also an Allan operation) for use in competition with the Richelieu Company on the profitable Montreal–Quebec City run: in 1874, after the Richelieu Company had rejected amalgamation with him, Allan sold the Union Navigation Company two more steamers. A year later the Richelieu Company, with its revenues plummeting, was forced to accept amalgamation with the Canadian Navigation Company to form the Richelieu and Ontario Navigation Company. Both Hugh and Andrew Allan were directors of the new company and Hugh was president for six years.

He continued his efforts to minimize competition in the St Lawrence valley. Lengthy negotiations and a sham bankruptcy by the Chambly and Montreal Navigation Company led to its purchase by the Richelieu and Ontario Navigation Company. The St Lawrence Steam Navigation Company, owned by the powerful Molson family, was a more formidable competitor and Allan settled for traffic arrangements with it. In 1879 his friends in the Conservative party, Macdonald and Charles Tupper*, arranged for the lowering of government tolls and the removal of boulders near the Richelieu and Ontario's Saint-Lambert docks. Despite mergers, consolidation, and government favours, business was not good and by 1878 the company's dividends had fallen to 2.5 per cent. There had been grumblings in 1876 about Allan's actions as company president, the wide distribution of free passes, the misuse of company funds, and the Allan family's growing monopoly of trade on the St Lawrence. Louis-Adélard SENÉCAL, a well-known Quebec City entrepreneur, received growing support for his plan to incorporate the Richelieu and Ontario Navigation Company and the Quebec, Montreal, Ottawa and Occidental Railway into a new, integrated transportation system in the lower St Lawrence valley. Senécal and his companies quietly bought up Richelieu and Ontario shares and just a few months before Allan's death succeeded in ousting him from the board.

Hugh Allan displayed an early and persistent interest in banking and credit institutions. While still in his thirties he became a director of the Bank of Montreal and remained on the board for ten years (1847–57). In 1856, in addition to 204 shares in the Bank of Montreal, he had shares worth £8,000 in the Commercial Bank of Canada, £1,000 in the Bank of Upper Canada, and £2,020 in the City Bank of Montreal. He was a director of the Montreal Credit Company (1871), held 100 shares in the Maritime Bank of the Dominion of Canada (1873), and was president of the Provincial Permanent Building Society (1871) which became the Provincial Loan Company in 1875. His most important banking endeavour began when, as a source of capital and to service his financial needs, he established the Merchants' Bank of Canada. Run as a family business, it was chartered in 1861 but did not open until 1864. Allan was routinely elected president until 1877 and then was re-elected president in 1882. Andrew Allan, who was on the board from 1861 to 1883, succeeded his brother as president in 1882 and their brother-in-law, Jackson Rae, was the bank's first cashier. In 1868 Hugh, the bank's largest shareholder, held 2,658 of its 12,176 shares while Andrew had 875 shares. By the late 1870s, however, there were other large shareholders in the bank, such as Robert Anderson whose 5,042 shares held in 1878 exceeded the combined holdings of the Allans.

In its first years the Merchants' Bank was dominated by Hugh Allan, who faithfully attended board meetings to approve bank policy, appointments, and major loans. He handled problems in England and when in Montreal often went to the head office on Saturdays to count the money and supervise the burning of mutilated bills. This was not an idle exercise. In 1868 he discovered a shortfall of $500 in bank funds: seven employees were dismissed and criminal charges were laid against the accountant and head teller. In 1873 the board, which routinely rubber-stamped Allan's decisions before 1877, wired him concerning the bank's biggest liability, the bonds of the Detroit and Milwaukee Railway: "Board approves: do best you can." And two years later it said: "Scheme set forth in [your letter] or any settlement approved by you will be satisfactory."

The Merchants' quickly established a reputation as one of Canada's most aggressive banks. Allan reported immediate and growing profits that averaged 10 per cent of the bank's paid-up capital: $30,502 in the first year of operation, $100,671 in 1867, and $726,120 in 1871. In 1868 the Merchants' took over Kingston's floundering Commercial Bank of Canada. According to Allan, who had been a Commercial Bank shareholder and handled the negotiations, it had liabilities of $1,170,960 and assets of $2,666,680, much of the latter being in stocks and bonds of doubtful value. Allan's offer of one Merchants' share for three Commercial shares was accepted; the takeover gave the Merchants' Bank 17 branches in the important Ontario hinterland and expansion in Ontario was rapid. In Quebec, however, the bank was hesitant to move beyond Montreal; in 1871 it had only two branches in Quebec outside Montreal, but there were 22 Ontario branches, 16 in towns of less than 5,000 inhabitants. By the mid 1870s the bank had opened a branch in London, England, had nine employees in New York, and had built a fine head office of Ohio stone on Montreal's Place d'Armes.

Allan's association with the Merchants' Bank brought benefits beyond special borrowing privileges, profits on shares, and his annual presidential salary ($4,000 in 1874). The bank was part of an expanding, interlocking commercial and industrial empire in which one sector generated business for another. It could be as simple as a $5,000 bill to the bank from Allan's shipping company for transporting Quebec bonds to the bank's London office. His Citizens' Insurance Company of Canada insured the bank's employees and invested $36,000 in its stock. His Montreal Telegraph Company rented space in the bank's Ottawa building, and the Montreal Elevating Company, of which he was a director, was voted overdraft privileges of $3,000 by the Merchants' board. In 1875 a contractor for one of Allan's railways defaulted and brought the Banque Jacques-Cartier to its knees, but the Merchants' helped prop it up with a time extension. Often the benefits to Allan were more direct. In April 1872 he was given 165 shares held by the bank in the Ontario Woollen Company and one month later the board authorized a credit line of $20,000 to the company. In 1876 he borrowed $300,000 from the bank (using his bank stock as collateral) to aid his Vale Coal, Iron and Manufacturing Company. Another of his companies, the Montreal Cotton Company, was given a $50,000 bank advance "on their own paper."

In 1877 the Merchants', by then Canada's second largest bank, nearly collapsed and it became clear that the handsome profits announced annually by Allan had been achieved by carrying losses forward. The bank was further weakened by sloppy inspection procedures and loans administration, over-expansion into small Ontario towns, and heavy losses on the New York gold market and on two major investments. From the Commercial Bank it had inherited Detroit and Milwaukee Railway bonds with a face value of $1,735,350. These bonds matured in 1875 but the bank was unable to redeem them for even 20 per cent of their face value. The bank made another questionable investment in May 1876 when Allan told the board that the bank had bought at par £4,185,333 of a Quebec government bond issue necessitated by the bankruptcy of Allan's Montreal Northern Colonization Railway and its sister project, the North Shore Railway. Faced with the reluctance of British financiers to invest in Canadian securities outside the public sector and the collapse of the province's two most important railway projects, the government had little choice but to raise construction money itself. Although Allan assured a worried bank stockholder that the loan to the province was "mutually advantageous," the bank's London manager reported that it would be "impossible" to place the Quebec bonds on the London market, even at 95 per cent of their face value.

In February 1877 Allan resigned as president because of what he called "absurd rumours" and "senseless" clamour raised by "a few interested Brokers, and by personal enemies of mine." The new president, John Hamilton, moved quickly to save the bank. The Bank of Montreal and the Bank of British North America lent the Merchants' $1,500,000 on the guarantee of the directors' promissory notes, and a new general manager, George Hague*, was hired from the Bank of Toronto. He wrote off $113,143 for losses in the Montreal office, $222,611 on branch losses, a $198,704 loss in the New York office, $633,000 in bad debts, $305,196 on the Detroit and Milwaukee bonds, $553,000 on losses in other securities, and $223,991 "from unanticipated difficulties in placing the [Quebec government] loan on the London Stock Exchange." Allan exhibited remarkable resilience by regaining the presidency of the bank in 1882.

His dealings with the Merchants' Bank show how he constructed a complex commercial and industrial empire by constantly expanding his interests. The telegraph was a natural adjunct to his steamship and rail communication. Allan was associated with the Canada Atlantic Cable Company, was president of the Montreal Telegraph Company (1852), and was a director of two American companies, the Troy Telegraph Company and the Western Union Telegraph Company. He was also an early participant in the development of the Canadian telephone industry; in 1878, using lines installed by the Montreal Telegraph Company, he made one of the first Canadian long-distance telephone calls, from Montreal to Princess Louise in Ottawa. Of more importance were the lengthy negotiations of the newly established Bell Telephone Company with Allan, resulting in its purchase of the Montreal Telegraph Company's "telephone plant" for $75,000. Allan was active in other transportation sectors that were directly related to his shipping interests: warehousing, elevator, station, bridge, and tunnel companies. President in 1870 of the Montreal Warehousing Company (established in 1865 to erect sheds and warehouses), which held its board meetings in the offices of the Montreal Ocean Steamship Company, he was also a director of the

Montreal Railway Terminus Company (1861), the Canadian Railway Station Company (1871), and the St Lawrence International Bridge Company (1875). As his dealings with the Grand Trunk illustrate, Allan knew the importance of the American Midwest. With prominent Americans James Frederick Joy and Henry Porter Baldwin of Detroit and Nathaniel Thayer of Boston, as well as important Canadian investors such as George Stephen* and William McMaster, Allan was on the incorporating board of the Detroit River Tunnel Company in 1870. Five years later, with four Montreal merchants (including his brother Andrew), he chartered the St Lawrence and Chicago Forwarding Company.

Allan also participated in at least five insurance companies. As well as an important source of capital, these companies provided fire and marine-loss protection for his interests. His entry into injury and life insurance for his workers allowed him to recoup a percentage of wages and may have been a reaction to the development of provident societies and other working-class protective organizations. He was associated with three marine insurance companies: he was a founding director of the Marine Mutual Assurance Company of Montreal in 1851, of the Canada Marine Insurance Company in 1868, and 14 years later (with Andrew) of the St Lawrence Marine Insurance Company of Canada. His most important insurance operation, however, was incorporated in 1864 as the Citizens' Insurance and Investment Company (after 1876 as the Citizens' Insurance Company of Canada). Hugh Allan was its first president and Andrew was a perennial member of the board. Citizens' bonded the employees at the Merchants' Bank and provided fire insurance for Hugh's companies. His stevedores on the Montreal docks had one per cent of their pay deducted for compulsory accident insurance with the company, which covered only "on-the-job" injuries and did not apply to sickness. Permanently injured employees received $5 a week, and in the event of death $500 was paid to the family. In 1872 Allan was listed as a director of the Canada Life Assurance Company and was named in the charter of the Manitoba Insurance Company. That same year Andrew was a director of the Confederation Life Association.

Manufacturing in Montreal took off in the period from 1861 to 1881 and Allan was active in organizing capital for dozens of companies in cotton and wool textiles, shoemaking, iron and steel, tobacco, and paper. The vehicle for the increasing concentration of capital was the developing business institution, marked by the separation of management and ownership and by the advent of the stock market. In textile production as in many other instances, Allan had the capital to get in on the ground floor, and he was able to benefit after 1878 from the National Policy. Canadian textile production had risen dramatically between 1861 and 1871, and grew even more sharply after 1878 when the tariff on woollen goods was doubled and the tax on imported cotton increased from 17.5 to 30 per cent. With tariff protection the value of Canadian cotton production tripled in four years to $1,753,500 in 1884. Allan was president of the Cornwall Woollen Manufacturing Company and owned 165 shares in the Ontario Woollen Company. George Stephen – fellow Scot, president of the Bank of Montreal, and the city's leading wholesale merchant – had interested Allan in cotton textiles and the two financiers capitalized on the willingness of Cornwall, Ont., to subsidize textile production. Allan became president of a Cornwall firm, the Canada Cotton Manufacturing Company, in 1872, and was an incorporator of the Stormont Cotton Manufacturing Company eight years later. He had also helped found the Montreal Cotton Company in Valleyfield, Que., in 1874. With dividends of 11 per cent in 1880, 20 per cent in 1881, and 14 per cent in 1882, Montreal Cotton stock sold at a premium of up to 60 per cent in 1881–82.

Profits were high but working conditions in the cotton mills were notorious. Allan, never noted as a model employer, was more concerned with profit than with the welfare of his employees, and his cotton mills were the subject of complaints concerning wages, drinking water, child labour, and industrial accidents. Weavers in the Canada Cotton and Stormont Cotton mills were paid $5 a week in 1888 and a dyer in Cornwall was paid $1.25 a day. In the Montreal mill ten-year-old children worked barefoot through the winter.

Allan took an early interest in the production of iron, steel, and rolling-stock. Impressed by the efforts of Toronto and Hamilton manufacturers to satisfy the Grand Trunk's needs, he and Stephen exhorted Montreal merchants in 1870 to show "enterprise and energy" by investing in the Canada Rolling Stock Company. Allan was also a director of the Canadian Railway Equipment Company (1872) and the Ontario Car Company (1882), and with Peter Redpath* and Stephen he owned the Montreal Rolling Mills. Specializing in nails, tacks, and pipe, this company, one of the four largest ironworks in Quebec, declared a 7 per cent dividend in 1878.

The interruption of American tobacco imports during the Civil War had given a boost to tobacco manufacturing in Montreal, and Allan served as president of the Adams Tobacco Company (1882). Pulp and paper was another growth industry, doubling its production twice between 1861 and 1881. Allan was a director of the Canada Paper Company, one of the first industrial companies to be listed on the Montreal Stock Exchange. A cheap labour base, access to capital, and improved transportation systems contributed to the rapid growth of shoemaking in Montreal in the decade 1861–71, the value of production rising from one to nine million dollars. Hides came from the west, tanning was done in Quebec City, and the finished leather was sent to Montreal. Allan was president (1882) of the Canadian Rubber Company of Montreal, one of the oldest shoe and boot makers in Montreal.

Allan was also active in exploiting natural resources such as land, fish, and mining. His interest in western land speculation may have developed from his Pacific railway project and the western operations of the Merchants' Bank. President of the Montreal and Western Land Company, he visited western Canada just a few months before his death in 1882. In that year he was also president of the North-West Cattle Company and the Canada and Newfoundland Sealing and Fishing Company. An active mining speculator, he was an original shareholder in the Montreal Mining Company founded in 1847. By 1855 the company was plagued with stock manipulation, haphazard bookkeeping, unwarranted dividends, and a debt of £19,340 to the Commercial Bank. In addition, that year the company was implicated in a scandal involving the transfer of 200 shares of stock to John Ross*, former attorney general of Canada West and president of the Grand Trunk Railway. Arranged by Cartier, Ross's quick profit of £1,000 was apparently necessary to facilitate the location of a county court-house at the site of a company mine in the Bruce Peninsula. Allan was furious at the deal which had not been entered on the company's books. He denied being the mysterious purchaser of the stock Ross obtained and, after leading an investigation which found "extreme irregularity," he resigned as president. Also associated with the Mulgrave Gold Mining Company, Allan was a director of the Vermont and Canada Marble Company and president of the Thunder Bay Silver Mining Company (1882).

Coal, the primary energy source for steamships, railways, and manufacturing industries, was Allan's most important mining interest. His investment in Nova Scotia's Pictou mines rose rapidly in the 1860s and he was the only Canadian director in 1865 on the founding board of the New York–based Acadian Coal Company. In 1873 he was involved in the establishment of the Vale Coal, Iron and Manufacturing Company. President of the company until his death, he placed the head office in Montreal and used $300,000 of his Merchants' Bank stock as collateral to construct the company's railway, wharf, surface plant, and miners' houses: his son Hugh Montagu Allan* later inherited the company presidency. The National Policy again benefited Allan. Its tax of 50 cents a ton on imported coal allowed the Vale Coal Company to retain large Montreal coal consumers such as the North American Glass Company and the New City Gas Company of Montreal (later the Montreal Gas Company).

Allan, in addition to land held by his companies, owned a substantial amount of property himself. By 1872 his holdings included Ravenscrag (his 609,260-square-foot estate on Mount Royal) and the 79,260-square-foot site of his former home on Rue Sainte-Catherine on which stood a dozen stores and a music hall. Aside from his summer estate, Belmere, on Lac Memphrémagog in the Eastern Townships, Allan, never a gentleman farmer like his brother Andrew, owned at least four properties on the outskirts of Montreal, each in an area of potential urban expansion. He held a 13,637-square-foot site in Hochelaga (now part of Montreal), a village on the eastern limits of the city, where one of his companies, the Montreal Northern Colonization Railway, proposed to locate its terminus and yards, and 30 acres on Côte Sainte-Catherine (now part of Outremont) on the northern extremity of the city. Near the Lachine Canal he held 79 acres himself plus 8 acres owned jointly with Robert James Reekie, with whom he also shared 26 acres in Saint-Henri (now part of Montreal), another potential area for manufacturing expansion. Besides his two residential sites Allan owned three properties within the city of Montreal, including an 11,637-square-foot site in the west-end ward of Saint-Antoine. He held two properties in the business core, a 9,553-square-foot property in the Place d'Armes banking district (probably the site of the Merchants' Bank) and a 26,850-square-foot site on McGill Street where his shipping company had its head office.

Although he was astute in obtaining what he wanted from governments, Allan's political influence was largely behind the scenes. Indeed, he apparently did not consider the act of voting to be of great importance, noting in 1873 that he had voted in only one parliamentary election. He had, however, volunteered for military service in the rebellions of 1837–38, reaching the rank of captain, and in 1849 he was a prominent anti-annexationist. A lifelong Conservative, he directed some $400,000 to the party's federal campaign in 1872 while pursuing the Pacific contract; his lawyer noted that Conservative policies were so favourable to Allan's interests that a contribution three times as large would have been justified. Campaign contributions were only one means of manipulating politicians: George-Étienne Cartier's constituents needed jobs in Allan's proposed railway shops, Francis Hincks's son wanted a position in the bank, and politicians sailed on Allan's ships and danced at his parties.

Controlling Canada's second largest bank increased his political power. The Merchants' Bank made loans to the provinces of Manitoba and Quebec, and to the city of Winnipeg. Favoured politicians were named by head office as solicitors for local branches and ex-finance minister John Rose became the bank's London solicitor. Future prime minister J. J. C. Abbott had a $1,000 annual retainer as the bank's Montreal lawyer in 1866. Sir Charles Tupper and Sir John A. Macdonald became special solicitors for the Winnipeg branch in 1883.

Even more dramatic evidence of the link between the state, politics, and business is provided by politicians who were among the Merchants' debtors. Although John Hillyard Cameron*'s large debt was the subject of board discussions in February 1870, Macdonald was probably the bank's most prominent debtor and it seems clear that the prime minister granted favours to his creditors. Macdonald and Allan had apparently not corresponded before 1868 when the Merchants' Bank inherited the former's debt of almost $80,000 to the Commercial Bank. Soon after, Allan jogged Macdonald's memory: "when quite convenient I will be glad to receive your proposals for settlement." Before settling his debts Macdonald did his best to cater to Allan. He helped him get favourable provincial legislation from Quebec, informed him of cabinet discussions on lighthouses, and accepted his choice as emigration agent, assuring him that the new agent would be as "friendly as possible" to his steamship operations. In November 1869 Macdonald asked the bank to accept the property held as collateral and his life insurance policies as payment. When the bank accepted these terms he wrote to Allan thanking him for his "kindness" and added that Francis Hincks was at work on banking policy. In February Macdonald apologized for not giving Allan's Montreal Telegraph Company a monopoly on government business; according to Macdonald it was "impolitic" to raise the matter. Despite the Pacific Scandal, the two men remained in touch. Allan wrote to Macdonald in 1878 asking for tariffs on rubber goods, shoes, hose, sewing machines, cottons, woollen goods, coal, and wrought iron.

Allan took a direct approach to what he described as "influencing" newspapers. He expedited European news via his telegraph and steamers to friendly newspapers, and his bank made loans to important publishers such as Georges-Isidore Barthe* of Sorel and John Lovell* of Montreal. The latter received a loan to publish the *Canada directory*, apparently on the condition that he handle the printing for Allan's telegraph and steamship interests. The Montreal *Gazette* was under Allan's influence for years. Although he sold his share of the paper to Richard and Thomas White in 1870, the new owners remained in debt to him and had a $20,000 "accommodation" at the Merchants' Bank, which also loaned money to their timber operations in Pembroke, Ont. Given this financial link, the *Gazette* usually paid careful tribute to Allan's activities and ideology as it did on 28 July 1871: "We mentioned yesterday a rumour to the effect that Mr. Hugh Allan had been honoured by the Queen in having had conferred upon him a Baronetcy. . . . That his eminent services in connection with ocean steam navigation have been thus recognized is matter for sincere congratulation among all classes of the people in Canada. No Knight in the Queen's galaxy of Knighthood, has more worthily won his spurs. And it is a subject of honest pride to Canadians that one who has done so much to develop the great interests of the St Lawrence route, has not only reaped the pecuniary rewards which enterprise and indomitable pluck, such as he has shown, richly deserve, but has also been honoured with well merited distinction by his Sovereign." The material basis of the *Gazette*'s legitimizing function could hardly have been made more direct than when Allan traded part of the Whites' debt for editorial support. During the 1872 campaign for a $1,000,000 subsidy for his Montreal Northern Colonization Railway, Allan deducted $5,000 from their loan. "Immediately after," his lawyer commented, "we noticed that the advocacy of the *Gazette* was all that could be desired."

Allan also took the direct approach in dealing with Quebec politicians such as Hector-Louis Langevin* and Cartier. He subsidized their campaigns, arranged for them to rub shoulders with the British élite, named their friends as company lawyers, and advertised in their newspapers. In return he received charters, favourable legislation, and the repeal of laws he disliked. His interference was blunt and the results usually swift. "Allan has telegraphed wishing the St. Lawrence navigation act repealed," Langevin wired Macdonald. "The Quebec government have promised me it shall be done."

Although a member of a Scottish shipping dynasty Allan never let ethnicity dominate over business sense. Dozens of Scots such as William Dow, George Burns Symes, and John Redpath* shared boardrooms with him, but others such as David Lewis Macpherson and John Young* never hesitated to sabotage his projects. The latter was perhaps Allan's most persistent opponent. They were members of two competing bourgeois groups in Montreal and their political and economic quarrels spanned a 25-year period. Young, as commissioner of public works, played a major role in blocking Allan's application to provide steamship service between Montreal and Liverpool in the early 1850s. A vociferous Liberal by the late 1860s, Young enraged Allan by attacking public subsidies to his railways and by advocating free trade with the United States. Allan, a manufacturer and protectionist, complained to the prime minister about Young's "annexationist" ideas. In 1873, however, he repaid old debts when the Merchants' Bank refused a $6,000 loan to the bankrupt Young. Nor did he show special leniency to other errant Scottish friends. Isaac BUCHANAN, a prominent Hamilton wholesaler, railway entrepreneur, and politician, owed Allan's bank $55,000 in 1872. Over a four-year period Buchanan tried, apparently without success, to ease the terms: his wife reminded Allan of their common heritage and Buchanan made courtesy calls to Allan's home and sent condolences on the death of his brother. As his interests spread across the continent Allan chose partners who brought him capital, local or ethnic prestige, political influence, or technical expertise.

Allan was cynical and astute in exploiting the Roman Catholic clergy and French Canadian bourgeoisie. While still a youth he had spent two winters in the villages of Sainte-Rose (now part of Laval) and Sainte-Thérèse where he learned to speak French, and as a young commission agent he had bought grain from French Canadian merchants along the Richelieu River. Publicly he was a model of tolerance: "I assure you, to whatever nationality you may belong, you will have full justice in everything I have to do with; I know nothing of nationality; I am desirous of getting the best man in the best places and of giving everybody fair-play." With the means and the power to placate, manipulate, or, if necessary, discipline his allies in the local French Canadian élite, he also knew which pockets to line and which priests to pamper, his aim being, he explained to an American colleague, to show French Canadians where "their true interest lay." When in 1871 he bought the controlling interest in and became president of the Montreal Northern Colonization Railway, an enterprise with important nationalist overtones, he went "to the country through which the road would pass, and called on many of the inhabitants. I visited the priests, and made friends of them, and I employed agents to go amongst the principal people and talk it up. I then began to hold public meetings, and attended to them myself, making frequent speeches in French. . . ."

Allan cultivated leading French Canadian clergymen. In 1870 he authorized a special stop of a company steamer for Louis-François Laflèche*, the new bishop of Trois-Rivières, permitting him to disembark in his own diocese on his return from Rome. Prominent Catholic laymen such as Louis Beaubien were named to his boardrooms; Joseph-Édouard Lefebvre* de Bellefeuille, a leading Ultramontane and friend of Bishop Ignace BOURGET, was secretary in several of his companies. François-Xavier-Antoine Labelle, the amiable curé of Saint-Jérôme who was Allan's favourite cleric, was described by one Quebec editor as "Sir Hugh's right arm." At a dinner held in his honour in February 1872 Allan interrupted toasts to pay tribute to Labelle. In November he invited Labelle to a Ravenscrag ball "for although I do not expect you would dance, and more especially the fast dances, you might like to see it. I expect to have about 500 people at it. Will you come?"

Like many of their English-speaking counterparts, French Canadian opinion-makers showed great respect for Allan. Bishop Bourget freed Labelle from his parish duties so that he could participate in the campaign to raise municipal subsidies for one of Allan's railways. In 1871 the bishop's newspaper, *Le Nouveau Monde*, praised the Montreal Northern Colonization Railway as "*une œuvre nationale*" and endorsed Allan's efforts to deepen the St Lawrence shipping channel and to build a new bridge over the river. *Le National*, founded in 1872 by Montreal Liberals, also supported his Pacific railway scheme and the $1,000,000 municipal subsidy which he sought from the city. *Le Journal de Québec* described him as "*le chevalier de* Ravenscrag" and *La Minerve* felt that his presence on a railway board gave "a moral guarantee."

But Allan was never free from criticism. The working conditions in his factories, his manipulation of government subsidies and policies, and his attempts to establish monopolies and purchase politicians all prompted objections from various elements in society. The most severe attacks, both from his contemporaries and from historians, concern his conduct during the negotiations for the Pacific contract. He was not, however, more corrupt than fellow Canadian businessmen or old political friends such as Cartier or Macdonald. Political payoffs, hidden backers, the use of foreign capital, the manipulation of contracts, and the diverting of public funds for private use were norms of the business morality of the day. The *chevalier* of Ravenscrag was resented more for his successes than for his methods, and his most powerful opposition generally came not from offended Canadian nationalists but from rivals in Montreal and Toronto. Many of the comments of his detractors, especially those concerning his close ties with French Canadians, were often repeated. "The contest [for the Pacific contract] has been, really, between Ontario and Quebec," a bitter D. L. Macpherson had written to Macdonald in 1872. "Quebec has secured the prize – thanks to *French domination*."

Allan's accumulation of wealth, climaxing in an estate estimated at between six and ten million dollars, enabled him, his family, and his heirs to live in privileged circumstances. The Allans hosted governors general and royalty, had 11 "live-in" domestics in their Montreal residence, and owned a private steam yacht, *Lady of the Lake*, for summer use on Lake Memphrémagog. In 1860 Allan had bought the Simon McTavish* estate on the slopes of Mount Royal and over the next three years built Ravenscrag, the mansion which in the opinion of one editorialist surpassed "in size and cost any dwelling-house in Canada, and looks more like one of the castles of the British nobility than anything we have seen here." Designed in Italian Renaissance style by the architectural firm of Hopkins and Wiley, the mansion's 34 rooms included a billiard room, a conservatory, a library, and a ballroom that could accommodate several hundred guests. From the 75-foot tower there was a fine view of the city, the port, and the distant Green Mountains of Vermont.

Little is known of Allan's personality or private life. Apparently a handsome man, he appears in photographs as a short, somewhat stocky individual with a full beard and moustache that offset his mid-life baldness. He was a member of the Tandem Club and the Montreal Citizens' Association (1868), an honorary member of the North British Society of Halifax (1871), and president of the St Andrew's Society (1848–50). A curler, presumably of some ability since he was named skip in 1852, he served as president of the Montreal Curling Club in 1846–47 and 1874–75. Described by his minister as a man of "little sentiment" who believed that "religion consisted mainly in a man doing his duty," Allan was accorded accolades and individual honours from the clergy, the military, and the crown: a Montreal-area priest described him as "a new Hercules," he was named a lieutenant in the Montreal 3rd Battalion (1847), and he was knighted by Queen Victoria's own hand in England in 1871.

His philanthropic activities seem restricted for one of his wealth and rank although it is not clear if this was typical of his Montreal peers. A lifelong Presbyterian, he attended St Gabriel Street Church and later St Andrew's Church. He served as the Presbyterian representative on the board which divided the clergy reserves, and was chairman of the church's temporalities board in the 1870s. He made minor donations, usually through his wife, to the Montreal Ladies' Benevolent Society and the Protestant Orphan Asylum, but his major philanthropic activity was the Montreal Sailors' Institute, of which his brother was president (1872) and of which the Allans were the primary patrons. Hugh did become a lifetime governor of the Montreal Protestant House of Industry and Refuge after making a $500 contribution in 1863, and he was a member of the first board of the Protestant Hospital for the Insane (1881).

In 1882, the year after his wife's death, Allan died of a heart attack while visiting his son-in-law in Edinburgh. The body of the "deceased knight" was returned to Montreal, placed in a highly polished oak coffin with silver handles, and laid out in Ravenscrag. The funeral, held on 27 Dec. 1882, caused the closing of the stock exchange for the afternoon. The hearse, preceded by a squad of city police and a detachment of firemen, was followed by his family; political, commercial, and industrial luminaries; "employees from the manager down to the workers on the wharves"; and some 2,000 citizens. After the service in St Andrew's, Allan was buried beside his wife in the family mausoleum in Mount Royal Cemetery.

It was symbolic that he should die in the land of his birth and be buried with honour in his country of adoption. A member of an important Scots shipping family, he had been trained by his father's colonial associates and, as a young man, promoted to partnership in a prominent Montreal merchant house. His operations were characterized by internationalism: he did business in London, Liverpool, Glasgow, New York, and Chicago; he transferred the ships he purchased from Canada to Scotland; and his Merchants' Bank had some of its most profitable activities in New York. At the same time, able in many instances to exploit both French and English Canadian nationalism, he remained a staunch anti-annexationist. Combining capital, international ties, and a willingness to invest in new forms of transportation, he had built Canada's most important steamship company. He increased his company's power by carefully attending to the protection of markets, soliciting favourable legislation, obtaining subsidies, and limiting competition.

From his shipping base Allan expanded vigorously into the industrial economy which developed after 1860, exploiting Montreal's growing metropolitan strength and widening markets brought by the transportation revolution. With improved technology, the increasingly bureaucratic nature of business, and the revised political structures of confederation, he became one of Canada's first monopoly capitalists. Despite some false starts and without the rationalization of later industrial organization, Allan developed an integrated financial, transportation, and manufacturing empire. His ships carried immigrants, his factories hired them and made the material for their clothes, his land companies sold them land, and his finanical agencies insured them and lent them money.

Capital was the key. Perhaps the most knowledgeable Canadian entrepreneur in the use of subsidies and public capital, he could tap both long- and short-term funds from his contacts in commercial banks, savings banks, insurance companies, and mortgage cooperatives. Rather than being just a model Canadian entrepreneur who profited in systematic fashion from the economic opportunities offered by Canada, Allan emphasized the importance of capital – and not management or technical skills – as the central factor in permitting the exploitation of emerging economic sectors in mid-19th-century Canada.

BRIAN J. YOUNG in collaboration with GERALD J.J. TULCHINSKY

AC, Montréal, État civil, Presbytériens, St Andrew's Church (Montréal), 27 Dec. 1882. Allan Memorial Institute of Psychiatry, McGill Univ. (Montreal), "The Allan Memorial Institute of Psychiatry: its history and foundation" (unpub. paper, n.d.). ANQ-M, Minutiers, James Smith, 27 May 1861; Testaments, Reg. des testaments prouvés, 13, 28 déc. 1882. AO, MU 500-15; MU 2095, John McLennan, "The early settlement of Glengarry." Baker Library, R. G. Dun & Co. credit ledger, Canada, 5: 61. Montreal Business Hist. Project (Montreal), J. Hutchison and P. Orr, "A study of Presbyterianism in Montreal, 1792–1850" (1979). PAC, MG 24, B25; D16; MG 26, A; MG 27, I, D11; MG 28, II3; MG 29, C37; RG 31, A1, 1871, Montreal, Saint-Antoine Ward. QUA, Canada Steamship Lines Ltd. records, La Compagnie du Richelieu, Procès-verbaux, 1869-75; Richelieu and Ontario Navigation Company, Minutes, 1875–81.

Allan Line Steamship Company, *Information & advice for emigrants* (Liverpool, 1878). Can., House of Commons, *Journals*, October–November 1873, app.I; Parl., *Sessional papers*, 1875, VI, no.7; VII, no.22: 236–67; 1878, IX, no.15: 169–208; Royal Commission on the Relations of Capital and Labor in Canada, *Report* (5v. in 6, Ottawa, 1889); Royal Commission on the Textile Industry, *Report* (Ottawa, 1938). Can., Prov. of, Legislative Assembly, *App. to the journals*, 1852–53; *Statutes*, 1852–53. *Extract of the official book of reference of the city of Montreal; west division: St. Antoine's Ward*, ed. L.-W. Sicotte (Montreal, 1870). *Extract of the official book of reference of the parish of Montreal . . .*, ed. L.-W. Sicotte (Montreal, 1872). Montreal Board of Trade, *Correspondence relating to ship channel in River St Lawrence . . .* (Montreal, 1871). Montreal Sailors' Institute, *Annual report* (Montreal), 1871–72. *Narrative of the proceedings of the St. Andrew's Society, of Montreal, from its formation on the 9th March, 1835, until the 1st January, 1844, to which is appended lists of the officers, members, and the constitution of the society* (Montreal, 1855). Alfred Sandham, *Ville-Marie, or, sketches of Montreal, past and present* (Montreal, 1870). *Canadian Illustrated News* (Montreal), 1872. *Le Franc-Parleur* (Montréal), 4 août 1876. *Gazette* (Montreal), 1838–82. *Globe*, 1882. *Le Journal des Trois-Rivières*, 1870. *La Minerve*, 1852–73; 14, 15 févr. 1882. *Le Monde*, 1875, 14 févr. 1882. *Montreal Daily Star*, 3 Aug. 1876; 15 June 1878; 4, 7 Feb., 9 Dec. 1882. *Montreal Daily Witness*, 13 Feb. 1872. *Montreal Herald and Daily Commercial Gazette*, 1881–82. *Montreal Witness*, 1871; 8, 15 Feb.; 18 Dec. 1882. *Morning Chronicle* (Quebec), 1870–82. *Le Négociant canadien* (Montréal), 1871–74. *La Patrie*, 11 déc. 1882.

Canadian biog. dict., II. Dent, *Canadian portrait gallery*, II. C. P. deVolpi and P. H. Scowen, *The Eastern Townships: a pictorial record; historical prints and illustrations of the Eastern Townships of the province of Quebec, Canada* (Montreal, 1962). H. W. Hopkins, *Atlas of the city and island of Montreal, including the counties of Jacques Cartier and Hochelaga, from actual surveys, based upon the cadastral plans deposited in the office of the Department of Crown Lands* ([Montreal], 1879). *Montreal directory*, 1842–82. North British Soc., *Annals of the North British Society of Halifax, Nova Scotia, for one hundred and twenty-five years . . .*, comp. J. S. Macdonald (Halifax, 1894). Notman and Taylor, *Portraits of British Americans*, II. *The year book and almanac of Canada . . .* (Montreal), 1870. H. G. J. Aitken, *The Welland Canal Company: a study in Canadian enterprise* (Cambridge, Mass., 1954). T. E. Appleton, *Ravenscrag: the Allan Royal Mail Line* (Toronto, 1974). Pierre Berton, *The national dream: the great railway, 1871–1881* (Toronto and Montreal, 1970); *The last spike; the great railway, 1881–1885* (Toronto and Montreal, 1971). F. C. Bowen, *A century of Atlantic travel, 1830–1930* (Boston, 1930). J. M. Cameron, *The Pictonian colliers* (Halifax, 1974). Campbell, *Hist. of Scotch Presbyterian Church*. Creighton, *Macdonald, old chieftain*. Currie, *Grand Trunk Railway*. Denison, *Canada's first bank*, II. Luc d'Iberville-Moreau, *Montréal perdu*, Michel Beaulieu, trad. ([Montréal, 1977?]). E. C. Moodey, *The Fraser-Hickson Library: an informal history* (London, 1977). R. T. Naylor, *The history of Canadian business, 1867–1914* (2v., Toronto, 1975), II. D. G. Paterson, *British direct investment in Canada, 1890–1914* (Toronto and Buffalo, N.Y., 1976). *The Royal Montreal Curling Club, 1807–1932* (Montreal, 1932). Joseph Schull, *100 years of banking in Canada: a history of the Toronto-Dominion Bank* (Toronto, 1958). O. D. Skelton, *The life and times of Sir Alexander Tilloch Galt* (Toronto, 1920; repub., ed. Guy MacLean, 1966). Alastair Sweeny, *George-Étienne Cartier: a biography* (Toronto, 1976). Tulchinsky, *River barons*. William Weir, *Sixty years in Canada* (Montreal, 1903).

Pierre Berton, "A priceless photo collection finds a home: *Maclean's* marks the hundredth anniversary of William Notman by helping to house his famous collection at McGill and make half a million irreplaceable portraits and views available to scholars," *Maclean's* (Toronto), 69 (1956), no.24: 15–27, 78–82. "'Ravenscrag': the historic residence of Sir Montagu and Lady Allan presented to the Royal Victoria Hospital," *Montreal Daily Star*, 14 Nov. 1940. J.-C. Robert, "Les notables de Montréal au XIXe siècle," *SH*, 8 (1975): 54-76.

ALLEYN, CHARLES JOSEPH, lawyer, politician, and public servant; b. 19 Sept. 1817 in County Cork (Republic of Ireland), son of Richard Israël Alleyn and Margaret O'Donovan; d. 4 April 1890 at Quebec City.

A descendant of a well-known Anglo-Irish family, Charles Joseph Alleyn attended school at Fermoy, Cork, and Clongowes Wood College in County Kildare, before his family immigrated to Quebec around 1837. He was called to the bar on 29 Sept. 1840 and became an outstanding lawyer who was respected especially by French Canadians as well as by the Irish. On 15 May 1849 at Quebec he married Zoé, daughter of Philippe-Joseph Aubert* de Gaspé, author of *Les anciens Canadiens*, and they had eight children.

By the end of October 1849 Alleyn had joined the annexationists of Quebec. In January 1850 he supported Joseph Légaré*, an annexationist candidate, at a by-election in Quebec City. *Le Canadien indépendant* (Quebec) spoke highly of Alleyn but other newspapers called him an empty prattler who lacked conviction and was only out to "acquire popularity." According to *Le Journal de Québec*, Alleyn stated in one of his speeches that he had been an officer in the volunteer troops during the 1837–38 disturbances, and that at that time he would have "joyfully [seen Légaré] mount the scaffold."

Although he had been defeated in the municipal elections of 1848 Alleyn was returned by acclamation as councillor for Champlain Ward on 4 Feb. 1851 and retained this office until February 1857. He was especially interested in public health; he worked on the health committee at regular intervals, and on 18 July 1854, during a serious cholera epidemic, he became a member of the local board of health. Through his work on the roads and elections committees he probably acquired experience useful for his future political career. On 13 Feb. 1854 the councillors chose him as mayor, but he was defeated the following year. This executive position had, however, enabled Alleyn, who was impartial as well as skilful in handling municipal affairs, to establish contact with provincial administrators.

Campaigning as a "progressive Reformer," Alleyn was elected to the Legislative Assembly for the constituency of Quebec City on 22 July 1854. In a letter to his constituents he declared himself in favour of the abolution of seigneurial tenure and the immediate settlement of the clergy reserves issue while at the same time safeguarding "vested interests." He considered an elective legislative council was necessary in the constitution of the country. He was further persuaded that in the matter of education the province needed separate schools, religion being, in his view, "the corner-stone of education." His opponents unsuccessfully contested the election, which according to them had been marred by irregularities. From 28 Nov. 1857 to 1 Aug. 1858 Alleyn served as commissioner in chief of public works in the government of John A. Macdonald* and George-Étienne Cartier*, and from 7 Aug. 1858 to 23 May 1862 as provincial secretary for Canada East in the new Cartier–Macdonald government. Although in April 1860 a committee of inquiry declared his 1857 election invalid, he was nonetheless re-elected by acclamation on 7 May 1860 at the by-election in the new constituency of Quebec West; he represented this constituency until just before confederation. In 1866, as a reward for service to his country and party, Alleyn obtained the lucrative post of sheriff of the district of Quebec, a post he retained until his death. He also took an interest in railways and was a director of the North Shore Railway and a signatory to the incorporation of the St Maurice Railway and Navigation Company (1857).

Ambitious, a realist and an opportunist, Charles Alleyn possessed all the qualities necessary for scaling the socio-political ladder, in both his city and country. By origin Irish and Catholic, an anglophone who spoke French, and a lawyer, he married a descendant of an illustrious French Canadian family. His desire to preserve his image in the eyes of society undoubtedly led him to join public associations and organizations. His involvement in the annexationist movement and the period he spent in municipal politics opened the door to a political career on the provincial level. Defining himself as a Canadian, he represented primarily the English-speaking element of Quebec. Both as an MLA and as a minister he knew how to promote the interests of his adopted city.

MARCEL PLOUFFE

A genealogy of the Alleyn family is in the possession of R. R. Alleyn (Quebec). AVQ, Procès-verbaux du conseil, juin 1850–mars 1858, novembre 1885. Québec, ville de, Bureau du trésorier, *Rapport annuel* (Québec), 1854, 1857. *L'Ami de la religion et de la patrie* (Québec), 21 janv., 31 oct. 1850. *Le Canadien*, 31 oct. 1849; 2, 21 janv. 1850; 3 févr. 1851; 6 févr., 7, 12, 21, 24 juill. 1854; 11, 16, 23, 30 déc. 1857; 18 avril, 7, 9 mai 1860; 1er juill. 1861; 8, 15 juin 1863; 5 avril 1890. *Le Canadien indépendant* (Québec), 19, 26 oct. 1849. *Le Courrier du Canada*, 7 avril 1890. *Le Journal de Québec*, 30 oct. 1849; 2, 19, 22 janv. 1850; 22 juill. 1854; 17 avril 1890. *Morning Chronicle* (Quebec), 21 Jan. 1850; 14 July, 4, 10, 14, 22, 28, 29 Dec. 1857. *Quebec Gazette*, 27 Oct. 1849; 15, 18, 20, 27 July, 2 Dec. 1857; 20 Aug. 1866. *Quebec Mercury*, 30 Oct. 1849; 25, 27 July 1854; 12, 15, 22 Dec. 1857. *Quebec directory*, 1844–45, 1847–56, 1860–61. P.-G. Roy, *Les avocats de la région de Québec*. F.-X. Chouinard et Antoine Drolet, *La ville de Québec: histoire municipale* (3v., Québec, 1963–67), III. P.-A. Dubé, "La crise annexionniste à Québec (1848–1850)" (thèse de MA, univ. Laval, Québec, 1974). Marcel Plouffe, "Quelques particularités sociales et politiques de la charte, du système administratif et du personnel politique de la cité de Québec, 1833–1867" (thèse de MA, univ. Laval, 1971). "Fifty years ago to-day", *Quebec Daily Telegraph*, 19 June 1911: 3.

ANDERSON, ALEXANDER CAULFIELD, HBC fur-trader and civil servant; b. 10 March 1814 near Calcutta, India, son of Robert Anderson and Eliza Charlotte Simpson; d. 8 May 1884 at Saanich, near Victoria, B.C.

Alexander Caulfield Anderson's father, a retired British army officer, operated an indigo plantation in Bengal in partnership with Alexander Caulfield. He prospered, returned to England in 1817, and settled in Essex, where his sons received a good education. In March 1831 Alexander joined the Hudson's Bay Company; his initial contract was for five years at an annual salary that increased progressively from £20 to £50. He sailed for Canada in April, accompanied by an older brother, James*, who had also joined the HBC.

Alexander spent his first year of service at Lachine, Lower Canada. In 1832 he was sent to Fort Vancouver (Vancouver, Wash.) where he arrived in November. The following year he was second in command of the party that built Fort McLoughlin (Bella Bella, B.C.) and in 1834 he was with Peter Skene Ogden* when the company's attempt to establish a post on the Stikine River was blocked by the Russians. In 1835 Ogden took charge of New Caledonia, the HBC department encompassing present-day north central British Columbia. Anderson evidently had impressed him favourably, for he too was transferred to that district, and spent the next five years there. His first assignment, which was to cross the Rockies to Jasper House, meet a party of new recruits, and bring back 40 packs of moose skins needed for shoe leather, nearly ended in tragedy. An early onset of winter forced the party to return to Jasper House, and a shortage of provisions there made a further retreat to Edmonton House (Edmonton) necessary. Anderson was severely criticized by some in the company for his management of the party, but an investigation exonerated him from all blame for its misfortunes.

In 1836 he took charge of the post on Fraser Lake where he remained until 1839. He was then stationed for a year at Fort George (Prince George, B.C.), after which he returned to Fort Vancouver. In 1840–41 he took temporary charge of Fort Nisqually (Wash.) and was there when the exploring expedition under Lieutenant Charles Wilkes of the United States Navy visited the post in May 1841 in the course of its survey of Puget Sound and the Columbia valley. In 1842 Anderson commanded the annual brigade to York Factory (Man.), and on his return was appointed to Fort Alexandria on the Fraser River where he was based until 1848.

Anderson is now best remembered as leader of three exploring expeditions carried out in 1846–47. It had been apparent for some time before the Oregon boundary settlement of 1846 that the boundary was likely to be the 49th parallel, in which case the HBC line of communication between the interior posts and Fort Vancouver by way of the Columbia River would be partly in the United States. A route to the ocean that would be entirely in British territory was essential, and Fort Langley on the Fraser River was the obvious alternative outlet. A year before the treaty was signed Anderson wrote to Sir George Simpson*, governor of the HBC, requesting permission to try to find a practicable travel route from the post at Kamloops (on the west bank of the Thompson River) to Fort Langley. Simpson asked Ogden to make the necessary arrangements. Ogden supported the proposal in a letter to Anderson's local superiors stating that because of Anderson's "active habits and experience in Caledonia I consider him fully competent to carry it into effect."

Ogden had suggested a route leading westward from Kamloops to the Fraser River in the vicinity of Cayoosh Flat (Lillooet), and then avoiding the canyons of the Fraser by travelling south by way of Seton, Anderson, Lillooet, and Harrison lakes and the Harrison River, which flows into the Fraser about 30 miles up-stream from Fort Langley. Leaving Kamloops on 15 May 1846, Anderson completed the journey by Ogden's route in nine days, but he considered it quite unsuitable for the company's purposes. On the return trip, which began on 28 May and occupied 13 days, he determined to leave the Fraser below the canyons and search for a way through the Cascade Mountains, which lie between the river and the interior valleys. Like many explorers before him, he followed water-courses – the Coquihalla River, Nicolum Creek, the Sumallo River, and Snass Creek, then, having crossed the height of land, descended by the Tulameen River to Otter Lake. There he had the good fortune to meet Blackeye, an Indian well acquainted with the country, who guided him north to Kamloops by way of Otter Creek and Nicola Lake. Anderson considered this route practicable, although in places snow might limit its use to a few months in the year.

Ogden and James Douglas*, the senior officers in charge of HBC operations west of the Rockies, hoped that a better route could be found and instructed Anderson to explore further in 1847. In May he set out once more from Kamloops, left his previous route at Nicola Lake, and by way of the Coldwater River and Uztlius Creek reached the Fraser about 13 miles up-stream from Yale. A pack trail was built to bypass the lower canyon and the HBC brigades used this route in 1848, but it proved too difficult and had to be abandoned. The company then fell back on a somewhat revised version of the route Anderson had followed in May 1846 via the Coquihalla and Tulameen rivers, and it served as the brigade trail from 1849 to 1860.

In 1848 Anderson was given charge of Fort Colvile (Colville, Wash.) and the surrounding district. He served there until 1851, after which he was stationed at Fort Vancouver as second in command to John Ballenden*. He retired on 1 June 1854 at the early age of 40. He had been appointed a chief trader in 1846 and would have been promoted chief factor had he continued in the service; but the promotion was contingent upon his accepting a post in New Caledonia, and he decided that he must make his home where a school would be available for his children. On 21 Aug. 1837 he had married Eliza Birnie, daughter of an HBC clerk, James Birnie; they were to have 13 children. Birnie had retired to Cathlamet (Wash.) on the lower Columbia and the Andersons settled nearby.

In 1858, curious to see something of the gold-rush, Anderson visited Victoria; James Douglas, by then governor of the colonies of Vancouver Island and British Columbia, urged him to move to Victoria and accept office. Anderson agreed and was appointed postmaster of Victoria, and served briefly as collector of customs of British Columbia. He also had business interests, including part-ownership of the Victoria Steam Navigation Company. In 1876 he was appointed dominion inspector of fisheries with jurisdiction over British Columbia coastal and inland waters. The same year the federal government asked him to act as its member on a dominion-provincial joint commission on Indian land in British Columbia. This proved a frustrating assignment for Anderson because the efforts of the commission to delimit Indian reserves were defeated by the hostility of the provincial government. The appointment ended in 1878. In 1882, when travelling on fisheries business, he was forced by an accident to spend a night on a sand-bar. He suffered severely from exposure and never fully recovered his health.

In addition to various reports and articles, Anderson wrote a *Hand-book and map to the gold region of Frazer's and Thompson's rivers*, and shortly after British Columbia joined confederation in 1871 he won a provincial government prize for an essay entitled *The dominion at the west; a brief description of the province of British Columbia.* In 1878 Hubert Howe Bancroft* visited Victoria in search of material for his *History of British Columbia* and Anderson wrote for him a substantial manuscript, partly autobiographical, entitled "History of the northwest coast." Bancroft considered him the "most scholarly" of all the HBC officers he interviewed and later penned this impression of him: "In personal appearance, at the time I saw him, he being then sixty-three years of age, Mr Anderson was of slight build, wiry make, active in mind and body, with a keen, penetrating eye, covered by lids which persisted in a perpetual and spasmodic winking, brought on years ago by snow-field exposures, and now become habitual. . . . In speech he was elegant and precise, and by no means so verbose as in his writings. . . ."

Anderson is commemorated in the naming of Anderson Lake, the Anderson River (a small tributary of the Fraser), and Anderson Island, in Puget Sound near Nisqually.

W. Kaye Lamb

A. C. Anderson was the author of *A brief account of the province of British Columbia, its climate and resources; an appendix to the British Columbia directory, 1882–83* (Victoria, 1883); *The dominion at the west; a brief description of the province of British Columbia, its climate and resources . . .* (Victoria, 1872); *Hand-book and map to the gold region of Frazer's and Thompson's rivers; with table of distances, to which is appended Chinook jargon – language used, etc., etc.* (San Francisco, [1858]); and *Notes on north-western America* (Montreal, 1876).

Brancroft Library, Univ. of California (Berkeley, Calif.), A. C. Anderson, "History of the northwest coast" (typescript at PABC, which also has the original journals of his exploring expeditions, some correspondence, and other papers). Univ. of British Columbia Library (Vancouver), Special Coll. Division, A. C. Anderson, "Writings of A. C. Anderson and other historical material," comp. E. A. Anderson (copy), which includes data from the Anderson family bible. [John McLoughlin], *The letters of John McLoughlin from Fort Vancouver to the governor and committee, [1825–46]*, ed. E. E. Rich and intro. W. K. Lamb (3v., London, 1941–44), II: 384–86. J. T. Walbran, *British Columbia coast names, 1592–1906 . . .* (Ottawa, 1909; repr. Vancouver, 1971), 20–21. H. H. Bancroft, *History of British Columbia, 1792–1887* (San Francisco, 1887), 157–70; *Literary industries* (San Francisco, 1890), 538. E. P. Creech, "Similkameen trails, 1846–61," *BCHQ*, 5 (1941): 256–62. Robin Fisher, "An exercise in futility: the joint commission on Indian land in British Columbia, 1875–1880," CHA *Hist. papers*, 1975: 75–94. J. C. Goodfellow, "Fur and gold in Similkameen," *BCHQ*, 2 (1938): 72–76. H. R. Hatfield, "On the brigade trail," *Beaver*, outfit 305 (summer 1974): 38–43. F. W. Howay, "The raison d'être of forts Yale and Hope," RSC *Trans.*, 3rd ser., 16 (1922), sect. II: 49–64.

ANDERSON, DAVID, Church of England priest and bishop; b. 10 Feb. 1814 in London, England, the only son of Captain Archibald Anderson; m. 1841 Miss Marsden, and they had three sons; d. 5 Nov. 1885 at Clifton (now part of Bristol), England.

David Anderson was educated at the Edinburgh Academy and at Exeter College, Oxford, where he graduated with a BA in 1836 and MA in 1838 (later receiving a BD and in 1849 a DD *honoris causa*). His academic career, however, was not outstanding. His attempt to win a fellowship at Exeter was such a strain that five days before his examination he collapsed from "nervous exhaustion." Instead he was forced, rather reluctantly, into the only other "respectable" calling – the church.

It was probably at Oxford that Anderson came to the attention of John Bird Sumner, the bishop of Chester. Sumner ordained him deacon at Clapham (now part of London) in 1837, and priest at Durham on 8 July 1838. Anderson's first charge was to Liverpool where he remained until 1841 when he was appointed vice-principal of St Bees College in the diocese of Carlisle. In 1847 Anderson became perpetual curate of All Saints' Church, Derby. When Sumner was raised to the see of Canterbury, it was not unexpected that he should offer his friend and protégé the recently established diocese of Rupert's Land, and on 29 May 1849 Sumner consecrated Anderson its first bishop. The diocese, which encompassed all of the enormous tract of land designated as Rupert's Land in the charter of the Hudson's Bay Company, was endowed by the estate of James Leith* and by the HBC. In addition to financial assistance, the latter provided a house and land at the Red River Settlement (Man.) for the bishop.

Anderson's incumbency was marked by religious and social controversy, resulting largely from the tensions which plagued the community. The settlement, moreover, could not support the aspirations of its sons and many succumbed to the beckoning of the open plains, alcohol, or the supposedly richer life in Canada and in the southern republic. Even upon his arrival at Red River, via York Factory (Man.), in October 1849 the bishop found himself involved in a rather hot debate with the settlement's Presbyterians. This group, remnants of the efforts of Lord Selkirk [Douglas*] to settle Scottish crofters on the plains early in the 19th century, thought they had too long suffered the ministrations of the clergy of the Church of England. After years of dispirited searching, the Presbyterians finally secured the services of a clergyman of their persuasion, John BLACK, who arrived in September 1851. Although they left the Anglican Upper Church (later St John's Church) peacefully, the Presbyterians demanded both compensation for their interest in the pews in which they had sat for some 20 years and the right to continue to bury their dead, according to Presbyterian practice, in the churchyard of St John's. The bishop, however, announced that he intended to make St John's his cathedral and to consecrate its graveyard, an act which would have prevented burial other than by Anglican practice. The resulting debate was so acrimonious that the London committee of the HBC, which governed Rupert's Land, had to intercede, and it advised the bishop to accommodate the Presbyterians. Although the bishop complied, his relations with them, the most prosperous element in Red River, were never to be improved. So bitter were his feelings that he refused the Presbyterian congregation the use of St John's while their church was under construction, declined all assistance from them after the great flood of 1852, and prevented Presbyterian students from attending his school.

Anderson did attempt to provide leadership in the years of discontent that followed his arrival in the settlement. He was a prime figure in the temperance movement, and he was at the forefront of the agitation to secure some change in Red River's constitutional status, arguing that the inhabitants of the settlement should have some direct involvement in their own government. One strategy, suggested by the Reverend Griffith Owen Corbett* and the Reverend John Chapman, was for the settlement to become a crown colony and the bishop supported this idea by signing a petition to the Colonial Office in 1862. A more radical movement led by William KENNEDY, Donald Gunn*, and James Ross* advocated annexation to Canada. When the fight between the two groups became bitter and their opposition to the HBC apparent, Anderson withdrew from the agitation.

The situation was further complicated in 1862 when the Sioux threatened the settlement [*see* Tatanka-najin*]. The Council of Assiniboia, of which the bishop was a prominent member, petitioned the Colonial Office for troops. But those pressing for a change in the political status of the settlement saw the petition as an insidious plot by a malevolent council dominated by the HBC to crush their movement. Then in December 1862, the Reverend Mr Corbett, who had opposed the request, was jailed for allegedly attempting an abortion on his maidservant; she, gossip had it, was pregnant with his child. Supporters of reform again argued that the charge was another HBC conspiracy, this time to get rid of the parson, a sympathizer. Anderson, who had initially advised Corbett to flee the settlement, held his own investigation and concurred with the finding of the court that Corbett was guilty [*see* James HUNTER]. In turn Anderson was condemned as an agent of the company conspiracy and his relations with his parishioners, always distant at best, were strained.

Anderson's problems in Red River were due in large part to his inability to control his divided and contentious clergy. His most prickly subordinate was the Reverend William Cockran* who had been in Red River since 1825 and had substantial influence in the settlement. Cockran also exerted considerable influence over Anderson and pressed the vacillating bishop to approve missions at Beaver Creek and at Portage la Prairie. It was also Cockran who in 1851 secured the resignation of the Reverend John Smithurst* because of allegations, unsubstantiated, of improprieties. Cockran and his considerable clerical and lay following considered themselves the settlement's watch-dogs against popery, Presbyterianism, and the native clergy, and managed to drag Anderson through an unending mire of contention and controversy.

In spite of these problems Anderson did have some successes. He placed the church on a firm footing and nurtured the roots of a creditable educational system. In 1849 there had been five Church of England clerics in Rupert's Land supported primarily by one missionary society in London, the Church Missionary Society; by 1864 there were 22, supported by the CMS, the Colonial and Continental Church Society, and the Society for the Propagation of the Gospel in Foreign Parts. Anderson was not able, however, to spread these clergy throughout Rupert's Land. In spite of short forays and the establishment of a few small missions the majority remained at Red River; HBC governor Sir George Simpson* had observed that the settlement had more clerics per person than any other part of the British empire. Although this concentration of clergy was due in part to Anderson's reluctance to press the HBC for further assistance, he was in fact too embroiled in events at Red River to direct his attention to the interior. He travelled only infrequently during his episcopacy, including visits to Moose Factory (Ont.) and Fort Albany (Ont.) in 1852, 1855, and 1860, and to the English River district (Ont.) in 1859.

The activity dearest to Anderson's heart was education. Shortly after his arrival in Red River he had purchased the Red River Academy from the estate of its former proprietor, the Reverend John Macallum*. Anderson renamed the academy St John's Collegiate School, introduced a rigorous course of classical studies, modern languages, and mathematics, and began a library which by 1855 numbered 800 volumes. The school, also a seminary, provided a thorough education and managed to send two scholars to the

University of Cambridge and one to the University of Toronto, as well as eight priests to interior missions. In 1855 Anderson turned over management of the college to Thomas Cochrane, William Cockran's son. Because of intemperate drinking habits, however, Thomas Cochrane was not popular in the community. His unpopularity, combined with easy access for the settlement's youth to American boarding-schools and an increasing dislike of the Church of England in the settlement, forced the closing of the school in 1859.

It must have been with some relief that Anderson quit Red River in 1864. The Corbett affair had rendered his position in the settlement untenable and he chose to retire to the serenity of Clifton, England. Here he could be close to his three sons who were in English boarding-schools. But his interest in Red River continued. As vicar of Clifton, and after 1866 as chancellor of St Paul's, London, he worked assiduously for the diocese of Rupert's Land collecting funds and speaking whenever asked. After a lengthy and debilitating illness, he died in 1885, leaving his sons a total of £674 10*s*.

FRITS PANNEKOEK

David Anderson was the author of *Britain's answer to the nations: a missionary sermon, preached in Saint Paul's Cathedral, on Sunday, May 3, 1857* (London, 1857); *A charge delivered to the clergy of the diocese of Rupert's Land, at his primary visitation* (London, 1851); *A charge delivered to the clergy of the diocese of Rupert's Land, at his triennial visitation in July and December, 1853* (London, 1854); *A charge delivered to the clergy of the diocese of Rupert's Land, at his triennial visitation, May 29, 1856* (London, 1856); *A charge delivered to the clergy of the diocese of Rupert's Land, in St. John's Church, Red River, at his triennial visitation, January 6, 1860* (London, 1860); *Children instead of fathers: a Christmas ordination sermon, preached at St. John's Church, Red River, on Sunday, December 25, 1853* (London, 1854); *The gospel in the regions beyond: a sermon preached in Lambeth Church, on Sunday, May 3, 1874, at the consecration of the bishops of Athabasca and Saskatchewan* (London, 1874); *The heart given to God and the work: an ordination sermon, preached in the Cathedral of Christ Church, Oxford, on Sunday, December 21, 1856* (London, 1857); *The net in the bay; or, journal of a visit to Moose and Albany* (London, 1854; 2nd ed., London, 1873; repr. [East Ardsley, Eng., and New York], 1967); *Notes of the flood at the Red River, 1852* (London, 1852); *The seal of apostleship: an ordination sermon preached at St. Andrew's Church, Red River, on Sunday, December 22, 1850* (London, 1851); *The truth and the conscience: an ordination sermon, preached at St. Andrew's Church, Red River, on Sunday, July 21, 1861* (London, 1861); *The winner of souls: a New-Year ordination sermon, preached at Saint John's Church, Red River, on Tuesday, January 1, 1856* (London, 1856).

CMS Arch., C, C.1, Rupert's Land inward, David Anderson to Henry Venn, 24 Jan. 1850. PAM, HBCA, A.11/96: f.339d; D.4/50: 64; D.5/30: ff.744–46; D.5/34: f.235; D.7/1: f.317; MG 2, C14, nos.29, 32, 33, 43, 56, 120. Somerset House (London), Probate Dept., Will of David Anderson, 7 Jan. 1886. USPG, E, 11, W. H. Taylor report, 12 Nov. 1862, pp.443–46. G.B., Parl., House of Commons paper, 1857, *Report from the select committee on the HBC*. William Knight, *Memoir of Henry Venn, B.D., prebendary of St. Paul's, and honorary secretary of the Church Missionary Society* (new ed., London, 1882). "Memorial of the late Bishop Anderson, of Clifton," *Gloucestershire Notes and Queries* (London), 3 (1887): 603–4. *Nor'Wester*, 1859–69.

Boon, *Anglican Church*. W. J. Fraser, "A history of St. John's College, Winnipeg" (MA thesis, Univ. of Manitoba, Winnipeg, 1966). Frits Pannekoek, "A probe into the demographic structure of nineteenth century Red River," *Essays on western history: in honour of Lewis Gwynne Thomas*, ed. L. H. Thomas (Edmonton, 1976), 81–95; "Protestant agricultural missions in the Canadian west to 1870" (MA thesis, Univ. of Alberta, Edmonton, 1970). C. F. Pascoe, *Two hundred years of the S.P.G.: an historical account of the Society for the Propagation of the Gospel in Foreign Parts, 1701–1900 . . .* (2v., London, 1901). Eugene Stock, *The history of the Church Missionary Society, its environment, its men and its work* (4v., London, 1899–1916). M. P. Wilkinson, "The episcopate of the Right Reverend David Anderson, D.D., first lord bishop of Rupert's Land, 1849–1864" (MA thesis, Univ. of Manitoba, 1950). T. C. B. Boon, "The archdeacon and the governor: William Cockran and George Simpson at the Red River colony, 1825–65," *Beaver*, outfit 298 (spring 1968): 41–49. Frits Pannekoek, "The Rev. Griffiths Owen Corbett and the Red River civil war of 1869–70," *CHR*, 57 (1976): 133–49.

ANDERSON, SAMUEL, royal engineer, boundary surveyor, and map-maker; b. 15 Nov. 1839 in London, England, son of Samuel Anderson; m. 10 Aug. 1876 Louisa Dorothea Brown; d. 11 Sept. 1881 at Bonnyrigg (Lothian), Scotland.

Samuel Anderson Sr, a writer to the signet, was registrar of affidavits at the Court of Chancery in London. There young "Sam" went to school, later going to St Andrews University and the Edinburgh Military Academy. He entered the Royal Military Academy at Woolwich (now part of London) on 11 Aug. 1857 in the first batch of cadets selected by competition. He won the sword for "exemplary conduct" and received a commission as lieutenant in the Royal Engineers on 21 Dec. 1858.

After a few months' service in England, Anderson was appointed to the staff of the boundary commission established under the Oregon Treaty of 15 June 1846 to survey and mark the 49th parallel from the Gulf of Georgia (Strait of Georgia) to the crest of the Rocky Mountains. The American party, under Archibald Campbell, had been at work since 1857 and the British land party, under Colonel John Summerfield Hawkins, RE, since July 1858. After intensive instruction in astronomy at the Ordnance Survey Office in Southampton, Anderson left England for Victoria, Vancouver Island, where he arrived on 2 Dec. 1859. He went inland at once to join the secretary of the British commission, Lieutenant Charles William Wilson, RE, who became a lifelong friend. Two years of zestful hard work and hard travelling followed. Anderson distinguished himself in reconnoitring ahead of the British working parties in wild and rugged country and in completing the determination and marking of difficult sections of the boundary line. In 1860–61 he was given charge of the survey office while the party was in winter quarters at Fort Colvile (Colville, Wash.). In 1862 the British party returned to England where Anderson, who succeeded Wilson as secretary, completed the maps and reports by 1864. After a delay of five years, he accompanied Hawkins to Washington, D.C., for the final joint meeting of the boundary commission, the maps being adopted by both governments on 24 Feb. 1870.

In the interval, Anderson served from November 1865 to June 1866 with Wilson under the aegis of the Palestine Exploration Fund, returning from the Holy Land with material for a detailed map of western Palestine. From 19 Nov. 1866 to 30 Nov. 1871 he held the appointment of assistant superintendent of the special schools for telegraphy and photography in the School of Military Engineering in Chatham, where he pioneered in using electricity for military purposes.

Meanwhile, a controversy about the latitude of the Hudson's Bay Company's Pembina post (West Lynne, Man.) had reopened the question of the unmarked gap in the Canadian-American boundary between the most northwestern point of the Lake of the Woods and the summit of the Rocky Mountains. Hawkins, Wilson, and Anderson were called upon to prepare an estimate of the cost of completing the survey, based on a careful plan of operation. A new joint commission was set up and in June 1872 Anderson was appointed chief astronomer to the British commission under the command of Captain Donald Roderick Cameron, RA. Anderson was the only member of the British party who had served with the earlier commission. While Cameron and Lieutenant Arthur Clitheroe Ward, RE, secretary of the British commission, went first to Washington to concert measures with Archibald Campbell, once more the American commissioner, and then on to Ottawa, Anderson completed the work of organization in England. He was promoted captain on 3 Aug. 1872 and brought out a party of Royal Engineers to join Cameron, arriving at Pembina on 18 Sept. 1872. There a contingent of Canadian government appointees also joined the party, among them George Mercer Dawson*.

Cameron and Anderson paid an official visit to Campbell. After that, Anderson was left for the most part to "bear the burden of organization." It proved difficult in the field to find the starting point for the work of the commission, since the reference monument on the Lake of the Woods erected by the joint commission of 1822–26 could not be found, until the Honourable James McKay* induced Indians to identify its site. Disagreement developed between Cameron and Anderson about the starting point of the survey and also about the method to be adopted in "running the line," Anderson concurring with the Americans. The British party worked through the winter of 1872–73, despite its severity, because the swamps west of the Lake of the Woods were accessible only when frozen. Anderson, at Pembina, cooperated in determining by telegraph the longitude of Pembina with Lindsay Alexander Russell*, assistant surveyor general of Canada, who had gone to the observatory at Chicago for this purpose. Anderson also made careful plans for the short summer seasons of 1873 and 1874 when, assisted by 30 mixed-blood scouts, he carried out advance reconnaissance to find possible transport routes and sites for camps and depots. The work of the British commission, pushed forward by Anderson with unremitting energy, was completed by 30 Aug. 1874, with 860 miles of boundary determined and marked west of Pembina. Anderson found the marker at the crest of the Rocky Mountains to connect with the work of the earlier commission. The most serious difficulties had been lack of water, wood, and grass; transport problems in rugged terrain; and, above all, mosquitoes.

The British commission worked in Ottawa on reports and maps from October 1874 to the summer of 1875, with a visit to Washington in January. On his return to London, Anderson completed the work on the record maps of the commission and on 29 May 1876 both commissioners and both chief astronomers signed the maps, reports, and protocol of agreement. Anderson's services were recognized by the award in 1877 of a CMG. He had been elected a fellow of the Royal Geographical Society in 1876.

Transferred on 1 Sept. 1876 to the War Office as assistant inspector of submarine defences, Anderson became inspector in June 1881, using his special knowledge of electricity to develop mines for defensive purposes. Promoted major on 13 Sept. 1879, he was detached for two more special assignments: as British commissioner for the delimitation of the Serbian frontier in 1879, and in July 1880 as a witness before Lord Morley's War Office committee on the pay and conditions of service for officers of the Royal Artillery and Royal Engineers.

Anderson died at his mother's home, Dalhousie Grange, in Scotland. His memory is perpetuated in the name of Anderson Peak in the Rockies. His zeal, outstanding ability, thoroughness, tact, and humanity gave him a leading role in the difficult and important work of establishing "boundary peace and permanence" for western Canada.

IRENE M. SPRY

Samuel Anderson, "The North-American boundary from the Lake of the Woods to the Rocky Mountains," Royal Geographical Soc., *Journal* (London), 46 (1876): 228–62.

Beinecke Rare Book and Manuscript Library, Yale Univ. (New Haven, Conn.), Samuel Anderson letters (uncatalogued western American mss.). PAC, RG 48, 29–32. PRO, FO 5/811, 5/814–15, 5/1466–68, 5/1474–77, 5/1505–6, 5/1532, 5/1666–70, 925/1566 (mfm. at PAC, National Map Coll.). Can., Dept. of the Interior, *Certain correspondence of the Foreign Office and of the Hudson's Bay Company copied from original documents, London, 1898*, [comp. O. J. Klotz] (Ottawa, 1899), pts. III-IV (copy at PAC, MG 30, C13, 7). [Albany] Featherstonhaugh, "Narrative of the operations of the British North American Boundary Commission, 1872–76," *Papers on Subjects Connected with the Duties of the Corps of Royal Engineers* (Woolwich, Eng.), new ser., 23 (1876): 24–69. G.B., Parl., Command paper, 1875, LXXXII, [1131], pp. 51–56, *North America, no. 1 (1875): correspondence respecting the determination of the north-western boundary between Canada and the United States*; 1876, LXXXII, [1552], pp.357–68, *North America, no. 8 (1876): further correspondence respecting the determination of the boundary between Canada and the United States*. . . . International Boundary Commission, *Joint report upon the survey and demarcation of the boundary between the United States and Canada from the Gulf of Georgia to the northwesternmost point of Lake of the Woods* . . . (Washington, 1937), 194–217. *Maps of the land boundary between the British possessions in North America and the United States, as established by the Treaty of Washington, 15th June, 1846, and surveyed and marked under the direction of the Joint Commission appointed to carry into effect the 1st article of the treaty* (Southampton, Eng., 1869). [Thomas Millman], "Impressions of the west in the early 'seventies, from the diary of the assistant surgeon of the B.N.A. Boundary Survey, Dr. Thomas Millman . . . ," Women's Canadian Hist. Soc. of Toronto, *Annual Report and Trans.*, 26 (1927–28): 17–55. North American Boundary Commission, 1872–1876, *Joint maps of the northern boundary of the United States, from the Lake of the Woods to the summit of the Rocky Mountains* . . . ([Washington, 1878]); *Reports upon the survey of the boundary between the territory of the United States and the possessions of Great Britain from the Lake of the Woods to the summit of the Rocky Mountains* . . . (Washington, 1878). *Royal Engineers Journal* (Brompton, Eng.), 11 (1881): 227–29. Royal Geographical Soc., *Proc.* (London), new ser., 3 (1881): 671. [C. W. Wilson], *Mapping the frontier: Charles Wilson's diary of the survey of the 49th parallel, 1858–1862, while secretary of the British Boundary Commission*, ed. G. F. G. Stanley (Toronto, 1970).

Marcus Baker, *Survey of the northwestern boundary of the United States, 1857–1861* (Washington, 1900). J. E. Parsons, *West on the 49th parallel: Red River to the Rockies, 1872–1876* (New York, 1963). Whitworth Porter, *History of the Corps of Royal Engineers* (2v., London and New York, 1889), II: 255–68. D. W. Thomson, *Men and meridians; the history of surveying and mapping in Canada* (3v., Ottawa, 1966–69), II: 162–76.

ANNAND, WILLIAM, farmer, politician, publisher, and businessman; b. 10 April 1808 at Halifax, N.S., son of William Annand and Jane Russell; m. first 19 Nov. 1830 Emily Cuff of Halifax, and they had two sons; m. secondly, in January 1834, Martha Tupper of Stewiacke, N.S., and they had four sons and five daughters; d. 12 Oct. 1887 in London, England.

William Annand's father, a Presbyterian from Banffshire, Scotland, immigrated in the mid 1780s to Halifax where he achieved modest success as a merchant. Annand Sr died in 1824 leaving to his two sons, William and James, an estate valued at £7,000. Dispatched to Scotland for further education, the Annand brothers returned to Nova Scotia in the late 1820s intent on becoming gentlemen farmers. They brought a "number of well bred cattle" with them to the several hundred acres of land they had inherited from their father in the upper Musquodoboit River valley. Although not initially profitable, their farm, with its "very handsome and commodious house . . . furnished in very excellent style," gave the Annands the rank of country squires.

Anxious to lay claim to a formal leadership role in community affairs, William in 1836 rallied support among his neighbours and secured nomination to a seat in the assembly. His candidacy had radical overtones, since the Musquodoboit area had traditionally been represented by members of the Halifax business and professional élite. Annand's challenge to convention was underscored when he issued an election card pledging to work for such reforms as assembly control over all public revenue, curtailment of official salaries, improvement of rural roads, and "a more efficient School system . . . [so] that the advantages of education may be extended to all classes of the community." By articulating rural alienation against the prevailing urban-commercial oligarchy, Annand became part of the reform movement then taking shape in Nova Scotia under the leadership of Joseph Howe*. Once elected, Annand rarely spoke in debates, but, by dutifully following Howe's lead, he consolidated his reputation as a Reformer. In 1843, however, he conspicuously called for an end to public financial grants to Nova Scotia's sectarian colleges in favour of establishing a single, non-denominational institution of higher education. The scheme died amidst sectional and sectarian rivalries, but by polarizing public opinion his proposals contributed to the disintegration of the coalition government led by Howe and James William Johnston*, thereby hurrying the coming of responsible government.

Annand was dumped from the Reform ticket in 1843 in favour of Laurence O'Connor Doyle*, a representative of Halifax's Irish Roman Catholic community, but in compensation Howe offered him a loan to buy and be editor of the *Novascotian*, Halifax's most widely read weekly newspaper. Annand's entry into publishing satisfied his personal ambition and relieved the domestic pressures caused by his second wife's desire to leave Musquodoboit and "play the lady instead of the farmer's wife," in Howe's words.

Within a year Annand founded the *Morning Chronicle*, a penny tri-weekly, while continuing the *Novascotian*. Reinforced by Howe's occasional services as editor, Annand's papers championed the cause of responsible government. In 1851, three years after the overthrow of oligarchy, he re-entered the assembly as member for Halifax County. Inside the house he acquired the nickname "Boots" for his unswerving loyalty to Howe through the various party realignments precipitated by railway and religious issues. Impeded by a "poor and thin" speaking voice and a "halting" oratorical style, Annand was nevertheless considered "an industrious committee man." His loyalty was rewarded in 1854 with the lucrative post of queen's printer. Although he lost the appointment in 1857 after ethnic and denominational feuding had brought the Conservatives to power, he retained his seat in the assembly. When the Liberals regained power in 1860 Annand's seniority in the party and friendship with Howe secured him the post of financial secretary.

By this time political opponents were describing Annand as a "slick, oily" individual who had been elevated to a position beyond his ability by obsequious loyalty to his party superiors. Circumstantial evidence confirms that Annand had attained only second-rank status in Halifax society. Although elected vice-president of the prestigious North British Society, he never attained the presidency nor did he appear as a director of other philanthropic or business organizations in the capital. Nevertheless, as proprietor of the *Morning Chronicle*, a daily by 1864, and as a rate-payer occupying premises valued at £1,800 in 1862, Annand was firmly established within Halifax's middle class. His political position proved to be less secure. In 1862 controversy erupted when Charles Tupper*, *de facto* leader of the Conservative party, disclosed that Annand had been speculating in land, allegedly in an effort to fleece British investors anxious to acquire gold mines in Nova Scotia. Although fraud could not be proven against Annand, the incident contributed to the defeat of the Liberal government in the general election of 1863. Paradoxically, Annand retained his seat and was able to establish himself as a leading figure among the small band of Liberals who survived the election.

In the autumn of 1864 Annand returned from a business trip to England to find Nova Scotia alive with controversy over the attempt by Tupper and several other members of the province's political and business élite to carry Nova Scotia into a British North American political union. The *Morning Chronicle* had come out in favour of union, but its editor, Jonathan McCully*, had acted on his own initiative. After a brief period of hesitation, Annand declared himself opposed to the federation scheme worked out at Quebec. Speaking at a public rally held at Halifax in December 1864, Annand declared that, while he favoured Maritime union, "the time for the consummation of the larger scheme had not arrived." This announcement was followed by McCully's dismissal from the paper and the publication of Howe's "Botheration" letters which maintained that only traitors and fools could advocate Nova Scotia's union with Canada.

Despite having established himself as a leading anti-confederate in the assembly debates in early 1865, events over the next few months suggested that Annand's opposition to colonial union lacked total conviction. With Howe temporarily absent from Nova Scotia and the imperial government exerting strong pressure to win converts to confederation, Annand began to equivocate. After an interview with the colonial secretary in London in the summer of 1865 he was convinced that the imperial authorities would "use every means in their power, short of [physical] coercion" to implement confederation. Significantly, Annand's return to Halifax was followed by the appearance of editorials in the *Morning Chronicle* proposing another intercolonial conference to work out revised terms of union. He later rationalized this seeming endorsement of the principle of union by insisting that his editorials had been written "in the hope that the delegates would not agree when they met, and, even if they did, that the question would be referred to the people for their ultimate approval." Many contemporaries concluded, however, that ambition had prompted Annand to edge toward union once its achievement became probable.

Before the 1866 session Annand again urged his anti-confederate allies to support a new conference on colonial union, but he remained evasive as to whether his ultimate objective was pure obstructionism or the negotiation of better terms. In all probability, Annand had not yet made up his mind. Under the circumstances his indecision proved disastrous for the anti-confederate forces. A number of assemblymen, anxious to curry favour with the ascendant unionist forces, bypassed Annand to make independent deals with the Tupper government. By the time the house convened Annand commanded no more than a weak minority and was powerless to defeat Tupper's pro-confederation resolution in April 1866 or to shape the Nova Scotian delegation sent to London to negotiate the final terms of union.

When Howe returned to Halifax in March 1866 he immediately supplanted Annand as anti-confederate leader and set about organizing a mass protest against Tupper's legislative coup. A delegation headed by Howe and including Annand went to London in July 1866 to lobby against Nova Scotia's inclusion in confederation. While in London Annand contributed a pamphlet to the anti-confederate cause, and then after the passage of the British North America Act in March

1867 returned home in May to lead a final but futile struggle against Tupper on the floor of the assembly. Annand declared that he had resolved to "dedicate the remaining years of my life" to the goal of extracting Nova Scotia from the "hateful and obnoxious" union. As an active campaigner in the joint federal and provincial elections held in September 1867, Annand could claim a measure of credit for the massive repudiation of the unionists at the polls. In March 1868 he and Howe were in London to protest Nova Scotia's inclusion in confederation. The imperial government's refusal to countenance more than minor revisions to the BNA Act plunged the anti-confederate movement into divisive debate, and launched Annand into the most controversial phase of his political career.

Although he had been defeated by Tupper in the September 1867 federal election in Cumberland, Annand was given a seat in Nova Scotia's appointed Legislative Council. With Howe removed to the federal scene, Annand became provincial treasurer and took command of the anti-confederate provincial administration. But leadership over a motley collection of ex-Liberals and ex-Conservatives, including such strong-minded individuals as Attorney General Martin Isaac WILKINS, presented Annand with a major challenge. Temperamentally incapable of more than cautious manipulation to maintain unity among his tempestuous followers, the new premier prudently avoided taking bold initiatives on controversial issues. Thus, when the anti-confederates met at Halifax in the summer of 1868 to plot future strategy, Annand let Howe speak first. Howe recommended negotiations with the Canadians for better terms, but Annand, fearing a revolt among his assembly supporters if he abandoned repeal, declared himself opposed to compromise. Simultaneously, however, the premier sought a "backstairs" interview with Sir John A. Macdonald* to ascertain what terms Nova Scotia might secure from the Ottawa government.

Late in 1868 Annand announced that his administration would petition Britain's new Liberal government to grant Nova Scotia release from confederation. At the same time he told Howe that should the petition fail, he would "go for annexation" with the United States. The prevailing atmosphere of diplomatic and military tension gave this empty boast sinister implications. Howe emotionally repudiated Annand and with Archibald Woodbury MCLELAN began negotiations for better terms with the federal government. Confronted by Howe's action, the provincial cabinet shifted course and pressed for inclusion of one of its members in the talks. Both Howe and Macdonald refused to allow provincial participation, and in January 1869 Nova Scotia was granted a modest increase in her financial subsidy from the federal treasury and Howe agreed to enter Macdonald's cabinet.

Rocked by Howe's defection and the simultaneous rejection of repeal by the imperial government, the Nova Scotia government sought retaliation. When Howe entered a by-election in Hants County to confirm his acceptance of federal executive office, Annand engineered a savage campaign designed to destroy the career of his lifelong associate. Howe's victory, combined with detailed revelations of what one contemporary described as Annand's "insincerity and wavering imbecility of purpose" might have been expected to demolish the premier's public reputation. He clung to office, however, extending his political career for another five years by identifying himself with the Nova Scotian majority which was reluctant to accept confederation.

Following the débâcle in Hants, the provincial executive placated their more extreme followers with defiant reaffirmations of the repeal cause. Rhetoric aside, however, Annand remained content to work within the existing constitutional framework, seeking greater autonomy for Nova Scotia, an expanded federal subsidy, greater Maritime representation in the House of Commons, and provincial nomination of senators. Ignored by Macdonald, the Nova Scotia government retaliated by disenfranchising federal employees and refusing to surrender possession of a new government building in Halifax. While frivolous, these gestures gave Annand the appearance of being a champion of provincial rights. In 1871, campaigning as the "Nova Scotia Party," his government secured re-election, albeit with a sharply reduced majority. During the federal election of 1872 the Annand government supported Alexander Mackenzie*'s Ontario-based Liberal party. The *Morning Chronicle* said this tactic would punish unionist "traitors" and help elect a party that would provide "moderately good government for the Dominion while we remain part of it." After the revelations of the "Pacific Scandal" brought Mackenzie to power in 1873, Annand's administration dropped talk of repeal and began stressing how Nova Scotia would profit from a close alliance with the new national government.

Annand's political metamorphosis was dictated more by considerations of expediency than principle. As public enthusiasm for the anti-confederate cause declined, the Nova Scotia government manœuvred to find alternate means of legitimizing its existence. Annand decided that his political survival required a commitment to resource development. Accordingly, his government in 1872 inaugurated a policy of subsidizing the construction of branch railways throughout the province. But a scarcity of private investment capital and regional demands for railway service hampered the programme and threatened to bring down Annand's government. By allying himself with Mackenzie's administration, Annand hoped to receive federal assistance for Nova Scotia's railways. In December 1874 he went to the electorate with a pledge of "immediate construction" of a line from New Glasgow to the Strait of Canso. Seemingly victorious at the polls, the government saw its majority dissolve after the federal government declared it would cooperate only in the construction of a railway reaching into the Cape Breton coal fields. This announcement devastated the province's development strategy since private contractors willing to build the longer line could not be found.

The collapse of his railway programme, persistent though unsubstantiated rumours of personal speculation in mining and railway stocks at the public expense, and his refusal to seek election to the assembly damaged Annand's position. Late in 1874, Philip Carteret Hill*, former leader of the anti-Annand forces in the assembly, joined the administration and in May 1875 replaced Annand as premier. Annand was appointed Canada's agent general in London, a post with little prestige which he was forced to vacate when Mackenzie's government was defeated in 1878. Annand continued to live in London and served as Nova Scotia's agent until his death in 1887.

William Annand possessed neither outstanding ability nor great depth of character. After leading an essentially prosaic business and political career, the confederation crisis gave him a leadership responsibility he could not discharge successfully. In his hands, the anti-confederate movement deteriorated into a parochial defence of the *status quo* and then expired amidst cynical inertia. Despite a remarkably long tenure as premier, Annand left no lasting imprint on provincial affairs and was remembered only as a mediocrity who lived in exciting times.

DAVID A. SUTHERLAND

William Annand was the author of *Confederation: a letter to the Right Honourable the Earl of Carnarvon, principal secretary of state for the colonies* (London, 1866), and editor of *The speeches and public letters of the Hon. Joseph Howe* (2v., Boston, 1858).

Halifax County Court of Probate (Halifax), A42 (original estate papers of William Annand Sr) (mfm. at PANS). Halifax County Registry of Deeds (Halifax), Deeds, 59, 65 (mfm. at PANS). PAC, MG 24, B29. PANS, MG 4, 48 (St Matthew's Church, Halifax), baptisms; RG 1, 203, 203a, 203b; RG 2, sect.2, 7, 1869–71; RG 32, 149–50; RG 35 A, 4. "[Four letters to William Garvie]," PANS *Report* (Halifax), 1948, app.C: 35–56. "Howe-Annand correspondence," PANS *Report*, 1957, app.C: 21–36. N.S., House of Assembly, *Debates and proc.*, 1855–75; *Journal and proc.*, 1836–75; Legislative Council, *Debates and proc.*, 1875; *Statutes*, 1867–75. *Acadian Recorder*, 1824, 1851, 1856, 1859–60. *British Colonist* (Halifax), 1851, 1854–55, 1859, 1869–73. *Christian Messenger* (Halifax), 1843. *Evening Express* (Halifax), 1859, 1865. *Halifax Evening Reporter*, 1865, 1874. *Morning Chronicle* (Halifax), 1844–75, 1887, 1909. *Morning Herald* (Halifax), 1875, 1877, 1887. *Novascotian*, 1836–43. *Times* (Halifax), 1843. *Unionist and Halifax Journal*, 1865.

Belcher's farmer's almanack, 1860–65. *Directory of N.S. MLAs*. R. J. Long, *Nova Scotia authors and their work, a bibliography of the province* (East Orange, N.J., 1918). North British Soc., *Annals, North British Society, Halifax, Nova Scotia, with portraits and biographical notes, 1768–1903*, comp. J. S. Macdonald ([3rd ed.], Halifax, 1905). *Standard dict. of Canadian biog.* (Roberts and Tunnell). Creighton, *Road to confederation*. G. M. Haliburton, "A history of railways in Nova Scotia" (MA thesis, Dalhousie Univ., Halifax, 1955). K. G. Pryke, "Nova Scotia and confederation, 1864–1870" (PHD thesis, Duke Univ., Durham, N.C., 1962). E. M. Saunders, *Three premiers of Nova Scotia: the Hon. J. W. Johnstone, the Hon. Joseph Howe, the Hon. Charles Tupper, M.D., C.B.* (Toronto, 1909). Waite, *Life and times of confederation*. Marguerite Woodworth, *History of the Dominion Atlantic Railway* ([Kentville, N.S.], 1936). L. J. Burpee, "Joseph Howe and the anti-confederation league," RSC *Trans.*, 3rd ser., 10 (1916–17), sect.II: 409–73. [Benjamin] Russell, "Reminiscences of a legislature," *Dalhousie Rev.*, 3 (1923–24): 5–16.

ARCHAMBEAULT (Archambault), LOUIS, notary and politician; b. 7 Nov. 1814 at Longue-Pointe (now part of Montreal), Lower Canada, son of Jacques Archambault, a farmer, and Catherine Raimondvert; m. first 9 Aug. 1839 Éloïse (Élise) Roy, at Saint-Roch-de-l'Achigan; m. secondly 17 July 1848 Marguerite-Élisabeth Dugal, at Terrebonne, and their children included Horace, politician and judge, and Joseph-Alfred, first bishop of Joliette; d. 3 March 1890 at L'Assomption, Que.

Louis Archambeault, who had only a primary education, was commissioned as a notary in 1836, and went into practice at Saint-Roch-de-l'Achigan, where he became mayor. On 18 March 1843 he was appointed registrar of Leinster County, divided in 1853 into L'Assomption and Montcalm. He was a warden of Leinster from 1848 and was re-elected by acclamation in L'Assomption County in September 1854 for a year, as he was again in 1877. In 1855 he left Saint-Roch-de-l'Achigan for the village of L'Assomption, where he was to be mayor from 1877 to 1882.

He took an intense interest in the question of the abolition of seigneurial tenure, and campaigned actively in the "anti-seigneurial convention of the district of Montreal." In 1853 this body adopted a plan for abolition, but Archambeault opposed the proposal because it involved redemption of seigneurial dues by the government. Archambeault asserted that "he considered it neither just nor equitable that public funds should be used to reimburse the *censitaires* to the detriment of workers in the city and the habitants of the Eastern Townships, who are not involved in the question and who also pay their quota into the public coffers." He put forward an alternative, which *Le Canadien* (Quebec City) considered preferable to the convention's proposal "as a plan for an immediate and general commutation." His participation in the debate earned him a reputation for competence; hence on 3 March 1855 he was appointed one of ten seigneurial commissioners to compile a land register.

In 1855 Rouge MLA Joseph Papin* accused him of having inadequately discharged his responsibility as a returning officer in the 1851 and 1854 elections. An inquiry in fact established that Archambeault had padded his accounts and improperly drawn a sum of about £150. Although this was a common practice at the time, he was relieved of his duties as registrar and seigneurial commissioner in January 1856; shortly after, he resigned as lieutenant-colonel in the militia. In the 1858 election Archambeault satisfied his desire for revenge by running against Papin, who was at a disadvantage because of the stand he had taken on denominational schools. To the surprise of most people, Archambeault defeated Papin by 18 votes. In 1861, however, over-confidence and poor organization led to his defeat by Alexandre Archambault, brother of Pierre-Urgel*. Since religious teaching in schools and Louis Archambeault's integrity were issues debated in the two elections, it seems possible that the voters had changed their minds about both matters. As compensation George-Étienne Cartier* reinstated him on 1 Feb. 1862 as lieutenant-colonel in the militia but on 6 September, after the Liberals had come to power, Archambeault was again relieved of his appointment. From this time election contests in L'Assomption became a kind of clan rivalry or feud between two families: according to *La Minerve* (Montreal), in the 1863 elections Louis Archambeault not only had to face the MLA who was outgoing but also "All the Archambaults, brothers, nephews, cousins of the great Alexandre . . . [who were] campaigning." *Le Pays* of Montreal contended that Archambeault regained his seat with the help of clerical intervention.

Louis Archambeault showed no enthusiasm for the Quebec resolutions in 1865. He thought they set out "a system closer to legislative than to federative union." But Cartier overcame his friend's reservations. On 15 July 1867 Archambeault was made commissioner of agriculture and public works in the government of Pierre-Joseph-Olivier CHAUVEAU in the new province of Quebec. From 2 Nov. 1867 he represented the division of Repentigny in the Legislative Council. The Conservative press approved, but *Le Pays* was shocked at the choice of a "legally convicted thief," of an "extortioner condemned by the highest authority in the country."

On the whole Archambeault proved an excellent minister. He was active in all of the many areas in his department, one of the most important in the Quebec government. With the help of assistant commissioner Siméon Le Sage* he made organizational changes, replacing the Board of Agriculture by an agricultural council controlled more closely by the executive. He protected the schools of agriculture of Sainte-Anne-de-la-Pocatière (La Pocatière) [*see* François PILOTE] and L'Assomption (which he had helped to found [*see* Pierre-Urgel Archambault]), against those who were pressing for a single school.

Increasing emigration to the United States was profoundly disturbing to the national conscience. Politicians turned to the only available solution – the settlement of new lands. Archambeault's work in this area is even more worthy of note than his work in agriculture. The laws which his efforts led to were to remain in force until the end of the century. Government financial assistance to settlement was greater between 1869 and 1873 than at any other time until 1900, except under the ministries of John Jones Ross* and Honoré Mercier*. To maintain the demographic balance within the Canadian federation, he sought to attract French-speaking immigrants, particularly rural people who were "moral and law-abiding," and had a little money saved; never has Quebec taken as much initiative in this sphere as it did during the early 1870s. The sums voted at that time were double what they would be in 1880–81, and five times as much as in 1898–99.

Beyond serving as legislative councillor and minister, Archambeault also ran in the federal elections of 1867, defeating Pierre-Urgel Archambault by 233 votes. After the double mandate was abolished by federal law, Archambeault resigned from the House of Commons on 2 Jan. 1874 and did not run in the 1874 elections. In that year he was implicated in the Tanneries scandal, which brought about the fall of the Gédéon Ouimet* cabinet and left him only the role of legislative councillor; he returned to practise as a notary. The Tanneries scandal, an episode in the land speculation fever raging in the Montreal region during the 1870s, was caused by the government's exchange of a plot of land for a less valuable one whose price had been artificially inflated. Speculators were thought to have shared part of the profit with their political associates. Archambeault persistently declared his innocence, but even the most sympathetic observer cannot avoid feeling uneasy. As commissioner of public works in the Ouimet government he was primarily responsible for the exchange. He did not manage to explain convincingly the famous $50,000 deposited in his name. His personal integrity was not, however, in question; the suspicion was that the transaction was designed to ensure the financial future of *La Minerve* and replenish the party's coffers. Archambeault disapproved of Ouimet's resignation, prompted by the departure of the three English-speaking members of his cabinet, and asserted: "I would have tried to fill the gaps [left by the ministers who resigned]. . . . On the supposition that no Englishman would want to enter the government, I would have called upon Canadiens instead. . . . This vigorous approach would have made these Englishmen reconsider, and would ultimately have brought them round to us." Like Ouimet he uncovered "odious plots, traitors, villains" at the bottom of the affair. One name in particular emerged, that of the former attorney general, George Irvine*, who had been the first to resign. In spite of his experience could Archambeault have been as much victim as accomplice?

Be that as it may, he did not re-examine his political allegiance. Circumstances and differences of opinion nevertheless did change his thinking. In the first place he was opposed to a new plan for the Quebec, Montreal, Ottawa and Occidental Railway which the cabinet of Charles-Eugène Boucher* de Boucherville advocated (that is, to abandon the Bout-de-l'Île line through L'Assomption for another passing through Terrebonne). After the 1878 *coup d'état* [*see* Luc LETELLIER de Saint-Just] Premier Henri-Gustave Joly* offered Archambeault a portfolio but he declined and remained in the Legislative Council, voting "for the ministerial proposals that appeared sound and worth adopting." He was in favour of the Joseph-Adolphe Chapleau* ministry at first but attacked it vehemently over the sale of the Quebec, Montreal, Ottawa and Occidental Railway to Louis-Adélard SENÉCAL and the Canadian Pacific syndicate. The Louis RIEL affair was the cause of the final stage in his evolution: he became a "National" Conservative, shoulder to shoulder with his former enemies, Liberals and Ultramontanes, in the same political movement. On 6 June 1888 he gave up his seat on the Legislative Council in favour of his son Horace, whom the press also labelled a National Conservative. Horace eventually completed the evolution in political allegiance begun by his father by becoming a Liberal minister; but when Louis left public life, *L'Étendard* of Montreal wrote that he had "always been an out-and-out Conservative."

Archambeault made a lasting name for himself not only in political history but also in the notarial profession. A member of the Montreal Board of Notaries from 1848 on, he sat on its executive from 1859 and was its president from 1865 to 1870. He held the same position on the Provincial Board of Notaries (1870–76). In both law and agriculture, Archambeault was a reformer. He was responsible in 1870 for the law which, chiefly through the creation of the single board, helped to raise the notarial profession from the depths to which it had sunk [*see* Louis-Édouard GLACKMEYER].

His career, fruitful but chequered, was overshadowed by the scandals of 1856 and 1874. Firm, energetic, and aggressive, he was one of the strong men of the Chauveau and Ouimet cabinets. According to an anonymous biographer, "his knowledge of constitutional law and his talents as an administrator should have ensured him a place in the cabinet even before confederation. His difficulty in handling the English language always led him to refuse offers made to him on various occasions." Had he mastered it, he could have asserted his claim to succeed Cartier, in preference to Hector-Louis Langevin*, a brilliant subordinate but a mediocre leader.

PIERRE and LISE TRÉPANIER

[No Louis Archambeault papers exist but various repositories hold separate items. Some of Archambeault's official correspondence is at ANQ-Q, in the public works records (PQ, TP) for the years 1867–74. This material includes a few of Archambeault's letters to officials in his department written in the course of his numerous absences; after having dealt with current concerns, he occasionally added personal comments on the politics of the day. The Siméon Le Sage papers (AP-G-149) contain one letter from Archambeault to Le Sage and several from the latter to him. At PAC, the Gédéon Ouimet papers (MG 27, I, F8, 1–2) in particular should be consulted for the Tanneries affair. There are also one or two items in the papers of John A. Macdonald* (MG 26, A), George-Étienne Cartier (MG 27, I, D4), and Francis-Joseph Audet* (MG 30, D1). The Joseph-Israël Tarte* papers (MG 27, II, D16), contain a lengthy and interesting letter on the confederation scheme written by Archambeault to Joseph-Guillaume Barthe*. ASQ holds a letter from Pierre-Joseph-Olivier Chauveau to Hospice-Anthelme-Jean-Baptiste Verreau* which mentions Archambeault (Fonds Viger-Verreau, carton 96: no.105). The collection Baby (P 58, U) at AUM has two of Archambeault's letters. For his militia career, *see* PAC, RG 9, I, C4; C5; and C6. P.T. and L.T.]

AC, Joliette, État civil, Catholiques, Saint-Roch-de-l'Achigan, 9 août 1839; Terrebonne (Saint-Jérôme), État civil, Catholiques, Saint-Louis (Terrebonne), 17 juill. 1848. ANQ-M, État civil, Catholiques, Saint-François-d'Assise (Montréal), 7 nov. 1814. Can., prov. du, Assemblée législative, *App. des journaux*, 1854–55, VIII: app.N; 1857, VII: app.43: VIII: app.51; Parl., *Doc. de la session*, 1862, IV: no.24; févr.–mai 1863, V: no.29. *Documents relatifs à l'échange des propriétés des Tanneries, près de Montréal* (n.p., n.d.). Qué., Commission royale, *Enquête concernant le chemin de fer de Québec, Montréal, Ottawa et Occidental* (4v., Québec, 1887), III: 78–90. Achintre, *Manuel électoral. Biographie de l'hon. Louis Archambeault, ministre de l'agriculture et commissaire des T. P. pour Québec, conseiller législatif et membre des Communes* (n.p., 1873). Anastase Forget, *Histoire du collège de L'Assomption; 1833 – un siècle – 1933* (Montréal, [1933]). M. Hamelin, *Premières années du parlementarisme québécois.* Christian Roy, *Histoire de L'Assomption* (L'Assomption, Qué., 1967), 321–22, 441–42, 462–63, 498. J.-E. Roy, *Hist. du notariat*, II: 548; III: 240, 247, 292–93, 321, 330–483; IV: 1–32, 71–75, 100, 121, 178–94, 269–71, 357–59, 426–40. J.-J. Lefebvre, "Les Archambault au Conseil législatif; quelques précisions sur sir Horace, l'hon. Louis et l'hon. Pierre-Urgel Archambault," *BRH*, 59 (1953): 23–28.

ARCHIBALD, Sir EDWARD MORTIMER, lawyer and office-holder; b. 10 May 1810 at Truro,

N.S., fifth son among 15 children of Samuel George William Archibald* and Elizabeth Dickson; m. 10 Sept. 1834 Katherine Elizabeth Richardson, and they had two sons and six daughters; d. 8 Feb. 1884 in London, England.

From the time that the Archibald family settled at Truro in 1762, it was prominent in the public life of Nova Scotia, particularly in the fields of law and politics. Edward Mortimer Archibald was to follow in this tradition. He attended private elementary schools at Truro and was enrolled in the newly established Halifax Grammar School when his father moved to Halifax to assume the offices of attorney general and surrogate of the Vice-Admiralty Court of the province. Edward was later a pupil at Thomas McCulloch*'s Pictou Academy before entering his father's office to study law. In 1831 he was called to the bar of Nova Scotia. On 10 October of that year he was appointed chief clerk and registrar of the Supreme Court of Newfoundland on the resignation of his brother Charles Dickson*. Edward did not arrive in St John's to assume office, however, until 8 Nov. 1832. He immediately began to practise as a barrister and attorney and so quickly demonstrated his competence that when, toward the end of 1833, there was a temporary vacancy in the Supreme Court, Governor Thomas John Cochrane* appointed Archibald acting assistant judge. He held that position through the ensuing term and during the midsummer term of 1834, discharging his duties efficiently.

Archibald had arrived in Newfoundland on the eve of the inauguration of representative government and he was to be close to the storm-centre of the tumultuous political events that led to responsible government in 1854. His role in these events was a significant one, not only because the judiciary was so closely involved with the politics of the early assemblies, but also because he held the additional office of clerk of the General Assembly.

Archibald became involved in the quarrel that erupted in January 1833 between the House of Assembly and the Council over the latter's power to amend revenue bills. He drew up the case for the assembly which, being sustained, led to the resignation of Chief Justice Richard Alexander Tucker*, president of the Council. His clerkship of the assembly being by crown appointment, it was inevitable that Archibald should eventually find it impossible to maintain a balance between loyalty to the executive and to the House of Assembly, both of which he was required to serve. The assembly's attitude towards Archibald cooled in 1837 when he was compelled to deny to a committee of the whole house access to certain documentary evidence that he had originally promised to produce and that, in its opinion, would have strengthened the case for the dismissal of Chief Justice Henry John Boulton*. The reason for Archibald's change of mind is apparent in a memorandum addressed to the assembly by Governor Henry Prescott* which stated categorically that "neither Mr. Archibald nor any other public functionary is at liberty to produce documents . . . committed to his charge without direction from the Executive Government." Although the radical chairman of the committee, John Valentine Nugent*, excused Archibald on the grounds that he was undoubtedly acting upon orders from the chief justice, the house, as a matter of principle, demanded and secured the right thereafter to appoint its own officers. Later that year Archibald's appointment as clerk of the General Assembly was terminated at his own request because he believed that he would find it impossible to tolerate the decided conflict of interest that would continue to exist.

In 1838 Archibald was again involved, though not directly this time, in a serious quarrel concerning the privileges and prerogatives of the House of Assembly. The culmination of the quarrel was the celebrated *Kielley* v. *Carson* case. Archibald assisted Mr Justice George Lilly* in preparing his dissenting opinion to the decision of the Supreme Court in support of the House of Assembly. Lilly's opinion was upheld by the Judicial Committee of the Privy Council which in 1843 reversed the decision and established, finally and authoritatively, the rule respecting the proper powers of colonial assemblies in the following terms: the House of Assembly of Newfoundland was "a local Legislature with every power reasonably necessary for the proper exercise of their functions and duties, but they have not what they have erroneously supposed themselves to possess – the same exclusive privileges which the ancient Law of England has annexed to the House of Parliament."

Because of Archibald's assistance to Lilly in 1838, his name was brought to the favourable attention of Lord Glenelg at the Colonial Office, and he thus added to his reputation for acumen and ability. Perhaps as a direct result, Archibald was summoned to appear before the imperial parliament in 1841 to give evidence upon the working of colonial constitutions. At the same time he was invited by the Colonial Office to assist in developing a new constitutional form for the government of Newfoundland that would avoid the seemingly inevitable deadlock between council and assembly which had rendered the 1832 model unworkable. The result was the Amalgamated Legislature, inaugurated in 1842 with Archibald as its chief clerk. Furthermore, in November 1841 he had been elevated to the office of attorney general for the colony, a position which gave him a seat in the Council and which he held concurrently with the office of clerk of the Supreme Court until his retirement and departure from Newfoundland in 1855.

Despite his Presbyterian upbringing, Archibald, while still a young law clerk in Halifax, had recognized the social advantages of regular attendance at the Anglican St Paul's Church. By 1840 he had become a pillar of the Anglican establishment in St John's. The position he had now attained in the political and social community of Newfoundland moved him even closer to the centres of conservatism and weakened what little sympathy he had possessed for those who were, with increasing frequency, designated in his correspondence as "rads." Nevertheless, he did not display that intransigent opposition to the idea of responsible government manifested by some of his colleagues, nor did the assembly ever come to regard him as one of its bitter enemies. Indeed, during the final negotiations of 1854 that led to responsible government, he joined with the Newfoundland colonial secretary, James Crowdy*, in urging and persuading the Council to accept the necessity of a representation bill which the Liberals in the House of Assembly, led by Philip Francis Little*, were determined to pass as the first act of the newly constituted legislature after responsible government.

Earlier in 1854 Archibald, along with William Bickford Row*, had argued in London the Council's case against responsible government, and the representation bill in particular; Hugh William HOYLES, representing the Central Protestant Committee, also fought the bill in London. It has been suggested, perhaps unkindly, that Archibald had been persuaded to modify his position by the promise of a substantial pension. Possibly he was sufficiently pragmatic to be willing to face the inevitable. In any event, stating that he could not continue to work with the type of radical who would control the executive government of Newfoundland after 1855, he submitted his resignation late in 1854 (effective the next year); he also refused a proffered seat on the bench, accepted his pension and a CB, and returned to the family home at Truro.

Although Archibald had perhaps intended to return to the private practice of law, he did not find the quiet life of a small town congenial. Consequently when he was offered the post of British consul at New York in 1857 he seized the opportunity with alacrity. For the next 26 years he held that position and in 1871 assumed additional responsibilities when he was named consul general for New York, New Jersey, Delaware, Rhode Island, and Connecticut. He performed his job skilfully and tactfully, particularly during the Civil War and throughout the heyday of Fenian activity. When he reached the "compulsory" retirement age of 70, Archibald was asked to remain and did so for an additional three years. He asked and was granted permission to retire on 1 Jan. 1883.

With a pension and a KCMG as rewards for his labours, Archibald again sought a quiet retirement, this time in Brighton, England. Once again he was unable to endure the peace and accepted a business appointment in London, but while house-hunting in that city contracted pneumonia and died.

LESLIE HARRIS

Sir Edward Mortimer Archibald's correspondence as British consul at New York with reference to negotiations for the renewal of the Reciprocity Treaty with the United States is published in Nfld., House of Assembly, *Journal*, 1866, app.: 787–92. Archibald published a *Digest of the laws of Newfoundland* . . . (St John's, 1847; repr. 1924).

PRO, CO 194, 1832–55. Nfld., *Blue book*, 1832–51; Executive Council, *Minutes*, 1848–55; House of Assembly, *Journal*, 1832–55. *Newfoundlander*, 1833–55. *Patriot* (St John's), 1834–55. *Public Ledger*, 1832–55. E. J. Archibald, *Life and letters of Sir Edward Mortimer Archibald, K.C.M.G., C.B.; a memoir of fifty years of service* (Toronto, 1924). Gunn, *Political hist. of Nfld.* Wells, "Struggle for responsible government in Nfld."

ARCHIBALD, THOMAS DICKSON, businessman and office-holder; b. 8 April 1813 in Onslow, N.S., son of David Archibald and Olivia Dickson; m. first 14 Nov. 1839 Susan Corbett of Pictou, N.S., and they had seven children; m. secondly 10 June 1867 Elizabeth Hughes of Boston, Mass.; m. thirdly 2 June 1874 Maria Louisa Burnyeat (*née* Goudge) of Dartmouth, N.S.; d. 18 Oct. 1890 at Sydney Mines, N.S.

Thomas Dickson Archibald was educated at Pictou Academy and then worked in the office of the General Mining Association at Albion Mines (Stellarton) in Pictou County. In 1832 he moved to Sydney Mines and engaged in merchandising, mining, and shipbuilding, principally in North Sydney. By 1841 he had joined the firm of Archibald and Company, founded in the 1830s by Samuel George Archibald*, his brother, and Peter Hall Clarke. Various Archibald and Dickson cousins were also involved in the firm, which acted as general and commission merchants, ship-brokers, agents for the sale of coal mined around Sydney, proprietors from 1861 of the Gowrie Coal Mines at Cow Bay (Port Morien), and agents for the North Sydney Marine Railway. Between 1841 and 1871 the company built 27 vessels at North Sydney, and engaged in shipping and in the fishery. In 1846 it opened a branch in Halifax as Archibald, Dickson and Company under the management of Charles W. Dickson. After 1853 Archibald and his cousin, Sampson Salter Blowers Archibald, were chief partners in the firm. Thomas Dickson Archibald himself became the agent at Sydney of one British and two American insurance companies and of the Bank of Nova Scotia.

In 1854 a seat on the Legislative Council of Nova Scotia became vacant, and as Cape Breton had only one representative in the appointed body at the time, the *Cape Breton News* supported the island's claim to the vacancy. The Liberal government of William YOUNG declared in favour of Archibald, who took his seat on 8 December. He remained in the Legislative Council until 1867, and was also a member of Joseph Howe*'s Executive Council from 3 Aug. 1860 to 5 June 1863.

In the upper house Archibald took a great interest in the arrangements made in 1857–58 to terminate the monopoly of the General Mining Association over the mines and minerals of Nova Scotia [*see* Richard Smith*]. Archibald's special concern was that the Cape Breton families who resided on lands covered by the GMA's former monopoly should be able to maintain the habit allowed by the GMA "of cutting the coal on their own lands with as much freedom as they use the water which runs before their doors." The 1858 law sanctioned the practice. This law also made it possible for other companies to compete with the GMA in opening new coalfields. One such firm was the Archibalds' Gowrie Mines, whose production rose from 2,800 tons in 1862 to 152,367 tons in 1891.

Archibald's interest in Cape Breton led him in 1859 to criticize as a "flagrant injustice" a provincial bill for equalizing the elective franchise in certain counties, because it proposed that "the old and venerated Township of Sydney . . . be swept away and abolished" while other "pet" townships on the mainland were to be "spared from the pruning knife." Other interests as a councillor were measures for the deaf and dumb and for education of the Micmacs at Shubenacadie, legislation on the currency, and the handling of public accounts. In 1860, defending Nova Scotia fishermen, he objected to a proposal which would have allowed French fishermen, who were subsidized by their government, to bring fish into Nova Scotia duty free. He was also chairman of a committee of the Legislative Council in 1861 which considered a bill to increase penalties for violation of the liquor licence law; Archibald considered the existing law "sufficiently stringent," and added, "we need only go a step further and make the violation a hanging matter."

Archibald favoured Nova Scotia's entry into confederation during the debates of the mid 1860s, and in October 1867 was appointed to the Senate, where he supported the government of Sir John A. Macdonald*. Archibald maintained his connection with the family firm and in the Senate continued his businessman's interest in commercial, industrial, and maritime development.

CHARLES BRUCE FERGUSSON

PAC, RG 31, A1, 1871 census, Nova Scotia. PANS, MG 1, 292; MG 4, 122; RG 1, 98: no.52; 214½G; 214½H; 361½; 448–50. Univ. of King's College Arch. (Halifax), Israel Longworth, "A history of the county of Colchester, Nova Scotia" (copy at PANS). Can., Senate, *Debates*, 1883. N.S., Legislative Council, *Debates and proc.*, 1858, 1860–61; *Journal of proc.*, 1854–67. *Cape Breton News* (Sydney, N.S.), 15, 22 April, 13 May, 17 June, 1 July, 2 Dec. 1854; 19 May 1855. *Cape Breton Spectator* (North Sydney, N.S.), 3 April 1847. *Morning Herald* (Halifax), 20 Oct. 1890. *North Sydney Herald*, 16 Nov. 1881. *Presbyterian Witness* (Halifax), 20 Oct. 1890. *Spirit of the Times* (Sydney), 19 July 1842.

Canadian biog. dict., II. *CPC*, 1867–90. *Hutchinson's N.S. directory*, 1864–67. *Lovell's N.S. directory*, 1871. *McAlpine's N.S. directory*, 1890–97. Wallace, *Macmillan dict.* M. J. Hart, *Janet Fisher Archibald . . . some account of her ancestry, environment and a few of her descendants* (Victoria, 1934). E. E. Jackson, *Windows on the past, North Sydney, Nova Scotia* (Windsor, N.S., 1974). Israel Longworth, *Life of S. G. W. Archibald* (Halifax, 1881). C. O. Macdonald, *The coal and iron industries of Nova Scotia* (Halifax, 1909). Thomas Miller, *Historical and genealogical record of the first settlers of Colchester County* (Halifax, 1873). J. P. Parker, *Cape Breton ships and men* (Aylesbury, Eng., 1967). C. W. Vernon, *Cape Breton, Canada, at the beginning of the twentieth century: a treatise of natural resources and development* (Toronto, 1903). A. W. H. Eaton, "The settling of Colchester County, Nova Scotia, by New England Puritans and Ulster Scotsmen," RSC *Trans.*, 3rd ser., 6 (1912), sect.II: 221–65.

ARMSTRONG, GEORGE, furniture manufacturer and undertaker; b. in 1821 in County Armagh (Northern Ireland), son of George Armstrong; m. about 1844 Margaret Longmoore; there were no children; d. 22 Sept. 1888 in Montreal, Que.

George Armstrong arrived in Montreal with his family at the age of 13. He was apprenticed to the firm of Bethune and Kittson, cabinet-makers and auctioneers, and on the expiry of his apprenticeship may have worked for a while as a journeyman. By 1851 he had managed to found his own business on St Urbain Street. He was burned out of his first premises, however, and moved to Victoria Square, one of the choicest business areas of Montreal in the 1860s. After another fire he erected in 1864 an impressive structure there, housing a factory, showrooms, and a funeral establishment. His three-storey, later four-storey, building with corner frontage was regarded as an architectural ornament to the square and a tribute to a man who had succeeded in Canada "by steady industry and perseverance."

Armstrong never achieved the reputation attained by John Hilton*, the acknowledged head of the Montreal cabinet trade. Armstrong, however, saw and met the need for furniture that was, as he himself described it, "really good and cheap." With Montreal's population expanding rapidly in the second half of the century, there was a growing market for the furniture Armstrong competently supplied. Though his output was by no means limited to inexpensive articles – "finely carved" chairs, "handsome" bookcases, and "very superior chamber sets" came from his workrooms – his increasing emphasis was on sturdy "cottage furniture" and such mass-produced goods as cane-bottomed chairs. At the Colonial and Indian Exhibition in London in 1886 his firm showed folding cots and Shaker chairs. This bid for overseas recognition proved successful: the exhibit was sold out and an English agent secured. Shaker chairs (plain, straight-backed chairs, with or without rockers) became so important a part of the firm's production that a slogan was painted on the factory declaring that no house was complete without one of Armstrong's Shaker chairs.

Like most Montreal furniture manufacturers Armstrong dealt also in imports, although the bulk of his stock was made on the premises. By holding winter sales he was able to clear his warerooms, and in his own words "to keep all hands working, as usual, during the severe winter months." The ensuring of steady employment for his men was a humane policy, in keeping with Armstrong's deep religious convictions. He was a trustee of St James Methodist Church and a supporter of the Irish Protestant Benevolent Society. The diary of another Montreal cabinet-maker, William Peacock, reveals it was at Armstrong's rooms that a group of Methodists met to pray on 26 Feb. 1871 before setting out on a 60-mile journey by sleigh to promote missionary work "in the country called the Gore or Lashuit" (Lachute). Armstrong himself accompanied the expedition.

George Armstrong died suddenly on 22 Sept. 1888. It was estimated after his death that he had "made a fortune of about $200,000," a far greater sum than most Montreal furniture manufacturers acquired at the time. Like many 19th-century cabinet-makers Armstrong was also engaged in the funeral business, and it was this side of his business that was to endure. He had admitted his nephew, William Armstrong, into partnership in 1877, and although William eventually gave up all connection with furniture manufacturing the funeral establishment remained in the family for over a century.

ELIZABETH COLLARD

The diary of William Peacock and family papers are in the possession of W. G. Armstrong (Montreal).

Arch. of the Irish Protestant Benevolent Soc. (Montreal), Annual reports, 1888–89. St James United Church (Montreal), Register of baptisms, marriages, and burials, 25 Sept. 1888. Charles Tupper, *Report . . . on the Canadian section of the Colonial and Indian Exhibition at South Kensington, 1886* (Ottawa, 1887), 44. *Gazette* (Montreal), 16 July 1860; 6 May 1863; 17 April 1865; 16 Feb., 19 Dec. 1867; 1 Sept. 1875; 1 Dec. 1876; 24 Sept. 1888. *Montreal Daily Witness*, 22, 24 Sept. 1888. *The Colonial and Indian Exhibition, London, 1886; official catalogue of the Canadian section* (2nd ed., London, 1886), 216. C. E. Goad, *Atlas of the city of Montreal from special survey and official plans, showing all buildings & names of owners* (Montreal, 1881), xii. *Montreal directory*, 1847–48, 1850–1976. *Industries of Canada; city of Montreal; historical and descriptive review; leading firms and moneyed institutions* (Montreal, 1886), 136. G. E. Jaques, *Chronicles of the St. James St. Methodist Church, Montreal, from the first rise of Methodism in Montreal to the laying of the corner-stone of the new church on St. Catherine Street* (Toronto, 1888), 8, 90. *Montreal business sketches with a description of the city of Montreal, its public buildings and places of interest, and the Grand Trunk works at Point St. Charles, Victoria bridge, &c., &c.* (Montreal, 1864), 136–37. Elizabeth Collard, "Montreal cabinet-makers and chairmakers, 1800–1850: a check list," *Antiques* (New York), 105 (January–June 1974): 1137, 1142.

ARMSTRONG, JAMES SHERRARD, lawyer and judge; b. 27 April 1821 at Sorel, Lower Canada, son of Captain Charles Logie Armstrong and Marjory (Margery) Ferguson; m. probably in 1847 Marie-Anne-Charlotte Olivier, niece of François Boucher, seigneur of Carufel and of part of the seigneury of Maskinongé; d. 23 Nov. 1888 at Sorel.

James Sherrard Armstrong descended from loyalists who had settled at Yamachiche, Que., in the autumn of 1778 [*see* Conrad Gugy*]. Called to the bar on 12 Feb. 1844, he practised law in Montreal for four years, and was soon interested in landed property. On 22 Sept. 1848 he bought the sub-fief of Hope (Saint-Didace, Que.) and rented from Charles Edward Dunn, owner of the seigneury of Lanaudière, the manor-house and mills in the concession of Crête-de-Coq (Sainte-Ursule, Que.). He went to live there at the end of 1848 but in 1857 decided to move to Sorel, where he remained for the major part of his career as a lawyer. In 1864 he was appointed deputy public prosecutor for the attorney general in the district of Richelieu, and in 1867 he formed a law partnership with Charles-Ignace Gill, who later became a judge of the Superior Court.

Legal practice did not keep Armstrong from a continuing interest in landed property. In addition to the Hope fief, which he retained until his death, in 1871 he bought the rights to *cens et rentes* from the Sorel seigneury, and in 1885 the same rights for the Gentilly seigneury. He sold these rights on 15 July 1886. For several years he was also president of the Montreal-Sorel railway.

His career, as sketched thus far, was not spectacular. It was that of a rural lawyer who had made the usual progress in his profession. Then, in November 1871, Armstrong was appointed chief justice of St Lucia in the West Indies. A former French colony ceded to Great Britain in 1803, St Lucia had kept a legal system derived from the custom of Paris. However, it lacked a civil code, and the modifications in the custom of Paris effected under Louis XVI as a result of republican pressures had not been adopted. The English judges appointed to St Lucia after the cession of the island had no knowledge of French laws. Thus at the time of Armstrong's appointment, the colony was in a state of legal chaos. With the help of Sir George William Des Vœux, the administrator of

St Lucia, Armstrong set to work to adjust the French civil laws of the province of Quebec for the island. He adapted the English version of the civil code of Lower Canada, and also drew up a code of procedure based on that of Lower Canada with minor modifications required by the local situation.

But Judge Armstrong had personal ambitions in Canada. After receiving the assurance of Prime Minister Sir John A. Macdonald* that he would obtain a similar post in Canada, he resigned as chief justice in December 1881. But Macdonald did nothing, and Judge Armstrong expressed his bitterness to some close friends, although he did not publicly show his dissatisfaction. In the end, loyalty to the Conservative party was partially rewarded by his appointment on 7 Dec. 1886 as chairman of the Royal Commission on the Relations of Capital and Labor in Canada.

Nothing in his background had prepared Armstrong to chair this commission of inquiry, one of the most important in the 19th century. His rural ancestry, his interests in the Montreal-Sorel railway, and his dependence on the Conservative party were scarcely conducive to objectivity, let alone an understanding of the problems of the urban proletariat and the beginnings of industrialization. Consequently he had difficulty in imposing his authority on the two factions into which the commissioners had split at the outset of the public hearings. The 16-member commission, set up by Macdonald, included a group of journalists and representatives of the business world on the one hand, and a group of representatives of the working-class milieu and of the Knights of Labor on the other. The latter, pro-worker faction accused the other one, which leaned towards liberalism, of favouring employers.

During the hearings there was open conflict on several occasions. Judge Armstrong, supported by commissioners Augustus Toplady Freed, a journalist and the editor of the *Hamilton Spectator* since 1881, and Michael A. J. Walsh, clashed with the secretary of the commission, Alfred H. Blackeby, and a member, Patrick Kerwin, at the sessions held in Montreal and Quebec. The confrontations were taken up by the press. Conservative newspapers such as *La Justice* and *La Vérité* sided with Armstrong, whom they regarded as an impartial judge. On the other hand, papers such as the Montreal *Canadian Workman* and the Toronto *Canadian Labor Reformer* vehemently attacked the chairman, accusing him of showing partiality to employers.

During the inquiry Armstrong attempted to moderate antagonism by personal intervention, doubtless fearing that employers especially might be attacked so that the displeasure of both the the business world and Macdonald's Conservative government would be aroused. He was not to complete his term of office as chairman of the commission, for he died suddenly on 23 Nov. 1888. He was replaced by Freed. In February 1889, unable to reach agreement, the two factions of the commission presented parallel but quite similar reports.

Armstrong's contribution to the work of the commission is difficult to evaluate, but it does not seem to have been a decisive one. Jules Helbronner* and some of the other commissioners made contributions of much greater significance, particularly in the drafting of the appendices to the commission's report. A conservative both politically and ideologically, Armstrong was violently criticized by the English-language working-class newspapers of Montreal and Toronto for favouring employers. Furthermore, at the beginning of 1888, a libel action was brought against him by the Hochelaga Cotton Manufacturing Company, for having made statements alleging immorality among their female workers, which by implication impugned the conditions in their factory. The incident is an illustration of the reactionary attitudes then held by employers concerning labour issues.

FERNARD HARVEY

James Armstrong was the author of *A treatise on the law relating to marriages, in Lower Canada* (Montreal, 1857), and of *Laws of intestacy, in the dominion of Canada* (Montreal, 1885).

AC, Richelieu (Sorel), État civil, Anglicans, Christ Church (Sorel), 27 April 1821, 23 Nov. 1888. PAC, MG 26, E, 7: 3158–61, 3175–77; MG 30, D1, 11: 424–28, 432. Can., Commission royale sur les relations du capital avec le travail, *Rapport* (5v. en 6, Ottawa, 1888–89), *Québec*, [II]. *Canadian Labor Reformer* (Toronto), 25 Feb., 10 March 1888. *Canadian Workman Newspaper* (Montreal), 18 Feb. 1888. *Gazette* (Montreal), 17 Feb. 1888. *La Minerve*, 26 nov. 1888. *La Presse*, 24 nov. 1888. *La Vérité* (Québec), 17 mars 1888. *Cyclopædia of Canadian biog.* (Rose, 1888), 325–26. "Références biographiques canadiennes," *BRH*, 48 (1942): 155–56. P.-G. Roy, *Inventaire des concessions en fief et seigneurie, fois et hommages et aveux et dénombrements, conservés aux Archives de la province de Québec* (6v., Beauceville, Qué., 1927–29), II: 272. Fernand Harvey, *Révolution industrielle et travailleurs; une enquête sur les rapports entre le capital et le travail au Québec à la fin du 19e siècle* (Montréal, 1978), 44–46. Duvern [Richard Lessard], "L'arrière-fief Hope," *BRH*, 33 (1927): 307–9; "James Armstrong, 1819–1888, juge," *L'Écho de Saint-Justin* (Louiseville, Qué.), 28 nov. 1940: 1.

ASH, JOHN, physician and politician; b. *c.* 1821 in Ormskirk, England, son of William Ash; d. 17 April 1886 in Victoria, B.C.

Little is known of John Ash's early life and education except that he attended Guy's Hospital in London, where he met Dr John Sebastian Helmcken*. In 1845 he became a member of the Royal College of Surgeons of England and a licentiate of the Society of Apothecaries. Ash apparently practised medicine in Coxwold (North Yorkshire), from 1849 to 1860, before deciding to emigrate; he arrived in Victoria in 1862. On 31 July 1863 the Victoria *Daily British Colonist* reported the birth of a daughter, Annie Freer, to his wife, Dorothy Agar, at the home of Dr John Helmcken in Esquimalt.

In 1865 Ash was elected to the House of Assembly of Vancouver Island as junior member for Esquimalt District. He owed his seat to his connection with Helmcken and the Hudson's Bay Company which controlled the riding because its employees made up a majority of the population. Ash supported the union of Vancouver Island with British Columbia, providing it was coupled with the granting of responsible government and of free port status for Victoria. He retained his seat until the abolition of the Island assembly upon the union of the two colonies in 1866. After British Columbia entered confederation in 1871, Ash was elected to the provincial legislature for Comox on northern Vancouver Island on 23 Dec. 1872. He was immediately appointed to the Executive Council as provincial secretary in the government of Amor De Cosmos*, serving until George Anthony Walkem*'s government resigned on 27 Jan. 1876. Ash also served as the first minister of mines of British Columbia when that portfolio was created in 1874, but received no additional salary. He remained in the assembly until 12 June 1882 when he decided not to seek re-election.

Modern political parties did not exist in British Columbia in Ash's lifetime, and alignments were based on personality coupled with regional and economic interests. Ash generally supported the faction led by De Cosmos, Walkem, and Robert Beaven*. Also, personal antipathy between Ash and John Robson*, whose *Daily British Colonist* regularly attacked him, probably played as great a part in determining the doctor's political alignment as did any regional or other interests.

Helmcken, in his reminiscences, describes Ash as "a hard-working clever man, noted for his short sight, tremendous breadth of shoulder and chest and – short temper. A very sensible companion, well read, when in good humour, but if in a bad one – keep clear." Ash's irascibility often involved him in quarrels, even with his political associates. Helmcken tells of an incident in which Ash and De Cosmos disagreed during a debate in the legislature. They met outside the house and "an altercation took place and blows were struck. De Cosmos always carried a stick and Ash asserted this had been used on his head. I came up at this time and with the aid of others induced them to go their way, for Ash had his 'monkey up' and was able to throw De Cosmos over the bridge." Sir James Douglas*, who had little liking for De Cosmos, later chided Helmcken for his intervention. Helmcken concluded that "Ash was honest and honourable almost to a fault – but let no one thwart him, either in opinion or action."

Ash's business career was unspectacular. In 1863 he had acquired land in the Metchosin District as part of a scheme to construct a dock at Pedder Inlet (now Pedder Bay). However, the project fell through and in 1870 Ash was released from his commitment. That year Ash also served as a trustee of the Victoria Cemetery Society, and in the year he died he became a founding director of the proposed Victoria and Saanich Railway.

Dr Ash's domestic life was shadowed by sadness. His only child, Annie, died of diphtheria in 1868 at the age of five, and his wife died in 1874. Late the following year, Ash married Adelaide Anne Amelia de Veulle, daughter of Sir John de Veulle, the high bailiff of the Island of Jersey. Their marriage was short; while they were visiting England, Adelaide Ash died of malaria on 13 July 1881 at Great Malvern (Hereford and Worcester). Dr Ash returned to Victoria and continued to practise medicine, specializing in ophthalmology, until his death of apoplexy at the age of 65 at his home in Victoria.

WENDY K. TEECE

Anglican Church of Canada, Diocese of British Columbia Arch. (Victoria), Christ Church Cathedral (Victoria), Register of marriages, entry no.225, 11 Dec. 1875, marriage of John Ash to A. A. A. de Veulle (mfm. at PABC). PABC, A. A. A. (de Veulle) Ash, Diary, 26 Aug. 1871–21 March 1872; Colonial corr., John Ash corr. B.C., Dept. of Mines, *Annual report* (Victoria), 1874; *Statutes*, 1874, no.16. [J. S. Helmcken], *The reminiscences of Doctor John Sebastian Helmcken*, ed. Dorothy Blakey Smith ([Vancouver], 1975). *Daily British Colonist* (Victoria), 4 Aug. 1863; 3, 21 Oct., 29 Nov. 1865; 26 Aug. 1868; 19 June 1870; 7 Nov. 1874; 14 Dec. 1875; 10 Aug. 1881; 24 Feb., 18, 21 April 1886. *The year book of British Columbia . . .*, comp. R. E. Gosnell (Victoria), 1911.

AUBERT, PIERRE (baptized **Joseph-Pierre-Blaise**), priest, Oblate of Mary Immaculate, and missionary; b. 3 Feb. 1814 at Digne, France, son of Jean-Joseph-Louis-Pierre Aubert, a businessman, and Laure-Modeste Castellan; d. 25 March 1890 in Paris.

Pierre Aubert entered the noviciate of the Oblates at Billens, Switzerland, on 1 Nov. 1830, where exactly one year later he took his perpetual vows. On Christmas Day 1836 he was ordained priest at Marseilles, France, by Charles-Joseph-Eugène de Mazenod, the coadjutor bishop of Marseilles and founder of the Oblates. Father Aubert had been a preacher at Aix-en-Provence since 1834; in 1840 he became director of the Notre-Dame-de-Lumières juniorate (minor seminary) of the Oblates at Goult, Vaucluse, a position he held until 1844.

That year Aubert left France with Father Joseph-Bruno Guigues*, the newly appointed superior of the Oblates in Canada, at Guigues' own suggestion. Settling in Longueuil, Canada East, Aubert devoted himself to preaching. In 1845 Joseph-Norbert Provencher*, the bishop at the Red River Settlement (Man.), who needed priests to extend the work of the church in his diocese, asked Guigues for the Oblates' help. Guigues, who himself faced a shortage of personnel, hesitated, but Bishop Mazenod appointed Aubert superior and founder of the first Oblate mission in the Red River Settlement, at St Boniface. Aubert and Father Alexandre-Antonin Taché*, who accompanied him, were the first Oblates sent to the west.

Leaving Lachine on 25 June 1845, the missionaries arrived at St Boniface on 25 August. Aubert was appointed priest of the cathedral at St Boniface and vicar general, posts he retained for five years. He immediately began to study the Chippewa language, under the direction of Abbé George-Antoine Bellecourt*, and in 1846 and again in 1847 he went to Wabassimong (Whitedog, Ont.). There he realized that the Chippewas were completely ignorant, as well as little disposed to accept religious instruction or receive priests. He agreed with Provencher that "less ploughing and more catechism" would have brought more results. The mission was soon abandoned. Aubert also visited Lac La Pluie (Rainy Lake, Ont.) in 1847, but with little more success.

Bishop Provencher held Aubert in high regard and consulted him on important questions such as the appointment of Louis-François Laflèche* as coadjutor to the bishop of Red River. He seems to have thought of him as his successor. But, given the opposition of the Hudson's Bay Company, "foreigners" could not be considered for the office of bishop.

Aubert left the west in 1850, and until 1857 resided at the bishop's palace in Bytown (Ottawa), where he was vicar general (1851–56), superior of the episcopal household (1854–57), and chaplain of the mother house of the Grey Nuns of the Cross (now Sisters of Charity, Ottawa) (1855–57). In this last capacity he worked on the constitutions of the community. In 1857 Aubert was appointed superior of the community of Saint-Pierre-Apôtre at Montreal, and served as theological adviser to Ignace BOURGET, the bishop of Montreal, at the third provincial council, held at Quebec in 1863. With the bishop's encouragement, he was one of the first to contribute to the *Revue canadienne* (Montreal), publishing in 1864 an essay on rationalism.

Having fallen ill, Aubert went back to France in 1865 and became superior of the sanctuary of Notre-Dame-de-Lumières. Elected assistant to the superior general two years later, he remained in Paris until his death. Aubert was a discreet counsellor, and was the intermediary between the superior general and Canadian authorities, and no important decision was made without consulting him. He took a particular interest in the activities of the Oblates in Canada and in the papal Zouaves. In 1870 Aubert accompanied Bishop Guigues to the Vatican Council as a theological adviser.

GASTON CARRIÈRE

Pierre Aubert was the author of "Du rationalisme," *Rev. canadienne*, 1 (1864): 40–46, 153–62. His "Notes pour servir à l'histoire de la province du Canada" is held by Arch. générales des Oblats de Marie-Immaculée (Rome) (copy at Arch. hist. oblates, Ottawa).

A.-A. Taché, *Vingt années de missions dans le nord-ouest de l'Amérique* (Montréal, 1866), 10–14, 34. Gaston Carrière, *Histoire documentaire de la Congrégation des Missionaires Oblats de Marie-Immaculée dans l'Est du Canada* (12v., Ottawa, 1957–75). J.-É. Champagne, *Les missions catholiques dans l'Ouest canadien (1818–1875)* (Ottawa, 1949), 71, 74, 93. Sœur Paul-Émile [Louise Guay], *Les Sœurs grises de la Croix . . .* (2v., Ottawa, [1945]-67), I: 169–72.

AUBIN, NAPOLÉON (baptized **Aimé-Nicolas**), journalist, publisher, playwright, and scientist; b. 9 Nov. 1812 at Chêne-Bougeries, a commune in the suburbs of Geneva (Switzerland), son of Pierre-Louis-Charles Aubin, a potter, and Élisabeth Escuyer; d. 12 June 1890 at Montreal, Que.

Little is known of Napoléon Aubin's childhood. We may surmise that during his adolescence at Geneva, the environment, his own temperament, and perhaps also his reading inclined him towards the progressive ideologies of his time and gave him an interest in natural science.

He left school when he was about 16, and set out for America in August 1829. The reasons for his departure are open to conjecture. The political and religious discussions which characterized his native milieu, and the attraction of America, a "land of success and freedom," no doubt influenced his decision. From 1829 to 1835 Aubin stayed in the United States. But, disappointed in the American way of life, he turned to Canada. He sent to *La Minerve* of Montreal articles in which he affirmed his support for the Patriote party. On his arrival in Canada, Aubin spent some months in Montreal, but at the end of October 1835 he settled in Quebec City and devoted himself to journalism. In addition to contributing to *L'Ami du peuple, de l'ordre et des lois* of Montreal, he was editor of *Le Canadien* of Quebec City from 1847 to 1849 and started several periodicals in Quebec City, whose brief lives did not dishearten him: *Le Télégraphe* (22 March–3 June 1837), *Le Fantasque* (published irregularly 1 Aug. 1837–24 Feb. 1849), *Le Standard* (November 1842), *Le Castor* (7 Nov. 1843–22 June 1845), *Le Canadien indépendant* (21 May–31 Oct. 1849), and *La Sentinelle du peuple* (26 March–12 July 1850). He also published, in 1842, the first newspaper in Canada devoted to working-class interests, the *People's Magazine and Workingman's Guardian* (Quebec). From

1853 to 1863 Aubin was again in the United States, then returned to Quebec, his adopted city.

There he contributed to *La Tribune* in 1863 and 1864, but in the latter year he retired to Longueuil, Canada East. In 1865 he launched another newspaper, *Les Veillées du Père Bon Sens* (Montreal) (1865–66 and 1873). In 1866 he finally settled in Montreal, and in 1868–69 wrote for *Le Pays*. His last contribution to the press was in 1876; at that time he was publishing in *Le National*, of which he had been editor from 1872 to 1874. A journalist by inclination, Aubin nevertheless earned his livelihood through his scientific and technical knowledge. In the end, the technician would overshadow the ideologue: he was appointed gas inspector for the city of Montreal in 1875, and he travelled all over Canada as a city lighting adviser.

Aubin is remembered particularly for his contributions to the life of his society as journalist, poet, story-teller, publisher, and playwright. His published journalism is impressive. Although in the 1830s he was in sympathy with the national cause, Aubin was sometimes hard on the leader of the Patriote party. He saw Louis-Joseph Papineau* as a tyrant and a coward, who was dragging the country on a dangerous downward path. Like Étienne Parent* he felt the Patriotes were going too far, and again like Parent warned the population on the eve of the uprising in 1837 to be on guard against its political leaders. *Le Fantasque* was then in its early days. Aubin drew the material for its satirical prose from the extremists, bureaucrats, and Patriotes. In the disturbed atmosphere of the late 1830s, he managed to bring a smile to faces that showed the strain of political conflict.

Well fitted to be a man of the opposition, Aubin kept an eye on the activities of Lord Durham [Lambton*]. He might approve of the amnesty granted by the British lord, but he found him a little too fond of fashionable gatherings. Balls were frequent at the governor's château. Did Durham work? Teasing aside, Aubin did offer the chief of state food for thought. With the governor in mind, he gave a sympathetic description of French Canadians. They must not be confused with their leaders. In Aubin's opinion, Durham in spite of everything remained insensitive to their grievances.

A liberal and a democrat, Aubin's assessment of the governors after the union was determined by their rejection or acceptance of the principle of ministerial responsibility. Charles Edward Poulett Thomson*, who carried through the project of union, was censured on several occasions by the editor of *Le Fantasque*. Tempered with irony, the criticism of the crown's representative was nevertheless severe. "When I think of how we are governed by a mere *poulet* [pullet], I begin to get *la chair de poule* [gooseflesh]." The colony's merchants saw it as logical that Canada West's debt should be shared by the taxpayers of the two united provinces. The nationalists of Canada East did not see it this way. Aubin made himself their spokesman in depicting the governor as a despoiler of the collective wealth of the French Canadians. Mixing irony with malice, he wrote: "When the knights of old went off to war, they were protected by their *écus* [a shield or coin]. Master Thomson launches forth covered with ours." Commenting on a rumour that the governor had "*rendu l'âme* [died, or yielded up his soul]," he remarked: "This is surely absurd. He would have quite enough trouble to *rendre* all he has taken from us let alone that [*âme*] which he never had." Sir Charles Bagot*, given a cool welcome by the humorist, found favour when Aubin perceived that the new governor had been won over to the idea of responsible government. On the other hand, Sir Charles Theophilus Metcalfe* was censured because he undid his predecessor's work.

The political ascension of Louis-Hippolyte La Fontaine* did not please Aubin. As the statesman moved closer to power, the journalist applied himself to rehabilitating Papineau, his favourite target before the armed uprising. Aubin considered La Fontaine intransigent when he refused the post of attorney general of Canada East in 1842 unless Robert Baldwin* was appointed to the Executive Council. Once in power La Fontaine became to him an intriguer who had wanted to climb to the leadership of the Patriote party. Not that Aubin disapproved of all the political moves made by the new leader of the French Canadians. The resignation of La Fontaine and Baldwin from Metcalfe's council in 1843 met with his full approbation; in his view the principle of responsible government must be upheld against the claims of authoritarian governors. But the principle of ministerial responsibility having been put into effect in 1848, Aubin argued that the Reform leader was now motivated by self-interest.

In the end, it was the Rouges who were most in line with Aubin's ideas. From 1847 to 1849, as editor for *Le Canadien*, he put forward his views on economic and social reform. He advocated land settlement efforts as a means of checking emigration to New England. Without condemning those who had carried on the struggle of the French Canadians solely on the basis of *survivance*, he considered that their full development could come only through economic emancipation. Deploring the lack of French-speaking entrepreneurs, he preached thrift and became a promoter of the textile industry. His social theories about methods of production were at times akin to some current in the Europe of 1848. He suggested enterprises financed by both workers and entrepreneurs, all French Canadians, who would share in the profits.

At the end of the 1840s, Aubin's political ideas were identical with those of Papineau and *L'Avenir* (Montreal). Had not the journalist himself drafted the *Manifeste adressé au peuple du Canada par le Comité constitutionnel de la réforme et du progrès* (Quebec,

1847)? It was with Papineau's support that Aubin left *Le Canadien* to start *Le Canadien indépendant* in 1849. In the columns of the new paper, separatism and annexationism had pride of place. To those who objected that his association with the annexationists was strange, Aubin replied that it was necessary to forget the past and redirect energies. Would not annexation to the United States carry the risk of eventual assimilation of the French Canadians? Aubin did not believe so. The local legislature would see that the national identity was protected. And if that did not happen, was it not better to set a high value on political and social progress, even if this might lead to the disappearance of the nation itself? In *La Sentinelle du peuple*, which replaced *Le Canadien indépendant*, Aubin continued to serve as spokesman for Papineau's political ideas, although he refused to back Papineau's opposition to the abolition of the seigneurial régime. On the other hand, he would unfailingly defend annexationism and loyalty to the political principles of the Rouges. Moreover, he would be president of the Institut Canadien of Montreal in 1869. Like many French Canadian Liberals, he considered confederation a plot hatched by the financial backers of the Grand Trunk, in league with scheming and venal politicians. The failure to offer a referendum on the 1867 constitution was to him a serious violation of the democratic principles he had always defended. As a nationalist, he was disturbed that French Canadians would be a minority in the new country. For him, annexation would have been preferable to the arrangement of 1867.

Aubin's career reflects the climate of suspicion, denunciation, and contempt for freedom of thought that prevailed during the early years of the union period. For publishing a poem by Joseph-Guillaume Barthe* dedicated to the political prisoners of 1837–38 deported to Bermuda, Aubin served 53 days in prison. Detention did not silence him. In the issue of 8 May 1839 of *Le Fantasque*, he spoke ironically about living conditions in a prison cell. Between 9 July and 1 October, Aubin published in the paper a short story entitled "Mon voyage à la lune." He used its plot as a cover for political and social criticism. "I dare not say anything more at the moment; people are so sensitive that they find allusions in everything. . . . If I laugh about an ass, Mr. Robert Symes [deputy chief of police at Quebec, well known for his contempt for French Canadians] insists that the ass is his emblem. . . . If I speak about decent people, the police imagine I am talking about them. . . . One can easily understand that with such limited freedom of the press a writer's only recourse is to . . . fly to the stars rather than lament longer on a prejudiced earth where in order to please and to live one must crawl . . . and lick the spurs of those who believe themselves great because they have their greatness proclaimed so often, who bear their rights in their scabbards and keep their hearts in their pockets."

In 1839, Aubin established a troupe of actors who played Voltaire's *La mort de César* at the Théâtre Royal of Quebec, as well as two short pieces of his own, *Le soldat français* and *Le chant des ouvriers.* The authorities became uneasy. For the *Quebec Gazette*, Voltaire's play was a revolutionary manifesto. The works of Aubin were judged subversive. Disturbed, Thomas Ainslie Young*, the chief of police of Quebec, wrote to the governor: "The entire performance had a decidedly political character, and its aim was to arouse the passions of the audience against the established order." At Young's request, the city council forbade any performance after 11 o'clock in the evening, so that Aubin's troupe ceased to perform for a while. The few plays by secondary authors which were put on in 1841 were harmless.

In 1842 Aubin published *Le rebelle, histoire canadienne*, by the Baron de Trobriand. According to the publisher's preface, the novel was intended to perpetuate the memory of the Patriotes. As with the theatrical performances staged by Aubin, the police were on the watch: a seller of *Le rebelle* was arrested in Montreal. At a time when the liberal nationalism of 1837 was being eclipsed by the initiative of those in power, a historian such as François-Xavier Garneau* could have found no better ally than Aubin. It was certainly no accident that he undertook to publish the first two volumes of the great historian's national history.

Versatility was one of Aubin's salient characteristics. His liking for science was not the least curious facet of this unusual individual. He gave public courses and lectures in popular science, and was one of the first professors of the Quebec School of Medicine (founded in 1845) where he was responsible for teaching chemistry. Two popular works on chemistry were written by him: *La chimie agricole mise à la portée de tout le monde . . .* (Quebec, 1847) and a *Cours de chimie* (Quebec, 1850). He gave his name to a widely used invention: during the decade he spent in the United States, from 1853 to 1863, he perfected a gas-lighting process which was patented in Canada, the United States, England, and France. The device was employed by several cities in North America, and was written up in an article in *Scientific American* (New York) in 1858. The journal explained how the device worked and pointed out that the invention was well thought of by its users.

Aubin is a fine example of an immigrant who succeeded, as a result not only of his talent but also of his adaptability in a cultural context quite foreign to his native environment. He was baptized a Calvinist, but kept it secret all his life. He found a place in the Roman Catholic community when, on 9 Nov. 1841 in the

Saint-Roch church in Quebec City, he married a girl from an established bourgeois family, Marie-Luce-Émilie Sauvageau, whose father, Michel-Flavien, was a notary in the city. It was a hasty marriage, the bride being pregnant, so there was no inquiry into Aubin's religious persuasion. The couple's four children were baptized Roman Catholics. The fact that a Presbyterian minister, Daniel Coussirat, delivered Aubin's funeral oration, and that he was buried in a Protestant cemetery, must have surprised many people. These events no doubt confirmed the conviction in uncompromising clerical-nationalist circles that Protestantism and liberalism were two sides of one and the same heresy.

Aubin's life in Canada somewhat weakens the myth of the xenophobia of French Canadians. As a man of the opposition, he might often have been reproached for not being a French Canadian. Joseph-Édouard CAUCHON made a stab at it, but he did not come off best in the bitter controversy in which the two men engaged. The majority of the intellectuals of Aubin's generation admired his talents without holding his origins against him, for at the very outset he made the national aspirations of his adopted country his own. The young generation of liberal intellectuals of the 1840s no doubt drew some of their vision of collective destiny from him. Easy of manner, Napoléon Aubin was a friend of many outstanding personalities of his day: Ludger Duvernay*, Philippe-Joseph Aubert* de Gaspé, Joseph-Guillaume Barthe, Étienne Parent, James Huston*, Louis-Joseph Papineau, and Joseph DOUTRE, to name only a few. At his funeral, the presence of an imposing number of prominent people – including diplomats, for Aubin had been honorary consul of Switzerland since 1875 – was evidence of the esteem he had won for himself among his compatriots.

SERGE GAGNON

[For a fuller understanding of the work of Napoléon Aubin the following studies by Jean-Paul Tremblay are useful: "Aimé-Nicolas dit Napoléon Aubin, sa vie et son œuvre" (thèse de PHD, univ. Laval, Québec, 1965), and *À la recherche de Napoléon Aubin* (Québec, 1969). S.G.]

Beaulieu et J. Hamelin, *Journaux du Québec*. Bernard, *Les Rouges*. Monet, *Last cannon shot*.

AUCLAIR, JOSEPH, Roman Catholic priest; b. 16 June 1813 at Jeune-Lorette (Loretteville), Lower Canada, son of Étienne Auclair, a farmer, and Marie-Jeanne Blondeau; d. 29 Nov. 1887 at Quebec City.

Joseph Auclair completed his studies at the Séminaire de Québec in 1836 and began his theology in the autumn of that year. Contrary to common custom, he does not appear to have had a parish ministry during his three years of theological training. He was ordained priest on 21 Sept. 1839, worked as a curate in the parish of Saint-Joseph (now in Lauzon), and in September 1841 was transferred to the parish of Saint-Roch in Quebec City, where he assisted parish priest Zéphirin Charest* until September 1847.

During this time Quebec City was still the principal port of entry in Canada for British immigrants, most of whom were Irish. When they were not stricken with cholera or typhoid, thousands of these poor wretches roamed the streets of Quebec in search of lodgings and employment. The labour market was glutted, all the more because the economy of Quebec, based almost exclusively on the timber trade and shipbuilding, was suffering from the impact of the abolition of the British protective tariffs and from the technological shift to iron and steam in the construction of ships. This overabundance of manpower and long periods of unemployment, particularly with the slackening of activity in the port during the winter, were the most tragic aspects of the prevailing social situation, especially in the working-class parish of Saint-Roch, where according to the clergy one of the consequences was an upsurge in alcoholism. The clergy attempted to combat this by creating on 15 Nov. 1840 the Société de Tempérance de la Paroisse Saint-Roch de Québec. Like the priests in the parish of Notre-Dame in Quebec City, they no doubt also kept a careful record of the poor and needy, and distributed food, clothing, and firewood.

The harsh misfortunes dogging Quebec during these years led the clergy to increase their activity. In May 1845 a terrible fire destroyed 1,630 dwellings, most of which were in Saint-Roch. Two years later a typhoid epidemic spread panic in Quebec, although it did not wreak as much havoc as had previous outbreaks of cholera. Stricken with the disease while carrying out priestly duties at the Marine and Emigrant Hospital, Auclair nevertheless agreed to become parish priest of Sainte-Marie in the Beauce region in September. He had no sooner arrived there than he had to return to the Hôpital Général in Quebec, where it took some weeks of care to prevent his death. After returning to Beauce Auclair continued the fight for temperance launched by the clergy. Early in 1849 he and a number of his parishioners signed a petition urging the government to take steps against drunkenness and to suspend tavern licences. In addition, like his colleagues in the other parishes, he maintained a close watch over teaching establishments.

In September 1851 the resignation of Abbé Louis Proulx* left vacant the perpetual office of priest of the parish of Notre-Dame in Quebec, the incumbents of which had for the most part acceded to the episcopate. This prestigious clerical post required someone with exceptional qualities because of the heterogeneous nature of the parish which included the Upper Town, where the bourgeoisie resided, and the working-class districts of the suburbs and the Lower Town. That year Archbishop Pierre-Flavien Turgeon* appointed Auclair to the post, probably with the expectation that his experience in a working-class environment, his education, and his unassuming ways would make him acceptable to all the parishioners.

Anxious to establish higher moral standards and to protect the Catholic faith from Protestant influence, Auclair took a particular interest in education. The public school system of Quebec City was managed by two institutions: the Quebec Education Society, which had been set up in 1821 by clergy and laity to support the first schools, and the Catholic School Commission. The parish priest of Notre-Dame closely observed and encouraged both these bodies. As a school commissioner and a member of the Board of Examiners for the teachers of the Quebec district, Auclair gave fresh impetus to the Quebec Education Society and invited the Society of St Vincent de Paul to organize evening classes in English and French. The instruction available in the fields of science and commerce apparently did not yet satisfy French Canadian aspirations: periodically Auclair deplored the fact that Catholics were enrolling in English-language Protestant schools. In 1862 he founded the Académie Commerciale de Québec in the belief that it would protect their faith. Auclair also saw education as a solution to the distress and poverty of some of his parishioners and considered that schools could be expected to improve the moral standards of the poor, that is to "reduce the number of vagrants and ne'er-do-wells." In one of his sermons written in 1866 to encourage the faithful to give generously to the Quebec Education Society he observed: "It is better to raise the moral standards of the poor today . . . than to have to pay for a large police force later."

Auclair was particularly sensitive to the destitution caused by the chronic unemployment in Quebec City at that time. The notebooks for his sermons provide detailed and moving descriptions of the predicament of underprivileged groups. He believed that by this means he could arouse the generosity of those who were more prosperous. In one instance he might announce a bazaar for the benefit of the female prisoners and the prostitutes of the Asylum of the Good Shepherd; in another he prepares for a collection for the Hospice Saint-Joseph-de-la-Maternité de Québec which he had founded in 1852 to provide temporary shelter for young unwed mothers and illegitimate children (thus preventing infanticide), or one for the poor and unemployed who lacked even firewood. Or again, he would draw a striking picture of the economic situation and launch a touching appeal to the faithful not affected by the recession, the seasonal slowdown of the port, or the rigours of winter – "an extremely bitter winter . . . ," he often repeated, "no work for a great many of the working class, extraordinarily high prices for the basic necessities of life." Moreover, in his opinion, the giving of alms was "just as much a duty as the commandment to keep the Sabbath holy."

Auclair seems to have been too conscious of the various consequences of unemployment in his parish to look favourably upon the formation of trade unions and the use of the strike as an instrument for bargaining. In any case he could not find words harsh enough to castigate such actions: "You are labouring for the damnation of your souls," he cried, "and you are completing the ruin of your city, which is already all too far advanced."

He remained parish priest of Notre-Dame until his death, having served for 36 years. Despite increasing blindness in the last 12 years of his life he obstinately refused to resign; he gave up his administrative tasks with reluctance and was most hesitant to accept the assistants appointed by his superior Elzéar-Alexandre Taschereau*. The archbishop did, however, succeed in persuading him in his final months to allow another priest to take over; Auclair then entered the Hôpital Général, where he passed away 11 days later.

During his ministry at Notre-Dame, Auclair held several other offices of distinction, which curiously enough were conferred on him largely after 1874, at a time when illness was beginning to affect him. He was appointed a member of the archbishop's general council for the period from 1851 to 1887, vicar general of the dioceses of Sherbrooke and Rimouski in 1874, and non-resident vicar general of the diocese of Chicoutimi in 1878. Finally in 1882 Archbishop Taschereau named him one of the assessors of the metropolitan officiality of Quebec. He owed at least two of his titles to his friendship with the bishops of Chicoutimi and Sherbrooke, Dominique RACINE and his brother Antoine*, with whom he went to stay each year for a rest from his labours in his parish.

RENÉ HARDY

Joseph Auclair was the author of *Le congrès* (Québec, 1875) and of *Les danses et les bals: sermons, notes et documents par le curé de N.-D. de Québec* (Québec, 1879).

AAQ, 61 CD, Sainte-Marie-de-la-Nouvelle-Beauce. ANQ-Q, État civil, Catholiques, Saint-Ambroise (Loretteville), 17 juin 1813. AP, Notre-Dame de Québec, Cahiers de prônes, 26 janv., 13 mai, 2 sept. 1855; 24 févr., 31 août, 7 déc. 1856; 10 oct. 1858; 30 janv. 1859; 6 mai, 7 oct. 1860; 14 avril 1861; 12 janv., 27 avril, 4 mai, 3 août 1862; 14 févr. 1863; 22 janv., 24 déc. 1865; 10 juin 1866; 27 janv., 7 juill. 1867; 1er mars 1868; 29 nov. 1869; 2 oct., 11 déc. 1870; 11 juin 1871; 10 nov. 1872; 14 nov. 1875. ASQ, MSS, 678; Polygraphie, L: 9, 15, 16; Séminaire, 9: no.4; Univ., carton 103: no.38. *Le Courrier du Canada*, 2 déc. 1887. *La Minerve*, 1er déc. 1887. *Catalogue de la bibliothèque de feu Rév. M. Joseph Auclair, curé de Québec* (Québec, 1888). André Simard, *Les évêques et les prêtres séculiers au diocèse de Chicoutimi, 1878–1968; notices biographiques* (Chicoutimi, Qué., 1969). Cyprien Tanguay, *Répertoire général du clergé canadien par ordre chronologique depuis la fonda-*

tion de la colonie jusqu'à nos jours (Québec, 1868), 141. G.-P. Côté, *Notice biographique sur le Révérend J. Auclair, curé de Notre-Dame de Québec, décédé le 29 novembre 1887* (Québec, 1888). Albert Faucher, *Québec en Amérique au XIXe siècle, essai sur les caractères économiques de la Laurentie* (Montréal, 1973). J. Hamelin et Roby, *Hist. économique*. René Hardy, "Aperçu du rôle social et religieux du curé de Notre-Dame de Québec (1840–1860)" (thèse de DES, univ. Laval, Québec, 1968). André Labarrère-Paulé, *Les instituteurs laïques au Canada français, 1836–1900* (Québec, 1965), 147. Sœur Marie-de-la-Joie [Jacqueline Picard], "La crèche Saint-Vincent-de-Paul et l'enfant né hors mariage (1901–1915)" (thèse de DES, univ. Laval, 1965). *L'œuvre d'un siècle: les Frères des écoles chrétiennes au Canada* (Montréal, 1937), 279–80. Ouellet, *Hist. économique*. Honorius Provost, *Sainte-Marie de la Nouvelle-Beauce: histoire civile* (Québec, 1970). René Hardy, "L'activité sociale du curé de Notre-Dame de Québec: aperçu de l'influence du clergé au milieu du XIXe siècle," *SH*, no.6 (November 1970): 5–32.

B

BABBITT, JOHN, jeweller, watchmaker, and scientist; b. 15 Oct. 1845 at Fredericton, N.B., son of Samuel Wellington Babbitt and Frances Maria Nealon; m. 9 June 1874 Margaret Turnbull (d. 1882), and they had two children; d. 10 Dec. 1889 at Fredericton.

In 1865 John Babbitt entered into partnership in Fredericton with the silversmith and jeweller, Alexander MacPherson. In 1868 he set up in business independently as a jeweller and watchmaker. He remained a craftsman all his life, but was at the same time keenly interested in scientific advances which were then being made. Babbitt seems to have had several sources of information concerning Alexander Graham Bell*'s invention, the telephone. He is believed to have seen an example of Bell's telephone at the Philadelphia Centennial International Exhibition in 1876, as well as a description in the *Scientific American*. Another source was three letters written between September and November 1877 to Babbitt's friend, Professor Loring Woart Bailey* of the University of New Brunswick, by his brother, William Whitman Bailey, professor of botany at Brown University in Providence, R.I.; these described a telephone constructed at his family's estate with the help of Bell's friend John Pierce, whose improvements Bell had adopted. Having gathered this information, Babbitt and Loring Bailey late in 1877 or early in 1878 made the first telephone in Fredericton, perhaps the first in the province. It was a magnetic telephone, the transmitters and receivers being wooden cylinders with vibrating plates of thin metal, and the magnets consisting of two iron bars around which wire was wound. This first telephone connected John Babbitt's house with that of his brother, George Nealon, and then with Professor Bailey's. It thus extended 200 yards. Babbitt later made telephone connections between various points in the city.

In 1879, when streets and places of business were lighted by gas and most houses by kerosene lamps and candles, Dr Loring Bailey imported from London, England, a 30- or 40-cell battery with which he and Babbitt produced the first electric light in Fredericton, and perhaps in the Maritimes. When such a light was placed in the portico of the university it was thrown by a parabolic reflector on the spire of Christ Church Cathedral and then on the Methodist church spire at Marysville three miles away, an event which produced a commotion among the inhabitants of both places. With some knowledge of Thomas Alva Edison's recent invention, particularly from a description in a scientific review, Babbitt also made what is believed to have been the first phonograph in New Brunswick.

Babbitt, it is clear, was strongly inclined to the study of mechanical laws, and indeed to many branches of physical science in both a theoretical and a practical way. He sometimes assisted in experimental work at the University of New Brunswick and Provincial Normal School, and in about 1880, together with Professor Bailey, he exhibited to a Saint John audience, for the first time, a heliostat, a large induction coil, and a phonograph.

ALFRED G. BAILEY

L. W. Bailey, "In memoriam, [John Babbitt]," *Univ. Monthly* (Fredericton), February 1890: 52. J. W. Bailey, *Loring Woart Bailey; the story of a man of science* (Saint John, N.B., 1925), 111–12. I. L. Hill, *Fredericton, New Brunswick, British North America* ([Fredericton, 1968]), 49–51. D. C. Mackay, *Silversmiths and related craftsmen of the Atlantic provinces* (Halifax, 1973), 91. A. G. Bailey, "The first telephone in Fredericton," *Atlantic Advocate* (Fredericton), 47 (1956–57), no.8: 77–78. *Daily Gleaner* (Fredericton), 12 Jan. 1925.

BABINEAU, FRANÇOIS-XAVIER, priest and teacher; b. 21 March 1825 at Saint-Louis-de-Kent, N.B., son of Joseph Babineau and Nathalie Le Blanc; d. 16 April 1890 at Saint-Hilaire, N.B.

Having received his early education at his birthplace, François-Xavier Babineau, son of one of the village's most prosperous farmers, entered in 1844 the college of Sainte-Anne-de-la-Pocatière, Canada East, for his classical education. In 1849 he went to the Grand Séminaire de Québec and on 18 Dec. 1851, at the age of 26, was ordained priest in the basilica at Quebec by Bishop Charles-François Baillargeon*. He was the first New Brunswick-born Acadian to become a Catholic priest.

Returning to his native province after a few weeks of rest in the Quebec region, Abbé Babineau ministered at Barachois and Cap-Pelé (1852), Grande-Digue and Cocagne (1852–54), Buctouche (1854–58), and again at Barachois and Cap-Pelé (1858–64). In January 1859, barely four months after his arrival at Cap-Pelé, a terrible epidemic of smallpox broke out. As the nearest doctor lived at Dorchester, about 45 miles away, Abbé Babineau improvised as a doctor himself, no one else daring to approach the dwellings of those "marked with the pox." The news of the "great pox" filled people with terror. Fearing the spread of disease among his parishioners, Abbé Babineau refused all assistance. Single-handed, he cared for the sick, changed their beds, prepared them for death, and saw to their burial in graves dug on their farms. Thus throughout the month and a half that the epidemic lasted he toiled unsparingly.

In 1864 François-Xavier Babineau became the first resident priest at Cap-Pelé; until this time the same priest had been responsible for the villages of Barachois and Cap-Pelé. Since the village had no school he set one up in the presbytery kitchen. His housekeeper, Marguerite Maillet, who had received some education, acted as teacher. In the autumn of 1868 Abbé Babineau was again appointed to Buctouche and the years he spent there were extremely happy ones for him; during his previous stay at Buctouche in the 1850s he had had a number of improvements made to the interior of the parish church. He was greatly disappointed in 1876 when the bishop of Saint John, John Sweeney*, moved him to the parish of Richibucto, and he could not help interpreting this change as an injustice. After only 15 months at Richibucto he obtained permission from Bishop Sweeney in March 1878 to leave his parish and go to live with his nephew, Abbé Joseph-Auguste Babineau, at Tracadie, in the diocese of Chatham. Six months later he left for Madawaska, where he retired permanently from active ministry.

A new career then opened up for him. In 1881 he entered teachers' college at Fredericton and obtained a primary teaching certificate. One of his classmates was Placide Gaudet*, the future Acadian genealogist. In 1884 his teaching certificate was re-assessed; it was now considered equivalent to a second level certificate. Teaching in the schools at Madawaska, particularly in the parishes of Saint-Hilaire and Saint-Jacques, he had the advantage of an education far superior to that of teachers of his day. Moreover, he became known as a highly competent schoolmaster. He died on 16 April 1890 at Saint-Hilaire. In the course of his life many of his contemporaries noted his great charity, his austere style of living, and his piety.

CORINNE LAPLANTE

Arch. de l'évêché de Bathurst (Bathurst, N.B.), Papiers et notes du père Armand Martin. Arch. of the Diocese of Saint John (Saint John, N.B.), Statement of sub-diaconat, F.-X. Babineau, 26 Oct. 1850. Arch. paroissiales, Saint-Hilaire (Saint-Hilaire, N.-B.), Reg. des baptêmes, mariages et sépultures; Saint-Louis-de-Kent (Saint-Louis-de-Kent, N.-B.), Reg. des baptêmes, mariages et sépultures. Centre d'études acadiennes, univ. de Moncton (Moncton, N.-B.), Fonds Placide Gaudet, 1.30-8; 1.57-2. PANB, RG 11, RS 115/7/5; RS 115/7/8; RS 117/1/9; RS 117/2/2. *L'Évangéline* (Weymouth, N.-É), 15 mai 1890. *Le Moniteur acadien* (Shédiac, N.-B.), 6 mai 1890. Cyprien Tanguay, *Dictionnaire généalogique des familles canadiennes depuis la fondation de la colonie jusqu'à nos jours* (7v., [Montréal], 1871–90), I: 21. L.-C. Daigle, *Les anciens missionnaires de l'Acadie* ([Saint-Louis-de-Kent, 1956]). D.-F. Léger, "Le père François-Xavier Babineau: premier prêtre acadien du N.-B.," *L'Évangéline* (Moncton), 21, 28 janv., 4 févr. 1937.

BACON, ELIZABETH NEWELL. *See* LOCKERBY

BADGLEY, WILLIAM, lawyer, judge, and politician; b. 27 March 1801 in Montreal, Lower Canada, son of Francis Badgley*, a merchant, and Elizabeth Lilly; brother of Francis*, doctor and professor, and of Elizabeth, wife of William Molson*; d. 24 Dec. 1888 in Montreal.

After attending private schools William Badgley completed his secondary education under the Reverend Alexander Skakel* at Montreal and for four years worked in the business world. He then studied law and on 20 Nov. 1823 was admitted to the Lower Canadian bar. He founded a successful law firm, Badgley and Abbott, and in 1828 was a co-founder of the library committee of the bar of Lower Canada. He had failed in 1826 to be appointed protonotary in Montreal. In 1830 ill health forced him to Europe, where in 1834 he married Elizabeth Wallace Taylor; they were to have six children.

When he returned to Canada in 1834, Badgley threw himself into politics, and in that year was a founder and, in 1837, secretary, of the Constitutional Association of Montreal which brought together opponents, principally merchants in the city, of the Patriotes. He assisted in preparing laws for the establishment of registry offices on the British model and also wrote a pamphlet, *Remarks on the registrar's office* (1837). Badgley's favourite project was the promotion of the union of Upper and Lower Canada to redress "the old system . . . of proscription by which the interests of those of British origin were disregarded." For this project he laboured unstintingly, producing newspaper articles and addresses. In 1837 Badgley and George Moffatt* went to England to present the grievances of Lower Canada's "British party" and to lobby for legislative union; they returned to Canada in 1838 after the rebellion.

Badgley's abilities had been recognized in England where he was offered an unsolicited post in the Colonial Office. In 1840 the new governor general of Canada, Lord Sydenham [Thomson*], appointed him commissioner of bankruptcy, a position he resigned in 1844 to become, on 29 April, a judge of the circuit court of the district of Montreal. He served as a judge until April 1847, when he returned to private practice, was named QC, and agreed to teach Roman and international law at McGill College, which in 1843 had conferred on him an honorary DCL. On 23 April 1847 he was appointed attorney general for Canada East in the government of William Henry Draper* and Denis-Benjamin Papineau*. The following month Draper resigned and Henry Sherwood* took over the leadership of a decidedly Tory Executive Council, in which Badgley continued as attorney general. On 10 June 1847 Badgley gained a seat in the legislature by defeating Bartholomew Conrad Augustus Gugy* in a by-election in the riding of Missisquoi. As attorney general Badgley personally conducted the business of the Canadian criminal terms, reputedly the last to do so. Parliament adjourned late in July and during the fall Sherwood and his ministers decided to call a general election. The Tories were soundly defeated in the December voting though Badgley personally was re-elected in the same riding, and on 10 March 1848 the triumphant Reformers under Robert Baldwin* and Louis-Hippolyte La Fontaine* took office.

Badgley was an acknowledged leader of the opposition in the new legislature, and with George Moffatt persuaded Montreal city officials to take effective measures to curb the violence during the Rebellion Losses riots in that city in 1849 [*see* James Bruce*, Lord Elgin]. In the elections of 1851 he was returned along with Reformer John Young* in the Montreal City riding. Over the next few years he ardently opposed Inspector General Francis HINCKS' financial schemes, agitated for the abolition of seigneurial tenure, presided over the private bills committee, tried generally to "do all in his power to assimilate the laws of Upper and Lower Canada," and, despite his thoroughly Conservative principles, won the admiration of Governor General Lord Elgin.

In 1854, with the realignment of the old parties and the Liberal-Conservative merger, Badgley decided to retire, but was prevailed upon to change his mind. He was then defeated in the Montreal riding by the Liberal candidate, Luther Hamilton Holton*. His exit from politics opened the way for a highly distinguished legal and judicial career. He served as *bâtonnier* of the Montreal bar from 1853 to 1855. From 1855 to 1857 he was professor of law at McGill College, where he was also the first dean of the law faculty. On 27 Jan. 1855 he was appointed to the Superior Court of Lower Canada, and in September 1863 he was promoted to the Court of Queen's Bench as temporary assistant judge; he resigned on 31 Dec. 1864. His most important appointment came on 17 Aug. 1866 when he was named puisne judge on the Court of Queen's Bench. In this post he distinguished himself as much as he had when practising law, especially in commercial cases. He was "systematic and methodical in habit, sober and discreet in judgment, calm in temper, diligent in research, conscientious . . . courteous and kindly in demeanour and inflexibly just." Because of deafness Badgley reluctantly retired from the bench on 2 March 1874, the same year his wife died. He continued to be active, however, and opened an office as a legal consultant.

In private life Badgley attained the rank of major in the militia, and was a prominent freemason, being named in 1850 provincial grand master of the grand lodge of the district of Montreal and William Henry. Bishop's College honoured him with his second doctoral degree in 1855. Badgley was also interested in scientific and charitable organizations, being two or three times president of both the Natural History Society and the St George's Society and an active member of the Church Society. In retirement he collected ferns and other botanical specimens.

One of the last of the old-style Lower Canadian Conservatives, Badgley's attachment to British culture, to a constitutional link with Britain, and to Protestantism was translated first into a preoccupation with achieving a union of the Canadas, and then with anglicising Lower Canada by reforming such French institutions as the registration of land and the seigneurial system of land tenure. He was also devoted to the development of Protestant McGill College and of the masonic order. Thus an obituary could refer to him as a "staunch Conservative" and, in the same breath, as an "earnest advocate of reform."

ELIZABETH GIBBS

William Badgley was the author of two pamphlets: *Remarks on the registrar's office* (Montreal, 1837) and *Representation against the title of the seminary to the seigniory of Montreal; and objections to the proposed ordinance for the extinction of seigniorial dues in the city and the island of Montreal* (Montreal, 1839).

AC, Montréal, État civil, Anglicans, Christ Church Cathedral (Montreal), 2 May 1801, 27 Dec. 1888. PAC, MG 30, D1, 3: 205–7. *Debates of the Legislative Assembly of United Canada* (Gibbs *et al.*), VI. *Elgin-Grey papers* (Doughty). *Montreal Daily Star*, 26 Dec. 1888. F.-J. Audet, *Les députés de Montréal*, 19, 68, 295–97. Borthwick, *Hist. and biog. gazetteer*, 190. Morgan, *Sketches of celebrated Canadians*. *Political appointments, 1841–65* (J.-O. Coté).

P.-G. Roy, *Les juges de la prov. de Québec*, 31. Wallace, *Macmillan dict.* Atherton, *Montreal*, III: 20–21. Pierre Beullac et Édouard Fabre Surveyer, *Le centenaire du Barreau de Montréal, 1849–1949* (Montréal, 1949), 34–37. Cornell, *Alignment of political groups*. Dent, *Last forty years*. Helen Taft Manning, *The revolt of French Canada, 1800–1835: a chapter in the history of the British Commonwealth* (Toronto, 1962). J. P. Noyes, "Hon. Judge Badgley, ex-M.P.P., for Missisquoi," Missisquoi County Hist. Soc., *Report* (St Johns [Saint-Jean-sur-Richelieu], Qué.), 4 (1908–9): 47–49.

BAILE (Bayle), JOSEPH-ALEXANDRE, Sulpician priest; b. 19 April 1801 at Saint-Genest de Bauzon, dept of Ardèche, France; d. 31 July 1888 at Montreal, Que.

In 1823, after studying under the Basilians, Joseph-Alexandre Baile entered the Sulpician *solitude* (noviciate) at Issy-les-Moulineaux, dept of Hauts-de-Seine, France; two years later he was sent to Canada. "I scarcely knew in what part of the world the country in question was," he later remarked. Ordained priest on 1 Oct. 1826, he became a professor of the final year in the classical programme (Rhetoric) at the Petit Séminaire de Montréal by 1827.

From 1830 to 1846 Baile held the position of director of the college. During this troubled period, he was keenly aware of both clerical and lay animosity towards the seminary, and criticized the superior of the Sulpicians in Canada, Joseph-Vincent Quiblier*, for his timorousness in this hostile atmosphere. The petty bourgeoisie, enamoured of revolution, accused the college of playing politics in preaching "blind submissiveness to the authorities." The director defended his teachers, alleging that their sole concern was to teach the doctrines of Pope Gregory XVI and refute the demagogues who dared to come to the very doors of the college to snatch signatures for their revolutionary petitions. He recommended stern disciplinary measures to counter these abuses. Baile also criticized Quiblier for his authoritarianism, on the grounds that the latter took decisions regarding the Petit Séminaire de Montréal without even consulting the director. Discouraged, Baile sought permission to return to France on several occasions, but his requests were denied. In 1845 hostility to Quiblier spread and the ecclesiastical authorities considered it imperative that the superior depart. Bishop Ignace BOURGET therefore urged Quiblier not to seek renewal of his five-year term and on 21 April 1846 Pierre-Louis Billaudèle* was elected superior of the Sulpicians in Canada.

In 1846 Baile went with Bourget to France to report to the superior general of the Sulpicians on the state of affairs in Montreal. Returning to Canada in 1847, he took over direction of the Grand Séminaire de Montréal, which had been founded seven years earlier. In his 20 years in office, Baile vigorously imparted the Sulpician spirit to the seminary. He was particularly concerned about the training of ecclesiastics, having deplored the multiplicity and very uneven quality of the theology courses at Montreal and the lack of theological knowledge among the Canadian clergy. According to him, the young ecclesiastics, who were for the most part impoverished, looked upon the seminary as a makeshift solution while they awaited a more remunerative post in a college. He held that the bishops encouraged this lamentable situation, thereby depriving those under their authority of a sound education. Baile proposed that seminarists should be admitted to orders only after a complete course in theology, a recommendation that Bishop George Conroy* was to adopt 30 years later when he was apostolic delegate to Canada. As to the theological teaching in the seminary, Baile kept a watchful eye on it. His innate conservatism clashed with the reforming zeal of Bourget, who considered the seminary's courses not sufficiently ultramontane; Baile, however, refused to make any changes.

Baile played a key role in the issue of the division of the parish of Notre-Dame which covered all of Montreal Island and which had been united with the Séminaire de Saint-Sulpice. The case, which led to a major confrontation between the seminary and the bishop of Montreal, began as an administrative dispute, became a political, and finally an ideological one, and lasted more than 15 years (1863–78) [*see* Ignace Bourget]. From May 1863 to February 1866, almost without pause, Baile defended the interests of his community before the court of Rome, where he argued for the *status quo* in both the administration of the parish and the relations between the bishop and the Séminaire de Saint-Sulpice. He suspected Bourget of wanting to destroy the seminary in order to acquire full control of its property, and threatened the Congregation of Propaganda with the removal of his community from Canada if Propaganda changed the established order. Rome settled the dispute in December 1865 by a pontifical decree allowing Bourget to divide the parish.

Three months later Baile succeeded Dominique Granet as superior of the Sulpicians in Canada. He then waged a relentless struggle against Bourget's administrative reforms. When he was back in Rome in 1867, he alleged that the division of the parish of Notre-Dame was contrary to civil law. He strongly defended his right to chair the parish council and reaffirmed the inviolability of the Sulpician properties. The seminary enjoyed the support of such powerful figures as George-Étienne Cartier*, Pierre-Joseph-Olivier CHAUVEAU, Thomas RYAN, and Thomas D'Arcy McGee*. All of them supported Baile's views, both in Canada and in Rome.

In 1871 the superior suggested to Archbishop Elzéar-Alexandre Taschereau*, the apostolic delegate in the conflict, a compromise which would leave the seminary with a single parish covering the city of Montreal and make its spiritual charge the responsibility of the Sulpician superior. Bishop Bourget vehemently rejected this solution [*see* Joseph DESAUTELS]. Finally, after bitter controversy over the independence of the Canadian church and three pontifical decrees, an understanding was gradually reached.

The Séminaire de Saint-Sulpice submitted to the new spiritual régime. The government therefore granted civil status to the five outlying parishes, which had been erected canonically by Bourget at the end of 1867, and in which the seminary had given up responsibility for the cure of souls. The churchwardens of Notre-Dame were charged with the temporal administration of the four other new central parishes. Baile renounced the chairmanship of the parish council. For his part, Bourget recognized the seminary's property rights but also acquired the use of some Sulpician properties in so far as they served parish purposes. However, the parish council's debts remained a source of discord, which gave Baile an opportunity to submit to Bishop Conroy in 1877 the plan he had once proposed to Taschereau.

Despite these distressing confrontations, Baile never lost the esteem of his bishop. In 1866 Bourget entrusted him with the spiritual guidance of the Sisters of Charity of the Hôpital Général in Montreal (Grey Nuns), an office he held for seven years. As well, the bishop often asked him to direct ecclesiastical retreats; he had the reputation of speaking simply, without pretence or literary affectation. With Bourget's approval, he supported setting up the Trappists at Oka. In 1878 Baile had the honour of presiding at the founding of the faculty of theology in the Université Laval at Montreal. He retired in 1881 and died on 31 July 1888.

Baile's contribution to the field of education is beyond dispute. He had always encouraged his lay and ecclesiastical students to engage in intensive study. On the administrative level, however, he displayed profound conservatism. Preferring tradition to innovation, lest the attempt to improve jeopardize present benefits, he frequently said: "The best is oftentimes the enemy of the good."

ROBERTO PERIN

ACAM, 465.101; 468.103; RLB, 13–25. ASSM, 21, Cartons 48–50, 63; 24, Dossier 2, Tiroir 71, no.2; Tiroir 75, no.3; 27, Tiroirs 100–4. *La Minerve*, 1er août 1888. Allaire, *Dictionnaire*, I. Louise Dechêne, "Inventaire des documents relatifs à l'histoire du Canada conservés dans les archives de la Compagnie de Saint-Sulpice à Paris," ANQ *Rapport*, 1969: 188–89. Henri Gauthier, *Sulpitiana* ([2e éd.], Montréal, 1926). Léon Pouliot, "Il y a cent ans: le démembrement de la paroisse Notre-Dame," *RHAF*, 19 (1965–66): 350–83.

BAILLIE HAMILTON, KER (he signed **Ker B. Hamilton**), soldier and colonial administrator; b. 13 July 1804 at Cleveland (North Yorkshire), England, son of the Reverend Charles Baillie Hamilton and Lady Charlotte, daughter of the 9th Earl of Home; m. 19 April 1834 Emma Blair, and they had five daughters; d. 6 Feb. 1889 at Tunbridge Wells (Royal Tunbridge Wells), England.

Ker Baillie Hamilton was educated at the Royal Military Academy, Woolwich (now part of London), and in 1822 entered the Indian military service. In the course of 1826 he was appointed a writer in the civil service and private secretary to the governor of Mauritius, thus beginning a career in colonial administration. He became clerk of the Executive Council and acting colonial secretary of the Cape of Good Hope in 1829, lieutenant governor of Grenada in 1846, and administrator of Barbados and the Windward Islands in 1851.

The following year Baillie Hamilton was named governor of Newfoundland. Despite his 30 years of colonial experience he was not prepared for the turbulent politics of Newfoundland. He was not used to dealing with colonial liberals, and, as an extreme evangelical churchman, he disliked not only Roman Catholics, such as Bishop John Thomas Mullock*, but also high church Anglicans, such as Bishop Edward Feild*. Moreover, his colonial experiences and his aristocratic and clerical connections (his father was an archdeacon and his brother-in-law a bishop) predisposed him to seek to direct political and church affairs in the colony. An impartial and mediating role was alien to his nature.

Baillie Hamilton arrived in Newfoundland in the midst of the Liberal campaign for responsible government. The Liberals, led by Philip Francis Little*, welcomed Baillie Hamilton's support of their proposals in 1853 for reciprocity with the United States but were quickly antagonized when they discovered his opposition to responsible government. The agitation for responsible government had started in the 1840s and had received the open and powerful support of Mullock. Hamilton's predecessor as governor, Sir John Gaspard Le Marchant*, however, had declared the colony unfit even for representative institutions. Baillie Hamilton in his first confidential dispatch (which the secretary of state for the colonies, the Duke of Newcastle, thought excellent) opposed any constitutional change in Newfoundland because its small, scattered fishing population had little education and no experience of self-government through municipal institutions. He stated that the other North American colonies had prospered for three-quarters of a century under the system that Newfoundland now had, and that Newfoundlanders were too busy discussing abstract theories to deal with actual problems. He also lamented that the parties had split on religious lines and that the Roman Catholics, although a minority, were united in political action and could triumph at the polls over Protestants who were divided by denominational differences.

To counteract Baillie Hamilton's dispatch, Little and Robert John PARSONS went to England to enlist the aid of the leading Radical, Joseph Hume, in persuading Newcastle to grant responsible government. They were successful and on 22 March 1854 news of Newcastle's decision reached the island. Newcastle felt that, although Newfoundland would perhaps be the severest test of responsible government, the colony should be allowed the same treatment as the rest of British North America. Baillie Hamilton's position was thus undermined. He sought to redeem it by insisting on implementation, in a manner not inimical to Protestant interests, of the three conditions set by Newcastle: the doubling of the number of seats in the assembly, an end to the payment of members' expenses from the colony's treasury, and the granting of pensions to colonial officials whose jobs were eliminated by the change in the governing system. When the assembly agreed in its representation bill to double the number of seats, but in such a way as to favour the Liberals, the Legislative Council rejected the measure with Baillie Hamilton's full support. Sir George Grey, the new colonial secretary, urged Baillie Hamilton to act as an impartial arbitrator and to mediate in the deadlock between the houses; Baillie Hamilton refused, despite the Colonial Office's displeasure. The assembly refused to conduct any business, and it was decided in June 1854 to send delegations to England. Little and Parsons represented the interests of the assembly, Edward Mortimer ARCHIBALD and William Bickford Row*, the council; Hugh William HOYLES, the leader of the opposition in the assembly, was sent by the Central Protestant Committee. The deadlock was finally broken on 9 November, not by the governor but by the office-holders in the council who feared losing their pensions if they did not agree to the original proposal. Peace was not immediately established, however, because Baillie Hamilton, thinking that winter elections would disenfranchise Protestant voters in the remote northern and southern areas, decided to postpone polling until May 1855. According to Baillie Hamilton, Little threatened him with "consequences injurious to himself personally" if elections were not soon held; however, Baillie Hamilton remained adamant, supported by the Colonial Office.

As well as battling with the Liberals, Baillie Hamilton had also entered enthusiastically and even with rancour into the conflict between Feild and a group of wealthy merchants of St John's and Harbour Grace led by the evangelical William Thomas. Three questions were at issue: the appointment of an incumbent to succeed the Reverend Charles Blackman* at St Thomas' Church, St John's; the refusal of sacraments to Anglicans unwilling to give financial support to their church; and the employment of clergymen whom the bishop refused to license. Baillie Hamilton saw himself as the evangelical Protestant champion facing the Tractarian bishop, and he complained about Feild to the Society for the Propagation of the Gospel. Letters appeared in 1854 in two religious newspapers in London, the *Record* and the *Guardian*, about the controversy, and Feild threatened to protest publicly to the colonial secretary about Baillie Hamilton's interference; comparative calm was restored only when he left Newfoundland. Although Baillie Hamilton was prepared to continue as governor under responsible government, the Colonial Office felt he would do better elsewhere and transferred him to Antigua in March 1855. Charles Henry Darling* succeeded him in Newfoundland.

Baillie Hamilton proved to be a successful governor for the next 12 years in Antigua and the Leeward Islands. In 1867 he retired to Tunbridge Wells, where he lived quietly until his death. The historian Daniel Woodley Prowse*, although commending his "liberal and enlightened views" on telegraphic and steam communication and his "very able despatches" on the French shore question, condemns Baillie Hamilton for being "as unfit a man as the British Government could possibly have selected to fill a difficult position." Newfoundland was clearly a difficult colony to administer, and there is no doubt that Ker Baillie Hamilton exacerbated any conflict into which he entered.

FREDERICK JONES

Guildhall Library (London), Commonwealth and Continental Church Soc., Newfoundland School Soc., Committee minutes, 1839–80; Reports, 1823–80. PRO, CO 194/139–42; CO 195/21–22. USPG, D9A, D9B. *The Church of England in Newfoundland, as indicated in a correspondence between Thomas E. Collett and the lord bishop of Newfoundland and the Rev. W. K. White* . . . (St John's, [1853]). H. W. Hoyles, *Case of the Protestant inhabitants against the unconditional concession of responsible government* (London, 1854). John Little, *The constitution of the government of Newfoundland, in its legislative and executive departments* . . . ([St John's], 1855). *Guardian* (London), 5, 12, 25 April, 24 May 1854. *Record* (London), 23, 30 March 1854. *Times* (London), 9 Feb. 1889. *Times and General Commercial Gazette* (St John's), 3 June 1854. Gunn, *Political hist. of Nfld.* Prowse, *Hist. of Nfld.* (1896). Wells, "Struggle for responsible government in Nfld." Frederick Jones, "The early opposition to Bishop Feild of Newfoundland," Canadian Church Hist. Soc., *Journal* (Glen Williams, Ont.), 16 (1974): 30–41.

BANNATYNE, ANDREW GRAHAM BALLENDEN (baptized **Andrew Grahme Balenden**), merchant and politician; b. 31 Oct. 1829 on South Ronaldsay, Orkney Islands, son of James Bannatyne and Eliza Balenden; m. in 1851 Annie, daughter of

Andrew McDermot; d. 18 May 1889 at St Paul, Minn.

Andrew Graham Ballenden Bannatyne was only three when his father, a British government fishery officer stationed at Stromness, Scotland, died. During his school years there, Andrew was deeply influenced by the family connection with the Hudson's Bay Company, in which both a grandfather and a great-grandfather had served. At 14, after completing "high school," Bannatyne entered the service of the HBC as an apprentice clerk, and was sent to Sault Ste Marie (Ont.) for two years, and then to Red River (Man.).

Bannatyne soon became keenly aware of the commercial possibilities at Red River and determined to leave the HBC when his contract expired on 1 June 1851. He set up as a general dry goods merchant and fur-trader and was immediately successful despite the prediction of the governor of Rupert's Land, Eden Colvile*, that "this youth will [not] be a very formidable opponent." His parting with the HBC was not amicable. Bannatyne later indicated to an acquaintance: "I am still in their black books. I wish the whole of them were now in McKenzie's River living on nothing but Jack Fish."

The 1850s were not an easy time for the HBC whose control over the civil government of Assiniboia and monopoly of the fur trade were being effectively broken, first by the events which culminated in the trial of Pierre-Guillaume Sayer* in 1849 [*see* Adam Thom], and increasingly by free traders such as Bannatyne and his father-in-law, Andrew McDermot. The company made a final attempt to protect its position in 1858 when George Barnston arrested Bannatyne at Norway House (Man.). But the HBC legal advisers decided his arrest had been illegal, and Bannatyne was quickly released and compensated by the company. All hope for the resurrection of its monopoly was destroyed. Bannatyne went on to great business success. In 1868 he formed a partnership with Alexander Begg* and their spring brigade that year consisted of over 300 carts carrying 1,000 pounds each. They were soon the largest retail and wholesale entrepreneurs in the Red River Settlement.

As one of the most successful businessmen in the area, Bannatyne had been expected to take part in public life. He did so with great enthusiasm. There were successive appointments as petty judge, postmaster, president of the petty court, and finally, in 1868, councillor of Assiniboia in which capacity he attended 12 meetings. His entrepreneurial activities did not blind Bannatyne to the clouded future of Red River. He knew that the settlement could not continue to exist in isolation. As early as 1863 he wrote to Edward Ellice* that "Old Red River is going to the Devil faster than ever, and God only knows what is to become of us if the English Government or some other friendly soul does not take us by the hand." The devil arrived in Red River with a survey crew led by John Stoughton Dennis in August 1869, and the insurgency led by Louis Riel was soon underway.

Bannatyne played an important role in the drama of 1869–70, not least in his attempt to bridge the gap of fear and apprehension between mixed-bloods and whites. The racial tension underlying the events in the settlement was illustrated in February 1869 when the often arrogant Charles Mair*, an ally of John Christian Schultz* and the Canadian party, insulted Bannatyne's wife Annie, a mixed-blood. "Mr. Mair got an awful overhauling from Mrs. Bannatyne – it is said she slapt his face and then struck him several times with a riding whip in Mr. B's store in presence of several persons." Bannatyne certainly saw himself as a conciliator in the conflict of 1869–70 but he did not conceal his sympathy for the Métis. Yet his links with the English-speaking community were broad. In September 1869, when Schultz had some furs seized by the sheriff, Henry McKenney, Bannatyne offered assistance to him in his "troubles" as a brother freemason. Even as late as 19 Nov. 1869, Schultz was attempting, unsuccessfully, to enlist Bannatyne's support in his anti-Métis cause. As a prominent member of the English-speaking community Bannatyne was called upon to chair many of the tense meetings of the winter of 1869–70, indicating his general acceptability to most residents of Red River. But Bannatyne's own position was clear. At a meeting of all factions on 26 November, called to determine Winnipeg's position at the convention of 1 December, Bannatyne was openly sympathetic to the Métis desire to secure terms from Canada.

Early in January 1870 Bannatyne agreed to become postmaster in Riel's provisional government on the condition that union with Canada would be actively sought. The acquisition of such a prominent non-Métis for Riel's government, despite his undisguised sympathies, greatly aided Riel's hopes for consensus in the distracted community. Bannatyne also served as secretary on the second day of the mass meeting of 19–20 January which heard Donald Alexander Smith*, Sir John A. Macdonald*'s emissary, make the dominion government's case for union.

Relations with the mercurial Riel, even for someone as well disposed as Bannatyne, were not always easy. Early in February 1870, when it appeared that the Métis leader's plans for a provisional government might not receive general assent, Riel flew into a rage and arrested several people, including Bannatyne. It was reported that for several days, until the provisional government was accepted, Bannatyne was "kept in the Mess room at Fort Garry and is very comfortable." He was then released from custody, appointed postmaster of the new government, and with Riel "took a good horn of brandy." Only a few days later, however, Bannatyne's store was stripped of arms and powder by a group of Métis. He did not make an issue of the break-in and, after his election as a councillor of the provisional government in February 1870, things went smoothly between the two men. Emotions subsided somewhat following the proclamation of the Manitoba Act in July, and Bannatyne wrote to Bishop Alexandre-Antonin Taché* in August that "my feelings are with Presid. Riel and I don't hide it while I know he is working for the good of the country." The hope of multi-racial unity as the only possible future for Red River had impelled Bannatyne to support Riel's programme.

His attitude was not generally popular in the English-speaking community. One prominent Manitoban, James Ross*, commented on 29 Sept. 1870 that he "did not approve of Bannatyne's course because [he was] too much with Riel." But the lieutenant governor, Adams George Archibald*, who had arrived on 2 September, was anxious to avoid extremes on both sides of the recent disputes. Early in January 1871 it was announced that "the first parliament of Manitoba will be held in the house of A. G. B. Bannatyne Esq., the best and most commodious building in Winnipeg." At the same time, the Canadian secretary of state for the provinces, Joseph Howe*, named Bannatyne as the postmaster of Winnipeg. It must have pleased Riel who wrote that "the result of your wise action amongst the people during last year will remain and become apparent. I hope the Post Office will not be taken from you."

Bannatyne continued to play an active role in the business and public life of the new province. The St Andrew's Society was founded in 1871 with Donald Smith as president and Bannatyne as first vice-president. These two men, along with Sir Hugh ALLAN, launched the Manitoba Insurance Company the same year, although little came of it. The ill-conceived Fenian raid in October 1871 [*see* John O'Neill*] brought a vigorous response from Bannatyne in his capacity as justice of the peace. He ordered two suspected Fenians arrested without a warrant or any written information, but they were quickly released by Lieutenant Governor Archibald who was put to some trouble explaining the precipitate action. Bannatyne's prominence in the newly opening western prairies made him an obvious choice as a member of the Executive Council of the North-West Territories and he was present at the inaugural meeting in March 1873.

Bannatyne was becoming more deeply involved in politics. On the death of Sir George-Étienne Cartier* in May 1873, Riel decided to seek election in the now vacant Provencher constituency and wrote to Bannatyne in August that he had heard "you had offered to use your influence in my election with the people at Oak Point. I accept the [nice?] offer." The next month, however, John Harrison O'Donnell*, a member of Manitoba's Legislative Council, signed a warrant for the arrest of Riel and Ambroise-Dydime Lépine* for the "murder" of Thomas Scott* in March 1870. Bannatyne hurried to St Boniface where he successfully warned Riel but Lépine was arrested on his farm and placed in custody. Although Riel was still in hiding, at a meeting at St Norbert in October he was nominated (seconded by Bannatyne) and won the riding by acclamation. Bannatyne, with Joseph-Noël Ritchot* and Joseph Dubuc*, was apparently part of a committee formed to assist Riel in reaching Ottawa; although the new member left the settlement for the east shortly after the election he did not make his brief but startling appearance in the house until after his re-election the following year.

While supporting Riel's political career Bannatyne also worked on behalf of Lépine. Shortly after the latter's arrest Bannatyne attended a protest meeting in St Boniface where, with Ritchot, Dubuc, and Robert Cunningham*, a member of parliament, he was chosen as part of the deputation which approached Lieutenant Governor Alexander MORRIS for the release of Lépine. When Morris announced that the law must take its course, Lépine's friends attempted to arrange bail, set at the rather high figure of $8,000. Bannatyne contributed one-quarter of this amount, most of the rest being raised by the Métis community. Lépine was finally released on bail on 22 Dec. 1873. At his trial in October 1874 he was convicted and sentenced to death, but the sentence was subsequently reduced to two years' imprisonment. In June 1876 Bannatyne, who had largely lost interest in local politics by that time, did approach Lieutenant Governor Morris with a delegation seeking Lépine's early release from prison.

In the general election of early 1874, Bannatyne followed a bewildering, if not mysterious, course, supporting both Riel and Donald Smith. He assisted Riel in his bid for re-election in Provencher, where he devised a clever stratagem to remove some of the Métis who were opposed to Riel by hiring them as carters at the appropriate moment. The device succeeded splendidly. Simultaneously, Bannatyne had been actively supporting Smith in Selkirk riding despite the fact that Smith was ostensibly a Conservative, although he had recently broken with Macdonald. Then abruptly, on 7 Feb. 1874, one week before the election, Bannatyne resigned his appointment as postmaster of Winnipeg. John Taylor, the Liberal candidate in Selkirk, withdrew from the contest and Bannatyne was nominated to oppose Smith. This surprising turn of events infuriated the *Manitoba Free Press*, no friend of Donald Smith. The editor, William Fisher Luxton, refused to support Bannatyne, since he was "one of those who sowed the seeds of rebellion." The affair is difficult to explain since Bannatyne was aware that Taché was committed to the support of Smith. In any event, Bannatyne lost and the *Free Press* alleged bitterly that there had been a conspiracy to ensure Smith's election; Bannatyne, in other words, had simply been a stalking horse.

The following year, however, Bannatyne did enter the House of Commons. Louis Riel had been declared an outlaw and expelled from the commons, leaving the Provencher seat vacant, and Bannatyne was elected by acclamation on 31 March 1875. Nevertheless he took little part in the business of the house, and apparently did not even attend the session of 1878. He declined to seek re-nomination for the general election called later that year.

Bannatyne seemed to lose interest completely in partisan disputes during these years. Local political affairs did not elicit much response from him, and more and more he devoted his energies to other public matters and his business career, which flourished during the 1870s. In 1874 he sold his dry goods business (the partnership with Begg had been dissolved earlier) and rented his store to a large wholesale concern. He was now turning to land speculation as immigration from Ontario began to gather strength.

There was little of a public nature in Winnipeg in which Bannatyne was not involved. In December 1872 he chaired the meeting which established the Winnipeg General Hospital, and he donated its first site. Ten years later he and Andrew McDermot gave to the city the permanent site of the hospital, and for 12 years Bannatyne served as president of the hospital's board. His experience and his place on the Council of the North-West Territories made him a valuable source of information for the Post Office Department which was attempting to establish service in the territories. He was a member of the council which established the University of Manitoba in 1877. But not all his pursuits were so serious: in December 1876 he played in the first curling match in Winnipeg. He was also president of the first snowshoe club, and vice-president of the Manitoba Cricket Club.

As a leader of the business community Bannatyne was instrumental in organizing, in 1877, the Manitoba Investment Association, of which he was an original director and later president. The prospects of this association would be conditioned by the rate of immigration to the west and particularly by the route of the Canadian Pacific Railway. The directors of the association lobbied strongly for Winnipeg as the entry to the west. Accordingly, Bannatyne became increasingly involved in land dealings as the railway came closer to reality. When the route was confirmed in June 1881, Manitoba boomed and Bannatyne's fortunes and reputation prospered. He was known as an "honest land agent" and "a thorough gentleman" in his business dealings, and other businessmen deferred to him as a financial power in the west. Unhappily, he lacked the foresight to take his profits and avoid the crash of the 1880s.

The frenzied land boom peaked in late 1881 and then began a precipitate decline. Bannatyne was absent from Manitoba during much of 1882, largely for reasons of health, and his affairs suffered. From Hot Springs, Ark., where he wintered, he wrote hopefully in January 1882 that "the land boom seems certainly like keeping up," and in London, in November, he was writing in the same vein. But in the end, like many others, Bannatyne lost virtually everything in the financial collapse. He nevertheless maintained his sense of humour, commenting ruefully to a fellow merchant that "the only thing my creditors can't take is my trip to Europe."

His participation in local affairs declined with his fortunes, but he continued his interest in development. He was especially concerned that the CPR should not run through the United States at any point. In November 1882 he was hoping that Premier John NORQUAY "will keep strong with all his faults. If we want to be Canadians, we require to have our own through road to Canada on our own territory no matter what the consequences are at present. Sir John [A. Macdonald] in this is right."

Bannatyne tried to recoup his finances by dealing in Métis scrip. He acted as intermediary between local Métis and the Canadian Department of the Interior with mixed success. There were some quite unsavoury aspects to the business although Bannatyne was never directly associated with fraud. Even if he never regained his wealth he was able to continue to winter in the south. On 18 May 1889, while returning from such a vacation, he died at St Paul, Minn. After a large civic funeral in Winnipeg, he was buried in Kildonan Cemetery.

J. E. REA

AASB, F623–26; T7811–12, 12763–64, 12862, 13597–98. PAM, MG 2, C6; C14; MG 3, D; MG 8, B52; B61, Journal; MG 12, E. Begg, *Red River journal* (Morton). Alexander Begg and W. R. Nursey, *Ten years in Winnipeg: a narration of the principal events in the history of the city of Winnipeg from the year A.D. 1870, to the year A.D. 1879, inclusive* (Winnipeg, 1879). HBRS, XIX (Rich and A. M. Johnson). *Daily Free Press* (Winnipeg), 2, 7, 14 Feb. 1874; 1 April 1875. *Manitoban* (Winnipeg), 21 Jan. 1871, 27 Sept. 1873. Alastair Sweeny, *George-Étienne Cartier: a biography* (Toronto, 1976).

BARBU. *See* KAMĪYISTOWESIT

BARKER, EDWARD JOHN, doctor, publisher, and editor; b. 31 Dec. 1799 at Islington (now part of London), England, son of William Barker and Margaret Greenwood; m. first in 1821 Elizabeth Phillips (d. 1859), and they had 13 children; m. secondly 8 May 1868 Ellen Griffiths; d. 27 April 1884 at Barriefield, near Kingston, Ont.

Edward John Barker went to South Carolina with his family in 1807. His father died soon after and Barker returned to Norfolk County, England, to attend school. In 1814 he joined the household of a distinguished uncle, John Barker, British consul at Aleppo (Haleb), Syria, before being apprenticed to a surgeon-apothecary in Malta. His service career began when he was appointed surgeon's mate on HM sloop *Racehorse* in 1819. Promoted surgeon on the death of his superior, he determined to devote his future to medicine, left the navy, and about two years later received his degree in London. He practised for ten years in the London district of East Smithfield before deciding to emigrate to Upper Canada. The Barkers arrived in Kingston in December 1832.

His skill and kindliness as a physician attracted popular support in Kingston, but Barker had developed a keen interest in journalism and he soon became editor of the moderate reform *Kingston Spectator*, which first appeared on 15 Jan. 1833. The following year he published the first issue of his own semi-weekly *British Whig*. This new venture required considerable courage. Kingston, with a population under 4,000, already supported three newspapers and although Barker's dedication to the British connection was well known and generally approved, his reform sympathies were not popular in what was still very much the conservative "King's Town." Nonetheless his vigorous editorials, his coverage of both domestic and foreign news, and his support of agricultural and mercantile interests initially won him many readers in Upper Canada.

The rebellion of 1837, however, not only threatened the future of the *Whig* but changed the political philosophy of its owner. His paper was boycotted, his press was wrecked, and he was physically assaulted. He refused to bow to intimidation, but could not condone armed rebellion, and early in 1838 transformed the *Whig* into a Conservative organ. The paper prospered in its new role, and during the years 1841–44, with Kingston the capital of Canada, it was known for its extensive reporting of parliamentary affairs. When the capital moved to Montreal the *Whig* was too securely established to be seriously affected.

Barker's special problems during the next two years seem to have been attacks from local rivals. In September 1845 the *Chronicle & Gazette* published a public apology to him to avoid a libel suit. In 1846 he successfully sued Dr John Stewart*, who had founded the *Argus* for the express purpose of "dissecting" Barker. His relations with other Canadian editors were normally cordial, yet when delegates gathered in Kingston in September 1859 to found an association "to promote the influence of the Press as a factor in the welfare of the State," he avowed that he could see no real value in the project although he would certainly not "throw cold water on the scheme at the proper time for action." In the event he became a founding-member of the Canadian Press Association, but later paid it scant attention.

Not long after launching the *Whig* Dr Barker had founded a job-printing establishment, the Atheneum Press. Its normal business was the production of pamphlets, tracts, commercial "flyers," and annual reports of local associations. At the Atheneum Barker printed the journals of the Legislative Assembly for 1843 on a one-year contract. He was also attracted to book-publishing; the first venture was probably *The military catechism . . .* by John Sidney Doyle, published in 1838. In May 1846 he launched his most ambitious venture, *Barker's Canadian Monthly Magazine*, which he intended to be conservative in tone but politically independent and entirely non-sectarian. Each issue featured an epitome of the history of the month, articles on Canadian agriculture and commerce, and "original tales, essays, and poems – as far as possible from native talent." The magazine achieved critical acclaim but failed in a market dominated by cheap American pirated editions of British periodicals. The last issue appeared in April 1847. The failure brought Barker close to bankruptcy, but he was resourceful and on 1 Jan. 1849 in a bold venture the *Whig* became a daily, the first successful daily in Upper Canada; 13 years later a weekly edition was added to what was henceforth one of the most influential newspapers in Canada.

Although himself cultured and kindly, Barker was also as an editor decidedly opinionated, consistently opposing the Liberal party, annexationists, religious extremists, and the proponents of total abstinence, and holding strong opinions on the conduct proper for the officers of the British garrison and other public figures. He used sarcasm and ridicule with devastating skill – often unjustly. He was, however, quick to apologize for errors and generous with praise. This combination of praise, attack, and retreat made the *Whig* all but irresistible reading.

Throughout his active years Barker was influential in the masonic lodge, the St George's Society, the mechanics' institute, and the Frontenac County agricultural and horticultural societies. He was also a founder of St Mark's (Anglican) Church, Barriefield. Although he never formally practised medicine after 1834 he was a forceful crusader for public health and sanitation. His prime interest, however, was the development of Kingston, nowhere more evident than in the columns entitled the "Spring walk of the British Whig," published annually for years as a chronicle of local developments. Dismayed by the coming of the railway, which effectively sealed the ruin of Kingston's lucrative forwarding business, and by the withdrawal of the imperial garrison in 1870, worth approximately £100,000 annually to the community, he nevertheless did not lose faith in the city's future. He also campaigned vigorously for the development of Kingston's hinterland. The subject had engaged his attention as early as the summer of 1834, when he published a series of articles about his travels on the Rideau Canal which he also issued as a pamphlet.

Barker was devoted to music and the theatre and his reviews stimulated public support for both amateur and professional performance. He persistently chided the city for its lack of a proper theatre and a suitable concert hall. He had delivered public lectures on vocal music in 1834, and in 1836 the *Whig* printed his one-act operetta, *The bridegroom*. For 30 years few public dinners in Kingston were not enlivened by his fine baritone voice which was his real claim to musical distinction, serious but also convivial.

In early autumn 1871 Dr Barker's monopoly of Conservative press and printing patronage in Kingston was challenged by younger, more partisan Conservatives who had purchased the *Daily News*. After some negotiation, Barker announced in October that he would relinquish control of the *Whig* to his grandson and long-time aide, Edward John Barker Pense, on 31 December. In mid December John Sandfield Macdonald* gave Dr Barker an appointment as registrar of Kingston, a patronage post he held until his death. When Pense assumed control of the paper as 1872 began, an era in political journalism ended; henceforth the *Whig* became an organ of the Liberal party and the *Daily News* represented Conservative interests.

Edward John Barker, a man of complex and fascinating character, had been a respected citizen and patriot and a great editor.

John W. Spurr

E. J. Barker was the author of *Observations on the Rideau Canal* (Kingston, [Ont.], 1834), and published *Barker's Canadian Monthly Magazine* (Kingston), 1846–47.

Daily British Whig, 1834–71; April 1884. *A history of Canadian journalism* . . . (2v., Toronto, 1908–59; v.2 by W. A. Craick). H. P. Gundy, "Publishing and bookselling in Kingston since 1810," *Historic Kingston*, 10 (1962): 22–36. Donald Swainson, "Alexander Campbell: general manager of the Conservative party (eastern Ontario section)," *Historic Kingston*, 17 (1969): 78–92. *Whig-Standard* (Kingston), 14 Jan. 1949.

BARLOW, ROBERT, cartographer and topographical draftsman; b. 18 Feb. 1813 at Margate, England; d. 16 Feb. 1883 at Montreal, Que.

Robert Barlow's career began with the Ordnance Survey of Great Britain with which he served, probably as a civilian, for 27 years. For the last five of these he superintended a survey district in the Isle of Lewis before coming to Canada with his family in 1855. He was recruited for the Geological Survey of Canada by William Edmond Logan*, the survey's founder and first director; Barlow received his permanent appointment as chief draftsman in June 1856. In November of that year his eldest son, Scott, was taken on as his assistant.

Barlow's chief contribution to the survey was his role in the production and preparation of topographical maps for its reports and publications. Considering the lack of adequate topographical maps at the time on which to enter the large quantity of geological detail being collected in the field, Barlow served an important function. His greatest work was the *Geological map of Canada* which bears the date 1865. Engraved on steel on a scale of one inch to 25 miles, it was, according to geologist Frank Dawson Adams*, "considered one of the finest maps of the kind . . . published in any country up to that time." It was exhibited at the Paris Exhibition of 1867, where it was awarded a prize. A reduced version, on a scale of one inch to 125 miles, had appeared in the atlas that was published in 1865 to accompany the monumental 1863 *Report of progress* of the survey.

Barlow was also responsible for the topographical drafting of the first of a series of maps, on the scale of one inch to four miles, which have since formed the basis of the survey's mapping enterprise. The project was announced in the 1863 report and the first map was planned for the Eastern Townships, Canada East. Barlow assembled data from a wide variety of sources, using boundary surveys, Crown Lands Department records, and maps of the British American Land Company. This map was finally published as a topographical map by private companies, in Toronto in 1875 and in Montreal in 1883, without acknowledgement of Barlow's work. Logan had intended him to prepare a geological map as well but, after Alfred Richard Cecil Selwyn* took over as director of the survey in 1869, Barlow was assigned to other work and the addition of geological features was postponed indefinitely. The decision not to produce the geological map, caused by the controversy surrounding Logan's interpretation of the Quebec group of strata, became a source of bitterness at the survey, as an 1884 parliamentary investigation of the organization revealed.

On 20 June 1880, a year before the office of the survey moved from Montreal to Ottawa, Barlow retired. He and his long-time colleague, James Richardson, were the first to take advantage of the civil service superannuation benefits which in 1877 were extended to all permanent employees of the survey under an act of 1870. Although Barlow apparently shared to some degree in the grievances voiced by the survey staff in this period, he retired gracefully with none of the public reluctance displayed by Richardson. Barlow died three years later in Montreal.

Three of his sons followed him into the survey and related fields. Scott succeeded him as chief draftsman and held the post until his own death in 1894. John Rigney trained with his father and spent three years with the survey before beginning a career with the city of Montreal; he became city surveyor in 1900. A third son, Alfred Ernest*, worked for the survey from 1883 to 1907 and achieved some prominence in Montreal as a consulting geologist.

Barlow's most significant contribution to the survey was in the area of cartography. His importance is best stated by a fellow employee, Robert Bell*, who referred to him as "probably the best topographical draughtsman in the Dominion, so far as we are aware," yet Barlow seems to have been one of those people who existed inconspicuously, leaving little trace although pursuing a useful life.

WILLIAM E. EAGAN

Robert Barlow prepared the *Geological map of Canada . . .* (n.p., 1865).

Can., House of Commons, *Journals*, 1884, app. 8: 66, 70, 83, 103–4, 117, 119, 165–67. Geological Survey of Can., *Report of progress from its commencement to 1863 . . .* (Montreal, 1863), xiii; *Report of progress from its commencement to 1863, atlas of maps and sections . . .* (Montreal, 1865); *Report of progress from 1866 to 1869* (Montreal, 1870), 1; *Report of progress for 1870–71* (Ottawa, 1872), 9–11; *Report of progress for 1871–72* (Montreal, 1872), 14; *Report of progress for 1875–76* (n.p., 1877), 31; *Report of progress for 1879–80* (Montreal, 1881), 9. *Free Press* (Ottawa), 17 Feb. 1883. *Dominion annual register*, 1883. F. D. Adams, "The history of geology in Canada," *A history of science in Canada*, ed. H. M. Tory (Toronto, 1939), 7–20. T. C. Weston, *Reminiscences among the rocks in connection with the Geological Survey of Canada* (Toronto, 1899). Zaslow, *Reading the rocks*, 88–89, 124.

BARNARD, FRANCIS JONES, businessman and politician; b. 18 Feb. 1829 at Quebec City, Lower Canada, son of Isaac Jones Barnard, harness maker, and Catherine Telfer; m. 6 July 1853 Ellen Stillman, and they had two sons, Sir Frank Stillman* and George Henry*, and a daughter, Alice, who married John Andrew Mara*; d. 10 July 1889 at Victoria, B.C.

Francis Jones Barnard, who came from a loyalist background, attended school in Quebec City until the age of 12 when he went to work to support his recently widowed mother. In 1855 he moved from Quebec City to Toronto, but three years later Barnard set out for the Fraser River gold-fields, travelling via New York and Panama. He reached Fort Yale (Yale, B.C.) in 1859. There he mined for gold without success, sold his claim, found work splitting cordwood, and then became a constable. In 1860 he was purser on the Fraser River steamer, *Fort Yale*; on 14 April 1861 the engines blew up near Hope. He then helped to build the trail from Yale to Boston Bar, and on its completion obtained a contract to clear and grade Douglas Street in Yale. Barnard and his family made their home in this town from 1861 until 1868.

In December 1861 Barnard acquired the business of Jeffray and Company, which carried the official mail from Victoria to Yale without charge; that winter he took the mail on foot from Yale to New Westminster and back, a distance of 200 miles. The next spring, charging two dollars a letter, he carried mail between Yale and the Cariboo, a round trip of 760 miles. In May 1862 Governor James Douglas* called for tenders for delivering the official mail from Yale to Williams Creek in the Cariboo. Barnard and his partner Robert Thompson Smith organized the British Columbia and Victoria Express Company, submitted a bid of £1,555 for one year, and on 25 June were awarded the contract for monthly delivery during the winter and bi-weekly at other times. On 1 July the establishment of regular service was announced, and on 7 July Barnard started out from Victoria with her majesty's mail.

During his first year Barnard had only a pony which he led on foot from Yale to Williams Creek. In 1863 he acquired two-horse wagons to use between Lillooet and Alexandria and entered into an arrangement with George Dietz and Hugh Nelson* to convey the government mail from Victoria and New Westminster to Yale, the start of the Cariboo Road, and to Douglas, the start of the Harrison–Lillooet Road. Commencing on 1 May 1864 Barnard's Cariboo Express left both Yale and Douglas every ten days, converged at Williams Lake, and then ran to Soda Creek; from there the mail was shipped by river steamer and saddle-train to Williams Creek. On 22 June, in conjunction with Dietz and Nelson, he obtained the government contract of £5,000 a year to make three deliveries of mail a month to Barkerville. In December he received another £2,000 for providing weekly service.

In addition to his mail and express business Barnard had established a stage-coach line earlier that year, using four-horse thorough-brace Concord stage-coaches from California. These vehicles proved so popular with the passengers transported by Dietz and Nelson from Victoria and New Westminster to Yale and Douglas that Barnard purchased larger, 14-passenger, 6-horse Concord coaches. By employing "crack whips" and having relays of fresh horses every 13 miles along the Cariboo Road, he was able to travel the 240 miles from Yale to Soda Creek in 48 hours. During the 1864 mining season Barnard's stage-coaches travelled some 110,000 miles, carried all the mail to the interior, transported 1,500 passengers to and from Soda Creek at the one-way fare of $130, and conveyed $4,619,000 worth of gold from the Cariboo to Yale. He employed 38 men, owned 400 horses, and had a way-station and stock ranch at 134 Mile House. When the full length of the Cariboo Road was completed to Barkerville in 1865, he had more property and way-stations, and in 1870 he acquired still more land in Lillooet and Lytton.

Late in 1865 the mining boom faltered, passengers grew fewer, and the volume of express freight declined, but by that time Barnard had established a monopoly over gold-carrying after the government in 1864 suspended its armed gold escort. Confident of Barnard's reliability and honesty, bankers and miners entrusted conveyance to him, sometimes in amounts of $10,000 and $20,000. He reduced his service to Williams Creek to once a week in 1866. There was a boom on the Big Bend of the Columbia River that year, but it, and Barnard's Kootenay express service, were short-lived.

In 1867, with a contract to deliver mail throughout the colony from January 1868 to October 1870 for $16,000 annually, he absorbed the express company of Dietz and Nelson and controlled all business between Victoria and Barkerville. He began to dream of a transcontinental transportation enterprise and in December wrote a friend that he planned to bring mustangs from California to breed stock in British Columbia "preparatory to running a coach from Yale to Lake Superior. Don't put me down for crazy." He sent his driver Stephen Tingley to purchase the horses. Near the northern end of Okanagan Lake he founded the B X Ranch, which his son Frank expanded in the 1880s until it had 2,000 head on 7,000 acres.

In 1867 he had been elected to the Legislative Council of British Columbia. In September of the following year, as the delegate from Williams Lake, he played a prominent part in the Yale Convention, which passed resolutions favouring immediate union with Canada. Later he urged the Legislative Council to include, as a term of union with Canada, the demand for a wagon road from Upper Fort Garry (Winnipeg) to British Columbia. When in 1870 the Canadian government promised instead a railway to the Pacific, Barnard realistically decided not to compete with the railway but to confine his business to the Pacific slope.

In 1870 Barnard resigned from the Legislative Council to avoid a charge of conflict of interest and organized the British Columbia General Transportation Company with Josiah Crosby Beedy. In October, after he was unsuccessful in a request for a $32,000 government subsidy to import from Scotland specially constructed steam carriages for the Cariboo Road, he lost the mail contract, but two years later the federal government awarded him the provincial mail contract and the traffic on the road increased as surveying for the railway began. In 1874 Barnard himself won the federal contract to build the 700-mile section of the Canadian Pacific Railway telegraph line from Fort Edmonton (Alta) to Cache Creek (B.C.) passing through the Yellowhead Pass. He invested so much of his money in this project that it became necessary to reduce his financial interest in his express company. In 1872 two of his drivers, Tingley and James Hamilton, had been made partners in F. J. Barnard and Company, and six years later, when the British Columbia Express Company was incorporated with a capital of $200,000, it included as additional partners Barnard's son, Frank, and his brother-in-law, George Andrew Sargison. Frank became the general manager in 1880 and the president in 1883.

Barnard suffered a grave financial reverse when the government of Sir John A. Macdonald* abandoned the Yellowhead Pass railway route and in 1879 cancelled his contract for the telegraph line. He brought suit against the crown for $225,000 in damages. His success in the federal by-election in Yale in July 1879 did not go unnoticed in the east. The Toronto *Globe* charged that his only interest was in a financial settlement, and that his claim was of "the most fraudulent character." During the inquiry into his claim, held in British Columbia early in 1880, George Anthony Walkem*, the premier and attorney general of the province, acted as counsel for the federal government against Barnard. Later, when his own political quarrel with the dominion was at its height, Premier Walkem conducted Barnard's case against the crown but failed to get compensation.

Worry over the matter affected Barnard's health and in 1880 he suffered a severe stroke. He was re-elected to the House of Commons in 1882 but was soon an invalid, and did not run in 1887. The following year he declined a seat in the Senate. On 10 July 1889 he died at Duval Cottage, his home in Victoria after 1868, leaving an estate of less than $30,000.

During the gold-rush period Barnard had successfully eliminated on mainland British Columbia the competition of the small American transport companies as well as the powerful Wells, Fargo and Company, and had established a virtual Canadian monopoly in the essential carriage of mail, express freight, passengers, and gold. His famous "B X" Company, which in 1874 delivered mail through Wrangel, Alaska, to the Cassiar mines (B.C.), was said to be the longest stage line in North America; it certainly was unrivalled for efficiency and dependability. Tingley took over the company in 1886 and it lasted, under various owners, until 1913 when automobiles replaced coaches on the upper Cariboo Road. An entrepreneur who envisioned further Canadian participation in the economic development of the Pacific seaboard, Barnard was one of the prime movers in obtaining British Columbia's union with Canada.

MARGARET A. ORMSBY

Francis Jones Barnard was the author of *To the electors of the district of Yale* . . . (n.p., 1879?).

PABC, Add. MSS 527; 696; B.C., Colonial secretary, Corr. outward, September 1861–November 1862; O'Reilly coll., Dewdney corr., F. J. Barnard to Edgar Dewdney, 18 March 1883; G. A. Sargison, Diaries, 1871–72. Private arch., A. B. Robertson (Vancouver), F. H. Barnard, "Canada's first stage coach; Frank Stillman Barnard, businessman and pioneer; Senator G. H. Barnard, the younger son" (typescript). B.C., *Statutes*, 1878, c.2. *British Columbian* (New Westminster, B.C.), 14 Dec. 1864. *Daily Colonist* (Victoria), 11 July 1889. *Government Gazette-British Columbia* (New Westminster), 10 Sept. 1864. *CPC*, 1880. J. B. Kerr, *Biographical dictionary of well-known British Columbians, with a historical sketch* (Vancouver, 1890), 91–94. A. S. Deaville, *The colonial postal systems and postage stamps of Vancouver Island and British Columbia, 1849–1871* . . . (Victoria, 1928). G. R. Elliott, *Quesnel: commercial centre of the Cariboo gold rush* (Quesnel, B.C., 1958). H. C. Hitt and G. E. Wellburn, "Barnard's Cariboo express in the colony of British Columbia, 1860–1871, and later expresses of F. J. Barnard," *The stamp specialist black book* (New York, 1945), 3–32. E. O. S. Scholefield and F. W. Howay, *British Columbia from the earliest times to the present* (4v., Vancouver, 1914), II, III. "Francis Barnard: from his broad back grew a mighty industry," *Province* (Vancouver), 19 July 1958: 15. W. J. West, "Staging and stage hold-ups in the Cariboo," *BCHQ*, 12 (1948): 185–209.

BARNSTON, GEORGE, HBC fur-trader and naturalist; b. *c.* 1800 in Edinburgh, Scotland; d. 14 March 1883 in Montreal, Que.

After apparently being educated as a surveyor and army engineer, George Barnston joined the North West Company as an apprentice clerk in 1820. He was taken into the Hudson's Bay Company following the union of the two companies in 1821, and served as a clerk at York Factory (Man.); he was described as having an excellent education, and showed great promise. During the 1825–26 season he was at Red River and Fort Bas de la Rivière (Man.), and in 1826 he was transferred to the Columbia District to help Æmilius Simpson* survey the Pacific coast. Finding Simpson an incompetent surveyor, he was obliged to conduct most of the work himself. He then helped James McMillan* establish Fort Langley (near present day Fort Langley, B.C.) in 1827, and served there and at forts Vancouver (Vancouver, Wash.) and Nez Percés (Walla Walla, Wash.).

The records for the period 1825 to the mid 1830s reflect Barnston's frustration and unhappiness. He had entered the fur trade with prospects of a £100 salary at the end of a six-year apprenticeship. A long way from this goal in 1825, he became, according to Governor George Simpson*, "touchy . . . and so much afflicted with melancholy or despondency, that it is feared that his nerves or mind is afflicted." In 1831, although he was then in charge of Fort Nez Percés and had reached the salary level he had sought, a sharp dispute with Simpson over his next appointment and rate of advancement caused him to resign. He attacked Simpson and accused the company's agents in the Indian country of "ingratitude and dishonorable conduct." Anxious not to lose Barnston, Simpson, despite "a half impertinent Letter" from him, was already in the summer of 1831 instructing that he be re-engaged "if he be at a loss to find employment in Canada." Barnston rejoined the service in 1832.

Barnston's frustration with his career was perhaps augmented by a concern for his family. In early 1829 he had taken as a wife "in the custom of the country," Ellen Matthews, a mixed-blood daughter of an American Fur Company employee; James, the first of their 11 children, was born in July 1831. Barnston's writings and other records of these years also reflect much personal sensitivity and introspection, and a strong moral sense which was respected by Simpson, who described him as "high Spirited to a romantic degree, who will on no account do what *he* considers an improper thing, but so touchy & sensitive that it is difficult to keep on good terms or to do business with him. . . . Has a high opinion of his own abilities which are above par. . . ." This portrait is reflected in the one Barnston gives of himself in his letters to his friend and fellow trader James Hargrave*.

In the ten years following his reunion with the HBC, Barnston served in the Albany District. After a season at Fort Albany, he founded Fort Concord in 1833 "on the Banks of Wawbickoobaw Lake" (Wapikopa Lake, Ont.) to extend the company's trade into the Winisk River area. In mid 1834 he was ordered to Martin Falls where he remained for six years; he then transferred to the charge of Fort Albany and was promoted chief trader. His long-continued discontent at Simpson's earlier treatment of him was followed, as a colleague James Douglas* wrote, by "a break in the clouds" and a developing friendship between them in the 1840s.

After a year's furlough in England, Barnston was appointed to Tadoussac in 1844. The move brought him nearer to means of "having my children better educated, an object ever near to my heart." James particularly gained: he had schooling in Lachine, and then in 1847 went to Edinburgh for a medical degree; at his death in 1858 he was a professor of botany at McGill College in Montreal. For his father, Tadoussac was "an extended, troublesome, and complicated" charge, as Simpson warned, one beset by free traders, smugglers, and encroaching settlement. But it was an opportunity for Barnston to prove his abilities and justify Simpson's confidence in him, and in March 1847 he was promoted to chief factor.

In 1851, after a year's furlough, Barnston replaced Donald Ross in charge of Norway House (Man.). Discouraged by the activities of free traders in the area, particularly those of Andrew Graham Ballenden Bannatyne, and the declining fortunes of the company, Barnston went on leave again in 1858–59, and then accepted charge of Michipicoten (Ont.) on Lake Superior where he remained from 1859 to 1862. After another year's furlough, he retired to Montreal in June 1863. That year the HBC was bought out by the International Financial Society, headed by Edward William Watkin*, and Barnston was much concerned for the future of the company. The company officers had not been consulted and were hostile to the change in management. Barnston corresponded with the London secretary in 1863 regarding the protection of the interests of commissioned officers of the company, and travelled to England the following year on what his friend James Hargrave called the "sleeveless errand" of telling the company directors that they had "treated their old officers of the Fur Trade very scurvily."

Retirement freed Barnston to pursue scientific research, primarily in botany and entomology, areas in which he had already done much work in the field and as a writer. His botanical interests probably began with his exposure to the studies of David Douglas* in the Columbia District in the 1820s; he greatly admired Douglas, corresponded with him, and published a detailed sketch of his travels and discoveries in the *Canadian Naturalist and Geologist* in 1860. At Martin Falls Barnston first studied insects and he also kept a journal of temperature, permafrost, flora, and fauna of the area for the Royal Geographical Society of London. On furlough in England in 1843–44, he visited several scientific societies. "Finding that I was kindly received at the British Museum," he wrote to George Simpson, "I handed over without reservation all my Collection of Insects to that Institution, at which the Gentlemen there expressed high gratification." Over half his specimens were new to the museum. He later gathered an extensive herbarium at Tadoussac, which he described in his correspondence with Hargrave, and in 1849–50 sent a collection of plants to Scotland. He also supplied specimens to the Smithsonian Institution (Washington, D.C.) and to McGill College. After 1857 he frequently published articles, mainly in the *Canadian Naturalist and Geologist.* An active member of the Natural History Society of Montreal, he served as its president in 1872–73 and later became a fellow of the Royal Society of Canada in 1882.

When Barnston died in Montreal in 1883, pallbearers and mourners at his "largely attended" funeral at Christ Church Cathedral included Donald Alexander Smith*, Dr Thomas Sterry Hunt*, John William Dawson*, and other prominent Montreal figures. The Royal Society of Canada paid tribute to Barnston as both a "diligent naturalist" and "a man of kind and amiable character, loved and respected by all who knew him."

JENNIFER S. H. BROWN and SYLVIA M. VAN KIRK

[A list of articles written by Barnston for the *Canadian Naturalist and Geologist* up to 1859 can be found in Morgan, *Bibliotheca Canadensis.* Among the more important of his articles are the following: "Abridged sketch of the life of David Douglas, botanist, with a few details of his travels and discoveries," *Canadian Naturalist and Geologist*, 5 (1860): 120–32, 200–8, 267–78; "On a collection of plants from British Columbia, made by Mr. James Richardson in the summer of 1874," *Canadian Naturalist and Quarterly Journal of Science*, new ser., 8 (1878): 90–94; and "Recollections of the swans and geese of Hudson's Bay," *Ibis: a Magazine of General Ornithology* (London), 2 (1860): 253–59. Barnston's correspondence with James Hargrave is at PAC, MG 19, A21. J.S.H.B. and S.M.V.K.]

AO, James McMillan file (unaccessioned). PAC, MG 19, A2, ser.2, 1. PAM, HBCA, A.16/42: f.254; A.34/1: f.62d; B.123/a/34–41, 42b; B.134/c/14: f.142a; B.135/c/2: 74; B.214/c/1: f.26; B.234/a/1; B.239/g/4: f.6; D.5/10: ff.28–29; D.5/11: ff.19–20, 85, 115–16, 129; D.5/12: ff.90–92, 206–7; D.5/31: ff.169–70. HBRS, XXX (Williams). *Minutes of Council, Northern Department of Rupert Land, 1821–31*, ed. R. H. Fleming (Toronto, 1940). RSC *Trans.*, 1st ser., 1 (1882–83): liv. *Montreal Herald and Daily Commercial Gazette*, 15, 17 March 1883. H. D. Munnick, "Louis Labonte," *The mountain men and the fur trade of the far west . . .*, ed. L. R. Hafen (10v., Glendale, Calif., 1965–72), VII: 191–99. [H.] B. Willson, *The life of Lord Strathcona & Mount Royal, G.C.M.G., G.C.V.O. (1820–1914)* (London and Toronto, 1915). G. A. Dunlop and C. P. Wilson, "George Barnston," *Beaver*, outfit 272 (December 1941): 16–17. G. L. Nute, "Kennicott in the north," *Beaver*, outfit 274 (September 1943): 28–32.

BARRETT, MICHAEL, physician and teacher; b. 16 May 1816, in London, England, son of Michael Barrett and Frances Scott; m. Ellen McCallum, and they had four sons and two daughters; d. 26 Feb. 1887 in Toronto, Ont.

Michael Barrett received the greater part of his early education at Caen, France. In 1833 his father, an English barrister, determined to emigrate and took the family to Upper Canada. Michael lived for a time at Penetanguishene serving as a sailor and engaging in fishing and trading activities on Georgian Bay. Later he taught school at Newmarket, where he turned out on the loyalist side during the rebellion of 1837. About this time his father moved to Natchez, Miss., where Michael later joined him.

About 1843 Barrett returned to Canada West and studied law in Toronto for two years. In 1845 he was appointed second English master at Upper Canada College and assistant master of the college boarding-house. Later he became first English master, and also taught French and geography, but eventually devoted his teaching mainly to physiology, chemistry, and anatomy. His active connection with the college lasted for 35 years. In 1846 he entered King's College, from which he received a BA in 1849 (he received an MA from the University of Toronto in 1853), and where he also studied medicine. In 1852 he was licensed by the provincial medical board, and in 1855 he was awarded the honorary degree of MD from Victoria College.

In 1852 Barrett joined the Toronto School of Medicine, then headed by John Rolph*, and lectured in chemistry and medical jurisprudence. In 1854 the school became affiliated with Victoria College in Cobourg as the medical department of the latter, and Barrett became one of its five professors. He became a member of the senate of the University of Toronto as a representative of the Toronto School of Medicine in 1855 and served in that capacity for some six years. In 1856, after a disagreement between Rolph and his staff, all of the latter, including Barrett, broke with Rolph and set themselves up as an independent proprietary school, taking with them the name, the Toronto School of Medicine, which affiliated with the University of Toronto. At the university Barrett also served as an examiner in medicine and arts in the late 1850s and early 1860s as well as examiner in physiology and comparative anatomy for about five years following 1862. He continued as a professor in the medical school until his death, serving as lecturer in physiology after Dr James Bovell*'s retirement in 1870. He also lectured in this subject at the Ontario Veterinary College in Toronto from the 1860s until his death.

In the last years of his life Barrett played an important part in the establishment of the Ontario Medical College for Women. At a time when women were being denied admission to existing medical schools, Augusta Stowe* Gullen, who would be the first woman to secure an MD in Canada, appealed to Barrett and other medical men for assistance. Barrett presided over a public meeting which endorsed plans for a women's medical school, and he also delivered the main address at the opening of the college in Toronto on 1 Oct. 1883. He was appointed dean and taught at the college until his death.

G. M. CRAIG

Academy of Medicine (Toronto), William Thomas Aikins papers. "Michael Barrett, M.A., M.D.," *Canadian Practitioner* (Toronto), 12 (1887): 94–95. *Globe*, 28 Feb. 1887. *Toronto Daily Mail*, 28 Feb. 1887. W. P. Bull, *From medicine man to medical man: a record of a century and a half of progress in health and sanitation as exemplified by developments in Peel* (Toronto, 1934). W. G. Cosbie, *The Toronto General Hospital, 1819–1965: a chronicle* (Toronto, 1975). Augusta Stowe Gullen, *A brief history of the Ontario Medical College for Women* (n.p., 1906).

BATES, ANNA HAINING. *See* SWAN

BAYFIELD, HENRY WOLSEY, naval officer and hydrographic surveyor; b. 21 Jan. 1795 in Kingston upon Hull, England, son of John Wolsey Bayfield and Eliza Petit; m. 2 April 1838 Fanny, daughter of Charles Wright, RE, and they had four sons and two daughters; d. 10 Feb. 1885 at Charlottetown, P.E.I.

It is not known how Henry Wolsey Bayfield was educated as a boy. At age 11 he entered the Royal Navy as a supernumerary volunteer 1st class. The boy "displayed presence of mind that would well become the greatest warrior" in a naval battle near Gibraltar in 1806 and was promoted volunteer 1st class. He was made midshipman in 1810 and master's mate in 1814; he served in the Mediterranean, off the coasts of France, Holland, and Spain, in the West Indies, and at Quebec and Halifax before joining the British flotilla on Lake Champlain in October 1814. Although promoted lieutenant in March 1815, he was acting as midshipman on the *Champlain* when he was transferred in January 1816 to the *Prince Regent*, stationed at Kingston, Upper Canada, naval headquarters for the province. There he became acting master and later acting lieutenant on the sloop *Star*, a vessel employed in the Royal Navy's surveying service on the Canadian lakes under the command of Captain William Fitz William Owen*.

Bayfield assisted Owen in the summer of 1816 in the survey of Lake Ontario and the upper St Lawrence from Kingston to the Galop Rapids at Edwardsburg (Cardinal), Upper Canada, and became lieutenant and assistant surveyor on the *Star* in September. This was his training period in nautical surveying and Owen commented on his remarkable talent for the work. When the *Star* was paid off that fall, Owen persuaded Bayfield to remain as assistant surveyor for the projected surveys of lakes Erie and Huron. The following June, when Owen returned to England, Bayfield, then 22, was placed in charge of the surveys. For financial reasons the Admiralty greatly reduced the surveying establishment. Bayfield had only one inexperienced assistant (Philip Edward Collins, midshipman) and two small boats. They completed the survey of Lake Erie in 1817, began work on Lake Huron that fall, and in 1820 made Penetanguishene their headquarters.

The large number of islands and bays in Lake Huron and Georgian Bay made this survey a four-year endeavour. On one stretch of the north shore, Bayfield reported that "we have ascertained the Shape, size & situation of upwards of 6,000 islands, flats and Rocks." Altogether, 20,000 islands, including Manitoulin, were charted in the Lake Huron survey. On this survey, and later on Lake Superior, the surveyors had to take provisions for six weeks at a time in their two small boats. Bayfield slept on a buffalo robe under the boat's mainsail in all kinds of weather. On warm summer nights the men were plagued by mosquitoes, and at times they suffered from ague and scurvy.

Early in 1823 Bayfield and Collins sailed for Lake Superior in a schooner, the *Recovery*, chartered from the Hudson's Bay Company, with Bayfield as acting commander. He found it quicker, however, to use the two small boats for surveying and to employ the schooner mainly for the transport of provisions. In three summers Bayfield and Collins circumnavigated Lake Superior, examining all its bays and coastal islands. Their winter headquarters were in Fort William (now part of Thunder Bay, Ont.), where in May 1825 they met Captain John Franklin* who had arrived to begin his second Arctic expedition. Bayfield returned to England in the fall of 1825 and spent nearly two years completing the charts of the three lakes, annotating them with comments on coastal features and geological formations. He also prepared plans from his own surveys of the connecting waters (Lake St Clair and River St Clair, Detroit River, St Joseph Channel, and St Marys River) and of Penetanguishene and some other harbours. Bayfield was promoted commander in 1826. While in England he persuaded the Admiralty that a survey was required of the St Lawrence River and Gulf, to be connected with the chain of surveys from Lake Superior eastward. He argued that there was no chart of the river between Montreal and Quebec, and that from Quebec to Anticosti Island there were only the "very incorrect" charts made more than 60 years earlier by Colonel Joseph Frederick Wallet DesBarres*, based on the surveys of Samuel Jan Holland*. (Charts had been made of the Gulf of St Lawrence in the 1760s by James Cook*.) The Admiralty appointed Bayfield superintendent of the St Lawrence survey in 1827.

He arrived in Quebec in September, bringing with him two assistants, Collins and Augustus Bowen, midshipman. Later Dr William Kelly joined the service as surgeon. Bayfield contracted for a 140-ton schooner, the *Gulnare*, fitted with two small boats, to be built in Quebec to his specifications, for hire to the Admiralty. This was the first of Bayfield's three survey vessels named *Gulnare*, launched in 1828, 1844, and 1852, of increasing size and strength. In addition Bayfield had two six-oared cutters built for the Admiralty in 1828. Other vessels and small boats were added in subsequent years. Bayfield devoted the next 14 years to a survey of the entire north shore of the St Lawrence River. Also systematically charted in these years were Lac Saint-Pierre, Quebec and Montreal harbours, the navigable portion of the Saguenay River, the northern Gaspé coast, the Strait of Belle Isle, the coast of Labrador from Belle Isle to Cape St Lewis, the Belle Isle coast of Newfoundland, Anticosti, the Îles de la Madeleine and other St Lawrence islands, Baie des Chaleurs, the New Brunswick coast of Northumberland Strait, the Miramichi, Restigouche, and Richibucto rivers, and the main harbours along these coasts.

During the winter months in Quebec the surveyors plotted their observations of the previous season, then sent the plans and charts to the Admiralty Hydrographic Office in London to be engraved. Bayfield examined the proof sheets with the eye of a perfectionist, insisting on accuracy of location and name, good style, and the most appropriate scale for each chart. He envisaged the charts as guiding ships to safe anchorage "instead of beating about the Gulf in thick fogs and uncertain tides as they hitherto have done," with resulting shipwrecks.

In summer the surveyors worked from daylight to dark, except when prevented by strong winds or fog. On one occasion, Bayfield and an assistant were marooned five days in a storm on a barren, granite island off the northeastern shore of the St Lawrence. "We began to day to catch Puffins & young Gulls & to collect muscles & clams to make our provisions run out as long as possible," Bayfield recorded on the fifth day. He complained frequently of mosquitoes; on one August day he recorded: "Never saw the Moschettoes & Black Flies more thick, their bites covered us with blood while observing & we could not open our mouths without swallowing them. The torment of them was beyond description." On the St Lawrence coast in 1833 Bayfield encountered John James Audubon who was studying and sketching the waterfowl for his *Birds of America*. A tragic event occurred in 1835 when Lieutenant Collins was drowned while surveying the Îles de la Madeleine. Collins was replaced by Lieutenant John Orlebar, who carried on Bayfield's work after his retirement.

Bayfield (promoted captain in 1834) was frequently consulted by the Admiralty and the government of Lower Canada on problems concerning navigation. In 1829 he testified before a committee of the assembly of Lower Canada that although there were three navigable channels in the St Lawrence River, the river pilots knew only one. Subsequently, in order to qualify, pilots were required to be able to take ships through each of the channels. When the rebellion in Lower Canada broke out in November 1837, the British government asked Bayfield to advise on the earliest date in the spring by which British troops would be able to land at Quebec. He was consulted on the best positions for lighthouses on the coasts and islands of the St Lawrence, and later on the coasts of the Maritime provinces, and at Cape Pine, Nfld. When the question of improving the St Lawrence ship channel in Lac Saint-Pierre came up in 1846, Bayfield was summoned to Montreal to advise the Canadian government on the best course for the channel, but because of the cost of his proposals they were only accepted in part.

Many aspects of science interested Bayfield. Though he lacked formal scientific training, he was observant, had an analytical mind, and read widely in scientific literature. He was one of the first to collect samples of rocks and minerals from Lake Superior; these were forwarded to the British Museum. He presented papers on the geology of Lake Superior and on coral animals in the Gulf of St Lawrence to the Literary and Historical Society of Quebec of which he was an original, and later an honorary, member. Bayfield contributed sets of geological and mineral specimens from the north shore of the St Lawrence and specimens of organic remains from the Mingan and Anticosti islands to this society and to the Geological Society of London, and a set of the mineral specimens to King's College, London. Papers by Bayfield on the geology of the north coast of the St Lawrence and Labrador appeared in publications of the Geological Society, and he published articles on navigational subjects in *Nautical Magazine*.

Bayfield practised astronomy in connection with his work, and he was keenly interested in such phenomena as tides, mirages, and the aurora borealis. Before establishing the first magnetic observatory in Canada, at Toronto in 1839, the Admiralty consulted him about the best location. (He recommended Toronto rather than Montreal or Quebec because of possible magnetic influence by mountains near the latter locations.) Five years later, he was consulted again when the first observatory in Quebec (built in 1854) was being considered. Bayfield was a fellow of the Royal Astronomical Society, a member of the Société géologique de France, and an honorary member of the Canadian Institute at Toronto.

In 1841 Captain Bayfield transferred his headquarters to Charlottetown, the centre of his future surveying activities. Before Bayfield left Quebec City, John Stewart*, the master of Trinity House (the body that regulated St Lawrence shipping and the conduct of river pilots), presented him with a testimonial expressing appreciation of his "talents and scientific acquirements" and thanks for the assistance he had rendered. Henceforth, Bayfield worked mainly on the coasts of Prince Edward Island and Nova Scotia. His staff gradually increased to include three assistant surveyors, a draughtsman, and a medical officer. One or two of his assistants customarily went off in surveying boats for a few days or weeks to work on a survey while Bayfield laboured elsewhere, but he was always in command. He gave his surveyors explicit instructions and they reported to him frequently in person or by letter. He set high standards which he expected his men to follow. He had little patience with carelessness, inaccuracy, or indolence, but he showed appreciation for good work and did not hesitate to recommend his assistants for promotions.

One of of Bayfield's special concerns was to obtain measurements of the distances between the meridians of Quebec, Halifax, and St John's. After establishing the longitude of Quebec, he made chronometrical measurements of the distances between the three centres. With the assistance of W. F. W. Owen, who in the 1840s was surveying the Bay of Fundy, and the co-operation of American authorities (the Cambridge Observatory at Boston and United States Coast Survey), Bayfield established the meridian distance between Boston and Halifax. In 1844 he and Owen "connected" their respective surveys by measuring with rockets the meridian distance across the Nova Scotia isthmus from Baie Verte to the Cumberland Basin.

By 1848 Bayfield had surveyed the entire coastline of Prince Edward Island including its bays and deeply indented harbours, the Northumberland Strait coast of Nova Scotia, and the northeastern extremity of the Gaspé. In the next five years, he concentrated on a survey of Cape Breton Island begun in 1847, its coast and harbours, the Strait of Canso, Isle Madame, and the Bras d'Or Lake with its bays and channels. At the request of the Admiralty Bayfield went to Sable Island in 1851 to verify its position and make recommendations for a lighthouse. Bayfield's last major project was a survey of Halifax harbour and adjacent headlands and bays in 1852–53. Afterwards, the survey was extended along the coast of Nova Scotia from Halifax to Cape Canso.

From 1832 to 1855, Bayfield had worked on his *Sailing directions for the Gulf and River of St. Lawrence,* writing it in the winter months, chapter by chapter, and sending each chapter to be printed when finished. The work was published in three stages, in 1837, 1847, and 1857. The entire work was revised and published in 1860 as *The St. Lawrence pilot*. A list of latitudes and longitudes, compiled laboriously by Bayfield, was published in 1857 as *Maritime positions in the Gulf and River St. Lawrence, on the south coast of Nova Scotia, and in Newfoundland*. Finally, Bayfield wrote *The Nova Scotia pilot* in two parts (1856 and 1860).

Bayfield, in declining health, retired from active surveying service in 1856 and became a rear-admiral. He was promoted vice-admiral in 1863 and admiral in 1867 and was granted a Greenwich Hospital pension of £150 annually as well as his regular pension. He lived quietly in Charlottetown until his death.

Bayfield's surveying methods were necessarily primitive and his charts have been supplemented or superseded. He measured depths of inshore waters by leadline and offshore waters by patent sounding-machine, and features of the coast (inlets, shoals, and rocks) by triangulation and the theodolite. His chief instruments for determining latitude and longitude were chronometers and the sextant. Bayfield's principal objective was to provide reliable guidance for the more than 1,000 sailing ships and steamers that travelled through the St Lawrence Gulf and River annually. He discovered many errors in the existing Admiralty charts which, he believed, had led to numerous shipwrecks with great loss of life. His own charts and sailing directions were as accurate as he could make them and for over 50 years they, and those for Lake Ontario and the upper St Lawrence which were partially his, guided innumerable ships through the treacherous waters of the St Lawrence system. Bayfield's hydrographic successors in Canada have built on his pioneering work. John George Boulton, the first Canadian hydrographic surveyor after confederation, paid him this tribute: "I doubt whether the British Navy has ever possessed so gifted and zealous a Surveyor as Bayfield."

Henry Bayfield was largely self-trained, but he was highly disciplined and exceptionally diligent. He was distinguished in appearance, courteous, and kindly, but formal in manner. An Anglican, he was devoutly religious (Sunday services were held on his ship), and he was devoted to his family. His service to Canada has been commemorated by plaques in Charlottetown, Owen Sound (shared with Captain Owen), and Penetanguishene, and by the adoption of his name for a variety of geographical sites in Ontario, Quebec, New Brunswick, Nova Scotia, and Prince Edward Island. The Canadian Hydrographic Service traditionally names one of its ships in his honour.

RUTH MCKENZIE

Henry Wolsey Bayfield was the author of: "Notes on the geology of the north coast of the St. Lawrence . . . ," Geological Soc. of London, *Trans.* (London), 2nd ser., 5 (1840): 89–102; "A notice on the transportation of rocks by ice . . . ," Geological Soc. of London, *Proc.* (London), 2 (1833–38): 223; "On rating chronometers," *Nautical Magazine and Naval Chronicle* (London), [12] (1843): 220–25; "On the errors of the sextant," *Nautical Magazine* ([London]), 2 (1833): 462–66, 519–23; "On the junction of the transition and primary rocks of Canada and Labrador," Geological Soc. of London, *Quarterly Journal* (London), 1 (1845): 450–59; "Outlines of the geology of Lake Superior," Literary and Hist. Soc. of Quebec, *Trans.*, 1 (1824–29); 1–43; "Remarks on coral animals in the Gulf of St. Lawrence," Literary and Hist. Soc. of Quebec, *Trans.*, 2 (1830–31): 1–7; "Remarks on the St. Lawrence," *Nautical Magazine and Naval Chronicle*, [7] (1838): 1–8; and "Terrestrial refraction in the St. Lawrence," *Nautical Magazine*, 4 (1835): 91–93. He compiled for the Hydrographic Office of the British Admiralty: *Maritime positions in the Gulf and River St. Lawrence, on the south coast of Nova Scotia, and in Newfoundland* . . . (London, 1857); *North American lights* ([London, 1847]); *The Nova Scotia pilot, from Mars Head to Pope Harbour, including Halifax harbour* (London, 1856); *The Nova Scotia pilot, south-east coast, from Mars Head to Cape Canso* . . . (London, 1860); and *Sailing directions for the Gulf and River of St. Lawrence* . . . (3v., London, 1837–[57]), republished as *The St. Lawrence pilot, comprising sailing directions for the Gulf and River* . . . (4th ed., 2v., London, 1860). He was also one of the compilers of *Sailing directions for the island of Newfoundland, the coast of Labrador, the Gulf and River St. Lawrence, and the coasts of Nova Scotia and New Brunswick to Passamaquoddy Bay* (London, 1851). His maps and charts are listed in: *The British Museum catalogue of printed maps, charts and plans; photolithographic edition to 1964* (15v., London, 1967), XII, columns 668, 673–76; *Catalogue of the National Map Collection, Public Archives of Canada, Ottawa, Ontario* (16v., Boston, 1976); *Maps and plans in the Public Record Office* (2v. to date, London, 1967–), II.

PAC, MG 24, F28; MG 40, I2. PRO, ADM 1/573–87; 1/2544; 1/2792; 1/3444–45 (copies at PAC); ADM 9/15; 107/46: 65–66; 196/3: 115. *Memoirs of hydrography, including brief biographies of the principal officers who have served in H.M. Naval Surveying Service between the years 1750 and 1885*, comp. L. S. Dawson (2v., Eastbourne, Eng., [1883]–85; repr. in 1v., London, 1969), I: 72–74. Morgan, *Sketches of celebrated Canadians*, 480–82. W. R. O'Byrne, *A naval biographical dictionary: comprising the life and services of every living officer in her majesty's navy* . . . (London, 1849), 57. Ruth McKenzie, *Admiral Bayfield, pioneer nautical surveyor* (Ottawa, 1976). G. S. Ritchie, *The Admiralty chart: British naval hydrography in the nineteenth century* (London and Toronto, 1967), x, 107, 190, 199. J. G. Boulton, "[Paper on Admiral Bayfield]," Literary and Hist. Soc. of Quebec, *Trans.*, new ser., 28 (1908–9): 27–95. Nazaire Levasseur, "L'Amiral Henry-Wolsey Bayfield: esquisse biographique," Soc. de géographie de Québec, *Bull.* (Québec), 15 (1921): 269–82. O. M. Meehan, "An outline of hydrography in Canada," *Soundings* (Ottawa), 4 (1965), no.1: 5–23.

BAYLE. *See* BAILE

BEARDY. *See* KAMĪYISTOWESIT

BEAUBIEN, PIERRE, doctor, politician, and landowner; b. 13 Aug. 1796 at Baie-du-Febvre (Baieville), Lower Canada, son of Jean-Louis Beaubien, a farmer, and Marie-Jeanne Manseau; d. 9 Jan. 1881 at Outremont, Que.

After studying at the Séminaire de Nicolet from 1809 to 1815, Pierre Beaubien entered the Petit Séminaire de Montréal for a year of philosophy. With the encouragement of Abbé Jacques-Guillaume Roque*, one of his teachers there, and the financial support of his father and some of his family who were in religious orders, Beaubien sailed for France to study medicine. He completed his classical studies in France and on 27 May 1819 received a *bachelier ès lettres* from the Académie de Paris. Having begun to study medicine around 1817, he was granted the title of doctor on 16 Aug. 1822, following his defence of a thesis on rheumatoid arthritis which he dedicated to Joseph-Claude Récamier, his professor in the academy's medical faculty. During the next five years he worked in France and travelled in Germany, Switzerland, and Italy. Beaubien returned to Lower Canada in the autumn of 1827 and was granted a licence to practise medicine in the province by the Montreal Board of Medical Examiners on 28 February. On 11 May 1829 at Quebec he married Marie-Justine Casgrain, daughter of Pierre Casgrain*, seigneur of Rivière-Ouelle, and widow of Charles Butler Maguire, a former naval surgeon. They were to have eleven children, but six died in infancy; one son, Louis*, became a famous politician, two others were ordained priests, and their only daughter became a nun.

Despite a diversity of interests, medicine remained Beaubien's principal activity. When he returned to Canada, Abbé Roque, his former teacher who was influential in Montreal religious circles, had him appointed doctor to the Sulpicians and the sisters of the Congregation of Notre-Dame, as well as to both the Hôpital Général and the Hôtel-Dieu of Montreal. He was the first professor to give clinical lectures at the Hôtel-Dieu, where he practised from 1829 to 1880. During these years devoted to medicine, Beaubien is reputed to have been amongst the first to bring the stethoscope into use in Canada. In 1849 the Montreal School of Medicine and Surgery recruited him, and doctors Eugène-Hercule Trudel, Bernard-Henri Leprohon, and Jean-Baptiste-Curtius Trestler, to replace Daniel Arnoldi*, Francis Badgley*, and William Sutherland, who had gone to McGill College. Beaubien taught medical theory and practice in the school, and early in the 1860s agreed to become its president. In this capacity he participated in the thorny discussions concerning the affiliation of the school with a university authorized to grant medical degrees. As a result of McGill College's opposition to such a step, and of the successive refusals of the University of Toronto and Université Laval, the school finally affiliated with Victoria College in Cobourg, Canada West, in 1866 [*see* Hector Peltier*]. Beaubien was also public health officer for Montreal from 1832 to 1836, and medical superintendent of the Montreal prison from 1849 until his death.

During the union period, Beaubien became active in politics. He represented Montreal in the Legislative Assembly of the Province of Canada from 22 Nov. 1843 to 23 Sept. 1844. He was defeated by George Moffatt* in 1844 but won again in Chambly in 1848 and represented it until July 1849. In the assembly he sat with the Reformers, and promoted the development of means of communication. During these years he was involved in municipal politics in Montreal, serving as a councillor from 1843 to 1846 and becoming an alderman in 1847.

Beaubien also had substantial land holdings at Côte-Sainte-Catherine, Côte-Saint-Louis, and Côte-des-Neiges on which the present Côte-des-Neiges cemetery is located and the town of Outremont was developed at the end of the 19th century. He was joint owner with Louis-Hippolyte La Fontaine* and Joseph Bourret* of the sub-fief of La Gauchetière, which had been made over to them by the Sulpicians on 1 June 1844. In 1868 Beaubien presented four of his lots at Côte-Saint-Louis to Bishop Ignace BOURGET, for the establishment of an educational institution for Roman Catholic children. The Clerics of St Viator built the Male Institution for the Catholic Deaf and Dumb of the Province of Quebec on this land in 1879. Three years before his death he gave to his son Louis the 22 lots he still owned in Côte-Saint-Louis.

Beaubien's role in the development of banking institutions in Quebec is not easy to determine but deserves mention. He helped set up the Banque du Peuple, being a member of its board of directors at its incorporation in 1835. In 1846 he also took part in the founding of the Montreal City and District Savings Bank, which had been started by Bishop Bourget, and was one of its directors until 1850. Beaubien also participated in the work of a number of organizations. By 1834 he had joined the Montreal Natural History Society. A member of the Association Saint-Jean-Baptiste de Montréal, he was elected its president in 1859.

Although Pierre Beaubien was not a prominent public figure, his diversified career and his wealth made him a person of note in 19th-century Montreal society.

JACQUES BERNIER

Pierre Beaubien was the author of *Dissertation sur le rhumatisme articulaire, présentée et soutenue à la faculté de médecine de Paris, le 16 août 1882* (Paris, 1822).

ANQ-M, Minutiers, Thomas Bédouin, 19 avril 1834; J.-J. Girouard, 23 juill. 1842, 15 mai 1844; L.-O. Hétu, 24 août 1878; Édouard Lafleur, 8 avril 1863; D.-É. Papineau, 6 févr. 1854. ANQ-Q, Minutiers, Louis Panet, 10 mai 1829. AP, Saint-Antoine-de-Padoue (Baieville), Reg. des baptêmes, mariages et sépultures, 13 août 1796. ASQ, Univ., Sér. U, Cartons 101, 8 déc. 1860, 9 janv. 1861; 102. Arch. privées, Pierre Beaubien (Hudson, Qué.), Certificat d'admission à la Soc. d'hist. naturelle de Montréal, 3 avril 1834; Corr., 8 janv. 1864, 23 janv. 1877, 8 mai 1880; Diplômes de l'académie de Paris, 1819, 1822; Licence to practice physic, surgery and midwifery in this province, 28 Feb. 1828. Bas-Canada, Chambre d'Assemblée, *Journaux*, 1835–36. "Le Dr Beaubien," *L'Union médicale du Canada* (Montréal), 10 (1881): 96. *La Minerve*, 6 nov. 1866. *Le Monde*, 10 janv. 1881. F. -J. Audet, *Les députés de Montréal*, 247, 270. C.-P. Beaubien, *Écrin d'amour familial: détails historiques au sujet d'une famille, comme il y en a tant d'autres au Canada qui devraient avoir leur histoire* (Montréal, 1914), 146–47, 149, 151, 163. H.-J.-J.-B. Chouinard, *Fête nationale des Canadiens-français célébrée à Québec en 1880: histoire, discours, rapports . . .* (Québec, 1881), 615. Cornell, *Alignment of political groups*, 11, 15–16, 24–28. *Histoire de la corporation de la cité de Montréal depuis son origine jusqu'à nos jours . . .* , J.-C. Lamothe *et al.*, édit. (Montréal, 1903). Robert Rumilly, *Histoire d'Outremont, 1875–1975* (Montréal, 1975), 14. T. T. Smyth, *The first hundred years: history of Montreal City District Savings Bank, 1846–1946* (Montreal, [1946]), 161. L.-D. Mignault, "Histoire de l'école de médecine et de chirurgie de Montréal," *L'Union médicale du Canada*, 55 (1926): 597–674.

BEAUCHEMIN, CHARLES-ODILON, printer and bookseller; b. 29 March 1822 at Sainte-Monique, Lower Canada, son of Antoine Picart, *dit* Beauchemin, a farmer, and Marguerite Fontaine; m. Louise Valois of Pointe-Claire, Canada East, and they had eight children; d. 29 Nov. 1887 in Montreal, Que.

At the Séminaire de Nicolet, which he entered in 1836, Charles-Odilon Beauchemin was not a poor student but he was a rather unusual one. Fascinated by machinery, he is said to have built the chapel organ and to have taken an interest in the various processes of bookbinding. In 1841, after his father's death, he had to leave the seminary to support his family.

Beauchemin spent some time with the Montreal printer John Lovell* (neither the date of his arrival nor the length of his stay is known). He was able to improve his knowledge of bookbinding and probably became acquainted with the business practices of the book trade. In 1842 he decided to try his luck in New England. With several hundred books purchased in Montreal, and in Quebec City in 1841, and with equipment for a bookbindery, he hoped to find a clientele among French-speaking people who had settled in the United States. An unfortunate accident near the present-day Victoria wharf in Montreal forced him to stay in the city until he had repaired some water-damaged books; he took up residence on Craig Street, near Saint-Denis. In a few days he sold his entire stock of books without having made any real effort, and decided to settle in Montreal. The house of Beauchemin was born.

Taciturn and straightforward in his dealings, Beauchemin was always interested in the technical aspects of his business. He assembled some of the machines himself and improved others. In addition he attached great importance to the training of his employees. As the firm expanded and diversified its operations, Beauchemin went into partnership in 1864 with his brother-in-law, notary Joseph-Moïse Valois, under the trade name of Beauchemin et Valois. In 1868 they added a printing-press to the bookstore. Valois attended to business matters and Beauchemin to the technical aspects of book production: the presses, stereotyping shop, and bindery. The partnership lasted 22 years. In 1886, after Valois' retirement, Beauchemin went into partnership with his son Joseph-Odilon, who had been the company's secretary since 1876. The firm was known from then as the Librairie C.-O. Beauchemin et fils.

After the death of Charles-Odilon, the house subsequently experienced remarkable growth, yielding its owners substantial profits. One observer noted that in 1920 Joseph-Odilon was a millionaire. The firm began publishing its famous *Almanach du peuple* in 1855. The *Almanach,* which at first came out irregularly, became an annual publication in 1870, and still occupies a notable place in the popular literature of Quebec.

JEAN-LOUIS ROY

ANQ-MBF, État civil, Catholiques, Saint-Jean-Baptiste (Nicolet), 29 mars 1822. *La Minerve*, 30 nov. 1887. "Références biographiques canadiennes," *BRH*, 49 (1943): 228. P.-M. Paquin, *La librairie Beauchemin, limitée, 125e anniversaire, 1842–1967* (Montréal, 1967). Rumilly, *Hist. de Montréal*, II: 278, 334. Léon Trépanier, *On veut savoir* (4v., Montréal, 1960–62), IV: 158–60.

BEAUDRY, JEAN-LOUIS, entrepreneur and politician; b. 27 March 1809 at Sainte-Anne-des-Plaines, Lower Canada, one of five sons of Prudent Beaudry and Marie-Anne Bogennes; m. 18 May 1835 in Montreal, Lower Canada, Thérèse, daugher of merchant Joseph Vallée, and they had one son and four daughters; d. 25 June 1886 at Montreal.

In 1823 Jean-Louis Beaudry, "a pushing, determined, industrious lad," left the family farm in Terrebonne County for the commercial world of nearby Montreal. There he quickly found work as a clerk in a dry goods store on Rue Saint-Paul, and he apparently remained in this position until 1826, perhaps acquiring in the mean time a working knowledge of English. He then moved to the new settlement of Isthmus (Newboro) in Leeds County, Upper Canada, where for the next four years he served as a storekeeper for Messrs Baraille and Company, a Montreal-based firm supplying goods to the labourers constructing the Rideau Canal. Upon his return to Montreal, Beaudry acquired a position with an English mercantile house from which he was subsequently dismissed in 1832 because of his activities supporting the Patriote party during the violent by-election in April and May for the assembly seat of Montreal West [*see* Daniel Tracey*]. Probably because of his considerable expertise in merchandising, Beaudry quickly found employment with yet another English merchant on Rue Saint-Paul, William Douglass.

In 1834 Beaudry and his younger brother Jean-Baptiste opened a dry goods store on Rue Notre-Dame. Through Jean-Louis's ceaseless work and considerable ability the store, featuring damaged goods and stock from bankruptcies at bargain prices, soon became an immense success. Although Beaudry handled the purchasing end of the business, making a dozen trips to Europe over the next 15 years, he also contributed a keen, early appreciation of popular advertising. The huge shutters of the building were painted in gaudy red, white, and blue stripes, quickly acquiring for the business a local notoriety as the "store with the striped shutters."

Beaudry was also making a name for himself in politics. His sympathies had been evident as early as 1827 when he signed the petition carried to England by John Neilson*, Denis-Benjamin Viger*, and Augustin Cuvillier* to express the opposition of the Patriote party to the proposed union of the Canadas. He subsequently identified himself readily with the aspirations of the party, in particular with the policies of Wolfred Nelson*, Cyrille-Hector-Octave Côté*, and Ludger Duvernay*. Although still relatively young and unsuited by his lack of education to assume a significant leadership role, Beaudry possessed the necessary tenacity and penchant for physical action to throw himself "body and soul" into the movement. By the late summer of 1837, when the situation had deteriorated to the point where paramilitary associations were being formed in the city, Beaudry had acquired sufficient popularity to be chosen a vice-president of the political wing of the Fils de la Liberté.

His prominence, however limited, had its drawbacks. Apparently fearing arrest following the street clash on 6 November between the Fils de la Liberté and the Doric Club, Beaudry left Montreal for the countryside. Whether he remained in the province long enough to participate in the first heady episodes of rebellion at Saint-Denis and Saint-Charles-sur-Richelieu later that month is unknown. By the end of November, however, he along with other Patriotes was safely in Vermont. As the Patriotes' "agent in Montpelier," Beaudry toured sympathetic American centres raising money and munitions for Robert Nelson* who was planning an invasion of Lower Canada. Beaudry's efforts, however, were soon hampered as a result of strict enforcement by American authorities of a neutrality act passed in March 1838. Some time following the general amnesty proclaimed by Lord Durham [Lambton*] in June, Beaudry, a "voluntary exile," not having been explicitly named as a leader of the rebellion and thereby not subject to arrest, returned to Montreal and quietly resumed his business career.

The rebellions left their mark upon Beaudry. Although a militant Patriote, he had never been particularly close to the wing of the movement led by Viger and Louis-Joseph Papineau*, and following the union of the Canadas in 1841 he easily accepted the leadership of Louis-Hippolyte La Fontaine* and Robert Baldwin* and their demand for responsible government. Beaudry's support, however, was not unwavering; in 1849, perhaps as a result of his business concerns, he signed the Annexation Manifesto. He remained a fixture in Montreal nationalist circles, taking part in virtually every patriotic movement that arose. Characteristically, he was instrumental, along with other local notables, in founding in June 1843 the Association Saint-Jean-Baptiste de Montréal. His conventional response to the politics and nationalism of the period was reflected as well in his attitude towards religion: he became, and remained, strongly identified with the Ultramontanes in the Roman Catholic Church in the province.

Beaudry was not a conventional businessman. By 1837–38 he had already realized a "respectable fortune" from his retail trade and, although he continued to be successful in this field, he also began speculating in land, becoming "one of the largest real estate owners in the city." More interestingly, however, Beaudry was also one of the most active of a group of French Canadians who participated in the burgeoning field of joint-stock ventures. Although he was involved in many such concerns during his career, including utilities, insurance companies, railways, and banks, his participation from 1853 to 1856 on the board of directors of the unsuccessful Montreal and Bytown Railway as "perhaps the most prominent of the French Canadian businessmen involved," and his founding of the Banque Jacques-Cartier in 1861 are the most important.

Beaudry's position in the city's business circles led to his appointment in the late 1840s as a warden of Trinity House, Montreal, the body whose main function was the regulation of navigation into the port. He retained this post until Trinity House was abolished in 1873 and its duties assumed by the Montreal Harbour Commission. Subsequently named a commissioner, he served until shortly before his death.

If Beaudry's business abilities and his nationalism won him general respect and a growing leadership role in the Montreal French Canadian community, his personality attracted considerable hostility. All sources tend to agree that he showed great energy, courage, and determination: that he possessed "backbone." A wide segment of the press, however, was quick to elaborate upon his shortcomings. He was stubborn to an extreme, hot-tempered, rude, and brutally candid. Although his personal honesty was never seriously questioned, there was some unflattering reference to his sharp business practices. An article in *L'Opinion publique* noted: "Beaudry is not well read. . . . This is not to say that he has no education. . . . But of all the books in the world, the one he is most fond of . . . is his cashbook." His later career in municipal politics would heighten public reaction, both positive and negative, but much of the city's English-language press exhibited strong animosity, a reaction based to a large extent on his personality and style rather than his policies. After his death one newspaper would refer casually to his four illegitimate children.

In 1854 and again in 1857 Beaudry presented himself in the three-member riding of Montreal as the Liberal-Conservative candidate for the assembly and on each occasion was easily defeated by his opponents. Rebuffed on the provincial level, he soon turned to Montreal municipal politics, where his involvement in numerous associations and his eminent business reputation left him with few rivals. It was also an area in which the city's English-speaking population tended to play a less significant role than their numbers warranted.

In June 1860, upon the resignation of the councillor

for St James Ward, Beaudry was returned to the city council of Montreal during a by-election. He was returned in St James by acclamation during the municipal elections of February 1861 and, two weeks later, elected an alderman by his fellow councillors. The following year Beaudry contested and won the mayoralty from the incumbent Charles-Séraphin Rodier* by 332 votes. His victory was decisive and it had been achieved against the determined opposition of the Montreal English-language press whose motivation was dislike of Beaudry rather than any particular fondness for Rodier. The Conservative *Pilot* led the assault: "better half a century of Rodier than half an hour of Beaudry." The mayoralty would offer him "almost unlimited opportunity for nice little money making transactions." Its pleas were in vain. While the "British portion" of the inhabitants absented themselves from the polls, Beaudry carried the French Canadian east-end suburbs and the west-end Irish vote, "which was almost unanimously thrown in his favour."

In 1863 Beaudry retained the mayoralty when his only opponent, Benjamin Holmes*, retired from the race, and he was again acclaimed in 1864. In 1865 he handily defeated an Irish Catholic candidate but the following year, perhaps sensing growing opposition to yet another year in office and seeing a strong candidate in Henry Starnes*, a former mayor, Beaudry took the *Gazette*'s advice: "If Mr. Beaudry . . . were to take a few years of rest from his public labours, we are sure he would meet with less strenuous and less effective opposition in another contest. . . ." Beaudry declined to run.

The position of mayor in 19th-century Montreal conferred prestige but little power upon the office-holder. Under the city charter the mayor acted as convenor, in effect speaker of the council. In 1852 the charter had been amended to allow the direct annual election of the mayor, thus removing from the council the right to select its own presiding officer. This amendment served to discourage capable individuals from going through the trouble and expense of annual election to a largely powerless position.

Beaudry was not deterred by these conditions. He compensated for the lack of direct powers to initiate or to veto bills by bullying or obstructing the council through his sheer force of character. As an inveterate conservative he had ample opportunity during his term of office in the 1860s to provide what a "Scottish Protestant" had described in his letter to the Montreal *Gazette* as "factious opposition to many of our most valuable public improvements." Furthermore, Beaudry possessed sufficient demagogic qualities to be attracted rather than repelled by the burden of annual elections. And the prestige and limelight surrounding the position were immensely attractive to a businessman who had heretofore existed on the fringe of political and public life.

Following confederation in 1867 he was appointed a provincial legislative councillor for Alma division, a position in which all commentators agree he served energetically and ably until his death to further the interests of Montreal. In 1868, after the lapse of only two years, he again presented himself for mayor, this time in opposition to the widely esteemed Liberal businessman, William Workman*. Beaudry accused Workman of being an accomplished swindler of the public purse. He also introduced religious and national antipathies into the campaign as well as unsubtle east end versus west end appeals. He badly miscalculated in his clumsy electioneering tactics against his genuinely popular Protestant opponent. Beaudry received fewer than 1,900 of the 5,000 votes cast. The contest had demolished his fragile reputation. He was now widely viewed as a man consumed by unrestrained political ambition who, according to Workman, had used "the most bitter, most violent, most unjust, and most unscrupulous means of obtaining the end at any cost." Lingering resentment contributed substantially to his absence from municipal office during the next ten years.

By the late 1870s, however, political animosities had sufficiently subsided to allow Beaudry to regain the mayoralty. In 1877 he won a crushing victory over Ferdinand DAVID, and the following year was returned by acclamation. His second mayoralty was marked by much the same conservatism and obstructionism as the first. His response, however, to the 12 July disturbances in 1877 and 1878 is significant. In 1877 members of Orange order who had attended a church service were attacked by a Catholic mob and during the ensuing mêlée Thomas Hackett, an Orangeman, was shot and killed. Beaudry bore the brunt of criticism in the city's English-language press for not having used the police to control the crowd. In 1878 he ignored the troops that had been called up to quell the expected riot and instead employed special constables to arrest the Orange leaders as they emerged from their hall for their customary march. Although the *Gazette* regretted his interference with civil liberties, it and the rest of the city's English-language press generally were grudgingly restrained in the light of Beaudry's successful defusing of an explosive situation.

His handling of the Orange crisis won him considerable support among the French Canadian and Irish Catholics of the city, but Beaudry was defeated in the mayoral election of March 1879. Sévère RIVARD, his opponent, had nationalist credentials also but, unlike Beaudry, he was a resident of the city's largely French-speaking east end and he was eminently acceptable as a candidate to the English-speaking west-end voters. Furthermore, Beaudry's business reputation had recently suffered from the financial troubles of his Banque Jacques-Cartier and he had not been able to gain re-election to its board of directors. All these factors contributed to his defeat.

Within two years, however, Beaudry bounced back, wedging himself firmly once more into the mayor's chair, this time for four consecutive terms from 1881 to 1885, defeating popular municipal politicians Horatio Admiral Nelson, John Layton Leprohon, and Henry Bulmer by respectable margins. Beaudry's successes resulted partially from his playing his nationalistic credentials against the confidence placed by his English-speaking opponents in the tradition of alternating English and French mayors for the city. He was also assisted by the annexation in 1883 of the *faubourg* of Hochelaga, which gave Montreal a comfortable majority of French Canadian electors. More interestingly, a growing body of Rouges at city hall and their popular newspapers, particularly Honoré Beaugrand*'s *La Patrie*, had since 1883 swung their support to Beaudry, the Conservative.

During the civic election of 1885, however, the intelligent, highly charismatic, and frankly brazen Beaugrand himself decided to run. Presented with the choice of a Rouge or a Conservative candidate and seeing the machinations of Liberal Senator Joseph-Rosaire Thibaudeau* behind an attempt by the Rouges to take over the city council, the Conservative *Gazette* swallowed years of frantic hostility and threw its support behind Beaudry. It and *La Minerve*, however, stood virtually alone in their support of the incumbent. Beaudry's demagoguery, his hostility to a much-needed programme of public sanitation, his notorious quarrels with council, and his general obstructionism had made him a nuisance, more and more irrelevant to the realities of an increasingly complex municipal administration. Against a lively, competent reformer and nationalist like Beaugrand, he stood little chance. Beaugrand emerged victorious by more than 400 votes.

Beaudry's municipal career was over. About a year later, on 15 June 1886, he took ill while attending the Legislative Council at Quebec. He was able to return to Montreal but ten days later he died of a paralytic stroke. He had been a prosperous businessman, leaving an estate valued at approximately $500,000, and certainly a successful Montreal mayoral candidate. His nationalism had interested him in politics in the 1820s and it remained an important force until the end. On 23 Nov. 1885 Beaudry delivered his last public address to the great crowd assembled on the Champ de Mars to protest the hanging of the Métis leader Louis RIEL. In recalling the event *L'Étendard* wrote: "That day he was one of the speakers most applauded and, while a conservative, he showed that, standing firmly for the national cause, he was first and foremost a French Canadian patriot."

LORNE STE. CROIX

AC, Montréal, État civil, Catholiques, Notre-Dame de Montréal, 28 juin 1886. PAC, MG 24, B2. Sylvain Forêt, "L'honorable J.-L. Beaudry," *L'Opinion publique*, 22 mars 1883. *L'Étendard*, 26 juin 1886. *Gazette* (Montreal), 8, 9 June 1860; 1, 12 March 1861; 24 Feb., 1 March 1865; 26 Jan., 7 Feb. 1866; 21 Jan., 11 Feb., 2 March 1868; 17 July 1878; 28 Feb. 1879; 21 Jan., 12 Feb., 3 March 1885; 26 June 1886. *La Minerve*, 18 mai 1835, 5 nov. 1867, 10 janv. 1885, 26 juin 1886. *Montreal Daily Star*, 25, 28 June 1886. *Montreal Herald and Daily Commercial Gazette*, 26 June 1886. *La Patrie*, 26 févr. 1883; 27 janv., 13 févr. 1885; 26 juin 1886. *Pilot* (Montreal), 22, 27 Feb., 1 March 1862. *Canadian biog. dict.*, II: 78–79. Fauteux, *Patriotes*. G. Turcotte, *Le Conseil législatif de Québec*. David, *Patriotes*. *Histoire de la corporation de la cité de Montréal depuis son origine jusqu'à nos jours . . .* , J.-C. Lamothe *et al.*, édit. (Montréal, 1903). Rumilly, *Hist. de Montréal*, II–III. Tulchinsky, *River barons*. R. M. Breckinridge, "The Canadian banking system, 1817–1890," *Canadian Banker*, 2 (1894–95): 443. Léon Trépanier, "Figures de maires," *Cahiers des Dix*, 20 (1955): 149–77.

BECHER, HENRY CORRY ROWLEY, lawyer, politician, and author; b. 5 June 1817 in London, England, youngest son of Captain Alexander Becher, RN, and Frances Scott; m. first 27 Oct. 1841 Sarah Evanson Leonard (d.1864), and they had eight children; m. secondly in 1874 Caroline Robertson, *née* Street; d. 6 July 1885 at Sidcup, England.

Henry Corry Rowley Becher immigrated to London, Upper Canada, in 1835. He began articling with John Wilson* in 1836 and was appointed registrar of the Surrogate Court of Middlesex County in 1839. Becher was admitted an attorney on 2 Nov. 1340 and was called to the bar on 2 Aug. 1841. He was elected a bencher of the Law Society of Upper Canada in 1853 and lectured a term at Osgoode Hall, Toronto, in 1856; the same year he was appointed QC on 4 October.

By the 1850s Becher was one of the busiest lawyers in the London area. Solicitor for Colonel Thomas Talbot* during the early 1850s, in 1852 he drew up the will that bequeathed most of the colonel's remaining estate to George Macbeth*, thereby causing an uproar in Talbot's family. Becher was also the municipal solicitor for London from 1849 to 1853. In April and May of 1855 alone he handled the crown business at the assizes at St Thomas, London, and Chatham, as well as submitting 27 civil briefs at St Thomas and 35 at London. In 1857 he became the solicitor of the Gore Bank and a director of the Great Western Railway. He had done legal business with the railway since 1852 but had refused the job of solicitor, and the £1,000 per annum plus staff that accompanied it. In the 1870s

Becher was again involved in a celebrated legal controversy which involved the settlement of an estate. The family of George Jervis Goodhue* objected to the stipulation in Goodhue's will that the majority of the estate was not to be distributed until after the death of his wife. The family managed to have a private bill passed in the Ontario legislature which supported their claims. Becher, however, refused to relent and on appeal his position was supported by a panel of nine judges. The estate was not distributed until after the death of Mrs Goodhue in 1880.

Becher's political career was almost the antithesis of his successful legal practice. He sat on the town council of London from 1850 to 1854 but his attempts to enter provincial politics were unsuccessful. In 1857 he failed to obtain the Conservative nomination in London which went to John Carling*, who later introduced the bill for the Goodhue family. In 1860 a by-election for the Legislative Assembly in Middlesex East promised to be an easy victory for the Conservatives. Becher managed to obtain the nomination for the Conservatives but Maurice Berkeley Portman, an unsuccessful candidate for the nomination, threw his support behind Francis Evans Cornish* who was running as a Conservative Orangeman. This split in Conservative forces allowed the Reformer to carry the riding. In 1861 Becher and Portman again vied for the Conservative nomination. Becher withdrew, after the intervention of John A. Macdonald*, with the promise of Portman's support in the election for the Legislative Council for Malahide. Portman won his contest but did not provide the expected support to Becher who lost to Elijah Leonard* Jr. After this defeat Becher never ran for public office but remained an active party organizer.

Becher was the victim of local Conservative rivalries, nominating conventions which he considered "immoral and democratic," and of his own reserved and proper manner. Although he was generally acknowledged as the most able candidate, the most polished speaker, and a man of "honor, intelligence and education," the fact that he was a lawyer hurt him in the predominantly rural areas in which he ran. This issue became explicit in the contest with Leonard when Becher suggested that the manufacturer of farm implements should "stick to his plough points," only to be met with the rejoinder that he should stick to his "law points." In 1860 John A. Macdonald advised Becher to canvass vigorously and thoroughly. "Lay aside your high-heeled boots for a while and take to proof whiskey. You can become a Tee-totaller the moment you are elected."

After giving up his political ambitions Becher made travel his major avocation. He crossed the Atlantic 20 times, made a number of trips to Florida, and travelled to Mexico in 1878; he wrote a book to assure people that Mexico was a good place to visit. His travels, however, confirmed his belief that Canada was the best place to live. Its people were "strong, hardy, energetic" because of the climate, God-fearing, and law-abiding. Its government was "the freest in the world" because it was "well understood and never lost sight of in practice, that the *rights* of men are equal."

In 1880 he became a fellow of the Royal Geographical Society and in 1882 a barrister of the Inner Temple, London, England. By the time of his death he owned considerable land, some in northern Ontario but chiefly in London. The most valuable was the 13 acres surrounding Thornwood, his impressive residence, which in 1970 was declared an historic site.

ELWOOD H. JONES

H. C. R. Becher was the author of *A trip to Mexico, being notes of a journey from Lake Erie to Lake Tezcuco and back . . .* (Toronto, 1880), and his diary, edited by M. A. Garland and Orlo Miller, has been published in *OH*, 33 (1939): 116–43. Letters from John A. Macdonald to Becher are in the possession of Mrs A. V. Becher (London, Ont.), and some have been edited by E. H. Jones in "Some letters from John A. Macdonald to H. C. R. Becher, 1857–63," *Western Ontario Hist. Notes* ([London]), 21 (1965), no.1: 26–33.

UWO, H. C. R. Becher papers. Macdonald, *Letters* (J. K. Johnson and Stelmack), I, II. "The Richard Airey–Henry C. R. Becher correspondence," ed. M. A. Garland, *Western Ontario Hist. Nuggets* (London), 36 (1969). *The Talbot papers . . .* , ed. J. H. Coyne ([Toronto], 1909). *London Free Press*, 1857–63. *Dominion annual register*, 1885.

BEDDOME, HENRY SEPTIMUS, physician and HBC employee; b.*c.* June 1830 in the parish of St Peter upon Cornhill, London, England, son of William Beddome; m. 11 July 1859 Frances Omand of the Red River Settlement (Man.), and they had eight children; d. 24 March 1881 at Headingley, Man.

In October 1848 Henry Septimus Beddome began the study of medicine at Guy's Hospital in London, shortly after significant educational reforms had been introduced. Clinical lectures, bedside teaching, case reporting, and the employment of senior students in the medical and surgical wards in positions of gradually increasing responsibility: all these were now characteristic features of Guy's. In June 1851, before completing the third and final year of his medical course, Beddome embarked as a surgeon on the Hudson's Bay Company's *Prince of Wales* for its annual voyage to York Factory (Man.). He returned to his studies in the fall of 1851 and on 3 May of the following year signed an agreement to return to York Factory as "Surgeon and Clerk" for five years at £100 per annum with return transportation guaranteed. Medical certificates dated 26 May show he qualified as a member of the Royal College of Surgeons of England; one week later he embarked on the *Prince of Wales*.

Upon landing on 11 September, Beddome found that he had under his immediate care 50 or more persons who wintered in the cluster of storehouses, workshops, and living quarters that was York Factory. Their life and work were wearing and hazardous. Although none of Beddome's medical journals survive, it is likely that he had to cope with the same sort of afflictions, disorders, and emergencies as his predecessor, including blurred vision and headaches, rheumatism, dysentery, sledding and other accidents, childbirth, scurvy, and influenza.

Beddome's responsibilities ranged far beyond the confines of the post. He was sent to Fort Churchill (Churchill, Man.) in 1854 to treat Postmaster William Anderson's ailments. He was also the public health and quarantine officer for the entire Northern Department of the HBC and for ships sailing to England. Epidemics could rage through a summer population swollen by interior boatmen, visiting natives, and ships' passengers.

In 1857, when Beddome's term of service ended, Bishop David ANDERSON of Rupert's Land apparently convinced him that he might earn £200 a year as a surgeon in the Red River Settlement. Beddome travelled to Upper Fort Garry (Winnipeg) with a detachment of Royal Canadian Rifles, sent out at the request of the HBC to buttress its authority among the residents of Red River as well as to counter Sioux movements to the south and American troops stationed at Pembina (N. Dak.). Sixteen York boats from Red River carried Beddome, 100 soldiers, 12 women, and a number of children over 700 miles and 34 portages south to the Red River Settlement. Beddome remained at Red River for two years and in June 1859 he signed another agreement with the HBC to serve as surgeon and clerk at York Factory for five years, first at £120 per year and then at £150. He took his bride to the north with him.

When typhus broke out among the 70-odd HBC recruits who arrived on the *Prince of Wales* in 1863, Beddome permitted only about a third of them to travel inland. From September until early December there were always 20 to 30 sick men: the outbreak was no doubt Beddome's greatest trial in his decade of doctoring on the bay.

In September 1864 Beddome and his family returned to Red River where he established a practice and a permanent residence, according to family tradition on the Red River just south of St Andrew's Church. Beddome rode on horseback to his calls or treated patients in his surgery. It is said that when Louis RIEL went into hiding in 1870, Beddome concealed him for a while in his dispensary.

Beddome and fellow doctors, John Harrison O'Donnell*, Curtis James Bird*, John Christian Schultz*, and J. B. Campbell, were the founders of the Medical Health Board of Manitoba, incorporated in 1871. It became the College of Physicians and Surgeons of Manitoba in 1877.

When smallpox broke out in November 1876 among the recently arrived Icelandic settlers at Gimli, Man., and spread among local Indians, a board of health was organized under the chairmanship of Lieutenant-Colonel William Osborne SMITH. Beddome, perhaps because of his York Factory experience, was chosen to make a tour of inspection of the east side of Lake Winnipeg during the winter. At Sandy River he buried the corpses of the HBC officer and two Indians, and he vaccinated the people at Fort Alexander on the Winnipeg River. In February 1877 Beddome took over the supervision of the Gimli district and stayed until spring, when the Icelanders began to abandon their winter dwellings and move into new ones built on their homesteads back from the lake. Beddome died at Headingley, on 24 March 1881, and was buried in the cemetery of St Andrew's Church.

THOMAS F. BREDIN

PAM, HBCA, A.32/21; B.239/a/103–8, 180; MG 7, B4; MG 12, B1, Corr., nos.1384, 1458, 1466, 1517; B2, Corr., nos.202, 211, 221, 255, 335. H. C. Cameron, *Mr Guy's hospital, 1726–1948* (London and Toronto, 1954). R. [B.] Mitchell, *Medicine in Manitoba, the story of its beginnings* (Winnipeg, [1955]). A. M. Johnson, "Life on the Hayes," *Beaver*, outfit 288 (winter 1957): 38–43. G. F. G. Stanley, "A soldier at Fort Garry," *Beaver*, outfit 288 (autumn 1957): 10–15.

BÉLANGER, FRANÇOIS-XAVIER, naturalist and museum curator; b. 1833 at Saint-Vallier, Lower Canada; m. Vitaline Fontaine; d. 19 Jan. 1882 at Quebec City.

François-Xavier Bélanger received a classical education at the Petit Séminaire de Québec from 1846 to 1853, and then worked as a schoolteacher for a few years. Finding himself lonely in his rural school district, he returned to Quebec and joined *Le Courrier du Canada*, where he became a proof-reader and later assistant editor. In 1868 he attracted attention when articles on certain species of Canadian silkworms appeared in the paper over his signature. His interest in natural history and talent for drawing caught the eye of Abbé Léon Provancher*, who invited him to prepare articles and prints for *Le Naturaliste canadien*, a monthly magazine launched in 1868. The following year, thanks to support from Provancher but particularly through the influence of Abbé Thomas-Étienne Hamel* (then professor of physics and dean of arts at the Université Laval), Bélanger received the title of curator of the university's zoological museum. With an annual salary of £100, he was responsible for the maintenance and development of the collections.

At that period the zoological museum contained a small number of unrelated pieces which had been assembled haphazardly by the priests of the Séminaire de Québec. The only items of value were specimens of American birds acquired through the Smithsonian Institution in Washington, and a small collection of North American coleoptera purchased from William COUPER in 1866.

His agreement with the Université Laval provided that Bélanger was to increase the number of indigenous species by collecting in the Quebec City region and travelling to other parts of the country. Similarly, through exchanges with naturalists and museums abroad, he was to build up the collections of exotic species. He was also to mount birds, fish, and mammals for exhibitions, to show visitors around, and to look after security in the museum. Evidently Bélanger discharged his many duties conscientiously: an 1875 inventory indicates that the museum owned more than 1,300 birds, about 100 mammals, a like number of reptiles and fish, and more than 12,000 insects (most of which were identified).

Abbé Hamel, who had become rector of the university in 1871, retained his interest in the museum's progress and encouraged Bélanger's endeavours. From 1874 to 1876 they both made a considerable effort to expand the entomological collections. In 1875 an announcement in *Le Journal entomologique de France* (Paris) invited naturalists of "good will" to engage in exchanges with the zoological museum at Laval. There was an immediate flood of correspondence from France, Belgium, and Switzerland, and the curator had to look after receiving and dispatching the pieces being exchanged as well as identifying and classifying the specimens. In 1876 he was given the additional task of preparing the sizeable zoological collection that the Université Laval wanted to exhibit at the Philadelphia Centennial International Exhibition. Bélanger went to Philadelphia with Hamel to take care of the display and make a few purchases for the zoological museum.

Apparently the supervision of the museum absorbed most of his energies, for Bélanger did not do much original research on Canadian fauna and published little. On occasion, however, he supplied such American entomologists as Alpheus Spring Packard and Ezra Townsend Cresson with specimens of rare and even new species. In addition to the articles in *Le Courrier du Canada*, Bélanger contributed a number of others on Canadian lepidoptera as well as numerous prints to *Le Naturaliste canadien*. He was also responsible for the first issues of the "Catalogue du musée zoologique de l'université Laval," which were published in the university's *Annuaire* from 1875. This was a work of wide scope which Bélanger was unable to finish and which Charles-Eusèbe Dionne, who succeeded him at the museum upon his death, had to bring to completion. Bélanger is also credited with having suggested to Provancher the establishment of the Société d'histoire naturelle de Québec which was set up in 1870.

RAYMOND DUCHESNE

François-Xavier Bélanger was the author of the following three articles published in *Le Courrier du Canada* in 1868 on 24 Feb., 26 Feb., and 4 March respectively: "Histoire naturelle: les insectes utiles"; "Le Polyphème et l'*Atacus luna*"; and "Le papillon vert, le cécropia, le prométhée." He was also responsible for the first issues of the "Catalogue du musée zoologique de l'université Laval," Univ. Laval, *Annuaire* (Québec), 1875–82. Finally, he wrote two articles for *Le Naturaliste canadien* (Cap-Rouge, Qué.): "Les Cynépides," 1 (1868–69): 56–58, and "Microlépidoptère," (1875): 45–48.

Arch. du séminaire de Chicoutimi (Chicoutimi, Qué.), Fonds Léon Provancher, Lettres de F.-X. Bélanger, 23 janv., 10 mars, 1er mai 1869; 25 févr. 1874; 6 nov. 1877. ASQ, MSS, 634; 636; Séminaire, 17, nos.311–31; Univ., Carton 79, no.81. "M. F.-X. Bélanger," *Le Naturaliste canadien*, 13 (1882): 26–28. [Léon Provancher], "Naturalistes canadiens," *Le Naturaliste canadien*, 5 (1873): 225. Victor Gaboriault, *Charles-Eusèbe Dionne, naturaliste, né à Saint-Denis-de-la-Bouteillerie* (La Pocatière, Qué., 1974). V.-A. Huard, *La vie et l'œuvre de l'abbé Provancher* (Québec, 1926), 139–40. Honorius Provost, "Historique de la faculté des arts de l'université Laval, 1852–1952," *L'Enseignement secondaire au Canada* (Québec), 31 (1951–52): appendix, 1–30; 32 (1952–53): appendix, 31–102.

BENNETT, CHARLES JAMES FOX, merchant and politician; b. 11 June 1793 at Shaftesbury, Dorset, England, son of Thomas and Leah Bennett; m. 1829 Isabella Sheppard of Clifton (now part of Bristol), England; d. 5 Dec. 1883 at St John's, Nfld.

That Charles James Fox Bennett's family had a connection with the West Country–Newfoundland trade is probable since he was sent to St John's in 1808, possibly as a clerk. Soon after the end of the Napoleonic wars he was in business on his own account in St John's and in the early 1820s formed a partnership with his elder brother Thomas*. The firm of C. F. Bennett and Company was engaged in the general trade of the colony, supplying planters (especially in St Mary's, Placentia, and Fortune bays), importing European merchandise, and exporting fish, usually on a commission basis. Unlike most Newfoundland trading firms, it seldom engaged in the seal-fishery, nor did it own many ships. The business prospered. By the mid 1820s the Bennetts owned a wharf and premises on Water St, and were becoming prominent citizens in St John's. Thomas represented the firm on the chamber of commerce though Charles was elected president in 1836. Since Charles had married into Bristol society – there was a branch of the firm in that city – it seems that he spent a portion of each year in England.

The two brothers took part in the agitation for a representative constitution in Newfoundland in the 1820s, reflecting the views of most St John's merchants. In January 1833 Charles became an aide-de-camp to Governor Thomas John Cochrane*, in June 1834 a justice of the peace, and in the same year a road commissioner. In the 1830s the brothers distinguished themselves from most Newfoundland merchants of the period by diversifying their business interests with a brewery, a distillery, and a sawmill. In 1847 they established a foundry at Riverhead, St John's. They also built ships on their waterfront property. On his own account, Charles commissioned extensive mineral explorations along the island's coast, and in the 1840s opened a slate quarry at Bay Roberts for which he brought in 12 to 14 Welsh miners; he also brought in a Welsh mining captain to search for potential mining sites in Placentia, Fortune, and Conception bays. In addition Charles was interested in farming, and in 1841 he was a founding member of the Agricultural Society. He eventually acquired 160 or more acres of land to the south of St John's, where he established something of a model farm with his valuable imports of horses and horned cattle. All these activities reflect Charles Bennett's life-long conviction that Newfoundland had considerable economic potential in addition to its fisheries, a point of view that was regarded as visionary in the first half of the 19th century. His capital, however, came from the traditional Newfoundland trade and his diversification coincided with a prosperous period for his firm which, in the 1840s and 1850s, became deeply involved in the lucrative Spanish trade, exporting fish in Spanish bottoms. The prosperity enabled the Bennett firm to experiment in the whale-fishery and to survive serious financial loss when their premises at St John's and on the Isle of Valen (Placentia Bay) were destroyed by fire in 1846. Thomas Bennett gave up an active role in the firm in 1848.

Charles Fox Bennett's political life began in 1842 when he announced his candidacy for St John's in the election to be held for the Amalgamated Legislature in December 1842. Governor Sir John Harvey*, however, felt that the more moderate Thomas would stand a better chance of winning a Catholic seat and, urging him to run, promised Charles a place on the Legislative Council. Charles joined the council in January 1843. In the same year he became a governor of the Savings Bank and in 1844 an auditor of accounts for the government. His role on the Legislative Council was not a prominent one. He was a member of the Conservative group and joined it in voting against John Kent*'s 1846 resolutions in favour of responsible government. With the return to a bicameral legislature in 1848, Bennett lost his seat on the Legislative Council, but was reappointed in 1850 when he also joined the Executive Council.

In the tense political climate between 1850 and 1854, Bennett emerged as a leading and vocal Conservative who opposed the introduction of responsible government with an intensity which, an obituary noted, was deemed unreasonable even in the fevered atmosphere of that time. He was one of the most obdurate councillors in the debates over the redistribution of seats that was to accompany the introduction of responsible government. The debates produced a deadlock between council and assembly: the Liberal majority in the assembly, which had strong Catholic support, wished to double the existing number of assembly seats; the Conservatives considered this increase would give the Catholics an automatic majority and sought a redistribution that would ensure Protestants the edge or at least remove the chance of a Catholic predominance. Bennett argued that responsible government was unsuited to Newfoundland, not only because the colony was small and underdeveloped, but also because it would consolidate the Roman Catholic interests in the government. In February 1852 he told the Commercial Society of St John's that a change in the constitution would hand over power to the Roman Catholic bishop, thus jeopardizing Protestant, particularly Anglican, rights.

For most of his life Bennett was active in the affairs of the Church of England in Newfoundland, and he was a keen supporter of Bishop Edward Feild*'s efforts to infuse the local church with Tractarian principles. He supported Feild's contention in the 1850s that Anglicans had a right to separate schools, and led a campaign in the Legislative Council with Bryan ROBINSON and Hugh William HOYLES for a subdivision of the Protestant educational grant among denominations, an issue as emotive as responsible government in that it split Methodists from Anglicans and further alienated Anglican low churchmen from their bishop. The political result was to drive non-Anglican Protestants and Roman Catholics into a tactical alliance in favour of responsible government; the Liberal party, led by Philip Francis Little*, was then able to present itself as non-sectarian. This development influenced the Colonial Office's decision in 1854 to grant responsible government to Newfoundland.

The introduction of responsible government in the following year was a Liberal triumph and Bennett suffered for his outspoken conservatism. He lost his seat on the Legislative Council, though not without a struggle. He challenged Governor Charles Henry Darling*'s right to remove him from the council, claiming his own right to a seat under the new constitution; his opinion, however, was rejected by both Darling and the Colonial Office. In 1856 when Bennett's foundry and mill burned down, possibly as a result of arson, a mob tried to prevent the fire companies from reaching the blaze and succeeded in perforating the water hoses. The Liberals in 1858 turned the attention of the house to Bennett's prospecting activities, in particular to his receipt between 1851 and 1854 of mining rights, with minimal obligations, to over a million acres of land situated in Bay d'Espoir, Fortune Bay, and the Burin Peninsula. The lease was referred to the imperial law officers who reported that it was *ultra vires*. In 1860 Bennett agreed to surrender the lease within two years if he could select in return ten mining locations from the initial grant. The agreement, however, was not incorporated in a local statute until 1904.

Bennett claimed that he was the victim of a "system of political and party persecution" which prevented him from forming a company, backed by English capital, to exploit minerals found within the lease area. Surveys and the trial shafts which had been started in the early 1840s had already cost him £20,000, and Bennett bore a lasting resentment against those who had thwarted his plans. He found compensation at Tilt Cove in Notre Dame Bay where in 1857 a rich deposit of copper ore had been discovered by Smith McKAY, a Nova Scotia prospector. McKay and Bennett went into partnership, using the latter's capital, to open the Union Copper Mine which began production in 1864. It was the colony's first significant mining venture, and by 1868 was providing employment for between 700 and 800 persons.

The dominant political issue of the 1860s in Newfoundland was confederation with the other British North American colonies. When the Quebec resolutions were published in St John's in December 1864, Bennett stood out as one of the most important opponents of the proposed scheme. In a series of letters to the press in 1864 and 1865, he set out his opinion that the colony had nothing to gain and much to lose in transferring control of its natural resources to Canadians who would inevitably raise taxes and thereby dislocate the traditional patterns of Newfoundland trade; he urged the opponents of confederation to organize themselves, raising the frightening prospect that in confederation Newfoundlanders would be drafted into a Canadian army and "leave their bones to bleach in a foreign land, in defence of the Canadian line of boundary." Although Bennett's opposition to confederation was shared by many Newfoundland merchants, he was the most outspoken and one of the few prepared to campaign actively against union. Bennett did not emerge immediately as a party leader, however, because much of his time was absorbed by his mining and business interests; he spent every winter and spring in England where his wife was living. In the fall of 1867 and again in 1868 he returned to his press campaigns against confederation, urging that the economic plight of the colony should not be used by the confederates to stampede it into union. He contended that Newfoundland had "a temporary but painful malady," and that it should wait for the cure which better times would bring. The confederates' position that union was the only remedy was unacceptable to him. If Newfoundland were wisely and economically administered, he argued, its fishing, mineral, and land resources would be ample to support its population. Still believing that responsible government was a mistake for Newfoundland, he went so far as to suggest that a return to crown colony status was preferable to confederation.

It was agreed by all sides that the question of confederation should be settled by a general election. As the election of 1869 approached, a feeling permeated the community that the terms of union already under discussion would inevitably be endorsed. Bennett did not share this apathy. Having urged the opponents of confederation in November 1868 to organize themselves and apparently having extracted a promise from the Conservative premier, Frederic Bowker Terrington Carter*, that the election would not be held until the fall of 1869, Bennett left for England early in that year, sure that no effective campaigning would begin until the summer. It was clear by this time that he was emerging as the leader of a party against confederation. Wealthy, respected, and still energetic at the age of 76, Bennett put aside plans to retire to England and prepared to fight the move which he was convinced would ruin the colony (and, his opponents remarked, his industrial and mining interests). He returned to Newfoundland late in July with Walter GRIEVE, another wealthy anti-confederate merchant, and a 140-ton steamer in which to canvass the outports. He purchased control of the *Morning Chronicle* in St John's and began a vigorous, outspoken campaign, aided by the confident atmosphere resulting from the best fishing season for a decade.

Bennett's party was a curious amalgamation of old enemies. He and a minority of Protestant merchants and professionals who were former supporters of the Conservative party found themselves allied with the Catholic Liberals, who were opposed to the extinction of the responsible government for which they had fought and who feared that Newfoundland might suffer under Canadian domination as Ireland had under English. The crusade against Carter's party and its pro-confederate platform gave Bennett's party a superficial unity, and its success was overwhelming. Playing on the ignorance and patriotism of rural voters, the anti-confederates won 21 of 30 seats. Bennett was elected for the Catholic district of Placentia–St Mary's, where his firm had once been active, and on 14 Feb. 1870 he became premier of Newfoundland. He did not hold a portfolio and did not take his salary as an assemblyman on principle.

Patrick Kevin Devine states that Bennett's anti-confederate government was long remembered as "the best we ever had." Its success was probably due to the relative economic prosperity of these years, which enabled the government to reduce taxes slightly, avoid borrowing, and increase expenditure – unique achievements for a Newfoundland administration. In accordance with Bennett's personal interests, mining royalties were abolished and the grant to the geological survey increased. More money was allocated to roads and public works. The coastal steam service was improved and a direct service to England instituted. A police force, modelled on the Royal Irish Constabulary, was formed when the imperial garrison was withdrawn in 1870. In external relations, Bennett's government cooperated with the imperial government. It acquiesced in the Treaty of Washington in 1871 and proved reasonably constructive over the difficult French Shore issue. But when Bennett started a lead mine at Port au Port on the west coast, an area in which he had long been interested, the inevitable protests from France claiming a breach of the treaty soured relations between Newfoundland and Britain. The Colonial Office saw Bennett's decision to open the mine as a deliberate attempt to force its hand, and eventually made him close it.

In general, the Bennett government was sensible and carefully progressive. Yet his party was composed of such disparate elements that any premier would have found it difficult to weld them into a coherent unit. A fine campaigner, Bennett was not a politician and found the task impossible. He was unable to establish a firm personal ascendancy in the party with the result that his following was inherently unstable and the government could not effectively counter opposition moves to undermine its position. Opposition to confederation was the only issue binding Bennett's party together. Realizing this, the Conservatives abandoned their advocacy of confederation about 1872, and concentrated on sectarian issues which would remove Bennett's Protestant support. They attacked his close relationship with Bishop Thomas Joseph Power* of St John's and his representing a Catholic district in the assembly. In the 1873 election Bennett could find no better platform than continued opposition to confederation; the Conservatives refused to take up the issue and instead accused him of selling out to the Roman Catholics. Furious, he launched a violent attack on the Orange order which played into his opponents' hands. He won the election with 17 anti-confederate seats against 13 Conservatives but almost immediately there were defections to the Conservative party. On 30 Jan. 1874 he resigned. Another election in the fall of 1874 gave Carter's Conservatives a clear majority. Bennett's party was reduced to 13 members from Catholic ridings in the house of 30. In effect, the anti-confederate party had reverted to the old Liberal party with Bennett as its aging, improbable, and titular leader.

Bennett remained in the assembly until 1878, an increasingly isolated figure. The Liberals tended to look to Joseph Ignatius Little* for leadership, especially once it became clear that Bennett was the only member of the house opposed to the construction of a railway from St John's to Halls Bay. His attitude in this matter was similar to his opinion about responsible government: railways were desirable *per se* and he had supported the construction of lines in the Tilt Cove and Betty Cove districts by mine owners, but Newfoundland was not ready for major lines. With a good sense that went unheeded, he argued that the colony needed more roads instead of an expensive railway which was certain to be its financial ruin and the cause of unbearable taxation for its fishermen. In this railway he saw a step towards confederation with Canada.

After 1878 Bennett's only political role was to make clear his opposition to the contract for the railway in 1881. He was fully occupied with his business affairs and with a lengthy lawsuit against his mining partner, Smith McKay. Bennett filed for a dissolution of partnership and the sale of the mine, claiming that McKay owed him £19,000. The final result was the latter's bankruptcy and Bennett's assumption of complete control over the Tilt Cove operation in July 1880. When Bennett died in 1883, control of C. F. Bennett and Company passed to his partner Thomas Smith, and to his brother Thomas' sons.

Aggressive and outspoken, politically conservative but economically progressive, Bennett did much to shape Newfoundland's future. He was one of the first businessmen to invest significantly in local industries and was the pioneer of the colony's mining industry. Above all, it was his stubbornness and determination which prevented Newfoundland from joining Canada in 1869. His electoral victory decided that for the foreseeable future Newfoundland would remain independent.

JAMES K. HILLER

PANL, GN 1/3A, 1850–74; GN 1/3B, 1855–58, 1868–74; GN 2/1, 32–69; GN 3/2, 1831–80. PRO, CO 194/68, 194/144, 194/154, 194/179–87. Supreme Court of Nfld. (St John's), Registry, Wills of C. J. F. Bennett, 1859, 1883. *Bennett* v. *McKay* (1874–84), 6 Nfld. R. 178, 241, 462. *Bennett* v. *McKay* (1884–96), 7 Nfld. R. 36, 44. *Evening Telegram* (St John's), 18, 21–24 March 1881; 6 Dec. 1883; 6 March 1900; 24 May 1904. *Morning Chronicle* (St John's), October–December 1867; October – December 1868; 31 July 1869. *Newfoundlander*, November 1827; 16 Dec. 1841; 19 Jan. 1843; 18 June, 30 July 1846; 2 Sept. 1847; 12 Jan. 1865. *Public Ledger*, December 1829; 4, 7 Nov. 1856; 30 Jan. 1857; 22 Feb. 1878. *Royal Gazette* (St John's), 15 Jan. 1833, June 1834, June 1835, June 1841, 11 Dec. 1883. *Times and General Commercial Gazette* (St John's), October–December 1867, October–December 1868.

A. E. Chaulk, "The Chamber of Commerce . . . 1827–1837" (unpublished graduate paper, Memorial Univ. of Newfoundland, St John's, 1969). Devine, *Ye olde St.*

John's. Garfield Fizzard, "The Amalgamated Assembly of Newfoundland, 1841–1847" (MA thesis, Memorial Univ. of Newfoundland, 1963). J. P. Greene, "The influence of religion in the politics of Newfoundland, 1850–1861" (MA thesis, Memorial Univ. of Newfoundland, 1970). J. K. Hiller, "Confederation defeated: the Newfoundland election of 1869" (unpublished paper presented to the CHA, Quebec, 1976). Frederick Jones, "Bishop Feild, a study in politics and religion in nineteenth century Newfoundland" (PHD thesis, Univ. of Cambridge, 1971). W. D. MacWhirter, "A political history of Newfoundland, 1865–1874" (MA thesis, Memorial Univ. of Newfoundland, 1963). E. C. Moulton, "The political history of Newfoundland, 1861–1869" (MA thesis, Memorial Univ. of Newfoundland, 1960). Philip Tocque, *Newfoundland: as it was, and as it is in 1877* (Toronto, 1878). Wells, "Struggle for responsible government in Nfld."

BENSON, WILLIAM THOMAS, manufacturer and politician; b. 20 April 1824 at Kendal, England, third son of Robert Benson and Dorothy Braithwaite, Quakers; m. 14 July 1858 Helen Wilson of Acton Grange, Cheshire, England, and they had one son and one daughter; d. 8 June 1885 in Cardinal, Ont., and was buried in Montreal, Que.

William Thomas Benson was educated in Kendal. In 1848 he began a career as a manufacturer of chemicals and entered into partnership with William Blythe, a Scot from whom he apparently received training in chemistry. Their firm, located in Accrington, produced chemicals used in finishing and dyeing textiles. Benson lived in Manchester and was probably in charge of the firm's business and sales office there. In 1858 he immigrated to Montreal where he met an Englishman, Thomas Aspden, who pointed out to Benson that there was no starch factory in Canada, even though starch was being used in the manufacture of textiles as well as in households, in food, and for laundry. Benson and Aspden, as partners, established a starch factory in 1858 in the village of Edwardsburg (Cardinal), Canada West, a site that offered excellent facilities for water-power and for transportation by water and rail to the markets of Montreal and Toronto. In 1860 Aspden left the firm which then became W. T. Benson, Canada Starch Works, though it was usually known as either W. T. Benson and Company or the Canada Starch Works. Benson managed the firm himself until 1865, when it was incorporated as the Edwardsburg Starch Company, a joint stock company in which he initially held 59 per cent of the shares and was managing director. The president of the company was Walter Shanly*, engineer and railway builder; other prominent original shareholders were Charles John BRYDGES, Peter Redpath*, and William Workman*. Benson ceased being managing director in 1875, when he took a two-year leave of absence because of ill health, but he retained the vice-presidency until his death. In 1875 also, the company increased its capital stock, reducing Benson's holding to 40 per cent.

Benson expanded his enterprises in Edwardsburg to include a grist-mill, a sawmill, box and barrel factories, and, for a time, a general store for the employees' use. He maintained an office in Montreal which served not only as a distributing centre for the starch factory but also as the headquarters of some of Benson's own enterprises, notably his commission merchant business in chemicals, oils, and wool. The waste gluten from the manufacture of starch was sold to farmers for cattle feed; Benson himself operated a large stock farm which eventually comprised 200 cattle, 200 sheep, and 25 horses.

The Edwardsburg Starch Company was the only Canadian supplier of corn and laundry starch until 1868, and its chief competitor was a firm in Oswego, N.Y. The success of the Canadian venture depended on the protective tariff on manufactured goods, such as starch, coming from the United States, and on free trade in corn, the firm's raw material. The tariff rates varied from time to time, and Benson viewed with alarm the free trade policy of Alexander Mackenzie*'s 1873–78 government. He supported Sir John A. Macdonald*'s National Policy, and was elected Conservative member for Grenville South in 1882, a seat he held until his death. In the 1870s and early 1880s the Edwardsburg Starch Company engaged in sporadic price wars with American competitors and with the British American Starch Company (later the Brantford Starch Works). In 1878 Benson's firm began marketing starch that did not bear the company name and sold it for less than the price of the Brantford product. In the following year the Brantford firm unsuccessfully suggested that both companies sell at the same price. The two firms finally agreed to maintain identical prices in June 1883 and by February 1884 Benson recommended a joint reduction in prices to meet new competition from a Cincinnati-based starch company. The price-fixing arrangement ended in 1885. In 1882 the Edwardsburg Starch Company had begun producing glucose and corn syrup; the decision to expand was made at least in part because of the fear of competition from the newly established Toronto Glucose Company. The factory's daily grinding capacity of 200 bushels in 1858 was gradually expanded to 2,500 bushels by 1900.

After Benson's death his son George Frederick Benson became president and managing director of the company. He continued in these positions after the firm amalgamated with two of its Canadian competitors in 1906 to form the Canada Starch Company.

Benson lived in a stone house built about 1800 by loyalist Hugh Munro, founder of Edwardsburg; he modernized it by adding more windows and a verandah, and it remained in the Benson family until 1921 when it was sold to the village for use as a senior level school. It was closed in the 1950s and was later destroyed by fire. Although an Anglican, Benson donated land in Edwardsburg for the Roman Catholic Sacred Heart Church built in 1875 as well as the Anglican St Paul's Church in 1873. The luxuriantly bearded W. T. Benson presented a striking figure. He was an astute and imaginative businessman, paternalistic towards his employees, public-spirited, conservative in outlook, and "of the highest integrity."

RUTH MCKENZIE

Gazette (Montreal), 9 June 1885. *The Canadian album: men of Canada; or, success by example . . .* , ed. William Cochrane and J. C. Hopkins (5v., Brantford, Ont., 1891–96), V: 139. *CPC*, 1885. *Historical record of the Edwardsburg and Canada Starch companies*, comp. G. F. Benson ([new ed., Montreal, 1959]). *A history of Cardinal*, [ed. F. B. Byers] ([Cardinal, Ont., 1967]).

BIBAUD, FRANÇOIS-MAXIMILIEN (he later added the given names of **Uncas** (an Indian name) and **Marie**; he occasionally used the inversion **Neilimixam Duabib** as a pseudonym, and often signed Bibaud, jeune), lawyer, professor of law, polygraph, and chronicler; b. 23 Oct. 1823 at Montreal, Lower Canada, son of Michel Bibaud*, a journalist and historian, and Élizabeth Delisle; d. unmarried on 9 July 1887 at Montreal.

François-Maximilien Bibaud undertook serious classical studies with the Sulpicians at the Petit Séminaire de Montréal from 1833 to 1843 and committed himself to a religious vocation. In 1842 he made his start as a writer in his father's *L'Encyclopédie canadienne*, which was published in Montreal, and in 1846 he contributed to the *Mélanges religieux* of Montreal as assistant editor. Shortly after deciding at the end of November of that year to give up a life in religion Bibaud resolved to become a lawyer. He worked in the offices of Joseph Bourret* and Toussaint Peltier*, taking the four years of legal training then required by law. During these years, in preparation for the bar admission examination, Bibaud drafted with care and unusual diligence four texts which recorded the juridical knowledge he had acquired through reading and experience: for English law, an abridged version of William Blackstone's *Commentaries on the laws of England*; for customary law, a clarification of the custom of Paris together with commentaries; and for Roman law, a translation of Justinian's *Institutes*, as well as a weighty volume entitled "Traités de Droit . . . ," on agreements and contracts. On 5 April 1851, proudly carrying this collection of manuscripts under his arm, he appeared for his examination for admission to the Montreal bar. With his usual vanity he later noted: "It was an outstanding examination in which I made my scholarship manifest." He greatly impressed his examiners by the tone of his replies and by the quality of his manuscripts. He was immediately asked to consider teaching law. In fact Bibaud had been thinking for two years about giving private classes, but his examiners suggested instead that he might help remedy the absence of organized teaching of law in Canada East by creating a proper school. The prospect of such a career was sufficiently pleasing to Bibaud for him to allow a small committee of nine lawyers to be set up centred around George-Étienne Cartier* and Augustin-Norbert Morin*; on 7 April this committee sent a letter to Bishop Ignace BOURGET and Father Félix MARTIN, rector of the new Jesuit Collège Sainte-Marie in Montreal, supporting a plan to establish a chair of law. Cartier and Morin skilfully emphasized to the bishop of Montreal the advantage of offering a programme for French Canadian students which could compete with the one McGill College was organizing. The two priests quickly concurred with the proposed plan and agreed to house the school in the Jesuit college. To launch his programme Bibaud delivered an "inaugural address" on 1 May 1851, but actual teaching did not begin until September with six pupils, only four of whom continued.

The programme lasted two years, and the students completed their period of probation at the same time. Lessons were given three mornings a week throughout the year, except for the month of August. For the first few years Bibaud undertook all the teaching himself. In 1858 he engaged Joseph-Achille-A. Belle as a "professor of the practice of law" for those aspiring to the bar, and later Léonard-Ovide Hétu to perform the same function for those intending to become notaries. Former pupils of Bibaud, both men gave instruction in their offices during the months of June and July. As for the man who pompously called himself "head professor" and "dean," he thought his own teaching had to be at one and the same time "historical, systematic, philosophical, and practical." His ambition was to see his school become "a true debating society, where the pupils raise all the objections they care to." Claiming to have based his methods on those used in German universities, he had his pupils participate regularly in review sessions, and originally twice, then once a year held "Solemn *Repetitoria*" during which a number of lawyers questioned the students on their studies. The session was conducted before jurists and ecclesiastics, to whom Bibaud was only too delighted to display the excellence of the training he was providing. And no doubt to ensure recruitment for the school the pupils of the senior classes at the college were also present. Because of the lack of suitable legal publications to back up his teaching Bibaud virtually had to dictate his courses. In order to have more time for discussion with his students he undertook in 1859 to publish at Montreal his *Commentaires sur les lois du Bas-Canada, ou conférences de l'école de droit, liée au collège des RR.*

PP. jésuites, suivis d'une notice historique. In both his curriculum and teaching methods Bibaud gave evidence of an originality that was particularly astonishing in a country without a long university tradition.

Enrolment slowly but steadily increased, reaching 40 in 1862, and Bibaud was able to boast that despite the creation of the faculties of law at McGill and Laval, his remained "the fashionable programme." In 1863 he published a list of all those who had attended his school: 140 candidates for the bar and 38 for the profession of notary; in addition, 86 of the 178 had received the "Bachelor of Laws" conferred by the school. Such well-known figures as George-Édouard Desbarats*, Hector Fabre*, Louis-Amable Jetté*, Ludger Labelle*, Siméon Pagnuelo*, and François-Xavier-Anselme TRUDEL were among the graduates.

On 1 Sept. 1867 Bibaud announced in the papers his decision to give up teaching. But the the closing of his school was actually only an episode in a conflict between Bishop Bourget and Université Laval. Bibaud proudly rejected any notion of affiliation with Laval, but the Collège Sainte-Marie did not have legal authority to confer, as Bibaud would have liked, degrees in law. The school therefore was unable to satisfy new requirements laid down in an act governing the admission of candidates to the bar.

Little is known about the last years of Bibaud's life, when he simultaneously ceased teaching law and writing on juridical matters. During the 16 years of his career as a jurist he had shown amazing vitality. Concurrently with his teaching duties and while continuing to produce an impressive number of works and short treatises of a historical nature, he published newspaper articles, many of them substantial, on the great legal reforms of his day, and delivered "lectures" to literary societies. He took care to have his presentations to these societies printed subsequently in order to consolidate his reputation, about which he was inordinately concerned. In his legal writings two works, however, occupy a special place. His *Essai de logique judiciaire*, published at Montreal in 1853, is a philosophical volume in which Bibaud analyses the different types of logical arguments as they apply to the interpretation of law; but his unnecessarily polemical style detracts from the value of the exposition. It was above all in his *Commentaires sur les lois du Bas-Canada, ou conférences de l'école de droit* that he revealed the astonishing range of his knowledge and his remarkable mastery of the manifold sources from which the Quebec law of the period derived, whether Roman or canonical law, customary law, English, French, or Canadian law. He had read widely; he can, however, be taken to task, here as elsewhere, for flaunting his knowledge. He could never resist the temptation to criticize authors, to call attention to the errors of judges, and to censure legislators, always in a cantankerous, unpleasant tone. These few defects have to be disregarded in order to appreciate the value of an otherwise remarkable work, the only original, systematic exposition of the law in Canada East to be published before the codification of the civil law in the 1860s.

His research and historical publications are just as important. These historical works, primarily encyclopædic, chronological, and biographical, represent an original contribution because of the attention that some of them give to the Indians. Bibaud was a knowledgeable bibliographer with a preoccupation for the great names; his works are considered landmarks in the history of intellectual development in French Canada and their influence was felt particularly in the teaching of law and the literature of jurisprudence.

ANDRÉ MOREL and YVAN LAMONDE

[François-Maximilien Bibaud wrote numerous works on various aspects of cultural life, including law, history, and religion. The following sources provide detailed inventories of both his printed works and his manuscripts: Concordia Univ. Library (Montreal), Special coll., D7 B5, MSS on hist., French Canada, law, and religion, 1847–84; *Guide to the manuscript collection in the Toronto public libraries* (Toronto, 1954): 12; É.-Z. Massicotte, "Quelques notes sur Maximilien Bibaud," *BRH*, 52 (1946): 90–93; Arthur Perrault, "Bibliographie des œuvres de Maximilien Bibaud," *Themis* (Montréal), 2 (1951–52): 31–34.

Space does not permit a full listing of all Bibaud's works, but those which have contributed most to an understanding of Canadian history are the following: *Biographie des Sagamos illustres de l'Amérique septentrionale, précédée d'un index de l'histoire fabuleuse de ce continent* (Montréal, 1848); *Les institutions de l'histoire du Canada, ou annales canadiennes jusqu'à l'an MDCCCXIX . . .* (Montréal, 1855); *Dictionnaire historique des hommes illustres du Canada et de l'Amérique* (Montréal, 1857); *Le panthéon canadien (choix de biographies), dans lequel on a introduit les hommes les plus célèbres des autres colonies britanniques* (Montréal, 1858); Adèle and Victoria Bibaud saw to the publication of a second edition in Montreal in 1891 under the title of *Le Panthéon canadien; choix de biographies*. The AUM holds a manuscript copy of this work (P 58, Q1/199). Other manuscripts are held by the AUM in P 58, M/15 and M/16. The Archives du collège de L'Assomption (Montréal) has the manuscript of "Nature canadienne ou mes pérégrinations" written in 1867.

Bibaud also published extensively in the newspapers. Sometimes signing them "Bibaud, jeune," he drafted a number of articles related to the existing civil laws in Canada East and to the teaching of law. In this connection the following papers should be consulted: *Le Colonisateur* (Montréal), 1862–63; *Mélanges religieux* (Montréal), 15, 18, 22 avril, 6 mai 1851; *La Minerve* (Montréal), mai-juill. 1851, 31 juill. 1852; *L'Ordre* (Montréal), 12 déc. 1858–16 févr. 1860.

In the course of his career, Bibaud become involved in two significant controversies. Articles about his dispute with the Institut canadien of Montreal on the subject of the apostasy of Commissioner François-Pierre Bruneau* are to be found in 1853 issues of the following Montreal papers: *La Minerve*;

Le Moniteur canadien; *Montreal Gazette*; *Le Pays*; and *Le Semeur canadien*.

For his controversy with Gonzalve Doutre* about apprenticeship and the practice of law, consult *L'Ordre*, 14–16 sept. 1863. A. M. and Y. L.]

ANQ-M, État civil, Catholiques, Notre-Dame de Montréal, 26 oct. 1823, 12 juill. 1887; M-72-41. PAC, MG 29, D29. *La Minerve*, 20 août 1867. Camille Bertrand, *La collection d'archives Baby* (Montréal, 1975), 10. *DOLQ*, I: 58, 390–91, 488. Le Jeune, *Dictionnaire*, I: 170. L.-O. David, *Mélanges historiques et littéraires* (Montréal, 1917), 282. Paul Desjardins, *Le collège Sainte-Marie de Montréal* (2v., Montréal, 1940–[44]), II: 60–103. Edmond Lareau, *Histoire du droit canadien depuis les origines de la colonie jusqu'à nos jours* (2v., Montréal, 1888–89). André Morel, "La codification devant l'opinion publique de l'époque," *Livre du centenaire du Code civil* (2v., Montréal, 1970), I: 27–45. Édouard Fabre Surveyer, "Une école de droit à Montréal avant le Code civil," *Rev. trimestrielle canadienne* (Montréal), 6 (1920): 140–50. Léon Lortie, "The early teaching of law in French Canada," *Dalhousie Law Journal* (Halifax), 2 (1975–76): 521–32.

BIG BEAR. *See* MISTAHIMASKWA

BIGSBY, JOHN JEREMIAH, doctor and geologist; b. 4 Aug. 1792 at Nottingham, England, son of Jacob Bigsby; m. probably in 1827 Sarah Beevor of Newark-upon-Trent, England, and they had two children; d. 10 Feb. 1881 in London, England.

John Jeremiah Bigsby, like his father, pursued a medical career, graduating from the University of Edinburgh in 1814 with an MD degree. In that same year he published his thesis and joined the Edinburgh Infirmary as a resident physician. On 14 March 1816 he joined the British army as an assistant surgeon, serving briefly in 1817 with the medical corps at the Cape of Good Hope.

In August 1818 Bigsby arrived in British North America as an assistant staff surgeon. Stationed at Quebec City, he was assigned to treat a typhus epidemic among Irish immigrants at Hawkesbury on the Ottawa River in September. On the steamship journey to Hawkesbury, Bigsby's developing interest in the geology of the St Lawrence region manifested itself in his remarks to Louis-Joseph Papineau*, a fellow passenger. After spending the winter in Quebec Bigsby received instructions in the spring of 1819 from the medical department to study the geology of Upper Canada. During that summer, travelling on the meagre retainer of £26, he collected geological specimens over a wide area encompassed by the Ottawa River and lakes Nipissing, Huron, Erie, and Ontario. That autumn he travelled with the head of the medical department from Quebec to Baie-Saint-Paul, Kamouraska, and La Malbaie, and closely observed the flora and fauna.

During the winter of 1819–20, Bigsby was appointed assistant secretary and medical officer to the British party of the international boundary commission, originally provided for under the terms of the Treaty of Ghent (1814). His appointment appears to have resulted from the fortuitous combination of the resignation of the British secretary and the favourable impression Bigsby may have made on the American party's chief agent, Major Joseph Delafield, during a chance meeting on the summer tour of 1819. Thus in the spring of 1820 Bigsby set out with the British party, which included David Thompson* as principal surveyor. In August they linked up with Delafield's party at St Joseph Island in northern Lake Huron and, after leaving the Americans, surveyed Manitoulin, Drummond, and other islands before severe weather forced them to return to Montreal in November.

In the spring of 1821 the commission assembled in the Niagara region, and Bigsby met formally with its board for the first time in May. That summer he took charge of the British party for the determination of the boundary in the Lake St Clair and Lake Erie area. In August, having completed the survey, Bigsby undertook a second tour of the north shore of the St Lawrence at La Malbaie before returning to Quebec for the winter. The commission was idle during the summer of 1822 and Bigsby took the opportunity to visit the Niagara Falls region with an international touring party. However, the next summer saw the survey resume its work with its most ambitious venture, the mapping of the vast region between Fort William (now part of Thunder Bay) and the Lake of the Woods. Bigsby's association with the commission had not only afforded him a vast area from which to collect geological specimens but also made possible personal associations within the British and American scientific communities.

Bigsby's reports of his field activities, mostly written during the winters, received public attention in several ways. From 1820 to 1825 he submitted several reports of his field experiences on the St Lawrence and the Great Lakes to Benjamin Silliman's prestigious *American Journal of Science, and Arts.* He prepared an account of his activities in the Lake Huron region for Governor Dalhousie [Ramsay*] which was read to the Geological Society of London in 1823 (and published in its *Transactions* the next year). Bigsby also contributed to the *Canadian Review and Literary and Historical Journal*, published briefly in Montreal. In 1824 the journal published anonymously "On the utility and design of the science of geology," which can be attributed to Bigsby because of its style and content; this essay, using evidence gathered in the Canadian field, is one of the first scholarly treatises on geology written in British North America. It shows knowledge of contemporary debates about the geological origins of the earth among the schools of Georges Cuvier, James Hutton, and William Buckland, but the author does not participate in them directly, and instead urges the "practical geologist" to ascertain, by extensive field work and exploration, the nature and composition of the elements of the earth's crust. The geologist should chronicle facts and collect specimens and secondarily observe in them "the goodness and wisdom of the great Architect; – and his power in the convulsions and consequent devastation which the elements have at intervals caused." During his years in Canada Bigsby was elected fellow of the Geological Society of London in 1823, an honorary member of the American Geological Society in 1824, and a member of the American Philosophical Society of Philadelphia in 1825.

In late 1826 or early 1827, either for personal reasons or because of the limited official interest shown in the exploitation of Canada's mineral potential, Bigsby departed for England. He settled in his native Nottinghamshire and established a medical practice in Newark-upon-Trent. There he served as alderman and mayor between 1827 and 1830 and became senior physician at the Newark Hospital in 1840. As part of his continuing interest in lecturing and publishing, from 1827 to 1829 he read several papers before the Geological Society of London on the geology of Canada which were published in the *Philosophical Magazine.*

With a modest income derived from his practice and his marriage, Bigsby was able to move to London in 1846 and devote more time to his literary and scientific avocations. In 1850 he published a two-volume memoir of his experiences with the boundary commission, *The shoe and canoe.* A highly readable travel account, it delightfully recaptures incident and accident in the survey, giving close attention to local colour and circumstance, and including his sketches of the landscape. From 1850 to 1864 he read and published numerous papers on North American geology. While in London, Bigsby also prepared an extensive glossary of fossils, the first part of which appeared in 1868 under the title *Thesaurus Siluricus.* In the book he repeatedly refers to the discoveries of Sir William Edmond Logan*, the first director of the Geological Survey of Canada, and acknowledges his debt to the work of Canadians Elkanah Billings* and John William Dawson*. The following year Bigsby was elected to the Royal Society and received its Murchison Medal. In 1877 he donated the Bigsby Medal to the Geological Society of London to be awarded biennally to a student of American geology under the age of 45. His second dictionary of fossils, *Thesaurus Devonico-Carboniferous,* was published in 1878 when he was in his mid 80s; a third volume, "Permian Thesaurus," was nearing completion at the time of his death. Bigsby's will bequeathed his library and geological works to the borough of Nottingham for the use of the students at the fledgling University College in Nottingham.

John Jeremiah Bigsby's contributions to Canadian mineralogy and palæontology were substantial, despite his brief sojourn in British North America. Logan, also a geologist who emphasized "facts then theories," respected both his facts and his theories; he stated in 1857 that Bigsby's 1823 essay on the geography and geology of Lake Huron was "the first essay of any importance upon the fossils of Canada." The Geological Survey of Canada report of 1863 also acknowledges Bigsby's vital role in the location of certain mineral deposits in the Lake Superior region. George Mercer Dawson*, another director of the Geological Survey and a recipient of the Bigsby Medal in 1891, honoured him in 1878 by giving his name to Bigsby Inlet in the Queen Charlotte Islands.

ANTHONY W. RASPORICH

J. J. Bigsby was the author of the following works: *Localities of Canadian minerals, with notes and extracts, chiefly collected from the writings of John Bigsby . . .* (Quebec, 1827); "Notes on the geography and geology of Lake Huron," Geological Soc., *Trans.* (London), 2nd ser., 1 (1824): 175–209; "On the utility and design of the science of geology, and the best method of acquiring a knowledge of it; with geological sketches of Canada," *Canadian Rev. and Literary and Hist. Journal* (Montreal), 1 (1824–25): 377–95; *The shoe and canoe, or pictures of travel in the Canadas, illustrative of their scenery and of colonial life; with facts and opinions on emigration, state policy, and other points of public interest . . .* (2v., London, 1850); *Thesaurus Devonico-Carboniferous: the flora and fauna of the Devonian and carboniferous periods . . .* (London, 1878); and *Thesaurus Siluricus: the flora and fauna of the Silurian period . . .* (London, 1868). For other publications by J. J. Bigsby see *Geologic literature on North America, 1785–1918,* comp. J. M. Nickles (2v., Washington, 1923–24), I: 100–1.

PAC, MG 18, H25, 2: no. 54; RG 8, I (C ser.), v.0. [Joseph Delafield], *The unfortified boundary: a diary of the first survey of the Canadian boundary line from St. Regis to the Lake of the Woods,* ed. Robert McElroy and Thomas Riggs (New York, 1943). Robert Etheridge, "Memoir: John Jeremiah Bigsby," Geological Soc. of London, *Quarterly Journal,* 37 (1881), [pt.II] : 39–41. *Quebec Gazette,* 29 May, 23 Oct., 26 Nov. 1820; 26 Nov. 1821. *Times* (London), 15 Feb., 13 April 1881. *DNB.* Zaslow, *Reading the rocks.*

BINNEY, HIBBERT, Church of England bishop; b. 12 Aug. 1819 in Sydney (N.S.), son of the Reverend Hibbert Binney and Henrietta Amelia Stout; d. 30 April 1887 in New York City.

The Binney family had emigrated to New England late in the 17th century, and in 1753 Jonathan Binney* arrived in Nova Scotia where he became a member of the first House of Assembly and later a councillor. Jonathan's son, the Reverend Hibbert Binney, was rector of St George's Church in Sydney, Cape Breton, at the time of his son's birth in 1819, but in 1823 left for England and by 1838 was rector of Newbury,

Berkshire. At age 19 the younger Hibbert entered King's College, London, and in 1842 graduated BA from Worcester College, Oxford, with 1st class honours in mathematics and 2nd class honours in classics. Hibbert followed his father into the ministry, being ordained deacon by the bishop of Oxford in 1842. In the same year he was appointed a fellow of Worcester College. He took his MA in 1844, was appointed tutor in 1846, and in 1848 became bursar of his college. At Oxford he was influenced by the Oxford Movement which was challenging the traditionally Erastian status of the established Church of England and which asserted the independence of the church from the state by emphasizing that the church's authority was based on Catholic order and tradition as it had been preserved in the Book of Common Prayer.

When the Anglican bishopric of Nova Scotia became vacant following the death of John Inglis* in October 1850, there was considerable feeling in the colony that laymen should have a part in choosing the next bishop. Many thought that he should be a Nova Scotian, and the fact that Hibbert Binney had been born in the colony argued for his appointment. In March 1851 Binney was named bishop by the imperial government and consecrated in London by the archbishop of Canterbury and the bishops of London, Oxford, and Chichester. There is some reason for believing that Joseph Howe* had advanced Binney's cause to Earl Grey, the colonial secretary, even though Binney would not have known much about missionary life in a colonial diocese. His father had spent most of his life in the colony and he belonged to an old and established Nova Scotia family, but Hibbert had left Nova Scotia at age four and had been educated as an English gentleman.

Thus Bishop Binney, steeped in Tractarian ideas, was sent at age 31 to a diocese characterized by latitudinarian and congregational sympathies. Of no such persuasion himself, he held, like his teachers at Oxford, that the Church of England contained within its tradition the truth concerning Catholic authority and spiritual grace. Coupled with this belief was an historical and theological conviction of the nature and power of the episcopal office. Bishop Binney firmly held that the church, being God's chosen instrument for dealing with his people, was unchangeable, and must remain firm and steadfast against all popular whims and fashions. As far as he was concerned, the church was divine and holy and, as such, had a unique role to play in the world, a role no other institution could fill. Such a concept involved a universal organization and one which could not compromise with local traditions. He would allow for parochial variations in small matters only, and would not permit any serious breach of ecclesiastical law or doctrine.

Coupled with his conception of a divinely founded institution was the opinion that the church should not be restrained by any civil authority, and he often pointed out the evils of the English establishment. The only proper authority ordained of God for governing his church was the bishop, who, as father in God, ordered the affairs of the church. He warned Nova Scotia Anglicans against the dilution of episcopal doctrine arising out of the institutional chaos rampant in the Nova Scotia church. He was an able scholar and his ideas were essentially Catholic and were steeped in the ancient traditions and thought of the Greek and Latin fathers of the church. They infused a foreign concept of worship into the rationalist and latitudinarian theories of the Nova Scotia church. Throughout his episcopate he attempted to inculcate his ideas by diplomacy and gradual teaching. He tried to avoid direct confrontation, but this was not always possible. His first step was to curb the power of local parishes. A major move toward this end would be the establishment of a diocesan synod under the guidance of the bishop.

Throughout the Anglican communion there was a general movement toward the formation of synods and convocations composed of clergy and laity to govern church affairs. Bishop John Inglis had stated that he thought this movement would cause division in the church and should be discouraged. The rural members of the Church of England in Nova Scotia were not accustomed to governing themselves, and the wealthy parishes in Halifax and the more prosperous towns in the Annapolis valley and the south shore felt a synod would give the smaller rural parishes an unprecedented voice in the decision-making processes of the Nova Scotia church. Bishop Binney, an advocate of well-ordered local church government, attended a meeting of bishops in London in 1853, which included Bishop Edward Feild* of Newfoundland and the archbishop of Canterbury, to discuss the problem. They wanted the imperial parliament to pass an act which would enable the colonial dioceses to govern themselves. However, that year the House of Commons defeated the Colonial Church Bill advanced by William Ewart Gladstone, after it had been passed in the House of Lords, because it felt that incorporation of synods in the colonies should be dealt with in the colonial legislatures.

Bishop Binney summoned his clergy and two delegates from each parish to a meeting in Halifax on 12 Oct. 1854 "in order that the Members of the Church may decide for themselves whether they will hold periodical Assemblies or not." Churchmen in Halifax suggested such a "convocation" would tend to strengthen the power of the bishop and that the whole design was a Tractarian plot. The old, established parishes of St Paul's and St George's in Halifax, with such influential members as Chief Justice Brenton Halliburton* and Henry Hezekiah Cogswell*, met in advance and decided not to support the proposal for a synod. Above all, they feared the desire in the rural parishes for a say in the affairs of the diocese. Despite this opposition, delegates from 23 of 36 parishes met in Halifax and decided "to hold periodical assemblies of the Clergy and Laity in this diocese" and to frame a constitution for a synod. On 11 Oct. 1855, with the older parishes maintaining a boycott, the parish delegates accepted a constitution giving the bishop the power of veto over all synodical measures. A third meeting held a year later, with only 12 of 50 parishes not adhering, gave a unanimous expression of loyalty to Bishop Binney. That year St Paul's in Halifax threatened to dismiss its curates, Edmund Maturin* and William Bullock*, if they attended the diocesan meeting.

In 1860, after spirited discussion, the diocesan assembly approved a proposed bill to incorporate the synod, provide for its organization, establish a system of ecclesiastical discipline over parishes and clergy, and ratify the episcopal veto. On 23 Feb. 1863 the bill was presented to the House of Assembly for approval, but on 2 March St George's in Halifax presented a petition condemning the provision for an episcopal veto. Binney, wary of opposition from both Anglicans and non-Anglicans, attempted to create a united Anglican front against the bill's opponents. But to achieve unity it was necessary to amend the bill to guarantee the right of parishes to nominate their own rectors and not to belong to the synod if they did not wish. This amended bill was passed in the assembly but not the Legislative Council, which felt the measure would create further dissension in the Church of England because of the intense opposition to Binney's views. Undaunted, Binney presented another bill which was passed on 29 April 1863; it incorporated the synod but did not confer on it any spiritual jurisdiction over parishes which did not choose to belong to it, nor did it extend to the bishop any coercive power to establish a form of worship. The diocese was divided into eight rural deaneries, and finally in 1878 St George's and St Paul's joined the synod, which continued with the episcopal veto. The opposition to Binney was similar to that encountered by other Canadian bishops, but he had accomplished his reorganization of the diocese with himself and the synod firmly in control.

But the church in Nova Scotia in order to be self-governing had to be financially self-supporting; it was not when Binney arrived in 1851. Anglican King's College at Windsor lost its favoured status in 1851 when on 7 April the provincial legislature passed an act to discontinue its preferential grant, though it continued to receive grants equal to those given to other denominational colleges. Still, the church's only institute of higher learning, founded in 1789, looked as if it might collapse. From 1851 to 1861 Binney and the Reverend George William Hill* campaigned both in Britain and in Nova Scotia to raise an endowment for the college. With this campaign and with the reconstitution of the board of governors as "Friends of the College," an endowment was established by 1861. But throughout Binney's episcopate King's was plagued by the unwillingness of local Anglicans to support it, lapses in discipline, and loss of scientific equipment, which finally led to the resignation of John Dart*, the president, in 1884. In 1881 the provincial government had threatened to withdraw financial support from all the denominational colleges if they would not form a provincial university in Halifax centred around Dalhousie. But Binney managed to rally enough support locally and in Britain for Canada's oldest English-speaking university to reopen in 1885 with the Reverend Isaac Brock* as president and Charles George Douglas Roberts* as one of its two professors.

Unlike the Methodists, Baptists, Presbyterians, and Roman Catholics in Nova Scotia, members of the Church of England were not accustomed to supporting their own church. From the days of Bishop Charles Inglis*, the diocese had been almost totally subsidized from England by the Society for the Propagation of the Gospel. On 1 Dec. 1850 the archbishop of Canterbury informed Binney that the SPG could no longer support the church in the colony and that money from England would be used instead for new missions in Africa and India. By 1860 Nova Scotia Anglicans still had done little to support their church, and Binney, this time in alliance with wealthy Haligonians, proposed an endowment scheme for the support of the diocesan clergy. Opposition came from rural parishes, especially that of Mahone Bay led by its rector, the Reverend William H. Snyder. Though gradually the people of the diocese began to contribute, Binney in 1870–71 repeatedly wrote to the SPG despairing of the unwillingness of the people to give support and of the harsh consequences of SPG policies. After a long struggle the Church Endowment Fund reached the point in 1872 where it could be used, and by 1880 the financial position of the diocese was secured.

Binney also wanted to improve the religious life of his diocese by emphasizing the sacramental life of the church. He frequently admonished his clergy to celebrate the Eucharist often and to emphasize the full theological significance of the offertory in the liturgy. He disliked the puritan and Calvinist leanings of the Nova Scotia clergy and reminded them to follow Anglican practice as set out in the Book of Common Prayer. This led him into difficulties with his clergy, in particular with the Reverend James Cuppaidge Cochran* of Halifax, who refused to give up his black Geneva gown for a white surplice, and also with the Reverend George William Hill, rector of St Paul's, Halifax, after 1865. In 1866 Hill was to attack the bishop publicly for destroying the Protestant Reformed faith of the Church of England. Binney took his *cathedra* out of St Paul's and on 21 Oct. 1864 established St Luke's, Halifax, as the diocesan cathedral. There Binney maintained high standards of worship, aided by the dean of the diocese, William Bullock, a Tractarian sympathizer.

During his episcopate Binney's Tractarian ideas gradually became accepted by the clergy and laity of the diocese as a whole, but his chief Tractarian venture was at Charlottetown. On 22 Aug. 1869 he preached at the opening service of St Peter's Cathedral, founded by him as a cathedral church for Prince Edward Island outside the normal jurisdiction of the parish church of Charlottetown, St Paul's. Here, as in Halifax, Binney appointed as his chaplain a devoted follower of the Oxford Movement, the Reverend George Wright Hodgson. From Charlottetown the Tractarian school planned an Anglo-Catholic mission to the whole diocese of Nova Scotia. Hodgson had close connections with Tractarians in Saint John, N.B., Montreal, and England, and his influence was felt in Halifax at St Luke's Cathedral and in the policy of the diocesan newspapers. Binney was in sympathy with Hodgson's aims but he was always sensitive to those of the opposite persuasion and never identified himself publicly with either of the contending schools. But Binney's Tractarian influence became so predominant that when the diocesan synod met in 1887 to select his successor, its first choice was the Reverend John Cox Edghill, a noted Tractarian and Anglo-Catholic.

Bishop Binney did not become closely involved in the political life of Nova Scotia. He did make comments which could be termed "political" on several occasions when decisions taken by government interfered with what he thought was the well-being of the Church of England. In the debate which surrounded the School Act of 1864 he stated that "no scheme of education which would omit religion from its plan, would be suitable." Again at the beginning of the confederation debate he seemed to favour federalism when he appeared at a public rally with Thomas Louis Connolly*, Roman Catholic archbishop of Halifax. By 1870, however, he saw that the economic policies of the federal government would adversely affect Nova Scotia and the financial position of the church, and he informed the SPG of his fears that "confederation from which great benefits were expected by many is really doing us serious injury." The difficulty he had in obtaining an act to incorporate the diocesan synod of Nova Scotia in 1863 indicates that his political influence was not very great, although he could count among his friends and family some of the most politically influential people in Nova Scotia. However, the day of a family compact was long gone, and the Anglican "party" was not nearly as powerful as the Roman Catholic and Presbyterian elements in Nova Scotia society.

When Binney came to the diocese in 1851 there were 36,482 Anglicans in Nova Scotia, comprising 10.3 per cent of the total population, who were served by 56 clergymen. When he died in 1887 the clergy had increased to 76, and in 1891 the Anglicans in Nova Scotia had risen to 64,410, making up 12 per cent of the total population. Binney left a permanent mark on the diocese. The diocesan synod with its episcopal veto still remains; the cathedral in Halifax came from his inspiration; above all, he raised the level of churchmanship in the diocese to the point where Anglicans began to feel a sense of responsibility for the support of their church.

Bishop Binney lived as one of the aristocrats of Halifax. Through his old and prominent family he inherited money, stocks, and property both in Nova Scotia and in England. He also inherited a great deal from his wife's family. On 4 Jan. 1855 Binney had married Mary Bliss, the daughter of William Blowers Bliss*, senior puisne judge of the Superior Court of Nova Scotia, and member of one of the oldest and most distinguished loyalist families of Saint John, N.B. In 1854 Binney had purchased from James Boyle Uniacke* a Georgian stone mansion on Hollis Street, Halifax, next to Government House, and this spacious edifice saw many social functions. After his death in New York City in 1887, Binney's estate was valued at between $400,000 and $500,000, most of which was left to his wife, three living children, and a granddaughter.

V. Glen Kent

[There are almost no personal papers of Hibbert Binney available. The most valuable primary source for reconstructing his life's work are the contemporary Halifax newspapers, particularly those of the Church of England. The papers of the Reverend George Wright Hodgson and Edward Jarvis Hodgson in St Peter's Cathedral, Charlottetown, shed a good deal of light on Binney's character. The only comprehensive research done on Binney is the following work: V. G. Kent, "The Right Reverend Hibbert Binney, colonial Tractarian, bishop of Nova Scotia, 1851–1887" (MA thesis, Univ. of New Brunswick, Fredericton, 1969). V.G.K.]

Hibbert Binney was the author of *A charge delivered to the clergy at the visitation held in the Cathedral Church of St. Luke, at Halifax, on the 3rd day of July, 1866* (Halifax, 1866); *A charge delivered to the clergy at the visitation held in the Cathedral Church of St. Luke, at Halifax, on the 6th day of July, 1870* (Halifax, 1870); *A charge delivered to the clergy at the visitation held in the Cathedral Church of St. Luke, at Halifax, on the 30th day of June, 1874* (Halifax, 1874); *A charge delivered to the clergy at the visitation held in the Cathedral Church of St. Luke, at Halifax, on the 6th day of July, 1880* (Halifax, 1880); *A charge delivered to the clergy at the visitation held in the Cathedral Church of St. Luke, at Halifax, on the 1st day of July, 1884* (Halifax, 1884); *A charge delivered to the clergy at the visitation held in the Cathedral Church of St. Paul, at Halifax, on the 20th day of October, 1858* (Halifax, 1859); *A charge delivered to the clergy of the diocese of Nova Scotia, at the visitation held in the Cathedral Church of St. Paul, at Halifax, on the 11th day of October, 1854* (Halifax, 1854); *Observations upon the mission held in the city of Halifax, November 11th to November 22nd, 1883, addressed to the clergy of his diocese, by Hibbert, bishop of Nova Scotia* (Halifax, 1883); *A pastoral letter, including a correspondence between the Rev. Geo. W. Hill and himself, by Hibbert, lord bishop of Nova Scotia* (Halifax, 1866); and *Remarks on diocesan synods, addressed to the clergy and laity of his diocese* (Halifax, 1864). The *Correspondence between the bishop of Nova Scotia and the Reverend Canon Cochran, M.A., touching the dismissal of the latter from the pastoral charge of Salem Chapel, Halifax, N.S.* (Halifax, 1866) was also published.

Halifax County Court of Probate (Halifax), no. 1555, will of Hibbert Binney, 3 July 1868; no.2121, will of William Blowers Bliss, 7 Nov. 1873. St Peter's Cathedral (Charlottetown), G. W. Hodgson papers; Service book, 13 June 1869. Univ. of King's College Arch. (Halifax), Minutes of the Board of Governors, 1851–87. Church of England, Church Soc. of the Diocese of N.S., *Report* (Halifax), 1850–57; Diocese of N.S., Synod, *Journal* (Halifax), 1864, 1866, 1868, 1870–71, 1873. *Proceedings and discussions connected with the introduction of a bill into the legislature of this province, by Bishop Binney, for the establishment of a Church of England synod in the diocese of Nova Scotia, and other papers relating thereto*, ed. W. T. Townshend (Halifax, 1864), 6, 9, 93–94. Univ. of King's College, Board of Governors, *Investigation of the recent charges brought by Prof. Sumichrast against King's College, Windsor, with letters, reports, and evidence* (Halifax, 1872). *Church Record* (Halifax), 13 Oct. 1860, 12 June 1861, 27 Oct. 1864. *Church Times* (Halifax), 20 Dec. 1850; 3, 31 Jan., 18 April, 9 May 1851; 16, 30 April 1853; 26 Aug., 16, 23 Sept., 19 Oct. 1854; 19 May, 13 Oct. 1855; 18 Oct. 1856; 12 Nov. 1863. *Halifax Catholic*, 13 May 1854. *Halifax Herald*, 2 May 1887. *Saint John Globe*, 13 June 1887.

Belcher's farmer's almanack, 1864. H. L. Clarke, *Constitutional church government in the dominions beyond the seas and in other parts of the Anglican communion* (London and Toronto, 1924). A. W. H. Eaton, *The Church of England in Nova Scotia and the Tory clergy of the revolution* (New York, 1891), 238–39. H. Y. Hind, *The University of King's College, Windsor, Nova Scotia, 1790–1890* (New York, 1890), 95. J. W. Lawrence, *Foot-prints; or, incidents in early history of New Brunswick, 1783–1883* (Saint John, N.B., 1883), 27. C. H. Mockridge, *The bishops of the Church of England in Canada and Newfoundland . . .* (Toronto, 1896), 141–42. *Two hundred and fifty years young: our diocesan story, 1710–1960* (Halifax, 1960). Judith Fingard, "Charles Inglis and his 'primitive bishopric' in Nova Scotia," *CHR*, 49 (1968): 247–66. D. C. Moore, "The late Bishop Binney of Nova Scotia," *Canadian Church Magazine and Mission News* (Hamilton, Ont.), 2 (1887): 283–86.

BIRCHALL, REGINALD (also known as **Lord Frederick A. Somerset**), convicted murderer; b. 25 May 1866 at Accrington, Lancashire, England, youngest son of the Reverend Joseph Birchall; m. in 1888 Florence Stevenson; d. 14 Nov. 1890 in Woodstock, Ont.

Reginald Birchall, after two years of private tutoring, spent six years in public schools, during which time he found delight in "whatsoever was against the rules and whatsoever was redolent of lawlessness and disorder." In the early spring of 1885 he entered Lincoln College at Oxford. Birchall had inherited £4,000 in 1878 from his father's estate to be held in trust until his 25th birthday. Nevertheless, he proceeded to live like a young aristocrat and through licentious activity, highlighted by his founding of the hedonistic Black and Tan Club at Oxford, fell heavily into debt. By 1888 he was forced to sell his future inheritance, at the discounted value of £3,000, to appease creditors and left Oxford without obtaining a degree. Birchall invested £500 in a farm at Woodstock, Ont., and eloped with the daughter of David Stevenson, master of transportation of the London and Northwestern Railroad. In November 1888 they set sail for Canada.

In Woodstock they found not the prosperous estate that had been advertised but a small farm. Undaunted, they took rooms in Woodstock, and, calling themselves Lord and Lady Somerset, established a line of credit and took the social life of the community by storm. Six months later, pressed by the local merchants to pay their bills, Lord and Lady Somerset suddenly disappeared from Woodstock and returned to London.

Birchall received an insider's tip on a sure thing in the 1890 English Derby. To raise capital he placed an advertisement in London newspapers posing as the owner of a prosperous Canadian horse farm and sales-yard who was looking for a partner to buy into the business for £500. Birchall planned to bet the money on the English Derby, take his partner to Canada, stall until the race was run, and then pay back the £500 with interest out of his winnings. Douglas Raymond Pelly invested £170 with Birchall. Separately, Frederick Cornwallis Benwell and his father Colonel F. Benwell of Cheltenham agreed to supply £500 but only after the son had seen the farm and examined the books.

Reginald and Florence Birchall, Pelly, and Benwell arrived in New York City on 14 Feb. 1890 and went on to Buffalo by train, arriving on the 16th. Early the next day Birchall and Benwell travelled by train to Eastwood, a station just east of Woodstock where Benwell expected to be shown the sales-yard. Instead, Birchall evidently led him into a heavily wooded area called Blenheim Swamp and shot him twice in the back of the head. That evening Birchall returned to Buffalo and told Pelly that Benwell had been unhappy with the farm and planned to return to England. Birchall avoided further questioning and the next day the party moved to the Canadian side of Niagara Falls.

On 20 February Birchall wrote Colonel Benwell that his son had examined the business, was well pleased, and had signed a deed of partnership. He requested that Colonel Benwell forward the £500 as soon as possible. Unfortunately for Birchall, Benwell's body was found in Blenheim Swamp four days after the murder. After Pelly noticed a picture of the victim in a newspaper, Birchall, accompanied by his wife, travelled to Princeton, Ont., and calmly identified the body. But, based on information supplied by Pelly and the suspicion of John Wilson Murray*, chief detective for the province of Ontario, Birchall was arrested at Niagara Falls on 2 March by the local police and was transferred to the Woodstock jail.

His trial opened on 22 Sept. 1890 and excited international attention. Since both Benwall and Birchall were members of the English upper class, there was speculation that the murder was part of a larger scheme to swindle and murder young Englishmen from prosperous families. Cable connections led directly from the court-house in Woodstock to London, England, and newspapers in France, Germany, and Italy covered the trial. Birchall steadfastly insisted that he was innocent but did not address the court. He was defended by George Tate Blackstock* and prosecuted by Britton Bath Osler* with Judge Hugh MacMahon* presiding. The circumstantial evidence was overwhelming; Birchall was found guilty and sentenced to hang. On 14 Nov. 1890, in the Woodstock jailyard, Birchall "went to his death ghastly white, but without a tremor."

JAMES W. NICHOL

During his imprisonment Reginald Birchall wrote *Birchall, the story of his life, trial and imprisonment as told by himself* (Toronto, 1890).

[J. W. Murray], *Memoirs of a great detective, incidents in the life of John Wilson Murray*, comp. Victor Speer (Toronto, 1905). *Evening Sentinel-Review* (Woodstock, Ont.), September–November 1890. W. S. Wallace, *Murders and mysteries, a Canadian series* (Toronto, 1931), 172–93.

BLACK, JAMES, a founder of the Disciples of Christ in Upper Canada; b. 15 Aug. 1797 in the parish of Kilmartin (Strathclyde), Scotland, son of John Black and Janet Campbell; m. 15 Feb. 1828 Lois Humphrey of Grimsby Township, Upper Canada, and they had nine children; d. 21 April 1886 in Eramosa Township, Ont.

As a youth James Black attended school in winter and herded sheep during the summer. At 15 he began teaching in a parish school at Bellanoch in Argyllshire. The district in which he lived was being influenced by an infant Scottish Baptist movement developed at the turn of the century by Robert and James Alexander Haldane, who had seceded from the Church of Scotland. Black was impressed by the "Haldanite" minister of nearby Lochgilphead, Dugald Sinclair, who later came to Upper Canada. Because of his questioning of Church of Scotland credal statements, Black was refused a further teaching position and in 1820 immigrated with his parents to Aldborough Township, Upper Canada, where he was soon engaged to teach and lead the worship of the Scottish Baptists and Presbyterians in the area. James moved with his family to Nassagaweya Township in 1825, but left his father's farm to teach at Martin's Mills (Milton) and later at Beamsville. In 1829, the year after he married, Black began to farm in Eramosa Township, where he lived until his death. Though noted for his strength, he did not enjoy farm work; he found time to act as a school trustee and municipal commissioner during the 1840s and to devote himself to evangelism.

Black gradually became associated with the Disciples of Christ movement, whose members sought to promote Christian union by rejecting the credal statements and ecclesiastical structures of existing churches. Their first meeting-house in western Upper Canada was built in the late 1820s on Black's farm. It appears that in the early 1830s Black began to absorb the writings of the spokesman for the American Disciples movement, Alexander Campbell, whose rejection of Calvinistic determinism he shared: like other adherents, Black avoided describing the complex origins of the Disciples and could not pinpoint the time when he had made the transition from Baptist to Disciple of Christ. The only authority the Disciples would acknowledge was the Bible, and they were reluctant to make doctrinal statements or even to engage in theological discussions. They looked forward to a day when all Christians would worship in small, independent, local churches joined together only informally. They hoped that a general dissatisfaction with existing churches would cause the old structures to melt away, leaving the field open for the restoration of New Testament Christianity. Some disenchantment with existing churches was evident in areas of rural Upper Canada where congregations of Disciples were established, but it never reached the scale the Disciples expected.

From the 1830s to the 1860s Black frequently journeyed from his farm to encourage the many congregations he helped to establish in Wellington County and to preach throughout the western portion of the province. Though Disciples were reluctant to pay a resident minister, they more willingly supported itinerant evangelists such as Black. He himself promoted the "co-operative movement" by which independent congregations in the 1840s began to join together to support evangelistic work. But there was strong internal criticism of efforts by Disciples to combine for any purposes on a larger than local level, thereby endangering the purity of their Christianity with ecclesiastical structures. Black in 1863 deplored the action of Disciples in Owen Sound who had joined the Baptist church there, even though the Baptists had adopted the Disciples' practice of weekly communion, because he felt that the Baptists were still an organized "sect, however orthodox." His suspicion of other churches is seen in his comment in 1858 when he referred to Satan preaching "as a minister of righteousness." Despite his suspicions Black shared in the work of the British and Foreign Bible Society. In 1854 he was chairman of a Canadian auxiliary to the American Bible Union, a Disciple organization, which was preparing a "pure version" of the Scriptures. In the early 1860s he was editor with Lazarus Parkinson of the *Adviser*, published monthly in Toronto and one of many short-lived Disciple magazines.

"In consequence of his advanced age" Black in 1871 limited his preaching travels to Wellington and Halton counties. By the time of his death in 1886 he had seen the Disciples movement grow to many congregations. His work had been of particular importance because the Disciples' suspicions of formal church structure made the success of individual congregations rest less on social circumstances than on the leadership of dedicated believers such as himself.

RICHARD E. RUGGLE

Emmanuel College Library (Toronto), Disciples of Christ coll., Proc. of the Wellington County Co-operation of Disciples of Christ, Record book 1, 31 Jan. 1869–5 July 1908. *Adviser* (Toronto), June 1862; March, May, December 1863; August 1864. *Ontario Evangelist* (Guelph, Ont.), May 1886. Reuben Butchart, *The Disciples of Christ in Canada since 1830* . . . (Toronto, 1949). Frank Day, *Here and there in Eramosa* . . . (Rockwood, Ont., 1953), 9, 11, 19, 26, 32, 51–52, 89–90, 141–42. *History of the Baptists in Scotland from pre-Reformation times*, ed. George Yuille (Glasgow, [1926]), 70, 116–17. Joshua Norrish, *The early history of Nasagiweya* (Guelph, 1889).

BLACK, JOHN, Presbyterian clergyman; b. 8 Jan. 1818 in the parish of Eskdalemuir (Dumfries and Galloway), Scotland, eldest son of William Black and Margaret Halliday; m. first 21 Dec. 1853 Henrietta (d. 1873), daughter of SALLY and Alexander Ross*, and they had four sons and three daughters; m. secondly 9 June 1874 Laurenda, sister of Andrew Graham Ballenden BANNATYNE; d. 11 Feb. 1882 in Winnipeg, Man.

John Black was educated by private teachers engaged by a group of families whose children lived too far from the parish school. His formal schooling began in 1825 when his father moved the family to a farm in the parish of Kilpatrick-Fleming (Dumfries and Galloway). There, after 1836, Black occasionally taught at the local school and in Cumberland. He had, according to his brother James, "very early manifested a deep interest in spiritual things and a strong desire for religious knowledge."

In the summer of 1841 his family emigrated to Bovina Township, N.Y., where two of John's married aunts were already living. He taught in the local school for a short period before enrolling in an academy in Delhi, N.Y., to prepare himself for the ministry. For the three years he was a resident in the United States, Black had a connection with a branch of Presbyterianism known as the Associate Church. He could not completely accept the teachings of this church and hesitated in his choice of theological schools. Following the disruption of the Church of Scotland and the formation of the Free Church of Scotland in 1843, Black decided to attend the Free Church's college (later Knox College) in Toronto; he was one of its first students when it opened in 1844. At the college he was active in the students' missionary society, and because he had some knowledge of French he was selected as the students' "French Missionary," serving in the summer of 1847 at Pointe-aux-Trembles near Montreal. At the close of his final college session in 1848 he proceeded to Canada East and was licensed to preach by the presbytery of Montreal. He expected to work among the French Canadians in Canada East but the shortage of Presbyterian ministers led him to supply English-speaking congregations as well.

In July 1851 he was ordained, and reluctantly agreed to serve the Presbyterian community in the Red River Settlement (Man.) on the understanding "that his stay in the North-West would be brief." He had no intention of remaining permanently, not wanting to be so far from his parents in New York. Though he recognized that Red River was "a very important mission" he felt he was being forced into it against his will. "Nobody else would go," he wrote his brother James in July, "and so I am called to go." Black arrived in September, the first Presbyterian minister in the northwest, and though he always hoped to return to eastern Canada he remained at Kildonan (now part of Winnipeg) until his death. During his three decades of service there Black was instrumental in the development of a number of Presbyterian churches and missions in Manitoba and the North-West Territories.

Just prior to his arrival in 1851 the Hudson's Bay Company had granted the Presbyterian community £150 and a plot of land at Frog Plain (about five miles north of Upper Fort Garry) in lieu of its rights in the Church of England's Upper Church (later St John's Church), where it had worshipped. On this site at Frog Plain the Kildonan church was completed in 1853. There was a protracted conflict over the consecration of St John's graveyard which would have ended the Presbyterians' rights to burial there. When the Anglican bishop of Rupert's Land, David ANDERSON, embittered that the Hudson's Bay Company had interceded on behalf of the Presbyterians, refused to accept Presbyterian students at his school, Black, an experienced teacher, established a Presbyterian school beside the Kildonan church.

Although his mission to Red River was primarily in response to requests from descendants of the settlers brought out by Lord Selkirk [Douglas*], the synod of the Presbyterian Church hoped that Black, with his knowledge of French, might also work among the Métis and Indians. Throughout his years in the west he "cherished a deep interest in the spiritual welfare of the Indians" and as a result of his leadership the Reverend James Nisbet* was sent out by the Foreign Mission Committee in 1862; within four years Nisbet had established the first Presbyterian Indian mission, at Prince Albert (Sask.). In 1868 Black built a church, later Knox Presbyterian Church, in the village of Winnipeg and three years later was instrumental in establishing Manitoba College, one of the colleges that federated with the University of Manitoba when it was incorporated in 1877.

Although the Kildonan church was used as an assembly point for forces opposing Louis RIEL in February 1870, Black was active with other clergymen in attempts to keep peace between the English- and French-speaking sections in the settlement. He was present at the mass meeting held at Upper Fort Garry (Winnipeg) on 20 Jan. 1870 and was appointed to a committee that was to arrange for the election of the English delegates to the "Convention of Forty," which met six days later.

When the first Board of Education of Manitoba was established in 1871 Black represented the Presbyterian parishes. He served until 1876 when he resigned in opposition to resolutions of the Protestant section of the board aimed at dissolving the denominational school system in the province. According to George Bryce*, one of his biographers, Black did not want "to interfere with the amity between Protestants and Roman Catholics, which had been a feature of the old days of the Red River Settlement."

In 1876 Queen's College in Kingston conferred an honorary DD upon Black. Six years earlier he had been elected the first moderator of the Presbytery of Manitoba. In 1881 he was offered the position of moderator of the Presbyterian Church in Canada, but was forced to decline because of illness; in April he went to the east in an attempt to restore his health but died less than a year later in Winnipeg. Black was described as a man of "strong intellect," an "indefatigable and gifted minister," whose "kindly disposition" made his name "a household word in the whole North West," and who was always in the "forefront in every movement for the advancement of education, temperance and morality."

HARTWELL BOWSFIELD

PAM, MG 2, C14. UCA, John Black, Corr. United Church of Canada, Manitoba Conference Arch. (Winnipeg), John Black papers. Begg, *Red River journal* (Morton). J. W. Bond, *Minnesota and its resources to which are appended camp-fire sketches or notes of a trip from St. Paul to Pembina and Selkirk settlement on the Red River of the north* (New York, 1853). HBRS, XIX (Rich and A. M. Johnson). A. Ross, *Red River Settlement*. George Bryce, *John Black the apostle of the Red River; or, how the blue banner was unfurled on Manitoba prairies* (Toronto, 1898). Olive Knox, *John Black of old Kildonan* (Toronto, 1958). J. P. Schell, *In the Ojibway country: a story of early missions on the Minnesota frontier* (Walhalla, N.Dak., 1911).

BLACKBURN, JOSIAH, publisher, journalist, and politician; b. 6 March 1823 in London, England, third son of the Reverend John Blackburn, a leading Congregational pastor, and Sarah Smith; m. 29 May 1851 Emma Jane Dallimore, and they had two sons and six daughters, including the journalist Victoria Grace; d. 11 Nov. 1890 at Hot Springs, Ark.

Josiah Blackburn was educated at the City of London and the Mill Hill schools before immigrating to Canada West in 1850. He joined his brother John at the Paris *Star* in 1852 and also became involved in the *Ingersoll Chronicle*. That same year he purchased the weekly *Canadian Free Press* from James Daniell, holder of a $500 mortgage against William Sutherland, who had founded the paper in London, Canada West, in 1849. From a small printing office at the back of a dry goods store, Blackburn acted as editor, reporter, proof-reader, bookkeeper, collector, and canvassing agent. Early in 1854 the operation was expanded, and on 5 May 1855 Blackburn began a daily edition, the *London Free Press and Daily Western Advertiser* (after 1872 the *London Free Press*) which has continued to the present. The weekly *Canadian Free Press* was maintained under various mastheads until the 1880s. Josiah's brother Stephen became a partner in 1858, assisting Josiah in reporting and in writing editorials, and was responsible for the business office until he left the firm in 1871. By 1860 the total circulation of all editions of the *Free Press* had reached 3,500 copies, second only to the *Globe* among Reform newspapers in Canada West. Although firmly established the journal nevertheless had a capital investment of only $2,000 in 1861; according to Blackburn, "My capital is felicity of expression." There were 22 employees on the staff.

The *Free Press*, with new quarters after 1868, continued to prosper despite brisk competition in London, and on 3 July 1871 Blackburn formed a joint stock company, the London Free Press Printing Company, with John K. Clare, Henry Mathewson, and William Southam* as his copartners; he himself was no longer involved with the day-to-day operation of the newspaper. The new arrangement led to many important innovations. By 1873 the journal had new type, a new press, and special features. An evening edition and pyramid headlines, summarizing news stories in bold print, were introduced. Blackburn was also ahead of his contemporaries in instituting a policy of avoiding editorializing in reports of speeches.

Blackburn was active in politics, and from its inception the *Free Press* had a reputation for supporting

Reformers. He was the Reform candidate for Middlesex East in the 1857–58 election, losing to Marcus Talbot, the editor of the rival London *Prototype.* Blackburn favoured reciprocity, retrenchment, temperance, and representation by population, and opposed separate schools and sabbath labour. According to the *Hamilton Spectator,* Blackburn would have been George Brown*'s "warming pan" in parliament.

The year 1858 was a frustrating one for Reformers, and by the year's end Blackburn was questioning Brown's leadership. In the furore caused by the celebrated "double shuffle" Blackburn took a different position from other Reform journalists, and from Brown and the *Globe* in particular. When the courts upheld the legality of the double shuffle he refused to impugn the motives of the judges [*see* William Henry Draper*], believing that, although it was unworthy and ill judged, it was not illegal. By April 1859 he was convinced that Brown was an impossible leader who could never achieve success especially since he had now alienated Lower Canadian Reformers. Blackburn's personal attack on Brown raised speculation in some quarters that he was seeking a party realignment under the leadership of Louis-Victor SICOTTE and John Sandfield Macdonald*, with the *Free Press* as official mouthpiece. By June a number of journals, notably the *Hamilton Times,* were supporting the *Free Press* position.

By July 1859, however, Brown had reasserted his leadership of the Reform party and by September he was advocating a party convention to reunite Reformers. The *Free Press* opposed suggestions that the union of the Canadas should be abandoned because traditional Reform goals seemed to be thwarted in it. Blackburn was also critical of the fact that the convention in November 1859 was to be an Upper Canadian affair at a time when cooperation with Lower Canadians was essential and when Reformers were criticizing Lower Canadian sectionalism. The convention organizers slighted Blackburn, who as a Reform candidate and editor should have been an ex-officio delegate, and did not admit him to the convention until proceedings were open to all journalists. The *Free Press* challenged the *Globe*'s interpretation of the major compromise of the convention, which called for the dissolution of the union and the creation of "some joint authority." Blackburn ridiculed the outcome of the convention, and in particular challenged the right of Brown to dictate to the Reform party as if the *Globe* and Toronto had a monopoly on truth. That Blackburn considered running as an independent candidate in the by-election for Middlesex East in 1860 is a reflection of his view that "the position of affairs is many-sided" and that Reformers came in different shades. By April 1860 he was defending and cooperating with Sandfield Macdonald, who had boycotted the Reform convention.

When Sandfield Macdonald and Sicotte formed a new administration in May 1862, the *Free Press* became the most official mouthpiece of the government in the western part of Canada West. In 1862 Blackburn went to Quebec to undertake the management of a government newspaper. In August the *Quebec Mercury* was leased; Blackburn became publisher and George Sheppard* editor. The *Mercury* was transformed into a daily on 12 Jan. 1863 and Blackburn continued with the newspaper until after the resignation of the government of Sandfield Macdonald and Antoine-Aimé Dorion* in March 1864.

Blackburn became a persistent advocate of coalition governments as the most effective means to pursue practical, short-term measures of reform. He readily accepted, therefore, the confederation coalition formed in June 1864, even though it included Brown and lacked the support of Sandfield Macdonald. The *Free Press* had reservations about confederation until the Charlottetown and Quebec conferences, when its practicality as a federal union with firm guarantees for Canada West was demonstrated. On the assumption that confederation meant independence, a favourable consequence of confederation, in Blackburn's view, would be non-involvement in British affairs and a chance to reduce defence commitments; attacks were then made on the *Free Press* as an advocate of annexation to the United States since many Upper Canadians felt annexation would follow independence.

The resignation of Brown from the coalition cabinet in December 1865 coupled with Sandfield Macdonald's selection as premier of Ontario in July 1867 reinforced Blackburn's views, and made his transition to the support of Sir John A. Macdonald* and the Conservatives a smooth one. Blackburn was henceforth an invaluable asset to Conservative party organization in western Ontario. He became a close personal friend of John Carling*, the Conservative member for London in both the dominion and the Ontario legislatures. The *Free Press* had a wide distribution throughout western Ontario, and had a reputation for sound political judgements, "never prejudicing party interests by haste or immature consideration." Blackburn was also relatively free to move where he was needed. One of the best examples of this occurred in 1872 when he went to Toronto to assist in establishing the Toronto *Mail* as an effective Conservative organ and foil to the *Globe,* thus meeting a need underlined by the defeat of the Sandfield Macdonald administration in December 1871. Blackburn remained chief of the staff at the *Mail* for about 15 months. But, though a strong Conservative publicist and organizer, Blackburn remained conscientious and independent in his approach to issues. A strong advocate of reciprocity in the 1850s, he gave only qualified support to the National Policy in the 1870s, after long argument.

Blackburn maintained an active interest in London.

In October 1875 he was on the executive committee of the London Musical Union. He was a promoter of the mechanics' institute and, in 1881, was a charter member of the reorganized London Board of Trade. He also supported efforts to establish a branch of the provincial university in London. Along with his entire family Blackburn was rebaptized an Anglican on 23 Aug. 1866 in St Paul's Cathedral, London.

During the 1880s Blackburn received two government appointments. In 1880 he was named census commissioner in western Ontario and in 1884 a commissioner for organizing a printing bureau at Ottawa. He investigated government printing establishments in Washington as well as some state capitals and his recommendations culminated in the establishment of the Department of Public Printing and Stationery in 1886.

At his death Blackburn left an estate with real and personal assets totalling nearly $20,000 and shares in the London Free Press Printing Company and Carling Brewing and Malting Company valued at an additional $35,000. He also owned 400 acres of Manitoba farm land.

Josiah Blackburn was one of the most important newspapermen of his day. He was also politically influential, whether as a supporter of George Brown, Sandfield Macdonald, or John A. Macdonald. His journalism and politics were both characterized by a conviction that rational discussion of the issues was important, and the belief that anything Toronto could do London could do as well.

ELWOOD H. JONES

Josiah Blackburn letters (copies at UWO) are in the possession of W. J. Blackburn (London, Ont.). [J. S. Macdonald], "A letter on the Reform party, 1860: Sandfield Macdonald and the *London Free Press*," ed. B. W. Hodgins and E. H. Jones, *OH*, 57 (1965): 39–45. *London Free Press*, 1852–90. *Mail*, 1872–73. *Quebec Daily Mercury*, 1862–64.

Cyclopædia of Canadian biog. (Rose, 1886). [Archie Bremner], *City of London, Ontario, Canada: the pioneer period and the London of to-day* (2nd ed., London, Ont., 1900; repr. 1967). C. T. Campbell, *Pioneer days in London: some account of men and things in London before it became a city* (London, Ont., 1921). *History of the county of Middlesex, Canada . . .* (Toronto and London, Ont., 1889; repr. with intro. D. J. Brock, Belleville, Ont., 1972). E. H. Jones, "The Great Reform Convention of 1859" PHD thesis, Queen's Univ., Kingston, Ont., 1971); "Political aspects of the *London Free Press*, 1858–1867" (MA thesis, Univ. of Western Ontario, London, 1964). [H.] O. Miller, *A century of western Ontario: the story of London, "The Free Press," and western Ontario, 1849–1949* (Toronto, 1949; repr. Westport, Conn., 1972). Fred Landon, "Some early newspapers and newspaper men of London," London and Middlesex Hist. Soc., *Trans.* (London, Ont.), 12 (1927): 26–34. H. O. Miller, "The history of the newspaper press in London, 1830–1875," *OH*, 32 (1937): 114–39.

BLAIN DE SAINT-AUBIN, EMMANUEL-MARIE, educator, song-writer, story-teller, and translator; b. 30 June 1833 at Rennes, France, son of Charles Blain de Saint-Aubin and Emmanuelle-Sophie-Jeanne Delamarre; d. 9 July 1883 in Ottawa, Ont.

Emmanuel-Marie Blain de Saint-Aubin began his secondary studies in 1844 and obtained his *bachelier ès lettres* at Rennes on 26 July 1851. Soon after he went to Paris to pursue higher education, but a passion for singing and music put an end to his original intentions. In 1857, at the age of 24, wishing to learn English, he considered going to England, but the fishing boat he boarded in Nantes took him instead to Saint-Pierre and Miquelon. For several months he earned his livelihood giving music and grammar lessons. He then went to Prince Edward Island where he became friendly with a number of English-speaking families and quickly mastered the mysteries of their language.

He then sailed to Gaspé, Canada East, where he was immediately charmed by the pleasant manners of the French Canadians and the correctness of their speech. In 1858 or 1859 he settled at Quebec City. Benjamin Sulte*, who knew Blain de Saint-Aubin well, described him in rather flattering terms. In this native of Rennes who had become a Québécois he detected great artistic and literary ability and the refinement of a man of the world. The lectures that Blain de Saint-Aubin occasionally gave, "without being remarkable," were "skilfully constructed." In one of his addresses, given at Kamouraska on 3 July 1861, while severely criticizing the great names of French literature, such as Honoré de Balzac, Eugène Sue, Alexandre Dumas, and George Sand, Blain de Saint-Aubin conceded the importance of the novel as a genre but suggested that in choosing reading material one should be selective.

The year 1862 was one of good fortune for Blain de Saint-Aubin: he obtained the post of assistant translator to the Legislative Assembly of the Province of Canada, and Governor General Lord Monck* invited him to give French lessons to his children. On 22 Nov. 1864, at Quebec, Blain de Saint-Aubin married Charlotte-Euphémie Rhéaume, a musician who was the elder daughter of lawyer Jacques-Philippe Rhéaume, later member for Quebec East in the provincial legislature; they were to have three children. This marriage presumably strengthened his ties with a city where his talent for song-writing and versification was constantly winning him more admirers. During this period he composed a patriotic song, "La Mère canadienne," dedicated to Lieutenant-Colonel Melchior-Alphonse de Salaberry* and set to music by Marie-Hippolyte-Antoine Dessane*, and on 7 Aug. 1865 *Le Courrier du Canada* printed one of his poems entitled "Honnête homme et chrétien" in homage to Sir

Étienne-Paschal Taché*. However, his post as translator obliged him to go to Ottawa when the government was transferred there that year.

Blain de Saint-Aubin immediately became a member of the Institut Canadien-Français of Ottawa and on 11 Jan. 1867 he gave a talk there on the past, present, and probable future of the French language in Canada. Having drawn his listeners' attention to the role of songs in sustaining French-Canadian nationality, he added that he had some apprehension about the consequences of confederation, for he prophesied that "the Anglo-Saxon majority will perhaps want to abolish the use of French in the confederate legislature."

Although his profession left him little spare time Blain de Saint-Aubin regularly attended the weekly receptions given by George-Étienne Cartier* and Joseph-Philippe-René-Adolphe Caron*. There he "organized the music, [and] composed occasional songs and even tunes." He tried his hand at the more dignified genre of the hymn and, when a poetry competition was sponsored by the faculty of arts of Université Laval in 1869, he submitted to the jury, which was chaired by Abbé Louis Beaudet, an anthem for the national festival of French Canadians, Saint-Jean-Baptiste Day. This anthem, whose epigraph was "Croire et combattre," earned him an honourable mention.

As a prose-writer, Blain de Saint-Aubin published neatly turned stories that were sparkling trifles in *L'Opinion publique* from January 1873 to December 1881. He contributed translations to the *Revue canadienne* of Montreal. One of the articles dealt with geological explorations in Canada in 1871, and in this connection he exhorted the French-speaking intellectuals to put aside barren controversies in order to "study the geography, topography and geology of our country, its agricultural resources, the best means of establishing in it a vast network of railways that will link the Atlantic to the Pacific, and of developing a trade that will soon amaze the descendants of Uncle Sam."

As a literary critic Blain de Saint-Aubin was no less anxious to advance letters in French Canada by making some of its authors known to English-speaking Canadians. As a critic, however, his major achievement was to have brought contemporary French-Canadian literature to the notice of the greatest literary critic of the day in France, Charles-Augustin Sainte-Beuve. When the latter died on 13 Oct. 1869, Blain de Saint-Aubin informed the readers of *Le Journal de Québec* that "Sainte-Beuve was thoroughly acquainted with the literary movement in Canada." For several years Blain de Saint-Aubin had been, anonymously, sending him the works of the following authors: François-Xavier Garneau*, Jean-Baptiste-Antoine Ferland*, Étienne Parent*, Pierre-Joseph-Olivier CHAUVEAU, Antoine GÉRIN-LAJOIE, Octave Crémazie*, Louis-Honoré Fréchette*, Léon-Pamphile Le May*, Henri-Raymond Casgrain*, Joseph-Étienne-Eugène Marmette*, and Narcisse-Henri-Édouard Faucher* de Saint-Maurice. But one day Blain de Saint-Aubin had sent him a lecture of his own on Canadian literature which had appeared among the miscellanea in *Le Journal de Québec*, and he took care this time to indicate his address. By return mail he received from Sainte-Beuve the following note dated Paris, 26 Jan. 1869: "Dear Sir, and I was about to say dear compatriot overseas, I have just received and read with interest the article on 'La littérature canadienne en 1868.' Nothing is more gratifying than to feel in touch, at so great a distance, through the mind, shared tastes, and goodwill: it is the most reliable of all transatlantic cables."

The absorbing profession of translator by which Blain de Saint-Aubin earned his livelihood prevented him from giving free rein to his admirable abilities as versifier, song-writer, story-teller, and literary critic; moreover, before he turned 50 he was in difficulties with his health. Soon after his 50th birthday he died suddenly, on the morning of 9 July 1883, at his home in Ottawa.

PHILIPPE SYLVAIN

[Nazaire Levasseur* has listed and described the characteristics of Emmanuel-Marie Blain de Saint-Aubin's songs in three articles: "Musique et musiciens à Québec," *La Musique* (Québec), 3 (1921): 50–53, 66–69, 82–83. The following should be added to Levasseur's list: "Chanson à Flora; chanson contre Crémazie," mentioned in Jeanne d'Arc Lortie, *La poésie nationaliste au Canada français (1606–1867)* (Québec, 1975), 304; "Chant patriotique," *Le Courrier du Canada*, 24 janv. 1862; "La chanson de la Saint-Jean-Baptiste" and "Chanson du Jour de l'An 1866," *Le Canadien*, 28 juin 1865 and 3 janv. 1866 respectively; "Le casque de mon père," "Serrons nos rangs; chant pour la Saint-Jean-Baptiste 1878," and "À l'hon. J.-A. Chapleau à l'occasion du dîner qui lui a été offert le 9 octobre 1878, à St-Henri," *La Minerve*, 19 mars 1870, 20 juin 1878, and 9 oct. 1878 respectively; and "De l'enseignement de la musique," *JIP*, 4 (1860): 26–27, 43, 62–63.

Blain de Saint-Aubin was also known as a skilled writer of verse. His work includes "Maman a toujours raison" and "Le cœur et la volonté," *Le Foyer canadien* (Québec), 2 (1864): 13–14, 374–75 respectively; "Le souvenir," *Rev. canadienne*, 2 (1865): 249; "Honnête homme et chrétien; hommage à la mémoire de l'honorable colonel sir Étienne-Paschal Taché," *Le Courrier du Canada*, 7 août 1865; "Hymne pour la fête nationale des Canadiens-français," a manuscript held at ASQ, Lettres, N, 181 (ASQ, Univ., Carton 29, no.66, contains the draft of Abbé Thomas-Étienne Hamel*'s letter informing Blain de Saint-Aubin that the "Hymne" had been awarded an honourable mention); and lastly, "Elzéar Labelle; In memoriam," *La Minerve*, 26 oct. 1875. His stories, which were published in *L'Opinion publique*, janvier 1873–décembre 1881, are analysed in Aurélien Boivin, *Le Conte littéraire québécois au XIX*[e] *siècle; essai de bibliographie critique et analytique* (Montréal, 1975), 68–69.

In addition to "De la lecture des romans," a manuscript held at ASQ, Fonds Viger-Verreau, Carton 35, no.2, several of Blain de Saint-Aubin's addresses were reprinted or published in contemporary newspapers and journals. These include: "Passé, présent et avenir probable de la langue française au Canada," *Le Journal des Trois-Rivières*, 22 janv. 1867; "Nos chansons et nos chanteurs," *L'Opinion publique*, 22, 29 déc. 1870; and "Quelques mots sur la littérature canadienne-française," *Rev. canadienne*, 8 (1871): 91–110. Guy Bouthillier and Jean Meynaud, *Le choc des langues au Québec, 1760–1970*, (2v., Montréal, 1970–71), I: 166, cites Blain de Saint-Aubin's account of his interview with Lady Monck. The authors confess in the introduction to their book that they had been unable to find any biographical information about Blain de Saint-Aubin.

As a translator, Blain de Saint-Aubin published a number of important articles including: [N. P. Wiseman], "Du perfectionnement intellectuel; discours prononcé par le cardinal Wiseman, à l'institution Hartley, Southampton, le 16 septembre 1863," and "Exploration géologique du Canada (rapport des opérations de 1871)," published respectively in *Rev. canadienne*, 1 (1864): 435–41 and 10 (1873): 188–97; also the text of an address by the Reverend Æneas McDonell Dawson*, "Les poètes canadiens-français," *JIP*, 13 (1869): 17–21. Blain de Saint-Aubin's article, "M. Sainte-Beuve et la littérature canadienne," was published in *Le Journal de Québec*, 19 oct. 1869.

The following studies and articles on Blain de Saint-Aubin were also used: Lareau, *Hist. de la littérature canadienne*; and Benjamin Sulte, "Blain de Saint-Aubin," *Canada-Rev.* (Montréal), 2 (1891): 52–54. Although, in writing his assessment, Sulte drew on a friendship of nearly 20 years' duration, some of his assertions must be approached with caution because Sulte too often relied on his own recollections and memory of events. Finally it should be noted that Levasseur made liberal use of Sulte's work in writing his own articles for *La Musique*. P.S.]

BLAKE, CATHERINE HONORIA. *See* HUME

BLANCHET (Blanchette), AUGUSTIN-MAGLOIRE, Roman Catholic priest, missionary, and bishop; b. 22 Aug. 1797 at Saint-Pierre-Montmagny, Lower Canada, son of Pierre and Marie-Rose Blanchette; d. 25 Feb. 1887 at Vancouver (Wash.).

Augustin-Magloire Blanchet followed in the footsteps of his older brother, François-Norbert. After studying Latin in his native parish, he enrolled at the Petit Séminaire, and then at the Grand Séminaire de Québec. Ordained priest on 3 June 1821, he acquired his early experience as a curate at Saint-Gervais (1821–22), and then as a missionary at Chéticamp, N.S., and on the Îles de la Madeleine (1822–26). He was recalled from there to take important posts as parish priest in the Montreal region: at Saint-Luc on the Richelieu river, also serving Saint-Jean-l'Évangéliste (1826–28); at Saint-Pierre-du-Portage (Assomption-de-la-Sainte-Vierge) (1828–30); and at Saint-Charles in Saint-Charles-sur-Richelieu (1830–38), ministering at Saint-Marc as well (1830–32). After considering entering the Séminaire de Saint-Hyacinthe, a proposal which caused strained relations with Bishop Jean-Jacques Lartigue*, Blanchet finally regained the confidence of the bishop, who appointed him an archpriest in 1835 and entrusted him with several important missions.

In 1837 political events in the Richelieu valley forced Blanchet, whose parish of Saint-Charles was the stronghold of the local Patriotes, to make a number of difficult choices. He acknowledged that the grievances of the party of Louis-Joseph Papineau* were justified, and, though he declined to engage actively in politics, he warned the governor, Lord Gosford [Acheson*], in a letter dated 9 Nov. 1837 that he might be misinformed, and that "if the government desires the happiness of the country, it should lose no time in complying with the just requests of the people." He added that "one could no longer count on the clergy to check the popular movement in the region," for "the shepherds cannot part company with their flocks." The morning of the battle at Saint-Charles, on 25 November, Blanchet, who was opposed to violence and bloodshed, went to the camp of the Patriotes, most of whom were his parishioners; he took the opportunity to bless them and get them to say prayers. His action was interpreted in varying ways: one Patriote, Siméon Marchessault*, saw in it only a desire to give a general absolution, but another, Simon Talon, *dit* L'Espérance, asserted that "the object of Messire Blanchet's prayer was to encourage the habitants to fight."

The British authorities and the supporters of the government leaned towards the latter interpretation. Blanchet was arrested for high treason and taken to Montreal where he was imprisoned on 16 December. After an inquiry conducted on the spot and a long explanation from Blanchet, the bishops of Montreal and Quebec, anxious not to compromise the clergy, gave their version of the events: Bishop Lartigue concluded that the parish priest had merely been "a little weak and imprudent," and Bishop Joseph Signay* considered that he had acted out of fear of the Patriotes. Consequently they both did all in their power, by speaking and writing, to intercede on his behalf with Gosford and even with Sir John Colborne*, the commander-in-chief of the forces in the two Canadas. Thanks to their efforts Blanchet was set free on 31 March 1838 on £1,000 bail.

When he left prison Blanchet became parish priest of Saint-Joseph, Les Cèdres, replacing his brother François-Norbert who was leaving for Oregon missions. Augustin-Magloire remained at Saint-Joseph until 1842 when he was summoned to the diocese of Montreal; he became a titular canon in 1844. Two years later a decision from Rome reunited the two

Blanchet brothers. It entrusted Augustin-Magloire with the direction of the diocese of Walla Walla, in the section of the Oregon Territory that is now the state of Washington, while his brother became archbishop of Oregon City (Oreg.). The new bishop was consecrated in the cathedral at Montreal on 27 Sept. 1846 and set out for Oregon on 4 March 1847. On 5 September, after a long, exhausting journey, Augustin-Magloire reached his destination and at the beginning of October his travelling companions, including four Oblate missionaries who had stopped at Fort Hall (Idaho), finally arrived also. At the Indians' request Blanchet and Jean-Baptiste-Abraham Brouillet, his vicar general, decided to take up residence among the Cayuses, some 25 miles from Walla Walla.

Tragic events obliged them to change their plans. A few days after the arrival of the Oblate missionaries, the Cayuses killed the Protestant missionaries and several settlers at Waiilatpu (Idaho). Bishop Blanchet himself met the Indian chiefs and pleaded the cause of those prisoners who had been saved thanks to an intervention by Abbé Brouillet. These actions did not placate the Americans, who accused the two Catholic missionaries of having instigated the attack, while the Cayuses received the exhortations and warnings with bad grace. In these circumstances Blanchet deemed it preferable to withdraw to St Paul (Oreg.), in the Willamette valley, leaving Brouillet behind; the latter remained until American soldiers arrived to avenge their fellow citizens in February 1848.

In 1850, at the request of the three bishops of Oregon, Rome created the diocese of Nesqually (later the diocese of Seattle, Washington) and transferred Augustin-Magloire to it; three years later the old diocese of Walla Walla was eliminated and part of its territory – Walla Walla and the lands of the Cayuse and the Dalles Indians – was annexed to the new diocese. In this expanse of nearly 100,000 square miles Blanchet laboured for more than 25 years, setting up missions, consecrating churches, instructing the faithful, and administering the sacraments, as did all the missionaries who worked with him. He also made a contribution to the first two provincial councils in Oregon City, in 1848 and 1861, and took part in the plenary councils at Baltimore, Md, in 1852 and 1866. Moreover, the 1852 council gave him the opportunity to visit Mexico, South America, and Europe, in order to collect funds for his diocese; he returned in 1856 with a few Sisters of Charity of Providence (Sisters of Providence).

An old man worn out by toil and illness, Augustin-Magloire Blanchet resigned from his post and became bishop of Ibora *in partibus infidelium* on 23 Dec. 1879; he remained in the diocese of Nesqually until his death in February 1887.

NIVE VOISINE

AAQ, 210 A, XI–XVIII; 26 CP, VI. ACAM, 420.041; RLB, 1; RLL, 8–9. ANQ-Q, QBC 25, Événements de 1837–1838, nos.292, 844. AP, Saint-Pierre-de-la-Rivière-du-Sud (Saint-Pierre-Montmagny), Reg. des baptêmes, mariages et sépultures, 22 août 1797. "Le curé de St-Charles, en 1837, se disculpe de trahison," François Beaudin, édit., *RHAF*, 22 (1968–69): 441–48. *Rapport sur les missions du diocèse de Québec . . .* (Québec), no.7 (juill. 1847): 1–34; no.8 (avril 1849): 1–33; no.9 (mars 1851): 1–28, 39–66. *L'Ami du peuple, de l'ordre et des lois* (Montréal), 20 déc. 1837. *Mélanges religieux* (Montréal), janv., août 1848. [O. B. Corrigan], "Chronology of the Catholic hierarchy of the United States," *Catholic Hist. Rev.* (Washington), 1 (1915–16): 367–89. C. H. Carey, *A general history of Oregon prior to 1861* (2v., Portland, Oreg., 1935). Richard Chabot, *Le curé de campagne et la contestation locale au Québec (de 1791 aux troubles de 1837–38): la querelle des écoles, l'affaire des fabriques et le problème des insurrections de 1837–38* (Montréal, 1975). E. V. O'Hara, *Pioneer Catholic history of Oregon* (Portland, 1911). Théophile Ortolan, *Cent ans d'apostolat dans les deux hémisphères: les Oblats de Marie Immaculée durant le premier siècle de leur existence* (4v., Paris, 1914–32), II. Sidney Warren, *Farthest frontier; the Pacific northwest* (New York, 1949; repr. Port Washington, N.Y., 1970).

BLANCHET, JOSEPH-GODRIC (Goderic), doctor, soldier, politician, and public servant; b. 7 June 1829 at Saint-Pierre-Montmagny, Lower Canada, son of Louis Blanchet, a farmer, and Marie-Marguerite Fontaine; m. 28 Aug. 1850 Émilie Balzaretti at Quebec City, and they had six children; d. 1 Jan. 1890 at Lévis, Que.

Joseph-Godric Blanchet received his secondary education at the Petit Séminaire de Québec from 1840 to 1844 and at the Collège de Sainte-Anne-de-la-Pocatière from 1844 to 1845. After training for four and a half years with his uncle, the surgeon Jean Blanchet*, he qualified as a doctor on 14 May 1850. He practised for a year at Quebec and a year at Saint-Nicolas, before settling into a practice in 1852 in the parish of Notre-Dame-de-la-Victoire (at Lévis).

Blanchet was soon initiated into politics by serving as mayor of the parish municipality of Notre-Dame-de-la-Victoire from 1855 to 1861. In this capacity, in 1857 he had several wharves, a covered market, and a market place built, and in 1861 he assisted in the incorporation of the town of Lévis. Having run unsuccessfully as a "Democratic" candidate for the Legislative Assembly in 1857, he was elected for Lévis in July 1861 as a Liberal-Conservative, was re-elected in 1863, and kept his seat until July 1867.

Conscious of the defence needs of the country and a supporter in 1862 of the Militia Bill which the assembly failed to pass, in 1863 Blanchet raised the 17th (Lévis) Battalion of Infantry and was appointed its lieutenant-colonel, retaining this post until 1884. In 1865 he took courses at the military school in Quebec City and obtained his 2nd and 1st class certificates.

That year he became commanding officer of the 3rd (Laprairie) Administrative Battalion after the Confederate raid on St Albans, Vt [*see* Charles-Joseph COURSOL]. In 1866 and 1870 he was given command of the militia on the south shore of the St Lawrence to guard the eastern borders of Quebec while there was a threat of a Fenian invasion.

That confederation was conceived and brought into being by the Conservatives proved opportune for Blanchet, who in 1867 obtained both federal and provincial seats in the riding of Lévis. Furthermore, on 27 Dec. 1867 he became the first speaker of the Quebec Legislative Assembly. As speaker, his duties included attending to the assembly's internal administration, defending its privileges, and maintaining order and dignity during debates. He also had the right to vote when the house divided equally on an issue. Blanchet exercised this prerogative twice: in 1872, when an amendment was made to a bill to secure the autonomy of the assembly, and three years later, when an amendment to an amendment was made to a bill legalizing certain notorial acts. In both instances, taking a stand opposite to that of the prime minister, he voted in favour of the proposed amendments. From 1867 to 1872 he chaired a committee whose major responsibility was to develop standing orders for the Legislative Assembly, and his familiarity with parliamentary procedure enabled him to carry out this task without difficulty. Re-elected to the provincial assembly in 1871 and to the federal parliament in 1872, Blanchet had to resign from the House of Commons in order to remain in the assembly when the double mandate was abolished by the federal government in 1873. He was again chosen speaker at the opening of the second legislature and held this office until he was defeated in the provincial election of 7 July 1875 by the sheriff of the district of Quebec, Étienne-Théodore Pâquet.

The years from 1867 to 1875 were the most active of Blanchet's career. In addition to duties as a federal member in Ottawa and as speaker at Quebec which kept him busy for more than half the year, Blanchet continued to practise medicine and he also took an interest in both business and the cultural life of the Quebec City region. He was vice-president of the Levis and Kennebec Railway Company in 1870, and its president from 1872 to 1876 [*see* Louis-Napoléon LAROCHELLE]. In 1871 he also took part in founding *L'Écho de Lévis*, a paper which served as his means of communication with his constituents. He belonged to a literary society, the Cercle de Québec, and was its president in 1870 and 1871. In 1873 he became a member of the Catholic committee of the Council of Public Instruction of Quebec.

After his defeat in the 1875 provincial elections he won the vacant federal seat of Bellechasse on 30 Oct. 1875. He was re-elected in 1878 and 1882 in the constituency of Lévis. Blanchet became speaker of the House of Commons on 13 Feb. 1879, and served in this office until 18 May 1882. He was the first and indeed the last parliamentarian to be the speaker at both federal and provincial levels. Blanchet resigned from the House of Commons on 4 Oct. 1883, after being appointed collector of customs for the port of Quebec. He held this post until his death in 1890.

FRANCES CAISSIE

Débats de l'Assemblée législative (M. Hamelin), [I–II]. Qué., Assemblée législative, *Journaux*, 1867–68. *Le triomphe de Joseph-Goderic Blanchet dans le comté de Lévis: une magnifique démonstration populaire, jeudi soir, 19 septembre 1878* (Québec, 1878). *Le Canadien*, 27 oct. 1871, 23 oct. 1874, 3 mars 1883, 3 janv. 1890. *La Minerve*, 4 janv. 1890. *Le Monde illustré* (Montréal), 8 mars 1890. *L'Opinion publique*, 20 févr. 1879. Achintre, *Manuel électoral. Canadian biog. dict.*, II. *Cyclopædia of Canadian biog.* (Rose, 1888). Dent, *Canadian portrait gallery.* J. Desjardins, *Guide parl.* P.-G. Roy, *Profils lévisiens* (2 sér., Lévis, Qué., 1948), I. Auguste Béchard, *Galerie nationale: l'honorable Joseph-G. Blanchet* (Québec, 1884). *Le Centenaire de Notre-Dame de Lévis* ([Lévis, 1950]). M. Hamelin, *Premières années du parlementarisme québécois.* "Les Blanchet," *BRH*, 38 (1932): 735–40. "Le premier orateur de l'Assemblée législative," *BRH*, 69 (1967): 63–64.

BLONDIN, ESTHER (Christine) SUREAU, *dit.* *See* SUREAU

BOIS, LOUIS-ÉDOUARD, Roman Catholic priest and historian; b. 11 Sept. 1813 at Quebec City, son of Firmin Bois and Marie-Anne Boissonnault; d. 9 July 1889 at Maskinongé, Que.

The parents of Louis-Édouard Bois lived in Quebec's Lower Town at the corner of Notre-Dame and Sous-le-Fort in a house said to have been built by Samuel de Champlain* in 1624. In 1819 they put their son in an English school, and four years later he entered the Petit Séminaire de Québec. In 1827 Louis-Édouard was sent to the new Collège de Sainte-Anne-de-la-Pocatière to finish his classical education; he then taught at the college while studying theology. Ordained priest on 7 Oct. 1837 at Quebec, he was immediately appointed curate at Saint-Antoine-de-Padoue, Rivière-du-Loup (Louiseville), to parish priest Jacques Lebourdais, *dit* Lapierre; from 1840 to 1843 he served as curate at Saint-Jean-Port-Joli to his uncle François Boissonnault. In 1843 he was named parish priest of Saint-François at Beauceville, where he gave a new stimulus to education, and opened in Tring, Forsyth, and Lambton townships chapels that later became the parishes of Saint-Victor, Saint-Éphrem, Saint-Évariste, and Saint-Vital. He left Beauce in 1848 to assume the office of parish priest of Saint-Joseph at Maskinongé, which he was to hold for 41 years.

A missionary and spiritual guide, Bois was also always a collector, a scholar, and a lover of history. While at Sainte-Anne-de-la-Pocatière (La Pocatière), he copied the manuscript of "Journal d'un voyage en Europe, 1819–1820," by Bishop Joseph-Octave Plessis*, and began to collect original documents, the first being the "Journal du Voyage" of Luc de La Corne*, which he received from his uncle François. At Saint-Jean-Port-Joli his acquaintance with Philippe-Joseph Aubert* de Gaspé prompted him to take a keener interest in history and to gather material. In 1842 he began compiling "Garde notes ou recueil de notes diverses relatives à l'histoire du Canada," in which he included a hodgepodge of notes on his readings, extracts of documents, and summaries of interviews; he left 19 notebooks, which are indexed. He also left 7 volumes of newspaper clippings entitled "L'Œuvre de mes ciseaux" ("The work of my scissors") and 14 volumes of original or copied "Manuscrits." In addition he put together a "Collection de seings, vues, armoiries, portraits" in three large in-folio albums, and a coin collection. But his greatest wealth was his library which at his death contained some 4,300 volumes and 1,013 pamphlets, mostly dealing with history, especially Canadian history.

Abbé Bois brought together this vast documentation for the specific purpose of writing a history of the first 12 bishops of Quebec. By 1845 he had finished a life of Bishop François de Laval*, a work of 371 pages in-quarto, with a large number of appended documents; from it he published an *Esquisse de la vie et des travaux apostoliques de Sa Grandeur Mgr. Fr. Xavier de Laval-Montmorency* . . . under the pseudonym of De Vapeaume. Two years later he put the final touches to a biography of the second bishop of Quebec, Jean-Baptiste de La Croix* de Chevrières de Saint-Vallier; Bois gave a summary of it in 1856, as the introduction to a reprint, published in Quebec, of Saint-Vallier's *Estat présent de l'Église et de la colonie française. . . .* Furthermore, by 1880 he had written studies of bishops Louis-François Duplessis de Mornay, Pierre-Herman Dosquet*, François-Louis de Pourroy* de Lauberivière, Henri-Marie Dubreil* de Pontbriand, Jean-Olivier Briand*, Louis-Philippe Mariauchau* d'Esgly, Jean-François Hubert*, Pierre Denaut*, Plessis, and Bernard-Claude Panet*, 2,100 pages in all, not including documents. Of this impressive labour only the biography of Bishop Mornay has been published in full, in 1912. Historian Henri Têtu*'s comment on the manuscript of this work explains why most of the writings of Abbé Bois remain unpublished: "his weakness is that he does not give sufficient indication of his sources of information, and does not quote often enough the authors he consulted. Furthermore . . . he obviously amplifies excessively, and a panegyrical tone prevails from beginning to end." Working under difficult conditions – access to sources was often impossible – Bois unhesitatingly made assertions often contradicted later by documents. He was not much concerned by all this, for in his opinion history should unveil only "deeds of heroism, true grandeur, unshaken integrity," in order to "foster emulation," and keep people "in the path of duty and honour."

Bois was the first to admit "that the task is far beyond the reach of my strength and capabilities," and that it would be better that his work remain in its boxes. But, while he was working at his major undertaking, he used the materials he collected to publish, again anonymously, a large number of brief historical accounts and some more substantial studies, for example on abbés Jean Raimbault* and Joseph-Onésime Leprohon*, Colonel François Dambourgès, Judge Adam Mabane*, and the French *émigré* clergy in Canada. He was also "the initiator and true compiler" of the 1858 edition of the *Relations des jésuites*, and he suggested to his protégé, Jean Blanchet, the publication of the *Collection de manuscrits contenant lettres, mémoires, et autres documents relatifs à la Nouvelle-France* . . . , for which he wrote the preface. In this way the "learned abbé" came to public attention. A number of Canadian intellectuals including James MacPherson Le Moine* and the abbé's great friend Jean-Baptiste Meilleur* regularly called upon his knowledge and his library; historian Francis Parkman twice went to Maskinongé to consult him. The Université Laval recognized his work by conferring on him the honour of *docteur ès lettres* in 1883; the Royal Society of Canada admitted him to membership in 1885. That year his bishop, Louis-François Laflèche*, appointed him a canon in recognition of his "industrious research" in history, particularly religious history. More than any other this honour must have gratified a scholar who considered discretion and charity the main attributes of an historian, and who dedicated to research all the time he could snatch from his ministry. The promotion did not change the way of life of this unusual parish priest, a man of commanding presence, who, often absent-minded and absorbed in thought, emerged from his meditations only to speak in maxims or mystify those with whom he talked.

His honours had come late, at a time when illness had almost incapacitated Abbé Bois and was to prevent him from continuing his research. He was able none the less still to direct the parish of Maskinongé, where he died on 9 July 1889; his funeral attracted priests and laymen from all parts of Quebec. In his will, dated 5 Feb. 1880, Abbé Bois bequeathed all his possessions, including his manuscripts and library, to the Séminaire de Nicolet.

NIVE VOISINE

[Among the published writings of Louis-Édouard Bois (some under pseudonyms), are the following: Un neveu, "Extraits du vieux livre de mon oncle," *Le Journal de Québec*, 1843; De Vapeaume, *Esquisse de la vie et des travaux apostoliques de Sa Grandeur Mgr. Fr. Xavier de Laval-Montmorency, premier évêque de Québec* . . . (Québec, 1845) (a review of this work appeared in *Le Journal de Québec*, 9 mars 1847); *Études et recherches biographiques sur le chevalier Noël Brulart de Sillery, prêtre, commandeur* . . . ([Québec, 1855]); "Notes sur Sa Grandeur Monseigneur de S. Vallier, second évêque de Québec . . . ," issued as an introduction to a reprint in Quebec in 1856 of the *Estat présent de l'Église et de la colonie française dans la Nouvelle-France* of Mgr Jean-Baptiste de La Croix de Chevrières de Saint-Vallier, first published in Paris in 1688; *Michel Sarrasin, médecin du roi à Québec, conseiller au Conseil supérieur, etc., etc.* ([Québec, 1856]); "Notice sur Mgr. Patrice Phelan, troisième évêque de Kingston," *Le Journal de Québec*, 20 juin 1857; *Le colonel Dambourgès, étude historique canadienne* (Québec, 1866); *Étude biographique sur M. Jean Raimbault, archiprêtre, curé de Nicolet, etc.* (Québec, 1869); *Notice sur M. Jos O. Leprohon, archiprêtre, directeur du collège de Nicolet, etc., etc.* (Québec, 1870); "Quelques observations à propos des notes historiques sur la paroisse Ste-Anne de la Pocatière . . . ," *L'Événement* (Québec), 11 févr.–4 mars 1870; Ruricola, "Les noms propres en Canada," *La Minerve*, 17 mars 1874 (this article was also issued as a preface to Pierre-Georges Roy*'s *Les noms géographiques de la province de Québec* (Lévis, Qué., 1906); Z, "Monseigneur Alexandre Macdonell," *Rev. canadienne*, 13 (1876): 8–20, 94–107, 352–74, 411–29; "Madame d'Youville et l'Hôpital Général de Montréal," *Le Journal de Québec*, 20 avril 1878; *Le juge A. Mabane, étude historique* (Québec, 1881); S. J. M., "Biographie du rév. père Emmanuel Crespel," *Le Journal de Québec*, 5, 7 févr. 1885, a text that was also published as a preface to a new edition in Quebec in 1884 of the *Voiages du R. P. Emmanuel Crespel, dans le Canada et son naufrage en revenant en France*, edited by Louis Crespel and first published at Frankfurt am Main (Federal Republic of Germany) in 1742; "L'Angleterre et le clergé français pendant la Révolution," RSC *Trans.*, 1st ser., 3 (1885), sect.I: 77–87; *L'île d'Orléans* . . . (Québec, 1895); "L'honorable Adam Mabane," *BRH*, 7 (1901): 42–46; "Mgr Duplessis-Mornay," *BRH*, 18 (1912): 246–56, 311–19.

The ASN has Louis-Édouard Bois papers (AP-G, L.-É. Bois), and a complete description is available through an inventory prepared by Thomas-Marie Charland (copy at PAC, MG 24, B26). The collection consists of about 44 volumes of historical notes and documents and more than 600 letters received by Abbé Bois from Jean-Baptiste Meilleur, Mgr Louis-François Laflèche, James MacPherson Le Moine, and Augustin Côté*. N. V.]

Le Canadien, 10 juill. 1889. *Le Journal de Québec*, 12 juill. 1889. *Le Monde illustré* (Montréal), 27 juill. 1889. J.-E. Bellemare, "L'abbé Louis-Édouard Bois," *L'Écho de Saint-Justin* (Louiseville, Qué.), 1er janv. 1923: 1–7. T.-M. Charland, "L'œuvre historique de l'abbé Louis-Édouard Bois," SCHÉC *Rapport*, 3 (1935–36): 13–24. "La paroisse de Saint-François de Beauce; quelques notes," *L'Éclaireur* (Beauceville, Qué.), 9 déc. 1909: 10. P.-G. Roy, "Les œuvres de M. l'abbé L.-É Bois," *BRH*, 6 (1900): 280–81. Henri Têtu, "Mgr Duplessis de Mornay," *BRH*, 4 (1898): 258–65.

BONAMI (Bonamis), *dit* **Lespérance (L'Espérance), ALEXIS**, HBC voyageur, guide, and boat brigade leader; b. 27 Nov. 1796 at Saint-Michel d'Yamaska (Yamaska, Que.), son of Pierre Bonami, *dit* L'Espérance, and Marguerite Gouin; m. in June 1825 his country wife, Marguerite Guernon (Grenon or Gouin), at the Red River Settlement (Man.), and they may have had a total of 18 children; d. 11 Dec. 1890 at St François Xavier, Man.

Alexis Bonami, *dit* Lespérance, was born into a fur-trade family, several members of which hired out as voyageurs to Montreal entrepreneurs. During the War of 1812 he served in a regiment commanded by Lieutenant-Colonel James Cuthbert*. Bonami probably began his career with the Hudson's Bay Company as a voyageur, paddling and portaging in the transport of bundles of furs and provisions. Although he had planned to return to Lower Canada after his initial contract, he remained in the west to perform a key role as a guide and brigade leader with the HBC for at least half a century. In 1826, at the age of 29, Bonami signed a three-year contract as a guide with the HBC at Norway House (Man.). Two years later he may have been chosen as a guide to accompany George Simpson* on his historic canoe trip to the west coast via the Fraser River.

Simpson had promoted the use of York boats following the union of the North West Company and the HBC in 1821 because of their large capacity relative to crew size, and they were soon used exclusively on the two main trunk routes from York Factory (Man.), to the Red River Settlement and to Fort Edmonton. By the late 1820s Bonami had risen to some prominence, and probably never served in the laborious and menial capacity of oarsman of a York boat.

Alexis Bonami became famous for leading the Portage La Loche brigade. York boats were first used on the route between York Factory and the Mackenzie River in 1823, and after experimenting with different routes to overcome the problems of transporting goods in and out of the Mackenzie River area as quickly as possible, the HBC finally settled on the complicated but efficient Red River route. In 1832 Bonami was brigade leader of the first Red River crew to make this journey, the longest and most difficult of the fur trade. The annual brigades left the Red River Settlement in four to six York boats as soon as the ice cleared from Lake Winnipeg at the end of May. They travelled down the Red River and across Lake Winnipeg to Norway House where they deposited their cargoes of furs and country provisions. Supplies kept in the warehouses at Norway House for the Mackenzie River were then taken along the Saskatchewan River, portaged to English River (now the Churchill River, Sask.), and on to Lac La Loche (Sask.). From there the cargoes were portaged to the middle of the Methy

Portage (Sask.) where a crew from the Mackenzie River District exchanged the incoming provisions for outgoing furs. Bonami's crew then retraced their route to Norway House and went down the Hayes River to York Factory, arriving in mid August, in time to meet the annual supply ship from Britain. After depositing their furs, they carried the new provisions back, leaving some at Norway House and bringing the rest to Red River by the middle or end of October. The Portage La Loche brigade travelled some 4,000 miles on a rigid schedule through dangerous waterways. The route continued in use until late in the century, but by the 1860s Red River carts were transporting cargo over the 12-mile Methy Portage.

Bonami was responsible for keeping the guides and tripmen who served under him to the schedule and for protecting his cargo and passengers. His fine qualities as brigade leader and his mastery of the route brought him considerable honour and respect among his fellows. Tripmen on a voyage worked up to 18 hours a day, seven days a week, and only bad weather kept them from the oars. An indiscretion or simple mishap could dump both crew and cargo into treacherous water. Disease or injury often impaired their work, and even as late as the 1860s the need to carry adequate provisions could pose a problem. The men for the Portage La Loche brigade were recruited annually at Red River and received somewhat less than the HBC's usual annual salary for transporters: middlemen earned £12, bowsmen £14, steersmen £16, and the guide £25. During the winter many of the La Loche tripmen lived in the Red River Settlement and they frequently supplemented their meagre incomes by hunting, hiring out as casual labour, and smuggling furs.

In 1835 the HBC granted Bonami 50 acres of land on the Assiniboine River near Upper Fort Garry (Winnipeg), across the river from a 70-acre lot which Bonami may have purchased himself. With the help of his family, he was able to work a surprisingly large farm. Within three years he owned livestock and had three acres under cultivation, and by the early 1840s he was cultivating 10 to 15 acres, well above the average for the settlement.

Upon his retirement, at an unknown date, Bonami is reputed to have been rewarded with an annual pension from the HBC. Shortly after his death, in December 1890, *Le Manitoba* of St Boniface eulogized his long career: "M. Lespérance . . . was an imposing figure among the host of intrepid voyageurs, whose hardships, dangers, and courage can only be appreciated by those who have shared them."

Carol M. Judd

AP, Saint-Michel (Yamaska), Reg. des baptêmes, mariages et sépultures, 28 nov. 1796. PAM, HBCA, B.235/b/3; B.239/k/1: 39, 101; B.239/u/1: no.70; D.4/102: 47; D.4/103: 22; E.6/7. R. M. Ballantyne, *Hudson's Bay; or every-day life in the wilds of North America, during six years' residence in the territories of the Honourable Hudson's Bay Company* (2nd ed., Edinburgh and London, 1848). *Le Manitoba* (Saint-Boniface), 17 déc. 1890. Carol [Judd] Livermore, *Lower Fort Garry, the fur trade, and the Red River Settlement* (Ottawa, 1977). R.[G.] Glover, "York boats," *Beaver*, outfit 279 (March 1949): 19–23. L.-A. Prud'homme, "Alexis Bonami dit Lespérance," *Rev. canadienne*, 29 (1893): 207–18.

BOOMER, MICHAEL, Church of England clergyman and educator; b. 1 Jan 1810 in Hill Hall, near Lisburn (Northern Ireland), eldest son of George Boomer, a linen manufacturer, and Mary Knox; m. first 18 May 1842 Helen Blair, *née* Adams, at Galt, Canada West, and they had four children; m. secondly Isabella Jemima Davidson (d. 19 Aug. 1876), widow of Absalom Shade*; and m. thirdly in November 1878 Harriet Ann Roche, *née* Mills; d. 4 March 1888 in London, Ont.

Michael Boomer, who was of Huguenot descent, was educated at the Royal Belfast Academical Institution where he was a foundation scholar for five years. On 22 Oct. 1832 he entered Trinity College, Dublin, and graduated with a BA in the spring of 1838; he later received an LLB and an LLD in 1859. Boomer came to Canada in 1840 and was immediately ordained deacon by Bishop John Strachan* of Toronto. The following year Strachan priested him and he settled in Galt where for more than 30 years he acted as a missionary for the Society for the Propagation of the Gospel in Foreign Parts. During his tenure at Little Trinity Church the congregation expanded greatly and Boomer was instrumental in the construction of the substantial stone church and brick parsonage as well as the stone schoolhouse.

In 1872 Boomer left Galt for London when he was appointed dean of the diocese of Huron by the new bishop, Isaac Hellmuth*. Hellmuth had for ten years been attempting to construct a varied Church of England educational system in London to rival that of Toronto. Shortly after Boomer's arrival, Hellmuth quarrelled with Isaac Brock*, the principal of the divinity school, Huron College, and the newly appointed dean soon replaced Brock as the principal and professor of divinity at Huron. Hellmuth was no doubt pleased with the change: Boomer, who had been on the council of Huron College since it was founded in 1863, wus already well acquainted with the college; having his dean as principal would allow the bishop to extend his influence; and, probably most important, the $2,000 salary and residence provided for Boomer by the college allowed Hellmuth to save the dean's stipend. Unfortunately, the numerous demands of the dual role were probably too much for one man.

As principal, Boomer had immediate difficulties. The general depression of the economy caused both a constant drop in enrolment and an increasing concern over the strength of the various endowments which supported the college financially. Problems with staff, one of which resulted in a lawsuit that went against the college to its financial loss, and problems with students, who objected to strict regulations as well as administrative shortcomings, increased; only half fees were charged for the first term of 1879 after the college was unable to replace a professor who had died the previous year. As dean, Boomer was unable to keep the college's graduates in the diocese; they were drawn away to surrounding dioceses where stipends were higher. Personal tragedy added to Boomer's worries. After the deaths of his son in China and of his second wife, Boomer asked for leave from his duties in September 1876; he was not to return to them for more than two years.

During this time, however, he presided at a meeting of alumni and students of Huron on 20 Feb. 1877 which pressed for the incorporation of a new university. On 7 March 1878 a charter was granted to the Western University of London, Ontario (now the University of Western Ontario) and on 9 May Boomer was elected vice-chancellor and provost, Hellmuth being chosen chancellor. The charter provided for the affiliation of Huron, and the council of the college decided on 20 May 1881 to join the university as soon as it opened. Classes in arts and divinity began at the university in October of that year with Boomer serving as professor of divinity; the affiliation with the university did not alter the character of the teaching of this subject. An amendment to the university's charter in 1882 provided that only members of the Church of England could sit on the senate, the purpose being to ensure grants from the Society for Promoting Christian Knowledge. Nevertheless, financial difficulties continued and were complicated by the departure of the university's most powerful supporter, Hellmuth, on his resignation as bishop in 1883. That year the first graduates completed their degrees in arts, but enrolment remained small.

In the midst of these struggles Boomer suffered a paralytic stroke in 1884 which prevented him from carrying out his duties. On 24 September he was granted six months' leave but his active involvement with university and college was finished. He resigned as principal of the college on 22 May 1885, one month after the college had decided to disaffiliate from the university; the resignation became effective 1 October. He did, however, remain dean of the diocese until his death. Boomer's third wife was active in fund raising for the college from her arrival in Canada and continued her philanthropic labours into the next century.

Boomer's 13-year principalship of Huron College, after a long and successful parish ministry, was not a happy period but he had struggled to carry the too heavy burden Hellmuth had given him and he had helped to establish what is now a major Canadian institution.

JAMES JOHN TALMAN

Church (Toronto), 21 May 1842. *Dominion Churchman* (Toronto), 15 March 1888. *London Advertiser* (London, Ont.), 5 March 1888. *London Free Press* (London), 6, 8 March 1888. *Alumni Dublinensis: a register of the students, graduates, professors, and provosts of Trinity College, in the University of Dublin*, ed. G. D. Burtchaell and T. U. Sadleir (Dublin, 1924), 81. *Canadian biog. dict.*, I: 327–28. Chadwick, *Ontarian families*, I: 87. J. J. Talman, *Huron College, 1863–1963* (London, 1963), 34–47. J. J. and R. D. Talman, *"Western" – 1878–1953: being the history of the origins and development of the University of Western Ontario during its first seventy-five years* (London, 1953).

BOTSFORD, BLISS, lawyer, landowner, politician, and judge; b. 26 Nov. 1813 at Sackville, N.B., the seventh son of William Botsford*, a politician and judge, and Sarah Lowell Murray, *née* Hazen; m. in 1842 Jane Chapman, and they had five children; d. 5 April 1890 at Moncton, N.B.

Bliss Botsford was the grandson of both Amos Botsford*, a distinguished loyalist who served as speaker of the New Brunswick House of Assembly from its inception in 1786 until his death in 1812, and William Hazen*, a prominent pre-loyalist merchant. Little is known of Botsford's childhood or early education; in 1829 he entered King's College (University of New Brunswick) in Fredericton and later left without taking a degree. Following in his father's footsteps, he studied law, under William End* of Gloucester County, and in 1838 was admitted to the bar. In 1836 Botsford moved to the Bend of Petitcodiac (Moncton) where he practised until 1870. When he arrived at the Bend it consisted of a few small shops, an inn, and less than 20 dwellings surrounded by marsh and forest. Botsford established for himself a large home with extensive grounds in the centre of the village, and as the settlement grew he began to acquire lands through purchase, mortgage, settlement of estates, and court judgements. In 1854, for example, he was assigned 100 acres of prime real estate in the town in payment of debts owed him by Jacob Trites, a grandson of the original land grantee. When the Anglican parish was established in 1851 Botsford donated land for the church and rectory and became one of the first church wardens.

Moncton, incorporated as a town in 1855, had expanded rapidly after 1850, chiefly because its shipbuilding industry was responding to the great demand for vessels caused by the Crimean War and the Australian gold-rush. By the late 1850s, however, the market for ships in Liverpool, England, was glutted and the operations of Joseph Salter*, Moncton's leading shipbuilder, were ruined in 1859. No new industry was found to replace shipbuilding, the Westmorland Bank (which was to fail in 1866) showed signs of weakness, real estate values dropped drastically, and the town debt could not be retired because many citizens were unable to pay their taxes. The completion in 1860 of the European and North American Railway from Saint John to Shediac did not offset these adverse economic factors, and the town settled into a deep depression. When Botsford was elected mayor of Moncton in March 1862 he successfully petitioned the legislature to repeal the town's incorporation act, thus reducing expenses by eliminating salaries for town officers and spreading the tax load among citizens over the whole of Westmorland County. Moncton was not to be reincorporated as a town until 1875, when its growing importance as a railway centre caused a resurgence. In 1870 the federal cabinet approved the recommendation of the commissioners of the Intercolonial Railway that Moncton be the site of the principal workshops of the publicly owned line. The city was also the junction-point of the Intercolonial and the European and North American Railway. Despite the national depression of the 1870s, railway activity at Moncton spurred further growth.

Botsford had been an active participant in Moncton's changing fortunes on the provincial as well as the local level. From 1851 to 1854 and again from 1856 to 1861 he had been a member of the assembly for Westmorland County, but he did not distinguish himself in the legislature. In 1865 he declared himself an opponent of New Brunswick's entry into confederation, and after his election in March of that year he became surveyor general in the anti-confederate government of Albert James SMITH. The following year Smith's government was defeated at the polls, but Botsford was personally re-elected and from 1867 to 1870 served as speaker of the New Brunswick assembly, a post previously held by both his father and his grandfather.

Botsford's impressive figure, well over six feet in height and more than 200 lbs in weight, coupled with personal magnetism and a vigorous and persuasive style of delivery, won for him a high place in the ranks of the legal profession. His greatest case was in 1852 when he represented Peter and John Duffy against Dr Abraham Gesner*, the celebrated geologist. On land 16 miles south of Moncton, the mineral and mining rights to which the Duffys had acquired and had then assigned to William Cairns, Gesner had discovered an outcropping of a glossy black substance with a high gas content which resembled soft coal. He called it albertite, but the Duffys claimed that the mineral was true coal and that, because of certain provincial regulations, it belonged to them. Gesner, supported by several scientists from Canada and the United States, claimed that the mineral was a new substance and that ownership was his by right of discovery. Botsford's defence included the use of expert testimony and a strong appeal to the principle of the "right of property owners," an argument which induced the jury to decide in favour of his clients. However, further research in later years proved that Gesner's argument had been correct.

By 1870 Botsford was one of Moncton's most respected citizens, and he was known for his hospitality. He was also an active freemason, and in 1870 the Royal Arch Masons named their new chapter after him. In the same year he was appointed judge of the county court for Westmorland and Albert, a post he held until his death. He was respected as a judge for his fairness, sympathetic treatment of young lawyers, logical and concise charges to juries, and the firmness of his decisions.

On 5 April 1890 Botsford was leaving his club rooms, located on the second floor of a building on Main Street, when he collapsed on the stairs and fell through a large window to the board sidewalk below. He died of massive fractures and internal haemorrhages a few hours later. On the day of Botsford's funeral, official mourning was declared in Moncton, which was to be incorporated as a city just two weeks later.

C. ALEXANDER PINCOMBE

St George's Anglican Church (Moncton, N.B.), "History of St George's Anglican parish," comp. J. J. Alexander (typescript, 1932). PANB, "This New Brunswick, a parade of places and people," comp. Ian Sclanders (clippings from the *Telegraph-Journal*, Saint John, N.B., 1937–38). Westmorland County Registry Office (Dorchester, N.B.), libro GG: 536–38. *Moncton Times*, 20 Jan. 1885, 11 Dec. 1889, 7, 9 April 1890, 15 June 1927. *Cyclopædia of Canadian biog.* (Rose, 1888), 603. *The register: being a list of former students and graduates of the College of New Brunswick, later King's College, and since 1859 the University of New Brunswick, Fredericton, N.B.* (Fredericton, 1924). E. W. Larracey, *The first hundred: a story of the first 100 years of Moncton's existence after the arrival in 1766 of the pioneer settlers from Philadelphia, Pa.* (Moncton, 1970), 122–23. L. A. Machum, *A history of Moncton, town and city, 1855–1965* (Moncton, 1965), 43, 107. MacNutt, *New Brunswick*, 432. C. A. Pincombe, "The history of Monckton Township (ca. 1700–1875)" (MA thesis, Univ. of New Brunswick, Fredericton, 1969), 141, 152, 167–68, 206–8. Waite, *Life and times of confederation*, 247. J. C. Webster, *A history of Shediac, New Brunswick* ([Shediac], 1928), 13.

BOURGEAU (Bourgeault), VICTOR, joiner, carpenter, woodcarver, and architect; b. 26 Sept. 1809 at Lavaltrie, Lower Canada, son of Basile Bourgeault, a master wheelwright, and Marie Lavoie; d. 1 March 1888 in Montreal, Que.

Bourgeau

Victor Bourgeau seems to have begun working in his father's business at an early age. During the 1820s he was employed at building sites in the region around Lavaltrie, as an apprentice joiner and carpenter to his uncle (also Victor Bourgeau). Little is known about his upbringing. When he married Edwidge Vaillant on 17 June 1835 he could not sign the register and his biographers attribute his lack of schooling to the precarious financial position of his father.

In the 1830s an event known by oral tradition, and recorded by his biographers, is believed to have changed the course of his career. Now an accomplished craftsman, Bourgeau is said to have met in Montreal the Italian painter Angelo Pienovi*, who being penniless offered to teach him the techniques of draughtsmanship. Although this story cannot be verified, something significant must have happened at this period because subsequently Bourgeau appears literate and skilled in draughting.

His first known works were executed in 1839 at Boucherville, where he received payment for the completion of altar carvings and other embellishments. These were unfortunately destroyed when the church of Sainte-Famille burned down in 1843. The craftsman, who still called himself a joiner and woodcarver, completed several projects for the church of Notre-Dame in Montreal, including a pulpit which was much lauded by his contemporaries and was described by his biographers as "a little masterpiece of elegance and strength."

Bourgeau entered seriously upon his long and fruitful career as an architect after 1847. He had come to Montreal in the 1830s in time to witness important architectural developments, which were increasingly influenced by neo-classical and neo-Gothic styles; it was the architect John Ostell* who, along with James O'Donnell*, John Wells, and William Footner, perhaps exemplified this trend most strongly and who in the 1840s exercised a preponderant influence. Several facts suggest that Bourgeau received his training under Ostell. Since the kind of work carried out by Ostell required numerous assistants it is likely that Bourgeau went to work as a trainee. This was the only way to enter the profession at that time; moreover, Ostell was his immediate predecessor in the field of religious architecture. After 1850 Bourgeau finished some of the work undertaken by Ostell, who had embarked on a business career, and took over his responsibilities in relation to the diocese and the religious communities. In addition, Bourgeau maintained a stylistic continuity, as his first architectural works demonstrate.

In 1849, when he was beginning to establish himself as an architect, the important project of enlarging the church of Sainte-Anne at Varennes gave Bourgeau an opportunity to display the general conformity to architectural tradition which was one characteristic of his art. Indeed, in commencing the enlargement of the nave between the towers and chapels, he reverted to a method of alteration which had been used in 1734 at Notre-Dame in Montreal. This type of modification was undoubtedly calculated to demonstrate that he was a practical architect thoroughly familiar with sensible, tested solutions. In 1850 the parish council of Sainte-Rose (now in the city of Laval) commissioned Bourgeau to build a new church. Here again, true to his architectural heritage, he constructed a neo-classical façade modelled on the church of Sainte-Geneviève at Pierrefonds, which had been designed by Thomas Baillairgé* and erected in 1839. The church at Sainte-Rose, Bourgeau's first large one, reveals also that he was sufficiently in command of his profession to be able to carry out major commissions and he used a technical approach which made a good impression on those who employed him.

Victor Bourgeau's success was now assured. He continued to draw up the plans for numerous buildings and to supervise the work on site. Olivier Maurault in *Marges d'histoire*, and Gérard Morisset* in his inventory of works of art, have already listed a substantial number of his accomplishments, but further detailed research alone will make it possible to do justice to the talent and industry of this prolific architect who, according to a study now in progress, designed some 100 buildings. After the church of Sainte-Rose (1850) Bourgeau prepared the plans for many buildings in which the influence of Thomas Baillairgé is noticeable. The church of Saint-Vincent-de-Paul (1857), now in the city of Laval, is an example of this continuation of a late form of neo-classicism. Testimony to the architect's ability to adapt himself to projects of a more modest scale can be found in the less elaborate churches of the Joliette region: Saint-Alexis (1852); Saint-Félix-de-Valois (1854); L'Assomption-de-la-Sainte-Vierge, in the village of L'Assomption (1863); and Saint-Antoine, at Lavaltrie (1869). All the edifices of this type have two characteristics: a façade on which ornamentation is developed regardless of the structure standing out behind it, and belfries of the usual octagonal or circular design but with two tambours superimposed and topped by a spire. Here we have what might almost be called Victor Bourgeau's signature. He copied these belfries, as well as some of the façades, from architectural texts. There is an obvious relationship between this type of building and certain edifices by the Americans Benjamin Henry Latrobe and Minard Lafever.

At the same time Bourgeau promoted the development of neo-Gothic architecture. The church of Saint-Pierre-Apôtre in Montreal, built in 1852–53, as well as the cathedrals of L'Assomption at Trois-Rivières, finished in 1858, and Saint-Germain at Rimouski, completed in 1862, are evidence of the architect's mastery of this new style. Bourgeau's neo-Gothic works were not, however, original creations, as the obvious affinity of the cathedral at Trois-Rivières with St Luke's in London makes clear. Bourgeau's debt to British and American architecture is substantial. His great neo-Gothic achievement remains the restoration of the interior décor of Notre-Dame in Montreal. The plans were submitted in 1857 but the work went on until 1880. Bourgeau set out to modify the building's appearance, which was deemed too severe, and the interior décor he created in Notre-Dame so well reflected Quebec tastes in architecture that it quickly became a model widely copied throughout the province.

But the use of neo-Gothic architecture inevitably resulted in confusion of Roman Catholic with Protestant churches in the province of Quebec. Indeed, after the earliest phase of this architecture (adopted for the symbolism of forms inherited from a glorious period of western Christian civilization), this structural affinity between the churches of the two religious groups gave rise to a quite violent reaction. In Montreal the Jesuits and Bishop Ignace BOURGET advocated a return to classical forms and baroque ornamentation. It was undoubtedly Bourget who led the way, with a plan worked out by 1852 for the reconstruction of the cathedral of Saint-Jacques (now the basilica of Marie-Reine-du-Monde) in Montreal, on the model of the basilica of St Peter's in Rome. Bourgeau was sent to Rome in 1857 to study and measure St Peter's, and initially opposed Bourget's plan because after seeing St Peter's he did not think it could be copied on a reduced scale. In 1871 the tenacious bishop of Montreal sent Father Joseph Michaud to Rome, and after taking the necessary measurements Michaud prepared a small-scale model. Work began in Montreal in 1875 and Bourgeau agreed to supervise it. The cathedral of Saint-Jacques was consecrated in 1885 but was not finished until 1890. This monument immediately became the symbol of the ultramontane movement and affirmed the supremacy of the neo-baroque style in the Roman Catholic religious architecture of Quebec.

Most of the churches erected by Bourgeau after 1865 were neo-baroque, particularly in their interiors. He followed the simplified model of St Peter's, with a boldly conceived coffered vault, a nave separated into three aisles by a colonnade, and a simple reredos as an integral part of the architecture, with space for the erection of that pre-eminently baroque feature, a baldachin. The interiors of Saint-Barthélémy (near Berthierville) and L'Assomption-de-la-Sainte-Vierge are two splendid examples of Bourgeau's architectural skill.

Bourgeau was also actively engaged in convent architecture. The convent of the Sisters of Charity of the Hôpital Général of Montreal (Grey Nuns), which led to some controversy (it was threatened with demolition in the 1970s), was built between 1869 and 1871 according to the plans of Bourgeau and his partner, Alcibiade Leprohon; they followed the main lines of the traditional architecture preserved in the religious communities, except for the façades to which they added a facing of rough-surfaced stone and openings framed in cut stone. The chapel, built between 1874 and 1878, has elements of Romanesque style. Elsewhere, as in the Hôtel-Dieu in Montreal, Bourgeau more directly adopted the neo-baroque style, particularly when he built the cupola over the chapel.

The Bourgeau–Leprohon partnership seems to have attracted a greater diversity of business. The partnership was formed about 1870, at the time when work was beginning on the convent of the Sisters of Charity of the Hôpital Général. The firm was subsequently commissioned to construct a number of buildings which are clearly more eclectic, in particular such commercial buildings as the hotel near the Bonsecours market, erected in 1861, and the examining warehouse in Montreal put up in 1875. One of Bourgeau's last important achievements was the preparation in about 1885 of the plans for the Canadian College in Rome, a building valued then at $200,000.

Bourgeau died on 1 March 1888 while on his way to make a business call on the Sisters of Charity; he was 78. He had lost his first wife in 1877, and also his two children, one having died in infancy and the other when he was a young lawyer. On 4 May 1878 at Montreal he had married Delphine Viau. His contemporaries remembered "old Bourgeau" as a demanding and relentless worker who had become a legend at the building sites he inspected, invariably sporting a top hat. His work, neglected in the midst of the vast productive activity of the latter half of the 19th century, is just beginning to be rediscovered and appreciated. It would, however, be a mistake to try to distinguish it too sharply from that of his contemporaries. His diversified and important contribution can be understood only in the context of his period and of the architectural climate of the 19th century.

LUC NOPPEN

AP, Saint-Antoine (Lavaltrie), Reg. des baptêmes, mariages et sépultures, 26 sept. 1809. IBC, Centre de documentation, Fonds Morisset, 2, B772.5/V64/1; 085/3/J65.5. *La Minerve*, 11 févr. 1857, 22 mars 1888. *Dominion annual register*, 1885: 217–18. M. A. Coyle, "Victor Bourgeau (1809–1888), architect: a biographical sketch" (paper presented at McGill Univ., Montreal, 1960). J.-C. Marsan, *Montréal en évolution; historique du développement de l'architecture et de l'environnement montréalais* (Montréal, 1974). Olivier Maurault, *Marges d'histoire; l'art au Canada* ([Montréal], 1929), 220–23; *La paroisse; histoire de l'église Notre-Dame de Montréal* (Montréal et New York, 1929); *Saint-Jacques de Montréal; l'église, la paroisse* (Montréal, 1923), 54–55. Luc Noppen, *Les églises du Québec (1600–1850)* (n.p.,

1977). Qué., Ministère des Affaires culturelles, "Église de Sainte-Rose . . . histoire, relevé et analyse" (Québec, 1974). Barbara Salomon de Friedberg, *Le domaine des sœurs grises, boulevard Dorchester, Montréal* (Québec, 1975). Franklin Toker, *The Church of Notre-Dame; an architectural history* (Montreal and London, Ont., 1970). John Bland, "Deux architectes du XIXe siècle," *Architecture, Bâtiment, Construction* (Montréal), 8 (juillet 1953): 20. G. Ducharme, "La maquette de la cathédrale de Montréal (œuvre du père Joseph Michaud, clerc de Saint-Viateur)," *Technique* (Montréal), 15 (février 1941): 85–91. A.-C. Dugas, "Le plan miniature de la cathédrale de Montréal et le R. P. Michaud, C.S.V., "*L'Action populaire* (Joliette, Qué.), 7 juin 1923: 3. Alan Gowans, "From Baroque to Neo-Baroque in the church architecture of Quebec," *Culture* (Québec), 9 (1949): 140–50. Olivier Maurault, "L'architecte Victor Bourgeau", *BRH*, 29 (1923): 306–7; "Projets de décoration de Notre-Dame," *Vie des arts* (Montréal), 9 (Noël 1957): 12–13. Gérard Morisset, "L'architecte Victor Bourgeau," *La Patrie*, 7 mai 1950: 26–27. Noël Paquette, "Le père Joseph Michaud C.S.V., architecte de la cathédrale de Montréal," *L'Estudiant* (Joliette), 6 (mai-juin 1942): 20–21. Émile Venne, "Victor Bourgeault, architecte (1809–1888)," *L'Ordre* (Montréal), 22, 23 mars 1935.

BOURGET, IGNACE, Roman Catholic priest and bishop; b. 30 Oct. 1799 in the parish of Saint-Joseph (now in Lauzon), Lower Canada, son of Pierre Bourget, a farmer, and Thérèse Paradis; d. 8 June 1885 at Sault-au-Récollet (Montréal-Nord), Que.

Ignace Bourget's forebear, Claude Bourget, was originally from the Beauce region around Chartres, France. On 28 June 1683 at Quebec City he married Marie, the daughter of Guillaume Couture*, a former *donné* of the Society of Jesus and a companion in captivity of Isaac Jogues*. Ignace was the eleventh of 13 children and in 1811, after a primary education about which little is known, he entered the preparatory class at the Petit Séminaire de Québec. His brother Pierre, who was 13 years older than he, had preceded him at the seminary and was ordained priest on 4 June 1814. Ignace proved a studious pupil but his assiduity did not earn him the highest academic rank. One of his fellow students was Étienne Chartier*, who was to become notable as "chaplain to the Patriotes," and his teachers included Charles-Joseph Ducharme*, subsequently a parish priest and founder of the Petit Séminaire de Sainte-Thérèse, and Antoine Parant*, later spiritual director and procurator of the Séminaire de Québec.

A pious youth, Bourget was admitted to the Congrégation de la Sainte-Vierge in 1812. Being clearly destined for the priesthood, he was tonsured on 11 Aug. 1818 in the cathedral at Quebec City and by the next month was at the Séminaire de Nicolet, where for three years he studied theology and taught first and second year classes in Latin elements and Syntax respectively. Joseph-Octave Plessis*, the archbishop of Quebec, conferred minor orders upon him on 28 Jan. 1821 and, at the parish church of Nicolet on 20 May, the subdiaconate. The next day Bourget left to assume his new appointment as secretary to Jean-Jacques Lartigue*, the auxiliary bishop at Montreal. He received the diaconate at the bishop's residence in the Hôtel-Dieu on 22 Dec. 1821 and was ordained priest on 30 November the following year.

The tasks facing the new priest soon multiplied. In addition to his duties as secretary to the bishop, Bourget took on supervision of the building of the episcopal residence and of the church of Saint-Jacques, the corner-stone of which was blessed on 22 May 1823. Construction, carried on at a brisk pace, was completed two years later and Archbishop Plessis consecrated the church on 22 Sept. 1825. Bourget was then appointed first chaplain of Saint-Jacques where he was responsible for organizing the pastoral ministry and seeing to the conduct of public worship. He also directed the Grand Séminaire Saint-Jacques which was housed with a primary school on the ground floor of the episcopal residence; there were never more than 20 students studying theology.

The duties entrusted to Abbé Bourget matched the complete confidence Bishop Lartigue had in his secretary. From the outset the young priest determined to be the unwavering disciple of the bishop, whose thinking reflected the ultramontane teachings to which such writers as Joseph de Maistre and Hugues-Félicité-Robert de La Mennais had recently attracted a great deal of attention in Europe, and whose authoritarian character was ill adapted to ambiguous situations and compromises. Thus it pained Lartigue to see his episcopal authority thwarted at times by the jurisdiction exercised over Montreal Island since the 17th century by the Sulpicians in their capacity as seigneurs and pastors of the single parish of Notre-Dame. He also found it scarcely tolerable that his superior, the archbishop of Quebec, was not more energetic in upholding the rights of the church with the civil power because he lacked boldness in his relations with the governors. "In the 70 years of conquest," Bourget wrote on 16 Jan. 1830, "religion in this country has almost always lost the advantage through fright, and I very much fear that we are not cured of it yet."

It was because Bourget showed himself to be Lartigue's spiritual heir and increasingly shared his views concerning church government that the bishop decided to propose him as his successor to the episcopal see in which he had been enthroned on 8 Sept. 1836. But this candidature, when it was submitted to Pope Gregory XVI, met with the opposition of the Sulpicians, who saw Bourget as an adversary because he shared Lartigue's suspicion of them, as well as that of certain parish priests in the Montreal region [*see* Jean-Baptiste Saint-Germain*]. These priests held that Bourget lacked the attainments essential for a bishop in an environment where there were many Protestants and considered him too preoccupied with rules and the minutiæ of discipline. But Pope Gregory overruled these objections and by an apostolic brief dated 10 March 1837 appointed Bourget bishop of Telmesse *in partibus infidelium* and coadjutor to the bishop of Montreal with right of succession. He was consecrated on 25 July in the cathedral of Saint-Jacques by Lartigue, assisted by Bishop Pierre-Flavien Turgeon*, the coadjutor of Quebec, and Bishop Rémi Gaulin*, the coadjutor of Kingston, Upper Canada.

Lower Canada was then passing through a difficult period. Faced with the rebel agitation in the Montreal region, Lartigue took a stand against the partisans of his cousin Louis-Joseph Papineau*. In a pastoral letter of 24 Oct. 1837 he resorted to the arguments of Pope Gregory's encyclical *Mirari vos* of 15 Aug. 1832 which condemned the propositions, deemed revolutionary, that La Mennais, who had shifted from ultramontanism to liberalism, had developed in his Paris paper *L'Avenir*. The young coadjutor, a model of loyalty to his hierarchical superior, adhered with the full force of mind and heart to the views expressed in the encyclical. This document provided the traditionalist and authoritarian answer to the great problem confronting the Roman Catholic Church since the beginning of the century: what attitude should be adopted to the world born of the intellectual and political revolution of the 18th century and particularly of the régime of civil and religious liberties proclaimed in the "Declaration of the Rights of Man and of the Citizen." Here, as Bourget himself later clearly indicated in his opposition to the liberal arguments of the Institut Canadien, was, at its origin, the explanation of the stance he would maintain throughout his episcopate.

But for the moment Bourget had to deal practically with the spiritual needs of a Catholic population scattered across a vast area bounded by James Bay on the north, the United States on the south, the border between Upper and Lower Canada on the west, and a line on the east which was halfway between Montreal and Quebec. Bishop Lartigue's declining health forced the coadjutor to undertake more and more of the administration of the diocese, which had 79 parishes, 34 missions at widely dispersed points, particularly in the Eastern Townships, and four missions to the Indians. With a total of 186,244 adherents of whom 115,071 were communicants, the diocese had 22,000 Catholics in Montreal itself – two-thirds of the town's inhabitants.

To inform himself as fully as possible of the needs of the diocese, Bourget set out to visit it. From 1 June to 14 July 1838 he was received by 16 parishes, and from 21 May to 5 July of the following year by a like number. In 1839, with the assistance of the Jesuit Jean-Pierre Chazelle*, rector of St Mary's College near Bardstown, Ky, he instituted a retreat for his priests; the success of this endeavour led him to make such week-long retreats an annual event. Thus, when Lartigue died on 19 April 1840, Bourget inherited a task with which he was thoroughly familiar. The plans conceived by Lartigue were to be realized by the person who had inherited both his see and his spirit.

In the autumn of 1840, as he continued to explore his vast diocese, Bishop Bourget went to the north shore of the Ottawa River. Its flourishing lumber industry [*see* Philemon Wright*] and the dynamism of some 5,000 settlers prompted him to lay the foundations of eight new missions, the nucleus of a religious structure which would lead in 1847 to the establishment of the diocese of Bytown (Ottawa).

To meet needs whose magnitude would have discouraged anyone else, the bishop of Montreal first consolidated the means already available to him. In November 1840 the training of ecclesiastics, conducted since 1825 in haphazard fashion at the Grand Séminaire Saint-Jacques, was entrusted to the Sulpicians of the Petit Séminaire de Montréal. A hospital was required at Saint-Hyacinthe: he detached four religious from the Hôpital Général to form a new community of Sisters of Charity [*see* Marie-Michel-Archange Thuot*]. Bishop Lartigue had long wanted to establish a religious journal independent of politics. This project was realized in December 1840 when the *Mélanges religieux* began publication in Montreal under the direction of Abbé Jean-Charles Prince*, superior of the Séminaire de Saint-Hyacinthe.

Up to this point the bishop of Montreal had called upon the internal resources of the diocese. In the period 1840–42 the preaching of Bishop Charles-Auguste-Marie-Joseph de Forbin-Janson*, a Bourbon supporter who had come to North America from France in 1839, marked the beginning of a contribution from elsewhere which would grow in the coming years. French-speaking circles in North America, from Louisiana to Lower Canada, in turn heard this fervent Legitimist. He gave free rein particularly in the Montreal region to a stirring eloquence which did not disdain the spectacular methods used in France during the celebrated Restoration missions 20 years earlier, and which now resulted in the erection of a gigantic cross – "the tallest and most beautiful in the world," as he proudly asserted to a compatriot – on Mount Belœil in October 1841. Less conspicuous but more lasting effects resulted from a trip Bourget made to Europe that year, from 3 May to 23 September. Personnel had to be recruited for the parishes to be supplied, the schools and colleges to be founded, the missions to be established or strengthened. In addition, thought had to be given to setting up an ecclesiastical province in order to unify the administration of the Canadian dioceses under a presiding metropolitan. The shortage of priests was a particular concern of the bishop of Montreal. The situation in Lower Canada had, it is true, improved since 1830. Nevertheless the diocese of Montreal, where needs were pressing and where Protestant proselytism had been making headway because of the presence of Swiss evangelical missionaries since 1834 [*see* Henriette Odin*], was in a less advantageous position than the diocese of Quebec.

Bourget's voyage overseas was fruitful. It coincided with the religious revival which was kindled in France during Louis-Philippe's reign by such men as Henri Lacordaire, Prosper Guéranger, Montalembert, and Louis Veuillot, and which inspired great fervour and rededication. Religious congregations of men and women grew rapidly. Thus in the course of his trip Bishop Bourget could channel towards his own diocese this swelling tide of apostolic activity; such indeed was the hope expressed by Veuillot's Paris newspaper, *L'Univers*, in its issue of 23 June 1841, when it learned that "Mgr de Montréal" had "come to Europe to seek a reinforcement of workers for the gospel."

Although the recruitment of secular priests met with a somewhat disappointing response from the bishops, apart from three Sulpicians who arrived in Montreal in the autumn of 1841 [*see* Rémi Carof*], the religious congregations reacted enthusiastically to Bourget's invitation. On 2 Dec. 1841 six Oblates of Mary Immaculate, four fathers and two brothers, landed in Canada [*see* Jean-Baptiste Honorat*]; on 31 May the next year it was the turn of the Jesuits, with six fathers and three lay brothers headed by Father Chazelle; on 26 December some sisters of the Society of the Sacred Heart of Jesus arrived to take over the direction of a school at Saint-Jacques-de-l'Achigan (Saint-Jacques); and finally, on 7 June 1844, four Sisters of Our Lady of Charity of the Good Shepherd from Angers came to give assistance to their colleagues who had already arrived in Montreal [*see* Jacques-Victor Arraud*].

Ably assisted by these reinforcements, Bourget added indigenous foundations: the Sisters of Charity of Providence (Sisters of Providence) [*see* Marie-Émilie-Eugénie Tavernier*], the Sisters of the Holy Names of Jesus and Mary [*see* Eulalie Durocher*], the Sisters of Mercy [*see* Marie-Rosalie Cadron*], and in 1850 the Sisters of St Anne [*see* Esther SUREAU, *dit* Blondin]. With the assistance also from 1844 of Bishop Prince as coadjutor, he was thus in a position to give a decisive stimulus to his diocese. A French priest, Abbé Charles-Étienne Brasseur* de Bourbourg, who during an enforced idleness in the Séminaire de Québec in 1845 made a study of the situation in Canada, could not resist comparing "the progress characteristic of great things" in the diocese of Montreal "under the influence of its bishop" with the inertia of the diocese of Quebec, which "has been merely existing, and vegetating like a sapless plant since the death of M. Plessis."

Bourget, whom a new pope, Pius IX, was to regard as the guiding spirit of the Canadian episcopate (as he said in confidence in 1847 to the founder of the Oblates, Bishop Charles-Joseph-Eugène de Mazenod), was not satisfied merely with promoting fruitful developments in his own diocese. He worked actively for the realization of projects that concerned the Canadian church, such as the establishment of the ecclesiastical province of Quebec, erected by a papal bull of 12 July 1844, and the conferring of the pallium on the metropolitan, Archbishop Joseph Signay*, a ceremony over which he presided on 24 November in the cathedral at Quebec.

Canada West also received his attention and watchful zeal. It was partly due to him that the diocese of Toronto, detached from that of Kingston, was created in 1841, and endowed with a cathedral which he consecrated on 29 Sept. 1848. Bishop Gaulin, who was unable to provide adequately for the administration of the diocese of Kingston, had received Bishop Patrick Phelan* as a coadjutor in 1843; the city of Kingston itself, chosen to be the capital of the Province of Canada, had little in the way of Catholic education and assistance to the sick. Accordingly Bourget invited the Congregation of Notre-Dame to set up a primary school in Kingston [*see* Marie-Françoise Huot*]. He also asked the Religious Hospitallers of St Joseph from the Hôtel-Dieu at Montreal to establish a hospital for the town and surrounding district; this was carried out in September 1845. On 12 February that year Bytown had received a group of Grey Nuns [*see* Élisabeth Bruyère*], this community having in the previous year sent a contingent of its members to the Red River region [*see* Marie-Louise Valade*], again at the prompting of Bourget.

The mere enumeration of these achievements is an eloquent testimony to the enthusiasm and energy of the tireless bishop. But his innovative measures both inside and outside his own diocese had in the end displeased his hierarchical superior, Archbishop Signay of Quebec, who was a procrastinator and little given to breaking new ground. Bourget had suggested to him in December 1844 that he should call a first provincial council in order to demonstrate that the title of archbishop was not merely honorific and that an important responsibility was attached to it. Signay was stung and his inertia became stubbornness. At the end of his tether, Bourget decided to go once more to Rome. There, with the encouragement of Abbé Charles-Félix CAZEAU, the archbishop's secretary, he sought – albeit in vain – his superior's resignation; he had already, with brutal frankness, written to Signay himself on 25 Sept. 1846: "For a long time I have been thinking that Your Grace should give up the administration of your archdiocese, contenting yourself with retaining the title of metropolitan. I shall use the occasion of my journey to Rome to put before the Holy See the reasons leading me to believe that it might be time for you to relieve yourself of this burden." Indeed in his opinion there were problems pending which only a concerted effort of the bishops in a provincial council could solve: non-observance of rituals, a complete revision of the catechism manual, and any number of other improvements in the organization of the Canadian church were all needed.

This second journey, in 1846, during which Bourget witnessed with delight the delirious demonstrations in Rome in favour of Pius IX, who had just succeeded the unpopular Pope Gregory, brought results as impressive as had his first. The decision was taken to create the diocese of Bytown, and its first bishop was his own candidate, Joseph-Bruno Guigues*, the superior in Canada of the Oblates of Mary Immaculate. Moreover, Bourget returned with some 20 labourers for the faith: his repeated invitations brought responses from the Congregation of the Holy Cross [*see* Jean-Baptiste Saint-Germain], the Clerics of St Viator [*see* Étienne CHAMPAGNEUR], the Jesuits, and the Sisters of the Society of the Sacred Heart of Jesus. When the great epidemic of 1847 swept Montreal, Bourget was able to detach several priests from his reinforced team to go to the aid of those stricken with typhus. He himself set the example and was fortunate to escape the ravages of the disease, unlike the nine priests and 13 religious sisters who were victims of their own dedication.

By the dawn of 1848 Bourget was justified in believing that the prediction he had shared with Bishop Turgeon in the dark days of 1837 had come true: "The people, seeing their clergy take up their interests at a time when their previous leaders abandon them to the mercy of an authority which they have insulted out of ignorance, will recover their feelings of affection and trust towards their pastors." During the decade just ended, a swing back towards the clergy had indeed occurred and the practice of religion had noticeably improved: the moving addresses of Bishop de Forbin-Janson had stirred hearts and minds, and the new clergy from Europe had sustained and consolidated the effects of his preaching. Moreover, one of the greatest paradoxes of this troubled period was the result produced by the French Canadian Missionary Society [*see* Henriette Odin], founded by English-speaking Protestants of Montreal in 1839, shortly after the ill-fated rebellion, to take advantage of a situation unfavourable to the Catholic clergy in order to recruit adherents. In fact, contrary to the expectations of the society's promoters, this same clergy, when put on the alert, made every effort to counteract the activity of the Swiss missionaries effectively and to recover "by dint of good offices," as Bourget had urged, the trust of the people which had been temporarily shaken. By 1848 "Christianization," to use the bishop's word, had gradually permeated all levels of French Canadian society. Religious congregations of men and women were given an increasingly important role in primary education, while the clergy, through the classical colleges which were under its sole direction, ensured the recruitment and training of the élite of the middle class. At the same time, the people of the towns, countryside, and settlements were fitted with a solid organization by parish priests and missionaries. Hospital and charitable assistance was dispensed by religious hands. Finally the *Mélanges religieux*, the Canadian counterpart of *L'Univers* though without the talent, and the Œuvre des bons livres, a library established in 1844 in Montreal [*see* Joseph-Vincent Quiblier*] on the model of one at Bordeaux and recognized in a pastoral letter of 20 Sept. 1845, proposed to inculcate "good principles" and sound doctrines.

These accomplishments were the fruit of unceasing labour. In the habit of allowing himself no more than five hours' sleep a day, Bourget seemed to contemporary witnesses to have taken a vow to waste no time. A man of action and authority, he nevertheless, like the most industrious and versatile of authors, left an impressive number of published and manuscript works. These manifest an extraordinary dedication to the task of composition, especially given that the written word never came easily to him. Bourget always commenced his pastoral letters well ahead of time and repeatedly revised his texts before sending them to the printer. Heavily burdened with all manner of tasks and worries, the bishop was none the less easy to approach. Even the inopportune visitor did not seem to irritate him. In intimate gatherings he had an inexhaustible fund of conversation and never missed the chance to make a teasing remark or to enjoy the apt retort, even at his own expense.

The prelate made an impression whenever he performed his episcopal duties. His mitre crowning his prematurely white hair, he would stride rather abruptly into the church to participate in liturgical rites with impressive dignity. When he undertook to speak, the conviction which enlivened his remarks made his lively blue eyes sparkle all the more and gave to his even features a ruddier hue.

The Roman liturgy which Bourget introduced into his diocese matched his reverence for the papacy, his exacting sense of order, and the effusive piety which fitted well with ultramontane devotional celebrations. Thanks to him, the formality and sedateness of the services conducted by the Sulpicians in Montreal, a true city of the north, gradually gave way to the Mediterranean warmth of Roman rites. As a result, new importance was accorded to gestures, to the public image, and to gatherings for magnificent ceremonies in immense churches. One thinks of the spectacular celebrations at Notre-Dame in Montreal when the Zouaves were departing, and the financial sacrifices that Bishop Bourget unhesitatingly imposed on his diocesan flock in order to erect a cathedral reminiscent of St Peter's in Rome. A similar emphasis was placed on processions, confraternities, the veneration of innumerable relics brought back from Rome (that "great reliquary," as he liked to term it), the observance of Forty Hours which he introduced to his diocese on 21 Feb. 1857, and such highly emotional devotions as those to the Seven Sorrows of Mary and to the Sacred Heart. As for the strict moral discipline applied in admission to the sacraments, this was softened as a result of the adoption in the Montreal diocese of the Ligourian ethical rules, as laid out by Bourget in his memorandum to the clergy on 25 July 1871: "Yes, St Alfonso has always been regarded as the [spiritual] director of this diocese, and his moral doctrines have always resolved the difficulties that were encountered in the course of the sacred ministry."

A churchman whose reputation for saintliness soon spread throughout the diocese, and whose sympathy and compassion for the moral and physical distress visible in Montreal, a city then experiencing rapid urbanization and the growth of a working class, Bourget was also a patriot whom the events of 1837 anchored to a conservatism antipathetic to any political or social adventure. It is significant that when the Institut Canadien, at the instigation of Jean-Baptiste-Éric Dorion*, founded on 5 April 1848 the Association des établissements canadiens des townships, the chairmanship of the central committee was given to Bourget, while Louis-Joseph Papineau had to be content with the vice-chairmanship. But in September the bishop resigned, and although the association survived it fell prey to ideological and political conflicts. No compromise was possible between the Ultramontane and the liberal, between the undisputed leader of his clergy as well as to a lesser but real degree of the conservative middle class which had rallied to the Reform party of Louis-Hippolyte La Fontaine* and Robert Baldwin*, and the former Patriote chief who since his return from exile had vehemently demanded the "repeal of the Union," a local variation of the liberal principle of "nationalities" (self-determination).

Following Papineau's example, the contributors to *L'Avenir*, a paper that began in July 1847 in Montreal, stood more and more aloof from the Reform majority. One of them, Papineau's nephew, Louis-Antoine Dessaulles*, moving in the wake of his uncle, proved a determined adversary of responsible government. Throughout May 1848 he argued passionately in *L'Avenir* that "the Union is undeniably the most flagrant injustice, the most infamous outrage upon our natural and political rights that could be perpetrated." The February revolution in Paris, and more importantly the seditious turn of events in Rome, inflamed men's minds. Pius IX, having shaken off his fleeting inclination towards liberalism after refusing to declare war on Austria for the liberation of the peninsula, had aroused the anger of the Italian patriots, and in face of the revolutionary ferment he deemed it prudent to flee Rome and take refuge in the kingdom of Naples. The question of the temporal power of the pope was from this moment a real one. The pope having failed to take up his task as leader of the national movement, the Roman republic, proclaimed on 5 Feb. 1849, took over the government of its territory by virtue of the right of a people to self-determination.

Bourget had not been slow to draw the parallel between the upheavals in Europe and the articles in *L'Avenir* that he termed "revolutionary." In his pastoral letter of 18 Jan. 1849 ordering "prayers for our Holy Father Pope Pius IX," he came down firmly on the side of the government against the supporters of Papineau and *L'Avenir*: "What recommendations can we make to you in order to escape the calamities that are besetting so many great and powerful nations? Here they are in brief: Be faithful to God and respect all legitimately constituted authorities. Such is the will of the Lord. Do not listen to those who address seditious remarks to you, for they cannot be your true friends. Do not read those books and papers that breathe the spirit of revolt, for they are vehicles of pestilential doctrines which, like an ulcer, have corroded and ruined the most successful and flourishing states."

The news of the proclamation in Rome of the Mazzini republic gave the young contributors to *L'Avenir* the chance to define their own position clearly: they were determined to draw all the logical inferences inherent in the liberal principle of nationalities. On 14 March 1849 they declared themselves against the maintenance of the temporal power of the pope with a bluntness reinforced by their observation that the clergy, headed by the bishop, sided openly with their political opponents. "Those of our readers who feel keenly the beauty and truth of the principles we are defending, will," their spokesman asserted, "understand our insistence, knowing that this revolution in Italy is the occasion for incessant attacks against democratic principles, coming from sources which are even more to be feared because they are more respectable."

There was no better way to cement the alliance between the clergy and the La Fontaine–Baldwin party. Through fear of possible upheavals, religion became the bulwark of political and social order. The Reform party, soon to call itself the Liberal-Conservative party, obtained appreciable political advantages from the clerical influence thus placed at its disposal. On the other hand their more liberal opponents, nicknamed the Rouges because of their radical arguments for the abolition of tithes, the secularization of education, the separation of church and state, and, on the strictly political side, annexation to the United States, attracted the persistent and unrelenting opposition of this same clergy, and especially of Bourget, particularly from the moment when the *L'Avenir* group seized control of the Institut Canadien, that is, in 1851.

The bishop of Montreal continued his tireless efforts in the field of social action. Because the first association set up to encourage the settlement of the Eastern Townships had failed to attain its goals in the circumstances already mentioned, Bourget personally took over the project, being behind the second association, dedicated to the same purpose, which the Canadian bishops recommended at their assembly in Montreal on 11 May 1850. Intemperance was a social evil in French Canada at that period. He entrusted the struggle against this scourge to the eloquence of Abbé Charles-Paschal-Télesphore Chiniquy* and in 1853 he founded the *Annales de la tempérance* at Montreal. His zeal encompassed the poor: convinced that each parish ought to see to their needs, he encouraged, with this intention, the expansion of the St Vincent de Paul Society, presiding over the founding of the Montreal conference on 19 March 1848. Among other unfortunates, the deaf-mutes required assistance: in 1850 there were about 1,100 in French Canada, 400 of whom lived in Montreal. For them, Bishop Bourget established the Hospice du Saint-Enfant-Jésus at Côte-Saint-Louis (now part of Outremont), and entrusted its management to Abbé Charles-Irénée Lagorce*, who was shortly succeeded by the Clerics of St Viator. The fire in Montreal on 8 July 1852, which destroyed 1,100 houses as well as the cathedral and the bishop's palace and which left about 10,000 destitute, grieved him deeply, and his words at the time testify to the charity and compassion he brought to all tragedies and disasters. By the role he played in social action he helped to sustain an ongoing broad movement of moral and religious renewal.

To his concern for these adversities was added his apprehension about the Institut Canadien, which since its foundation in 1844 had become increasingly influential in every sphere of French Canadian life, political, social, or religious. This institute brought together the young intellectual élite of Montreal to discuss the most advanced ideas of the time, and its library had been built up with no obvious regard for the rules of the Index of Forbidden Books. Bourget judged the institute eminently subversive of the moral and spiritual well-being of his flock and believed it expedient to issue a first warning. At the second provincial council, held in Quebec City in June 1854, he used his influence with the other bishops to get a disciplinary regulation drawn up indicating to the priesthood and the faithful the attitude to be adopted towards "literary institutes." Its explicit text was clearly aimed at the Institut Canadien: "When it is an established practice that a literary institute has books harmful to faith or morals, that readings are given there which are anti-religious, that immoral and irreligious newspapers are read there, one cannot admit to the sacraments those who are members of it, unless there is reason to hope that, given the strength of good principles, they may continue to effect reforms within [the institutes]."

This document, dated 4 June 1854, did not prevent the institute from getting 11 of its members elected to the Legislative Assembly that summer. Its success allowed "the brilliant pleiad of 1854," as Arthur Buies* called it, to abandon pure speculation for action, having been restricted heretofore to the institute's own platform or to *Le Pays*, which had replaced *L'Avenir* two years earlier. While Charles Daoust*, the member for Beauharnois and editor of *Le Pays*, demanded in his paper the separation of church and state, Joseph Papin*, the member for L'Assomption, constituted himself the interpreter in parliament for his liberal colleagues with the aim of obtaining a particularly important consequence of that separation, non-denominational schools.

No doubt contemplating future battles against those who held these views, which could not but give offence to him as an Ultramontane, Bourget set off a third time for Rome, on 23 Oct. 1854. Turgeon, the archbishop of Quebec, who had succeeded Signay at his death on 3 Oct. 1850, had invited him to represent the ecclesiastical province at the proclamation of the dogma of the Immaculate Conception, set for 8 December. Bourget spent his leisure in Italy and France studying in detail the particular characteristics of the Roman liturgy, which the Benedictine Prosper Guéranger had been zealously restoring in France since 1840, and in 1856 he published in Paris a substantial volume of 569 pages entitled *Cérémonial des évêques commenté et expliqué par les usages et traditions de la sainte Église romaine avec le texte latin, par un évêque suffragant de la province ecclésiastique de Québec, au Canada, anciennement appelé Nouvelle-France*. He presented complimentary copies of his book to all the bishops of France, a courteous gesture which did not, however, make the work a best-seller; it was seldom read. Nevertheless, when Bourget returned to Montreal on 29 July 1856, he hastened to apply to the last detail the conclusions he had drawn from his newly acquired erudition in liturgy. In his ultramontane fervour he sometimes acted with a haste and intransigence which ran counter to what certain subordinates such as Abbé Charles La Rocque*, parish priest of Saint-Jean (Saint-Jean-sur-Richelieu), believed feasible, and to their conviction that one should not sweep away time-honoured usages. Probably realizing that the young generation of ecclesiastics would be more receptive to his views, Bourget wanted the Séminaire de Montréal to adopt manuals of Roman theologians instead of those of the Gallican Jean-Baptiste Bouvier being used by the Sulpicians.

The bishop regretted "that here as in France, the Society of Saint-Sulpice, which in many ways is so worthy of respect, is not at the head of this splendid movement which is taking place throughout the world in favour of the sound doctrines of Ultramontanism." Even the details of priestly garb were not a matter of indifference: in 1858 he made it obligatory for his clergy to wear the Roman collar instead of the French band. Finally, as one more of the indirect results of his last voyage to the banks of the Tiber, his cathedral, destroyed by fire in 1852, was to be rebuilt on no less a model than St Peter's in Rome.

His nearly two years overseas reinforced Bishop Bourget's ultramontane convictions. What he saw in Italy, in the state of Piedmont which had remained clerical for so long and where the liberals had since 1850 been pursuing their task of secularization, contributed in no small measure to confirming his aversion to liberalism. Back in Montreal, he found himself again confronted by those liberals whose principles and activities had seemed so detestable to him in Europe. But he did not act immediately.

To counteract the influence of the Institut Canadien, a group of its moderate members had in 1852 started a rival association, the Institut National, which they had placed under the patronage of the bishop of Montreal; its success had not, however, lived up to the expectations of the founders and their protector. On 2 Feb. 1857, no doubt thinking that they would be more fortunate, the Sulpicians set up the Cabinet de lecture paroissial with spacious premises near the Place d'Armes, "in opposition to the Institut Canadien" according to a contemporary, Laurent-Olivier David*; a literary centre which was attached to it in October subsequently became the Cercle Ville-Marie. In September 1854 the Jesuits, who had founded the Collège Sainte-Marie in 1848, had forestalled the Sulpicians in the battle against the common foe by setting up in their college the Union Catholique, first a congregation and then an academy, which on 23 Nov. 1858 started the newspaper *L'Ordre* espousing the views of Louis Veuillot [*see* Cyrille Boucher*].

Whether or not the two enterprises, Sulpician and Jesuit, had produced the anticipated results, Bishop Bourget decided to take drastic action. He did so in three pastoral letters on 10 March, 30 April, and 31 May 1858, which followed a well-developed plan. In the first letter, he described the disastrous effects of the French Revolution and, generally, of all revolutions, which he attributed to the circulation of evil books; in the second, he indicated that revolutionary propaganda could be prevented in Canada through the enforcement of the rules of the Index; and in the third, he stigmatized those whom he considered the harbingers of revolution in Canada, the liberals of the Institut Canadien.

The institute, brought under attack by the first pastoral letter, in which it was likened to "a seat of pestilence" for the whole country, met on 13 April. The majority of its members, in accord with the liberalism it professed, refused to yield to the bishop's threatening text. Indeed, for a liberal, each person has the power to choose his intellectual sustenance as he wishes; cases of poisoning that may result are merely accidental inconveniences, amply compensated for by a higher good: liberty. But the minority, following its leader Hector Fabre*, although as desirous as the radical majority of not finding itself under the thumb of the clergy, was ready to compromise. Fabre and his friends realized that most of the institute's members lacked the necessary maturity and culture to tackle indiscriminately the reading of certain works in their association's library. They believed "that if society has the right to regulate the sale of poison, the institute should have the right to forbid its members to poison themselves." Since no agreement could be reached, a separation followed. On 22 April 1858, 138 of the some 700 members tendered their resignations to the president of the Institut Canadien, Francis Cassidy*. On 10 May they formed an opposing association which they named the Institut Canadien-Français.

In his second pastoral letter, dated 30 April, Bishop Bourget called the Institut Canadien specifically to account. "Against the evil books" in its library he brought forward the rules of the Index. The summons was to submission, otherwise "it would follow that no Catholic could henceforth belong to this institute; that nobody could read the books in its library, and that no one could in future attend its sessions or go to listen to its readings," for by virtue of the regulations of the Council of Trent the mere fact of possessing, reading, selling, or passing on prohibited books was so grave an offence that it resulted *ipso facto* in excommunication.

Having dealt with the library of the institute and its readers, the bishop of Montreal in his third letter attacked the principles of its leaders. Wishing to make his censure of French Canadian liberalism as authoritative and effective as possible, he took his arguments from the encyclical that had determined the direction of his thinking once and for all at the beginning of his priestly career, Gregory XVI's *Mirari vos*. Using this blunt pontifical text, he accentuated its forcefulness by giving it an extreme interpretation whose categorical and absolute precepts can only occasion profound astonishment today. Having censured liberal views he turned to the newspaper which transmitted them, *Le Pays*. After singling out amongst the "bad papers," the "irreligious paper," the "immoral paper," and the "heretical paper," Bourget came to the anticlerical paper; this he termed "impious," for "each priest being the representative of Jesus Christ," and "the authority which is vested in him being that of Jesus Christ himself, any attempt to destroy the influence of the clergy is tantamount to attacking this divine authority." Clearly, for the prelate's pen the "impious paper" was another term for the "Liberal paper," since the Liberals had always been opposed to clerical interference in the political sphere. Indeed Bourget himself immediately confirmed this identity: "The Liberal paper is the one that claims, among other things, to be *free* in its religious and political opinions; that would like the church to be separate from the state; and that in a word refuses to recognize the right of religion to have anything to do with politics, even when the interests of faith and morals are at stake." In order to prove that "no one is permitted to be *free in his religious and political opinions*," the churchman started from the principle that Jesus Christ has "given his church the power to teach all peoples the *sound doctrine*," namely "that pure doctrine which instructs them to govern themselves, as all truly Christian peoples must do. Here obviously is a moral point of high import. Now, any moral point comes within the domain of the church and essentially derives from its teaching. For its divine mission is to teach sovereigns to govern with wisdom and subjects to obey in gladness."

In this way the bishop's thinking led directly to theocracy, which in the opinion of a contemporary of Veuillot, Abbé Henri Maret, dean of the faculty of theology at the Sorbonne, was the epitome of the social and political doctrine of ultramontanism. And in fact, according to the Ultramontanes, "the Sovereign Pontiff, in addition to his spiritual authority, [which is] sacred for all Catholics, possesses by *divine right* a true political jurisdiction throughout the world, a jurisdiction which renders him an arbiter of the great social and even political questions; and, in certain respects, kings and heads of nations are only his deputies." From this theocratic principle follow "social and political privileges for the clergy of each nation," and the fact that "civil intolerance is raised to the rank of religious dogma."

The intransigence of the bishop clashed again with the intransigence of the liberals over the war launched by Piedmont which was the start of the unification of Italy. From 1859 Austria was gradually forced out of the Italian peninsula: principalities and the kingdom of Naples disappeared, the Papal States broke up, and the kingdom of Italy was brought to completion by virtue of the principle then entering into international public law: the right of peoples to self-determination.

For Catholics these dramatic years were a distressing period. In their view the movement for the unification of Italy was nothing short of a concerted attempt on the part of forces hostile to the Roman Catholic Church to reduce it to impotence. Nobody was more convinced than the bishop of Montreal. Consequently, from 1860, he sent out an increasing stream of pastoral letters and memoranda to his clergy concerning "the independence and inviolability of the Papal States." For him the revolution was first attacking the papacy "in order next to overthrow unimpeded the rest of the universe," including Canada, where liberal books and newspapers were serving as a means of spreading the "forces of evil." *Le Pays*, whose editor after 1 March 1861 was Louis-Antoine Dessaulles, was naturally a target, as is apparent from the seven long letters ablaze with ultramontane fervour which Bourget addressed to the newspaper in February 1862. The owners of the liberal paper having refused to publish them, Dessaulles replied to the bishop on 7 March. In the course of his remarkably lucid letter, he came to the central problem which divided Ultramontanes and liberals: which group would impose its ideology on the community? He had suspected that the bishop of Montreal wanted "to intermingle the spiritual and temporal spheres, in order to control and dominate the latter by means of the former," while the ambition of the "laymen" was to "avoid confusion between these two orders of ideas" and to require "that the spiritual order be entirely distinct from the temporal order." He concluded: "In a word, my lord, in the purely social and political order we insist on our entire independence from the ecclesiastical power."

The apprehensions of Dessaulles and those who shared his liberal convictions about the crushing preponderance of the ecclesiastical structures in French Canadian society, particularly in the Montreal region, can be understood in the light of facts about Bishop Bourget's diocese in this period. (These are taken from historian Serge Gagnon.) The diocese had 128 parishes and 322 priests to serve a Catholic population of 342,654, of whom 210,654 were communicants: hence one priest for every 1,064 persons or 623 communicants. Of this total, 121 parish priests and 48 curates were assigned to pastoral duties. Thus almost every parish had a resident priest and some 40 per cent of the parish priests were assisted by a curate. About one-third of the clergy exercised their ministry as chaplains or teachers; apart from 52 secular clergy, all of these belonged to the various communities of regular clergy settled in the diocese. The great majority of secular clergy, who did not work at the parish level, taught the 811 pupils of the four classical colleges in the diocese, where many of the 127 candidates for priesthood in the diocese directed classes while pursuing theological studies. The lay religious taught 5,943 boys. "As for the 10 communities of women, they comprise, in addition to 1,033 religious, 148 novices and 152 postulants. Seven of these women's communities teach 9,705 children. The other three attend to 36,463 poor, sick and infirm, etc."

The Catholic population, suitably endowed with these structures in large part attributable to the ability and zeal of Bishop Bourget, was on the whole amenable to the directives given by its pastors and committed to the realization of the objectives suggested to it. There is no better indication of this than the recruitment and enlistment of 507 Zouaves, in seven detachments, who went to assist the papacy from 1868. Historian René Hardy, who has minutely analysed all aspects of this important episode of Canadian religious history in the 19th century, estimates that the amount expended in sending the Canadian volunteers to Rome was at least $111,630, no trivial sum since it was raised in years of financial hardship. As historians Jean Hamelin and Yves Roby show, the financial crisis in England and the difficulties of reconstruction after the American Civil War had a negative impact on the economy of Quebec, so that all sectors of the economy were adversely, though unevenly, affected. Most Canadian Catholic bishops were hesitant about fitting out soldiers and instead exhorted their dioceses to contribute to the charity known as Peter's pence, but thanks to Bishop Bourget, despite all pecuniary and other difficulties, French Canada stood with France, Belgium, Holland, Ireland, and others in recruiting volunteers for the defence of the Papal States. The stakes, already considerable by reason of the objective that was directly and publicly pursued, were perhaps higher still because of the accompanying tactics calculated to disseminate ultramontane ideology throughout the various strata of society. "The function of the Zouaves in clerical strategy as a whole," writes Hardy, "was principally to legitimate the cause of the Holy See, which the French Canadian clergy used as a pretext to justify its opposition to the section of the bourgeoisie that was contending with it for power. Whatever the needs of Rome might be, Bishop Bourget and his associates wanted Canadians to serve in the pope's army, for in their judgement these soldiers were an even more powerful means of combatting the ideas diffused by the liberals of *Le Pays* and of the Institut Canadien than the organizing of public demonstrations and prayers or the circulation of newspapers and pamphlets favourable to the cause. In short, it was a matter of involving the population directly in this struggle of 'truth against error' by getting [their] compatriots to fight in it, increasing in this way information favourable to the papal viewpoint, fostering affection for Pius IX by constantly publicizing his misfortunes, arousing fear and hatred for his enemies, and, in the Roman tradition, forging on the battlefields and in the papal city an ultramontane élite which in the future would serve as a bulwark against the introduction into Canada of 'subversive and revolutionary ideas' such as those condemned in the *Syllabus*."

Concurrently with the expansion of ultramontanism, which the Zouave movement powerfully assisted, liberalism as represented by the Institut Canadien met with one defeat after another. Attempts at reconciliation with the bishop of Montreal in 1864, a petition addressed to Pius IX by 17 Catholic members of the institute in 1865, unfavourable reports by Bourget to the Holy Office in 1866 and 1869, all these proceedings finally resulted in the *Annuaire de l'Institut Canadien pour 1868* [*see* Gonzalve Doutre*] being placed on the Index in July 1869. The Guibord affair [*see* Joseph Guibord*; Alexis-Frédéric Truteau*], with its succession of sudden developments between November 1869 and 1874, really marked the final decline of the association, even though the Privy Council in London appeared to give victory to the liberals over the ecclesiastical authority. Joseph Doutre in particular, who with Dessaulles was one of the institute's most influential associates, never forgave the clergy for having subjected him to relentless opposition as a member of it, and especially whenever he aspired to a political role in his country's government.

This conflict was not the only one in which the bishop of Montreal was involved. An Ultramontane and a churchman *par excellence*, he was paradoxically led by circumstances to wage exhausting and endless struggles against the two most impressive religious institutions of the Canadian church at that period, the Séminaire de Québec and the Séminaire de Saint-Sulpice at Montreal.

The founding in 1852 of the Université Laval by the Séminaire de Québec stemmed from Bishop Bourget's initiative [*see* Louis-Jacques Casault*]. But this initiative was based on a misunderstanding. According to the bishop the new university was to be a provincial one for which all the bishops of the ecclesiastical province took responsibility. It was not long, however, before he was forced to sound a different note, since the organization and management of the university were taken over entirely by the seminary and the archbishop of Quebec. An attempt was made to allay Bourget's apprehensions by introducing an affiliation clause making the extension of university privileges to affiliated institutions possible, but this clause proved inoperative in his diocese. In 1858 none of the local classical colleges was affiliated with Laval, and an application from the Montreal School of Medicine and Surgery was twice turned down [*see* Hector Peltier*]. From 1862 Bishop Bourget thought of establishing another university in his episcopal city. He was impatient to do this because of the increasing numbers of Catholic students who had to enrol in the faculties of law and medicine at McGill College and elsewhere. In 1865 he based an application to Rome on statistics: in 1863–64 Laval had only 72 registered students. Few of those who enrolled came from Montreal, which had 530 Catholic students at the university level, counting those attending the "grand séminaires." For its part the Séminaire de Québec stressed that in 10 years it had spent more than $300,000 to maintain the university, whose future would be irrevocably compromised by an institution at Montreal. Rome concluded that it was not expedient to create a second university at Montreal. In 1870 Laval suggested a branch in Montreal, but as the authority of its bishop was virtually ignored, Bourget rejected the project. Two years later the Montreal bar started negotiations which came to naught. The Jesuits attempted in their turn to obtain university privileges for the law school of their Collège Sainte-Marie from the government, but the bishop, at Rome's request, asked them to withdraw their petition [*see* François-Maximilien BIBAUD]. A provisional epilogue in the dénouement of this 25-year university crisis came in a resolution of Propaganda dated 1 Feb. 1876 stating that a branch of the Université Laval should be established at Montreal. The costs were to be paid by Montrealers, but the university authority would remain at Quebec, the bishop of Montreal being at most permitted to approve the appointment of the vice-rector. Bourget, however, tendered his resignation as bishop soon after, and thus avoided having to implement such a decree.

Another conflict, no less bitter, had pitted Bourget against the Séminaire de Montréal over the thorniest problem with which he had to deal as an administrator: the division of the parish of Notre-Dame. At the time of his resignation the feelings aroused by this incident had only just subsided.

"The Parish," as the expression went, covered all of Montreal Island and in 1864 it had a population of 100,000. Its status had not changed since Bishop François de Laval* had erected the parish of Ville-Marie canonically in 1678, and united it for all time to the Séminaire de Montréal. A few years later an ordinance of Bishop Saint-Vallier [La Croix*] had decreed that the superior of the seminary should be *ex officio* the parish priest. In 1863 the superior general of Saint-Sulpice in Paris presented a report to the Holy See in which he begged that the established order be maintained. Asked to reply to him, Bourget stated: "I grant that the superior of Saint-Sulpice should be the priest in perpetuity of the parish of Montreal. But, at the same time, I expect him to be *entirely subordinate to the bishop. This entire subordination to the bishop* on the part of the parish priest of Montreal must be that which is required by the holy canons for the good government of souls." The two parties were summoned to Rome. The superior proved conciliatory on certain points but adamant as to a method of dismissal for the parish priest; he even threatened the bishop that he would withdraw from Montreal his entire community of 57 priests, of whom 42 were assigned to pastoral ministry. Finally in 1865 the superior accepted the following decisions of Propaganda: the bishop obtained authorization to divide the parish of Montreal; the new parishes would be offered first to the Sulpicians; the parish priest of Notre-Dame would be nominated by the seminary but would receive his investiture from the bishop; he could be dismissed by either the superior or the bishop [*see* Joseph-Alexandre BAILE; Joseph DESAUTELS].

Within the boundaries of the parish of Notre-Dame, Bourget hastened to erect ten new canonical parishes between September 1866 and December 1867. But he had to have them incorporated by the civil authority so that, by virtue of the law, they would have a legal existence. It was on this point that the Sulpicians lay doggedly in wait for him. They urged the government not to recognize the autonomy of the new parishes, which in their eyes were merely succursal chapels of the parish of Notre-Dame. To uphold their cause they could count on the advice of their former pupil, George-Étienne Cartier*, who was then at the summit of his political power, and on the legal skill of a protégé of Cartier, lawyer Joseph-Ubalde Beaudry*, the legal adviser to the council of the parish of Notre-Dame. For his part Bourget had the eminent lawyer Côme-Séraphin CHERRIER to assist him. The result was an endless series of disputes, punctuated by frequent appeals to Rome, during the course of which Cartier brought his authority to bear to such an extent that the bishop of Montreal's patience, legendary though it was, almost reached the breaking point. "What then," he wrote on 19 Feb. 1871, "is the nub of this inextricable difficulty? It is M. Cartier, who exercises his right to [use] pressure, or rather oppression."

By this time the battle was raging on all fronts. *Le Nouveau Monde*, begun in 1867, identified itself with the causes supported by Bourget, who on 28 Sept. 1872 condemned *La Minerve*, Cartier's journal, "because of the insults it continually hurls at the editor of *Le Nouveau Monde*, that is to say at me." The ultramontane paper had conducted a relentless campaign for four months against the work Beaudry had published at Montreal in October 1870, *Code des curés, marguilliers et paroissiens accompagné de notes historiques et critiques*. A new St George, Canon Godefroy Lamarche, the editor of *Le Nouveau Monde*, seems not to have been able to crush the dragon of "Gallicanism" in Beaudry, for in 1872 Siméon Pagnuelo*, a young lawyer who was Lamarche's legal adviser and associate, in his turn published *Études historiques et légales sur la liberté religieuse en Canada* [*see* Desautels] which attacked Beaudry's arguments.

Pagnuelo had already helped draft the *Programme catholique* [*see* François-Xavier-Anselme TRUDEL], which Bourget considered "the strongest safeguard of the true Conservative party and the firmest support for the right principles that must govern a Christian society." Repudiated by the new archbishop of Quebec, Elzéar-Alexandre Taschereau*, the programme struck a blow at the hitherto uncontested authority of Cartier over the Conservative party, and he suffered a resounding defeat in Montreal East in the federal elections of 1872. Bourget denied having contributed to the defeat but this was not the opinion of Charles La Rocque, the bishop of Saint-Hyacinthe, who might be viewed as the prototype of the symbiotic alliance existing between clerics and French Canadian politicians in the 19th century. He wrote to Cartier on 1 Sept. 1872: "May I tell you in friendly fashion that I feel humiliated when I reflect whence came the blow that succeeded in striking you down." For the Ultramontanes it was evident that the bishop of Montreal, whose golden anniversary of ordination had been celebrated in great style from 27 to 30 Oct. 1872, had finally triumphed over his Sulpician adversaries and their powerful ally, since early in January 1873 all the canonical parishes obtained their civil registration. "The immense popularity of the great statesman," Bishop Louis-François Laflèche* observed on 31 January, "shattered in Montreal against the firmness of this worthy bishop, like a clay vase against rock."

Weighed down by so much labour, and often sick, Bourget had secured Canon Édouard-Charles Fabre*, Cartier's brother-in-law, as a coadjutor. The archbishop of Quebec presided at his consecration on 1 May 1873 in the church of the Collège Sainte-Marie. All the bishops had assembled around the archibishop and Bourget, the dean of the Canadian episcopate.

At first sight this ceremony symbolized a harmony that seemed to exist in the episcopal body. But appearances were deceptive. Archbishop Taschereau, in particular, was not very fond of the bishop of Montreal. As former rector and chancellor of Université Laval he had been unalterably opposed to the attempts to set up another university. On the question of the division of the parish of Notre-Dame, he had often sided with the Sulpicians. But, above all, the extremism of the Ultramontanes in Montreal offended his innate realism, and his close friends did not look kindly upon the "rabid men of Montreal." He also reproached Bourget for welcoming into his diocese priests whom Quebec had got rid of without regret: the Jesuit Antoine-Nicolas Braun, for example, who on the recent occasion of the 50th anniversary of Bourget's ordination as priest had delivered in the archbishop's presence a sermon railing against liberalism and Gallicanism, the archbishop himself, in Montreal eyes, being far from free of their taint. But Taschereau was particularly annoyed about Abbé Alexis Pelletier*. The latter, a Gaumist, had been obliged to resign as auxiliary priest at the Séminaire de Québec, and had taken refuge in the diocese of Montreal. There, from the safe cover of the inner offices of *Le Franc-Parleur*, a subsidiary of *Le Nouveau Monde*, he vented his ill temper on Taschereau, the person whom he saw as "the perfect example of domination, arrogant superiority, imperious, arbitrary autocracy, and a cold ill-concealed disdain for any grandeur other than his own."

The apparent unison among the bishops was shown once more when they published a collective letter on 22 Sept. 1875 denouncing Catholic liberalism, which the Conservatives used as a weapon against their Liberal adversaries. The province was in an uproar. "One hears talk only of politics," Abbé Jean-Baptiste-Zacharie Bolduc, procurator of the archdiocese of Quebec, observed on 21 Jan. 1876 to his friend Benjamin Pâquet*. Bourget himself entered the fray when a pastoral letter sent with a memorandum to his clergy on 1 February in its turn condemned Catholic liberalism. To his great regret he was unable to form a precise notion of what Catholic liberalism really was: he would have to ask Rome for a definition! The bishop of Montreal attacked those who reviled the clergy, especially the parish priests who deserved respect and obedience: "I listen to my parish priest, my parish priest listens to the bishop, the bishop listens to the pope, the pope listens to our Lord Jesus Christ." Feeling that this pastoral was "bound to stir up trouble," the archbishop of Quebec was alarmed. In Taschereau's immediate circle men like Abbé Louis Pâquet believed Bourget had lost his senses. "Frankly," he added, "this is the most charitable opinion." The Capuchin Ignazio Persico, a good observer who had been parish priest of Sillery since 1873, thought too many bishops were ardent political partisans, as he intimated on 20 April 1876 to Cardinal Alessandro Franchi, the prefect of Propaganda: "It is obvious that many bishops not only prove to be party men, but also take matters to extremes; and [they do] this not to defend religious values but simply for political or personal motives."

Archbishop Taschereau judged it his duty to straighten things out. In his pastoral letter of 24 May 1876, he stated that it was necessary to discriminate between the liberalism which had been condemned and the liberalism which had not. He enjoined his priests not to speak of politics in the pulpit or elsewhere, and to show no preference for any candidate. But Bishop Persico believed the archbishop could no longer control the situation. Rome would have to institute an inquiry on the spot: this would be the mission of Bishop George Conroy*.

Bishop Bourget thought that his resignation at this time would quell the storm. Such was his wish when on 28 April 1876 he asked Cardinal Franchi "to persuade the Holy Father, by accepting my resignation, that I be cast into the sea, so that perfect calm might be restored." On 15 May he learned that his resignation had been accepted by the pope, to take effect in September.

Bourget was appointed archbishop of Martianopolis, the former capital of Moesia Inferior, a region that partly corresponds to present-day Bulgaria, and retired to the residence of Saint-Janvier de Sault-au-Récollet in the spring of 1877, together with his loyal secretary of more than 30 years, Abbé Joseph-Octave Paré*. Ill and exhausted, Bourget had, as he said many times, but one desire: to "meditate on the years of eternity." Only twice did he come out of his seclusion for any substantial period. The first time, urged by the die-hard supporters of an independent university at Montreal, the old man, then nearly 82, embarked on yet another journey to Rome from 12 Aug. to 30 Oct. 1881. He was unsuccessful, for Propaganda confirmed its decree of 1 Feb. 1876: there would be only one Catholic university in the province of Quebec. The second time, to help pay off the diocese of Montreal's enormous debt of some $840,000, he travelled through the parishes, in all seasons regardless of the weather, to collect donations. In his memorandum to the clergy on 11 Oct. 1882 he announced that his trip had yielded the grand total of $84,782. This sum was no more than a tenth of the amount necessary to extinguish the debt but, in the words of one of his friends, "he reestablished the confidence which seemed temporarily to have ebbed in the possibility of meeting the diocese's monetary crisis." On 9 Nov. 1882, at Boucherville, concluding his diocesan collection he celebrated the diamond anniversary of his ordination.

This occasion really was the end of his public life. Sick and growing ever weaker, he passed away on 8 June 1885. After an impressive funeral in the church of Notre-Dame, his body was placed in a vault of the unfinished cathedral in Montreal. A commemorative statue by artist Louis-Philippe Hébert*, a former Papal Zouave, has stood in the parvis of the building since 24 June 1903. His remains were finally transferred on 20 March 1933 to another part of the cathedral, the mortuary chapel for bishops and acchbishops; his mausoleum, which stands in the centre, is the visual symbol of his pre-eminent place in the history of the diocese.

Even today the personality and work of the second bishop of Montreal still inspire intense feelings. One has only to look through recent historical works to realize that there are fewer devotees than there were 10 or 20 years ago, and that his religious and political conceptions are being scrutinized more and more critically. It is impossible to think of Ignace Bourget as other than a man of the church, but it was an authoritarian, uncompromising, intolerant church, in short the church of the last phase of the pontificate of Pius IX, whose anathema against the modern world in the end confined Roman Catholics as a body to a kind of ghetto. On the other hand, to do justice to the bishop, one must stress the tireless worker he proved to be despite an often deplorable state of health; the leader who awakened the devotion of so many; the man of prayer whose saintliness inspired a veritable cult; and finally the effective administrator who set up or helped to set up so many lasting institutions within and beyond his diocese. That is why Bishop Bourget remains, despite his inadequacies, one of the great architects of the province of Quebec.

PHILIPPE SYLVAIN

[The ACAM is of course the principal source for information on the life and work of Bishop Ignace Bourget. In particular, the Registres des lettres de Mgr Bourget (RLB) and the valuable file on the Institut Canadien (901.133; 901.134; 901.135) were used. In 1965, when the file was first opened, its contents had not yet been classified. A perusal of the file revealed that there was a wealth of information in the material from the institute's members or about them; in particular, the numerous letters from Louis-Antoine Dessaulles to Bourget on the difficulties arising between the institute and the bishop proved most important and useful for defining the existing liberal and ultramontane ideologies and delineating the conflict between lay and clerical forces at that time.

The *Mandements, diocèse de Montréal*, I-VIII, are an essential printed primary source. The most complete list of Bourget's writings is to be found in Léopold Beaudoin's thesis, "Bio-bibliographie de Monseigneur Ignace Bourget" (thèse de Bibliothéconomie, univ. de Montréal, 1950). Danielle Boisvert's recent work, *Inventaire sommaire d'une collection de mandements, lettres pastorales et circulaires de Mgr Ignace Bourget (P 66), 1840–1858* (Montréal, 1979), prepared as one of the publications of AUM, is also useful.

Father Léon Pouliot spent more than 40 years studying the life and work of Bishop Bourget. He published numerous studies in various reviews and periodicals, and then synthesized these in his principal work: *Monseigneur Bourget et son temps* (5v., Montréal, 1955–77). He also wrote *Les dernières années (1876–1885) et la survie de Mgr Bourget* (Montréal, 1960). Anyone who writes on Bourget is inevitably indebted to this remarkable accumulation of information on the second bishop of Montreal. Volume IX of Arthur Savaète's major study of ecclesiastical matters in Canada, *Voix canadiennes, vers l'abîme* (12v., Paris, 1908–22), also proved useful. In addition to Lucien Lemieux's fine scholarly and detailed history of the diocese of Montreal, *L'Établissement de la première province ecclésiastique au Canada, 1783–1844* (Montréal et Paris, 1968), the following works were used: Serge Gagnon, "Le diocèse de Montréal durant les années 1860," *Le Laïc dans l'Église canadienne-française de 1830 à nos jours* (Montréal, 1972), 113–27; René Hardy, "Les zouaves pontificaux et la diffusion de l'ultramontanisme au Canada français, 1860–1870" (thèse de PHD, univ. Laval, Québec, 1978); Robert Perin, "Bourget and the dream of a free church in Quebec, 1862–1878" (PHD thesis, Univ. of Ottawa, 1975); and Sylvain, "Libéralisme et ultramontanisme." Unfortunately it has not been possible to consult the PHD thesis which Mme Huguette Lapointe-Roy is currently preparing at Université Laval on various aspects of the social history of mid-19th-century Montreal. P.S.]

BOURINOT, JOHN, merchant and politician; b. 15 March 1814 at Grouville, Jersey; m. in 1835 Margaret Jane Marshall, and they had 11 children; d. 19 Jan. 1884 in Ottawa, Ont.

John Bourinot was educated in Caen, France, and

came to Nova Scotia as a young man. He carried on business as a ship-chandler in Sydney, supplying mainly French ships, and shortly after his arrival he was appointed French vice-consul there. He also became an agent of Lloyd's of London and a justice of the peace. Marriage in 1835 into the "blue-blooded" Marshall family aided his rise to prominence in the colony. Mrs Bourinot was the daughter of John George Marshall*, MLA for Sydney County for almost 12 years and chief justice of the Court of Common Pleas in Cape Breton from 1823 to 1841. A cousin, John Joseph Marshall*, MLA, was to be financial secretary in James William Johnston*'s administration and speaker of the assembly in the 1860s. It seems that Judge Marshall opposed his daughter's marriage to a newcomer, several years younger than herself.

In 1840 Bourinot took an active part in the "independence agitation" in Sydney. A number of its residents believed that the interests of Cape Breton Island had been neglected by the Nova Scotia government, especially in the matters of roads and the administration of justice. They unsuccessfully petitioned London that year for a return to independent status for the island. In 1851, with other citizens, Bourinot advocated Sydney as a terminus for the projected European and North American Railway. Eight years later the voters of Cape Breton County sent him to Halifax as a Conservative MLA. In the assembly, as later in the Senate of Canada, he chose to devote himself to regional interests and became the champion of Cape Breton Island. Changing ground several times during the debates over confederation in the early 1860s, Bourinot eventually joined the "whiskered rats" who, deserting Joseph Howe*'s cause, voted for Charles Tupper*'s union resolution in 1866. In so doing he likely reflected the views of his constituents, but the most important factor in his decision to support the Quebec resolutions may well have been the interests and attitudes of his family. One son, Marshall, was a mining promoter who looked to central Canada to replace the coal markets in the United States which would decline with the passing of reciprocity; another son, Sir John George Bourinot*, was an ardent advocate of colonial federation and an owner of the strongly pro-confederate *Halifax Evening Reporter*.

Bourinot's appointment to the Canadian Senate in 1867 was regarded by many people as a reward for bolting the anti-confederate ranks, but he was never a strong party man, was not particularly popular with Tupper and his "crew," and had already favoured colonial federation in the early 1860s.

Bourinot's career in the Senate was not spectacular, and his only involvement was in committee work and in negotiations for grants to aid the development of Cape Breton. His role of elder statesman and retired gentleman was ended by a paralytic stroke in Ottawa, where he had gone to attend the opening of parliament in 1884.

A. A. MACKENZIE

[R. J. Uniacke], *Uniacke's sketches of Cape Breton and other papers relating to Cape Breton Island*, ed. C. B. Fergusson (Halifax, 1958). *British Colonist* (Halifax), 10 Nov. 1863. *Cape Breton Advocate* (Sydney, N.S.), 1840–41. *Royal Gazette* (Halifax), 22 June 1859. *Directory of N.S. MLAs*. *Dominion annual register*, 1884. B. D. Tennyson, "John George Bourinot, M.H.A. and senator," *Essays in Cape Breton history*, ed. B. D. Tennyson (Windsor, N.S., 1973), 35–48; "Economic nationalism and confederation: a case study in Cape Breton," *Acadiensis*, 2 (1972–73), no.1: 39–53.

BOURNE, ADOLPHUS, engraver, lithographer, publisher of Canadian views, and merchant; b. April 1795 in Staffordshire, England; married and had ten children; d. 14 July 1886 in Montreal, Que.

Adolphus Bourne was born into a family which had connections with the pottery trade. Trained in England as an engraver, he first appears in Montreal directories in 1820, the year in which he started business modestly by engraving the lettering for the title-page of a book of verse. Three years later he engraved a map of the city but little else is known of his work during the 1820s. In 1830 Bourne printed and published six Montreal scenes, engraved by William Satchwell Leney* after water-colours by Robert Auchmuty Sproule*, which comprised the first set of single-sheet engravings of a Canadian city to be printed in Canada. He travelled to London, England, two years later to have four views of Quebec City and portraits of Denis-Benjamin Viger* and Louis-Joseph Papineau* lithographed by the famous firm of Charles Joseph Hullmandel. Returning a few months later with a lithographic press, Bourne advertised as "A. Bourne's London Branch Lithographic Establishment," at the same time noting that he would also continue with copperplate engraving and printing. Over the next 18 years he printed more than 20 Canadian views, a significant proportion of the pictorial material printed in Canada before 1850. From about 1845 to 1865 Bourne also carried on a modest china, glass, and earthenware importing business, wholesale and retail, until it was declared insolvent in 1865; a fire on his property was one of the causes of his losses. Credit reports of this business describe him as of good character, but "rather crotchety in bus[iness] Matters," his wife being the better business "man" of the two. Although no longer listing himself as a printer in his later years, he reissued the early Montreal and Quebec sets of views as chromolithographs in 1871 and 1874, and in 1878 published a view of Montreal by James D. DUNCAN.

The quality of Bourne's prints varies, from accomplished professional works to expressive but naïve productions, corresponding to the ability of the artists, engravers, and lithographers with whom he collaborated. His own work, especially as a lithographer, does not achieve the highest standard within the whole range of his publications, but he is important for his effort to establish a pictorial printing trade in Montreal.

MARY ALLODI

Two of Adolphus Bourne's engravings appear as the title-pages of *Hours of childhood, and other poems* (Montreal, 1820) and *A plan of the city of Montreal* (Montreal, 1823).

Baker Library, R. G. Dun & Co. credit ledger, Canada, 5: 96. PAC, MG 24, B2: 1431–32. *Canadian Courant* (Montreal), 13 June 1832. *Gazette* (Montreal), 16 July 1886. Harper, *Early painters and engravers*. *Montreal directory*, 1842–86. *Printmaking in Canada: the earliest views and portraits*, comp. Mary Allodi *et al.* (Toronto, 1980). F. St.G. Spendlove, *The face of early Canada: pictures of Canada which have helped to make history* (Toronto, 1958).

BOWLES, GEORGE JOHN, administrator and entomologist; b. 14 June 1837 at Quebec City, the eldest son of John Bowles, a shoemaker, and Margaret Cochrane; m. there 31 Oct. 1861 Isabella Patterson, the daugher of a British army officer, and they had one son and two daughters; d. 16 June 1887 at Montreal, Que.

Having spent his early childhood at Quebec, George John Bowles went with his family to Trois-Rivières in 1844. He began formal studies in a school there, but lacking the financial means to continue them had to acquire a knowledge of literature and science on his own. In 1851 his family returned to Quebec, and the following year he took a job as a clerk in the Quebec Provident and Savings Bank. He remained with this establishment for nearly 20 years, during which he rose to the position of assistant cashier (assistant general manager). In 1872 Bowles left Quebec to settle in Montreal, joining the British American Bank Note Company as secretary treasurer, a post he retained for the rest of his life.

At Quebec, some time around 1863, Bowles developed a liking for natural history, and began to interest himself in entomology. In 1864, with William COUPER (then assistant secretary of the Literary and Historical Society of Quebec) and Abbé Louis-Ovide Brunet* (a professor of natural history at Université Laval), he organized the Quebec City branch of the Entomological Society of Canada, which had been founded at Toronto the previous year. The Quebec branch remained active until about 1872, meeting in the rooms of the Literary and Historical Society whose small natural history museum it used.

One of the most active members of the little society from 1864 to 1872, Bowles collected and studied the insects of the Quebec region, especially lepidoptera. He also showed particular interest in species harmful to crops and gardens, as his articles in the *Canadian Naturalist and Geologist* and the *Canadian Entomologist* indicate. The first of these, which appeared in the former journal in 1864, marks an important step in the development of applied entomology in Canada. In this article Bowles noted the arrival in North America of the cabbage white butterfly (*Pieris rapæ*), a European species especially harmful to market garden crops. Probably brought by ocean liners docking at the port of Quebec, the first specimens had found the environment suitable and had greatly multiplied. Bowles predicted that unless steps were taken to destroy the caterpillars each season the species, which was still confined to the Quebec region, would soon spread throughout Canada and cause extensive crop damage.

Settling at Montreal in 1872, Bowles retained his interest in entomology. The following year he helped found the Montreal branch of the Entomological Society of Ontario, which in 1871 had replaced the Entomological Society of Canada [*see* William Couper]. He was to remain a principal figure in this branch, serving as president from 1875 to 1881 and again from 1884 to 1887. In 1875 he took advantage of his first election to the presidency to try to guide the development of the little Montreal society and raise the scientific standards of its work. Its members were amateurs, mainly engaged in collecting lepidoptera and coleoptera on Montreal Island. Bowles urged them to diversify their interests and broaden their studies, pointing out that entomology was bound to play a part in solving the major problems of biology, especially that of the origin of species. He further reminded them that entomology was a practical science of considerable importance to agriculture, forestry, and medicine. Consequently he advised the members of the Montreal branch to collect all categories of insects, and to study not only the forms but also the stages of their individual development, the influence of environment and food, the role of instinct, the behaviour and geographical distribution of the species, indeed, all aspects of the natural history of insects. Practising what he preached, Bowles published in the *Canadian Entomologist* and in the annual reports of the Montreal Horticultural Society and Fruit Growers' Association of the Province of Quebec numerous articles on widely diverse questions dealing with taxonomy and systematics, the behaviour of species, and applied entomology.

In addition to being a member of the Entomological Society of Ontario, Bowles belonged to the Natural History Society of Montreal, the New York Entomological Society, and the American Association for the Advancement of Science. For several years he held the post of assistant editor of the *Canadian Entomologist*. His correspondence, still not collected, shows that he maintained close relationships with American entomologists such as John Lawrence LeConte, Samuel Hubbard Scudder, and William Henry Edwards, and with Canadian naturalists, in particular James Fletcher, William Saunders*, and Abbé Léon Provancher*. After his death his impressive entomological collections were placed in the Redpath Museum of McGill University, Montreal.

George John Bowles was no mere collector: a skilled entomologist, he was able to grasp the potential importance of the study of insects for elucidating the great scientific questions of the time, and the practical role that entomology could play in the development of agriculture in Canada through the identification of harmful species. By his contributions to entomological literature and by his efforts to organize learned societies, he earned a place of honour in the small band of naturalists who in the 19th century interested themselves in the flora and in the fauna of Canada.

RAYMOND DUCHESNE

[George John Bowles wrote numerous articles as an active member of various scientific associations. These include: "On the occurrence of *Pieris rapæ* in Canada," *Canadian Naturalist and Geologist*, new ser., 1 (1864): 258–62; "Address of the incoming president of the Montreal branch of the Entomological Society of Ontario," Entomological Soc. of Ontario, *Annual report* (Toronto), 6 (1875): 10–13; "The importance of practical entomology," Montreal Horticultural Soc. and Fruit Growers' Assoc. of the Prov. of Quebec, *Report* (Montreal), 3 (1877): 95–98. A dozen articles also appeared under his signature in the *Canadian Entomologist* (London, Ont.) between 1869 and 1887; several of these analyse lepidoptera, migratory insects, and new species of butterflies. R. D.]

Arch. de la Soc. entomologique du Québec (dép. de biologie, univ. Laval, Québec), Minute books of the Montreal branch of the Entomological Soc. of Ontario, 1873–87. Arch. du séminaire de Chicoutimi (Chicoutimi, Qué.), Fonds Léon Provancher, Letters of G. J. Bowles, 8 Oct. 1867, 17 Dec. 1874, 16 Dec. 1878, 16 Jan. 1882, 14 Aug. 1884. ASQ, MSS-M, 474–77; 479; 484. F. W. Goding, "*In memoriam*: George John Bowles," Entomological Soc. of Ontario, *Annual report*, 20 (1889): 20–21. E.-J. Leroux et R.-O. Paradis, "Histoire et perspectives de la protection des plantes au Québec: aspect entomologique," *Phytoprotection* (Ottawa), 51 (1970): 99–123. J.-M. Perron, "Histoire des sociétés d'entomologie au Québec," Soc. entomologique du Québec, *Annales* (Sainte-Foy), 19 (1974): 18–27.

BOWRING, CHARLES R. (his middle name may have been Rennie), merchant, politician, and office-holder; b. 1840 in St John's, Nfld, grandson of Benjamin Bowring* and second son of Charles Tricks Bowring and Harriet Harvey; m. Laura, daughter of John Henry WARREN, probably *c.* 1869, and they had six sons and one daughter; d. 31 Jan. 1890 in St John's.

In 1841 Charles R. Bowring's family moved to Liverpool, England, where he was educated and raised as a Unitarian. On the completion of his formal education, Charles entered the Liverpool office which his father ran for the family firm (after 1839 called Bowring Brothers). He received a commercial training and in 1864 was sent to St John's as a junior partner to his uncle, John, who administered the office there. When John retired to England in 1869, Charles became the manager and senior partner in Newfoundland and remained so until his death. In 1875 his cousin, Edgar Rennie Bowring*, joined the St John's office as his junior partner.

Under Charles, the St John's operation became one of the leading firms in the seal- and cod-fisheries and in the transportation of foodstuff to the coastal communities. In 1876 the company was awarded the Newfoundland government's mail contract, which required the addition of two more ships to its already extensive fleet, by this time numbering 57 sailing and steam vessels. By the 1880s the firm had established clear primacy in the seal-fishery and in the middle of the decade was also making its mark in whaling. It had diversified as well by acting as Newfoundland agent for several shipping and insurance companies, including Lloyd's of London from 1866. In 1884 the firm established the Red Cross Line, a passenger and freight service.

In 1873 Bowring had been elected as a Conservative to the House of Assembly for the district of Bonavista Bay, and was re-elected the next year following the defeat of the anti-confederate government led by Charles James Fox BENNETT. After the 1874 election, protests were lodged against Bowring's appointment as a non-official member of the Board of Revenue and an action against him was taken to the Supreme Court of Newfoundland. The case was dismissed. He again offered himself as a candidate in Fortune Bay in the election of 1882, but was defeated.

In 1886 Bowring was appointed to the Legislative Council by Prime Minister Robert Thorburn*, succeeding his father-in-law, John Henry Warren. Bowring served on the council until his death and he was apparently an active and able legislator. He consistently opposed the incorporation of the city of St John's when it came before the council and in 1886 he refused to support a bill to provide a sewage system for the city proposed by the government. Yet his father, a few years before, as chairman of the Liverpool Corporation Health Committee, had instigated some of the more advanced social reforms and sanitary improvements of 19th-century England. Although the father had fought valiantly against the property holders in Liverpool to effect his reforms, the son closed ranks with his fellow property owners to stifle, for a time, necessary social change.

For several years Bowring was a director of the Commercial Bank in St John's. By 1885 the economies of both Great Britain and Newfoundland were in the grip of a trade recession and it was possibly this situation which motivated him in the same year to resign in protest against the bank's extravagant loan policy. When the bank refused to accept his resignation, he sold his holdings and thus became ineligible to serve on the board. His foresight was justified because in 1894 the bank was compelled to suspend payments, and economic chaos ensued for many Newfoundland firms and employees. The Bowring company escaped.

Charles was also a member of the St John's Chamber of Commerce, chairman of the St John's Gas Light Company, and one of the largest shareholders in the Atlantic Hotel. As a prominent member and president of the Athenæum Society, he was closely involved in the cultural and intellectual life of the city. It is probable that he converted to the Church of England, since their orphanage benefited from his largesse and he was actively involved in the completion of the Cathedral of St John the Baptist, a project undertaken in 1880.

CALVIN D. EVANS

Wilcox v. *Bowring* (1864–74), 5 Nfld. R. 403. *Greene* v. *Bowring; Pinsent* v. *Ayre* (1874–84), 6 Nfld. R. 6. *Pinsent* v. *Ayre; Greene* v. *Bowring* (1874–84), 6 Nfld. R. 82. *Noseworthy* v. *Bowring* (1884–96), 7 Nfld. R. 78. *Murray* v. *Bowring* (1884–96), 7 Nfld. R. 143. *Daily Colonist* (St John's), 31 Jan. 1890. *Evening Herald* (St John's), 3 Feb. 1890. *Evening Telegram* (St John's), 4 Oct. 1883; 13 Oct., 3, 15 Nov. 1884. *Royal Gazette* (St John's), 4, 11 Feb. 1890.

Business and general directory of Nfld., 1877. *Directory for the towns of St. John's, Harbor Grace, and Carbonear, Newfoundland, for 1885–86*, comp. John Sharpe (St John's, 1885). *Newfoundland men; a collection of biographical sketches . . .*, ed. H. Y. Mott (Concord, N.H., 1894), 41. Melvin Baker, "The government of St. John's, Newfoundland, 1888–1902" (MA thesis, Memorial Univ. of Newfoundland, St John's, 1975); "Origins of St. John's municipal council, 1880–1888" (unpublished graduate paper, Memorial Univ. of Newfoundland, December 1974), 2, 7, 10–15. Thomas Land, "Bowring Brothers Limited," *Book of Nfld.* (Smallwood), IV (advertisement section). David Keir, *The Bowring story* (London, 1962). A. C. Wardle, *Benjamin Bowring and his descendants; a record of mercantile achievement* (London, 1938). Edward Morris, "The growth of municipal government in St. John's," *Newfoundland Quarterly* ([St John's]), 7 (1907–8), no.1: 5–8.

BRAUN, ANTOINE-NICOLAS, Jesuit priest and writer; b. 5 Feb. 1815 at Saint-Avold, dept of Moselle, France, son of Antoine-Nicolas Braun and Marguerite-Victoire Simonet; d. 1 Feb. 1885 at Sault-au-Récollet (Montréal-Nord), Que.

After completing his secondary education in his native parish Antoine-Nicolas Braun began theological studies at the Grand Séminaire de Metz, entered the noviciate of the Society of Jesus at Tronchiennes, Belgium, and in 1846 was ordained priest at Laval, France. He became curate at Laprairie (La Prairie) upon his arrival in Canada East in 1851, and four years later was appointed to serve at Quebec City, where he worked for 15 years. He was spiritual director of the Sisters of Charity of Quebec (1856–70), and at the request of Charles-François Baillargeon*, bishop of Quebec, drafted the community's rules [*see* Marie-Anne-Marcelle Mallet*]. He was also director of the Congrégation des Hommes de la Haute Ville and a retreat preacher. On more than one occasion the bishop of Quebec delegated Lenten preaching at the cathedral to him. After hearing Father Braun's lectures on Christian marriage in 1866 Bishop Baillargeon suggested that he publish the series. A letter from the general of the society, Father Pierre Beckx, finally persuaded Braun, and the *Instructions dogmatiques sur le mariage chrétien* was published at Quebec in 1866 and at Montreal in 1873. The book, which refuted the Gallican arguments of the French legal authority, Robert-Joseph Pothier, then being taught at Université Laval, led to pressures for Braun's removal from the diocese of Quebec from which he was ousted in 1870.

Accepted by the Collège Sainte-Marie at Montreal, he was made a lecturer, and then devoted himself to preaching at the church of Le Gesù and in various parishes of the diocese. On the occasion of Bishop Ignace BOURGET's 50th anniversary in the priesthood, Braun preached a sermon on 29 Oct. 1872 and it provoked a protest which the newspapers helped stir up across the province. The reactions of the congregation and the public can largely be accounted for by unforeseen circumstances. It had been planned that Father Braun would preach to Bishop Bourget's staff at the bishop's palace, and that Bishop Louis-François Laflèche* would preach to the clergy and the public at the church of Notre-Dame. But when, at the last moment, Laflèche was unavailable Father Braun was assigned to Notre-Dame and was replaced for the sermon at the palace by Abbé Alexis Pelletier*, who after difficulties with the Quebec diocesan authorities had been accepted into the diocese of Montreal. A rigorist and strict Ultramontane, Father Braun extolled his bishop's zeal for "sound principles": the freedom of the church, the right enjoyed by a bishop to act independently of civil authority in erecting parishes, the struggle against Gallicanism and liberalism which endangered the faith. Since many priests and laymen did not give these "sound principles" as broad an interpretation as did Bishop Bourget, Braun aroused considerable animosity. On 10 Nov. 1872 Father Jean Bapst, the Jesuit superior of the province of New York, wrote Father Braun that his sermon appeared to him to be beyond reproach. The Holy Office expressed the same opinion in 1873, on the occasion of a trip Braun made to Rome with Bishop Laflèche. Seen in perspective, the sermon deserved, in the words of Racine's *Britannicus*, "neither this undue honour, nor that affront." It was but one incident in Father Braun's life.

In 1869 the superiors of the society had asked Father Braun to study the Jesuits' estates question, and to advise the legislators thereon. The issue had remained unsettled since the death in 1800 of Father Jean-Joseph Casot*, the last Jesuit in New France. England had then taken over the Jesuits' estates, which it later gave to the united Province of Canada. Since all the land was in Quebec, the province had assumed responsibility for the estates at confederation, although the Jesuit order had returned to Canada in 1842. Braun published his *Mémoire sur les biens des jésuites en Canada, par un jésuite* in 1874, a learned treatise on ecclesiastical law, in which he made a case for the inalienability of the properties the church possessed or of those that had belonged to it but whose donors or owners were dead. He held that the church had the right and even the duty to repossess the latter properties if this were possible, and it was for the church, in the person of the Pope, to redistribute them in the closest possible conformity to the wishes of the deceased. Father Braun set forth the principles that led to the settlement of the Jesuits' estates question. In 1888 the Quebec government of Honoré Mercier* and the Jesuit order in Canada, which was delegated *ad hoc* by the Holy See, reached an agreement. Then Pope Leo XIII portioned out the compensation deemed equitable by both parties: by a papal brief of 15 Jan. 1889 the Society of Jesus was granted $160,000 and land at Laprairie, the Université Laval received $100,000 and its affiliate in Montreal $40,000, and a further $100,000 was to be divided among the bishops in the province.

In 1875 Father Braun's long-cherished project of establishing a Carmelite convent at Montreal was carried out. That year, to help recruiting and to introduce the public to the Discalced Carmelite Nuns, he published *Une fleur du Carmel; la première carmélite canadienne, Marie-Lucie-Hermine Frémont, en religion sœur Thérèse de Jésus*. The book is the story of a girl from Lévis, Que., who, believing she was called to the Carmelite life, went to Rheims, France, in 1872 to undertake her noviciate. She died there about six months later and the Carmelites of Rheims then decided to go to Montreal, arriving in May 1875. With Father Braun's support Mother Séraphine du Divin Cœur de Jésus, the superior at Montreal, expected the convent to be surrounded by a stone wall in accordance with the rules of her order; the lay administrators thought the plan wasteful and held Father Braun responsible for it. To restore calm in a situation which had roused strong feelings, Bishop Bourget requested Father Braun to stay away from the convent. None the less Father Braun, a bold fighter, had judged there was room in Canada for this contemplative order, and time has proved him right. Two other Carmelite convents have been founded, one at St Boniface (Man.) in 1912, which was transferred to Trois-Rivières in 1929, and another at Quebec City in 1950.

From 1875 to 1885 Father Braun was attached to the church of Le Gesù as a preacher and confessor; in addition, he conducted retreats both in the town and in the country. Bishop Édouard-Charles Fabre*, who had a high opinion of Braun, often invited him to preach at the cathedral in Montreal. He was already exhausted when he was appointed to the noviciate at Sault-au-Récollet, then the home for aged and sick Jesuits; he died there on 1 Feb. 1885. Antoine-Nicolas Braun had been as inflexible in his personal life as in the guidance and preaching he had offered to others.

LÉON POULIOT

The principal writings of Antoine-Nicolas Braun are the following: *Instructions dogmatiques sur le mariage chrétien* (Québec, 1866; reimpr. Montréal, 1873); *Mémoire sur les biens des jésuites en Canada, par un jésuite* (Montréal, 1874); *Une fleur du Carmel; la première carmélite canadienne, Marie-Lucie-Hermine Frémont, en religion sœur Thérèse de Jésus* (Montréal, 1875; 3e éd., Québec, 1881).

Arch. de la Compagnie de Jésus, prov. du Canada français (Saint-Jérôme, Qué.), Fonds général, 1092, 5274; sér. A-1, 7; sér. BO37. *L'Étendard* (Montréal), 2 févr. 1885. *Le Nouveau Monde* (Montréal), 30 oct. 1872. *Le Carmel au Canada français: mère Séraphine du Divin Cœur de Jésus, 1816–1888, fondatrice et prieure du Carmel de Montréal* (nouv. éd., Montréal, 1944). R. C. Dalton, *The Jesuits' estates question, 1760–1888: a study of the background for the agitation of 1889* (Toronto, 1968). Paul Desjardins, *Le Collège Sainte-Marie de Montréal* (2v., Montréal, 1940–[44]), II: 186. Lareau, *Hist. de la littérature canadienne*. "Chronique diocésaine et provinciale," *La Semaine religieuse de Montréal*, 6 (1885): 105–6.

BRENNAN, MARGARET, named **Sister Teresa**, member of the Congregation of the Sisters of St Joseph; b. 1 July 1831 in Kingston, Upper Canada, second child of Michael Brennan, a merchant, and Mary Begley; d. 23 Aug. 1887 at Port Arthur (now part of Thunder Bay), Ont.

When Margaret Brennan received the religious habit of the Sisters of St Joseph in Toronto on 15 Oct. 1852, the community in Canada West had nine members, four of them the founders who had come the previous year from Carondelet (St Louis, Mo.) and Philadelphia [*see* Maria Bunning*]. Born into a fairly well-educated family of moderate means, she entered a poor community which cared for orphans, the indigent, and the sick. The convent was located on land donated to the diocese by John Elmsley* in a building which Mrs Elmsley and her sister Mrs John King had fitted up as an orphanage. When Margaret Brennan began her noviciate, the sisters and 55 orphans lived in this small duplex house.

In 1853 Sister Teresa began to teach at St Paul's cathedral school, one of three institutions in which the Sisters of St Joseph taught at the time. The following year, after she had made her final profession, overcrowding at the convent necessitated the building of a noviciate and boarding-school near St Paul's Church. The first superior general of the congregation, Marie-Antoinette Fontbonne*, named Sister Delphine, fell victim to typhus in 1856 and was replaced by Caroline Struckhoff, named Sister Teresa. Sister Teresa Brennan took over the latter's charge as local superior of the orphanage until she was herself appointed superior general by Bishop Armand-François-Marie de Charbonnel* in 1858. The first Canadian-born member of the congregation, she now became the first Canadian-born superior general.

During the first year of her term of office Sister Teresa opened a convent and school in Oshawa. In 1862, when John Elmsley donated to the sisters two acres of his Clover Hill estate for the erection of a new motherhouse in Toronto, she supervised the planning and completion of the building, which included a boarding-school and noviciate. After five years she resigned as superior general and was appointed mistress of novices, an office which required special spiritual and intellectual qualities for the training and forming of new members. Sister Teresa also served as local superior in St Catharines (1865–66, 1869–72), in London (1868), and in Barrie (1875–78). From 1878 to 1887 she acted as assistant to the superior general, an office she had filled at various times after 1866.

Sister Teresa devoted her life with utter selflessness to the interests of the congregation, but she also had concern for those outside it. The enrolment in the Catholic schools in Toronto had steadily increased, and by 1881 the sisters were engaged in eight elementary schools. They also taught in one high school, with some financial assistance from the separate school trustees, and in their private boarding-school. In the House of Providence, opened in 1857, the orphans, the poor, the old and the young, men and women, Catholic and non-Catholic, were harboured, cared for, and even taught if they were of school age. In addition, the sick of the city were visited in their homes, although hospital work *per se* was not begun until St Michael's Hospital was opened in 1892. Sister Teresa had a share in organizing and directing all these undertakings. In 1876 she even went on a fund-raising tour to the United States in order to keep the institutions running and to make it possible to have qualified sisters in the field of education.

Sister Teresa's health was never robust. After beginning her noviciate in 1852, she became ill and was given an unheard-of permission by Bishop Charbonnel to return to her home while wearing the religious habit. Her recovery was deemed miraculous, but at times during her 35 years in religion her health obliged her to withdraw from some of her activities. Finally, in February 1887, she suffered a severe heart attack. To recuperate she went to Port Arthur, where the congregation, now 200 strong, had opened a mission in 1881. On 23 August she died suddenly, away from the motherhouse where she had spent most of her life.

Sister Teresa had amply fulfilled her mission as teacher, administrator, counsellor, and friend, and her contribution to Canada lies in the example of a life devoted to the needs of others. She also helped lay the foundation of the Sisters of St Joseph, who still carry on an apostolate in the fields of education, health care, and social work, not only in Ontario but in the western provinces and the Northwest Territories.

MARY BERNITA YOUNG

St Mary's Cathedral (Kingston, Ont.), Register of baptisms, burials, and marriages, July 1831. Sisters of St Joseph of Toronto Arch. (Toronto), Reception and profession books. Sisters of St Joseph of Toronto, *Community annals*, [1851–1956] (3v., Toronto, [1968]), I: 6, 53, 56, 154–56. *Kingston Chronicle* (Kingston, [Ont.]), 2 July 1831. W. P. Bull, *From Macdonell to McGuigan, the history of the growth of the Roman Catholic Church in Upper Canada* (Toronto, 1939). *Jubilee volume, 1842–1892: the archdiocese of Toronto and Archbishop Walsh*, [ed. J. R. Teefy] (Toronto, 1892), 156. Sister Mary Agnes, *The Congregation of the Sisters of St. Joseph: Le Puy, Lyons, St. Louis, Toronto* (Toronto, 1951).

BRISEBOIS, ÉPHREM-A., soldier, NWMP officer, politician, and civil servant; b. 7 March 1850 at South Durham, Canada East, son of Joseph Brisebois, a hotel keeper and JP in Drummondville, Canada East, and Henriette Piette; m. *c.* 1876–80 Adelle Malcouronne, and they had no children; d. 13 Feb. 1890 in Winnipeg, Man.

Éphrem-A. Brisebois was a member of a well-educated, bilingual, and deeply religious Roman Catholic family. Though an excellent student he left school at 15 to fight with the Union Army during the final phase of the American Civil War, and then served for almost three years with other Quebec volunteers in the courageous "Devils of the Good Lord" unit of the Papal Zouaves in Italy.

In 1873, when the federal government was creating the North-West Mounted Police to bring Canadian law to the west [*see* Patrick ROBERTSON-ROSS], Brisebois, a highly capable soldier and a strong Conservative, was appointed one of nine commanding officers by Prime Minister Sir John A. Macdonald*. Brisebois helped to recruit men for the new force and led a contingent on a 110-mile march through blizzards from Port Arthur (now part of Thunder Bay, Ont.) to Lower Fort Garry (Man.). There, he trained the raw recruits all winter. On 8 July 1874, in command of one of the six divisions, and having recently been promoted inspector, he embarked on the 900-mile trek westward. At Fort Benton (Mont.), he and his superior officer James Farquharson Macleod* purchased supplies and hired legendary mixed-blood scout Jerry Potts* as a guide.

Brisebois helped erect Fort Macleod (Alta), and then, following a disagreement with Macleod, was sent with a small detachment to establish Fort Kipp (Kipp, Alta). In the summer of 1875 he took charge of building Fort Brisebois. He often clashed with Macleod, his popular superior. The winter of 1875–76 was bitterly cold, one of the worst on record, and Brisebois frequently did not punish his men when they shirked duties or disobeyed orders because of the weather. Discipline and morale deteriorated. His orders to build cabins for two interpreters in a nearby Métis camp were not carried out. He himself fell in love with a Métis girl, and in frontier fashion took her to his quarters as his common-law wife, thereby enraging Roman Catholic and Protestant missionaries alike. His expropriation of the fort's only cook-stove to heat his draughty room was the final straw; the insubordination of the whole division approached mutiny. Brisebois was sharply criticized by his superiors and, on the suggestion of Macleod, Fort Brisebois was renamed Fort Calgary in June 1876.

Concerned with the disappearance of the buffalo which he knew would mean starvation for many Indians, he tried while at the fort to enforce strict hunting regulations. He warned in 1875 that unless these were enforced "the Buffalo will disappear in less than 10 years. These Indians will then be in a starving condition and entirely dependent upon the Canadian Government for subsistence." Within five years the Indians had become dependent on the government for food.

In August 1876 Brisebois resigned from the NWMP and rode alone 1,200 miles to Winnipeg via Fort Edmonton and the Carlton Trail. He failed to find employment in Ottawa and returned to Quebec where he flung himself into politics against the Liberals. During a by-election in 1877 in the riding of Drummond and Arthabaska, Brisebois, according to Louis-François-Roderick Masson*, "more than any other man" contributed to the victory of the Conservative candidate, Désiré-Olivier Bourbeau, over cabinet minister Wilfrid Laurier*. Brisebois fought in three more election campaigns. In December 1880 he was appointed land titles registrar of the Little Saskatchewan district with headquarters in Minnedosa, Man. He and his bride Adelle were popular in the predominantly Anglo-Saxon Protestant Minnedosa; the snowshoe club they founded became an important part of the social life of the community and Roman Catholic church services were held in their home.

During the North-West rebellion of 1885, when a dispute between the town's chief of police, John Cameron, and the Indians of a neighbouring reserve threatened to lead to open hostilities, Brisebois quickly organized two companies of white and Métis home guards to prevent bloodshed. He also recruited the 92nd Light Infantry Company of the Winnipeg Rifles to help suppress the insurrection led by Louis RIEL; he himself joined the 65th Battalion of Rifles (Mount Royal Rifles) of Quebec, as part of the Alberta Field Force. In Alberta he served as sub-commander at Fort Edmonton which was threatened at one point by the Crees of Big Bear [MISTAHIMASKWA]. After the rebellion Brisebois returned to Minnedosa where he strove to make sure that Ottawa did not forget the soldiers' services. As registrar he settled hundreds of land claims, but late in 1889 the land titles office was phased out. Unemployed, Brisebois moved to Winnipeg where a few weeks later, at the age of 39, he died of a heart attack. He was buried in the cemetery in St Boniface, Man.

PETER L. NEUFELD

PAC, RG 2, 1, P.C.988, 28 July 1874; P.C.759, 16 Aug. 1876; RG 18, A1, 610, nos.70, 96, 111; B7, 3436, regimental number O–8. *Minnedosa Tribune* (Minnedosa, Man.), 7 Dec. 1883–1890. H. A. Dempsey, "Brisebois: Calgary's forgotten founder," *Frontier Calgary: town, city, and region, 1875–1914*, ed. A. W. Rasporich and H. C. Klassen (Calgary, 1975), 28–40. S. W. Horrall, *The pictorial history of the Royal Canadian Mounted Police* (Toronto, 1973). E. C. Morgan, "The North-West Mounted Police, 1873–1883" (MA thesis, Univ. of Saskatchewan, Regina Campus, 1970). P. L. Neufeld, "Brisebois: forgotten Mountie pioneer," *Canadian Frontier Annual* (Surrey, B.C.), 1977: 80–83.

BRONSON, HENRY FRANKLIN, lumber manufacturer; b. 24 Feb. 1817 in Moreau Township, Saratoga County, N.Y., son of Alvah Bronson and Sarah Tinker; m. 5 Nov. 1840 Editha Eliza Pierce, and they had three sons and one daughter; d. 7 Dec. 1889 at Ottawa, Ont.

Henry Franklin Bronson, a member of a family well known in the northeastern United States, was educated at Poultney Academy in Vermont where he specialized in agricultural science and rudimentary forestry. During his early youth he had spent a good deal of time with the family of lumberman John J. Harris in Queensbury Township, Washington (Warren) County, N.Y., and when he completed his education he joined Harris' lumber and forwarding business as a clerk. In 1840 Harris purchased large stands of white pine in the upper Hudson lakes region, erected mills there, and made Bronson a junior partner. The new firm, Harris and Bronson Company, developed good markets for its lumber in the growing cities of Boston and New York but by 1848 found its timber supplies becoming increasingly restricted. Consequently, in the summer of 1848 Bronson undertook an exploratory journey up the Ottawa valley to investigate its timber and water-power resources. He was impressed with the area and recommended that the business be transferred north.

Harris, reluctant to move the mills into a foreign colony, was more inclined to invest in the pine lands of Michigan. Nevertheless, when it was announced in 1852 that the fine hydraulic sites at the Chaudière Falls near Bytown (Ottawa) were for sale he decided to visit the area. Harris was treated to a civic banquet by the eager burghers who were anxious to attract new industry to their town and who promised that if his company invested in any of the hydraulic lots no competitive bids would be accepted from other companies. With this guarantee the Harris and Bronson Company acquired hydraulic lots on Victoria Island adjacent to the Chaudière Falls for 1*s*. per lot above the upset price of £50, and a water-power rental charge of £5 per annum for each run of stones operated in their mills. Bronson became a full partner at this time.

In late 1852 the company erected a modern mill using a gang saw, a device with several saws set in a frame which could be operated by one man (Bronson was the first to use iron rather than wood for the frame or gate). A new partner, James Coleman, joined the business and in 1853 Harris, Bronson and Coleman Company obtained timber limits along the Gatineau River. Nearly 700 square miles of new limits were acquired along the Dumoine River and in several other areas in 1857. In 1864 the firm made arrangements with the Canadian Land and Emigration Company to cut timber from the latter company's pine groves along the York branch of the Madawaska River.

With a new mill and first quality timber limits, the company was in an excellent position to supply its traditional markets in the northeastern United States, and the signing of the Reciprocity Treaty between the United States and British North America in 1854 promoted its development and expansion. Despite temporary depressions in 1857–58 and 1861–62 caused by stagnation in the American market, the partners were able to increase their production each year until by 1870 it had reached over 25 million board feet annually. In 1866 Harris retired and Abijah Weston of Painted Post, N.Y., and Bronson's eldest son Erskine Henry joined to form Bronsons and Weston Lumber Company. Weston was a large lumber wholesaler with offices in Michigan, New York, and Vermont who brought important new capital into the firm enabling the partners not only to enlarge their lumbering and milling operations in Canada but also to set up their own wholesale outlets at Albany, Boston, and Burlington, Vt. Rough lumber was resawn and dressed at these outlets which were operated under a separate corporate entity, Bronson, Weston, Dunham and Company. In 1871 Bronsons and Weston acquired large tracts of redwood timber in California which were developed later by Erskine Henry Bronson. In the late 1870s or the early 1880s the partners also set up their own bank at Painted Post to help finance the company's various operations.

H. F. Bronson had moved his family to Bytown in 1853 and had soon become a prominent member of the "American community," a name applied to American entrepreneurs such as William Goodhue PERLEY and Ezra Butler Eddy* who had moved north between 1852 and 1854 to set up the sawmilling industry in the town. Bronson, however, did not long remain a member of a foreign clique. Although he never gave up his American citizenship, he moved easily into community affairs and rapidly became respected in Ottawa. He was a dominant influence in St Andrew's Presbyterian Church and a founder of Ottawa Ladies' College in 1869. He and his wife were charter members of the Protestant Orphans' Home in Ottawa, and took an active interest in many other philanthropic organizations. In 1868 with Perley and James SKEAD he promoted the Upper Ottawa Steamship Company. He was also not reluctant to become involved in Canadian politics, and the Reform party gained his sympathy. After the termination of the Reciprocity Treaty in 1866 Bronson lobbied hard and long to have it restored. By 1870 he had become a major supporter of the federal and provincial Liberals in eastern Ontario and he used his company as a political machine in every constituency in which it did business; indeed its woods managers served as Liberal poll bosses.

Before his death in 1889 Henry Franklin Bronson had built an impressive empire which stretched from Mattawa, Ont., to New York City and as a corporate entity did over one million dollars worth of business each year. The Ottawa mills alone employed more than 300 men. His legacy was his share in helping establish the sawn lumber industry which dramatically changed the social and economic structure of the Ottawa valley. Bronsons and Weston Lumber Company was managed by E. H. Bronson until 1899 when it was dissolved and replaced by a holding company, the Bronson Company.

ROBERT PETER GILLIS

PAC, MG 27, II, D14, 5; MG 28, I37, 1–6; III26; RG 1, E1, 75: 264; RG 31, A1, 1871 census, 893: schedule 7, Bronson, Weston and Company. Can., Prov. of, Legislative Assembly, *App. to the journals*, 1857, V: app.25. *Ottawa Citizen*, 18 Jan. 1894. *Cyclopædia of Canadian biog*. (Rose, 1886). H. R. Cummings, *Early days in Haliburton* (Toronto, 1963), 131–52, app.IV. J. E. Defebaugh, *History of the lumber industry of America* (2v., Chicago, 1906–7), I: 158. A. R. M. Lower, *The North American assault on the Canadian forest: a history of the lumber trade between Canada and the United States* . . . (Toronto and New Haven, Conn., 1938; repr. New York, 1968), 123–47.

BROUSE, WILLIAM HENRY, physician and politician; b. 15 June 1824 in Matilda Township, Dundas County, Upper Canada, second son of Lieutenant-Colonel Jacob Brouse and Nancy Parlow; m. 28 Jan. 1857 Frances Amelia Jones of Prescott, Canada West, who was from an established, influential family, and they had one son and one daughter; d. 23 Aug. 1881 at Ottawa, Ont.

William Henry Brouse's ancestors, the Krausse family, emigrated from Germany to the 13 Colonies in the 1750s and changed their name to Brouse. At the close of the American revolution they left for British territory, settling on the banks of the St Lawrence River in Dundas County. William was raised on his father's farm and attended local schools, taking time off to assist with the planting and harvesting. His father, however, was determined that William would receive a better education than his own and in September 1839 William entered the Upper Canada Academy in Cobourg, Canada West. He continued on into Victoria College, but left in 1845 without a BA. He received an honorary MA in 1849 and later served as a member of the college's senate for many years.

After leaving Victoria, Brouse studied medicine with John Rolph* in Toronto for one year before attending McGill College in Montreal, where he earned an MD degree in the spring of 1847. Later that year he was appointed to head the fever hospital at Iroquois Point, Canada West, which in that year contained some 300 immigrants. In 1848 Brouse moved to Prescott where he began a highly successful practice on both sides of the St Lawrence. He was elected to the medical examining board for Upper Canada in 1850 and from 1866 to about 1878 was a member by election of the Medical Council of Ontario, serving as its president in 1870. An appointment as the professor of surgery at the Toronto School of Medicine, affiliated with the University of Toronto, was refused by Brouse in 1878. Throughout his life medicine remained his chief interest and he practised until his death.

Professional success led to contact with the business community and Brouse served with the Toronto Life Assurance and Tontine Company as chief medical officer and as a director. During the 1870s he continued to develop business interests. By 1879 he was a director of the Ottawa Agricultural Insurance Company and by 1880 a director of the Prescott and Brockville Macadamized Road Company.

Brouse was also politically involved, and served as reeve, mayor, and postmaster of Prescott. His first attempt to enter provincial politics was unsuccessful. In 1858, running as a Liberal (described in 1872 by important Conservative John HAMILTON as an "extreme grit"), Brouse was defeated by Conservative George Crawford* in a close election to represent the St Lawrence division in the Legislative Council. However, in the federal election in 1872 Brouse was returned for the riding of Grenville South, a seat he held until he was called to the Senate on 9 Aug. 1878, just before the return of a Conservative government. In 1872 and 1874 Brouse had defeated the prominent Conservative Walter Shanly*, who had held the seat from 1863 to 1872 and held it again from 1885 to 1891. Shortly before his death Brouse moved to Ottawa where he continued to sit in the Senate and also practised medicine.

Although not a major politician, Brouse was certainly an active one. Patronage problems were given diligent attention, and he was always vigilant about the best interests of St Lawrence shipping and the maintenance of the natural beauty of the Thousand Islands area. He intervened regularly in debate and his speeches on public health were based on impressive research into conditions in the United States, Great Britain, and Europe. Brouse favoured a dominion sanitation bureau to educate people concerning public health. Having served for years as surgeon for the 56th Battalion of Infantry, he was also interested in the militia and military matters. He brought before the house, and successfully campaigned for, a $50,000 annual grant for the veterans of the War of 1812; he also proposed, unsuccessfully, that some recognition be granted to the loyalist veterans of the rebellions of 1837–38. He agitated for the introduction of a systematic drill in schools as "an early initiation to all that is implied in the term discipline: viz., duty, order, obedience to command, self-restraint, punctuality and patience."

A man of obvious professional prestige who represented important sections of the élite within the Liberal party, Brouse held a difficult seat for two parliaments. Familiar with some areas of the business community, he could boast strong local ties as well as contacts and influence beyond his region, especially in Toronto. Brouse was, therefore, a useful party member, if not a distinguished politician.

DONALD SWAINSON

AO, MU 469–87. PAC, RG 31, A1, 1871 census, Grenville County, Prescott; MG 26, A; B, Letterbooks 3, 6, 7. Can., House of Commons, *Debates*, 1875–78; Senate, *Debates*, 1879–81. *Daylight through the mountain: letters and labours of civil engineers Walter and Francis Shanly*, ed. F. N. Walker (Montreal, 1957). *Globe*, 24 Aug. 1881. *Ottawa Daily Citizen*, 24 Aug. 1881. *Canadian biog. dict.*, I. *Canadian directory of parl.* (J. K. Johnson). *CPC*, 1872–73, 1875, 1879. William Canniff, *The medical profession in Upper Canada, 1783–1850 . . .* (Toronto, 1894). T. W. H. Leavitt, *History of Leeds and Grenville, Ontario, from 1749 to 1879 . . .* (Brockville, Ont., 1879; repr. Belleville, Ont., 1972). Swainson, "Personnel of politics."

BROUSSEAU, LÉGER (baptized **Joseph**), bookseller, publisher, and printer; b. 21 May 1826 at Quebec City, son of Jean-Baptiste Brousseau and Nathalie

Doré; m. first 12 June 1860 at Quebec Catherine Rose Bennett; m. secondly 27 Nov. 1866 Georgiana Garneau of Cap-Santé, Canada East, and they had ten children of whom three were still alive at the time of his death; d. 8 Feb. 1890 at Quebec.

Little is known about Léger Brousseau's early life. He is thought to have learned the trade of typographer at the *Quebec Mercury* before entering into partnership with his elder brother Jean-Docile*; the elder Brousseau, whose bookstore and printing works were on Rue Buade, had been the official printer for the archdiocese of Quebec since 1855 and the owner of *Le Courrier du Canada* since 1858. Léger looked after the operation of the press and began using his name as publisher in 1861 when his brother embarked on a political career. He compiled the synodical and episcopal enactments of the diocese of Quebec, and in 1871 he published *Le Journal des jésuites . . .*, edited by abbés Charles-Honoré Laverdière* and Henri-Raymond Casgrain*. After the printing works burned down in 1872 copies of this latter work became extremely rare, as did those of Théophile-Pierre Bédard's *Histoire de cinquante ans (1791–1841), annales parlementaires et politiques du Bas-Canada, depuis la Constitution jusqu'à l'Union* (1869). Brousseau undertook the second edition in 1876 of the *Mémorial de l'éducation du Bas-Canada* by Dr Jean-Baptiste Meilleur*, and also published school texts. He printed newspapers and journals: *Journal de l'Instruction publique* (1871–79), *Journal of Education for the Province of Quebec* (1872–79), and the *Annales de la bonne Sainte-Anne-de-Beaupré* from 1873. Having published the "Causeries du dimanche" by Judge Adolphe-Basile Routhier* in *Le Courrier du Canada* in 1870 and 1871, he made widely known Routhier's judgement concerning the "undue influence" at the time of the 1876 election between Hector-Louis Langevin* and Pierre-Alexis Tremblay* in Charlevoix. He printed books and biographies by Stanislas Drapeau*, a prolix author, and published the numerous pamphlets of Narcisse-Eutrope Dionne*, a versatile writer whose inexpensive works sold well.

During the 1860s catechisms, pious pamphlets, and diocesan almanacs constituted the bulk of Brousseau's sales to his ecclesiastical clientele, to whom he also supplied wine, registers, and stationery. From 1875, however, there was an increasing demand for souvenirs of retreats and pilgrimages, communion certificates, and holy pictures, all signs of a devotional revival. In 1880 Brousseau became the printer of the almanac of the diocese of Rimouski for a five-year period, and during these years his press seems to have functioned at maximum capacity, with orders booked four months in advance.

A member of the Cercle catholique de Québec and the Association des typographes de Québec, as well as an honorary member of the Union Allet of papal Zouaves in 1878, Brousseau was in the main a man who undertook charitable endeavours for the religious communities, to which he was asked to supply stationery free. Thanks to his good relations with Stanislas Drapeau and Joseph-Charles Taché*, who were federal officials, and with Langevin, a federal cabinet minister, he enjoyed considerable influence in Ottawa. More important, however, the fact that his brother-in-law, Pierre Garneau*, was a minister in the Quebec government from 1875 brought him printing contracts for the private and public bills of the legislature, the *Statuts de la province de Québec*, and the professional and municipal corporations. In 1880, during an era when conflicts of interest went unheeded, Brousseau received contracts from the city of Quebec for such items as notices and minutes of meetings during the tenure of his brother, Jean-Docile, as mayor.

During the 1860s the archdiocese of Quebec, through Vicar General Charles-Félix CAZEAU, played a part in the editing of *Le Courrier du Canada* and also reserved the right to "approve" the editor, but in the 1870s Brousseau apparently had a free hand. In 1872 he purchased the paper and three years later dismissed reporter Guillaume Amyot because of an article in which he had drawn attention to the contracts awarded without tender by Quebec when Jean-Docile Brousseau was a member of the city council; in 1879 Amyot's successor, Roch-Pamphile Vallée, was also relieved of his duties. At this prosperous stage in its development *Le Courrier du Canada* had a solid network of subscription agents, correspondents, and readers, even in the United States, but Brousseau did not consider any changes in the form of his paper. A tri-weekly edition was, however, added to the daily, and in 1882 he launched *Le Journal des campagnes.* From 1884 he seems to have gradually relinquished the task of publishing *Le Courrier du Canada* to Thomas Chapais* in order to become the Quebec agent of several renowned European publishers, including Desclée, De Brouwer et Compagnie of Bruges, Belgium, and Poursin-Escande and Gustave Guérin et Compagnie of Paris.

What Brousseau had built during his life was broken up soon after his death. On 27 Jan. 1891 Thomas Chapais acquired *Le Courrier du Canada* and *Le Journal des campagnes* for $6,000. In February Mme Brousseau, the sole heir, sold the bookshop and printing works to Léger Brousseau Jr for $22,000, but financial difficulties obliged him to sell it a few years later.

Léger Brousseau had made himself supplier to the clergy; official printer for two dioceses, the legislature, and the city of Quebec; and also an administrator who although punctilious allowed enormous credit to a touchy and neglectful clientele. He owed part of his fortune to favourable political and ecclesiastical circumstances and to improved communications and postal services. He owed his fortune also to his knowledge of his trade, his unremitting labour, and his ability as a businessman and publisher.

ELZÉAR LAVOIE

AAQ, CD, Diocèse de Québec, IX: 2ff.; 20 CG, II; 33CR, B: 19; I: 71. AC, Québec, État civil, Catholiques, Sainte-Famille (Cap-Santé), 1882; Minutier, P.-É. Bélanger, 3 avril 1890; 27 janv., 4, 19 févr. 1891; 12 juin 1897. ANQ-Q, AP-G-16; État civil, Catholiques, Notre-Dame de Québec, 21 mai 1826, 12 juin 1860; Sainte-Famille (Cap-Santé), 27 nov. 1866. BE, Québec, Reg. B, 162, no.82508.

Le Canadien, 10, 13 févr. 1890. Beaulieu et J. Hamelin, *Journaux du Québec*, 185. Claude Poirier, "Inventaire analytique du fonds Léger Brousseau," ANQ *Rapport*, 1972: 159–253. André Labarrère-Paulé, *Les laïques et la presse pédagogique au Canada français au XIXe siècle* (Québec, 1963). Réjean Robidoux, "*Les Soirées canadiennes* et le *Foyer canadien* dans le mouvement littéraire québécois de 1860" (thèse de DES, univ. Laval, Québec, 1957). Elzéar Lavoie, "La clientèle du *Courrier du Canada*," *Culture* (Québec), 30 (1969): 299–309; 31 (1970): 40–57. Romain Légaré, "Apôtre de l'Évangile au Canada," *Le Souvenir* (Trois-Rivières), 17 (1970), no.1: 4–10. Raoul Renault, "Le journal des jésuites," *BRH*, 5 (1899): 52. Philippe Sylvain, "Les débuts du *Courrier du Canada* et les progrès de l'ultramontanisme canadien-français," *Cahiers des Dix*, 32 (1967): 255–78. R. G. Thwaites, "Le journal des jésuites," *BRH*, 5 (1899): 22.

BROWN, MICHAEL SEPTIMUS, silversmith and jeweller; b. 22 Dec. 1818 in Halifax, N.S., son of William Brown and Joanna Bessonett, *née* Stairs; d. unmarried on 29 Nov. 1886 in Halifax.

Michael Septimus Brown was a cousin of the noted chronometer-maker, Richard Upham Marsters*, and two of his elder brothers learned the watch, clock, and hardware trade from their half-brother, John Stayner Bessonett. Brown himself, however, was apprenticed in 1833 to the talented silversmith and goldsmith, Peter Nordbeck*. In 1840 Brown established an independent jewellery and silver business in Halifax; in addition to wares made with the skills learned from Nordbeck, he relied heavily upon imported British speciality items, such as watches, toys, and eyeglasses. Brown became increasingly ambitious as his skills attracted new clients, but the real success of his firm appears to date from the mid 1850s when he commenced regular buying trips to England to improve the quality of his imported stock.

Brown was able to attract many of Nordbeck's customers following the latter's death in 1861, and in new quarters the firm became the most prominent enterprise of its type in Halifax. Inferior stock was discontinued and the emphasis was placed on quality, reliability, and honesty. Brown was respected for his integrity and at one time his watches carried this guarantee: "Wind me up and use me well, and let me have fairplay / And I to you will try to give the precious time of day / But if by chance that I should stop, or fail to give the hour, / Take me back to M. S. Brown, and he will give me power." Brown himself was noted for his superb silver flatware and jewellery, but the firm's workshops produced several other talented artisans, including David Hudson Whiston and Brown's nephew Thomas, who was apprenticed to the business in 1851 at age 14.

Brown and his nephew formed a partnership in 1871 and the following year, in failing health, Brown retired in favour of Thomas. The firm then became M.S. Brown and Company. The public saw little more of the generous, lively, and intelligent founder of the business, since Michael Brown spent his last years as an invalid. When he died of apoplexy without a will, his estate of some $60,000, accumulated through property and investment in Halifax banks, was divided among his family. His firm, continued by a succession of owners until it was purchased by Henry Birks and Sons in 1919, maintained its founder's record for quality and integrity.

LOIS K. KERNAGHAN

Halifax County Court of Probate (Halifax), no.3541, estate of M.S. Brown. PANS, MG 1, 160A. *Acadian Recorder*, 3 July 1882, 29 Nov. 1886. D. C. Mackay, *Silversmiths and related craftsmen of the Atlantic provinces* (Halifax, 1973). Harry Piers and D. C. Mackay, *Master goldsmiths and silversmiths of Nova Scotia and their marks*, ed. U. B. Thomson and A. M. Strachan (Halifax, 1948).

BROWN, THOMAS STORROW, hardware merchant, journalist, Patriote, and writer; b. in 1803 at St Andrews, N.B., son of Henry Barlow Brown, a merchant, and Rebecca Appleton; m. in 1829 Jane Hughes (d. 1833), and m. secondly in 1860 Hester Livingstone; d. 26 Dec. 1888 in Montreal, Que.

Thomas Storrow Brown's father, a loyalist who had taken refuge in New Brunswick in 1776, returned to the United States in 1811, settling in Woodstock, Vt. In 1818, Thomas Storrow Brown went to Montreal to live with his uncle Thomas Storrow, who found him work with the ironmonger J. T. Barrett, on Rue Saint-Paul. In 1825 Brown is believed to have opened a hardware store on the same street, probably with the assistance of the Barrett family. He does not seem to have been successful, for after being in partnership with François-Benjamin Blanchard* for some time, he went bankrupt in 1835. He then turned to land speculation. In 1833, with Jacob De Witt*, Brown had taken part in negotiations for the incorporation of the City Bank, and in the organization of the Banque du Peuple, of which he was a director. In 1834, when the cholera epidemic was raging in Montreal, Brown served on a committee to help the victims; it set up a hospital and provided funds to cover initial expenses.

It is difficult to determine the date at which Brown joined the Patriote party. He allegedly belonged to the Society of the Friends of Ireland, an organization which helped found in 1828 a Montreal newspaper, the *Irish Vindicator and Canada General Advertiser*; in 1832 it became the *Vindicator and Canadian Advertiser* [*see* Edmund Bailey O'Callaghan*]. But, if this is true, it is surprising that his name is not on the list of militant Patriotes who organized support for Daniel Tracey* in the election in the west riding of Montreal in 1832. Perhaps at that date Brown, like his partner Blanchard who would also become a Patriote, was supporting the Tory Stanley Bagg. But from 1836 Brown committed himself openly. He worked with the most radical members of the Patriote party, some of whom were anglophones; these radicals were dissatisfied with the control exercised by the most powerful men of affairs, and were receptive to either American democratic ideas or the views of the radicals in England. In 1836–37 Brown contributed to the *Vindicator*, and forwarded a dozen or so open letters, under the pseudonym L.M.N., to the *Express* (New York). In 1837, he preached revolution to the Fils de la Liberté, and when the members of the Doric Club sacked the offices of the *Vindicator* during a riot on 6 November, Brown was seriously wounded in one eye.

Ten days later he left Montreal for Varennes, after the government had issued warrants for the arrest of Patriote leaders. Accompanied by Dr Eugène-Napoléon Duchesnois, Dr Henri-Alphonse Gauvin*, and Rodolphe Desrivières*, he then set out for Saint-Charles where he arrived just as an entrenched camp was being established. Brown made a great impression since he had just come from the city and was practically a war casualty. With the approval of Louis-Joseph Papineau*, he was appointed general, but in reality he did not have the makings of a leader, lacking both a sense of organization and the ability to inspire his men. This lack did not prevent him from forging blithely ahead, certain of victory. However, on 25 November when the fight against the government forces under George Augustus Wetherall* had scarcely begun, Brown left in search of reinforcements, disappearing ingloriously from the battlefield. He went to Saint-Denis before fleeing to the United States, reaching Berkshire, Vt, on 10 December.

He was imprisoned for nearly a month for debts contracted in Canada, and then apparently experienced difficulty in integrating himself into the group of political refugees. In April 1838 he published a long article on the rebellion in the *Vermonter* (Vergennes, Vt) and shortly after left for Florida where he edited the *Florida Herald* in Key West. When this venture failed, he found himself a post as an auditor but when amnesty was proclaimed in 1844, he returned to Montreal and went back to hardware. Two years later, Louis Perrault* wrote to Edmund Bailey O'Callaghan: "T. S. Brown is a clerk at [Charles Wilson*'s] hardware store. He is behaving properly now. He will make his way if he doesn't take to drink again." On the evidence of the *Montreal directory*, Brown apparently set up his own business on Rue Saint-Paul about 1854. In 1862 with William Bristow* and George Sheppard*, he was appointed to the Financial and Departmental Commission "to enquire into the prevailing mode of keeping the Public Accounts of this Province, and the items of receipt and disbursement of money by every department of the public service, and how the same have been and are now checked and audited." Two years later he left the hardware store following his appointment as official assignee responsible for applying the new bankruptcy law. He kept this post until he became completely blind, some ten years before his death.

FERNAND OUELLET

[In addition to articles and letters published in various newspapers in the 1830s, Thomas Storrow Brown wrote a number of pamphlets. Some of these related to the events occurring in 1837–38: *Brief sketch of the life and times of the late Hon. Louis-Joseph Papineau* ([Montreal, 1872]; *1837; my connection with it* (Quebec, 1898). Others are linked to his role in public life: *A history of the Grand Trunk Railway of Canada, compiled from public documents* (Quebec, 1864); *Montreal fifty years ago* (Montreal, 1868). In his capacity as a commissioner, he co-authored Can., Prov. of, Financial and Departmental Commission, *Report* (2v., Quebec, 1863–64). He also wrote a more personal short book entitled *Strong drink, what it is and what it does* (Montreal, 1884). F. O.]

ANQ-Q, AP-G-417; QBC 25, Événements de 1837–1838. ASQ, Fonds Viger-Verreau, Sér. O, 0139–52. McGill Univ. Libraries (Montreal), Dept. of Rare Books and Special Coll., MS coll., CH443.RBR box. PAC, MG 24, B2; RG 31, A1, 1831, Montreal. *An alphabetical list of the merchants, traders, and housekeepers, residing in Montreal; to which is prefixed, a descriptive sketch of the town*, comp. Thomas Doige (Montreal, 1819). Borthwick, *Hist. and biog. gazetteer*, 277–79. Fauteux, *Patriotes*. John Boyd, "Thomas Storrow Brown et le soulèvement de 1837 dans le Bas-Canada," *Rev. canadienne*, nouv. sér., 18 (juillet–décembre 1916): 50–69, 110–29. Émile Chartier, "Après 'l'Affaire de Saint-Denis,' 1er–12 décembre 1837, d'après un mémoire de Brown," *BRH*, 56 (1950): 130–47.

BROWNE, GEORGE, architect; b. 5 Nov. 1811 in Belfast (Northern Ireland); d. 19 Nov. 1885 in Montreal, Que.

George Browne's Belfast years are obscure, and research has failed to confirm his personal or architectural parentage. He was part of the great British migration to America following the Napoleonic wars and was probably attracted to Quebec City, as were other architects, because of its prosperity caused by the flourishing lumber trade. John Douglas Borthwick*, who presumably knew Browne in his later years, states that he was the son of an architect of the same name and that he came to Quebec in 1830. The following year "G. Browne & Co." advertised in the *Quebec Mercury*, claiming they had "gone through their usual term and probation of their profession, besides having superintended the most eminent Buildings." Whatever his background and connections Browne was active in Quebec during the years 1830–35, judging from advertisements for contracts and surviving contracts themselves.

Connecting buildings with their architects in this period has proved a difficult task. In 1966, 9 Rue Haldimand was identified as one of "two houses with cut stone fronts in Haldimand Street" which were tendered for in the *Quebec Mercury* of 15 Dec. 1832. It has since been attributed to Henry Musgrave Blaiklock*, but on stylistic grounds this attribution seems highly unlikely. The old customs house, Rue Champlain, documented as by Blaiklock (1830–39), shows similarities in the basic architectural vocabulary but has none of the sculptural sense nor the differentiation of textures which one finds in 9 Haldimand. Another possible candidate for the design of the latter house is Frederick Hacker, who arrived in Quebec in 1832. His 43 Rue d'Auteuil of 1834 uses some of the same architectural forms but shows a very different sense of proportion. Buildings at 73 Rue Sainte-Ursule (built in 1831 and now a convent) and 56 Rue Saint-Louis (1832–34) can quite rightly be associated with 9 Haldimand. All three appear to be by the same hand, showing subtleties in the handling of projections and recessions, as well as textures – qualities which Browne was to develop further in his Kingston period.

In October 1835 Browne announced that he was proceeding the following spring to the United States "to superintend several very extensive buildings," but nothing is known of these. He seems to have returned to Canada by the time of the rebellions in 1837–38; Borthwick states that he held a commission in the militia and "took an active part"; he also states that Browne moved to Montreal in 1840.

Browne's introduction to government service, which was crucial since it indirectly provided him with the greatest opportunities of his career, may have come from the provincial secretary, a fellow-Irishman, Dominick Daly*, for whom he had built a Gothic villa (probably the building now known as Benmore at Sillery) in 1834 and two town houses the following year. In February 1841 Lord Sydenham [Thomson*] proclaimed the union of the Canadas and chose Kingston, Canada West, as the new capital. Browne was sent to provide facilities for the government by extending or altering existing structures: adding a wing to Alwington House for the governor general, fitting up the recently completed hospital as a parliament building, and erecting offices for the civil service. None of this work survives. Despite Browne's employment with the government he was free to accept private commissions. In the *Chronicle & Gazette* on 17 February he solicited clients, describing himself as an "architect, measurer, and landscape gardener." During his three years in Kingston he carried out much domestic and commercial work as well as the greatest project of his career, the Kingston Town Hall and Market Building.

Two of his most interesting surviving works, a stone manse for St Andrews Presbyterian Church and a stucco country villa, Rockwood, for John Solomon Cartwright*, were domestic commissions carried out in 1841. The former shows a sensitive use of the native limestone, in both texture and mass. The treatment of the walls in broad panels, which were cut back at the corners and in the central bay, makes one think of Sir John Soane's buildings in Britain, but the manse is blockier and heavier, as if in response to the coarse nature of the local stone. Rockwood is massive and symmetrical, with Tuscan columns *in antis*. It is also "picturesque," the light columns playing against the dark recessed porch and the heavy cornice making strong shadows against the walls, which, as for the manse, were modelled in receding planes. The picturesque element must have been even greater when the original landscaping and outbuildings, which included a lodge and stable, were intact, especially since the front was approached obliquely. Internally, the villa shows a varied and sophisticated use of rectangular and curving shapes and vaultings, and a two-storey octagonal tribune. The sequence of rooms from front to back originally culminated in a breath-taking view of islands and Lake Ontario. There is a feeling of confidence and triumph in Rockwood, appropriate in the boom town atmosphere of Kingston at this period.

The physical and spiritual qualities of the villa are found on a grander scale in the town hall and market building, a commission which Browne won against 11 competitors in 1842. The structure, perhaps the largest of its kind in North America at the time, was to contain two great halls, one a meeting-place to be used as well for grand entertainments and the other a merchants' exchange; a library and reading-room for the mechanics' institute; a large market to the rear; and a host of other facilities, including auction rooms and a restaurant. It was a veritable community centre, possibly unique on the continent at that date. It was originally intended to cost £10,000 but the final bill was over £25,000. As designed, the exterior of the building suitably expressed its varied functions yet was coherent and majestic, a fitting symbol of the town's pride as capital of the united Canadas. Despite two fires and additions, the city hall (recently renovated and partly restored) remains one of the finest pieces of 19th-century architecture in Canada.

Other structures in Kingston which, on stylistic grounds, appear to be by Browne are: the Stuart mausoleum and the Forsythe monument in St Paul's churchyard; a former country house, known as Ashton (826 Princess Street); two parts of what may have been originally designed as a three-sectioned residential and commercial complex (165–67 Princess); and the Hales cottages (311–17 King Street West). Drawings suggest that Browne designed the Tuscan-pilastered block at William and King, built as a Bank of Montreal and now the Frontenac apartments. Browne also built three round-cornered commercial buildings, the Mowat Building (now destroyed), Wilson's Buildings, and Commercial Mart. All are Tuscan and "primitive" in style, and the last two have the massive scale seen in the city hall and all Browne's later Kingston work. This interest in the Tuscan style was taken up by later architects who worked in Kingston, for example William HAY.

In the spring of 1844, when the capital was moved to Montreal, Browne moved too, to superintend new quarters for the legislature and executive. His work included the fitting up of St Ann's Market as a parliament building (destroyed in the riots of 1849) and additions to the vice-regal mansion, Monklands.

In his later years Browne executed a large number of commissions. He worked for the government at least into the 1850s, hence at times in Quebec City. He remodelled Spencer Wood, the governor general's residence, and also made alterations to the Parliament Buildings. Neither of these stands, but his Chalmers Church of 1852–53 remains on Rue Sainte-Ursule, a sober affair which suggests that Browne's heart was not with the Gothic Revival. Some of his most splendid late Montreal buildings have been destroyed: Wellington Terrace (1855–56) which filled the south side of Sainte-Catherine Street between McGill College Avenue and Mansfield Street, and the Prince of Wales Terrace of 1861 which stood on Sherbrooke Street until 1972. As David Hanna has recently pointed out, Browne was not only the architect of these buildings but also their first owner. In other words he was following a pattern set by earlier British speculative builder-architects such as Thomas Cubitt or the Adam brothers. One very grand building by Browne does survive in Montreal, Molsons Bank (now the Bank of Montreal) at Rue Saint-Jacques and Rue Saint-Pierre (built 1864–66), a superb essay in the Second Empire style in contrast to Browne's earlier neo-classicism. Yet the architect retains his own sense of ponderous mass combined with urban scale, as well as the ability to think of a building "in the round," rather than as an assemblage of façades.

Any final assessment of Browne must await a detailed study of him and his contemporaries, among whom he will probably rank high. But it seems likely that the buildings of his Kingston period, especially the city hall, will be regarded as his greatest achievements. As a young man, only 29 when he arrived in Kingston, he created buildings that were intensely personal in nature yet responsive to peculiar local circumstances, and at the same time "national" in symbolism and ambition. He was also aided by a splendid medium, the austere, grey Kingston limestone, which responded perfectly to his large ideas.

Browne seems to have given more time to other activities in his later years. In 1854 he was unanimously elected to represent the Central Ward of Montreal, and in 1857 he was appointed a commissioner of the peace. He was apparently also in the real estate business.

When he died in 1885 Browne was buried in the Mount Royal Cemetery beneath a splendid neo-baroque monument which he had designed for his first wife, Anna Maria Jameson (d. 1859) of Dublin. The monument also commemorates four children who died in infancy, his eldest son, Thomas Richardson, and his second wife, Helen Kissock. Also buried in this plot are his youngest son, George, a prominent architect in Winnipeg, and John James, another son, who became a well-known Montreal architect. John James's son, Fitzjames, continued the family tradition and became an architect and real estate dealer in Montreal.

J. DOUGLAS STEWART

ANQ-Q, Cartothèque, Plans by Browne for government buildings (mfm. at Qué., Ministère des travaux publics, Planothèque). ASQ, Fonds Viger-Verreau, Sér. O, 0165–0171 (mfm. at PAC). Bibliothèque de la ville de Montréal, Salle Gagnon, Fonds Jacques Viger, "Souvenirs canadiens." PAC, National Map Coll., Kingston, 1841, Alwington House plans; Kingston, 1842, Town Hall and Market plans. *Chronicle & Gazette*, 17 Feb. 1841. *Quebec Mercury*, 2 June 1831, 15 Dec. 1832, 13 Oct. 1835. Borthwick, *Hist. and biog. gazetteer*, 259; *Montreal*, 50. *The Canadian album: men of Canada; or, success by example . . .*, ed. William Cochrane and J. C. Hopkins (5v., Brantford, Ont., 1891–96), III: 222. *Inventaire des marchés de construction des Archives civiles de Québec, 1800–1870*, G.-G. Bastien *et al.*, compil. (3v., Ottawa, 1975). A. J. H. Richardson, "Guide to the architecturally and historically most significant buildings in the old city of Quebec with a biographical dictionary of architects and builders and illustrations," Assoc. for Preservation Technology, *Bull.* (Ottawa), 2 (1970), nos.3–4.

Margaret Angus, *The old stones of Kingston: its buildings before 1867* ([Toronto], 1966). André Bernier, *Le Vieux-Sillery* ([Québec], 1977). *City of Kingston, Ontario: buildings of historic and architectural significance* (2v., [Kingston, Ont.], 1971–73), I: 3–9, 40–43, 70–73, 88–90, 100–4; II: 5–8, 136–38. Peter Fraser, "George Browne: architect" (unpublished paper, Queen's Univ., Kingston, 1966). D. B. Hanna, "'The new town of Montreal': creation of an upper middle class suburb on the slope of Mount Royal in the mid-nineteenth century" (MA thesis, Univ. of Toronto, 1977). Marion MacRae and Anthony Adamson, *The ancestral roof: domestic architecture of Upper Canada* (Toronto and Vancouver, 1963). Nick and Helma Mika, *Kingston City Hall* (Belleville, Ont., [1974]). Luc Noppen *et al.*, *Québec:*

trois siècles d'architecture ([Montréal], 1979). J. D. Stewart, "Architecture for a boom town: the primitive and the neo-baroque in George Browne's Kingston buildings," *To preserve & defend: essays on Kingston in the nineteenth century*, ed. Gerald Tulchinsky (Montreal and London, 1976), 37–61. J. D. Stewart and I. E. Wilson, *Heritage Kingston* (Kingston, 1973). Margaret Angus, "Architects and builders of early Kingston," *Historic Kingston*, no.11 (1963): 25–27; "John A. lived here," *Canada: an Hist. Magazine* (Toronto), 2 (1974–75), no.2: 8–21. *Journal of Canadian Art Hist.* (Montreal), 1 (1974), no.2: 43 (letter to the editor by Douglas Richardson). Luc Noppen, "L'utilisation des maquettes et modèles dans l'architecture du Québec," *Journal of Canadian Art Hist.*, 1 (1974), no.1: 8–9. J. D. and Mary Stewart, "John Solomon Cartwright: Upper Canadian gentleman and Regency 'man of taste,'" *Historic Kingston*, no.27 (1979): 61–77.

BRUNEL, ALFRED (his name appears on his death certificate as **Alfred Varnell Brunell**), engineer, militia officer, and public servant; b. in 1818 in England; d. 17 April 1887 at Tivetshall St Margaret, Norfolk, England.

In his capacity as a civil engineer, Alfred Brunel was first employed on various public works for the Province of Canada beginning in 1844. In 1851 and 1852 he conducted the surveys for the Victoria Bridge in Montreal with Thomas Coltrin Keefer*. He was then appointed assistant engineer for the Ontario, Simcoe and Huron Railroad Union Company (after 1858 the Northern Railway Company of Canada) and served as its superintendent from 1853 to 1856. Also during this period he was an active member of the Canadian Institute, serving as secretary 1852–53 and as a member of the council 1853–55. He served as an alderman for St George's Ward in Toronto, 1857–59 and 1861–62; for two years, 1859 and 1860, he also acted as city engineer.

Brunel began his second career when he took a leading part in organizing the 10th Battalion Volunteer Militia Rifles in Toronto formed on 14 March 1862, a contribution to the general mobilization which took place in the British American colonies in response to the strained relations between Britain and the United States after the *Trent* affair in 1861. He was gazetted major in 1862 and with the Fenian troubles brewing in 1865 he rose to the command of his regiment as lieutenant-colonel on active duty. He retained this rank after his resignation from active service in 1871.

Military duties did not interfere with Brunel's third career as a public servant. On 28 Oct. 1862 he had been appointed to a royal commission to inquire into the customs ports of the Province of Canada, with special reference to the free ports of Gaspé, Canada East, and Sault Ste Marie, Canada West. This experience led to his appointment as inspector of customs, excise, and canals in 1863. It was then a natural transition to his appointment, in 1867, as assistant commissioner of inland revenue in the new federal civil service. Four years later he was promoted commissioner, or permanent deputy head, a rank he retained until he was superannuated in December 1882.

The Department of Inland Revenue over which Brunel presided for more than a decade was not a large department, even by early standards, but it embraced a curious variety of tasks that required a far-flung, dispersed staff. Its officials collected a host of miscellaneous excise duties as well as sundry fees and charges from the users of public works, from the measurement of timber (the culler's office), and from the canal system. Early consumer protection services were also assigned to this department, including inspection of food and drugs, control over suppliers of gas, and testing of the weights and measures used in retail trade. It was a special burden of responsibility on Brunel and his small headquarters staff to ensure the integrity of such a dispersed staff, many of whom were constantly on the move. The detailed statistical tabulations which made up the bulky annual reports of this department suggest that Brunel's training as an engineer served him in good stead during the period in which he had to control and coordinate these varied operations.

As the highest ranking civil servant in his department Brunel testified in 1877 before a select committee of the commons investigating the relationship between the political heads of departments and the permanent deputy heads. He informed the committee that he had been "treated well by both political parties" and stated: "It is a matter of perfect indifference to me which is in power." Not surprisingly, he was one of the public servants chosen as a member of a royal commission, established in 1880, to undertake a thorough review of the civil service. Moreover, his *ex officio* position on the civil service examining board as well as the board of audit placed him among that small number of senior permanent officials who played such a notable, but on the whole unnoticed, role in preparing the new civil service of the dominion to face the more demanding tasks waiting in the wings of the 20th century.

J. E. HODGETTS

Can., House of Commons, *App. to the journals*, 1877, app.7; Parl., *Sessional papers*, 1867–82 (annual reports of the Dept. of Inland Revenue); *Sessional papers*, 1880–81, X: no.113. *CPC*, 1877–81. *The Colonial Office list* . . . (London), 1876, 1882. *Dominion annual register*, 1880–83. *Political appointments and judicial bench* (N.-O. Coté). Hodgetts, *Pioneer public service*. *The Royal Canadian Institute, centennial volume, 1849–1949*, ed. W. S. Wallace (Toronto, 1949).

BRUSH, GEORGE, shipbuilder and industrialist; b. 6 Jan. 1793 at Vergennes, Vt, son of Elkanah Brush and Alathea Frink; m. Eliza Maria Seymour of

Vergennes, and they had nine children, six of whom survived him; d. 21 March 1883 at Montreal, Que.

After a common school education in Vergennes and six years of employment in a country store, George Brush became one of the earliest steamboat entrepreneurs on Lake Champlain; in 1815 he commanded the *Champlain*, the second steamboat built on the lake. Two years later Brush moved to Montreal where he became a captain and engineer on steamboats operated by the Torrance family [*see* David Torrance*]. Although Brush may have continued to command steamboats until 1834, he became increasingly involved in their construction. In 1823 he supervised the building of the *Hercules*, which under his command was the first tow-boat to bring ocean-going vessels through the difficult Sainte-Marie current near Montreal. Other important steamboats on the St Lawrence, the *British America*, the *St. George*, and the *Canada*, were also built for the Torrances under Brush's watchful eye. In 1834 he was hired by the Ottawa and Rideau Forwarding Company, of which Peter McGill [McCutcheon*] was one of the principal owners, to manage their operations in Kingston, Upper Canada.

While supervising the construction of steamboats at various towns along the St Lawrence, Brush probably came in contact with the Ward brothers, John D.*, Lebbeus B., and Samuel, also originally from Vergennes, who built steamboat engines at the Eagle Foundry in Griffintown (now part of Montreal). By 1838 Brush was back in Montreal as a one-third partner with the Wards in the Eagle Foundry. In that same year the firm constructed an engine for the *Sydenham*: commissioned by the Royal Navy through Hugh ALLAN's company, this ship proved to be the fastest steamboat in the fleet. Within seven years Brush was sole proprietor of the firm, having purchased the remaining Ward interest.

From shipbuilder, captain, and engineer, Brush successfully made the transition to owner-manager of a substantial business in the very competitive engine-building industry [*see* Augustin Cantin*]. Joined in 1852 by his eldest son, George S., Brush expanded and diversified his business to meet the competition of the new foundries attracted to the banks of the Lachine Canal where cheap hydraulic power was available. Brush and his son manufactured "steam engines, steam boilers, hoisting engines, steam pumps, circular saw mills, bark mills, shingle mills, ore crushers, mill gearing, shafting, hangers and pullies, hand and power hoists for warehouses," and numerous other products. Although the Eagle Foundry remained relatively small, it was evaluated at between £10,000 and £25,000 in 1866. By the early 1880s it employed a modest-sized work-force of 60 to 100 skilled workmen and made products, worth approximately £70,000 to £100,000 annually, which were sold across the country.

Brush was a member of the American Presbyterian Church in Montreal. A "man of immense energy," "great determination of spirit," and "of the most scrupulous honour," he was successful in the city's business community although he seems to have restricted his entrepreneurial activities to his own firm, not diversifying his interests as did most Montreal industrialists.

GERALD J. J. TULCHINSKY

AC, Montréal, État civil, Presbytériens, American Presbyterian Church (Montréal), 23 March 1883. *Montreal in 1856; a sketch prepared for the celebration of the opening of the Grand Trunk Railway of Canada* (Montreal, 1856), 47. *Montreal Daily Star*, 22 March 1883. Borthwick, *Hist. and biog. gazetteer*, 314. *Canadian biog. dict.*, II: 99–100. *Dominion annual register*, 1883: 302. Terrill, *Chronology of Montreal*. James Croil, *Steam navigation and its relation to the commerce of Canada and the United States* (Toronto and Montreal, 1898; repr. Toronto, 1973), 310–11. Tulchinsky, *River barons*, 213–18.

BRYDGES, CHARLES JOHN, railway official, civil servant, and HBC land commissioner; b. February 1827 in London, England; m. in 1849 Letitia Grace Henderson, and they had two sons and one daughter; d. 16 Feb. 1889 in Winnipeg, Man.

The names of Charles John Brydges' parents are unknown, but during his successful middle years he claimed a connection with the barony of Chandos, then much in dispute. His father died before he was two and his mother five years later. With no siblings or close relatives, he entered boarding-school for nine years – dependent for his future upon only a small legacy, driving ambition, and an extraordinary capacity for work.

In 1843 Brydges was appointed a junior clerk in the London and South-Western Railway Company. During his ten years there he served a varied apprenticeship that helped to prepare him for his managerial career in Canada. Although not a trained scientist or engineer, he admired such contemporary British railway experts as Isambard Kingdom Brunel of the Great Western Railway; he was also attracted to schemes for the self-improvement and financial welfare of railway employees. As honorary secretary of the railway's literary and scientific institution he provided leadership to an employees' library, donated a collection of mechanical drawings, gave lectures for adult improvement, and supported a children's school. Already appreciating personal connections, Brydges initiated a "friendly society" to benefit the railway's workmen, and, knowing the need for financial prudence, he pressed on the company and its employees the urgency of contributory superannuation provisions. In 1852 he published these and other views in a pamphlet, *Railway superannuation: an examination of the scheme of the General Railway Association for providing superannuation allowances to worn out and disabled railway employés.* Brydges continually demonstrated his concern for employees' welfare and self-respect; he often clashed with his managerial peers, but throughout his career he won respect and affection from the rank and file.

Brydges' years with the London and South-Western culminated in his appointment as assistant secretary. He was not content, however, to await indefinitely the final promotion possible from within company ranks. In 1852 he was offered the post of managing director of the Great Western Rail Road Company of Canada. Notwithstanding a hasty offer of the secretaryship and efforts by the directors to obtain his release after he had accepted the overseas post, Brydges was off to Canada. Although only 26, he was determined to strike out afresh, putting his apprenticeship to the test in a promising managerial challenge.

Brydges' new appointment illustrated the problems inherent in the development of huge ventures by colonial promoters who were heavily dependent upon external capital. With favourable provincial legislation and local supporters such as Sir Allan Napier MacNab*, as well as Peter* and Isaac BUCHANAN, earlier schemes for a southwest rail network in Canada West had finally been parlayed into the Great Western. The project depended upon private British investors for more than 90 per cent of its capitalization, however, and the Canadian board was shadowed by a London corresponding committee. Brydges was the committee's appointee; this factor, combined with his youth, compromised his position. Yet, with characteristic energy and confidence, he soon played skilfully to both sides of the house.

Three characteristics marked Brydges' performance at the Great Western. First, he operated comprehensively rather than concentrating on a few issues. He began by improving administrative efficiency and by reducing slipshod contracting and accounting; even legal matters received his careful attention. For two years he had only a single departmental superintendent (in traffic), responsibility for all other departments and their coordination falling directly upon himself. At the time of his arrival in Canada early in 1853, however, his most immediate challenge was construction.

Against the advice of his chief engineer, John T. Clarke, he rushed the poorly built line to technical completion as a running line within the year. He thus placated his Canadian board, stole a march on other Canadian railway projects in the region (notably the Grand Trunk), and could impress potential American through lines with the Great Western's value as a Canadian "short cut" to the Midwest. The legacy of his precipitate action would be severe maintenance and financial problems, as well as an alarming accident rate. On balance, however, this calculated gamble was probably warranted if the line was to be recognized as a major operation with important American connections.

Brydges' drive for consolidation was the second characteristic that shaped the development of the railway. Technically, this led to varied, sometimes doubtful projects such as the railway deck on the Niagara Gorge bridge, expensive car-ferry and ice-breaker facilities on the Detroit River, and the fruitless acquisition of steamers for the run from Hamilton, Canada West, to Oswego, N.Y. Territorial acquisition in the southwestern traffic area was, in contrast, vital. His British committee assumed that absorption of small lines, such as the London and Port Sarnia, must be unprofitable. However, Brydges, like the Canadians, recognized their tactical importance in forestalling Grand Trunk and American competition. Playing a dangerous game, with his loyalties divided between British and Canadian interests, he advised Peter Buchanan, the road's sole agent in London, against "the sending out of two directors from England to sit at our Board." His position on the board gave him great leverage over the inexperienced Canadian promoters and his distance from London was opportune. With sharp traffic increases and enthusiastic support from affected communities, Brydges' confidence soon carried him too far.

Evidence of his headstrong ways was provided by his grandly optimistic prediction of profits. Brydges was still dangerously unfamiliar with road-bed and rolling-stock deterioration in Canada, and this inexperience supplemented the board's indifference to heavy indebtedness. Consequently, their joint decision to repay government advances was unwise, politically unnecessary, and alarming to expectant British shareholders. Brydges' attempt to lease the Buffalo and Lake Huron as well as to purchase the bankrupt Detroit and Milwaukee, combined with the financial panic of 1857, precipitated the establishment of an internal stockholders' committee in Britain, headed by H. H. Cannan, to inquire into the line's management.

The investigation focused upon Brydges' third quality, his authoritarianism. Even Peter Buchanan had earlier remarked upon his wilfulness: "Brydges requires a master over him and that party ought to be President with a couple of thousand a year *and nothing else* to do." Although this view was held by many on both sides of the Atlantic by 1858, it was not entirely fair because Brydges' authoritarianism was exacerbated by the weakness of his executive and the available personnel. Attempts had been made from 1854 by London to outflank him by creating more senior administrative posts. Divisions between the board and the corresponding committee together with inexperience and petulance among the English appointees only confirmed his indispensability. By attempting to lay all the faults of the line at his feet, the Cannan committee created a backlash in his favour. Brydges and the directors received a firm vote of confidence from the stockholders on 11 April 1861.

Accordingly, he turned with renewed confidence to an earlier project of "fusion" with the less aggressive Grand Trunk Railway. Anticipating this merger, in December 1861 he became the Grand Trunk's superintendent while remaining managing director of the Great Western. Amalgamation might appeal to his wavering Canadian directors but it was still unacceptable to London, and to the Canadian legislature it smacked of unbridled monopoly (the lines did finally amalgamate in 1884). Rebuffed, still under suspicion in London for his apostasy, and resented by many Canadian colleagues for his wilfulness, Brydges reviewed his position. The directors of the Great Western had never recognized the Detroit and Milwaukee venture as a stage in the line's progress to the west. The Grand Trunk was a company of grander scope and, as he had learned after the severing of MacNab's connection with the Great Western, one with firmer political support. If politics and vision were necessary ingredients of successful Canadian railroading, he would move with the winners. Late in 1862, he resigned his post with the Great Western to become general manager of the Grand Trunk.

Brydges might have had to struggle with an undiminished and hopeless legacy of errors in Grand Trunk construction, maintenance, and operation. Fortunately, his predecessor as manager, soon to be president, was Edward William Watkin*. Most of Brydges' years with the Grand Trunk were spent in Watkin's shadow, but because Watkin was his sort of comprehensive, consolidating manager Brydges was satisfied to be his hard-driving lieutenant. Rooting out inefficiency, seeking technical improvements, expanding capacity, and importuning government for larger postal and military subsidies, they made a strong team. Brydges also assisted by beginning a long career as a Tory counsellor, patronage agent, and self-appointed adviser to John A. Macdonald*. He courted Montreal business leaders; he engaged prominently, and with conviction and dedication, in civic affairs, especially poor relief and hospitals, and in Anglican causes. On the job he built up the employees' morale and loyalty by supporting reading-rooms, education for workers, and improved benefits. As a lieutenant-colonel, with his popular older son as aide-de-camp, he organized the Grand Trunk Railway Regiment, on 27 April 1866, to meet the Fenian threat [*see* John O'Neill*]. The move further aroused the men's loyalty – and recommended the railway to the government for its responsibility. Brydges also aided Watkin's campaign for trunk expansion by helping to arrange the series of exchanges between Canadian and seaboard leaders which allowed the regional representatives to become acquainted with one another and assisted in preparing the way for confederation.

When Watkin was forced out in 1869, by circumstances and pressures not unlike those Brydges had experienced at the Great Western, the best days were over. The new president, Richard Potter, was never to show the same confidence in Brydges, nor could he as ably turn away shareholders' criticisms. By 1872 Potter's faith was shaken by two developments: his belief that if Brydges had not obtained kickbacks on rentals of rolling-stock he had at least set these rentals at exorbitant rates; and the realization that Brydges still could not delegate authority and was responsible for alarming administrative lapses by over-extending himself. Potter, like the Great Western committee, tried to force new senior colleagues on him, and Brydges' resentment grew throughout 1873 and 1874.

Meantime, since 1868 he had represented Ontario and Quebec on the supervisory Board of Railway Commissioners, a federal body, with provincial representatives, which was established to superintend the construction of the Intercolonial Railway. Having gained unusual power because of the other commissioners' inexperience, as he had on the Great Western board, he was preparing for a new career as government adviser on railway matters. His clashes with the Intercolonial's presiding engineer, Sandford Fleming*, gave him increasing prominence and authority. His resignation from the Grand Trunk in March 1874 was therefore not a desperate decision.

Brydges' break was further softened by two developments. First, he received severance pay of 4,000 guineas and a $10,000 bond from Quebec friends and especially from Grand Trunk employees. Secondly, in 1874, when the Board of Railway Commissioners was removed and the Intercolonial was placed under the direct control of the federal Department of Public Works, the new Liberal prime minister, Alexander Mackenzie*, chose Brydges to oversee the remaining construction of the road and appointed him general superintendent of government railways. Unswervingly honest, Mackenzie, by appointing a confidant of Macdonald and an allegedly dishonest manipulator, raised doubts about the charges against Brydges. Mackenzie's obsessive moral concern should have prevailed even over his anxiety to get an experienced railway assistant. Although Brydges chafed at Mackenzie's caution and piecemeal approach to the proposed Pacific railway, they worked together effectively for four years.

Simultaneously, however, Brydges alienated Maritimers of both parties. Following Mackenzie's instructions he reduced the Intercolonial staff and costs by 25 per cent and appointed capable men of whatever party. Liberal patronage agents were outraged but Conservatives were also affected by Brydges' attacks (Tory workers dismissed from the railway, Sandford Fleming, and especially Charles Tupper*, who was accused of receiving kickbacks connected with the Intercolonial). Maritimers were briefly united in demanding Brydges' dismissal. In 1878, with Macdonald's return to power and Tupper as minister of public works, only the timing of Brydges' firing was at issue. It came in January 1879.

In that year, through his managerial reputation and continuing connections within the Tory party, Brydges began a new career in the Hudson's Bay Company. Nominally land commissioner of the HBC, he was secretly authorized by the governor, the deputy governor (Sir John ROSE), and the board of the company to follow the principle of consolidation in a new context. He should progressively take over all company operations, including land, furs, supplies, and stores, thus supplanting Donald Alexander Smith* and others and creating what was in effect a more varied and comprehensive chief commissionership. Ironically, Brydges' company years coincided with Smith's rise as liaison officer between Ottawa, the HBC, and the Canadian Pacific Railway, climaxed by Smith becoming the HBC's largest shareholder and governor. As Brydges' most exacting assignment, his connection with the HBC produced strains which would precipitate his death but it also held its triumphs.

His arrival in Winnipeg in May 1879 was like that of a great administrative juggernaut. Extensive surveys began in prospect of a "Manitoba fever"; new administrative, legal, accounting, and advertising machinery emerged; contracts for supplies to Indians and the North-West Mounted Police became competitive; new hotel and milling facilities enhanced the value of HBC lands; a subsidiary bridge company for the Red and Assiniboine rivers at Winnipeg was formed; the retail stores were reorganized under new men, not those only "accustomed to the barter system with the Indians"; supervision of barge and steam transport of goods and passengers was wrenched from the hands of "incompetents"; and, finally, executive operations were permanently moved from Montreal to Winnipeg in November 1880. Within a year the HBC was recognized as the most reliable source for information on settlement and commerce in Manitoba and the North-West Territories.

Brydges held that the HBC should erase the image of the old fur-trading company which was speculative and passive in its social and regional concerns – intent on incremental profits from the industry of others. It should instead identify with the northwest, even at the risk of offending vested political and economic interests. This boldness would eventually prove his undoing.

Brydges himself assumed a leading role in the rapidly expanding town of Winnipeg. As in Montreal he was prominent in civic activities: energetic chairman of the general hospital, president of the board of trade and of the Manitoba Board of Agriculture, an outstanding diocesan figure, and a determined advocate of retrenchment in municipal proliferation and taxation throughout Manitoba. Although a supporter of the property owners' association, he acted independently of the "Citizen's Ticket" urban reform movement – perhaps because it was dominated by CPR figures. He was determined to make the HBC a part of the growing regional consciousness in Manitoba and the west.

His forthrightness exasperated many people and he could not escape charges of partisanship. He was a major investor in Alexander Tilloch Galt*'s North-Western Coal and Navigation Company, formed to develop coal deposits on the Belly and Bow rivers (Alta), and this involvement alarmed the CPR, particularly in view of the old Grand Trunk connections of Galt and Brydges. Advocating Winnipeg over Selkirk for the CPR crossing of the Red River earned him the gratitude of Bishop Alexandre-Antonin Taché* and the Winnipeg business interests, but further alienated Sandford Fleming and the CPR hierarchy, and eroded Brydges' good relations with Ottawa. Although pressured to establish policies for the promotion of immigration as well as for the development and sale of land jointly with the CPR, he demurred, for he foresaw inherent complications and competition. He felt that the HBC should remain free to criticize the CPR's monopolistic rates and branch lines policies, thereby lining up with western interests. Inevitably, these tactics alarmed CPR supporters such as George Stephen*, Donald Smith, and perhaps even Sir John A. Macdonald. This was Brydges' dilemma. Even Smith's rising power in the HBC did not deter Brydges from joining the Winnipeg Board of Trade and the Manitoba Board of Agriculture in condemning the CPR's branch lines monopoly. The suspicions of the railway and the government were exacerbated by unfounded rumours that he was helping the Grand Trunk undermine the CPR's bond sales prospects by feeding information critical of the CPR to agents of the Grand Trunk who used it on the money markets in New York and London.

To retaliate, in 1882 Smith forced a review by the HBC of Brydges' land administration, and the investigating committee included his old rival, Sandford Fleming. Brydges was mildly reproved for laxity when the committee discovered extensive speculation by several of his associates but he was himself cleared and granted a generous purse for his competence and forbearance. Nevertheless, Smith won the last round. For more than two years, beginning in May 1884, Brydges was saddled with a supervisory "Canadian Sub-Committee," consisting of Smith and Fleming, which was largely ineffectual and which only hamstrung him in meeting the severe challenges of the Manitoba "bust" following the massive speculation connected with the arrival of the CPR.

Brydges' success in recovering company land and maintaining payments between 1882 and 1889 was perhaps his finest managerial achievement. By carefully pressing for payments when economic conditions improved and relaxing demands during hard times he countered the effects of the crash, and retained many original settlers on company lands. The HBC would realize nearly $900,000 in collections and recoveries of unpaid early instalments, while retaining its reputation for efficiency and fair dealing. Brydges obviously expected warm commendation for his efforts. Instead, he soon faced Smith's most effective attack yet.

Although Brydges had sharply criticized the CPR, he had always preferred the Canadian syndicate to American railway incursions into Manitoba. By 1888, however, he so sympathized with Manitoba's battles with Ottawa over disallowance of provincial branch lines [*see* John NORQUAY] that his headstrong actions plunged him into a new crisis. Miscalculating Smith's strength on the HBC board, he pushed the directors to grant an American line, the Northern Pacific Railroad, access to company land in Winnipeg to provide competition for the CPR and improve HBC property in the centre of the city. Rebuffed by the board, Brydges entered a period of great defensiveness and agitation, which precipitated his sudden collapse and death from a heart attack on 16 Feb. 1889. He died on Saturday afternoon when, characteristically, as founding chairman he was making his weekly inspection of the Winnipeg General Hospital.

Brydges was never as significant in Canadian public life as he liked to assume. However, his association with large enterprises and his aggressive, usually efficient ways brought him considerable prominence. His early managerial positions in central Canadian railways had provoked much controversy and his career as a watchdog over government railways had made him the object of bitter partisanship. During his years in the west his deserved reputation for enterprise continued and his attempts to deal fairly with the settlers and to align the interest of his employers more closely with local needs enhanced that reputation. On balance, he had discharged his duties forthrightly and responsibly. Representing a middle level of public and private entrepreneurship in Canada, Brydges was too abrasive to be totally effective, yet strong enough to gain respect from a later generation, removed from the particular forms of intolerance and suspicion through which he had lived.

ALAN WILSON and R. A. HOTCHKISS

Charles John Brydges was the author of *Grand Trunk Railway of Canada; letter from Mr. Brydges in regard to trade between Canada and the lower provinces* (Montreal, 1866); *Great Western Railway of Canada; Mr. Brydges' reply to the pamphlet published by Mr. H. B. Willson* (Hamilton, [Ont.], 1860); *Hudson's Bay Company (Land Department): report . . .* (London, 1882); *Mr. Potter's letter on Canadian railways, reviewed, in an official communication addressed to the Hon. Alexander Mackenzie, premier of the dominion* (Ottawa, 1875); and *Railway superannuation: an examination of the scheme of the General Railway Association for providing superannuation allowances to worn out and disabled railway employés* (London, 1852). His letters as land commissioner, in PAM, HBCA, A.12/18–26, have been published in *The letters of Charles John Brydges, 1879–1882, Hudson's Bay Company land commissioner*, ed. Hartwell Bowsfield with an intro. by Alan Wilson (Winnipeg, 1977).

AO, MU 1143; MU 2664–776. N.B. Museum, Tilley family papers. PAC, MG 24, D16; D79; MG 26, A; B; F; MG 29, B1; B6; RG 30. Sandford Fleming, *The Intercolonial: a historical sketch of the inception, location, construction and completion of the line of railway uniting the inland and Atlantic provinces of the dominion . . .* (Montreal and London, 1876). Notman and Taylor, *Portraits of British Americans*, I. P. A. Baskerville, "The boardroom and beyond; aspects of the Upper Canadian community" (PHD thesis, Queen's Univ., Kingston, Ont., 1973). Currie, *Grand Trunk Railway*. Douglas McCalla, "Peter Buchanan, London agent for the Great Western Railway of Canada," *Canadian business history; selected studies, 1497–1971*, ed. D. S. Macmillan (Toronto, 1972), 197–216. G. R. Stevens, *Canadian National Railways* (2v., Toronto and Vancouver, 1960–62), I. Alan Wilson, "Fleming and Tupper: the fall of the Siamese twins, 1880," *Character and circumstance: essays in honour of Donald Grant Creighton*, ed. J. S. Moir (Toronto, 1970), 99–127; "'In a business way': C. J. Brydges and the Hudson's Bay Company, 1879–89," *The west and the nation: essays in honour of W. L. Morton*, ed. Carl Berger and Ramsay Cook (Toronto, 1976), 114–39.

BRYDONE-JACK, WILLIAM. *See* JACK

BUCHANAN, ISAAC, merchant, politician, and pamphleteer; b. 21 July 1810 at Glasgow, Scotland, fourth son of Peter and Margaret Buchanan; m. in January 1843 Agnes Jarvie at Glasgow, and they had 11 children; d. 1 Oct. 1883 at Hamilton, Ont.

Isaac Buchanan's father was a successful manufacturer who later became a merchant in Glasgow. During the Napoleonic wars Peter acquired Auchmar, an historic 1,378-acre estate in Buchanan parish, Stirlingshire, possession of which entitled him to add "of Auchmar" to his name. He was an elder of the Church of Scotland, and his Glasgow home was often visited by leading lay and clerical figures in the evangelical wing of the Kirk. The family valued education, and Isaac, after attending the Glasgow Grammar School, began preparing for university and a profession. Then, instead, in October 1825, he began an apprenticeship with the Glasgow firm of William Guild and Company, West Indian merchants. Buchanan always said this decision was entirely his own, and entirely impromptu; his father, however, had recently lost heavily in the depressed Caribbean trade, and the set-back to the family's fortunes may well have prompted the change in plans.

William Guild had branches in Jamaica and Honduras, but he decided that Montreal might be a better place to launch his own son, William Jr, in business. In March 1830 he and his son formed William Guild Jr and Company of Montreal, dry goods importers; Buchanan, whose energy and enthusiasm had greatly impressed the elder Guild, was made junior partner, to receive one-quarter of the profits. Buchanan left home for the first time early in April, travelling to Montreal via Liverpool and New York. To compete with established firms, the new business sought out merchants arriving in Montreal for the first time, most of them from Upper Canada. Because these merchants lacked capital, sales to them could be made only on 12 months' credit. This use of credit alarmed the elder Guild, who feared his capital would be locked up in Canada; accordingly, Buchanan suggested that the firm be relocated farther from their competition and closer to their customers in order to try to secure cash business. In December 1831 Buchanan moved to York (Toronto) and in 1832 opened William Guild Jr and Company, possibly the first and certainly the largest exclusively wholesale firm in the town. But again sales could be made only on a long-term credit basis.

Despite periods of loneliness and depression, Buchanan was confident of Upper Canada's future. He speculated in land, bought some steamboat shares, and then, with his only surviving brother, Peter*, agreed to buy the Guilds' share in the York business. In 1834, using their two-thirds share of their parents' estate, about £12,000 sterling (much of it realized from the sale of the Auchmar estate in 1830), the brothers opened Peter Buchanan and Company in Glasgow, to handle finances and purchases, and Isaac Buchanan and Company in Toronto, to manage sales and credit. The two brothers jointly owned each company. An important ally was Robert William Harris*, dry goods manager of the Guild firm in Toronto, who in 1835 became a partner in Isaac Buchanan and Company.

Isaac Buchanan quickly became a figure of some note in Toronto. He helped found in 1835 the city's board of trade, of which he was president from 1835 to 1837, the St Andrew's Society in 1836, of which he was also president, and the Toronto Club, the city's first men's club; and he was chairman of the trustees of the Presbyterian St Andrew's Church. He found himself resented by the city's Tory oligarchy, which he in turn regarded as extremely provincial. He was particularly aggrieved by the inferior position of his church, the Church of Scotland, in Upper Canada, and in 1835 published a newspaper extra to demand that it be given a share of the revenues from the clergy reserves. Like most of his later pamphlets and open letters, this was important more as a symptom of local problems than as a contribution to their solution; Buchanan seldom had strikingly original ideas to present, and his strident rhetoric did little to persuade the unconvinced.

On the outbreak of rebellion in Upper Canada in early December 1837, Buchanan accepted a commission in the local militia and served in Toronto and then on the Niagara frontier. He saw his chief problem as being the troops he commanded, all Irishmen, "incarnate devils," but, he pledged, "if I do get to close Quarters with these infernal Rebels and Yankees I am prepared to sell my Life as dearly as I can." In February 1838, back in Toronto, he published a warning that "the selfish principles of the high church party" would soon provoke another rebellion unless changes were made to provide equal distribution of funds from the clergy reserves. That month, however, he left for Britain, to place the 1838 orders for Isaac Buchanan and Company and to take charge of the Glasgow office for 18 months; meanwhile Peter came to Upper Canada.

In 1839, inspired by high profits for 1838 at Toronto and by low prices in Britain, Isaac Buchanan decided to increase Peter Buchanan and Company's shipments vastly, borrowing heavily to finance this venture from their Glasgow bank and a number of mercantile firms in Glasgow and in England. To sell these goods, Peter Buchanan and Harris had to expand the firm's clientele rapidly. But now the business, with its heavy accounts outstanding in the western part of Upper Canada, could, Isaac Buchanan feared, be outflanked by a strong firm based in Hamilton, and rumour had it that several Montreal firms were planning such branches. To anticipate them he went to Hamilton in the spring of 1840, rented a very large warehouse nearing completion, and with John Young*, Hamilton's leading merchant, founded a new business known as Buchanan, Harris and Company. To help attract customers to so small a centre a grocery department was opened and to buy its supplies an office was needed in Montreal. Using the firm's western connection, the man hired to manage this Montreal office, James Law, soon built it into a highly successful operation, known from 1845 as Isaac Buchanan and Company (the Toronto firm of this name having ceased to exist); it had a warehouse on the Lachine Canal and to its substantial grocery trade were added iron, hardware, and grain. Buchanan's decisions to expand were taken largely without consulting his brother, but backed by rapid Upper Canadian expansion and his partners' business abilities, they succeeded handsomely. By the end of 1843, Peter and Isaac's original capital had increased fivefold. But Isaac found little pleasure in business routines, which offered an unsatisfactory outlet for his "superabundant vitality."

In 1841, under the auspices of a new governor

general, Lord Sydenham [Thomson*], Upper and Lower Canada were united in one province. Although when he was in Glasgow Buchanan had protested the appointment of Thomson because of the governor's links to the Baltic trade, he soon agreed entirely with him on the union and the clergy reserves, and on the importance of pursuing policies for economic development that would transcend older colonial issues. Hence Buchanan readily accepted nomination in the governor's interest in the election of 1841 to represent Toronto, citadel of the compact Tories, and he contributed £1,000 to help his cause. In a bitter campaign, which Buchanan's speeches did nothing to calm, Buchanan and John Henry Dunn* won a narrow victory, receiving strong support from many Toronto merchants.

At the first session of the post-union assembly, Buchanan claimed to "have been very *instrumental* in all thats going on." Most notably, he helped to block Sydenham's proposed provincial bank of issue, which would, he feared, shrink the money supply in Canada West and, by destroying many businesses (though not his own), reduce commerce there to total dependence on Montreal merchants. But it was not his nature to seek or to understand compromises and alliances, and he found the role of private member ultimately uncongenial. Thus he returned to Glasgow while his brother again came to Canada; after missing the 1842 session, he resigned his seat early in 1843, convinced that his basic aims, the union and "responsible government," had now been safely achieved.

Buchanan was not an original or a leading theoretician on constitutional matters, and his opinions here were typical of many moderates. In essence he thought the term "responsible government" implied that the oligarchical rule of the 1820s and 1830s had ended and that a majority in the Legislative Assembly would now dictate the complexion of the government. But the term need not imply the full application of the principles of cabinet government as Robert Baldwin* understood them. Specifically Buchanan considered that the governor had a central responsibility to work to preserve the British connection and to prevent the spread of American ideas in Canada; the governor was entitled to act independently to fulfil this responsibility. To Buchanan and many like him, such as William Henry Draper*, Baldwin was a dangerously doctrinaire extremist who, while personally above reproach, was surrounded by potentially subversive influences; Baldwin's ideas were seen as leading inevitably to a breaking of the imperial tie.

While in Glasgow, Buchanan courted and married Agnes Jarvie, the daughter of a Glasgow merchant, who was half his age. Throughout their life together she was a vital and loyal support to him. In mid 1843 they returned to Canada, planning that Isaac would earn enough for them to retire eventually to Scotland. In keeping with this more conservative objective, he agreed to his brother's plan to close the Toronto store at the end of 1844 and to consolidate the Upper Canadian business at Hamilton, the more successful branch; another department, hardware, was now added. Thus, Buchanan, Harris and Company became full-fledged general wholesale merchants, with the intention of monopolizing the trade of those customers whom they chose to support with credit.

Despite his resignation as MLA, Buchanan never really left politics; while in Britain, for example, he advocated legislation along the lines of the Canada Corn Act of 1843, for the passage of which he always claimed some credit. Back in Toronto, he strongly criticized the Reform ministers, led by Louis-Hippolyte La Fontaine* and Baldwin, for resigning from the Executive Council in late 1843. Their actions, he said, were too narrowly partisan and indeed, because more than a few of their followers were republicans, threatened the British connection. Principally in the columns of Hugh Scobie*'s Toronto newspaper, the *British Colonist*, he engaged in an increasingly acrimonious correspondence with several Reform leaders, including James Hervey PRICE, James LESSLIE, and Francis HINCKS; it was published in February 1844 under the title *First series of five letters, against the Baldwin faction*. During the election of 1844 he campaigned widely in Canada West in support of Governor Sir Charles Theophilus Metcalfe*.

Buchanan was in Glasgow as the disruption of the Church of Scotland built up in the early 1840s, and, following events closely, he unhesitatingly took the evangelical side. On his return to Canada West, he became "one of the key lay figures" in the establishment of the Free Church of Scotland. He was chairman of its Sustentation Fund board; neutralized Scobie's newspaper, the voice of moderate Presbyterianism, by using subsidies; and contributed a total of at least £650 to the foundation of churches bearing Knox's name in Toronto, Hamilton, and eight to ten other locations in Canada West. Within the Free Kirk, he took a moderate stand, opposing both clerical control of church property or the press and complete congregational control (which he regarded as an American principle), and he advocated that the Free Kirk obtain a fair share when funds from the clergy reserves were distributed.

Late in 1844, the Buchanans and their newborn son, Peter, moved to Hamilton. At once Isaac took steps to found the Hamilton Board of Trade and in April 1845 he was elected its first president. Yet by summer he was once more on the move, journeying to New York in response to the first Drawback Law of the United States, which remitted duties on foreign goods being re-exported to Canada. There in August he opened an office, similar in purpose to the earlier Montreal one, to buy and sell on the firm's behalf in the New York market.

Buchanan was still in New York when repeal of the Corn Laws was announced early in 1846; immediately he took ship for England, to lobby and to write widely to newspapers and politicians both there and in Canada. Repeal, he predicted, would, in a "fiery ordeal," lead to Canada's annexation to the United States. His partners, his brother especially, doubted the acuteness of the danger and the wisdom of his alarmist talk, and there is no evidence that his views were heeded. Nevertheless, determined to continue his crusade, he quit the business in 1848, sold his Hamilton house, and returned to Scotland where he lived first in Edinburgh and then in Greenock. A pamphlet, which appeared in 1850 as an extra edition of the *Greenock Advertiser*, is representative of his views. Entitled *Moral consequences of Sir R. Peel's unprincipled and fatal course*, it argued that free trade would not only cost Britain her colonies but also, without monetary reform, sharply increase imports over exports, thereby drastically increasing unemployment in Britain. The same year, with the issue of free trade in mind, Buchanan organized an essay contest for working men on "their own interests," offering prizes totalling £200 for the best essays.

Britain's prosperity in the 1850s belied Buchanan's predictions, while in Canada West the business he had left also prospered remarkably. His crusading activities having been costly, Isaac decided in 1850 to return to business, probably in Liverpool. Peter, doubting his ability to succeed alone, persuaded him instead to rejoin the old business at Hamilton. Discussion of Isaac's return set in motion major changes in the business, beginning in 1851 with the opening of a new branch at Liverpool, known as Buchanan, Harris and Company, and another at London, Canada West, in partnership with Adam HOPE, and known as Adam Hope and Company. With his wife and five children, Buchanan moved back to Hamilton in late 1851. His readmission to the partnership, however, led to arguments that culminated at the end of 1853 in the establishment by Young and Law of a separate business, competing directly with that of the Buchanans and Harris. To defend their position, the Buchanans further expanded their trade as the Upper Canadian boom of the mid 1850s rushed to its peak. By the end of 1856, their firms' total assets, principally outstanding accounts in Canada West, exceeded $3,000,000; liabilities were just over half this figure. Isaac Buchanan's share of the firm's capital, though much smaller than his brother's or Harris', exceeded $200,000; he was rich, and his business was among Canada's largest.

Signalling his intention to live permanently in Hamilton, Buchanan built between 1852 and 1854 a large and attractive house, called "Auchmar," on an 86-acre estate and farm that he named "Clairmont Park," situated on the mountain outside the city. He sought to improve the local schools (though his sons received much of their schooling at a private academy in Galt and his older daughters were sent to Edinburgh for their later education) and he was a leader in the "Hamilton Educational Movement," which in 1855 secured a charter for a college in the city; lack of funds prevented further progress on the project. He also gave the land and £25 for the new MacNab Street Presbyterian Church. Indeed, although he made enemies by a somewhat high-handed manner, his generosity was legendary, and few local causes can have gone entirely unpatronized by him.

To Buchanan, his most important cause was Hamilton's Great Western Railway. He was a director of it in 1853–54 and, for longer periods, of some of its subsidiary lines. But his real power in the Great Western was informal, the result of his relationship with his brother and with Harris who were more central figures in the company. In 1854 it became plain that the member for Hamilton, Sir Allan Napier MacNab*, was abandoning the Great Western for its rival, the Grand Trunk. Ignoring a written pledge to his brother to eschew active politics, Buchanan ran for election. His aim, he said, was only to compel MacNab to change his views on the railway and on the clergy reserves, which Buchanan now felt should be secularized because it was impossible to divide the funds equitably among the churches. MacNab, easily evading these issues, won re-election convincingly.

In 1856 Buchanan sought to persuade the Great Western to take control of the "Southern route," the most direct route between Michigan and Buffalo, N.Y. Charters for the Amherstburg and St Thomas Railway and the Woodstock and Lake Erie Railway and Harbour Company had been granted by parliament in 1855 and 1847 respectively and together they covered this route. The former charter had not been acted upon by its promoters and the latter project was stalled for lack of funds, but in the summer of 1856 Buchanan learned that Samuel Zimmerman*, the great contractor, was moving to take full control of both charters. He was convinced that Zimmerman, with Grand Trunk backing, would build the line, and capture the valuable American through trade, thereby destroying the Great Western and with it Hamilton's commercial independence. With John Smyth Radcliff, vice-president of the Great Western, Buchanan set out to battle Zimmerman, ignoring the unfavourable state of capital markets, the resistance of shareholders in the Great Western to new expenditure, and the opposition of Charles John BRYDGES, the powerful managing director of the Great Western, and also without consulting Peter Buchanan and Harris, who were in England. First, without immediate expenditure, Buchanan secured control of one of two competing boards of the Amherstburg and St Thomas. He then paid £25,000 to one or more of the directors of the Woodstock and Lake Erie to induce them to resign from its board in favour of his nominees and gave a bond to that company's bank, guaranteeing to pay its debts. Radcliff issued drafts to reimburse Buchanan, but these the Great Western's board in London, England, refused to accept. Attempting, unsuccessfully, as it turned out, to have the board reverse this decision, Buchanan rushed to England. There he also faced his brother and Harris, who were appalled that he had committed himself to pay more than $1,000,000; in order to protect their credit they demanded his resignation from the business. Nominally no longer a partner, Isaac remained active in the business, when time permitted, because Harris was too ill to manage at Hamilton alone.

Two committees of the provincial assembly explored aspects of the tangled Southern railway issue in 1857. To both, Buchanan told his story candidly, for he had, he said, acted from the highest of motives, and had not sought personal profit. Remarkably, although he was sharply criticized for bribery, Buchanan's reputation for honesty, affluence, and even business competence apparently survived almost unscathed. Nevertheless his experience before these committees convinced him that he needed to be in the assembly to protect his Southern interests. Stressing the need to build the Southern line under the auspices of Hamilton businessmen and politicians, he again ran for Hamilton in 1857, and, aided by the usual large outlay of funds, won handily. Once in the assembly he helped to secure passage in 1858 and revision in 1859 of the charter for a company called the Niagara and Detroit Rivers Railway Company. This consolidated the Amherstburg and St Thomas and the Woodstock and Lake Erie railways, and its provisions defined the legal relationships in such a way that Buchanan was cleared from further liabilities. Ultimately, Buchanan's 1856 venture into the Southern cost him over $200,000, but the wounds to his honour and self-esteem haunted him more in the years to come, and in an effort to vindicate his judgement and to secure some return from his outlay he later sank still more money into the Southern project when William Alexander Thomson* took it up. Yet he really had little to do with the ultimate creation of the Canada Southern Railway, which was finally built after 1870. The episode is revealing of Buchanan's overestimation of his power and his lack of perspective on the feverish railway politics of the 1850s.

In 1857 the great boom of the 1850s ended in a sharp crash. In response, Buchanan early in 1858 led in the formation of the Association for the Promotion of Canadian Industry, an organization of manufacturers and merchants in Canada West who pressed for tariff protection. Tariffs did rise in 1858 and 1859, but despite Buchanan's later claim to have been the father of Canada's protective tariff, the government's need for revenue, not this association, was probably the major cause of the decision to raise them; nor are the links between this increase and the later National Policy tariff strong enough to support his claim.

The collapse of 1857 left the city of Hamilton effectively bankrupt as a result of its heavy borrowing for railways and waterworks. With others from the city, Buchanan sought to negotiate a refinancing with the creditors (most of them in Britain) and then to see it through the assembly. In 1864 he at last secured passage of a law that reorganized the city's debts and allowed it to resume payments. Throughout this period Buchanan continued to patronize Hamilton organizations. Closest to his heart were the Hamilton Board of Trade, for which, as its current president, he secured a charter of incorporation in 1864, and the 13th (Hamilton) Battalion of Infantry (later the Royal Hamilton Light Infantry), of which he was founder in 1862 and lieutenant-colonel for about two years.

Buchanan's career in the legislature was genuinely independent: no party, he said, was sufficiently patriotic. Yet his intense opposition to "political economy" pushed him towards the Conservatives, and for three months in the spring of 1864 he became president of the council in the short-lived government of Sir Étienne-Paschal Taché* and John A. Macdonald*. Buchanan is, however, remembered more for his economic writings in these years, notably *The relations of the industry of Canada, with the mother country and the United States* (1864), edited by Henry James Morgan* whose *Sketches of celebrated Canadians* Buchanan had recently subsidized. Like most of his works, *Relations* was largely compiled from his speeches, previously published letters, and extracts from favourite authorities such as Henry Charles Carey, an American economist, and John Barnard Byles, a British jurist. Still regretting the victory of Manchester-style liberalism in Britain, he spared no opportunity to criticize those in Canada, particularly George Brown*, who held similar views. In arguments that were distinguished more for repetition and forceful language than for political insight, analytic rigour, thoroughness, or subtlety, he dwelt on the need for reform of the tariff and the currency.

A protective tariff, he argued, would limit imports of goods that could be manufactured locally, put the many unemployed to work, encourage immigration, and keep in circulation in the province money that would otherwise have flowed abroad. Unlike Canadian protectionists of later periods, he strongly advocated a Canadian-American *zollverein*, that would extend reciprocity to manufactured goods and erect a common Canadian-American tariff against outside goods. Revealing his continuing concern with imperial issues, he argued that a *zollverein* would help to decentralize the manufactures of the empire, for both British working poor and British capitalists and their capital would then come to Canada to secure full access to the American market. The increased urban population in Canada which would have to be fed would free agriculture in Canada West from dependence on a single crop and hence from soil exhaustion. Thus, protection was in the interest of all producers, including the farmer and the working man; convinced that the latter would agree, he had long advocated universal manhood suffrage. Representation by population in the union parliament he opposed, however, because the present tariff was being sustained with the help of votes from Canada East.

On the currency question, Buchanan called for the issue of irredeemable paper currency, "*emblematic* money instead of money *containing in itself intrinsic value*. . . ." This would free Canada from the "*sudden expansions and contractions*" that foreign trade and purely monetary factors induced. "Our error lies in this, that the circulation is based upon and in proportion to GOLD, the rich man's property, instead of upon LABOUR, the poor man's property – that this basis is therefore a thing that can be sent away instead of a thing that cannot be sent out of the country. . . ." In this case, he said, the desired object could be achieved simply by eliminating the "*vicious interference of* [monetary] *legislation, militating against the laws of nature*."

Buchanan's ideas derived from wider bodies of protectionist and currency thought. Though in some ways internally inconsistent, as his opponents often noted, they were informed, finally, by a conservative outlook on society, and he was better at criticizing than at proposing convincing alternatives. Although it is doubtful if his writings were widely read or attracted many consistent supporters, they do have a place in the limited literature of social criticism in mid-Victorian Canada.

Buchanan's publishing and politics cost him much time and money (indeed his expenditures from 1860 to 1864 averaged the enormous sum of $25,000 annually) and the Buchanan enterprises, which he had formally rejoined in 1858, had also been severely struck by the crash of 1857. Only months before his death in 1860, Peter Buchanan had drastically reorganized their business to enable it to recover from its problems if given careful management. But, although he was aware of the situation, Isaac gave little time to his business, and his decisions, when he could be brought to make them, were often harmful to it. Thus the main Hamilton and Glasgow business, despite large annual sales, ran increasingly deeper into debt. Only a narrow escape from failure in 1864 induced Buchanan to resign from the assembly on 17 Jan. 1865 and to turn all his energy to saving the business. Most important, he persuaded the very capable Adam Hope to move to Hamilton in 1865, but it was now too late. In the fall of 1867, Buchanan, Hope and Company and Peter Buchanan and Company failed.

By offering his creditors more than did his two erstwhile partners, Hope and Robert Wemyss (the Glasgow manager since Peter's death), Buchanan secured control of the business estate. Although he reopened an importing business in 1868 at Hamilton, under the name Buchanan and Company, the firm dealt only in dry goods because Buchanan now lacked the capital to do a general business. He did not reduce expenditures sufficiently for the smaller scale of his business, and Hamilton had become less and less an ideal location for a dry goods importer. In 1871 he could not pay the last two instalments due to his old creditors. Endeavouring to protect a position in the business for one son, he transferred control of the Hamilton firm to John I. Mackenzie in 1872. Two years later he was ousted from the Montreal firm by the other partners there, Robert Leckie and F. B. Matthews, as they sought, ultimately unsuccessfully, to avoid bankruptcy themselves. The New York and Glasgow offices expired for lack of business. A variety of highly speculative ventures failed to yield profits, and businesses into which Buchanan put his four older sons, who had received modest bequests from their uncle, likewise lost money.

By 1876 Buchanan had sold the mountain estate, given such assets as remained to him to his creditors, and was living in rented quarters in Hamilton. Though he still wrote and held some honorific local positions, he was now entirely dependent for income on a testimonial organized by friends at his urging. He applied to the Liberal government of Alexander Mackenzie* for a postmastership, but, not surprisingly, was refused. The creditors, some of whom were aggrieved by Buchanan's recurrent promises since 1860 that his financial situation would soon improve, would not give him his final discharge from his second bankruptcy until 1878. Early in 1879 the Macdonald government appointed him an official arbitrator for disputed property expropriations in connection with public works, and this appointment enabled him to live his last years in modest but once more secure circumstances. Although the careers of his three oldest boys did not prove successful, his fourth son, James, after an early bankruptcy in Hamilton in the 1870s, went on to earn a fortune in Pennsylvania. In 1900 he bought back the old family home in Hamilton, and some of his sisters lived there for almost 30 years thereafter.

Isaac Buchanan is remembered chiefly for his writings and his role as a grandee in Hamilton, but also for his careers in politics, railways, the church, and early Toronto business. He was a leader within Upper Canada's Scottish community particularly before 1846, and though the focus of his concerns shifted thereafter, his values and activities continued to reflect his links to Scotland and to indicate the importance of the Scots in Upper Canadian life. Yet he was probably most important as a businessman, for here he had his greatest success and earned the wealth that underlay his other roles. Although his very range of activities made him scarcely a "typical" entrepreneur, his confidence in the future of Upper Canada, his willingness to take risks, and the success he gained thereby exemplify the intertwined processes of Scottish expansion overseas and Upper Canadian business development in the provincial economy's formative years. If in the end his business failed, that too was far from an unusual outcome.

DOUGLAS MCCALLA

Isaac Buchanan was the author of the following works: . . . *Britain the country, versus Britain the empire: our monetary distresses – their legislative cause and cure* (Hamilton, [Ont.], 1860); *Can the British monarchy be preserved?* (n.p., 1848); *First series of five letters, against the Baldwin faction, by an advocate of responsible government, and of the new college bill* (Toronto, 1844); *A government speciepaying bank of issue and other subversive legislation, proposed by the finance minister of Canada* (Hamilton, 1866); *Letters illustrative of the present position of politics in Canada, written on the occasion of the political convention, which met at Toronto, on 9th Nov., 1859* (Hamilton, 1859); *Moral consequences of Sir R. Peel's unprincipled and fatal course, disquiet, overturn and revolution* (Greenock, Scot., 1850); *The patriotic party versus the cosmopolite party; or, in other words, reciprocal free trade, versus irreciprocal free trade* (Toronto, 1848); *The real state of things in Canada; explained in a few rough sketches on financial and other vital matters in both the Canadas . . .* (Toronto, 1837); *The relations of the industry of Canada, with the mother country and the United States . . .*, ed. H. J. Morgan (Montreal, 1864); *A thoroughly British legislature wanted, or, in other words, legislation combining patriotism and popularity . . .* (Greenock, 1850). Among the extra issues of newspapers he published was one of the *Albion of U.C.* (Toronto) in 1835.

AO, MU 1876, file 3854. HPL, M. H. Farmer, "Calendar of the Buchanan papers, 1697–1896 . . ." (typescript, 1962); Hamilton biog., Buchanans (newspaper clippings). PAC, MG 24, D16; RG 30, 1, 2, 11, 326, 327, 329, 361. Scottish Record Office (Edinburgh), Court of Session, Unextracted process, CS 249/493; Office of Court, Concluded sequestration process, CS 318/12, 1869, no.56. *The Arthur papers; being the Canadian papers mainly confidential, private, and demi-official of Sir George Arthur, K.C.H., last lieutenant-governor of Upper Canada, in the manuscript collection of the Toronto Public Libraries*, ed. C. R. Sanderson (3v., Toronto, 1957–59), III. Can., Prov. of, Legislative Assembly, *Journals*, 1841, 1857–64; *Statutes*, 1864, c.71, c.72. "Parl. debates" (CLA mfm. project of parl. debates, 1846–74), 1858–64. W. J. Rattray, *The Scot in British North America* (4v., Toronto, 1880–84), II: 541–43. [Hugh Scobie], "Letters of 1844 and 1846 from Scobie to Ryerson," ed. C. B. Sissons, *CHR*, 29 (1948): 393–411. *British Colonist* (Toronto), 1838–44. *Canadian Merchants' Magazine and Commercial Rev.* (Toronto), 1857–59. *Dominion annual register*, 1883: 302–4. *Hamilton directory* (Hamilton), 1853–80. Morgan, *Sketches of celebrated Canadians*, 553–81. *Notes on the members of the Buchanan Society, nos. 1–366 (1725–1829)*, comp. R. M. Buchanan (Glasgow, 1931), nos.84, 89, 96, 102, 123, 131. Notman and Taylor, *Portraits of British Americans*, I: 381–400. T. M. Bailey, *Traces, places and faces: links between Canada and Scotland* ([Hamilton], 1957). P. A. Baskerville, "The boardroom and beyond; aspects of the Upper Canadian railroad community" (PHD thesis, Queen's Univ., Kingston, Ont., 1973). H. J. Bridgman, "Isaac Buchanan and religion, 1810–1883" (MA thesis, Queen's Univ., 1969). M. F. Campbell, *A mountain and a city: the story of Hamilton* (Toronto, 1966). Careless, *Brown*, I: 33–40, 59–60, 259. Dent, *Last forty years*, I: 105, 125, 138, 307, 362; II: 295, 365, 392–93, 435, 443. C. D. W. Goodwin, *Canadian economic thought: the political economy of a developing nation, 1814–1914* (Durham, N.C., and London, 1961), 49–51, 82–83. C. M. Johnston, *The head of the lake: a history of Wentworth Country* (Hamilton, 1958). M. B. Katz, *The people of Hamilton, Canada West: family and class in a mid-nineteenth century city* (Cambridge, Mass., and London, 1975), 190–95. Douglas McCalla, "The Buchanan businesses, 1834–1872: a study in the organization and development of Canadian trade" (DPHIL thesis, Univ. of Oxford, 1972); "Peter Buchanan, London agent for the Great Western Railway of Canada," *Canadian business history; selected studies, 1497–1971*, ed. D. S. Macmillan (Toronto, 1972), 197–216; *The Upper Canada trade, 1834–1872: a study of the Buchanans' business* (Toronto, 1979). Marion MacRae and Anthony Adamson, *The ancestral roof: domestic architecture of Upper Canada* (Toronto and Vancouver, 1963), 179–81. Walter Neutel, "From 'southern' concept to Canada Southern Railway, 1835–1873" (MA thesis, Univ. of Western Ontario, London, 1968). J. D. Barnett, "An election without politics – 1857 – I. Buchanan," *OH*, 14 (1916): 153–62. Douglas McCalla, "The Canadian grain trade in the 1840's: the Buchanans' case," CHA *Hist. Papers*, 1974: 95–114; "The decline of Hamilton as a wholesale center," *OH*, 65 (1973): 247–54.

BUCK, WALTER M., civil engineer and railway contractor; b. in December 1826 in Dublin (Republic of Ireland); he married and had eight children; d. 15 May 1881 in Fredericton, N.B.

Walter M. Buck received his training as a civil engineer in Ireland. Around 1855 he immigrated to St Andrews, N.B., and worked as an engineer for the Department of Public Works for a few months in 1856. He was then hired as chief engineer of the New Brunswick and Canada Railway and Land Company, which was to build a line from St Andrews northwest through Charlotte and York counties to Debec, Carleton County, near the Maine border. Buck's duties were to survey the proposed route, estimate the cost of construction, and supervise the contractors engaged to do the work. The railway, the second in New Brunswick, was completed in 1862. In 1866 the company finished construction of a branch line running from the main line at Watt, Charlotte County, to St Stephen and in 1868 another branch from Debec to Woodstock in Carleton County. Buck apparently supervised the laying of the branch lines and as chief engineer also involved himself in the railway's operation.

In 1867 Buck joined the controversy over the route the Intercolonial Railway was to take through New Brunswick to link Halifax with the Grand Trunk Railway at Rivière-du-Loup, Que. He rejected proposed routes through central New Brunswick or along the Baie des Chaleurs in favour of a "Frontier Route" which would run from Rivière-du-Loup along the Maine border to Woodstock, N.B., and then along the existing New Brunswick and Canada Railway to its intersection with the proposed Western Extension Railway from Bangor, Maine, to Saint John, N.B. From Saint John connection would be made by steamer across the Bay of Fundy to Digby County, N.S., and from there to Halifax over lines then under construction. Although the "North Shore" route was eventually chosen for strategic reasons, Buck argued that "the most suitable position for a railroad is along the line of defence, and not at an inaccessible distance to the rear of it." He added that his "Frontier Route" was shorter, would cost $7,500,000 less to construct, and would serve not only prosperous western New Brunswick but growing Aroostook County in eastern Maine as well. His plan rejected, Buck in 1868 nevertheless joined the staff of the Intercolonial's location survey directed by Sandford Fleming*. The following year Buck was appointed resident engineer for a 20-mile section of the line in Northumberland County. The section he supervised was built over rough terrain, necessitating heavy earthworks, but only one small river, the Bartibog, had to be bridged. His section was completed in December 1874 and in July 1876 the entire Intercolonial was opened from Halifax to Rivière-du-Loup.

Following his work on the Intercolonial, Buck began a new involvement in railways by himself becoming a contractor. In 1874 he and a partner were awarded the construction contract for the 44-mile Albert Railway, which was to run from Salisbury on the Saint John–Moncton line along the shores of Shepody Bay to the town of Albert. The line, completed in 1877, prospered in its first years of operation because significant quantities of gypsum mined near Hillsborough were transported over it. In addition to these major engineering and construction functions, Buck also worked in the early to mid 1870s on preliminary surveys of the Chatham Branch Railway, completed in 1876 between Chatham and Passmore on the Intercolonial line, and the "Miramichi Railway," probably the Northern and Western Railway completed between Fredericton and Chatham only in 1887.

Buck, who had moved from St Andrews to Moncton, in 1878 joined the federal Department of Public Works, apparently as an engineer in the office of the chief engineer of government railways who in turn was subordinate to General Superintendent Charles John Brydges. In 1879 Buck became an employee in the newly organized Department of Railways and Canals. Much of his work appears to have involved the arbitration of claims that had arisen between contractors and the federal government during the construction of the Intercolonial in the early 1870s. While investigating one of these claims, Buck died suddenly in Fredericton in May 1881.

Christopher Andreae

W. M. Buck was the author of *The best route for the Intercolonial Railway through the provinces of Quebec and New Brunswick* (Saint John, N.B., 1867).

Can., Dept. of Railways and Canals, *Annual report* (Ottawa), 1879–81. Canadian National Railways, Hist. Research Branch (Montreal), "Synoptical history of organization, capital stock, funded debt and other general information as of December 31, 1960." *Daily Sun* (Saint John, N.B.), 17 May 1881. *Moncton Times*, 18 May 1881. *Statutory hist. of railways* (Dorman). G. R. Stevens, *Canadian National Railways* (2v., Toronto and Vancouver, 1960–62). M. L. Bladen, "Construction of railways in Canada to the year 1885," *Contributions to Canadian Economics* (Toronto), 5 (1932): 43–60.

BUCKLAND, GEORGE, agriculturalist, editor, and educator; b. 10 Dec. 1804 in England; d. 27 Feb. 1885 at Toronto, Ont. He and his wife Amelia had one son and three daughters.

George Buckland was a prominent English agriculturalist and a member of the Royal Agricultural Society of England when he toured parts of Canada and the United States in the early 1840s. In Toronto he became acquainted with William G. Edmundson*, editor of the *British American Cultivator*, and continued corresponding with him after his return to England. Buckland considered establishing a model farm and agricultural school near Toronto but decided the venture was too risky for one individual. In 1847, however, Robert Baldwin* and agriculturalist Adam Fergusson* persuaded Buckland to return to Canada on the understanding that he would be named professor of agriculture at King's College in Toronto; he finally received the appointment when the chair of agriculture was created in 1851, two years after King's College had become the University of Toronto.

In October 1847, shortly after his arrival, Buckland joined Edmundson as co-editor of the *British American Cultivator* and served as the editor of various agricultural journals until 1864. Buckland was a strong advocate of scientific agricultural methods including the cultivation of high-grade seeds, the importation of pure-bred livestock, and the use of improved agricultural implements. He succeeded Edmundson as secretary of the Board of Agriculture of Upper Canada when the latter left the province in 1849. The position dovetailed nicely with his work as co-editor, with William McDougall*, of the *Canadian Agriculturist*, begun in January 1849, which contained the transactions of the board and reported extensively on its activities and projects. Buckland spent much time, especially before 1852, giving lectures around the province, attending meetings of agricultural societies, and reporting on their activities. He also helped organize the annual provincial exhibition, begun in 1846.

After receiving his appointment at the university Buckland immediately set up a 25-acre experimental farm on the campus and planted 16 acres of wheat. He had seeds sent from England to help determine how to adapt English methods and products to Canadian climate, soil, and markets. In addition to lecturing on the science, history, and practice of agriculture, he directed the landscaping of the university grounds. Although the agricultural journals publicized the programme and the university provided five scholarships of £30 each, his classes were poorly attended. Only one or two students received diplomas in agricultural science, and in 1855 the classrooms were "almost tenantless." By 1860 the experiment was an acknowledged failure although Buckland probably held the chair of agriculture until his death when it was abolished. His critics laid the responsibility, in part at least, on his shoulders, accusing him of neglecting his duties at the university. From 1859 to 1865 he served as first dean of residence at University College.

Buckland had resigned in 1859 as secretary of the Board of Agriculture. Before doing so, he had arranged for Andrew Smith* to come from Scotland to be the veterinary surgeon for the board. Smith became the director of the Upper Canada Veterinary School (later the Ontario Veterinary College), established as a result of the efforts of Buckland and Adam Fergusson, and he gave the first lectures in Toronto in 1862. Buckland also lectured on the history, breeding, and management of animals.

He was also instrumental in the establishment of the Ontario Agricultural College for which William F. Clarke, editor of the second *Canada Farmer*, had procured 400 acres near Guelph in 1871. In spite of opposition because of the expense, notably from William Weld, editor of the *Farmer's Advocate and Home Magazine*, the college opened on 1 May 1874. Buckland gave his time freely to the college and, had it not been for the devotion which he and a few others showed, the institution might not have survived. Until January 1876 he lectured there, as often as three times a week, on the theory and practice of agriculture as well as the anatomy and physiology of farm animals.

Buckland suffered a heart attack in February 1885 on the way to his home at Upper Canada College after attending services at St Luke's (Anglican) Church with his son. He was taken to the central police station where he died. At the time of his death he was assistant commissioner of agriculture for Ontario.

Ann MacKenzie

PAC, RG 31, A1, 1861 census, Toronto, St Patrick's Ward. UTA, A-73-0026, Dept. of Graduate Records, George Buckland file. York County Surrogate Court (Toronto), no.5548, Will of George Buckland, 17 March 1885 (mfm. at AO). *Agriculturist & Canadian Journal* (Toronto), 1 (1848): 61–72. *British American Cultivator* (Toronto), 2 (1843): 129–44. *Canada Farmer* (Toronto), 1 (1847): 85–92. *Canada Farmer* (Toronto), 1 (1864): 1–16. *Canadian Agriculturist* (Toronto), 1 (1849): 1–28; 5 (1853): 65–96, 129–60, 321–52; 8 (1856): 261–88; 11 (1859): 241–64. *Farmer's Advocate and Home Magazine* (London, Ont.), 9 (May 1874); 20 (April 1885): 97. *Globe*, 2 March 1885. *Dominion annual register*, 1885. F. E. Gattinger, *A century of challenge: a history of the Ontario Veterinary College* (Toronto, 1962). R. L. Jones, *History of agriculture in Ontario, 1613–1880* (Toronto, 1946; repr. 1977). G. E. Reaman, *A history of agriculture in Ontario* (2v., Toronto, 1970). A. M. Ross, *The college on the hill: a history of the Ontario Agricultural College, 1874–1974* (Vancouver, 1974). *The University of Toronto and its colleges, 1827–1906*, [ed. W. J. Alexander] (Toronto, 1906). Wallace, *Hist. of the Univ. of Toronto*.

BURPEE, ISAAC, merchant, entrepreneur, and politician; b. 28 Nov. 1825 at Sheffield, Sunbury County, N.B., eldest child of Isaac Burpee and Phoebe Coban; m. in 1855 Henrietta Robertson, and they had eight children; d. 1 March 1885 in New York City.

Isaac Burpee, the descendant of pre-loyalist settlers from Massachusetts, was educated at the Sheffield Grammar School and in 1848 moved to Saint John, N.B. There, with his brother Frederick, he established a flourishing hardware business which by 1872 had become a "wholesale only" establishment selling not only small wares but also significant quantities of imported and domestic iron and steel. In the 1860s he purchased valuable property in Saint John and a home in the suburb of Portland (now part of Saint John), and by 1872 the assessed value of his personal and real estate in the city was $70,000.

As Burpee's fortune grew, he began investing in a variety of industrial enterprises based on his hardware company in Saint John. In partnership with Howard Douglas Troop [*see* Jacob Valentine Troop], he established in 1882 a steamship line between London, Halifax, and Saint John, but the endeavour failed when the sole boat operated by the partners was wrecked on its second voyage. In 1883 Burpee and some associates purchased the Coldbrook Rolling Mills north of Saint John to produce iron and steel forms, nails, and spikes. His other interests were in the Confederation Life Association, the New Brunswick Land and Lumber Company, the Red Granite

Company, which held property in Saint John and Charlotte counties, the Victoria Coal Mining Company, and the Saint John Cotton Company. Beginning in the early 1870s Burpee was heavily involved in the financing, construction, and operation of railways in the province. The Central Railway Company, with which his brother, Egerton Ryerson Burpee, and his uncle, Charles Burpee*, were also involved, was to link Fredericton with Saint John, but construction was not begun until 1887. The New Brunswick Railway Company was to link Fredericton with Edmundston, via Woodstock, and opened for service in 1878. Burpee felt that not only would his hardware company and rolling-mills supply materials for the railways' construction, but that the lines would run through lumber and coal-bearing lands he owned throughout the province. However, Burpee's attempt to create an extended economic empire was not particularly successful; by 1884 he had made valuable investments but was struggling to show an operating profit on his holdings. Perhaps the demands of his wide-ranging business activities, coupled with an active career in federal politics, were too great for his energies and financial resources.

Burpee had first entered political life when he led the movement to incorporate Portland and became the first chairman of the town council in 1871. The following year he was elected member of parliament for the City and County of Saint John with an overwhelming majority. Originally an independent who supported Sir John A. Macdonald*'s government, Burpee became convinced over the summer and fall of 1873 of the government's culpability in the Pacific Scandal and on 31 October joined the ranks of the Liberal opposition. A week later he was sworn in as minister of customs in Alexander Mackenzie*'s cabinet, after Protestant members of parliament for New Brunswick, including three of Burpee's relatives, had pressured Mackenzie into appointing him rather than the Irish Catholic, Timothy Warren Anglin*. As customs minister until 1878, Burpee appears to have been efficient, knowledgeable, and conscientious. Although he was easily re-elected in Saint John in 1874, 1878, and 1882, he was not a notably skilful politician; Mackenzie thought him "a model office man but not good for six sentences in the House and no parliamentary knowledge."

Burpee looked upon public service as an obligation to be fulfilled and concerned himself in politics mainly with business matters. His economic philosophy was typical of the 19th century *laissez-faire* school. He believed that individual enterprise and energy, not government legislation and protection, were the keys to personal and national progress. Like his colleagues in the Reform party in the 1870s, he accepted that depressions were natural, if unfortunate, and that the government's role was to pare expenditures, keep down the public debt, and maintain tariffs at the lowest possible levels. Burpee apparently had no doubts, therefore, about opposing the protectionist National Policy of the Macdonald Conservatives during and after the 1878 federal election. He argued that the protective tariff was unfair to consumers, especially the poor and labourers, that it aided the interests of Ontario and Quebec at the expense of the Maritime provinces, that it was antithetical to the British connection, and that it would promote urbanization at the expense of rural, agricultural interests. Perhaps most important, he felt the high tariff favoured not the majority of manufacturers but only a specific few such as sugar refiners and cotton and woollen manufacturers. Burpee's efforts to promote industrial activity in New Brunswick in the 1880s may well have been, therefore, a defensive and unwilling response to the protective tariff, and his lack of any great success in his own endeavours probably confirmed his negative opinion of the National Policy.

Although his being an important businessman undoubtedly aided Burpee's political career, it also presented problems. In November 1873 a cry was raised about the propriety of selecting a large importer as minister of customs, and as a result Burpee retired, at least pro forma, from his hardware firm. This was but one of several conflict of interest accusations levelled at him while he was minister. Even after the defeat of the Liberals in 1878, Burpee was accused by newspapers opposed to him in the 1882 election of attempting to manipulate import duties imposed by Washington on incoming lumber in such a way as to injure the sawmilling industry of Saint John and increase traffic on the New Brunswick Railway, of which he was vice-president. The significance of business affairs in Burpee's political career can also be seen in the fact that James Domville*, Conservative MP for Kings County from 1872 to 1882, was Burpee's most consistent political antagonist as well as a business competitor.

Besides his activities in business and politics, Burpee gave of his time and money to a number of charitable or social agencies, including the New Brunswick Deaf and Dumb Institute, the Saint John Industrial School, the Portland Free Public Library, the Saint Paul's Sunday School House, and the Marysville Methodist Church. He showed an interest in such community endeavours as the Saint John centennial celebrations in 1883 and the New Brunswick Historical Society, founded in 1874. He also held executive positions on the Congregational Union of New Brunswick and Nova Scotia and the Evangelical Alliance of New Brunswick during the 1870s.

The last two years of Burpee's life were unhappy. Aside from business problems, his second son was drowned in July 1883 and his younger brother was killed in a train accident the following year. These tragedies gave Burpee a feeling of impending doom. "The sad bereavements we have passed through," he wrote Edward Blake*, "has made me feel as if something harder would soon come again. I have been tending more to my private affairs in consequence, and almost feel afraid to leave my family." His sense of foreboding proved correct for, after putting his affairs in order, he died of either liver or heart disease in New York City in March 1885.

Though not a politician of major significance, Burpee was a notable example of the involved 19th-century Canadian entrepreneur. As a hard-working, efficient, and upstanding businessman, he had managed to accumulate an estate valued at his death at approximately $200,000.

WILLIAM M. BAKER

[There is no manuscript collection of Isaac Burpee papers, but useful information may be gleaned from N.B. Museum, Isaac Burpee, estate papers, 1887–1907; Scrapbooks C9, C58; and the Reverend Robert Wilson's scrapbook. *See also* PAC, MG 23, D1; MG 26, B; E; and PANB, York-Sunbury Hist. Soc. coll., Burpee family papers. AO, MU 136–273, contains letters from Burpee, and the records of the Registrar of Deeds (Saint John, N.B.) provide evidence of Burpee's land transactions. Useful unpublished materials include PANB, I. M. McQuinn, "Histories and origins of the railways of New Brunswick" (typescript), and "N.B. political biog." (J. C. and H. B. Graves), I: 59. W.M.B.].

Can., House of Commons, *Debates*, 1875–85. N.B., *Acts*, 1864–89. *Daily Sun* (Saint John, N.B.), 1882, March 1885. *Daily Telegraph* (Saint John, N.B.), 11 July 1883. *Globe*, 1873, 1875, 29 Sept. 1876, 1885. *New Dominion and True Humorist* (Saint John, N.B.), 1872–74. *Ottawa Daily Citizen*, 1873–74. *Ottawa Times*, 1873–74. *Saint John Globe*, 1867–73, 14 Dec. 1901. *Canadian directory of parl.* (J. K. Johnson). *CPC*, 1873; 1879. Dent, *Canadian portrait gallery*, IV: 25–26. *Encyclopedia Canadiana*, II: 143. Wallace, *Macmillan dict.* Michael Bliss, *A living profit: studies in the social history of Canadian business, 1883–1911* (Toronto, 1974). K. J. Donovan, "New Brunswick and the federal election of 1878" (MA thesis, Univ. of New Brunswick, Fredericton, 1973). Thomson, *Alexander Mackenzie.* Waite, *Canada, 1874–96.* T. W. Acheson, "The national policy and the industrialization of the Maritimes, 1880–1910," *Acadiensis*, 1 (1971–72), no.2: 3–28. C. M. Wallace, "Saint John, New Brunswick (1800–1900)," *Urban Hist. Rev.* (Ottawa), [4] (1975–76), no.1: 12–21.

BURTIS, WILLIAM RICHARD MULHAREN, lawyer, author, journalist, and temperance advocate; b. 1818 in Saint John, N.B.; d. 12 Dec. 1882 in York County, N.B.

William Richard Mulharen Burtis received his early education at the Saint John Grammar School, and in 1832 began studying law in the Saint John office of William Boyd Kinnear*. Admitted to the bar as attorney in 1839 and as barrister in 1841, Burtis gradually built up a large and successful legal practice in Saint John. He was appointed common clerk of Saint John in 1855, but resigned in 1863 because of ill health, and later acted as a valuator of land damages on the Intercolonial Railway until his retirement in 1878. His major contributions, however, were made in the fields of literature, journalism, and the New Brunswick temperance movement.

In 1837 Burtis was a principal organizer of the Young Men's Debating Society of Saint John, and in the same year he was awarded that society's gold medal for his essay on "The rise and progress of New Brunswick." At the society's request, Burtis' essay was printed in October 1837 in the sole issue of the *Literary and Historical Journal* (Saint John), intended by its editor, John Henry Crosskill*, to be a pioneer literary magazine in New Brunswick. Although relying heavily upon the recently published works of the early New Brunswick historians, Peter Fisher* and Robert Cooney*, Burtis' article also reveals the zeal of the amateur historian, for he rhapsodizes on the virtues and sufferings of New Brunswick's loyalist founders and revels in the province's subsequent material progress. Between 1841 and 1843 he contributed several works of folklore and historical fiction concerning the early settlement of New Brunswick to *Amaranth* (Saint John), the first significant literary magazine in the province.

During the early years of his legal practice in Saint John, Burtis played a major role in the New Brunswick temperance movement. In 1843 he became a principal organizer of the Saint John Young Men's Total Abstinence Society, and lectured frequently in support of the moral crusade to eradicate the evil of strong drink. When the New York–based Sons of Temperance spread into New Brunswick from Maine in 1847, Burtis became a member and in the summer of the same year was chosen patriarch of the Saint John–based Gurney Division of the organization. His major contribution to the temperance movement, however, was made as associate editor of Christopher Smiler's *Temperance Telegraph* (Saint John), which commenced publication on 25 Jan. 1844 and was devoted to the cause of total abstinence. When the *Telegraph* became the official organ of the Sons of Temperance in New Brunswick in early 1848, Burtis became its editor and from 1850 until its demise in April 1851 he shared editorial duties with the Reverend J. D. Casewell. The weekly's formidable influence under Burtis was indicated by the New Brunswick legislature's decision early in 1849 to propitiate it with a special grant of £50.

Burtis resumed his literary activities in 1860, entering a competition sponsored by the Saint John Mechanics' Institute for the best essay on "New Brunswick, as a home for emigrants." In a field of 18, Burtis' intensely patriotic and fervently anti-American entry was judged fifth, and, along with the four ranking above it, was published and distributed throughout the province and the United Kingdom on the orders of the New Brunswick government. Burtis' essay, whose purpose was to attract immigrants to New Brunswick and away from the United States, emphasized the cruel treatment the province's loyalist founders had suffered from their American compatriots, the extreme democracy of the republican system of government in contrast to the superior British constitutional system, and the social disorders said to be characteristic of American life. Encouraged by this partial literary success, Burtis contributed several articles during 1860 to the Saint John *Guardian*, a short-lived literary monthly dedicated to stimulating an indigenous New Brunswick literature. Perhaps the most significant of Burtis' contributions was "Grace Thornton, a tale of Acadia," published in 12 chapters. In 1867, in celebration of the advent of confederation, Burtis exercised his poetic talents in *The new dominion, a poem*, prophesying with patriotic grandiloquence the future affluence of New Brunswick and greatness of Canada under the British constitution, in sharp contradistinction to the United States, torn by civil war. Following confederation, Burtis withdrew from literary ventures to his law practice, but his enduring enthusiasm for New Brunswick's past found expression in the New Brunswick Historical Society, formed on 25 Nov. 1874. He became a charter member and the first secretary-treasurer of the society. Upon his retirement from the legal profession in 1878, he moved to his country residence on the north branch of the Oromocto River in York County, where he died four years later.

William R. M. Burtis' legal career, literary endeavours, amateur historical interests, and strong temperance advocacy reflected significantly much of New Brunswick's literary, intellectual, and social concerns and development during the mid 19th century.

MURRAY BARKLEY

W. R. M. Burtis was the author of "The rise and progress of New Brunswick . . ." published in October 1837 in the *Literary and Hist. Journal of New Brunswick and Nova Scotia* (Saint John, N.B.); *New Brunswick, as a home for emigrants: with the best means of promoting immigration, and developing the resources of the province* (Saint John, 1860); "Grace Thornton, a tale of Acadia," published in the *Guardian, a Monthly Magazine of Education and General Literature* (Saint John), 1860; and *The new dominion, a poem* (Saint John, 1867).

N.B. Museum, W. R. M. Burtis papers; Tilley family papers. G. E. Fenety, *Political notes and observations; or, a glance at the leading measures that have been introduced and discussed in the House of Assembly of New Brunswick*... (Fredericton, 1867). *Amaranth* (Saint John), 1841–43. *Daily Telegraph* (Saint John), 14 Dec. 1882. *New Brunswick Courier* (Saint John), 1837–51. *Temperance Telegraph* (Saint John), January 1844–April 1851. *Dominion annual register*, 1882. Harper, *Hist. directory*. W. G. MacFarlane, *New Brunswick bibliography: the books and writers of the province* (Saint John, 1895). Morgan, *Bibliotheca Canadensis*. J. K. Chapman, "The mid-nineteenth century temperance movement in New Brunswick and Maine," *CHR*, 35 (1954): 43–60.

BUTCHER, MARK, cabinet-maker; b. in 1814 at St James, Suffolk, England, son of William and Patience Butcher; m. first in 1836 Margaret Chappell, and they had six children; m. secondly in 1849 Catherine Hooper, and they had seven children; d. 2 June 1883 in Charlottetown, P.E.I.

Mark Butcher, a member of a family of cabinetmakers, immigrated with his parents to Prince Edward Island in 1829. In February 1835 he announced the opening of a workshop in Charlottetown to specialize in all types of woodworking and turning. The business grew steadily. His competent workmanship, the continual exhortation of the public by politicians and newspapers to encourage home manufacture, and the extraordinary economic prosperity of the period from 1855 to 1865, combined to make the Butcher factory a flourishing enterprise. It was patronized by all classes of society. Even shipbuilding families whose vessels sailed regularly to more fashionable centres bought furniture from Butcher's shop. An important part of the business was to provide furniture for public institutions such as government offices, Government House, the Central Academy, Prince of Wales College, and the Charlottetown Court House.

Every article of household furniture was executed at the Butcher factory, from drawing-room Grecian or French sofas to butlers' trays, bidets, and washing machines; significant quantities of church and school furniture were also produced. At least one carver specialized in figure-heads for ships. Imported woods such as rose, zebra, satin, mahogany, and black walnut were used extensively, as well as native birch, pine, and bird's-eye and curled maple.

By 1867, the year he switched from horse-drawn power to steam machinery to turn his lathes, Butcher was employing 40 men in his factory. In 1874 he sought 20 additional joiners and cabinet-makers. As well as maintaining a retail store in Charlottetown, he had branch stores in Cardigan and Georgetown and shipped his products to New Brunswick and Newfoundland. He exhibited with the Island contingent at the 1862 exhibition in London, England, but he also showed his furniture locally, usually winning first prize in competitions.

Butcher's early designs reflect the transition from Regency to Victorian styles. Labelled or stamped furniture remaining from the earlier period include a desk, reading chair, chest of drawers, Regency-style sofa, gentleman's dressing mirror, and some chairs inspired by Grecian prototypes. He then progressed into the mid-Victorian style. Again labelled pieces, exquisitely carved in a wide variety of designs, are extant. The carvers were familiar with English style-books and with English and American imports, but according to tradition they copied from examples produced by Butcher or his foreman which hung on the walls near their work-benches. One of Butcher's less expensive items, a simple chair, appears to have been a design unique to him. The crossbar in the centre back, carved from a single piece, is designed to look like three separate pieces.

Though furniture-making was Butcher's main vocation, he pursued other business interests as well. In his early years he operated a thriving livery stable. Like most cabinet-makers, he was an undertaker; as such, he advertised coffins and caskets in rosewood, mahogany, walnut, and imitation woods. In the 1860–70 period he was the architect of a market building in Charlottetown, a brick engine-house for a woollen mill, and at least one dwelling. In conjunction with Thomas Alley, he designed a powder-magazine and Prince Street Methodist Church. He also built railway cars for the Prince Edward Island Railway in 1873–74. Butcher took part in community affairs, serving as a member of the Charlottetown City Council from 1865 to 1869, as a member of the mechanics' institute, and from 1863 until his death as a trustee of the Methodist church.

Mark Butcher was Prince Edward Island's most proficient and prolific cabinet-maker in the second half of the 19th century, and he produced furniture which compared in quality with any manufactured in British North America. Following his death in 1883, the business was taken over by his nephew, Mark Wright, who continued it under his own name.

IRENE L. ROGERS

Charlottetown City Hall, City Council, Minutes, 1864–69. Trinity United Church (Charlottetown), Church records, 1863–83. P.E.I., House of Assembly, *Journal*, 1836, 1848, 1850, 1855, 1861–65. *Colonial Herald, and Prince Edward Island Advertiser* (Charlottetown), 2 Oct. 1841. *Examiner* (Charlottetown), 15 May 1865; 19 April, 8 July 1867; 17 May 1869; 3 Aug. 1874; 2 June 1877; 2 Jan. 1878; 12 July 1880; 18 March 1881; 10 March 1882. *Herald* (Charlottetown), 6 June 1883. *Island Argus* (Charlottetown), 11 Aug. 1874. *Islander*, 6 July 1849, 6 June 1853, 19 Feb. 1864, 15 Feb. 1867, 14 Feb. 1868, 15 Oct. 1870. *Patriot* (Charlottetown), 6 March, 6 May 1869; 9 July 1870; 24 July 1880. *Royal Gazette* (Charlottetown), 17 Feb. 1835; 12 Jan., 23 Feb. 1836; 7 March, 4 July 1837; 3 July 1838.

C

CADDY, JOHN HERBERT, soldier, engineer, teacher, and artist; b. 28 June 1801, in Quebec City, Lower Canada, son of Colonel John Thomas Caddy of the Royal Artillery and Hannah Godard (Goddard); d. 19 March 1883 at Hamilton, Ont.

John Herbert Caddy was born into a family of military engineers. His grandfather had been sent to Newfoundland in the 18th century to build a fort. In about 1796 his father left Kent, England, for a posting in Lower Canada and in 1808 was transferred to the garrison at Fort Malden, Amherstburg, Upper Canada. John Herbert began his schooling at Amherstburg and in 1815 he was sent to England for military training at the Royal Military Academy, Woolwich (now part of London). In March 1816 he was enlisted at the academy as a gentleman cadet in the Royal Artillery and received training as an engineer and cannoneer. Like George Heriot*, James Pattison Cockburn*, Philip John Bainbrigge, and other English military artists who painted Canadian scenes, Caddy was trained at Woolwich in topographical sketching and painting. Much of his free time was spent at the home of a family friend, Colonel Richard Hamilton, at Woolwich Common. Caddy was commissioned 2nd lieutenant on 29 July 1825 and promoted 1st lieutenant in 1827. In 1828 he married Colonel Hamilton's daughter Georgiana, shortly before he left for duty in Tobago.

He returned to England in 1831, but after two years left his family for his second West Indian posting, at St Lucia. In May 1834 he was transferred to St Vincent where he was joined later by his wife and family. Diary fragments describe the social rounds, the hunting, and the sketching which were possible with light military duties. Before he left for St Vincent Caddy had prepared for publication a series of four folios of scenes, largely of the West Indies. The pictures of the first folio were engraved in London and were published in 1837 by Ackermann; the other three folios never appeared.

Caddy returned with his family to Woolwich in July 1837. After a year of relaxation he was posted to British Honduras (Belize) in December 1838 where he served as harbour-master at the town of Belize, the capital. In November 1839 he and Patrick Walker, secretary to the settlement's superintendent, led a hastily organized official expedition to the ruins of the Mayan city of Palenque, not far inland from Belize. On his return Caddy prepared from his diary and sketches a text and illustrations for their official report to Westminster which he intended to publish as a book, but John Lloyd Stephens and Frederick

Catherwood, leaders of a rival American expedition to Palenque, managed to get out a popular account first. Caddy's Palenque diary, text, and illustrations, along with fragments of earlier diaries, were finally collected and published in 1967 by David Michael Pendergast.

Caddy returned to Woolwich in 1841 as a captain. He was appointed to Malta the next year, but exchanged that posting for one to London, Canada West. Two years later he was assigned another West Indian tour of duty, but, deciding to remain in London, he retired on half pay. His family of eight children was to include three born in Canada. As civil engineer for London, Caddy laid out plans for the growing community, and he acquired considerable land in the centre of the town. He also began to paint Canadian landscapes.

In 1851 Captain Caddy disposed of his land in London and moved to Hamilton where he lived for the next 32 years until his death. After a brief employment as a civil engineer on the Great Western Rail Road, he had turned to painting as his profession. He opened a studio, gave private lessons, and served as art instructor at Wesleyan Female College (later renamed Hamilton Ladies' College).

Caddy was a painstaking artist who worked slowly and carefully from pencil sketches made on the scene, through sepia drafts, to the finished picture. Apparently he sometimes completed several versions of the finished landscape but rarely, if ever, signed his work. He exhibited water-colours and oils in the annual provincial exhibitions from 1858 to 1868, winning awards for his meticulous landscapes, marines, and animal and flower studies. In London he had painted a portrait of Colonel Thomas Talbot*, but his strength was not in portraiture or in the figure. While in Canada he copied some scenes of Great Britain, Ireland, and the West Indies he had painted earlier. He did landscapes of scenes in and around Hamilton, Toronto, Brantford, Queenston, Niagara, and London, as well as farther afield, in the regions of Lake Huron, Georgian Bay, Muskoka, Lake Superior, the St Lawrence River, and New Brunswick. He also painted scenes of the Kawartha Lakes; his father and two younger brothers had taken up land in Douro Township in 1834 and were neighbours of the Stricklands, Traills, and Moodies. Caddy visited his family in Douro in 1841 where he likely met Samuel Strickland* but by that time the Traills and Moodies had moved. Other members of Caddy's family, including his brothers Edward C. and Douglas T. as well as one of his own sons, were also amateur or professional artists.

GORDON ROPER

The most complete list of the institutions holding works by J. H. Caddy appears in Harper, *Early painters and engravers*. Other works are held in private collections, in Dundurn Museum (Hamilton, Ont.), and by the Warnock-Hersey Company (Montreal). A typed draft of a dictation by H. G. Caddy and family letters are in the possession of Helen Caddy Roper (Peterborough, Ont.). For his expedition to Palenque see: *Palenque: the Walker-Caddy expedition to the ancient Maya city, 1839–1840*, ed. D. M. Pendergast (Norman, Okla., 1967).

Canadian Illustrated News (Hamilton), 24 Oct. 1863. *Hamilton Spectator*, 21 June 1883. Mary Allodi, *Canadian watercolours and drawings in the Royal Ontario Museum* (2v., Toronto, 1974). *Landmarks of Canada: what art has done for Canadian history* . . . (2v., Toronto, 1917–21; repr. in 1v., 1967). *Painters in a new land: from Annapolis Royal to the Klondike*, ed. Michael Bell (Toronto, 1973). Mabel Burkholder, "Retired artillery officer becomes local artist," *Hamilton Spectator*, 15 April 1952. "Hamilton in the fifties," *Hamilton Spectator*, 14 Feb. 1942.

CALDWELL, WILLIAM BLETTERMAN, soldier and colonial administrator; b. probably in 1798; d. 29 Jan. 1882 in London, England. He is known to have married and had five children.

William Bletterman Caldwell's family background is unknown but it may be assumed to have been English. Caldwell made the army his career, and began as ensign in the 60th Foot in September 1814. He served in various regiments during the following years, being promoted captain in 1831 and major in 1846. In September 1848 he arrived at the Red River Settlement as the officer commanding a small body of out-pensioners of the Royal Hospital, Chelsea, as well as governor of the District of Assiniboia. Caldwell was nominated for the post of governor by the colonial secretary, Lord Grey, but appointed and paid by the Hudson's Bay Company.

The first governor not previously associated with the HBC, Caldwell was appointed in an attempt to solve the basic anomaly in the government of the colony at Red River: the HBC enjoyed a monopoly of the fur trade and at the same time appointed the members of the government and the courts. It was hoped as well that the pensioners under his command would have a stabilizing effect on the colony, made restless by the approach of American settlement and by demands from its inhabitants for self-government and free trade, but this attempt by the HBC to give the settlement an impartial government, with some force at its disposal, failed. The settlers continued to regard the governor and the Council of Assiniboia as creatures of the HBC, and the pensioners were too few in number and their habits too unmilitary to instil the respect that the previous military unit in the settlement, the 6th Foot, had imposed [*see* John ffolliott CROFTON].

It was under these circumstances that Caldwell, as governor, had to preside over the trial of Pierre-Guillaume Sayer* in the General Quarterly Court of Assiniboia in May 1849. Sayer was a Métis who, along with three others, was charged with trading in furs with the Indians. The action was apparently instigated by John Ballenden*, HBC chief factor at Red River, in an attempt to obtain a clear judicial decision that trading in furs with the Indians by private individuals was illegal. Unfortunately for Ballenden, although Sayer was found guilty he was not sentenced; this result was interpreted by most as freeing the trade [*see* Adam THOM]. The trial was, in fact, the company's last attempt to enforce its monopoly.

Caldwell emerged from the affair with the reputation of being a weak and ineffectual governor. The Métis, led by Louis Riel* *père*, had attended the trial *en masse* and armed, yet Caldwell had not called out the pensioners to protect the court. He defended himself by arguing that he had not been given a force of 200 as promised; only 56 men, with 42 women and 57 children, had arrived in Red River in September 1848. His force, he declared, could man the walls of Upper Fort Garry (Winnipeg) but could not police the settlement. When he had inquired of the members of the Council of Assiniboia and the leading settlers if reliable men would serve as special constables, the reply had been that they would not in a matter relating to the fur trade because they feared a reaction by the Métis. He had therefore decided that calling out the pensioners could not be a success and might prove to be a provocation, a decision that demonstrates his common sense, if nothing else.

Opposition to Caldwell reached a climax in July 1850 with the celebrated *Foss* v. *Pelly* case, which arose out of rumours of an indiscretion by Sarah McLeod*, the wife of Chief Factor John Ballenden, and Captain Christopher Vaughan Foss, Caldwell's second-in-command. The gossip increased until Foss sued Augustus Edward Pelly, the HBC accountant at Red River, and his wife, along with John Davidson, the mess steward, and his wife, for conspiracy to slander. Because all the magistrates in the settlement refused to sit with him, Caldwell was forced to hold court alone. The three-day trial which followed was a disorderly affair. When the legal complexities overcame Caldwell, he called upon Adam Thom, the recorder, to assist him. Thom, who had advised Foss and Mrs Ballenden before the case and strongly supported them, appears to have taken every opportunity to ensure Pelly's conviction, including stepping down from the bench to testify on behalf of the plaintiff, before charging the jury. In the end, the court found in favour of Foss, and Caldwell awarded him damages.

Caldwell's irregular handling of the trial in the *Foss* v. *Pelly* case brought to a head the dissatisfaction of the English-speaking settlers with him. Led by Alexander Ross*, 500 of them petitioned for Caldwell's dismissal. The situation was defused when the new governor of Rupert's Land, Eden Colvile*, arrived a month after the trial, in August 1850, took up residence in the settlement, and with Caldwell's consent presided over council and court until quiet was restored.

Though Colvile considered him unfit to be governor, Caldwell resumed his duties in 1851 and remained in Red River until 1855 when he returned to England. He was succeeded by Francis Godschall Johnson*. Caldwell had been promoted lieutenant-colonel in 1854, and he retired from the army in 1857. He was called before the select committee of the British House of Commons held in 1857 to investigate the renewal of the HBC licence, and gave evidence favourable to the company. He died in London in 1882.

W. L. MORTON

PAM, HBCA, A.11/95, 2 Aug. 1849, 24 March 1850; D.4/42, 25 June 1840; D.5/22, 26 May 1848. PRO, CO 42/608, Caldwell to Merivale, 31 March 1856. *Canadian North-West* (Oliver), I: 352. G.B., Parl., House of Commons paper, 1857, *Report from the select committee on the HBC*. HBRS, XIX (Rich and A. M. Johnson). *Hart's army list*, 1846; 1854; 1857. Rich, *Hist. of HBC*, II: 544.

CALVIN, DILENO (Deleno) DEXTER, lumber merchant, forwarder, businessman, and politician; b. 15 May 1798 at Clarendon, near Rutland, Vt, the fourth of five children of Sandford Jenks Calvin and Abigail Chipman; m. first in 1831 Harriet Webb (d. 1843); m. secondly in 1844 Marion Maria Breck (d. 1861); m. thirdly in 1861 Catherine Wilkinson (d. 1911); there were six children of each of the first two marriages and two children of the third, but only six of the fourteen survived to adulthood; d. 18 May 1884 at Garden Island, Ont.

Dileno Dexter Calvin's father, an unsuccessful lawyer before becoming a farmer, died when Dileno was eight; he had provided little for his son in the way of education or inheritance. In 1818 Dileno left Vermont and settled at Rodman, N.Y., where he was a labourer for three years. An ambitious man, he became a pioneer farmer and lumberman near La Fargeville, N.Y. On his first serious lumbering operation in 1825, he and a neighbour squared some timber which they transported by raft down the St Lawrence for sale at the timber coves near Quebec City. Calvin eventually decided he should concentrate on lumbering and in 1835 moved to nearby Clayton; the core of his business was rafting timber for delivery at Quebec City, where it was trans-shipped to British markets.

Clayton proved to be an inadequate base and in 1844 Calvin relocated on land rented at the eastern end of Garden Island, two miles south of Kingston, Canada West, where he could operate within the British trading system. His new base was at the foot of the Great Lakes navigation system at a point on the river where, until into the 20th century, it was convenient and economic to form into rafts the timber arriving by ship from the Great Lakes basin. The island provided Calvin with a sheltered bay for easy access by sailing craft and for building rafts. It was thus crucial in the development of Calvin's operations.

Calvin had actually become active on the island even before he left Clayton. In 1836, with partners John Counter* and an American, Hiram Cook, he formed the Kingston Stave Forwarding Company which rented land on Garden Island. The company became Calvin, Cook and Counter in 1838 (afterwards, Calvin and Cook) and Quebec City merchant James Bell Forsyth*, who was later to profit from the company's success, assisted in its establishment. After the island became its base in 1844, Calvin controlled the company, usually with at least one partner. It established a branch in Hamilton (which lasted until 1854), in addition to the one already set up in Quebec City, and also agencies in a variety of places including Liverpool, Glasgow, and Sault Ste Marie. The company maintained 12 to 15 ships to deliver square timber and staves, chiefly oak and pine, to Garden Island from as far afield as Michigan and Indiana. Although Calvin purchased some timber for resale and on occasion financed independent timber producers, the bulk of the wood delivered at Quebec City by his firm did not belong to it but to various timber entrepreneurs. The timber was carried the 350 miles to Quebec City for a fee. Calvin was therefore shielded from some market vicissitudes, because he charged his fee regardless of his customers' profit margins. In order to maximize profits and maintain a permanent and stable work-force (during peak periods it numbered 700), Calvin sought business opportunities apart from the lumber trade; he and his partners operated as general merchants, manufacturers, forwarders, common carriers, wharfingers, warehousemen, and shipbuilders. The partnership also operated a lucrative government-subsidized tugboat service on the St Lawrence above Montreal from 1858 to 1874. The firm's assets increased from $216,000 in 1854 to $460,000 in 1871; in 1880 it had $75,000 invested in its towing and wrecking business alone. Apart from his involvement in the firm Calvin had large holdings of land in the United States and served as director of the Kingston and Pembroke Railway. In 1865 the firm was one of the biggest dealing in timber in Canada and controlled the largest single timber operation at the coves of Quebec City. At his death, Calvin owned over 92 per cent of his company (known as Calvin and Son after 1880) and left an estate conservatively valued at more than $324,000.

Perhaps the most interesting aspect of Calvin's career is his role as a benevolent patriarch. In 1848 Calvin and Cook purchased 15 acres at the foot of Garden Island and by 1862 owned the entire island; in 1880 Calvin bought his partner's share. Referred to by his employees as "the Governor," Calvin dominated the little society that developed on Garden Island. From 1860 to 1885, the years of the company's greatest prosperity, as many as 750 people lived and worked there. Most were company employees. It was an entirely self-contained community, which had its own school subsidized by the firm, a mechanics' institute with an excellent library, its own post office, and several fraternal societies. Despite the divergent origins of its inhabitants, French Canadian, Scottish, English, Irish, American, and Indian from the Caughnawaga Reserve near Montreal, the island avoided ethnic or religious conflict. Visitors described it as "a simple well-ordered village" and found it "fascinating"; modern studies confirm that the firm sought the welfare of the island's inhabitants. Calvin's paternalistic approach to his workers had several consequences. During the recession following the panic of 1873 he had to cut wages but refused to lay off workers; he also raised wages when he could, and allowed senior workers to purchase small portions of the business. He did, however, maintain strong opposition to organized labour. After sailors on his ships had been organized by the Seamen's Union in the late 1870s and early 1880s, he went to great lengths to break the union (he imported sailors from Glasgow) and eventually fired most of its members. By converting schooners into barges for towing on Lake Ontario, he reduced his need for sailors.

Calvin was also a leader in public life. He was commissioned a magistrate in 1845 soon after he became a naturalized Canadian. By 1865 he was reeve of Wolfe Island and the surrounding islands, and served as the first warden of Frontenac County after it was separated from the county of Lennox and Addington in 1863. Three years later Garden Island was incorporated as a village and Calvin was routinely acclaimed reeve for the remainder of his life. He was a perennial member of the Frontenac County Council and served as county warden four times. In 1870 Sir John A. Macdonald* appointed Calvin, along with Hugh ALLAN and Casimir Stanislaus Gzowski*, to a canal commission, which urged the improvement of the St Lawrence canals; Calvin, no doubt thinking of his forwarding business based in the Kingston area, opposed making the river navigable for ocean shipping.

In 1868 Calvin entered provincial politics, running as the Conservative candidate, with the reluctant support of Macdonald, in the by-election for Frontenac necessitated by the death of Sir Henry Smith*. He won an easy victory over Byron Moffatt Britton. In 1871 he was acclaimed. Although he lost the nomination for Frontenac in 1875, he easily re-entered the house in 1877, after the death of the sitting Conservative member, Peter Graham. Calvin repeated his success in the general election of 1879 but did not stand in 1883. He had enjoyed the benefit of almost all the votes from Garden Island since he owned the land and employed virtually all the inhabitants; as his grandson noted: "the men . . . wisely voted . . . Conservative."

Although not a major politician, Calvin was an active member and presented his views with vigour. He worked hard to obtain patronage appointments for his constituents. He was passionately interested in tax reforms, disagreeing with the principle of exemption for holdings such as stocks or wild lands. Curiously enough, he sided with agriculture against lumber when their interests clashed; he advocated vesting timber rights with landowners and opposed granting extensive timber limits which might retard the settlement necessary for the development of the country. As well, Calvin favoured minor reforms in the electoral and judicial systems. He enforced prohibition, a lifelong passion about which he regularly spoke, on the residents of Garden Island. Seventy years old at the time he entered provincial politics, Calvin was regarded as "one of the eccentrics of the early days of the Ontario Parliament"; he gave up provincial politics only a year before his death. His eccentricities, in fact, were numerous; his grandson notes that he was suspicious of men who bit their finger nails, disliked short men "for no better reason than because they were short," and had an abiding contempt for dogs and their owners. When "a man's poor," noted the elder Calvin, "he gets a dog, if he's very poor he gets two."

He was never to lose his affection for his American home. During the winter of 1842–43, when he was living in Clayton, N.Y., he became involved in a religious revival and was baptized as a Baptist in 1844 after the death of his first wife. He was to remain a devout member of the church. Although he had become a British subject and a monarchist (commenting to Macdonald on one occasion, "I can *holler* for the Queen as loud as you can"), he maintained the Calvin homestead at La Fargeville and was buried at Clayton beside his mother and first wife.

DONALD SWAINSON

Calvin family papers are in the possession of Meg and John d'Esterre (Garden Island, Ont.), and this collection includes valuable scrapbooks of newspaper clippings and other items.

AO, MU 500–15. Ont., Legislative Library, Newspaper Hansard, 1868–82 (mfm. at AO). PAC, MG 26, A. QUA, Calvin Company records; Calvin legal papers. *By-laws of Elysian Lodge, no.212, A.F.A.M., Garden Island, Ontario* (Hamilton, Ont., 1872). *Ottawa Daily Citizen*, 12 June 1880, 19 May 1881. *Catalogue of books contained in the library of the Garden Island Mechanics' Institute* (Kingston, Ont., 1883). *CPC*, 1872; 1874; 1877; 1878; 1881; 1883. *Kingston directory* (Kingston), 1857–58, 1865, 1867, 1885–86. M. C. Boyd, *The story of Garden Island*, ed. M. A. Boyd (Kingston, 1973). A. A. Calvin, "Timber trading in Canada, 1812–1849: special emphasis on forwarding, 1836–1849" (BA thesis, Queen's Univ., Kingston, 1930). D. D. Calvin, "Rafting on the St. Lawrence," *Patterns of Canada*, ed. W. J. Megill (Toronto, 1966), 119–25; *A saga of the St. Lawrence: timber & shipping through three generations* (Toronto, 1945). Beverley Doherty, "Real wage changes as revealed in the manuscripts of the shipyard of the Calvin Company: selected years, 1848–1884" (BA thesis, Queen's Univ., 1973). Sarah Edinborough, "Garden Island: a unique community seen through its social institutions" (unpublished paper, Queen's Univ., 1978). T. R. Glover and D. D. Calvin, *A corner of empire: the old Ontario strand* (Toronto and Cambridge, Eng., 1937). A. R. M. Lower, *Great Britain's woodyard: British America and the timber trade, 1763–1867* (Montreal and London, 1973). Christian Norman, "A company community: Garden Island, Upper Canada at mid-century," *Canadian papers in rural history*, ed. D. H. Akenson (2v. to date, Gananoque, Ont., 1979–), II: 113–34. Adam Shortt, "Down the St. Lawrence on a timber raft," *Queen's Quarterly*, 10 (1902–3): 16–34. Donald Swainson, "Benevolent patriarch ruled an island and an industry," *Whig-Standard* (Kingston), 28 April 1979: 9; "Garden Island and the Calvin Company," *Historic Kingston*, no.28 (1980): 35–56.

CAMERON, GEORGE FREDERICK, poet, lawyer, and journalist; b. 24 Sept. 1854 in New Glasgow, N.S., eldest son of James Grant Cameron and Jessie Sutherland; m. 22 Aug. 1883 Ella Amey, and they had one daughter; d. 17 Sept. 1885 at Millhaven, Ont.

George Frederick Cameron received his early education in New Glasgow and appears to have excelled in both academic and athletic pursuits. An early love affair was disrupted when George moved with his family to Boston in April 1869. The young couple nevertheless considered themselves engaged and corresponded regularly. For three years Cameron devoted much of his energy to writing on the subject of freedom, especially the struggle which was taking place in Cuba. He contributed poems and articles on this struggle to local newspapers and journals. In 1872 news that his fiancée was engaged to another suitor, whom she later married, seriously affected George's physical and emotional health. Two years later, returning to Boston after a recuperative vacation, he learned of the death of his former fiancée and travelled to Nova Scotia to visit her grave. The stress of these years provided the material for much of his early poetry.

Cameron returned to Boston in the autumn of 1874 and enrolled in the Boston School of Law. He graduated in 1877 at the head of his class and entered the local firm of Dean, Butler and Abbot. During his five years with the firm he continued to submit literary pieces to local journals. In June 1882 he left Boston and in the fall of that year enrolled in Queen's College in Kingston, Ont. Although he did not excel at his studies, he was a member of a group of poets at Queen's which included Thomas Guthrie Marquis*, and he won the poetry prize at Queen's in 1883 for "Adelphi." In March of the same year he left the university to become editor of the *Daily News* in Kingston. He held this position, and continued to write poetry, until his early death, of heart failure, two years later.

A selection of his verses, *Lyrics on freedom, love and death*, was published posthumously at Boston and Kingston in 1887 by his brother Charles John Cameron, whose laudatory preface has provided the basis for subsequent biographical notices. Charles also published Cameron's libretto for a military opera, *Leo, the royal cadet*, which appeared in 1889 over the joint names of George and composer Oscar F. Telgmann. The opera, set at the Royal Military College of Canada in Kingston, is a lighthearted piece about love and war, faintly reminiscent of Gilbert and Sullivan and the contemporary Savoy operas. It was performed in 1889 in Kingston and several other Ontario cities.

Cameron's poetry was discovered by Archibald Lampman*, who referred to him as a "poet of most genuine and fervid poetic energy" and recommended ten of his poems for inclusion in James Elgin Wetherell*'s *Later Canadian poems* (1893). Wetherell selected 15 of Cameron's poems, including seven recommended by Lampman, and they have since become standard anthology material. Lampman had elaborated his assessment of Cameron as a writer "of rare spontaneity" and "genuine poetic impulse" in a lecture on Cameron and Charles George Douglas Roberts* given at Ottawa in 1891, which was published posthumously as "Two Canadian poets."

Of Cameron's published verse, his juvenilia, "Lyrics on freedom," have not outlasted their political occasions; his "Lyrics on love," indicative of the influence of several real or imaginary emotional upheavals, are brooding, melancholy, and misogynic; his "Lyrics in pleasant places and other places" and "Lyrics on death" commemorate personal impressions. Cameron modelled himself poetically after Sappho and Shelley but owed most, especially in the two longer poems in *Lyrics*, to the young Tennyson. "Adelphi" is a verse tale of the affections of two brothers for the same woman to the point of self-sacrifice in the manner of Tennyson's "Enoch Arden." "Ysolte," the highly imaginative account of an unhappy love, resembles Tennyson's "Maud." It demonstrates, in tone and substance, the duality of Cameron's attitude to life, which he sees throughout his work in extremes of love and hate, romance and truth. The melancholy in Cameron's poetry was in part the conventional elegiac mood evident in the more sombre poems of Lampman but was also attributable to the genuine emotion of a man who suffered deep depression. His work on the whole is metrically competent and introspective, forsaking originality in imagery and emotion for a fondness for conventional poetic diction which romanticizes events of little lasting appeal and thus does not rise above the level of verse.

Cameron's reputation has suffered most from later uncritical panegyrists who praised him for what they would have liked him to be rather than for what he was: a competent verse writer representative of his time.

ALEXANDER H. BRODIE

G. F. Cameron's poetry can be found in *Lyrics on freedom, love and death*, ed. C. J. Cameron (Kingston, Ont., and Boston, 1887; repr. Toronto and Buffalo, N.Y., 1973), and in *Later Canadian poems*, ed. J. E. Wetherell (Toronto, 1893); with Oscar F. Telgmann he wrote *An entirely new and original military opera in four acts, entitled: Leo, the royal cadet* ([Kingston], 1889).

QUA, Richard Albert Wilson papers. A. S. Bourinot, *Five Canadian poets . . .* (Montreal, 1954), 22–26; "George Frederick Cameron," *Canadian Author and Bookman* (Toronto), 29 (1953–54), no.4: 3–5. L. J. Burpee, *A little book of Canadian essays* (Toronto, 1909), 73–87. S. W. Dyde, "The two Camerons," *Queen's Rev.* (Kingston), 3 (1929): 196–98. E. C. Kyte, "George Frederick Cameron," *Educational Record of the Province of Quebec* (Quebec), 63 (1947): 117–22. Archibald Lampman, "Two Canadian poets: a lecture," *Univ. of Toronto Quarterly* (Toronto), 13 (1943–44): 406–23. J. M., "Who's who in Canadian literature: George Frederick Cameron," *Canadian Bookman* (Toronto), 13 (1931): 179–80. Geoffrey Vivien, "A forgotten Canadian poet," *Canadian Author and Bookman*, 23 (1947), no.3: 57.

CAMERON, JOHN (known as **Cariboo Cameron**; also known as **John A. Cameron**), prospector; b. 1 Sept. 1820 in Charlottenburg Township, Glengarry County, Upper Canada, son of Angus Cameron and Isabella McDougal; m. first 20 Feb. 1860 Margaret Sophia Groves; m. secondly 1 March 1865 Christina Adelaide Wood; d. 7 Nov. 1888 at Barkerville, B.C.

John Cameron spent much of his early life in Glengarry County. In the 1850s he was in California, apparently as a prospector, but had returned to Glengarry by 1860. When gold was discovered that year in the Cariboo district of the British Columbia interior, Cameron decided to go there. He arrived at Victoria, Vancouver Island, in February 1862 with his wife and an infant daughter who died soon after. In Victoria, Cameron met Robert Stevenson, another native of Glengarry County, who backed him in his first venture in British Columbia, that of transporting supplies into the Cariboo gold district. Cameron was also a partner in a small company which in August staked a claim on Williams Creek in the Cariboo – the famous Cameron Claim.

On 22 Dec. 1862 the miners on the Cameron Claim "struck it very rich at 22 feet." The claim soon became one of the largest operations in the Cariboo district and its success made Cameron a wealthy man. But prior to the strike, on 23 October, Margaret Sophia Cameron had died of typhoid fever and Cameron was determined to take his wife's body back to Canada West for burial. On the last day of January 1863 Cameron and Stevenson, escorted for a time by other miners, set out on a gruelling 400-mile journey to Victoria, hauling Sophia's body on a toboggan. They reached Victoria on 7 March and the body was buried there in an alcohol-filled coffin, pending its removal to the east. Cameron then returned to Williams Creek where he spent the summer working his claim.

In October 1863 Cameron left the Cariboo and, taking the coffin with him, travelled by way of the Isthmus of Panama and New York, reaching Cornwall, Canada West, before the end of the year. In December he had the coffin reburied. In March 1865 Cameron married Christina Adelaide Wood of Osnabruck Township and in July he laid the cornerstone of his imposing new residence, Fairfield House, at Summerstown in Glengarry County. In this period of prosperity, Cameron's often rash behaviour, extravagance, and arrogance tended to foster hostile speculation on how he had obtained his fortune. This speculation included references to the first Mrs Cameron, and there was much gossip about the contents of the mysterious sealed coffin. It was even suggested that an appearance of death was contrived and that Cameron had actually sold his wife to an Indian chief for gold. In 1873, more than ten years after his first wife's death, Cameron could bear his tormentors no longer and had the coffin raised. The face of Mrs Cameron, almost perfectly preserved in the alcohol, was exposed to the scrutiny of the public.

His windfall melted away, Cameron returned to British Columbia in 1886 or 1887. He died a poor man at Barkerville, the scene of his gold-mining success, and was buried nearby in the cemetery at Camerontown, a village named after him.

ROYCE MACGILLIVRAY

AO, MU 535, Cornwall, St John's Presbyterian; MU 539, Williamstown, St Andrew's Presbyterian; RG 8, I-6-B, 65. PABC, Add. MSS 6, Francis Dickie, "'Cariboo' Cameron's funerals' saga, with suggested amendments, &c by Duncan Cameron" (typescript); Add. MSS 315, Robert Stevenson diary and memo book, 1863–76 (copy); [James Cumming], "John A. ('Cariboo') Cameron"; GR 216, 34–41. PAC, MG 24, I3, 14: 14–15, 462, 808, 813–14, 825, 839–40. [W. B. Cheadle], *Cheadle's journal of trip across Canada, 1862–1863*, ed. A. G. Doughty and Gustave Lanctot (Ottawa, 1931), 244, 249. Viscount [W. F.] Milton and W. B. Cheadle, *The north-west passage by land: being the narrative of an expedition from the Atlantic to the Pacific . . .* (6th ed., London, [1865]; repr. Toronto, 1970), 360, 373. *Advertiser* (Cornwall, [Ont.]), 12 July 1865. *British Columbian* (New Westminster, B.C.), 21 March, 18 April, 2 May, 6 June, 1, 5 Aug., 21 Oct. 1863. *Cornwall Standard* (Cornwall, Ont.), 24 April 1903. *Daily British Colonist* (Victoria), 28 Feb. 1862; 9 March, 7 Sept., 21, 22, 28 Oct. 1863. *Daily Union* (Ottawa), 2 March 1865. *Freeholder* (Cornwall), 15, 22 Dec. 1865. *Glengarry News* (Alexandria, Ont.), 16 Nov. 1928. *Mainland Guardian* (New Westminster), 10 Nov. 1888. *Montreal Herald*, 26 Aug. 1873.

H. H. Bancroft, *History of British Columbia, 1792–1887* (San Francisco, 1887). J. G. Harkness, *Stormont, Dundas and Glengarry: a history, 1784–1945* (Oshawa, Ont., 1946), 405–8. W. P. Morrell, *The gold rushes* (2nd ed., London, 1968). Ormsby, *British Columbia.* W. W. Walkem, *Stories of early British Columbia* (Vancouver, 1914), 243–87. Charles Clowes, "Cariboo Cameron: a true saga of the romantic west," *Maclean's* (Toronto), 49 (1936), no.1: 26, 28, 30. A. D. Kean, "Dragged body on toboggan 320 miles, took 47 days," *Toronto Daily Star*, 31 March 1934. Robert Stevenson, "The true story of the death of 'Cariboo' Cameron's wife," *B.C. Saturday Sunset* (Vancouver), 3 April 1909: 5, 14.

CAMERON, Sir MATTHEW CROOKS, lawyer, politician, and judge; b. 2 Oct. 1822 in Dundas, Upper Canada, youngest child of John McAlpine Cameron of Inverness-shire, Scotland, and Nancy Foy of Northumberland, England; m. 1 Dec. 1851 Charlotte Ross Wedd (d. 14 Jan. 1868) of Hamilton, Canada West, and they had three sons and three daughters; d. 25 June 1887 in Toronto, Ont.

Matthew Crooks Cameron's parents came to Upper Canada in 1819, and settled in Dundas where his father became a merchant and postmaster. The family moved to Hamilton in 1826, when John McAlpine Cameron was made deputy clerk of the crown for the Gore District, and Matthew received his first education at a local school. He attended the Home District Grammar School when his family moved to York (Toronto). His father was appointed first permanent clerk in the House of Assembly and by 1834 had entered the service of the Canada Company in its Toronto office. Matthew was thus the son of a family with some means and status in Upper Canada.

Cameron went to Upper Canada College in 1838, but his studies there were interrupted in 1840 by an accident while he was out shooting with two school friends. His ankle shattered by a careless shot, he suffered complications that led to the amputation of his leg and caused him pain for the rest of his life. David Breakenridge Read*, who was in residence at the college while Cameron was a "day boy," recalled the change in his temperament. From being lively, fond of sports, and not particularly studious, he became "of a serious turn of mind." After a period of convalescence and adjustment to the use of crutches and an artificial limb, he decided not to return to the college but to pursue a legal career as his two older brothers had done.

Cameron articled with Joseph Clarke Gamble* and William Henry Boulton* in Toronto, and proved a diligent student with an aptitude for law. He was called to the bar in 1849 and began practice as Boulton's partner. In 1850 he was in partnership with William CAYLEY, who served as inspector general in the Conservative ministries from 1845 to 1858. Although he practised with Cayley at times during the 1850s and early 1860s, from 1859 to 1878 Cameron was also the senior partner in important law firms that included Daniel McMichael, Edward Fitzgerald, and Alfred Hoskin. Moreover, Cameron had begun to go on circuit as soon as he was admitted to the bar, and had quickly gained a high reputation throughout Canada West as an honest and skilful lawyer in both civil and criminal cases. He was unusually successful even against such formidable rivals as John Hillyard Cameron*, Philip Michael Matthew Scott VanKoughnet*, or John Hawkins Hagarty*. Cameron was tall and slender, with a commanding presence and impressive manner of speaking. He had a tremendous capacity for work despite his physical disability. These qualities, combined with his air of sincere conviction, mastery of the law, and power of logical analysis, made him particularly effective before a jury. John Charles DENT called him "for many years the best-known *Nisi Prius* lawyer" in the province. He was created a QC on 27 March 1863, and elected a bencher of the Law Society of Upper Canada in April 1871.

Cameron gave his whole attention to his legal work for ten years after 1849, except for his service in 1852 as a government commissioner to inquire into the frequent accidents on the Great Western Rail Road. His first interest in public life was shown in 1859 when he was elected to represent St James' Ward on the Toronto City Council. Two years later he was defeated as a candidate for mayor of Toronto but was elected to the Legislative Assembly for Ontario North, defeating the incumbent Joseph GOULD. Reflecting his family background, education, and associations with men such as Boulton and Cayley, Cameron was a strong Conservative. He supported the government of George-Étienne Cartier* and John A. Macdonald*, voting for the Militia Bill of 1862, the defeat of which brought about the downfall of that government. He opposed the Reform ministry then formed by John Sandfield Macdonald* and Louis-Victor SICOTTE. As an amendment to the address from the throne in 1863 he proposed a motion favouring representation by population to remedy the injustice suffered by Canada West in the present system. Although the motion failed to pass, it was a shrewd move tactically for it divided the Upper Canadian Reformers who were eager for "rep by pop" from Sandfield Macdonald who was pledged to the counter principle of a "double majority."

In the elections of June 1863, Cameron was defeated in Ontario North by William McDougall*, a Reformer. McDougall became provincial secretary in the coalition of June 1864 formed to work for federal union and, when he sought the necessary re-election in Ontario North, Cameron decided to run against him. In the by-election of 30 July Cameron regained the seat although government leaders including John A. Macdonald and George Brown* used their influence on behalf of McDougall. In a letter to Macdonald on 9 July 1864 Cameron explained his motive in running: "While I admit the propriety of your doing nothing against a colleague, I regret you should have thought it necessary, actively, to interfere to the prejudice of a Conservative who seeks nothing in the contest except to relieve your Government and the country from the reproach of having so objectionable a politician in your Council." Another probable motive for his candidacy was his opposition to the coalition and its proposed federation which he distrusted; he was to remain an anti-confederate Conservative while in the assembly from 1864 to 1867.

When the federal scheme took shape at the Charlottetown and Quebec conferences of 1864, Cameron confessed his dilemma to John A. Macdonald, with whom his friendship remained firm. Macdonald, like Cameron, strongly preferred a legislative union but tried to reassure him that federation was the "only practicable plan" to protect local interests. Cameron was never convinced that confederation was the solution to the colonies' problems. When the Quebec Resolutions were before the Canadian legislature in early 1865, he condemned confederation as an "extravagantly expensive arrangement" as compared with a legislative union. Constitutional change he held to be unnecessary; material progress and provisions for defence could be achieved in the existing system if assemblymen would cease impeding the "wheels of government" by their "factious conduct." He was not "dazzled" by the prospect of a great nation: "We can never be so great in any way as we can by remaining a dependency of the British Crown." The resolutions, he claimed, "individualized" the provinces, increasing the elements of contention as well as the possibility of dismemberment from the empire and drift "into the vortex of annexation" to the United States which would be the "greatest injury" that could happen. When the legislature approved the resolutions on 11 March of that year, Cameron was alone among the Conservatives from Canada West in opposition. He then seconded an unsuccessful motion by John Hillyard Cameron to submit the scheme to the people before its enactment.

With confederation an accomplished fact in 1867, Cameron felt it his "duty" to make it work. He accepted office on 20 July 1867 as provincial secretary and registrar in the first Ontario coalition ministry under Sandfield Macdonald and in August ran both provincially in Toronto East and federally in Ontario

North. Although he assisted the coalition candidate, Thomas Nicholson GIBBS, in defeating George Brown in Ontario South, Cameron was himself unsuccessful in Ontario North. He was returned in Toronto East, however, and retained the seat in the elections of 1871 as well as those of 1875 when he defeated provincial treasurer Adam CROOKS. His quick perception of issues and clear, straightforward speech made him as powerful in legislative debate as in pleading at the bar. Representing, along with John Carling* of London, the Conservative interests in Sandfield Macdonald's coalition, Cameron quickly became the chief Conservative spokesman in the assembly, though he declared that he had taken office to "quell the partisan spirit which in the past had done a great deal of mischief in the country." In 1868 he opposed an extension of suffrage on the basis of income as "revolutionary": property had always been the basis.

Cameron was both a strength and a weakness to the Macdonald administration. He assisted in passing legislation to promote settlement and mining in northern Ontario and especially in piloting through the house the controversial School Act of 1871, which aimed at making elementary education free and compulsory. He took a sensible stand when Edward Blake*, leader of the Liberal opposition, introduced a motion in 1871 which would in effect have chided the Canadian government for its inaction in the "cold blooded murder" of Thomas Scott* by Louis RIEL at the Red River Settlement. Cameron argued that the offence was beyond the jurisdiction of Ontario and that it would be "unwise" to interfere with another government's prerogative. His amendment was carried.

On the other hand, he caused the premier embarrassment by accepting a retainer on behalf of Patrick James Whelan*, on trial in 1868 for the murder of Thomas D'Arcy McGee*; his action precipitated a resolution by Blake that "No Minister of the Crown shall act as Counsel against the Crown, on a Crown prosecution." Blake's resolution was withdrawn after Sandfield Macdonald promised no further "offences of this kind." Cameron's avowed conservatism, coupled with the independence inherited from his Highland ancestors, contributed to tensions within the government and made it hard for Macdonald to preserve the "Patent Combination." A debate of 1868 over the request by the Toronto, Grey and Bruce Railway Company to use a narrow gauge is a prime example of the ministers in public disagreement. Arguing against Edmund Burke WOOD, the provincial treasurer, Cameron insisted that the narrow gauge be permitted because it was less expensive and the area the railway would serve needed transportation.

Transferred to the Crown Lands Department on 25 July 1871, Cameron left office on 19 Dec. 1871 with his colleagues after defeat in the house on their railway policy. Coalition government was at an end in Ontario. Macdonald had lost ground in the spring elections of 1871. Faced by strengthened Liberals and several independents, he had been unable to maintain control of the legislature. Discouraged and gravely ill, he seldom appeared in the house before his death on 1 June 1872. The formation of a Liberal ministry by Blake in December 1871 and its reorganization by his successor Oliver Mowat* in October 1872 marked the permanent establishment of party government in the province. The Conservatives assumed the role of official opposition. With Sandfield Macdonald dead and John Carling gone to the House of Commons, Cameron was unquestionably their ablest member. He became the first leader of the Ontario Conservatives.

Their weakness in the assembly put the burden of criticizing government measures largely on Cameron. He assailed vigorously Mowat's "desecration" of the bench in returning to politics, the political favouritism he detected in the sale of timber limits, and the move of the agricultural college (later the Ontario Agricultural College) from Mimico to Guelph which he alleged took place for political reasons. He charged that the reservation by the lieutenant governor of bills to incorporate the Orange order was inspired by the premier's desire to "stand well with both the Roman Catholics and Orangemen" and "put a difficulty in the way" of John A. Macdonald in Ottawa. Reservation transferred the problem to the prime minister who had to be as careful as Mowat in avoiding the alienation of either Catholic or Protestant voters. When Mowat later provided for incorporation of the Orange order by a general act, Cameron called it an affront to Protestants, and as the dispute dragged on he felt it had become a "struggle for civil and religious liberty" against undue Catholic influence.

The chief issue in his campaign of 1875, the first straight party fight in Ontario, was the government's extravagance in contrast with the earlier economy of Sandfield Macdonald. But Cameron was handicapped both by the discouragement of the Conservatives over their federal defeat in 1874 and by his own failure to present a positive policy. The electorate showed its approval of Mowat's increased provincial spending by returning him to office with a safe majority. In the new house Cameron nevertheless returned to the cry for economic retrenchment. When asked to approve the creation of a department of education he deplored the expense of adding a minister. He feared, too, that the connection of politics and education would lead, as had recent liquor licensing changes, to an increase in the evils of patronage, and his "Conservative principles led him to oppose altering any system which had worked well in the past." Similarly, "out of true Conservative principles," he always defended the privileges of the University of Toronto and Upper Canada College.

Cameron was not the antiquated bigot depicted by

the *Globe*. He supported reform to enable the payment of witnesses in criminal cases and to provide better protection to married women in conveying their property. Although he disapproved of secret voting in principle, he did not divide the assembly on the bill which introduced the ballot in 1874. Still, the belief was growing that he was too much the old high Tory for late 19th-century Ontario. The Toronto *Nation* commented on the decadence of the Conservatives under his leadership. Even the Conservative *Leader* acknowledged his shortcomings as a party leader, complaining that he spent too much time on his "briefs" and not enough in the legislature, and that he did not consult the caucus sufficiently. Moreover, some of his tactical moves had turned out to be blunders: his 1872 motion for an inquiry into a possible offer by Blake to induce Wood's resignation from the Sandfield Macdonald government in 1871, and his suggestions of impropriety on the part of Archibald McKellar*, first following the "Proton Outrage" investigation of 1872 [*see* Abram William LAUDER], and again in 1874 concerning mismanagement of the agricultural college at Guelph. An incident in 1876, however justified, when Cameron led the Conservative members into the lobby to protest proposed amendments in the election law, became something of a joke when it was dubbed the "March of the Cameron Men."

Very different was the satisfaction felt in both political and professional circles when Cameron was sworn in on 27 Nov. 1878 as a puisne judge of the Court of Queen's Bench, and when he was made the chief justice of the Court of Common Pleas on 13 May 1884. According to D. B. Read, he brought insight and conscientiousness to his judicial work, and rendered several judgements of historic importance. On 5 April 1887 he was created a KB. Less than three months later he died.

Cameron's many activities had been an expression of his Scottish and intellectual heritage, and of his political and business interests. He had been a member of the Caledonian and St Andrew's societies, president of the Ontario Literary Society, first president of the Liberal-Conservative Association of Toronto, and a director of the Dominion Telegraph Company, Confederation Life Association, and Isolated Risk Fire Insurance Company of Canada.

Cameron's forte had been law. His eminence at the bar or on the bench was unquestioned. As a politician he had set an example of the highest personal integrity. But for all his ability and devotion to his party he had fallen short of being a successful leader. Although in private life kindly and possessed of "the magnanimity of a Scottish Chief," he could not bring himself to employ the hand-shaking and other arts likely to win votes. In the house he often seemed unnecessarily blunt. Thus his opposition to a tile drainage bill in 1878 because it would benefit only a few, and his comment in 1876 that the Conservatives would give justice but no more than justice to Roman Catholics, were less than conciliatory to the farmers who still made up the majority, and the Catholics who formed one-sixth, of the Ontario electorate. Most important, in his attachment to Britain and the empire, his Anglicanism, his preference for the proven system over the new, and his aristocratic temper, he was distinctly in the old Tory tradition. This had gone out of fashion in the post-confederation era of more moderate and flexible parties, broadly based and capable of comprehending diverse interests, such as John A. Macdonald's at Ottawa and Oliver Mowat's in Ontario.

A. MARGARET EVANS

Ont., Legislative Library, Newspaper Hansard, 1867–77 (mfm. at AO). PAC, MG 26, A. Can., Prov. of, Parl., *Confederation debates*, 448–63, 744–45, 975–77. *Canada Law Journal*, new ser., 23 (1887): 243–44. *Globe*, 11 July 1874, 27 June 1887. *Leader*, 14 Dec. 1874. *Nation* (Toronto), 31 Dec. 1874, 15 Jan. 1875. *Canadian biog. dict.*, I: 740–42. *CPC*, 1877. Dent, *Canadian portrait gallery*, III: 100–3. Read, *Lives of judges*, 404–24. A. M. Evans, "Oliver Mowat and Ontario, 1872–1896: a study in political success" (PHD thesis, Univ. of Toronto, 1967). B. W. Hodgins, *John Sandfield Macdonald, 1812–1872* ([Toronto], 1971). Joseph Pope, *Memoirs of the Right Honourable Sir John Alexander Macdonald, G.C.B., first prime minister of the dominion of Canada* (2v., Ottawa, [1894]).

CAMPBELL, COLIN, merchant, shipbuilder, shipowner, and politician; b. 7 Aug. 1822 at Shelburne, N.S., son of Colin Campbell and Maria Taylor; m. 9 Dec. 1845 Phoebe Ann Seely of Saint John, N.B., and they had ten children; d. 25 June 1881 at Weymouth, N.S.

Colin Campbell's grandfather, also named Colin Campbell*, immigrated to New York from Scotland in 1776 and moved to Shelburne, N.S., with other loyalists in 1783. The family moved to Weymouth shortly after Colin's birth in 1822, and he was educated there and at Digby, N.S. In the early 1840s he established himself as a merchant with a general store in Weymouth and also became a shipowner; his first vessel was the *Cygnet*, a 60-ton schooner built by Henry Barr at Weymouth in 1848. Two years later Campbell became the master and owner of a small brigantine. The next year he obtained a quarter share of the *Maria*, a 136-ton brigantine built at Weymouth by George Taylor. In 1854 Campbell established his own shipyard near his general store, in which over the next quarter century he built a number of vessels. He acquired timber lands in Digby County to guarantee a supply for his shipyard, and he also exported timber to the United States and Britain. All but one of his vessels were built at his yard with Reuben Hankinson as the master builder, and all were named for members of his family.

The first vessel built in the Campbell yard was the *Colin Campbell*, a brig of 169 tons launched in July 1854. In 1857 Campbell built the *Douglas*, a 110-ton brigantine, and in 1859 the *Charlotte*, a 71-ton schooner. He launched his first barque, the *Helen Campbell*, 274 tons, in August 1860. After 1860 both the number and the size of his vessels steadily increased. His first large barques were the 599-ton *Susan L. Campbell*, launched in July 1863, and the 664-ton *Minnie Campbell*, launched in November 1865. Over the next ten years six more barques and a brigantine were added to the Campbell fleet. These vessels averaged 688 tons, the largest being the *Agnes Campbell* built in 1870 at a cost of $29,559, the *Harriet Campbell* in 1873 at $30,872, and a second *Susan L. Campbell* in 1875 at $34,336. Three more large barques were added to the Campbell fleet in the late 1870s: the *Douglas Campbell*, 875 tons, the 1,112-ton *Harry Campbell*, and the 1,132-ton *Campbell*, the largest and the last of the Campbell vessels, built in 1879.

Colin Campbell was sole owner of all the vessels from 1854 to 1873, when his son George Douglas obtained a quarter share in three of them. Another son, John, acted as his father's agent in London, where he arranged charters, cargoes, and insurance for the vessels. Campbell enjoyed considerable success with his vessels. Although a few only lasted three or four years, he retained over half from eight to 13 years. At the time of his death eight vessels, a brigantine and seven barques totalling 6,000 tons and valued at over $80,000, flew the Campbell house flag.

In 1871 Campbell went into partnership with George Johnson to carry on a dry goods and grocery business at Weymouth Bridge (Weymouth). The partnership was known as Colin Campbell and Company, with Campbell holding three-quarters of the shares, and continued until his death. In addition, Campbell was agent at Weymouth for the Merchants' Bank of Halifax, founded in 1869. In April 1872 he formed the Weymouth Marine Insurance Company of which he was president. The company ran into financial difficulties in October 1878 and was dissolved the following year.

Campbell also had an active political career, serving in the House of Assembly as the member from Digby County from 1859 to 1867 and as a member of the Executive Council from 30 Nov. 1860 until 5 June 1863 in the government of Joseph Howe*. Again from 19 June 1875 until 15 Oct. 1878 he was a member without portfolio in the Executive Council of Philip Carteret Hill*. During his time in the assembly Campbell supported railway construction, free schools, and Nova Scotia's entry into confederation .

After Campbell's death in 1881 the majority of shares in the vessels were held by the women of the family and John Campbell managed the shipping business. No new vessels were constructed, however, and the existing fleet was gradually lost or sold. The store at Weymouth Bridge was continued and the lumber business was expanded and operated until after World War I.

CHARLES A. ARMOUR

Dalhousie Univ. Arch., MS 4-1, Colin Campbell, Daybooks, ledgers, letterbooks, and misc. papers, 1859–81; Campbell papers, Estate records, 1881–85; G. D. Campbell and Sons, Daybooks, ledgers, and letterbooks, 1881–90. Digby County Court of Probate (Digby, N.S.), Will of Colin Campbell, 28 Dec. 1875 (mfm. at PANS). PAC, RG 42, ser.I, 98–99, 240, 242, 248, 263–65. *Morning Chronicle* (Halifax), 27 June 1881. *Novascotian*, 2 July 1881. *Yarmouth Herald* (Yarmouth, N.S.), 30 June 1881. *Yarmouth Tribune*, 29 June 1881. *Directory of N.S. MLAs*. J. S. McGivern, *Truly Canadian* (5v., Toronto, 1968–69), III.

CAMPBELL, DUNCAN, journalist and historian; b. 3 April 1818 at Oban, Scotland, youngest son of the Reverend John C. Campbell, Congregationalist minister; m. Mary Stewart, and they had two sons and three daughters; d. 26 Aug. 1886 at Halifax, N.S.

Duncan Campbell began his career in journalism as editor of the Glasgow *Argus* and editorial writer for the *Daily Bulletin*, the first penny daily established in Scotland. In 1862, on a commission of the Glasgow Road Reform Association, he lectured throughout Scotland on the abolition of the archaic toll system.

Shortly before confederation the government of Nova Scotia, headed by Charles Tupper*, was earnestly engaged in recruiting settlers from Britain and the Continent, primarily as a remedy for the shortage of labour in mining and agriculture. Through the auspices of an agency in Glasgow established by the colony, Campbell conducted a large group of Scottish emigrants to Halifax early in the summer of 1866. He was shortly afterwards commissioned by Tupper to survey Nova Scotia as a potential home for immigrants and completed his report, a highly readable and informative document, in time for the 1867 session of the legislature.

The survey aroused in Campbell a profound interest in Nova Scotia history and he proceeded to give it serious and thorough study. Beamish Murdoch*'s three-volume treatise had carried the province's history only to 1827 and the intervening half century had not been covered. Campbell set out to update Murdoch's history and his *Nova Scotia, in its historical, mercantile and industrial relations* was published by John Lovell* in Montreal in 1873. Devoting the initial chapter primarily to the manners and customs of the Micmacs, he followed the history of the province to the death of Joseph Howe*, whom he interviewed at

Government House a few days prior to Howe's death in June 1873. The volume concludes with a series of chapters dealing with existing agricultural and industrial conditions, which provide a comprehensive but by no means impartial account of the Nova Scotian economy in the years immediately following confederation. Though Campbell's style was attractive and the content itself of considerable interest, the volume was not an unqualified success, being uneven in treatment and somewhat lacking in significant subject-matter.

Campbell was more fortunate with his *History of Prince Edward Island*, published in the autumn of 1875, for he had the time and opportunity to study and absorb his subject. To prepare himself he spent some time in Prince Edward Island studying all original records available, having received the generous support of local authorities in his research. This account spans the period from 1763, when the island became a British possession, to confederation. Campbell's profound concern for immigration prompted him to devote considerable space to the controversial land question and, casting aside any pretence of impartiality, he vehemently condemned the imperial government for its action in restricting land grants [*see* George Coles*].

During the two decades in which he resided in Nova Scotia Campbell was engaged in a variety of occupations. After a brief period with the immigration service of the federal Department of Agriculture he worked as a reporter on the Halifax *Morning Chronicle* during 1869 and 1870, and then served as secretary of the Halifax Industrial Commission for a short time. He worked as a bookkeeper, but eventually devoted himself wholly to historical writing. He was also a frequent contributor to the local press of articles and letters dealing with topics of public interest.

In the local North British Society Campbell was reported to be "a great favorite. . . . His eloquence and intellectual ability charmed his fellow-countrymen. . . ." He was an active supporter of St Matthew's Presbyterian Church and the Young Men's Christian Association, as well as other similar organizations. The *Morning Chronicle*, paying tribute to his accomplishments as a journalist and historian, described him as "moral, upright and honest . . . a genial, pleasant, courteous gentleman, but not without the egotism of the Scot."

In addition to his histories of Nova Scotia and Prince Edward Island, Campbell edited his father's autobiography. His history of Nova Scotia, adapted for use in the schools of the province under the title *History of Nova Scotia, for schools* (1877), was included in the curriculum for many years. He was also the author of a prize essay which was published in the *Nova Scotian Journal of Agriculture*.

SHIRLEY B. ELLIOTT

Duncan Campbell was the author of "Historical account of the rise and progress of agriculture in Nova Scotia," *Nova Scotian Journal of Agriculture* (Halifax), 4 (1881): 173–78; *History of Nova Scotia, for schools* (Montreal, 1877); *History of Prince Edward Island* (Charlottetown, 1875; repr., Belleville, Ont., 1972); and *Nova Scotia, in its historical, mercantile and industrial relations* (Montreal, 1873); and he was the editor of [J. C. Campbell], *Missionary and ministerial life in the Highlands, being a memoir of the Rev. John Campbell* (Edinburgh, 1853).

PANS, MG 5, Camp Hill Cemetery (Halifax), Register of burials, 1886. North British Soc., *Annals, North British Society, Halifax, Nova Scotia, with portraits and biographical notes, 1768–1903*, comp. J. S. Macdonald ([3rd ed.], Halifax, 1905), 354–55. *Morning Chronicle* (Halifax), 27 Aug. 1886. *Morning Herald* (Halifax), 27 Aug. 1886. *Canadian biog. dict.*, II: 540. *McAlpine's Halifax city directory* . . . (Halifax), 1869–70, 1886–87. *Literary history of Canada: Canadian literature in English*, ed. C. F. Klinck *et al.* (2nd ed., 3v., Toronto and Buffalo, N.Y., 1976), I: 236.

CAMPBELL, GEORGE WILLIAM, physician, educator, and businessman; b. 19 Oct. 1810 in Roseneath (Strathclyde), Scotland, son of Robert Campbell, chamberlain, and Catherine Campbell; m. Margaret Hutchison, stepdaughter of William LUNN, and they had four children; d. 30 May 1882 in Edinburgh, Scotland, and was buried 16 June 1882 in Montreal, Que.

George William Campbell, a superior student, was educated by a tutor at his home in Roseneath before studying medicine for one year in Dublin. He completed his training at the medical school in Glasgow, graduating MD in 1833. In May of that year he immigrated to Montreal, where he practised medicine for the remainder of his life. In 1835 Campbell joined the founders of the medical faculty of McGill College and became professor of surgery, an appointment he retained until 1875 (when he received an honorary LLD from the college), and professor of midwifery (a chair he relinquished in 1842). In 1835 he was also elected attending physician and surgeon to the Montreal General Hospital, a valuable position for a young doctor building a practice. He served actively in the hospital until 1853 when, now thoroughly established, he resigned and was placed on the consulting staff. One of his patients in the late 1850s was James Barry*, whose death in 1865 began a curious controversy concerning his sex. In 1860, when the first dean of the McGill medical faculty, Andrew Fernando Holmes*, died, Campbell succeeded him and continued in that office until his death.

As a teacher Campbell was dry and direct, and was much respected by his students. He strongly supported lecturing as a mode of teaching. Campbell published only a few case reports and addresses. His strengths in his medical career were surgical skill and administrative ability, and he is especially remembered for the latter. His effectiveness as dean was enhanced by his remaining aloof from the fierce political struggles within the profession and the faculty. Through the quality of Campbell's administration and the work of noted physicians on its staff such as Robert Palmer HOWARD and William Osler*, the medical faculty of McGill College came to be recognized as one of the top three or four medical schools on the continent.

The management of a large fortune amassed during an unusually successful surgical career involved Campbell actively in business. From 1869 until his death he was a director of the Bank of Montreal, and he was vice-president of that institution from 1876 to 1882. He also held directorships in the Montreal Telegraph Company and the Montreal Gas Company, and was associated as an active stockholder in a large number of local and national business ventures.

CHARLES G. ROLAND

Among G. W. Campbell's publications was an "Introductory lecture," *Canada Medical Journal and Monthly Record of Medical and Surgical Science* (Montreal), 6 (1869): 145–64.

PAC, RG 30, 10484–85. *Canada Medical and Surgical Journal*, 10 (1882): 699–703. *Canada Medical Record* (Montreal), 10 (1882): 213–15. G. P. Girdwood, "Introductory lecture delivered on Friday, 1 October 1875, at the opening of the forty-third session of the medical faculty of McGill University," *Canada Medical and Surgical Journal* (Montreal), 4 (1876): 193–94. R. P. Howard, *A sketch of the life of the late G. W. Campbell, A.M., M.D., LL.D., late dean of the medical faculty, and a summary of the history of the faculty* (Montreal, 1882). *Montreal Daily Star*, 15 June 1882. *Dominion annual register*, 1882: 334–35. H. [W.] Cushing, *The life of Sir William Osler* (2v., Oxford, 1925; repr. London and Toronto, 1940). Heagerty, *Four centuries of medical hist. in Can.*, II: 71. [F. J. Shepherd], "Biographical note: Geo. W. Campbell," *McGill News* (Montreal), 6 (1925): 2.

CAMPBELL, STEWART, lawyer and politician; b. 5 May 1812 in Jamaica, son of Colonel John Campbell, a soldier and politician, and a Miss Stewart; m. in 1837 Georgina McIntosh Richardson of Halifax, N.S.; d. 20 Feb. 1885 in Guysborough, N.S.

Stewart Campbell received his early education and studied law in England. He completed his legal training in Halifax, probably under William YOUNG, and was called to the bar in 1835. He practised law in Halifax prior to moving, some time before 1842, to Guysborough where he was associated with Judge Joseph Marshall*. During his residence in Guysborough he was a surrogate judge of the Court of Vice-Admiralty of Nova Scotia and a lieutenant-colonel of the Guysborough reserve militia, and held the offices of judge of the court of probate and coroner for the county.

Having developed a large and varied legal practice, Campbell in 1851 successfully entered the political field as a Liberal candidate for the assembly in Guysborough, and was re-elected in 1855, 1859, and 1863. Considered a political moderate by his peers, he served from 31 March 1854 to 31 Jan. 1861 as speaker of the assembly under both Liberal and Conservative governments, and from 1863 to 1865 he was a commissioner for consolidating the statutes of Nova Scotia. Though he was speaker, Campbell was active in looking after his constituents' interests and was necessarily involved in the distribution of patronage in Guysborough. The destitution facing the fishermen of his constituency during certain years deeply concerned him; in 1856, for example, he wrote Provincial Secretary William Alexander HENRY that 150 families would be reduced to starvation unless measures were adopted for their relief. Campbell also sought improvements in the educational facilities in his county. He survived the bitter religious feuds which split the Liberal party during the late 1850s and the disputed election of 1859 to remain the representative for Guysborough until 1867.

Campbell was included among the moderates who during the debates of the mid 1860s opposed Nova Scotia's entry into confederation. In September 1867 he was elected as Guysborough County's first member of the House of Commons. Although elected as a moderate anti-confederate, once in Ottawa Campbell generally supported the government of Sir John A. Macdonald* and was the first member of parliament from Nova Scotia to quit the repeal and annexation movements when it became obvious in 1868 that these would fail. It was probably his support for Macdonald which provoked an Antigonish crowd to pelt Campbell with eggs at a social occasion in September 1868. Re-elected in 1872, Campbell's 23 years in political office as an influential provincial and federal member ended with his defeat by John Angus Kirk in the 1874 general election.

Campbell had been named a QC in 1860 and in 1876 was appointed a county court judge for an area comprising the present-day counties of Antigonish, Guysborough, and Inverness; he served on the bench until his death in 1885. A local historian wrote in 1950 that Campbell was remembered in eastern Nova Scotia as "a scholarly and distinguished old gentleman, a devotee of cricket, which he had learned on the playing fields of Eton."

R. A. MACLEAN

PANS, MG 2, 733, nos.374, 379; 734, nos.911, 1022; 735, nos.1193, 1198; MG 4, 37; RG 1, 206; RG 5, E, 16; GP, 11; Vert. MSS file, Campbell, Stewart. St Paul's Anglican Church (Halifax), Marriage register, 1757–1863, 7 June 1837 (mfm. at PANS). *Morning Herald* (Halifax), 21 Feb. 1885. *Novascotian*, 14 Sept. 1868. *Belcher's farmer's almanack*, 1837. *Canadian directory of parl.* (J. K. Johnson). *CPC*, 1873. *Directory of N.S. MLAs*. *Dominion annual register*, 1885. *Political appointments, 1841–65* (J.-O. Coté). H. C. Hart, *History of the county of Guysborough, Nova Scotia* (2nd ed., [Windsor, N.S., 1895?]). A. C. Jost, *Guysborough sketches and essays* (Guysborough, N.S., 1950).

CAPREOL, FREDERICK CHASE, businessman and promoter; b. 10 June 1803 at Bishop's Stortford, Hertfordshire, England, second son of Thomas and Fanny Capreol; m. in 1833 Miss Skyring, and they had 11 children; d. 12 Oct. 1886 in Toronto, Ont.

Frederick Chase Capreol received a "commercial education" in England before arriving in Canada in 1828. For the next two years he resided in Montreal and participated in "settling up the affairs of the North West Fur Company." Capreol went back to England in 1830 but returned to Canada in 1833. He landed in New York where he married a woman he had met during the crossing and the couple continued to York (Toronto), Upper Canada; there they settled.

Although Capreol pursued various careers, such as real estate agent and pedlar of portraits of Queen Victoria and Sir Francis Bond Head*, his main occupation was the operation of an auction room which he opened in 1833 and continued until about 1850. In November 1833 he purchased a large amount of wild land near the Credit River. But because the original owner, an alcoholic of unsound mind, had been plied with liquor for two days at Capreol's home during the negotiation of the agreement, the Court of King's Bench overturned the transaction. Henceforth the financial and social élite of Upper Canada regarded Capreol with suspicion. His impetuosity was displayed in 1843, when the police refused to act immediately after the murder of his friend Thomas Kinnear. Chartering a steamer in the middle of the night, Capreol pursued and captured the murderers, Grace Marks and James McDermott, near Lewiston, N.Y. He was never reimbursed for the expense he incurred.

In July 1848 Capreol began to promote the building of a railway from Toronto to Georgian Bay. Undaunted by the failure of both the Great Western and the City of Toronto and Lake Huron railway companies to attract money, he was supremely confident. When the administration of Robert Baldwin* and Louis-Hippolyte La Fontaine* reserved for royal assent legislation passed by the assembly granting the road a charter, "mad Capreol" rushed to England and acquired the queen's approval. He returned in August 1849 and took his place as a director at the first meeting of the board of the Toronto, Simcoe and Lake Huron Union Rail-road Company, later renamed the Northern Railway Company of Canada.

Earlier railway construction in Canada had been seriously impeded by lack of capital. In hopes of overcoming this obstacle Capreol sponsored a "Grand Canadian Railroad Lottery" with prizes of land and stock valued at $2,000,000. In January 1850 he petitioned the Toronto City Council to invest £100,000 in tickets by means of debentures but, persuaded by alderman John George Bowes*, it decided to hold a referendum on the debenture issue. Capreol's plans evoked contrary reactions. Young patricians such as James McGill Strachan* and George William Allan* and rising financiers such as John Cameron, Ezekiel Francis Whittemore*, and James Mitchell supported him. Others, including many merchants, manufacturers, and workers, felt that the lottery fed on "a strong temptation to attain wealth without labour" and believed that anyone who could conjure up such a "demoralizing device" must have private gain in mind. Unfortunately for Capreol, the public did not share his confidence. The lottery collapsed after the debenture plan was decisively defeated. However, "the City took Stock in the Railway to an amount of £50,000 . . . [and] the Company was able to go on with the work."

Late in 1850, while he was arguing with the company's board of directors over suitable remuneration for expenses incurred in the promotion of the railway, Capreol concluded a contract with a New York firm of railway contractors, Storey and Company, to build the road. The public impact of this event made the board more receptive to Capreol's requests and in December he received £11,000 in company bonds payable over a seven-year period, bearing interest from 1 Jan. 1852. Yet he was still regarded with suspicion by the financial élite of Toronto. Through their mouthpiece, the board of trade, the merchants supported the railway, but not Capreol. The directors of the railway fired him from his position as manager two days before the sod-turning ceremony on 15 Oct. 1851. He had done well financially but he was denied the prestige, which to Capreol was more important, that would have accompanied the position of manager of Toronto's first successful railway.

Although his involvement with the Northern Railway was the high point of his public life, Capreol continued to be so busy that he once confided: "I have scarce time for the necessary calls of nature." In 1853 he became the first president of the newly chartered Metropolitan Gas and Water Company, and in 1863, along with Malcolm Cameron* and John Willoughby Crawford*, he incorporated the General Manufacturing Company of Peel. After the failure of this attempt at the manufacturing of cotton products, he turned to the final and possibly the grandest promotional scheme of his career. From 1865 until the 1880s he was obsessed with the idea of building a canal to link lakes Huron and Ontario. Capreol turned the first sod at the formal commencement of the Huron and Ontario Ship Canal on 17 Sept. 1866. He hoped world-wide recognition would accompany a successful project but his single-handed attempt to promote the multi-million-dollar enterprise failed.

The consistency of Capreol's failure in politics was only interrupted once. He ran repeatedly after 1843 in St George's Ward for election to the Toronto City Council. Until 1853 he always lost, generally finishing last. But in a by-election late in that year, occasioned by the resignation of Edward Graves Simcoe Wright, Capreol was finally elected to the council. He sat on council for only two months and attended infrequently. In 1842, running as an independent in Toronto, Capreol had made his first foray into provincial politics. He finished last. After confederation he attempted twice, without success, to gain election to the Ontario legislature. In his first attempt, in 1872, Capreol arrived at the nadir of his undistinguished political career when he failed to receive a single vote.

For Capreol the 1880s were years of bitterness and disappointment. He informed Sir John A. Macdonald* that he had spent 52 years of his life on great projects for which he "had crossed the Atlantic 23 times," but he had never received a proper reward. Even a card imprinted with a basket of forget-me-nots sent to Macdonald did not result in the knighthood he had requested. Although Capreol died a man of means, his career did not bring him the acclaim and public honours he so deeply coveted. The only memorial to him is a small railway junction town in northern Ontario that bears his name.

PETER BASKERVILLE

CTA, Toronto City Council papers, 1847–52 (mfm. at AO). MTL, Robert Baldwin papers. PAC, MG 24, B30; D16; MG 26, A; RG 30, 1414; RG 31, A1, 1861, Toronto, St George's Ward.

Doe ex dem. Jones v. *Capreol* (1834/35), 4 U.C.Q.B. (O.S.) 227. *British Colonist* (Toronto), 1839–54. *Globe*, 1845–61; 14 Oct. 1886. *Leader*, 1853–60. *Patriot* (Toronto), 1835–39, 1850–54. *Toronto Daily Mail*, 13 Oct. 1886. Morgan, *Sketches of celebrated Canadians*. P. A. Baskerville, "The boardroom and beyond; aspects of the Upper Canadian railroad community" (PHD thesis, Queen's Univ., Kingston, Ont., 1973). B. D. Dyster, "Toronto 1840–1860: making it in a British Protestant town" (1v. in 2, PHD thesis, Univ. of Toronto, 1970). A. F. Hunter, *A history of Simcoe County* (2v., Barrie, Ont., 1909; repr. 1948), I. Masters, *Rise of Toronto*. W. H. Pearson, *Recollections and records of Toronto of old . . .* (Toronto, 1914). *Robertson's landmarks of Toronto*, I. C. C. Taylor, *Toronto "called back," from 1894 to 1847 . . .* (Toronto, 1894). Elwood Jones and Douglas McCalla, "Toronto waterworks, 1840–77: continuity and change in nineteenth-century Toronto politics," *CHR*, 60 (1979): 300–23. R. D. Smith, "The Northern Railway: its origins and construction, 1834–1855," *OH*, 48 (1956): 24–36.

CAREY, DANIEL, lawyer, journalist, and author; b. 19 Nov. 1829 at Quebec City; m. about 1855, probably to Mary Murphy of Quebec, and one son was born of the marriage; d. 5 Jan. 1890 in Winnipeg, Man.

Little is known about Daniel Carey's early career. According to an obituary in the *Manitoba Daily Free Press* in 1890, Carey studied law in Montreal before he took up journalism, working first as an employee with the *Montreal Transcript* and then as editor of the *Quebec Argus*. However, the *Montreal directory* lists him as an assistant accountant (1850–53) and editor (1853–54) of the short-lived *Monitor* (also published in French as the *Moniteur*). In 1855, according to the *Quebec directory*, he lived in Quebec City and owned a bookshop on Rue Saint-Jean. On 9 Dec. 1857 Carey started the *Vindicator*, a literary paper of Reform bent that sought to defend the interests of the Irish of the city; it ceased publication in 1865. He was very active in Irish circles at Quebec, and in 1860 had been one of the incorporators of the St Bridget's Asylum Association of Quebec, an organization established to assist orphans and poor immigrants.

Carey gave up journalism about 1864 and entered the Department of Crown Lands at Quebec as a clerk in the office of the superintendent of cullers at an annual salary of $800. In 1870 he became a junior clerk in the federal Department of Public Works. Two years later, moved by a sense of adventure, he set out for Winnipeg, leaving his wife behind; he was called to the Manitoba bar that year and started a practice. Appointed protonotary of the Court of Queen's Bench in 1873, he combined the duties of librarian and interpreter to the court, his years in Quebec City having enabled him to master French. In addition the lieutenant governor of Manitoba, Alexander MORRIS, regularly consulted him on important criminal cases.

In 1874 Carey was the interpreter in the celebrated trial of the lieutenant of Louis RIEL, Ambroise-Dydime Lépine*, who had been charged with the murder of Thomas Scott*. He was relieved of his post as protonotary in 1878 because, according to the attorney general, Joseph Royal*, he had hindered the crown and unduly favoured the defence during the assizes of October 1877. It seems indeed that this dismissal stemmed from a divergence of views about the nature of a protonotary's office, for in addition to performing the duties of clerk of court and interpreter during proceedings Carey was also on occasion required to deliver certain judgements, and his legal knowledge could be called upon. Carey probably believed that he was to serve both the defence and the crown, his sole responsibility being to ensure respect for the law. On the other hand, the attorney general felt the protonotary was a law officer answerable to the crown rather than to the court. The latter opinion prevailed and Carey was obliged to give up his post.

He then returned to private law practice, with a brief venture into politics. In the 1883 provincial elections in Manitoba he stood as Liberal candidate in St Francis Xavier riding but was defeated by Conservative Edward Francis Gigot (72 to 36). The St Boniface paper *Le Manitoba* came out against him during the campaign, as the following passage published just before the election indicates: "Mr. Carey is not one of us, by either sentiment or sympathy: he is our most deadly enemy and his election would be a disaster." Carey was a partner in the legal firm of Carey and O'Reilly in 1883 but seems to have gone into partnership with his son, John Francis Xavier, the following year, for *Henderson's directory of the city of Winnipeg* includes the firm of Carey and Carey. From 1885 to 1890 the elder Carey apparently practised on his own, and at one point held the post of secretary-treasurer to the Catholic section of the Winnipeg School Board. In a letter of 3 Aug. 1885 which he sent from Regina to Archbishop Alexandre-Antonin Taché*, Carey mentioned a discussion with the crown officers of the pending cases of Métis involved in the rebellion of 1885; he expressed his pessimism as to the fate of the accused who refused to plead guilty to the charge of treason-felony.

A journalist and lawyer, Daniel Carey also gained recognition as a writer and poet. He published a collection of legal judgements which constitutes the first printed volume of law reports in the Canadian west. According to Henry James Morgan* he also composed three epic poems, "The battle of St. Foye," "Confederation," and "Pioneers of Canada," the first of which would have appeared in the *New Era* (Montreal) published by Thomas D'Arcy McGee*. Morgan also wrote in 1867 that Carey was preparing a popular history of Canada; it does not seem to have been published.

JOCELYN SAINT-PIERRE

[As well as having been editor of the *Monitor* (Montreal), 1853–54, Daniel Carey founded on 9 Dec. 1857 the *Vindicator*, an organ of the Irish community of Quebec City; he continued to work on this paper, which later became the *Quebec Vindicator*, until 1864. Regrettably, it is impossible to track down a complete collection of this paper but a few issues are held at ANQ-Q. In addition, Carey compiled and wrote the introduction to *Judgments in the Queen's Bench, Manitoba* (Winnipeg, 1875; repr. Calgary and New York, 1918). This work, better known as "Carey's Manitoba reports, 1875," constitutes the first volume of Manitoba law reports. J. ST-P.]

AASB, T 19982–85, 30966, 31877–78, 32556. PAC, RG 2, 1, P.C.216, 5 Oct. 1870; P.C.1255, 25 July 1871; P.C.684, 20 June 1872; RG 11, B1(b), 753–54. PAM, MG 12, B1, Corr., nos.557, 879, 1304; LB/J, nos.300, 305. *Le Manitoba* (Saint-Boniface), 15, 19, 22 déc. 1882; 4, 8, 19, 25 janv. 1883; 8 janv. 1890. *Manitoba Daily Free Press*, 6 Jan. 1890. *Morning Chronicle* (Quebec), 5 Dec. 1857. *Quebec Vindicator*, 29 Sept. 1863. Beaulieu et J. Hamelin, *La presse québécoise*, I. *CPC*, 1883: 312–13. *Dominion annual register*, 1882: 428. *Henderson's directory of the city of Winnipeg* . . . (Winnipeg), 1881–90. Manitoba Library Assoc., *Pioneers and early citizens of Manitoba; a dictionary of Manitoba biography from earliest times to 1920*, [comp. Marjorie Morley *et al.*] (Winnipeg, [1971]), 44. *Montreal directory*, 1842–64. Morgan, *Bibliotheca Canadensis*, 62. *Quebec directory*, 1844–64. P.-G. Roy, *Les avocats de la région de Québec*, 73. George Gale, *Quebec twixt old and new* (Quebec, 1915). [R.] D. and Lee Gibson, *Substantial justice: law and lawyers in Manitoba, 1670–1970* (Winnipeg, 1972). B. B. Cooke, "Famous Canadian trials; V: Ambroise Lépine, Riel's lieutenant," *Canadian Magazine*, 45 (May–October 1915): 57–61.

CAREY, ELIZABETH. *See* FIELD

CARRIER, CHARLES WILLIAM (baptized **Charles-Guillaume**), businessman; b. 20 Jan. 1839 at Saint-Henri, Lower Canada, son of Ignace Carrier and Marie-Louise Dallaire; m. 1 June 1864 Henriette, daughter of Louis Carrier, merchant and mayor of Lévis, Canada East; d. 18 Sept. 1887 at Lévis.

The youngest of a family of 14 children, Charles William Carrier entered the Collège de Lévis in 1853, the year of its opening [*see* Joseph-David DÉZIEL]. In 1855 he commenced an apprenticeship in the local commercial firm of Louis Carrier, his future father-in-law. There he was given full rein to learn business practices. In 1861 he took over the management of the firm, and, following his marriage in 1864, he was given complete control. Successful in this endeavour, he was able that same year to accept the proposal of a young mechanic, Damase Lebon, *dit* Laîné, to establish an iron foundry at Lévis. It was a major venture for these years. Wooden shipbuilding had been given a temporary stimulus by the American Civil War just at the time it had started to give way to iron shipbuilding in the rest of the world. The boom years of 1862 and 1863 for wooden ships therefore concealed the reality that their days were numbered. Carrier and Laîné saw beyond this activity and realized the need for the establishment of competent iron works, manufacturing a variety of products such as steam pumps, engines, and boilers. With this purpose in mind, in 1864 they formed the Fonderie Canadienne at Lévis, which was managed by the firm of D. Laîné et Compagnie. Six years later, with the acceptance of a third associate, Pierre-Sévère Riverin, the original partnership was dissolved and replaced by the firm of Carrier, Laîné et Compagnie. According to *Le Canadien* of 4 Nov. 1872, the foundry, which occupied 13,000 square feet near the Quebec-Lévis ferry landing and already employed over 100 workers, was busily expanding its operations. In addition to manufacturing domestic commodities, such as stoves, and mechanical instruments, the company had ventured into shipbuilding on a small scale, constructing barges and river ferries.

By 1873, Carrier, Laîné et Compagnie was soundly established and justifiably well known, and in that year steps were taken to incorporate it as the Quebec Iron Works. A prospectus was issued on 22 May proposing a joint stock company with a capitalization of $100,000. There were some extraordinary clauses in this prospectus, not the least of which were a personal guarantee from the promotors for three years of an 8 per cent annual dividend for shareholders and a rapid schedule for the calling of shares. The company proposed refitting its workshops to meet the construction needs of the rapidly developing railway system around Quebec, and planned to begin the manufacture of more sophisticated products such as wheels, axles, and ancillary equipment for railway rolling-stock. Capitalists may have had doubts about the future of railway development – this was the year of the Pacific Scandal – or about the ability of the partners to cope with such a large-scale undertaking; in any case, the idea seems to have died. No evidence has been found that the Legislative Assembly of the province of Quebec was approached for an act of incorporation. None the less, by 1880 Carrier, Laîné et Compagnie had added a new building to their works, measuring 200 feet by 80 feet, for the manufacture of locomotive and other types of engines. The following year the company signed a contract with the Intercolonial Railway for the construction of 100 railway cars.

Carrier was an employer of the old stamp who took a paternal interest in his workmen. He was credited with rejuvenating Lévis just when the shipyards were starting their decline, and he established training programmes for his employees in the skills of ironworking. To this end he had brought over from Europe French and Belgian specialists abreast of the latest technological innovations in metallurgy. He also did everything in his power to obtain the best possible environment for his firm, and became involved in the formation of various societies for the advancement of local industry: he was one of the founders of the Permanent Building Society of Lévis in 1869, president of the Board of Trade of the town of Lévis in 1873, director of the Société de prêts et de placements de Québec in 1878, and president of the Board of Arts and Manufactures of the province of Quebec from 1882 to 1887. This board, created in 1857, was charged with the establishment of technical schools in the principal industrial centres of the province; as a result of Carrier's influence, Lévis was granted a technical school in 1873. He also supported other projects affecting his community; in 1877, for example, he was listed among the shareholders of the Levis and Kennebec Railway Company [*see* Louis-Napoléon LAROCHELLE] and, in 1881, among those of the Quebec and Levis Telephone Company. Constantly on the look-out for new projects, he became one of the administrators of the North Shore Railway Company in 1882.

In 1886 Carrier contracted tuberculosis, and in the winter of 1886–87 he left for California to seek a cure. His journey was to no avail, and he returned to Lévis to die. As befitting one who had given so much to his community, Carrier was accorded "one of the most largely attended" funerals ever seen at Lévis. People of all classes of society came to pay homage to the man who had kept the city prosperous and busy throughout the 1870s and early 1880s while other towns suffered depression and unemployment. Of Carrier's three sons, only Charles-Henri continued his father's interest in the foundry; finally, in 1908, Carrier, Laîné et Compagnie was sold to the Bank of Montreal for $380,000.

KENNETH S. MACKENZIE

ANQ-Q, État civil, Catholiques, Notre-Dame (Lévis), 1er juin 1864; Saint-Henri, 21 janv. 1839. Baker Library, R. G. Dun & Co. credit ledger, Canada, 8. *Le Canadien*, 4 nov. 1872. *Morning Chronicle* (Quebec), 27 May 1873. *Cyclopædia of Canadian biog.* (Rose, 1888). P.-G. Roy, *Dates lévisiennes* (12v., Lévis, Qué., 1932–40), I-III. Gervais, "L'expansion du réseau ferroviaire québécois." P.-G. Roy, "Un industriel canadien-français: Charles-William Carrier," *Cahiers des Dix*, 13 (1948): 187–223.

CARROLL, JOHN SALTKILL (he never used his middle name), Methodist clergyman and author; b. 8 Aug. 1809 in a fishing hut on Saltkill's Island, Passamaquoddy Bay, N.B., the elder of twin sons of Joseph Carroll and Molly Rideout; m. in 1833 Beulah Adams of Perth, Upper Canada, and they had one son; d. 13 Dec. 1884 at Leslieville (now part of Toronto), Ont.

John Carroll's father, a saddler originally from County Down (Northern Ireland), was shipwrecked on the coast of New Brunswick after service on the British side in the American revolution and he settled in that province for some years. John was born in the course of a move by the family to Upper Canada and spent his first years in the Niagara peninsula and along the Grand River. His father served in the War of 1812, and in 1814 the family settled in York (Toronto) where John's mother ran a boarding-house. His early formal education was much interrupted and virtually ended in the winter of 1817–18 when the York school, first conducted by William Barber, closed. In 1822–23 he spent an unhappy year on a brother's bush farm north-west of York, and with his return to town became an apprentice in Jesse Ketchum*'s tannery.

Although religion seems to have been little practised in the home during Carroll's childhood, the New Light revival of Henry Alline* in New Brunswick had made a strong impression on several members of the family. Carroll's mother suffered for some years from religious melancholy, and an older brother underwent an impressive conversion towards the end of his brief life. John was enrolled in the first Methodist Sunday school in York at its inception in 1818; he was converted under Methodist preaching on 24 Aug. 1823, and a few weeks later experienced "persuasion that God had cleansed my inmost heart." In 1827, after a short period of teaching in the town of Scarborough, he was received on probation as a preacher, and in 1833 was ordained by the Canadian Wesleyan Conference which had just come into being through the affiliation of Canadian and British Methodists.

With the exception of the 1839–40 season, when because of ill health he was assigned the post of tutor at Upper Canada Academy, Cobourg, Carroll held a number of pastorates in Upper and Lower Canada until his superannuation in 1870. He then lived in Leslieville and at the time of his death was still engaged in founding suburban congregations around Toronto. He served as a chairman in ten different districts over a period of 27 years. In 1863 he was elected co-delegate or vice-president of the annual conference of the Wesleyan Methodist Church, the highest Methodist office open to a Canadian. The following year he addressed the Methodist Episcopal general conference in Philadelphia, and in 1876 the University of South Carolina conferred on him an honorary DD. He seems to have been a man who enjoyed the confidence of his fellow ministers rather than one distinguished for outstanding gifts of administration or leadership. Essentially Carroll was an effective revivalist, most at home in a camp-meeting or on a new circuit, and in his later years he came to symbolize an era of "happy" Methodism that was rapidly disappearing in such centres as Toronto with its settled congregations.

In the controversies that frequently convulsed Upper Canadian Methodism, Carroll always stood with the main Wesleyan body of the Canadian conference. He took this position in disputes with the followers of Henry Ryan* who in the late 1820s were opposed to links with American Methodism; he did so again with the Methodist Episcopals who objected to the 1833 union with the British Wesleyan Conference. From 1845, however, he also worked continuously for the union of all branches of Canadian Methodism, and on one occasion issued a scheme of his own that offered concessions to minority groups. His *Reasons for Wesleyan belief and practice, relative to water baptism* (1862), an exposition of the Wesleyan Methodist position on the subject, was endorsed by officials of all Canadian Methodist groups.

Carroll is chiefly remembered, however, neither as a preacher nor as a controversialist, but as a chronicler of early Methodism and of pioneer life in Upper Canada. He began in 1837 to send historical sketches to the *Christian Guardian* (Toronto), and between 1867 and 1877 published *Case and his cotemporaries*, a laborious five-volume compilation of facts about early Canadian Methodism that is not only indispensible to the historian but is also interesting to the general reader for the anecdotes of saddle-bag preachers scattered through it. Carroll's admiration for William Case* as a kind of hero figure is reflected in the title. *The stripling preacher* (1852) and "*Father Corson*" (1879) are works of pious remembrance. Of greatest literary interest among Carroll's writings are *My boy life* (1882), a series of sketches of his childhood and youth in York, most of which had originally appeared as instalments in *Pleasant Hours*, a Sunday school paper, *Past and present* (1860), a series of "crayons" of Methodist worthies reprinted from the *Canadian Methodist Magazine*, and *The school of the prophets* (1876), a frank account of Methodist personalities in the Perth area at the time of his pastorate there in the early 1830s, in which his talent for humorous description is least restrained by concern for denominational respectability.

Carroll's works abound with the clichés and conceits of the self-educated writer. He could on occasion be tedious or over-earnest, but at his best he was a skilful unmasker of pious foibles and pomposities. Few other writers have described 19th-century Canadian Methodism from within, and none with such irreverent yet sympathetic wit.

JOHN WEBSTER GRANT

J. S. Carroll was the author of: *The besiegers' prayer; or, a Christian nation's appeal to the God of battles, for success in the righteous war: a sermon . . . preached in St. Johns Canada East, on the occasion of the "General Fast," April the 18th, A.D. 1855* (Toronto, 1855); *Case and his cotemporaries; or, the Canadian itinerants' memorial: constituting a biographical history of Methodism in Canada . . .* (5v., Toronto, 1867–77); *The "exposition" expounded, defended, and supplemented* (Toronto, 1881); *"Father Corson"; or, the old style Canadian itinerant: embracing the life and gospel labours of the Rev. Robert Corson . . .* (Toronto, 1879); "Ministerial experience thirty years ago," *Wesleyan Repository, and Literary Record* (Toronto), 1 (1860–61): 9–13, 46–50; *My boy life, presented in a succession of true stories* (Toronto, 1882); *A needed exposition; or, the claims and allegations of the Canada Episcopals calmly considered, by one of the alleged "seceders"* (Toronto, 1877); *Past and present, or a description of persons and events connected with Canadian Methodism for the last forty years . . .* (Toronto, 1860); *Reasons for Wesleyan belief and practice, relative to water baptism . . .* (Peterborough, [Ont.], 1862); *The school of the prophets; or, Father McRorey's class, and 'Squire Firstman's kitchen fire, a fiction founded on facts* (Toronto, [1876]); *The stripling preacher, or a sketch of the life and character, with the theological remains of the Rev. Alexander S. Byrne* (Toronto, 1852); *Thoughts and conclusions of a man of years concerning churches and church connection* (Toronto, [1879]). J. W. Grant edited *Salvation! O the joyful sound: the selected writings of John Carroll* (Toronto, 1967).

PANB, Genealogical reference files, "Nicholas and Sarah Oliver Rideout family, Maugerville, N.B." (typescript). UCA, Matthew Richey papers, 1841–54, John Carroll to Matthew Richey, 3 July 1848. Methodist Church (Canada, Newfoundland, Bermuda), Toronto Conference, *Minutes* (Toronto), 1885: 14–15. *Canada Christian Advocate* (Hamilton, Ont.), 13, 27 March, 22 May, 12 June 1872. *Christian Guardian*, 10, 17 Dec. 1845; 2 Feb. 1848; 2, 9 July 1862; 5 Aug. 1863; 25 May 1864; 11 Oct. 1865; 5 Jan. 1877; 17 Dec. 1884; 4 Feb. 1885; 31 Dec. 1902. Cornish, *Cyclopædia of Methodism*, I: 39, 75, 750; II: 74. [W. H. Withrow], "Memories of the late Rev. Dr. Carroll," *Canadian Methodist Magazine*, 24 (July–December 1886): 550–53.

CARTWRIGHT, HARRIET. *See* DOBBS

CARY, LUCIUS BENTINCK, 10th Viscount FALKLAND, colonial administrator; b. 5 Nov. 1803, eldest son of Charles John Cary, 9th Viscount Falkland, a captain in the Royal Navy, and Christiana Anton; m. first 27 Dec. 1830 Amelia FitzClarence, natural daughter of William IV, and they had one son; m. secondly 10 Nov. 1859 Elizabeth Catherine Gubbins, widow of the 9th Duke of St Albans; d. 12 March 1884 at Montpellier, France.

Little is known of the early life of Lucius Bentinck Cary, who succeeded to the Falkland viscountcy in 1809 after his father's death in a duel. Possibly through his father's acquaintance with the Duke of Clarence during their naval careers, Falkland became sufficiently intimate with the royal household to be appointed lord of the bedchamber and to marry the natural daughter of the duke after the latter succeeded to the throne as William IV in 1830. Falkland also launched his political career in 1830 by publishing a pamphlet advocating parliamentary reform; the following year he sat in the House of Lords as a representative peer for Scotland and was created GCH. To his Scottish title he added in 1832 that of Baron Hunsdon of Scutterskelfe, Yorkshire, in the peerage of the United Kingdom. By 1837 he was chief government whip in the Lords and in that year was made a privy councillor. On Victoria's accession in 1837 he served first as lord-in-waiting and after 1838 as lord of the bedchamber.

Somewhat unexpectedly, Falkland was appointed in August 1840 lieutenant governor of Nova Scotia at a critical time in the province's history. A fierce, protracted political battle had just culminated in a successful demand by the assembly for the recall of the lieutenant governor, Sir Colin Campbell*. As a titled aristocrat, practised courtier, and political manipulator, Falkland was sent to calm these troubled waters by introducing the system of administration which Lord Sydenham [Thomson*] had developed in the Canadas. In the aftermath of the rebellions and the Durham Report, British ministers were not prepared to jeopardize imperial interests by conceding the controversial principle of responsible government which the British North American Reformers demanded. Nevertheless, as a step towards a more harmonious and acceptable form of government in Nova Scotia, Falkland was instructed to reconstitute the Executive Council, hitherto a Tory oligarchy, so that it included able, influential members from both houses of the legislature, irrespective of party affiliations. Working closely with such a body the governor would play an active part in formulating policies and in pushing through a vigorous legislative programme of much-needed reforms, as if he were prime minister of a coalition government.

Initially, fortuitous circumstances enabled Sydenham in the Canadas and Falkland in Nova Scotia to proceed along these difficult lines. With an appeal to the public spirit of provincial politicians, Falkland in October 1840 constructed an executive of both Conservatives and Reformers. Although shunned by die-hard Tories of the old official and merchant clique, whose upstart pretensions the aristocratic governor loathed, moderate Conservatives like James William Johnston* expressed a willingness and felt an obligation to offer their services to the crown. Joseph Howe* and several fellow Reformers, still elated about the triumph over Campbell and reassured by Falkland's liberal credentials, also accepted office in the coalition because they saw it as a practical step toward responsible government.

At first the anomalous arrangement prospered and Falkland established an intimate working relationship with Howe based on personal friendship and an apparent similarity of outlook. They conferred on policy, patronage, and protocol, and plotted to ensure that Howe succeeded Hibbert Newton Binney* as collector of excise at Halifax. Nevertheless, such an uneasy political compromise, which gave the elected politicians enhanced influence but denied them real power, could not long survive the reawakening of personal rivalries and controversial issues. During the contentious session of 1843 the question of provincial subsidies to denominational colleges set the anti-sectarian Howe and the Baptist Johnston at each other's throats. Falkland brought matters to a head when he incautiously appointed to the legislative and executive councils Mather Byles Almon*, Johnston's brother-in-law and a prominent Conservative merchant and banker. Howe and his friends angrily resigned and took up the cry of single-party government. From that moment the intimacy between Falkland and Howe was irretrievably shattered and the two intemperate, unforgiving men drifted into a remorseless, unedifying feud. Through the press Howe scathingly attacked Falkland and in an exasperated outburst in the assembly in 1846 declared that someone would "hire a blackfellow to horsewhip a Lieutenant-Governor." Hypersensitive to criticism and irritated by defiance, Falkland championed ever more staunchly the principle of coalition. His failure after the 1843 election to persuade Reformers to rejoin the executive meant that in practice Falkland fell into the clutches of the Conservatives, thereby hastening the advent of the party government he so deprecated.

Local Reformers alleged that the governor's abandonment of liberal for tory sympathies was intended to curry favour with Sir Robert Peel's ministry in England and win him preferment elsewhere. Nevertheless, Falkland's antipathy to the whole concept of government by a cabinet formed from the majority party in the assembly was the result not so much of personal calculation or political convictions, as of an instinctive distaste for the prospect of being ingloriously reduced to a cipher, like "a King at a Tournament," as Howe had described it, "who had nothing to do but to remain neuter during the Contest and then distribute the prizes among the Victors." This degrading possibility offended Falkland's *amour propre* more than his principles. Frenzied, alarmist dispatches home warned of the threatened destruction of the royal prerogative and of Britain's ties with Nova Scotia, but Falkland's cautious superiors refused to intervene or explicitly proscribe party government. After three years of unavailing struggle, Falkland asked to be relieved of his post and left for England in August 1846.

Although there was talk of him succeeding Lord Elgin [Bruce*] as governor of Jamaica, Falkland spent the next two years more congenially as captain of the Yeomen of the Guard, and possibly as government whip in the Lords. In 1848 he was appointed governor of Bombay. After an uneventful, undistinguished period of service in India he returned to England in 1853. He subsequently served as a magistrate and deputy lieutenant for the North Riding of Yorkshire.

Falkland was a tall, distinguished-looking man with a stately bearing and a severe, disdainful countenance which mirrored his aristocratic conceit and sensitive self-esteem. His administration in Nova Scotia was marked by courteous good humour when things went favourably, but adverse circumstances brought out an injudicious impulsiveness and an imperious, irritable temper ill suited to smoothing the difficult transition from representative to responsible government. Whatever his success in handling fellow peers, he lacked the adroitness, pliancy, and self-effacing detachment to be an adept manager of colonial politicians or a skilful moderator of their factional rivalries. Although he tended to view provincial politics in terms of personalities rather than political principles, the passage of events exposed his much vaunted liberalism as a shallow faith masking an instinctive conservatism and an egocentric temperament.

PETER BURROUGHS

PAC, MG 24, B29. PANS, RG 1, 116–19. PRO, CO 217/175–93; CO 218/32–34. [Joseph Howe], *Joseph Howe, voice of Nova Scotia*, ed. J. M. Beck (Toronto, 1964); *The speeches and public letters of Joseph Howe*, ed. William Annand (2v., Boston and Halifax, 1858); *Speeches and letters* (Chisholm). N.S., House of Assembly, *Journal and proc.*, 1840–46. *Illustrated London News*, 22 March 1884. *Times* (London), 14 March 1884. W. R. Livingston, *Responsible government in Nova Scotia: a study of the constitutional beginnings of the British Commonwealth* (Iowa City, 1930). W. S. MacNutt, *Atlantic provinces: the emergence of colonial society, 1712–1857* (Toronto, 1965). C. [B.] Martin, *Empire & commonwealth: studies in governance and self-government in Canada* (Oxford, 1929). D. A. Sutherland, "J. W. Johnston and the metamorphosis of Nova Scotian conservatism" (MA thesis, Dalhousie Univ., Halifax, 1968).

CASSELS, ROBERT, banker and businessman; b. 21 Feb. 1815 at Leith, Scotland, son of Walter Gibson Cassels and Janet Scougall; d. 18 Feb. 1882 at Montreal, Que.

Robert Cassels began his banking career in 1831 when he joined the National Bank of Scotland at Leith. He then worked in England until 1837 when he immigrated to Nova Scotia and opened a branch of the Bank of British North America at Halifax. During the next 24 years he managed branches at Chatham, N.B. (1838–41), Quebec City (1841–55), and Montreal (1855–61). By 1861 he was one of the more respected and experienced bankers in British North America. Wooed to Toronto in March of that year by Alexander Tilloch Galt*, Cassels became chief cashier (general manager) of the faltering Bank of Upper Canada, succeeding Thomas Gibbs Ridout*. Cassels' decision to accept the post was a fateful one. The bank, which had enjoyed a long, if overly respected, career since 1822, was virtually insolvent. In the words of a perceptive contemporary, David Lewis Macpherson*, it was managed by two "old men" (Ridout and William Proudfoot*) and assorted "cantankerous noodles." The bank had failed to master a series of problems in the late 1850s and was forced by the recession of 1857 to reap the harvest of careless credit policies; it had to accept useless securities and unsaleable real estate from debtors, thus severely restricting its cash flow.

Into this financial morass stepped Cassels, attracted in part by the board's guarantee of $10,000 annually for eight years and the promise of absolute control as manager. Before all else, he had to increase the bank's working capital and convince the public that the institution had a future. Since it was the government bank, Cassels looked to Galt, the Canadian minister of finance, for aid. Conditional on an optimistic report from Cassels concerning the bank's position, Galt privately promised both an increase in the government's deposit, which had already reached $1,200,000, and a guarantee to Glyn, Mills and Company, the bank's London agents, for future debts. In April 1861 Cassels supplied the requisite report to Galt. The public, however, did not learn about the government support, and the large amount owed Glyn, Mills and Company was included in the bank's annual statement for 1861 under the entry "cash deposits bearing interest." Believing on the basis of Cassels' report that the bank was worth saving, the stockholders accepted a reduction in capital from $50 to $30 per share, thus freeing some $1,200,000 to cover outstanding bad debts.

Cassels also initiated an overhaul of the decrepit managerial structure: head office activities were separated from branch business, loans and discounts were severely curtailed, and a land department was created to collect outstanding mortgages, terminate hopeless debts, and sell all land belonging to the bank. Cassels took a number of small creditors to court, and he forced large debtors such as the Kingston Brewery and Distillery (owing $210,000) [*see* James Morton*], the Lyn Tannery near Brockville ($124,000), and the Chippewa Distillery and Tannery at St Catharines ($128,000) into trusteeship to be managed on behalf of the bank. He himself acted as trustee or co-trustee of the three firms. The bank received little from these arrangements but Cassels, as trustee, did, in the form of commissions and inside information. His brother, Richard Scougall, a branch manager for the bank at Ottawa, purchased the Lyn Tannery in the late 1860s, and with Robert, who also owned flour and woollen mills, operated it until 1879.

Cassels had particularly to maintain good relations with several associates: with the Canadian government because its account enabled the bank to remain solvent; with the Grand Trunk Railway which had a debt of about $200,000 and was reluctant to pay it off; and especially with the Bank of Montreal which could at any time demand that its transactions with the bank be made in specie rather than notes – such a demand, attempted in the early 1860s, would have drained the bank of its holdings and precipitated collapse. In May 1862 a reform-oriented government, headed by John Sandfield Macdonald* and Louis-Victor SICOTTE, replaced the Conservative ministry of John A. Macdonald* and George-Étienne Cartier* of which Galt had been a member. Cassels' government connections crumbled. Luther Hamilton Holton* from Montreal, who became minister of finance in 1863, had long despised the Bank of Upper Canada which he considered a Conservative tool. Ignoring what he thought was Cassels' "bullying, coaxing and whining," Holton transferred the government account to the Bank of Montreal, effective January 1864. Despite considerable parliamentary lobbying Cassels failed to get the Grand Trunk to grant the bank preferential status for repayment of its large loans. Finally, late in 1866, the Bank of Montreal, managed by Edwin Henry King*, Cassels' former employee at the Montreal branch of the Bank of British North America, demanded redemption of the bank's notes in gold. The Bank of Upper Canada suspended payment on 18 Sept. 1866 and was placed under trusteeship on 12 Nov. 1866. Cassels was one of the trustees.

Perhaps Cassels had been, as Bank of Montreal director John ROSE claimed in 1866, excessively "sanguine." But he himself stood to gain much in salary and commissions by the bank's continuance; after the collapse and a legal battle with the rest of the bank's trustees (he resigned from the posts of trustee and manager on 10 July 1867) he lost the remaining years of his guaranteed salary and in 1868 he had also to arrange a payment of $20,000 to the bank to clear off claims made by the trustees about his use of its funds.

By 1867 Cassels had been, in addition to a banker, a successful negotiator for the city of Hamilton with London bondholders in 1863, a director of the Grand Trunk Railway from 1858 to 1866, the Canada Landed Credit Company of Toronto in 1866, and the Northern Railway Company of Canada during the 1860s, president of the St Andrew's societies of Quebec City, 1854, and Toronto, 1865, and the St James Club of Montreal, a Queen's College of Kingston trustee in 1866, and a militia officer, retiring in 1862 as the senior major in the Montreal Garrison Artillery Brigade. Despite this background and his requests for assistance from Sir John A. Macdonald, Cassels could not overcome his association with the Bank of Upper Canada and never again worked for a publicly owned bank. He left the Lyn Tannery around 1879, relocating in Montreal where he operated as a private banker until his death three years later, virtually unnoticed.

On 7 Aug. 1838 Cassels married Mary Gibbens, daughter of James MacNab, receiver general of Nova Scotia. They had five daughters and nine sons including Hamilton* and Robert*, prominent Toronto lawyers, and Walter Gibson Pringle* who became a judge of the Exchequer Court of Canada.

PETER BASKERVILLE

PAC, MG 24, B40, 3–4; D16, 21; D21, 3; D36; MG 26, A, 304; MG 27, I, D8, 7; RG 19, C1, 1192; 1210. QUA, M. L. Magill papers. *Gazette* (Montreal), 1882. *Globe*, 1866, 1882. Chadwick, *Ontarian families*, I: 26–29. *Dominion annual register*, 1882: 335–36. R. M. Breckenridge, *The history of banking in Canada* (Washington, 1910). Denison, *Canada's first bank. Money and banking in Canada; historical documents and commentary*, ed. E. P. Neufeld (Toronto, 1964), 132–48. "Glyns and the Bank of Upper Canada," *Three Banks Rev.* (Edinburgh), 55 (September 1962): 40–52. E. C. Guillet, "Pioneer banking in Ontario: the Bank of Upper Canada, 1822–1866," *Canadian Banker*, 55 (1948), no.1: 115–32. Shortt, "Hist. of Canadian currency, banking and exchange: the passing of the Upper Canada and Commercial banks," *Canadian Banker*, 12: 193–216.

CASTLE, JOHN HARVARD, Baptist clergyman and educator; b. 27 March 1830 in Philadelphia, Pa, son of Robert Castle of County Antrim (Northern Ireland); m. 15 Sept. 1853 Mary Antoinette Arnold of Rochester, N.Y., and they had two daughters and three sons; d. 11 June 1890 in Philadelphia.

John Harvard Castle was the son of a Scottish-Irish family which had emigrated to the United States and settled in Pennsylvania in 1825. Upon being converted and baptized at about 16, he decided to enter the Baptist ministry. To that end, after completing his early education in Philadelphia, he enrolled in 1847 at the newly established university at Lewisburg (later

Bucknell University) where he completed his studies in 1851 as a member of the first graduating class. (He was awarded a DD in 1866.) He then proceeded to the Rochester Theological Seminary; following his graduation from this Baptist institution and his ordination in 1853 at Pottsville, Pa, he served a number of pastorates in Pennsylvania and New York. In the process he became actively involved in the educational and missionary work of American Baptists serving, for instance, on the boards of the university at Lewisburg and the Crozer Theological Seminary. This experience stood him in good stead during his subsequent career in Canada.

Apparently Susan Moulton, the American-born second wife of Senator William MCMASTER of Toronto, a financier and businessman, was largely instrumental in having Castle, one of her former pastors, called in 1873 to fill the pulpit of the Bond Street Baptist Church in that city. Under Castle's vigorous leadership the church flourished and its congregation rapidly increased to the point where new quarters had to be planned. A campaign spearheaded by Castle's initiative and the McMasters' financial contributions led to the completion of the Jarvis Street Baptist Church in 1875. At once this successor to the Bond Street Church became a prominent landmark in Toronto and the show-piece of the Baptist community.

Subsequently Castle played a crucial role in the founding of the Toronto Baptist College, the immediate forerunner of McMaster University. The school was the outgrowth of a scheme to remove to Toronto the theological department of the Canadian Literary Institute in Woodstock, Ont. Founded by Baptists in 1857, and opened in 1860, the institute furnished instruction in the arts and for the ministry under the principalship of Robert Alexander Fyfe* (in 1883 it was renamed Woodstock College). The move of the theological department was undertaken in the belief, shared by Castle and Senator McMaster, that the growing city of Toronto would provide a more stimulating and challenging environment for the training of Baptist clergymen than the small town of Woodstock. Throughout, Castle skilfully shouldered the difficult task of convincing the Baptist constituency of the need for this new urban venture in education, one that would lead to the dismemberment of the much respected literary institute. Through his efforts opposition to the proposal was overcome at a special educational convention called by the Baptists in April 1879, and two years later the Toronto Baptist College was opened in the building known as McMaster Hall, on a site purchased for it on Bloor Street by McMaster. Predictably Castle was named president of the new institution, an appointment that necessitated his resignation from Jarvis Street Church.

From the beginning, Castle occupied the chair of systematic theology and pastoral theology. Well regarded by the Baptist community as both a theologian and a teacher, he sought, with the support of the McMasters and his colleagues, Theodore Harding Rand* and Malcolm MacVicar*, to train a ministry that could cope not only with traditional rural concerns but with the strong forces of industrialization and urbanization in Canada. He also hoped that the Toronto Baptist College would become Canada's principal centre for educating prospective Baptist pastors, a move in keeping perhaps with the city's own metropolitan ambitions in the late 19th century. But administrative difficulties and financial problems combined to frustrate this latter ambition and, as a result, sister institutions such as Acadia University in Nova Scotia continued to produce their own theological graduates.

Although the college was affiliated with the University of Toronto from its inception, Castle took a decisive part in blocking plans to have it federate with the university, an arrangement being contemplated by other denominational institutions in Ontario such as Victoria and Trinity. In 1884 representatives of these various denominational colleges and universities met to discuss plans for federation. As the discussions continued, Castle and MacVicar appeared to draw a sharp distinction between federation and affiliation. Affiliation could be for the college a means of preserving its arts courses, particularly philosophy, which had been introduced to supplement the curriculum, whereas federation with the provincial university, it began to seem certain, would emasculate the arts programme. These serious reservations about union were reinforced by the opposition of a vocal element within the denomination whose moral and financial support Castle and MacVicar had no desire to forfeit. This element was already convinced of the need for an independent university under Baptist auspices as a "Christian alternative" to the arts programme which federation promised. In the spring of 1887, Castle, accompanied by Rand, appeared before the private bills committee of the Ontario legislature in an effort to demonstrate the viability of an independent venture. McMaster University received its charter later that year, absorbing the Toronto Baptist and Woodstock colleges. In 1930 the university moved to Hamilton.

The Toronto Baptist College became McMaster University's faculty of theology although it continued in its previous role until the university actually opened in 1890. Castle taught and presided as principal of the faculty until failing health, which had ruined his chances of becoming the university's first chancellor in 1887, forced him to retire in 1889. He returned to the United States to take up residence in Rochester after a productive career of 16 years in Canada, In the summer of 1890 he died in his native Philadelphia, where he had recently completed a term preaching in a local church.

In an obituary Thomas Trotter*, clergyman and

educator, remarked upon Castle's engaging personality, and upon his great ability as an administrator and conciliator which had been shown to such advantage at the Toronto Baptist College. He was a man of "tact, and resource, and Christian devotion."

CHARLES M. JOHNSTON

Canadian Baptist Arch., Biog. file, J. H. Castle; Toronto Baptist College, Corr., 1881–85; Board of Trustees, Minute book, 12 April 1881–28 April 1887; Toronto Baptist College, Executive Committee, Minute book, 21 June 1881–28 Oct. 1887.

[William Davies], *Letters of William Davies, Toronto, 1854–61*, ed. W. S. Fox (Toronto, 1945). Toronto Assoc. of Baptist Churches, *Minutes* (Toronto), 1875–80. *Canadian Baptist* (Toronto), 26 June 1890: 4–5. *The Baptist year book* . . . (Toronto), 1873–90, especially the annual reports of the president of the Toronto Baptist College and principal of the faculty of theology for 1882–89. Robert Hamilton, "The founding of McMaster University" (BD thesis, McMaster Univ., Hamilton, Ont., 1938). C. M. Johnston, *McMaster University* (2v., Toronto and Buffalo, N.Y., 1976–81). A. L. McCrimmon, *The education policy of the Baptists of Ontario and Quebec* (Toronto, 1920). *McMaster University, 1890–1940* . . . (Hamilton, 1940). D. C. Masters, *Protestant church colleges in Canada: a history* (Toronto, 1966). Thomas Trotter, "John Harvard Castle," *McMaster Univ. Monthly* (Toronto), 1 (1891–92): 145–50.

CAUCHON, JOSEPH-ÉDOUARD, journalist, businessman, and politician; b. 31 Dec. 1816 at Quebec City, son of Joseph-Ange Cauchon, *fils*, and Marguerite Valée; d. 23 Feb. 1885 in the Qu'Appelle valley (Sask.).

Joseph-Édouard Cauchon was a descendant of one of the oldest families in the colony. His ancestor Jehan Cochon, originally from Dieppe, in Normandy, France, is thought to have arrived in Canada with his family, including a son named Jean, about 1636. Having come as a settler rather than an indentured employee, Jehan obtained a land grant in the Beaupré seigneury which the Compagnie des Cent-Associés was then making special efforts to settle. His son secured a similar grant in the same period, and from 1652 to 1667 held the office of seigneurial attorney. He was thus a member of the "public service bourgeoisie" which was concentrated in the region around Quebec City and engaged in both agriculture and administration. In 1680, for unknown reasons, the name Cochon was written Cauchon, and the more elegant form remained in use. The family established itself on the Beaupré shore and apparently did not move to the city until the sixth generation. It is known that Joseph-Ange was a dairyman at Quebec when he married Marguerite Valée on 14 April 1814. Their son Joseph-Édouard was born two years later in Saint-Roch parish in Quebec City.

Joseph-Édouard Cauchon received his classical education at the Petit Séminaire de Québec from 1830 until 1839 when he began to study law in the office of James George Baird. In 1841 he published at Quebec a handbook, *Notions élémentaires de physique, avec planches à l'usage des maisons d'éducation*, which was of limited scientific and pedagogical value but which drew attention to its youthful author. From 1841 to 1842 he also worked as a journalist for *Le Canadien*, a paper then printed by Jean-Baptiste Fréchette; Cauchon replaced Étienne Parent*, who as representative for Saguenay County had to go to Kingston, Canada West, for the first two sessions of the Legislative Assembly of united Canada. Cauchon's experience with the paper profoundly influenced his future. Although he was called to the bar in 1843, he never practised law, and was to be a journalist and politician.

With his brother-in-law Augustin Côté*, Cauchon launched *Le Journal de Québec* on 1 Dec. 1842. This paper replaced the French edition of the *Quebec Gazette* which after a number of interruptions had ceased publication on 29 October as a result of insuperable financial difficulties. Cauchon was proprietor from 1842 to 1862 and editor from 1842 to 1875, except for the years 1855 to 1857 and in 1861 when he was a member of the government. Orginally a bi-weekly, in folio of two pages, *Le Journal de Québec* resembled other 19th-century newspapers, particularly in the columns it carried. It mainly discussed politics and religion, and tended to support the Reform position. It took its provincial and international news from Canadian and foreign papers and gave extensive coverage to municipal, economic, and literary activities of the Quebec region. According to a circular of 5 Nov. 1842 *Le Journal de Québec* aspired to be a "palladium of liberty." It declared itself independent of men and parties, and would extend support to one or the other "solely for the sake of principles." Both nationalist and unionist, it would convey French Canadian views first and foremost but was ready to offer "a willing hand to all . . . who desire the advancement and prosperity of [our] common native land." This ideal would be eroded by the impetuous personality, ambition, and personal interests of Cauchon, who for almost all his political career was its guiding spirit.

It is difficult to gauge Cauchon's work as a journalist since *Le Journal de Québec* has not yet been systematically studied. Furthermore, contemporary testimony concerning Cauchon was always tainted by party passions. In the opinion of Liberal Laurent-Olivier David*, Cauchon was "ambitious, violent, enamoured of money, honours, and luxury, lacking in scruple, enterprising, full of shifts and expedients." On the other hand Alfred Duclos* De Celles, a friend of the Conservatives, admired Cauchon who had "read everything, retained everything – history, constitutional law, political economy." Again, for *La*

Patrie of Montreal, Cauchon was an unpredictable journalist able to disconcert the most unruffled opponent – the only one "who ever succeeded in driving the wise and worthy Étienne Parent into a rage." From all these testimonies, although in many ways contradictory, Cauchon emerges as a journalist who made an impact with his keen intelligence, violent and energetic nature, and scathing pen.

Cauchon and his influential *Journal de Québec* entered into all the public discussions of the day, which in the final analysis were political. As examples one might cite articles written to counter his opponents: George Brown* and the *Globe* (Toronto) on educational and religious questions and on the principle of "rep by pop"; Télesphore Fournier and Marc-Aurèle Plamondon of *Le National* (Quebec) on the radical ideology of the Rouges (the name, taken by Cauchon from the French radicals, was to become the accepted one); Louis-Antoine Dessaulles* and *Le Pays* (Montreal) on the democratic nature of the government; and Joseph-Charles Taché* and the *Courrier du Canada* (Quebec) on the principle of confederation and on school reform.

The most famous of these debates was on confederation, a subject which inspired Cauchon to write two pamphlets. In 1858 he came out against an initial plan in a series of articles which he published at Quebec as a brochure entitled *Étude sur l'union projetée des provinces*. The scheme was still quite vague, and the author examined it on the basis of 27 hypotheses which summed up the problems of the union. In July 1864, when the coalition of George Brown and Sir Étienne-Paschal Taché* had just been formed, Cauchon returned to the subject in a series of articles published at Quebec between 12 Dec. 1864 and 28 Jan. 1865. This series constitutes the political essay entitled *The union of the provinces of British North America*, published in both French and English; its value as a document has been confirmed by historians studying the confederation period. In it the author first gradually cleared away his arguments of 1858 and, having pointed out the important steps in the constitutional history of Canada since 1840, he established that the union of the provinces, as one or on a federal basis, had become a political necessity. He then declared himself in favour of a centralized federal system, resembling a legislative union rather than the American constitution. Finally he defended each of the 72 Quebec Resolutions, which the parliament of Canada would soon be invited to ratify, and concluded that the proposed confederation would guarantee the protection of the privileges, long-standing rights, and special institutions of Canada East. This work, which supported those favouring confederation, revealed Cauchon's political affiliation. Indeed in 1864, after 20 years of political life, he had become one of the most powerful Conservatives in Canada East.

Cauchon had entered politics in 1844. That year he was elected for Montmorency County, defeating Frédéric-Auguste Quesnel*. He represented this constituency throughout his political career, being elected "by acclamation" in 1848 and 1861 and facing opponents in 1851, 1854, 1857, and 1863. As was customary, some of these elections were marked by corruption and violence.

In the parliament of united Canada, Cauchon immediately associated his name with the politicians who would be called upon to play a decisive role in the country's history. He supported the Reform policy of Louis-Hippolyte La Fontaine* and Robert Baldwin*; with Pierre-Joseph-Olivier CHAUVEAU, he fought to get Augustin-Norbert Morin* elected speaker of the house because he was bilingual; he waged war on Louis-Joseph Papineau*, whom he categorized as one of those "men who are powerful destructive [forces], but who have never built anything on the ruins they have made." In parliament Cauchon therefore supported the great political compromise that followed the failure of the 1837–38 rebellion and led to ministerial responsibility. Moreover, in a debate in 1849 on the repeal of union Cauchon defended union because it ensured equal representation in parliament and thus guaranteed the institutions and laws of each section of the province. But Cauchon expressed his opposition in 1851, disapproving of the alliance of the government, then under Francis HINCKS and Augustin-Norbert Morin, with Brown's Clear Grits, whose "democratic, socialist and anticatholic" principles he condemned. He even refused the offer Hincks made him of the post of assistant provincial secretary without a seat in the cabinet. Cauchon's distrust of the government, an attitude he expressed both in parliament and in his *Journal de Québec*, helped to weaken the government and the Reform party.

Cauchon, with his "brother in arms" Louis-Victor SICOTTE, was responsible for the defeat of the Hincks–Morin government in 1854 which signalled the formation of the Liberal-Conservative coalition. He enthusiastically welcomed the events of 1854, even though they blighted his well-known hopes of becoming prime minister. Indeed those hopes were bound up with the political crisis of 1854, which the Liberal-Conservative coalition resolved. Under the government of Sir Allan Napier MacNab* and Morin in 1854 Cauchon firmly supported the bills abolishing the seigneurial régime and secularizing the clergy reserves.

When the government was reconstituted under MacNab and Étienne-Paschal Taché in 1855, Cauchon made his presence felt by introducing a bill to make the Legislative Council elective. Appointed commissioner of crown lands for Canada East that year, he retained this post under the new government of Taché and John A. Macdonald* but resigned in

April 1857 over the issue of the North Shore Railway. The story of this railway really began in 1852 when the era of Canadian railways had just dawned. It was incorporated in 1853, at the time the government decided to subsidize the building of the Grand Trunk from Montreal to Lévis, on the south shore. The promoters of a railway on the north shore between Montreal and Quebec asked for similar assistance. The government refused, asserting that this railway was of local rather than provincial interest. Convinced that only a north shore railway could improve the economic situation of Quebec City, Cauchon devoted his energies to the project from 1855; time and again, as his correspondence shows, he approached Quebec City, the north shore municipalities, and London financiers for the necessary funds. In 1857 the plans and estimates were ready but there was still no capital. Cauchon then gave the government an ultimatum: he asked for a grant of land for the railway and threatened to resign as commissioner if it was not made. The government accepted Cauchon's resignation, but a few months later granted 1,500,000 acres of uncultivated land to the venture. It should be pointed out that land transferred by the government to the railways served in that period as a guarantee for loans which the companies would have had to negotiate in the financial markets. For its part Quebec City voted a subsidy of $50,000. However, the project had to be suspended when approaches to London financiers proved unsuccessful. It was obvious that the obstacle was the Grand Trunk Railway [*see* James Bell Forsyth*], a fact unlikely to give Cauchon warm feelings towards such colleagues such as Étienne-Paschal Taché, who was personally involved in the Grand Trunk venture. Consequently Cauchon showed himself particularly jealous of his political autonomy after 1857, and when voting in the house fluctuated between the right and the left.

He even became an opponent of the government of John A. Macdonald and George-Étienne Cartier* in 1858, openly supporting the principle of double majority [*see* Thomas-Jean-Jacques LORANGER]. During a parliamentary debate on this question Cauchon asserted that the federal principle, which was the basis of the union of the two Canadas and had been ratified in 1848 by the government, "can be real only to the extent that the executive councillors from one section of the province enjoy the express confidence of the majority of its representatives." On two major matters, the seat of government and the bill on customs duties, introduced by Alexander Tilloch Galt*, Cauchon also voted against the Cartier–Macdonald government, and in his *Journal de Québec* he opposed the confederation scheme which had been included in the government's platform at Galt's insistence.

In short Cauchon displayed certain liberal leanings. Officially, however, he was still a supporter of the Liberal-Conservative party. During the 1860s, when party lines became strongly drawn, he always backed the Conservative government. He was even minister of public works from 1861 to 1862, and in 1864, although he had been opposed to any constitutional change, as noted earlier, he became one of the most ardent advocates of confederation. During the subsequent debates he devoted a great deal of time in particular to explaining the clauses pertaining to the Senate, judicial organization, marriage, and divorce. He also made himself the defender of a provincial legislative council but vigorously objected to the clause giving special protection to certain counties in Canada East which were predominantly English-speaking; he considered it an affront to French Canadians, who had always respected the rights of Protestant minorities. The support he had given to the federative plan, the authority he enjoyed at Quebec, and the respect he commanded in political circles made him the natural choice in 1867 as prime minister of the new province of Quebec.

Immediately after confederation Cauchon was called upon to form the government. He set to work, but encountered a major obstacle which led to his failure. In order to secure in the government adequate representation of the various social groups, Cauchon offered the portfolio of provincial treasurer to Christopher DUNKIN, a converted opponent of confederation. At Galt's suggestion, Dunkin accepted on condition that the education bill of Hector-Louis Langevin* be revived in the Quebec legislature. This bill had given the last government of united Canada some trying moments in 1866. In effect the 1866 Langevin bill was designed to give the Protestant minority in Canada East the independence it had long desired in the field of education, and was financially favourable to the Roman Catholic majority. That same year Robert Bell*, a young Irishman in Canada West with a lofty sense of strategy, introduced an education bill which was favourable to the Catholic minority of Canada West but which had no chance of being passed. In his *Journal de Québec* Cauchon supported the claims of the Catholic minority in Canada West and censured the ministers who refused to introduce Bell's bill as a corollary to Langevin's; although he favoured a recognition of the rights of the Protestant minority, he objected to the creation of a Protestant superintendent of education in Canada East. Faced with this dilemma Langevin had withdrawn his own bill to avoid exposing the government of John A. Macdonald and Narcisse-Fortunat Belleau* to defeat. In 1867, Cauchon could not reintroduce a bill which took no cognizance of his earlier objections. Consequently Dunkin was ruled out. Yielding to the obvious fact that under Galt's influence, any Protestant representative would act as Dunkin had, Cauchon abandoned the idea of forming a government and becoming prime minister of Quebec. He did, however, continue as the member for Montmorency in the Legislative Assembly of the province from 1867 to 1874.

But a man of Cauchon's calibre and ambition could not be content with a mere representative's seat in the Quebec parliament. In October 1867 he accordingly issued an ultimatum to his friends in Ottawa: he wanted "the lucrative post of senator and speaker of the senate." This explicit demand precipitated the resignation of Belleau from his seat for the division of Stadacona within six days; Cauchon was appointed to succeed him and then to the speakership of the Senate, a post he held from November 1867 to May 1869. This move was looked upon with disfavour in political circles, whether they were hostile or friendly to the government. The government's "underhand dealing" was denounced in terms sometimes verging on insult. Thus Senator George Crawford* upbraided the government for sending to the Senate "the only 'Cochon' in the House": "he is a 'cochon' [pig] in his appearance, in his bearing, in his table manners and in parliament." The appointment, made despite wide opposition, is fairly indicative of the pressure Cauchon brought to bear and indeed of his ascendancy within the Conservative party, not only in the Quebec region but also at the provincial and federal levels.

His power was exerted in another sphere. He was mayor of Quebec City from 1865 to 1867 but it is difficult to assess what he accomplished since he never published a report, for which he was rightly blamed by his political enemies. The major event during his term of office was the fire on 14 Oct. 1866 which totally destroyed the suburbs of Saint-Roch and Saint-Sauveur; nearly 3,000 houses were lost and 15,000 persons were left homeless. Cauchon organized a permanent fire brigade with a telegraphic alarm system at a cost of $38,120. To this end he raised the budget of the municipal fire committee from $4,000 to $9,000. In addition he is said to have collected more than $500,000 for the disaster victims. But he was overwhelmingly defeated in the municipal elections of December 1867 by John Lemesurier who had the support of the working class.

Ousted from both the provincial government and the Quebec City Council, Cauchon had therefore to direct most of his energies to the Senate. But the upper house was much too calm and peaceful an arena for him. Consequently he resigned on 30 June 1872, to return on 7 Aug. 1872 to the House of Commons where he had briefly held a seat in 1867. This time he came as an independent member for the riding of Quebec Centre. The opposing candidate had been James Gibb Ross, who represented the Protestant English minority in the city. The campaign, "the fiercest that has ever been seen at Quebec," had developed into a struggle between nationalities, and had been marked by a pistol fight in the Protestant cemetery on Rue Saint-Jean. This fight had left numerous casualties in both camps and one of Ross's supporters had been killed. Because he had a great deal of influence at Quebec as the president of the North Shore Railway Company, a director of a number of banks, and the owner of the Asile de Beauport (Centre hospitalier Robert-Giffard) and *Le Journal de Québec*, Cauchon had emerged the electoral victor. He was evidently economically well situated; he was in addition one of the directors of the Interoceanic Railway Company of Canada (1872–73). At Quebec he was said to be rich. In fact he lived like a pasha. The stone house at 63 Rue d'Auteuil which he had bought in 1855 was like a palace-cum-museum. Its architecture was sumptuous and there were rooms set aside for the numerous works of art that Cauchon had brought back from his frequent trips to Europe.

Cauchon, who with his brother-in-law formed the firm of A. Côté et Compagnie, had a good credit rating with R. G. Dun and Company of New York. According to the brief comments in the handwritten register for Quebec City for the years 1855–63, it is clear that the two men possessed next to nothing in 1855, although they had been in business for 15 years. At that time their credit rating was based only on the official patronage *Le Journal de Québec* enjoyed. But in the years after 1857, when the patronage had ceased temporarily, they were still given the same rating by R. G. Dun because they were recognized as "reliable businessmen who have sufficient capital at their disposal." In 1861 the register mentions that the two men also had in their favour the support of the clergy and their influence with the government, Cauchon being at that time minister of public works and well looked after by governmental patronage. But it is certain that Cauchon acquired wealth by other means and that land speculation was his most lucrative source, as is evident in the numerous notarial acts which have been located.

In 1873 Cauchon's ambition and hopes were reawakened by a number of events. Belleau's term of office as lieutenant governor was expiring, and Cauchon coveted the post. But he had far too many enemies and his prestige was declining, so there could be no question of conferring this office on him. Indeed the Beauport asylum affair had seriously undermined his standing in the province. Despite skilful subterfuge on his part, it had been proved that Cauchon had been the real owner of the asylum since 1866, the physicians Jean-Étienne LANDRY and François-Elzéar Roy serving him as figureheads, and that Cauchon was reaping all the profits from the business. The asylum had been subsidized before 1867 by the government of united Canada, and after that date by the government of Quebec, which created a conflict of interest for Cauchon who was then a member of the Legislative

Assembly. But it was not until 1871 that the opposition in the Quebec assembly tried to develop this into a scandal which would overthrow the government. Cauchon, however, continued to outwit his enemies. His electoral mandate was challenged during the session of December 1871 but the investigating committee was unable to reach a conclusion in the absence of one important witness. Meanwhile Cauchon sold all his interests to Dr Roy. The committee resumed its inquiry in the 1872 session and reported to the assembly. On 10 Dec. 1872, at the moment when the representatives were to decide the validity of Cauchon's election, he tendered his resignation to the speaker. He again ran for election in Montmorency County, resumed his seat in the assembly at the end of the session, and kept it until 1874; he then resigned from his post for good as a result of the abolition of the double mandate permitting members of the House of Commons to sit also in a provincial legislature.

When Cartier died in May 1873 Cauchon was eager to succeed him as leader of the Quebec wing of the Conservative party, but nobody in Montreal or Quebec wanted him. Following this new disappointment he allied himself tacitly with the Liberal opposition in the House of Commons. During the Pacific Scandal he openly proclaimed his change of allegiance and became one of the bitterest foes of his former political friends.

That year Cauchon also encountered difficulties in the management of the North Shore Railway. As a result of the lobbying of several representatives from constituencies in the region between Quebec and Montreal, the company had been reconstituted in 1870 by an act which granted more land and money, and Cauchon had become its president. With characteristic vigour he devoted much energy to his task. He launched a veritable campaign in the municipalities and obtained numerous promises of subsidies from Quebec City (a sum estimated at $1,000,000), Trois-Rivières, and other localities. But he was less successful in the countryside. L'Assomption and Champlain counties, under pressure from the Ultramontanes, opposed any contributions, and thus broke the unanimity required among the north shore counties if the project were to be carried out. Specifically, the resistance was related to the proposed layout of the system, but it can be explained by differences of opinion and conflicts of interest. The aim behind the railway was to encourage trade and industry on the north shore, whereas according to the conservative ideology reigning in some regions settlement was the first priority for the provincial economy. Hence the Ultramontanes, who had been attacked by Cauchon when the *Programme catholique* was made public [*see* François-Xavier-Anselme TRUDEL], seized the opportunity to indulge in political revenge at the expense of the undertaking which Cauchon headed, despite its undeniable financial advantages. Nevertheless Cauchon went ahead quickly with construction, giving the contract to a Chicago firm. The latter, however, was unable to obtain the necessary capital on the London market. Consequently Cauchon once again met with a setback and himself suffered the ridicule he had so often turned against all and sundry. In May 1873 he was ousted from the company by the machinations of a group of Quebec financiers who successfully manipulated the election of the directors. James Gibb Ross, whom Cauchon had so "savagely" beaten in the preceding federal elections, became the new president.

It was, then, a man disappointed in many undertakings, embittered and more aggressive than ever, who was received into Liberal ranks at the end of 1873, during the Pacific Scandal. There is no doubt that Cauchon, in this volte-face, was an opportunist. He could not believe seriously in political liberalism. He would shortly advocate a union embracing all men of the same principles, whether Liberal or Conservative; he was even to have been the leader of this party of union, which in fact never came into existence.

However Cauchon, who was not compromised by a Liberal past and had ready access to the clerical milieux of Quebec, was of great assistance to Alexander Mackenzie*. He helped to settle the thorny issues of the general pardon for the Métis leaders, including Louis RIEL, and of the New Brunswick schools. He served as an intermediary between the Liberal party and the Roman Catholic Church. Thus he helped, in particular by sending an address to Rome, to rehabilitate the party in the province. At a time when "undue influence" was raising the question of the relations of church and state in Canada, he drafted, at the clergy's request and with the support of the Liberal members of the federal parliament, another factum which certainly influenced Rome's attitude after the inquiry of Bishop George Conroy*. Taking into account Cauchon's influence and experience, Mackenzie made him president of the Privy Council in December 1875. He tried in vain to appoint him minister of justice but did manage to make him minister of internal revenue on 8 June 1877. Unfortunately Cauchon, who was invariably peremptory, surly, and argumentative, quickly became a liability for the Liberal government. He was even behind the dissensions among the Quebec Liberals. Wilfrid Laurier* asserted that their happiness "will be complete when old Joe has been driven out of the temple." With an eye to the general elections of 1878 Mackenzie therefore found himself obliged to dismiss Cauchon in order to make room for Laurier in the government and thus rebuild the unity of the party's Quebec wing. He gave a clear explanation of this to George Brown: "I told Cauchon that I could not maintain him any longer, that his advent had done us harm everywhere; and whether just or unjust the feeling was so strong and universal against him that I had resolved not to go to the elections with him."

Cauchon, however, was not one to submit to a rebuff without compensation, even if it meant exile: on 4 Oct. 1877 he accepted the post of lieutenant governor of Manitoba. The appointment gave rise to widely divergent comment. In the province of Quebec a few justified it on the grounds of Cauchon's long parliamentary experience, extensive knowledge of constitutional law, and bilingualism. But in general Mackenzie was blamed for having chosen Cauchon in preference to better candidates solely in order to clean up the government in preparation for the general elections. The appointment received more criticism in Ontario. Thus in Toronto the *Mail* offered its sincere condolences "to the people of Manitoba, who deserve a better fate," and the *Grip* likened Cauchon to an unwanted child "left on Manitoba's doorstep by his frustrated mother, the Mackenzie administration." In Manitoba itself Cauchon's appointment awakened racial antagonism and sparked a nationalist quarrel between the *Manitoba Daily Free Press* of Winnipeg and *Le Métis* of St Boniface. Between 1871 and 1875 English immigration, particularly from Ontario, had steadily increased so that English-speaking people were in the majority in Manitoba and held the balance of power. There were fears among the English that Cauchon would not respect the wishes or even the laws of the majority but would work on behalf of the French-speaking minority. In short, there were fears of a dictatorship. In the French community his appointment produced "a glimmer of hope," for, as Archbishop Alexandre-Antonin Taché* observed, "The appointment of a French Canadian is as extraordinary as the arrival of the railway."

Cauchon took up his duties on 2 Dec. 1877. The death of his wife, Marie-Louise Nolan, four days later, subdued the critics so that he was able to begin his term of office quietly. Moreover he had the opportunity to make his peaceful intentions known: "I am not the representative of a faith or a nationality. . . . My duty is to ensure that the law is upheld, to bestow special favour on no citizen but to render justice to all." In fact Cauchon restricted himself to the role assigned to him by the constitution. He allowed those charged with the responsibility to govern to do so and generally served as no more than the intermediary between the federal government and the province. In 1878 he reserved for the governor general's assent the act to abolish the publication in French of the province's official documents. Commenting on his action in a letter to Archbishop Taché, he revealed his own commitment regarding the future of French in Manitoba: "I have done all I can, I have even gone beyond my sphere in order to remedy the evil. . . . The French language is secure. For how long I do not know, for I am not sure that the Manitoba Act, which in any case is very vague, cannot be attacked by your provincial legislature when the latter desires. . . . The only remedy is an immigration of the French from Lower Canada, which the clergy should encourage with all its influence and all its energy. Is it not better that our compatriots come here rather than go to the United States?" Disappointed by what they have called a "policy of indifference," some people, such as Frank A. Milligan in his study of the lieutenant governors of Manitoba, have seen in Cauchon a "do-nothing king," and asserted that during his term of office the prestige of the lieutenant governor was at its lowest ebb. But the most commonly voiced reproach, namely Cauchon's lack of influence at Ottawa, first with Mackenzie and then with Macdonald, suggests a false notion of the function of a lieutenant governor. All things considered, one can concur in Joseph Dubuc*'s judgement that "Cauchon administered the government with justice and impartiality." He left his post on 1 Dec. 1882.

Cauchon was overtly engaged in business in Manitoba, and this activity may more deeply have shocked those who did not appreciate his discreet role in politics. He arrived in Winnipeg at the time of the economic boom resulting from the building of the railway and continued the game of speculation which had already made him rich in Quebec. According to Dubuc, he realized a profit of some $500,000. The *Manitoba Daily Free Press* asserted in March 1882 that it had learned from an authoritative source in Ottawa that Cauchon had already made a profit of $1,000,000. His speculation included such deals as the sale of 120 lots in three evenings for $15,243.50 at Point Douglas (now part of Winnipeg), and of 470 acres for $283,000 at St Boniface. In December 1880 he had bought a lot for $60,000 in the heart of Winnipeg, opposite the large new Hudson's Bay Company building. On it he built a splendid four-storey edifice in Grecian style for offices and stores. Known as the Cauchon Block, it cost $100,000 to build. But caught unawares and ruined by the crash of 1882, Cauchon had to abandon his "palace" to his creditors in September 1884; he had lived in it for a few months, having decided to remain in Winnipeg at the end of his term of office. Then he retired with his son to a homestead called Whitewood in the Qu'Appelle valley. He lived there on "hard-tack and bacon," and died on 23 Feb. 1885.

Cauchon had been married three times, a fact which prompted Robert Rumilly to remark that he had "the physique of Bluebeard." On 10 July 1844 at Quebec he married Julie Lemieux, and they had two children, Joseph and Joséphine; then in 1866 he married Marie-Louise Nolan, and they had a son, Nolan; on 1 Feb. 1880 in Chicago, he took as his third wife Emma Lemoine of Ottawa.

Cauchon had made his will in Winnipeg on 12 Feb.

1884. After disposing of personal possessions, he left his wife half his property; to his son Nolan, a minor, he bequeathed $2,500 plus a third of the balance, and the remainder was shared equally between his other two children. No notarial contract has been found of his possible assets in the province of Quebec at the time of his death. Thus his inheritance was probably limited to his Manitoba assets valued officially at $150, and to the indemnity of £1,329 12*s.* (or approximately $6,500) which the Colonial Life Assurance Company paid to his heirs on 26 June 1885.

More than anyone else, or at least in a more visible fashion, Cauchon stuck to intrigue, even "corrupt intrigue," in his *Journal de Québec*, his political career, and his financial activities. It is beyond doubt that he knew how to reconcile his principles with his interests, that he made journalism the stepping-stone for his political career, and his political career the crossroads for his financial operations. For 30 years he was the strong man of the district of Quebec, ruling supreme in various branches of human activity. While Cauchon was studying at the Séminaire de Québec, a priest had advised him to give up his name because it left him open to ridicule, and to adopt the second family name, Laverdière. His reply was: "I shall call myself Cauchon and nothing else, and I shall force the mockers to lower their heads when [they hear] that name." Such was the stormy life of Cauchon: a constant challenge, a ceaseless battle.

ANDRÉE DÉSILETS

Joseph-Édouard Cauchon was the author of: *Aux électeurs du Bas-Canada* (Québec, 1863); *Étude sur l'union projetée des provinces britanniques de l'Amérique du Nord* (Québec, 1858); *Notions élémentaires de physique, avec planches à l'usage des maisons d'éducation* (Québec, 1841); and *The union of the provinces of British North America* (Quebec, 1865).

AASB, T22052–57. ANQ-Q, AP-P-134; AP-G-344. ASQ, Fichier des anciens; Fonds C.-H. Laverdière, no.54; Fonds Viger-Verreau, Sér. O. Baker Library, R. G. Dun & Co. credit ledger, Canada, 8. BE, Québec, Reg. B, 44, no.17288; 46, no.18313; 55, no.22775; 64, no.27268; 67, no.28673. PABC, Crease coll., Henry Pering Pellew Crease, Corr. inward, Sir Hector-Louis Langevin, 1872–96. PAC, MG 26, A; B; MG 27, I, C8; D4; D11; F3; MG 29, C10. PAM, MG 3, D1; MG 12, B1; C; MG 14, B26. Surrogate Court of Eastern Judicial District (Winnipeg), no.97, will of J.-É. Cauchon, 12 Feb. 1884. Alexander Begg and W. R. Nursey, *Ten years in Winnipeg; a narration of the principal events in the history of the city of Winnipeg from the year A.D. 1870, to the year A.D. 1879, inclusive* (Winnipeg, 1879). Can., chambre des Communes, *Journaux*, 1867-68, 1872–77; Parl., *Doc. de la session*, 1867–77; Sénat, *Débats*, 1868–72. Can., Prov. du, Assemblée législative, *Journaux*, 1844–66; Parl., *Débats parl. sur la confédération*. *Canada Gazette*, 1867–77. Québec, Assemblée législative, *Journaux*, 1867–74. Québec, ville de, Bureau du trésorier, *Comptes* (Québec), 1865–67. *L'Aurore des Canadas* (Montréal), 8 nov. 1842. *Le Canadien*, 1841–42. *Le Courrier du Canada*, 1857–58, déc. 1867, 1873, févr. 1885. *Le Journal de Québec*, 1842–89. *Manitoba Daily Free Press*, 20 Aug. 1881, 1 March 1882. *Le Métis* (Saint-Boniface, Man.), 1877–85. *Le Nouvelliste* (Québec), 26 févr. 1885. *La Patrie*, 28 févr. 1885. *Le Pays* (Montréal), juin 1855, déc. 1867.

Achintre, *Manuel électoral*. Beaulieu et J. Hamelin, *Journaux du Québec*; *La presse québécoise*, I: 123–26. Charles Beaumont, *Généalogie des familles de la côte de Beaupré* (Ottawa, 1912). Dent, *Canadian portrait gallery*, IV: 138–44. J. Desjardins, *Guide parl. DOLQ*, I: 738–39. *Encyclopedia Canadiana*, II: 289. Le Jeune, *Dictionnaire*, I: 329. *The makers of Canada; index and dictionary of Canadian history*, ed. L. J. Burpee and A. G. Doughty (Toronto, 1911). Morgan, *Sketches of celebrated Canadians*, 609–12. J. P. Robertson, *A political manual of the province of Manitoba and the North-West Territories* (Winnipeg, 1887). P.-G. Roy, *Les avocats de la région de Québec*, 83. Cyprien Tanguay, *Dictionnaire généalogique des familles canadiennes depuis la fondation de la colonie jusqu'à nos jours* (7v., [Montréal], 1871–90), I: 133–34. Dom [J.-P.-A.] Benoît, *Vie de Mgr Taché, archevêque de Saint Boniface* (2v., Montréal, 1904). Careless, *Union of the Canadas*. Chapais, *Hist. du Canada*, V–VIII. F.-X. Chouinard et Antonio Drolet, *La ville de Québec, histoire municipale* (3v., Québec, 1963–67), III. Cornell, *Alignment of political groups*. L.-O. David, *Au soir de la vie* (Montréal, [1924]); *L'Union des deux Canadas, 1841–1867* (Montréal, 1898). Alfred Duclos De Celles, *Cartier et son temps* (Montréal, 1913); *La Fontaine et son temps* (Montréal, 1912). Désilets, *Hector-Louis Langevin*. M. Hamelin, *Premières années du parlementarisme québécois*. F. A. Milligan, "The lieutenant-governorship in Manitoba, 1870–1882" (MA thesis, Univ. of Manitoba, Winnipeg, 1948), 230–45. Rumilly, *Hist. de la prov. de Québec*, I-III. Soc. hist. de Saint-Boniface, *Les francophones dans le monde des affaires de Winnipeg, 1870–1920* (Saint-Boniface, 1974). L.-P. Turcotte, *Le Canada sous l'Union*. P. B. Waite, *Canada, 1874–1896; arduous destiny* (Toronto and Montreal, 1971). B. J. Young, *Promoters and politicians: the North-Shore railways in the history of Quebec, 1854–85* (Toronto, 1978). Andrée Désilets, "Une figure politique du XIXe siècle; François-Xavier Lemieux," *RHAF*, 20 (1966–67): 572–99; 21 (1967–68): 243–67; 22 (1968–69): 223–55. "Feu l'honorable Joseph Cauchon," *Rev. canadienne*, 21 (1885): 177–81. "Les maires de Québec de 1833 à 1894," *La Presse*, 31 mars 1894. F. [A.] Milligan, "Reservation of Manitoba bills and refusal of assent by Lieutenant-Governor Cauchon, 1877–82," *Canadian Journal of Economics and Political Science* (Toronto), 14 (1948): 247–48.

CAYLEY, WILLIAM, lawyer and politician; b. 26 May 1807 at St Petersburg (Leningrad, U.S.S.R.), second son of John Cayley, British consul and merchant, and his second wife, Harriet Raikes; m. 12 April 1836 Emma Robinson, daughter of D'Arcy Boulton*, and they had 11 children; d. 23 Feb. 1890 at Toronto, Ont.

William Cayley completed his education in England. He entered Christ Church, Oxford, in 1826 and graduated with a BA in 1830. He obtained an MA in 1833 and was called to the bar from Lincoln's Inn in

1835. Some time between 1835 and 1838 he immigrated to Upper Canada, and was admitted as a barrister to the Law Society of Upper Canada during the Easter term in 1838. He was to practise law in Toronto at various times over the next 30 years when not holding public office. In 1850 he was in a partnership with Matthew Crooks CAMERON; Daniel McMichael later joined the firm. The Toronto city directory of 1862–63 lists him as a barrister in partnership with Cameron and McMichael. In 1864–65 he disappears from the city listings but he reappears as clerk of the surrogate court in 1866.

Connected by marriage to the Boultons, a prominent Tory family, Cayley was chosen on 6 Aug. 1845 by William Henry Draper* to succeed William Benjamin Robinson* on the Executive Council as inspector general. A safe seat in the Legislative Assembly was opened for him in the constituency of Huron for which he was returned on 28 Feb. 1846. In the ensuing decade Cayley was viewed by Tory leaders as a loyal and trustworthy associate specializing in public finance. When he took up office, heavy expenditures on public works and unexpected expenses incurred as a result of the Irish famine immigration brought major problems for Cayley, who at the same time had to raise funds on a sluggish money market. One recourse was to sell British consols, in which funds from the clergy reserves were invested, and replace them with Canadian government debentures. Cayley's personality marked him more as a hard-working lieutenant than a party leader, yet he was high in the Tory party councils in the late 1840s, conducted the negotiations in April 1847 with René-Édouard Caron* seeking to enlarge the French Canadian wing of the ministry, and journeyed to England with Sir Allan Napier MacNab* in 1849–50 to lobby against the policies of the governor, Lord Elgin [Bruce*]. In 1849 Elgin referred to "Cayley & Co" in describing the Tory party.

In the general election of 1847–48 Cayley retained his seat for Huron, but went out of office on 10 March 1848 with the defeat of the Tory ministry. He was in the front bench of the opposition and led the fight against the government's proposed clergy reserve settlement. He favoured the implementation of the provisions of the imperial statute of 1841 whereby the share of the income not allotted to the Church of England would be divided proportionately among the Roman Catholic, Presbyterian, and other Christian bodies. He was out of the assembly for one term following his defeat by Malcolm Cameron* in the election of December 1851.

Returned for Huron and Bruce in 1854 he once more became inspector general on 11 September in the ministry of MacNab and Augustin-Norbert Morin*, as well as a member of the Board of Railway Commissioners. Although defeated in the general election of 1857, he held these offices until August 1858. From 3 Nov. 1854 until 28 July 1857 he was the government director on the Grand Trunk Railway Company board. In 1854–55, when a committee of the house led by William Lyon Mackenzie* launched a strong attack condemning the accounting methods of government departments, Cayley, at the prompting of John A. Macdonald* who was attorney general for Canada West, brought in the Audit Act of 1855. This legislation was a landmark in Canadian public administration because it created a new office, auditor of public accounts, and a new department of government, the Audit Board. In 1857 a bill made the use of the decimal currency mandatory in all government accounts after 1 Jan. 1858. Cayley's 1857 budget, which Alexander Tilloch Galt* saw through the house in 1858, increased significantly the level of customs duties on selected items and earned for Cayley the reputation of initiating a protectionist policy in Canada.

Policies which had been inaugurated by Francis HINCKS before Cayley's return to office in 1854 were to result in important activities during his term. In three years of economic prosperity, 1854–56, a number of new banks were chartered, towns were enabled to borrow heavily through the Municipal Loan Fund, and large capital grants were made to the Grand Trunk and the Bank of Upper Canada. Cayley, who was described by a contemporary as "too timid a hand for any efficient reform," did little either to police the trend towards large increases in government spending or to control other inflationary influences in the economy. When the onset of a sharp recession in 1857 contracted the world's money market, Canadian land values fell disastrously, banks were hard pressed to maintain liquidity [*see* Robert CASSELS], and government revenues shrank dramatically.

Once Cayley lost his seat in the general election of 1857 his usefulness to the government was ended. During the ministerial crisis of 1858 he was replaced in the Executive Council by Galt as inspector general and by George Sherwood as representative of the Toronto Conservatives in the reconstructed government of George-Étienne Cartier* and Macdonald. Cayley had, however, been returned for Renfrew in a March 1858 by-election, and sat for that riding until he retired from politics in 1861.

Cayley had been associated as director with the Bank of Upper Canada from at least 1839, but when he joined the bank as assistant manager in 1859 he wrote to George Carr Glyn of Glyn, Mills and Company that he was "as little prepared as the gardeners for the frost of Saturday last." His promotion within the bank, however, was rapid; he was appointed inspector (manager of agencies) and then, at a board meeting on 17 April 1861, he replaced William Proudfoot* as president. His banking career came to an abrupt end at the annual general meeting of 25 June 1861. Angry shareholders were beginning to realize the full extent of the bank's financial difficulties and neither Cayley nor Proudfoot was re-elected as director. When the bank failed in 1866 Cayley presumably suffered significant personal losses. A group of businessmen including Cayley, Angus MORRISON, Joseph Curran MORRISON, and Frederic William CUMBERLAND, had obtained a charter for a Bank of Canada in 1858 but it was never acted upon and was purchased by William MCMASTER, president of the Canadian Bank of Commerce, in 1866. From 1866 to 1869 Cayley was clerk of the surrogate court for York County. Perhaps because of his involvement with the Audit Act he was appointed auditor of the province of Ontario in 1870 and continued in that office until 1877.

Cayley was an adherent of the Church of England but he could show independence. In 1860, for instance, as a member of a select committee named by parliament he joined George Brown* in defending the non-sectarian position of the University of Toronto in opposition to the stand taken by John A. Macdonald and Malcolm Cameron. He was an amateur painter and a president of the Toronto Club and the Toronto Curling Club. In politics his intense partisanship earned the enmity of Reformers. Lord Elgin felt Cayley "well qualified to give a cause any gloss that may suit his interests." Macdonald explained to a colleague, "There is an opinion very prevalent . . . that he is insincere & scheming. This arises altogether from his manner, which he is conscious of but cannot amend. . . . his merits far outweigh his faults." For Macdonald, "trustworthiness & ability as a Statesman" were Cayley's chief attributes and for many years he relied on his judgement and administrative ability in framing and implementing public financial policy.

PAUL G. CORNELL

William Cayley was the author of *Finances and trade of Canada at the beginning of the year 1855* (London, 1855). See also *Correspondence between the Hon. Wm. Napier, on behalf of the English shareholders of the Grand Trunk Railroad Company, and the Honble. Wm. Cayley (inspector general)* . . . (Toronto, 1856).

AO, MU 500–15; RG 1, A-I-6, 31. MTL, Robert Baldwin papers, 35, no.107; 39, no.73; 50, no.89; 55, no.46; 64, no.24; 74, no.53. PAC, MG 24, D36. *Elgin-Grey papers* (Doughty). [John Langton], *Early days in Upper Canada: letters of John Langton from the backwoods of Upper Canada and the Audit Office of the province of Canada*, ed. W. A. Langton (Toronto, 1926). Macdonald, *Letters* (J. K. Johnson and Stelmack), I, II. *Toronto Daily Mail*, 24, 27 Feb. 1890. [J.] B. Burke, *A genealogical and heraldic history of the colonial gentry* (2v., London, 1891–95), II: 750–53. *Canada, an encyclopædia* (Hopkins), I: 493. Chadwick, *Ontarian families*, I: 51–54. *Toronto directory*, 1843–70. Wallace, *Macmillan dict. Canada and its prov.* (Shortt and Doughty), V: 277–83, 288–91; IX: 133; XVIII: 448–49. Careless, *Brown*. Cornell, *Alignment of political groups*. Creighton, *Macdonald, young politician*. Joseph Pope, *Memoirs of the Right Honourable Sir John Alexander Macdonald, G.C.B., first prime minister of the dominion of Canada* (rev. ed., Toronto, 1930). Edward Porritt, *Sixty years of protection in Canada, 1846–1907, where industry leans on the politician* (London, 1908).

D. F. Barnett, "The Galt tariff: incidental or effective protection?" *Canadian Journal of Economics* (Toronto), 9 (1976): 389–407. Peter Baskerville, "Donald Bethune's steamboat business: a study of Upper Canadian commercial and financial practice," *OH*, 67 (1975): 135–49. "Glyns and the Bank of Upper Canada," *Three Banks Rev.* (Edinburgh), 55 (September 1962): 40–52. George Metcalf, "Draper conservatism and responsible government in the Canadas, 1836–1847," *CHR*, 42 (1961): 300–24. Shortt, "Hist. of Canadian currency, banking and exchange," *Canadian Banker*, 10–13.

CAZEAU, CHARLES-FÉLIX, Roman Catholic priest and vicar general; b. 24 Dec. 1807 at Quebec City, son of Jean-Baptiste Cazeau, a wheelwright, and Geneviève Chabot; d. there 26 Feb. 1881.

Charles-Félix Cazeau began classical studies in 1819 at the Collège de Saint-Roch in Quebec City, which had been founded the previous year by Bishop Joseph-Octave Plessis*; Charles-François Baillargeon*, later archbishop of Quebec, was one of his teachers. In 1822 Cazeau entered the Séminaire de Nicolet, where he pursued his education until 1825 when Plessis, who had paid for his stay at Nicolet, chose him as his under-secretary. While learning about the administration of the diocese, Cazeau continued theological studies at the Grand Séminaire de Québec. The day after his ordination to the priesthood by Bishop Bernard-Claude Panet* on 3 Jan. 1830, he was given the post of secretary of the diocese of Quebec and became chaplain to the Congrégation des Hommes de Notre-Dame-de-Québec. He remained responsible for the spiritual direction of the congregation until April 1849, and served as secretary of the diocese until October 1850.

At the time Cazeau was appointed secretary in 1830, the Roman Catholic Church in Canada was suffering from a severe shortage of priests so that, as soon as they were ordained, most were sent to a parish or mission. Cazeau and Ignace BOURGET were the only priests ordained in the first three decades of the 19th century to hold solely administrative posts throughout their priesthood.

From his earliest years as secretary, Cazeau gave evidence of the qualities that would mark his long administrative career in the archdiocese of Quebec. His particular responsibility while Panet was bishop was to carry out decisions related to the temporal government of the diocese: establishing new and dividing old parishes, assigning priests to new offices or duties, building churches, and handling petitions from parishioners. Although he was only 22 at the time of his appointment, his bishop already seemed to have great confidence in him. Abbé Narcisse-Charles Fortier*, who had been secretary to Plessis and Panet, was not unaware of this confidence when he suggested to his friend Charles-François Painchaud* in September 1830 that he work through Cazeau to get the bishop to accept Painchaud's choice of a director for the Collège de Sainte-Anne-de-la-Pocatière: "Through Cazeau, you will succeed in this endeavour." At the same time Cazeau was learning the role which was to become his major responsibility – that of spokesman to the government for the episcopate. In the autumn of 1831 he attended the sessions of the House of Assembly of Lower Canada when a parish council bill was being debated, and he apparently conveyed the bishops' desiderata in the matter to representative Jean-François-Joseph Duval. Cazeau was also becoming aware of the importance of the press as a vehicle to serve the interests of the church. In 1831 he attempted without success to interest Panet and Bishop Jean-Jacques Lartigue* in launching a newspaper, to be edited by a competent priest, a venture which Cazeau believed "necessary to counter the anti-political and anti-religious doctrines . . . coming from abroad." Despite this setback, he none the less indirectly influenced the press through his efforts to avert possible conflict between politicians and members of the clergy. At the end of 1831 Cazeau took the initiative of advising Lartigue to remove from an article the bishop was about to publish in a Quebec newspaper a reproof directed at two members of the assembly; he thought Lartigue should avoid setting these two against the clergy since the latter might in future have need of their support.

When Bishop Joseph Signay* succeeded Panet in February 1833, he probably only retained Cazeau as secretary because of his thorough knowledge of diocesan affairs, for during his 16 years in office the bishop displayed a great deal of distrust of him. By August Signay's new coadjutor, Bishop Pierre-Flavien Turgeon*, urged him to show more confidence in Cazeau and suggested he should not humiliate him too much. Turgeon further emphasized that it was especially in Signay's interest to treat his secretary with consideration since "one cannot do without his services." The situation apparently did not improve much, for on 16 July 1834 Cazeau's friend, Bishop Joseph-Norbert Provencher*, urged him to remain in office until he was driven out, otherwise "everything is going to go topsy-turvy in the diocese." Cazeau therefore decided to perform his duties without recriminations against his superior, until such time as the future of the bishopric, which was made an archdiocese in 1844, seemed to him compromised by Signay's behaviour. At the beginning of 1846 Cazeau secretly conveyed his concern to Bishop Bourget, inviting him to come and see for himself the sorry state of affairs in the archdiocese, a situation he attributed to Archbishop Signay's incompetence. Shortly before Bourget left for Rome in the autumn of that year, Cazeau suggested that he should intercede with the Holy See and request Signay's resignation. He also provided Bourget with the requisite information to justify such a step. Rome delayed its decision, and from 1846 to 1848 Cazeau repeatedly pressed Bourget to reiterate his request for the resignation to the Holy See at the same time urging him to persuade the archbishop of Quebec to resign. But in November 1848 Cazeau found out that, without the knowledge of his entourage, Signay had already tendered his resignation to Rome on 17 March. He immediately informed Bourget, exhorting him to intervene again with the Holy See, but this time to see that Signay's request would be denied, since the financial terms attached to it were such that his successor would find it impossible to meet the administrative needs of the archdiocese. Signay finally reached an understanding with his immediate associates as to the terms of his resignation, and on 10 Nov. 1849 turned over the administration of the archdiocese to his coadjutor, Bishop Turgeon. Less than a year later, on 8 Oct. 1850, Turgeon took possession of the metropolitan see of Quebec following Signay's death. The next day he conferred on Cazeau the title of vicar general.

During Signay's episcopal tenure, the diocese of Quebec, one of the most extensive in the world, was run by four people – the bishop, his coadjutor, a secretary, and an under-secretary – with occasional aid from one or two others. Cazeau was thus led to undertake a large part of the management of affairs, especially since illness often forced Turgeon, the coadjutor, to take more or less prolonged periods of rest. In these years Cazeau, whose power increasingly surpassed his status as the bishop's authorized representative, took particular care to see that both the canonical erection and the incorporation of new parishes were valid, and often intervened to settle conflicts between parishioners or churchwardens and their parish priest. Exceeding somewhat his authority as secretary, he at times took certain priests to task for rebelling against their bishop. On matters of ecclesiastical discipline he was, moreover, uncompromising; Signay's incompetence in this area was one of the reasons Cazeau urged Bourget to request the archbishop's resignation. "The Clergy," he wrote to Bourget in 1846, "is becoming accustomed to not respecting its leaders, and it will take many years to restore things to their normal state." Cazeau did not hesitate to remind even ecclesiastics with a rank above his of their duty to respect and obey the bishop of Quebec. In 1836, on the occasion of Bishop Lartigue's assumption of episcopal office in Montreal, he reproached Lartigue for his offhand attitude towards Signay. Ten years later he reprimanded Vicar General Alexis Mailloux* when he accused Signay of ill will towards him. All the same, Cazeau maintained cordial relations with the clergy as a whole, and it was not uncommon for a priest to go through him to obtain some particular authorization from the bishop or his coadjutor.

Cazeau played an important role in the missionary thrust that developed within the Canadian church from the 1840s, after a notable increase in its ranks. In 1844, thanks to Cazeau and Turgeon, Provencher obtained for the northwest a number of Oblate missionaries whom Bourget had recruited in France. In Canada East the priests in charge of the Saguenay and north shore missions, in particular fathers Jean-Baptiste Honorat* and Flavien Durocher*, corresponded frequently with Cazeau, informing him of their endeavours and seeking his services in practical matters: financial transactions, approaches to the government about land grants to the Indians, the hiring of labourers, the purchase of various objects required for worship, and the supervision of the printing of a prayer book. When missionaries complained about being harassed by certain agents of the Hudson's Bay Company, Cazeau negotiated the settlement of these disputes with James Keith*, a company official in residence at Lachine, or with the governor, Sir George Simpson*; he came to an agreement with them about the terms upon which numerous missionaries might travel westward in company canoes. But Cazeau's principal role was to manage the funds earmarked for missionary activity by the Society for the Propagation of the Faith. It was a tedious job, as he admitted to Provencher in April 1850, requiring him to keep a strict record of the money he distributed to the missions in Canada East and in the northwest. He was also obliged to maintain voluminous correspondence, not only with the many missionaries but also with the boards of the society in Lyons and Paris and with Abbé Mailly, the procurator in London of certain Canadian bishops.

Officially the titular bishops communicated directly with government representatives, but in the 1840s Cazeau, although only a secretary, became a key figure in the relations between church and state. He kept a close watch on the proceedings in the legislature, and regularly intervened when the interests of the church were at stake. Acquainting himself with bills likely to affect the legal status of any religious corporation, he consulted the bishops concerned and, when necessary, made rough drafts of amendments. He then passed these on to the member or minister responsible for steering the bill through the assembly, supplying him if need be with arguments to counter opposition that might arise during the debate. Cazeau thus took an active part in legislation dealing with parishes, the incorporation of religious, educational, and charitable institutions, the recognition of bishops as corporate entities, immigration, and the licensing of taverns. He also approached government officials and commissioners appointed to put various enactments or laws into effect when their decisions might be detrimental to the acquired rights of the church. Furthermore, he reached agreements with the governors general, either directly or through their associates, concerning the appointment and working conditions of priests in institutions under the control of the British army, such as the military hospitals and the quarantine station on Grosse-Île in Canada East. Finally, numerous clergy and even some laymen who sought favours from the government or had petitions to submit to it secured Cazeau's intervention on their behalf, thus increasing their chances of success.

Immediately following his accession to the see at the end of 1850, Turgeon greatly increased the number of his advisers and assistants; hence Cazeau was freed of some of his administrative tasks and was able to give more attention to his role as the Canadian bishops' emissary to governmental authorities. Cazeau's numerous initiatives were no longer intended solely to protect the interests of the church, but were also conducive to securing for the church a measure of ecclesiastical control. Thus in 1851 he urged Louis-Hippolyte La Fontaine*, the attorney general for Canada East, to entrust the operation of a teachers' college that the government was planning to set up to a board of education rather than a government department, to enable the episcopate or persons selected by it to direct the institution. Two years later, as a result of Cazeau's influence with the ministers, the superior of the College of Bytown (Ottawa) was included on the senate of the University of Toronto. In December 1854 he considered securing the appointment to the Legislative Council of a candidate favourable to the episcopate. Two months earlier he had even asked a minister to eliminate a sentence in the preamble to a bill to secularize the clergy reserves, claiming it might suggest that the state wanted to free itself "from all religious control." In his opinion, societies could not govern themselves "without the help of religion." At that moment Cazeau's influence with politicians was such that Joseph-Bruno Guigues*, the bishop of Ottawa, considered him practically a minister of the crown.

Cazeau's political interventions, always discreet and unofficial, had the unobtrusive character of operations behind the scenes. His place in the clerical hierarchy hardly equipped him for sensational deeds or resounding utterances. "A good vicar general," as Bourget so rightly remarked to him at the time of his appointment to this office, " is duty-bound to work in the shadow of his bishop." Cazeau found this advice quite acceptable. He rarely signed public pronouncements: he only published a few corrections and clarifications in the newspapers when he felt personally attacked, such as in 1850 when Jean-Baptiste-Éric

Dorion* of *L'Avenir* and Édouard-Louis PACAUD in *Le Moniteur canadien* of Montreal accused him of "intriguing" on behalf of ministerial candidates in the ridings of Quebec and of Mégantic. His comments in the newspapers, appearing first in the 1830s, became more numerous and consequential as his relations developed with eminent members of the Liberal-Conservative party – La Fontaine, Augustin-Norbert Morin*, René-Édouard Caron*, Étienne-Paschal Taché*, Jean-Charles CHAPAIS, George-Étienne Cartier*, Pierre-Joseph-Olivier CHAUVEAU, and even "dear brother" John A. Macdonald*. His influence upon a part of the clerical and conservative press (for instance *Le Courrier du Canada* during the 1860s [*see* Léger BROUSSEAU]), his fierce, determined opposition to liberalism, and his unshakeable support of the Liberal-Conservative party can be traced to the alliance forged between the clergy and the moderate Patriotes after the rebellions of 1837–38. This alliance gave rise to the definition and maintenance within Quebec society of a conservative and defensive nationalism focused on survival.

Throughout the episcopacies of Turgeon and Baillargeon from 1850 to 1870 Cazeau did not abandon his role as advocate to the civil government of the interests of the church. He made unofficial representations concerning the bill presented by Thomas-Jean-Jacques LORANGER on the chairing of parish council meetings (1860), the separate school bills (1861 and 1866), the bill concerning registers of marriage, baptisms, and burials (1862), and the *Code civil* (1865) [*see* René-Édouard Caron]. He performed this role in addition to continuing to deal with the ordinary business of the diocese. He was chaplain to the Congregation of the Sisters, Servants of the Immaculate Heart of Mary (known as the Sisters of the Good Shepherd) at Quebec, and he saw to the installation of religious communities in parishes such as Saint-Patrice at Rivière-du-Loup, Saint-Louis at Lotbinière, and Saint-François-Xavier at Chicoutimi. During this period he supervised the creation of new dioceses in the ecclesiastical province of Quebec and, as the agent of Bishop Alexandre-Antonin Taché* of Manitoba and the procurator of Bishop Edward John Horan* of Kingston and Bishop Guigues of Ottawa, he found time to make profitable investments for them in banks or with friends such as businessman Thomas McGreevy*.

Cazeau's interest in education naturally led him to foster its development. He attended the opening of the École Normale Laval on 12 May 1857, and the following month addressed the teachers' banquet at which his brother Vincent, himself a teacher, was no doubt present. It was through his endeavours that the College of Bytown in Ottawa, St Michael's College in Toronto, and Father Flavien Durocher's school in Saint-Sauveur Ward at Quebec regularly received their government grants. He gave unceasing support to the Université Laval. Adhering to the policies of the archdiocese of Quebec and the rector of Laval, he, too, unhesitatingly exerted pressure, even on the Vatican, in order to block the proposal to set up a rival university at Montreal [*see* Charles-François Baillargeon].

Over the span of his career, it is clear that Cazeau's political militancy assumed exceptional importance at the time of confederation. From the "Great Coalition" of June 1864 [*see* George Brown*] to the eve of the elections in the summer of 1867, during which few months the parliaments in Ottawa and London took the steps to adopt the new constitution, the clergy officially kept silent. There was no need for the clergy to address publicly a question upon which the electorate did not have to declare itself. Whenever its interests seemed threatened, the clergy invariably responded privately, exerting pressure on parliamentarians and journalists. Cazeau carried out this task with tact, firmness, and speed.

On 23 June 1864, after the coalition ministry had been formed, George Edward Clerk* of the *True Witness and Catholic Chronicle* of Montreal vigorously denounced the union "with the fanatical and anti-clerical [George] Brown." The vicar general rebuked him that very day, and two days later complained to the bishop of Montreal: "To protect ourselves against anarchy, indecision had to be avoided; it was necessary to resort to this union, however lacking in balance it may seem." Bourget refused to intervene with the journalist. Cazeau returned to the charge in November. At his suggestion the bishops, assembled at Trois-Rivières to celebrate Bishop Thomas Cooke*'s 50 years of priesthood, addressed to Bourget their complaints against the *True Witness*, which was now opposing the too liberal aspects of confederation. This meeting was on November 7, and by then the specific content of the resolutions of the Quebec conference was already known; that same day Antoine-Aimé Dorion* denounced them in a manifesto to his electors in Hochelaga County.

Months before confederation was brought before the legislature on 3 Feb. 1865, the bishops of Canada East, with the exception of Bourget, had, therefore, decided to support it. The ministers and members supporting the coalition lost no time in getting the clergy behind them. When Cartier announced in the assembly on 7 February the adhesion of the clergy, it was to the great displeasure of Vicar General Alexis-Frédéric Truteau* of Montreal, but no anxiety was occasioned in the bishopric of Quebec. "Silence gives consent," Bishop Baillargeon confided to the bishop of Kingston. Cazeau was of the same opinion.

The debate raised two delicate questions for the clergy: divorce and minority rights. With regard to the first, it should be recalled that the delegates to the Quebec conference anticipated inserting in the new constitution a clause on marriage and divorce, placing them under the jurisdiction of the federal government. As divorce was not allowed in Canada East, there was controversy among ecclesiastical leaders – the religious authorities of Quebec were accommodating, whereas those in Montreal, modelling themselves on Pius IX in his encyclical *Quanta cura*, proved uncompromising. In Cazeau's opinion Catholic legislators owed it to themselves "to tolerate an evil that they cannot forestall," a contrast to the attitude he would take in 1870 to an analogous bill permitting divorce in New Brunswick. At that time he adopted the view of the bishopric of Montreal and asked Cartier, in a letter dated 3 March 1870, to withdraw the bill, in obedience to the *Syllabus*. It is true that in the archdiocese of Quebec in 1865 the plan of confederation "had become a matter of dogma, and an attempt was being made to see how to circumvent that of marriage" in order to preserve the overall scheme.

On the question of minority rights in Canada East and West, an issue debated in the assembly in the summer of 1866, the bishops agreed unanimously, and found it hard to accept the spinelessness of their Conservative allies. The bishops wanted to know what the Conservatives proposed for the Roman Catholics in Canada West to compare with what they were already providing for the Protestants of Canada East (protected counties, bilingualism, and the make-up of the Legislative Council). Robert Bell*, the representative for Russell, sponsored a bill on separate schools in 1866 similar to one presented on 31 July by Hector-Louis Langevin* on behalf of the Protestants of Canada East; given the context, the hostility of the members from Canada West verged on insult and outrage [*see* Joseph-Édouard CAUCHON]. The bishopric of Quebec was greatly disturbed. "What are we to tell our friends and enemies to vindicate you?" Cazeau asked Cartier on 3 Aug. 1866. Cartier withdrew the Langevin bill. Cazeau immediately congratulated him, but not without holding him "responsible for what will be settled" in London concerning the privileges of the English-speaking minority in Canada East.

From June 1864, and especially during the constitutional debates of 1865 and 1866, the political and religious powers had collaborated spontaneously, despite a few differences of opinion which never seriously affected their mutual trust. This cooperation was so close that in the autumn of 1865 at Cartier's request Cazeau and Horan, the bishop of Kingston, went to the Maritimes on a mission to persuade the Roman Catholics of New Brunswick and Nova Scotia to accept confederation. In the March 1865 election in New Brunswick the Conservative government of Samuel Leonard Tilley* had been defeated on the issue of confederation. This reverse was attributed to the defection of the Roman Catholics, including the Acadians, and of the clergy who, like the bishops of Saint John and Chatham, were opposed to the plan. These were the circumstances that prompted Tilley and Cartier to seek the assistance of Cazeau and Horan. "The more events unfold," Cartier wrote to Cazeau, "the more we must be aware of the needs of Confederation, in order not to be engulfed in the *horrible*, *vulgar* and anti-Catholic *democratic system* of our neighbours." This was also Cazeau's conviction. Were these the arguments that won the support of James Rogers*, the bishop of Chatham, and of the whole Catholic hierarchy in the Maritimes? Curiously enough, it seems that Tilley's victory in 1866 was due to the return of some of the province's Catholic vote.

Until the spring of 1867 the political role played by Cazeau was of prime importance. It was he who directed what might be called the secret interventions of the church on behalf of confederation, for the archbishop of Quebec had been crippled for more than 10 years and his coadjutor, Bishop Baillargeon, feeling that political affairs were beyond him, merely ratified the positions adopted by his associates. Thus, led to play a decisive role, Cazeau filled the vacuum that attracted neither Bourget, for ideological reasons, nor bishops Joseph LA ROCQUE of Saint-Hyacinthe and Thomas Cooke of Trois-Rivières, for health reasons. After Bishop Louis-François Laflèche* was elevated to the office of coadjutor in the diocese of Trois-Rivières in 1867, Cazeau left to him the task of convincing the episcopate to take official steps in favour of the new régime. Laflèche had proposed that each bishop prepare a special pastoral letter on the confederation scheme. With the exception of Bourget, all the bishops welcomed this idea with enthusiasm.

When Elzéar-Alexandre Taschereau* acceded to the office of archbishop of Quebec in 1870, Cazeau, while remaining active, seemed to keep more in the background. On two occasions, from October 1870 to March 1871 and from December 1872 to April 1873, he ran the archdiocese in the archbishop's absence. During this period he became a target for more overt criticism. In 1871 Alphonse Villeneuve, the author of *La Comédie infernale ou conjuration libérale aux enfers, par un illuminé*, published in Montreal, accused him of having deliberately distorted Archbishop Taschereau's thinking towards a disavowal of the *Programme catholique* [*see* François-Xavier-Anselme TRUDEL]. The following year Bourget denounced Cazeau's intervention in the matter of the law on registers of births, marriages, and deaths, because an amendment had resulted that favoured the Sulpicians in their claim to the parish of Notre-Dame in Montreal [*see* Joseph DESAUTELS].

The evolution of thinking in the church and in society also was of great concern to Cazeau. The victory of the Liberals in the federal elections of 1874, the legal proceedings resulting from the role of the clergy in the elections and the condemnation of the undue influence it exercised [*see* Pierre-Alexis Tremblay*], the Gaumist quarrel [*see* Charles-François Baillargeon] and the progress of Catholic liberalism even within the clergy [*see* Luc DÉSILETS], despite Taschereau's pastoral letter of 22 Sept. 1875, saddened him to the point that, as he said, he almost wished "to reach the end of [his] career." His reflections on the history of liberalism in Canada matched the official opinion of the church since the conquest: in both were found the same references to "law and order," and both drew the same analogies between atheism and disloyalty to England, and between democracy and anarchy. This was in essence what he confided to the publisher of *L'Événement* on 10 March 1877 and it was the substance of an article which he published under the pseudonym of an English-speaking Catholic in the *Quebec Daily Evening Mercury* in March and April of that year.

In December 1879 Cazeau ended his career and went to live at the Asylum of the Good Shepherd in Quebec City, which he had directed since 1862. Here he celebrated his jubilee as a priest on 3 Jan. 1880 and here he died on 26 Feb. 1881. The testimonies that poured in from all sides on the occasion of these two events evoked in their own way the qualities of refined courtesy, politeness, simplicity, and charity that the vicar general seems to have cultivated throughout his life. The Irish community of the province of Quebec had lost a protector, who had succoured some 700 orphans during the epidemics of 1847 and 1849. And the people of Quebec, also sorely tried by these epidemics and by the fires of 1849, 1854, 1860, and 1866, mourned a man whose devotion had become proverbial.

A member of the Institut Canadien and the St Patrick's Literary Institute of Quebec, Cazeau was also remembered in intellectual circles. Various historians and archivists, such as Jacques Viger*, Henry de Courcy, Edmund Bailey O'Callaghan*, abbés Jean-Baptiste-Antoine Ferland* and Louis-Édouard BOIS, and even Francis Parkman, considered him an associate. The poet Octave Crémazie* was in some measure his protégé.

No better witness to this man, whom some contemporaries termed the Cardinal Giacomo Antonelli of Canada (recalling the secretary of state under Pius IX) and the *éminence grise* haunting the very corridors of parliament, can be found than his own words: "My life, for the 55 years that I have lived in the presence of the archbishops of Quebec, has been in no way extraordinary. My merit consists entirely in having done my best to help the prelates who have honoured me with their confidence to administer the diocese."

MARCEL BELLAVANCE and PIERRE DUFOUR

AAQ, 12 A, I : 130r.; K: 45r., 86r., 120r., 121r.; 20 A, VII: 13; 1 CB, VII: 83; VIII: 41–42, 82, 84–85; XIV: 23–25; XVI: 1–3, 7, 9, 11, 14–20, 28–29, 32–34, 49, 49a, 50, 58, 78–80, 84, 86, 90, 93, 97, 99–100, 104, 107–10, 119, 131, 135, 148, 151–52, 154, 173, 229, 240–41, 250–55; 515 CD, II: 218; CD, Diocèse de Québec, I: 207; 53 CF, I: 12, 14; 321 CN, I: 58; 60 CN, XI: 139; 26 CP, XI: 84. AASB, P 0257–58, 0680–83, 0857–60, 1860–66, 1872–76; T 4500–3, 5917–19, 54905–7; Ta 3871–73. AC, Québec, État civil, Catholiques, Notre-Dame de Québec, 1er mars 1881. ACAM, 295.098, 830–1; 295.099, 834–5; 295.101, 831–69, –75, –77, 836–48, –60, –69, –70, –71, –72, –77, 837–9, –18, –50, 839–15, –22, 840–5, 842–30, 846–2, –7, –10, –17, –18, –34, –37, 847–5, 15, –17, –18, –19, –20, –28, 848–5A, –8, –9, –13B, –28, –35, –36, 849–9, –11, –25, –26, –43, 850–20, –32, –46, 851–22, –71, –72A, –72B, 854–3, –6, –28, 860–27, 862–8, 864–14, 865–1, –4; 752.704, 872–39. ANQ-Q, AP-G-134; État civil, Catholiques, Notre-Dame de Québec, 24 déc. 1807. Arch. de l'archevêché de Sherbrooke (Sherbrooke, Qué.), Fonds Antoine Racine, VII, B1, 8 oct. 1851. Arch. de l'évêché de Nicolet (Nicolet, Qué.), Brouillons de lettres envoyées à C.-F. Cazeau par J.-C. Canac-Marquis, 1848–49, et par Jean Harper, 1832–67. Arch. de l'évêché de Trois-Riviéres, Fonds L.-F. Laflèche, Corr. reçue, C.-F. Baillargeon, 14 mai 1867; Jean Langevin, 16 oct. 1870. Arch. of the Archdiocese of Kingston (Kingston, Ont.), 1D8, Envelope no.10, C.-F. Cazeau à E. J. Horan, 28 mars, 13 juin, 26 août, 2 nov. 1866; 2D8, Envelope no.11, Cazeau à Horan, 10 janv. 1866, 31 mars, 9, 15 avril 1867; 4D9, Envelope no.7, C.-F. Baillargeon à Horan, 15 févr. 1865; Félix Buteau à Horan, 17 févr. 1865; Cazeau à Horan, 3 mars 1865. Archivio della Propaganda Fide (Rome), Scritture riferite nei Congressi: America Settentrionale, 8 (1865): 992. ASQ, Fonds Viger-Verreau, Cartons 59, nos.155–203; 62, nos.228, 233, 262, 303; 68, no.5; 70, no.7. BNQ, MSS-101, Coll. La Fontaine, R.-É. Caron à La Fontaine, 22 mars 1850; C.-F. Cazeau à R.-É. Caron, 22 mars 1850; C.-F. Cazeau à La Fontaine, 22 mars 1850 (copies at PAC). PAC, MG 24, K3; MG 27, I, D8. L.-N. Bégin, *L'Église, le progrès et la civilisation: conférence donnée à l'institut le 5 janvier 1880, à l'occasion du 50e anniversaire de prêtrise de Mgr Cazeau, A.I.C.Q.* (Québec, 1880). *L'Abeille* (Québec), 3 mars 1881. *L'Opinion publique*, 21 avril 1881. Ivanhoë Caron, "Inventaire de la correspondance de Mgr Bernard-Claude Panet, archevêque de Québec," ANQ *Rapport*, 1933–34: 235–421; 1934–35: 321–420; 1935–36: 157–272; "Inventaire de la correspondance de Mgr Joseph Signay, archevêque de Québec," ANQ *Rapport*, 1936–37: 125–330; 1937–38: 23–146; 1938–39: 182–357. Gaston Carrière, "Au Centre de recherches en histoire religieuse du Canada (Ottawa): quelques sources d'histoire religieuse canadienne à Paris et à Rome," *Archives* (Québec), [1] (juillet–décembre 1969): 62–65. Monique Signori-Laforest, *Inventaire analytique des archives du diocèse de Saint-Jean, 1688–1900* (Québec, 1976). André Simard, *Les évêques et les prêtres séculiers au diocèse de Chicoutimi, 1878–1968: notices biographiques* (Chicoutimi, Qué., 1969). Henri Têtu, *Notices biographiques: les évêques de Québec* (Québec, 1889). Lorenzo Angers, *Chicoutimi, poste de traite, 1676–1856* (Montréal, 1971). J.-C. Bonenfant, *La naissance de la Confédération* (Montréal, 1969). J. M. S. Careless, *Colonists and Canadiens, 1760–1867* (Toronto, 1971). Gaston Carrière, *Histoire documentaire de la Congrégation des Mission-*

naires Oblats de Marie-Immaculée dans l'Est du Canada (12v., Ottawa, 1957–75), I-V; *L'université d'Ottawa, 1848–1861* (Ottawa, 1960). Creighton, *Road to confederation,* 373. E. A. Mitchell, *Fort Timiskaming and the fur trade* (Toronto and Buffalo, N.Y., [1977]). Monière, *Le développement des idéologies,* 171, 179–80. Henri Têtu, *Histoire du palais épiscopal de Québec* (Québec, 1896). Nive Voisine *et al., Histoire de l'Église catholique au Québec, 1608–1970* (Montréal, 1971). Armand Gagné, "Le siège métropolitain de Québec et la naissance de la Confédération," SCHÉC *Sessions d'étude,* 34 (1967): 41–54. L.-E. Hamelin, "Évolution numérique séculaire du clergé catholique dans le Québec," *Recherches sociographiques* (Québec), 2 (1961): 189–241.

CHAMPAGNEUR, ÉTIENNE, Roman Catholic teaching brother and priest; b. 8 Aug. 1808 in the village of Recoules, dept of Aveyron, France; d. 18 Jan. 1882 at Camonil-sous-Rodez, France; in 1905 his remains were brought back to Joliette, Que., where they were buried the following year.

Although almost nothing is known about Étienne Champagneur's family, they must have been landowning farmers. He evidently did well in his preparatory studies for the priesthood, but he left the seminary to become a lay teacher for six years. His indecision can no doubt be attributed to timidity, conscientiousness, and introspection but also to a desire to develop himself through ascetic practices and by the eventual exercise of authority. In December 1844 he entered the noviciate of the Clerics of St Viator at Vourles, Rhône, France; twice, however, he interrupted his stay there, first to settle family affairs, and then to join the Trappists, where, despite the attraction for him, he stayed only six or eight weeks. In January 1847 Champagneur took his first vows, and in April, as a consequence of a visit to France by Bishop Ignace BOURGET who sought to bring the Clerics of St Viator to Canada, he left France charged with the task of establishing the Viatorians in Canada. He was accompanied by two other teaching brothers, Augustin Fayard and Louis Chrétien.

They were the first of the Viatorians in Canada. Reaching Montreal with Bishop Bourget at the end of May, they were immediately sent to the village of L'Industrie (Joliette). There they took charge of the parish school and of a college which had opened the year before through the combined efforts of parish priest Antoine Manseau* and businessman Barthélemy Joliette*. The Collège de Joliette claimed to be breaking new ground in education through a five-year study programme centred around industrial arts and science, liberal arts, and the modern languages, French and English.

The Viatorians, usually assigned to small country schools in France, were ill prepared for this task, since only Brother Champagneur was well enough educated and could give leadership. However, the somewhat unexpected arrival of reinforcements in the persons of Thérèse Lahaye and Antoine Thibaudier, two French religious who had been working in the United States since 1841, and the presence of two tonsured clerics among the nine Canadian recruits to the community (five from the newly founded Brothers of the Holy Cross in Chambly), helped to ensure the college's success in its first year.

Deprived of some of his authority by the "Americans," who had recently been ordained priests, Brother Champagneur withdrew to devote himself to training the Canadian recruits, a task which Thibaudier and Lahaye considered a waste of time. Indeed he believed that "not being a priest, it was better . . . to remain in the background and give wide latitude to the new Fathers." In 1849 he accepted the priesthood that Bishop Bourget offered him, and soon after resumed the office of superior, and held as well the posts of principal of the college and novice master. However, in 1852 his direction of the Collège de Joliette led to a "rebellion" of the staff: the French religious were unable to fit themselves into the tradition of classical colleges, since most of them had not pursued studies at an advanced level. Abbé Pascal Lajoie succeeded him as principal that year. By that date the bishop of Montreal had entrusted two other colleges to the Viatorians, one at Chambly [*see* Pierre-Marie Mignault*] in 1849 and the other at Rigaud in 1850. At Rigaud, the modern teaching programme of Joliette served as model and inspiration, but in both colleges instruction in Latin was also offered.

In 1852 the congregation agreed to teach deaf and dumb boys, and so had the opportunity to establish itself in Montreal, as Bishop Bourget had wanted [*see* Charles-Irénée Lagorce*]. After this development Father Champagneur steered those he trained mainly towards the primary schools. Bourget, who spent six weeks at the mother house of the congregation at Vourles at the end of 1855, encouraged this orientation. He also busied himself strengthening the congregation's links with France; meanwhile Father Champagneur was hoping to have some freedom in the choice of work to be undertaken in Canada. The bishop ordered him to send some religious to Victoria on Vancouver Island in 1858, in fulfilment of his promise to Bishop Modeste Demers*, and others to Bourbonnais, Ill., in 1865, in order to undo the "harm" that Abbé Charles-Paschal-Télesphore Chiniquy* had done to the Franco-American population. Five years later, in response to his repeated requests, Champagneur was replaced as superior by Pascal Lajoie; he still retained the post of novice master.

The Canadianization and "clericalization" of the Clerics of St Viator were soon ensured by a small number of French brothers (never more than five), the recruitment of at least ten Canadians every year, the collaboration of parish priests such as Antoine Manseau, and the guidance of a bishop regarded in some ways as a co-founder. Nevertheless, Abbé Champagneur's contribution was not insignificant. Bishop Joseph La Rocque might declare in 1855 that he had never seen "a man so inept, as far as the direction of various institutions is concerned," yet Champagneur's numerous "resignations," his desire to join the Trappists, and his abortive plan for a community of colonizing hermits at Saint-Côme, called the solitaries of St Viator, reveal not only his difficulty in adapting but also his desire for a new kind of society. The fact that he was born in France no doubt helped him to maintain himself at the head of this congregation for more than a generation, but more can be said: young Canadians discerned in him a true master of the spiritual life.

From 1847 to 1874, when he returned to France, Abbé Champagneur initiated into religious life the 250 or so young men who entered the noviciate, most of whom subsequently taught either within or outside the Viatorians. He knew all of its members intimately, so his real influence cannot be evaluated in terms of the administrative difficulties he encountered at one time or another. His *Cours de méditations*, published between 1871 and 1874, gives only an imperfect notion of a narrow spirituality centred around conversion, asceticism, and holiness of life. Those who committed themselves to these practices were enabled to gain a reputation at least within their community (and often outside). Étienne Champagneur is a fine example of this, though he himself had felt obliged to enter the priesthood in the pursuit of his special aims.

Benoît Lévesque

[The central directorate of the Clerics of St Viator (Rome) has published many series of the records held in the different repositories of the congregation in Rome, Joliette, Que., and Outremont, Que. The location of the original is given in marginal notes accompanying the published documents. In particular, the following were consulted: *Circulaires du père Étienne Champagneur, fondateur et supérieur: 1847–1848, 1850–1870* (Outremont, 1972); *Documents: le père Louis Querbes, fondateur des Clercs de Saint-Viateur, 1793–1859* (14v., Côteau-du-Lac, Qué., 1955–60); "Dossier: Amérique," (6v. duplicated, Côteau-du-Lac, 1955–59), II–VI; *Dossier Querbes; correspondance reçue par le père Louis Querbes* (33v. to date, n.p., 1960–).

Also consulted were the following sources held in the repository in Rome: vol. I of Reg. matricule de tous les sujets ordonnés au noviciat de Vourles, France, depuis la fondation jusqu'au 1er oct. 1876, and the Reg. des religieux; in the archive at Joliette, a number of Father Louis Querbes's letters, documents relating to the college in that city, and a copy of Champagneur's *Instructions pour le noviciat des C. S. V.*; in the archives at Outremont, RL-1, RL-2, RL-3, RL-4, RD, RG-1 (there is an incomplete notebook for 1847–48 attributed to Champagneur), another copy of the *Instructions pour le noviciat*, and the "Conférences du noviciat des Clercs de Saint-Viateur."

Also used were: *Le Clerc de Saint-Viateur élevé à la perfection par la pratique de l'oraison . . .* (3v., Joliette, 1869–72), and the *Annuaires de la Congrégation des Clercs de Saint-Viateur*, 1918, 1925, 1931, 1943 (the archives of the Clerics of St Viator in Outremont holds a complete collection of the year-books which bear various titles and places of publication). B. L.]

ACAM, 420.080; 465.105; 901.055; 990.027. Arch. de la Soc. hist. de Joliette, Cartable Antoine Manseau, curé. Arch. de l'évêché de Joliette, Cartable collège de Joliette; Cartable Saint-Charles-Borromée-de-L'Industrie, I. *Mélanges religieux* (Montréal), 25, 28 sept. 1846; 2 juin, 24 août 1847. Allaire, *Dictionnaire*. Antoine Bernard, *Vie du père Champagneur: fondateur au Canada de l'Institut de Saint-Viateur* (Montréal, 1943). Benoît Lévesque, "Les communautés religieuses françaises au Québec: une immigration utopique (1837–1874)? Étude de sociologie historique," *Éléments pour une sociologie des communautés religieuses au Québec*, Bernard Denault et Benoît Lévesque, édit. (Montréal et Sherbrooke, Qué., 1975); "D'un projet primitivement utopique à une congrégation religieuse: sociologie génétique des Clercs de Saint-Viateur (1793–1859)" (thèse de doctorat, univ. de Paris V, 1975); "Naissance et implantation des Clercs de Saint-Viateur au Canada, 1847–1870" (thèse de MA, univ. de Sherbrooke, 1971). J.-C. Robert, "L'activité économique de Barthélemy Joliette et la fondation du village d'Industrie (Joliette), 1822–1850" (thèse de MA, univ. de Montréal, 1971), 127–64. Pierre Robert, *Vie du père Louis Querbes, fondateur de l'Institut des Clercs de Saint-Viateur* (1793–1859) (Bruxelles, 1922), 392–93. François Prud'homme, "Étude sur les divers recueils: instructions pour le noviciat," *Feuillets querbésiens* (Côteau-du-Lac), no.46 (1960): 502–4; no.47 (1960): 517–20. J.-C. Robert, "Un seigneur entrepreneur, Barthélemy Joliette, et la fondation du village d'Industrie (Joliette), 1822–1850," *RHAF*, 26 (1972–73): 375–95.

CHANDONNET (Chandonnais), THOMAS-AIMÉ, priest, educator, and writer; b. 26 Dec. 1834 at Saint-Pierre-les-Becquets (Les Becquets), Lower Canada, fifteenth child of Joseph Chandonnais, a farmer, and Angèle Bibeau; d. 5 June 1881 in Montreal, Que.

In 1848 Thomas-Aimé Chandonnet entered the Séminaire de Québec where he took his first baccalaureate examination in 1853. He then taught there while studying theology and was ordained priest on 23 Feb. 1861. His courses in philosophy from 1859 to 1865 became progressively firmer in structure but developed little in content; his pupils no doubt derived a philosophical and moral justification of the supremacy of heaven over earth, faith over reason, the spiritual over the temporal, the church over the state, and the "eternal kingdom" over the "earthly kingdom." Chandonnet also made use of these themes in a speech on Saint-Jean-Baptiste Day (24 June) in 1865.

As a graduate of the Séminaire de Québec, Chandonnet took part in the Gaumist controversy [*see* Charles-François Baillargeon*] over the use of pagan or Christian authors for teaching purposes; he was chiefly opposed to the intransigence displayed by those defending censorship on the basis of Christian principles. While in Rome from August 1865 to September 1867 to study for the doctorates he received in theology, canon law, and philosophy, Abbé Chandonnet continued to collaborate with Bishop Baillargeon, the agent and procurator of the Canadian bishops in Rome, in attempts to settle the Gaumist controversy.

Appointed principal of the École Normale Laval in Quebec City in 1867, the learned abbé delivered a number of lectures there between 10 Dec. 1867 and 30 March 1868 in which he again tackled the "Thomist" question of the connections between faith and reason. In a second series he defended the supremacy of the church and the thesis of the "free state in the free church," and took a stand against Charles Forbes, Comte de Montalembert. By 1868 he was preoccupied with founding a Catholic journal and also took up again the Gaumist quarrel through his opposition to George Saint-Aimé [Alexis Pelletier*], professor at the Collège de Sainte-Anne-de-la-Pocatière and a leading Gaumist. But in 1871, shortly after the death of Bishop Baillargeon, Chandonnet left his position at Quebec to serve as a priest in New England. There he concerned himself with the French Canadian emigrants who had made their homes at Worcester and New Bedford, Mass. He returned to Canada in 1874 and spent the next two years at the Séminaire de Sainte-Thérèse. In Montreal from 1877, he founded that year and directed until 1881 *La Revue de Montréal*, a scholarly publication with a religious tone which promoted moderate ultramontane studies while at the same time supporting the diocese of Quebec in a new ecclesiastical wrangle over the establishment of a branch of the Université Laval in Montreal [*see* Joseph DESAUTELS].

After a sojourn in Ottawa, Thomas-Aimé Chandonnet died on 5 June 1881 in Montreal, at the age of 46. For reasons which are not indicated in archival records he was buried in the Côte-des-Neiges Cemetery "in unconsecrated ground and without religious rites."

YVAN LAMONDE

[Thomas-Aimé Chandonnet was the author of a number of works including *Discours prononcés à Notre-Dame de Québec au triduum de la Société St-Vincent-de-Paul les 21, 22 et 23 décembre 1863* (Québec, 1864); *La Saint-Jean-Baptiste à Québec en 1865* (Québec, 1865); *Notre-Dame-des-Canadiens et les Canadiens aux États-Unis* (Montréal, 1872); *L'Abbé Joseph Aubry* (Montréal, 1875); *L'Université Laval à Montréal* (Montréal, 1878). He also contributed articles to the *Rev. de Montréal* in the years 1877 to 1881, in some inshances under the pseudonym of T.-A. de Saint-Claude. The journal is held by the library of the Dominican monastery of Notre-Dame-de-Grâce, in Montreal. Y.L.]

AP, Notre-Dame de Montréal, Reg. des baptêmes, mariages et sépultures, 6 juin 1881. ASQ, Fonds Viger-Verreau, Cartons 23, nos.344, 348; 24, no.181; 26, no.360; Sér. O, 0136–0138; MSS, 34, I, 30 août, 5 oct. 1853, 23 févr. 1861; MSS-M, 183; 220; 222; 230; 586; 775; 1112; Univ., Carton 84, no.88. Alexis Pelletier wrote an article and two books under pseudonyms: L. S. J., "Nouveaux documents sur la question de l'enseignement des classiques chrétiens et païens au Canada, lettre à M. Bonnetti," *Annales de philosophie chrétienne* (Paris), 5e sér., 19 (1869): 7–32; George Saint-Aimé, *Résponses aux dernières attaques dirigées par M. l'abbé Chandonnet contre les partisans de la méthode chrétienne . . .* (Québec, 1868); and *La question des classiques en présence des rectifications et des critiques de M. l'abbé Chandonnet par un "Chrétien"* (Québec, 1865).

L'Abeille (Québec), 10 juin 1860. *Le Courrier de Saint-Hyacinthe*, 6 août 1868. *Le Courrier du Canada*, 16, 18, 19, 23, 25, 28, 30 nov., 2, 5, 7, 14, 16, 19 déc. 1864; 22 févr. 1869. *L'Écho du cabinet de lecture paroissial* (Montréal), 1er, 15 août, 1er sept. 1865. *L'Événement* (Québec), déc. 1867–avril 1868, 28 juill., 1er, 4 août 1868. *L'Opinion publique*, 16 juin 1881. *Le Journal de Québec*, 6, 13 juin, 4 juill. 1865. L.-A. Fortier, *L'université Laval affiliée au Collège royal des chirurgiens de Londres (Ang.) contre l'école de Médecine et de Chirurgie de Montréal affiliée à l'université du collège Victoria (Cobourg, Ontario), affiliée au Collège royal des chirurgiens de Londres et l'abbé T. A. Chandonnet* (Montréal, 1879). M.-A. Lavigne, *L'abbé T.-A. Chandonnet, docteur en philosophie, théologie et droit canon* (Montréal, 1950). Thomas Charland, " Un gaumiste canadien; l'abbé Alexis Pelletier," *RHAF*, 1 (1947–48): 195–236. É.-Z. Massicotte, " Quelques librairies montréalaises d'autrefois, " *BRH*, 50 (1944): 171. Pierre Trudel, "La protection des Anglo-Québécois et la presse conservatrice," *Rev. de l'univ. d'Ottawa*, 44 (1974): 137–57.

CHAPAIS, JEAN-CHARLES, businessman and politician; b. 2 Dec. 1811 at Rivière-Ouelle, Lower Canada, son of Jean-Charles Chapais, merchant, and Julienne Boucher; m. 30 June 1846 Georgina Dionne, whose uncle, Charles-Paschal-Télesphore Chiniquy*, performed the ceremony; they had six children, including Thomas*, a politician and historian, and Jean-Charles*, an author of several books and pamphlets on agriculture; d. 17 July 1885 at Ottawa, Ont., and was buried 22 July in the church of Saint-Denis-de-la-Bouteillerie at Saint-Denis, Que.

Jean-Charles Chapais's ancestors came from Normandy. François and Jean Chapais left Brécey for New France around 1740, after Intendant Gilles Hocquart* had decided a new levy of settlers was needed. Jean established himself on land in the seigneury of La Bouteillerie (or Rivière-Ouelle), first opened for settlement in 1672. The economic and social ascent of the Chapais family took several generations. Jean-Charles was born into a reasonably well-to-do family that took an interest in the political life of the country as well as in the social problems of the parish. He was given a superior education, the prerogative of young men of social standing at that time. After studying at Rivière-Ouelle with Rémi Béchard, an experienced teacher "selected and engaged" by the Chapais and Boucher families "for the training of their sons," he received a classical education at the Séminaire de Nicolet from 1824 to 1830. He then spent two years in Quebec City where to satisfy his father's ambitions he took private English lessons from the Reverend Daniel Wilkie* and endeavoured "to make the best possible contacts in Quebec society."

In 1833 Jean-Charles Chapais bought two plots of land for his son in the fief of Saint-Denis, between the La Bouteillerie and Kamouraska seigneuries. There the young man became a "smallwares retail merchant," as well as being a farmer and a wholesaler. His business concerns grew rapidly, in response to the needs of those in the surrounding countryside. During the 1840s Chapais was a member of the two firms of Chapais et fils and Chapais et frères. He also raised cattle and farmed, and in addition exploited the "Pêche à Belle," a concession for a net fishery which he had leased in 1839. Through these various economic activities, as well as the substantial dowry of his wife Georgina Dionne, he was soon in comfortable circumstances and was even reputed to be extremely rich. These factors also made him the pivot of economic and social development in Saint-Denis. Chapais's business interests attracted settlers and people of all trades to Saint-Denis and he provided a livelihood for a fair number of employees through his general store, farm, and fishery. He fought tenaciously for the canonical establishment and incorporation of the parish, and was involved in building a chapel in 1839 and a parish church between 1840 and 1856. Active in organizing education and in setting up a public library, he took part in the incorporation of the municipality, becoming its first mayor in 1845 and its first postmaster in 1849. Saint-Denis grew in a few decades from a sparsely populated village into a prosperous, well-organized centre as a result of Chapais's efforts.

In the 19th century such an influential person was bound to have a political career, and in 1851 the second phase of Jean-Charles's life began. His father-in-law, Amable Dionne*, a Kamouraska merchant, a member of the Legislative Council for Canada East, and one of the richest and most influential French Canadians of the time, dreamed of making his son-in-law a political leader in the district. When the Legislative Assembly seat for Kamouraska became vacant in 1850, Chapais, who confessed he had "never wanted to become a member of the legislature," yielded to Dionne and to pressure from his friends, and stood for election. He thought he would be unopposed, but the Rouges ran Luc LETELLIER de Saint-Just, a notary in Rivière-Ouelle, against him. Letellier won. Chapais and Letellier were adversaries on five occasions between 1850 and 1857 and their electoral contests became legendary for their bitterness and violence, with the results often disputed and sometimes declared invalid. Chapais, who took the seat in 1851, represented Kamouraska until confederation. He supported Conservative leaders Augustin-Norbert Morin*, Étienne-Paschal Taché*, and George-Étienne Cartier*, although he also sympathized deeply with Louis-Victor SICOTTE. In 1863 he refused to join the government of George Brown* and Antoine-Aimé Dorion*, because, as a friend commented, he would not agree "to tarnish 13 years of good political life in a single day."

Chapais was rarely in the forefront in the house, but did have some influence on legislation which concerned Canada East relating to agriculture, settlement, education, and the abolition of the seigneurial system, as well as the laying out of the Intercolonial Railway and the development of the Grand Trunk, of which he was appointed a director by the government. In 1864 Chapais became commissioner of public works; it was as a member of the cabinet that he took part in the work that prepared the way for confederation. However, his active participation was limited to the Quebec conference, and for a while he was cool towards Hector-Louis Langevin*, who, though younger than he, was a delegate not only at Charlottetown but also in London.

Appointed in July 1867 to Sir John A. Macdonald*'s cabinet as minister of agriculture, Chapais sought the federal and the provincial seats for Kamouraska in the general elections held that year. However, as a result of electoral illegalities, the riding lost its right to both provincial and federal representation for two years. The provincial seat of Champlain, vacated in November 1867, provided Chapais with an alternative and he was returned by acclamation. Two months later he was appointed to the Senate for the division of La Durantaye. He remained minister of agriculture until 1869 when he became receiver general, a post he held until 1873. As an MLA at Quebec and a senator and minister at Ottawa, Chapais was one of the politicians who monopolized power following confederation. When the double mandate was abolished in 1871 he withdrew from the provincial scene. Two years later he resigned from the federal government. Historians have usually linked Chapais's resignation to the New Brunswick separate schools question, but it seems clear that a pretext has been interpreted as a decisive cause. Pressure was certainly brought to bear on Chapais to give up his ministerial post and this was, in his wife's words, a source of "sorrow" and "disappointment" to him. In 1869 Macdonald had already transferred Chapais from the important ministry of agriculture to the post of receiver general, and thereby set him on the path which sooner or later would lead to his withdrawal from the government. In 1873 Macdonald's party was in crisis and he endeavoured to improve the status of his ministry by bringing in new and stronger figures who were both competent and flexible. He also sought to strengthen his position in the House of Commons by introducing into the cabinet more representatives from the house itself. With this in mind, Macdonald insisted on the resignation of the man whom, in a pejorative but significant fashion, he called "my nun"; he chose Théodore Robitaille*, who was a member of the House of Commons, as Chapais's successor.

In his *Manuel électoral: portraits et dossiers parlementaires du premier parlement de Québec*, Auguste ACHINTRE notes that Chapais "is still, at the present date [1871], a minister whose modesty and unselfishness seem to limit his value and diminish his influence." Admittedly, Chapais's whole political career with the exception of the electoral contests in Kamouraska deserves this judgement, despite the fact that historians, influenced by the preoccupations of traditional historiography, have attached more importance to that part of his career than to his economic and social activity in Saint-Denis. The name of Jean-Charles Chapais is just a shadowy watermark in the political history of the 19th century but it is written with bold, indelible strokes in the institutions and history of Saint-Denis.

ANDRÉE DÉSILETS

[The following newspapers were consulted regarding the important events in the career of Jean-Charles Chapais: *Le Courrier de Saint-Hyacinthe, Le Courrier du Canada, Le Journal de Québec, La Minerve, Le Pionnier de Sherbrooke* (Sherbrooke, Qué.), and *L'Union des Cantons de l'Est* (Arthabaska, Qué.). A.D.]

ANQ-Q, AP-G-36; AP-G-134; AP-G-242. PAC, MG 26, A. Can., Sénat, *Débats*, 1868–85. Can., prov. du, Assemblée législative, *Journaux*, 1851–66. Qué., Assemblée législative, *Journaux*, 1867–71. Achintre, *Manuel électoral*. *CPC*, 1867–79. J. Desjardins, *Guide parl*. Le Jeune, *Dictionnaire*. *Municipalités et paroisses dans la province de Québec*, C.-E. Deschamps, compil. (Québec, 1896). Terrill, *Chronology of Montreal*. Wallace, *Macmillan dict*. Julienne Barnard, *Mémoires Chapais; documentation, correspondance, souvenirs* (4v., Montréal et Paris, 1961–64). P.-B. Casgrain, *Étude historique: Letellier de Saint-Just et son temps* (Québec, 1885). Chapais, *Hist. du Canada*. H. M. Miner, *St. Denis; a French-Canadian parish* (Chicago, 1939). Rumilly, *Hist. de la prov. de Québec*, I. Henri Têtu, *Histoire des familles Têtu, Bonenfant, Dionne et Perrault* (Québec, 1898). C.-E. Rouleau, "L'honorable Jean-Charles Chapais," *BRH*, 5 (1899): 368–70.

CHAUVEAU, PIERRE-JOSEPH-OLIVIER, lawyer, man of letters, politician, sheriff, and professor; b. 30 May 1820 at Charlesbourg, Lower Canada, son of Pierre-Charles Chauveau and Marie-Louise Roy; m. 22 Sept. 1840 Marie-Louise-Flore Masse at Quebec; d. there 4 April 1890.

The Chauveau family was one of the oldest in Charlesbourg. Pierre, a cooper from Bordeaux, France, had settled there at the beginning of the 18th century. On 22 Aug. 1707, at Beauport, he married Marie-Charlotte Lavallée, and they had 12 children. Pierre-Joseph-Olivier was of the fifth generation of Chauveaus in Canada. He scarcely remembered his father, a prosperous merchant of Charlesbourg, who had died prematurely when Pierre-Joseph-Olivier was only four. His maternal grandfather, Joseph Roy, a rich grain merchant who lived at the corner of Rue Sainte-Anne and Rue du Trésor in Quebec City, assumed the father's responsibilities, taking his daughter and her small son into his home. According to one of his biographers, Louis-Michel Darveau*, Chauveau enjoyed an "extremely pampered" existence in this household, for attention was lavished on him by his mother, two aunts, and grandfather. Darveau thinks this hot-house atmosphere fostered Chauveau's desire to please and need to be flattered.

In Quebec Chauveau attended the primary school near the garden of the fort on the Plains of Abraham. At nine he entered the Séminaire de Québec, where he proved a brilliant pupil with obvious literary talent. Chauveau said little about these years, when his fellow students were Elzéar-Alexandre Taschereau*, later a cardinal, and Luc LETELLIER de Saint-Just, who became lieutenant governor of Quebec. Two teachers, the abbés Jean Holmes* and Jérôme Demers*, are thought to have kept an attentive eye on his progress.

At 17, after hesitating between law and the priesthood, Chauveau finally chose law. He articled in the law office of his two maternal uncles, André-Rémi Hamel*, the advocate general for Lower Canada, and Louis-David Roy*. He had much in common with Roy who, at 29, was a friend of François-Xavier Garneau* and, as Chauveau noted, was "in his [own] generation one of the men who had the greatest talent for and dedication to the sciences and arts." Both were keenly affected by the tragic events which culminated in the collapse of the rebellions of 1837 and 1838, and Chauveau, full of fire and ambition, was determined not to remain on the sidelines. On 6 April 1838 *Le Canadien* published his first poem, "L'Insurrection," which exalted the heroism of the Patriotes. He subsequently sent occasional articles to this newspaper, including the poem "Adieux à Sir John Colborne," on 23 Oct. 1839, which again expressed his patriotic fervour. In the turmoil of this period, which he judged "cruel" and "hard to weather," Chauveau still managed to continue his legal studies, finishing under George Okill STUART, whose firm was reputed one of the best in Quebec City. There he improved his English, acquiring an exceptional mastery of the language. On 30 Aug. 1841 he was called to the bar.

Chauveau began to practise law with considerable backing. His uncle Louis-David Roy invited him to become a partner in his firm, replacing Roy's brother-in-law, André-Rémi Hamel, who had been appointed a judge on 1 May 1839. This offer was especially attractive since Chauveau had married on 22 Sept. 1840 and could not afford the luxury of a prolonged wait for clients. He practised with his uncle until 24 Dec. 1849, when Roy too was appointed a judge. Chauveau then went into partnership with a young lawyer, Philippe-Baby Casgrain.

It was the practice of law that assured Chauveau of an income, but it was politics and literature that intrigued him. Like most young people of Quebec, he was against the proposed union of the Canadas, but rallied, with Augustin-Norbert Morin* and Thomas Cushing Aylwin*, to support the "Adresse aux électeurs de Terrebonne," delivered by Louis-Hippolyte La Fontaine* on 28 Aug. 1840, which argued that union could under certain circumstances benefit French Canadians. For Chauveau, La Fontaine was, however, only a political leader. His intellectual mentors were Étienne Parent* and Morin, who to counteract the defeatism spreading through French-speaking circles constituted themselves "the initiators of the national and literary movement among young people"; in addition, Napoléon AUBIN, the editor of *Le Fantasque* in Quebec, had acquired a strong hold upon the younger generation through his free and easy manner, humour, and liberalism. With Joseph-Charles Taché*, Télesphore Fournier, and James Huston*, Chauveau frequented the learned and patriotic circles and societies of Quebec. These educated young men gathered regularly at the Hôtel de la Cité, the Hôtel de Tempérance, or the offices of *Le Fantasque*, to meet Aubin, their intellectual leader. Eager to foster literary and scientific movements, Chauveau helped found the Société Saint-Jean-Baptiste de Québec in 1842, and the Société Canadienne d'Études littéraires et scientifiques the following year. At their gatherings he found audiences for his first great speeches, such as the one he gave to the Société Saint-Jean-Baptiste in 1842 on liberal ideas, in which he took the opportunity to denounce absolutism and colonialism. His dynamic contribution to the intellectual life of the city gained him the presidency of the Literary and Historical Society of Quebec in 1843. Chauveau's fame was beginning to spread beyond Quebec, since letters he had written were published by French journalist Théodore-Frédéric Gaillardet, owner of *Le Courrier des États-Unis* (New York), from 20 May 1841 and reprinted in Canadian newspapers. In these letters – which were to appear at irregular intervals until 1855 – Chauveau analysed the situation in Canada, usually in the context of British colonial policy. His tone was restrained and polite and his interpretations were often apt and always shrewd. In his early writings he outlined the problems of a colony dominated by a narrowly mercantilist mentality and immured in "its middle ages," as demonstrated by the "growing influence" of the clergy, " the remarkable piety of the upper classes [and the] superstitions persisting among the people." In ensuing months he refined his thinking and modified his outlook. At the height of the crisis occurring under Governor Sir Charles Theophilus Metcalfe* in 1844, Chauveau denounced in *Le Courrier* the impracticality of the confederation scheme advanced by Lord Durham [Lambton*]: England rejected the plan because she was afraid of promoting the independence of the colonies as did the colonials because they feared excessive centralization.

The young man who spoke with such authority in *Le Courrier des États-Unis* in 1844 was 24 years old. Married and living in the residence which had belonged to his grandfather Roy and which he would inherit in 1851, he earned his living in the court room and his laurels in patriotic and literary circles. Lively and witty, Chauveau liked to charm and to display his brilliance, and he enjoyed both good books and the company of intellectuals. He was fiery, but not aggressive. Chauveau had a well-stocked, even encyclopædic mind and a reliable memory. He had definite ideas on literature and history which he developed in 1847 in a lecture entitled "État de la littérature en France depuis la Révolution," published in the third of the four volumes of *Répertoire national, ou recueil de littérature*, brought out in Montreal in 1848–50 by James Huston. From Abel-François Villemain, a specialist in comparative literature at the Sorbonne who greatly admired Mme de Staël, Chauveau took the concept of linking literary movements to social realities: "the literature of a people is its history; it is the whole body of the writings of its most distinguished citizens." This sociological vision of literature was matched by a vision of history which was free of any idea of divine providence. He argued that history was the resultant of two forces, the first an inward one "of concentration . . . , which tends to draw towards a common centre the public power, wealth, knowledge," and the other an outward one of expansion which "tends to spread and universalize all these things, to make them as far as possible common to all and equal for all." Philosophically, Chauveau was a liberal imbued with the idea of progress, for whom the French revolution represented "one of the progressive developments of Christian societies," and constitutional monarchy "order united to liberty." But he was also a patriot who felt keenly his status as a colonized subject. In his poem "Adieux à Sir John Colborne" he wrote of the French Canadian people: "Alms and kicks, [it] accepts everything with a dejected air." He took great pride in his French origins, was chauvinistically dedicated to his native town, and pondered the fate of the French Canadian people anxiously.

Chauveau's political opinions placed him with La Fontaine, although he had never accepted the union which, to him, was "an act of political oppression" and a "financial operation," as he stressed in "L'Union des Canadas ou la Fête des Banquiers," a poem published in *Le Canadien* on 5 April 1841. This young man, who was well educated and aware of contemporary events, had a future. He felt he had literary talents, but he knew he resided in a country where the cultivated man had to resign himself to living in the world "of scruples [the priesthood], chicanery [the law] [or] illness [medicine]." There was no secure future in Canada for a man of letters. Politics was a faster route to success and prestige. Moved more by ambition, vanity, and patriotic duty than by inclination and aptitude, he chose this course in 1844. It was a difficult decision which left him deeply embittered, as he confessed to the French literary critic, Adolphe de Puibusque six years later: "How I love your lot and prefer it to mine! You follow your natural bent. . . . [My life] is a stream diverted from its source and forced to fulfil a prosaic destiny."

Circumstances weighed heavily in the choice Chauveau made. At the time of the political crisis precipitated in 1844 by Governor Metcalfe on the question of ministerial responsibility, Chauveau supported La Fontaine. In September, Metcalfe dissolved the houses and plunged the province into a difficult electoral campaign. In the riding of Quebec, La Fontaine's supporters were looking for someone to provide a threat to the incumbent, John Neilson*, who was being criticized for his support of the government of William Henry Draper* and Denis-Benjamin Viger*. Thomas Cushing Aylwin suggested Chauveau, and Joseph-Édouard CAUCHON approved. Chauveau launched his campaign on 1 October, on the steps of the church of Saint-Roch in Quebec City, unveiling a three-point programme: responsible government, the advancement of education, and the development of industry. He summed up his plans in a maxim: "The greatest good for the greatest number." On 12 November, he won a resounding victory by 1,000 votes.

When the session opened in Montreal on 28 Nov. 1844, Chauveau sat in opposition with La Fontaine's supporters, since electoral support in Canada West had returned the Draper–Viger ministry to power. Like any other new member, Chauveau had to learn the ropes, but he lost no time in converting his ideas, which were strongly tinged with liberalism, into practical politics. He entered the arena bent on denouncing in his turn the injustices of the union of 1841, which he considered "the most monstrous of iniquities." He employed all his eloquence to defend the use of French in the Legislative Assembly, responsible government, representation by population, and the economic needs of the Quebec City region, and he gave serious attention to the problem of the emigration of French Canadians to the United States. Not a party man, he took the line of the free thinker who primarily acts according to his principles and, leaving partisan wrangles to others, prefers to rally to the defence of important causes. He was not therefore an unconditional ally of La Fontaine. As a citizen of Quebec City, he distrusted La Fontaine and the Montrealers around him. Their differences of opinion reflected the old rivalry between Quebec and Montreal which for a time divided the Reform party. But these internal struggles were suppressed when questions of national interest were involved. For the immediate future, the Draper–Viger government was the real adversary. On 27 June 1846 Chauveau delivered against it one of the best indictments of his career, raging against the defects of the electoral map, the pillaging of revenues for the benefit of Canada West, government patronage, and the ousting of French-speaking officials from the public service. Opposition to the government was growing in Quebec and, in order to channel the discontent and keep a close watch particularly over the material interests of the region, the Comité Constitutionnel de la Réforme et du Progrès was set up under the chairmanship of René-Édouard Caron*. On 29 July 1846, when the public meeting to found it was held in Quebec City, Chauveau indicated his support for the movement, which published a manifesto in November. Among the important demands advanced in the manifesto were responsible government, representation by population for the two sections of the province, a redrawing of the electoral map, free trade, free navigation on the St Lawrence, and the granting of lots for settlement at low rates. The December 1847 elections proved favourable to the Reform coalition under La Fontaine and Robert Baldwin*; Chauveau, who had the full backing of his constituents to present the grievances set out by the committee, was re-elected by acclamation. The make-up of the new Reform cabinet, however, left some unhappy: both Louis-Joseph Papineau*, who had returned from exile and coveted the speakership of the assembly, and Chauveau, who wanted a portfolio, were disappointed. Convinced he was one of the architects of the victory and the natural spokesman for the citizens of the Quebec City region, Chauveau behaved like a spoiled child and his friends were barely able to persuade him not to resign his seat.

Chauveau remained a member, but one could sense he was deeply wounded. He lent an attentive but sceptical ear when Papineau launched the movement to repeal the union on 14 March 1848. As events progressed, some people in Quebec City invited Papineau to assume the leadership of a new party and to speak there on 11 May. He was applauded by an audience of more than 8,000, which prompted him to say in *L'Avenir* of Montreal on 15 May: "Yes, at Quebec there is life and a sense of honour. In Montreal, it's another matter." Public opinion in Quebec City was, however, divided: Aubin in *Le Canadien* backed Papineau but Cauchon and the *Journal de Québec* defended La Fontaine's position. At no point did Chauveau exploit this situation to play the leader.

Moreover, in the house on 20 March he had declared to Papineau that he shared his idea of electoral reform, judging it an "indispensable development of the institutions we have been given," but also asserted that he had confidence in the present government's ability to effect it: "I feel sure that in time we will obtain from a Liberal administration what we had dared to ask of a hostile administration." He was on the platform at the meeting on 11 May, and after Papineau's speech said a few words "about the present situation of the country." At that time he seemed to want to take advantage of the unrest to hasten reform, rather than to present himself as one of Papineau's true supporters. Chauveau's attitude therefore expressed his desire to "take back what belonged to us by means of what had been left to us."

Although he sometimes fought beside Papineau on questions such as the eligibility of those deported in 1838 for compensation, Chauveau primarily served the cause of the Comité Constitutionnel de la Réforme et du Progrès. During the 1849 session he brought before the assembly a petition from the businessmen of Quebec City requesting "the repeal of duties on flour, grain and supplies in general," and demanded the construction of the Halifax and Quebec and the Quebec and Saguenay railways, as well as the improvement of the docks on the Rivière Saint-Charles. He also found himself on occasion chiding the government over matters of patronage. Using the debate on the bill to regulate representation in the Legislative Assembly, he moved the adoption of resolutions severely denouncing the Act of Union, which earned him La Fontaine's antipathy. His position, midway between the radical Liberals and the moderate Reformers, was difficult to maintain and he was led to depend increasingly upon the regional sections of the constitutional committee with which he remained in constant touch through his friend Luc Letellier de Saint-Just. During the summer of 1849, he decided not to support the Annexation Manifesto [*see* Luther Hamilton Holton*], and in the autumn refused to sign the "Protest against the separation of Canada from England" even though 2,000 from Quebec City had endorsed it. He justified his position by asserting to Louis-Joseph Massue*: "If the annexationists were to have the upper hand, we would be placing ourselves in a compromising position." During this disturbed period, emigration of French Canadians to the United States remained his principal concern and he put forward radical measures to open up uncultivated land in Canada East to settlers.

In 1849 the Montreal riots [*see* James Bruce*] did not shake the Reform party, which Baldwin and La Fontaine controlled with an iron hand. But this strength would not last long. By 1850, the appearance in Canada West of the Clear Grits on the political chessboard heralded the crumbling of the coalition. This new faction demanded secularization of the clergy reserves, the separation of church and state, and elective democratic institutions on the American model. Feeling themselves challenged, Baldwin and La Fontaine handed in their resignations the following year and Francis HINCKS and Morin formed a new ministry. Wanting ministers who enjoyed wide popularity in the Quebec City region, they offered the post of solicitor general to Chauveau. In the elections held in November and December 1851 he was returned by acclamation on a programme which was drawn from that of 1847, with the further objectives of the abolition of the seigneurial system and an elected rather than appointed legislative council – two projects Morin had borrowed from the Rouges.

The post of solicitor general was not one of the more important ones, but it gave Chauveau the recognition, prestige, and income he badly needed. As a minister, he had to adapt himself to the directions chosen by his leader and play down certain of his own ideas that were judged too liberal. With all his eloquence he supported Morin, who set up the procedures for abolishing the seigneurial system and making the Legislative Council elective. In August 1853 Morin appointed him provincial secretary. In this capacity he was charged with carrying out the recommendations of the commission on education established in 1853 and chaired by Louis-Victor SICOTTE [*see* Jean-Baptiste Meilleur*]. But the members of the legislature were little concerned about such matters, so the recommendations were not implemented. The secularization of the clergy reserves and the abolition of seigneurial tenure split the various political forces into ungovernable factions in 1854. The Clear Grits, the Rouges, and the ten or so representatives aligned with Cauchon refused to postpone dealing with these questions. Chauveau, whose enemies suspected him of being close to the Clear Grits, was not really satisfied with the government's performance and from January 1854 periodically threatened, in private, to resign. From the outset of the session on 13 June, the various factions formed an alliance which brought down the government within ten days. The elections failed to produce a solid majority. Hincks resigned in September and in an unprecedented realignment, Morin's Reformers joined the Conservatives led by Sir Allan Napier MacNab*. This political shuffle did not affect Chauveau, who for the time being retained his portfolio. But in January 1855 Étienne-Paschal Taché*, Morin's successor, chose Cauchon and George-Étienne Cartier* for the ministry instead of Chauveau, who once more became merely a representative. He confided to his friend Abbé Hospice-Anthelme-Jean-Baptiste Verreau* that he had the feeling he had been shown the door, since as compensation he had been offered only "the chairmanship of the Commission to revise the Statutes, with a kind of understanding that I would be appointed a judge after that." Chauveau's impression was that the blow came from Lewis Thomas DRUMMOND, but it seems more logical to suppose that Cauchon – who was very influential in the house and among the clergy – would give more credibility and weight to the cabinet than Chauveau.

The loss of his ministerial portfolio was a hard blow to Chauveau's vanity, as well as to his financial security. Although Letellier de Saint-Just supplied him with clients, his income as a lawyer was inadequate for the needs of his family, who went through a difficult period. In 1852 death deprived him of his grandmother, mother, and mother-in-law. One daughter, Olympe, suffered from tuberculosis and another, Annette, was not well. His wife experienced periods of despondency and he himself was worried about his sons Pierre and Alexandre, who were in college. Abbé Verreau, the family confidant, endeavoured to alleviate his misfortunes by lending him money, comforting his wife, and keeping an eye on the children at boarding-school. These troubles were kept secret and in public Chauveau projected the image of a man for whom everything was going well. His work "Charles Guérin: roman de mœurs canadiennes," which appeared anonymously in *Album littéraire et musical de la revue canadienne* between February 1846 and March 1847, and was published as a book under his name in 1853 by Georges-Hippolyte Cherrier*, brought him renown. This novel, which in its form reflects the influence of Balzac, is a realistic portrayal of the manners and customs of French Canadian society around 1830. Behind a conventional love story that is psychologically rather improbable, the real plot is developed and brought to an indefinite conclusion: the struggle of French Canadians to ensure their individual and collective fulfilment. In the book, the English hold all the high offices in the government and monopolize commerce, and the liberal professions are described as crowded with "idle, starving and desperate men." All that is left is farming, but good land is becoming scarce. To realize their ambitions, the young Canadiens in this novel are tempted to leave their country or to ingratiate themselves with the high and mighty. Jean Guilbeault, a fiery young patriot, proposes to build a new country and Charles Guérin joins in his friend's plan. Together they set out to carve from the forest in the Eastern Townships a land where industry and commerce will belong to French Canadians, the habitant will no longer be exploited, the virtues of their ancestors and traditional customs will be kept alive. The novel is not a literary masterpiece – it has been rightly criticized for its lack of unity – and it suffers from comparison with works published in France in the same period. It nevertheless established Chauveau as the best prose writer of his generation in French Canada, and he conferred on a literary genre just taking form there a social and political significance which influenced the character of subsequent works in this field. Combined with his success as a speaker, both on the hustings and in academic lecture halls, this novel placed him at the heart of intellectual life in Quebec City. Since 1848 he had been a frequent visitor to the bookstore of Octave Crémazie*, at 12 Rue de la Fabrique, where a dozen years later the "Quebec school" came into being. He attended regularly the Institut Canadien of Quebec, where he was much in demand as a lecturer, and he served as its president from 1851 to 1852. For some years he was also vice-president of the Quebec Library Association.

Conscious of his own worth and facing a difficult family situation, Chauveau put pressure on the MacNab–Taché cabinet for compensation. The resignation of Jean-Baptiste Meilleur as superintendent of the Board of Education on 19 June 1855 relieved his friends of an embarrassing situation. Chauveau resigned his seat in the assembly on 1 July and the following day was appointed superintendent. Although he did not feel ready at first to fill this post, which would oblige him to move to Montreal, he accepted it as a makeshift. Yet his salary would be £750, and his duties would be suited to his reputation and culture. He bade Quebec farewell in a resounding address at the ceremony on 18 July commemorating the heroes who had fallen on the Plains of Abraham. To a crowd of 10,000 assembled before a special platform on which were seated the governor, Edmund Walker Head*, Commander Paul-Henry de Belvèze*, and religious and lay dignitaries, Chauveau delivered a eulogy of the brave men who had died on the battlefield and a defence of the existing concord between France and England. Inspired by the beauty of the setting, the solemnity of the event being remembered, and the emotion of the crowd, he gave a speech charged with a passion and eloquence rarely equalled in Canada. This address, which became a standard piece in anthologies, established Chauveau's reputation as a national orator and won him praise from French literary critics.

In the autumn of 1855 Chauveau settled with his family in Montreal, where he undertook the arduous task of putting into operation the school system which Meilleur had set up in 1841 and ironing out the difficulties in it. In February 1856 he presented his first report, outlining his plan of action: a statutory budget for the Board of Education, a special fund to subsidize certain schools and improve the working conditions of teachers, greater uniformity in school texts, and increased powers for both the superintendent and a Council of Public Instruction, notably in respect of regulations concerning the internal management of schools and the treatment of teachers. There was nothing very innovative in this report, since Meilleur, and Sicotte in his 1853 report, had demanded these reforms in the past. But the man now proposing these measures had panache, friends in the government, and experience in politics: he was also addressing a public more sensitive to educational matters than in earlier years and he could count on the vigorous parliamentary opposition of the Rouges to prompt the government to act.

These circumstances explain the speed and effectiveness of Chauveau's action. During the spring of 1856 Cartier steered through the assembly a set of measures designed to create two pedagogical journals, establish a pension fund for teachers, and set up the Council of Public Instruction. The government was also to make £22,000 available to the universities, colleges, and specialized institutions, £5,000 of which would be earmarked for establishing three normal schools (teachers' colleges) – Jacques-Cartier and McGill at Montreal and Laval at Quebec City. The creation of these schools, which posed the problem of the prerogatives of the Catholic church in matters of education, gave rise in 1856 and 1857 to private discussions between Chauveau and the ecclesiastical authorities; they resulted, in the words of Jean-Charles Magnan, in "the 1857 agreement." The Catholic normal schools were to be run by the superintendent, with the assistance of university representatives, and the bishops were to appoint the principals of these colleges. Historian Louis-Philippe Audet has stressed the confessional, "separate," and national character of these teaching institutions, which were intended for young men and women 16 and over who held a certificate of good conduct. Although retired, Meilleur followed these innovations closely, and confided to Abbé Louis-Édouard BOIS: "It is a victory for my opinions and recommendations." During 1857 the opening of these schools was marked by a series of festivities at which the superintendent made himself highly visible.

The *Journal of Education for Lower Canada* and its counterpart in French, the *Journal de l'Instruction publique*, were launched that year. The two journals were the official organs of the Department of Public Instruction, and the French edition was in fact identified with Chauveau, who managed it and was virtually its sole author until 1867. The regular column in the French edition, "Revue mensuelle," in which Chauveau revealed a rare mastery of the French language and a wide culture, was the delight of the literary men of the time. However, teachers showed scant interest in the publication and in 1864 even launched a much more vigorous rival, *La Semaine* (Quebec) [*see* Norbert THIBAULT]. Thus the *Journal de l'Instruction*, which lasted until 1879, began to decline in 1865. The contents of the journal, together with the annual reports of the department, enable us to identify Chauveau's principal pedagogical ideas: the competence of teachers, the necessity of modern teaching materials, the development of libraries, the importance of a pedagogical journal, and the urgency of establishing an adequate budget. His work as superintendent from 1855 to 1867 was based on these ideas.

On 17 Dec. 1859, through Chauveau's efforts, the government set up the first Council of Public Instruction, a key component of the school system. The mandate of this council, which had 15 members (4 Protestants, 10 Catholics, and the superintendent), was to supervise the management and classification of schools as well as the qualifications and recruitment of teachers and also to approve school texts and prepare regulations for boards of examiners. The council held its first meeting on 10 Jan. 1860 and Chauveau, its guiding spirit, established an order of priorities: the competence of teachers, subsidies to higher education, and "the introduction of military training in teachers' colleges." As superintendent, Chauveau was involved with daily administrative problems that often degenerated into political questions. Thus English-speaking Protestants, who wanted to have their own school system, were a powerful pressure group which Chauveau, and Cartier, had to take into account when grants were allotted for education.

The Department of Public Instruction did not at that time have a heavy bureaucratic structure, and Chauveau was able to diversify his own activities. An *ex officio* member of the Board of Agriculture and vice-president of the Board of Arts and Manufactures of Lower Canada, he conducted an inquiry into the schools of agriculture in 1857 at the request of these two bodies. He also took part in a convention of American scholars held the following year at the Marché Bonsecours in Montreal, and contributed to the proceedings of various literary societies. On 16 April 1858, with his friend Verreau, he became a member of the Société Historique de Montréal, which had been founded five days earlier by Jacques Viger*. In 1861, at the time of the *Trent* affair [*see* Sir Charles Hastings DOYLE], he enrolled the students of the École Normale Jacques-Cartier in what was apparently the 4th battalion (Chasseurs Canadiens), with himself as captain. Apart from contributions to the *Journal de l'Instruction*, he published little. According to Abbé Gustave Bourassa, he apparently preferred a new role, making "our national [French Canadian] life known to literary and scholarly Europe, particularly to France." By 1859 he had maintained a regular correspondence with Victor Duruy and Charles Forbes, Comte de Montalembert, and, as the years went by, he added François-Edmé Rameau* de Saint-Père, Monseigneur Félix Dupanloup, Xavier Marmier, and a dozen others to his list of correspondents. Chauveau, who liked to comment on the political events and the progress of literature and the arts in Canada, proved an effective publicist, and his activity was not unconnected with the interest European circles took in Canada in the

1880s. This correspondence also reveals one of his great passions: bibliophily. His extensive library, containing 6,723 titles at his death, included the great works by ancient and modern authors as well as impressive volumes on history, literature, the arts, and jurisprudence, a considerable collection of Canadian works, and a large number of rare books from the most famous publishers of Europe in the early years of printing.

On 10 Oct. 1866, with the object "of improving our system of public instruction as much as possible," the council recommended that Chauveau should visit Europe and the United States. On 12 November he embarked on the *Austrian* with Cartier and John A. Macdonald*. He was in search of ideas, they sought ratification of confederation in London. After spending time in Great Britain, Italy, Germany, and France, Chauveau returned on 18 June 1867, proud to have ascertained that Canada East was not terribly backward in the field of education, and enriched by an experience he intended to be of benefit to his compatriots. In particular, he did not forget the efforts of many European countries to develop a form of teaching to prepare young people for commerce and industry. As for agriculture, the example of Ireland prompted the idea of a project to endow the teachers' colleges with model farms.

From the time of his return, Chauveau was worried about his personal situation. He wanted to sell his house in Quebec City in order to pay off his debts and start a newspaper. Not eager to be removed from the political scene, he declined Cartier's invitation to take the place of Judge Joseph-André Taschereau*. Obviously he could not suspect at that time what awaited him. The Conservative strategists had everything planned: after the British North America Act came into effect, Cauchon would form the first cabinet of the province of Quebec. But no one had foreseen that the very name of Cauchon would unleash the hostility of the English-speaking Protestant electorate of Quebec; in fact, Cauchon had compromised himself during the summer of 1866 by opposing the bill of Hector-Louis Langevin* which gave guarantees concerning schools to the Protestant minority of Canada East [*see* Christopher DUNKIN] and by imposing while mayor of Quebec an income tax which proved unpopular with English-speaking merchants. Under these conditions, if Cauchon were premier, a favourable result in the elections which were to come would be jeopardized. The Conservatives managed to persuade Cauchon to resign and replaced him with Chauveau, a reassuring figure for both Catholics and Protestants. Thus on 1 July 1867 he took the oath of office at the residence of Lieutenant Governor Narcisse-Fortunat Belleau*. Anxious to preserve unity within the Conservative party of Quebec, he retained in his cabinet the men approached a few days earlier by Cauchon. In addition to the duties of first minister, he assumed responsibility for the office of provincial secretary and, from 1868, for that of minister of public instruction. This accumulation of offices brought him an annual income of $4,750, $1,000 more than for ordinary ministers.

Chauveau had taken on a difficult mission, with a slim margin for manœuvring. Basically, the dice were loaded: the ablest public servants and the most outstanding politicians had been drawn to Ottawa, and by the working of the double mandate the members of the federal parliament could exercise a guardianship over the Legislative Assembly of Quebec. The division between Quebec and Ontario of the debts contracted under the union – some $10,600,000 – was an unknown factor that paralysed governmental action. Chauveau was not the unchallenged leader but the man chosen through compromise, catapulted to the head of a coalition of factions, each with its hungry chief: Cauchon demanded compensation for having resigned, the English-speaking Protestants wanted the explicit guarantees for their own schools which Chauveau had secretly made in 1865 provided that similar guarantees were granted to the Catholics of Canada West [*see* Robert Bell*], and the Montrealers, feeling underrepresented at the provincial level, feared they would be at a disadvantage in the dispensing of patronage. Chauveau was conscious of the precariousness of his position, and on 27 Sept. 1867 wrote to Rameau de Saint-Père: "I shall get out of this only by dint of prudence and patience, if I get out of it at all."

After his appointment to the post of premier, Chauveau hastily gathered together a few legal officers and clerks to form an embryonic public service and began preparing his troops for the general elections scheduled for September 1867. Only a small number of candidates were put forward by the Liberal party; Chauveau was re-elected by acclamation and the Conservative party won 54 of the 65 seats in the assembly. This resounding victory did not, however, ensure cohesion among the elected majority, which was still based on the ability of one man to satisfy particular interests.

Chauveau had no programme, and he had to face formidable problems: the establishment of an administrative structure, the sharing of the debt of the old Province of Canada, the school question, and the massive emigration of French Canadians to the United States. The first problem was the major subject of debate in the first parliamentary session, which opened on 27 Dec. 1867. The government passed a set of bills establishing the basis for the public service (which still had only 92 employees), the Treasury Department, and the Department of Public Instruction. During the second session, in 1869, the departments of Crown Lands, Agriculture, and Public

Works were organized. The problem of the public debt was referred to an arbitration commission, before which jurist Charles Dewey DAY pleaded on behalf of Quebec for a settlement determined by the standards (of equal responsibility) imposed upon ordinary commercial companies when they shared liabilities, rather than according to the population or the assets of each province, as Ontario wanted. Day presented a well-documented report, but the arbitrators were more responsive to the arguments of Ontario – their decision on 5 Sept. 1870 required Quebec to pay $5,000,000, at least $2,000,000 more than it wanted to, and Ontario $5,600,000.

The extremely complex school question necessitated several bills, the most important being the one passed on 5 April 1869, after 18 months of pressure from the Protestants who had formed a powerful lobby. At stake were the incorporation and administrative autonomy of the Protestant school system. Chauveau was trapped at the outset, with 14 Protestant representatives, including some ministers, threatening to withdraw their support from the government. After consulting the clergy and the Catholic representatives, Chauveau reached a compromise by means of the 1869 bill: the Council of Public Instruction would have 21 members, 14 of them Catholics, and would be divided into Protestant and Catholic committees [*see* Louis GIARD]; the minister or the superintendent would have a Protestant and a Catholic assistant; the government would allocate education grants in proportion to the population of the two groups involved; and, finally, at the request of a majority of its members, the Council of Public Instruction could divide into two distinct bodies. The Protestants, who had avenged the withdrawal of the Langevin bill in 1866, loudly voiced their satisfaction, but a good many French-speaking representatives, including Cauchon and Joseph-Adolphe Chapleau*, judged the concessions, in confirming the division of the school system into two official sectors, to be excessive.

Finally, the emigration question was symptomatic of a general malaise and required an overall approach. The ability to deal with the problem was partly beyond the Chauveau cabinet, because the means to control economic conditions lay elsewhere. On 21 Feb. 1868 the permanent committee on agriculture, immigration, and colonization gave its assessment – emigration resulted from the weakness of the manufacturing sector, the continued use of outmoded agricultural techniques, and the absence of roads in regions suitable for settlement. Many representatives considered that only a rise in tariffs could stimulate industry but this was an area under the jurisdiction of the federal government. Unable to develop a long-term strategy, Chauveau was reduced to applying limited measures, such as the reorganization of the agricultural societies, the creation of settlement associations, and the acceleration of road construction. Understandably, excitement was aroused in 1868 when the American contractor Jerome B. Hulbert claimed he could build roadbeds with wooden rails at a cost within reach. Old dreams were reborn, and the railways became the great panacea. Companies formed in the 1850s were revived and new ones created. Henri-Gustave Joly* founded the Quebec and Gosford Railway Company, Abbé François-Xavier-Antoine Labelle* recommended a line joining Montreal and Saint-Jérôme, and Cauchon proposed to link Quebec to Montreal by way of the north shore of the St Lawrence. Railways unleashed wild speculation. The assembly resembled a boxing ring: 15 members of the legislature were on the governing bodies of railway companies and 35 were associated in some way with a railway project. Besieged by requests for subsidies, Chauveau got a blueprint law passed in 1869. He wanted to subsidize the companies by making grants of crown lands but in the face of opposition from the Liberal representatives he fell back on direct payments to railways equal to 3 per cent of their building costs over a period of 20 years. Cauchon was not satisfied, and by means of ultimatums to the provincial government obtained 2,700,000 acres of land in November 1870 for the North Shore Railway Company.

Clearly Chauveau did not have the funds to satisfy every appetite nor did he have the clout to stifle demands. The sombre forecasts made by Langevin in 1868 were proving increasingly accurate: "Chauveau is not very likeable, nor [is he] liked . . . he is such a child. . . . He will not last." By 1869 he had already lost much of his credibility. Joly, who organized the Liberal opposition, criticized him openly, and certain journalists, such as Hector Fabre* in *L'Événement*, made him a prime target. The 1871 elections, much tougher than those of 1867, gave him a majority, divided by local interests, on which he could not rely. Cauchon defended the Quebec City region, Langevin the lower St Lawrence, and Cartier the Montreal region. In January 1870 *Le Courier de Saint-Hyacinthe*, the spokesman for a dozen Conservative representatives, raised the standard of revolt and in April 1871 the Ultramontanes, grouped around the *Programme catholique* [*see* François-Xavier-Anselme TRUDEL], followed suit. The latter, who were still few in number, were noisier than a whole regiment and their intrigues revealed the profound split within the Conservative party. In 1872 the rift widened as a result of the discussions on bills to establish a Jesuit-controlled university and to regulate the keeping of registers of births, marriages, and deaths. Ignace BOURGET, the bishop of Montreal, and the Ultramontanes supported these two bills but Chauveau and George Irvine* were opposed. The first was withdrawn, and the second amended at the request of Charles-Félix CAZEAU, the vicar general of the archdiocese of Quebec. The factions were becoming ungovernable. Harassed by private debts and overwhelmed on all sides, Chauveau confided to his friend Verreau on 2 October: "I see before me less clearly than ever in my political affairs and in my personal affairs." Langevin took the initiative of helping him to clarify his intentions and advised him to resign. Chauveau demanded compensation in return, and on 21 Feb. 1873, with difficulty, Langevin obtained for him the office of speaker of the Senate. Chauveau submitted his resignation two days later, on the pretexts of "urgent need of rest," weariness of the "burden of public affairs," and "personal misfortunes." There was much truth in these official statements: his finances were exhausted and he had been sorely tried by the death of two of his daughters, Henriette in 1870 and Flore in the following year. But these were not the only reasons for his resignation, which must be attributed chiefly to his failure to show leadership and his inability to establish himself in the Conservative party. He took his seat in the Senate, leaving behind him the image of a distinguished man, but also of a sorry strategist who had succumbed to the influence of the federal government.

At 53 he was already in his decline, and more difficult years lay ahead. The speaker's office in the Senate was merely a fleeting episode, since the accession to power of the Liberal party on the federal scene, following the Pacific Scandal, forced him to tender his resignation as speaker on 8 Jan. 1874; he resigned his seat at the same time to seek election in Charlevoix County for the House of Commons. Defeated by Pierre-Alexis Tremblay*, Chauveau faced a void: Cartier, his protector, was dead, and the Ultramontanes, among them bishops Bourget and Louis-François Laflèche*, were opposed to his being reinstated as superintendent of public instruction. However, he declared himself ready to do "whatever the episcopate would ask." He was even reduced to appealing to his friends for a job. In these circumstances he was obliged to run again into debt to provide for necessities and to secure medical care for his wife, who never recovered from the deaths of her daughters and passed away quietly on 24 May 1875. That year Chauveau considered returning to political life. He got in touch with the archbishop of Quebec, Elzéar-Alexandre Taschereau, with the hope that the church would bless and encourage this return. But Taschereau kept his distance and the Ultramontanes promised him a fierce battle. Charles-Eugène Boucher* de Boucherville even attempted to offer him a post as justice of the peace to keep him out of the fray. Despite the lack of support, Chauveau thought of standing for Dorchester in the next provincial elections but the death of his daughter Éliza led him to abandon this plan.

The beneficial rest Chauveau found in the intimacy of his study prompted him to take up his pen again while he was without a post. At the end of 1874 he wrote a 60-page article on the system of education in Canada, which was published in German in the *Encyklopädie des gesammten Erziehungs und Unterrichtswesens* at the beginning of 1876. At a convention held at the Collège Sainte-Marie on 24 June 1874 he delivered a long speech on the evolution of the school system of Quebec which, although well documented, did not have the loftiness of thought, the emotion, or the oratorical flow of the speech made seven years before at the grave of his friend François-Xavier Garneau. During 1875 he took an interest in various sidelights of history, such as the first marriage in New France, the life of Bertrand de Latour*, the departure of Jean Talon* in 1672, and the shipwreck of the *Éléphant.* While waiting to find a position, Chauveau wrote articles for which he was paid; for instance he published a column called "Revue européenne" in *L'Opinion publique* in 1876 and in *La Revue de Montréal* the following year. In March 1876 he was appointed a member of the Quebec Harbour Commission and a few weeks later became its chairman. Learning the good news, his creditors went after him. He had to sell part of his library to McGill College and borrow once more from his friend Verreau. Though not lucrative, this new post left him plenty of leisure. He took advantage of it to publish *L'Instruction publique au Canada: précis historique et statistique*, in which he expounded the main arguments of the article that had appeared in the German encyclopædia in greater detail and updated them with recent statistics. He also found the time to address the members of the Institut Canadien of Quebec: on 13 Oct. 1876, about the advancement of letters, and on 16 Jan. 1877, when he revived tales of his childhood in a lecture entitled "Souvenirs et légendes."

Chauveau's chairmanship of the Quebec Harbour Commission was only one step on the way to more prestigious employment. In September 1877 Boucher de Boucherville offered him the post of sheriff of Montreal. This senior official named judges, saw to the execution of the judgements of the police and assize courts, imposed fines, ordered the seizure of possessions and property, and also administered the court-house and prisons. For want of something better, Chauveau accepted this position. In 1878 he was offered the opportunity of returning to politics, but he said he was "too encumbered with debts and too bruised" by past experiences. He did choose that year to accept the invitation to teach in the law faculty at Université Laval in Montreal. This new post restored his fortunes but increased his worries. He gave a great deal of time to preparing courses which the students did not seem to appreciate. The latter petitioned the university authorities, complaining that Chauveau "lacks method, and spends too much time on insignificant details." They even demanded his dismissal, but did not obtain it. Despite all these complaints, Chauveau was dean of the faculty from 1884 to 1890.

When the fourth edition of Garneau's *Histoire du Canada depuis sa découverte jusqu'à nos jours* was published, Chauveau prepared a detailed biography of the author which came out as part of the fourth volume in 1883. In it he painted a lively and accurate portrait of Garneau, enlivened with critical remarks on his writings: in this regard, just as he had as a youth, he showed himself less distrustful than Garneau of English-speaking Canadians and less harsh towards the Patriotes who had rallied to the union of 1841. Meanwhile Chauveau found in the Royal Society of Canada an intellectual centre worthy of him. As vice-president from 1882 to 1883 and president from 1883 to 1884, he delivered several lectures before it.

Chauveau was prevented from undertaking a complete edition of his own works by "the responsibilities, anxieties, dangers and annoyances" inherent in his office of sheriff of Montreal. He was also subjected to continual harassment by the Ultramontanes. In 1884 and 1885 Jules-Paul Tardivel* and Father Joseph Grenier led a smear campaign against Chauveau because he had previously corresponded with Victor Duruy and had accepted decorations from a so-called masonic French government. They accused him of having spread "poisonous ideas" and perverted "even the Christian notion of education" throughout his life: "he has sown in our school laws and system the germ of . . . all the ideas of the masonic programme." In the face of such inquisitorial remarks, Honoré Beaugrand* and Alphonse Lusignan* undertook Chauveau's defence in *La Patrie*. Cares and illness prevented him from producing much in this period. The speech he delivered at Quebec on 24 June 1889, at the inauguration of the monument to Jacques Cartier* and Jean de Brébeuf*, was his last. Four months later he wrote to Rameau de Saint-Père: "I think the machine is beginning to break down, and frankly I should not be sorry; for life has not been very pleasant for me for some years and the future – if one can speak of future at my age – promises to be more sombre still!" Stricken with paralysis, he retired to his residence on Rue Sainte-Anne in Quebec City, where he died on 4 April 1890.

JEAN HAMELIN and PIERRE POULIN

[Pierre-Joseph-Olivier Chauveau left numerous writings, the most important, in our opinion, being: *Charles Guérin: roman de mœurs canadiennes* (Montréal, 1853), serialized in *Album littéraire et musical de la rev. canadienne* (Montréal), February 1846–March 1847 (a detailed analysis of this novel and a description of the various editions up to the present can be found in *DOLQ*, I: 101–5); *La Pléiade rouge: biographies humoristiques* (Montréal, 1854), written in collaboration with Joseph-Charles Taché under the pseudonym of Gaspard Le Mage; *L'Instruction publique au Canada: précis historique et statistique* (Québec, 1876), first published in German in the *Encyklopädie des gesammten Erziehungs und Unterrichtswesens* . . . , ed. K. A. Schmid *et al.* (2nd ed., 10v., Gotha and Leipzig, [Democratic German Republic], 1876–87); *François-Xavier Garneau: sa vie et ses œuvres* (Montréal, 1883), published first as part of the fourth volume of the 1882–83 edition of Garneau's *Histoire du Canada depuis sa découverte jusqu'à nos jours* (4e éd., 4v., Montréal), published through the efforts of the historian's son, Alfred Garneau*. A complete inventory of Chauveau's work has been compiled by T.-L. Hébert, "Bio-bibliographie de Pierre-Joseph-Olivier Chauveau" (thèse de bibliothéconomie, univ. de Montréal, 1944); this compilation, together with its descriptive commentary, is useful for identifying the scope of Chauveau's publications. Mention must also be made of the systematic study in *DOLQ*, I, of Chauveau's principal writings.

Articles, poems, and reprints of speeches by Chauveau can be found in the newspapers and journals of the period: *Le Canadien*, 1838–41, 1847–51, *Le Courrier des États-Unis* (New York), 1841–55, *Le Castor* (Québec), 1843–45, *Le Journal de Québec*, 1844, 1854, 1871, and the *JIP*, 1857–73.

Chauveau's contemporaries produced numerous biographies of him. The following proved useful: Achintre, *Manuel électoral*, 3–4; L.-M. Darveau, *Nos hommes de lettres* (Montréal, 1873), 124–53; and L.-O. David, *Biographies et portraits* (Montréal, 1876), 189–99. More recently, historians have emphasized certain specific aspects of his career; *see*: J.-A. Pelletier, "L'Union des Canadas et P.-J.-O. Chauveau dans la tourmente," *Mosaïque québécoise* (Québec, 1961), 88–97; Maurice Lebel, "P.-J.-O. Chauveau, humaniste du XXe siècle," *Rev. de l'univ. Laval* (Québec), 17 (1962–63): 32–42; L.-P. Audet, "P.-J.-O. Chauveau et l'éducation," RSC *Trans.*, 4th ser., 4 (1966), sect.I: 13–40; "P.-J.-O. Chauveau, ministre de l'Instruction publique, 1867–73," RSC *Trans.*, 4th ser., 5 (1967), sect. I: 171–84; and Gérard Parizeau, *La Société canadienne-française au XIXe siècle: essai sur le milieu* (Montréal, [1975]), 233–52.

The ANQ-Q holds the personal papers (correspondence, draft bills, and official lists) of Chauveau in AP-G-41. It also has a good many of his letters in various collections such as in the Fonds Côme-Séraphin Cherrier (AP-G-43), the Fonds Hector-Louis Langevin (AP-G-134), and the Fonds Jean-Baptiste Meilleur (AP-G-184). The records of the provincial secretary (QBC 6), the Department of Public Instruction (QBC 27), and the Department of Education (PQ-É) contain the official correspondence, minutes, and financial records of the various governmental bodies during Chauveau's tenure of office. The article, "De quelques testaments," J.-J. Lefebvre, édit., ANQ *Rapport*, 1960–61: 168–74, included Chauveau's will.

Correspondence with Chauveau is also held at the PAC in the John A. Macdonald papers (MG 26, A, 202, 226, 340–50, 513–24), the Alexander Mackenzie papers (MG 26, B), the Joseph-Adolphe Chapleau papers (MG 27, I, C3), and the George-Étienne Cartier papers (MG 27, I, D4). In addition, the ASQ has an important collection of letters written by Chauveau from 1850 to 1890 in the Fonds Viger-Verreau, Cartons 94–96, and Univ., Carton 106, nos.35–36, 70–71,

87, 100. In addition to the Chauveau papers deposited at the PAC (MG 24, B54) and the Fonds Alphonse Desjardins at the Fondation Lionel-Groulx, Institut d'hist. de l'Amérique française (Montréal), some items of lesser importance on Chauveau can be found in the following collections: ASN, AP-G, L.-É. Bois; J.-A.-I. Douville; and AUM, P58, H3/81; I2/58. Researchers will also find Francine Hudon, *Inventaire des fonds d'archives relatifs aux parlementaires québécois* (Québec, 1980), 39–41, a useful work. J. H. and P. P.]

Can., prov. du, Assemblée législative, *App. des journaux*, 1855–59 (reports of the superintendent of public instruction); Parl., *Doc. de la session*, 1860–66 (reports of the superintendent of public instruction). *Debates of the Legislative Assembly of United Canada* (Gibbs *et al.*), IV-XI. *Débats de l'Assemblée législative* (M. Hamelin), [I-II]. Qué., Parl., *Doc. de la session*, 1869–74 (reports of the Department of Public Instruction). *L'Événement*, 1868–73. L.-P. Audet, *Hist. de l'enseignement*, II; *Histoire du conseil de l'Instruction publique de la province de Québec, 1856–1864* (Montréal, 1964). Désilets, *Hector-Louis Langevin*. M. Hamelin, *Premières années du parlementarisme québécois*. André Labarrère-Paulé, *Les instituteurs laïques au Canada français, 1836–1900* (Québec, 1965); *Les laïques et la presse pédagogique au Canada français au XIXe siècle* (Québec, 1963). Monet, *Last cannon shot*. L.-P. Audet, "Le premier ministère de l'Instruction publique au Québec, 1867–1876," *RHAF*, 22 (1968–69): 171–222.

CHERRIER, CÔME-SÉRAPHIN, lawyer, politician, and businessman; b. 22 July 1798 at Repentigny, Lower Canada, son of Joseph-Marie Cherrier, a farmer and merchant, and Marie-Josephte Gaté; m. 18 Nov. 1833 at Montreal, Que., Mélanie Quesnel, widow of the merchant Michel Coursol, and they had four children; d. 10 April 1885 in Montreal.

Côme-Séraphin Cherrier belonged to the powerful network of the Viger, Papineau, Lartigue, and Dessaulles families. One of his father's sisters had married Joseph Papineau*, the father of Louis-Joseph*, and another Denis Viger*, the father of Denis-Benjamin*. Following his mother's death in 1801, Côme-Séraphin was brought up by the Viger family. After attending the Petit Séminaire de Montréal from 1806 to 1816, he studied law under Denis-Benjamin Viger and was called to the bar of Lower Canada on 23 Aug. 1822.

Cherrier practised law until the beginning of the 1860s. He retired at that time but according to contemporary accounts maintained his legal office on Rue Saint-Vincent as a private adviser. His first partnership was with Louis-Michel Viger*, and later he worked with Denis-Aristide Laberge (1832–34), Charles-Elzéar Mondelet* (1835–41), and Antoine-Aimé Dorion* and Vincislas-Paul-Wilfrid Dorion* (1841–60). In general, contemporary accounts agree on the importance of his legal career. He made his mark primarily in political trials. Following the 1827 elections the attorney general, James Stuart*, defeated by Wolfred Nelson* in the riding of William Henry, prosecuted a large number of voters for perjury. Stuart claimed they had falsely sworn that they met the property qualifications but Cherrier managed to disprove that there had been perjury. The following year, with his colleagues William Walker* and Dominique Mondelet*, he successfully defended the publisher and editor of the *Canadian Spectator* (Montreal), Jocelyn Waller*, who had been accused of libelling the administration of Lord Dalhousie [Ramsay*]. On this occasion Cherrier demonstrated a thorough grasp of the fine points of a jury trial. In 1836 he offered his services to the residents of Saint-Benoît, who were charged with having cut off the tails and manes of several horses belonging to government officials. That year he defended Ludger Duvernay*, who had been indicted for his attack in *La Minerve* upon a report made by a grand jury of the Court of King's Bench. At the time of the abolition of the seigneurial system [*see* Lewis Thomas DRUMMOND] he argued one of the last of his famous cases. Chosen with Christopher DUNKIN and Robert Mackay to represent the seigneurs and establish their claims for compensation, he drafted a detailed, elaborate speech (published in 1855) which earned him the warm thanks of the seigneurial commission. Finally, he was called upon to advise Bishop Ignace BOURGET of Montreal in the quarrel over the division of the Montreal parish of Notre-Dame which developed between the bishop and the Sulpicians around 1866 [*see* Joseph-Alexandre BAILE; Joseph DESAUTELS].

The various honours and offices conferred upon Cherrier over the years testify to his fame. To recognize his assistance in 1851 in establishing a law course at the Collège Sainte-Marie [*see* François-Maximilien BIBAUD], the Jesuits of St John's University at Fordham, N.Y., awarded him an honorary LLD in 1855. Having been the president of the library of the barristers' society of Lower Canada for many years, in 1855 and 1856 he held the office of *bâtonnier* of the Montreal bar. In addition, in 1877 he became titular professor and dean of the law faculty of the Montreal branch of Université Laval of Quebec City.

His participation in political trials, as well, no doubt, as his family ties with the Montreal nucleus of the Patriote party, inevitably led Cherrier into politics. Yielding to pressure from his associates, according to his biographers, he ran in the riding of Montreal in 1834 and was elected to the assembly. He took part in the 1835 and 1836 sittings, but ill health prevented him from joining in the stormy debates prior to the 1837 rebellion. However, he did sometimes appear that year, and Fernand Ouellet without hesitation ranks him among the star performers of the Patriote party. In August 1837 he was one of the members of the house who disembarked at Quebec dressed in clothes of local fabric, out of respect for the Patriote leaders' instructions to wear no imported garments.

Although Cherrier's speeches sought to further the struggle by constitutional means and were not the most violent to be delivered, he was nevertheless arrested and imprisoned on 1 Dec. 1837. His incarceration proved distressing; he fell seriously ill but was finally released to house-arrest in March 1838. Cherrier subsequently re-entered politics only once, in an unsuccessful bid for the mayoralty of Montreal in 1859 [*see* Charles-Séraphin Rodier*]. He turned down all other proposals, invariably for reasons of health: in 1842 when Sir Charles Bagot* offered him the post of solicitor general in order to conciliate French Canadians hostile to union, and again in 1844 when Denis-Benjamin Viger, to whom Cherrier owed a great deal, invited him to join the government. On three occasions he declined appointment to the bench, the final offer, in 1864, being that he should succeed Sir Louis-Hippolyte La Fontaine* as chief justice of the Court of Queen's Bench of Canada East.

Although he withdrew from the political fore-stage after the rebellion Cherrier none the less continued to play an influential role. He belonged to the group of moderate Liberals, and through family ties was also in contact with the former Patriotes in Montreal, where in 1840 he participated in the first "anti-unionist" gathering. Subsequently, he seems to have supported La Fontaine's alliances and plans for reform, at least on the evidence of their correspondence. Cherrier was likewise involved in the Association de la Délivrance, which bookseller Édouard-Raymond Fabre* set up in 1843 to facilitate the return of the political exiles. As one of Cherrier's last political acts he gave a speech in 1865 to the Institut Canadien-Français against the confederation project. He cited four reasons for his opposition: the lack of consultation with the people; the surrender of local authority, in favour of a thinly disguised legislative union; the imminent danger of difficulties in the relations between provincial and federal governments; and the loss of taxation powers for Canada East.

By the mid 1850s Cherrier seemed to be a kind of sage, participating in the establishment of every organization, attending every meeting, and being consulted about everything. *La Presse* of Montreal on 10 April 1885 noted that "all the present generation had acquired the habit of seeing him wherever religious, patriotic or charitable endeavour was involved." His reputation for wisdom stemmed at one and the same time from his moderation, his acknowledged legal erudition, his legendary indecisiveness, and, indeed, his obstinate refusal to make up his mind unequivocally. He was thus a complex individual, capable both of advising Bourget in his struggle against the Sulpicians and later of opposing his ultramontanism and also supporting his opponents at Université Laval.

Cherrier became an active member of the Association Saint-Jean-Baptiste de Montréal upon its reorganization in 1843, and served as vice-president in 1852 and president in 1853. In 1860 he gave a remarkable address in defence of the temporal power of the papacy at Notre-Dame in Montreal and hence in 1869 was proclaimed a knight of the Order of St Gregory the Great. This stand on behalf of the church no doubt brought him the favourable attention of the apostolic delegate Bishop George Conroy*; Cherrier wrote a letter to the bishop on 15 Sept. 1877 explaining the nuances differentiating the liberalism of French Canadians from the liberalism condemned by the *Syllabus* of 1864. Cherrier also belonged to the St Vincent de Paul Society of Montreal and was its vice-president for a time. His contribution to public charity was widely recognized and *La Patrie* of Montreal on 10 April 1885 even claimed that "the poor have lost in him a most tender father." He was a member of the Council of Public Instruction in 1859 and again after 1867.

It is difficult to pin down the origin of Cherrier's fortune, which at his death was valued by the *Montreal Daily Star* at more than $1,000,000. According to some of his biographers, his legal practice brought him a comfortable living, and in addition Denis-Benjamin Viger is thought to have made him a sizeable gift before 1844. Most of his landed property also came from Viger, who at his death in 1861 bequeathed to Cherrier all his personal chattels and real estate, including several properties in the Saint-Jacques district. Hence around 1870 Cherrier owned in this locality an area estimated at more than 770,000 square feet, as well as smaller lots in other districts of Montreal and on Île-Bizard, the seigneury which had belonged to Viger. Apart from his real estate Cherrier owned stock in a number of companies. During the 1840s, for example, he acquired (with George-Étienne Cartier*, George Moffatt*, and Alexandre-Maurice Delisle*) a block of shares in the St Lawrence and Atlantic Railroad. In 1865 he was listed as one of the 10 major shareholders of the Banque du Peuple which he served as a director from 1865 to 1877 and as president from 1877 to his death. In the conduct of his affairs Cherrier apparently drew criticism for unwillingness to take risks with his property, which was left an undeveloped stretch in the urban landscape to the east of Rue Saint-Denis in Montreal. His biographers have excused him on the grounds that he lacked business sense, but no doubt his legendary indecisiveness was also a factor. Cherrier was, however, well aware that his land would inevitably increase in value and seems to have deliberately waited as long as possible. His occasional sales of property as well as certain other sources of revenue, for example the rent from the mill on Île-Bizard, enabled him to live comfortably in his residence on Rue Lagauchetière.

Wilfrid Laurier* has probably best described Cherrier's complex and contradictory nature: "Côme-Séraphin Cherrier, one of the most eminent members of the bar of Lower Canada . . . , was himself a man of an exceptional kind. He scarcely belonged to our time, even to our continent. One would indeed have taken him for a living anachronism, for the incarnation of those remarkable figures who, at once powerful and affable, were the ornament of the *parlement de Paris* in the 17th century. A man of inflexible principles masked by an unfailing kind-heartedness, of liberal instincts restrained by conservative customs, of austere piety tempered by the most chivalrous spirit, he combined the most refined Attic wit with the simplicity of a child."

JEAN-CLAUDE ROBERT

Côme-Séraphin Cherrier was the author of *Discours . . . prononcé dans l'église paroissiale de Montréal, le 26 février 1860, dans la grande démonstration des catholiques en faveur de Pie IX* (Montréal, 1860); *L'Honorable F.-A. Quesnel* (Montréal, 1878); *Mémoire . . . sur les questions soumises par l'honorable Lewis Thomas Drummond, procureur général de Sa Majesté pour le Bas-Canada, à la décision des juges de la Cour du banc de la reine et de la Cour supérieure, en vertu des dispositions de l'Acte seigneurial de 1854* (Montréal, 1855); *Présidence des assemblées de fabrique de N.-D. de Montréal . . . ou réponse à la consultation de l'honorable procureur général Cartier, dans laquelle on prétend que le supérieur du séminaire de Montréal a ce droit de présider les assemblées de fabrique de la paroisse de Notre-Dame, à l'exclusion du curé de cette paroisse* ([Lyon, France, 1866]); and contributed to *Discours sur la confédération* (Montréal, 1865).

ANQ-M, État civil, Catholiques, Notre-Dame de Montréal, 18 nov. 1833; M-72-148; Minutiers, Joseph Belle, 22 oct. 1859; N.-B. Doucet, 12 déc. 1821; D.-É. Papineau, 16 nov. 1870, 27 juin 1873; Testaments, Reg. des testaments prouvés, 13, 7 oct. 1873. ANQ-Q, AP-G-43; AP-G-417. BNQ, MSS-30; MSS-101, Coll. La Fontaine (copies at PAC). PAC, MG 24, B46, 1. *Extracts of the books of reference of the subdivisions of the city of Montreal*, ed. L.-W. Sicotte (Montreal, 1874). Honoré Mercier, *Feu Côme-Séraphin Cherrier: conférence faite à la salle de "La Patrie" . . .* ([Montréal], 1885). *Montreal Daily Star*, 10 April 1885. *La Patrie*, 10 avril 1885. *La Presse*, 10 avril 1885. F.-J. Audet, *Les députés de Montréal*, 411–16. Borthwick, *Hist. and biog. gazetteer*, 257–58. *Canadian biog. dict.*, II: 334–36. L.-O. David, *Biographies et portraits* (Montréal, 1876), 208–19. *Dominion annual register*, 1885: 252–53. Fauteux, *Patriotes*, 176–78. *Montreal directory*, 1842–85. R. S. Greenfield, "La Banque du Peuple, 1835–1871, and its failure, 1895" (MA thesis, McGill Univ., Montreal, 1968), 4, 133–34. [Wilfrid Laurier], *In memoriam: sir A.-A. Dorion, chevalier, juge-en-chef de la Cour d'appel, ancien ministre de la justice* (Montréal, 1891). André Lavallée, *Québec contre Montréal, la querelle universitaire, 1876–1891* (Montréal, 1974), 25–27, 54. Monet, *Last cannon shot*, 42, 100–1, 128, 146. Fernand Ouellet, *Le Bas-Canada, 1791–1840: changements structuraux et crise* (Ottawa, 1976), 441. Léon Pouliot, *Mgr Bourget et son temps* (5v., Montréal, 1955–77), V: 53. J.-L. Roy, *Édouard-Raymond Fabre, libraire et patriote canadien (1799–1854): contre l'isolement et la sujétion* (Montréal, 1974), 157–58. Robert Rumilly, *Histoire de la Société Saint-Jean-Baptiste de Montréal: des Patriotes au fleurdelisé, 1834–1948* (Montréal, 1975), 51, 54, 68.

CHIEF JOSEPH. *See* ONASAKENRAT, JOSEPH

CHINIC, GUILLAUME-EUGÈNE, businessman; b. 26 Oct. 1818 at Quebec City, son of Joseph-Martin Chinic and Julie Measam; d. there 28 April 1889 and was buried 30 April in the Belmont cemetery (now in Sainte-Foy, Que.).

Martin Dechinique*, who founded the Canadian branch of the family, came from Saint-Pierre in the diocese of Bayonne, France, to Quebec City in 1740 and worked as a ship's captain and pilot. The only son to survive him, Martin Chinic*, went into business; he had a son, Joseph-Martin, a merchant and shipbuilder, who died prematurely leaving two boys, one of whom died when he was eight. The other, Guillaume-Eugène, an orphan from an early age, had to be brought up by his grandparents. According to Pierre-Georges Roy*, Chinic, "while still quite young, became an employee of the Méthot firm" at Quebec probably around 1833 or 1834. François-Xavier Méthot*, having founded the firm in 1808, was at that time at the peak of his business career. He ran a wholesale and retail hardware store on Rue Saint-Pierre, and to increase his profits engaged in what economists call vertical integration. Thus he set up a nailery at Beauport in 1834, known as the Ventadour mill, a mastic factory in 1835, and later a factory for making millstones. These small establishments were still in operation in 1873 but by then belonged to Chinic. Sole heir of a family that was moving up in society, the young clerk of the 1830s, with his business ability and initiative, had succeeded in winning the affection and confidence of Méthot, who had gradually brought him into his firm. It is not known when the partnership of Méthot et Chinic began. According to the *Quebec directory* it existed in 1847 – the date 1845 is given in a brochure put out by the company – and ended in 1853 with the death of François-Xavier Méthot; Chinic then became the principal partner and head of the firm.

The hardware trade remained the backbone of Chinic's activities until he retired. The firm was not a family one and over the years its name changed with the partners; however, in 1880 his son, Eugène-Philéas-Nowlan, joined the business. Seven years later Chinic relinquished his interests in the company following a transaction the real reasons for which remain a mystery. In the autumn of 1887 the stock of Beaudet et Chinic was sold to English-speaking financiers, who formed a joint stock company capitalized at $100,000 but with a potential of $150,000; the *Montreal Herald and Daily Commercial Gazette* attributed the move to an increased volume of business, while *La Justice*, of Quebec, claimed it was due to a bankruptcy. The Chinic Hardware Company Limited (Compagnie Chinic de quincaillerie Limitée) was run by Edwin Jones as president, George Taylor Davie* and Winceslas Méthot as directors, William Shaw as manager, Eugène-Philéas-Nowlan Chinic as assistant manager, and Hector-Edmond Dupré as secretary. The new owners also acquired the nailery at Beauport and a stone-cutting works which used rough-hewn stone imported from France to produce millstones and blocks for flour-milling. According to *Le Canadien* of 30 Sept. 1887, Chinic intended to start a new business establishment with one of his former employees, but it is not known whether this project ever came to anything.

During the 1840s Chinic firmly secured his position in society. On 1 Feb. 1844, at Montreal, he married Marie-Anne-Claire, the daughter of Joseph Leblond, a merchant, and they were to have 12 children. Repeatedly bereaved by the deaths of six of their children, four in infancy, the Chinics also had their consolations. Through felicitous marriages, their surviving children formed alliances with such well-known families as the Taschereaus, Angers, Wurteles, Navarros, Knights, and Chagnons – clear evidence of the considerable reputation enjoyed by the Chinics. At the outset of his married life Chinic resided in the building that housed the hardware store. Around 1850 he moved to a magnificent residence on the Chemin Sainte-Foy, where he lived until his death. He was already a prominent figure in Quebec City. He had taken part in the founding of the Institut Canadien in 1848, and the next year was one of the citizens who sought the incorporation of the Société Saint-Jean-Baptiste de la Cité de Québec. He was fond of sport, particularly yachting, and in 1869–70 was commodore of the Quebec Yacht Club.

With the wealth he had inherited from his family and the income from the hardware store Chinic was soon in easy circumstances. He was kind and generous by nature and supported philanthropic causes, as is shown by his role in the founding of the Caisse d'Économie de Notre-Dame de Québec [*see* François VÉZINA] and his position as its vice-president (1854–56) and director (1857–59, 1872–73, 1875–76). But he was also concerned, as a businessman, with getting a good return on his capital, an endeavour in which he was engaged as early as 1847. That year his name appeared on the act incorporating the District Bank of Quebec. He does not seem to have been very active in this bank, probably being content to treat it as a good investment. Between 1850 and 1880 his financial ventures increased greatly. He associated himself with Francophone businessmen such as François Vézina, Isidore Thibaudeau*, Pierre Garneau*, and Ulric-Joseph Tessier* who were attempting to break into the business world and who were competing with their Anglophone compatriots in the development of Quebec City. The city was entering a difficult period of transition. In the 1850s it suffered the consequences of the building of canals on the St Lawrence and the construction of the Grand Trunk; these reduced its use as a port and benefited Montreal, Toronto, and Portland, Maine. Furthermore, the advent in the 1860s of iron steamships spelled the end of its shipyards, and the declining demand for squared timber in the 1870s meant fewer sailing vessels in port and fewer raftsmen in the coves along the river. Joined together in the Quebec Board of Trade, businessmen strove vainly to protect the city's interests. The majority finally came to see Quebec as the economic centre of a region, with its prosperity hinging on a network of railways to link it to the hinterland and a network of credit institutions to channel savings into the hands of entrepreneurs.

These developments throw light on Chinic's involvement in both railway construction and banking institutions. He invested in the Quebec Building Society, which under François Vézina's management became a powerful credit instrument with dividends of 10 per cent a year. In this society he played an active part, and agreed in 1851 to be one of its directors. He played an even more decisive role in the creation of the Banque Nationale, which opened in April 1860: he had been a member of the founding committee since 1858, and with his friends Vézina and Isidore Thibaudeau, Chinic provided leadership for the enterprise; subsequently he proved one of the most energetic shareholders of the bank, of which he was vice-president from 1860 to 1863 and president from 1864 to 1876. Concurrently with these financial activities Chinic continued to take an interest in railway construction. When the North Shore Railway Company was formed in 1853, to link Quebec to Montreal, Chinic, although not prominent in the company, seemed to be involved; in addition, in 1854 the *Quebec directory* listed him as one of the Quebec Northern Railway directors. The promoters were planning to build a railway with wooden tracks which in its first phase would link Quebec to the Rivière Sainte-Anne, with its abundant reserves of firewood. But the promoters' enthusiasm failed to persuade investors, who refused to take up 8,000 shares of £10 each. Nevertheless, Chinic remained interested in railways. He was secretary of the North Shore Railway Company in 1857–58 and his name appeared on the act of incorporation of the St Maurice Railway and Navigation Company in 1857; he was a central figure in the negotiations, and probably also in the political moves, that resulted in 1858 in the amalgamation of these two companies to form the North Shore Railway and St Maurice Navigation and Land Company. A visit in 1868 by the American engineer Jerome B. Hulbert, a specialist in wooden track railways, created interest in a scheme for a railway to link Quebec City and Lac Saint-Jean, the first section of which was to follow the route already put forward to join Quebec City and Portneuf County. The Quebec and Gosford Railway was incorporated in 1869 and work began during the summer of 1870; in November the section was opened. Chinic, one of the directors of the company, was jubilant. But disenchantment set in immediately. With use the wooden tracks quickly proved vulnerable to the Quebec thaw. By the spring of 1873 the track was unusable and the shares of the Quebec and Gosford plummeted to 10 cents each. It was the end of wooden track railways, but not of a railway to Lac Saint-Jean. These disappointments, the international economic depression which paralysed Quebec from 1874, and political rivalries combined to delay the project. Chinic did not succumb to discouragement. The *Quebec directory* listed him as vice-president of the Quebec and Lake St John Railway Company (another name for the Quebec and Gosford Railway which in 1870 had obtained authorization to extend its track to Lac Saint-Jean) in 1875–76 and in 1879–80, a period in which the company obtained a number of grants but did not manage to organize itself on a sound basis or to meet the standards laid down by the province. Moreover the provincial government, which in 1875 undertook the construction of the Quebec, Montreal, Ottawa and Occidental Railway, had only limited funds for the Quebec–Lac Saint-Jean project. Illness prevented Chinic from completing his work. The Quebec and Lake St John Railway Company, which was reorganized in 1882 by Élie Saint-Hilaire, an MLA, established the first link between Quebec and Lac Bouchette on 29 Aug. 1887.

Chinic liked politics but did not care much for electoral battles. In contrast to other business friends he never sought election either as an alderman or as an MLA. He was a man who worked behind the scenes. He had friends among both the Bleus and the Rouges and he had helped all of them in various ways. In 1875 the Liberals appointed him to the Senate and in January 1876 the Conservatives of Quebec appointed him, together with George Irvine* and Henri-Gédéon Malhiot, a commissioner of the Quebec, Montreal, Ottawa and Occidental Railway. He held these posts only a few years: the provincial cabinet abolished the railway commission in 1878 and illness forced Chinic to resign from the Senate the next year. In these two posts he accomplished nothing noteworthy. It is possible that the recurrent economic crisis of the years 1874–78, one of the most severe in the 19th century, obliged him to concentrate his energies on his hardware business and on the management of La Banque Nationale of which he was president. Both these establishments survived, but Chinic was being slowly worn out by illness. He passed away on 28 April 1889.

HUGUETTE FILTEAU and JEAN HAMELIN

The records of the Chinic firm no longer exist for the period before 1940, and Guillaume-Eugène Chinic's biography had to be written mainly from printed sources and studies.

AC, Québec, État civil, Catholiques, Notre-Dame de Québec, 30 avril 1889. ANQ-Q, État civil, Catholiques, Notre-Dame de Québec, 26 oct. 1818. Can., prov. du, *Statuts*, 1847, c.113; 1848, c.17; 1849, c.148; 1852–53, c.100; 1857, c.149; 1858, c.56; 1859, c.108; 1861, c.85. Qué., *Statuts*, 1869, c.53; 1875, c.2; 1880, c.46. *Le Canadien*, 7 nov. 1853; 5, 30 sept. 1887; 29 avril 1889. *Le Journal de Québec*, 3, 29 sept. 1887. *La Justice* (Québec), 23 déc. 1887. *Montreal Herald and Daily Commercial Gazette*, 4 Nov. 1889. *Morning Chronicle* (Quebec), 30 Jan. 1854, 3 Dec. 1872, 7 May 1879, 24 Dec. 1887. *La Patrie*, 15 janv. 1889. *CPC*, 1880. *Quebec almanac*, 1825–35. *Quebec directory*, 1847–90. P.-G. Roy, *Fils de Québec* (4 sér., Lévis, Qué., 1933), IV: 30–31. Auguste Béchard, *Histoire de la Banque nationale . . .* (Québec, 1878). F.-X. Chouinard et Antonio Drolet, *La ville de Québec, histoire municipale* (3v., Québec, 1963–67), III: 85. *Une page d'histoire de Québec: magnifique essor industriel* (Québec, 1958), 40–43. François Vézina, *Récit historique de la progression financière de la Caisse d'économie de Notre-Dame de Québec* (Québec, 1878). J. H. Bartlett, "The manufacture of iron in Canada," American Institute of Mining Engineers, *Trans.* (New York), 14 (1885–86): 508–42. "Les Méthot," *BRH*, 39 (1933): 80–81. Léa Pétrin, "Industrie et commerce à Québec: un morceau du vieux Québec," *Le Soleil* (Québec), 21 sept. 1947. P.-G. Roy, "La famille Chinic," *BRH*, 45 (1939): 207–10.

CICOT. *See* SICOTTE

CIMON (Simon), SIMON-XAVIER, merchant, contractor, and politician; b. 4 Dec. 1829 at La Malbaie, Lower Canada, son of Hubert Simon and Angèle Simard; m. 9 Nov. 1848 Marie-Claire, daughter of Pierre Garon of Rivière-Ouelle, Canada East, who represented Rimouski in the Legislative Assembly of Quebec; d. 26 June 1887 at La Malbaie.

Simon-Xavier Cimon studied at the Petit Séminaire de Québec from 1841 to 1843. He dabbled in business in Quebec City before he became a building contractor. As a builder he was known particularly for the construction of the Parliament Building at Quebec City in 1878. That same year he found himself involved in a general strike of construction workers. This strike, which affected more than 1,000 men, was sparked by the plan of contractors such as Cimon to reduce daily wages from 60 to 50 cents. The strikers resorted to violence and damaged the property of a number of contractors. Cimon announced his intention of suing the city for each day of work lost because of inadequate police protection. The demonstrations subsequently escalated into riots, and the militia was called in to restore order. The workers immediately returned to their jobs, but received substantial pay increases. Cimon was actually to be accused of inciting the strike by a political opponent, Charles Langelier*, who asserted that his attachment to provincial Conservative leader Joseph-Adolphe Chapleau* had led him to bribe workers to strike in order to embarrass the government of Henri-Gustave Joly*. In the 1880s Cimon set up a pulp and paper mill at La Malbaie, and at the end of his life he was reputed to be very wealthy.

In 1867 Cimon had been elected to the House of Commons for Charlevoix as a Conservative, but in 1872 was defeated by the independent candidate Pierre-Alexis Tremblay*. He ran unsuccessfully in the provincial general election of 1875 and in the February 1879 by-election in Charlevoix. He was eventually elected a federal representative for Charlevoix in a by-election on 19 March 1881 and continued to serve until his death, although in parliament he was always a secondary figure.

Cimon was co-owner, with Edmund James Flynn*, of the *Journal de Québec*, which served the Conservative party's interests after 1880. However, irritated because Sir John A. Macdonald*'s government had granted contracts to Liberals, Cimon during the 1887 session voted with the opposition, thus earning himself the designation "independent Conservative." Further, a month before his death, he threatened the prime minister that he would take Wilfrid Laurier*'s musket and fight. But, while preparing to go to welcome Honoré Mercier* and his colleagues, he was stricken with apoplexy and died on 26 June 1887 at his residence. His son, Simon Cimon, succeeded him as Conservative member for Charlevoix in the House of Commons, serving from 28 Sept. 1887 to 3 Feb. 1891.

LOUISETTE POTHIER

AC, Saguenay (La Malbaie), État civil, Catholiques, Saint-Étienne (La Malbaie), 1829. ASQ, Fichier des anciens. PAC, MG 26, A, 442. *Le Canadien*, 1867–87. *Le Courrier du Canada*, 1867–87. *Le Journal de Québec*, 21 mars 1881, 26 juin 1887. Beaulieu et J. Hamelin, *Journaux du Québec*, 198. *Canadian directory of parl.* (J. K. Johnson), 121. *CPC*, 1887: 105; 1889: 113. Jean Hamelin *et al.*, *Répertoire des grèves dans la province de Québec au XIXe siècle* (Montréal, 1970), 43–45. Charles Langelier, *Souvenirs politiques* [de 1878 à 1896] (2v., Québec, 1909–12). Rumilly, *Hist. de la prov. de Québec*, III: 36–37, 56–57; V.

CLARKE, HENRY JOSEPH (he also at times added the middle names **Hynes** or **O'Connell**), lawyer and politician; b. 7 July 1833 in Donegal (Republic of Ireland), eldest son of Francis Clarke; d. 13 Sept. 1889 near Medicine Hat (Alta).

Henry Joseph Clarke came to Lower Canada with his parents at the age of three. His father was employed by the customs department in Montreal, where he later became a councillor and alderman. Henry was educated at Montreal Academical Institution and Collège Sainte-Marie and was called to the bar in 1855. A Roman Catholic, he had command of both English and French. He practised law in Montreal until 1858 when he was attracted to California by the gold rush. He became a journalist with the *Alta California* (San Francisco), and went to San Miguel (El Salvador) in the early 1860s, where he learned to speak Spanish and collected Central American curios. On his return to Montreal, he established a reputation as a criminal lawyer, and in the general election of 1863 unsuccessfully contested the Châteauguay riding as a Liberal-Conservative against the minister of finance, Luther Hamilton Holton*. Clarke served as a captain of the 1st Battalion (Prince of Wales's Regiment) of Volunteer Rifles, during the Fenian raids of 1866; in 1867 he was made a QC. In these years he became a close friend of Thomas D'Arcy McGee*, acting as secretary of his successful election committee in Montreal West in 1867 and writing a "short sketch" of his life, published in 1868.

Clarke came to Manitoba in November 1870 to assist Lieutenant Governor Adams George Archibald* in establishing the provincial government, having been encouraged to do so by Sir George-Étienne Cartier* and Bishop Alexandre-Antonin Taché*. Archibald had arrived on 2 September, shortly after the military expedition led by Colonel Garnet Joseph Wolseley*. Louis RIEL, whose provisional government had won provincial status for the region, had fled prior to the arrival of the troops. In the weeks that followed, particularly after the departure of Wolseley and the British regulars early in September, some of the militia volunteers from Ontario sought to avenge the shooting of Thomas Scott* by bullying and persecuting Riel's followers. Several Métis were killed without criminal proceedings being taken against their assailants, even when, as in the death of Elzéar Goulet*, these were known. It was to this lawless situation that Archibald endeavoured to bring law and order.

Elections for the first Legislative Assembly of Manitoba were held and Clarke was chosen by acclamation for St Charles on 30 Dec. 1870. On 3 Jan. 1871 he was appointed attorney general. His debating skill enabled him to take the lead in piloting government legislation through the house, and this activity may be responsible for mistaken references to him as the first premier of Manitoba. The minutes of the Executive Council make no mention of a first minister during these early years, and a letter from Archibald to Sir John A. Macdonald* on 16 Jan. 1871 makes clear that it was the lieutenant governor who provided leadership: "I gave the Council a memo. of 32 Bills which would be absolutely necessary to form the sketch of a Provincial

Constitution, and have set them to work to get their hands in." When Archibald's successor, Alexander MORRIS, was forming a new ministry in July 1874, he wrote to the secretary of state, Richard William Scott*: "I would call your attention to the fact that in forming the government I did so through the intervention of a premier [Marc-Amable Girard*] thus introducing responsible government in its modern form into the Province – the previous ministry was selected personally by my predecessor and none of its members were recognized as first minister."

Clarke's relations with Lieutenant Governor Archibald steadily deteriorated. They clashed over two issues in particular: legislation which would govern admission to the bar of Manitoba and the establishment of courts in the province. Archibald complained to Cartier in May 1871 that Clarke wanted "to constitute himself the Bar of Manitoba, and to shut the door to every person else he did not think fit to admit." Clarke also proposed a provincial supreme court comprising a chief justice and two puisne judges. Aspiring to be one of these judges himself, he persuaded his colleagues on the Executive Council in 1872 to support him, but Archibald had warned Macdonald in May 1871: "Bad as he is where he is, he would be greatly worse on the Bench. Whoever else you think of, don't think of him." Archibald conceded in August 1871 that there was something in Clarke's "devil may care style" which impressed ignorant people, but he had "seldom seen a man so void of anything like discretion – or common sense."

Alexander Morris took office as lieutenant governor on 2 Dec. 1872. His reaction to the attorney general was more mixed. Early in 1873 he refused Clarke's request to be made premier and told him that "he must be content with being the acknowledged leader of the Govt. in the House." "With all his faults," Morris wrote to Macdonald in February 1873, "he is the best man I have, & has a strange streak of good & chivalrous loyalty running through his strange composition. In other words he is an Irishman. . . ." Yet barely two weeks later Morris is writing to Macdonald that Clarke was "unprincipled." It is apparent that quite apart from the difficulties which he created by his unruly temperament, Clarke was an embarrassment to the government because his marital affairs had become something of a public scandal. Shortly after his wife, Ann Hynes, joined him in Winnipeg in the summer of 1871 he had left her for a married woman, Mrs Maria Merrick Sinclair, whom he later married in California.

Clarke was attorney general during turbulent times. In October 1871 tension was generated by the abortive Fenian raid at Pembina (N. Dak.) led by John O'Neill* and the arrest of three Métis for complicity. While the "ultra loyal" element among the newcomers from Ontario assailed Clarke for being pro-Métis and threatened to hang him if he did not commit the prisoners to trial, Joseph Royal*'s *Le Métis* bitterly attacked him for alleged unfairness and discrimination against them. The Métis were tried and one of them, Oiseau Letendre, was convicted in December 1871. Royal became a member of the Executive Council in March 1872, and a rival there of Clarke, their quarrels erupting especially in *Le Métis* of St Boniface, and in the *Weekly Manitoban* of Winnipeg which supported Clarke. A bilingual Roman Catholic, Clarke became the spokesman in the house for those Métis (including Pascal Breland*, Joseph Hamelin, and John Bruce) who regarded the leadership of Riel as detrimental to their cause. Royal spoke for the much larger group which continued to look to Riel for leadership.

The presence of Riel in the settlement (he had returned to St Vital in May 1871) was a constant temptation to vengeful Orangemen, especially after February 1872 when Premier Edward Blake*'s government in Ontario offered a reward of $5,000 for the arrest of any of the "murderers" of Thomas Scott. Nevertheless, Riel decided to seek a federal seat in the general elections of 1872. Clarke tried to dissuade him on the grounds that his candidature would not only be an embarrassment to the government at Ottawa but also personally dangerous. Failing to convince Riel, Clarke accepted nomination in Provencher in opposition to him. Their confrontations threatened to become violent, Clarke even challenging Riel to a duel on one occasion. Both men, however, withdrew from the contest in September so that Cartier, who had been defeated in Montreal East, could be elected for Provencher by acclamation. Macdonald commended Clarke's action as "very wise and patriotic." He added, obviously in response to a request from Clarke, that "you are too young and active a politician to be laid on the shelf as a Judge just now."

During the federal elections of 1872 mobs destroyed the printing establishments of both *Le Métis* and the *Manitoban*, and in the ensuing months the same unruly element, which Lieutenant Governor Morris described as "fanatical Orangemen" instigated by "scoundrels," agitated for the arrest of the murderers of Scott. Then, following the death of Cartier in May 1873, and in spite of Clarke's efforts to dissuade him, Riel persisted in being a federal candidate and was elected by acclamation on 13 Oct. 1873. Meanwhile, in September, a warrant issued by Dr John Harrison O'Donnell* (a member of Manitoba's Legislative Council) on an information laid by William A. Farmer, had been served on Ambroise-Dydime Lépine*, Riel's adjutant-general at the time of Scott's execution in March 1870. It was generally believed that Clarke had connived with Francis Evans Cornish*, who instigated the Lépine arrest, but Clarke denied this rumour, assuring Morris under oath that he had had nothing to do with the warrant. At the assizes in November 1873 a true bill for murder was found against Lépine by a grand jury; Clarke acted for the crown and Royal for the defence. Released on bail, Lépine went to trial on 13 Oct. 1874; he was convicted and sentenced to death, but the sentence was commuted to a short prison term in January 1875 by the governor general, Lord Dufferin [Blackwood*].

Clarke had represented the provincial government at a conference on immigration held in Ottawa in September 1871 and published a lengthy report. In March 1873 Clarke, Royal, and Thomas Howard* were sent to negotiate with the federal government for better terms for the province. They particularly wanted an increase in the subsidy, financial assistance for the erection of public buildings, a federal police force, an enlargement of provincial boundaries, and a continuation of Manitoba's special four per cent customs tariff beyond 1 July 1874. These negotiations were renewed in December 1873 but brought little result beyond an additional $25,000 to meet the province's most pressing needs. When the Law Society of Manitoba was formally constituted in 1872 Clarke served as its first president.

The demise of the ministry in which Clarke served came in July 1874. There are indications that he himself planned to retire from the government even before its defeat. A redistribution bill of 1873 had reduced the number of provincial electoral districts in which French-speaking constituents were in the majority, but this bill failed to satisfy the demands of the growing English population. When the 1874 session opened on 2 July, Clarke announced that since the bill had been based on incomplete surveys the government would introduce a new one. The next day a motion of non-confidence in the ministry was carried, 15 to 7, and Clarke, Royal, Howard, John NORQUAY, and James McKay* tendered their resignations to Lieutenant Governor Morris on 4 July.

Following his resignation Clarke went to California; when passing through St Paul (Minn.) he suffered a beating from an American he had prosecuted in 1873 for the attempted kidnapping of Lord Gordon Gordon*. He remained in California until 1877 when he returned to Winnipeg and resumed his law practice. He unsuccessfully contested the riding of Rockwood in the provincial elections of December 1878 and December 1879. Whereas formerly he had courted the French-speaking and Roman Catholic vote, Clarke now favoured the abolition of French as an official language and the adoption of a school system similar to that in Ontario. This switch may be explained by the fact that Clarke was running in Rockwood, an English-speaking constituency, and that the English were by then a majority of the population of Manitoba. It is also possible that clerical displeasure with his marital conduct may have been a further factor in this change. Following the North-West rebellion of 1885, Clarke acted as counsel for 25 of Riel's followers; they pleaded guilty to treason-felony, Clarke spoke eloquently for clemency, and in the event seven received no sentence and the rest one to seven years.

Clarke died in September 1889 on the train while *en route* west for his health. He was buried at Pembina in accordance with his wishes but his widow later had his remains moved to Volunteer Park, Seattle, Wash. Twice married, he had no children of his own.

A controversial figure, Clarke was reckless, intemperate, and opportunistic, and made many enemies. His detractors said that he used his office to enrich himself and that any concern for the Métis was pure opportunism. Yet he deserves credit for helping to lay the foundations of law and government in Manitoba, and for supporting the Métis at a time when it took some courage for an English-speaking politician to do so.

LOVELL C. CLARK

H. J. Clarke was the author of *A short sketch of the life of the Hon. Thomas D'Arcy McGee, M.P., for Montreal (West)* . . . (Montreal, 1868), and *Report of the honourable the attorney-general to His Excellency the Hon. A. G. Archibald, lieutenant-governor of the province of Manitoba and the North-West Territories, on the immigration conference held at Ottawa, 18th Sept., 1871* (n.p., 1871).

AASB, T 7815–16, 7865–66, 8051–53. PAC, MG 26, A (mfm. at PAM). PAM, MG 3, D1; MG 12, A; B; MG 14, C54. *Manitoba Daily Free Press*, 16 Nov., 2 Dec. 1878. *CPC*, 1870–74. Alexander Begg, *History of the North-West* (3v., Toronto, 1894–95). [R.] D. and Lee Gibson, *Substantial justice: law and lawyers in Manitoba, 1670–1970* (Winnipeg, 1972). Stanley, *Louis Riel*. Frances Ebbs-Canavan, "Manitoba's first premier and attorney-general: Henry Joseph Clarke, Q.C., 1871–1874," *Manitoba Hist.* (Winnipeg), 1 (1946–49), no. 3: 1–11.

CLARKE, LAWRENCE, HBC fur-trader and office-holder; b. 26 June 1832 in Fermoy (Republic of Ireland); m. first in 1859 Jane (d. 1870), daughter of John Bell*, and they had five children; m. secondly in 1874 Catherine (Katherine) McKay, and they had nine children; d. 5 Oct. 1890 in Prince Albert (Sask.).

Lawrence Clarke joined the Hudson's Bay Company in Montreal in 1851, after spending several years in the West Indies. He was immediately sent to Fort McPherson (N.W.T.) on the Peel River, and there was promoted to clerk. In 1863 Clarke was transferred to Fort-à-la-Corne (Sask.), then HBC headquarters on the lower Saskatchewan River. Four years later he went to Fort Carlton as chief trader; he was made factor in 1868 and chief factor in 1875. Three years later, as chief factor of the Saskatchewan District, he moved to Prince Albert where he served until his death. While at Fort Carlton he became an honorary member of the Smithsonian Institution of Washington, D.C., to which he shipped large quantities of Indian artifacts. He is mentioned by such travellers as

Sir William Francis Butler*, the Earl of Southesk [Carnegie*], Sir Sandford Fleming*, and the Marquess of Lorne [Campbell*] as having been a generous host during their tours of the North-West Territories. In 1875 he provided crucial assistance to the North-West Mounted Police during their first winter on the North Saskatchewan.

Holding a senior HBC position, Clarke regarded himself as the most important man in the Saskatchewan District, with responsibilities extending beyond the fur trade, and was active in cultural and commercial affairs. He worked to gather support for Bishop John McLEAN's efforts in 1879 to establish Emmanuel College in Prince Albert, which it was hoped would develop into a university of Saskatchewan. Clarke himself donated money for its construction and for scholarships. He also supported the development of steamboat traffic on the North Saskatchewan River and provided financial assistance with the bringing of telegraph and railway services to Prince Albert. In 1881 his public career reached a climax when he became the first man from the North-West Territories to be elected to a legislative post, taking his place on the Council of the North-West Territories for the new District of Lorne. The council sat only 17 days during Clarke's two-year term, and although he was an active member his sole contribution of importance was a resolution calling on the federal government to extinguish Métis land claims. The establishment of a land office in Prince Albert shortly afterward is usually seen as a consequence of his work.

Clarke's interest in the land titles question had been of long standing, and until the outbreak of the rebellion in 1885 [*see* Louis RIEL] he continued his attempts to resolve a problem that caused dissatisfaction among white settlers and Métis alike. Arrogant and peremptory, however, he was considered by some of his contemporaries to be temperamentally unsuited for dealing with the large and restive Indian and Métis population of his district. He was actively disliked by many, and was even suspected of hoping to speculate profitably in the Métis land scrip which would be distributed by the government if his efforts were successful. The suspicion seems unfounded. Yet clearly his sympathy did not extend beyond those Indians and Métis who had abandoned their nomadic habits for farms and the white man's way of life. Clarke was always intensely suspicious of any attempt by the Métis to organize themselves and over-reacted to efforts such as that of Gabriel Dumont* in 1875 to establish an informal Métis "government." Because of Clarke's alarms on this occasion, 50 North-West Mounted Police had been sent to Fort Carlton and Dumont was called before the magistrates there, one of whom was Clarke, to explain his actions. As the relations between whites and Métis deteriorated over the next ten years, so did Clarke's with Métis activists. Indeed, it was widely held in the territories that his rash behaviour was partly responsible for the outbreak of rebellion in 1885. Two particularly damaging rumours were attached to Clarke's name. The first, current among the Métis, reported a provocative warning by him that their petitions to the government were to be answered not by redress but by the strengthening of the NWMP detachment. Although Clarke consistently denied this charge, modern historians agree that it was probably well founded. The second rumour suggested that it was largely due to his urgings that Superintendent Leif Newry Fitzroy Crozier* marched on Duck Lake on 26 March without awaiting the arrival of Colonel Acheson Gosford Irvine* with NWMP reinforcements. Clarke never commented on this charge. He was present during the first stages of the ensuing confrontation, but fled precipitately when the fighting broke out. His health collapsed immediately thereafter, and though he was appointed a supply officer of the Canadian expedition to suppress the rebellion, he was unable to fulfil his duties.

Clarke had not stood for re-election to the Council of the North-West Territories in 1883. His connection with the HBC had been an issue in 1881, and in 1883 there were strong suspicions that he was using his political influence to persuade the government to locate the new land office and telegraph office on HBC property and not in Prince Albert itself. In November the issue of the location of the telegraph office actually burst into a riot. Although he served as president of the Prince Albert Board of Trade between 1887 and 1889, his health remained poor until he died in 1890 at the age of 58.

STANLEY GORDON

Glenbow-Alberta Institute, C. D. Denney papers (mfm.). PAC, MG 26, A; MG 27, I, C4. PAM, HBCA, D.20/35. Saskatchewan Arch. Board (Regina), Campbell Innes papers. *Prince Albert Times and Saskatchewan Rev.* (Prince Albert), 1882–90. *Saskatchewan Herald* (Battleford, [Sask.]), 1878–90. *McPhillips' alphabetical and business directory of the district of Saskatchewan, N.W.T. . . . ,* [comp. H. T. McPhillips] (Qu'Appelle, [Sask.]), 1888. G. W. D. Abrams, *Prince Albert: the first century, 1866–1966* (Saskatoon, Sask., 1966). N. F. Black, *History of Saskatchewan and the North West territories* (2v., Regina, 1913; 2nd ed., 1v., 1913). J. K. Howard, *Strange empire; a narrative of the northwest* (New York, 1952). D. G. Lent, *West of the mountains: James Sinclair and the Hudson's Bay Company* (Seattle, Wash., 1963). Stanley, *Birth of western Canada*. George Woodcock, *Gabriel Dumont: the Métis chief and his lost world* (Edmonton, 1975).

COCKBURN, JAMES, lawyer, businessman, and politician; b. 13 Feb. 1819 at Berwick upon Tweed, England, son of James Cockburn, a merchant, and Sarah Turnbull; m. 14 Dec. 1854 Isabella Susan Patterson (d. 1862), and they had three children; d. 14 Aug. 1883 at Ottawa, Ont.

James Cockburn's family was of Scottish Presbyterian origin although Cockburn himself was a member of the Church of England by the 1860s. He received his early education at a grammar school in Berwick upon Tweed. In 1832 he came with his family, which seems to have had some financial resources, to Montreal, Lower Canada, where his father died of cholera in the same year. Sarah Cockburn then moved her family to York (Toronto), Upper Canada, and in 1832–33 James continued his education at Upper Canada College.

Cockburn began to study law in 1841 and was admitted to the bar in 1846. He then moved to Cobourg and in July of that year began to practise in partnership with D'Arcy Edward Boulton. Cockburn was also involved in other business activities in Cobourg and the surrounding area. In 1856 he was employing men for the construction of a dam, slide, booms, and piers at Campbellford on the Trent River and he was also the Cobourg agent for the Colonial Life Assurance Company. From 1864 to 1870 he acted as mortgage and land agent for Richard John Cartwright*.

Meanwhile Cockburn's legal practice was declining. In 1863 he had been appointed a QC and the following year was elected a bencher of the Law Society of Upper Canada. By then, however, he was involved in politics and these accolades were probably more political than professional honours; he was not a prominent lawyer. His business affairs also ran into difficulties. In 1864 he tried to borrow money on the security of his Cobourg properties but land values had fallen sharply. By 1866 he was virtually bankrupt and he was never able to restore his financial position. In 1869, admitting that his legal career was in jeopardy, he explained his plight to Cartwright: "I have come to grief and have been made to feel very poor and very penniless. . . . I am trying to work up my professional practice again, but it needs time, and time though it may heal will also kill."

Cockburn was more successful in politics. He served on the Cobourg Town Council in 1855–56 and in 1859. In 1861 he successfully contested Northumberland West against Sidney SMITH, postmaster general in the government of George-Étienne Cartier* and John A. Macdonald*. Cockburn was described by Macdonald in 1861 as "a Tory of the old school. In fact, [you] might say he belonged to the old fossil party – a Tory of the old Family Compact. . . ." Promising in the campaign that "If elected my vote shall be given unhesitatingly against [the ministry] on every question involving want of confidence," Cockburn endorsed representation by population and sought unity of political opinion in Canada West in order to accomplish for it "the objectives we frequently desire." Although he voted in favour of the government's militia bill, on which the Cartier–Macdonald ministry was defeated in May 1862, he explained that this support was not an expression of "his confidence" in Macdonald. He endorsed portions of the policy of the new administration formed by John Sandfield Macdonald* and Louis-Victor SICOTTE but never committed himself to the Reform ministry. After his election by acclamation in 1863 he emerged as a supporter of John A. Macdonald and remained a Liberal-Conservative for the rest of his career. On 30 March 1864 he was appointed solicitor general in the government of Étienne-Paschal Taché* and John A. Macdonald.

Cockburn was not a distinguished parliamentarian nor was he an important regional politician. He administered his portfolio in a routine manner, and attended to the patronage problems of his constituents. With the instability of union politics, which meant frequent change in cabinets, men such as Cockburn who would otherwise have remained obscure rose to ministerial rank. Cockburn had the good fortune to be in office when the "Great Coalition" was formed in 1864 [*see* George Brown*] and as a minister of the government became a delegate to the Quebec conference. His contributions to the proceedings and to the subsequent debates on confederation in the Legislative Assembly were negligible. Nevertheless, "an inferior man," as Alexander Mackenzie* privately called him, is remembered as a father of confederation.

Cockburn was elected by acclamation to the first federal parliament in 1867. There was no place for him in the cabinet; as compensation he was chosen speaker of the House of Commons. Leading Liberals held the first speaker in low regard and his inability to speak French was resented by some members from Quebec. In 1873, however, he was re-elected to the post. His fortunes declined rapidly after the fall of the Macdonald government in November 1873. He lost Northumberland West in 1874 and was unsuccessful in Northumberland East in a by-election later that year. He moved his family to Ottawa to re-establish himself as a lawyer. The *Toronto Daily Mail* claimed that he built "a good practice in the Supreme Court," but he remained destitute. In 1878 he secured the Conservative nomination in Northumberland West after a bitter struggle and won a narrow victory in the general election of that year. However, his political career was virtually over. Cockburn was seriously ill after 1878; his major interest was in securing a patronage post to obtain financial security for himself and his children. In 1871 he had tried to persuade Macdonald to appoint him lieutenant governor of British Columbia. He asked for the speakership again in 1878 and was refused. In 1881 Macdonald finally employed the sick and worried man on the consolidation of the statutes. Cockburn pursued the task informally until ill health forced him to resign his seat on 15 Nov. 1881. He was immediately appointed to the commission for the codification of dominion statutory law. By 1882 Cockburn was too ill to leave his lodgings, but he continued to press Macdonald for patronage until his death.

DONALD SWAINSON

AO, MU 132, P. L. Climo, "The Honourable James Cockburn . . ." (typescript); MU 506–7. PAC, MG 26, A. QUA, Alexander Mackenzie papers. Can., House of Commons, *Debates*, 1875–81. "Parl. debates" (CLA mfm. project of parl. debates, 1846–74), 1861–74. *Globe*, 11 Nov. 1874, 15 Aug. 1883. *Ottawa Daily Citizen*, 15 Aug. 1883. *Toronto Daily Mail*, 15 Aug. 1883. *Canadian directory of parl.* (J. K. Johnson), 128. *CPC*, 1862, 1864, 1871, 1873, 1879. Notman and Taylor, *Portraits of British Americans*, III. W. F. Dawson, *Procedure in the Canadian House of Commons* (Toronto, 1962). Donald Swainson, "'Forgotten men' revisited – some notes on the career of Hon. James Cockburn, a deservedly neglected father of confederation," *OH*, 72 (1980): 230–42; "Personnel of politics."

CODERRE, JOSEPH-EMERY. *See* EMERY-CODERRE

COFFIN, THOMAS, merchant, shipbuilder, and politician; b. 1817 in Barrington, Shelburne County, N.S., son of Thomas Coffin and Margaret Homer; m. first in 1840, Sarah Doane; m. secondly in 1870, Adeline Coffin; several children were born of each marriage; d. 13 July 1890 in Barrington.

Thomas Coffin's family had been engaged in farming, shipbuilding, fishing, and general trade since its arrival in Shelburne County from Nantucket (Mass.) in the 1760s. His father trained his sons to carry on in these occupations, and when an adult Thomas conducted lengthy trading voyages as captain. He prospered sufficiently to build a large store in 1856 on one of the two wharves his father owned at Shelburne. Like many other merchants in the 1850s Coffin was attracted to shipbuilding, and in 1853 he and his brother James joined with James Sutherland and his sons to acquire timber lands and sawmills on the upper reaches of the Clyde River. From 1854 until the late 1870s they operated a shipyard on the river, producing several barques, brigantines, and schooners, including two ships over 1,000 tons each.

As a member of a well-established family and a prosperous businessman in his own right, Coffin considered it his duty to perform public service. Though his own formal education was apparently limited, he was appointed commissioner of schools for the western district of Shelburne County in 1849, and again from 1854 to 1857; he was also school commissioner for the Barrington district in 1857–58 and 1864. He had been named a justice of the peace in 1855, and despite his lack of any legal training he served on the court of probate from 1861 to 1865.

Coffin's most prominent public role began in 1851 when he was elected as a Reformer to represent Shelburne County in the House of Assembly. He rarely spoke in the house, did not take an active part on committees, and introduced only a few bills pertaining to shipping or trade. In 1851, in one of his rare speeches, he defended Joseph Howe*'s proposal for constructing a railway from Halifax to Windsor because it would "give to those engaged in the prosecution of the fisheries an increased market." Coffin's support was surprising to Howe since the other western county members, particularly Thomas Killam* of Yarmouth, denounced the project as a threat to the fisheries. Coffin usually voted, however, with other merchants to reduce tariffs and oppose the extension of aid to railway construction and manufacturing industries. In the general election of 1855 Coffin lost his seat, but he regained it in 1859. Although frequently absent from the assembly, probably because he was at sea, Coffin supported Howe's sorely pressed administration when he was present. In the general election of 1863 Coffin was one of only 14 Liberals returned to a house of 55 members. He was soon caught up in the debate over union of the British North American colonies and joined with members from the western counties in opposing the scheme. Coffin apparently saw in union threats of increased tariffs and emphasis on the development of the upper provinces.

Coffin's opposition to confederation was undiminished by the passage of the British North America Act, and in the federal election in September 1867 he was elected by acclamation to represent Shelburne in the House of Commons. He attempted to remain neutral when in 1868 bitter strife broke out between Howe and the anti-confederate provincial administration of William ANNAND. Sir John A. Macdonald*, refusing to recognize Annand's government as the legitimate voice of the province, had chosen instead to deal with Howe and the other federal members of parliament. Howe, who had come to accept union as inevitable, was negotiating with Macdonald to improve the financial terms of Nova Scotia's entry into confederation. The split between the federal and provincial anti-confederates elected in 1867 was put to political advantage by Coffin: in Ottawa he became identified as a supporter of Macdonald's government, a position useful for patronage purposes, while at the county level he retained ties with the supporters of the anti-confederate provincial ministry. This tactic helped him win the 1872 general election, again by acclamation.

Coffin and other Nova Scotia members of parliament became dissatisfied, however, with Macdonald's policy of arbitrarily choosing members of his cabinet, who in turn were expected to direct the votes of the members of their respective provincial caucuses. The Nova Scotians wanted themselves to select and dismiss their cabinet representatives and to be involved in decision making. Howe's resignation in May 1873 opened up a cabinet post coveted by several members, including Coffin. Disappointed in his pursuit of office, Coffin pledged his support to the leader of the opposition, Alexander Mackenzie*. When the Pacific Scandal forced the resignation of Macdonald's cabinet in November 1873 and a Liberal government was formed, the ten Nova Scotia supporters of Mackenzie decided that the two members of parliament with the longest records of parliamentary service, Coffin and William Ross*, should become ministers. Unable to resist the dictates of the Nova Scotia group, Mackenzie reluctantly appointed Coffin receiver general.

Returned by acclamation in the ensuing by-election and in the general election of February 1874, Coffin soon revealed his deficiencies as a parliamentarian and minister. His position was made secure, however, when Mackenzie dismissed William Ross because he doubted his judgement and honesty. The Nova Scotia caucus denounced Mackenzie's action as arbitrary; the appointment to the cabinet in September 1874 of William Berrian Vail*, who represented a Halifax faction, was equally resented. In such circumstances, Mackenzie felt he could not afford to remove Coffin, whom he thought had "neither talent, tongue or sense," but he briefly considered abolishing the office of receiver general as a means of ridding himself of his unsatisfactory colleague. Coffin's downfall finally came in the federal election of 1878 when he was soundly defeated by Thomas Robertson*, a prominent provincial Liberal. Coffin never again ran for political office and, embittered by what he considered treachery on the part of both provincial and federal Liberals, supported the Conservatives until his death in 1890.

Coffin's attempts to fulfil his self-conceived ideas of social responsibility required political abilities he did not possess. His insistence on remaining in the cabinet prevented Mackenzie from searching for a Nova Scotian who could have contributed to cabinet decisions and acted as a spokesman for government policies in the province at a time when the Liberals sorely lacked both political leadership and public appeal. It was fortunate for Coffin's self-esteem that he did not realize that by clinging to office he had betrayed the interests of his own party and helped to cause the Liberal defeat in 1878.

KENNETH G. PRYKE

PANS, MS file, Coffin family. Shelburne County Court of Probate (Shelburne, N.S.), Book 3, Will of Thomas Coffin. *Acadian Recorder*, 8 Sept. 1870. *Morning Chronicle* (Halifax), 1864–74. *Morning Herald* (Halifax), 1878, 15 July 1890. *Novascotian*, 1851–67. *Yarmouth Herald* (Yarmouth, N.S.), 15 July 1890. *CPC*, 1876. Edwin Crowell, *A history of Barrington Township and vicinity, Shelburne County, Nova Scotia, 1604–1870; with a biographical and genealogical appendix* (Yarmouth, [1923]; repr. Belleville, Ont., 1974). K. G. Pryke, *Nova Scotia and confederation, 1864–74* (Toronto, 1979). Thomson, *Alexander Mackenzie*. K. G. Pryke, "The making of a province: Nova Scotia and confederation," CHA *Hist. papers*, 1968: 35–48.

COLLINSON, Sir RICHARD, naval officer and Arctic explorer; b. 1811 in Gateshead, England, third son of John Collinson, rector of Gateshead; d. 13 Sept. 1883 in Ealing (now part of Greater London), England.

Richard Collinson went to school until the age of 12 when Captain Thomas Maling, RN, offered to recruit him as a midshipman. He entered the Royal Navy on 2 Dec. 1823 and began his career with a long voyage on Maling's ship, *Cambridge*, to the Pacific coast of South America. After his return home in June 1827, he spent a few months of inactivity on board *Gloucester* until his father obtained a post for him on *Chanticleer*, commanded by Captain Henry Foster, which was then fitting out for an important surveying voyage to the Atlantic coast of South America. During this voyage, which lasted from April 1828 to May 1831, Collinson took an active part in the scientific work and was praised by both Foster and Horatio Thomas Austin* (who took command on Foster's death in February 1831) for his diligence and for the accuracy of his observations. His conduct on the voyage won him numerous admirers, notably Captain Francis Beaufort, hydrographer of the navy, whose personal guidance was to establish him in a successful career as a surveying officer.

In December 1831 Collinson joined *Ætna*, commanded by Captain Edward Belcher*, for a two-year surveying cruise on the west coast of Africa. In September 1833 he was again under Austin's command for a voyage on the steamer *Salamander*, replaced a few months later by *Medea*, to Portugal and the Mediterranean. During the voyage he received the long awaited news of his promotion to lieutenant on 23 March 1835. In December he joined *Sulphur*, commanded first by Captain Frederick William Beechey* and later by Belcher, for a surveying expedition to the west coast of America between Cape Horn and Mount St Elias (Alaska). Towards the end of the voyage he fell into dispute with Belcher, a common experience for subordinates of that quarrelsome officer, and in June 1838 was transferred to the British flagship in the Pacific. He returned to England in November 1839.

At the outbreak of the 1st Chinese War in 1840, Beaufort secured for Collinson an important post as surveying officer to the fleet. His main task in China was to survey and mark with buoys a number of rivers, notably the Yangtze (Chang Jiang), which were then unknown to European navigators, enabling the British fleet to penetrate with safety to the inland cities. His great success was rewarded with promotion to commander on 18 June 1841 and to post-captain on 23 Dec. 1842, and with nomination as CB. After the conclusion of the war in 1842, he remained in China for four years, surveying the coast from Zhoushan to Hong Kong. In summer 1846 he finally returned home to Durham for a long period of rest.

Collinson was still on leave at his father's home in autumn 1849 when the government decided upon an intensive search for Sir John Franklin*'s missing ships, following the failure of Sir James Clark Ross*'s attempt in 1848–49. A major expedition under Austin was to search the eastern Arctic by way of Baffin Bay, and *Enterprise* and *Investigator* were fitted out for an expedition to the western Arctic by way of Bering Strait. In December 1849 the Admiralty, again at Beaufort's instigation, offered command of the latter expedition to Collinson.

The two ships sailed from the Thames on 11 Jan. 1850, with Collinson on *Enterprise* and Robert John Le Mesurier McClure*, his second in command, on *Investigator.* During the long outward voyage *Investigator* proved to be much the slower ship and trailed behind. Collinson allowed her to catch up in the Strait of Magellan but the ships soon parted again in the Pacific. He waited a further five days at Honolulu, then sailed north on 30 June hoping to rendezvous in Bering Strait.

Displaying a characteristic concern for the safety of his ship and crew, Collinson chose to avoid the potentially dangerous waters of the Aleutian Islands chain by sailing around its western extremity. This decision, made in spite of Henry Kellett*'s commendation of Seguam Pass as a wide and safe route through the Aleutians and in full knowledge of the urgency of reaching the ice at the beginning of August, proved disastrous for the expedition's immediate progress. It added a considerable distance to Collinson's route, delayed his arrival in the ice by a decisive two weeks, and allowed McClure to steal a march on him. McClure had left Honolulu four days after Collinson, but sailed through the Seguam Pass, rounded Point Barrow on 7 August, and went on to winter in Prince of Wales Strait. Collinson entered the ice nine days later, searched unsuccessfully for a clear passage through the pack for a further fortnight, and then abandoned the attempt. He chose instead to winter in Hong Kong, and try afresh in 1851.

On the voyage from Honolulu in 1850, Collinson's extreme caution had begun to exasperate some of his officers, who already showed signs of the indiscipline and unrest that were to bedevil this expedition more than most. They were baffled by his course around the Aleutians. They queried his insistence on seeking a route directly across Beaufort Sea towards Banks Island, instead of attempting an inshore route around Point Barrow. And some of them clearly resented his decision to return to Hong Kong rather than to winter near Point Barrow. They may have been justified in showing some frustration at the loss of a whole season, but instances of overt criticism and other signs of unrest recurred so frequently throughout the voyage that, on later occasions, Collinson was driven to placing officers under arrest in order to keep them in check.

After the long voyage south, Collinson had only six weeks at Hong Kong to re-stock the ship and rest his crew before setting out northward again on 2 April 1851. This time he arrived in the ice in good season, passed around Point Barrow on 25 July, and, after coasting to Franklin Bay, set his course for Banks Island, hoping to rejoin *Investigator.* He entered Prince of Wales Strait on 26 August, unluckily just 10 days after *Investigator* had emerged from wintering there. Half-way through the strait, Collinson found evidence that McClure had explored it before him, but he continued to its northeastern extremity hoping, like McClure, to pass through into Melville Sound and thus complete the discovery of a northwest passage. But both found the sound choked with ice and turned back. Collinson wanted now to find a winter harbour on the west coast of Banks Island. At Cape Kellett on 6 September he found evidence that he was still following *Investigator.* The next day he met heavy pack and, considering the west coast to be too dangerous for wintering, turned south again, having little doubt that McClure had been forced to do likewise. In fact, *Investigator* was still far to his north and was about to become inextricably beset in Mercy Bay. Collinson returned to the southern end of Prince of Wales Strait where, in Walker Bay, Victoria Island, he found a safe winter harbour.

In contrast with several other naval searching expeditions, Collinson attempted little exploration by sledge in spring 1852, but he did lead a sledge party up Prince of Wales Strait between 16 April and 6 June to examine the north coast of Victoria Island. He explored it to Wynniatt Bay although, again, he had been preceded a year earlier by a party from *Investigator.*

Enterprise was released on 5 August and Collinson determined on exploring Prince Albert Sound, then thought to be a strait dividing Victoria Island into three parts. He demonstrated that the three parts were, in fact, a single island. This important discovery, however, far from satisfying him, left him uncertain as to what to do next. Almost despairingly, he chose to continue eastward through Dolphin and Union Strait, Coronation Gulf, and Dease Strait (a dangerous, rocky channel previously believed to be navigable by boat only), and made his way to Cambridge Bay, Victoria Island, where he wintered. More than 50 years later he was to win high praise for his skill in negotiating these straits from Roald Amundsen*, who took his little ship *Gjöa* through in 1905: "His soundings and surveys of this narrow and foul channel were very helpful. . . . Sir Richard Collinson appears to have been one of the most capable and enterprising sailors the world has ever produced. He guided his great, heavy vessel into waters that hardly offered sufficient room for the tiny 'Gjöa.'"

In spring 1853 Collinson organized only one extended sledge journey, to examine the east coast of Victoria Island northward to Gateshead Island. This choice proved unfortunate because, as he approached his farthest north, he found a note from Dr John Rae* indicating that he had searched the same stretch of coast two years earlier. Time after time on this expedition Collinson had searched a supposedly unknown region, only to find that another explorer had beaten him to it. Worse still, though, he was later to learn that this infuriating duplication of effort had almost certainly cost him the honour of discovering the fate of the Franklin expedition. On the 1853 sledge journey, like Rae before him, Collinson had unwittingly passed within 30 miles of the last relics of Franklin's retreating crews, lying just across Victoria Strait on King William Island. Unlike Rae, he had had every opportunity to make the crossing to where the relics lay. The Inuit at Cambridge Bay had tried to direct him there, he had even planned to send one of his sledges in that direction, and he had finally been deterred only by his uncertainty about what the Inuit were trying to tell him, the inaccuracy of the map they drew for him, and the roughness of the ice in Victoria Strait. Had he known earlier that on Victoria Island he was merely following in Rae's footsteps, he would almost certainly have gone to King William Island. In the early summer one of Collinson's men picked up a wooden fragment, possibly a relic of the Franklin expedition, near Cambridge Bay. Now, however, it was too late to follow up such a clue. The ice was about to break up and, after two years in the Arctic and with fuel supplies low, Collinson was compelled to take the first opportunity to sail back to Bering Strait and home.

The expedition, hampered by ice and weather, was forced to spend one more winter in the Arctic at Camden Bay on the north coast of Alaska. In August 1854 *Enterprise* finally rounded Point Barrow and met the awaiting crew of *Plover*, their first contact with Europeans for three years. *Enterprise* arrived back in England on 5 May 1855. In the mean time, *Investigator* had been abandoned in Mercy Bay, Banks Island. McClure and his crew had been rescued in 1853 by Kellett and taken home in 1854 on the ships of Sir Edward Belcher, Kellett's superior.

In spite of his disciplinary problems and his rather limited discoveries, Collinson won high praise from both contemporary and later navigators, notably for his excellent seamanship in negotiating notoriously difficult channels and his perseverance throughout so long an expedition. But the acclaim of his colleagues was not matched at the Admiralty where he received a distinctly frosty reception. He annoyed them by electing to resurrect the matter of indiscipline on board his ship and urging them to court-martial some of the officers. The Admiralty, taking a kinder view of the behaviour of men subjected to the stresses of such a testing voyage, preferred to let the matter rest – an attitude Collinson regarded as a personal affront. Further disappointment came when a select committee of the House of Commons sat to adjudicate the claims to an award for the discovery of a northwest passage submitted by McClure, by Henry Kellett on the basis of his rescue of McClure, and by Collinson. Collinson's case was undoubtedly strong. He had independently discovered the same northwest passage as McClure – through Prince of Wales Strait – though admittedly a year later. Moreover, he had come close to completing the discovery of another northwest passage, south of Victoria Island, which, as he said in evidence, was at least navigable whereas McClure's was not. But when the committee reported, Collinson and Kellett were passed over with an honourable mention, while McClure and his men received the £10,000 award.

Collinson was deeply hurt by the absence of any official recognition for his achievements; the only real token of appreciation came from the Royal Geographical Society, which awarded him its Founder's Medal in 1858. And so embittered was he by the Admiralty's rebuff in the matter of discipline that he never again approached them for a command.

He maintained an active interest in exploration and the sea. He advised Lady Franklin [Griffin*] on the preparation of her *Fox* expedition of 1857–59, and he began to involve himself closely in the work of the United Services Institution and the Royal Geographical Society, of which he became a fellow in 1855 and vice-president from 1857 to 1875. In 1861, after the outbreak of the American Civil War, he visited Canada for a short time charged with examining defence establishments along the frontier from the Atlantic Ocean to Lake Superior. Later, he edited an account of Sir Martin Frobisher*'s voyages for the Hakluyt Society.

Collinson also began to develop a new career in maritime affairs. In 1858 he procured an appointment in London as younger brother at Trinity House, the establishment responsible for the maintenance of aids to navigation, such as lights and buoys, on Britain's coasts and rivers. He became increasingly involved in the work of Trinity House in his later years; he was elected elder brother in 1862, and in 1875 he rose to become deputy master, the working head of the establishment. In that same year, the Admiralty at last offered him full recognition for his services by recommending his nomination as KCB and by promoting him to the rank of admiral (he had already attained flag rank in 1862 and had become a vice-admiral in 1869). Collinson spent the rest of his working life at Trinity House, and retired in 1883, just five months before his death.

Collinson was one of the most highly esteemed

naval officers of his day. His early successes as a surveying officer, his excellent work during the Chinese war, and his fine achievements in the Arctic set him on a brilliant naval career that deserved a more honourable end. That he allowed a seemingly minor dispute over discipline to cut short his career shows that he had a stubborn nature, but it also displays some of his finer qualities as an officer. It was not malice that drove him to seek courts martial for his officers so long after the events had occurred, but a strict regard for discipline and justice which, he believed, was "essential to comfort" on board ship. Although his strong commitment to discipline gave him, in his brother's words, a "somewhat severe manner," he was otherwise described as kind-hearted, modest, and good-humoured. And, stubborn though he was, he was not a man to bear a grudge. During and after the Arctic expedition McClure, his subordinate, stole much of the glory that was due to Collinson, but Collinson would not join those who condemned him. As a fellow officer, Sir George Henry Richards*, wrote: "he was far too generous and unselfish not to concur and to rejoice in the honours which were bestowed on his second, who, but for his chief's unsuspicious and trusting nature would never have had the opportunity of making himself famous."

CLIVE A. HOLLAND

Richard Collinson edited: [George Best], *The three voyages of Martin Frobisher, in search of a passage to Cathaia and India by the north-west, A.D. 1576–8* (London, 1867). His *Journal of H.M.S. Enterprise, on the expedition in search of Sir John Franklin's ships by Behring Strait, 1850–55*, was edited by his brother Thomas Bernard Collinson and published in London in 1889.

Albany Museum, 1820 Settlers' Memorial Museum (Grahamstown, Republic of South Africa), Francis Skead, Private journal kept on board HMS *Enterprise*, 1849–52. Gunnersbury Park Museum (London), Collinson papers, corr., 1826–57. National Maritime Museum (London), CLS/1-54 (papers and journals of Vice-Admiral Sir Richard Collinson, 1811–83). Scott Polar Research Institute (Cambridge, Eng.), MS 248/355–60 (Richard Collinson, corr. with Lady Franklin, John Barrow, and the Admiralty). Roald Amundsen, "*The north west passage*": *being the record of a voyage of exploration of the ship "Gjöa," 1903–1907* . . . (2v., London, 1908). G. B., Parl., Command paper, 1852, L, [1449], pp. 671–892, *Arctic expedition: further correspondence and proceedings connected with the Arctic expedition*; House of Commons paper, 1851, XXXIII, 97, pp.195–307, *Arctic expeditions: return to an address of the Honourable the House of Commons, dated 7 February 1851; – for, copy or extracts from any correspondence or proceedings of the Board of Admiralty in relation to the Arctic expeditions* . . . ; 1854–55, VII, 409, pp.1–60, *Report from the select committee on Arctic expedition; together with the proceedings of the committee, minutes of evidence, and appendix.* Royal Geographical Soc., *Proc.* (London), new ser., 5 (1883): 606–9. W. H. B. Webster, *Narrative of a voyage to the southern Atlantic Ocean, in the years 1828, 29, 30, performed in H.M. sloop Chanticleer, under the command of the late Captain Henry Foster, F.R.S. &c.* (2v., London, 1834). *DNB*. W. R. O'Byrne, *A naval biographical dictionary: comprising the services of all living naval officers* . . . (new ed., London, 1861), 225–36.

COOPER, JAMES BARRETT, printer, newspaper publisher, and office-holder; b. 4 Nov. 1811 in London, England, son of James Cooper and Ann Skeet; m. 5 June 1833 Jane Bagnall, and they had 12 children; d. 12 April 1888 in Upper Stewiacke, N.S.

James Barrett Cooper, son of a captain of a vessel trading between London and Newfoundland, moved to Newfoundland as a boy. After his father's death there, Cooper and his two brothers went to Charlottetown, P.E.I., with their mother, who married William Cullen, clerk of the House of Assembly. As a young man, Cooper apprenticed to James Douglas Haszard*, an established newspaperman. At the age of 26 he began his own newspaper, the *Colonial Herald, and Prince Edward Island Advertiser*, with the assistance of John S. Bremnar; the first issue appeared on 5 Aug. 1837. The *Colonial Herald* prided itself on its independent principles and, as a result, Cooper's early political affiliations are difficult to ascertain. An enlarged edition of the *Colonial Herald* was begun on 3 Jan. 1841, both Cooper and Bremnar then being described as publishers. They also published the *Prince Edward Island almanack*, the 1841 census, and a sheet almanac, did bookbinding and printing, and operated a store which sold a wide variety of stationery, books, and medicine. In addition, they were printers to the House of Assembly.

The partnership was dissolved by mutual consent in March 1844 and the paper and printing business was carried on by Cooper. Four months after striking out on his own, Cooper ceased publication of the *Colonial Herald*, auctioned his home and business, and moved to Meadow Bank where he began farming. He supplemented his probably meagre income by acting as agent on the Island for "Moffat's life pills" and "Phoenix bitters" and as a commissioner for the small debts court in the Crapaud and De Sable area. He was also appointed justice of the peace for Queens County in 1847, a position he held for 36 years, and in 1848 was commissioned a lieutenant in the 1st Regiment, Queens County militia, in which he eventually became a major.

In March 1850 he became a 2nd clerk in the House of Assembly, which had a Liberal majority, and in 1853 was again residing in Charlottetown. When he was not reappointed as assistant clerk in September 1854, Cooper toured the United States, apparently giving temperance lectures, until the fall of 1856. The following May Cooper launched the Charlottetown *Monitor* which gradually emerged in support of the Tory party, perhaps because of his unhappiness with the Liberals at not having been reappointed to his post in 1854. His advocacy of the Tory party paid off, however, when in 1860 he accepted a position from the government of Edward PALMER as clerk of the Legislative Council, a post he filled for almost seven years. In 1860 the *Monitor* became extreme in its support of Protestantism, Toryism, and the Orange order, presumably because Cooper was influenced by men who were providing him with financial support. After he was appointed clerk, Cooper may have surrendered most of his editorial duties to his associate editor, Donald Currie*; his opponents charged that Palmer, the Reverend George Sutherland*, and the Reverend David Fitzgerald* also provided him with editorial assistance, but the extent of their involvement is uncertain.

Cooper's hard work in support of the Tories was in vain; although they were successful in the election of 1863, the office of queen's printer which Cooper's friends in the Orange order had wanted him to have was once again given to John Ings, publisher of the *Islander*. This was a hard blow to Cooper who sorely needed the government's financial support to stay in business and, despite assistance from some Presbyterian individuals, the *Monitor* had to cease publication in 1865. During its seven-year existence the *Monitor* had been involved in continual exchanges with Edward Whelan*'s *Examiner* and from 1862 to 1864 it had engaged in heated debate with Edward Reilly*'s Roman Catholic *Vindicator*. Cooper also discussed such issues as responsible government, financial and legislative reform, the criminal code, and education. As a result of editorials he wrote in the fall of 1863 several major improvements were made to Prince of Wales College. Before 1864 the *Monitor* advocated federal union of the British North American colonies and printed articles in favour of Maritime union, but when confederation became an issue in that year Cooper shied away from expressing any definite opinions. By 1866 he had joined the ranks of those opposed to union.

Cooper had taken a special interest in the land question; he drew up a petition in 1859 asking the British government for a solution in favour of the tenants. In 1860 he served on a committee which prepared a memorial for the commission appointed by the Palmer government, presenting the grievances of descendants of the loyalists and disbanded soldiers to whom land had been promised in 1790. Cooper was always a strong advocate of temperance; he gave lectures on the topic and took a leading role in local organizations. He was secretary of the Charlottetown Temperance Society in 1840; an organizing member in 1841 and office-holder in 1843–44 of the Prince Edward Island auxiliary to the New British and Foreign Temperance Society; and in August 1850 became the first president of the Prince Edward Island Benevolent Total Abstinence Society. In addition he was for many years grand scribe and grand worthy patriarch of the Sons of Temperance, serving as a representative to other British North American divisions for over 20 years, and he was a director of the Temperance Hall Company for over 10 years. In 1843 and 1859 he was vice-president of Charlottetown Mechanics' Institute and was its secretary in 1853. A strong supporter of the Orange order, he was grand master in 1867 and lectured on Orangeism. In addition he did some preaching for the Methodists.

In October 1865 the *Monitor* was superseded by the *Weekly Bulletin*, published by Cooper's two sons, James and Henry, the latter having earlier been in partnership with his father. The *Weekly Bulletin* lasted only a short time but the printing business was carried on by Henry until his death in 1877. In 1870 Cooper was referred to by the *Patriot* as the "*Islander* scribe," but his connection with the *Islander* is not known. Cooper's life was not without hardship and sadness: he constantly struggled to keep his newspapers in print and only two of his 12 children survived him. Around 1883 he moved to Upper Stewiacke, N.S., where he died in 1888.

JEAN LAYTON MACKAY

PAPEI, RG 1, Commission books, January 1855–May 1862: 340; RG 18, 1841 census, 1881 census. Prince Edward Island Heritage Foundation (Charlottetown), J. B. Cooper file. P.E.I., House of Assembly, *Journal*, 1838; 1852; Legislative Council, *Journal*, 1860; 1867. *Colonial Herald, and Prince Edward Island Advertiser* (Charlottetown), 5 Aug. 1837–27 July 1844. *Examiner* (Charlottetown), 25 May, 15 June, 24 Aug., 12 Oct. 1857; 6, 13 Sept. 1858; 14 Feb. 1859; 5 June, 2, 24 Dec. 1860; 25 March, 24 June, 28 Oct. 1861; 5 Jan., 2 Feb., 26 Oct. 1863; 30 Oct. 1865; 17 Dec. 1877, 28 March 1884. *Herald* (Charlottetown), 1 Nov. 1865. *Islander*, 8 Jan., 12 Feb. 1847; 5 June 1857; 3 Nov. 1865; 13 July, 19 Oct. 1866. *Monitor* (Charlottetown), 23 May 1857–8 Dec. 1864. *Patriot* (Charlottetown), 24 Sept., 27 Oct. 1870. *Vindicator* (Charlottetown), 14 Nov., 19 Dec. 1862; 16 Jan., 6 Feb., 3 July 1863. *The Prince Edward Island almanack . . .* (Charlottetown), 1853, 1869–71, 1873–83. *The Prince Edward Island calendar . . .* (Charlottetown), 1847, 1850–51; 1855–59; 1861–68; 1870–72. *Past and present of P.E.I.* (MacKinnon and Warburton), 114, 118. Robertson, "Religion, politics, and education in P.E.I."

CORBY, HENRY, distiller, businessman, and politician; b. in 1806 at Hanwell (now part of Greater London), England, son of James Corby; d. 25 Oct. 1881 at Belleville, Ont.

Henry Corby, after serving as an apprentice to a baker in London, married Alma Williams in 1832 and immigrated to Belleville, Upper Canada. With a small amount of capital, he invested in merchandise, operated a small general store, and by 1838 had established a bakery. He had accompanied the Hastings Rifle

Brigade on patrol during the rebellion in Upper Canada in December 1837, and he procured a profitable contract to supply local troops with provisions. The contract was extended through 1838 and the bakery also flourished, but Corby suddenly disposed of his enterprises after the tragic drowning of his wife and two of their three children on 27 Dec. 1838. He then purchased the lake steamer *Queen* and became involved in the forwarding trade, buying and selling grain at ports from Belleville to Kingston. In 1842 he sold the vessel and returned to Belleville where he continued to market grain. The same year he married his late wife's sister, Matilda; they were to have 12 children.

Planning to establish a new milling operation, Corby in 1855 purchased Salyer Reed's grist-mill located north of Belleville at Hayden's Corner (the name was changed to Corbyville in 1882), and he added a distillery four years later. During his ownership the milling activity remained the dominant part of the business. The local demand for whisky led to the establishment of the distillery but its annual production was comparatively low and it did not compete with other distilleries such as that of Gooderham and Worts [*see* William GOODERHAM Sr]. The business remained essentially a family enterprise; Henry Jr, George, and Edward all joined their father in the firm.

By 1840 Corby had developed a lasting interest in municipal politics. He had been a member of Belleville's first police board in 1839 and was a village councillor from 1842 to 1847 and again in 1849. He also served both as reeve of Belleville and as a councillor from 1857 to 1860; he was re-elected to the latter post in 1862. Having acquired a large amount of experience in municipal affairs, Corby ran for mayor of Belleville in 1863 but was defeated by James Brown, who was to become the federal member for Hastings West in 1867. Corby was not discouraged from participating in public events; in 1865 he was among five founding directors, including Mackenzie Bowell*, appointed to the local board of trade. He was elected mayor of Belleville in 1867 and again the following year.

Corby's popularity was evident. As an independent Conservative, he was elected the first member for the Ontario legislature in Hastings East in 1867, and enjoyed two consecutive terms of office, sitting from 1867 to 1875. In the assembly, Corby supported Stephen Richards*' land grant policy in 1868 and helped persuade the government to establish the Ontario School for the Deaf which opened on 20 Oct. 1870 at Belleville. He was also a long-time promoter and director of the Grand Junction Railway which was to run from Belleville through Peterborough to Toronto, and he assisted in securing a charter in 1871 for its construction. In 1874 he supported the act of incorporation for the Belleville and North Hastings Railway which amalgamated with the Grand Junction five years later. Corby retired from public life in 1875 because of failing health.

He then devoted time to his milling and distillery business. In 1876, after the death of his second wife, he married Isabel Metcalfe of Kingston. He continued to be active in business affairs and such fraternal organizations as the Sons of England and the St George's Society until August 1881 when his health finally collapsed; he then sold the distillery, the mills, and a wine importing business to his son Henry for $10,000. It was Henry Jr's modernization of the business which helped it attain a prominent position in the distilling industry around the world.

DAVID M. CALNAN

AO, MU 470, A. A. Campbell to Alexander Campbell, 8 Jan. 1872. Belleville Public Library (Belleville, Ont.), Hastings County Hist. Soc. Arch., Henry Corby, files 210-1, 916, 916-1, 917, 919-22, 924-27. Corby Distilleries Limited (Corbyville, Ont.), Henry Corby file. Ont., Legislative Library, Newspaper Hansard, 1874 (mfm. at AO). PAC, MG 26, E14; F; MG 29, D61. *Intelligencer* (Belleville), 1862–73. *Weekly Intelligencer* (Belleville), 27 Oct. 1881. *Directory of the county of Hastings . . .* (Belleville), 1859–60: 73, 158, 185. G. E. Boyce, *Historic Hastings* (Belleville, 1967). William Canniff, *History of the settlement of Upper Canada (Ontario), with special reference to the Bay Quinté* (Toronto, 1869; repr. as *The settlement of Upper Canada*, intro. D. W. Swainson, Belleville, 1971), 493, 496. W. C. Mikel, *City of Belleville history* (Picton, Ont., 1943), 25–30, 50–53. W. F. Rannie, *Canadian whisky; the product and the industry* (Lincoln, Ont., 1976), 125–30.

CORBY, JOHN. *See* HOWARD, JOHN GEORGE

COTÉ, GABRIEL. *See* MĪMĪY

COTÉ (Côté), JOSEPH-OLIVIER, notary, public servant, and author; b. 8 April 1820 at Quebec City, Lower Canada, son of Olivier Côté, a blacksmith, and Louise-Charlotte Sasseville; m. 12 Nov. 1851 at Montreal Marie-Julie-Léocadie Leprohon (d. 1900), and they had four sons and two daughters; d. 24 April 1882 at Ottawa, Ont.

Joseph-Olivier Coté studied at the Séminaire de Québec from 1831 to 1835 when he left to study law first under René-Gabriel Belleau until 1838 and then under Louis-Édouard GLACKMEYER. He was admitted as a notary in 1841. In 1842–43 he was deputy registrar of Berthier County and in June 1845 the governor, Sir Charles Theophilus Metcalfe*, appointed him clerk in the Executive Council Office of the Province of Canada; the office was then headed by William Henry Lee*. Coté's duties included maintenance of the registers of commissions for all the known official appointments from 1651 and supervision of the compilation of manuscript indexes to the registers; these indexes were completed to confederation. He also compiled two editions (1860 and 1866) of a most useful handbook, *Political appointments and elections in the Province of Canada*, which covered the years 1841 to 1865. This project was extended by his son, Narcisse-Omer, who published a supplement in 1918 carrying the work to confederation, and added two further volumes continuing the tables to 1917. Joseph-Olivier also wrote periodically in both French and English newspapers under various *noms de plume*. His articles covered a wide variety of political and economic subjects, such as balance of trade, capital punishment, secularization of the clergy lands, and a parliament of all nations.

At confederation the Executive Council Office became the Privy Council Office of the dominion. In 1872 Lee retired and William Alfred Himsworth, who had joined the office shortly before Coté, was appointed to the clerkship and Coté to the deputy clerkship. In late 1879 Coté was appointed deputy governor general to sign letters patent for dominion and other lands, even though he was having trouble with his eyes and his health was failing. When Himsworth died at the opening of the next year Sir John A. Macdonald* appointed Coté clerk of the Privy Council on 13 Jan. 1880 and his annual salary was increased by $1,000 to $3,200. At the end of 1880 he was appointed a commissioner *per dedimus potestatem* to administer the oaths of office for the government. In spite of increasing ill health, which at times necessitated his working from his home, he was able to carry on until his death in 1882. Henry James Morgan* described him as a "most painstaking, discreet, courteous and efficient public officer" and his appointments gave general satisfaction. The tables prepared by him and his son remain invaluable references for the historian and political scientist to this day.

FREDERICK H. ARMSTRONG

Joseph-Olivier Coté compiled *Political appointments and elections in the Province of Canada from 1841 to 1860* (Quebec, 1860) and a second edition, . . . *from 1841 to 1865* (Ottawa, 1866); a third edition was edited by N.-O. Coté: . . . *and appendix from 1st January, 1866, to 30th June, 1867, and index* (Ottawa, 1918).

PAC, MG 26, A; RG 68, 88: 336; 320: 257; 412: 662. *Free Press* (Ottawa), 24 April 1882. *Ottawa Daily Citizen*, 25 April 1882. *Canadian men and women* (Morgan, 1912), 262. *CPC*, 1881: 24. *Dominion annual register*, 1882: 336–37.

COTTER, JAMES LAURENCE, HBC fur-trader and photographer; b. 24 Dec. 1839 at Jaulna (Jalna), India, son of Colonel George Sackville Cotter and Agnes Kilgour; m. 13 Sept. 1868 at Sault Ste Marie, Ont., Frances Symington Ironside, daughter of George Ironside*, and they had 11 children; d. 6 Aug. 1889 at Sault Ste Marie.

James Laurence Cotter, a descendant of an Irish baronet, was brought up by his grandmother near Edinburgh, where he attended Loretto School. He arrrived in Canada in 1857 and joined the Hudson's Bay Company that fall as an apprentice clerk. Governor George Simpson* described him as "a young gentleman of good education" and sent him to Fort La Cloche (Ont.) on Lake Huron, where he was to be kept "actively engaged" and pick up the "French & Indian" languages. Cotter served two seasons at Bersimis (Betsiamites, Que.) and another at Fort Chicoutimi (Que.) as a clerk and was then transferred to Moose Factory (Ont.), the administrative headquarters of the HBC's Southern Department. At Moose Factory, where he arrived in October 1867, Cotter was initiated into the complexities of a large fur-trading centre. In 1872 he was assigned to the Eastmain District and made junior chief trader the following year. He recommended to George Simpson McTavish, officer-in-charge at Moose Factory, that the district headquarters be moved from Little Whale River (Petite rivière de la Baleine, Que.) to Fort George (Que.). McTavish agreed, and the move was made in the summer of 1874. Cotter was promoted to chief trader in 1875, and remained at Fort George for another year, until he was sent to Rupert's House (Fort-Rupert, Que.) to take charge of Rupert's River District.

In 1879 Cotter returned to Moose Factory to take charge of the Southern Department, which comprised the districts of Albany, Rupert's River, Eastmain, Moose Factory, New Post (on the Abitibi River), and Kenogamissi (on the Moose River). The 1880s were a period of important changes in the development of northern Ontario: the building of the Canadian Pacific Railway and the opening up of the northwest to settlement were, in Cotter's words, "beginning to have their effect in unsettling the minds of the people." This general instability was reflected in the difficulty Cotter experienced in retaining qualified staff, especially skilled mechanics and boat builders. He was, however, successful in obtaining higher wages and better pensions for the men. He also succeeded, despite the restrictions on space in company ships, in having the wives and families of his staff brought out and housing provided for them. As settlement advanced to the north and west, the Indians too were affected. They were exposed to epidemics of whooping cough and influenza, which invariably meant death and sorrow, a decrease in fur returns, and an increase in their debts. To protect the Indians, Cotter prevailed upon them not to travel in areas afflicted by contagious diseases. During this unsettling period, Cotter, who attained the rank of chief factor in 1883, kept the fur returns for the Southern Department reasonably stable. His interests went beyond the fur trade. He established a sawmill for the HBC at Moose Factory, brought in livestock to improve the company's herd, and planted several productive vegetable gardens.

It is perhaps as a photographer, however, and not as a company officer that Cotter is best remembered. He made his own camera, and took some of the first photographs of the area around Hudson Bay. Nine drawings in *Harper's Weekly* (New York) of 7 June 1879, for instance, were based on Cotter's photographs. Historians and anthropologists are particularly interested in the artistically composed, sharp, clear photographs of people, buildings, and transportation. One of his photographs, taken at Moose Factory in 1871, shows a flat-roofed building which probably dates from 1762. Others show the Moose Factory bell tower, double-masted coastal vessels, the fort cannon pointing out to James Bay, and Indians and canoes. His pictures capture scenes reminiscent of a life which had changed little since the establishment of the fort in 1673. Cotter's photographs of the Inuit of the Eastmain District at Little Whale River, with their skin tents and kayaks, are probably the first photographs from that area.

During the winter of 1888–89 Cotter was too ill to work. He and his family left Moose Factory for Sault Ste Marie, where he died on 6 August.

SHIRLEE ANNE SMITH

Some of J. L. Cotter's photographs are reproduced in "The Eskimos of Eastmain," *Beaver*, outfit 260 (1929–30), 301–6 and 362–65, and in the photo essay of J. L. Cotter and C. P. Wilson, "Moose Factory today and yesterday," *Beaver*, outfit 277 (June 1946), 22–29.

PAM, HBCA, James Cotter file; George Simpson McTavish file; George Simpson genealogical table; A.1/71: 74; A.1/149: 204; A.6/13: ff.72d–73d; A.6/52: 320–21; A.6/53: 93, 523; A.6/55: 259; A.11/43: f.128d; A.11/47: ff.217, 229d, 234, 262b, 266b, 272, 280, 280d, 281, 289d, 291, 292, 293d, 294, 294b, 294d, 303, 408, 414; A.11/149: 104; A.44/8: 212; B.17/a/1: f.9d; B.77/a/39: ff.20d, 21; B.77/a/40: f.6d; B.134/g/39: f.13d; B.134/g/40: f.14d; B.135/a/181: f.18d; B.186/a/99: ff.13, 25d, 26, 31d, 72d; B.373/a/5: ff.56d, 70, 72; B.373/a/6: f.6d; B.373/c/2: f.44d; D.4/53: ff.65d, 88, 88d; D.14/2: f.510; D.14/5: f.262; D.14/8: f.79; D.20/15: f.275d; D.20/29: f.326d. H. M. S. Cotter, "Chief factor and photographer," *Beaver*, outfit 264 (December 1933): 23–26.

COUPER, WILLIAM, entomologist and naturalist; fl. 1860–86.

Nothing is known of William Couper's youth but he is believed to have arrived in Canada in 1843 and established himself in Toronto. He worked as a typographer in the printing shop of Henry ROWSELL. Couper seems to have followed this trade for much of his life, as well as giving private instruction in taxidermy. After a brief stay at Trois-Rivières in 1860, he lived in Quebec City until 1869, in Ottawa from 1869 to 1870, in Montreal from 1871 to 1884, and, lastly, in New York City from 1884 to 1886. He probably died at his son's residence in Troy, N.Y., about 1890.

At a time when the natural sciences especially were not well developed in Canada, Couper took an interest in ornithology, ichthyology, and botany. His most important contribution, however, was undoubtedly to entomology. He first became known in this field because of his excellent and original collections which won him praise and awards at exhibitions in Toronto in 1852 and 1856. Couper did not confine his interests to the insects themselves; his collections also included nests, cocoons, and various structures which both illustrated the building instinct of hexapods and facilitated the identification of species. In 1863 he announced that he had assembled more than 6,000 specimens, mostly vegetable matter, bearing traces of activity by insects in the larval or adult stages.

Couper wrote many articles and notes which were published particularly in Canadian and American periodicals. Taking up a number of subjects, his writings are still of much interest because they were the result of personal observation and experience. He noted the arrival and departure of migrating birds, reported the presence of rare species in various places, and wrote extensively about insect-eating birds. Contained in his writing on his favourite subject, entomology, are some of the first references to the different species of insects found near Quebec City, at locations on the north shore of the St Lawrence, and on the island of Anticosti, as well as discussions of insects harmful to crops, such as the apple borer, the cabbage butterfly, and the onion fly. Couper also established a list of the hymenoptera found on Montreal Island, and took a special interest in coleoptera, publishing taxonomical descriptions of 15 new species. In the *Canadian Sportsman and Naturalist*, a journal he began in Montreal in 1881 and published for three years, he focused particularly on types of game in Canada as well as hunting and fishing regulations; in one series of articles he even described Canadian museums of the period.

Whenever the occasion arose William Couper was an enthusiastic supporter of entomology. He became a corresponding member of the Entomological Society of Philadelphia, and in 1864, a year after the Entomological Society of Canada was organized in Toronto, he helped to establish a branch in Quebec City. In 1873 he became a founder and first president of the Montreal branch of the society which in 1871 had become the Entomological Society of Ontario. For several years its monthly meetings were held at his house. Unlike the Quebec branch, the one at Montreal developed steadily, and in 1951 became known as the Entomological Society of Quebec.

RODOLPHE O. PARADIS

In addition to the articles which he wrote for his own journal, the *Canadian Sportsman and Naturalist* (Montreal), 1881–83, William Couper was the author of a large number of notes and articles in the *Canadian Journal*, 1853–56, the *Canadian Entomologist* (London, Ont.), 1869–80, the *Canadian Naturalist and Geologist*, 1857–65, the *Proc.* of the Entomological Soc. of Philadelphia, 1863, the *Trans.* of the Literary and Hist. Soc. of Quebec, 1864–65, and the *Annual report* (Montreal) of the Montreal Horticultural Soc. and Fruit Growers' Assoc. of the Prov. of Que., 1879.

Morgan, *Bibliotheca Canadensis*, 83. R.-O. Paradis, "Étude biographique et bibliographique de William Couper, membre fondateur et premier président de la Société entomologique du Québec," Soc. entomologique du Qué., *Annales* (Québec), 19 (1974): 4–15. C. J. S. Bethune, "The rise and progress of entomology in Canada," RSC *Trans.*, 2nd ser., 4 (1898), sect.IV: 155–65. Léon Provancher, "Naturalistes canadiens," *Le Naturaliste canadien* (Cap-Rouge, Qué.), 5 (1873): 131.

COURSOL, CHARLES-JOSEPH (baptized **Michel-Joseph-Charles**), lawyer, office-holder, politician, and businessman; b. 3 Oct. 1819 at Fort Malden, Amherstburg, Upper Canada, only child of Michel Coursol and Mélanie Quesnel; m. 16 Jan. 1849 at Montreal, Émilie-Hélène-Henriette, daughter of Étienne-Paschal Taché*, and they had two sons and two daughters; d. 4 Aug. 1888 at Montmagny, Que.

Charles-Joseph Coursol's father, who died the year after the birth of his son, was an officer with the Hudson's Bay Company stationed at Fort Malden. Charles-Joseph was subsequently adopted by his uncle, Frédéric-Auguste Quesnel*, and enjoyed a comfortable upbringing in Montreal; he was also to share with his cousin the considerable fortune left by Quesnel on his death in 1866. From 1828 to 1834 he was educated at the Petit Séminaire de Montréal and later studied law with Côme-Séraphin CHERRIER, a prominent member of the Viger–Papineau family who became his stepfather in 1833.

Although Coursol apparently took no part in the rebellions of 1837–38, by the time he was called to the bar on 24 Feb. 1841 the cause of reform, coalescing in Canada East around Louis-Hippolyte La Fontaine*, had seized the youth with, as one contemporary, John Fennings TAYLOR, claimed, "the violence of a moral epidemic." His early political career, whether as the leader of a mob of 600 bludgeon-armed toughs supporting Reform candidate James Leslie* in Montreal during the election of March 1841, or as a defender of La Fontaine's Montreal home in August 1849 from a Tory mob enraged by the Rebellion Losses Bill, suggests he was attracted by the more physical, organizational side of the struggle for responsible government.

An extroverted, passionate activist, related both by birth and by marriage to notable families in the province, Coursol moreover acquired a distinguished legal reputation. As a consequence he won local popularity and secured election as a city councillor for Saint-Antoine Ward from 1853 to 1855. The same attributes had made possible for Coursol the more propitious rewards of patronage from the ministry of La Fontaine and Robert Baldwin* and later of Taché and Sir Allan Napier MacNab*. On 30 June 1848 he was appointed coroner, with Joseph Jones, for the district of Montreal; in January 1856 he was commissioned a captain in the 2nd Company of Militia Cavalry, Montreal; and, most important, on 2 Feb. 1856 he was named inspector and superintendent of police for Montreal: by virtue of this last appointment he also served as chairman of the quarter sessions and judge of the sessions of the peace for the district.

Toward the end of the American Civil War, Judge Coursol severely aggravated the already poor relations between the United States and Canada with a decision which was one of the factors in the abrogation of the Reciprocity Treaty of 1854. On 19 Oct. 1864 a group of about 20 Confederate soldiers, who had gathered in Canada East, launched an attack on the border town of St Albans, Vt, looting and firing it. Pursued back across the border by a local posse, 14 of the raiders were arrested by Canadian authorities and were held in Saint-Jean (Saint-Jean-sur-Richelieu) on six charges of extraditable offences. Coursol was sent from Montreal to act as the presiding magistrate when the preliminary examinations opened in the last week of October. Shortly after the trial began, Coursol changed the venue to Montreal. On 13 December, after a prolonged trial, he discharged the prisoners and most of them fled the country. Ignoring the question of the legal status of "raiders" under British law, and without referring the case either to the attorney general for Canada East, George-Étienne Cartier*, or to a higher court, Coursol, "this wretched prig of a police magistrate" (in John A. Macdonald*'s view), argued that he lacked the jurisdiction to pass judgement owing to the fact that the Canadian extradition act of 1861 had not been proclaimed by the British parliament. Coursol, however, was in error, the act having indeed been recognized in England by an order in council. The governments of the two countries were outraged. He was suspended from the office of police magistrate on 26 Jan. 1865. The report of the commissioner in charge of the inquiry into the proceedings connected to the raid, Frederick William Torrance, found Coursol, as a servant of the crown, liable to an indictment "for malfeasance" in office. Nevertheless, on 9 April 1866, after tensions and memories had faded, Coursol was reinstated at the urging of Cartier on the grounds that the error had been made in good faith: a politically astute decision.

Throughout the 1860s and 1870s Coursol's continued interest and participation in a wide variety of Montreal's cultural, social, and business affairs increased his popularity. A director of the Banque du

Peuple and president of the Crédit Foncier du Bas-Canada, he found the time and enthusiasm during the *Trent* crisis of 1861 to raise a militia regiment, the Canadian Chasseurs. As lieutenant-colonel, he commanded the unit along the Canadian-American border during the Fenian threat of 1866. Three years later Coursol received two federal appointments: police commissioner for the dominion and commissioner under the Canadian statute of 1868 concerning the extradition provisions of the Webster-Ashburton Treaty of 1842. His local aspirations peaked when he was elected mayor of Montreal by acclamation in 1871 and again in 1872, followed by four consecutive terms, 1872–76, as president of the Association Saint-Jean-Baptiste de Montréal. On 24 June 1874 the association held the largest demonstration ever seen in the city to that date in an attempt to encourage the repatriation of French Canadians who had gone to live in the United States [*see* Ferdinand GAGNON]. Coursol was a member of the Montreal Harbour Commission from 1871 to 1873 and was also prominent in the movement organizing the Papal Zouaves [*see* Ignace BOURGET]. He was created a knight of the Order of Charles III of Spain in 1872 and on 28 February of the following year was named a QC.

Not surprisingly, in the second half of the 1870s, while the federal Conservatives regrouped to assault Prime Minister Alexander Mackenzie*'s Liberal government, the Montreal Tory organization viewed Coursol favourably although perhaps as a somewhat unreliable ally. "He is desperately ambitious," wrote Thomas WHITE to Macdonald, "and that trait in his character is one to play upon." Sir John was urged to dangle vague promises of political preferment before him. Whatever stratagem Macdonald used, Coursol, championing the National Policy, won the constituency of Montreal East by almost 1,400 votes in the general election of 1878. In the next contest of 1882 he won the seat by acclamation. However, the North-West rebellion of 1885, and possibly his disappointed aspirations for a seat in the Senate, led him and several others in March 1886 to break Conservative ranks to support the motion made by Auguste-Charles-Philippe-Robert Landry* deploring the government's stance on the hanging of Louis RIEL. In the subsequent election of 1887, Coursol, "an old Conservative" and still a supporter of the National Policy, accused the Conservative party of having betrayed its duty and traditions, and ran as an independent Conservative. The party members recognized the hopelessness of opposing the popular renegade and did little to dramatize his disaffection while the Liberal press supported him as an oppositionist. On 15 Feb. 1887 he again won by acclamation. He died 18 months later, having taken little part in the parliamentary session.

LORNE STE. CROIX

AC, Montréal, État civil, Catholiques, Notre-Dame de Montréal, 7 août 1888. PAC, MG 24, B125; MG 26, A, 19, 203, 296, 434; MG 30, D1, 9: 112–18. [J. A. Macdonald], *Correspondence of Sir John Macdonald . . .* , ed. Joseph Pope (Toronto, 1921), 19. *Canada Gazette*, 1 July 1848; 19 Jan., 2 Feb. 1856; 4–5 Dec. 1869. *Gazette* (Montreal), 28 Jan. 1856, 5 Sept. 1865, 17 Feb. 1887, 6 Aug. 1888. *La Minerve*, 6 août 1886, 16 févr. 1887. *Montreal Herald and Daily Commercial Gazette*, 15, 16 Feb. 1887; 6 Aug. 1888. *Canadian directory of parl.* (J. K. Johnson), 139. *CPC*, 1887: 198. *Cyclopædia of Canadian biog.* (Rose, 1886), 665. Notman and Taylor, *Portraits of British Americans*, II: 325–28. Wallace, *Macmillan dict.*, 157. Creighton, *Macdonald, old chieftain*, 448–49; *Macdonald, young politician*, 195; *Road to confederation*, 212. *Histoire de la corporation de la cité de Montréal depuis son origine jusqu'à nos jours . . .* , J.-C. Lamothe *et al.*, édit. (Montréal, 1903), 210–11, 291–93. Monet, *Last cannon shot*, 75, 131, 241, 342. P.-G. Roy, *La famille Taché* (Lévis, Qué., 1904), 41, 56–57, 61–62. Rumilly, *Hist. de Montréal*, III. L. B. Shippee, *Canadian-American relations, 1849–1874* (New Haven, Conn., and Toronto, 1939). Léon Trépanier, "Figures de maires," *Cahiers des Dix*, 22 (1957) : 163–92.

COUTURE, GEORGE, merchant and politician; b. 4 June 1824 in the parish of Saint-Joseph (now in Lauzon), Lower Canada, son of Ignace Couture, a carpenter, and Anastasie Lefebvre, *dit* Boulanger; d. 4 Nov. 1887 at Lévis.

George Couture belonged to the fifth generation of descendants of the youngest son of Guillaume Couture*. In 1836, after studying briefly with an elderly teacher, George embarked on a commercial career, becoming a clerk with P. Lachance, a crockery merchant on the Rue du Palais in Quebec City. Five years later, armed with his meagre savings and the encouragement of his former employer, he went into business for himself in a small house in Lévis where he sold pottery and flour. This new enterprise was in an excellent location, at the intersection of the Côte du Passage, which led to the St Lawrence, and the "King's Road." Businesses such as those of Étienne Dalaire and Louis Carrier were already well established there.

In 1844 Couture established himself in his father's home at the same crossroads, where 20 years later he erected an impressive stone building to house the firm of "George & Ed. Couture," general merchants. In a short time George, who had taken his younger brother Louis-Édouard into partnership in 1861, was in control of most of the trading on the south shore. He amassed a sizeable fortune and became one of the largest landowners in Lévis. In the 1850s he had become interested in the ferryboat service between Quebec and Lévis, bought two boats (one from his brother Ignace, an enterprising businessman), and also built wharves. In 1863, when the town councils of Quebec and Lévis decided to assume direct control of the river crossing in order to end excessive competition, Couture formed a company with Pierre Barras, James Tibbits, and François-Théodule Foisy which obtained the contract to operate the ferry service for ten years.

His prominent position in the economic affairs of the region led Couture to take an interest in public life. In 1865 he was elected to the Lévis municipal council for the first time; from 1870 to 1881 he held the office of mayor; only in 1884 did illness force him to retire from municipal activities. From 1857 he had been a member of the toll-roads commission for the south shore, and was its chairman for several years. He was leader of the Conservative party for the counties of Lévis and Dorchester, and on 28 April 1881 was appointed to the Legislative Council of Quebec by the government of Joseph-Adolphe Chapleau*. He was remembered in the council as a man of few words who possessed an eminently practical mind.

George Couture ranked as one of the most generous benefactors of charitable works in Lévis. He was a churchwarden in 1852 when the parish of Notre-Dame-de-la-Victoire was created, and agreed that year to take part in the syndicate appointed by the archbishop of Quebec, Pierre-Flavien Turgeon*, to superintend the building of the Collège de Lévis [*see* Joseph-David DÉZIEL]. Each year he distributed his salary as legislative councillor among the religious communities of Quebec and Lévis. Thus in 1882 he gave $300 to the Hospice Saint-Joseph-de-la-Délivrance, $250 to the convent at Lévis, and $250 to the convent of the Sisters of the Good Shepherd at Quebec. In 1884 he was made a knight of the Order of the Holy Sepulchre in appreciation of his services to charitable organizations. His philanthropy has been compared to that of Joseph Masson*, Barthélemy Joliette*, and George Manly Muir.

George Couture left no descendants. On 3 Feb. 1846 he had married Marie, daughter of Pierre Roy, a farmer at Saint-Charles; the couple's four children died in infancy. After the death of his first wife he married Geneviève Jelly, the widow of Pierre Saint-Hilaire, on 5 June 1854 at Lévis, but they had no children.

George Couture, who was still to be seen behind his counter in his sixties, when he was at the height of his fortune and laden with honours, had already been held up to his contemporaries as a model of how to succeed by dint of hard work and perseverance.

PIERRE SAVARD

ANQ-Q, AP-G-239. *Le Canadien*, 7, 9 nov. 1887. *La Minerve*, 7 nov. 1887. P.-G. Roy, *Dates lévisiennes* (12v., Lévis, Qué., 1932–40), I–IV. J.-E. Roy, *Biographie de l'honorable George Couture, représentant au Conseil législatif la division de Lauzon* (Lévis, 1884).

COWESSESS. *See* KIWISĀNCE

COWLEY, ABRAHAM, Church of England clergyman and missionary; b. 8 April 1816 at Fairford (Gloucestershire), England, son of Robert and Mary Cowley; m. 26 Dec. 1840 Arabella Sainsbury of Marlborough, England, and they had three sons and a daughter; d. 11 Sept. 1887 at Selkirk, Man.

Abraham Cowley was admitted to Farmor's Endowed School in Fairford in November 1821 and he remained there until October 1828 when he was recorded as being "past age." Little is known of his life in these years and during the next decade, although the vicar of Fairford, Francis William Rice, later Lord Dynevor, maintained an interest in him. In 1839 he was admitted to the Church Missionary Society College in Islington (now part of London), England, where he was prepared for missionary work abroad. On 5 Jan. 1841, less than a fortnight after their marriage, Abraham and Arabella Cowley set out for Montreal on their way to the Red River Settlement in Rupert's Land. This unusual route was taken in the belief that the Cowleys would be able to travel with Bishop George Jehoshaphat Mountain* of Montreal who was planning a visitation of Rupert's Land. The couple arrived in Montreal on 28 February, and Cowley was ordained a deacon on 7 March. Bishop Mountain's visit to the northwest was postponed, however, and the Cowleys, seeing no hope of reaching the Red River Settlement from Montreal, returned to England and took ship almost immediately for Hudson Bay. They arrived in Red River on 28 Sept. 1841, having made three crossings of the Atlantic in nine months.

Cowley had assumed that on his arrival he would be ordained to the priesthood by Mountain, and that he would at first assist William Cockran* at Red River and then succeed him when he retired. This plan was scotched by Adam THOM, the recorder of Rupert's Land, who chose to challenge the competence of the bishop of Montreal in Rupert's Land [*see* John Smithurst*] and affirmed that Cowley's ordination as priest would be invalid in such circumstances. Cockran and Cowley agreed that until the matter was resolved Cowley should establish a mission among the Indians at some place away from Red River. Looking for "a suitable place for farming, abounding with wood and adjoining a good fishery," Cowley chose a site on the Little Dauphin River (now Dauphin River) between lakes Manitoba and St Martin where there was a considerable band of Saulteaux Indians. This mission was known as Partridge Crop, but in 1851, on his initial visit, David ANDERSON, the first bishop of Rupert's Land, changed the name to Fairford (Man.) as being more appropriate. On 7 July 1844, the controversy with Thom having blown over, Cowley had been ordained a priest at Red River by Bishop Mountain.

In his dealings with the Indians, Cowley does not seem to have been as understanding or considerate of their condition as some of his contemporaries. He railed at them for their failure to conform to a code of ethics which was foreign to them and therefore could have little meaning for them. On 28 Sept. 1846 he commented in his diary that now he felt he understood the Indians better and could talk more firmly to them. Yet his speaking of the love of God and at the same time threatening them with the pains and punishments of hell puzzled and distressed the Indians. He quoted one of them as saying of him: "we can understand when the blackcoat interprets the Word of God and when he speaks of life but when he turns it to the Indians and goes round afterwards bringing us all as it were into hell . . . we cannot understand it." Cowley was more successful in helping his charges to come to terms with agricultural life. A good farmer himself, he may have introduced a new strain of wheat to the region, and he encouraged the Indians in the raising of livestock and helped them to build houses. As did most of his peers, he took it for granted that the nomadic life was no longer practical for them.

The Cowleys left Fairford in 1854 to assist Cockran at the Indian Settlement (now Dynevor, Man.); they remained there until Cowley's death. He served for many years as secretary of the corresponding committee of the Church Missionary Society. In 1867 he received an honorary DD from St John's College in Winnipeg and succeeded Cockran, who had died two years earlier, as archdeacon of Cumberland. Also in 1867 his eldest son, serving with the Hudson's Bay Company in the Yukon, was drowned. The other children maintained the family association with the west.

F. A. PEAKE

CMS Arch., C, C.1/I, C.1/L, C.1/M, G1, C.1/P, and especially C.1/O, Journals of Abraham Cowley (mfm. at PAC). PAC, MG 19, E9. Church Missionary Soc., *Register of missionaries (clerical, lay, & female), and native clergy, from 1804 to 1904* ([London?, 1905?]), 55. A. Ross, *Red River Settlement*, 290. T. C. B. Boon, "St Peter's Dynevor, the original Indian settlement of western Canada," HSSM *Papers*, 3rd ser., no.9 (1954): 16–32. W. L. Morton, "Agriculture in the Red River colony," *CHR*, 30 (1949): 305–21.

CRAMP, JOHN MOCKETT, Baptist minister, author, and educator; b. 25 July 1796 at St Peter's (St Peter Extra), Isle of Thanet, England, son of Thomas Cramp and Rebecca Gouger; m. first 25 Sept. 1820 Maria Agate, and they had one daughter; m. secondly 1 Feb. 1826 Anne Burls, and they had eight children, one of whom, THOMAS, became a prominent Montreal businessman; d. 6 Dec. 1881 at Wolfville, N.S.

John Mockett Cramp was the son of a Baptist minister and was baptized and received into his father's church in September 1812. He was educated at Canterbury and then, for three years, at Stepney Theological Institute in London. On 7 May 1818 he was ordained minister and took charge of Dean Street Baptist Church, Southwark (now part of London); until 1844 he held pastorates in several parts of England. Cramp, however, was by inclination more the scholar than the pastor. His reading was both catholic and voluminous and was reflected in his writings. His first sermon was published in 1819 and he wrote extensively for most of the rest of his life – sermons, church history, biography, theological works, and hundreds of newspaper articles. From 1825 to 1828 he edited the *Baptist Magazine* and he became a partner in a publishing business, a venture that ended in financial disaster.

His growing reputation as a Baptist scholar led in 1844 to the offer of the presidency of the Canada Baptist College in Montreal, operated by the Canada Baptist Missionary Society. In spite of Cramp's efforts to establish the struggling college on a sound financial and scholastic footing, it collapsed in 1849 because it lacked strong denominational support. During his presidency, Cramp edited the *Montreal Register* and, after 1849, the *Colonial Protestant, and Journal of Literature and Science* and the *Pilot.* Cramp also took an active part in the affairs of both the denomination and the colony. He early became interested in the efforts of Henriette Feller [Odin*] to evangelize French Canadian Catholics, and in both Canada East and the Maritimes forged permanent links between Baptists and Madame Feller's Grande-Ligne mission.

In 1850 the board of governors of the newly formed Acadia College, the Baptist institution of higher learning opened early in 1839 in Wolfville, N.S., selected Cramp as president to succeed the Reverend John Pryor*. When he arrived at Acadia in June 1851, Cramp found the college on the verge of collapse, having only one professor, Isaac Chipman, few students, and no money; the Baptist community in the Maritimes had decided in 1850 that it was inconsistent with their advocacy of the separation of church and state to accept further government grants for Acadia College. Cramp, however, energetically set out to revive the institution and earned for himself the title "second founder" of Acadia. He launched a successful campaign among Maritime Baptists for endowment funds to provide a sound financial base for the college. In addition to his duties as president Cramp taught classical languages, history, philosophy, theology, logic, political economy, and even geology. His activities outside the college were equally wide ranging: he delivered a monthly public lecture, preached every Sunday evening, acted as unofficial assistant pastor of the Wolfville Baptist church, became actively involved in the temperance movement, edited the *Abstainer*, and the *Athenæum, and Journal of Temperance*, and still found time to read extensively and to write.

That Acadia College survived the disastrous 1850s is largely a result of Cramp's efforts, but his early years at Acadia were disappointing for him. He wrote sadly in his journal that "My services in the College were not so acceptable as I had hoped, and there was, besides, a strong desire for the return of [Edmund Albern CRAWLEY] to the College." Crawley, Acadia's founder and a professor there until his resignation in 1847, would, however, return only as president, so Cramp resigned his post in September 1853 to assume a position created for him as principal of the theological institute of the college. The major emphasis at Acadia remained, however, the education of laymen, who during Cramp's years at the college were twice as numerous as those studying theology.

It must have been with some bitterness that Cramp watched as Crawley mismanaged the newly established endowment fund, losing £3,410 (nearly one-third of the total) in mining stock speculation. After Crawley's resignation in September 1856, Cramp was appointed "chairman of faculty" and finally reappointed president on 18 Jan. 1860, a post he occupied until his retirement in 1869. It was during Cramp's second term as president that Acadia was placed on a secure footing. The college's endowment fund was enlarged to guarantee the salaries of the professors, and enrolment rose sharply. Cramp was able to attract able professors, among them James De Mille*; Crawley returned to teach in 1866.

Cramp spent his years of retirement actively furthering the interests that had preoccupied much of his life. Among his many published works are *Paul and Christ! A portraiture and an argument* (1873) and *A memoir of Madame Feller, with an account of the origin and progress of the Grande Ligne mission* (1876). He also wrote extensively for newspapers and magazines in both North America and Britain. Throughout his life one of the major forces in Cramp's thought was his aversion to tyranny and oppression, in whatever form they might appear. The "tyranny" imposed by rum would thus be opposed as strongly as political or military oppression. These same fears were the basis of his strong anti-Catholicism. His study of history, and especially of the Reformation, had led him to conclude that "Popery is friendly to that arbitrary power of the state, which it exercises in the church; and where its influence is unrestrained, free institutions cannot prosper." According to Cramp, "The popish system is a grand conspiracy against the authority of Christ and the rights of men; it tends to universal slavery, crouching man's industry, fetters his mind and corrupts his morals." For him, the lines were clearly drawn between ignorant superstition on the one hand and intelligent Christianity on the other. Catholicism, then, "must be swept from the face of the earth." His roles as writer and educator clearly were defined by his strong desire to free men's minds so that higher goals could be attained. His strongly held views often led him into controversy over such issues as public schooling, temperance, the Jamaica rebellions in 1865, and Baptist missions to Catholic communities.

His success in his chosen role of educator can be best measured by the prominence of the students who graduated from Acadia during his years there. Ministers such as Edward Manning Saunders*; educators of the calibre of Theodore Harding Rand* and Charles Frederick Hartt*; lawyers and politicians such as Sir Robert Linton Weatherbe*, Wallace Graham*, and Neil McLeod* all attest to the fact that Cramp's emphasis on education brought tangible results beyond even his expectations. Thus it is his work as an educator that remains Cramp's chief claim to recognition.

BARRY M. MOODY

[J. M. Cramp's works include: *Baptist history: from the foundation of the Christian church to the close of the eighteenth century* (London, 1868); *A catechism of Christian baptism* (Halifax, 1866); *The lamb of God* (London, 1871); *A memoir of Madame Feller, with an account of the origin and progress of the Grand Ligne mission* (London and Montreal, [1876]); *Paul and Christ! A portraiture and an argument* (London, 1873); *Scripture and tradition: a reply to Mr. Maturin's letter on "The claims of the Catholic Church," addressed to "the parishioners of St. Pauls, Halifax, Nova Scotia"* (Halifax, 1859); *A text-book of popery . . .* (London, 1831). Other works are listed in *Baptist authors: a manual of bibliography, 1500–1914*, comp. W. E. McIntyre (3v., Montreal and Toronto, [1914]), III: 170–71, *British Museum general catalogue*, and *National union catalog*. B.M.M.]

Acadia Univ. Arch. (Wolfville, N.S.), Acadia College endowment, List of subscribers, 1 Jan.–20 Sept. 1853; Board of Governors, Minutes, I, 1850–83. Atlantic Baptist Hist. Coll., J. M. Cramp, Journal (typescript). [S. W. DeBlois], *Historical sketch of the 1st Horton Baptist Church, Wolfville, for the period of one hundred years, from A.D., 1778, to A.D., 1878* (Halifax, 1879). *The Acadia record, 1838–1953*, comp. Watson Kirkconnell (4th ed., Wolfville, 1953). *Canadian literature in English*, comp. V. B. Rhodenizer (Montreal, 1965), 331–32. *The Baptists of Canada: a history of their progress and achievements*, ed. E. R. Fitch (Toronto, 1911). I. E. Bill, *Fifty years with the Baptist ministers and churches of the Maritime provinces of Canada* (Saint John, N.B., 1880). A. C. Chute and W. B. Boggs, *The religious life of Acadia* (Wolfville, 1933). T. A. Higgins, *The life of John Mockett Cramp, D.D., 1796–1881 . . .* (Montreal, 1887). *Jubilee of Acadia College, and memorial exercises* (Halifax, 1889). G. E. Levy, *The Baptists of the Maritime provinces, 1753–1946* (Saint John, 1946). R. S. Longley, *Acadia University, 1838–1938* (Wolfville, 1939); *The Wolfville United Baptist Church* (Kentville, N.S., 1954). E. M. Saunders, *History of the Baptists of the Maritime provinces* (Halifax, 1902). Sons of Temperance of North America, *Centennial, Sept. 29th 1942: the pioneer total abstinence order of North America, 1842–1942: one hundred years of service* ([Halifax, 1942]), 126, 191.

CRAMP, THOMAS, merchant and shipowner; b. in April 1827 on the Isle of Thanet, England, son of the Reverend John Mockett CRAMP, Baptist minister, and Anne Burls; m. 21 Jan. 1866 at Montreal, Canada East, Marianne Dunn, and they had a son and a daughter; d. 18 Feb. 1885 at Montreal.

Thomas Cramp was raised at St Peter's (St Peter Extra), Isle of Thanet, where his grandfather had been a Baptist minister and farmer. In April 1844 the family sailed for Canada when Thomas' father was appointed president of the Canada Baptist College in Montreal. Shortly after his arrival, Thomas entered the auction and commission brokerage firm of John Leeming and Company and he later joined John Torrance and Company, shippers, tea importers, grocers, and general merchants. When John Torrance* retired in 1853 his nephew David Torrance* succeeded him; Cramp's ability made him a partner in the firm which was now called David Torrance and Company, and by the 1870s he largely ran the business. A closely allied Toronto firm, Cramp, Torrances and Company, was opened in 1870, composed of Cramp and David's sons, John at Montreal and David at Toronto (the latter was replaced in 1873 by another brother George William). The Toronto firm purchased a large warehouse and had sales of nearly $1,000,000 in 1872.

Like most leading Montreal merchants in the mid-19th century, Cramp was involved in the incorporation of a good number of companies in association with his business partners and such other Montreal luminaries as Luther Hamilton Holton*, Hugh ALLAN, Edwin Atwater*, John Young*, and Charles John BRYDGES. These companies included the Canadian Inland Steam Navigation Company in 1857, the Montreal Railway Terminus Company and the Montreal Hydraulic and Dock Company in 1861, the Consumers' Gas Company of the City and District of Montreal in 1874, and his farthest flung venture, the Assiniboine Bridge Company in 1880 set up to build a bridge over the Red River in Manitoba. Unfortunately, several were hardly profitable enterprises. Cramp simultaneously sat on the boards of some of these companies, as well as on the boards of the Canada Guarantee Company; the Liverpool, London and Globe Insurance Company; the Union Bank of Canada; the Kingston and Montreal Forwarding Company; the North Western Colonization Company; and, most important, Molsons Bank, of which he was a director from 1872 until 1876. In addition, he was involved with real estate, owning a large residence on upper St Urbain Street, land on Dorchester and St Catherine streets, a block of brick stores, and nine villa lots.

Naturally interested in improving the commercial facilities of the city, Cramp was active on the board of trade; he was frequently a member of its council or of its board of arbitration from the 1850s until his death and was elected its president in 1863. He was a member of the Montreal Harbour Commission in 1860–61, 1863–66, and 1874–79 and became president on the death of John Young in 1878, but, being a staunch Liberal, was not reappointed by Sir John A. Macdonald*'s government in 1879 [*see* Andrew ROBERTSON]. From 1882 until his death Cramp participated in the Montreal Corn Exchange Association, where he began some much needed reforms.

Cramp's charitable activities paralleled his business interests in variety and scope. He helped incorporate the Montreal Library Society in 1859 and the Protestant Institution for Deaf-Mutes and for the Blind a decade later [*see* Joseph MACKAY]. In 1874 he became one of the incorporators and a life director of the Western Hospital of Montreal which had connections with Bishop's College and he was active in the Boys' Home of Montreal, founded in 1870. His wife also concerned herself with a number of benevolent organizations.

In 1876, on the death of David Torrance, Cramp became president of David Torrance and Company which was valued at about $500,000 (the Toronto firm was valued at $100,000). The business had been undergoing difficulties in previous years, partially connected with the depression, and since neither Cramp nor Torrance's sons possessed extensive personal capital, reorganization after Torrance's death was a problem. The difficulties came partly from the major involvement of the firm in the Mississippi and Dominion Steamship Company, founded in 1870 to trade with Liverpool from Montreal in the summer and from New Orleans in the winter. The New Orleans route was soon dropped and the firm became the Dominion Steamship Company Ltd, but the combination of depression, competition, and a series of accidents put the business in an uncertain position.

When Cramp died suddenly of a throat infection, his home, valued at $15,000, had to be sold to cover debts. John Torrance succeeded him as president of the Montreal firm, which continued for many years. The Dominion Steamship Company was sold in 1894, the shares realizing less than one-tenth of their original cost.

Cramp was popular in Montreal, where he helped incorporate the St James Club in 1858 and the Montreal Club in 1866. With such leading Liberal figures as Honoré Mercier* and Joseph-Raymond Fournier*, *dit* Préfontaine, he incorporated the Reform Club in 1881. He became an adherent of the Church of England and was a member and benefactor of St Martin's Church. By businessmen he was regarded as a person who carried out his commitments and his calm temper was a great aid in difficult negotiations. His career demonstrates how a young man with ability could work his way up in the commerce of Montreal in the second half of the 19th century.

FREDERICK H. ARMSTRONG

Thomas B. Cramp (Montreal) has papers of the Cramp family. Baker Library, R. G. Dun & Co. credit ledger, Canada, 5: 361; 7: 188; 27: 249–60. Can., *Statutes*, 1873, c.109; 1874, c.90; 1880, c.61. Can., Prov. of, *Statutes*, 1857, c.169, c.178; 1859, c.120; 1861, c.82, c.96. Que., *Statutes*, 1869, c.89; 1871, c.36; 1873–74, c.40, c.53; 1878, c.42; 1880, c.90; 1881, c.58. *Gazette* (Montreal), 19 Feb. 1885. *Montreal Daily Witness*, 21 Feb. 1885. *Montreal Herald and Daily Commercial Gazette*, 19 Feb. 1885. *Times* (Montreal), 18 Feb. 1885. *Dominion annual register*, 1885: 253–54. T. A. Higgins, *The life of John Mockett Cramp, D.D., 1796–1881* . . . (Montreal, 1887), 381–96.

CRAWFORD, ISABELLA VALANCY, author and poet: b. 25 Dec. 1850 in Dublin (Republic of Ireland), daughter of Dr Stephen Dennis Crawford and Sydney Scott; d. unmarried 12 Feb. 1887 at Toronto, Ont.

Of all the literary lives of her generation in Ontario, the life of Isabella Valancy Crawford is the most obscure. How she came to write in such a variety of styles, with such a range of subject matter, when she was isolated from fellowship with other authors is a matter of wonderment and speculation. Before 1972, when Mary F. Martin published "The short life of Isabella Valancy Crawford," the only biographical information available was offered by John William Garvin* in his preface to *The collected poems* (1905). His wife Katherine Hale added to that but neither biographer verified the poet's birthdate or origins. However, research at universities gained momentum in the 1970s. A reprint of the collected poems in 1972, with an introduction by poet James Reaney, made Crawford's work generally available; six of her short stories, edited by Penny Petrone, appeared in 1975; and in 1977 the Borealis Press published a book of fairy stories and a long unfinished poem, "Hugh and Ion." The poem had been discovered in the Queen's University Archives (Kingston, Ont.) by Dorothy Livesay, who named it "The Hunter's Twain." She also found, in Dublin Castle Archives, a genealogy of the Crawford family from 1616, when one William Crawford left "Cunningburne," Scotland, to settle in County Antrim (Northern Ireland). His direct descendent, Stephen Crawford, was listed as a voter in Donnybrook, Dublin, from 1836 but did not live there until 1845 (the year of his death). It is therefore possible that he also had apartments above his place of business on Grafton Street, and that his second son, Dr Stephen Dennis Crawford, may have brought his wife, Sydney Scott, to that address. No record has been found of that marriage or of the birthdates and birthplaces of at least six children, of whom Isabella wrote that she was the sixth.

Epidemics in Ireland may have led to the deaths of the first five children and to the decision to emigrate to Wisconsin. The parents' arrival date there and whether the infant Isabella accompanied them are not as yet known. But it is certain that another daughter, Emma Naomi, was born in Wisconsin in 1854, whereas a son, Stephen Walter, was born in 1856 in Ireland. In a history of the Crawford family being written by a direct descendant of this son, Mrs Catherine Humphrey, the author propounds the theory that Mrs Crawford returned to Dublin for the birth of her son whilst the doctor went to Canada in search of a home. Penny Petrone has found in the registry office at Walkerton, Ont., a record of an 1858 transaction in Paisley, Canada West, which concerned a domicile in the name of "Mrs Sydney Crawford."

The only existing account of Crawford's early childhood in Paisley tells of the genteel style of living of this Scots-Irish family, a style that must have been a cover for poverty. In a letter, a neighbour of the Crawfords reports that in an outlying settlement like Paisley a doctor's duties were largely those of midwifery, and that payment was often in kind; however, "women were afraid to have him [Dr Crawford] as he was a heavy drinker, but very clever if sober." An anonymous account (probably emanating from one of the Strickland family) records how the family left the pioneer farming community in 1864 for the more established settlement of Douro Township: "They seemed to be very poorly off and we felt real sorry for them in Canada amidst such unsuitable surroundings. My brother, knowing that there was no resident physician in the village of Lakefield, made to them the following offer. That they move to Lakefield and make use of his home during the months in which he would be away from the village." Lakefield was a more sophisticated community, containing as it did Samuel Strickland*'s "Farm School" for gentlemen agriculturalists. But it was his sisters, the writers Susanna Moodie [STRICKLAND] and Catharine Parr Traill [Strickland*], who must have fascinated the young Crawfords. Mrs Traill's daughter Katie (Katharine Agnes) is thought to have been a close companion of Isabella. Moreover the Traills had a summer cottage near a Stony Indian reserve where the young girl might have picked up her interest in Indian legends and beliefs. The image of the canoe is recurrent in Crawford's poetry and she must have delighted in canoeing on the Otonabee River and Kawartha Lake, where the Indians hunted and fished amongst the water lilies. In direct contrast to this wilderness was the bustling market town of Peterborough, where Dr Crawford set up practice in 1869.

In the Peterborough years Crawford began sending poems and stories to newspapers which she would have found in the mechanics' institute. The Toronto *Mail* was the first known publisher of a poem by Crawford, "The Vesper Star," on 24 Dec. 1873. When Dr Crawford died, on 3 July 1875, the three women became dependent on Isabella's literary earnings. There had been a quarterly stipend from the doctor's youngest brother, Dr John Irwin Crawford, in Ireland, but this ceased at some time, perhaps as early as the move to Peterborough. Isabella's only living brother, Stephen Walter, had left home at 16 to seek work in northern Ontario and, though from time to time he visited his widowed mother and apparently endeavoured to help, he married in 1886 and had a family of his own to care for. Another blow had come when Emma Naomi died in 1876 at 21 "from consumption." Faced with all their difficulties, the poet must have persuaded her mother that Toronto, the publishing centre of English Canada, was the place where she could best earn a living. When they left Peterborough is not known.

The story of Isabella Valancy Crawford's literary struggles has been vividly sketched by Katherine Hale in the introduction to her anthology. Crawford published one book of poetry, *Old Spookses' Pass, Malcolm's Katie and other poems*, at her own expense in 1884. For this she received scant reward in her lifetime (only 50 copies were sold), although there were notices in such London journals as the *Spectator*, the *Graphic*, the *Leisure Hour*, and the *Saturday Review*. These articles pointed to "versatility of talent," and to such qualities as "humour, vivacity, and range of power," which were impressive and promising despite her extravagance of incident and "untrained magniloquence." In the 20th century critics have given the work increasing respect and appreciation.

In Toronto from 1883 until her death in 1887 the poet lived with her mother in boarding-houses on Adelaide Street, then in rooms at 180 Adelaide Street West, and then at 57 John Street, sending out a quantity of "occasional" verse to the Toronto papers, a number of serialized novels and novellas for Frank Leslie's New York publications, and articles for the *Fireside Monthly*. In 1886 she became the first local writer to have a novel, *A little Bacchante*, serialized in the *Evening Globe*. For the most part Crawford's prose followed the fashion of the *feuilleton* of the day. It was romantic-Gothic "formula fiction." Yet there are indications that the young woman possessed other gifts, such as the ability to write *contes* concerning pioneer life in Canada West. Her fairy stories written in Lakefield reveal a youthful delight in music, poetry, and nature.

A woman of brilliant intellect, well acquainted with world culture, Isabella had grown up not in her parents' Dublin but in a pioneer society. It must have become clear to her early that there would be few sympathizers with her imaginative gifts, and she would have to leave them aside to earn a living for herself and her mother. The only avenue open was the popular magazines and newspapers, and for them she wrote light "homely" verse, humorous sketches, short romantic stories, and melodramatic novelettes. Her creative life was far from that of Emily Dickinson who perfected her poetry in seclusion.

Yet Isabella's poetry has survived. Although no comprehensive critical analysis of her work has yet been published, the poetry is now receiving serious study. She was, in one sense, a Victorian poet, for whom Tennyson was the guide and idol. But in her long poems, "Malcolm's Katie," an idyll recreating the backwoods life of farm and forest, and "Old Spookses' Pass," relating a stampede during a cattle drive through the Rockies, she displays a remarkable flair for narrative, and for combining plot, theme, and characterization with an exuberant and arresting use of imagery. In the former poem she presents a new myth of great significance to Canadian literature: the Canadian frontier as creating "the conditions for a new Eden," not a golden age or a millennium, but "a harmonious community, here and now." Crawford's social consciousness and concern for humanity's future committed her, far ahead of her time and milieu, to write passionate pleas for brotherhood, pacifism, and the preservation of a green world. Her deeply felt belief in a just society wherein men and women would have equal status in a world free from war, class hatred, and racial prejudice dominates all her finest poetry regardless of whether she was using Graeco-Roman, Vedantist, Scandinavian, or North American Indian sources. These are sources that Longfellow too used but one has only to consider the imaginative intensity and the originality of language in her Indian "South Wind" sequences or in "Gisli, the Chieftain" to recognize how great was her talent and how well her poetry stands up to comparison with the work of her contemporaries.

DOROTHY LIVESAY

[Although only one book, *Old Spookses' Pass, Malcolm's Katie, and other poems* ([Toronto], 1884), was published during her lifetime, Isabella Valancy Crawford's contributions to newspapers and journals consisted not only of numerous poems but also of many prose works including: "A five-o'clock tea" which appeared in volume 17 (January-June 1884): 287–91, of *Frank Leslie's Popular Monthly* (New York); "Extradited" which was published in the *Globe*, 4 Sept. 1886, and was republished in volume 2 (1973), no. 3: 168–73, of the *Journal of Canadian Fiction* (Montreal); and "A little Bacchante" which was serialized in the *Evening Globe* in 1886. J. W. Garvin edited the first posthumous collection of her poetry, *The collected poems of Isabella Valancy Crawford* (Toronto, 1905); 18 years later his wife, Katherine Hale, published *Isabella Valancy Crawford* (Toronto), an anthology of poetry which also included biographical information. The 1970s saw a rebirth of interest in the work of Crawford, and Garvin's collection was reprinted in 1972 (Toronto and Buffalo, N.Y.) with an introduction by James Reaney. Three years later *Selected stories of Isabella Valancy Crawford*, edited by Penny Petrone and published in Ottawa, appeared and, in 1977, a previously undiscovered poem, named *Hugh and Ion*, was published by Glenn Clever.

More complete descriptions of Crawford's works can be found in "Annotated bibliography of Isabella Valancy Crawford," comp. Lynne Suo, *Essays on Canadian Writing* (Downsview, Ont.), 11 (summer 1978): 289–314, and "A preliminary checklist of the writings of Isabella Valancy Crawford," comp. Margo Dunn, *The Crawford symposium*, ed. F. M. Tierney (Ottawa, 1979), 141–55.

Most of Crawford's unpublished writing is held by the Queen's University Archives and is described in *A catalogue of Canadian manuscripts collected by Lorne Pierce and presented to Queen's University*, [comp. Dorothy Harlowe, ed. E. C. Kyte] (Toronto, 1946), 100–4. D.L.]

Evening News (Toronto), 13 June 1884. *Evening Telegram* (Toronto), 12 June 1884, 14 Feb. 1887. *Globe*, 14 June 1884, 14 Feb. 1887. *Graphic: an Illustrated Weekly Newspaper* (London), 4 April 1885. *Illustrated London News*, 3 April 1886. *Leisure Hour* (London), 34 (1885): 165. *Mail* (Toronto), 24 Dec. 1873. *Saturday Rev. of Politics, Literature, Science, and Art* (London), 23 May 1885. *Spectator* (London), 18 Oct. 1884. *Varsity* (Toronto), 23 Jan. 1886. *Week* (Toronto), 11 Sept. 1884, 24 Feb. 1887. *The Crawford symposium*, ed. F. M. Tierney (Ottawa, 1979). Roy Daniells, "Crawford, Carman, and D. C. Scott," *Literary history of Canada: Canadian literature in English*, ed. C. F. Klinck *et al.* (Toronto, 1965), 406–10. Margo Dunn, "The development of narrative in the writing of Isabella Valancy Crawford" (MA thesis, Simon Fraser Univ., Burnaby, B.C., 1975). Pelham Edgar, "English-Canadian literature," *The Cambridge history of English literature*, ed. A. W. Ward and A. R. Waller (15v., Cambridge, Eng., 1907–27), XIV: 343–60. S. R. MacGillivray, "Theme and imagery in the poetry of Isabella Valancy Crawford" (MA thesis, Univ. of New Brunswick, Fredericton, 1963). C. F. MacRae, "The Victorian age in Canadian poetry" (PHD thesis, Univ. of Toronto, 1953). Patricia O'Brien, "Isabella Valancy Crawford," *Peterborough, land of shining waters: an anthology* (Peterborough, Ont., 1967), 379–83. James Reaney, "Isabella Valancy Crawford," *Our living tradition, second and third series*, ed. R. L. McDougall (Toronto, 1959), 268–88.

Frank Bessai, "The ambivalence of love in the poetry of Isabella Valancy Crawford," *Queen's Quarterly*, 77 (1970): 404–18. L. J. Burpee, "Isabella Valancy Crawford: a Canadian poet," *Poet Lore: A Magazine of Letters* ([Boston]), 13 (1901): 575–86. H. W. Charlesworth, "The Canadian girl: an appreciative medley," *Canadian Magazine*, 1 (March–October 1893): 186–93. J. M. Elson, "Pen sketches of Canadian poets: Isabella Valancy Crawford," *Onward: a Paper for Young Canadians* (Toronto), 5 March 1932. Dorothy Farmiloe, "I. V. Crawford: the growing legend," *Canadian Literature* (Vancouver), 81 (summer 1979): 143–47. Northrop Frye, "Canada and its poetry," *Canadian Forum* (Toronto), 23 (1943–44): 207. Robert Fulford, "Isabella Crawford: grandmother figure of Canadian literature," *Toronto Star*, 10 Feb. 1973: 77. J. W. Garvin, "Who's who in Canadian literature: Isabella Valancy Crawford," *Canadian Bookman* (Toronto), 9 (1927): 131–33. E. J. Hathaway, "How Canadian novelists are using Canadian opportunities," *Canadian Bookman* (Sainte-Anne-de-Bellevue, Que.), 1 (1919), [no.31]: 18–22; "Isabella Valancy Crawford," *Canadian Magazine*, 5 (May–October 1895): 569–72. K. J. Hughes, "Democratic vision of 'Malcolm's Katie,'" *CVII: Contemporary Verse Two* (Winnipeg), 1 (1975), no.2: 38–46. K. J. Hughes and Birk Sproxton, "'Malcolm's Katie': images and songs," *Canadian Literature*, 65 (summer 1975): 55–64. Donald Jones, "Canadian poetess' home discovered on King Street," *Toronto Star*, 29 Nov. 1980: H8. Dorothy Livesay, "The hunters twain," *Canadian Literature*, 55 (winter 1973): 75–98; "Tennyson's daughter or wilderness child? The factual and the literary background of Isabella Valancy Crawford," *Journal of Canadian Fiction*, 2: 161–67. M. F. Martin, "The short life of Isabella Valancy Crawford," *Dalhousie Rev.*, 52 (1972–73): 390–400. J. B. Ower, "Isabella Valancy Crawford: 'The canoe,'" Canadian Literature, 34 (autumn 1967): 54–62. E. M. Pomeroy, "Isabella Valancy Crawford," *Paisley Advocate* (Paisley, Ont.), 12 Feb. 1930; "Isabella Valancy Crawford (December 24th, 1850–February 12th, 1887)," *Canadian Poetry Magazine* (Toronto), 7 (1943–44), no.4: 36–38. "A rare genius recalled," *Globe*, 13 March 1926. C. S. Ross, "I. V. Crawford's prose fiction," *Canadian Literature*, 81: 47–59. M. M. Wilson, "Isabella Valancy Crawford," *Globe*, Saturday magazine sect., 15, 22 April 1905. Ann Yeoman, "Towards a native mythology: the poetry of Isabella Valancy Crawford," *Canadian Literature*, 52 (spring 1972): 39–47.

CRAWLEY, EDMUND ALBERN, lawyer, Baptist minister, businessman, and educator; b. 20 Jan. 1799 at Ipswich, England, son of Thomas Crawley, a captain in the Royal Navy, and Esther Bernal; m. first in 1833 Julia Amelia Wilby, and they had one son; m. secondly in 1843 Elizabeth Johnston, and they had six children; d. 27 Sept. 1888 at Wolfville, N.S.

When he was five years old, Edmund Albern Crawley's family moved from England to settle near Sydney, Cape Breton Island, where his father held the position of crown surveyor. In 1816 Crawley entered King's College in Windsor, N.S., and was graduated BA in 1820. He then studied law in James William Johnston*'s Halifax law office and was admitted to the bars of both Nova Scotia and New Brunswick in 1822. He became identified with the Halifax group of socially prominent Anglican evangelicals, including Johnston and James Walton Nutting*, who in 1825 left the Anglican St Paul's Church and in 1827 founded the Granville Street Baptist Church. Crawley, who was baptized by immersion on 1 June 1828 and joined the church, soon felt called to the ministry. Giving up his law practice, from 1828 to 1830 he studied in Massachusetts at the Congregationalist Andover Theological Seminary and then in 1830–31 at Baptist-dominated Brown University in Providence, R.I. He was ordained minister at Providence on 16 May 1830 and the following year returned to Halifax to become pastor of the Granville Street Baptist Church, a post he held until 1839.

It was in the field of education, however, that Crawley made his most significant contributions to Nova Scotian development. Early in 1828, together with Edward Manning*, Charles TUPPER, and Nutting, he spearheaded the drive to provide educational facilities for the Nova Scotia Baptist community. Crawley later wrote that at this time Baptists "were regarded as occupying the lowest rank in religious estimation – were in fact despised as an ignorant and deluded sect." To help raise the educational level of the Baptist community, and especially of its ministers, Crawley and his associates in June 1828 presented resolutions to the meeting of the Nova Scotia Baptist Association urging the establishment of Horton Academy at Wolfville, N.S. As a result, the Nova Scotia Baptist Education Society was established to found the academy and Crawley was elected one of the society's two secretaries, a position he filled until 1837.

Baptists continued to be excluded from the Anglican King's College in Windsor, and were forced to send their Horton Academy graduates to the United States for a college education, where many of them stayed permanently. To alleviate this problem Crawley in the mid 1830s supported the efforts of Thomas McCulloch*, a Free Church Presbyterian minister and educator in Pictou, N.S., to reconstitute Dalhousie College in Halifax as a non-denominational institution of higher learning. It would appear to have been Crawley who persuaded the Baptists, some of whom wanted to elevate Horton Academy to college status, to support instead the Dalhousie plan. However, when in September 1838 he was denied a promised teaching position in the new "provincial" college because of his Baptist affiliation, his anger knew no bounds. Outraged at this "betrayal," Crawley joined with John Pryor*, Ingraham E. Bill*, and others to persuade the Nova Scotia Baptist Association to proceed with the establishment of a Baptist college in Wolfville. By early 1839 Queen's College (renamed Acadia College in 1841) was operating with Crawley and Pryor sharing the teaching and administrative duties. Until 1847, when he returned to pastoral work in Halifax, Crawley was one of the major driving forces behind the institution.

In 1853 Crawley reluctantly agreed to leave his Halifax church and return to the college, which was suffering from financial difficulties and a small enrolment. However, he would accept no subservient position, and thus forced the recently appointed president, John Mockett CRAMP, to relinquish that office. Crawley's term as president was a disaster from which the college very nearly did not recover. On his advice the board of governors invested £3,410 (approximately one-third of the recently raised endowment fund) in the West Columbia Mining and Manufacturing Company of Cincinnati, Ohio, a speculation to which Crawley and many other leading Baptists were already heavily committed. During a trip to the United States in December 1854, he found the company on the verge of ruin, and on the basis of his own heavy investment and that of his friends, he assumed the presidency of the company early in 1855. A deeply divided and embittered Acadia board of governors gave him a one year's leave of absence. This period proved insufficient and Crawley severed his ties with Acadia in September 1856.

The years that followed were disastrous ones for Crawley himself. In spite of his best efforts, the mining company collapsed, carrying with it the Crawley family fortunes and the Acadia investment. Crawley was reduced to near destitution and his misery was compounded when his nephew and close associate, Thomas Henry Crawley, was stabbed to death on the streets of Cincinnati. A girls' school, Mount Auburn Female Seminary, established by Crawley in 1856 on the outskirts of Cincinnati, also proved a failure. Through the intervention of an old friend, he was appointed in 1860 joint president of Lime Stone Springs Female College in Spartanburg County, S.C., but the outbreak of civil war the following year forced the closing of the college. Crawley spent the war years teaching in a private school in Shelby, N.C.

In 1865 he was invited to return to Acadia College where he taught from 1866 to 1882, the last 13 years as principal of the college's theological institute. He had been awarded the honorary degree of DD by Brown University in 1844 and was given a DCL by King's College, Windsor, in 1887.

Crawley was without doubt one of the most ambitious and aggressive of the Maritime Baptist leaders of the 19th century. He was an early proponent of a system of public schools supported by compulsory tax assessment, instituted by the government of Charles Tupper* in 1866, and a frequent adversary of Joseph Howe*, whose plans for making Dalhousie a provincial university dictated his attacks on denominational colleges such as Acadia. Vitally interested in education, foreign missions, and general denominational progress, Crawley was none the less also interested in his own advancement. The founding of Acadia itself was to some extent a result of this characteristic. He could at times be rather high-handed in his drive for proper recognition, as is seen in his relations with J. M. Cramp. Crawley was a man who engendered either great loyalty among his supporters or great animosity among his opponents. Throughout his life, he remained generally unpopular within the Baptist denomination as a whole, except among a small circle of influential leaders. For many he remained too much the upper-class, urban intellectual within a denomination that was still predominantly lower class and rural.

BARRY M. MOODY

Acadia Univ. Arch. (Wolfville, N.S.), Board of Governors, Minutes, I, 1850–83. Atlantic Baptist Hist. Coll., E. A. Crawley, Corr. and letterbook; Edward Manning, Corr., 1778–1859.

Origin and formation of the Baptist church in Granville-Street, Halifax, N.S. . . . (Halifax, 1828). *Christian Messenger* (Halifax), 1838. *Novascotian*, 1838. *The Acadia record, 1838–1953*, comp. Watson Kirkconnell (4th ed., Wolfville, N.S., 1953). Andover Theological Seminary, *General catalogue, 1808–1908* (Boston, Mass., 1909). I. E. Bill, *Fifty years with the Baptist ministers and churches of the Maritime provinces of Canada* (Saint John, N.B., 1880). A. W. H. Eaton, *The history of Kings County, Nova Scotia . . .* (Salem, Mass., 1910; repr. Belleville, Ont., 1972). *Jubilee of Acadia College, and memorial exercises* (Halifax, 1889). G. E. Levy, *The Baptists of the Maritime provinces, 1753–1946* (Saint John, 1946). R. S. Longley, *Acadia University, 1838–1938* (Wolfville, 1939). E. M. Saunders, *History of the Baptists of the Maritime provinces* (Halifax, 1902).

CREIGHTON, JOHN, bookseller, publisher, municipal politician, and prison administrator; b. 19 Aug. 1817 near Clandeboye, County Down (Northern Ireland), son of Hugh Creighton and Mary Young; m. 8 Oct. 1850 Frances Coverdale, sister of Kingston carpenter and architect William Coverdale*, and they had eight children; d. 31 Jan. 1885 at Portsmouth (now part of Kingston), Ont.

The eldest of four brothers, John Creighton came with his family to Kingston, Upper Canada, in 1823. He attended the Midland District Grammar School along with John A. Macdonald* who remained a life-long friend. After serving as an apprentice printer to John Lovell* in Montreal, he worked for the Kingston *Chronicle & Gazette* and rose to press foreman. In 1846 he transferred to the Kingston *Argus* as printer and manager and also contributed articles on mercantile affairs. He became an elder of St Andrew's Presbyterian Church, served on church committees, and taught Sunday school. In 1844 he was elected president of the Kingston Typographical Society, an early trade union, and during his term sought to prevent the employment of apprentices in place of journeymen printers.

Creighton moved to New York State in 1848 but returned to Kingston the following year, and in 1851 became a clerk in a book and stationery store which he soon purchased. By 1853 he had added a job printing department and bookbindery which were both managed by his brother, James Moore Creighton, until his death in 1865. Some publications were issued under his own imprint, "John Creighton," others under his brother's, "James M. Creighton." Together they published many pamphlets, sermons and religious tracts, the Botanical Society of Canada *Annals*, at least three volumes of verse, including Charles Sangster*'s *The St. Lawrence and the Saguenay, and other poems* (1856), some prose fiction, and local history.

From 1859 to 1862, John Creighton served on the Kingston City Council as alderman for Victoria ward; in 1863 he was elected mayor, and was returned by acclamation in 1864 and 1865. As mayor he enlarged City Park, improved sanitary conditions in the town market place, and, after urging public support for poor relief, was voted $800 by council to disburse as he saw fit. When fire destroyed the market wing of the city hall in January 1865, Creighton received authorization to rebuild it and to procure a clock for the dome.

Although Creighton was appointed police magistrate in 1866 and acting warden of the Kingston Penitentiary in October 1870, he continued in private business until the government of Sir John A. Macdonald named him warden in January 1871. He was the most respected warden in the history of the institution, and was also perhaps the most successful. He was an efficient administrator, and a humane and far-sighted leader in penal reform. His primary aim was not punishment but rehabilitation. He impressed upon his staff that even the worst offenders deserved compassion and four-fifths of them would respond to firm but kindly treatment. He considered lashings degrading to the prisoners and repugnant to his own feelings, though necessary as a last resort to restrain unruly convicts. On the few occasions when he did order the lash, he attended with the prison doctor and often remitted part of the punishment.

Creighton believed that the first step towards moral reformation of the inmates was improvement of their physical condition. His changes included improved lighting, heating, and ventilation, better shoes, uniforms, and bedding, close inspection of all kitchen supplies, and a more varied diet. Exercise periods were doubled in length and extended to all prisoners. He ate his own meals in the prison dining hall, personally heard complaints, and visited the men in their cells, in the workshops, on the penitentiary farm, and in the stone quarries. He started a lending library, improved the school equipment, began night classes, and inaugurated prison entertainment by the inmates on holidays.

In October 1873, after visiting six of the larger American penal institutions including Sing Sing Prison in New York State, Creighton noted with satisfaction that "in none of these Institutions are the convicts so well fed or clothed as with us." Among the convicts at Kingston were Fenian prisoners arrested in 1866. One of them when released invited Creighton to his wedding; another testified that he "could not say anything but what was gentlemanly towards that noble Warden Creighton for I love and esteem him as if he were my own Father or Brother." James George Moylan*, federal prisons inspector, had an equally high regard for Creighton's achievements. In his report for 1881–82 to Sir Alexander Campbell*, the minister of justice, Moylan noted that the buildings and improvements carried out by convict labour during Creighton's term of office amounted in value to $120,000, but cost less than $20,000, "tangible and convincing proof . . . of experience and good judgment in administering the Penitentiary." In 1884 Moylan pointed out that although Creighton had served under seven ministers of justice, there had never been an inquiry into his administration. The prisoners' high regard for him was reflected in their "admirable discipline" during an enforced absence when stricken with a heart attack "by too close attention to his work." Despite a second attack in 1884 he continued working until a few days before his death.

H. PEARSON GUNDY

Correctional Staff College (Kingston, Ont.), Canadian Penitentiary Service Museum, Warden John Creighton's journal, 1870–74 (mfm. at QUA). PAC, RG 31, A1, 1861 census, Frontenac County. QUA, Corporation of the City of Kingston, Minutes of council, 1852–66; Reports of committees, 1852–66; A. E. Lavell papers, Unpub. hist. of Kingston penitentiary; Midland District School Soc., Board of Trustees, Minutes. St Andrew's Church (Kingston), Marriage registers.

Can., Parl., *Sessional papers*, 1871–84 (reports of the inspector of penitentiaries of the Dominion of Canada). *Chronicle and News*, 6 Oct. 1865. *Daily British Whig*, 31 Jan. 1885. *Daily News* (Kingston), 3 Jan. 1871, 31 Jan. 1885. *Globe*, 2 Feb. 1885. *Weekly British Whig*, 5 Feb. 1885. J. A. Edmison, "The history of Kingston Penitentiary," *Historic Kingston*, no. 3 (1954): 26–35.

CREVIER, JOSEPH-ALEXANDRE, doctor and naturalist; b. 26 Feb. 1824 at Cap-de-la-Madeleine, Lower Canada, son of Frédéric-François Crevier, *dit* Bellerive, a merchant, and Louise Rocheleau; m. in 1850, at Saint-Hyacinthe, Canada East, Zoé-Henriette Picard, *dit* Destroismaisons, and they had two sons and four daughters; d. 1 Jan. 1889 in Montreal, Que.

After studying with his uncle Édouard-Joseph Crevier, who later became vicar general of the diocese of Saint-Hyacinthe and founder of the Collège Sainte-Marie-de-Monnoir, Joseph-Alexandre Crevier received a classical education at the Collège de Chambly, then at the Séminaire de Saint-Hyacinthe. One of the first students of the Montreal School of Medicine and Surgery, he received his licence to practise in 1849 and took up residence at Saint-Hyacinthe. From 1861 to 1872 he practised at Saint-Césaire, where he began a long series of scientific and popular publications. A tall man, with a broad brow and a bushy beard, whose timidity probably stemmed from a speech defect, Crevier was an eccentric, more at home in his laboratory, in his workshop (shaping wood and metal, or polishing the mirrors of his telescopes), and on geological expeditions in the field, than he was in society. In a somewhat slipshod manner, he wrote on most of the sciences, for his curiosity and erudition ranged from interest in the infinitely small to astronomy. Léon Provancher*, who chided him in a friendly way for spreading himself too thin, rated him highly and made him a member of his ephemeral Société d'histoire naturelle de Québec, and named two insects, the *Meniscus* and the *Epyrhissa Crevieri*, after Crevier, the discoverer of the *Ichneumon Marianapolitensis*, of the same genus. Crevier's collection contained 1,443 specimens, mainly of Canadian minerals, fossils, molluscs, insects, and plants, as well as 656 microscopic preparations.

Crevier gained a reputation as a scientist through his articles in *Le Naturaliste canadien* and in newspapers before he went to Montreal in 1872. He was essentially a popularizer and a naturalist whose knowledge of taxonomy was not comparable to that of his compatriot, Augustin De Lisle*. Although in practising his art he displayed the researcher's bent, he was self-taught and unaccustomed to the rigorous discipline of the scientific method. Hence his study on bufonine (a venom contained in the warts of the toad) whose toxicity he claimed to have demonstrated through subcutaneous injections that killed animals, is interesting but inconclusive. In 1866 he had published an *Étude sur le choléra asiatique*, which was as remarkable as it was debatable. Through microscopic examination of the faeces of cholera victims of the 1854 epidemic, he had discovered a micro-organism which was unknown to him. In four years of observing microzoa and microphytes collected in rivers, lakes, and ponds he found none resembling it. This confirmed his opinion that a bacterium was the agent of the cholera. His contemporaries, such as Jean-Gaspard Bibaud, attributed the contagion to unexplained emanations from plants or sick animals. A distinction was not always made between *cholèra morbus*, an infinitely more serious disease, and relatively benign diarrhœic infections. Thus, the remarkable therapeutic efficacy of "Dr. Crevier's celebrated anticholeric and antidyspeptic drops" made diagnosis of the disease and identification of its cause even more uncertain. But this modest country doctor's assertion that a contagious disease was microbial in origin makes him one of the numerous obscure forerunners of Louis Pasteur.

In 1873 Crevier pointed out the presence of pathogenic animalculae in the stagnant waters of certain districts of Montreal, delivered a lecture on infusoria, and gave a course on "micrology" at the Montreal School of Medicine and Surgery. He asserted in *L'Album de la Minerve* (Montreal) that he had discovered *Bacterium variolare*. the agent of smallpox (which is in fact a viral disease). It was soon raging in Montreal, and Crevier came out against compulsory vaccination. At the height of the 1875 epidemic, he even proposed that a league be formed to fight vaccination. Because the needles were often inserted in one arm after another without being re-sterilized, or were used with undiluted vaccine, he had reason to fear that vaccination would transmit smallpox and other serious diseases. He set little store by the contrary opinions of his colleagues, especially those who had founded the Montreal Medical Society and were publishing *L'Union médicale du Canada*. Its editor was Dr Jean-Philippe Rottot and the journal called to order doctors who resorted to publicity to ensure the sale of their own patent remedies.

Crevier's lectures and articles on geology and the origin of the earth won him a reputation as a materialist and free-thinker; he joined the Institut Canadien of Montreal at the time of the last reverberations of the Joseph Guibord* affair. With journalist Auguste ACHINTRE, he published an interesting monograph on the Île Sainte-Hélène, and, with Dr Guillaume-Sylvain de Bonald* and some other Frenchmen, he taught at the Institut National des Beaux-Arts at Montreal directed by the mysterious Abbé Joseph Chabert*. Crevier was at the height of his fame when Elkanah Billings*, the palaeontologist to the Geological Survey of Canada, died in 1876. He was proposed as the successor to Billings, to whom he had supplied numerous fossils, including a new species of gastropod which he had called *Pleurotomaria Crevieri*. Despite exaggerated praise of Crevier by Chabert, who assumed he was as good as appointed, and the unanimous backing of the French-language press in Montreal, he did not obtain the post. Joseph Frederick Whiteaves*, a member of the survey who enjoyed the support not only of the English-language press but also of the director, Alfred Richard Cecil Selwyn*, was chosen by the government.

The following year, the Montreal School of Medicine and Surgery opened the chair of histology and microscopy to competition. Crevier drafted part of the discourse required for the examination, but as the date of the competition was not announced for a long time, he lost interest. His scientific activity slowed as publicity increased for his blood and hair restorer drops. He planned to present his remedy for cholera to the Académie Nationale de Médecine in Paris, and reworked his study on the question. Louis-Honoré Fréchette*, a friend of 25 years' standing, urged him to communicate his work to the recently founded Royal Society of Canada. For some years before his death he was cultivating and studying the tuberculosis microbe. Two years after his death, a species of mollusc discovered by him was named *Unio Provancheriana*.

Fréchette aptly described Crevier: "He was like certain unschooled artists, who, forced to educate themselves by puzzling out even the most elementary methods involved in their work, sometimes achieve a masterpiece without ever attaining full mastery of their art."

LÉON LORTIE

[The Crevier collection was willed to the Collège Saint-Laurent in Montreal, but was apparently lost because there is no mention of it in the chapter on the college's museum in *Sainte-Croix au Canada, 1847–1947* (Montréal, 1947).

In addition to articles published in *La Minerve*, *Le Monde canadien* (Montréal), *Le National* (Montréal), *Le Naturaliste canadien* (Québec), *L'Opinion publique*, *La Patrie*, *La Presse*, *L'Union médicale du Canada* (Montréal), and other periodicals in the years from 1859 to 1885, Joseph-Alexandre Crevier published two pamphlets: *Étude sur le choléra asiatique* ([Saint-Césaire, Qué.], 1866); *Le choléra, son historique, son origine, sa nature* (Montréal, 1885). In collaboration with Auguste Achintre, he wrote: *L'Île Ste. Hélène: passé, présent et avenir; géologie, paléontologie, flore et faune* (Montréal, 1876). L.L.]

J.-G. Bibaud, *Quelques considérations sur les causes et l'hygiène des maladies contagieuses et le choléra en particulier* (Montréal, 1866). Joseph Chabert, *Le premier Canadien nommé à l'éminente charge de paléontologiste de la Commission géologique du Canada* (Montréal, 1877). L.-H. Fréchette, "Mémoires intimes; le docteur Crevier," *Le Monde illustré* (Montréal), 10 nov. 1900: 434–35; 17 nov. 1900: 450; 24 nov. 1900: 467. Jacques Rousseau, "Le docteur J.-A. Crevier, médecin et naturaliste (1824–1889)," Assoc. canadienne-française pour l'avancement des sciences, *Annales* (Montréal), 6 (1940): 173–269.

CROFT, HENRY HOLMES, professor of chemistry and author; b. 6 March 1820 in London, England, youngest son of William Croft; m. in 1844 Mary Shaw, and they had seven children; d. 1 March 1883 at Las Hermanitas, near San Diego, Tex.

Henry Holmes Croft, after attending London schools, became a clerk in the Ordnance Office (his father was deputy paymaster general of ordnance) and attended University College, London, as an occasional student. There he developed an intense interest in experimental chemistry, which he pursued in a home-built laboratory in the family residence. Observing this preoccupation, his father sought advice from a friend, Michael Faraday, who advised that the youth should be sent to Germany to further his studies. Accordingly, in 1838 Croft entered the University of Berlin, where he studied for some three and a half years under several eminent professors, particularly the noted Eilhard Mitscherlich. In addition to his studies in chemistry, he acquired a broad scientific training in such subjects as mineralogy and geology, botany and zoology, physics, and entomology; the last became one of his special interests. He did not take a PHD, although he was awarded an honorary DCL at the University of Toronto in 1853.

In 1842 the cornerstone of King's College was laid at Toronto and it became the responsibility of the governor general, Sir Charles Bagot*, as chancellor, to select the first members of the teaching staff. After consultation with leading English scientists he offered Croft the chair of chemistry and experimental philosophy. At the end of 1842, at the age of 22, Croft left for Canada and took up his new duties in Toronto in the following year.

Despite his youth, Croft immediately entered briskly into the controversies swirling about King's College concerning its control by the Church of England. In his first year he opposed the president of the college, Bishop John Strachan*, and in association with the professor of anatomy and physiology, Dr William Charles Gwynne*, petitioned the provincial legislature for amendments to weaken church control. Gwynne and Croft were a minority on the college council at first, but by the end of the decade they had won over most members. When the University of Toronto replaced King's College in 1850, Croft became vice-chancellor (until 1853), and after 1857 he was a member of the university senate.

Croft was an effective teacher who encouraged his students in experimental approaches; his broad scientific training stood him in good stead at a time when a small teaching staff put a premium on versatility. He continued research of his own, particularly on the double salts of cadmium, but was not much interested in publishing his results. He was, however, a founder, and a president, of the Canadian (later Royal Canadian) Institute, and several of his papers were published in its journal. When the School of Practical Science was established at Toronto in 1877 he was appointed professor of chemistry and chairman of the board. He also supported the establishment of what became the Ontario Agricultural College at Guelph [*see* William JOHNSTON].

Croft took a keen interest in various phases of community life. He was an accomplished pianist, and a member of the Quintette Club and of the Philharmonic Society. He was active in various societies, especially those related to agriculture, horticulture, and entomology, as well as the mechanics' institute. But his most enthusiastic extracurricular interest was aroused following the *Trent* affair of 1861 [*see* Charles Hastings DOYLE] when the threat of war with the United States led to the formation of corps of volunteer militia in the Province of Canada. A university rifle corps was raised, which became the 9th Company, Queen's Own Rifles, and Croft was elected its captain. He continued in the company for several years, attaining the rank of major before retiring.

Croft acquired a considerable reputation in the field of toxicology. He became skilled in detecting the presence of poisons and was frequently consulted in cases where homicide was suspected.

His long-time colleague, Daniel Wilson*, who was not noted for his charitable judgements, described Croft as "most genuinely transparent, honest, and straightforward," one who "instinctively hat[ed] shams." Croft's last years were darkened by several family tragedies and in 1880 he retired on two-thirds salary to live on his son's farm in Texas, where he died not long afterward.

G. M. CRAIG

Henry Holmes Croft was the author of *Course of practical chemistry, as adopted at University College, Toronto* (Toronto, 1860). A list of his other works appears in Morgan, *Bibliotheca Canadensis*, 85–86.

UTA, Daniel Wilson, Journal. *Examiner* (Toronto), 20 Dec. 1843. John King, *McCaul, Croft, Forneri: personalities of early university days* (Toronto, 1914). *University College: a portrait, 1853–1953*, ed. C. T. Bissell (Toronto, 1953). Wallace, *Hist. of Univ. of Toronto*. C. R. Young, *Early engineering education at Toronto, 1851–1919* (Toronto, 1958). W. H. Ellis, "Henry Holmes Croft, D.C.L.," *Univ. of Toronto Monthly* (Toronto), 2 (1901–2): 29–32.

CROFTON, JOHN FFOLLIOTT, soldier; b. 9 Oct. 1800 in Dublin (Republic of Ireland), eldest son of the Reverend Henry Crofton and Frances ffolliott; m. 15 Oct. 1845 Anne Agnes Addison, and they had four sons and one daughter; d. 17 July 1885 in London, England.

Born into a prominent Irish family, John ffolliott Crofton was educated privately and at Trinity College, Dublin, receiving a BA in 1824. Later that year he enlisted as an ensign in the 6th Foot, then stationed at the Cape of Good Hope and under orders for India. In 1832 he was appointed interpreter to a force operating against the desert tribes at Parkur (Nagar Parkar, Pakistan). In 1840–41 Crofton was employed in the defence of Aden against the Arabs. The regiment then returned to England and was quartered at Preston until it was moved to Mullingar (Republic of Ireland) in December 1844. Crofton had been promoted lieutenant in 1826, captain in 1835, and major in 1842.

In 1845 Crofton was assigned command of a detachment to be sent to the Red River Settlement (Man.). The Hudson's Bay Company governor, Sir George Simpson*, had secured these troops for the settlement by stressing to the British government American threats arising from the Oregon boundary dispute, but in fact he wanted to use them to enforce measures protecting the HBC monopoly against free traders such as Andrew MCDERMOT and James Sinclair*. These measures, which had been enacted by Alexander Christie*, governor of Assiniboia, included a proclamation requiring traders to declare that they would not use goods they imported for the illegal traffic in furs. Another proclamation "required authorized importers to bring their outgoing mail to Fort Garry, addressed but not sealed, for inspection of the company's officers." Simpson also refused space on company ships to traders. Such measures, however, increased the resentment against the company and, because it lacked a means of enforcement, did little to stop illicit trade.

Crofton's detachment consisted of 307 officers and men of the 6th Foot, 28 officers and men of the Royal Artillery, one sergeant and 11 men of the Royal Sappers and Miners, and 15 women and 17 children. The party sailed from Cork on 26 June 1846, disembarking at York Factory (Man.) on 9 August and arriving at the settlement on 10 September. The detachment was divided between Lower Fort Garry and Upper Fort Garry (Winnipeg) where Crofton, now a lieutenant-colonel, made his headquarters. The Oregon dispute had been settled before the troops reached Red River but clearly they would stay over at least one winter. Crofton took steps to maintain discipline and morale among them. He purchased additional equipment and clothing, laid down rules to safeguard his men against the rigours of a severe season, and court-martialled deserters. He also encouraged sports and recreations, especially reading.

Although he undertook his duties assiduously, the recently married Crofton wished to leave the settlement at the first opportunity. He disliked the local society, recording in his diary that he was "much disgusted with the vulgar and ill-bred folk here," and thought his posting of no value to his future career. The effect of the troops on the settlement was, however, dramatic. The illicit trade diminished and open defiance of the company abated. Perhaps more important, the troops provided a significant stimulus to the local economy. Alexander Ross* noted: "During their short stay, the circulation of money was increased by no less a sum than 15,000*l.* sterling; no wonder then that they left the colony deeply regretted."

As commander, Crofton was appointed an ex-officio member of the Council of Assiniboia presided over by Governor Christie. He first attended on 15 Jan. 1847 and was present at two subsequent meetings. In fact, Simpson intended appointing Crofton governor of Assiniboia because many settlers objected to an HBC man in the position; though this appointment was not made, apparently because of Crofton's unwillingness to remain in the colony, it set the conditions upon which the next governor, William Bletterman CALDWELL, was selected.

Crofton formally handed over command to Major Thomas Griffiths (1798–1876) of the 6th Foot on 16 June 1847 and left for England via Montreal two weeks later. Griffiths did not impress Simpson, who decided that he was "altogether disqualified, as well from inaptitude for business as from temper" for the governorship. When the detachment was recalled, Griffiths returned with it to Great Britain in 1848.

Crofton was subsequently employed in the War Office but his involvement with the problems of Red River continued. Long-standing complaints by the Métis against HBC rule had led to a petition of grievance, presented by Alexander Kennedy ISBISTER to the colonial secretary, Lord Grey, on 17 Feb. 1847, calling for an inquiry into conditions at the settlement. Crofton's views, which he had previously given in two meetings with Governor General Lord Elgin [Bruce*] in Montreal, were solicited by the Colonial Office. He maintained that "the government of the Hudson's Bay Company is mild and protective, and admirably adapted, in my opinion, for the state of society existing in Prince Rupert's Land," and he disputed the petition's specific charges of maladministration of justice. As he had by his own admission taken little interest in the society of the settlement, it is unlikely that Crofton had any real understanding of the views of the traders and Métis, but, on the basis of his and other evidence, the colonial secretary decided against a parliamentary inquiry.

In 1857, when the approaching expiry of the HBC trading monopoly caused the House of Commons to establish a select committee to consider the continuance of company rule and the suitability of the Red River area for settlement, Crofton gave evidence. He again supported HBC rule, which he characterized as "patriarchal"; he also favoured further settlement and improved communication with Canada.

Promoted colonel in 1854, Crofton was appointed major-general in 1861, lieutenant-general in 1870, and general in 1877. He retired from the army in 1881 to London where he later died.

KEITH WILSON

PAM, HBCA, D.4/33, 24 Oct. 1845; D.5/18, 14 Dec. 1846; D.5/19, 20 March, 14 May 1847; D.5/21, 1 March 1848. PRO, WO 25/786. Winnipeg Public Library, "Winnipeg in 1846: copy of the diary of the late Colonel J. F. Crofton . . ." (typescript).

Canadian North-West (Oliver), I: 48, 327–45. *Elgin-Grey papers* (Doughty), I: 65. G.B., Parl., House of Commons paper, 1849, XXXV, 227, pp.509–627, *Hudson's Bay Company (Red River Settlement)* . . .; 1857, *Report from the select committee on the HBC*. HBRS, XIX (Rich and A. M. Johnson). Mactavish, *Letters of Letitia Hargrave* (MacLeod), 230. A. Ross, *Red River Settlement*, 364–65. *Hart's army list*, 1842, 1844, 1854, 1868, 1870, 1877, 1881. C. L. Kingsford, *The story of the Royal Warwickshire Regiment, formerly the Sixth Foot* (London, [1921]), 81–97. A. S. Morton, *Sir George Simpson, overseas governor of the Hudson's Bay Company; a pen picture of a man of action* (Toronto and Vancouver, 1944), 194–99, 217–19. Morton, *Manitoba* (1957). W. D. Smith, "The despatch of troops to Red River, 1846, in relation to the Oregon question" (MA thesis, Univ. of Manitoba, Winnipeg, 1951), 114–20. Roy St G. Stubbs, *Four recorders of Rupert's Land; a brief survey of the Hudson's Bay Company courts of Rupert's Land* (Winnipeg, 1967), 23–24. C. P. Stacey, "The Hudson's Bay Company and Anglo-American military rivalries during the Oregon dispute," *CHR*, 18 (1937): 281–300.

CROOKS, ADAM, lawyer and politician; b. 11 Dec. 1827 in West Flamborough Township, Upper Canada, the fourth son of James Crooks* and Jane Cummings; m. 4 Dec. 1856 Emily Anne (d. 1868), daughter of General Thomas Evans*, and they had no children; d. 28 Dec. 1885 at Hartford, Conn.

Adam Crooks was raised in the privileged, well-to-do atmosphere of the Homestead, the family farm a few miles west of Dundas, Upper Canada. His father was a prosperous paper-mill owner and politician; his mother came from a loyalist family. After attending common schools near Dundas and in Hamilton, Adam entered Upper Canada College in Toronto at the age of 11 and was a pupil until 1846. His brilliance as a scholar was immediately evident; he stood first in his class every year. Academic success followed Crooks through his years at the University of Toronto. He received a BA in 1852, with first prize medals in both classics and metaphysics, and an MA in 1853.

Crooks studied law concurrently with his university work; he received a BCL from the University of Toronto in 1851 and was called to the bar in the same year. Practising in Toronto, he soon specialized in the remunerative field of equity law. His most famous case, in 1862, the *Commercial Bank of Canada* v. *the Great Western Railway Company*, was a $900,000 civil suit. The bank, for which Crooks was one of the counsel, successfully appealed a lower court decision before the Judicial Committee of the Privy Council and Crooks was in England during much of 1864 and 1865 in connection with the case. He had received a DCL from the University of Toronto and was named a QC in 1863. After having been in several law partnerships during the 1850s he emerged in 1864 as the senior partner in the firm of Crooks, Kingsmill and Cattanach which continued until 1883. In 1871 he was elected a bencher of the Law Society of Upper Canada for which he had served as lecturer and examiner in commercial law and equity for several years.

Crooks had continued to take an interest in the affairs of the University of Toronto following his graduation. In 1863 he joined Edward Blake* and other graduates on its senate to defeat recommendations of a commission established by the legislature to divide a major portion of the government endowment among the denominational colleges of Canada West. With support from the public and from within the senate Crooks was elected vice-chancellor the following year; he held this office for nine years. After his entry into the provincial cabinet in 1871, he sponsored legislation which gave graduates more representation on the university's senate and provided for the chancellor to be elected by convocation rather than appointed by the government. He consistently adhered to the principle of a strong, central provincial university, with control shared by faculty and graduates.

Prominent in the city's legal circles and in university government, Crooks enjoyed the additional accoutrements of a professional upper-middle-class life. He was a member of the corporation of Hellmuth College in London, Ont., founded by his brother-in-law, Isaac Hellmuth*, and belonged to the Toronto Club. In 1869 he became the first Canadian to be elected a fellow of the Royal Colonial Institute, London, England. In May of that year he read to the institute its first paper dealing with Canada, "On the characteristics of the Canadian community," in which he depicted a "distinctive, intelligent, educated, and self-reliant" population, "devoted to the development of the great resources of the country."

Scattered references in speeches after 1870 indicate that Crooks had had a long association with railways, and in particular with the promotion of narrow gauge railways, during the 1850s and 1860s. He was apparently instrumental in obtaining railway charters and in 1868 he was a provisional director of at least one railway, the narrow gauge Toronto, Grey and Bruce. He was also a director of the proposed Toronto and Georgian Bay Canal Company (after 1865, the Huron and Ontario Ship Canal Company) and an enthusiastic supporter of projects to develop northwestern Ontario.

Politics attracted the attention of this talented lawyer. At a meeting of the Reform Association of Upper Canada in Toronto in April 1867 Crooks was appointed to fill one of the vacancies on the central executive committee as the association prepared for the coming elections. He was unsuccessful later that year in his first attempt for the provincial riding of Toronto West but secured the seat for the Liberals in 1871. Running in Toronto East in the 1875 election, he lost to Matthew Crooks CAMERON, but subsequently was returned in an Oxford South by-election after the original returns electing Adam OLIVER were nullified. He retained Oxford South in 1879 with a large majority and again in 1883 despite failing health.

Crooks's scholarship and legal background quickly won him a prominent place in the Liberal cabinet. He took office as attorney general in the government of Edward Blake on 20 Dec. 1871 and soon began the consolidation of Ontario municipal law which resulted in the Municipal Institutions Act of 1873. On 25 Oct. 1872 Crooks became provincial treasurer in the reconstituted Liberal administration of Oliver Mowat*. "He had no previous experience with matters of finance," wrote Charles Robert Webster Biggar in his sketch of the Mowat government in 1905, "but his untiring industry, and his capacity in mastering details . . . soon enabled him to master the subject of our provincial finances. His 'budget speeches' are models of lucidity." During the 1870s Crooks steered a number of bills through the legislature including, in 1873, the Mechanics' Lien Act, providing security to workers for unpaid wages, and the Married Women's Real Estate Act, under which married women could hold property in their own right. As provincial treasurer, he was chairman of the Private Bills and Railway Committee at a time of active railway expansion, and he directed government funding for service and development projects.

Crooks's name became publicly associated with the Mowat government's attempt to control the sale of alcoholic beverages in the province. The liquor licence act of 1876, popularly known as the Crooks Act, required skilful drafting and piloting through the legislature, because provincial jurisdiction in this area was a matter of dispute and also because it tried to find a middle ground between the extreme camps of "drys" and "wets." The act transferred licensing power from municipalities to provincially appointed commissioners, restricted the number of licences that could be issued in each community, increased licence fees, and provided for the inspection of licensed premises. Although it succeeded in introducing order to a chaotic system of licensing, the Conservative opposition objected to the legislation on the grounds that it opened the door to provincial patronage, a criticism the Mowat administration was unable to dispel entirely. The constitutionality of the act was challenged in the well-known case *Hodge* v. *the Queen* [*see* John Godfrey SPRAGGE], but was upheld in 1883 by a decision of the Judical Committee of the Privy Council. This move towards regulation by the government of social and economic activities was Crooks's most difficult assignment as provincial treasurer.

Crooks was sworn in as Ontario's first minister of education on 19 Feb. 1876, although he continued as provincial treasurer until March 1877. Egerton RYERSON's retirement provided Mowat with an opportunity to replace an appointed superintendent with a minister of education directly responsible to the legislature. The choice of Crooks came as no surprise. His previous portfolios had given him the necessary seniority to bring status to this new cabinet position and his association with the University of Toronto gave him the confidence of the personnel of the universities in the province. Moreover, despite their being on opposite sides during the University of Toronto debate in 1863, Crooks was virtually handpicked by Ryerson. "He is most cordial and seems to be thoroughly at one with me on all educational matters," Ryerson wrote his daughter Sophia Howard early in 1876. Most important to Ryerson was Crooks's decision to make long-time deputy superintendent John George Hodgins* the new deputy minister. Ryerson observed that Crooks "takes upon himself only what requires the action or policy of government, & places the whole management of the Department . . . under Dr. Hodgins, who is virtually installed in my place."

Crooks approached his new portfolio with enthusiasm, but even in the month of his appointment he gave Mowat cause for concern because of his "overworking himself." Mowat wrote that he must "relieve" Crooks of the treasurer's office as soon as the session ended and expressed the hope that Crooks "may continue to give sufficient attention to the Department of Education without injury to himself." Crooks recovered temporarily, continued briefly as treasurer, and displayed considerable energy as minister of education. During his first year he visited teachers' meetings and trustees' conferences throughout the province, gaining "practical knowledge of the condition and working of the educational system under my charge." Thus armed, he introduced a number of changes in 1877: stricter certification requirements for teachers, a provincial network of county model schools for teacher training, and a reduction in the number of required subjects on the elementary school curriculum. But with the exception of certification, these changes were practical concessions to the reality of local control of schools, rather than bold advances of provincial power. Crooks realized that local taxation, management, and control were of paramount importance for education in Ontario in the 1870s. "The principal functions of the Education Department are those of supervision," he told the legislature in 1879. The department must "strictly refrain from taking upon itself, or interfering with powers and duties entrusted to local managment, and which local experience can more intelligently deal with than any central authority at a distance."

Thus elementary and secondary schools changed little during Crooks's seven years as minister. He saw a decidedly limited role for elementary schools, referring to them as "the fifth of the essential institutions of civilized life," coming after the family, civil society, the state, and the church. The true place of the school was "misapprehended," he warned, if it trespassed on the prerogatives of the other four, particularly if it attempted to supply "what the family alone can adequately give." Also suggesting a traditional role for Ontario high schools, Crooks declared in his first annual report as minister that they "constitute the necessary stepping-stone between the Public Schools and the University." As a graduate of Upper Canada College, he favoured the continuation of a strong role for private schools in secondary education. As a supporter of the University of Toronto, Crooks was able to avoid the embittered university-government relations that characterized the administration of his successor, George William Ross*.

Questions of church-state relations in education frequently surfaced during Crooks's years as minister. The withdrawal in 1882 of Sir Walter Scott's poem *Marmion* from the high school literature curriculum under pressure from the Roman Catholic hierarchy, including Archbishop John Joseph LYNCH, annoyed the Toronto *Mail* and militant Protestant clergymen who charged Crooks with subservience to the Catholic Church. Further concessions, such as Roman Catholic model schools, the easier transfer of Quebec teaching certificates to Ontario, the appointment of a Catholic separate school inspector, and less cumbersome arrangements for Catholic ratepayers to place their names on the separate school tax roll, similarly annoyed Protestants while failing to satisfy growing Catholic demands. Crooks managed to avoid any direct confrontation with either side, but the church-state question would increase in intensity after his retirement. John Morison Gibson*, a political colleague, referred to this and other lingering educational questions when he wrote the new minister of education, George William Ross, in December 1883: "You will now have made a slight examination of the nooks and crannies of Dr. Ryerson's den. Some of them poor Crooks never saw into, and some he did see he had to wink at."

Provincial initiative in educational policy was severely compromised by the pitiful decline in Crooks's mental and physical health. Hodgins had observed such deterioration as early as 1878, and by the early 1880s it was evident to his close colleagues that the minister was succumbing to the ravages of cerebral paresis. Finally, in January 1883, Crooks collapsed after an evening sitting of the legislature, and Mowat had no choice but to relieve him of his cabinet responsibilities. Crooks nevertheless ran in the election of March 1883 and retained his seat. However, the committee on privileges and elections reported him to be "incurably insane" and declared the seat vacant. Then friends and business associates spirited him off to Europe in search of a cure. By the fall of 1884 he was confined to an asylum in Hartford, Conn., where he died in December 1885.

The assessment of Crooks as minister of education by his contemporaries and by historians is generally unfavourable. "He followed and never ventured to anticipate popular demands," wrote William Pakenham. In her study of the Mowat administration, A. Margaret Evans concluded that "the strong leadership that was desirable in Ontario's first Minister of Education seems not to have been given by Crooks." But the shadow of Ryerson in the guise of Hodgins as deputy minister, the continuing adherence to local control of schools, plus his declining health, limited Crooks's leadership as education minister. His significance rests more with his contributions to the practice of law and to the University of Toronto, and with his work as attorney general and provincial treasurer.

ROBERT M. STAMP

[Letters by Adam Crooks were published in *Correspondence arising out of the pastoral letter of the Right Reverend Francis Fulford* . . . (Toronto, 1862), and Crooks was the author of "On the characteristics of the Canadian community," Royal Colonial Institute, *Proc.* (London), 1 (1869): 162–74, and of the election address, *Reform government in Ontario: eight years' review* . . . (Toronto, 1879). Some of his speeches, including budget speeches and a few which he gave as minister of education in 1879, and election addresses were also published. The records of the Department of Education while he was minister are at AO, RG 2; series D-1 to D-4 are of particular importance. His reports as minister of education were published both separately and in Ont., Legislature, *Sessional papers*. R.M.S.]

AO, MU 158, Oliver Mowat to Edward Blake, 18 Jan. 1876. Ont., Legislative Library, Newspaper Hansard, 2 Feb. 1876 (mfm. at AO). *Commercial Bank of Canada* v. *Great Western Railway Co.* (1862–64), 22 U.C.Q.B. 233. Ontario Educational Assoc., *Proc.* (Toronto and Hamilton, Ont.), 1876–83, 1919. [Egerton Ryerson], *My dearest Sophie: letters from Egerton Ryerson to his daughter*, ed. C. B. Sissons (Toronto, 1955). *Globe*, 12 April, 24 Aug. 1867; 7, 10, 13 March 1871; 8 Jan. 1875; 29 Dec. 1885. *Canadian biog. dict.*, I: 52–55. *Cyclopædia of Canadian biog.* (Rose, 1886), 168–69. Dent, *Canadian portrait gallery*, II: 139–43. *Toronto directory*, 1850–83. J. G. Althouse, *The Ontario teacher: a historical account ofprogress, 1800–1910* . . . (Toronto, 1967). C. R. W. Biggar, *Sir Oliver Mowat . . . a biographical sketch* (2v., Toronto, 1905). *Canada and its prov.* (Shortt and Doughty), XVIII: 227–341. A. M. Evans, "Oliver Mowat and Ontario, 1872–1896: a study in political success" (PHD thesis, Univ. of Toronto, 1967). V. E. Parvin, *Authorization of textbooks for the schools of Ontario, 1846–1950* ([Toronto], 1965). R. M. Stamp, "The campaign for technical education in Ontario, 1876–1914" (PHD thesis, Univ. of Western Ontario, London, 1970). F. A. Walker, *Catholic education and politics in Ontario: a documentary study* ([Don Mills, Ont.], 1964; repub., Toronto, 1976). Wallace, *Hist. of Univ. of Toronto*.

CROWFOOT. *See* ISAPO-MUXIKA

CUDLIP, JOHN WATERBURY, merchant and politician; b. probably in 1815 in Saint John, N.B., son of John Cudlip, a retired British naval officer, and Rebecca Waterbury; m. in 1852 Emily Allison, and they had seven children; d. 22 Nov. 1885 in Saint John.

John Waterbury Cudlip attended school in Saint John and possibly in England, and while still in his teens began working in a variety of positions for John Robertson*, a prominent Saint John businessman with wide-ranging interests. He became a licensed auctioneer and by 1850 had entered a partnership with George E. Snyder, specializing in shipping, trading with the West Indies, and wholesaling.

Cudlip early showed an interest in community affairs. He was made a freeman of Saint John in 1836 and a militia officer in the Saint John City Light Infantry the previous year, but his main contribution was as commander of the "famous No. 5" volunteer fire-engine company which battled valiantly against a series of Saint John blazes in the 1830s and 1840s. Cudlip also was active in the mechanics' institute and the chamber of commerce, both vital bodies in Saint John in that period. By the later 1840s he was one of a group of aggressive and successful business and professional men, including Robert Jardine*, Samuel Leonard Tilley*, and John Hamilton GRAY, who made Saint John into a dynamic commercial city. He served in the Rail-Way League of 1849 and later that year became secretary of the league's successor, the New Brunswick Colonial Association. These organizations lobbied for the construction of a railway from Saint John to Shediac and urged reforms in government, including increased colonial autonomy, British North American union, and numerous internal changes, not the least of which was more influence over provincial matters for the businessmen of Saint John.

Active in politics throughout the 1850s and 1860s, Cudlip was elected as a "thorough" Reformer to the Saint John City Council in May 1852. He had already worked for candidates sponsored by the Colonial Association in the 1850 general election, all six of whom were elected in Saint John. As a key organizer, he aided the rise to power of Charles Fisher*'s Reform government in the 1854 election, and in 1855 was himself a candidate in a Saint John by-election. His unsuccessful campaign was supported by Tilley, now provincial secretary and the author of the 1855 prohibitory liquor law, despite the fact that Cudlip was a wholesale liquor dealer. Defeated again in the 1856 election, Cudlip was successful as a Liberal in 1857 and easily led the poll in the general elections of both 1861 and 1865. In the assembly his speeches were never long but were usually blunt and strongly independent. As one would expect of a vice-president of the chamber of commerce, Cudlip was a Saint John stalwart, and Tilley came to depend upon him in matters concerning the city as well as questions of trade, manufacturing, and currency. Sweden and Norway took advantage of his experience as well by appointing him their vice-consul from 1864 to 1876.

The negotiations among New Brunswick, Canada, and the imperial government over the Intercolonial Railway in 1862 and 1863 alarmed Cudlip. He wanted the railway to follow a more westerly route to aid Saint John's trade with the United States rather than the North Shore route championed by the British for reasons of defence. The railway question forced Cudlip to break with Tilley and the Liberals. "If the British Government want a Military Road, let them build it themselves," he said in 1863. He became a leading critic of government policy, especially after Tilley in 1864 united the construction of the Intercolonial with New Brunswick's entry into confederation as the grand design of the province's future. In the 1865 election he stood as an anti-confederate and received more votes than any other candidate in the province. Tilley and his government were defeated, and in 1866 Cudlip joined Premier Albert James SMITH's Executive Council.

Another election over confederation was forced in 1866, and the anti-confederates, including Cudlip, were routed at the polls. After the reorganization of federal and provincial governments in 1867, there were numerous vacancies in the New Brunswick legislature, and in March 1868 Cudlip stood unopposed in a Saint John by-election, even though his platform called for a repeal of the British North America Act and the annexation of New Brunswick to the United States. A year later he shocked loyalist sensibilities by proposing that New Brunswick do "what our people are doing individually, and ask the United States to admit us into the Union on fair and equitable terms." Cudlip was labelled "treasonable and disloyal" and his motion was not permitted to be entered in the assembly's journal. His political career was ended.

Whatever disgrace Cudlip may have incurred through his support of annexation, he remained popular in Saint John and carried on a successful business career. He was president of the chamber of commerce in 1869 and was one of the directors of the ill-fated Maritime Bank of the Dominion of Canada begun in Saint John in 1872. When the federal Liberal party gained power in 1873, Prime Minister Alexander Mackenzie* chose two of Cudlip's friends, A. J. Smith and Isaac BURPEE, for his cabinet. Burpee as minister of customs subsequently appointed Cudlip inspector of customs for New Brunswick and Prince Edward Island. The defeat of the Liberals in 1878 should have caused the dismissal of Cudlip, but Tilley, now finance minister in Sir John A. Macdonald*'s new government, used his influence to permit him to retain his post, which he did until 1885.

He died on 22 Nov. 1885 from injuries suffered in a fire in his home the previous day. Obituaries in the Saint John newspapers noted his unwavering advocacy of the city's interests and said that John Cudlip, though "impulsive and outspoken," died "without an enemy in the world."

C. M. WALLACE

N.B. Museum, Saint John, Register of voters, 1785–1869, esp. 1836; Tilley family papers, Corr. PAC, MG 27, I, D15. PANB, "N.B. political biog." (J. C. and H. B. Graves). Trinity (Anglican) Church (Saint John, N.B.), Baptismal and marriage registers (copies at N.B. Museum).

N.B., House of Assembly, *Reports of the debates*, 1865. *Daily Sun* (Saint John), 23 Nov. 1885. *Head Quarters* (Fredericton), 12 March 1856. *Morning News* (Saint John), 1849–50. *Morning Telegraph* (Saint John), 14 March 1868. *New Brunswick Courier* (Saint John), 1849–50. *New Brunswick Reporter and Fredericton Advertiser*, 18 March 1869. *Saint John Globe*, 23 Nov. 1885. *Weekly Telegraph* (Saint John), 25 Nov. 1885. *CPC*, 1868. *Dominion annual register*, 1885. *New Brunswick almanac* (Saint John), 1851, 1856, 1865. *Hutchinson's St. John directory . . .* (Saint John), 1863–64. MacNutt, *New Brunswick*. C. M. Wallace, "Saint John boosters and the railroads in mid-nineteenth century," *Acadiensis*, 6 (1976–77), no.1: 71–91. J. R. H. Wilbur, "The stormy history of the Maritime Bank (1872) to 1886," N.B. Hist. Soc., *Coll.* (Saint John), no.19 (1966): 69–76.

CUMBERLAND, FREDERIC WILLIAM, engineer, architect, railway manager, and politician; b. 10 April 1820 in London, England, son of Thomas Cumberland; m. 30 Sept. 1845 Wilmot Mary Bramley, and they had four daughters and three sons, including Frederic Barlow*; d. 5 Aug. 1881 in Toronto, Ont.

Although the family of Frederic William Cumberland claimed descent from a bishop of Peterborough, England, they would appear to have had more humble origins. Cumberland's father was servant to the vicar of Kippax (West Yorkshire) until about 1819 when he became a messenger at the Irish Office, first in London and later, from 1828 to 1833, in Dublin. He then had the post in London of office-keeper for the Colonial Office until 1839. Frederic was educated by a minister who probably ran a parish school in Dublin. In 1834–35 he studied at King's College School, the junior school of King's College, University of London, before apprenticing with William Tress, civil engineer, for five years. Some time after 1834 he met Sir Charles Barry, for whom he may have worked on the Houses of Parliament at Westminster.

Part of Cumberland's work as an apprentice was to prepare surveys for the Tithe Commutation Commission and for various railways. He soon obtained posts as assistant engineer on the Plymouth branch of the Great Western Railway and later on the London and Birmingham Railway, and he may also have designed some railway stations. By 1843, on Lord Stanley's recommendation, he had been appointed to the engineering department of the Admiralty as first assistant at the dockyards at Chatham, and he was later promoted to the larger Portsmouth dockyards; in these positions he constructed both dry docks and fortifications, attaining such expertise in the building of permanent foundations that he continued to be consulted on the subject for a decade after coming to Canada. From 1845 to 1847, while at the dockyards, he may have assisted in editing and he contributed to the professional journal of the Royal Engineers.

Cumberland's marriage in 1845 connected him with Toronto and was probably a major factor in his emigration. One of his wife's sisters, Matilda Ann, was the second wife of Thomas Gibbs Ridout*, first cashier (general manager) of the Bank of Upper Canada. Another sister, Julia Elizabeth, married as her second husband, Joseph Davis RIDOUT, prominent businessman of the city; after Julia Elizabeth's death in 1852 Joseph married Cumberland's sister, Caroline. In 1847 the Cumberlands came to Toronto via New York City and the Erie Canal. Soon after his arrival Cumberland worked as a surveyor laying out the intersection of Bloor and Yonge streets, as an evaluator for the British America Fire and Life Assurance Company, and as county engineer for the united counties of York and Peel from 1848 to 1854.

Cumberland's primary profession, however, was that of architect. Before 1850 he probably constructed the wall around the Provincial Lunatic Asylum at Toronto (999 Queen Street West), a building which John George HOWARD had designed and built in 1845–49. In 1850 he formed a partnership with Thomas Ridout, a son of Thomas Gibbs Ridout. Before the partnership was terminated in 1852, Cumberland and Ridout designed a number of important buildings. The first of these was St James' Cathedral in Toronto, a commission Cumberland himself had won in competition with ten other entrants in 1849. The cathedral, of white brick with stone trim, as were most of Cumberland's buildings, was Gothic in style. The main part of the work was completed by 1853; lack of funds caused a delay in the completion of the tower and spire until 1874. Cumberland also designed the now demolished St James' School for the cathedral. A second commission received by the partnership was for a series of interconnected buildings to house the Normal and Model schools at Toronto, built in 1851–52 (now demolished except for the main façade). The structure had a Roman exterior and a Gothic interior; a third storey was later added which somewhat spoiled the design. In 1851 Cumberland also designed the York County Court House. On this commission he ran into a dispute over fees; he had charged only two and a half per cent instead of the customary five per cent because he was county engineer. As soon as the building was completed his office was abolished and he then demanded the full fee; a compromise was eventually effected. About the time the partnership was dissolved in 1852, Cumberland designed another important Toronto building, the seventh Post Office, in classic style with Ionic columns; it still stands on Toronto Street.

In 1852 Cumberland formed a new partnership with William George Storm*, a pupil of Toronto architect William Thomas*. Storm had already begun to work for Cumberland in 1850 on St James' Cathedral. Their partnership lasted until 1866–67, when Cumberland became totally occupied with railway management, and it is difficult to separate their work while the partnership lasted. Their first major commission was the now demolished Toronto Mechanics' Institute (after 1883 the Toronto Public Library), which was built in 1853–54 in the Renaissance *palazzo* style. As a member of the executive of the institute, Cumberland did not charge either for drawing plans or for superintending construction. The magnetical observatory followed in 1854–55 (still on the grounds of the University of Toronto) as well as various offices such as the York Chambers (now demolished) and alterations to Government House (also now demolished).

In 1856 came the commission for what was probably to be his major work, University College in the University of Toronto. As preparation for designing the building, the university authorized Cumberland to tour the British Isles and France where he was able to see the main ideas being developed in architecture; he was greatly influenced by art historian John Ruskin's theories, particularly as they were being applied in the new University Museum at Oxford. Despite the attempts by Governor General Edmund Walker Head* to suggest alterations in the design, University College is largely Norman in style, but it nevertheless represents the introduction into Canada of the High Victorian era of architecture, which incorporated ideas from many periods to achieve picturesque effects. The building, which was constructed in 1856–59, was so successful and so well in advance of the ideas of the era in incorporating stylistic innovations with a functional design that, after it was severely gutted by fire in 1890, it was restored on much the same lines. Financially, the project was less successful, for Cumberland ran into major difficulties with the university over costs.

Meanwhile he had become involved in several other buildings of importance in Toronto, including the Queen Street Methodist Church (1857), the beautiful Gothic chapel of St James-the-Less in St James' Cemetery (1857–61), and the imposing centre portion of Osgoode Hall (1857–60) with its magnificent library, one of the finest rooms in a Canadian building. Storm played an increasing part in the construction of these buildings. Cumberland designed many large residences in the city, all of which are now demolished, including homes for Professor George Templeman KINGSTON, Casimir Stanislaus Gzowski*, Thomas Gibbs Ridout, John Ross*, and other prominent citizens; he also designed his own spacious home, Pendarves (1860), still standing in the University of Toronto grounds. Many of these residences were pleasing, spacious, mid-Victorian houses, in the style of Tuscan villas.

Outside Toronto Cumberland was also active. With Thomas Ridout he had a branch operation in Hamilton in 1850–51 and he designed buildings across the province. These included the Haldimand County Court House at Cayuga and the Gothic Church of the Ascension at Hamilton (both 1850–51), the Hamilton Central School (1851–53), and the Ontario County Court House at Whitby (1853), a fine Doric-domed structure. The Hamilton Post Office (1854–56) was one of other buildings that no longer stand.

Any evaluation of Cumberland's work would place him as one of the most important Canadian architects. A man of great imagination, who could implement the familiar styles demanded by his clients, he was also instrumental in introducing High Victorian picturesque eclecticism to Canada. His work was as successful financially as it was architecturally. His average income in the early 1850s ranged from $8,000 to $12,000 and one year went as high as $16,000. Thus when he abandoned the architectural profession he did so not because of any lack of success. The difficulties he had frequently encountered over fees were part of the reason. The recession of 1857, moreover, had halted construction and by 1860 Toronto, the site of the majority of his commissions, had erected most of the principal structures that it would need for some time.

Cumberland was also attracted by the challenge and excitement of railways and thus gradually moved from architecture to full-time railway management. In 1852 the floundering Ontario, Simcoe and Huron Railroad Union Company (renamed the Northern Railway Company of Canada in 1858) appointed Cumberland chief engineer. He held this post for two years and then joined the company again: as a director in 1857, as vice-president in 1858, and then from 1859 until his death as general manager or managing director. He was also agent for the Port Hope, Lindsay and Beaverton Railway (1860), director of the North-West Navigation and Railway Company (1863) and of the Interoceanic Railway Company (1872), and manager of the Northern Extension Railways (1870–75) prior to its merger with the Northern and of the Hamilton and North Western Railway (1879–81) which also combined with the Northern. Along with Charles John BRYDGES of the Great Western and Grand Trunk railways, and Thomas Swinyard of the Great Western, Cumberland was an early example of the professional manager in an era dominated by amateurs. In part because he could learn from his mistakes, he also ranks as one of the more successful managers in 19th-century Canada.

As chief engineer of the Ontario, Simcoe and Huron from 1852 to 1854 Cumberland, in order to satisfy the Board of Railway Commissioners, renegotiated existing open-ended contracts and instituted a system in which fixed-price contracts were obtained by tender. The engineering staff, previously controlled by the contractors, was placed under the supervision of the chief engineer who reported to the company's board of directors. Control was thus shifted from the contractors to the Canadian directors. Cumberland also encouraged through traffic rather than local trade and he assured the directors that he had upgraded the standards of construction. Stepping back from active involvement in 1854, he watched the railway slide towards bankruptcy by 1857. The directors lacked managerial experience, construction remained shoddy, and the through traffic ran at a loss. In 1859 Cumberland returned as general manager. The Canadian government, in order to protect its investment of

£578,000 in a mortgage on the Northern, removed control of the railway from the company on 4 May 1859. A week later, after the company agreed to meet conditions demanded by the government, an order in council returned control of the railway to the company (an act passed in 1860 confirmed the transfer). Among the stipulations of the agreement between the company and the government was the negotiation of a financial arrangement between the two largest investors, the government and the British bondholders; in exchange for an additional £250,000 investment, the bond-holders were given votes in the election of directors proportionate to their investment, and thereby acquired control of the railway.

As general manager, Cumberland. given a free hand by the bondholders and aware of past mistakes, instituted a number of operational changes which formed the basis for his later claim that no railway in Canada had been better managed. Since he held the bondholders' proxies Cumberland appointed and controlled the Canadian directorate and was able to streamline the entire managerial structure. One of the first managers to de-emphasize through traffic, he cultivated instead the remunerative local trade. To guarantee high quality construction, he closely supervised all renovations, new construction, and purchases of rolling-stock. He expanded only when forced to by competition or by the depletion of lumber, the road's main freight, near existing track. In part because of Cumberland's sound and conservative management, the Northern played an important role in opening Toronto's rich hinterland.

Unlike his operational methods, Cumberland's financial policy met with much criticism. To discourage excessive expansion, the Northern's capital account, money invested in the railway through stocks and bonds, had been closed in 1860 by the act passed that year. This closing forced Cumberland to pay for all rail and stock maintenance and for expansion out of current working expenses. As a result he quickly re-established a sizable floating liability which he attempted to reduce only after the annual payment of the principal and interest to British bondholders; the payment of interest on various provincial government loans and also the payment of dividends to shareholders followed after the liability in priority. The bondholders profited from this system and increased their investment at crucial times, but the provincial government and shareholders saw little direct return. Aware of the importance of the bondholders' investment, the government gave the arrangement its "tacit concurrence." The private shareholders, who owned half of the shares, and the governments of Toronto and Simcoe County, who owned the other half, could only fume; they too desired the expansion of the road for economic and political reasons, and realized the need for capital from the London market. After Cumberland's death, the government, despite strong pressure from the bondholders, refused to grant any further public assistance to the road. Bereft of Cumberland's advocacy and managerial ability, the Northern lost its independent status and became part of the Grand Trunk system in 1888.

Cumberland's railway interests greatly affected the political activities he took up. Indeed, the railway, not the electorate, was his constituency. Although he represented Algoma as a Conservative in the Legislative Assembly of Ontario from 1867 to 1875 and in the House of Commons in 1871–72, he rarely visited the constituency and had little contact with the local electorate. He spent Northern money to finance his own elections as well as the election of the Northern's president, John Beverley Robinson*, to succeed him in the House of Commons for Algoma in 1872 and that of their ally, Sir Francis HINCKS, for Renfrew North in 1869. He also used Northern money for donations to the Conservative party, for such purposes as testimonials to Sir John A. Macdonald* and the founding of a Conservative newspaper, the *Mail*, in 1872. He casually defended the spending of over $16,000 in this way by stating that "in those matters" he was regarded as a representative of the railway.

Parliamentary and community support was also acquired by wining and dining MPs and prominent businessmen, hiring a federal deputy minister of justice to expedite legislation for the railway in 1868, distributing bribes for municipal bonuses, and promising townships kickbacks from government subsidies. Of questionable ethics, too, was Cumberland's use of over $7,000 of the Northern's money to purchase personal shares in the steamboat *Chicora*. None of this conduct was particularly unusual. When these details surfaced, during a federal Liberal government investigation in 1877, George LAIDLAW felt they were just "a little point gained by the Ministerialists" which would not harm the Conservatives in the ensuing elections. He was right. Cumberland's personal image, however, was tarnished. Despite many attempts, he never regained the position of provincial aide-de-camp to the governor general, an office he held from 1865 until 1878. Nor, despite hints from Cumberland, did Macdonald provide a remunerative position to which the beleaguered manager could retire in his last years.

Cumberland's interests in architecture, railway management, and politics would seem to have been enough to occupy any man; he was, however, also involved in an amazing variety of activities around Toronto. He was a promoter and director of the Niagara Navigation Company, along with his son Barlow and Frank Smith*, as well as a director of the Merchants' Express Company and the Rama Timber Transportation Company. Active in banking, he was an incorporator and director of the unsuccessful Bank of Canada in 1858, along with Angus MORRISON, William CAYLEY, and William Henry Boulton*; a director of the Imperial Guarantee and Loan Society; and a director of the Canadian Bank of Commerce from 1871 to 1877. Attracted to military life, he organized the 10th Battalion Volunteer Militia Rifles (later the Royal Grenadiers) in 1861–62 and became its first lieutenant-colonel. When the battalion ran into difficulties in 1880, he reassumed the lieutenant-colonelcy to reorganize it. In 1866 he had also been active in arranging military transportation by rail during the Fenian raids.

A member of the Church of England, Cumberland was active in synod affairs and he generously allowed the congregation of St Stephen's-in-the-Fields to use his house for a year after the church burned in 1865. He held numerous honorific posts: for example, on the local committee of the Agricultural Association of Upper Canada, as Canadian commissioner to the Great Exhibition in London in 1851, and as organizer of the reception for the Prince of Wales during his visit to Toronto in 1860. He became a life member of the mechanics' institute in 1848 and held many posts with it, including the presidency in 1852–53. In 1849, together with Sandford Fleming*, Kivas Tully*, and others, he organized the Canadian Institute, of which he was corresponding secretary in 1851–52, vice-president in 1852–53, and recording secretary in 1854–56.

Cumberland was a member of the Toronto Board of Education and wrote a column for his friend Egerton RYERSON in the *Journal of Education for Ontario* for many years. He was also a member of the corporation of Trinity College in 1869–70 and of the governing body of Trinity College School, Port Hope, from 1870 until his death. In spite of his disagreements over the costs of University College, he was a member of the senate of the University of Toronto from 1853 until he died. In 1864 he was admitted as a student to Osgoode Hall, but did not complete a legal education.

Cumberland was prominent in the St George's Society of Toronto and was its president in 1855–56. He was a noted freemason, reorganizing St Andrew's Lodge and becoming its master about 1878, as well as becoming deputy grand master of the Toronto District. A keen sportsman, he was an active cricketer and president of the Toronto Cricket Club when he died. In 1881 he also helped incorporate the Ontario Jockey Club and became its first president. Any man as active as Cumberland, however, would naturally arouse opposition. As the *Globe* noted in its obituary, "he was a man of strong individuality, and in the positions which he occupied necessarily excited a good deal of antagonism." Cumberland's exact wealth is impossible to determine as he placed most of his funds under a deed of trust in 1870 and the evaluation of his estate, which excluded all real estate, amounted to only $36,965. Certainly his home was not only one of the major social centres but also one of the most impressive dwellings in the city. Cumberland made substantial contributions to almost every aspect of life in Toronto, designing many of its important buildings, developing its communications, and extending the range and improving the quality of its educational, cultural, and sporting activities.

FREDERICK H. ARMSTRONG and PETER BASKERVILLE

[The AO acquired in 1979 the Horwood collection of architectural drawings which includes a substantial number by the Cumberland and Storm partnership. A full evaluation of each individual's contribution to the partnership must await an analysis of these drawings. F.H.A. and P.B.]

Frederic William Cumberland was the author of "Iron roofs erected over building slips, nos 3 and 4, in Her Majesty's Dockyard, Portsmouth," *Papers on Subjects Connected with the Duties of the Corps of Royal Engineers* (London), 9 (1847): 59–65; and of "Some notes of a visit to the works of the Grand Trunk Railway, west of Toronto, February, 1855," *Canadian Journal*, 3 (1854–55): 225–27.

AO, Frederic William Cumberland letters (uncatalogued); Diaries of Mrs Frederic William Cumberland (uncatalogued); MU 469–87; 2390–98; 2697, 2700, 2702, 2749, 2752; RG 49, I-7-B-3, 4, Northern Extension Railways, folder 1. MTL, Sir Thomas Galt papers; John Harvie papers; Northern Railway of Canada papers; T. A. Reed scrapbooks. PAC, MG 24, E17, 2; RG 30, 121, 167, 197. UTA, A70-0005, Senate, Minutes, 1850–73. UWO, Thomas Swinyard papers. York County Surrogate Court (Toronto), no. 3122, Will and inventory of F. W. Cumberland, 13 Aug. 1881 (mfm. at AO). Can., Parl., *Sessional papers*, 1877, VII: no.10. *Globe*, 2 Feb. 1855, 6 Aug. 1881. *Toronto Daily Mail*, 6 Aug. 1881. *Canadian directory of parl.* (J. K. Johnson), 146. Chadwick, *Ontarian families*, I: 36–37, 42–43. *Cyclopædia of Canadian biog.* (Rose, 1886), 705–7. *Dominion annual register*, 1880–81: 404. W. H. Smith, *Canada: past, present and future, being a historical, geographical, geological and statistical account of Canada West* (2v., Toronto, [1851–52]), I: 165. Alfred Sylvester, *Sketches of Toronto, comprising a complete and accurate description of the principal points of interest in the city, its public buildings . . .* (Toronto, 1858). [G. P. Ure], *The hand-book of Toronto; containing its climate, geology, natural history, educational institutions, courts of law, municipal arrangements . . .* (Toronto, 1858). Eric Arthur, *Toronto, no mean city* ([Toronto], 1964). M. E. Arthur, "The frontier politician," *Aspects of nineteenth-century Ontario: essays presented to James J. Talman*, ed. F. H. Armstrong *et al.* (Toronto and Buffalo, N.Y., 1974), 278–96. Currie, *Grand Trunk Railway*. Alan Gowans, *Building Canada: an architectural history of Canadian life* (Toronto, 1966). *Hist. of Toronto and county of York*, II: 36–37. S. G. Morriss, "The church architecture of Frederic William Cumberland" (2v., MA thesis, Univ. of Toronto, 1976). *Robertson's landmarks of Toronto*, I: 163, 165, 325; II: 801–7; IV: 35. [Brian Winter], *A town called Whitby* ([Whitby, Ont., 1967]). F. [H.] Armstrong, "Fred's buildings . . . ," *Heritage Canada* (Ottawa), 3 (1977), no.3: 44–47. Crawford Grier, "The right place," *Varsity Graduate* (Toronto), 12 (1965–66), no.1: 97–101. S. G. Morriss, "The church architecture of Frederic

William Cumberland (1820/21–1881)," Ontario Museum Assoc., *Newsletter* (Toronto), 4 (1975), no.3: 17–25; "The nine-year odyssey of a high Victorian Goth: three churches by Fred Cumberland," *Journal of Canadian Art Hist.* (Montreal), 2 (summer 1975): 42–53. [F. N. Walker], "A doorway made him famous," *Univ. of Toronto Bull.* (Toronto), 54 (1953–54): 99–100; "Doorways that welcome," *Canadian Banker*, 66 (1959), no.1: 64–79.

CURRIER, JOSEPH MERRILL, lumberman, businessman, and politician; b. in 1820 in North Troy, Vt, seventh son of Ezekiel Currier; m. in 1846 Christina Wilson, and they had one son; m. secondly in 1861 Anne (Annie) Crosby (she died later that year); and m. thirdly in 1868 Hannah (d. 1901), daughter of Ruggles Wright of Hull, Que.; d. 22 April 1884 in New York City.

Joseph Merrill Currier, a Presbyterian of French Canadian descent, obtained some education at North Troy before moving to Canada in 1837. He entered the lumber trade in the Ottawa valley as an employee. Later he managed Levi Bigelow's mills at Buckingham (Que.), and then the lumber business of Thomas McKay* and John McKinnon in New Edinburgh (now part of Ottawa), where he made his home. About 1850 he entered into partnership with Moss Kent Dickinson*, a prominent forwarder, lumberman, and politician, and they built a sawmill and grist-mill complex at Manotick, Canada West, which supplied sawn lumber for the American market; Currier withdrew from the firm in 1863. In addition Currier had a lumber business of his own at New Edinburgh on the Rideau River from 1853 until he sold out in the late 1860s. He was also a partner in the firm of Wright, Batson and Company (later Wright, Batson and Currier) of Hull. In 1868 this firm constructed a steam sawmill in Hull and by 1871 was producing 30 million board feet of lumber annually.

Currier had extensive business interests beyond the lumber industry. From 1872 to 1877 he was president of the Citizen Printing and Publishing Company, which owned the *Ottawa Daily Citizen*, although it did not control the paper's editorial policy. He moved to incorporate this firm in 1873. He served as president of the Ottawa and Gatineau Valley Railway Company and of the Ontario and Quebec Railway Company, and as a director of the Ottawa City Passenger Railway Company [*see* William Goodhue PERLEY]. Currier was also involved in the Upper Ottawa Improvement Company, in the Victoria Foundry with Horace MERRILL, and in "a host of other enterprises," including tannery, insurance, and banking companies. During the mid 1870s, however, his business career foundered and by 1878, when the Wright, Batson and Currier mill burned down, he was, according to his friend and colleague, Alonzo Wright*, "hopelessly bankrupt." He managed, nevertheless, to retain the house he had built in 1868 at 24 Sussex Drive, Ottawa, which eventually became the official residence of the prime minister of Canada. In 1873 he had been made president of the Ottawa Valley Immigration Society.

In the decade preceding confederation Currier developed an interest in politics and represented By Ward on the Ottawa City Council. In 1863 he was elected to the parliament of the Province of Canada for Ottawa, defeating Richard William Scott*. Although elected as a supporter of John Sandfield Macdonald*, Currier consistently voted with the Conservatives in the house and supported confederation in the debates of 1865. He represented Ottawa in the federal house until 1882, along with a second member after 1872. He was a loyal Conservative federally, but his party identification was not as strong at the provincial level. In 1871, when Edward Blake* formed his provincial Liberal administration, Ottawa district leaders were anxious to have R. W. Scott, Currier's old opponent, in the new Liberal government to protect distinctive Ottawa valley interests such as timber and railways; Currier supported these regional economic concerns, advising Scott in a telegram, "Go in by all means."

Although Currier was devoted to the interests of the people of Ottawa, he was "one of the silent kind" and not particularly active in the legislature. His interventions in debate were usually short and concerned with a small number of matters. Anxious to see Ottawa an effective capital, during his first session in 1863 he moved a resolution calling for the speedy completion of the parliament buildings. Over the years he regularly showed his concern with various business enterprises as well as Ottawa River shipping and the lumber trade. Although a Presbyterian, Currier was solicitous for his Roman Catholic supporters, and in 1875, when advocating relief for New Brunswick Catholics who were being denied the right to their own schools, he stated in the House of Commons that they should not be refused "the same privileges and laws that the Protestant minority in Quebec and the Roman Catholic minority in Ontario, enjoyed." Two years later he supported the reading of prayers in the House of Commons in both English and French.

On 16 April 1877 Currier resigned his seat as a result of a violation of the "independence of parliament" act, revealed to the house by Liberal Wilfrid Laurier*. The ensuing debate about sales agreements between the government and several firms to which Currier belonged reveals that the violation was only technical, and the Liberal high command was motivated by partisan interests. Currier explained that "the firm of T. W. Currier & Co. (of which I was at that time a partner, though not an active one) on 21st May 1874, received an order from the Director of Penitentiaries for goods . . . which were supplied in June, 1874. . . . I also find that the firm of [Batson] & Currier, of which I am a member, fulfilled several small orders for lumber for the Library of Parliament . . . , but in each case without my personal cognizance." In a vigorously fought by-election on 9 May 1877, Currier was re-elected, but he was unable to pay his election expenses and a disgruntled Conservative organizer was left $700 in arrears.

Upon the return of the Conservatives to power in 1878, an attempt was made to secure a cabinet post for Currier. Alonzo Wright suggested to Sir John A. Macdonald* that Currier was in "a difficult plight" because of his bankruptcy and should be given a "refuge" in the form of a cabinet seat. Joseph Tassé*, Currier's fellow member of parliament for Ottawa, strongly urged his colleague's claim: "Mr. Currier has made large sacrifices for the party, and his appointment as minister would be generally well received." Currier was apparently convinced that he was about to receive his political reward, but he was wrong; he never did serve in cabinet. He did not contest the election of 1882. On 23 May 1882 he was appointed postmaster of Ottawa, a position he held until his death.

Joseph Merrill Currier, an immigrant with little formal education, became a highly successful businessman until his difficulties in the mid 1870s. Undistinguished as a politician, he was really a businessman in politics, a loyal Conservative who received his patronage reward when in need. Politics for Currier was thus a successful form of bankruptcy insurance.

DONALD SWAINSON

PAC, MG 24, B40; MG 26, A; MG 27, II, D14. Can., House of Commons, *Debates*, 1875–82. *Free Press* (Ottawa), 22 Nov. 1878, 22 April 1884. *Ottawa Daily Citizen*, 11 Nov. 1873; 12 Jan. 1874; 23, 25 April 1884. *Canadian directory of parl.* (J. K. Johnson). *CPC*, 1873. *Dominion annual register*, 1884. J. W. Hughson and C. C. J. Bond, *Hurling down the pine; the story of the Wright, Gilmour and Hughson families, timber and lumber manufacturers in the Hull and Ottawa region and on the Gatineau River, 1800–1920* (Old Chelsea, Que., 1964). Swainson, "Personnel of politics." H. [J. W.] and Olive Walker, *Carleton saga* (Ottawa, 1968).

CUSHING, ELIZA LANESFORD. *See* FOSTER

CYGNE, LE. *See* ONASAKENRAT

D

DALLAS, ALEXANDER GRANT, HBC administrator and businessman; b. 25 July 1816 in Berbice region, British Guiana (Guyana), son of Murdoch Dallas, MD, and Helena Grant; d. 3 Jan. 1882 in London, England.

Alexander Grant Dallas belonged to the Galcantray branch of the family. He was still a child when his father died and the family returned to Scotland; Alexander's grandfather, John Dallas, was a merchant at Inverness, and Alexander was educated at Inverness Academy, where he won a gold medal. He entered business in Liverpool in 1837. About 1842 he joined the famous trading firm of Jardine, Matheson and Company and spent five years in China. He prospered, but an attack of fever made it necessary for him to leave the Orient, and he returned to Scotland where he purchased the estate of Dunain, near Inverness.

His health restored, Dallas soon became active in London financial circles. In April 1856 he was elected to the committee of the Hudson's Bay Company which at that time was worried about the state of its affairs on the Pacific coast. James Douglas* was serving as both governor of Vancouver Island, for which the company was responsible, and officer in charge of the company's Western Department, and it was felt that he was favouring the colony at the expense of the company. In addition, the affairs of the subsidiary Puget's Sound Agricultural Company were in disarray. Dallas was asked to conduct an investigation and take remedial measures. He left England on 2 Jan. 1857 and arrived in Victoria in May, after stops in San Francisco and Fort Vancouver (Vancouver, Wash.). His arrival was naturally unwelcome to Douglas, but personal relations were sufficiently good to permit Dallas' marriage to the governor's second daughter, Jane, on 9 March 1858.

After successfully organizing the affairs of the Puget's Sound Agricultural Company, Dallas was preparing to return to England when in April the Fraser River gold-rush suddenly erupted. Douglas, the only British governing official in the region, was compelled to extend his authority arbitrarily to the mining areas; it soon became obvious that one early result of the influx of thousands of miners would be the end of the company's trading monopoly on the mainland. In the early stages of the rush the only resources Douglas had available to deal with this population increase were often those of the company, and thus the conflict of interest inherent in his dual position was intensified. His differences with Dallas, who had stayed to protect the interests of the company, seem to have been sharpest over the land question; in Victoria and at forts Langley, Hope, and Yale the needs of the government clashed with the claims of the company. A few years later, in an outspoken private letter, Dallas recalled "the unscrupulous way in which Douglas wished to saddle all the expenses on the Company," and "his attempts to deprive us of the lands which he himself [had] made over to me as Company's property. . . ."

In August 1858, when the crown colony of British Columbia was created, Douglas was offered the governorship on condition that he sever his connection with the HBC. Anticipating Douglas' acceptance, the company sent Dallas a commission naming him "representative of the Company for the Western Department." The new colony was duly proclaimed on 19 November and Douglas became its governor, but he chose to ignore the direction to cease acting for the company. "Mr. Douglas," Dallas wrote on 14 December, "has I think little idea of giving up control of the Company's business." With considerable forbearance Dallas held his commission in abeyance, but in March 1859 the company sent specific instructions to both Douglas and Dallas ordering the transfer of authority to Dallas.

Sir George Simpson*, the company's governor-in-chief in North America, died on 7 Sept. 1860. Some months before his death Simpson had suggested that Dallas should succeed him, and the company decided to act upon the recommendation. Dallas, anxious to discuss matters with the committee, left Victoria for London on 24 March 1861. In London he was busy with various company affairs, notably its land claims in British Columbia, until the end of the year. The fair and reasonable terms he proposed in a memorandum submitted in August became the basis for a formal settlement between the crown and the company in November.

Dallas' commission as "President of Council and Governor in Chief in our Territory of Ruperts Land" was dated 3 Feb. 1862. He left for Canada in March, arrived at Upper Fort Garry (Winnipeg), where he was to make his headquarters, in May, and presided over his first council at Norway House in June. Later in the year, and again in 1863, he made far-ranging inspection tours of the company's establishments that were comparable with Simpson's celebrated travels. Dallas saw clearly that great changes would soon take place in the west. Population would flood in, and he was anxious to see the company relieved of its responsibility to govern Rupert's Land. In July 1863, in a letter to the company's governor, he emphasized "the importance . . . of the immense districts . . . suitable for settlement being administered as a Crown Colony"; and, in the light of his experience with Douglas, he also emphasized "the impropriety of allowing the offices of Crown Governor and Hudson's Bay Company representative to be held by the same individual. . . ." In a second letter, in October, he raised the question of Indian land claims, which would be the basic cause of the Red River disturbance six years later, and warned that there would be "serious trouble hereafter with the Indians and half-breeds unless the local government is better supported. . . ."

By 1864 Dallas was anxious to retire to his estates in Scotland, and he sailed from Quebec on 9 July. To have the benefit of his advice, the company retained his services in an advisory capacity until 31 May 1866. He continued to take a lively interest in the affairs of Vancouver Island. When it was proposed that the island colony should be absorbed by British Columbia, with Gilbert Malcolm Sproat* and Donald Fraser* he formed the London Committee for Watching the Affairs of British Columbia in an unsuccessful effort to defeat the plan. He met with better success later when he was a member of an influential lobby that secured the transfer of the capital of the united colony from New Westminster to Victoria in 1868.

Dallas spent his last years on the Dunain estate, which he improved greatly. He was interested in sport and particularly enjoyed riding and hunting. He is said to have been an accomplished water-colour painter. One of his nine children, Major-General Alister Grant Dallas, who was born in Victoria, had a distinguished military career in India, the South African War, and World War I.

W. Kaye Lamb

[Alexander Grant Dallas' activities for the Hudson's Bay Company may be traced in the HBCA at PAM, notably in series A.1 (minutes), A.7 (London locked private letterbooks), A.11 (London inward correspondence), D.8 (Dallas' inward and outward correspondence), and F.12 (correspondence of the Puget's Sound Agricultural Company). See also James Dallas, *The history of the family of Dallas, and their connections and descendants from the twelfth century* (Edinburgh, 1921); E. W. Watkin, *Canada and the States; recollections, 1851 to 1886* (London and New York, [1887]); F. W. Laing, "Hudson's Bay Company lands on the mainland of British Columbia, 1858–1861," *BCHQ*, 3 (1939): 75–99; and B. A. McKelvie, "Successor to Simpson," *Beaver*, outfit 282 (September 1951): 41–45. W. K. L.]

DALTON, SARAH. *See* Holman

DALY, THOMAS MAYNE, businessman, politician, and office-holder; b. 17 Feb. 1827 at Hamilton, Upper Canada, son of John Corry Wilson Daly* and Leonora Mayne; m. 19 June 1846 Helen McLaren Ferguson, and they had at least one daughter and three sons, including Thomas Mayne*; d. 4 March 1885 at Stratford, Ont.

Thomas Mayne Daly attended Upper Canada College at Toronto in 1841 and later received some training in medicine. For most of his life he resided in Stratford. He was a member of the Church of England. In 1848–49 he became active in local politics when he served on the Huron District Council, and in 1850 he was a member on the council of the united counties of Huron, Perth, and Bruce. Daly was one of the leaders in the struggle to establish Perth as a separate county with Stratford the county town; a goal finally achieved in 1853. Daly also attended to various business interests, his main occupation being contracting. He built roads in Perth County and was a contractor for railways and public works in both Canada and the United States. He also operated a stage-coach company and a grain mill, published the *Stratford Examiner* in the 1850s, and speculated extensively in land. By 1854, at the age of 27, Daly shared with his father the distinction of being "the leading property owners and largest taxpayers in Stratford."

Provincial politics attracted the young businessman and in August 1854, running as an independent Reformer in the new constituency of Perth, he became the county's first member of the Legislative Assembly. He apparently changed his political views soon after his election and in September absented himself from the assembly when the Reform government of Francis HINCKS and Augustin-Norbert Morin* was defeated. He then supported the administration formed by Sir Allan Napier MacNab* and Morin and continued thereafter as a Liberal-Conservative follower of John A. Macdonald*. He was re-elected in 1857 but was defeated by Michael Hamilton Foley* in the general election of 1861 before successfully contesting the by-election when the constituency became vacant in 1862. After losing in the general election of 1863 as well as in the federal election of 1867 he returned briefly to municipal politics, serving as mayor of Stratford in 1869–70 and as reeve of North Easthope Township in 1872. Entering federal politics again in 1872, he won the seat of Perth North and acted as whip in Macdonald's government until its resignation in 1873. Daly then successfully contested Perth North in a provincial by-election and served as a member of the Ontario legislature until he was defeated in 1875. From 1876 to 1878 he again served as mayor of Stratford.

Daly was not an important parliamentarian and he rarely spoke in the house. His relationship with the Conservative party during the 1860s and 1870s is, however, of interest. During the late 1850s his business empire had collapsed. Heavy speculation in land led him deeply into debt and he was unable to meet the demands of his creditors during the panic of 1857. His contracting firm declined because of mismanagement and by 1858 was under new ownership. At the end of the decade Daly was $250,000 in debt and without assets; he remained in financial distress for the rest of his life. For years Daly corresponded regularly with Macdonald on a constant theme: he was a loyal servant of the Liberal-Conservative party and in return he expected a remunerative post. In 1864 he explained to Macdonald that although he had doubts about the scheme of confederation he had nonetheless worked for it within the Orange order, of which he was provincial grand master, and in return sought the post of sheriff. When the post was not forthcoming Daly insisted that "times are so bad here that if I have to starve it out much longer, I am afraid of myself." In 1866, because of his extensive contacts in the United States, he was employed to spy on Fenians in New York State by Macdonald, to whom he presented an extensive report. Unfortunately Daly's contribution to the Conservative party had never been significant enough to warrant much patronage and he got no permanent post during the 1860s. After his provincial legislative service in 1874–75 he became desperate once more. In 1877 he obtained the federal nomination for Perth North, to the dismay of Conservative organizers who were convinced that he would lose the election. Daly agreed to withdraw, in return for the promise of an appointment if the Conservatives were successful. The Conservatives did win in 1878 but Macdonald did not find Daly a post until 1884. Then, despite his being described by the minister of customs, Mackenzie Bowell*, as "a useless encumbrance," he was appointed deputy collector of customs at Stratford. He held this post until his death the following year.

DONALD SWAINSON

Ont., Legislative Library, Newspaper Hansard, 1875 (mfm. at AO). PAC, MG 24, B60; MG 26, A. "Parl. debates" (CLA mfm. project of parl. debates, 1846–74), 1854–63, 1873. *Globe*, 8 Jan. 1874, 5 March 1885. *Canadian directory of parl.* (J. K. Johnson), 149. *CPC*, 1873. *Dominion annual register*, 1885. W. S. Johnston and H. J. M. Johnston, *History of Perth County to 1967* (Stratford, Ont., 1967). Swainson, "Personnel of politics"; "Thomas Mayne Daly and patronage as welfare," *OH*, 72 (1980): 16–26.

DARLING, WILLIAM, merchant and capitalist; b. in 1819 in Edinburgh, Scotland; m. Mary Davidson, also of Edinburgh, and they had eight children; d. 1 Nov. 1885 in Hochelaga (now part of Montreal), Que.

William Darling, the eldest son of an Edinburgh fancy goods merchant, emigrated in 1840 to Montreal, where he opened a small commission business for his father. After a short time he founded his own firm under the name of William Darling and Company and built up an extensive wholesale trade in hardware and iron goods, writing and printing papers, and fancy goods, all imported from England and Germany. Succeeding in his business, Darling eventually opened a branch of the firm in Toronto and took his four sons into the company; the eldest, William, was attached to the firm in Montreal with his brother James, while Andrew and Thomas J. worked in the Toronto branch.

Although his principal interest was in commerce, Darling was also active in Montreal's financial community. In 1865 he was one of the provisional directors of the Sun Insurance Company of Montreal (known after 1882 as the Sun Life Assurance Company of Canada) but withdrew from the company soon after its incorporation. Three years later he was listed among the shareholders of the Bank of British North America, holding a small block of 13 shares. In 1875, with Malcolm Cameron*, Robert CASSELS, Joseph GOULD, and others, Darling sat on the provisional board of directors of the Bank of the United Provinces, which had received its charter in 1874 under the name of the London and Canada Bank. This bank, however, never opened its doors and the charter eventually lapsed. In 1875 he was one of the founding directors of the Canada Land Investment Guarantee Company (Limited). With investments in both the Royal Canadian Insurance Company and the Merchants' Marine Insurance Company of Canada, he served as president of the latter in 1876. Darling also had substantial investments in the Merchants' Bank of Canada (200 shares), the Canadian Bank of Commerce (20 shares), the Bank of Montreal (35 shares), and the Consolidated Bank of Canada (38 shares). In the reorganization of the Merchants' Bank following its near collapse in 1877 [*see* Sir Hugh ALLAN], Darling was unanimously elected to the board of directors and was largely responsible for the appointment of George Hague* as general manager that year. Darling was recognized as Hague's right-hand man on the board and remained active as a director until his death in 1885.

As a prominent member of the commercial community, Darling took an active interest in the Montreal Board of Trade, serving on the council from 1864, as vice-president from 1871 to 1874, as president for the year 1874–75, and then, for the remainder of his life, as a member of the board of arbitration. In 1868 he was also listed among the members of the Board of Brokers, later incorporated as the Montreal Stock Exchange. Although not formally trained in law he possessed a mind proper to a judge, and his opinions on legal questions relating to trade and commerce were held in high regard. As a result, he was frequently called upon to settle disputes. During the 1870s he was named arbitrator by the Liberal government of Alexander Mackenzie* in the expropriation of land for the enlargement of the Lachine Canal, and he was retained in that office by Sir John A. Macdonald* after the Conservative victory of 1878. The Liberal administration also called upon Darling to help in the framing of the Insolvent Act of 1875.

In politics Darling was a lifelong Liberal and a close associate of Mackenzie, Edward Blake*, and Luther Hamilton Holton*. Standing as a Liberal candidate for Montreal West in 1878 he advocated free trade, contending that the imposition of tariffs burdened the working man. The Conservative candidate, Mathew Hamilton GAULT, who was an ardent supporter of Macdonald's National Policy, accused Darling of not having any capital invested in Canadian industry and therefore of being little interested in promoting native manufacture. With the support of a large section of Montreal's business community Gault roundly defeated Darling by more than 1,500 votes in an election that brought the Conservatives back to power. Three years later, in 1881, Darling was appointed a justice of the peace, an office he occupied until his death.

Darling was closely associated with the Presbyterian St Gabriel Street Church, becoming a member of the board of trustees in 1864 and from 1871 serving as its chairman. Taking a particular interest in the church's financial affairs, he was active from 1867 as a member of the Board for the Management of the Temporalities Fund of the Presbyterian Church of Canada; as chairman of the board from 1875 he presided over the fund, from which annual stipends were paid to the ministers of the Presbyterian Church in Canada. Because of the failures of the Commercial Bank of Canada in 1867 and the Consolidated Bank in 1879 and through losses incurred in the troubles of the Merchants' Bank in 1877, the fund had lost $154,143 since its incorporation in 1858. The decisions to invest in the Merchants' and Consolidated banks were apparently made before Darling took over as chairman, and "not a dollar of the fund was lost by unfortunate investments" under his direction. He was also involved in the administration of the Ministers' Widows' and Orphans' Fund.

Unlike most English-speaking, Protestant merchants of his day, Darling resided in the predominantly French-speaking community of Hochelaga, where he devoted his leisure hours to farming and gardening. It was at his home, Bloomfield House, that he died on 1 Nov. 1885 of inflammation of the lungs. His eldest son, William, succeeded him as head of the family firm, William Darling and Company, and in his turn became involved in the administration of the St Gabriel Street Church.

GLADYS BARBARA POLLACK

Montreal Board of Trade Arch. (Montreal), Minute books, 1864–88 (mfm. at ANQ-M). PAC, RG 31, A1, 1871, Montreal. Can., Parl., *Sessional papers*, 1867–68, VI, no.12; 1872, VI, no.13; 1877, VII, no.12; 1878, IX, nos.14, 15; 1880, VIII, no.12; 1884, X, no.32; 1885, VIII, no.14; IX, no.17; *Statutes*, 1874, c.91; 1875, c.60, c.63. Can., Prov. of, *Statutes*, 1864, c.161; January–March 1865, c.43. *The Canadian Bank of Commerce: charter and annual reports, 1867–1907* (2v., Toronto, 1907), I. *Extract of the official book of reference of the parish of Montreal . . .* , ed. L.-W. Sicotte (Montreal, 1872), 4. [Montreal] Board of Trade and Corn Exchange Assoc., *Statements relating to the home and foreign trade of the Dominion of Canada; also, annual report of the commerce of Montreal . . .* (Montreal), 13 (1876)–18 (1886). Que., *Statutes*, 1873–74, c.54. *Gazette* (Montreal), 4, 5, 11, 13, 18 Sept. 1878; 2, 3, 5 Nov. 1885. *Journal of Commerce* (Montreal), 30 Aug., 13 Sept. 1878, 6

Nov. 1885. *Monetary Times*, 27 Nov. 1885. *Montreal Herald and Daily Commercial Gazette*, 5 Nov. 1885. Borthwick, *Hist. and biog. gazetteer. Cyclopædia of Canadian biog.* (Rose, 1886), 753–54. *Montreal directory*, 1863–69; 1871–75; 1881–85. *The year book and almanac of Canada* . . . (Montreal), 1876. R. M. Breckenridge, *The Canadian banking system, 1817–1890* (Toronto, 1894). Campbell, *Hist. of Scotch Presbyterian Church.*

DAVID, ELEAZAR (Eleazer) DAVID, cavalry officer, lawyer, and civil servant; b. 8 June 1811 in Montreal, Lower Canada, eldest son of Samuel David, a prominent Montreal merchant, and Sarah, daughter of Aaron Hart* of Trois-Rivières, Lower Canada; d. 1 Feb. 1887 at Coaticook, Que.

Eleazar David David, whose parents belonged to two of the most prominent Jewish families in Lower Canada, studied law and was admitted to the bar in 1832. He practised in Montreal and became legal adviser to the trustees of the Spanish and Portuguese Synagogue. From the 1820s David served in the Royal Montreal Cavalry, and by the time of the outbreak of the rebellion in 1837 he was senior captain. His younger brother, Moses Samuel, served under him as troop cornet and adjutant, while another brother, Dr Aaron Hart David, the future dean of the medical faculty of Bishop's College at Lennoxville, was assistant surgeon in the Montreal Rifles.

At the battle of Saint-Charles-sur-Richelieu Captain David was in command of 20 troopers who acted as dispatch bearers and reconnaissance men. David's command of both French and English and his resourcefulness made him invaluable to the British military authorities. His horse was shot from under him and his services were mentioned in dispatches by Sir John Colborne*, who shortly after the battle promoted him major. On 14 December, at the battle of Saint-Eustache, David was in command of 95 troopers of the Royal Montreal Cavalry and the newly raised Queen's Light Dragoons.

After the rebellion, David resumed his law practice and continued his rise in the provincial military establishment. In October 1839 he was appointed extra assistant adjutant-general. However, in May 1840 he forfeited his social, legal, and military position in Montreal by eloping with Eliza Locke Walker, the wife of Captain Henry William Harris of the 24th Foot. David had formed a liaison with Mrs Harris early in 1838, and when they fled to the United States they took with them her month-old baby, whom David later acknowledged to be his child. There followed ten years of exile in the United States, France, Italy, and the West Indies, during which David apparently lived on private means.

David returned to Montreal in 1850 with Eliza, his wife after Harris' death in 1849, and their five children. He was welcomed as a prodigal son, resuming his rank as major in the Montreal Cavalry, his law practice, and his role as legal adviser to the synagogue. For a time he practised law in partnership with the future Judge Thomas Kennedy RAMSAY, but they quarrelled, probably over the financial arrangements of the partnership, and separated after litigation. From 1858 until 1863 David was registrar and treasurer of Trinity House, Montreal. He had been promoted lieutenant-colonel of the Montreal Cavalry by 1860 and, despite an accusation by troopers that he had subjected them to ridicule by giving wrong orders while on parade, a charge which was subsequently proved groundless and malicious, David was appointed assistant adjutant-general of cavalry in 1866.

David had always been extravagant and careless about money, and by the 1860s was impecunious. His independent means had likely been depleted by the ten years spent abroad, and it appears that when he returned to Montreal he was placed under considerable financial strain by several lawsuits against him for non-payment of promissory notes. The culmination of his difficulties came in 1873 when he was convicted of embezzling money from the Montreal Decayed Pilots Fund, a type of pension fund for retired pilots, which had been entrusted to him while he was treasurer of Trinity House. He was sentenced to two years in the penitentiary, which provoked his cousin, Fanny David, daughter of Abraham JOSEPH, to speak bitterly of him as "a thorn to my family." Upon his release from prison in about 1876, he retired with his family to Coaticook where he lived until his death in 1887. Of his 11 children by Eliza, only four daughters survived him. His wife died in Coaticook in 1896.

David's conduct during the rebellion gave him a place in history as a distinguished officer. His notoriety as the usurper of another man's wife and his involvement in a fraud twice put him beyond the pale of Montreal society. Yet the affection, loyalty, and continued respect bestowed upon him during his long life indicate a man to whom much was forgiven and from whom much was expected and received.

ELINOR KYTE SENIOR

McCord Museum (Montreal), Hale family papers; Military papers, Misc. no.2, M5728. PAC, MG 24, I61; RG 8, I (C ser.), 749: 40; 1272: 180; RG 9, I, C4, 12; C7, 1; C8, 6. Spanish and Portuguese Synagogue (Montreal), Minutes of the meetings of trustees, 1832–73. "Items relating to congregation Shearith Israel, New York," American Jewish Hist. Soc., *Pubs.* (Baltimore, Md.), 27 (1920): 76. *Gazette* (Montreal), 24 Oct. 1839, 19 May 1840, 3 Feb. 1877, 1 Aug. 1896. J.-J. Beauchamp, *Répertoire général de jurisprudence canadienne* . . . (4v., Montréal, 1914–15), I: 675. *The Lower Canada jurist* (35v., Montreal, 1857–91), VI: 295. Michel Mathieu, *Rapports judiciaires révisés de la province de Québec* . . . (28v., Montréal, 1891–1903), XXIII: 279–80. *Montreal directory*, 1856–62. *The Jew in Canada; a complete record of Canadian Jewry from the days of the French régime to the present time*, ed. A. D. Hart (Toronto and Montreal, 1926), 503. Sack, *Hist. of the Jews in Canada* (1945), 123, 138. "Les Israélites au Canada," *Arch. israélites de France* (Paris), 3 (1842): 295–96.

DAVID, FERDINAND (baptized **Ferdinand-Conon**), painter, coach-builder, building contractor, and politician; b. 30 May 1824 at Sault-au-Récollet (Montréal-Nord), Lower Canada, son of David-Fleury David*, a master sculptor, and Cécile Poitras; m. first 8 Oct. 1844 Olive Boyer, *dit* Quintal, in the church of Notre-Dame in Montreal, Canada East; m. secondly 29 Oct. 1868, in the same place, Sophie Homier, widow of Joseph Papin*; seven children were born of these two marriages; d. 16 July 1883 in Montreal.

Ferdinand David received his primary education in his native village, where he also learned the trade of carpentry. His father, who was quite well known for his decorative carvings in various churches, apparently was always in a precarious financial position and decided around 1835 to emigrate to the United States, where he died at Troy, N.Y., six years later. It is not known whether Ferdinand followed his parents and he may instead have established himself in Montreal, probably as an apprentice. In any case, he was married in Montreal in the fall of 1844. The *Montreal directory* for the following year lists David as a coach-builder and painter but these activities did not bring him public recognition. In fact his name never appears in the business section of the city's directories, which indicates his lack of importance in these fields and may imply that he worked for an established coach-builder. Judging by newspapers, David owed his reputation more to his work on the city council of Montreal. First elected by popular vote in 1861, he represented the Saint-Louis Ward until 1864. The following year the councillors chose him as alderman, a post he held until his resignation in 1877. As a member and chairman of the roads committee he seems to have played an important role in the areas of highways and public transport; it may be assumed that he was one of the initiators of the horse-drawn tramway system which was introduced in Montreal on 27 Nov. 1861. In 1877 he stood as a candidate for the office of mayor of the city, but Jean-Louis BEAUDRY defeated him by 2,780 votes to 812.

At the time of his election to the city council David began to work as a building contractor. Little is known about his activities in this connection until the 1870s when he joined with lawyers Sévère RIVARD and Gustave-Adolphe Drolet* and architect Michel Laurent in the firm of David, Rivard, Laurent et Drolet which specialized in real estate speculation and housing construction. At the beginning of 1872, acting through this company, David bought a huge estate belonging to Benjamin-Godfroi Comte, situated in the Saint-Louis and Saint-Jacques wards of Montreal and in the village of Saint-Jean-Baptiste (now part of Montreal). Shortly after making the purchase the partners sold a section of the land in small lots. The most important speculative venture was in the village of Saint-Jean-Baptiste: David and his partners owned parcel number 15, which they subdivided into 1,298 lots of about 20 or 25 feet by 200. The group obviously took an active part in the development of the village for on 13 June 1872 David and his associates gave the bishop of Montreal, Ignace BOURGET, 20 lots for the building of a Catholic church, on the understanding that henceforth they would be exempted from church tax. Also around that time they undertook the construction of several houses, particularly on Rue Drolet. David himself owned several lots and buildings in Saint-Antoine and Saint-Louis wards.

In the political sphere, apart from his participation on the city council, David briefly entered provincial politics. He was elected to the Legislative Assembly in 1871 on the Conservative party ticket in the riding of Montreal East, which he represented until 1875. During his term of office he sat on the special committee for industries appointed in 1871 [*see* Louis-Napoléon LAROCHELLE]. In the interests of integrity he demanded that in the "Tanneries scandal," which had implicated the government of Gédéon Ouimet* in a fraudulent deal with Montreal speculators in 1873, a bill be introduced requiring a secret vote and the holding of an impartial inquiry [*see* Louis ARCHAMBEAULT].

Active in other concerns, David was involved in the temperance campaigns around 1845, was vice-president of the Association Saint-Jean-Baptiste de Montréal, and in 1868 was president of the Société de l'Union Saint-Joseph de Montréal. During the 1870s he held office as president of the Société de Colonisation de Montréal, and as director of the Montreal Northern Colonization Railway Company. His defeat in his bid to become mayor of Montreal apparently was the beginning of a period of semi-retirement. This enabled him about 1878–79 to embark on a long journey abroad which took him to such places as Nice and Paris in France.

Ferdinand David's career illustrates an interesting phenomenon: the development during the 19th century of an urban bourgeoisie which was not exclusively professional and whose members had in common a modest social origin and an ability to seize upon opportunities for acquiring wealth during the process of urban growth – whether in the course of the expansion of the city's area, as in David's case, or of the urban market, as in the case of Louis Boyer*. The author of an obituary in *La Minerve* of Montreal said of David: "He was a *self made man* in the full sense of the term. He was indeed one who owed everything to his own efforts."

JEAN-CLAUDE ROBERT

AC, Montréal, État civil, Catholiques, Notre-Dame de Montréal, 19 juill. 1883. ANQ-M, État civil, Catholiques, La Visitation-de-la-Bienheureuse-Vierge-Marie, Sault-au-Récollet (Montréal), 30 mai 1824; Notre-Dame de Montréal, 8 oct. 1844, 29 oct. 1868; Minutiers, E.-P. Fréchette, 13 juin, 6 nov. 1872, 3 déc. 1873, 26 mai 1875, 10 août 1880. AVM, Documentation, Biog. des conseillers, F.-C. David; Membres des conseils municipaux, 1833–99. Bibliothèque de la ville de Montréal, Salle Gagnon, Minutes de l'Union Saint-Joseph de Montréal. PAC, MG 30, D1, 9: 887.

Extract of the official book of reference of the parish of Montreal . . . , ed. L.-W. Sicotte (Montreal, 1872). *Extracts of the books of reference of the subdivisions of the city of Montreal*, ed. L.-W. Sicotte (Montreal, 1874). *L'Aurore des Canadas* (Montréal), 28 août 1841. *La Minerve*, 17 juill. 1883. *Le Monde* (Montréal), 16 juill. 1883. *Montreal Daily Star*, 19 July 1883. *L'Opinion publique*, 19 juill. 1883. Borthwick, *Hist. and biog. gazetteer*, 178; *Montreal*, 67. *CPC*, 1874: 386–87. *Dominion annual register*, 1883: 307–8. *Montreal directory*, 1842–83. É.-J.[-A.] Auclair, *Saint-Jean-Baptiste de Montréal; monographie paroissiale, 1874–1924* (Québec, 1924). *Histoire de la corporation de la cité de Montréal depuis son origine jusqu'à nos jours* . . . , J.-C. Lamothe *et al.*, édit. (Montréal, 1903).

DAVIE, ALEXANDER EDMUND BATSON, lawyer and politician; b. 24 Nov. 1847 in the parish of St Cuthbert, Wells (Somerset), England, son of Dr John Chapman Davie and Anne Collard Waldron; m. 3 Dec. 1874 Constance Langford Skinner, and they had three sons and four daughters; d. 1 Aug. 1889 in Victoria, B.C.

Alexander Edmund Batson Davie was educated at Silcoate's School in Wakefield (West Yorkshire), England. In 1862, leaving his mother, a brother, and a sister behind, Alexander immigrated with his father and three brothers to Vancouver Island; they were among the first to settle in the Cowichan River valley (near present-day Duncan, B.C.). Shortly after his arrival Davie began articling in Victoria with Robert Bishop, and after June 1865 with Robert Edwin Jackson. The chief justice of Vancouver Island, Joseph Needham*, enrolled Davie as a solicitor for the island on 25 Nov. 1868, and the following year Matthew Baillie Begbie* enrolled him on the mainland. Davie became active in the Law Society of British Columbia, and was elected its secretary in July 1869. He was called to the bar in February 1873, the first lawyer to have received his complete legal education on Vancouver Island. On 31 March 1874 he was elected a bencher in the law society, a position he held for most of his life.

With a law practice in Victoria and also from about 1870 in the Cariboo, Davie turned to politics. His father had been a member of the Legislative Council for a short time, and his own experience as law clerk to the Legislative Assembly between 1872 and 1874 whetted his appetite for political office. In the provincial election in the fall of 1875 he ran in the Cariboo constituency, there being no seat available in his home, Victoria. He stood as an independent, but like other candidates in the Cariboo agreed with the government of Premier George Anthony Walkem* concerning the pressure it applied on the Canadian government to fulfil three crucial promises made to the province when it joined confederation in 1871: to take over its debt, to lend it money to build a dry dock, and to begin construction on the Canadian Pacific Railway. Walkem reciprocated Davie's support; without it Davie would not likely have been elected as there was much opposition to him among the miners "on the grounds that that gentleman has no claim on the constituency and has only a very temporary interest in their welfare." There was also speculation that Davie's support for Walkem was only feigned. He did vote with Walkem on issues about which they agreed but otherwise he remained an independent. When Walkem lost the confidence of the assembly and Andrew Charles ELLIOTT became premier in February 1876, Davie voted with Elliott, but such shifts were not unusual at a time when political parties were unknown.

In May 1877 Davie accepted Elliott's offer of the provincial secretaryship, but the necessary by-election, which took place on 22 June 1877, proved to be disastrous for him. He failed to convince the voters that a cabinet minister would best serve their interests, and Walkem was determined to defeat his imagined betrayer. Davie did not run in the 1878 election, having returned to full-time law practice in Victoria with Montague William Tyrwhitt Drake and Robert Edwin Jackson. In 1879 he formed a partnership with Charles Edward Pooley which lasted until his death.

But although he continued to practise law, the lure of politics was too strong. Davie was elected for Lillooet in the provincial election of July 1882. The following January, when William SMITHE formed a government, Davie became attorney general, and he was returned by acclamation in the subsequent by-election on 15 Feb. 1883. The appointment recognized his legal ability, and a further honour came in September 1883 when he was made a QC. In 1884 he headed a three-man commission, on which Elliott also sat, to investigate the disturbances at William Duncan*'s mission at Metlakatla (B.C.) caused by the demands of the Tsimshian Indians, which included compensation for their land. The commission did not even consider land claims but recommended the provincial government assert its authority over the land in the area by surveying it.

As attorney general, Davie in 1884 forcefully argued for provincial rights before the Supreme Court of Canada regarding the Canada Temperance Act of 1878, claiming that British Columbia, like the other provinces, had the right under the British North America Act to regulate its own liquor sales; the Supreme

Court ruled in favour of the provinces. His most significant contribution, however, was in legal reform. The chaos of the gold-rush era had resulted in many hasty, ill-conceived laws which had to be modernized and consolidated. Davie sponsored a large number of new laws, most of which met with little opposition in the assembly. He also established regular sittings of the various courts.

Premier Smithe died on 28 March 1887, and on 1 April the lieutenant governor, Hugh Nelson*, asked Davie to form a new government. On becoming premier, Davie retained the post of attorney general. His health soon broke down and on 11 October he left Victoria for California and the southwestern United States to recuperate. At the request of the provincial secretary, John Robson*, the assembly granted permission for Davie's prolonged absence so that he did not have to forfeit his seat. Although Robson ran the government during his absence, Davie attempted to direct policy by outlining his views on current issues in letters to Robson. Government *in absentia* was unsatisfactory; it was fortunate that Davie's ministry had a considerable majority and was not faced with any contentious issues. This tranquillity, and Davie's brief active service, makes it difficult to evaluate his effectiveness as premier.

Upon his return from the United States on 21 May 1888, Davie attempted to be an active premier but it was obvious his health was little improved. In July 1889 he declined the position of justice of the Supreme Court of Canada which had been offered to him on Robson's advice by Sir John Sparrow David Thompson*, the Canadian minister of justice, and stayed on as premier.

On 1 Aug. 1889 he died of phthisis in Victoria after receiving the last rites of the Roman Catholic Church, which he had joined in 1882. He did not die a wealthy man, leaving an estate of $14,000 and a lot worth $1,500. The *Vancouver Daily World* paid tribute to him as a "true Christian gentleman" devoted to his family.

ZANE H. LEWIS

PABC, Add. MSS 525, A. E. B. Davie to John Robson, 23 Nov. 1887–30 April 1888; Colonial corr., A. E. B. Davie corr.; Crease coll., A. E. B. Davie to H. P. P. Crease, 4 April 1870, 16 Nov. 1883, 1 July 1889; A. E. B. Davie, Petition to be called to the bar, 1873; Law Society of British Columbia, Minutes, 1869–1915; O'Reilly coll., Peter O'Reilly to Edgar Dewdney, 27 March 1887; Premier, Corr. inward, no.746/87, Honoré Mercier to A. E. B. Davie, 24 Sept. 1887. Supreme Court of British Columbia in Probate, Victoria Registry (Victoria), will no.1834 (A. E. B. Davie); file no.1014, 5 Aug. 1889. B.C., Legislative Assembly, *Journals*, 1873–89; *Sessional papers*, 1885, ". . . Metlakatlah inquiry, 1884: report of the commissioners, together with the evidence." *Cariboo Sentinel*, 12, 19 June, 3 July, 9 Oct. 1875. *Daily Colonist* (Victoria), 26 Nov. 1868; 5 Dec. 1874; 16, 29 May, 3 July 1877; 3 Oct. 1883; 16 Oct. 1884; 1, 4 Aug., 1 Dec. 1889. *Vancouver Daily World*, 1 Aug. 1889. F. W. Howay and E. O. S. Scholefield, *British Columbia from the earliest times to the present* (4v., Vancouver, 1914), II: 401, 445–48; IV: 326, 329. S. W. Jackman, *Portraits of the premiers: an informal history of British Columbia* (Sidney, B.C., 1969), 71–72, 74.

DAY, CHARLES DEWEY, lawyer, politician, judge, and educationalist; b. 6 May 1806 in Bennington, Vt, son of Ithmar Hubbell Day and Laura Dewey; m. first in 1830 Barbara Lyon, and they had three children; m. secondly in 1853 Maria Margaret, daughter of Benjamin Holmes*; d. 31 Jan. 1884 while visiting England.

Charles Dewey Day's father, "Capitain" Ithmar Day, probably worked with the North West Company before moving his family from Vermont to Montreal in 1812 to begin a retail business in drugs and provisions. Some time after 1828 he moved to Hull where he established a sawmill, fulling-mill, and blacksmith shop. His eldest son, Charles Dewey, was educated in Montreal and, after studying law for five years under Samuel Gale*, was admitted to the Lower Canadian bar on 25 May 1827. Although Day maintained offices in Montreal, he was most active in the Ottawa valley where he acted as counsel for such timber barons as Ruggles and Philemon Wright*. On 4 Jan. 1838 Day was appointed QC.

Day's growing political prominence may explain his rapid professional advancement. He had begun his political career in April 1834 by publicly protesting the House of Assembly's endorsement of Louis-Joseph Papineau*'s 92 Resolutions. Papineau's opponents soon formed constitutional associations and Day became a prominent spokesman in the one at Montreal. At the Montreal Constitutionalists' initial meeting Day was not only placed on the committee of correspondence, but was chosen to second Augustin Cuvillier*'s resolution endorsing "the continuance of the existing connection between the United Kingdom and this Province." The commercial bias of Day's political philosophy is clearly revealed in the speech he gave on this occasion. After condemning the "band of mad revolutionalists" desirous of starting a Canadian civil war, he adamantly defended the continuance of British immigration to Canada and the reputation of the British American Land Company, which the Patriotes had attacked. Subsequently he was among those who favoured the abolition of feudal tenure, equal sharing of the clergy reserves among Protestant denominations, and the establishment of an office of land registry. In 1836 he won a closely contested election to serve as a delegate to a convention called to petition the king and parliament on the state of politics in Lower Canada.

The outbreak of rebellion accelerated Day's political ascendancy. In1838 he was appointed deputy judge advocate to preside over the trials of Patriote prisoners, and in May 1840 he entered the appointed Special Council as solicitor general, taking the place of the late Andrew Stuart*. Given Day's long-standing commitment to a legislative union of Upper and Lower Canada, it is not surprising that Governor General Lord Sydenham [Thomson*] invited Day to continue as solicitor general in the Executive Council constituted to carry union. In the subsequent general election held early in 1841 Day successfully contested the Ottawa constituency, a contest which cost his election committee, composed of timber men like Ruggles Wright, some £1,580. But Day's Tory past proved obnoxious to the Reform members of Sydenham's coalition cabinet and in February 1841 Robert Baldwin* demanded Day's resignation as a condition of his group's support of Sydenham's government. In the end Baldwin, not Day, left the cabinet. Yet Day's victory proved short-lived. On 28 June 1842 Governor General Sir Charles Bagot*, in an effort to make his Executive Council more representative of the will of the lower house, named Day to the Court of Queen's Bench.

Out of office, Day's differences with the Reform party were soon resolved. On 1 Jan. 1850 he was raised to puisne judge of the Superior Court by the Reform government of Baldwin and Louis-Hippolyte La Fontaine* and in the mid 1850s he became a strong supporter of the prominent Liberal, John Young*, and of his schemes to improve transportation facilities on Lac Saint-Pierre. As a judge, one of Day's most exacting tasks was to help untangle the complex claims created by the abolition of seigneurial tenure in 1854 [*see* Lewis Thomas DRUMMOND]. In 1859 the Conservative government of George-Étienne Cartier* and John A. Macdonald* named Day to the commission to codify the civil law of Lower Canada, a task which he shared with Augustin-Norbert Morin* and René-Édouard Caron* and which occupied the next six years of his life. Accepting particular responsibility for drafting sections of the code relating to commercial matters, Day accomplished for the commission what probably constitutes his most significant legal contribution. In 1865 he was appointed to a commission to determine the amount of government subsidy to be paid railway companies carrying the provincial post, and in that same year became the Hudson's Bay Company's attorney in a lengthy case in which the company pressed claims against the United States government arising out of the Oregon treaties of 1846 and 1863. Meanwhile, in 1868 Day became the province of Quebec's arbitrator to divide and adjust "the credits, liabilities, properties and assets" resulting from the former union of the two Canadas. Finally in 1873 John A. Macdonald appointed Day to the royal commission to report on Lucius Seth HUNTINGTON's charges of corruption against the Conservative government for its handling of the proposed Canadian Pacific Railway charter.

Apart from law and politics, Day's principal interest was education. In 1836 he had joined the executive of a small Montreal committee to improve provincial education, which counted among its members many who would become Patriote leaders. In 1841, as solicitor general, he introduced a bill to establish and maintain government-assisted common schools in the united province along the lines first suggested in the Durham Report. One of the original incorporators of the Advocates' Library and Law Institute of Montreal, he served as its president in 1847–48. He also helped organize the Montreal meeting of the American Association for the Advancement of Science in August 1859. In 1869 Day was named to the Quebec Council of Public Instruction and served as chairman of its Protestant committee from 1869 to 1875; in the following year he was reappointed to the reconstituted council. Even his tenure as vice-president of the Anglican Church Society from 1842 to 1852 may have been motivated by that society's educational objectives.

But Day's most important educational work was with the Royal Institution for the Advancement of Learning, the provincial body responsible for higher education. A member of the institution's board of governors, he served as its president from 1852 to 1884, and as principal *pro tempore* of McGill College from 1853 to 1855 and chancellor of the university from 1864 to 1884. With Christopher DUNKIN he engrafted the faculty of law onto McGill in 1848, and affiliated to it as well the High School of Montreal, the McGill Normal School (Montreal), St Francis College (Richmond), and Morrin College (Quebec). It was Day, too, who in 1852 insisted on amending the Royal Institution's statutes, thereby ending the old antagonism between it and McGill College's directors [*see* John Bethune*]. Day pressed for the inclusion of science and modern literature in the curriculum and was responsible for the selection in 1855 of McGill's most distinguished principal, John William Dawson*, who established the university's academic reputation. Not only was Day the architect of McGill's mid-century revival, but he also guided it through numerous legal and political difficulties. At his death in 1884 the university's board of governors declared that McGill's "progress and present prosperity in a great measure are due to his eminent ability and wise counsel."

CARMAN MILLER

ANQ-M, État civil, Presbytériens, St Andrew's Church (Montreal), 1830–36; Unitariens, Messiah Unitarian Church (Montreal), 1853; Minutiers, G. D. Arnoldi, 1828–36. McGill Univ. Arch., Minutes of the board of governors, 1848–84. PAC, MG 24, D8. *The Arthur papers; being the Canadian papers mainly confidential, private, and demi-*

official of Sir George Arthur, K.C.H., last lieutenant-governor of Upper Canada, in the manuscript collection of the Toronto Public Libraries, ed. C. R. Sanderson (3v., Toronto, 1957–59). Can., Prov. of, Legislative Assembly, *Journals*, 1841–45. Church of England, Church Soc. of the Diocese of Quebec, *Annual report* (Quebec), 1843–52. [C. E. P. Thomson], *Letters from Lord Sydenham, governor general of Canada, 1839–1841, to Lord John Russell*, ed. Paul Knapland (London, 1931). *Bytown Gazette* [Ottawa], February 1836–September 1837. *Canadian Courant and Montreal Advertiser*, 13 Aug. 1814–15 April 1816. *Gazette* (Montreal), January–May 1834, April–July 1836, January–March 1884. *An alphabetical list of the merchants, traders, and housekeepers, residing in Montreal; to which is prefixed, a descriptive sketch of the town*, comp. Thomas Doige (Montreal, 1819). F.-J. Audet, "Commissions d'avocats de la province de Québec, 1765 à 1849," *BRH*, 39 (1933): 584. *Canada, an encyclopædia* (Hopkins). [G. E. Day], *A genealogical register of the descendants in the male line of Robert Day . . .* (2nd ed., Northampton, Mass., 1848). J. Desjardins, *Guide parl. Montreal directory*, 1842–59. Notman and Taylor, *Portraits of British Americans*. *Political appointments, 1841–65* (J.-O. Coté). P.-G. Roy, *Les juges de la prov. de Québec*. Atherton, *Montreal*, I-II. N. F. Davin, *The Irishman in Canada* (London and Toronto, 1877). Dent, *Last forty years*. R. S. Longley, *Sir Francis Hincks; a study of Canadian politics, railways, and finance in the nineteenth century* (Toronto, 1943). C. W. New, *Lord Durham; a biography of John George Lambton, first Earl of Durham* (Oxford, 1929). Rich, *History of HBC*, II. L.-P. Audet, "La surintendance de l'éducation et la loi scolaire de 1841," *Cahiers des Dix*, 25 (1960): 147–69. J. E. C. Brierley, "Quebec's civil law codification; viewed and reviewed," *McGill Law Journal* (Montreal), 14 (1968): 521–89. Olivier Maurault, "Louis-Hippolyte La Fontaine à travers ses lettres à Amable Berthelot," *Cahiers des Dix*, 19 (1954): 129–60. Maréchal Nantel, "En marge d'un centenaire," *Cahiers des Dix*, 17 (1952): 233–44.

DEARIN, JOHN JOSEPH, druggist and politician; b. probably in 1818 at St John's, Nfld, son of William Dearin and Elizabeth King, and baptized 15 May 1819; d. 25 July 1890 at St. John's.

After serving an apprenticeship to a pharmacist in St John's, John Joseph Dearin worked as a druggist-clerk in Harbour Grace before returning to the city in the late 1840s. In partnership with his brother George, he opened an apothecary shop on Water Street and soon gained a reputation as an excellent counter-prescriber. Like many others in his trade, Dearin adopted the title "doctor," by which he was always known. His business appears to have flourished; he was, for instance, the sole agent in Newfoundland for J. C. Ayer and Company of Lowell, Mass., a large firm manufacturing patent medicines. Dearin occasionally practised dentistry as well as dispensing medicines, and was also interested in daguerreotype. He became well known in the east end of St John's as "an original character very free in his speech."

Dearin's political attitudes were typical of those held by most Roman Catholic tradesmen in St John's. In the 1850s he supported the campaign for responsible government, contributing letters to Robert John PARSONS' *Patriot*, and in the 1860s he opposed confederation, as he was to do all his life. Dearin did not enter public life until the 1870s, however, probably for personal reasons. His first wife, Catherine, had died in 1864. He had married on 4 June 1866 Bessie Josephine Stanislaus Furlong, but she died in 1868, and in 1869 a daughter by his first marriage also died. Only a son by his second marriage was left.

In 1873 Dearin was first elected for St John's East as a member of the victorious anti-confederate party led by Charles James Fox BENNETT. The party disintegrated soon after the election, however, and Dearin found himself a member of the Liberal opposition. With confederation no longer an issue, the Liberals were prepared to support the government of Frederic Bowker Terrington Carter* in any progressive legislation it might propose. Dearin, for example, encouraged the Conservatives to press forward with the building of a railway from St John's to Carbonear, which he saw as the first stage of the trans-island line they were cautiously considering. "Build this road," he said, "and a glorious future will dawn on the country." In the 1876 session Dearin chaired a select committee whose report endorsing the project was accepted by the assembly, and he continued to speak enthusiastically about the government's proposal for a trans-island railway in the 1877 and 1878 sessions. Although Dearin was a hard-working member both inside and outside the assembly, he was defeated in the 1878 election by Robert John Parsons Jr, whose father had once held the seat. Construction of a railway to Harbour Grace was started in 1881, when Dearin was out of the assembly. He helped perpetuate an impression that he was the railway's progenitor, but credit in fact should have gone to Premier Sir William Vallance Whiteway*. Dearin's role was solely that of an effective propagandist; nevertheless, as the *Evening Telegram* remarked, his voluble advocacy of a controversial scheme certainly "had the effect of breaking the ground" for its eventual acceptance.

Dearin was re-elected in 1882 in support of Whiteway's Conservative government, which had fought the election in a pro-railway alliance with the Liberals against the "New Party." In the complicated sectarian manœuvrings of the mid 1880s, however, Dearin seems to have become estranged from the Catholic political hierarchy led by Sir Ambrose Shea*, and he was defeated in the election of 1885. Four years later, with Shea out of politics, Dearin was adopted as a candidate by the revived Whiteway party which was committed to completing the trans-island railway. He was re-elected for St John's East in 1889. The campaign was too much for him, however, and he died less than a year later.

JAMES K. HILLER

Nfld., House of Assembly, *Journal*, 1876. *Colonist* (St John's), 2 Aug. 1890. *Evening Mercury*, 2 Nov. 1885, 9 Nov. 1889. *Evening Telegram* (St John's), 26 July 1890. *Harbour Grace Standard* (Harbour Grace, Nfld.), 10 March 1877. *Newfoundlander*, 6 June 1864, 4 June 1866, 9 June 1868, 24 Feb. 1869, 8 Nov. 1878, 7 Nov. 1882. *Patriot* (St John's), 7 Jan. 1854, 15 Nov. 1873. *Public Ledger*, 14 March, 14 May 1878. *Times and General Commercial Gazette* (St John's), 30 July 1890. Frank Cramm, "The construction of the Newfoundland railway, 1875–1898" (MA thesis, Memorial Univ. of Newfoundland, St John's, 1961). Devine, *Ye olde St. John's*.

DEASE, ELLEN, named **Mother Teresa**, of the Institute of the Blessed Virgin Mary in America; b. 4 May 1820 at Naas (Republic of Ireland), daughter of Oliver Dease and Anne Nugent; d. 1 July 1889 at Toronto, Ont.

Ellen Dease was the youngest of five children whose parents were both from ancient and distinguished families. Orphaned while young, she went to live with her grandmother in Dublin and received most of her early education at home. She attended a seminary for young ladies in Dublin before furthering her education in Europe, mainly in Paris. Fluent in French and Italian, she was also an accomplished musician who for a time participated in the social life of Dublin. At the age of 25 Ellen entered the novitiate of the Roman Catholic Loretto (now Loreto) Abbey, Rathfarnham (County Dublin), and became known as Mother Teresa.

The Dublin abbey, established in 1822, is the Irish branch of the Institute of the Blessed Virgin Mary, founded in the 17th century by Mary Ward. She had seen the need for a more ordinary manner of religious life for women, allowing them freedom to go when and where they could serve the church, but in time a more monastic life was adopted, with religious names being introduced in 1810. The institute had quietly opened a school for girls in York in 1686, long the only such Catholic school in England.

Within 25 years of its foundation, Loretto-Rathfarnham had sent out new foundations, including those in India and Mauritius. At the request of Bishop Michael Power* of Toronto, Rathfarnham sent five sisters, Mother Teresa being one, to his diocese in 1847. Years later she wrote about the delay in their ship's departure from Ireland: "One day longer in the cherished land of our birth . . . was a balm to the heart . . . especially to one Sister T. whom obedience rather than zeal sustained under the sacrifice which she felt almost as great as that of life would have been."

Bishop Power apparently did everything possible to ensure a good journey for the sisters, and all went well until their arrival in Toronto on 16 September. Seeing at once they were not expected, they took a cab in some embarrassment to the bishop's house, and then were further dismayed by his worried manner. The travellers had been unaware that malignant typhus was raging in the city. Bishop Power, occupied with tending the sick, the dying, and the bereaved, in what Henry Scadding* called "the terrible season of 1847," had no place prepared for them. The sisters were made welcome in a private home until a house was rented on Duke Street; classes began there for nine boarders on 29 September with Mother Teresa teaching languages and music. Meanwhile the bishop had contracted fever, and on 1 October he died.

Bishop Power's death was a near disaster to the Loretto sisters who now found themselves, some two weeks after arriving, deprived of their patron. The newly formed diocese did not have the means to provide for them, and no help could be expected from the hard pressed motherhouse in Ireland. With great determination and often at the expense of their well-being, the sisters, led by Mother Ignatia (Anne Hutchinson), threw themselves into their work. In 1848 they moved to a larger but less expensive house. The income from their private boarding- and day-school, Loretto House, enabled them to open a free school for poor children in the cathedral parish with Mother Gertrude (Mary Fleming) as teacher, the first sister to teach in the separate schools of the city.

When Bishop Power's successor, Armand-François-Marie de Charbonnel*, arrived in Toronto in 1850, he was alarmed at the plight of the sisters and immediately wrote on their behalf to Dublin: "Deprived of a bishop, of a house, and of many other things during three years, I am amazed at their having got through the numberless difficulties. . . . The members of the house are too few . . . in fact they are overwhelmed." However, the rigours of the climate and overwork continued to take their toll. Mother Ignatia lived only long enough to find renewed hope for the survival of the Canadian foundation. By the time of her death on 9 March 1851 the little group of five had lost two others, including Mother Gertrude. On 19 March 1851 Mother Teresa was named superior and entered on the long term of office that gave her the title of foundress of the institute in America.

In September classes resumed with new hope. Numbers had increased in the Roman Catholic community and its schools and there was a contagious mood of success in the atmosphere of Toronto, now increasing its influence with the expansion of industry and the railways. As education became more important in the new prosperity, Loretto grew. During her administration Mother Teresa opened 13 houses. The sixth, Loretto-Niagara at Niagara Falls, remained her favourite; the seventh, Loretto House on Bond Street, was the first home the sisters owned in Toronto; and the ninth, on Wellington Street, was the first considered suitable to bear the name Loretto Abbey. The last foundation made by Mother Teresa was in 1880, at Joliet, Ill., the first of several opened in the United States.

The Lindsay school, opened in 1874, has particular significance. The parish priest, Father Michael Stafford, aware of the career-oriented curricula in the public schools, insisted that pupils in his pastoral care follow like courses and write the examinations of the provincial Department of Education. Teachers were therefore required to have professional certificates but, although the institute had many new members, few had normal school training and certificates when they entered. In the 19th century, education of young ladies emphasized character training based on religious and ethical principles, artistic and social accomplishments, and competence in the management of a home; both within and without the community there were strong objections to any changes. Some thought it deplorable to descend to competition in education, not to mention the indignity of girls entering the business world to earn their own living. Even Mother Teresa, always insistent that her teachers be competent in their field and well prepared for their classes, wrote in a letter to Ireland: "Education here is carried to excess." However, before long the sisters were attending the Toronto Normal School, and china painting and "plain and fancy needlework" along with fluency in foreign languages vanished into the history of education.

On 6 June 1881 the Institute of the Blessed Virgin Mary was established in America by papal decree as a generalate in its own right, separate from Rathfarnham. Mother Teresa, who had travelled to Ireland in 1860 and 1870, both to obtain needed funds and volunteers and to ensure that the Canadian houses were following the life-style of the Dublin abbey, thus became the superior general of the institute in America. Though she outlived the other sisters who came in 1847, Mother Teresa's health had long been delicate, and in her 70th year she died at Loretto Abbey in Toronto. Her grave is in the grounds of the place she loved, Loretto-Niagara.

Mother Teresa was given affection and respect by countless friends, both Roman Catholic and Protestant; by pupils, who at the time of her death numbered thousands; and by the sisters of the institute in Ireland and in Canada. Dearly loved by young children, she had the gracious and gentle manner of a Victorian lady, but like all leaders and founders she had to cope, sometimes firmly, with people and problems both in and outside of her communities. That she did so with a minimum of friction was owing to her own serenity, and to the faith, hope, and love that supported her fortitude. Perhaps her quiet greatness is best seen in the self-mastery of learning to live with loneliness for her homeland, with privation and hardship, and even with harrowing situations. She was able to adapt herself and the institute to the changing needs of the church. She gave her life to Canada and earned a place of honour in its history.

KATHLEEN MCGOVERN

Arch. of the Archdiocese of Toronto, Bishops Power and de Charbonnel letterbook and de Charbonnel letters; Bishops Power and de Charbonnel letterbook and Power letters. Loretto Abbey Arch. (Toronto), Annals; Corr.; Doc.; Memoranda. M. C. E. Chambers, *The life of Mary Ward (1585–1645)*, ed. H. J. Coleridge (2v., London, 1882–85), II: 465. *St. Mary's convent, Micklegate Bar, York*, ed. H. J. Coleridge (London, 1887), 77–90. Henry Scadding, *Toronto of old*, ed. F. H. Armstrong (Toronto, 1966), 48. Eric Arthur, *Toronto, no mean city* ([Toronto], 1964), 120–21. *Joyful mother of children: Mother Frances Mary Teresa Ball* (Dublin, 1961), 65, 214–15. L. K. Shook, *Catholic post-secondary education in English-speaking Canada: a history* (Toronto and Buffalo, N.Y., 1971), 156. M. Margarita, "The Institute of the Blessed Virgin Mary," CCHA *Report*, 12 (1944–45): 69–81.

DEBLOIS, GEORGE WASTIE, businessman, land agent, and politician; b. 12 July 1824 at Halifax, N.S., eldest son of Stephen Wastie DeBlois*; d. 14 Aug. 1886 in Charlottetown Royalty, P.E.I.

Little is known of the early life of George Wastie DeBlois. He is thought to have worked for his father, a prosperous Halifax merchant, from whom he received an inheritance of approximately £3,000 upon the latter's death in 1844. DeBlois moved to Charlottetown in May 1847 and in August of that year married Sarah Frances, daughter of Thomas Heath Haviland* Sr; they were to have 13 children. Since the DeBlois family and that of Samuel Cunard* were friends and business associates in Halifax, it is not surprising that George DeBlois became land agent for the extensive Cunard holdings in Prince Edward Island in 1853, continuing in that capacity until the estate was purchased by the Island government of James Colledge POPE in July 1866. He was also agent for Lawrence Sullivan and Lady Cecilia Georgiana Fane, and was thus responsible for estates totalling more than one-quarter of a million acres. At a time when land agents generally were unpopular, DeBlois enjoyed a reputation for fairness and humanity; it was said that he gave the "utmost possible satisfaction to his clients without unduly harassing the tenantry." His career as land agent ended in 1875 when the large estates were purchased with funds supplied by the federal government under the 1873 terms of the Island's entry into confederation. He continued his business agencies for insurance and coal and was a director of the Charlottetown Gas Light Company; for many years he served as a justice of the peace for Charlottetown and as lieutenant-colonel of the 6th Regiment of Queens County militia, and he was a trustee of Prince of Wales College in 1877 and 1878.

A firm adherent of the Church of England, DeBlois

was intensely interested in the debate on education which frequently disturbed the provincial political scene. In 1876 a legislative committee chaired by Louis Henry Davies* submitted a report making it clear that the Island's educational system was in a deplorable state. The election held in August of that year was fought on the education issue, but not on the usual party or religious lines. There were alignments of those who favoured government assistance to denominational schools, known as the "Denominationalists" or "Sectarian School Party," and those opposed to public funding of denominational schools, referred to as the "Free Schoolers" or the "Non-Sectarian School Party." Although all Catholics generally supported the Denominationalists, not all Protestants supported the Free Schoolers. The town ridings were considered crucial to the outcome of the election, and DeBlois and Davies were chosen to contest the Charlottetown seats for the Free Schoolers. The incongruity of this duo running together demonstrated the intensity of the feeling over the school question. Davies, a Liberal, was the lawyer who had represented the interests of the tenants at the land commission proceedings in 1875. DeBlois, a life-long Conservative, was the land agent who contested the compensation awarded to proprietor Charlotte Sulivan under the Land Purchase Act of 1875. Thus DeBlois was running with a former adversary and against a friend and fellow Conservative, James Colledge Pope. The campaign was long and bitter. Davies and DeBlois were victorious in Charlottetown and the Free Schoolers won 19 of 30 seats. Davies headed the coalition government and appointed DeBlois provincial secretary and treasurer.

Davies soon after antagonized the Conservative members of his coalition government by campaigning on behalf of the Liberal candidate in the November 1876 federal by-election in Queens County. DeBlois was needled by the *Examiner* into declaring his support for J. C. Pope, the Conservative candidate. As soon as the assembly met in 1877, the leader of the opposition, William Wilfred Sullivan*, attempted to widen the rift between Davies and DeBlois by emphasizing the past differences of opinion among the members of the current coalition. Once the Public Schools Act was passed in 1877, there was no longer any unifying purpose to hold the coalition together and on 20 Aug. 1878 DeBlois and three other Conservatives resigned their seats in the Executive Council, citing Davies' campaigning in the federal by-election as the reason. Shortly after the house was called into session in 1879, Davies was defeated on a want of confidence motion, DeBlois voting with the other Conservatives to bring Davies down. W. W. Sullivan formed the new government in March 1879 and called for dissolution and an election in April. DeBlois was once again a candidate in Charlottetown and won on a straight party ticket, with the Conservatives taking 26 of 30 seats. Having been single-minded on the education question, DeBlois had little reason to expect that the Catholic Sullivan would reward him with a seat on the Executive Council. He remained a back-bencher throughout the remainder of his brief political career and did not run in the election of 1882.

DeBlois was not a politician at heart, having been persuaded to enter the political arena only because of his interest in the school question, and he was better known as a Tory businessman. He was generally conceded to be a man of integrity.

ELINOR BERNICE VASS

Halifax County Court of Probate (Halifax), no.113, will of S. W. DeBlois (mfm. at PANS). PAPEI, RG 16, Land registry records, Conveyance registers, liber 66: ff.86, 112. St George's Anglican Church (Halifax), Parish records (mfm. at PANS). St Paul's Anglican Church (Charlottetown), Marriage registers, 26 Aug. 1847 (mfm. at PAPEI). St Paul's Anglican Church (Halifax), Parish records (mfm. at PANS).

Abstract of the proceedings before the Land Commissioners' Court, held during the summer of 1860, to inquire into the differences relative to the rights of landowners and tenants in Prince Edward Island, reporters J. D. Gordon and David Laird (Charlottetown, 1862). P.E.I., House of Assembly, *Debates and proc.*, 1877–82. *Report of proceedings before the commissioners appointed under the provisions of "The Land Purchase Act, 1875,"* reporter P. S. MacGowan (Charlottetown, 1875). *Examiner*, May–August 1876; March–April 1879. *Islander*, May–August 1876; March–April 1879. *Patriot* (Charlottetown), May–August 1876; March–April 1879. *Canadian biog. dict.*, II. *Directory of N.S. MLAs*. *The Prince Edward Island almanack* . . . (Charlottetown), 1853–54, 1868–69, 1871, 1875, 1877, 1881, 1884–86. *The Prince Edward Island calendar* . . . (Charlottetown), 1862–63, 1865–66, 1870. *Prince Edward Island directory* . . . (Charlottetown), 1864. A. H. Clark, *Three centuries and the Island, a historical geography of settlement and agriculture in Prince Edward Island, Canada* (Toronto, 1959). Robertson, "Religion, politics and education in P.E.I." A. W. H. Eaton, "Old Boston families; the Deblois family," *New England Hist. and Geneal. Register* (Boston), 57 (1913): 16–20.

DELANEY (Delany), JOHN, public servant, politician, and meteorologist; b. in 1811 in Ireland; m. Elizabeth Troy, and they had five sons and three daughters; d. 26 April 1883 at St John's, Nfld.

Little is known of John Delaney's early life, but his later career indicates that he received at least some education. He immigrated from Ireland to St John's in 1831 with his wife, a sister of Father Edward Troy*. At St John's, Delaney, like most Roman Catholics, attached himself to the Liberal party and in 1835, with the support of Patrick Morris* and other Liberal politicians, was appointed door-keeper of the House of Assembly, a position he retained until 1843. In 1848 he was elected to the House of Assembly for the district of Placentia–St Mary's.

Although Delaney often voted with the Liberal party, he was not active in the movement for responsible government. Perhaps in appreciation Governor Ker BAILLIE HAMILTON, on the advice of the Conservative administration, appointed him keeper of the House of Assembly in 1852 and surveyor of roads in 1853. However, Delaney's lack of enthusiasm for responsible government had cost him the support of the powerful Roman Catholic politician Ambrose Shea*; in the election of 1852 Delaney lost his seat to George James Hogsett*. Delaney regained the seat in 1855, was re-elected in 1859, and chose not to run in 1861.

Early in his legislative career Delaney had shown an interest in improving internal communications in Newfoundland. In 1851 he had been active in obtaining passage of the Postal Act which reorganized the mail service in the colony, and on 17 Feb. 1860 he was appointed by Governor Sir Alexander Bannerman* to succeed William Lemon Solomon, Newfoundland's first postmaster general. Delaney believed that cheap postage and improved communications were essential to the social and economic development of Newfoundland and worked energetically to expand and modernize the postal system. By the early 1880s he had established mail service to all parts of the island and to the Labrador coast using steamships, initiated door-to-door delivery in St John's, introduced a money-order system, and negotiated uniform postal rates with Great Britain and continental North America.

Although Delaney made an important contribution to Newfoundland as a public servant, his work as an amateur scientist is of almost equal significance. He was interested in astronomy, electricity, and telegraphy, and was competent enough as a civil engineer to survey a number of roads in St John's and on the Avalon Peninsula. His main scientific achievement, however, was in the field of meteorology. From 1857 to 1864, Delaney, assisted by two of his sons, John Joseph and Edward Magdalene Joseph, recorded observations of the temperature, atmospheric pressure, and rainfall at St John's, and submitted them to the Smithsonian Institution in Washington, D.C., for its compilation of statistics on the climate of North America. Although the two sons died in 1866, from 1871 to 1873 Delaney contributed another series of observations to the Smithsonian. In 1871 when the Meteorological Office (later the Meteorological Service) of Canada was formed by George Templeman KINGSTON, Delaney organized a network of six stations along the Newfoundland coast, manned by volunteer observers, which provided the Canadian meteorologists with important data on weather conditions in the approaches to the Gulf of St Lawrence. In spite of failing health Delaney spent his last years attempting unsucessfully to persuade the Newfoundland government to extend the Canadian storm-warning system to the island. He had become a fellow of the Royal Meteorological Society, London, in 1873.

As a politician John Delaney was undistinguished, but as a public servant he was vigorous and far-sighted. In his efforts to improve communications in Newfoundland he was generally in harmony with the aspirations of the St John's commercial community and the governments of the day. At times, however, his plans for the postal system and for a more elaborate meteorological service were thought to be too expensive and were ignored. Delaney's persistent advocacy of progressive measures reveals his confidence in his own judgement and independence of mind. His meteorological work gave climatologists their first accurate, long-term measurements for Newfoundland, and the link he initiated with the Meteorological Service of Canada continued almost unbroken until Newfoundland entered confederation in 1949.

IAN M. STEWART

Can., Atmospheric Environment Service (Downsview, Ont.), Letterbook of the superintendent of the Meteorological Service, 1873–83. PAC, RG 93, A2, 1874–78. Nfld., *Blue book*, 1855–60; House of Assembly, *Journal*, 1837–61. Smithsonian Institution, *Annual report* (Washington), 1858–64. *Terra Nova Advocate and Political Observer* (St John's), 28 April 1883. *Times and General Commercial Gazette* (St John's), 1, 29 Dec. 1852; 7 April 1860; 21 Aug. 1975. Gunn, *Political hist. of Nfld.* William Smith, *The history of the Post Office in British North America, 1639–1870* (Cambridge, Eng., 1920).

DÉLÉAGE (Deléage), JEAN-FRANÇOIS-RÉGIS, priest, Oblate of Mary Immaculate; b. 15 Dec. 1821 at Crossac, commune of Sainte-Sigolème, dept of Haute-Loire, France, son of François Deléage and Jeanne Romeyer, farmers; d. 1 Aug. 1884 at Ottawa, Ont.

Jean-François-Régis Déléage attended the Petit Séminaire de Monistrol-sur-Loire, Haute-Loire, and the Grand Séminaire du Puy. On 24 Feb. 1847 he entered the noviciate of the Oblates at Notre-Dame de l'Osier, Isère, and made his profession on 27 Feb. 1848. He completed theological studies in Montreal, and was ordained priest on 29 Oct. 1848 by Joseph-Bruno Guigues*, bishop of Bytown (Ottawa).

Although Déléage spoke little English, he worked first from 1848 to 1853 in the parish of Our Lady of the Visitation at South Gloucester, Canada West, which at that time included about 2,000 Irish among its members. Despite violent opposition from Orangemen, he built a church there, and he ministered to this parish and to various missions including Osgoode, Metcalf, and Embrun.

Father Déléage was then sent to Canada East as priest to the newly created parish of L'Assomption-de-Maniwaki (L'Assomption-de-la-Sainte-Vierge), which in 1853 comprised about 200 families, and as superior of the Oblates in this region. He erected a fine parish church, encouraged the building of schools, and in 1870 arranged for assistance from the Sisters of Charity of Ottawa. He set out to promote settlement on the land that the government had assigned to the Oblates in order to encourage the Algonkins to take up farming but he met with scant success. The priest also arranged for several families from South Gloucester to move to his parish, and they were followed by some French Canadian families, who settled on the banks of the Lièvre. In 1854 Déléage set up a sawmill at the Chute des Eaux and then in 1860 a sawmill and a flour-mill on the Rivière Joseph (Saint-Joseph) which was the beginning of the parish of Moulin des Pères or Sainte-Famille-d'Aumond. He persuaded the government to build roads and grant a post office. He was also responsible for setting up the parishes of Saint-Gabriel, Sainte-Philomène, and La Visitation in the Maniwaki region.

In addition to his work as a parish priest, Father Déléage served the missions in the Témiscamingue region for several years, and in 1859–60 he and Father Jean-Marie Pian were among the first Catholic priests to winter at Fort Albany (Ont.) on James Bay. He also visited the missions on the Saint-Maurice River and those in the lumber camps, particularly on the Gatineau. Through this work he got to know Alonzo Wright*, the king of the Gatineau River region, who called him "my old friend." The parish priest was popular among both whites and Indians. He was said to have mastered eight Indian dialects.

A financial setback caused by difficulties in selling timber from the mills led Déléage to ask to be relieved of the post of superior. After a brief period (1879–81) in the parish of Sainte-Anne at Mattawa, Ont., he spent his last years at the mission of Témiscamingue, which had been founded at his request in 1863 to provide him with closer contact with the northern missions and place him in a better position to learn the various Indian dialects.

All his life Jean-François-Régis Déléage was a devoted missionary who never hesitated to make the sacrifices necessary to ensure the spiritual and material well-being of his flock. He belonged to the family of great missionaries of the last century, among whom were Nicolas Laverlochère, Jean-Marie Pian, and Louis-Étienne-Delille Reboul*, all of whom also worked in these missions.

GASTON CARRIÈRE

AP, L'Assomption-de-la-Sainte-Vierge (Maniwaki), *Codex historicus* (copy at Arch. hist. oblates, Ottawa). *Notices nécrologiques des membres de la Congrégation des Oblats de Marie-Immaculée* (8v., Paris, 1868–1939), V: 409–50. Gaston Carrière, *Histoire documentaire de la Congrégation des Missionnaires Oblats de Marie-Immaculée dans l'Est du Canada* (12v., Ottawa, 1957–75), II-VII; IX; XI. Sœur Paul-Émile [Louise Guay], *Les sœurs grises de La Croix . . .* (2v., Ottawa, [1945–] 67), I: 325–26.

DENNIS, JOHN STOUGHTON, surveyor, militia officer, civil servant, and entrepreneur; b. 19 Oct. 1820 in Kingston, Upper Canada, eldest son of Joseph Dennis and Mary Stoughton; m. 13 Sept. 1848 Sarah Maria Oliver, and they had several children; d. 7 July 1885 at Kingsmere, Que., and was buried at Kingston.

John Stoughton Dennis was born into a family of relative affluence in which military virtues and loyalty counted for much. During the American revolution his grandfather, John Dennis*, supported the British and left his home in Philadelphia, eventually settling on the Humber River near York (Toronto); during the War of 1812 his father, Joseph, a lake captain, was captured and imprisoned by the Americans. About 1822 Joseph moved his family from the Kingston area to York, and then in 1830 to Weston. Here the Dennis family were to play a prominent role in the economic life of the community.

John Stoughton was educated at Victoria College in Cobourg, Upper Canada, and, after apprenticing with Charles Rankin, he qualified as a land surveyor on 4 Jan. 1842. His surveying career was an active one. Over the next two decades he surveyed a number of town sites along the projected routes of the Grand Trunk and Great Western railways; he registered the plan for Weston on 18 July 1846. He surveyed the Bruce Peninsula in 1855, and townships and colonization roads in the Muskoka, Haliburton, Parry Sound, and Nipissing districts between 1860 and 1865. In 1861 he began laying out ten townships for the Canadian Land and Emigration Company in the Minden-Haliburton area. He also surveyed various Indian reserves on the shores of lakes Huron and Superior. His professional competence had been recognized when he was appointed to the board of examiners for provincial land surveyors in 1851.

Although he lived in Toronto, Dennis maintained a keen interest in Weston, helping to secure the passage of the Grand Trunk Railway through it; he was also a member of the first board of the local grammar school. His concerns extended beyond local matters, to the institution for the deaf, dumb, and blind in Hamilton and to the Canadian Institute. Dennis was especially interested in the militia, believing himself "descended of martial ancestors." In 1855 he was made a lieutenant of a cavalry troop, and in the following year commander of the Toronto Field Battery. In 1862 he was appointed brigade-major of the 5th Military District (with the rank of lieutenant-colonel), and he held the post until 1871.

Dennis first saw active service in June 1866 during the Fenian invasion. Somehow he secured temporary command of the 2nd Battalion, Queen's Own Rifles [*see* William Smith DURIE], which was sent on 1 June to Port Colborne where Dennis was second in command to Lieutenant-Colonel Alfred Booker*. Colonel George John Peacocke, the commander of the imperial troops on the Niagara frontier, instructed Booker to bring his force to Stevensville (now part of Fort Erie, Ont.) to await the Fenian attack. Dennis, believing the Fenians drunk and disorganized, beseeched Booker to attack immediately, but this scheme was rejected, though Booker later agreed to take independent action. Dennis commandeered the tugboat *W. T. Robb*, and began patrolling the Niagara River in an attempt to stop Fenian movements. On 2 June, Booker's force, proceeding towards Stevensville, was attacked and defeated at Ridgeway by a force of Fenians led by John O'Neill*. In the afternoon of the same day, Dennis landed 70 of his men at Fort Erie in an attempt to find out where the Canadians were and to dispose of the prisoners he had taken. Some 150 Fenians appeared, but, confident of victory and unaware that more Fenians were coming up, Dennis urged his men forward. Following an exchange of fire, he ordered a retreat; the tugboat cast off without him and he was forced to disguise himself as "a labouring man." He escaped, but 34 of his men did not.

An officer who had served at Fort Erie subsequently demanded an investigation into Dennis' conduct, and another, who had lost a leg in the battle, publicly labelled him "a coward" and a "Poltrooney scoundrel." Dennis requested a court of inquiry which examined charges by the officers, mostly of endangering his men unnecessarily but also of deserting them in the face of enemy fire. The court exonerated him completely but its president, George Taylor Denison* II, privately felt Dennis culpable of disobeying orders and published a dissenting opinion questioning his judgement.

After the embarrassments of 1866 Dennis returned to his surveying career. In 1869 he was sent by William McDougall*, Canadian minister of public works, to the Red River Settlement (Man.) as a temporary employee of the Canadian government to survey lots for prospective settlers. The Métis of Red River, who had not wanted the surveys undertaken in the first place, were doubly suspicious of Dennis when he stayed with Dr John Christian Schultz*, whom they heartily distrusted, after his arrival in August. The surveys, based on the American section system, seemed to threaten existing river lot holdings and, despite Dennis' reassurances to them, the Métis under Louis RIEL obstructed a survey team on André Nault*'s farm on 11 Oct. 1869. Dennis attempted in vain to persuade William Mactavish*, the governor of Assiniboia and of Rupert's Land, to punish the perpetrators. Prime Minister Sir John A. Macdonald* deemed this pressure by Dennis "exceedingly injudicious." Dennis, he continued in a letter to McDougall, was "a very decent fellow and a good surveyor" but quite without a "head." Surveys in the Métis area stopped but those elsewhere continued.

McDougall, as lieutenant governor designate of the North-West Territories, arrived in Pembina (N. Dak.) on 30 October, and Dennis journeyed south to meet him. On 21 October the National Committee of the Métis of Red River had ordered McDougall not to enter the settlement and Dennis and McDougall were turned back to Pembina by a Métis patrol on 3 November. They remained at Pembina until 29 November when Dennis returned to the colony with two proclamations, one announcing McDougall's assumption of authority on 1 December, the supposed date of the transfer of the colony from the Hudson's Bay Company to Canada, and the other naming himself McDougall's "Lieutenant" and "conservator of the peace."

The colonel established his headquarters at Lower Fort Garry and attracted "a motley crowd of 300"; he tried to ensure order among the volunteers by prohibiting liquor, but the attempt collapsed when he exempted himself. On 6 December a call "to all loyal men" produced a few more volunteers. Then, the following day, Schultz and a band of followers, barricaded in his Winnipeg warehouse, were forced to surrender to Riel, who proclaimed a provisional government on 8 December. Dennis, without either seeing or paying his men, disbanded them on 9 December and fled the colony two days later. His surveyors, who had been brought into the fort, were instructed to go back to their work, one of them being told specifically not to survey "beyond the limits of the English portions of the settlement." Dennis returned to Ottawa with McDougall, leading Macdonald to reflect sourly that they had "done their utmost to destroy our chance of an amicable settlement" with the Métis. On 12 Feb. 1870 Dennis reported to Hector-Louis Langevin*, the minister of public works, that the people of Red River had not allowed the surveyors to proceed for fear of the Métis; he nevertheless took pride in the fact that they had surveyed 20,000 acres of farmland along the Red and Assiniboine rivers, ascertaining "present actual boundaries (but making no change whatever)." Two days later he assured Macdonald in a letter that he had "discharged" his duty "with prudence and judgment."

On his return to Ontario Dennis served for a time as Lieutenant Governor William Pearce Howland*'s private secretary, and on 7 March 1871 his professional qualifications secured his appointment as Canada's first surveyor general and head of the new Dominion Lands Branch. He made solid contributions as surveyor general. In March 1872 he produced a report which optimistically outlined the agricultural possibilities of the northwest. His office pushed ahead with the Manitoba surveys and after 1874 extended the base and meridian lines north from the 49th parallel to the North Saskatchwan River and west from Red River to the Rocky Mountains. For the most part Dennis remained in Ottawa, providing for corrections in the surveys already run, planning new and more detailed surveys, allocating the HBC lands, and trying to reassure the Indians and the Métis, as well as the few white settlers, that their rights would be respected. The possibilities of the west had clearly seized Dennis' imagination, and he busily formulated a grand scheme in which Hudson Bay was to become a great commercial artery, funnelling people and produce in and out of the west.

On 14 Nov. 1878 Dennis became the deputy minister of the interior under Macdonald as minister. He won the post on merit; he had been no party war-horse, for, as he later informed Sir John, "I have never upon principle, since I have been in receipt of a salary from the Government, either as a staff officer of Militia or since I entered the regular Civil Service, cast a single vote." Dennis did not toady to his minister, and in July 1879 they had a heated disagreement over the details of the disposition of the 100,000 acres of western railway lands. Macdonald proposed that the land be sold in 80-acre units, while Dennis argued for the new American system of 160 acres. Apparently Dennis carried the day, for the homestead units were raised to 160 acres. Macdonald praised Dennis' work, which the latter found almost as gratifying as "a compliment (if such a thing could be imagined) coming from the Queen herself."

As deputy minister, Dennis kept a sharp eye on the northwest; concerned over the depressed condition of the Indians and Métis, he urged the government to assist the Métis in becoming settled farmers by giving them cattle, technical training, and whatever else they needed, in the belief that they could then help civilize the Indians. His advice was ignored. In 1880 Dennis travelled to England with the Canadian delegation which was attempting to finance the Canadian Pacific Railway. The following year he joined Sir Alexander Tilloch Galt* on a tour of inspection of the west; it was a tiring journey for the ailing deputy minister who subsequently resigned his office on 31 December. He took comfort from the fact that he had helped to formulate public lands policy at a time "when the country was as a *white* sheet" and from the knowledge that his services were appreciated. On 24 May 1882 he was created a CMG.

During his retirement Dennis maintained close relations with his "dear old chief," even contributing to Macdonald's campaign fund in 1882. Although he had insisted that he had left office "poor and involved in debt," he was able to invest in several private business concerns, including a consumers' cooperative and a mining venture in what is now Alberta. His most cherished enterprise was Dennis, Sons and Company, established in 1882, with offices in England, to tender advice to prospective colonizers and immigrants. John Stoughton Dennis Jr, also a prominent surveyor, was a member of the firm, and the company became involved in surveys in the northwest; political influence helped secure contracts.

Dennis was active until his death in July 1885. Although he may be remembered as a militia officer who was prone to leap upon his horse and ride off in all directions at once, he should also be recalled as an able administrator who made significant, lasting contributions to Canada.

COLIN FREDERICK READ

AO, MU 1131, Skirving and Dennis families, W. W. Duncan, "Narrative of the Skirving and Dennis families" (typescript, March 1967); MU 2399. PAC, MG 26, A; MG 29, E74; RG 9, I, C8, 7. PAM, MG 3, B5; B11; B16-2; D1; MG 12, A; B.

Can., Parl., *Sessional papers*, 1870, V: no.12. W. McC. Davidson, *Louis Riel, 1844–1885; a biography* (Calgary, 1955). G. T. Denison, *History of the Fenian raid on Fort Erie; with an account of the battle of Ridgeway* (Toronto, 1866), v, 22–91; *Soldiering in Canada; recollections and experiences* (2nd ed., Toronto, 1901). J. K. Howard, *Strange empire; a narrative of the northwest* (New York, 1952). J. A. Macdonald, *Troublous times in Canada; a history of the Fenian raids of 1866 and 1870* (Toronto, 1910). E. B. Osler, *The man who had to hang: Louis Riel* (Toronto, 1961). Stanley, *Birth of western Canada*. D. W. Thomson, *Men and meridians; the history of surveying and mapping in Canada* (3v., Ottawa, 1966–69). V. B. Wadsworth, *History of exploratory surveys conducted by John Stoughton Dennis, provincial land surveyor, in the Muskoka, Parry Sound and Nipissing districts 1860–1865 . . .* (n.p., 1926) (copy at AO). H. F. Wood, *Forgotten Canadians* (Toronto, 1963). Charles Unwin, "Col. John Staughton Dennis," Assoc. of Ontario Land Surveyors, *Annual report* (Toronto), 29 (1914): 57–58.

DENT, JOHN CHARLES, lawyer, journalist, author, and historian; b. 8 Nov. 1841 at Kendal, England, son of John Dent and Catherine Mawson; m. 17 Oct. 1866 Elsie McIntosh, and they had two sons and three daughters; d. 27 Sept. 1888 in Toronto, Ont.

John Charles Dent immigrated with his family to Canada West as a small child. He studied law in the Brantford office of Edmund Burke WOOD, later treasurer of Ontario and chief justice of Manitoba. Dent was called to the bar in 1865 but, disliking the practice of law, he returned to England to embark on a new career in journalism.

Dent learned his trade working for the *Daily Telegraph* in London. At this time the extension of the franchise, the advance of literacy, and technological innovations were transforming part of the British press into media of mass communications, creating a new and larger reading public, and altering reportorial style. The *Telegraph*, founded in 1855 and taking its name from the invention which had recently accelerated the transmission of news, was priced at 1*d.* when competitors were selling at 4*d.* In search of a mass public, it was pioneering the field of "sensational journalism." Dent is also reported to have contributed "a series of articles on interesting topics" to *Once a Week*, an intellectually undemanding periodical catering to the interests of the lower middle class. Dent's contributions cannot be identified, but his later fiction is of the sort favoured by this magazine. In 1867 he moved to the United States. He is said to have been employed on the Boston *Globe*, founded in 1872 as a "commercial and business journal of the first class," but driven to sensationalism when it neared bankruptcy in the competitive Boston market.

In 1876 Dent's experience as a popular writer was of interest to Goldwin Smith* who, with John Ross Robertson* as proprietor, was about to found the Toronto *Evening Telegram*, an organ intended to support Edward Blake* and the Liberal party. This was Smith's only venture with a journal catering to popular taste, and he himself did not intend to direct editorial policy. He did, however, reserve the right of appointing the first editor, who was Dent. The *Telegram* soon departed from the liberal convictions of Smith to pursue the imperialist and conservative enthusiasms of Robertson; within a year Dent resigned his position to become editor of the reform-minded *Weekly Globe*. Whether these facts were related is unknown but Dent's later political views certainly coincided with those of the *Globe* and its owner George Brown* rather than with the *Telegram*'s. Dent remained with the *Globe* until shortly after Brown's death in 1880, when he became a freelance writer of popular history.

Within a year he began two major undertakings. The first was *The Canadian portrait gallery* in four volumes containing biographical sketches of 204 leading figures in Canadian history. Some had already been written for the *Weekly Globe* and a few were written by other contributors; Dent's own work amounted to 185 biographies or some 888 pages. Also in 1881, he began publishing *The last forty years: Canada since the union of 1841*, which, like the *Portrait gallery*, was issued serially. Consisting of 735 pages of text in two volumes, it long remained the leading account of the period in English.

In achieving so much so quickly, Dent owed a great deal to Sir Francis HINCKS who, as he acknowledged, possessed an invaluable knowledge of the past, being the last leading politician of the 1840s still alive. Hincks, moreover, had a keen interest in history, particularly with regard to the role he and other "Baldwinite" Reformers had played in it. In 1877 he had published a short *Political history of Canada between 1840 and 1855* and he was then at work on his more lengthy *Reminiscences of his public life* which appeared in 1884. Both books were highly tendentious, aimed at correcting errors of fact and interpretation being made by historians, at assailing what were taken to be mistaken views of old political opponents, and at establishing Hincks's own view of the past. At one time he had hoped to assist Louis-Philippe Turcotte* in bringing out a "corrected" edition of *Le Canada sous l'Union, 1841–1867* (1871–72) which he himself had intended to translate into English. Turcotte, however, died before this project could be accomplished. Dent's undertakings therefore provided the old man with just the sort of opportunity for which he had long been waiting. He now advised Dent closely as to factual detail, and even contributed an article on an old enemy, Sir Dominick Daly*, to *The Canadian Portrait gallery*. His most important contribution, however, probably lay in providing the basic conceptual framework of *The last forty years.*

Donald Swainson, a close student of the latter book, has remarked that while the chapters on the 1840s seem carefully researched and well organized, Dent's treatment of the period from 1850 to the 1870s resembles "a hasty and annalistic 'history of his own times.'" It appears more than coincidental that the good work corresponds with a period in which Dent's mentor was active in politics and, more especially, with the period covered in Hincks's *Political history.* Up until the 1880s, moreover, most historians believed that "responsible government" had been achieved not in 1848 (the date now generally, if misleadingly, accepted) but in 1840, a conviction which corresponds with that of old opponents of Hincks such as Egerton RYERSON; Hincks was still seeking to undermine that belief. In this regard, Dent employed Hincks's "Baldwinite" concept, and it governed his understanding of early Canadian politics to a truly remarkable extent. As Swainson observes, he "was obsessed with the issue of responsible government and in *The Last Forty Years* devoted considerable space and great passion to it. It is the book's major preoccupation."Yet the "struggle for responsible government" was more than a preoccupation; it is the book's single unifying theme, in the absence of which the later chapters fall into conceptual disarray.

Dent returned to this theme, to project it into a more distant past, in his last major work, *The story of the Upper Canadian rebellion*, published in two volumes in 1885. The second volume, which deals with the immediate causes and events of the rising, is of some enduring value in that it contains information which does not survive elsewhere, and because its author displayed a more reasonable regard for evidence here than elsewhere in his text. The first volume, which in treating long term causes deals with almost the whole of the colony's political history, is a mixture of fact and fantasy amounting to historical myth.

Partly inspired by models derived from English "Whig" history, this volume contains the story of a "struggle for liberty" which partakes of melodrama. Its heroes are moderate Reformers standing in the evolutionary tradition of "responsible government"; its villains are British officials and local Tories opposed to this tradition and radicals who departed from it by embracing republicanism and taking up arms in 1837. Dent's many critics early took note of his simplistic, black and white presentation of the politics of the period and, more especially, of his savage characterizations of those he saw as villains. John King*, son-in-law of William Lyon Mackenzie*, in his rancorous rebuttal of Dent, *The other side of the "Story,"* observed: "In one chapter we find the late Chief Justice [Sir John Beverley Robinson*], and the late Bishop [John Strachan*], compared to 'half famished tigers of the jungle.' In another [Robert Fleming Gourlay*'s] description of the Bishop as 'a lying little fool of a renegade Presbyterian' is approvingly quoted. Here, there and everywhere the most offensive epithets are applied to William Lyon Mackenzie, while [John Rolph*] is little short of an angel of light." Dent's critics, and Dent himself, however, seem not to have realized that they were dealing less with a product of historical research than with symbols, or dramatis personae, which emerged from, and reinforced, a preconceived thesis treated as a plot.

It is therefore instructive to compare Dent's historical writing with some of his purely imaginative work which was published posthumously in 1888 in *The Gerrard Street mystery and other weird tales*. As with *The story of the Upper Canadian rebellion*, these tales contain symbols which, within the context of particular plots, give expression to a noteworthy historical point of view. In the 1880s Dent was caught up in the emotively charged debate as to "the political destiny of Canada": whether it would become federated with the British empire, be annexed to the United States, or develop into an independent nation. He did not pretend to know what the outcome would be, but he had a marked preference for independence. This bias, which was related to his pervasive concern for "responsible government," is also apparent in his fiction, most notably with respect to his use of English, Canadian, and American symbols.

"The haunted house on Duchess Street" is a tale of Gothic horror in which the Horsfalls, a terrorized family of Americans, including a George Washington Horsfall, are driven from an ancient Canadian house, associated with old compact Tories, by the ghost of the autocratic Captain Bywater, an Englishman as the name was intended to suggest, who had perished there of his own immoral excesses. The symbolic implications of the plot and the curiously evocative names Dent tended to assign to his characters are even more apparent in "Sovereen's disappearance." Callously abandoned by a dissolute English husband called Sovereen, a Canadian heroine is befriended by an upright American, Thomas Jefferson Haskins. When the husband, broken and ruined, returns, he is tenderly nursed on his deathbed by Mrs Sovereen who resolves to live out the rest of her life in virtuous widowhood. And of the same order is "Gagtooth's image," wherein a central image, representing disappointed hopes for the future in the United States, is transferred from an American to a Canadian context, there to be cherished by the narrator.

The symbolic content of these stories is similar to that of Dent's histories. They are also suggestive of how literature functioned in relation to history in the mind of their author. As a popularizer Dent sought to make dry-as-dust history interesting by means of literary techniques. In the introduction to his posthumously published short stories we are told that, like Macaulay, he believed "the incidents of real life, whether political or domestic, admit of being so arranged, without detriment to accuracy, to command all the interest of an artificial series of facts; that the chain of circumstances which constitute history may be as finely and as gracefully woven as any tale of fancy." Yet Dent's powers of fancy, even unfettered by historical fact, were governed by borrowed stereotypes. In his short stories, however, he did manage to manipulate his own symbols, whereas in his imaginative projections upon the screen of history he appears rather to have been manipulated by them, to have become, in effect, symbol-bound.

In 1884 Dent edited and introduced the collected speeches of Alexander MORRIS in *Nova Britannia; or, our new Canadian dominion foreshadowed*, which, as the title suggests, reflected a nationalist point of view he fully shared. That same year he published some largely rehashed material in *Toronto, past and present*, which he wrote in collaboration with Henry Scadding*. In 1887 he founded and edited *Arcturus: a Canadian Journal of Literature and Life* where he published some of his fiction and gave expression to the dim view he had come to take of national politics. Addressed to "a wide circle of readers . . . [to] deal with questions of general interest in a readable and popular manner," this weekly collapsed within half a year of its founding.

Dent was honoured for his contributions to Canadian letters by election to the Royal Society of Canada in 1887. This election was bitterly resented by certain Conservatives who remembered him as having written in 1883 "foul libels on [Sir Charles Tupper*] and on Goldwin Smith in the Toronto *News*"; nor can it have been any more to the taste of Liberals who yet regarded themselves as standing in the tradition of William Lyon Mackenzie; nor to French Canadian historians such as Henri-Raymond Casgrain* who, reacting against Dent's Anglo-Protestant biases, had delivered a stinging critique of *The last forty years* before the Royal Society in 1884. Oddly enough, he seems to have owed his election to the support of Colonel George Taylor Denison* III, a prominent imperialist. While sharing some of Dent's nationalist fervour Denison must have been completely out of sympathy with his hankerings after independence. It was perhaps in the hope of wooing Dent from these that he acted as sponsor. In any event nothing came of it for Dent died of a heart attack in the following year.

In his time Dent was assailed by critics of all political stripes who were far from accepting his interpretation of Canadian history and whose criticisms, on the whole, were quite well taken. Dent, however, published several stout volumes, as they did not, and over the years his views tended to win out. Thus as a popularizer of a point of view, his achievement was a great one.

G. H. PATTERSON

J. C. Dent was the author of *The Canadian portrait gallery* (4v., Toronto, 1880–81), *The story of the Upper Canadian rebellion; largely derived from original sources and documents* (2v., Toronto, 1885), and *The last forty years: Canada since the union of 1841* (2v., Toronto, 1881). An abridged edition of the last work was published under the title, *The last forty years: the union of 1841 to confederation*, ed. Donald Swainson (Toronto, 1972). With Henry Scadding, Dent wrote *Toronto, past and present: historical and descriptive; a memorial volume for the semi-centennial of 1884* (Toronto, 1884), and he edited Alexander Morris' speeches in *Nova Britannia; or, our new Canadian dominion foreshadowed* . . . (Toronto, 1884); he was also the editor of the journal *Arcturus: a Canadian Journal of Literature and Life* (Toronto), 1887. His short stories were published in *The Gerrard Street mystery and other weird tales* (Toronto, 1888).

PAC, MG 29, D60; MG 30, D37. [H.-R.] Casgrain, "Les quarante dernières années: le Canada depuis l'union de 1841, par John Charles Dent; étude critique," RSC *Trans.*, 1st ser., 2 (1884), sect.I: 51–61. Francis Hincks, *The political history of Canada between 1840 and 1855: a lecture delivered on the 17th October, 1877, at the request of the St. Patrick's National Association, with copious additions* (Montreal, 1877); *Reminiscences of his public life* (Montreal, 1884). "How history is written: the Hincks to Dent letters," ed. Elizabeth Nish, *Rev. du Centre d'Étude du Québec* (Montréal), no.2 (avril 1968): 29–96. [John King], *The other side of the "Story," being some reviews of Mr. J. C. Dent's first volume of "The story of the Upper Canadian rebellion," and the letters in the Mackenzie-Rolph controversy* . . . (Toronto, 1886). *Standard dict. of Canadian biog.* (Roberts and Tunnell), II: 107. G. [H.] Patterson, "An enduring Canadian myth: responsible government and the Family Compact," *Journal of Canadian Studies*, 12 (1977), no.2: 3–16.

DESAUTELS, JOSEPH, Roman Catholic priest and vicar-general; b. 26 Oct. 1814 at Chambly, Lower Canada, son of Joseph Desautels and Madeleine Fréchette; d. 4 Aug. 1881 in Salem, Mass., buried 9 August at Varennes, Que.

A student at the Petit Séminaire de Montréal from 1828 to 1830, Joseph Desautels subsequently acquired a knowledge of canon law under the direction of Bishop Jean-Jacques Lartigue* before being ordained priest on 29 April 1838. After serving as curate at Sainte-Martine (1838), Saint-Hyacinthe (1838–39), and Sainte-Marie-de-Monnoir (Marieville) (1839–40), he accompanied Bishop Ignace BOURGET on an extensive visitation of the Ottawa valley in 1840. Struck by the lack of pastoral services in this region, Bourget erected its first canonical parish, Saint-Paul in Aylmer, and put Desautels in charge of it. The young parish priest also assumed responsibility for the lumber camps nearby. After eight years of intensive missionary activity, he was transferred to the parish of Sainte-Madeleine in Rigaud. There, with the help of his churchwardens, he set up the Collège Bourget in 1850, entrusting its management to the Clerics of St Viator. The next year he accompanied bishops Jean-Charles Prince* and Alexandre-Antonin Taché* to Rome to secure ratification of the decrees of the first Provincial Council of Quebec.

Bourget recognized Desautels's dedication to duty and in 1855 appointed him to one of the most prestigious parishes in the diocese of Montreal, Sainte-Anne in Varennes. Desautels soon increased the number of religious organizations in his parish, founding the boarding-school of Notre-Dame-du-Sacré-Cœur in 1855, the industrial college at Varennes in 1857, and the Hospice de La Jemmerais for the poor, the aged, and orphans in 1859. In 1860 he was involved in a lawsuit brought by Pierre Jarret, *dit* Beauregard, against Michel Sénécal; Jarret sought to invalidate Sénécal's election as churchwarden because it had taken place at a meeting chaired by Desautels, the parish priest, rather than by a member of the parish council. Desautels gave advice on canonical matters to Sénécal's lawyer, Côme-Séraphin CHERRIER, one of the most famous of the profession in Canada East. Cherrier won the case for Sénécal, judgement being given by Louis-Hippolyte La Fontaine*, the chief justice of the Superior Court. In 1860 a law entitled "An act to regulate the presidency at *fabrique* meetings in the Catholic parishes of Lower Canada" embodied La Fontaine's ruling. Even though this statute supported Desautels's position, he strongly opposed the state's encroachment on religious liberties. He set forth his arguments systematically in *Manuel des curés pour le bon gouvernement temporel des paroisses et des fabriques dans le Bas-Canada*, published in 1864. The church, he maintained, had the power in Canada to legislate on all matters within its sphere since Canadian law unquestionably recognized this authority. In 1862 Bishop Bourget appointed him honorary canon of the Cathedral of Saint-Jacques (Montreal) and that year he was one of the small group accompanying the bishop to Rome to discuss such matters as the establishment of a Catholic university in the diocese of Montreal. At this time Bourget secured him the title of honorary privy chaplain from the ecclesiastical authorities in Rome.

From 1865 to 1875 Desautels played a vital role in the major religious controversies in French Canada. When the parish of Notre-Dame in Montreal was divided in 1866 [*see* Joseph-Alexandre BAILE; Ignace Bourget], he encouraged his bishop to disregard the rich and powerful opposition to the episcopal plan. He even advised the use of canonical sanctions to bring the Séminaire de Saint-Sulpice back into line. In 1867 he and canons Alexis-Frédéric Truteau* and Étienne-Hippolyte Hicks were sent to Rome to defend the interests of the diocese. Desautels quickly assumed leadership of the delegation, determining strategy, making the written submissions, and ingratiating himself with the cardinals and their advisers. In the dispute with the Séminaire de Saint-Sulpice Desautels claimed that episcopal prerogatives were simply a question of rights based on civil and canon law. He took occasion to accuse the Sulpicians of Gallicanism, insubordination towards episcopal authority, and bad management of parish funds. At the beginning of 1868 he returned to Montreal, satisfied with his mission. Soon after, Bourget made him a vicar general.

In 1870 Judge Joseph-Ubalde Beaudry*, who had been the lawyer for the parish council of Notre-Dame, published in Montreal his *Code des curés, marguilliers et paroissiens accompagné de notes historiques et critiques*, which in some sense was a justification of the Sulpician claims. Worried that it had been written by such an eminent and influential jurist, Bourget commissioned Desautels to find a competent layman to refute its argument. Desautels chose Siméon Pagnuelo*, a young lawyer who had endorsed the *Programme catholique* [*see* François-Xavier-Anselme TRUDEL], and supplied him with the requisite arguments to meet Beaudry's challenge. Hence a work entitled *Études historiques et légales sur la liberté religieuse en Canada* appeared in Montreal in 1872, transforming a simple issue of parish government into an ideological confrontation. The book defended the idea that the Canadian church had full jurisdiction over religious questions; in the minds of those who upheld it, the denial of this right led directly to Gallicanism. The debate had a strong nationalist character and deeply divided the Quebec clergy. Simultaneously, other religious controversies arose over such issues as the New Brunswick schools question, the amnesty of Louis RIEL, and the establishment of a Catholic university in Montreal.

At the conclusion of a canonical inquiry into the dismemberment of the Montreal parish, occasioned by a rescript issued by the Sacred Congregation of Propaganda on 8 March 1871 and conducted by the archbishop of Quebec, Elzéar-Alexandre Taschereau*, Desautels left again for the Eternal City, where he remained for two years. He conceived his mission to be to defend and ensure the continuance of the religious endeavours, and Bourget, seriously ill in 1872, thus had a helper and successor in Rome who could pursue his objectives. Desautels wanted to dissuade Propaganda from accepting the recommendations of Taschereau's report, which he knew was sympathetic to the Sulpician arguments. He also attempted to capitalize on the political and religious issues being debated in Quebec in order to induce the cardinals to decide the university question in favour of Montreal. Finally, he wished to get official approval for the course of action the diocese had adopted in respect of the *Programme catholique*, the civil code, the New Brunswick schools question, and the diocesan newspapers. In order to accomplish these objectives, he endeavoured to discredit the religious hierarchy in Quebec by denouncing its willingness to accommodate politicians. He told Propaganda that, except for Bourget and the bishop of Trois-Rivières, Louis-François Laflèche*, the bishops were influenced by a network of family connections or friendships with political leaders; in this instance Desautels was alluding particularly to Archbishop Taschereau and to Jean Langevin*, the bishop of Rimouski. According to him their bias rendered them powerless to preserve the independence and integrity of the church. Finally, Desautels placed the *Code des curés* before the Catholic authorities in Rome to secure an explicit condemnation of it. Rome, however, never acted on his proposal.

As long as the vicar general stayed in Rome the balance beween the dioceses of Montreal and Quebec was maintained. It is true that the canonist Filippo de Angelis publicly approved Bourget's arguments in the major political and religious discussions, but the cardinals, to help restore religious peace in Quebec, scrupulously avoided taking sides. Although Propaganda showed great concern for the prerogatives of the archdiocese of Quebec in relation to the university question, it also supported the episcopal interests of the diocese of Montreal in the division of the parish of Notre-Dame. In 1874 the deterioration of the diocese's financial position forced Desautels to return to Canada after the promulgation of the fourth papal decree on the dismemberment. From then on Benjamin Pâquet*, the representative of the archdiocese of Quebec, gained increasing ascendancy in Propaganda.

In 1875 Monsignor Cesare Roncetti came to Canada as an ablegate to investigate the university question. Desautels accompanied him throughout his stay and made such a favourable impression on him that

Roncetti had him appointed domestic prelate. For Desautels this was the summit of his career. The growing influence of Pâquet nevertheless became obvious early in 1876 when Rome settled the university question. The decision taken – to create a Montreal campus of the Université Laval – was diametrically opposed to Bourget's cherished idea of an independent university in Montreal. Crushed by this move the bishop resigned. Desautels, like most Montreal canons, thought that Bourget's resignation jeopardized the very future of Catholicism. Although the other bishops accepted the 1876 decree, they had differing interpretations of the right it conferred on the episcopate to supervise the professors. The suffragan bishops composed one petition in which they described this right, while Taschereau and the authorities of the Université Laval drew up another favourable to the existing rights of the university.

Rome communicated its decision through the apostolic delegate, Bishop George Conroy*, who remained in Canada from May 1877 to June 1878. Conroy relied on specific instructions which called upon him to calm the state of political and religious agitation in Quebec and to secure the bishops' acceptance of the plan proposed to Rome by Taschereau and the Université Laval. Moreover, in accordance with the 1876 decree, the diocese of Montreal found itself obliged to assume the heavy financial burden of establishing the Montreal branch of the university while the Université Laval enjoyed the exclusive right of appointing the professors. Furthermore Bourget's friends were excluded from the new law faculty, and Sulpicians were favoured. As for the division of the parish of Notre-Dame in Montreal, Bishop Conroy opted for a compromise and ignored various important claims advanced by Bourget. Desautels saw in these developments the total destruction of Bourget's endeavours and the consequent subjection of the church to the politicians. No longer received at the bishop's palace, he spent his last days at Varennes among his parishioners.

A zealous disciple of Lartigue and Bourget, Desautels was a practical man who had a realistic view of human nature. "I have the misfortune," he once boasted, "of not seeing the Pope or God in every employee of the Congregations." His shrewdness and enthusiasm were of great importance when the interests of the diocese of Montreal had to be defended in Rome. On the other hand, his words and actions often betrayed a lack of judgement and restraint that in turn led to the failure of some of the causes he had championed all his life.

ROBERTO PERIN

Joseph Desautels was the author of *Manuel des curés pour le bon gouvernement temporel des paroisses et des fabriques dans le Bas-Canada etc., etc. avec un chapitre sur la dîme* (Montréal, 1864). ACAM, 901.086; 901.136; RCD, 41–44; RLB, 16–25. Arch. du diocèse de Saint-Jean-de-Québec (Longueuil, Qué.), 6A/202–488. *La Minerve*, 6 août 1881. Allaire, *Dictionnaire*, I. Wallace, *Macmillan dict.* Antoine Bernard, *Les Clercs de Saint-Viateur au Canada* (2v., Montréal, 1947–51), I. Lareau, *Hist. de la littérature canadienne.* Hector Legros et sœur Paul-Émile [Louise Guay], *Le diocèse d'Ottawa, 1847–1948* (Ottawa, [1949]). Robert Perin, "Bourget and the dream of the free church in Quebec, 1862–1878" (PHD thesis, Univ. of Ottawa, 1975).

DESILETS, LUC, Roman Catholic parish priest and vicar general; b. 23 Dec. 1831 at Saint-Grégoire (now part of Bécancour), Lower Canada, eldest son of François Désilets, a farmer, and Marguerite Hébert; d. 30 Aug. 1888 at Trois-Rivières, Que.

The Desilets family were descendants of Antoine Desrosiers, who arrived at Trois-Rivières in 1645 and whose children followed the contemporary custom of taking the name of the land they occupied: Lafrenière, Du Tremble, Dargis, and Desilets. One of them, Jean-Baptiste Desrosiers, *dit* Desilets, settled at Bécancour in the area that became the parish of Saint-Grégoire-le-Grand (Saint-Grégoire) in 1835. François Désilets, who came from this branch of the family, was a prosperous farmer: nearly all of his eight children received an education and they were prominent in the Trois-Rivières region in the late 19th century.

Luc Desilets began his classical studies at the Séminaire de Nicolet on 17 Sept. 1845; having decided to become a priest, he entered upon his chosen vocation on 8 Sept. 1852. Except for a short period at the Séminaire de Sainte-Thérèse, he received his theological training at Nicolet where he also taught (1852–54) or served as librarian (1855–56). He was made a deacon on 22 Sept. 1855 but a serious psychological and physical illness kept his ecclesiastical superiors from ordaining him to the priesthood until 25 Sept. 1859.

Desilets was immediately appointed assistant priest of the cathedral in Trois-Rivières and secretary to Thomas Cooke*, the first bishop of the diocese. He quickly demonstrated great initiative, and a tendency to exceed the bounds of his office or at least claim credit for the success of various steps taken by his superior. A case in point was in the appointment of Louis-François Laflèche*, the superior of the Sèminaire de Nicolet, to the bishopric of Trois-Rivières as vicar general and diocesan procurator in 1861. After two years of service, Desilets, whose health was still frail, was sent to work in quieter parishes: Saint-Eusèbe in Princeville from 1861 to 1862, and Saint-Frédéric in Drummondville from 1862 to 1864. Bishop Cooke then called him to the parish of Sainte-Marie-Madeleine in Cap-de-la-Madeleine where he remained until 1888.

At the time of Desilets's arrival the parish, which

had 1,100 inhabitants, was considered difficult to run, both because it had been without a resident parish priest from 1792 to 1844 and because there were frequent clashes between the villagers, labourers who came from the surrounding vicinity to work in the lumber industries, and the old farming families on the concessions. He engaged in a severe, corrective ministry yet was remembered as a charitable man who was pious and devoted, especially to the sick. Exercising control with a firm hand, he was rigorous and indeed punctilious. It was even said that he forced reconciliation upon quarrelling parishioners who nevertheless were consistently divided into two camps, particularly at election time. In fact his political interventions only led to renewed disunity, discord, and incidents of aggression in his parish.

The parish was also divided for a long time over the construction of a new church. The old stone building, erected between 1715 and 1719, was clearly too small and the diocesan authority ordered a larger one built. Desilets's frequent illnesses and the difficulty of dividing the costs between the day labourers and the property owners, who claimed they were "assessed more heavily," led to a delay of several years. The decision to build was finally taken in 1878 and the stone was cut at Sainte-Angèle-de-Laval across the river from the parish. Both priest and parishioners counted on a bridge of ice forming in the winter of 1878–79 over which they could transport materials more cheaply. Despite special prayers – every Sunday the parish made supplications to Our Lady of the Rosary, to whom the priest showed great devotion – the whole winter passed without their being able to cross the river on the ice, and the month of March was already under way when they realized that only a "miracle" would bring about the formation of an ice bridge. Prayers were intensified and on Friday 14 March 1879 the river began to freeze over as a result of an ice jam. On Sunday and the succeeding days the assistant priest, Louis-Eugène Duguay, and a group of men set to work to strengthen the bridge and mark the route. By 26 March, with the help of a corvée of parishioners, friends, and people from other parishes, enough stone had been transported for construction to begin. When the last load had been brought across, the ice bridge immediately became too dangerous for further use. As a result of what became known as the "miracle of the bridge of rosaries," the new church opened for worship on 3 Oct. 1880.

The "miracle" attracted a certain number of pilgrims who came individually to pray in the old chapel, which had been preserved out of gratitude and had become the meeting place of the Confrérie du Très-Saint-Rosaire. The first public pilgrimage took place on 7 May 1883. Year by year the number of pilgrims slowly increased; they came from Trois-Rivières and Champlain and, after a dock was built in 1887, from some of the parishes on the south shore such as Saint-Grégoire-le-Grand. On several occasions Desilets himself went to urge pilgrims to come.

But Desilets was known more for his active interest in political life than as a parish priest and founder of the pilgrimage of Notre-Dame-du-Cap. Having come to the parish at the time when confederation was under discussion, he opted for the Quebec Resolutions and its promoters. Similarly when the Guibord affair arose [*see* Joseph Guibord*], when the Université Laval and a number of political figures were accused of Gallicanism, and when a group of intransigents launched the *Programme catholique* [*see* François-Xavier-Anselme TRUDEL], the parish priest Desilets was invariably and vociferously on the side of the "right principles." An Ultramontane and a supporter of the Conservative party, he sometimes claimed the role of political organizer for his parish and even for the constituency of Champlain. No doubt when speaking to politicians and even to his bishop he exaggerated his influence, but it must be admitted that he pursued the Liberals relentlessly and that the candidate he supported was usually victorious. The best example is his report of his intervention at the time of the election of the sole "Programmist," François-Xavier-Anselme Trudel, in 1871: "Anselme would not have got a single vote in Cap-de-la-Madeleine, not one, . . . if I had not made three or four pronouncements to the parishioners explaining their duties according to the Encyclical, the Councils, and the Bishop's letters."

In 1872 Desilets joined his brothers Pierre, Alfred, and Gédéon in purchasing the *Journal des Trois-Rivières*, even boasting that he ran up a debt of $3,000 to settle the transaction. More important, despite his persistent and vigorous denials, he was a regular contributor to the paper; although it is not always easy to attribute a specific article to his prolix pen there is no doubt that he was responsible for several texts on theological and political matters, as Laflèche, bishop of Trois-Rivières, acknowledged in 1877 in a letter to Bishop George Conroy*, the apostolic delegate. In addition to writing anonymous articles, he kept up a voluminous correspondence with politicians such as Sir George-Étienne Cartier*, Sir Hector-Louis Langevin*, and Trudel, as well as with religious authorities. His lengthy, well-written letters denounced the Gallican and liberal evils and proposed drastic action. He himself joined in veritable crusades bearing on political problems more or less connected to religion; for example he fought the public loan to the North Shore Railway [*see* Joseph-Édouard CAUCHON].

Desilets made special efforts, however, to exercise a decisive influence on Bishop Laflèche. A frequent visitor to the bishop's palace in Trois-Rivières, he got himself selected for special missions, such as negotiating the sale of the buildings of the Collège de Nicolet to the federal government in 1868–69, and in

1871 evaluating the orthodoxy of Judge Joseph-Ubalde Beaudry*'s *Code des curés, marguilliers et paroissiens accompagné de notes historiques et critiques*, which had been published in Montreal the year before. He plunged into these tasks with such enthusiasm that on almost every occasion he was reprimanded by the bishop. Despite the confused nature of his relations with Laflèche, Desilets was one of those who induced the bishop of Trois-Rivières to abandon his cautious stand in the conflict between Quebec City and Montreal, particularly in regard to a Catholic university in Montreal, and to side with Bishop Ignace BOURGET against Archbishop Elzéar-Alexandre Taschereau*. An avowed opponent of Taschereau, the former rector of the Université Laval, the parish priest of Cap-de-la-Madeleine denounced him to Laflèche as a Catholic liberal who was responsible for the advance of liberalism in Quebec. His accusations became increasingly violent as conflict over politics and religion grew more acrimonious; it was heightened at the time of the elections in Charlevoix [*see* Pierre-Alexis Tremblay*] and Bonaventure which were disputed on grounds of clerical interference; it also increased as a result of the episcopal declarations unconditionally denouncing Catholic liberalism (22 Sept. 1875), and then recognizing the legitimacy of a kind of non-doctrinal political liberalism (11 Oct. 1877). The apostolic delegate, Bishop Conroy, did not escape the condemnation of Desilets who considered him a friend of the liberals and deemed his visit to Canada "a disaster." Desilets's intervention, together with the pressure from the dioceses of Montreal and Rimouski, convinced Laflèche that it was his duty to denounce to Rome Taschereau's administration and Conroy's mission, a step he took on 7 Oct. 1878.

In 1883, at the time of a second attempt to split the diocese of Trois-Rivières, Desilets mobilized the forces of the north against those of the south; he particularly attacked Abbé Joseph-Calixte Canac, *dit* Marquis, and the directors of the Séminaire de Nicolet, as the principal supporters of the division. That year he went to Rome with Laflèche and remained there as the bishop's procurator. He entered into many negotiations and drafted numerous reports which he faithfully outlined to his superior in a weekly letter of 20 to 40 pages. He stayed in Rome until the summer of 1885 when Propaganda announced the division of the diocese and the appointment of Elphège Gravel as the first bishop of Nicolet.

In 1885, in recognition of all his services, Bishop Laflèche appointed Desilets titular canon and vicar general; the preceding year the bishop had promoted him to the important parish of Saint-Antoine at Baie-du-Febvre (Baieville) but the division of the diocese prevented him from filling this post. The indefatigable fighter remained at Cap-de-la-Madeleine to devote his last years to spreading the practice of the rosary. Stricken with a heart attack during the summer of 1888 he went to live with his brother Alfred, in whose home he died suddenly on 30 August. Laflèche officiated at his funeral and delivered a moving eulogy.

Luc Desilets's private papers and pastoral work show him to have been a man of staunch faith as well as a charitable and devoted priest who fervently preached devotion to the Virgin Mary. On the other hand his political activism was based on a Manichean vision of the world which had little relationship to the true state of Canadian society at the time, and some of his interventions revealed at the least a certain lack of balance. This judgement had been reached years before by his teachers at Nicolet, and the historian of today finds it hard to reject their opinion.

NIVE VOISINE

AAQ, 33 CR, I: 96, 102, 104. ACAM, 295.104. ANQ-Q, AP-G-134. Arch. de l'archevêché de Rimouski (Rimouski, Qué.), Corr. avec Trois-Rivières. Arch. de l'évêché de Trois-Rivières, Fonds L.-F. Laflèche, Corr. reçue, Narcisse Pelletier, 15 déc. 1861; Luc Desilets, 16 oct. 1870, 27 juin, 14 juill. 1871, 15 févr. 1873, 23 sept. 1878; Paroisses, Sainte-Marie-Madeleine (Cap-de-la-Madeleine, Qué.); Reg. des lettres envoyées: L.-F. Laflèche, Giovanni Simeoni, 7 oct. 1878. Arch. du sanctuaire Notre-Dame-du-Cap (Cap-de-la-Madeleine), D7, chemise 4; D27; D28, chemise 3; D43, I: 16–28, 157–73. Archivio della Propaganda Fide (Rome), Scritture riferite nei Congressi: America Settentrionale, 18 (1877): f.480. Arch. du séminaire de Trois-Rivières, Mauriciana, Les villes et localités, Cap-de-la-Madeleine. *Le Journal des Trois-Rivières*, 7 avril 1879, 4 sept. 1888, 7–22 mars 1889.

P.-É. Breton, *Cap-de-la-Madeleine, cité mystique de Marie* (Trois-Rivières, 1937). Alfred Désilets, *Souvenir d'un octogénaire* (Trois-Rivières, 1922). [Arthur Joyal], *Deuxième centenaire du sanctuaire national de Notre-Dame du Cap, 1715–1915* (Trois-Rivières, 1915). Romain Légaré, *Un apôtre des deux mondes, le père Frédéric Janssoone, O.F.M., de Ghyvelde* (Montréal, 1953). [Eugène Nadeau], *Notre-Dame-du-Cap, reine du Très Saint Rosaire; son histoire, ses prodiges, ses foules* (Cap-de-la-Madeleine, [1947]). Robert Rumilly, *Monseigneur Laflèche et son temps* (Montréal, [1945]). Frédéric Janssoone, "Le sanctuaire du Cap-de-la-Madeleine; notice historique sur ses origines et son développement," *Le Souvenir* (Trois-Rivières), 3 (1955), no.1: 1–22. Hermann Morin, "Le curé Désilets, fondateur du pèlerinage de Notre-Dame du Cap (1831–1888)," *Notre-Dame du Cap, reine du Très Saint Rosaire* (Cap-de-la-Madeleine), numéro spécial (avril 1955): 1–26. Albert Tessier, "Luc Désilets, un des 'fanaux de tôle' de Mgr Laflèche," *Cahiers des Dix*, 19 (1954): 161–86; "Messire Luc Désilets, apôtre du rosaire et fondateur du sanctuaire national du Cap-de-la-Madeleine (1831–1888)," SCHÉC *Rapport*, 21 (1953–54): 67–77.

DE SOLA, ALEXANDER ABRAHAM, clergyman, professor, author, editor, and publisher; b. 18 Sept. 1825 in London, England, the sixth child of

David Aaron de Sola and Rebecca Meldola; m. 30 June 1852 Esther, youngest daughter of Henry Joseph* and Rachel Solomons, and they had at least three sons; d. 5 June 1882 in New York City, and buried in Montreal, Que.

Alexander Abraham de Sola was born into an accomplished Jewish family of Spanish and Portuguese extraction which had come to London via Amsterdam in the early years of the 19th century. His maternal grandfather, Dr. Raphäel Meldola, was chief rabbi of the Sephardic congregation of London, and his father was an author and *hazan* (the title for a non-ordained Jewish reader or leader in the Sephardic tradition) of the same congregation. Endowed with his father's intellectual interests and versatility, Abraham was educated first at the City of London Corporation School, and later under the direction of his father and Louis Loewe, an Oriental scholar. After a year's service as a tutor Abraham applied for and received the office of *hazan* to the Montreal Jewish congregation of Shearith Israel in 1846. Arriving in January of the following year he was to serve this congregation until his death.

Having been active in literary societies in London, as co-editor of the *Voice of Jacob* and as director of the Sussex Hall Literary Institution, de Sola soon established himself at the centre of Montreal's English-speaking intellectual community. An eloquent, popular, and prolific lecturer and a man of broad interests, he frequently addressed the Montreal Mercantile Library Association, the Montreal Literary Club, the Numismatic and Antiquarian Society of Montreal (of which he was elected an honorary member), the Montreal Mechanics' Institute, and the Natural History Society (which he served as president in 1867–68), as well as several organizations associated with McGill College. Many of his speeches and sermons, delivered in English, were published in periodicals and the contemporary Jewish press. Although he was chiefly concerned with the reconciliation of religion and science, the articles' diverse subjects reflect the eclectic nature of his intellectual interests. He wrote on the history of Jews in England, Persia, Poland, and France; reported on cosmography and Sinaitic inscriptions; examined botanical and zoological references in the Scriptures; and drew critical acclaim from European scholars for his articles on prominent Jews such as Sir Moses Montefiore, a contemporary philanthropist, and R. Abram Peritsol, who contributed to the development of the arts and sciences. De Sola also wrote medical studies, on the rabbinical dietary laws and the use of anaesthetics, which appeared in major medical journals and were reprinted as pamphlets. His chief works include: *Behemoth hatemeoth*, a 16-page pamphlet published by John Lovell*, containing an annotated catalogue of the animals pronounced unclean by the book of Leviticus as determined by Jewish and Christian authorities; *A Jewish calendar for fifty years*, a 177-page volume, prepared with New York rabbi Jacques Judah Lyons, and also published by Lovell, containing an introductory essay on the Jewish calendar system together with historical notes on various Jewish congregations in North America and elsewhere; a *Biography of David Aaron de Sola*, a short, 61-page sketch of his father; *The form of prayers according to the custom of the Spanish and Portuguese Jews*, a five-volume collection, based on earlier versions published by his father and Isaac Leeser, which he revised, edited, and republished. In 1853 he also edited a small booklet entitled *The Jewish child's first catechism of Bible history*. Rounding out his versatile literary career, de Sola became a book distributor in 1873 when he, together with his brother-in-law Jesse Joseph, purchased the copyright of Leeser's translation of the 24 books of the Holy Scripture as well as the distribution and copyright of a long list of works issued by Leeser's Philadelphia publishing house.

As minister of the Shearith Israel congregation he sought to organize the educational, benevolent, and fraternal life of his religious community. In 1849 de Sola established a Sunday school which one year later boasted some 35 students, and in 1854 he opened a private Jewish day- and boarding-school, for boys and girls. When the Protestant school board was reorganized in 1875 the school claimed and received public support for the employment of a teacher, thereby helping to establish the claim of the Montreal Jewish community for publicly supported separate schools. Soon after he arrived in Montreal he and Moses Judah Hayes* had been instrumental in founding the Hebrew Philanthropic Society to care for the poor, sick, and needy "Israelite in Montreal," including a growing number of immigrants. De Sola subsequently helped establish the Young Men's Hebrew Benevolent Society (1863), the *Yod Beyod* or Jewish Mutual Aid Society (1872), and the Ladies' Hebrew Benevolent Society (1877). A member of the Ancient Jewish Order of Kesher Shel Barzel, he gave his name in 1872 to its first Canadian lodge, known as De Sola Lodge no.89 as a tribute to its distinguished leader. Two years later he was named district grand *saar* for the dominion of Canada, a position which brought him in close contact with the Jewish communities of Toronto, Hamilton, and London, Ont. Although of orthodox doctrine and strict Sephardic tradition, de Sola went out of his way to cooperate with the Ashkenazi Jewish community by supporting their schools and social organizations, and in 1878 he even considered devising a common ritual to permit the union of the congregations, which would join together Montreal's two rich Jewish traditions. In touch with the larger international Jewish community and with its chief philanthropists such as Montefiore, de Sola pleaded publicly the cause of his co-religionists in Persia, Morocco, Palestine, and Russia and organized funds for their relief which attracted support from the gentile community. He also attempted to interest working-class Portuguese Jews residing in London, England, in emigrating to Canada.

Outside his religious community de Sola enjoyed a wide reputation as a scholar, teacher, and public citizen. Of broad liberal sympathies, he not only belonged to the literary societies of the city but supported its educational and benevolent institutions as well. In July 1848, a year after he arrived in Canada, McGill College appointed him a lecturer in Hebrew and rabbinical literature, and in November 1853 a professor of Hebrew and Oriental literature, a position which he held until his death. He also taught philology and Chaldean and Spanish language and literature at McGill as well as Hebrew at the Presbyterian College. In recognition of his service and his growing international reputation, particularly after the publication of his authoritative study on "Sanatory institutions," in 1858 McGill made him an honorary doctor of laws, the first time a Jewish minister had received the honour in England or North America. While at McGill de Sola also worked closely with the eminent scientists John William Dawson* and Sir William Edmond Logan*. A tolerant, public-spirited man, he participated in and supported several institutions. He sent his sons to the High School of Montreal and the Catholic Commercial Academy, supported the Montreal Eye and Ear Institution, and in 1850 joined the management committee of the Montreal Dispensary. In 1869 he played a prominent part in attempting to have the Canadian government alter its copyright laws to afford greater protection to Canadian authors. Although he received many testimonies of public esteem during his lifetime, one of his greatest honours came on 9 Jan. 1872 when he opened the House of Representatives of the United States with prayer, the first British subject to do so. His participation, coming shortly after the signing of the Treaty of Washington, received wide publicity and letters of congratulation from many public men including William Ewart Gladstone, the British prime minister, and Sir Edward Thornton, the British minister at Washington.

In 1876 de Sola's health began to decline and he spent a year in Europe trying to recuperate. Upon his return he resumed his work, but the strain proved too much and he finally died on 5 June 1882 while in New York City visiting his sister. The class de Sola belonged to, his Protestant and anglophilic sympathies, and his intellectual interests in science and religion gave him easy access to influence and recognition. At his death he enjoyed a wide reputation as a translator, author, editor, publisher, teacher, and public and spiritual leader, not only among his co-religionists and the local community but also among scholars and public men in Canada and abroad. Two of de Sola's sons, Clarence I. and Meldola, followed in his footsteps; the former was one of the leading Canadian Zionists; the latter was a minister and one of the most prominent scholars and exponents of orthodox Judaism in North America.

CARMAN MILLER

Alexander Abraham de Sola was the author of *Behemoth hatemeoth: the nomenclature of the prohibited animals of Leviticus, as determined by the most eminent authorities, both Jewish and Christian . . .* (Montreal, 1853); *Biography of David Aaron de Sola, late senior minister of the Portuguese Jewish community in London* (Philadelphia, [1864]); "Critical examination of Genesis III. 16; having reference to the employment of anæsthetics in cases of labour," *British American Journal of Medical and Physical Science* (Montreal), 5 (1849–50): 227–29, 259–62, 290–93; "The Day of Atonement: a sermon delivered in the synagogue Shearith Yisrael, Montreal," *Occident, and American Jewish Advocate* (Philadelphia), 6 (1848–49): 322–33; "A few points of interest in the study of natural history," *Canadian Naturalist and Geologist*, new ser., 3 (1868): 445–53; "God's judgments on earth: a sermon delivered in the synagogue 'Shearith Yisrael' Montreal, during the prevalence of Asiatic cholera," *Occident, and American Jewish Advocate*, 7 (1849–50): 348–62; "Hebrew authors and their opponents," *Jewish Chronicle* (London), 13, 27 July, 10 Aug., 2 Nov., 7 Dec. 1849; "History of the Jews of France, after Bégin and Carmoly," *Jewish Messenger* (New York), 27 Jan.–17 March 1871; "History of the Jews of Poland," *Jewish Messenger*, 14 Jan.–4 March 1870; "An inquiry into the first settlement of Jews in England," *Occident, and American Jewish Advocate*, 6: 208–11, 247–51, 294–98, 349–55; "Life and writings of Saadia Gaon," *Hebrew Rev.* (Cincinnati, Ohio), 2 (1881–82): 208–39; "The Mosaic cosmogony," *Jewish Messenger*, 11, 18, 25 March 1870; "Notes on the Jews of Persia under Mohammed Shah, obtained from one of themselves," *Occident, and American Jewish Advocate*, 7: 504–7, 549–54, 596–601; 8 (1850–51): 43–48, 141–45; "Observations on the sanatory institutions of the Hebrews as bearing upon modern sanatory regulations," *Canada Medical Journal and Monthly Record of Medical and Surgical Science* (Montreal), 1 (1852–53): 135–41, 203–11, 325–40, 464–68, 529–32, 589–99, 654–66, 728–41; also issued in part under title: *The sanatory institutions of the Hebrews . . .* (Montreal, 1861); "The Passover: a sermon delivered in the synagogue Shearith Israel, Montreal, on Passover, 5608," *Occident, and American Jewish Advocate*, 7: 72–86; "The Pentecost: a sermon, delivered at the synagogue Shearith Israel, Montreal, on Pentecost, 5607," *Occident, and American Jewish Advocate*, 5 (1847–48): 229–40; "The revelation at Sinai; its possibility and necessity: a sermon delivered in the synagogue, Shearith Yisrael, Montreal, on Pentecost 5608," *Occident, and American Jewish Advocate*, 6: 226–36; *The righteous man: a sermon commemorating the bestowal of public honors on Sir Moses Montefiore, by the city of London; preached in Montreal, on Sabbath Noah 5625* ([Montreal, 1865?]); *The study of natural science: an address . . . at the conversazzione held in the hall of the Natural History Society of Montreal, on Wednesday, 9th March, 1870 . . .* (Montreal, 1870); *Valedictory address to the graduates in arts of the University of McGill College,*

Montreal, delivered at the annual convocation, Tuesday, 3rd May, 1864 (Montreal, 1864); and "Yehuda Alcharizi and the book Tachkemoni," *Jewish Record* (Philadelphia), 7 Nov. – 5 Dec. 1879. De Sola also edited *The form of prayers according to the custom of the Spanish and Portuguese Jews* . . . (new ed., 5v., Philadelphia, [1878]) and *Voice of Jacob* (London), 1841–48; and he compiled *The Jewish child's first catechism of Bible history: adapted [from Pinnock] to the capacity of young minds* (Montreal, 1853; repr. 1866; repr. Philadelphia, 1877) and, with J. J. Lyons, *A Jewish calendar for fifty years . . . from A.M. 5614 till A.M. 5664* . . . (Montreal, 1854). He translated "Life of Shabethai Tsevi, the pseudo-Messiah . . . ," *Jewish Messenger*, 26 March–6 Aug. 1869. Other works by de Sola are listed in Morgan, *Bibliotheca Canadensis* and *Printed Jewish Canadiana, 1685–1900* . . . , comp. R. A. Davies (Montreal, 1955).

AC, Montréal, État civil, Juifs, Shearith Israel Congregation (Montreal), 8 June 1882. Atwater Library (Montreal), Mechanics' Institute of Montreal, Minute books, 1847–82. McGill Univ. Arch., Abraham de Sola papers (for a description of the these papers see *Abraham de Sola papers: a guide to the microfilm*, comp. Evelyn Miller (Montreal, 1970)). *Gazette* (Montreal), 3 June 1882. Borthwick, *Hist. and biog. gazetteer. Canada, an encyclopædia* (Hopkins). *Canada directory*, 1851; 1857–58. *Cyclopædia of Canadian biog.* (Rose, 1888). *Encyclopædia Judaica* (16v., Jerusalem, 1971–72), V. *Montreal directory*, 1851–59. *Quebec directory*, 1847. Atherton, *Montreal. The Jew in Canada: a complete record of Canadian Jewry from the days of the French régime to the present time*, ed. A. D. Hart (Toronto and Montreal, 1926). Sack, *Hist. of the Jews in Canada* (1945). Evelyn Miller, "The 'learned Hazan' of Montreal: Reverend Abraham de Sola, LL.D., 1825–1882," *American Sephardi* . . . (New York), 7–8 (1975): 23–43.

DEVINE, THOMAS, surveyor and cartographer; b. in County Westmeath (Republic of Ireland), probably in 1818; m. Jane Molloy, probably in 1866, and they had two sons, including James Arthur, a prominent physician and playwright in Winnipeg, Man.; d. 14 Nov. 1888 in Montreal, Que.

Thomas Devine was to state that he had acquired practical knowledge of his profession on the Ordnance Survey of Ireland under the Royal Engineers, and he may have attended an engineers' academy. After immigrating to Canada, he was appointed a provincial land surveyor on 11 June 1846, becoming a surveyor and draftsman in the Crown Lands Department, Upper Canada surveys branch, on 7 July 1846. However, he made only one field survey, of the York branch of the Madawaska River in 1847. Afterwards he was employed in the office which, as part of the peripatetic government, relocated six times during the union period. By 1857 he had succeeded Andrew RUSSELL in charge of the branch although his position as head of surveys, Upper Canada, was not confirmed until 22 July 1859. His duties, which remained substantially unchanged until his retirement, required him to project surveys of crown lands, to supervise the work and reports of the surveyors, to copy and compile plans for district agents, municipal councils, and the public, and to see to the preservation of original plans, field books, and reports.

From 1857 Devine was responsible for the compilation and publication of an important group of maps. His *Map of the north west part of Canada, Indian territories & Hudson's Bay* (1857) was the first map of the west compiled and printed in Canada and has been described as "an outstanding consolidation of cartographic material on the West." Portraying the topography, geology, and climatic zones as then known, the map stressed the capacity of the land for agriculture and settlement. It accompanied the annual report of the Crown Lands Department for 1856 by Joseph-Édouard CAUCHON and was intended to support claims for Canadian expansion into the prairies. Devine's *Government map of Canada, from Red River to the Gulf of St. Lawrence* (1859), the first official map of the province, has been shown to be the first reasonably accurate map of the area, and more accurate than those that followed in the 1860s. Three other important maps, *Topographical plan of the north shore of Lake Huron* (1858), *Plan of the north shore of Lake Superior* . . . (Toronto, 1860), and the *Government map of part of the Huron and Ottawa territory* . . . (New York, 1861), each went into several editions and were designed to provide information for intending settlers, lumbermen, and emigration agents.

Devine did not ignore the surveying side of his responsibilities. In 1859 he submitted a new form of field notebook for surveyors employing the "split-line method" in which the important distance measurements were placed clearly between the lines and more space was provided for pictographic and written representations of landmarks, the intention being to provide a clear, standardized system of describing a surveyed line. He noted in his report for 1861 that much surveying was of a low calibre and recommended various improvements, including examination of surveyors' work in the field. To speed up the publication of maps he had recommended in 1860 that a lithograph press be installed in his office, but the department rejected his suggestion. In 1864 he was called before the committee examining the suitability of the region between the Ottawa River and Georgian Bay for settlement and lumbering; he provided the first land classification map of the area which he compiled from surveyors' reports on timber and soil. Though he admitted that these reports were inclined to be more accurate in estimating timber, he indicated that the value of the land for settlement had always been underrated and that "in numerous instances the lands condemned by the surveyors as unfit for settlement have since been settled with a thriving population."

Devine continued with the Ontario Crown Lands Department after confederation and in 1872 he became deputy surveyor general of Ontario. In 1877 he produced his last major map, covering North America and designed to show all historical boundaries that would have a bearing upon the impending decision on Ontario's northern and western boundaries. This map, compiled from the analysis of 186 earlier maps acquired by the federal and provincial governments, was referred to by representatives of both during the arbitration proceedings of 1878. Although the matter was finally decided in Ontario's favour, it was not resolved until 1889 [*see* James Andrews MILLER].

Before poor health forced him to retire in 1879 Devine had also given of his time to provincial and local matters. After 1858 he was a member of the board of examiners of land surveyors for the Province of Canada and was chairman of the Ontario board at his retirement. He also became a member of the Toronto Separate School Board in 1867 and was its chairman in 1877 at the height of the struggle for control of school property between the board, consisting of laymen, and Archbishop John Joseph LYNCH.

Devine returned to Ireland on retirement but came back to Canada in 1884, settling in Montreal where he remained until his death. During the union period the government had rewarded his efforts by paying him, at times, less than his predecessor and his counterpart in Canada East, despite his accomplishments. In 1860 these were acknowledged when he was elected a member of the Royal Geographical Society; he was also a corresponding member of the Geographical Society of Berlin and the American Geographical and Statistical Society.

JOAN WINEARLS

Thomas Devine was the author of "Description of a new Trilobite from the Quebec group," *Canadian Naturalist and Geologist*, 8 (1863): 210–11, and the compiler of *Government map of Canada, from Red River to the Gulf of St. Lawrence* (Quebec and Toronto, 1859); *Map of the north west part of Canada, Indian territories & Hudson's Bay* (Toronto, 1857); *Official documents relating to the early survey & settlement of Ontario [U.C.] from the Treaty of Peace in 1783 to the separation of Ontario (UC) from the province of Quebec in 1792* (n.p., [1873?]) (copy at AO); Ont., Ministry of Natural Resources, Survey Records Branch (Toronto), "Map of part of North America, designed to illustrate the reports and discussions relating to the boundaries of the province of Ontario . . . , 1877"; *Topographical plan of the north shore of Lake Huron shewing P.L.S. Albert P. Salter's recent survey* (Toronto, 1858).

AO, RG 1, A-I-2, 49: 118; 50: 28, 375–76, 399–400; A-I-4, 34; A-II-2, 5; A-II-6, 3, 12–14; A-VII, 49. Ont., Ministry of Natural Resources, Survey Records Office, Instructions to land surveyors, 5: 58–60, 397–98 (mfm. at AO). PAC, RG 31, A1, 1871, Toronto, St George's Ward (mfm. at AO). "Biographical sketch of the late Thomas Devine, F.R.G.S.," Assoc. of Provincial Land Surveyors of Ontario, *Proc.* (Toronto), 1889: 129–30. Can., Prov. of, Legislative Assembly, *App. to the journals*, 1857–59, Reports of the commissioner of crown lands of Canada; 1859, III: app.19; *Journals*, 1860, app.4; 1861, app.1; 1862, app.1; February–May 1863, app.3; August–October 1863, app.1; 1864, apps.7, 8; August–September 1865, app.6; Parl., *Sessional papers*, 1860–66, Reports of the commissioner of crown lands of Canada; 1862, III: no.11, app.26. Ont., Legislature, *Sessional papers*, 1879, V, no.31: 133–40, 417. *Report of proceedings before the arbitrators, in the matter of the boundaries of the province of Ontario* (Toronto, 1880). *Gazette* (Montreal), 16 Nov. 1888. *Globe*, 16 Nov. 1888. *Toronto Daily Mail*, 16 Nov. 1888. *Manitoba historical atlas: a selection of facsimile maps, plans, and sketches from 1612 to 1969*, ed. J. [H.] Warkentin and R. I. Ruggles (Winnipeg, 1970). Morgan, *Sketches of celebrated Canadians*. R. S. Lambert and Paul Pross, *Renewing nature's wealth; a centennial history of the public management of lands, forests & wildlife in Ontario, 1763–1967* ([Toronto], 1967), 61–149. M. B. MacK. Olsen, "Aspects of the mapping of southern Ontario, 1783–1867" (MPHIL thesis, Univ. of London, 1968). W. F. Weaver, *Crown surveys in Ontario* ([Toronto], 1962), 15.

DÉZIEL, JOSEPH-DAVID, Roman Catholic parish priest; b. 21 May 1806 at Saint-Joseph in Maskinongé, Lower Canada, son of Gabriel Déziel, *dit* Labrèche, and Marie Champoux; d. 25 June 1882 at Lévis, Que.

After studying at the Petit Séminaire de Montréal (1819–21) and the Séminaire de Nicolet (1821–27), Joseph-David Déziel taught at the latter (1827–30). He continued theological studies and on 5 Sept. 1830 was ordained priest by Bishop Joseph Signay* in the church of Saint-Jean-Baptiste at Nicolet. Déziel served as curate successively at Saint-Antoine-de-Padoue in Rivière-du-Loup (Louiseville, Que.), Saint-Édouard in Gentilly, and Saint-Joseph in Maskinongé, and then was appointed parish priest of Saint-Patrice in Rivière-du-Loup in 1835. He transferred on 29 Sept. 1837 to Saint-Pierre-les-Becquets (Les Becquets). Here he succeeded in restoring harmony among the parishioners who had been split since 1830 on the issue of the site and dimensions of their future church; the church opened in 1839. In October 1843 Abbé Déziel was appointed parish priest of Saint-Joseph at Pointe-Lévy (Lauzon), a parish of more than 4,000 persons that stretched from Beaumont to the Rivière Etchemin, and from the St Lawrence to the parish of Saint-Henri-de-Lauzon (Saint-Henri). There was no lack of work for a dynamic young priest. Since 1784 the parishioners had been asking for a new church located nearer to the centre of the territory it had to serve. In 1845 this question and plans for dividing the parish were brought up again; indeed in the next five years there were at least 15 petitions and counter-petitions to the bishop for permission to build a new church, each suggesting a different site. On 18 April 1850 Bishop Pierre-Flavien Turgeon*, the administrator of the archdiocese of Quebec, gave authorization for a chapel of ease to be built in the commune or village of Aubigny on a piece of land situated on the edge of the cliff facing Quebec that the government had granted for this purpose in 1848. The parish councillors of Saint-Joseph, however, viewed such a division of the parish with disfavour, perhaps because it would lead to reduced revenues. Abbé Déziel did not back down; through seven generous donors he obtained land adjoining the lot given by the government. There the church was to be built, in accordance with Bishop Turgeon's enactment of 17 July 1850 which also specified it should be named Notre-Dame-de-la-Victoire. The new church was opened on 20 Nov. 1851, and in October 1852 Déziel came to take charge of the new parish, leaving the parish of Saint-Joseph to Abbé Joseph-Honoré Routhier. Two years later, following a decree of Bishop Turgeon on 23 Nov. 1854, the presbytery was built and the church enlarged.

Déziel had further plans: by January 1851 his wish was to build a college close to the proposed church. In June 1851 three parishioners, Pierre Carrier, Thomas Fraser, and Marie Couture, gave part of their lands adjoining the church for a college, and on 12 Sept. 1851 a subscription was started. Under the priest's direction the parishioners began to cut timber, quarry stone and sand, and cart them, by corvée, to the proposed site of the college, which became truly a cooperative endeavour. The new Collège de Lévis opened on 15 Sept. 1853. The Brothers of the Christian Schools agreed to take on the teaching there, after the Jesuits and the Clerics of St Viator refused. The college initially offered a commercial course, but in 1859 Abbé Déziel wanted to introduce Latin classes. The superior general of the Christian Brothers opposed this suggestion, and they returned control of the college to its founder. The priests of the Séminaire de Québec then agreed to run the college, beginning in September 1860. Two Latin classes were provided, but they were dropped at the end of 1870 because there were not enough pupils, and in 1874 the seminary gave the college back to Abbé Déziel. The annals of the Séminaire de Québec state: "Henceforth we shall have nothing to do with the Collège de Lévis. Up to now the moral and intellectual aspects have been our concern; but through a combination of circumstances M. Déziel, the parish priest of Notre-Dame-de-Lévis, who was responsible for the temporal aspects, has come to think a full [and independent] corporation should be set up, and thus the Collège de Lévis will be on its own." Still parish priest of Notre-Dame-de-la-Victoire, Déziel became the first superior of the college when it was incorporated on 23 Feb. 1875. That year the council of the college, chaired by Déziel as superior, undertook a building programme which roughly doubled the size of the 1853 structure. Déziel had to struggle until 1879 to get permission for a classical course: the Séminaire de Québec and the Collège de Sainte-Anne-de-la-Pocatière feared the loss of some of their students. Bishop Elzéar-Alexandre Taschereau* finally gave his consent, and on 24 May 1879 Abbé Thomas-Étienne Hamel*, rector of Université Laval, announced the university council was affiliating the Collège de Lévis with the faculty of arts.

The education of boys had been assured, but Abbé Déziel had also long been concerned about the education of girls. In 1852 he had begun efforts which were to lead to the opening of the convent of Lévis and the Hospice Saint-Michel in the same building in 1858. The site of this building was the land granted by the government in 1848 for the church of Notre-Dame-de-la-Victoire. In 1852 the parish councillors of Notre-Dame asked the government for use of the site; however, the land was not finally given over until January 1857, largely as a result of the opposition of the parish councillors of Saint-Joseph. Déziel wanted not only to ensure the education of young girls by building a "convent," but also to provide for the needs of old and infirm priests. In 1856 a subscription was launched among the priests, and by 1861 it had brought in 1,761 louis. However, the Sisters of Charity of Quebec did not arrive to take charge of both hospice and convent until 22 Sept. 1858.

Déziel wanted to endow the convent with a boarding-school, but Bishop Charles-François Baillargeon* was opposed, as he had entered into an agreement with the parish priest of Saint-Joseph and with the Religious of Jesus and Mary that there would be no other boarding-school for young girls in the region until the one at Saint-Joseph was well established. The letters exchanged by Abbé Déziel and Bishop Baillargeon reveal the priest's tenacity, as well as his financial difficulties, particularly in 1859 when he saw no alternative but to give up his parish: "My spirit of self-denial is not great enough to permit me to witness with my own eyes the ruin of a work so dear to me which has cost me so much toil . . . a new parish priest will, I hope, be better able than I to enter into the views of your Excellency and those of my neighbour [the parish priest of Saint-Joseph]." Apparently his resignation was not accepted. In 1861 the parish council made over the hospice and convent to the Sisters of Charity on condition that they support both; finally, in 1863 Bishop Baillargeon, "yielding to the urgent pleas of the parish priest of Notre-Dame-de-Lévis," allowed the sisters "to take up to 20 boarders."

Such work and worry had undermined Déziel's health, and in 1865 he took a rest-cure of 11 months, during which he visited Europe, journeying twice to Vichy, France, to take the waters; since he possessed nothing, the generous parishioners of Notre-Dame-de-la-Victoire had raised a fund to cover his expenses. Completely recovered, Abbé Déziel took up his work again, with unremitting and ubiquitous activity. Since

1851 the population had increased appreciably: the 1861 census gives 6,694 inhabitants in the parish of Notre-Dame-de-la-Victoire at Lévis, and Lévis itself as the third largest town in Canada East, its incorporation as a town having in fact occurred that year. The parish priest took part in all developments in his town, and even helped draft the municipal regulations. The charitable organizations he founded or supported were numerous and varied. However, Déziel was forced to think of dividing the parish of Notre-Dame because of the increase in its population, which had reached 9,032 by 1871. A new parish, west of Notre-Dame, was erected canonically on 21 Aug. 1875, under the name of Saint-David-de-Lauberivière (Saint-David), partly to honour Déziel and partly to commemorate the fifth bishop of Quebec, François-Louis de Pourroy* de Lauberivière. When Notre-Dame was divided, Abbé Déziel, who had had to face many objections, wrote to Taschereau: "I believe I have done my duty before God and man, in all things bearing in mind only the glory of God and the spiritual good of my parishioners. . . ."

It was also in 1875 that Déziel dedicated his zeal and energy to yet another charitable endeavour, the building of a hospice-orphanage, which he had long had in mind. A piece of land was given to him by Louis-Édouard Couture; the Sisters of Charity of Quebec agreed to handle this project also and one of them drew up the plans. Déziel prepared the estimates and himself directed the work on site. Construction, begun in 1877, was completed two years later; management of the establishment was entrusted to the Sisters of Charity from the convent, but in 1881 the two houses, and the two endeavours of education and orphanage, were separated. The Hospice Saint-Joseph-de-la-Délivrance was incorporated the following year. When it opened in 1879, the hospice had taken in 40 girls; six years later it took in 300. The first group of orphans were in fact already students at the convent, by virtue of the system of " industrial schools" set up by the government in 1870 to provide orphans with "a shelter and preparation for an honest and useful future"; the convent at Lévis had been selected as one of these schools and allotted 40 scholarships for this purpose.

In 1880 solemn celebrations were held at Lévis to mark the golden jubilee of the ordination of the venerable parish priest of Notre-Dame-de-la-Victoire, who received from Rome the title of privy chamberlain to Leo XIII. Worn out by toil and care, Abbé Déziel died in his presbytery on 25 June 1882, at the age of 76. A builder, leader of men, priest, and citizen, he had participated in the shaping of the religious and civil life of Lévis from its earliest years, and he is rightly considered the founder not only of a parish but also of the town of Lévis. In 1885, only three years after his death, the citizens of Lévis erected a magnificent monument to their founder, created by sculptor Louis-Philippe Hébert*.

Georges-Étienne Proulx

[There are numerous references to Joseph-David Déziel in the annals of the Couvent de Lévis (Lévis, Qué.) for the years 1857–82. G.-É. P.]

AAQ, 210 A, XXIV: 602; XXVII: 660; 211 A, K; 258r, 279–99; 511 CD, II: 16; 61 CD, Lauzon, II: 9, 16; Notre-Dame de Lévis, I: 3–7, 18–21, 30, 43, 46, 72, 73, 75, 83, 84, 101, 107, 108, 113, 115, 124; Saint-David, I: 3, 3c-f, 8, 10, 11. Arch. du collège de Lévis, Fonds J.-D. Déziel; Fonds G.-É. Sauvageau, I. ASQ, Séminaire, 68: no.3. PAC, RG 31, A1, 1861 census, Notre-Dame-de-la-Victoire de Lévis. P.-G. Roy, *Dates lévisiennes* (12v., Lévis, 1932–40). I–III; X. J.-E. Roy, *Mgr Déziel, sa vie, ses œuvres* (Lévis, 1885). P.-G. Roy, *Glanures lévisiennes* (4v., Lévis, 1920–22). Julien Déziel, "Mgr Jos.-David Déziel (1808–1882), sa vie et son ascendance familiale," *BRH*, 68 (1966): 27–36.

DICK, ROBERT, Baptist minister, journalist, reformer, and inventor; b. 12 Jan. 1814 in Bathgate (Lothian), Scotland, ninth child and fourth son of James Dick and Janet Brown; m. 11 Jan. 1838 Mary Muir, and they had five children; d. 9 Dec. 1890 in Buffalo, N.Y.

Robert Dick's family immigrated to Upper Canada in 1821 with several hundred other Lowland Scots through the Trongate Society of Lanarkshire for whom land had been reserved in Johnstown District. Both parents died on the journey, but the children took possession of lot 13 in the 9th concession, Lanark Township, and Robert helped in the felling, fencing, farming, and potash-making.

Although from a Presbyterian background, four of the five boys became ministers in the Free Will Baptist Church, so named because it rejected the doctrine of predestination. Robert may have been licensed by the church to preach as early as his 17th year, and soon after began to study classics and mathematics for college entrance. In 1836 he and his sombre brother, William (1812–53), entered the Hamilton Literary and Theological Institution (later Colgate University) in Hamilton, N.Y. They were among the first Free Will Baptist preachers to attend college after half a century of their sect's existence. Asked to leave in their first year because they organized an anti-slavery society amongst the students, they transferred to Hamilton College in Clinton, N.Y. William graduated in 1841 but Robert apparently left without graduating (an honorary AM was conferred by the college in 1875), perhaps because he had married in 1838. In 1839 Robert was ordained in Ames, Montgomery County, N.Y., serving there and in Middleville, Herkimer County, N.Y., until 1843.

In the "Burned-over District" of upper New York State Dick's zest for controversy was fanned into a blaze. He wrote a pamphlet on behalf of the Clinton quarterly meeting of Free Will Baptists in 1842, *Close communion, the offspring of arrogance*, in which he argued that the communion table should be open to all evangelical believers, whether Baptist or not. He campaigned against slavery and for total abstinence. He was corresponding secretary of the New York Education Society, under which grandiose title the Clinton quarterly meeting set up the evangelical and abolitionist Clinton Seminary in 1841 (later Whitestown Seminary), thus helping to shift the emphasis from inspiration to education in the formation of Free Will Baptist preachers. Dick returned to Canada and between 1843 and 1847 he ministered to his home church in Lanark village, preached as an itinerant in nearby areas, taught to earn income, and helped William to establish the Baptist cause in Bytown (Ottawa). From 1847 to 1849 Robert and William ran a school in Brockville. There, in June 1848, the brothers founded the first Canadian lodge of the Sons of Temperance, an American benefit society based on principles of total abstinence; its grand division for Canada West convened in Brockville in April 1849. There, too, Robert began publishing the *Unfettered Canadian* in 1849, representing the Canadian Eclectic Medicine Society, a body following a system of medical treatment developed by the American physician Samuel Thomson. The journal sought the defeat of legislation which would have given graduates of conventional medical schools sole right to practise in Canada; it hoped to secure "to every man who claims it the untrammelled right of choice to 'the philosophy and means of health.'"

As Toronto was temporarily the provincial capital, Robert moved there with the *Unfettered Canadian* in 1849. His brother Alexander (1817–1901) came at about the same time. Within two years Robert had founded about 60 lodges of the Sons of Temperance in and near Toronto. But he and Alexander soon lost leadership in the order because they unsuccessfully advocated separation from American lodges which excluded blacks from membership, and because Robert insisted on receiving 15*s*. to cover the expenses for each lodge he opened. After 1851 he supported himself as a colporteur selling books and tracts, some of which he published himself, as a lecturer on temperance, and as a preacher in the countryside around Toronto, dropping in as an unannounced evangelist on picnics and funerals alike. In the summer of 1855 the Canada Baptist Union, which had collapsed in 1848, was reorganized, partly at his instigation, chiefly for evangelical Baptists. Dick became, appropriately, its superintendent of colportage.

To further a complex of issues Dick published monthly in Toronto, between 1854 and 1858, the *Gospel Tribune, for Alliance and Intercommunion throughout Evangelical Christendom*, later subtitled the *Christian Communionist*. It advocated church union of all evangelicals, total abstinence, and ostracism of all churches and other organizations which excluded blacks and Indians. Although he claimed almost 7,000 subscribers in 1856, 1,500 subscriptions were unpaid in 1858, the depression year in which the journal ceased publication. It was in wrestling with the recalcitrant subscription list that Dick hit on the inventions that made his fortune. Frustrated by the time required to write addresses on wrappers and to check the currency of subscriptions, he devised ways of speeding both processes. He invented an addressing machine which could fix thousands of prepared labels in an hour and act as a ledger and running record at the same time. In later years he refined the patents for the "Union Mailer" with its ancillary processes and added patents for locking type in printers' forms. By 1868 he claimed that over 300 papers and journals in North America used his system under patent; the 12 in Canada included the Toronto *Globe* and *Leader*.

Dick moved permanently from Toronto to Buffalo, N.Y., in 1859, probably so that he could establish his patent in the United States. Although his inventions made him wealthy he continued to proselytize in laneways and chapels until age and affluence drew him into the more exalted Congregationalist connection in the 1880s. He formed the Buffalo Law and Order Society which fought the Sunday opening of saloons but he refused to join the Prohibitionist party as he thought abstinence should be voluntary. His politics were Republican; his two sons had joined the United States Army during the American Civil War, the eldest dying in uniform.

Dick died of pneumonia in 1890, survived by his wife and a widowed daughter. His patents passed to his brother and business partner, Alexander, who had moved with him to Buffalo; Alexander himself made improvements to the "Matchless Mailer," as Robert's invention was now known, and was a patentee in his own right of the "Fairy Nest Cradle," a suspended basket for babies which was rocked by means of a foot treadle.

Robert Dick was an unequivocating, declamatory man, riding through the countryside and striding through the towns with satchels full of improving literature, much of which was written, or published, by himself. His evangelism was grounded on a belief in free will, which he logically extended to advocate open communion for all believers, total abstinence but not legislative prohibition, free choice and simplicity in medical care, and demolition of barriers based on race. His thoroughness, however, made him a difficult and isolated man, despite his penchant for inaugurating institutions and attending meetings. But among the fruits of his impatience and reforming zeal were the inventions which brought him wealth.

BARRIE DYSTER

[Robert Dick was the author of *Close communion, the offspring of arrogance: answer of the Clinton quarterly meeting to the circular letter of the Onondaga Association . . .* (Utica, N.Y., 1842) and publisher of the *Unfettered Canadian* (Brockville, [Ont.], and Toronto), 1849–50 (?), the *Gospel Tribune . . .* (Toronto), 1854–58, and the quarterly *Dick's Patent Expositor* (Buffalo, N.Y., and Fort Erie, Ont.); a copy of the latter for November 1868 has survived at the Burke Library, Hamilton and Kirkland Colleges (Clinton, N.Y.), as an enclosure to a letter from Dick to Edward North, 19 Jan. 1869. B. D.]

General Register Office (Edinburgh), Register of births and baptisms for the parish of Bathgate, 1814. PAC, RG 1, L3, 295, L20/32; 296, L21/61; 297a, L2/54; 299, L4/18. Anti-Slavery Soc. of Can., *Annual report* (Toronto), 1857. Canada Baptist Union, *Annual report*... (Montreal), 1844–46. *The Canadian Baptist Register* (Toronto), 1856–60. Hamilton College, *Letter of the half century annalist for the year 1891 . . .* (n.p., [1891]). *A memorial of the semi-centennial celebration of the founding of Hamilton College, Clinton, N.Y.* (Utica, 1862). Sons of Temperance, Grand Division of Canada West, *Proc.* (Brockville and Hamilton, [Ont.]), 1850–52. *Globe*, 27 Aug., 14 Sept., 28 Nov. 1850. *Watchman* (Toronto), 9 Sept., 11 Nov. 1850. *Free Baptist cyclopædia*, ed. G. A. Burgess and J. T. Ward (Chicago, 1889). *The Free Baptist register and year book . . .*, 1842–1902. Hamilton College, *Complete alumni register, 1812–1922* (Clinton, 1922). Morgan, *Bibliotheca Canadensis*, 106. W. R. Cross, *The Burned-over District; the social and intellectual history of enthusiastic religion in western New York, 1800–1850* (Ithaca, N.Y., 1950). Andrew Wilson, *A history of old Bytown and vicinity, now the city of Ottawa* (Ottawa, 1876).

DICKENS, FRANCIS JEFFREY, NWMP officer; b. 15 Jan. 1844 at London, England, fifth child and third son of Charles Dickens and Catherine Hogarth; d. unmarried 11 June 1886 at Moline, Ill.

Francis Jeffrey Dickens inherited none of his famous father's literary talent. He was educated at a school for English boys at Boulogne, France, but did poorly, perhaps because he stuttered and was partially deaf. After a short stay in Germany in 1859, where he began studies in medicine, he returned to London and was employed for a time as a clerk in a commercial firm. He then worked in a minor editorial capacity on his father's magazine, *All the Year Round* (London). This arrangement suited neither father nor son, and after failing the Foreign Office examination Francis obtained a commission in the Bengal Mounted Police in February 1864, largely through family influence.

Dickens spent the next seven years in India, returning to England in 1871 after the death of his father. The next three years were spent dissipating his inheritance and quarrelling with his family. By 1874 he was penniless, and his sister appealed to the governor general of Canada, Lord Dufferin [Blackwood*], a family friend, to find him a position with the recently formed North-West Mounted Police. Prime Minister Alexander Mackenzie* was able to oblige and Dickens was appointed sub-inspector (the title was later changed to inspector) on 19 Oct. 1874.

Dickens was assigned to D division, then stationed at the temporary headquarters of the NWMP at Dufferin, Man. For the next six years he moved with the headquarters from Dufferin to Swan River Barracks (Livingstone, Sask.) and Fort Macleod (Alta), and finally to Fort Walsh (Sask.). To be kept under the eye of the commissioner this long could mean either that an officer was marked for promotion or that he was considered a bad risk for an independent command. Dickens' fitness reports leave no doubt that those in charge were reluctant to trust him. His superiors consistently rated him as lazy, alcoholic, and unfit to be an officer in the NWMP.

The accuracy of these evaluations was amply demonstrated after Dickens was finally posted away from headquarters. Taking charge of a 12-man detachment at Blackfoot Crossing (Alta), Dickens, between June 1881 and January 1882, was involved in three incidents which nearly resulted in the annihilation of his detachment by Blackfoot Indians. In all three, Dickens, acting on complaints from whites, attempted to arrest Indians accused of crimes without the customary effort to hear their side of the story and secure the cooperation of the tribal leaders. In each case the Indians resisted arrest and a perilous armed impasse was reached. The first time Dickens was rescued by the quick thinking of a subordinate; the second time by the intervention of Chief Crowfoot [ISAPO-MUXIKA]. The third and most serious incident required not only Crowfoot's influence but the summoning of reinforcements under Superintendent Leif Newry Fitzroy Crozier*. Crozier was forced to back up Dickens' ill-considered actions, but relations between the police and the Blackfoot were permanently impaired.

Dickens was subsequently placed under the close supervision of Crozier. When Crozier was given command of D division at Battleford (Sask.) in September 1883, Dickens accompanied him and was assigned to command Fort Pitt. It was here during the rebellion of 1885 that Dickens was involved in the most famous incident of his career. After the opening of hostilities at Frog Lake (Alta) on 2 April 1885, some 28 civilians sought refuge in Fort Pitt. Eleven days later Big Bear [MISTAHIMASKWA] and his followers led by Wandering Spirit [KAPAPAMAHCHAKWEW] and Āyimīsis appeared and demanded the surrender of the fort. Dickens refused and two days of negotiations followed which came to an end when a scouting party of three policemen stumbled onto the Cree camp. In the ensuing gun-fight one constable was killed, a second was wounded, and the third was taken prisoner. At this point the civilians in the fort decided to give themselves up to Big Bear because Fort Pitt was poorly sited for defence and lacked an internal water supply. Dickens then decided to abandon the post and retreat down-river to Battleford. A scow was hastily constructed and after six days Dickens and his men reached safety.

Dickens took no further part in the rebellion. Until September 1885 he acted as a justice of the peace at Battleford and presided over the preliminary hearings of some of the rebel prisoners. He left the force in spring 1886, the government declining to find him employment elsewhere in the public service. After a lengthy dispute over the size of his retirement gratuity, Dickens headed in June for the United States to begin a lecture tour. On 11 June, just before he was to deliver his first lecture at Moline, he died, apparently of a heart attack.

Francis Dickens made a definite, if negative, impact on the Canadian west. He was partly responsible for the serious deterioration in relations between the NWMP and the Blackfoot in the 1880s. His misadventures also contributed to the strong prejudice against English officers that existed in the mounted police in the late 19th century.

RODERICK CHARLES MACLEOD

PAC, MG 27, I, B3; RG 18, A1, 5, 6, 9, 12. Royal Canadian Mounted Police Arch. (Ottawa), Service file 0/29 (Francis Jeffrey Dickens). Can., Parl., *Sessional papers*, 1882, VIII, no.18; 1886, VI, no.8a. Ronald Atkin, *Maintain the right: the early history of the North West Mounted Police, 1873–1900* (London and Toronto, 1973). P. A. W. Collins, *Dickens and education* (London and New York, 1963). S. W. Horrall, *The pictorial history of the Royal Canadian Mounted Police* (Toronto, 1973). J. P. Turner, *The North-West Mounted Police, 1873–1893 . . .* (2v., Ottawa, 1950). Vernon LaChance, "The diary of Francis Dickens," *Queen's Quarterly*, 37 (1930): 312–34. James McCook, "Inspector Dickens, N.W.M.P.," *Blackwoods' Magazine* (Edinburgh), 311 (January–June 1972): 122–33. John Manning, "Inspector Frank Dickens of the North West Mounted," *Colorado Quarterly* (Boulder, Colo.), 8 (1959–60): 63–75.

DICKIE, JOHN BARNHILL, teacher, farmer, shipbuilder, and politician; b. 30 March 1829 at Cornwallis, N.S., eldest son of Isaac Patton Dickie and Rebecca Barnhill; m. first on 7 Oct. 1850 Ellen Putnam, and they had three children; m. secondly in 1858 Harriet Dickson, and they had eight children; d. 5 June 1886 at Truro, N.S.

John Barnhill Dickie's ancestors had come from Londonderry (Northern Ireland) to Cumberland County, N.S., about 1763. John was educated at Canard and Wolfville, N.S., then from 1847 to 1851 at the Mount Allison Wesleyan Academy in Sackville, N.B., and finally at the Halifax Free Church College. While attending the Wesleyan academy, Dickie taught in a comfortable schoolhouse at Middle Stewiacke, N.S., giving instruction in book-keeping, surveying, mensuration, algebra, and Latin to an average of 30 students. He also ran a farm in Middle Stewiacke. Later he taught mathematics at the Halifax Academy.

In 1854 Dickie was appointed coroner for Colchester County. By 1856 he had moved to Onslow where he operated both a farm and a store. He served from 1858 to 1859 as treasurer for the poor in the district of Onslow, became a justice of the peace in 1861, and for a short time in 1863 was a militia major. In 1866 he was the founder and first president of the Onslow Agricultural Society, and was appointed *custos rotulorum* of Colchester and a trustee of school lands in Onslow in 1868. In 1871 Dickie moved to Truro where he had been named manager of the Merchants' Bank of Halifax, the first financial institution in that village. Between 1872 and his death he also owned shares in six vessels built along the Minas Basin shore; one, the *Colchester*, was reputed to have been the fastest vessel ever launched in the Bay of Fundy. He formed the Truro Marine Insurance Company in 1872 to protect his investments.

In December 1874 Dickie was elected to the assembly as an independent member for Colchester County, although his political sympathies had generally been with the Liberals. The results of the election made it uncertain whether the Liberal government of William ANNAND could still command a majority in the assembly, and when on 11 March 1875 Dickie accepted Annand's offer of the speakership a furore resulted. For Annand, the appointment of Dickie eliminated a potential negative vote, and rumours persisted that Dickie had sold his principles for money, prestige, or the promise of a seat in the Legislative Council. One newspaper praised Dickie at this time as "sagacious, clear-headed and able," but another described his acceptance as corrupt and treacherous. His Colchester colleague, William Albert Patterson, who left the house rather than vote against his friend, was later to refer to "the sale of the Speakership," and when Dickie was appointed to the Legislative Council three years later, the *Colchester Sun* labelled the appointment "The Last Act."

Dickie lacked the parliamentary training essential to rule over an almost equally divided house. In trying to satisfy all, he satisfied none. On at least three occasions his actions or rulings caused violent controversy. When, on 30 April 1875, he broke a tie vote on an amendment to a railway bill, the opposition's frustration exploded. For the first and only time in Canadian parliamentary history a resolution was carried by a vote of 20–12 requesting the speaker to resign, which he did the following day. "He had to listen to certain whereases, impeaching him of the high crimes of ignorance and incompetence, of drawing a salary under false pretences and filling a position given him as the price of treachery." His inexperience condemned him: a correct ruling would have been that the fatal motion required 48 hours notice. The Toronto

Mail observed that the incident was "peculiar to Nova Scotian politics which are indeed inscrutable and past finding out."

Dickie retained his seat in the assembly until 1878, and from that year until his death sat in the Legislative Council. A quiet man, he never publicly commented upon the humiliating experience of 1875, and from his correspondence with his brother James there emerges a serene individual. An active Presbyterian, in his last years Dickie concentrated on his business and when he died of intestinal cancer in 1886 he left an estate in excess of $61,000.

ALLAN C. DUNLOP

Dalhousie Univ. Arch., MS 4–63. *Canadian biog. dict.*, II. A. W. H. Eaton, *The history of Kings County, Nova Scotia* . . . (Salem, Mass., 1910; repr. Belleville, Ont., 1972).

DICKSON, JOHN ROBINSON, surgeon and educator; b. 15 Nov. 1819 at Dungannon (Northern Ireland), son of David Dickson and Isabella Robinson; m. 8 May 1839 Ann Benson of Kingston, Upper Canada, and they had four sons and four daughters, including Dr Charles Rea* and Anne, one of the first female medical graduates in Ontario; d. 23 Nov. 1882 on Wolfe Island, near Kingston.

John Robinson Dickson was apprenticed to an apothecary in 1829. He did not complete his six-year term and spent some time at the Royal Belfast Academical Institution before entering Anderson's College in Glasgow to study medicine. In 1837, before he had finished his studies, the Dickson family immigrated to Upper Canada and John was apprenticed to Dr John Hutchinson of Peterborough. Dissatisfied with country practice Dickson considered emigrating to the United States. From October 1841 to March 1842 he studied at the University of New York, receiving an MD degree. However, because of increased prospects Dickson returned to Canada and in April 1842 was licensed by the Medical Board in Canada West; he opened his practice in Kingston, then the capital of the united provinces. Late in the 1840s John A. Macdonald* became a patient and a close friend. Dickson took his turn as "medical man for the month" between 1846 and 1849 at the hospital (later Kingston General Hospital) organized by the Female Benevolent Society [*see* Harriet DOBBS].

Dickson was vitally interested in improving medical training in Upper Canada, then acquired mostly by apprenticeship and hospital attendance. So that the hospital might offer better advantages to medical students Dickson joined Dr Horatio YATES in seeking election in 1853 as alderman to serve on the hospital board, then limited to elected municipal officials. They were both successful, and Yates took over reorganization of the hospital. Dickson issued invitations to local doctors to meet at John A. Macdonald's house in February 1854 to discuss the formation of a medical school. The next month doctors Dickson, James Sampson*, John Stewart*, and Orlando Sampson Strange met with trustees from Queen's College to propose the plan that led to the organization of the Queen's faculty of medicine later that year. Dr Dickson was appointed professor of the principles and practice of surgery, and in 1861 became vice-president of the faculty (the title was changed to dean two years later). He received an MD degree from Queen's in 1863.

In 1864 after a year of feuding, first with Dr John Stewart, secretary of the faculty, concerning personal and fiscal matters, and later with William Leitch* and the trustees concerning regulatory demands, Dickson submitted his resignation to Queen's. Two years later he organized a new medical school, the Royal College of Physicians and Surgeons of Kingston, affiliated with Queen's for the granting of degrees, which was staffed by former Queen's professors who had left the university rather than accede to the trustees' demand that they declare their belief in the doctrines of the Westminster Confession of Faith. Dickson was professor of clinical surgery and president of the new college. In his inaugural address in October 1866 he strongly encouraged the creation of a central examining body in the province to ensure uniform medical qualifications. He managed to have the courses of medical study recognized by the royal colleges of surgeons in both Edinburgh and London, two colleges from which he held degrees. In 1880 the college began a series of medical lectures for women to be given by Dickson and Yates. Unfortunately, largely because of protests from male students, it was short-lived.

In September 1865 the Medical Board became the Council of Medical Education and Registration of Upper Canada, and when it met in June 1866 Dickson served as its first president. He followed James Sampson as surgeon to the provincial penitentiary and at Rockwood Asylum. For some years Dickson had been a member of the provincial commission on lunacy and in December 1869 was appointed medical superintendent of the asylum. An elder of the Presbyterian Church and a strong advocate of temperance he abolished the use of alcohol at the asylum. He served as vice-president of the Canadian Medical Association and was a member of the council of the Botanical Society of Canada.

Dr Dickson organized the Cataraqui Medical Society, which met to hear papers each month, and served as president from September 1880 until May 1881 when he became ill. He retired to his son's home on Wolfe Island where he died in 1882.

MARGARET SHARP ANGUS

A number of articles by J. R. Dickson appeared in the *British American Journal* . . . (Montreal), 1860–62.

QUA, Queen's Univ. medical faculty records, II, box 2, folder 16; X, box 8, vols.1, 8; XI, box 11, vol.1. Macdonald, *Letters* (J. K. Johnson and Stelmack), II: 163. *Chronicle & Gazette*, 8 May 1839, 13 May 1842. *Daily British Whig*, 2 Jan. 1854, 23 Nov. 1882. *Canadian biog. dict.*, I: 348–49. Margaret Angus, *Kingston General Hospital, 1832–1972: a social and institutional history* (Montreal and London, Ont., 1973). William Canniff, *The medical profession in Upper Canada, 1783–1850 . . .* (Toronto, 1894).

DINNING, HENRY, shipbuilder; b. *c.* 1830 probably in Ireland, son of James and Isabella Dinning; m. in 1864 Etta Carpenter, and they had at least nine children; d. 15 Feb. 1884 at Quebec City.

Henry Dinning immigrated to Quebec City with his family in 1832 and received his education there. On 1 Sept. 1850 he became a partner in a shipbuilding firm with William Henry Baldwin*, who in the previous year had leased the Anse au Foulon shipyard originally owned by George Black*. Their partnership agreement, signed for an 8-year term, provided that Baldwin would receive a credit of £1,000 for stock, furniture, and accounts receivable, and that he would superintend the shipyard while Dinning concerned himself with the office work. The partners built the 1,034-ton *Birmingham* in 1851 and the 1,203-ton *Countess of Elgin* the next year. In 1853 Baldwin and Dinning built four vessels: the 1,294-ton *Annie Jane*, the 1,237-ton *Argonaut*, the 476-ton *Chance*, and the 755-ton *Meteor*, followed by at least one vessel, the 1,032-ton *Ocean Monarch*, in 1854. In May 1856, however, the partnership was dissolved and Dinning took over the outstanding accounts and the yard at Anse au Foulon.

In 1858 Dinning formed a partnership with his father and the following year the firm of H. Dinning and Company, "shipbuilders, dock proprietors and repairers," constructed the 1,236-ton *Prince Consort*. Four years later it produced the 1,236-ton *Annie Frost* and the 1,154-ton *Etta*. The shipyard reached a high level of activity in 1866 when it built two ships and a barque, and carried out major repairs on a fourth vessel. H. Dinning and Company was considered one of the busiest shipyards on the St Lawrence River that year, and the credit agents of R. G. Dun and Company estimated its worth at between $25,000 and $50,000; it received a good credit rating.

The Quebec shipbuilding industry, which had weathered financial crises in 1854–55 and 1862–64, encountered yet another during the years 1866 and 1867, and the Dinning firm laid down no vessels in the latter year. The removal of protectionist duties by France from 1864 to 1870 could not compensate for the loss of markets caused by the commercial depression in England and the American tariffs on Canadian-built vessels. High interest rates contributed to the firm's rising production costs, as did a strike by ship's carpenters, who were organizing to seek protection from the competition of non-specialized labour. Together with the growing obsolescence of wooden ships in competition with steam and iron, these factors created numerous difficulties for shipbuilders such as Dinning. Nevertheless, his firm recovered in 1868, building two vessels. In May 1870 he launched the 550-ton barque *Lady Young*, whose quality workmanship and materials earned it "the highest class that has been given to any colonial vessel" by Lloyd's Register of British and Foreign Shipping, and in August he launched the *Guinevere*, the first composite ship built at Quebec, with an iron frame instead of the usual wooden one. Dinning continued his innovations the following year by launching what the *Morning Chronicle* described as "the first iron ship built in Quebec," actually a lightship built in Britain, dismantled, and then reassembled at his yard. The early 1870s were among the most ambitious years of Dinning's career.

He was also heavily involved in salvaging and repairing vessels that had been wrecked in the approaches to the St Lawrence and he travelled as far as Saint-Pierre and Miquelon in search of likely prospects. Sometimes he undertook to salvage vessels for their underwriters but on other occasions he bought the wrecks at auctions, gambling that he could repair them and recover a profit. In these risky ventures Dinning was not always successful; he lost three vessels between 1870 and 1871. By 1877 he was insolvent and legal proceedings were filed by rival groups of creditors who sought to have their various claims recognized. Dinning nevertheless remained in business until his death. He continued to build wooden vessels although, as he explained at a meeting of Quebec City merchants in 1879, their construction involved a loss of 20 to 30 per cent. By 1881 his debts were discharged; however, he never again demonstrated the innovative spirit of his earlier days.

Dinning followed his father's example by becoming involved in various economic, political, and social activities in the city. Both men were among the incorporators of the Quebec Street Railway Company in 1863, a group which also included businessman Guillaume-Eugène CHINIC. Like his father, Henry Dinning served on the city council. He represented Champlain Ward as a councillor from 1872 to 1874, during which time he sat on the fire, roads, and by-laws committees, and as alderman from 1874 to 1877, when he served on the finance and aqueduct committees. At a council meeting in 1874, he was suggested as a possible candidate for the mayoralty but received only one vote. A member of the city's board of trade from at least 1865 to 1867, and again from February 1870 until his death, he occasionally sat on its council and its board of arbitration. He was also a member of the Quebec Yacht Club and its vice-commodore in

1868. His funeral cortège was said to have been one of the largest seen in the city.

In collaboration with KENNETH S. MACKENZIE

AC, Québec, État civil, Méthodistes, Chalmers Wesley United Church (Quebec), 18 Feb. 1884. ANQ-Q, Fichier protestant, Henry Dinning et famille; Minutiers, J. G. Clapham, 27 March 1851. AVQ, Procès-verbaux du conseil, 1872–77. PAC, RG 4, C1, 395, files 1667, 1734; RG 31, A1, 1871, Quebec City, Montcalm Ward, p.82. Can., Prov. of, *Statutes*, August–October 1863, c.61. *In re Dinning, insolvent, and Samson* et al., *petitioners* (1878), 4 Q.L.R. 26. *In re Dinning, insolvent, and Wurtele* et al., *petitioners* (1878), 4 Q.L.R. 37. *Watson* et al., *and Samson*, in re *Dinning* (1878), 4 Q.L.R. 365. *Canada Gazette*, 23 Aug. 1856. *Morning Chronicle* (Quebec), 4 Aug., 31 Oct. 1863; 2 May, 15 Aug. 1870; 1 June 1871; 5 May 1876; 16, 19 Feb. 1884. *Quebec Official Gazette*, 18 Jan., 16 Feb., 15 March 1878; 8 July 1881. *Dominion annual register*, 1884. Jean Hamelin *et al.*, *Répertoire des grèves dans la province de Québec au XIXe siècle* (Montréal, 1970), 19. *The mercantile agency reference book . . .* (Montreal and Toronto), 1866. *Quebec directory*, 1848–80. Fernand Ouellet, *Histoire de la Chambre de commerce de Québec, 1809–1959* (Québec, 1959). Narcisse Rosa, *La construction des navires à Québec et ses environs; grèves et naufrages* (Québec, 1897; réimpr., Montréal, 1973). F. W. Wallace, *Wooden ships and iron men: the story of the square-rigged merchant marine of British North America, the ships, their builders and owners, and the men who sailed them* (Boston, 1937; repr. Belleville, Ont., 1973).

DOBBS, HARRIET (Cartwright), humanitarian and artist; b. 27 Aug. 1808 in Dublin (Republic of Ireland), daughter of Maria Sophia and Conway Edward Dobbs, QC; m. 21 Nov. 1832 in Dublin the Reverend Robert David Cartwright, son of Richard Cartwright* of Kingston, Upper Canada, and they had one daughter and four sons, including Sir Richard John Cartwright*; d. 14 May 1887 at Portsmouth (now part of Kingston).

Harriet Dobbs grew up in Ireland as one of eight children in an upper class, religious family. She received a good education including drawing lessons which encouraged her considerable talent for sketching and painting. She sketched daily in Ireland and produced drawings, water-colours, and "likenesses" after she came to Canada.

On 5 June 1833 Harriet arrived in Kingston with her husband as the newest member of one of the town's founding families. Shortly after entering the new stone mansion that was to be her home she received the élite of Kingston who came to welcome her in "the ceremony of cake and wine . . . a Canadian custom it seems." In addition to the status of the family in the community, her husband's position as assistant minister to Archdeacon George Okill Stuart* at St George's Church encouraged her inclination towards charitable work.

Harriet immediately joined the Female Benevolent Society, an interdenominational group of women who since 1820 had been providing, in an abandoned blockhouse, the only hospital care for the poor in Kingston. The hospital, actually a hostel for the sick and their families, opened in November and closed in May each year. During the summer the remaining patients were placed in boarding-houses. Harriet Cartwright, as one of the managers of the society, took her turn in a rotation system, being responsible for the management of the hospital for a week at a time.

To raise badly needed funds for the society she organized a sewing group in December 1833, acting as secretary for the ladies who produced items for sale at an annual bazaar. She also painted "likenesses" to raise funds for charity. Not satisfied with just the physical care of the poor, in April 1834 she organized the first FBS school in a room attached to the hospital. Classes ceased later that year when she was forced to limit her charitable activities because of the birth of her first child and the care required by her ailing husband. After the blockhouse hospital burned in December 1835, the society became dormant, expecting a general hospital to be opened in the new building constructed for that purpose.

In 1839 Harriet Cartwright reorganized the FBS as "a society for giving out work to employ the poor . . . by directing industry into the right channels." The members collected funds, appointed visitors, purchased sewing and knitting materials, and distributed work to the unemployed and to fatherless families. The finished products were given to the poor or sold at the annual bazaar. With the materials the society also handed out advice and dire warnings about "the evil of strong drink."

In 1840 the FBS took an activist role in the fight for temperance, which was very unusual for women's groups at that time, especially in Canada. Harriet wrote that the society "ventured so far out of place as to get up a petition to the magistrates to diminish the licenses and look after the unlicensed dram shops abounding in every quarter." A waterfront fire in Kingston in April 1840 had burned 14 taverns on one block and the petition succeeded in bringing about a limit on the number of liquor licences issued. In November Harriet wrote that the FBS had "had some effect." Late that year Harriet also organized a Church of England district visiting society to investigate cases of distress and "to create a more friendly intercourse with those in the lower class, who often feel themselves overlooked & neglected by their superiors." The men of St George's visited in the district, the women visited in the town.

The general hospital, expected to commence in 1835, never opened and the FBS began a temporary hospital again late in 1842, this time in an old warehouse. Harriet's time, however, was spent caring for her sick husband who died 24 May 1843. After a short visit to Ireland with her four children, Harriet returned to her work in Kingston. In November 1845 the society opened two wards in the hospital building, which had been vacated by the parliament, and Harriet Cartwright's name headed the list of "visitors" who took responsibility for running the hospital. Its operation became too expensive and time-consuming for the FBS and after 1846 they were assisted by a male volunteer committee until the hospital was incorporated under municipal management in 1849 [*see* Horatio YATES].

During this time as frequent epidemics, especially the typhus epidemic of 1847, left more widows and orphans in Kingston, the FBS formed the Widows' and Orphans' Friends Society. Harriet Cartwright was the secretary, and the society concentrated on providing shelter for unfortunates. A house of industry, opened in 1847 and assisted by city funds after 1852, provided accommodation for widows but not for orphans. The society was reorganized and in 1856 the Orphans' Home and Widows' Friend Society, incorporated in 1862, began to concentrate on providing a home for "destitute orphans and homeless children." In February 1857 the ladies bought a small house, and architect William Coverdale* donated the plans for a dormitory and school building. The "ladies' school" which had been held at the house of industry from 1848 moved to the home in 1857. The salaries of the teachers were paid by the trustees of the common schools, and 70 orphans and children from destitute families were enrolled.

For 31 years Harriet served as corresponding secretary of the Orphans' Home and Widows' Friend Society. She sought funds from business and government as well as by personally canvassing homes in the village of Portsmouth, where she had moved after her return from Ireland. She interviewed prospective employers, adoptive parents, and the fathers of abandoned children, and as well investigated apprentice bonds and working conditions of the wards of the FBS. A new orphans' home was opened in 1863; in her final years Harriet was planning to establish a kindergarten.

As a manager of the FBS Harriet was also involved in the care of women in the provincial penitentiary, which had opened in 1835. Dr James Sampson*, surgeon at the penitentiary and the Cartwrights' family physician, persuaded her to be one of the first regular visitors to the prison. She was especially troubled by the incarceration of mentally ill women for whom there was no other institution until the Rockwood Asylum was opened in 1856. She also assisted her brother, the Reverend Francis William Dobbs, who was chaplain at the penitentiary after 1875, in organizing Christmas parties for women prisoners.

Harriet Cartwright faced the sorrows of her life, the death of her first son at 14 months and her husband's death after 11 years of marriage, as "deserved chastisement" to be accepted "with a truly humble heart." She typified the spirit of Victorian humanitarianism and her obituary in the *Daily Whig* of Kingston said: "She was a good old lady, full of piety and much given to good work and her reward is certain."

MARGARET SHARP ANGUS

The letterbook of Harriet Dobbs (Cartwright) is in the possession of her descendants and some of her sketches are held at the PAC.

Canadian Penitentiary Service Museum, Arch. Section (Kingston, Ont.), Kingston Penitentiary, Inspector's letterbook, 23 April 1835–1 May 1866; Warden's letterbook, 2 Aug. 1834–8 Sept. 1843. QUA, Cartwright family papers, H. D. Cartwright, letters, 1832–43 (transcripts); House of Industry records; Orphans' Home and Widows' Friend Society records. *Daily British Whig*, 16 May 1887. *Daily News* (Kingston), 5 Sept. 1856, 20 April 1857. *Kingston Spectator*, 22 Jan. 1833. M. I. Campbell, *100 years: Orphans Home and Widows Friend Society, 1857–1957* ([Kingston, 1957?]). J. D. Stewart and I. E. Wilson, *Heritage Kingston* (Kingston, 1973). Margaret Angus, "A gentlewoman in early Kingston," *Historic Kingston*, no.24 (1976): 73–85. H. L. Cartwright, "The Cartwrights of Kingston," *Historic Kingston*, no.16 (1968): 41–47.

DONKIN, JOHN GEORGE, soldier, NWMP constable, author, and journalist; b. 7 June 1853 at Morpeth, England, son of Arthur Scott Donkin, MD, and Mary Moor; d. 3 Jan. 1890 at Alnwick, England.

As a young man John George Donkin apparently intended to follow his father into the medical profession. He was employed for a time as a locum tenens for medical practitioners in the north of England but failed to complete his formal studies. He then tried his hand at journalism before joining the army and serving for two years as an enlisted man in the 17th Lancers.

Donkin came to Canada in April 1884 with little money and no plans. Hearing of the farming opportunities in Manitoba, he joined a group of immigrants and proceeded to Brandon where he hired himself out to a local farmer. Donkin soon found that the pursuit of husbandry was "not my forte." He decided to "try my luck" in the North-West Mounted Police and enlisted as a constable at Winnipeg on 30 Sept. 1884. Donkin probably received a few lectures on the duties of a peace officer, although training at this time largely consisted of foot drill, small arms practice, and instruction in the care and management of horses. After his few weeks of training in Regina, Donkin was moved north to Prince Albert (Sask.) in December 1884. As he remained there throughout the North-West rebellion, he did not take part in the fighting. He did, however, get the chance to use his earlier medical experience when he was appointed hospital steward to the post.

Following the rebellion, Donkin returned to Regina, where he formed part of the guard responsible for Louis RIEL in the weeks before his execution in November 1885, an event Donkin did not witness. In 1886 he was promoted corporal, and spent the remainder of his service at the isolated posts of Wood Mountain, Carlyle, and Souris River, all in present-day Saskatchewan. After nearly four years in the NWMP Donkin applied for permission to purchase his discharge before the end of his five-year term. Permission was not always given, especially if the force was under strength, but Donkin was granted his release on 12 March 1888. Shortly afterwards he returned to England where he again worked as a journalist.

Donkin would have passed into obscurity had he not published, a year after his return to England, an account of his experiences under the title *Trooper and redskin in the far north-west: recollections of life in the North-West Mounted Police, Canada, 1884–1888.* As an ordinary constable he had served during the rebellion, come into close contact with Riel, and lived the life of a mounted policeman in the early years of western settlement. His book, however, contains little of the self-glorification, heroism, and romance that is characteristic of most literature of the period on the NWMP. From the moment he arrived on the prairies, Donkin was struck by the contrast between his own experience and the way the country was portrayed by those "journalist globetrotters" who had set forth its "wondrous glories." The result was an unembellished account of the daily routine of mounted police life, the harshness of the climate, the rude prairie settlements, and the loneliness of police detachments. With an eye for detail, Donkin described his experiences in a candid and critical manner, leaving behind a valuable record not only of the NWMP but also of western Canada at an important period in its development.

Donkin became addicted to alcohol, a condition that probably contributed to the instability of his career. His premature death came within a few months of the publication of his book. Penniless and ill, he died in the workhouse at Alnwick from "inflammation of the lungs accelerated by excessive drinking."

S. W. HORRALL

J. G. Donkin was the author of *Trooper and redskin in the far north-west: recollections of life in the North-West Mounted Police, Canada, 1884–1888* (London, 1889; repr. Toronto, 1973).

General Register Office (London), Death certificate, J. G. Donkin, 3 Jan. 1890. Royal Canadian Mounted Police Arch. (Ottawa), Service file 1094 (John George Donkin). *Manitoba Daily Free Press* (Winnipeg), 12 March 1890.

DORWIN, JEDEDIAH HUBBELL, merchant and manufacturer; b. 25 May 1792 at New Haven, Vt, son of Philo Dorwin and Mary Hubbell; m. 7 April 1817 Isabella Williamson, and they had at least one son and one daughter; d. 12 Nov. 1883 at Montreal, Que.

Jedediah Hubbell Dorwin's life is more completely recorded than those of most other 19th-century entrepreneurs who operated on a small scale because of the records and journals he kept from 1811 until the day before he died in 1883. From this collection he preserved eight large volumes of journals, reminiscences, newspaper clippings, and weather reports for their possible interest to "someone that may come after me."

Dorwin left his father's farm in New Haven in 1811 without capital or special training, thereafter living by his wits, always ready to change direction in pursuit of some new opportunity. From 1811 to 1814 he was in the Oswego area of New York State residing with his mother's relatives and employed, for the most part, in various aspects of the salt trade. His stay was marred by illness and he returned home to recuperate.

In the spring of 1815 Dorwin became involved in the long-established provisions trade between Vermont and Lower Canada, fully restored now that the war was over. He made several trips to Montreal taking pork, cheese, and butter and, on at least one occasion, arranged to smuggle tea and loaf sugar back across the border. The following March he settled permanently in Montreal. For the next two years he operated small grocery and provision stores, first in the *faubourg* Sainte-Marie and later closer to the centre of the city. He gave up this line of business during the recession of 1818–19. In the spring of 1819 he subcontracted from Oliver Wait and Abner Bagg* the levelling of the northern section of Citadel Hill. Using Irish immigrant labourers, Dorwin completed by the fall what proved to be only "a moderate paying contract."

In December he found a more promising career when he bought cod from "some men from near Boston" and took it by sleigh to sell in Quebec City. For the next year or two, he continued buying and selling cod during the winters while also dabbling in trade with the American farmers in the Eastern Townships. During the spring and summer, however, he ventured farther afield and bought fish on the Labrador coast in exchange for unspecified goods; he also briefly entered the whaling trade in 1822 with the purchase of a ship in Labrador. Dorwin's maritime interests and profits were growing, and he now conducted what he considered to be a very lucrative trade in fish with the Quebec City firm of Ware and Gibb. By 1825 he was shipping wheat to Chatham, N.B., in his own schooner. Later in the year his vessel assembled a cargo in the ports of Sydney, N.S., Halifax, and Saint John, N.B., for the West Indies and returned to Quebec with sugar in June 1826. Having profited immensely from this excursion, Dorwin increased his involvement in the maritime trade in subsequent years. However, he was probably not a major trader.

It is more difficult to reconstruct Dorwin's later years. During the 1830s he, like other Montreal produce dealers, made trips into the Midwest of the United States to buy wheat and packed meats. Unspecified interests in the United States kept Dorwin away from Montreal, except for brief visits, from the autumn of 1836 until 23 May 1840 when he returned from Jonesville, Mich., "for good." Although still listed as a commission merchant in the Montreal directory for 1842–43, he was associated with Peter McGill [McCutcheon*] in the lumber trade as early as 1840. His commission business in Montreal may have been continued for a time by his brother Lewis who had been associated with him in some of his earlier ventures. For the next two decades, Dorwin played a central role in developing the lumber trade of Rawdon, a town north of Montreal, and in 1850 was president of a proposed railway from the village of L'Industrie (Joliette) to the township of Rawdon, which would be a 12-mile extension of the line then under construction from Lanoraie on the St Lawrence to the village of L'Industrie. Difficult terrain and a shortage of funds delayed the opening of the extension and, if it ever operated, its life was short. Dorwin's success as a timber merchant is difficult to gauge; in any event he did not have sufficient resources to re-establish himself after a major fire in his mills at Rawdon in 1859.

After 1860 Dorwin acted for three or four years as a Montreal agent of the Royal Naval Military and East India Life Assurance Company. From the mid 1860s to 1869–70 he was listed in the directories as a inventor and manufacturer of barometers. Dorwin, always a man of parts, had turned to a life-long avocation for his livelihood. There are indications of further financial reverses in the journals. It is possible that Canfield Dorwin, a Montreal broker who failed in questionable circumstances in 1869, was his brother and that, although Canfield may have been able to restore to some degree his own fortunes, he did not aid his older brother. Certainly Jedediah felt his losses from this period deeply. Although his financial position probably remained unsatisfactory, by about 1880, the year in which he turned 88, he seems to have recovered his spirits and returned to Rawdon with another unsuccessful railway scheme. He had a moment of triumph in February 1881 when "Montreal in 1816," an article based on his recollections and his "well known journal," was credited with selling the largest printing of the *Montreal Daily Star* to that date as well as causing a limited second printing. The manuscript journals he left give an inside view of the small community of American businessmen who settled in Montreal after the War of 1812, as well as glimpses of the thoughts and interests of Dorwin as a member of that community.

In collaboration with GERALD J. J. TULCHINSKY

Jedediah Hubbell Dorwin was the author of "Montreal in 1816: reminiscences of Mr. J. H. Dorwin . . . ," *Montreal Daily Star*, 5 Feb. 1881. His journals are at PAC, MG 24, D12 and his "Antiquarian autographs" are at McCord Museum (Montreal).

AC, Montréal, État civil, Anglicans, Christ Church Cathedral (Montreal), 15 Nov. 1883. PAC, RG 4, C1, 120, file 130. *Montreal Daily Star*, 1, 7, 26 Feb. 1881. *Dominion annual register*, 1883: 308–9. *Montreal directory*, 1842–83. Marcel Fournier, *Rawdon: 175 ans d'histoire* (Joliette, Qué., 1974). Tulchinsky, *River barons*. R. R. Brown, "The St. Lawrence and Industrie Village Railway," Railway and Locomotive Hist. Soc., *Bull.* (Boston), 70 (August 1947): 39–43. Albertine Ferland-Angers, "La citadelle de Montréal (1658–1820)," *RHAF*, 3 (1949–50): 493–517. W. A. Mackintosh, "Canada and Vermont: a study in historical geography," *CHR*, 8 (1927): 9–30.

DOUGALL, JAMES, merchant, horticulturist, and politician; b. 21 Sept. 1810 at Paisley, Scotland, son of John Dougall, manufacturer and merchant, and Margaret Yool (Yuil); m. first in 1832 Susanne (1814–63), daughter of François Baby*, and they had five sons and two daughters; m. secondly in 1864 Elizabeth Maçon, *née* O'Neill, and they had two daughters; d. 5 April 1888 in Windsor, Ont.

In the mid 1820s James Dougall's father, whose family had long been established in the muslin trade, decided that economic conditions in Scotland necessitated emigration to Canada. In 1826 Dougall sent his son JOHN to Canada followed by James with a consignment of dry goods to sell. The two brothers established wholesale dry goods stores first at Quebec and then in Montreal. John Sr joined his sons and in 1828 he opened with James a branch in York (Toronto). A fire destroyed the York establishment and in mid 1830 John Sr and James moved to Sandwich (Windsor) where they opened the first general store in the region. John Jr, who remained in Montreal, was a partner in the business, named J. and J. Dougall. The location of the store, on the communication lines between Detroit and Upper Canada, guaranteed its success; John Sr returned to Montreal (he died in 1836) and James soon built a larger store and a wharf. His marriage, in 1832, connected him to some of the political and commercial leaders of the district, including James Baby* and William Hands*. About 1834 Dougall became the agent for the Commercial Bank of the Midland District, and in 1837 he was appointed a magistrate and notary public, posts he retained for the rest of his life. According to tradition, Dougall was responsible for choosing the name of Windsor in 1836.

In January 1838, shortly after the outbreak of the

rebellions, Upper Canada was threatened by a Patriot invasion from Detroit under Dr Edward Alexander Theller*. To help in the defence of the region, Dougall loaned $12,000 to the defending forces to purchase arms, flour, and pork. He also provided $14,000 worth of clothing and blankets at cost. In December 1838 the Patriot army finally crossed the river into Canada, and Dougall, after removing $24,000 from his safe in case the store was looted, participated in the battle of Windsor under Colonel John Prince*. Although he did not support Prince's decision to shoot prisoners taken in the battle, he did condone the action in later years.

Following the rebellion Dougall gave up the Commercial Bank agency, but shortly after became an agent of the People's Bank (later purchased by the Bank of Montreal), and moved his residence to Anderdon Township in Essex County, just north of Amherstburg, where he operated a branch store. His estate, Rosebank, became noted for its crops and pure-bred cattle and horses imported from Scotland. In 1850 he opened the Windsor Nurseries. Throughout his life he wrote articles for various agricultural journals in the United States and for his brother's papers, the *Montreal Witness* and the *Daily Witness* in New York.

By 1839 J. and J. Dougall had become a flourishing wholesale and retail business and operated two vessels. The firm became Dougall and Redpath in 1840 when John married the daughter of Montreal merchant John Redpath*. In 1842 James Dougall hired Charles Hunt* to expand the firm's provision business, supplying meat to the British market and corn, biscuits, and fish to the Hudson's Bay Company. The conversion of John, by 1832, and then James to the temperance cause, however, ended the lucrative liquor trade in their stores.

By the late 1840s the firm had overextended its credit in Montreal and was suffering following the depression of 1847. In a fire in downtown Windsor, on 16 April 1849, the firm lost buildings and goods valued at $25,000, only part of which were insured. Arrangements were made to repay creditors, however, and by 1853 R. G. Dun and Company was able to report "both good business men bear excellent characters & may be depended on for liabilities they will assume."

In the early 1850s James had returned to Windsor, where a land boom accompanied the construction of the Great Western Railway. He developed the land owned by his father-in-law, and in 1856 he and Charles Hunt also purchased land and subdivided it. Although Dougall and Redpath had pulled through the worst of its difficulties from the 1840s it never regained its former prosperity. The partnership, which was heavily in debt, was dissolved in March 1858 but John and James remained responsible for its obligations. James then joined his sons, John and Francis, to form a new partnership which was moderately successful despite the current depression. The old debts, however, could not be paid off and by April 1865 James, brother John, and the new partnership were forced into bankruptcy with some $82,000 in unsecured debts, the Bank of Montreal being a large creditor. Discharge from bankruptcy was not granted until April 1869; James was then able to continue a nursery business on a limited scale, while his sons established their own store.

Dougall had always been active in community affairs. He was elected warden for Anderdon in 1845 and, after Windsor was incorporated as a village in 1854, sat on the first council. He was a member of the first town council in 1858 and the next year was elected mayor, an office he held until 1861. He sat as an alderman from 1863 to 1865 and was mayor for part of 1867 as well as the following two years. He also contributed to the development of educational facilities. In 1845 he had donated the funds for the construction of a school to educate both white and black children in Anderdon and later he built a schoolhouse opposite his Windsor residence. By the mid 1850s he had become a grammar school trustee and with the amalgamation of the school-boards in Windsor in 1864 he was elected chairman, an office he retained until his death 24 years later. He had less success in provincial politics, losing elections for the Legislative Council in 1856 and 1860.

After the passing of the Ontario Liquor Licence Act of 1876 [*see* Adam CROOKS], Dougall was appointed to the provincial board of licence commissioners. He was also active in the Windsor Board of Trade, and served as its president for some years. He was frequently its delegate to the Dominion Board of Trade and gave papers on trade development on the Windsor frontier.

Dougall was a member of the Presbyterian Church in Windsor and also in Detroit where he had excellent social connections. When he died after a lingering illness, he left personal and business effects worth only $450. His career, however, is not summed up by his business difficulties, but rather by his funeral eulogy, which stated that a sketch of his life "in this section of country would be to relate the history of this Western Peninsula."

FREDERICK H. ARMSTRONG

James Dougall was the author of "Battle of Windsor: James Dougall's account," ed. Francis Cleary, Essex Hist. Soc., *Papers and addresses* (Windsor, Ont.), 2 ([1915]): 25–29; *The Canadian fruit-culturist; or letters to an intending fruit grower* . . . (Montreal, 1867); and "My recollections of Toronto forty years ago," *New Dominion Monthly* (Montreal), July 1869: 1–4. A *Descriptive catalogue of fruit trees, grape vines, small fruits, &c., cultivated and for sale at the Windsor Nurseries, Windsor, Ontario, Canada, established 1850, James Dougall, proprietor* (Montreal, 1874) (copy at AO) was also published.

AO, Hiram Walker Hist. Museum coll., 20–135 (G. F. Macdonald papers). Baker Library, R. G. Dun & Co. credit ledger, Canada, 15: 13, 24–25, 39. Essex County Surrogate Court (Windsor), grant book H, no.471 (will of James Dougall; inventory of estate, 23 July 1888). PAM, HBCA, D.4. E. A. Theller, *Canada in 1837–38 . . .* (2v., Philadelphia and New York, 1841). *Canadian Emigrant* ([Windsor, Ont.]), 20 Sept. 1836. *Northern Messenger and Sabbath-School Companion* (Montreal), 24 Sept. 1886. *Commemorative biographical record of the county of Essex, Ontario, containing biographical sketches of prominent and representative citizens and many of the early settled families* (Toronto, 1905), 69, 137. Richardson Dougall, *James Dougall of Glasgow (1699–1760) and his descendants through Dougall and McDougall lines in the United States and Canada* (Ann Arbor, Mich., 1973), 3, 149–50, 159–62, 170–71, 174–75, 357. "Charles Hunt, 1820–1871," ed. G. W. H. Bartram, *Centennial review, 1967* (London, Ont., [1967]), 55–85. R. A. Douglas, "The battle of Windsor," *OH*, 61 (1969): 137–52. J. M. Hitsman, "Please send us a garrison," *OH*, 50 (1958): 189–92.

DOUGALL, JOHN, merchant, journalist, and publisher; b. 8 July 1808 in Paisley, Scotland, elder of the two sons of John Dougall, manufacturer and merchant, and Margaret Yool (Yuil), and brother of James; d. 18 Aug. 1886 at Flushing, N.Y.

In his youth John Dougall received significant intellectual and literary stimulus from his father, but his first ventures in the adult world were commercial. He immigrated to Canada in 1826 and, using his ties with Scottish merchants, established with James a commission business for the distribution of textiles in Quebec and in Montreal and its hinterland. A branch office was begun in York (Toronto), but failed. When James then established a store at Sandwich (Windsor) with their father, John was a partner. In Montreal John's commission business and a book and stationery shop provided a moderate income, and tied him to the economic aims of the Montreal business community. In the 1840s Dougall was a director of the Montreal Provident and Savings Bank. In addition, his marriage in 1840 to Elizabeth Redpath, eldest daughter of John Redpath*, gave him a commercial partnership with the Redpath family and an important entrée into the English-speaking upper class of Montreal.

Dougall's activities were largely determined by an impressive personal philosophy of Christianity. A Calvinist by birth and conviction, an evangelical, and an individualist, he had strongly held views of right and wrong. In 1831 he left the Presbyterian Church to join the Congregational Church. He sought to carry his ideas to all classes of society in a variety of ways. He was a founding member in 1839 and executive officer of the French Canadian Missionary Society, an anti-Roman Catholic organization aimed at evangelizing French Canadians and converting them to Protestantism [*see* Henriette Odin*]. He himself took to the streets, particularly in working class and harbour districts, talking and preaching to those he met, and in the 1860s and 1870s was an active supporter of the Young Men's Christian Association.

It was as a journalist and publisher that Dougall had his greatest impact. He had long had literary ambitions, and had attempted various writing ventures in his youth. In the late 1820s he published a number of pieces of prose and poetry in the *Montreal Herald*. In 1835 Dougall accepted the editorship of the *Canada Temperance Advocate*, the organ of the Montreal Temperance Society of which he had been a founding member in 1832. As editor he assumed the active leadership of the temperance movement in the Canadas, writing, travelling, and speaking throughout Upper Canada and parts of Lower Canada. In the 1840s and 1850s Dougall was involved in the publication of several other smaller journals devoted to the Sunday school movement, evangelism, and current affairs.

Dougall resigned as editor of the *Advocate* in 1845 and one year later established his greatest paper, the weekly *Montreal Witness*. The *Witness* grew steadily and a daily edition was added in 1860. The paper achieved a sufficiently large circulation in the English-speaking areas around Montreal to ensure moderate financial success despite the dissolution in 1858 of the Dougall and Redpath partnership. The paper was a stern champion of "right" ideas: evangelical Christianity, temperance, Sabbatarianism, economic progress, and free trade. Sermons were often reprinted and objectionable advertisements, such as those for alcoholic beverages, were refused. John Dougall believed that a newspaper must be politically independent, but the *Witness* was generally on the side of Reform or Liberal politicians. It was so aggressive and so intolerant of Catholics, Irish, and French Canadians that it directly stimulated the establishment in 1850 of a rival paper, the *True Witness and Catholic Chronicle* [*see* George Edward Clerk*], as a voice for the English-speaking Catholics of Montreal. Later, in 1875, when the newspaper was under the editorship of Dougall's eldest son, John Redpath, the *Montreal Witness* was placed under ecclesiastical ban by Bishop Ignace Bourget.

Dougall was convinced of the need for inexpensive (a penny per issue), daily, religious newspapers, particularly for the working class, in every urban centre in North America and Europe. In June 1871 he was looking for "new fields to conquer," now that several of his Canadian projects were well established. He left the *Montreal Witness* in the charge of his son, and with support and capital from Manhattan residents moved to New York City. Here he established the *Daily Witness* to embody his ideas. The *Daily Witness* was only briefly successful and failed in 1877, but the New

York *Weekly Witness* which he also founded in 1871 achieved considerable circulation and continued after Dougall's death.

John Dougall was an energetic, aggressive, and tireless worker. His views and forceful personality combined to antagonize people easily, but he also had much personal magnetism and a wide circle of friends. He had six daughters and three sons, several of whom were imbued with their father's moral fervour.

J. G. SNELL

John Dougall was the author of *Essay upon the nature of the wine and strong drink mentioned in the Scriptures* (Montreal, 1837).

PAC, MG 29, C34. Can., Prov. of, Legislative Assembly, *Report of the select committee . . . appointed to inquire whether any, and what measures can be adopted, to repress the evils of intemperance* (Montreal, 1849), 7, 54. French Canadian Missionary Soc., *Annual report* (Montreal), 1845: 4, 33. *Canada Temperance Advocate* (Montreal), 1835–45. *Montreal Witness*, 1845–86. Beaulieu et J. Hamelin, *La presse québécoise*, I: 132, 147–50. Richardson Dougall, *James Dougall of Glasgow (1699–1760) and his descendants through Dougall and McDougall lines in the United States and Canada* (Ann Arbor, Mich., 1973), 3, 149–50. J. A. Johnston, "Factors in the formation of the Presbyterian Church in Canada, 1875" (PHD thesis, McGill Univ., Montreal, 1955), 400, 475–78. J. I. Cooper, "The early editorial policy of the *Montreal Witness*," CHA *Report*, 1947: 53–62.

DOUGLAS, JAMES, doctor; b. 20 May 1800 at Brechin (Tayside), Scotland, son of George Douglas, a Methodist minister, and Mary Mellis; d. 14 April 1886 in New York City.

After serving a five-year apprenticeship under Dr Thomas Law of Penrith, England, James Douglas went in 1818 to study surgery in Edinburgh where there were highly renowned surgeons and medical schools. In March 1819, he enlisted as surgeon on a whaler and went to Spitsbergen, but resumed his studies in August and obtained his diploma as a surgeon from the Royal College of Surgeons in Edinburgh in April 1820. During his training he had diligently taken the anatomy classes of dynamic young Robert Liston, as well as those of John Barclay, whose lively style of teaching Douglas appreciated. In May, having attended lectures in London by John Abernethy and Sir Astley Paston Cooper, he received a diploma from the Royal College of Surgeons of that city. He spent a year in India, and upon his return in the autumn of 1822 accepted a position as director of medical services in a settlement on the Mosquito Coast in Honduras. But by the following autumn, seriously ill with the yellow fever he had picked up in that unhealthy climate, he had to go to Boston, Mass., for treatment. On his recovery, he thought of going back to Scotland, but not before paying a visit to John Stephenson* and Andrew Fernando Holmes*, former colleagues who lived in Montreal. On the way, he was forced to stop unexpectedly at Utica, N.Y., because of repairs to the Erie Canal. He decided to settle in Utica where in 1824 he married Hannah Williams. He also brought his young brother, George Mellis Douglas*, over from Scotland to serve as his assistant and begin medical training. For two years he lectured in anatomy and surgery at the medical college in Auburn; he also received an honorary doctorate in medicine from the Berkshire Medical Institution of Williams College in New York State.

After two bold experiments in dissection on corpses he had managed to obtain clandestinely, Douglas had to flee in midwinter 1825–26 to avoid the legal consequences. In Montreal his friends Stephenson and Holmes, who were aware of his surgical skill, strongly advised him to stay in Canada and establish himself in Quebec City. Arriving there on 13 March 1826, he quickly acquired a large clientele, being successful, it seems, in correcting strabismus and club-foot. He also won the esteem of Quebec's foremost doctors, including Joseph Morrin* and Joseph Painchaud*. The latter offered Douglas a room in his house on Rue de l'Arsenal, to use for dissection at his convenience. For many years the mortal remains of convicted criminals were taken there after execution. Douglas nearly died of typhus in the winter of 1828–29 but resumed work after a long convalescence. In September 1830 his wife died of tuberculosis; the couple's two children had died in infancy. A year later, he married Elizabeth, daughter of Archibald Ferguson, of Quebec City.

In 1832 during a serious cholera epidemic in Quebec City construction had begun on the naval hospital; two years later, when cholera had again broken out, this became the Marine and Emigrant Hospital. After the doctor in charge, William Augustin Hall, died in 1837, Douglas agreed to take his post provided he could have an experienced doctor such as Painchaud to work with him. The hospital, which had been mismanaged, was in a sorry state. Douglas was strict, authoritarian, methodical, and self-disciplined, and demanded the same qualities in his subordinates. Under his direction this 300-bed hospital, dedicated to the care of sick sailors and immigrants, quickly became famous, and the training given gained wide recognition. Positions there were sought by medical students who, in order to obtain a licence to practise in that period, had to demonstrate the level of their knowledge before a committee appointed by the governor. A student was sure to make a favourable impression if he had worked under Douglas, Painchaud, and their team. When Joseph Morrin opened his Quebec Medical School in 1848, the Marine and Emigrant Hospital became the centre for clinical teaching.

At the turn of the 19th century, the care of the mentally deranged in Lower Canada was deplorable. They were scattered throughout hospitals and prisons in Quebec City, Montreal, and Trois-Rivières where they were shut up in "cells" like prisoners. In 1824 a commission set up under John Richardson* to investigate their situation had recommended a complete revision of the system. Nothing had been done to implement this report prior to 1843 when the new governor, Sir Charles Theophilus Metcalfe*, strongly urged the Legislative Assembly to recommend that a special organization be established to undertake the care of the mentally ill. Two years later Metcalfe asked Douglas to assume responsibility for the insane in the province under the existing contract system (a system by which the government paid a specific sum for each patient in the hospitals and the latter remained private institutions). Douglas accepted and served for three years. In partnership with doctors Joseph Morrin and Charles-Jacques Frémont*, he bought Robert Giffard* de Moncel's manor-house at Beauport and had it converted for his new patients. On 5 Sept. 1845 the Asile de Beauport (Centre hospitalier Robert-Giffard) was opened, and Metcalfe then took steps to ensure that the 81 insane persons rotting in the prison of Montreal and in the hospitals at Trois-Rivières and Quebec were transferred to it. Many of them had not seen the sun for years and they rediscovered themselves, living together and working on the farm or doing domestic chores. This therapy produced excellent results, many of the patients becoming well enough to return to their families.

Douglas had taken his role seriously, devoting himself to his patients, but in so doing had neglected the Marine and Emigrant Hospital where the situation had deteriorated; it became necessary for a royal inquiry to be instituted in 1852. The inquiry was directed by doctors Wolfred Nelson* and Robert Lea MacDonnell* and by Zéphirin Perrault, a lawyer from Kamouraska, Canada East. Dr Anthony von Iffland* was its secretary. It left no doubt as to Douglas' professional competence but his tyrannical behaviour was censured. After this he gradually gave up the practice of medicine but he renewed his contract at the Beauport asylum.

Douglas had suffered from respiratory disorders since 1850, and had spent winters in Egypt, Italy, and Palestine, from which he brought back numerous souvenirs, in particular several mummies now housed in the museum of Université Laval and the Metropolitan Museum of Art in New York. With the deaths of Dr Morrin in 1861 and Dr Frémont in 1862, Dr Jean-Étienne LANDRY, through the purchase of some of their shares, became co-owner of the asylum at Beauport. When Douglas left for Europe in 1865, he authorized his son to liquidate his share, and it was bought by Joseph-Édouard CAUCHON on behalf of Dr François-Elzéar Roy. Douglas' fortune was vanishing. He had speculated in mining properties that had proved worthless, and he was even obliged to auction off his property at Beauport.

In 1875 he went to Phoenixville, Penn., to live with his son James*, the sole remaining member of his immediate family. Two of the four sons of his second marriage had died in infancy, and another, George, had died in 1861, just after obtaining a commission in the British army; his wife had died in 1859. Douglas spent the last 11 years of his life in the United States. On 10 April 1886 he had a cerebro-vascular stroke and died four days later. He was buried in Mount Hermon Cemetery, at Sillery, Que., which he himself had helped to establish.

SYLVIO LEBLOND

James Douglas was the author of "Account of the attempt to form a settlement on the Mosquito shore in 1823," Literary and Hist. Soc. of Quebec, *Trans.*, new ser., 6 (1869): 25–39; *Journals and reminiscences*, ed. James Douglas Jr (New York, 1910); and "A whaling voyage to Spitzbergen in 1818," Literary and Hist. Soc. of Quebec, *Trans.*, new ser., 10 (1873): 21–67. Correspondence is in the possession of Mrs. F. N. Douglas (Lakefield, Ont.).

ANQ-Q, État civil, Anglicans, Cathedral of the Holy Trinity (Quebec), 1 Oct. 1830; Presbytériens, St John's Church (Quebec), 19 Oct. 1831. R. B. Douglas, "Biographical sketches of James Douglas, M.D., 1800–1886, and James Douglas, LL.D., 1837–1918" (speech delivered at an unveiling ceremony at the Pavillon Perry of Douglas Hospital, Verdun, Que., 1971). H.H. Langton, *James Douglas: a memoir* (Toronto, 1940). Sylvio Leblond, "Anatomistes et résurrectionnistes en Grande-Bretagne," Canadian Medical Assoc., *Journal* (Toronto), 93 (1965): 73–78, 113–20; "Le docteur George Douglas (1804–1864)," *Cahiers des Dix*, 34 (1969): 145–64; "L'hôpital de la Marine de Québec," *L'Union médicale du Canada* (Montréal), 80 (1951): 616–26; "James Douglas M.D. (1800–1886)," Canadian Medical Assoc., *Journal*, 66 (1952): 283–87; "Joseph Painchaud," *L'Union médicale du Canada*, 82 (1953): 182–87; "Québec en 1832," *Laval médical* (Québec), 38 (1967): 183–91; "William Marsden (1807–1885), essai biographique," *Laval médical*, 41 (1970): 639–59. C.-A. Martin, "Le premier demi-siècle de la psychiatrie à Québec," *Laval médical*, 12 (1947): 710–38. C. K. Russel, "Dr. James Douglas, 1800–1886, adventurer: famous as a physician, surgeon and alienist – a leader among men," American Neurological Assoc., *Trans.* ([New York]), 61 (1935): 2–6.

DOUTRE, JOSEPH (baptized **Joseph-Euloge**), journalist, writer, and lawyer; b. 11 March 1825 at Beauharnois, Lower Canada, son of François Doutre and Élisabeth Dandurand, *dit* Marcheterre; d. 3 Feb. 1886 in Montreal, Que.

Joseph Doutre spent his childhood in the village of Beauharnois which was in the seigneury of the same name. His father was a shoemaker and the sexton of the church of Saint-Clément there. That Joseph

Doutre, the most determined adversary of the church in Quebec during the latter half of the 19th century, was brought up in the shadow of the altar is not the least paradoxical aspect of his eventful life. He probably attended primary school in Beauharnois before beginning classical studies at the Petit Séminaire de Montréal in September 1836. The principal of the seminary at that time was Joseph-Alexandre BAILE, a French Sulpician. It is worth noting that even at the height of his anti-clerical campaigns Doutre never disparaged his former teachers in any way. At the seminary he met young people whom he would re-encounter later, such as Toussaint-Antoine-Rodolphe Laflamme*, his colleague at the bar, Magloire Lanctôt*, and William Oscar Dunn, father of Oscar DUNN, a journalist who was a follower of the French ultramontane author, Louis Veuillot. When he left the seminary in 1843, Doutre studied law under Norbert Dumas, Augustin-Norbert Morin*, and finally Lewis Thomas DRUMMOND.

Doutre began to write and publish even before he was called to the bar on 30 April 1847. He contributed articles first to the *Mélanges religieux* and *L'Aurore des Canadas*, both published in Montreal. On 17 and 21 Nov. 1844 he had a short story entitled "Faut-il le dire! . . ." in *Le Ménestrel* (Quebec). The first two instalments of his novel, *Les fiancés de 1812*, were also distributed to subscribers at this time. Through Doutre, Montreal was suddenly exposed to the same literary currents as Paris in the field of the novel. On the banks of the St Lawrence, the law student was endeavouring to imitate Eugène Sue, whom Charles-Augustin Sainte-Beuve considered the novelist most in vogue in France and Europe. Sue owed his success to his "Mystères de Paris," first published in *Le Journal des Débats* (Paris) from 19 June 1842 to 15 Oct. 1843. The editor of *Le Courrier des États-Unis*, Théodore-Frédéric Gaillardet, republished Sue's novel in the *Semaine littéraire*; hence Montreal bookseller Édouard-Raymond Fabre* could deliver the episodes of "Mystères de Paris" to eager readers as they were printed in New York. Sue's novel had a truly seminal influence on Doutre. Reading it led him to self-knowledge; four years after the publication of *Les fiancés de 1812* he recalled: "I responded to the vitality in me that rebelled against the indifference of the times." In 1844, at the age of 19, with Sue as his model, he began his struggle against the prejudices, ignorance, and apathy of French Canadians as well as against a religion too often degenerating into Pharisaism. He attacked religious intolerance, the hypocrisy of "those sanctimonious knaves, who spend their lives in a church or robed in a priest's cassock," but who were none the less shady in their business dealings. Hence for him the reading of novels such as "Mystères de Paris" provided "an enlightened school of private and public discipline," for it effectively revealed "the vices of the social system, [and] the lack of public institutions for the encouragement of virtue."

Doutre begged public indulgence for his work. His ambition was "to give some stimulus to literature amongst us." But the final product did not come up to the young man's aspirations; in expressing his ideas, which were very modern from the social point of view, he had to rely on his as yet undeveloped natural talent, and he offended many sensitive readers. The result was that the *Mélanges religieux* judged *Les fiancés de 1812* to be "a sufficiently immoral work that fathers would forbid their children to read it, and that a woman who began reading it could not but blush and cast away such a production." Two years later, in 1846, Doutre published "Le frère et la sœur," a short story obviously inspired by Chateaubriand's *René*, but with the theme of incestuous temptation watered down. In it he looked back on his years at Beauharnois when he had "more than once trodden the shady paths of the seigneurial domain. More than once also its woods had echoed with the harmless sound of [his] inexpert gun." Doutre wasted no further time on purposeless experiments with the pen; the practice of law and the activities of politics were henceforth to demand all his attention.

Despite the assertions of a number of historians, he was not one of the young men who, on 17 Dec. 1844, had laid the foundations of the Institut Canadien. But he soon joined this group, became one of its acknowledged leaders, and in July 1847 was amongst the 13 young men who formed the initial nucleus of contributors to *L'Avenir* of Montreal. Doutre at first favoured the Reform party; indeed in April 1848 he and his friends were in a position to boast in their paper that they had helped Louis-Hippolyte La Fontaine* to get elected and they called themselves "the true friends of the government." But the next month the "Thirteen" rallied behind Louis-Joseph Papineau* who was attacking the union of Upper and Lower Canada and was bringing the revolutionary principle of "nationalities" (self-determination) to bear upon Canadian affairs. From that date Doutre stood out as one of the most persistent opponents of the ministerial party. When *L'Avenir* in August 1848 published "La tuque bleue," a satirical piece probably written by Louis-Antoine Dessaulles* but attributed to Charles Daoust* by George-Étienne Cartier*, it was Doutre who fought a duel with Cartier, the latter considering himself to have been ridiculed by this scurrilous document.

The clergy, convinced that *L'Avenir* was seeking "to spread revolutionary principles," as Bishop Ignace BOURGET wrote in his pastoral letter of 18 Jan. 1849, began to support the party of La Fontaine and Robert Baldwin* in an increasingly open fashion. When *L'Avenir* advocated annexation to the United States and demanded the suppression of tithes, clerical opposition to the Rouges stiffened and became so marked that Doutre believed, or was determined to believe, that there existed a letter from Lord Elgin [Bruce*] to the bishops, asking them to suppress the annexationist movement. Doutre published a diatribe in *L'Avenir* on 24 Nov. 1849 with the provocative title "Proposition infâme! Le peuple au marché!" A year later, under the heading of "Chronique religieuse," he published a long screed in which he gave vent to his anticlericalism with a vehemence almost unparalleled in French Canadian literature. Doutre was getting even with the "mixed, politico-religious party," which counted on the people's ignorance stopping them from casting "every four years a disinterested vote for the management of our public affairs." He felt that the source of this ignorance was the religious instruction given in schools and colleges in the grip of the clergy: "it is the sole cause; for here in brief are the social guide-lines of the mass of our population: eat and pray to God. . . . They are taught to scorn and flee all the rest."

Clerical hostility to the arguments of *L'Avenir* accounts for the exasperated tone of this statement. The evolution of Canadian politics since 1848 had decisively influenced Doutre's thinking: in 1850 he had reached the point where he upheld the essential tenet of political liberalism, separation of church and state, and as a consequence supported the exclusion of the clergy from politics and non-denominational, secular education. At 25 years of age, Doutre had adopted the line of action from which he would never deviate.

On 17 Dec. 1850, at the sixth anniversary of the founding of the Institut Canadien, he gave a speech outlining the goal of a truly modern education. Pointing out that a young man leaving college had no understanding of real life and of words such as income, taxes, trade, politics, elections, and public law, or even of words relating to sport, fashions, dancing, and the theatre, he stressed that thanks to the Institut Canadien this same young man could henceforth find his place in society immediately. According to Doutre, the institute had opened to all, without distinction of class, "the prospect of human greatness and of the honours attaching to high rank in public life"; hence one saw young people engaged in technical trades competing with men from the liberal professions. The use of the spoken word was no longer the sole preserve of members of the bar, the art of writing was within the reach of all, "and everywhere," he added, "you will find the immense influence of the press in the hands of young men whose appearance in the world of politics only dates from the formation of our societies for meetings and discussions."

It was because the Institut Canadien was a lay creation, free of clerical domination, that it was on the road of progress. Doutre had given proof of this *a contrario*, when in *L'Avenir* of 6 April 1850 he condemned a "minor coup d'État" of the library committee of the Institut Canadien in Quebec City which had voted to cancel its subscription to *L'Avenir*. This committee included the abbés Louis Proulx*, Jean Langevin*, and Elzéar-Alexandre Taschereau*, representatives of the clerical party, and the "Reverend" Joseph-Édouard CAUCHON, representative of the ministerial party: thus in composition it reflected what Doutre branded as "the mixed, politico-religious party." "The pulpits and the confessional," he protested, "were not enough for it; it has seized control of a public institution, founded on the example of the efforts of the youth of Montreal; it has done so in order to repress thought and opinion there, to forbid discussion and examination of them, to stop the spread of doctrines which are too sound not to be understood and accepted, finally to give [this institution] the appearance of a gathering of ignoramuses which they know so well how to do."

When *L'Avenir* temporarily ceased publication in January 1852, Doutre began to take an increasingly prominent role in the Institut Canadien, whose president from May 1852 was "citizen" Pierre Blanchet*. The progressives prevailed over the moderates; the latter finally decided to set up a rival association, the Institut National, for which they secured Bishop Bourget's patronage. This secession in no way stayed the progress of the Institut Canadien, if we are to judge by the Olympian detachment with which Doutre noted in the "eighth annual report," published in December 1852, that during the course of the year nine members had left the institute, two "to join a new society formed last spring."

Doutre was active in a variety of ways. On the occasion of a competition organized by the Institut Canadien in 1851, he had won a prize given by Legislative Councillor Pierre-Amable Boucher de Boucherville for an essay entitled "Du meilleur emploi qu'un citoyen peut faire de son existence tant pour la société que pour sa famille." The following year he published "Les sauvages de Canada en 1852," a talk on the Iroquois of Caughnawaga which he had given to the institute; he characterized this talk as "observations rather superficially assembled over two or three years, and tacked together in a twenty-four hour study carried out on the spot and copied from life." His forceful thinking and zeal for work so impressed his colleagues that in November 1852 they elected him president of the institute for a one-year term; it was under his presidency that the association was incorporated. At the beginning of 1854 it was able to acquire a large building on Rue Notre-Dame and a journalist and friend then claimed: "The Institut Canadien is now built on solid ground."

That year was to be particularly auspicious for the

group. Although Doutre was not among the 11 members of the institute elected to parliament, he distinguished himself at its "convention" on the abolition of seigneurial tenure. Doutre had been urging the abrogation of tenure since 1849, and had clearly indicated in *L'Avenir* of 4 May 1850 that on this question he parted company with Louis-Joseph Papineau and Louis-Antoine Dessaulles, who were themselves seigneurs. He had lived in a village that was part of a seigneury, and this may have been the origin of his opposition to such a system. But it was in educational issues that he was particularly active. When bookseller Édouard-Raymond Fabre, a close friend of Papineau and a founder of the Liberal newspaper *Le Pays* (Montreal), died in July 1854, Doutre spoke in his praise to the members of the institute. He emphasized Fabre's strength of character in acquiring a businessman's training at a time when "commercial education establishments still had to be created." "Even today," Doutre went on, "the necessity for an education derived from sources other than Greek or Latin authors is barely appreciated."

Doutre wanted not only the practical training he had already demanded in the columns of *L'Avenir* but also non-denominational instruction in schools, as was being advocated by another "convention" of the institute, focused this time on education. However, it was an inopportune time to insist on non-denominational teaching. The bishop of Toronto, Armand-François-Marie de Charbonnel*, and the Catholics of Canada West were fighting fiercely for the *de jure* recognition of separate schools. Consequently Doutre, who probably foresaw that he would enter politics in the near future, deemed it prudent to ease off a little. Therefore, during the sessions at the "convention," he showed admirable moderation; while supporting the principle of non-denominational schools, he prudently decided to shelve the thorny question of existing denominational schools and wait "until the public complains about the present system."

Doutre no doubt had his eye on a seat in the Legislative Council, now that it was an elective body. In September 1856 he ran in the division of Salaberry, but lost to the ministerial candidate, Louis Renaud*. He tried his luck again in 1863, running in Laprairie County for election to the Legislative Assembly. He met with another defeat, this time at the hands of Conservative candidate Alfred Pinsonnault. Doutre then gave up the attempt at elective office, but now harboured a much stronger hatred for the clergy, to whose opposition he attributed his successive defeats.

Meanwhile the bishops had come down hard on the Institut Canadien. Following the publication of Bishop Bourget's three pastoral letters on 10 March, 30 April, and 31 May 1858, 138 members resigned from the institute to set up a rival society, the Institut Canadien-Français. The bishop of Montreal vigorously rejected the free-thinking opinions of the leading members of the Institut Canadien, singling out Doutre and his brother-in-law Charles Daoust in particular.

At a banquet given in February 1858 by political friends of Daoust, who was editor of *Le Pays* and Liberal representative for Beauharnois County from 1854 to 1857, Doutre had returned to the question of non-denominational schools, stating that "the principle of mixed schools" seemed to him "the most rational, and the one that must some day prevail." But the right moment for attaining this objective was not at hand; "I do not think," Doutre continued, "that the state of our public education is such that one should apply this principle as an absolute rule, or as the main basis of our system." This was a public declaration, printed in *Le Pays* of 16 Feb. 1858, but Doutre had revealed what he really thought in a letter written to George Brown* five days earlier: the Catholics were overly excited and the "Jesuits must be met with their own arms – diplomacy." Doutre was certain that one day it would be possible to give Canada the non-denominational system advocated by Brown, for, he added, the success the Jesuits were enjoying was nearing its end.

Bishop Bourget obviously was unaware of the contents of this letter, but Doutre had shown his hand sufficiently in his public speech for the bishop to detect the obstinate champion of the liberal tenet of separation of church and state. If there had been the slightest ambiguity, Daoust dispelled it on this same occasion by declaiming "that the church and the state ought to have a separate existence, each live its own life, and not identify with each other in a common action." The bishop quoted this extremely explicit declaration; he indignantly called it "impious language," and to stigmatize his liberal opponents more effectively he resorted to arguments elaborated a quarter of a century earlier in Gregory XVI's encyclical *Mirari vos*.

Ostracized by the clergy and unable to enter politics, Doutre concentrated almost exclusively on his legal practice. One of his first partners was Joseph Lenoir*, *dit* Rolland, a talented poet. Among the lawyers who subsequently became his partners were his brother-in-law Charles Daoust, his brothers Gonzalve* and Jean-Baptiste, his cousin Raoul Dandurand*, and Médéric Lanctot*; others trained under his direction, notably Wilfrid Laurier*.

His competence and passion for work placed him in the forefront of his profession. He was made a QC on 15 Aug. 1863, under the administration of George Brown and Antoine-Aimé Dorion*, and was often a member of the council of the bar and of its library committee; from 1864 to 1866 he was an examiner and from 1867 to 1868 *bâtonnier*. He was a corresponding member for the Société de Législation Comparée of Paris from 1872, and contributed regularly to legal publications such as the *Lower Canada Jurist* and the *Legal News* in Montreal. In 1880 John Lovell and Son published his *Constitution of Canada: the British North America Act, 1867, its interpretation, gathered from the decisions of courts, the dicta of judges and the opinions of statesmen and others; to which is added the Quebec Resolutions of 1864, and the constitution of the United States*; the contents of its 414 pages are clearly indicated by the title.

Doutre argued a number of important cases. In 1857 he had become counsel for the *censitaires* appearing before the court established to settle the consequences of the abolition of seigneurial tenure. Three years later he agreed to defend a French bank cashier by the name of Lamirande who was guilty of misappropriating funds and who had taken refuge in Canada. But the case that brought him most sharply to public attention was undoubtedly the Guibord affair, to which his name is still attached.

From 1858 the rift between the Institut Canadien and the bishopric of Montreal had continued to widen. Despite the archbishop of Quebec's counsel of prudence, Bourget in that year rigorously applied to the library of the Institut Canadien the rules of the Index, the violation of which *ipso facto* entailed excommunication; in so doing he clashed with liberal opinion which denied any one the right of surveillance and prohibition in respect of books and reading materials. Liberals held that every individual had the right to choose his own intellectual fare; the cases of poisoning that might result were only accidental inconveniences, amply compensated for by the superior blessing of liberty.

Doutre, whose literary career had begun under the ægis of Eugène Sue, and who, because of his liberalism, found himself barred from the political office to which his talents and aspirations entitled him, must have felt this act of episcopal authority as a stinging blow. Hence it is perhaps surprising to find him on the committee appointed in October 1863 to "inquire into the means best suited to smooth out the difficulties that have arisen between His Lordship the Bishop of Montreal and the Institut." This encounter, which took place under the bishop's roof, proved fruitless and although Doutre and 16 other members of the institute applied to Pius IX on 16 Oct. 1865 to have the censure removed, the Institut Canadien, of which Doutre again became president in May 1867, saw its 1868 *Annuaire* put on the Index by the Holy Office on 7 July 1869.

Shortly after sending to Rome a second appeal, signed by Doutre, the Institut Canadien lost one of its members, printer Joseph Guibord*, who died suddenly on 18 Nov. 1869. Confronted with the refusal of the ecclesiastical authorities to grant the deceased a Catholic burial, his widow, through Adolphe and Joseph Doutre, as well as Toussaint-Antoine-Rodolphe Laflamme, instituted proceedings in the Superior Court of Montreal against the parish council of Notre-Dame. The case gave Doutre, one of the two counsel for the plaintiff, the opportunity not only to arouse national interest in the Liberal opinions he had been proclaiming for nearly a quarter of a century, but also to mount a violent, occasionally truculent, verbal attack against his ultramontane enemies, represented by the Jesuits whom he, and in Raoul Dandurand's view many influential Liberals, suspected of being the instigators of Bishop Bourget's attack. Had not the Jesuit Firmin Vignon set up the Union Catholique at the Collège Sainte-Marie in September 1854 to thwart the Institut Canadien?

Doutre carefully excluded from the Guibord affair "the venerable priests of Saint-Sulpice, among whom was the parish priest then in office"; he poured his concentrated venom into tirades reminiscent of the most famous anti-Jesuit diatribes. "There is in the world," he exclaimed, "a circle of men who are in permanent conspiracy against all that constitutes the material and spiritual happiness of humanity, a circle of men who call themselves Catholics and who have been proscribed thirty-seven times by the Pope and the princes of all Catholic countries." Rising to further heights, he burst into an invective worthy of Michelet: "Let honour be rendered to the Indians of this continent, who had begun to rid the land of Canada of the first seed of the holy Society of Jesus!" And what was the result of the Jesuits' influence since their return to Canada? "A few years sufficed to condemn our population to the most abject ignorance. They seized possession of everything, with the most innocent air possible. The Bishop of Montreal enrolled in their service. As a Jesuit? As a blind tool? We do not know. Through the Bishop of Montreal, they controlled the Board of Public Instruction, the choice of school texts [and] that of institutions, the direction of studies and courses in the primary and model schools." Against the advancing conquest of the ultramontane troops in the field of education, and, more generally, in secular structures, there remained one dyke, one bastion which "alone" was left "standing": the Institut Canadien. Therefore upon it alone "all efforts" had been "concentrated" for years.

Thus, in his argument as counsel, Doutre pinpointed the central problem beneath the antagonism between the Liberals and the Ultramontanes – the attitude that should be adopted to a world born of the intellectual and political revolution of the 18th century, and especially of the programme of civil and religious liberties proclaimed in the Declaration of the Rights of Man and of the Citizen. If Guibord, the target of ecclesiastical censure, received burial in a Catholic cemetery, it would be a victory for the Institut Canadien, and the liberalism it embodied, over religious authority; if he did not, his burial would be a variant of the custom of "burial in unconsecrated ground," which at this same period liberals in Belgium saw as further confirmation of the political domination of the clergy.

The rest is well known. Guibord's widow, or more precisely the Institut Canadien, won its case in the Superior Court on 2 May 1870 with Judge Charles-Elzéar Mondelet* presiding. This judgement was reversed by the Court of Revision and the Court of Appeal, but was upheld on 21 Nov. 1874 by the Judicial Committee of the Privy Council. On 16 Nov. 1875 Guibord's remains, which had been in the vault of the Protestant cemetery at Mount Royal since November 1869, were solemnly transported to the Catholic cemetery of Côte-des-Neiges with an escort of cavalry and foot-soldiers.

It was a Pyrrhic victory for Doutre. In fact the Institut Canadien, which he saw as the last rampart of radical liberalism, was slowly breaking up under the irresistible force of the mounting tide of ultramontanism. Several of its best-known members had died or made their submission to the church, so that by the beginning of 1886 *La Presse* could claim that the Institut Canadien no longer existed except "in name."

But Doutre did not surrender. According to the testimony of Laurent-Olivier David*, he was one of the few liberals who, having withdrawn from the church, did not recover the faith of his childhood. "I had ambition," he admitted to his colleague Rodolphe Laflamme, "I thought I had enough talent and energy to make my way; I saw [others] pass in front of me and my friends, and rise to honours, men who were of no merit; we were ostracized as a result of political opinions and reforms that were very questionable; I cannot pardon the clergy for the wrong it has done us."

On 28 Sept. 1858, at Montreal, Doutre had married Angéline, the daughter of Jean-Baptiste Varin and Hermine Raymond. Widowed the following year, he married Harriet Green, a native of Vermont, and they had six children, three boys and three girls. He died on 3 Feb. 1886 in Montreal, and was buried in the Protestant cemetery at Mont-Royal. When one considers his life, marked by so much activity and conflict, one notes with surprise that Doutre was but 60 years old.

Less than a year earlier his unbending ultramontane opponent, Bishop Ignace Bourget, had passed away. "With a little more conciliatory spirit on both sides," Doutre confided to his cousin Raoul Dandurand and to Honoré Mercier*, "perhaps we would have found some common ground." To be sure, but, even when the characters and intractable convictions of the two men are left out of account, it must be noted that a diehard ultramontanism and an uncompromising radicalism had clashed. If these two ideologies were in such opposition, it was not, essentially, because their religious or non-religious principles were contradictory but because each wanted to impose itself on the community.

PHILIPPE SYLVAIN

Joseph Doutre was the author of *Constitution of Canada: the British North America Act, 1867, its interpretation, gathered from the decisions of courts, the dicta of judges and the opinions of statesmen and others; to which is added the Quebec Resolutions of 1864, and the constitution of the United States* (Montreal, 1880), and of a speech printed in *Cour supérieure, Montréal; plaidoiries des avocats*: in re *Henriette Brown* vs. *la fabrique de Montréal; refus de sépulture* (Montréal, 1870), 35–64. He is known to have written one novel, *Les fiancés de 1812; essai de littérature canadienne* (Montréal, 1844), and some novellas: "Le frère et la sœur" and "Faut-il le dire! . . . ," printed in *Contes et nouvelles du Canada français, 1778–1859*, John Hare, édit. (lv. to date, Ottawa, 1971–), I: 168–92. Doutre also wrote "Du meilleur emploi qu'un citoyen peut faire de son existence tant pour la société que pour sa famille," published in *L'Institut canadien en 1852*, J.-B.-É. Dorion, édit. (Montréal, 1852), 144–92; "Les sauvages du Canada en 1852; Caughnawaga; les Iroquois; leur constitution politique et sociale; leur langue; usages, coutumes, superstitions," and "Notice biographique sur le feu Édouard R. Fabre, Esr. . . ." in *L'Institut canadien en 1855*, J.-L. Lafontaine, édit. (Montréal, 1855), 190–225 and 117–49 respectively.

AP, Saint-Clément (Beauharnois), Reg. des baptêmes, mariages et sépulture, 11 mars 1825. Arthur Buies, *Une évocation: conférence faite à la salle de "La Patrie" jeudi, le 6 décembre 1883* ([Québec, 1883]). L. C. Clark, *The Guibord affair* (Toronto and Montreal, 1971). Raoul Dandurand, *Les mémoires du sénateur Raoul Dandurand (1861–1942)*, Marcel Hamelin, édit. (Québec, 1967). *L'Avenir*, 16 juill. 1847–janv. 1852. *La Patrie*, 4 févr. 1886. *La Presse*, 3 févr. 1886. *La Vérité* (Québec), 13 févr. 1886. Bernard, *Les Rouges*. Pierre Beullac et Édouard Fabre Surveyer, *Le centenaire du barreau de Montréal, 1849–1949* (Montréal, 1949). Thomas Chapais, *Mélanges de polémique et d'études religieuses, politiques et littéraires* (Québec, 1905), 93–94. L.-O. David, *Histoire du Canada depuis la Confédération* (Montréal, 1909). Achille Erba, *L'esprit laïque en Belgique sous le gouvernement libéral doctrinaire (1857–1870), d'après les brochures politiques* (Louvain, Belgique, 1967), 677–78. J.-T.-D. Fortier, "La seigneurie de Beauharnois et la famille Ellice" (a talk given to the Soc. hist. de Rigaud, Rigaud, Qué., 21 mars 1958). Lareau, *Hist. de la littérature canadienne*, 281–82. Augustin Leduc, *Beauharnois; paroisse Saint-Clément; 1818–1919; histoire religieuse, histoire civile; fêtes du centenaire* (Ottawa, 1920). Olivier Maurault, *Le collège de Montréal, 1767–1967*, Antonio Dansereau, édit. (2e éd., Montréal, 1967). Léon Pouliot, *Mgr Bourget et son temps* (5v., Montréal, 1955–77), IV: 26, 94. N. S. Robertson, "The Institut Canadien; an essay in cultural history" (MA thesis, Univ. of Western Ontario, London, 1965). Sylvain, "Libéralisme et ultramontanisme"; *La vie et l'œuvre de Henry de Courcy (1820–1861), premier historien de l'Église catholique aux États-Unis* (Québec, 1955). Marguerite Maillet, "Joseph Doutre et l'éducation," *Co-incidences* (Ottawa), 4 (1974), no.2: 5–16. Philippe Sylvain, "Un adversaire irréductible du clergé canadien-français du dix-neuvième siècle: Joseph Doutre," *Cahiers des Dix*, 41 (1976): 109–25.

DOYLE, Sir CHARLES HASTINGS, soldier and colonial administrator; b. 10 April 1804 in London, England, the eldest son of Lieutenant-General Sir Charles William Doyle and Sophia Cramer Coghill; d. unmarried on 19 March 1883 in London.

Charles Hastings Doyle, like his father, attended the Royal Military College at Sandhurst, England, before entering the army as an ensign on 23 Dec. 1819. Doyle's rise through the ranks was gradual; on 16 June 1825 he purchased his captaincy, and while holding this rank through the 1830s he served as an aide-de-camp at Quebec. By 1841 he had been promoted to major. Doyle, who had served in both the East and the West Indies, purchased his lieutenant-colonelcy in 1846 and by 1854 had become a full colonel. From 1846 to 1856 he was on the staff of the quartermaster general and served in the Crimean campaign where at Varna he was invalided. For the next four and one-half years he was inspector general of militia in Ireland. Finally on 15 Sept. 1860 Doyle was appointed major-general and a year later was posted to the North American command.

Doyle arrived in Halifax on 16 Oct. 1861 to assume command of the British troops in the Atlantic area, which included the Maritime colonies, Newfoundland, and Bermuda. The outbreak of the American Civil War the previous April had spurred the imperial authorities to re-evaluate the defences of British North America, and Doyle busied himself with analyses of defence works and military personnel. After the Northern seizure of Confederate agents on the British steamer *Trent* on 8 Nov. 1861, relations between Britain and the North became strained and military preparations were stepped up. Britain dispatched troops to reinforce her garrisons in central Canada, but winter had closed the St Lawrence and it became necessary to re-route the reinforcements through Halifax. Responsibility for transporting the troops fell upon Doyle. Working closely with the lieutenant governor of New Brunswick, Arthur Hamilton Gordon*, Doyle by 17 March 1862 had dispatched almost 7,000 British regulars overland through New Brunswick to the eastern terminus of the Grand Trunk Railway at Rivière-du-Loup, Canada East. The speed and efficiency of the operation brought much credit to him. Diplomatic tensions eased in the spring, however, when the Northerners released the prisoners taken from the *Trent.*

One of Doyle's main concerns during these years was the Atlantic area militia. An inspection tour had shown that the militia existed only "on paper" and that the local legislatures had "repeatedly refused to provide money for the purpose of Defence." He urged upon the Maritime lieutenant governors the necessity of a thorough reorganization of the militia and made an improved training system for officers the "key stone" of his efforts. In the summer of 1864 almost 35,000 militiamen received a week's military training in Nova Scotia alone.

As commander of the British forces, it was Doyle's responsibility to assume the position of administrator whenever a lieutenant governor was out of the province or in the interim between appointments. It was during the absence from Nova Scotia of the Earl of Mulgrave [PHIPPS] in the fall of 1862 that Doyle made one of his most important political contacts. A strong supporter of the projected Intercolonial Railway, Doyle offered to aid Joseph Howe*'s advocacy of the line by writing to the home authorities "showing the great utility the railroad will be in a military point of view." As a result of correspondence concerning the railway, a warm friendship developed between Doyle and Howe.

In December 1863 Doyle, as administrator of Nova Scotia, again found himself in the midst of a diplomatic conflict. The *Chesapeake*, a steamer with Northern registry, had been seized by Southern agents with the help of some British Americans, but was soon recaptured by Northern gunboats in neutral British American waters and brought into Halifax. Doyle demanded that the ship be surrendered to him, along with three Nova Scotians on board whom he claimed were illegally detained. The Northern commander complied, but the anger of numerous Southern sympathizers in Halifax had been aroused by the Northerners' actions and they aided the escape of one of the three Nova Scotians whom Doyle wanted arrested for piracy in the original seizure of the *Chesapeake*. Doyle managed to defuse the troubled situation by impartially pursuing the three Nova Scotian wrongdoers in the courts. He was commended by all sides for his judicious handling of the affair, and even the American secretary of state, William Henry Seward, praised Doyle for his "just and friendly proceedings."

Doyle devoted his next few years in command almost entirely to military matters. By April 1866 the menace of a Fenian invasion of New Brunswick was at its most serious, and Doyle quickly responded to Lieutenant Governor Gordon's request for military aid. On 17 April he left Halifax with Royal Navy warships carrying over 700 British regulars and proceeded to Passamaquoddy Bay where the Fenian force was concentrated. This show of British armed might discouraged the Fenians,and the invaders dispersed.

Doyle remained in New Brunswick following the Fenian scare and in October 1866, with the departure of Arthur Gordon, became administrator of the province. The defeat of Albert James SMITH's anti-confederate government in general elections the previous June had been decisive in a successful move toward a Canadian union, but Doyle's first months in office were devoted entirely to undermining the still considerable opposition to confederation. As a result of his efforts, on 1 July 1867 he was named the province's lieutenant governor, a post he held until the following October. His ability to mediate and to remain on good terms with all political extremes had made Doyle one of the most respected figures in Maritime political circles by this time. Charles Tupper*, now a leading force behind Sir John A. Macdonald*'s federal government, realized that Doyle might be useful in the troubled political situation in Nova Scotia, where only one pro-confederate among 19 federal members of parliament and two pro-confederates among 38 members of the provincial assembly had been elected in September 1867. After repeated appeals from Tupper, Doyle finally consented to accept an appointment as lieutenant governor of Nova Scotia.

Doyle lamented that he was facing "odds that would beat the Angel Gabriel if sent here to govern." On the one side he faced the recently elected assembly committed to the repeal of the British North America Act, and on the other the federal government which was urging strong action against the unruly repealers. His main problem was to prevent an open split between the two levels of government. For this reason, even before entering the province, Doyle turned to his old friend Joseph Howe, now a member of parliament and the principal leader of the anti-confederate movement, and urged him not to "kick us when we are down." Doyle offered Howe his services as a "contact-man" with Macdonald's federal government and Howe assured Doyle that "you may not only rely on my personal aid but on every friend I have to smooth your path and make your administration successful."

The most pressing problem facing Doyle after his swearing in on 28 October was the formation of a new provincial ministry. Early in November he accepted the resignation of the pro-confederate government of Hiram Blanchard* which had been in office since the previous July. This move did not please Sir John A. Macdonald who wanted the confederates to stay in office until they were defeated in the assembly. Acting on the advice of Howe, Doyle summoned Richard A. McHeffey to form a ministry from among the anti-confederate majority. Immediate and widespread opposition was soon voiced by William ANNAND and Martin Isaac WILKINS, both anti-confederate leaders with considerable cabinet experience in previous Liberal and Conservative governments. Annand, who had no seat in the assembly but was soon appointed to the Legislative Council, was then selected premier by the anti-confederate caucus, and McHeffey was forced to become minister without portfolio. The incident illustrated not only that Doyle had a much better working relationship with Howe than with the provincial anti-confederates, but also that a serious rift was developing between Howe and the more radical Nova Scotia repealers.

In the interval between Doyle's appointment and the first meeting of the legislature on 30 Jan. 1868, the relationship between him and his ministry began to take form. Conflict first arose over the appointment of legislative councillors. Before leaving the province Sir William Fenwick WILLIAMS, Doyle's predecessor, had appointed six councillors who supported confederation. The anti-confederate ministry now tried to have these appointments revoked, but Doyle held firm, claiming the appointments were legal and he had no right to overturn them. Politically, he realized that it would be hard enough to control the "Antis" without losing his majority support in the Legislative Council. The ministry quickly realized that Doyle could not be easily manipulated.

Confrontation also appeared likely over the contents of the throne speech. What could Doyle say about confederation that would not alienate his government, yet would reiterate his own support for the new union? He informed Macdonald that "nothing will make me advocate repeal in my speech from the Throne, as I cannot afford to sacrifice either my honour or consistency, so that a crisis is likely to arrive here. . . . I think the general opinion is that they will give way upon this point, *I* most certainly *will not.*" A solution to Doyle's dilemma came from a familiar source, Howe, who assured him that "I have talked with most of [the anti-confederate assemblymen] and am assured that there is no disposition to press you unfairly." He even suggested the actual wording of Doyle's speech. One crucial phrase submitted by Howe read: ". . . and I beg to assure you of my cordial co-operation within the limits of law and the constitution in the maturing of such measures as may appear to you calculated to promote the general welfare." The avenue for compromise had been opened. By employing Howe's vague and temperate phraseology, a complete break was prevented between Doyle and his government. By the end of the short session which followed, the "Antis" were convinced Doyle had earned the "confidence of your Sovereign, the respect of your Council and the affection of the people of the province."

Attention next shifted to England where a repeal delegation led by Howe was presenting its case to the British authorities. Doyle journeyed to London after the close of the provincial legislature and wholeheartedly threw himself behind the confederation cause. He undoubtedly was pleased when the repeal case was formally rejected by the British parliament on 4 June 1868. However, the rejection left Howe in a difficult position. He would not encourage insurrection in Nova Scotia or its annexation to the United States, but neither could he completely abandon his former position. The solution to his dilemma seemed to lie in seeking "better terms" for Nova Scotia than it had received on entering confederation in 1867. Throughout the summer and fall of 1868 Sir John A. Macdonald and Howe negotiated "better terms." In the early stages when direct correspondence between the two men would have been indelicate, Doyle maintained personal contact with both and passed on information. Macdonald confided to Governor General Lord Monck* that while in Halifax in August to address the repeal convention he had received "most valuable assistance from General Doyle" and had consulted him "in every step we took." Doyle became the weather-vane for the federal government in the stormy atmosphere of Nova Scotia politics. Of most concern to him was the widening split between Howe and the provincial anti-confederates because the fight with the "locals" made it difficult for Howe to concentrate on the negotiations with the federal government. Nevertheless, by January 1869 the details of better terms, including increases in Nova Scotia's debt allowance and its annual subsidy from the federal government, had been worked out. Howe then entered Macdonald's cabinet.

While Doyle was playing an important role as "middle man" between Howe and Macdonald he also took dramatic action to bring his hostile local ministry under control. In a fiery speech on repeal, Attorney General Martin Isaac Wilkins insinuated that if Britain remained unsympathetic to Nova Scotia's pleas then the province might have "to appeal to another nation to come to our aid." Doyle regarded Wilkins' statement as treasonous and sought to have him censored. A confrontation quickly developed between Doyle and his ministers over the issue, but Doyle forced his council to back down. He thus clearly showed his determination to deal decisively with any disloyal actions on the part of the local administration.

With Howe's entrance into the federal cabinet Macdonald felt the "heart" had been removed from the anti-confederate movement. The task was now to convince the still obstinate "locals" that their cause was hopeless. Macdonald urged Doyle to use all his influence with them. Of utmost importance was Howe's re-election in Hants County, necessitated by his acceptance of the cabinet post. Doyle repeatedly emphasized to Macdonald that Howe's popularity in Nova Scotia was at a low ebb and that many of his former friends were deeply angered by his abandonment of the anti-confederate cause: "Their ire is now turned towards Howe, and I know they intend to use every *possible effort* to defeat his election. Tupper and Company will afford him every assistance, but you *must do the same* . . . for, if he is reelected they *must* give up the Ghosts." Nevertheless, Doyle was not worried by the "abuse which is being poured upon the devoted head of our friend Joe," because he felt Howe could handle it. Howe himself was confident of victory, the prospects of which greatly pleased Doyle: "I shall then be able to talk to my locals *pretty loud*, as the Yankees say, and force them . . . to accept the situation, or *smash* them up."

One of the first manœuvres of the confederates was to assure an election day that would allow enough time for an effective campaign. By working closely, Tupper and Doyle were successful in delaying the date of the by-election in Hants. Jeremiah Northup*, Howe's campaign manager, also asked Doyle to speak with Archbishop Thomas Louis Connolly* of Halifax and "make him put 'both spurs in' to some of his Priests in Hants." Connolly informed Doyle that he would be meeting with the clergymen in question and that "all will be right." On 20 April 1869 Howe emerged victorious by 383 votes. Doyle was only one of many to heave a sigh of relief when the results were officially confirmed.

Howe's election greatly strengthened Doyle's hand; at the opening of the new session he again forced his ministers to delete any mention of repeal from the speech from the throne, and he even added a few moderate statements of his own. The government was under tremendous pressure concerning their future policy towards confederation, but Doyle decided that rather than force the issue he would allow his ministers to withdraw gradually from the repeal policy. Macdonald supported Doyle's manœuvring: "I think you have been quite right in rejecting all idea of coercion. They will find their level fast enough without any direct agency of yours, and without your appearing to act as a despot." Doyle's wisdom was rewarded, since by the end of the session the repeal cause was practically dead.

Doyle's remaining two and a half years in Nova Scotia were anticlimactic. With the disappearance of the repeal issue, his main task had been completed. As early as June 1869 Doyle urged Macdonald to replace him. He felt that he was no longer a "political necessity," especially after the confederates made substantial gains in both the provincial election of 1871 and the federal contest of 1872. Among his "routine" final duties was to act as administrator of the Dominion of Canada in June of 1872 on the departure of Baron Lisgar [Young*].

Archbishop Connolly's assessment of Doyle seems fair: "I know of no public man in England or in this country who under every phase of difficulty between two great contending parties, could have exhibited more unbending principle, more energy, more tact, or more honorable forebearance; no one man who could have blended stern principle and sound policy so happily together." From his arrival in 1861 Doyle had been a man "on the spot," compelled to deal with the *Trent* affair, the *Chesapeake*, the Fenians, and the anti-confederate movement: "I no sooner get rid of one difficulty here than up starts another." Yet meeting these challenges provided Doyle with his political education, and forced him to develop a style and character all his own which in time became his most valuable asset. Not one of the incompetent imperial figures who had characterized the early 19th century of "Wellington's Generals," Doyle was qualified to perform both the military and the political tasks demanded of him. Had it not been for his attempt "to steer . . . by the pole-star of impartiality" and his firm, yet just, handling of a hostile provincial government, it is unlikely that Nova Scotians would have accepted the fact of confederation as soon or as gracefully as they did.

Doyle left Nova Scotia in May 1873 and spent his remaining years in England in relative peace and tranquillity. In 1869 he had been appointed KCMG and promoted lieutenant-general. From April 1874 to May 1877 he commanded the southern district at Portsmouth, England, and in the latter year was promoted general and placed on the retired list. He died suddenly of heart disease in London in 1883.

RONALD H. MCDONALD

PAC, MG 24, B29; MG 26, A, 114–15. PANS, RG 1, 105–10, 126–28, 128A; RG 2, sect. 2, 1–8. N.S., House of Assembly, *Debates and proc.*, 1861–73; *Journals and proc.*, 1861–73. R. H. Campbell, "Confederation in Nova Scotia to 1870" (MA thesis, Dalhousie Univ., Halifax, 1939). R. G. Dickey, "Party government in Nova Scotia, 1867–1878" (MA thesis, Dalhousie Univ., 1941). D. A. Muise, "Elections and constituencies: federal politics in Nova Scotia, 1867–1878" (PHD thesis, Univ. of Western Ontario, London, 1971). K. G. Pryke, "Nova Scotia and confederation, 1864–1870" (PHD thesis, Duke Univ., Durham, N.C., 1962).

DRUMMOND, LEWIS THOMAS, lawyer, politician, and judge; b. 28 May 1813 at Coleraine (Northern Ireland), son of Lewis Drummond; d. 24 Nov. 1882 in Montreal, Que.

Lewis Thomas Drummond, the son of a prominent Irish attorney, immigrated to Lower Canada with his widowed mother in 1825 and was educated at the Séminaire de Nicolet. He then studied law in the Montreal office of the prominent Tory attorney, Charles Dewey DAY, and in 1836 was admitted to the bar of Lower Canada. Drummond established his own practice in Montreal where he quickly gained renown with his able defence of the Lower Canadian rebels in 1838. His oratorical abilities in both English and French (Joseph-Édouard CAUCHON was to say that he combined the Irish richness of imagination with the cold reason of the German) led him to politics as early as 1840, when he became a supporter of the Reformers under Louis-Hippolyte La Fontaine*. In September 1842 Governor Sir Charles Bagot* chose La Fontaine to lead the government of the united province, and the latter entrusted the dispensation of patronage in Montreal to his lieutenant, Drummond. In the municipal elections of December 1842 held to replace the city council appointed by Lord Sydenham [Thomson*], the La Fontaine party emerged with a majority of two members, though Drummond was personally defeated.

The political strategy of La Fontaine, who united his forces with the Upper Canadian Reformers led by Robert Baldwin* in the pursuit of responsible government, met with difficulty after Bagot was replaced in March 1843 by Sir Charles Theophilus Metcalfe*. In November of that year La Fontaine and the members of the cabinet, with the exception of Dominick Daly*, resigned *en bloc* after serious disagreements with Metcalfe, and Montreal became a testing ground for Lower Canada's adherence to the political struggle for responsible government. A faction led by Denis-Benjamin Viger* and Denis-Benjamin Papineau* supported Metcalfe because they felt that French Canadian interests would be better served not by an alliance with Upper Canadian Reformers but by trusting in a benevolent and open-minded governor to make decisions based on a clear distinction between the wishes of the parliamentary majorities from Canada East and Canada West.

Both sides regarded the Montreal by-election of April 1844 as a prelude to the general election expected later that year. Drummond became the La Fontaine candidate, while Viger's followers allied themselves with the Tory candidate, William Molson*, thus seriously compromising their "autonomiste" and nationalist appeal. In the violent election which ensued, Drummond and his organizer, Francis HINCKS, united two groups of arch-rivals, the French Canadian and the Irish workers on the Lachine Canal and on the docks, and used the latter to rule the polling stations physically; Drummond was declared the winner by a large majority.

La Fontaine's party won an easy victory in the 1844 general elections, but Drummond ironically lost his seat in Montreal, in part because the fickle Irish canal workers had sold their services to the Tory side. Cauchon found him an uncontested seat in Portneuf, near Quebec City, and Drummond continued to campaign among the Montreal Irish in the interests of his party. In the assembly Drummond, who had been appointed to a commission inquiring into riots among workers on the Lachine Canal, championed the cause of Irish labourers whose oppression by employers, he said, goaded them into violence. Nevertheless he supported the mobilization of a mounted police force to keep the peace at public works projects and argued that since canal workers had no property to protect they should be deprived of arms. When he demanded compensation for pardoned Lower Canadian rebels of 1837–38 who had suffered loss of property, he argued that they had been ignorant of the implications of their actions, in an admittedly unjustified armed uprising. His cultural and religious identification with these groups (no doubt strengthened by political opportunism) was clearly not accompanied by any radical tendencies on his own part. In fact Drummond allied himself with the conservative French Canadian élite in 1842 by marrying at Saint-Marc Josephte-Elmire, the eldest daughter and heiress of Pierre-Dominique Debartzch*, a seigneur and former legislative and executive councillor,

Drummond also became a favourite of the Roman Catholic hierarchy. To help counterbalance the influence of his opponent Viger at the bishop's palace, in 1846 he defended the church's claim to the Jesuits' estates and in 1852 was instrumental in overcoming Upper Canadian opposition to the incorporation of the Jesuits' Collège Sainte-Marie in Montreal. (Drummond's sons, Lewis and Charles, attended the college and eventually joined the Jesuit order.) At the same time Drummond was an enthusiastic advocate of commerce and industry. Already an investor in some valuable Montreal real estate, in 1842 he became one of three directors of the Montreal City and District Savings Bank, which was seen by French Canadians as a step towards their sharing in the return of prosperity. Three years later he bought shares in the Société de Navigation de la Rivière Richelieu, which grew into a major St Lawrence River shipping firm by the 1850s [*see* Jacques-Félix Sincennes*]. In 1847 he became a shareholder in the St Lawrence and Atlantic Railroad and helped found the Garden River Mining Company. During the late 1850s he was president of the Stanstead, Shefford and Chambly Railroad, and finally, in 1859, he was an incorporator of the Transmundane Telegraph Company. Though Drummond did occasionally find himself in straitened financial circumstances, he was at least a junior member of Montreal's business élite.

To a certain degree, Drummond embodied the post-rebellion alliance between those French Canadian nationalists who became the "bleus" and the English-speaking business community. But he did not fit neatly into either group, nor was he able to marshal a unified Irish following, which may explain why he never again represented a Montreal constituency after 1844. In 1848, when Baldwin and La Fontaine were returned to power, Drummond was elected in Shefford, an isolated, English-speaking, Protestant county in the Eastern Townships. Still, he continued to handle patronage in Montreal. From 7 June 1848 he was solicitor general for Canada East without a cabinet seat, and he ruthlessly used the patronage power to deprive annexationists in Montreal and the Eastern Townships of their public offices. He grew so concerned about the spread of annexationist sentiment that he advocated the dispatch of a greater number of British troops to Canada and the mobilization of a mounted police force to reinforce the local magistrates.

Drummond had not, in fact, forgotten his liberal principles for, after the annexation crisis dissolved in 1850, he played a key role in the long overdue reforms of the land-holding system in Canada East, particularly when he became attorney general for Canada East in the Hincks–Augustin-Norbert Morin* government formed in October 1851. The previous year he actually came into conflict with La Fontaine by advocating the secularization of the clergy reserves; he worked on bills to reform municipal institutions and road construction, as well as the seigneurial system. Under existing legislation, *censitaires* could voluntarily switch to freehold tenure, but they had to compensate the seigneurs for loss of their dues and services. Though himself a seigneur through his wife, Drummond proposed legislation in 1852 which would limit certain seigneurial privileges and place a ceiling on the steadily increasing *cens et rentes* (annual rent). The seigneurs would be indemnified from public funds for some of their losses. The English-speaking commercial group objected that the lower dues would not only drastically reduce the value of their seigneuries, but would perpetuate a system which interfered with commerce and industry by removing the incentive for *censitaires* to commute to freehold tenure. Drummond's bill was accepted by the assembly but rejected by the Legislative Council in May 1853. In September 1854 the Hincks–Morin government was succeeded by a new administration formed by Morin and Sir Allan Napier MacNab*, and later that year Drummond, who retained the post of attorney general East, and his French Canadian colleagues were forced by pressure from Canada West to accept extensive modifications in the bill.

The new provisions literally turned Drummond's bill upside-down by abolishing seigneurial tenure, while doing little to improve the financial situation of the habitants. Rather than being lowered as initially proposed, the current *cens et rentes* and casual dues (whose value on each seigneury was to be fixed by a commission) became the basis for the price which a former *censitaire* would have to pay to the seigneur in order to gain full ownership of his farm. Because the vast majority could not afford such a price, they paid in its stead an annual constituted rent (the annual interest charge against the value of their property), thereby remaining in basically the same subservient position as before. The true beneficiaries were the commercial and industrial entrepreneurs of Canada East: as former seigneurs, under the 1854 law their annual rents would not diminish and a government indemnity fund would compensate them for loss of the *lods et ventes* (the charge of one-twelfth the selling price exacted to the benefit of the seigneur when a *censitaire*'s farm changed hands); as capitalists, it was now easier for them to speculate in land, to control timber reserves, and to build mills at water sites within the old seigneuries.

Drummond's inability to have the seigneurial system reformed as he would have liked had inevitable political consequences. In failing to aid the *censitaires* he could no longer appear as a "friend of the people," nor, on the other hand, could he take credit for the legislation among the English-speaking business interests who ultimately benefited from it. The Anglo-Protestant community had been further alienated in 1853 when neither Montreal municipal authorities nor Drummond's office of the attorney general succeeded in controlling Catholic rioters who were protesting the presence of the crusading apostate, Alessandro Gavazzi. Not surprisingly, therefore, John A. Macdonald* had little difficulty in blocking Drummond's attempt to become co-premier with him in May 1856, and formed instead a ministry with Étienne-Paschal Taché*. When Drummond carried through his threat to resign as attorney general, Macdonald and Taché simply replaced him with George-Étienne Cartier* in the new government. Drummond's disaffection with the "bleu" party grew until 1858, when he switched sides to become attorney general for Canada East in the short-lived ministry of George Brown* and Antoine-Aimé Dorion*. By this time, local grievances in his riding of Shefford, such as his failure to win a judicial district for the area, had culminated in a vocal demand for representation by a Townships resident. Drummond was defeated in Shefford by Asa Belknap Foster* in August 1858 and forced to take a seat in Lotbinière.

During Drummond's later years in opposition to the Macdonald–Cartier government, his strong identification with Canada East occasionally brought him into conflict with George Brown, the powerful leader of the Reformers. In 1859, for example, Drummond was spokesman for 12 Lower Canadian Reformers who expressed resentment at Brown's vociferous attack on Cartier's bill to apply additional common revenues for the compensation of seigneurs. In spite of growing coldness between the two wings of the Reform party, however, Drummond was never willing to support a return to separate status for the two sections of the province. Instead he became a champion of their federation.

In 1862 Drummond was able to support a ministry more in tune with his middle-of-the-road political philosophy, that of John Sandfield Macdonald* and Louis-Victor SICOTTE. However, in May 1863 he was asked to join A.-A. Dorion and his Rouge supporters in replacing Sicotte and his moderate followers in the cabinet; he thus took over from Thomas D'Arcy McGee*, the previous Irish representative. Unfortunately for Drummond he had to resign his public works portfolio when he failed to win in two by-elections in Rouville, which he had represented since 1861. This loss effectively ended his political career. In March 1864 the Macdonald–Dorion government appointed Drummond to a long-coveted position as a puisne judge of the Court of Queen's Bench. After a notable judicial career, Drummond was forced to retire in 1873 because of ill health. He subsequently was active in the St Vincent de Paul Society until his death from chronic bronchitis in 1882.

J. I. LITTLE

BNQ, MSS-101, Coll. La Fontaine (copies at PAC). DCB, Fichier André Garon. McGill Univ. Libraries (Montreal), Dept. of Rare Books and Special Coll., "Legislative bills and newspaper discussions concerning seigniorial tenures act, 1851–54." MTL, Robert Baldwin papers. PAC, MG 24, B40.

Can., Prov. of, Legislative Assembly, *Journals*, 1854–55; *Statutes*, 1854–55, c.3. *Debates of the Legislative Assembly of United Canada* (Gibbs *et al.*), I–VIII. *Documents relating to the seigniorial tenure in Canada, 1598–1854*, ed. W. B. Munro (Toronto, 1908). Christopher Dunkin, *Address at the bar of the Legislative Assembly of Canada, delivered on the 11th and 14th March, 1853, on behalf of certain proprietors of seigniories in Lower Canada* . . . (Quebec, 1853). [Francis Hincks], *The seigniorial question: its present position* (Quebec, 1854). *Commercial Advertiser* (Montreal), 1853. *Le Courrier de Saint-Hyacinthe*, 1854. *L'Ère nouvelle* (Trois-Rivières), 1853. *La Minerve*, 1854. *Montreal Gazette*, 1851, 1853–54. *Montreal Herald and Daily Commercial Gazette*, 1853, 1882. *Morning Chronicle* (Quebec), 1853. *Toronto Patriot*, 1851.

Borthwick, *Hist. and biog. gazetteer.* J. Desjardins, *Guide parl.* J. P. Noyes, *Sketches of some early Shefford pioneers* ([Montreal], 1905). P.-G. Roy, *Les juges de la prov. de Québec.* R. B. Burns, "D'Arcy McGee and the new nationality" (MA thesis, Carleton Univ., Ottawa, 1966). Careless, *Brown; Union of the Canadas.* Dent, *Last forty years.* R. C. Harris and John Warkentin, *Canada before confederation; a study in historical geography* (Toronto, 1974). D. A. Heneker, *The seigniorial regime in Canada* (Quebec, 1927). Monet, *Last cannon shot.* W. L. Morton, *The critical years: the union of British North America, 1857–1873* (Toronto, 1964). O. D. Skelton, *The life and times of Sir Alexander Tilloch Galt* (Toronto, 1920). T. P. Slattery, *Loyola and Montreal* (Montreal, 1962). G. J. J. Tulchinsky, *The river barons: Montreal businessmen and the growth of industry and transportation, 1837–53* (Toronto and Buffalo, N. Y., 1977). G.-É. Baillargeon, "À propos de l'abolition du régime seigneurial," *RHAF*, 22 (1968–69): 365–91; "La tenure seigneuriale a-t-elle été abolie par suite des plaintes des censitaires?" *RHAF*, 21 (1967–68): 64–80. J.-C. Bonenfant, "La féodalité a définitivement vécu," *Rev. de l'univ. d'Ottawa*, 47 (1977): 14–26. Jacques Monet, "*La Crise Metcalfe* and the Montreal election, 1843–1844," *CHR*, 44 (1963): 1–19.

DUCHESNAY, HENRI-JULES JUCHEREAU. *See* JUCHEREAU

DUDER, EDWIN, merchant and shipowner; b. c. 1822 at St Mary Church, Devon, England, youngest of the nine children of Thomas Duder and Ann Congdon; m. first Mary Elizabeth Edgar, and they had one son, Edwin John; m. secondly Ann Blackler, and they had two daughters and one son, Arthur; d. 20 Feb. 1881 at St John's, Nfld.

Edwin Duder's family immigrated to Newfoundland in 1833 and, through enterprise and marriage, established itself in the commercial, social, and political life of the colony for the remainder of the century. The family's arrival in St John's coincided with the rapid decline in the outports of many of the old English-based mercantile establishments such as the Slade family firm, and their replacement by St John's–based entrepreneurs, well placed to seize emerging opportunities. The career of Edwin Duder is a signal illustration of the process.

At St John's, Edwin Duder established an import-export business which had, by the mid 1850s, spread along the northeast coast of the island to settlements such as Greenspond, Joe Batt's Arm, Herring Neck, Change Island, Barred Islands, and Twillingate, centres of the inshore and Labrador fisheries and sealing. At these and other settlements, Duder owned extensive premises, supplied the fishermen in exchange for their catch, and owned and managed about 4,500 tons of shipping for the period from 1840 to 1889, being second only to Punton and Munn [*see* John Munn*] of Harbour Grace.

Throughout the same period, Duder's fleet (excluding boats and skiffs) consisted of a maximum of 100 sailing ships in any one year. They were, for the most part, Newfoundland-built schooners engaged in the fisheries and coastal trade. He also owned a small number of foreign-going brigs and brigantines, not more than half a dozen vessels, possibly supplemented by chartered bottoms; with these he engaged in the export of salt fish to the West Indies, Brazil, Great Britain, and continental Europe. Although he seems not to have prosecuted the seal-fishery on a large scale, Duder was advantageously placed to reap the harvest of the inshore hunt through his dense network of northeast coast establishments. In the spring of 1862 he and his associate James Landers Muir received a windfall of £25,000 from the catch by landsmen.

Muir was in partnership with Duder from about 1858 to 1865. In 1871 Edwin Duder Jr entered his father's firm and its name was subsequently amended to Edwin Duder and Sons. Edwin Sr died in 1881. "Not slothful in Business, Fervent in Spirit – serving the Lord," reads the inscription on the memorial plaque to him in St Peter's Anglican Church at Twillingate; and it describes him as "a merchant of this place." He was a merchant of many places in Newfoundland, but above all a merchant of St John's.

The end of Duder's business empire came not long after his death, and it was the subject of a thoughtful analysis by the prime minister of Newfoundland, William Vallance Whiteway*, in the House of Assembly on 11 May 1897. Speaking to the general economic problems of the decade, he used two once-great firms, those of Duder and Munn, to illustrate the shattering impact of the failure of the Commercial Bank in 1894. The common pattern he sketched in his speech was the division of an estate on the death of the principal, which left the business without adequate capital. Edwin Duder had made several large bequests to family, church, and charitable organizations; the business was divided between his two sons. Arthur died within a year of Edwin Sr, and Edwin John, the surviving partner, was obliged to pay half the value of the family firm in cash to his brother's widow. The great Duder enterprise continued during the recession of the 1880s, but it did so without adequate capital. When the Commercial Bank crashed, Edwin John, who had begun business in 1882 with a capital stock of $128,000, owed it $668,600 on current account alone. On 24 May 1895 the Duder northeast coast premises, upon which the meteoric rise of the enterprise had been based, were sold by the creditors.

G. M. Story

A Duder genealogical tree is in the possession of Janet Story (St John's).

Maritime Hist. Group Arch., Board of Trade, ser. 107–8; Duder name file. PANL, Duder coll. *Evening Telegram* (St John's), 21, 22 Feb. 1881; 2 May, 1, 2 June 1897. *Newfoundlander*, 28 March 1879. *Royal Gazette* (St John's), 31 Aug. 1835; 17 Aug. 1852; 22 Feb., 27 Dec. 1881. *Twillingate Sun* (Twillingate, Nfld.), 17 March 1881. *Business and general directory of Nfld.*, 1877: 9. *Family names of the island of Newfoundland*, comp E. R. Seary and S. M. P. Lynch (St John's, 1976). H. Y. Mott, *Newfoundland men, a collection of biographical sketches* (Concord, N.H., 1894). *Notable events in the history of Newfoundland; six thousand dates of historical and social happenings*, comp. P. K. Devine and J. O'Mara (St John's, 1900), 39, 156. *A "who was who" of families engaged in the fishery and settlement of Newfoundland, 1660–1840*, comp. Keith Matthews (St John's, 1971). *Book of Nfld.* (Smallwood), V: 561. [E. M. Manuel], *St. Peter's Anglican Church, Twillingate, one hundred and twenty-five year history, 1845–1970 . . .* (n.p., 1970?), 12–13, 36. Prowse, *Hist. of Nfld.* (1895), 491–92. G. M. Story, *George Street Church, 1873–1973* (St John's, 1973).

DUNCAN, JAMES D., painter, lithographer, and teacher of drawing; b. in 1806 in Coleraine (Northern Ireland); m. in 1834 Caroline Benedict Power of Sorel, Lower Canada, and they had three sons and two daughters; d. 28 Sept. 1881 in Montreal, Que.

James D. Duncan spent the first 19 years of his life in Ireland. In 1825, after having received some artistic training, he immigrated to Lower Canada, and by

1830 was established in Montreal as a professional artist and teacher of drawing. During the rebellion of 1837 Duncan held a commission as lieutenant in a light infantry regiment.

Numerous views in oil, gouache, and water-colour of Montreal life and scenery, presenting landscape and enlivened with the anecdote of genre painting, established Duncan as a recorder *par excellence* of that city over several decades. He also painted a few Quebec landscapes and in 1848 travelled to Niagara and London, Canada West, in search of new subject-matter. That Duncan's early water-colours were influenced by the British tradition in water-colours is demonstrated in a series of views of Montreal commissioned by Jacques Viger* in 1831, which range from a purely topographical approach as in "Ruins of Fort Senneville" to a more picturesque rendition in his view of "St. Genevieve."

Duncan met the Victorian demand for picturesque topographical views of known scenes, and this pictorial convention established early in his career remained constant throughout his life. "View of Montreal from St. Helen's Island" (1852) is typical of his work: in the foreground is the island from which the viewer sees the city, with trees as a frame and with an element of genre anecdote. The depiction of the city, in the middle ground, is by detailed rendering of its buildings. In the background, the undulating profile of Mount Royal gives a pleasingly picturesque horizon line.

Numerous studies of genre subjects were part of Duncan's pictorial method. His earliest sketch-book for 1840 to 1845 has scenes of Montreal streets and its markets, hunters, and Indians. Such sketches are the source for the genre anecdotes Duncan always included in his more finished water-colours. He was one of the pioneers among English-speaking Canadian artists in his use of genre, and as such has an artistic link with Cornelius Krieghoff* whose influence upon him is highly probable but still to be worked out in detail.

After the early 1850s Duncan's water-colour views began to demonstrate a growing interest in autumn colouring. Although the subject-matter in such works as "Montreal from the mountain" (1858) is still the detailed depiction of a panoramic Montreal, much of the artist's attention is concentrated on the autumn landscape in the foreground, with subtle handling of the foliage in pure yellows, roses, salmon tans, and greens placed side by side. This ordered, naturalistic rendering of landscape, combined with clear, consistent colouring, is characteristic of Duncan's water-colours during the latter part of his career.

Duncan used many of his water-colours of Montreal life and city views as illustrations in such magazines as the *Canadian Illustrated News* (Montreal) and the *Illustrated London News*. He also produced the drawings for Newton Bosworth's *Hochelaga depicta*, a Montreal guide book published in 1839 and 1846; these illustrations, in which architectural detail is reproduced with great exactness, are significant because they are among the few remaining original sources of Montreal architecture of the time.

In contrast to Duncan's prolific output of water-colour landscapes, only four major landscapes in oil by him are known. The earliest, a "View of Montreal" (*c.* 1826), shows the influence of classical idealism in the dramatic lighting and careful ordering of the Montreal scenery. This style gives way to a picturesque topographical approach in "Montreal from the mountain" and "Montreal from St. Helen's Island" (1838), where Duncan pictured the most prosperous aspects of the city with great architectural detail. The fourth, a large "View of Montreal from the mountain" (*c.* 1843), was possibly a trial painting for a projected series of panoramas.

As a portrait painter Duncan was most active prior to the late 1850s. His portraits included oils, miniatures in water-colour and pastel, and silhouettes, and he also took photographs. Their style is uneven and inconsistent, and the few attributions of portraits to him may result from a failure to recognize his erratic mannerisms. The best examples are the series of historical Canadian portraits commissioned by Jacques Viger between 1839 and 1845.

Duncan also painted a number of works based on historical themes. In 1845 Viger commissioned him to illustrate sections of his "Ma Saberdache" in which the artist portrays the "First encounter with the Illinois," "Montreal in 1693," and similar subjects. In addition, Duncan provided the water-colour illustrations for Viger's "Costumes des communautés religieuses de femmes en Canada . . ." presented by Viger to Mgr Cajetan Bedini in memory of the latter's visit to Montreal in 1853. Duncan's other historical works such as "Burning of Hayes House, Montreal" (1852) and "Gavazzi riot" (1853) depict contemporary events.

Duncan was one of Canada's first lithographic draughtsmen; he again looked to both Montreal and Quebec for his subject-matter. In 1847 he published a *Panoramic view of Montreal*, which was engraved by W. S. Barnard. A set of six views of Montreal was drawn on stone by Duncan and published in 1849 in Montreal. In these works Duncan reveals the same pictorial organization and concerns as in his water-colour views.

Throughout his career Duncan was a part-time teacher of drawing at various Montreal institutions such as the high school of the McGill Normal School and the High School of Montreal. In 1845 he collaborated with M. G. H. Gordon in establishing drawing classes at Place d'Armes, Montreal. Duncan had the reputation of being an accomplished and conscientious teacher, who tried to provide his students with a basic knowledge of drawing and water-colour techniques and to introduce them to the major aesthetic trends current in Europe.

In later life Duncan achieved financial as well as artistic success. In 1864 he became involved in a profitable commercial enterprise, Duncan and Company, "lithographic printers and engravers and draughtsmen." He displayed his work at the Great Exhibition in London, England, in 1851, the provincial exhibitions at Montreal 1863–65, the Art Association of Montreal 1865–79, the Society of Canadian Artists 1867–71, and with the Royal Canadian Academy in 1881. In 1879 he travelled to England and Scotland, evidently to purchase works of art for himself and for such collectors in Montreal as George Alexander Drummond*. Late in 1880 he returned to Montreal where he died the following year.

Recognized as an artist of distinction, in 1847 Duncan had been a founding member, along with Krieghoff, and treasurer of the Montreal Society of Artists, and he was elected a member of the Society of Canadian Artists at Montreal in 1867 and an associate of the Royal Canadian Academy in 1880. In the works he produced for sale Duncan catered to the artistic demands of the rapidly growing middle class. In his career and his works he is the epitome of the successful mid-19th-century Canadian artist.

PATRICIA A. TODD

Over 40 works by Duncan are at McCord Museum, Montreal.

ASQ, Fonds Viger-Verreau, Sér.O, 095–0125. Bibliothèque de la ville de Montréal, Salle Gagnon, Fonds Jacques Viger, "Costumes des communautés religieuses de femmes en Canada . . . en 1853." McGill Univ. Arch., McGill High School arch.; McGill Normal School arch. Royal Ontario Museum (Toronto), Canadiana Dept., Sigmund Samuel coll., James Duncan, Sketchbook. George Alexander Drummond letters in the possession of G. M. Drummond (Montreal) were also consulted.

Canadian Illustrated News (Montreal), 5 July 1873. *Illustrated London News*, 7 Aug. 1852; 19 March, 16 April 1859. *La Minerve*, 16 oct. 1845, 4 juill. 1854. *Montreal Gazette*, 1 Nov. 1856. Mary Allodi, *Canadian watercolours and drawings in the Royal Ontario Museum* (2v., Toronto, 1974), I: 691–726. C. P. de Volpi and P. S. Winkworth, *Montréal: a pictorial record . . . 1535–1885* (2v., Montreal, 1963), I: 85, 89–94. J. R. Harper, *Everyman's Canada; paintings and drawings from the McCord Museum of McGill University* (Ottawa, 1962), 43–44; *Painting in Canada*, 124, 189. Gérard Morisset, *La peinture traditionnelle au Canada français* (Ottawa, 1960), 148–50. P. St. G. Splendlove, *The face of early Canada: pictures of Canada which have helped to make history* (Toronto, 1958), 65–66. Jules Bazin, "L'album de consolation de Jacques Viger," *Vie des arts* (Montréal), 17 (1959): 26–30. É.-Z. Massicotte, "L'illustrateur du vieux Montréal," *BRH*, 46 (1940): 139–41.

DUNKIN, CHRISTOPHER, lawyer, politician, and judge; b. 25 Sept. 1812 at Walworth (now part of London), England, son of the Honourable Summerhays Dunkin and Martha Hemming; d. 6 Jan. 1881 at Knowlton, Que.

Christopher Dunkin came from a well-to-do English family and hence was given a good education. He studied at the universities of London and then Glasgow from 1829 to 1831. Following his mother's marriage to Jonathan Barber, a doctor and professor of literature who lived in Massachusetts, Dunkin came to the United States. He studied at Harvard University until 1833, when he was appointed a Greek and Latin tutor there. Throughout his university education the courses he took in Latin, Greek, mathematics, and logic had developed his two greatest assets: his exceptional intelligence and his ability to reason. He resigned his tutorial post in 1835 and married Mary, one of the daughters of Jonathan Barber. The latter's professorial activities were increasingly being divided between Massachusetts and Lower Canada, and this probably provided an incentive for Dunkin to move to the Canadian metropolis, Montreal, in 1837. Dunkin's ambition and Tory sentiments presumably played a part in his decision to emigrate to the city in a period when patriotic fervour was at a peak. He served as a correspondent for the *Morning Courier* from May 1837 to June 1838, and then turned to public administration. He held the post of secretary first to the education commission, which was set up in 1838 [*see* Sir Arthur William Buller*], and then to the postal service commission [*see* Thomas Allen Stayner*], before becoming deputy provincial secretary for Canada East, an office he retained from 1 Jan. 1842 until 19 May 1847. He had no difficulty in serving under the governments of William Henry Draper* and of Robert Baldwin* and Louis-Hippolyte La Fontaine*. Meanwhile he studied law with Alexander Buchanan* and then Francis Godschall Johnson*, receiving his commission as a lawyer in 1846.

In partnership with William Collis Meredith and Strachan Bethune*, Dunkin went into practice in Montreal. He then pursued his career in the Eastern Townships, a region that offered promising financial prospects because of its rapid economic growth and scarcity of talented lawyers. When St Francis College was founded at Richmond in 1854, Dunkin was appointed its legal counsel to negotiate an affiliation with McGill College of Montreal. In this capacity he sat on the councils of these institutions, and in 1859 he also sat on the Council of Public Instruction.

Dunkin also gained renown as a result of his brilliant *Address at the bar of the Legislative Assembly of Canada . . .* , published at Quebec in 1853, and his defence of 35 seigneurs before the special tribunal set up in 1855 to adjudge the claims made following the passage of the 1854 act dealing with the seigneurial system [*see* Lewis Thomas DRUMMOND]. Using well-researched documentation he put forward a solid, logical argument, demonstrating by extensive historical analysis that the seigneurs exercised an absolute right of property over their domains, for which they could legitimately claim compensation equal to the market value. His successful defence in this difficult case quickly brought him into the front ranks of the legal profession, and the substantial fees he received from it enabled him to finance future ventures.

Following the example of many lawyers who had attained professional success, Dunkin had gone into politics. He failed in his first try in 1844, in Drummond, but was elected as a Conservative in Drummond and Arthabaska in 1857, defeating Jean-Baptiste-Éric Dorion*. He held this seat until 1861, then served as the member for Brome from 1862 to 1867, and represented the riding both provincially and federally from 1867 until 1871. His success in elections was probably due more to his organizational skill and tactical sense than to personal warmth or imagination. He apparently acquired a reputation for coldness, conceit, and inflexibility. It was he who sponsored the temperance bill of 1864, which became known as the Dunkin Act. It is not possible to ascertain whether Dunkin introduced this coercive measure out of moral conviction or mere political opportunism, since there were innumerable petitions demanding the strict control of liquor in this period, indeed as many as there would later be in opposition to confederation. No doubt ambitious to serve as a minister in a new government, Dunkin was the only English-speaking Conservative in Canada East to vote against the government of Sir Étienne-Paschal Taché* and John A. Macdonald* on 14 June 1864; the loss of his vote denied the ministry a majority, thus bringing about its fall and precipitating the crisis that was to lead to confederation.

Dunkin attracted attention during the parliamentary debates on confederation in 1865 by delivering a speech against it which many regarded as the best given – it was certainly the longest and best researched. He expressed doubts concerning the functioning of the proposed system, calling it a bad mixture of the British and American constitutions; his principal opposition was to the inadequate guarantees of fair representation for the provinces in the Canadian Senate, and to the establishment of the party system. Dunkin, although he represented Brome County, made little reference to the fears of the Protestant minority in Canada East concerning education on the eve of confederation, and he said nothing when Hector-Louis Langevin*'s bill on education was withdrawn in 1866. Had it been passed, this bill would have given the Protestants of Canada East the right to run their own schools independently.

In 1867 Joseph-Édouard CAUCHON, who had been called to form the first Quebec provincial government, offered Dunkin a cabinet post. Wishing to regain credibility with his English-speaking constituents, and drawing on the advice of the federal member for Sherbrooke, Alexander Tilloch Galt*, Dunkin agreed to accept this offer, provided Langevin's education bill would be taken up again in the provincial house. Cauchon, who had previously opposed the bill, could not accept this condition; thus Dunkin turned down the portfolio. Realizing that he could not secure the support of the English-speaking members, Cauchon had no alternative but to withdraw.

Following Cauchon's failure to create a cabinet, the first government of the province of Quebec was formed by Pierre-Joseph-Olivier CHAUVEAU, who had worked with Dunkin on the Council of Public Instruction. The two men knew each other well and because Chauveau was reputed to be more willing to listen to the difficulties of English-speaking Quebeckers, negotiations between the two were easier. Dunkin was slated to be provincial secretary, but after various ministerial deals he replaced Gédéon Ouimet* as provincial treasurer. As preparation for this office he had only his capacity for work and his sense of detail. His appointment inaugurated a political tradition in Quebec that lasted for more than a century: the office of provincial treasurer went to an English-speaking member.

Dunkin now tackled a triple task – to create his department, prepare the province's first budget, and negotiate a sharing of the debt of the former Province of Canada with Ontario. He performed the first task well, bringing the management of income and expenditures under a single department and thus getting rid of the duplication existing under the union. On the other hand he failed to find a quick solution to the problem of debt-sharing [*see* Pierre-Joseph-Olivier Chauveau], and his budgetary plans were jeopardized as a result. At the same time he lost the confidence of the business community, which criticized him for his inexperience in financial administration. Furthermore he never managed to reconcile his roles as the representative of Protestant interests in the government and as the man chiefly responsible for the financial stability of the province. Protestants expected that he would act as a protector and even press his French-speaking colleagues for legislation to guarantee them a privileged position in the field of education. He failed to satisfy Anglophone public opinion, and he was even accused of collaboration with and subservience to the French-speaking majority. The Montreal *Gazette* and the *Evening Star* condemned him roundly.

As a minister, however, Dunkin had a Quebecker's view of politics and the new constitution. In his first budget speech in 1868 he defended the doctrine of the equality of provincial and federal powers and the necessity of involving the provincial government in fostering the economic development of Quebec. He backed down on the question of autonomy when he presented his budget in 1869, being obliged at that time to recognize the financial dependency of the provinces on the federal government, which absorbed almost all public revenue. But his attitude none the less led the Quebec City newspaper *L'Événement* to regard him as a faithful representative of Quebec's interests. The newspapers of the time sometimes referred to the "Chauveau–Dunkin" government as they had formerly said the "Macdonald–Cartier" government [*see* George-Étienne Cartier*], an eloquent testimony both to the part he played in this government and to his importance as a target for the opposition papers.

Finding himself impotent as provincial treasurer and having lost his credibility in Quebec business circles, Dunkin agreed to enter the federal cabinet in 1869, although still a member of the provincial assembly. Sir John A. Macdonald, who was reshaping his ministry that year, was looking for an English-speaking representative from the Eastern Townships to replace John ROSE and Galt, the latter having been kept on the sidelines since the failure of the Commercial Bank of Canada in Kingston. Apparently Macdonald's first choice was John Henry POPE, an eminent businessman who in fact was to succeed Dunkin in 1871; when Pope refused him, Macdonald undertook negotiations which finally brought Dunkin into the Department of Agriculture on 16 Nov. 1869. This appointment was not surprising since Dunkin was well versed in agriculture. He had a 316-acre property, valued at $10,000 in 1871, at Knowlton on Lac Brome, where farming was conducted as an industrial operation, organized and managed like a factory. The reports of the agricultural exhibition of Brome County mention that Dunkin often won first prize for his livestock. He seems to have been a competent minister of agriculture. On 25 Oct. 1871 he left politics for the bench, becoming a judge of the Superior Court of Quebec for the district of Bedford.

Dunkin had several reasons for resigning from his post. Because of his health he was finding it progressively harder to assume political and administrative duties. In 1869 he had announced to his constituents that he was not well enough to continue after the next elections to hold both federal and provincial seats, and at most would remain their member in Ottawa. In addition, a strong current of opposition had been surfacing in Brome; it was therefore wiser for Dunkin to withdraw from the political scene and accept judicial appointment before a general election was called.

As his past brilliance as a lawyer presaged (he had been made a QC in 1867), Dunkin proved a good judge, his decisions being generally well received. Displaying a certain conservatism in his decisions, he left no legal precedents. Until the end of his life he continued to give attention to his agricultural operation and to his interests in the South Eastern Counties Junction Railway Company. He died in January 1881 at his residence in Knowlton.

In addition to wide-ranging knowledge Dunkin seems to have possessed great intellectual capacity and might have been expected to have become a more outstanding figure in Quebec or Canadian politics. It is possible that he never realized his powers to the full. He may have suffered from a lack of imagination in the exercise of power. In any case he did not succeed in imposing his authority as forcefully as did Pope. He was never feared as was Cauchon, even though he helped to thwart him in 1867. Finally, he never managed to adopt a political stance as independent as Galt's. In spite of everything, including poor health, he did, however, make an important contribution in the field of public administration.

PIERRE CORBEIL

Christopher Dunkin was the author of *Address at the bar of the Legislative Assembly of Canada, delivered on the 11th and 14th March, 1853, on behalf of certain proprietors of seigniories in Lower Canada* . . . (Quebec, 1853); *Address . . . before the Legislative Assembly of Canada, on behalf of certain seigniors, petitioners of the honorable house against a bill introduced by the Hon. Mr. Attorney General Drummond* . . . ([Quebec?, 1853?]); *Case (in part) of the seigniors of Lower Canada, submitted to the judges of the Court of Queen's Bench and of the Superior Court for Lower Canada* . . . (Montreal, 1855); *Chronological list or index of grants in fief and royal gratifications of grants in fief, made in New France to the time of its session to the British crown in 1760* (Quebec, 1853); and . . . *Speech delivered in the Legislative Assembly . . . during the debate on the subject of the confederation of the British North American provinces* (Quebec, 1865).

Brome County Hist. Soc. Arch. (Knowlton, Que.), Christopher Dunkin papers. Can., prov. du, Parl., *Débats parl. sur la confédération. Débats de l'Assemblée législative* (M. Hamelin), [I]. *Advertiser and Eastern Townships Sentinel* (Waterloo, Que.), 1864–69. *Evening Star*, 27 Oct. 1869. *Gazette* (Montreal), October–November 1869. *Montreal Herald and Daily Commercial Gazette*, 10 Jan. 1881. *Morning Chronicle* (Quebec), 16 June 1864. *Canadian biog. dict.*, II: 64–66. Dent, *Canadian portrait gallery*, IV: 209–11. *Political appointments, 1841–65* (J.-O. Coté). P.-G. Roy, *Les juges de la prov. de Québec*, 191. Désilets, *Hector-Louis Langevin*. André Labarrère-Paulé, *Les instituteurs laïques au Canada français, 1836–1900* (Québec, 1965).

DUNN, OSCAR, journalist and public servant; b. 14 Feb. 1845 at Coteau-du-Lac, Canada East, son of William Oscar Dunn and Marie-Anne-Mathilde Beaudet; m. 5 Sept. 1876, at Montreal, Marie-Mathilde Leblanc; d. 15 April 1885 in Quebec City.

Oscar Dunn's ancestor Charles Dunn was a Protestant loyalist of Scottish origin who was prompted to leave the United States by the American revolution, and settled in the parish of Sainte-Ursule, near Rivière-du-Loup (Louiseville, Que.). William Oscar Dunn studied medicine at McGill College and practised at Coteau-du-Lac. He married in 1844, was widowed in 1851, and died in December that year in Bermuda. The guardianship of his children, Oscar and Donalda, was a contentious issue. The Dunns won a first lawsuit, but in the conflict of family influences the French-Catholic Beaudets finally prevailed. In 1855 the Court of Appeal set aside the judgement of the court of first instance.

From 1855 to 1864 Oscar Dunn studied at the Séminaire de Saint-Hyacinthe, where he made friends with the man who would later be his mentor and whom he was to call his adopted father, Abbé François Tétreau. The student was already incapacitated by the sporadic recurrence of a chronic infection which was probably tubercular. His disability made it even harder for him to choose a career and left him perplexed about his future for a long time. Coupled with the traumatic experience of being an orphan whose guardianship had been in dispute, it predisposed him to seek security and understanding.

While still at the seminary, Oscar Dunn contributed to *Le Courrier de Saint-Hyacinthe*, edited by Honoré Mercier*. His schooling finished, he began legal training under Francis Cassidy* and Charles-André Leblanc*, his future father-in-law, but quickly abandoned law for journalism. In June 1866 he was editing *Le Courrier de Saint-Hyacinthe* and remained with the paper until March 1868, when he sailed for Europe to complete his training as a journalist.

As Paris correspondent for *La Minerve* of Montreal, he sent articles recording the shifts of public opinion in France and telling readers as much about the Parisian way of life as about his own thinking. Like his predecessor Elzéar GÉRIN, he also contributed to the Liberal newspaper of Jean-Jacques Weiss, the *Journal de Paris*. The diocesan journal in Montreal, *Le Nouveau Monde*, expressed fear concerning the baneful influence of free-thinkers on the Canadian journalist. He suffered petty annoyances, such as insinuations in a series of articles that he was leading "the Parisian life," and reproaches for the bantering and somewhat derisive tone of his articles. Having had enough of "the study of free-thinking journalism," Dunn then turned to *L'Univers* (Paris) for which the ultramontane journalist Louis Veuillot invited him to write an article on Canadian literature, but the draft was abandoned half-way through. In December 1868 and the beginning of 1869 Dunn visited Rome and the Canadian Zouaves, whom he had dreamed of joining. He had an audience with Pius IX, who urged him as a journalist to be upright at all times in order to avoid error.

Refreshed by almost a year spent at the very sources of French culture and of Catholicism, Dunn returned to Canada. However, he did not receive the position that *La Minerve* had seemed willing to reserve for him and he remained only a contributor. In April 1870 he resumed the editorship of *Le Courrier*, but retired six months later because of a disagreement with Camille Lussier, the owner of that regional newspaper. The latter considered Dunn was "not religiously minded enough for *Le Courrier*," and "too readily accepted the French Republic." After Dunn had contributed sporadically over a lengthy period to the illustrated journal *L'Opinion publique* (Montreal), he seriously thought of going to France, for Quebec journalism did not offer him secure employment. However, in September 1872 he agreed to join the editorial staff of *La Minerve*. He remained a member until the autumn of 1873, and then replaced Laurent-Olivier David* at *L'Opinion publique*. In December 1874 Dunn abandoned the role of committed journalist and became co-owner of the *Revue canadienne* in Montreal, which he left a year later; shortly after, he became a civil servant.

In the period preceding his trip to Europe in 1868, Dunn had not yet departed from conventional ideas; the views he expressed were fundamentally of a didactic and apologetical character and supported the ultramontane scheme. Dunn's zeal to proselytize – which was equalled only by his patriotic concern – prompted him, among other things, to give a favourable press to the cause of the Zouaves and, almost without realizing what he was doing, to provoke a quarrel between Abbé Joseph-Sabin RAYMOND of the Séminaire de Saint-Hyacinthe, and Louis-Antoine Dessaulles*, mainly about the participation of the teachers at the seminary in political struggles and in the editing of *Le Courrier*. In politics Dunn was dedicated to the cause of the Conservative party, which he never abandoned; he supported the new confederation by expressing anti-Americanism and a confusing mixture of religion with politics. Soon after his return from Europe the type of article for which he would develop a predilection began to appear under his signature: a short, concise, lively text, always urbane, sometimes humorous, and marked by a preference for reason over wit. Dunn discussed all the major questions of the day. To mention only the best known, these included the Pacific Scandal, the North West Territories, the New Brunswick schools question, and in particular the current politico-religious disputes. Dunn held certain ideas firmly, and these were in line with the stand he took in the name of union, order, and respect. Dunn had an intuitive grasp of the precarious balance of political and social forces. Whether it was the Métis cause, aversion to legislative union or annexation, the redefinition of colonial ties, the attempted amalgamation of the Institut Canadien of Montreal and the

Institut Canadien-Français (Montreal), the political union of Catholic forces or that of political parties in Quebec – a subject about which he made one of his most significant contributions to current political thought – Dunn constantly attempted to define the roles and to ensure the survival of Catholic and French-speaking citizens. Religion and *patrie*: here was his *leitmotiv*, an inseparable pair. He was one of the first journalists to raise them to the level of values to be protected. Yet his conservatism in no way detracted from his lucidity. Before Benjamin Pâquet*, Joseph-Sabin Raymond, or Wilfrid Laurier*, he made needed distinctions in the unduly confused notion of liberalism; also he did not hesitate to call in question certain tenets which were not integral to it. He spoke readily of compulsory education and universal suffrage. In sum, Oscar Dunn's thinking during his years as a journalist was that of a conservative with a mind open enough to understand new situations and to benefit from experience.

Fascinated by politics, for him the logical outlet from journalism, Dunn twice entered the electoral fray. But he was inclined to be haughty, and failed to win the support of the voters in the constituency of Saint-Hyacinthe in 1872 or in Soulanges in 1875. The second defeat, which was appealed, was followed by another change in his career for Dunn left Montreal and went to Quebec, where as he said he found himself a "public servant and happy." He succeeded Napoléon Legendre* as editor of the official *Journal de l'Instruction publique* (Quebec), and held the post until this pedagogical journal ceased publication in 1879. He then went into the secretariat of the Department of Public Instruction, taking Louis GIARD's post in 1882. Public service by no means consigned the former political journalist to oblivion. In 1876 he published *Dix ans de journalisme* and in 1878 *Lecture pour tous*, collections of the essays and articles he considered his best, drawn principally from *La Minerve*, the *Revue canadienne*, and *L'Opinion publique.* In 1877, as a logical consequence of his enthusiasm for the teaching of drawing, he published a *Manuel de dessin industriel à l'usage des maîtres d'écoles primaires.* As opportunity arose he wrote a small number of articles for the *Journal de l'Éducation, L'Opinion publique*, and the *Nouvelles Soirées canadiennes*, all published in Montreal. Only once, in 1882, did he attend the meetings of the Royal Society of Canada, of which he was a member, and he did not contribute to its work. Throughout his life he attached considerable importance to linguistic questions. This interest led in 1880 to the *Glossaire franco-canadien*, a work which despite imperfections was the first to point out the contribution made by French dialects to the French spoken in Canada. He was unable to complete a revised edition of this study: he died suddenly on 15 April 1885, at the age of 40, at the Garrison Club in Quebec.

Beneath his aristocratic bearing, abrupt manner, ready sarcasm and irony, and dedication to serious study – for example, to bibliophily – this rather diminutive man hid a generous nature and a dry humour that delighted his friends, some of whom were the scholars of the time. His repartee and his anecdotes, deftly handled, seemed to be tossed off to see what effect they would have on his listeners.

GUY PROVOST

[Oscar Dunn was the author of *Pourquoi nous sommes Français* (Montréal, 1870); *L'Union des partis politiques dans la province de Québec* (Montréal, 1874); *Dix ans de journalisme; mélanges* (Montréal, 1876); *Manuel de dessin industriel à l'usage des maîtres d'écoles primaires* (Montréal, 1877); *Lecture pour tous* (Québec, 1878); *Glossaire franco-canadien et vocabulaire de locutions vicieuses usitées au Canada* (Québec, 1880); and *Une disparition mystérieuse* (Montréal, 1884), which he signed as Charles de Soulanges. G.P.]

ANQ-M, État civil, Catholiques, Notre-Dame de Montréal, 1er août 1859; Saint-Ignace (Coteau-du-Lac), 15 janv. 1844, 14 févr. 1845, 15 janv. 1847, 3 juill. 1851; Saint-Joseph (Soulanges), 21 avril 1823; Minutiers, Louis Adam, 20, 30 oct. 1851. ANQ-MBF, État civil, Anglicans, Saint Andrew de Rivière-du-Loup (Louiseville), 7 July 1822; Saint-Joseph (Maskinongé), 8 juill. 1786; Minutier, Eustache Sicard de Carufel, 26 mars 1852. PAC, MG 18, H6, 4: 444; MG 29, D40, 2: 1431–32, 1435; MG 30, D1, 12: 10–103. *Décisions des tribunaux du Bas-Canada* (17v., Montréal et Québec, 1851–67), V. *Catalogue d'une bibliothèque canadienne, ouvrages choisis en particulier sur l'Amérique et le Canada, 2000 volumes, collectionnés par feu M. Oscar Dunn* (Québec, 1885). *Catalogue d'une bibliothèque canadienne, ouvrages sur l'Amérique et en particulier sur le Canada collectionnés par M. Oscar Dunn* (Québec, 1880). L.-P. Bender, *Literary sheaves, ou la littérature au Canada français* (Montreal, 1881). Jean Bruchési, *Rappels* (Montréal, 1941). Guy Provost, "Oscar Dunn, sa vie, son œuvre" (thèse de D. ès L., univ. Laval, Québec, 1973). F.-J. Audet, "Oscar Dunn" and "Encore Oscar Dunn" in *BRH*, 34 (1928): 291–94 and 406 respectively. L.-P. Bender, "Quebec City thirty years ago . . . sketch of Oscar Dunn," *Quebec Daily Telegraph*, 18, 25 April, 2 May 1908. Jean Bruchési, "À propos d'Oscar Dunn" and "La famille d'Oscar Dunn" in *BRH*, 34 (1928): 344–46 and 571–74 respectively; and "Oscar Dunn et son temps," *Rev. trimestrielle canadienne* (Montréal), 14 (1928–29): 183–204. Alfred Duclos De Celles, "Oscar Dunn," RSC *Trans.*, 1st ser., 4 (1886), sect.I: 65–70.

DUNSMUIR, ROBERT, coal-miner, entrepreneur, and politician; b. 31 Aug. 1825 near Kilmarnock (Strathclyde), Scotland, the son of James Dunsmuir; m. in 1847 Joanna (Joan) Olive White, and they had ten children; d. 12 April 1889 at Victoria, B.C.

Robert Dunsmuir was the son and grandson of

Ayrshire coal-masters. He received his early education at the Kilmarnock Academy and at about age 16 entered the mines as an apprentice to his uncle and guardian, Boyd Gilmour. By 1850 Gilmour was overman at the Hudson's Bay Company coal-mine near Fort Rupert (near present-day Port Hardy) on northern Vancouver Island. On Gilmour's urging, Dunsmuir indentured himself to the company, arriving at Fort Rupert with his wife and three children in September 1851.

Dunsmuir entered a difficult situation, for despite dedicated efforts by men such as Gilmour and John Muir the mines were failing. The coal was limited in extent and quality, poor management by the HBC officers in charge had caused much unrest among the miners, machinery and skilled labour were in short supply, and hostile natives were a continual threat. During 1851–53 the HBC transferred its mining apparatus to the newly discovered coalfields at Nanaimo. The Dunsmuirs joined in the move to Nanaimo, though several miners, including Gilmour, soon returned to Scotland.

In 1855 Dunsmuir refused to join a strike of dissident miners, earning for his apparent loyalty to the HBC a free-miner's licence to work an abandoned HBC shaft. In 1862, when the HBC sold its coal mining operation to the Vancouver Coal Mining and Land Company, he contracted to work as a mines' supervisor for the new firm. Two years later, his record of independence, initiative, skill, and productivity brought him to the attention of Horace Douglas Lascelles* and three other naval officers at Esquimalt who persuaded Dunsmuir to become resident manager of their newly formed Harewood Coal Mining Company. The company encountered difficulty in starting production, chiefly because of lack of capital, and was absorbed by the VCMLC; Dunsmuir, recognized as the most knowledgeable miner on the island, was hired once again by this company as mines' supervisor.

After joining the VCMLC Dunsmuir conducted clandestine explorations for coal on surrounding lands. He continued his secret surveys until 1869 when he discovered the Wellington seam, five miles northwest of Nanaimo harbour, the thickest and most extensive of the coal measures found until then in the Nanaimo basin. After laying claim, he was able to arrange short-term financing from San Francisco but was soon forced to seek more capital. He obtained £32,000 to develop the colliery from another group of naval officers, which included Lieutenant Wadham Neston Diggle. In addition to the claim Dunsmuir's contributions to the enterprise would be his expertise and his willingness to build and operate the colliery. He insisted upon and received half the shares plus full control over all operations. In 1873 the mine was incorporated under the name Dunsmuir, Diggle Limited, a ten-man partnership that included the naval officers, Dunsmuir, and his sons James* and Alexander.

Dunsmuir's first years as a colliery owner were devoted to establishing a basic mining operation – a high risk venture given the economic recession of the time. He had to take into account the VCMLC's large plant, and to create the vital elements of several shafts for mining, a skilled work-force, and an efficient three-mile transport link from pit-head to wharves, which after 1870 meant a steam railway. Newspapers reported each step in the colliery's advance, and editorials were soon stressing the significance of Dunsmuir's efforts to the region's economy. By the end of 1874 the British Columbia minister of mines, John Ash, reported that "The Departure Bay [Dunsmuir] Mines are now in full operation," the returns from which "illustrate the value of the seams." That year Dunsmuir's coal output totalled 29,818 tons, of which only 2,384 tons were unsold. This production figure was more than half the VCMLC's output, and in the following year Dunsmuir's operation came within 10,000 tons of its chief competitor. By 1878 Dunsmuir had overtaken the other colliery's production, raising 88,361 tons of coal compared to 82,135.

Although the company had had sufficient financial backing from its partners to begin mining, it was mainly Dunsmuir who had taken the risks, and who had provided the management necessary to create, maintain, and expand the operation from a mere claim to British Columbia's foremost colliery. Until 1878 it appears that Dunsmuir ploughed most of the profits back into the firm; no additional shares were issued and there is no evidence indicating other sources of financing were necessary. His business success is even more impressive when it is realized that he kept pace with technical developments. Dunsmuir described his works in 1879 as having "4¾ miles of railway; 4 locomotives; over 400 waggons; 4 [hauling] engines and 2 steam pumps; 3 wharves for loading vessels, with bunkers, etc." In 1879 Dunsmuir, Diggle Limited purchased another colliery in the same seam, the South Wellington, to the south of Nanaimo. Together, the two operations provided underground access through one pit (160′ deep) and two main shafts (one reaching 310′). The purchase gave the firm a further "4½ miles of railway; 1 locomotive; over 50 waggons; 1 steam pump; 2 large winding engines; 1 small engine"; the combined labour force was now 418.

The purchase of the South Wellington proved both a logical and a profitable move, as the output, work-force, and plant value of Dunsmuir, Diggle, all rose sharply. In 1881 Dunsmuir claimed that his coal operations were worth $245,000. Equally significant, he was by then employing 547 men (more than half of whom were Chinese) and his annual output had reached 181,048 tons of coal, fully 84.4 per cent of which was exported. Further expansion occurred in 1882 when Dunsmuir sank two additional main shafts; eventually a total of five mines were in production on the Wellington deposit. What probably gave Dunsmuir his greatest satisfaction, however, was his step-by-step purchase of the holdings of the non-family partners. Before the 1870s had ended, he had bought all but Diggle's interests. Then on 14 Sept. 1883 Victoria's *Daily British Colonist* reported that Diggle had sold his holdings to Dunsmuir for $600,000, and that henceforth the firm would conduct business "under the name and style of R. Dunsmuir & Sons."

Dunsmuir was a shrewd and opportunistic coal proprietor. Compared with other coal entrepreneurs of the 1870s and 1880s, he was not particularly lucky or especially ruthless, but he made the most of the important advantages he had over his competitors. He had been a thoroughly knowledgeable coal-miner and a highly experienced mines' supervisor before starting his own colliery, and by being the sole claimant of the island's richest coal seam when he began his first venture as a coal-mine proprietor, Dunsmuir's potential as a producer was the greatest on the island. Furthermore, although he was a latecomer to the province's coal trade, his entry occurred at a time when speculative coal enterprises were most profitable. What distinguished him above all from other promoters, the majority of whom failed to secure sufficient start-up capital, was his astute move in turning for support to the naval officers who had both an awareness of the value of the coalfields in the region and the financial means to make substantial investments. Also important was Dunsmuir's proximity to the colliery: as his usual residence was Nanaimo, nothing to do with the operation escaped his attention and day-to-day management decisions were made with ease. Finally, he was able to recruit and train as his chief subordinates his two sons, who were also in the original partnership, and a son-in-law, John Bryden; not only did he fix the colliery's management in the family's grip, he also ensured that as the company prospered the financial position of the family was correspondingly strengthened. Thus it was that most of Dunsmuir, Diggle's power and wealth came to be concentrated in the Dunsmuir family's hands. He was dedicated to the new coal industry and determined to dominate if not monopolize it.

Within ten years of starting operations Dunsmuir had generated sufficient capital from sales to build a colliery operation that surpassed in size and output the combined value of all other British Columbia coal mines, to purchase extensive holdings of coal-bearing lands in the Comox district, and to construct and operate a fleet of colliers; he also invested heavily in real estate on Vancouver Island and in an iron foundry, a theatre in Victoria, agricultural lands, and a mainland diking scheme. Most of Dunsmuir's wealth was in the form of equity capital, but it none the less gave him all the security he needed to continue making acquisitions whenever and wherever he chose. This was, after all, a time in Canadian history when neither corporate nor income taxes existed, and what coal royalties there were had little impact on profits. Indeed, it was a period in which governments appeared more eager to give money to men like Dunsmuir than to take it from them. A case in point is his involvement in the building of a railway on Vancouver Island.

A rail link between Nanaimo and Victoria had been planned as early as 1873, but no serious effort to start construction was made until December 1883 when the province transferred to the federal government sufficient crown lands for the project. To safeguard control of the island's economic future, and prevent the possibility of the Northern Pacific Railroad gaining the contract, many businessmen and politicians urged Dunsmuir to build the line. Dunsmuir was reluctant to accept the task, thinking it of little benefit to his colliery operations. He submitted a proposal to the Canadian government, however, and despite the severity of his terms he emerged as the sole acceptable alternative to foreign builders. After much shrewd bargaining in Ottawa Dunsmuir agreed to construct the railway in return for a subsidy of $750,000 in cash and a parcel of land comprising some two million acres – fully one-fifth of Vancouver Island. Significantly, the land grant came with "all coal, coal oil, ores, stones, clay, marble, slates, mines, minerals, and substances whatsoever in, on or under the lands so to be granted." He received also all foreshore rights for the lands, all mining privileges (including the right to mine under adjacent seabeds), and the retention of all coal and other minerals taken from the land. Additionally, as contractor he was permitted to cut whatever timber and erect whatever structures he saw fit to build the line. To promote settlement, provision was made for the sale of farmlands to homesteaders at one dollar per acre. Squatters of at least one year's residence were allowed to buy up to 160 acres, and those settlers with title were allowed to retain their holdings, but virtually all else would go to the contractor in right of performance. It was, in short, a major give-away of British Columbia's natural resources.

Although Dunsmuir had been chosen to prevent the Americans from gaining control of the railway, the lands, and the area's mineral rights, he was not averse to exploiting American talent and experience in constructing the railway. The contract which Dunsmuir drew up for the Esquimalt and Nanaimo Railway named himself, his son James, and his son-in-law John Bryden as contractors, and Charles Crocker, Mark Hopkins, Leland Stanford, and Collis Potter

Huntington, all officials of the Southern Pacific Railroad, as subcontractors. Construction began at Esquimalt on 26 Feb. 1884 and proceeded on schedule. Sir John A. Macdonald*, prime minister of Canada, drove the "last spike" at Shawnigan Lake on 13 Aug. 1886, and by September trains were running into Victoria along lines laid from Esquimalt across Indian lands Dunsmuir had managed to have expropriated for his use.

Building the railway was Robert Dunsmuir's last major entrepreneurial effort. James Dunsmuir and John Bryden were now the driving forces behind further expansion of the family's business, and their time was filled with consolidating and operating the huge industrial, transportation, and commercial activities created chiefly by the elder Dunsmuir. Robert was content to leave such matters to his successors, busying himself more with his other investments, particularly those in Victoria where he then resided. He had already built a mansion in Nanaimo; he now busied himself with plans to build a sandstone castle (Craigdarrock), a task that both challenged his remaining energies and suited his image as British Columbia's leading 19th-century industrialist.

Part of Robert Dunsmuir's notoriety stemmed from his business acumen, but a greater part resulted from his approach to labour relations. He believed the mines he owned were his to do with as he chose. In his mind, he alone had been responsible for raising the capital, building the collieries, opening the markets, and maintaining the plant. He had tended always to pay lower wages than his competitors, and he had preferred to employ Orientals who were willing to work for half the pay other miners would accept. His coal operations were generally safer than those of his main competitor, the VCMLC, though like all colliery owners of the time the Dunsmuirs resisted many of the demands for safety improvements made by provincial inspectors of mines, thereby perpetuating the hazardous conditions that led to accidents, including the 1876 disaster at Wellington. In 1877 when all the island colliers were threatening to strike over wages [*see* Samuel H. MYERS], Dunsmuir was to be struck first, but before the threatened work-stoppage could spread to Nanaimo, Robert locked out his employees, claiming he alone would break the resistance. Four months were lost before the miners, harassed by both police and militia sent north from Victoria at Robert's demand, and plainly destitute, agreed to return to work. Yet Dunsmuir, clearly victorious, chose also to be vindictive, and offered the men a maximum daily wage of $2.50 – a rate one-third lower than his best-paid employees were earning before the strike. He effectively had broken the most significant attempt up to that time to organize mine workers in British Columbia, and he never faced another major rebellion by labour. For this action especially, Robert Dunsmuir gained a reputation as the province's most ruthless, avaricious employer.

Yet, to the middle and upper levels of island society, Dunsmuir symbolized wealth, success, and moral authority, a circumstance which encouraged him when he was extricating himself from direct management of the collieries to pursue new interests. He entered politics in the provincial election of 1882 as a candidate for Nanaimo. He was elected and returned again in July 1886, but, apart from becoming president of the Executive Council in the administration of Alexander Edmund Batson DAVIE in 1887, Dunsmuir left no appreciable mark as a politician.

For much of his later life, Robert was alienated from his wife, though she inherited his entire estate. The Dunsmuir children were educated and treated in a fashion befitting their father's wealth. He made the collieries a family business, drawing the menfolk in first as workers and then as managers. They, in turn, retained control until 1910, when the main Dunsmuir interests were sold to William Mackenzie* and Donald Mann*. James Dunsmuir was premier of British Columbia from 1900 to 1902 and lieutenant governor from 1906 to 1909.

Robert Dunsmuir was and has remained the most controversial person in the province's history. He has been recognized by most historians as a great builder, a pioneer industrialist intent upon shaping his province as much as increasing his personal fortune. He has, on the other hand, been more recently presented, by writers probing the province's early industrial activities, as British Columbia's chief symbol of unbridled capitalism, and a ruthless exploiter of men and material. The most recent research reveals that neither view is fully accurate, and suggests strongly that a full-scale study of his personal and business career and the social context in which he lived is needed.

DANIEL T. GALLACHER

PABC, Add. MSS 436, ser.A; Add. MSS 523; GR 86; GR 184; Albion Iron Works, Minutes of meetings of directors, 7 Nov. 1882–29 June 1904; B.C., Dept. of Lands and Works, Coal prospecting licences, Register and index, 1883–1906; Corr. with Robert Dunsmuir and W. N. Diggle re coal claims, 1869–71; Mining licences under mineral ordinance, 1869: coal lands, 1872; John Bryden, Diary and letter book, 1878–80; Colonial corr., C. S. Nicol corr.; Robert Dunsmuir, Family tree; Fort Nanaimo corr., August 1852–September 1853 (transcript); Fort Nanaimo journal, August 1855–March 1857 (transcript); G.B., Colonial Office, Despatches to Vancouver Island, 21 July 1849–16 Aug. 1858 (duplicates); Vancouver Coal Mining and Land Company, Director's diary, 1 July 1880–30 Sept. 1881; Vancouver Island, Governor (Blanshard), Despatches to London, 26 Dec. 1849–30 Aug. 1851 (copies); Governors Blanshard and Douglas, Corr. outward, 22 June 1850–5 March 1859 (copies); Vert. file, James Dunsmuir; Robert Dunsmuir; Fort Rupert; Nanaimo. PAM, HBCA, A.11/72–78.

Articles of association of the Albion Iron Works Company (Limited) . . . (Victoria, 1883). B.C., Dept. of Mines, *Annual report* (Victoria), 1874–89. Can., *Census of Canada, 1880–81* (4v., Ottawa, 1882–83). HBRS, XIX (Rich and A. M. Johnson). [John McLoughlin], *The letters of John McLoughlin from Fort Vancouver to the governor and committee, [1825–46]*, ed. E. E. Rich and intro. W. K. Lamb (3v., London, 1941–44). *Daily Colonist* (Victoria), 1858–89. *Nanaimo Free Press* (Nanaimo, B.C.), 1874–89. *Nanaimo Gazette*, 10 July 1865–July 1866. *Nanaimo Tribune*, August 1866–31 Aug. 1867. *Vancouver Daily World*, 18 April 1889. *Victoria Daily Times*, 5 Oct. 1908, 8 June 1920.

J. B. Kerr, *Biographical dictionary of well-known British Columbians, with a historical sketch* (Vancouver, 1890), 152–54. *Standard dict. of Canadian biog.* (Roberts and Tunnell), II. *The year book of British Columbia* . . ., comp. R. E. Gosnell (Victoria), 1897: 322. J. [G. P.] Audain, *From coalmine to castle: the story of the Dunsmuirs of Vancouver Island* (New York, 1955). H. H. Bancroft, *History of British Columbia, 1792–1887* (San Francisco, 1887). J. N. G. Bartlett, "The 1877 Wellington miners' strike"(BA essay, Univ. of British Columbia, Vancouver, 1975). William Bennett, *Builders of British Columbia* . . . (Vancouver, 1937). R. E. Cail, *Land, man, and the law: the disposal of crown lands in British Columbia, 1871–1913* (Vancouver, 1974), 138–41. C. H. Clapp, "Coal-fields of Vancouver Island," *The coal resources of the world: an inquiry made upon the initiative of the executive committee of the XII International Geological Congress, Canada, 1913* . . ., ed. William McInnes *et al.* (3v. and atlas, Toronto, 1913), II: 509–13. *Cumberland, British Columbia, 1871–1971* (Cumberland?, B.C., 1971?). D. T. Gallacher, "Men, money, machines: studies comparing colliery operations and factors of production in British Columbia's coal industry to 1891" (PHD thesis, Univ. of British Columbia, 1979). F. W. Howay and E. O. S. Scholefield, *British Columbia from the earliest times to the present* (4v., Vancouver, 1914), III: 666–70. P. M. Johnson, *A short history of Nanaimo* (Nanaimo, 1958), 33–48. Gustavus Myers, *History of Canadian wealth* (Chicago, 1914; repr. New York, 1968; Toronto, 1972), 301–8. P. A. Phillips, *No power greater: a century of labour in British Columbia* (Vancouver, 1967), 2–12. Martin Robin, *The rush for spoils: the company province, 1871–1933* (Toronto, 1972). R. D. Turner, *Vancouver Island railroads* (San Marino, Calif., 1973). A. F. Buckham, "The Nanaimo coal field," Canadian Institute of Mining and Metallurgy, *Trans.* (Montreal), 50 (1947): 460–72. B. A. McKelvie, "The founding of Nanaimo," *BCHQ*, 8 (1944): 169–88. J. D. MacKenzie, "The coal measures of Cumberland and vicinity, Vancouver Island," Canadian Institute of Mining and Metallurgy, *Trans.*, 25 (1922): 382–411. T. A. Rickard, "A history of coal mining in British Columbia," *Miner* (Vancouver), 15 (1942), no.6: 30–34; no.7: 28–30. R. H. Roy, "'. . . in aid of a civil power,' 1877," *Canadian Army Journal* (Ottawa), 7 (1953), no.3: 61–69. J. T. Saywell, "Labour and socialism in British Columbia: a survey of historical development before 1903," *BCHQ*, 15 (1951): 129–50.

DURIE, WILLIAM SMITH, militia officer; b. in 1813 at Gibraltar, son of William H. Durie, an army surgeon, and Helena Lee, sister of Sir Francis Lee; he and his wife Anna had one son and daughter; d. 3 June 1885 at Toronto, Ont.

William Smith Durie graduated from the Royal Military College, Sandhurst, England, in 1828. He was commissioned ensign in the 94th Foot on 20 Jan. 1832 and transferred to the 83rd Foot on 11 Aug. 1837 when it was ordered to Canada. On 18 May 1838 he obtained permission to sell his lieutenant's commission on the grounds of ill health. He received a largely honorific commission as captain in the sedentary Canadian militia on 28 Nov. 1838.

After serving in Canada, Durie's father had retired from the army and as an assistant inspector of hospitals on 14 June 1836. He obtained land grants in Upper Canada in the townships of Collingwood, Sunnidale, and Plympton in recognition of his rank and his 38 years of service. From 1838 to 1855 William Smith Durie lived in Thornhill, Toronto, and Barrie, presumably managing his own land and that of his father, but little is known of his life in these years. In 1856 he was affluent enough to own a schooner valued at £300 which he docked on Lake Simcoe.

In 1855 Durie had resumed more active military life as captain of the Barrie Rifle Company, an early unit in Canada's new volunteer militia. Inspired by the military excitement of the Crimean War and modelled on militia systems in some American states, the volunteer units were expected to fulfil a police role. In September 1856 Durie and 20 of his men rushed to Collingwood when sailors rescued a comrade from the authorities. The sailors escaped on their vessel but Durie and his men received official thanks for their efforts. Because of his seniority Durie was promoted lieutenant-colonel on 11 Dec. 1856.

That year, in preparation for the visit of the Prince of Wales, militia companies in Montreal and Toronto were formed into battalions. Durie assumed command of the Toronto corps which included companies in Barrie and Whitby as well as six in Toronto (two of which wore Highland dress). Since companies elected their own officers and purchased their own uniforms and equipment, Durie needed tact and patience as well as military experience to unify his command. The unit, created 26 April 1860, was first known as the 2nd Battalion Volunteer Militia Rifles; Durie secured the title 2nd Battalion, Queen's Own Rifles of Toronto on 18 March 1863. He drafted standing orders, badgered authorities for a drill shed, which was completed in June 1864, and struggled to standardize uniforms and arms.The result was probably the best organized militia unit in Canada.

Durie's task was made easier by the recurrent alarms of the 1860s, from the *Trent* affair to the Fenian raids. In the winter of 1864–65 he was chosen to command a battalion of embodied militia at Niagara-on-the-Lake. His success as an administrator and disciplinarian helped to win him the appointment of assistant adjutant-general for Canada West on 15 Nov. 1865. He did not formally relinquish command of the Queen's Own until 14 Sept. 1866 but he was performing only staff duties in Toronto when the battalion was part of the militia force under Alfred Booker* which suffered a humiliating defeat by the Fenians at Ridgeway on 2 June 1866.

In the post-confederation militia, Durie was appointed deputy adjutant-general for the 2nd Military District which included Toronto, Hamilton, and central Ontario. This area had a heartier appetite for patriotic military activity than did most other parts of Canada, and whereas many staff officers treated their positions as sinecures Durie was regarded as conscientious and popular. In 1871 he was almost alone among militia staff officers in urging that the volunteer system remain the basis for recruiting: "The record of the past shows that the existing force has cheerfully met all the active service duties required of it and that, too, with no ordinary sacrifice to a large proportion of the members composing the force."

Durie's own zest for service had to be satisfied by commanding the militia during disturbances at Toronto in the fall of 1875, known as the "Jubilee Riots," when Protestant roughnecks attacked Catholic processions on two successive Sundays, and also by participation in an expedition by part of his old regiment to Belleville in early January 1877 to oppose the striking locomotive engineers of the Grand Trunk Railway. In 1880, over his bitter objections, he was superannuated at the age of 67 with two years pay but without a pension. Four years later, the old soldier was father to a daughter.

At some sacrifice to his private fortune, Durie showed that Canada's volunteer militia system could work but that it would depend on the willing sacrifice of a minority. In the Queen's Own Rifles he gave the volunteers a model unit.

DESMOND MORTON

PAC, RG 8, I (C ser.), 769: 41, 45; 1000: 125, 136; RG 9, II, A1, 149: no.6885. Queen's Own Rifles Regimental Museum (Toronto), William Smith Durie papers. Can., Dept. of Militia and Defence, *Report on the state of the militia* (Ottawa), 1868–80. *Globe*, 4 June 1885. *Northern Advance and County of Simcoe General Advertiser* (Barrie, [Ont.]), 7 Aug., 11 Sept. 1856. *Toronto Daily Mail*, 4 June 1885. W. T. Barnard, *The Queen's Own Rifles of Canada, 1860–1960: one hundred years of Canada* (Don Mills, Ont., 1960). Desmond Morton, *The Canadian general: Sir William Otter* (Toronto, 1974).

E

EARLE, SYLVESTER ZOBIESKI (the second name sometimes appears as **Sobieski**, **Zolieski**, and **Solieski**, but he signed Zobieski), physician and municipal politician; b. 7 Aug. 1822 at Kingston, Kings County, N.B., son of Sylvester Zobieski Earle and Maria Hughson; m. in 1847 Catherine McGill Otty, and they had eight children; d. 1 March 1888 in Saint John, N.B.

Sylvester Zobieski Earle, the grandson of a loyalist merchant and the son of a doctor and assemblyman, received his early education in Kings County. He then chose his father's profession and studied medicine at the University of the City of New York. Awarded the degree of MD in 1844, Earle visited a number of medical centres in Europe before he returned to New Brunswick in 1845 and received his practitioner's licence. He joined his father in practice at Hampton, Kings County, was married in 1847, and ten years later was appointed county coroner. Earle also became involved in the militia. When he moved to Saint John in 1864 he joined the 62nd Saint John Fusiliers, and after being commissioned surgeon to the unit in February 1866, saw active service during the Fenian raid that year.

Earle had a successful medical practice in Saint John and played a significant role in such fraternal societies as the masonic order as well as in the militia. In April 1877 he was elected mayor of the city and soon after encountered some jurisdictional difficulties with members of the common council, caused primarily by his lack of experience in civic government. This skirmish was quickly forgotten, however, in the total disruption caused by the great fire which ravaged Saint John on 20–21 June 1877.

The fire was first discovered on a wharf in the city's waterfront and business district. Before it was contained the next day it had destroyed the most densely populated and prosperous part of the city and spread through more than nine miles of streets containing 1,612 buildings. Thirteen thousand people were left homeless, 19 people were thought dead, and contemporary estimates put the material loss at $27 million, only $7 million of which was covered by insurance. Cash donations and supplies soon arrived from throughout North America and the British Isles and Mayor Earle, whose home and office had escaped the conflagration, benefited from the advice of the chairman of the Chicago relief committee which had been formed in the aftermath of that city's destructive fire a few years earlier. Earle reorganized the Saint John Relief and Aid Society which housed citizens in a skating rink and in "tent cities" and disbursed money, food, clothing, and furniture to the destitute. Looting was widespread, with the police discovering large quantities of goods concealed in houses outside the city, and rumours circulated that ships "laden with spoils from the fire" were heading towards other Maritime ports. On 22 June Earle appealed for help directly to the military commander at Halifax, Lieutenant-General William O'Grady Haly*, and approximately 140 soldiers were dispatched to Saint John. The general pointed out, however, that Earle's request should have been transmitted through New Brunswick's lieutenant governor, Samuel Leonard Tilley*.

The citizens of Saint John praised Earle's efforts, and in 1878 he was re-elected mayor. A highlight of the reconstruction campaign was the laying of the corner-stone of the new city hall on 29 May 1878. But many residents left the city, and it has been estimated that Saint John did not recoup its loss in population until 40 years after the fire. Moreover the calamity occurred at a time when wooden shipbuilding, Saint John's major industry, was being surpassed by the new technology of steam and steel. It is possible that the economic and social dislocation caused by the 1877 fire simply accelerated the decline which the city underwent in the late 19th century. Mayor Earle was criticized, especially by the merchant community, for not acting more quickly in rebuilding the city's vital waterfront, and it was said that he lacked economic acumen in his discussions with the federal government over financial relief for the port. No immediate federal assistance was provided for its reconstruction. When Earle sought a third term as mayor in 1879 he was defeated.

Earle continued to act as a coroner for Saint John County, a position he had held since 1867, and in 1882–83 was president of the New Brunswick Medical Society. At his death in 1888 he was a commissioner of the General Public Hospital and of the board of health and the president of the New Brunswick Council of Physicians and Surgeons.

ELIZABETH W. MCGAHAN

N. B. Museum, M. G. Otty coll., Earle family papers, geneal.; Otty family papers; Tilley family papers. PANB, Common Council of Saint John, Minutes and papers, 1841–1955. St Paul's Anglican Church (Hampton, N.B.), Records (mfm. at PANB). *Historical records of the 62nd St. John Fusiliers (Canadian militia)*, comp. E. T. Sturdee (Saint John, N.B., 1888). Saint John, *Annual report of the corporation of the city*, 1877–79. *Morning News* (Saint John), 1877–78, 2 March 1888. *Saint John Daily Sun*, 2 March 1888. *Saint John Globe*, 2 March 1888. *Canadian biog. dict.*, II. *Hutchinson's New Brunswick directory for 1865–1866 . . .* , comp. Thomas Hutchinson (Montreal, [1866]). *McAlpine's St. John city directory* (Saint John), 1876, 1887–88. W. F. Bunting, *History of St. John's Lodge, F. & A.M., of Saint John, New Brunswick, together with sketches of all Masonic bodies in New Brunswick, from A.D. 1784 to A.D. 1894* (Saint John, 1895). Esther Clark Wright, *The loyalists of New Brunswick* (Fredericton, 1955; repr. Moncton, 1972). R. H. Conwell, *History of the great fire in Saint John* (Boston, 1877). K. F. C. MacNaughton, *The development of the theory and practice of education in New Brunswick, 1784–1900: a study in historical background*, ed. A. G. Bailey (Fredericton, 1947). George Stewart, *The story of the great fire in St. John, N.B., June 20th, 1877* (Toronto, 1877). W. B. Stewart, *Medicine in New Brunswick . . .* (Moncton, N.B., 1974). *The University of New Brunswick memorial volume . . .*, ed. A. G. Bailey (Fredericton, 1950).

EDSON, ALLAN AARON, artist; b. 18 Dec. 1846 in Stanbridge Township, Canada East, son of Hiram Edson and Elvira Gilmore; m. in 1871 at Montreal Mary Stewart, and they had four sons; d. 1 May 1888 in Glen Sutton, Que., and was buried 3 May in Mount Royal Cemetery, Montreal.

Allan Aaron Edson moved with his family to Stanbridge village when he was young. His father ran a hotel which was close to the bank of John Carpenter Baker, a patron of the arts who later helped finance Allan's studies abroad and became an important purchaser of his work. A second move in about 1861 took the family to Montreal. Here Allan, who had received a commercial training, worked in several business houses, including, it is said, that of Augustus J. Pell, a well-known picture frame manufacturer and art dealer. At Pell's he would have met professional artists.

According to his obituaries Edson was briefly, in these early years, a pupil of Robert Stuart Duncanson*, and by 1864 he had given up his regular employment and was preparing to go abroad for further art training. When he returned to Montreal about two years later he began at once to make a name for himself. One of his paintings was among the prizes offered in 1866 in an art lottery sponsored by the Art Association of Montreal. His name appeared at this time with those of established artists, including Otto Jacobi and James D. DUNCAN. Futher study in both Great Britain and continental Europe followed. In all, Edson made at least four trips overseas. He went for the last time in the 1880s, and remained in France for five years; during part of this period he was a pupil of Léon-Germain Pelouse, the teacher who had the greatest influence upon him. Though he had considerable success by the 1880s, Edson was never free from financial strains. In a letter written to his wife from Paris in 1881 he spoke of the difficulties of painting with fingers stiff from cold (a fire in his room was too expensive), and of dining on "dish-watery" soup in cheap cafés.

Contemporaries described Edson as unusually modest. He was, none the less, conspicuous in professional organizations: a founding member of the Society of Canadian Artists in 1867, an early member of the Ontario Society of Artists, founded in 1872, and a charter member in 1880 of the Royal Canadian Academy of Arts. At the first academy exhibition in March 1880, Princess Louise, Marchioness of Lorne, purchased works by Edson for her mother, Queen Victoria, and for herself. The queen lent an Eastern Townships landscape by him to the Colonial and Indian Exhibition in 1886.

From the 1860s until his death Edson exhibited regularly in Canada. His work was also shown at the Royal Academy of Arts in London and the Paris Salon; it was seen at world fairs in Philadelphia (1876) and Antwerp (1885). He taught composition and landscape painting at the Art Association of Montreal, and provided illustrations for publications such as the *Canadian Illustrated News* and *L'Opinion publique*.

In his earlier period Edson had traits in common with the Hudson River school of painting; his later style showed strongly the effects of his years in France. He was not, however, a mere product of European training, returning home to portray Canada in a foreign spirit. Edson proved able to adapt what he had learned abroad to the essential ruggedness of the Canadian landscape. Typical of his subjects are the early "Sheep in landscape" (the National Gallery of Canada, Ottawa); "The coming storm over Lake Memphremagog" (Musée du Québec); "A trout brook" (exhibited at Philadelphia in 1876 and owned, at that time, by Augustus J. Pell); "Cow-path in the woods" and "In the mountains, Glen Sutton" (both in his studio at the time of his death). His favourite subjects were found in his native Eastern Townships. All his life he was preoccupied with the effect of sunlight filtering through leaves in the interior of woodlands. How early this theme absorbed his attention is evident from a contemporary account of an 1868 Montreal exhibition: "Edson's latest work . . . and his best . . . shews a woodland where the sunlight steals through the green boughs of opening glades. . . ."

He was successful in both oils and water-colours, but his water-colours generally commanded the highest praise. J. E. Hodgson, RA, a professor at the Royal Academy Schools, who was commissioned by the government of Canada to report on the Canadian art shown at the Colonial and Indian Exhibition in London, declared that "in point of colour" there was nothing finer in the whole collection than Edson's water-colour landscape. Though at the time of his death, Edson was only beginning to realize his full powers, he was described as the best landscape painter Canada had yet produced.

ELIZABETH COLLARD

[Works by Allan Aaron Edson are held in a number of public collections including the National Gallery of Canada (Ottawa), the Musée du Québec, the Montreal Museum of Fine Arts, the Art Gallery of Ontario (Toronto), and the Edmonton Art Gallery. Some information concerning Edson was provided by the late T. A. Knowlton of Montreal. Mrs Ruby Moore of Stanbridge East, Que., has Gilmore family papers. E.C.]

McGill Univ. Libraries (Montreal), Blackader Library, H. G. Jones and Edmond Dyonnet, "History of the Royal Academy of Arts" (typed copy, 1934), chapter 5. Montreal Museum of Fine Arts, Reference Library, Album de coupures, 1863–82; Classeur canadien, Dossier A. A. Edson; MS Watts. National Gallery of Canada, A. A. Edson, Acc. nos.131, 1398, 9648, 15379, 17556, 18161. Missisquoi County Hist. Soc., *Report* (St Johns [Saint-Jean-sur-Richelieu], Que.), 6 (1960): 47–48. Charles Tupper, *Report . . . on the Canadian section of the Colonial and Indian Exhibition at South Kensington, 1886* (Ottawa, 1887), 64. *Canadian Illustrated News* (Montreal), 11 March 1871; 4 May, 10 Oct. 1874; 24 April 1880; 25 June, 2 July 1881. *Gazette* (Montreal), 13 Nov. 1867, 23 Dec. 1868, 26 June 1873, 26 Nov. 1880, 3 May 1888. *Montreal Daily Star*, 3, 28 May 1888. *Montreal Daily Witness*, 2, 19, 25 May 1888. *L'Opinion publique*, 2 mai 1872. *La Patrie*, 3 mai 1888. *The Colonial and Indian Exhibition, London, 1886: official catalogue of the Canadian section* (2nd ed., London, 1886). Harper, *Early painters and engravers*, 103.

J. H. S. Bugeia and T. C. Moore, *In old Missisquoi; with history and reminiscences of Stanbridge Academy* (Montreal, 1910), 121–24. W. [G.] Colgate, *Canadian art: its origin & development* (Toronto, 1943; repr. 1967), 35, 121–24. Harper, *Painting in Canada.* Gérard Morisset, *La peinture traditionnelle au Canada français* (Ottawa, 1960), 171–72. "Allan Aaron Edson, R.C.A.," Missisquoi Hist. Soc., *Report* (St Johns [Saint-Jean-sur-Richelieu]), 7 (1961): 105–9. "Allan Edson – R.C.A. – 1884–1888, Canadian landscape painter," *News and Eastern Townships Advocate* (St Johns [Saint-Jean-sur-Richelieu]), 28 Jan. 1960. "Art in continental states," *Art Journal* (London), new ser., 10 (1871): 8. Elizabeth Collard, "Eastern Townships artist: Allan Edson," *Canadian Antiques Collector* (Willowdale, Ont.), 5 (1970), no.1: 13–15. A. de C. Gilmour, "[Letter to the editor]," *News and Eastern Townships Advocate*, 11 Feb. 1960. A. J. Graham, "The Ontario Art Society's exhibition," *Rose-Belford's Canadian Monthly and National Rev.* (Toronto), 5 (1880): 99. John Horn, "Allan Aaron Edson, R.C.A.," *Dominion Illustrated* (Montreal), 1 (1888): 94.

ELDER, WILLIAM, Presbyterian clergyman, journalist, and politician; b. 22 July 1822 at Malin, County Donegal (Republic of Ireland); d. 23 July 1883 in Saint John, N.B., and was survived by his wife and two daughters.

William Elder received an excellent theological education at Belfast College, the universities of Glasgow and Edinburgh, and New College in Edinburgh. His education was reflected in the high literary quality of his later writings and speeches. Elder greatly distinguished himself academically, excelling especially in metaphysics and the classics. Thus trained for the Free Church Presbyterian ministry, he came to New Brunswick as a missionary. In 1853 he briefly occupied the pulpit of the Saint John Presbyterian Church, and early in 1854 was called to the pastorate of the Presbyterian church at St Stephen, where he remained until 1863. But his literary inclinations had soon led him into denominational journalism, and in March 1856 he had founded the *Colonial Presbyterian and Protestant Journal*, which he continued to publish and edit after moving back to Saint John in 1863. Elder did not continue as an active minister, although he occasionally preached at his former parish in the city.

Perceiving that a much wider influence could be exercised during the confederation era through secular rather than denominational journalism, Elder founded the tri-weekly *Morning Journal* in Saint John on 1 May 1865. As its publisher and editor, Elder united scholarly attainments with marked journalistic ability in his dignified but forceful editorials in favour of confederation, at the very moment when the fortunes of the pro-confederates had reached their lowest ebb in the province. While opposing Samuel Leonard Tilley* on the question of the Western Extension railway from Saint John to Maine, the *Morning Journal* played a significant role in helping Tilley achieve the confederate victory over Albert James SMITH in the crucial New Brunswick election of June 1866. As early as 1867 Henry James Morgan*, commenting upon Elder's "bold, earnest and logical" editorials and "cultivated and refined taste," observed that he already occupied "a first position amongst British American journalists."

On 2 July 1869 Elder's *Morning Journal* amalgamated with John Livingston's tri-weekly *Morning Telegraph* (Saint John), to form the *St. John Daily Telegraph and Morning Journal*, with Livingston as proprietor and Elder as editor. Simultaneously, Elder's *Colonial Presbyterian* merged with the *Presbyterian Advocate* (Saint John), under similar arrangements. In 1871 Elder purchased Livingston's interests in both newspapers, and continued as publisher and editor of the *Presbyterian Advocate* until it was discontinued in 1876, and of the *St. John Daily Telegraph and Morning Journal* (the title was abbreviated to the *Daily Telegraph* in September 1873) until his death. Under Elder's skilful proprietorship, the *Daily Telegraph* rose to unprecedented prominence in the Maritime provinces. Its circulation was more than double that of any daily in New Brunswick, and that of the *Weekly Telegraph* was equal to the combined circulation of its three leading rivals in the Maritimes. The *Presbyterian Advocate* and the *Daily Telegraph* together had a circulation of 20,000 each week, the largest output for an advertising medium in Canada east of Montreal.

Much of the *Telegraph*'s success is attributable to Elder's complete reorganization of its editorial staff, which included James Hannay*, Elder's assistant editor from 1872 to 1883, who was the *Telegraph*'s editor between 1893 and 1901 and New Brunswick's most prominent historian before World War I. But it was principally William Elder's own character and vigorous, articulate editorship that made the *Daily Telegraph*, between 1871 and 1883, according to the Toronto *Globe*, one of the "most enterprising, most ably conducted, and most influential journals in the Dominion. . . ."

Through the *Daily Telegraph*'s well-reasoned and conscientious editorials on federal politics, Elder warmly supported Sir John A. Macdonald*, Tilley, and the Conservatives until disillusioned by the Pacific Scandal in 1873. Thereafter, he aligned the *Telegraph*'s editorial policy with Alexander Mackenzie*'s Liberals in dominion politics, but maintained that provincial politics should be divorced completely from federal. During the New Brunswick school controversy of the early 1870s, he was a strong supporter of the free, non-sectarian school system which was inaugurated against Roman Catholic objections in January 1872. On the local level the *Telegraph*, with zealous civic pride, devoted much attention to the commercial, industrial, social, and intellectual advancement of Saint John in particular, and New Brunswick in general. Elder's editorials on such topics combined an articulate literary style and careful logic with high-minded integrity.

William Elder himself first entered politics in the federal general election of 1872 as a Conservative candidate for the City and County of Saint John. The members elected were Isaac BURPEE and Acalus Lockwood Palmer*, but the contest had little political significance since all the candidates presented themselves as moderate Conservatives. On the provincial scene, the *Daily Telegraph*'s spirited support of the Common Schools Act, 1871, had contributed much towards the carrying of the measure by the government of George Luther Hatheway* in May 1871. When a vacancy occurred in Saint John County through the death of Joseph Coram, Elder was elected to the provincial assembly in a by-election on 6 Nov. 1875. He was re-elected in 1878 and 1882. Although there were no firm dividing lines between parties in New Brunswick provincial politics before 1883, Elder was generally seen as a supporter of the government of George Edwin King* and he became, both through the *Telegraph*'s influential editorials and his polished oratory in the house, one of the strongest defenders of John James Fraser*'s administration formed in 1878. After Fraser resigned as premier and William Wedderburn as provincial secretary prior to the June 1882 general election, the government was reorganized under the leadership of Daniel Lionel Hanington* and Pierre-Amand Landry*. Elder was shocked at being excluded from the reconstituted administration. The new government, which depended for its support on the 22 conservative assemblymen elected in June 1882, soon faced an opposition of the more liberal supporters of the previous King and Fraser administrations, among whom Elder and Andrew George Blair* were most prominent. When the Hanington–Landry government was forced to resign following defeat on a non-confidence motion on 24 Feb. 1883, Blair formed a Liberal government on 3 March, the first distinct "party" administration following confederation. Elder was appointed provincial secretary, president and chairman of the board of agriculture, and a commissioner of the provincial lunatic asylum. He died less than five months later, but during his brief tenure in office he revealed himself to be an able and industrious administrator.

While he was actively engaged in journalism and politics, Elder also served as an elected director of the Saint John Grammar School Board and of the Saint John Board of Trade; he frequently represented the latter at the annual meetings of the Dominion Board of Trade. He considered himself a member of the Saint John business community and was a director of the Saint John Cotton Company and the principal organizer of the Dominion and Loyalist Centennial Exhibition held in Saint John in October 1883. His unceasing labours as the exhibition's executive chairman possibly contributed to his death a few months before it opened. Between April 1867 and October 1872 he had been a frequent contributor to *Stewart's Quarterly* (Saint John), one of the highest quality literary magazines in Canada in the immediate post-confederation era. In educational matters, Elder was primarily responsible for the establishment of the Fredericton Normal School in the late 1870s and he frequently addressed university convocations. These orations, several of which were published, exhibited refined scholarly eloquence. In recognition of his services to education in the province, the University of New Brunswick conferred upon him the honorary degree of LLD in June 1883.

Elder's sudden death occasioned great public mourning throughout New Brunswick and brought forth eulogistic tributes from across Canada. As a Presbyterian clergyman, the leading orator of the New Brunswick assembly from 1875 to 1883, and briefly a prominent member of the Blair government, he had gained widespread recognition, but he was best known for his successful career as New Brunswick's most influential journalist after confederation. The dignified publisher and editor of the Saint John *Daily Telegraph* became, as the *Dominion annual register* observed, commenting upon his enlightened public spirit and indomitable energy, "one of the ablest and most worthy newspaper writers in the Dominion."

MURRAY BARKLEY

William Elder was the author of *Meliora: an oration delivered before the "Alumni" of Mount Allison Wesleyan College, Sackville, on the 1st of June, 1880* ([Saint John, N.B., 1880]) and *The university: medieval and modern; an oration, delivered at the encœnia of the University of New Brunswick, on the 21st of June, 1871* (Saint John, 1871).

Colonial Presbyterian and Protestant Journal (St Stephen, N. B., and Saint John), March 1856–June 1869. *Daily Sun* (Saint John), 24, 27 July 1883. *Daily Telegraph* (Saint John), 2 July 1869–27 July 1883. *Globe*, 25 July 1883. *Morning Journal* (Saint John), 1 May 1865–30 June 1869. *Presbyterian Advocate* (Saint John), 1869–76. *Stewart's Quarterly* (Saint John), April 1867–October 1872. *CPC*, 1883. *Dominion annual register*, 1883. Harper, *Hist. directory*. W. G. MacFarlane, *New Brunswick bibliography: the books and writers of the province* (Saint John, 1895). Morgan, *Bibliotheca Canadensis*. Hannay, *Hist. of N.B.*

ELLIOTT, ANDREW CHARLES, lawyer, judge, and politician; b. *c.* 1828 in Ireland, the son of John Elliott; d. 9 April 1889 at San Francisco, Calif.

Andrew Charles Elliott, though raised in Ireland, was admitted to Lincoln's Inn, London, on 11 Nov. 1851 and called to the bar in 1854. In 1858 he was in chambers at Inner Temple Lane, but the following year he obtained from Sir Edward Bulwer-Lytton a letter of introduction to Governor James Douglas* of British Columbia, and left England to practise in the gold colony. He was admitted to the bar of British Columbia in June 1859. To his disappointment he discovered that no county court system had been organized and he anticipated a short stay in the colony. In September, however, Elliott learned from Douglas that he intended to establish county courts, and Elliott accepted the appointment of county court judge for the district of Yale and Hope at a salary of £200 plus fees. His commission was issued on 10 Jan. 1860 and in the execution of his duties he proved to be fearless among the turbulent miners at Yale. At the conclusion of the mining season Elliott requested leave to return to England. When he arrived back in the colony in July 1861 he was accompanied by his wife Mary and their daughter.

Douglas now offered to appoint Elliott gold commissioner and stipendiary magistrate for the Lillooet district at a salary of £400. Elliott was "in no way enthusiastic" about moving his family to the tiny settlement of Lillooet which was at the terminus of the Harrison–Lillooet Road to the Cariboo goldfields. Once at Lillooet, however, he found companions among the scattered ranchers, and formed a good opinion of the local native people whom he considered industrious and enterprising. When he marked out the Indian reserves he saw to it that they obtained large holdings of well-watered pastoral land. Although Elliott's health and constitution were poor, he was, in Douglas' view, "an active popular Magistrate." He was appointed to the Legislative Council by Governor Frederick Seymour*, Douglas' successor, and was a member in 1865 and 1866.

After the union of British Columbia and Vancouver Island in November 1866, Elliott was one of the supernumerary officials for whom Seymour wanted to find a place. During this period of extreme financial stringency, Seymour asked Elliott to hold the position of high sheriff, and promised to restore his judgeship when conditions improved. Elliott agreed in March 1867, and soon took up residence in Victoria. At confederation with Canada in 1871, Elliott was still high sheriff. Twice in 1872 he applied to the Canadian government for a judgeship, but received no satisfaction. In 1873 the office of high sheriff was abolished by the provincial legislature and the following year Elliott became police magistrate of Victoria.

In the autumn of 1875 Elliott was elected to the Legislative Assembly as a member for Victoria and eventually became the leader of the opposition [*see* William SMITHE]. After the government of George Anthony Walkem* was defeated on 25 Jan. 1876, Elliott was summoned by Lieutenant Governor Joseph William Trutch* to form a ministry, assuming office on 4 February. Unlike his predecessor, who was accused by the *Daily British Colonist and Victoria Chronicle* of "extravagance, dishonesty, tyranny and arrogance," Elliott when he became premier had a reputation for honesty and gentlemanly behaviour. "Nearly twenty years in office and not rich!" exclaimed David William Higgins*, the editor of the paper.

In his subsequent election campaign for endorsement Elliott promised to obtain complete fulfilment of the Carnarvon Terms. These terms, a compromise between the governments of British Columbia and Canada, were proposed in 1874 by the colonial secretary, Lord Carnarvon, after Canada had become delinquent in fulfilling the railway promise of 1871. They included the offer from the federal government of a railway from Esquimalt to Nanaimo, on Vancouver Island, in return for the province's agreement to extend the ten-year limit for the completion of the transcontinental railway. Elliott won a victory at the polls on 21 Feb. 1876, but by the time the legislature opened on 15 April, a critical juncture had been reached in the province's relations with the federal government. In January Walkem had forwarded to the queen a memorial endorsed by the legislature which outlined the province's grievances and threatened secession from Canada. The petition echoed the general exasperation in the province with the policies of the Alexander Mackenzie* government; the legislation for the island railway proposed by Lord Carnarvon had been defeated in the Senate on 5 April 1875, and on 25 September the Privy Council, accepting Edward Blake*'s argument that the island railway was a mere local work which had been intended as compensation for the unavoidable delay in construction of the transcontinental, offered in its place a cash bonus.

With the appeal to the imperial government resting at the Colonial Office, Elliott turned his attention to provincial fiscal matters. He discovered that Walkem had handled finances so irresponsibly that the Bank of British Columbia had cut off the government's credit, that a temporary loan from Sir James Douglas had been arranged, and that federal subsidy and debt allowance payments for 1876 had been drawn and expended. Despite the federal guarantee for support provided in the terms of union, the Esquimalt dry dock, then being constructed, was such a sink-hole for provincial funds that an approach for more assistance had to be made to Ottawa, and in July 1877 Elliott invited the imperial government to take over the work. To replenish the empty treasury and obtain funds for rising school costs, repairs to the Cariboo Road, and the expense of the Indian reserve commission, Elliott instituted real estate, income, and school taxes, as well as a tax on wild lands, and re-imposed the road tolls abolished in 1871. By these measures Elliott succeeded in putting the province's finances on a sounder basis which in turn allowed him to secure the release of the federal subsidy, at this time some $213,000. But his heavy impositions were unpopular; the property and income taxes caused "great discontent," and the federal minister of justice, Blake, disallowed the act reimposing tolls on the Cariboo Road on the grounds that they interfered with trade and commerce.

In the matter of the railway dispute with the federal government, Elliott was a moderate who welcomed the news in June 1876 that Governor General Dufferin [Blackwood*] intended a goodwill visit to the province. Unfortunately, Lord Dufferin's first impression of Elliott was not favourable: Elliott seemed "a Dublin lawyer of respectable, but I should say of no more than respectable ability. . . ." By the time of Dufferin's departure, the premier appeared in a better light: he was "a very reasonable man," whose ministers had "made up their minds not to go on crying out any more for the Esquimalt & Nanaimo Railway, and the secession folly *on that account*, was also knocked on the head." In March 1877, when Elliott agreed to a season's delay in starting the construction of the island railway, the governor general credited him with "allaying all local impatience" and extinguishing "the firebrands." No strong protest issued from Victoria when in December 1877 Mackenzie announced that the Fraser River route had been chosen for the Canadian Pacific Railway. But when in May 1878 there was a further announcement to the effect that Esquimalt had definitely been eliminated as the terminus of the transcontinental, Elliott's popularity was destroyed in his own riding of Victoria.

Though as a magistrate Elliott had been "brave to a fault," as a politician he was a poor disciplinarian. In 1876 he had to dismiss Thomas Basil HUMPHREYS, his finance minister, for being uncooperative, and Ebenezer Brown, president of the Executive Council, for advocating a railway policy contrary to his own. Under the loose system of personal alliance which characterized British Columbia's politics of this period, Elliott's support continued to wane. He had inherited many problems from Walkem, and on the floor of the house he was no match for that wily politician, who cast Elliott in the role of traitor to his province. "A genial, whole-souled gentleman of generous impulses," Elliott found it difficult to deny favours to prominent men or old friends. Thus in 1876 he yielded to pressure and endorsed a policy to exclude Chinese immigrants. When a labour dispute occurred at the Wellington coal mine, he agreed with the owner, Robert DUNSMUIR, that the militia should be called out. But despite failings of this sort, Elliott made an important contribution in the sphere of dominion-provincial relations through his temperate stand in the railway dispute. In 1879 when Walkem, back in office, attempted to rouse the population to secession, he was unsuccessful.

The Elliott ministry was defeated on a redistribution bill, the legislature was dissolved on 12 April 1878, and only eight of Elliott's supporters were returned in the May election. Elliott resigned on 25 June 1878 and left political life. His last public service to his province was as one of the three commissioners appointed on 28 Oct. 1884 to investigate the Indian troubles at Metlakatla following William Duncan*'s dismissal [*see* Alexander Edmund Batson DAVIE].

After his retirement as premier, Elliott made every effort, including a visit to Prime Minister Sir John A. Macdonald* in Ottawa in 1882, to obtain from the Canadian government the pension he felt he was entitled to as a former colonial official. His efforts were to no avail. Elliott was in London in 1881, arranging support for his pension claim, when his wife died suddenly in Victoria. Two years later, having returned to Victoria, he served as pallbearer on 14 Nov. 1883 at the funeral of his son-in-law, James William Douglas, the only son of his old friend Sir James Douglas. Elliott himself continued to suffer poor health, and, when he was in San Francisco in March 1886, three physicians advised that it would be dangerous for him to return to the northern coastal climate. He took up residence in San Francisco and died there on 9 April 1889. His daughter brought his body back to Victoria, where on 17 April he was buried.

MARGARET A. ORMSBY

Bancroft Library, Univ. of California (Berkeley), A. C. Elliott, "British Columbia politics . . . information given at San Francisco 1880" (copy at PABC). PABC, B.C., Colonial Secretary, Corr. outward, 1859–70 (copies); GR 495; Colonial corr., A. C. Elliott corr; Crease coll., H. P. P. Crease, Corr. inward, 1868; A. C. Elliott papers. PAC, MG 26, B.

B.C., Legislative Assembly, *Journals*, 1875–78; *Sessional papers*, 1876–77. Can., Parl., *Sessional papers*, 1871, IV: no.18; 1875, VII: no.19; 1885, X: no.34. *Dufferin–Carnarvon correspondence, 1874–1878*, ed. C. W. de Kiewiet and F. H. Underhill (Toronto, 1955). *Daily Colonist* (Victoria), 10, 13 Feb. 1874; 27 Jan., 22 Feb., 2, 12 April, 6 May 1876, 15, 17 Dec. 1881; 11, 18 April 1889. *Mainland Guardian* (New Westminster, B.C.), 1877–78. *Victoria Daily Standard*, 1877–78. Thomson, *Alexander Mackenzie*. Edith Dobie, "Some aspects of party history in British Columbia, 1871–1903," *Pacific Coast Hist. Rev.* (Glendale, Calif.), 1 (1932): 235–51. R.E. Gosnell, "Prime Ministers of British Columbia: Andrew Charles Elliott," *Vancouver Daily Province*, 23 March 1921. J. A. Maxwell, "Lord Dufferin and the difficulties with British Columbia, 1874–1877," *CHR*, 12 (1931): 364–89. M. A. Ormsby, "Prime Minister Mackenzie, the Liberal Party, and the bargain with British Columbia," *CHR*, 26 (1945): 148–73; "Some Irish figures in colonial days," *BCHQ*, 14 (1950): 61–82.

ELWYN, THOMAS, public servant; b. in 1837 or 1838 in Ireland, eldest son of Lieutenant (afterwards Lieutenant-General) Thomas Elwyn, RA; d. 11 Sept. 1888 at Victoria, B.C.

Thomas Elwyn came from a military and naval family, and he himself served in the Crimean War as lieutenant in the 30th Foot. In 1858 he left England "on speck" for the newly proclaimed gold colony of British Columbia, and travelling by the Panama route arrived in Victoria, Vancouver Island, on Christmas Day. Being "well recommended from home" he was soon attached by Governor James Douglas* to the police force under Inspector Chartres Brew*, and after five months as chief constable at Yale he was appointed, on 8 June 1859, assistant gold commissioner and stipendiary magistrate for the district of Lillooet [*see* John Carmichael HAYNES]. Here he remained until the spring of 1861 when he was given command of the gold escort from the Cariboo mines, Douglas considering him "peculiarly fitted for the task" by reason of his knowledge of the country and his previous military experience. When the gold escort was rejected by the miners because the government could not guarantee safe delivery, Elwyn was posted to the Cariboo district as gold commissioner on 21 April 1862. On 30 October, however, he resigned because of a conflict of interest: he owned a share in a claim on Williams Creek which had now "become so valuable," he said, "that I cannot in justice to myself abandon it." The governor expressed his "high appreciation . . . of the manner in which [Elwyn had] conducted the responsible duties entrusted" to him and regretted the loss of his "experience and ability."

When the gold escort was temporarily revived in 1863 Elwyn was made second in command to Philip Henry Nind and brought the treasure safely to New Westminster. In 1864 Elwyn was second in command of the party recruited in New Westminster by Brew for an expedition sent out to capture the Chilcotin Indians who had killed Alfred Penderell Waddington*'s road construction crew at the head of Bute Inlet. During the mining season of 1865 Elwyn was working on White Horse Creek in the Kootenay, and the following spring he accompanied, as the agent of the government, the Western Union Telegraph expedition during its extension of the line north from Quesnel. When work was suspended for the winter he was left in charge of a mining party exploring on the Stikine River, but in the spring of 1867 the telegraph project was abandoned and Elwyn returned to civilization. In 1868 he was appointed to the Legislative Council, acting (for that session only) as magistrate for the Cariboo district where he seems to have tried his luck again at mining during the next few years. In 1871 he was in charge of a band of cattle being driven from Barkerville towards Tête Jaune Cache, B.C., as winter provisions for a Canadian Pacific Railway survey party. Subsequently he is said to have been "engaged in the [Hudson's Bay Company]'s service on the steamer Otter and other vessels"; he was undoubtedly purser on the *Otter* from 1873 to 1876. Finally, on 7 Nov. 1877, he was appointed deputy provincial secretary and gave great satisfaction in that office until his death.

Elwyn was one of the earliest supporters of the Pioneer Society of British Columbia, serving as its president in 1878 and 1879. On 4 Oct. 1879 he married Rebecca, daughter of Captain William Henry McNeill*, and they had two daughters, one of whom died in infancy. Elwyn himself died after over a year's illness from "consumption" in 1888.

When all debts were paid Elwyn's estate amounted to less than $100. His friends mourned him as a man "ever courteous, considerate and generous," "of boundless sympathy and charity," "noble all through," who bore himself towards women "with unvarying chivalrous courtesy, hating the flippant fashion of to-day." And yet in his pursuit of fortune in the successive gold excitements of British Columbia, he had borrowed money from friends and relations of both sexes, "to carry him through." Nind, who left the colony in 1866, commented soon after, in private letters, on Elwyn's "youthful indiscretions" as a magistrate in Cariboo and roundly asserted that he had been "proved to be a scamp." On the other hand, though Elwyn resigned as gold commissioner in 1862 the government continued to employ him in positions of trust; and ten years as deputy provincial secretary confirmed his public reputation as "a shrewd, clear-headed man," with considerable executive ability and an untarnished record for "probity, sincerity and manliness."

DOROTHY BLAKEY SMITH

PABC, Add. MSS 218; Add. MSS 412; B.C., Colonial Secretary, Corr. outward, 1859–67 (copies); Colonial corr., M. B. Begbie corr.; Chartres Brew corr.; Thomas Elwyn coll., Corr. outward, 1865; O'Reilly coll., Peter O'Reilly diary, 1865. Supreme Court of British Columbia in Probate, Victoria Registry, Elwyn estate papers (copy at PABC).

B.C., *Blue book*, 1859–62; Legislative Council, *Journals*, 1868. [A. T. Bushby] "The journal of Arthur Thomas Bushby, 1858–1859," ed. Dorothy Blakey Smith, *BCHQ*, 21 (1957–58): 83–160. *British Columbian* (New Westminster, B.C.), 27 Oct. 1866. *Cariboo Sentinel*, 19 Aug. 1871. *Daily Colonist* (Victoria), 5 June 1863; 17 April 1866; October 1873–October 1876; 12, 14 Sept., 7 Oct. 1888. *Hart's army list*, 1858.

EMERY-CODERRE, JOSEPH, doctor; b. 23 Nov. 1813 at Saint-Denis, on the Richelieu, Lower Canada, son of Marc Coderre, a farmer, and Marie-Angélique Desgranges; m. in 1843 Héloïse-Euphémie Dasylva, and they had 11 children; d. 9 Sept. 1888 in Montreal, Que.

At the age of 14, Joseph Emery-Coderre began working as a clerk in the store of a Saint-Denis merchant before being employed by businessman Jean-Baptiste Trudeau in Montreal, on Rue Notre-Dame. He saved enough to buy a business in his birthplace but in 1836 returned to Montreal to enter into a partnership with Benjamin Ouimet, the brother of André*, who would become president of the Fils de la Liberté. His return to Montreal gave Emery-Coderre the opportunity to take up medical studies. His membership in the Fils de la Liberté and his sympathy for the cause of the Patriotes attracted the attention of the civil authorities, who judged it prudent to arrest him on 6 Nov. 1838. He was held in prison in Montreal for 38 days. It seems that, like a good medical student, he treated fellow prisoners suffering physical or psychological distress; Dr Daniel Arnoldi*, the prison doctor, is said to have appreciated his help.

Once released, Emery-Coderre wrote articles for the bi-weekly *L'Aurore des Canadas* (Montreal), owned by François Cinq-Mars, which first appeared on 15 Jan. 1839 and was dedicated to restoring social and political peace in Lower Canada. But Emery-Coderre did not abandon his medical studies and on 13 Aug. 1844, after two years of "training" under Dr Olivier-Théophile Bruneau, he obtained his licence to practise.

The Montreal School of Medicine and Surgery, which was incorporated in 1845, appointed him professor in 1847. He taught materia medica (the art of treatment through medication) and botany, and also agreed to serve as the school's secretary, a post he was to hold for nearly 40 years. When the College of Physicians and Surgeons of Lower Canada was founded in 1847, Dr Emery-Coderre, together with his colleague Francis Badgley*, launched a protest movement which two years later resulted in valuable amendments to the existing medical law; the main object of the amendments was to establish the election of the college's board of governors on a basis of representation proportional to the number of doctors in each region. In 1857 Emery-Coderre joined the medical staff of the Hôtel-Dieu. Working with colleagues from the school – doctors Pierre-Antoine-Conefroy Munro, Louis Boyer, Jean-Gaspard Bibaud, and Pierre BEAUBIEN – and with the Religious Hospitallers of St Joseph at the Hôtel-Dieu, he had begun in 1849 to act as a link in order to secure the agreement of 1850 which elevated the hospital to the rank of a clinical teaching centre.

On 10 Sept. 1866 the Montreal School of Medicine and Surgery, having met with two refusals from the Université Laval at Quebec, became the faculty of medicine of Victoria College at Cobourg, Canada West [*see* Hector Peltier*]. Ten years later, when Laval was authorized to establish itself in Montreal and sought to affiliate with the Montreal School of Medicine and Surgery, the members of the school categorically refused, so emphatically that in June 1883 Archbishop Elzéar-Alexandre Taschereau* of Quebec excommunicated them. Two months later, however, under pressure from Rome, Archbishop Taschereau was forced to lift the excommunication. As secretary of the school, Emery-Coderre welcomed the news that the sanction was lifted. Nevertheless, until his death in 1888, he was unequivocally opposed to any *rapprochement* between the school in Montreal and the Université Laval.

Emery-Coderre was an active medical man. In 1853 he was president of the Institut Canadien of Montreal, an appointment which earned him the severe disapproval of Bishop Ignace BOURGET who suspected the members of this new cultural association of nefarious designs. He was a contributor to the *Traité élémentaire de matière médicale et guide pratique des sœurs de charité de l'asile de la Providence*, published in 1869, and a founder of the Medical Association of Canada (1867), the Medical Society of Montreal (1871), and the Medical Union of Canada (1872). In 1885 Emery-Coderre bitterly opposed compulsory vaccination, and in December launched the journal *L'Antivaccinateur canadien-français* (Montreal). However, when the smallpox epidemic that was then raging in Montreal subsided, his vehemence moderated somewhat. The journal ceased publication after three issues.

Definitely given to disputation, Joseph Emery-Coderre played a prominent role after 1847 in the struggle to establish the rights of rural French-speaking doctors. In the conflict between the Ultramontanes and the Institut Canadien he took a reasonable stance, and in the conflict about the university he behaved with integrity and dignity.

ÉDOUARD DESJARDINS

Joseph Emery-Coderre contributed to *Traité élémentaire de matière médicale et guide pratique des sœurs de charité de l'asile de la Providence* (Montréal, 1869), and founded in December 1885 *L'Antivaccinateur canadien-français* (Montréal).

AC, Montréal, État civil, Catholiques, Notre-Dame de Montréal, 12 sept. 1888. ANQ-M, État civil, Catholiques, Saint-Denis, 24 nov. 1813. Fauteux, *Patriotes.* Abbott, *Hist. of medicine*, 65, 69, 72. J.-B.-A. Allaire, *Histoire de la paroisse de Saint-Denis-sur-Richelieu (Canada)* (Saint-Hyacinthe, Qué., 1905). Heagerty, *Four centuries of medical hist. in Canada*, I-II. André Lavallée, *Québec contre Montréal, la querelle universitaire, 1876–1891* (Montréal, 1974), 46, 48, 67, 144, 153. Rumilly, *Hist. de la prov. de Québec*, IV: 57–58, 89–90, 92; V: 85. Philippe Constant [J.-J. Lefebvre], "À propos du Dr Coderre," *Le Devoir* (Montréal), 1er févr. 1938. Docteur Frank [ ], "Médecins d'autrefois: notes biographiques sur le Dr J.-Emery Coderre," *Le Docteur* (Montréal), 1 (1922–23), no.8: 14–19. Paul Dumas, "Les médecins de l'Hôtel-Dieu et la littérature médicale canadienne," *Le Journal de l'Hôtel-Dieu de Montréal* (Montréal), 11 (1942): 479–87. "Memento nécrologique: le docteur J. E. Coderre," *L'Union médicale du Canada* (Montréal), 17 (1888): 558–59. L.-D. Mignault, "Revue historique; histoire de l'école de Médecine et de Chirurgie de Montréal," *L'Union médicale du Canada*, 55 (1926): 597–674.

ENTREMONT, SIMON D', agriculturist, politician, and office-holder; b. 28 Oct. 1788 at West Pubnico, N.S., third child of Bénoni d'Entremont* and Anne-Marguerite Pothier; d. 6 Sept. 1886 at East Pubnico, N.S.

Philippe Mius* d'Entremont, lieutenant to Charles de Saint-Étienne* de La Tour, the governor of Acadia, was granted the barony of Pobomcoup, near Cape Sable, by the latter in 1651 or 1653. During the expulsion of the Acadians by Governor Charles Lawrence*, Simon d'Entremont's father was driven out of Pobomcoup some time between 1756 and 1758; he was one of the first to return to this region, settling at West Pubnico around 1766.

According to George Stayley Brown*, Simon d'Entremont did not go to school, there being none at the time, but he nevertheless managed to learn to express himself in writing in both French and English and to acquire the rudiments of Latin and Micmac. On 20 June 1810 Simon married Elizabeth Larkin, of East Pubnico. He then took up residence on the east side of Pubnico harbour, where he had received quite a large piece of property from his father. Nine children were born of the marriage. His first wife died on 16 Feb. 1830, and the next year he married Élisabeth Thériault, of Meteghan, N.S.; they also had nine children.

In the provincial elections of 1836, Simon d'Entremont stood for Argyle Township, established as a constituency that year. The population of this township in Yarmouth County was largely Acadian. D'Entremont won the election and, according to Clarence J. d'Entremont, he and Frederick Armand Robicheau, of Corberrie in Digby County, were the first Acadians in North America elected to a house of assembly.

In 1823 the Legislative Assembly of Nova Scotia passed a resolution permitting Catholics who were elected members to assume their seats without taking the oaths under the Test Act, which denied tenets of the Roman Catholic faith. However, tradition has it that at the opening of the 15th session on 31 Jan. 1837, when Simon d'Entremont stepped forward to take his place, the test oath apparently was brought to him. After reading it, he said: "You can take back your document. . . . I would rather swallow a dogfish, tail first, than swear that." Moreover, he well knew that he was right to refuse to take the oath, for it had been abolished eight years earlier by the British parliament. Simon d'Entremont was allowed to take his seat after swearing a simple oath of loyalty to the laws of the land. He sat from 1837 until dissolution in 1840.

D'Entremont stood again in the 1840 elections but was defeated by John Ryder of Argyle; he then withdrew from the political arena but not from public life. Two years earlier, in 1838, he had been appointed a justice of the peace for Yarmouth County, and he held this office to an advanced age. He had also been appointed supervisor of sewers in Canton Township in 1839. From 1854 to 1864 he was customs officer for the ports of Argyle.

D'Entremont ended his long career in public service on 6 Sept. 1886. Four days later the parish priest of West Pubnico, Father William McLeod, noted: "I have today inhumed Simon d'Entremont, Esq. with all the rites of the Church he served so well. He had a large funeral, attended by many English-speaking families." He left 136 descendants – children, grandchildren, and great-grandchildren.

LOUIS R. COMEAU

Arch. paroissiales, Saint-Pierre (Pubnico-Ouest, N.-É.), Reg. des baptêmes, mariages et sépultures, 10 sept. 1886. Centre acadien, Collège Sainte-Anne (Church Point, N.-É.), Paroisse Sainte-Marie (Meteghan, N.-É.), Reg. des baptêmes, mariages et sépultures, 1818–29. Centre d'études acadiennes, univ. de Moncton (Moncton, N.-B.), Fonds Placide Gaudet, "Notes généalogiques sur les familles acadiennes, c.1600–1900" (mfm. at the Centre acadien, Church Point). *Le Moniteur acadien* (Shédiac, N.-B.), 16 sept. 1886. *Directory of N.S. MLAs*, 90. G. S. Brown, *Yarmouth, Nova Scotia: a sequel to Campbell's history* (Boston, 1888), 482. H. L. d'Entremont, *The baronnie de Pombcoup and the Acadians: a history of the ancient "Department of Cape Sable," now known as Yarmouth and Shelburne counties, Nova Scotia* (Yarmouth, N.S., 1931), 54. C. J. d'Entremont, "À la mémoire de Simon d'Entremont," *Le Petit Courrier* (Pubnico-Ouest), 9 mars 1967; "Simon d'Entremont de Pubnico-Est, 1788–1886 . . . ," Soc. hist. acadienne, *Cahiers* (Moncton), 2 (1966–68): 233–35.

ESPRIT ERRANT. *See* KAPAPAMAHCHAKWEW

EWING, JULIANA HORATIA. *See* GATTY

EYNON, JOHN HICKS, Bible Christian minister; b. 6 May 1801 in Gloucester, England; m. first Elizabeth Dart (d. 1857); m. secondly in 1865 Mrs Ann Down from Exeter, Canada West; there were no children by either marriage; d. 22 March 1888 at Exeter.

Little is known of John Hicks Eynon's early life. He was converted through the preaching of his future wife, Elizabeth Dart, a preacher in the Bible Christian Church; this Methodist sect was found largely in Devon and Cornwall. In 1826 he entered the ministry of the church and was appointed to Penzance, and then to brief ministries in Falmouth and Truro as well as on the Isles of Scilly. He became secretary of the missionary society of the church in 1831, at a time when requests from Bible Christian settlers in North America prompted the English conference to send Francis Metherall* to Prince Edward Island and John Glass to Upper Canada. Discouraged by numerous difficulties, Glass resigned and opened a school; Eynon was appointed to replace him.

Arriving in Cobourg in 1833, Eynon began work among the West Country immigrants around Cobourg, Oshawa, and Bowmanville. He had inherited from Glass a 200-mile circuit, extending through Darlington to Dummer Township, and received help in his duties from his wife, Elizabeth. Faced with an unsettled political situation, inadequate assistance, scarcity of funds, transportation difficulties, the rigours of the climate, and a shortage of church buildings, Eynon found progress slow and the work discouraging. In 1834 he declared: "I have such a sense of my ignorance and nothingness, that I am tempted to give up preaching altogether." The lack of visible results persuaded Eynon to hold his first "protracted meeting" in Hope Township in 1838. This nightly revival meeting, which continued for four weeks, proved somewhat successful in recruiting new members. But in 1840 the Bible Christian mission in Upper Canada reported only 256 members.

Throughout its history the Bible Christian Church in Canada was to consist almost entirely of West Country immigrants. Thus Eynon's ministry received its greatest impetus from the migration of people from Devon and Cornwall into the Huron Tract near present-day Exeter. In 1845 Eynon set off on a 600-mile tour of western Upper Canada "to find out where the people were, and how they were furnished with the means of grace." As a result of this survey the church began work in the area, work which accounted for much of its growth from 633 to 2,113 members between 1845 and 1855.

From 1842 to 1847 Eynon served as district superintendent of the Bible Christian mission, but his arduous labours led to a deterioration of his health and in 1848 he agreed that he would take advantage of a visit to England to serve as a "missionary deputation" for a year and report on his work in Canada. He drew large crowds on the circuits in Devon and Cornwall. Returning to Canada in 1849, Eynon served on the Darlington, Cobourg, and Mariposa circuits, before resuming the position of district superintendent in 1852. The following year the Canadian mission became a self-governing conference, independent of the English conference. In 1864 the small Prince Edward Island District merged with the Upper Canada District. By 1860 membership had risen to 3,986. Illness forced Eynon to retire in 1859.

He lived in retirement in Bowmanville until he moved to Exeter in 1883. In 1884 the Bible Christian Church, with 6,807 members, joined other Methodist bodies to form the Methodist Church of Canada. Eynon died on 22 March 1888 after almost 62 years as a Christian minister, and was buried in Zion Church Cemetery, Hope Township.

ALBERT BURNSIDE

Bible Christian Church in Canada, Annual Conference, *Minutes* (Bowmanville, Ont.), 1857–84. Bible Christians, Annual Conference, *Minutes* (Shebbear, Devon, Eng., and London), 1819–66. *Bible Christian Magazine* . . . (Shebbear), 1833–71. *Christian Guardian*, 1888. *Observer* (Bowmanville), 1867–84. *United Methodist ministers and their circuits . . . 1792–1932*, comp. O. A. Beckerlegge (London, 1968). F. W. Bourne, *Bible Christians; their origins and history, 1815–1900* ([London], 1905). Albert Burnside, "The Bible Christians in Canada, 1832–1884" (THD thesis, Emmanuel College, Victoria Univ., Toronto, 1969). George Eayrs, *Our founders and their story; a short history of three churches and their union as the United Methodist Church* (London, 1907). Richard Pyke, *The early Bible Christians* (London, 1941). Thomas Shaw, *The Bible Christians, 1815–1907* (London, 1965).

F

FAFARD, LÉON-ADÉLARD (baptized **Léon-Dollard**), Oblate of Mary Immaculate, priest and missionary; b. 8 June 1850 at Saint-Cuthbert, Canada East, son of Dr Charles Fafard and Tersile (Alexine) Olivier; d. 2 April 1885 at Frog Lake (Alta).

Léon-Adélard Fafard studied at the Collège de L'Assomption from 1864 to 1872. After a year's noviciate with the Oblates at Lachine, which ended on 27 June 1873, he took his perpetual vows on 29 June 1874. Recruited by Father Albert Lacombe* to serve in the west, he arrived on 5 Sept. 1875 at the Saint-Albert mission (Alta) where he was ordained subdeacon on 21 September, deacon on 30 November, and priest on 8 December. A week later he was sent to the Buffalo Lake mission (Alta), a wintering post for Métis coming from distant points to hunt buffalo. He spent the remainder of the winter there before returning to Saint-Albert; he went back to Buffalo Lake on 30 Oct. 1876. The buffalo having vanished from the Canadian prairies, this mission was now abandoned, and on 4 July 1877 Vital-Justin Grandin*, the bishop of Saint-Albert, sent Fafard to found the mission of Saint-Alexandre-de-Rivière-qui-Barre on Lake La Nonne (Alta), where he built a combined house and chapel. He returned to Saint-Albert, then set off with his superior, Jean-Marie-Joseph Lestanc, for Fort Pitt (Sask.); they arrived in August and established the Saint-François-Régis mission among the Woodland Crees.

Fafard accompanied Métis groups on their buffalo hunt during the summer and autumn of 1878 and 1879. When these expeditions proved disappointing he tried to persuade the Métis to turn to raising crops and livestock, even setting an example by tilling the soil at Saint-François-Régis, but he had little success with the Métis. Fafard and Lestanc spent the winters visiting the mission's outposts. In addition they attempted to pacify the disgruntled and restless Métis and Indians, who, given the federal government's lack of response to all their requests for help, were facing starvation.

Having worked for six years at Fort Pitt, Fafard moved to Frog Lake on 5 May 1883. He had probably foreseen that Fort Pitt would soon be abandoned: by Treaty no.6, signed in 1876, the Crees had been granted reservations some distance away, and so the importance of Fort Pitt had diminished. On 10 Aug. 1883 Fafard was appointed superior of the Frog Lake mission, as well as of those at Long and Onion lakes. He settled at roughly the spot where Abbé Jean-Baptiste Thibault* had chosen to build a hut with a mansard roof in 1843. The unpretentious residence at Frog Lake also served as a school, where Fafard, while undertaking numerous other tasks, taught some 20 pupils. A log church, well, shed, and stable were added nearby. In the autumn of 1883, as Fafard's work-load was becoming too heavy, Félix-Marie Marchand was appointed his assistant. Marchand remained with him until October 1884 in order to learn the Cree language and run the school. He was then sent to Onion Lake to build a permanent mission; he returned to Frog Lake late in March 1885, bringing some Indians from Onion Lake to take part in the religious ceremonies of Holy Week.

At that time there was a concentration of three bands of Woodland Crees on the reservation at Frog Lake.

Big Bear [MISTAHIMASKWA], the great chief of the Plains Crees, and some 20 families came to settle there also, although they did not officially belong to the reservation. On 31 March, five days after Louis RIEL's victory at Duck Lake (Sask.), and despite warnings of serious danger, the whites and the Métis at Frog Lake expressed their unwillingness to take refuge at Fort Pitt and Fafard categorically refused to leave his flock. Emboldened by the victory of Riel's Métis, Big Bear's men, under the leadership in particular of their war chieftain, Wandering Spirit [KAPAPAMAHCHAKWEW], decided to follow the Métis example and take the offensive. On 2 April they burst into the church at Frog Lake during a Maundy Thursday service. Wandering Spirit ordered the people of the mission to accompany him to Big Bear's camp. Fafard and Marchand marched at the head of the column, praying as they went. Thomas Trueman Quinn, the Indian agent, refused to follow and was shot. The result was an outburst of violence. Charles Gouin (a Métis), John Williscroft, John Gowanlock, and John Delaney were killed. Responding to Theresa Delaney's cry for help, Fafard ran to grant absolution to her husband. He had scarcely finished when he was mortally wounded by a bullet; Marchand, William Gilchrist, and George Dill suffered the same fate.

Some Métis placed the bodies of the two missionaries and of Gowanlock and Delaney in the burial vault of the church. Subsequently interred in the cemetery, the bodies of the priests were transferred in 1891 to the cemetery of the new mission opened at Onion Lake in 1887 and finally, many years later, were buried in the Oblate cemetery at Saint-Albert.

E. O. DROUIN

[V.-J. Grandin], "Les martyrs du Nord-Ouest: lettre de Mgr Grandin au père et à la mère du R. P. Fafard, martyrisé au lac La Grenouille," *Missions de la Congrégation des missionnaires oblats de Marie Immaculée* (Paris), 23 (1885): 417–30. [Hippolyte Leduc], ["Lettres au révérend père Aubert"], *Missions de la Congrégation des missionnaires oblats de Marie Immaculée*, 16 (1878): 465; 22 (1884): 24. Allaire, *Dictionnaire*. W. B. Cameron, *The war trail of Big Bear* . . . (Toronto, 1926), 13. Jules Le Chevalier, *Batoche, les missionnaires du Nord-Ouest pendant les troubles de 1885* (Montréal, 1941), 99, 101–19. A.-G. Morice, *Histoire de l'Église catholique dans l'Ouest canadien du lac Supérieur au Pacifique (1659–1915)* (3v., Winnipeg et Montréal, 1912), III: 78–88. Théophile Ortolan, *Cent ans d'apostolat dans les deux hémisphères: les Oblats de Marie Immaculée durant le premier siècle de leur existence* (4v., Paris, 1914–32).

FAFARD, THÉOGÈNE, physician, druggist, and professor of botany; b. in 1855 probably in Montreal, Canada East, son of Norbert Fafard and Appoline Claude; m. 28 Nov. 1882 Anna-Séphora Germain at St Boniface, Man., and they had one daughter who survived infancy; d. 4 Jan. 1890 at St Boniface.

Théogène Fafard's family was well established in the Montreal area in the early 1870s. In 1872, after three years at the Collège de Montréal, Fafard began to study at the Montreal School of Medicine and Surgery, which was affiliated with Victoria College at Cobourg, Ont. His brother Abel, who was to follow him to Manitoba, was an undertaker, and another brother, Norbert, a physician, was with the Montreal firm of Fafard et Daoust, chemists and druggists. In 1876 Théogène graduated and for the next two years practised medicine in Montreal.

What brought the young physician to Manitoba in November 1878 is not known, but he arrived at a time when hundreds of French Canadian families were moving into the province. Within a week of his arrival Fafard had a patient at the hospital operated by the Sisters of Charity of the Hôpital Général of Montreal (Grey Nuns), and thus began an association with the Hôpital de Saint-Boniface that lasted until his death. The records of the hospital, founded in 1871 by the Grey Nuns as an extension of the charitable institutions established by the order after its arrival at Red River in 1844 [*see* Marie-Louise Valade*], show that Fafard cared for hundreds of patients during his 11 years as resident doctor. According to an 1887 report, he visited "the sick every day and gives his services at no charge."

In the bustling climate of St Boniface in 1878–79, and as a member of a small Franco-Manitoban élite, Fafard soon involved himself in community affairs. He became a director of the Société de Colonisation de Manitoba, a member of the Roman Catholic section of the Board of Education of Manitoba, and the official physician for the Société Saint-Jean-Baptiste. He failed in his only attempt to win election to the St Boniface municipal council in 1880, and was content to take charge of the enumeration for the St Boniface provincial constituency in 1881.

When it became apparent that Fafard could not distinguish himself in political life, he focused his energies on medicine, and during the 1880s he gained recognition as the foremost French Canadian doctor in the province. In 1880 he was appointed a coroner for the province of Manitoba, a position he held until his death. In 1882, in partnership with his brother Abel, now a contractor in St Boniface, he opened a pharmacy which he sold seven years later to Dr Joseph-Honoré-Octavien Lambert. When St Boniface was incorporated as a town in 1883, Fafard was chosen as its first medical officer over his rival, Dr Lambert.

Fafard was one of the incorporators of the privately operated Manitoba Medical College in April 1884 and he joined the faculty as professor of botany on 1 October for the second session. He occupied this position until his untimely death in January 1890.

ROBERT PAINCHAUD

PAM, MG 7, D8. *Le Manitoba* (Saint-Boniface, Man.), 1881–90. *Le Métis* (Saint-Boniface), 1878–81. Élisabeth de Moissac, "Le soin des malades à la Rivière-Rouge et le premier hôpital de Saint-Boniface," *Les Cloches de Saint-Boniface* (Saint-Boniface), 70 (1971): 82–87, 140–48.

FAHEY, JAMES A., journalist and politician; b. in 1849 or 1850 in Smithville, Canada West, the son of F. Fahey, an Irish Catholic cooper; m. and had seven children; d. 2 June 1888 in Toronto, Ont.

James A. Fahey grew up in the towns of York (Haldimand County), Grimsby, and Dundas, Canada West, before apprenticing as a printer on James Somerville's Reform newspaper, the Dundas *True Banner*. Fahey made his first contributions as a reporter to the *True Banner*; he left it some time before 1870 when he appeared briefly in Toronto as a "city news reporter." By this time he had become a steadfast Conservative, which he remained for the rest of his life, and had also acquired a reputation as an effective platform speaker in Irish national circles in Hamilton. In early 1872 he founded the *Hamilton Standard*. It shortly afterward became the organ of the Nine Hour movement in Hamilton because of what the movement's corresponding secretary, James Ryan*, termed the journal's "protective spirit and conservative proclivities." The *Standard* soon perished, along with the movement for shorter hours which Fahey had supported although some members of the Hamilton Typographical Union had accused the *Standard* of not paying its printers union scale.

Fahey then moved to the *Guelph Daily Herald*, where he probably worked with Alexander Fraser Pirie*, and he became editor of the newspaper in 1874 when Pirie moved on to Toronto. While spending the winter of 1874–75 in California in an attempt to combat the consumption from which he had suffered since youth, Fahey came to doubt the salubrity of the climate and returned to Ontario claiming that those who remained in California for their health were the "dupes of emigration agents." He joined the staff of the *Hamilton Spectator* in mid 1875, where he was probably engaged in general news gathering; in August 1876 he began to send regular letters to the Toronto *Mail*, using the pseudonym Rupert, in which all manner of affairs were discussed in a light, humorous vein. By 1877 he had moved from Hamilton to Stratford where he became editor of the *Stratford Weekly Herald*. He was a vigorous supporter of the Conservative party in the 1878 federal election and acquired a reputation as a willing stump orator. In his only attempt to gain elective office he was an unsuccessful Conservative candidate in the 1879 provincial election in Grey South.

Fahey reached the highest point in his brief career when he left the *Herald* in December 1880 to join the editorial staff of the Toronto *Mail*. He was chosen to conduct the editorial page of the *Mail*'s new evening daily, the *Evening News*, which began publication in May 1881. Although its opponents referred to it as a "sewer" journal, it made an attempt to offer a livelier, more accessible sort of journalism. Fahey was accomplished in most of the forms of this new journalism for an expanding reading public, including such genres as humorous letters, police court reporting, satirical and topical verse, and stories in dialect. His writing was always characterized by an appreciation of the textures of urban life and a detached, ironic style. Fahey's outspoken anti-temperance stance confirmed him as a member of the journalistic bohemia of central Canada in the 1870s and 1880s; he counted among his friends and associates Robert Kirkland Kernighan* ("The Khan"), Alexander Whyte Wright* (who began as a journalist under Fahey at the Guelph *Herald*), and Edward Farrer*, as well as Pirie. His colleagues recalled him as "always coughing, thin to a skeleton, little of appetite," "grey-haired," and "aged in appearance." Yet even the poor health that gave rise to this condition served him as material for ironic humour; he confessed to his readers that he took amusement in his cough which could "scare a hyena out of a graveyard."

Fahey stayed at the *News* for less than a year, because of uncertain health or friction with management. He spent the winter of 1881–82 in Winnipeg as editor of the *Sun* but, upon discovering that the *Sun* was in poorer health than he was, returned to Toronto later that year to take up an editorial position on Patrick Boyle*'s *Evening Canadian*. He stayed with this paper until 1886 when he became an editorial writer at William Findlay Maclean*'s *Toronto World*, the least prestigious and lowest-paying of the Toronto dailies. He spent his last years in declining health, beset by worries about money and the fate of his seven children whose mother had died in 1885. He unsuccessfully sought political favours for his "unpurchased loyalty" to the Conservative party and complained to his friends that Conservative politicians, including Sir John A. Macdonald*, stood by "with averted eyes" in his hour of need. After catching a cold, he died of complications on 2 June 1888. His friends in the Toronto press organized a fund for his orphaned children.

One of the pioneers of the new journalism aimed at the expanding newspaper readership in late 19th-century Canada, Fahey became expert in breaking up editorial matter into shorter, more pointed paragraphs, thus introducing new techniques of persuasion that would transform publicity in the early 20th century. The columns, or "paragraphs" as they were called by contemporaries, in which Fahey and others specialized proved a lighter, more digestible fare than the more formal editorial pages of established political organs. Humour, poetry, and anecdote were important components of Fahey's journalism and his appeal as a writer stemmed in part from his willingness to share his ironic views on life. As one of the many colourful figures whose personalities became familiar to readers of the English Canadian press of the 1870s and 1880s, Fahey played a small but important role in making the Canadian newspaper more generally accessible to a mass readership.

RUSSELL G. HANN

AO, MU 2307, James Fahey to T. C. Patteson, 1 Sept. 1876. PAC, MG 26, A; MG 30, C97. *Evening News* (Toronto), 2 May, 8 July 1881; 6 June 1888. *Globe*, 4, 5 June 1888. *Grip* (Toronto), 11 Dec. 1880. *Hamilton Spectator*, 29 Jan. 1872. *Irish Canadian* (Toronto), 16 Feb. 1882. *National* (Toronto), 26 Aug., 23 Sept. 1875. *Stratford Weekly Herald* (Stratford, Ont.), 4, 25 Aug. 1880. *Toronto Daily Mail*, August 1876–January 1877; 4–6 June 1888. *Toronto World*, 16 March; 2, 13, 21, 26 April; 14 May; 4–6 June 1888. P. D. Ross, *Retrospects of a newspaper person* (Toronto, 1931). P. F. W. Rutherford, "The people's press: the emergence of the new journalism in Canada, 1869–99," *CHR*, 56 (1975): 169–91.

FAIRBANKS, SAMUEL PRESCOTT, lawyer, politician, and civil servant; b. 31 Jan. 1795 at Halifax, N.S., son of Rufus Fairbanks and Ann Prescott, and brother of Charles Rufus Fairbanks*; m. 28 Sept. 1820 Charlotte Ann Newton, a granddaughter of Simeon Perkins*, and they had several children; d. 7 Dec. 1882 at Darmouth, N.S.

Samuel Prescott Fairbanks attended King's College, at Windsor, N.S., to which he matriculated on 3 Sept. 1810, a classmate of Thomas Chandler Haliburton*. Fairbanks was admitted to the bar at Halifax in 1818, and then moved to Liverpool, N.S., where he practised until 1845. He built a large double house and was active in the affairs of Trinity Church (Anglican) as vestryman and later warden. From 1836 to 1845 he represented Queens County in the Nova Scotia House of Assembly as a Conservative; he acted as registrar of the court of probate from 8 Nov. 1842 to 1847 and was appointed a QC on 1 May 1845.

In 1845 Fairbanks was asked by Lord Falkland [CARY], lieutenant governor of Nova Scotia, to become provincial treasurer, and he accepted on condition that the office not become a political appointment. Fairbanks thus was guaranteed the security of his appointment regardless of which party controlled the assembly. Falkland, however, had no justification for extending any promise about the nature of the appointment. In October 1839 Colonial Secretary Lord John Russell had written Governor Sir Colin Campbell* explicitly singling out the office of provincial treasurer as one which was to be dependent upon the confidence of the assembly.

The Liberals won the election of 1848 and no Tory appointee could hope for magnanimity from them. The matter of the provincial treasurer was aired in the legislature, the Colonial Office, and the Nova Scotia and British press. On 1 April 1848 the assembly gave third reading to a bill to abolish the post of provincial treasurer and create instead the two offices of financial secretary and receiver general. Fairbanks ceased to be provincial treasurer in July 1848, but he persistently petitioned the Executive Council for redress of what he considered a breach of faith on the part of government, and sought an appointment to some other public but non-political office.

The Liberal *Acadian Recorder* (Halifax) led the press in the fight against Fairbanks, boldly declaring in January 1849 that Fairbanks' appointment in March 1845 had been conceived in the mind of the Conservative leader James William Johnston* "in his anxiety to destroy Responsible and Departmental Government, and fasten his friends on the Treasury for Life." From the Colonial Office Earl Grey, in a dispatch of 1852, agreed that Fairbanks had been victimized but stated that any compensation was the responsibility of the provincial legislature. Thus, without becoming directly involved, Grey upheld the principle of responsible government while at the same time counselling, by implication, an end to the problem through magnanimous provincial action. Replying in September 1852 to a petition from Fairbanks presented by Sir John Harvey*, the Executive Council passed a motion declaring that while it did not "admit that any wrong has been done to Mr. Fairbanks" it was "disposed should a suitable opportunity offer to make provision for him." But the provincial secretary, Joseph Howe*, was unsympathetic, and Fairbanks met with little success. He was to wait a full decade before he could look to the provincial government for an appointment.

In 1857 the Conservatives were returned to office under J. W. Johnston, and on 31 December Fairbanks was appointed commissioner of crown lands with a salary of £500 per annum. In addition, he received an annual stipend of £400 as commissioner of mines, an arrangement which the colonial secretary, Henry Labouchere, viewed with "much gratification." The remainder of Fairbanks' career seems to have been relatively tranquil. In 1859 he applied for an increase in his stipend as commissioner of mines, saying that correspondence during his tenure had amounted to some 12,000 letters. On 26 August of the same year he was given added responsibility as commissioner for the protection and disposal of Indian lands. When he retired in 1872 the Liberal government granted him an annuity of $1,200 "during his life." A decade later he died at his Dartmouth home.

Fairbanks' career could hardly be termed colourful, yet it provides an interesting example of a man who was caught in the transition from executive to responsible government and who reacted in a very human way. Despite the *Acadian Recorder* his complaint seems sincere, and he himself must have realized there could be no turning back of the clock for he never asked to be reinstated as provincial treasurer. The fact that he served as a civil servant under three Liberal governments, one of them led by Howe, would seem to vindicate him in the face of those who initially opposed his requests for compensation.

JOHN G. LEEFE

Holy Trinity Anglican Church (Liverpool, N.S.), Registers (mfm. at PANS). PANS, RG 1, 102, 198–203a, 214½ G; RG 5, GP, 2. Private arch., Seth Bartling (Liverpool), R. J. Long, "The annals of Liverpool and Queen's County, 1760–1867" (1926) (typescript at Dalhousie Univ. Library, Halifax; mfm. at PANS). [John Inglis], *Memoranda respecting King's College, at Windsor, in Nova Scotia; collected and prepared for the purpose of making evident the leading object in suggesting and establishing that institution* (Halifax, 1836), 25. *Acadian Recorder*, 29 Jan., 30 April 1849. *Directory of N.S. MLAs*, 114. *Dominion annual register*, 1882: 196. T. B. Akins, "History of Halifax City," N.S. Hist. Soc., *Coll.*, 8 (1895); repub. as *History of Halifax City* (Belleville, Ont., 1973), 151, 234.

FALARDEAU, ANTOINE-SÉBASTIEN, painter; b. 13 Aug. 1822 at Cap-Santé, Lower Canada, son of Joseph Falardeau, a farmer, and Isabelle (Élizabeth) Savard (Savarre); drowned 14 July 1889 at Florence, Italy, when his horse bolted, throwing him into the river.

Antoine-Sébastien Falardeau apparently ran away from home at about 14 years of age and went to try his luck in Quebec. Thanks to an aunt, he found work at the house of Dr James Arthur Sewell. The nature of his artistic apprenticeship remains a mystery; it is known only that young Falardeau took courses in painting and that in 1841 he was an apprentice sign-painter with Robert Clow Todd* while also working as a clerk in Quebec. The Italian painter G. Fassio*, who had been at Quebec since 1835, may have turned Falardeau's thoughts towards Italy and even taught him the rudiments of Italian. It is possible that the merchant Abraham Hamel, brother of Théophile*, supported his projects financially. But his relations with Théophile Hamel probably had little artistic significance.

On 14 Nov. 1846, with meagre resources, Antoine-Sébastien Falardeau left Quebec for Florence where he was to spend most of his life. It is thought that he studied at the academy of fine arts there, and that he won the first prize at the academy of fine arts in Parma for a copy of Correggio's *Il Giorno.* After some difficult years, he gained a reputation as a skilled artist and also some degree of wealth. Appointed a knight of the order of Saint-Louis on 17 Jan. 1852 by Charles III, Duke of Parma, on 7 Sept. 1861 he married Caterina Mannucci-Benincasa, daughter of the Marquis Francesco Mannucci-Benincasa Capponi; the couple had at least three children.

The comments of artist Napoléon Bourassa*, who lived near Falardeau in Florence in 1852, suggest that he was a meticulous man, devoted to work, enthusiastic, and resolute. "I have been surprised to see the strength of his character. . . . He is cheerful, and has the turn of mind to rouse the gravest of men to laughter. . . . He is the most scrupulously careful man imaginable." Finally, "he is quite as inflexible as I [am] in [his ideas], and does not understand how someone can think differently from himself." A year later, Bourassa wrote to Théophile Hamel: "Falardeau is doing well in Florence; he has set himself up this spring in accommodation which certainly suggests his taste, work, and thrift. . . . I believe that within ten years he will succeed in duplicating the contents of the galleries in Florence." Falardeau was above all a copier; Carlo Dolci and Guido Reni apparently were his favourites. He also did "excellent drawings from nature." We know that he painted portraits. In 1882, for example, the Canadian government commissioned him to do a portrait of former Quebec Premier Joseph-Adolphe Chapleau* for $500. In his book on the artist, Émile Falardeau expressed the opinion that he executed more than 300 original paintings. There is, however, no evidence to support the assertion.

Falardeau's career in Italy was followed with interest by his compatriots in Canada. He made two brief visits to Canada in 1862 and 1882, on both occasions exhibiting his work. Montreal and Quebec newspapers pointed with pride to his success abroad and encouraged "art lovers to go and admire the works of a Canadian artist who brings such honour to Canada." The public response was enthusiastic enough that Antoine Plamondon*, who could brook no rival, took the offensive and denounced copies made by artists in Italy.

Antoine-Sébastien Falardeau's paintings have been so widely dispersed that a study of his work is likely to remain impossible. There certainly are a number of works in Italy; others, bought by tourists, have gone into oblivion, a common fate for copies. Are there many in Canada? According to newspaper articles published during his visits to Canada he brought more than 100 paintings in 1862 and sold them at Quebec and Montreal, and in 1882 sold 75 canvases at prices ranging from $20 to $250. He also did a collection in 1857 for Dr George Ansel Sterling Ryerson* of Toronto, and completed portraits and original works commissioned during his two stays and by visitors to Italy. Hence it can be asserted there were more than 200 paintings by Falardeau in Canada.

Although no assessment can be made of Falardeau's work as a whole, his talents as a copyist must be acknowledged. Napoléon Bourassa, who visited him every day, stated that "he has few equals at Florence among those who make copying their profession." His copies were "irreproachable," and his drawings from nature "excellent." Falardeau's marvellous little picture representing *Beatrice Cenci* (Guido Reni), now held by the Musée du Québec, gives a good idea of his talent. In the words of Henri-Raymond Casgrain*, he "has more charm than boldness, more subtlety and elegance than vigour, more exquisite delicacy and feeling than energy. He excels in perfection of finish, in poetry of execution. His miniatures have a truthfulness of tone, a purity of line, a transparency and freshness, a harmony of style and often a naïvety, that are delightful." Several of the 20 or so pictures held at the Musée du Québec are of this high quality.

RAYMOND VÉZINA

Private arch., Anne Bourassa (Montréal), Lettre de Napoléon Bourassa à Charles Laberge, 19 déc. 1852; Madeleine Hamel (Québec), Lettre de Napoléon Bourassa à Théophile Hamel, décembre 1853. IBC, Centre de documentation, Fonds Morisset, 2, F177/A634.7.

Le Canadien, 16 nov. 1846. *Le Journal de Québec*, 22 août 1862. *La Minerve*, 2, 17, 19, 22 juill. 1862; 10, 18 juill. 1882. Georges Bellerive, *Artistes-peintres canadiens-français; les anciens* (Québec, 1925). H.-R. Casgrain, *A. S. Falardeau et A. E. Aubry* (Montréal, 1912). Émile Falardeau, *Un maître de la peinture: Antoine-Sébastien Falardeau* (Montréal, 1936). A. H. Robson, *Canadian landscape painters* (Toronto, 1932).

FALKLAND, LUCIUS BENTINCK CARY, Viscount. *See* CARY

FARAUD, HENRI, priest, Oblate of Mary Immaculate, missionary, bishop, and author; b. 17 June 1823 at Gigondas, dept of Vaucluse, France, the youngest of the six children of François-Xavier Faraud and Madeleine Faurye; d. 26 Sept. 1890 at St Boniface, Man.

Henri Faraud received a classical education at the minor seminary of Notre-Dame-de-Lumières at Goult. He took his perpetual vows in 1844 and then spent two years studying for the priesthood at Notre-Dame de l'Osier, Isère. When Bishop Joseph-Norbert Provencher* sought additional missionaries to work with him in the northwest, Charles-Joseph-Eugène de Mazenod, the bishop of Marseilles and founder of the Oblates of Mary Immaculate, named Faraud to the missions in America. Leaving on 3 June 1846, Faraud reached St Boniface on 8 November after an arduous journey. While continuing his theological studies he worked with Abbé George-Antoine Bellecourt* until June 1847 to familiarize himself with Indian customs and the Ojibwa language. Made a sub-deacon in late April 1847 and a deacon on 1 May Faraud was ordained priest seven days later. That summer he went with Pierre AUBERT, the Oblate superior of the region, to minister to the Ojibwa Indians of Wabassimong (Whitedog, Ont.). However, the mission was quickly abandoned because of the apathy of the Indians, and by the end of July the two priests were back at St Boniface.

In June 1848 Bishop Provencher sent Faraud to replace Louis-François Laflèche* at Île-à-la-Crosse (Sask.); he worked there with Alexandre-Antonin Taché* who became a close friend. A year later he was appointed missionary in charge of the vast Lake Athabasca district. Faraud travelled from Île-à-la-Crosse over the Portage La Loche (Sask.) route, one of the Hudson's Bay Company's canoes taking him on board. By September he had reached Fort Chipewyan (Alta), where he established the first Catholic mission in the region, naming it La Nativité. For 10 months in 1849–50, Faraud laboured alone in the mission which served an area stretching from the Peace River to the Arctic Ocean. Then, feeling the need for personal renewal through contact with his fellow priests, he made the 750-mile return trip from La Nativité to Île-à-la-Crosse. In October 1852 his first companion, Father Pierre-Henri Grollier*, arrived at Lake Athabasca. Faraud set up a permanent mission at Fort Resolution (N.W.T.), on Great Slave Lake. When Bishop Provencher died in 1853, Taché succeeded him as superior of the Oblates in the west, and he chose Faraud as one of his councillors.

Foreseeing the Hudson's Bay Company's loss of its monopoly of the fur trade, and subsequent refusal to transport missionaries and their stores, in 1855 Bishop Taché got Faraud to agree that the mission at Lake La Biche (Alta) should become the supply base and point of departure for journeys to the north. Fathers Jean Tissot and Augustin Maisonneuve were dispatched to the mission in order to move it to a more suitable location six miles from Fort Lac-la-Biche and put it on a firm footing; they introduced farming on a large scale, and in 1856 even laid a 100-mile corduroy road to Fort Pitt (Sask.) for Red River carts. In 1855 Father Vital-Justin Grandin* and Brother Patrick Bowes had received their authorizations to come to the Athabasca district, and Brother Alexis Reynard* arrived the following year. These new recruits made it possible for Faraud to carry the gospel ever farther afield and in the course of time some 20 other missions were established.

Without Faraud's knowledge Taché and Grandin joined the archdiocese of Quebec in 1860 to request Rome to detach the Athabasca–Mackenzie district from the diocese of St Boniface as a vicariate apostolic, and to appoint Faraud its first incumbent. To facilitate matters Faraud was summoned in 1861 to Île-à-la-Crosse, which was closer to St Boniface, and Grandin undertook a three-year tour of the northern missions. Taché, when he went to Paris to attend the general chapter of the Oblates, also paid a visit to the Vatican, where his plan was adopted and the papal bulls were signed on 13 May 1863. In August Faraud left for Europe, and on 30 November he was consecrated bishop of Anemour.

On his return Faraud stayed in Montreal for a couple of weeks to supervise the printing of some books in Indian languages which he had put together over the years. He had also taught reading in syllabic signs to many of his flock. At the end of the summer of 1865 he made his way to his vicariate via the Portage La Loche. His life as a missionary did not change significantly, but his responsibilities increased. Anticipating his inability to cope with them single-handed, he had secured permission from Pius IX on 3 Aug. 1864 to select an auxiliary without right of succession; he was to make his choice in consultation with the vicariate's staff and to consecrate him in the north. Isidore Clut*, who had been his assistant at La Nativité since 1858, was selected and appointed bishop of Arindel in 1864.

Faraud spent the next two decades at Lake La Biche, which became his episcopal see in 1869. He left it only three times: in 1872 he travelled to Europe where he spent two years begging for help to ensure the survival of his missions; in 1879–80 he undertook a visitation of his vicariate; and in 1889 he was summoned to St Boniface by Taché for the first council held in western Canada. Taché found him so aged by 40 years of hardship and by the liver disease which had long undermined his health that he persuaded him to ask for Father Émile-Jean-Baptiste-Marie Grouard* as a successor and to submit his resignation; Faraud complied on 20 March 1890.

During an ordination at the Collège de Saint-Boniface on 26 Sept. 1890 Faraud was overcome by faintness and died a few hours later. He was buried in the crypt of the cathedral of St Boniface, beside Bishop Provencher.

E. O. DROUIN

Henri Faraud was the author of [*Petite histoire sainte, en montagnais et en caractères syllabiques*] (Paris, 1876; réimpr., Montréal, 1932), and *Dix-huit ans chez les sauvages: voyages et missions . . . dans l'extrême nord de l'Amérique britannique d'après les documents de Mgr l'évêque d'Anemour*, [F.-F.] Fernand-Michel, compil. (Paris et Bruxelles, 1866; réimpr., East Ardsley, Angl., et New York, 1966). Other works, both published and in manuscript, are available at Arch. hist. oblates (Ottawa).

A.-A. Taché, *Vingt années de missions dans le Nord-Ouest de l'Amérique* (Montréal, 1866). P.-J.-B. Duchaussois, *Aux glaces polaires; Indiens et Esquimaux* (Lyon, [1921?]); *Les sœurs grises dans l'Extrême-Nord: cinquante ans de missions . . .* (Montréal, 1917). A.-G. Morice, *Histoire de l'Église catholique dans l'Ouest canadien du lac Supérieur au Pacifique (1659–1915)* (3v., Winnipeg et Montréal, 1912). Théophile Ortolan, *Cent ans d'apostolat dans les deux hémisphères: les Oblats de Marie Immaculée durant le premier siècle de leur existence* (4v., Paris, 1914–32).

FAREWELL, ABRAM (Abraham), merchant, contractor, and politician; b. 21 Dec. 1812 at Harmony, Whitby Township, Upper Canada, the fifth child of Acheus Moody Farewell and Elizabeth Annis; m. 18 Jan. 1837 Caroline Stone; d. 8 Feb. 1888 at Oshawa, Ont.

Abram Farewell received his early education at a local school in Whitby Township, and became an avid reader, particularly of political and constitutional works. He taught school in Whitby Township before joining his father's mercantile and produce business at Harmony in 1830. Seven years later he built a large store there. The business prospered, and later he entered the grain export trade; he was also part-owner of several ships which carried grain to American ports. In 1852 Farewell was an incorporator and shareholder of the Oshawa Manufacturing Company, a large-scale maker of agricultural implements. Three years later he joined the syndicate of millers, including William GAMBLE and James Gooderham WORTS, which founded the Bank of Toronto. By 1860 he had sold his shares in the bank and owned instead 200 shares worth $8,000 in the Ontario Bank. The latter, chartered in 1857, was controlled by Montreal financiers such as John Starnes from the Montreal City and District Savings Bank.

Farewell was an early advocate of the development of Ontario County through the construction of gravel roads and railways. In particular in the 1840s he advocated improving Simcoe Street by making it a toll-road so that the Oshawa–Harmony area would be better able to handle trade in grain and timber coming from Port Perry, the collection centre for the northern part of the county; Whitby had such an advantage with Port Perry because of a separate toll-road. In the 1850s he also predicted that unless a railway was built from Georgian Bay to Whitby, control of the inland grain and timber trade would be seized by Toronto and Port Hope interests. Although ridiculed at first by the ratepayers in Pickering and Whitby townships and Oshawa, who would have had to support the costly railway with their taxes, by 1867 Farewell's ideas were being taken up in response to the impending construction of the Toronto and Nipissing Railway. In 1868 he was one of the incorporators of the Port Whitby and Port Perry Railway Company; although construction was completed on 31 Aug. 1870 the line was too late to prevent the loss of trade funnelled to Toronto by the Toronto and Nipissing. In later life Farewell was a member of the contracting firm of Sifton, Ward and Company which built about 130 miles of the Canadian Pacific Railway track between Fort William (now part of Thunder Bay), Ont., and Selkirk, Man.

Throughout his life, Farewell took an active part in local Reform politics. Although a "radical," he had joined other Whitby Township Reformers in severing relations with William Lyon Mackenzie* over the constitutional issue in September 1837, and in December refused to follow Mackenzie in open rebellion. The next year, the steamer on which Farewell was making his semi-annual buying trip to Montreal was sunk by rebels in the canal at Beauharnois and he was held captive on the seigneury of Edward Ellice* for several weeks. This experience made him a lifelong enemy of Mackenzie and a strong advocate of constitutional methods to achieve political change.

Farewell entered public life in 1843 when he was elected to the Home District Council; he remained in office until 1849. Although opposed to the separation for administrative purposes of Ontario County from York, which came about in 1851, because he feared higher taxes would be imposed, Farewell was elected to the Ontario County Council, and was deputy reeve for Whitby Township, in 1854, 1856, and 1857. He was also a perennial candidate for parliament, but enjoyed little success. Too radical a Clear Grit to receive support from the "practical" Reformers, he was usually defeated by "moderates" who could command both Reform and Conservative support. He was defeated in the riding of Ontario South by John M. Lumsden in 1854, and in 1857, when the constituency's Reform association split between radical and moderate factions, Farewell withdrew in favour of Oliver Mowat* who was elected in 1858. In 1860 he contested King's Division for the Legislative Council, but lost to David Reesor of Markham.

When Mowat was appointed vice-chancellor of the Court of Chancery in Canada West in 1864, Farewell contested Ontario South on an anti-confederation platform, but was narrowly defeated in an extremely corrupt election by Thomas Nicholson GIBBS, who was supported by John A. Macdonald*. In 1871 Farewell finally won the provincial seat of Ontario South, defeating Dr William McGill, the sitting member; however, he lost to Nicholson William Brown, a Whitby industrialist, in 1875.

Farewell was a member of the Disciples of Christ Church and was a strong supporter of all aspects of its work. Also actively involved in the temperance movement, in 1855 he toured several American states which had enacted prohibitory liquor laws and interviewed leading public figures concerning the results. His findings were published that year in a pamphlet written jointly with George P. Ure entitled *The Maine law illustrated.* Afterwards he campaigned on behalf of the Canadian Prohibitory Liquor Law League and as president was primarily responsible for the establishment of a number of temperance organizations in Ontario County.

LEO A. JOHNSON

Abram Farewell was the author, with G. P. Ure, of *The Maine law illustrated: being the result of an investigation made in the Maine law states* (Toronto, 1855).

AO, MU 2576, Scrapbook 11: 99. PAC, MG 24, B40, 7: 1620; MG 26, A. *Globe*, 16 Jan. 1857. *North Ontario Observer and General Advertiser* (Port Perry, [Ont.]), 12 Dec. 1857, 20 June 1867, 9 March 1871, 31 Dec. 1874, 24 Feb. 1876. *Oshawa Reformer* (Oshawa, Ont.), 22 Jan. 1875, 4 Oct. 1878, 13 Feb. 1880. *Oshawa Vindicator* (Oshawa), 28 Aug. 1867; 18 March 1869; 15, 22 March, 7 June 1871. *Pickering News* (Pickering, Ont.), 13 April 1883. *Whitby Chronicle* (Whitby, Ont.), 10 Dec. 1857, 20 June 1867, 13 April 1883. J. E. [C.] Farewell, *County of Ontario; short notes as to the early settlement and progress of the county . . .* (Belleville, Ont., 1973; first pub. with: Ontario County, *By-laws of the council . . .* (Whitby, 1907)). W. H. Higgins, *The life and times of Joseph Gould . . .* (Toronto, 1887; repr. Belleville, 1972). M. M. Hood, *Oshawa . . . a history of "Canada's motor city"* (Oshawa, 1968). L. A. Johnson, *History of the county of Ontario, 1615–1875* (Whitby, 1973), 142, 147, 187, 217, 237, 239, 241, 248. J. D. Ross, *Education in Oshawa from settlement to city* ([Oshawa?], 1970).

FARRAR, GEORGE WHITEFIELD (Whitfield), potter; b. 29 April 1812 at Fairfax, Vt, son of Isaac Brown Farrar and Alma Lawrence; m. 25 Sept. 1836 Sophia Adams Winslow at Barre, Mass., and they had three sons and one daughter; d. 28 Jan. 1881 at Iberville, Que.

George Whitefield Farrar came of a family whose roots in North America went back to the 17th century, to Jacob Farrar, who emigrated from England to Massachusetts in or about 1653. In the 18th century George's father settled in Vermont and eventually established a pottery at Fairfax. It was at this pottery that George received his training.

He continued as a potter in Fairfax until the 1850s, when he crossed the Canadian border to Saint-Jean (Saint-Jean-sur-Richelieu). Other members of the extensive Farrar clan had for some years been engaged in potting there and had introduced the making of stoneware to the area. In 1857 he entered into a partnership in Saint-Jean with his potter-brother, Ebenezer Lawrence Farrar. The partnership was announced in the Saint-Jean *News and Frontier Advocate* as effective from 13 April 1857. It was short-lived, for less than three months later Ebenezer lost his life in the burning of the steamboat *Montréal* on the St Lawrence. George W. Farrar carried on the business in Saint-Jean, and across the Richelieu River at Iberville after fire destroyed the Saint-Jean plant in 1876. He was joined, when they were old enough, by his sons; the two who had most to do with the pottery were George Henry and Ebenezer Lawrence. At various periods the pottery was officially operated under his sons' names, but he always maintained an interest in it. After his death it continued in the family name until 1926 when George H. Farrar sold it. The pottery closed in the early 1930s.

The Farrars' products were the common earthenware and stoneware of the North American potter.

Articles produced were almost entirely utilitarian: snuff jars, bottles, spittoons, jugs, teapots, butter pots. Within this range, quality was good. George W. Farrar was awarded a medal for earthenware at the provincial fair in Montreal in 1860; under his sons' names the factory's stoneware was exhibited abroad, at Philadelphia (1876) and Paris (1878). In 1861 the pottery used up some 500 tons of clay (stoneware clay was imported from New Jersey) and employed 18 hands. By the 1870s steam power had been installed and 40 persons were on the payroll; the pottery was now one of the largest in Canada.

But George W. Farrar's accomplishments did not end with the production of dark-bodied earthenware and salt-glazed stoneware. He was the promoter of the St Johns Stone Chinaware Company, the first whiteware pottery in Canada, established in 1873. Because, like most Canadian potters, Farrar never made much money, he lacked capital to embark on such an ambitious venture as the formation of the company on his own, but his was the moving spirit behind it. Much of the required capital came from Edward C. MACDONALD, the company's president and a "merchant prince" of Saint-Jean, who bought the company outright when it slipped into bankruptcy in 1877. Farrar himself was connected with it for only a brief period – he withdrew early to take back the management of his own pottery – yet his had been the vision of a new dimension in Canadian potting: the first commercial production of whiteware.

The *News and Frontier Advocate* summed up his importance when George W. Farrar, a former councillor of Saint-Jean, died in 1881: "Mr. Farrar encountered many difficulties in this country but he was . . . ever enthusiastic in his schemes. He was undoubtedly the promoter of the St. Johns Chinaware . . . factory, which is at present doing such a large and flourishing business and as he was but a short time connected with the concern, its lack of success at the outset cannot certainly be laid to his charge."

ELIZABETH COLLARD

[Examples of wares from the pottery operated by George Whitefield Farrar and his sons are to be seen in a number of Canadian museums, including the National Museum of Man (Ottawa), the Musée du Québec, the Montreal Museum of Fine Arts, the McCord Museum (Montreal), and the Royal Ontario Museum (Toronto). Farrar family papers are in the possession of Mrs Effie Farrar Sutherland (Montreal). E.C.]

AP, St Johns United Church (Saint-Jean-sur-Richelieu), Register of acts of civil status, I: 197. PAC, RG 31, A1, 1861, 1871 censuses, Saint-Jean, Que. Can., Canadian Commission at the International Exhibition of Philadelphia, 1876, *Report* (Ottawa, 1877). *Montreal Gazette*, 5 Oct. 1860, 23 Sept. 1863. *Morning Chronicle* (Quebec), 4 July 1857. *News and Frontier Advocate* (Montreal and St Johns [Saint-Jean-sur-Richelieu]), 24 April 1857. *Quebec Mercury*, 23 July 1857. *Canada directory*, 1857–58. *Eastern Townships gazetteer & directory, for the years 1875–76 . . .* (Montreal, 1875). J.-B.-A. Allaire, *Histoire de la paroisse de Saint-Denis-sur-Richelieu (Canada)* (Saint-Hyacinthe, Que., 1905). C.H. Chandler and S.F. Lee, *The history of New Ipswich, New Hampshire, 1735–1914, with genealogical records of the principal families* (Fitchburg, Mass., 1914). Elizabeth Collard, *Nineteenth-century pottery and porcelain in Canada* (Montreal, 1967). H.H. Lambart, *Two centuries of ceramics in the Richelieu valley: a documentary history*, ed. Jennifer Arcand (Ottawa, 1970), 5–14. Lura Woodside Watkins, *Early New England potters and their wares* (Cambridge, Mass., 1950). Donald Webster, *Early Canadian pottery* (Toronto, 1971).

FAUQUIER, FREDERICK DAWSON, Church of England clergyman and bishop; b. probably 29 July 1817; m. *c.* 1846 Sarah Burrowes (Burroughs), and they had at least two sons; d. 7 Dec. 1881 in Toronto, Ont.

Records concerning Frederick Dawson Fauquier are few and little is known of his antecedents. He is said to have been born in Malta, where, presumably, his father was in the service of the British government. At the time of his death it was stated that he had been orphaned in childhood and sent to England as the ward of an aunt "who had rooms allotted to her in Hampton Court Palace"; Thomas Fauquier, a member of the royal household who with his wife had apartments in this palace until his death around 1841, was probably an uncle. Fauquier seems to have been educated in England, perhaps in Richmond (now part of Greater London) at an academy for boys whose parents were serving abroad. Some basis for the suggestion that he was an orphan is provided by the fact that he did not proceed to university but in 1836 immigrated to Upper Canada, where he farmed at East Zorra, near Woodstock.

While at East Zorra, Fauquier came under the eye of Edward Huntingford, whose father had built a church for the settlers and who himself ministered in it after his arrival from England in 1844. It has been claimed that when Huntingford returned to England in 1845 he urged Fauquier to seek ordination so that he might succeed to the charge, but this story does not seem completely in accord with the evidence. Fauquier went to study under Alexander Neil Bethune* at the Diocesan Theological Institution, opened in Cobourg in January 1842. Its curriculum required a three-year residence and, if Fauquier spent the full three years there, he must have been one of the institution's first students as he was made deacon in 1845. He was ordained priest in 1846 by Bishop John Strachan*, his stipend being paid by the Society for the Propagation of the Gospel. He continued to farm and seems to have married about this time. His ministry in East Zorra, his only parochial charge, seems to have been quiet and effective but not otherwise outstanding.

When the establishment of the diocese of Algoma was being discussed in 1872, Fauquier was nominated by the Canadian bishops for election as bishop, apparently on the suggestion of his diocesan in Huron, Isaac Hellmuth*. A contemporary noted that few would have considered "this gentle, simple, modest incumbent of a small country parish" for a bishopric. That Hellmuth, "a professed Low Churchman, should have put forward in so marked a manner almost the only High Churchman in his diocese, spoke volumes in his favour." But it was a time when tensions over churchmanship were strong and sometimes bitter. Fauquier was remembered to have been a pupil of Bethune, then bishop of Toronto, and he was rejected by the laity. John Philip DuMoulin*, rector of St Thomas' Church, Hamilton, was elected, but after the synod had dispersed he declined the honour. A second session of the electoral synod was held in 1873, and Fauquier, who in the mean time had been created archdeacon of Brant, was elected on the third ballot.

The new bishop of Algoma was consecrated in Toronto by the metropolitan of Canada, Ashton Oxenden*, on 28 Oct. 1873 in St James' Cathedral. Trinity College, Toronto, conferred an honorary DCL upon Fauquier the following year. Immediately after his consecration he left for Collingwood and, travelling by lake steamer, arrived at Sault Ste Marie on 6 November. His diocese comprised a vast area stretching from the head of Lake Superior to the Muskoka region, within a hundred miles or so of Toronto. The population was sparse and missionary work had been intermittent, concentrated chiefly in the vicinity of Prince Arthur's Landing (later renamed Port Arthur and now part of Thunder Bay, Ont.), Sault Ste Marie, Manitoulin Island, and Muskoka. There were but seven clergy and nine churches.

Partly because of his wife's chronic ill health, but also for convenience, Fauquier lived during the winter months in Toronto. Thence he was able to visit the southern part of his diocese and to carry on the fund-raising tours which plagued the lives of missionary bishops. One of his constant complaints was that an adequate endowment fund had not been established for the diocese before its foundation. While in residence at Sault Ste Marie, Fauquier continued his practice of farming the property surrounding his home with the help of a hired man. He travelled regularly throughout his huge diocese, and on going into a community visited all the inhabitants, by whom he came to be well known and greatly loved.

It is difficult to glean much of Fauquier's thought and teaching. His diaries, for the years 1878, 1880, and 1881, are concerned with day-to-day events, mainly ecclesiastical, and contain little reflection on the issues of the time. Although he frequently preached extemporaneously, he also kept written sermon notes but these have disappeared. A solid churchman, although not a ritualist, he emphasized the sacramental life, as was to be expected of one trained under Bethune. In his parochial ministry he usually celebrated the Eucharist monthly. In his episcopal visits, particularly to isolated places, he stressed the sacraments of baptism and Eucharist and did all he could to provide opportunities for their reception. Concerned with the well-being of the Ojibwas, he encouraged the building of a combined school and chapel at Batchawana, north of Sault Ste Marie, but the venture was short-lived. More enduring were the Shingwauk and Wawanosh schools, for Indian boys and girls respectively, opened in 1873 and 1879. Their chief architect was the Reverend Edward Francis Wilson, but they had the warm support of Bishop Fauquier and his wife. Like most of his contemporaries, Fauquier saw the interests of the native peoples as being best served by assimilation to the white majority. He perceived the Indian schools as training grounds: "It is thought that they [the Indians], when properly prepared, will be able to work with their red brethren, and work more effectually amongst them, both for *evangelization* and *civilization*, than white men can be expected to do."

Fauquier's wife fell seriously ill in the fall of 1881 and they set out for the south in search of warmer weather. The journey was never completed; she died on 4 November at her brother's home at Mount Vernon, N.Y. The distraught bishop returned to Toronto, where he himself died on 7 December. A few hours before his death he wrote sadly to Wilson of the deepening void created by his wife's passing: "How true it is that we seldom appreciate our blessings and privileges until they are taken from us." The bodies of Bishop and Mrs Fauquier were taken to Sault Ste Marie, and were interred in the Shingwauk cemetery on 22 May 1882.

During his brief episcopate Fauquier laid the foundation for later work. By the time of his death there were 34 churches, seven parsonages, and an impressive see house at the Sault, the house built largely through the generosity of the Baroness Burdett-Coutts. Perhaps more important, he had gathered around him 13 clergy and a number of lay workers who shared his vision for the church in Algoma. He was succeeded as bishop of Algoma by Edward Sullivan*.

F. A. PEAKE

Anglican Church of Canada, Diocese of Algoma Arch. (Sault Ste Marie, Ont.), F. D. Fauquier, Diaries, 1878, 1880, 1881. A. N. Bethune, *Memoir of the Right Reverend John Strachan, D. D., LL.D., first bishop of Toronto* (Toronto and London, 1870). Church of England, Ecclesiastical Prov. of Canada, Synod, *Journal of the proc.* (Quebec and Montreal), 1874, 1877, 1880. *Algoma Missionary News and Shingwauk Journal* (Sault Ste Marie), 1877–81. *Evangelical Churchman* (Toronto), 15 Dec. 1881. C. H. Mockridge, *The bishops of the Church of England in Canada and Newfoundland* . . . (Toronto, 1896). C. F. Pascoe, *Two hundred years of the S.P.G.: an historical account of the Society for the Propagation of the Gospel in Foreign Parts, 1701–1900* . . . (2v., London, 1901). O. R. Rowley *et al.*, *The Anglican episcopate of Canada and Newfoundland* (2v., Milwaukee, Wis., and Toronto, 1928–61). D. M. Landon, "Frederick Dawson Fauquier: pioneer bishop of Algoma," Canadian Church Hist. Soc., *Journal* ([Toronto]), 11 (1969): 75–87.

FERRIER, JAMES, merchant, politician, railway promoter, and capitalist; b. 22 Oct. 1800 in Fife, Scotland; m. Mary Todd, and they had at least two sons and two daughters; d. 30 May 1888 in Montreal, Que.

James Ferrier emigrated from Scotland to Montreal in 1821 after several years of employment in a Perth mercantile house. He worked 18 months for a Montreal merchant and then opened the first store on Rue Notre-Dame, a residential street which soon became part of the city's commercial hub. By 1836, when he withdrew from full-time involvement in trade, Ferrier had accumulated a substantial fortune not only from his store but also from the extensive real estate holdings he had acquired in the city. With Joseph Masson* and Harrison STEPHENS he was considered among the wealthiest Montrealers of the mid 19th century.

Using capital acquired during his early career, James Ferrier turned to larger financial ventures. With Augustin Cuvillier*, Albert Furniss, and William Edmonstone he was on the Montreal board of directors of the Bank of British North America, a British-based bank that began operations in Upper and Lower Canada under royal charter in the spring of 1837 with a nominal capital of £1,000,000. Ferrier was one of the incorporators of Molsons Bank in 1855 along with Montreal businessmen such as William Molson*, and he was a shareholder in several other Canadian banks. A promoter and long-time director of the New City Gas Company from its foundation in 1847, he was also active in the Montreal Fire Assurance Company, serving as its president for six years, an incorporator of the Montreal Credit Company with Hugh ALLAN in 1871, and in later years a director of two other insurance companies, the Guarantee Company of North America and the Accident Insurance Company of North America.

By 1847 Ferrier had considerable investments in his son James's hardware firm, Bryson and Ferrier. In 1851 that partnerhsip was dissolved and James Jr was joined by his brother George Davies in the wholesale and retail hardware firm of Ferrier and Company. The credit agents of R. G. Dun and Company reported in 1856 that the young men were "brought up to & understand their bus[iness] well." "The firm is called hot here, both on acct of good char[acter] & ability of the Partners, & the belief is that in case of any difficulty, the father would protect their paper." James Ferrier Sr was reported to have advanced from $30,000 to $35,000 to his sons, and he retained undisclosed investments in the firm at least until it began to encounter financial difficulties in the mid 1870s. Ferrier continued to help his son James by purchasing partnerships for him in the Horse Nail Works, Ausable Chasm, N.Y., at $25,000 and the Horse Nail Works, Pointe-Saint-Charles (now part of Montreal), at $31,000. His son began to diversify his business interests in later years, and, after that, it becomes increasingly difficult to distinguish the financial involvements of father and son.

Venturing into industrial development in Canada East, James Sr leased and operated the Saint-Maurice ironworks from 1847 to 1851 and was a promoter and president of the Montreal Mining Company. Not surprisingly, his extensive business, financial, and industrial connections led to active involvement in two of Montreal's most important railways, the Montreal and Lachine and the Grand Trunk. The former, chartered in 1846, was the first line built on the island of Montreal, and Ferrier was elected its president. Under his direction £75,000 in share capital was raised and the seven-mile line was in operation by mid November 1847. The Montreal and Lachine became the launching pad for an ambitious programme of railway expansion: the St Lawrence and Ottawa Grand Junction (never constructed) to go northwest from Lachine into the hinterland of the St Lawrence and Ottawa rivers, and the Lake St Louis and Province Line, united in 1850 with the Montreal and Lachine to form the Montreal and New York Railroad, to go south through Plattsburgh to New York City. After a series of costly and inconclusive battles with rival railways the Montreal and New York was brought into the Champlain and St Lawrence Railroad, which then became the Montreal and Champlain Railroad in 1857, and was soon in turn absorbed by the Grand Trunk. Although Ferrier had resigned from the presidency of the Montreal and Lachine and its branches in 1851, perhaps because of its increasing financial difficulties, he served as chairman of the Canadian board of directors of the Grand Trunk until his death, and was as well a director of the International Bridge Company, a Grand Trunk venture. He was also involved in other transportation projects such as the Canadian and West Indian Royal Mail Steamship Company and the Waterloo, Magog and Stanstead Railway. For Ferrier and Montreal businessmen like him, railways were a source of power and profit for their promoters, the financial institutions they represented, and the Montreal community at large.

In the political life of Montreal during the 1840s, Ferrier played an important role, first as an appointed member of the municipal council in 1841. After council positions became elective, he was alderman for East Ward in 1844. In 1845 he became mayor of the city; during his term in office he organized relief for the citizens of the Quebec City *faubourg* of Saint-Roch who were suffering the effects of a severe fire. On 27 May 1847 Ferrier was appointed to the Legislative Council where he remained until confederation. In 1867 he became a member of the dominion Senate and represented Victoria in the Legislative Council of Quebec; he held both posts until his death and was particularly active on the council's private bills and railway committees. Like many other prominent businessmen of the era, Ferrier served as a justice of the peace and held the post of lieutenant-colonel in the local militia.

He also took an active part in religious and philanthropic endeavours. Several times president of the St Andrew's Society, he also played a leading role at McGill College, as a member from 1845 until his death and as president from 1845 to 1852 of the Royal Institution for the Advancement of Learning, which in the latter year became the college's governing body. The restoration of financial stability and order to McGill's affairs after a period of great difficulty and uncertainty during the 1840s has been attributed largely to his efforts. In September 1884 he was appointed chancellor of McGill. He had travelled extensively throughout Europe, Africa, and Asia, and souvenirs of his travels were donated to the Natural History Society of Montreal and to McGill. Although he was originally a member of the Presbyterian St Gabriel Street Church, his numerous associations with John Torrance* and his sympathies for the Methodists led to his becoming a member of the St James Street Methodist Church, which he devoutly attended and where he regularly taught a Sunday school class. In addition he advanced the cause of Methodism throughout the city by contributing generously to the building of churches in Griffintown and in several suburbs. Ferrier filled almost every office open to a layman and served often as a delegate to its many conferences where he spoke strongly in favour of union of all Methodist churches. He took an interest in the Wesleyan Theological College in Montreal, was a member of the senate of Victoria College at Cobourg, Ont., was president of the Montreal Auxiliary Bible Society, and was an officer in both the Sabbath School Association of Canada and the French Canadian Missionary Society. He was, as well, active in the Montreal Protestant House of Industry and Refuge and in several temperance and prohibition societies, serving as president of the Quebec Temperance and Prohibitory League.

Ferrier died in Montreal following a brief illness; he was survived by his son James and one daughter, Margaret Watson, who had married John, son of David Torrance*. A sermon delivered at his funeral noted that "by his diligence and enterprise, combined with the strictest integrity, with clear intellect, a well-balanced judgment," and "a prompt and untiring energy," Ferrier had achieved commercial success. "He had deep convictions, firm Christian principles, and he shaped his life by them."

GERALD J. J. TULCHINSKY

AC, Montréal, Minutiers, J. W. Trenholme, 1 Jan. 1887. ANQ-Q, AP-G-134, Boîte 12. Baker Library, R. G. Dun & Co. credit ledger, Canada, 5: 35; 6: 35. McCord Museum (Montreal), J. H. Dorwin, "Antiquarian autographs." *Débats de la législature provinciale* (G.-A. Desjardins *et al.*), [III]: 254–57; [IV]: 385–86; IX: 327–29. Hugh Johnston, *Death abolished: a sermon preached . . . in St. James Street Methodist Church, Montreal, Sunday morning, October 9th, 1881, on the occasion of the death of Mrs. James Ferrier* (Montreal, 1881); *Memorial of the late Hon. Senator Ferrier, of Montreal: a sermon preached in St. James Street Methodist Church, on Sunday, June 3rd, 1888 . . .* (Toronto, 1888). Myles Pennington, *Railways and other ways: being reminiscences of canal and railway life during a period of sixty-seven years . . .* (Toronto, 1896). W. J. Rattray, *The Scot in British North America* (4v., Toronto, 1880–84), II: 602.

Gazette (Montreal), 31 May 1888. *La Minerve*, 12 mars 1853, 1 juin 1888. *Montreal Witness*, 8 June 1888. *La Patrie*, 1 juin 1888. Borthwick, *Hist. and biog. gazetteer*. *Canada, an encyclopædia* (Hopkins), I: 443–44, 478–90. *Canadian biog. dict.*, II: 242–47. *Canadian directory of parl.* (J. K. Johnson), 201. *CPC*, 1877: 92–93. Dent, *Canadian portrait gallery*, IV: 93–94. *Montreal directory*, 1852: 352. Notman and Taylor, *Portraits of British Americans*, I. Terrill, *Chronology of Montreal*. G. Turcotte, *Le Conseil législatif de Québec*, 291–92. Campbell, *Hist. of Scotch Presbyterian Church*. S. B. Frost, *McGill University: for the advancement of learning* (1v. to date, Montreal, 1980–). *Histoire de la corporation de la cité de Montréal depuis son origine jusqu'à nos jours . . .*, J.-C. Lamothe *et al.*, édit. (Montréal, 1903).

FIELD, ELIZABETH (Eliza) (Jones; Carey), author and painter; b. 1 June 1804 at Lambeth (now part of London), England, the eldest daughter of Charles Field, a wealthy soap and candle manufacturer, and Elizabeth Carter; m. first 8 Sept. 1833 Peter Jones [Kahkewaquonaby*]; m. secondly in 1858 John Carey of Muncey, Canada West; d. 17 Aug. 1890 at Brantford, Ont.

Eliza Field, a member of an affluent family, "spent eight happy years" in a boarding-school in Surrey, England, where she exhibited a talent for painting. After her mother's death in 1820 she returned home to assist in raising her six younger brothers and sisters. An intensely religious individual, she worshipped with her family at the evangelical Surrey Chapel and began teaching Sunday school there in 1823. Although she led a comfortable life, throughout her youth she felt "impatient" to do God's work, and as she recorded in her diary on 2 July 1832, she wanted "to be more useful – to be more entirely employed for the benefit of others." She had already met the man with whom she would undertake this endeavour.

In June 1831 Eliza had visited the home of friends in Bristol where Peter Jones, an Indian preacher from Canada touring England to raise money for Methodist Indian missions, was recuperating from illness. After he recovered he resumed his work and visited her in Lambeth. They saw one another constantly during the winter and in February Peter proposed. Eliza, deeply in love with the handsome Ojibwa and anxious to assist him in converting the North American Indian to Christianity, eagerly accepted. Her father and step-mother as well as many of her friends opposed her decision but, with the aid of character references for Peter, including one from his friend Egerton RYERSON (who was in England in 1833), the objections of her parents were eventually removed. After being separated for more than a year (Peter had returned to Canada in April 1832), the two were married in New York City on 8 Sept. 1833 by the Reverend Nathan Bangs.*

They took up residence in a small cabin on the Credit River Indian Reserve and Eliza's first years proved extremely difficult. Wherever she went with her husband they aroused great curiosity and her diary entry for 6 Sept. 1834 suggests her distress: "I desire to be enabled to feel charity to such who from the want of education or refined delicacy towards the feelings of a stranger make me an object of general observation." She also found it difficult to adjust from the luxury she had known in England to the hardships of life on an Indian reserve. A small woman, of delicate health, she frequently came down with fevers and between 1834 and 1836 she suffered two miscarriages and two still births. Nevertheless, she instructed the children on the reserve in Christianity and also taught the Indian girls sewing, a skill she had hastily acquired shortly before leaving Britain.

Elizabeth visited England with her niece Catherine Bunch Sonego [Nahnebahwequay*] in 1837–38 and after her return gave birth to a son, the first of four who survived infancy. In 1841 Peter was posted to the Muncey mission (near London, Canada West) where they remained until 1849. Following a brief stay in London they moved into a substantial brick house, Echo Villa, in Brantford in 1851; Peter was to die there five years later. Although the 1840s and 1850s were marked by Peter's severe illnesses as well as by the rejection on the part of some Ojibwas, led by Oominewahjeween (William Herchmer), of the Joneses' efforts to "Europeanize" the Indians and create "brown Englishmen," they were the years of greatest domestic happiness for the growing family.

During this time Eliza also pursued artistic and literary interests. In 1838 she published a *Memoir of Elizabeth Jones, a little Indian girl*, an account of the death of her pious niece, which was intended as a lesson for use in Sunday schools. She continued her painting and sketching, and won a prize at the Upper Canada Provincial Exhibition in 1854 for her miniature water-colours. After Peter's death she gathered together his diaries and an unfinished history of the Ojibwa; *Life and journals* appeared in 1860 and *History of the Ojebway Indians* appeared in 1861. She later wrote a sketch of Joseph Brant [Thayendanegea*], which ran serially in the *New Dominion Monthly* late in 1872, under her Ojibwa name Kecheahgahmequa (the lady from beyond the blue waters). Her diaries for various periods between 1829 and 1883 have been preserved, and offer, among other things, an opportunity to study her comments on Upper Canada as well as her impressions of her husband's people.

In 1858 Eliza had married John Carey, a white farmer from New York who had been the school teacher on the Muncey Reserve during the 1820s. The marriage was unhappy and Eliza may have left her second husband within several years. In one of her notebooks she recorded "my own tastes, & feelings & sympathies, were not and never could be in union with my husbands"; Carey did not have Peter's "natural refinement & amiable qualities." Continuing to make trips to England, she taught painting in Brantford, in addition to her writing, before she lost her sight about 1880. The last years of her life were spent in Lambeth Cottage, her home in Brantford, where she died on 17 Aug. 1890. She deserves to be remembered today for defying the social pressures against an inter-racial marriage and marrying the man she loved.

DONALD B. SMITH

Elizabeth Field was the author of *Memoir of Elizabeth Jones, a little Indian girl, who lived at the River-Credit Mission, Upper Canada* . . . (London, 1838; rev. ed., New York, 1841), and, as Ke-che-ah-gah-me-qua, "Sketch of the life of Captain Joseph Brant, Thayendanagea," *New Dominion Monthly* (Montreal), July–December 1872: 198–203, 276–82. She was also the author of "Brant's school-days," *New Dominion Monthly*, July–December 1872: 349–51.

Victoria Univ. Library (Toronto), Peter Jones coll., Eliza Jones Carey papers. Peter Jones (Kahkewaquonaby), *History of the Ojebway Indians; with especial reference to their conversion to Christianity* . . . , [ed. Elizabeth Field] (London, 1861). [Kahkewaquonaby], *Life and journals of Kah-ke-wa-quo-nā-by (Rev. Peter Jones), Wesleyan missionary*, [ed. Elizabeth Field] (Toronto, 1860). *Christian Guardian*, 5 Nov. 1890. D. B. Smith, "Eliza and the Reverend Peter Jones," *Beaver*, outfit 308 (autumn 1977); 40–46; "Peter and Eliza Jones: their last years," *Beaver*, outfit 308 (winter 1977); 16–23; "The transatlantic courtship of the Reverend Peter Jones," *Beaver*, outfit 308 (summer 1977): 4–13.

FINLAYSON, ISOBEL GRAHAM. *See* SIMPSON

FISBACH (Fitzbach, Fisbacht), MARIE (baptized **Marie-Joseph**; also known as **Marie-Geneviève**), named **Marie du Sacré-Cœur (Roy)**, founder of the Congregation of the Sisters, Servants of the Immaculate Heart of Mary (known as the Sisters of the Good Shepherd), and of the Asylum of the Good Shepherd; b. 16 Oct. 1806 at Saint-Vallier, Lower Canada, daughter of Charles Fisbacht, a day-labourer originally from Luxembourg, and Marie-Geneviève Nadeau; d. 1 Sept. 1885 at Quebec.

Marie Fisbach, whose father had died when she was very young, lived in a poverty-stricken home. While still a girl, she entered the service of the family of François-Xavier Roy, a merchant in Quebec's Upper Town; she married him on 17 April 1828 at Cap-Santé after the premature death of his wife. Five years later she was widowed and left in sole charge of her three daughters. Cheated of most of her assets by the guardians of her two step-children, she was obliged to become a "servant" once more, this time at the presbytery of Saints-Gervais et Protais (Saint-Gervais), in order to secure her children's future. In May 1846 her youngest daughter died, and the following September the two remaining daughters entered the ranks of the first postulants of the Grey Nuns of Quebec. A few weeks later Marie joined them as a boarder. There it was suggested that she take charge of a charitable organization "to help women in moral and social distress." The initiator of the project was an Irish lawyer, George Manly Muir, clerk of the Legislative Assembly; he was a militant Catholic, active in the Society of St Vincent de Paul. During the course of numerous visits to Quebec prisons, Muir had concluded that there was an urgent need to establish houses which would attempt to rehabilitate women after their release.

On 11 Jan. 1850 Marie Fisbach and a companion, Mary Keogh, a young Irish orphan, set up the Asile Sainte-Madeleine (later the Maison Marie-Fitzbach) in the *faubourg* Saint-Jean. They were joined by six helpers and took in 20 penitents in the first year; they then moved the home to larger quarters at the corner of Lachevrotière and Saint-Amable streets in the Saint-Louis district, at the time one of the poorest and most disreputable sections of the city. Here the work of the Sisters of the Good Shepherd of Quebec would establish itself. In 1852, convinced that social and moral education were needed to complete this initial work, the director of the home started two classes, one English and one French, for 90 pupils. For income the two endeavours relied on sewing, public collections, gifts and a weekly subscription of $2.50 from the Society of St Vincent de Paul, as well as aid in kind from the seminary, the Ursuline convent, and the Hôtel-Dieu.

In 19th-century Canada East, it was normal that a social service should lead to the founding of a religious community. On 30 May 1855 the Asylum of the Good Shepherd of Quebec was incorporated, and on 2 Feb. 1856 the sisters were established canonically as the Congregation of the Sisters, Servants of the Immaculate Heart of Mary. On this occasion seven women took the first perpetual vows in a ceremony under the direction of Marie Fisbach, who had become Sister Marie du Sacré-Cœur. To the public the nuns would always be the Sisters of the Good Shepherd, from the initial name of the home. They were often confused with the Sisters of the Good Shepherd of Angers, who had arrived in Canada in 1844 and directed several houses of re-education and rehabilitation in the Montreal region. In 1867 Rome recognized the existence of the new community; its constitutions received final approval in 1921.

At the first elections in 1856 Marie Fisbach, the founder, was elected superior; she had in fact acted in this capacity during the initial phases. But she did not command unanimous support and in 1859 she took the rank of assistant; one of her earliest companions, Marie de Saint-Vincent de Paul, succeeded her as superior. Some years later Marie Fisbach renounced elective office in order to live in solitude, relieved of an active apostolate. However, she followed with interest the expansion of her work, which continued throughout her lifetime and after her death.

A whole series of social welfare services developed from Marie Fisbach's activities. The religious sisters visited women prisoners and gave them shelter when they left prison; in addition, at the government's request, they founded a number of reformatory houses in 1870, and eventually in 1931 they assumed full responsibility for the women's prison. From 1874 they took unmarried mothers into "homes" for the duration of their pregnancies and then into hospitals set aside for them. They also opened the Crèche Saint-Vincent-de-Paul at Quebec for children slated for adoption, as well as the Marie-du-Temple nursery school at Pointe-aux-Trembles (Neuville, Quebec) to look after the intellectual and psychological development of these children. Finally, the sisters organized residences for elderly married women and, at Quebec, a Maison Béthanie where women pledged themselves, by a vow of constancy, to end their lives in prayer and atonement. And while they were providing a growing number of welfare services, the sisters were also extending their educational work with children who were economically and socially underprivileged.

The Sisters of the Good Shepherd early expanded their endeavours beyond Quebec City into various areas of the province, and even into the United States (1882). In time the congregation established itself in countries where there were missions – for instance, in the Union of South Africa in 1935, on the island of Grande Comore in 1958, and in Tunisia in 1965. Hence the statistics of the congregation for the 100 years or so from its foundation to 1950 are impressive.

In 1856 the Good Shepherd order numbered seven sisters, 31 protégées, and 150 pupils. By 1950 there were 1,283 sisters, 2,396 protégées, and 16,805 pupils. In 1975, 1,296 sisters were still looking after a large number of protégées and pupils but the growing socialization and secularization of social and educational services make it impossible to determine exactly the extent of their work.

ANDRÉE DÉSILETS

AC, Montmagny, État civil, Catholiques, Saint-Vallier, 17 oct. 1806. Arch. de la Maison généralice des sœurs du Bon-Pasteur de Québec, Statistiques, 1955, 1975. *Le Canadien*, 2 sept. 1885. Le Jeune, *Dictionnaire*, I: 205–7. Papin Archambault, *Sur les pas de Marthe et de Marie, congrégation de femmes au Canada* (Montréal, 1929). L.-P. Audet, *Le système scolaire*, I: 77–86. [H.-R. Casgrain], *L'asile du Bon-Pasteur de Québec d'après les Annales de cet institut* (Québec, 1896). [Angèle Barabé, dite sœur Sainte-Henriette], *Le Bon-Pasteur de Québec; un siècle d'histoire* (Québec, 1949). [Georgianna Juneau, dite sœur Saint-Paul de la Croix], *Mère Marie du Sacré-Cœur (1806–1885), fondatrice du Bon-Pasteur de Québec et ses collaboratrices* (Québec, 1935). [Émilie Langlois, dite sœur Marie du Carmel], *Les temps héroïques de notre histoire, 1850–1856* (Québec, n.d.). Sœur Marie d'Israël [Marguerite Jean], "Marie-Geneviève Fitzbach & le Bon-Pasteur de Québec," Assoc. des religieuses enseignantes du Québec, *Bull.* (Québec), 3 (1964): 239–49. Sœur Saint-Antoine de Jésus [Irma Deschênes], "Une communauté du Québec," *L'Action* (Québec), 12 déc. 1967: 9.

FORGUES, MICHEL, priest and teacher; b. 13 Feb. 1811 at Saint-Michel, Lower Canada, son of Michel Forgues and Marie-Anne Denis; d. 28 Nov. 1882 at Saint-Laurent, Île d'Orléans, Que.

Michel Forgues entered the Petit Séminaire de Québec as a boarder in 1826 and completed classical studies in 1834 with a brilliant record. As seminarist he taught literature classes from 1834 to 1840; during this period he was ordained priest on 23 Sept. 1837. Leaving the seminary in 1840, he served in the parish of Sainte-Marguerite-de-Dorchester for five years and then in Sainte-Marie-de-la-Nouvelle-Beauce (Sainte-Marie) from 1845 to 1847. Abbé Forgues supervised the incorporation of the latter parish in 1846 and began the construction of a new presbytery. In the summer of 1847 he and several other priests devoted themselves to helping those stricken with typhus at the quarantine station on Grosse Île [*see* George Mellis Douglas*], and he was obliged to spend time recuperating in the Hôpital Général of Quebec. He returned to the seminary as assistant bursar in 1847 but continued to serve as a parish priest on occasion. Perhaps in an attempt to ensure his attachment to the seminary, he was made a member of the house and brought into the council as titular bursar, a position he held from 1849 to 1859. However, in 1859 he accepted the parish ministry at Saint-Germain-de-Rimouski (Rimouski). After two years there he rested for four years at his family's home at Saint-Michel, and in 1865 ended his wandering career at Saint-Laurent on the Île d'Orléans. There he built the present church and a convent. He also compiled a genealogy of families on the Île d'Orléans which was published in the report of the Public Archives of Canada for 1905.

As bursar of the seminary, Forgues had immediately effected a double reform in the accounting system: to conform with the Canadian economy, he substituted British currency for the *livres*, *deniers*, and *sols* the seminary was still using in its accounts; to the primitive systems of the "Brouillard" (day-book) and the "Journal du séminaire" (seminary account book), he added a more rational, indexed "Grand Livre" (ledger), in which details could be verified quickly. His most significant contribution, however, was to make a striking improvement in the institution's finances by getting rid of the annual deficit of a number of farms and mills, by making timely sales of land, and by collecting debts and outstanding seigneurial dues; in all these transactions he conducted business with strict fairness and firmness. Thanks to his skilful stewardship, the seminary, with a cash surplus of £6,600 and an enviable credit rating, was able in 1852 to assume responsibility for founding the Université Laval, as well as for the costs of its first three buildings [*see* Louis-Jacques Casault*]. Forgues was one of the nine directors of the seminary to sign the petition to Queen Victoria for a university charter. The years of construction, from 1854 to 1857, took about £50,000 from the seminary's coffers and obliged it to borrow funds. But in 1857 it was possible to begin to repay the debt by utilizing a small financial surplus. The abolition of seigneurial tenure in 1854 was fought by the seminary along with many other seigneurs; Forgues himself drafted a report on the subject. Nevertheless the change meant substantial payments in compensation after a few years, and enabled the seminary to make sizeable loans in its turn.

After his departure in 1859 Forgues remained on good terms with the seminary; he transacted business with it (including selling potatoes which he received as a tithe in his parish) and he supported as patron certain pupils at the seminary who were his parishioners. At the time of his death the "Journal du séminaire" wrote: "to its former bursar the seminary owed the good order now established in the bursar's office. He was also a benefactor of the seminary, to which he bequeathed $8,000 for the board of pupils" – they came from Saint-Laurent, his last parish.

HONORIUS PROVOST

Michel Forgues compiled a "Genealogy of the families of the island of Orleans," published in the PAC *Report*, 1905, II, pt. II.

AAQ, 210 A, XXI: 603; 61 CD, Sainte-Marie-de-la-Nouvelle-Beauce. ASQ, MSS, 12: f.88; 13, 27 nov. 1874; 34, I, 5 juill. 1849; Séminaire, 34, nos.11–14. *Le Courrier du Canada*, 2 déc. 1882. *Annuaire de l'université Laval pour l'année académique 1883–84* (Québec, 1883), 92–93. *Dominion annual register*, 1882: 342. Wallace, *Macmillan dict.* David Gosselin, *Figures d'hier et d'aujourd'hui à travers Saint-Laurent, I.O.* (3v., Québec, 1919), I: 25–36. J.-E. Roy, *Souvenirs d'une classe au séminaire de Quebec, 1867–1877* (2v., Lévis, Qué., 1905–7).

FORTIN, PIERRE-ÉTIENNE, surgeon and politician; b. 14 Dec. 1823 at Verchères, Lower Canada, son of Pierre Fortin, carpenter, and Marie-Anne-Julie Crevier, *dit* Duvernay, sister of Ludger Duvernay*; he did not marry, but left his estate to his natural daughter, Suzanne-Marie; d. 15 June 1888 in Laprairie (La Prairie), Que.

Pierre-Étienne Fortin spent his youth in Laprairie, and then studied at the Petit Séminaire de Montréal, graduating in 1841. He later studied medicine at McGill College, and after his graduation in 1845 returned to Laprairie where he practised for two years. He spent his time in Montreal and at Grosse Île, Canada East, during the typhus epidemic of 1847–48, when he himself became ill. His medical practice was interrupted in 1849 when he formed and led a troop of mounted constabulary which helped quell the rioting that followed the passage of the Rebellion Losses Bill in April 1849 [*see* James Bruce*].

In 1852 Fortin was appointed stipendiary magistrate and given responsibility for the protection of fisheries in the Gulf of St Lawrence; he was the first to hold such a position and he retained it until 1867. His duties included preparing annual reports, discouraging illegal fishing by foreign fishermen, issuing permits and collecting fees, and gathering statistics concerning catches and the production of fish oil. Fortin was also sent to Saint-Pierre and Miquelon and the French shore of Newfoundland to examine the fishing techniques used there. While travelling in his ship, *La Canadienne*, along the St Lawrence coastline, Fortin compiled a book containing descriptions of 80 species of marine animals and fish which inhabited the Gulf of St Lawrence, and prepared a collection of birds, both of which he intended to donate to the Université Laval.

Fortin succeeded in endearing himself to the Gaspesians through his sincerity and interest in protecting fishermen's rights against foreign vessels and through his efforts to have measures passed which would improve their working conditions, such as the construction of lighthouses along the gulf coast. Concerned that the Gaspesians should not become wholly dependent on fishing, Fortin attempted to instruct them in agricultural methods. He also attempted to establish an oyster-bed in the village of Gaspé, Canada East, using imported oysters, but the project was not successful. Along with the regular functions of his office, Fortin provided free medical services in Gaspé.

In 1867 when John Le Boutillier*, member of the Legislative Assembly for Gaspé County, was named to the Legislative Council, the Conservatives asked Fortin to be their candidate for both the House of Commons and the Quebec assembly; he was elected to both. The provincial administration of Gédéon Ouimet* appointed him commissioner of crown lands in February 1873, but along with the other members of the government he resigned from the Executive Council in September 1874 because of the Tanneries scandal [*see* Louis ARCHAMBEAULT]. As commissioner of crown lands Fortin had shown initiative by establishing fire protection and conservation programmes to preserve provincial forests. Following his re-election in 1875 Fortin was appointed speaker of the assembly. In this capacity he founded in 1876 the marine section in the Legislative Assembly library; the library was destroyed by fire on 18 April 1883. Fortin was forced to resign as speaker on 10 Nov. 1876 when Edmund James Flynn*, his Liberal opponent in the election, charged that clerical interference had helped him win. Although an investigation exonerated Fortin, he had already been replaced as speaker by Louis Beaubien*.

In addition to being member for Gaspé in the House of Commons, Fortin was chairman of its special committee on navigation and the fisheries. In 1868 he attended the Maritime Exposition at Le Havre, France, to study ways of benefiting the fisheries, and sent reports on the exposition to *La Minerve* (Montreal). During this trip he also visited the electric lighthouses at Cap de la Hêve and Le Havre and the military ports and naval yards of Cherbourg, Portsmouth, and Glasgow. He retired from federal politics with the abolition of dual representation in 1874, but he was re-elected to the House of Commons on 17 Sept. 1878 and served until 15 Jan. 1887. Fortin was called to the Senate on 12 May 1887 to represent Kennebec but his health was failing and he died the following year.

Fortin's significant achievements were the successful promotion of the Baie de Chaleur Railway (incorporated in 1872) and the establishment of a telegraph which more closely connected Gaspé and Bonaventure counties with the rest of province; the erection of lighthouses along the gulf coast; the establishment of navigation schools; and the institution of postal service in the wide-ranging Gaspé region. He strongly opposed reciprocity because he believed the United States would benefit from the agreement at Canada's expense. He also concentrated on reducing the advantages of Newfoundland fishermen who charged Canadian fishermen lighthouse dues whenever they sailed to or from Newfoundland and who were exempt from the rigid laws concerning inspection of herring to which Canadian fishermen were subject. Fortin's strenuous efforts to improve the fishermen's situation were the beginning of a serious and organized attempt to protect Canadian fishing rights.

Fortin was responsible for the founding of the Société de Géographie de Québec, incorporated on 9 April 1879, to spread the study of geography throughout Quebec and Canada and to acquaint foreigners with Canada's economic richness. He served as its first president. His cultural pursuits were broad, and he had a reputation as a musician, artist, and singer.

IRENE BILAS

AP, La Nativité-de-la-Très-Sainte-Vierge (La Prairie), Reg. des baptêmes, mariages et sépultures, 1er févr. 1877, 19 juin 1888; Saint-François-Xavier (Verchères), Reg. des baptêmes, mariages et sépultures, 14 déc. 1823. "Parl. debates" (CLA mfm. project of parl. debates, 1846–74), 1867–74. *Le Courrier du Canada*. 1869–71, 16 juin 1888. *L'Électeur* (Québec), 16 juin 1888. *La Minerve*, 29 déc. 1865. 1867–68, 1872–73, 16 juin 1888. *Le Monde* (Montréal), 18 juin 1888. *Montreal Daily Star*, 16 June 1888. *L'Opinion publique*, 23 déc. 1875.

Achintre, *Manuel électoral*. *Canadian directory of parl.* (J. K. Johnson), 211. *CPC*, 1867, 1872–79. J. Desjardins, *Guide parl.* Wallace, *Macmillan dict.* Damase Potvin, *Les oubliés: le commandant Pierre Fortin . . .* (Québec, [1943]); *Le roi du golfe: le Dr P.-É. Fortin ancien commandant de la "Canadienne"* (Québec, n.d.). Philippe Constant [J.-J. Lefebvre], "Le sénateur Pierre Fortin (1823–1888), son ascendance – ses alliés," *BRH*, 68 (1966): 87–96. "Les disparus," *BRH*, 35 (1929): 252. [N.-H.-É.] Faucher de Saint-Maurice, "Louis-Zéphirin Joncas, député de Gaspé," *Rev. d'hist. de la Gaspésie* (Gaspé, Qué.), 6 (1968): 58–68. "L'honorable Pierre Fortin, fondateur de la Société de géographie de Québec," Soc. de géographie de Québec, *Bull.* (Québec), 4 (1910): 347–50. Michel LeMoignan, "Les députés de la Gaspésie," *Rev. d'hist. de la Gaspésie*, 1 (1963): 139–43. Firmin Létourneau, "L'histoire d'un Gaspésien," *Rev. d'hist. de la Gaspésie*, 5 (1967): 67–86. G.-É. Marquis, "La Société de géographie de Québec," *La Rev. de l'univ. Laval* (Québec), 2 (1947–48): 67–77.

FOSTER, ELIZA LANESFORD (Cushing), writer and editor; b. in 1794 at Brighton, Mass., daughter of John Foster, pastor of the Congregationalist Unitarian Church in Brighton, and Hannah Webster, novelist; d. 4 May 1886 at Montreal, Que.

Before her marriage to Dr Frederick Cushing in 1828, Eliza Lanesford Foster had written two historical romances, *Saratoga* and *Yorktown*, published anonymously in Boston in the 1820s. In 1833 Eliza moved to Montreal with her husband. He established a successful medical practice in the city, but succumbed to ship-fever in 1846 while treating immigrants. Eliza Foster Cushing lived on in Montreal for 40 years. Her financial status remains a mystery: she did not move in the circles of the well-to-do, nor did she keep servants in her house; and yet she had sufficient means for the occasional lengthy trip. To an advanced age she enjoyed what she called providence's grant of "much sound health of body and mind as permit [me] to enjoy without diminution the friendships and blessings with which he still brightens [my] later days."

From 1838 to 1851 Eliza Foster Cushing, while also contributing regularly to magazines in the United States, wrote some 70 short stories, poems, and historical romances for the *Literary Garland* of Montreal. This magazine, begun in December 1838 by John Gibson* and John Lovell*, was the first Canadian literary journal to survive longer than three years. Few of Mrs Cushing's pieces have any Canadian content or interest; only one (published in *Godey's Magazine* of Philadelphia) even hints that she was aware of living in exciting times in Lower Canada. But all the tales have a distinct flavour and a decided moral lesson. In the fashion of the polite literature of the day, the settings are pastoral and upper class, the activities languid; emotions abound as women swoon, blush, weep, and have palpitations while dashing young men flirt with temperamental belles but settle for self-sacrificing, principled, sweet young ladies, and dark, sinister gamblers ruin the lives of innocent women. The reading public was apparently eager for her stories. But by 1851 Mrs Cushing, now herself editor of the *Garland*, was forced to admit that American competition and declining public favour clearly spelled the end for what she called "the only magazine published in British North America."

Mrs Cushing had already found another literary outlet, for in 1847 she and her sister Harriet launched the first periodical in Canada East to be devoted exclusively to children. A tiny magazine, *Snow Drop* was full of "amusement and instruction," and was devoted to the "progress and improvement" of middle- and upper-class young people through short stories, poems, history and nature lessons, "conundrums," and games. The editors invited participation from their readers but it came only from girls. Indeed girls seem to have been the object of most of the moral lessons which again imbued all the tales: they were the ones who had to learn truthfulness, reliability, goodness, obedience, filial respect, perseverance, thrift, orderliness, integrity, and self-reliance. As future guardians of the morals of their families, perhaps they did have the most to learn.

In the hopes of attracting a wider audience, Mrs Cushing expanded *Snow Drop* in 1850 into another series, larger and more varied. But her publisher, it seems, had grandiose plans for launching another magazine and for dislodging the two widowed sisters as editors. A new publisher, Robert W. Lay, took over in 1852, but by the following year both *Snow Drop* and Eliza Cushing disappear from public view.

Through the *Literary Garland* and the *Snow Drop*,

Eliza Foster Cushing contributed to the tone of moralizing sentimentality in 19th-century Canadian letters, a tone that would not vanish entirely until the 1920s. The religious and moral sentiment which pervades her writings may have been inherited from her father, but her literary taste and talent undoubtedly stemmed from her mother, an early American novelist. Mrs Cushing's literary pieces were in marked contrast to the partisan polemics of most newspapers of the 19th century. But the very existence of her work, and that of Susanna Moodie [STRICKLAND] and Rosanna Eleanora Leprohon [Mullins*], may be taken as evidence of the growth of a leisured, apolitical, genteel (and perhaps distaff) reading public. The failure of the two periodicals to last longer suggests, however, either that the reading public was not yet large in Canada or that it preferred American and British magazines to Canadian copies of them.

SUSAN MANN TROFIMENKOFF

Eliza Lanesford Foster (Cushing) was the author of *Saratoga, a tale of the revolution* (2v., Boston, 1824); *Yorktown, an historical romance* . . . (2v., Boston, 1826). J. S. Cushing papers are in the possession of Marjorie Harbert of Montreal.

PAC, RG 31, A1, 1871 census, Montreal, Saint-Antoine Ward: 40. *Gazette* (Montreal), 5 May 1886. *Literary Garland* (Montreal), 1838–51. *Montreal Daily Star*, 5 May 1886. *Snow Drop; or, Juvenile Magazine* (Montreal and Toronto), 1847–53. M. M. Brown, *An index to the "Literary Garland," (Montreal, 1838–1851)* (Toronto, 1962), 5–6. J. S. Cushing, *The genealogy of the Cushing family, an account of the ancestors and descendants of Matthew Cushing, who came to America in 1638* (Montreal, 1905), 308–9. *Dominion annual register*, 1886: 264. S. J. Hale, *Woman's record ; or sketches of all distinguished women, from "the beginning" till A.D. 1850* (New York, 1853), 825–26. Morgan, *Bibliotheca canadensis*, 73. F. C. Pierce, *Foster genealogy; being the record of posterity of Reginald Foster, an early inhabitant of Ipswich, in New England* . . . (Chicago, 1899), 238–39. Watters, *Checklist*, 270, 430. J. G. Brierley, "A study of literature in English produced in the province of Quebec prior to confederation, with its historical background" (MA thesis, McGill Univ., Montreal, 1929), 128. *Literary history of Canada: Canadian literature in English*, ed. C. F. Klinck *et al.* (Toronto, 1965), 188, 193, 229. L. J. Loggie, "*The Literary Garland*: a critical and historical study" (MA thesis, Univ. of New Brunswick, Fredericton, 1948). R. L. McDougall, "A study of Canadian periodical literature of the nineteenth century," (PHD thesis, Univ. of Toronto, 1950). *British American Journal of Medical and Physical Science* (Montreal), 3 (1847–48): 138. Carole Gerson, "*The Snow Drop* and *The Maple Leaf*: Canada's first periodicals for children," *Canadian Children's Literature* (Guelph, Ont.), 18–19 (1980): 10–23.

FOSTER, WILLIAM ALEXANDER, barrister and essayist; b. 16 July 1840 at Toronto, Upper Canada, son of James Foster and Mary Morrison; m. in 1877 Margaret, daughter of John George Bowes*; d. 1 Nov. 1888 at Toronto, survived by two children.

William Alexander Foster remains a somewhat enigmatic figure in Canadian history although many of his contemporaries and some modern scholars share the opinion that he was a man of great intellectual capacity whose political ideas contributed to the definition of liberal nationalism in Canada. He was educated at the Toronto Academy and at the University of Toronto where he received an LLB in 1860. After articling with Adam Wilson*, he was called to the bar in 1861. In 1867 Foster formed a partnership with Caleb E. English; John Roaf, QC, joined the firm in 1870. The following year Foster became a partner of Thomas Moss and Featherston Osler* and from 1872 to 1875 worked with them in the firm of Harrison, Osler and Moss. Foster also devoted much energy to his duties as a member of the senate of the University of Toronto. As a writer he contributed to two London papers, the *Westminster Review* and the *Times*, as well as to several in Toronto, the *Daily Telegraph*, the *Canadian Monthly and National Review*, the *Grumbler*, and the *Monetary Times*; he was a founder of this last paper in 1867 and its editor.

Foster's name is most frequently associated with the Canada First movement. Self-consciously patriotic in its defence of political purity in the wake of the Pacific Scandal in 1874, of national self-interest and equality within the British empire in the aftermath of the negotiations which led to the Treaty of Washington in 1871, and of a distinctly Canadian interpretation of the history and national character of Canadians in the first blush of the confederation experiment, Canada First gave the appearance of marking the initial incursion of young, urbane, liberal intellectuals into the mainstream of Canadian political devleopment. But the public movement had evolved out of more secret, even clandestine activities of a group of young men which had, in contrast with the gentler aspirations and pronouncements of Canada First, been part of Ontario's hysterical reaction to the Red River uprising of 1869–70 led by Louis RIEL.

Foster and four or five of his friends had idolized Thomas D'Arcy McGee*'s perception of the new Canadian nation, as found in his writing and political stance from the late 1850s until his death in 1868, and they agreed to use their talents, collectively or individually, to promote the goals of confederation. This group included Henry James Morgan*, Charles Mair*, George Taylor Denison* III, and Robert Grant Haliburton*. Each had particular interests: Morgan, a biographer, collected facts about prominent Canadian public men; Mair, a poet, was an enthusiast on behalf of Canadian literature; Denison, lawyer and cavalry officer, wrote extensively on national defence; Haliburton, a Nova Scotian essayist and businessman, was interested in the effects of environment on the shaping of national character; Foster had written extensively and perceptively on the economic background and purpose of confederation. In two articles prepared for the *Westminster Review* in 1865 and 1866 Foster convincingly argued that the political and economic cohesion and interdependence imposed upon the British North American colonies by their common geography would, with the growth of population, guarantee their independence as a nation in spite of Britain's waning presence and the need for their continued economic cooperation with the United States.

The "old five of the corner room" – Morgan's rooms in an Ottawa hotel – met in the nation's capital in the spring of 1868. Haliburton was in Ottawa to confer with McGee on the government's policy toward the Nova Scotia coal industry. Denison was lobbying for the post of assistant adjutant-general of cavalry. Mair was doing research for the government connected with the annexation of the Hudson's Bay Company lands in the northwest. Morgan, a career civil servant, introduced Foster and Denison, the Torontonians, to Mair and Haliburton, and the five became fast friends who shared a mutual interest not only in the great political issues of the day but in the somewhat more sophomoric pursuits of young comrades on the loose in a strange city. "Chamber maids . . . orgies! Oh me!" Foster protested when reminded later of their eclectic interests. What cemented their friendship, however, was their mutual concern for both the pace of Canada's development as a nation and the quality of its national life defined in terms of the attributes of nationalism, especially a national identity. In these matters they took their lead from McGee's romantic vision of a new nationality destined to rival both its neighbour to the south and its British parent by virtue of the superior moral fibre and intellectual vigour of its young men.

The informal programme of lectures and essays sponsored by the group was set aside in favour of more direct action when the people of the Red River area resisted unilateral annexation of Rupert's Land to the dominion in 1869. Mair, who was serving at the time as accountant and paymaster of a Canadian government survey crew in Red River, eluded capture by the Métis, and with Dr John Christian Schultz*, the leader of the Canadian party in Red River, made his way to Toronto. Foster and Denison, who had corresponded continuously with Mair, had augmented the group with new members, creating the "Twelve Apostles." They arranged the public meetings and disseminated much of the propaganda which in Ontario lionized Mair and Schultz as heroes and vilified the Métis who had executed Thomas Scott* by depicting them as relics of a medieval society whose values were inconsistent with and inimical to the goals of confederation. Foster's role in these events is not precisely clear, but there is evidence to suggest that in conjunction with George Roden Kingsmill, an editor and one of the "Apostles," he penned the editorials in the *Daily Telegraph* which announced the news of Scott's death to Torontonians and demanded that the government deal peremptorily and harshly with the "few hundred dirty, ignorant, miserable half-breeds" who had defied Canadian authority. In effect, the "Apostles" defended the Upper Canadian contention that Manitoba was Ontario's frontier and that one of the purposes of confederation was to ensure that Ontario's territorial ambitions were realized. To reinforce this defence, in the summer of 1870 the "Apostles" created the North West Emigration Aid Society. Ostensibly the society existed to offer advice to intending emigrants about the climate, topography, and agricultural potential of Manitoba, about the availability of land, and about travel arrangements and required gear. In fact, they made a pamphlet available on request, but its technical contents barely disguised the society's express purpose of promoting an unarmed invasion of Manitoba by anglophone settlers who would soon submerge the Métis population. No evidence about the society's success survives, and in any case events quickly propelled the attentions of the "Apostles" toward yet another crisis of nationality.

In 1871 the Manitoba crisis gave way to the events surrounding the negotiations for the Treaty of Washington during which Britain, anxious to cement relations with the United States after the animosity generated during the Civil War, forced the Canadian government to accept a treaty that was harmful to its interests. Foster responded with a pamphlet entitled *Canada First; or, our new nationality*. He defended the proposition that the imperial relationship had to be redefined in terms of equality among nations. This development, he argued, presupposed two others: that Canadians had to embrace their new nationality with a patriotism which effectively demonstrated that national pride had replaced colonial inferiority and that the idea of a Canadian national sentiment had form and substance which distinguished it from colonial loyalties. Conversely, Britain had to recognize the existence of these feelings, and their basis in fact, before dependence could give way to equality. In Foster's opinion, the process of developing a national sentiment would be a slow one because of the new nation's racial, religious, and political diversity which tended to promote disunity and disharmony. But he maintained, using a concept borrowed from Haliburton, that a common nationality inevitably would evolve out of contact with the northern environment which all Canadians shared and which would make them the "northmen of the New World."

Both the title and the patriotic sentiments of Foster's pamphlet became the watchwords of a formal political movement which emerged in Toronto in the wake of the Pacific Scandal. Led by Foster and Goldwin

Smith*, a group of political activists including many former "Apostles" decided to test the strength of a new party in Canadian politics, a party ostensibly more "nationalistic" than the older parties which they accused of self-interest. Smith was to be the Canada First party's candidate in the Toronto West by-election held in December 1873, but he was in England at the time of the nomination meeting and the Canada Firsters endorsed the Liberal candidate for the riding, Foster's law partner, Thomas Moss, who was victorious.

The Canada First party subsequently was subjected to a great deal of ridicule by the national press, and Foster therefore took it upon himself to establish the party on a firm basis by creating in 1874 the Canadian National Association with its own headquarters, the National Club, and its own journal, the *Nation.* Foster was also the author of the association's manifesto, a programme consisting of 11 points concerned with political reform, economic development, and external relations, which seemed to foreshadow, in some respects, the later National Policy of Sir John A. Macdonald*. For example, the manifesto called for a national policy of protective tariffs to encourage industrial growth and the establishment of a system of free homesteads in the public domain to encourage immigration. Similarly, the association's call for the introduction of the secret ballot anticipated one of Prime Minister Alexander Mackenzie*'s important political reforms. The association also advocated the representation of political minorities who went unrepresented in parliament because they were unable to elect spokesmen through the usual democratic processes: an idea which became somewhat more current during the third party protest movements of the next century. But the remainder of the planks were at best platitudinous, at worst vacuous. Compulsory voting, reorganization of the Senate, abolition of the property qualification for members of the House of Commons, and an income franchise were all intended as liberal democratic antidotes to what the Canada Firsters regarded as a political system too susceptible to abuses of power and privilege. The association, however, never detailed how it proposed to implement these reforms. "Pure and economic administration of public affairs," the 11th point of the platform, was clearly intended to distinguish the new association from the evidently corrupt older parties, especially the Liberal-Conservatives. But it was this plank more than any of the others which opened the platform to the resounding ridicule of the partisan press who correctly pointed out that honesty, economy, and patriotism were every politician's stock-in-trade and that for one party to claim to have a monopoly on these virtues was evidence of political simple-mindedness.

To Foster's chagrin, the platform of the Canadian National Association attracted attention from all the wrong quarters. The newspapers tore it to pieces; but worse, Edward Blake*, the theoretician of the Liberal party, publicly embraced and embellished some of the association's positions in an address at Aurora in October 1874, leaving the movement with neither a platform nor a constituency. The *Nation* ceased publication in 1876, and the National Club's political function was swiftly replaced by a social one. After the collapse of the Canada First movement, Foster devoted himself to his law practice. Working alone initially, in 1877 he formed a partnership with James B. Clarke and in 1882 his brother-in-law, Robert H. Bowes, joined the firm. Foster was commissioned a QC on 26 Oct. 1885.

Foster's death in 1888 marked the beginning of the debate over the importance of the Canada First movement. Schultz, Denison, Mair, Haliburton, and Morgan saw Canada First's importance, and Foster's contribution to it, in terms of the secretive, aggressively nationalistic phase of the "Apostles' " activities before 1873. Goldwin Smith, and the later supporters of the party, eulogized Foster as the "animating spirit" of an intellectual movement pledged to "elevate the character of a nation" through its lofty principles of liberal nationalism. Until recently, the latter interpretation has predominated among historians, perhaps as a reflection of scholarly preoccupation with the search for a Canadian identity, a search in which the Canadian National Association has appeared as an obvious beacon on an uncharted horizon. Canada First has also been explained as a genuine third-party movement. The current consensus, however, is that the Canada Firsters were Canadian "imperialists" whose actions and attitudes reflected the hopes and frustrations of the national quest for power, status, and security inherent in the process of confederation but rooted in the entire Canadian historical experience.

Of all the men involved in the Canada First movement, Foster was the least public personality and perhaps the most original intellect. He is known almost solely on the basis of his published essays which characterize him as a perceptive commentator whose clarity, insight, and judgement were frequently clouded by vague and unduly romanticized intimations of the political possibilities of a national *volksgeist.*

DAVID GAGAN

Essays by William Alexander Foster are contained in *Canada First: a memorial of the late William A. Foster, Q.C.*, intro. Goldwin Smith (Toronto, 1890). The volume includes Foster's *Canada First; or, our new nationality; an address*, originally published in 1871 at Toronto.

AO, MU 1058. "Canada First movement: scrapbook of clippings relating to that movement and to its founder and leader William Alexander Foster" (Canadian Library Assoc. mfm. project, 1956). MTL, Denison family papers. PAC, MG 29, D61; E29. QUA, Charles Mair papers. *Daily Tele-*

graph (Toronto), 4–11 April 1870. *Globe*, 2 Nov. 1888. *Commemorative biog. record, county York*. Carl Berger, *The sense of power; studies in the ideas of Canadian imperialism, 1867–1914* (Toronto and Buffalo, N.Y., 1970). G. T. Denison, *The struggle for imperial unity; recollections & experiences* (Toronto and London, 1909). D. P. Gagan, *The Denison family of Toronto, 1792–1925* (Toronto, 1973). [F.] N. Shrive, *Charles Mair, literary nationalist* (Toronto, 1965). F. H. Underhill, *The image of confederation* (Toronto, 1964; repr. 1967, 1973). W. S. Wallace, *The growth of Canadian national feeling* (Toronto, 1927). D. P. Gagan, "The relevance of 'Canada First,'" *Journal of Canadian Studies*, 5 (1970), no.4: 36–44. G. M. Houghman, "Canada First: a minor party in microcosm," *Canadian Journal of Economics and Political Science* (Toronto), 19 (1953): 174–84.

FRASSE DE PLAINVAL, LOUIS (also known as **Louis Nathal**), soldier, police chief, singer, actor, and impresario; b. 1841 or 1842 in Ardennes, France; d. 2 Jan. 1890 in New York City.

Nothing definite is known about the family, education, or early career of Louis Frasse de Plainval, but he seems to have been well born and to have had some military training before he arrived in Canada. The title of "Vicomte" appears to have been bestowed on him posthumously.

Knowledge of Plainval's Canadian career begins with his enlistment on 27 May 1870 as a sergeant in Captain Jacques-O. La Branche's company of the 2nd battalion, Quebec Rifles, recruited as part of the military expedition to the Red River Settlement (Winnipeg) under Colonel Garnet Joseph Wolseley*; from July to December 1870 Plainval served as colour sergeant of this unit. In August 1870 he arrived in the new province of Manitoba and quickly made a reputation for himself in concerts and theatricals as well as in military affairs. Plainval was married at the time he enlisted; his wife, May Susee Van Nostrand, joined him at Upper Fort Garry (Winnipeg) in February 1871 and shortly after opened a private boarding-house in St Boniface, Man. He was officially discharged from the militia on 1 May 1871 and received a land grant in Manitoba.

Before his discharge Plainval had become involved in the establishment of the Manitoba provincial police force and in June 1871 he was appointed assistant chief. He was promoted to chief of police on 5 Aug. 1872 after the first chief, Captain Frank Villiers, had been dismissed for "great irregularities not satisfactorily explained." As chief, Plainval served most conspicuously in directing the attempt to quell riots during the dominion election of September 1872 which led to the destruction of poll books and the wrecking of the offices and printing presses of both the *Weekly Manitoban* (Winnipeg) and *Le Métis* (St Boniface). The leader of the mob, Francis Evans Cornish*, later the first mayor of Winnipeg, abused Plainval at the height of the violence as "a toad-eating Communist who ought to be banished." These alleged communist sympathies seem unlikely in the light of reports that one of Plainval's brothers had lost his life in April 1871 fighting communist insurgents at Versailles.

In March 1873 the Manitoba government reduced the provincial police from 15 to 7 men as an economy measure, and Plainval resigned in protest on 1 April. Before this time he is said to have submitted a plan to Sir John A. Macdonald* for a mounted constabulary force for service in the North-West Territories, a prototype of what became the North-West Mounted Police.

Immediately after his resignation Plainval left Manitoba in mysterious haste. He hired two horses and a cutter to travel to Pointe-de-Chêne (Sainte-Anne-des-Chênes, Man.), but drove instead directly to the United States border. Monetary difficulties and fears of a capias were rumoured as reasons for his departure to meet his wife in St Paul, Minn.

For the next seven years Plainval's activities and whereabouts remain unknown, but it seems likely he began a theatrical career in the United States. Bearing the new name of Louis Nathal, he staged a brief but triumphant return to Manitoba in 1880. From 4 to 23 October the Nathal Comic Opera Company performed at Winnipeg's City Hall Theatre, where Louis and his leading lady, Louise Lester, starred in *The chimes of Normandy*, Lecocq's *Giroflé-girofla*, von Suppe's opera *Fatimitza*, a Gilbert and Sullivan double bill of *Cox and box* and *H.M.S. Pinafore*, and Offenbach's *La grande-duchesse de Gérolstein*. The company was warmly received. Lieutenant Governor Joseph-Édouard CAUCHON attended some performances, and benefits were given to Nathal and Miss Lester. On 18 October Andrew Graham Ballenden BANNATYNE read a eulogistic address after the final curtain call and presented Plainval with a handsome gold watch. On 22 October Miss Lester was given a beautiful pair of moccasins filled with gold coins, a presentation "evidently as gratifying to the audience as the recipient."

After this triumph Plainval is not known to have returned to Canada. He lived principally in New York devoting his talents to the adaptation of French plays to the American stage, the most successful being *Monbars, The suspect*, and *A prisoner for life*. He died in the French Hospital at New York on 2 Jan. 1890, from the prevailing "grippe."

JOHN A. BOVEY

PAC, RG 9, II, B4, 16: f.20. PAM, RG 2, A1, 11 March, 5 Aug. 1872. *Manitoba Daily Free Press*, 6–25 Oct. 1880. *Manitoba Gazette* (Winnipeg), 2 April 1873. *Le Métis* (Saint-Boniface, Man.), 15 juin 1871. *New York Times*, 4 Jan. 1890. *Weekly Manitoban* (Winnipeg), 11 Feb., 17 June 1871; 21 Sept. 1872. Alexander Begg, *History of the North-West* (3v., Toronto, 1894–95), II: 161. Frances Ebbs-

Canavan, "He planned the R.N.W.M.P.," *Maclean's* (Toronto), 47 (1934), no.6: 50–51.

FRENCH, JOHN, soldier and NWMP officer; b. 1843 in Ireland, the youngest son of John French and Isabella Hamilton; m. Frances Mary Chapman, and they had four children; d. 12 May 1885 at Batoche (Sask.).

John French, a militia captain in Ireland for 16 years, came to Canada and in 1874 joined the North-West Mounted Police, then being organized by his brother George Arthur French*, the force's first commissioner. John French was given the rank of sub-inspector (the title was later changed to inspector), at a salary of $1,000 per annum, and attached to D division under Inspector James Morrow Walsh* for the NWMP march to western Canada. Assigned routine postings at Swan River Barracks (Livingstone, Sask.), Fort Walsh (Sask.), and Battleford (Sask.), French does not seem to have had the opportunity to distinguish himself. Major-General Edward Selby Smyth* described him in 1875 as simply "an Irish Militia Officer, with no conspicuous judgement, but active. . . ." In 1876 French received a sharp reprimand from his brother for borrowing money from a subordinate to move his family west, an action Commissioner French considered "subversive of proper discipline." These reactions, however, say more about the extraordinarily strict standards of the NWMP than about the individuals involved. French remained on the force until 1883 when, with the rank of inspector, he retired, probably to take advantage of the government's offer of a free quarter-section to NWMP officers with three years' service. He took up farming near the Qu'Appelle River and was soon one of the area's leading citizens, serving a term as churchwarden and as a municipal councillor of Qu'Appelle. He was described as a "tall, powerful soldierly looking man with jet black hair and beard."

In 1885, with the outbreak of rebellion in the west, French was authorized by Major-General Frederick Dobson Middleton* to raise a troop of mounted scouts. This corps, which became known as French's Scouts, consisted of one other officer, Lieutenant W. Brittlebank, and 33 men. During the campaign Middleton had nothing but praise for French, describing him as "full of pluck and energy" and a "first-rate rider and scout." Prior to the battle at Fish Creek (Sask.), French reportedly captured three Sioux Indians single-handed. In the battle of Batoche French again distinguished himself when he risked his life to rescue a wounded constable. Later, French and his scouts took part in the main attack on Batoche on 12 May 1885, an assault inspired by the pell-mell charge of Colonel Arthur Trefusis Heneage WILLIAMS and his Midland Battalion. French and his men reached the village and approached the house of Xavier Letendre, but while French was "standing in the door directing his men a bullet fired from the opposite side of the river entered his breast killing him instantly." The shot was said to have been fired by Métis Alexander Ross, himself killed during the battle. Lieutenant Brittlebank assumed command of the scouts until they were disbanded in June.

French received much posthumous praise for his actions at Batoche, including a comparison in the *Qu'Appelle Vidette* to Charles George Gordon of Khartoum. Lord Melgund [Elliot*, later Lord Minto], Middleton's chief of staff, reported "he had done so well and was such a fine leader." Two of French's sons were to serve in the NWMP.

JOHN N. JENNINGS

Royal Canadian Mounted Police Arch. (Ottawa), Service files, John French. *Telegrams of the North-West campaign, 1885*, ed. Desmond Morton and R. H. Roy (Toronto, 1972). *Qu'Appelle Vidette* (Fort Qu'Appelle, [Sask.]), 14 May 1885. A. L. Haydon, *The riders of the plains; a record of the Royal North-West Mounted Police of Canada, 1873–1910* (Toronto, 1910; repr. 1918; repr. Edmonton, 1971), 252. Nora and William Kelly, *The Royal Canadian Mounted Police: a century of history, 1873–1973* (Edmonton, 1973).

FULLER, THOMAS BROCK, Church of England clergyman and bishop; b. 16 July 1810 at Kingston, Upper Canada, son of Major Thomas Richard Fuller of the 41st Foot and Mary O'Brien England; d. 17 Dec. 1884 at Hamilton, Ont.

Thomas Brock Fuller was named after a godfather, Sir Isaac Brock*. Both of his parents were dead by 1817 and he was adopted by his mother's sister Margaret, who later married William Leeming, a Church of England missionary in the Niagara District. After studying with the Reverend Thomas Creen in Niagara, Thomas enrolled at the Hamilton Grammar School and then at the Home District Grammar School at York (Toronto) where John Strachan* was schoolmaster. A scholarship awarded in 1828 by the Society for the Propagation of the Gospel enabled Fuller to attend Joseph Braithwaite's seminary at Chambly, Lower Canada, until 1833 when he was ordained deacon. He served as assistant minister at Montreal and Lachine until 1835, being priested that January. On 14 May he married Cynthia Street of Chippawa (now part of Niagara Falls), daughter of merchant Samuel Street*. In character "the ideal parson's wife," she also "brought him a large fortune." They were to have six sons and three daughters.

When Fuller was appointed rector at Chatham, Upper Canada, in 1836 the financial prospects of the Church of England in Canada did not look promising. Grants from the SPG for the church in the Canadas had recently been cut, and the clergy reserves were not an assured source of future income. In an anonymous pamphlet Fuller warned churchmen not to "depend upon the favor of government, or trust to the property we now hold." He felt the church must enlist lay support and allow laymen some voice in disbursing church funds; Fuller later boasted of having been the first to suggest synodical government in the Canadian church, but John Strachan had broached the topic in 1832.

Convinced that the climate at Chatham was bad for his health, Fuller in 1840 accepted the rectorship at Thorold, Upper Canada, and he was named rural dean of Niagara by Bishop Strachan in 1850. At Thorold, Fuller became prominent in local affairs. He promoted the establishment of the Niagara District Agricultural Society, and was a vice-president of the Thorold Township Agricultural Society in 1847. In 1845 he had compiled the *Canadian agricultural reader*, and 13 years later became the first president of the mechanics' institute in Thorold.

In Fuller's view, preaching was an important aspect of the minister's task. In 1879 he would state that he had seen the style of sermons change during his lifetime from elaborate, learned, dry essays to plain, earnest, practical addresses. His own voice was gentle and patient, and he advised others not to use manuscripts but to speak from the heart to the heart. Yet occasionally he himself must have used notes, for many of his sermons from the 1840s on were published. They frequently were concerned with disputes among religious bodies.

Fuller had declared in 1836 that clergy should be educated in Canada rather than in Europe and had urged the establishment of a theological school in Upper Canada. Although he had no formal university training and later in life felt unfairly criticized for his lack of learning (after 1856 he added to his signature his honorary doctorate from Hobart College, Geneva, N.Y.), he always maintained a lively interest in education. At Chatham he sought to establish a church school, and at Thorold he became in 1857 one of the first trustees of the town's grammar school. In 1867 Egerton RYERSON appointed him a member of the Council of Public Instruction for Canada West despite objections from the *Globe* because of his earlier advocacy of Anglican separate schools.

Fuller also gave support to Trinity College in Toronto. In 1852 he donated 200 acres of land in Sarnia to the college, and he gave $1,000 towards its endowment. The campaign begun by Wesleyan Methodists and members of the Church of Scotland to bring the colleges they had established under a single provincial university in order to obtain larger shares of available public funds was supported by Fuller who felt that his church should join them. As chairman of the synod's committee on university education he tried unsuccessfully in 1862 to convince the synod that Trinity should become part of a reformed University of Toronto endowed by the government. Fuller was long a member of the Trinity College Council and often a member of its committees though at one point he felt "systematically *excluded.*" When Trinity sought to increase its endowments in the early 1880s, he angrily refused to help, but a few days before his death made a generous donation. The college had conferred an honorary DCL on him in 1857.

In 1861 Fuller had moved to Toronto to become rector of St George the Martyr. When Strachan in September 1866 sought the election of a coadjutor, Fuller drew enough support from laymen and the evangelical clergy to be a leading contender. Alexander Neil Bethune* was elected on the ninth ballot, but the defeat of an evangelical candidate was a factor which led to the founding of the Church of England Evangelical Association in 1868 [*see* Henry James GRASETT]. Fuller was made a vice-president but later remained aloof from groups such as this set up in opposition to official bodies of the church.

By 1868 the diocese of Huron and Ontario had been set apart from Toronto, and a further division of the Toronto Diocese was suggested in 1869. It was not until 17 March 1875, however, that delegates from parishes in the counties of Lincoln, Welland, Wentworth, Haldimand, Wellington, and Halton met at Hamilton to choose a bishop. Fuller, archdeacon of Niagara since 1867, was elected over his closest rival, John Gamble Geddes*, on the first ballot, receiving 32 of the 51 clerical votes and 33 of the 44 lay votes. Fuller was consecrated first bishop of the diocese of Niagara in St Thomas' Church, Hamilton, on 1 May 1875, and he designated Christ's Church, where Geddes was rector, as the cathedral.

One of the most pressing concerns for the new bishop was the form of public worship. He viewed with dismay many of the changes in it and sought to enforce uniformity; he warned his clergy against extempore prayer and disapproved of newly introduced liturgical practices. When in 1881 he discovered four of his younger clergy using alb and chasuble, he insisted on adherence to the legal decisions of the British courts regarding "ornaments."

Fuller appreciated the contribution the SPG had made to the Canadian church, and when he attended the second Lambeth conference in 1878 he made an extensive speaking tour on behalf of the society. Yet he always stressed the need for people to support their church, and had set an example by paying the £2,305 debt on St John's Church in Thorold when he left it and by donations to the cathedral in Hamilton. His wife's wealth enabled him to compensate for the inability of his parishes, or even of the new diocese, to pay an adequate stipend. About half the parishes of his diocese were mission parishes, and Fuller made great efforts to see his missionaries adequately paid. In the bitter negotiations over the division of funds between the dioceses of Toronto and Niagara, Fuller was particularly watchful that his mission parishes not suffer.

Although Fuller appears to have been reserved and formal, he received many expressions of appreciation from those who knew him. He seems to have found it difficult to acknowledge points of view other than his own; yet his idealism and untiring efforts, despite the physical infirmities which he suffered late in life, did much to strengthen the diocese of Niagara and the Anglican Church in Ontario.

RICHARD E. RUGGLE

T. B. Fuller was the author of *The Canadian agricultural reader . . .* (Niagara, [Ont.], 1845); "Christian unity," *Canadian Methodist Magazine*, 19 (January–June 1884): 50–58, 138–50, 246–56; *Diocese of Niagara: selections from the address of the lord bishop of Niagara, delivered at the annual session of the Synod of the Diocese of Niagara, on the 31st May, 1881 . . .* (Hamilton, Ont., 1881); *Extracts from the judgment of the Judicial Committee of the Privy Council of England, in certain ecclesiastical cases* (Hamilton, 1881); *Memoir of Mr. John Beatty . . .* (Toronto, 1861); *A nation's mercy vouchsafed to a nation's prayers: a sermon preached in St. George's Church, Toronto, on Sunday, 25th February, 1872 . . .* (Toronto, 1872); *Thoughts on the present state and future prospects of the Church of England in Canada . . .* ([Detroit], 1836; repr. Hamilton, 1887). References to other works by T. B. Fuller may be found in *Biblio. of Canadiana* (Staton and Tremaine).

AO, Strachan (John) papers, Letterbooks. St John's Anglican Church (Thorold, Ont.), Fuller letters. Trinity College Arch. (Toronto), Trinity College records, A/II/3, 12 July 1870; A/II/4, 6 Aug. 1877, 25 June 1879, 29 Jan. 1880, 15 Dec. 1881. USPG, C/CAN/Tor, V, 45: f.519. Church of England, Diocese of Niagara, Synod, *Journal* (Hamilton), 1875–85; Diocese of Toronto, Synod, *Journal* (Toronto), 1865–75; *Proc.* (Toronto), 1853–64. Ecclesiastical Prov. of Canada, Synod, *Journal of the proc.* (Montreal), 1862. [Alexander] Dixon, *Useful lives . . . a sermon . . . preached in Christ Church Cathedral, Hamilton, September 7th, 1883 . . .* (Toronto, 1884). *Doc. hist. of education in U.C.* (Hodgins), I: 229; XIV: 254; XVI: 61, 227–28; XVII–XX. *Christian Guardian*, 2 March, 27 April, 18, 25 May, 1 June 1842. *Church* (Cobourg, [Ont.], and Toronto), 29 July 1837; 30 March 1839; 23 April, 18 June 1842. *Hamilton Spectator*, 17, 18 March, 1, 3 May 1875; 17 Dec. 1884. *St. Catharines Journal* (St Catharines, [Ont.]), 10 Sept. 1857. Chadwick, *Ontarian families*, I: 49–50. Dent, *Canadian portrait gallery*, IV: 125–26. J. L. H. Henderson, "John Strachan as bishop, 1839–1867" (DD thesis, General Synod of Canada, Anglican Church of Canada, 1955). *Jubilee history of Thorold, township and town . . .* (Thorold, 1897–98), 100–3, 113–17, 135–41, 163–68. John Langtry, *History of the church in eastern Canada and Newfoundland* (London, 1892), 245–49. *Some men and some controversies; published on the occasion of the centennial of the diocese of Niagara*, ed. R. [E.] Ruggle (Erin, Ont., 1974). R. [E.] Ruggle, "Thomas Brock Fuller: first bishop of Niagara," *Wentworth Bygones* (Hamilton), 10 (1973): 23–36.

FULTON, JOHN, physician, educator, author, and editor; b. 13 Feb. 1837 near St Thomas, Upper Canada; m. January 1864 Isabella Campbell of Yarmouth Township, Canada West, and they had one son and three daughters; d. 15 May 1887 in Toronto, Ont.

John Fulton was raised on the family farm and began his education at an early age; his teachers described him as being one of their best-behaved and most advanced students. At the age of 18 when his health was considered unsuited for the robust life of the farm he became a schoolteacher and displayed a capacity to provide information in a clear and simple manner for his students. After a few years, however, he decided upon a career in medicine.

Fulton studied with a practising physician before entering John Rolph*'s Toronto School of Medicine, which was affiliated with Victoria College, Cobourg. He graduated in 1863 with an MD and in 1864 received an MB from the University of Toronto. Fulton worked briefly in Bellevue Hospital in New York City, and then travelled to London, Paris, and Berlin where he visited hospitals. He received a licence from the Royal College of Physicians of London and membership in the Royal College of Surgeons of England. In 1864 he returned to Fingal, Canada West, where he established his practice. Within a few months his former teacher, John Rolph, invited him to be professor of anatomy at the school. Fulton continued in that position until 1871, combining lectureships in physiology and botany during 1869–70. In March 1871, after Rolph's death and because of the diminishing importance of the Toronto School of Medicine, Fulton resigned from the school and accepted the professorship in physiology at Trinity Medical College in Toronto, a position he held until the early 1880s when he succeeded Dr Norman Bethune* in the chair of surgery. He retained this chair until his death. He was also surgeon to the Toronto General Hospital.

Fulton's most significant contribution was in the field of professional medical communications. In 1868 he published *A manual of physiology*, one of the early medical texts written in Canada by a Canadian. The book is derivative but has the virtue of brevity, being intended particularly for medical students. The work is interesting historically although it is difficult to assess what its practical value was to contemporaries.

Fulton's contribution as an editor was unquestionably valuable. In 1870 he purchased the *Dominion Medical Journal* (Toronto), changed its name to the *Canada Lancet*, and edited the journal for the remainder of his life. Its growth in circulation in the first decade from a few hundred to more than 3,000 attests to its acceptance. Before the *Lancet* Canadian medical journals were, in general, either a pallid imitation of British models or a means of partisan support for a particular medical school or party. But Fulton's journal was vigorous and fair, at least by contemporary standards. Furthermore, although in the beginning it reprinted much material from other sources, it soon began to publish original material by Canadian, if mainly Ontarian, physicians. Fulton's editorials became the sinew that bound the rest of the journal together and gave resilience to the whole. He fought against quackery and government interference in the practice of medicine and, on occasion, wrote on topics such as women's rights in a manner that has a surprisingly modern ring.

Early in May 1887 Fulton caught a cold from which pneumonia developed, and symptoms of typhoid fever also appeared before his death on 15 May. Many of his students at the Toronto General Hospital attended his funeral at Knox Presbyterian Church, where Fulton had been a member and trustee, and doctors Walter Bayne Geikie*, Charles William Covernton*, and Joseph Workman* were pallbearers.

Fulton, although active in what were turbulent years for medical education in Ontario, seemed able to avoid becoming embroiled in the major confrontations and virulent contests of personality. He had a reputation as a clear-headed, persevering, thorough, and kindly physician who set an example as a painstaking and eminently fair medical editor.

CHARLES G. ROLAND

John Fulton was the author of *A manual of physiology* (Toronto, 1868), repub. as *A text book of physiology* (2nd ed., Philadelphia and Toronto, 1870).

"The late Dr. Fulton," *Canada Lancet* (Toronto), 19 (1886–87): 313–14. *Evening Telegram* (Toronto), 16, 18 May 1887. *Globe*, 29 Oct. 1884; 17, 19 May 1887. *Cyclopædia of Canadian biog.* (Rose, 1886). H. A. Kelly and W. L. Burrage, *American medical biographies* (Baltimore, Md., 1920), 417–18. *The Ontario medical register . . .* (Toronto), 1882. *A history of the University of Trinity College, 1852–1952*, ed. T. A. Reed ([Toronto], 1952). Wallace, *Hist. of Univ. of Toronto.*

G

GAGNON, FERDINAND, journalist and newspaper owner; b. 8 June 1849 at Saint-Hyacinthe, Canada East, son of Jean-Baptiste Gagnon and Élizabeth Marchessault; d. 15 April 1886 at Worcester, Mass.

Little is known about Ferdinand Gagnon's childhood. In 1859 he entered the Séminaire de Saint-Hyacinthe, where he completed his final year (Rhetoric) in 1865. He is reported to have distinguished himself there "by his outstanding talent and industry." One of his childhood friends, Dr Omer Larue, noted that his interest in journalism became apparent during this period. His single-sheet publications "circulated from row to row, to the great delight of the pupils and the great displeasure of the masters." In June 1865 he went to work in Saint-Hyacinthe in the law office of Arthur-Prisque Letendre and Honoré Mercier*, where he remained until 7 Jan. 1868. Paying a visit then to his parents, who had been living in Concord, N.H., for some months, he decided to take up residence in the United States himself.

Gagnon, not yet 19, was one of some 200,000 French Canadians who left Quebec between 1860 and 1870. At the time of his arrival, those in the New England states were just beginning to coalesce. Their small settlements of several hundred families were disorganized and scattered across the foreign and sometimes hostile land. Educated young men facing the possibility of unemployment in Quebec found good prospects in New England for using their talents and realizing their ambitions. Gagnon stayed only a few months in Concord, where he secured employment in the legal firm of Marshall and Chase and studied American law. He settled at Manchester, N.H., in October 1868 and taught French there until March 1869. From the time of his arrival in the United States, Gagnon had taken an interest in the problems of his fellow *émigrés*. The French Canadians in Concord appointed him their delegate to the fourth French Canadian convention in the United States, held at Springfield, Mass., on 7–8 Oct. 1868. His role in drafting a constitution for the Union Canadienne de Secours Mutuel, a federation of charitable organizations in the United States, caught the attention of observers, especially journalist Médéric Lanctot*, who was there to represent the Montreal press. Young Gagnon was captivated by Lanctot's personality and the ideas he advanced in favour of the independence of Canada from Britain and its annexation to the United States, especially since, having been raised in a staunchly nationalist milieu, Gagnon despised the British. In a speech in 1866 he had declared that "wherever England has pushed her way in she has always left bloody and humiliating traces of her passage," and he had not failed to mention the events of 1837–38.

After the convention the two men remained in contact. On 25 Feb. 1869 in Manchester Gagnon founded a weekly, *La Voix du peuple*, with the financial assistance of Dr Adolphe-Louis Tremblay, an influential member of one of the clubs in sympathy with Lanctot's ideas. The four-page paper, whose motto was "Wait and hope," ceased publication on 15 Sept. 1869, when Dr Tremblay left New England. *La Voix du peuple* disappeared at about the same time as

L'Idée nouvelle, the first paper launched by Lanctot to spread the idea of Canadian independence; it was published first at Burlington, Vt, and then at Worcester.

On 16 Oct. 1869 Gagnon married Malvina Lalime, who was born at Saint-Hyacinthe, and that year he did not attend the fifth annual convention of French Canadians in the United States, again held in mid-October. Hence he played no part in the efforts of Lanctot and his friends to infiltrate the convention and get it to favour Canadian independence. Nevertheless he continued to advocate Lanctot's ideas, long after the latter had returned to Montreal disillusioned. The newlyweds settled in Worcester, where nearly 2,000 French Canadian *émigrés* lived. There Gagnon founded *L'Étendard national,* the first issue of which appeared on 3 Nov. 1869; on 7 November of the following year *L'Opinion publique* of Montreal purchased the paper and it became the Montreal journal's American edition. Gagnon continued to write for *L'Étendard,* which was published until 1874, and on 18 March 1873 he also founded *Le Foyer canadien* with Frédéric HOUDE. During the summer of 1874 Gagnon sold his interests in *Le Foyer* to his partner and on 16 October founded *Le Travailleur,* which was to be his major achievement. With a team of excellent contributors, including Benjamin Sulte* and Aram J. Pothier, Gagnon set out to uphold causes dear to him: religion, family, language, and brotherhood. As journalism was not one of the more lucrative professions, he went into partnership with one of his brothers-in-law, Alfred-G. Lalime, a manufacturer of flags, banners, and badges for national and charitable organizations.

It was during this period that Gagnon, despite his youth, began to establish himself as a leader in the French Canadian community in New England. He owed his success to his great talent and unremitting efforts, of course, but also to the friendship and enlightened counsel of the founder of the parish of Notre-Dame-des-Canadiens in Worcester, Abbé Jean-Baptiste Primeau. Like many young, educated French Canadians who came to test their skills in the United States but still cherished the notion of returning to their country, Gagnon remained profoundly attached to French Canada. "Any upright man must love his country, and, if he is far away from it, must feel a desire to live there," he claimed. "If we no longer have this desire . . . we are worthless creatures, we are racial degenerates." Thus patriotism required all French Canadians, even *émigrés,* to combat emigration to the United States. In 1871 he asserted it was no longer necessity that made people emigrate, but rather caprice. After all, prosperity had returned to the homeland. It was good to fight emigration, he said at Worcester in September 1871, but even better to encourage *émigrés* to return to Quebec; otherwise French Canadians would soon be no more than "the pale shadow of a people." However, to the substantial number of *émigrés* who had permanently severed their ties with Quebec Gagnon commended the advantages of naturalization, unless they wanted to remain second-class citizens. At the same time he urged them never to repudiate their national identity, whose two essential elements were the Catholic faith and the French language.

Some were surprised that anyone could advocate naturalization and encourage repatriation in the same breath. But Gagnon dreamed of a "national union [of the French Canadians in Canada and the United States] which must take place sooner or later." Like the delegates to the tenth annual convention of French Canadians in the United States, held in New York in 1874, he wanted *émigrés* to be seen as "the spearhead" of the French Canadian nation, not as its "fugitives or deserters." He therefore welcomed enthusiastically an invitation to the *émigrés* to take part in the celebrations of the 40th anniversary of the Association Saint-Jean-Baptiste de Montréal in 1874.

Those arranging the celebrations entrusted the responsibility for organizing Franco-American participation to a committee that included Abbé Primeau, Lalime, Houde, and Gagnon. They received a response beyond all expectations; 18,000 *émigrés* invaded Montreal. Their presence prompted Charles Thibault, a lawyer in the Eastern Townships, to exclaim: "There is such a multitude of our own people beyond the 45th parallel that one can hardly tell where the motherland now is. It is as if French Canada had extended its frontiers." Gagnon, Houde, and Honoré Beaugrand* praised their fellow *émigrés,* asked that repatriation agents be dispatched to the United States, and tried in vain to get the delegates to take an official stand on the issue of amnesty for Louis RIEL. The Franco-Americans, to whom "abandoning" Riel meant denying the solidarity of all French Canadians, found their Montreal brothers very timorous.

The presence in Montreal of thousands of visitors flaunting their prosperity and taking a malicious delight in ostentation had a magical effect on the people of Quebec. In 1875 there was a mass desertion, "a small-scale evacuation of the province of Quebec," as Alexandre Belisle noted in his *Histoire de la presse franco-américaine.* The appointment of Ferdinand Gagnon as a repatriation agent in March 1875 was one of the steps the Quebec government took to put a halt to the exodus. It was a good choice. Gagnon had the support of influential members of the clergy, and had a good propaganda instrument at his disposal in *Le Travailleur.* He set to work enthusiastically to recruit new settlers from amongst the expatriates. He distributed pamphlets describing the Eastern Townships, obtained tickets at reduced rates for those applying to return to Canada, gave lectures in various places, replied to hundreds of requests for information, and corresponded with Pierre Garneau*, the commissioner of agriculture and public works, as well as with Siméon Le Sage*, the deputy commissioner, and Jérôme-Adolphe Chicoyne, the settlement agent at Sherbrooke. The French Canadians who wished to use Gagnon's services to return to Quebec received certificates of recommendation from him which they had to present to Chicoyne on arrival at Sherbrooke. It was Chicoyne's task to direct them to La Patrie in the Eastern Townships, where there was still undeveloped land. They were offered 100-acre lots at low prices, payable over a period of several years.

Despite Gagnon's efforts, the repatriation attempt was a failure. For every *émigré* who returned, five or ten persons crossed the border in the opposite direction. The invitation extended by Quebec had almost no appeal for a person who had already succumbed to the attraction of the United States and left everything. In addition, Gagnon granted certificates only to those who had some capital to meet initial expenses. Moreover, repatriation aroused growing opposition among the Franco-American élite, for according to them it impeded the movement towards naturalization. Some opponents openly made fun of Gagnon's "disinterestedness." Out of sheer weariness he relinquished his post in 1879.

Yet he did not propose to give up the struggle. There was so much to be done to ensure the future of the French fact in the United States. What he observed there worried him. The progress of assimilation among French Canadian *émigrés* was disturbing. In 1882 Gagnon announced that it was time to fight. He did admit that being in the midst of a Protestant, English-speaking population represented a heavy handicap, but much could be expected from a race of heroes. For the *émigrés* to forget their origin would be tantamount to forfeiting their honour. To all and sundry he stressed that allegiance to a particular government changed only the political status of a person, not his origin. In 1882, the very year in which he took out naturalization papers, Gagnon declared: "History for history, traditions for traditions, I prefer those of my native soil . . . I am happy to be a loyal citizen of this country, but I am equally proud and gratified to be a French Canadian." There was a "spiritual homeland," which was transmitted from generation to generation, shaped by respect for historical memories and traditions, religious faith, and the language of one's forefathers. Gagnon argued that to ensure the survival of this "country" the élite, and in particular the clergy, must use every possible means to recreate in the United States the image of the French Canadian homeland with its churches, schools, societies, and newspapers, its national holiday (Saint-Jean-Baptiste Day), and its teaching of Canadian history. Gagnon did not merely hand out advice, he was present at every fight. As evidence one need only mention the part he played in relation to the Wright report.

Colonel Carroll Davidson Wright, chief of the Massachusetts Bureau of Statistics of Labor, drawing on the invidious observations of certain investigators, alleged in his annual report for 1881 that the Franco-Americans constituted an obstacle to the adoption of a 10-hour work day. Expressing prejudices already widely held, the report used the term "Chinese of the Eastern States" to designate French Canadians, adding that they were "a horde of invaders of industry, not a flow of stable migrants," whose only ambition was to return to their homeland when they had accumulated enough money. The Franco-American leaders were indignant; they called meetings and circulated petitions. Gagnon led the fight in Worcester. He published articles in *Le Travailleur*, and headed a group of prominent people from Worcester who with other compatriots met Colonel Wright in Boston on 25 Oct. 1881. There he delivered a speech in which he stressed the remarkable contribution made to the history of the United States by the French Canadian element, solemnly declared his loyalty, and demanded that the report be recognized as a malicious libel.

Gagnon had made his presence felt as a leader. He enjoyed great prestige, although some of his compatriots would reproach him for his behaviour at the time of Riel's execution and the incidents related to Notre-Dame-de-Lourdes in Fall River, Mass. The Franco-American community was infuriated by the sentencing and hanging of Riel in 1885 and by the hostility of Irish American bishops to French-speaking clergy which was revealed by Bishop Thomas Francis Hendricken's refusal to appoint one of them to the parish of Notre-Dame-de-Lourdes. These events were seen as signs of the danger to which a Protestant and Anglo-Saxon environment exposed the expatriate French Canadians. Although Gagnon shared the feelings of his compatriots, particularly in regard to clergy of their own tongue and origin, he was afraid the militants would go to extremes. He censured the "hot-heads" who "allow themselves to be carried too far by their sympathies for the Métis," and once the decision concerning Fall River had been pronounced by the Sacred Congregation of Propaganda, he castigated those who persisted in seeing all the Irish bishops in New England as unrelenting enemies of the Franco-Americans. In certain circles Gagnon was violently condemned and even some of his friends found it hard to accept this "lapse of patriotism."

Death came suddenly to this man of imposing physique, who in 1885 weighed nearly 340 pounds. He was struck down by Bright's disease on 15 April 1886, when he was only 36 years old. He left his wife and seven children to mourn him.

YVES ROBY

Ferdinand Gagnon's most important writings are to be found in *Ferdinand Gagnon: biographie, éloge funèbre, pages choisies*, M.-E. Martineau, édit. (2e éd., Manchester, N.H., 1940). The first edition, which was published in Worcester, Mass., under the title of *Ferdinand Gagnon, sa vie et ses œuvres*, soon after his death in 1886, included a short biography by Benjamin Sulte.

L'Étendard national (Worcester), 1869–74. *Le Foyer canadien* (Worcester), mars 1873–septembre 1874. *Le Travailleur* (Worcester), 1874–86. *La Voix du peuple* (Manchester), 25 févr.–15 sept. 1869. Belisle, *Hist. de la presse franco-américaine*. P.-P. Charette, *1834–84; noces d'or de la Saint-Jean-Baptiste; compte-rendu officiel des fêtes de 1884 à Montréal* (Montréal, 1884). Rosaire Dion-Lévesque [L.-A. Lévesque], *Silhouettes franco-américaines* (Manchester, 1957). Félix Gatineau, *Historique des conventions générales des Canadiens-français aux États-Unis, 1865–1901* (Woonsocket, R.I., 1927). Robert Rumilly, *Histoire des Franco-Américains* (Montréal, 1958). Donald Chaput, "Some *repatriement* dilemmas," *CHR*, 49 (1968): 400–12.

GAMBLE, WILLIAM, merchant, miller, and land developer; b. 5 Aug. 1805 at Kingston, Upper Canada, son of John Gamble*, surgeon of the Queen's Rangers, and Isabella Elizabeth Clarke; m. 10 Dec. 1833 Elizabeth Bowles Brenchley, and they had one daughter; d. 20 March 1881 in Toronto, Ont.

Educated in Kingston, William Gamble came to York (Toronto) in 1820 with his widowed mother and younger brother, Joseph Clarke Gamble*. William became a partner with another brother, John William*, in a general store about 1822 and its sole owner in 1827. He sold it to Henry Hamilton in 1828. Taking Thomas William Birchall as partner, Gamble opened a general store and a commission agency for grain, flour, pork, and ash, exporting the surplus to Britain either on commission or on his own account, and importing manufactured goods. In 1835 he sold his share in the store to Birchall and bought the King's Mill on the Humber River, in Etobicoke Township, from Thomas Fisher* with whom he continued to have many business dealings. The establishment, which Gamble renamed Milton Mill, consisted of a sawmill, nail factory, inn, stables, and store. In 1837–38 Gamble added a grist-mill and distillery, expanded the stables, and built a hotel in place of the inn. The grist-mill was destroyed by fire in 1847 and rebuilt on a larger scale. Gamble also acquired ships to transport his neighbours' excess cereals and his own and Fisher's flour to Toronto. Here he and a partner had established the Milton Depository, apparently a combined granary and store for the sale of British products. Gamble also advertised various fine qualities of wheat seed. He exported to England in ships which he either owned outright or in which he held substantial shares. In 1840 he bought a lot at the mouth of the Humber, where, in association with Fisher, he built a wharf, stores, and a house. In 1843 he was placed in charge of building a swing bridge at the mouth of the Humber; he rebuilt it in 1866 probably to handle the increasing traffic. In 1846 he leased a woollen mill on the Humber at Dundas St, purchasing it in 1851 from Duncan Murchison with whom he had participated in developing the village of Milton (renamed Lambton in 1840 and now in Etobicoke).

From 1835 Gamble was associated with his brother John William in the development of Mimico, south of Lambton, on lands granted to their father, where John William had made his home. William also leased the surrounding clergy reserves. As pathmaster of Etobicoke Township and on his own initiative, he built roads, some of which he planked and which helped to open the township.

His milling business was crippled by the repeal of the British Corn Laws in 1849 and a flood in 1850 which washed out most of the mill dams on the Humber. Although practically bankrupt, he continued his milling operations on a diminished scale until 1862 when the Bank of Upper Canada foreclosed his mortgages. He presumably continued to live at Milton Mill and, in 1873, as one of the trustees of John William's bankrupt properties, he drew up new plans for the development of Woodbridge on the Humber in Vaughan Township.

Over the years William Gamble had held a number of public offices. In 1833 he was appointed to the town of York Board of Health, established that year in anticipation of an outbreak of cholera. He was made a justice of the peace the same year and served on the Court of Quarter Sessions in 1842. He refused a commission in the 3rd York Regiment of militia in 1836, probably because his business enterprises required so much of his time. Gamble became a director of the Bank of Upper Canada in 1829, and of the British America Fire and Life Assurance Company in 1834. In 1846 he donated the site for an Anglican church, St George's-on-the-Hill (Islington), and served as warden from 1846 to 1848 and from 1851 to 1852. His financial difficulties did not diminish the business community's respect for him: he was active in founding the Bank of Toronto, incorporated in 1855, and was vice-president of its provisional board.

William Gamble's career illustrates the important role of the merchant miller who, by providing a base for one or two villages and, with or without government aid, building roads and bridges, helped to open up townships for rapid settlement. The repeal of the Corn Laws and the new transportation patterns established by the developing railway networks had much to do with placing this kind of pioneer enterprise in jeopardy.

NORAH STORY

[MTL, Humber Valley Arch., contains copies and extracts of documents in the PAC, AO, and York County Registry Office and Surrogate Court (Toronto), as well as extracts from newspapers, gazetteers, and related books. There is a card index and a typescript copy of Norah Story, "The merchant millers of the Humber." N.S.]

GATTY, JULIANA HORATIA (Ewing), author; b. 3 Aug. 1841 at Ecclesfield (South Yorkshire), England, daughter of Alfred Gatty, the vicar of Ecclesfield, and Margaret Scott, a well-known children's writer; m. 1 June 1867 Alexander Ewing, and they had no children; d. 13 May 1885 at Bath and was buried at Trull, near Taunton, England.

Juliana Horatia Gatty was educated at home, as were her three sisters. Stories by Hans Christian Andersen, the brothers Grimm, and Frederick Marryat were among those read and remembered by the Gatty children. Juliana's nickname, "Aunt Judy," given to her by her brothers and sisters because of a talent for story-telling and mimicry, was used by her mother in the titles of both her popular book, *Aunt Judy's tales* (1858), and the children's monthly she established in May 1866, *Aunt Judy's Magazine.* As well as acting as the family story-teller, Juliana promoted family theatricals and presided over their imaginative games.

Juliana's earliest literary involvement was as the editor and "principal contributor" to an unpublished family magazine; it continued from 1856 until the early 1870s under various titles but was known mainly as "The Gunpowder Plot Magazine." Her first published story, "A bit of green," appeared in Charlotte Mary Yonge's *Monthly Packet* in July 1861; it was also one of the stories in her first book, *Melchior's dream and other tales* (1862), illustrated by her elder sister and edited by her mother. Most of her subsequent stories and verses were to appear first in *Aunt Judy's Magazine.*

Shortly after her marriage on 1 June 1867, Juliana Horatia Ewing, as her name would appear on future literary efforts, sailed for Canada with her husband. Major Ewing, attached to the 22nd Foot, was posted in Fredericton where the couple remained until their return to England in October 1869. It is clear in her many letters home that, although occasionally homesick, Juliana enjoyed her life in Fredericton, where she lived initially in a large home she named Reka Dom, meaning "house by the river." She reports in a letter her husband's delight in discovering that Fredericton was at about the same latitude as the garden of Eden and one gathers that it became a kind of Eden for them in the first two years of married life. Mrs Ewing was fascinated by Canadian flora and fauna, planted a garden, painted water-colours of New Brunswick scenes, learned to canoe on the river and to snow-shoe on the surrounding hills, studied Hebrew with Bishop John Medley*, attended the nearby cathedral, and became acquainted with the local Malecite Indians, as well as collecting their handicrafts.

While in Canada she continued to write. In September 1867 *Aunt Judy's Magazine* published "An idyll of the wood" which contained a description of the New World: "A country of pine woods was near; and light was in sight. . . . Not home, but yet a land of wondrous summer beauty." In December of that year "Three Christmas trees," set "in the small town of a distant colony," appeared in the same magazine. *Mrs. Overtheway's remembrances* (1869), often considered her best book, was originally published in *Aunt Judy's Magazine* and the final two of its four parts were completed while she was in Fredericton. The third part ran in the journal from June to October 1868 with the name of her house Reka Dom as the title; the fourth part, "Kerguelen's Land," inspired by a book belonging to Bishop Medley, also appeared in the October 1868 issue. Some of her works written after her return to England in 1869 reflect experiences in Canada. Indigenous flowers such as the trillium and jack-in-the-pulpit are mentioned in stories, and she included descriptions of several dogs she had in Canada, of which she was very fond. A poem, "Canada home," appeared in *Aunt Judy's Magazine* in 1879 and in the 1895 edition of *Verses for children.* It was published again, along with a memoir of Mrs Ewing, eight of her Canadian water-colours, and 22 of her letters from Fredericton, in *Leaves from Juliana Horatia Ewing's "Canada home"* (1896).

After her return to England Juliana had not only continued her work as an author but had also briefly become involved in the editing of *Aunt Judy's Magazine.* When her mother died in 1873, she and her sister, Horatia Katharine Frances Eden, continued the journal; after two years Juliana withdrew and her sister carried on alone until 1885, the year in which Juliana, her most important contributor, died. In the final decade of her life, although plagued by delicate health, Juliana had managed to publish books almost at a rate of one each year. *Six to sixteen* (1876) was remembered by Rudyard Kipling in his autobiography: "I owe more in circuitous ways to that tale than I can tell. I knew it, as I know it still, almost by heart." In 1877 she dedicated *A great emergency* to Bishop Medley and his wife "in pleasant and grateful memory of New Brunswick." Henry James called *Jackanapes* (1884) "a genuine little masterpiece, a wonderful little mixture of nature and art." Some of her other well-known works are *Lob Lie-by-the-fire* (1874), *Jan of the windmill* (1876), *The story of a short life* (1885), and a posthumously published collection, *Verses for children* (1888). An authorized version of her works appeared in 18 volumes from 1894 to 1896.

Juliana Horatia Ewing's writing was marked by genuine human feeling. Her greatest strengths were her ability to convey the normal pleasures of childhood in an unaffected, unpatronizing manner; her gift for detailed, accurate description of country life; her gentle, lightly ironic humour; and her simple, practical common sense and piety. Her stories may have the manner of the Victorian era, but they have a permanent place in the history of children's literature.

DESMOND PACEY with additions by JUDITH ST. JOHN

J. H. Gatty (Ewing) was the author of "A bit of green," *Monthly Packet* (London), 22 (July–December 1861): 80–91; *Melchior's dream and other tales*, ed. Mrs Alfred Gatty [Margaret Scott] (London, 1862); "An idyll of the wood," *Aunt Judy's Christmas volume for young people* (London), 3 (May–October 1867): 257–66; "Three Christmas trees," *Aunt Judy's May-Day volume for young people* (London), 4 (November 1867–April 1868): 80–88; "Mrs. Overtheway's remembrances," *Aunt Judy's Christmas volume for young people*, 5 (May–October 1868): 67–74, 162–67, 195–206, 259–75, 323–47; *Mrs. Overtheway's remembrances* (London, 1869); *Lob Lie-by-the-fire, or the luck of Lingborough; and other tales* (London, 1874); *Jan of the windmill; a story of the plains* (London, 1876); *Six to sixteen: a story for girls* (London, 1876); *A great emergency, and other tales* (London, 1877); *Jackanapes* (London and New York, 1884); *The story of a short life* (London, [1885]); *Verses for children and songs for music* (London, 1888; enlarged ed., London and New York, [1895]); [*Works*] (18v., London, 1894–96). *Leaves from Juliana Horatia Ewing's "Canada home,"* comp. E. S. Tucker (Boston,1896), was also published. For more complete lists of her works see: *British Museum general catalogue; National union catalog; The Osborne collection of early children's books, [1476]–1910: a catalogue*, comp. Judith St John (2v., Toronto, 1958–75); H. K. F. [Gatty] Eden, *Juliana Horatia Ewing and her books* (London and New York, 1885).

G. [E.] Avery, *Mrs Ewing* (London, 1961). Marghanita Laski, *Mrs. Ewing, Mrs. Molesworth and Mrs. Hodgson Burnett* (London, 1950). Christabel Maxwell, *Mrs Gatty and Mrs Ewing* (London, 1949). [M. O.] Oliphant *et al.*, *Women novelists of Queen Victoria's reign: a book of appreciations* (London, 1897), 298–312. A. I. Hazeltine, "Aunt Judy: Mrs. Gatty and Mrs. Ewing," *Horn Book Magazine* (Boston), 16 (1940): 320–30, 457–66. "Juliana Ewing's world: morality with fun; interpreter of Victorian childhood," *Times Literary Supplement* (London), 9 Aug. 1941: 380. Marjorie Thompson, "Mrs. Ewing in Fredericton," *Atlantic Advocate* (Fredericton), 55 (1964–65), no.6: 38–42.

GAUDET (Godet), JOSEPH, farmer and politician; b. 10 May 1818 at Gentilly (now part of Bécancour, Que.), son of Charles Godet, a farmer, and Marguerite Panneton; m. 23 Feb. 1846 Deneige Levasseur at Bécancour, and they had 16 children, including Athanase, who also became a farmer and represented Nicolet in the House of Commons from 1884 to 1888; d. 4 Aug. 1882 at Gentilly.

Joseph Gaudet received only an elementary education before becoming a farmer in his native village. However, according to those who heard him during election campaigns, he was an exceptional public speaker who used polished French. These natural gifts were an important asset in the course of his long political career. He entered parliament in the elections of 1857–58 as representative for Nicolet County, and in 1861 and 1863 he was returned by acclamation as a Liberal-Conservative and solid supporter of George-Étienne Cartier*. Shortly after confederation, yielding to the pleas of his electors and probably of Cartier himself, who promised him a seat on the Legislative Council as compensation, he stood as a candidate in Nicolet County and was elected to both the House of Commons and the Legislative Assembly of Quebec.

But Gaudet remained in the Quebec assembly for only a brief period. As one of the group of Conservatives who judged the economic and social policy of Pierre-Joseph-Olivier CHAUVEAU inadequate, he unhesitatingly voted on several occasions against the government, even at the risk of causing its defeat. In 1871, when public opinion had become critical of the double mandate (which would be abolished by the province in 1874), Gaudet opted for the federal level. Since he supported the *Programme catholique* in 1871 [*see* François-Xavier-Anselme TRUDEL], he was backed by the clergy as well as the *Journal des Trois-Rivières*. He won with a large majority at the federal elections of 1872, and again in 1874 even though his party was defeated. In October 1877 he was appointed legislative councillor for the division of Kennebec. According to Andrée Désilets, this appointment represented a government concession to the agricultural class, rather than a personal reward; it revealed that party leaders were obliged to attempt to satisfy every group in society in order to maintain their own political strength. Thus Gaudet ended his parliamentary career in the Legislative Council.

Among members of the Quebec legislature, Joseph Gaudet typified the average farmer who enjoyed prestige in his own environment but who in the house was not the real spokesman of agricultural interests. Naturally he was even less effective on the federal scene.

LOUISETTE POTHIER

ASN, AP-G, J.-C.-C. Marquis, nos.13–15. Can., Chambre des communes, *Debats*, 1875–77. "Parl. debates" (CLA mfm. project of parl. debates, 1846–74), 1870–74. *Le Canadien*, 5 août 1882. *Le Courrier du Canada*, 1857–82. *L'Ère nouvelle* (Trois-Rivières), 1857–63. *Le Journal des Trois-Rivières*, 1867–82. *Le Messager de Nicolet* (Nicolet, Qué.), 19 août 1882. *Le Nouveau monde* (Montréal), avril, mai 1871. *Quebec Daily Mercury*, 20 Jan. 1869. Achintre, *Manuel électoral*. *CPC*, 1862: 29; 1873: 175. J. Desjardins, *Guide parl.* Cyprien Tanguay, *Dictionnaire généalogique des familles canadiennes depuis la fondation de la colonie jusqu'à nos jours* (7v., [Montréal], 1871–90; réimpr. New York, 1969), I: 273; IV: 310–12. G. Turcotte, *Le Conseil législatif de Québec*, 194. Désilets, *Hector-Louis Langevin*, 176, 214–15. M. Hamelin, *Premières années du parlementarisme québécois*. Rumilly, *Hist. de la prov. de Québec*, III: 176–77. Raymond Douville, "Charles Boucher de Niverville, son ascendance, sa carrière politique," *Cahiers des Dix*, 37 (1972): 104. Albert Tessier, "Luc Désilets, un des 'fanaux de tôle' de Mgr Laflèche," *Cahiers des Dix*, 19 (1954): 170.

GAULT, MATHEW (Matthew) HAMILTON, financier and politician; b. 18 July 1822 in Strabane (Northern Ireland), eldest son of Leslie Gault, a merchant and shipowner, and Mary Hamilton; m. in May 1854 in Montreal, Canada East, Elizabeth J. Bourne, and they had 16 children; d. 1 June 1887 at Montreal.

Mathew Hamilton Gault was educated at the private school of the Reverend Charles Allan, a Presbyterian minister who was considered to be one of the best classical scholars in Ireland. Gault's formal education ended when, at age 15, he injured his spine in a fall from a horse and was confined to bed for a year. Financial losses suffered by his father in the early 1840s, resulting from the loss of a number of ships at sea, the decline in the grain trade, and the removal of duty on Baltic timber, led the family to immigrate to Canada. They arrived in 1842, settling in Montreal, but Mathew's mother soon fell ill and returned to Ireland on the advice of her doctors; within nine months of arrival his father died of cholera. Mathew Hamilton Gault found himself, at the age of 20, the head of a large family.

For the first years after its arrival in Canada the family was sustained by the sale of properties in Ireland, although heavy losses were incurred with the failure of a Montreal savings bank. Mathew and his brothers attempted farming but abandoned it after losing about $7,000 in three years, and from 1844 to 1848 Mathew was a grocer in Montreal. In 1851 he became an agent in Montreal for insurance companies, representing the Mutual Life Assurance Company of New York and the Western Assurance Company of Toronto; the next year he also became agent for the British America Fire and Life Assurance Company of Toronto. By the early 1860s he was the secretary-treasurer of the Montreal Permanent Building Society, which became the Montreal Loan and Mortgage Company in 1875; he was named its president in 1877 or 1878, a position he retained until his death. Many of the investors in the syndicate which controlled the society were to remain associated with Gault in other enterprises; they comprised a cross-section of Montreal merchants, bankers, and industrialists. From 1866 to 1870 he was the manager in Montreal of the Royal Canadian Bank of Toronto and from 1879 he was a director of the Royal Insurance Company of England.

In 1865 Gault assembled a syndicate of bankers and merchants, including Alexander Walker Ogilvie*, who petitioned the legislature for a charter of incorporation for the Sun Insurance Company of Montreal. Parliamentary assent was obtained on 18 March 1865 but difficulty in raising funds under the terms of the original charter, as well as general economic uncertainty, postponed the actual commencement of operations until 27 Dec. 1871 as the Sun Mutual Life Insurance Company of Montreal (it became the Sun Life Assurance Company of Canada in 1882). Gault became the company's first managing director and with 500 shares, worth approximately $5,000, its largest shareholder. Much of the firm's initial success was due to Gault's technical skill, actuarial acuteness, and organizational talent.

In 1873 Gault assumed the presidency of the Exchange Bank of Canada, founded the previous year, many of whose shareholders were board members or shareholders of the Sun Life. Gault resigned as managing director of the Sun Life on 31 March 1879 when he and Robertson Macaulay*, the firm's secretary, disagreed over the company's investment policy, especially with regard to holdings in the Exchange Bank and the Montreal Loan and Mortgage Company, but on 10 September Gault was elevated to vice-president of the Sun Life. However, he had to resign this post in 1883 when the Exchange Bank failed and the Montreal Loan and Mortgage Company temporarily collapsed. Gault was president of both and had been instrumental in inducing Sun Life to invest substantially in them. As a result Macaulay, then Sun Life's managing director, and a group of rebellious shareholders forced Gault to resign. His brother, Andrew Frederick Gault*, an important Montreal dry goods merchant and textile manufacturer, replaced him as vice-president. In 1887, when he failed in his bid to gain control of the company, A. F. Gault sold all but 43 of the shares held by the Gault family in the Sun Life, receiving $39,000 for the 1,300 shares. Soon after the 1883 failure, shareholders of the Exchange Bank had brought suit in an attempt to make Mathew Gault, as president, responsible for the recovery of funds borrowed by the bank's directors. The courts, however, placed full responsibility upon the bank's manager, Thomas Craig, Mathew's brother-in-law and an associate in the Montreal Loan and Mortgage Company, who, at the height of the scandal, absconded to New York.

Gault also held directorships in such diverse organizations as the Montreal Mining Company, of which he was vice-president from 1872 to 1887, the Richelieu and Ontario Navigation Company [*see* Sir Hugh ALLAN], the Dominion Telegraph Company, the Windsor Hotel Company of Montreal (the hotel opened in 1878), the Railway and News Advertising Company, the Canadian Navigation Company, and several cotton companies. In addition he had been, in his early days, an active member of the militia and retired from it with the rank of captain in the Montreal Garrison Artillery Brigade. For many years he was a justice of the peace of the city of Montreal and a warden of Christ Church Cathedral. He was a founder and the first president of the Irish Protestant Benevolent Society of Montreal, a trustee of the Mount Royal Cemetery Company, a member of the board of management of the Montreal Protestant House of Industry and Refuge, and a director of the Montreal General Hospital and of the Montreal Sailors Institute.

Gault numbered among his intimates many members of the Conservative party, including Sir John A. Macdonald* and Sir George-Étienne Cartier*. Active in several federal election campaigns in Montreal, Gault was himself induced to run for the Conservatives in 1878. Cognizant of the importance of the votes of workingmen and the weakness of Alexander Mackenzie*'s appeal to them, Gault campaigned vigorously in the working class districts of the Montreal West riding as a supporter of the National Policy. He enjoyed the endorsement of Montreal mayor Jean-Louis BEAUDRY and several local businessmen, and defeated his opponent, merchant William DARLING. In the House of Commons he was not active in debate, his chief concern being the maintenance of the protective tariff. He took a keen interest in party matters, however, and was in frequent communication with Macdonald about various patronage questions and issues affecting Montreal's prosperity. Although ill in 1882 he was re-elected in Montreal West with a large majority.

After a protracted illness Gault died on 1 June 1887. A tall (6 foot, 1 inch), handsome man, with fashionable mutton chops, he was, in spite of the Exchange Bank disaster, a respected and highly esteemed member of the Montreal business community. About 1869 he had acquired Braeside, a mansion on McTavish Street, high on the slope of the mountain near McGill College, which commanded a superb view of the city and the surrounding countryside. In addition he had a summer residence, Rockcliffe, at Cacouna, Que.

GLADYS BARBARA POLLACK and
GERALD J. J. TULCHINSKY

AC, Montréal, État civil, Anglicans, Christ Church Cathedral (Montreal), 4 June 1887. Baker Library, R. G. Dun & Co. credit ledger, Can., 5: 15, 293; 6: 121. PAC, MG 26, A. Sun Life Assurance Company of Canada Arch. (Montreal), Card index to minutes, 1870–1931; Directors' files, M. H. Gault, "Notes on the subject of Leslie Gault"; "First original list of shareholders, Sun Mutual Insurance Company of Montreal"; "First 200 policy applications"; Minutes, 29, 31 Dec. 1883; 4, 11 March 1884.

Can., House of Commons, *Debates*, 1875–87, especially 1879: 1435, 1441; 1880: 42, 215, 969, 1295; 1884: 1215; 1885: 49, 1305; 1886: 668, 704, 1198; Parl., *Sessional papers*, 1878–82 (reports of the superintendent of insurance, 1876–80); *Statutes*, 1880, c.68; 1882, c.63, c.104. Can., Prov. of, *Statutes*, February–May 1863, c.61, c.62. Que., *Statutes*, 1873–74, c.40; 1881, c.50. Sun Life Assurance Company of Canada, *Report of the directors* (Montreal), 1876, 1883. *Gazette* (Montreal), 20, 29 Aug., 20 Sept. 1878; 5, 7, 8 Dec. 1883; 14 May 1884; 2 June 1887. *La Minerve*, 2 juin 1887. *Monetary Times*, 14, 24, 28 Sept., 12 Oct., 7, 14, 21 Dec. 1883; 7, 14 March 1884; 14 Jan. 1887. *Montreal Daily Star*, 12 March 1884, 1 June 1887. *Montreal Herald and Daily Commercial Gazette*, 14 March 1884. Borthwick, *Hist. and biog. gazetteer*. *Canadian biog. dict.*, II: 400. *Canadian directory of parl.* (J. K. Johnson). *CPC*, 1880. *Cyclopædia of Canadian biog.* (Rose, 1886), 431–32. *Montreal directory*, 1852, 1854–55, 1858–59, 1863–70, 1871–75, 1877–78, 1881–83. *The year book and almanac of Canada . . .* (Ottawa), 1873: 43; 1875: 73. G. H. Harris, *The president's book; the story of the Sun Life Assurance Company of Canada* (Montreal, 1928). Joseph Schull, *The century of the Sun: the first hundred years of Sun Life Assurance Company of Canada* (Toronto, 1971). "The founder of the company," *Sunshine* (Montreal), March 1896: 34.

GAUVREAU, PIERRE, carpenter, mason, building contractor, architect, and civil engineer; b. 8 April 1813 at Quebec City, son of Pierre Gauvreau, a carter, and Angèle Ouvrard, *dit* Laperrière; m. there 8 Sept. 1835 Marie-Luce Simard; d. 16 May 1884 at Quebec.

After studying at the Séminaire de Québec between 1825 and 1835 Pierre Gauvreau learned carpentry and masonry on building sites and in the workshop. In this activity he was carrying on family tradition since his ancestors Guillaume and Girard-Guillaume Deguise*, *dit* Flamand, became recognized as masons during the French régime, and his cousin, Jean-Baptiste Roy-Audy*, worked as a carpenter and artist. Gauvreau's career went through three stages. He acquired experience as a carpenter, mason, and contractor from 1835 to 1844. He then became an architect, and from 1848 to 1867 held the post of architect and engineer in the Department of Public Works of Canada East. From 1867 to 1882 he performed the same duties in the office of the commissioner of agriculture and public works for the province of Quebec.

Gauvreau is first listed as a contractor in 1837 when he secured the contract to rebuild the church of Notre-Dame-de-l'Annonciation in Ancienne-Lorette; the following year he and Jean-Baptiste Paquet undertook to demolish the walls of the Château Saint-Louis in Quebec City which had been destroyed by fire. Then, with Joseph and Toussaint Vézina, Jean Patry, and other builders, he constructed some 20 houses and edifices in or near Quebec City, the most important being the stone building on the corner of Rue Sainte-Famille and Côte de la Fabrique (1838) (later occupied by a branch of the Provincial Bank of Canada), Bishop Joseph Signay*'s school on the Chemin du Foulon (1841), and William Sheppard*'s house at Sillery (1843). With few exceptions most of these buildings reflected either rudimentary design (being erected without benefit of an architect) or a more elaborate conception (because of the use of plans by such architects as the partners Frederick Hacker and Edward Taylor Fletcher, Goodlatte Richardson Browne, or Richard John Cooper).

From 1844 Gauvreau, working as an architect, prepared plans and estimates for other building contractors or sometimes for himself. He was from this time using a style with more sober, austere lines suited to the architectural traditions of Quebec; however, his buildings have a few ornamental features in the style fashionable in the 1840s. In five years he designed in this manner more than 30 houses and a few commercial buildings.

When in the employ of the Quebec Department of Public Works from 1848 to 1882, as already noted, Gauvreau supervised a number of government building projects. At the outset his services were mainly used in the improvement of existing public buildings; then in the 1850s and 1860s he was asked to put up many wharves and a few lighthouses in the tiny settlements scattered along the St Lawrence from Rimouski to Montreal. During this period Gauvreau directed the building of some 12 court-houses from plans drafted by architect Frederick Preston Rubidge*. By 1870 he began to draw up the plans of certain public edifices in Quebec City; the post office on Rue Buade (1870), with a 108-foot façade in the French neo-Renaissance style, and the observatory in the park of the Champs de Bataille (1873) have been attributed to him. From 1877 to 1879, together with Eugène-Étienne Taché, he prepared the plans for the Quebec Parliament Buildings (Édifice A).

As an architect Gauvreau seems only once to have worked with a religious institution. In 1846 the parish council of Saint-Roch-des-Aulnaies turned to him after the plan submitted by Charles Baillairgé* for a new church was judged too similar to that of Sainte-Anne-de-la-Pocatière (La Pocatière, Que.). Hence it was under Gauvreau's direction that a neo-Gothic church was erected in 1849–50. This building, as is true of Gauvreau's work as a whole, has certain features in common with the work of Charles Baillairgé. There is every indication that each in turn drew on Thomas Baillairgé*'s legacy and that they perfected their skills as architects and engineers at the same time.

Although rarely innovative from the point of view of form, Gauvreau was a good builder who apparently was more concerned with the structural qualities of a building than with its lines. It was probably this preoccupation that led him in 1854 to patent a cement he had just invented. "Gauvreau cement," made with stone from Cape Diamond, was used especially in stonework exposed to water and humidity. It was employed in the three forts at Lévis built about 1870 and subsequently in various public works projects across the country. The factory disappeared with the advent of American cement factories at the beginning of the 20th century.

Gauvreau was active in civic affairs in Quebec City. He was a councillor for Saint-Jean Ward (1856–62), chairman of the aqueduct committee during his term as councillor, and a member of the Board of Trade (1864). He had eight children. Three sons engaged in building operations: Louis-Petrus was to succeed his father as architect in the Department of Public Works; Théophile-Elzéar and Théophile-Alfred took over the cement factory and also manufactured plaster of Paris at Quebec. The Gauvreau family lived in the suburb of Saint-Jean on Rue d'Aiguillon, where the cement factory was located. Paralysed for the last 18 months of his life by an apoplectic seizure Gauvreau died on 16 May 1884 at Quebec.

A public servant for a long time, Pierre Gauvreau was primarily an architect working on site, participating more often in the actual task of construction than in the creation of designs. The few buildings he planned were only copies modelled on traditional architecture. Gauvreau was conservative and scrupulously careful; as his annual reports to the office of the commissioner of agriculture and public works confirm, he made few innovations in civil architecture.

LUC NOPPEN and A. J. H. RICHARDSON

ANQ-Q, État civil, Catholiques, Notre-Dame de Québec, 8 avril 1813, 8 sept. 1835; Minutier, Henri Bolduc, 9 oct. 1866; E. G. Cannon, 18 oct. 1845; 14 août, 14 oct. 1847; 21, 28 févr., 6 juill., 7 sept. 1850; 14 avril 1851; C.-M. De Foy, 9 janv. 1844; Josiah Hunt, 30 janv. 1830, 2 avril 1839; Alexandre Lemoine, 27 oct. 1849; C.-S. L'Espérance, 24 avril 1862; E. B. Lindsay, 9 août 1849; Joseph Petitclerc, 27 févr. 1839; 24, 25 avril, 8 mai 1857; J.-B. Pruneau, 10 mars 1866; A.-B. Sirois-Duplessis, 8 oct. 1864; Félix Têtu, 17 juin 1844. AP, Saint-Roch-des-Aulnaies, Reg. des délibérations du conseil de la fabrique, 1846, 1849. AVQ, Procès-verbaux du conseil, 1856–62. PAC, RG 11, A1, 8, no.1017.

Can., Parl., *Doc. de la session*, 1883, VI: no.10; VII–VIII: no.10a. Qué., Parl., *Doc. de la session*, 1870, no.17, app.11; 1882, I, no.2. *L'Événement* (Québec), 19 mai 1884. *Canadian biog. dict.*, II: 164–65. *Quebec directory*, 1853–84. P.-G. Roy, *Fils de Québec* (4 sér., Lévis, Qué., 1933), III: 181–82. M. Hamelin, *Premières années du parlementarisme québécois*, 103. Gérard Morisset, *Peintres et tableaux* (Québec, 1936), I: 241–42. Marcel Plouffe, "Quelques particularités sociales et politiques de la charte, du système administratif et du personnel politique de la cité de Québec, 1833–1867" (thèse de MA, univ. Laval, Québec, 1971). "Le ciment Gauvreau," *BRH*, 47 (1941): 216–17.

GEEZHIGO-W-ININIH. *See* KEZHEGOWINNINNE

GENDRON, PIERRE-SAMUEL, notary and politician; b. at Sainte-Rosalie, Lower Canada, and baptized 31 Aug. 1828 at Saint-Hyacinthe, son of Simon Gendron, a farmer, and Marie-Louise Dion; m. in May 1850 his cousin Louise Fournier, and they had several children; d. 11 June 1889 at Saint-Hyacinthe, Que., and was buried in his native village.

Pierre-Samuel Gendron studied briefly at the Séminaire de Saint-Hyacinthe, but had to leave for reasons of health. In 1847 he turned to teaching, and for about ten years taught in the parishes of Saint-Simon and Sainte-Rosalie. He then entered the office of notary Louis Taché at Saint-Hyacinthe as a clerk and was admitted to the profession in 1860, establishing himself in his native parish. He had been secretary-treasurer of the school district and the village since 1855.

Gendron was a candidate for the Conservatives in the riding of Bagot in the 1867 election; he sat in both the provincial and the federal legislatures until the double mandate was abolished by the federal government in 1873. He then decided to continue in provincial politics and was re-elected by acclamation in 1875. The next year, however, he resigned to become protonotary of the Superior Court in Montreal, an office he held until 1887 when he returned to Saint-Hyacinthe.

In politics, Gendron had defeated such illustrious opponents as Maurice LAFRAMBOISE and François Langelier*. Well informed about his electors' needs, as a parliamentarian he was active in the house and also in his constituency. He was secretary of the agricultural society in his county, and was concerned about the stagnation in the farming sector and about emigration to the United States. Taking advantage of a law passed during the government of Pierre-Joseph-Olivier CHAUVEAU to establish and encourage societies to promote colonization, in 1869 he founded the Société de Colonisation du Comté de Bagot, becoming its first president. As part of its work this body attempted to repatriate French Canadians by helping them to establish themselves, particularly in the region of Compton. During the debate on a bill to revise the municipal code in 1870, he got an amendment carried despite cabinet opposition. Gendron was aware of economic trends and in the 1871 session of the Quebec legislature proposed a special committee to study ways of developing and encouraging industry; in 1873 this committee was made a permanent one. In 1875 he became president of the Lake Champlain and St Lawrence Junction Railway Company (previously the Philipsburg, Farnham and Yamaska Railway Company); he had taken effective steps to ensure that this railway would run through his county when a private bill had been debated in 1871.

The Conservative newspapers often suggested Pierre-Samuel Gendron for important posts, but he was the typical representative of a rural constituency. He never neglected personal contacts with his constituents and often participated in the many local festivities. Remaining close to his origins, he lived in his riding throughout his entire political career. His extensive knowledge of local institutions and viewpoints, as well as his sustained effort, ensured his electoral successes.

MARIE-PAULE R. LABRÈQUE

PAC, MG 26, A, 345: 158300–1; 371: 172392–95; 523: 571; RG 4, B26, 137: no.5324. Québec, Parl., *Doc. de la session*, 1869–70. *Le Courrier de Saint-Hyacinthe*, 22 juill., 7 oct. 1869; 13 juin, 1er juill. 1876; 13 juin 1889. *Canadian directory of parl.* (J. K. Johnson), 225. P.-S. Gendron, *La famille Nicolas Gendron; dictionnaire généalogique* (Saint-Hyacinthe, Qué., 1929). J.-B.-O. Archambault, *Monographie de la paroisse de Sainte-Rosalie* (Saint-Hyacinthe, 1939). M. Hamelin, *Premières années du parlementarisme québécois*. Edmond Chartier, "La colonie de rapatriement," *Rev. canadienne*, nouv. sér., 13 (janvier–juin 1914): 406–15.

GÉRIN, ELZÉAR (baptized **Édouard-Elzéar**), journalist, lawyer, and politician; b. 14 Nov. 1843 at Yamachiche, Canada East, son of Antoine Gérin, *dit* Lajoie, and Amable Gélinas; m. 14 Oct. 1873 at Trois-Rivières Marie-Agathe-Élodie Dufresne; d. during the night of 18–19 Aug. 1887 at Montreal, Que.

Elzéar Gérin spent his childhood in the family home in the region of Yamachiche called Petites-Terres. He followed his elder brother ANTOINE to the Séminaire de Nicolet in 1857 for the usual secondary studies, which he completed in 1863. He was strongly influenced there by Abbé Louis-François Laflèche*, who from 1856 to 1861 was teacher in mathematics and philosophy, prefect of studies, and superior of the college.

His classical studies finished, Elzéar Gérin soon joined his elder brother in Quebec and made his start in journalism with *Le Journal de Québec*. Antoine Gérin-Lajoie was at that time seriously overworked; he was not only the deputy parliamentary librarian, but also the manager, treasurer, and secretary of *Le Foyer canadien*. Hence he asked Elzéar (already known through his publication of a history of the *Quebec Gazette* in 1864) to enliven the periodical by writing a monthly column, which the paper was to carry from 10 January to 15 June 1866. In his column Gérin reflected on the plan for confederation, the United States, which had just "laid down arms," and European politics, to which he thought the Canadian press did not attach enough importance. In the July 1866 issue of *Le Foyer canadien*, Hector Fabre* took over the column from Gérin, who had accepted the editorship of the recently established Ottawa newspaper, *Le Canada*.

Elzéar Gérin left Quebec without regret. At the Institut Canadien-Français of Ottawa, in a talk on "Québec jadis et aujourd'hui," he admitted it openly: "I am not one of those who miss everything they have left at Quebec, everything including the northeast wind. I should like to talk to you about Quebec as a man who lived there without becoming attached to it, who no doubt sometimes had a pleasant time there, but who was more often bored there."

The first issue of *Le Canada* had come out on 21 Dec. 1865. A tri-weekly, the paper became what its owners, the brothers Louis-Napoléon and Ludger Duvernay*, wanted it to be, "the advocate of our faith and of our distinct nationality in the capital." Gérin, who on 13 May 1866 was elected to the management committee of the Société Saint-Jean-Baptiste in Ottawa, decided to ensure that the national festival would be especially spectacular by bringing together volunteers through the columns of his paper. The climax of this patriotic festival in 1866 was obviously Laflèche's sermon in the cathedral at Ottawa in which he went over briefly the arguments of his book, *Quelques considérations sur les rapports de la société civile avec la religion et la famille*, whose publication Gérin had announced in his paper. Certain passages of the address by Laflèche aroused enthusiasm in some, but filled others, such as Liberal member of the Legislative Assembly Jean-Baptiste-Éric Dorion*, with explosive indignation. "So I say again," stressed Laflèche, "the heaviest tax imposed upon us by the conquest is the necessity to learn English. Let us pay it honourably, but only as required. . . . It has been my privilege to travel in the United States. There I met compatriots who received me hospitably. I spoke in French to the small children clustering round their mother; they did not understand me."

"All would have been for the best in the best of all worlds," Gérin wrote in his paper, "if M. Éric Dorion had not permitted himself to make the most unseemly remarks concerning the situation of French Canadians in the United States." Dorion, the "Enfant Terrible" whose opposition to confederation was strengthening his annexationist sympathies and admiration for the great neighbour to the south, was in Ottawa for the parliamentary session and he reacted vehemently to Laflèche's assertions. He, also, had visited many towns and villages in the United States where thousands of Canadians were settled, and he was proud to report favourably on their prosperity and their love for the beautiful French language.

A friend of Dorion's was offended by Gérin's remark and, under the pen-name of "Pic Dur," on 23 July sent Dorion's paper, *Le Défricheur* (L'Avenir, Que.), a playful description of a picnic that he alleged had taken place the previous Sunday, at the time of high mass, on the banks of the Ottawa River. Besides Gérin, those present included Joseph Royal*, "a writer *of high principles*," Joseph-Alfred-Norbert PROVENCHER, "editor of the holy and devout *Minerve*," and Magloire McLeod, "editor of *Le Journal des Trois-Rivières*, the great church newspaper." Accompanying them were "two of the actresses of the French theatrical troupe from New York, who happened to be passing through Ottawa." Gérin was furious and vowed to have his revenge: on the evening of Tuesday 31 July when Dorion went to the Library of Parliament Gérin was already there. A violent altercation took place that degenerated into combat; for Dorion, who had a weak heart, it could have been fatal if others had not put an end to it. Back in the assembly Dorion invoked the parliamentary privilege of immunity. Gérin was arrested and imprisoned on Parliament Hill. *Le Défricheur* of 8 August announced mockingly: "M. Gérin has the honour to be the first prisoner of the great legislative palace." His confinement ended at the close of the session a week later.

No doubt satisfied with his work at *Le Canada*, the Duvernay brothers sent Gérin to England as correspondent of *La Minerve* to cover the London conference, which opened officially on 30 Nov. 1866. Gérin obtained his information about the developing plan of confederation from a reliable source, Hector-Louis Langevin*, who reserved the right to inspect his communications to the Montreal paper.

From England Gérin went to France, to complete his "literary and political education." While continuing to send material to *La Minerve*, he helped edit the *Journal de Paris*, which had been launched a few months earlier by Jean-Jacques Weiss and Édouard Hervé, opponents of the imperial régime. Gérin made it clear on his return to Canada in early July 1868 that he was quite proud of having published his "modest articles" in a paper whose patrons included the most illustrious representatives of the liberal Catholic school, Bishop Félix Dupanloup, Frédéric, Comte de Falloux, and Charles Forbes, Comte de Montalembert.

On 16 July 1868 the subscribers to *La Minerve* read in its pages the following solemn and intriguing lines: "We present to Canadian readers today a document not yet published in Europe that we guarantee is authentic." There followed a lengthy text of four large closely printed columns of material from which, as lines of dots indicated, passages had been omitted. The text was highly critical of the liberal and Gallican principles of the person to whom it was addressed; its introductory sentence intimated that it was a brief sent by Pius IX to his "venerable brother" Georges Darboy, archbishop of Paris, and its final sentence, that the brief had been issued from St Peter's in Rome on 26 Oct. 1865.

There was no indication of how *La Minerve* had obtained this confidential text, whose publication would eventually prevent Archbishop Darboy from being created a cardinal, despite Napoleon III's requests to Pius IX for a crown-cardinal. It was only when this issue of *La Minerve* was copied by the French newspapers in Europe that the government of France became disturbed and asked its consul at Quebec, Abel-Frédéric Gautier, to make discreet inquiries on behalf of the minister of public worship about the origins of this "leak." On 18 May 1869 the consul forwarded the information he had "been able to collect." He told the minister that the pope's letter to Darboy was to have been printed in the *Journal de*

Paris, and that only the intervention of the nuncio in Paris had prevented its publication. "But the type had already been set up," the consul added, "and one or two proofs had been obtained for the proof-reader before the authorization to print. At that time in Paris there was a Canadian named Elzéar Gérin, who was attached, I do not know in what capacity, to the editorial staff of the *Journal de Paris*. This Gérin . . . apparently took and kept one of these proofs, which on his return to Lower Canada he handed over to the newspaper *La Minerve*, of which he had been the correspondent in Paris." The consul was accurately informed. This was how Gérin played a decisive role in an episode of the struggle in France between "liberals" and "ultramontanes."

On his return to Canada, Gérin was called to the bar and went to Trois-Rivières to practise law; on 21 Sept. he also became editor of *Le Constitutionnel*, started on 4 June by Télesphore-Eusèbe Normand. As its title indicated, the new paper intended to follow the political line of the Conservative party which had secured the adoption of the new Canadian constitution in 1867.

In this post Gérin, who was a born journalist, showed how much strength and flexibility he had gained from his association with European masters. In addition, he was giving freer rein to his gifts as a lively writer and as a keen observer of nature, for example in "Le Saint-Maurice; notes de voyage," which appeared in the *Revue canadienne* (Montreal) in January 1872.

As a journalist Gérin had on several occasions dealt in *Le Constitutionnel* with two aspects of the economy of Quebec that he considered vital for the development of the province, lumbering and railway building. When he was elected as member of the Legislative Assembly for Saint-Maurice County in the provincial elections of 1871, he undertook to enlighten his colleagues about the importance of timber as a main source of provincial revenues and to expose those profiteering from the system of private sales of timber limits on crown lands. As it was the period of "railway fever," Gérin also commanded attention through speeches that favoured the development of regional railway networks but with the help of the latest technical improvements and the consequent abandoning of wooden rails.

In 1868 Gérin had also been a candidate for Saint-Maurice in the federal elections but had been defeated by Dr Élie Lacerte. Lacerte was again successful in 1875, this time in the provincial elections. Gérin returned to journalism. In 1882, to reward him for his many services to the Conservative party, the government of Joseph-Alfred MOUSSEAU named him to the Legislative Council as representative for the division of Kennebec.

A frail man long in indifferent health, Elzéar Gérin died prematurely at the age of 43 in Montreal. He was one of those gifted men who, especially in the 19th century, were unable to fulfil their exceptional promise of mind and spirit in the service of their fellow Canadians.

PHILIPPE SYLVAIN

Elzéar Gérin was the author of *La Gazette de Québec* (Québec, 1864); "Relations commerciales entre les États-Unis et le Canada," *Rev. canadienne*, 2 (1865): 748–57; 3 (1866): 108–22; "Chroniques," *Le Foyer canadien* (Québec), 4 (1866): 47–57, 165–76, 243–72, 316–24; "Québec jadis et aujourd'hui: causerie lue devant l'Institut canadien-français d'Ottawa," *Le Canada* (Ottawa), 15, 17 févr. 1866; and "Le Saint-Maurice; notes de voyage," *Rev. canadienne*, 9 (1872): 33–57.

ANQ-MBF, État civil, Catholiques, Immaculée-Conception (Trois-Rivières), 14 oct. 1873; Sainte-Anne (Yamachiche), 14 nov. 1843. *Le Canada* (Ottawa), 21 déc. 1865–décembre 1866. *Le Défricheur* (L'Avenir, Qué.), 4 juill.–14 août 1866. Beaulieu et J. Hamelin, *La presse québécoise*, II: 115. F.-L. Désaulniers, *Les vieilles familles d'Yamachiche* (4v., Montréal, 1898–1908), I: 109–10. Henri Vallée, *Les journaux trifluviens de 1817 à 1933* (Trois-Rivières, 1933). Désilets, *Hector-Louis Langevin*. J.-A.-I. Douville, *Histoire du collège-séminaire de Nicolet, 1803–1903, avec les listes complètes des directeurs, professeurs et élèves de l'institution* (2v., Montréal, 1903). M. Hamelin, *Premières années du parlementarisme québécois*. Réjean Robidoux, "*Les Soirées canadiennes* et *le Foyer canadien* dans le mouvement littéraire québécois de 1860" (thèse de DES, univ. Laval, Québec, 1957), 81–100. P.-G. Roy, "Elzéar-Gérin-Lajoie et l'enfant-terrible," *BRH*, 7 (1901): 125. Philippe Sylvain, "Le rôle de *La Minerve* dans l'échec au cardinalat de Monseigneur Darboy," *Cahiers des Dix*, 33 (1968): 193–213.

GÉRIN-LAJOIE, ANTOINE, journalist, lawyer, writer, and public servant; b. 4 Aug. 1824 at Yamachiche, Lower Canada, son of Antoine Gérin, *dit* Lajoie, and Amable Gélinas; d. 4 Aug. 1882 in Ottawa, Ont.

Antoine Gérin-Lajoie was so strongly attached to his native land that in introducing him one must first evoke the bit of it his family occupied and owned. His great-grandfather, Jean Jarin (Jarrin or Gérin), who originally came from the diocese of Grenoble, France, arrived in Canada around 1750 as a sergeant in the colonial regulars and took part in the Seven Years' War. He subsequently settled in the region of Yamachiche. His high spirits and good humour earned him the nickname of "Lajoie," which was added to his family name. This surname was not, however, used by all his descendants. Thus two of Antoine Gérin-Lajoie's brothers, Elzéar GÉRIN and Mgr Denis Gérin, did not adopt the full surname; nor did four of his five children.

The Gérins were diligent and prosperous farmers in the Yamachiche region. Antoine Gérin-Lajoie's parents cultivated a stretch of land in the concession of Petites-Terres, on the south side of the King's Road.

Rooted in his native soil, Antoine admired his parents, work on the land, and the traditional values of which he saw himself as both beneficiary and guardian. The eldest of 16 brothers and sisters, he was a quiet, obedient, and sensitive child. At the age of eight he was attending the village school, where he obtained "a number of prizes and a great many compliments." He then entered a secondary school in Yamachiche, where he learned a little Latin. When the local parish priest, Sévère-Nicolas Dumoulin*, suggested that he should receive a classical education, his parents proudly agreed. In 1837 he entered his second year (Syntax) at the Séminaire de Nicolet.

At that time the seminary was one of the most respected institutions of secondary education in Lower Canada. Abbé Jean-Baptiste-Antoine Ferland*, a director, quickly became a friend of this impressionable and gifted pupil who surpassed his classmates in talent, creativity, and achievement. Antoine had a passion for literature and by the age of 15 had begun to write poetry. One evening in 1842, when he was in his sixth year (Rhetoric) at the seminary, he composed a song in memory of the Canadians deported to Australia after the 1837–38 rebellion; called *Un Canadien errant*, and put to the tune of *Par derrière chez ma tante*, it was taken up by the whole seminary. The song spread throughout Canada East, and was to remain one of the most popular ballads in Quebec. Shortly after, Gérin-Lajoie founded a literary and debating society, becoming its secretary and leading spirit, and with classmate Raphaël Bellemare he edited a weekly paper, *Le Moniteur* (Nicolet). Towards the end of his school years, he composed a three-act tragedy in verse, *Le jeune Latour*; one of the earliest plays in French Canadian theatre, it was given a special performance in July 1844. In the style of Corneille, the drama is set at the time of the conquest and deals with the conflict between a young Canadian officer, who is holding an Acadian fort for the French, and his Anglophile father. It was reprinted in *L'Aurore des Canadas* and brought him further celebrity.

This formative period in Gérin-Lajoie's life reveals what would later be his concerns, and also his disillusionments, hesitations, and renunciations. He was idealistic and sensitive, as imaginative as he was talented; from the moment he left the seminary he was caught up in utopian fantasies – for instance he dreamed of going to Paris for 15 or 18 months to study literature, politics, and journalism, then returning to his country to start a French newspaper and play an important role in politics. His first attempts were disappointing. He contemplated taking a diploma in law, but decided to try his luck in the United States with a friend, Guillaume Vassal, and hoped to find a teaching post there. He left on 13 Aug. 1844 with $15, and was back 17 days later; he had been to New York, Stoningen (Mass.), Providence (R.I.), and Boston, but had encountered only refusals and polite advice to return to his own country. Then began what would be the most dynamic and laborious four years of his youth. Having first knocked on several doors without finding a job, Gérin-Lajoie joined *La Minerve* in 1845. This liberal and democratic paper corresponded to his ideology and, although he was simultaneously proof-reader, translator, and occasional writer, he felt honoured to be working in the office where Augustin-Norbert Morin*, Louis-Hippolyte La Fontaine*, and Léon Gosselin* had "wielded the pen." His weekly salary was, however, hardly adequate: first 2 piastres, then 3, and then 5, a ceiling never exceeded during his two and a half years with the newspaper. His clothes were so shabby that he did not dare to walk around town in daylight, much less to appear in society. Despite adversity he was able to sense opportunities which would enable him to realize the patriotic ambitions he cherished. Having started a literary society at college, he now decided to set up a similar one for French Canadian society. In 1844 he proposed the founding of the famous Institut Canadien of Montreal and became its first secretary; he delivered several addresses to the members and was elected president in the summer of 1845, serving until November 1846. He was also appointed secretary of the Association Saint-Jean-Baptiste in Montreal in April 1845 and retained this post for several years.

Abandoning journalism towards the middle of 1847, Gérin-Lajoie devoted himself to the study of law, at the same time maintaining a close interest in politics. An unwavering admirer of La Fontaine, he was opposed to the Conservative government of Henry Sherwood* and Denis-Benjamin Papineau*, formed in May 1847 under Governor Lord Elgin [Bruce*]. When the ministry failed to win the support of French Canadians, elections appeared inevitable. In order to ensure the defeat of Joseph-Édouard Turcotte*, the candidate in Saint-Maurice County, Gérin-Lajoie initiated political meetings to secure the nomination of Louis-Joseph Papineau*, who had returned from Europe two years earlier. In the elections held at the end of 1847 and the beginning of 1848 the government lost to the Reformers; La Fontaine was called to form the new ministry, the first responsible government. Gérin-Lajoie's brief political adventure had lasted long enough for his liking. Having completed his legal studies, he was called to the bar on 20 Sept. 1848 and opened a law office. Nevertheless, rightly or wrongly, he did not believe he possessed the gifts that make a good lawyer. "I like the study of law," he remarked, "but chicanery and trials thoroughly bore me." In January 1849 he accepted his first post in the public service, becoming a transcriber in the Department of Public Works and subsequently, in April, treasurer and paymaster.

Gérin-Lajoie belonged to the first generation of

French Canadian intellectuals to find themselves drawn to the public service. From then on, as his son Léon Gérin* wrote, he was "an intellectual in abeyance," by turns a ministerial or editorial secretary, political writer, and public servant in various capacities. Yet he contemplated settling near Nicolet and becoming "an educated farmer." "Ah, if I were a farmer! . . . ," he exclaimed, at the beginning of his "Mémoires," a kind of journal to which he confided his desires, whims, and memories from 1849 until his death. He also thought once more of going to Paris, becoming a journalist, and "trading in books" there. In 1850 he prepared a short documentary work on Canadian political institutions, which he published in 1851 under the then fashionable title of *Catéchisme politique*. The sub-title, *Élémens du droit public et constitutionnel du Canada, mis à la portée du peuple*, clearly indicates the book's content and purpose. In 1850, when the seat of government had been transferred to Toronto after the burning of the parliament building in Montreal the previous year, Gérin-Lajoie decided to resign from his public works post. After briefly practising law, he returned to the Department of Public Works as a secretary to provincial adjudicators and then in September 1851 made a second trip to the United States, to study English. A few months after his return, finding himself obliged to "earn his living," Gérin-Lajoie accepted in November 1852 a post as supernumerary in the translators' office of the Legislative Assembly. (The government had recently moved to Quebec.) On 24 Sept. 1854 he was appointed a translator.

The following year, after the assembly recommended a second transfer of the seat of government to Toronto, Gérin-Lajoie reluctantly moved to that city. On 31 March 1856 he was appointed deputy librarian of the assembly, with special responsibility for the French section of the library. Undertaking this task with single-minded devotion, he assembled the first *Grand catalogue raisonné* of the library, published in 1857. "Learned and helpful as a Benedictine," as Alfred Duclos* De Celles described him, he always made an effort to place his vast and unpretentious erudition at the disposal of parliament and of those who came to consult him. In Toronto he met Étienne Parent* and a firm friendship developed between the two men. Parent had been under-secretary of the Province of Canada since 1847 and, having spent the winter of 1855–56 alone, decided to bring his family to Toronto in May. They lived in the same boardinghouse as Gérin-Lajoie, who met the eldest of Parent's three daughters, Joséphine-Henriette, and on 26 Oct. 1858 married her in St Michael's Cathedral, Toronto.

The seat of government was again transferred to Quebec during the summer of 1859. Gérin-Lajoie's next six years there coincided with the first noteworthy phase of French Canadian literary history. It was the period of what has been called the "Quebec School," with which Gérin-Lajoie was intimately associated. In poet Octave Crémazie*'s bookshop on Rue de la Fabrique, men who already had or would acquire a name in politics, history, and literature met regularly. Among them were Étienne Parent, François-Xavier Garneau*, Abbé Ferland, Pierre-Joseph-Olivier CHAUVEAU, François-Alexandre-Hubert LA RUE, Joseph-Charles Taché*, and a young priest, Abbé Henri-Raymond Casgrain*. Garneau's *Histoire du Canada depuis sa découverte jusqu'à nos jours*, published between 1845 and 1848, had already impressed them, and Abbé Casgrain had no difficulty in convincing them of the necessity for a French Canadian literature. On 21 Feb. 1861 they founded a journal that Gérin-Lajoie had planned, *Les Soirées canadiennes* (it lasted until 1865). Soon after, a second journal was launched, *Le Foyer canadien*, which remained in publication from 1863 to 1866. It was in *Les Soirées* that Gérin-Lajoie published the first part of his novel *Jean Rivard, le défricheur canadien* in 1862, and in *Le Foyer* that the sequel, *Jean Rivard, économiste*, appeared in 1864. This work now seems too rhetorical and apologetical. But it struck a chord among contemporaries, for its message responded to their hopes. Indeed it was precisely in this that its real merit lay. The story is well known: the hero of the novel, Jean Rivard (the surname of the spouse of Gérin-Lajoie's grandfather, Ursule Rivard-Laglanderie), goes off into the dense forests south of Lac Saint-Pierre to set up a village (that is, a "small republic") which he will head and which could be a religious, educational, economic, and political model for French Canadians. Much of the novel consists of correspondence between Rivard and a former college friend who practises law in Montreal, Gustave Charmenil (Gérin-Lajoie believed this was the surname of the wife of his maternal ancestor Jean Gélinas). Charmenil's letters, even more than Jean Rivard's, exalt the virtues and dignity of rural life. "There have always been two men in me," Gérin-Lajoie had written at the beginning of his "Mémoires"; it seems not unreasonable to suppose that Charmenil is a barely veiled portrait of the man Gérin-Lajoie must have been, while Jean Rivard is the incarnation, almost to the point of myth, of the ideal person he would have liked to become. In any case, for three-quarters of a century *Jean Rivard* was a classic of the ideology of both church and state, which extolled the prime importance for French Canadians of a rural destiny. It also brought Gérin-Lajoie his most widespread fame.

Early in November 1865 Gérin-Lajoie and his family had to make another and final move, this time to Ottawa, the new capital. He now had two sons, Henri, and Léon who would become the first Canadian sociologist. A third son was born in Ottawa, and then two daughters. For Gérin-Lajoie, life in Ottawa was uneventful. From 1867, he complained of his health and of premature old age. His family burdens increased, and financial worries were added to his responsibilities as a librarian. This office increasingly took up more of his time, especially during parliamentary sessions. Yet he carried on extensive correspondence with his friends, and from 1872 to 1874 was a principal contributor to *L'Album littéraire et musical de la Minerve*. He also turned his attention to history. Friends and parliamentary representatives had urged him to recount the political life of Canada during the period following union because, as a journalist and public servant, and as an occasional participant, he had studied events closely and had known all those who played significant roles. He accepted, and began to draft what was to be his second major work: *Dix ans au Canada, de 1840 à 1850. . . .* The study would be published posthumously, largely for a reason that may be worth recalling. By a curious coincidence, one of Gérin-Lajoie's colleagues, Louis-Philippe Turcotte*, had also, at the same time, written a book on the history of the union period in Canada. Fearing competition would be harmful to him, he asked Gérin-Lajoie to defer publication of his history. The latter consented readily and put his manuscript away. The first part of Turcotte's book, *Le Canada sous l'Union, 1841–1867*, appeared in 1871, the succeeding parts in 1872. Not until 1888, after Gérin-Lajoie's death, did Abbé Casgrain begin to publish his former collaborator's text in the Université Laval's journal *Le Canada-français*. The work has neither the lyricism nor the style of Garneau's *Histoire*, of which in its own way it is an extension. Using numerous official documents unknown at the time, Gérin-Lajoie minutely and dispassionately recapitulates the history of the establishment of responsible government in Canada. In disciplined fashion he achieves his purpose to "recount the facts exactly and impartially . . . in the service of no interest other than that of justice and truth."

These are his own words, and they express what undoubtedly was the objective of every one of his multifarious activities. A patriot with an almost religious fervour, obsessed with the notion of duty, he was haunted all his life by the image of the soil and of work on the farm. Each spring during his years in Ottawa, once the parliamentary session was over, he would nostalgically take his family back to his homestead in Yamachiche. In delicate health, he succumbed prematurely under the weight of his professional responsibilities. He suffered a paralytic stroke in 1878 and then a second. He did not survive the third which occurred on 4 Aug. 1882, his birthday. In 1924, at Yamachiche, official celebrations rightly commemorated the centenary of the birth of this man who throughout his life had remained loyal to his motto: "Rather honour than honours."

JEAN-CHARLES FALARDEAU

[The most comprehensive bibliography of Antoine Gérin-Lajoie's literary output and of secondary works dealing with him is in René Dionne, *Antoine Gérin-Lajoie, homme de lettres* (Sherbrooke, Qué., 1978). Many of Gérin-Lajoie's letters and unpublished writings, as well as some other documents, are held in various archival repositories, including ANQ-Q, PAC, ASJCF, ASQ, the National Library (Ottawa), and the Centre de recherche en civilisation canadienne-française (Université d'Ottawa).

In addition to the articles (generally unsigned) that he wrote as a reporter for *La Minerve* (Montréal) from 1845 to 1849 and in 1852, Gérin-Lajoie published many lectures and articles in Canadian periodicals and newspapers in the 1840s, in particular in the *Revue canadienne* (Montréal). His other most noteworthy works are: *Le jeune Latour*, a three-act tragedy which was published in *L'Aurore des Canadas* (Montréal) on 10, 13, and 17 Sept. 1844, in *Le Canadien* (Québec) on 16, 18, and 20 Sept. 1844, and also as a small book in 1844 and in 1848 in *Le Répertoire national, ou recueil de littérature canadienne* (Montréal), edited by James Huston*; "Éloge de l'honorable Joseph Rémi Vallières de St. Réal, juge en chef du district de Montréal," an address delivered to the Institut Canadien de Montréal on 25 Feb. 1847, which was published in the *Album littéraire et musical de la Minerve* in 1847; *Catéchisme politique; ou élémens du droit public et constitutionnel du Canada, mis à la portée du peuple . . .* (Montréal, 1851); *Jean Rivard, le défricheur canadien*, first published in *Les Soirées canadiennes* (Québec), 2 (1862): 65–319, and reissued in numerous editions in the period up to 1958, either by itself or with *Jean Rivard, économiste*. The latter, a novel, was first published in *Le Foyer canadien* (Québec), 2 (1864): 15–371. Gérin-Lajoie also wrote "L'abbé J.-B.-A. Ferland," *Le Foyer canadien* (Québec), 3 (1865); i–lxxii; *Dix ans au Canada, de 1840 à 1850; histoire de l'établissement du gouvernement responsable* (Québec, 1888). His manuscript memoirs have never been found.

The tenth issue of *BRH*, 30 (1924), was entirely devoted to Antoine Gérin-Lajoie and his works. The authors contributing to this number were: Pierre-Georges Roy*, Henri-Raymond Casgrain, Joseph-Guillaume Barthe*, Sir Hector Fabre*, Edmond LAREAU, Ernest Gagnon*, Édouard-Zotique Massicotte*, Alfred Duclos De Celles, Louis-Michel Darveau*, and Benjamin Sulte*. The issue also came out as a pamphlet entitled *Le Centenaire de Gérin-Lajoie* (Québec, 1924). J.-C. F.]

J.-G. Barthe, *Souvenirs d'un demi-siècle; ou mémoires pour servir à l'histoire contemporaine* (Montréal, 1885). *Chansons populaires du Canada, recueillies et publiées avec annotations . . .*, Ernest Gagnon, édit. (2e éd., Québec, 1880). H.-R. Casgrain, *Œuvres complètes* (3v., Québec, 1873–75), II: 431–542. Léon Gérin, *Antoine Gérin-Lajoie; la résurrection d'un patriote canadien* (Montréal, 1925). Séraphin Marion, *Les lettres canadiennes d'autrefois* (9v., Hull, Qué., et Ottawa, 1939–58), IV. Camille Roy, *Manuel d'histoire de la littérature canadienne-française* (Québec,

1918). [C.-G. Testard de] Louvigny de Montigny, *Antoine Gérin-Lajoie* (Toronto, 1926). Mason Wade, *Les Canadiens français de 1760 à nos jours*, Adrien Venne et Francis Dufau-Labeyrie, trad. (2v., Ottawa, 1963). Camille Roy, "Le centenaire de Gérin-Lajoie," *Le Canada-français* (Québec), 2e sér., 11 (1923–24): 780–89.

GERVAIS, GUALBERT, Papal Zouave and teacher; b. 23 Sept. 1844 at Berthier-en-Haut (Berthierville), Canada East, son of Nicolas Gervais, a farmer, and Catherine Tellier; d. 12 April 1888 at Montreal, Que., and was buried two days later in the cemetery of Sainte-Geneviève-de-Berthier parish in his native village.

After completing his secondary education in his native village, Gualbert Gervais entered the École Normale Jacques-Cartier at Montreal in September 1860. He remained there until 1865 and obtained the three diplomas (elementary, model, and academic) awarded by that institution. During this period Gervais maintained with the school's principal, Abbé Hospice-Anthelme-Jean-Baptiste Verreau*, a relationship marked by respect and gratitude; indeed, throughout his career Gervais would enjoy Verreau's support. In the beginning Verreau saw him as a candidate for the priesthood. In 1866, after many invitations, he asked Gervais to come to a decision: "I have often told you that I do not believe you were made for the world. Was I wrong? Once and for all write to me . . . plainly on this matter. I will not bother you again." Probably influenced by his failing health, Gervais took this occasion to renounce any notion of seeking orders. In August 1867, having failed to find a teaching post, he accepted the position of secretary to the principal offered by Verreau; in addition to board, lodging, and laundry, he received the meagre salary of $4 a month.

In December 1867 Gervais enlisted in the battalion of Zouaves then being organized in Montreal to aid the Papal States, which were being threatened by the movement for Italian unity [*see* Ignace BOURGET]. His principal motive in joining the papal army was not the difficulty of finding employment. Like most of his Zouave compatriots, Gervais was convinced above all that the future of Catholicism depended on maintaining, in Rome, the temporal power of the pope. This cause was so sacred that, in letters to his parents the following year and to the parish priest of Sainte-Geneviève-de-Berthier, he said he would not be averse to giving up his life for its sake. Hence he approached his mission in a spirit of piety and devotion. Promoted corporal in November 1869, he was assigned administrative tasks which enabled him to stay permanently in Rome; the majority of his compatriots had to pack their gear frequently and move from garrison to garrison. In other respects his life as a Zouave was quite like that of the others: after work he went to the premises fitted up for the Canadians by Chaplain Louis-Edmond Moreau, where he could make use of a games room, library, and restaurant. The numerous letters to his parents and to his benefactor Verreau, who paid for his stay in Rome, express deep admiration for Pius IX; Gervais venerated the pope as a saint. After the capitulation of Rome in September 1870 Gervais was deported to England and then repatriated with the other Canadian volunteers, who with rare exceptions had had no more opportunity than he to defend the papal territory in combat. With a touch of both regret and irony, he noted that he had served "as a hero, in an office."

In September 1872 Gervais was taken on at the École Normale Jacques-Cartier as an assistant master, with a salary of $400 a year, plus board and lodging. From 1875 he taught arithmetic in addition to the history of Canada and the United States, and also held the post of secretary-treasurer. His salary was increased in that year to $600, and then in 1883 to $700. He received the latter sum until his death even though he had more than 15 years' experience in the field of education. This remuneration was roughly equivalent to that received by Montreal bookbinders and printers with the same number of years of experience, judging by the average annual wages for these trades of $558 and $546, respectively, in 1891. But being a self-effacing, discreet, and meek man, he apparently did not complain. When Gervais died, Gédéon Ouimet*, superintendent in the Department of Public Instruction, observed: "Poor Gervais has made the mistake of letting himself die. All the same, he is well rid of the troubles of [this] life." His lack of interest in the material aspects of existence and his attitude of submission in the face of death seem to have sprung from the religious faith that inspired him. As his younger brother Oscar testified: "Wherever he might be, his life was very tranquil; he lived it without ostentation, with eternity always on his mind."

RENÉ HARDY

AP, Sainte-Geneviève-de-Berthier (Berthierville), Reg. des baptêmes, mariages et sépultures, 23 sept. 1844. Arch. de l'univ. du Québec à Montréal, 2P, Brouillard, 1867, 1875–88; Corr., Gualbert Gervais à ses parents, 27 déc. 1867; Napoléon Legendre à H.-A.-J.-B. Verreau, 17 sept. 1872; Verreau à Legendre, 19 juill. 1875; Gédéon Ouimet à Verreau, 13 avril 1888; Reg. des professeurs, 3: 115. ASQ, Fonds Viger-Verreau, Cartons 29, nos.223–25; 30, nos.173, 180–82, 219, 225, 249; 34, no.157. Jean De Bonville, *Jean-Baptiste Gagnepetit: les travailleurs montréalais à la fin du XIXe siècle* (Montréal, 1975), 90. [L.-]A. Desrosiers, *Les écoles normales primaires de la province de Québec et leurs œuvres complémentaires; récit des fêtes jubilaires de l'école normale Jacques-Cartier, 1857–1907* (Montréal, 1909), 336, 377. René Hardy, "Les zouaves pontificaux et la diffusion de l'ultramontanisme au Canada français, 1860–1870" (thèse de PHD, univ. Laval, Québec, 1978).

GIARD, LOUIS, doctor and office-holder; b. 1 Nov. 1809 at Saint-Ours, Lower Canada, son of François Giard, a farmer, and Marie-Charles Daigle; m. 22 June 1840 at Saint-Pie, Lower Canada, Lucille, daughter of Joseph-Toussaint Drolet, a Patriote, and they had four children; d. 4 Jan. 1887 at Montreal, Que.

After receiving an education at the Séminaire de Saint-Hyacinthe from 1821 to 1830, Louis Giard taught as a cleric at the Collège de Chambly until 1834. Because he did not feel called to the priesthood he left teaching in that year and went to Montreal to study medicine. During this period he was also on the editorial staff of the Montreal paper *La Minerve*. In April 1837 he obtained his licence and went into practice at Saint-Pie.

In 1848 Giard accepted the post of secretary to the Education Office for Canada East (the predecessor to the Department of Public Instruction established in 1856), bringing him into association again with a medical colleague, Jean-Baptiste Meilleur*, the superintendent of education. Giard was to work in the field of education for 34 years. He was closely connected with the events marking Meilleur's service as superintendent: the *guerre des éteignoirs* after the school act was passed in 1846, the appointment of the first school inspectors, and the inquiry of Louis-Victor Sicotte in 1853 which resulted in Meilleur's departure in 1855. Despite the latter's resignation Giard continued to collaborate with his three successors: Pierre-Joseph-Olivier Chauveau, who was superintendent of education until 1867 and minister of public instruction for the province of Quebec from 1868 to 1873; Gédéon Ouimet* (1873–74); and Charles-Eugène Boucher* de Boucherville (1874–75).

In his position as secretary to the department Giard's duties were primarily those of comptroller general and included responsibility for distributing government subsidies for education to the school commissions, and for ensuring that each municipality raised as much by taxation as the government supplied. In addition he was required to assist the superintendent in drafting the annual report on all the schools in the system, expenditures undertaken, and suggested improvements. When he began in 1848 Giard received an annual salary of £175 which was increased the following year to £225.

Louis Giard was acting superintendent of public instruction for the province of Quebec from 15 July 1867 to 24 Feb. 1868 when an act defining the duties of the minister of public instruction was passed, after which time he resumed the position of secretary under the new ministry. On 17 Dec. 1859 he had been appointed recording clerk to the Council of Public Instruction for Canada East which, like the department, had been established in 1856, and in August 1869 he was also appointed one of the secretaries for the new provincial council. This body was divided into two committees on the basis of religion; Giard was secretary to the 14-member Catholic council and Henry Hopper Miles secretary to the 7-member Protestant one. The council made most of the important decisions concerning education, which the ministry then had to implement. During the years immediately following confederation the council adopted measures to develop a denominational structure for schools, to standardize instruction in normal schools, to set up boards of examiners, to improve the salaries of teachers, and to promote the teaching of agriculture and the sciences.

In 1875 the ministry of public instruction again became a department (Ouimet was to serve as its superintendent from 1876 to 1895). The council also underwent an important change; all Roman Catholic bishops with dioceses in the province of Quebec were allowed to sit on the council and determine the direction given to teaching. The Catholic committee thus had seven bishops and eight lay members, including the superintendent, while the Protestant committee was composed of a number equal to the lay section of the Catholic one. It may be surmised that Giard played an essential role in the reorganization. Probably for this reason he submitted a petition about this time, requesting monetary compensation for his many years of voluntary service on the council. However, it is not known what result his action had.

In September 1882 Jules Ferry, the minister of public instruction in France who was responsible for the secularization of the public school system, appointed Giard an *officier d'académie*. Despite the fact that this was an honorary title, Ultramontanes in Quebec decried it as a national dishonour and accused Giard of being a freemason. That year Giard resigned as secretary to the department (and probably to the council) on grounds of advanced age. In 1880 he had been assigned a deputy, Oscar Dunn, who succeeded him and held the post until 1885.

Giard also contributed to the *Journal de l'Instruction publique*, published at Quebec City, and served as its editor from 1868 with assistance of Pierre Chauveau, the prime minister's son. According to André Labarrère-Paulé, "Giard's role appears to have been purely nominal. As secretary to the ministry of Public Instruction he is a safeguard, nothing more." Responsibility for the paper seems to have fallen more upon Abbé Hospice-Anthelme-Jean-Baptiste Verreau*, the principal of the École Normale Jacques-Cartier. Nonetheless, when Giard and Chauveau came to the paper, its content became more diverse, and the reader could find articles on pedagogy and general culture, studies on settlement, biographies, and practical arithmetic exercises suggested for teachers. After Chauveau left in 1872, the quality of the paper deteriorated and partisanship and prejudice began to shape the tenor of too many of its articles. It ceased publication in 1879.

Louis Giard was a key official in the field of education and on several occasions was able to influence the decisions of ministers and superintendents in political and legislative matters. He died in January 1887 at the age of 77 at the home of his son-in-law Louis-Wilfrid Sicotte.

LOUIS-PHILIPPE AUDET

J.-B. Meilleur, *Mémorial de l'éducation du Bas-Canada . . .* (2e éd., Québec, 1876), 354. *Procès-verbaux du conseil de l'Instruction publique* (2v., Québec, s.d.), I. *Le Canadien*, 17 avril 1837; 3 juill. 1840; 23 août 1869; 22 sept. 1874; 5, 15 janv., 8 oct. 1877; 15 sept. 1882; 10 mai 1883; 4, 5 mars, 3 juill. 1886. *La Minerve*, 5, 8 janv. 1887. L.-P. Audet, *Hist. de l'enseignement*, II: 350–51; *Histoire du conseil de l'Instruction publique de la province de Québec, 1856–1964* (Montréal, 1964); *Le système scolaire*, V. [Pierre] Boucher de La Bruère, *Le conseil de l'Instruction publique et le comité catholique* (Montréal, 1918). André Labarrère-Paulé, *Les laïques et la presse pédagogique au Canada français au XIXe siècle* (Québec, 1963), 7–35, 83-121. Georges Côté, "Le département de l'Instruction publique," *Contact* (Québec), no.11 (octobre 1952): 63.

GIBBS, THOMAS NICHOLSON, miller, merchant, manufacturer, banker, and politician; b. 11 March 1821 at Terrebonne, Lower Canada, the eldest son of Thomas Gibbs and Caroline Tate; m. in August 1843 Almira Ash, and they had seven children; d. 7 April 1883 at Oshawa, Ont.

Thomas Nicholson Gibbs was educated in Lower Canada and also in England at a school run by his uncle. In 1832 the family moved to Oshawa, Upper Canada, where Thomas Gibbs entered the grain and produce business. Two of his sons, Thomas Nicholson and William Henry, formed the firm of Gibbs and Brother in 1842 and built a grist-mill south of Oshawa. To this business were soon added fulling-, oatmeal, and barley mills, a distillery, and a tannery; Gibbs and Brother quickly became large-scale exporters of grain and produce. When their chief milling competitor, John B. Warren, failed, the two brothers took over his mill in 1865, thereby consolidating their local dominance in the grain and milling trade.

In 1852, in partnership with Oshawa and Montreal businessmen including Abram FAREWELL, Gibbs became a major investor in and director of the Oshawa Manufacturing Company, a maker of agricultural implements capitalized at $75,000. The firm, headed by an American, Algernon Sidney Whiting, employed New England craftsmen brought to Oshawa. The company declared bankruptcy in 1858. Ten years later the brothers purchased the Oshawa Cabinet Company from the estate of Edward Miall, its founder. This firm was operated separately from Gibbs and Brother, with Thomas as president. He was intensely disliked by his employees because of his harsh labour practices in such matters as suspensions, firings, and forced voting in municipal and provincial elections. In the federal election campaign of 1872, one of the Oshawa company's men, James Brown, on the basis of his working experience, fought hard to prevent an alliance in Ontario between labour and the Conservatives, the party for which Gibbs was standing. Letters opposing the alliance that appeared in the *Ontario Workman* and the *Oshawa Vindicator* under the pseudonym Heather Jack were actually written by Brown.

Because the grain trade required access to large amounts of credit, Gibbs joined the consortium of millers, including Farewell and James Gooderham WORTS, which founded the Bank of Toronto in 1855. Henceforth he would become deeply involved in banking and finance. When the Ontario Bank was being sponsored by John SIMPSON of Bowmanville in 1857, Gibbs was both an incorporator and an early investor, and served as director and vice-president. The economic boom of the early 1870s marked the apex of Gibbs's fortunes. In 1871 he was an incorporator and director of both the Confederation Life Association and the Dominion Telegraph Company. Two years later, in cooperation with other Oshawa businessmen, he founded the Ontario Loan and Savings Company and he was named president in 1874. The following year the directors of the St Lawrence Bank (incorporated in 1872) elected Gibbs president, hoping that he could stave off its impending collapse. Although the other banks in Toronto refused assistance, Gibbs used his political connections with Sir John A. Macdonald* to obtain a loan of $150,000 from the Bank of Montreal, and the St Lawrence Bank survived the crisis. Renamed the Standard Bank of Canada in 1876, and with a greatly reduced capital, it eventually prospered; in 1880 Gibbs owned $30,000 worth of shares. With his associates in the Ontario Loan and Savings Company Gibbs founded the Western Bank of Canada, based in Oshawa, in 1882. In addition to these business interests, he was a lifelong director of the Sydenham Harbour Company (its name was changed in 1878 to the Oshawa Harbour Company), which had been founded by his father, and was chairman of the Canadian board of the London and Canadian Loan and Agency Company and also of the English and Scottish Investment Company of Canada. The firm of Gibbs and Brother failed in 1878 after an unsuccessful foray into speculation in barley, but the other Gibbs enterprises continued to prosper and in 1880 the Oshawa Cabinet Company, with sales of $167,000, employed 125 men.

As Oshawa's chief businessman and financier, Gibbs dominated local politics in the 1850s and 1860s. He held few abstract philosophical theories, but rather saw politics as an extension of his business interests.

In the 1850s he was described as a moderate Reformer by local Conservatives, but after confederation was clearly identified as a supporter of Sir John A. Macdonald. Gibbs had begun his public career in 1850 when he was elected the first reeve of the village of Oshawa. He retained that office until 1854 and won it again in 1857. As Oshawa's representative to the council of the united counties of York, Ontario, and Peel, he vigorously opposed their separation because of the expense that would be involved as well as the likelihood that Whitby, and not Oshawa, would be named the county town of Ontario County. Once separation became inevitable, however, he threw his support behind it, and in 1854 was named the first warden. In the general election held that same year he contested Ontario North as a Reformer but ran third to Joseph GOULD and Ogle Robert Gowan*.

When a by-election was called in Ontario South after Oliver Mowat*, the Liberal incumbent, was appointed vice-chancellor of the Court of Chancery in Canada West in 1864, local Conservatives backed Gibbs as a moderate Reformer against Farewell, a radical Grit. Gibbs's correspondence with Macdonald makes it clear that his narrow victory was won by large-scale vote buying and patronage. In the federal election of 1867 Gibbs fought the most notable campaign of his career. Local Reformers nominated George Brown*, while Gibbs was backed by the Conservatives and the John Sandfield Macdonald* "Bureaucratic Liberals." Again Gibbs won by corrupt practices. With Brown's narrow defeat the way was opened for Alexander Mackenzie* to assume the leadership of the federal Liberal party. Because Gibbs was the only successful Conservative candidate in the area, he became Sir John A. Macdonald's confidant and "fixer" in dealings with Toronto capitalists such as William GOODERHAM Sr as well as during the Canadian Pacific Railway negotiations held in the city.

As a legislator, Gibbs made few contributions. When he spoke it was generally on the practical aspects of banking or tariffs. Although he initially had supported the principle of reciprocity, the abrogation of the treaty in 1866 and the acquisition of the Oshawa Cabinet Company two years later changed his perspectives and he now favoured retaliatory tariffs and protection for manufacturers. On 14 June 1873 Sir John A. Macdonald named Gibbs secretary of state for the provinces and superintendent general of Indian affairs. He was moved to the Department of Inland Revenue on 1 July 1873 but the Pacific Scandal and the defeat of Macdonald's government on 6 Nov. 1873 ended his cabinet career almost before it had begun. Gibbs had been re-elected in the general election of 1872 and again in the by-election necessitated by his elevation to the cabinet on 14 June 1873. Defeated in 1874 by Malcolm Cameron*, he was returned in 1876 after Cameron's death necessitated another by-election. He lost his seat in the general election of 1878 but two years later was appointed to the Senate.

LEO A. JOHNSON

PAC, MG 24, B30, 2: 1108, 1115; B40, 7: 1610–24; 8: 1852; MG 26, A. United Counties of York, Ontario, and Peel, Municipal Council, *Minutes* ([Toronto]), 1853. *Canadian Statesman* (Bowmanville, Ont.), 6 June 1872. *Globe*, 4, 7 Sept. 1874. *Mail*, 2 Sept. 1874. *Monetary Times*, 3, 24 Sept. 1868. *North Ontario Observer and General Advertiser* (Port Perry, Ont.), 12 April 1883. *Ontario Observer* (Prince Albert, Ont.), 26 July 1866; 20 June, 25 July, 1, 29 Aug. 1867; 4 July 1868; 29 June, 6 July 1871; 16 Aug. 1872; 19 June 1873. *Ontario Workman* (Toronto), 11 July, 1 Aug., 21 Nov., 12 Dec. 1872; 16 Jan. 1873. *Oshawa Reformer* (Oshawa, Ont.), 21 June 1872; 14 March, 2, 9 July 1873; 28 Jan., 6 Feb., 31 July 1874; 12, 19 Feb., 14 May 1875; 7 Jan., 10 March, 14 April, 7 July 1876; 20 Sept., 4 Oct. 1878; 28 March, 6 June 1879; 13 Feb., 15 Oct. 1880. *Oshawa Vindicator* (Oshawa), 23 June 1858; 3 July, 7, 28 Aug., 4 Sept. 1867; 3, 10 Oct. 1894. *Whitby Chronicle* (Whitby, Ont.), 20 June 1867; 20, 27 Feb. 1873; 18 June 1874.

Canada, an encyclopædia (Hopkins), I: 281. *Canadian biog. dict.*, I: 295–96. J. E. [C.] Farewell, *County of Ontario; short notes as to the early settlement and progress of the county . . .* (Belleville, Ont., 1973; first pub. with: Ontario County, *By-laws of the council . . .* (Whitby, 1907), 74–75, 77. W. H. Higgins, *The life and times of Joseph Gould . . .* (Toronto, 1887; repr. Belleville, Ont., 1972), 126, 139, 163, 166–87, 191–212, 263–65, 267–68, 271–72. M. M. Hood, *Oshawa . . . a history of "Canada's motor city"* (Oshawa, 1968), 57, 64–65, 69, 71–72, 75, 83–84, 87–92, 96–97, 109. L. A. Johnson, *History of the county of Ontario, 1615–1875* (Whitby, 1973), 92, 135, 142, 147–48, 180–87, 191, 211, 226, 237, 239, 247–50, 328, 335–36. V. Ross and Trigge, *Hist. of Canadian Bank of Commerce*, III: 205–6, 223–31, 297, 306–7.

GIDNEY, ANGUS MORRISON, teacher, journalist, and poet; b. 4 May 1803 at Jemseg, N.B., son of Joshua Gidney and Phoebe Morrison; m. Experience Beals, and they had one son and three daughters; d. 20 Jan. 1882 at Bridgetown, N.S.

As a child Angus Morrison Gidney moved with his parents to a farm east of Bridgetown where he devoted his early years to self-education and farming. In his late teens he began to contribute prose and verse to the periodical press of the province, meanwhile embarking on a teaching career, mainly in Wilmot and Annapolis townships, in which he was engaged for the next two decades. In the primitive single-room schools of the era preceding free schooling in the province Gidney would have as many as 50 pupils at one time. In the spring of 1843 he became editor of the *Novascotian* (which Joseph Howe* had sold in 1841) and assistant editor in the autumn of that year when William ANNAND bought the newspaper. He was also at this time parliamentary reporter for both the

Novascotian and Annand's *Morning Chronicle*, established in 1844.

In August 1845 he severed his connections with these two newspapers and purchased from Alexander Lawson* the *Yarmouth Herald*, then the only newspaper in Nova Scotia west of Halifax. As its managing editor he vehemently supported reform in the Nova Scotian government, the paramount issue at that time being the struggle for responsible government, which finally became a reality in February 1848. Titus Smith*, the eminent botanist and scholar, contributed a weekly column on agriculture to Gidney's newspaper until shortly before his death in 1850. Gidney appears to have temporarily abandoned journalism in 1851, moving to Sandy Cove, Digby County, where he resumed teaching, while contributing articles and poetry to the periodical press of the Maritime provinces.

On 30 Jan. 1843 the *Novascotian* had carried the first chapter of an historical novel by Gidney entitled "The refugee's daughter: a legend," published under the pseudonym "Clifton Hughes, a Novascotian." Publication of the novel ceased abruptly on 17 April 1843 after ten instalments, probably because Gidney's new duties as editor of the *Novascotian* prevented him from completing the work at this time. Fourteen years later all 44 chapters of Gidney's highly romanticized tale of a loyalist army officer and his young daughter were published in the *Liverpool Transcript*, between 5 Feb. and 24 Dec. 1857. Though he had originally planned to issue the novel in a single volume he ultimately decided against the plan, "the times not being auspicious for such an enterprise." The product of a vivid imagination stimulated by extensive reading in history and literature, the story's setting ranges from the bleak coastal settlements of Nova Scotia across the Atlantic to the court of St James, with a series of improbable events taking place in rapid succession.

In 1859 Gidney began to edit the Digby *Acadian*, a weekly newspaper established by his son, Ingraham, who two years later also purchased the Bridgetown *Register*. The elder Gidney, following the discontinuation of the *Acadian* in 1862, joined his son at the *Register*, renamed the *Free Press*, in 1863. Father and son continued to publish it until 1872. Throughout this decade the Gidneys' newspaper violently opposed confederation, denouncing it regularly in the strongest terms and calling for its repeal. During his years as a journalist in Halifax and Yarmouth, Gidney had firmly supported Howe and his political beliefs, but when Howe joined forces with Sir John A. Macdonald* and his government in 1869 Gidney did not hesitate to condemn him as a traitor to the province.

A figure of formidable appearance, Gidney served as sergeant-at-arms of the Nova Scotia House of Assembly during the Liberal régime from 1868 to 1878. He was postmaster in Bridgetown for a brief period but lost the position, probably because of politics, in 1865. He was apparently a voracious reader and derived considerable pleasure from presenting lectures on literary and historical topics to local reading societies.

Described as a "teacher, journalist and poet . . . [with] powers far above mediocrity," Gidney was highly regarded in the community, where he gave devoted service to the local Baptist church and actively campaigned for the temperance movement. In 1835 he had published anonymously a temperance tract, *The effects of alcohol; a poem descriptive and moral.* As a political journalist he expressed himself with facility and conviction, freely employing caustic satire with marked success. His poetry, often published under a pseudonym, embraced a wide range of topics, from the death of a daughter to reflections on Henry Ward Beecher and a tribute to Halifax. No doubt influenced by English poets of the previous century, his style is stilted and characterized by florid language and frequent allusions to classical and literary subjects.

SHIRLEY B. ELLIOTT

In addition to his contribution to the *Novascotian*, 1843–45, *Morning Chronicle* (Halifax), 1844–45, *Yarmouth Herald* (Yarmouth, N.S.), 1845–51, *Acadian* (Digby, N.S.), 1859–61, *Register* (Bridgetown, N.S.), 1861–63, and *Free Press* (Bridgetown), 1863–72, Angus Morrison Gidney was the author of the novel "The refugee's daughter: a legend," first published in part in the *Novascotian* from 30 Jan. to 17 April 1843, then in full in the *Liverpool Transcript* (Liverpool, N.S.) from 5 Feb. to 24 Dec. 1857.

PANS, RG 14, 70. *Dominion annual register*, 1882: 340. R. J. Long, *Nova Scotia authors and their work, a bibliography of the province* (East Orange, N.J., 1918). Morgan, *Bibliotheca Canadensis*. G. E. N. Tratt, "A survey and listing of Nova Scotian newspapers with particular reference to the period before 1867" (MA thesis, Mount Allison Univ., Sackville, N.B., 1957). D.C. Harvey, "Newspapers of Nova Scotia, 1840–1867," *CHR*, 26 (1945): 279–301.

GILMOUR, ALLAN, timber merchant, shipbuilder, and shipowner; b. 29 Sept. 1805 at Craigton, Mearns (Strathclyde), Scotland, the son of John Gilmour, a farmer, and Margaret Urie; m. in 1839 Agnes Strang of St Andrews, N.B., and they had one son; d. 18 Nov. 1884 at Glasgow, Scotland.

Allan Gilmour attended the Mearns parish school, where he received a good grounding in mathematics and the elements of bookkeeping. Through his uncle, Allan Gilmour Sr, principal partner in the timber-importing firm of Pollok, Gilmour and Company, established in Glasgow in 1804 as a loose partnership and in 1812 as a registered co-partnership, he secured in 1819 a clerk's position in the company's head office. Industry and a rapid grasp of the workings of the business led to his promotion in 1821 to a clerkship in the booming Miramichi branch in New Brunswick. In 1824 Gilmour was transferred to the Bathurst, N.B., branch, where he took regular French lessons from the local priest, acquiring considerable fluency in that language. In 1825, at his uncle's suggestion, he returned to Scotland and spent a year in Greenock, then a rising shipbuilding centre, where he learned ship-draughting and the principles of ship construction. From 1826 to 1828 he served in Saint John, N.B., with Robert Rankin and Company, a Pollok, Gilmour branch firm which had been established in 1822 by Robert Rankin*. The Saint John operation was enlarged from the export of timber to include the importing of textiles, foodstuffs, and building supplies, and the construction of ships, to which Gilmour devoted himself. By branching out into shipbuilding the firm found a ready use for some of its timber and increased profits through the sale in Liverpool of the ships as well as their timber cargoes.

Gilmour's chance to assume a leading position in the business came early in 1828 when, in conjunction with Allan Gilmour Sr and William Ritchie* of Montreal, he made a survey of the timber-producing potential of the upper St Lawrence and Upper Canada. As a result of this survey, it was decided to establish a firm in Quebec under the name of Allan Gilmour and Company, the partners being the two Allan Gilmours, members of the Pollok family of Glasgow, and Ritchie. Operations commenced at Wolfe's Cove (Anse au Foulon) in July 1828, and they soon extended to the Lévis side of the river at Indian Cove (Anse aux Sauvages) as the firm under the junior Gilmour's direction rapidly rose to be a leading purchaser of timber rafts. In its New Brunswick operations Pollok, Gilmour had advanced money to operators in the field and thereby guaranteed itself a timber supply each spring, but the custom among timber merchants at Quebec was to bid for the rafts brought down the St Lawrence by independent operators. Many merchants maintained up-river agents, often innkeepers, who would alert them to the approach of timber rafts. In 1832, at the instigation of Allan Gilmour Sr, an attempt was made to secure a "corner" in timber by pre-empting rafts coming downstream, and it was so successful that a large profit was made. By 1835, 150 men were employed receiving rafts at the firm's coves. Gilmour, who was assisted by his younger brother John*, also commenced shipbuilding operations at Wolfe's Cove, specializing in large, stoutly built vessels for the timber trade, an example being the *Advance* of 1,466 register tons, "a leviathan of her day."

From Quebec Allan Gilmour and Company carried mostly square timber in the company's ships, though some deals and staves were also exported. Until 1830 the major port of destination was Greenock, but after that date the ships unloaded at Liverpool. There the company maintained huge storage yards for the square timber and itself sold the wood to builders who, recognizing its excellence as construction material, used it for beams in the buildings then being erected in a construction boom in Britain.

Gilmour was the favourite nephew of Allan Gilmour Sr, after whom he had been named, and his success at Quebec further commended him to his uncle, who intended that he should succeed not only to his partnership in the central firm in Glasgow but also to his considerable fortune and landed property in Scotland. Unfortunately for this plan, in 1837–38 a violent dispute arose between Gilmour Sr and his associates, the nephews of his original partners, John and Arthur Pollok. Gilmour Sr left the firm, withdrawing his capital and urging his nephew to do likewise. Gilmour refused to follow his uncle, thus losing his chance of a considerable inheritance. Late in 1838 the Glasgow partners asked him to return to Scotland and, in effect, to become manager of Pollok, Gilmour. When he did so it was decided to split the company's operations between two principal head offices, one in Liverpool, specializing in the timber trade and headed by Robert Rankin, and the other in Glasgow, headed by Gilmour and concerned chiefly with the shipping side. Since Rankin and Gilmour were close friends, the arrangement worked well.

There can be little doubt, from John Rankin's account in *A history of our firm*, that Robert Rankin was the head of the concern, but Gilmour's role as "marine superintendent" was a crucial one. He ran his sailing fleet efficiently and economically; in John Rankin's words, "he was active, of rare determination, impetuous, passionate (though only momentarily so), but he could be obdurate." Until his retirement in 1870, by which time the business was essentially a shipping firm rather than a timber importing concern, Gilmour was rated as one of Scotland's principal shipowners and a leading expert in the Canadian timber trade. He had also given important evidence to parliamentary committees from 1846 to 1848 on the navigation laws and in 1853–54 on the tonnage measurement of ships and other maritime matters.

In Glasgow Gilmour resided in fashionable St Vincent Street, and as his fortune grew he leased and later purchased landed estates where he could indulge his taste for an outdoor life. In Canada he had hunted moose, and in Scotland he fished and shot on his estates of Lundin and Montrave in Fifeshire. He retained his partnerships in the various Pollok, Gilmour branch firms in Canada until his death in 1884, and among the considerable number of businessmen in Glasgow who had commenced their careers in Canada he was regarded as one who had been particularly successful. He was certainly in the first rank of the great timber magnates of the 19th century, and his good fortune in this most lucrative of fields for the British entrepreneur may be attributed not only to his astuteness as a businessman but also to the fact that the various Pollok, Gilmour concerns in British North America had been well established and were served by competent personnel from the very beginning of the timber trade era.

DAVID S. MACMILLAN

[The bulk of the records of the various Pollok and Gilmour concerns were destroyed after the publication in 1921 of John Rankin's history of the firm, but some early family and business papers can be found at the Univ. of Glasgow Arch., Adam Smith Business Records Store, UGD/36. D.S.M.]

Canadian business history; selected studies, 1497–1971, ed. D. S. Macmillan (Toronto, 1972). A. R. M. Lower, *Great Britain's woodyard: British America and the timber trade, 1763–1867* (Montreal and London, 1973). MacNutt, *New Brunswick*. John Rankin, *A history of our firm, being some account of the firm of Pollok, Gilmour and Co. and its offshoots and connections, 1804–1920* (2nd ed., Liverpool, 1921). *The Scottish tradition in Canada*, ed. W. S. Reid (Toronto, 1976). D. M. Williams, "Merchanting in the first half of the nineteenth century: the Liverpool timber trade," *Business Hist.* (Liverpool), 8 (1966): 103–21.

GIROUARD, GILBERT-ANSELME, merchant and politician; b. 26 Oct. 1846 in Sainte-Marie-de-Kent, N.B., son of Anselme Girouard and Suzanne Jaillet; m. in 1872 Sophia Baker, and they had three children; d. 13 Jan. 1885 in Buctouche, N.B.

Gilbert-Anselme Girouard, like most prominent New Brunswick Acadians of the late 19th century, was educated in a local parish school and then pursued a classical training at the Collège Saint-Joseph in Memramcook, N.B. It was at the college, established by Father Camille Lefebvre* in 1864, that Girouard became fluently bilingual and developed his oratorical skills as an active member of the Société Saint-Jean-Baptiste. After graduating in 1868, he taught school in his native parish at a salary of $10 per month. In 1870 he moved to nearby Buctouche where he established himself as a general merchant.

Business flourished in Buctouche and Girouard gained considerable respect in the community. A Liberal-Conservative by political persuasion, he was eventually approached to seek election as member of parliament for Kent County. Girouard agreed to stand, and in the general election of 1878 he defeated the incumbent Liberal, George McLeod, and three other English-speaking candidates. The Conservatives under Sir John A. Macdonald* won a decisive victory nationally, but the Liberals in New Brunswick under Sir Albert James SMITH and Isaac BURPEE retained all but five of the 16 seats. The second Acadian to sit in the House of Commons, Girouard was easily re-elected in 1882 when he received almost twice as many votes as his opponent, George Valentine McInerney.

As a member of parliament until 1883, Girouard actively pressed for local improvements in his constituency and worked on behalf of the entire Acadian people. He was one of the most vocal proponents of a railway, opened in 1885, between Buctouche and the mercantile centre of Moncton. The people of the Buctouche area were thus freed from relying on transportation by horse cart or packet-boat from the existing rail terminus at Shediac. He spoke out in favour of an Acadian senator, and in March 1885 Pascal Poirier* was appointed. Girouard also wrote letters of recommendation for Placide Gaudet* who was trying for a position at the national archives, and was responsible for the selection in 1885 of Auguste Renaud, the first Acadian member of parliament, as collector of customs for Buctouche.

In 1880 Girouard joined 40 other clerical and lay Acadian leaders in attending the Société Saint-Jean-Baptiste convention in Quebec City to which French-speaking peoples from across Canada had been invited. Inspired by the resulting realization of themselves as a special group within the larger francophone population, the Acadian leaders decided to organize a similar convention for themselves. Almost 5,000 Acadians assembled in convention at Memramcook in late July 1881, an occasion described as the "rebirth of the Acadian nation." Declaring their intention to "live as a separate entity [and] to forge their own identity and heritage," the Acadians chose a national feast day and established the Société Nationale de l'Assomption to represent them. Girouard, who was secretary of the convention's executive committee, laid particular emphasis in his speeches on the importance of education for young Acadians and on the preservation of an Acadian heritage. He continued to be active in the movement and was an executive member for a local convention held in Buctouche in August 1883.

In the House of Commons Girouard made lengthy statements only twice. The first, in 1880, concerned his belief that the Maritime provinces were entitled to a portion of the fisheries compensation to be paid Canada by the United States as a result of the Treaty of Washington of 1871. The second speech which he delivered in 1881 was of much greater significance in Girouard's career for it ultimately led to his resignation in the summer of 1883. It dealt with his claim for losses sustained in 1872 in fulfilling a contract from the federal government to deliver railway ties to Bathurst, N.B., for the Intercolonial Railway. Confusion had developed over the place of delivery and some of the ties were lost at sea while being rafted from Bathurst to Petit-Rocher. Girouard claimed that delivery had been made and that the government owed him a considerable sum of money. Timothy Warren Anglin*, Liberal MP for Gloucester, charged Girouard with conflict of interest, and against Macdonald's wishes he resigned. Girouard's health was also precarious, and Pierre-Amand Landry*, a leading figure in the New Brunswick government, had been pressing for some months to take over his seat. Girouard was appointed collector of customs for Richibucto immediately prior to his resignation, and Landry assumed his seat after winning a by-election on 22 Sept. 1883.

Girouard's health continued to deteriorate, and he was rarely seen in public after the spring of 1884. He died from tuberculosis in January 1885 at age 38.

DELLA M. M. STANLEY

Centre d'études acadiennes, Univ. de Moncton (Moncton, N.-B.), Fonds Placide Gaudet, 1.64-6, 8, 9; Fonds Pierre-Amand Landry, 5.1-1. PAC, MG 26, A, 226.

Can., House of Commons, *Debates*, 1880–81. *Daily Sun* (Saint John, N.B.), 14 Jan. 1885. *Le Moniteur acadien* (Shédiac, N.-B.), 15 janv. 1885, 1 juill. 1890. *Weekly Transcript* (Moncton), 4 July 1883. *CPC*, 1879, 1883. *Dominion annual register*, 1883–85. *Album historique, 1864–1939, publié à l'occasion des fêtes du 75e anniversaire, 13–14 juin 1939* ([Moncton, 1939]). *L'album souvenir des noces d'argent de la Société Saint-Jean-Baptiste du collège Saint-Joseph, Memramcook, N.B.* ([Moncton, 1894]). Conventions nationales des Acadiens, *Recueil des travaux et délibérations des six premières conventions*, F.-J. Robidoux, compil. (Shédiac, 1907). É.-L. Léger, *L'histoire de la paroisse de Saint-Antoine, les débuts jusqu'à l'année 1967* ([Shediac Bridge, N.-B.], 1967). Marguerite Michaud, *La reconstruction française au Nouveau-Brunswick: Bouctouche, paroisse-type* (Fredericton, 1955). D. M. M. Stanley, *Au service de deux peuples: Pierre-Amand Landry* (Moncton, 1977).

GIRROIR, HUBERT, Roman Catholic priest and teacher; b. 18 July 1825 at Tracadie, N.S., son of Captain Joseph Girroir and Angélique Le Blanc; d. 25 Jan. 1884 at Havre Boucher, N.S.

Hubert Girroir received his early education in Tracadie, but left there in 1841 to attend the newly founded St Mary's College in Halifax. The following year he returned home and during 1842–43 received private academic instruction from the parish priest, Louis-Modeste Anssart. His education was then interrupted until 1850, but during the interval he became skilled at boatbuilding and blacksmithing. In September 1850, with funds supplied by Bishop William Fraser* of Arichat, he entered the Grand Séminaire de Québec and was ordained priest on 19 Feb. 1853. At Quebec Girroir demonstrated his talent for speed-skating by defeating an American champion in a race. His superiors, at first reluctant to allow such a contest, relented when Girroir promised to donate his winnings to the seminary.

Following ordination Girroir served for about six months as an assistant in the parish of Notre-Dame-de-la-Victoire (at Lévis, Que.). In August 1853 he returned to Nova Scotia and was appointed an assistant at the cathedral in Arichat. Girroir also began to teach Christian doctrine and French at St Francis Xavier College in Arichat, recently established by Bishop Colin Francis MacKinnon*. In 1855 the seminarians and senior students of the college were transferred to a new location at Antigonish which was to become St Francis Xavier University in 1866. Father Girroir remained in Arichat as rector of the cathedral and principal of the renamed Arichat Academy which taught younger students in preparation for their entry into college. The only Acadian priest in the diocese until 1860, he worked zealously to promote education and the French language and culture among the many Acadians of the area. He was largely responsible for bringing the French-speaking Christian Brothers to Arichat in 1860 and he supported the teaching efforts of the sisters of the Congregation of Notre-Dame from Montreal.

In 1863 Girroir was appointed pastor at Little Arichat (West Arichat) where he continued to serve the interests of his Acadian parishioners and students. However, the regulations included in the Free School Act of 1864 required that teachers take qualifying exams in English if a school was to receive public funding. The language provision made it virtually impossible for the French-speaking brothers to continue teaching in the area, and they left the district in 1866. Girroir felt that Bishop MacKinnon and some of his own parishioners had not whole-heartedly supported his efforts in French language education. His unhappiness over the language stipulations prompted him to complain bitterly to Premier Charles Tupper* in March 1866 that "whenever an Acadian community is on the point of taking a position among others, there must be something to thwart the efforts of many years." In June 1867 MacKinnon attempted to resolve the continuing split in the Little Arichat parish by transferring Girroir, who resisted by appealing to Archbishop Thomas Louis Connolly* of Halifax and to Rome.

It was not until June 1868 that Girroir took up his next post at Chéticamp, a French-speaking community on the northern shore of Cape Breton Island. There he established a number of schools and supported the temperance movement. He was also largely responsible for having the harbour dredged, a project which was of great economic benefit to the fishing community. In June 1875 he was appointed to Havre Boucher, on the mainland of eastern Nova Scotia, another community with a large Acadian population. He remained there until shortly before his death in January 1884. Despite his successes in the cause of Acadian cultural survival and French language education in Nova Scotia, Girroir also met many setbacks and in 1866 gloomily speculated that there was "a fatality attached to the Acadian race."

R. A. MacLean

Casket (Antigonish, N.S.), 29 Aug. 1858, 15 March 1861, 18 Feb. 1892, 4 Jan. 1934. Allaire, *Dictionnaire.* Anselme Chiasson. *Chéticamp, history and Acadian traditions* (Moncton, N.B., 1961). A. A. Johnston, *A history of the Catholic Church in eastern Nova Scotia* (2v., Antigonish, 1960–71), II: 253–54, 301, 423–31, 458, 526. A. A. MacDonald, *Centenary, Saint Paul's parish* (Havre Boucher, N.S., 1961). Éphrem Boudreau, "L'abbé Hubert Girroir, 1825–1884," Soc. hist. acadienne, *Cahiers* (Moncton, N.-B.), 6 (1975): 69–81.

GLACKMEYER, LOUIS-ÉDOUARD, notary and municipal councillor; b. 7 Dec. 1793 at Quebec City, son of Frédéric-Henri Glackmeyer*, a music teacher, and Marie-Anne O'Neil; d. 9 Feb. 1881 at Quebec.

Louis-Édouard Glackmeyer's father, a native of Hanover (Federal Republic of Germany), came to Canada in 1776 as bandmaster of a regiment of auxiliary troops of Brunswick and Hesse. His mother was the sister of Jean-Baptiste O'Neil, the well-known verger of the cathedral at Quebec who was famous for the pranks and practical jokes recounted by Louis-Honoré Fréchette* in his *Originaux et détraqués* (Montréal, 1892). Louis-Édouard Glackmeyer studied at the Petit Séminaire de Québec and on 13 Dec. 1815 was admitted to the profession of notary. Employed in 1815 as an assistant in the office of the law clerk of the crown, it was not long before he grew sick of the minutiæ of the bureaucracy; a few months later he opened his own office on Rue Saint-Pierre, in Quebec.

When George IV died in 1830, James Stuart*, the attorney general of Lower Canada, maintained that all public officers and all members of the liberal professions must renew their commissions and pay the same charges as were required when they were originally granted. During the 1831 session Glackmeyer complained to the assembly; shortly thereafter the house decided to call for Stuart's resignation. "He was accused of certain acts committed during the election at William-Henry [in 1827], the unwarranted collection of certain fees for the renewal of notarial commissions, and practices aimed solely at increasing his emoluments. . . ." Lord Aylmer [Whitworth-Aylmer*] suspended Stuart in 1831, and Lord Goderich, the colonial secretary, permanently relieved him of his office in 1832.

On 7 July 1840 Roger Lelièvre chaired a meeting of 25 notaries of the Quebec region who founded the Association des Notaires du District de Québec. The principal aims of the association were to attend to all the profession's concerns from the point of view of both the members and the public, and to supervise the studies of clerks aspiring to the profession. A committee of seven, including Glackmeyer, was instructed to draft the association's rules; however, as things did not go to his liking, Glackmeyer resigned.

When three boards of notaries for Quebec, Montreal, and Trois-Rivières were set up by law in 1847, Glackmeyer at first expressed some doubts about the outcome but finally supported this development. Through this law, the boards obtained by royal sanction powers to appoint, reject, and discipline their members themselves. On 20 Sept. 1847 Glackmeyer was appointed *syndic* of the Quebec Board of Notaries. At the elections for the second triennium (1850–53), he was chosen president of this board. In 1851, when an application was made for amendments to the statute relating to the notarial profession in Canada East, Glackmeyer was summoned before a committee of the Legislative Assembly concerned with notaries' fees. In his testimony, Glackmeyer affirmed that the majority of notaries considered the act permitted the boards to fix maximum, but not minimum, fees. According to him, such a regulation could only operate to the advantage of the profession, but it would not prevent notaries from working for a mere song.

In spite of the hostility being roused by the measure, Glackmeyer expressed his approval of an act adopted in 1860 which the attorney general for Canada East, George-Étienne Cartier*, championed. The act regulated everything related to certificates given by the registrars and provided for the method of cancelling mortgages, for the registration of proxies, and for the building of safety vaults in registry offices. In addition, the act ordered the compiling of a land register for the whole province and the renewal, once the register was completed, of all titles involving mortgages. That year, the Quebec Board of Notaries, with Glackmeyer as president, rejected a bill then before the Legislative Council to have all notarial acts countersigned by witnesses. Despite these protests, the council adopted the measure.

By 1862, as a result of the passing of the 1847 and 1859 laws permitting the creation of new boards of notaries, these institutions had increased in Canada East from three to ten. The admission examinations, which varied from one board to another, allowed almost anyone to become a notary. Furthermore, each district had its own regulations, rates, and procedures. In 1869, in order to clear up some of the confusion, notary Louis Archambeault, of the Montreal board, introduced a bill to create a single board of notaries as well as to fix the number of notaries and their place of residence. This last point aroused sharp opposition; Glackmeyer saw in it an attack on the freedom of the individual to choose his profession and to practise it in the setting of his choice. Archambeault modified his bill along these lines and it was adopted in 1870; thus a single board of notaries was created for the province of Quebec.

At the election for its first triennium on 5 Oct. 1870, Glackmeyer was chosen vice-president of the Provincial Board of Notaries. In 1873, at the elections for the second triennium, he became president. He was re-elected for a second term in 1876 but resigned because of advanced age. In his final report, Glackmeyer stressed the efforts made by the board to set stricter examinations for the admission of candidates and thereby improve the reputation of the profession throughout the province. He declared himself opposed to a statute reducing the period of training for students from four to three years. He had been the first to suggest a list recording the names and addresses of all notaries practising in the province of Quebec. In 1876, when he retired, 756 notaries in Quebec were on record.

On 6 Aug. 1822, at Quebec, Louis-Édouard Glackmeyer had married Marie-Henriette, the daughter of Étienne-Claude Lagueux*, a rich Quebec merchant who long represented Northumberland County in the Lower Canadian House of Assembly. Thus Glackmeyer was soon involved in the great political discussions of the day and closely connected with the Bédards and the Nelsons. He even had fleeting inclinations from time to time to stand for election: in the Saguenay, or in Montmorency, or in Quebec County. He supported Wolfred Nelson* when the latter broke with Louis-Joseph Papineau*, but rejoined Papineau in 1848 and fought with him for the end of the union of the two Canadas. According to a letter in *Le Canadien* in 1848, it was at this time that he thought of standing in Quebec County. But Glackmeyer rapidly abandoned politics. He was, however, a member of the Quebec City Council from 1833 to 1845 and from 1854 to 1856, representing in turn the wards of Saint-Charles and Saint-Pierre. He was also municipal assessor for the city in 1833, then one of the justices of the peace in charge of municipal administration from 1836 to 1840.

A more enduring passion was music. He played the flute in a quartet directed by Chief Justice Jonathan Sewell*, and later he was president of the Septette Club, which was formed in 1857 and included his sister Angélique-Henriette Glackmeyer, the notary Chavigny de La Chevrotière, Alfred Paré, Archibald Campbell*, and the three Pfeiffer brothers. Glackmeyer lived in turn at Quebec, La Canardière, Charlesbourg, and Beauport. At Charlesbourg, where he owned a rural property, he could give free rein to his interest in botany, a science about which he was well informed. From 1844 to 1859, at Beauport, he made numerous meteorological observations, recording them in a book still extant in the Public Archives of Canada.

Louis-Édouard Glackmeyer did not move in society; and he seldom left his office on Rue Saint-Pierre, with its large clientele. He was even considered by his contemporaries to be somewhat eccentric; but his goodness and sound qualities earned him the confidence and respect of his colleagues and fellow citizens.

CLAUDE VACHON

Arch. du séminaire de Chicoutimi (Chicoutimi, Qué.), Fonds Provancher, Ernest Gagnon, "Notes sur le notaire Glackmeyer"; Lettres de L.-É. Glackmeyer. PAC, MG 30, D1, 14; 18; MG 24, I94.

"Mémoire sur la partie occidentale du Canada, depuis Michillimakinac jusqu'au fleuve du Mississippi," *BRH*, 26 (1920): 25. P.-V. Charland, "Notre-Dame de Québec; le nécrologe de la crypte ou les inhumations dans cette église depuis 1652," *BRH*, 20 (1914): 305. Le Jeune, *Dictionnaire*, II: 666. P.-G. Roy, *Fils de Québec* (4 sér., Lévis, Qué., 1933), III: 56–58. Georges Monarque, *Un général allemand au Canada: le baron Friedrich Adolphus von Riedesel* (Montréal, 1946), 143–45. J.-E. Roy, *Hist. du notariat*, II–IV. P.-G. Roy, *La famille Glackmeyer* (Lévis, 1916). André Vachon, *Histoire du notariat canadien, 1621–1960* (Québec, 1962), 79–155. P.-B. Casgrain, "Une autre maison Montcalm à Québec (1759)," *BRH*, 8 (1902): 337. *La Musique* (Québec), I (1919): 74. P.-G. Roy, "La famille Glackmeyer," *BRH*, 22 (1916): 195–205.

GLEN, THOMAS, merchant and politician; b. 1796 at Greenock, Scotland, son of Alexander Glen, Glasgow merchant; m. 29 Aug. 1829 Jane Reed (d. 1834) of Bay Bulls, Nfld, and they had one son; d. 28 April 1887 at St John's, Nfld.

Thomas Glen was educated in Scotland and came to Newfoundland about 1811 to work as a clerk for Miller, Fergus and Company. This firm was a general supply firm at Bay Bulls, one of the important fishing settlements south of St John's. He subsequently went into partnership with James Fergus. The partnership was not, however, a financial success. The Bay Bulls business became insolvent in 1826 and Fergus and Glen moved to St John's to start a West Indies trading company. In January 1837 they formed a partnership with Eugenius Harvey; Fergus withdrew in December 1838, and in December 1841 Glen and Harvey dissolved their association. Glen then acted as a commission merchant and auctioneer, activities he maintained along with a political career through the 1860s.

Glen entered public life in 1842 when he was elected by a narrow majority to the Amalgamated Legislature as the representative for Ferryland. A member of the majority Conservative party within the legislature, he received several patronage posts, becoming a governor and later auditor of the government-controlled Savings Bank and a commissioner for the construction of the Colonial Building in St John's; he retained these posts probably until 1848 and 1850 respectively. After the great fire of 1846, which devastated much of St John's including his own business premises, Glen was appointed a relief commissioner and re-building appraiser. He was also an active member of the Scottish Society of St John's, serving as its president in 1845.

Glen, along with Walter GRIEVE, was one of the few Conservatives in the Amalgamated Legislature to support John Kent*'s 1846 resolutions in favour of introducing responsible government to Newfoundland. By 1848 the members had divided along sectarian lines, the Catholic Liberals being proponents of responsible government and the Protestant Conservatives being opponents, and Glen's position as a Congregationalist representing a Catholic constituency became difficult. He was defeated in 1848 and did not run again until 1855. By that year Philip Francis Little* had worked out a political alliance between the Catholics and non-Anglican Protestants. Peter Winser, the Liberal who had defeated Glen in 1848, moved to contest the new district of St John's West and Glen was nominated as the Liberal candidate for Ferryland, now a two-member riding. He was returned with Edward Dalton Shea*. Glen remained a member for this constituency until 1874.

The introduction of responsible government immediately followed the election of 1855, and Glen became receiver general in the Liberal administrations of Little (1855–58) and John Kent (1858–61). Daniel Woodley Prowse* describes Glen as "a heaven-born Receiver General, one of the best party men that ever sat in a cabinet," and one of the most active and important members of both governments. Glen also managed the Liberal party funds. Had it not been for the issue of confederation with the other British North American colonies, it is quite possible that Glen would have drifted over to the Conservatives during the 1860s, as did several Liberals. He believed, however, that union would ruin the colony's economy and fought strongly against it from the opposition benches. He argued that retrenchment and reform would be of far greater benefit, and that responsible government could not be judged a failure so soon after its inception. With the electoral victory in 1869 of the anti-confederation party led by Charles James Fox BENNETT, Glen became once again receiver general. Although he was not a dominant figure in the Bennett government, he did manage to fulfil the party's campaign promises of reduced taxation and government expenditure, helped by the prosperity of the colony during this period. In July 1874, Glen retired from active politics, and because of his personal financial need he accepted the post of auditor of public accounts from the Frederic Bowker Terrington Carter* administration. Though his last report was published in 1885, Glen nominally held the post until his death in 1887.

Throughout his political career Glen was recognized as an able, if conservative, financial administrator. He believed in strict economy and a minimum of government intervention, opinions not always shared by his colleagues. He was especially wary of government subsidies to industries and transportation. As a public figure his behaviour and speech were independent, sharp, and crusty. Had he been more pliable, his political success might well have been greater.

JAMES K. HILLER

Nfld., Amalgamated Legislature, *Journal*, 1843; *Blue book*, 1874. *Evening Mercury*, 29 April 1887. *Newfoundlander*, 20 Dec. 1838; 23 Dec. 1841; 9 Jan. 1845; 27 Aug. 1846; 29 April, 20 May 1847; 30 Nov. 1848. *Public Ledger*, December 1827, 7 Oct. 1842. *Royal Gazette* (St John's), September 1843, February 1849. Garfield Fizzard, "The Amalgamated Assembly of Newfoundland, 1841–1847" (MA thesis, Memorial Univ. of Newfoundland, St John's, 1963). J. P. Greene, "The influence of religion in the politics of Newfoundland, 1850–1861" (MA thesis, Memorial Univ. of Newfoundland, 1970). W. D. MacWhirter, "A political history of Newfoundland, 1865–1874" (MA thesis, Memorial Univ. of Newfoundland, 1963). Prowse, *Hist. of Nfld.* (1895).

GLENN (Glen, Glyn), JOHN, soldier, prospector, trader, and farmer; b. 1833 in County Mayo (Republic of Ireland); d. 9 Jan. 1886 in Calgary (Alta).

John Glenn was 16 when he emigrated to the United States. He was living in Waco, Tex., when the American Civil War started in 1861 and he became a Confederate soldier. However, he deserted in a protest against slavery and fought with the Union forces until the end of the war in 1865. He then began prospecting for gold and later claimed he had travelled from "the Rio Grande to the Peace River." In 1872 he was traversing the Yellowhead Pass en route from the Cariboo (B.C.) gold-fields when he met the expedition of Sandford Fleming* which was inspecting the proposed route for the Canadian Pacific Railway. A solitary traveller, Glenn greatly impressed the party with his "self reliant individualism" and courage.

By the summer of 1873 Glenn was prospecting on the North Saskatchewan River. That September he married Adélaïde Belcourt, a Métis, at the Roman Catholic mission at St Albert near Fort Edmonton. During the next two years he developed a trading business with the Indians. While returning from Fort Benton (Mont.) in the fall of 1874 with his wagon of goods he overtook the first detachments of North-West Mounted Police to reach the northwest, and sold them such luxuries as flour and syrup at a "pretty stiff price." In July 1875 he settled permanently on Fish Creek at its junction with the Bow River (Alta), and later that year, when the NWMP, led by Éphrem-A. BRISEBOIS, arrived to establish Fort Calgary, he was on hand to build stone fireplaces in the barracks and to sell them hay. In 1876 Glenn and a man named Sam Livingston started farming, the first to do so in the area. Glenn sold his farm in 1879 to Indian commissioner Edgar Dewdney* who planned to operate it as a supply farm. The holdings, two log buildings and two small fields of oats and barley, together with a milk cow and calf, were sold for $360.

Glenn then moved farther west and became a squatter on the south side of Fish Creek east of the Macleod trail crossing. It was here that Glenn instituted the first irrigation scheme on the Canadian prairies, locating his own point of diversion and laying out the system himself. It irrigated his fields and those of Samuel William Shaw who also used the diversion for the operation of a woollen mill.

Glenn became an active, respected, and prosperous member of the Fort Calgary area. His farm was a "show place" which all visiting notables came to see, including the Marquess of Lorne [Campbell*] in 1881. Glenn was the first permanent local resident to purchase property in the CPR's sale of lots for the townsite of Calgary in 1883 (the town of Calgary was incorporated in 1884) and he was a founder and vice-president of the Calgary District Agricultural Society in 1884. An unfailing champion of the country's agricultural possibilities, he was an organizer, along with Livingston, of a protest meeting of settlers held on his own farm on 6 April 1885. The Alberta Settlers Rights Association was formed and strong resolutions were drafted and directed to Ottawa protesting regulations governing range leases, homestead restrictions, Métis grievances, and the lack of western representation in government.

On 17 Oct. 1885 Glenn was injured in an accident caused by a runaway team of horses. He died a few months later, leaving his widow and six children.

SHEILAGH S. JAMESON

Glenbow-Alberta Institute, Canada North West Land Company papers, CPR townsite sales books, XXIV; Simon John Clarke diaries, 1876–86; Frank M. Crosby papers, 1863–84; Patrick and William Glenn, "Biography of John Glenn, pioneer of pioneers (of Calgary and Mindapore district from 1873 to 1886)"; Irrigation papers, W. L. Jacobson project, 1961–64, f.167; Samuel W. Shaw papers, 1885–98.

Calgary District Agricultural Soc., *District of Alberta: information for intending settlers* (Ottawa, 1884). Can., Parl., *Sessional papers*, 1879, VI: no.7. G. M. Grant, *Ocean to ocean: Sandford Fleming's expedition through Canada in 1872 . . .* (Toronto and London, 1873; repr. Toronto, 1970), 267–68. *Calgary Herald*, 1883–86. *Globe*, 4 April 1885. *Macleod Gazette and Alberta Livestock Record* (Fort Macleod, [Alta.]), 1882–86. J.[C.] McDougall, *On western trails in the early seventies: frontier pioneer life in the Canadian north-west* (Toronto, 1911).

GLOVER, Sir JOHN HAWLEY, naval officer and colonial administrator; b. 24 Feb. 1829 at Yateley, Hampshire, England, son of the Reverend Frederick Augustus Glover and Mary Broughton; m. November 1876 Elizabeth Rosetta Scott, and they had at least one child; d. 30 Sept. 1885 in London, England.

John Hawley Glover's father had planned that his son would enter the Royal Engineers but instead, with the help of his mother, the daughter of an admiral, he joined the Royal Navy on 4 Dec. 1841 as a first class volunteer serving under Admiral Sir Edward Campbell Rich Owen. Glover's prospects were bright, but the sudden death of his mother and his estrangement from his father when the latter quickly remarried deprived him of the essential financial means to further his career. Withdrawal from naval service was, however, avoided when Owen encouraged Glover to enter the Surveying Branch; he joined it in May 1842 and with his pay was able to support his own advancement. Until 1852 he served on surveying ships in the Mediterranean and along the west coast of Africa. In 1853 Glover took part in the war in Burma and was mentioned twice in dispatches. After his recovery from a wound received in Burma, surveying duties took him to the Baltic and to the Elbe and Weser rivers until March 1857 when he was sent with the Niger expedition to survey the lagoons at Lagos and a portion of the Niger River. His career at sea ended in 1862 with the completion of this tour and with his advancement to the rank of commander at the age of 33. He was later placed on the retired list, and in 1877 promoted captain.

On 21 April 1863, Glover was appointed administrator of Lagos; in 1864 he became colonial secretary of the colony, and in 1866 he again assumed the duties of administrator until 9 July 1872. In his second term as administrator he was actively involved in suppressing marauding Ashantis, and in 1873 he volunteered to serve against the Ashantis when war appeared imminent. His instructions were to raise a native force with which to act at his discretion under the leadership of Sir Garnet Joseph Wolseley*; with Hausa tribesmen he accompanied the main force proceeding into the Ashanti country, and showed skill in raids and movement of military supplies. He was largely responsible for the peace reached on 14 Feb. 1874 and received the thanks of the British parliament and a GCMG for this service. His actions were long remembered by the Hausas.

Glover was offered the post of governor of Newfoundland on Christmas Eve 1875 and he arrived there on 7 April 1876. The colony, he found, had matured considerably since the rowdy days following the opening of the first legislature in 1833 under Governor Thomas John Cochrane*. The Liberal premiers Glover worked with during his terms in office, 1876–81 and 1883–85, Frederic Bowker Terrington Carter* and William Vallance Whiteway* respectively, were both talented men and prominent lawyers, who ably guided Glover in his administration of the colony. During Glover's first term, Carter and particularly Whiteway sought to diminish external influence over the colony's affairs and policies.

The French government was aware that its hold on the west coast, also called the French shore, depended upon the restriction of private and commercial settlement and complained to the British government at every attempt by Newfoundland to place settlers on it. Nevertheless, by the time Glover left Newfoundland in 1881, the colony had made significant progress towards control of the west coast. In 1877 Commander William HOWORTH became the first magistrate on the west coast appointed by Newfoundland and customs officers began collecting dues for use by the colony. The area gained representation in the assembly in 1881 and France conceded the right "in principle" for the Newfoundland government to make land grants for settlement, mining, and industrial enterprises in the same year. These changes were representative of the substantial easing of British control over the colony. The greatest threat to French ambitions was the Railway Act of 1880 which provided for the construction of a line to run from St John's to Halls Bay, a mining region in Notre Dame Bay. This railway would connect the centres of population, open land in the valleys of the Gambo, Gander, and Exploits rivers, and facilitate lumbering and mining operations in the interior. The government hoped to continue the line all the way down the west coast to Port aux Basques where it would connect by ferry with the mainland railway system, but after complaints to Britain from the French government, the imperial government forced the colony to accept the shorter line to Halls Bay. Yet for the colony, overly dependent upon the fishery, the diversification promised by the completion of the longer railway was too strong a need to be denied forever.

Glover, at first unaccustomed to the complexities of responsible government, soon adopted a policy of following the advice of his ministers in colonial matters while trying to prevent a serious breach with the home government which had the responsibility for fishery treaties with France. The Newfoundlanders' success with the French shore problem eased the political atmosphere in the colony, and made the positions of the governor, British naval personnel, and officers on the treaty coast less onerous. The governor's role of liaison between the colony and the home government was also aided in 1878 by the satisfied feeling in Newfoundland following the negotiation by Whiteway of an award from the Halifax Commission: Newfoundland received $1 million as its share of funds paid by the United States to Great Britain as compensation for advantages gained in the Atlantic fisheries through the Treaty of Washington in 1871.

Glover was happiest when travelling throughout the island with his wife. Together they visited fishermen's homes, inspected working establishments, ventured down mines, and holidayed in popular resorts and remote outports. Glover was the first governor to cross a large part of the island when in 1878 he went on a two-month trip between Halls Bay and the Bay of Islands accompanied by the famous geologist, Alexander MURRAY, and, for part of the way, by Moses Harvey*, a clergyman and historian who published *Across Newfoundland with the governor* the following year. Glover thus knew more about the people and the personalities of the colony than many of the government ministers. When he opened the legislature in 1879 he could say with conviction that he had been impressed with the agricultural resources and forest lands in the western part of the island which would attract settlers; it afforded "such facilities for the construction of a main highway that this great work might be accomplished at a very modest cost." The speech was a mixture of truth and exaggeration, which presaged the railway age of Newfoundland.

On a visit to England during the London season of 1881, Glover accepted the governorship of the Leeward Islands and was instructed to travel there quickly because of urgent problems. Sir Henry Berkeley Fitz-Hardinge Maxse succeeded him in the autumn of 1881. The Glovers were not reluctant to leave Newfoundland; they were equally content to depart from the Caribbean in 1883. Sir John contracted malaria in Antigua, and while waiting for a better posting, rested in Germany, Ireland, and England. Maxse, who had arrived in Newfoundland in poor health, died in September 1883 and the colony was without a governor at a time when negotiations with France over fishery treaty rights were taking place. The Colonial Office persuaded Glover to take up the governorship again for a short term. Before going to St John's, he went to Paris to participate in the treaty talks, acting in an advisory capacity to the British ambassador. This visit enabled him to nurse his health further and when the negotiations were over Glover took a holiday in Sussex. He received an urgent message in late May 1884 from Premier Carter asking him to come to Newfoundland immediately to deal with colonial matters so that Carter could fulfil his obligations as chief justice and preside at the trials of Roman Catholics charged with the murder of several Protestants during riots at Harbour Grace in 1883. Despite the religious tension in the colony, Glover was well received when he arrived in June accompanied by two Colonial Office officials who were sent to persuade the government of Newfoundland to accept the terms of the recent Paris negotiations.

Glover stayed in Newfoundland long enough to see the latest French shore terms rejected by the colony and the completion of the railway to Harbour Grace, the second largest community on the island. In late 1884 he and Lady Glover opened the new graving docks in the St John's harbour. Glover, however, had not fully recovered his health and he collapsed on 2 March 1885. Rest cures in Topsail, Nfld, and in Homberg (Federal Republic of Germany) did not help him and he died at his home in London on 30 Sept. 1885. A monument was later raised to his memory in St Paul's Cathedral, London, with a replica in the Anglican Cathedral of St John the Baptist in St John's, completed during Glover's second term.

In her private diary Glover's wife has provided considerable background detail to his career of a kind not normally included in political histories. She considered the proper role of her husband as paterfamilias to backward and primitive colonies, a view which was condescending but not without truth. However, in Daniel Woodley Prowse*'s judgement, "No more honourable, generous, kind hearted, or active ruler ever presided over our government."

FREDERIC FRASER THOMPSON

PRO, CO 194/193–202, 194/248. Royal Commonwealth Soc. (London), Sir John Hawley Glover papers. Moses Harvey, *Across Newfoundland with the governor: a visit to our mining region; and this Newfoundland of ours: being a series of papers – the natural resources and future prospects of the colony* (St John's, 1879). *Illustrated London News*, 25 April 1874. *Times and General Commercial Gazette* (St John's), 2 Oct. 1885. *The annual register: a review of public events at home and abroad* (London), 1885. *DNB*. G.B., Adm., *Navy list*, 1874–86. Henry Brackenbury, *The Ashanti war; a narrative prepared from the official documents by permission of Major-General Sir Garnet Wolseley, C.B., K.C.M.G.* (2v., London, 1968). J. K. Hiller, "A history of Newfoundland, 1874–1901" (PHD thesis, Univ. of Cambridge, Eng., 1971). E. R. [Scott] Glover, *Life of Sir John Hawley Glover, R.N., G.C.M.G.*, ed. Richard Temple (London, 1897); *Memories of four continents: recollections grave and gay of events in social and diplomatic life* (London, 1923). F. F. Thompson, *The French shore problem in Newfoundland: an imperial study* (Toronto, 1961).

GODET. *See* GAUDET

GOLD. *See* GOULD

GOOD, JAMES, ironmonger, machinist, manufacturer, and politician; b. probably some time between 1814 and 1818 in Ireland; m. in 1839 Eleanor Bull, and they had at least six daughters and one son; d. 12 Sept. 1889 at Toronto, Ont.

It is possible that James Good, on his arrival at York (Toronto) from Dublin in 1832, found employment in the firm of either Amos Norton or Reason Williams, ironworkers in the city. In 1840, with the financial backing of his father-in-law, Bartholomew (Bartley) Bull, an Irish-born Methodist and Orangeman with useful real estate holdings, Good was able to acquire the Union Furnace Company. The business was to be known by various names including the Toronto Engine Works, the Toronto Locomotive Works, and James Good and Company.

Shortly after a fire in 1841 levelled the firm's buildings and threw 50 employees out of work, Good entered into a short-lived partnership with James Rogers Armstrong*; Good was later said to have "tricked" his partner. In 1845 R. G. Dun evaluated Good's worth to be $5,000 to $6,000 and considered his firm safe for moderate credit even though Good was dilatory in meeting his obligations. Seven years later Good was reported as worth $50,000 and "perfectly safe" for credit.

As the proprietor of a large iron foundry Good was able to bid on contracts for several locomotives at the beginning of the first major railway boom in Canada. Between 1853 and 1855 he built nine engines, at an average cost of $5,000, for the Ontario, Simco, and Huron Railroad Union, the first passenger service in Canada West. He also produced at least five locomotives for other Canadian railways.

Good's *Toronto*, the first locomotive built in Canada West and possibly in any British colony, was designed in the United States tradition of engine construction and was completed in April 1853. It weighed 25 tons and the width and stroke of its cylinders were 16 inches and 22 inches. Canadian railways, built by British engineers, had originally used British made locomotives. However, these were found to be far too light and sensitive for the operating conditions in North America. As a result a rugged, relatively crude (by British standards), but eminently more suitable locomotive design evolved during the 1840s and 1850s in the United States and became known as the "American" locomotive. All of Good's engines were built to the common Canadian railway gauge of 5′6″. Most, if not all, of his locomotives were scrapped when the various railways converted to the North American standard gauge of 4′8½″ in the late 1870s and 1880s.

Early in 1856 Good sold his business. He returned to the engine-building trade about four years later, after the recession that began in 1857 had abated. Despite previous debts, he arranged the ownership of his property and machinery in such a way that he was able to avoid suit for former liabilities. The Montreal firm of Frothingham and Workman [*see* Thomas WORKMAN] accepted a chattel mortgage worth $1,200 in 1860, but it would appear that for the next 30 years Good had "no credit locally." Nevertheless he remained in business until his death. In 1867 he employed 45 people, and in that year his company contained machine, moulding, blacksmith, and pattern shops, as well as a stove-mounting shop, warehouse, and counting room. It manufactured machinery for grist- and sawmills; stoves; hollow-ware; tin, copper, and iron ware; and potash kettles. In 1875 the firm survived a second fire which again levelled the premises.

Good was an artisan of undoubted capabilities, but his talent for management was questioned by his contemporaries. It is recorded in the Dun entry for 23 May 1855 that he "has got into a more extensive [business] than he knows how to manage. There are any number of [executions] now lying in the [Sheriff's hands against him]. . . ." He was popular in Toronto, however, and in 1854 he was elected a councilman for St James' Ward. The next year he won the election for alderman in the same constituency. Good was also active in the Methodist community until 1879 when he was forced to take a more passive role after his hearing failed. He died suddenly at home on 12 Sept. 1889 while preparing to go to work.

Good's share in locomotive building followed a typical North American pattern. During the early years of railway construction, up to the 1860s, small iron foundries and machine shops throughout the continent were engaged in the building of a limited number of locomotives. The technology was simple and required relatively inexpensive equipment. As the demand for engines increased, small shops could no longer handle it. Some companies lacked the capital to expand; others decided to remain in the manufacture of their traditional products. Good's firm would appear to have been in the second category.

GEORGE GRAHAM MAINER

[I should like to acknowledge with gratitude the assistance provided by Chris Andreae in the preparation of this biography. G.G.M.]

Baker Library, R. G. Dun & Co. credit ledger, Canada, 26: 16, 54; 27: 91. PAC, RG 30, 1597: 225; 2028: 98, 385. Henry Scadding, *Totonto of old*, ed. F. H. Armstrong (Toronto, 1966). W. S. and H. C. Boulton, [*Plan of Toronto*] (Toronto, [1858?]). C. E. Goad, *Atlas of the city of Toronto and suburbs from special survey and registered plans showing all buildings and lot numbers* (Montreal, 1884). *Toronto directory*, 1867. F. R. Berchem, *The Yonge Street story, 1793–1860: an account from letters, diaries and newspapers* (Toronto, 1977). W. H. Pearson, *Recollections and records of Toronto of old . . .* (Toronto, 1914). *Robertson's landmarks of Toronto*. J. H. White, *American locomotives: an engineering history, 1830–1880* (Baltimore, Md., 1968), 449–58. R. R. Brown, "British and foreign locomotives in Canada and Newfoundland," Railway and Locomotive Hist. Soc., *Bull.* (Boston), 43 (April 1937): 6–22. John Loye, "Locomotives of the Grand Trunk Railway: recollections of the picturesque engines that served the great Canadian railway together with historic notes in passing," Railway and Locomotive Hist. Soc., *Bull.*, 25 (May 1931): 12–31. R. D. Smith, "The Northern Railway: its origins and construction, 1834–1855," *OH*, 48 (1956): 24–36.

GOODERHAM, WILLIAM, distiller, businessman, and banker; b. 29 Aug. 1790 at Scole, Norfolk, England, second son of James and Sarah Gooderham; m. Harriet Tovell Herring, and they had eight sons and five daughters; d. 20 Aug. 1881 at Toronto, Ont.

When William Gooderham was 12 years old he left his father's farm in Norfolk to work in the London office of his mother's brother, an East Indies trader. During the Napoleonic wars he joined the Royal York Rangers and saw action in the capture of Martinique in 1809 and Guadeloupe in 1810. Before he was 21 he was invalided home after contracting yellow fever. Gooderham became a recruiting officer for the duration of the war, and thus acquired the means both to pay off an £800 mortgage on his father's farm, which he was soon to inherit, and to secure a modest income for himself. He became a gentleman farmer, although his estate suffered from the general decline in values of agricultural property after the war.

In 1831 Gooderham's brother-in-law, James Worts, began a large immigration of their two families to Upper Canada. Worts established himself as a flour miller at the mouth of the Don River near York (Toronto) and began construction of a windmill. In 1832 Gooderham brought over to York a company of some 54 persons: members of his own and of Worts's family, as well as servants and 11 orphans. Gooderham invested the £3,000 which he had brought with him in Worts's milling business and the two brothers-in-law formed the partnership of Worts and Gooderham. It ended with Worts's death in 1834. Gooderham continued the firm but changed its name to William Gooderham, Company.

In 1837 he added a distillery to make efficient use of surplus and second-grade grain. Four years later he introduced gas for illumination and converted the entire plant from wind- to steam-power. Shipments on consignment to Montreal in the early 1840s illustrate his growing interests in the harbourfront area and in distant markets. In 1846 the firm built its own wharf and by the 1860s owned schooners on the Great Lakes. His nephew, James Gooderham WORTS, had joined him as a full partner in 1845 and the firm's name was then changed to Gooderham and Worts. During the 1860s and 1870s it enjoyed a pre-eminence in Toronto's industry, transportation, and finance, as well as on the stock exchange, and in the council and the board of arbitration of the Toronto Board of Trade.

The complex of buildings owned by Gooderham and Worts, designated the Toronto City Steam Mills and Distillery in 1845, grew to become an industrial show-place and made its owners the city's largest taxpayers. A major expansion was began in 1859 with a new, five-storey distillery built under the direction of Toronto architect David Roberts and with local suppliers. It was acknowledged as the largest distillery in Canada West: in 1861 it could produce 7,500 gallons of spirits in a day and the firm had begun exporting to the English market. In early 1862 the costs of new buildings, which included storehouses and an engine house, and of equipping the old windmill with modern machinery were estimated at $200,000. A brick malthouse was later added. After 1862 the windmill was used for further distilling the firm's premium brands, "Toddy" and "Old Rye," which enjoyed both an English market and large sales in Canada East, as well as "common whiskey" which was popular in Canada West. A spectacular fire destroyed a storehouse and a lumber pile and gutted the interior of the main milling and distillery building on the evening of 26 Oct. 1869, causing approximately $100,000 worth of damage. The company was not covered by insurance. Undeterred, Gooderham and Worts rebuilt, and their business continued to grow. In 1874–75 the company produced over 2,000,000 gallons, or one-third the total amount of proof spirits distilled in the country. By the late 1870s, Gooderham and Worts, in common with other Canadian distillers, had withdrawn from the English market and had turned increasingly to selling grain alcohol for the manufacture of such products as vinegar and methylated spirits, as well as the scent "Florida Water." Although Gooderham and Worts delegated direct management and some degree of ownership in the 1860s and 1870s, they were primarily responsible for the success of the firm.

Visitors to the Gooderham and Worts establishments after 1861 were struck by their massive size, by their cleanliness, by the fully automatic milling machinery which further distinguished the operation from most others in the province, and by the shelters for the livestock alongside the distillery. Just as the distillery had grown out of the mill, a livestock operation, begun in the 1840s, was an offshoot of the distillery business. Gooderham first raised pigs and then cattle, fattened on the nutritious swill that was a by-product of distilling. A dairy herd numbering 22 in 1843 grew into a dairy and beef operation which by 1861 was fattening about 1,000 animals a year, but at that time the herd was probably no longer owned by Gooderham and Worts. When improved transportation opened an English market, only beef was produced and by the end of the decade there were sheds for 3,000 animals near the distillery. Farms in Peel County near Streetsville and Meadowvale (both now part of Mississauga), listed among Gooderham's assets in 1881, may have been used to raise supplementary feed.

In 1845 Gooderham and Worts had taken a 14-year lease on flour mills at Norval, Halton County, and they invested in a woollen and linen mill at Streetsville some time before January 1868, when it burnt down. At Gooderham's death, the firm had mills and general stores at Pine Grove, on a branch of the Humber River, and at Streetsville and Meadowvale. They imported corn for the distillery from the western states, advertised locally for rye (which was, however, largely imported), oats, and barley, and looked to the hinterland of Toronto for supplies of grain.

In the expansion of their facilities after 1859, Gooderham and Worts included a siding to the Grand Trunk Railway large enough to hold 14 cars, and they were to be prominent among Toronto businessmen interested in the narrow gauge railways promoted by George LAIDLAW, a former employee. The partners' interest in railways grew naturally out of the needs of their mills and of the Toronto flour-mill and distillery complex. In 1870, on terms favourable to themselves, they advanced a loan large enough to give the bonds of both the Toronto, Grey and Bruce and the Toronto and Nipissing railways a market value. Thereafter their influence increased in the operation of the two lines, especially the Toronto and Nipissing of which William Gooderham Sr had become a provisional director upon its incorporation in 1868. Even before William GOODERHAM Jr replaced John Shedden* as president of the Toronto and Nipissing Railway Company in 1873, the Gooderham interests were the railway's main customer, and the Toronto terminal of this line was established conveniently near the distillery and cattle sheds. Although family control of a railway built with much public funding did not escape criticism, defenders of the line pointed to the need for Gooderham's capital to launch the enterprise and to finance its chief activity, which involved buying cordwood in the north and storing it to season before transporting it for sale in the city.

When Gooderham became president of the Bank of Toronto in 1864, a post he held until his death, he embarked on the last of several careers. Gooderham and Worts was the only firm in the Millers' Association of Toronto, which obtained a charter for the bank in 1855. Until he took over as president, Gooderham left Worts to look after the partners' interests in the bank. Although he had also been a director of the Bank of Upper Canada in 1860, Gooderham probably had viewed this role as serving his other interests more than those of banking. The Bank of Toronto was fortunate in having George Hague* as cashier (general manager) for 13 of the 17 years of Gooderham's presidency. Nevertheless, the bank's combination of conservative investment policy with internal efficiency and innovative management bore the mark of Gooderham's stamp. Under him the bank achieved an enviable reputation for stability which brought it a growing share of the business from the staple industries. Its stocks remained at a relatively high price, even during the recession in the 1870s. The Bank of Toronto was also a leader in expounding the interests of Ontario banks and its directors saw several of the operating principles of their managers, notably the maintenance of an unusually large reserve, incorporated into dominion regulations established by the bank acts of 1870 and 1871 [*see* Sir Francis HINCKS].

As it must have reflected his views on the relative value of banks and savings companies, the inventory of Gooderham's estate provides an interesting footnote to his banking career: he held shares worth $42,000 in the Bank of Toronto as opposed to $122,000 in loan and savings companies, $90,000 of this sum in the Canada Permanent and $32,000 in the Western Canada Loan and Savings companies.

Although his conservative views were well known, Gooderham avoided the public eye, and even if he was on the first publicly elected school board in 1850, his only real venture into politics was as city alderman for St Lawrence Ward in 1853 and 1855. He chaired the committee on wharves and harbours which accepted Casimir Stanislaus Gzowski*'s tender, later overturned, to build the Esplanade development. A staunch evangelical Anglican, Gooderham was a leading member of Little Trinity Church (which was near the distillery) and a warden from 1853 to 1881. He was a lifelong freemason, and served as president of the York Pioneer Society from 1878 to 1880. His charitable activities were both personal (he took a growing number of orphans under his protection) and institutional. He represented the board of trade on the trust of the Toronto General Hospital, and along with Worts and William Cawthra* he contributed the $113,500 needed to build a new wing for patients with infectious diseases.

In the last three or four years of his life, Gooderham turned much of his business over to his third son, George*, who became a full partner in Gooderham and Worts before his father died. His eldest son, William, president and managing director of the Toronto and Nipissing Railway from 1873 to 1882 after an inglorious career in other businesses, died in 1889; his second son, James, had been killed in an accident on the Credit Valley Railway in 1879. Three other sons, Henry, Alfred Lee, and Charles Horace, were employed in branches of the family concerns. The Reverend Alexander Sanson of Little Trinity Church eulogized Gooderham as a type of patriarch.

Even after providing for his children, Gooderham left an estate which amounted to approximately $1,550,000 at first valuation. Obituaries stressed the breadth of his influence in the business community and his contribution to the city's growth from a town of "three or four thousand inhabitants, and little wealth" to the metropolis in 1881. Gooderham built his empire by combining the principle of dealing in articles of widespread consumption with a sensitivity, which he retained as he grew older, to the opportunities offered by new techniques and new markets. In the fluctuating marketplace of Toronto in the mid 19th century, this combination proved highly successful.

DIANNE NEWELL

MTL, Biog. scrapbooks, VII: 481; XXIX: 25; Toronto scrapbooks, VII: 127; XII: 41. York County Surrogate Court (Toronto), no.3236, will of William Gooderham, 9 Sept. 1881 (mfm. at AO).

Bank of Toronto, *Reports and proc. of annual meetings* (Toronto), 1857–81. Can., Parl., *Sessional papers*, 1876, III: no.3. "Canadian railways, no.XXV: Toronto and Nipissing Railway," *Engineering; an Illustrated Weekly Journal* (London), 28 (July–December 1879): 295–98. Toronto Board of Trade, *Annual report* ... (Toronto). 1860–63; *Annual review of the commerce of Toronto* . . . , comp. W. S. Taylor (Toronto), 1867, 1870; *Annual statement of the trade of Toronto* . . . , comp. J. M. Trout (Toronto), 1865. *Daily Mail and Empire*, 23 Oct. 1933. *Globe*, 7 Feb. 1862, 22 Aug. 1881, 21 June 1882, 6 March 1885. *Monetary Times*, 1869–83. *Toronto Daily Mail*, 22 Aug. 1881, 21 June 1882. *Canadian biog. dict.*, I: 62–70. Chadwick, *Ontarian families*, I: 154–57. *Dominion annual register*, 1882. Masters, *Rise of Toronto*. Middleton, *Municipality of Toronto*. *Robertson's landmarks of Toronto*. Joseph Schull, *100 years of banking in Canada: a history of the Toronto-Domion Bank* (Toronto, 1958). E. B. Shuttleworth, *The windmill and its times; a series of articles dealing with the early days of the windmill* (Toronto, 1924). Shortt, "Hist. of Canadian currency, banking and exchange: some individual banks," *Canadian Banker*, 13: 11, 184–91.

GOODERHAM, WILLIAM, businessman and philanthropist; b. 14 April 1824 at Scole, Norfolk, England, eldest son of William GOODERHAM and Harriet Tovell Herring; d. 12 Sept. 1889 at Toronto, Ont.

William Gooderham accompanied his father when the latter moved to York (Toronto), Upper Canada, in 1832. After receiving a grammar school education, probably in Toronto, he refused to join his father's milling and distilling firm and instead moved to Rochester, N.Y., in 1842 where he took up a mercantile career. Born into an evangelical Church of England family, Gooderham was converted to Methodism while at Rochester and became a strong temperance advocate. On 14 April 1847 he married Margaret Bright whose sister, Sarah, had married his cousin, James Gooderham WORTS, in 1840. There were no children.

About 1850 Gooderham and his brother James opened a general store at Norval, Halton County, Canada West. The business was not profitable and closed in 1859. William then became the Toronto-based partner in the Boston grain firm of Taylor Brothers, but when his misjudgements proved costly, the partnership was ended. Other ventures were equally unsuccessful and several times Gooderham had to be rescued by friends and relatives. An obituary in the *Toronto World* commented: "His record as a business man tells of confidence placed in talents he did not possess."

In the 1870s Gooderham was, however, named

vice-president and managing director, and in 1873 became president and managing director, of the Toronto and Nipissing Railway Company, then controlled by Gooderham and Worts. He remained head of the railway until its heavy losses forced an absorption in 1882 into the group of lines consolidated as the Midland Railway of Canada. In 1871 he was an incorporator of the Confederation Life Association and represented family interests on its board of directors until 1872. Failing health and his wife's illness caused him to withdraw gradually from active business management in the early 1880s.

Two events shaped the last decade of Gooderham's life. First, his own illness and that of his wife (who had become an invalid in 1875) brought about a reconversion to Methodism, and, secondly, in 1881 he received some $300,000 from his father's estate. With this money Gooderham launched himself into careers in finance and philanthropy. He invested large sums in the shares of several corporations and was elected to their boards. He was director of the Great North-Western Telegraph Company of Canada, the Canadian Bank of Commerce, the Western Assurance Company, the Canada Permanent Loan and Savings Company, the Toronto General Trusts Company, and the British America Assurance Company. Of his investments, only the Central Bank of Canada proved to be a serious misjudgement. When that institution failed in 1888, Gooderham was named a liquidator, probably because of his known rectitude and the fact that he owned a large number of shares. With double liability, his losses exceeded $40,000. Nevertheless, his estate was valued at approximately $450,000 at his death.

With his religious reconversion Gooderham had entered upon a career of evangelism which lasted to the day he died. In spite of his eccentric behaviour, which included importuning strangers in public places to proclaim the Word of God, his generosity to religious organizations was admired. He personally supported missionaries in India, the Canadian northwest, and in the South Sea islands; assembled a quartet of young people with whom he paid regular preaching visits to hospital wards; gave sermons in various Protestant churches; and financially supported numerous charities. He was a director of the Toronto Willard Tract Depository, a member of the Toronto General Hospital Trust, and chairman of the executive of the China Inland Mission. In 1888 he gave $25,000 to erect the Toronto Christian Institute. He died the next year preaching to destitute men at a Salvation Army haven.

Gooderham's will created a sensation. Instrumental in ending the delay in the implementation of the act of 1887 for the federation of Victoria University at Cobourg with the University of Toronto, it provided, in addition to a $75,000 permanent endowment, for $125,000 to be paid to Victoria on the condition that it move to Toronto. Federation with the University of Toronto was proclaimed on 12 Nov. 1890 and the transfer was completed in October 1892. In addition Gooderham bequeathed $150,000 to organizations such as the Upper Canada Bible Society, the Young Men's and Young Women's Christian associations, the Boy's Home, Girl's Home, and homes for infants, the Toronto Home for Incurables, the House of Industry, and the Salvation Army.

LEO A. JOHNSON

York County Surrogate Court (Toronto), no. 7660, will of William Gooderham, 18 Jan. 1890 (mfm. at AO). Can., *Statutes*, 1871, c.54. *Christian Guardian*, 18, 25 Sept. 1889. *Globe*, 13 Feb. 1888, 13, 17–20 Sept. 1889. *North Ontario Observer and General Advertiser* (Port Perry, Ont.), 17 Oct. 1872. *Toronto Daily Mail*, 13, 17 Sept. 1889. *Toronto World*, 13, 19, 20, 22 Sept. 1889. *Canadian biog. dict.*, I: 62–70, 730–32. Chadwick, *Ontarian families*, I: 154. W. H. Higgins, *The life and times of Joseph Gould . . .* (Toronto, 1887; repr. Belleville, Ont. 1972), 202–12. L. A. Johnson, *History of the county of Ontario, 1615–1875* (Whitby, Ont., 1973). A. H. Raynar, "The arts colleges: Victoria College," *The University of Toronto and its colleges, 1827–1906*, [ed. W. J. Alexander] (Toronto, 1906), 124–36. G. R. Stevens, *Canadian National Railways* (2v., Toronto and Vancouver, 1960–62), I: 450–53.

GORDON, JOHN, manufacturer, merchant, and railway promoter; b. in 1828 at Latheron (Highland), Scotland; d. unmarried 29 May 1882 at Paris, France.

John Gordon, his father, mother, and sister joined the flood of Scots who left the Highlands for North America. They landed in 1841, eventually settling at Grenville, Canada East. Perhaps they received information on the country through their kinsmen, JOSEPH and Edward Mackay, who were establishing what would prove to be a successful dry goods business in Montreal. It is not known what the elder Gordon did for a living or how long the family remained in Grenville before moving to Peterborough, Canada West.

Following the death of the father in 1851, the remaining members of the family moved to Hamilton. John Gordon formed a partnership in that year with his uncle, Donald Mackay, under the name of Gordon, Mackay and Company, Gordon being the senior partner. Mackay had been a merchant-tailor in Hamilton and the firm continued this retail activity, also branching out extensively into the importing and wholesale dry goods trade. Because firms were not required to identify all partners until 1869, it is uncertain if anyone else participated in this business. In view of the later involvement of Joseph and Edward Mackay in Gordon's business endeavours, and the value to a new firm of the transoceanic business connections the brothers undoubtedly possessed, it is possible that they were involved in Gordon, Mackay and Company.

The 1840s and 1850s were years of commercial growth for Hamilton, but the depression of 1857 revealed how precarious this prosperity was. The city's commercial community, with an infrastructure of debt and over-extended credit, suffered many failures. Although Gordon, Mackay and Company managed to weather the 1857 depression, its move to Toronto in 1859 was a sound decision, and evidence of the rise of Toronto and the decline of Hamilton. Donald Mackay, however, remained in Hamilton to operate a tailoring and retail clothing store in his own name until 1866.

The move to Toronto must have been successful for Gordon and the firm. In 1861 its operations were significantly diversified with the establishment of a cotton mill on the Welland Canal at Merriton (now part of St Catharines). This development allowed Gordon, Mackay and Company to offer a good selection of Canadian-made cottons of their own and other manufacture, unlike most of their competitors. From the beginning the Lybster Mills, as it was called, specialized in cheaper cotton goods, lines of production in which British and American manufacturers had less competitive advantage.

The expansion occurred at a fortunate time: the American Civil War effectively protected the Canadian market by disrupting the northern cotton industry and causing a cotton famine among English manufacturers. Inevitably the return to peace revitalized competition from the United States; the operations of the Lybster Mills were upset and indeed for several months in 1869 its works were shut down completely. In the following three years, however, the dry goods business prospered, creating handsome profits for both branches of Gordon, Mackay and Company. The firm opened new and larger premises in Toronto in 1870 and by 1872 Lybster Mills was booming, returning ten per cent on invested capital. Since the opening of the mill, the productive capacity had doubled with new machinery bought in England and with workers and managers attracted from the United States. Gordon and Mackay reorganized the firm in 1872 as a joint-stock corporation under the name of the Lybster Cotton Manufacturing Company in order to finance its expansion into a new stage of production, the bleaching of cotton goods. The company initially was capitalized at $250,000, with one-fifth retained by Gordon, Mackay and Company. The provisional directors of the new company were Donald Mackay, John MACDONALD from Toronto, and, from Montreal, Edward Mackay, Andrew ROBERTSON, and John Rankin.

The depression which began in 1873 had an adverse effect on this new departure. The Lybster Cotton Manufacturing Company continued to pay dividends of eight per cent on its stock, but its spinning and weaving capacity did not expand significantly as much larger cotton mills with financial connections in the Montreal commercial community were established on the St Lawrence River. The wholesale business of Gordon, Mackay and Company suffered as well during the depression. The dumping of British and American textiles on the Canadian market and attempts by British manufacturers in particular to bypass Canadian wholesalers through commercial travellers caused many of the smaller and less established concerns to go under. Gordon, Mackay and Company, however, was able to weather the crisis, if not to prosper as in its recent past.

Although the affairs of Gordon, Mackay and Company occupied much of his time, Gordon was president of the Toronto, Grey and Bruce Railway from 1868 to 1880 and controlled the largest block of stock in it. Beginning in 1867, Gordon, with James Gooderham WORTS, John Shedden*, and George LAIDLAW among others, actively promoted narrow gauge railways as an inexpensive form of transportation and as an alternative to the Grand Trunk Railway. To Gordon's subsequent embarrassment, the financial and operational realities of the Toronto, Grey and Bruce did not fulfil the optimistic projections for it. The dependence upon municipal bonuses and the difficulty of negotiating loans in Canada and of selling bonds at favourable discounts in England were aggravated by unforeseen construction costs and the depression of the mid 1870s. These problems put a considerable burden upon the railway and upon Gordon who took complete charge of the financial arrangements and made frequent trips to maintain the confidence of English investors. Probably the strain imposed upon Gordon by these financial difficulties contributed to the breakdown of his health that eventually forced him to retire from business during the last years of his life.

Of Gordon's life outside business few details are known. While in Hamilton, he had been on the executive of the Hamilton Highland Society and he later became president of the Ontario Rifle Society. His religious affiliation was Presbyterian. In the 1870s he was politically active, one of the significant minority of Liberals who argued in defence of a protective tariff policy. He expressed this concern as early as March 1870 at a protectionist meeting in Toronto and to the Toronto Board of Trade the following year. In 1872 he ran unsuccessfully as the Liberal candidate in the riding of Peterborough West.

The career of John Gordon is an illustration of 19th-century links between a successful commercial enterprise and other business endeavours. The Lybster Mills, by providing a supply of textiles, and the Toronto, Grey and Bruce Railway, by extending the limits of Toronto's market, contributed to the commercial prosperity of Gordon's company and to his personal fortune. Upon his death Gordon left an estate valued at $94,000 of which $40,000 was real property and $54,000 was personal property, principally stock in his businesses and railway shares.

DAVID G. BURLEY

York County Surrogate Court (Toronto), no.4692, will of John Gordon, 26 Oct. 1882 (mfm. at AO). Can., House of Commons, *Journals*, 1876, app.3, Evidence of Andrew Robertson. Ont., Legislature, *Sessional papers*, 1871–72, II: no.29; 1874 (1st session), III: no.13; 1874 (2nd session), II: no.5; 1875–76, III–IV: no.33; 1877, IV: no.41; 1878, IV: no.26. *Globe*, 6 July 1872, 20 May 1882. *Mail*, 15 July 1872. *Monetary Times*, 28 Nov. 1867; 25 June, 15 Oct., 19 Nov. 1868; 29 April, 12 Aug., 3 Sept. 1869; 1 April, 26 Aug., 2, 16, 23 Sept. 1870; 13 Jan., 3 Feb., 25 Aug., 22 Sept., 10 Nov., 22 Dec. 1871; 12 Jan., 6, 13 Sept. 1872; 17 Jan., 19 Sept., 21 Nov. 1873; 6 Feb., 18 Sept. 1874; 10 Sept. 1875; 3 March 1876; 2 June 1882. *Dominion annual register*, 1882. Masters, *Rise of Toronto*, 105, 110, 145.

GOSSE, PHILIP HENRY, naturalist and religious writer; b. 6 April 1810 in Worcester, England, second of four children of Thomas Gosse, miniature portrait painter, and Hannah Best, domestic servant; m. first in 1848 Emily Bowes (d. 1857), and they had one son; m. secondly in 1860 Eliza Brightwen; d. 23 Aug. 1888 at St Mary Church, near Torquay, England.

Philip Henry Gosse was educated at local schools in Poole, Dorset; he especially valued the classical training he received from 1823 to 1824 at a nearby boarding-school in Blandford. "From infancy my tastes were bookish," he recalled, and so when he left school at 15 his academic interests did not end. He developed a delight for the study of natural history long before his formal education ceased and throughout his life he was an adherent of the natural theology tradition. As well he was influenced by his father's strong belief in evangelical Christianity, and inherited from him a keen interest in painting and drawing. After quitting school Gosse held a number of odd jobs until 1827 when a clerkship was obtained for him in the counting-house of Slade, Elson and Company in Carbonear, Nfld.

Arriving in Newfoundland in June 1827, Gosse found a colony divided into two warring classes, merchants and fishermen [*see* William Carson*]. This tension was exacerbated by the concomitant local and historical hostility between English Protestants and Irish Catholics, each vying for the upper hand in light of the prospect of representative government. Nevertheless, Gosse was able to pursue his chores at the counting-house, outfitting and tallying the catch of the seal fleets in March and April and the cod trade in June and October as well as copying letters and ledgers the rest of the year. This activity left plenty of spare time and Gosse participated in the local intellectual life, which included a book club and a debating society.

The year 1832 was Gosse's *annus mirabilis.* Though his first few years in Newfoundland had been pleasant his life lacked direction. In May 1832 he purchased George Adams' *Essays on the microscope* (London, 1787) which served to focus his hitherto diffuse though eager interest in natural history. Then in the next month a letter from home announcing that his sister Elizabeth was on the verge of death stirred his conscience and raised the issue of his relationship with God once again, resulting in an evangelical conversion. Thus Gosse commenced the two activities which dominated the remainder of his life, the study of nature and the practice of evangelical Christianity.

In November 1832 Gosse began systematically to collect insects and to enter scientific observations in journals. Extracts from his meteorological record were published in the *Conception-Bay Mercury.* In the following summer he commenced filling a volume ("Entomologia Terrae Novae") with coloured drawings of butterflies, moths, beetles, and other insects; despite an unusually high level of scientific accuracy, it has remained unpublished. Meanwhile, he had joined the Methodist society in Carbonear, read the theological works of John and Charles Wesley, become a member of the chapel choir, participated in public prayer-meetings, and was eventually persuaded to act as a local preacher with Philip Tocque* and others.

In June 1835 Gosse left Newfoundland. He had fulfilled the terms of his indenture at the counting-house, and the mounting tension between the Irish Catholics and English Protestants following the granting of representative government in 1832 was making life unbearable for him. Moreover, he had "pretty well exhausted Entomology in Newfoundland; it was a cold barren unproductive region." One of Gosse's close friends, George Edward Jaques, and his wife had heard some "very flaming accounts" about Canada and were intent on moving there. Gosse decided to join them and together they purchased 110 partially cleared acres just north of Compton, Sherbrooke County, Lower Canada.

For the next three years Gosse worked his 60 acres of the land in the face of constant hardship. Although Compton was situated in an area reputed to be rich agriculturally, the short seasons often forced settlers to work at trades more profitable than farming; in the winter months Gosse taught school to supplement his income. Jaques and Gosse farmed separately and without the help of agricultural labourers who were in short supply; through inexperience, they grew crops which were sold only with difficulty. In spite of an initial wave of optimism it soon became apparent that the experiment was a failure, and Gosse left the colony in March 1838, spending seven months in Alabama before returning to England early in 1839. Except for an 18-month sojourn in Jamaica he remained in England for the rest of his life.

During his years in Canada Gosse's spiritual life was at a low ebb, with nourishment coming only from the irregularly held Methodist services in Compton and the winter prayer-meetings. On the other hand, his scientific pursuits gradually became "from the mere salt, the condiment, of life, almost its very pabulum." He was often seen in the field collecting insects, and people spoke of him as "that crazy Englishman who goes about collecting bugs." During his first winter in Canada he had assembled his scientific journals and composed "The entomology of Newfoundland," apparently the companion to the volume of illustrations. Although excerpts from these journals were subsequently published, Gosse realized that the book itself was unworthy of publication and it remained in manuscript. Modest recognition was given to his scientific pursuits in 1836 when he was elected a corresponding member of two societies to which he sent papers, the Literary and Historical Society of Quebec and the Natural History Society of Montreal. In May 1837, after five years of accumulating data, Gosse decided to bring his observations together into a general work on Canadian natural history. Three years later, *The Canadian naturalist: a series of conversations on the natural history of Lower Canada* was published in London, with his own illustrations.

In the years that followed Gosse wrote more than 40 books and pamphlets as well as 230 articles on religious and scientific themes. As a naturalist he is best known for his original, often pioneering, works on invertebrate marine zoology, ornithology, rotifera, and lepidoptera. He was the foremost popularizer of natural history in mid-Victorian England, and was elected a fellow of the Royal Society of London in 1856. His religious works, in which he was deeply influenced by the Plymouth Brethren, include prophetic, hortative, and exegetical essays, as well as attempts to resolve the conflict between religion and science.

Gosse made no impact on the religious life of either Newfoundland or Canada. In the history of entomology in Newfoundland, however, he occupies a special place, for in a day when the colony did not possess any men of science, scientific institutions, or even cabinet collections, he was the first person systematically to investigate and to record the entomology of that island. No such status can be assigned to his Canadian investigations, especially since he himself recognized his deficiency in the systematic knowledge of natural history. *The Canadian naturalist*, presented as a conversation between a father and son, was old-fashioned in format and addressed to a popular rather than to a learned audience. Yet Gosse brought together much accurate and original information about the flora and fauna of the Eastern Townships, focusing his attention on ecology rather than taxonomy, and the book and its illustrations were well received "[F]rom this book," Charles James Stewart Bethune* wrote in 1898, "many Canadian entomologists of note received their first lessons, and learned the names of some of our common butterflies and moths."

DOUGLAS WERTHEIMER

Gosse was the author of *The Canadian naturalist: a series of conversations on the natural history of Lower Canada* (London, 1840; repr. Toronto, 1971); "List of butterflies taken at Compton, in Lower Canada," *Entomologist* (London), 1 (1840–42): 137–39; "Notes on butterflies obtained at Carbonear Island, Newfoundland, 1832–1835," *Canadian Entomologist* (London, Ont.), 15 (1883): 44–51; "On silk produced by diurnal Lepidoptera," *Intellectual Observer* (London), 10 (1866–67): 393–94; "The Y-shaped organ of Papilio larvæ," *Hardwicke's Science-Gossip* (London), 8 (1871): 224. For other works by Gosse and a study of his life see D. L. Wertheimer, "Philip Henry Gosse: science and revelation in the crucible" (PHD thesis, Univ. of Toronto, 1977).

National Museums of Canada Library (Ottawa), P. H. Gosse, "Entomologia Terrae Novae," *c.*1835. PAC, MG 24, I63. PANL, T. B. Browning papers, Sketchbook of Newfoundland scenes, apparently by William Gosse. S. H. Scudder, "Gosse's observations on the butterflies of North America," *Psyche* (Cambridge, Mass.), 3 (1881): 245–47. R. B. Freeman and Douglas Wertheimer, *Philip Henry Gosse: a bibliography* (Folkestone, Eng., 1980). E. W. Gosse, *Father and son; a study of two temperaments* (London, 1907); *The life of Philip Henry Gosse, F.R.S.* (London, 1890). C. J. S. Bethune, "The rise and progress of entomology in Canada," RSC *Trans.*, 2nd ser., 4 (1898), sect.IV: 155–65. F. A. Bruton, "Philip Henry Gosse's entomology of Newfoundland; introductory note," *Entomological News* (Philadelphia), 41 (1930): 34–38. T. W. Fyles, "A visit to the Canadian haunts of the late Philip Henry Gosse," Entomological Soc. of Ont., *Annual report* (Toronto), 23 (1892): 22–29.

GOSSIP, WILLIAM, publisher, bookseller, and journalist; b. in 1809 in Plymouth, England, son of William G. and Mary Ann Gossip; m. Anne Catherine Coade, and they had four sons and three daughters; d. 5 April 1889 at Halifax, N.S.

Early in the 1820s William Gossip accompanied his parents and sister to Halifax where his father, a 2nd lieutenant in the Corps of Royal Engineers, was stationed. It would appear that young Gossip received a sound general education. About 1831 Gossip moved to Pictou where, in the strongly partisan religious and political climate of the day, he published and edited the *Pictou Observer*. A Conservative organ sympathetic to the Burgher section of the Presbyterian church, the *Observer* faced stiff competition from the *Colonial Patriot*. George Munro*, who was to become a benefactor of Dalhousie University, served as an apprentice on Gossip's paper. By 1834 Gossip had discontinued the *Observer* and returned to Halifax. He established a stationery, bookselling, and publishing business there and in June 1834, with his brother-in-law John Charles Coade as a partner, he began a new weekly, the *Times*. During its 14 years of life, it was undoubtedly the most highly regarded, moderate, and influential of the Conservative newspapers in Nova Scotia. In 1847, at a time of heated arguments over the granting of responsible government to the colony, Gossip and Coade started another more partisan weekly, the *Standard and Conservative Advocate*, which was meant primarily for readers outside the capital. Both newspapers stopped publication in 1848.

From 1848 to 1858 Gossip published the Anglican *Church Times* as well as continuing with his stationery and bookselling business. The *Church Times* spoke with a less certain voice than Gossip's earlier publications: the major battles against religious and political privilege had subsided, and the paper's editorial voice reflected the contributions of several clergymen as well as those of Gossip. A member of the Nova Scotian Institute of Natural Science, he served on its council in various capacities. He was also the first editor of the institute's annual *Proceedings and Transactions*, serving from 1863 until his death. He published several papers on such topics as anthropology and the geology of Nova Scotia. On occasion he lectured to the Halifax Mechanics' Institute and in 1883 he presented a paper before the Royal Society of Canada. His work was scholarly and he possessed a clear and uncluttered writing style.

Many of Gossip's views and opinions can be gathered from his newspapers, especially the *Times*. Politically he considered himself "decidedly Conservative, in the proper sense of the term." He valued tradition and the British connection. Yet he could accept change or even call for reform if he saw the need, and realized that the political turmoil of the 1830s and 1840s reflected a deep social and economic malaise among Nova Scotians. Human behaviour fascinated him and he was tolerant of other races and religions; he disliked wrangling and abhorred violence. Gossip took pride in his province and its resources, human and material, and in 1838 he saw the scheme of federal union proposed by Lord Durham [Lambton*] as a threat to both. In religion Gossip was a faithful member of the Church of England, although he did not favour its privileged position. He put great store by family ties and loyalty and had both a deep sense of responsibility to individuals as well as to society and an abiding belief in honesty. Photographs of Gossip reflect a kindly, serene, and alert personality. Normally a rather quiet man, he could be righteously indignant with individuals or practices which he considered unfair. He gave unstintingly of his time and talents to numerous community activities.

In an age of reforming zeal, the role of a moderate conservative such as Gossip might not seem to stand out, but his newspapers were important in Nova Scotian politics and their survival shows he must have spoken to a sizable cross-section of public opinion. Having achieved a modest degree of financial success he left a flourishing stationery business, a tidy sum of money, and stock (valued at about $14,500) to his wife, surviving children, and a sister living in the United States. He seems to have been universally liked and respected.

GERTRUDE E. N. TRATT

William Gossip published the following papers in the Nova Scotian Institute of Natural Science, *Proc. and Trans.* (Halifax): "The affinity of races," 3 (1871–74): 288–315; "Anniversary address, 1876," 4 (1875–78): 225–32; "Anniversary address, 1879," 5 (1879–82): 99–111; "Enquiry into the antiquity of man," 1 (1863–66), no.3: 80–102; "On the antiquity of man in America," 2 (1867–70), no.3: 35–77; "On the occurrence of the Kjoekkenmoedding, on the shores of Nova Scotia," 1 (1863–66), no.2: 94–99; "Paper," 6 (1883–86): 155–66; and "Report . . . May 1883," 6 (1883–86), no.2, app.: i–xii.

Halifax County Court of Probate (Halifax), no.3833, original estate papers of William Gossip. PANS, MG 9, no.41: 67; Photograph coll., W. H. Gossip. St Paul's Anglican Church (Halifax), Registers of baptisms, burials, and marriages, 8 April 1889 (mfm. at PANS). J. G. MacGregor, "Opening address," Nova Scotian Institute of Natural Science, *Proc. and Trans.*, 7 (1886–90): 319–20. *Church Times* (Halifax), 1848–58. *Evening Mail* (Halifax), 13 March 1896. *Halifax Evening Reporter*, 3 Sept. 1867. *Halifax Herald*, 13 Aug. 1883, 6 April 1889, 29 July 1896. *Novascotian*, 19 July 1852. *Pictou Observer* (Pictou, N.S.), 1831–34. *Standard and Conservative Advocate* (Halifax), 1847–48. *Times* (Halifax), 1834–48. D. A. Sutherland, "J. W. Johnston and the metamorphosis of Nova Scotian conservatism" (MA thesis, Dalhousie Univ., Halifax, 1967). G. E. N. Tratt, "A survey and listing of Nova Scotian newspapers with particular reference to the period before 1867" (MA thesis, Mount Allison Univ., Sackville, N.B., 1957). D. C. Harvey, "Newspapers of Nova Scotia, 1840–1867," *CHR*, 26 (1945): 279–301. J. S. Martell, "The press of the Maritime provinces in the 1830's," *CHR*, 19 (1938): 24–49. Harry Piers, "A brief historical account of the Nova Scotian Institute of Science, and the events leading up to its formation; with biographical sketches of its deceased presidents and other prominent members," Nova Scotian Institute of Science, *Proc. and Trans.* (Halifax), 13 (1910–14): lxxxiv.

GOULD (Gold), JOSEPH, farmer, miller, businessman, politician, and philanthropist; b. 29 Dec. 1808 in Uxbridge Township, Upper Canada, near the present town of Uxbridge, the third of ten children of Jonathan Gold and Rachel Lee; m. 1 Jan. 1839 Mary James, and they had 11 children; d. 29 Jan. 1886 at Uxbridge.

Joseph Gould (he changed his name from Gold while he was in school) was born in the sparsely settled township of Uxbridge three years after his family arrived from Germantown, Pa. He received little education at the local school and was largely self-taught. He took up carpentry briefly before acquiring a farm with the help of a loan from a neighbour, Ezekiel James, his future father-in-law. He also bought a sawmill, and after initial difficulties it was soon operating profitably. Gould prospered as the population of the area grew over the next decades.

Always interested in the well-being of his fellow man, Gould was introduced to events in the outside world by a visit to York (Toronto) in 1830 and by the reading of William Lyon Mackenzie*'s *Colonial Advocate.* He became a strong supporter of Mackenzie and the Reform movement in the 1830s. In 1837, Gould, who believed in a peaceful solution to the grievances of the people, was nevertheless persuaded by approximately 50 of his neighbours to lead them to Montgomery's Tavern on Yonge Street, headquarters for the planned attack on Toronto. He fought in the battle near the inn and was caught while fleeing to the United States. He was sentenced to transportation to Van Diemen's Land (Tasmania), but his sentence was reduced to nine months' imprisonment. In October 1838 he was pardoned under the general amnesty granted by Lord Durham [Lambton*].

Once released, Gould returned to farming and business. As a farmer he built up a large holding and at one time worked between 600 and 700 acres. He also speculated in land, owned mills and commercial property in the village of Uxbridge, and ran the Whitby, Lake Scugog, Simcoe and Huron Road from 1865 to 1876, the first two years in partnership with Chester Draper. In the 1860s he supported the proposed railway from Whitby to Lake Huron and paid for a large share of the survey's costs himself. This railway met opposition from many farmers in the county because they would have borne most of the cost without benefitting from the line. While the route was being debated, the Toronto and Nipissing Railway was built. Seeing that the Whitby and Lake Huron would fail, Gould had also promoted vigorously the Toronto and Nipissing and bought a considerable amount of stock in it as well.

Gould first held political office in 1836–37 when he served as township commissioner for Uxbridge. From 1842 to 1854 he was district councillor and, as a member of the provisional county council established in 1851, he was instrumental in the creation of Ontario County the following year. He became the first reeve of Uxbridge Township in 1853, the first warden of Ontario County in 1855, and finally reeve of the village of Uxbridge. As a Reformer, Gould campaigned three times for the seat of Ontario North in the Legislative Assembly. He defeated Ogle Robert Gowan* in 1854 and 1857 even though the riding contained many Orangemen, but lost by 99 votes to Matthew Crooks CAMERON in the third attempt in 1861. He voted with the reform group of Francis HINCKS and Augustin-Norbert Morin* and the Morin and Sir Allan Napier MacNab* coalition of 1854 until measures for the abolition of seigneurial tenure and secularization of the clergy reserves were passed. He then opposed such Hincksite proposals as the Grand Trunk aid bill of 1857 and became, in the main, a supporter of the policies of George Brown*. By 1861, however, he had antagonized a number of groups in his riding, including the Roman Catholics. After his defeat that year he asked that his name not be put forward again, but continued to work for the Reform cause, and he was president of the Reform Association of Ontario North for a quarter of a century.

Maintaining a concern for his fellow man, Gould aided financially troubled local farmers, made considerable donations to various denominations for church buildings (he himself was born a Quaker), and gave generously to the agricultural societies and to educational projects such as the village's first grammar school built in 1856. He also served as chairman of the Uxbridge Township school board for 20 years. Although he supported primary schools and compulsory education, he opposed higher education which, as a self-made man, he felt to be of no use.

When Gould died in 1886, his estate was valued at approximately $250,000, despite the fact he had already given a great deal to charity and to his children. Much of his wealth had been acquired through shrewd commercial dealings which some contemporaries criticized as too cold-blooded. At his death, however, he was remembered for his service to the area, not for his hard-nosed business undertakings.

RONALD J. STAGG

PAC, RG 5, A1, 4 May 1838. *Constitution* (Toronto), 13, 20 Sept. 1837. W. H. Higgins, *The life and times of Joseph Gould . . .* (Toronto, 1887; repr. Belleville, Ont., 1972).

GOW, PETER, businessman, politician, and office-holder; b. 20 Nov. 1818 at Johnstone (Strathclyde), Scotland, second son of John Gow (a descendant of Niel Gow, a well-known 18th-century Perthshire violinist) and Agnes Ferguson; m. 29 Dec. 1857 Mary Maxwell Smith of Kirkcudbright (Dumfries and Galloway), Scotland, and they had nine sons and three daughters; d. 24 Feb. 1886 in Guelph, Ont.

After education at a private school, Peter Gow worked with his father, a shoe manufacturer. Immigrating to Canada West in 1842 to improve his position, he spent two years at Brockville and then settled in Guelph. He built woollen and oatmeal mills on the Speed River to serve the developing area, but leather was his chief interest. By 1853 he had a tannery "in full operation" and a store stocked with boots and shoes which he sold "cheap for cash" or exchanged for country produce. Gow remained in business until 1868 when he leased his factories and retired in comfortable circumstances.

Gow was active in municipal affairs in Guelph as a member of the committee founding a mechanics' institute in 1850, as an elected school trustee in 1852, and as a town councillor in 1855. He accompanied the reeve to Toronto in December 1855 to obtain incorporation and establish ward divisions for Guelph. He was elected alderman for the south ward, deputy reeve, and representative to the county council in 1856. The next year Gow became reeve and in 1858 was again elected alderman, but he lost the mayoralty contest of 1859. Re-election as alderman for the south ward in 1863, 1864, and 1865 was followed by two terms as mayor in 1866 and 1867, during which time the town of 6,000 persons erected its first street lights and observed its 40th birthday.

Elected for Wellington South to the first Ontario Legislative Assembly in 1867, Gow firmly opposed John Sandfield Macdonald*'s coalition government, condemning the "mawkish cry" of "no politics" and declaring that "the only correct government was a party government." Although he spoke little in the legislature, dedicated attention to the needs of his constituents won him re-election by acclamation in 1871 and 1875, while political loyalty earned him the office of provincial secretary in December 1871 in the new liberal government of Edward Blake*. He was replaced in that post by Timothy Blair PARDEE on 25 Oct. 1872 when Oliver Mowat* succeeded Blake as premier. Conservatives complained that "poor Peter Gow," the "only honest man in the late Ministry," had been cast aside "like an old glove." They later suggested that his departure from the cabinet was eased by transferring the site of the proposed agricultural college (later the Ontario Agricultural College) from Mimico to Guelph in 1873. In the assembly, however, Gow claimed that he had opposed the move until convinced of the unsuitability of the former Mimico site; he also insisted that his retirement from the cabinet was an entirely unrelated "personal matter." The premier may have preferred the more influential Pardee as provincial secretary, but there is no evidence of a bargain between Mowat and Gow. The latter probably had asked, as the *Globe* reported, for relief from responsibility because of health problems which eventually caused him to resign his seat in 1876. He then accepted the less demanding shrievalty of Wellington County. He continued as sheriff until his death.

True to his Scottish heritage, Gow was a Presbyterian, and a curling club president. He was a charter member in 1868 and a manager of Chalmer's Church. Charles Clarke* described him as a splendid organizer and effective worker, "essentially a man of the people." Gow contributed to the commercial prosperity and social progress of Guelph in the mid 19th century. He helped revive party government in Ontario after confederation and establish the long Liberal administration beginning in 1871.

A. MARGARET EVANS

Ont., Legislative Library, Newspaper Hansard, 1867–77 (mfm. at AO). *Globe*, 31 Dec. 1867, 26 Oct. 1872, 11 March 1873. *The annals of the town of Guelph, 1827–1877*, comp. C. A. Burrows (Guelph, Ont., 1877), 63–158. *Canadian biog. dict.*, I: 752–55. *CPC*, 1876: 387. *DNB* (entry for Niel Gow). Charles Clarke, *Sixty years in Upper Canada, with autobiographical recollections* (Toronto, 1908), 159, 180–81.

GRASETT, HENRY JAMES, Church of England clergyman and educator; b. 18 June 1808 at Gibraltar, the eldest of the 14 children of Henry Grasett, surgeon to the 48th Foot, and Ann Bligh Stevenson; m. 17 Oct. 1837 Sarah Maria, daughter of John Stewart*, president of the Executive Council of Lower Canada, and they had eight children; d. 20 March 1882 in Toronto, Ont.

Henry Grasett brought his family to Quebec City in 1814 and Henry James was educated there at the Royal Grammar School. From about 1825 to 1830, supported by a scholarship from the Society for the Propagation of the Gospel, Grasett studied theology under Bishop Charles James Stewart*. In 1830 he enrolled at St John's College, Cambridge, from which he received his BA in 1834 (MA in 1842, BD in 1853, and an honorary DD in 1877). He returned to Quebec the same year and was ordained deacon on 19 May 1834 and priest on 8 June 1835 by Bishop Stewart. In 1835 Grasett began his long career in Toronto as curate to the rector at St James, John Strachan*. Grasett became domestic and examining chaplain to Strachan in 1839, rector and chaplain to the garrison in 1847, and dean in 1867. Despite differences in their churchmanship, during all these years Grasett worked closely with Strachan. Both men – the first bishop and the first dean of Toronto – are buried beneath the altar of St James'.

Like many 19th-century clerics, Grasett was deeply involved in education. Probably through Strachan's influence he joined the Home District Board of Education in the 1840s and was its chairman by annual election from 1851 until his death. Two of its noteworthy achievements were the establishment in 1871 of the Toronto (later Jarvis) Collegiate Institute and the appointment of Archibald MacMurchy* as "rector" of the school which became known for its academic excellence. Grasett also participated in education at the provincial level. On Strachan's recommendation to Egerton RYERSON, Grasett was appointed in 1846 to the newly established Board of Education for Upper Canada (renamed the Council of

Public Instruction in 1850), which was to assist the superintendent of education in organizing and operating the public school system. He remained on the council until it was replaced by the Department of Education in 1875, and was occasionally its chairman. In 1872 Grasett, as chairman, summarized the achievements of the council on the occasion of an official visit to Toronto by the governor general, Lord Dufferin [Blackwood*]: the establishment of normal and model schools, the preparation of laws and regulations to govern the school system, the selection and authorization of textbooks and prizebooks, the inauguration of school libraries, and immense improvements in school accommodations and in the character, qualifications, and pedagogical methods of teachers. Throughout, Grasett said, "it has been our aim to devise and develop a System of sound universal Education on Christian principles, imbued with a spirit of affectionate loyalty to the Throne and attachment to the unity of the Empire."

Grasett's tall, slightly stooping figure hurrying along Toronto streets was a familiar sight, and his kindness and generosity made him many friends. Yet he was shy and diffident in his public manner, and almost inarticulate in extemporaneous address. His sermons, while clear and flowing, were designed to appeal to the intellect rather than the emotions. It was his churchmanship that accounted for his wide popularity with Anglican laymen in Toronto. At a time when most of the clergy in the Toronto diocese were high church, Grasett had a low church orientation, which he probably owed to his early training by Stewart and to the religious atmosphere of St John's College. He served in the 1850s and 1860s as a prominent executive member of the non-denominational Upper Canada Tract and Upper Canada Bible societies, both of which were shunned by high churchmen. The Protestant atmosphere and furnishings of St James' Cathedral in Toronto, for which he was responsible, were sources of annoyance to high churchmen. As a member of the corporation of Trinity College, Grasett supported Bishop Benjamin Cronyn* of the diocese of Huron in his attack on the high church theology of Provost George WHITAKER. In 1866 Grasett was an unsuccessful low church candidate in the election of a coadjutor bishop for the diocese.

As the diocese's most outstanding cleric in the low church group, Grasett became a leader of a new, militant campaign to counter the progress of ritualism. He was president of the Evangelical Association established in 1869 to arouse the protestantism of laymen. When the Evangelical Association was superseded in 1873 by the Church Association of the Diocese of Toronto, he helped write its constitution and served as the only clergyman among the three vice-presidents. The Church Association included some of Toronto's most prominent Anglican laymen of the time: William Henry Draper*, Casimir Stanislaus Gzowski*, Daniel Wilson*, Edward* and Samuel Hume Blake*, George Taylor Denison*, and John George Hodgins*. In the 1870s their efforts were remarkably energetic and successful. A massive propaganda campaign was undertaken, as part of which the *Evangelical Churchman* was established in 1876 and a mission fund set up to support new evangelical ministers. The fund was outside the control of the diocesan synod despite the protests of the bishop, Alexander Neil Bethune*. Grasett was a member of the fund's committee, and in the spring of 1875 Bethune singled him out for investigation before a commission, appointed by the bishop, on charges of "depraving" the doctrine and discipline of the church. The charges were eventually dropped because no canon law had been broken, but only after months of violent newspaper controversy.

When Bethune died in 1879 the Church Association could claim credit for the choice of his successor. It organized a large block of lay delegates at the episcopal election, in which a candidate had to win a majority of both lay and clerical votes. For the first 23 ballots, with first George Whitaker and then Joseph Albert LOBLEY receiving about 80 per cent of the votes from the clergy, the laymen prevented the selection of a high church candidate. Arthur Sweatman*, a moderate evangelical, finally obtained a majority from the clergy on the understanding that following his election the Church Association would be disbanded. During the election Grasett had provided St James' parish hall to the association for rallies and meetings.

Grasett was no doubt gratified by the election of Sweatman, but he had probably received more satisfaction from having been chosen chairman of a Church Association committee on clerical education in the fall of 1874. Distrusting Trinity College, evangelicals wanted a seminary of their own. Under Grasett's anxious guidance and despite Bethune's hostility, the committee made the Protestant Episcopal Divinity School a reality by October 1877. Principal James Paterson Sheraton* and a small staff had begun conducting classes in St James' that summer for nine ordination candidates. Grasett was one of the trustees of the school and taught pastoral theology. At the time of his death the institution (renamed Wycliffe College in 1885) was about to move into its own new buildings on Queen's Park.

The founding of the divinity college brought together the two strands of Grasett's public life, education and Protestant Christianity. Although an Anglican clergyman, he rejected historical and theological arguments thrusting in the direction of Catholicism. He firmly repudiated the doctrine of apostolic succession, and defined the visible church of Christ in broad and comprehensive terms. Wycliffe College was intended to perpetuate evangelical Protestantism within the church, and it was precisely because he shared this orientation that Grasett was able to associate in Toronto and on the provincial council with men of all other Protestant denominations in constructing the public school system of Ontario on the basis of their common Christian principles.

H. E. TURNER

AO, RG 2, B-3; Strachan (John) papers. Toronto Board of Education, Education Centre Library, Reference Services, Hist. Coll., County Grammar School Board, Minutes, 1851–82. A. N. Bethune, *Memoir of the Right Reverend John Strachan, D.D., LL.D., first bishop of Toronto* (Toronto and London, 1870). Church Assoc. of the Diocese of Toronto, *Occasional paper* ([Toronto]), [1873–75]. *Doc. hist. of education in U.C.* (Hodgins), I, IX, XXIV, XXVIII. *Dominion Churchman* (Toronto), 1875–79. *Echo and Protestant Episcopal Recorder* (Port Hope, [Ont.], and Toronto), 1853–63. *Evangelical Churchman* (Toronto), 1876–79. *Globe*, 1850–82. *Toronto Daily Mail*, 1860–82. Chadwick, *Ontarian families*. *Centennial story: the Board of Education for the city of Toronto, 1850–1950*, ed. H. M. Cochrane (Toronto, 1950). T. R. Millman, *The life of the Right Reverend, the Honourable Charles James Stewart, D. D., Oxon., second Anglican bishop of Quebec* (London, Ont., 1953). V. E. Parvin, *Authorization of textbooks for the schools of Ontario, 1846–1950* ([Toronto], 1965). H. E. Turner, "The evangelical movement in the Church of England in the diocese of Toronto, 1839–1879" (MA thesis, Univ. of Toronto, 1959).

GRAY, JOHN HAMILTON, soldier and politician; b. 14 June 1811 at Charlottetown, P.E.I., son of Robert Gray* and Mary Burns; m. first Susan Pennefather (d. 1866), and they had at least two children; m. secondly in 1869 Sarah Caroline Cambridge, and they had three children; d. 13 Aug. 1887 at Charlottetown.

John Hamilton Gray's father emigrated from Glasgow to Virginia in 1771 and during the American revolution fought on the loyalist side. When the war ended he sought refuge in Shelburne, N.S., and in 1787 was invited by Lieutenant Governor Edmund Fanning* to assume several important official functions on Prince Edward Island. The elder Gray later married the daughter of Lieutenant George Burns, a proprietor and prominent public figure who had come to the Island in 1764. Thus, by the time of the birth of John Hamilton in 1811, the Gray family was established solidly within the ruling upper class of the Island, and his career, both as soldier and as politician, was to a great extent predetermined by family tradition.

In his middle or late teens Gray was sent to England to complete his education. According to an obituary in the Charlottetown *Patriot* he had, from his childhood, "evinced a desire for military life." In his early twenties he joined the 7th Dragoon Guards of the British army and served with them for 21 years, much of his time being spent in India and South Africa. His career in the army appears to have been distinguished but unspectacular, and in later years one of his favourite remembrances of his military life seems to have been that he had had a daughter born in each quarter of the globe.

Gray retired to Prince Edward Island in 1852 with the rank of colonel and quickly became involved in public life. Although he had been absent from the colony as an adult, upon his return he demonstrated a lively interest in local affairs and seemed to adjust readily to the restricted compass of Island political life. Gray's public statements reveal that his experience in the British army had created in him a loyalty to Britain and a sense of empire which were exceptional on the Island at the time; and yet, like other Islanders of the period, he was capable of alluding patriotically to Prince Edward Island as his "native land."

On 12 April 1854 Gray was appointed to the Legislative Council by the Conservative government of John Myrie Holl*, but his new career as a politician was cut short by the outbreak of the Crimean War. Feeling the call of duty, Gray resigned from office and returned to military life, and though he failed to reach the actual scene of conflict he was absent from the Island for about two more years.

Shortly after his second return to the Island, Gray became embroiled in the dispute over religion which was brewing in the colony and which would bedevil Island politics for the next 20 years. An elder of Charlottetown's kirk of St James since 1853, he believed strongly that the Bible ought to be a regular part of the school curriculum, a practice vigorously opposed by the large Roman Catholic minority. Gray soon emerged as one of the champions of the Protestant cause and served as chairman of the "Great Protestant Meeting" held in Charlottetown on 13 Feb. 1857 at which it was decided to establish a Protestant newspaper, the *Protector and Christian Witness*. The paper was merged with the *Protestant and Evangelical Witness* in 1858, at which time Gray had to deny charges that he had written secretly for it or had directed its editorial policy. He again showed his deep involvement in religious disputes by chairing a second Protestant meeting in February 1858, although his participation did not reveal a rancorous or narrowly sectarian attitude. Yet, it is also clear that his religious views were an asset to him in his political career. In the "Bible Elections" of 1858 and 1859, in which Protestant voters deserted George Coles*'s Liberal party, Gray was elected with sizable majorities as Conservative member for the predominantly Protestant riding of Queens, 4th District.

Following the 1859 election the Conservatives under Edward PALMER formed an all-Protestant government and soon introduced a scheme in which Gray was to play a key role. On 5 May 1859 Gray proposed in the assembly that the British government appoint a commission to inquire into the land question with a view to achieving the eventual abolition of the rental system. The Liberals accused the Conservatives of insincerity and pointed, with some justification, to the Tories' previous lack of support for measures designed to assist the cause of the tenants, such as the Land Purchase Act of 1853. Eventually, however, a three-man commission was appointed and Gray, the leading proponent of the scheme, stated optimistically that "never in the history of this Island was there a brighter prospect opened to us for a fair and equitable settlement." He seems to have believed sincerely that the land commission might be the solution to the problem of landlordism, and he was extremely bitter when in 1862 the British government heeded the objections of landlords and disallowed Island legislation which would have allowed a tenant "the right to purchase the land on which he lives." Having been absent from the Island during the tumultuous 1830s and 1840s, Gray had not participated in the struggles related to land tenure led by William Cooper* or in George Coles's fight for responsible government. It thus took him some time to perceive that British colonial policy and the best interests of Prince Edward Island were not always identical.

Identification with the land commission might have seriously impaired Gray's political credibility, but by the time of the provincial election of January 1863 the religious controversy over education had become the dominant issue in Island politics and he succeeded in being re-elected. Gray had become government leader in the assembly in 1860 when Edward Palmer moved to the Legislative Council; after the election, he resigned from the Executive Council in mid February and precipitated a crisis which forced Palmer out of the Conservative leadership. Gray assumed the premiership by 2 March 1863.

The British government's dismissal of the land commission's recommendations propelled Gray towards the belief that, if united, the British North American colonies "would have more power and be in a better position to approach the British throne. . . ." It is not surprising, therefore, that in the discussions regarding union of the Maritime colonies and confederation which came to the fore in the early 1860s, Gray was quite sympathetic to the notion of political amalgamation. In 1863 and 1864 he endorsed the Island's participation in discussions of a Maritime union, though he seemed to prefer the idea of a broader federation. He argued that a form of British North American federation would present a strong united front to possible American expansionism in addition to improved relations with Britain. Gray was clearly committed to union, though not without reservations. Most Islanders, on the other hand, were quite evidently opposed to a union of any sort.

When the Charlottetown conference convened on 1 Sept. 1864, Gray, as premier of the host colony, was selected chairman. The conference was dominated by the persuasive delegates from Canada, and Gray, along with the rest of the Maritime delegates, appears to have been satisfied for the most part merely to listen to the arguments for a general British North American union. He needed little convincing, and by the time the conference ended he had become an ardent supporter of the scheme. After leaving Charlottetown the delegates made their way to Nova Scotia and New Brunswick, and although Gray's speech in Halifax appears from the reports to have been rather non-committal, in Saint John he expressed enthusiastic support for confederation.

At the Quebec conference the following month Gray continued his support. However, the Prince Edward Island delegation, especially Edward Palmer, soon became a thorn in the side of the conference, expressing disapproval of almost every major resolution. Though Gray did not relinquish his support for confederation, he joined with his fellow delegates from the Island in arguing that the arrangements proposed regarding such matters as the composition of the Senate and representation in the House of Commons were inimical to the best interests of the Island.

The entire conference must have been an extremely difficult exercise for Gray because as a committed supporter of confederation he was anxious that the experiment not flounder, but as an Island politician he could not support measures which were clearly unacceptable to the Island populace. Nonetheless, he joined many of the "Fathers" on the banquet circuit following the Quebec conference. In Ottawa he stated his conviction that the new nation would soon take its place "among the first nations of the world," and in Belleville predicted that the colonies would soon be united "in the bonds of brotherhood which shall never be severed." It was the kind of talk that went over particularly well in Canada West, but its reception in his home province was quite another matter.

By the time Gray returned to Charlottetown on 10 Nov. 1864, Attorney General Palmer had already launched a peremptory and damaging attack against confederation. Gray responded by submitting to the newspapers an impassioned defence of the proposed union, arguing principally that confederation would offer a permanent solution to the vexatious land question by making compulsory the sale of lands and by providing the Island government with funds to purchase them. The sharp public difference of opinion between the premier and his attorney general placed Gray in an extremely awkward position, especially when it became increasingly clear that the overwhelming majority of Islanders were on Palmer's side of the dispute. Palmer could see no advantages for the Island in confederation and his rather churlish behaviour during this episode may also be explained by his personal animosity towards Gray, who in 1863 had deposed him as Conservative leader and premier. Feeling deserted and isolated, Gray resigned on 20 Dec. 1864, thereby bringing a sudden and permanent end to his political career. For a man of Gray's disposition and honour it must have been an extremely bitter and regrettable stroke of misfortune. The resignation was an unexpected and, to some, a rather precipitous decision, and it is possible that the illness of his wife had some bearing on the decision. Susan Gray had been too ill to accompany her husband to the Quebec conference and, after a lingering illness, died on 12 Nov. 1866. In 1868 the Charlottetown *Herald* attributed Gray's exit from the political scene to an "irreparable family affliction."

The internecine feuding within the Conservative party which surrounded Gray's departure and Palmer's simultaneous resignation from the Executive Council created a serious crisis of leadership. Early in January 1865 Gray was invited by the party to return to the position he had vacated, but he declined to lead a party which did not share his commitment to the Quebec Resolutions. Instead, James Colledge POPE, whose position on confederation was ambiguous, became premier.

In 1867 Gray's urge for political involvement apparently returned. However, he was defeated by David Laird*, an anti-confederate, in his attempt to secure the Conservative nomination in his old riding of Queens, 4th District. In 1873 he managed to win the nomination, but was defeated soundly at the polls. It would appear that Gray's role in the confederation controversy did irreparable damage to his political career, though this assessment is difficult to substantiate.

Gray's removal from the political scene allowed him to become more deeply involved with another of his great interests, the militia. He had been since 1862 the commanding officer of the volunteer brigade of the Island, and in 1867 was appointed adjutant general of the militia of the Island. In 1873 he accepted a position as deputy adjutant general of the newly formed Military District no.12 of the Dominion of Canada.

The comments of contemporaries reveal that Gray was a private, serious man whose reserve probably bordered on severity. There were few who would have questioned his integrity and rectitude, but he inspired respect rather than affection. In many ways he remained very much the soldier, possessing, by all accounts, a disciplined and somewhat officious manner, and being, in the words of the Charlottetown *Examiner*, "punctual to a fault." His comments in the legislature were generally of a practical, commonsensical nature, with a fine command of detail. He usually spoke clearly and to the point, and had little patience with the "useless repetitions" of some of his more garrulous colleagues. He was easily provoked by those members who, in his words, insisted on "serving up the same viands, hot, cold, hashed and rehashed." In debate he exhibited little in the way of rhetorical flair, but was very much the infantryman, advancing relentlessly and logically from one point to the next. Apart from the occasional sardonic gibe he lacked the gift of wit, and whereas the official reporter would often record "Laughter" following the remarks of a witty member, on one occasion, when Gray had attempted to be humorous, the reporter recorded simply "A laugh."

Though somewhat grave, Gray was not a harsh or vindictive man. In a period when the language in the Island legislature was frequently shrill and acerbic, he refrained from abuse and was seldom even sarcastic. Neither was he a narrowly partisan person, and when in 1869 a drive was begun to raise funds for the erection of a monument in honour of the Liberal journalist and politician Edward Whelan* who had died in December 1867, and to raise support for his widow and child, Gray did not hesitate to endorse the campaign. This is remarkable inasmuch as Whelan had been one of the most outspoken of his political opponents. In the *Examiner* Whelan had frequently criticized Gray, and on occasion held him up to ridicule. At Gray's death in 1887, obituaries also mentioned his Christian charity towards the poor of the city of Charlottetown.

Today in Prince Edward Island, John Hamilton Gray is possibly better known than any of the other talented public figures of the lively and eventful 1850s and 1860s. Though he is most often remembered as a politician, it is clear that he was above all a soldier. His years in public office were but a brief interlude between his service in the British army and with the Island volunteers and the Canadian militia. Indeed, his chairmanship of the Charlottetown conference and role as a father of confederation were something of a happenstance, and it is interesting that his obituaries almost completely pass over this aspect of his life. They suggest that by the time of his death the Island public had practically forgotten his participation in the confederation movement. It would appear, therefore, that the recognition Gray has received for his role as a father of confederation has been the result of the increased Canadianization of the Island's self-image in the decades since his death.

DAVID E. WEALE

P.E.I., House of Assembly, *Debates and proc.*, 1858–65. *Examiner* (Charlottetown), 1858–65, 19 Nov. 1866, 15

Aug. 1887. *Islander*, 1858–65. *Patriot* (Charlottetown), 15 Aug. 1887. *Prince Edward Island Register* (Charlottetown), 26 Feb. 1828. *Canada's smallest prov.* (Bolger). Robertson, "Religion, politics, and education in P.E.I." Edward Whelan, *The union of the British provinces* . . . (Charlottetown, 1865; repr. Summerside, P.E.I., 1949).

GRAY, JOHN HAMILTON, lawyer, politician, and judge; b. in 1814 at St George, Bermuda; d. 5 June 1889 at Victoria, B.C.

John Hamilton Gray's paternal grandfather, Joseph, was a loyalist from Boston who settled in Halifax; his father, William, was the naval commissary at Bermuda and later, from 1819 to 1845, the British consul at Norfolk, Va. John Hamilton received a classical education and acquired a BA from King's College, Windsor, N.S., in 1833. After articling under William Blowers Bliss*, he was admitted as an attorney in New Brunswick on 6 Feb. 1836 and as a barrister on 9 February of the following year. He settled in Saint John and recognition as a successful young advocate followed quickly, largely because of his spectacular courtroom oratory. In 1853 he was created a QC.

After law Gray was most active in the militia. On 25 May 1840 he was appointed a captain in the New Brunswick Regiment of Yeomanry Cavalry. By January 1850 he was a major in the Queen's New Brunswick Rangers, and on 20 May 1854 he was appointed their lieutenant-colonel, a rank he treasured. Through his military connections he met Lieutenant-Colonel Harry Smith Ormond who commanded the 30th Foot in New Brunswick. After Ormond went to Ireland in December 1843 Gray visited him there, and married his daughter, Elizabeth (Eliza), in Dublin in 1845; they had seven children. Gray's military interests later led him to membership in the Dominion Rifle Association of which he became vice president.

Perhaps as a result of his close attachment to the military and his family background Gray felt comfortable with the traditional establishment of New Brunswick. A "Conservative of the old school" was the way Liberal newspaperman George Edward Fenety* described him and he meant the phrase to be taken in the best sense. Gray was "very gentlemanly in his manners, and of a forgiving disposition." His entrance into politics on the Reform side has, however, led to some confusion.

The city of Saint John was dogged by innumerable problems in 1848–49, including economic dislocation related to Britain's adoption of free trade practices, depression, riots over parades by members of the Orange order, enormous fires, and the rejection of a railway scheme by which it had hoped to gain economic dominance on the northeastern Atlantic seaboard. These difficulties united people of all political leanings in the New Brunswick Colonial Association formed in 1849 [*see* Charles Simonds*]. At a meeting early in September Gray moved a motion in favour of a "*Federal Union of the British North American colonies, preparatory to their immediate independence.*" This startling proposal for independence, from the very proper Gray, was rejected by the association, but it anticipated the acceptance of the idea of a federal union; the association also adopted a progressive reform platform which provided the basis for a strong campaign during the 1850 provincial election. Gray and five other Saint John members of the association (Simonds, Robert Duncan Wilmot*, William Johnstone Ritchie*, Samuel Leonard Tilley*, and William Hayden Needham*), all committed to the platform and the defeat of the "compact" government at Fredericton, were elected. Gray apparently was elected as a Liberal, possibly as a radical. He was certainly a Saint John stalwart. In the assembly he proved to be highly effective, moving immediately to the front ranks of the opposition. When he spoke the house was full, for Gray was a orator "of the most finished and classic type." It was later claimed that he "was perhaps the most polished speaker on the floors of the House, as though he had prepared his speeches over the midnight oil, and set phrases to music . . . his impromptu replies to opponents being of equal polish."

Lieutenant Governor Edmund Walker Head*, finding his Executive Council inept and moribund, gave its "compact" government one last gasp of life by offering council positions to Wilmot and Gray. They accepted, and the Liberal opposition was robbed of much of its sting. When Wilmot, who was appointed solicitor general, succeeded in his by-election, three of the Saint John members of the New Brunswick Colonial Association, Ritchie, Tilley, and Simonds, saw no course but to resign from the assembly, their cause having been rejected by the people. Fenety later commented that a "terrible bomb-shell was thrown into the Liberal wigwam in St. John" by the Wilmot–Gray defection, and Gray's conscience bothered him. In a public letter of 2 Aug. 1851 he claimed that he had accepted the offer of a council seat in order to obtain the construction of the European and North American Railway from Saint John to Shediac. It was "*distinctly understood that the Government will accept no proposal for building* [the Intercolonial to bypass Saint John] *which shall not embrace in an equally favourable and explicit manner the European and North American Railway.*" Within two years the railway was approved. What Gray did not say was that, being a gentleman who honoured tradition, he could not possibly refuse to serve his governor when asked. Gray's desertion of his colleagues, however, was to haunt him for the rest of his political career. More and more he came to be regarded as a weathercock with great plumage and little substance.

For the next two decades Gray remained deeply involved in New Brunswick politics. Soon after his entry into office, he became the leader of the Conservatives in the assembly, a role which suited his training and temperament. In 1854 he also chaired a commission of inquiry into the affairs of King's College, Frederiction, then under threat of abandonment [*see* Edwin Jacob*], and he valiantly supported the college through its difficult evolution into the University of New Brunswick under president William Brydone JACK. The university thanked him with an honorary degree in 1866.

When the general election of 1854 ended the "compact" government by returning a clear majority of Reformers, Gray found himself leading the opposition to the government of Charles Fisher*. Lieutenant Governor John Henry Thomas Manners-Sutton* disliked his Reform council, and choosing for an issue the controversial prohibitory liquor law of 1855 introduced by Tilley, the provincial secretary, he arbitrarily dismissed them from office in May of the following year, replacing them with a Gray–Wilmot government. The governor had stretched his powers by the action, but Gray, the new attorney general, did not hesitate to accept the office when it was offered. He appeared to be justified when he won a provincial election in June 1856, and he had the liquor law repealed. The temporary nature of the support the Conservatives had garnered from that question became obvious as members drifted back to Fisher. Gray tried to carry on, but he could no longer command a majority in the house and after Fisher's victory in the elections of May 1857 he resigned and was replaced at the end of that month. Gray had led his last government. He remained clearly identified as a Conservative by opposing a Liberal school bill in 1858 and being dubbed "Archbishop Gray" for his efforts.

Over the next few years Gray's major contribution was as chairman of three committees of inquiry into the construction of the European and North American Railway, in 1858, 1859, and 1860. Politics, patronage, graft, and spiralling costs had made the railway a natural centre of controversy after it was taken over by the government in 1856. The report of 1858 did point to some irregularities in finance and in awarding of contracts. The second report, in 1859, concluded that the railway would be "a first class Road, of superior description, well and solidly built," but there was a suggestion that it might have been more cheaply constructed. The final inquiry in 1860 was forced by the Conservatives over Gray's objections. He declared the railway a "thoroughly constructed road" and condemned his colleagues for their pettiness. During the session of 1860 he dissociated himself from his colleagues and afterwards generally supported Tilley, who became premier in 1861. In the election held that year, however, Gray paid the penalty for political fickleness by being soundly thrashed.

Always in demand as a lawyer, Gray settled back into his practice and also held a number of official posts. From 1857 to 1859 he had been umpire between the fishery commissioners of the United States and Great Britain [*see* Moses Henry Perley*] acting under the Reciprocity Treaty of 1854, and in 1860–61 he was chairman of the three-man commission, which included Joseph Howe* and John William RITCHIE, appointed to investigate the tenant question in Prince Edward Island. In 1864 Gray achieved great popularity in Saint John by defending three New Brunswickers who were among those participating in the seizure of the American steamship *Chesapeake* during the American Civil War. After depositing passengers and crew at Saint John, the *Chesapeake* had been captured off Nova Scotia by a Northern cruiser. The leader of the conspirators, John C. Braine, and the three Saint John area men were eventually brought before the New Brunswick courts; Braine, a strong supporter of the Confederacy, was released. Gray, whose brother had been killed while fighting for the Confederacy, successfully defended the other three with the assistance of Ritchie, a Nova Scotian attorney.

Following a short rest after his political defeat in 1861, Gray soon began once again to make his views known. On one occasion, in February 1863, he called for a British North American union in a speech entitled "The practical application of passing events to our country" and on another he pressed for the construction of the Intercolonial Railway, with Saint John as the eastern terminal. Tilley decided to support him even though he was warned that "parties will be in a queer mess . . . 'Greek meeting Greek.'" Although others had not forgotten the desertion of 1851, Tilley had forgiven Gray. Tilley had also realized that the old political alliances of the 1850s were giving way to new ones, and he began to form a new Liberal-Conservative coalition, with Gray as a member.

Gray won the by-election and was subsequently chosen by Tilley as a New Brunswick delegate to the Charlottetown conference of 1864. As far as can be determined, Gray did not have much influence. He did insist on clearly defined powers for the provinces. "I think it best to define the powers of the Local Governments," he said at Quebec, "as the public will then see what matters they have reserved for their consideration, with which matters they will be familiar, and so the humbler classes and the less educated will comprehend that their interests are protected." Gray's *Confederation: or, the political and parliamentary history of Canada* (1872), of which only the first volume was published, is little more than a compilation of speeches and newspaper articles of the time, offering no insights into his role or into the success of confederation.

Gray and the other New Brunswickers encountered great hostility when they returned home from Quebec, and in a public meeting Gray's oratory mysteriously failed him, as he "had not devoted sufficient time to his rehearsals." Albert James SMITH, in the mean time, was leading a crusade against confederation, gaining converts among members of the assembly and the populace. Tilley was in a quandary. He did not believe he could get the Quebec Resolutions through the house, but he was required by law to go to the polls by June of 1865. In January 1865, Gray wrote Tilley that defeat in the assembly was likely. "The chance is too great, and our honour is at stake." Wait a month for the people to be educated before calling the election, he suggested, "then – Gentlemen, walk the plank."

Tilley followed that advice and early in March he, Gray, and a majority of the New Brunswick pro-confederates went off the plank together in a landslide anti-confederate victory. Trying to explain what had happened, Gray wrote John A. Macdonald* that the merchants, manufacturers, and intelligent classes had supported them, a point that is ignored by historians who have made the following Gray's most quoted statement: "Again the Banking interests united against us – they at present have a monopoly and their directors used their influence unsparingly. They dreaded the competition of Canadian Banks coming here and the consequent destruction of that monopoly – and many a businessman now in their power felt it not safe to hazard an active opposition to their influence." About two weeks later, in a letter to George Brown*, Gray wrote that the people had rejected them "from their hatred to the Govt. and from the desire to oust Tilley who they thought had been too long in power."

This explanation may be an indication that the relationship with Tilley had cooled, for Gray was not again to play a central role in the confederation movement. He worked hard for the idea, was successful in the 1866 election that reversed the decision of 1865, and served as speaker of the assembly in 1866 and 1867. But he was not invited to the London conference, nor did he gain prominence at Ottawa, though he sat for Westmorland in the House of Commons from 1867 to 1872. Chairman of the committee of supply, he was also appointed dominion arbitrator under section 142 of the British North America Act to settle the division of debts, liabilities, and assets between Quebec and Ontario in 1867. In 1871 he presented a preliminary report on the uniformity of statutory law in Ontario, New Brunswick, and Nova Scotia. His speeches in the house became infrequent, but he started with a good one in 1867. It was humorous, literate, and moving. "That to be a Canadian, not in its former limited sense, but in the sense of the new Dominion," the report of the speech noted, "was to belong to a country of which any man might be proud. This national sentiment must be fostered, must be encouraged. He was an Englishman in every fibre of his frame, and every pulsation of his heart. He loved England still, but he loved Canada more."

Gray realized in 1872 he had no political future and he was not a candidate in the elections held that year. He sought and was granted a puisne judgeship in the Supreme Court of British Columbia on 3 July 1872, an appointment resented in that province where George Anthony Walkem* referred to Gray as an "empty-headed favourite." Gray none the less served his term with great distinction, providing a balance and specialized skills that would otherwise have been lacking. As late as 1883, however, Attorney General John Roland Hett accused Gray in the *Victoria Daily Standard* of being in collusion with counsel during a hearing on an election which Hett had recently lost. Gray was vindicated in the courts.

As a judge Gray was to become involved in two controversial subjects, the treatment of the Chinese and the boundary between British Columbia and Alaska. Discrimination against the Chinese in British Columbia began shortly after the arrival of the first immigrants in the 1850s. In 1878 Gray ruled in *Tai Sing* v. *Maguire* that the intention of the provincial Chinese Tax Act, 1878, was to "drive the Chinese from the country, thus interfering at once with the authority reserved to the Dominion Parliament as to the regulation of the trade and commerce, the rights of aliens, and the treaties of the empire." The act, according to Gray, was "unconstitutional and void." Undoubtedly this decision led to his appointment on 4 July 1884, along with Joseph-Adolphe Chapleau*, as a commissioner on the Royal Commission on Chinese Immigration. Their report identified three "phases of opinion" in the province: the first, "of a well meaning, but strongly prejudiced minority, whom nothing but absolute exclusion will satisfy"; the second, "an intelligent minority, who conceive that no legislation whatever is necessary – that, as in all business transactions, the rule of supply and demand will apply and the matter regulate itself in the ordinary course of events"; and the third "of a large majority, who think there should be a moderate restriction, based upon police, financial and sanitary principles, sustained and enforced by stringent local regulation for cleanliness and the preservation of health." Though Gray appeared personally to support the second opinion, he recommended the third.

Gray also became an authority on the boundary problems between British Columbia and Alaska. In 1876 his involvement in a case in which a prisoner, Peter Martin, had been transported over contested territory led to a diplomatic incident and to Gray's writing Prime Minister Alexander Mackenzie* with recommendations for a solution to the jurisdictional question. His suggestions, in time, became the cornerstone of the Canadian position. In 1884 he wrote a paper on the limits of the Canadian claim, which was officially adopted by the province. Though Gray's contentions would eventually be repudiated by the Alaskan Boundary Tribunal of 1903, he was so highly regarded that a Canadian delegation at Washington in 1888 to try to settle the dispute postponed its deliberations until he could join them.

Gray actively publicized his opinions on the boundary question and other issues through lectures and articles in magazines and journals. One subject that interested him intensely was the controversy surrounding the Bering Sea seal-fishery. Another was the Imperial Federation League and he helped to organize a local branch of the movement in British Columbia. In 1889, when he was planning to receive Tilley, his old New Brunswick colleague, for whom he had promised "*a right Royal Reception*" in Victoria, he was struck by paralysis and died on 5 June. His wife, Eliza, unfortunately was left no inheritance.

Gray had several careers, as lawyer, politician, judge, and arbitrator. That he was an excellent lawyer is unquestioned, yet it is as a New Brunswick politician that he is remembered, despite his limited accomplishments. Usually overlooked are his activities as a jurist and negotiator, in which he made significant contributions.

C. M. WALLACE

[Though John Hamilton Gray was a renowned orator and leading figure in New Brunswick politics for two decades, he has not as yet attracted a biographer nor did he leave any private papers to encourage one. His short and undistinguished stint as head of the government offered little in the way of substance and his grand speeches have suffered with the passage of time. As a father of confederation he has received token piety, but his *Confederation; or, the political and parliamentary history of Canada, from the conference at Quebec, in October, 1864, to the admission of British Columbia, in July, 1871* (Toronto, 1872) is a disappointing collection of speeches and newspaper articles that offers no insights into either his role in the movement or the nature of the problems. One of his reports for the House of Commons was published separately as *Extracts from the Hon. J. H. Gray's preliminary report on the statutory laws: Ontario, New Brunswick, and Nova Scotia* (Ottawa, 1871), and for his work on the Royal Commission on Chinese Immigration see its *Report* (Ottawa, 1885). Speeches delivered by Gray were published in the newspapers of the day and as pamphlets.

Despite his imposing manner, Gray ranked well below Edward Barron Chandler*, Charles Fisher, and Samuel Leonard Tilley in influence. Since he was a long-time associate of Tilley's, there are many Gray letters in N.B. Museum, Tilley family papers, and in PAC, MG 27, I, D15 (S. L. Tilley papers), as well as in PAC, MG 26, A (John A. Macdonald papers), and B (Alexander Mackenzie papers). With the exception of one letter, J. H. Gray to W. H. Gray, 5 July 1848, there is no correspondence by him in PAC, MG 24, D63 (Gray family papers).

In the secondary literature George Edward Fenety and James Hannay*, the Whiggish newspaper-historians of the era, both condemned Gray as shallow and opportunistic because of his desertion of the Liberal cause in 1851, though Fenety came to respect him as a gentleman, as can be seen in his "Political notes," published in *Progress* (Saint John, N.B.), 1894. More recently, historians of New Brunswick, such as William Stewart MacNutt*, have pictured Gray as a bit player in an imperial pageant. MacNutt's *New Brunswick* stands out as having largely superseded all previous studies, especially that of Hannay, *Hist. of N.B.* MacNutt had written a preliminary draft biography of Gray for the *DCB* shortly before his death, but he was unable to complete it. In it he empathized with Gray's gentlemanliness, his conservatism, and his deference. C.M.W.]

PAC, MG 24, B40. PANB, RG 2, RS 6, 1851–67. PRO, CO 188; CO 189. UNBL, MG H12a. B.C., Legislative Assembly, *Sessional papers*, 1885, "Alaska boundary question. . . ." *Documents on the confederation of British North America: a compilation based on Sir Joseph Pope's confederation documents supplemented by other official material*, ed. G. P. Browne (Toronto and Montreal, 1969). G. E. Fenety, *Political notes and observations; or, a glance at the leading measures that have been introduced and discussed in the House of Assembly of New Brunswick . . .* (Fredericton, 1867). [J. H. Gray], "Mr. Justice Gray to the Hon. A. Mackenzie," Alaskan Boundary Tribunal, *Proc.* (7v. and 3v. atlas, Washington, 1904), III: 256–58. N.B., House of Assembly, *Journal*, 1860–67; *Reports of the debates*, 1850–67. "Parl. debates" (CLA mfm. project of parl. debates, 1846–74), 1867–72. *Tai Sing* v. *Maguire* (1867–89), 1 B.C.R. (part 1), 101. *Daily Colonist* (Victoria), 6 June 1889. *Daily Sun* (Saint John), 7 June 1889. *Morning Freeman* (Saint John), 1860–72. *Morning News* (Saint John), 1849–72. *Morning Telegraph* (Saint John), 1864–69. *New Brunswick Courier*, 2 Aug. 1851. *St. John Daily Telegraph and Morning Journal* (Saint John), 1869–72. *Saint John Globe*, 1858–72. *CPC*, 1867–72. *New-Brunswick almanac*, 1851. Wallace, *Macmillan dict.* J. K. Chapman, *The career of Arthur Hamilton Gordon, first Lord Stanmore, 1829–1912* (Toronto, 1964). M. O. Hammond, *Confederation and its leaders* (Toronto, 1917). D. G. G. Kerr, *Sir Edmund Head, a scholarly governor* ([Toronto], 1954). Ormsby, *British Columbia*. E. O. S. Scholefield and F. W. Howay, *British Columbia from the earliest times to the present* (4v., Vancouver, 1914), III: 932–35, 986–90. L. B. Shippee, *Canadian-American relations, 1849–1874* (New Haven, Conn., and Toronto, 1939). C. C. Tansill, *Canadian-American relations, 1875–1911* (New Haven and Toronto, 1943). Waite, *Life and times of confederation*. C. M. Wallace, "Sir Leonard Tilley: a political biography" (PHD thesis, Univ. of Alberta, Edmonton, 1972). H. C. Wilkinson, *Bermuda from sail to steam: the history of the island from 1784 to 1901* (2v., London, 1973). D. R. Williams, '. . . *The man for a new country': Sir Matthew Baillie Begbie* (Sidney, B.C., 1977). R. W. Winks, *Canada and the United States: the Civil War years* (Baltimore, Md., 1960). A. G. Bailey, "The basis and persistence of opposition to confederation in New Brunswick," *CHR*, 23 (1942): 374–97. Georgiana Ball, "The Peter Martin case and the provisional settlement of the Stikine boundary," *BC Studies*, 10 (summer 1971):

35–55. C. M. Wallace, "Saint John boosters and the railroads in mid-nineteenth century," *Acadiensis*, 6 (1976–77), no.1: 71–91.

GRIEVE, WALTER, merchant and office-holder; b. *c.* 1809, son of Robert Grieve and Margaret Johnston of Killater (Strathclyde), Scotland; m. in April 1846 Jane Richardson, and they had two sons; d. 26 March 1887 at Greenock, Scotland.

Walter Grieve apparently came to St John's, Nfld, in the late 1820s to join his elder brother James Johnston. James, who had arrived in Newfoundland in 1828, was working for the firm Baine, Johnston and Company in which their maternal uncle, William Johnston, was a partner. This firm was engaged in the traditional import-export trade and had branches in Greenock and St John's. Walter joined it, and after the death of William Johnston in 1837 he effectively ran the St John's branch, with James usually resident in Greenock. The brothers gained full control of the firm when Walter Baine died in 1851. Four years later Walter Grieve relinquished the management of Baine, Johnston and Company to his nephew Robert Grieve, and established his own firm, Walter Grieve and Company, at St John's, and another firm in partnership with Alexander Bremner at Trinity. During the 1860s Grieve began to spend most of the year in Scotland, and he therefore transferred the management of Walter Grieve and Company to another nephew, Robert Thorburn*, who was also made a partner. In 1863 the two firms, Baine, Johnston and Company and Walter Grieve and Company, combined to send the first steamers to the seal-fishery from St John's. Although no longer directly involved in management, Grieve maintained an active interest in both firms.

Walter Grieve had held various local offices in St John's: road commissioner in the late 1830s, justice of the peace, president of the Chamber of Commerce of St John's for the years 1847–48, 1855–56, and 1857–58, president of the Scottish Society, one of the four-member Board of Revenue in 1855, and director of the privately owned gas and water companies. Through choice he did not play a prominent role in elective politics. He had refused to run for the legislature in 1842, despite the fact that a large number of St John's citizens had tried to conscript him. He was, however, appointed by Governor Sir John Harvey* to the Executive Council as surveyor general, though he sat only for a short period between the years 1845 and 1848. His retirement from the council coincided with the introduction of the bicameral legislature. His political attitudes appear to have been liberal; he had supported the campaign for the grant of a constitution in the late 1820s, and his friendship with Philip Francis Little*, leader of the Liberals in the 1850s, suggests that unlike most St John's merchants he favoured the granting of responsible government. He made his one noteworthy entry into Newfoundland politics in 1869 when he joined Charles James Fox BENNETT in his anti-confederation campaign. His influence in the mercantile community and among those fishermen and planters who dealt with his firms, as well as his money, were important factors in Bennett's electoral victory.

Though a Presbyterian, Grieve was sympathetic towards the aspirations of the local Roman Catholic church. Non-Anglican Protestants and Catholics of Newfoundland often aligned to oppose the Church of England. They supported each other over such contentious issues as the educational grant, responsible government, and patronage. A friend of Catholic Bishop Michael Anthony Fleming*, Grieve contributed generously to the building of the Cathedral of St John the Baptist, completed in St John's in 1855. Patrick Kevin Devine records that Grieve donated all the ropes and scaffolding, and in gratitude Fleming gave Grieve his farm, Carpasia, located outside St John's.

Grieve emerged from his Newfoundland career wealthy and popular. The native prejudice against businessmen who viewed their stay in Newfoundland as temporary was mitigated by his public spirit, generosity, and refusal to become embroiled in local quarrels. An anonymous diarist noted in 1863 that "As a merchant and as a man, Walter Grieve, Esq., has, in my opinion, no competitor in this community. He is one of nature's noblemen."

JAMES K. HILLER

Maritime Hist. Group Arch., Baine, Johnston & Company papers; Bremner papers; Grieve name file.

Nfld., *Blue book*, 1840–50. *Evening Telegram* (St John's), 15 June 1883. *Newfoundlander*, 22 Sept. 1842; 12 Jan., 30 April 1846. *Royal Gazette* (St John's), 1838; August 1843; April, August 1847; February 1851. *Chafe's sealing book* (1923). Devine, *Ye olde St. John's*. Prowse, *Hist. of Nfld.* (1895).

GROS OURS. *See* MISTAHIMASKWA

GURNEY, EDWARD, iron-founder; b. in 1817 in Steuben Township, Oneida County, N.Y., son of Byrem Gurney; m. Nancy, and they had one son and one daughter; d. 21 Nov. 1884 in Hamilton, Ont.

When Edward Gurney was a young man his family moved to Utica, N.Y., where he and his brother Charles learned the iron-moulding trade. In December 1842 the family immigrated to Hamilton, Canada West. The next year Edward and Charles, each supplying $1,400 capital, began a stove manufacturing business. Initially, employing only one man and one boy, the company produced two stoves per day. In the early years sales were excellent, but payments were slow and there is a legend that on one occasion the firm was saved financially by John Fisher, who with Calvin

McQuesten operated a threshing machine factory in Hamilton. The Gurney brothers' business prospered, however, and in 1847 Edward and Charles formed a partnership with Alexander Carpenter, a Hamilton businessman who held a patent on a new cooking stove design. Originally established as Carpenter, Gurney and Company, the firm soon became Gurneys and Carpenter and expanded into the production of a wide variety of iron products. By 1856 it was estimated that the worth of the firm was approximately $200,000. In 1859 the partners took a patent on the new Protectionist stove and the next year built a larger foundry. In 1861 Carpenter retired; the new firm, E. and C. Gurney and Company, continued to grow and soon employed some 100 men and produced a greatly increased variety of products. By the early 1870s the estimated capital of the company was between $750,000 and $1,000,000. In 1875 the factory was enlarged to cover almost a city block.

Success led to the opening of branches. In 1868 the Gurneys had purchased John McGee's Phoenix Foundry in Toronto and made Edward Gurney* Jr manager. The Toronto operation prospered and by 1875, carrying lines similar to those of the Hamilton factory, had equalled the business of the parent plant. Branches were also opened in Montreal and Winnipeg. This expansion allowed the ageing Gurney brothers to bring Charles's son George into the business, as well as a nephew, John H. Tilden. In August 1883 the partnership was incorporated as E. and C. Gurney Company (Limited), with a capitalization of $300,000 and Edward as president.

Edward Gurney was also involved in numerous other enterprises. In 1856 Elijah W. Ware had established a scale factory in Hamilton and the Gurneys were soon associated with him, forming Gurney, Ware and Company. A decade later the Provincial Scale Works, their trade name, had annual sales of $20,000 and employed 15 men; ten years after that its value exceeded $250,000. Ware was later bought out by the Gurney family and the business continued in operation until the 1960s. The Gurneys were also owners of the Gurney Manufacturing Company in Dundas, Ont., which made agricultural implements. Edward was a director of many concerns including the Canada Screw Company, the Landed Banking and Loan Company, the Ontario Cotton Mills, and the Hamilton and North Western Railway Company. He was also a vice-president of the Hamilton and Lake Erie Railway Company. In 1872 he helped establish the Bank of Hamilton and remained a director for the rest of his life.

Edward never sought political office: "He had too much business to attend to." He did, however, sit on the council of the Hamilton Board of Trade and was a strong proponent of tariff protection long before Sir John A. Macdonald*'s National Policy of 1878. Edward was a member of the Centenary Methodist Church and sat on the board of directors of the Wesleyan Female College at Hamilton.

When Gurney arrived in Hamilton the population was under 3,500 and when he died it exceeded 35,000; correspondingly the increase in his wealth had greatly exceeded the growth of his adopted city. At his funeral 500 to 600 of his employees followed the coffin, and his estate, not including real estate, was valued at $456,500. Descriptions of Edward invariably include the same adjectives; keen, shrewd, and careful. An obituary in the *Hamilton Spectator* stated: "His life was essentially a business life; it knew no such word as rest."

Frederick H. Armstrong

Baker Library, R. G. Dun & Co. credit ledger, Can., 25: 101, 238, 240, 267. HPL, Scrapbooks and clipping files. MTL, Biog. scrapbooks, I: 468, 483. Wentworth County Surrogate Court (Hamilton, Ont.), will, codicil, and inventory of Edward Gurney, 9 Sept., 28 Oct. 1884; 21 Dec. 1885.

Dundas True Banner (Dundas, Ont.), 27 Nov. 1884. *Hamilton Spectator*, 22, 25 Nov. 1884; August 1889 (summer carnival ed.). *Dominion annual register*, 1884: 226–27. *The mercantile agency reference book for the British provinces . . .* (Montreal and Toronto), I (1864): 136. *Hamilton city sketches*, ed. T M. Thomson ([Hamilton, 1954]), 47–48. *Hamilton, the Birmingham of Canada* (Hamilton, 1892). Marcel Moussette, "Répertoire des fabricants d'appareils de chauffage du Québec (1760–1867)," Can., Direction des parcs et des lieux hist. nationaux, *Travail inédit numéro 125* (Ottawa, 1972), 41–42. V. Ross and Trigge, *Hist. of Canadian Bank of Commerce*, III: 66, 88, 152, 351.

H

HAMILTON, JOHN, businessman and politician; b. 1802 at Queenston, Upper Canada, youngest son of Robert Hamilton* and Mary Herkimer, widow of Neil McLean*; d. 10 Oct. 1882 at Kingston, Ont.

John Hamilton was born into a wealthy and influential family. He received a classical education at Queenston and Edinburgh, Scotland, before working as a clerk from 1820 to 1824 for Desrivières and Blackwood, wholesale merchants in Montreal. John's father had died in 1809, but because of his youth and the complicated nature of the will, he did not receive his share of the estate until 1824. The final settlement, although not totally satisfactory to John, did enable him and his stepbrother Robert to found the Queenston Steamboat Company.

The brothers purchased a used steamboat, the

Frontenac, from Henry Gildersleeve* for about £1,500 in January 1825 to add to a new but smaller steamer which they had built, the *Queenston*. The *Frontenac* sailed between Kingston and Niagara, stopping at York (Toronto) on its return, and the *Queenston* sailed between Prescott and Niagara, with stops at Kingston and York. Robert left the partnership probably in the late 1820s. John Hamilton repeatedly utilized technical innovations to succeed in the financially hazardous and extremely competitive inland shipping business. In 1830–31 he had the *Great Britain*, a new model steamer, built at Prescott at a cost of over £20,000. He also owned the *Lord Sydenham*, the first large steamer, and the *Passport*, the first iron steamer, to run the Lachine rapids. A shrewd manager, he generally owned only two or three steamboats and leased others, which allowed him to keep his overhead costs down and to react more quickly than many of his competitors to sharp fluctuations in the economy. He avoided competitive wars and instead sought rate agreements which guaranteed all operators a profitable return.

In the early 1840s, partly because of the reckless competitive practices of his Lake Ontario rivals, Donald Bethune* and Hugh Richardson*, Hamilton temporarily stopped the Lake Ontario runs and concentrated on the St Lawrence trade. Transferring his home and business from Queenston to Kingston, he began a forwarding business between that place and Montreal. By 1850, Richardson was bankrupt and Bethune was floundering. That year, associated with the large forwarding firms of Macpherson and Crane, and Hooker and Holton, Hamilton re-entered the lake business. In 1857, as the main proprietor of the Canadian Lake and River Line, he operated most of Bethune's old boats which he had probably purchased after Bethune's bankruptcy. The "debilitating" competition of the Grand Trunk Railway forced Hamilton into a brief retirement in 1862 but he recommenced operations in 1865 and by 1868 he was the Kingston manager for the Canadian Navigation Company. A multipartnership, like its predecessors in the 1840s and 1850s, the company was also called the Royal Mail Line.

Hamilton was less successful in his career as a banker. After a period as vice-president of the Commercial Bank of the Midland District, he succeeded John Macaulay* as its president in 1847, a position he held until the early 1860s. Hamilton used his position with the bank to strengthen his steamboat business. He persuaded the bank to end its business with Donald Bethune and in 1847 it initiated proceedings against him to recover an overdue loan. In areas separate from his interest in shipping, Hamilton's administration was extremely lax. By June 1859, for example, the bank had allowed the Detroit and Milwaukee and the Great Western railway companies to borrow amounts totalling $942,672, more than the companies could repay. Decisions such as these led to the demise of the bank.

Although never his major interest, Hamilton's political career was exceptionally long. In 1831 he accepted an "unexpected . . . [and] undesired" appointment to the Legislative Council of Upper Canada. His initial reluctance soon disappeared and he sat in the Legislative Council of the Province of Canada from 1841 to 1867 and served in the Senate from 1867 until his death. His 51-year career as a Conservative councillor and senator was marked by dependable, rather than innovative, legislative service.

His involvement with Queen's College at Kingston was of a more positive nature. Despite a belief that Canada West lacked the money to support a separate Presbyterian institution and that only one "United College" giving instruction in every area but divinity should be created, Hamilton was a co-founder of Queen's and provided respectability and solidity in its troubled early years. His business contacts and his political position were used to the advantage of the college. An ardent Presbyterian, he none the less agreed with William Morris*, co-founder and chairman of the board of trustees, that the laity, not the clergy, should control the board. When Morris resigned late in 1842, Hamilton, characterized by a Queen's historian as a "competent" layman, became chairman and remained so until he died.

By the mid 1870s, Hamilton, "one of those thoroughly aristocratic men," was a patriarchal figure in the Kingston area. He had been an incorporator of the Wolfe Island, Kingston and Toronto Railroad Company in 1846 and the Union Forwarding and Railway Company in 1859 as well as a director of the Kingston Fire and Marine Insurance Company and the Life Association of Scotland. For a short period of time he operated a stage-coach line and during most of his life, like many of his contemporaries, he speculated in land. He was at one time president of the Kingston St Andrew's Society. Some time before 1830 he had married Frances Pasia (d. 1873), sister of David Lewis Macpherson*, a Conservative ally of John A. Macdonald*, and one of his 11 children married a son of William Henry Draper*.

PETER BASKERVILLE

AO, MU 1143. MTL, James Van Cleve, "Reminiscences of early sailing vessels and steam boats on Lake Ontario" (typescript). PAC, MG 24, D24; I26, 4–6; 65. QUA, William Morris papers, 1–2; Queen's Univ. letters, Hugh Allan to Hamilton, 11 April 1854; Hamilton to Allan, 24 April 1854; Hamilton to McIver, 16 June 1854; James Sutherland papers. *Canadian Merchants' Magazine and Commercial Rev.* (Toronto), 1 (April–September 1857): 58, 327–28; 3 (April–December 1858): 239. *Commercial Bank of Canada*

v. *Great Western Railway Co.* (1862–64), 22 U.C.Q.B. 233. *Counter* v. *Hamilton* (1839–40), 6 U.C.Q.B. (O. S.) 612. *Great Western Railway Co.* v. *Commercial Bank of Canada* (1862–65), 2 U.C.E. & A. 285. *Henderson et al.* v. *Graves* (1862–65), 2 U.C.E. & A. 9. *Holcomb* v. *Hamilton* (1862–65), 2 U.C.E. & A. 230. *McDonell et al.* v. *Bank of Upper Canada* (1850–51), 7 U.C.Q.B. 252. *British Colonist* (Toronto), 4 May 1842. *Chronicle & Gazette*, 20 May 1837. *Daily British Whig*, 11 Oct. 1882. *Globe*, 12 Oct. 1882. *Hamilton Spectator*, 15 Oct. 1851. *Leader*, 26 March 1857. *Queen's College Journal* (Kingston, Ont.), 25 Oct. 1882. *Toronto Daily Mail*, 9 Dec. 1882. *The Canadian mercantile almanack . . .* (Niagara, [Ont.], and Toronto), 1846–47. *CPC*, 1880. *Cyclopædia of Canadian biog.* (Rose, 1886). *Dominion annual register*, 1882. Donald Swainson, "Kingstonians in the second parliament: portrait of an élite group," *To preserve & defend: essays on Kingston in the nineteenth century*, ed. Gerald Tulchinsky (Montreal and London, 1976), 261–77. Peter Baskerville, "Donald Bethune's steamboat business: a study of Upper Canadian commercial and financial practice," *OH*, 67 (1975): 135–49. A. L. Johnson, "The transportation revolution on Lake Ontario, 1817–1867: Kingston and Ogdensburg," *OH*, 67: 199–209.

HAMILTON, JOHN, lumberman, financier, and politician; b. 16 Dec. 1827 at Hawkesbury, Upper Canada, son of George Hamilton* and Lucy Susannah Christina Craigie; d. 3 April 1888 in Montreal, Que.

John Hamilton's father, one of the most successful early lumbermen in the Canadas, bequeathed to his sons upon his death in 1839 a large, integrated timbering operation, including numerous timber berths, mills at Hawkesbury, and his own timber cove at New Liverpool, Lower Canada. In 1843, after completing his education in Montreal, John Hamilton entered the lumber trade with his two elder brothers, Robert and George Jr.

A new partnership, called Hamilton and Thomson, was formed at this time with John Thomson, former manager of John Caldwell*'s Etchemin Mills Company, and his sons Andrew and John. Robert Hamilton became the firm's permanent agent in Quebec City and supervised the New Liverpool timber cove, while John Hamilton learned the milling business in Hawkesbury. The new company produced squared pine and oak as well as pine deals for the British market. Timber was acquired from limits along the lower Ottawa River and from the Gatineau, Rideau, Rouge, and South Nation rivers, and this supply was supplemented by wood bought from smaller contractors at the Hawkesbury mills. Hamilton and Thomson quickly expanded its operations by purchasing L. G. Bigelow's mill on the Rivière du Lièvre, and with these new facilities the company was able to take a dominant part in the timber trade.

Around 1849 the Hamiltons bought out the Thomson interest in the business and Robert, George Jr, and John set up a new partnership called Hamilton Brothers. At this time John Hamilton took over sole responsibility for the management of the up-country cutting operations and the milling activities at Hawkesbury and on the Rivière du Lièvre. Thus established, he married Rebecca Lewis in 1852. During the late 1850s the company continued to acquire new limits at Rapides des Joachims on the upper Ottawa in Canada East and along the Dumoine and Noire rivers. In 1860 R. G. Dun and Company appraised the firm's worth at between $320,000 and $400,000, and by 1871 its production had climbed to 40 million board feet of pine annually, amounting to nearly $550,000 worth of business. After Robert Hamilton's death in 1872 John carried on alone and the company remained the principal basis of the Hamilton family's wealth until it was sold in 1888.

John Hamilton had inherited more than a business from his father. He had also been inculcated with George Hamilton's staunch ultra-Tory views and his intense and partisan interest in public affairs. Such an interest he amply demonstrated in 1858 when he was elected as Hawkesbury's first reeve. Hamilton remained reeve until 1864, and served as warden of the United Counties of Prescott and Russell three times. In 1860 he was elected for the Inkerman division (counties of Argenteuil, Ottawa and Pontiac, Canada East) to the Legislative Council supporting the Conservative ministry of George-Étienne Cartier* and John A. Macdonald*. Hamilton tried to establish himself as a political power in "the Ottawa country," but was not particularly successful in his endeavours. He greatly resented the influence which Richard William Scott*, member of the Legislative Assembly for Ottawa City, wielded with the government, especially with the Crown Lands Department, in policy and patronage matters. After the administration's defeat in 1862, Macdonald used Hamilton as a rallying point amongst the Ottawa valley lumber community for Conservative support against John Sandfield Macdonald*. For services rendered at this time Hamilton was appointed to the new Canadian Senate on 28 Oct. 1867.

Hamilton's political prestige began to wane considerably after confederation. The Conservative party in the Prescott County area was divided into two factions: English-speaking individuals, with whom Hamilton was closely associated, and French-speaking. The rapidly growing French Canadian population in Prescott forced Hamilton to enter into an agreement in 1867 with the parish priest, Antoine Brunet, stipulating that the Conservatives would endeavour to elect a French Canadian to the House of Commons and an English-speaking member to the Ontario legislature. Because of party considerations Hamilton was forced to give his support to Thomas D'Arcy McGee* as a candidate in Prescott for the first Ontario legislature. The Protestants, annoyed by

Hamilton's agreement with Brunet, were further alienated by his assistance to an Irish Catholic, and he finally found it necessary to support the minority English-speaking Conservative group over the majority French-speaking group. Hamilton's agreement with Brunet was respected at the provincial level, so that an English Canadian went to the assembly, but from 1867 until 1878 an English Canadian was also elected for Prescott to the House of Commons. When a French Conservative, Félix Routhier, was elected federally in 1878 despite Hamilton's open opposition, his influence among the English Canadian Conservatives was destroyed.

Finding his political power base being eroded and himself somewhat "off the political track," Hamilton had been turning to other interests after confederation. In 1869 he was appointed colonel of the 18th (Prescott) Battalion of Infantry in Prescott and he took a lively interest in local and national militia matters. It was, however, his involvement in an ever widening group of corporate and financial ventures which diverted Hamilton's attention from immediate political affairs. During the 1860s and early 1870s he earned a reputation as a sound businessman not only for his management of Hamilton Brothers but also as a director of several transportation companies closely related to the lumber industry, including the Union Forwarding and Railway Company, the Canada Central Railway, the North Shore Railway, and the St Maurice Navigation and Land Company. Hamilton's business reputation was complemented by his prestige as a senator; he became involved in other corporate enterprises, and made a concentrated effort to establish himself in the Montreal financial community by accepting in 1872 directorships in the Reliance Mutual Life Assurance Society of London, the Canada Investment and Agency Company, and the Coldbrook Rolling Mills Company of Nova Scotia.

The key to John Hamilton's success in these new areas of business was his association with the Merchants' Bank. It had been founded in 1861 by Hugh ALLAN (president from its opening in 1864), Andrew Allan*, Edwin Atwater*, and Louis Renaud*, among others; both John and his brother Robert had bought shares in the bank and used its credit to finance their own business activities. In 1874 John was elected to the board of directors, and the following year was honoured with the vice-presidency. Hamilton, however, was not completely happy with his new situation. The depression which followed the economic crash of 1873 weighed heavily on Canadian business, and the Merchants' Bank was particularly vulnerable. While quickly increasing its capital, the rapid expansion in business had also brought the bank questionable Detroit and Milwaukee Railway bonds acquired with the take-over of the Commercial Bank in 1868, losses in floating a Quebec government loan in London, losses in the New York gold market, and numerous bad or doubtful debts at home, which now threatened to pull it under. As early as the annual meeting of 1874 concern was expressed regarding circulation and deposits not keeping pace with the bank's increase of capital. As well Hamilton himself suspected that the Allans were using the bank for their own speculative purposes and not for the good of the institution. The matter came to a head in early 1877 when, because business conditions were not improving, a special meeting of stockholders was called to discuss the affairs of the bank. As a result Jackson Rae, the Merchants' general manager, resigned on 21 February, and a day later Hugh Allan stepped down as president.

At this crucial point John Hamilton, as vice-president, took over direction of the affairs of the second largest bank in Canada and was named president. George Hague*, the recently retired general manager of the Bank of Toronto, was persuaded to take over the management of the troubled institution and his full investigation, confirmed by a committee of Hamilton, his vice-president, and Hugh Allan (who had continued as director), revealed that the bank faced losses totalling nearly 3 million dollars. Hague imposed harsh retrenchment policies, such as the elimination of operations which showed losses in New York and London as well as of unprofitable branches at home, and rebuilt the bank's internal structure. The directors guaranteed a 1.5 million dollar loan from the Bank of Montreal and the Bank of British North America, and Hamilton went to the banking committee of the federal parliament with a proposal to devalue each of the bank's shares by 25 per cent: the act, which reduced the capital stock from nine to a little more than six million dollars, was passed in early 1878. With this help and Hague's expert management the bank was back in excellent shape by 1882. That year, at the annual meeting of 21 June, Hamilton, with some bitterness, surrendered the presidency to Hugh Allan, who had once again captured the support of the majority of directors and shareholders.

John Hamilton's handling of the Merchants' Bank affair earned him high esteem throughout the entire Canadian business community. In 1884 he was invited to join the powerful and illustrious group which formed the board of directors of the Bank of Montreal. He accepted this position gladly and the influence and prestige it bestowed enabled him to divest himself of all his other business duties, except his interest in the management of Hamilton Brothers. He even resigned as president of the Canada Timber and Lumber Association, a position he had held since 1876. Once again he had reached a turning-point in his life. Putting behind him the bustle of Montreal finance, he devoted a great deal more time to the Hawkesbury mills and his family concerns. Indeed his domestic life had been extremely active. Rebecca Hamilton had died during the early 1860s and John had remarried. When his second wife, Ellen Marion Wood, died in January 1872 he married, on 3 June of the same year, a widow, Jean Major. From his first two marriages a family of three sons and five daughters survived to adulthood; its activities were centred at Evandale, his island estate, and long his chief residence, near the Hawkesbury mills, and at his Montreal home, Tyrella House.

Hamilton retired honourably from the Senate early in 1887 when his seat was needed for his old friend, John Joseph Caldwell Abbott*, whom Sir John A. Macdonald wished to become government leader in the upper house and a member of the Privy Council. Hamilton was not loath to step down since he had never found the satisfaction in politics he had hoped would be forthcoming and he was beginning to despair of politicians ever finding the solution to Canada's grave economic problems. Unfortunately he did not live long enough to enjoy his more relaxed pace of life; on 3 April 1888 at 60 years of age, John Hamilton died at his home in Montreal.

ROBERT PETER GILLIS

AO, MU 1197–223. PAC, MG 24, D7; MG 26, A, 222; MG 29, E24; RG 31, A1, 1871, Prescott sub-district and Hawkesbury village. Can., Prov. of, Legislative Assembly, *Journals*, 1854–55. Chadwick, *Ontarian families*. *CPC*, 1871–84. *Cyclopædia of Canadian biog*. (Rose, 1886). *List of the shareholders of the Merchants' Bank of Canada as of 1 June 1882* (Montreal, 1882). Notman and Taylor, *Portraits of British Americans*, III. Atherton, *Montreal*, III. Lucien Brault, *Histoire des comtés unis de Prescott et de Russell* (L'Orignal, Ont., 1965). M. S. Cross, "The dark druidical groves: the lumber community and the commercial frontier in British North America, to 1854" (PHD thesis, Univ. of Toronto, 1968). J. E. Defebaugh, *History of the lumber industry of America* (2v., Chicago, 1906–7), I: 134, 537. Denison, *Canada's first bank*. S. J. Gillis, *The lumber trade in the Ottawa Valley, 1806–54* (Ottawa, 1975). R. M. Breckenridge, "The Canadian banking system, 1817–1890," *Canadian Banker*, 2 (1894–95): 105–96, 267–366, 431–502, 571–660. Shortt, "Hist. of Canadian currency, banking and exchange: some individual cases," *Canadian Banker*, 13: 272–88.

HAMILTON, KER BAILLIE. *See* BAILLIE

HANNAN, MICHAEL, Roman Catholic priest and archbishop; b. 20 July 1821 at Kilmallock, County Limerick (Republic of Ireland), son of James Hannan and Mary Carroll; d. 17 April 1882 at Halifax, N.S.

Michael Hannan was educated at Kilmallock and Kilfinnane in County Limerick and began the study of Latin and Greek at a very young age. In 1840 he came to Halifax where he finished his philosophical and theological studies at St Mary's College, while teaching classics to the younger students. He was ordained to the priesthood by Archbishop William Walsh* on 27 April 1845 and was appointed parish priest at Windsor, N.S. The following year he took up duties as a parish priest in Bermuda, which at that time came under the jurisdiction of the archbishop of Halifax, before returning to St Mary's Cathedral in Halifax in 1847.

In the early 1860s Hannan first began serving as vicar-general of the archdiocese of Halifax, a post he filled regularly from 1868 to 1877. As spokesman for Archbishop Thomas Louis Connolly* and the large Catholic population of Halifax, Hannan wielded no small amount of influence. His position was especially significant in relation to his service from 1865 to 1874 as an active member of the Halifax Board of School Commissioners. In 1864–65 the government of Charles Tupper* instituted a system of non-denominational public schools supported by compulsory taxation, but Archbishop Connolly considered religious training an integral part of the education of Catholic children and was worried that Catholics would be unable to "control" the schools attended by their children. Connolly pressured Tupper to create separate Catholic schools in law, but Tupper adamantly refused. A compromise was reached which resulted in the establishment of one school system with separate school buildings for Catholic teachers and students. Roman Catholic involvement in the direction of the school system was guaranteed by the inclusion of Catholics on the provincial Council of Public Instruction and on local school commissions.

Hannan's work as a Halifax school commissioner in the first decade of the new educational system's operation was particularly delicate and earned wide praise. He dealt directly with Tupper, sometimes without the approval or prior knowledge of Archbishop Connolly, for Tupper seemed to find Hannan's reactions less emotional than those of the archbishop. Hannan none the less criticized Theodore Harding Rand*, the superintendent of education from 1864 to 1870, for his public comments opposing religion in the schools and sought to have him removed. Hannan was also active politically as a supporter of Tupper and the federal Liberal-Conservative party. Unlike Connolly, who was criticized for his overt political partisanship, Hannan did not proclaim his support for the party's policies, publicly preferring instead to work behind the scenes in the 1872 federal election.

On 20 May 1877 Hannan was consecrated archbishop of Halifax in succession to Connolly who had died the previous year. During his five years as archbishop Hannan maintained his interest in education, overseeing the construction of numerous schools and working diligently to consolidate the informal but increasingly accepted Catholic presence in the educational system.

DAVID B. FLEMMING

Halifax County Court of Probate (Halifax), no.2975, will of Michael Hannan, 22 April 1882. PAC, MG 26, D, 2, 13, 25; F, 4, 5; RG 31, A1, 1871, census, Nova Scotia. *Morning Chronicle* (Halifax), May 1877, April 1882. *Canada, an encyclopædia* (Hopkins), II. Dent, *Canadian portrait gallery*, III. *Standard dict. of Canadian biog.* (Roberts and Tunnell), II: 194–95. Wallace, *Macmillan dict.* Sister Maura [Mary Power], *The Sisters of Charity, Halifax* (Toronto, 1956).

HANS HENDRIK (called **Hans Christian** by Elisha Kent Kane*), Greenlander (Inuk) hunter, guide, and dog-driver; b. *c.* 1834 in Fiskenæsset, Greenland, the second of five children of Benjamin and Ernestine; d. 11 Aug. 1889 at Godhavn, Greenland.

Hans Hendrik spent his youth in Fiskenæsset where he was educated by Moravian missionaries. In July 1853 he was engaged as a hunter on Dr Kane's expedition in search of Sir John Franklin* and sailed on board the *Advance* to Rensselaer Harbour, northwest Greenland, where the expedition spent two winters. In June 1854 Hans accompanied William Morton on a sledge journey north along the Greenland coast where they discovered and explored the Kennedy Channel as far as Cape Constitution. Kane found Hans a valuable addition to his crew, especially during the second, enforced, wintering. With morale low and provisions almost exhausted, Hans remained cheerful and continued to hunt when all but he and Kane were sick or injured. Kane repeatedly paid tribute to Hans's labours and at one point wrote: "If Hans gives way, God help us." In April 1855 Hans ran away from the expedition, it seems because of a growing fear of Kane whose arrogance upset him. He went to live with the Inuit at Etah, remaining in the north for several years.

In August 1860 Dr Isaac Israel HAYES's expedition, which was attempting to prove the existence of an open polar sea, landed at Cape York to hire Hans as a hunter. Hans agreed to go and took his wife, Merkut, and his baby son on board Hayes's ship, the *United States.* They sailed to Foulke Fjord where the expedition wintered. Hayes had considerably less respect for Hans than Kane, and was continually mistrustful, describing him as "a type of the worst phase of the Esquimau character." He even accused Hans of being responsible for the deaths from exposure of two members of the expedition, though it is clear from Hans's account of the incidents that he did his utmost to save both men.

Hans returned south after the expedition, in the summer of 1861, and worked for the Greenland Trading Company in the region of Upernavik. He was at Prøven, Greenland, in August 1871 when Charles Francis Hall* asked him to join his north polar expedition. By this time Hans and Merkut had three children and they were allowed to take them on board Hall's *Polaris.* Hans and his family were members of the party of 19 which was carried away from the *Polaris* on an ice floe in October 1872. The party survived a remarkable six-month drift southward through the Davis Strait, and was picked up off the coast of Labrador in April 1873. The survival of all 19 members was entirely due to the efforts of Hans and Ipilkvik (Joe Ebierbing), a Canadian Inuk; the seamen of the party were despondent and ill-tempered and refused to help themselves, whereas Hans and Ipilkvik hunted tirelessly. The leader of the party, George Emory Tyson*, rather unfairly criticized Hans for being a less proficient hunter than Ipilkvik and considered him "a little foolish." Hans was, nevertheless, acclaimed a hero on landing at St John's, Nfld, and later during a tour of several cities in the United States.

Returning to Upernavik, Hans rejoined the Greenland Trading Company, but in 1875 was again called on for his services, this time by the British Arctic expedition of George Strong Nares*. Hans joined the expedition and sailed on board *Discovery* to Discovery Harbour on the northeast coast of Ellesmere Island. It appears that Captain Henry Frederick Stephenson of the *Discovery* had great faith in Hans and used his skills extensively; Nares recorded that "all speak in the highest terms of Hans . . . who was untiring in his exertions with the dog-sledge, and in procuring game." In 1876, after the expedition, Hans returned to the trading company at Godhavn. His last involvement in an Arctic expedition was in 1883 when he accompanied Alfred Gabriel Nathorst on a scientific exploration of west Greenland.

Inuit were frequently employed on 19th-century polar expeditions and received both cash and goods for their services. But Hans was unusual among them not only because of the number of expeditions he took part in, but also because his memoirs were published. These present a rare insight into the Greenlanders' impressions of explorers and into the brutal treatment the native people often received. It is difficult to make a fair assessment of Hans from the conflicting expedition narratives: some of the explorers found him trustworthy, hard-working, and cheerful; others, notably Hayes, considered him unreliable, incompetent, and morose. The memoirs, however, show him to have been sensitive, responding warmly to affection and fair treatment, but bemused and distressed by the taunting and bullying that was all too often meted out to him and other Inuit.

CLIVE A. HOLLAND

Hans Hendrik's memoirs were published under the title *Memoirs of Hans Hendrik, the Arctic traveller, serving under Kane, Hayes, Hall and Nares, 1853–1876*, trans. H. [J.] Rink, ed. George Stephens (London, 1878).

[C. F. Hall], *Narrative of the north polar expedition, U.S. Ship Polaris, Captain Charles Francis Hall commanding*, ed. C. H. Davis (Washington, 1876). I. I. Hayes, *The open polar sea: a narrative of a voyage of discovery towards the North Pole, in the schooner "United States"* (London,

1867). E. K. Kane, *Arctic explorations: the second Grinnell expedition in search of Sir John Franklin, 1853, '54, '55* (2v., Philadelphia and London, 1856). G. S. Nares, *Narrative of a voyage to the polar sea during 1875–6 in H.M. ships "Alert" and "Discovery"* (2v., London, 1878). [G. E. Tyson], *Arctic experiences: containing Capt. George E. Tyson's wonderful drift on the ice-floe, a history of the Polaris expedition, the cruise of the Tigress, and the rescue of the Polaris survivors*, ed. Euphemia Vale Blake (New York, 1874). Dan Laursen, "Grønlændere i forskningens tjeneste II: 'Hans Hendrik' fra Fiskenæsset," *Grønland* (Charlottenlund, Sweden), 4 (April 1956): 144–49. Mads Lidegaard, "Hans Hendrik fra Fiskenæsset," *Grønland*, 8 (August 1968): 249–56. H. [J.] Rink, "Om Grønlænderen Hans Hendriks Deltagelse i Nordpolsexpeditionerne, 1853–1876, under Kane, Hayes, Hall og Nares . . . ," *Geografisk Tidskrift* ([Copenhagen]), 1 (1877): 24, 186–92. C. [H.] Ryder, "Grønlænderen Hans Hendrik," *Geografisk Tidskrift*, 10 (1889–90): 140–43.

HARDISTY, RICHARD CHARLES, HBC fur-trader and politician; b. *c.* 1832, probably at Fort Mistassini (Baie-du-Poste, Que.), fourth son of Richard Hardisty and Margaret Sutherland, and brother of William Lucas HARDISTY; m. in 1866 Eliza, daughter of George Millward McDougall*, Methodist clergyman and missionary, and they had three children; d. 15 Oct. 1889 at Winnipeg, Man.

Richard Charles Hardisty's father, a Hudson's Bay Company chief trader, was a native of London, England, and his mother was of Indian and Scottish parentage. Hardisty spent nine years at the Red River Academy before joining the HBC in 1849 as an apprentice post master in the Red River District (Man.). Five years later he was appointed clerk and assumed charge of Cumberland House District (Sask.). This was a small district with only three posts, but it was a promotion for the "efficient young officer." During the year that Hardisty served at Cumberland House he increased the returns by £250, which pleased Governor George Simpson*. From 1855 to 1861, Hardisty served at Carlton House (Sask.) where he had been sent to counteract increasing competition from free traders. In 1862 he was appointed chief trader and took charge of the Saskatchewan District during the temporary absence of Chief Factor William Joseph Christie*. Christie took a strong fatherly interest in Hardisty, encouraged him in his work, treated him as an assistant, and wrote him long informative letters closing with the paternal blessing, "May a kind Providence watch over & Protect you."

In 1864 Christie sent Hardisty to re-establish Rocky Mountain House (Alta) which had been closed in 1861 because of the threatening attitude of the Blackfoot Indians. Hardisty built a new post and remained there until 1867 when he was transferred to Fort Victoria (now Pakan, Alta). Each spring he was sent to Carlton or Norway House (Man.) with the annual returns, and once back in Fort Edmonton supervised the transshipment of trade goods and supplies for the various posts before retiring to his own station.

Having been granted furlough for the 1869–70 season, Hardisty left Edmonton in April with his family, probably for Montreal. On 27 Dec. 1869, however, he arrived at Upper Fort Garry (Winnipeg) with his brother-in-law, Donald Alexander Smith*, a special commissioner from the government of Canada to the provisional government established by Louis RIEL. The HBC fort had been seized by Riel and his party on 2 November, and when Hardisty and Smith were admitted to the fort by Riel they were put under house arrest. Smith had taken the precaution of leaving his official papers at Pembina (N. Dak.) to avoid any danger of their being confiscated by Riel. The Métis leader, interested in seeing Smith's actual commission, gave Hardisty permission to travel to Pembina, escorted by two of his men, to collect Smith's documents. Smith's supporters did not trust Riel with regard to the papers; they had Hardisty intercepted on his return journey and escorted him to the fort. With Smith in possession of the documents, Riel was forced to recognize his official status and allow him to call a general meeting of the people in the Red River Settlement on 19 Jan. 1870 to state the views of the government of Canada about its future intentions towards the northwest. For Hardisty, who lacked neither courage nor stamina, the trip from Pembina to Scratching River (now Morris River) where he was intercepted, had been "as hard a one as he ever had experienced."

With Smith, Hardisty left Upper Fort Garry on 19 March for eastern Canada but returned to Fort Victoria that fall. In 1872 he was made a chief factor and was appointed to the charge of the Upper Saskatchewan District with headquarters at Fort Edmonton. For the next 17 years Hardisty travelled his large district, ministering to the needs of Indians and settlers. They were years of constant change and adjustment. The Indians and Métis suffered because of the retreat of the buffalo, and were frequently bewildered by the results of treaty negotiations. Hardisty also realized that new fur-trading posts would not meet the competition of free traders. Instead, he closed unprofitable posts and proposed that the HBC buy furs from these traders. His abilities as a trader were unquestioned but he was not good at accounts, as a number of expressions of concern by HBC commissioners show.

Noting in 1882 that as many as 300 heads of families were arriving in the northwest in a year, Hardisty concentrated on the new settlements which were springing up close to the railways. To control the grain and timber market, he purchased a mill in 1881 with his own capital, and explained his actions to the HBC commissioner in Winnipeg, James Allan Grahame*, by saying "If Edmonton gets built up into a town as is expected, the sale of lumber will then come into play."

The HBC saw a conflict of interest here and Hardisty relinquished the mill at its request in 1885. To meet the competition of American traders who were swarming along the Bow River, in 1874 he had sent John Bunn to select a site for Bow Fort, 40 miles from modern Calgary.

In the first general election of 1887 for the District of Alberta, Hardisty ran as an independent after having been refused the Conservative nomination. Two points in his programme reveal his progressive thinking: he wanted the rights of the Métis upheld and a highway built between Edmonton and the Mackenzie River. Better known in the northern, less populated part of his constituency than in the south, he was defeated by his Conservative opponent, Donald Watson Davis.

In January 1888, while visiting England, Hardisty was appointed an acting inspector of the Northern Department of the HBC with an increase in salary of £100 per annum. On 23 Feb. 1888 he was called to the Senate of Canada, the first senator from the District of Alberta. He died in Winnipeg on 15 Oct. 1889 from injuries received when thrown from a buggy at Broadview (Sask.).

SHIRLEE ANNE SMITH

Glenbow-Alberta Institute, Richard Hardisty papers. PAC, MG 26, A. PAM, HBCA, A.1/177: f.57d; A.1/183: ff.92d, 103d; A.6/37: f.59d; A.6/57: f.605; A.11/99: f.152d; A.12/7: ff.142d, 484d; A.12/8: f.116; A.12/27: ff.18, 407; A.12/28: f.529; A.12/29b: f.416; A.12/45: ff.356, 372; A.31/9: f.31; A.34/1: f.72; A.64/38: f.35; B.60/a/31: f.76; B.60/a/32: ff.2, 36d; B.60/a/33: ff.2, 44d; B.60/a/34: ff.32d, 34, 85; B.60/a/36: f.26; B.60/a/37: ff.12, 82d; B.60/a/38–41; B.60/b/2: 517, 583; B.60/b/3: 62, 63d, 92, 93d, 101, 102d, 105, 128d; B.60/c/11: f.4d; B.133/a/14; B.135/g/1: 4; B.135/z/3: f.259; B.186/b/22: f.10; B.239/g/51; B.239/k/12: 250; B.239/k/13: no.30, 1862; B.239/k/14: no.23, 1867; D.5/10: f.108; D.5/22: f.378; D.13/5: 372; D.13/11: ff.26, 567d; D.14/8: f.701d; D.20/34:36. Begg, *Red River Journal* (Morton). *Edmonton Bulletin*, 26 Feb., 19 March 1887. *Manitoba Daily Free Press*, 16, 19 Oct. 1889. J. G. MacGregor, *Senator Hardisty's prairies, 1849–1889* (Saskatoon, Sask., 1978). J. E. Nix, *Mission among the buffalo: the labours of the Reverends George M. and John C. McDougall in the Canadian northwest, 1860–1876* (Toronto, 1960). Iris Allan, "The McDougalls, pioneers of the plains," *Beaver*, outfit 304 (summer 1973): 14–19. Edmund Taylor, "Reminiscences of H.B.C. pioneers," *Beaver*, 4 (1923–24): 174–75.

HARDISTY, WILLIAM LUCAS, HBC fur-trader; b. *c.* 1822 probably at Waswanipi House (Que.), on Waswinipi Lake in the Rupert River district, second child of HBC Chief Trader Richard Hardisty and Margaret Sutherland, and brother of Richard Charles HARDISTY; m. Mary Allen, and they had three sons and two daughters; d. 16 Jan. 1881 at Lachine, Que.

William Lucas Hardisty was educated at the Red River Academy, and in 1842 entered the Hudson's Bay Company as a post master (a rank below that of clerk). He was posted to the Mackenzie River District, and in 1843 was sent to Frances Lake (Yukon) to serve under Robert Campbell*. The next summer Hardisty was left in charge of the post during the absence of Campbell who, upon his return, reported: "the Fort & every thing about it in the best possible order . . . I could not be more highly satisfied. . . ."

In November 1844 Hardisty left Frances Lake for Pelly River Post to collect provisions and to trade with the "gens des Couteaux," a branch of the Salish, and other local bands. After a "highly satisfactory" trading trip he was obliged to return to Frances Lake in January 1845 because, as Campbell wrote, of "our constant enemy [–] want of provisions." In March Hardisty again attempted to trade with the Indians of the Pelly River area, but lack of food forced his return to Frances Lake in April.

In 1846 Hardisty was once more left in charge of Frances Lake during Campbell's absence. Illness in 1847–48 forced him to winter at Fort Simpson (N.W.T.). Recovered by June 1848, he helped Augustus Richard Peers construct new buildings on the Peel River, taking charge there while Peers travelled to Fort Simpson. In November Hardisty took over the "lonely abode" of Lapierre's House at the junction of the Bell and Rat rivers, an outpost on the route to Fort Yukon (Alaska). During the summer of 1849 he again assisted at Peel River, and then took charge during Peers's absence. In September Hardisty and his men were surprised by the arrival of Lieutenant William John Samuel PULLEN and 14 others from the ship *Plover* who had travelled down the Mackenzie River in search of Sir John Franklin*. Food being short at Peel River, the visitors soon left to winter at posts that were better supplied.

In 1851 Hardisty left Lapierre's House to replace Alexander Hunter Murray* in charge of Fort Yukon. That winter Hardisty was successful in opening trade with new Indian groups, receiving "warmest Commendations" from his superior James Anderson*. Hardisty applied for a leave of absence for 1853–54, apparently having in mind some private business with retired HBC officer George Gladman*, but Governor Sir George Simpson* responded by warning that as a clerk Hardisty did not have tenure, adding that "the withdrawal of clerks from duty on the ground of ill health private business and other reasons more frivolous . . . is attended with serious inconvenience." Thus denied sure readmittance to the HBC, Hardisty kept his Fort Yukon position.

Situated among the Kutchin or Loucheux Indians, themselves active traders, Hardisty continued to please his superiors and was promoted chief trader in 1858. He greatly encouraged trade and experimented with substituting direct trade for the system of having the Indians accumulate debts to the company. In 1859–60, after taking charge of Fort Resolution on Great Slave Lake, he assisted Robert Kennicott of the Smithsonian Institution in collecting birds, thus beginning a lengthy affiliation with the institution as a contributor of specimens and later as an author; his detailed account of the Loucheux Indians was published by the Smithsonian in 1867.

After spending 1860–62 at Fort Liard (N.W.T.), Hardisty moved to Fort Simpson and took charge of the Mackenzie River District, replacing Bernard Rogan Ross*. Pressed by the need to accommodate missionaries, by threats of free traders, by provisioning problems, and, in 1864–66, by widespread syphilis, scarlet fever, and measles among the Indians, Hardisty earned a commendation for good management in difficult times. He was particularly praised for his "judicious and well timed" change in the debt system along the lines of his Fort Yukon experiment. In 1868 Hardisty was promoted chief factor.

From 1869 until retirement Hardisty remained in charge of the Mackenzie District. Following the American purchase of Alaska he was obliged to cope with the American take-over of Fort Yukon in the fall of 1869; the HBC men there were ordered to cease trading or face penalties for smuggling. By November 1870 the Mackenzie trade was beginning to show a deficit, and Hardisty wrote to Donald Alexander Smith*, his sister's husband, that the company appeared "to have lost ground entirely in that quarter. The Americans are carrying all before them, they have goods similar to our own which they are selling more than 200 p cent cheaper than we can afford to do – also supply the Indians gratuitously with Tea, Sugar, Rice, Raisins & Flour." Hardisty consequently urged the division of his district into two, to ease management and to enable the company to oppose free traders more effectively. He also proposed periodic trading trips to the Indians of the Yukon and the use of the Bering Strait as a shipping route for goods being brought into the area.

Hardisty retired from the HBC in 1878, and after passing the winter of 1878–79 in Winnipeg, he took up residence in Lachine. He died there on 16 Jan. 1881.

JENNIFER S. H. BROWN

W. L. Hardisty was the author of "The Loucheux Indians," Smithsonian Institution, *Annual report* (Washington), 1866: 311–20.

AO, Moose Factory Anglican and Methodist missions, 1780–1906 (mfm.). PAM, HBCA, A.34/1: f.122; A.36/7: ff.62–64; B.85/a/13: f.7; B.200/b/15: f.21; B.200/b/17: f.4; B.200/b/20: 9, 21, 50; B.200/b/21: f.13; B.200/b/22: f.37; B.200/b/23: f.12; B.200/b/26: f.30; B.200/b/28: 3, 108–12; B.200/b/30: 6, 16; B.200/b/32: 5; B.200/b/33–36; B.200/b/38: 42, 100, 109; B.200/c/1: f.37; D.4/82: ff.175–78. PAC, MG 19, A29; D12. HBRS, XIX (Rich and A. M. Johnson). [John Rae], *John Rae's correspondence with the Hudson's Bay Company on Arctic exploration, 1844–1855*, ed. E. E. Rich and A. M. Johnson (London, 1953). *Montreal Herald and Daily Commercial Gazette*, 18 Jan. 1881. *Winnipeg Daily Times*, 18 Jan. 1881. W. J. Healy, *Women of Red River: being a book written from the recollections of women surviving from the Red River era* (Winnipeg, 1923). [H.] B. Willson, *The life of Lord Strathcona & Mount Royal, G.C.M.G., G.C.V.O. (1820–1914)* (London and Toronto, 1915). G. L. Nute, "Kennicott in the north," *Beaver*, outfit 274 (September 1943): 28–32.

HARRIS, AMELIA. *See* RYERSE

HARRIS, JAMES STANLEY, blacksmith, manufacturer, merchant, and office-holder; b. 25 Oct. 1803 in Annapolis County, N.S., the son of Benjamin Harris and Rachel Bolscomb (Balcomb); m. in 1837 Louisa Ann Wilson of Dorchester, N.B., and they had one son and eight daughters; d. 11 June 1888 in Portland (now part of Saint John), N.B.

James Stanley Harris received little formal education and at age 15 apprenticed as a blacksmith. In 1823 he moved to Saint John, N.B., where he finished his apprenticeship and became an expert edge-tool maker under the direction of James Wood, one of the most experienced ironworkers and the first edge-tool manufacturer in the city. In 1828 Harris and Thomas Allan (Allen), also an expert machinist, formed the firm of Harris and Allan to produce tools. With starting capital of about $5,000 they set up shop in Portland Bridge and also opened a hardware store to sell their products. Three years later they established the first foundry in New Brunswick. The foundry, located in Portland, was small. It smelted imported pig-iron in a furnace whose blast, originally produced by two large bellows worked by men in relays, became more powerful after the introduction of steam power. The partners pioneered the casting of Franklin stoves and were the first in New Brunswick to make cut nails and a set of mill castings. As their sales increased, Harris and Allan enlarged their buildings and added new ones, all of wood. By the early 1840s their plant comprised a foundry, machine, blacksmith, pattern, and fitting shops, and a large warehouse.

A fire in 1845 destroyed the moulding and machine shops, as well as other buildings, and a steam engine, lathes, and a large quantity of materials and manufactured stock were ruined. The uninsured loss to Harris and Allan was $30,000, but work was resumed in a new casting shop within 15 days of the fire. About 1856 another fire destroyed the machine and steam shops and a warehouse – again with a loss of $30,000. A three-floor, brick machine shop was immediately built, but other buildings were replaced in wood and were destroyed in a third fire in 1871; on this occasion the loss was $40,000, representing a warehouse, stove shop, and a shed containing a number of railway cars under construction.

For many years Harris and Allan did a large business in the manufacture and sale of stoves and agricultural machinery, grates, mantelpieces, nail plate, bar iron, ship's iron knees, shafting, and all kinds of hammered shapes. The firm also operated a shop devoted to slate materials which they marbled and sold for home decoration. Their household products and agricultural machinery were sold at the firm's store in Saint John. During the shipbuilding boom in Saint John in the 1850s the company made healthy profits from ship work, but Harris foresaw that land transportation would grow in importance and the company gradually decreased the manufacture of stoves and agricultural machinery to devote itself to the production of railway cars and parts. During the 1850s Harris and Allan had also been part-owners of the York and Carleton Mining Company, a New Brunswick concern which produced pig-iron. From 1855 to 1870 Harris was a major shareholder in the Saint John Manufacturing Company, which operated a woollen mill at Mispec, near Saint John.

When Thomas Allan died (either in 1860 or 1861) Harris purchased his interest in the business. The new firm, James Harris and Company, then began the manufacture of railway car wheels, and by keeping pace with improvements in manufacturing processes built itself a reputation as good as that of any wheel maker in North America. It soon began producing, as well, railway running gear and passenger, box, and platform cars. In 1870 Harris purchased large rolling-mills in Saint John which, combined with the existing plant, enabled the company to undertake heavy work beyond the capacity of any rival firm in Canada. Indeed, the history of the Harris works is coincident with the railway construction boom in New Brunswick which had begun in the 1850s. During the 1860s and 1870s the company did a large amount of work for the Intercolonial and Western Extension railways, and when the Intercolonial switched to a narrow gauge in 1875 Harris' firm in six months completed a $300,000 contract which consumed 500 tons of wrought iron for axles, 1,500 tons of cast iron for trucks, and 1,000 tons of iron in other related works. In the early 1880s the firm's shops were consuming more than 4,000 tons of iron annually, of which one-half was charcoal iron imported from the United States to produce car wheels, and the rest pig-iron and malleable iron imported mainly from England.

In 1881 Harris' firm employed 230 men and had annual sales of $200,000; by 1888 its staff had increased to 282 in the railway car works and 78 in its rolling-mill. In the latter year the company was advertising that it manufactured railway cars of every description, steel tires, chilled car wheels, hammered railway car axles, steam engines, mill machinery, turbine water wheels, pump, bridge, fence, and ship's castings, tapered and parallel bars for ship's knees, nail plate, and shafting and shapes of all kinds. Harris personally supervised the operations of his company until a few months before his death in June 1888. His son-in-law, James C. Robertson, had been taken into partnership in December 1887 and assumed the management when Harris stepped down. In accordance with one of the terms of Harris' will, the company was sold within three years of his death and in 1892, when the federal government expropriated its five-acre site in Saint John for $200,000, the company moved to Amherst, N.S., and merged with Rhodes Curry and Company.

Harris had played a modest role in local affairs, serving as a member of the Portland Town Council from 1871 to 1876 and as a justice of the peace for Saint John County from 1866 to 1884. He was a trustee of the Portland Methodist Church and at one time president of the Portland branch of the British and Foreign Bible Society. In 1875 he was both president of the Manufacturers' and Mechanics' Exhibition, held in Saint John in the fall, and chairman of the local advisory board for the Philadelphia Centennial International Exhibition, held the following year. He also served on the board of the Dominion and Loyalist Centennial Exhibition of 1883.

Harris' business sense and acumen are evident in his rise from a blacksmith's apprentice to become a leading Canadian manufacturer; he left an estate valued at $235,000.

D. RIK WHITTAKER

Fernhill Cemetery (Saint John, N.B.), Burial records, J. S. Harris. N. B. Museum, Allan's Foundry, Ledger, 1866–70. Portland United Church (Saint John), Burial records, June 1888. N.B., *Acts*, 1847; 1849; 1854–55. *St. John and its business: a history of St. John . . .* (Saint John, 1875), 128. *Daily Sun* (Saint John), 13 Dec. 1887–15 June 1888. *Daily Telegraph* (Saint John), 1 Oct. 1875–1 Oct. 1885. *Saint John Globe*, 25 Jan. 1892. *Canadian biog. dict.*, II: 684–87. P. G. Hall, "A misplaced genius," *New Brunswick Magazine* (Saint John), 1 (July–December 1898): 247–56.

HARRIS, JOHN, manufacturer; b. 21 July 1841 in Townsend Township, Norfolk County, Canada West, eldest son of Alanson Harris* and Mary Morgan; m. October 1863 Jane Tufford of Beamsville, Canada West, and they had nine children; d. 25 Aug. 1887 at Brantford, Ont.

John Harris received his education at the Beamsville Grammar School and by working in his father's sawmill at Whiteman Creek from an early age. When Alanson Harris sold the mill and in 1857 bought a small factory in Beamsville to manufacture farm tools, John was probably one of the five mechanics he employed. In 1863 Alanson took John into partnership as

A. Harris and Son. A second son, Thomas, was to join the firm later.

As with the Massey family, it was the founder's son who presided over the transformation of the firm from a primitive business into a large company manufacturing agricultural implements. In his history of the Massey-Harris firm, Merrill Denison* credits John Harris with establishing the association with D. M. Osborne and Company of Auburn, N.Y., which led to the Harris company's manufacture under licence of the Kirby mower and the Kirby reel-rake reaper, its chief products in the 1860s and 1870s. An inventor himself, John Harris took out a number of patents on improvements to the firm's machines. The most important of these were innovations in the design of self-binding harvesters. The Brantford binder (advertised as "The Little Brantford Beauty") became one of the firm's staple lines in the 1880s.

Having outgrown its Beamsville factory, the company had relocated in Brantford in 1872 and begun to use the trade name of A. Harris, Son and Company. By 1877 the firm's capacity had to be doubled and in 1882 a new plant constructed. In 1883 approximately 4,500 mowers, reapers, and binders were produced; by 1887 the company was employing 300 men and was probably Canada's second largest manufacturer of agricultural implements. Its agencies in western Canada dated from 1879 when branches were opened in Manitoba at Winnipeg, Emerson, and Portage la Prairie. It thus preceded the Massey Manufacturing Company in western expansion by a few years but in 1879 had only just begun to follow the larger firm into exporting.

As president of A. Harris, Son and Company (Limited), incorporated in 1881, John Harris became one of Brantford's more prominent citizens. He was an alderman from 1881 to 1883, licence commissioner for South Brant for several years, and continually active in local Reform politics (at his death he was president of the Reform Association of South Brant, and it was thought he was on the verge of a political career). A devout Baptist, who at one time thought seriously of becoming a minister, he led one of the largest Bible classes in Brantford, served as president of the local Young Men's Christian Association, and enjoyed discussing religion with his employees both on and off the job. The workers seem to have liked and respected the affable son, John, considerably more than the gruff, uneducated father, Alanson.

Already suffering from tuberculosis, John Harris contracted malaria while watching harvester trials in Texas in the spring of 1887. Two months later, in the words of a testimonial from his employees, "The Great Reaper . . . stepped in and silenced the active brain and life."

Young men like Lyman Melvin Jones* and John's son Lloyd* were already active in the business and would become prominent in later years. But the loss of the managing heir to the company may well have influenced Alanson Harris' decision to agree to merge with his larger competitor, the Massey Manufacturing Company, in 1891.

MICHAEL BLISS

Massey-Ferguson Limited Arch. (Toronto), "A. Harris & Son Co." (typescript, 1937); "In memory of John Harris . . ." (privately circulated memorial obituary, 1887). *Brantford Weekly Expositor* (Brantford, Ont.), 2, 9 Sept. 1887. *Globe*, 25 Aug. 1887. Merrill Denison, *Harvest triumphant: the story of Massey-Harris* (Toronto, 1948). *The history of the county of Brant, Ontario* . . . (Toronto, 1883).

HARRIS, JOSEPH HEMINGTON, Church of England clergyman and educator; b. in 1800, son of Joseph and Cordelia Anne Harris of London, England; d. 25 June 1881 at Torquay, Devon, England.

Little is known about Joseph Hemington Harris' early life save that he came from a middle class family and received a preparatory education at Mill Hill and St Paul's schools in London. In 1817 he entered St John's College, Cambridge, where he had a distinguished career as a classical scholar, receiving a BA in 1822 and an MA in 1825. In 1824 he was elected a fellow of Clare College, Cambridge, and was made a deacon in the Church of England; he was priested the following year.

In 1829, the year Harris was awarded a Lambeth DD, Sir John Colborne*, lieutenant governor of Upper Canada, decided to establish a school in York (Toronto) to be known as Upper Canada College, modelled after English public schools. He requested a brother-in-law who was the vice-chancellor of the University of Oxford, a cousin who was a master at Eton College, and the former headmaster of Elizabeth College in Guernsey, Colborne's previous posting, to seek a suitable candidate for the principalship of the new institution. Their choice was Harris. He readily accepted the appointment and arrived in the colony late in the autumn of that year to prepare for the inauguration of the school.

It opened under favourable auspices on 8 Jan. 1830 with 89 boys. In Harris it had a noted scholar as principal and classics master, the provincial government had granted it a lavish 66,000-acre endowment, and most groups in the colony favoured the project. Opposition came only from Tories such as John Strachan* and John Beverley Robinson*, who feared the college might become a rival to the projected University of King's College, chartered in 1827.

Although Harris possessed a cold and distant personality, he proved himself a good teacher and administrator. He was often rigid and unyielding in his opinions but soon realized that the conditions of the colony demanded some modifications of the traditional English school practices. Because of the delay in opening King's College he added a seventh form which imparted what might be described as an introductory university year. For those boys whose parents preferred that their sons be prepared for business he instituted a "partial course" which taught subjects of a commercial nature, notably bookkeeping. He also established a boarding-house for students who could not travel daily to the school.

Upper Canada College prospered under Harris' regime, which lasted until 1838. It saw slow but steady growth (there were some 133 students in 1838) and earned a reputation for academic excellence. Increasingly, however, it came under attack for its apparent catering to the needs of the upper classes, its seemingly narrow classical curriculum, and its lavish endowment. In 1836 Harris published *Observations on Upper Canada College* in which he defended the school as a public institution, but his pamphlet did not allay criticism.

Harris immersed himself in the activities of the Church of England at York. He took services and preached in the churches of the town and the surrounding countryside, and assisted the Society for Promoting Christian Knowledge and the Sunday School Society of the Diocese of Quebec. His support of the York Auxiliary Bible Society, however, brought him into further conflict with Strachan, who in 1832 published a pamphlet on John Henry Hobart, Episcopalian bishop of New York, in which he repeated Hobart's harsh strictures on non-denominational Bible societies and condemned Anglicans who participated in them. Harris was provoked into composing a rejoinder in which he defended the activities and purposes of these organizations.

Harris' first wife, Charlotte Ann, died in 1834 and he married Jane Yonge, sister-in-law of Sir John Colborne, in 1837. In July, perhaps dismayed by the continued criticism of the college, Harris submitted his resignation as principal to take effect on 1 April 1838. He returned to England. In 1845 he became curate of Cockington, Devon, and in 1848 was presented to the living of Tormoham-with-Torquay, where he remained as vicar until 1879. He retired in that year to Torquay where he died in 1881.

J. D. PURDY

J. H. Harris was the author of *A letter to the Hon. & Ven. Archdeacon Strachan in reply to some passages in his "Letter to Dr. Chalmers on the life and character of Bishop Hobart," respecting the principles and effects of the Bible Society* (York [Toronto], 1833); *Observations on Upper Canada College* (Toronto, 1836); and *A sermon, preached at St. James's Church, York; on Sunday, March, 17th 1833, in aid of the Sunday School Society, for the Diocese of Quebec* . . . (York, n.d.). Other works by Harris are listed in *British Museum general catalogue.*

AO, Strachan (John) papers, Letterbooks, 1812–34, 1827–34. PAC, RG 5, B11, 4. UTA, A73-0015/001, Upper Canada, General Board of Education, Minutes, 14 June 1823–11 March 1833 (copies at AO); A74-0018, Upper Canada College records. *Doc. hist. of education in U.C.* (Hodgins), I: 284–90; II: 94–96, 171–74; III: 184. *The Town of York, 1815–1834: a further collection of documents of early Toronto*, ed. with intro. E. G. Firth (Toronto, 1966). *Patriot* (Toronto), 1834, 1837. *Upper Canada Gazette* (York), 1829. *Alumni Cantabrigienses* . . ., comp. John and J. A. Venn (2 pts. in 10v., Cambridge, Eng., 1922–54), PT.II, vol. III: 255. *Dominion annual register*, 1880–81: 410–11. *The roll of pupils of Upper Canada College, Toronto, January, 1830, to June, 1916*, ed. A. H. Young (Kingston, Ont., 1917), 54. Wallace, *Macmillan dict.*, 301. *A history of Upper Canada College, 1829–1892; with contributions by old Upper Canada College boys, lists of head-boys, exhibitioners, university scholars and medallists, and a roll of the school*, comp. George Dickson and G. M. Adam (Toronto, 1893), 25–30, 50–64. R. B. Howard, *Upper Canada College, 1829–1979: Colborne's legacy* (Toronto, 1979).

HART, THEODORE, businessman; b. 7 May 1816 in Montreal, Lower Canada, son of Benjamin Hart* and Harriot Judith Joseph and grandson of Aaron Hart*; d. 28 May 1887 in Mézières, France.

Theodore Hart began his business career in his father's firm, Benjamin Hart and Company, a Montreal insurance agency and mercantile business. His cousin, Abraham JOSEPH, was also associated with the firm. After his father's death in 1855 Theodore established a similar but separate business which was to include large land holdings and extensive corporate interests. His mercantile business consisted of a general wholesale and retail trade and a part interest in at least one ship that traded between Britain and Canada East. As an insurance agent Hart handled marine, life, and fire insurance, and represented the Equitable Fire Insurance Company of London, the Sun Mutual Life Insurance Company of Montreal, the Mercantile Insurance Company, the Security Insurance Company of New York, Minerva Life of London, and the New York Underwriters. His land holdings included 6,400 acres of mining lands north of lakes Huron and Superior, the Le Closse fief in the centre of Montreal bought from the Sulpicians in 1845, and other valuable real estate in the city, including over 200 houses. One of the incorporators of the Grand Trunk Railway in 1851 and a provisional director of the Montreal and Bytown Railway established in 1853, Hart also served as a director of the Richelieu Company, the Consumers' Gas Company, the Montreal Railway Terminus Company, the Montreal Permanent Building Society, the Montreal and Lachine Railroad Company, the Anglo-Canadian Telegraph Company, and the Canadian board of the International Life Assurance Society of London; he also held shares in the Bank of Montreal and the City Bank. Hart was particularly active as an investor in such mining concerns as the Upper Canada Mining Company, the Echo Lake Mining Company, and the Montreal Mining Company. His deep involvement in railways with termini in Montreal may have been motivated by a desire to increase the value of his extensive land holdings in the city's east end and in its central business district around Place d'Armes.

Hart also participated actively in and contributed generously to the life of his community. A member of the militia, he served during the 1837 rebellion and by 1846 had attained the rank of captain in the 3rd Battalion of Montreal militia. He served as director of the Montreal Horticultural Society in 1853–54, was a member of the St James Club, and held executive offices in both the Montreal Merchants' Exchange and Reading Room and the Montreal Board of Trade. Along with his father he signed the Annexation Manifesto of 1849 and later became a political partisan of Luther Hamilton Holton*, a Liberal and the man he felt would serve the "best commercial interests" of the city. Hart made generous financial donations to McGill College's general endowment, the Montreal Protestant House of Industry and Refuge, and the Montreal General Hospital, which he served as a governor for several terms; in recognition of his philanthropy the hospital made him a life governor in 1878.

Although a member of one of Montreal's most prominent Jewish families and an early, active participant in the Shearith Israel congregation, Hart became estranged from his religious community in the late 1840s. The cause of his estrangement may have been his second marriage, to Mary Kent Bradbury, a Unitarian from Boston. His first marriage on 4 Jan. 1842 to Frances Michael David, his first cousin, ended with her death in 1844 after she had given birth to two daughters, who died in infancy. By his second marriage Hart had three sons and a daughter. Like several of his business contemporaries, including his friend Luther Holton, both Hart and his wife joined the Unitarian Church of the Messiah.

In 1872 Hart gave up business and five years later retired to Europe for health reasons, although he visited Montreal periodically. He died of stomach cancer on 28 May 1887 at the home of his daughter, the wife of a French prefect.

A man of external piety, philanthropy, public spirit, and wealth, who made the transition from a family mercantile firm to large corporate interests, Hart possessed all the stereotyped qualities of the successful, mid-19th-century Montreal businessman.

CARMAN MILLER

AC, Montréal, État civil, Unitariens, Messiah Unitarian Church (Montreal), 30 June 1887; Minutiers, L. A. Hart, 7 March 1888. ANQ-M, État civil, Juifs, Shearith Israel Congregation (Montréal), 4 janv., 13 oct. 1842; 4 mars, 13 oct. 1844. Bibliothèque Atwater (Montréal), Mechanics' Institute of Montreal, Minute books, 1829–35. McCord Museum (Montreal), Hart papers; Militia lists, 1846. McGill Univ. Libraries (Montreal), Dept. of Rare Books and Special Coll., W. N. Evans, "History of the Church of the Messiah: Montreal, 1892" (typescript). PAC, MG 24, D16.

Can., Prov. of, Legislative Assembly, *Journals*, 1849–57. Can., Prov. of, *Statutes*, 1859–67. *Elgin-Grey papers* (Doughty). Montreal General Hospital, *Annual report* (Montreal), 1861–87. *Gazette* (Montreal), May, June 1887. *La Minerve*, mai 1873. *Montreal Transcript*, January 1863. *Canada directory*, 1851; 1857–58. *The Jewish encyclopedia . . .* , ed. Isidore Singer (12v., New York and London, 1901–6), VI. *Montreal directory*, 1847–59. *Montreal pocket almanack and general register* (Montreal), 1845–59. Terrill, *Chronology of Montreal.* Atherton, *Montreal*, I–III. Camille Bertrand, *Histoire de Montréal* (2v., Paris et Montréal, 1935–42). *The Jew in Canada: a complete record of Canadian Jewry from the days of the French régime to the present time*, ed. A. D. Hart (Toronto and Montreal, 1926). Joseph Kage, *With faith and thanksgiving: the story of two hundred years of Jewish immigration and immigrant aid effort in Canada (1760–1960)* (Montreal, 1962). Sack, *Hist. of the Jews in Canada.* Gérard Malchelosse, "Les Juifs dans l'histoire canadienne," *Cahiers des Dix*, 4 (1939): 167–95.

HARVEY, ALEXANDER, merchant; b. 2 June 1827 at Aberdeen, Scotland, eldest child of Alexander Hervey (Harvey) and Ann Charleton; m. in 1864 Margaret Stuart of Hamilton, Canada West, and they had two sons and two daughters; d. 7 March 1886 at Hamilton.

Alexander Harvey immigrated to Hamilton with his parents and younger brother John in 1854. He worked as a clerk first at Mount Healy, Canada West, and then in Hamilton, where he opened his own retail flour and feed store about 1858. R. G. Dun and Company quickly gave him a sound rating, and within two years he had doubled his worth to $4,000 and had broadened his business into wholesale groceries. In 1864 he and John Stuart, his wife's brother, formed a partnership, Harvey, Stuart and Company. Stuart brought $12,000 into the firm which had a total estimated worth of over $25,000. In 1869, with assets of $178,000 and liabilities of only $66,000, the partnership purchased additional premises and expanded into the wholesaling of crockery.

In the early 1870s Stuart grew progressively more interested in railway development and paid less attention to the details of the business. He became involved in the capitalization of the Hamilton and Lake Erie Railway Company, and was joint security for a large amount. In 1876 Harvey decided to withdraw from the partnership, taking $40,000 as his portion. He then formed a successful business, Alexander Harvey and Company, with Robert Nicholson Sterling, who invested $3,000, as junior partner. Harvey's assets at this time were estimated at $130,000 and included his home and two commercial buildings.

Harvey was involved in various other developments

in Hamilton. He was a director of the Wellington, Grey and Bruce Railway Company, but, in connection with his brother John, was mainly concerned with insurance and financial institutions. Both brothers held directorships in the Dominion Fire and Marine Insurance Company, the Mutual Life Association of Canada, and the Hamilton Provident and Loan Society, which Alexander helped to found in 1859. In 1872 he was one of the founders of the Bank of Hamilton and became a provisional director. He was an early supporter and member of the council of the Hamilton Board of Trade and was also a director of the Commercial Travellers' Association of Canada in Toronto.

A Presbyterian, during most of his life Harvey supported the MacNab Street (Presbyterian) Church. At his death his estate, exclusive of real estate, was valued at $61,400. The estimate of his qualities as a business man by R. G. Dun and Company at the time of the dissolution of the partnership in 1876 may well stand as his epitaph: "a very reliab[le], capable man, inexpensive & cautious & free from enta[n]glements & is believed to be quite good for anything he will undertake."

FREDERICK H. ARMSTRONG

Baker Library, R. G. Dun & Co. credit ledger, Canada, 25: 208F, 228P, 241, 299. Scottish Record Office (Edinburgh), Old Machar parish (cathedral) baptismal register, Aberdeen, 2 June 1827. Wentworth County Surrogate Court (Hamilton, Ont.), will and inventory of Alexander Harvey, 26 June 1884, 3 May 1886. *Hamilton Spectator*, 8 March 1886. *Hamilton directory* (Hamilton), 1856–73. *The mercantile agency reference book for the British provinces* . . . (Montreal and Toronto), I (1864): 136. V. Ross and Trigge, *Hist. of Canadian Bank of Commerce*, III: 64–65, 67, 152.

HAY, ROBERT, cabinet-maker, furniture manufacturer, and politician; b. 18 May 1808 in the parish of Tibbermore, Newbigging (Tayside), Scotland, the youngest child of Robert Hay and Bettrice Henderson; m. 18 Nov. 1847 in Toronto, Canada West, Mary Dunlop (1828–71), of Glasgow, Scotland, and they had eight children; d. 24 July 1890 at Toronto.

Robert Hay began working as an apprentice cabinet-maker in Perth, Scotland, at age 14. In September 1831 he immigrated with his family to York (Toronto) where shortly thereafter his parents died of cholera. Hay and another Toronto cabinet-maker, John JACQUES, entered into partnership in 1835 to produce cabinetware, purchasing William Maxwell's shop on King Street. The firm of Jacques and Hay, and its successor in 1871, Robert Hay and Company Limited, had its principal outlet in the same city block until the company was dissolved in 1885. From a small operation employing two artisans and producing goods to order, the partners built their company into the leading furniture manufacturer in the Province of Canada by 1850. The firm maintained its primacy until at least 1882, when the last in a series of major fires temporarily crippled its manufacturing capacity.

The growth in the volume of production of the firm was accompanied by a profound transition from the artisan mode to that of highly mechanized mass production of standardized furniture parts. Jacques and Hay were among the first in the Canadas to employ steam-power for their machinery, and in 1854 set up a branch plant and sawmill in the village of New Lowell in Simcoe County, Canada West, to manufacture components for items of furniture. The village of New Lowell was built on part of the 1,100 acres the company held in Sunnidale Township. Although the original plan to attract a variety of industries to the site failed, Jacques and Hay built their own plant as well as employees' houses, an inn, a schoolhouse, a church, and a railway station for the Toronto, Simcoe and Lake Huron Union Rail-road of which Hay was one of the original promoters and which ran through the property.

By the 1860s Jacques and Hay were exporting to Glasgow large numbers of chairs and assorted wooden pins for the textile industry. The company reported annual sales of $500,000 in 1870, and two years later the wholesale trade of Robert Hay and Company in chairs alone was nearly $150,000; no other furniture manufacturer in Ontario had anything approaching this volume of trade. The company was the largest employer in the Canadian furniture industry, with nearly 500 employees on its pay-roll in the 1870s.

Although it was the leader in mass production furniture, the company maintained a reputation for the high quality of its solid walnut cabinetware throughout nearly 50 years of operation. Machine production eliminated much of what had previously been the artisans' work, but many operations still required craftsmanship of the first order. It appears likely that the firm distinguished between the production of elegant drawing-room pieces and higher volume cottage furniture.

Hay was the entrepreneur of the business, while Jacques supervised the daily operations of the factory and warehouse in Toronto; after Jacques's retirement in 1870, the junior partners, George Craig and Charles Rogers, assumed his responsibilities. The peripatetic Hay spent much time cultivating business and political acquaintances, contacts which were undoubtedly at the root of his firm's persistent winning of contracts to supply imperial, provincial, and local governments with military, school, and hospital furniture. Severe credit shortages, currency restraints, and the market fluctuations of a staple-producing economy compelled the firm to turn intermittently to making interior fittings for such notable buildings as Osgoode Hall, University College, and the Queen's Hotel in Toronto, and at least one early steamer. The company supplied a great deal of timber from its stands near New Lowell to Ontario railways during the building boom of the post-confederation years, and it shipped millions of board feet to Chicago and Troy, N.Y. During slack periods the firm also produced a wide variety of wooden commodities such as broom handles and clothes pins, as well as haircloth for furniture coverings and mattress filling.

In pursuit of a favourable business climate Hay was an early advocate of tariff protection. He participated in the founding of the Association for the Promotion of Canadian Industry in 1858, and was active in its successor in 1866. He was also elected for Toronto Centre in the federal election of 1878 as a Liberal-Conservative and an advocate of the National Policy defeating John MACDONALD. He held the seat until the dissolution of parliament in January 1887, but was an extremely reticent member in the House of Commons. In local politics he was much involved with politicians in lobbying for development important to New Lowell such as a post office, a telegraph, and a railway stop.

While garnering a personal fortune, Robert Hay helped to propel the Ontario furniture industry into a new age of mass production and he was among the first to exploit the possibilities in exporting manufactured products. But the firm did not survive his participation in it. When he retired in 1885, he insisted on winding up the business because of disagreement over its valuation. His only surviving son, John Dunlop, was trained as a merchant and gentleman farmer and took no active interest in the furniture business, and his sons-in-law were bankers or merchants.

Hay's interests had shifted in later life. He had been a founder and provisional director of the St Lawrence Bank in 1872 and he was elected a director of the Credit Valley Railway in 1875 and president of the Canadian Lumber Cutting Machine Company. In the 1880s he speculated in lands in the North-West Territories, briefly operated a wholesale lumber business in Medonte Township with his son, and spent increasing amounts of time with his prize-winning livestock on his farm near New Lowell.

As a leading Toronto business man, Hay had been active in the community as a member of the St Andrew's (Presbyterian) Church, the St Andrew's Society, and the mechanics' institute. Upon his death in July 1890, his estate, valued at nearly $350,000, was divided among his four surviving children..

STANLEY POLLIN

AO, RG 31, Declarations of partnerships, 1: nos.250, 377; 2: nos.3527, 4581. CTA, Toronto assessment rolls, St George's Ward, 1835–90. Land Registry Office for the Division of Toronto, Deeds, instrument no. 4198[B]. Royal Ontario Museum (Toronto), Canadiana Dept., Sigmund Samuel Coll., S. M. Smith, "Jacques and Hay, 1835–85, cabinet-makers" (typescript, n.d.). Scottish Record Office (Edinburgh), Tibbermore parish register, 1808. Simcoe County Arch. (Minesing, Ont.), Jacques and Hay Furniture Company papers. Simcoe County Registry Office (Barrie, Ont.), Abstract index to deeds, Medonte Township (mfm. at AO, G.S. 5435); Sunnidale Township (mfm. at AO, G.S. 5511–13). Toronto Boroughs and York South Registry Office (Toronto), Abstract index to deeds (mfm. at AO, G.S. 6033–34). York County Surrogate Court (Toronto), no.8052, will of Robert Hay, 6 Sept. 1890 (mfm. at AO).

Isaac Buchanan, *The relations of the industry of Canada, with the mother country and the United States* . . . , ed. H. J. Morgan (Montreal, 1864). Can., House of Commons, *Debates*, 1878–83, 1891. *Banner* (Toronto), 16 Feb. 1844. *Daily Leader* (Toronto), 30 Dec. 1854. *Globe*, 1847–56, 2 Feb. 1882. *Toronto Daily Mail*, 1886–90. *Toronto World*, 25 July 1890. *Canadian biog. dict.*, I: 192–96. *Commemorative biog. record, county York*. *CPC*, 1879. *Cyclopædia of Canadian biog.* (Rose, 1886), 293. Joan MacKinnon, *A checklist of Toronto cabinet and chair makers, 1800–1865* (Ottawa, 1975). Middleton, *Municipality of Toronto*. Philip Shackleton, *The furniture of old Ontario* (Toronto, 1973).

HAY, WILLIAM, architect; b. 17 May 1818 at Dikeside, parish of Cruden, near Peterhead, Scotland, son of William Hay, a grain merchant, and Jean Alexander; d. 30 May 1888 at Joppa, near Edinburgh, Scotland.

William Hay, who had been apprenticed as a joiner, broke a leg in a fall while working and at his doctor's suggestion decided to study architecture while he was convalescing. He was raised as a Scottish Episcopalian and his first commission was appropriately St James Episcopal Church at Cruden in 1843. The next year he went to Edinburgh as assistant in the office of the prominent architect John Henderson. In 1846 George Gilbert Scott, one of the best-known Gothic Revival architects of the day, retained Hay as clerk-of-the-works in the construction of the new Anglican Cathedral of St John the Baptist for Bishop Edward Feild* at St John's, Nfld. Late in that year and early in the next Hay travelled extensively in the British Isles retaining skilled workers and arranging for the supply of materials.

In April 1847 he sailed for St John's accompanied by his wife, Janet Reid (1819–60), whom he had married in 1844, and her brother Thomas, their ward, who later went on to a prominent political career in Bermuda. Hay remained in St John's until after the completion of the cathedral's nave in 1850; it was gutted in the great fire of 1892 but was subsequently rebuilt within its shell. While in Newfoundland he also drew plans for a proposed church at St Francis Harbour in Labrador. In 1848–49 Bishop Feild, who had become a close friend, consulted him about the rebuilding of the pro-cathedral in Hamilton, Bermuda, then part of the diocese of Newfoundland.

Hay returned to Scotland in 1850, but his movements during the next three years are rather obscure. He was architect of St John's Church at Longside, near Peterhead, in 1853, and he apparently visited Montreal and Chicago with the idea of establishing a practice. He finally settled at Toronto where he quickly became one of the leading architects. There he designed the Toronto General Hospital and Gould Street United Presbyterian Church, 1855; the House of Providence, 1855–58; the original parts of St Basil's Church and St Michael's College, 1856; the school addition to Holy Trinity Church, 1858; and the Yorkville Town Hall, 1859–60. He also worked for the provincial government, extending the Parliament Buildings on Front Street and remodelling the old hospital on Gerrard Street for the Executive Council offices in mid decade; as well he designed a wooden church for the garrison. He favoured for churches and church-related commissions Gothic architecture in the high church style preferred by the English architect, Augustus Welby Pugin; Hay's institutional buildings were often mansard-roofed and were in the eclectic style now called Second Empire. Believing that utility and convenience should be basic requisites of architecture, he incorporated the latest ideas in heating, ventilation, and sanitation. Of all these commissions only the work at Holy Trinity and much-remodelled versions of St Basil's and St Michael's survive. Hay also designed numerous dwellings including the parsonage of Holy Trinity Church (1861) and the adjacent Scadding House, built about 1860 for Henry Scadding*, rector of Holy Trinity. Although the latter has since been remodelled and moved a few feet, they can both still be seen. Outside Toronto he was responsible for several surviving buildings: the Commercial Bank (now the Empire Life) at Kingston in 1853, and the churches of St George's (Anglican) at Newcastle in 1857, St Andrew's (Presbyterian) at Guelph in 1857–58, and St Paul's at Southampton in 1861. He also prepared designs for other structures.

Hay was active in the social life of Toronto, a member (and vice-president, 1859–61) of the Toronto Mechanics' Institute, and on the council of the Canadian Institute, 1858–60. Concerned with provincial organizations as well, he was on the executive committee of the Board of Arts and Manufactures for Upper Canada and was secretary of the Association of Architects, Civil Engineers, and Provincial Land Surveyors of Canada. An ardent freemason, he was associated with many masonic organizations.

After the death of his wife in 1860 he determined to leave Toronto and, probably early in 1862, turned his practice over to his recently acquired partner Thomas Gundry and to Henry Langley*, who had studied with him for seven years. Hay's activities then again become uncertain. In that year he visited Bermuda, working on the nave of the church for Feild, but in 1863 he appears to have settled briefly in Edinburgh before proceeding to Halifax, N.S., where he was listed in partnership with David STIRLING of that city and was architect of the mansion of Alexander Keith*, Keith Hall. Shortly afterwards, perhaps after visiting other parts of the empire, Hay returned to Scotland, opening a practice in Edinburgh, and established his residence, Rabbit Hall, in the suburb of Joppa. Once again an active freemason, he eventually became a member of the grand committee of the grand lodge of Scotland. In 1870 he married Jemima Huddleston (d. 1905) of Ryde, Isle of Wight, and they were to have one daughter.

Hay's most important work following his departure from Canada was the restoration of St Giles's Cathedral in Edinburgh between 1872 and 1883. In this he was assisted by George Henderson, son of his old master: the younger Henderson became his partner about 1878 after practising in Australia for many years. The partnership carried out many works at Edinburgh, Peterhead, and Galashiels; they also worked across the border in Cumberland.

Hay visited Bermuda in 1883 to arrange for repairs on the pro-cathedral and to design Government House. He and his family then made an extensive tour of North America, during which they visited his former residences in Canada. In 1884, when the cathedral in Bermuda burned, Hay was asked to design the replacement, the present Cathedral of the Most Holy Trinity.

When Hay died in 1888, after eight months' illness, he left a personal estate of some £7,500 and a flourishing practice. Described as a man of "kindly and genial disposition," he played an influential role in Canadian architecture in the mid century, although few of his Toronto buildings survive today. His career provides a good example of how the Victorian empire was united not only by soldiers and administrators but also by professionals who made use of the opportunities provided by its many territories.

FREDERICK H. ARMSTRONG

William Hay was the author of "Architecture for the meridian of Canada" and of "The late Mr. Pugin and the revival of Christian architecture" in the *Anglo-American Magazine* (Toronto), 2 (January–June 1853): 253–55 and 70–73 respectively. A photocopy of the "Hart family diary" covering the period from 1842 to 1966 is held by F. H. Armstrong of London, Ont.

General Register Office (Edinburgh), Register of births and baptisms for the parish of Cruden, 1818; SC 70/1/270: 211–23, Inventory of estate of William Hay, 20 Nov. 1888; SC 70/4/234: 703–23, Marriage contract of William Hay, 3 June 1870, and testamentary deed of William Hay and Jemima Huddleston or Hay, 20 Nov. 1888. Royal Commission on the Ancient and Historical Monuments of Scotland (Edinburgh), Buildings of Scotland Research Unit papers. "Ecclesiastical architecture: village churches," *Anglo-American Magazine*, 4 (January–June 1854): 20–22. "The editor's shanty," *Anglo-American Magazine*, 4 (January–June 1854): 211–13. "New churches," *Ecclesiologist* (London), 11 (1850): 200–1. "The late Mr. William Hay, architect," *Builder* (London), 54 (January–June 1888): 414. "The late Mr. Wm. Hay, architect," *Canadian Architect and Builder* (Toronto), 1 (1888), no.7: 11. D. M. Lyon, *History of the Lodge of Edinburgh (Mary's Chapel) no. 1: embracing an account of the rise and progress of freemasonry in Scotland* (Edinburgh and London, 1873), 349, 353. T. S. Reid, *Trinity Church, Bermuda; a sketch of its history, drawn from various sources* ([Hamilton, Bermuda?], 1886), 8–9, 11, 15–16. *Hutchinson's N.S. directory*, 1864–65: 138–39. *Toronto directory*, 1859–60: 212, 273, 276, 278–79. [G. P. Ure], *The hand-book of Toronto; containing its climate, geology, natural history, educational institutions, courts of law, municipal arrangements* . . . (Toronto, 1858), 234–36, 258-59, 268–70. Wallace, *Macmillan dict.*, 307.

Eric Arthur, *Toronto, no mean city* ([Toronto], 1964), 85, 114, 116–17, 124–25, 142, 247, 249. B. F. L. Clarke, *Anglican cathedrals outside the British Isles* (London, 1958), 55–56, 126–27. William Dendy, *Lost Toronto* (Toronto, 1978). T. A. Reed, "Toronto's early architects: many fine buildings still standing," Royal Architectural Institute of Canada, *Journal* (Toronto), 27 (1950): 46–51.

HAYES, ISAAC ISRAEL, physician and Arctic explorer; b. 5 March 1832 in Chester County, Penn., son of Benjamin Hayes and Ann Barton; d. unmarried 17 Dec. 1881 in New York City.

Isaac Israel Hayes was a descendant of an Oxfordshire family which had settled in Chester County in the 18th century. He attended Westtown Academy from 1838 to 1848, and in 1852 became a medical student at the University of Pennsylvania where he earned a doctorate in medicine. He had become interested in Arctic exploration and in May 1853 volunteered to serve as surgeon under Elisha Kent Kane* aboard the brig *Advance* on the second expedition supported by Henry Grinnell, a New York merchant, to search for Sir John Franklin*. Hayes led the party that in 1854 discovered and explored Grinnell Land (Ellesmere Island). He was also in charge of a party that attempted unsuccessfully to reach Upernavik, the nearest Inuit settlement, after Kane had been forced to spend a second winter in the Arctic. When the expedition returned to New York in 1855, Hayes had a permanently mutilated foot. In *An Arctic boat journey* he gave a graphic description of the hardships he had experienced and an excellent clinical account of the various forms of scurvy that had killed many of the crew.

In July 1860 Hayes took command of the schooner *United States* at Boston for another expedition financed by Grinnell. He hoped to approach the pole via the open sea which he believed to exist north of the 85th parallel. The expedition's scientific endeavours were, however, badly hurt by the death of its astronomer, August Sonntag, who with HANS HENDRIK, an Inuit guide, attempted a futile trip to obtain more dogs after their pack had been hit by an epidemic of Arctic rabies. Hayes made one of the earliest clinical studies of this epizootic, which has not yet been completely explained; clearly an affection of the central nervous system, Arctic rabies had a high morbidity among dog teams, with loss of discipline, temper, and control of motor activity but no hydrophobia. Hayes managed to complete the survey of Grinnell Land as far as what he thought was 81°35′ where he saw open sea.

Returning to New York in 1861, Hayes joined the Union army and was in command of Satterlee Army Hospital, West Philadelphia, during the Civil War. He rose from the rank of major to brevet-colonel. After demobilization he went into business in a shipping company in New York, giving up the practice of medicine. He did, however, maintain his interest in the Arctic, giving much of his time to writing and lecturing. In 1867 he published *The open polar sea*, and in 1868 *Cast away in the cold*, a book for children.

Hayes's third and last Arctic expedition was to Greenland in 1869 aboard the brig *Panther*. The trip was financed by William Bradford, a well-known artist of marine and Arctic scenes, who assumed charge of photography and illustration on the expedition. Hayes looked after the geographical and geological observations, especially those of glaciology, and published an account of the expedition's findings in *The land of desolation* in 1871. He also presented illustrations and photographs of the expedition, including those of William Bradford, in *The Arctic regions* (London, 1873).

After this Greenland expedition Hayes was busy as a lecturer, newspaper reporter, free lance writer, and politician. From 1875 until his death in 1881 he was a Republican member of the New York State assembly. He never lost touch with exploration, being an active member of the American Geographical Society of New York and a close associate of its president, Charles Patrick Daly. He was influential in the decision of the society to sponsor its first Arctic expedition, a search for the records and logs of the lost Franklin expedition. Although Hayes may have been disappointed when he was not chosen to lead this expedition, he gave his fullest support to the man chosen, Lieutenant Frederick Schwatka*.

The Arctic achievements of Dr Hayes were substantial and he received gold medals from the Société de Géographie (Paris) and the Royal Geographical Society (London). Although his observations have been shown to be not always completely accurate with regard to detail, in their broader scope, and in their account of Greenland's glaciers, they were sound. Hayes was an advocate of the theory of the open polar sea, but in this error he was in good company. We know now that the Kennedy Channel, which he had visited in 1860, and other parts of the Arctic Ocean are at unpredictable times open in the winter. Hayes and others merely extrapolated from their data the conclusion that the Arctic Ocean is always open near the pole. Perhaps Hayes's most important achievement was that, like Charles Francis Hall* and Elisha Kent Kane, he explored what might be called the "American route" which was later used by Robert Edwin Peary to reach the North Pole.

ROBERT E. JOHNSON

I. I. Hayes was the author of "Address on Arctic exploration, delivered November 12, 1868," American Geographical and Statistical Soc., *Journal* (New York), 2, PT.II (1870): 1–31; *An Arctic boat journey, in the autumn of 1854* (Boston, Mass., 1860); *Cast away in the cold; an old man's story of a young man's adventures, as related by Captain John Hardy, mariner* (Boston, [1868]); *The land of desolation: being a personal narrative of adventure in Greenland* (London, 1871); "Lecture on Arctic explorations," Smithsonian Institution, *Annual report* (Washington), 1861: 149–60; *Observations upon the relations existing between food and the capabilities of men to resist low temperatures* (Philadelphia, 1859); *The open polar sea: a narrative of a voyage of discovery towards the North Pole, in the schooner "United States"* (New York, 1867); "Physical observations in the Arctic seas . . . ," ed. C. A. Schott, *Smithsonian Contributions to Knowledge* (Washington), 15 (1867), article V; *Pictures of Arctic travel . . . Greenland* (New York), [1881]); "Remarks," American Geographical Soc. of New York, *Journal* (New York), 12 (1880), 258–73; and "[Report of Dr Hayes' Arctic expedition]," American Philosophical Soc., *Proc.* (Philadelphia), 8 (1861–62): 383–93.

American Geographical Soc. (New York), C. P. Daly corr., 1859–99. National Arch. (Washington), RG 94, Personal papers of medical officers and physicians prior to 1912, I. I. Hayes file. G. W. Cullum, "Biographical sketch of Doctor Isaac I. Hayes," American Geographical Soc. of New York, *Journal*, 13 (1881): 110–24. W. H. Gilder, *Schwatka's search; sledging in the Arctic in quest of the Franklin records* (New York, 1881). E. K. Kane, *Arctic explorations: the second Grinnell expedition in search of Sir John Franklin, 1853, '54, '55* (2v., Philadelphia and London, 1856). [Frederick Schwatka], "Address," American Geographical Soc. of New York, *Journal*, 12 (1880): 246–58. *New-York Tribune*, 18 Dec. 1881. *DAB*. *The national cyclopædia of American biography* (57v. to date, New York, [*et al.*], 1892–), III: 280. J. S. Futhey and Gilbert Cope, *History of Chester County, Pennsylvania, with genealogical and biographical sketches* (Philadelphia, 1881). [S. C. Harry *et al.*], *Proceedings of the bi-centennial gathering of the descendants of Henry Hayes . . .* (West Chester, Pa., 1906). *Arctic Pilot* (London), III (5th ed., 1959).

HAYNES, JOHN CARMICHAEL, public servant and rancher; b. 6 July 1831 at Landscape, County Cork (Republic of Ireland), eldest son of Jonas Haynes and Hester Carmichael; m. 6 Sept. 1868 Charlotte Moresby (d. 1872) at Hope, B.C., and they had one son; m. secondly 14 Jan. 1875 Emily Josephine Pittendrigh, at Osoyoos, B.C., and they had three sons and three daughters; d. 6 July 1888 at Princeton, B.C.

John Carmichael Haynes left Ireland in 1858, hoping to join the police force which Chartres Brew*, a friend of his uncle, expected to establish in British Columbia. On board the *Sonora* from Panama, he became acquainted with Colonel Richard Clement MOODY, Arthur Thomas Bushby*, and Thomas ELWYN. "Paddy" Haynes made a good impression: Bushby considered him "a decent sort of a fellow." They arrived in Victoria on Christmas Day 1858, and early in January 1859 Governor James Douglas* appointed Haynes and Elwyn special constables to accompany Brew on an expedition to quell disturbances among the gold-miners at Hills Bar. After order was restored Brew employed Elwyn and Haynes briefly to collect miners' licences. They were not particularly successful but Brew was satisfied that they were competent and would perform any duty "with zeal and fidelity." Haynes then served at Yale as a constable under Magistrate Edward Howard Sanders, and in November 1859 was promoted to acting chief constable.

The next year Governor Douglas chose Haynes to assist William George Cox*, the justice of the peace, assistant gold commissioner, and deputy collector of customs at Rock Creek, inland near the international boundary line, where gold had been found. In this open range country around the Kettle River, it was easy for American traders, cattlemen, and mule-drivers to gain access. Douglas, to divert commerce to British hands, ordered the Hope–Princeton Trail built over the Cascade Mountains and stationed Cox and Haynes at Rock Creek. Haynes arrived there on 15 Oct. 1860. Six weeks later Cox sent him to Similkameen, the scene of another gold flurry, where he opened a customs house in December. That same month Douglas imposed along the southern boundary customs duties and tolls on imported animals. In 1861 the Cariboo gold rush drew miners northward and by November the last had left Rock Creek. Inland traffic into British Columbia from American territories now passed through the Okanagan valley and Haynes was moved to Osoyoos Lake where he assumed responsibility for the whole area of Rock Creek, Okanagan, and Similkameen. He became deputy collector of customs in March 1862, a year in which 800 men and over 9,000 cattle, horses, and mules passed through his station, and he collected more than £ 2,200 in revenue. The heavy movement of men and animals continued throughout 1863 and into the early months of 1864, but then cattle ranches, established by drivers in the interior valleys, began to supply the food requirements of the Cariboo District and the cattle drives declined.

Haynes was transferred to the Kootenay District as justice of the peace and assistant gold commissioner in June 1864. After an arduous 20-day trip by way of Fort Colvile (Colville) and Fort Spokane (near Spokane) in Washington Territory, he arrived on 10 August at

Wild Horse Creek (Wild Horse River, B.C.) where a camp of 1,000 miners, shopkeepers, and labourers had sprung into existence. In this predominantly American community lawlessness prevailed, but Haynes vigorously applied the colony's mining and revenue laws. Six weeks after his arrival, when Arthur Nonus Birch*, the colonial secretary of British Columbia, and Arthur Bushby made an official visit to the camp, they found "no pistols to be seen, and everything as quiet and orderly as it could possibly be in the most civilized district of the colony." Haynes turned over to them 75 lbs of gold, the revenue collected on imports he had found when he arrived. In recognition of his work, Governor Frederick Seymour* appointed him a member of the Legislative Council.

Attendance at the 1865 and 1866 sessions of the council strengthened Haynes's ties with government officials. These associations proved helpful: in 1865 he obtained permission to reduce the size of the two large Indian reserves at the head and foot of Okanagan Lake, thus making meadow and range lands available for white settlement. That year Haynes also supervised the construction of a new customs house at "the narrows" of Osoyoos Lake, but he spent most of that year and the following spring at Fort Shepherd on the Columbia River. In August 1866 during the brief rush at Big Bend he was appointed district court judge at French Creek, but soon returned to Osoyoos as collector of customs. In November, when the colonies of British Columbia and Vancouver Island were united, Haynes remained on the civil list as deputy collector of customs for the southern boundary.

Unexpectedly Haynes was ordered to return to Wild Horse Creek as magistrate and district court judge in the summer of 1870. He protested being sent to "the most out of the way & unpleasant station in the colony," the "great Personal inconvenience" of the move, and the salary of £450, which was less than that received by other magistrates. He travelled to Victoria in the winter of 1870–71 to seek an adjustment. Governor Anthony MUSGRAVE, who was then making recommendations on the future of the colony's public servants after its entry into confederation, privately felt that Haynes's appointments as magistrate and judge had been "temporary" and that he should be superannuated though allowed to transfer to the federal customs department. But Haynes was needed in Kootenay, and remained at Wild Horse Creek as a magistrate and district court judge until 1872, when he returned to Osoyoos as justice of the peace and also served in the federal customs department until his death.

His income assured, Haynes rapidly expanded his land holdings after 1872. In August 1869, with his partner, Constable William Hamilton Lowe, he had acquired 160 acres of land at the head of Osoyoos Lake, to which he added an adjoining 480-acre tract the following year. In 1872, after Lowe suffered a severe accident, Haynes absorbed his lands, and further acquisitions between 1874 and 1888 increased his holdings to 20,756 acres. He established a horse ranch but could not find a market, and turned to cattle ranching, eventually increasing his herd to 4,000 head and acquiring the title of "The Cattle-King of the South Okanagan." He made cattle drives over the Hope Trail to New Westminster and over the Dewdney Trail to Kootenay and Calgary (Alta). After he built a fine house on the eastern shore of Osoyoos Lake in 1882, it was rumoured that his properties had a value of $200,000.

In 1888, while returning over the Hope Trail with his two sons who had been at school in Victoria, Haynes was taken ill. He died on 6 July at the home of John Fall Allison at Princeton and was buried at Osoyoos. His lands and cattle passed to Thomas Ellis whom Haynes had earlier befriended as a young Irish immigrant. Haynes had carried out his duties in Osoyoos and the Kootenay firmly and yet without offence to American miners, traders, and drivers. With other Irish landed proprietors he later shared a comfortable life as a country squire in a pastoral setting and with them established cattle ranching as the first industry of the Okanagan.

MARGARET A. ORMSBY

PABC, Add. MSS 180; B.C., Colonial secretary, Corr. outward, 1859–69 (letterbook); Dept. of Lands and Works, Corr. outward, 1865–66; Colonial corr., Chartres Brew corr.; W. G. Cox corr.; J. C. Haynes corr.; GR 112; GR 495; Herald Street coll.; O'Reilly coll., Emily Haynes to Peter O'Reilly, 3 Aug. 1888; Vancouver Island, Governor (Douglas), Corr. outward, 27 May 1859–9 Jan. 1864 (letterbook).

[Susan Allison], *A pioneer gentlewoman in British Columbia; the recollections of Susan Allison*, ed. M. A. Ormsby (Vancouver, 1976). B.C., *Blue book*, 1859–70; Legislative Assembly, *Journals*, 1877. [A. T. Bushby], "The journal of Arthur Thomas Bushby, 1858–1859," ed. Dorothy Blakey Smith, *BCHQ*, 21 (1957–58): 83–198. Matthew Macfie, *Vancouver Island and British Columbia: their history, resources, and prospects* (London, 1865), 255–62. *Daily Colonist* (Victoria), 11 July 1888. *Government Gazette–British Columbia* (New Westminster, B.C.), 5 Nov. 1864. *Kelowna Courier and Okanagan Orchardist* (Kelowna, B.C.), 12 March 1908. R. E. Cail, *Land, man, and the law: the disposal of crown lands in British Columbia, 1871–1913* (Vancouver, 1974). M. A. Ormsby, "Some Irish figures in colonial days," *BCHQ*, 14 (1950): 61–82. H. E. White, "John Carmichael Haynes: pioneer of the Okanagan and Kootenay," *BCHQ*, 4 (1940): 183–201.

HÉBERT, NICOLAS-TOLENTIN, priest and colonizer; b. 10 Sept. 1810 at Saint-Grégoire (now part of Bécancour), Lower Canada, son of notary Jean-Baptiste Hébert and Judith Lemire; d. 17 Jan. 1888 at Kamouraska, Que.

Nicolas-Tolentin Hébert received a classical and theological education at the Séminaire de Nicolet and was ordained priest on 13 Oct. 1833 at Quebec City. A curate there until 1840, he became parish priest first of Saint-Pascal, Lower Canada, and then of Saint-Louis in Kamouraska; the latter post he held from 1852 until his death.

It is as a colonizer that Nicolas-Tolentin Hébert deserves attention. In the late 1840s the clergy was endeavouring to stimulate large-scale colonization in Canada East in order to slow down the exodus of its Catholic population to the United States. In support of this effort, the priests of the constituencies of L'Islet and Kamouraska met at Sainte-Anne-de-la-Pocatière (La Pocatière) at the end of 1848 and decided to set up the Association des Comtés de L'Islet et de Kamouraska pour Coloniser le Saguenay. They entrusted the responsibility for this undertaking to Hébert who was known for his practical mind and organizational ability.

The association was something of a prototype for the land settlement societies of Quebec in the 19th century. It had the structure of a cooperative, with the parish as the basic unit. Each of the participating parishes (there would be eight in all) had a committee representative of the number of its shareholders. Shares were sold at the unit price of £12 10*s*. (about $50) but, if parish committees so recommended, the society could accept payment in work; a shareholder could hold no more than three shares. A share entitled its owner to a 100-acre lot. After five years the society was to be dissolved and the properties distributed by a drawing of lots. The society reached its peak in 1851, when 296 shareholders held 360 shares. In theory, the money collected was to be used for the purchase of land, the opening of access routes, and, wherever possible, the partial clearing and building of a house on each lot. There was no requirement that shareholders take possession of their property. In reality, the shareholders were divided into two fundamentally different categories: those (largely from the clergy or the local *petite bourgeoisie*) who sponsored settlers, and those who were themselves settlers; in 1851 the second group represented only 31 per cent of the membership and held but 20 per cent of the shares. These figures give a striking picture of what the Association des Comtés de L'Islet et de Kamouraska pour coloniser le Saguenay really represented: an alliance of clergy and rural bourgeoisie serving a 19th-century ideology focused on God and the land.

Hébert's organization was not the first to enter the Saguenay area. In 1846 Jean-Baptiste Honorat*, the superior of the Oblates in the Saguenay, had founded the first colonizing settlement at Grand-Brûlé (Laterrière). A year later the people of La Malbaie founded another at the Rivière aux Sables (Jonquière). In 1848, pushing farther west, two societies attempted to gain a foothold to the east of Lac Saint-Jean: that of Baie-Saint-Paul, in the township of Signay, and another, initiated by parish priest François Boucher, in the adjoining township of Caron. The difficulties encountered by these organizations strongly influenced Abbé Hébert. At Laterrière, settlement had been greatly hampered by the desperate struggle waged by the superior of the Oblates against the brutal methods of capitalists William Price* and Peter McLeod* who headed a vast timber monopoly in the region. Furthermore, the townships of Signay and Caron were doomed to stagnate, if not die, for want of support. Hébert concluded that only an efficient organization could ensure a durable settlement, and also that it was in the interests of any colonizing organization to know how to come to terms with those holding the timber monopoly of the region. After his settlement had begun, confrontations occurred with McLeod's men who were attempting to strip the association's land of commercial timber. Hébert succeeded in making Price's partner see reason, and the latter bought logs and agricultural produce from the society, thus supplying it with some income. Such, in brief, are the factors that ensured the success of the work of his association. Hébert did not, properly speaking, open the Lac Saint-Jean region to settlement, but it was he who broke the terrible isolation of the area and hence cleared the way for colonization to move westwards from the Saguenay.

Throughout the period of its operations, and indeed after its dissolution in 1856 (a few years later than intended), the association was able to rely on the leadership of the Collège de Sainte-Anne-de-la-Pocatière through Abbé François PILOTE. The plan of settlement to be carried out by the association, of which Pilote was the last president, was undoubtedly developed in the college. The society had in Pilote both an effective political mediator and a no less skilful publicity agent. In 1852 he published at Quebec *Le Saguenay en 1851* . . . , a work designed to make both the Saguenay area and the society's activities there known.

On 14 Feb. 1849 an order in council granted the association the townships of Labarre and Métabetchouan near Lac Saint-Jean. The society was to meet the cost of surveying the land; the price of the land was fixed at a preferential rate of 1*s*. per acre until 1 Jan. 1850, when it would rise to 2*s*. Early in June 1849, Abbé Hébert explored the area with a view to settlement. His final choice was the township of Labarre. On 21 August the occupation and clearing of the new property started; two years later the settlement had 120 permanent residents.

The greatest obstacle the new settlement had to face was the complete absence of access routes: without a road it was in danger of suffocating. After numerous petitions, the government agreed to release £1,500 (approximately $6,000) for the construction of a regional road to link the Upper Saguenay to Lac Saint-Jean. In 1855, one year after work had begun, the funds were exhausted; the road was finally completed after the dissolution of the society. Distance and transport difficulties were a heavy burden on the finances of the new settlement. Moreover, the association had fallen far short of its promises. In 1855 about 100 of a possible 337 lots were occupied. But, more serious still, the society had accumulated debts of $6,800 with merchants, and the government would only issue property titles *en bloc* for land occupied either by shareholders or by the settlers they had recruited. Surprisingly the greatest recruiting effort took place after the dissolution of the society although it was not until 1871 that all the lots were occupied. The absenteeism of the shareholders who sponsored settlers was quickly denounced by the new settlers as a serious impediment to the colonization process, and only numerous interventions by Hébert and Abbé Pilote prevented the government from revoking the sale of long-vacant lands.

To facilitate the taking over of the land, Hébert had granted the settlers large credit margins on the purchase of lots and merchandise. In order to wipe out the society's debt, and particularly to reimburse the shareholders sponsoring settlers for their expenses, Hébert changed all the settlers' debts into mortgage loans. On 26 Aug. 1857 he gave to the general creditor of the society, Jean-Baptiste RENAUD, a Quebec merchant, approximately £1,253 11*s.* in partial payment of the debt of £1,720 7*s.* 11*d.* Nine years later he made over further amounts to the Collège de Sainte-Anne-de-la-Pocatière, which assumed responsibility for the remainder of the debt to Renaud. In this way the affairs of the society were liquidated. Collection of the debts continued until the end of the century and resulted in the ruin of many settlers.

Although Nicolas-Tolentin Hébert's efforts were not totally successful, they nevertheless made possible a colonizing thrust to the west of the Saguenay. Since 1857 the settlement established in the township of Labarre has borne the name of Hébertville, and in 1925 a monument was erected there in honour of the parish priest Hébert.

NORMAND SÉGUIN

Arch. du Collège de Sainte-Anne-de-la-Pocatière (La Pocatière, Qué.), 38-XIV. BE, Chicoutimi, Lac-Saint-Jean-Est (Hébertville). PAC, MG 24, I81. Qué., Ministère de l'Agriculture, Reg. des lettres, Corr. de N.-T. Hébert. Michèle Le Roux, "La colonisation du Saguenay et l'action de l'Association des comtés de l'Islet et de Kamouraska" (mémoire de DES, univ. de Montréal, 1972). François Pilote, *Le Saguenay en 1851; histoire du passé, du présent et de l'avenir probable du Haut-Saguenay, au point de vue de la colonisation* (Québec, 1852). P.-M. Hébert, "Un Acadien ouvre la vallée du Lac-St-Jean," Soc. hist. acadienne, *Cahiers* (Moncton, N.-B.), 3 (1968–71): 224–36.

HENDERSON, ALEXANDER, merchant and municipal politician; b. 3 Nov. 1824 in Pitsligo parish (Grampian), Scotland, son of John Henderson and Catherine Udny; he and his wife Margaret had nine children; d. 3 June 1887 in Toronto, Ont.

Alexander Henderson, a boy with hair "as red as a carrot," attended school at Peterhead, Scotland, before immigrating to Canada with his family in April 1835. Henderson's father "was completely strapped on arrival at Quebec," and had to borrow money from a fellow immigrant, George Brodie, to make the trip to Toronto. John tried his hand at coopering and farming before settling in the city. "Sandy," as Alexander was called, began working as a clerk in William Mather's general store and by 1842 had established his own store dealing in groceries, liquor, and dry goods. By the late 1840s, however, he dealt exclusively in dry goods. He sold the business in 1854 to his head salesman, John Rowland, and went into partnership with his brother John in a wholesale dry goods business.

By this time Alexander had become a large investor in Toronto properties and in 1857 he relinquished control of the partnership to his brother in order to devote more attention to real estate. In 1859 he was a director of two short-lived corporations, the Metropolitan Building Society and the Toronto and Ontario Building and Investment Building Society. He was also a director of the Union Permanent Building and Savings Society as well as the Toronto, Grey and Bruce Railway Company.

Henderson served as an alderman for St James Ward from 1868 until he retired in 1876. He chaired the city's board of works during 1871 and 1872 and the committee on finance and assessment during 1874. In later years he served as a justice of the peace. In addition, Henderson was a director of the Toronto House of Industry and a long-time member of both the St Andrew's and the Caledonian societies. "A staunch Liberal in politics," Henderson was also a member of the secessionist Presbyterian congregation of the Reverend John Jennings* before the disruption of 1844 when he aligned himself with the Free Church and was a "consistent member of the Knox Presbyterian Church."

Perhaps the basis of Henderson's success in business is revealed in a boyhood trait described by a former classmate and chum, Alexander Anderson Brodie, a son of George: "He knew well there was nothing to be gained by endangering himself where there was nothing to be gained." Brodie, a farmer in York County, also discloses something of Henderson's social attitude after becoming a prosperous merchant: "he could not do otherwise than give me a very little contenance, with a sickly smile when I met him in Toronto or happened to call into his store. His demeanour indicated there was a great gulf between us, that my company was unsavoury to him was quite palpable."

DANIEL JAMES BROCK

The author used the reminiscences of Alexander Anderson Brodie in the possession of Mrs Ronald Hutcheson, Ingersoll, Ont. (copy at UWO). Baker Library, R. G. Dun & Co. MS reports, 26: 50, 84, 151, 206, 351. General Register Office (Edinburgh), Register of births and baptisms for the parish of Pitsligo, November 1824. *Commemorative biog. record, county York. Toronto directory*, 1837–73. *Hist. of Toronto and county of York*, II: 63–64.

HENDRIK. *See* HANS HENDRIK

HENRY, WILLIAM ALEXANDER, lawyer, politician, and judge; b. 30 Dec. 1816 at Halifax, N.S., son of Robert Nesbit Henry, an Irish-born merchant, and Margaret Forrestall, *née* Hendricken; m. first in 1841 Sophia Caroline McDonald, who died in 1845, leaving an infant son; m. secondly in 1850 Christianna McDonald, and they had 7 children; d. 3 May 1888 at Ottawa, Ont.

William Alexander Henry's father moved from Halifax to Antigonish, N.S., following the War of 1812 to operate a timber business and store. He was taught there by the Reverend Thomas Trotter*. During the late 1830s he studied law with Alexander McDougall, and he was admitted to the bar as attorney in 1840 and barrister in 1841. Henry was active in politics and in the 1840 election successfully opposed McDougall to gain election as the representative of Sydney (Antigonish) County in the assembly, thus entering the house at a time when the council of Lieutenant Governor Lord Falkland [CARY], led by James William Johnston* and Joseph Howe*, was making a strained attempt at coalition government. In the assembly Henry was described as an opportunist, a dull and prosy speaker who delivered a speech like "a tired boy turning a grindstone." He was, however, personally popular, "a great mixer," admired as a sportsman, and noted for looking after the interests of his constituents.

Henry was defeated in 1843, after the collapse of the coalition, but was re-elected in 1847 when he supported the Reformers' call for responsible government. The Reformers had a margin of seven seats in the new assembly, and on 26 Jan. 1848 Henry seconded the non-confidence motion of James Boyle Uniacke* which forced Johnston's resignation and the formation of the first responsible government under Uniacke and Howe. Re-elected in 1851, Henry became minister without portfolio in April 1852 at a time when prominent Liberals such as Thomas Killam* were criticizing the government for endorsing Howe's scheme for a publicly financed railway from Halifax to Windsor, N.S. When in April 1854 William YOUNG replaced Uniacke as leader of the Liberal government, he chose Henry to succeed Alexander McDougall as solicitor general.

In August 1856 Henry switched portfolios to become provincial secretary, but on 9 Feb. 1857 he resigned from the government, explaining that he could not accept his colleagues' dismissal of William Condon from his position as gauger for the port of Halifax. Condon, a Roman Catholic and president of the Charitable Irish Society, had publicly disclosed Joseph Howe's illegal campaign to recruit Americans for the British army in the Crimea: Condon had also taken part in a Halifax public meeting at which Howe and others thought disloyal statements had been made, and he had become involved in a newspaper controversy in which he went beyond the conduct suitable for a civil servant. The Condon–Howe affair took place during a period of bitter feeling in Nova Scotia between Roman Catholics and Protestants, and led to massive defections from the Liberal party by Catholics. Henry, a Presbyterian with Catholic relatives, represented a predominantly Catholic constituency and claimed in the assembly that Condon's dismissal was persecution on religious grounds.

Ten days after Henry resigned from the cabinet, Young's government was defeated in a Conservative non-confidence motion supported by all the Roman Catholic members and two Protestant Liberals, John Chipman Wade* and Henry. His switch from Liberal to Conservative did not affect Henry's popularity; he was re-elected in May 1859, a month after joining Johnston's government as solicitor general. Although the Liberals gained a majority in the 1859 election, the Conservatives did not resign because Johnston and Henry maintained that some Liberals elected were legally disqualified from taking their seats. The British law officers did not agree, and on 7 Feb. 1860 the Johnston government yielded to the Liberals. When the Conservatives were returned to power in 1863 Henry again became solicitor general and on 11 May 1864 attorney general in the government of Charles Tupper*, who had succeeded Johnston as Conservative leader. Henry strongly supported Tupper's free school legislation in 1864 and 1865 and opposed Isaac LeVesconte*'s efforts to have Roman Catholic separate schools established in law, believing with Tupper that Catholic representation on the Board of Public Instruction, as constituted by the cabinet, would protect Catholic interests.

There is no evidence that Henry was interested in the union of British North America before the Charlottetown conference in September 1864, which he attended as attorney general of Nova Scotia. Also a delegate to the Quebec conference the following month, he took an active part in its deliberations as well as in its social activities. He was a supporter of broad and unspecified federal powers and specific, limited fields of jurisdiction for the provincial legislatures, with a supreme court to decide questions of jurisdictional competence. He reiterated his belief that the people of Nova Scotia would benefit commercially from union, especially after his journey to Washington in 1866 as one of the British North American delegates who attempted unsuccessfully to persuade the Americans not to abrogate the Reciprocity Treaty of 1854. Henry also emphasized the necessity to unite for defence and to complete the Intercolonial Railway between Halifax and Quebec. His campaign in support of confederation was pursued in the face of the mounting opposition to the Quebec scheme nurtured by Howe and William ANNAND.

Henry was a delegate to the London conference in December 1866 at which the form of confederation was finalized, and was one of the attorneys general who helped frame the language of the British North America Act. Here may lie the source of the unproved tradition that he drafted the BNA Act. The Nova Scotia delegates in London voted to accept the Quebec Resolutions, but Henry objected to the limitation on the number of Senate seats, fearing that its members could thereby frustrate popular measures with impunity. He also supported Archbishop Thomas Louis Connolly*'s unsuccessful efforts to have the existence of Roman Catholic separate schools in Nova Scotia entrenched in the BNA Act; the separate schools of the religious minorities in Ontario and Quebec were guaranteed in the act. In the federal election of 18 Sept. 1867, when only one pro-confederate MP was elected in Nova Scotia, Henry was defeated in Antigonish County by Hugh McDonald*, one of his former law students and a leading anti-confederate. After this loss, his first in 24 years, and another defeat in a federal by-election in Richmond in April 1869, Henry returned to the practice of law at which he was highly skilled. In 1870 he was elected mayor of Halifax and in 1873–74 president of the Charitable Irish Society.

Although nominally a Conservative, Henry felt more affinity for the federal Liberal party led by Alexander Mackenzie* than he did for the Liberal-Conservative party of Sir John A. Macdonald*. His estrangement from Macdonald, who had rewarded other pro-confederate leaders with appointments to the Senate or the bench, was coupled with the distance he maintained between himself and the anti-confederate government of William Annand in Nova Scotia. In 1873, when he was again defeated in a by-election in Antigonish, Henry switched his party allegiance from the Conservatives to the Liberals, ostensibly because of Conservative involvement in the Pacific Scandal, but in fact because he deeply resented the recent appointment of his rival Hugh McDonald as a county court judge. In October 1875, two years after the federal Liberals had come to power, the minister of justice, Edward Blake*, appointed Henry one of the judges of the newly created Supreme Court of Canada. It was felt that Henry, as one of the fathers of confederation, knew the intentions of the framers of the BNA Act, especially with respect to the division of powers between the federal and provincial legislatures.

In its first decade the Supreme Court, under Chief Justice William Buell RICHARDS, was plagued by serious problems concerning its credibility and importance. Blake's wish that appeals to the Judicial Committee of the Privy Council should end was not politically acceptable to the Conservative party or to the British government, both of which wanted to maintain an imperial link by permitting such appeals. The Supreme Court was often bypassed when appeals were made directly from the courts of last resort in the provinces to the JCPC, and the Supreme Court's decisions were frequently overturned by the English law lords. In parliament the court was subjected to many criticisms of its procedures. Henry diligently attended court, frequently dissented from the opinions of his fellow justices, and often had his judgements upheld by the JCPC. But Sir Robert Laird Borden* was to describe him as an "able" rather than a "great student," and in 1880 fellow justices John Wellington Gwynne* and Samuel Henry Strong* complained to Sir John A. Macdonald that Henry's judgements were "long, windy, incoherent masses of verbiage, interspersed with ungrammatical expressions, slang and the veriest legal platitudes inappropriately applied." Henry continued to serve until his death in 1888, and contributed to the administrative reforms which led to greater respect and utility for the Supreme Court. His 13 years on the bench were, however, overshadowed by his more than 20 years of political activity in his native province; an obituary described him and Tupper as the men who had led Nova Scotia "by the nose into Confederation."

PHYLLIS R. BLAKELEY

AO, MU 159–62. PANS, MS file, William Alexander Henry, Commissions, 1854–75; Doc., 1848, 1851; MG 9, no. 102; RG 1, 200: 3 April 1852, 4 April 1854, 14 Aug. 1856, 24 Feb. 1857, 15 April 1859; 201: 11 June 1863; 202: 11 May 1864; 262: ff.2, 7–21; RG 7, 36–37. *Documents on the confederation of British North America: a compilation based on Sir Joseph Pope's confederation documents supplemented by other official material*, ed. G. P. Browne (Toronto and Montreal, 1969). N.S., House of Assembly, *Debates and proc.*, 1855–61, 1864–67; *Journal and proc.*, 1840–67. *Casket* (Antigonish, N.S.), 1857–58; 1864–65; 31 Oct. 1935; 9 Jan., 20 Feb. 1936. *Morning Chronicle* (Halifax), 5 Jan. 1876; 4, 7 May 1888; 16 Feb. 1900. *Morning Herald* (Halifax), 4, 7 May 1888. John Doull, *Sketches of at-*

torney generals of Nova Scotia, 1750–1926 (Halifax, 1964), 70–74.

The courts and the Canadian constitution: a selection of essays, ed. W. R. Lederman (Toronto, 1964). *Leading constitutional decisions; cases on the British North America Act*, ed. P. H. Russell (Toronto, 1965). G. [G.] Patterson, *Studies in Nova Scotian history* (Halifax, 1940); *More studies in Nova Scotian history* (Halifax, 1941). D. G. Whidden, *The history of the town of Antigonish* (Wolfville, N.S., 1934), 89–90, 102–5. P. R. Blakeley, "William Alexander Henry, a father of confederation from Nova Scotia," N.S. Hist. Soc., *Coll.*, 36 (1968): 96–140. J. B. Brebner, "Joseph Howe and the Crimean War enlistment controversy between Great Britain and the United States," *CHR*, 11 (1930), 300–27.

HENSON, JOSIAH, fugitive slave, Methodist preacher, author, and founder of the settlement at Dawn (near Dresden), Canada West; b. 15 June 1789 in Charles County, Md, to slave parents; m. first *c.* 1811 Charlotte, a slave (she probably died October 1852), and they had at least 12 children; m. secondly *c.* 1856 Mrs Nancy Gamble, a free black widow; d. 5 May 1883 at Dresden, Ont.

Josiah Henson was given the Christian name of his first master, Dr Josiah McPherson, and the surname of his master's uncle. According to his autobiography, the only known source for his early life, Josiah was five when McPherson died and he was sold to less benign masters, first to a tyrant named Robb, and shortly thereafter to Isaac Riley in whose service he was reunited with his mother. As a young man Henson was "maimed for life," having an arm and both shoulder blades broken by the white overseer of a neighbour of his master. Faithful in his obligations, Henson was a trusted slave, travelling extensively on his master's business. In 1825, because of financial difficulties, Riley transferred his slaves to the farm of his brother Amos in Kentucky. Henson was charged with the supervision of the journey, and, refusing an opportunity to escape into Ohio, he delivered his charges. At 18 Henson had become a Christian after hearing his first sermon and during his three years in Kentucky he became a Methodist preacher. In September 1828, on the advice of a white Methodist preacher, Henson used a trip to see his master in Maryland as an excuse to tour the country as a preacher and earn money to buy his freedom. In 1829 he arranged the purchase but was betrayed by his master and was taken to New Orleans that same year to be sold. Saved only by the illness of his transporter, his master's son, which necessitated their return to Kentucky, Henson decided to flee, taking with him his wife and four children. After a long trek through Indiana and Ohio, they sailed to Buffalo whence, crossing the Niagara River, they finally reached Upper Canada on 28 Oct. 1830.

For approximately four years Henson worked as a farm labourer in the Waterloo area where he preached occasionally and began to learn to read. Then in 1834, having planned an exclusively black settlement, he led about a dozen of his associates to Colchester where they rented government land. Shortly after their arrival the group was freed from rent because of a mistake in the conditions of allotment; Henson had planned that they remain only a short time, but after this advantageous happening the settlers remained seven years. Here Henson met Hiram Wilson, the missionary sent by the American Anti-Slavery Society in 1836 to minister to Canadian blacks. Aided financially by Wilson's friend, James Cannings Fuller, a Quaker philanthropist of Skaneateles, N.Y., Henson decided to establish a more formally organized black community for fugitive slaves where they could prove their capacity for freedom. With Wilson and a silent partner (probably Fuller), he purchased 200 acres in Dawn Township, Upper Canada, "for the alone purpose . . . of Education Mental Moral and physical of the Coloured inhabitants of Canada not excluding white persons and Indians"; he also purchased 200 adjoining acres for himself to which he moved his family in 1842. The Canada Mission, a group originally composed of Wilson's friends in Ohio and later of philanthropists in upstate New York, provided continuing support.

Central to Dawn, as a living and working community, was the British-American Institute. Established in 1842 as a manual labour school for students of all ages, it was designed both to train teachers and to provide a general education "upon a full and practical system of discipline, which aims to cultivate the *entire being*, and elicit the fairest and fullest possible development of the physical, intellectual and moral powers." Throughout Dawn's existence, the institute remained its principal focus.

Until 1868 Henson served regularly on the institute's executive committee, which not only directed the school but oversaw the farms, grist-mill, sawmill, brickyard, and rope-walk which the settlement undertook. Yet he was never the community's official administrative head, a role always filled by a white man: first Wilson (1842–47), then Samuel H. Davis of the American Baptist Free Mission Society (1850–52), and finally John Scoble*, former secretary of the British and Foreign Anti-Slavery Society (1852–68). Throughout, however, Henson functioned as patriarch of Dawn and as a spokesman for Canada's growing black population. In both capacities, he raised funds by tours of the American Midwest, New England, and New York between 1843 and 1847 as well as England in 1849–51 and 1851–52.

Henson was also persistently involved in Dawn's internal dissensions and consequent investigations of the institute's effectiveness and financial management. In 1845 William P. Newman was appointed secretary of the executive committee to reorganize the management and he soon charged the committee, Henson included, with maladministration. Although two years later a Negro convention at Drummondville (now part of Niagara Falls, Ont.) cleared Henson of wrongdoing, in 1848 the trustees of the institute condemned the whole executive committee as "unfit" to direct the affairs of the school. Similarly, investigations in Britain in 1849 and 1852 produced equivocal findings which nourished doubts about Henson's aptitude.

Much of the tension was generated by conflicts between Henson, as spiritual and symbolic leader, and the official administrators. Spreading throughout the community, these dissensions racked Dawn and nearby centres of black settlement. They caused the resignation of Wilson in 1847, the failure of an attempt to rule by committee from 1847 to 1850, and the brevity of Davis' tenure. Even Scoble, who stayed at Dawn for 16 years, tangled increasingly with Henson over property sales and in subsequent lawsuits Scoble emerged victorious. In 1868, when the institute closed and after Scoble had left Dawn, the assets of the school were used to establish the Wilberforce Educational Institute in nearby Chatham. After this time the settlement died out and Henson, though he stayed on in Dresden until his death, had lost his role as a black leader.

In 1849 Henson had published his autobiography, which underwent numerous editions and modifications during his lifetime. Three years after the first edition appeared, Harriet Elizabeth Beecher Stowe's *Uncle Tom's cabin; or, life among the lowly* (2v., Boston and Cleveland, Ohio, 1852) was published. Stowe acknowledged that she had met Henson and read his book; thereafter, Henson was the putative prototype of the fictional "Uncle Tom." For some years he made lecture tours as the "real life Uncle Tom" and in 1876 he returned to England to raise funds to support himself, his resources having been depleted in his long court battle with Scoble. He also returned to his old slave home in Maryland briefly in 1877–78, but thereafter spent his last years quietly.

Although Josiah Henson had been a participant in abolitionist activity in the United States, his importance in Canadian history lies in his work at Dawn. It was here that he contributed significantly to Canada's role in the North American anti-slavery crusade.

WILLIAM H. PEASE and JANE H. PEASE

Josiah Henson's autobiography was published under the title: *An autobiography of the Rev. Josiah Henson ("Uncle Tom") from 1789 to 1881 . . .*, ed. John Lobb (rev. ed., London, Ont., 1881; repr., intro. R. W. Winks, Reading, Mass., 1969).

Amistad Research Center, Dillard Univ. (New Orleans), American Missionary Assoc. papers. Boston Public Library, Anti-slavery coll. Kent County Land Registry (Chatham, Ont.), Records (mfm. at AO). Massachusetts Hist. Soc. (Boston), G. E. Ellis papers, 1846; A. A. Lawrence papers, 1850–51. UWO, Fred Landon papers. Canada Mission, *Report* (Rochester, N.Y.), 1844. Colonial and Continental Church Soc., Mission to the Coloured Population in Canada, [*Report*] (London), 1867. *Report of the convention of the coloured population, held at Drummondville, Aug., 1847* (Toronto, 1847). *Scoble* v. *Henson* (1861–62), 12 U.C.C.P. 65. *A side-light on Anglo-American relations, 1839–1858, furnished by the correspondence of Lewis Tappan and others with the British and Foreign Anti-Slavery Society*, ed. A. H. Abel and F. J. Klingberg (Lancaster, Pa., 1927). *British and Foreign Anti-Slavery Reporter* (London), 1841, 1844, 1846, 1851–52, 1856. *Liberator* (Boston), 1842–43, 1845, 1848, 1851–52, 1858. *Massachusetts Abolitionist* (Boston), 1841–42. *National Anti-Slavery Standard* (New York), 1841, 1851. *North Star* (Rochester), 1846–47, 1849, 1852, 1854. *Oberlin Evangelist* (Oberlin, Ohio), 1845. *Planet* (Chatham), 1859, 1861. *Provincial Freeman* (Windsor, Toronto, and Chatham), 1854–55, 1857. *Voice of the Fugitive* (Sandwich and Windsor, [Ont.]), 1851–52. *DAB*. J. L. Beattie, *Black Moses: the real Uncle Tom* (Toronto, 1957). J. H. Pease and W. H. Pease, *Black Utopia: Negro communal experiments in America* (Madison, Wis., 1963); *Bound with them in chains: a biographical history of the antislavery movement* (Westport, Conn., 1972), 115–39. R. W. Winks, *The blacks in Canada: a history* (Montreal, 1971).

HERBOMEZ, LOUIS-JOSEPH D', Roman Catholic missionary, priest, and bishop; b. 17 Jan. 1822 at Brillon, dept of Nord, France, son of Louis d'Herbomez and Marie-Alexandrine Bricquet; d. 3 June 1890 at New Westminster, B.C.

Louis-Joseph d'Herbomez worked with his father as a shoeing-smith until he was 17 years old, when he began attending the Cambrai diocesan seminary. On 20 Nov. 1847 he entered the Oblates of Mary Immaculate noviciate at Nancy. He made his perpetual profession on 21 Nov. 1848 and on 14 Oct. 1849 Charles-Joseph-Eugène de Mazenod, bishop of Marseilles and founder of the Oblates, ordained him priest.

Sent to the Oblate missions in the Oregon Territory of the United States in 1850, d'Herbomez served under Father Pascal Ricard, the Oblate superior at Olympia (Wash.). From 1851 to 1853 he worked among the Yakima Indians and established the mission of St Joseph d'Ahtanum; during the last year he moved to Puget Sound to work with the Coast Salish. In 1856 d'Herbomez was appointed *visiteur extraordinaire* of the Oblate missions in Oregon and in 1858 he succeeded Ricard as missionary vicar.

During their stay in Oregon the Oblates were not able to establish good relations with local American government agents who disliked their working in Indian languages. Even after the Oblates had withdrawn from the Yakima Indian missions in 1855, relations with these agents did not improve; consequently in 1858 the Oblate superiors authorized d'Herbomez to move his headquarters north to Esquimalt (B.C.) in British territory. The Oblates, now under the protection of Modeste Demers*, the French-speaking bishop of Vancouver Island, and the friendly Hudson's Bay Company officers, planned missions both on the island and on the mainland. On Vancouver Island they started work with the Irish sailors of the Royal Navy, the white settlers, and the Indians from the mission they established at Esquimalt. On the mainland they began to work with the whites and Indians of the Fraser River mines and with the Indians of the Okanagan valley. Despite the influx of miners during the Fraser River gold-rush in 1858, the Indians remained numerically superior to the white population and were the focus of the Roman Catholic missionary efforts.

D'Herbomez's long-range plan for his missions to the Indians was to establish agricultural villages modelled on the reductions established by the Jesuits for the Indians of Paraguay in the 17th century. In these church-centred villages, separate from the debauched gold-rush towns, the Indians could live a temperate life, learn Christianity and agricultural methods, do public penance for sins, celebrate Catholic feasts instead of traditional Indian ones, and have their children educated in an industrial school. In the early 1860s the Oblates founded several reductions, as well as mission posts at New Westminster, Esquimalt, and Fort Rupert (near present-day Port Hardy) on northern Vancouver Island. From these posts the missionaries travelled to surrounding areas for instructional and liturgical gatherings. For the white population the Oblates, under d'Herbomez's direction, established parishes and schools, including St Louis College at Victoria.

On 22 Dec. 1863 d'Herbomez was appointed titular bishop of Miletopolis and vicar apostolic of the newly established vicariate of British Columbia. He was consecrated on 9 Oct. 1864 at Victoria by François-Norbert Blanchet and took up his seat in New Westminster a week later. D'Herbomez also retained his position as Oblate superior in British Columbia and over the next year, in an attempt to make the work of his congregation on the mainland autonomous from that of Bishop Demers, removed the Oblate missionary priests and brothers from the island diocese. In 1865 the Oblates established St Louis College at New Westminster. D'Herbomez encouraged the Sisters of St Anne to establish a school for girls there, and, in 1868, another at St Mary's Mission. By 1869 d'Herbomez had opened 55 chapels in Indian villages, begun developing mission districts such as those at William's Lake, Stuart's Lake, and Cranbrook, and made extensive pastoral tours. His health failing from the strain of his work, he had appointed Father Pierre-Paul Durieu*, the director of St Mary's Mission, as his assistant in 1867.

In 1869 d'Herbomez travelled to Europe to attend the Vatican Council. When he returned to British Columbia he recommended that the federal government set aside reserves for the Indians in existing villages, extinguish Indian title to the lands of the province, give them annual grants for agricultural implements, clothes, and blankets, and appoint Catholic agents for Catholic Indians. He especially requested the establishment of industrial and agricultural boarding-schools for Indian children pointing out that the Oblates had founded some schools of this type and intended to establish one in each mission district.

In June 1875 Durieu was appointed coadjutor bishop. Though still in poor health, d'Herbomez remained active and further expanded his missionary efforts to the Indians of Kamloops in 1878, to the construction crews of the Canadian Pacific Railway in the 1880s, and to the newly incorporated city of Vancouver in 1886. Despite the expansion of Roman Catholic missionary work and the praise given the Oblates for their work among the Indians, the success of the effort was ephemeral. Methodist and Church of England missionaries provided strong competition, and the apparent acceptance of the Oblates by the Indians was belied by their maintaining traditional religious practices and social activities. Moreover, mill and cannery work gave the Indians the funds for maintaining these traditions, and discouraged parents from allowing their children to attend the schools instead of adding to the family income. Although the huge devotional gatherings of Indians during the 1880s seemed to fulfil the early plans of d'Herbomez, the Oblate schools failed to enrol many Indian pupils or, if they did, to train them for long.

By 1887, when d'Herbomez went to Rome to attend the Oblates' general chapter, his ill health was more pronounced. In 1888 Durieu relieved d'Herbomez of his functions as missionary vicar. Two years later d'Herbomez died of stomach cancer and was buried at St Mary's Mission. Although it was Durieu rather than d'Herbomez who became known, through the writing of Father Adrien-Gabriel Morice*, as the founder and architect of the Oblate Indian mission villages such as Sechelt, contemporaries of d'Herbomez viewed these mission villages as "the fulfilment of all his dreams."

JACQUELINE GRESKO

L.-J. d'Herbomez was the author of "Letter from his lordship the bishop of Miletopolis and vicar apostolic of British Columbia . . . ," published in [H.-L. Langevin], *British Columbia: report of the Hon. H. L. Langevin, C.B., minister of public works* (Ottawa, 1872), 158–60, and of *Secular schools versus denominational schools* (n.p., 1881).

Arch. hist. oblates (Ottawa), G-LPP, d'Herbomez à Joseph Fabre, 4 févr., 1er juin 1864; 12 août 1867; 12 déc. 1873; 27 sept. 1884; d'Herbomez aux Conseils centraux de la Propagation de la Foi, 12 déc. 1864 (typescript); HPK 5001,

"Acte de visite de la maison de Ste Marie du 18 au 25 septembre 1882"; HPK 5241, Paul Durieu à LeJacq, 27 nov. 1883; 23, 25 févr. 1884; HPK 5282, Paul Durieu à d'Herbomez, 14 févr., 15 mars, 1er juin, 25 sept. 1869 (typescript). Can., Parl., *Sessional papers*, 1873, V: no.23; 1874, VI: no.17; 1875, VII: no.8; 1876, VII: no.9; 1877, VII: no.11; 1878, VIII: no.10; 1879, VI: no.7. *Consecration of the Right Rev. Dr. D'Herbomez, O.M.I., which has taken place in the Cathedral of St. Andrews, Victoria, V.I., October 9th, 1864 (21st Sunday after Pentecost)* (n.p., n.d.). *Missions de la Congrégation des missionnaires oblats de Marie Immaculée* (Marseille et Paris), 1 (1862), 2 (1863), 3 (1864), 4 (1865), 6 (1867), 9 (1870), 11 (1873), 17 (1879), 18 (1880), 19 (1881), 22 (1884), 24 (1886), 27 (1889), 28 (1890), 31 (1893). Robert Cooke, *Sketches of the life of Mgr. de Mazenod, bishop of Marseilles, and founder of the Oblates of Mary Immaculate, and of the missionary labours and travels of members of that society* . . . (2v., London and Dublin, 1879–82), I: 329–46. Kay Cronin, *Cross in the wilderness* (Vancouver, 1960). Gabriel Dionne, "Histoire des méthodes missionnaires utilisées par les Oblats de Marie Immaculée dans l'évangélisation des Indiens du 'versant Pacifique' au dix-neuvième siècle" (thèse de MA, univ. d'Ottawa, 1947). M. M. Down, *A century of service, 1858–1958: a history of the Sisters of Saint Ann and their contribution to education in British Columbia, the Yukon and Alaska* (Victoria, 1966). Wilson Duff, *The Indian history of British Columbia* (1v. to date, Victoria, 1964–), I: *The impact of the white man*. J. J. [Kennedy] Gresko, "Roman Catholic missionary effort and Indian acculturation in the Fraser valley, 1860–1900" (BA essay, Univ. of British Columbia, Vancouver, 1969). Sœur Marie-Rollande, *Mère Marie-Angèle, deuxième supérieure générale des Sœurs de Sainte-Anne, 1828–1898* (Montréal, 1941), 182–85. A.-G. Morice, *History of the Catholic Church in western Canada from Lake Superior to the Pacific (1659–1895)* (2v., Toronto, 1910), II.

"Hommes et choses d'autrefois; un champ d'apostolat trop peu connu: les Oblats dans l'Orégon et la Colombie Britannique," *Petites annales des missionnaires oblats de Marie Immaculée* (Paris), 37 (1932): 7, 73. E. M. Lemert, "The life and death of an Indian state," *Human Organization* (New York), 13 (1954–55), no.3: 23–27. Wayne Suttles, "The persistence of intervillage ties among the coast Salish," *Ethnology* (Pittsburgh, Pa.), 2 (1963): 521–25.

HIBBARD, ASHLEY, manufacturer, importer, railway contractor, and militia officer; b. 27 March 1827 at Stanstead, Lower Canada, son of Pliny V. Hibbard and Hannah Labaree; d. 23 March 1886 at his home near Frelighsburg, Que.

Although originally from New England, Ashley Hibbard's family was one of the oldest at Stanstead, his grandparents having arrived in the region from New Hampshire by 1807. About his education and early pursuits little is known.

During the first half of the 19th century the Stanstead area experienced rapid economic development – commercial operations expanded at an increasing rate and numerous industries, unusually specialized for the time, were established. These developments led to an intitial accumulation of capital which was often diverted away from regional channels of circulation. Thus by 1849, when Ashley Hibbard is first known to have been in Montreal, he already owned a hardware business. Five years later he invested £6,000 in a rubber footware factory, an enterprise in which he was involved with two partners, William Brown and George Bourn, in the firm of Brown, Hibbard, Bourn and Company. In 1856 their factory consisted of six buildings and was equipped with complex machinery driven by a steam engine; 158 workers produced daily more than 1,500 pairs of boots and shoes and half a ton of springs (for vehicles) and straps. These goods, intended partly for a local market, were also periodically shipped on the *Sarah Sands*, a steamship belonging to the company, to customers in Canada West, the Maritimes, the United States, and England.

In 1862, for reasons that are still obscure, Hibbard left the enterprise, then known as the British American Manufacturing Company (in 1910 it was to merge with other rubber manufacturers to form the Dominion Rubber Company Limited), and settled in England where he set up a large rubber factory in Manchester. Following his departure from Canada charges of embezzlement appear to have been brought against him. He returned to Canada in 1865, and the following year was indicted in Montreal by a grand jury in the Court of Queen's Bench. At this time he published the only pamphlet that he is known to have written, *A narrative and exposure of the evil of secret indictments, by grand juries*. The Montreal directories of 1866 to 1869 describe Hibbard as a merchant engaged in importing rubber, with offices on Rue Saint-Paul near the harbour.

In the ensuing years Hibbard became involved in railway construction. His name is listed in 1871 as one of the directors of the Montreal, Chambly and Sorel Railway Company, which in 1875 became the Montreal, Portland and Boston Railway Company. After this reorganization the company awarded the contract for the construction of the section between Saint-Lambert and Farnham to Francis A. Hibbard, a civil engineer. He gave Ashley power of attorney by notarial act, and the latter in fact became the builder of this section, which was to open in 1877. Meanwhile, the journeymen on this part of the road protested against the despotic measures being used by the company which was refusing to pay their outstanding wages even though it had obtained subsidies from the provincial government. But by 1877 the Montreal, Portland and Boston Railway Company was in bankruptcy and two different boards of directors were struggling to get possession of the line. Early in 1878 Hibbard appealed to the Quebec government to intervene to save the railway. He had borrowed $75,000 from the Bank of Montreal to finance the building of the section between Saint-Lambert and Farnham-Ouest and had also endorsed a loan of $2,000 obtained by the former president of the railway company. During the summer of 1878 the provincial government transferred $20,419 to the Bank of Montreal to cover part of the advance made to Hibbard. Late in 1878 and again early in 1879 Hibbard submitted reports to the government on the state of the company. By means of additional subsidies the section from Farnham-Ouest to Stanbridge was finished in 1879 and Hibbard continued to operate it until 1883. However, the Montreal, Portland and Boston Railway project was never completed, and the sections actually constructed were gradually abandoned by their respective owners. The Saint-Lambert to Farnham section built by Hibbard was closed by the government as too dangerous; in 1878 it ended up as part of the Grand Trunk.

Hibbard also dabbled in public affairs during the course of his career. In 1849 he signed the Annexation Manifesto [*see* Luther Hamilton Holton*] and in 1858 he ran for election to the Legislative Council in the division of Alma but was defeated by Joseph-François Armand. In 1863, two years after the *Trent* affair [*see* Charles Hastings DOYLE], Hibbard formed the 6th Battalion of militia (Hochelaga Light Infantry), and commanded it as lieutenant-colonel until his death. In 1870 this battalion was called up to counter the Fenian invasion at Eccles Hill, Quebec [*see* John O'Neill*].

Hibbard was reputed to be wealthy at the time of his death in 1886. He was then living on the family estate, Commeston, near Frelighsburg in the Eastern Townships. Early in the 1860s he had married Sarah Ann Lane, a native of Manchester, England, and later there was a second marriage. From these two marriages, 16 children survived him.

GAÉTAN GERVAIS

Ashley Hibbard was the author of *A narrative and exposure of the evil of secret indictments, by grand juries* (Montreal, [1866]), and of a report on the Montreal, Portland and Boston Railway Company at ANQ-Q, PQ, TP, Bureau des chemins de fer.

PAC, RG 30, 2790–93. *Débats de l'Assemblée législative* (M. Hamelin), [III], 2: 51. *Montreal in 1856; a sketch prepared for the celebration of the opening of the Grand Trunk Railway of Canada* (Montreal, 1856). *Gazette* (Montreal), 25 March 1886. Atherton, *Montreal*, III: 198–99. *Canadian men and women of the time* (Morgan, 1912), 531. *Dominion annual register*, 1886: 271. *Montreal directory*, 1842–71. P.-G. Roy, *Les juges de la prov. de Québec*, 569. Gaétan Gervais, "L'expansion du réseau ferroviaire québécois (1875–1895)" (thèse de PHD, univ. Laval, Québec, 1978). M. Hamelin, *Premières années du parlementarisme québécois*, 195–96. B. F. Hubbard, *Forests and clearings; the history of Stanstead County, province of Quebec, with sketches of more than five hundred families*, ed. John Lawrence (2nd ed., Montreal, 1963), 91–92, 96, 120–21. Leslie Roberts, *From three men* (n.p., 1954). G. F. G. Stanley, *Canada's soldiers; the military history of an unmilitary people* (rev. ed., Toronto, 1960), 229–30.

HIGGINSON, Sir JAMES MACAULAY, soldier, office-holder, and colonial administrator; b. in 1805 in Ireland, son of Major James Higginson and Mary Macaulay; m. first Louisa Shakespear and secondly Olivia Dobbs; d. 28 June 1885 in County Wicklow (Republic of Ireland).

James Macaulay Higginson was educated at Trinity College, Dublin, before entering the Bengal army in 1824. He served in several campaigns and came to the notice of Sir Charles Theophilus Metcalfe* at the siege of Bhurtpore in 1825–26. When Metcalfe was appointed deputy governor of Bengal in 1829 Higginson became a member of his personal staff; the association lasted until Metcalfe's death in 1846. Higginson acted as military secretary to Sir Charles on his various postings in India, 1833–37, and by 1838 had risen to the rank of captain in the Bengal army. Although his later appointments in the imperial service were civil ones, he continued to use his military title until 1846.

Higginson sailed from India for Bristol with Metcalfe on 15 Feb. 1838 and spent the next year in England. When Sir Charles was made governor of Jamaica on 11 July 1839 Higginson, accompanied by his family, went along as his private secretary; the governor formed affectionate and long-lasting ties with Higginson's children. After his return to England with Metcalfe in 1842, Higginson was at "loose ends." Although he seems to have continued to be involved in Metcalfe's affairs, he was also engaged in a commercial venture in India on his own; it was unsuccessful and Metcalfe made good his losses.

Sir Charles accepted the governorship of Canada in January 1843 and early in March Higginson was appointed his civil and private secretary. After their arduous winter journey overland from Boston to Kingston, Canada West, in part in horse-drawn sleighs, Metcalfe began a tenure of office in Canada which was to be unhappy, not only because of his differences with the Reformers about the implications of responsible government but also because of his constantly worsening cancer of the cheek. He resigned in the autumn of 1845 and returned home in December.

Metcalfe's illness caused a heavy administrative load to fall upon the shoulders of Higginson, who had to conduct government business almost single-handed. His correspondence for 1843 covers a wide range of subjects: the disturbances on the Welland Canal, the St Lawrence ice-bridge at Quebec City, measures pertaining to quarantine ships, furnishings of the provincial lunatic asylum at Toronto, the land grant for King's College in Toronto, civil service pensions, and projects of the Board of Works. Higginson became the governor general's adviser, political spokesman, and messenger, often dealing with disgruntled Reformers. As early as May 1843 Higginson had a long conversation with Louis-Hippolyte La Fontaine* on the nature of responsible government. One of their chief disagreements arose over patronage; Higginson maintained that some appointments were the prerogative of the governor general while La Fontaine argued that patronage "ought to be bestowed exclusively on us." Higginson's report of this conversation to Metcalfe did not endear him to the Reformers. When in November a crisis arose leading to the resignation of La Fontaine, Robert Baldwin,* and the other ministers, except Dominick Daly*, Higginson received some of the odium bestowed on Metcalfe. Reformers suspected Higginson of misleading Metcalfe and derisively labelled him "the everlasting secretary."

Higginson's other major concern in Canada was the Indian Department. On 22 Jan. 1844 the report of a royal commission established by Sir Charles Bagot* in 1842 recommended major administrative changes in departmental structure and personnel, including the suggestion that "the management of the Indians be placed under the Civil Secretary." Higginson became superintendent general of Indian affairs on 15 May. Under him the recommendations made by the commissioners "were for the most part carried into effect," including, on 1 July 1845, the abolition of the office of chief superintendent for Canada West. At that time this office was held by Samuel Peters Jarvis*, who had been suspected of having mismanaged department monies.

Scurrilous rumours began to circulate about the nature of the relationship between Higginson and Metcalfe; one even suggested that Higginson's wife, Olivia, was Metcalfe's illegitimate daughter. He survived these innuendoes and remained in Canada until the spring of 1846 when he departed for the West Indies. After Metcalfe's death in September gossip-mongers doubtless took pleasure in the terms of his will: his former secretary was one of its chief beneficiaries, inheriting £20,000. Higginson served as governor of Antigua and the Leeward Islands, 1846–50, and of Mauritius and the Seychelles, 1850–57. He retired to Ireland in the autumn of 1857, living there until his death. He was made a CB in March 1851 and raised to a KCB in 1857.

The career of James Macaulay Higginson, at the second or third level of the imperial service, is typical of those of thousands of men who worked diligently and unobtrusively throughout the 19th century to run the far-flung empire. The study of such careers casts clearer light not only on events but also on the nature of colonial relationships during this important period.

DOUGLAS LEIGHTON

J. M. Higginson papers are in the possession of T. B. Higginson (Scarborough, Ont.).

BNQ, MSS-101, Coll. La Fontaine (copies at PAC). MTL, Samuel Peters Jarvis papers. PAC, MG 24, A33; RG 7, G1, 405; RG 8, I (C ser.), 60, 79; RG 10, A4, 508–9; A5, 263, 510–12, 622–23, 752–53; A6, 116–18; B8, 766–67. [T. T. Higginson], *Diaries . . .* , ed. T. B. Higginson (London, 1960). J. W. Kaye, *The life and correspondence of Charles, Lord Metcalfe* (rev. ed., 2v., London, 1858). *Times* (London), 7 July 1885. T. B. Higginson, *Descendants of the Reverend Thomas Higginson* (London, 1958). S. [B.] Leacock, *Baldwin, LaFontaine, Hincks; responsible government* (Toronto, 1907). J. D. Leighton, "The development of federal Indian policy in Canada, 1840–1890" (PHD thesis, Univ. of Western Ontario, London, 1975). E. [J.] Thompson, *The life of Charles, Lord Metcalfe* (London, 1937). C. B. Sissons, "Ryerson and the elections of 1844," *CHR*, 23 (1942): 157–76.

HILL, HENRY GEORGE, carpenter, architect, and entrepreneur; baptized 8 Dec. 1805 at Halifax, N.S., son of Henry and Sarah Hill; m. Hester Maria before 1833; no children are known; d. 7 Jan. 1882 at Somerville, Mass.

Henry George Hill's father was a carpenter and Hill probably learned from him the basic trade skills on which he built his ambitious career. By 1833 Hill was well established in Halifax as a house-carpenter and joiner. After a brief period of cabinet-making, upholstering, and interior decoration, he devoted himself in 1836 exclusively to architectural designing and "Plain and Ornamental Building." By then Hill, an active Methodist, had already designed and built Brunswick Street Wesleyan Methodist Chapel (1833–34) and during the late 1830s he apparently erected at least two other Methodist chapels in Halifax. These churches and his neo-classical designs for the Bank of Nova Scotia (1836), a private school façade (1842), a suburban cottage (1842), and a villa (1843, occupied in 1859 by the Institution for the Deaf and Dumb) gave Hill a solid reputation in architecture. He concentrated on domestic work but also designed commercial and public buildings, which included Temperance Hall (1849), the Halifax County Court House (1854 but not to Hill's design), and the city's Rockhead Prison (1855). Although Hill's plans were undoubtedly based upon British and American pattern-books, he was regarded locally as "an architect of judgment and taste."

Hill's principal working material was wood and, backed by a construction section under master carpenter John Mumford, he appears to have been Halifax's most active designer before such formally trained architects as William Thomas* and David STIRLING began executing commissions there in the 1850s. This competition, the increasing use of stone, brick, and cast iron in Halifax buildings, and financial strain occasioned Hill's gradual withdrawal from active participation in the design field. His only known design after 1857 was the elegant store built in 1859 for the Halifax dry goods firm of John Doull and William

Miller, but he performed architectural tasks of a supervisory and evaluative nature for the Nova Scotia government in the 1860s and the federal government in the early 1870s.

The critical event in Hill's career was the wharf contract undertaken for the Ordnance department at Halifax in 1849. After his coffer-dam failed, Hill sued the department on the grounds that its inaccurate specifications had prevented his fulfilment of the contract. In the case heard by the Supreme Court of Nova Scotia in 1856, Hill had overwhelming public sympathy. This legal confrontation gave focus to Haligonian grievances against the military's stinted contracts and bureaucratic manner. The court awarded Hill a substantial sum (about half of his £20,000 claim) but the government obtained a rule nisi against the decision. Heavy financial loss led to Hill's decision to rechannel his building interests. As a builder he had developed a wood-product supply business, which he now pursued as his principal concern. In 1860 he established the Prince Albert Steam Saw Mill where, five years later, he installed advanced planing machinery imported from the United States. By the early 1870s the mill was the largest sash, door, and blind factory in Nova Scotia.

Hill's other major business activity was speculative development, which supplemented his contract work. Between 1833 and 1873 he bought numerous Halifax properties, many in the city's expanding suburbs. On some lots he built houses which he either sold or rented; others he held, anticipating advantageous sales for building purposes, and a few he resold for immediate profit. Among Hill's creditors for his various business transactions were fellow Methodists Edward Jost of Halifax and several members of the prominent family of the Reverend William Black*.

Hill's financial situation was always precarious. The depression of the 1870s led to the assignment of his property to creditors in 1873 and the resulting litigation failed to relieve his pecuniary distress. Hill continued to describe himself as an architect, however, and he probably prepared plans from time to time until he left Halifax in 1880.

Closely related to his professional and religious interests were Hill's public activities. He was a member of the Halifax Temperance Society and a director of the Nova Scotia Benefit Building Society, founded in 1850. Elected to Halifax City Council in October 1862, Hill subsequently chaired the property, streets, and city prison committees, where his building experience was particularly applicable. He resigned from council in March 1865.

Henry G. Hill was remarkable for his success, however uncertain, in sustaining himself as a native-born designer and entrepreneur in mid-19th-century Halifax. His ambition and industry, coupled with a capacity to sustain risk and to adapt, account for his achievements as an architect, manufacturer, and developer.

SUSAN BUGGEY

Bank of Nova Scotia Arch. (Toronto), Directors' minute book, 1832–75. Can., Parks Canada (Ottawa), Canadian Inventory of Historic Building, Group D, H. G. Hill. Halifax County Registry of Deeds (Halifax), Deeds, 1833–89 (mfm. at PANS). PAC, RG 8, I (C ser.), 1814–15, 1839; RG 11, D2, 3840; 3841–42; 3848; RG 31, A1, 1871, Halifax, Ward 1; Yarmouth. PANS, H. G. Hill, Plan of Rockhead Prison, Halifax, May 1855; MG 4, Brunswick Street United Church (Halifax), Minnie Bell, "History of the Brunswick Street Wesleyan Chapel, 1834–1934" (mfm.); Registers, 23 Sept. 1804, 8 Dec. 1805 (mfm.). PRO, WO 1/551: ff.1–15, 775–85; 49/2, pt.1: ff.760–61. Duncan Campbell, *Nova Scotia, in its historical, mercantile and industrial relations* (Montreal, 1873), 511–12. Halifax, *Annual report of the several departments of the city government . . .* (Halifax), 1862–64. N.S., House of Assembly, *Journal and proc.*, 1851, app.52; 1854–55, app.15; 1857: 371; 1865: 88, 90; 1866, app.9; 1867, app.4. *Acadian Recorder*, 6 April, 7 Dec. 1833; 16 Dec. 1854; 1, 15 Dec. 1855; 17 Jan., 3 Oct., 7 Dec. 1857; 5 Aug. 1859; 13 April 1861; 4, 11 Oct. 1862; 1, 27 March, 6 May 1865; 17 Nov., 1 Dec. 1866; 2 Jan. 1867. *British Colonist* (Halifax), 4 Sept. 1849; 9 Feb., 4 June 1850; 27 June 1862. *Evening Express* (Halifax), 17 Sept., 20 Oct. 1862; 13, 27 May 1863; 23 Dec. 1864; 27 March, 19 May 1865. *Halifax Evening Reporter*, 18 Dec. 1860; 31 Jan., 4 May 1861; 3 Dec. 1862; 25 March 1865; 13 Sept. 1871; 1 July 1879. *Halifax Morning Sun*, 30 Nov. 1859. *Morning Herald* (Halifax), 13 Jan. 1882. *Novascotian*, 5 Feb. 1836; 2 June, 1 Sept. 1842; 5 June 1843; 13 May 1844; 23 June 1845; 15 June 1846; 28 Aug. 1848; 19 March, 6 Sept., 10 Dec. 1849; 11 March 1850; 1 Nov. 1852; 1 Sept., 22, 29 Dec. 1856; 6, 12, 19, 26 Jan., 2 Feb., 7 Dec. 1857; 15 Feb., 17 May 1858; 5 Sept. 1859; 24 Sept., 26 Nov. 1860. *The Halifax, N.S. business directory . . .*, comp. Luke Hutchinson (Halifax), 1863. *McAlpine's Halifax city directory . . .* (Halifax), 1869–78. *Nugent's business directory for the city of Halifax . . .* (Halifax), 1858–59. T. W. Smith, *History of the Methodist Church within the territories embraced in the late conference of Eastern British America . . .* (2v., Halifax, 1877–90), II: 208–12. Susan Buggey, "Building Halifax, 1841–1871," *Acadiensis*, 10 (1980–81), no.1: 90–112.

HINCKS, Sir FRANCIS, banker, journalist, politician, and colonial administrator; b. 14 Dec. 1807 in Cork (Republic of Ireland), the youngest of nine children of the Reverend Thomas Dix Hincks and Anne Boult; m. first 29 July 1832 Martha Anne Stewart (d. 1874) of Legoniel, near Belfast (Northern Ireland), and they had five children; m. secondly 14 July 1875 Emily Louisa Delatre, widow of Robert Baldwin Sullivan*; d. 18 Aug. 1885 in Montreal, Que.

Francis Hincks's father was a Presbyterian clergyman whose interest in education and social reform led him to resign his pastorate and devote himself full time to teaching. His elder sons, of whom William* was one, became university teachers or clergymen, and it was assumed that Francis would follow in their footsteps. However, after briefly attending the Royal Belfast Academical Institution in 1823, he expressed a strong preference for a business career and was apprenticed to a Belfast shipping firm, John Martin and Company, in that year.

In August 1832 Hincks and his bride of two weeks departed for York (Toronto), Upper Canada. He had visited the colony during the winter of 1830–31 while investigating business opportunities in the West Indies and the Canadas. Early in December he opened a wholesale dry goods, wine, and liquor warehouse in premises rented from William Warren Baldwin* and his son Robert*; the two families soon became close friends. Hincks's first advertisement in the *Colonial Advocate* offered sherry, Spanish red wine, Holland Geneva (gin), Irish whiskey, dry goods, boots and shoes, and stationery to the general merchants of Upper Canada.

Because his wholesale business was frequently in financial difficulties, Hincks readily accepted the invitation of George Truscott* and John Cleveland Green in 1835 to join them in founding the joint-stock Farmers' Bank and to serve as cashier (general manager). When the bank's directors elected Tories as president (John Elmsley*) and solicitor, several prominent Reformers, such as James LESSLIE, James Hervey PRICE, and Dr John Rolph*, withdrew and in the same year formed the Bank of the People. Hincks cast his lot with the Reformers and became cashier of the new bank. He welcomed other opportunities in new enterprises: in 1836 he was a founder of the Home District Mutual Fire Insurance Company of Upper Canada and its first secretary.

From the outset of his political career Hincks was, like Robert Baldwin, a moderate Reformer, with misgivings about the radical wing of the movement led by William Lyon Mackenzie*. After the Reform victory in the provincial election of 1834 Hincks was one of two auditors chosen by a select committee of the assembly investigating the Welland Canal Company to examine its books. Most of the Reformers, including Hincks, received well the news of the appointment of Sir Francis Bond Head* as lieutenant governor of Upper Canada in December 1835. They quickly became disillusioned, however, for Head's conduct, especially during the election campaign of 1836, convinced them they could not hope to achieve responsible government while he remained in office. In the autumn of 1837 Hincks was alarmed to learn that some Reformers led by Mackenzie were plotting rebellion. He was not in their confidence, but suspected that some of the directors of his bank were still associated with Mackenzie and he knew that Rolph was deeply involved. The attempt at rebellion in December was easily crushed but a decided reaction against the Reform movement followed. Amid accusations and rumours, Hincks went into hiding for a week until the hysteria cooled. Some Reformers, including Peter Perry*, Thomas Parke*, Price, and Lesslie, despaired of obtaining reform and thought of leaving British North America. Sharing this pessimism, Hincks joined the Mississippi Emigration Society which planned to organize a mass migration to Iowa, and on its behalf went to Washington to investigate the possibility of securing a large block of land. By the time he returned to Upper Canada in early 1838 Lord Durham [Lambton*] had been appointed to investigate the causes for the rebellions in Upper and Lower Canada. Hope was rekindled among the Reformers, and the society decided to postpone definite plans until Durham had submitted his recommendations.

Anxious to promote their cause while awaiting Durham's arrival, Reformers such as Hincks and Price travelled to the villages north of Toronto with a strong Reform tradition. They were conscious of the need for a newspaper to explain the implications of responsible government and to emphasize that moderate Reformers rejected rebellion and sought to attain their ends by following British examples. Hincks resigned in June 1838 from the Bank of the People to establish the *Examiner* in Toronto.

Its first issue was published on 3 July with the motto "Responsible Government" to which the words "and the Voluntary Principle" were soon added. For the next four years, while Hincks remained proprietor and editor, these were its predominant editorial themes: parliamentary government on the British model, and support of religious bodies only by the voluntary contributions of their adherents. Possibly Hincks's editorials helped persuade Durham that responsible government was the basic reform needed to establish harmony between the executive and the assembly.

Hincks and his contemporaries did not have a uniform and cohesive notion about what they meant by responsible government, but generally they meant the parliamentary form of government that was evolving in Great Britain. Following this model they urged that the governor's advisers should be chosen from among the group which could command a majority in the assembly and that the governor should act on their advice. Thus they could be held responsible by the assembly for the governor's actions. They saw responsible government as the means of wresting control of Upper Canada from the Tories and of obtaining the power they needed to implement a reform programme. But there was no general agreement as to what that programme should be. In the 1840s most Upper Canadian Reformers agreed that the clergy reserves should be secularized, but it is doubtful whether a majority of French Canadian Reformers shared this view. By the 1850s, Hincks would give top priority to using political power to forward railway projects and developmental schemes.

Durham's report, containing the recommendations

that Upper and Lower Canada should become a single colony, that expenditures should be introduced in the legislature by members of the executive, and, most particularly, that responsible government should be introduced in the Canadas, stimulated a Reform revival in Upper Canada after it reached the colony early in April 1839. Through the *Examiner* Hincks soon became recognized as the principal political spokesman and strategist of the Upper Canadian Reformers although Baldwin was the acknowledged leader. Hincks perceived immediately that if Upper Canadian Reformers joined forces with their French Canadian counterparts the united party might be wellnigh invincible. Taking the initiative, on 12 April 1839 he wrote an exploratory letter to Louis-Hippolyte La Fontaine*, leader of the Lower Canadian Reformers. "Lord Durham ascribes to you national objects," he observed. "If he is right, union would be ruin to you, if he is wrong, & that you are really desirous of liberal institutions & economical government, the union would in my opinion give you all you desire. . . ." His background and bias led Hincks to think only in terms of individual political and social liberty; he likely shared Durham's assumption that the assimilation of French Canada was inevitable. However, through their correspondence and association, Hincks and La Fontaine came to understand the hopes and fears of Reformers in each other's province. For his part, Hincks constantly stressed two basic ideas: responsible government was the means by which any desirable reform could be attained; and a union of the Canadas offered the best opportunity to obtain responsible government because it would enable the Reformers of the two provinces to cooperate in achieving their aims. It was typical of Hincks that it was he, rather than Baldwin, who had established contact with La Fontaine. But in spite of his most persuasive arguments he failed in his attempt at having the Reformers work together; the French Canadian Reformers did not believe they could rely on the support of their counterparts in Upper Canada. It remained for Baldwin and La Fontaine to consummate an alliance on the basis of personal friendship in the early 1840s, although Hincks had contributed greatly to the understanding that made the alliance possible.

The first election after the union of the Canadas in February 1841 took place in March and Hincks was pleased with the results. He was elected in Oxford County, and, according to his analysis, in Canada West the Reformers had won 19 seats, the supporters of Governor Sydenham [Thomson*] 17, and the Tories 5. The results from Canada East were less promising. French Canadian Reformers had elected a majority, but gerrymandering, the governor's influence, and violence at the polls had deprived them of seats they had fully expected to win. Hincks began to fear that in their resentment French Canadians might adopt an uncooperative, anti-union stance. To counteract this danger he wrote to La Fontaine's lieutenant, Augustin-Norbert Morin*, proposing strategy to gain responsible government when the legislature met.

To his surprise Hincks found, when the session began in June, that it was the Reformers of Canada West who did not remain steadfast to the cause of a united Reform group. Baldwin and Hincks knew that evidence of good faith must be given to La Fontaine and his followers. But most Upper Canadian Reformers were aware that their constituents wanted the public works promised by Sydenham and they refused to risk losing these projects by supporting the French Canadians in their opposition to the governor. When it became apparent that an alliance would not materialize during the session, Hincks's basic pragmatism led him to reassess his own position. Rather than constantly opposing the government, he decided to support measures of which he approved. Soon he came to feel that there were liberal men connected with the administration, such as Charles Dewey DAY and Henry Black*, and that "practical responsibility" had been conceded, if not the full theory of responsible government. Before the session ended Hincks had voted against Baldwin and the French Canadians on a number of measures including a bill to establish municipal councils in Upper Canada, and had become interested in Sydenham's proposal to create a government bank of issue. Bitter words were exchanged and a rift developed between Hincks and Baldwin. Ironically, after the session ended the prospects for a united Reform party improved. Largely through Baldwin's efforts La Fontaine was elected for the 4th riding of York on 23 Sept. 1841. And, as errant Reformers returned to Baldwin's leadership, it appeared the government would not be strong enough to carry its measures in the next session.

Advised by the Colonial Office to strengthen his government, Sir Charles Bagot*, Sydenham's successor, offered Hincks the office of inspector general of public accounts in June 1842. Hincks readily accepted and thereby earned the reputation of being a political opportunist. He sold the *Examiner* to Lesslie upon taking office. Bagot's expectation that Hincks would align moderate Reformers from Canada East and West with the government did not materialize and the governor soon realized he must obtain the support of the French Canadian bloc in the assembly. He entered into negotiations that culminated in La Fontaine and Baldwin joining the administration in September 1842. Hincks was thus reunited with his former colleagues, but he was still regarded as a traitor by many Upper Canadian Reformers who agreed with Price that his presence "polluted" the administration. Hincks had never ceased to consider himself a Reformer; he showed no hesitation now in resuming an active role in the movement and was soon advising Baldwin on political tactics. As inspector general he took steps to improve the collection of customs duties and to establish more efficient accounting practices in the office of the receiver general, John Henry Dunn*.

Bagot had sought the support of La Fontaine and his followers in order to maintain harmony between the executive and the assembly, but before he could judge the success of his "great measure" he became ill and asked to be replaced. At the end of March 1843 his successor, Sir Charles Theophilus Metcalfe*, arrived. Hincks was initially impressed by the new governor. Bagot had been instructed by the colonial secretary, Lord Stanley, to resist any attempt by the Reformers to alter the civil list established by the imperial act of union. None the less, when his council objected to the imperial government's determining the civil list, Metcalfe asked Hincks to prepare a memorandum and used it to renew Bagot's proposal to the British parliament that the Canadian legislature be permitted to pass a civil list of its own. On the question of control of patronage Metcalfe was obviously sensitive. Both his own inclinations and Stanley's instructions led him to resist any attempt by the Reformers to gain acceptance of their claim that the Executive Council must be consulted on all appointments. But even on this question Hincks observed to Baldwin that the governor was "really . . . acting very well and is I think improving." Anxious to meet Metcalfe half way, Hincks advised Baldwin that the Executive Council ought to appoint a reasonable number of Tory magistrates in the Home District to show the governor that the Reformers were fair and that they appreciated his "not objecting to a single name" among the officials they nominated for the districts of Gore and Simcoe.

Such impressions were short lived. Soon after his arrival in Canada Metcalfe began to suspect that his Executive Council probably intended to force a test of responsible government by tendering advice he could not accept and resigning *en masse* when he refused it. He hoped the test would come over control of patronage, which he felt he could defend, rather than over other contentious issues such as the civil list, the location of the capital, or an amnesty for those exiled for their involvement in the rebellions of 1837–38. The crisis occurred on 26 Nov. 1843. The entire council, with the exception of Dominick Daly*, announced their intention to resign because Metcalfe would not agree that the council was responsible to the assembly and consequently that it must always be consulted before an appointment was made. On 12 December Daly, William Henry Draper*, and Denis-Benjamin Viger* were sworn in as members of council, but the governor was unsuccessful in forming a new council that would have the support of a majority in the assembly. Finally, he appealed to the province and called a general election in September of 1844. The new assembly contained a slight majority of the governor's supporters, but most of these were elected from Canada West. Among the Lower Canadian members his supporters were in a decided minority, with virtually no French Canadians. This imbalance continued until the La Fontaine–Baldwin administration was formed after the general election in 1848.

Throughout the crisis, Hincks had remained steadfast to the Reform cause. In the midst of it Baldwin's father died and, in a state of depression, the Reform leader decided to withdraw from politics. Hincks's friendship with Baldwin, and his insistence that Baldwin's resignation would seriously damage the Reform movement, helped persuade him to remain at his post.

In February 1844 Hincks was given an opportunity once more to combine his political career with journalism. Despite Baldwin's misgivings, La Fontaine and Theodore HART, a Montreal Reformer, invited Hincks to take over as editor of the Montreal *Times and Commercial Advertiser* in order to make it a reliable Reform organ. He accepted and, upon moving to Montreal, became active in the Unitarian community. Hincks soon found that the proprietor of the paper, Hutton Perkins, would neither give him a free hand editorially nor sell the paper to him. Consequently, with financial assistance from Hart, Baldwin, and La Fontaine, he established a new newspaper in Montreal, the *Pilot*, whose first issue was published on 5 March. Completely at home with the vituperative journalism of his day, Hincks was soon writing editorials that provoked heated responses from Tory editors. Having frequently witnessed the intimidation of Reformers in Canada West by Tory mobs, he could now not resist encouraging the use of Irish canal workers to disrupt Tory meetings. Speaking at every election meeting, and sometimes providing a brass band, stressing that the Tories were the traditional enemies of the French Canadians, and playing on Irish prejudices, Hincks worked diligently at cementing the alliance between the Irish and the French Canadians. His efforts contributed to the victory of Reform candidate Lewis Thomas DRUMMOND in the by-election in Montreal in April 1844 – a significant rebuff to Metcalfe and the Tories since Montreal had been regarded as a Tory stronghold. Hincks was confident that in his short time in Montreal he had united French and Irish, and this, he informed Baldwin, "will secure us in future from much trouble."

Thoroughly engrossed with his newspaper, Hincks began to doubt whether he would wish to hold office again. "My *Ambition* is satisfied, and I really have no desire personally to go back, and I think to be of the most service to the party, I had better remain as I am," he advised Baldwin in May. Still, he sought re-election when Metcalfe dissolved the legislature in September 1844. He attributed his unexpected defeat in Oxford County by Robert Riddell to the Scots of Zorra Township whose Presbyterian conscience he had offended when he supported John Prince*'s bill permitting hunting of game on Sunday. Baldwin suspected that the *Pilot*'s wide-ranging attacks on the Scottish Tory merchants of Montreal were probably an additional factor.

Hincks soon realized that the *Pilot* required numerous subscriptions from Upper Canada's Reformers in order to survive: most Reformers in Canada East were French and not likely to subscribe to an English paper, and most of the Montreal merchants were Tories and unlikely to advertise in it. But Hincks's efforts in Canada West soon brought him into conflict with George Brown* who naturally felt that subscriptions to the *Pilot* should not be encouraged at the expense of the *Globe*. Their newspapers were not the only source of friction between the two men. Hincks suspected Brown of aspiring to replace him as the Reform candidate in Oxford at the next election. Brown, he confided to Baldwin in September 1845, "has been there exerting himself *not only against the Pilot* but against *me* personally. His object is to unseat me for that Co & as my friends think *to substitute himself*. He proposes also to substitute [Edward Blake*] for you as a leader. My information *can be relied on*." Brown, in correspondence with Baldwin, denied having any political aspirations, and all the evidence indicates that Hincks's suspicions were unwarranted. Isolated as he was from Upper Canadian politics and having lost his seat in the assembly, Hincks was prone to believe any rumour he heard. He was becoming critical of the leadership provided by Baldwin and La Fontaine and bitter over the failure of Lower Canadian Reform leaders to provide adequate support for the *Pilot*.

He frequently considered selling the paper and almost did so in 1847 when a profit of $4,500 on investments in the Echo Lake Mining Company and the Lake Huron Silver and Copper Mining Company gave him sufficient funds to satisfy his creditors. But in the end he decided to keep it; he enjoyed journalism and the *Pilot* enabled him to serve as the link between Reformers from Canada East and West. Hincks also knew that he had considerable influence with the French Canadian leaders. Between 1845 and 1847 when, under the guise of recognizing the equity of the double majority principle, Draper sought to separate the French Canadian members from La Fontaine's leadership and from their alliance with the Upper Canadian Reformers, Hincks's influence and advice were important factors in keeping the Reformers from Canada East united and steadfast to the cause.

The legislature was dissolved and an election called in late 1847 while Hincks was in Ireland, his first visit since his arrival in Canada. After briefly investigating prospects in both Canada East and Canada West, Baldwin decided Hincks's best chance for re-election was still in Oxford County and asked Brown to campaign on his behalf. Though Hincks returned to Canada before the election, urgent private business prevented him from leaving Montreal to make even a token appearance in his constituency: Theodore Hart had been unable to meet a note valued at £450 held by Hincks, and the latter had had subsequently to borrow money on the note. He owed his election to the efforts of Brown and of Thomas Strahan Shenston*, his political agent in Oxford. But such knowledge, rather than improving relations between Hincks and Brown, likely increased Hincks's sense of insecurity and his suspicions of Brown.

Despite his past doubts Hincks sold the *Pilot* and readily accepted the office of inspector general in the ministry formed by La Fontaine and Robert Baldwin in March 1848. He soon became aware of the extent to which rumours of political instability together with mismanagement and over-expenditure had undermined the financial reputation and credit of the province which had been borrowing heavily to finance public works without making adequate provisions to repay debts. His predecessor as inspector general, William CAYLEY, had not established a sinking fund and had failed to pay either interest or principal on a loan of £140,000 he had floated in 1846. Yet, Hincks found when he took office, expenditures for public works were still increasing. Canadian debentures could only be sold in London at a large discount and financial institutions were reluctant to handle them at all. Hincks set to work to restore the province's credit. Largely as a result of his efforts both Baring Brothers and Glyn, Halifax, Mills and Company took on the role of Canadian financial agents in England, and soon the debentures were selling at a premium. In the session of the legislature which opened in January 1849, Hincks sponsored a bill which created a sinking fund for the eventual retirement of the provincial debt.

Hincks's other great interest in this session was the Railway Guarantee Act. Intended to stimulate railway construction in Canada, the act authorized a government guarantee of six per cent interest on half the bonded debt of any railway over 75 miles in length after half the line had been built. Hincks was convinced that railways were the key to Canadian economic development and was pleased when his act encountered little opposition within the legislature despite the prevailing depression. The government's Rebellion Losses Bill, however, generated a violent storm in the legislature, abuse of Governor General Lord Elgin [Bruce*], and a riot in Montreal which resulted in the burning of the Parliament Buildings and attacks on the houses of Hincks and La Fontaine. When the Tories sent Sir Allan Napier MacNab* and Cayley to England to urge the disallowance of the act, the government chose Hincks to counteract their efforts. Upon his arrival in England he found there was no possibility of the act being disallowed, and he concentrated instead on promoting Canadian securities as an attractive investment.

Just as his efforts began to bear fruit, reports arrived of agitation in Canada for annexation. Hincks realized that under such conditions Canadian bonds had little attraction for British investors and, feeling completely frustrated, he left for Canada. He arrived back in Montreal to find that an annexation manifesto had been signed by many business and professional men, predominantly from Canada East, including the Reform leaders Luther Hamilton Holton* and Antoine-Aimé Dorion*. In correspondence with Baldwin he was soon criticizing him and La Fontaine for their weak leadership in a time of crisis. "Had *prompt* measures been taken with the annexationists," he declared to Baldwin, "they would have been down by this time instead of increasing in influence & numbers." He urged that those who had signed the manifesto be stripped of offices and honours. In this mood he considered his retirement from office. However, by the spring of 1850, with the annexation movement in decline, Canada's reputation on the London money market improved. Possibly, too, Britain's recovery from the financial crisis of 1847–48 helped to create a more favourable climate for the sale of Canadian debentures. Before the end of May 1850 the balance of a £500,000 Canadian loan had been negotiated and the debentures had been sold slightly above par.

It was with considerable misgivings that Hincks learned in the spring of 1851 that Brown was contemplating running for the assembly in a by-election in Haldimand. For some time he had feared that Brown's extreme voluntaryism could threaten the Reform alliance with La Fontaine and his followers. Moreover, since December, when the *Globe* had reported fully on the "papal aggression question" in Great Britain and given it Canadian implications, Brown had become the symbol of Upper Canadian "no popery" fanaticism in the eyes of most Roman Catholics. When Mackenzie decided to run in this by-election, Hincks and his cabinet colleagues declined to endorse Brown for fear of creating further division in the Reform ranks. With the Catholics of Haldimand arrayed against him, Brown went down to defeat. Henceforth, he became increasingly disillusioned with the Reform party and the rift between Hincks and himself widened. Brown began to share the Clear Grits' suspicion that French Canadian influence was causing the government to have second thoughts about secularizing the clergy reserves and he feared that this influence was undermining the voluntaryist principles of the Reform party. Hincks also considered himself a voluntaryist, but his views were much less extreme than those of Brown. "My notions of civil and religious liberty," he explained to Shenston, "lead me to allow each Christian Community to manage its affairs in its own way. I would give them no state support but I would not deprive them of the power of managing their affairs."

The rift between Hincks and Brown widened on 30 June 1851 when Baldwin suddenly decided to resign from the cabinet after a majority of the members from Canada West in the assembly supported Mackenzie's attack on the Court of Chancery that Baldwin had recently reformed. Hincks was his logical successor, and although he offered to resign with Baldwin, he had no real desire to do so. He had been critical of Baldwin's leadership and he probably felt he could provide Upper Canadian Reformers with more positive and more dynamic direction. But he was assuming the leadership of the western section of the party at a difficult time. Reform unity was threatened by both the Clear Grits in Canada West and the Rouges in Canada East; and, at the same time, Brown's *Globe* was increasingly critical of compromises made by Baldwin and La Fontaine for the sake of unity. Yet if the union of the Canadas was not preserved, the province's credit would be seriously impaired.

Aware that the *Globe*'s intolerant voluntaryism threatened the Reform alliance, Hincks, upon taking over from Baldwin, indicated his intention to insist that its editorial policy be in accord with the policy of the party. But Brown, finding the prospect of Hincks's leadership intolerable, severed his connection with the party early in July. He regarded Hincks as a mere political opportunist who valued power more than principles. Hincks, however, seeing himself as a political realist, considered Brown to be a governmental impossibility because he refused to recognize the significance of French Canadian political strength. Anxious to reunite the party, Hincks welcomed William McDougall*'s proposal that two Clear Grits, John Rolph and Malcolm Cameron*, be taken into the government in return for support of McDougall's newspaper, the *North American* of Toronto. This arrangement made it impossible to give Solicitor General John Sandfield Macdonald* a seat in the cabinet (he was offered the post of commissioner of crown lands), let alone the post of attorney general west which he wanted. In his disappointment Macdonald vowed, "I will make Hincks pay for it if I can. . . ." Hincks was faced with the fact that less than six months after he had assumed the leadership two influential Reformers, Brown and Macdonald, had been alienated.

Baldwin's resignation had led La Fontaine to consider his own position and he soon announced his intention to resign also. On 28 Oct. 1851 Hincks and Augustin-Norbert Morin became the new co-premiers, with a programme which included secularization of the clergy reserves, abolition of seigneurial tenure, an elective Legislative Council, increased representation in the assembly, extension of the franchise, and the encouragement of railway construction.

Upon taking office they advised the governor, Lord Elgin, to dissolve the house. The ensuing election, held in December, returned the Reformers in approximately the same numbers as in the previous parliament. Because of the friction caused by the Clear Grits and by Brown's personal opposition to himself, Hincks chose to run in both Oxford and Niagara to ensure that he won a seat. He was successful in both constituencies, and chose to sit for Oxford.

Convinced that railways would bring a new era of prosperity to British North America, Hincks was anxious to encourage further railway building. When Baldwin had announced his intention to resign as premier, Hincks was in discussions with Edward Barron Chandler* and Joseph Howe* concerning the joint financing by Canada, New Brunswick, and Nova Scotia of a railway from Halifax to Windsor or Sarnia on Canada's western boundary. They reached an agreement and in August 1851 Hincks piloted a bill through the legislature authorizing Canadian participation in the scheme. But late in the year he was dismayed to learn that the project was in danger. There had been a misunderstanding: the imperial government was willing to guarantee the interest on a loan to build the railway only if it followed a defensible route through northern New Brunswick along the south shore of the Gulf of St Lawrence. Because New Brunswick was interested only in a line that would provide service for the Saint John valley, the arrangement was about to collapse.

Hoping to work out a compromise, Hincks and two cabinet colleagues, Étienne-Paschal Taché* and John Young*, visited New Brunswick and Nova Scotia early in February 1852. A new plan was worked out, which Howe opposed because it would use the Saint John valley and thus give Saint John a direct rail link with the Canadas, enabling it to compete with Halifax as the principal ocean port for British North America during the winter shipping season. In a masterful speech in Halifax, Hincks appealed directly to the merchants and people of Nova Scotia and won general support for the plan. Howe capitulated and agreed to do "all that a Nova Scotian ought, to bring this matter to a successful issue." Hincks still had to persuade the imperial government to reverse its stand and guarantee the interest on the loan for a railway that, because of its proximity to the American border, would be vulnerable in the event of war. When the colonial secretary, Lord Grey, gave some encouragement to the idea of a delegation to promote the scheme in England, Hincks left at the end of February, and it was agreed that Howe and Chandler would join him.

The railway was the main reason for his mission to England, but Hincks also hoped to see the imperial parliament repeal its Clergy Reserve Act of 1841 and thus clear the way for the Canadian legislature to solve the reserves problem on its own terms. He also intended to press for negotiations for a reciprocity treaty with the United States. But he encountered one frustration after another. Howe did not come to England, although in the end his absence made little difference. The Whigs had been defeated in parliament before Hincks arrived and the attitude of the new colonial secretary, Sir John Somerset Pakington, soon convinced Hincks that, though the government was procrastinating regarding the railway, the Saint John valley route would ultimately be denied the imperial guarantee. Determined that Canada should at least have a main trunk line from Quebec to its western boundary, he concluded an arrangement with the British firm of Peto, Brassey, Jackson and Betts to build a line approximately 330 miles long from Montreal to Toronto and Hamilton as a private, rather than a publicly owned, enterprise.

Before he returned home in late spring, Pakington had come to personify for Hincks the exasperation he had experienced in England. Ignoring Hincks, Pakington informed Lord Elgin in Canada that the imperial Clergy Reserve Act would not be repealed in the current session. Upon learning indirectly of Pakington's dispatch, Hincks hastened to warn him that "there will be no end of agitation in Canada if the attempt be made to settle this question permanently according to public opinion in England instead of that of the province itself." Finally, Pakington rejected Hincks's proposal to encourage the United States to enter a reciprocity agreement (thus enabling Canada to gain more revenue from canal tolls) by granting American vessels free navigation of the St Lawrence River. The colonial secretary insisted that the Americans must make an equivalent concession.

In the parliamentary session which began late in the summer of 1852 Hincks's main priorities were to have his railway arrangements approved and to obtain endorsement of his warning to Pakington concerning the clergy reserves. His resolutions asserting that the Canadian parliament had the constitutional right to settle the reserves question without interference from England passed without difficulty despite objections from Brown and Henry John Boulton*. In the hands of Hincks and William Mather Jackson, a partner in the firm of Peto, Brassey, Jackson and Betts who accompanied him back to Canada, plans for the Grand Trunk were expanded during the fall and winter of 1852–53 into a line stretching from Sarnia to the year-round port of Portland, Maine. Jackson, aided by Hincks, who entered into personal negotiations with Alexander Tilloch Galt*, purchased or leased charters, rights, and partially completed railways, and committed his firm to build some 1,100 miles of track. The Grand Trunk was to be financed by an issue of stocks and debentures floated in April 1853 by Baring Brothers and Glyn, Mills and Company on the London exchange. The contractor agreed to hold an equal amount of stock for later sale, and the Canadian government was to guarantee bonds worth £3,000 for every mile completed. When his Grand Trunk bills came up in the house in 1852, 1853, and 1854, Hincks, as he confidently expected, obtained solid majorities in favour.

Hincks's Municipal Loan Fund Bill was another measure for his special attention. He was convinced that municipalities in Canada West were excellent sources of funds for investment in railways and other important communication links, but he knew how difficult it was for them to sell their debentures in Britain. In an effort to make credit more readily available he introduced his bill in 1852 which authorized the provincial government to sell municipal loan fund debentures and to lend the proceeds to municipalities for investment in railway, canal, and road companies. As security for such loans the province would accept the municipalities' own debentures. Although the measure led several cities and towns to overextend their financial base, this danger was apparently not foreseen, for the bill encountered little opposition either in the legislature or in the press.

Though he had attended his first session as a member in 1851, Brown had soon emerged as the government's most aggressive critic on church-state matters and on questions of representation within the assembly. He felt Hincks was betraying Baldwin's ideal of a single, well-endowed provincial university by his bill in 1853 to transform the University of Toronto into an examining authority and to give its teaching functions to church and non-denominational colleges which would be affiliated with the university. He saw the government's Ecclesiastical Corporations Bill of 1853 as an even greater evil, one which would result in numerous incorporated religious bodies with large land holdings locked up forever in mortmain and capable of exercising extensive power that could pose a threat to the country's liberties. For Brown this bill and legislation introduced in 1853 to expand the provisions for separate schools in Upper Canada showed that Morin and his followers controlled the Reform alliance. Brown saw the solution in representation by population: if the principle of equal representation in the assembly for each section of the province gave way to representation based on population, the danger for Canada West would disappear because it now had the larger population. Hincks knew "rep by pop" was a threat to the Reform alliance and to the Canadian union itself. "The truth," Hincks was reported as declaring in the assembly in rejecting Brown's arguments, "was that the people occupying Upper and Lower Canada were not homogeneous: but they differed in feelings, language, laws, religion and institutions, and therefore the union must be considered as between two distinct peoples, each returning an equal number of representatives."

In September 1853 the implications of a transaction entered into by Hincks in 1852 became a public concern. Shortly after his return to Canada, Mayor John George Bowes* of Toronto had proposed that they purchase jointly city of Toronto debentures which the contractors building the Ontario, Simcoe and Huron Railroad Union Company were willing to sell at a 20 per cent discount. Confident that he could arrange a profitable resale of the debentures through his contacts in London, Hincks readily agreed. He soon received, through Glyn, Mills and Company, an offer to purchase the debentures if they were issued in sterling and made payable in London. These requirements presented no problem. The government of Canada had just consolidated the city's municipal debt, in which these debentures were included, through an act in 1852; Toronto City Council, unaware that the mayor and Hincks now owned the securities, issued new debentures in sterling payable anywhere. Hincks and Bowes were thus able to exchange the debentures they bought for £40,000 for new ones that could be readily sold for £50,000. After deducting expenses they cleared a profit of slightly more than £8,000. But the city now entered a suit against Bowes and it was revealed that Hincks was indeed his partner in the stock manipulation of the "£10,000 job." In his own mind Hincks did not believe he had acted dishonestly, but he was powerless to stem the rising tide of innuendo. As a result he was also suspected of having profited from his position and inside knowledge in a whole series of nefarious schemes.

Brown claimed that prior knowledge of the amalgamation in 1854 of the St Lawrence and Atlantic Railroad with the Grand Trunk had enabled Hincks to make a profit by investing in depressed shares of the former company. Actually, he had not bought St Lawrence and Atlantic shares until after the amalgamation had been announced and their price had risen considerably. The rumour also circulated that Hincks had received a commission for arranging a loan in England for the city of Montreal. In fact the negotiations he was conducting on behalf of Montreal collapsed, but Hincks refused to admit that he had acted improperly in this assignment and also stated that had he been successful he would have expected a commission. Malfeasance was suspected when it was learned that some 1,000 shares of Grand Trunk stock had been entered in Hincks's name on the company's books and that the initial deposit on the shares had been paid by Sir Samuel Morton Peto of the contracting firm. The donation of railway shares appeared to his enemies to be an obvious bribe. The company's explanation, not very convincing, was that the stock was allotted to Hincks in trust for distribution in Canada, thereby permitting Canadian investors to acquire it at par, and that Hincks never personally received any of the stock.

Numerous other charges, which began to appear in September 1853 and continued until June 1854, were added as the *Globe*, the *Montreal Gazette*, and other newspapers labelled Hincks the "arch-corruptionist." It was suggested that his opposition to the incorporation of a company to build a canal on the Canadian side of the border at Sault Ste Marie was due to his financial interests in the area which would be adversely affected. He was accused of using political influence on behalf of a land speculation syndicate, to which Samuel Sylvester Mills* and James Morris* also belonged, to enable it to acquire government property at prices much below its true value. Subsequent investigations would reveal that these charges were based on rumour and misinformation rather than hard fact.

Hincks returned from a voyage to England and to the United States, where he participated in the negotiation of the Reciprocity Treaty, in June 1854. The assembly met soon after, on 13 June, and he was confronted by a hostile house determined to drive the Hincks–Morin administration out of office. The government was accused of corruption and extravagance and of procrastination in dealing with seigneurial tenure and the clergy reserves (the imperial act having finally been repealed in late 1852). When a motion of censure was carried, Hincks and Morin advised Elgin to dissolve parliament. In the election in August 1854, Hincks, again afraid of being defeated in Oxford, ran in Renfrew as well. Although elected in both ridings, he sat for Renfrew as had been pre-arranged with John Egan*, who had supported his nomination on that condition. Hincks and Morin won the largest number of seats, but failed to obtain a clear majority. Their minority government was defeated shortly after parliament met in early September and the leaders submitted their resignations on the 8th.

Hincks knew that Brown and John Sandfield Macdonald aspired to reconstruct the Reform party in Canada West, and he feared that Brown's influence might destroy the alliance with Morin's followers and thus imperil both the union and Canada's economic prospects. He tried to form alternative alignments. The alignment which occurred differed from any he had envisaged, but it was one of which he fully approved; MacNab approached Morin and proposed a coalition of Liberals and Conservatives. It was agreed by both groups that the coalition's programme would include secularizing the clergy reserves, abolishing seigneurial tenure, and making the Legislative Council elective. At Morin's request MacNab agreed to include Hincks's followers in the coalition and, after further discussion with Hincks, Robert Spence* and John Ross* were named to represent the Hincksites in the cabinet.

Once the new government had taken office the actions of Hincks and his associates were investigated. Select committees of both the assembly and the Legislative Council met from 26 Oct. 1854 until the end of April 1855. As a member of the assembly's committee Brown appeared, at times, to be both judge and prosecutor. But, in spite of his determined efforts, the committee reported that the evidence presented to it would not support a charge of corruption against any member of the late administration. Indeed the committee expressed its amazement that after all the rumours no one appeared before it to make formal charges or to offer evidence. To the committee Hincks insisted that the acceptance of office did not deprive a man of his right to participate in legitimate investments; such a position was bound to result in suspicion and rumours of scandal, but no evidence was presented to prove that he had ever used the powers of his office or inside information for personal gain. He maintained that his speculation in Toronto debentures was a legitimate transaction, in which any investor might have participated. The Court of Chancery had ruled that, as mayor, Bowes could only have acted as a trustee of Toronto and must therefore give his half of the profit to the city. There were no grounds to sue Hincks for the other half.

Not intending to remain in politics Hincks resigned his seat on 16 Nov. 1855. He planned a visit to England and Ireland and, upon his return, to accept the offer of the presidency of the Grand Trunk Railway. However, in the spring of 1856, while still in Great Britain, Hincks accepted appointment as governor of Barbados and the Windward Islands; after the accusations he had faced in Canada such an appointment, at the hands of Queen Victoria, was the ultimate vindication. During his term as governor he worked to improve the social conditions and educational facilities on the islands and won the approbation both of their inhabitants and of the authorities in England. He established a nonsectarian board of education and urged that the number of schools be increased. His concern over the poor living conditions of the native population led him to propose that large numbers should be relocated on unoccupied lands on other islands and that each family be given land on which to maintain themselves. His plans were only partially successful because the planters, fearing a reduction in the labour supply, opposed them. In September 1861, Hincks was appointed governor of British Guiana (Guyana) with an increase in salary and rank and, at the same time, was created a CB. But he soon clashed with a group of business and professional men whose leaders, known as the "Bermuda Clique," wished to wrest power from the planters and the governor and demanded a more representative form of government as a means to this end. Because he felt the colony was not yet ready for such a system, Hincks opposed the move. His quarrels with the chief justice of the colony, William Beaumont, who was determined to reduce the power and authority of the governor and his executive, together with the constant stream of plaintive appeals each addressed to the Colonial Office, probably explain why Hincks did not receive a reappointment when his term ended in 1869. He was, however, recommended for a knighthood which he received in that year.

While Hincks was visiting Canada in 1869, Sir John A. Macdonald* offered him the post of minister of finance as a replacement for John Rose whose resignation had followed a cabinet decision to withdraw his banking bill. Hincks accepted, and upon taking up his office on 9 Oct. 1869 he turned to the difficult unfinished business of regulating the banks and currency of the country. He was elected to the house for Renfrew North on 13 November.

Rose had hoped to do away with the notes issued by all Canadian banks and to replace them by dominion notes. He had been defeated by the combined opposition of Liberal politicians and Ontario businessmen and financiers such as Senator William McMaster. Hincks personally preferred a bank of issue, but he knew he must compromise. On 15 Feb. 1870 he stated that the special status of the Bank of Montreal, which had become the sole issuer of government notes, was to be terminated after a six-month period of notice. He then obtained the agreement of bankers from Ontario, including McMaster, to a bill which defined the concurrent circulation of bank and government notes: notes issued by banks were limited to amounts of $4.00 and higher; dominion notes only were to be issued for smaller denominations. Although the bankers had won the most lucrative share of the business, Hincks improved the government's position with a requirement that each bank normally should hold one-half and never less than one-third of its cash reserve in dominion notes. His first bank act encountered some opposition but passed both houses in 1870.

The next year the main provisions in the act were extended and a new bank act consolidated the 1870 and earlier acts. The spirit of compromise was kept alive: in the face of opposition from spokesmen for small banks, Hincks reduced the minimum capital for banks starting up from $1,000,000 to $500,000 with 20 per cent paid up. All the provisions of the act would apply to the 19 banks whose charters it renewed and to future bank charters, but special provisions were inserted to govern banks whose charters were not up for renewal and to meet the particular needs of some institutions. Hincks had succeeded in ending the stalemate he had inherited in 1869 and in establishing the principle of general legislation applying equally to the banks and currency in the country.

As minister of finance Hincks performed his duties ably, but he was losing his zest for politics and, in addition, was disturbed by his cool reception from many coalition Liberal-Conservatives. Although he was re-elected for the constituency of Vancouver in the general contest of 1872 he longed to be free of his cabinet responsibilities. On 21 Feb. 1873 he resigned as minister but retained his seat in the house. He did not run in the 1874 general election, and with the defeat of Macdonald's government he moved to Montreal and began to contribute editorials to the *Journal of Commerce*. In 1871 he had become the first president of the Toronto-based Confederation Life Association and retained that position until 1873 (he sat on the board of directors until 1879). He assumed the presidency of the Consolidated Bank of Canada in 1875, but age and infirmity led him to neglect his duties and to sign documents without adequate scrutiny. When the bank failed he was indicted on 6 Feb. 1879 under his own banking legislation for making a "wilfully false and deceptive return." Hincks was found guilty by Samuel Cornwallis Monk of the Queen's Bench, but on a motion by the defence Monk reserved the case for the full court. The original verdict was over-turned and Hincks acquitted, but he was censured for his negligence. At a special general meeting of the shareholders of the bank held on 18 September, he was voted out of office.

Though retired, he remained active and in 1878 served as the federal government's representative on the Ontario-Manitoba boundary commission. He also enjoyed assisting John Charles Dent, the historian, in the preparation of his *Canadian portrait gallery* and *The last forty years*, and subsequently began working on his own reminiscences. Unfortunately, he had left it too late and the book he published in 1884 fell far short of the work he might have produced earlier. His second wife died in 1880 and he spent his last years living with his daughter, Ellen Ready. In August 1885 he contracted smallpox when an epidemic struck Montreal, and he died on the 18th of the month.

It was during the years before he became premier that Hincks was most productive. In this period he acquired the business and banking experience upon which his reputation as a financial administrator rested, and through the *Examiner* became the leading spokesman for the Upper Canadian Reform movement. His political astuteness and foresight led him to realize that, given the permanence of the French fact in Canada, some form of consociational democracy was the key to political power. He was one of the first Reformers to see that an English-French alliance would become a basic factor in Canadian politics and he took the initiative to achieve such an alliance. Ironically, in 1841, when his political pragmatism and his willingness to compromise led him to separate temporarily from Baldwin and La Fontaine, he became permanently labelled as a political opportunist.

Upon moving to Montreal in 1844 he hoped to make the *Pilot* a link between Reformers in both sections of the province, but he never attained his objective. He exercised considerable influence with La Fontaine and his French Canadian followers, but he had isolated himself from the Reformers in Canada West. As Brown's influence grew in the western half of the province, Hincks's declined, a fact he deeply resented. It was probably his business and banking background that led him to regard responsible government as a means of obtaining the power not only to secularize the clergy reserves and solve the seigneurial tenure problem, but also to promote railway building and economic expansion. He was the first Reformer to commit himself deeply to the development of Canada's economic potential.

Despite the enthusiasm with which Hincks and Morin took office in 1851, they failed to achieve their primary objectives with regard to the clergy reserves and seigneurial tenure. Hincks contributed in an important way to the creation of the Grand Trunk Railway, but because of the difficulties it soon encountered it became a political liability rather than an asset. He had hoped to reunite the diverse elements of the Reform party in Canada West, but his efforts were unsuccessful. He then worked to form a new political alignment that would preserve both the English-French alliance and the union of the Canadas, and thus contributed to the formation of the Liberal-Conservative coalition even as he was forced out of office in 1854. Hincks undoubtedly saw the years that followed as a vindication of his reputation – in reality they were an anticlimax. Although he served successfully as a colonial governor and then as a minister of finance under John A. Macdonald, he never regained his former enthusiasm for politics and economic development.

Tradition has it that Hincks was a financial genius – it would be more accurate to say that he was a successful financial administrator. His banking skill kept the Bank of the People solvent during a period of economic crisis, and as inspector general he helped to restore Canada's financial reputation by putting the province's finances on a sound footing. Baring Brothers and other British financial houses held him in high regard. He was given credit by Samuel Zimmerman* and many other Canadian entrepreneurs for establishing a favourable economic environment for railway building and development. But he was apparently incapable of applying his talents to his own private affairs. At no time was he a wealthy man, and he rarely made sizable profits on his investments. He was frequently hard pressed by the want of relatively small sums of money, and late in life, when he came to draw up his will, he did not expect much to be left of his estate after his debts were paid.

WILLIAM G. ORMSBY

The most important writings of Sir Francis Hincks are the following: *The political history of Canada between 1840 and 1855: a lecture delivered on the 17th October, 1877, at the request of the St. Patrick's National Association, with copious additions* (Montreal, 1877); *Religious endowments in Canada: the clergy reserve and rectory questions: a chapter of Canadian history* (London, 1869); and *Reminiscences of his public life* (Montreal, 1884). Other publications are listed in *National union catalog* and *Biblio. of Canadiana* (Staton and Tremaine) and its *First supp.* (Boyle and Colbeck), or can be found in the AO pamphlet collection. Hincks was also the editor of the *Examiner* (Toronto) from 3 July 1838 to June 1842, and of the *Pilot and Journal of Commerce* (Montreal) from 5 March 1844 to 27 March 1848.

BNQ, MSS-101, Coll. La Fontaine (copies at PAC). MTL, Robert Baldwin papers; Thomas Strahan Shenston papers. PAC, MG 24, B30, 1; B68. Can., Prov. of, Legislative Assembly, *App. to the journals*, 1854–55, XIV: app.A.A.A.A. *The Consolidated Bank of Canada: a compilation*, comp. J. F. Norris (Montreal, 1879). "How history is written: the Hincks to Dent letters," ed. Elizabeth Nish, *Rev. du Centre d'Étude du Québec* (Montréal), no.2 (avril 1968): 29–96. Dent, *Canadian portrait gallery*. *DNB*. Notman and Taylor, *Portraits of British Americans*. G. E. Boyce, *Hutton of Hastings: the life and letters of William Hutton, 1801–61* (Belleville, Ont., 1972). R. M. Breckenridge, *The history of banking in Canada* (Washington, 1910). Careless, *Brown*, I; *Union of the Canadas*. G. M. Craig, *Upper Canada: the formative years, 1784–1841* (Toronto, 1963). Dent, *Last forty years*. S. [B.] Leacock, *Baldwin, LaFontaine, Hincks: responsible government* (Toronto, 1907); new ed. issued under title: *Mackenzie, Baldwin, LaFontaine, Hincks* (London and Toronto, 1926). R. S. Longley, *Sir Francis Hincks: a study of Canadian politics, railways, and finance in the nineteenth century* (Toronto, 1943). Monet, *Last cannon shot*. W. G. Ormsby, *The emergence of the federal concept in Canada, 1839–1845* (Toronto, 1969). Adam Shortt, "Founders of Canadian banking: Sir Francis Hincks, most notable of Canadian ministers of finance," *Canadian Banker*, 33 (1925–26): 25–38; "Hist. of Canadian currency, banking and exchange," *Canadian Banker*, 10–13.

HIND, WILLIAM GEORGE RICHARDSON, painter; b. 12 June 1833 at Nottingham, England, son of Thomas Hind and Sarah Youle; d. unmarried 18 Nov. 1889 at Sussex, N.B.

William George Richardson Hind, the son of a lace manufacturer, immigrated to Canada in 1851 and joined an elder brother, Henry Youle Hind*, who had settled in Toronto earlier and was establishing a reputation as an intellectual. Henry played a major role as constant mentor to William who apparently lacked his brother's stability of temperament. Details of William Hind's art training are unknown since statements reporting study in Nottingham, London, and on the Continent cannot be confirmed. However, his education was such that on his arrival in Toronto at the age of 18 he was appointed "Drawing Master" at the Toronto Normal School (probably at Henry's instigation) where he served from November 1851 to November 1857. During this time he maintained a studio in Toronto and exhibited paintings at the Upper Canada

Provincial Exhibition of 1852. No paintings executed in Toronto have been located but the titles of two, *Reading the news* and *Waiting for the bat*, indicate that they were in the popular narrative genre style, consistent with a strain developing in England and the United States and paralleled in Montreal by Cornelius Krieghoff* and James D. DUNCAN. Hind revisited England at the end of the decade, presumably to familiarize himself with the latest developments in British art.

The artist returned to Canada in May 1861. After this time Hind's movements, traceable through the subject matter of his paintings, can be confirmed in the few ephemeral references which are available. When William disembarked at Quebec in 1861 he discovered his brother already in that city *en route* to explore the little known Moisie River which flows into the lower St Lawrence. William joined the party as expedition artist. He sketched landscapes in this region, made detailed botanical and ethnological studies, and recorded the customs of the local Naskapi and Montagnais Indians. Over 100 of these sketches survive; some were used, without retouching, as woodcut illustrations in Henry's published report, *Explorations in the interior of the Labrador peninsula* (1863). After the party's return to Toronto, William used other field studies as a basis for painting an important series of large finished water-colours; 16 of these were made into coloured lithographs for inclusion in the same report. One of them, *The game of bones*, epitomizes his artistic approach. The painting is highly romantic in subject matter: two Indians, intensely absorbed, gamble away their belongings in a rocky northern setting. But Hind treats the subject with the cold detachment and objectivity found in certain Pre-Raphaelite paintings. A few of the expedition studies illustrate mythological Naskapi tales; evidently the artist drew on his imagination in painting these and they lack the realistic conviction evident in other studies which portray actual incidents. The unemotional realism found in *The game of bones* also characterizes his six known self-portraits, and is particularly evident in the finest of these in which the artist with his palette sits before his studio easel.

During the winter of 1861–62 rumours of sensational gold discoveries in British Columbia swept Toronto. Hind joined an "Overlanders" group [*see* Thomas McMicking*] and set out for the Cariboo in April 1862. The party purchased Red River carts at Upper Fort Garry (Winnipeg) and followed the old fur traders' trails across the prairies. During the trip Hind made himself so objectionable that his comrades ostracized him and he was forced to travel alone for several days before he was forgiven. Between Fort Garry and Jasper House (Alta) Hind kept a sketch-book which records the party winding across the open prairie, fording swollen streams, hunting duck and buffalo, and passing the hours in camp. A parallel series of finished water-colours details other incidents on the prairies as well as some farther west: threading through formidable forests and muskeg in the foothills, scaling steep mountains, and arriving in Victoria after a cursory look at the Cariboo gold fields. Realism and skilful use of the water-colour medium characterize the group.

Hind lived in Victoria for the next seven years. There are few references to his life there but on 25 Feb. 1863 the *Daily British Colonist* noted his talent as a sign painter; it was an era when trade and tavern signs overhanging wooden sidewalks were a characteristic of the local scene. Two years later the *Colonist* praised him lavishly for his views of British Columbia destined for display in England to encourage emigration. As well he occasionally painted scenes of the activities of the local Indians. Historically his most significant oil and water-colour paintings of these years picture mining life in the Cariboo and probably date from a visit in 1864.

Hind appears to have left Victoria for the east in 1869. He arrived at Winnipeg in the fall and did not leave until at least the following autumn when the settlement was being designated as the capital of the new province of Manitoba. Several oil paintings which depict homestead life in the area vary tremendously in quality. The finest, picturing an ox pulling a Red River cart along a country road, is executed in a highly realistic, almost *trompe-l'œil*, manner. In contrast, other Fort Garry oils, particularly studies of Indians, are weak in composition, lack texture, and are undistinguished in subject matter. In June 1870 two woodcuts of Cree and Ojibwa Indians appeared in the *Illustrated London News* as the first of a series to illustrate life in "the new province," but no further work by Hind was published.

Henry Youle Hind had moved to Windsor, N.S., in 1866 and William followed him to the Atlantic region late in 1870 where he seems to have abandoned professional artistic ambitions. He spent his later years in Nova Scotia and New Brunswick and probably worked as a draughtsman for the International Railway Company. But as an avocation he continued to sketch vignettes in pencil, water-colour, and oil, picturing life in smaller centres such as Shediac, N.B., Matapédia, Que., as well as Pictou and Windsor, N.S. The most delightful, which include Pictou streets, port activities, the repairing of undersea cables, and the building of wooden ships, appear in an 1876 diary converted into a sketch-book. These gentle paintings contrast with the subdued but nevertheless evident excitement and spirit of adventure in his earlier western works. A belated honour for Hind was the inclusion of one of his paintings in the Colonial and Indian Exhibition in London in 1886. His last six years were spent in Sussex, N.B., where, at the time of his death, a local newspaper commented on his artistic ability, fondness for sports, well-informed mind, and "grand and occasionally eccentric habits."

Realism in Hind's paintings is of a quality rarely found in Canadian art but characteristically Victorian in mood. Detail is added to detail to create an aesthetic attuned to the Victorian search for analytical knowledge and concern with materialism. By outlining every stone on the beach, every leaf on the tree, and by rendering birds and flowers with an exactitude which makes the species readily identifiable, he sees with the eyes of Darwin or of Audubon. Even such subjects as Cariboo tavern scenes are treated with the detachment of Dutch or Flemish genre which makes their subject matter acceptable in a moralizing age.

J. RUSSELL HARPER

The most complete list of institutions holding work by Hind is in Harper, *Early painters and engravers*. Other works are held in the National Gallery of Canada (Ottawa) and in Dalhousie University (Halifax).

PABC, Stephen Redgrave, Journals, and sundry papers, 1872–75 (typescript). PANS, MS file, W. G. R. Hind, letters, 1870. H. Y. Hind, *Explorations in the interior of the Labrador peninsula, the country of the Montagnais and Nasquapee Indians* (2v., London, 1863). *Daily British Colonist* (Victoria), 25 Feb. 1863, 19 April 1865. *Catalogue of a collection of drawings and watercolours by the Canadian artist William George Richardson Hind . . . which will be sold by auction by Messrs. Sotheby & Co. . . .* ([London, 1967]). J. R. Harper, *Everyman's Canada; paintings and drawings from the McCord Museum of McGill University* (Ottawa, 1962). *William G. R. Hind (1833–1888); a confederation painter in Canada: an exhibition organized and circulated by Willistead Art Gallery of Windsor for centennial year, 1967* ([Windsor, Ont., 1967]). J. R. Harper, *Painting in Canada; William G. R. Hind* (Ottawa, 1976). M. S. Wade, *The Overlanders of '62*, ed. John Hosie (Victoria, 1931). G. F. G. Stanley and L. C. C. Stanley, "The brothers Hind," N.S. Hist. Soc., *Coll.*, 40 (1980): 109–32.

HOGG, SIMON JACKSON, miller, lumber merchant, and municipal politician; b. in 1845 in Halton County, Canada West, to a farming family of Scottish extraction; d. 6 Dec. 1887 in Calgary (Alta).

Simon Jackson Hogg apprenticed early in his life as a miller in the village of Nottawa, near Collingwood (Ont.). Following the completion of his training, he worked for a while in a flour-mill in Creemore, and then became part owner of a mill in New Lowell. A hard-working and shrewd manager, he did well in the flour-milling business. During the 1870s, however, he had the misfortune of losing his substantial savings in wheat speculation. Closing his business at New Lowell, he moved to Mansfield, where he undertook to manage a flour-mill for D'Alton McCarthy*.

In 1881 Hogg decided to seek his fortune in the Canadian west. Leaving his wife and children in Ontario, he went to Manitoba, settling first in Minnedosa and then in Brandon. By the spring of 1883 he was in Medicine Hat (Alta), operating a lumber yard in partnership with J. A. Deacon. Later that year the partners moved their business to Calgary, arriving just before the Canadian Pacific Railway. Hogg and Deacon, now operating as S. J. Hogg and Company, were immediately caught up in the building boom in the frontier town. With a large stock of goods they helped meet the ever-rising demand for lumber and building supplies. In addition, Hogg and his partner sold wagons, ploughs, rakes, mowers, binders, and binding twine to the settlers who were taking up land in the Calgary district. The growing volume of trade, coupled with the inflated prices for lumber and farm implements, made their operation highly profitable. Once again Hogg was beginning to feel economically secure. Accordingly he had a modest but comfortable frame dwelling house built for $1,500 and in the late fall of 1885 his family came from Ontario to join him.

From the outset, Hogg had played a leading role in the development of the western community. One month after the incorporation of Calgary as a town in November 1884, he was elected to the first town council, topping the polls with 183 votes. Although he did not serve a full one-year term, he was an active and influential councillor. Along with Mayor George Murdoch and Joseph Henry Millward, Hogg became a member of the important standing committee on by-laws, and thus helped to shape the structure of Calgary's government. As a member of this committee Hogg kept in mind the needs of the townspeople, but also his own. For example, although he was concerned about providing adequate fire protection for the town, which in the mid 1880s consisted mainly of wooden structures, he persuaded the council to modify a proposed fire by-law so that he would not have the expense of buying additional land to ensure that his lumber yard was a safe distance from the nearest downtown buildings.

In 1886 and 1887 Hogg was the chairman of the Calgary Public School Board which had been established in March 1885. An effective administrator, he won the confidence of his fellow trustees and the ratepayers, and on 25 Nov. 1887, less than two weeks before his death at age 42, he was named chairman of the board for another year.

Hogg died as a result of an attack of pleurisy, leaving his wife and seven children. According to an obituary, he "was a man of the kindliest disposition," and "his sound judgment and high intelligence made his presence felt in whatever company he found himself." During his illness Hogg had put his business affairs in order. He left a fairly sizeable estate which included his life insurance policies valued at $10,500.

HENRY C. KLASSEN

Calgary Board of Education Arch., Calgary Public School Board, Minute book, 1885–92: 18–57. Glenbow-Alberta Institute, City of Calgary papers, Minutes, 1884–85: item 5, p.103. *Calgary, Alberta, Canada: her industries and resources*, comp. and ed. [T. S.] Burns and [G. B.] Elliott (Calgary, 1885; repr. 1974), 12, 19, 48. *Calgary Herald*, 1883–87. *Calgary Tribune*, 1885–87. *Illustrated atlas of the county of Simcoe* (Toronto, 1881; repr. Port Elgin, Ont., 1970), 50. *Illustrated historical atlas of the county of Halton, Ont.*, comp. J. H. Pope (Toronto, 1877; repr. Port Elgin, 1971), 71. M. L. Foran, "The Calgary town council, 1884–1895: a study of local government in a frontier environment" (MA thesis, Univ. of Calgary, 1970), 38–55. H. C. Klassen, "Life in frontier Calgary," *Western Canada: past and present*, ed. A. W. Rasporich (Calgary, 1975), 42–57. R. M. Stamp, *School days: a century of memories* (Calgary, 1975), 9–23.

HOLMAN, SARAH (Dalton) (known as **Sallie Holman**), singer and actress; b. probably 24 June 1849 at Lynn, Mass., daughter of George W. Holman and Harriet Phillips, *née* Jacobs (Jackson); m. in 1879 James T. Dalton; d. 7 June 1888 in London, Ont.

Sallie Holman was the undisputed star of the Holman opera company which toured the eastern United States and Canada from the late 1850s to the early 1880s. Her parents were active in the theatre in New York throughout the 1840s and 1850s. By 1858 the four Holman children were touring as members of the Holman Juvenile Opera Troupe. Sallie, the elder daughter, was the leading lady in all of the Holman productions; an attractive girl, she won the hearts of audiences with her pleasing soprano voice and her dramatic skills. Benjamin Phillips Holman, Harriet's son by an earlier marriage, was the comedian of the group, while Alfred took the dramatic male roles. Julia, the youngest, sang the contralto roles and Harriet Holman served as coach, accompanist, and musical director.

One of the Holmans' earliest Canadian performances, in August 1858, was in London, Canada West, George's home since the 1830s as well as the Holmans' summer home for many years. In its early years the company appeared at Barnum's Museum and the Hope Chapel Theatre in New York (1859 and 1860), at the Prince of Wales Theatre in Toronto (May 1860), and in Montreal (1861). During the 1860s, the company's tours extended south to Nashville and west to St Louis. Following Benjamin's untimely death in 1864, his place was taken by William Henry Crane, who became one of America's best-loved comedians.

In 1867 George Holman took over the management of the Royal Lyceum Theatre in Toronto. The Holmans performed there until 1872, while continuing to tour, under the name the Holman English Opera Troupe; the company changed names repeatedly, however, with eight variations recorded between 1858 and 1878. Their repertoire consisted primarily of English versions of French operettas in vogue during the period, such as Offenbach's *La grande-duchesse de Gérolstein* and Lecocq's *Giroflé-Girofla*. Other favourites included Balfe's *The Bohemian girl*, Auber's *Fra Diavolo*, and Donizetti's *La fille du régiment*. The Holmans also performed farce as well as dramatic works, such as *The streets of New York*, *Under the gaslight*, and *The coleen Bawn*. The company was composed of actors, comedians, and singers, including Canadian comedian Harry Lindley, Joseph Brandisi, a French Canadian, and Blanche Bradshaw, the wife of Alfred Holman. Sallie, however, was the main attraction. One Toronto critic described her as "the bright star of the constellation"; others noted her sprightly manner, finely expressive face, and "the thorough abandon with which she entered the spirit of the role."

In 1872 the company moved to Montreal where George took over the management of the Theatre Royal. One year later he bought the Music Hall in London, renovated it, and renamed it the Holman Opera House; the company opened there on 25 Dec. 1873, performing *La grande-duchesse*. Until 1880 the Holmans opened each season in London before setting out on tour. Other engagements included the opening of Gowan's Opera House in Ottawa in February 1875 and the Canadian *première* of Gilbert and Sullivan's *H.M.S. Pinafore* at the Royal Opera House in Toronto on 13 Feb. 1879. Sallie played the role of Josephine; Captain Corcoran was played by James T. Dalton, an English baritone who had joined the Holmans around 1877. Dalton and Sallie Holman were married during 1879.

Following Julia Holman's death in the same year, the troupe's success began to wane; Sallie's death in June 1888 was the final blow to the company. She had fallen ill in February of that year prior to an evening performance at Glencoe, Ont., and after a brief recovery suffered a relapse. Her father died four months after her death.

An obituary which appeared in the Montreal *Gazette* bears witness to Sallie Holman's successful career. She is referred to as "the soul" of her company and "one of the most amiable and gifted of Canadian artists." William Henry Crane considered her to be an exceptional performer yet one born perhaps too early to receive the recognition which she deserved.

MURRAY D. EDWARDS and FRANCES R. HINES

MTL, Theatre Dept., Vertical file, Royal Lyceum file. *Gazette* (Montreal), 12 June 1888. *Globe*, 8 Oct. 1867, 14 Feb. 1879. *London Advertiser* (London, Ont.), 23 Dec. 1873, 24 Sept. 1877, 7 June 1888, 24 Feb. 1936. *London Free Press* (London, Ont.), 20 Aug. 1858, 27 Dec. 1873, 18 Feb. 1888. G. C. D. Odell, *Annals of the New York stage* (15v., New York, 1927–49). *Types of Canadian women and of women who are or have been connected with Canada*, ed. H. J. Morgan (1v. publ., Toronto, 1903), I: 161. W. H.

Crane, *Footprints and echoes* (New York, 1927). Franklin Graham, *Histrionic Montreal; annals of the Montreal stage with biographical and critical notices of the plays and players of a century* (2nd ed., Montreal, 1902; repr. New York and London, 1969). Carl Morey, "Canada's first opera ensemble," *Opera Canada* (Toronto), 11 (1970), no.3: 15, 75.

HONEYMAN, DAVID, Presbyterian minister, geologist, teacher, and curator; b. in 1817 in Fifeshire, Scotland; m. Mary Donaldson of Dundee, Scotland, and they had three daughters; d. 17 Oct. 1889 in Halifax, N.S.

David Honeyman was educated in Scotland at Dundee High School and at the University of St Andrews where he combined a specialization in Oriental languages with the study of natural science. He was expert enough in the latter discipline to act as a collector of specimens for the Watt Institution in Greenock. In 1836, however, Honeyman relegated science to the background and entered the theological hall of the United Secession Church. After studies in Glasgow and Edinburgh, he was licensed to preach in 1841. Following the disruption in the Church of Scotland in 1843, Honeyman joined the Free Church and under the auspices of its colonial committee accepted a position as professor of Hebrew at the Free Church College in Halifax, N.S. He arrived in September 1848. Honeyman taught at the college until 1850 when he left the Free Church, abandoned his tentative plans to move to the United States, and joined the Presbyterian Church of Nova Scotia, a body more voluntaryist and disestablishmentarian than the Free Church. In the first half of 1851 he did missionary work at Canso and on 19 August was ordained before taking charge of the congregations of Gays River, Shubenacadie, and Lower Stewiacke. In June 1852 he became a member of his church's Board of Home Missions and in September 1853 accepted a charge from the Presbyterian congregation at Antigonish, where he lived for the next 15 years.

The interest in science which Honeyman had shown as a student had not disappeared, however, and the publication of John William Dawson*'s *Acadian geology* . . . (Edinburgh and Pictou, N.S., 1855) inspired in him a determination to investigate the little-known rock structures around him. So involved did he become in geological studies that in 1858 he left the active ministry. He continued, however, to preach and assist in church work until his death and he remained serenely untroubled by the scientific/religious paradoxes that wrought havoc with the theological convictions of so many of his contemporaries.

Honeyman's resignation as minister was followed the next year by his first publication, in the *Transactions* of the Nova Scotia Literary and Scientific Society, which dealt with the fossiliferous rocks of Arisaig (Antigonish County). The article, the first of many, established his reputation as a serious contributor to the virtually pristine field of the geology of Nova Scotia. His timing was opportune because of the growing realization of the potential mineral wealth of the colony. He was, therefore, well placed to lobby for and then in August 1861 to accept a commission to prepare and take to England an exhibit of Nova Scotia minerals for the London International Exhibition of 1862. He was to represent Nova Scotia again as commissioner at the Dublin International Exhibition (1865), as executive commissioner at the universal exposition in Paris (1867), and at the Philadelphia Centennial International Exhibition (1876). In 1882 he represented Canada at the International Fisheries Exhibition in London.

Honeyman's major goal was systematically to investigate and record the province's geology by means of a government-sponsored survey such as had existed in the Province of Canada since 1842. Pressure had been applied to the Nova Scotia government to establish a similar survey as early as 1861, and the hurried efforts to collect exhibits for the 1862 and 1865 international exhibitions increased the realization of the inadequacy in the province's knowledge of the importance of its mineral resources. Honeyman clearly saw himself as director of the survey and was bitterly disappointed when action promised by Charles Tupper*'s administration came to naught in 1864. Perennial financial restrictions and the strong possibility that such a survey would be integrated into the Geological Survey of Canada with the achievement of confederation probably prevented the creation of an independent enterprise. Honeyman in the mean time was consoled with a commission in 1864–65 to prepare a brief overview of Nova Scotia geology. In this project he worked closely with Henry How*, professor of natural history and chemistry at King's College, Windsor, N.S., which in 1864 awarded Honeyman an honorary DCL. In 1868 he also worked briefly for the Geological Survey of Canada under Sir William Edmond Logan*.

Honeyman had more success in establishing the Provincial Museum in Halifax (now the Nova Scotia Museum). Aided particularly by John Robert Willis* and Andrew MacKinlay*, Honeyman persuaded the provincial government to provide room to house the collections so painfully gathered for the international exhibitions, as well as those of the defunct Halifax Mechanics' Institute. The museum opened in 1868 with Honeyman as curator. Its early years were difficult, however, because the museum did not receive legislative sanction or appropriations until 1872. During Honeyman's tenure as curator, from 1868 to 1889, the museum's annual budget (which included his salary) rarely exceeded $1,300. Hampered by lack of funds and space, he was nevertheless able to expand the collections significantly, particularly in geology, and through his prolific writings to add to his own reputation and to that of the museum. His published articles on Nova Scotia geology number approximately 58.

Honeyman's meticulous geological collections won him medals at the international exhibitions of the 1860s and 1870s and his encounters with leading scholars led to his election in 1862 to such scientific organizations as the Société géologique de France, and the Society of Arts and Letters, the Horticultural Society, and the Geologists' Association of London. He also became a fellow of the Geological Society of London and an original member of the Geological Society of America; in addition he received the Mantuan Medal for scientific merit and in 1882 was one of the original fellows of the Royal Society of Canada. His writings appeared in respected international journals, but his preferred vehicle was the *Proceedings and Transactions* of the Nova Scotian Institute of Natural Science, of which he became a member in 1866 and in whose establishment in 1862 he had probably assisted. He enhanced the institute's reputation by joining its council in 1870, becoming its secretary in 1871, and by accepting the editorship of its *Proceedings* in 1887; he held all these positions until his death. In his later years Honeyman demonstrated a growing interest in marine biology. He was active as well in the field of education, endeavouring unsuccessfully in the constrained financial climate of the 1870s to establish schools of mines, of science, and of technology. He did help establish the first science faculty at Dalhousie University in 1878 and without salary taught geology there, as well as giving courses at the museum.

Like so many of his 19th-century contemporaries, David Honeyman was an amateur who elevated himself to the position of scholarly expert and in the process helped to lay the foundations of a new science. He did much to popularize the field of geology in Nova Scotia, both through his publications and through the provincial museum. Perhaps equally important in an age of religious conformity, throughout his career he was able to combine unimpeachable religious and clerical credentials with a scientific attitude which made him an appropriate publicist for a nascent science still subject to suspicions of heresy by the religious majority.

William D. Naftel

David Honeyman was the author of *Giants and pigmies, geological* ([Halifax, 1887]). A complete bibliography of his works may be found in *Bibliography of the geology of Nova Scotia*, comp. D. J. Gregory (Halifax, 1975).

Dalhousie Univ. Arch., MS 1–1, A, 1–4. PANS, MG 9, no.213, "Exhibition memoranda of the Rev. David Honeyman, D.C.L., F.G.S."; RG 5, P, 50, 1872; RG 7, 50, 23 Feb., 19 April, 29 Nov. 1864; RG 14, 70, 1885. Dalhousie Univ., *Calendar and examination papers . . .* (Halifax), 1878. Free Church of N.S., *The missionary record* (Halifax), 1851–52. Edwin Gilpin, "The geological writings of Rev. D. Honeyman, D.C.L.," Nova Scotian Institute of Natural Science, *Proc. and Trans.* (Halifax), 7 (1886–90): 357–62. J. G. MacGregor, "Opening address," Nova Scotian Institute of Natural Science, *Proc. and Trans.*, 7 (1886–90): 320–32. N.S., House of Assembly, *Journal and proc.*, 1861–90; Legislative Council, *Journal of proc.*, 1865, 1872. Presbyterian Church of Nova Scotia, *Missionary register* (Pictou, N.S.), 1850–53.

Acadian Recorder, 1869, 1889. *Dalhousie Gazette* (Halifax), 7 Nov. 1889. *Eastern Chronicle* (New Glasgow, N.S.), 1903. *Morning Chronicle* (Halifax), 1876, 1889, 1903. *Morning Herald* (Halifax), 1889. *Novascotian*, 1865. *Presbyterian Witness* (Halifax), 1848, 1853, 1889. *Dominion annual register*, 1882. Zaslow, *Reading the rocks*. F. W. Gray, "Pioneer geologists of Nova Scotia, the men and their times," N.S. Hist. Soc., *Coll.*, 26 (1945): 153–72. Harry Piers, "A brief historical account of the Nova Scotian Institute of Science, and the events leading up to its formation; with biographical sketches of its deceased presidents and other prominent members," Nova Scotian Institute of Science, *Proc. and Trans.*, 13 (1910–14): liii-civ. "Three directors in ninety-eight years," *Nova Scotia Museum Newsletter* (Halifax), 4 (1964–65): 48–49.

HOOPER, EDMUND JOHN GLYN, lumberman, merchant, and politician; b. 7 July 1818 at Dock (Devonport), England, son of John G. and Sarah Hooper; m. first in 1839 Isabel Richmond of Milton, Vt; m. secondly in 1851 Cynthia Ham of Fredericksburgh, Canada West; d. 5 Oct. 1889 at Napanee, Ont.

Edmund John Glyn Hooper immigrated with his parents to Quebec City in 1819, and studied at the Petit Séminaire de Québec from 1831 to 1833. In 1843 he moved to what later became Lennox and Addington County, Canada West, where, with his brother Augustus Frederick Garland Hooper, he engaged in lumbering operations on the Napanee River. He later built his own sawmill at Fifth Depot Lake in Frontenac County which was destroyed by fire in 1855. Hooper then became a general merchant in Camden East until 1863, when he moved to Napanee and with his two sons, William Henry and Cavalier, established a dry goods business. While in Quebec, Edmund Hooper had served as a lieutenant in the Royal Quebec Voluntary Artillery during the 1837–38 rebellions. From 1866 to 1881 he was captain of the Napanee Battery of Garrison Artillery which he raised and commanded. During the Fenian alarms of 1866 and 1870 he commanded the gunboat *Rescue*, operating out of Kingston.

In 1863 Edmund Hooper was appointed treasurer of the provisional council of the county of Lennox and Addington, newly separated for judicial and administrative purposes from Frontenac County. The appointment was arranged by Richard John Cartwright*, who had just defeated Augustus Hooper in the riding of Lennox and Addington for a seat in the Legislative

Assembly. Both Hoopers were staunch Conservatives and the appointment was intended to assuage supporters of Augustus' unsuccessful attempt to have Newburgh named the county seat; John STEVENSON and others had successfully backed Napanee.

In 1873 Edmund Hooper ran against Cartwright in a federal by-election in Lennox caused by the latter's entry into Alexander Mackenzie*'s Liberal cabinet following the Pacific Scandal and the resignation of Sir John A. Macdonald*'s Conservative government. The riding became the arena for a bitter struggle between Macdonald and the Liberal "renegade" Cartwright, which left the two men implacable enemies. Despite the efforts of Macdonald and Alexander Campbell* to secure Hooper's victory, Cartwright won with a large majority.

In the federal election of 1878 Hooper again received the Conservative nomination for Lennox after such outsiders as Lewis WALLBRIDGE, William McDougall*, and Macdonald himself had declined to stand. He was not expected to win; in Kingston the *Daily British Whig* labelled him a "party scapegoat" and even the Tory *Daily News* conceded Cartwright's re-election to be "beyond doubt." The contest, as in 1873, was an abusive one in which the editor of the *Napanee Express*, Cartwright's organ, was charged with writing and distributing in Napanee a scurrilous address attributed to Hooper. Once again Macdonald made every effort to unseat Cartwright, sending Campbell, Wallbridge, Mackenzie Bowell*, and McDougall into the riding to stump for Hooper, in addition to holding his own rallies there. Hooper won with a slim majority, largely as a result of the excellent organization of the Conservatives in the county, Macdonald's efforts, and Cartwright's extended absence during the campaign while he helped the ailing Mackenzie in the Maritimes and western Ontario.

The year 1879 brought to Hooper political and financial ruin. In September a group of "ratepayers" petitioned the provincial government for an investigation of the financial affairs of the county. The inquiry revealed that over $48,000 was missing. Though Hooper, the county treasurer, escaped criminal charges, his sureties (required by his position) were forced to forfeit bonds to the amount of $20,000, he himself was declared indebted to the county for more than $32,000, and he was obliged to resign the post he had held since 1863. In December Hooper and his two sons declared bankruptcy and his house, property, and dry goods store were seized in an effort to pay his debts. He nevertheless retained his seat in the House of Commons and attended sessions until the dissolution of parliament in 1882. His debts, however, compelled him to borrow $4,000, for which he pledged his sessional allowances. In 1880 he had moved to Gauthier, Man., to live with his stepdaughter. In the 1882 federal election, Macdonald himself was elected for Lennox, but was unseated the following year after an election bribery trial of some of his local agents at Napanee.

In late 1886 Hooper returned to Napanee, where he continued to implore Macdonald in vain for patronage: "My defeat of your *Mortal* enemy Cartwright was my ruin & that of my family." His career in fact provides an interesting glimpse of patronage in the Macdonald era. In a final letter to Macdonald just prior to his death he applied for the position of caretaker at the new Napanee post office, and complained: "I must say without meaning any offence that after 40 years adherence and after all I have done for our party, I have little reward for it." The position, he learned, had already been promised.

JAMES A. EADIE

MTL, Patullo family papers, Reply to questionnaire from Lennox riding, 1878. PAC, MG 26, A, Lewis Wallbridge to Macdonald, 17 Dec. 1877, 2, 16 March 1878; M. J. Pruyn to Macdonald, 15 Feb. 1878; E. J. G. Hooper to Macdonald, 6 Oct. 1879, 28 March, 24 May 1880, 12 Aug. 1882, 5 March 1885, 10, 12 Dec. 1888. *Daily British Whig*, 13 Dec. 1877; 12 March, 18 April 1878; 11, 12, 15 Oct. 1889. *Daily News* (Kingston, Ont.), 16 April 1878, 12 Oct. 1889. *Napanee Express* (Napanee, Ont.), 12 July 1878, 24 Dec. 1880. *Napanee Standard* (Napanee), 28 April 1870; 28 Feb., 21 March, 17 Oct. 1878; 29 Jan., 5 Feb., 4 March, 10, 17 June 1880; 25 March, 1 April, 26 Aug. 1882; 13 Oct. 1883. *CPC*, 1879, 1881. J. A. Eadie, "Politics in Lennox and Addington County in the pre-confederation period, 1854–1867" (MA thesis, Queen's Univ., Kingston, 1967). W. S. Herrington, *History of the county of Lennox and Addington* (Toronto, 1913; repr. Belleville, Ont., 1972). W. M. Alkenbrack, "The financial crisis in Lennox and Addington County, 1879–1880: the Hooper investigation," Lennox and Addington Hist. Soc., *Papers and Records* (Napanee), 14 (1972): 23–37.

HOPE, ADAM, merchant and politician; b. 8 Jan. 1813 at West Fenton, Dirleton parish (Lothian), Scotland, son of Robert Hope and Christian Bogue; m. in 1840 at St Thomas, Upper Canada, Hannah White (1821–1916), and they had three sons and one daughter who survived infancy; d. 7 Aug. 1882 at Hamilton, Ont.

Adam Hope came from a well-known Scottish agricultural family; his father's farm, Fenton Barns, was noted as a model of progressive agriculture, and his older brother George was a prominent agricultural writer, opponent of the Corn Laws, and defender of the rights of tenants. Adam Hope, however, pursued a career in trade. Following education at Dirleton Parish School and in Edinburgh, he spent six years in a mercantile firm in Leith. In 1834 he came to Upper Canada and soon secured employment at Hamilton in the firm of Young and Weir [*see* John Young*] which handled dry goods, groceries, and hardware. After three years he took the course of many ambitious young mercantile clerks at the time and opened his own general store and produce business at St Thomas. He operated it in partnership with Thomas Hodge and with the support of John Young and, after 1840, of Young's new firm, Buchanan, Harris and Company [*see* Isaac BUCHANAN].

With the encouragement of Buchanan, Harris and Company, Hope dissolved the St Thomas business in 1845 and moved to London to become a partner in the general store of John Birrell*, under the name of Hope, Birrell and Company. Hope and Birrell drew heavily on their credit to become Buchanan, Harris and Company's largest customer and London's leading general merchants. Indeed, the account became so large that Peter Buchanan* and Robert William Harris* of the Hamilton firm decided to transform their advances into majority ownership and to use Hope's business as a base to expand their wholesaling activities in the rapidly developing London region. The Hope-Birrell partnership was dissolved in 1851; Birrell kept the retail dry goods business, and Hope opened London's first essentially wholesale business, selling dry goods, groceries, and hardware (the last department, managed by his younger brother Charles James, sold also at retail). Adam Hope and Company quickly developed a large clientele in the small centres north and west of London, and by 1856 Hope estimated the net value of his capital in the business at £10,000. Like most Upper Canadian businesses, this one suffered reverses in the 1857 depression, but Hope proved a canny manager, writing off many bad debts, scouring the countryside for new accounts, and closely scrutinizing his costs and profit margins.

By 1865 Hope, still with the support of Buchanan, Harris and Company, had put his London business on an excellent footing. But Isaac Buchanan, whose Hamilton business had not recovered as had Hope's, offered the latter a partnership in his Hamilton and Glasgow firms; Hope's job was to do for the Hamilton business what he had done in London since 1857. He leapt at the chance of a partnership in what had long been Canada West's largest wholesale house. Only after he had liquidated most of his London business, become a partner in Buchanan, Hope and Company of Hamilton and in Peter Buchanan and Company of Glasgow, and moved the retail hardware department to Hamilton, did he discover that he had been misled by Isaac Buchanan's usual business optimism and his own ambition. Despite his best efforts, he could not avert bankruptcy. Buchanan, Hope and Company failed in 1867, with fierce quarrelling among its partners. Hope, his brother Charles, and Robert Wemyss (who had been Isaac Buchanan's and Hope's Glasgow partner) acted to keep Adam Hope and Company, the hardware firm, which legally was partially distinct, from failing as well. They were obliged to pay $95,000 owed to Buchanan, Hope and Company and bills of Peter Buchanan and Company. The bills, which totalled nearly £35,000 sterling, were due mainly to the Union Bank of Scotland, and Adam Hope and Company stood as their guarantor. The only resources left to Adam Hope and Company were Charles Hope's modest capital, established customers in western Ontario, and the high confidence of another creditor, Henry Rogers, Sons and Company, hardware merchants of Wolverhampton, England, in the Hope brothers now that their operations were divorced from Isaac Buchanan's.

Remarkably, the Hopes and Wemyss paid all their debts, though the brothers eventually broke with Wemyss. They were fortunate that the iron and hardware business would be the strongest trade in the next phase of Hamilton's development, yet even so their recovery was a great achievement. They opened a branch in Toronto in 1868, but closed it in 1871; a Montreal branch, A. and C. J. Hope and Company, also opened in 1868, did better. When he died, Hope was able to leave to his brother and sons a successful iron and hardware firm.

Adam Hope shared the liberal outlook and Unitarian religion of his family. After the Upper Canadian rebellion of 1837 in which he fought as a private in the St Thomas Volunteers, he became an influential figure in the developing Reform party in western Upper Canada, though he never stood for election. It was a fitting climax to a lifetime of committed party activity in London and Hamilton that he was named to the Senate in 1877. There he was a partisan Liberal who spoke mainly on business issues. He denounced the National Policy with special passion; a lifelong free trader, he had remained true to his faith even through his long association with and dependence on that ardent protectionist, Isaac Buchanan.

Despite breaks in his career caused by changes in location and bankruptcy, Hope was an important figure in the business communities of London and Hamilton. He was president of the City of London Building Society throughout its existence, and, before leaving London in 1865, was briefly president of the newly organized Huron and Erie Savings and Loan Society, later to be one of the principal business institutions of western Ontario. He was first president in 1857 of the London Board of Trade. In 1872 he helped found and became first president of the Hamilton Provident and Loan Society, a mortgage and savings company that, by drawing on British capital, grew rapidly into one of the largest of the almost 50 such companies then operating in Ontario. He remained president until his death. In 1874 he was elected a director of the Canadian Bank of Commerce, a post he also held until he died; he was the bank's vice-president from 1876 to 1879.

Having come to Canada alone and without capital,

Adam Hope had made his own way by hard work, ability, and integrity. His life was a clear affirmation of the liberal values in which he so strongly believed.

DOUGLAS MCCALLA

HPL, Adam Hope letters, 1834–37 (typescript); Hamilton biog., Adam Hope; Hope family. PAC, MG 24, D16. Can., Senate, *Debates,* 1877–82. *The Canadian Bank of Commerce: charter and annual reports, 1867–1907* (2v., Toronto, 1907), I. *Evening Times* (Hamilton, Ont.), 8 Aug. 1882. *Globe,* 9, 11 Aug. 1882. *Monetary Times,* 1868–82.

CPC, 1880. *Cherrier & Kirwin's Hamilton directory for 1872–73 . . .* (Montreal, 1872). *City of Hamilton directory for 1871–2 . . . ,* comp. H. N. McEvoy (Hamilton, 1871). *DNB* (entry for George Hope). *Dominion annual register,* 1882: 346. *Railton's directory for the city of London, C.W. . . . 1856–1857* (London, [Ont.], 1856). *Sutherland's city of Hamilton and county of Wentworth directory for 1868–9,* comp. James Sutherland (Hamilton, n.d.). *History of the county of Middlesex, Canada . . .* (Toronto and London, Ont., 1889; repr. with intro. D. J. Brock, Belleville, Ont., 1972). P. D. W. McCalla, "The Buchanan businesses, 1834–1872: a study in the organization and development of Canadian trade" (DPHIL thesis, Univ. of Oxford, 1972).

HOUDE, FRÉDÉRIC, journalist and politician; b. 23 Sept. 1847 at Saint-Antoine-de-la-Rivière-du-Loup (Louiseville), Canada East, son of Antoine Houde, farmer, and Angèle Descoteaux; d. 15 Nov. 1884 at his birthplace.

Frédéric Houde received his secondary education at the Séminaire de Nicolet and in 1868 became an assistant editor of *Le Constitutionnel* in Trois-Rivières. In 1869 he emigrated to New England and was associated with various newspapers in the new parishes then being established for French Canadian immigrants. He worked briefly for *L'Étendard national* of Worcester, Mass. (a special edition of *L'Opinion publique* of Montreal), and then moved to *Le Protecteur canadien* of St Albans, Vt. When the latter ceased publication in September 1871 after a fire in the printing shop, Houde joined forces with Antoine Moussette to found *L'Avenir national* at St Albans in October 1871. Later he went into partnership with Ferdinand GAGNON to launch *Le Foyer canadien* in Worcester on 18 March 1873. In August 1874 Houde bought Gagnon's share and moved the paper to St Albans, where in June 1875 he arranged a merger with *Le Nouveau Monde* of Montreal.

During his six years in New England, Houde was extremely active in Franco-American associations and in the annual Francophone conventions held in American cities. He was one of the principal organizers of the huge French Canadian and Franco-American congress held in Montreal on 24 June 1874 to celebrate the 40th anniversary of the Association Saint-Jean-Baptiste de Montréal and to reunite the "brother emigrants" whose exodus was deplored [*see* Ferdinand Gagnon]. On this occasion, Houde vigorously defended Siméon Pagnuelo*'s resolution in support of Louis RIEL. Riel went to Worcester to thank Houde and spoke at a public meeting there (18 July 1874).

Houde returned to Canada in 1875 and played a prominent part in ultramontane journalism as editor of *Le Nouveau Monde*, the unofficial organ of Bishop Ignace BOURGET of Montreal. In July 1879 Houde became its sole proprietor, while retaining his connection with *Le Foyer canadien*. Houde's journalistic career came to a sudden end in 1882 as a result of his involvement in the ecclesiastical dispute over the Montreal rights of Université Laval. On 24 January *Le Monde* received from Archbishop Elzéar-Alexandre Taschereau* of Quebec a letter, to be published "without comment," written by Cardinal Giovanni Simeoni, prefect of the Sacred Congregation of Propaganda, which denounced "the individuals who claim to be defending Montreal" in the quarrel. *Le Monde* published the letter, but two days later (26 January) Houde wrote a strong article accusing Archbishop Taschereau of "making undue use of his influence" with the cardinal to secure the latter's statement in favour of Université Laval. Immediately Bishop Édouard-Charles Fabre* of Montreal communicated to Houde his disapproval of the article and ordered him to repudiate it. Convinced that he could not in conscience retract what he had written, yet unwilling to oppose his bishop, Houde promptly announced (27 January) his intention to sell his newspaper and to abandon journalism.

Houde had, however, other irons in the fire. On 17 Sept. 1878 he had been elected a Conservative member of the House of Commons for Maskinongé ; he was re-elected 20 June 1882 and served until his death. In the house he was a frequent speaker, his remarks being moderate and informed. He spoke against patronage and in favour of protectionism. He also did not hesitate to oppose Wilfrid Laurier* in April 1882 when he was convinced that Laurier was being unfair to his French Canadian compatriots in attributing the failure to elect many Liberals to the manipulation of popular prejudices by the press and the Conservative party. Houde was also president of the Club Cartier of Montreal and lieutenant-colonel commanding the 86th battalion of Trois-Rivières militia. In 1880 he published in *Le Nouveau Monde* a historical novel, "Le manoir mystérieux, ou les victimes de l'ambition," which appeared in book form with an introduction by Casimir Hébert in 1913. Subsequently, Lionel Léveillé, in 1914, and Abbé Albert Dandurand, in 1937, showed that Houde's novel was in reality a skilful transposition into a Canadian setting of Sir Walter Scott's *Kenilworth*.

A tireless defender of French Canadian rights, one of the founders of Franco-American journalism, and a devout Roman Catholic whose convictions sometimes brought him into conflict with the hierarchy, Houde was astonishingly active despite a tubercular condition. He died at the age of 37, after delivering a long speech to his constituents in a cold autumn rain. He was survived by his wife, Catherine Dougherty, whom he had married on 28 June 1874, and by two sons and a daughter.

DAVID M. HAYNE

Frédéric Houde was the author of the novel "Le manoir mystérieux, ou les victimes de l'ambition," first serialized in *Le Nouveau Monde* (Montréal), from 20 Oct. to 14 Dec. 1880, and then published in part in *La Lyre d'or* (Ottawa), 2 (1889), nos.4–6. The novel was published as a separate volume in Montreal in 1913.

L'Étendard (Montréal), 18 nov. 1884. *Dominion annual register*, 1884: 229. Belisle, *Hist. de la presse franco-américaine*. Josaphat Benoît, *L'âme franco-américaine* (Montréal, 1935), 139. T.-A. Chandonnet, *Notre-Dame-des-Canadiens et les Canadiens aux États-Unis* (Montréal, 1872), 72, 99, 100. Albert Dandurand, *Le roman canadien-français* (Montréal, 1937), 100–1. *Ferdinand Gagnon: biographie, éloge funèbre, pages choisies*, M.-E. Martineau, édit. (2e éd., Manchester, N.H., 1940), 18–19. Germain Lesage, *Histoire de Louiseville, 1665–1960* (Louiseville, Qué., 1961), 236, 241, 259–60. Rumilly, *Hist. de la prov. de Québec*, III: 145–51; *Histoire des Franco-Américains* (Montréal, 1958), 67–75, 81. H.-L. Auger, "Frédéric Houde," *L'Écho de Saint-Justin* (Louiseville), 1er févr. 1923. Charles Drisard, "Frédéric Houde," *L'Écho de Saint-Justin*, 1er févr. 1927. Edmond Léo, "Causerie littéraire: *Le manoir mystérieux*, roman canadien inédit, par Frédéric Houde," *Le Devoir* (Montréal), 6 sept. 1913. "Frédéric Houde," *BRH*, 33 (1927): 456. [Lionel Léveillé], "Curiosités littéraires: roman canadien inédit par . . . Walter Scott," *Le Nationaliste* (Montréal), 10 mai 1914.

HOWARD, HENRY, doctor; b. 1 Dec. 1815 at Nenagh (Republic of Ireland); d. 12 Oct. 1887 in Montreal, Que.

After studying in Dublin and at the Royal College of Surgeons in London, Henry Howard immigrated to Kingston, Canada West, in 1842. He remained there until 1845 when he moved to Montreal, where he obtained a post at the Montreal Eye and Ear Institution and soon became a specialist in ophthalmology. Displaying considerable interest in scientific questions, from 1845 to 1851 he regularly sent articles to English medical journals and to the *British American Journal of Medical and Physical Science* (after May 1850 the *British American Medical and Physical Journal*) which was published in Montreal. In 1850 his reputation as a first-rate eye specialist spread throughout North America as a result of the publication in Montreal and London of his book *The anatomy, physiology and pathology of the eye*.

As a doctor Howard was involved in a wide variety of concerns in his field: he took an active role in organizations which from 1840 had concentrated on the interests of the medical profession and the advancement of medicine in Canada. From 1844 he belonged to the Montreal Medico-Chirurgical Society, founded the previous year to promote contact among and exchanges between the members of the Montreal School of Medicine and Surgery, and by the time of his death he had numerous friends within this society, of which he was the senior person. In 1851 the St Lawrence School of Medicine opened; Howard lectured there in ophthalmology and otology, but his role was a minor one because of the school's brief existence.

In the next phase of his career Howard made a further contribution to the development of medicine in Canada East. In June 1861 the governor general appointed him medical superintendent of the new insane asylum at Saint-Jean, the establishment of which represented a unique experiment in Canada East. The government had been unable to commit itself to financing construction of the Beauport asylum (the Centre Hospitalier Robert-Giffard) when it was founded in 1845 [*see* James DOUGLAS] and had adopted a leasing system with management turned over by contract to private individuals who eventually became the owners of the buildings. In contrast, Saint-Jean was wholly financed by the government.

In 1872 Laurent-David Lafontaine, a physician who was a member of the Legislative Assembly of Quebec, questioned certain expenses incurred by the asylum, especially for the purchase of spirits, and recommended that the care of the insane be entrusted to a religious community. Howard defended his administration, and indignantly protested against the government's desire to put all the psychiatric institutions of Quebec in the hands of private owners, whether professed religious or members of the laity. In his opinion the supervision of the asylums must of necessity be a matter for the medical profession in order to avoid any exploitation of the mentally deranged. In this regard Howard asserted that a system of state asylums offered better protection for the insane; using statistics, he demonstrated a higher percentage of cures at Saint-Jean than at Beauport, where the proportion of incurable patients had become alarmingly high as a result of the economy measures applied to the treatment of mental illness. Aware that the government was prepared to abandon its state asylum system to realize substantial savings, both in capital and operating costs, Howard proposed a compromise formula. While pursuing the objective of putting medical interests before financial ones in the care of the insane, he undertook to meet the cost of building an asylum on condition that the government would grant him a leasing contract similar to the one in effect at the Beauport asylum, which included provision for an annual government allowance of $143 per patient up to 650 patients, and $132 for each additional patient. Despite his plea the government decided in 1875 to transfer the patients of Saint-Jean to Longue-Pointe Lunatic Asylum (Hôpital Louis-H. LaFontaine, Montreal), opened in 1873 and run by the Sisters of Charity of Providence (Sisters of Providence).

Howard himself worked at the Longue-Pointe asylum from 1875 to 1887. During these years he represented the government as either a visiting physician or a member of the medical board which was set up in 1885. The government's measures in the 1880s to regain medical control of the mental institutions, which had thus far been in the hands of the owners, probably gave him considerable satisfaction. Indeed, in 1885 the government of John Jones Ross*, following criticisms about the leasing system and the state of the asylums in Quebec as well as accusations of failure to institute reforms levelled by the opposition, decided to enact a law giving the government medical control of insane asylums. There were, however, violent confrontations between the members of the medical board and certain owners of asylums who opposed the "secularizing" measures of the government.

The administrative wrangles in which Howard was involved did not adversely affect his work as an alienist. His invention of a ventilation system is evidence of both the precarious state of Canadian asylums during the 19th century and the importance that he attributed to physical treatment in the cure of insanity. Howard defined insanity as "a physical disease caused by a pathological change in the sensory nerves and the organ of consciousness. . . ." Using the resources of logic and rhetoric, he expressed the conviction that any effective treatment would have to come from the application of natural laws, otherwise only the symptoms were being tackled. Moral derangement constituted the second essential element of Howard's theory about mental illness. The natural order was to a morally sound society what the body was to an intellectually mature mind. In his opinion the ideal remedy would be for the intellectual and moral élite to contrive to isolate the insane in order to control the evolution of society, particularly by preventing such persons from reproducing.

Howard's ability probably commanded respect. However, several of his colleagues, especially the French-speaking ones, criticized the dogmatic nature of his pronouncements and the implacable logic of his reasoning. In 1881, during a criminal trial, Howard corroborated the case for the defence which rested on the contention that the accused was not responsible by reason of insanity. According to the majority of the other specialists Howard's arguments were not unassailable, and in their opinion the accused was of sound mind. The verdict of guilty shows the conservative attitude of the authorities in matters of insanity.

Howard's participation in several Canadian and American medical associations, his political activities in the St Patrick's Society, and his administrative and professional pursuits show he was an ambitious man with great intellectual energy. His most outstanding endeavour was the management of the Saint-Jean asylum. Thanks to his extensive experience as a mental specialist, he recommended administrative reforms of benefit in the treatment of the insane. On the other hand his theory about mental and moral derangement must be treated with some reservation, especially in view of its empirical nature.

RODRIGUE SAMUEL

[Henry Howard was the author of *The anatomy, physiology and pathology of the eye* (Montreal and London, 1850) and *A rational materialistic definition of insanity and imbecility, with the medical jurisprudence of legal criminality, founded upon physiological, psychological and clinical observations* (Montreal, 1882). He also published many articles for the *British American Journal of Medical and Physical Science* (Montreal) from 1845 to 1851 and the following articles for *Canada Medical and Surgical Journal* (Montreal): "Mental and moral science; with some remarks upon hysterical mania," 6 (1877–78): 439–53; "Some remarks on the medical jurisprudence of insanity," 6: 210–20; and "Responsibility and irresponsibility in crime and insanity . . . ," 7 (1878–79): 347–58.

Information on conditions in asylums during the period may be found at ACAM which holds the correspondence between the archdiocesan authorities, the sisters of Longue-Pointe Lunatic Asylum, and the provincial government concerning the laws related to insane asylums, 1880–85; in the annual reports of the inspectors of prisons and asylums, reprinted in Can., Prov. of, Parl., *Sessional papers*, from 1860 to 1867, and in Qué., Parl., *Doc. de la session*, 1869 to 1888. R.S.]

Borthwick, *Hist. and biog. gazetteer*, 144–45. Fernand Harvey and Rodrigue Samuel, *Matériel pour une sociologie des maladies mentales au Québec* (Québec, 1974). Heagerty, *Four centuries of medical hist. in Canada*, II: 92–112, 119. H. E. MacDermot, *One hundred years of medicine in Canada, 1867–1967* (Toronto and Montreal, 1967).

HOWARD, JOHN GEORGE (originally named **John Corby**), architect, surveyor, civil engineer, and artist; b. 27 July 1803 in Bengeo, Hertfordshire, England; m. 7 May 1827 to Jemima Frances Meikle in London, England; d. 3 Feb. 1890 at Colborne Lodge, Toronto, Ont.

According to the parish registers of Bengeo, John Corby was the fourth of seven children of John and Sarah Corby. After attending a boarding-school in Hertford and spending two years at sea before the mast, John Corby became a carpenter and joiner. In 1824 he was articled for three years to a London architect, William Ford, who married his older sister in 1825. Except for a brief period as resident engineer on the Cromford Canal in Derbyshire, Corby remained with Ford until his departure for Canada, latterly transacting business for himself.

Despairing of success in his profession in England, Corby had resolved to emigrate and in September 1832 he and his wife arrived in York (Toronto). It was at this time that he changed his name to John George Howard. He himself gave two explanations; one conflicts with the evidence of the Bengeo parish registers, and the other is unsubstantiated and unlikely. On 11 Feb. 1834 when his change of name was revealed in a court case Howard wrote to Lieutenant Governor Sir John Colborne*'s secretary, explaining that he was illegitimate, that when he was about 18 he had adopted the name Corby after the man his mother had subsequently married, and that he had assumed "his proper name" when he left England. Later in life he claimed direct descent from Thomas Howard, the 4th Duke of Norfolk, through a 17th-century Howard who had adopted the name Corby from the ancestral estate Corby Castle, because of a family quarrel. All his life Howard was proud of this alleged connection with the great Howard family.

In March 1833 a selection of Howard's architectural drawings was brought to the attention of Colborne, and Howard was appointed to teach geometrical drawing at Upper Canada College with a salary of £100 a year. As well as teaching 12 hours a week, he did some professional work at the college so that the students could view the practical side. Appointed first drawing master in 1839, Howard remained at the college until about 1856. In 1833 he had also been commissioned by the Anglican bishop of Quebec, Charles James Stewart*, to prepare plans and specifications for small churches; these were lithographed and distributed throughout the diocese of Quebec, which then included Upper Canada. In the absence of suitable designs for such projects in architectural books of the period Howard's suggestions would have been extremely important. Unfortunately none of these plans have been identified.

With such signs of official favour, Howard soon began to receive commissions, especially in Toronto, and in the 1830s and 1840s he was one of the busiest architects in Upper Canada. Working in the wide range of styles characteristic of versatile architects of the late Georgian period, he designed a great many houses, shops, and offices, ranging from tiny labourers' cottages to the Chewett buildings (1833), Woodlawn, the home of William Hume Blake* (1840), and the Bank of British North America (1845). He also built about a dozen churches throughout the province, generally for the Church of England and in early Gothic Revival style, including St John's, York Mills, and Christ Church, Tyendinaga (both 1843). He won six competitions for public buildings throughout the province, including Queen's College at Kingston, but only one of these was actually built to his design. This was his major work, the Provincial Lunatic Asylum in Toronto, built 1845–49, which was an immense building in the local white brick that he had introduced into practice; it was demolished by the provincial government in 1976. He did, however, build a number of other public buildings, such as Toronto's third jail (1840), the Brockville court-house and jail (1841–43), and the Toronto House of Industry (1848). His prize-winning plans were probably not built because of their size and expense; for example, his design for the government house in Toronto (1834) was a huge domed and porticoed neoclassical building with an estimated cost of £50,000. It was this plan that he later exhibited as a charter associate of the Canadian Academy of Arts (later the Royal Canadian Academy of Arts) in its first exhibition in 1880.

Although Howard had been a surveyor in England, he was not licensed in Canada until 26 Jan. 1836, after he had served a six-month apprenticeship and passed the local examinations. Much of his surveying and engineering work was performed for the city of Toronto on sidewalks, streets, sewers, and bridges. He surveyed the harbour, laid out the Esplanade on the waterfront, and subdivided the peninsula (now Toronto Island). On 1 May 1843 he succeeded Thomas Young* as city surveyor, and held this part-time position, paid by commission, until he was replaced by William Kingsford* as a full-time salaried city engineer and surveyor in June 1855. Besides his work for the city, Howard was employed by other institutions and private developers. For example, in 1842 he laid out St James' Cemetery, an interesting and early example of picturesque planning. In the following years he subdivided some of the Toronto properties of Henry John Boulton*, Samuel Peters Jarvis*, and Thomas Gibbs Ridout* in a more straightforward gridiron fashion.

In 1834 Howard was on the committee of the short-lived Society of Artists and Amateurs of Toronto, and in 1847 was a founding member, vice-president, and treasurer of the Toronto Society of Arts. He painted a number of water-colours, mostly Toronto scenes or copies of European paintings; many of them as well as paintings by his wife are on exhibit in the Howards' home after 1837, Colborne Lodge.

By 1855 Howard was virtually retired. He spent his time working on the extensive grounds of Colborne Lodge, land bought in 1836 for a sheep farm. The house, now restored and open to the public as a museum, is an early North American example of the small suburban villa popularized in Britain at the beginning of the 19th century. In 1873, in return for a yearly pension of $1,200, Howard deeded 120 acres of this property to the city as a public park to be called High Park; the remaining 45 acres and Colborne Lodge became city property at his death (the city added 170 acres to the park in 1875 and a further 71 acres in 1930). Howard was appointed forest ranger by the city in 1878, with responsibility for improving the park. In 1885 Howard published *Incidents in the life of John G. Howard, esq.*, based, with some discrepancies, on his journals. The Howards were childless, but Howard had three children by Mrs Mary Williams. At his death his estate was valued at $48,379, much of it real estate, in which he had speculated throughout his life in Canada.

Howard was one of the first professional architects in Upper Canada. His work represents the transitional period between the earlier and more provincial phase of Georgian style and the later exuberance and sophistication of Victorian work. From the evidence of more than 700 of his drawings that have survived, it is apparent that he favoured neoclassical designs and tended to rely heavily on London practice of the 1810s and 1820s, which was not always suited to Canadian conditions. Because he was cut off from metropolitan contacts and sources of inspiration, his work did not progress beyond its late Georgian roots. However, he did bring a new level of achievement and breadth of experience to the province before the arrival of other professionally trained architects around the mid century. He is now best remembered for the charm of his Regency cottages and villas, of which Colborne Lodge is the most significant example, and for the massive splendour and ingenious engineering of his lunatic asylum.

EDITH G. FIRTH

J. G. Howard was the author of *Incidents in the life of John G. Howard, esq., of Colborne Lodge, High Park, near Toronto; chiefly adapted from his journals* (Toronto, 1885).

Guildhall Library (London), MS 7498/36–7 (St Leonard Church, Shoreditch, London, Record of marriages, 7 May 1827). Hertfordshire County Record Office (Hertford, Eng.), D/P17 1/3 (St Leonard's Church, Bengeo, Register of baptisms, 11 Sept. 1803). MTL, John George Howard papers; Shirley McManus, "The life of John G. Howard." PAC, RG 5, A1, 138: 75372–77. Canadian Academy of Arts, *Annual exhibition* (Ottawa), 1880. Royal Canadian Academy of Arts, *Report of council* (Toronto), 1882–90. Soc. of Artists and Amateurs, *Catalogue of the first exhibition* . . . (Toronto, 1834). Toronto Soc. of Arts, *First exhibition, 1847* ([Toronto?, 1847?]). *Catalogue of paintings in the gallery at Colborne Lodge, High Park; a donation from John G. Howard, esq., J.P., to the corporation of the city of Toronto, May 7th, 1881* (Toronto, 1885). *Landmarks of Canada: what art has done for Canadian history* . . . (2v., Toronto, 1917–21; repr. in 1v., 1967). Eric Arthur, *Toronto, no mean city* ([Toronto], 1964), 120–21. *Hist. of Toronto and county of York*, II: 69–81. Marion MacRae and Anthony Adamson, *The ancestral roof: domestic architecture of Upper Canada* (Toronto and Vancouver, 1963); *Hallowed walls: church architecture of Upper Canada* (Toronto and Vancouver, 1975). George Baird and Robert Hill, "999 Queen, a collective failure of imagination," *City Magazine* (Toronto), 2 (1976–77), no.3–4: 34–59. Eric Hounsom, "An enormous building for its time," Royal Architectural Institute of Canada, *Journal* (Toronto), 42 (1965): 63–65. T. A. Reed, "Toronto's early architects: many fine buildings still standing," Royal Architectural Institute of Canada, *Journal*, 27 (1950): 46–51.

HOWARD, ROBERT PALMER, physician and educator; b. 12 Jan. 1823 in Montreal, Lower Canada, son of Robert Howard, merchant, and Margaret Kent; m. first in 1855 Mary Frances Chipman, and they had one son; m. secondly in 1872 Emily Severs, and they had four children; d. 28 March 1889 in Montreal.

After leaving school and working for a short time in his father's merchandise business, Robert Palmer Howard attended McGill College, receiving an MD degree in 1848. Following graduation he studied in Dublin, London, Edinburgh, and Paris. In Dublin he took instruction from doctors Robert James Graves and William Stokes, an experience which contributed greatly to his subsequent success as a physician and educator.

Late in 1849 Howard returned to Montreal and commenced medical practice. The following year the Montreal Dispensary was founded and he was appointed one of its attending physicians. Howard's outstanding career as an educator began modestly in 1851 when he became an instructor in chemistry at the St Lawrence School of Medicine of Montreal, a rival to the McGill medical faculty, which lasted only from 1851 to 1852. Howard then joined the staffs of the McGill medical faculty and its teaching hospital, the Montreal General. He was appointed demonstrator of anatomy and curator of the Medical Museum at McGill and an attending physician at the Montreal General.

Howard's ability as a teacher was quickly recognized by rapid academic advancement. In 1854 he assumed the post of professor of medical jurisprudence and two years later the professorship of clinical medicine. In 1860 he relinquished these chairs to assume the professorship of the theory and practice of medicine, which he held until his death. At the Montreal General Hospital his exceptional abilities led in 1858 to his election as chairman of the medical board and secretary of the board of governors, offices which he occupied for 30 years. He was promoted to consulting rank at the Montreal Dispensary in 1864 and at the Montreal General Hospital in 1874. After the death of George William CAMPBELL, Howard was in 1882 made dean of the McGill medical faculty, a post he held until his death. McGill University honoured him in 1886 by an LLD.

His qualities of leadership were also appreciated beyond his university and hospital. He was president of the Canadian Medical Association (1879–80), president of the College of Physicians and Surgeons of the Province of Quebec (1880–83), and twice president of the Montreal Medico-Chirurgical Society (1872–73 and 1879–80). In all these posts he used his considerable influence to raise the standards of premedical and medical education not only in Montreal but throughout Canada. For example, he advocated a four-year medical course with annual sessions of nine instead of six months, an unusually high standard at that time. One of his deepest concerns was the introduction of a federal bill to establish uniformity of qualifications for a licence to practise medicine in the various Canadian provinces. Here his labours were in vain. Medical licensing was under provincial jurisdiction and Howard was frustrated by lack of agreement among the provincial bodies concerned. It was left to one of his students, Thomas George Roddick*, to achieve such an agreement in 1912, after prolonged and difficult negotiations.

Throughout his professional life, from 1849 until only two weeks before his death, Howard maintained an active medical practice. For many years he included surgery in it, but his talents did not lie in this field and in 1880 he withdrew from all surgical work. His reputation as a physician grew steadily and at the time of his death he was described as one of the leading consultants in Canada. He was as well an associate fellow of the College of Physicians of Philadelphia and a vice-president of the Association of American Physicians. His reputation was further enhanced by his publications. Howard was neither a prolific writer nor a highly original investigator but he did contribute sound articles to medical publications in Canada and the United States and was widely regarded as an authority on pulmonary tuberculosis and other diseases of the chest. His publications also shed light on such varied subjects as appendicitis, anaemia, heart disease, cirrhosis of the liver, nephritis, leprosy, tumours of the uterus, aneurysm of the aorta, and paralysis of the eye muscles.

Although Howard rendered distinguished service in many areas he is probably best remembered as a superb teacher. His lectures and instruction at the bedside were based on a thorough knowledge of medicine gained not only by practice but also by careful postmortem examinations and familiarity with the medical literature. Combining enthusiasm with earnestness and dignity, he inspired his pupils with his own zeal and love for medicine. One of these pupils was William Osler*, who took every opportunity to express his admiration and affection for his former teacher. "I have never known one in whom was more happily combined a stern sense of duty with the mental freshness of youth." After Howard's death in 1889, both the Montreal General Hospital and McGill University commissioned Robert Harris* to paint memorial portraits of him, which they still display. Two of Howard's sons, Robert Jared Bliss and Alan Campbell Palmer, became physicians, and the latter was to occupy many of the posts in Montreal previously held by his father.

EDWARD HORTON BENSLEY

[In addition to his *Notes on practice of medicine* (Montreal, 1891), Robert Palmer Howard published a large number of articles in several Canadian and American journals from 1852 to 1889. E.H.B.]

McGill Univ. (Montreal), Medical Library, R. P. Howard, Collected reprints, 1855–89. [William Osler], *Selected writings . . .* (London and Toronto, 1951), 191. *Medical News, a Weekly Medical Journal* (Philadephia), 6, 13 April 1889. Borthwick, *Hist. and biog. gazetteer*, 376. *Canadian biog. dict.*, II: 318–19. *Cyclopædia of Canadian biog.* (Rose, 1888), 511–12. H. A. Kelly, *A cyclopedia of American medical biography, comprising the lives of eminent deceased physicians and surgeons from 1610 to 1910* (2v., Philadelphia and London, 1912), II: 16–17. H. A. Kelly and W. L. Burrage, *American medical biographies* (Baltimore, Md., 1920), 567. Abbott, *Hist. of medicine*, 67, 70, 88. H. [W.] Cushing, *The life of Sir William Osler* (2v., Oxford, 1925). H. E. MacDermot, *History of the Canadian Medical Association* (2v., Toronto, 1935–58).

HOWLEY, THOMAS, physician, surgeon, and office-holder; b. *c.* 1840 at St John's, Nfld, son of Richard Howley and Eliza Burke; m. 26 April 1869 Mary St John of St John's, and they had two sons and one daughter; d. 21 Aug. 1889, near St John's.

Thomas Howley came from a well-known Roman Catholic family of St John's. His Irish-born father, a fish merchant, farmer, and civil servant, encouraged the education of his children with a view to their becoming leaders in colonial society. Thomas became a doctor, James Patrick a government geologist and an historian of the Beothuks, Richard Vincent a priest and educator, and Michael Francis* an author and archbishop of St John's.

Thomas received his early education in St John's under John Valentine Nugent*, a local educator and politician. In 1853 he began working with Thomas McMurdo, a druggist of St John's, and became interested in medicine. He received a medical degree in Ireland in May 1862 and was a licentiate of the King's and Queen's College of Physicians of Dublin and the Royal College of Surgeons of Ireland. After another year of study in Edinburgh Howley worked briefly as a surgeon on a transatlantic passenger liner, before enlisting in the United States Army late in 1863. He was assigned as a surgeon to the 25th United States Coloured Troops' Regiment which fought in Florida. There Howley developed malaria and, although he recovered, the side-effects remained with him. When the Civil War ended, Howley spent the winter of 1865–66 working in several New York hospitals before returning to Newfoundland in April 1866 to establish a general practice at Harbour Grace. Three years later he married and moved his practice to St John's.

Howley was one of eight doctors practising in the city which in 1869 had a population of some 23,000. In 1867 the doctors of St John's had organized a medical society specifically to enforce a new fee structure: instead of patients giving their doctors an annual payment for medical services, they were required to pay for each visit and also for the medicines used. To supplement their private practices, doctors held various government offices: the more senior and experienced were given the positions of visiting physician to the St John's Hospital and the three posts of district surgeon, while the more junior doctors could obtain appointments as city health officers or at the harbour when quarantine was imposed to prevent epidemics spreading from foreign ports. Practitioners were also paid for consultations given to the hospital physician and for services rendered at the hospital. Howley's first major appointment was on 23 April 1872 as one of the two health officers for St John's and he became responsible for maintaining a quarantine establishment at the port. His second major appointment, on 20 May 1879 as a district surgeon for St John's East at an annual salary of $231, made him responsible for the treatment of its sick and poor. He held both positions until his death.

As one of the principal doctors on the island, Howley wrote several medical reports for the government. In 1874 he was asked by the administration of Frederic Bowker Terrington Carter* to head an inquiry into a dysenteric disease prevalent among children in several Notre Dame Bay settlements. Howley attributed the disease to an outbreak of measles and typhoid in the area; in his report he deplored the unsanitary conditions in these settlements and criticized the inhabitants for their lack of concern about individual health and welfare. Following the lead of Sir Edwin Chadwick and other reformers in England, Howley stressed the need for improvements in sanitation and better housing for the poorer classes as the most effective measures against epidemic diseases. Such suggestions generally went unheeded because the politicians disagreed as to how sewage facilities could be provided without the direct taxation opposed by citizens. Howley's warnings proved prophetic: a diphtheria epidemic from 1888 to 1891 resulted in 3,183 cases and 624 deaths. In a report to the government on the epidemic in 1889 Howley blamed its spread in St John's on the city's "wretchedly constructed and located dwellings"; houses were "built in defiance of all sanitary laws; damp sodden foundations; rotting timber sills; mouldy cellars; earth piled up against the bared walls preventing all chances of dryness; no house drains at all in the great majority of instances, necessitating the throwing out of the house slops out of doors, to still further saturate and poison the surrounding soil; and where house-drains do exist, they often are defective. . . ." Characteristically, Howley's report included references to professional studies on the treatment of diphtheria, and he had the 1888 annual report of the New York Board of Health on diphtheria published in the local newspapers.

Howley gave invaluable service to the board of health, which considered him "the ablest authority here on contagion." But illness forced him to retire in 1889 and he spent the last few months of his life in a country residence outside St John's. He had been a diligent doctor, respected for his unselfish devotion to his profession. He was also "a most entertaining conversationalist," "well read," and able to "talk on any subject."

MELVIN BAKER

Centre for Newfoundland Studies, Memorial Univ. of Newfoundland (St John's), J. St P. Knight, "History of the fever hospital; a lecture delivered before the Newfoundland Historical Society, March 27th, 1941" (typescript). PANL, GN 2/2, 1889. Nfld., *Blue book*, 1866–89; House of Assembly, *Journal*, 1866–89. *Daily Colonist* (St John's), 22 Aug. 1889. *Evening Mercury*, 28 March 1889. *Evening Telegram* (St John's), 24 Aug. 1889. *Lovell's province of Newfoundland directory . . .* (Montreal), 1871. *When was that? A chronological dictionary of important events in Newfoundland down to and including the year 1922 . . .*, comp. H.M. Mosdell (St John's, 1923). Paul O'Neill, *The story of St. John's, Newfoundland* (2v., Erin, Ont., 1975–76), I. W. D. Parsons, "The Newfoundland Medical Association, 1924–1974," Nfld. Medical Assoc., *Newsletter* ([St John's]), 16 (1974), no.3.

HOWORTH, WILLIAM, naval officer and office-holder; m. and had two children; d. 23 Feb. 1881 in Newfoundland.

Little is known of William Howorth's early life. He joined the Royal Navy and is first mentioned in naval records as acting mate. He was promoted lieutenant in 1856 and commander in 1867. He had an active and varied naval career serving on the west coast of Africa, in the Pacific Ocean, and in European and Australian waters. As part of his service in the Crimean War he was present at the bombardment of Sveaborg in 1855, and he was honourably mentioned in dispatches. Between the years 1859 and 1863 Howorth was stationed in Chinese waters following the *Arrow* incident of 1856; he again distinguished himself in action, on one occasion by undertaking a hazardous expedition into North China in search of coal deposits.

From 1873 to 1875 Howorth served on the West Indies and North Atlantic station, which was responsible for the protection of British fisheries in Newfoundland waters. The Treaty of Paris of 1815 and the Convention of 1818 with the United States had defined the fishing rights of the various nations off Newfoundland. The most difficult aspect of Howorth's duties was maintaining peace among the nationals who had fishing rights along the west coast of the island, including the fishermen of Newfoundland, France, and the New England states. Although the Americans did not send naval vessels to patrol their treaty shore, the French did, and their presence led to dangerous confrontations, made worse by the sour diplomatic relations between Britain and France.

Aside from policing the fisheries, Howorth was one of the two British naval officers on the Newfoundland station commissioned by the colonial government to act as justices of the peace for the duration of the fishing season. In addition, as the senior naval officer on the station he supplied medical aid to residents in the Bay of Islands and the St George's Bay area, heard complaints against the extortive practices of the merchants, and swore in special constables to preserve order when the need arose. The undeveloped and neglected state of the treaty shore led Howorth to look into the general condition and potential resources of the area. In 1874 he carried out an important survey of the French shore and Labrador fisheries. He also studied the state of agriculture, mineral locations, and lumbering. His report concluded that the deposits of coal, iron, limestone, and gypsum were more important to the future of the area than the fisheries and urged the establishment of a more thorough magisterial system to prevent possible encroachments by foreign powers.

Howorth's report influenced the British government's decision to begin relinquishing to the colony some of the functions it had been fulfilling on the west coast. In 1877 Howorth was appointed the first full-time stipendiary magistrate at St George's Bay by the administration of Frederic Bowker Terrington Carter* and the imperial government. The choice reflected Howorth's reputation for having a considerable grasp of the social conditions, complications arising from the treaties, and the natural resources of the region as well as for firm but fair handling of the cases brought before him as senior naval officer on the treaty coast. For the years 1879 and 1880 he was one of John DELANEY's volunteer observers at the meteorological station at the Bay of Islands.

Howorth officially retired from the Royal Navy in 1879 and in the next year visited England with his family to seek medical assistance. He returned to Newfoundland early in 1881, probably to wind up his affairs, but died on 23 Feb. 1881 shortly after his arrival. Declining health had prevented Howorth from establishing a full and permanent system of civil government including magistrates and collectors of customs, and representative government did not come to the west coast until the election of 1882. However, the *Royal Gazette* commented on the general regret at the death of Howorth who had had the area's "best interests at heart."

FREDERIC FRASER THOMPSON

William Howorth was the author of *Report on the Newfoundland and Labrador fisheries, 1874* (St John's, 1874). *Newfoundlander*, 30 Nov. 1875, 25 Feb. 1881. *Royal Gazette* (St John's), 22 March 1881. F. F. Thompson, *The French shore problem in Newfoundland: an imperial study* (Toronto, 1961).

HOYLES, Sir HUGH WILLIAM, lawyer, judge, and politician; b. 17 Oct. 1814 at St John's, Nfld, son of Newman Wright Hoyles* and Lucretia Brown; m. 7 Sept. 1842 Jean Liddell of Halifax, N.S., and they had three sons and three daughters; d. 1 Feb. 1888 at Halifax.

Hugh William Hoyles was educated at Pictou Academy in Nova Scotia, received his legal training under Samuel George William Archibald*, attorney general of Nova Scotia, and was called to the bar in 1837. Hoyles returned to St John's some time before 1842 and quickly established a reputation and a large practice as a result of his excellent mercantile and family connections and his talents as a lawyer. He gained some popularity as a supporter of the Natives' Society, as a member of the managing committee of the Newfoundland Church Society, organized by Bishop Aubrey George Spencer*, and as a keen sportsman (excelling at rowing).

In 1848 Hoyles was elected to the assembly as a Conservative for Fortune Bay, the constituency his father had represented. He soon emerged as a dominant figure in his party and became well known particularly for his views on the school issue and on responsible government. Hoyles was critical of the secular General Academy, established in St John's in 1845 for secondary education in opposition to Bishop Edward Feild*'s St John's Collegiate School (later Church of England Academy) founded in September 1844. Hoyles supported the bishop, alleging that the academy was crippled by its failure to give religious education, and in 1850 he succeeded in having the General Academy dissolved and its government allowance divided among three separate academies. Hoyles was also hostile to the elementary school system, which had been set up on a non-denominational basis in 1836 but was modified in 1843 to allow the establishment of separate Roman Catholic schools. Until 1853 he campaigned with Feild, by means of speeches, resolutions, petitions, and public meetings, for the division of the state grant to the Protestant elementary schools so that the Anglicans could set up their own system. The other Protestant denominations did not necessarily agree with this proposal and

Hoyles was unsuccessful, but his campaign had an important effect on the issue of responsible government.

The cause of responsible government had been taken up by the Liberal party which had controlled the assembly since 1848 and had been led since 1852 by the able politician Philip Francis Little*. Although it maintained publicly a non-denominational pose, privately its leader spoke of "the Catholic Party"; it could command a solidly Roman Catholic vote and had the outspoken support of Bishop John Thomas Mullock*. The Protestants of Newfoundland, however, comprised a majority of the population and if they could remain united, given the political divisions along religious lines, the Conservatives would be able to control the assembly. By following Bishop Feild, however, Hoyles alienated many Methodists, who supported the *status quo* in education, from the Conservative party which appeared to be dominated by high church Anglicans. As a result these Methodists and some evangelical Anglicans supported the Catholic Liberals.

Hoyles came to realize that Feild was an electoral liability and in 1853 he dropped the demand for elementary church schools in an attempt to rally all Protestants in a grass roots, anti–Roman Catholic campaign. It was too late. Little had won some Protestant support in the house and through Joseph Woods*'s *Courier*, and he portrayed the opposition as sectarian bigots when he went to London in 1854 to discuss the issue of responsible government with the colonial secretary, the Duke of Newcastle. Newcastle decided that responsible government could no longer be withheld and was prepared to grant it in that year, subject to conditions which included making representation in the House of Assembly more equitable. Hoyles established a Protestant committee to fight the decision by preparing a petition, signed by 1,600 of a possible 6,210 Protestant males of St John's, and he published a pamphlet entitled *Case of the Protestant inhabitants*. He was sent to London in July 1854 by the Central Protestant Committee to plead the case against responsible government which he, the governor, Ker BAILLIE HAMILTON, and the new colonial secretary, Sir George Grey, viewed as unsuitable for Newfoundland because of the religious divisions in the colony [*see* Edward Mortimer ARCHIBALD; William Bickford Row*]. All of his efforts were to no avail; the British government was determined that a settlement be reached. Thus responsible government was granted to the colony late in 1854. In November Hoyles returned to London to defend the governor's actions in postponing an election until May 1855. By this election Little became the first premier. Despite his failure, Hoyles had established himself as an outstanding politician: he had been at the forefront of the Conservative campaign, speaking in the House of Assembly, addressing public meetings, and lobbying the Colonial Office.

Hoyles learned from his mistakes. During the next six years, as leader of the opposition, he carefully strove to restore the Protestant unity which his educational campaign had destroyed. In 1857 he joined the corresponding committee of the Colonial Church Society, an Anglican evangelical body which had maintained schools in Newfoundland since 1823. In 1859 he accepted the vice-presidency of the Bible Society, an organization dominated by Methodists, which was frowned upon by Feild, and in the election of that year Hoyles ran with Edward Evans, a Methodist, for the two assembly seats representing Burin, a key constituency. They were defeated, however, by Ambrose Shea* and James J. Rogerson.

During these years Hoyles continued to take a prominent part in the affairs of his own church. He was a committee member of the Church Society, a director of the Church of England Academy, and a sponsor of the Church of England Asylum for Widows and Orphans. His legal practice flourished in the 1850s, and he was a principal figure in two well-publicized libel cases: in 1856 he prosecuted Magistrate Ollerhead for slandering the Reverend Henry Lind* and in November 1858 he prosecuted the Spanish consul, unsuccessfully, on behalf of Walter GRIEVE, a wealthy merchant. He became a director of the St John's branch of the International Life Assurance Company and a committee member of the Water Company. Hoyles also played a prominent role in spearheading a Newfoundland protest against the Fishery Convention of 1857. He moved a hostile resolution in the assembly and joined Little, Laurence O'Brien*, and James William TOBIN in a delegation to London in March 1857.

In the early 1860s the Liberals were divided and charged with corruption and inefficiency. Bishop Mullock was discontented with politicians who were using him to keep themselves in office while neglecting the causes for which he stood. Indeed in 1860 Ambrose Shea, a moderate Liberal, was making tentative offers of a coalition with Hoyles. The opportunity for change came with dramatic suddenness in February 1861. The government, now headed by John Kent*, brought in a bill to pay official salaries in the lower-valued colonial currency rather than in British currency. The judges objected and on the advice of Hoyles petitioned the governor, Sir Alexander Bannerman*, to suspend the legislation. Kent thereupon accused the governor of conspiring with the opposition. Bannerman, who had never liked the Liberals and had been waiting patiently for them to discredit themselves, demanded an apology from Kent. When none was forthcoming he consulted Hoyles in his legal capacity, proceeded to dismiss the ministry, and invited Hoyles to form the next government. The new administration was composed of Anglicans Robert Carter* and Hoyles, Methodists John Bemister* and Nicholas Stabb, Laurence O'Brien, a Roman Catholic, and John Henry WARREN. Ambrose Shea was asked to join but declined. Defeated in the assembly on a vote of non-confidence, Hoyles called an election on 2 May 1861. His hopes of a non-sectarian contest were frustrated when both Feild and Mullock entered the fray. The election gave Hoyles a majority of two; Harbour Main's return was disputed and violence prevented any return from Harbour Grace. The more extreme Liberals then attempted to force their candidates for Harbour Main, George James Hogsett* and Charles Furey, upon the House of Assembly. In the riots that ensued in St John's three people were killed, property, including Hoyles's country cottage, was set on fire, and Feild was stoned. Hoyles stood firm, however, and his refusal to permit the two men to be seated as members eventually restored comparative calm. After the by-election in Harbour Grace of November 1861, the Conservatives had a more comfortable majority of four in the house of 30.

Safely in power, Hoyles worked to divide his opponents. He realized that once religion ceased to be a cause of party difference, class and economic interest would grow in importance and the wealthier Liberals would drift towards the Conservative party. He therefore began a policy of distributing patronage strictly according to the numerical strengths of the denominations and also made a determined though unsuccessful attempt to persuade Kent and Shea to join his administration. In going along with the Methodists, who had in 1859 decided in favour of denominational schools and now changed their mind again to oppose them, Hoyles offended Feild. He attempted to cut expenditures on poor relief, with little success, and followed a policy of careful reform, increasing the police establishment, banning mumming, appointing customs officers for the Labrador coast, and consolidating the public debt as a means of dealing with the poor economic condition of the colony. When confederation became an issue he carefully involved the opposition and invited not only the Conservative Frederic Bowker Terrington Carter* but also the Liberal Shea to represent Newfoundland at the Quebec conference in 1864. Hoyles was in poor health by this time and retired from politics to become chief justice of Newfoundland in 1865. Carter then became prime minister and Shea and Kent joined the government.

As chief justice, Hoyles soon won general esteem and affection. Daniel Woodley Prowse* describes him as "a model judge, the most painstaking, able and impartial administrator that ever graced the Bench of any British colony. . . ." In August 1869 Anthony MUSGRAVE, who had been governor since 1864, left for British Columbia to assume the governorship there. He had believed that Newfoundland was about to enter confederation and had designated Hoyles as the new lieutenant governor. Late in 1869 the anti-confederates won the general election. Hoyles's hopes were frustrated, but he was consoled by a knighthood which he had received from Queen Victoria that year. In 1875 denominational schools were established in Newfoundland, something Hoyles had fought for in his youth but which he strongly opposed by the 1870s.

In 1876 Hoyles was the administrator of Newfoundland in the absence of Sir John Hawley GLOVER. In 1880 he retired to Nova Scotia where he lived on his pension with his married daughter, although he maintained his connections with Newfoundland by continuing to contribute to its charities and the Church Society. When he died in 1888, the St John's *Royal Gazette* obituary said that "His name had become a synonym for uprightness and integrity, and is respected, one might say revered, beyond that of any other native of the Colony." Prowse summarized the general feeling in the colony towards Hoyles: "We are all proud of Sir Hugh as the most distinguished Newfoundlander of our day." He deserves these words of praise; through his political experience Hoyles, the young Conservative Anglican, came to see the danger of religion in politics, and in the early 1860s he began the attempt to separate them. The ultimate result was the defusing of the extreme and violent nature of mid-19th-century Newfoundland politics.

FREDERICK JONES

H. W. Hoyles was the author of *Case of the Protestant inhabitants against the unconditional concession of responsible government* (London, 1854).

Guildhall Library (London), Commonwealth and Continental Church Soc., Newfoundland School Soc., Committee minutes, 1839–80; Reports, 1823–80. PAC, MG 24, B51 (mfm. copy). PRO, CO 194/116–78; CO 197/4–63. USPG, D9A, D9B, D27, D39. Church of England, Nfld. Church Soc., *Annual report* (St John's), 1842, 1850–55, 1863. Edward Feild, *Remarks on the sub-division of the legislative grant for the encouragement of education in this colony* (St John's, 1852). John Little, *The constitution of the government of Newfoundland, in its legislative and executive departments . . .* ([St John's], 1855). R. B. McCrea, *Lost amid the fogs: sketches of life in Newfoundland, England's ancient colony* (London, 1869). Henry Winton, *A chapter in the history of Newfoundland for the year 1861* (St John's, 1861). *Newfoundlander*, 1855–59, 1864–76. *Patriot* (St John's), 1839–53, 1864–66. *Public Ledger*, 1839–60, 1862–64. *Royal Gazette* (St John's), 1842–53, 1864–76. *Times* (London), 3 Feb. 1888. *Times and General Commercial Gazette* (St John's), 1842–55, 1864–76.

Gunn, *Political hist. of Nfld.* Alfred Morine, *Sir Hugh Hoyles, prime minister (1861–1865), chief justice of Newfoundland (1865–1880)* (n.p., n.d.). E. C. Moulton, "The political history of Newfoundland, 1861–1869" (MA thesis, Memorial Univ. of Newfoundland, St John's, 1960). S. J. R.

Noel, *Politics in Newfoundland* (Toronto, 1971). Prowse, *Hist. of Nfld.* (1896). Wells, "Struggle for responsible government in Nfld." Frederick Jones, "John Bull's other Ireland – nineteenth century Newfoundland," *Dalhousie Rev.*, 55 (1975–76): 227–35; "Religion, education and politics in Newfoundland, 1836–1875," Canadian Church Hist. Soc., *Journal* (Sudbury, Ont.), 12 (1970): 64–76.

HUME, CATHERINE HONORIA (Blake), b. 1804 or 1805 at Kiltegan, County Wicklow (Republic of Ireland), daughter of Joseph Samuel Hume; m. in 1832 in Ireland William Hume Blake*, and they had two sons, Edward* and Samuel Hume*, and two daughters; d. 3 Feb. 1886 at London, Ont.

Catherine Honoria Hume, although born into the prosperous landed gentry of Protestant Ireland, enjoyed little of the comfort and elegance of other branches of the Hume family. Her father, the second son of William Hume, a wealthy and influential landowner, inherited only a small portion of the family estates and entered the army in pursuit of a professional career. Catherine was born at the family seat, Humewood, and began her education in Dublin where her father was stationed. After his premature death, however, the family evidently returned to County Wicklow. Despite changing family fortunes, Catherine's education was genteel and refined. She played the piano and harp, read classical literature in Latin, and was fluent in French and Italian.

In the spring of 1832 she married William Hume Blake, a childhood friend and first cousin who was five years her junior. Only months later they immigrated to Canada as part of an impressive group of relatives and friends, dominated by clergymen lured by the prospect of better appointments with the Church of England in Upper Canada. Hume Blake, still unsettled about a career, accompanied his elder brother Dominick Edward* to Adelaide Township, Middlesex County, in 1833, where he settled at Bear Creek, near Strathroy, in the hope of becoming a gentleman farmer. But Catherine soon tired of the drudgery of pioneer life and according to family legend confronted Hume, questioning whether the hands of her newly born son Edward had no greater future than to become as calloused and weather-beaten as his father's. In 1835 at Catherine's insistence the Blakes moved to Toronto.

After Hume Blake's enrolment as a student-at-law, Catherine operated a private girls' school to supplement the family's income. Following Hume's admission to the bar in 1838, she transferred her abundant energies to charitable societies, and then to the support of Hume's diverse interests in legal reform, education, and politics. Catherine played an influential and frequently decisive, albeit private, role in Hume's flourishing career, and in the 1850s, when Hume's health deteriorated and he was forced to resign positions of influence and prestige, she asserted her dominant role as the Blake matriarch. Throughout the 1860s she accompanied Hume on frequent trips abroad in search of healthier climates. After his death in 1870, she resided chiefly in London, Ont., at the home of her elder daughter, Sophia Cronyn, where she died in 1886 as a result of injuries sustained in a fall.

Catherine Blake was motivated by an uncompromising evangelical Christian faith which had mixed effects on her offspring. Edward did not share his mother's emotional commitment to Christianity, and was chronically depressed by a sense of guilt often reinforced by her stern admonitions. Samuel, however, became a devout and equally uncompromising leader of Toronto's low church faction of the Church of England. As well as playing an integral role in the education of her children, even after they had been enrolled in private schools, Catherine also instilled in them the desire to attain in Canada the status which her branch of the Hume family had lost in Ireland. Edward, especially, bore the burden of his family heritage and strove to achieve goals which Catherine had once set for her husband. Many of the ambitions of William Hume, Edward, and Samuel can be traced to the influence of Catherine Blake.

In one sense, Catherine Blake was the archetypal wife of a successful Victorian businessman and politician. She ran an efficient household and belonged to the proper charitable and religious societies, while remaining unobtrusively off the stage of public events. In another sense, however, Catherine's life demonstrated the tensions inherent in a social role which provided 19th-century women with little hope of fulfilling their aspirations. Denied a meaningful career she transferred her ambitions to her husband, and, after his chronic illness, to her sons. Strong-willed, intelligent, and ambitious, Catherine Blake was a domineering mother whose family provided her main source of self-fulfilment.

J. Daniel Livermore

Writings by Catherine Hume Blake were published as "The riots of 1849 in Montreal," *CHR*, 15 (1934): 283–88; and "Edward Blake: a portrait of his childhood," ed. M. A. Banks, *Profiles of a province: studies in the history of Ontario* . . . (Toronto, 1967), 92–96.

AO, MU 136–273. MTL, Robert Baldwin papers. J. D. Livermore, "Towards 'a union of hearts': the early career of Edward Blake, 1867–1880" (PHD thesis, Queen's Univ., Kingston, Ont., 1975); "The personal agonies of Edward Blake," *CHR*, 56 (1975): 45–58.

HUMPHREYS, THOMAS BASIL, politician, gold seeker, conveyancer, and auctioneer; b. 10 March 1840 in Liverpool, England, son of John Basil Humphreys and Mary Elizabeth Morgan; m. 3 Nov. 1873 Caroline (Carrie) Watkins, and they had a son and three daughters; d. 26 Aug. 1890 in Victoria, B.C.

Thomas Basil Humphreys was educated at Walton-on-the-Hill (now part of Liverpool) but other details of his early life are vague. Although his obituary claims he had served in the East India Company there is no reference to him in the company's surviving records. Humphreys arrived in British Columbia from California aboard the steamer *Oregon* on 26 July 1858. He later described himself as having "come out as a needy adventurer." Success in the gold-fields seems unlikely for he was hired in March 1859 as a constable at Fort Hope (Hope, B.C.) at a salary of $80 a month. He was soon transferred to Port Douglas (Douglas, B.C.) where he remained until he resigned on 4 Dec. 1860. As a constable Humphreys displayed the independence of authority and intemperance of languge which were to characterize his political career. Following his resignation, "couched in a vile and libelous manner," as an official noted, he returned to mining until August 1864, then became an auctioneer and conveyancer at Port Douglas; within a year he moved to Lillooet where he combined auctioneering with mining. Despite this variety of occupations Humphreys was listed on the electoral rolls as a labourer for his entire life. Business was clearly secondary to politics in Humphreys' life. T. B. Humphreys and Company, auctioneers, ceased to advertise after 1874, and the last ten years of Humphreys' life were a period of almost continual financial difficulty.

In November 1868 Humphreys was elected to the Legislative Council of British Columbia for Lillooet as a pro-confederation candidate, holding the seat until 1871 when British Columbia entered confederation and the council was abolished. He was a strong supporter of responsible government and during the confederation debates his chief concerns were its immediate introduction and the retention of as many offices as possible in the hands of British Columbians. But his views and means of advancing them brought him into conflict with the other members of the Legislative Council. At a public meeting on 11 April 1870 he accused Joseph William Trutch*, the chief commissioner of lands and works, of fiscal mismanagement, implying that $500,000 had been embezzled; he also denounced the Legislative Council as an "infamous, rascally arrangement" and stated that he had no confidence in the executive. As a result of this speech Humphreys was suspended from the council for breach of privilege on 19 April. A petition calling for his reinstatement gathered 160 signatures, but neither it nor Humphreys' letter of apology produced the desired result. As a further show of support, a public meeting in Victoria on 13 May, chaired by Amor De Cosmos*, presented Humphreys with a gold watch and chain. In November the constituents of Lillooet returned him to the Legislative Council.

Following confederation Humphreys represented Lillooet in the Legislative Assembly of British Columbia from 1871 to 1875. He was one of the most vocal opponents of the government of John Foster McCreight* and moved the non-confidence motion which brought De Cosmos to power in December 1872. But De Cosmos did not give Humphreys a cabinet post, despite their long association, and he immediately joined the opposition. From September 1875 to July 1882 Humphreys sat for the riding of Victoria District. When Andrew Charles ELLIOTT formed a government in February 1876 he did not repeat De Cosmos' mistake but gave Humphreys the finance and agriculture portfolio. On 26 July, however, Humphreys resigned because of a disagreement with the rest of the cabinet over financial matters and again crossed the floor, supporting George Anthony Walkem* with as much vigour as he had previously attacked him. Following Walkem's return to power in June 1878 Humphreys served as provincial secretary and minister of mines, portfolios he retained when Robert Beaven* succeeded Walkem as premier in June 1882.

In the general election the following month, Humphreys lost his seat and spent the next several years in the political wilderness. He unsuccessfully contested a by-election in Yale in October 1882, and in July 1886 he was defeated in his old riding of Victoria District. The following February he unsuccessfully sought election to the Canadian House of Commons from Victoria. Finally, in December 1887 he was returned to the Legislative Assembly for Comox in a by-election but his health began to fail. He went to San Francisco in August 1889 for medical consultation but his condition continued to decline. Unable to attend the 1890 session of the legislature, he died on 26 Aug. 1890.

An acid-tongued demagogue, the "Destroyer of Governments," Humphreys was one of the earliest professional politicians in British Columbia. He played an important role in the provincial legislature of the first decades after confederation, especially in the struggle for responsible government.

MICHAEL F. H. HALLERAN

City of Victoria Arch., British Columbia Land and Investment Company, Limited, Letterbooks outward, 1872–92. PABC, Colonial corr., T. B. Humphreys corr.; C. S. Nicol corr., C. S. Nicol to R. C. Moody, 17 March 1859; Petitions, 18 April 1870; GR 224, 6, 8; T. B. Humphreys, Notes for election speech at Comox. B.C., Legislative Assembly, *Sessional papers*, 1875–90 (list of voters, Victoria City and Lillooet); Legislative Council, *Journals*, 1870. *Cariboo Sentinel*, 21 Nov. 1868, 19 Nov. 1870. *Daily Colonist* (Victoria), 12 April 1870; 4 Nov. 1873; 5 July 1874; 27 July 1876; 24 July, 24 Oct. 1882; 17 Feb., 7 July, 4 Dec. 1886; 4 Jan., 29 April 1888; 8, 23 Aug. 1889; 24 Jan., 27, 28 Aug. 1890. *Gazette* (Victoria), 28 July 1858. *Government Gazette–British Columbia* (Victoria), March, May 1870.

J. B. Kerr, *Biographical dictionary of well-known British Columbians, with a historical sketch* (Vancouver, 1890). *The year book of British Columbia . . .*, comp. R. E. Gosnell (Victoria), 1911.

HUNTER, JAMES, Church of England clergyman and missionary, translator, and philologist; b. 25 April 1817 at Barnstaple, England; d. 12 Feb. 1882 in London, England.

James Hunter, after some experience as a schoolmaster, entered the Church Missionary Society College at Islington (now part of London), England, to train for the ministry. He also acquired some medical knowledge in London hospitals in anticipation of missionary work for the society. Ordained a priest in the Church of England in 1844, Hunter sailed with his wife Ann on 1 June in a Hudson's Bay Company ship. On 13 August they reached York Factory (Man.) and on 26 September, having travelled by York boat, they arrived at Cumberland Station, the new Indian mission at The Pas (Man.) on the Saskatchewan River. The missionaries spent an uncomfortable winter because a careless boatman had lost part of their stove *en route*.

By 1846 Hunter was raising cattle, horses, pigs, and sheep as well as crops of wheat, barley, and potatoes on the mission farm. After 1847 some of the Indians, following his example, built log houses, cleared land, and planted crops, and even adopted European clothes. In 1845–46 Hunter had engaged a carpenter for three years to erect a church, manse, and school, but construction progressed slowly as all lumber had to be hand sawn from local timber. In 1848, when members of the expedition led by Sir John Richardson* and John Rae* in search of Sir John Franklin* wintered at Cumberland House (Sask.), three carpenters donated three months' labour to building the mission manse at The Pas. The church, with a 70-foot spire, was consecrated by the bishop of Rupert's Land, David ANDERSON, in the summer of 1850.

Hunter was energetic in converting Indians to Christianity, and each year reported many baptisms. In 1845 he sent James Beardy, a young Christian Indian from The Pas, to Lac la Ronge (La Ronge, Sask.); the next year a native catechist, James Settee*, joined Beardy. In the summer of 1847 Hunter went by canoe to Lac la Ronge where he baptized 124 Indians, and in 1848 this mission was placed on a permanent basis with the arrival of the Reverend Robert Hunt and his wife. Two other stations were established as outposts of the Cumberland mission: in 1850 Hunter sent a catechist, John Humpherville, to Moose Lake (Sask.), and in 1853 the Reverend Henry Budd*, another Indian, who had preceded Hunter at The Pas, to Nepowewin (Nipawin, Sask.).

Even before he had acquired a proper knowledge of Cree, Hunter began translating religious literature. He advocated Roman characters rather than the syllabic script developed for the Crees in 1840 by the Reverend James Evans* at Rossville (Man.). Hunter's scholarly mind could not accept the imprecision of the syllabic system which he regarded as merely a kind of shorthand. Yet formal schooling was essential to master the Roman alphabet whereas the mnemonic features of the syllabic script could be learned by a nomadic people within a day. Hunter's competence in Cree grew after his marriage on 10 July 1848 to Jean (Jane) Ross, eldest daughter of Donald Ross, the HBC factor at Norway House (Man.); she had learned the language in infancy, and she now joined Hunter in his work. Impatient to see translations in print, Hunter proposed their printing in England as early as 1848. Bishop Anderson, however, advised further revision, as he found inconsistencies in Hunter's orthography, and as late as 1853 the bishop wrote that "his translation is still, I tell him, a little over spelt, rather too many letters. . . ." Copies of the Gospel of St Matthew, printed in England by the Church Missionary House, had arrived at York Factory on the supply ship of 1853. When the Hunters went to England on furlough in the autumn of 1854 they saw a large number of their translations through the press. Among their publications in 1855 were the Gospels of St Mark and St John, the Book of Common Prayer, Jean Hunter's translation of the first epistle general of St John, and a catechism. Most of these were reprinted in the late 1870s, and many are still in use. Some of the Hunters' translations were issued eventually in syllabic script. Jean Hunter also compiled hymns. In recognition of his work as a translator Hunter was granted an MA by the archbishop of Canterbury in 1854.

In September 1855, on their return from England, the Hunters travelled to the Red River Settlement again by York boat. Ten days out from York Factory the party stopped long enough for Jean to give birth to a child. Two weeks later her eldest child and sister narrowly escaped drowning and a young English woman was lost when the boat capsized in a wind storm on Lake Winnipeg. Jean Hunter was in delicate health for many months thereafter. The hardships of frequent childbirth for women in the wilderness are exemplified by the story of Hunter's two wives. His first wife had died on 20 Nov. 1847 following childbirth, and only the first of her three children lived. Jean also lost two children at birth; in her third confinement, at St Andrews parish on Red River in the winter of 1851–52, Dr John Bunn* gave her chloroform, probably one of the first uses of the anæsthetic in the west.

Hunter was stationed at St Andrews from 1855 to 1865. In 1854 Bishop Anderson had made him an archdeacon of Cumberland, with responsibility for secular and financial matters relating to the more distant missions. Further, as corresponding secretary to the Church Missionary Society, he was the liaison between the local clergy and the headquarters in England. He was indefatigable in these duties as he was in the spiritual leadership of his parish. One last missionary venture, in 1858–59, saw him travelling with the HBC brigade to Fort Simpson (N.W.T.) on the Mackenzie River to investigate the feasibility of missions there. On his recommendation the Reverend William Kirkby set off in 1859 for that distant country. In 1860 appeared an eight-page ordination sermon by Hunter, *God's charge to Zion's watchmen*, the first booklet printed in the Red River Settlement.

The winter of 1862–63 saw the trial of the Reverend Griffith Owen Corbett* on a charge of attempting to induce an abortion on a 16-year-old servant-girl in his house. There was great public excitement in the settlement. Corbett denied both the charge and the paternity of the child. A popular medical missionary, he was believed by many to have been framed by the civil authorities for his vigorous opposition to the HBC. The Church of England clergy remained aloof, which was interpreted by some as tacit support of the authorities and by others as an example of missionary rivalry since Corbett was sponsored by the Colonial and Continental Church Society. Archdeacon Hunter, acting as the bishop's examiner, interviewed the girl in late November, and satisfied himself that Corbett was guilty as charged. In mid January 1863, before Corbett's trial, a rumour spread suggesting that Hunter was guilty of moral turpitude, apparently in relation to the paternity of the child. Shocked that such a calumny should be circulated in his own parish, Hunter responded emotionally by offering his resignation to the bishop but withdrew it when the author of the rumour, John Tait, a miller and carpenter, admitted two weeks later that it was without substance. The incident adversely affected Hunter's chances of being named bishop of Rupert's Land in 1864. When Bishop Anderson resigned Hunter expected to be named on his record as administrator, missionary, and translator, but unease in England that he might not be acceptable to the laity in Red River caused him to be passed over in favour of Robert Machray*.

In the summer of 1865 the Hunters returned to England. He continued to work for the CMS until 1867 when he accepted the important charge of vicar of St Matthew's Church, Bayswater, London, which he retained until his death. So popular was he as a preacher that a new church had to be built to accommodate the worshippers. In 1875 his great study, *A lecture on the grammatical construction of the Cree language*, was published by the Society for the Propagation of Christian Knowledge. Much of the 265-page volume is given over to paradigms of the Cree verb. It remains a basic source in the study of the language. The archbishop of Canterbury awarded him a DD in 1876.

The tombstone of James and Jean Hunter in Highgate Cemetery, London, bears this tribute: "By their joint labours they gave the Bible and the Prayer Book in their native tongue to the Cree Indians of North-west America."

BRUCE PEEL

James Hunter was the author of *A lecture on the grammatical construction of the Cree language . . .* (London, 1875). His other works, and those of his wife, Jean Ross, can be found in Peel, *Biblio. of the Prairie prov.* (1973), and J. C. Pilling, *Bibliography of the Algonquian languages* (Washington, 1891), 243–48.

CMS Arch., C, C.1/I; C.1/L; C.1/M; and esp. C, C.1/O, Journals of James Hunter (mfm. at PAC and Univ. of Alberta, Edmonton). *Church Missionary Intelligencer and Record* (London), new ser., 7 (1882): 180–81. Mactavish, *Letters of Letitia Hargrave* (MacLeod). Church Missionary Soc., *Register of missionaries (clerical, lay, & female), and native clergy, from 1804 to 1904* ([London?, 1905?]), 62. *Crockford's clerical directory . . .* (London), 1867–81. Boon, *Anglican Church.* [J. A.] Mackay, "James Hunter," *Leaders of the Canadian church*, ed. W. B. Heeney (2nd ser., Toronto, 1920), 79–85.

HUNTINGTON, LUCIUS SETH, lawyer, journalist, businessman, politician, and author; b. 26 May 1827 at Compton, Lower Canada, the son of Seth Huntington, a farmer, and Mary Hovey; d. 19 May 1886 in New York City.

Both the paternal and the maternal ancestors of Lucius Seth Huntington moved from New England to the Eastern Townships at the turn of the 19th century. Because they were part of a wave of settlers more attracted by cheap and plentiful land than by British political institutions, it was perhaps natural that Huntington would become an "advanced Liberal" and warm admirer of the United States. Educated in local grammar schools and at Brownington Seminary in Vermont, Huntington studied law under John Sewell Sanborn*, Sherbrooke's annexationist MLA. To support himself while studying, he became principal of Shefford Academy in Frost Village. After his admission to the bar in 1853 he married Miriam Jane Wood. The legal profession in the western section of the Townships was overcrowded, so Huntington decided to supplement his income by becoming a merchant. Commerce had begun to boom in the Townships after the construction of the Grand Trunk Railroad in 1852.

The railway freed the region from economic isolation, and each town clamoured for a branch line in order to partake in the prosperity. The Montreal politicians who represented the area found themselves unable to satisfy the demands of their "backwoods" constituents, who also requested local courts, financial institutions, and higher education facilities. The voters of the Townships resolved to elect local residents to gain these improvements. The ambitious young Huntington quickly put himself at the head of the regional protest movement by founding the *Advertiser and Eastern Townships Sentinel* in Knowlton, Canada East, in January 1856. He was assisted by a local entrepreneur, Hiram Sewell Foster, and given full support by the county's two members of the Legislative Council, Paul Holland Knowlton* and Philip Henry Moore*. As a Conservative, Knowlton allayed suspicions that the newspaper was simply a Liberal organ. The *Advertiser*'s main goals were to develop a sense of local pride in the human and natural resources of the region and to have that spirit forcefully expressed in political life. When George-Étienne Cartier*'s law reform bill of 1857 decentralized the courts, the *Advertiser* boasted that it was "the direct result of Eastern Townships agitation for practical reform" and proof that the people could "redress the social and political evils which oppress them."

In 1857 the newspaper moved from Knowlton to Waterloo, Canada East, because Huntington had become secretary of the Stanstead, Shefford and Chambly Railroad Company. Huntington's political sympathies clearly lay with the Liberals, but they did not interfere with his ambitions for the region and himself. In 1858 he successfully supported Asa Belknap Foster*, a local candidate in a by-election in Shefford County, against Lewis Thomas DRUMMOND, who had just been appointed attorney general in the short-lived Liberal ministry of George Brown* and Antoine-Aimé Dorion*. Publicly Huntington claimed that Drummond's only sin was that he was from Montreal, but like Foster he probably felt that Drummond had jeopardized the Stanford, Shefford and Chambly Railroad (of which he was president) by joining the Liberals.

Drummond's defeat in Shefford marked the end of absentee representation in the western section of the Townships. When Foster resigned in 1860 to seek election to the Legislative Council, Huntington decided to become a candidate in the by-election himself. But like most Townships people sympathetic to the Liberals, he found it difficult to defend a party which under George Brown advocated the sectional interests of Canada West. Huntington's solution was to launch the Eastern Townships Party. The Montreal Tories, frustrated by Huntington in their attempts to represent the Townships directly, turned to the francophone population, now two-thirds of the Shefford electorate, as a source of voting strength. They offered as their candidate Michel-Adrien Bessette, the popular mayor of North Stukely, who embittered the campaign by declaring that the French Canadian majority should elect one of their own nationality and religion. The result was a tie vote, and before the matter could be settled, the legislature was dissolved. In the 1861 general election Huntington managed to win a comfortable majority over Flavien-R. Blanchard, the mayor of Ely.

In the house, Huntington became a regular supporter of the Liberal party. He was an effective speaker, and by 1863 had proved himself a capable enough parliamentarian to be appointed solicitor general in the John Sandfield Macdonald*–Dorion government. In 1864 he, like the other Lower Canadian Liberals, refused to support the Great Coalition [*see* George Brown] and its confederation project. No guarantees, he felt, could ensure the future of the English-speaking minority should Canada East acquire its own legislature.

The return of the Liberals to the opposition benches in 1864 enabled Huntington to devote more time to his private interests. By this time he had stopped managing the *Advertiser* and had moved to Montreal where he wrote occasional editorials for the *Montreal Herald*, edited by Edward Goff PENNY. But his financial interests continued to be centred in the Eastern Townships, especially after 1865 when the demand which had been created by the American Civil War enabled him to profit from copper mines he owned in Bolton Township. His personal economic well-being and that of his region clearly depended upon trade with the Americans. In 1867 he declared that confederation would prematurely sever the Canadian connection with England, but by 1870 he agreed with Alexander Tilloch Galt* and the French-speaking Liberals that the continuing diplomatic tie with Great Britain was hindering the renewal of a reciprocal trade agreement with the United States such as had existed between 1854 and 1866. For such a purpose he was particularly anxious that Canada acquire independent treaty-making powers.

Huntington had reason to be concerned for by 1871 his fortunes had reached a low ebb. The short wooden railway built to his mine proved to be impracticable, the bottom fell out of the copper market, and his wife and one of his sons died in rapid succession. Furthermore, his stand on Canadian independence did little except embarrass the Liberal party hierarchy. Huntington was fading into political obscurity when in 1873 he uncovered the famous Pacific Scandal. In the House of Commons he charged that the government of Sir John A. Macdonald* had granted Sir Hugh ALLAN's American-financed company the charter to build the Canadian transcontinental railway in return for contributions toward the Conservatives' 1872 general election campaign. Macdonald suspected that Huntington's old partner in the Eastern townships railway, the Conservative Asa Foster, had played a key role in publicizing certain incriminating documents. These suspicions were reinforced after the Conservatives resigned in November 1873 and met defeat at the polls, for Foster, Huntington, and George Stephen* soon formed a syndicate to acquire the Pacific railway construction contract. Huntington planned to resign his post as president of the Privy Council in Alexander Mackenzie*'s newly formed cabinet in order to devote all his energies to this project, but he soon became involved in a scandal of his own. The Conservatives, anxious for revenge, charged that Huntington had made false representations in selling his and other Townships copper mines in Great Britain. Luther Hamilton Holton*, a powerful Montreal Liberal, persuaded Huntington not to step down as the cabinet's Protestant Quebec representative because to do so might be interpreted as a confession of his guilt. The British company involved eventually dropped a law suit it had instituted, and Huntington remained in the cabinet as postmaster general after October 1875. Because he continued as a minister, he ended his involvement in the syndicate seeking the railway construction contract.

Huntington soon precipitated another national controversy. During the Argenteuil by-election of December 1875, which came amid the controversy following the death of Joseph Guibord* in 1869, Huntington warned Quebec's Protestants that they could not hope to defend themselves against the encroachments of ultramontane Catholics unless they supported the Liberal party. A. T. Galt poured oil on the resulting fire by endorsing and elaborating upon this theme in two published pamphlets. This episode was the beginning of the end of Huntington's political career, because Holton had now decided that he wanted Huntington's cabinet post. Using the Argenteuil speech as his lever, Holton informed Alexander Mackenzie that Huntington should be forced to resign if the ministry did not share his views and then demanded in the House of Commons that the government make a public announcement on the issue. Mackenzie confided to George Brown that he indeed agreed with Huntington's sentiments, "but I fear we are not strong enough with the English in Quebec hostile to us to carry that principle into effect." Although the Catholic hierarchy demanded, and the Liberal government eventually delivered, an official disavowal of Huntington's speech, he did remain in the cabinet.

The rift in the Quebec wing of the party was not quickly healed, nor could Huntington live down the suspicion that he was a less capable minister than Holton would have been. In spite of the Liberal defeat nationally in 1878, he managed to retain his seat against both Conservative and French Canadian Liberal opponents. However, he was continually hounded as a hypocrite and a francophobe, and personal misfortunes drew him further away from active politics after 1879. He felt deeply the loss of his second son, Russell, who had been a member of the *Montreal Herald*'s editorial staff, and a severe throat infection kept him from speaking either in parliament or during his 1882 election campaign. When the Conservatives in Shefford united behind the French Canadian Liberal candidate, Huntington was defeated at last. He then moved to New York, the home of his second wife, Mrs Marsh, in order to receive special medical attention. During his remaining four years of life he made only brief visits to Canada, in order to oversee his business interests in the Laflamme, Huntington and Laflamme law firm and the Mutual Life Association of Canada.

Partly to help pass the time, and partly to keep his views before the public, Huntington in 1884 published a rather prosaic novel entitled *Professor Conant* in which he stressed the importance of what he called an independent public opinion. Not surprisingly, ultramontanism was singled out as one of its greatest enemies. Abstract as Huntington's arguments were, it is nevertheless clear that his liberal philosophy was tailored to fit his own social and economic interests as an English Canadian entrepreneur in the Eastern Townships. In fact the declining influence of the anglophone population in the region had a good deal to do with his ultimate failure as a politician.

J. I. LITTLE

[Lucius Seth Huntington was the author of *The independence of Canada; the annual address delivered before the Agricultural Society of the County of Missisquoi, at Bedford, Sept. 8, 1869* (Montreal, 1869) and of *Professor Conant: a story of English and American social and political life* (Toronto, 1884). Among the papers of politicians, the most useful for Huntington's career are the following: at PAC, the George Brown papers (MG 24, B40) and the Alexander Mackenzie papers (MG 26, B); and at AO, the Blake (Edward) papers (MU 136–273). J. I. L.]

Can., House of Commons, *Debates*, 1867–69, 1876–82. *Advertiser and Eastern Townships Sentinel* (Knowlton and Waterloo, Que.), 1856–60. *Montreal Herald and Daily Commercial Gazette*, 20, 22 May 1886. *Canadian directory of parl.* (J. K. Johnson). *CPC*, 1867–81. Dent, *Canadian portrait gallery*, IV: 56–61. J. P. Noyes, *Sketches of some early Shefford pioneers* ([Montreal], 1905), 15–64, 77, 83. R. P. Frye, "Resident representation; a political problem of the Eastern Townships of Quebec as seen from the pages of the *Waterloo Advertiser and Eastern Townships Sentinel*" (MA thesis in preparation, Univ. of Ottawa). W. R. Graham, "The Alexander Mackenzie administration, 1873–78: a study of Liberal tenets and tactics" (MA thesis, Univ. of Toronto, 1944). O. D. Skelton, *The life and times of Sir Alexander Tilloch Galt* (Toronto, 1920). Thomson, *Alexander Mackenzie* (Toronto, 1960). J. S. Willison, *Sir Wilfrid Laurier and the Liberal party; a political history* (2v., Toronto, 1903). Y.-F. Zoltvany, "Les libéraux du Québec, leur parti et leur pensée (1867–1873)" (thèse de MA, univ. de Montréal, 1960). T. A. Burke, "Mackenzie and his cabinet, 1873–1878," *CHR*, 41 (1960): 128–48.

HYMAN, WILLIAM, exporter and politician; b. in 1807 in Russia; m. Amelia Hart, and they had five daughters and three sons; d. 8 Dec. 1882 in Montreal, Que.

William Hyman's parents, who were of the Jewish faith, fled Russia at the beginning of the 19th century to escape Czarist oppression. They took refuge at Lódź, Poland, but their circumstances never improved and they both perished. In 1835 Hyman managed to get out of Poland with his young wife, Amelia Hart, and, attracted by its Jewish community, found asylum in Norwich, England. He entered the service of a jeweller named Hart, who sent him to New York in 1840 to represent his firm.

Hyman's stay in the United States was brief; by 1843 he was living at Gaspé, Canada East, where he was developing an interest in the cod trade. It was not, however, until 1845 that he acquired from the Guernsey captain Francis Ahier his first fishing establishment, at Grande-Grève. At that time his immediate neighbour was Frederick Janvrin, who owned the largest fishing room on the Baie de Gaspé as well as several fishing posts on the north shore of the Gaspé. In 1855 Janvrin's enterprises passed into the hands of the Jersey-based firm of William Fruing and Company, Hyman's principal competitor for the rest of his life.

The large Jersey companies operating in the Gaspé sent agents there, but Hyman managed his business himself on the spot. It was not until 1875 that he officially gave his eldest son Isaac Elias responsibility for managing his establishments and renamed the firm William Hyman and Sons, while retaining until his death control of certain financial operations. From its beginnings in the 1840s, Hyman's business experienced a steady and relatively rapid growth, considering the limited capital initially invested (£220). With the number of producers of dried cod increasing through the use of a credit system, he acquired fishing establishments, collecting posts, and warehouses in the major settlements of the Forillon peninsula and, farther away, on the north shore of the Gaspé. He exported more than 2,000 quintals of cod from the port of Gaspé in 1855 and 11,000 quintals in 1880. Hyman's business ranked fourth in total exports from the port of Gaspé in the second half of the 19th century; it accounted for nearly 10 per cent of the shipments, a quantity half what his principal competitor, William Fruing and Company, exported, even though that firm had substantial capital at its disposal. At his death, Hyman bequeathed to his heirs a dock, storehouses and a warehouse at Gaspé, a hotel and several properties and mortgages in the Forillon peninsula region, and six fishing establishments – two at Grande-Grève, two at Rivière-au-Renaud, one at Cap-des-Rosiers, and one at Cap à l'Ours. He had also accumulated many securities in banks at Quebec City and Montreal, and owned a Montreal residence where he had spent the winters since 1874.

The major exporters in the Gaspé peninsula at that time were almost all Jersey islanders. They were the most important element in the economy of the cod trade. In fact, they were simultaneously financiers, brokers, exporters, ship-owners, and buyers of supplies in the Mediterranean. Hyman consequently depended on the Jersey men for the smooth operation of his business, whether for the financing of his cargoes, the supply of goods, or the sale of his produce. For the shipping and sale of his cod, he tried several times to get round the Jersey network by using agents at Halifax, N.S., or in Liverpool, but without success. However, the depositing of his capital in Canadian rather than European banks probably enabled him to come through the financial crisis that severely affected the Jersey companies from 1873. William Fruing and Company was unable to weather the storm and its holdings were finally acquired by William Hyman and Sons in 1918 and 1925.

Like the Jersey firms, the Hyman company based its power and wealth on the extension of both advances and credit to the fishermen. It not only exported cod but also imported the goods needed for the fishermen's work and subsistence. From the outset, the establishment of a comprehensive credit system seemed desirable because of insufficient yield from the short fishing seasons and the special features of the production of dried cod which ensured that the fishermen would constantly turn to the company for supplies of salt, fishing tackle, and food. Thus indebtedness was integral to the way of life of Gaspé fishermen. The "committed" nature of their production guaranteed a regular supply of dried cod to companies such as William Hyman's from the communities dependent upon the firm.

Brought to the fore by his position within the local society, Hyman was given various political and legal responsibilities. He was reeve in Cap-des-Rosiers Township from its formation in 1858 until 1882, the first Jew in Canada to hold such an office. In this capacity he promoted the installation of a telegraphic system, and then the building of the Cap Gaspé lighthouse which was completed in 1871. He also became a member of the county council (established in 1869), a justice of the peace, and a militia captain.

William Hyman's death in 1882 coincided with the end of an era in which Jersey men ran the fisheries in the Gaspé. Four years later the powerful Paspébiac firm of Charles Robin and Company ran into serious financial difficulties and, with the turn of the century, the flow of Jersey capital to the Gaspé dried up. William Hyman's business was able to adjust to the 20th century, thanks to his son Isaac Elias, who took it over, and to his grandson Percy, who ensured its continued existence until 1967.

MICHEL LE MOIGNAN and ROCH SAMSON

David Hyman of Lahr, German Federal Republic, possesses private letterbooks of Isaac Elias Hyman, 1882–84, and letterbooks of William Hyman, 1864–66, 1874–77.

Arch. de la Soc. hist. de la Gaspésie (Gaspé, Qué.), Livre des minutes de la municipalité de Cap-des-Rosiers, 1858–82. BE, Gaspé (Percé), Reg. B, 1, no.252; 2, no.159. PAC, RG 16, A2, 467. *Canadian Jewish reference book and directory, 1963*, comp. Eli Gottesman (Ottawa, 1963), 309. Sack, *Hist. of the Jews in Canada* (1945), 146. E. C. Woodley, "The Hymans of Gaspé," *Rev. d'hist. de la Gaspésie* (Gaspé), 11 (1973): 74–78.

I

IRUMBERRY DE SALABERRY, CHARLES-RENÉ-LÉONIDAS D', militia officer and office-holder; b. 27 Aug. 1820 in Chambly, Lower Canada, the third son of Lieutenant-Colonel Charles-Michel d'Irumberry* de Salaberry, hero of the battle of Châteauguay, and Marie-Anne-Julie Hertel de Rouville; m. first 30 Jan. 1849 Marie-Victorine-Cordélia Franchère (d.1855), and they had three children; m. secondly 1 Sept. 1869 Louise-Joséphine Allard (d.1877), and they had four children; m. thirdly 3 Nov. 1880 Marie-Louise Baby; d. 25 March 1882 at L'Assomption, Que.

The ancestry and marriages of Charles-René-Léonidas d'Irumberry de Salaberry go far to explain his character and career. He grew up in a family accustomed to private means and public service. As a younger son he was perhaps more than usually dependent on public employment to which he and his friends came to feel he was reasonably entitled. His background may explain his lack of professional training: contrary to statements often made, there is no evidence that he was an engineer or even a land surveyor. He belonged to the class, already disappearing by the mid 19th century, whose members might expect to live on their name.

In 1852 he was a lieutenant-colonel in the 2nd Battalion of the Rouville militia. He served with the same rank in the Voltigeurs de Québec, his commission being signed in 1862 at the height of the *Trent* affair [*see* Sir Charles Hastings DOYLE]. Salaberry then attended the School of Military Instruction of Quebec, established as part of a programme to improve the militia of Canada, especially as a result of the pressures leading to the American Civil War; he received a 1st class certificate in 1865. In becoming a qualified militia officer, Salaberry had continued the military traditions of his famous father and also of his mother's family. What other employment he may have had in the 1850s and 1860s, and what means he used to support his family, are not known. He was, however, briefly in the public service.

In 1857 Salaberry was appointed to the hastily organized Canadian exploration expedition, led by George Gladman* and including Simon James Dawson* and Henry Youle Hind*, charged with exploring the route between Fort William (Thunder Bay, Ont.) and the Red River Settlement (Man.), and providing detailed information for the Canadian government on the feasibility of using this route. Salaberry and G.-F. Gaudet, the only French Canadians appointed to the expedition, were listed as "assistants under the charge" of Dawson, but were paid only 7*s.* 6*d.* a day, the wages of chainmen and less than the assistants of Gladman and Hind received. There was clearly mismanagement of some sort, especially as Gaudet had some professional training as an engineer, and they protested. It may well be that the two French Canadians were a belated appointment.

At Red River in 1857 Salaberry's name and language made him useful in hiring French-speaking members of the community and in buying supplies from them for the survey of the route from Upper Fort Garry (Winnipeg) to the Lake of the Woods. Moreover, veterans of the War of 1812 who lived in Red River, remembering his father, sought his aid in applying for pensions in recognition of their service. Late that fall Salaberry went to Toronto with other members of the expedition, and he returned to Red River ahead of the main party for the expedition of 1858 led by Dawson and Hind. That summer he worked under Dawson's direction and was commended for his skill in encouraging the boatmen during the exploration on the Saskatchewan and Assiniboine rivers. A third expedition in 1859 did not materialize.

Salaberry then dropped out of public view, apparently living by private means. In February 1868 a petition prepared by friends was submitted to the Legislative Assembly of Quebec requesting an appointment for him. No action was taken that year but in July 1869 he was appointed superintendent of woods and forests in the district of Montreal.

In the fall of 1869, however, the Red River rebellion broke out under the leadership of Louis RIEL. The federal government, seeking to reassure the people of Red River of its good intentions, decided in December to dispatch emissaries. It appointed Abbé Jean-Baptiste Thibault*, who had served in the northwest for 35 years, and Salaberry, who was probably chosen on the recommendation of Sir George-Étienne Cartier* because of his experience in the northwest in 1857 and 1858.

On Christmas Eve 1869 Salaberry arrived in Pembina (N. Dak.) with Thibault, who continued on alone to the Red River Settlement where he was kept under surveillance by Riel's men at Bishop Alexandre-Antonin Taché*'s palace in St Boniface. Early in January Salaberry joined his colleague and they appeared before the Métis council of the provisional government. Riel, who had insisted upon seeing their instructions, declared that these did not empower Thibault and Salaberry to negotiate on behalf of Canada and politely dismissed them. The two commissioners had not succeeded in persuading the inhabitants of Red River to stop resisting the Canadian government but they did manage to soothe the feeling in St Boniface.

Donald Alexander Smith*, a commissioner appointed by Sir John A. Macdonald* after Thibault and Salaberry had been selected, had arrived in the Red River Settlement with Richard Charles HARDISTY on 27 December. It was evident on 19 January, the first day of a two-day convention held at Upper Fort Garry, that Smith had succeeded in weakening support for Riel among the people of Red River by using the influence and funds of the Hudson's Bay Company. However, the next day the convention decided, on Riel's suggestion, that a council of the settlement be elected to prepare terms for their own delegates to take with them to Canada. Smith had wanted to negotiate a settlement himself and blamed this setback on Thibault, whom he accused of helping rally Riel's supporters. It is to be presumed that Salaberry concurred with the sending of delegates, for when questioned by the meeting he firmly assured those present that the Canadian government would pay the expenses of these delegates to Ottawa. This was Salaberry's sole contribution to the proceedings at Red River; his other activity during his three-month sojourn at St Boniface was to organize and train a boys' band.

On 24 March 1870 Salaberry left Red River with Joseph-Noël Ritchot*, one of the provisional government's delegates, for Ottawa, where he introduced him to Cartier and Joseph Howe*, the secretary of state for the provinces. Salaberry later returned to Quebec and resumed his duties as superintendent of woods and forests in the Montreal district. He retained the post until his death in 1882.

W. L. MORTON

PAC, MG 24, G45, 5: 1468–72; 9: 2023; MG 27, I, C6, Le Moine to Salaberry, 19 Dec. 1869. PAM, HBCA, D.5/44, 9 Sept. 1857; D.5/46, 21 Jan. 1858. Begg, *Red River journal* (Morton). Can., Prov. of, Legislative Assembly, *App. to the journals*, 1858, II: app.3; 1859, IV: app.36. *Manitoba: the birth of a province*, ed. W. L. Morton (Altona, Man., 1965). P.-G. Roy, *La famille d'Irumberry de Salaberry* (Lévis, Qué., 1905). Stanley, *Louis Riel.*

ISAPO-MUXIKA (Crowfoot, occasionally known in French as **Pied de Corbeau)**, Blackfoot chief; b. *c.* 1830 near the Belly River in what is now southern Alberta, son of Blood Indians Istowun-eh'pata (Packs a Knife) and Axkyahp-say-pi (Attacked Toward Home); d. 25 April 1890, near Blackfoot Crossing (Alta).

Crowfoot was born into the Blood tribe of the Blackfoot Confederacy, which at the time also included the Blackfoot and Piegan tribes. As an infant he was given the name Astohkomi (Shot Close). When he was five his father was killed by Crow Indians and within a year Crowfoot's mother married Akaynehka-simi (Many Names), a member of the Blackfoot tribe. Taken to the Blackfoot tribe the boy was given the name of Kyi-i-staah (Bear Ghost), and later received his father's name of Istowun-eh'pata.

As was customary, Crowfoot began when in his teens to accompany older warriors on raids against enemy tribes. During a raid for horses on a Crow camp, he performed bravely and was wounded, for which he was given his adult name Isapo-muxika, a name that had been owned by a relative killed several years earlier. Properly, the name Isapo-muxika translates as "Crow Indian's big foot," but it was shortened to Crowfoot by interpreters.

Although Crowfoot was not from a family of chiefs and was from another tribe, he soon demonstrated his leadership abilities among the Blackfoot Indians. Perhaps more important, he continued to establish himself as a formidable and respected warrior. Before he was 20 years old he had been in 19 battles and had been wounded six times. His most serious wound occurred during a winter raid upon the Shoshoni Indians; he was shot in the back and the lead ball was never removed. In later years this wound made it difficult for him to ride horses or to travel long distances. Crowfoot seldom went to war after he reached manhood. Instead, he became involved with raising horses, which made him wealthy, and in the affairs of the tribe. In 1865, with the death of the chief of his band, No-okskatos (Three Suns), Crowfoot became a minor chief of the Blackfoot tribe, leading a band of about 21 lodges. At first his followers were known as the Big Pipes band but later were renamed the Moccasin band.

It was in 1865 also that Crowfoot first came to the attention of the local white population after his dramatic role in a battle at Three Ponds, which occurred just east of the present village of Hobbema, Alta. Father Albert Lacombe*, an Oblate missionary, was visiting a Blackfoot camp there when it was attacked by Crees. Although greatly outnumbered and despite casualties, the Blackfeet held off the raiders for several hours during the night. Just before dawn Father Lacombe tried to get between the lines to call a truce, but he was not recognized by the Crees and was wounded by a ricocheting bullet. When the battle seemed lost, Crowfoot arrived with a large number of warriors and the enemy was soon routed.

Crowfoot, as a minor chief, tried to establish friendly relations with white fur-traders and missionaries. Late in 1866 he prevented a number of Blackfoot warriors from looting a train of Hudson's Bay Company carts and killing its Métis drivers. Then, defying a number of warrior chiefs, he provided a safe escort for the Métis back to Fort Edmonton. He also became a good friend of HBC trader Richard Charles HARDISTY who was in charge of Rocky Mountain House.

In the smallpox epidemic of 1869–70 several Blackfoot leaders died and Crowfoot emerged as one of the three head chiefs of the tribe. In 1872, with the death of Akamih-kayi (Big Swan), the leadership was reduced to Crowfoot and Natosapi (Old Sun), an elderly warrior chief.

In 1873 Crowfoot's eldest son was killed in a raid on a Cree camp, and the chief led a large revenge party which succeeded in killing an enemy warrior. This was Crowfoot's last warlike deed. Some months later during a temporary peace treaty between the Blackfeet and Crees, Crowfoot met a Cree who bore a startling resemblance to his dead son. He adopted the man, who was known to the Crees as Poundmaker [PĪTIKWAHANAPIWĪYIN], and gave him his dead son's name, Makoyi-koh-kin (Wolf Thin Legs). Poundmaker returned to the Crees where he became a chief, but he remained close friends with Crowfoot for the rest of his life.

During the 1870s American traders were invading the Canadian west selling whisky and repeating rifles to the Indians. As a result, hundreds of Indians were dying from the liquor and the intertribal warfare it precipitated. When Crowfoot was informed in 1874 that the North-West Mounted Police were being organized and were coming to his hunting grounds he welcomed the police as a needed solution to a serious problem. He told the Reverend John Chantler McDougall*: "If left to ourselves we are gone. The whiskey brought among us by the Traders is fast killing us off and we are powerless before the evil. . . . Our horses, Buffalo robes and other articles of trade go for whiskey, a large number of our people have killed one another and perished in various ways under the influence, and now that we hear of our Great Mother sending her soldiers into our country for our good we are glad."

In December 1874 Crowfoot first met James Farquharson Macleod*, assistant commissioner of the NWMP, and the two became friends. It was largely through their influence that white settlement in Blackfoot territory occurred without violence. Macleod insisted that Blackfoot rights be respected, while Crowfoot encouraged his people to maintain friendly relations with the police. Although he was actually one of two head chiefs of the Blackfoot tribe, the police considered him to be the leader of the entire Blackfoot nation. In fact, the Bloods were a larger tribe than the Blackfeet and all three tribes in the confederacy had independent leadership, but the confusion between "Blackfoot tribe" and "Blackfoot nation" – which included the Blood, Piegan, and Blackfoot tribes and their allies the Sarcees and the Gros Ventres – as well as Crowfoot's impressive role as diplomat and politician, often caused whites to place him in a position that he did not in fact occupy. Crowfoot, for his part, was careful to consult his fellow chiefs in such situations.

In 1876, when the wars were raging in the United States between the Plains Indians and the American cavalry, a Sioux messenger came to Crowfoot's camp asking the Blackfeet to join the fight. After the Sioux had defeated the Americans, the messenger said, they would help the Blackfeet exterminate the NWMP. Crowfoot not only rejected the offer but said he would join the police to fight the Sioux if they ever came north. (News of Crowfoot's stand was forwarded to Ottawa and eventually to England where Queen Victoria praised the chief for his loyalty.) A short time later, when the Sioux fled to Canada after the battle at Little Bighorn River (Mont.), Crowfoot realized they came as refugees. He met Sitting Bull [TA-TANKA I-YOTANK] during the chief's exile in Canada, and when he learned that Sitting Bull's tribe sought peace with the Blackfeet he was pleased to accept the chief's offer of tobacco. The great Sioux leader was so impressed that he named his own son Crowfoot.

In 1877 David Laird*, the new lieutenant governor of the North-West Territories, invited the Blackfoot, Blood, Piegan, Sarcee, and Stony tribes to negotiate Treaty no.7 with the Canadian government. These tribes included those living in what is now southern Alberta south of the Red Deer River, and no.7 was the last of the treaties to be negotiated by the Canadian authorities in the 1870s in a programme to obtain the surrender of all Indian claims to the western Canadian prairies. At the outset an argument arose as to a meeting-place for the negotiations, the Bloods and Piegans preferring Fort Macleod and Crowfoot insisting on Blackfoot Crossing in the centre of his own domain away from any of the white man's forts. The government acceded to Crowfoot's demands, but the leading chiefs of the Blood and Piegan tribes threatened not to attend. Negotiations began on 16 September with Crowfoot as the principal chief in attendance, and for the next four days he led the discussions. When the Bloods and Piegans finally arrived they joined Crowfoot in an all-night session to receive his account of the treaty and his recommendations. By dawn, all the leading chiefs had agreed to the terms of the treaty and, because of Crowfoot's role during the negotiations and his favourable attitude towards the pact, he was asked to respond for the entire Blackfoot nation: "While I speak, be kind and patient. I have to speak for my people, who are numerous, and who rely upon me to follow that course which in the future will tend to their good. The plains are large and wide. We are the children of the plains, it is our home, and the buffalo has been our food always. I hope you look upon the Blackfeet, Bloods and Sarcees as your children now, and that you will be indulgent and charitable to them. . . . The advice given me and my people has proved to be very good. If the Police had not come to the country, where would we be all now? Bad men and whiskey were killing us so fast that very few, indeed, of us would have been left to-day. The Police have protected us as the feathers of the bird protect it from the frosts of winter. I wish them all good, and trust that all our hearts will increase in goodness from this time forward. I am satisfied. I will sign the treaty."

Shortly after taking treaty, many Indians began to doubt the wisdom of their actions. The deaths of three prominent chiefs, the destruction of extensive grazing lands by prairie fires, and the disappearance of the buffalo were considered to be ill omens. By summer 1879 hunting was so poor that many Blackfeet were starving and were forced to follow the last buffalo herds into the United States. Crowfoot took his tribe into Montana where, without the presence of the NWMP, they were again subjected to the problems of whisky pedlars, horse thieves, and intertribal warfare. During this time the Blackfoot treaty with the Sioux ended – with a horse raid on Crowfoot's camp. To add to the unsettled conditions, Louis RIEL and his followers spent a winter camped by the Blackfeet, attempting to spread discontent. As the buffalo herd was destroyed, the Blackfeet faced starvation, and in 1881 hunger forced the tribe to return to Canada.

Upon his return Crowfoot learned that the government agency responsible for his people had changed from the NWMP to the newly established Department of Indian Affairs. Over the next months he found the new administrators to be callous in their treatment of the Indians. Angry and disillusioned, he openly defied the police for the first time early in 1882 when they tried to arrest a minor chief of the Blackfoot tribe. Crowfoot was becoming distrustful of the government and the NWMP, and when Cree and Métis agitators began to visit his camp, he learned that his problems were shared throughout the west.

In 1884, after one of Riel's followers had been arrested in the Blackfoot camp, the Indian commissioner, Edgar Dewdney*, invited Crowfoot and other Blackfoot chiefs to visit Regina and Winnipeg. As the commissioner had hoped, the visit to the large white settlements shattered the Indians' belief that they were more numerous than the whites. This knowledge had a great impact upon Crowfoot's behaviour during the North-West Rebellion of 1885. Undoubtedly his sympathies were with the Crees, led by Big Bear [MISTAHIMASKWA] and Crowfoot's own adopted son, Poundmaker, but he believed they could not win. In addition, neither the Piegans nor the Bloods would support their hereditary enemy, the Crees, and the Blood tribe even offered to send warriors to fight for the government. Actually, for the first several days of the rebellion, Crowfoot was non-committal, both to rebel runners who visited his camp and to government officials. Only after he had ascertained the continued hostility of the Bloods and Piegans, as well as hearing promises of the government, did he finally pledge his loyalty to the crown.

Nevertheless, considerable alarm was expressed during the rebellion regarding the loyalty of the Blackfoot nation. At one point, Calgary inhabitants feared they would be attacked, and Father Lacombe was sent to Crowfoot's camp to investigate. He was told by Crowfoot that in spite of frequent messages from the Crees and the fact that Poundmaker was in the centre of the conflict, the Blackfeet did not intend to rise. When this news was transmitted to Ottawa, the governor general, Lord Lansdowne [Petty-Fitzmaurice*], expressed his thanks to Crowfoot on behalf of the queen, and the cabinet of Sir John A. Macdonald* gave the Blackfoot chief a round of applause. In the following year Crowfoot and his foster brother Nookska-stumik (Three Bulls) were taken on a tour of Montreal and Quebec by Father Lacombe in recognition of their loyalty. Crowfoot was lionized by the press and public, his tall stately appearance and classic Indian features fulfilling everyone's romantic image of "the noble Indian." On his return from Quebec, Crowfoot stopped in Ottawa where he met Macdonald and gave him the Indian name for "Brother-in-Law."

Although Crowfoot had become a notable Canadian figure, he was an unhappy man during the last decade of his life. He was increasingly disillusioned about the treatment of his people by government employees and officials, his own health was deteriorating, and his personal life was struck by a series of tragedies. Crowfoot had a total of ten wives during his lifetime – usually three or four at one time – his favourite wife being Sisoyaki (Cutting Woman). She accompanied him on trips to other reserves and occupied the honoured place beside him in his teepee. But in spite of the large number of wives, only four of Crowfoot's children ever reached maturity. In a tribe where boys were highly favoured, Crowfoot had only one blind son, Kyi-i-staah (Bear Ghost), and three daughters who survived their childhood years. Many of the others died of tuberculosis. To add to his grief, his adopted son Poundmaker was sent to prison for his part in the rebellion; released in 1886 as a favour to Crowfoot, he died suddenly in Crowfoot's camp only four months later.

The last three years of Crowfoot's life were spent quietly, visiting old friends on neighbouring reserves. In 1887 he assisted Red Crow [Mekaisto*], head chief of the Bloods, in preventing his warriors from raiding the Gros Ventre Indians, and in the following year he travelled to Montana where he tried unsuccessfully to arrange a peace treaty with the Assiniboins. Ill and with failing eyesight, Crowfoot remained on his reserve during the winter of 1889–90, and died during the spring. His chieftainship was assumed by his foster brother, Three Bulls, but neither he nor succeeding chiefs achieved the prestige or greatness of Crowfoot.

HUGH A. DEMPSEY

Can., Parl., *Sessional papers*, 1876, VII, no.9: 23–24. Morris, *Treaties of Canada with the Indians*. *Macleod Gazette and Alberta Livestock Record* (Fort Macleod), 22, 29 May 1890. H. A. Dempsey, *Crowfoot, chief of the Blackfeet* (Edmonton, 1972). C. E. Denny, *The riders of the plains: a reminiscence of the early and exciting days in the north west* (Calgary, 1905). Katherine Hughes, *Father Lacombe, the black-robe voyageur* (Toronto, 1911). J. [C.] McDougall, *On western trails in the early seventies; frontier pioneer life in the Canadian north-west* (Toronto, 1911).

ISBISTER, ALEXANDER KENNEDY, HBC fur-trader, educator, and lawyer; b. June 1822 at Cumberland House (Sask.), son of Thomas Isbister and Mary Kennedy; d. 28 May 1883 at Barnsbury (now part of Greater London), England.

Alexander Kennedy Isbister was born at the Hudson's Bay Company post of Cumberland House in Rupert's Land where his father, an Orkneyman, was employed as a clerk. His mother was the daughter of Chief Factor Alexander Kennedy* and his Cree wife Aggathas. Kennedy provided that young Alexander be sent to school at St Margaret's Hope in the Orkney Islands. The boy showed promise during his four years there, but the death of his grandfather appears to have occasioned his return to Rupert's Land, where he attended the Red River Academy in the Red River Settlement (Man.), from 1833 to 1837.

At age 16, Isbister entered the service of the HBC at the rank of assistant postmaster and was sent to Fort Simpson (N.W.T) in the Mackenzie River District. In 1840 he helped John Bell* establish Fort McPherson (N.W.T.), on the Peel River, which for many years was the company's most northerly post. During the following season he explored the Peel River area, and later published scientific papers based on his observations. Already, however, Isbister was beginning to chafe at his lack of advancement in the company's service. In the 1830s the prejudices of George Simpson*, governor of the HBC, against mixed-bloods had become evident, with the result that they had little chance of being promoted to the officer class even when they possessed a good education. Isbister resigned at the beginning of the 1841 outfit and spent the rest of the season in Red River with his family before sailing to Great Britain in the fall of 1842 at the age of 20.

From 1842 to 1844 Isbister attended King's College (University of Aberdeen), and spent the following year at the University of Edinburgh. He was described by one of his professors as a young man "of great intelligence and energy." He excelled in chemistry, mathematics, natural history, and Greek. For a time he assisted the surgeon at the Royal Dispensary in Edinburgh, but he was soon in London to begin a remarkable career as an educator. In 1849 he was 2nd master of the East Islington Proprietary School and by 1851 was headmaster. He was appointed to Jews' College in 1855, and three years later became the first headmaster of Stationers' Company School. He gave distinguished service to the College of Preceptors, the supervisory body of the English teaching profession, as editor of its organ, *Educational Times*, for over 20 years, and as dean of the college from 1872. During his career, Isbister wrote over 20 school textbooks, principally on English grammar, arithmetic, and geometry. Somehow he also found time to further his own education; in 1858 he received an MA from the University of Edinburgh and in 1866 an LLB from the University of London, becoming barrister-at-law of the Middle Temple.

Isbister's accomplishments reveal an exceptional intellect, but he also possessed "a singularly simple and attractive manner, high character and benevolent disposition." There is no evidence that the question of race was ever a hindrance to Isbister's English career. Understandably, he became an ardent champion of the rights of his native countrymen whom he felt were prevented from realizing their potential because of the tyrannical monopoly imposed by the HBC in Rupert's Land. An active supporter of the campaign for free trade rights in Red River, Isbister headed a delegation in 1847 which presented a petition against the HBC to the British government on behalf of approximately 1,000 inhabitants of Red River [*see* George-Antoine Bellecourt*]. He lobbied members of parliament, wrote pamphlets, and conducted an extensive correspondence with the Colonial Office, presenting evidence to support the petitioners' claims that the company was neglecting the welfare of the Indians, as well as stifling the economic development of the colony and challenging the legal validity of the company's charter. The colonial secretary, Lord Grey, however, accepted the company's refutation of the charges, and after months of bureaucratic delay the issue was dropped when Isbister was informed that the responsibility and expense of proving a case against the HBC would have to be borne by the petitioners. Isbister's hoped-for parliamentary inquiry finally came in 1857; he testified that the HBC was not governing or developing Rupert's Land in the interests of its people. Fearful of an American takeover, he recommended that the whole area be annexed to Canada. Ever the champion of the underdog, Isbister, after the HBC signed over Rupert's Land to Canada in 1869, supported in vain the claims of the HBC officers in the field that they were entitled to a direct share in the £300,000 compensation paid to the company.

Isbister showed his concern for education in Rupert's Land in a practical manner. As early as 1867 he endowed a prize for the winner of an open competition among scholars from the common schools of Red River. He left a generous bequest to the fledgling University of Manitoba: his collection of nearly 5,000 books to provide the basis for "a permanent Educational Library" (unhappily most were lost in a fire in 1898) and a trust fund to establish university scholarships for "meritorious Students and Scholars in the various places of education in the Province for both sexes . . . where the highest education is given without any distinction of race, creed or nationality."

After living for over 20 years in London, where his widowed mother and a sister joined him, Isbister moved to Barnsbury in Middlesex. His distinguished career in England had never interfered with his active interest in the development of western Canada, and especially the welfare of its native people. His concern and his generosity brought tribute to him in 1883 from the Historical and Scientific Society of Manitoba as one of the finest scions of old Manitoba.

SYLVIA M. VAN KIRK

Alexander Kennedy Isbister was the author of: *A few words on the Hudson's Bay Company, with a statement of the grievances of the natives and half-caste Indians, addressed to the British government through their delegates now in London* (London, 1847); and *A proposal for a new penal settlement, in connexion with the colonization of the uninhabited districts of British North America* (London, 1850). Other writings are listed in the *British Museum general catalogue* and the *National union catalog.*

PAM, HBCA, B.80/a/17; B.200/b/14: ff.3, 14; C.1/935: f.40; D.4/23: f.122; D.4/24: f.5; MG 1, D2; MG 2, C1; C4. [George] Bryce, "In memoriam: late A. K. Isbister . . . ," HSSM *Trans.*, [8] (1883–84): 1–4. *Educational Times and Journal of the College of Preceptors* (London), 36 (1883): 189–90. G.B., Parl., House of Commons paper, 1849, XXXV, 227, pp.509–627, *Hudson's Bay Company (Red River Settlement)* . . . ; 1857, *Report from the select committee on the HBC.* HBRS, XXX (Williams). *DNB.* Isaac Cowie, *The company of adventurers: a narrative of seven years in the service of the Hudson's Bay Company during 1867–1874 on the great buffalo plains* . . . (Toronto, 1913). H. C. Knox, "Alexander Kennedy Isbister," HSSM *Papers*, 3rd ser., no.12 (1957): 17–28.

J

JACK, WILLIAM BRYDONE (his middle name was originally **Bryden** and his surname has frequently been given as **Brydone-Jack**), mathematician, astronomer, natural scientist, and educator; b. 23 Nov. 1817 at Trailflatt in the parish of Tinwald (Dumfries and Galloway), Scotland, son of Peter Jack, a stonemason and master builder, and Janet Bryden; m. first 19 Dec. 1844 Marian Ellen, daughter of Charles Jeffery Peters*, and they had four daughters and one son; m. secondly in 1859 Caroline Disbrowe (Disbrow), and they had one daughter and four sons; d. 23 Nov. 1886 at Fredericton, N.B.

William Brydone Jack received his early education in parish schools and at Hutton Hall Academy near the town of Dumfries. In 1835 he was admitted to the University of St Andrews in Fife, and in 1840 was graduated MA. As an undergraduate, his course of study included Latin, Greek, mathematics, physics, and philosophy; he was a consistent scholarship winner in the humanities as well as in his major areas of study, mathematics and the natural sciences. Although he was influenced by several distinguished professors, it was Sir David Brewster, a leading mathematician and the principal of United College at St Andrews, who became his mentor. On Brewster's recommendation, Jack in September 1840 accepted the post of professor of mathematics and natural philosophy at King's College, Fredericton, intending to stay in New Brunswick only a few years to gain teaching experience.

King's College, established by royal charter in December 1828, was the successor to an academy founded by loyalist petitioners in 1787 which was chartered as the College of New Brunswick in 1800. University-level education had been offered only since the early 1820s under Principal James Somerville*, and after the reorganization of 1829 the college under Principal Edwin Jacob* provided a course of study on the Oxford model restricted to mathematics, classical languages, and philosophy. With an average enrolment of only a dozen students, the college was continually attacked for its élitist character and its narrow curriculum. Jack, having been educated in the Scottish tradition which combined empirical and practical studies with the classics, wanted to adapt the college curriculum to the "exigencies of the times & the country" by teaching the "art of observing and the art of experimenting." He soon developed a close and lasting association with a fellow Scot, Dr James Robb*, who had taken up his appointment as first professor of chemistry and natural history at King's College in 1837. Together they submitted a letter to the college council early in 1847 suggesting that the teaching of sciences would be improved if the sum of £1,000 were provided for the purchase of scientific apparatus to assist the professors in illustrating their branches of study. The college council provided £550, designating £300 for the purchase of "a good seven feet achromatic telescope." Jack, after obtaining sound advice, carefully selected a suitable telescope, but a group of council members objected to the magnitude of this expenditure and tried to have his order cancelled. Jack persevered in his efforts and obtained the desired instrument. This confrontation had just been concluded when he entered a second delicate negotiation to persuade the council that, instead of utilizing a room in the college building, a separate observatory should be built to house the telescope. Again he was successful; the first astronomical observatory in British North America was completed at Fredericton in 1851 through his persistence.

In addition to his collaboration with James Robb on scientific and educational matters, Jack also established a close working relationship with Dr J. B. Toldervy, a Fredericton physician, who owned a private observatory. It is probable that all three men were members of the Fredericton Athenæum, a society founded by Robb for the promotion of literary and scientific research. Early in 1855 Jack and Toldervy determined the exact longitude of Fredericton with reference to Boston by exchanging telegraphic signals with Harvard College Observatory. This important achievement of mid-19th-century astronomy was facilitated by the advantageous location of Toldervy's observatory near the telegraph office. Encouraged by the success of their new approach, Jack and Toldervy later that year determined the longitudes of other locations in the province with reference to Fredericton and forwarded their findings to Astronomer Royal George Biddell Airy. As it turned out, the values of longitude they had determined for Grand Falls and Little Falls agreed with those established in 1842 by the American commissioners who had surveyed the New Brunswick–Maine boundary, rather than those of the British commissioners. Jack and the astronomer royal disagreed as to which longitudinal values should be adopted, and their forthright correspondence was terminated abruptly. Jack nevertheless continued to receive valuable publications on Airy's astronomical work at Greenwich which influenced his scientific pursuits at Fredericton. The introduction in 1854 of a course in civil engineering at King's College must be attributed largely to Jack's interest in the practical subject of surveying and to his knowledge of the accurate triangulation of the British Isles carried out under the astronomer royal.

During the 1850s King's College's critics in the assembly, among them Albert James SMITH, redoubled their attacks on its exclusive nature and Principal Jacob's abhorrence of "practical education." Repeated demands were made for its conversion into an agricultural school or for the cessation of its annual public grant. To prevent the college's destruction, Lieutenant Governor Sir Edmund Walker Head* appointed a commission of eminent British North American educators to make recommendations on how the college could better serve New Brunswick [*see* Edwin Jacob]. As an outcome of the commission's report, the college in 1859 was converted into the secular University of New Brunswick and all religious tests for students and professors were discontinued. The lieutenant governor and Professor Jack worked closely to transform the college from a traditionalist, classical institution into a university offering "practical" training in the sciences as well as the arts.

Dr Joseph R. Hea was appointed first president of the newly constituted university in 1860, but after only one year he was succeeded by Jack. As president, Jack, realizing that the image of the university needed improvement, travelled throughout the province during the summers to inform audiences of the education the university could provide for their sons and of the role he envisaged for it in the development of the province. The death in 1861 of James Robb, whose assistance in this public endeavour would have been valuable, was a serious loss to the new president.

During the 1860s Jack assembled a competent teaching staff at the university. George Montgomery Campbell, a graduate of Cambridge, taught classics; Loring Woart Bailey*, a Harvard graduate, lectured in chemistry, physics, geology, and other natural sciences; Joseph Marshall* d'Avray, who had taught at King's College in the 1850s and was a former chief superintendent of education, was professor of English and French language and literature; Jack himself taught mathematics, natural philosophy, and astronomy. Students received a bachelor's degree after completing three 40-week sessions in which they had studied all the subjects offered. Tuition and accommodation were a modest $160 per session, but still the enrolment did not grow as quickly as Jack would have liked. Though his efforts to popularize the university met with some success, prejudices lingered, the denominational colleges in New Brunswick continued to attract both students and endowments, and the inadequate funding provided by the legislature hindered his attempts to build "a truly provincial university with every opportunity for expansion and fruitful service."

Moreover, the prosperity, growth in population, and development of provincial resources which were anticipated with confederation in 1867 did not materialize. Although Jack had envisaged the inclusion of navigation, law, medicine, engineering, and agriculture, nearly five years elapsed after his retirement in 1885 before any new chairs were established. But, despite its problems, the University of New Brunswick during Jack's tenure as president produced graduates of outstanding ability. In the 1860s they included James Mitchell*, George Robert Parkin*, and George Eulas Foster*; in the 1870s William Odber Raymond*, John Douglas Hazen*, and Charles George Douglas Roberts*; and in the early 1880s Bliss Carman* and Walter Charles Murray* were students.

During the 1840s and the 1850s Jack could direct his attention to the teaching of mathematics, physics, and astronomy, and to his scientific pursuits within these disciplines. After 1861 his responsibilities as president, coupled with his teaching, left him little opportunity for scientific work, although in the 1870s he assisted the surveyor general of the province in improving the standard of surveying. Jack has, however, the distinction of being the first Canadian astronomer, with contributions to this field in four phases: the building and equipping of the first astronomical observatory in British North America, the application of "galvanism" or the electric telegraph to the measurement of longitude, the preparation and presentation of the first public lectures on astronomy in Canada, and the development of methods for standardizing surveyors' chains and checking magnetic compasses. His pioneering scientific work ensures him a place as one of the builders of the science of astronomy in Canada.

William Brydone Jack's contributions to education in New Brunswick extended over 45 years, and included service on the provincial board of education from 1872 to 1885. To the intellectual life of the university and the province he brought the best traditions of his ancestry and education. On his retirement in 1885 the university senate awarded him a pension and in high tribute to his dedicated service appointed him one of its members. His death within the next year, however, deprived the university of his continuing sound advice.

J. E. KENNEDY

W. B. Jack was the author of "[Uniform weights, measures, and moneys]," Soc. of Arts, *Journal* (London), 1 (1852–53): 157–62, and, with J. B. Toldervy, "Account of the operations for determining the longitude of Fredericton, New Brunswick, by galvanic signals," Royal Astronomical Soc., *Monthly Notices* (London), 15 (1854–55): 190–94.

General Register Office (Edinburgh), Register of births and baptisms for the parish of Tinwald, 1817. UNBL, RG 61, U.N.B. Observatory, Corr., 1854–62, W. B. Jack and J. B. Toldervy, "Synopsis of a report on the determination by electric telegraph of the longitudes of the Grand and Little Falls of the River Saint John . . ."; RG 109, Report of committee approving expenditures on telescope, 23 March 1847; Report of committee on the erection of the observatory, 19 March 1851; Request from Robb and Jack for additional equipment, 22 Feb. 1847; Resolution attempting to annul order for telescope, 5 April 1848. *Cyclopædia of Canadian biog.* (Rose, 1888), 260. Dent, *Canadian portrait gallery*, IV: 108–9. *Standard dict. of Canadian biog.* (Roberts and Tunnell), II: 52–54. A. F. Baird, "The history of engineering at the University of New Brunswick," and F. A. Firth, "King's College, Fredericton, 1829–1859," *The University of New Brunswick memorial volume . . .* , ed. A. G. Bailey (Fredericton, 1950), 75–81 and 22–32 respectively. *The University of New Brunswick: a retrospect and a prospect* (Fredericton, 1925). [A. G. Bailey], "History of the University of New Brunswick," Univ. of New Brunswick, *Calendar* (Saint John, N.B.), 1941: 11–16. W. O. Raymond, "The genesis of the University of New Brunswick: with a sketch of the life of William Brydone-Jack, A.M., D.C.L., president from 1861–1885," RSC *Trans.*, 3rd ser., 12 (1918), sect.II: 95–108.

JACOBS, PETER. *See* PAHTAHSEGA

JACQUES, JOHN, cabinet-maker, furniture manufacturer, and financier; b. 9 Nov. 1804, probably in the county of Cumberland, England, son of Thomas Jacques; m. Mary Quinton (1808–95), and they had one son and one daughter; d. 14 Feb. 1886 in Toronto, Ont.

John Jacques is believed to have apprenticed in cabinet-making at Wigton (Cumbria), England, and he spent some years at his trade in London. In 1831 he immigrated to York (Toronto) and worked as a cabinet-maker first for Elisha Benjamin Gilbert and later for William Maxwell. Jacques entered into partnership with Robert HAY to buy Maxwell's business in 1835. Their firm, Jacques and Hay, was to set the pace for furniture manufacturing in the Canadas for the following half century.

Jacques and Hay produced in much greater quantity than their rivals, but they also led in quality. Pioneers in mass production techniques in the Upper Canadian furniture industry, they catered to the constant demands of immigrants with functional, machine-worked furniture in pine and basswood. They also served many middle class people and tended the needs of the wealthy leaders of taste who had first supported their venture. Their products were of considerable significance in the development of what might be called a southern Ontario furniture style in the middle decades of the 19th century. Firms such as Jacques and Hay, it is true, had to follow successive international fashions in Empire, Gothic, Rococo, and Eastlake styles, but into these fashions Jacques and Hay particularly blended the element of the regional style and thus perpetuated it. The principal characteristics of this regional variation on a general North American theme were solidity, a virtual absence of veneer, the large use of black walnut, and ornamentation which though it reflected the fussiness of the age never reached the point of vulgarity; the finished product bore a high gloss.

By the 1840s Jacques and Hay and other early Upper Canadian cabinet-makers had weaned many of the élite away from a dependence on imported furniture, although such customers in Montreal clung tenaciously to imports from Britain and the United States. Mahogany and rosewood were still thought to be materials of quality in Montreal, but in Canada West walnut, abundant in the region and virtually absent in Canada East, and to a lesser extent other native hardwoods such as maple and oak, were raised in status. Jacques and Hay were assisted in Canada West by the antipathy of many members of their upper class clientele to American products and by the costs of transporting bulky items from Britain.

Patrons of Jacques and Hay for their first-class work included leaders in public life and business in Canada West, and they supplied some of the finest institutional furnishings of their time. Sword's Hotel and Osgoode Hall in Toronto, and Rideau Hall in Ottawa, were fitted with the firm's best products. Like most of the leading makers of quality cabinetware, Jacques and Hay exhibited frequently and their winning of prizes in local, provincial, and international competitions further enhanced their reputation. Descriptions of their craftsmanship in exhibition pieces suggest a high degree of skill and taste; furthermore, extant pieces of their furniture, such as those made in 1867 for the splendid collection by James Austin* in his Spadina House in Toronto, testify to qualities of endurance and elegance. In the 1860s mention of their name was a special mark of distinction in lists of household effects being put up for auction.

Jacques's role in the firm was the supervision of practical day to day production in the shop and warehouse. He did not fail to delegate responsibility, and his retirement from the firm on 26 Dec. 1870 was effected smoothly and speedily. He was financially successful in the years following his retirement, and invested in banks, railways, and mortgages. At his death Jacques left over $250,000, 80 per cent of it invested in mortgages. He had led an active public life, being at one time a member of the York Pioneer Society, the Toronto Mechanics' Institute, the Canadian Institute, and the St Andrew's (Presbyterian) Church of Toronto. A supporter of the Reform cause, he never held political office.

Today, a lack of understanding of the true place of machine-assisted production of furniture in the 19th century, the absence of unquestioned provenance, and the current taste for pre-Victorian furniture, have combined to reduce the place of Jacques and Hay in the history of our industrial arts. As craftsmanship is recognized for its intrinsic worth and the depreciation of Victoriana lessens, the contribution of Jacques and Hay will be fully recognized.

STANLEY POLLIN

AO, RG 31, Declarations of partnerships, 1: nos.250, 377. CTA, Toronto assessment rolls, St George's Ward, 1836. Land Registry Office for the Division of Toronto, Deeds, Instrument no.4198[B]. Simcoe County Arch. (Minesing, Ont.), Jacques and Hay Furniture Company papers. York County Surrogate Court (Toronto), no.5917, will of John Jacques, 24 Feb. 1886 (mfm. at AO). William Chambers, *Things as they are in America* (Edinburgh, 1854). *British Colonist* (Toronto), 1838–54. *Globe*, 1844–70, 16 Feb. 1886. *Leader*, 5 March 1856. *Toronto Patriot*, 1838–44. *Toronto Daily Mail*, 15 Feb. 1886. Joan MacKinnon, *A checklist of Toronto cabinet and chair makers, 1800–1865* (Ottawa, 1975).

Alan Gowans, "The Canadian national style," *The shield of Achilles: aspects of Canada in the Victorian age*, ed. W. L. Morton (Toronto and Montreal, 1968), 208–19. *Hist. of Toronto and county of York*. R. H. Hubbard, *Rideau Hall: an illustrated history of Government House, Ottawa; Victorian and Edwardian times* (Ottawa, 1967). Jeanne Minhinnick, *At home in Upper Canada* (Toronto, 1970). S. C. Parker, *The book of St. Andrew's; a short history of St. Andrew's Presbyterian Church, Toronto* (Toronto, 1930). Philip Shackleton, *The furniture of old Ontario* (Toronto, 1973). G. F. Stevens, *Early Ontario furniture* (Toronto, 1966). A. S. Thompson, *Spadina: a story of old Toronto* (Toronto, 1975). Phil Ives, "The charm of old walnut," *Canadian Magazine*, 37 (May–October 1911): 565–73.

JAMOT, JEAN-FRANÇOIS, Roman Catholic missionary and bishop; b. 23 June 1828 at Châtelard, dept of Creuse, France, son of Gilbert Jamot, a farmer and landowner, and Jeanne Cornabat; d. 4 May 1886 at Peterborough, Ont.

Jean-François Jamot received his elementary education in his native town and in July 1849 graduated *bachelier ès lettres* from the Académie de Bourges of the Université de France. He then began studies in theology at the Grand Séminaire de Limoges and on 9 Oct. 1853 was ordained priest. The following year, while teaching classics at the Collège d'Ajain, Jamot met the French-born bishop of Toronto, Armand-François-Marie de Charbonnel*, and expressed to him a desire to work as a missionary in Canada. Charbonnel advised him to learn English, and Jamot spent eight months at All Hallows College in Dublin, Ireland, before arriving in Toronto on 10 May 1855.

A month after his arrival Jamot was appointed parish priest in Barrie, with additional responsibility for Catholics in nine surrounding townships. During his eight years in this charge Jamot displayed an aggressive and conscientious approach to the work of the church despite the frustrations of insufficient staff and finances. He built two schools and in 1857 recruited the Congregation of the Sisters of St Joseph of Toronto as teachers, bought and exchanged income properties and sites for prospective churches and schools, built churches in the outlying missions and a presbytery in Barrie, visited the missions and closely directed the spiritual life and work of the few assistant priests he had, and cultivated the support of laymen capable of helping his work. He kept his superiors in Toronto fully informed of his activities and problems, and despite his protest that he would "like rather to have nothing to do with money matters," he left the Barrie post in September 1863 both well established and solvent, though at considerable cost to his own pocket.

In 1860, while still in Barrie, Jamot had been appointed vicar-general and chancellor of the diocese of Toronto by Bishop Charbonnel's successor, John Joseph LYNCH, who late in 1863 also named Jamot rector of St Michael's Cathedral, Toronto. The Catholic population of the city of Toronto in 1860 had numbered over 12,000, of whom one-third were Jamot's parishioners. The diocese, although it stretched east and west of the city, and far north, was overwhelmingly urban, Irish, and working class. Besides his work as vicar-general on what Lynch called "the organization of church machinery," Jamot supervised the fund raising and construction for the completion of St Michael's Cathedral and in 1866 served as chaplain to the forces on the Niagara frontier during the Fenian raids. In 1869–70 he accompanied Lynch to the Vatican Council. While in Rome Lynch argued for the creation of a separate diocese for the northern reaches of the diocese of Toronto.

The efforts of Lynch and Joseph-Bruno Guigues*, bishop of Ottawa, to have a diocese created in northern Ontario were finally successful when on 25 Jan. 1874 Pope Pius IX created the vicariate of Northern Canada and appointed Jamot its vicar apostolic; his episcopal consecration took place at Issoudun, France, on 24 Feb. 1874, and in July he returned to Toronto.

Jamot's vicariate was bordered on the south by the Muskoka River, from Georgian Bay east to the Lake Huron–Ottawa River watershed; it then stretched north and northwest to the extent of the political boundaries of Ontario, and included the Canadian islands in lakes Superior and Huron. He estimated that there were approximately 8,000 Catholics in a total population of over 20,000; the inhabitants previously had been Indians, French Canadians, and Métis, but the federal and Ontario governments were encouraging immigration and the building of railways in the area, and an influx of construction workers and settlers of varied ancestry had already begun. Jamot had the help of ten priests, including six Jesuits, who manned 13 chapels in the Algoma District, but in the districts of Parry Sound and Muskoka there were no churches and no priests; the total value of church property he estimated at less than $3,000. Five schools were run by religious orders of men and women – two at Wikwemikong on Manitoulin Island, one at Garden River, and two at Fort William (now part of Thunder Bay) – with 200 Indian students.

Jamot installed himself at Sault Ste Marie in September 1874 and, having started the construction of a church there, began to cast around for sources of support. He fixed upon the Society for the Propagation of the Faith in Paris, and did not hesitate to play upon the sympathies or prejudices of its directors. For the vicariate's first full year of operation Jamot estimated the costs of personnel and of building maintenance and construction at $4,500, with income of only $240. He also alerted the society to the activities of missionaries of the Church of England who were attempting to undermine the faith of Catholic Indians and to the recent election of a "Huguenot" Anglican bishop, Frederick Dawson FAUQUIER. Jamot argued that the conversion of the nomadic Indians could best be achieved by encouraging them to settle in Catholic tribal communities; but to do this, more priests were needed, and books and catechisms in native languages were essential. The Paris organization responded to Jamot's appeals with generous grants, and from 1874 to 1883 annually supplied between $4,000 and $5,000, almost half of his financial requirements. He also made fund-raising tours of southern Ontario dioceses in winter, when travel throughout his vast territory was impossible.

In 1876 Jamot moved his headquarters to Bracebridge, the chief town of the districts of Parry Sound and Muskoka which were being rapidly populated by free grant settlers. He was instrumental in encouraging this settlement by publishing letters in newspapers and working closely with Ontario government officials; in December 1877 Jamot reminded Timothy Blair PARDEE, the commissioner of crown lands, that through public meetings and his visits to parishes to southern Ontario he had had "a great deal to do" with attracting the "immense number of people who have come in." In return for aiding settlement policy and for discreet help during elections, the Liberal government of Oliver Mowat* often appointed surveyors and land agents whom Jamot recommended and who he thought would encourage settlement by Catholics. But friction also characterized the relationship: Jamot attacked the government for not opening up lands on the south shore of Lake Nipissing to settlers he had recruited in Waterloo County, and Pardee was shocked in 1877 by Jamot's "open and direct threats of determined opposition to the government unless certain requests made were not immediately acceded to."

During the late 1870s and the early 1880s the feverish activity of settlement in the southern districts of his vicariate and of railway construction and logging in Algoma, though gratifying to Jamot, greatly increased the demands on his already insufficient funds and harried priests. As early as 1877 he had urged the apostolic delegate in Canada, Bishop George Conroy*, to recommend attaching to his vicariate part of the heavily populated and generously endowed diocese of Kingston, and in 1879 the bishops of Ontario unanimously endorsed the suggestion. On 11 July 1882 Pope Leo XIII appointed Jamot bishop of the new diocese of Peterborough, adding the counties of Durham, Northumberland, Victoria, Peterborough, and part of Haliburton to the existing vicariate. Jamot's diocese now stretched from Port Hope to the Manitoba border; to the 27 churches, 22 schools, 14 priests, and 10,000 Catholics of the former vicariate the five counties added 20,000 members, 11 priests, 13 schools, 20 churches, and debt-free church property valued at over $200,000. From his cathedral of St Peter-in-Chains in Peterborough, which he enlarged in 1884, Jamot attacked his work with a new vigour.

Jamot strengthened the well-established church in the southern counties by creating new missions, building churches, establishing separate schools and recruiting religious orders to teach in them, and supervising the education of seminarians, six of whom were ordained for service in his diocese between 1883 and 1886. But the problems of the northern part of the diocese required more unconventional methods. The education of native children continued to concern Jamot: he repeatedly argued with the federal government for larger grants, better salaries for teachers, and Indian involvement in school administration. He also denounced as bureaucratic folly the selection of teachers and textbooks by Indian agents and the attempts to make compulsory both attendance and English as the language of instruction. When a Jesuit at Port Arthur (now part of Thunder Bay) complained to Jamot in 1883 that the Indians, "the little ones who were crushed by the mighty ones," were cheated of the timber rights on reserve lands, Jamot tackled the federal government, dismissing Sir John A. Macdonald*'s charge that the Indians were engaged in a "conspiracy" to revoke a legal surrender. Political action in the pursuit of Christian goals was risky since, as another missionary at Fort William suggested, Macdonald was "dissatisfied at seeing the friendly relations which exist between the Episcopacy and the clergy of Ontario and the Ontario Government."

Jamot showed special concern for the welfare of the thousands of men who worked in lumber camps, mines, railway construction, and public works projects in the north. He encouraged the Sisters of St Joseph to establish a hospital at Fort William, opened in 1884, to treat injured workers, and in 1883 he stationed a priest on the railway line between the construction camps of North Bay and Sudbury. During his last extensive tour of the diocese late in 1884 Jamot saw new settlements, churches, schools, and orphanages throughout the north. When on 10 Nov. 1885 he left Peterborough for Rome to report to Leo XIII on the condition of his diocese, Jamot represented a church still hard-pressed for resources yet one which had successfully met numerous and unique challenges.

Jamot resumed his work after his return from Rome in March 1886, but contracted pneumonia and died in Peterborough on 4 May. Relentless in his commitment to his goals and adept at marshalling and manipulating any means of furthering his work, Jamot was a builder of heroic proportions whose devotional workbooks also reveal the vibrant spiritual life that those around him always felt.

ALAN STILLAR

Arch. of the Archdiocese of Toronto, Barrie, Sacred Hearts of Jesus and Mary, general corr. 1849–99; Edward Kelly, "Biographical notes of some interest to me probably not so to anybody else" (copy at Univ. of St Michael's College Arch., Toronto); Peterborough; St Michael's Cathedral, 1866–73. Arch. of the Diocese of Peterborough (Peterborough, Ont.), Bishop J. F. Jamot corr., 1862–81; 1882–86; Diocese of Peterborough, Canada, Memorandum book; Personal effects of Bishop Jamot. *Daily Evening Review* (Peterborough), 6, 7 May 1886. *Daily Examiner* (Peterborough), 4–6 May 1886. E. J. Boland, *From the pioneers to the seventies: a history of the diocese of Peterborough, 1882–1975* (Peterborough, 1976). H. C. McKeown, *The life and labors of Most Rev. John Joseph Lynch, D.D., Cong. Miss., first archbishop of Toronto* (Montreal and Toronto, 1886). J. S. Moir, "The problem of a double minority: some reflections on the development of the English-speaking Catholic church in Canada in the nineteenth century," *SH*, no.7 (April 1971): 53–67.

JOE BEEF. *See* MCKIERNAN, CHARLES

JOHNSON, GEORGE HENRY MARTIN (Onwanonsyshon), Six Nations chief and interpreter; b. 7 Oct. 1816 at Bow Park, near Brantford, Upper Canada, eldest son of John "Smoke" JOHNSON and Helen Martin; d. 19 Feb. 1884 at Chiefswood, near Brantford, Ont.

George Henry Martin Johnson was born in the ancestral home of his mother's family on the Grand River. According to Mohawk custom his parents had lived with his mother's parents until the birth of their first child but soon after George's birth they settled on their own farm some one and a half miles to the north and it was here that George spent his childhood. In the early 1830s he was educated at the Mohawk Institute, the school established for Indian children on the outskirts of Brantford by the New England Company and run by the Reverend Abram NELLES. During this period the young Mohawk displayed an amicable personality and an "aptitude for learning," being especially proficient in languages.

In 1838 the Reverend Adam Elliot* became the

Church of England missionary to the Grand River Indians, an event that was to have a great impact on George Johnson's personal and public life. When Elliot could not master the intricacies of the Mohawk language and required the services of an interpreter, he and Nelles agreed on Johnson for the position. In 1840 George was formally appointed interpreter for the Anglican mission on the reserve, the first of a series of posts, including interpreter to the superintendent, timber ranger for the reserve, and various positions on the Six Nations Council, which made him an important figure in the conduct of local white-Indian relations for the next 40 years. Johnson's position as interpreter necessitated his living with the Elliot family, where he met the missionary's young sister-in-law, Emily Susanna Howells, apparently a cousin of American novelist William Dean Howells. Her family had emigrated from Bristol, England, to the United States and in 1845 Emily had come to live with her sister Eliza Beulah at the Anglican mission near Brantford.

By the early 1850s, George Johnson and Emily Howells had decided to marry, a decision that roused opposition from both families. George's family, indeed the Indian community, did not approve of his marrying a white woman because she would then acquire Indian status and the right to a portion of her band's annuities and other benefits, and Emily's relatives were scandalized by her desire to marry a "savage." Both attitudes illustrate the gulf which separated the Indian and white communities in the mid 19th century. When Elliot refused to perform the ceremony, the couple sought out a more sympathetic Anglican priest, the Reverend William Greig, who married them at Barriefield, near Kingston, Canada West, on 27 Aug. 1853. As a wedding present for his bride, George had a new house, Chiefswood, built on a 200-acre plot on the east bank of the Grand River. The relative opulence of this Regency villa is reflected in Johnson's Indian name, Onwanonsyshon, translated as "lord of the great house." In this house, which stands today, restored, the four Johnson children, two sons and two daughters, grew up. The youngest, Emily Pauline* (Tekahionwake), became well known as a poet and lecturer.

In 1862, Jasper Tough Gilkison* was appointed superintendent to the Six Nations Indians, a post he held until 1891. He became a frequent guest in the Johnson household and relied upon George's judgement in the administration of affairs on the reserve. The upshot of this close association was Johnson's appointment as government interpreter for the Six Nations. Shortly before this appointment he had been elected Teyonhehkon, one of the 50 great chiefs of the Iroquois Confederacy, to succeed his maternal uncle, Henry Martin. Such a chieftainship descended matrilineally and Johnson's mother, as chief matron of the Mohawks, had nominated George. Her choice had been quickly ratified by the great council but George's acceptance of the government post led many chiefs to wonder if it was proper to have an employee of the imperial government on their council. After much discussion the council decided to displace him. The power of the chief matron then became apparent; Helen Martin appeared before the council and, after soundly berating its members, threatened that she would not nominate a successor if her son were removed. A compromise was effected. George remained a hereditary chief but a council resolution, which usually required a unanimous vote, would be valid without his assent. His status as a chief combined with his government connections, his family's position, and his ties with the Anglican presence on the reserve to make Johnson a powerful figure in the community.

The Grand River Reserve had long been plagued by "groups of white ruffians" who sold liquor to the Indians and by the more respectable timber plunderers who, in collusion with members of the reserve, illegally used Indian lands as a source for prized varieties of timber sought by the lumber companies now that farmland had replaced much of the hardwood forest in southern Ontario. The Indian Department had customarily appointed local notables as timber rangers or special constables but after 1860 Johnson took a leading part in the attempts to suppress both the illicit timber trade and the ready traffic in liquor. The success of his efforts, and the desperation of his opponents, finally led to violence. In January 1865 Johnson was unconscious for five days after being beaten by two men, one of whom was later imprisoned for five years for his part in the affair. In October 1873 the chief was again severely injured when six men shot him and left him for dead on the road near his home. He recovered from his wounds but his health was permanently affected and he frequently suffered from neuralgia and erysipelas. This last attack, however, "aroused a flame of popular indignation" amongst whites as well as Indians; although the six assailants were not tried, many of those exploiting the reserve either ceased or were punished.

In the last decade of his life Johnson was occupied with the affairs of the reserve's agricultural society which he had helped found; he was also a member of the Provincial Horticultural Society. A well-known figure, he was often invited to official functions as a representative of his people and government representatives invariably called on him when visiting the area. On 10 Aug. 1876 he was present in Brantford at Alexander Graham Bell*'s first demonstration of the telephone. Students of Iroquois culture and society generally received a hospitable welcome from Johnson and in the years before his death he formed a warm friendship with the American philologist, Horatio Emmons Hale.

George Johnson's life was not a spectacular one; his daughter's fame far eclipsed his own. Yet his career is important and instructive for it elucidates the difficulties, and the possibilities, experienced by the Six Nations of the Grand River in their relationships with the surrounding white community.

DOUGLAS LEIGHTON

PAC, RG 10, CI, 6, 803–93. UWO, Gilkison papers. H. [W.] Charlesworth, *Candid chronicles; leaves from the note book of a Canadian journalist* (Toronto, 1925). Mrs W. G. Foster [A. H. Foster], *The Mohawk princess, being some account of the life of Tekahion-wake (E. Pauline Johnson)* (Vancouver, 1931). Katherine Hale [A. B. Garvin], *Historic houses of Canada* (Toronto, 1952). *The history of the county of Brant, Ontario* ... (Toronto, 1883). E. P. Johnson, *Flint and feather, the complete poems of E. Pauline Johnson (Tekahionwake)* (Toronto, 1931); *The moccasin maker* (Toronto, 1913). C. M. Johnston, *Brant County: a history, 1784–1945* (Toronto, 1967). Marion MacRae and Anthony Adamson, *The ancestral roof: domestic architecture of Upper Canada* (Toronto and Vancouver, 1963). Walter McRaye [W. J. McCrea], *Pauline Johnson and her friends* (Toronto, 1947). F. D. Reville, *History of the county of Brant* (2v., Brantford, Ont., 1920). H. E. Hale, "Chief George H. M. Johnson – Onwanonsyshon: his life and work among the Six Nations," *Magazine of American Hist.* (New York), 13 (January–June 1885): 131–42; "An Iroquois condoling council," RSC *Trans.*, 1st ser., 1 (1883), sect.II: 45–65. E. H. C. Johnson, "The Martin settlement," Brant Hist. Soc., *Papers* ([Brantford]), 1908–11: 55–64.

JOHNSON, JOHN (Sakayengwaraton, Shakoyen'kwaráhton, usually known as **Smoke Johnson)**, pine tree chief of the Mohawks; b. 2 or 14 Dec. 1792 at the Johnson settlement, northwest of Cainsville, Upper Canada, son of Tekahionwake (Jacob Johnson) and his first wife; m. in 1815 Helen Martin, daughter of Mohawk chief George Martin* and Catherine Rollston (Wan-o-wen-re-teh), a white woman of Dutch ancestry captured by the Mohawks as a girl; they had a large family, including George Henry Martin JOHNSON; d. 26 Aug. 1886 on the Grand River Reserve, near Brantford, Ont.

John "Smoke" Johnson's father and his aunt were baptized at Fort Niagara (near Youngstown, N.Y.) in the presence of Sir William Johnson*, the superintendent of northern Indians, who evidently suggested his own name as a suitable surname for the children and acted as their godfather. Nevertheless, Jacob used his Indian family name, Tekahionwake, throughout his life; John "Smoke" Johnson was the first of his family to use the English name. His Indian name translates as "he has made the mist disappear for them." This mist, known to the Mohawks as smoke, provided Johnson with the name by which he was generally known.

A full-blooded Mohawk of the bear clan, Johnson in his youth was well acquainted with Joseph Brant [Thayendanegea*] and they were both regular attendants at the Mohawk Church, near Brantford. Johnson fought with the British in the War of 1812 as a young warrior, probably under John Norton*, in battles at Queenston Heights, Stoney Creek, and Lundy's Lane. Apparently Johnson was the man who kindled the fire that burned Buffalo on 30 Dec. 1813. For these military services he was later awarded a pension of $20 per month.

Johnson's personality and oratorical gifts gave him a leading role in the Grand River community after the war. His familiarity with both English and Mohawk made him indispensable to the successive superintendents of the Six Nations Indians, including Jasper Tough Gilkison*, superintendent from 1862 to 1891, with whom his son had close relations. These associations led to Johnson's becoming a chief on the advice of the British government acting through the Indian Department. A speaker of the Grand River Council for over 40 years, his splendid rhetoric in the traditional Iroquois oratorical style earned him the title "The Mohawk Warbler."

In 1869, when the young Prince Arthur* was inducted as an honorary Six Nations chief, Johnson and Skanawati (Chief John Buck) were appointed by the great council to conduct the ceremony, at which Johnson's son, George, acted as interpreter. In a sense, this marked the end of Johnson's active public career, in his 77th year. Physically and mentally active until his death at 93, he became the "grand old man" of the Six Nations community.

Long interested in his people's traditional ways, though a staunch Anglican all his life, by the early 1880s Johnson was reputed to be the only man left who knew the meaning of the entire Iroquois Book of Rites. His last years were marked by the unfortunate loss of the last manuscript of that work. In 1832 he had made a copy of the Book of Rites at the request of the elderly owner of the only extant copy. This action was fortunate, because soon afterwards the first copy was lost in a fire. In 1883 the philologist Horatio Emmons Hale published a work about the Book of Rites, using the Johnson copy. The following year, an American, Mrs Erminnie A. Smith, bought his copy from Johnson for $10 and refused to reconsider the purchase even though several of the younger Johnsons objected that the old chief had been deceived. The copy was sold at a great profit to the Smithsonian Institution in Washington, D.C., where it remains today.

Early in 1886 Johnson was asked to preside at the laying of the cornerstone of a memorial to Joseph Brant in Brantford but refused the honour because of Iroquois traditions regarding the dead. Although he did attend the ceremony on 11 August, he did not live to see the unveiling on 13 October. He died on 26 Aug. 1886 while gardening in the summer heat.

John "Smoke" Johnson's youth was spent during a

happy age in the history of the Six Nations. His long adult life ran from the last period of Indian warfare in eastern Canada over years when new types of threats developed to endanger Indian culture.

DOUGLAS LEIGHTON

AO, MU 1143. *The Iroquois book of rites*, ed. H. [E.] Hale (Philadelphia, 1883; 2nd ed., Toronto, 1963). *The valley of the Six Nations: a collection of documents on the Indian lands of the Grand River*, ed. C. M.Johnston (Toronto, 1964). Mrs W. G. Foster [A. H. Foster], *The Mohawk princess, being some account of the life of Tekahion-wake (E. Pauline Johnston)* (Vancouver, 1931). C. M. Johnson, *Brant County: a history, 1784–1945* (Toronto, 1967). Walter McRaye [W. J. McCrea], *Pauline Johnson and her friends* (Toronto, 1947). F. D. Reville, *History of the county of Brant* (2v., Brantford, Ont., 1920). A. I. G. Gilkison, "Reminiscences of earlier years in Brant," *OH*, 12 (1914): 81–88. E. H. C. Johnson, "Chief John Smoke Johnson," *OH*, 12 (1914): 102–13; "The Martin settlement," Brant Hist. Soc., *Papers* ([Brantford]), 1908–11: 55–64.

JOHNSTON, WILLIAM, educator and lawyer; b. 24 July 1848 in Lockerbie, Scotland, son of David Johnston; d. unmarried 7 Jan. 1885 in Guelph, Ont.

William Johnston's family immigrated to Canada in 1851 and settled in Cobourg, Canada West, where his father taught in a public school. William enrolled in Victoria College, Cobourg, at the age of 14, and after a year he left to teach school in Northumberland County. In 1869 he entered Knox College, Toronto, but because of ill health had to drop out and seek medical advice in Edinburgh. In 1872 he returned to the University of Toronto and graduated in 1874 with the gold medal for metaphysics.

In August 1874, shortly after his graduation, Johnston became rector and then acting principal of the School of Agriculture and Experimental Farm at Guelph which had accepted its first students in May; he became principal in 1876. Under the short tenures of the first two principals, Henry McCandless and Charles Roberts, the school had quickly attracted criticism from politicians and suspicion from farmers. During the five years that Johnston headed the school he managed to end the bad publicity and to win support from Ontario farmers. Between 1874 and 1879 the school's enrolment grew from 28 to 89.

In his reorganization of the school, Johnston, for administrative purposes, separated the farm and the school. William Brown, the professor of agriculture, became the first farm manager while Johnston, as principal, controlled the school. The conflict resulting from this "double headship" eventually led to Johnston's resignation in 1879 and continued to cause endless friction for ten years after his departure.

Within the school itself Principal Johnston established an academic programme which emphasized both the scientific and the practical aspects of farming. The requirement of manual labour for all students remained a characteristic of campus life until 1920. Johnston was interested in that "miscellaneous medley of youths, whose natural place is the plough, the bench, the forge, or the mine." He was opposed to the example set by the American land grant colleges whereby liberal arts and engineering developed side by side with the colleges of agriculture. Likewise he refused to accept the pattern of European agricultural schools, which he said trained "peasants," made "stewards and managers of farms," and hardly ever turned out "the peasant proprietor holding his own plough" or the manager "controlling his own business."

More than anyone else Johnston must be regarded as the founder of the Ontario Agricultural College and Experimental Farm, as the school became known in 1885. He gave it a philosophy of education, both theoretical and practical, which may still be discerned, and convinced at least some farmers in Ontario that the school could be important to the success of agriculture in the province. He hired competent men, such as James Hoyes Panton*, whose lectures in chemistry and geology ensured that the science as well as the practice of agriculture would flourish at Guelph. Also he was the first to recommend that the School of Agriculture and Experimental Farm should be removed from the control of the provincial government.

Principal Johnston resigned on 30 Sept. 1879 to enter the law office of Blake, Kerr and Boyd in Toronto, and in February 1882 he was called to the bar of Upper Canada. He was secretary of the Central Reform Association during the federal election of 1882 and the provincial election of 1883. Unfortunately Johnston's second career as a lawyer interested in reform politics was cut short by his untimely death at the age of 36. "His ability and judgment" were praised in an obituary notice, which also singled him out "as one of the rising young men of the Liberal Party." It is, however, as an educator and as the architect of the Ontario Agricultural College at Guelph that William Johnston deserves historical note.

ALEXANDER M. ROSS

Ont., Agricultural Commission, *Report of the commissioners . . .* (Toronto, 1881), app.O: 17–47; app.P: 14–80; Legislature, *Sessional papers*, 1874 (2nd session), I, no.1: xi–xiii, app.F. Ontario School of Agriculture and Experimental Farm, *Annual report* (Toronto), 1874–79. A. M. Ross, *The college on the hill: a history of the Ontario Agricultural College, 1874–1974* (Vancouver, 1974).

JONES, ELIZABETH. *See* FIELD

JOSEPH, ABRAHAM, commission merchant, banker, and municipal politician; b. 14 Nov. 1815 in Berthier-en-Haut (Berthierville), Lower Canada, third son of Henry (Harry) Joseph*, shipowner and trader, and Rachel Solomons (Solomon), daughter of

Lucius Levy Solomons*; m. 18 Nov. 1846 Sophia David, granddaughter of Aaron Hart* of Trois-Rivières, Canada East, and they had five sons and eight daughters; d. 20 March 1886 in Quebec City, and interred in Montreal, Que., in the cemetery of the Spanish and Portuguese Synagogue.

Abraham Joseph received a thorough training in the principles and traditions of the Jewish faith from his parents, but little is known of his formal education except that he attended the Académie de Berthier where he was head of his class in 1828. Two years later the family, which included nine children, left Berthier-en-Haut for Montreal. In 1832, after Henry Joseph and his eldest son both died the same day from cholera, the eldest surviving son, Jacob, adopted his father's name and was thenceforth known as Jacob Henry. He inherited his father's extensive tobacco and snuff import business, begun by the Solomons more than 30 years earlier, and operated it with the assistance of Abraham and their mother. The tobacco was purchased in the United States on regular buying trips. In 1836 Abraham moved to Quebec City to oversee the firm's interests there, and on 1 April 1837 he became a partner in the firm with a one-fifth interest. The business in Montreal was described in 1844 as H. Joseph and Company, "wholesale manufacturers and importers of Tobacco, 144 St. Paul Street." By 1851 the office in Quebec City was listed in the city directory as A. Joseph and Company, general merchants, and in 1854 it was described as "dealers in tobacco, general agents and commission merchants, on Napoleon Wharf." The partnership was terminated on 31 March 1859; Jacob Henry then carried on business on his own in Montreal and Abraham took charge of the company in Quebec City.

Joseph was also interested in shipping and with his brother Jacob Henry and his cousin Theodore HART was an owner of the barque *Benjamin Hart*, built in Quebec City in 1839. In addition, Joseph was one of the incorporators of the St Lawrence Navigation Company in 1861, serving as its president in 1879–80, and he was active for many years in the Quebec Marine Insurance Company (founded in 1862) and the St Lawrence Tow Boat Company (1863), holding the offices of president, director, and then vice-president of the latter from at least 1867 to 1873. In 1866 he was appointed a provisional director of the British American Steamship Company, established to carry mail weekly between Quebec City and Pictou, N.S.; the company represented an attempt by Quebec City merchants to establish shipping links with the Maritime colonies at the time of the impending union of the British North American colonies. In 1871 he was appointed a director of the Quebec and Gulf Ports Steamship Company (in service from 1867), and he continued as a director when the firm became the Quebec Steamship Company in 1880.

Joseph was also active in the development of the financial institutions of Quebec City. His first involvement was with the District Bank of Quebec, a small savings bank established in 1847 by 40 members of the Quebec business community, both English-speaking and French-speaking. We then find Joseph as a director, from 1854 to 1858, and as president, from 1859 to 1865, of the Union Building Society which handled mortgages and provided long-term capital for property acquisitions. In 1860 he was elected to the board of directors of the Banque Nationale which he had helped to establish two years before [*see* François VÉZINA]; he and six other directors remained on the board for 14 years. He resigned in 1874 to become president of the Stadacona Bank which had been accorded a capital reserve of $1,000,000 when it was incorporated in 1873.

To safeguard his commercial interests Joseph became a member of the Quebec Board of Trade in 1848. His election as president in 1863 was recognition of his importance in the city's business community. As president he chaired the dinner on 15 Oct. 1864 attended by the delegates from the Atlantic colonies to the Quebec Conference. The *Quebec Mercury* reported that in his speech he stated that "the merchants of Quebec . . . all heartily desired some change in our present position – they desired a thorough commercial union – they desired that the unequal and hostile tariffs of the several provinces should disappear. . . . We wanted a commercial union in order to bring about closer ties, and we wanted that union under one flag. . . ." On the death of his wife in 1866, he refused re-election as president of the board of trade; however, he remained active in it, and was to become vice-president, from 1876 to 1878, of the Dominion Board of Trade, formed in 1873.

Joseph never took part in provincial politics. In 1837, although he was of the opinion that Louis-Joseph Papineau* was "as far as his private conduct goes . . . a good enough fellow, far from being haughty," he volunteered with the Quebec Light Infantry at the outbreak of the rebellion and attained the rank of major before resigning in 1839. On 27 Sept. 1846 he became a justice of the peace and in January 1847 a magistrate. He was also involved in municipal politics. Elected to the Quebec City Council in Saint-Louis Ward in 1854, he was to serve on the roads, waterworks, and finance committees. On two occasions, in 1858 and in 1860, he unsuccessfully contested the mayoralty; he retired from politics after his second attempt. In 1856 he became the vice-consul at Quebec City for Belgium (his younger brother Jesse had been consul at Montreal since 1850) and he retained the post until his death. He was also a member of the St George's Society and served as its president in 1855–56.

By the end of the 1860s Joseph had become a

well-established businessman in Quebec City, with a wholesale grocery specializing in imported foods and whisky, its principal customers being shipping companies, militia units, and country grocers. He was, however, severely affected by the economic depression which began in 1874. The Stadacona Bank lost $75,000 because of bad debts and had to draw upon its reserves and lower its dividends by 6 per cent in 1876 and by 2 per cent in June 1879. One month later the bank liquidated its assets at the request of the shareholders, who were paid in full. His own business was also transformed in 1878: two sons, Montefiore and Andrew Cohen, acceded to the management of the firm and its name was changed to A. Joseph and Sons. The two sons carried on the business after Abraham's death. Also in 1878, at the age of 63, Abraham resigned many of his directorships but retained interests in shipping and banking. In addition, at various times after 1871, he was president of the De Léry Gold Mining Company, and he owned considerable property, especially in Quebec City. When he died in 1886 the Montreal *Gazette* noted that death had claimed one of Quebec City's "oldest citizens" who would be "greatly missed in business and social circles."

ANNETTE R. WOLFF

[Abraham Joseph kept a diary from 1834 to 1876 which provides a great deal of information on political, economic, and social life in Quebec during this period. The PAC has a copy as well as other documents on the Joseph family in MG 24, I61. Genealogical information was supplied by the Jewish Public Library in Montreal. A. R. W.]

AC, Québec, Minutiers, E. G. Meredith, 29 March, 31 May 1886; 13 Jan., 26, 27 May, 18 June, 6 Dec. 1887; 28 April 1891. ANQ-M, Minutiers, G. D. Arnoldi, 6, 25 avril 1836; I. J. Gibb, 6 avril 1837. Can., prov. du, *Statuts*, 1847, c.113; 1861, c.99; 1862, c.71; février–mai 1863, c.59. Can., *Statuts*, mars–août 1873, c.66, c.73, c.108; 1880, c.62. *Gazette* (Montreal), 22 March 1886. *Quebec Daily Mercury*, 17 Oct. 1864. *Cyclopædia of Canadian biog.* (Rose, 1888), 274–75. *Quebec directory*, 1847–86. *The Jew in Canada: a complete record of Canadian Jewry from the days of the French régime to the present time*, ed. A. D. Hart, (Toronto and Montreal, 1926). E. C. Woodley, *The house of Joseph in the life of Quebec: the record of a century and a half* (Quebec, 1946). Martin Wolff, "The Jews of Canada," *American Jewish year book* (Philadelphia), 27 (1925–26): 154–229.

JUCHEREAU DUCHESNAY, HENRI-JULES, lawyer, magistrate, and politician; b. 6 July 1845 at Sainte-Marie-de-la-Nouvelle-Beauce (Sainte-Marie), Canada East, son of Elzéar-Henri Juchereau* Duchesnay, a lawyer and politician, and Élisabeth-Suzanne Taschereau, daughter of the Honourable Jean-Thomas Taschereau*; d. 6 July 1887 at Sainte-Marie.

Henri-Jules Juchereau Duchesnay's ancestor, Jean Juchereau* de Maur, who had arrived in New France in 1634 with his wife and four children, was the first seigneur of Saint-Augustin. During the next two centuries, the Juchereau family became connected with the other nobility in the Quebec region through marriage.

Juchereau Duchesnay received a classical education at the Petit Séminaire de Québec, and studied law at Université Laval in Quebec City and McGill College in Montreal. On 14 Sept. 1866 he was called to the bar, and practised at Quebec with Honoré-Cyrias Pelletier for some months before taking up residence in his native parish. On 19 May 1871 he was appointed lieutenant-colonel of the militia and on 3 Jan. 1874 stipendiary magistrate for Beauce County. In 1875 he accepted the post of inspector of mines for the Beauce area, which included the 1,500-square-mile basin of the Rivière Chaudière considered to be a gold-bearing region. The most intensive mining was being carried out on the Rivière Gilbert, a tributary of the Chaudière; in October 1882 Juchereau Duchesnay listed 16 companies prospecting on the Gilbert alone. Joseph Obalski*, a mining engineer working for the provincial government, noted in his report in 1898 that gold was to be found there in "commercial quantities."

In 1882 Juchereau Duchesnay, who devoted part of his time to agriculture, collaborated in establishing a creamery designed to teach butter manufacturing; there was at that time only one other similar operation in Quebec, at Saint-Denis-de-la-Bouteillerie. As president and managing director of the Société de Fabrication de Beurre et de Fromage de la Paroisse de Sainte-Marie, he imported from Denmark two centrifugal separators, the first to be installed in Canada and indeed in North America. They yielded unexpectedly good results, but unfortunately the suspicious farmers did not provide the requisite daily quota of milk. Observing that the company was operating at a loss, despite an annual grant of $1,000 from the provincial government, the shareholders withdrew in July 1883, leaving Juchereau Duchesnay to run the undertaking by himself; he continued until "his financial resources were exhausted." Two years after his death the butter-factory was reorganized as a cooperative.

Politics also interested Juchereau Duchesnay. In 1885, according to *L'Électeur* of Quebec City, he was one of the speakers who "in energetic terms stigmatized the cowardly and criminal servility of the federal ministers" who had voted for the execution of Louis RIEL. At a meeting of the Société Saint-Jean-Baptiste he secured the adoption of a motion "that the society's flag have a black border during the celebration of the national holiday on 24 June." In 1887 he stood as "National" Conservative candidate in Dorchester County, dissociating himself from his leader, Sir John A. Macdonald*, because of the Riel affair. On 22 February he defeated Dr Charles-Alexandre Lesage, the Conservative incumbent. Juchereau Duchesnay served for only a few months before he died of typhoid fever on 6 July 1887. His brother-in-law, Honoré-

Julien-Jean-Baptiste Chouinard*, won the subsequent by-election on 8 Jan. 1888.

On 21 Sept. 1869, at Quebec, Henri-Jules Juchereau Duchesnay had married Caroline, daughter of Cirice Têtu, a Quebec merchant, and they had ten children. Juchereau Duchesnay led an active life in the Beauce region, where he was held in high esteem. Although he had many abilities his premature death deprived him of the time to acquire the standing and respect his father had enjoyed.

MADELEINE FERRON

AP, Sainte-Marie-de-la-Nouvelle-Beauce (Sainte-Marie), Reg. des baptêmes, mariages et sépultures, 8 juill. 1887. Qué., Parl., *Doc. de la session*, 1882, I: no.2; 1883–84, IV: nos.22, 22a, 22b, 23. *L'Électeur* (Québec), 24, 26 nov. 1885. *CPC*, 1887. P.-G. Roy, *Les avocats de la région de Québec*, 146. Frère Éloi-Gérard [Talbot], *Recueil des généalogies des comtés de Beauce-Dorchester-Frontenac, 1625–1946* (11v., Beauceville, Qué., 1949–55), I. Joseph Obalski, *Or dans la province de Québec* (Québec, 1898). Honorius Provost, *Sainte-Marie de la Nouvelle-Beauce; histoire civile* (Québec, 1970). P.-G. Roy, *La famille Juchereau Duchesnay* (Lévis, Qué., 1903); *La famille Taschereau* (Lévis, 1901). Rumilly, *Hist. de la prov. de Québec*, X. Errol Bouchette, "Les débuts d'une industrie laitière et notre classe bourgeoise," RSC *Trans.*, 3rd ser., 6 (1912), sect. I: 143–57.

JUNEAU, FÉLIX-EMMANUEL, teacher, school inspector, and author; b. 27 May 1816 at Quebec City, son of Nicholas Juneau, a merchant, and Josephte de Villers; d. there, unmarried, 17 Feb. 1886.

Félix-Emmanuel Juneau studied at the Petit Séminaire de Québec from 1831 to 1833, and again in 1836–37 after attending the Collège de Sainte-Anne-de-la-Pocatière the previous year. Forced to abandon his studies, apparently as a result of his father's financial difficulties, he took up teaching. Around 1840 he opened his own school in the *faubourg* Saint-Roch in Quebec City; called the Académie commerciale et littéraire, it eventually had up to 160 pupils.

From an early stage Juneau set his mind on advancing his profession and raising the standards of teachers. In *Le Castor* of March 1845 he announced, as interim secretary, the creation of a committee to set up an association of schoolteachers of the district of Quebec. Soon after a general meeting at his school, the Library Association of the Teachers of the District of Quebec (incorporated in 1849) was formed. The founders of this first organization of teachers included Antoine Légaré*, Clément Cazeau, Charles Dion, and Benoît Marquette. A similar association was also established at Montreal in 1845. The members of the Quebec association met once a month "to learn from each other, to fit themselves the better to meet the needs of society, and to give the status of the teacher all the importance it has in other nations." They set as their goal, among other things, the standardization of teaching methods, of subjects taught, and of material used, as well as of discipline. Through numerous petitions to the government, the Quebec association promoted measures designed to improve teaching: the appointment of school inspectors from 1852, the setting up of a retirement fund in 1856, and the creation of three normal schools (teachers' colleges) the following year. It had about 60 members at the outset and grew steadily until 1854, when a fire destroyed Juneau's house where the records and part of the association's library were kept. The meetings then became less frequent and were poorly attended. However, in 1857 the superintendent of the Department of Public Instruction, Pierre-Joseph-Olivier CHAUVEAU, while opening the three normal schools, also set up three associations which were actually a continuation of the 1845 organizations. On 21 July 1857 Juneau was elected president of the Association des Instituteurs de la Circonscription de l'École Normale Laval. He regularly attended its meetings for the rest of his life, frequently contributing to discussions and occasionally giving lectures.

A member of the board of examiners of the district of Quebec from 1849, Juneau was appointed a teacher in the practical division of the École Normale Laval upon its opening in 1857. He remained there only two years, however; on 2 Dec. 1859 he was appointed school inspector for the counties of Lévis and Dorchester. This was a particularly heavy responsibility, since inspectors were legally required to visit their districts twice a year and make reports to the superintendent. In 1859 Juneau had under his charge 99 schools, with an enrolment of 6,837 children, for which he received an annual salary of $700. His reports indicate that the quality of the teaching was generally good and indeed he noted steady improvement every year. On 16 June 1868 he was entrusted with another inspection district, which included the counties of Montmorency, Quebec, and Portneuf, as well as the Catholic schools of Quebec City. Because of its size, his district was subdivided in 1875. A year before his death Juneau had under his jurisdiction 130 schools, with some 8,237 pupils, and his annual salary had increased to $1,000.

Because of his concern to improve the status of the schoolteacher and the quality of teaching, Juneau published several works to assist his colleagues and make schooling more pleasant for children. Thus in 1847 he brought out at Quebec a *Dissertation sur l'instruction primaire, dans laquelle on propose de réunir à la fois les avantages pratiques de l'enseignement mutuel, du simultané et de l'individuel*, one of the first pedagogical texts by a French Canadian lay teacher. Having to deal with the problem of small, ill-ventilated schools, too many pupils, and often archaic teaching materials, he proposed resorting to the Lancaster system, which was based on the use of monitors but left the teacher an active role in the instruction. That year at Quebec he republished *La Nouvelle Méthode pour apprendre à bien lire* by the Frenchman Jean Palairet; according to Charles-Joseph Magnan*, "this method was laborious, illogical and devoid of interest," but it long remained on the list of books recommended by the Council of Public Instruction. In 1866 Juneau published at Quebec a *Traité de calcul mental à l'usage des écoles canadiennes*, which in Edmond LAREAU's view had the great advantage of finally giving the pupils "exercises in dollars and cents." Two years later, in collaboration with Napoléon Lacasse, he published at Quebec an *Alphabet ou syllabaire gradué, d'après une nouvelle méthode*, which was designed to be more sensible and better suited to the minds of children than similar earlier works.

After devoting nearly half a century to the field of education, Félix-Emmanuel Juneau passed away at Quebec in 1886. He could lay claim to having been one of the first lay teachers who worked unremittingly to enhance the dignity of his profession and the quality of teaching.

HUGUETTE FILTEAU

In addition to the works mentioned in the biography, Félix-Emmanuel Juneau was the author of *Ode à mon âme* (Québec, 1874) and *Livret des écoles ou petites leçons de choses* (Québec, 1877).

AC, Québec, État civil, Catholiques, Saint-Roch (Qué.), 20 févr. 1886. ANQ-Q, État civil, Catholiques, Notre-Dame de Québec, 28 mai 1816. ASQ, Fichier des anciens. Can., prov. du, *Statuts*, 1849, c.145. *JIP*, 1857–79. Joseph Letourneau, "Notice nécrologique: feu M. F. E. Juneau," *L'Enseignement primaire* (Québec), 6 (1886): 54–56. *Catalogue des anciens élèves du collège de Sainte-Anne-de-la-Pocatière, 1827–1927*, [François Têtu, compil.] (Québec, 1927). *Quebec directory*, 1854–86. P.-G. Roy, *Fils de Québec* (4 sér., Lévis, Qué., 1933), IV: 10–12. [L.-]A. Desrosiers, *Les écoles normales primaires de la province de Québec et leurs œuvres complémentaires; récit des fêtes jubilaires de l'école normale Jacques-Cartier, 1857–1907* (Montréal, 1909), 83, 148–52. André Labarrère-Paulé, *Les instituteurs laïques au Canada français, 1836–1900* (Québec, 1965), 119–33. C.-J. Magnan, "Éducateurs d'autrefois – anciens professeurs de l'école normale Laval – IV – F.-E. Juneau: 1816–1886," *BRH*, 48 (1942): 44–50.

K

KACHENOOTING, GEORGE. *See* STEINHAUER

KAH-PAH-YAK-AS-TO-CUM. *See* KĀPEYAKWĀSKONAM

KAMĪYISTOWESIT (Beardy, literally little moustache, known in French as **Barbu**), chief of the Willow band of the Plains Cree; b.*c.* 1828 probably near Duck Lake (Sask.); d. 16 April 1889 at the Beardy Reserve (Sask.).

The members of the Willow band were related to, or allied with, the mixed-blood descendants of George Sutherland*, who had been an employee of the Hudson's Bay Company at the end of the 18th century. Little is known of Beardy's early life except that he was said to possess spiritual powers or "medicine." He became a chief about 1870 and a few years later was one of the Plains Cree chiefs who welcomed the news that the government of Canada intended to make treaty with the Indians of the Saskatchewan River district. However, he refused to attend the major council on 23 Aug. 1876 at which Treaty no.6 was negotiated by Alexander MORRIS because the treaty commissioners would not respect a vision Beardy had had as to where this council should take place. Finally, to obtain Beardy's adhesion, a special meeting was held on 28 August with his people near Duck Lake [*see* KĀPEYAKWĀSKONAM].

On learning the terms of the treaty, Beardy expressed his dissatisfaction with what the government offered the Cree. He thought the sections relating to assistance were inadequate in view of the crisis caused by the depletion of the buffalo herds. In addition, he wanted a provision for the management of the remaining buffalo. Although his recommendations were not accepted, Beardy saw no alternative for his people and signed.

As stipulated in the terms of the treaty Beardy selected as his reserve a site surrounding Duck Lake. When the agricultural equipment and animals promised in the treaty failed to arrive Beardy protested to the lieutenant governor of the North-West Territories, David Laird*, in September 1877. He also continued his efforts to modify the treaty so that his band would receive sufficient assistance to survive the economic crisis Beardy foresaw. Receiving no satisfaction from local officials, Beardy wrote to the governor general of Canada, Lord Dufferin [Blackwood*], in January 1878.

Beardy was a source of anxiety to government officials. In 1878 he argued that he was entitled to additional presents and that his annuities and treaty goods should be brought to his reserve. When officials finally did go to see him and failed to bring the presents and food he expected, he refused to accept the annuities and provisions they did bring. By December Beardy's people were destitute and he announced his intention of taking what his people needed from the local merchants. A unit of the North-West Mounted Police was sent to Duck Lake and Beardy's people were given their treaty money to purchase the much needed goods. The crisis passed, but Beardy protested further when he did not receive all he had been promised by the treaty commissioners.

Beardy's belief that the government was not honouring Treaty no.6 was further reinforced when the band's reserve was surveyed. Rather than allotting the band all the lands they wanted, the government excluded those parcels claimed by the local Métis, and threatened Beardy with loss of treaty entitlement if he did not accept the exclusions. Land grievances aside, hunger continued to be the band's principal problem in the early 1880s, and Beardy is alleged to have killed some treaty cattle to feed his people despite the fact they were intended for stock raising. When Governor General Lorne [Campbell*] visited the area in 1881 Beardy spoke to him about the need for more assistance and for the full and immediate implementation of the treaty. This appeal had no effect; Beardy and other Cree chiefs including Poundmaker [PĪTIKWAHANAPIWĪYIN], Big Bear [MISTAHIMASKWA], Kāpeyakwāskonam (One Arrow), and Little Pine [MINAHIKOSIS] then came together at a meeting on his reserve in August 1884. The treaty was discussed and plans were made for future action if demands for the redress of grievances continued to be ignored. Beardy, Little Pine, and Big Bear began organizing a meeting of all Plains Cree chiefs which was to be held in 1885.

When rebellion broke out in the northwest in March 1885, however, Beardy remained neutral, though promises of food and aid did attract a small number of his band to join Louis RIEL. Beardy met Major-General Frederick Dobson Middleton* at Batoche (Sask.) and explained that he could not restrain his young men. After the rebellion, because Beardy and other members of his band had left their reservation despite a proclamation forbidding such movements, the entire band was suspended from treaty. Moreover, Beardy was no longer officially recognized by government officials as the spokesman for his people, although his band continued to regard him as their leader until his death in April 1889.

Beardy, at times dismissed as a gadfly and nuisance, was a man of some foresight regarding the fate of his people and their culture. He recognized the inadequacy of the treaty he signed, and from the beginning he sought to have it modified to provide the aid the Cree needed in a period of crisis. Finding the government indifferent, he joined other Plains Cree leaders in a movement to pressure the government, but before they could achieve their goal they were overtaken by the events precipitated by the Métis.

JOHN L. TOBIAS

PAC, RG 10, B3, 3185, file 41783/1; 3576, file 309; 3577, file 429; 3582, file 949; 3584, file 1130; 3636, file 6694/1; 3656, file 9030; 3697, file 15423; 3768, file 33642; 3777, file 37642; 3785, file 41783; 3793, files 45948, 46008; 3809, file 53828/1; 3820, file 57325; 3831, file 62987; 3874, file 10508; 7768, file 27109/2. PAM, HBCA, B.27/a/1–17. Morris, *Treaties of Canada with the Indians*. C. P. [Mulvany], *The history of the North-West rebellion of 1885 . . .* (Toronto, 1885; repr. 1971). Stanley, *Birth of western Canada*; *Louis Riel*. D. G. Mandelbaum, "The Plains Cree," American Museum of Natural Hist., *Anthropological Papers* (New York), 37 (1941): 155–316.

KAPAPAMAHCHAKWEW (Papamahchakwayo, Wandering Spirit, occasionally known as **Esprit Errant**), war chief of a band of Plains Cree; b. *c.* 1845; d. 27 Nov. 1885 by hanging at Battleford (Sask.). He was survived by at least one daughter.

From the fragmentary evidence concerning Wandering Spirit's earlier life, he seems to have been the ideal Plains Cree warrior. In appearance he was tall and lithe with an arresting countenance distinguished by large piercing eyes, a long straight nose, and thick curly hair. His voice had a smooth, velvet quality and though usually soft could rise to ringing tones. A member of the band that followed Big Bear [MISTAHIMASKWA], he attained the prestigious position of war chief, an office separate from the social chieftainship held by Big Bear, as a result of his daring battle exploits. He was reputed to have killed between 11 and 13 warriors of the Blackfeet, hereditary enemies of the Crees – more than any other member of the band. His unique war bonnet was made of a whole lynx skin looped double with the head fixed to the tail, open at the top, and decorated with five eagle plumes. As war chief, Wandering Spirit was also head of the warrior society, especially important during the summer hunts and festivities. Among its functions were policing the tribal camps, keeping guard against enemies, and carrying out special duties in connection with the buffalo hunt.

For warriors such as Wandering Spirit the collapse of the Plains Cree way of life in the 1870s, resulting from the disappearance of the buffalo and the signing of the treaties, engendered particular bitterness and despair. The band of dissidents who gathered around Big Bear tried to resist the new order but eventually starvation forced them to adhere to Treaty no.6 in December 1882. During the winter of 1884–85 Big Bear's destitute band camped in the vicinity of the small settlement of Frog Lake (Alta), which was an agency for the Department of Indian Affairs and a Roman Catholic mission. Resentful of Indian agent Thomas Trueman Quinn's strict enforcement of the "no work, no ration" policy, militants such as Wandering Spirit grew increasingly hostile. The band had, in fact, been exposed to the ideas of Louis RIEL, whom they had met in Montana in the early 1880s when they had been following the remaining buffalo herds. Riel urged that through concerted action the Métis and the Indians could drive the Canadians from their country and regain their freedom and independence. The signal for action came in late March 1885 with the news that the Métis had risen and routed the

North-West Mounted Police at Duck Lake (Sask.). By this time, Big Bear was powerless to prevent Wandering Spirit and the other warriors from attacking Frog Lake.

Early on the morning of 2 April the 12 whites and mixed bloods at Frog Lake were rounded up while the Indians ransacked the stores of the Hudson's Bay Company post and the police barracks. Quinn's defiant refusal to proceed to the Indian camp with the other prisoners so infuriated Wandering Spirit that he shot him and then shouted for the death of all whites, most of whom were killed within a few minutes. Nine men died. Only the two women, Theresa Gowanlock and Theresa Delaney, and William Bleasdell Cameron*, an HBC employee, were spared.

Wandering Spirit played a prominent role in subsequent events. His hatred of the Canadian government and its agents, the police, was manifest in his speeches prior to the fall of Fort Pitt (Sask.) in mid April: "We are tired of him [the government] and all his people and we are going to drive them out of the country." Only Big Bear's intervention at Fort Pitt prevented another violent outburst, which might have resulted in the deaths of the white captives, whom Wandering Spirit rightly suspected of sowing dissension between the Plains Crees and their reluctant Wood Cree allies. As Big Bear's band began to move toward Poundmaker [PĪTIKWAHANAPIWĪYIN] at Battleford, the war chief worked actively to heal the breach and therefore held a Thirst Dance near Frenchman Butte (Sask.). When the advance of Major-General Thomas Bland Strange*'s forces interrupted the ceremony, Wandering Spirit rallied the camp for war and entrenched his men in rifle pits in a strategic position on Frenchman Butte. During the battle of 28 May, Wandering Spirit evinced good generalship as he "moved up and down the rifle-pits, haranguing his warriors, buoying up their courage," and they repelled General Strange's attack.

As the Indians withdrew to the north after this inconclusive engagement, a dramatic change seems to have come over Wandering Spirit. The war chief sought refuge with the Wood Crees, who had seized an opportunity to desert Big Bear shortly after the battle. According to one account Wandering Spirit had experienced such traumas that within a few months his hair had turned almost white. In any case, burdened with remorse at the havoc he had wreaked, he attempted to atone for his actions by trying to commit suicide as the Wood Crees came in to surrender at Fort Pitt. He later explained to Cameron: "I knew there was no hope for me. Perhaps, I thought, if I sacrificed myself the government would not be so hard on the rest." Wandering Spirit did not die from his self-inflicted chest wound but was carried by stretcher to Battleford to stand trial.

The trials of the Crees arrested for their action at Frog Lake were short, and, in retrospect, justice seems to have been arbitrarily dispensed. None of the Indians was given legal counsel; all were tried by stipendiary magistrate Charles-Borromée Rouleau*. Wandering Spirit admitted that he shot Quinn, but refused to explain his actions. On 22 September he was summarily sentenced to hang. The next person found guilty of murder was Paypamakeesit (Round the Sky), who was accused of shooting Father Léon-Adélard FAFARD after the latter was wounded by Wandering Spirit. According to one account, Paypamakeesit, who had been cared for by the priest, was provoked into the shooting by the taunts of his comrades, but no evidence of this nature was presented in court. On 3 October Kittimakegin (Miserable Man) and Manachoos (Bad Arrow) were tried for the murder of Charles Gouin. Both pleaded not guilty, and Miserable Man asked Cameron to back his alibi that he had been in the HBC store at the time of the murder. Cameron, however, who loathed Miserable Man, had already helped secure for the crown testimony of Indian witnesses claiming that Wandering Spirit had ordered Bad Arrow to shoot Gouin and that Miserable Man had also shot him. The case against Apaschiskoos (Little Bear) and Nabpace (Iron Body) for the murder of George Dill appears in retrospect unconvincing: Iron Body was convicted on the evidence of Little Bear, who was then also convicted of the killing, but both stoutly denied that they had fired the fatal shot and Iron Body maintained that an Indian who had escaped custody had shot Dill. It seems that the federal government was determined to make an example of these Indians. When the cases were reviewed by the minister of justice, John Sparrow David Thompson*, no mitigating circumstances were taken into consideration and the death sentences were upheld.

Wandering Spirit, morosely silent throughout his imprisonment, granted Cameron an interview the day before his execution. He regretted having believed that the Indians could resist the encroachments of the whites and restore the old way of life. The proud war chief declared he was not afraid to die, but he begged that he not be buried with the humiliating ball and chain which shackled him. As the eight Indians stood on the scaffold, Wandering Spirit was the only one who had no last words. While some of the others shouted war cries and defiance of the whites, Wandering Spirit, according to legend, softly chanted a love song to his wife. The bodies were buried in a common grave, later covered by an unmarked concrete slab.

SYLVIA M. VAN KIRK

PAC, RG 13, C1, 1421. *The Frog Lake 'massacre' : personal perspectives on ethnic conflict*, ed. Stuart Hughes (Toronto, 1976). Stanley, *Birth of western Canada*. R. S. Allen, "Big Bear," *Saskatchewan Hist.* (Saskatoon), 25 (1972): 1–17. D. G. Mandelbaum, "The Plains Cree," American Museum of Natural Hist., *Anthropological Papers* (New York), 37 (1941): 155–316.

KĀPEYAKWĀSKONAM (Kah-pah-yak-as-to-cum, One Arrow, known in French as **Une Flèche)**, chief of a band of Willow Crees, b. *c.* 1815 probably in or near the valley of the Saskatchewan River; d. 25 April 1886 at St Boniface, Man.

One Arrow was the chief of a band of Willow Crees which, until the disappearance of the buffalo from the Canadian prairies in the 1870s, traditionally hunted in the region bisected by the South Saskatchewan River and stretching from near Duck Lake in the north to Little Manitou Lake and Goose Lake to the southeast and southwest respectively. After a last desperate trek to the Cypress Hills in search of bison in 1879, the great majority of the band settled permanently on their reserve four miles east of the South Saskatchewan River, behind the Métis settlement of Batoche (Sask.). After the 16-square-mile site was surveyed in 1881, the hunting operations of the band appear to have shifted to the east, into the wooded and parkland areas of the Carrot River valley where small game could still be found.

One Arrow's followers did not initially impress the officials of the Department of Indian Affairs with their efforts towards agricultural self-sufficiency, but the department also took little notice of the fact that, as late as 1884, the band had not received from the government many of the implements and some of the livestock which it had been promised in 1876 under the terms of Treaty no.6. Nor did it receive, until 1884, the instruction and supervision in farming given to most other bands; once it was begun, the band made rapid progress.

Chief One Arrow himself did not come into prominence until the outbreak in 1885 of the North-West rebellion. In 1876 he had been associated with chiefs Beardy [KAMĪYISTOWESIT] and Saswaypew (Cut Nose) in an attempt to obstruct the negotiation of Treaty no.6 at Fort Carlton (Sask.), but on 28 August, five days after the treaty had been concluded, One Arrow and the other two chiefs signed a formal adhesion to the agreement. In 1880 the same three chiefs were arrested on a charge of inciting their followers to butcher government cattle. A jury refused to convict them, however, much to the disgust of the officials of the Department of Indian Affairs. Four years later, in August 1884, One Arrow attended a large council of chiefs along with Big Bear [MISTAHIMASKWA] and Papewes (Papaway, Lucky Man) to discuss Indian grievances. He seems to have joined in the charges that the "sweet promises" made at the time of the treaty, "in order to get their country from them," had not been kept, and in the threats of unspecified but non-violent measures that would be taken in order to force the government to act. In all of these activities, however, One Arrow does not seem to have played more than a minor role.

His part in the North-West rebellion is, in many respects, unclear. Since his reserve was the closest to the Métis settlement on the South Saskatchewan River, his Indians were, naturally, most susceptible to Métis influence. On 17 March 1885 Métis leader Gabriel Dumont* visited the band and invited them to a meeting two days later. On 18 March, Indian Agent John Bean Lash arrived and obtained a profuse profession of loyalty from the chief. As he left the reserve Lash was taken prisoner by Louis RIEL and an armed mob of about 40 Métis in one of the first overt acts of the rebellion. One Arrow and his band probably had no part in the capture but the following day, under the guidance of their Métis farm instructor, Michel Dumas, One Arrow's men butchered all of their cattle and joined the rebels, apparently becoming the first Indian band to do so. The chief and his men were subsequently seen by the captive Indian agent, Lash, and others, armed and in the company of Riel and his Métis, immediately following the battle at Duck Lake on 26 March and in and around the settlement of Batoche until its capture on 12 May.

In fact, One Arrow appears to have been too old and feeble to have taken an active part in the hostilities. As early as 1882 he had attempted to resign his chieftainship on grounds of old age and infirmity, but had been dissuaded from doing so by an official of the Department of Indian Affairs. Nevertheless, One Arrow was arrested on a charge of treason-felony, and tried at Regina on 13 Aug. 1885. The old man was utterly confused by the entire proceedings. His lawyer confessed that he was unable to gain One Arrow's confidence, and thus could not present a coherent defence. The sole defence witness called to testify to the chief's good character did not appear, and the greater part of the prosecution's evidence was not translated into Cree for the benefit of the prisoner, who spoke no English. Only after a verdict of guilty had been rendered did One Arrow speak. He denied that he had actively participated in the rebellion, and explained that he had been coerced by Gabriel Dumont into leaving his reserve and joining the rebels at Batoche. He claimed that he had shot no one and had never had any intention of doing so. His explanations were to no avail, and he was sentenced to three years in the Stony Mountain Penitentiary in Manitoba.

In prison his health rapidly deteriorated and on 10 April 1886, after serving only a little more than seven months of his sentence, he was released. Such was his condition, however, that he was unable to proceed to his home, or even to walk. During his incarceration his conversion to Roman Catholicism brought him to the attention of the archbishop of St Boniface, Alexandre-Antonin Taché*, and upon his release One Arrow was carried to the archbishop's palace, where he lingered between life and death for a fortnight before expiring on Easter Sunday, 25 April 1886. During his imprisonment the Department of Indian Affairs had unsuccessfully attempted to starve the members of his band into abandoning their reserve and moving to Duck Lake, where they would be under closer supervision from the Indian agent and other officials. Among One Arrow's last acts was a plea to Indian Commissioner Edgar Dewdney* against the mistreatment of the members of his band.

One Arrow was not an extraordinary chief. He did not take a leading role in the movement to promote the settlement of the claims and grievances of the Indians of the northwest against the Canadian government, but few doubted his support for that movement. Although he was one of only three chiefs from the northwest imprisoned for his part in the rebellion of 1885, his ambiguous and ineffective actions in concert with the Métis seem hardly to have been sufficient to justify his conviction. Indeed, during the entire affair and its aftermath, he gave the appearance of a tragic old man, destroyed by forces over which he had no control and which he could not understand.

KENNETH J. TYLER

Can., Dept. of Indian Affairs and Northern Development, Central Registry files (Ottawa), Treaty annuity paysheets for treaties 4, 6, and 7, 1879–90. Glenbow-Alberta Institute, W. A. Fraser, "Plains Crees, Assiniboine and Saulteaux (Plains) bands, 1874–84" (typescript, 1963). PAC, MG 26, A, 210: 89419–26; MG 27, I, C4; RG 10, B3, 3584, file 1130; 3697, file 15423; 3719, file 22685; 3746, file 24549; CII, Duck Lake Agency, 1591–1601; RG 13, B2, 816: 2444. Can., Parl., *Sessional papers*, 1880–86 (annual reports of the Dept. of Indian Affairs, 1880–85); 1886, XIII, no.52: 13–33. Morris, *Treaties of Canada with the Indians*. *Daily Manitoban* (Winnipeg), 1886. *Le Manitoba* (Saint-Boniface), 1886. S. E. Bingaman, "The North-West rebellion trials, 1885" (MA thesis, Univ. of Saskatchewan, Regina, 1971).

KATZMANN, MARY JANE (Lawson), poet, editor, and historian; b. 15 Jan. 1828 at Preston, N.S., daughter of Christian Conrad Caspar Katzmann and Martha Prescott; m. 31 Dec. 1868 William Lawson, a prominent merchant in Halifax, N.S., and they had a daughter; d. 23 March 1890 in Halifax.

Mary Jane Katzmann's father, a native of Hanover (Federal Republic of Germany), was a graduate of Göttingen University. He obtained a commission in the 60th Regiment of the British army during the Peninsular War, and then settled in Nova Scotia. His wife was descended from a prominent New England planter family. Living amid cultured surroundings, Mary Jane displayed a precocious intelligence and an early interest in literature. She could read at the age of three, and, with the guidance of her family, was largely self-educated. Her early poetical efforts, which Joseph Howe* is said to have encouraged, appeared in various local newspapers.

In January 1852, at age 24, Mary Jane Katzmann became editor of the *Provincial, or Halifax Monthly Magazine*, and under her expert guidance it became possibly the best of the early Nova Scotian periodicals. The format and printing were superior, and the quality of the contributions was commendable. Unlike Mary Eliza Herbert*, whose *Mayflower, or Ladies' Acadian Newspaper* (Halifax) had immediately preceded the *Provincial*, Mary Jane Katzmann tailored her publication to attract a wide audience, both male and female; she also strove to include articles of regional origin rather than selected reprints. Devoted to "advancing the welfare of mankind, by ministering to their cultural improvement, and consequently, their social happiness," the magazine stressed material "of a purely Literary and Scientific character, nothing merely Sectarian or Political." A true expression of the late Romantic and early Victorian intellect, the *Provincial* carried poetry and prose on such diverse topics as foreign travel, local history, rural idylls, science, and social conditions. It was well received by its readers but sufficient subscriptions were not forthcoming, and publication ceased with the December 1853 issue. Nothing further is known of the editor until 1866, when she was operating the Provincial Bookstore in Halifax; evidence indicates that she was an astute and capable businesswoman.

Following her marriage, Mrs Lawson relinquished the bookstore to her younger sister, and assumed the role expected of a Victorian wife. Much of her free time was devoted to charitable and social causes, particularly those associated with the Church of England; she was revered for her kindness and judicious guidance.

Her later literary efforts included the *History of the townships of Dartmouth, Preston and Lawrencetown, Halifax County, N.S.*, for which she received the Thomas Beamish Akins Historical Prize from King's College, Windsor, in 1887. This collection of vignettes concerning early individuals and settlement in the Dartmouth area was based on an earlier series carried in the *Provincial*; it remains her enduring contribution to Canadian literature. Although it relies heavily on description and anecdote, and reads much like a Victorian travelogue, the book nevertheless reveals a fine sense of historical detail and comprehension. It also succeeds in being something more than a mere recitation of dates and names; although it can in no way be compared to a modern sociological study, it does convey, in a fashion which many early regional histories lack, a colourful sense of the people and the times. Following Mrs Lawson's death, the history was published in 1893, along with a volume of her verses, entitled *Frankincense and myrrh.* These poems, covering a 40-year period, reveal a woman of sympathy, sincerity, and piety. They lack, however, the keen wit of her earlier efforts, and much of their quality is marred by sentimentality and effusiveness.

Although Mrs Lawson has been remembered primarily for her single volume of social history, the significance of her earlier career cannot be overlooked. In an age when women accomplished little beyond the circle of home and charity, her success, although limited to the provincial sphere, was threefold: as the capable and youthful editor of a successful, if short-lived, periodical, as an able businesswoman in a circle dominated by male initiative, and as one of the first native Nova Scotian women to achieve literary recognition, and certainly the first to make an enduring impression. Her contribution to the colonial intellectual scene is one which cannot be ignored.

LOIS K. KERNAGHAN

[Mary Jane Katzmann was the editor of the *Provincial, or Halifax Monthly Magazine*, 1852–53. Her *History of the townships of Dartmouth, Preston and Lawrencetown, Halifax County, N.S.*, was edited by Harry Piers and published in Halifax in 1893. Piers and Constance Fairbanks edited *Frankincense and myrrh, selections from the poems of the late Mrs. William Lawson (M.J.K.L.)*, also published in Halifax in 1893. An obituary published in the *Acadian Recorder*, 24 March 1890, and a paper by P. R. Blakeley, "Some forgotten women writers of Nova Scotia," read before the Halifax Library Club, 8 March 1950, were also useful. L.K.K.]

KA-WE-ZAUCE. *See* KIWISĀNCE

KEEFER, SAMUEL, civil engineer and public servant; b. 22 Jan. 1811 at Thorold, Upper Canada, fourth son of George Keefer* and Catherine Lampman; m. first 13 May 1840 Anne E. Crawford (d. 1876), second daughter of Senator George Crawford*, of Brockville, Upper Canada; m. secondly in December 1883 Rosalie E. Pocock, also of Brockville; d. there 7 Jan. 1890.

Politics and engineering were necessarily related in mid-19th-century Canada since most big projects were public works in which the key jobs were political appointments. Samuel Keefer's apprenticeship from 1827 to 1833 in the Welland Canal Company, which was interrupted by two years at Upper Canada College, was an ideal preparation for an engineering career in such a world. Under the guidance of his father, who was president of the company, William Hamilton Merritt*, its driving force, and the Erie Canal veterans who engineered the work, Keefer learned the technical and political lessons of his craft. Expertise and political influence eventually carried Samuel Keefer to the top of his chosen profession, from which he fell in disgrace, only to be rescued by grateful political friends.

In 1833, after the completion of the Welland Canal, Keefer managed to secure an appointment as secretary to a commission established by the government of Lower Canada to recommend ways of improving navigation on the St Lawrence River near Montreal. When the House of Assembly ignored the commission's report it became apparent that no work would result from it and Keefer returned to Upper Canada in 1834 as an assistant engineer on the Cornwall Canal. This much interrupted project remained unfinished when the money ran out in 1838 and Keefer and the rest of the staff were dismissed. Nevertheless, Keefer recovered from this setback. A year later, no doubt with some help from his friends, he was appointed secretary to the newly established Board of Works of Lower Canada and with the reorganization of the board following the union of 1841 he became its chief engineer. By the age of 30 Keefer held one of the most important engineering appointments in British North America.

The Board of Works (after 1846 the Department of Public Works) was the largest department in the provincial bureaucracy. In 1842 its headquarters staff of four administered a field staff of 92, which included many engineers. A decade later the field staff numbered over 200 and by confederation had reached 500. The board built and maintained many of the roads and bridges of the province (although these were being turned over to local authorities wherever possible); it also looked after the timber slides, harbours, and lighthouses, and it was responsible for housing the peripatetic provincial government and its departments. But in the 1840s by far its greatest and most costly responsibility was the completion of the St Lawrence canal system. In the 1850s oversight of the planning and construction of the provincial railway system would be added to these responsibilities.

Hamilton Hartley Killaly*, a boisterous Irish eccentric, ruled over this vast transportation empire, and a proud and sober Samuel Keefer served as his second in command and chief rival. Each hired and trained his own "school" of engineering protégés, and naturally the professional jealousy at the top of the department permeated the struggle for place and preferment that went on below. In the early 1840s at least, there was enough work for everyone. During his tenure as chief engineer Samuel Keefer laid out the Beauharnois Canal, directed the enlargement of the Lachine Canal, rebuilt the lock at Sainte-Anne-de-Bellevue and the canal at Saint-Ours on the Richelieu River, and carried out preliminary surveys for a canal at Sault Ste Marie. He designed the suspension bridge over the Chaudière Falls at Bytown (Ottawa), completed in 1844, and introduced economical solid-timber gates on the St Lawrence locks in 1850. From 1846 to 1848 he was placed in direct charge of enlarging and re-aligning the Welland Canal.

Keefer also managed to negotiate the difficult transition from one transportation technology to another. When the railway era arrived in earnest he left the Department of Public Works in 1853 to take up more lucrative employment as a divisional engineer on the

Grand Trunk Railway under Alexander McKenzie Ross. There he acquired the knowledge and experience that laid the groundwork for the second half of his career. He supervised construction of the line between Montreal and Kingston (which he had previously surveyed for the government), including two important bridges at Sainte-Anne-de-Bellevue and Kingston Mills. He also decided upon the location of the great Victoria Bridge at Montreal, preliminary work for which had been done by his half-brother, Thomas Coltrin Keefer*. When the railway opened for business, in 1856, he served briefly as superintendent of its eastern division while simultaneously acting as chief engineer for the projected Brockville and Ottawa Railway.

He was called back into public service by the government of John A. Macdonald* and Étienne-Paschal Taché*. In the aftermath of the horrible Desjardins Canal wreck of 12 March 1857, which claimed 60 lives, including that of Samuel Zimmerman*, the assembly had passed an Act for the Better Protection of Accidents on Railways which required regular inspection of the road-bed, cuttings, embankments, bridges, rolling-stock, engines, and operating procedures of every railway in the province. Samuel Keefer was appointed as the first inspector of railroads. His surviving letterbooks attest to his stern attention to detail and the seriousness with which he conducted himself as protector of the public safety. But the correspondence also shows the practical difficulty of enforcing proper procedures and imposing expensive improvements upon financially shaky railway companies. Safety regulation became, in practice, a trade-off between pliant and accommodating politicians and earnest but powerless officials, all too frequently punctuated with disaster.

When in 1859 Hamilton Killaly's career as deputy of the largest spending department of government had to be sacrificed to the universal demand for retrenchment and restraint, Samuel Keefer had the duties of deputy commissioner of public works added to his responsibilities as inspector of railroads on 6 May. The most immediate task facing the new deputy was the design and construction of permanent parliament and departmental buildings at Ottawa. He devised an elaborate scheme to determine the best design submitted in the architectural competition and his recommendation of the plan of Thomas Fuller* and Chilion Jones* for the centre block and the designs of Frederick Warburton Stent and Augustus Laver for the flanking buildings met with general approval. However, with the choice of Thomas McGreevy* as principal contractor and in the supervision of his work, Keefer began the trial of his life. With construction already in progress, designs had to be altered to provide for heating and ventilation among other things. Expenditures vastly exceeded estimates. Communications broke down completely between the commissioner of the department until 1861, John Rose, and his deputy amidst mutual frustration and embarrassment. Hamilton Killaly was called back to pass judgement upon the work of his successor. Finally, with a change of government and governors general, a royal commission was appointed by the government of John Sandfield Macdonald* and Louis-Victor Sicotte to investigate what had become the Parliament Buildings scandal.

In 1863 the royal commission reported that the Department of Public Works had not examined the site properly before calling for tenders. Instead of being a level site, as the architects and contractors had assumed, it was a hill of solid rock. More shocking still, the commissioners discovered that McGreevy's successful bid had been drawn up by departmental officials from the schedules submitted with the competing tenders. Notwithstanding this collusion, when the contractors and the government could not agree upon what was to be done under the tendered rates and what was to be charged as more expensive "extra" work, Keefer appeared to have consistently given McGreevy the benefit of the doubt. As deputy commissioner, Keefer naturally bore the brunt of these charges which he took without accusing his equally culpable political superiors. His competence in question and his character besmirched, Samuel Keefer retired to private practice in 1864.

He returned to the Niagara district to begin the reconstruction of his career. There he built the second suspension bridge across the gorge which, when it was opened to traffic in 1869, was the longest bridge of its kind in the world. For this achievement he ultimately won a gold medal in the engineering competition at the 1878 universal exposition in Paris. Alas, the bridge blew down in the great storm of 1889 after the bridge company directors had doubled its width without consulting their engineer.

Keefer's political friends never forgot his ordeal and sacrifice, and in gratitude sought to redeem his reputation. "I have long been waiting my opportunity to reconnect you in some way with the Public Service," Sir John A. Macdonald wrote in November 1870, "and now I think the time has come." Macdonald appointed Keefer secretary to the canal commission, chaired by Hugh Allan, in the hope, he said, that some work might rebound to him from its report. Keefer did conduct some surveys for the still-born Baie Verte canal in 1872, but during the dark days of Liberal rule he was reduced to building bridges for the city of Ottawa. His main achievement for the city was the construction of the Dufferin Bridge across the Rideau Canal at Confederation Square. After the Conservatives returned to power, Keefer also returned, in 1880, as one of three royal commissioners appointed to investigate the conduct of the Alexander

Mackenzie* administration in Canadian Pacific Railway affairs. Now that the former victim had become judge, it might be said that his vindication was complete.

Keefer spent his remaining years in semi-retirement in Brockville where he was active in the Church of England and in local Conservative political affairs. He also took a hand in attempting to elevate engineering above immediate political and commercial servitude to proper professional status. Since 1860 he had been a member of the Institute of Civil Engineers in London and in 1869 joined the American Society of Civil Engineers. In 1887 Keefer helped found the Canadian Society of Civil Engineers, serving as its second president (T. C. Keefer was the first). A lifelong Conservative, Samuel Keefer obviously suffered for his partisanship, but because of it he survived.

H. V. NELLES

AO, MU 2664–776. PAC, MG 24, E1; I106; MG 26, A; MG 29, A2; D61; RG 11, A1, 1–39; B1, 828–43; RG 43, ser. B4b, 91, 93–94. Can., Canadian Pacific Railway Royal Commission, *Report* (3v., Ottawa, 1882); Parl., *Sessional papers*, 1871, VI: no.54. Can., Prov. of, Parl., *Sessional papers*, 1862, II: no.3; February-May 1863, II: no.3. Canadian Soc. of Civil Engineers, *Trans.* (Montreal), 1 (1887) – 4 (1890). *Daylight through the mountain: letters and labours of civil engineers Walter and Francis Shanly*, ed. F. N. Walker (Montreal, 1957). Lower Canada, House of Assembly, *Journals*, 1834: app.E.

Cyclopædia of Canadian biog. (Rose, 1886). H. G. J. Aitken, *The Welland Canal Company: a study in Canadian enterprise* (Cambridge, Mass., 1954). *Canada and its prov.* (Shortt and Doughty), X: 475–624. D. [G.] Creighton, *The empire of the St. Lawrence* (Toronto, 1956). Currie, *Grand Trunk Railway*. J. P. Heisler, *The canals of Canada* (Ottawa, 1973). Hodgetts, *Pioneer public service*. Robert Keefer, *Memoirs of the Keefer family* (Norwood, Ont., 1935). T. C. Keefer, *The old Welland Canal and the man who made it* (Ottawa, 1911); *Philosophy of railroads and other essays*, ed. H. V. Nelles (Toronto and Buffalo, N.Y., 1972). R. A. J. Phillips, *The east block of the Parliament Buildings of Canada: some notes about the building, and about the men who shaped Canada's history within it* (Ottawa, 1967). A. H. Armstrong, "Profile of parliament hill," Royal Architectural Institute of Can., *Journal* (Toronto), 34 (1957): 327–31. C. C. J. Bond, "The Canadian government comes to Ottawa, 1865–66," *OH*, 55 (1963): 23–34.

KELLY, MICHAEL JOHN, politician and office-holder; baptized 20 May 1815 at St John's, Nfld, son of Gilbert Kelly and Margaret Knee; m. 1 Dec. 1842 Bridget Doohan (Droohan), and they had at least one daughter; d. 25 March 1890 at Brigus, Nfld.

Michael John Kelly first comes to notice on 22 May 1855 when he was elected to the Newfoundland House of Assembly as one of the representatives from Placentia–St Mary's. He was acting colonial secretary from 9 March to 9 May 1857, receiving £250, and that year was also honorary magistrate of the French shore from Cape Ray to Quirpon. On 15 May 1857 he replaced Patrick Hogan as the appointed representative for the district of Placentia to the Roman Catholic board of education. The same year Kelly and James Luke Prendergast became acting superintendents of the fisheries of Newfoundland, and after four months of preparation presented reports to the House of Assembly. Kelly was paid £200 for his report on measures for the protection of the fisheries and on the settlements in Labrador and along the Strait of Belle Isle.

The Act for the Encouragement of Education, passed on 10 May 1858, empowered Sir Alexander Bannerman*, as governor, to appoint two competent school inspectors, one Protestant and one Roman Catholic. On 25 May Kelly was named the first Roman Catholic inspector of schools for the colony at an annual salary of £200 plus expenses and John Haddon became the Protestant inspector. Kelly resigned his seat in the assembly immediately upon accepting the post, but was sworn in once more for Placentia–St Mary's on 27 Jan. 1859. The duties of the two inspectors included visiting all the grammar and commercial schools in the colony, submitting annual or semi-annual reports to the legislature on such matters as number of scholars in attendance, subjects taught, kinds of texts used, state and size of school houses, amount of government allowance and tuition fees received by each teacher and their qualifications, as well as the general effectiveness of the system. The school boards, appointed by the governor according to the act, were required to return statements on the amount of funding received under the act to the inspectors for inclusion in their reports. In 1860 reports were received from 90 Roman Catholic schools with 4,639 registered pupils (there was an average daily attendance of 3,195); in 1864 the total number of schools in Newfoundland was 292 with 15,798 students.

The reports of the first inspectors, Kelly and Haddon, were frank and, because they described the level of teaching as perfunctory and poor, at times they received chilly receptions from the chairmen of school boards, teachers, and parents. Certain problems reappear frequently in Kelly's reports: some of the schools were "unprovided with sufficient school furniture" and lacked "sufficient books," others were "perfectly inoperative for portions of the winter." Reasons cited for the poor quality were the subdivision of education grants and the "apathetic indifference exhibited . . . by the people to everything connected with education." Kelly suggested that prizes be given at annual school examinations to students who attended regularly or who demonstrated progress in their studies, and that libraries be established in the principal schools.

Kelly retired early in 1879, and he submitted his last report in March. His final salary stood at £1,333 annually and he drew a pension of £650 from the government of Newfoundland. Maurice Fenelon was appointed his successor on 20 May 1879.

BARBARA J. EDDY

PANL, GN 2/1, 1857–59; GN 2/2, 1857–59. Nfld., *Blue book*, 1857–59; House of Assembly, *Journal*, 1855–75, esp. 1858, app., "Protection of the fisheries, taking the census, &c., at the Labrador and Straits of Belle Isle, during the summer of 1857," 436–43. *Harbour Grace Standard* (Harbour Grace, Nfld.), 2 April 1890. *When was that? A chronological dictionary of important events in Newfoundland down to and including the year 1922 . . .*, comp. H. M. Mosdell (St John's, 1923), 69. Arthur Barnes, "The history of education in Newfoundland" (D. PÆD. thesis, New York Univ., 1917), 99–109. *Book of Nfld.* (Smallwood), IV: 543. F. W. Rowe, *The development of education in Newfoundland* (Toronto, 1964), 140–41.

KELLY, WILLIAM MOORE, businessman and politician; b. 1827 in Moncton, N.B., son of J. M. Kelly; m. first Eliza Ann Long of Cocagne, N.B.; m. secondly Margaret Fraser of Chatham, N.B.; five sons and two daughters were born of the two marriages; d. 12 Dec. 1888 in Montreal, Que.

William Moore Kelly's father immigrated from Belfast to New Brunswick in 1798 and settled at the Bend of Petitcodiac (Moncton). The eldest of a large family, William while still in his teens operated a stage-coach line between Moncton and Chatham. After the death of his first wife in 1856, he moved to Chatham where he expanded his business by extending his coach line into the Miramichi River valley and by obtaining contracts to deliver mail there.

Kelly's political career began in June 1867 under powerful auspices. When John Mercer Johnson* resigned from the provincial legislature to enter the first dominion parliament, he nominated Kelly as his successor in the two-member riding of Northumberland County. Kelly was elected by acclamation, but another aspirant charged that Kelly's influential supporters, Johnson and Peter Mitchell*, had pressured the county sheriff to close nominations early. In the brief election campaign, Kelly, a Conservative who favoured confederation, had proposed such policies as free education, the improvement of roads, and the construction of the Intercolonial Railway. In April 1869 Kelly became chief commissioner of public works in the cabinet of Andrew Rainsford Wetmore*, a post he held until 1878. He was re-elected in the 1870, 1874, and 1878 general elections.

Kelly became deeply involved, in both his official capacity as a dispenser of subsidies and as a private investor, in the railway construction then occurring in New Brunswick. In 1870 he introduced legislation to incorporate the Chatham Branch Railway Company which planned to link Chatham with the Intercolonial Railway; as a shareholder and director of the railway, Kelly supported the company's successful request for additional provincial government aid in 1873. Criticism of his business dealings first arose in 1871 when Kelly answered opposition demands that he not accept mail contracts from the government while he held office by arguing that he had as much right to continue his long-standing business as did the lawyers who also served in the government.

For the most part, Kelly was able to avoid involvement in the bitter debate on the Common Schools Act of 1871 which divided Roman Catholics and the advocates of non-denominational education [*see* George Luther Hatheway*]. However, in July 1873 Jabez Bunting Snowball*, one of the province's most powerful lumbermen, who had nominated Kelly in the 1870 general election and who opposed the schools act, publicly criticized him for circulating a petition which pledged the signers to support direct taxation for the maintenance of public schools. A few weeks later Kelly was criticized in the Chatham press for supporting subsidies for rail lines in the western counties in preference to similar requests for lines in his own Miramichi area. In retreat from criticism, Kelly repeatedly failed to appear at public meetings called in the ensuing months to discuss public works and other government undertakings.

In March 1878 Henry O'Leary*, an opposition member of the legislature, accused Kelly and Robert Young* of having used their positions as chief commissioner of public works and president of the Executive Council respectively to make an improper deal in 1874 with Joseph Cameron Brown, the railway contractor who had built the Chatham line. It was alleged that Brown gave Kelly $13,000 and relinquished certain claims against Kelly, Young, and the Chatham Branch Railway in return for promises that he would receive the construction contract for the Kent Northern line and that he would be paid a balance owing him of more than $16,000. Brown, who got the contract but not the $16,000, revealed the details of the deal. A special legislative committee exonerated Young of wrongdoing, but a minority report severely criticized Kelly for in effect extracting a kickback. None the less, Kelly was re-elected at the general election held in June of the same year. He had, however, resigned as chief commissioner prior to the election.

During his first years as commissioner Kelly had been regarded as the most influential and popular member of the government. His later political decline mirrors the stormy years of the early 1870s when New Brunswickers argued vehemently, sometimes violently, over the Common Schools Act and were divided by jealousies aroused during frenzied railway construction. Shortly after the legislative criticism of his railway dealings and his re-election in 1878, Kelly retired to the seclusion of the Legislative Council, where he sat until, suffering from ill health, he moved to Toronto in 1882. He died in 1888 while visiting a son in Montreal.

RICHARD WILBUR

PANB, Williston family MSS., Chatham Branch Railway; "N.B. political biog." (J. C. and H. B. Graves), XI: 47. N.B., House of Assembly, *Journal*, 1867–78; *Reports of the debates*, 1867–71; *Synoptic report of the proc.*, 1874–78. *Daily Sun* (Saint John, N.B.), 13 Dec. 1888. *Gleaner and Northumberland Schediasma* (Chatham, N.B.), 1867–73. *New Brunswick Reporter and Fredericton Advertiser*, 15 Dec. 1888. *Canadian biog. dict.*, II: 668. *CPC*, 1878.

KEMP, ALEXANDER FERRIE, Presbyterian clergyman, scholar, and administrator; b. 28 June 1822 at West Greenock (Strathclyde), Scotland, only son of Simon Kemp, a teacher, and Grace Ferrie; d. 3 May 1884 in Hamilton, Ont., and was survived by his wife and three children.

Alexander Ferrie Kemp received his education at the University of Edinburgh and the Presbyterian College, London, England. He was appointed chaplain to the 26th Foot stationed in Bermuda by the Colonial Committee of the Church of Scotland (Free). In November 1850, before sailing for Bermuda, he was ordained into the Free Church by the Presbytery of Lancashire.

In 1855 Kemp accepted a call to the St Gabriel Street Church in Montreal, the mother church of Scottish Presbyterianism in Canada. The ten years he spent in Montreal were probably the most productive of his career. In addition to his duties as minister of an active congregation and as clerk of the Presbytery of Montreal, Kemp, with the Reverend Donald Fraser*, edited the *Canadian Presbyterian* from 1857 to 1858, and in 1861 he published a valuable *Digest of the minutes of the Synod of the Presbyterian Church of Canada.* In 1863 Kemp was chairman of a committee of the Synod of the Canada Presbyterian Church (formed in 1861 by the union of the Presbyterian Church of Canada and the United Presbyterian Church in Canada) which was requested to examine the Reverend Charles-Paschal-Télesphore Chiniquy*'s application to be admitted along with his congregation at St Anne's, Ill., into connection with the Canada Presbyterian Church. Chiniquy, in trouble with the Presbytery of Chicago over his administration of charity funds and a college, sought a new connection in order to avoid an expensive presbytery trial. After conducting an inquiry, Kemp suggested that Chiniquy's congregation be admitted to the Canadian synod.

Kemp contributed frequently to the *Canadian Naturalist and Geologist*, published by the Natural History Society of Montreal of which he was a member and occasionally on the executive. He wrote an article on marine algæ in Bermuda, another on shore plants on the northeast coast of the United States, and several on marine and freshwater algæ in Canada. McGill College granted him an honorary MA in 1863.

Possession of the St Gabriel Street Church had been in dispute since the disruption of the Church of Scotland in Canada in 1844 [*see* Robert Burns* and Henry Esson*], and as a result its manse was not occupied by the church's minister. In 1856 legal action was taken in Kemp's name by the Free Church congregation, but in a countersuit the opposing Church of Scotland party laid claim to the church. A compromise reached in 1864 gave both the church and the manse to the Church of Scotland and £1,450 to Kemp's Free Church congregation to enable it to secure another church. Because he was unable to rally full support behind plans for building a new church, and because the old church was to be vacated in November 1865, Kemp felt it his duty to resign, which he did in June 1865.

In 1866 Kemp was called to the newly created St Andrew's Church in Windsor, Canada West. There he published *A review of the state and progress of the Canada Presbyterian Church since the union in 1861*, saying that during its short life of five years the church had made little or no progress and that radical changes in structure were necessary to ensure its future. The critical reviews his pamphlet elicited, including two published by the Reverend John Mark King* of Toronto and the Reverend David Inglis of Hamilton, received tart rejoinders from Kemp, in one of which he wrote that "If the discussion only beget a little more tolerance of personal liberty and public debate in ecclesiastical minds, it will not have been without its use." Possibly piqued by the attitudes of his Canadian brethren, Kemp resigned his charge in 1870 and spent the next four years teaching in the United States, first at Olivet College in Michigan, during which time Queen's College, in Kingston granted him an LLD, then at Knox College in Galesburgh, Ill.

Kemp returned to Ontario in 1874 and continued his work in education. In that year he was made the first principal of the Young Ladies' College in Brantford, a position he held for four years, and from 1878 until his retirement in 1883 he was principal of the Ottawa Ladies' College.

ELIZABETH ANN KERR MCDOUGALL

[Alexander Ferrie Kemp was the author of *Digest of the minutes of the Synod of the Presbyterian Church of Canada, with a historical introduction and an appendix of forms and procedures* (Montreal, 1861); *A reply to the "Review reviewed" of the Rev. D. Inglis . . .* (Sarnia, Ont., 1867); *The Rev. C. Chiniquy, the presbytery of Chicago, and the Canada Presbyterian Church* (n.p., 1863); *A review of the state and progress of the Canada Presbyterian Church since the union in 1861* ([Windsor, Ont., 1867?]). He was also author of some articles in the *Canadian Naturalist and Geologist*:

"Notes on the Bermudas and their natural history with special reference to their marine algæ," 2 (1857): 145; "The fresh water algæ of Canada," 3 (1858): 331–45, 450–66; "A classified list of marine algæ from the lower St. Lawrence, with an introduction for amateur collectors," 5 (1860): 30–42; "On the shore zones and limits of marine plants on the north eastern coast of the United States," 7 (1862): 20–34. Kemp edited with Francis Wallace Farries and James B. Halkett, the Presbyterian Church in Canada, *Hand-Book . . . , 1883* (Ottawa, 1883). E.A.K.McD.]

Presbyterian Church in Canada Arch. (Toronto), Knox Church (Montreal), Session records, 1864–78; Presbyterian Church in Canada, Minutes of the Presbytery of Montreal, 1853–59; St Gabriel Street Church (Montreal), Minutes of the session, 1846–63; Records of the deacon's court, 1848–58. *Canada Presbyterian* (Toronto), 14 May 1884. *Hamilton Spectator*, 5 May 1884. Campbell, *Hist. of Scotch Presbyterian Church.* William Gregg, *History of the Presbyterian Church in the Dominion of Canada . . .* (Toronto, 1885).

KENNEDY, Sir ARTHUR EDWARD, soldier and colonial administrator; b. 5 April 1809 in County Down (Northern Ireland), the fourth son of Hugh Kennedy and Grace Dorothea Hughes; m. 18 May 1839 Georgina Mildred Macartney, and they had three children; d. 3 June 1883 off Aden in the Red Sea.

Born of Irish gentry, Arthur Edward Kennedy was privately tutored and in 1823–24 attended Trinity College, Dublin. In 1827 he entered the British army and served in infantry regiments in the Ionian Islands from 1828 to 1837, and in British North America from 1838 to 1839 and again from 1841 to 1844. Kennedy sold his captaincy in 1847 and accepted the position of poor law inspector in the Irish relief mission of General Sir John Fox Burgoyne. In Kilrush Union, County Clare, Kennedy faced the task of administering relief for almost half the 82,000 inhabitants of the district. Testifying before a House of Commons select committee on poor relief in 1850, he concluded that the relief mission in his charge had accomplished little. Years later he was still to recall "that there were days in that western county when I came back from some scene of eviction so maddened by the sights of hunger and misery . . . that I felt disposed to take the gun from behind my door and shoot the first landlord I met."

In 1851 Kennedy's office was abolished and he applied for a position in the colonial service. In May 1852 he was appointed governor of Gambia, but before assuming office he obtained the governorship of Sierra Leone. In the capital, Freetown, he found a corrupt and inefficient government and was forced to make many administrative changes. This reformist zeal earned Kennedy a number of local enemies but the Colonial Office supported him and in 1854 appointed him, in addition, consul general for the adjacent Sherbro district (now part of Sierra Leone).

Having "earned his credit in the Colonial Service by his courage in grappling with abuses," Kennedy was promoted in the fall of 1854 to the governorship of Western Australia where he continued his vigorous administrative approach to colonial government. He also encouraged an economic revival by increasing revenue and immigration, promoting land sales, and sponsoring explorations for arable land and mineral resources. Like Sierra Leone, Western Australia had no popular assembly and the strongly executive character of the constitution raised the possibility of the governor exceeding his powers; Kennedy was overruled at least once by the Colonial Office. Nevertheless, by the end of his term in 1862, Kennedy was regarded as one of the "best governors" in the colonial service.

The fierce competition for governorships delayed Kennedy's re-employment until July 1863. His appointment, made public in December, was to the comparatively insignificant colony of Vancouver Island. After six years of joint governorship under Sir James Douglas*, the island and mainland British Columbia were now each to have a separate governor; Frederick Seymour* was appointed for the mainland in January 1864. Kennedy and his party arrived at Victoria on 25 March 1864 and were received with great flourish. The press hailed Kennedy's appointment as a long-awaited change from the Hudson's Bay Company's influence, and from the nepotism and authoritarianism that it thought the colony had suffered under Douglas. However, the House of Assembly was worried that the appointment of a separate governor for the mainland colony would jeopardize Victoria's favoured position. Just prior to Kennedy's arrival the assembly had refused to vote a permanent appropriation for the civil list in return for control of the extensive crown lands of the colony, an arrangement requested by the Colonial Office. Now, it threatened to withhold Kennedy's salary, and it denied him supplies, an appropriate office, and clerical assistance. In the absence of a government house, the new governor and his family were confined to a hotel. The shabby treatment of the governor was denounced at a "monster meeting" by the citizens of Victoria but the assembly was not persuaded to make amends, although in the matter of his salary and those of his officials an uneasy truce was concluded in July 1864 when the assembly agreed to indemnify the executive for any loss incurred in paying the salaries.

Early in his administration Kennedy pledged his support for universal, government-financed, non-sectarian education, a goal that was realized in 1865 by the Common School Act. He also drew attention to the general ignorance of the hinterland and its resources, and promised government aid to any private concern searching for minerals on southern Vancouver Island. In June 1864 a consortium of local interests organized and dispatched a party headed by Dr Robert Brown*, and in July the expedition discovered gold at

Sooke, about 20 miles from Victoria. There appeared to be "payable diggings," and, as one Victorian commented, "Everyone here has gone cracked about the Sooke mines and the place is becoming depopulated." The Sooke discovery created a sudden appreciation in the value of crown lands, and encouraged Kennedy to reintroduce the Colonial Office's proposal to convey the lands to the assembly in return for the vote of a civil list. The assembly again refused.

Kennedy also found himself at odds with the assembly with regard to a proposal to unite the colony with British Columbia. The terms of the resolutions passed by the assembly emphasized the interests of the island, but Kennedy argued that any prospective union must encompass the interests of both colonies. In January 1865, however, the assembly was persuaded by Amor De Cosmos* that union would revitalize Vancouver Island's sagging economy: it resolved to accept any form of union with British Columbia that the Colonial Office might grant, a position which could not have pleased Kennedy more.

In matters of public administration Kennedy devoted himself, predictably, to correcting the numerous irregularities he encountered and to improving efficiency. Believing in the value of a competent, well-paid, and respectable civil service, he insisted on the resignation of several corrupt or unqualified officials. He also ordered that the public accounts be audited and that delinquent real estate taxes be collected. The budget for 1865, which totalled $390,000, reflected Kennedy's desire to increase the size and emoluments of the civil service. Although the assembly did not enact the entire budget, it voted salaries for the governor's staff, rent for Kennedy's residence, and even appropriated $50,000 for a permanent government house, probably to improve Victoria's chances of being designated the capital of the proposed united colony.

Because of his experience in Africa and Australia, Kennedy considered himself a competent judge of Vancouver Island's native people. He believed that their contact with Europeans invariably brought drunkenness, prostitution, and violence and that their "very lamentable condition" was caused by the brisk and illegal trade in alcohol carried on by Europeans, such as the former police commissioner, Horace Smith. Kennedy advocated the separation of Indians from whites, and, with the acting attorney general, Thomas Lett Wood, he tried to facilitate the conviction of whisky traders by strengthening the prohibitions against the trade and by permitting Indians to testify on oath in court. These measures were, however, blocked by the assembly, as was Kennedy's proposal to employ qualified Indian agents. He urged the crown to recognize native ownership of land and to permit alienation of Indian land only after "fair consideration," but the Colonial Office deemed that compensation for Indian lands should be made by the colonists, which in effect meant that "fair consideration" might never be paid.

Although Kennedy was convinced that the successful government of Vancouver Island's native people depended on the impartial application of the law, he approved, however unhappily, of the Royal Navy's bombardment of the Ahousahts of Clayoquot Sound in 1864. In this raid, purportedly carried out in retaliation for the murder of the crew of the trading vessel, *Kingfisher*, the guns of the Royal Navy demolished nine Indian villages and killed 13 Indians.

With the advent of economic depression Kennedy's popularity declined and his problems with the assembly, which demanded retrenchment, increased. When the governor introduced his estimates for 1866, totalling $193,000, the *Daily British Colonist*, controlled by assemblymen De Cosmos and Leonard McClure*, intimated that Kennedy was "deranged." Kennedy's low opinion of the assembly appeared to be justified when De Cosmos introduced a wild scheme to repeal taxes and borrow huge sums for operating expenses and public works; Kennedy rejected the scheme. In May 1866 the government's overdraft at the Bank of British North America stood at $80,000 and the bank refused further credit. In the face of collapsing finances the assembly expressed "non-confidence" in the governor and it expired in September without having sent the governor a bill of supply. Kennedy managed to keep the government functioning until the news arrived of the impending union of the colonies. According to the imperial act of union the governorship of the united colony devolved upon Seymour, and Kennedy was perforce unemployed.

In sharp contrast to his arrival, Kennedy's departure from Victoria on 23 Oct. 1866 was a disheartening affair. The disastrous economic condition of the colony and the unfavourable and unpopular terms of union were conditions only too apparent to the Victorians who bade him and his family a perfunctory farewell. However, Kennedy's misfortunes in Vancouver Island were caused largely by peculiar and local circumstances, in particular by an aggressive assembly fully poised to challenge the predominance of the executive. Kennedy, unable to develop a rapport with what the Colonial Office called a "lunatic House of Assembly," discredited his régime early by promoting costly plans to enlarge the bureaucracy and by appointing officers who had little or no influence beyond the executive. The confrontation between Kennedy and the assembly was exacerbated by severe economic depression and compounded by increasing anxiety concerning the union question, the resolution of which lay entirely with the Colonial Office in London. When news of the seemingly adverse settlement reached Victoria in September 1866, the last vestiges of public confidence in Kennedy vanished.

Kennedy's governorship of Vancouver Island, however, was merely a brief unhappy interlude in an otherwise successful public career that spanned 56 years. In December 1867, having returned to London, he was rewarded for his recent trials in Vancouver Island by a knighthood and the governorship of the West African settlements. After his term there, he received two important appointments, the governorships of Hong Kong (1872–77) and Queensland (1877–83). When returning home from Sydney, Kennedy died on board the *Orient* and was buried at sea. At the time of his death his estate consisted of nearly £11,000. His public services had been acknowledged by various honours: CB (1862), KCB (1867), KMG (1871), and KCMG (1881).

ROBERT L. SMITH

PABC, Crease coll., Henry Pering Pellew Crease; Arthur Stanhope Farwell, Diary (typescript); Vancouver Island, Executive Council, Minutes, 26 March 1864; Governor, Despatches to London, 1864–66 (letterbooks). PRO, CO 60/17: ff.176–92v. (transcripts at PABC); 60/19: 474; 60/31: 298–302; 305/22: 21, 99, 167–71; 305/23: 477; 305/25: 471; 305/28: 63–80, 175; 305/30: 340; WO 25/787: f.29. Univ. of Nottingham Library (Nottingham, Eng.), Manuscripts Dept., Newcastle MSS, Letterbooks, 1859–64 (mfm. at PAC). W. F. Butler, *Sir William Butler, an autobiography* (London, 1911), 12. G.B. Parl., Command paper, 1867, XLVIII, [3852], pp. 281–332, *Further papers relative to the union of British Columbia and Vancouver Island. . . .* [J. S. Helmcken], *The reminiscences of Doctor John Sebastian Helmcken*, ed. Dorothy Blakey Smith ([Vancouver], 1975), 208. *Daily British Colonist and Victoria Chronicle*, 4, 21 April, 29 July, 27 Aug. 1864; 21, 22 Feb., 26 April, 13 May, 7 July, 29 Nov., 23 Dec. 1865; 27 Jan., 8 Feb., 24 July, 23 Aug. 1866. *Illustrated London News*, 16 June 1883. *Lagos Times and Gold Coast Colony Advertiser* (Lagos), 25 July 1883. *Times* (London), 11, 15 Nov. 1854; 5 Dec. 1863; 25 Dec. 1867; 13 June 1883. *Victoria Daily Chronicle*, 27 March, 8, 12 April, 3 July, 28 Aug., 23 Nov. 1864; 31 March, 30 Nov. 1865; 8 Feb. 1866.

F. B. Archer, *The Gambia colony and protectorate: an official handbook* (London, 1906; repr. with intro. J. M. Gray, 1967), 336. *The Colonial Office list . . .* (London), 1879. *DNB*. G. B. Endacott, *A history of Hong Kong* (London, 1958). Robin Fisher, *Contact and conflict: Indian-European relations in British Columbia, 1774–1890* (Vancouver, 1977). Christopher Fyfe, *A history of Sierra Leone* (London, 1962), 266–72, 275, 306. H. C. Gilliland, "The early life and early governorships of Sir Arthur Edward Kennedy" (MA thesis, Univ. of British Columbia, Vancouver, 1951). J. M. Gray, *A history of the Gambia* (London, 1966), 435. Ormsby, *British Columbia*. P. F. Palmer, "A fiscal history of British Columbia in the colonial period" (PHD thesis, Stanford Univ., Calif., 1932). A. B. C. Sibthorpe, *The history of Sierra Leone* (4th ed., New York, 1970), 70. R. L. Smith, "Governor Kennedy of Vancouver Island and the politics of union, 1864–1866" (MA thesis, Univ. of Victoria, 1973). H. C. Gilliland, "Arthur Kennedy's administration of the colony of Western Australia examined as a background to the initiation of the Vancouver Island exploration expedition of 1864," *BCHQ*, 18 (1954): 103–15. R. L. Smith, "The Hankin appointment, 1868," *BC Studies*, 22 (summer 1974): 26–39; "The Kennedy interlude, 1864–66," *BC Studies*, 47 (autumn 1980): 66–78.

KENNEDY, WILLIAM, HBC fur-trader, sailor, explorer, and magistrate; b. in April 1814 at Cumberland House (Sask.), fifth child of Chief Factor Alexander Kennedy* and his Cree wife, Aggathas; m. 29 Nov. 1859 in London, England, Eleanor Eliza Cripps, and they had one son and one daughter; d. 25 Jan. 1890 at St Andrews, Man.

William Kennedy was sent to school in his father's hometown, St Margaret's Hope, Orkney Islands, in 1825; over the next eight years he was taught French as well as other subjects. In 1833 he joined the Hudson's Bay Company and spent five years in the Ottawa valley, mainly at Fort Coulonge, Lower Canada. Transferred to the Ungava and Labrador area, he then served at forts Chimo, Trial, and Nascopie on Lake Petitsikapau (Labrador). Kennedy's religious convictions led him to disagree with the HBC policy of selling liquor to the Indians and he resigned in 1846. He moved to Canada West, where he began a lobby against the HBC monopoly, arguing that the Province of Canada should be allowed to expand into Rupert's Land. In 1848 he started a fishery at the mouth of the Saugeen River, and was thus one of the founders of Southampton, Canada West. From 1848 to 1850 he was captain of a boat on Lake Huron.

On the suggestion of ex-Chief Trader John McLEAN, Kennedy was accepted, in 1851, by Lady Franklin [Griffin*] as commander of her second private expedition in search of her husband Sir John Franklin*, whom Kennedy had met in 1819 at Cumberland House. Shortly before the expedition sailed, Kennedy was joined by Joseph-René Bellot*, a sub-lieutenant in the French navy; he had insisted on having Bellot as his second in command in spite of opposition from the British Admiralty. This Arctic expedition was the best prepared of any up to that time. Kennedy was well acquainted with the perils of the north after his service in Ungava and Labrador; he chose a nucleus of men experienced in the Canadian wilds, and he insisted his crew protect themselves with native clothing. His ship, the 89-ton *Prince Albert*, had a very shallow draught, making it a poor sea vessel, but it proved highly manœuvrable in the Arctic ice.

In May 1851 the *Prince Albert* and its crew of 17 left Aberdeen, Scotland. In July, near Upernavik, Greenland, the expedition encountered the *Advance* and the *Rescue* which had been sent out under the command of Edwin Jesse De Haven* the previous year by New York merchant Henry Grinnell to search for Franklin. The three ships became locked in ice and Kennedy and Dr Elisha Kent Kane*, the medical officer of the American expedition, became friendly and later corresponded. Kennedy succeeded where the Americans had failed in penetrating Lancaster Sound into Prince Regent Inlet. Here Kennedy made use of blasting powder, which he had learned to use at the arsenal at Woolwich (now part of Greater London), in April 1851, to break through the ice.

In September, while attempting to reconnoitre Port Leopold on the northeast shore of Somerset Island, Kennedy and four men were separated from the *Prince Albert* by a shift in the ice which carried the ship south. Bellot put it into winter headquarters at Batty Bay. Unfamiliar with Arctic travel, he succeeded in reaching Kennedy only on a third attempt after Kennedy had been marooned for more than five weeks.

With the *Prince Albert* locked in the ice at Batty Bay, Kennedy, Bellot, and 12 crewmen set out at the end of February 1852 to explore the Boothia Peninsula area. After a stop at Fury Beach, the group continued south on 29 March and reached Brentford Bay on 5 April. Eight of the crewmen then returned to the *Prince Albert*, while Kennedy, Bellot, and the remaining four men headed southwest; on 7 April they discovered a new channel which Kennedy later named Bellot Strait. At this crucial time an error seems to have been made, perhaps because of snow-blindness, and the party did not explore Boothia Peninsula to the southwest as ordered, but moved west to Prince of Wales Island, crossing the frozen Peel Sound and Franklin Strait without realizing it. They returned safely to the Prince Albert on 30 May, having completed a journey of some 1,100 miles, and on 28 Aug. 1852 sailed from Beechey Island, arriving in Aberdeen about 40 days later. Although unsuccessful in his search for Franklin, Kennedy contributed to the knowledge of the Canadian Arctic and brought his crew back to Britain without the loss of a single man.

A second expedition under Kennedy supported by Lady Franklin was organized in 1853 to search the western and Russian Arctic via the Bering Strait. This mission was aborted when the crew mutinied in Valparaiso, Chile, and Kennedy had them jailed. Replacements were unavailable because of the impending Crimean War and Kennedy returned to Britain. When a third expedition did not materialize, he came back to Canada in 1856, living for a time in Toronto.

Kennedy joined the agitation for annexation of Rupert's Land to Canada, resuming his lobby against the HBC. He wrote several articles on the "western question" for newspapers, and was associated with George Brown* who printed excerpts from at least one of his letters in the *Globe*. Kennedy became a director of the North-West Transportation, Navigation and Railway Company and made a journey from Toronto to the Red River Settlement (Man.) in February 1857 to prove the possibilities of the route, even in the worst weather. In Red River he circulated a petition requesting union with Canada which 575 settlers signed. The following year, Kennedy carried the first mail from Toronto to Red River for the North-West Transportation, Navigation and Railway Company, which held the contract from the Canadian government.

Kennedy settled permanently at Red River in 1860 where he built his home, the Maples, at St Andrews (the house is now the Red River House Museum). There he operated a store with his brother George. He became a member of the Board of Education of Manitoba in 1878 and a magistrate the following year. On 13 Feb. 1879 he read the first scientific address to the Historical and Scientific Society of Manitoba. During the 1880s Kennedy argued for a railway to Churchill (Man.) on Hudson Bay to break the monopoly of the Canadian Pacific Railway. A fighter to the end, he died on 25 Jan. 1890. In his eulogy of Kennedy, Canon Samuel Pritchard Matheson* said "he was a man who never got his due. While other men far less deserving received honour and emolument, he was passed over."

EDWARD CHARLES SHAW

William Kennedy was the author of *A short narrative of the second voyage of the Prince Albert, in search of Sir John Franklin* (London, 1853).

PAM, HBCA, A.12; B.38/a/7; C.1/806; MG 2, C1; MG 7, C12; MG 10, F2, Minutes, 1879. Scott Polar Research Institute (Cambridge, Eng.), MS 248/105, 14 Jan. 1851; MS 248/107, 2 May 1851. J.-R. Bellot, *Memoirs of Lieutenant Joseph René Bellot . . . with his journal of a voyage in the polar seas, in search of Sir John Franklin*, [ed. Julien Lemer] (2v., London, 1855), I: 93, 136, 198; II: 14, 180. *Globe*, 16 Sept. 1848, 22 Jan. 1857. *Manitoba Morning Free Press*, 27 Jan. 1890, 30 April 1910. *Times* (London), 3 Nov. 1853. *Manitoba directory . . .* (Winnipeg), 1878–79. W. S. Fox, *The Bruce beckons; the story of Lake Huron's great peninsula* (Toronto, 1952). W. J. Healy, *Women of Red River: being a book written from the recollections of women surviving from the Red River era* (Winnipeg, 1923). L. H. Neatby, *The search for Franklin* (Edmonton, 1970). Noel Wright, *Quest for Franklin* (London and Toronto, 1959). E. C. Shaw, "Captain William Kennedy, an extraordinary Canadian," HSSM *Papers*, 3rd ser., no.27 (1970–71): 7–18.

KENNEDY, WILLIAM NASSAU, house painter, soldier, politician, civic official, and entrepreneur; b. 28 April 1839 at Newcastle, Upper Canada, second of six children of John Kennedy, a lieutenant-colonel in the militia, and Catharine Lambert; m. Mary Anne Chambers, and they had four sons and one daughter; d. 3 May 1885 in London, England.

William Nassau Kennedy left school at an early age and worked as a contractor for a brief period. He then trained for two years with David William Dumble, a barrister at Peterborough, but subsequently took up his father's occupation of house painter and interior decorator. The Kennedy family had a distinguished military tradition; in February 1857 William enlisted as a private in the newly organized 1st Company, Peterborough Rifles. With his father and brothers he took part in the formation of the 1st Company, Peterborough Infantry, five years later. After progressing through several non-commissioned ranks, Kennedy earned a 1st class certificate from the Toronto Military School and was commissioned ensign on 7 July 1865. The new subaltern accompanied his father's unit for the defence of the Niagara peninsula during the Fenian invasion of June 1866 but the Peterborough volunteers never saw action. The next year Kennedy was gazetted temporary adjutant and drill instructor as captain of the newly formed 57th (Peterborough) Battalion of Infantry. Subsequently he obtained a 1st class certificate from the Military Riding School in Toronto, rating special mention for proficiency in horsemanship and swordsmanship. Like his father, who had been a justice of the peace and an assessor for Peterborough, William was public spirited, and served on the Peterborough Town Council for six years.

Late in 1869 came the news that the Métis at the Red River Settlement (Man.) were offering armed resistance to the annexation of Rupert's Land by Canada. To Captain Kennedy went the coveted vacancy allotted to the 57th Battalion for one officer on the Red River expedition dispatched west under the command of Colonel Garnet Joseph Wolseley*. Kennedy journeyed to Upper Fort Garry (Winnipeg) as a lieutenant in the 1st Battalion of Infantry (Ontario Rifles), gaining experience and the warm friendship of Colonel Wolseley, a bond which later would prove beneficial to him.

Kennedy elected to stay in Manitoba, and when in October 1871 a Fenian raid led by William Bernard O'Donoghue* and John O'Neill* was launched into Manitoba from adjacent American territory, he raised a temporary volunteer unit, the Winnipeg Rifle Company, to help the small Winnipeg garrison repel the invaders. The event stressed the value of maintaining a local force of citizen-soldiers, and exactly one week after the invasion Kennedy helped to found the Winnipeg Field Battery of which he became adjutant. The following year he rose to command the unit, an appointment he was to hold until 1883.

In the 1870s Kennedy became a leading citizen of Winnipeg. He was made registrar of deeds for Selkirk County and Winnipeg and city clerk in 1873, posts which it is believed he held as late as 1881. In 1874 he became a member of the first Executive Council of the North-West Territories and in 1875 was elected the second mayor of Winnipeg. He held the former office for one year and the latter for two consecutive one-year terms. His family eventually joined him in Winnipeg in 1876. He was a member of the Protestant section of the Board of Education of Manitoba from 1876 until at least 1881, serving as chairman in 1876.

As a prominent booster of Manitoba, Kennedy was active in some 11 railway charter groups between 1875 and 1883, was involved in the affairs of the Manitoba South-Western Colonization Railway, and was vice-president of the Manitoba and Hudson's Bay Railway in 1884. He also seems to have dealt in real estate. His inclination toward community life led him to join the Orange order, the Foresters, and many other fraternal organizations. A charter member of the Prince Rupert's Lodge, Kennedy became deputy grand master in the freemasons' Grand Lodge of Manitoba when it was formed in 1875. His other interests ranged from competition rifle shooting to music.

The west in 1883 was troubled by economic difficulties, labour disputes in the construction crews of the Canadian Pacific Railway, and unrest among the Métis and Indians who felt threatened by the advancing railway. The North-West Mounted Police were too few and the militia corps on the prairies not well enough trained and equipped to handle any widespread disturbances. An apprehensive group of Winnipeggers led by Captain Kennedy resolved to raise a full battalion of rifles. On 9 Nov. 1883 the 90th Winnipeg Rifles was organized. Kennedy was chosen to command and was accordingly promoted to major and brevet lieutenant-colonel.

In the midst of organizing his battalion, Colonel Kennedy learned that his old commander and colleague, now Major-General Sir Garnet Joseph Wolseley, was seeking Canadian boatmen to transport a British military expedition up the Nile River into the Sudan to rescue Major-General Charles George Gordon trapped in Khartoum. Kennedy swiftly raised a contingent from Manitoba, but his personal offer to go was refused by British recruiting authorities. Major Frederick Charles Denison*, of the influential Toronto military family and commander of the Canadian voyageurs, did not relish taking as his subordinate an officer senior to himself. The Manitoba volunteers, on the other hand, exhibited such displeasure at the prospect of proceeding overseas without Kennedy that the impasse was avoided by promoting Denison to brevet lieutenant-colonel and allowing Kennedy to go to Egypt in the civilian capacity of foreman. Once there, Denison recruited Kennedy to act as temporary paymaster to the Canadian contingent, whereupon the latter exploited his old friendship with General Wolseley in the interest of having himself appointed permanent paymaster.

Apart from his professional qualifications, Kennedy proved himself on more than one occasion among the ablest manipulators in the patronage-ridden militia of the time. When recruiting for the voyageur contingent, Kennedy, quite against explicit instructions from the British authorities to hire only experienced men, included some of Winnipeg's young business and professional élite. These youthful imperialists were genuinely imbued with a spirit of adventure and patriotism, but knew next to nothing about the handling of boats. Kennedy accompanied the voyageurs throughout the journey up the Nile, taking every opportunity to favour his Manitobans in the face of Denison's criticism of their questionable performance as boatmen. On the return voyage to England, he contracted smallpox and was hospitalized in London where he finally succumbed to the disease.

William Nassau Kennedy was a characteristic 19th-century Canadian civic leader, entrepreneur, and militia commander. In a competitive frontier environment where opportunities abounded for the enterprising, most men found little in the militia establishment to attract them. Some, like Kennedy, imbued with an intense patriotism for Canada and the empire, were not above manipulating men and circumstances, or employing patronage and the privileges of office, in the interests of keeping up a force of citizen soldiers as a symbol of order and authority – a force which would be tested in the North-West rebellion of 1885.

J. A. Rodger Letourneau

PAM, MG 14, B59. *Records of the Nile voyageurs, 1884–85: the Canadian voyageur contingent in the Gordon relief expedition*, ed. C. P. Stacey (Toronto, 1959). George Young, *Manitoba memories; leaves from my life in the prairie province, 1868–1884* (Toronto, 1897). *Manitoba Daily Free Press*, 4 May, 24 Oct. 1885. *Peterborough Examiner* (Peterborough, Ont.), 7 May 1885. E. J. Chambers, *The 90th Regiment: a regimental history of the 90th Regiment, Winnipeg Rifles* ([Winnipeg], 1906). Roy MacLaren, *Canadians on the Nile, 1882–1898: being the adventures of the voyageurs on the Khartoum relief expedition and other exploits* (Vancouver, 1978).

KEZHEGOWINNINNE (Geezhigo-w-ininih, Kezigkoenene, Kishigowininy, literally skyman, man of the sky, or one who is exalted; also known as **David Sawyer**), Ojibwa chief, member of the Eagle totem, Methodist lay preacher, teacher, and farmer; b. probably in 1812 at the head of Lake Ontario in Upper Canada, eldest son of Chief Joseph Sawyer [Nawahjegezhegwabe*] and his wife Wetosy (Jane); m. probably in 1830 Anna Springer, and they had at least three sons and one daughter; d. 11 Nov. 1889 at the New Credit Reserve, Tuscarora Township, Ont.

Kezhegowinninne grew up during a period of crisis for his people, the Credit band of Mississaugas (Ojibwas). Having ceded almost all of their land to the British crown, the band wandered aimlessly in search of ever-diminishing reserves of fish and game. The ranks of the Ojibwas had been reduced by European diseases, such as smallpox and tuberculosis, against which they had no natural immunity. Their numbers on the northwest shore of Lake Ontario, over 500 in 1787, had fallen to approximately 200 by 1819. Many members of the tribe believed it would soon be extinct.

In the early 1820s the band's fortunes dramatically improved. Peter Jones [Kahkewaquonaby*] was converted to Methodism in 1823 and the following year returned to his mother's people to preach the gospel. Conversion to Christianity not only offered hope to the dispirited band but also aided in the adoption of a new life-style based on farming and education in the ways of the white man. One of Jones's first converts was his cousin, Kezhegowinninne, who in 1825 was baptized as David Sawyer by the Reverend Alvin Torry and thus entered the Methodist Episcopal Church (after 1833 he was in the Wesleyan Methodist Church) to which he would devote his life. Once he had accepted Christianity Sawyer immediately brought his parents to the Grand River Reserve where they too became part of the growing Indian Church. The Sawyers settled in the Methodist Indian village which was being built at the mouth of the Credit River during the winter of 1825–26 and David attended the mission school taught by John Jones [Thayendanegea*], brother of Peter.

By the late 1820s Peter Jones had persuaded almost all the band to become Christians. After he finished school Sawyer became one of his most trusted assistants. In July 1829 he received his first appointment as a teacher at the Lake Simcoe mission school and the following year he was stationed at the Methodist school for the Matchedash band on Georgian Bay. He also acted as an interpreter for the white Methodist missionary in the area and occasionally preached to the Indians in Ojibwa. In the summer of 1832, Sawyer and two members of the Credit band were entrusted with a special mission to the Indians around Sault Ste Marie. Sawyer's journal of the trip, later translated in the *Christian Guardian*, is a fascinating document describing the hardships they had to overcome: "An Indian is not at a loss what to do in whatever condition he is in," wrote Sawyer with pride. In 1833 he was sent to the Saugeen settlement on Lake Huron and the following year, pleased with his work, the church dispatched him to Muncey in Middlesex County. At both missions Sawyer acted as a teacher and an interpreter for the white missionary. After two years at Muncey he returned to the Credit Mission, where the band council immediately voted to appoint him as their paid employee.

From the limited documentary evidence that has survived Sawyer appears to have been a capable and highly independent individual. A devoted Methodist, he attacked any preacher he considered too lax in spreading the gospel. On one occasion in 1840 he told the Credit band council that he "saw no difference between the British and Canadian [Methodist preachers] . . . they love ease and were afraid to go into the backwoods for fear [of] wetting their feet." He was equally severe towards Indians whom he felt did not make an honest attempt at farming. In a letter to Peter Jones on 1 May 1849, Sawyer stated that "if the place did literally flow with milk and honey, it would not keep some of them [the Indians] from starving who have disgraced the place for they would never take time or pains to gather it as long as they could get whiskey." The Wesleyan Methodist Church was to receive Sawyer on trial in 1851 and he was ordained "for special purposes" the following year.

By 1847 the pressure from settlers and lumbermen on their lands at the Credit River had forced the Credit band to seek a more isolated area. Early that year Sawyer with other members of the band moved north to the Owen Sound area, intending to establish farms on lands which still belonged to the Ojibwas. Once they saw the poor quality of the area, however, most of them returned south and settled in the fertile southwest corner of the Grand River Reserve near Brantford, offered to them by the Six Nations council; in 1848 they named the reserve given to them New Credit. Sawyer and a handful of others remained with the Newash band near Owen Sound. Recognizing his abilities, the Newash band asked him to act as their agent and to help them in transacting business with the government. In return the band adopted him and his family, gave him 43 acres for his private use, and aided him in building a house.

Sawyer had settled in an Indian community badly split into factions: religious (Methodist, Roman Catholic, and non-Christian) and tribal (Ojibwa and Potawatomi). The Indian Department opposed Sawyer's appointment as the band's agent partly because as a fervent Methodist he might increase religious tension. When he left the Newash for one year in 1851 to help the Methodist missionary at the neighbouring Saugeen mission, the Indian Department quickly replaced him with Charles Keeshick (Kezicks), a Potawatomi recently adopted into the band, who was the brother-in-law of Chief Peter Jones Kegedonce, a leader of the Potawatomi and largely Roman Catholic faction. During Keeshick's term of office the band ceded to the government in 1854 almost all of the Bruce peninsula, and after the surrender native opposition to the Roman Catholic faction mounted quickly. On 9 March 1855 the band passed a resolution that David Sawyer replace Kegedonce as chief and also act as its writer and interpreter. The Indian Department would not accept his election despite a letter sent to the superintendent general of Indian affairs, Lord Bury, on 30 June 1855 by the Reverend Conrad Vandusen*, the Methodist missionary at Newash and Colpoys Bay since 1852. He pointed out that, of the 106 adult Indians in the Owen Sound and Saugeen area with legitimate claim to the land, 78 endorsed the petition for the removal of Keeshick and Kegedonce, both of whom were supported only by a number of Potawatomis recently adopted into the tribe. But the Indian Department, undoubtedly satisfied with the tractable Indians then holding office, left them in power.

When Sawyer was absent from the Owen Sound area in 1856 the Indian Department secured the surrender of the Newash reserve which the band had retained for their own use in 1854. A "few Indians" invited to Toronto signed a treaty in February 1857 by which they surrendered all the land, including Sawyer's farm. He found he had no legal recourse because Indians, considered by the government to be minors, could not own property individually. By making a special journey to London, England, one Indian woman, Catherine Sutton [Nahnebahwequay*], was able to have her title restored but Sawyer's several petitions went unanswered.

Having no means of subsistence without his farm, Sawyer finally moved to New Credit in October 1861, where he became head chief after his father's death two years later. Under his capable leadership for 25 years, New Credit became one of the leading Indian agricultural settlements in North America. Sawyer helped to achieve at New Credit his original goals for an Indian settlement at Owen Sound. At his death the local Methodist minister, the Reverend Thomas S. Howard, paid tribute to "his Christian integrity in every department of life."

Ojibwas educated at the Methodist mission schools in the 1820s and 1830s, like David Sawyer, were the exceptions among the native people, most of whom had scant knowledge of the white man's ways. The Indian Department often clashed with the Europeanized Indians, who frequently protested against whatever they considered to be unjust treatment of their people. Suspecting their fervent Methodism and independence, the department worked on occasion to counteract their influence, as the career of David Sawyer suggests.

DONALD B. SMITH

Kezhegowinninne's "Journal" was translated by John Jones and published in the *Christian Guardian*, 13 Feb. 1833.

PAC, RG 10, A6, 1011. UCA, Mission register for the Credit River Mission. Victoria Univ. Library (Toronto), Peter Jones coll., Anecdote book, no.4. Woodland Indian Cultural Educational Centre (Brantford, Ont.), New Credit registry, 1847–74, Sawyer to Peter Jones, 1 May 1849. Enemikeese [Conrad Vandusen], *The Indian chief: an account of the labours, losses, sufferings, and oppression of Ke-zig-ko-e-ne-ne (David Sawyer), a chief of the Ojibbeway Indians in Canada West* (London, 1867). T. S. Howard, "David Sawyer," *Christian Guardian*, 19 March 1890. Peter Jones (Kahkewaquonaby), *History of the Ojebway Indians; with especial reference to their conversion to Christianity . . .*, [ed. Elizabeth Field] (London, 1861); *Life and journals of Kah-ke-wa-quo-nā-by (Rev. Peter Jones), Wesleyan mis-*

sionary, [ed. Elizabeth Field] (Toronto, 1860). P. S. Schmalz, *The history of the Saugeen Indians* ([Toronto], 1977).

KINGSTON, GEORGE TEMPLEMAN, meteorologist, author, professor, and public servant; b. 5 Oct. 1816, son of Lucy Henry Kingston and Francis Sophia Rooke and brother of author William Henry Giles Kingston; m. in 1851 Henrietta Malone, and they had one son; d. 21 Jan. 1886 at Toronto, Ont.

George Templeman Kingston was born near Oporto (Porto), Portugal, where his father, an English wine merchant, periodically resided. At age 14, after an elementary schooling in England, he went into the Royal Navy as a midshipman and won a gold medal for mathematics at the naval college in Portsmouth. But at age 26, finding a seafaring life not suited to his constitution, he left the navy and became a student at Gonville and Caius College, Cambridge. He graduated with honours in mathematics in 1846, taking a position among the wranglers, and was awarded an MA in 1849. After teaching at Eton College for some time, he came to Canada in 1852 to become the first principal of a nautical college in Quebec. When that school closed in May 1855 he began his association with the University of Toronto.

In 1839 the British Government had established a magnetic observatory at Toronto where meteorological observations were also taken. The observatory was operated by British military personnel, after 1842 under John Henry LEFROY, until 1853 when Professor John Bradford Cherriman* of the University of Toronto assumed control of it on behalf of the Legislative Council of the Province of Canada. In May 1855 Cherriman was made professor of meteorology and director of the observatory and at the same time Kingston was appointed professor of natural philosophy at the University of Toronto. But before Kingston could take up his position, Cherriman, who was Kingston's brother-in-law, somehow managed to obtain what he apparently considered the more desirable appointment for himself, and when Kingston arrived in Toronto in August he was forced to accept the now vacant position of professor of meteorology and director of the observatory. The combined offices brought Kingston a salary of £450, one-third payable by the university and two-thirds by the province.

During the decade prior to confederation, Kingston appears to have been occupied with administering the observatory and lecturing on meteorology at the university and at the local normal school. In 1858, with the cooperation of Egerton RYERSON, chief superintendent of education for Canada West, he instituted a programme of weather observing at some 12 grammar schools. The programme lasted less than two decades but it did provide a base for future climatological surveys. However, during the pre-confederation period in Canada observations and other scientific work were not considered to be of great value to the public and it was difficult to obtain the necessary funds to maintain the observatory. From 1855 to 1864 Kingston published the annual mean meteorological results at Toronto in the *Canadian Journal*; he also pursued other related interests, contributing many articles to the journal and serving as a member and twice as vice-president of the Canadian Institute which published it.

In 1867 ownership of the observatory passed to the dominion government but it continued to be administered by the University of Toronto. Kingston deplored this anomaly and noted that there were too few meteorological observers, that there was no true description of Canada's climatology, and that existing agencies were inadequate to remedy the situation. National meteorological services were being organized in other countries, and after the United States Congress established a service early in 1870, Kingston managed to impress on Peter Mitchell*, minister of marine and fisheries, the advantages of a network of stations to observe and issue storm warnings. Consequently, on 1 May 1871, expenditures of $5,000 were approved for meteorological and climatological purposes within the Department of Marine and Fisheries over one year. This was the beginning of a national meteorological service, although there had been no act or order in council specifically creating it. Kingston immediately began to organize a small network of observing stations, adding locations in Kingston, Port Dover, and Port Stanley to Toronto, and in January 1872 the first exchange of meteorological data took place between Canada and the United States. Later in the same month Kingston, as acting superintendent, filed the "first report of the Meteorological Office of the Dominion of Canada" (after 31 Dec. 1876 the Meteorological Service).

At first, daily weather observations were obtained from the four stations in southern Ontario, but by late 1872 the network extended from Winnipeg to Halifax. As part of the exchange of Canadian and American data, the U.S. service gave storm warnings for Canada. Additional staff members, including Charles Carpmael*, Kingston's eventual successor, were added; one of the trainees issued the first storm warning prepared in Canada in October 1876, and another, in 1877, the first general forecast. Storm warnings were the more important of the two then and were displayed to mariners and sailors by combinations of wicker baskets hung on poles at ports and harbours on the Great Lakes, the St Lawrence waterway, and the Atlantic coast. The weather predictions were telegraphed to 75 cities and towns in Canada each day and bulletins were then posted.

Suffering from ill health, Professor Kingston retired from his posts in 1880. Because of his role in promoting and organizing the national meteorological service Kingston could be called the "Father of Canadian Meteorology."

MORLEY K. THOMAS

A list of G. T. Kingston's publications can be found in Morgan, *Bibliotheca Canadensis*.

Can., Atmospheric Environment Service (Downsview, Ont.), Letterbooks of the superintendent of the Meteorological Service, 1870–80. Can., Parl., *Sessional papers*, 1872, IV, no.5, app.13; 1873, IV, no.8, app.16; 1874, III, no.4, app.27; 1875, V, no.5, suppl.4; 1876, V, no.5, suppl.3; 1877, V, no.5, suppl.3; 1878, II, no.1, suppl.3; 1879, III, no.3, app.46; 1880, VI, no.9, app.34. Royal Meteorological Soc., *Quarterly Journal* (London), 13 (1887): 122–23. *Dominion annual register*, 1886. John Patterson, "A century of Canadian meteorology," Royal Meteorological Soc., *Quarterly Journal*, 66 (1940), suppl.: 16–33. A. D. Thiessen, "The founding of the Toronto Magnetic Observatory and the Canadian Meteorological Service," Royal Astronomical Soc. of Can., *Journal* (Toronto), 34 (1940): 308–48. M. K. Thomas, "A century of Canadian meteorology," Can., Atmospheric Environment Service, *Annual report of operations* ([Toronto]), 1971–72: 1–20. Andrew Thomson, "Professor George T. Kingston, 1817–1886," Canadian Meteorological Service, *Monthly report* ([Toronto]), April 1971: [1]–5.

KISHIGOWININY. *See* KEZHEGOWINNINNE

KITTSON, NORMAN WOLFRED, fur-trader, merchant, steamboat owner, and entrepreneur; b. 5 March 1814 in Chambly, Lower Canada, son of George Kittson and Nancy Tucker; m. Élise Marion, a Métis of St Boniface (Man.); d. 10 May 1888 en route to St Paul, Minn.

Norman Wolfred Kittson was educated at the grammar school in William Henry (Sorel, Que.). He was drawn to the fur trade by the stories he heard from traders, including Alexander Henry*, the elder, who had been active among the Indians in the Saskatchewan country. Entering the American Fur Company in 1830 as an apprentice, Kittson was soon associated with Henry Hastings Sibley, one of the company's senior clerks in the area that would become the state of Minnesota. In 1843, though he would maintain his connection with Sibley and the company for another decade, Kittson achieved a large degree of independence and made Pembina (N. Dak.) the headquarters of his own operations. Kittson soon found himself competing against the Hudson's Bay Company for the furs in the Red River valley.

Kittson's success at Pembina, 70 miles south of the Red River Settlement, represented a threat to the trading monopoly of the HBC in the Red River valley area, and enabled him to play a significant part in bringing free trade to the settlement in 1849. Of the free traders at Red River from whom he obtained furs, the most important were Andrew MCDERMOT and James Sinclair*. Through his wife Kittson became strongly attached to the Métis people of the settlement and in the early 1850s he usually hired them as tripmen to load his Red River carts with furs and buffalo robes, drive them to St Paul, and return with supplies for himself at Pembina and for Red River.

Kittson was a member of the Minnesota Territorial Legislative Council for the Pembina district between 1852 and 1855. He moved from Pembina to St Paul in 1854, became one of the city's influential businessmen, with large real estate holdings and investments, and in 1858–59 served as mayor of the city. A "sprightly, fine-looking man," "elegantly dressed" and "genial in nature," he became closely identified with St Paul's metropolitan aspirations, and was committed to the development of the city's northwest hinterland, which in his view included the Red River. In 1856 Kittson opened a general store in St Boniface, a sign of the reality of free trade and the interest of St Paul capital in the area. The following year he and other merchants shipped over $120,000 of furs from the Red River Settlement to St Paul. Although he sold his establishment at St Boniface in 1861, Kittson continued to import furs from the settlement and provide it with supplies.

The transportation system between St Paul and the Red River Settlement required much improvement, and in 1858–59, as a leading St Paul entrepreneur, Kittson was instrumental in opening steamboat service on the Red River. In the latter year, HBC Governor Sir George Simpson* described Kittson as "the most extensive and respectable of the American traders doing business at Red River." Simpson's successor, Alexander Grant DALLAS, converted Kittson "from an opponent into an ally," and in 1862, when the HBC had been using the St Paul route for freighting for a few years, appointed him shipping agent at St Paul and at Georgetown (Minn.), the head of navigation on the Red River. Kittson retained the agency for the remainder of the decade, and the HBC benefited from his extensive experience. He coordinated the importing of trade goods from England, and the exporting of furs by cart brigades between St Paul and Georgetown and on the company's steamboat, the *International*, between Georgetown and the Red River Settlement. Red River carts were often used over the entire route because the water level on the Red River was frequently not high enough for steamboat travel.

In 1872, two years after the province of Manitoba was created, Kittson joined a competitor, James Jerome Hill of St Paul, in organizing a steamboat line, the Red River Transportation Company, in which he had invested $75,000 by 1873. The line, with Kittson as manager but run by Hill, had five steamboats. Its monopoly on the Red River during the 1870s, in the transport of immigrants and supplies to Winnipeg and the homesteads of southern Manitoba, made it an important factor in the development of the area.

Kittson's last major venture was in 1879 when he was in poor health. With Hill, George Stephen* of the Bank of Montreal, and Donald Alexander Smith* of the HBC, he bought the St Paul and Pacific Railroad and reorganized it as the St Paul, Minneapolis and Manitoba Railway. It provided the first railway connection between St Boniface and St Paul. During a meeting with Stephen in Montreal in 1877, Kittson had expressed his confidence in the success of the railway: "The settlement of the Red River Valley, both in Minnesota and Manitoba, has been very rapid during the past two years, and the early development of that section, together with the increase of traffic from the Black Hills and the upper Missouri, will make this railway one of the very best paying roads in this country." Kittson's confidence was not misplaced, and by 1881, when he sold all of his stock in the railway, he was a wealthy man.

A busy transportation agent most of his life, Kittson died on 10 May 1888 in a lower berth on a Chicago and Northwestern train speeding through the night towards St Paul.

HENRY C. KLASSEN

PAM, HBCA, A.12/10, 16 May, 21 June 1859; A.12/42, 1 July, 23 Aug. 1861; A.12/43, 28 May 1862; A.12/45, 24 Aug. 1869; D.9/1, 2 June 1867. *Manitoba Daily Free Press*, 11 May 1888. *Nor'Wester*, 15 March, 1 April 1861; 28 May 1862. *DAB*. A. C. Gluek, *Minnesota and the manifest destiny of the Canadian northwest: a study in Canadian-American relations* (Toronto, 1965). Albro Martin, *James J. Hill and the opening of the northwest* (New York, 1976). Morton, *Manitoba* (1967). C. W. Rife, "Norman W. Kittson, a fur-trader at Pembina," *Minnesota Hist.* (St Paul, Minn.), 6 (1925): 225–52.

KIWISĀNCE (Cowessess, Ka-we-zauce, Little Child, literally boy), chief of a mixed band of Plains Cree and Saulteaux; d. probably in April 1886.

Kiwisānce was the leader of a mixed band of Plains Cree and Saulteaux which was said to have camped regularly in the vicinity of Leech Lake (Sask.) and followed the way of life based upon the buffalo hunt. He signed Treaty no.4 at Fort Qu'Appelle in September 1874, but does not seem to have taken any active part in the negotiations. Neither he nor his band was anxious to select a reserve and commence farming as contemplated by the terms of the treaty. They were determined to cling to their traditional means of livelihood for as long as possible.

The diminishing herds of buffalo led Kiwisānce and his band to the Cypress Hills (Sask.) in 1876. Other Indians from all parts of the Canadian prairies congregated in the same district in a desperate quest for the last of the buffalo to be found north of the 49th parallel. By 1878 Chief Kiwisānce had come to realize that he and his followers would soon be faced with starvation. Through Major James Morrow Walsh* of the North-West Mounted Police, he pleaded with the Canadian government to send someone who could instruct his band in farming. Before this request was met, the Kiwisānce band was reduced to selling its horses, eating its dogs, and begging for food from the NWMP.

Edgar Dewdney*, newly appointed as Indian commissioner, visited the Cypress Hills in June of 1879, bringing agricultural instructors with him. He assisted Kiwisānce in selecting a reserve site at Maple Creek (Sask.) beside the followers of Chief Piapot [Payipwat*]. By 1881 the two groups were reported to be making excellent progress in agriculture, and Kiwisānce had asked the government to send a school teacher for his band.

Instructions had been issued as early as 1879 to have Kiwisānce's reserve surveyed, but this work was never completed and the chief was much concerned about the insecurity of his band's title to the land on which his followers were residing. On one occasion he demanded a deed for the reserve from the Indian agent at Fort Walsh. When he failed to get it, Kiwisānce resigned his chieftainship to emphasize his anxiety, though he resumed his position shortly thereafter. His concern was apparently in response to a dissident movement within his band, led by one of his headmen, Louis O'Soup*, who was well known for his oratory and intrigues. In 1877 O'Soup had persuaded a faction of the band to abandon the Cypress Hills and return to the Qu'Appelle River valley in the hope of having himself recognized as chief in Kiwisānce's place. O'Soup then attempted to lure other band members away from the Cypress Hills, and in 1880 succeeded in having a reserve for the entire band surveyed at Crooked Lake (Sask.), 300 miles east of Maple Creek where the majority of the band were still settled with Kiwisānce. The chief's apprehensions about the land which had been promised to him were confirmed in the winter of 1881–82. Fearing a conflict between the Plains Indians in the Cypress Hills and the American Indians or authorities, the Canadian government concluded that all the Cree and Saulteaux Indians in the Cypress Hills area should be prevailed upon to move north or east. The food rations distributed by the Department of Indian Affairs, upon which these Indians depended for survival, were ordered discontinued to effect the removal. The bitter pill was sweetened considerably by Indian agent Allan McDonald*, who confronted O'Soup and persuaded him to resign as headman, cease his intrigues, and welcome Kiwisānce to the reserve at Crooked Lake. The chief came east with a portion of his band in the summer of 1882, and then returned with McDonald to the Cypress Hills in an attempt to persuade the more obstinate of his followers – and those of other bands – to accompany him. Although a number refused, Kiwisânce did bring another 100 persons out of the district in the spring of 1883, increasing the population on his reserve at Crooked Lake to 345. His cooperation with government officials was of significant assistance in enabling the authorities to remove the great majority of the Plains Indians from the vicinity of the Cypress Hills.

Once settled on his reserve in the Qu'Appelle valley, Kiwisânce worked energetically on his farm and encouraged other members of his band to do likewise. In 1883 McDonald declared that these Indians were the most advanced of all in Treaty no.4, and, in 1884, Kiwisânce was awarded a yoke of oxen as the chief of the band that had progressed most in agriculture. The Department of Indian Affairs was also pleased with Kiwisânce because of his unwavering support of the NWMP. He had met Colonel James Farquharson Macleod* in 1874 and believed that the law enforcement officials would assist his people in times of trouble. In 1877 a group of Assiniboin attacked his camp, but he went to the police instead of retaliating. When starving Indians from the adjacent Sakimay Reserve looted a government ration house in 1884 and defied the police force dispatched to arrest them, Kiwisânce condemned the looters and offered his son as a guide for the authorities.

Later in 1884, Chief Piapot called a meeting of all Treaty no.4 Indians to promote his allegations that the written text of the treaty did not contain all of the promises made at the treaty negotiations. Kiwisânce refused to participate, and personally retrieved a few members of his band who attended surreptitiously. Moreover, while O'Soup and a few others sympathized with the actions of Louis RIEL and the Métis and Indians who rose in rebellion in 1885, Kiwisânce was able to counteract the influence of Riel's runners and keep his band loyal to the Canadian government. The exact date and circumstances of his death soon after were not recorded, but it probably occurred in April 1886 when he was succeeded as chief by his perennial rival, O'Soup.

Kiwisânce was a prominent Plains chief who, once he had come to realize that the nomadic life style of the buffalo hunters was no longer viable, did his utmost to cooperate with Canadian government officials in adapting his band to an agricultural base. His efforts and example were doubtless a great contribution to the transformation of the Kiwisânce band into one of the most successful agricultural communities on the Prairies.

KENNETH J. TYLER

Can., Dept. of Indian Affairs and Northern Development, Central Registry files (Ottawa), file 73/30-2-73; Treaty annuity paysheets for treaties 4, 6, and 7, 1874–86. PAC, MG 26, A, 213; RG 10, B3, 3573, file 154/2; 3577, file 444; 3584, file 1130/3; 3585, file 1130/3B; 3625, files 5470, 5489; 3637, file 7088; 3640, file 7452; 3649, file 8280; 3666, file 10181; 3668, file 10490; 3671, file 10836/2; 3682, file 12662; 3686, file 13168; 3716, file 22541; 3730, file 26219; 3745, file 29506/4; 3751, file 30034; 3768, file 33642; 4103, file 29188. Can., Parl., *Sessional papers*, 1875–80 (Dept. of the Interior, Annual reports of the Indian Branch, 1874–79); 1880–87 (Annual reports of the Dept. of Indian Affairs, 1880–86). R. B. Deane, *Mounted Police life in Canada: a record of thirty-one years' service* (London and Toronto, 1916; repr. Toronto, 1973). Morris, *Treaties of Canada with the Indians*. *Opening up the west; being the official reports to parliament of the activities of the Royal North-West Mounted Police force from 1874–1881* (Toronto, 1973). *Settlers and rebels: being the official reports to parliament of the activities of the Royal North-West Mounted Police force from 1882–1885* (Toronto, 1973). I. A. Andrews, "The Crooked Lakes reserves: a study of Indian policy in practice from the Qu'Appelle treaty to 1900" (MA thesis, Univ. of Saskatchewan, Regina, 1972). K. J. Tyler, "A history of the Cowessess band" (unpublished paper prepared for the Federation of Saskatchewan Indians, 1975).

KOOPMAN, LEVI. *See* MARCHAND, LOUIS

KUKATOSI-POKA (**Starchild**, sometimes referred to as **Kucka-toosinah**), Blood Indian and NWMP scout; b.*c.* 1860, probably in what is now southern Alberta; d. in December 1889 on the Blood Indian Reservation (Alta).

Little is known of Starchild's early life. He was about 14 years old when, in 1874, the North-West Mounted Police arrived on the Canadian prairies to maintain law and order and establish the institutions of Canadian civil government. In the years that followed, the disappearance of the buffalo herds and the influx of white settlers led to profound changes in the tribal life of the plains Indians. The Blood tribe, which was a part of the Blackfoot Confederacy, signed Treaty no.7 with representatives of the Canadian government [*see* ISAPO-MUXIKA; Alexander MORRIS] in 1877. By signing the treaty, the Indians agreed to give up their nomadic way of life and settle on reservations.

Starchild achieved prominence as a result of the murder of a NWMP constable in the Cypress Hills (Sask.). On 17 Nov. 1879 Marmaduke Graburn, a 19-year-old who had enlisted the preceding June, was shot and killed while riding out alone near Fort Walsh. No witnesses to the killing could be found, but from tracks discovered at the scene the police believed the murder had been committed by two Indians. Graburn was the first mounted policeman to be murdered since the arrival of the force in the west and the authorities were worried that unless his killers were quickly apprehended the NWMP would lose the respect of the Indians. All attempts to solve the crime came to nothing until the winter of 1880–81 when two Indians incarcerated at Fort Walsh informed the police that a Blood named Starchild had boasted of shooting Graburn. Starchild was believed to be in Montana and it was not until May 1881 that the NWMP learned he had returned to the Blood reservation near Fort Macleod (Alta). Shortly afterwards Starchild was arrested and charged with the murder of Graburn.

The trial took place at Fort Macleod on 18 Oct. 1881 and attracted a great deal of attention throughout the North-West Territories. The Indians saw it as a test of the impartiality of the white man's laws. Many white settlers, on the other hand, assuming that Starchild was guilty, hoped for a verdict that would discourage any repetition of such acts. They believed that a verdict of not guilty would be interpreted by the Indians as a sign of weakness. The case was tried before Lieutenant-Colonel James Farquharson Macleod*, a magistrate and the commissioner of the NWMP, and Superintendent Leif Newry Fitzroy Crozier*, a justice of the peace. The jury of six white men, including former mounted policemen, deliberated for nearly 24 hours before returning a verdict of not guilty.

The decision of the jurors was felt by some to have been influenced by their fear of retaliation by the Indians. As one of the jurors pointed out later, however, the crown's case rested entirely upon Starchild's own boastful statement that he had killed Graburn. There was no corroborating evidence. Moreover it was not unusual for young Indians (Starchild was about 19 years old at the time of Graburn's murder) to boast of deeds they had not actually committed in order to gain recognition. Most historians of the NWMP, however, have assumed that Starchild was the murderer. The truth of the matter will never be known.

In July 1883 Starchild was arrested for bringing stolen horses into Canada from the United States. Once again he appeared before Macleod. On this occasion he was convicted and given four years' imprisonment with hard labour, a sentence which, by contemporary standards, was not unduly harsh. Starchild served his sentence at Stony Mountain Penitentiary in Manitoba. He was pardoned for good behaviour on 5 July 1886.

After his release from prison he returned to live on the Blood Indian reservation. Strangely enough, he was later employed by the NWMP as a scout. In 1888 two whisky traders were arrested as a result of his resourceful and determined action. "Out of several Indian scouts that I have tried none have proved to be worth their salt but Starchild," wrote Richard Burton Deane*, the officer commanding the police post at Lethbridge (Alta). "He did some good work for us, and I do not expect to replace him." Unfortunately, between April and December 1889 Starchild became involved in an affair with the Indian wife of a white man and the same officer had to discharge him.

Starchild believed that his life was protected by "strong medicine," and that no harm could come to him as long as he did not take a woman. It was shortly after his romance with the white man's wife that he died. His death, like those of so many of his fellow tribesmen, was caused by tuberculosis.

S. W. Horrall

Glenbow-Alberta Institute, Elizabeth Bailey Price papers, 1922–36. Royal Canadian Mounted Police Arch. (Ottawa), Service file 335 (Marmaduke Graburn); R. N. Wilson papers. Can., Parl., *Sessional papers*, 1879, IX, no.52; 1880–81, III, no.3; 1883, X, no.23; 1889, XIII, no.17. S. B. Steele, *Forty years in Canada: reminiscences of the great North-West . . .* , ed. M. G. Niblett (Toronto, 1915; repr. 1972). J. P. Turner, *The North-West Mounted Police, 1873–1893 . . .* (2v., Ottawa, 1950). H. A. Dempsey, "Starchild," *Western Canada Police Rev.* (Vancouver), 7 (1953); reprinted in 15 (1961): 6–16.

L

LAFRAMBOISE, MAURICE (baptized **Maurice-Alexis**), lawyer, politician, newspaper proprietor, and judge; b. 18 Aug. 1821 at Montreal, Lower Canada, son of Alexis Laframboise, a merchant, and Lucie-Angélique, daughter of Gabriel Cotté*; d. 1 Feb. 1882 at Montreal.

After classical studies at the Petit Séminaire de Montréal from 1831 to 1840, Maurice Laframboise articled in law and was called to the bar on 9 Dec. 1843. He settled at Saint-Hyacinthe and in 1846 married Rosalie, daughter of the seigneur Jean Dessaulles* and Rosalie Papineau, sister of Louis-Joseph*. Laframboise attended to the affairs of the Dessaulles seigneury until 1852 at which time the seigneury was divided among the Dessaulles children, Louis-Antoine*, the eldest, receiving half, and Rosalie and Georges-Casimir a quarter each.

Laframboise practised law at Saint-Hyacinthe in partnership with both Jean-Baptiste Bourgeois and Augustin-Cyrille Papineau, son of Denis-Benjamin Papineau*. From 1857 to 1860 he was mayor of Saint-Hyacinthe, succeeding his brother-in-law Louis-Antoine Dessaulles who had held the office since the town's incorporation in 1849. Laframboise ran for the Liberals in the general elections of 1857–58 and was elected in Bagot, the county adjoining Saint-Hyacinthe, where Dessaulles, an important member of the Rouges, had lost by a narrow margin in 1854. Re-elected in the general elections of 1861 and 1863, Laframboise had to go to the polls again in the latter year after accepting the post of commissioner of public works in the government of John Sandfield Macdonald* and Antoine-Aimé Dorion*; he received 58 per cent of the votes, defeating Dr Jean-Baptiste Desrosiers, the brother-in-law of George-Étienne Cartier*. The Macdonald–Dorion government had to give up office in the spring of 1864 and on 29 March Laframboise left his post. That same year the Laframboise family left Saint-Hyacinthe for Montreal.

As an opposition member, Laframboise was one of the most important opponents of confederation, and therefore belonged to the Saint-Jean-Baptiste Club [*see* Ludger Labelle*] as did Médéric Lanctot*, the editor of *L'Union nationale*, and Joseph-François Perrault and Alexandre Dufresne, members of the assembly for Richelieu and for Iberville. Laframboise delivered major speeches about confederation during the debates in the house in 1865. He argued that a question of this magnitude must be referred to the people, that the authority of a central government and the addition of the Maritime provinces would be dangerous for the "religion," "nationality," and "institutions of Lower Canada," and that the plan of confederation was consistent with the means outlined in the report of Lord Durham [Lambton*] for "the annihilation of French nationality in this country."

In the federal elections which followed confederation in 1867, Laframboise, standing as the Liberal candidate in Bagot County, polled 43 per cent of the votes and had to concede defeat to Pierre-Samuel GENDRON. Despite this reverse he remained influential in the Liberal party. In the provincial elections of 1871 he campaigned with Liberal members Pierre Bachand* and Félix-Gabriel Marchand* (elected in 1867 for Saint-Hyacinthe and Saint-Jean) in the Yamaska and Richelieu region, and was himself elected in Shefford. At the end of 1871, when the Parti National was formed, largely by moderate Liberals and a few Conservatives, and when *Le Pays*, a newspaper still associated with the Rouges, ceased publication, Laframboise laboured to establish *Le National* to provide a voice for the new movement. Its first issue appeared on 24 April 1872 and he became its owner-publisher. Laframboise and the paper's editor, Charles Laberge*, a former contributor to *L'Ordre*, made it their policy to defend the position of the "*Nationaux*" and of the moderate Liberals.

In the assembly, Laframboise and other Liberals declared themselves in favour of both reform of the electoral law and commercial and industrial training. At the same time he took an interest in the economic development of the Saint-Hyacinthe region, where it was felt in business circles that progress would come through industry and railways. In 1872 he was one of the promoters of the Philipsburg, Farnham and Yamaska Railway, but the project eventually failed. With his brother-in-law, Georges-Casimir Dessaulles, who was the town's mayor, and Pierre Bachand, he was a principal shareholder of the Maison de Banque R. St-Jacques et Cie, a limited partnership formed to "trade in money" at Saint-Hyacinthe; in 1873 the firm was incorporated as the Banque de Saint-Hyacinthe.

With the provincial elections of 1875 approaching, the Liberals, to counterbalance the Club Cartier of the Conservatives, founded in Montreal the Club National where politics were discussed and publicity campaigns organized. Laframboise gave a library to the club, which primarily brought young people together. That year Conservative newspapers alleged that Liberal leaders, in particular Toussaint-Antoine-Rodolphe Laflamme* and Louis-Amable Jetté* but also Laframboise, had attempted to take advantage of a plan to enlarge the Lachine Canal in 1874 and of the Liberal party's being in power in Ottawa to profit from a speculation (the so-called "Lachine Canal job"). Laframboise was nevertheless re-elected unopposed for Shefford.

Maurice Laframboise was mentioned as a candidate for the lieutenant governorship of Quebec when René-Édouard Caron* died on 13 Dec. 1876, but Luc LETELLIER de Saint-Just was chosen. Similarly his name came up for the post of lieutenant governor of Manitoba before the appointment of Joseph-Édouard CAUCHON. When Letellier brought about the resignation of the provincial Conservative government of Charles-Eugène Boucher* de Boucherville in 1878, the Liberal leader, Henri-Gustave Joly*, did not select Laframboise for his cabinet, but it was the latter who announced the composition of the Liberal government in the Legislative Assembly. At that time Laframboise aspired to become speaker of the house; disappointed, he then entertained thoughts of succeeding Letellier as lieutenant governor, but once again his hopes were dashed.

However, before resigning at the end of 1878 the government of Alexander Mackenzie* appointed Laframboise judge of the Superior Court for the Gaspé district. On 22 Feb. 1879 *Le National*, which was now in financial difficulty, published its last issue and the cause of Liberal journalism in Montreal was taken up by Honoré Beaugrand* in *La Patrie*. Maurice Laframboise died on 1 Feb. 1882 in Montreal at the age of 60.

Laframboise had six children. One of his daughters married Louis-Onésime Loranger, attorney general in the Quebec government of Pierre-Joseph-Olivier CHAUVEAU, and one of his sons, Jules, was manager of the Canadian Bank of Commerce at Saint-Hyacinthe from 1895 to 1924.

For many years the Parc Laframboise, with its racetrack, reminded the citizens of Saint-Hyacinthe that Maurice Laframboise had been the first to promote the

Turf Club, which had attracted to the town British officers stationed in Montreal until 1871 as well as members of the important families of the region.

JEAN-PAUL BERNARD

ANQ-M, État civil, Catholiques, Notre-Dame de Montréal, 18 août 1821. PAC, MG 30, D1, 17: 304–6. Can., Prov. du, Parl., *Débats parl. sur la confédération*. *Gazette* (Montreal), 2 Feb. 1882. *Le Journal de Saint-Hyacinthe* (Saint-Hyacinthe, Qué.), 13 août 1863. *La Minerve*, 2 févr. 1882. *Montreal Herald and Daily Commercial Gazette*, 2 Feb. 1882. *L'Opinion publique*, 28 nov. 1878, 9 févr. 1882. Beaulieu et J. Hamelin, *La presse québécoise*, II: 188–89. J. Desjardins, *Guide parl. Dominion annual register*, 1882. P.-G. Roy, *Les juges de la prov. de Québec*, 70–71, 290–91, 424–25.

Album souvenir; St-Hyacinthe, 1748–1948 (s.l., s.d.), 69, 99. J.-P. Bernard, "La pensée des journalistes libéraux de Saint-Hyacinthe, 1853–1864" (thèse de MA, univ. de Montréal, 1958); *Les Rouges*, 146–50, 188–92, 221, 225–30, 233–34, 295–311. C.-P. Choquette, *Histoire de la ville de Saint-Hyacinthe* (Saint-Hyacinthe, 1930), 58, 262–69, 413–14, 474–75. M. Hamelin, *Premières années du parlementarisme québécois*, 122–31, 194–95, 210–11, 218–21, 232–33, 252, 276, 304, 309. Laurent Lapointe, "La formation de la Banque de St-Hyacinthe et le développement économique régional (1850–1875)" (thèse de MA, univ. de Montréal, 1976), 102, 131. Rumilly, *Hist. de la prov. de Québec*, I: 51, 53–54, 193, 196, 205, 207, 216; II: 17, 63, 94, 108, 134–35, 165, 177; III: 149; *Hist. de Montréal*, II: 381; III: 28–29, 64–67, 92–93, 97. É.-Z. Massicotte, "Une société politique secrète à Montréal; le Club Saint-Jean-Baptiste," *BRH*, 21 (1915): 134–38.

LAIDLAW, GEORGE, grain merchant, forwarder, and railway promoter; b. 28 Feb. 1828 in Sutherland (now part of Highland), Scotland, son of George Laidlaw; m. in June 1858 Ann Middleton of Toronto, Canada West, and they had five sons and three daughters; d. 6 Aug. 1889 near Coboconk, Ont.

George Laidlaw's youth indicates an adventurous and anti-establishment spirit: law studies in Edinburgh abandoned in favour of joining the rebels of Don Carlos in Spain, participation in the Mexican-American War of 1848, and an expedition to the goldfields of California a year later. After returning to Scotland for five years the young man who journeyed to Canada in 1855 was rather more subdued. He arrived in Toronto during a wave of prosperity and obtained a position as wheat buyer in the firm of Gooderham and Worts, grain merchants and distillers. By 1865, despite seven years of economic instability, he had established his own forwarding firm.

It was through the grain trade that Laidlaw became familiar with the shortcomings of the Ontario inland transport system. In 1867 he published two pamphlets setting forth his views. In the first, *Reports & letters on light narrow gauge railways*, Laidlaw advocated cheaper railway lines, built to the narrow gauge of 3′6″, compared with the provincial gauge of 5′6″, and proposed construction by means of a system of small contracts let to local residents, each for the grading and laying of a few miles of track. He further visualized using indentured immigrant labourers, who would pay for their passage from overseas and for grants of land by building the railways. He predicted that a narrow gauge railway, built and fully equipped for 60 per cent of current railway construction costs, would serve for 50 years.

In the second pamphlet, *Cheap railways*, Laidlaw suggested using narrow gauge track for the construction of two lines. The Toronto, Grey and Bruce was to run northwest from Toronto to Orangeville and Lake Huron, with a branch to Owen Sound; the Toronto and Nipissing was to follow a course northeast from Toronto to Markham and the Kawartha lakes region to a point on Lake Nipissing. "Your summer sky is darkened with the smoke of burning money," Laidlaw reminded residents of regions to be served by the lines. While trees were being burned in remote corners of the province, Toronto residents were victims of monopolistic rates for firewood. Time and time again Laidlaw urged that new railway charters should prohibit excessive charges for the transport of firewood. Laidlaw also levelled a volley at the Grand Trunk and the Northern, for carrying American traffic in bond across Ontario at rates lower than those charged for local Ontario traffic.

The two proposed railways provided a focus for anti–Grand Trunk sentiment, thereby appealing to Torontonians as well as to isolated settlers. Breaking the cordwood monopoly would reduce fuel prices, and the Toronto, Grey and Bruce could possibly divert bonded traffic, destined for international markets, from the Erie Canal system to the St Lawrence system. Both developments would enhance Toronto's position as a metropolitan centre, and influential businessmen, including George Gooderham*, James Gooderham WORTS, and John GORDON, endorsed Laidlaw's proposals. Until he broke with the Grits he had a close ally in George Brown*; the *Globe* called Laidlaw a prophet and was quick to publish excerpts from "the vigorous pamphlet" as well as letters written by him.

During 1867 and 1868 Laidlaw stumped untiringly on behalf of the companies and in 1868 statutes creating the Toronto, Grey and Bruce Railway Company and the Toronto and Nipissing Railway Company were passed by the Ontario legislature. Both charters provided for the carriage of firewood at low, fixed rates, and stipulated that no foreign traffic could be charged less than traffic in the corresponding local product.

The sod-turning ceremonies for both lines took place in October 1869 at intermediate points, Weston and Cannington. South of those points the routes remained in doubt and access to downtown Toronto became the single most pressing problem for the lines throughout the 1870s. Access to the Toronto harbour was essential if the Toronto, Grey and Bruce was ever to be an alternative route for American bonded traffic. Although both it and the Toronto and Nipissing did reach the harbour by 1873, they were away from the centre of the city, so that the easy exchange of rolling-stock and the sharing of repair facilities was prevented.

The narrow gauge lines effectively broke the firewood monopoly and contributed significantly to the growth of Toronto in the 1870s. Not surprisingly, Grand Trunk officials were critical of the narrow gauge concept, and friction between Laidlaw and Frederic William CUMBERLAND, managing director of the Northern Railway, was severe for many years. Locked into a power struggle for control of the hinterland of Toronto, these rival groups showed a hint of unity only when the ascendancy of Toronto was threatened by an outside interest, such as the Wellington, Grey and Bruce Railway, of Guelph and Hamilton.

Laidlaw did not take part in the construction of the two lines but transferred his attention to the Fenelon Falls region where in 1870–71 the Toronto and Nipissing was being constructed. He proposed a colonization scheme in which a railway, running north from the Toronto and Nipissing, would be built by indentured immigrants who would be paid in land along the route. However, the plan failed to gain favour with the provincial legislature and the Fenelon Falls railway and settlement scheme never materialized. But Laidlaw could not put the idea of building north into the Precambrian shield out of his mind. His observation, that land 200 miles north of Lake Nipissing was certain to be good agriculturally because it was no farther north than the English Channel, is naïve by modern assessments, but commanded serious attention a century ago. In addition to opening the area for settlement Laidlaw also hoped to provide a link between Toronto and the transcontinental railway, then being discussed in parliament, which appeared likely to pass through the Nipissing region. Thus, in 1872, with the support of Toronto businessmen, Laidlaw became president of the Victoria Railway, an extension of the Toronto and Nipissing, from Lindsay to the upper Ottawa River valley. Track reached the town of Haliburton in 1878 but went no farther, and the line became a mineral and timber carrier. Laidlaw had given up active participation in the Victoria in 1876 and his dream of Toronto as the eastern terminus of the Pacific railway faded. But two colleagues, James Ross* and George Stephen*, whose first taste of railway building was on the Victoria, later achieved prominence with the Canadian Pacific Railway Company of 1881.

The Credit Valley Railway, incorporated in February 1871, was yet another Laidlaw scheme. The line was to run from Toronto westward to St Thomas, with branches through the Credit River valley to local termini at Orangeville and Elora. Laidlaw's relationship with the Credit Valley Railway differed from those with his other railway enterprises in that he stayed with it through construction and remained its president for ten years. Through the mid 1870s he conducted rural fund-raising campaigns and lobbied in Ottawa and London, England. In London, in 1877, he floated a bond issue at the height of the depression, despite alleged efforts by the Grand Trunk to subvert the attempt; the success won for him the accolade, "The Prince of Bonus Hunters."

The construction of the Credit Valley was, however, a continuing tale of frustration and setback. In 1874 the province had decided upon 4′ 8½″ as the standard railway gauge for Ontario, and made its adoption a condition of financial support. Thus the cost-saving features espoused by Laidlaw were lost. The increased expenses came at a time of declining prosperity and local contractors could not undertake the big projects. Finally, there was the continuing thorny issue of access to downtown Toronto, where Laidlaw pressed "with dogged resolution" against the Grand Trunk and then against the city council in 1879–80. In 1883, two years after Laidlaw gave up the struggle, the Credit Valley finally found its way through Toronto, but on an alignment two miles inland along what was then the fringe of the city.

Laidlaw's frustration with the Toronto situation and his rebuff by city officials no doubt contributed to one last railway scheme. In 1880 he presented his idea for a system of railways – the Credit Valley, the Toronto, Grey and Bruce, and the Northern, plus a new line between Toronto and Ottawa – to join with a north shore route linking Quebec, Montreal, and Ottawa as a rival to the Grand Trunk. In this plan, Toronto would share the role of Canada's major city with Montreal. The proposed system (excluding the Northern) eventually became the base of the CPR in southern Ontario but Laidlaw was not involved.

Laidlaw retired from his railway career in 1881. Vicissitudes and heart trouble had taken their toll, and his alleged secret ambition to be a gentleman farmer was also said to have influenced him. In 1871 he had bought several thousand acres of land in Bexley Township, on Balsam Lake. This land was traversed by the Toronto and Nipissing line, and undoubtedly served as a source of wood for Toronto. During the 1880s he raised beef cattle and enjoyed his retirement.

He was a visionary more than a businessman. Even his fund-raising activities convey the impression of an energetic man caught up in his dreams of a prosperous agricultural yeomanry, of a city in its ascendancy, and of a nation gaining control over its territory. The Toronto, Grey and Bruce and the Toronto and Nipissing were both converted to standard gauge within ten years, long before the 50 years Laidlaw had predicted. Far from being technically ill-conceived, these lines as built were admirably suited to a pioneering nation with little capital. Standard gauge drew them into an integrated rail network in the 1880s and demonstrated their continuing importance as traffic grew. Speeches and fund raising by Laidlaw produced 500 miles of railway radiating from Toronto. When he retired his achievements were unrecognized, although acknowledgement did come later. He appears not to have made money from his ventures, and George Stephen had to help him in 1883 when he experienced personal financial difficulty. Obituaries describe Laidlaw as modest, unassuming, and scrupulously honest. He was "far and away the boldest railway promoter," "life and soul" of the Toronto railway movement, and by all appearances the catalyst in a crucial period in the growth of Toronto and her hinterland.

THOMAS F. MCILWRAITH

George Laidlaw was the author of *Cheap railways: a letter to the people of Bruce and Grey, showing the advantages, practicability and cost of a cheap railway from Toronto through these counties* . . . (Toronto, 1867), and commented on *Reports & letters on light narrow gauge railways* . . . by Charles Fox *et al.* (Toronto, 1867), which he compiled.

AO, MU 20, Laidlaw to J. C. Bailey, 9 Dec. 1874; 30 May, 9 Aug. 1876; 16 April, 6, 8, 11, 15 Sept. 1877; 28 March, 17 May, 9, 17, 26 June 1879. *Evening Telegram* (Toronto), 7 Aug. 1889. *Globe*, February–July 1867, May 1869, March 1871, September 1879, February–March 1880, 8 Aug. 1889. *Toronto World*, 14 June, 8, 9 Aug. 1889. Masters, *Rise of Toronto*, 64, 75, 110–14, 149. Alfred Price, "George Laidlaw – pioneer railway builder," *Canadian Magazine*, 68 (July–December 1927), no. 6: 21–23, 34–37.

LAING. *See* LANG

LAJOIE. *See* GÉRIN-LAJOIE

LANDRY, JEAN-ÉTIENNE, doctor, surgeon, and professor; b. 25 Dec. 1815 at Carleton, Lower Canada, son of Sébastien Landry and Émerence Painchaud; m. 31 Aug. 1841 Caroline-Eulalie, daughter of notary Roger Lelièvre of Quebec City, and they had 11 children, of whom three survived infancy; d. 17 June 1884 at Quebec City.

Jean-Étienne Landry was an Acadian by descent and a Gaspesian by birth. His father, a leading citizen in Carleton, was well regarded by Abbé Charles-François Painchaud*, who since 1806 had served as a missionary in the Baie des Chaleurs region and resided in Carleton. Thus, after Sébastien Landry was widowed, Painchaud had no qualms about blessing his marriage to his own sister Émerence on 31 Oct. 1813. On Christmas Day 1815 their first child, Jean-Étienne, was born.

The previous year Painchaud had left Carleton to take charge of the parish of Sainte-Anne-de-la-Pocatière (Sainte-Anne). In 1827, realizing that an institution for secondary education was needed for the people in the lower St Lawrence region, he added responsibility for the establishment of a classical college to his parish duties. He invited his nephew, Jean-Étienne, whose sharpness of mind he had quickly noted, to become a student in it. The young Gaspesian arrived in 1831 when the Collège de Sainte-Anne-de-la-Pocatière was going through a difficult initial period. The first director, Abbé Étienne Chartier*, whose pedagogical theories allowed the students excessive freedom, had bequeathed to his successor, Abbé Louis Proulx*, a situation which had to be rectified, if its disastrous moral and disciplinary results were to be corrected. The college's 75 students were taught by seminarists who had just received the habit. There was extensive improvisation. The most gifted pupils would occasionally skip a year. Hence in July 1834, just three years after his arrival, Landry completed his sixth year (Rhétorique), winning second prize. Anxious to keep his nephew at the college, and having visions of a career in the church for him, Abbé Painchaud got him to enter ecclesiastical life in September 1835 and put him in charge of a first-year Latin class. But the attempt misfired. After only a few months Jean-Étienne left the village of Sainte-Anne-de-la-Pocatière (La Pocatière) for Quebec, where another uncle, Dr Joseph Painchaud*, who had been in practice in that city for five years, agreed to take him on as a medical student.

Landry was attached as an intern to the Marine and Emigrant Hospital, an institution for transient seamen and immigrants. His experience as a student in this hospital was unhappy and, when offered the opportunity to leave Quebec City, he did not hesitate. In 1839 when dispute over the boundary between Canada and Maine exacerbated the long-standing quarrel between the British and the Americans, troops were sent to the Madawaska region to counter any forays the Americans might make. Landry donned military uniform as a "Medical attendant of a detachment of the 24th Regiment," according to *Le Canadien* of 22 July 1839, which announced his forthcoming departure. His stay in the disputed frontier region in fact passed without incident. At the beginning of February 1840 he came back to Rivière-du-Loup to take over the hospital. Released from the army in April, he returned to Quebec, took his examinations on 8 July, and a week later was licensed to "practise medicine, surgery and obstetrics in the province of Lower Canada."

He went into practice at Pointe-Lévy (Lauzon and Lévis). Then in April 1844 he was appointed surgeon to the Marine and Emigrant Hospital. As instructor in anatomy, Landry was authorized on 4 Dec. 1845 to open a dissecting room. The most tangible proof of his growing reputation as a skilful surgeon was his appointment in September 1849 as a professor in the Quebec School of Medicine, which had been incorporated in 1845 but was not officially opened until 15 May 1848. Its president was Joseph Morrin*, a Scot who already presided over the College of Physicians and Surgeons of Lower Canada and was affiliated with the Hôtel-Dieu. The principal professors of the school, apart from Morrin, were Joseph Painchaud, Charles-Jacques Frémont*, Pierre-Martial Bardy*, Jean Blanchet*, and James DOUGLAS. The school lasted only a short while; it closed on 30 April 1854 and was succeeded by the faculty of medicine of Université Laval, whose chairs had been granted to the professors associated with Morrin, among them Landry.

On 10 Dec. 1853, immediately after his appointment as professor at Laval, Landry had been selected for an important mission in Europe and he left Quebec on 18 December with Octave Crémazie*. After his return on 20 April, Landry gave the capital's newspapers a succinct report of the results of this mission. *Le Journal de Québec* of 2 May reported that on his "special assignment" for the university Landry had visited the University of Oxford, University College and King's College in London, the universities of Liège, Louvain, Ghent, and Brussels in Belgium, and had attended the Faculté de Médecine in Paris during his stay in that city. At these institutions he studied procedures and their practical application, "gleaning whatever might be helpful to the Université Laval." For its medical faculty he purchased "books, instruments, anatomical preparations necessary for teaching," and reportedly put to good use the money available to him. "At his request, the seminary also agreed to allow him to acquire a superb collection of natural pathological specimens (more than 500 items), which he has added to a sizeable purchase of prepared specimens to be used in the study of [both] skin and other diseases. The instruments were made by one of the foremost Parisian craftsmen."

In his medical teaching Landry demonstrated abilities which his students highly appreciated: clarity of exposition, precision in details, and a competence vitalized by the daily practice of surgery at the Hôtel-Dieu and at the Marine and Emigrant Hospital where he was still giving instruction in medicine as applied to outpatient clinics. In addition to teaching at Laval, treating an ever-growing clientele, and practising surgery, Landry gave much of his energies to the Asile de Beauport (Centre hospitalier Robert-Giffard), of which he became one of the owners in 1863. With the passing years, however, his medical activity diminished as a result of crippling rheumatism and increasing deafness. In 1880 he turned over the direction of the Asile de Beauport to his son Philippe, who was then the federal member for Montmagny county, and to his son-in-law Dr Georges-Antoine Larue. Then in April 1881 he asked Université Laval for permission to retire.

It was with the serenity of duty well done and the esteem of the community that Landry was ending his fruitful career when suddenly a storm as violent as it was unexpected burst over his head. By around 1880 the Catholic world had become haunted by the spectre of freemasonry. When in 1870 the papacy had lost the last of its territory with the entry of the Italian troops into Rome, most of the faithful had attributed this catastrophe to the efforts of Italian freemasonry, which hoped that the emergence of Rome as the capital of a united Italy would also signify the end of Roman Catholicism. In other Catholic countries such as Belgium and France, freemasonry had also adopted an anti-Catholic attitude. In France especially, the advent of the Third Republic saw the rise of an aggressive form of freemasonry which lent support to all the forces interested in fighting Catholicism.

It is not surprising that in French Canada, which was so attuned to France, the masonic menace was quickly detected. At Quebec the Cercle Catholique was outspoken in its denunciations. The president of this circle, founded on 26 May 1876, was Clément Vincelette, manager of the asylum at Beauport since 1853. Its members were militant Ultramontanes, the most prominent being Joseph-Israël Tarte*, editor of *Le Canadien*, Jules-Paul Tardivel*, his associate, bookseller Joseph-Alfred Langlais, Narcisse-Eutrope Dionne* and Roch-Pamphile Vallée, both staff writers of *Le Courrier du Canada*, and Landry's son Philippe, the political opponent of François Langelier* who was a professor of law in Université Laval. The university was the target of the Cercle's attacks. The members joined forces with the Montreal Ultramontanes, who were engaged in a desperate struggle there and in Rome to get the branch institution Laval had set up in Montreal in 1876 [*see* Joseph DESAUTELS] replaced by a university independent of Quebec and uncontaminated by the defects apparent to them at Laval: Gallicanism, liberalism, and ties with freemasonry.

With the last point the opponents of the Quebec university were striking their enemy in a vulnerable spot, for some of the Protestants in the professorial ranks at Laval were freemasons. One, Dr James Arthur Sewell, had even been dean of the medical faculty since 1863 and thus sat on the university council. Jean-Étienne Landry considered such a situation unacceptable in a Catholic university. The rector, Abbé Thomas-Étienne Hamel*, who was also vicar general of the archdiocese of Quebec, thought differently, at least if we accept the version Landry gave some years later of a conversation between them on Hamel's return from a trip to Rome in 1873. Hamel had allegedly told Landry that he "had done all he could in Rome to make it understood that the freemasons in Canada were (without exception) not as malicious or as dangerous as those in Europe, since they were considered only as members of benevolent or mutual benefit societies, but that in Rome they refused to see reason on this point, and became infuriated when such remarks were made to them." To which Landry replied, according to his account, "the freemasons *are everywhere the same* regarding the Church and society."

Landry had informed the members of the Cercle Catholique of the opinion which, in his view, Hamel held concerning freemasonry, and he repeated this version to priests who came to his house to say mass once illness confined him to his room; the story spread so widely that the bishop of Saint-Hyacinthe, Louis-Zéphirin Moreau*, wrote to Quebec to ask for an explanation. The archdiocese reacted swiftly and in April 1883 deputed Abbé Louis-Nazaire Bégin*, the promoter of justice in the archdiocesan tribunal, to question Landry. Asserting that secret societies were making "great progress in Canada, with some priests reported to be affiliated with these societies hostile to the church," Landry repeated to Bégin his account of the conversation with Hamel in 1873. Hamel subsequently told Bégin that "M. Landry had a *mania* of which no one in the world can cure him."

On 30 April 1883 Hamel wrote to Landry to protest against the remarks attributed to him and to demand that he retract the malicious gossip he had started. Hamel suggested that Landry publish in the press a declaration which he himself had drawn up: Landry would admit that as a result of "precise information" he now realized he had "interpreted in a completely erroneous manner" a conversation dating back ten years, and that he was pleased to say that "no credence" should be given to "all the rumours" of Vicar General Hamel having expressed "objectionable ideas concerning freemasonry" to him. Unwilling to "dishonour" himself Landry flatly refused to sign this document, as he indicated in a letter of 7 June to Abbé Pierre Roussel, secretary of Université Laval.

However, the archbishop of Quebec had already come to the rescue of his vicar general, for, on 1 June, Elzéar-Alexandre Taschereau* had published a pastoral letter on secret societies which was immediately reprinted in the press. Stating that, according to the church's teaching, it was "always a very grave error to join secret societies properly so called, known under the generic name of freemasonry," the archbishop enunciated "a precise and practical rule for putting an end to the fatal blindness" to which "too many persons who did not reflect sufficiently on the consequences of their actions and of their words" were succumbing. "With reference to a Catholic," he stated, "the accusation of freemasonry is certainly grave enough by its very nature to give rise to calumny or scandal, or a rash, serious judgement. Circumstances may lend an extra degree of maliciousness, if for example a priest, a vicar general, a bishop, a cardinal . . . or the reputation of a Catholic institution is involved." Cruel though the archbishop's blow was, Landry remained silent but he behaved otherwise when on 5 June Université Laval, through its secretary, notified him that by unanimous resolution of the council it was withdrawing the title of "professor emeritus" conferred on him two years earlier. Replying on 7 June to Roussel, Landry showed that his deepest sensitivity had been offended: his honour as a man who had devoted the best of himself to an institution which now ignominiously cast him aside as if he were a common backbiter. By then he was confined to his room as an invalid and was almost totally deaf. Indeed, Bégin had found him unable "to hear a word, unless it was shouted into his ear." Consequently he was glad to hand things over to his son Philippe, a born polemicist, who vigorously took up his father's cause.

With no hope of obtaining justice for his father at home, despite his appearance on 23 July 1883 before the diocesan court, Philippe left for Rome on 4 August with two purposes: to denounce in the name of the Cercle Catholique Taschereau's pastoral letter concerning secret societies, and to present his father's case with supporting documents to the cardinals of Propaganda. But Propaganda, exasperated by the endless complaints from Quebec and not too sure how to solve these political-religious problems from a distance, dispatched the Belgian Cistercian Dom Joseph-Gauthier-Henri Smeulders to Canada as an apostolic commissary; he left Rome on 20 Sept. 1883. Philippe Landry returned to Quebec soon after to submit his report against Hamel to him. Hamel replied with a counter-report dated 13 June 1884.

Thus matters stood when Dr Jean-Étienne Landry died on 17 June. His will showed that he had a large fortune, especially for that period. In addition to substantial legacies to religious and charitable institutions, he left about $100,000 to each of his three children.

Philippe Landry was persistent and strove more earnestly than ever to rehabilitate fully his father's good name. Even a brief account of the conflict of statements in Quebec and Rome would be too long. Any tentative agreement always met the insurmountable obstacle: did Dr Landry repeat accurately the remarks of Rector Hamel concerning freemasonry? Yes, maintained Philippe Landry; no, vehemently replied Hamel. Even after the latter's death on 16 July 1913, Philippe, who had become the speaker of the Canadian Senate, would not let the matter drop. In September 1915 he appealed to the archbishop of Quebec, Cardinal Louis-Nazaire Bégin, who was then chancellor of Université Laval, to have "struck" from the records of the Université Laval council the "resolution of expulsion" which was "a blot" on his father's honour. In vain! On 20 Dec. 1919, the very day of Senator Landry's death, Mgr Amédée-Edmond Gosselin*, archivist of the Séminaire de Québec, closed the Landry–Hamel case with a note certainly not charged with religious charity: "The affair is well and truly ended. . . . The honour of the university is worth at least as much as the honour of Dr Landry."

Jean-Étienne Landry's career had been an integral part of the first quarter-century of Université Laval. An illustration of the heroic and promising beginnings of that institution, it finally became lost in the maze of ideological struggles which drew too many fine minds away from creative work. The historian cannot but contemplate with profound sadness the tangled skein of those unending and unrelenting controversies that all too effectively and for too long made scientific advance within this small French-Canadian community a vain hope.

PHILIPPE SYLVAIN

[This biography is a résumé of my essay entitled "Jean-Étienne Landry [1815–1884], l'un des fondateurs de la faculté de médecine de l'université Laval," published in the *Cahiers des Dix*, 40 (1975): 161–96. Where necessary, *Le Journal de Québec*, *Le Courrier du Canada*, and *L'Électeur* of Quebec were consulted to check statements from *Le Canadien*. The *Annuaire* of Université Laval was used for the years 1856 to 1883. P. S.]

ASQ, Univ., Cartons 34–35. A.-C.-P.-R. Landry, *Landry vs Hamel: sommaire, mémoire, documents et pièces justificatives* (Rome, 1883). *Le Canadien*, 22 juill. 1839–18 juin 1884. C.-M. Boissonnault, *Histoire de la faculté de médecine de Laval* (Québec, 1953). M. Hamelin, *Premières années du parlementarisme québécois*, 134, 284–86. Jules Landry, "Le docteur J. É. Landry" (a lecture to the Soc. hist. de Québec and the Soc. canadienne d'hist. de la médecine, Québec, 1965). Wilfrid Lebon, *Histoire du collège de Sainte-Anne-de-la-Pocatière* (2v., Québec, 1948–49), I. *Trois siècles de médecine québécoise* (Québec, 1970).

LANG (Laing), GEORGE, mason and builder; b. *c.* 1821 in Roxburghshire (now part of Borders), Scotland; m. in 1844 Susan Johnston in Edinburgh, and they had no children; d. 2 July 1881 at Shubenacadie, Hants County, N.S.

Trained in Scotland as a mason, George Lang is said to have worked on the Scott Monument in Edinburgh, erected between 1841 and 1846, and then to have immigrated to St John's, Nfld, to work on the Anglican cathedral constructed between 1847 and 1850. There he may have met David STIRLING, an architect from Roxburghshire, and worked with him on buildings erected after the great fire of 1846. In 1851 Lang and Stirling began operating the Albert Freestone Quarries in Albert County, N.B., where Lang remained as manager until 1858. Financed and promoted by Charles Dickson Archibald* and British associates, the quarries supplied sandstone – the popular brownstone of New York – to the American market.

In 1858 Lang moved to Halifax, where he successfully tendered on principal government and commercial contracts. These works made him one of the leading Halifax builders of the early 1860s. His first building was the Halifax County Court House, designed by William Thomas* of Toronto and erected between 1858 and 1860. Lang's second commission, a monument in St Paul's Cemetery, commemorated Halifax's fallen sons of the Crimean War, especially Augustus Frederick Welsford and William B. C. A. Parker. Lang repeated the monument's lion motif on several later buildings. His third undertaking involved four important contracts for rebuilding Granville Street after the destructive fire of September 1859.

Although Lang erected other stores and offices in 1862–63, his building activities were largely institutional and governmental. In 1860–61 he undertook work for the British army at Fort Massey and the Wellington Barracks in Halifax, and in 1862 for the Church of England at St Luke's School House in Halifax and with the hall and library of King's College, Windsor. In 1862–63 he built the impressive Halifax Club, designed by Stirling.

Unlike his principal competitors, Lang was not involved in building houses and tenements on speculation. In 1863, again with Stirling, he built Keith Hall for the brewer and politician, Alexander Keith*, and a group of cottages in Bowery Street; in 1864 Lang constructed the Quinlan House. His experiments with patent roofing, his periodic but unsuccessful tenders, and his purchase of building lots, mainly in 1864, suggest that it was promising opportunity elsewhere rather than lack of interest which kept Lang largely out of the busy domestic construction field.

Early in 1864 Lang's low tender won the contract for the new Provincial Building, designed by Stirling, to house the customs department and post office. Lang began ambitiously with the purchase of a 40-horsepower steam-engine. Soon, however, he encountered labour combinations, critical commissioners, and financial over extension. By August 1865 it was "rumoured that each separate brick and stone is to be marked with the date of the year it was put in." Later in 1865, after having assigned all his property to his principal creditor, James Forman*, Lang was relieved of the contract. The slate quarry, financed by Forman, which he had opened in 1863 at Douglas

(Douglas Road), Hants County, was turned over with his other assets.

For his remaining 15 years Lang operated a brick manufactory in Shubenacadie, initially with Halifax carpenter James Thompson. An honorary member of the North British Society from 1858, Lang served as a volunteer in the Chebucto Greys from 1860 to 1865 and as vice-president of the Caledonia Curling Club in 1862. The Nova Scotia building stones he collected and displayed at the international exhibitions of 1862 (London) and 1865 (Dublin) won him honorary mention at the latter.

A builder's situation in mid-19th-century Halifax was continually unstable. Although Lang's ambition, energy, and skills proved insufficient to establish him permanently in this precarious milieu, a number of his buildings and his Crimean War monument survive today.

SUSAN BUGGEY

Colchester County Court of Probate (Truro, N.S.), Original estate papers, 1880, no.921 (mfm. at PANS). General Register Office (Edinburgh), Registers for St Cuthbert's Church, Edinburgh, 12 Aug. 1844. Halifax County Registry of Deeds (Halifax), Deeds, 1861–81 (mfm. at PANS). PANS, MS file, Halifax – Provincial Building (new); RG 39C, nos. 1278, 1281–82, 1314–15, 1515, 1653–54, 3155, 3631, 4390, 4426. QUA, David Stirling, Notebook (copy at PANS). St Paul's Anglican Church (Halifax), Registers of baptisms, burials, and marriages, 6 July 1881 (mfm. at PANS). Westmorland County Registry Office (Dorchester, N.B.), libro E: f.530; F: 71; G: 25 (mfm. at PANB).

Duncan Campbell, *Nova Scotia, in its historical, mercantile and industrial relations* (Montreal, 1873), 390–92. N.S., *Statutes*, 1854, c.68; 1857–58, c.70. N.S., House of Assembly, *Journal and proc.*, 1860; 1864; 1866; 1869. *Acadian Recorder*, 9 Oct. 1858; 28 May, 24 Dec. 1859; 2 Aug. 1862; 19 Dec. 1863; 6 Feb., 10 Dec. 1864; 26 Aug. 1865; 20 Jan. 1866; 24 Aug., 15 Sept. 1870; 6 July 1881. *British Colonist* (Halifax), 4 Feb., 19 June 1862; 31 Dec. 1863. *Evening Express* (Halifax), 31 Dec. 1859; 13 Nov. 1861; 28 March, 21 May, 20 June, 25 July, 12 Sept., 29 Oct. 1862; 29 April, 4 May, 15 June, 9 Nov. 1863; 13, 15 Jan., 3 Feb., 23 March, 20 April, 4 May, 5 Dec. 1864; 27 March, 5 April, 23 June, 22, 24 Nov., 8 Dec. 1865. *Halifax Reporter*, 3, 24 Nov. 1860; 11 June 1864. *Morning Journal* (Halifax), 27 June 1864. *Morning News* (Saint John, N.B.), 8 May 1854. *Novascotian*, 13 Sept., 25 Oct. 1858; 31 Oct., 26 Dec. 1859; 2 Jan., 25 June, 16 July 1860. *Belcher's farmer's almanack*, 1862. *The Halifax, N.S. business directory . . .*, comp. Luke Hutchinson (Halifax), 1863. *Hutchinson's N.S. directory*, 1864–65. *Lovell's N.S. directory*, 1871: 361. *McAlpine's Maritimes provinces business directory . . .* (Saint John and Halifax), 1880–81: 250, 465. North British Soc., *Annals of the North British Society of Halifax, Nova Scotia, for one hundred and twenty-five years . . .*, comp. J. S. Macdonald (Halifax, 1894). Harry Piers, "Artists in Nova Scotia," N.S. Hist. Soc., *Coll.*, 18 (1914): 160.

LANGEVIN, EDMOND (baptized **Edmond-Charles-Hippolyte**), priest and vicar general; b. 30 Aug. 1824 at Quebec City, son of Jean Langevin, a businessman and public servant, and Sophie Laforce; d. 2 June 1889 at Rimouski, Que.

Edmond Langevin came from a lower middle class family prominent in Quebec. After receiving a classical education from 1833 to 1842 at the Petit Séminaire de Québec, where he was a "distinguished and model pupil," he entered the Grand Séminaire. While studying theology, he held the office of under-secretary of the archdiocese of Quebec. He was ordained priest on 18 Sept. 1847 and continued to serve in the secretariat of the archdiocese, becoming assistant secretary on 28 Sept. 1849 and secretary on 10 Oct. 1850. He retained this post of "confidential adviser" to the incumbents of the archdiocese until 30 April 1867, when Bishop Charles-François Baillargeon* selected him as vicar general. The following day, his brother Jean Langevin*, bishop of the new diocese of Rimouski, entrusted him with the same duties and brought him to his cathedral city.

Three of the Langevin family were to be famous. Jean, the eldest son, had distinguished himself as principal of the École Normale Laval before becoming a bishop. Hector-Louis*, Edmond's younger brother, chose the legal profession and would become leader of the Quebec wing of the Conservative party after 1873. Edmond was "the guiding spirit of the Langevin trio, just as he [was] its centre by birth." Although he was self-assertive, as were his brothers, his personality "was more conciliatory, more adaptable." The Langevin brothers certainly formed a curious triumvirate, with Jean in the upper ranks of the church, Hector in those of politics, and Edmond between them, playing the less conspicuous role of their confidant and counsellor. This role is revealed in Edmond's regular correspondence with Hector, which contains advice on corrections to the second edition (published in 1878) of the *Droit administratif ou manuel des paroisses et fabriques*, written by Hector at the suggestion of Jean Langevin to help his priests with parish administration; counsel on how to win the Holy See's gratitude by taking the initiative to secure an address of homage to the pope from the Canadian parliament; and advice on how to solve his difficulties with certain politicians such as Joseph-Édouard CAUCHON: "In these parts when piglets go over fences, they are hobbled and a nail is put through their snouts. I recommend this remedy to you for the *other*."

The correspondence gives us an idea of Edmond's thinking. His opinions, which invariably were clear and reasonable, without a doubt influenced his two brothers. A conservative at heart, he zealously advocated respect for the established order. He told a parish priest who asked him about the Métis rebellion: "Naturally the ministers have no sympathy for the law-breakers; on the contrary, the protection of society demands that terror be instilled in those who . . . might be disposed to play the same game." Of Louis RIEL he wrote: "I abominate his career as much as I do the stupid and impious end of another so-called patriot [Louis-Joseph Papineau*]." An Ultramontane, he was alarmed by the "spreading spirit of secularism" and by the "obvious tendency of civil courts to encroach on the rights of the church." He said of liberals: "They are tyrants . . . small minds, whom history will treat as they deserve, [they] have destroyed ecclesiastical influence in Canada."

In the diocese of Rimouski, he played an important role in support of his brother Jean. "Religion, education, agriculture, settlement, industry, nothing was unfamiliar to him." He took on the management of two congregations of nuns, a conference of the Society of St Vincent de Paul (which he brought into the diocese of Rimouski), the Society of St Francis de Sales, the Apostleship of Prayer, the Third Order of St Francis of Assisi, and the Société d'Agriculture of Rimouski. His experience in the chancery of Quebec had made him indispensable to his bishop, who appointed him administrator of the diocese on 21 May 1875, and then provost of the cathedral chapter in 1878; he held the latter post until 1889. He was a remarkable theologian, and taught theology and the scriptures at the Grand Séminaire de Rimouski. He enjoyed the esteem of most bishops and was chosen as a vicar general by a number of them including Antoine Racine* of Sherbrooke in 1874, Louis-Zéphirin Moreau* of Saint-Hyacinthe in 1876, and Elzéar-Alexandre Taschereau* of Quebec. In addition he served for many years as secretary in the provincial councils.

Interested in the humanities, Langevin did some historical research. In 1874 he published a biography of Bishop François de Laval* which, according to his brother Jean, for no apparent reason met with "sarcasm and scorn" from the "Messieurs" of the archdiocese of Quebec.

His lifelong goodness, piety, and devotion earned him the title of protonotary apostolic *ad instar*, conferred in an imposing ceremony on 2 May 1888 at Rimouski, with Cardinal Taschereau officiating. This honour, "fully deserved," was welcomed "with general satisfaction throughout the whole country." It had, however, been slow in coming; the worthy prelate passed away on 2 June 1889, after a few days of illness.

GÉRALD GARON

Edmond Langevin was the author of *Notice biographique sur François de Laval de Montmorency, 1er évêque de Québec* . . . (Montréal, 1874).

ANQ-Q, AP-G-36. Arch. de l'archevêché de Rimouski (Rimouski, Qué.), Dossier Agriculture, I; Dossier Edmond Langevin, Lettres d'Edmond Langevin et de Jean Langevin, notes biographiques; Lettres particulières, 1873–88; Livre de corr., 1er mai 1867–31 janv. 1891. *Visite à Rimouski de son éminence le cardinal Taschereau, archevêque de Québec; les 30 avril, 1 et 2 mai 1888* (Rimouski, 1888). A.-C. Morin, *Dans la maison du père; nécrologie sacerdotale du diocèse de Rimouski, 1867–1967* (Rimouski, 1967). Désilets, *Hector-Louis Langevin*. Gérald Garon, "La pensée socio-économique de Mgr Jean Langevin" (thèse de MA, univ. de Sherbrooke, Sherbrooke, Qué., 1977). Albert Tessier, *Les sœurs des petites-écoles, 1874–1894* (Rimouski, 1962).

LAREAU, EDMOND (baptized **Pierre-Bénoni-Evremond**), lawyer, teacher, author, journalist, and politician; b. 13 March 1848 at Mount Johnson (Mont-Saint-Grégoire), Canada East, son of Pierre-Bénoni Lareau and Odile Sylvestre; m. 9 Feb. 1880 Marguerite Robillard in Montreal, Que.; d. there 21 April 1890.

Edmond Lareau received his secondary education at the Collège Sainte-Marie-de-Monnoir and then studied at Victoria College in Cobourg, Ont., receiving a diploma of bachelor of law in 1870. In 1874, Lareau was granted a bachelor of civil law, *ad eundem*, in recognition of work he had done in civil law, by McGill College in Montreal, where in the same year he became a professor of law; he retained this position for the rest of his life. Admitted to the bar of the province of Quebec on 27 Sept. 1870, he practised as a lawyer in Montreal, particularly with Calixte Lebeuf, a Liberal sympathizer.

Lareau took an early interest in politics. In 1875 he became the first president of the Club National, an organ of the Quebec Liberal party [*see* Maurice LAFRAMBOISE]; his lecture to the club on *Libéraux et Conservateurs*, in some measure complementing the famous speech on Canadian Liberalism made by Wilfrid Laurier* in 1877, attracted wide attention. In 1882 Lareau ran as a Liberal in the federal elections in Rouville, but was defeated by George-Auguste Gigault. The following year he successfully sued the newspaper *La Minerve* for libel during the election and won $600 in damages. Maintaining his association with the party organization, Lareau in 1883 became counsel for the Association Libérale de Montréal. Two years later, at the time of the Louis RIEL affair, he was one of the 28 citizens who organized the great rally on the Champ de Mars in Montreal, a prelude to the formation of Honoré Mercier*'s Parti National. Lareau stood again in Rouville in the provincial elections of 1886 and this time was successful. During the three subsequent sessions in the Legislative Assembly of Quebec he argued for a pragmatic concept of liberalism. He often spoke in the house and his comments were greatly enriched by his legal knowledge.

In constitutional matters Lareau was a defender of provincial autonomy along the lines of Mercier; he commended the latter's initiative in summoning the 1887 interprovincial conference, a gathering roundly condemned by Sir John A. Macdonald*'s party in Ottawa and the Conservative opposition in Quebec. He was especially in favour of transferring the federal right of disallowance to London and he urged the necessity of increasing federal subsidies to the provinces to guarantee provincial autonomy. Also devoted to defending the rights of the English-speaking minority in Quebec, in 1887 he noted that the Quebec provincial boards of examiners favoured French Canadians in their tests for admission to study for the liberal professions by asking questions too closely related to the content taught in French institutions and failing to consider the different training given to English-speaking candidates.

In fiscal and commercial matters Lareau held classical liberal views. He particularly opposed a bill put forward in 1887 to institute an income tax to finance insane asylums, fearing that taxpayers would be forced to make a sworn declaration of their income. When a bill was introduced that year to abolish the right of municipalities to tax commercial travellers, Lareau gave it his support and delivered a lengthy speech in defence of freedom of business and the rights of the consumer. In his opinion this tax penalized consumers who were not near urban centres, since it encouraged commercial travellers to narrow their field of operation. He based his argument on Canadian case-law and the example of the Supreme Court of the United States, which had "just ruled in favour of commercial travellers." As for another issue, Lareau favoured restricting the tax exemption of religious communities to the buildings where public services were dispensed without monetary gain; their other properties should be subject to the special tax for municipal services and calculated solely on the value of the land on which the edifice was built. In support of this view Lareau pointed to the fact that buildings belonging to a religious community "do not necessarily have a market value." This opinion represented a middle ground between legislators committed to ultramontanism and the young Liberal intellectuals of *Canada-Artistique* (Montreal), who towards the end of the 1880s were expressing indignation at the tax exemptions accorded the church. Lareau also adopted an intermediary position on the condition of the working class. In 1887 he declared himself opposed to the complete abandonment of the right to garnishee wages: "It would be dangerous both for the supplier and for the worker. The former would be deprived of a serious moral guarantee for the money owed him. As to the latter, the very person you are trying to protect, you would be taking away his credit, which would be a grave step." Hence Lareau proposed that a quarter of the pay should be liable to garnishment.

During his political career Lareau also gave his attention to journalism, contributing in the 1880s to a number of Liberal papers such as *La Patrie* and *Le Temps*, which was founded in Montreal by Honoré Mercier in 1883. In his articles Lareau gave evidence of openness of mind and of a moderation which contrasted with the anticlericalism of Benjamin Sulte* and Arthur Buies*. In *La Patrie* of 3 Jan. 1889 he observed of the United States: "In no country is the Roman Catholic religion more free. But this liberty given the Catholic faith is equally guaranteed by the constitution to all the others. The State is not sectarian: all men are equal before the law." Nothing could better sum up his opinion about the relationships that the state should maintain with the various religious persuasions. Lareau also contributed to periodicals, and from 1875 regularly wrote articles on literature for the *Revue canadienne*. From 1884 to 1890, as a legal specialist, he was co-editor with John Sprott Archibald of the *Lower Canada Jurist* (Montreal), a vast compendium of judicial rulings issuing from courts having jurisdiction in civil matters in the province of Quebec.

Lareau produced two major works, a history of literature and a history of law. The *Histoire de la littérature canadienne*, which came out in 1874, is a veritable encyclopædia of letters, and more than a century after publication it is still being consulted. Lareau had a concept of literature that was unusually broad for his time; far from confining himself to the classic literary works, he also commented on journalism as well as writings on the law and natural science. How he managed to produce such a monument of erudition at an early age remains a mystery. In one 133-page chapter devoted to Canadian historiography he makes his philosophy of history clear. After a brief exposé of ancient and mediæval historiography from the works of Geoffroi de Villehardouin and Jean Froissart, he turns to a discussion of the "first glimmers of positivism": "cold reason blazed the trail, trusting in its own strength: from then on humanity took a step in its forward march." Both English- and French-speaking Canadian historians appear in this chapter, the author never questioning whether their works properly belong to the historical genre. Pierre Du Calvet* wins praise for his liberal ideas and Dr Jacques Labrie* is nicknamed the "Canadian Livy." Michel Bibaud* is judged "inferior" to Jean-Baptiste-Antoine Ferland* as a "philosopher-historian," to François-Xavier Garneau* as a "political historian," and to Étienne-Michel Faillon* as a "narrator," and he is said to "not follow, as [does] Garneau, the American social movement."

Lareau also made a study of the broad syntheses developed by French Canadian historians in the mid 19th century. In accordance with his own ideological system, Lareau expressed a preference for the first edition of Garneau's *Histoire du Canada depuis sa découverte jusqu'à nos jours* published in three volumes between 1845 and 1848 (there would eventually be seven more editions) as the version which readers were bound to prefer because of its advanced liberal views. This original edition, and in particular its first volume, had been attacked by the clerical-Conservative group, but Lareau nevertheless comments without rancour upon their condemnation. He prefers to give a context for Garneau's later changes, suggesting that social forces obliged him to revise his original version "in order to make his book more acceptable to the majority of Canadian readers." This concern for the relationship between the writer as producer and the reader as consumer more than once enabled Lareau to avoid making value judgements of the uncompromising and categorical kind so often found in the 19th century, when articulate analysis was overridden by dogmatism. Although he does not hesitate to acknowledge his preferences, he does so in a spirit of tolerance quite rare in his day. As an example, Lareau considers Faillon a historian who epitomizes belief in the workings of providence, who usually seeks "causes in supernatural or legendary explanations, neglecting natural or physical causes. . . . M. Faillon too often forsakes the real to take flight in the conjectural." Here Lareau clearly shows his bias. But he concludes his assessment: "Consequently his history will have a more welcome place in the libraries of religious communities."

Ever mindful of the readership for literary works, Lareau commented particularly on the writings of François Daniel and Louis-Philippe Turcotte*. Daniel's *Histoire des grandes familles françaises du Canada* . . . (1867) is described as a "luxury volume intended to grace salons and libraries." As for Turcotte's *Le Canada sous l'Union, 1841–1867* (1871–72), Lareau judges it a tool useful for men actively engaged in politics, or for young people contemplating a political career.

Despite the moderate tone of this history of Canadian literature, the clerical-Conservative faction did not spare Lareau. Just as they had with Garneau and Charles-Étienne Brasseur* de Bourbourg, the Conservative critics emphasized defects in his presentation in order to discredit the author and his ideas. Thus Narcisse-Henri-Édouard Faucher* de Saint-Maurice criticized him for inaccuracies, a lack of literary style, and an excess of typographical errors, in an attempt to condemn his liberalism more thoroughly. In 1879 critic Rémi Tremblay published under the pseudonym of Father Louison an eight-page pamphlet entitled *Chansonnier politique du canard, avec musique*, with a dialogue between master and pupil: the pupil is questioned about Lareau's literary history in a sequence that brings out its grammatical errors. The critic concludes that "before writing one must learn to think, and . . . to constitute oneself the historian of a country's literature, one must at least have some idea of spelling, style and grammar." As Lareau's friends recalled at the time of his death, the history of literature was a "sin of youth" which according to Faucher de Saint-Maurice he began to commit as soon as he left college.

Lareau's second major work is undoubtedly his two-volume *Histoire du droit canadien depuis les origines de la colonie jusqu'à nos jours*, published in 1888 and 1889. In 1872 with Gonzalve Doutre*, Lareau had produced a similar synthesis which went up to 1791 and was primarily designed as a more or less methodical compilation of facts. This second attempt proved a much more thorough study and remains a classic of Canadian historiography which is still frequently consulted for its scientific value. In the first volume the author deals with the period of the French régime, and in the second with that of the English régime up to 1887. He seldom lets his ideological perspectives distort the scientific exposition of his subject. It is true that Lareau, who admired British liberties, trial by jury, and *laissez-faire* economic policies, did not fail to contrast New England in its rapid progress with a New France stifled in its development by the absolutism of the state and an autocratic system of criminal justice. But the author does not hesitate to use more objective factors to explain the economic stagnation of New France, for example the absence of specie and the deficit in the balance of trade. He also weighs his judgement carefully when dealing with the seigneurial régime. In discussing the relations between church and state in New France, however, Lareau reveals his ideology more explicitly. Those who followed the example of Governor Frontenac [Buade*] and wanted to ensure the supremacy of the state over the church, or to set up mechanisms for popular consultation such as the convocation of the states general, win the historian's admiration, whereas Bishop François de Laval* is judged severely for having supposedly exceeded his authority. To make this point, Lareau conjures up the image of a dominating, absolutist bishop, thus coming close to Garneau's interpretation in his first edition of the *Histoire*. Garneau is moreover not the only liberal writer upon whom Lareau draws. Contrary to the predominant historiography of the second half of the 19th century, Lareau on occasion makes use of the views of abbés Guillaume Raynal and Brasseur de Bourbourg.

The volume devoted to the British régime is freer from ideological discussions. Less nationalistic than Garneau or Sulte, Lareau describes the development of the political and constitutional structure of Canada, drawing on the work of Théophile-Pierre Bédard and Louis-Philippe Turcotte. In this section the legal historian also takes the opportunity to come to the defence of lawyers. He indignantly rejects the epithet of "vermin" which Lahontan [Lom*] bestowed on them. Lareau, who according to *La Patrie* was a lawyer with a large practice, enlivens his remarks with a slight touch of corporatism. Thanks to the law, "the weak find protection against the encroachments of the strong"; the lawyer "has fought against all those who sought to make one man the slave of another. . . . He has done more for the human race than all the philosophical sects put together."

This history by Lareau was not, however, entirely to the liking of the clerical Conservatives. Thomas-Étienne Hamel*, a critic of the journal *Le Canada-français* (Quebec), reproached him for his "prejudices" concerning the status of the church and for his effort to ridicule certain persons and certain questions such as the quarrel over precedence or the discussion to determine whether the tithe was a matter of divine or positive law. But it is none the less true that Lareau gave evidence of a critical spirit that was well above the level usual in 19th-century Quebec.

Throughout his career Lareau never betrayed the ideas defended in his articles or books, with the result that he was not afraid to show his independence towards the "Mercierist" coalition when, beginning in 1889, doubt was cast upon the government's integrity in questions involving corruption and fraud. By his legal, historical, and literary works, Edmond Lareau belonged clearly to the liberal element of his generation, at least to the extent that this group was committed to freedom of thought as against an ultra-conservative attitude of the ultramontane type. Nevertheless, his thinking was never doctrinaire, and he maintained a tolerant attitude towards ideologies opposed to his own.

SERGE GAGNON

[Edmond Lareau was the author of the following works in law, history, and literature: *Tableau des délais fixes contenus dans le Code civil, le Code de procédure civile, les règles de pratique et l'acte de faillite, 1869* (Montréal, 1870); *Le droit civil canadien suivant l'ordre établi par les codes, précédé d'une histoire générale du droit canadien* (Montréal, 1872), which he wrote with Gonzalve Doutre; *Hist. de la littérature canadienne*; *Mélanges historiques et littéraires* (Montréal, 1877); *Libéraux et Conservateurs* (Montréal, 1879); *Réformes judiciaires: examen du rapport de la commission de codification des statuts* (Montréal, 1882); *Histoire abrégée de la littérature* (Montréal, 1884); *Le Code civil du Bas-Canada* (Montréal, 1885); and *Histoire du droit canadien depuis les origines de la colonie jusqu'à nos jours* (2v., Montréal, 1888–89). He also wrote articles for the *Rev. canadienne*, to which he contributed regularly as early as 1875. S.G.]

Débats de la législature provinciale (G.-A. Desjardins *et al.*), IX: 533–36, 629–30, 695–97, 813–15, 1113–16. *Le Canadien*, 6 nov. 1889, 23 avril 1890. Beaulieu et J. Hamelin, *La presse québécoise*, I-III. Borthwick, *Hist. and biog. gazetteer*, 150. *CPC*, 1889: 262. *DOLQ*, I: 316–18, 362–64, 472–73. *Dominion annual register*, 1882–84. Marguerite Gauthier, "Bibliographie d'Edmond Lareau" (thèse de DES, univ. de Montréal, 1943). Le Jeune, *Dictionnaire*, II: 74. Serge Gagnon, *Le Québec et ses historiens de 1840 à 1920: la Nouvelle-France de Garneau à Groulx* (Québec, 1978). Rumilly, *Hist. de la prov. de Québec*, VI. É.-Z. Massicotte, "Notes généalogiques et bibliographiques sur Edmond Lareau," *BRH*, 29 (1923): 69–72.

LAROCHELLE, LOUIS-NAPOLÉON, manufacturer, railway contractor, and politician; b. 14 Nov. 1834 at Saint-Anselme, Lower Canada, son of Siméon Gautron*, *dit* Larochelle, and Sophie Pomerleau; m. there 12 Dec. 1876 Georgiana Plante; d. 27 Oct. 1890 at Saint-Anselme.

After studying at the Petit Séminaire de Québec from 1847 to 1856, Louis-Napoléon Larochelle embarked on a business career. He was the son of an enterprising industrialist who owned a sawmill, foundry, and textile factory; when his father died in 1859, Louis-Napoléon took over his interests. Although little is known about his activities in the local economy of Saint-Anselme, they seem to have made him fairly prosperous. His ability to raise money apparently was good enough to enable him to invest substantial sums in 1873 and 1874 in the Levis and Kennebec Railway Company. In 1885 he lost $20,000 when a carding mill he owned burned down. These facts suggest that Larochelle had considerable resources at his disposal.

It was probably the Levis–Kennebec affair that made Larochelle famous, particularly as a result of his disputes with his partner, Charles Armstrong Scott. Because of his involvement in the local economy, Larochelle was quickly attracted to the Levis and Kennebec Railway Company, incorporated in 1869 to link the town of Lévis with the Atlantic coast by a line through the Beauce region and the state of Maine. In 1870 Larochelle joined such influential politicians as Joseph-Godric BLANCHET, Hector-Louis Langevin*, and Christian Henry POZER on the company's board of directors; the president was Alexandre-René Chaussegros* de Léry. Taking advantage of the political pressure it could bring to bear, the company obtained substantial subsidies from the Quebec government. On 31 Dec. 1870 the contract to build the first 50 miles was awarded to a well-known American promoter of roads with wooden rails, Jerome B. Hulbert, who began the work of levelling in 1871. By the next year the route was ready for the wooden rails but, feeling that these were not likely to stand up to spring thaws, the company opted for iron rails, and consequently had to put up more capital. A new building contract was then granted to Hulbert's previous foreman, Charles Armstrong Scott, and to Louis-Napoléon Larochelle, who was to be the contractor: by its terms they could operate the line for 99 years and were to have a certain number of shares in the company. To further these interests, the two men entered into partnership on 8 Jan. 1873. Acting as guarantor for the necessary credit, Larochelle advanced $30,000 for the construction of the line to encourage English capitalists to supply the rest. At the end of 1873 Scott and Larochelle went to New York to buy a locomotive and 600 tons of rails, paid for by Larochelle, with money borrowed from Judge Joseph-Noël Bossé and James Gibb Ross.

At that time the company decided to issue debentures to provide financial backing for the contractors and commissioned Scott to negotiate these securities. Scott went to London and signed a contract with British broker John Langham Reed for the sale of debentures of the Levis–Kennebec company in the amount of £100,000. Reed, who paid only £55,000 for the debentures, secured the right to resell this issue, bearing 7 per cent interest over a 20-year period, as well as first claim to purchase the next two issues. Because the broker made various deductions Scott and Larochelle actually received only £48,000 (instead of £55,000) on the first debenture sale, and by 1874 the Levis–Kennebec company was saddled with a debt of £100,000 and annual interest payments of £7,000. On 20 June 1875 only the section from Lévis to the Scott junction (28 miles) was put in service, but a provincial subsidy of $4,000 a mile the following year enabled the company to complete the 15½-mile section connecting Scott with Saint-Joseph in the Beauce region. Having laid only 43½ miles of track by 1876, the Levis–Kennebec company was not yet legally authorized to issue the second series of debentures. Reed already had these securities in hand, having got the documents signed in advance by the company's president, Joseph-Godric Blanchet, and he now asked for the third series. Failing in the attempt, Reed demanded to be reimbursed for the entire amount already paid to the Levis–Kennebec company, and this brought its operations to a standstill. Scott and Larochelle declared themselves insolvent. The two contractors became embroiled in a quarrel when Scott transferred to Reed the 65,000 Levis–Kennebec shares he had acquired under the terms of the construction contract; Reed thus gained control of the company.

Anxious to present his version of the facts, Scott in 1877 published a pamphlet entitled *The Levis and Kennebec Railway, and its difficulties*, which prompted Larochelle to defend himself similarly in a pamphlet also brought out that year entitled *Chemin de Lévis et Kennebec; réfutation de la brochure de C. A. Scott*. In it Larochelle attempted to show how Scott had shirked his responsibilities by making over his shares to Reed without requiring him to acknowledge a personal debt of $40,000 to the workers and suppliers of the Levis–Kennebec company. Larochelle further reproached Scott for acting from the outset as a servant of the English capitalists, regularly accepting their "one thousand dollar gifts" and readily submitting to their terms, while pocketing $1,800 annually for representing the company's interests in London. Initially without financial resources, Scott had quickly made a fortune for himself in this operation, which by now had seriously depleted Larochelle's assets.

Meanwhile the Levis–Kennebec company insisted that Reed hand over to it the second series of debentures and at its annual meeting in February 1877 deprived him of the right to exercise his power as principal shareholder. The British bondholders then brought some dozen actions against the company; the result was a complete financial impasse at the beginning of the 1880s when the company was unable to pay the interest on its borrowed capital. The Levis and Kennebec Railway Company went bankrupt, and on 22 March 1881 was finally auctioned by the sheriff, on the steps of the church of Notre-Dame-de-la-Victoire at Lévis, for $192,000. James Robertson Woodward purchased it for the Quebec Central Railway Company.

A supporter of the Quebec Conservative party, Larochelle held many posts in the course of his political career. One of the most distinguished citizens of the region, he served as mayor of Saint-Anselme from 1870 to 1878 and again from 1881 to 1889. In the provincial elections of 1867 he stood in Dorchester County against an influential opponent, Hector-Louis Langevin. In this contest between two Conservatives, Langevin had the advantage of having represented the county for 10 years in the Legislative Assembly of the Province of Canada. In addition Langevin intended to seek the federal seat as well in order to help establish the new federal system, and he promised if elected to devote his salary as an MLA to the needs of the county. Larochelle agreed to withdraw provided that Langevin promised to resign his provincial seat after one year and to give Larochelle his support in the subsequent by-election. Having finally decided to ignore Larochelle's demands Langevin went after and won both seats. In the 1871 provincial elections Langevin stood in the riding of Quebec Centre, leaving the field clear for Larochelle, who was returned for Dorchester by acclamation. That year he was appointed to the legislature's select committee for industrial development. He was re-elected in the elections held four years later.

Larochelle's tendency to independent views became evident when the provincial government of Charles-Eugène Boucher* de Boucherville committed itself in 1875 to building the Quebec, Montreal, Ottawa and Occidental Railway on the north shore of the St Lawrence. The member for Dorchester and four ministers of the Conservative cabinet opposed the government's railway policy, fearing that public subsidies for the railways on the south shore would be reduced. After this quarrel with the party leadership Larochelle did not run in the elections of 1878.

He returned to political life in 1881 but was beaten by Nicodème Audet in the provincial elections in

Dorchester; he finally won the seat, by acclamation, in 1886. At that time the Conservative party of Quebec, led by John Jones Ross*, was the victim of the backlash against Ottawa's refusal to commute the death sentence imposed on Louis RIEL. A few months after his election Larochelle was one of the five "National Conservatives" who withdrew their confidence from the Ross government and thus held the balance of power in the Quebec Legislative Assembly. On 20 Dec. 1886 he and Ferdinand Trudel published a statement in *La Presse* calling on Ross to resign. Honoré Mercier* came to power early in 1887 and the following year appointed Larochelle to the Legislative Council, usually the final stage in a political career.

Larochelle died on 27 Oct. 1890, after some weeks of illness; he was survived by his wife and five children. His funeral, attended by many political figures, was held at Saint-Anselme.

GAÉTAN GERVAIS

Louis-Napoléon Larochelle was the author of *Chemin de Lévis et Kennebec; réfutation de la brochure de C. A. Scott* (Québec, 1877), which was written as a reply to the charges levelled at him by Charles Armstrong Scott some months earlier in a work entitled *The Levis and Kennebec Railway, and its difficulties: a brief history of Larochelle & Scott's connection with the line from its commencement to the present time* (Quebec, 1877).

AC, Beauce (Saint-Joseph de Beauce), État civil, Catholiques, Saint-Anselme, 12 déc. 1876; 30 oct. 1890. ANQ-Q, PQ, TP, Bureau des chemins de fer (mémoires rédigés par L.-N. Larochelle sur les affaires de la Compagnie du chemin de fer de Lévis et Kennebec). ASQ, Fichier des anciens. *Le Canadien*, 28 oct. 1890. *Le Courrier du Canada*, 29, 31 oct. 1890. *La Presse*, 20 déc. 1886. *CPC*, 1889: 246. *Dominion annual register*, 1885: 371; 1886: 366. P.-G. Roy, *Dates lévisiennes* (12v., Lévis, Qué., 1932–40), I–IV. Adrien Bouffard, *Saint-Anselme de Dorchester . . . une paroisse coopérative* (n.p., [1946]), 22, 45. Désilets, *Hector-Louis Langevin*. Gervais, "L'expansion du réseau ferroviaire québécois." M. Hamelin, *Premières années du parlementarisme québécois*. Honorius Provost, *Chaudière Kennebec; grand chemin séculaire* (Québec, 1974). Rumilly, *Hist. de la prov. de Québec*, II–VI. "Les disparus," *BRH*, 39 (1933): 435.

LA ROCQUE (Larocque), JOSEPH, Roman Catholic priest, professor, and bishop; b. 28 Aug. 1808 at Chambly, on the Richelieu River, Lower Canada, son of Timothée-Amable La Rocque and Marie-Angèle Paré; d. 18 Nov. 1887 at Saint-Hyacinthe, Que.

Joseph La Rocque obtained a classical education at the Collège de Saint-Hyacinthe, aided, as was his cousin Charles La Rocque*, by a bursary from the Association pour faciliter les moyens d'éducation dans la Rivière-Chambly. From 1821 to 1829 his love of study, sharp intelligence, and sound judgement always put him at the top of his class. Having first completed the philosophy programme, La Rocque, during his final year of the classical programme (Rhetoric) under Abbé Joseph-Sabin RAYMOND, was asked to replace philosophy instructor Abbé Louis Proulx*, who had unexpectedly been appointed director of the college. "Because of the preparation he put into it, his teaching," according to that institution's historian, "was enjoyed and was completely satisfactory."

La Rocque entered ecclesiastical life in August 1829 and, while studying theology, taught literature at the college either in Saint-Hyacinthe or in his native village. When he returned to the Collège de Saint-Hyacinthe, he taught calligraphy, stenography, and drawing as well as literature. With his friend and former teacher of rhetoric, Raymond, he became involved in a controversy concerning the philosophical basis of certainty, taking the position expounded in France some years earlier by Hugues-Félicité-Robert de La Mennais. A papal condemnation of La Mennais's propositions abruptly ended a lively debate in which the two friends supported each other with more bluster than reason [*see* Isaac-Stanislas Lesieur-Désaulniers*].

Ordained priest on 15 March 1835 by Bishop Jean-Jacques Lartigue*, La Rocque continued to teach at the Collège de Saint-Hyacinthe, with abbés Raymond, Lesieur-Désaulniers, and Jean-Charles Prince*. He was appointed director on 22 July 1840, and superior two years later when Bishop Ignace BOURGET changed the college to a seminary by canonical decree.

In August 1847 Bishop Bourget summoned him to the diocese of Montreal to receive the office of canon in the cathedral chapter. In particular, La Rocque was given the task of editing the *Mélanges religieux*, succeeding Hector-Louis Langevin* when he resigned on 20 July 1849. The *Mélanges* was the official organ of the diocese and at the bishopric people thought that during his two years as editor Langevin had given the journal a marked political bias; this bias was to be emphasized again in the political column for which Langevin was asked to be responsible after his resignation. "Since the *Mélanges* now has a more ecclesiastical character," La Rocque wrote to him on 1 Oct. 1849, "it would appear that as far as possible it should avoid making an assault upon men's passions. . . . I believe you will draw the same conclusion, if you recall how unwelcome priests are when they want to give advice to political partisans." The peace-loving La Rocque, with the collaboration on the paper until December 1849 of Abbé Joseph-François Cénas (a native of Lyons), was obliged despite his inclinations to take up the cudgels against *L'Avenir*; the latter had mounted a scathing attack on the tithe system and, in general, on the clergy's influence, which the Rouges deemed excessive in both politics and education. La Rocque's toughest adversaries were Louis-Antoine

Dessaulles* and Joseph DOUTRE. In September 1851 La Rocque was happy to hand over his position to François-Magloire Derome*, a lawyer. A reluctant journalist, La Rocque was certainly more at ease as spiritual director of the nuns of Notre-Dame de Charité du Bon-Pasteur and the Sisters of Charity of Providence (Sisters of Providence) who were entrusted to his care.

La Rocque accompanied Bishop Prince as his secretary on a trip to Rome in 1852. When in France briefly, La Rocque saw the famous Henri Lacordaire, and their meeting had some bearing on a proposal to establish a Dominican institution at Saint-Hyacinthe. On 6 July 1852, in Rome, Pius IX appointed La Rocque bishop of Cydonia *in partibus infidelium* and coadjutor in Montreal to succeed Bishop Prince, who had been named on 8 June to the new diocese of Saint-Hyacinthe. On his return home, La Rocque was consecrated bishop on 28 October in the church of his native parish. Not content to devote all his energies to the diocese of Montreal, he also undertook the administration of the diocese of Saint-Hyacinthe from 13 Nov. 1856 to 15 July 1857 during Bishop Prince's illness. These heavy strains undermined La Rocque's health, and he began to feel the effect of the disabilities that later forced him to give up his episcopal duties prematurely.

Prince died on 5 May 1860 and La Rocque was his successor, taking possession of the see on 3 September. During his administration of the diocese of Saint-Hyacinthe, six parishes were set up by canonical decree, two new missions were established, and 31 priests were ordained. He visited parishes and missions to ascertain their needs and administer confirmation. Various confraternities were formed, construction was began on the Hôtel-Dieu of Saint-Hyacinthe, and churches and other religious buildings were erected or repaired.

But the bishop's chief accomplishment, with the help of Vicar General Joseph-Sabin Raymond, was the founding on 14 Sept. 1861 of the order of the Sœurs Adoratrices du Précieux-Sang. In the words of Elphège Gravel, a local ecclesiastic who was to become the first bishop of Nicolet, this foundation was a "work of prayer and expiation in the town of Saint-Hyacinthe," destined to counterbalance "the sneers and attacks" of the Institut Canadien, whose president at the time by coincidence was an important citizen of Saint-Hyacinthe, Louis-Antoine Dessaulles.

Bishop La Rocque treated this recalcitrant member of his diocese so leniently that he was rather severely reprimanded by Bishop Bourget of Montreal. Dessaulles, held up to public scorn by an "announcement" read from all the Montreal pulpits on 18 Jan. 1863 concerning his lecture at the Institut Canadien on 23 December, was only too happy, in a letter of 1 Feb. 1864 to Bourget, to contrast "the gentleness and spirit of charity, indulgence, and impartiality" of the bishop of Saint-Hyacinthe with the harshness of the bishop of Montreal. He asserted that La Rocque's comments on his lecture on "progress," and on his other writings, had singled out neither "the frightful monster of rationalism," "its hideous head," or "its poisonous venom," nor "the blasphemies" of the "tribune of pestilence" that Bishop Bourget had branded as infamous in his "announcement." La Rocque admitted that this information, transmitted to him the next day by Bishop Bourget, was "a bitter pill" for his spirit, and he sought to exonerate himself in a letter of 3 Feb. 1864. He noted that the "opinion" Dessaulles was quoting as his authority had been "written with extreme moderation of both *substance* and *form*." "Your Excellency," he continued, "will understand the motive if he reflects on the friendly zeal that makes me desire to see M. Dessaulles return to the principles he acquired in infancy from his devoted mother. But, nevertheless, I certainly have not failed to censure the writer's rationalist tendencies. It is true that I tell readers I am going to pass quickly over this part of the lecture, as over some other parts. My sole intention has been to smother the fire that had set men's minds aflame, and to try to restore the peace we desire."

Bishop La Rocque, in poor health for many years, suffered from sciatica which increasingly confined him to his room; he also had an antipathy to the details of an administration encumbered with a debt of about $44,000, an enormous sum for the period. He begged Pius IX to relieve him of the crushing burden. By a rescript dated 17 Aug. 1865, he was authorized to resign his bishopric and was transferred to the see of Germanicopolis *in partibus infidelium*. In July the following year he handed over the direction of the diocese to his cousin and successor, Bishop Charles La Rocque, and went to live with the Sœurs Adoratrices du Précieux-Sang.

His retirement was a fruitful one. It enabled him to strengthen the congregation he had founded and to draft its fundamental laws. In addition he was the author of *Dévotion au Précieux Sang* and of *L'Année ecclésiastique et liturgique*, a compilation of reflections for Sundays throughout the year and the principal solemn ceremonies of the church; he also wrote a series of meditations for the *Retraites annuelles*. He celebrated the 50th year of his ordination on 19 March 1885. Two years and eight months later, on 18 Nov. 1887, he died, surrounded by his religious family, at the age of 79. He was buried in the cemetery of the Sœurs Adoratrices du Précieux-Sang.

"Bishop Joseph," as he was familiarly called by a small circle of close friends, was noted for his shrewd mind, conversational charm, and polished manners. For Louis-Thomas Bourgeois, a French Dominican who had known him at Saint-Hyacinthe, "his generosity and noble mind and spirit made him one of the most likeable of men."

PHILIPPE SYLVAIN

Joseph La Rocque was the author of *L'Année ecclésiastique et liturgique, comprenant toute l'année chrétienne depuis la XXIVe semaine après la Pentecôte jusqu'à la fin de l'année ecclésiastique suivante* (Montréal, 1887) and of *Dévotion au Précieux Sang, spécialement préparé pour le mois du Précieux Sang (juillet)* (4e éd., Saint-Hyacinthe, Qué., 1897).

ACAM, 901.135, 864-1, -2. *Mandements, lettres pastorales et circulaires des évêques de Saint-Hyacinthe*, A.-X. Bernard, édit. (8v., Montréal, 1888–98), II: 5–16. *Mélanges religieux* (Montréal), juillet 1849–septembre 1851. É.-J.[-A.] Auclair, *Mère Catherine-Aurélie; histoire de mère Catherine-Aurélie du Précieux-Sang, née Aurélie Caouette, fondatrice de l'Institut du Précieux-Sang au Canada, 1833–1905* (Québec, 1923), 422ff. C.-P. Choquette, *Histoire du séminaire de Saint-Hyacinthe depuis sa fondation jusqu'à nos jours* (2v., Montréal, 1911–12), I. Désilets, *Hector-Louis Langevin*, 49. Monet, *Last cannon shot*, 133. A.-J. Plourde, *Dominicains au Canada* (3v. to date, Montréal, 1973–), I, no.1. Claude Galarneau, "L'abbé Joseph-Sabin Raymond et les grands romantiques français (1834–1857)," CHA *Report*, 1963: 85.

LA RUE (Larue), FRANÇOIS-ALEXANDRE-HUBERT, doctor, professor, chemist, and writer; b. 24 March 1833 at Saint-Jean, Île d'Orléans, Lower Canada, son of Nazaire Larue and Adélaïde Roy; m. 10 July 1860 Marie-Alphonsine, daughter of Judge Philippe Panet*, and they had ten children; d. 25 Sept. 1881 at Quebec City and was buried in the cemetery of his native village.

François-Alexandre-Hubert La Rue received a classical education at the Petit Séminaire de Québec before he entered the Quebec School of Medicine, which gave place to the faculty of medicine of the Université Laval organized in 1853. In 1855 La Rue was the first person, and the only one that year, to receive a bachelor of medicine from the faculty. He was immediately selected by the Séminaire de Québec to go to the university at Louvain to study medical jurisprudence and chemistry. Realizing that he was wasting his time at Louvain, La Rue went to the École de Médicine in Paris, where he obtained sound scientific training. On his return in 1859 he defended the first doctoral thesis in medicine at Université Laval, and taught there, first forensic medicine and chemistry, then histology and toxicology. In 1862 he succeeded Thomas Sterry Hunt* as professor of inorganic chemistry in the faculty of arts, which in 1867 conferred an MA on him. In 1875 the federal government appointed him analytical chemist for the Quebec region under the provisions of the 1874 act to prevent the adulteration of food, drink, and drugs.

La Rue was a pioneer in several fields. His thesis on suicide is a remarkable work which interprets statistics and includes a medical and philosophical study of the moral responsibility of both rational and insane persons committing suicide. Gifted with a sharp mind and ready pen, the author frequented the bookshop of Octave Crémazie*, the meeting-place of the Quebec literary school. In 1861, with Abbé Henri-Raymond Casgrain* as moving spirit, Antoine GÉRIN-LAJOIE, and Joseph-Charles Taché*, La Rue founded *Les Soirées canadiennes*, and he afterwards contributed to *Le Foyer canadien*. Although he had some skill as a writer, La Rue is of interest more for the number of subjects with which he was able to deal than for his literary style. His shrewd observations of material and psychological realities are well conveyed by his clear, concise, picturesque, and, when necessary, vigorous style. These qualities characterize both his didactic and his popular works, as well as his literary writings such as the "Voyage autour de l'Île d'Orléans" in *Les Soirées canadiennes* (1861), "Les Chansons populaires et historiques du Canada" in *Le Foyer canadien* (1865), *Voyage sentimental sur la Rue Saint-Jean . . .* (1879), and the articles, speeches, and lectures gathered in the two-volume *Mélanges historiques, littéraires et d'économie politique*.

La Rue was a man of medium height, with a thick head of hair that receded with the years, making his high, broad brow more prominent. His strong jaw and piercing eyes gave him a look of severity which his moustache softened. His gait was quick and he spoke in a curt and abrupt manner. Although he demanded a high standard at examinations, his students remembered him as a professor who knew how to humanize his learning. He was a clever conversationalist and was much sought after as a lecturer; his wit made his lessons pleasant. Yet he was anxious to give guidance and stimulus to his fellow-countrymen.

A practical man, La Rue sought reforms in education and in agriculture. His article, "De l'éducation dans la province de Québec," which appeared in the second volume of the *Mélanges* among other places, was an indictment of the elementary schools, which he felt were accomplishing nothing. He hoped that in the old parishes these schools would disappear and be replaced by model schools whose programmes appeared more satisfactory to him, although he was severely critical of their teaching methods and textbooks. Secondary teaching also left much to be desired, because of a lack of competent teachers and an undue emphasis on memory rather than reason. He suggested remedies and, practising what he preached, wrote textbooks for his own children on Canadian and American history, arithmetic, and grammar, which he published. He also addressed himself to adults, who spoke in a language which was deteriorating, who had ceased to read after leaving school, and who were indifferent to learning.

After his thesis was published, La Rue did not resume his scientific work, which was to be his major achievement, until 1867. From that time he was increasingly absorbed in it. He became interested in metallurgy, and also wanted to improve the prevailing old-fashioned farming customs by the use of methods based on chemistry, physics, and botany. Instead of the settlement of distant territories, he wanted to see restored the value of already depleted lands closer to home, and to set an example he worked his father's land with his brothers. He also began to publish manuals. In 1868 he and Abbé François PILOTE recommended that agricultural teaching be entrusted to specialized schools, rather than being left to normal schools as Pierre-Joseph-Olivier CHAUVEAU advocated. In 1870 Chauveau offered the Université Laval a grant for applied science courses. La Rue had already drawn up the programme, with Abbé Thomas-Étienne Hamel*, and given a course on agricultural chemistry when the university decided to refuse the grant in order to avoid any political interference. In 1873 the commissioner of agriculture and public works for the province of Quebec instructed him to draft a *Petit manuel d'agriculture à l'usage des cultivateurs*; by 1877 his *Petit manuel d'agriculture à l'usage des écoles élémentaires*, first published in 1870, was in its 13th edition.

In 1868 and 1869, about 12 years before Thomas Alva Edison patented a similar device, La Rue had obtained Canadian and American patents for a magnetic sand separator which he had invented with Quebec clockmaker Cyrille Duquet and improved with Abbé Isidore-François-Octave Audet. The invention was developed to assist William Markland Molson's Moisie Iron Works in mining the magnetic sands on the north shore of the St Lawrence. La Rue had earlier worked in Pittsburgh, Pa, with Louis Labrèche-Viger*, the inventor of Viger's steel, on processes for extracting iron and manufacturing steel from these ores in a single operation. As their processes differed, each had patented them in Canada and in the United States, and in 1874 La Rue had also obtained a patent for a process for concentrating pyrites to extract their magnetite. The Molson company exported iron, mostly to the United States, until it went bankrupt in 1875 [*see* William Molson*]. La Rue was one of those who in 1876 supported Dr Joseph-Alexandre CREVIER for the post of palæontologist on the Geological Survey of Canada. But it is La Rue rather than Crevier who deserves the title of the first French Canadian scientist.

La Rue was not active in politics but, as a friend and colleague of François Langelier*, he was considered a liberal by the Ultramontanes. During the university dispute [*see* Ignace BOURGET; Joseph DESAUTELS], Bishop Louis-François Laflèche*, in a report to the Holy See in 1873, quoted testimony of Joseph-Édouard CAUCHON gratuitously accusing the Laval professors of being free-thinkers. However, when La Rue treated the sensitive subject of suicide he clearly showed his religious convictions, as he did in many other writings. He also intervened to prevent religious congregations from being subject to municipal taxes which he deemed unfair. In 1882, a year after La Rue's death, Abbé Hamel was to take up Cauchon's charges and to defend vigorously the reputation of his friend.

LÉON LORTIE

[François-Alexandre-Hubert La Rue published many works in addition to his articles in *Le Foyer canadien* (Québec), *Les Soirées canadiennes* (Québec), and *L'Événement* (Québec). In 1859 he issued in Quebec, under the pseudonym Isidore de Méplats, *Le Défricheur de langue; tragédie bouffe en trois actes et trois tableaux*. His other writings were signed Hubert La Rue or F.-A.-H. La Rue, and include the following published at Quebec: *Du suicide* (1859); *Réponse au mémoire de MM. Brousseau, frères, imprimeurs des "Soirées canadiennes"* (1862); *Éloge funèbre de M. l'abbé L.-J. Casault, premier recteur de l'université Laval, prononcé le 8 janvier 1863* (1863); *Éléments de chimie et de physique agricoles* (1868); *Les corporations religieuses catholiques de Québec* (1870), translated as *The Catholic religious corporations of the city of Quebec* (1870); *Études sur les industries de Québec* (1870); *Mélanges historiques, littéraires et d'économie politique* (2v., 1870–81); *Petit manuel d'agriculture à l'usage des cultivateurs* (1873); *Histoire populaire du Canada, ou entretiens de Madame Genest à ses petits-enfants* (1875); *Les corporations religieuses catholiques de Québec et les nouvelles taxes qu'on veut leur imposer* (1876), translated as *The Catholic religious corporations of the city of Quebec and the proposed new taxations* (1877); *Petit manuel d'agriculture, d'horticulture et d'arboriculture* (1878); *De la manière d'élever les jeunes enfants du Canada, ou entretiens de Madame Genest à ses enfants* (1879); "Éloge de l'agriculture, rapport du docteur Hubert LaRue sur le concours d'agriculture ouvert par l'Institut canadien de Québec," Institut canadien de Québec, *Annuaire* (Québec), 1879: 83–101; *Voyage sentimental sur la Rue Saint-Jean, départ en 1860, retour en 1880, causeries et fantaisies aux 21* (1879); *Petite arithmétique très élémentaire à l'usage des jeunes enfants* (1880); *Petite grammaire française très élémentaire à l'usage des jeunes enfants* (1880); *Petite histoire des États-Unis très élémentaire ou entretiens de Madame Genest à ses petits-enfants* (1880). With Michel-Édouard Méthot*, he also wrote *Souvenir consacré à la mémoire vénérée de M. L.-J. Casault, premier recteur de l'université Laval* (1863). L.L.]

L'Opinion publique, 13 nov. 1881. C.-M. Boissonnault, *Histoire de la faculté de médecine de Laval* (Québec, 1953). Yolande Bonenfant, "Le docteur Hubert Larue (1833–1881)," *Trois siècles de médecine québécoise* (Québec, 1970), 83–97. Merrill Denison, *The barley and the stream: the Molson story; a footnote to Canadian history* (Toronto, 1955). Jean Du Sol [Charles Angers], *Docteur Hubert LaRue et l'idée canadienne française* (Québec, 1912). Jean Piquefort [A.-B. Routhier], *Portraits et pastels littéraires* (Québec, 1873). Léon Lortie, "Siderurgical inventions in early Canada," *Canadian Patent Reformer* (Montreal), 2nd ser., 18 (1975): 65–68. Arthur Maheux, "P.-J.-O. Chauveau, promoteur des sciences," RSC *Trans.*, 4th ser., 1 (1963), sect.I: 87–103.

LAUDER, ABRAM (Abraham) WILLIAM, lawyer and politician; b. 6 June 1834 at Bewcastle (Cumbria), England, son of Thomas D. Lauder; d. 20 Feb. 1884 at Toronto, Ont.

Abram William Lauder received his early education at Canonbie and Langholm (Dumfries and Galloway), Scotland. It is not known when he came to Canada but in 1853 he received a provincial certificate from the Toronto Normal School. He taught for four years in Ontario County. In 1856 Lauder married Maria (Marie) Elise Toof of Whitby, who was later to write travel books. Their only child, William Waugh*, became an outstanding pianist.

In 1857 Lauder and his wife moved to Toronto where he became a law student. He articled with the firm of Ross, Crawford and Crombie and was called to the bar in 1864. He and John Ross*, senior member of the firm in which he had articled, established the firm of Ross and Lauder. Lauder remained in partnership with Ross until the latter's death in 1871. He continued a successful law practice in Toronto until he died.

Lauder first entered the political arena in September 1867 when he successfully stood for election to the Ontario legislature in the riding of Grey South. He took a non-partisan position in his first election and supported the coalition government of John Sandfield Macdonald*. However, as his political career progressed he clarified both his loyalty and his ideology, becoming a supporter of the Conservative party. His re-election on 21 March 1871 was based on his constant attention to his constituency, a predominantly farming community. Thus he argued against land policies that favoured speculation and supported land reform legislation in 1868. He also favoured expansion of railways to his riding and in 1869 took an active role as the government trustee of the municipal bonds for the development of the Toronto, Grey and Bruce Railway.

Lauder, in speeches in the legislature, regularly condemned corrupt practices at all levels of government. It was ironic, therefore, and probably extremely painful, that he himself should be accused of corruption. Following the election of 1871, a constituent, Alexander Hunter, filed a petition against Lauder on 26 April. A trial was begun in Owen Sound in September, and then adjourned until November when Oliver Mowat*, who presided, declared that Lauder had not been duly elected. Although Mowat found that one of Lauder's workers had contravened the Election Act of 1868 by using bribery, travel expenses, and "entertainment," in the form of liquor, to obtain votes, neither candidate was found guilty of corrupt practices. Lauder was able to stand in the by-election and was again returned, in January 1872. The campaign for this contest provided him with an opportunity for revenge.

In the house he produced affidavits from five of his constituents which charged John W. Lewis, a government land valuator, with influencing voters in Proton by promising that the new Liberal government under Edward Blake* would take a "liberal policy" in dealing with the residents of Grey County. Lauder also implicated such prominent Liberals as Archibald McKellar*, Adam Oliver, Blake, and Blake's law partner James Kirkpatrick Kerr*. A select committee (headed by John Charles Rykert, "an unswerving Conservative") assembled on 9 Feb. 1872 and the "Proton Outrage" investigation began. McKellar, Oliver, and Kerr all testified, as did Thomas Hall Johnson, the assistant commissioner of crown lands. Blake also appeared briefly to deny any complicity. Lauder, although not a member of the committee, conducted most of the questioning. The unanimous report delivered on 29 February found Lewis culpable and implicated Oliver, McKellar, and Kerr, but absolved all others. Lauder's political success then continued unabated; after the redistribution of the Grey County ridings in 1874 he was elected for Grey East until his death.

Perhaps the most dramatic moment in Lauder's life occurred shortly after the investigation, during the Toronto printers' strike of 1872. Lauder was one of the lawyers hired by the Toronto Typographical Union to defend its strike committee which had been charged with conspiracy by the Master Printers' Association under an English law of 1792 constraining labour combinations. At a protest rally on 16 April which followed the arrests of the union leaders, Lauder delivered a moving impromptu address in which he rejected the master printers' exploitation of the confused condition of Canadian law concerning labour organizations. He condemned these unwarranted arrests for being "at variance with freedom and equality." As a Conservative, he was perhaps encouraged in his defence of civil liberty by the fact that George Brown*, the prominent Liberal, had initiated the legal action.

Lauder's contribution was that of an intelligent, principled member of the community whose consciousness of responsibility is reflected in both his professional and his non-professional duties. He was also secretary treasurer for Canada of the Star Life Insurance Company, based in Britain, and, with John Ross, was a promoter and initial shareholder of the Dominion Bank. A Methodist, he negotiated with Egerton Ryerson the purchase of the land on which the Metropolitan Church in Toronto was built and he was a member of the senate of Victoria College at Cobourg.

SALLY F. ZERKER

Ont., Legislative Library, Newspaper Hansard, 30 Dec. 1867 (mfm. at AO); Legislative Assembly, *Journals*, 1867–68; 1871–73; Legislature, *Sessional papers*, 1873, III: no.49; *Statutes*, 1868, c.8; 1868–69, c.20, c.21; 1870–71, c.3. *Globe*, 21 Feb. 1884. *Ontario Workman* (Toronto), 18 April, 9 May 1872. *Canadian biog. dict.*, I: 90–92. *Canadian men and women of the time* (Morgan, 1898), 564. *CPC*, 1873: 331; 1881: 249.

LAURASON. *See* LAWRASON

LAURIN, JOSEPH, author, notary, trade unionist, politician, and public servant; b. 18 Oct. 1811 at Quebec City, son of Joseph Laurin and Catherine Fluet; m. 3 Sept. 1839, in the parish of Saint-Joseph (now in Lauzon), Lower Canada, Marie-Louise, daughter of merchant Étienne Dalaire (Dallaire); d. 3 March 1888 at Ancienne-Lorette, Que.

After completing a classical education at the Petit Séminaire de Québec from 1824 to 1833, Joseph Laurin remained there for a year to study theology and to teach. In 1834 he was transferred as a teacher to the Collège de Sainte-Anne-de-la-Pocatière but he gave up the idea of becoming a priest that year and sought training in the office of notary Fabien Ouellet at Quebec City. Obliged to pay for his studies, Laurin drew on his pedagogical experience to put together five works designed to remedy the lack of school texts at this period. Thus between 1836 and 1839 he published *Traité d'arithmétique, Livre destiné à l'instruction de l'enfance, Traité sur la tenue des livres, Le chansonnier canadien, ou nouveau recueil de chansons*, and *Géographie élémentaire.* These books, which according to *Le Fantasque* of Quebec showed a sometimes questionable scholarly rigidity, reveal the author's belief in the necessity of training the mind: "Without education, a man cannot do for his fellows all the good they have a right to expect from him in society, nor can he hold the distinguished rank that enlightenment always ensures for the person possessing it. It is therefore each person's duty . . . to use his influence to encourage men to cultivate their minds."

Laurin was admitted to the notarial profession on 20 Aug. 1839 and established himself on Rue Couillard in Quebec City. An examination of his minute book, which contains more than 9,197 acts for the period 1839 to 1888, shows that he had a large clientele, which was drawn particularly from the working classes. A year after he opened his office, one of the first great strikes in the history of the working-class movement in Canada broke out in the shipyards along the Rivière Saint-Charles at Quebec City. More than 800 shipwrights stopped production to show their dissatisfaction with the owners of the shipbuilding yards, who had for some time been trying, through a coalition, to keep salaries as low as possible. In December 1840 the workers, wanting to organize their defence effectively, founded the Société Amicale et Bienviellante des Charpentiers de Vaisseaux de Québec. On this occasion Laurin, who was sympathetic to the aspirations of the workers, was elected secretary and legal adviser to the society; in this capacity he drafted both its request for incorporation and its by-laws. At a meeting on 21 December Laurin declared he "would make every endeavour to uphold the shipwrights in their noble determination to oppose vigorously and unremittingly the hateful monopoly of the master shipbuilders, who, not content with having exploited the toil and sweat of the poor shipwrights to amass wealth, also want in this harsh season to rob them and their families at one fell swoop of all means of subsistence by offering them a mere pittance, while they sell their ships at a good price on the other side of the Atlantic." As a result of this organized response, the owners of the shipyards bowed to the workers' demands in a few days and raised their wages from 3 to 4 shillings a day. This first victory added strength to the new trade union.

Laurin was also active in politics, In the 1836 elections he ran in Saguenay as a candidate favouring the 92 resolutions; although he was motivated by a restrained patriotism, he was confronted with a campaign to discredit him led by the *Quebec Gazette.* He failed to obtain enough support and withdrew his candidature after 13 days. Nevertheless in 1844 he was elected for Lotbinière to the Legislative Assembly of the Province of Canada ; he retained this seat until 1854 when he was defeated by John O'Farrell, a Quebec lawyer, in an election declared fraudulent. During his ten years in the house Laurin struggled against instances of oppression of French Canadian people. Thus in 1844 he protested against English being used almost exclusively in the assembly and called for enforcement of the parliamentary regulation that all statutes and associated documents be translated into the two languages. But in the following year a motion made by Laurin was declared inadmissible by the speaker, Sir Allan Napier MacNab*, because it was written in French. Louis-Hippolyte La Fontaine* tried unsuccessfully to have the speaker's decision overturned. In 1849, during the debate on a bill for electoral reform, the young notary put forward a motion to bring in a system of proportional representation in order to correct the electoral injustices experienced by Canada East since 1840; when this motion was defeated, he joined those calling for the repeal of the union. Laurin's name is associated particularly with the 1847 act to organize the notarial profession in Canada East; the bill incorporated a concept Laurin had put forward, the setting up of three boards of notaries (at Montreal, Trois-Rivières, and Quebec) authorized to issue certificates to candidates and to supervise professional practice.

Concerned about the proper conduct of his profession, Laurin in 1840 helped found the Association des Notaires du District de Québec [*see* Louis-Édouard GLACKMEYER]. He also served as the first secretary of the Quebec Board of Notaries from 1848 to 1862, was its treasurer from 1862 to 1868, and became its president in 1868, retaining this office until 1870. During these years, Laurin concentrated on dealing with the board's current business and at times sat on its committees, such as one to study the bill embodying the new civil code in 1865 [*see* René-Édouard Caron*] and another which in 1868 was to draft a bill to amend the 1847 legislation relating to the notarial profession. This last bill was adopted in 1870 by the Quebec Legislative Assembly, and brought the members of the profession together in a single corporation, the Quebec Provincial Board of Notaries.

Throughout his career Laurin carried out diverse administrative, legal, and military duties. Thus he represented Saint-Roch Ward on the municipal council of Quebec City from 1843 to 1846, and later served as mayor of the village of Ancienne-Lorette. For several years he was a commissioner on the Court of Queen's Bench and justice of the peace for the district of Quebec. Laurin, who was described as physically robust, was given in 1847 the rank of captain in the local militia and in 1858 became a lieutenant-colonel. Three years earlier he had accepted a commission as crown lands agent and also as agent for the conversion of land tenure in the *censive* (seigneurial area) of Quebec. In 1868 he became superintendent of waterside lots in the province of Quebec and agent for the Lauson seigneury; he retained these posts until 1887.

Laurin died on 3 March 1888 at the residence in Ancienne-Lorette which he had purchased in 1845 from his friend, the musician and notary Louis-Édouard Glackmeyer. This house had been named Montebello, in honour of Louis-Joseph Papineau*, whom Laurin greatly admired.

LUCIE BOUFFARD and ROBERT TREMBLAY

Joseph Laurin was the author of *Traité d'arithmétique, contenant une claire et familière explication de ses principes, et suivi d'un traité d'algèbre* (Québec, 1836); *Livre destiné à l'instruction de l'enfance, ou nouvel alphabet français à l'usage des enfans* (Québec, 1837); *Traité sur la tenue des livres, en partie simple et en partie double, rédigé pour la classe mercantile* (Québec, 1837); *Le chansonnier canadien, ou nouveau recueil de chansons* (Québec, 1838); and *Géographie élémentaire, par demandes et par réponses, à l'usage des écoles* (Québec, 1839). His minute books (1839–88) are at the ANQ-Q.

ANQ-Q, État civil, Catholiques, Notre-Dame de Québec, 18 oct. 1811. *Debates of the Legislative Assembly of United Canada* (Gibbs *et al.*), VIII: 189–90, 349–50, 1427–28. *Le Canadien*, 13 janv. 1836, 21 déc. 1840, 20 janv. 1841. *Le Fantasque* (Québec), 3 juin 1839, 10 déc. 1840. *DOLQ*, I: 244. Ouellet, *Hist. économique*, 500–1. J.-E. Roy, *Hist. du notariat*, III: 57, 137–46, 148, 227, 317, 351, 436–37, 446. S. B. Ryerson, *Le capitalisme et la Confédération: aux sources du conflit Canada-Québec (1760–1873)*, André d'Allemagne, trad. (Montréal, 1972), 231–35. Réal Bertrand, "Le notaire Joseph Laurin", *Vie française* (Québec), 15 (1960–61): 218–28. Lionel Groulx, "Faillite d'une politique," *RHAF*, 2 (1948–49): 81–96.

LAVIGNE, AZARIE, cabinet-maker and furniture dealer; b. in March 1841, son of Hippolyte Lavigne and Lucie Brodeur; d. unmarried on 10 Feb. 1890 in Montreal, Que.

Where Azarie Lavigne was born is not clear, but he served his apprenticeship in Montreal under John Hilton* and his son William. Hilton was the acknowledged leader of the Montreal cabinet trade until his death in 1866, and Lavigne used the connection with him as a recommendation. Lavigne opened his business in 1865, at age 24. From the beginning he was a cabinet-maker and a furniture dealer, selling both his own and other makers' furniture. He also offered furniture-repairing services.

Lavigne soon acquired a reputation for his own furniture, particularly his custom-made pieces; at the Provincial Agricultural and Industrial Exhibition, held in Montreal in 1873, he won first prize for a set of furniture in Louis XVI style, specially made for one of his clients. He also made the mayor's chair for the Montreal City Hall opened in 1878.

By the mid 1880s Lavigne was involved in the production of art furniture and had named his firm the Dominion Art Furniture Factory. Theoretically, the claim to art furniture production implied a manifest distinction between a common furniture factory and one that retained the services of an art director or an artist-designer. In practice the term was used loosely. Some cabinet-makers with an eye to business seized on the fashionable phrase to boost sales but simply continued with ordinary mass production. There was in any event no clear definition of art furniture; it presumably met standards of taste adhered to by followers of the Aesthetic movement, which had begun in England and which made a cult of the science of beauty. From the 1870s the movement had its followers in Montreal. At the Dominion Art Furniture Factory, Lavigne turned out a wide variety of fashionable goods, some of which were probably ebonized and showed traces of the Japanese-inspired asymmetrical lines dictated by the aestheticism of the period. There is nothing to suggest he made any original or significant contribution to the trend, but he did demonstrate initiative in keeping abreast of the times.

Lavigne's business was small compared to that of Montreal competitors such as Owen McGarvey*, who did ten times as great a volume of trade. None the less, between 1881 and 1887 Lavigne managed to raise his credit rating from fair to good. His success was attained in the face of difficulties. On 15 Sept. 1881 his factory was destroyed by fire and three of his carvers were seriously injured. Only a fraction of the loss, estimated at about $20,000, was covered by insurance.

Upon Lavigne's death in 1890, his business was taken over by Rasmus Tombyll, who had previously operated a furniture factory on Rue Notre-Dame.

ELIZABETH COLLARD

AC, Montréal, État civil, Catholiques, Notre-Dame de Montréal, 13 févr. 1890. *Gazette* (Montreal), 17 Sept. 1873, 16 Sept. 1881. *Montreal Daily Witness*, 4 Dec. 1867, 18 Dec. 1890. *Montreal Herald*, 17, 19 Sept. 1873. *La Patrie*, 11 févr. 1890. *La Presse*, 12 févr. 1890. *Toronto Daily Mail*, 16 Sept. 1881. *The mercantile agency reference book . . .* (Toronto and Montreal), 1881; 1887. *Mitchell & Co's Canada classified directory*, 1865; 1866. *Montreal directory*, 1865–90. Léon Trépanier, "Nos hôtels de ville," *Cahiers des Dix*, 25 (1960): 231.

LAVIGUEUR, CÉLESTIN (baptized **Jean-Célestin**), musician and composer; b. 19 Jan. 1831 at Quebec City, son of Jean Delage, *dit* Lavigueur, and Marguerite Douglass; d. 11 Dec. 1885 at Lowell, Mass.

Célestin Lavigueur showed a talent for music at an early age and seems to have devoted himself entirely to studying it after he terminated his classical studies at the end of his second year at the Petit Séminaire de Québec. Although introduced to the violin through lessons from notary François Huot, Lavigueur quickly acquired the essential musical skills by himself. He gave violin recitals in salons and musical groups, and at 22 his reputation earned him an invitation to the Petit Séminaire de Québec, where he taught piano, violin, and wind instruments from 1853 to 1881. He also did keyboard and orchestral arrangements for the seminary band.

Lavigueur enjoyed considerable success as a concert artist. The public was charmed immediately by his tall, elegant figure, and by the magnetism he exuded from the moment his bow touched the strings. Critics did not hesitate to call this musician who had acquired an ability to play in a stirring and engaging fashion a genius. With Marie-Hippolyte-Antoine Dessane* he organized concerts in which both performed. His repertoire, as was common in the province of Quebec at the time, probably consisted mostly of airs transcribed from Rossini, Donizetti, or Meyerbeer; to these he occasionally added works of his own composition.

A self-taught composer, Lavigueur usually wrote songs for specific occasions. "La huronne," like "Au Canada, beau pays, ma patrie," was intended for patriotic celebrations and "Donnez" gave an invitation to assist the victims of the fire that devastated the wards of Saint-Roch and Saint-Sauveur in Quebec City in 1866. "Pas de Thibault, c'est Laurier qu'il nous faut," a political song, supported the cause of Wilfrid Laurier* in the 1877 federal election in the county of Quebec East. Lavigueur also composed a sentimental song, "Soyez les bienvenus," dedicated to the Marquess of Lorne [Campbell*] and his wife Princess Louise, as well as others such as "Amour," "Thérèse la blonde," "Le petit ramoneur," "Le nom de sa sœur," and "La fauvette du canton." He wrote three operas, which were favourably received by the Quebec public: *La fiancée des bois* was based on a text by Léon-Pamphile Le May*; for *Un mariage improvisé* and *Les enfants du manoir* he himself wrote the libretti.

In 1881, at the invitation of one of his sons, Lavigueur settled with his family in Lowell. No doubt he hoped to find more opportunities there to use his gifts, and perhaps he was seeking material security as were so many other musicians emigrating from Quebec at that time. His Franco-American compatriots did have the chance to enjoy his work, but death caught him in mid career putting the finishing touches to his opera *Les enfants du manoir*.

Lavigueur had married Mary Childs of Quebec on 19 Jan. 1863, and they had four children, including Émile, a violinist, and Henri-Edgar*, who was mayor and MP of the city of Quebec. Lavigueur's contemporaries have described him as impressionable, gentle, and above all sensitive to the beauty of nature and the poetry of life. It was probably his enthusiasm and artistic sincerity that brought this self-taught man his great public acclaim and the honour of being elected to the Académie des Muses Santones of France in 1885.

ANTOINE BOUCHARD

ANQ-Q, État civil, Catholiques, Saint-Roch (Québec), 20 janv. 1831, 19 janv. 1863. ASQ, Fichier des anciens; MSS, 433; Séminaire, 183, nos.5e, 5j, 6b, 10a. Canadian Music Library Assoc., *A bio-bibliographical finding list of Canadian musicians and those who have contributed to music in Canada* (Ottawa, [1961]). *Catalogue of Canadian composers*, ed. Helmut Kallmann (2nd ed., Toronto, 1952; repr. St Clair Shores, Mich., 1972), 151. *Dictionnaire biographique des musiciens canadiens* (2e éd., Lachine, Qué., 1935). *Grove's dictionary of music and musicians* (5th ed., ed. Eric Blom, 9v. and 1 suppl., London, 1954–61), V: 89. Helmut Kallmann, *A history of music in Canada, 1534–1914* (Toronto and London, 1960), 93. Nazaire Levasseur, "Musique et musiciens à Québec," *La Musique* (Québec), 1 (1919): 111; 2 (1920): 47, 50, 186; 3 (1921): 98–100; 4 (1922): 143. Antoine Roy, "Célestin Lavigueur," *BRH*, 38 (1932): 710–12.

LAWRASON, LAWRENCE (the name often appears as **Laurence Laurason**), merchant and politician; b. 10 Aug. 1803 in Ancaster Township, Upper

Canada, youngest child of Lawrence Lawrason and Rachel Pettit; m. 21 May 1827 Abigail Lee, and they had four children; d. 14 Aug. 1882 at London, Ont.

At age 14 Lawrence Lawrason became a clerk for the dry goods merchants James Hamilton and John Warren, working at the mouth of the Grand River, at Queenston, and finally at Sterling (St Thomas). In 1819 Lawrason returned to his father's farm but three years later purchased, with two of his brothers, over 550 acres in London Township, a few miles northwest of the land reserved for the town of London. In addition to farming he established a general store, ashery, and distillery in imitation of the activities of Hamilton and Warren. In 1825 Lawrason was appointed London's first deputy postmaster, a position he held until 1828 when the post office moved closer to the town.

In 1832 Lawrason moved into London and in September opened a general store and dry goods business, both retail and wholesale, in partnership with George Jervis Goodhue*. Like many of the early London merchants Lawrason engaged in large-scale land speculation in the region. He was also involved in attempts to promote local projects. Throughout the 1830s he unsuccessfully supported a scheme to make the Thames River navigable between London and Chatham. Lawrason was also an original shareholder in the London and Gore Rail Road Company incorporated in 1834. He was commissioned a justice of the peace in 1835 and three years later was appointed one of three boundary line commissioners for the London District to adjudicate both public and private boundary disputes.

Goodhue left the partnership in 1840 but Lawrason continued on his own until 1845 when he formed a partnership with his wife's nephew, Hiram Chisholm. From 1842 to 1850, with the exception of 1846, Lawrason was one of the representatives of London Township on the London District Council. In a provincial by-election for London in January 1844, necessitated by the resignation of Hamilton Hartley Killaly*, Lawrason, a staunch Conservative, overwhelmed the Reform candidate, Simeon Morrill*. In the general election in October he defeated a more liberal Conservative opponent, John Duggan of Toronto. Lawrason, however, relinquished his seat to William Henry Draper* in January 1845 so that Draper would be able to lead the government party from within the assembly. Also in that year Lawrason was named a rebellion losses claims officer for the London District.

During the 1850s Lawrason continued to be involved in local affairs. In 1850 he was elected to the town council in London for St Patrick's Ward. He also served as president of the London and Port Stanley Railway Company from 1853 to 1857 and was honoured by having the first locomotive purchased by the company named the *L. Lawrason*. As well Lawrason was a director of the Bank of Upper Canada, a trustee of the London Savings' Bank, and president of the Proof Line Road Company and the London Building Society. He retired from his partnership with Chisholm in 1855 at which time the business was dissolved. According to R. G. Dun and Company he had "retired rich."

After his retirement, Lawrason lent large sums of money to his son-in-law, Lionel Augustus Ridout*, a hardware merchant in London (brother of George Percival* and Joseph Davis RIDOUT), and also gave security for a further $72,600 in loans and credit received by Ridout. The combination of the depressed economy in the late 1850s and the death of Ridout in 1859 seriously injured Lawrason's financial position. Finally, in 1864, he declared bankruptcy. During the late 1860s and early 1870s he was the local agent of the Edinburgh Life Association Company and further supplemented his income by serving as London's first full-time police magistrate.

An active member of the Church of England, Lawrason served as rector's warden of St Paul's Church in London and had played a leading role in the erection of both the original church, which was officially opened in 1834, and the second church (now the cathedral) in 1846. He was also active in the local militia and by 1856 had risen to the rank of lieutenant-colonel in the 1st Battalion of London militia. Although Lawrason was to suffer bankruptcy he had been a cautious and successful businessman who placed a high value on fairness, selflessness, and compassion.

DANIEL JAMES BROCK

Baker Library, R. G. Dun & Co. MS reports, 19: 26. UWO, Laurason, Ridout, Penington families papers; Middlesex County Court, Insolvency cases, 1864, docket no.4; Lionel Ridout papers. Can., Prov. of, Legislative Assembly, *Journals*, 1844–45; Parl., *Sessional papers*, February–May 1863, III: no.9; January–March 1865, III: no.9. *London Advertiser* (London, Ont.), 15 Aug. 1882, 1 April 1886. *Canadian biog. dict.*, I: 519–20.

LAWRENCE, WILLIAM DAWSON, shipbuilder, shipowner, and politician; b. 16 July 1817 at Gilford (district of Banbridge, Northern Ireland), son of William Dawson Lawrence and Mary Jane Lockhart; m. in 1839 Mary Hayes, and they had ten children; d. 8 Dec. 1886 in Maitland, N.S.

William Dawson Lawrence's parents came to Nova Scotia while he was still an infant and settled at Five Mile River, Hants County. As a child he was taught by his mother and later attended a school at Five Mile River. In 1838 Lawrence went to Dartmouth where he apprenticed in the shipyards of Alexander Lyle and John Chappell. In 1847 Lawrence designed the *Wanderer*, a barque of 568 tons built by John Chappell for the firm of Fairbanks and Allison of Halifax and launched in April 1849.

Lawrence soon became involved in the design, construction, ownership, and operation of his own vessels. His first was the *St. Lawrence*, a brigantine of 170 tons built in 1852 at Five Mile River in partnership with his brother James. The vessel was owned by Lawrence, his brothers, James and John, and Alexander MacDougall. Lawrence operated the *St. Lawrence* until 1855, at which time he moved to Maitland, sold the vessel, and launched the *Architect*, a barque of 348 tons. In 1859 he launched the *Persia*, a barque of 285 tons, which he operated until 1865. In 1860 he built the 117-ton brigantine *Clyde*. In 1862 he sold the *Architect* and launched the *William G. Putnam*, a barque of 716 tons, and the next year built the *Mary*, a barque of 642 tons.

Lawrence's deep sea vessels were not involved to any extent in the coastal trade, but carried general cargoes to all parts of the world. He often imported tea, flour, and molasses which he exchanged in Maitland for shipbuilding materials. From the early 1850s Lawrence, though operating the vessels he built, had shared ownership with other Maitland merchants. By 1867, however, he was ready to proceed on his own. He sold the *William G. Putman* and *Mary* and in September of that year launched the *Pegasus*, a ship of 1,120 tons built at a cost of £9,640, and at the time the largest vessel constructed in the Maitland area. The *Pegasus*, under Captain James Ellis, Lawrence's son-in-law, was not profitable at first because of a general depression, but by the end of 1868 freight rates had risen and the ship became engaged in the profitable trade in guano, a natural fertilizer found especially in the Pacific islands off Peru.

In the fall of 1872 construction began on an even larger vessel; William's brother Lockhart was master builder and William's son John helped mould the frames and did much of the interior work. In August 1874 the *Pegasus* was sold and in September the *William D. Lawrence*, a ship of 2,459 tons, was launched. The vessel was 262 feet long, 48 feet wide, and had a 29-foot hold. It had cost $107,452 to build. As a result, Lawrence found himself in debt for more than $27,000. He owned 60 of her 64 shares, and Captain Ellis the rest. On a voyage of almost three years Lawrence sailed in the ship with Ellis and other members of his family, and when he returned to Nova Scotia he published an account of the interesting places and people he had encountered. The *William D. Lawrence* had many profitable voyages before its sale for £6,500 to a group of Norwegians in 1883. In 1884 Lawrence recounted that in a period of eight and a half years he had cleared the $27,000 debt and made a profit of $140,848.

Although the *William D. Lawrence* was the largest wooden vessel ever built in the Maritimes, the ship was in fact only slightly larger than the 2,377-ton *Morning Light* built at Saint John, N.B., by Richard and William Wright* in 1855. Contrary to popular belief, the *William D. Lawrence* was not the largest square-rigged vessel built in British North America. That honour belongs to the 5,294-ton *Baron of Renfrew* built by Charles Wood* at Quebec in 1825.

Lawrence had also been active in politics throughout the 1860s. In December 1859 he had been appointed a justice of the peace for Hants County, a post he held until his death. In May 1863 he had been elected to represent Hants in the provincial assembly, where he supported free education and adamantly opposed confederation. Re-elected in the provincial election of 1867 as an anti-confederate, Lawrence felt betrayed when Joseph Howe* deserted the cause and accepted a position in the federal cabinet early in 1869. In the 1871 election Lawrence again made the repeal of confederation a key issue, but he was defeated by William Henry Allison. Although he retained an active interest in politics until his death in 1886, Lawrence never again sought political office.

William Lawrence was representative of the many hundreds of Maritimers in the 19th century who built, owned, and operated their own ships. Many fortunes were made through good management and the shrewd acquisition of profitable cargoes, but a great deal also depended on having the good luck to escape shipwreck.

CHARLES A. ARMOUR

William Dawson Lawrence was the author of an untitled pamphlet which describes a lengthy voyage and was published at Maitland, N.S., in 1880.

Nova Scotia Museum (Halifax), Judith Boss, "Notes on William D. Lawrence" (typescript, 1975); William D. Lawrence, Letterbook and vessel's cost accounts, 1870–74. PAC, RG 42, A1, 44–53, 55, 66, 80–85, 307–12, 368. PANS, Biog., William D. Lawrence, Docs., 1835–1908 (mfm.); MS file, William D. Lawrence. *Novascotian*, 12 Jan. 1884, 18 Dec. 1886. *Directory of N.S. MLAs*.

LAWSON, MARY JANE. *See* KATZMANN

LEACH, WILLIAM TURNBULL, clergyman, in the Church of Scotland and then in the Church of England, and educator; b. 1 March 1805 in Berwick upon Tweed, England, son of Robert Leach and Elizabeth Turnbull; m. first Jessie Skirving (d. 21 Feb. 1848); m. secondly Eliza Margaret Easton (d. 7 June 1866); and m. thirdly Louisa Gwilt (d. 24 June 1935); d. 13 Oct. 1886 in Montreal, Que., survived by a son and two daughters.

William Turnbull Leach was educated in his native town and at Stirling, Scotland, and in 1827 graduated MA from the University of Edinburgh. After studying theology he was licensed a minister of the Church of Scotland and in the early 1830s came to Upper Canada under the auspices of the Glasgow Colonial Society. In 1835 he accepted a call to be minister of St Andrew's Church (Kirk) in Toronto. He also served as chaplain of the 93rd Highlanders, the St Andrew's Society, and the St Andrew's Lodge of Freemasons. Leach demonstrated his zeal for education by playing an active role in the establishment of a Presbyterian college at Kingston. He was a trustee of Queen's College when it was granted a charter in 1841 and opened under its first principal, Thomas Liddell*.

At this time, however, Leach began to doubt Presbyterian doctrines such as predestination and to challenge the legitimacy of all forms of Presbyterianism because they lacked apostolic succession. In 1842 he resigned from St Andrew's and was tried for his heretical opinions by the presbytery of Toronto. He then turned to the Church of England and early in 1843 was ordained priest by Bishop George Jehoshaphat Mountain* of Quebec. On 20 Feb. 1843, on the recommendation of Bishop John Strachan* of Toronto, the proprietors of the newly formed St George's Church in the west end of Montreal chose Leach as their first incumbent. He gained the respect of Montrealers during the typhus epidemic of 1847 by risking his life to help the stricken Irish immigrants who were crowded into hospital sheds on the waterfront.

In 1846 Leach established a connection with McGill College which was to last until his death. Over the course of 40 years he held a series of important appointments: professor of classical literature and lecturer in mathematics and natural philosophy, 1846–53; fellow and vice-principal, 1846–86; lecturer in logic, rhetoric, and moral philosophy, 1853–72; dean of the Faculty of Arts, 1853–86; and Molson professor of English language and literature, 1872–83. Leach's responsibilities at McGill were carried out under laborious conditions, often with discouraging prospects of success and meagre recompense. From 1847 to 1855, for example, in the absence of a permanent principal, he did much to keep McGill functioning in his capacity as vice-principal. Leach supported the Reverend John Bethune*, acting principal of the college since 1835, in his struggle "earnestly to connect McGill College as closely as possible" with the Church of England. Bethune's goal of exclusive Anglican control clashed with that of the trustees of James McGill*'s endowment, and in 1846 he was dismissed. The principalship would then have gone to Leach had he not been a clergyman. But Leach came to recognize the impossibility of trying to maintain a denominational connection and "cordially acquiesced" in the appointment in 1855 of John William Dawson*, a layman, as principal. Dawson later described Leach as "a man of rare gifts and of warm attachment to the college." As a leading educator, Leach was also appointed in 1876 one of eight members of the Protestant school committee of the Council of Public Instruction for Quebec, and thus helped to organize a Protestant school system for the province.

Leach's duties at McGill became too heavy to be combined with those of incumbent of St George's Church. The congregation would have retained him on whatever conditions he might propose, but he resigned in 1862. He did not, however, altogether retire from parochial work. From 1865 to 1867 he had charge of St Stephen's Church in Lachine, Canada East. In 1854 Leach had been appointed a canon of Christ Church Cathedral by Bishop Francis Fulford* of Montreal, and in 1865 he was named domestic chaplain to the bishop and an archdeacon. McGill awarded him an honorary DCL in 1849 and an honorary LLD in 1857, and in 1867 Bishop's College, Lennoxville, Quebec, awarded him an honorary DCL.

Archdeacon Leach's career was important for his work as a teacher. He achieved an immense amount of steady, unpretentious work of high scholarly quality, conscientiously performed under generally difficult circumstances. At the time of his death Bishop William Bennett Bond* (formerly his assistant at St George's) spoke of the "natural reserve of character" that had prevented Leach from assuming "that prominence . . . to which his experience and high qualifications entitled him."

EDGAR ANDREW COLLARD

William Turnbull Leach was the author of several pamphlets: *A discourse delivered in St. Andrew's Church, Toronto, on the thirtieth day of November, 1838 (St. Andrew's Day)* (Toronto, 1838); *A sermon, preached in St. Andrew's Church, Toronto, on the thirtieth day of November, 1837 (St. Andrew's Day)* (Toronto 1838); *A discourse delivered in St. Andrew's Church, Toronto, on the fourteenth day of December, 1838, being a day of public fasting and humiliation, appointed by authority* (Toronto, 1839); *Discourse on the nature and duties of the military profession, delivered in Saint Andrew's Church, Toronto, to the 93d Highlanders, on the eve of their departure from Toronto garrison* (Toronto, 1840); *A discourse, delivered to St. Andrew's Lodge (no.1) of Freemasons, on Monday, the 28th December, 5840: being the annual festival of St. John the Evangelist* (Toronto, 5841 [1841]); *An address on Rechabitism, delivered at the quarterly meeting of the members of the Independent Order of Rechabites, in the hall of the Spring of Canada tent, on the 18th July, 1845* (Montreal, 1845); *Sermon preached in St. George's Chapel, Montreal, on Advent Sunday, 1851, appointed, by authority, for the celebration of the third semi-centennial jubilee of the Society for the Propagation of the Gospel in Foreign Parts* (Montreal, 1851); *A great work left undone; or the desideratum in systems of education; a lecture delivered on the 26th January, 1864* (Montreal, 1864).

Anglican Church of Canada, Diocese of Montreal Arch. (Montreal), Francis Fulford papers. McGill Univ. Arch., Board of Governors, Minute books. *Gazette* (Montreal), 14 Oct. 1886. *Montreal Daily Star*, 14 Oct. 1886. *Cyclopædia of Canadian biog.* (Rose, 1888), 134. John Bethune, *A narrative of the connection of the Rev. J. Bethune D. D. with M'Gill College* . . . (Montreal, 1846), 56. J. D. Borthwick, *History of the diocese of Montreal, 1850–1910* (Montreal, 1910), 103–4. D. D. Calvin, *Queen's University at Kingston: the first century of a Scottish-Canadian foundation, 1841–1941* (Kingston, Ont., 1941), 26, 302. J. W. Dawson, *Fifty years of work in Canada* . . . (London and Edinburgh, 1901), 96; *Thirty-eight years of McGill* . . . (Montreal, 1894), 7. A. P. Gower-Rees, *Historical sketch of St. George's Church, Montreal, and its constitution* (Granby, Que., 1952), 10–11, 529. *The history of St. Stephen's Anglican Church, Lachine, Quebec, Canada, 1822–1956*, comp. George Merchant (n.p., [1956]), 128. Cyrus Macmillan, *McGill and its story, 1821–1921* (London and Toronto, 1921), 195–96, 204. S. C. Parker, *The book of St. Andrew's; a short history of St. Andrew's Presbyterian Church, Toronto* (Toronto, 1930). O. R. Rowley, "St. George's Church, Montreal . . . ," *Canadian Churchman* (Toronto), 70 (1943): 308–11. "Vice-principal Leach," *McGill Univ. Magazine* (Montreal), 4 (1905): 14–15.

LEAHEY, RICHARD HENRY, longshoreman, union organizer, and labour leader; b. in 1852 or 1853 in County Cork (Republic of Ireland), son of Robert and Mary Leahey; m. 27 Nov. 1876 Julia Doyle at Quebec City; d. there 19 Sept. 1889.

Richard Henry Leahey came to Quebec City as a child, probably with his mother and stepfather, the trade unionist Joseph Kemp. Leahey must have had some formal education because his first employment was apparently as a clerk to Dr John L. Wherry of Rue Champlain in the Lower Town. He then worked as a cabinet-maker before becoming a longshoreman. Leahey performed various semi-skilled jobs on the docks, such as winch-man, hatch-man, and stower, but never worked in the supervisory capacity of stevedore. As a labourer, he was representative of the Irish Catholics who immigrated to Quebec City in the 1850s. By 1860 they accounted for approximately 40 per cent of the population, forming a large pool of unskilled labour for local capitalists. Most of these immigrants settled in the suburb along Rue Champlain, near the docks that were their principal locale for employment. Historical circumstances influenced the division of labour along ethnic lines in 19th-century Quebec; French Canadians had a monopoly of the skilled jobs in shipbuilding, an industry which had begun during the French régime, and the Irish had to be content with the unskilled and semi-skilled work of longshoring.

Timber, the main export of the port of Quebec in the 19th century, was potentially the most dangerous product to load. The size of the deals, the speed with which the vessels had to be charged to take advantage of the tides, poor and faulty equipment, and adverse weather conditions, all combined to create an extremely hazardous working environment. As well, the seasonal nature of the port, which was open for only seven months of the year, did not allow dockers a stable and reliable income. Once the ice came the longshoremen were unemployed. Leahey, who was apparently one of the more experienced and busy workers on the Quebec docks, earned $245 for 27 weeks of work in 1887. Evidence given before the Royal Commission on the Relations of Capital and Labor the following year indicated that the annual income of dock workers in Quebec City averaged between $160 and $170. To supplement their low wages, most harbour workers sought other jobs during the winter. Some stayed in the city to shovel snow or work as tradesmen's assistants, but the majority, including Leahey, were forced to leave Quebec City to work either in lumber camps or in year-round ports such as Savannah, Ga, and New York City, where they easily found employment: the Quebec dockers enjoyed a reputation as steady and trustworthy workers.

The uncertainties facing longshoremen led them to organize themselves for self-protection. In 1857 they founded the Quebec Ship Labourers' Benevolent Society which was incorporated five years later. During a period when trade unions operated clandestinely as benevolent associations because of a federal law which prohibited their formation, this society soon dedicated itself to defending the interests of longshoremen. The monthly dues were originally spent mostly to help workers injured on the job, or families whose main wage-earner had died, naturally or by accident. As the QSLBS grew, moneys collected were also used to build a strike fund and to cover expenses incurred in suing employers. The association was transformed into a true union by a period of crisis which threatened the livelihood of longshoremen in the Quebec region. In the 1860s the port of Quebec began to decline and by the 1880s was superseded by Montreal as a result of the replacement of the square timber trade by grain, the improvements of the shipping channels of the St Lawrence River, and the undisputed supremacy of steamships which could more easily navigate against the current of the St Lawrence River than could sailing vessels.

It is not known when Leahey joined the QSLBS, but by 1888 he was president of one of its five sections; the members of his section worked primarily at the coves near Cap Diamant. The approximately 2,000 members in the union represented virtually all of the dockers who worked in the area and they strove to protect themselves from the repeated attempts by the Quebec Board of Trade to prevent all forms of group action among maritime labourers. As early as the 1860s the society had been powerful enough to insist on certain working conditions. For example, the "donkey engine," a steam-powered engine used in such ports as Montreal to stow timber in the holds of ships, was forbidden in Quebec because the union felt it was too dangerous. In addition, by the time Leahey was president in 1888 the union had secured agreements on the number of men to form gangs. Unlike their counterparts in Montreal and Halifax, the men had also won overtime pay-rates of time-and-a-half after eight hours and double-time on Sundays and holidays. Furthermore, the men could refuse to work more than a normal shift without jeopardizing their chances of being rehired. The wage rate at Quebec was also the highest in Canada: at 37½ cents per hour in 1887 it was nearly double the 20 cents per hour paid in Halifax and higher even than the 30 cents per hour paid in New York City. These benefits were won in part through recourse to general strikes such as those in 1866 and 1867 which completely shut down the port of Quebec and to sporadic strikes against such ship owners as Narcisse Rosa*.

Leahey, like his stepfather, was involved in organizing the Knights of Labor in Quebec City. From 1887 to 1888 he replaced Kemp as the master workman of district assembly 114, a mixed assembly, espousing industrial union principles, in which longshoremen predominated. Many dockers belonged to the Knights of Labor, but they endeavoured to maintain the QSLBS as a separate entity because they felt that their particular needs might be overlooked in the myriad reforms advocated by the Knights. Leahey was indefatigable in his efforts for the Knights, organizing working men despite the hostile pastoral letters of the Roman Catholic Church [*see* Elzéar-Alexandre Taschereau*] which forbade Catholics to join any secular labour association. However, in July 1888 the district assembly which encompassed Quebec City voted 17 to 3 to withdraw Leahey's organizer's commission after he refused to organize the *bateaux*-men of Quebec as Knights. He felt that these men, who unloaded and transported goods from off-shore ships to shore, might then "work against" the QSLBS, competing with the longshoremen and taking their jobs.

On 19 Sept. 1889, at about 7:30 p.m., several thousand tons of rock broke off from the cliff near the Dufferin promenade and crashed down onto the houses on Rue Champlain. Leahey, his wife, mother, stepfather, and three other members of his immediate family were among the 52 killed; the Leaheys' canary was the sole survivor in their house. The avalanche was the third in 50 years to ravage the working-class areas at the foot of the cliffs at Quebec City. The coroner's inquest blamed the government of Sir John A. Macdonald* for not constructing buttresses below the cliffs as recommended by the city's chief engineer, Charles Baillairgé*, in 1881.

Leahey and his wife and 16 other victims were buried on 22 September in Woodfield Cemetery, St Patrick's parish, Quebec City. Over 700 members of the QSLBS marched in the funeral cortège. On the day after the tragedy, Daniel John O'Donoghue*, a prominent labour figure in Ontario, introduced a motion in the Toronto Trades and Labor Council offering condolences to the QSLBS in "the loss it has sustained in the death of Brother Richard Leahey and several others of its members through the occurrence of the catastrophe."

Leahey's death was a misfortune for the QSLBS, which none the less remained one of the strongest unions in the country into the 20th century. Its influence and prosperity were only to wane with the further decline of the port. Although union leadership was not solely responsible for improving working conditions, men such as Leahey must be credited with focusing the grievances of their fellow labourers and bequeathing to the workers the necessary tools of resistance in the struggle against their employers. In the vanguard of the workers' movement in the 19th century, Leahey, like so many others, recognized the necessity of unifying and coordinating the actions of labourers to deal effectively with their employers.

CATHERINE A. WAITE and ROBERT TREMBLAY

AC, Québec, État civil, Catholiques, St Patrick's Church (Québec), 27 Nov. 1876, 22 Sept. 1889. Catholic Univ. of America Arch. (Washington), Terence V. Powderly papers (mfm. at PAC). PAC, MG 28, I44, 1: 174a. Can., Royal Commission on the Relations of Capital and Labor in Canada, *Report* (5v. in 6, Ottawa, 1889); *Evidence: Quebec*, esp. 744–49. *Globe*, 20 Sept.–1 Oct. 1889. *Le Journal de Québec*, 20–26 sept. 1889. *Quebec Morning Chronicle*, 20, 26 Sept. 1889. *Toronto World*, 20 Sept.–1 Oct. 1889. Jean Hamelin *et al.*, *Répertoire des grèves dans la province de Québec au XIXe siècle* (Montréal, 1970), 16–17, 25–26, 40–41, 95–96. *Quebec directory*, 1877–90. J. Hamelin et Roby, *Hist. économique*, 309–10. Fernand Harvey, "Les Chevaliers du travail, les États-Unis et la société québécoise, 1882–1902," *Aspects historiques du mouvement ouvrier au Québec*, Fernand Harvey, édit. (Montréal, 1973), 33–118. *Les travailleurs québécois* (J. Hamelin). C. A. Waite, "The longshoremen of Halifax, 1900–1930; their living and working conditions" (MA thesis, Dalhousie Univ., Halifax, 1977). J. I. Cooper, "The Quebec Ship Labourers' Benevolent Society," *CHR*, 30 (1949): 336–43.

LEBLANC, AUGUSTIN, cabinet-maker, wood-carver, gilder, and building contractor; b. 11 March 1799 at Yamachiche, Lower Canada, son of Étienne Leblanc, a farmer, and Marie Tessier; m. 9 Feb. 1830 Julie Hébert at Saint-Grégoire (now part of Bécancour), Lower Canada; d. 26 Feb. 1882 at Saint-Hugues, Que.

Nothing is known about Augustin Leblanc's childhood and training. Presumably, however, he apprenticed as a cabinet-maker and wood-carver with a craftsman who was either established at Yamachiche or in the region for a time. Leblanc could have learned his trade in the workshop of Joseph Milette, a wood-carver, or been an apprentice to Joseph's son, Alexis*, who was six years his senior. His apprenticeship may have been served on the building site of the church of Sainte-Anne, where construction went on sporadically from 1815 to 1858.

During his training Leblanc apparently gave particular attention to the gilding of wood. At any rate, it was in this field that he began his career, when on his own in 1831, and in association with Damase Saint-Arnaud the following year, he undertook to gild the interior of the church at Bécancour. In 1832, he embarked on the same task in the church at Saint-Grégoire, the village where he seems to have settled. His career assumed some importance in 1833 when he signed a contract with the parish council of Saint-Pierre, at William Henry (Sorel), as a master wood-carver, "to see that the interior of the church is completed and decorated."

His growing reputation brought him some large-scale projects. In 1835 he installed a carved vault at Deschaillons, and beginning in 1841 he also decorated the interior of the church at Grondines (Saint-Charles-des-Grondines). But Leblanc always followed an architect's plans. Thus in 1839 he and Alexis Milette started to work on the interior of the church at Baie-du-Febvre (Baieville), using designs by Thomas Baillairgé*. Four years later Baillairgé supplied him with plans for his work on the church at Saint-Zéphirin. Leblanc completed the vault of the church at Saint-Denis on the Richelieu River in 1844 from designs attributed to the priest of the parish. In 1850 Victor Bourgeau prepared the plans he used to enlarge the church at Saint-Grégoire.

On a few occasions, Leblanc acted as a contractor for buildings of minor importance. In 1835 he worked on the construction of both a stone presbytery at Saint-Denis on the Richelieu and the first chapel at Saint-Aimé (Massueville). He was given the task of erecting the seigneurial manor-house in Saint-Aimé the following year, and he was provided with the plans. After he helped to enlarge the church at Saint-Grégoire, where construction work began in 1850 and dragged on for some time, Leblanc became less active. From 1872 until at least 1880 he was at Saint-Hugues, where he was engaged in decorating the interior of the church (following Bourgeau's plans) and worked on the vault and presbytery. By 1875 Augustin Leblanc Jr seems to have begun to take over from his father, but his career apparently did not last long, since there is no trace of him after his father's death.

By the nature of his work, Augustin Leblanc established himself as head of a wood-carving enterprise. Although he always followed the plans of the prominent architects of his time, first Thomas Baillairgé and then Victor Bourgeau, he did not become an outstanding craftsman. Moreover, his personal contribution to the large projects executed with several apprentices or associates cannot be clearly identified. Nevertheless, through his work, Leblanc (like André Paquet*, *dit* Lavallée, Alexis Milette, and the brothers Joseph and Georges Héroux) enabled the architect to free himself from the building site. It was this generation of craftsmen-builders who put an end to the prevailing confusion between foreman and architect, performer and creator. The change was clearly a sign of the industrial age, when new technology and the fashions of the day would make obsolete the small family enterprise which sought to create works of art.

Luc Noppen

AC, Saint-Hyacinthe, État civil, Catholiques, Saint-Hugues, 1er mars 1882. ANQ-MBF, État civil, Catholiques, Sainte-Anne (Yamachiche), 11 mars 1799. AP, Saint-Grégoire (Nicolet), Reg. des baptêmes, mariages et sépultures, 9 févr. 1830. IBC, Centre de documentation, Fonds Morisset, 1, 15868/884; 2, L445.2/A923.8/1–4. J.-E. Bellemare, *Histoire de la Baie-Saint-Antoine, dite Baie-du-Febvre, 1683–1911* (Montréal, 1911), 213–18, 603–5. Napoléon Caron, *Histoire de la paroisse d'Yamachiche (précis historique)* (Trois-Rivières, 1892). Azarie Couillard-Després, *Histoire de Sorel de ses origines à nos jours* (Montréal, 1926), 188. O.-M.-H. Lapalice, *Histoire de la seigneurie Massue et de la paroisse de Saint-Aimé* (s.l., 1930), 154–56, 425–28.

LECLERC, NAZAIRE, Roman Catholic priest, author, and journalist; b. 21 July 1820 at Sainte-Anne-de-la-Pocatière (La Pocatière, Que.), son of Jean-Benoît Leclerc and Anastasie Perrault; d. 31 Oct. 1883 at Cap-Rouge, Que.

After studying at the Collège de Sainte-Anne-de-la-Pocatière from 1831 to 1842, Nazaire Leclerc was ordained priest on 28 Sept. 1845 at Quebec City. He served as curate in the parish of Saint-François (at Beauceville) from 1845 to 1848, as first parish priest of Saint-Vital at Lambton for the next three years, and again as curate in Saint-Jean-Baptiste on Île-Verte (1851–52), in Saint-Pierre-de-la-Rivière-du-Sud (Saint-Pierre-du-Sud, at Saint-Pierre-Montmagny) (1852–56), and in Notre-Dame-de-la-Victoire (at Lévis) (1857–60). In 1861, after 15 years of pastoral endeavour, he returned to the college to live and became editor of *La Gazette des campagnes*, a newspaper founded that year by Émile Dumais to popularize practical instruction related to farming and settlement. In April 1862 he was authorized by notarial agreement to acquaint himself with the teaching in the college's new school of agriculture [*see* François Pilote] so that he could publicize in *La Gazette des campagnes* the "good results [obtained] at this school, from the theoretical as well as from the practical point of view."

During his stay at the college from 1861 to 1868, Leclerc did not always make life easy for his superiors, or, indeed, for the archbishop of Quebec,

Charles-François Baillargeon*. He soon deflected *La Gazette* from its original purpose by using it as a political forum. Nor did he always respect the rules governing the ecclesiastical staff of the college. In 1868 he left the institution in bad odour, after being ousted from *La Gazette*. "Poor priest! What course will he take? May God counsel and guide him," sighed Archbishop Baillargeon, who had always considered the college an "asylum" and "haven of refuge" for Leclerc. Perhaps the latter had been guilty of some escapade before being charitably taken into the college in deference to the bishop in 1861. Louis-Antoine Dessaulles*, who kept a notebook detailing the amorous adventures of the Quebec clergy, recorded some evidence incriminating Leclerc on this count.

Leclerc's departure from the college not only created a sensation but also had further repercussions. He had sold the institution some land on credit and now gave notice that he wanted what he was owed. In the summer of 1868 his attorney called upon the college to pay eight per cent interest on the sum involved but, because it was in financial difficulties, the college ignored the request. In the autumn Leclerc threatened, through his notary, to prosecute the college if the capital was not repaid, and the college was obliged to borrow $800 to discharge the $924 debt to him.

Withdrawing to Saint-Jean-Chrysostôme from 1868 to 1873, then to Cap-Rouge from 1873 to 1883, Abbé Leclerc, who had substantial capital, decided to become a writer on his own account. In 1868 he published 5,000 copies of the *Catéchisme d'agriculture* which was intended for primary school teachers who were to have their pupils learn it by heart. The following year at Quebec he started a 24-page bimonthly, *La Gazette des familles canadiennes et acadiennes*. As both owner and editor, Leclerc busied himself with the journal until 1874; in September of that year he suspended publication, citing reasons of health, and in November he sold the periodical to Abbé Ferdinand Bélanger.

An analysis of *La Gazette des familles* from 1869 to 1874 reveals certain recurring themes, especially in the leading articles which were chatty pieces on farming, parish life, and the family. Reports on national and European events informed the reader about the Louis RIEL and the Joseph Guibord* affairs, the first Vatican council, and the papal Zouaves [*see* Ignace BOURGET], and they also contained reprints of the official declarations of Pius IX. Finally, there were notices of ordinations and deaths of the clergy as well as articles with a moral message on such topics as blasphemy, alcoholism, and proper behaviour at election time. Leclerc's successors seem to have deviated little from this subject-matter.

In contrast, the layout of *La Gazette des familles* was innovative and foreshadowed the style he later adopted for annals. The reduced format, short articles, and unusually low subscription rate of one *écu* per year made it a suitable periodical for a populace which was becoming increasingly literate. The readership, of rural origin, was drawn especially from within the diocese of Quebec, although the publication reached as far as Acadia. It was generally the priest, but sometimes a schoolteacher or notary, who undertook the distribution. In this way Leclerc worked to accomplish one of the journal's objectives: to counter the effects of literature judged dangerous. Although according to various indications there were probably about 3,000 subscribers, the irregularity of subscription payments seems to have caused increasing difficulty with accounts receivable during the five years of Leclerc's direction. In his efforts to cover production and distribution costs he showed no lack of ingenuity. From time to time he published a record of subscribers broken down by institution and locality, a sort of prize list designed to promote sales. He lowered costs by producing double numbers, thus publishing less frequently and reducing postal charges. He also sought advertisers: an insurance company and one of his agents in Montreal, a merchant of church ornaments, both paid him for a page. Later he obtained a contract from the Quebec government to publish private bills. Leclerc did not hesitate to offer spiritual rewards to his readers; thus he announced that he would celebrate mass on the first Friday of each month on behalf of his subscribers except, as he specified, those in arrears. Occasionally he threatened to resort to a lawyer to force them to pay. Even the sale of the first bound volumes, which were offered to parish priests for their libraries, did not enable him to get rid of his deficit. Furthermore, when Archbishop Elzéar-Alexandre Taschereau*, extending patronage, sought to increase the demand for the paper by the announcement that Leclerc had undertaken to give half of the subscription payments to the nearly bankrupt Collège de Sainte-Anne-de-la-Pocatière, the expected results failed to materialize. To satisfy his creditors Leclerc had to borrow. In September 1873 he received notice to pay his printer $130; but he had already launched a second periodical, the *Annales de la bonne Sainte-Anne-de-Beaupré* (Cap-Rouge) in April, and the income from this venture enabled him to clear his deficit.

In fact, because the new periodical gradually became the major medium of communication of an important centre of pilgrimage, the *Annales* ensured Nazaire Leclerc's financial success. The number of visitors to the village of Sainte-Anne-de-Beaupré (nearly 40,000 by 1877) was growing rapidly and this growth brought a staggering increase in subscribers to the *Annales*, from 11,000 in 1879 to 30,000 in 1883. When Leclerc sold the periodical to the Collège de Lévis in 1877, it was already earning a profit, as the terms of the transaction indirectly indicate: the purchaser was to pay the founder (or his heirs) half of the profits for the next 20 years. The maximum to be paid was, however, set at $800 per year. The Collège de Lévis respected this agreement until 1897 when it turned over the *Annales*, with more than 50,000 subscribers, to the Redemptorists (the Congregation of the Most Holy Redeemer) for the sum of $60,000.

Leclerc spent the last years of his life at Cap-Rouge. It would be hard to say whether it was luck, his business talents, or the social and religious situation that created the exceptional success of the *Annales* in the 19th century. However, the progressive elimination of illiteracy following the establishment of a primary school system in the 1840s led to the growth of a market for ideas. This cultural revolution, still too little known, may explain the proliferation and success of a literature for popular consumption; *La Gazette des familles* and the *Annales* were amongst the most widely distributed examples of this genre. Leclerc had perhaps realized that the ability to receive a message by reading might now extend beyond the restricted confines of the élite.

SERGE GAGNON

Nazaire Leclerc was the author of two pamphlets: *Catéchisme d'agriculture ou la science agricole mise à la portée des enfants*, published at Quebec in 1868, and of *Le Mois de Ste. Anne et de St. Joachim*, also published at Quebec, in 1874. In addition he was the editor of *La Gazette des campagnes* (Sainte-Anne-de-la-Pocatière [La Pocatière], Qué.), 1861–68, and owner of *La Gazette des familles canadiennes et acadiennes* (Cap-Rouge, Qué.), 1869–74, and of the *Annales de la bonne Sainte-Anne-de-Beaupré* (Cap-Rouge), 1873–77.

Arch. de la basilique Sainte-Anne-de-Beaupré (Sainte-Anne-de-Beaupré, Qué.), P 22 A, b 6, nos.2583–85. Arch. du collège de Sainte-Anne-de-la-Pocatière, 30–VII; 30–XLIII; 57–XXX; 57–XXXI; 58–X; 59–C; 60–IX; 62–LXXVI; 64–XXXII; 64–XXXVIII; 66–LXXIII; 122–XI; 122–XLIX; 122–CI; 123–XIII; 123–XIV; 123–XLVII; 123–LI. PAC, MG 24, B59, Cahier de notes. Allaire, *Dictionnaire*, I: 328. Albert Faucher, *Québec en Amérique au XIXe siècle, essai sur les caractères économiques de la Laurentie* (Montréal, 1973). Wilfrid Lebon, *Histoire du collège de Sainte-Anne-de-la-Pocatière* (2v., Québec, 1948–49), I: 202, 312, 484. Gérard Tremblay, "N.-A. Leclerc, fondateur des *Annales*, 1873; 100 ans dans le bon vent," *Sainte-Anne-de-Beaupré*, 101 (1973): 165–66.

LE CYGNE. *See* ONASAKENRAT, JOSEPH

LEFROY, Sir JOHN HENRY, soldier, scientist, and colonial administrator; b. 28 Jan. 1817 in Ashe (Hampshire), England, the fourth son and sixth child of the Reverend John Henry George Lefroy and Sophia Cottrell; m. first 16 April 1846 Emily Merry (d. 1859), daughter of Sir John Beverley Robinson*, and they had two sons and two daughters; m. secondly 12 May 1860 in London, England, Charlotte Anna Mountain, *née* Dundas; d. 11 April 1890 in Lewarne, Cornwall, England.

John Henry Lefroy was educated in private schools before entering the Royal Military Academy in Woolwich (now part of London) in January 1831. Upon graduation he was appointed a 2nd lieutenant in the Royal Artillery on 19 Dec. 1834. A deeply religious man throughout his life, while he was stationed at Woolwich for the next few years he joined with fellow officers in weekly Bible readings and prayer meetings and in conducting a Sunday school for soldiers' children. He displayed an early aptitude for science, describing himself as a "zealous labourer in a field of real interest," and during a three-month posting at Chatham in 1837 he studied practical astronomy at the Royal Engineers Establishment.

In 1839 the British government began in earnest to create a network of colonial observatories and to launch a series of expeditions to study terrestrial magnetism, both under the direction of Edward SABINE. Lefroy was one of the first three officers chosen for the observatories planned for Upper Canada, St Helena, and the Cape of Good Hope. Shortly after their selection they proceeded to Dublin for instruction from Britain's foremost expert in magnetism, Professor Humphrey Lloyd of Trinity College. On 25 Sept. 1839 Lefroy embarked for St Helena.

The Toronto observatory, which was to become the foremost post in the imperial network, had been in operation for about two years when Lefroy arrived in October 1842 to take up the superintendency. He found that "the work had fallen terribly in arrears." Nevertheless, planning began almost immediately on an expedition to the northwest to ascertain the geomagnetic characteristics of British North America and to attempt to locate the magnetic north pole. With his assistant, William Henry, RA, and in the company of a brigade headed by John MCLEAN, Lefroy left Lachine, Canada East, on 1 May 1843, beginning a 5,000-mile trek which was to last 18 months and bring him back to Toronto in November 1844.

Lefroy and his assistant took magnetic observations at more than 300 stations. While wintering at Fort Chipewyan (Alta) they took observations every hour from 16 Oct. 1843 to 29 Feb. 1844, and every two minutes, for hours at a time, during high magnetic disturbances. Later at Fort Simpson (N.W.T.), from 26 March to 25 May, Lefroy "carried on hourly observations as assiduously . . . as I had at Fort Chipewyan." He travelled as far north as Fort Good Hope (N.W.T.) on the Mackenzie River and as far west as Fort Simpson. In *Notes of a twenty-five years' service* McLean noted "his gentlemanly bearing and affable manners [which] endeared him to us all" and also called him "the ablest *mangeur de lard* [novice] we have had in the country for a number of years." The scientific findings of the trip were communicated to the Royal Society by Sabine and later published jointly in 1855 with findings of Sir John Richardson* at Fort Confidence (N.W.T.); in 1883 Lefroy published his *Diary of a magnetic survey* thus providing a personal account of his most significant scientific work.

During his travels in the northwest Lefroy met some of its leading and most colourful figures including Sir George Simpson* and the Reverend James Evans*, and he became interested in the "general condition of the Indians," especially "the strong desire which pervades many of them for Christian Instruction." His journals of the expedition are filled with notes on geology, people, customs, and traditions. His personal observations, moralistic and anecdotal, were recorded in his *Autobiography*, which was published posthumously by his widow "for private circulation only," and can be found as well in *In search of the magnetic north*, a collection of his letters from the northwest edited for publication in 1955.

Shortly after his marriage in 1846 Lefroy and his wife left Toronto, accompanied by George William Allan* and his bride (also a daughter of Sir John Beverley Robinson), to honeymoon in Europe. While in England Lefroy visited Sabine who was "very hot" to introduce photography to magnetic registration at Toronto; Lefroy, however, felt that it was "altogether premature." It was not their first disagreement. In his autobiography Lefroy complains that Sabine had given him no credit for the intense effort involved in the hourly observations at Fort Chipewyan and that when the trip's expenses were much higher than expected Sabine "threw the blame on me, even to the extent of denying that he had ever authorized me to winter in the north-west." Nevertheless Lefroy returned to Toronto on 21 Nov. 1846 and spent the next few years "endeavouring to reduce the registration of magnetic phenomena by photography to a practical certainty" as well as carrying on the current work of the observatory. The observations at Toronto during Lefroy's tenure were perhaps the most complete of any taken throughout the British network. Before he returned to England in April 1853 he was involved in the transfer of the observatory to the provincial government on 31 March 1853; as president of the Canadian Institute he worked with the members to persuade the government to purchase the observatory's instruments and books, and to continue at its expense the high standard of the operation which occasioned intense local pride [*see* George Templeman KINGSTON].

During his sojourn in Toronto Lefroy carried on a host of activities, mostly connected with the scientific community. On 9 June 1848 he was elected a fellow of the Royal Society; he was later elected a fellow of the Royal Geographical Society, the Geological Society of London, and the Society of Antiquaries. He was 1st vice-president in 1851–52 and then president in 1852–53 of the Canadian Institute, the founding of which in 1849 was a major sign of the scientific ferment in Canada at the time. Toronto's first book club, whose membership included some of the city's leading citizens, was founded and managed by Lefroy. On travels to the United States he became acquainted with some of the leading American scientists, including Alexander Dallas Bache, Joseph Henry, and Jean Louis Rodolphe Agassiz. Lefroy also published papers in American and Canadian journals on scientific subjects and on the Indian population.

Back in England with a reputation based on his work in Toronto, Lefroy became a scientific adviser on artillery to the War Office during the Crimean War, was involved in reform of the armed forces, and served on numerous military committees before being appointed inspector-general of army schools and later director-general of the Ordnance Office (from 1868 to 1870). During this period he became increasingly involved in the activities of the Royal Artillery Institution and contributed to its professional journal. Following his retirement from the army on 1 April 1870 with the honorary rank of major-general, he served as governor of Bermuda (1871–77) and briefly, beginning in 1880, as governor of Tasmania. After his return to England he published a number of papers on a wide range of subjects, mainly military. He was awarded a CB in 1870 and a KCMG in 1877.

Lefroy returned to Canada twice, the first visit being a brief one in 1877 when illness forced him to leave Bermuda for England. His final visit was in 1884 when as president of the geographical section of the British Association for the Advancement of Science he delivered the presidential address at its annual meeting in Montreal. While there he was awarded an LLD from McGill College, "so that I have at last the right to a cap and gown, the object of my ambition." He and his second wife were entertained by Governor General Lord Lansdowne [Petty-Fitzmaurice*] at Quebec City and by Lieutenant Governor John Beverley Robinson*, his brother-in-law, in Toronto. Lefroy journeyed to the Canadian west with the object of viewing the Rockies, but in Winnipeg his strength waned and he had to return to England. Conditions on this trip were significantly different: the crossing of Lake Superior, which had earlier taken him a week, was accomplished in one day by steamer. He was taken sick the day he landed in England, from "heart weakness" and bronchitis. His remaining days were marked with frequent attacks of illness "always borne with patience and cheerfulness."

Perhaps the most significant appraisal of Lefroy's importance to science came in 1874 from his former mentor, Humphrey Lloyd, who described his work as "probably the most remarkable contribution to our knowledge of the phenomena of magnetic disturbances." Although his scientific accomplishments were more the result of diligence than inspiration, his work at Toronto and in the northwest earned a great deal of admiration for both himself and the observatory, in Britain as well as in Canada.

CAROL M. WHITFIELD and RICHARD A. JARRELL

Sir John Henry Lefroy was the author of *Autobiography of General Sir John Henry Lefroy, C.B., K.C.M.G., F.R.S., etc., colonel commandant Royal Artillery*, ed. [C. A.] Lefroy (London, [1895]); *Diary of a magnetic survey of a portion of the dominion of Canada chiefly in the north-western territories executed in the years 1842–1844* (London, 1883); *In search of the magnetic north: a soldier-surveyor's letters from the north-west, 1843–1844*, ed. G. F. G. Stanley (Toronto, 1955); "The president's annual address," *Canadian Journal*, 1 (1852–53): 121–24; "Sir Henry Lefroy's journey to the north-west in 1843–4," ed. W. S. Wallace, RSC *Trans.*, 3rd ser., 32 (1938), sect. II: 67–96; and, with John Richardson, of *Magnetical and meteorological observations at Lake Athabasca and Fort Simpson, by Captain J. H. Lefroy, Royal Artillery; and at Fort Confidence, in Great Bear Lake, by Sir John Richardson, C.B., M.D.* (London, 1855).

PAC, MG 24, H25. PRO, Meteorological Office, BJ 3 (Sabine papers) (mfm. at PAC). John McLean, *Notes of a twenty-five years' service in the Hudson's Bay territory* (2v., London, 1849; repub. as *John McLean's notes of a twenty-five year's service in the Hudson's Bay territory*, ed. W. S. Wallace, Toronto, 1932). "Memorial of the Canadian Institute to the three branches of the legislature to continue the Royal Magnetic Observatory under provincial management," *Canadian Journal*, 1 (1852–53): 145–47. "The observatory," *Canadian Journal*, 1: 282–83. *DNB*. Morgan, *Bibliotheca Canadensis*, 220–21. W. S. Wallace, "A soldier-scientist in the north-west," *Queen's Quarterly*, 45 (1938): 394–400.

LEGGE, CHARLES, civil engineer and patent solicitor; b. 29 Sept. 1829 at Silver Springs, near Gananoque, Upper Canada; d. 12 April 1881 in Toronto, Ont.

Charles Legge received his early education at the village academy in Gananoque. In 1846 he entered Queen's College in Kingston, but he left soon after to study engineering under Samuel KEEFER, chief engineer of the Department of Public Works for the Province of Canada, who was supervising the enlargement of the Welland Canal. Legge moved to the Montreal headquarters of the department in 1848; there he worked with Keefer for four more years before being appointed staff engineer on the Williamsburg Canals, a series of canals along the St Lawrence River between Prescott and Dickinson's Landing, near Cornwall. In 1853 Legge's duties concerned primarily the engineering of the Junction Canal (one of the Williamsburg Canals), then under construction.

When Keefer left the Department of Public Works to join the Grand Trunk Railway in 1853, Legge went with him. Working on the construction of the Montreal–Kingston line he surveyed the stretch between Kingston and Brockville and was involved in the construction of the Cornwall, Canada West, section. In 1856 Legge was appointed superintending engineer for the completion of the south end of the Victoria Bridge at Montreal, the Grand Trunk's most ambitious project. A bridge across the St Lawrence of almost two miles in length was necessary to tie the Grand Trunk system together and, following plans drawn up by Thomas Coltrin Keefer*, Robert Stephenson, and Alexander McKenzie Ross, James Hodges* had begun construction from Pointe-Saint-Charles on Montreal Island in 1854. Legge directed the building of the weirs and coffer-dams for the piers and the erection of the tubular structure of the southern portion of the bridge; he was also in charge of the quarries at Pointe-Claire, Montreal Island, and at Lake Champlain, Vt. When the bridge was completed on 30 Nov. 1859 it was the world's longest bridge, and to eulogize the engineers engaged on the project Legge wrote *A glance at the Victoria Bridge, and the men who built it* (1860), detailing the many tribulations encountered in its construction.

During the following decade Legge developed a civil engineering consulting business, specializing in harbour improvements and hydraulic power projects. In 1861 the chairman of the Montreal Harbour Commission, John Young*, engaged him to prepare a plan for enlarging Montreal's harbour and exploiting the water-power of the Lachine Rapids. In short order Legge produced two pamphlets outlining a complete plan for massive docks and for an extensive hydraulic power system combined with an aqueduct from above the rapids. However, as a result of the economic and political problems surrounding the management of the harbour commission this project was never realized. In 1864 Legge published a scaled-down version of his plan, addressed to private interests, but was still unable to have the project carried through. In later years Legge acted as a consultant on water-power development in Chambly, Saint-Jérôme, and Richmond, Que., and in Gananoque, Ont. His reports, written in a readable style and clearly explaining the financial and technical details of the projects, described the topography and resources of each area, the possibilities for water-power as well as the strategy for its development, and the economic benefits that would accrue. Characteristic of his reports were the different financial and engineering options prepared for the consideration of investors.

During these years Legge was also active in the field of patents. In 1864 he opened a patent-soliciting office in Montreal under the name of Charles Legge and Company, securing Canadian patents for inventors and entrepreneurs. A pamphlet written by Legge in 1867 advocated changes in the 1849 patent laws, and with the passage of a new Patents of Invention Act in 1869 he prepared a second pamphlet outlining the procedure for obtaining patents in Canada and in foreign countries. Legge's agency, the second largest in North America and the largest in Canada, apparently carried on an international business with representatives in the United States and Europe, and it operated successfully until 1878.

In 1869 Legge turned his attention to the Montreal Northern Colonization Railway, both as a founding member of the board of directors and as chief engineer. The railway was chartered by the provincial government to link Montreal with the Laurentians, and Legge surveyed a line to run from the harbour at Hochelaga through Mile End (both now part of Montreal) to Saint-Jérôme. Dominated by a group of Montreal capitalists led by Hugh ALLAN, who became president of the company in 1871, the proposed railway soon began to appear more as part of a transcontinental system than as a mere colonization railway. In 1871 Legge co-authored a *Report on exploration of routes north and south sides of Ottawa River, for the Montreal Northern-Colonization Railway from Grenville to Ottawa city* and by 1874 he had made surveys as far as Georgian Bay. However, although the line had the support of powerful commercial interests and generous land grants from the Quebec government, its construction was stymied by financial problems and the opposition of the Grand Trunk. Under these pressures Legge had suffered a mental breakdown in 1872; he was to endure a second in March 1875, before the railway finally collapsed a few months later. In November of that year the Quebec government announced that it was taking over the charter of the Montreal Northern Colonization, as part of the Quebec, Montreal, Ottawa and Occidental Railway.

In the early 1870s Legge surveyed a number of other railway lines in Quebec and Ontario and was engineer-in-chief on such projects as the Toronto, Simcoe and Muskoka Junction Railway, the Gananoque and Rideau Railway, the Montreal, Chambly and Sorel Railway, and the Yamaska Valley Railway. Two of the surveys he made at this time, one for the Montreal and City of Ottawa Junction Railway and the other for a line in Prince Edward County, Ont., were published. Unfortunately Legge had no more success with these lines than with the Montreal Northern Colonization, and all of the projects were either aborted or postponed.

Legge's last major project was the Royal Albert Bridge, originally proposed by the Montreal Northern Colonization Railway to cross the St Lawrence in the east end of Montreal and provide an alternative to the Grand Trunk's Victoria Bridge. The project was vigorously pushed by John Young in the face of strong opposition from other members of the Montreal Harbour Commission as well as from the Montreal Board of Trade, and in 1876 Legge was named engineer. The promoters of the project, however, withdrew their request for a federal charter in October 1876, and the bridge was never built.

Little is known of Legge after this last set-back. By 1880 he seems to have left Montreal and he died unnoticed in Toronto on 12 April 1881. The cause of his early death, at the age of 51, is not clear, but the mental and physical strain of his work had taken its toll as it did with other engineers of his time.

Although he helped engineer one of Canada's greatest construction projects, the Victoria Bridge, Legge left few other engineering works. His importance as a consulting engineer and pamphleteer, with 23 published papers on water-power, railways, bridges, and patents, is, however, seen in the success of many of his projects after his death. Furthermore, he was recognized as a pioneer in the field of patent soliciting, having successfully established the second largest agency in North America.

LARRY S. MCNALLY

Charles Legge wrote 23 pamphlets between 1860 and 1874 including the following: *A glance at the Victoria Bridge, and the men who built it* (Montreal, 1860); *Preliminary report and plans shewing the necessity of hydraulic docks at Montreal, with manufacturing facilities in connection with a city terminus, for the Grand Trunk Railway . . .* (Montreal, 1861); *Suggestions with reference to the proposed new act; respecting letters patent for inventions, in the Dominion of Canada* (Montreal, 1867); *Report on Montreal Northern Colonization Railway, Montreal to city of Ottawa, with branch line to St. Jerome* (Montreal, 1872), translated into French as *Rapport sur le chemin de fer de colonisation du Nord, Montréal à Ottawa avec embranchement à St. Jérôme* (Montréal, 1872). For a more complete list of his writings *see*: Dionne, *Inventaire chronologique des livres, brochures, journaux et revues publiés en langue française dans la province de Québec depuis l'établissement de l'imprimerie au Canada jusqu'à nos jours* (4v. et supp., Québec, 1905–12; réimpr., 2v., New York, 1969); Philéas Gagnon, *Essai de bibliographie canadienne . . .* (2v., Québec et Montréal, 1895–1913; réimpr., Dubuque, Iowa, [1962]); as well as the *Catalogue of pamphlets, journals and reports in the Public Archives of Canada, 1611–1867, with index*, comp. Norman Fee (2nd ed., Ottawa, 1916), and the *Catalogue of pamphlets in PAC* (Casey), I.

PAC, RG 11, A1, 19, no.19767. Québec, *Statutes*, 1869, c.55. *Canadian Illustrated News* (Hamilton, Ont.), 16 Jan. 1864. *Canadian Illustrated News* (Montreal), 12 Feb., 1 April 1876. James Hodges, *Construction of the great Victoria Bridge in Canada* (2v., London, 1860). *Dominion annual register*, 1880–81: 415–16. *Montreal directory*, 1859–80. Michel Stewart, "Le Québec, Montréal et Occidental: une entreprise d'État" (thèse de PHD en cours, Univ. Laval, Québec). B. J. Young, *Promoters and politicians: the North-Shore railways in the history of Quebec, 1854–85* (Toronto, 1978).

LEPAGE, JOHN, teacher, businessman, and poet; b. 28 Dec. 1812 at Pownal, Queens County, P.E.I., third child of Andrew LePage and Elizabeth Mellish;

m. first in 1847 Alice Foster, and they had three children who died in infancy; m. secondly in 1852 Charlotte McNeill, and they had five children; d. 8 or 9 Jan. 1886 at Charlottetown, P.E.I.

John LePage, whose father had immigrated to Prince Edward Island from the Channel Islands about 1807, was educated in Island schools and then became a teacher. He taught first at Lot 49, Queens County, and then for many years at Malpeque, Prince County, before becoming third master of the Central Academy in Charlottetown about 1848. His last post, in which he taught students at the elementary level, was abolished in 1860 when the Central Academy began restricting itself to post-elementary education. He then joined the newly formed Bank of Prince Edward Island as a clerk, but soon left to become secretary-treasurer of the Charlottetown Gas Light Company, a position he held until his retirement in 1883.

LePage was best known publicly for his poetry, published in two substantial volumes: *The Island minstrel, a collection of the poetical writings of John LePage* (1860) and *The Island minstrel . . . volume II* (1867). The 1867 edition reprints a number of poems from the earlier book, but the two volumes contain substantially different material. LePage also published at least two pamphlets and a number of poetic broadsheets, and frequently contributed verse to the local press under the initials P.L.I. or P.L.J.

He was very much a public poet in that his verse generally dealt more with subjects drawn from the world he and his readers knew from personal experience than with the exploring and articulating of his personal feelings and values. He wrote verses for special occasions, odes, eulogies to military heroes, and elegies on local notables, but his most interesting poetry lies in his comic-satiric treatment of certain social and political aspects of Island life. In these poems, he often employed doggerel rhythms and verse patterns to help deflate the inherent pretentiousness and pomposity of public figures and events. The most striking poem of this sort is his pamphlet *(Flies in amber): an authentic history of the land commission and other stirring events in Prince Edward Island* (1862) which deals with the ineffectual efforts of the royal commission of 1860–61 established by the government of Edward PALMER to solve the land tenure problem in Prince Edward Island. In the poem, LePage uses an Indian maiden (his muse) as a narrator and, in describing the activities of the commission, parodies the style of Longfellow's *Song of Hiawatha*. By structuring the poem this way, LePage is able to use the perspective and pseudo-Indian dialect of the young Micmac girl to insinuate devastating satiric commentary into her ostensibly innocent narration of events.

LePage did not pretend to write "great" poetry, but described his efforts as "homemade verse," which "if not so fine as some of the imported articles . . . may nevertheless be considered passable." This description appears to be a just estimation of his poetic talents, but to it one must add LePage's observation that "trifles help to form the sum of human things."

THOMAS B. VINCENT

John LePage was the author of *Shipwreck of the "Fairy Queen," in Northumberland Strait, October 7th, 1853* [and] *Fate of Sir John Franklin . . .* (Charlottetown, 1853); *The spirit of English poetry: a lecture delivered before the Mechanics' Institute, Charlottetown, on the evening of Tuesday, 21st April, 1857* (Charlottetown, 1857); *The Island minstrel: a collection of the poetical writings of John LePage . . .* (Charlottetown, 1860); *Rhymes for the times and reason for the season; or, a rhyming rhapsody on American revolutions* (Charlottetown, 1861); *An address to America* (Charlottetown, 1862); *Farewell to 1862* (Charlottetown, 1862); *(Flies in amber): an authentic history of the land commission and other stirring events in Prince Edward Island* (Charlottetown, 1862); *Rifle shooting at Truro, N.S., Friday, Sept. 12, 1862* (Charlottetown, 1862); *The calling out of the posse comitatus* (Charlottetown, 1865); *The Island minstrel: a collection of some of the poetical writings of John LePage . . . volume II* (Charlottetown, 1867); *Visits of distinguished personages to Prince Edward Island, duly chronicled* (Charlottetown, 1869); *Loss of H.M. ironclad turret-ship 'Captain,' off Cape Finnisterre, on the night of 6th September, 1870* (Charlottetown, 1870); *Choral symphonies, at an entertainment given in the basement of the Wesleyan Chapel, Charlottetown, P.E. Island, February 3rd, 1871* (Charlottetown, 1871); *The Island minstrel, miscellaneous papers* (Charlottetown, 1885).

Examiner (Charlottetown), 9 Jan. 1886. *Islander*, 16 Sept. 1859, 27 Dec. 1861. *Patriot* (Charlottetown), 9 Jan. 1886. Wallace, *Macmillan dict*.

LEROY, PIERRE-AUGUSTE, teacher and author; b. 20 Feb. 1846 at Mauves (Mauves-sur-Loire, Loire-Atlantique), France, son of Pierre Leroy, a doctor, and Marie-Anne-Rosalie Lebreton; d. after 1886 in France or Switzerland.

Pierre-Auguste Leroy arrived at Quebec on 6 March 1874, intent upon introducing a reform of classical education. Nearing the age of 30, he meditated on his past, which appeared to him to be a succession of failures and hardships. From earliest childhood he had wanted to be a missionary so that he could die a martyr to his Roman Catholic faith. It was for this reason, he asserted, that at the age of 14 he had vainly begged his father to let him join the ranks of the papal army after its defeat at Castelfidardo, Italy. He had then entered the Collège de Couet, in the department of Loir-et-Cher in France, to complete his classical education but in 1867, having reached the age of majority, he abandoned the medical studies he had taken up at his father's insistence and after the battle of Mentana enrolled in the 3rd battalion of Papal Zouaves. In May 1868, at the end of his six-month term of service, he joined the Cistercians at the Abbaye d'Aiguebelle near Donzère, France, believing he was taking up his vocation. Less than a year later, however, his superiors made him resume life as a lay person to recover his health, which he had undermined by excessive privations. It was then that Leroy turned his mind to education.

The evidence suggests that he was a teacher for a few years, since at the beginning of 1874 he published at Lyons a pedagogical work, *Commentarii de bello Helvetio; nouvelle méthode pour apprendre le latin en peu de temps.* On 2 February he asked the minister of public instruction to try out his teaching methods which, he argued, could shorten secondary studies by one half. Experience had led him to consider the system of classical teaching an obstacle in his search for the way laid out for him by Providence. Hence he conceived the idea that each man had a particular mission to fulfil which was indicated to him in childhood by "virtually unquestionable signs." In his view the system of classical teaching took no account of the vocations of children. Authoritarian and too restrictive, it placed excessive emphasis on memorizing; learning useless material consumed much of the time that a child should be devoting to exercising creativity and learning a trade, thus coming to realize what it was that Providence intended for his life. Rejected in France, Leroy turned his attention to Canada, which he had heard about during the 1867 universal exposition at Paris, in the hope that his "invention" would be welcomed there.

As soon as he reached Quebec in March 1874, Leroy went to see Abbé Thomas-Étienne Hamel*, the superior of the Séminaire de Québec, and suggested that he be given a class where he could test his method of teaching Latin. He was invited to give a lecture on the subject to the seminary's teachers on 8 April but, despite the interest aroused by what he said, his request was refused. He then appealed to Gédéon Ouimet*, the prime minister and minister of public instruction for Quebec. No doubt interested, the latter agreed to chair a second lecture by Leroy, given on 30 April at the École Normale Laval in Quebec City in the presence of the mayor, the leading citizens, and numerous journalists. The next day many newspapers praised Leroy's system, and Napoléon Legendre*, associate editor of *Le Journal de l'Instruction publique*, even expressed the hope that the government would assist him. In fact, Ouimet did give Leroy the grant and the premises he had requested. Leroy therefore announced that from September 1874 he would offer an experimental three-year course covering, with the exception of philosophy, all the subjects required in France for the examination for the *baccalauréat ès lettres*, which marked the end of secondary studies.

The encouragement Leroy received in Quebec was not unconnected with the desire entertained in certain circles there since 1840 for a reform of classical education to adapt it to the exigencies of the industrial age. For example, when the members of the Institut Canadien at Montreal pointed to the gap in technology and in wealth between French Canadian and Anglo-Saxon society in North America, they denounced the education given in the classical colleges as the cause of this backwardness. In this respect Leroy's system, which cut the time for Latin and Greek studies in half but maintained an adequate initiation in them, seemed a desirable compromise between the abolition of these subjects and their retention unchanged. Henceforth more time would be given to useful learning. However, some teachers considered this new system too demanding, since it forced them to offer instruction on almost an individual basis. Leroy responded to them in newspaper articles couched in aggressive and argumentative language. To prove he was right he proposed to give his 30 or so students examinations in public every three months to show the progress accomplished. So successful were these examinations that Leroy was again commended for his system. In December 1874 Joseph-Édouard CAUCHON of *Le Journal de Québec* lauded the man and his work, and Napoléon Legendre continued to show enthusiasm. Abbé Antonin Nantel, the superior of the Séminaire de Sainte-Thérèse, predicted an early triumph for Leroy and hoped the power of public opinion would overcome all resistance. Abbé Dominique RACINE, the superior of the Séminaire de Chicoutimi, after a trial of the system in his institution, testified to its positive results. But Ouimet's government was defeated in the wake of the Tanneries scandal [*see* Louis ARCHAMBEAULT] in September 1874 and Leroy's grant was not renewed for 1875. This blow, and the overload of work Leroy had imposed upon himself for the sake of establishing his reputation at Quebec, affected his mental health. He retired from teaching and began a life of writing, controversy, and wandering.

Convinced he had to reform teaching if he were to accomplish his God-given mission, Leroy returned to France at the end of 1875. His object was to interest the superior of the Abbaye d'Aiguebelle in founding in Quebec a college which Leroy himself would run on the model of a monastery; its students would live by the Rule of St Benedict, adapted and somewhat relaxed. Such an environment would permit him to apply his system and would help to spread its use. The students would be admitted without fees, would spend part of their time apprenticing to a trade, and would leave the institution prepared to take the places for which they were predestined.

Unable to find encouragement in France, in 1876 Leroy returned to Quebec, where he experienced the same refusal from Archbishop Elzéar-Alexandre Taschereau*. He then went to Chicoutimi and met Father Charles Arnaud, an Oblate of Mary Immaculate, who was apparently sympathetic to his plan. Leroy immediately took various steps to get Arnaud appointed first bishop of the diocese of Chicoutimi. He wrote of receiving miraculous proofs that Arnaud was designated by God to hold this post and to become the agent of Providence for the reform that he proposed. On this theme, he pestered the archbishop of Quebec and the apostolic delegate, Bishop George Conroy*, all the time drafting pamphlets and newspaper articles about the subject. But in spite of these initiatives, Dominique Racine was named head of the diocese of Chicoutimi in 1878.

Leroy lost a great deal of his credibility in Quebec City after his return in 1876. The papers refused to publish what he wrote and he had to start his own, *La Volonté*, which was distributed without charge and appeared irregularly in 1876 and 1877. An outcast, he wrote that he was now termed a "black sheep," whom "the good women of Quebec look upon as a real devil," on a par with a "Protestant minister." This reputation was not due solely to his extravagant behaviour but also to the fact that from the moment the clergy had refused to support his plan they had become the target of his attacks. As an example, he railed against the absolute power that the church exercised over education.

In 1878 Leroy left Quebec City penniless and on foot. He wound up at Saint-François-du-Lac in Yamaska County, where he was given shelter by a local farmer whose son he undertook to teach. In the spring of 1879 he went to Saint-Hugues and took a post in the primary school, where for a year or so he experienced great satisfaction in trying out his method with young pupils. But there his obsessions still haunted him and he left the institution to rededicate himself to his vocation – the total and radical reform of the educational system.

An unexpected inheritance enabled Leroy to return to France towards the end of 1881. He continued to seek a college where he could institute his reform, and with this in mind he vainly requested the bishop of Nantes to entrust him with the position of superior of the Collège de Couet. He was back in the province of Quebec by the end of 1883 and the following year tried to convince the new apostolic delegate, Mgr Joseph-Gauthier-Henri Smeulders, of the necessity of replacing Bishop Racine with Father Arnaud as head of the diocese of Chicoutimi. In 1885 he even went to Rome to intercede in favour of Arnaud, claiming that in this Oblate missionary he could recognize the future pope "of whom the prophecies speak." Failing to win his case, he returned to Quebec late that year. He then became convinced he was being spied on by the police of the French Republic, and in 1886 returned to his native land to live like a fugitive. Accounts of this period in his life suggest that his mind was completely unhinged: revolver in pocket, he made his way along the roads of France and Switzerland, seeking to evade the secret agents who in countless disguises were following him. No doubt he ended his days in a lunatic asylum.

René Hardy

Pierre-Auguste Leroy wrote numerous works dealing with pedagogy and with his mystical visions including : *Études de langues; réforme de l'enseignement . . .* (Québec, 1874); *Thèmes, règles et vie d'Agésilas: nouvelle méthode pour apprendre le latin en peu de temps* (Québec, 1874); *Pour et contre, réforme de l'enseignement: nouvelle méthode pour apprendre les langues en peu de temps* (Québec, 1875) (an account of this work can be found in "Bulletin bibliographique," *JIP*, 19 (1875): 46); *L'enfant et l'Éducation* (Québec, 1877); *Ensemble du système* (Québec, 1877); *Gage de la victoire* (s.l., 1878); *Lumen in cœlo, le mot de l'énigme: explication de la prophétie de St. Malachie* (Québec, 1881); *Lumen in cœlo, la fin du monde: nous sommes aux derniers jours du monde* (Québec, 1885); *Lumen in cœlo, le futur pape: laissez passer la justice de Dieu* (Nantes, France, 1885); *En avant, Œdipe; où est l'étoile?* (s.l., [1886]). Leroy also founded a newspaper, *La Volonté*, at Quebec in 1876; however, it ceased publication at beginning of the following year.

Arch. départementales, Loire-Atlantique (Nantes), État civil, Mauves, 20 févr. 1846. Gédéon Ouimet, "Rapport du ministre de l'Instruction publique de la province de Québec, pour l'année 1872 et en partie pour l'année 1873," *JIP*, 19: 36–37. *Le Journal de Québec*, 28 févr., 13 juin 1876; 1877. Bernard Lippens, *Pierre Leroy: son système, sa marotte, ses luttes homériques et ses travaux herculéens* (Québec, 1874). J.-C. Drolet, "Monseigneur Dominique Racine fondateur de l'Église saguenéenne," SCHÉC *Rapport*, 31 (1964): 55–64. Ægidius Fauteux, "Les carnets d'un curieux: Pierre Leroy ou les navrantes étapes d'une folie," *La Patrie*, 2 déc. 1933: 32–33, 35.

LESPÉRANCE (L'Espérance), ALEXIS BONAMI, *dit*. *See* Bonami

LESPÉRANCE (Rocheleau, *dit* **Lespérance), PIERRE**, silversmith; b. 19 Dec. 1819 at Quebec City, son of André Rocheleau, *dit* Lespérance, a cabinet-maker, and Charlotte Sasseville; m. first 20 Feb. 1865 Catherine Bélanger (d. June 1868); m. secondly 23 Feb. 1870 Elizabeth Hill; d. 23 April 1882 in Quebec City.

Through an agreement made by his father on 20 June 1836, Pierre Lespérance was engaged "in the capacity of an apprentice silversmith to M. Laurent Amiot [*], master silversmith, for the entire period that remains until he attains the age of twenty-one years." Lespérance "binds himself to do all the tasks that may be demanded of him, whether by the said Sieur Amiot or by any other persons supervising ~~his shop~~ his workshop." Amiot always insisted that a notary use the exact word intended, and the result sheds light on his personality and on the organization of work in his establishment. In this instance he crossed out the word "shop," implying the store where customers came to buy products, and replaced it with "workshop," meaning the place where craftsmen laboured; he also crossed out the word "trade" of silversmith, substituting the "art" of silversmithing. Amiot was not in sole charge of his atelier: in fact Lespérance would have to obey "other persons." His own uncle, François Sasseville*, who rented Amiot's workshop and store after his death in June 1839, comes immediately to mind. Since the apprenticeship contract did not expire until December 1840, it may be assumed that Lespérance continued his training under Sasseville.

The professional links between the two silversmiths are still obscure. In October 1850 the Provincial Industrial Exhibition in Montreal awarded a prize of £3 5*s.* to "Sasseville and Lespérance" for a chalice they had entered. Yet if Lespérance was Sasseville's associate and shared the prize, one must ask why his name was not mentioned in the glowing appreciation of this object that appeared in *Le Journal de Québec* on 17 October. Sasseville left the old shop of Laurent Amiot, on Rue de la Montagne, around 1852 and established himself on Côte du Palais. This move may have coincided with a change in the relationship between Sasseville and Lespérance. John E. Langdon has, indeed, suggested that the two formed a partnership in 1854. In 1856 Lespérance also had a store on Rue du Palais; hence one is tempted to assume that they shared the same establishment. However, Lespérance seems to have enjoyed some degree of professional autonomy, for he asserted that he himself had made articles of church silver which he sold to the parish of Saint-Joseph at Pointe-Lévy (Lauzon). He quickly recognized these articles when a burglar who had stolen them attempted to resell them to him in 1856, and he immediately turned the culprit over to the authorities.

Lespérance's name was again associated with Sasseville's in 1858; that year Lespérance used the technique of electroplating to gild for the Cathedral of Notre-Dame in Quebec City a monstrance which had "come from the workshop of M. Sasseville" six years earlier. These circumstances indicate the degree to which the career of Lespérance is inseparable from that of Sasseville until the latter died in 1864. Sasseville's will attests to the close bond between the two men; by its terms Lespérance received 100 shares in the Banque du Peuple, as well as Sasseville's workshop, store, and all his movables. The sole condition attached to this inheritance was that Lespérance should "fulfil all the obligations and complete all the works" to which Sasseville had committed himself and which were unfinished at the time of his death. Lespérance was also to have full authority over the financial operations of the enterprise. In March 1864 Lespérance announced in the papers "that the silversmith's establishment previously belonging to the late M. François Sasseville, on Rue du Palais, will be carried on in the name of the undersigned . . . [who] will continue to execute, as in the past, all the church silver and will do everything he can to deserve the patronage with which the clergy has always honoured this ancient establishment."

Lespérance was 44 years old when he embarked on this new chapter in his life, to last 18 years. The man remained as inconspicuous and unknown as he had been during Sasseville's lifetime. The main events of his private life in this period were his marriage, the birth of a son in January 1867, the death of his first wife in June 1868, and his remarriage. Apart from numerous liturgical vessels furnished to the clergy, and a few drawings and water-colours painted under the direction of his teacher, artist John Murray, his career was marked by the production of two articles of silver of a commemorative character. According to *Le Journal de Québec*, the first, a rather unusual piece executed in 1864, was an "exact miniature copy, on a scale of half an inch to the foot, of the column raised on the heights of Sainte-Foye to the heroes of the two nations who fought in 1759, one for the conquest, and the other for the defence of Canada. All [the details] of this work are exquisitely finished and the artist's skill is manifest in every part of this gem of a monument." This "magnificent work" was offered to the French consul at Quebec, "Baron [Charles-Henri-Philippe] Gauldrée-Boilleau, in memory of his services and of his benevolence." The second commemorative object was a trowel "presented to Her Royal Highness Princess Louise . . . at the laying of the foundations of the Kent Gate," at Quebec City in 1879. *Le Journal de Québec* of 14 June praised the engraver Torcapel, who had done the decorative details, commenting only briefly on the silversmith: "For the work of preparing [it, we are] indebted to M. Lespérance, whose ability in this type [of endeavour] is known." Commemorative silver was very popular at the end of the 19th century yet very little is known about objects of this type made by French-speaking Quebec craftsmen.

Ambroise-Adhémar Lafrance, who had worked as an apprentice under Sasseville, continued his training with Lespérance. After the latter's death in 1882, Lafrance ran the enterprise on his own, with the tools and models that had come down from Amiot's time. Lespérance and Lafrance, living anachronisms, were guardians of the traditional craft of church silver in an era of full-blown industrialization and commercialization. Thus, the silversmith Cyrille Gingras, who from 1888 worked in the important atelier of Cyrille Duquet, declared in an interview published in 1938 that "the other important shop in the city [of Quebec] during this period [1882-1905] was that of Father

Lafrance, who operated under the name of l'Espérance . . . in a house belonging to the nuns of the Hôtel-Dieu on the corner of Rue Charlevoix and Côte du Palais."

ROBERT DEROME
with the collaboration of SYLVIO NORMAND

[Articles crafted by Pierre Lespérance can be found in major public and private collections, in particular at the Musée du Québec (Québec) and in the Henry Birks Collection of Silver at the National Gallery of Canada (Ottawa). Several parish councils of the Quebec City region own pieces of his work. R.D. and S.N.]

ANQ-Q, État civil, Catholiques, Notre-Dame de Québec, 20 déc. 1819, 20 févr. 1865, 23 févr. 1870; Minutiers, A.-A. Parent, 20 juin 1836, 2 juill. 1839; A.-B. Sirois-Duplessis, 30 nov. 1863. IBC, Centre de documentation, Fonds Morisset, 2, A517/L382; G492.5/C997.5; L169.5/A495.1; R673/P622. Musée du Québec, A-53.85-d. *Le Journal de Québec*, 17, 22, 26 oct. 1850; 14 juin 1853; 3 avril 1855; 6 sept. 1856; 27 mars 1858; 17 mars, 23 août 1864; 23 févr. 1865; 12 janv. 1867; 16 juin 1868; 23 févr. 1870; 14 juin 1879; 24 avril 1882. *Quebec directory*, 1854–62. J. E. Langdon, *Canadian silversmiths, 1700–1900* (Toronto, 1966). Gérard Morisset, *Le Cap-Santé, ses églises et son trésor* (2e éd., C. Beauregard *et al.*, édit., Montréal, 1980). G.-H. Dagneau, "La fabrication des vases sacrés se fera à Québec," *L'Action catholique* (Québec), 14 avril 1938: 24. Gérard Morisset, "Nos orfèvres canadiens: Pierre Lespérance (1819–1882)," *Technique* (Montréal), 22 (1947): 201–9.

LES PRAIRIES. *See* PASKWĀW

LESSLIE, JAMES, merchant, publisher, and politician; b. 22 Nov. 1802 in Dundee, Scotland, the third of 12 children of Edward Lesslie and Grace Watson; d. 19 April 1885 at Eglinton (now part of Toronto), Ont.

James Lesslie's father was a well-to-do stationer, bookbinder, and bookseller in Dundee, and was able to provide his offspring with a good education. When, in 1819, Edward decided to emigrate to Canada to open a new business that would offer greater opportunities to his large family, his funds allowed him to plan to charter a brig to carry them and his stock. First, however, he sent out his second son, John, with a supply of goods to launch the enterprise. Arriving in 1820, John chose the town of York (Toronto) as the best business site in fast-arising Upper Canada. He had come out on the same ship as William Lyon Mackenzie*, also from Dundee and an acquaintance of his father, and the two young men began a general store together, in a building opposite St James' Church, which pioneered at York in selling books and drugs – the profit from the former going to Lesslie, the latter to Mackenzie. The following year they opened an additional store, Mackenzie and Lesslie, at the prosperous milling village of Dundas, dealing again in drugs, books, hardware, and general merchandise.

Meanwhile, ill health delayed the main Lesslie immigration. Consequently, Edward's third son, James, then 19, was sent on the chartered brig in charge of the family's goods and supplies as well as his 17-year-old sister and his 11-year-old brother, Charles. They landed at Quebec in the fall of 1822, after a 70-day passage through heavy gales. Since the stock he had brought was not now needed at York, James was advised to open a shop at Kingston instead. He did so, and ran the Kingston store for the next four years. By that time his parents and the rest of the family had arrived and settled in Dundas, where Mackenzie and John Lesslie had dissolved their partnership early in 1823, the former taking his share of the goods and moving to Queenston to establish a store there. The Dundas establishment then fell largely to the direction of another Lesslie brother, William, slightly younger than James. But all three stores, John's in York, James's in Kingston, and William's in Dundas, operated under the name of Lesslie and Sons.

This three-branch undertaking even had its own "coinage" struck in Birmingham, England, in the form of copper tokens in halfpenny and twopenny values, as was frequent practice in a day of inadequate currency in the colony and mongrel, dubious coins in circulation. Lesslie and Sons thrived with the expanding settlement boom of the 1820s, and in York they moved to larger quarters on King Street. There were also shifts in management. John took over the Dundas store and William the one in Kingston, while from 1826 James was in control at York – clearly still the main enterprise – assisted by his father and the youngest Lesslie brother, Joseph. Only the eldest brother, Edward, does not seem to have been closely engaged in the family business and presumably was farming. In 1828 Edward Sr died, but the firm continued under the same title. In York, indeed, with the growing specialization of increased trade, Lesslie and Sons became designated "Stationers and Druggists"; one side of their large brick store was mainly given over to books and stationery, the other to pharmaceuticals.

As the leading figure in this significant business, James Lesslie was becoming affluent and prominent. From 1829 he gradually acquired highly valuable real estate especially in the emerging centre of the town, some of which remained with his heirs till the 1950s. He was also entering into civic-minded activities. In 1831 he played a major part in establishing the mechanics' institute. Joseph Bates, an English watchmaker who was a tenant of Lesslie and Sons and who had been a member of the original London society, was eager to transplant to Canada this scheme for educating and elevating the working classes. James Lesslie heartily approved, issued circulars for a founding meeting, and worked actively thereafter to promote the institute and secure it a parliamentary grant. In

1834, when York was incorporated as the city of Toronto, he ran in the first civic elections, and was returned as alderman for St David's Ward, as was William Lyon Mackenzie. In 1836, he was one of a small key group of Toronto Reformers who pressed for and obtained a House of Industry to deal with the increasing problems of poverty in the swelling city.

James Lesslie was assuredly a Reformer, almost by definition. An earnest Scots Baptist who saw any "state Religion" as a "horrible delusion," he was an aspiring business exponent of self-help and progress, a well-read, reform-minded bookseller who looked for an enlightened democratic public to bestow "rational freedom upon our land," and a family friend of William Lyon Mackenzie to boot. James, in the rising political clashes of the 1830s in Upper Canada, quite naturally upheld civil liberty and religious equality, and opposed what he viewed as the despotic powers of hidebound Toryism or the unjust pretensions of a privileged Church of England. A close supporter of Mackenzie, Lesslie seconded his nomination as mayor in Toronto's first civic administration of 1834. He also became president of the Canadian Alliance, founded late in 1834 with Mackenzie as its corresponding secretary, which was intended to spread more advanced Reform ideas, such as a written, elective constitution on the American model, the secret ballot, the abolition of all monopolies, and the full separation of church and state.

Then in 1835 Lesslie was instrumental in the establishment of the Bank of the People, a Reform response to the government-associated Bank of Upper Canada, being named its first cashier (general manager) and shortly afterwards succeeding the first president, John Rolph*, when Francis HINCKS was appointed cashier. Under good management the "People's Bank," despite having no limited liability, weathered the financial crises of 1836 without having to suspend payments like the other Toronto banks. Yet its limited capital and unlimited risk were drawbacks which brought about its sale to the Bank of Montreal in 1840, all its stockholders having been paid off, as Lesslie could proudly record.

In the mean time, political discord in Upper Canada had led to the brief outburst of rebellion in 1837, which unhappily involved James Lesslie. He had gained considerable public exposure (and, in Tory eyes, notoriety) by this time, as an ardent member of the radical wing of the Reform movement, that associated with Mackenzie and Peter Perry*, rather than the moderates linked with William Warren Baldwin* and his son Robert*. For instance, in 1836 James and another advanced Reformer, Jesse Ketchum*, had delivered to Lieutenant Governor Sir Francis Bond Head* a decidedly "stinging" Reform address, a rejoinder to the governor's no less sharp answer to an initial address from Toronto citizens. While radical in leanings, however, Lesslie was in no way implicated in the rebellion itself and repudiated the appeal to force. Nevertheless, in the turmoil that accompanied the crushing of the Yonge Street rising, whether impelled by anger, suspicion, or plain vengefulness, an armed loyal band descended on James's house on 8 Dec. 1837, arrested both him and his brother William, and thrust them in jail. There they were held for 13 days, without warrant, examination, or appeal to habeas corpus. When finally released, still uncharged, they were bound over to keep the peace on sureties of £500 each. A hotly indignant petition by James and William was carried to the imperial parliament and to the Colonial Office, but accomplished little more than to relieve their feelings.

Indeed, in the period of harassment and frustration which followed the rebellion many despondent radicals grew ready to give up Canada and move to the United States. For this purpose the Mississippi Emigration Society was formed in Toronto early in 1838. Three delegates – two Reform members of the assembly, Peter Perry and Thomas Parke*, and James Lesslie – were selected to choose and negotiate for land to settle. Near Davenport, Iowa, they found a desirable tract, although James fell ill from the ordeals of a long journey into a wilderness of swamps and prairie. On their return, however, they learned of the mission to Canada of Lord Durham [Lambton*], a new, liberal governor general who offered high promise of reforming the colonial political system. James decided to stay. In fact, the Mississippi venture lost impetus, though some did emigrate, including his brother Charles, who spent the rest of his days at Davenport.

In the next few years, James Lesslie busied himself with the campaign by a reinvigorated, though more moderate, Reform movement for responsible government, a campaign which found strong endorsement in the recommendations of Durham's report in 1839, and which was led by Robert Baldwin with the vigorous backing of Francis Hincks's new party organ, the Toronto *Examiner*. At the same time the Lesslie business went on growing and changing. The old partnership was dissolved; John retained the Dundas store; William merged his Kingston business into James's at Toronto; and in 1841, now under the name of Lesslie Brothers, the Toronto firm built and occupied a fine brick store. Here Joseph would also work, but the enterprise really remained with James, especially after William died in 1843.

By then, moreover, a very different undertaking had been added. In 1842 Francis Hincks gave up the *Examiner* on entering the government. Lesslie took it over, and published it from the rear of his extensive store buildings. It was not a strange departure for him. Well-versed in public affairs, and a bookseller linked to the realm of popular publishing, he was only doing what William Lyon Mackenzie had done earlier when he had moved into journalism; and James had every reason to want to keep the influential Reform journal going. Still, he also had a sizeable commercial business as well as job-printing activities to manage. Joseph helped as assistant editor for a time, but it was not till 1846, when James obtained the services of a bright young English immigrant, Charles Lindsey*, as editor, that he might feel running the *Examiner* was no longer a problem.

By then, his journal faced a different sort of problem, sharpening competition from another rising Toronto Reform paper, the *Globe*, founded by George Brown* in 1844. Moreover, this ably managed journal had the backing of the leaders of Baldwin's party. When the Reformers won power in 1848 under Baldwin and Louis-Hippolyte La Fontaine*, the *Globe* became the recognized ministerial organ for Upper Canada, and the older *Examiner* was shunted to the side. Perhaps Lesslie's erstwhile radical reputation had helped shape the decision of the ascendant Baldwin moderates in the party. At any rate, his radical sentiments now markedly revived, both in the hope of pushing Reform achievements still further and in resentment of the Baldwinites who were leaving true "Old" Reformers out in the cold. This attitude was expressed in his paper, which moved on through 1849 from minor quarrelling with the *Globe* and the ministerial leaders to outright support of a newly emergent left-wing faction in Upper Canada Reform, soon to be dubbed the Clear Grits.

From the autumn of 1849, Lesslie's paper began pouring scorn on the inadequate and "aristocratical" achievement of responsible government, calling for a completely democratic and elective constitution on the American model, and also for the abolition of all remaining ties between church and state, notably featured in the clergy reserves of Upper Canada. Lesslie, in fact, entered zealously into a mounting voluntaryist crusade to make all churches purely voluntary bodies with no state aid or recognition. Accordingly, he played a prominent role in founding the Anti-Clergy Reserves Association in Toronto in May 1850. He also worked closely with the group that had shaped the initial, idealistic Clear Grit movement by 1850, which included old radical Reform associates Peter Perry, Malcolm Cameron*, and John Rolph, as well as younger democratic enthusiasts William McDougall* and Charles Clarke*.

But now his *Examiner* was to be passed on the left as well, when in 1851 McDougall aided by Clarke began the Toronto *North American* as a more effective popular Clear Grit organ. Then in 1852 the Toronto *Leader* appeared, a well-funded moderate journal which rapidly became influential and which also lured away the *Examiner*'s editor, Charles Lindsey (replaced by Daniel Morrison*). Beset by vigorous rivals all around it, Lesslie's paper thus went into decline during the early 1850s. It was viewed by regular party men as having become rather eccentric, and too inclined to ride its publisher's disestablishment hobby-horse. Lesslie was probably losing interest in any case, perhaps influenced by the fact that left-wing Reform had now expended much of its zeal and had not produced a democratic Utopia – although, on the other hand, he did see the battle to abolish the reserves achieve success in 1854. After the Reform ministry of Francis Hincks and Augustin-Norbert Morin* fell from power in that year, moreover, the Clear Grits and a more centrist group of Upper Canadian Reformers, who were increasingly influenced by George Brown, began coming back together. One sign of this was the growing party press hegemony built up by the *Globe*, which was marked further by Lesslie selling the *Examiner* to Brown in 1855, at a loss of some $8,000 in unpaid subscriptions.

During the 1840s and into the 1850s, Lesslie had continued his involvement in civic affairs in Toronto, notably in regard to non-sectarian public education, a cause close to his heart. In 1843 he was appointed a member of a committee reporting under the city's board of examiners to design a system of tuition and supervision in Toronto's common schools devoid of sectarian content or church connection. In 1851 he was elected a school trustee for St David's Ward, and was an ardent advocate of free schooling in a lively public debate the next year, an aim that was subsequently achieved for the city. He himself, however, was defeated in the school elections of 1853 (the victim of Roman Catholic votes, said the *Globe* darkly), but served again as trustee from 1854 to 1857. He was also a justice of the peace for the Home District after 1842, and for York County in 1850–51, yet does not seem to have been prominent in this capacity.

In any event, he sold off his stationery, book, and drug business about the time that he closed out the *Examiner*. Although only in his mid 50s, he was evidently anxious to retire. Hence he took up residence on a 28-acre farm estate north of Toronto at the village of Eglinton, which he had purchased from an old Reform associate, James Hervey PRICE – and which, incidentally, was adjacent to the site of Montgomery's Tavern, Mackenzie's headquarters during the rebellion. Lesslie's friendship with the leader of that ill-fated enterprise continued through their later lives, both while Mackenzie was in exile and after his return to Canada in the early 1850s. Indeed, in 1859, James served on the committee which drafted the appeal for funds for the "Mackenzie Homestead," the house on Bond Street, Toronto, given to the erstwhile "Little Rebel" as a public testimonial.

Nevertheless, Lesslie otherwise remained largely in retirement with his books and his farm after moving to Eglinton. He was, however, no recluse. He stayed in close touch with his family, spread from Dundas to Davenport, Iowa; his former political friends were frequent visitors; and he had valuable properties still to attend to in Toronto through business agents. In 1869, for example, he concluded a jointly advantageous transaction with George Brown by opening up "Globe Lane" between their adjoining King Street properties. Lesslie spoke at the Reform Convention of 1859 to urge the dissolution of the union between Upper and Lower Canada – an enduring radical position. But generally he kept out of politics and the public eye. Thus he passed some 30 years at Eglinton, living with his wife, Jacqueline, and their only child, an adopted daughter, and a small farm staff. There he died survived by two brothers and three sisters from the large Lesslie clan that had come to Canada over 60 years before.

J. M. S. CARELESS

AO, MU 1720; MU 1805–1949; MU 2020, James Lesslie to W. Edwards, 12 Jan. 1884. Dundas Museum (Dundas, Ont.), James Lesslie diaries. MTL, James Lesslie, Résumé of events and people in Toronto, 1822–1838 (typescript, 1880). *Evening Telegram* (Toronto), 17 Aug. 1889. *Examiner* (Toronto), 19 Sept., 10 Oct., 14 Nov. 1849; 15 Sept. 1855. *Globe*, 27 April, 9 May 1850; 31 July 1851; 10 Jan. 1852; 13 Jan. 1853; 11 Nov. 1859; 21, 24 April 1885. *Weekly Globe*, 29 Aug. 1855. Careless, *Brown*, I: 41–42, 62–65, 77, 107, 123–24.

LETELLIER DE SAINT-JUST, LUC (baptized **Luc-Horatio**), notary and politician; b. 12 May 1820 at Rivière-Ouelle, Lower Canada, son of François Letellier de Saint-Just, a notary, and Marie-Sophie Casgrain; m. 9 Feb. 1848 Eugénie-Éliza Laurent; d. 28 Jan. 1881 at Rivière-Ouelle.

Luc Letellier de Saint-Just's ancestor, François, who came from the small town of Saint-Just, near Saint-Quentin, France, arrived in Canada with the colonial regular troops some time before 1740; that year he left the army to marry and settle in Quebec. One of his sons, Michel, represented Hertford County in the House of Assembly from 1800 to 1804. Michel's son, François, was licensed as a notary on 29 June 1811, and took up residence at Rivière-Ouelle, where in 1814 he married Marie-Sophie Casgrain, the eldest daughter of the seigneur of La Bouteillerie. A gentleman of parts who was prominent in the social and political life of the region, François died prematurely in April 1828 of "a chest illness"; Luc, his eldest child, was not yet eight.

After attending primary school in Rivière-Ouelle and Kamouraska, Luc Letellier de Saint-Just studied at the Collège de Sainte-Anne-de-la-Pocatière from 1830 to 1836. Though inclined as a student to be rather indolent, he was cheerful and impulsively generous, capable moreover of firmness and tenacity when he set his mind on a particular goal. At the college he began to demonstrate unusual ability as a speaker. He went to the Petit Séminaire de Québec to complete his education, graduating with Pierre-Joseph-Olivier CHAUVEAU in the tragic year of 1837.

His maternal uncle, Judge Philippe Panet*, had taken him under his wing, and on his advice Luc began a training period with Pierre Garon, a notary at Rivière-Ouelle, who treated him as a son. He was commissioned a notary in 1841, and soon acquired a clientele among those prominent in the district of Rivière-Ouelle. An accomplished horseman and a sportsman who liked hunting and fishing, he led the life of a country squire, taking a growing interest in politics which he followed in *Le Courrier des États-Unis* (New York) and other sources, and discussed in the drawing-rooms of leading citizens. At that period the local élite, the Letelliers, Casgrains, Chapais, and Dionnes, supported the Reform group led by Louis-Hippolyte La Fontaine*. On 6 Dec. 1847 Luc Letellier de Saint-Just assembled these families in his office to form an electoral organizing committee for the parish of Rivière-Ouelle. According to his biographer, Philippe-Baby Casgrain, about 1848 he thought of practising as a notary in Quebec, for "his clientele at Rivère-Ouelle [was] not very lucrative"; it is not certain that he carried out this plan to move. A "young aristocratic dandy," Letellier was, according to Mgr Henri Têtu*, "idle and easy-going," preferring politics to horses and horses to his professional practice. In December 1850 he was at Rivière-Ouelle, fully determined to succeed Pierre Canac, *dit* Marquis, the representative for Kamouraska who had died on 26 Nov. 1850. Political unanimity no longer existed. By January there were two candidates: businessman Jean-Charles CHAPAIS and notary Letellier de Saint-Just. Both drew their support from family connections and local rivalries, some of which dated from the division of the parish of Rivière-Ouelle in 1840. Both candidates had similar programmes based on a manifesto approved by the electors on 31 December, apparently through the initiative of the supporters of *L'Avenir* of Montreal. But Chapais was closer to the clergy and the ministerialists, and Letellier to *L'Avenir* and the Reform party organizers of Kamouraska. This campaign was the beginning of the legendary battles between the Chapais and the Letelliers, which in the coming decades were marked by brawls, corrupt practices, sensational interventions by parish priests, and electoral contests that eventually were incorporated into the political folklore of Quebec. On 1 Feb. 1851 Letellier beat Chapais by 59 votes. According to his opponent, the young "dandy" had transformed himself into "a sort of clown wearing a hooded greatcoat of grey cloth, and armed with a stubby, black pipe, [who went about] dispensing handshakes." But Letellier held his seat for only a few months. Chapais had his revenge in the general elections of December, and retained his seat in 1854 and 1857 through the support of the parish priests who suspected Letellier of *rougisme*.

Letellier was elected legislative councillor for the division of Grandville in 1860, and on 16 May 1863 was appointed minister of agriculture in the Liberal cabinet of John Sandfield Macdonald* and Antoine-Aimé Dorion*. Ministerial instability was a characteristic of the political life of the period; ministries crumbled like houses of cards. On 29 March 1864 the Liberal government fell, the Conservatives returned to power, and it was Chapais rather than Letellier who obtained a portfolio.

A change in the form of government was advocated, largely to escape the deadlock. Chapais became one of the builders of confederation. Letellier, on the other hand, was one of those who fought the project, to no avail, for the sake of both the autonomy of all the provinces and the future of French culture, and in opposition to the centralizing nature of the new régime. "I frankly admit," he stated, "that I would prefer a legislative union between Upper and Lower Canada, with inequality of representation in the Lower House and equality in the Upper House accepted in order to ensure to the two provinces reciprocal guarantees for their respective institutions." Once confederation was achieved, however, he rallied to it as did most of its opponents, and on 23 Oct. 1867 he agreed to represent the division of Grandville in the Senate.

As leader of the Liberal party in the Senate, Letellier still hankered after electoral battles. He entered the political fray indirectly by supporting the candidacy of Charles-Alphonse-Pantaléon Pelletier* against Chapais in the provincial elections of 1867; this electoral campaign degenerated into a general free-for-all. Letellier would not have been averse to sitting in the Quebec Legislative Assembly, particularly as leader of the Liberal party, but to realize his dream he had first to get elected. Dogged by ill luck, however, he suffered his fifth consecutive defeat in the Kamouraska by-election on 11 and 12 Feb. 1869; this was followed by another defeat in L'Islet in the 1871 general election. Until 1875 Letellier had to content himself with being the secret power behind the Quebec Liberals. In the 1872 federal elections he was the Liberal organizer for the south shore, where he succeeded in getting all his candidates elected, from Lévis to Gaspé.

In November 1873 the Liberals under Alexander Mackenzie* took office in Ottawa, following the resignation of Sir John A. Macdonald*'s cabinet on the 7th. Finally Letellier was to know success. Mackenzie appointed him minister of agriculture and co-leader, with Richard William Scott*, in the Senate. More a politician than an administrator, Letellier de Saint-Just was one of the most dreaded foes of the Conservative party. As a minister, he was instrumental in securing the decision of Governor General Lord Dufferin [Blackwood*] to commute the death sentence pronounced upon Ambroise-Dydime Lépine*, Louis RIEL's right-hand man. He also played an important part in obtaining the dispatch to Rome of a report protesting clerical meddling in the elections, and in the repatriation to Manitoba of Canadians who had emigrated to the United States. His term of office was, however, darkened by the death in May 1876 of his wife, who left him with several children and two nieces they had adopted in 1861. Letellier never fully recovered from the shock.

Late in 1876 the lieutenant governor of Quebec, René-Édouard Caron*, passed away after a long illness. On 15 December Alexander Mackenzie, after some hesitation, appointed Letellier lieutenant governor rather then Joseph-Édouard CAUCHON because of the latter's unpopularity. Mackenzie parted reluctantly with such a brilliant second in command. Letellier took his new duties seriously. He enjoyed the ceremonies and the fashionable life at Spencer Wood (Bois de Coulonge, Sillery, Que.), the lieutenant governor's official residence, where he lived in princely style. But he had a predilection for active political life and party strife. The tranquillity of Spencer Wood did not really suit him. He meddled in the political contests of the lower St Lawrence River counties, criticized on occasion the decisions of the Conservative cabinet of Charles-Eugène Boucher* de Boucherville, and even refused to sign an order in council. Where Letellier de Saint-Just claimed to be acting on principle, the Conservatives saw only partisan motivation. Boucher de Boucherville endeavoured to conceal the latent conflict; the attorney general, Auguste-Réal Angers*, a blunt man who had already been involved in the electoral confrontations down river, came to the point of curtly refusing invitations to Spencer Wood. The mutual distrust between Angers and Letellier surfaced over railway policy, which was of crucial importance at that period and was creating difficulties for the government of Boucher de Boucherville. Every region and town was clamouring for a railway, considered the key to economic progress, but the government, with its small budget, could not subsidize all the lines. Municipalities, dissatisfied with the routes proposed, refused to pay their share. Angers's announcement that he intended to take a tough line provoked indignant reaction.

Letellier did not agree with his ministers on the railway question. Without consulting the federal government to which he was subject, but probably aware that he would have the support of the Liberals in the legislature, he dismissed Boucher de Boucherville's Conservative government on 2 March 1878. And he entrusted the Liberal leader, Henri-Gustave Joly*, who did not have a majority in the house, with the task of forming a new government. It was a partisan act; it also created a sensation. The Conservatives protested that it was a *coup d'état*. The Ottawa Liberals were dumbfounded: Mackenzie and Wilfrid Laurier* privately condemned Letellier's action, and Luther Hamilton Holton* turned down a post in Joly's cabinet. The province was in a state of turmoil. A general election would be necessary to settle this great dispute. Joseph-Adolphe Chapleau* opened the campaign with his famous cry: "Silence the voice of Spencer Wood and let the mighty voice of the people speak." However, despite the fire and eloquence of Chapleau, the electors gave their approval to Letellier.

All was well as long as the Liberals were in power in Ottawa, but in September 1878 Macdonald and the Conservatives were returned in strength. The Bleus of the province of Quebec, furious with the author of the *coup d'état*, demanded his removal from office. That would be another act of grave significance. Macdonald hesitated, temporized, and sent two of his ministers to England to consult the imperial government, which dumped the matter back in his lap. Chapleau's friends persisted; they virtually engaged in conspiracy, with Joseph-Alfred MOUSSEAU, the member for Bagot in the House of Commons, as their principal spokesman, and he proved tenacious. Finally, the Macdonald government removed Letellier, and on 25 July 1879 appointed a Conservative, Théodore Robitaille*, as his successor.

Letellier retired, financially ruined and physically broken. He had been stricken with a heart attack in May and given last rites, and had only partially recovered his health. But he was a fighter. He sent his family to Rivière-Ouelle, and went to Quebec to live in a friend's house. He remained near his doctors, and especially his friends, with whom he was ready to continue the struggle by meeting with the Liberal organizations of Quebec and Ontario. But his health no longer matched his courage. He suffered a second heart attack and retired, a sick man, to his son-in-law's house in Ottawa. In May 1880 he returned to Rivière-Ouelle, where he died on 28 Jan. 1881.

ROBERT RUMILLY

Almost all the papers of the chief political figures of the period from 1876 to 1880, as well as the newspapers, contain references to the *coup d'état* and to Luc Letellier de Saint-Just. These should be consulted for a full examination of his career.

AP, Rivière-Ouelle, Reg. des baptêmes, mariages et sépultures, 13 mai 1820, 9 févr. 1848, 2 févr. 1881. Qué., Assemblée législative, *Journaux*, 1877–80. *Le Canadien*, 5–17 févr. 1881. *Montreal Herald and Daily Commercial Gazette*, 31 Jan. 1881. *L'Opinion publique*, 4, 11 janv. 1877; 7 août 1879; 3, 17 févr. 1881. *CPC*, 1873–78. J. C. Dent, *Canadian portrait gallery*, I: 47–53. Julienne Barnard, *Mémoires Chapais; documentation, correspondance, souvenirs* (4v., Montréal et Paris, 1961–64). P.-B. Casgrain, *Étude historique: Letellier de Saint-Just et son temps* (Québec, 1885). M. Hamelin, *Premières années du parlementarisme québécois*. P.-H. Hudon, *Rivière-Ouelle de la Bouteillerie; 3 siècles de vie* (Ottawa, 1972). Rumilly, *Hist. de la prov. de Québec*, I–II. Henri Têtu, *Histoire des familles Têtu, Bonenfant, Dionne et Perrault* (Québec, 1898), 401–5. Alpheus Todd, *Parliamentary government in the British colonies* (London, 1880). J.-C. Bonenfant, "Destitution d'un premier ministre et d'un lieutenant-gouverneur," *Cahiers des Dix*, 28 (1963): 9–31.

LITTLE, JAMES, lumberman and conservationist; b. in 1803 near Londonderry (Northern Ireland); m. in 1832 Anne Youell, and they had at least three sons; d. 2 Oct. 1883 at Montreal, Que.

James Little immigrated to British North America in 1823 and settled near St Catharines, Upper Canada. He became acquainted with William Hamilton Merritt*, worked on the Welland Canal, and, at Merritt's urging, became a contractor on the project. When he encountered financial difficulties and was imprisoned for debt in 1832, Merritt secured his release and in 1833 employed him in the Grand River Navigation Company. Little surveyed the river for dam and lock sites, participated in construction, and managed the company from 1835 to 1840. In 1834 he purchased land at Seneca, Haldimand County, for his home and built a general store there. By 1840 he appears to have become an independent and established businessman and land speculator; in 1842 he applied for a large amount of Indian land in the area, including lots in the prosperous nearby community of Caledonia. Little offered to pay a set amount for each lot regardless of its value, and tried to have the Crown Lands Department establish the selling price. The chief superintendent of Indian affairs, Samuel Peters Jarvis*, opposed the sale, suspecting that Little wanted the land for speculation. In 1846 a compromise was reached and Little purchased the land for £1,300 which went to the Six Nations trust fund. In 1854 he purchased more town lots in Caledonia.

In 1844 Little had built a flour-mill on the south side of the Grand River at Caledonia and by 1848 he had entered the timber trade. From his own lands and from limits leased in Brant, Elgin, Norfolk, and Wentworth counties he took out square timber and naval stores including masts for the British market, and he manufactured sawn lumber for the American market at a mill in Caledonia. After the signing of the Reciprocity Treaty with the United States in 1854 his business with Buffalo, N.Y., and Toledo and Cleveland, Ohio, dominated his operations. Little expanded his lumbering activities during the late 1850s until he had several mills in the counties in which he had timber limits, and in the 1860s he even operated in the southern Georgian Bay area. He also established carding- and fulling-mills at Caledonia.

In addition to his business interests Little took an

active role in community affairs. He was a founding member of the Wesleyan Methodist chapel at Seneca in 1843 and postmaster for the area from 1839 until 1860. In an effort to get railway facilities for Caledonia, Little persuaded the Hamilton and Port Dover Railway in 1853 to run its line through the village. The outcome of his endeavour was unfortunately not satisfactory. The village of Caledonia was obliged to pledge £10,000 in debentures to the line although actual construction of the railway was not started until 1873, and the citizens were left with a heavy tax burden.

By the late 1860s Little found that timber supplies were running out in southwestern Ontario. He blamed this problem on the Reciprocity Treaty which he contended had both stimulated production and driven down prices. The Americans, he charged, had taken Canadian supplies at a low cost and saved their own forests for future use. Faced with exhausted pineries he transferred his operations to the Rivière Saint-Maurice region of Quebec and in 1873 he moved to Montreal where he became a timber broker and speculated in timber limits. The realization that southwestern Ontario had been gutted of pine, and his forced relocation, profoundly affected his thinking. He began to reflect upon the wasteful practices of Canadian lumbermen and the possibility that wood supplies in North America would soon be exhausted.

The results were two pamphlets, *The lumber trade of the Ottawa valley* and *The timber supply question, of the dominion of Canada and the United States of America*. Both booklets carried basically the same message: the timber supplies of North America were being destroyed by fire and reckless lumbering, and strict government regulation of the remaining forest areas was necessary if a perpetual yield was to be maintained. Little's greatest fear was that once the Americans had used up all their available sources they would turn to Canada for lumber, and gut all the forests of Ontario and Quebec within five years. He wanted classification of land for agricultural or forest use, forest reserves, reforestation, and strict protection of young trees. Most Canadians greeted Little's suggestions with scepticism and considered him a crank. Only in the lumbering community did his ideas elicit support. Many operators did not agree that the United States would become dependent on Canada for wood products, but they did sympathize with his call for more government regulation to reverse the steady decline in the quality of their timber resources.

Little was undeterred by the cool response. He studied American conservationist thought and in 1874 began to correspond with Franklin Benjamin Hough, the pioneer protagonist of forestry in the United States. Hough invited him to give a paper on "The white pine forests of Canada" to the founding meeting of the American Forestry Congress, held at Cincinnati, Ohio, in April 1882. Little accepted and also formed an unofficial delegation from Quebec, including Henri-Gustave Joly*, to attend the meeting. In Cincinnati the Quebec group was joined by members of the Ontario Fruit Growers' Association which was part of the official Ontario delegation. The Canadians in attendance were in the forefront of those who asserted that fire, wasteful cutting practices, poor wood utilization, and improper land clearance were wiping out the forests of North America. Indeed so enthusiastic was the response of the Canadian delegates that the Americans agreed to meet again soon in Montreal.

Little threw himself into organizing the Montreal conference. He pressed the Quebec Limitholders' Association to have a good attendance of its members. He was successful in gaining the association's support and consequently the three-day conference in August 1882 provided an excellent platform for discussions between conservationists and lumber operators. The conference's committee on forest fires, chaired by Pembroke lumberman Peter White*, and including James Kewley Ward, John Bryson, and Little's son William, all prominent lumbermen, was particularly effective. The committee recommended that all pine and spruce lands unfit for settlement should be reserved for lumbering, that brush burning by settlers be prohibited in the summer and autumn, and that fire districts be established and policed by officers with magisterial powers. The committee also suggested that the cost of maintaining this fire prevention system be met by a moderate tax on the timber operators. Little was proud that the forest industry had taken such a positive approach to forest protection.

Unfortunately he did not live to see the immediate results of the Montreal conference, which included the enactment of forest fire regulations in Ontario modelled largely on the committee on forest fires' recommendations, and the appointment in 1883 of a federal forestry commissioner, J. H. Morgan, to study forest conservation problems.

ROBERT PETER GILLIS

James Little was the author of *Information for the public: the case of the Indian Department, in reference to the Grand River settlers . . .* (Hamilton, [Ont.], 1852); *The lumber trade of the Ottawa valley, with a description of some of the principal manufacturing establishments* (Ottawa, 1871; 3rd ed., 1872); "The timber question," Montreal Horticultural Soc. and Fruit Growers' Assoc. of the Prov. of Quebec, *Report* (Montreal), 6 (1880): 14–19; and *The timber supply question, of the dominion of Canada and the United States of America* (Montreal, 1876).

PAC, MG 24, E1, 7: 800–1; 8: 922–25; 10: 1210–13; 13: 1964; MG 28, III26, 102; RG 1, E1, 68: 102; L3, 297, L 2/4; RG 10, A1, 7: 3592–612; RG 15, DII, 1, v.298, file 62441; RG 68, Index to Indian and Ordnance land, 1845–67. Can., Prov. of, Legislative Assembly, *App. to the journals*, 1846,

I: app.F. Ont., Commissioner of Agriculture and Arts, *Annual report* (Toronto), 1882, app.C. *Montreal Herald and Daily Commercial Gazette*, 1883. *Canada directory*, 1851. Can., Prov. of, Dept. of the Postmaster General, *List of post offices in Canada, and the names of the postmasters* (Quebec and Toronto), 1854–60.

Canadian men and women of the time (Morgan, 1912). J. E. Defebaugh, *History of the lumber industry of America* (2v., Chicago, 1906–7), II: 148. R. S. Lambert and Paul Pross, *Renewing nature's wealth; a centennial history of the public management of lands, forests & wildlife in Ontario, 1763–1967* ([Toronto], 1967), 178–79. A. R. M. Lower, *The North American assault on the Canadian forest: a history of the lumber trade between Canada and the United States* . . . (Toronto and New Haven, Conn., 1938; repr. New York, 1968), 146. R. B. Nelles, *County of Haldimand in the days of auld lang syne* (Port Hope, Ont., 1905). A. D. Rodgers, *Bernhard Eduard Fernow: a story of North American forestry* (Princeton, N.J., 1951). *A short history of Caledonia*, ed. A. H. Arrell (Caledonia, Ont., n.d.). R. P. Gillis, "The Ottawa lumber barons and the conservation movement, 1880–1914," *Journal of Canadian Studies*, 9 (1974), no.1: 14–30. B. E. Hill, "The Grand River Navigation Company and the Six Nations Indians," *OH*, 63 (1971): 31–40.

LITTLE CHILD. *See* KIWISĀNCE

LITTLE PINE. *See* MINAHIKOSIS

LOBLEY, JOSEPH ALBERT, Church of England clergyman and educator; b. 10 Feb. 1840 in Liverpool, England, son of Benjamin Lobley, a joiner and builder, and Mary Harrison; m. in 1867 Elizabeth Ann Mais, and they had at least one daughter; d. 6 Jan. 1889 at Sedbergh, England.

Joseph Albert Lobley received his early education at the Collegiate Institution in Liverpool, matriculated to the University of Cambridge in 1859, and obtained his BA in 1863. In the latter year he was ordained deacon and in 1864 priest. From 1863 to 1866, while still resident at Cambridge, he was curate of nearby Bourn, an ecclesiastical benefice of which Christ's College, Cambridge, was the patron. His academic distinction led to his election in 1865 as a fellow of Trinity College, Cambridge, a post he soon resigned to become curate of Hamer, near Rochdale (now part of Greater Manchester); he was vicar there from 1867 to 1873. While at Hamer he was designated bishop of Victoria, Hong Kong, but declined the post on medical advice. Through his interest in the missionary work of the Society for the Propagation of the Gospel, he probably familiarized himself at this time with the state of the Church of England in Canada.

In 1873 Ashton Oxenden*, Anglican bishop of Montreal, invited Lobley to come to Canada as principal of the proposed Montreal Diocesan Theological College. Bishop's College at Lennoxville, Quebec, had provided clergy for Montreal since the founding of the diocese in 1850 and the bishop of Montreal was, *ex officio*, vice-president of Bishop's. Yet Oxenden was aware that Bishop's had "earned the character (somewhat unjustly perhaps) of nurturing extreme opinions in its students" and he therefore resolved, for this and other reasons, to establish a training school of his own. The Montreal college opened under Lobley's guidance on 22 Sept. 1873 with only two students, but at the end of the second academic term had increased their number to ten. The college was not incorporated until 1879 and was without its own quarters until 1881, but it received strong support from Oxenden and prominent laymen. Lobley, who gave the entire course in theology, also taught general introductory subjects to those whose early education was inadequate and encouraged those who were qualified to secure a bachelor's degree at McGill College or Bishop's. In the four years Lobley headed the college, 12 students were prepared for ordination, among them Lewis Norman Tucker*, later general secretary of the Missionary Society of the Church of England in Canada, Elson Irving Rexford*, principal of the college from 1904 to 1928, and Jervois Arthur Newnham*, successively bishop of Moosonee and of Saskatchewan. Bishop Oxenden praised Lobley's "great efficiency" and in 1891 wrote of him: "He was a little too much of a Churchman for some of my friends at Montreal, but he was a good and able man."

Lobley had originally intended to stay in Canada only five years, but late in 1877 he handed over the principalship of the Montreal college to the Reverend William Henderson* and agreed to become head of Bishop's following the death of its first principal, Jasper Hume Nicolls*. For the next seven and a half years Lobley led a busy life as an administrator and able teacher particularly of classics and mathematics. Although the number of students at Bishop's never exceeded 40 during his tenure, he was occupied with expanding the curriculum to include science and law, laying out a scheme for a new library, maintaining strict discipline, adding to the chapel, and directing the college's religious services. From 1883 to 1885 he assumed as well the rectorship of Bishop's College School, a closely allied preparatory school founded in 1836 by Lucius Doolittle*. Lobley, who served the mission of Milby throughout this period, was an excellent preacher and had a good singing voice which helped him both at social occasions and in the conduct of services.

His outstanding work both at Montreal and at Lennoxville earned him speedy recognition in the church. In the episcopal election of 1879 to choose a successor to Alexander Neil Bethune*, bishop of Toronto, Lobley received a majority of the clerical votes but failed, if only by a few votes, to receive the approval of the laity. In March 1880 he was asked to succeed George WHITAKER as provost of Trinity College, Toronto, and later was offered posts as dean of Quebec's Cathedral of the Holy Trinity and of Kingston's St George's Cathedral, but he declined these offers. On his return to England in 1885 he lived first in Cambridge and was employed by the SPG as organizing secretary for the dioceses of Ely and Peterborough from January 1886 to July 1887. In August of the latter year he became vicar of Sedbergh, a living in the gift of Trinity College, Cambridge, but he died in January 1889 at age 48.

Joseph Albert Lobley left a fine record as an educator during his 12 years in Canada. The institutions he served are still active and attest to the soundness of his work. Although a few conservative evangelical Anglicans in Montreal and Toronto entertained doubts about his churchmanship, Lobley was not a party man. His personal charm was great, and the important positions which were offered to him in his comparatively short lifetime reflect his character and ability.

THOMAS R. MILLMAN

Joseph Albert Lobley was the author of *The church and churches in southern India: a review of the Portuguese missions to that part of the world in the sixteenth century, etc.* (Cambridge, Eng., 1870), of two sermons published in the *Church Guardian* (Montreal), 9 Aug. 1882 and 8 July 1885, and of a report on Bishop's College published in *Mission Field* (London), 1 April 1879.

Anglican Church of Canada, General Synod Arch. (Toronto), Mountain-Roe-Jarvis coll., sect. 2, Roe papers, B, diaries and journals, Fannie Roe diaries, 14 Dec. 1876; 24 Oct., 15, 23, 25 Dec. 1877; 3, 14 Jan., 11, 20, 29 Oct. 1878; 3 March 1879; 8 March 1880. Bishop's Univ. Arch. (Lennoxville, Que.), Alumni Assoc., Minutes, 1878; College Council, Record of meetings, 1876–95; Corporation, Minutes, 1877–90; Trustees, Minute books, 1875–90. Church of England, Diocese of Toronto, Synod, *Journal* (Toronto), 1879. *Educational Record of the Province of Quebec* (Montreal), 5 (1885): 100, 162–63, 183. Ashton Oxenden, *The history of my life, an autobiography* (London, 1891); *My first year in Canada* (London, 1871). [A. C. Scarth], *Memoir of the Rev. Archibald Campbell Scarth, M.A., D.C.L., rector of St George's Church, Lennoxville . . .*, [ed. Henry Roe] (Sherbrooke, Que., 1904). *Evangelical Churchman* (Toronto), 7 Feb. 1889. *Gazette* (Montreal), 1873–74. *Sedbergh and District Parish Magazine* (Sedbergh, Eng.), February 1889.

Alumni Cantabrigienses . . ., comp. John and J. A. Venn (2 pts. in 10v., Cambridge, 1922–54), pt.II: IV. George Abbott-Smith, *I call to mind: recollections and impressions of the last three-quarter century* (Toronto, [1947]). Oswald Howard, *The Montreal Diocesan Theological College, a history from 1873 to 1963* (Montreal, 1963). D. C. Masters, *Bishop's University, the first hundred years* (Toronto, 1950).

LOCKERBY, ELIZABETH NEWELL (Bacon), poetess; b. 12 Sept. 1831 at Cavendish, Queens County, P.E.I., sixth of 12 children of John Lockerby and Margaret Forbes; m. in 1874 Hiram Bacon; d. 6 Dec. 1884 at Indianapolis, Ind.

Elizabeth Newell Lockerby's parents had immigrated from Scotland to the Miramichi River in New Brunswick in 1820 before settling the following year in Cavendish. There her father farmed and worked as a blacksmith. In 1862 John Lockerby retired from farming and moved to Charlottetown, accompanied by his wife and his 31-year-old daughter. Elizabeth, who had been writing poetry since her early teens, soon began to pursue a life of her own. In 1863 she attended the Provincial Training Seminary at Truro, N.S., and from 1864 to 1867 travelled frequently to Nova Scotia and New Brunswick to visit friends and relatives.

In 1866 Elizabeth Lockerby published, probably at her own expense, a volume of poetry which evidence suggests she then sold door-to-door in Charlottetown. She seems to have nurtured hopes of pursuing a career as a professional writer and to this end went to New York City in 1868, but her meagre talents and lack of literary connections and intellectual sophistication soon proved to her that she would not succeed. The following year she went to Portland, Maine, to study the life insurance business. This career was also short-lived, for in 1872 she was in Chatham, N.B., assisting her brother in his mercantile business.

In 1873 her life took a dramatic turn when she became "companion to a lady whose husband is Cashier in the National Bank of Chicago." The following year she met and married Hiram Bacon in Chicago. Bacon, 73 years old and twice widowed, was a retired lawyer and landowner from Indianapolis, and it was in that city that the couple lived until his death in 1881. They had no children.

Elizabeth Lockerby's reputation as a writer rests on two publications: a book of poems, *The wild brier: or, lays by an untaught minstrel* (Charlottetown, 1866), and a collection of poetry and prose, *Oak leaves* (Halifax, 1869). The first volume was reprinted in Indianapolis in 1881 and 1883, and the second was also reprinted there in 1882, all at her own expense. She may also have written some pieces for magazines and journals. The prose pieces in *Oak leaves* contain sentimental tragedy, lush description, or speculations on the marvel of human creation. Of her known works, the poems are most interesting. The early poems, written between 1843 and 1852, are heavily sentimental in tone and mood, with a marked tendency toward melodramatic description and narration of events. Her best known piece, "George and Amanda," written during this period, deals with the death of a young New England sailor in the terrible hurricane of October 1851 which virtually destroyed an American fishing fleet on the north shore of Prince Edward Island. It has some effective descriptive passages:

Some boldly stood to sea, and vainly hoped
To leave the dreadful storm behind, but found

That it more fiercely broke on all sides round, –
And creaking, crashing, foundered far at sea.
Some sought to gain the sheltering ports, but failed,
And on the rocks were driven, and there, with all
Their complement of men, to death went down!

Lockerby's early poetry, though it frequently reveals the young author's lack of artistic control over the emotional elements of her verse, does show a flair for versification and narration, and a sensitivity for human feeling. Unfortunately, she never developed the artistic skills and intellectual perceptions necessary to go significantly beyond the sentimental approach of her youthful verse. In her later poems, written between 1853 and 1869, she tempered her propensity for sentimentalism by developing a strong didactic element in her verse, as did many poets of her day. Almost inevitably, she turned to religion and morality as her main subjects. These later poems, while technically competent, are indistinguishable from the great mass of mid-19th-century religious verse published in North America and Britain.

THOMAS B. VINCENT

[Elizabeth Newell Lockerby was the author of *Oak leaves* (Halifax, 1869; repr. Indianapolis, 1882) and *The wild brier: or, lays by an untaught minstrel* (Charlottetown, 1866; repr. Indianapolis, 1881, 1883). John Lockerby of Toronto supplied the author with written information on E. N. Lockerby, copies of which have been deposited with the *DCB/DBC*. T.B.V.]

LONGLEY, AVARD, farmer, merchant, orchardist, temperance advocate, and politician; b. 22 Feb. 1823 at Paradise, Annapolis County, N.S., son of Asaph Longley and Dorcas Poole; m. first in 1848 Hannah Maria Whitman; m. secondly in 1855 Charlotte Augusta Troop, and they had at least three children; d. 22 Feb. 1884 in Paradise.

Avard Longley's ancestors came to Nova Scotia from New England. From the beginning his life was greatly influenced by his family's attachment both to the land they farmed and to the Baptist Church in which they worshipped. He was educated in his home town and became a successful farmer and merchant there. Through the influence of the local Baptist church and his father-in-law, William Henry Troop, he became increasingly convinced of the evils of alcohol and of the necessity of total abstinence. The temperance cause became the glasses through which he viewed many issues of the day, and he frequently held positions of importance in local, provincial, and national temperance organizations.

It was apparently Longley's involvement in the temperance movement that first drew him into politics. In 1859, on a platform of opposition to rum and railways, he was elected a Conservative member of the Nova Scotia assembly for Annapolis County. Among the candidates opposing him were his brother Israel, and his successful running mates included James William Johnston*, the incumbent premier. Johnston's government was subsequently ousted by William YOUNG and the Liberals early in 1860. Longley was re-elected in 1863 when the Conservatives under Johnston and Charles Tupper* resoundingly defeated the Liberals. He gave his full support to Tupper's controversial bill in 1864 which established a public school system supported by compulsory assessment, although many of his Annapolis County constituents opposed the plan. His stand on the other key issue of the day, union of the British North American colonies, is less clear. In 1864, referring to the choice between a union of the Maritime colonies or a general union, Longley was recorded as having made the curious and ambivalent statement: "Somehow or other it appeared to be inadvisable to include Canada in the arrangement; but he was inclined to think, if there is to be any union at all, it should be one of the whole of the Provinces." In the ensuing discussion of union over the next three years he wisely refrained from again entering the debate.

In late 1864 Longley was appointed commissioner of railways, a post he occupied until 1869; under his direction, railway lines were constructed between Truro and Pictou and between Windsor and Annapolis. Having resigned his assembly seat in 1867 to run, unsuccessfully, in the federal election of that year, he failed in his attempt to re-enter provincial politics in 1871. He was, however, again elected for Annapolis in 1874 and served until 1878. In the Nova Scotia house he was considered a major spokesman for the temperance cause and the Baptist Church.

Longley's first attempt at entering federal politics was as the pro-confederate candidate in Annapolis County in 1867. In this election, in which Joseph Howe*'s anti-confederate forces triumphed, Longley was soundly defeated, probably as much by resentment over Tupper's Free School Act as by opposition to confederation among the voters. He was defeated again in 1872, but was finally elected to the House of Commons in 1878. During the brief period he spent in Ottawa, Longley once reminded a somewhat startled (or amused) Sir John A. Macdonald* and his fellow members that the temperance question was worth ten National Policies. He also attempted unsuccessfully to have the House of Commons bar permanently closed. Ill health forced his retirement at the time of the 1882 general election.

Politics by no means dominated Longley's life. As an increasingly prominent orchardist and a pioneer in the important Annapolis valley apple industry, he saw the potential in the export of apples to overseas markets and in 1863 was one of the founders of the Nova Scotia Fruit Growers' Association. He served the association in numerous executive capacities and was its president from 1883 until his death the following year. Church affairs also occupied much of his time. He had joined the Baptist church in Paradise in May 1842 and from 1870 until his death served as its clerk. In 1876 and again in 1878 he was elected president of the Maritime Baptist Convention, and from 1874 until his death he was an elected member of the board of governors of Acadia College in Wolfville, N.S., despite the fact that he had had very little formal education himself.

Neither a significant politician nor a brilliant public speaker, Avard Longley as a spokesman for the Baptist Church and the temperance cause nevertheless represented important social forces in 19th-century Nova Scotia. He clearly saw politics in such terms, although the causes he championed often put him out of step with the major political trends and politicians of his day.

BARRY M. MOODY

Annapolis County Court of Probate (Annapolis Royal, N.S.), L77, Administration of estate of Avard Longley, 13 May 1884 (mfm. at PANS). Atlantic Baptist Hist. coll., Paradise and Clarence Baptist Church records, 1827–69. PANS, MG 4, Wilmot Township, Township book, 1749–1894 (mfm.). Can., House of Commons, *Debates*, 1879. N.S., House of Assembly, *Debates and proc.*, 1864. *Acadian Recorder*, 23 Feb. 1889. *The Baptist year book of Nova Scotia, New Brunswick, and Prince Edward Island . . .* (Saint John, N.B.), 1876. *The Baptist year book of the Maritime provinces of Canada . . .* (Saint John), 1880. *Directory of N.S. MLAs*. *Historical records and general catalogue of Acadia College, August, 1888* (Halifax, 1888). W. A. Calnek, *History of the county of Annapolis . . .*, ed. A. W. Savary (Toronto, 1897; repr. Belleville, Ont., 1972). [S. N. Jackson], *Historical sketch of the Paradise and Clarence United Baptist Church read at the centennial services held Sept. 10–13, 1910: 1810–1910* (n.p., [1910?]). R. S. Longley *et al.*, *Three Avard Longleys of Annapolis County* (n.p., 1943).

LONGWORTH, FRANCIS, merchant, shipbuilder, and politician; b. 3 Oct. 1807 in Charlottetown, P.E.I., third son of Francis Longworth* and Agnes Auld; m. 3 Aug. 1835 Sarah Parker Watts, and they had 12 children; d. 12 June 1883 in Charlottetown.

Francis Longworth's father, a member of an Anglo-Irish, Anglican, land-owning family, in the early 1790s immigrated from County Westmeath (Republic of Ireland) to Charlottetown, where he became prominent in local society, holding several public offices, including that of high sheriff for Queens County. Little is known about the younger Francis' upbringing and education. He first appears in 1833 as the Island agent for a variety of American magazines. The following year his older brother, Robert, took him into his Charlottetown store which dealt "in all manner of British and Foreign goods." The firm of R. and F. Longworth apparently prospered, for by 1839 the brothers were making their first initiatives in the expanding Island shipbuilding industry. The partnership ended by mutual consent in November 1842 and Francis proceeded to open his own Charlottetown store with Albert Hinde Yates. Longworth's primary activity was as a general commission merchant, but he continued his involvement in shipbilding and brokerage, owning individually or in partnership a total of 47 vessels with a tonnage of 6,352 between 1840 and 1855. His business interests would often compete with his dedication to a political career.

In common with all the members of his family, Longworth moved easily in the society of Charlottetown's élite, thereby joining an interlocking Family Compact which dominated the economic and political life of both the town and the Island. In 1838 this élite chose him to be, with Edward PALMER, a representative for Charlottetown and Royalty to the Island House of Assembly. For promoting the interests of Charlottetown and defending the propertied class from the inroads of the Escheat agitation led by William Cooper*, and later resisting the advance of responsible government, Longworth was returned without interruption through nine elections. Indeed, Longworth and Palmer often ran unopposed, a fact Edward Whelan*'s *Palladium* attributed to the fear the Family Compact instilled in both the electorate and possible Reform candidates. In 1847 Francis Longworth featured in Whelan's "Black Watch" editorial outlining the commercial and familial connections of the Compact system.

Longworth served his political apprenticeship under the Conservative leaders Joseph Pope* and Edward Palmer, and he emerged as a partisan. His tactics, according to his Reform adversaries, "attempted not to convince," and he "scarcely threw out any thing but volleys of abuse." Unfortunately for the Conservative cause, Longworth's usefulness in the assembly was limited by his lengthy business sojourns abroad. In 1846 he missed an entire session, and for the elections of 1842 and 1850 he trusted surrogates to win him re-election. Moreover, Longworth's performance in the house was rarely brilliant; he seldom spoke, even on contentious issues, and when he did break his silence it was usually to little effect. Only during the debates over responsible government, notably in the sessions of 1847 and 1849, did he make anything approaching a formidable display for the Conservatives. Contrary to the account of the historian Walter Ross Livingston, at no time could Francis be termed "the skillful leader of the Conservative party." This inflated view of the role of Francis Longworth (repeated by William Stewart MacNutt*) is largely explained by Livingston's erroneously crediting to Francis the moderate responsible government amendments proposed in the late 1840s by his brother

JOHN. By combining one man's conservative views with another man's moderate amendments, Livingston invented a single character more complex and Machiavellian than Francis ever was. In fact, Francis Longworth provides a straightforward example of the Family Compact's attitude toward responsible government.

The meaning and significance of responsible government in Prince Edward Island was the object of confused debate [*see* George Coles* and John Longworth]. Francis Longworth found that "none of its admirers appear to know what it really is." If the Reformers meant by responsible government the complete control by the assembly of the Executive Council, and through that body control of the lieutenant governor, then Longworth could see only calamity ahead. If the line of demarcation between the liberties of the people and the prerogatives of the crown was not maintained, that happy balance which best protected the people from themselves would be lost and the cause of liberty retarded. He baulked at the prospect of giving government over to those lacking property, a seditious tenantry who would easily fall under the spell of the "political speculator . . . , the glib tongued mob-orator." Not only would such a change upset the stability of society, it would also inevitably, in Longworth's opinion, provide the engine "that would ultimately sever the connexion that . . . subsists between the mother country and the British Provinces." Francis was one of three members of the assembly who refused to vote for responsible government in 1847, and although he was forced by events to support his brother John's moderate version of the idea in 1849, "he was afraid injury and destruction would be the consequence." Francis would not give up even after the institution of responsible government in 1851. He supported the Tory plan of "non-departmental" government in which elected Tories would sit on the Executive Council and non-elected Tories would hold salaried positions as the supposedly "non-political" heads of government departments. This bid to consolidate the Tory hold on political and administrative office was coupled with a plan to make the appointed Legislative Council elective, in the hope of reducing the existing dominance of it by the Liberals. By these means Longworth and the Tories might, in the words of Daniel Cobb Harvey*, "recapture the substance of power while leaving to the ostensible victors the shadow."

Longworth reached the inner corridors of Executive Council power as colonial secretary in the government of John Myrie Holl* which took office in February 1854. When Lieutenant Governor Sir Alexander Bannerman* dissolved the assembly in June without the consent of the Executive Council, Longworth openly accused him of improper conduct. Bannerman dismissed him for this impertinence, but Longworth refused to resign until the Holl government was forced out by the voters in the ensuing election.

Longworth did not run in the election of 1859, which the Tories won. The new government, however, rewarded him with a position as controller of customs and navigation laws, and collector of customs for the port of Charlottetown. In 1873 he became appraiser of customs for the port, a position he held until his superannuation in 1880. A justice of the peace, he was thrice appointed high sheriff of Queens County and in April 1869 officiated at a public execution which was so marred by badly measured and broken ropes that it proved to be one of the last executions held in public on the Island. Longworth was also on occasion president of the Benevolent Irish Society, and was a founding member of the Island's mechanics' institute. He took an active interest in the commercial life of Charlottetown and was on many boards of directors, including those of the Charlottetown Gas Light Company and the Steam Navigation Company.

Although a member of the assembly for over two decades, Francis Longworth was preoccupied with his business interests and lacked the skills necessary to become a major force in Island politics. None the less, as a strong partisan for the Conservative cause he articulated a firm belief in the right of the propertied class to rule. As time passed, his continued belief in such principles removed him from the mainstream of political life in Prince Edward Island.

M. BROOK TAYLOR

[The author is indebted to L. R. Fischer for providing statistics concerning Francis Longworth's shipbuilding activities. The most important sources for Longworth's political career are the reports of the assembly and contemporary newspapers. P.E.I., House of Assembly, *Debates and proc.*, 19, 29 March 1855; 11 April 1857; *Journal*, 18 March 1847; 17, 30 March, 18 April 1849. For his appointment to the Executive Council and the office of high sheriff see PAPEI, RG 1, Commission books, 5 May 1848, 22 April 1854, 12 April 1859, 7 May 1867, 6 May 1868; RG 5, Minutes, 17, 18 Feb. 1854; 11 April 1859. For electoral debates, public meetings, and the assembly debates prior to 1855 see *Royal Gazette* (Charlottetown), 30 Oct. 1838; 11 Feb. 1840; 17 May 1842; 14 July, 11 Aug. 1846; 13 April 1847; 30 March 1849; 15 Jan. 1850; *Islander*, 25 Feb., 22 July 1853; 2, 16, 23 June 1854; *Examiner* (Charlottetown), 14 Aug. 1847; 5, 12 June 1854; *Palladium* (Charlottetown), 15 Feb. 1844. For aspects of his business career see *Royal Gazette*, 29 Oct. 1833; 30 Dec. 1834; 3 May, 1 Nov. 1842; 1 Aug. 1843; 24 June 1853; 4 June 1858; *Islander*, 4 Feb. 1853. There is an obituary in the *Examiner*, 13 June 1883.

For the major issues and problems of Longworth's era, the most relevant secondary sources are Duncan Campbell, *History of Prince Edward Island* (Charlottetown, 1875; repr. Belleville, Ont., 1972); Basil Greenhill and Ann Giffard, *Westcountrymen in Prince Edward's Isle: a fragment of the great migration* (Newton Abbot, Eng., and Toronto, 1967), especially chap. 10; D. C. Harvey, "Dishing the Reformers," RSC *Trans.*, 3rd ser., 25 (1931), sect.II: 37–44; W. R. Livingston, *Responsible government in Prince Edward Island: a triumph of self-government under the crown* (Iowa City, 1931), 27–28, 49–50; MacKinnon, *Government of P.E.I.*, chap. 3–5; W. S. MacNutt, "Political advance and social reform, 1843–1861," *Canada's smallest prov.* (Bolger), 116–19, 121; J. B. Pollard, *Historical sketch of the eastern regions of New France . . . also, Prince Edward Island: military and civil* (Charlottetown, 1898), 201. M.B.T.]

LONGWORTH, JOHN, lawyer, land agent, politician, and judge; b. 19 Sept. 1814 at Charlottetown, P.E.I., fourth son of Francis Longworth* and Agnes Auld; m. 31 Aug. 1847 Elizabeth White Tremaine, and they had six children; d. 11 April 1885 in Charlottetown.

Born into an affluent Anglican family, John Longworth was educated at Alexander Brown's grammar school in Charlottetown and then studied law under Attorney General Robert Hodgson*. Admitted as an attorney of the Supreme Court of Prince Edward Island in October 1837, Longworth became a notary public and opened his own Charlottetown law office the following year. He quickly built a reputation as a land conveyancer and acted as agent for a variety of British and American insurance firms. By the mid 1840s John Longworth was, by both birth and qualifications, a rising member of Charlottetown society.

In 1846 he won a seat in the Island House of Assembly. Unlike the riding represented by his brother FRANCIS in Charlottetown, John's constituency in the rural 2nd District of Queen's County could not be guaranteed by the Charlottetown oligarchy or Family Compact. Thus, although elected as a Conservative, John was conscious that as a representative of tenant farmers in a rural riding he could not afford to give unqualified support to a party dominated by an urban or propertied class. The tensions inherent in such a situation rendered his position in the house difficult, especially during the debates over responsible government in 1847 and 1849.

In Prince Edward Island, responsible government was less a political principle than a means for asserting the rights of the small freeholders and tenantry against absentee landowners and the local oligarchy. The precise method by which the goal was to be achieved remained ill defined, but the problem eventually came to focus on the Executive Council and its ultimate responsibility to either the lieutenant governor, as the representative of the crown, or to the assembly, as the representative of the people. In this debate Longworth occupied a position considerably more moderate than that of some of the extreme Conservatives, including his brother Francis. Unlike them, John was willing to give wider representation in the assembly to the tenantry by increasing the number of rural ridings. He was also ready to concede the assembly's right to select at least four members of the nine-man Executive Council. However, he was not as willing as the Reformers to see the lieutenant governor become a tool of the assembly, and he wanted to reserve the crown's right to appoint and retain on the Executive Council the treasurer, colonial secretary, and attorney general, even if they could not command a majority in the assembly. John Longworth embodied his thoughts in an 1847 assembly resolution which became known as the Longworth amendment (and which is often mistakenly attributed to his brother Francis). As a compromise it was attractive enough to win several Reform votes in 1847 and again in 1849, but as the Reformers grasped the need for the assembly's complete control over the Executive Council, and as the Conservatives hardened in their opposition to significant change, John Longworth found himself occupying a lonely position in the middle. Others found his proposals "neither one thing nor the other . . . , [a] mongrel system."

Longworth was defeated in 1850 in the electoral sweep by the Liberals led by George Coles*. Subsequently, attempts were made to win him over to the Liberal cause. When in April 1853 Coles needed a lawyer for the office of solicitor general, Joseph Hensley*, the attorney general, recommended Longworth for the position. He took the office but only on condition that it not be regarded as a political appointment and that he not sit on the Executive Council. In the partisan atmosphere of the times such an arrangement could not be maintained and Longworth quickly resigned in order to run as a Conservative candidate in the July election. When he lost again, this time badly, he temporarily removed himself from politics. His law practice was building a fine reputation; by now he was a deputy judge of the Vice-Admiralty Court and a master and examiner in chancery. He was also increasing his interest in the commercial life of the colony. In 1856 he was chosen a founding director of the Island's first bank, the Bank of Prince Edward Island, and later became a shareholder, then director, of the Charlottetown Gas Light Company. He also helped to form the local mechanics' institute, was a trustee of the Central Academy, and was active in several religious societies.

In 1858 a Conservative resurgence permitted Longworth to recapture Queen's County, 2nd District. When Edward PALMER formed a Tory government in April 1859, Longworth was appointed to the Executive Council, a position he maintained until his and his party's defeat in the election of 1867. During his eight years in power three issues were to be of special interest to him: educational reform, confederation, and the tariff. In all three areas he was motivated by a practical concern for the economic well-being of the

Island. In 1863 he sponsored an act to reduce by £15 the government grant to each school district, arguing that the free education system absorbed an inordinate 38 per cent of the £42,000 annual revenue and that parents would take a more active interest in the schools if they paid directly for their support. The same concern for economy made him an opponent of reciprocity, and later union, with the other colonies of British North America. Prince Edward Island was an agricultural colony and Longworth could see no benefit in joining with Canada, whose unbounded agricultural capabilities would render the Island industry redundant. American trade was the natural complement to the produce of the Island, and he worked hard to keep alive the Reciprocity Treaty of 1854 with that nation. He sought to promote free trade with the Americans as a delegate to the Detroit Convention in 1865 and, after Prince Edward Island joined confederation in 1873, he split with the federal wing of the Conservative party over its high-tariff National Policy.

In 1865 riots occurred in Queens County when the new and radical Tenant League withheld payments of rent to landlords. Longworth had been sympathetic to the plight of the tenants, many of them his constituents, but as a member of the government he could not condone violence. In 1866 he acted as a prosecutor of the agitators, and the following year was defeated at the polls. He never ran for political office again.

John Longworth had an active public life outside of politics. Appointed QC in 1863, he was active in many important cases tried before the Island's supreme court, a body for which he became protonotary in 1883. Continuing his interest in education, he was made chairman of the newly formed Charlottetown Board of School Trustees in 1878. He also acted as aide-de-camp to several lieutenant governors between 1863 and 1879. His last years were marred by the collapse in 1882 of the Bank of Prince Edward Island, whose presidency he had recently assumed. The cashier (general manager) had given false reports of the bank's transactions and had absconded when discovered. Longworth bore the ultimate responsibility for the collapse, and while he was foremost amongst his co-directors in rendering assistance to those most seriously affected, the collapse broke his health and spirit and hastened his death.

John Longworth was an able and intelligent debater and a definite asset to the Conservatives in the assembly. He did not enter into the religious controversies vehemently argued by William Henry Pope* and Father Angus McDONALD, and by maintaining the moderate proprieties of a gentleman, he avoided the opprobrium of the partisan. Longworth was greatly respected in the legal profession and it was felt that his work was always thorough and correct.

M. BROOK TAYLOR

PAPEI, Bank of Prince Edward Island, Minute book, 1856–82; RG 1, Commission books, I–V; RG 5, Minutes, 1853–67; RG 16, Land registry records, Conveyance registers, 1767–1885. Prince Edward Island Heritage Foundation (Charlottetown), Longworth geneal. St Paul's Anglican Church (Charlottetown), Register of baptisms, 1827–1929; Register of burials, 1827–72 (mfm. at PAPEI). *Abstract of the proceedings before the Land Commissioners' Court, held during the summer of 1860, to inquire into the differences relative to the rights of landowners and tenants in Prince Edward Island*, reporters J. D. Gordon and David Laird (Charlottetown, 1862). P.E.I., House of Assembly, *Debates and proc.*, 1859–67; *Journal*, 1859–67. *Examiner* (Charlottetown), 1860–67, 1881–85. *Islander*, 1850–60. *Royal Gazette* (Charlottetown), 1832–55. *Canadian biog. dict.*, II. *Cyclopædia of Canadian biog.* (Rose, 1888). *Dominion annual register*, 1886. F. W. P. Bolger, *Prince Edward Island and confederation, 1863–1873* (Charlottetown, 1964). W. R. Livingston, *Responsible government in Prince Edward Island: a triumph of self-government under the crown* (Iowa City, 1931). MacKinnon, *Government of P.E.I. Past and present of P.E.I.* (MacKinnon and Warburton). J. B. Pollard, *Historical sketch of the eastern regions of New France . . . also, Prince Edward Island: military and civil* (Charlottetown, 1898). Robertson, "Religion, politics, and education in P.E.I." Waite, *Life and times of confederation*. David Weale and Harry Baglole, *The Island and confederation: the end of an era* (n.p., 1973). D. C. Harvey, "Confederation in Prince Edward Island," *CHR*, 14 (1933): 143–60; "Dishing the Reformers," RSC *Trans.*, 3rd ser., 25 (1931), sect. II: 37–44. I. R. Robertson, "The Bible question in Prince Edward Island from 1856 to 1860," *Acadiensis*, 5 (1975–76), no.2: 3–25.

LORANGER, THOMAS-JEAN-JACQUES, politician, judge, and writer; b. 2 Feb. 1823 at Yamachiche, Lower Canada, son of Joseph Rivard, *dit* Loranger, a farmer and later an innkeeper, and Marie-Louise Dugal; d. 18 Aug. 1885 at Sainte-Pétronille, Île d'Orléans, Que.

Thomas-Jean-Jacques Loranger, the eldest of 13 children, received a classical education at the Séminaire de Nicolet where he was a brilliant student. In 1842 he became a law student in the office of Antoine POLETTE in Trois-Rivières, and was called to the bar on 22 April 1844. After practising on his own at Trois-Rivières for some years, he went into partnership with Pierre-Richard Lafrenaye, a fellow student in Nicolet, and finally entered the Montreal office of Lewis Thomas DRUMMOND, who was then attorney general of Canada East. In 1853 he formed a law partnership with François-Pierre Pominville, and in 1858 Loranger and his two brothers, Louis-Onésime, who would later become a judge, and Jean-Marie, opened their own law office.

Thomas-Jean-Jacques Loranger had an active legal career. He took a notable part in the legal discussions relating to the abolition of the seigneurial régime. As one of the attorney general's deputies to the Seigneurial Court, he presented a long report, *Mémoire com-*

posé de la plaidoirie de T. J. J. Loranger, which was published in 1855 and completed the next year by *Suite du mémoire de M. Loranger*. He maintained that the French feudal system had not been introduced into Canada in its entirety, and that in particular the seigneurs had obtained land grants only on condition they make sub-grants. In order to encourage settlement, the *cens* and *rentes* had been fixed at a very low rate, since their "maximum was not to exceed two sous per *arpent*"; as a result they had limited capital value at the time of the abolition of the seigneurial system. The court accepted the main lines of his argument. On 18 Dec. 1854 he was appointed a QC.

On 10 Aug. 1854 he had been elected as a Reformer to represent Laprairie in the Legislative Assembly. Re-elected in 1857, he became provincial secretary for Canada East in the government of John A. Macdonald* and George-Étienne Cartier*. During the 1858 session, in an important debate on a motion relating to the double majority, he declared that "any attempt at legislation affecting one section of the province, against the wishes of the majority of the representatives of that section, would be fraught with dangerous consequences for the well-being of the province, and would give rise to many injustices." Yet, according to Louis-Philippe Turcotte*, Loranger "was of the opinion that the question of the double majority must not be raised. How could the majority from Lower Canada act in concert with that from Upper Canada, when the latter wanted mixed [non-denominational] schools and increased representation? To admit the principle that a majority in [each of] the two sections was required on general questions would be to run the risk of very frequent changes of government. A small majority would then prevail over a large one; and in the present situation, when the government is in the minority by three votes in Upper Canada and is supported by virtually all the members from Lower Canada, it would be an insignificant minority that would override the large total majority."

During the same session, Loranger was among those who opposed Cartier's choice of Ottawa as the capital and expressed a preference for Montreal. He voted against Cartier; the government resigned, and thus Loranger ceased to be a minister on 1 Aug. 1858. The Macdonald–Cartier government was replaced by that of George Brown* and Antoine-Aimé Dorion* which, however, lasted only 48 hours. The Conservatives returned to power and in the "double shuffle" [*see* George-Étienne Cartier] that then occurred Cartier did not offer Loranger a cabinet post. According to Laurent-Olivier David*, this was the beginning of an estrangement between the two men. As an illustration, when a bill relating to registry offices was under discussion on 16 May 1860, Loranger accused Cartier of wanting to anglicize his compatriots. Cartier got angry and asked Loranger if he knew how he had had to work and to struggle against certain prejudices to carry through a host of measures favourable to French Canadians. In 1862 Loranger helped defeat the Conservatives on the militia bill, and the government of John Sandfield Macdonald* and Louis-Victor SICOTTE took office. Loranger remained an MLA until he was appointed a Superior Court judge on 9 March 1863.

As a judge, Loranger sat successively at Beauharnois, Saint-Jean, and Sorel; he was often called to the Court of Appeal as an *ad hoc* judge as well. He retired in 1879 and became professor of administrative law at the Montreal branch of Université Laval.

In 1873 Loranger had published the first volume of his *Commentaire sur le Code civil du Bas-Canada*. A publisher's note announced that the work would eventually consist of a large number of volumes, and would be "a complete treatise, much more complete than any book of this type previously published in Canada, on all the subjects in this code, as well as on all the subjects connected with it." In his preface the author stressed the theoretical and practical nature of the work he was undertaking. But he was unable to finish the project. In the first volume he could only cover the first 114 articles of the code, ending with curatorship. In the second volume, published in 1879, he dealt solely with marriage. The author used his foreword to state his deep personal conviction that canon law and civil law recognize marriage "as a religious and sacramental act and as a civil contract," and that "the church alone has jurisdiction over the marriage tie and the impediments to its validity, and that the state alone has authority over its civil aspects." Loranger's incomplete treatise has now been superseded, but at the time its publication was an important event in legal circles in Quebec.

In 1879 Loranger and a number of Montreal jurists started a legal journal, *La Thémis*, which was published monthly until December 1884. The journal contained articles on various subjects, and in particular carried sections continuing Loranger's *Commentaire sur le Code civil du Bas-Canada* and others completing *La bibliothèque du Code civil* by Charles Chamilly de Lorimier. In 1869–72 Loranger also contributed to *La Revue légale* (Montreal and Sorel, Que.), which had just been started.

In addition, Loranger's *Lettres sur l'interprétation de la constitution fédérale*, published in two volumes in 1883 and 1884, made him one of the first French Canadians to publish in the field of constitutional law. In this work he formulated the theory of a federative pact, which would later be taken up by several authors, particularly from Quebec. He thus became one of the great defenders of provincial autonomy. "The confederation of the British Provinces," he wrote, "was the result of a compact entered into by the provinces and the Imperial Parliament, which, in enacting the British North America Act, simply ratified it." Further on, he added: "In the reciprocal sphere of their authority, there exists no superiority in favour of Parliament over the provinces, but, subject to Imperial sovereignty, these provinces are quasi-sovereign within their respective spheres, and there is absolute equality between them."

In 1876 the Quebec legislature had passed an act calling for the codification of the province's general statutes. For this task, four commissioners were appointed on 16 Aug. 1877, with Judge Loranger as chairman. The commission set to work immediately and on 15 Feb. 1878 presented an initial report to the government describing what it had accomplished to date. However, at the beginning of March Charles-Eugène Boucher* de Boucherville was dismissed from office by Lieutenant Governor Luc LETELLIER de Saint-Just, Henri-Gustave Joly* came to power, and as a result the commission was set aside. According to Loranger this suspension was "a regrettable fact from all points of view." In 1880, by virtue of a new act, the work of codification was resumed under the sole direction of Loranger, and in 1881 he presented the *Report of the commission appointed to revise and consolidate the statutes of the province of Quebec*. In it he outlined his ideas on the nature of Canadian federalism, as well as a plan of codification. Loranger proposed the creation of a permanent commission "whose functions would be to ensure consistency in the statutory laws and to protect the code of the statutes from the incoherence and confusion of new laws." In 1882 the *Judicial reforms proposed by the commission for the codification of the statutes* was published with a foreword by Loranger. But he was unable to complete his work, for he died on 18 Aug. 1885 at Sainte-Pétronille on the Île d'Orléans, where he was spending the summer with his family.

On 17 Dec. 1859 Loranger had been appointed to the first Council of Public Instruction. He had been president of the Association Saint-Jean-Baptiste de Montréal in 1880 and 1884, and thus had presided at the great celebrations in Montreal marking the 50th anniversary of the association. He was also among those who took the initial steps to have the Monument National raised, and he presided at the laying of the corner-stone. His funeral was held on 21 August in Notre-Dame, Montreal, with all the pomp called for by the death in office of a president of the Association Saint-Jean-Baptiste, an event which the newspapers stressed had not occurred since the death of Ludger Duvernay* in 1852. The burial took place at the Côte-des-Neiges cemetery. Loranger was a commander of the order of Saint-Grégoire-le-Grand.

On 13 May 1850, in Montreal, Loranger had married Sarah-Angélique Truteau, the niece of vicar general Alexis-Frédéric Truteau*, and they had one child. His wife died in 1858 and on 6 July 1864, at Quebec, he married Zélie-Angélique Borne, granddaughter of Philippe-Joseph Aubert* de Gaspé, and they had seven children. Laurent-Olivier David described Loranger as "one of the most scholarly, eloquent and witty men of his time, with a mind quintessentially French, serious in nature and lively, sparkling, and graceful in expression: a star of the first magnitude in the Pleiad of talents that shone with such brilliance from 1848 to 1867."

JEAN-CHARLES BONENFANT

[The major works of Thomas-Jean-Jacques Loranger are: *Mémoire composé de la plaidoirie de T. J. J. Loranger, c.r., un des substituts du procureur-général, devant la Cour seigneuriale* (Montréal, 1855); *Suite du mémoire de M. Loranger contenant sa réplique devant la Cour seigneuriale* (Montréal, 1856); *Commentaire sur le Code civil du Bas-Canada*, A. E. Brassard, édit. (2v., Montréal, 1873–79). As president of the commission he published the Qué., Royal Commission, *First report of the commissioners appointed to classify, revise and consolidate the general statutes of the province of Quebec* (Quebec, 1878); *Report of the commission appointed to revise and consolidate the statutes of the province of Quebec ...* (Quebec, 1881); and *Judicial reforms proposed by the commission for the codification of the statutes: first report* (Quebec, 1882). The last two works were also issued in French. In addition, he wrote *Lettres sur l'interprétation de la constitution fédérale, dite l'Acte de l'Amérique britannique du Nord, 1867* (2v., Québec, 1883–84), which was translated into English and published under the title of *Letters upon the interpretation of the federal constitution known as the British North America Act (1867)* (2v., Quebec, 1884). For a fuller description of Loranger's works and of articles about him in various periodicals, the reader should consult Ursule Loranger, "Bio-bibliographie de l'honorable juge Thomas-Jean-Jacques Loranger ..." (a paper presented to the École de bibliothéconomie de l'univ. de Montréal, 1943). J.-C. B.]

AC, Montréal, État civil, Catholiques, Notre-Dame de Montréal, 21 août 1885. *L'Événement*, 18 août 1885. *Gazette* (Montreal), 19–22 Aug. 1885. *La Minerve*, 19 août 1885. *Le Monde illustré* (Montréal), 29 août 1885. *Montreal Herald and Daily Commercial Gazette*, 19 Aug. 1885. *La Presse*, 20 août 1885. Beaulieu et J. Hamelin, *La presse québécoise*, II. Charles Chamilly de Lorimier, *La bibliothèque du Code civil de la province de Québec* (21v., Montréal, 1871–90). L.-O. David, *Tribuns et avocats ...* (Montréal, 1926). *Dominion annual register*, 1885: 267. P.-G. Roy, *Les juges de la prov. de Québec*, 507. L.-O. David, *Mes contemporains* (Montréal, 1894), 255–60; *Souvenirs et biographies* (Montréal, 1911), 60–66. É.-Z. Massicotte, *Processions de la Saint-Jean-Baptiste en 1924 et 1925; accompagnées de biographies et portraits des présidents généraux de la Société Saint-Jean-Baptiste de Montréal ... (1834–1926)* (Montréal, 1926). L.-P. Turcotte, *Le Canada sous l'Union*, II: 344–45.

LORD, WILLIAM WARREN, merchant, shipbuilder, and politician; b. 11 Feb. 1798 in Tryon, Prince County, P.E.I., son of John Lord, a farmer, and Charlotte Gouldrup; m. in 1825 Annie Lea, and they had no children; d. 9 May 1890 in Charlottetown, P.E.I.

William Warren Lord, the son of a loyalist, received a rudimentary education in the Tryon area. During his teens he worked on the family farm and in 1817 moved to the Miramichi River in New Brunswick to work as a lumberman. Around 1825 he returned to Tryon, married, and within a few years had set up an inn and tavern. He also entered the shipbuilding business and acted as an insurance agent; his prominence in the community was shown by his appointments as justice of the peace, fence viewer and constable, member of the board of health, and commander of a small militia unit.

In the spring of 1841 Lord left Tryon for Charlottetown. His move was regretted by the people of his home town who, at a special meeting, gave him credit for directly and indirectly helping to improve the economic state of the area since the late 1820s. In Charlottetown he opened a general store, constructed a wharf, and had built under his own direction numerous brigs, barques, clippers, schooners, and steamers. In the more than 20 years he spent in business in Charlottetown, he owned approximately 42 vessels which made regular trading voyages to Dublin, Liverpool, and London, often accompanied by Lord himself. An important figure in the Charlottetown business world, he was a shareholder and director for many years of the Bank of Prince Edward Island, a founder and director of the Union Bank of Prince Edward Island, and a director of the Charlottetown Mutual Fire Insurance Company and the Marine Insurance Company of Prince Edward Island. He was, as well, part-owner of the Charlottetown *Advertiser*. In April 1856 he took into his business his wife's relative, John Lea, and his nephew, Artemus Lord. The latter, whom he and his wife had adopted as a son, carried on the business after Lord's retirement in 1864.

Lord combined his business activities with a lively interest in provincial politics. A Liberal, he was first elected to the assembly to represent Prince County in 1835, serving until 1838. In 1850 he re-entered the assembly as member for Prince County, 3rd District, and with such colleagues as George Coles*, Edward Whelan*, Joseph Pope*, and James Warburton* successfully established the Island's first responsible government in 1851. Lord was a member of Coles's Executive Council from 1851 to 1857, with the exception of a few months in 1854, but when he accepted the paid office of commissioner of public lands in May 1857, he was obliged by law to seek re-election. He was defeated by the Conservative James Colledge Pope, whose victory presaged the Liberal government's difficulty in handling the contentious issue of religion in publicly supported schools. Lord was returned for Prince County, 4th District, in 1858 but in the following year was not a candidate in the election in which Protestant voters deserted the Liberal party and elected an all-Protestant, Tory government under Edward Palmer.

In the assembly Lord consistently advocated free schools, abolition of the leasehold system of land tenure, protection of agriculture and the fisheries, and vigilant economy in the expenditure of public funds. Although a faithful Liberal, he prided himself on his independence in the legislature and did not hesitate to offer his opinions and suggestions or to defend his character against attacks by the Tory press. Lord was active in assembly committees and during periods when the Liberals were in power frequently served in such posts as trustee of the lunatic asylum, commissioner for the government-run poor asylum, official representative to the Royal Agricultural Society (which he had helped organize) and commissioner for its model farm, member of the Charlottetown Board of Health, commissioner for the small debts court, and road justice for Charlottetown.

Shortly after his defeat in the 1857 by-election, Lord declined to stand as Liberal candidate for the mayoralty of Charlottetown, but from 1863 to 1870 he represented Prince County, 1st District, in the Island's elected Legislative Council. When Coles and the Liberals returned to power in 1867, Lord again became a member of the Executive Council, serving under Liberal premiers Joseph Hensley* and Robert Poore Haythorne*, until his defeat in the 1870 election. Like the majority of Island politicians and electors he had opposed the Island's entry into confederation in the 1860s because he felt that the colony's loss of independence could not be compensated by any terms of union, no matter how advantageous.

Lord often administered estates, executed wills, and conducted sales and auctions. He belonged to the Central Liberal Society and the Royal Agricultural Society, and after 1853 was a lieutenant-colonel in the Island militia. He and his wife were both active workers in the Methodist Church, to which he bequeathed money. Lord retained close links with his home town of Tryon (to which he donated a town hall) and he was buried there after his death in 1890. In a biography published in 1881, his neighbours were said to "give him credit for having lived an unblemished life," a judgement which reflected the high standards he set for himself in both business and politics.

Jean Layton MacKay

PAPEI, Bank of Prince Edward Island, Minute book; Indenture of amalgamation between the Bank of Nova Scotia and the Union Bank of Prince Edward, 26 Sept. 1883 (mfm.); Prince Edward Island shipping registers, 1824–69 (mfm.). Supreme Court of Prince Edward Island (Charlottetown), Estates division, liber 12: f.409 (mfm. at PAPEI). P.E.I.,

House of Assembly, *Debates and proc.*, 1855–57; *Journal*, 1835–38, 1850–60; Legislative Council, *Debates and proc.*, 1867–70; *Journal*, 1863.

Examiner (Charlottetown), 1855–64, 3 Jan. 1876, 9 May 1890. *Islander*, 15 Oct., 19 Nov. 1847; 31 Oct. 1851; 4, 11, 18 March 1859; 15 Jan. 1864; 16 July 1869; 11, 18 March, 17 June, 26 Aug., 2 Sept., 14, 28 Oct. 1870. *Prince Edward Island Register* (Charlottetown), 1823–30. *Royal Gazette* (Charlottetown), 1831–53. *Canadian biog. dict.*, II. *Cyclopædia of Canadian biog.* (Rose, 1888). *The Prince Edward Island almanack . . .* (Charlottetown), 1853–54; 1864; 1869; 1873–80. *The Prince Edward Island calendar . . .* (Charlottetown), 1857; 1862–68; 1870–71. *Past and present of P.E.I.* (MacKinnon and Warburton), 481, 698. W. H. Warren, "Pioneers of Tryon and North River," *Prince Edward Island Magazine* (Charlottetown), 1 (1899–1900): 410–14.

LUNN, WILLIAM, businessman, politician, and educator; b. 18 July 1796 at Devonport, England, eldest son of William Lunn and Elizabeth Heard; m. 1 Feb. 1821 Margaret Fisher, the daughter of Duncan Fisher* and the widow of William Hutchison, and they had four children; d. 19 June 1886 in Montreal, Que.

William Lunn was educated in Devonport and began working at the naval dockyard there. In 1819 he was sent by the Admiralty to Kingston, Upper Canada, to take charge of stores. The following year he settled in Montreal, and when the British naval establishment was withdrawn in 1834 he chose to remain there.

Lunn's interests were diverse and his energies great. He was one of the original subscribers to the Montreal General Hospital, and served as a member of the committee of managers intermittently from 1824 to 1886. In 1872 six of the original founders and governors of the institution, the Reverend John Bethune*, Anglican dean of Montreal, James Leslie*, William Molson*, William Lunn, William Ferguson, and John Mackenzie, were praised in the hospital's 50th annual report as men "deserving of the congratulations and thanks of the society. . . ." Lunn was also active in civic and business affairs, and was a member of the board of governors of the Bank of Montreal (1829–49), a director of the Montreal Committee of Trade (1829) and of the Montreal Library (1829), a justice of the peace in Montreal (1826–30), a commissioner of the port of Montreal (1839–40), a municipal councillor (1842–45), and an alderman (1846).

His most enduring contribution to the life of his adopted city was in the field of education. At a time when instruction for Catholic children was provided mainly by the church, education for Protestants depended heavily on private schools operated by individual teachers, schools supported by British missionary groups such as the Society for the Propagation of the Gospel, and those promoted by the cooperative efforts of citizens. One of these cooperative ventures opened in 1773 under the direction of John Pullman and a second was organized by William Lunn in 1822 when he helped establish the British and Canadian School Society of which Horatio Gates* was president and Louis-Joseph Papineau* and Charles William Grant* vice-presidents. The school, supported by popular subscriptions and government aid, admitted both boys and girls, and followed the Lancastrian monitorial system. Teachers were brought from England and Joseph Lancaster himself was invited to teach in 1829. Lunn's school later became a centre for the distribution of school materials and for the training of elementary teachers. Its enrolment exceeded 500 when, in 1866, it came under the control of the Protestant Board of School Commissioners for the city of Montreal. Lunn was secretary-treasurer of the British and Canadian School Society throughout the 44 years of the school's existence and his wife was, for a time, president of the Female Department.

Lunn's other educational affiliations were numerous. He was secretary-treasurer of the Society for the Advancement of Education and Industry which he and John Molson* organized in 1826; secretary-treasurer of the Protestant Board of School Commissioners (1846–71) and member of the board (1871–83); a member of the original board of directors of the High School of Montreal established in 1843; and chairman of the Protestant Educational Association (1864), a citizens' group for "the promotion and protection of the educational interests of Protestants in Lower Canada." In recognition of Lunn's work the Protestant Board of School Commissioners named in his honour an elementary school which existed from 1908 to 1941.

His son Alexander Hutchison Lunn, who was head boy at the High School of Montreal in 1847 and 1848, became a lawyer and partner in the firm of Cramp and Lunn. His stepdaughter, Margaret Hutchison, married Dr George William Campbell. Lunn died in 1886, as one of his contemporaries said, "full of years and good deeds."

Margaret Gillett

ANQ-M, État civil, Méthodistes, East End (Montréal), 1 Feb. 1821. McGill Univ. Arch., Montreal General Hospital records, Register of proc., 1822–32. British and Canadian School Soc., *Annual report* (Montreal), 2 (1824). Can., Prov. of, *Statutes*, 1859, c.122. *A few remarks on the meeting at Montreal for the formation of an association for the promotion and protection of the educational interests of Protestants in Lower Canada* (Montreal, 1864). Montreal General Hospital, *Fiftieth annual report . . . with a synopsis of its history to the present time* (Montreal, 1872). Borthwick, *Hist. and biog. gazetteer*, 420. *Canadian biog. dict.*, II: 170–74. *Montreal directory*, 1848–49; 1859; 1884–85. Terrill, *Chronology of Montreal*. L.-P. Audet, *Le système scolaire*, VI: 215–18. G. M. Burnett, "The High School for

Girls, Montreal, 1875–1914" (MA thesis, McGill Univ., Montreal, 1963). Denison, *Canada's first bank*. H. E. MacDermot, *A history of the Montreal General Hospital* (Montreal, 1950), 13. E. I. Rexford *et al.*, *The history of the High School of Montreal* (Montreal, 1950).

LYALL, WILLIAM, Presbyterian clergyman, author, and professor; b. 11 June 1811 in Paisley, Scotland, the third son of William Lyall, merchant; d. 17 Jan. 1890 in Halifax, N.S.

William Lyall was educated at Paisley Grammar School and at the universities of Glasgow and Edinburgh. Early in life he was attracted to the study of philosophy and, although ordained a minister of the Free Church of Scotland, he made his mark as a philosopher rather than as a theologian. After serving Free Church congregations in Broxburn, West Lothian, Uphall, and Linlithgow, he immigrated to British North America in 1848. For the next two years he was tutor at Knox College, Toronto. He resigned in 1850 to become professor of mental and moral philosophy and classical literature at the Free Church College in Halifax. In 1860, following a union of Presbyterian churches, he was transferred to the Theological Seminary in Truro, N.S. When this institution closed in 1863 Lyall became professor of logic and psychology at Dalhousie College in Halifax, a position he held until his death.

During Lyall's years as a student the "philosophy of common sense" as developed by Thomas Reid and Dugald Stewart was pre-eminent in Scotland and it was to this school that he belonged. When Lyall wrote *Intellect, the emotions, and the moral nature* (1855), he was greatly influenced by Sir William Hamilton under whom he may have studied at Edinburgh. Although largely a synthesis of philosophical thought and not highly original, the work merits recognition as one of the first Canadian books in this field. For Lyall, philosophy was the handmaiden of religion, and he never strayed from currently held theological views. "In the scriptures," he wrote, "we have the only, the authoritative statement of man's apostacy. Philosophy may speculate: the Bible reveals – not the mode or nature of change, but the circumstance of change. The great fact is told, the modus of it is left unexplained." His book attracted widespread attention and for a number of years was in vogue as a text in metaphysics.

On the strength of this work, the *West of Scotland Magazine* in 1856 suggested Lyall as the successor to Sir William Hamilton in the chair of logic and metaphysics at Edinburgh. The magazine claimed that Lyall "had done much to confirm and strengthen the principles of Scottish philosophy" and that his writing displayed the erudition and talent which "eminently fitted him to succeed the great champion," Hamilton. Nothing came of the proposal and Lyall remained in Nova Scotia. On 3 May 1864 he was awarded an honorary LLD from McGill College in Montreal and when the Royal Society of Canada was established in 1882 Lyall was named a founding fellow.

In addition to his teaching duties, for which he was "in his own person a whole faculty of arts," Lyall dabbled in poetry, cultivated a wide interest in English literature, and did occasional supply preaching. During the summer of 1852 he ministered to the congregation of St Andrew's Free Church, St John's, Nfld, and he held office in 1852–53 as moderator of the Free Church presbytery in Halifax. Above all, he enjoyed teaching, his objective being "to evoke in students a taste and zeal for philosophical investigation."

WILLIAM B. HAMILTON

[There is no known collection of William Lyall papers and his major published works are the most important sources of information for his biography: *Strictures on the idea of power; with special reference to the views of Dr Brown, in his "Inquiry into the relation of cause and effect"* (Edinburgh, 1842); *The philosophy of thought: a lecture delivered at the opening of the Free Church College, Halifax, Nova Scotia, session 1852–3* (Halifax, 1853); and *Intellect, the emotions, and the moral nature* (Edinburgh and London, 1855). Scattered references to Lyall may be found in Free Church of Nova Scotia, Synod, *Minutes* (Halifax), 1850–60; Presbyterian Church of the Lower Provinces of British North America, Synod, *Minutes* (Halifax), 1860–75; Presbyterian Church in Canada, Synod of the Maritime provinces, *Minutes* (Halifax), 1875–90.

A few lectures, poems, and other articles were published in the *Dalhousie Gazette* (Halifax), the most important being "Wordsworth: a criticism," 23 (1890–91): 135–37, 158–63, and in the *Presbyterian Witness* (Halifax), 6, 13 Nov. 1852; 1 Aug. 1868, 2 Feb. 1878. Obituary notices may be found in: *Morning Herald* (Halifax), 20 Jan. 1890; *Presbyterian Witness*, 25 Jan. 1890; and *Dalhousie Gazette*, 22 (1889–90): 93–94. Secondary sources include the following: William Gregg, *History of the Presbyterian Church in the dominion of Canada . . .* (Toronto, 1885); D. C. Harvey, *An introduction to the history of Dalhousie University* (Halifax, 1938); A. B. McKillop, *A disciplined intelligence: critical inquiry and Canadian thought in the Victorian era* (Montreal, 1979); and Watters, *Checklist*. W.B.H.]

LYNCH, JOHN, farmer, brewer, office-holder, real estate broker, and essayist; b. 9 Nov. 1798 in Gorham, N.Y., son of David Lynch who was a native of Ireland; d. 12 Oct. 1884 in Brampton, Ont.

John Lynch immigrated with his family from New York State to the Cornwall, Upper Canada, area in 1813. Six years later he homesteaded his own farm in Chinguacousy Township, on land which is now part of Brampton. In 1832 he put his farm out to rent and began a new career in York (Toronto) as a brewer. The next year he was appointed a justice of the peace, a commission he held for the rest of his life. After a few years in the city he returned to his farm, but by 1839 he had joined John Scott, his neighbour and brother-in-law, in a brewery and ashery in the Brampton area. In 1859 he left the business and established himself as a real estate broker and land conveyancer in Brampton. By that time he had acquired several town lots in addition to his own land on the edge of the growing village.

Lynch threw himself into the municipal life of Brampton and its locality. In 1852 he was elected reeve of Chinguacousy Township and after Brampton was incorporated as a village in that year he served as the first reeve. The next year he helped found the County of Peel Agricultural Society in which he remained active as the secretary treasurer from 1853 to 1869. His leadership abilities were recognized in 1855 when he was appointed commander of the local militia unit, the 6th Peel Battalion, in which he rose to the rank of lieutenant-colonel. Throughout these decades Lynch was part of the campaign which achieved the complete separation of Peel County from York County in 1866 and the incorporation of Brampton as the county town.

Although Lynch had little formal schooling, he succeeded in gaining a modest reputation as an essayist and compiler. Between 1856 and 1858 he submitted five prize-winning essays to the *Journal and Transactions* of the Board of Agriculture of Upper Canada. Four of the essays, models of careful research and thorough if optimistic analysis, related the farming methods being used in the counties of Peel, Simcoe, Grey, and Bruce. The other essay, "Agriculture and its advantages as a pursuit," printed in the journal in 1856, is a typical example of 19th-century agricultural "boosterism." It concludes that the "pursuit of agriculture may be considered as desirable to the higher classes, or the affluent, as a source of healthful recreation and rational enjoyment; profitable to the middle classes as the best means of acquiring and retaining a competency; and necessary to the lower classes, as affording the means of subsistence, and almost the only pursuit by which they can ever hope materially to improve their condition." In 1874 he compiled a directory of Peel County, enlivened with historical sketches and personal reminiscences. Lynch's last literary effort of note was the publication as a pamphlet of a lecture he had given before the mechanics' institute in Brampton in 1867, *Canada: its progress and its prospects* (1876). It epitomized his guiding philosophy: Canada is a great land with the capability of outstripping even the United States in material development if its people have the fortitude to take advantage of the opportunities so abundantly offered.

Lynch's personal life, like that of many a pioneer, was marked by tragedy. A devout Roman Catholic (he donated the land for the local church), in 1832 he married Susan Monger, the daughter of a prominent Methodist, but the union ended with her untimely death the following year in childbirth. In 1845 he married Anna McCormick, who died nine years later, leaving an infant daughter.

Abstemious, respected, and full of the earnest dignity of the self-made man, Lynch earned a prominent place in Peel society. He symbolized that class of pioneer whose patriotic faith, local pride, and personal initiative forged communities and made their institutions work.

DOUGLAS A. LAWR

John Lynch wrote "Agricultural report on the county of Peel – 1853"; "Agriculture and its advantages as a pursuit"; "Report of the agricultural condition and prospects of the county of Bruce"; "Report on the industrial condition, resources, prospects, extent and boundaries of the county of Simcoe"; and "Report of the state of agriculture, &c., in the county of Grey – 1853" in vols. 1 (1856) and 2 (1858) of Upper Canada, Board of Agriculture, *Journal and Trans.* (Toronto). He also wrote *Canada: its progress and its prospects; a lecture . . . for the Brampton Mechanics' Institute on the 10th of April 1867 . . .* (Brampton, Ont., 1876), and compiled the *Directory of the county of Peel, for 1873–4* (Brampton, 1874); the section on Brampton in the latter was reprinted in 1973.

Peel County Surrogate Court (Brampton), no. 873, will of John Lynch, 14 Nov. 1885 (mfm. at AO). PAC, RG 68, General index, 1841–67: 472. United Counties of York and Peel, Municipal Council, *Minutes* ([Toronto]), 1854. United Counties of York, Ontario, and Peel, Municipal Council, *Minutes* ([Toronto]), 1852–53. *Conservator* (Brampton), 24 Oct. 1884. *Canadian biog. dict.*, I: 711–12. *Brampton's 100th anniversary as an incorporated town, 1873–1973* (Brampton, 1973), 152–54. W. P. Bull, *From Brock to Currie: the military developments and exploits of Canadians in general and of the men of Peel in particular, 1791 to 1930* (Toronto, 1935), 207; *From Macdonell to McGuigan: the history of the growth of the Roman Catholic Church in Upper Canada* (Toronto, 1939), 283–84, 388–89.

LYNCH, JOHN JOSEPH, Lazarist, Roman Catholic priest, and archbishop; b. 6 Feb. 1816, probably in County Fermanagh (district of Fermanagh, Northern Ireland), son of James Lynch and Ann Connolly; d. 12 May 1888 in Toronto, Ont.

Although commonly thought to have been born in Clones (Republic of Ireland), John Joseph Lynch was probably born in nearby County Fermanagh. He received his early education in Lucan, County Dublin, before attending the Academy of St Joseph in Clondalkin and, in 1835, the Lazarist St Vincent's College at Castleknock. In 1837 he entered the seminary of Saint-Lazare in Paris and four years later took the vows of the Congregation of the Mission (whose members are also called Lazarists or Vincentians). Having committed himself to a missionary society, Lynch expected an overseas posting; consequently he was dismayed at being sent to labour for the church in his native land. He returned to Ireland where he was raised to the priesthood at Maynooth, County Kildare, in June 1843. His earlier disappointment evaporated when, in 1846, after three years of work at St Vincent's College and as a missionary in various parts of Ireland, he was sent to Texas.

Lynch served as a saddle-bag preacher in that state at the time of the Mexican-American War. Unfortunately, the life of an itinerant preacher left him vulnerable to typhoid fever. Experiencing an attack from which he could not completely recover in the deep south, he was moved to one of the Lazarist institutions, St Mary's of the Barrens, Perryville, Mo. After a brief recuperative stay, he was named superior of this seminary in 1848, a position he held until 1856. He then took up the assignment, which he had sought, of establishing a seminary for his congregation at Niagara Falls, N.Y. When the necessary land and funds had been acquired he founded Our Lady of Angels (later Niagara University).

During the mid 1850s the second bishop of Toronto, Armand-François-Marie de Charbonnel*, a vigorous battler for Catholic expansion, had been seeking relief from his episcopal duties. Lynch was suggested as a possible successor and he was invited to Toronto in 1858 for a summer mission and, obviously, for careful scrutiny. What made Lynch attractive to Charbonnel, in addition to his administrative and preaching abilities, was his Irish background, a matter of no small consequence considering the ethnic composition of Toronto's Catholic population at that time. Lynch was consecrated as coadjutor bishop on 20 Nov. 1859, with rights of succession. The following year Charbonnel finally obtained release from his post in order to pursue a monastic life in France; Lynch became the third bishop of Toronto on 26 April 1860.

The situation Lynch inherited was an encouraging one. In Toronto's population of 45,000, the Catholics, largely of Irish birth, numbered 12,000, their strength exceeded only slightly by members of the Church of England. More positive still, Catholic numbers were increasing at a greater rate than the population as a whole. Thanks in part to his predecessor's efforts, Roman Catholic separate schools, financed by government grants and taxes from supporters, were well established legally, notably by the act passed by the government of Sir Allan Napier MacNab* and Étienne-Paschal Taché* in 1855, known as the Taché Act. Furthermore Charbonnel had supervised the establishment of St Michael's College under the Basilian direction of Jean-Mathieu Soulerin* and had brought in members of the Christian Brothers and the Sisters of St Joseph to serve as instructors in the separate schools.

Yet there were problems. The seemingly aggressive growth of Catholicism and its institutions in the 1850s had evoked a Protestant response; harsh words, bitter politics, and spilled blood were also features of that decade. The increase in Catholicism had also outstripped the resources of the church in Canada West, with the result that in 1859 in the diocese of Toronto, which included the counties of Ontario, Peel, Simcoe, York, Lincoln, and Welland, there were only 43 churches and approximately 36 priests. So while prospects might be bright, Bishop Lynch, who was no fool, knew that the future would not present clear sailing.

The growing strength of Irish Catholicism, and of the Protestant reaction, forced Lynch into the public limelight in subsequent years, just as surely as it was a factor in his appointment as a prelate assistant to the papal throne in 1862 and in his elevation to first archbishop of Toronto on 15 March 1870 while he was attending the Vatican Council in Rome. (As a result of Lynch's appointment, the diocese of Toronto became a metropolitan see with the bishops of the dioceses of Kingston, Hamilton, and London as suffragans.) Thus Lynch was consulted by Egerton RYERSON on the separate school legislation proposed by Richard William Scott* in 1863, which in its final form remedied some of the deficiencies of the Taché Act. Lynch supported the new legislation and with its passage declared himself "quite satisfied," but when confederation approached he hoped for fresh arrangements for separate schools in Ontario. The Scott Act, however, formed the basis of the province's separate school system. Lynch's consultations with Ryerson also led to his appointment to the Council of Public Instruction, on Ryerson's recommendation.

After 1867 Lynch simply sought improved conditions for separate schools, but he did not pursue this goal as aggressively as had Charbonnel. He would have preferred the establishment of separate high schools and separate normal schools in Ontario, but he was conscious of the fact that Catholic ratepayers, many of them of the working class, would not be able to bear an additional burden. In any event, to his conservative eyes, a high school education might raise student expectations beyond a warranted level. Consequently the bishop was satisfied with minor amendments to the school law in 1877, 1879, and 1886 which facilitated the assessment of Catholic ratepayers as separate school supporters and increased the borrowing powers of separate school trustees. For his apparent contentment and his warm relationship with Oliver Mowat*, Liberal premier of Ontario after 1872, Lynch was subjected to criticism by fellow Catholics including bishops James Vincent Cleary* of the diocese of Kingston and John Walsh* of the diocese of London who wanted a tougher stand for concessions to separate schools. His lack of aggressiveness came from his understanding that in a strongly Protestant province no government dared show excessive generosity to Catholics. In addition, he probably questioned the wisdom of a return to the heated and often unproductive exchanges of the 1850s. Lastly, he recognized that separate schools, whatever their constitutional safeguards, existed on Protestant sufferance and after 1867 without the support of the Catholic majority in Quebec which they had received under the Union. The percentage of Toronto's population that was Catholic was slowly decreasing during the 1870s and 1880s; Catholics had declined to 19 per cent of the total population by 1881 and were outnumbered not only by members of the Church of England but also by the Methodists. The archbishop was careful; his chief concern would be cautiously nurturing growth, not vigorously seeking conquest.

Despite his caution, Lynch was dragged into battles with both Catholics and Protestants. In March 1876 members of the "lay party" of the Toronto Separate School Board, including its chairman, Remigius Elmsley, began to call for an accounting by the archbishop of the episcopal corporation's management of school properties and were supported in their efforts by Patrick Boyle*'s *Irish Canadian.* This assault was followed by demands in 1879, 1882, and 1887-88 for the use of the ballot to replace open voting in separate school board elections. In his dual capacity as archbishop and separate school superintendent, Lynch fought back against the rebels. His tough, conservative stance was not simply inspired by a desire to remain the unchallenged chieftain of Toronto Catholics; he was deeply worried lest divided Catholicism lend itself to a successful Protestant assault which could place the separate schools in jeopardy. Accordingly, he viewed the malcontents as more than mischievous; they were wicked. He used every weapon in his considerable arsenal – his position, sermons, letters, and the refusal of absolution – to defeat the rebellious element in the lay party on both issues.

These quarrels invited Protestants to enter the fray, particularly in the cause of the secret ballot. The interference of militant Protestants, such as Robert Bell, Conservative member of the Legislative Assembly for Toronto West from 1875 to 1879, was motivated, in part, by the desire to shape an issue which would defeat Oliver Mowat who, they charged, was closely allied with, if not dictated to by, Archbishop Lynch. Thus, in 1882, when the Catholic leader suggested the withdrawal of Sir Walter Scott's poem, *Marmion,* from study for matriculation on the grounds that it was offensive to Catholics, and the minister of education, Adam CROOKS, temporarily complied, provincial Conservatives and the *Mail* were quick to scream papist domination. In 1884-85 Lynch was made privy to education minister George William Ross*'s selections from the Bible which were to be used in public schools, and his editorial and administrative suggestions were accepted. The Conservatives under William Ralph Meredith* raised this issue, particularly during the course of the provincial election campaign of 1886. The bishop once more found himself in the centre of a storm, largely because of his concern for Catholic children who were being educated in public schools. The archbishop would have preferred to avoid being dragged into political debate and would rather have worked quietly with Mowat, a man whom he admired and no doubt favoured, especially in the light of the behaviour of provincial Conservatives during the later years of his episcopacy. The archbishop's preference for Mowat must have had an impact upon the province's Catholic voters.

Lynch kept a watchful eye on other political developments: urging patronage appointments for Irish Catholics at provincial and federal levels, pressing John A. Macdonald* to consider Catholics as political candidates and senators in March 1867, arguing with George Brown* on "the advisability of taking an Irish Catholic into the new Cabinet of the Liberal party" being formed by Edward Blake* in 1871, and denouncing to Blake's successor, Mowat, the probable passage of a bill to incorporate the Orange order in 1873. Lynch's relationship with the federal Conservatives was never as consistent as with the Ontario Liberals; Macdonald none the less actively sought his support on several occasions and received cautious but favourable replies.

His Irish background and his desire for the well-being of his church provided the inspiration for the archbishop's political activities. His frequent lectures on Catholic doctrine and belief were widely attended by both Catholics and Protestants. Soon after his return from Rome in 1870 he spoke about the Vatican Council and his support for the doctrine of papal infallibility during the council's proceedings. An able if somewhat autocratic administrator, he oversaw the rapid expansion of his diocese. During his incumbency 70 priests were ordained; two priests of the diocese, Jean-François JAMOT and John Walsh, were elevated to the episcopacy; and, in addition, 40 churches, 30 presbyteries, and 7 convents were established. Lynch convoked diocesan synods in 1863 and 1882, as well as a provincial council in 1875 which passed decrees regarding devotions, administration, and finances. Furthermore, he struck out in new directions in the development of benevolent institutions: enlarging the House of Providence, creating the St Nicholas Home for Working Boys, founding the Sunnyside Orphanage for boys, and establishing the Notre Dame Institute, a boarding-home for working girls and female students attending Toronto Normal School. All of these institutions were under the supervision of the

Congregation of the Sisters of St Joseph. In encouraging these developments, the archbishop was not only protecting Catholic souls but was sensitively responding to the developing social problems attendant upon Toronto's urban growth.

Archbishop Lynch was deeply concerned about Ireland, advocating Home Rule for his native land on the grounds that in North America the Irish had shown themselves to be remarkably responsible citizens. But the Irish people were more than that to him: they were a chosen people destined to preserve and extend the true faith throughout the world. Given this providential destiny, he was most anxious that the Irish should appear well in the eyes of all, and yet he knew only too well the less than flattering stereotype that existed in Ontario. An Irishman who did half the wrong of others received twice the blame. So, although not an abstainer himself, he urged the Irish to practise temperance, believing that under the influence of alcohol "the Irishman becomes more unreasonable than men of other and more plodding temperaments." He also pleaded for workers to reclaim the victims of alcohol. Lynch's experiences in Texas and in Canada had convinced him that Irish immigrants should be discouraged from movement to locations lacking sufficient Roman Catholic clergy. Mass migration, he argued, frequently stripped his people of their religion. He demonstrated these concerns throughout his career, addressing open letters to the clergy of Ireland in 1865 and 1883, and fighting vigorously for the protection of separate schools in Ontario.

Never a robust man, Lynch became ill in 1882 and acquired the assistance of Timothy O'Mahony as auxiliary bishop. Yet he remained to the end a warrior for his church and his people. In 1884, when he celebrated his jubilee as bishop of Toronto, prominent civil and ecclesiastic figures paid tribute to the achievements of the past 25 years. A mark of his devotion is that when he died he left an estate of less than $500.

CHARLES W. HUMPHRIES

John Joseph Lynch was the author of several published pastoral letters as well as *Questions and objections concerning Catholic doctrine and practice: answered by John Joseph Lynch, archbishop of Toronto* (Toronto, 1877).

Arch. of the Archdiocese of Toronto, Lynch papers. PAC, MG 26, A, 228. [J. J. Lynch], "Archbishop Lynch and the Knights of Labor," ed. G. J. Stortz, Committee on Canadian Labour Hist., *Bull.* (Halifax), 6 (autumn 1978): 2–3. *Globe*, April–May 1888. *Cyclopædia of Canadian biog.* (Rose, 1886), 691–92. Dent, *Canadian portrait gallery*, I; 141–45. *Standard dict. of Canadian biog.* (Roberts and Tunnell), II: 245–48. Daniel Conner, "The Irish-Canadian: image and self-image, 1847-1870" (MA thesis, Univ. of British Columbia, Vancouver, 1976). *Jubilee volume, 1842–1892: the archdiocese of Toronto and Archbishop Walsh*, [ed. J. R. Teefy] (Toronto, 1892). H. C. McKeown, *The life and labors of Most Rev. John Joseph Lynch, D.D., Cong. Miss., first archbishop of Toronto* (Montreal and Toronto, 1886). J. S. Moir, *Church and state in Canada West: three studies in the relation of denominationalism and nationalism, 1841–1867* (Toronto, 1959). F. A. Walker, *Catholic education and politics in Ontario: a documentary study* ([Don Mills, Ont.], 1964; repub. Toronto, 1976); *Catholic education and politics in Upper Canada: a study of the documentation relative to the origin of Catholic elementary schools in the Ontario school system* (Toronto and Vancouver, 1955; repub. Toronto, 1976).

M

MCARTHUR (Macarthur), ALEXANDER, HBC employee and businessman; b. 5 June 1843 at Nairn (Highland), Scotland, son of John Macarthur and Sarah Dallas; m. 22 June 1880 Hannah May Hutchins, and they had two sons, both of whom died in infancy; d. 21 Aug. 1887 in Winnipeg, Man.

Alexander McArthur was educated in Nairn, where he became the secretary of the Nairn Literary Institute. He worked in a local law office before coming to Canada in 1861. Between 1864 and 1868 he was employed as a clerk by the Hudson's Bay Company in the Montreal Department; he then worked in banking in both Montreal and Toronto.

In October 1869 McArthur went to the Red River Settlement (Man.), possibly as an agent of McArthur and Martin, general commission merchants in Montreal. His role in the Red River disturbance is uncertain and has been confused with that of his brother Peter who was one of those arrested with John Christian Schultz* by Louis RIEL on 7 Dec. 1869. Nevertheless, Alexander may have been among those arrested and imprisoned in early December. Before the year was out he had established a general merchandise operation in Winnipeg; the following year he bought a sawmill on the Winnipeg River and set up a retail lumber business in Winnipeg. He apparently sold the sawmill in 1876, and the lumber business in 1878. In the latter year McArthur helped establish the Manitoba Investment Association, of which he was vice-president and general manager until 1885; Andrew Graham Ballenden BANNATYNE was president. In conjunction with his other activities, McArthur became the agent for the North West Navigation Company, organized in 1880 by his brother Peter, who sold out in 1883.

McArthur made several attempts at elective office.

In January 1874 he ran unsuccessfully for the Winnipeg City Council, and two years later, in a provincial by-election in St Paul's, he was defeated when he ran as an opponent of the government of Robert Atkinson Davis*, a moderate French-English coalition. McArthur finally achieved political success in 1879, when he was elected a Winnipeg alderman. He was among the founders of the Historical and Scientific Society of Manitoba in 1879 with George Bryce* and Alexander Begg* and served on its executive council and as president. He also contributed historical and zoological papers to the society. In the late 1870s he was a financial supporter as well as the secretary treasurer of the fledgling Winnipeg General Hospital.

The 1880s were disastrous for McArthur, both financially and personally. In 1882–83 the so-called boom in Winnipeg collapsed, and McArthur was one of the many speculators and investors who were hard hit. In January 1886 his wife and second son died within a week of each other. By December of that year his financial distress forced the sale of his 300-volume personal library, his paintings, and his well-known collection of stuffed birds; the latter went to James Jerome Hill in St Paul, Minn.

Undaunted, McArthur announced in mid February 1887 a plan for an expedition to the Arctic to explore and collect ornithological specimens. Planning to proceed by pony to Norway House (Man.) and then by dog team to Chesterfield Inlet (N.W.T.), he hoped to reach the magnetic pole by whaling ship and, after wintering near King William Island, investigate unexplored territory. The Smithsonian Institution, which agreed to help with expenses, would receive ornithological specimens. McArthur and his two companions, a drug clerk and a servant, were, however, back in Winnipeg in March after having got no farther than a point between Norway House and Oxford House (Man.) when they heard that plans for Inuit assistance had fallen through. He made plans for a second attempt but died on 21 Aug. 1887 before he could set out.

McArthur appeared to be a man desperate for some achievement which would bring him recognition. In 1878 he had tried unsuccessfully to import reindeer from Norway to the Canadian northwest, to areas where deep snow and a lack of roads made transportation and communications difficult. His scheme for exploring in the Arctic was also short-sighted in both its planning and its execution. His ability was not always equal to his imagination.

JOHN D. INGRAM

Alexander McArthur was the author of the following papers published in HSSM *Trans.*: "The causes of the rising in the Red River Settlement, 1869–70," 1 (October 1882); "A tragedy on the plains: the fate of Thomas Simpson, the Arctic explorer," 27 (December 1886); and "Our winter birds," 28 (January 1887).

PAM, HBCA, B.134/g/38–43; MG 7, B7-1, Marriages, no.146; Burials, no.19; MG 14, C20; C66. Begg, *Red River journal* (Morton). Alexander Begg and W. R. Nursey, *Ten years in Winnipeg: a narration of the principal events in the history of the city of Winnipeg from the year A.D. 1870, to the year A.D. 1879, inclusive* (Winnipeg, 1879). Peter MacArthur, "The Red River rebellion," *Manitoba Pageant* (Winnipeg), 18 (1972–73), no.3: 22–24. *Manitoba Daily Free Press*, 11, 17–22 Nov. 1876; 3 June 1878; January, 24 Feb. 1879; 5 Jan., 4 May 1880; 3, 8 Feb. 1881; 26 Feb. 1883; 15 Feb., 31 March, 22 Aug. 1887. *Winnipeg Daily Times*, 1880–81. J. A. Jackson, *The centennial history of Manitoba* (Toronto, 1970). Morton, *Manitoba* (1967).

McBEATH (McBeth), ROBERT, farmer, businessman, and office-holder; b. 14 April 1805 in Kildonan (Highland), Scotland, the fifth of eight children of Alexander McBeath and Christian Gunn; m. 19 Jan. 1832 Mary McLean, and they had 11 children; d. 20 Aug. 1886 at Kildonan (now part of Winnipeg), Man.

Robert McBeath came to Canada with his parents as a member of the fourth party of colonists brought out by Lord Selkirk [Douglas*] in 1815. Sailing on the *Hadlow* from Gravesend, England, to York Factory (Man.), they reached the Red River Settlement on 5 November. The colony was in ruins, having been pillaged by the North West Company, and the McBeaths had to sustain themselves over the winter near Pembina (N. Dak.) by hunting and fishing. They returned to the colony in 1816 but when on 19 June Robert Semple*, the governor of the Hudson's Bay Company, and 20 of his men were killed at Seven Oaks by a group of Nor'Westers under Cuthbert Grant*, the colonists' houses and goods were ransacked and they were forced to seek refuge at Jack River House, at the northern end of Lake Winnipeg. The McBeaths spent the next two years at Pembina when grasshoppers ravaged the colony.

Alexander McBeath was given a farm lot near Kildonan in 1817 by Lord Selkirk in consideration of the hardships, losses, and misfortunes he had suffered. Robert McBeath later farmed this lot, and between 1839 and 1854 he purchased additional lots from the HBC, until, at the time of his death, he possessed over 400 acres. In the late 1850s McBeath opened a general store in Kildonan and carried on a freighting business between the Red River Settlement and York Factory.

McBeath was sworn in as a councillor of Assiniboia on 29 March 1853, the first Selkirk colonist to receive that honour. He attended 60 of a possible 77 council meetings and served on four committees before the council ceased operation in 1869. In 1859 he was appointed to a committee to draft regulations on the importation of liquor into the Red River Settlement. As a result of the committee's recommendations, importation was limited, a schedule of fines and licence fees was drawn up, and the sale of liquor to the Indians was forbidden. McBeath was also on committees appointed in 1863 and 1864 to mark the main public roads in the settlement and to study the question of a public ferry. In 1865 he was a member of a committee to distribute seed wheat purchased from the HBC.

As a prominent figure in the settlement, McBeath was frequently called upon for jury duty and was appointed a justice of the peace on 19 Nov. 1852. In 1863 he was one of four justices of the peace who sent a petition to Governor Alexander Grant DALLAS. Deploring the lack of a sufficient military force in the settlement to prevent jail breaks and to guard against Indian disturbances, the petitioners requested a renewal of negotiations with the Sioux as well as a warning to them to keep away from the settlement. In 1866 the governor was authorized to raise a body of 50 to 100 mounted men to meet any emergency. McBeath served as a magistrate at 38 sessions of the General Quarterly Court of Assiniboia. His decisions were fair and impartial, although his knowledge of French was inadequate. One of the most important questions which came before McBeath for settlement was the investigation, in 1870, into the death of Elzéar Goulet*, one of Louis RIEL's lieutenants, who was killed while fleeing from supporters of the Canadian party. Although the inquiry ended inconclusively, racial conflict was avoided.

McBeath was a prominent member of the Presbyterian Church, first at Frog Plain (now part of Winnipeg), then at Kildonan, and was one of 80 Kildonan signatories who petitioned the Council of Assiniboia to ratify the constitution of their congregation and declare it a corporate body. The request was refused in 1854 because the council claimed not to possess such power. McBeath's sons provided hay for the horses and cows of the Reverend John BLACK, who was the Presbyterian minister at Kildonan for over 30 years. During the disturbance at Red River in 1869–70, Black preached law and order and tried to discourage open resistance to Riel. His influence may partially explain the passivity of the Kildonan settlers throughout the disturbance.

McBeath did not take an active part in the disturbance, although he was present at the meeting on 20 Jan. 1870 to hear Donald Alexander Smith*, the special commissioner from the government of Canada, and when John Christian Schultz* escaped from Upper Fort Garry (Winnipeg) on 23 Jan. 1870 McBeath gave him shelter for the night. In the first provincial election of December 1870, McBeath voted for the opponent of the successful candidate, John Sutherland*, who had represented Kildonan at the convention of January 1870 [*see* Riel]. This support may have been McBeath's way of expressing his disapproval of the actions of the convention.

In his later years McBeath's interests centred around his family, his farm, his garden, and his church. He died at his residence on 20 Aug. 1886, a respected member of the community, who had given freely of his time and means to further projects for the general welfare of the Red River Settlement. Smith wrote that he "was one of my most esteemed friends . . . who so materially aided in the opening up of the great North-West."

BARRY E. HYMAN

PAM, MG 2, B1, 29 March, 6 Dec. 1853; 22 June 1854; 10 March, 26 May 1859; 28 April, 19 Dec. 1863; 12 March, 3 Nov. 1864; 21 March 1865; C40. *Canadian North-West* (Oliver), I: 68, 80, 83–84. *Manitoba Sun* (Winnipeg), 23 Aug. 1886. R. G. MacBeth, *The Selkirk settlers in real life* (Toronto, 1897). F. H. Schofield, *The story of Manitoba* (3v., Winnipeg, 1913).

McCAUL, JOHN, clergyman in the Church of Ireland, professor, educational administrator, and author; b. 7 March 1807 in Dublin (Republic of Ireland); m. in October 1839 Emily Jones, and they had seven children; d. 16 April 1887 at Toronto, Ont.

Born into a scholarly family, John McCaul received careful early training in White's School, Dublin, and the Moravian School, Antrim (Northern Ireland), before entering Trinity College, Dublin, in 1820. Over a period of eight years of study, first in mathematics and later in the classics, he received numerous prizes and medals for superior scholarship, especially in the Greek language. In 1828 he was awarded the degree of MA; he continued to reside at Trinity, as scholar and tutor, for another decade, and also served as university examiner in classics. He was admitted deacon in the Church of Ireland in 1831 and priest in 1833. In 1835 the university awarded him the degrees of LLB and LLD. During these years McCaul published several textbooks, treatises, and editions with classical themes and authors.

In 1838 Upper Canada College in Toronto was engaged in a search for a new principal to succeed Joseph Hemington HARRIS and asked the archbishop of Canterbury to seek out a suitable candidate. The choice fell on John McCaul, who accepted at once. He arrived in Toronto on 25 Jan. 1839 and was installed in office four days later. He proved to be both popular and successful in his new duties, and his place in provincial society was further secured when, in October 1839, he married a daughter of Jonas Jones*, a judge and prominent member of the old Family Compact. At this time, before a university had been started in the province, Upper Canada College was the leading educational institution and McCaul had fair scope for his abilities, both administrative and scholarly. He took particular interest in the 7th form, which provided the closest approximation to university-level training available in the province.

In 1842, under the leadership of the governor general, Sir Charles Bagot*, and Bishop John Strachan*, plans were finally under way for the opening in Toronto of King's College, for which a charter had been obtained in 1827. Strachan was its president. Members of staff were appointed, headed by John McCaul as vice-president and professor of classics, logic, rhetoric, and *belles-lettres*. When classes began in June 1843 he resigned as principal of Upper Canada College and became, owing to Strachan's duties as bishop, the effective working head of King's College. With Strachan's resignation as president in 1848, McCaul assumed the post. During these years he took some part in the increasingly acrimonious debate over King's College; in particular, in 1845, under the pseudonym "A Graduate," he published a pamphlet, *The university question considered*, defending the college against the charges of Anglican exclusiveness.

It might have been expected that McCaul would join with Strachan in adamant opposition to Robert Baldwin*'s 1849 bill which remodelled King's College into the secular University of Toronto. In fact McCaul did sign a minority petition of protest (the majority of the college council supported the bill), but when the bill became law he remained at the university as president and as professor of classics. In 1853, by an act of the provincial legislature, the University of Toronto was reorganized to become solely an examining and degree-granting institution, with instruction in the arts and sciences assigned to the newly established University College. McCaul became president of University College, and remained in that post until his retirement in 1880. In 1853 he was also elected vice-chancellor of the university, but was defeated for re-election in 1855 by John Langton*.

During an academic career spanning some 40 years McCaul consciously sought to introduce and maintain the best standards of British universities in Canada's provincial society. On one level he was concerned with form and ceremony: in 1853 the newly arrived Daniel Wilson* saw him as "quite a magnificent fellow, having, in addition to his gown and square cap, his clerical bands and his *scarlett hood* as a LL.D. of Trinity College, Dublin." Wilson also found him to be "a bit of a martinet in all matters of College discipline. It is a high crime and misdemeanour to appear in College hours otherwise than in cap and gown." McCaul was especially effective at the annual convocations, which became prominent Toronto events under the influence of his dignified bearing, his ready eloquence, and his skill at finding apt quotations from the Greek and Roman classics. He was always turned to for the devising of academic documents and for framing appropriate mottoes.

McCaul was not a notable educational innovator – the circumstances of the time probably made such a role impossible in any event – but he did help bring about two changes of considerable importance. Undergraduates at King's College and University College, as in most colleges and universities, followed a prescribed course of study, with little or no choice of subjects. In the 1850s, however, University College began to permit students to select courses from among various "options" after they had fulfilled basic requirements; that is, they could pursue some degree of specialization in the areas of their preference. This change, in line with what was beginning to happen in some other colleges and universities, was heavily attacked, especially by Egerton RYERSON, but it survived. It led eventually, at the University of Toronto, to the system of "honour" and "pass" courses, which for over 75 years was a distinctive feature of the arts programme. Secondly, McCaul, despite his own background in classics, contributed to the enlargement of the curriculum of University College at its outset in 1853 by helping to secure the appointment of two professors in science, Edward John Chapman* and William Hincks*, one in English and history, Daniel Wilson, and one in modern languages, James Forneri.

McCaul also played some part in the cultural life of Toronto and of Canada. For a time he was president of the Canadian (later the Royal Canadian) Institute. He was also editor of *The Maple Leaf; or Canadian Annual, a Literary Souvenir*, and he wrote articles and reviews for various periodicals. He helped organize the Philharmonic Society in Toronto with John Ellis*, and served as its president both in the 1840s and in the 1870s when the orchestra was conducted by James Paton Clarke*; McCaul also composed several anthems and vocal musical works.

The duties of a college president left little time for research, but McCaul managed to continue the interest in epigraphy he had acquired in Dublin. In 1863 he published a work on Britanno-Roman inscriptions, and in 1869 one on Christian epitaphs of the first six centuries.

Although McCaul's powers had markedly declined even before his retirement, he played a valuable role at the University of Toronto at a crucial time. During nearly all his years there, the university and University College were the focus of sharp and often bitter controversy and attack. McCaul, who was not of a combative nature, took little direct and visible part in these controversies, in contrast for instance, to Daniel Wilson, but his support for the concept of one strong provincial university never wavered. Moreover, it was of inestimable value to the institution to have at its head a man of deep scholarship who strove constantly for high academic standards. Others, such as Wilson, Edward Blake*, and Adam CROOKS, made it possible for the University of Toronto to survive during this difficult generation; McCaul helped it to survive with some scholarly distinction.

G. M. CRAIG

John McCaul was the author of *Britanno-Roman inscriptions, with critical notes* (Toronto and London, 1863); *Christian epitaphs of the first six centuries* (Toronto and London, 1869); *Emigration to a better country: a sermon, preached in the cathedral church of St. James, Toronto, on Saint Patrick's day, 1842, before the societies of St. George, St. Patrick, & St. Andrew* (Toronto, 1842); and *"Love of God and of our neighbour": a sermon, preached in the cathedral church of St. James, Toronto, on Tuesday, March 17, 1840, before the societies of St. George, St. Patrick, & St. Andrew* (Toronto, 1840). Under the pseudonym "A Graduate" he wrote *The university question considered* (Toronto, 1845) and he was co-author of *Letters on King's College* (Toronto, 1848) with John Macara. A list of papers written by McCaul appears in Morgan, *Bibliotheca Canadensis*, 254–55, and other works are listed in the *British Museum general catalogue*.

UTA, Daniel Wilson, Journal. *Toronto Daily Mail*, 18 April 1887. *A history of Upper Canada College, 1829–1892; with contributions by old Upper Canada College boys, lists of head-boys, exhibitioners, university scholars and medallists, and a roll of the school*, comp. George Dickson and G. M. Adam (Toronto, 1893). John King, *McCaul, Croft, Forneri: personalities of early university days* (Toronto, 1914). *University College: a portrait, 1853–1953*, ed. C. T. Bissell (Toronto, 1953). *The University of Toronto and its colleges, 1827–1906*, [ed. W. J. Alexander] (Toronto, 1906). Wallace, *Hist. of Univ. of Toronto*. T. A. Reed, "President McCaul's inscriptions," *Univ. of Toronto Monthly* (Toronto), 27 (1926–27): 61–62, 114–15, 158–59. William Wedd, "The Rev. John McCaul, LL.D.," *Univ. of Toronto Monthly*, 2 (1901–2): 2–5.

McCORD, ANDREW TAYLOR, public servant and philanthropist; b. 12 July 1805 in Belfast (Northern Ireland), son of Andrew and Margaret McCord; m. Charlotte Taylor, and they had six daughters and one son; d. 5 Sept. 1881 in Toronto, Ont.

Andrew Taylor McCord attended the Royal Belfast Academical Institution at the same time as Francis HINCKS before immigrating to Upper Canada with his family at the age of 26. His sisters launched a ladies' seminary in York (Toronto) in July 1831 and he apparently opened a dry goods business there before relocating shortly thereafter in Dundas. He returned to York and in June 1834, after failing to obtain the post of first city chamberlain (treasurer) which went to Matthew Walton, he was appointed collector for St Patrick's Ward. Walton died of cholera in August of that year and Alderman James LESSLIE, lately of Dundas, and the mayor, William Lyon Mackenzie*, nominated McCord to succeed Walton. The mayor, however, was soon bitterly opposed to McCord, apparently on no more substantial grounds than that he was "personally obnoxious to him." Nevertheless, with support from both Tory and Reform factions on the council (Lesslie personally signed his bond of surety) McCord assumed the office he would hold for the next 40 years. Thereafter his position was relatively free from political controversy, despite his Reform sympathies. Through the years of Tory ascendancy in municipal politics, McCord stayed above factionalism by maintaining a scrupulously neutral public position. As Mayor George Monro* testified before the commission inquiring into the city administration's conduct during the election of 1841, "The City Chamberlain would not vote for one; he did not vote at all: he still retains his situation from which he is not likely to be removed."

The responsibilities of the city chamberlain grew substantially during McCord's career. Originally the rate of pay for the chamberlain, anticipated to be a part-time post, was set at four per cent of the monies passing through his hands. As the volume of financial transactions increased dramatically, the terms were altered to a straight salary and by the mid 1850s McCord had become the highest paid city official except for the mayor. Feeling hampered by insufficient staff, McCord struggled to accommodate the city's mushrooming demands. Until 1871 the office of chamberlain was charged with overseeing all municipal property and establishing the financial credit of the city for major capital ventures. It was in the area of debenture transactions that McCord served the city with the greatest distinction. In 1856, in connection with the Esplanade development, he successfully negotiated the sale of £119,000 of municipal debentures at par in London. However, in the early 1870s the increasing complexity of the city's business and revelations of embezzlement by clerks in the chamberlain's office prompted the appointment of a city commissioner in 1871, a board of valuators in charge of assessment in 1872, and an assessment commissioner in 1873. But while McCord's relations with the council's finance committee became increasingly strained between 1871 and 1873 during a controversy over the auditing of his department's records and by two cases of embezzlement, his reputation for securing the most favourable arrangements on the London money market hardly dimmed. The resignation which he felt was forced upon him by adverse publicity was postponed until 1874 by the request of the water works commission that he be sent to London in connection with the sale of $600,000 in debentures. Later that year McCord's political career began and ended when he ran for mayor against the incumbent Francis Henry Medcalf* and Angus MORRISON. Supported by local Reformers as well the *Globe* and calling for economic restraint and good government, McCord ran a respectable second to Medcalf but never again stood for elective office.

As a philanthropist, McCord gave generously of his time and money to many religious and civic causes. Following his sisters, McCord, his wife, and parents left the Church of Scotland to become active members in the Zion (Congregational) Church in 1836–37. In 1847 McCord, alone, was baptized a member of Bond

Street Baptist Church; he assumed a leading role in local Baptist activities and was treasurer (1851–58) and vice-president (1867–75) of the Baptist Convention of Canada. For over 30 years he was secretary and vice-president of the Upper Canada Religious Tract and Book Society, and prominent in the Upper Canada Bible Society, the Toronto City Mission, and the Toronto Temperance Reformation Society. Strenuously active during an era which relished a myriad of charitable ventures, he was a member of the managing committee of the Toronto Athenaeum; a trustee of the Toronto General Burying Grounds for 25 years; sometime president of the Irish Protestant Benevolent Society; and a director of the House of Industry, the Newsboys' Lodging and Industrial Home, and the Home for Incurables.

At his death McCord's reputation as a public servant and benefactor obviously remained secure since his obituaries mention a long-forgotten bankruptcy early in his career as evidence of "the sterling honesty of his character." With the difficulties of his last years as chamberlain forgotten, his death was noted as leaving "a vacancy not readily filled" in the ranks of the city's philanthropic and religious workers.

SUSAN E. HOUSTON

CTA, Toronto City Council, Minutes, 1834–58; Toronto City Council papers, 1834–96 (mfm. at AO). York County Surrogate Court (Toronto), no.4361, will of A. T. McCord, 22 Sept. 1881 (mfm. at AO). Can., Prov. of, Legislative Assembly, *App. to the journals*, 1841, app.S. Toronto City Council, *Minutes of proc.*, 1859–74. *Globe*, 6 Sept. 1881. *The Baptist year book . . .* (Toronto, etc.), 1856–80. *Toronto directory*, 1833–69. B. D. Dyster, "Toronto 1840–1860: making it in a British Protestant town" (lv. in 2, PHD thesis, Univ. of Toronto, 1970). Middleton, *Municipality of Toronto*.

McCORMICK, ROBERT, naval surgeon, Arctic explorer, and naturalist; b. 22 July 1800 at Runham, near Great Yarmouth, Norfolk, England, the only son of Robert McCormick, RN; d. 25 Oct. 1890 at Wimbledon (now part of Greater London), England.

Robert McCormick spent his childhood near Great Yarmouth and was educated by his mother and sisters. His father, a naval surgeon, had encouraged young Robert to become a naval executive officer, but his death in the wreck of the *Defense* in December 1817 left his son without the necessary influence and means. In 1821 Robert decided to enter the Royal Navy as a surgeon. He was accepted as an apprentice by the famous Sir Astley Paston Cooper, originally from Norfolk, and after study in London at Guy's and St Thomas's hospitals he became a member of the Royal College of Surgeons on 6 Dec. 1822. In 1823, as assistant surgeon, he was assigned to the flagship *Queen Charlotte*.

McCormick's first duty was in the Caribbean where he served until 1825 when he contracted yellow fever and was invalided home. He then spent two years as medical officer to shore stations. McCormick's first experience in the Arctic was in 1827 with William Edward Parry* aboard the *Hecla* to Spitsbergen, although he was not a member of Parry's unsuccessful polar sledge party. He contributed significantly to the expedition by keeping the crew healthy and by studying the plants, animals, and geology of Spitsbergen. Following the expedition he was promoted to the rank of surgeon on 27 Nov. 1827.

After a year on half pay, McCormick was assigned to the *Hyacinth* and Caribbean duty, but in 1830 he was again invalided home, from Rio de Janeiro. Posted once more to the Caribbean, he suffered yet another attack of yellow fever, for which he was sent home in 1834. For the next four years he was unattached except for one month aboard the *Terror* in relief of ice-bound whalers.

In 1839 McCormick successfully applied for duty with the expedition of James Clark Ross* to the Antarctic as surgeon and zoologist aboard the *Terror*. The expedition was out from September 1839 until September 1843 and did important work in all branches of science in the Antarctic, Australia, and New Zealand. The large collections of zoological materials were worked up later, however, not by McCormick, but by John Edward Gray and Sir John Richardson*, on orders from the Admiralty after the task had remained undone for some time after the expedition. McCormick apparently lacked the drive and skill, and also the scientific ability, to cope with the massive collections. He did gain some recognition with election in 1844 as an honorary fellow of the Royal College of Surgeons. In 1845 McCormick received what he thought was a life appointment as a surgeon to the yacht *William and Mary*, but to his dismay the commission was changed and he was assigned to the Woolwich Dockyard, east of London. Even in this post he was disappointed; he was superseded in 1849.

McCormick was a proponent of the search for Sir John Franklin*, and was one of the first to lay detailed plans for it before the Admiralty and the House of Commons. He advocated the use of small boats and sledges to explore Wellington Channel and then go south to Boothia Peninsula and King William Island. His suggestions, well based on Arctic and Antarctic experience, were unofficial, coming from a medical officer and not a line officer, and were rejected. (Francis Leopold McClintock* was later to prove him correct.)

In 1851, however, McCormick was appointed surgeon on the *North Star* in the search fleet of Sir Edward Belcher*; in February 1852 William John Samuel PULLEN received the command of the *North Star*. At last McCormick's life-long ambition was realized: during this expedition he became officer in command of a party. In August and September 1852 he explored the Wellington Channel, in a boat named *Forlorn Hope*, covering 240 statute miles. He did not find any trace of Franklin's ships, *Erebus* and *Terror*, but did map the east side of the channel and establish the probability of a connection between Baring Bay and Jones Sound, virtually proving that Franklin had proceeded westward from Beechey Island.

McCormick was awarded the Arctic Medal in 1857. In 1859 he was finally promoted deputy inspector-general, his last rise in rank. He was placed on the retired list in 1865, and in 1876 received a Greenwich Hospital pension of £80 per annum through the good offices of his friend, the medical director-general, Sir Alexander Armstrong*, himself an old Arctic hand. In 1884 McCormick published *Voyages of discovery in the Arctic and Antarctic seas, and round the world*. Despite excellent illustrations, sound scholarship, and an interesting narrative, it came too late to arouse much interest for most of the information was already well known and the incidents were too remote for acclamation.

McCormick, in fact, spent the last 20 years of his life in relative obscurity. He had failed either to reach the top in the naval medical service or to become a distinguished biologist. He displayed stamina and competence in exploration but had little opportunity to engage in it except, perhaps, during the *North Star* expedition. His troubles in the Admiralty have been attributed to a lack of tact and a strong individualism which resulted in frequent disagreements with each of the medical directors-general of his time, especially Sir William Burnett. The yellow fever he contracted and his dislike of small ships led him to avoid assignments to the Caribbean, even to the point of insubordination. However, these characteristics do not explain the scientific failure. McCormick was on good terms with many influential scientists of the day, including Sir John Barrow, Sir Joseph Dalton Hooker, and Sir Charles Lyell, and had opportunities to make his mark, but he did not display the single-mindedness, patience, and learning which in these years gave men like Hooker and Francis Beaufort distinguished careers.

McCormick's name was given to several natural features: in the Antarctic, to Cape McCormick by Ross; in the Arctic, to McCormick Bay by Beaufort and McCormick Inlet by McClintock; and in north-west Greenland, to a valley. McCormick was proud of having his portrait painted in 1853 by Stephen Pearce, one of a series planned on the commanders in the Franklin search. He thought it a harbinger of a distinguished future, but, in the event, the *Forlorn Hope* was his first, last, and only command.

ROBERT E. JOHNSON

Robert McCormick was the author of *Narrative of a boat expedition up the Wellington Channel in the year 1852 . . .* (London, 1854) and *Voyages of discovery in the Arctic and Antarctic seas, and round the world . . .* (2v., London, 1884).

PRO, ADM 11/104. H. Berkeley, "Naval biography: Deputy Inspector-General Robert McCormick, R.N., F.R.G.S.," *Illustrated Naval and Military Magazine* (London), new ser., 1 (1889): 607–11. Frederic Boase, *Modern English biography . . .* (6v., Truro, Eng., 1892–1921; repr. London, 1965), II: 576. *DNB*. [V. G. Plarr], *Plarr's lives of the fellows of the Royal College of Surgeons of England*, ed. D'Arcy Power *et al.* (2v., Bristol, Eng., and London, 1930), I: 100. *Arctic Pilot* (London), III (5th ed., 1959): 295, 575, 595, 631. J. J. Keevil, "Robert McCormick, R.N., the stormy petrel of naval medicine," Royal Naval Medical Service, *Journal* (London), 29 (1943): 36–62.

McCURDY, JAMES MACGREGOR, bookseller and schoolmaster; b. in 1830 in Truro, N.S., eldest son of Isaac McCurdy; d. 12 Oct. 1886 at Newcastle, N.B.

Little is known of the early life of James MacGregor McCurdy, but it is thought that he was educated at Pictou Academy in Pictou, N.S., and then obtained a teaching licence. McCurdy taught school in his native province for a time, but by 1854 had moved to the Bend of Petitcodiac (Moncton), N.B., where he successfully operated McCurdy's Book and Stationery Store. There he sold books and musical supplies and instruments, and operated a reading-room and circulating library. The settlement at the Bend, whose petition for incorporation McCurdy signed on 30 Jan. 1855, was experiencing a period of economic growth due mainly to the active shipyards operated by Joseph Salter*. But the town showed little appreciation for cultural pursuits, and it was in this area, especially in education, that McCurdy struggled to make a contribution.

In his report for 1854 on the schools of the Bend, Inspector John S. Sayre suggested that cattle were better cared for than school children and that greater economic prosperity seemed to be accompanied by a declining concern for the quality of education. In the face of public apathy and without a system of compulsory tax assessment for the support of public education, New Brunswick schools suffered from insufficient and inadequate textbooks, ugly and uncomfortable school buildings, irregular operation, and incompetent teachers whose poor training was coupled with salaries lower than those paid in almost any other occupation. The Grammar Schools Act of 1846 and the Parish Schools Act of 1847 had established a provincial training school for teachers and a system of school inspection under a provincial board of education, but financing of the educational system was left to voluntary local initiative with limited allowances provided by the provincial government. As a well-educated man with a 1st class teaching certificate,

James McCurdy was a valuable asset to the people of Moncton, and by 1857 he had closed his bookstore and resumed teaching. In 1858 the Westmorland County Grammar School with its meagre provincial funding was moved from Moncton to Shediac, so McCurdy opened in Moncton a "Superior School" offering students a high school curriculum which included algebra, geometry, navigation, English, French, classics, and mathematics. In that year he instructed 50 male and 8 female students and was paid £71. McCurdy's high reputation as a teacher increased the attendance at his school despite the distressed state of affairs in Moncton after 1861, and by 1868 he had a teaching staff of four.

In 1871 the government of George Luther Hatheway* passed the Common Schools Act which revolutionized education in the province by creating a free, non-sectarian school system supported by direct assessment and administered by elected trustees in well-defined school districts. When the act became effective on 1 Jan. 1872 McCurdy joined the new public system and continued as a respected member of the teaching profession until his death in 1886. He pursued his innovative work by establishing a night-school for adults in 1879.

McCurdy had also been active in other worthy activities in the town. He taught in the Sunday school and served as an elder of St John's Presbyterian Church, was a charter member in 1870 of the Moncton YMCA, and was active in the temperance movement. At the time of his sudden death from typhoid fever, McCurdy was hailed in obituaries as "the father of education" in Moncton, but his accomplishments had been achieved despite the indifference of the population toward the education of their own children.

C. Alexander Pincombe

N.B., Board of Education, *Annual report on the parish schools of New Brunswick* (Fredericton), 1855; 1859; House of Assembly, *Journal*, 1855; Legislative Council, *Journal*, 1861, app.21; 1870, app.18. *Moncton Times*, 14, 17 Oct. 1886; 15 June 1927. *Westmorland Times* (Moncton, N.B.), 27 Sept. 1855. A. M. Anderson, "Education in the city of Moncton" (MA thesis, Univ. of New Brunswick, Fredericton, 1935). E. W. Larracey, *The first hundred: a story of the first 100 years of Moncton's existence after the arrival in 1766 of the pioneer settlers from Philadelphia, Pa.* (Moncton, 1970). L. A. Machum, *A history of Moncton, town and city, 1855–1965* (Moncton, 1965). *125th anniversary, 1838–1963, St. John's United Church, Moncton* ([Moncton, 1963]). C. A. Pincombe, "The history of Moncton Township (ca. 1700–1875)" (MA thesis, Univ. of New Brunswick, 1969), 183–84, 196–97, 218, 316–17.

McDERMOT, ANDREW, HBC employee, merchant, and office-holder; b. in 1790 at Belanagare, County Roscommon (Republic of Ireland), the eldest son of Miles MacDermot and Catherine (Kitty) O'Connor; m. *c.* 1814 Sarah McNab (d. 1875), and they had 17 children; d. 12 Oct. 1881 at Winnipeg, Man.

Andrew McDermot was educated at home by the "hedge-schoolmasters" who taught Roman Catholic children in secret during the penal times in Ireland. As there were few opportunities for advancement in Ireland, McDermot joined the Hudson's Bay Company and sailed from Sligo on 24 June 1812, arriving at York Factory (Man.) 26 August on the *Robert Taylor*. A mutiny broke out when the steerage passengers protested about insufficient provisions, and McDermot signed their manifesto. There were further problems when discontent developed between Irish passengers and a party of settlers sent out by Lord Selkirk [Douglas*]. McDermot learned to speak Gaelic from Scottish Highlanders during the two-month voyage.

Engaged by the HBC as a writer for three years at £30 per annum, McDermot spent the first two seasons in the East Winnipeg District. For the 1814–15 trading season, he was promoted to assistant writer and trader and placed in charge of the small HBC post on the Berens River, where he remained until 1816. He was described as "Sober. Honest. Ready and willing in the discharge of his duty. Obedient & respectful of his superiors. . . . He has a tolerably good knowledge of the Indian language."

In 1816 he was promoted to clerk and transferred to Big Point House, approximately nine miles south of Lake Dauphin, to oppose the North West Company in the Lake Manitoba area. Two years later he was made a trader with a salary of £40 per annum, and following the union of the HBC and the NWC in 1821, McDermot was moved to the Lower Red River District with a salary of £45 per annum. At the expiry of his contract in 1824, he was permitted to retire.

McDermot disliked the slow advancement offered by the fur trade and, wanting to be his own master, opened a store just north of the HBC reserve at Fort Garry. The company considered it desirable to have stores run by private individuals to supply the settlers' demands for articles it did not provide, and McDermot was also allowed to import goods in the company's ships via York Factory. He prospered and soon acquired his own brigade of York boats to carry goods between York Factory and the Red River Settlement. In an attempt to keep furs from going to the rival American post at Pembina (N. Dak.), the HBC gave McDermot a special licence to engage in the fur trade, and he resold his furs to the company at a profit. His friendship with Governor George Simpson* secured him contracts with the HBC for freighting goods, exporting tallow to England on company ships, importing rum, supplying Upper and Lower Fort Garry with firewood and provisions for horses, and importing cattle from the United States. His business increased with the arrival of the 6th Regiment of Foot in

1846 under the command of John ffolliott CROFTON, and that year he sent Simpson £2,000 sterling to invest for him. Simpson continued to manage McDermot's investments in subsequent years.

McDermot also speculated profitably in land. The executors of the Selkirk estate granted him a lot in the parish of St John's in 1824 and he acquired additional lots in the parishes of St James, St Charles, and St Boniface. He constructed water-mills at his home, Emerald Lodge, and at Sturgeon Creek and Rowlings Creek, and a steam-mill at Portage la Prairie. Emerald Lodge, often referred to as McDermotown, became the nucleus of Winnipeg, and the McDermot Avenue of today marks the northern boundary of this property.

In anticipation of the passing of the ownership of the District of Assiniboia from the Selkirk estate to the HBC in 1836, the membership of the Council of Assiniboia was increased from 5 to 15 to make it more representative. McDermot, as an important member of the community, was invited to attend the first meeting of the reorganized council on 12 Feb. 1835. He was appointed to the public works committee which was responsible for the construction of roads and bridges, surveying, the operation of ferries, and public improvements. He became a councillor of Assiniboia in 1839.

McDermot and James Sinclair* were the moving force behind the free trade movement that culminated with the trial of Pierre-Guillaume Sayer* in 1849. In an effort to curb the activities of the two leaders, Chief Factor Duncan Finlayson* had refused to renew their freighting contract with the HBC in 1843, and the following year Chief Factor Alexander Christie*, governor of Assiniboia, issued a proclamation against the illegal traffic in furs and stated that all mail would be censored. In 1845 goods ordered from the United Kingdom by McDermot and Sinclair were refused space in company ships. Christie, supported by Adam THOM, continued to tighten his restrictions, but by the end of the year acknowledged that the private trade could no longer be checked by such measures. In April 1846 Christie wrote to Simpson that the dispute would be a real test of the company's power and determine whether it or a confederacy of smugglers would be paramount. The influenza epidemic of 1846, together with the arrival of the 6th Regiment, eased the threat of rebellion. An understanding was reached whereby McDermot received a partial payment for his losses and was allowed to sell his furs and to use the company's ships again for export and import through York Factory.

McDermot had resigned from the Council of Assiniboia over his dispute with Governor Christie. Persuaded to return, he took the oath of office on 15 Jan. 1847. He was appointed *ex officio* president of the General Quarterly Court of Assiniboia in August 1849. In May 1851 he resigned from both offices, stating that he had more than he could manage with his own private affairs, but the real reason was his lack of confidence in Major William Bletterman CALDWELL, the new governor of Assiniboia, whom he claimed was unacquainted with both business and the art of government. McDermot refused further offers of public office but was persuaded to become a justice of the peace for Manitoba in 1871.

When the disturbances of 1869–70 came to upset the settlement, McDermot was an old man, retired from business since 1866. His sons-in-law, Andrew Graham Ballenden BANNATYNE and Thomas Bird, and his son Henry McDermot managed his business interests. Though McDermot did not approve of Louis RIEL's actions, he took no active part in events.

As a senior resident of the province, McDermot was given the honour of heading the deputation and addressing congratulations to Lieutenant Governor Adams George Archibald* upon his departure from Manitoba in 1872. The recommendation by Donald Alexander Smith* in 1872 which led to McDermot's appointment as Manitoba's representative among the provisional directors of the Canadian Pacific Railway was yet another tribute. McDermot was regarded as a remarkable man. He was reputed at his death on 12 Oct. 1881 to have been the wealthiest man in Manitoba and one of the most generous. He donated the land for Winnipeg's first post office, and, with Bannatyne, the land for the Winnipeg General Hospital. He was sociable and always kept an open house, and his personal charm as well as a somewhat erratic and roguish temperament, seemed to draw all and sundry to him.

Born a Roman Catholic, McDermot had left that Church in 1866, and even Archbishop Alexandre-Antonin Taché*'s efforts could not win him back. He was buried in the Church of England cemetery of St John's Cathedral.

BARRY E. HYMAN

PAM, MG 2, A6; C8; C14: nos.100, 287, 513; HBCA, D.5. HBRS, XIX (Rich and A. M. Johnson). A. Ross, *Red River Settlement*. W. J. Healy, *Women of Red River: being a book written from the recollections of women surviving from the Red River era* (Winnipeg, 1923). D. G. Lent, *West of the mountains: James Sinclair of the Hudson's Bay Company* (Seattle, Wash., 1963).

McDONALD, ANGUS, paper manufacturer; b. *c.* 1807 at Roslin (Lothian), Scotland, son of Mrs Jean McDonald; d. 16 Nov. 1887 in the village of Portneuf, Que.

Angus McDonald was only seven years old when his father died. Soon afterwards his mother married John Smith, a paper manufacturer and son of the owner of Alex. Pirie and Sons of Aberdeen, a well-known firm that had been manufacturing paper since 1770. Young McDonald, who was to learn his stepfather's trade, finished his apprenticeship in 1828. Determined to make his own way he set off for North America, probably that year, with William Miller, the son of another paper manufacturer, and Alexander and John Logan, brothers who were also trained apprentices. The four travelling companions became employees in a paper-mill near Philadelphia.

In 1833 one of them saw a notice in a newspaper that the paper-mill in Jacques-Cartier, a village in Portneuf County, was for sale. This mill had been developed for George Waters Allsopp* in 1817 by Artemas Jackson, who had set up the first paper-mill in Lower Canada at Saint-André-d'Argenteuil (Saint-André-Est) between 1804 and 1806. The Scotsmen came to Jacques-Cartier and rented the mill from the Allsopps from 7 May 1833 to 1 July 1841, operating under the name of Miller, McDonald and Logan. However, paper was made by hand there and the partners were soon looking for a place where they could build a machine-operated mill. While retaining the mill at Jacques-Cartier, the Logan brothers and McDonald established themselves at Portneuf at an excellent site some eight miles upstream on the Rivière Portneuf about 1837. In 1843, under the name of McDonald and Logans, they enlarged the second mill, equipping it with the first Fourdrinier machine in Canada. This machine, built in Glasgow by John Brown whose son Colin installed it at Portneuf, had cylinders 72 inches in diameter, run by hydraulic power, and produced sheets of paper 24 inches wide from the pulp poured onto a cloth conveyer belt travelling over a horizontal frame. This pulp was made of rags, the sole material from which paper was produced until the middle of the century.

In 1845 Angus McDonald acquired several sites on Rue Saint-Paul in Quebec City. He moved with his family to Quebec and from there managed McDonald and Logans. In 1851 his business was going so well that he bought the barony of Portneuf from the Ursulines of Quebec for more than £3,350. By then McDonald owned yet another paper-mill (under the firm name of McDonald and Smith), a flour-mill, a sawmill, a carding-mill, the largest nail factory in Canada East, a general store, and a farm, all at Portneuf. In the same period he also fitted out a fleet of schooners for transport between Newfoundland and Quebec City, as well as the steamer *New Liverpool*, which plied between Portneuf and Quebec City. According to the 1851 census, 51 people were employed at the two paper-mills in Portneuf, both of which were steam operated by then. One, owned by McDonald and Logans, made newsprint while the other, owned by McDonald's stepbrother Peter Smith, produced packing paper. The working capital for the two was £1,500 and the annual value of their products £4,500. McDonald and Logans bought Smith's mill the following year. In 1856 the paper industry at Portneuf is said to have produced 600 tons of paper, valued at $100,000; a third of this was sold in Quebec City and the remainder in Montreal.

A member of the Quebec Board of Trade, Angus McDonald was also a director of the Quebec Provident and Savings Bank in 1847. He was a shareholder of the Quebec and Richmond Railway Company, and in addition had important interests in the planned North Shore Railway [*see* Joseph-Édouard CAUCHON], serving as the company's vice-president in 1854. It may indeed have been the latter venture which led to a bankruptcy in 1857. George Burns Symes*, the "prince of merchants" of Quebec, then undertook to purchase all of McDonald's enterprises but retained him at the head of the paper-mills. In 1862 Symes sent him to England to study a new process of manufacturing paper from straw and four years later he went to the American Wood Paper works in Royersford, Penn., to investigate the method of using soda to make wood pulp.

About 1869 Alexander Logan, Angus' brother-in-law and former partner, brought him to Windsor Mills in the Eastern Townships, where for ten years he managed the mill belonging to the firm of Angus, Logan and Company, which utilized the soda process. In 1881 McDonald went to help his nephews, William T. and Peter Miller, build a paper-mill at Glen Miller in Ontario. Subsequently, while enjoying a well-earned retirement, he took a trip to his native Scotland. On his return he stayed for a while in Portneuf County, where he died suddenly on 16 Nov. 1887. His body was interred in Thorold Township, Ont.

On 26 Oct. 1838 at Quebec McDonald had married Margaret Logan, the sister of Alexander and John, and they had one daughter. A seigneur and justice of the peace at Portneuf, an entrepreneur and businessman, McDonald had also involved himself – in the spirit of *bourgeois oblige* – in municipal politics. He served as an alderman in Quebec City for two terms, from 1851 to 1855, attending all the council meetings and sitting on committees dealing with finance, incorporations, markets, fires, and regulations. He also took an interest in charitable works, as a director of the Mount Hermon Cemetery at Sillery, a trustee of Chalmers Free Church (Chalmers-Wesley United Church) on Rue Sainte-Ursule, and a founding member of both the Temperance Hall Association and the Victoria Hospital at Quebec.

Angus McDonald is one of the finest examples of the Scottish artisans who arrived in Canada early in the 19th century with little capital and devoted their energies to trade and industry. For more than 70 years he engaged in the making of paper, mainly in Canada but also in Scotland and the United States. He was one of the pioneers of paper manufacturing, an industry acknowledged to be of vital importance to Quebec and Ontario.

CLAUDE GALARNEAU

ANQ-Q, État civil, Presbytériens, St John's Church (Quebec), 26 Oct. 1838, 5 Jan. 1843. ASQ, C 43: 27. AVQ, Procès-verbaux du conseil, 1850–55. BE, Québec, Reg. B, 13, nos.5271, 5282; 16, nos.6216, 6423. Can., Prov. du, *Statuts*, 1852–53, c.62; 1854–55, c.224. *L'Abeille* (Québec), 19 déc. 1850. *Le Canadien*, 20 juill. 1834, 24 juill. 1857. *Le Journal de Québec*, 31 juill. 1852. *Morning Chronicle* (Quebec), 17 Nov. 1887. *Canada directory*, 1851; 1857–58. *Lovell's Canadian dominion directory*, 1871. *Quebec directory*, 1847–56. George Carruthers, *Paper-making* (Toronto, 1947). [Lucien Gauthier], *Album souvenir: 1861–1961; centenaire de Portneuf, 8, 9, 10, 11, 12 juillet 1961* (s.l., s.d.). J. Hamelin et Roby, *Hist. économique*. François Hardy, "Étude d'une papeterie de type familial et de son impact économique local" (thèse de MA, univ. Laval, Québec, 1972). Ouellet, *Hist. économique*. Robert [Philippe] Sylvain, *Clerc, garibaldien, prédicant des deux mondes: Alessandro Gavazzi (1809–1889)* (2v., Québec, 1962), II: 344–83.

McDONALD (MacDonald), ANGUS, Roman Catholic priest, educator, and journalist; b. 4 Nov. 1830 at the Inlet (Fairfield), Lot 47, Kings County, P.E.I., son of Angus McDonald and Mary Campbell, both natives of the Island; d. 29 April 1889 in Charlottetown, P.E.I.

Born in a rural area at the eastern extremity of Prince Edward Island, it is probable that Angus McDonald passed his first years in humble circumstances. Despite the irregular nature of his early education in various Kings County schools, the youngster must have excelled, for in 1845 he was able to enrol in Charlottetown's Central Academy, a grammar school with relatively few rural pupils. McDonald remained at the academy, where he was soon recognized as an outstanding student, until 1852, when he proceeded to the Séminaire de Québec. He returned to Prince Edward Island in 1853 or 1854, apparently because of ill health, and resumed his theological studies "in an intermittent kind of way, according as his health would permit him," at the residence of Bishop Bernard Donald MacDonald* in Rustico. When in January 1855 Bishop MacDonald founded a new "diocesan Seminary," St Dunstan's College in Charlottetown, he named Angus McDonald rector, although the latter had not yet been ordained, being under canonical age. The college opened with 18 students, seven of whom would eventually become priests. Although he had an assistant from the beginning, the strain of his new duties caused McDonald to suffer a severe relapse; he recovered over the summer of 1855 and on 21 November was ordained at Rustico.

As rector of St Dunstan's, "Father Angus" became a well-known figure in Island public life. Political parties in the late 1850s and early 1860s were divided largely along religious lines, with Protestants supporting the Conservatives, and the Roman Catholic minority supporting the Liberals. McDonald was the leading Catholic spokesman in a series of "religious" disputes which erupted in the local press of the early 1860s over such topics as the temporal power of the papacy, the "Index Prohibitory," and comparative levels of morality and education in Roman Catholic and Protestant countries. His major adversaries were David Laird*, the editor of the *Protestant and Evangelical Witness*, and William Henry Pope*, the Tory colonial secretary and editor of the *Islander*. McDonald was particularly annoyed with Pope who he thought was cynically exploiting the religious prejudices of the more credulous Island Protestants for political motives. In the summer of 1862 the rector appealed, directly or indirectly, to Lieutenant Governor George Dundas*, the local Tory government, and the British secretary of state for the colonies, the Duke of Newcastle, to dismiss Pope (who was not an assemblyman) as colonial secretary because of his virulent attacks upon Roman Catholic doctrines and institutions. Pope remained in office but, privately, Newcastle virtually ordered Dundas to silence him.

The quarrel was renewed in late September when Pope claimed that the Roman Catholic clergy, since 1860 led by Peter MacIntyre*, bishop of Charlottetown, were united in a determination to obtain public endowment for St Dunstan's College, and that the way to prevent this was to keep the Tories in office at the next election. Father Angus and Edward Whelan*, the Irish Catholic editor of the *Examiner*, retaliated by accusing Pope of reneging on a promise made the previous year to obtain a public grant for the college as a Roman Catholic institution. Pope then made clear that any grant would have been conditional upon the secularization of St Dunstan's and he also revealed the incautious threat made by MacIntyre, when he had learned that a grant was not possible, to do all in his power to defeat the Tory government. These disclosures had an explosive impact on the local political scene and led directly to the Tory victory, based exclusively on Protestant support, in the general election of January 1863.

On 17 Oct. 1862, in the midst of the bitter dispute, a militantly ultramontane newspaper, the *Vindicator*, had appeared. Father Angus was widely believed to be its editor, although on 13 Feb. 1863, after much equivocation, this was denied in its editorial column. Nevertheless, his signed correspondence in other papers had suddenly ceased, and much of the *Vindicator*'s material closely resembled McDonald's former contributions to the press: essays on the rates of crime and illegitimacy in Protestant England, ardent defences of the papacy against the claims of Victor Emmanuel II and Giuseppe Garibaldi, and attacks upon such public educational institutions as Prince of

Wales College (successor to the Central Academy) and the Normal School as "Protestant." The *Vindicator* was particularly prone to personal abuse. In addition to Dundas, Pope, and Laird, targets included the Reverend David Fitzgerald* and school visitor John Arbuckle Sr, both militant Orangemen, and Joseph Harding Webster*, master of the Normal School. Attacks on Webster for alleged impropriety led to a successful libel suit against the *Vindicator*'s publisher, Edward Reilly*, and on 5 Oct. 1864 it ceased publication. Father Angus had also continued privately to press his case against Pope at the Colonial Office, but the major result, aside from further angering Pope (who had been informed of the charges against him), was to wear out McDonald's welcome at Downing Street. To the chief clerk of the Colonial Office, he had by May 1863 become "that unscrupulous ecclesiastic."

Political issues revolving around "religion and education" subsided in the mid 1860s, and Father Angus appears to have confined his energies to more conventional activities. When the question of a grant to St Dunstan's College arose again in 1868, he took no public part in discussion of it. In June of the same year he was named by the Liberal government to the board of education, as one of two examiners of teachers, with power to exempt candidates for licences from attendance at the Normal School. His health appears to have been failing again by 1869. He was replaced as rector of the college, and in October he was summoned to Rome by Bishop MacIntyre to the Vatican Council, to serve as "Theologian to the Bishop." When he returned to Prince Edward Island in the summer of 1870, his health showed little improvement. He was assigned to the parish of Fort Augustus, Queens County, his first pastoral charge, and he remained there until 1877, with the exception of a lengthy period in 1873–74 which he spent in New York, again for reasons of health. During the rest of his life he appears to have been a semi-invalid; he spent his time in different parts of rural Prince Edward Island (Grand River West, West River, Tignish, Rustico), sometimes assisting other priests. His symptoms suggest that he suffered from a form of chronic rheumatoid arthritis. Following a winter at the Hôtel-Dieu Hospital in Montreal, he returned to Charlottetown on 19 April 1889 and died ten days later of stomach cancer.

Angus McDonald achieved his greatest success as founding rector of St Dunstan's College. He was, in the words of Laurence K. Shook, "without any specialized academic training." But although it is difficult to be precise about the academic standing of the college, there can be no doubt that, from the first, it fulfilled its primary purpose: to provide preliminary training for future priests of the diocese of Charlottetown. McDonald himself appears to have been a man of superior intellectual capacity, and during his rectorship he was a popular public lecturer, particularly at the Catholic Young Men's Literary Institute, on topics ranging from the classics to the contemporary Polish question to intemperance. As a journalist and polemicist he was less successful, and it is conceivable that Bishop MacIntyre removed him from St Dunstan's partially because, by the end of the 1860s, MacIntyre was becoming dissatisfied with the Liberal leadership and the possibility was arising of an alliance with the rector's old enemies in the Conservative party now led by W. H. Pope's brother, James Colledge.

Ian Ross Robertson

[The author is grateful to Professor Paul Potter of the Department of History of Medicine and Science, University of Western Ontario (London), for his diagnosis of the medical symptoms ascribed to Father Angus McDonald in surviving reports.

Almost all issues of the *Vindicator* (Charlottetown), 1862–64, are available on microfilm. The author believes that Father Angus was its major contributor, but in the event that he was not, examples of his polemical writing will be found in his letters to the *Islander*, 1, 8, 22 Feb., 8, 22 March 1861, and to the *Examiner* (Charlottetown), 16 Dec. 1861; 13, 27 Jan., 3, 17, 24 Feb., 3, 10, 17, 24, 31 March, 7, 14, 21 April, 5, 26 May, 14 July, 29 Sept., 6 Oct. 1862. For an indication of the sort of atmosphere which McDonald wished to create at St Dunstan's College, see his advertisement in the *Vindicator*, 14 Aug. 1863. I.R.R.]

PAPEI, Central Academy, Note-book, 1844–53. PRO, CO 226/96: 248–302; 226/98: 29–39, 66–75, 221–30. Univ. of Nottingham Library (Nottingham, Eng.), Manuscripts Dept., Newcastle MSS, Letterbooks, B-4: 81–82, 230–32 (mfm. at PAC). P.E.I., House of Assembly, *Debates and proc.*, 1870: 41. *Examiner*, 22 Jan. 1855; 16 Jan. 1860; 9 Jan., 24 July 1865; 29 April, 1 May 1889. *Herald* (Charlottetown), 23 Jan., 1, 15 May 1889. *Island Argus* (Charlottetown), 6 Jan., 7 July 1874. *Islander*, 27 Dec. 1845, 24 July 1846, 16 July 1847, 22 Oct. 1869. *Island Farmer* (Summerside, P.E.I.), 2 May 1889. *Island Guardian and Christian Chronicle* (Charlottetown), 3 May 1889. *Monitor* (Charlottetown), 22 Oct. 1863. *Patriot* (Charlottetown), 29 April 1889. *Prince Edward Island Agriculturist* (Summerside), 6 May 1889. *Summerside Journal and Western Pioneer*, 12 Aug. 1869, 2 May 1889. [A.-E. Arsenault], *Memoirs of the Hon. A. E. Arsenault, former premier and retired justice, Supreme Court of Prince Edward Island* ([Charlottetown, 1951]), 17. J. C. Macmillan, *The history of the Catholic Church in Prince Edward Island from 1835 till 1891* (Quebec, 1913), chap.13–17 and pp.102–6, 117–18, 248–49, 258, 260–61, 282, 285, 291, 301, 305, 307, 318, 397, 408, 425, 455, 460–62. I. R. Robertson, "Highlanders, Irishmen, and the land question in nineteenth-century Prince Edward Island," *Comparative aspects of Scottish and Irish economic and social history, 1600–1900*, ed. L. M. Cullen, and T. C. Smout (Edinburgh, [1977]), 234–36; "Religion, politics, and education in P.E.I.," chap.4–6. S. N. Robertson, "The public school system," *Past and present of P.E.I.* (MacKinnon and Warburton), 365a–66a, 369a. L. K. Shook, *Catholic post-secondary education in English-*

speaking Canada: a history (Toronto and Buffalo, N.Y., 1971), 39–42. M. O. McKenna, "The history of higher education in the province of Prince Edward Island," CCHA *Study Sessions*, 38 (1971): 33–35. I. R. Robertson, "The Bible question in Prince Edward Island from 1856 to 1860," *Acadiensis*, 5 (1975–76), no.2: 16–17, 21; "Party politics and religious controversialism in Prince Edward Island from 1860 to 1863," *Acadiensis*, 7 (1977–78), no.2: 29–59.

MACDONALD, EDWARD C., merchant, financier, and industrialist; b. in 1810 or 1811, son of William Macdonald, a British army officer; d. unmarried on 25 Jan. 1889 at Saint-Jean (Saint-Jean-sur-Richelieu), Que.

Edward C. Macdonald came of military stock: his great-grandfather had served under General James Wolfe* at the taking of Quebec and his grandfather with the British forces in the American Revolutionary War; his father did garrison duty in Nova Scotia, New Brunswick, and Upper and Lower Canada. Where Edward was born is obscure, his birthplace being variously given as New Brunswick and Upper Canada.

It was at Saint-Jean, where his father had once been barrack master, that Macdonald pursued a remarkably successful business career. In the mid 1830s he opened a general store and drug store in partnership with his younger brother Duncan. The brothers, operating under the firm name of E. and D. Macdonald, gained a reputation as sound businessmen. They remained partners for over 50 years in a multiplicity of enterprises and were known locally as "the merchant princes of St. Johns." The 1830s were a propitious time for Macdonald to go into business, for the village of Saint-Jean was about to enter into new economic prospects. A port of entry, advantageously situated on the Richelieu River at the foot of the navigable waters of Lake Champlain, it was connected in 1836 to Laprairie, Lower Canada, by the Champlain and St Lawrence Railroad, the first to open in Canada. The Chambly Canal, under construction in the 1830s, placed it in further direct communication with inland ports. It was not long before the Macdonalds were among the largest shippers of grain in the province.

While continuing as merchants, the brothers acquired real estate holdings. In the 1850s they opened a private bank. They were speculators, their money undoubtedly behind many a Saint-Jean venture, including the town's first woollen mill, the St Johns Woollen Manufacturing Company, of which Edward Macdonald was president in the early 1870s. The mill was not rebuilt when it burned in the fire which swept through Saint-Jean on 18 June 1876, levelling almost the entire business section of the town.

What has given Macdonald a lasting place in Canadian industrial history was his backing of the St Johns Stone Chinaware Company. It was the first pottery in Canada to concentrate on the production of "whiteware" for the table, and the only one to remain in existence for any length of time; Edward Macdonald made possible its lifespan of some 25 years.

The man who originally promoted the idea of making whiteware in Saint-Jean was George Whitefield FARRAR, the potter, but he lacked the capital to launch the audacious project and it was the Macdonalds who provided the major part of the $50,000 required. Edward Macdonald, who became the company's first president in 1873, reported to the shareholders in 1875 that the company had satisfactorily disposed of an average output of 100 crates per month from the date of the initial shipment on 28 Aug. 1874. Optimism, however, was premature. It was a time of economic depression, and by 1877 Canada's first whiteware pottery was bankrupt. Its history might well have ended at this point had Edward Macdonald not decided to buy the company outright. As proprietor he hired a new manager and brought in experienced designers such as Philip Pointon, an English-born potter who had worked previously at the Cap Rouge Pottery near Quebec City. In the first year of Macdonald's ownership more than half the workers at the St Johns Stone Chinaware Company were Staffordshire men, bringing their experience and traditional skills to a struggling Canadian industry.

The company had been founded to make in Canada the tough, high-fired earthenware that had first been produced in Staffordshire in Regency times, and which was known by a variety of names, including "ironstone china," "stone china," and "white granite." Plain, undecorated stone china of good quality accounted for the major part of the output, but the pottery also produced a considerable amount of hand-painted stone china. A specialty was a blue ware in which the body itself was coloured. In 1880 Macdonald copyrighted a design for a popular jug (produced in both blue and white) whose moulded decoration featured "A Fern sprigg running down each side. . . . Faced and reared with fleur-de-lis." Orders were also executed for monogrammed table services and for presentation pieces. The company did a growing business in hotel and institutional table and toilet wares, competing, on a modest scale, with crockery imports.

Sustained by Macdonald money and benefiting from Edward's complete freedom of direction, which he was able to exercise as proprietor, Canada's pioneer whiteware pottery finally achieved financial success. From a bankrupt enterprise it was turned into one with a high credit rating, employing some 400 workers, and equipped with modern machinery. This venture into the unlikely field of potting – an industry notoriously unprofitable in Victorian Canada – highlights Edward Macdonald's shrewd, effective pertinacity in business. Money alone, even when it could procure skilled technical assistance, would not have been enough to see the St Johns Stone Chinaware Company out of its early difficult years. The vision of whiteware potting in Saint-Jean had been George Farrar's, but it was Macdonald who made it a commercial success. Within a decade of his death, after the company had been sold to a group of ceramists from France, it was again bankrupt.

The key to Edward Macdonald's character was pin-pointed in the *News and Frontier Advocate* at the time of his death. A man who could never be prevailed upon to accept any public office (he left that to his brother, who was mayor of Saint-Jean), Edward was "at his office early and late . . . never so happy as when at work . . . it was with reluctance that he left his business for even a day's recreation."

ELIZABETH COLLARD

[Much of the family information was obtained from the Macdonald family papers which were in the possession of the late Robert Howard of Montreal. E.C.]

AP, St James Anglican Church (Saint-Jean-sur-Richelieu), Registers of baptisms, marriages, and burials, 28 Jan. 1889. PAC, MG 8, F77; RG 31, A1, 1861, 1871, Saint-Jean, Que. W. M. Ryder, *Memoirs* ([Saint-Jean-sur-Richelieu], 1900), 68. *Gazette* (Montreal), 19, 20 June 1876; 28 Jan. 1889. *La Minerve*, 31 mars 1896. *Montreal Daily Witness*, 19, 22 June 1876. *News and Frontier Advocate* (St Johns [Saint-Jean-sur-Richelieu]), 22 June 1876. *County of Missisquoi and town of St. Johns directory for 1879, 1880, and 1881* . . . (Montreal, 1879). *The Eastern Townships business and farmers directory for 1888–89* . . . (St Johns, 1888). *Eastern Townships gazetteer & directory, for the years 1875–76* . . . (Montreal, 1875). *The Eastern Townships gazetteer and general business directory* . . . (St Johns, 1867). *Illustrated atlas of the Dominion of Canada* . . . (Toronto, 1881). J.-D. Brosseau, *Saint-Jean-de-Québec; origine et développements* (Saint-Jean, [1937]), 250. Elizabeth Collard, *Nineteenth-century pottery and porcelain in Canada* (Montreal, 1967), 269–90. H. H. Lambart, *Two centuries of ceramics in the Richelieu valley: a documentary history*, ed. Jennifer Arcand (Ottawa, 1970), 13–16. Elizabeth Collard, "The St. Johns Stone Chinaware Company," *Antiques* (New York), 110 (July–December 1976): 800–5.

MACDONALD, JOHN, merchant, churchman, philanthropist, and politician; b. 27 Dec. 1824 in Perth, Scotland, son of Elizabeth Nielson and John Macdonald; m. in 1850 Eliza Hamilton (d. 1856); m. secondly in 1857 Annie Elizabeth Alcorn; d. 4 Feb. 1890 at Toronto, Ont.

Raised on floggings and Presbyterian prayer-meetings to be an intensely serious lad, John Macdonald came to Canada in 1837 when the regiment in which his father was an officer was sent out in response to the colonial disturbances. He briefly attended Dalhousie College in Halifax, then Bay Street Academy in Toronto, before entering the firm of C. and J. McDonald of Gananoque as a clerk in 1840. In 1842 he joined the Toronto dry goods house of Walter Macfarlane whereupon he fell into worldly habits until his conversion to Methodism in 1843 through the influence of a fellow clerk. He became a local preacher, but instead of entering the ministry as planned he left his job in 1847 and went to Jamaica for reasons of health. After a year, during which he was appalled by the licentiousness of life there, he returned to Toronto and opened his own retail dry goods business in September 1849.

Macdonald moved into wholesaling through jobbing, and in 1853 sold his retail business. He prospered in the 1850s by close accounting, a reluctance to extend credit, and the departmentalization of his house to maximize responsibility and accountability. None of these practices were as yet common in Canadian business. By the 1860s John Macdonald and Company was the largest dry goods house in Canada, and probably the largest wholesale house of any kind. Its Gothic five-storey warehouse running from Wellington to Front Street was one of the adornments of Toronto's commercial district. In the 1870s the business was estimated to be worth $500,000 and to have annual sales of $1,000,000. Approximately 100 clerks were employed in the house, whose operations the owner likened variously to a British regiment and an anthill. One of the few retailers to whom he extended substantial credit was a struggling fellow Methodist, Timothy Eaton*.

In 1863 John Macdonald defeated John Beverley Robinson* Jr for the Toronto West seat in the assembly. He was one of seven Reformers who stayed out of the coalition of 1864 and he opposed confederation as an ill-considered, expensive scheme unsuited to advance the interests of Canada West. Defeated in the 1867 federal election, he was returned by acclamation for Toronto Centre in an 1875 by-election. As an independent Liberal in the House of Commons he supported Sir John A. Macdonald* on the need for moderate protection in 1876, but opposed a protective tariff in 1878 and was defeated by Robert HAY in that year's general election. Not an active or partisan member of parliament – rather the independent gentleman who served as a public duty – in 1877 he had moved the resolution introducing opening prayers to the House of Commons and spoke often to his biographer of "the foul and fetid atmosphere" of Ottawa politics.

Macdonald gained greatest prominence as a devout and generous Methodist. He preached almost every Sunday and at one time or another held virtually every office open to a layman in the Methodist Church. He was the ubiquitous corner-stone layer during the Methodist church-building boom in Ontario in the 1870s and 1880s, collecting some 30 trowels and contributing substantially to building funds. He supported the Methodist unions of 1874 and 1884 and was a member of the board of regents of Victoria College and one of the strongest proponents of its move from

Cobourg to Toronto. He was also a member of the senate of the University of Toronto. Tending to conservatism in faith and doctrine, he favoured aggressive missionary and evangelical work. In spare hours he distributed tracts, visited the sick, and exhorted his employees and business associates to abstain from alcohol. An obsessive fear of death heightened the sense of urgency with which he went about his good works.

Macdonald's extant diaries confirm charitable donations of roughly one-fifth his annual income. As well as supporting the church he was a major patron of the Young Men's Christian Association and Toronto General Hospital. He also encouraged and donated to the Salvation Army. A stream of needy men and women passed through his office, ranging from collectors for charity to "tramps in every stage of dilapidation"; they received financial help, prayers and tracts, and, on occasion, a share of his lunch. He was fond of giving uplifting addresses to aspiring young businessmen and his long 1872 pamphlet, *Business success: what it is and how to secure it*, is one of the few 19th century Canadian success manuals. It is typical of the genre in stressing industry, integrity, sobriety, and careful accounting, as well as warning that wealth and true success are not synonymous. Macdonald contributed a number of articles to the *Globe* and the *Canadian Methodist Magazine* on church matters, his travels, and his business life. He also enjoyed translating Latin poetry, versified for his own amusement, and as the father of 12 children became an accomplished player of marbles.

John A. Macdonald appointed John Macdonald to the Senate in November 1887. This highly unusual honouring of a known Grit was in recognition of the wholesaler's occasional support for Macdonald and the Tories in the 1870s and his important opposition to commercial union in the Toronto Board of Trade's debate earlier in the year, during which he had urged extended trade with the West Indies as an alternative.

Macdonald seems to have been genuinely respected as a Christian gentleman; he had made few enemies in business and politics. Not a man to hide his light, however, Macdonald lived in one of Toronto's finest houses, Oaklands, and was not always successful in wrestling to avoid the sins of pride and love of self. He was an autocratic employer who could be offensively persistent in attempting to improve other men's morals. In the fullest sense he seems to have tried to live the role his biographer assigned to him as Toronto's "Merchant Prince."

John Macdonald was one of the most prominent of the great wholesalers who dominated Toronto business in the 1870s and 1880s. Channelling most of his surplus energy into Christian good works, he made little attempt to diversify his business interests. His sons were not able to prevent the family firm from finally being made uneconomic by the direct purchasing practices of Eaton's and other large retailers. The firm lasted into the 1920s only because it had been built on strong foundations.

The churches whose foundations Macdonald laid survived longer, and their strength would have pleased him. Always fearful that the time allotted to him would be brief, he had tried to use it to create in Toronto a community of prosperous, God-fearing, and sober Christians. As well as anyone he personified capitalism and Christianity in the early years of "Toronto the Good."

MICHAEL BLISS

There are daily journals of John Macdonald for 1871 and 1882–84 in the possession of Mrs F. H. Lytle, Toronto, and for 1886 at the Academy of Medicine (Toronto). He was the author of *Business success: what it is and how to secure it; a lecture delivered before the Toronto Young Men's Christian Association* (Toronto, 1872); *Elements necessary to the formation of business character* (Toronto, 1886); and "Leaves from the portfolio of a merchant," *Canadian Methodist Magazine*, 22 (July–December 1885): 68–75, 131–39; 23 (January–June 1886): 318–26, 428–40.

Baker Library, R. G. Dun & Co. credit ledger, Canada, 27: 237, 254, 299. PAC, MG 26, A. Can., House of Commons, *Debates*, 1875–78; Senate, *Debates*, 1887–90. Can., Prov. of, Parl., *Confederation debates*, 760–65. *Globe*, 5 Feb. 1890. *Commemorative biog. record, county York*. C. P. Mulvany, *Toronto: past and present: a handbook of the city* (Toronto, 1884; repr. 1970). Cornell, *Alignment of political groups*. Hugh Johnston, *A merchant prince: life of Hon. Senator John Macdonald* (Toronto, 1893).

MACDONELL (McDonell), ALLAN, lawyer, office-holder, prospector, and pamphleteer; b. 5 Nov. 1808 at York (Toronto), Upper Canada, son of Alexander McDonell* (Collachie) and Anne Smith; d. 9 Sept. 1888 at Toronto.

Allan Macdonell's grandfather, also named Allan, was a loyalist officer who settled in Glengarry County in 1784. His father was the first sheriff of the Home District, a member for Glengarry, and after 1831 also a legislative councillor. In York, Allan attended the Home District Grammar School and then studied law. Upon completion of his legal training in the office of Henry John Boulton*, he was called to the bar in 1832 and entered into partnership with Allan Napier MacNab*. It would seem that Macdonell did not find legal practice congenial for he apparently quit the profession in 1837 except for one last foray in 1858, when he acted on behalf of George Brown* in contesting, unsuccessfully, the legality of the "double shuffle" performed by John A. Macdonald*.

In 1837 Macdonell was appointed to succeed William Munson Jarvis as sheriff of the Gore District. As a major in the Queen's Rangers he raised and equipped a troop of cavalry at his own expense during the rebellion of 1837–38. After the rebellion he resumed his shrievalty, but resigned the post about 1842. Macdonell obtained a government licence in 1846 for "exploring the shore of Lake Superior for mines" and the following year he and several associates commenced work, prospecting primarily for copper. He was to devote more than ten years of his life to this project, being instrumental in organizing the Quebec and Lake Superior Mining Association in 1847 and active in the Victoria Mining Company (he served as the first president in 1856). In 1865 he was managing director of the Upper Canada Mining Company. During his years of involvement in mining Macdonell supported the Indians of the Great Lakes area in their attempts to obtain compensation from the government for their lands. He may well have been one of the "certain interested parties" to whom William Benjamin Robinson* referred in his report on treaty negotiations as having advised the Indians to demand what Robinson considered "extravagant terms." The agitation proved successful and the Indians obtained better terms in the Robinson treaties of September 1850, at the signing of which Macdonell was present.

By the 1850s Macdonell's chief passion had become westward expansion, the annexation of the lands of the Hudson's Bay Company, and the destruction of that company's trade monopoly in the west. His interest in the northwest can be traced not only to his bent for promotion but to other sources as well: connections within his family – his uncle Miles Macdonell* had been governor of the district of Assiniboia; politics – as a Toronto Reformer Macdonell distrusted the HBC and its monopoly; and personal interest – the company had tried to restrict his mining explorations in the 1840s. In 1851 Macdonell and a group of associates, including his brother Angus Duncan, applied to the Canadian assembly for a charter to build a railway from the Province of Canada to the Pacific. The petition was denied because the promoters had not completed adequate preparatory work: they did not have the agreement of the imperial government which was sovereign in the northwest, of the HBC which governed the area, or of the Indian tribes which inhabited the territory. Moreover they had no capital. This preliminary effort prompted Macdonell to write *Observations upon the construction of a railroad from Lake Superior to the Pacific* (1851) which, according to the historian Gerald E. Boyce, "for the next ten years served as the text for promoters of the Pacific Railway and Northwest annexation." It was an extravagant document in which Macdonell argued that this railway would be a better link between Britain and the Orient than a Central American canal. Undeterred by the set-back, in 1852 Macdonell and his brother applied, unsuccessfully, for a charter to build a canal at Sault Ste Marie. Such a canal, which was shortly after built by the Americans, would link lakes Huron and Superior, thereby providing easier access to the Lake Superior mining area, and form part of a communications network between Canada and the west. Further attempts to obtain a Pacific railway charter in 1853 and 1855 also failed.

By the mid 1850s opinion in Canada West was, however, shifting in favour of the annexation of the HBC lands: arable land was vanishing in the province and the completion in 1855 of the Ontario, Simcoe and Huron Railroad [*see* Frederic William CUMBERLAND] from Toronto to Collingwood made logical an attempt to penetrate the upper lakes region and beyond. Macdonell did what he could to push public opinion along. In 1856 he gave an enthusiastic speech to the Toronto Board of Trade in which he assaulted the claims of the HBC and proclaimed that "British subjects, and above all Canadians, will exercise a right of trade" in the west; the following year he amplified his views before an assembly committee that was investigating the firm's monopoly. His grandiose planning was now meeting more receptive ears. To the general mania for railway development, prospecting, and commercial expansion was added a desire for a share of the gold discovered in British Columbia in 1858. Moreover, information on the northwest was more widespread as a result of the British expedition led by John PALLISER, the Canadian one dominated by Henry Youle Hind* and Simon James Dawson*, and the emergence of a Canadian party led by Dr John Christian Schultz* in the Red River Settlement.

Macdonell and his associates, such as William MCMASTER, Adam Wilson*, and Thomas Clarkson*, were finally successful in 1858 when they secured a charter for the North-West Transportation, Navigation and Railway Company. The charter granted normal corporate powers but the company also acquired some valuable privileges. For example, the government was permitted to authorize the "Company to enter upon any ungranted lands of the Crown" and to establish transportation and trade facilities "from any place or places on the shores of Lake Superior, to any point in the interior, or between any navigable waters within the limits of Canada" as long as such projects were "in one single continuous line of communication extending westward from Lake Superior." Capital stock, originally 20,000 £5 shares, could be increased by £7,500 for each mile of portage railway constructed in units of five miles or more. The company was also permitted to procure timber, stone, fuel, and other necessary material from crown lands. The government was to be able to purchase back any company possession except wharves and warehouses for the investment value plus six per cent. A survey was to be completed within two years; the charter would lapse in 1860 unless major progress was recorded.

Macdonell was elected a founding director of the North-West Transportation, Navigation and Railway

Company along with such leading business figures as McMaster, Wilson, MacNab, Jean-Charles Chapais, John Gordon Brown*, William Pearce Howland*, and William Kennedy. This directorship Macdonell retained for the life of the company and he was one of the most active members of its board, but perhaps his most important contribution was as its chief propagandist. Three of Macdonell's pamphlets were published by the company: *Memoranda and prospectus of the North-West Transportation and Land Company*; *The North-West Transportation, Navigation, and Railway Company: its objects*; and *Prospectus of the North-West Transportation, Navigation, and Railway Company*. The pamphlets attacked the HBC monopoly and stressed the benefits of opening the west. The first, published just before the company was incorporated and concentrating on prospects for trade and on communication, proposed a mail service to Red River and a transportation system based largely on water routes. The second, published after the company's charter was passed, emphasized the benefits in trade and employment the company would bring and described in detail the proposed transportation system, which would be a combination of railways, canals, and steamboats. In the third pamphlet, which stated the objectives of the company, he set out the "opening of a route to the rich prairie lands West of Red River" and the company's desire for a railway eventually to the Pacific. Amid the constant animosity towards the HBC and the incessant boosterism in these writings, the evolution of a transportation scheme is evident.

The operations of the North-West Transportation, Navigation and Railway Company were to be described in 1871 by Joseph James Hargrave*, son of James*, a chief factor of the HBC, as "quixotic" and "abortive"; the firm was, in fact, premature and underfunded, and had no authorization from the HBC or the imperial government to operate west of Canada. In the fall of 1858 the company entered into a major deal which ultimately destroyed it. The Canadian government, perhaps affected by Macdonell's first pamphlet, had decided early in the year to subsidize a mail route connecting Canada with Red River and awarded the contract to Captain Thomas Dick*, who was associated with Macdonell and his colleagues. The key to Dick's operation was the ship *Rescue*, operating between Collingwood and Fort William (now part of Thunder Bay), Canada West. This he sold, along with the mail contract, to the North-West Transportation, Navigation and Railway Company in October 1858 for the inflated price of £6,000, paid in company stock. When it was revealed that Dick had owned the vessel jointly with some of the directors of the firm, a group of dissident shareholders successfully brought suit against the company. Affected adversely both by the recession of 1857, which had dried up capital, and by the lawsuit brought by the shareholders, the company began to come apart in 1859. In March the firm was reorganized as the North-West Transit Company with headquarters in England and an executive committee in Toronto. The new company nevertheless lost the contract for the mail service, which had been run in an inefficient and expensive manner. Adequate capital could not be found in Britain and in 1860 the firm lost a second suit to a group of shareholders. Its mandate not having been fulfilled, its charter expired in that year.

In December 1856 the Toronto *Leader*, no doubt correctly, had called Macdonell a "monomaniac" who possessed an "unconquerable penchant for magnificent schemes." After 1860 he fades from public view and little is known of him other than that in the mid 1880s he was residing in Toronto, where he died. Although he was not an important business figure, Macdonell was nevertheless a prophet of Toronto's metropolitan or imperialistic ambitions to control and exploit the vast territories of western British North America.

Donald Swainson

Allan Macdonell was the author of *The North-west Transportation, Navigation, and Railway Company: its objects* (Toronto, 1858); "Observations upon the construction of a railroad from Lake Superior to the Pacific," in Can., Prov. of, Legislative Assembly, *App. to the journals*, 1851, III, app.U.U., repub. in *Project for the construction of a railroad to the Pacific, through British territories . . .* (Toronto, 1852), 5–36; and *A railroad from Lake Superior to the Pacific: the shortest, cheapest and safest communication for Europe with all Asia* (Toronto, 1851).

PAC, MG 24, I8, 37–40; RG 5, A1, 201. Can., Prov. of, Legislative Assembly, *App. to the journals*, 1857, IV, app.17; *Statutes*, 1858. J. J. Hargrave, *Red River* (Montreal, 1871). Morris, *Treaties of Canada with the Indians*. North-West Transportation and Land Company, *Memoranda and prospectus of the North-West Transportation and Land Company . . .* (Toronto, 1858). North-West Transportation, Navigation and Railway Company, *Prospectus of the North-West Transportation, Navigation, and Railway Company . . .* (Toronto, 1858). W. J. Rattray, *The Scot in British North America* (4v., Toronto, 1880–84), IV. E. W. Watkin, *Canada and the States: recollections, 1851 to 1886* (London and New York, [1887]). *Globe*, 1848–60. [J.] B. Burke, *A genealogical and heraldic history of the colonial gentry* (2v., London, 1891–95), II. *Toronto directory*, 1859–62. Wallace, *Macmillan dict.*

G. E. Boyce, "Canadian interest in the Northwest, 1856–1860" (MA thesis, Univ. of Manitoba, Winnipeg, 1960). Careless, *Brown*, I. J. S. Galbraith, *The Hudson's Bay Company as an imperial factor, 1821–1869* ([Toronto], 1957). A. S. Morton, *A history of the Canadian west to 1870–71 . . .* (2nd ed., ed. L. G. Thomas, Toronto and Buffalo, N.Y., 1973). Douglas Owram, *Promise of Eden: the Canadian expansionist movement and the idea of the west, 1856–1900* (Toronto, 1980). Rich, *Hist. of HBC*, III. Donald Swainson, "Canada annexes the west: colonial status confirmed," *Federalism in Canada and Australia: the early years*, ed. B. W. Hodgins *et al.* (Waterloo, Ont., 1978), 137–57. A. M. Wright, "The Canadian frontier, 1840–

1867" (PHD thesis, Univ. of Toronto, 1943). W. L. Scott, "A U.E. loyalist family," *OH*, 32 (1937): 140–70. Donald Swainson, "The North-West Transportation Company: personnel and attitudes," HSSM *Papers*, 3rd ser., no.26 (1969–70): 59–77.

MACDONNELL, Sir RICHARD GRAVES, colonial administrator; b. 3 Sept. 1814 in Dublin (Republic of Ireland), eldest son of the Reverend Richard MacDonnell, provost of Trinity College, Dublin, and Jane Graves; m. in 1847 Blanche Anne Skurray of Brighton, England; d. 5 Feb. 1881 at Hyères, France, and buried at Kensal Green, London, England.

After a strict upbringing in an Irish Protestant family, Richard Graves MacDonnell attended Trinity College, where he graduated BA (1835), MA (1836), LLB (1845), and LLD (1862). Called to the Irish bar in 1838 and admitted to the English bar at Lincoln's Inn in 1841, his professional career took him in July 1843 to the colony of Gambia, in west Africa, as chief justice. In October 1847 he became governor of the British settlements on the Gambia River, where he indulged his passion for exploration and organized punitive campaigns against unruly native tribes. In 1852 he was nominated lieutenant governor of St Lucia in the West Indies but was sent instead in January 1853 to administer St Vincent, where he first encountered the rabid parochialism of a colonial assembly. With a reputation for forthrightness and intolerance, he became governor of South Australia in June 1855 at a time when a new constitution, which would give the colony local self-government, was under discussion. Never loath to speak his mind, MacDonnell drafted his own constitutional proposals and declared that South Australians were not ready for responsible government, a conviction unshaken by subsequent experience of its operation in that colony. He engaged in public debate on religious matters and, in advocating federation in Australia, championed personal policies even after the governor had supposedly surrendered this constitutional right. His reward was two years' enforced leisure in Britain when Sir Dominick Daly* succeeded him in March 1862.

Neither MacDonnell's sardonic contempt for the degeneracy of colonial politicians nor his dour determination to wield effective gubernatorial authority had diminished when he was appointed lieutenant governor of Nova Scotia in May 1864 on the recommendation of his predecessor, the Earl of Mulgrave [PHIPPS]. Although MacDonnell was sent to foster a union of the maritime colonies, which he heartily favoured as a cure for petty provincialism, he arrived at the moment when the Canadian ministry was suggesting a wider federation. He criticized the proposed distribution of power between federal and provincial authorities, the continuation of provincial governments given to corruption, and the downgrading of the post of lieutenant governor. At the Quebec conference in October 1864 he bluntly told John A. Macdonald*: "You shall not make a mayor of me, I can tell you." In view of his unabashed criticism of the Canadian proposals as premature and ill-contrived, MacDonnell was placed in something of a dilemma when the Colonial Office subsequently decided to endorse confederation. His embarrassment was short-lived, however, because of the devious stratagem he employed to prevent popular hostility to confederation in Nova Scotia from jeopardizing the new imperial policy. Both before and after the New Brunswick election of 1865 had returned an anti-confederate majority, he wanted to postpone an appeal to the Nova Scotian electorate as well as a vote in the legislature on confederation, since both recourses seemed certain to produce an adverse declaration. As a calculated expedient he proposed to Premier Charles Tupper* in the spring of 1865 that the ministry should introduce in the assembly a pious resolution favouring maritime union which would facilitate an inconsequential airing of opinion. Despite the governor's explanations, the reasoning behind this unexpected revival of the now discarded scheme of maritime union was misunderstood in London and official confidence in him fatally undermined. MacDonnell's position had clearly become invidious, and he predicted that imperial support for confederation would speed "my departure from this unlucky 'cul de sac' in which I have got myself pouched." Much to his joyous relief, the Colonial Office promoted him in October 1865 to the governorship of Hong Kong.

In this more congenial clime MacDonnell found a pliant council which accorded him the freedom to embark on an ambitious programme of administrative and social reforms, until ill health forced him in 1872 to retire from public service. He was gazetted CB in 1852, knighted in 1856, and created KCMG in 1871.

A career administrator of indifferent abilities overlaid by an innate cleverness, MacDonnell had the faults of his virtues: his purposeful energy and easy self-assurance were matched by an overbearing manner, a disdainful superiority, and a waspish tongue. His immediate successor, Sir William Fenwick WILLIAMS, dismissed him as "Governor McPotato," and Sir Charles Hastings DOYLE, commander of the British forces in North America, said he was "*au fond* a charlatan." Disparaged by other contemporaries as a middle-class snob, his proconsular temperament was better suited to crown colonies than to mature self-governing settlements where he was expected passively to defer even to those politicians whose small-mindedness and corrupt practices he despised.

PETER BURROUGHS

Letters and addresses by Richard Graves MacDonnell were published in two works: Thomas Binney *et al.*, *The church of the future, as depicted in the Adelaide correspondence, examined and estimated* . . . (Hobart Town and Launceston, Tasmania, [1859]), and [Augustus Short] *et al.*, *Christian union: if not, why not? As discussed by the lord bishop of Adelaide, his excellency the governor, the Rev. T. Binney and others* (London, 1859). He also published "Australia" in *Lectures delivered before the Dublin Young Men's Christian Association, in connexion with the United Churches of England and Ireland, during the year 1863* (Dublin, 1864), 329–96, and "Our relations with the Ashantees" in Royal Colonial Institute, *Proc.* (London), 5 (1873–74): 71–102.

PANS, RG 1, 108–9; RG 2, sect. 2, 3–5. PRO, CO 217/234–37. UNBL, MG H 12a. F. E. O. [Cole] Monck, *My Canadian leaves, an account of a visit to Canada in 1864–1865* (London, 1891). *Solicitors' Journal and Reporter* (London), 25 (1880–81): 300. *Illustrated London News*, 5 March 1881. *Times* (London), 8 Feb. 1881. *ADB*. *DNB*. Notman and Taylor, *Portraits of British Americans*, I: 197–216. J. K. Chapman, *The career of Arthur Hamilton Gordon, first Lord Stanmore, 1829–1912* (Toronto, 1964). Creighton, *Road to confederation*. G. B. Endacott, *A history of Hong Kong* (London, 1958). W. M. Whitelaw, *The Maritimes and Canada before confederation* (Toronto, 1934; repr. 1966).

MacDOUGALL, DUGALD (Donald) LORN, stockbroker and capitalist; b. 12 Aug. 1811 in Auchdoonan (Western Isles), Scotland, son of Peter MacDougall, major in the 25th Foot; m. in 1857 Lucy Boston, daughter of John Boston*, sheriff of the Montreal District, and they had four children; d. 13 Nov. 1885 at Montreal, Que.

Having passed his youth in Devon, England, Dugald Lorn MacDougall immigrated to Lower Canada in 1840. He settled in Montreal where, in partnership with John Glass, he opened a stockbroker's office, reputedly the first in the city. With still relatively few companies offering shares to the public, MacDougall and Glass apparently conducted a commission business in produce and livestock as well as stocks and bonds. In 1849 both associates were among the Montreal merchants who signed the Annexation Manifesto. The *Montreal directory* for 1849–50 lists MacDougall as a produce and bill broker in the firm of MacDougall Brothers, probably a partnership with his brother George Campbell.

Thomas Davidson, the son of David Davidson*, cashier (general manager) of the Bank of Montreal, joined the firm in 1859, but a few years later D. L. MacDougall and Davidson retired from the partnership to open their own brokerage. Through Davidson's connections with the Bank of Montreal and his family ties with James FERRIER, a prominent local capitalist, the new firm developed important contacts in the Montreal business community. In the 1860s MacDougall and Davidson became general agents for the North British and Mercantile Insurance Company, based in Edinburgh, Scotland, and both partners were appointed to the company's Canadian board of directors.

While continuing his stock-trading business with Davidson, MacDougall formed a partnership with Ferrier, Edward Martin Hopkins, Ferdinand McCulloch, and Thomas Reynolds to speculate in stocks and bonds. Incorporated as the Montreal Investment Association in 1865, the company had a capital reserve of $1 million, divided into 5,000 shares of $200, and anticipated opening an office in London, England. Active into the 1880s, the association bought and sold bonds, stocks, real estate, and debentures, and occasionally invested in loans and mortgages.

MacDougall played a role of considerable importance during the formative years of the trade in stocks and bonds in Montreal. A councillor on the Montreal Board of Trade during the 1850s, he was chairman of the Montreal Merchants' Exchange and Reading Room in 1860. He was active on the Board of Stock and Produce Brokers for a number of years and in 1863 was among those responsible for the reorganization which led to the creation of the Board of Brokers. Separated from the trade in produce, subsequently carried on at the Montreal Corn Exchange Association, the new board was an informal association designed to govern brokerage rates, the sale of shares, and the certification of brokers. The board, which was in certain aspects as much a private club as a financial institution, used the first fee charged for listing a company to purchase champagne and, in the first dispute between members, ruled that the party at fault provide a case of champagne as a fine.

Ten years later, in 1873, MacDougall was a central figure in transforming the Board of Brokers into the Montreal Stock Exchange. With his brothers (Hartland St Clair and George Campbell), Frank Bond, and James Burnett, he was among the principals named in the act of incorporation granted the exchange in 1874 and was subsequently elected its first chairman, a post he held until illness forced him to resign in 1883. His brother Hartland St Clair served as chairman in 1894–95 and 1897–99, and, continuing the family tradition, his nephew Hartland Brydges, son of George Campbell MacDougall, was elected to the same post in 1914–15. Following the 1874 reorganization, membership on the Montreal Stock Exchange rose from 28 to 42. The cost of a seat was set at $1,000 and by 1883 this fee had risen to $4,500.

Aside from his activity as a broker, MacDougall made a place for himself in the circle of Montreal businessmen speculating in railways, mines, and other sectors of the economy. With such prominent capitalists as Hugh ALLAN, Louis Renaud*, and John Joseph Caldwell Abbott*, MacDougall was among the founding directors of the Canada Marine Insurance Company in 1856. Two years later he participated in the formation of the Montreal Mountain Boulevard

Company, as did William Dow*, Mathew Hamilton Gault, Luther Hamilton Holton*, Peter Redpath*, and others, and with many of the same investors he was behind the formation of the Montreal Railway Terminus Company in 1861.

MacDougall was also a major investor in a number of companies formed to extract and refine mineral deposits in various parts of Quebec and Ontario. In association with Alexander Tilloch Galt* and others he set up the Orford Mining and Smelting Company of Lower Canada in 1863; with Harry Braithwaite Abbott, Thomas Reynolds, and Thomas Ryan, the Kennebec Gold Mining Company in 1864; with Sir Narcisse-Fortunat Belleau*, Renaud, Reynolds, Ryan, and William McNaughton, the Gaspé Lead Mining Company in 1866; with William Cunningham, Thomas Cramp, Ryan, and William Henry Allan Davies, the Canada Plumbago Company, for mining in Buckingham Township near Ottawa, also in 1866; and with James Hodges*, Walter Shanly*, William Dow, and John Redpath*, the Canada Peat Fuel Company, with its works in the counties of Napierville, Beauharnois, Huntingdon, and Châteauguay, in 1867. In later years he had interests in the Montreal Mining Company, the Huron Copper Bay Company, and several silver mines in the Lake Superior area. Among his other interests should be mentioned his participation in the formation of the Consumers' Gas Company of the City and District of Montreal in 1873, directorships in the Guarantee Company of North America and the Accident Insurance Company of North America, partnership in the Touchwood Qu'Appelle Land and Colonization Company Limited in 1883, and considerable investments in the Bank of Montreal, the Merchants' Bank of Canada, the Bank of Toronto, and the Metropolitan Bank.

MacDougall lived in a sumptuous residence on Sherbrooke Street valued at $10,000 in 1881. Both he and his wife were involved in various charitable associations: he, most notably, was a founding subscriber in the Montreal Protestant House of Industry and Refuge in 1863; Lucy MacDougall was active in the Montreal Ladies' Benevolent Society. A respected member of the congregation of the Anglican Christ Church Cathedral, MacDougall lent his assistance in the founding of the Mount Royal Cemetery Company.

Outside of these philanthropic and religious interests MacDougall led an active social life, and when the prestigious St James Club of Montreal was founded in 1858 he was one of the 93 original members, in company with such notables as his father-in-law John Boston, Peter McGill [McCutcheon*], John Young*, Robert Cassels, Thomas Cramp, and the brothers Thomas and William Workman*. One of the incorporators of the Montreal Skating Club, founded in 1861, MacDougall also took a strong interest in the activities of the Montreal Hunt Club, serving as master of the hounds from 1854 to 1858. During the period of tension in American-British relations following the seizure of the *Trent* by the United States Navy in November 1861, MacDougall organized and commanded the Royal Guides Governor General's Body Guard for Lower Canada, a militia unit based in Montreal. In 1866 he led the troop against the Fenian invaders at Saint-Armand-Centre and Pigeon Hill, in the county of Missisquoi. The Royal Guides were disbanded three years later.

Despite his failing health MacDougall was still active in business at the time of his death in 1885. His funeral, presided over by William Bennett Bond*, Anglican bishop of Montreal, was held on 16 November and as a tribute to the late chairman the Montreal Stock Exchange adjourned its activities for the day. In recognition of his leadership in establishing the exchange, a portrait of MacDougall still hangs in the boardroom of the Stock Exchange Tower, Victoria Square, Montreal.

Charles Doyon

AVM, Doc. administratifs, Rôles d'évaluation, 1881. PAC, RG 68, 240. Can., Parl., *Sessional papers*, 1867–68, VI, no.12; 1872, VI, no.13; 1877, VII, no.12; 1878, IX, no.15; 1880, VIII, no.12; 1885, IX, no.17; *Statutes*, 1873, c.103; 1874, c.54. Can., Prov. of, *Statutes*, 1841, c.66; 1856, c.124; 1858, c.19, c.22; 1861, c.82, c.123; February–May 1863, c.62; August–October 1863, c.78; 1864, c.111; January–March 1865, c.42. *Elgin-Grey papers* (Doughty), IV: 1487–94. Que., *Statutes*, 1873–74, c.54. *Gazette* (Montreal), 14 May 1873; 14, 16 Nov. 1885. *Montreal Herald and Daily Commercial Gazette*, 14, 16 Nov. 1885. *Canada directory*, 1857–58. *The Canadian army, 1855–1965; lineages – regimental histories*, comp. C. E. Dornbusch (Cornwallville, N.Y., 1966), 106–7. *Canadian men and women of the time* (Morgan, 1898), 687. *Canadian men and women of the time* (Morgan, 1912), 301–2, 687. *Dominion annual register*, 1883: 342; 1885: 267. J.-J. Lefebvre, "Présidents, Bourse de Montréal, 1874–1959," *BRH*, 67 (1961): 57–61. *Montreal directory*, 1842–43; 1850; 1857; 1860; 1862–68; 1870–85; 1893–94. *A register of the regiments and corps of the British army: the ancestry of the regiments and corps of the regular establishment*, ed. Arthur Swinson (London, 1972), 119. E. A. Collard, *Chalk to computers: the story of the Montreal Stock Exchange* ([Montreal], 1974).

MACGEORGE, ROBERT JACKSON, journalist, author, editor, and clergyman of the Episcopal Church of Scotland; b. 19 Dec. 1808 in the parish of Gorbals (now part of Glasgow), Scotland, the son of Andrew Macgeorge, "a well known and much respected solicitor of Glasgow," and Elizabeth Jackson; m. first 13 June 1841 Elizabeth Stevenson MacBrayne (d. 1842), and they had one daughter; m. secondly 4 Sept. 1844 Elizabeth MacIntosh Grant, and they had one daughter; d. 14 May 1884 in Orcadia, Rothesay, Scotland.

Robert Jackson Macgeorge was educated at the

universities of Glasgow and Edinburgh before becoming a law clerk, poet, and dramatist. In 1830 he wrote a farce, "The students," and a drama, "A legend of Carrick," which were performed in Glasgow the same year. He submitted material to *Fraser's Magazine for Town and Country* as well as the *Scottish Monthly Magazine*, and, when poor health sent him abroad, accounts of his travels in Asia appeared in the Scottish *Literary Gazette*. In 1839 Macgeorge was ordained deacon in the Scottish episcopal church and was priested the following year. He served briefly in Glasgow before immigrating to Canada West in September 1841. Bishop John Strachan* was pleased with the new arrival and Macgeorge took over the incumbency of Streetsville (now part of Mississauga), where he was to remain until 1858. His literary interests, however, quickly reappeared.

Macgeorge soon became editor of the Streetsville *Weekly Review* and under his direction it became one of the most widely read, popular, and oft-quoted journals in the province. Using the pseudonym "Solomon of Streetsville," Macgeorge, with "good-natured sarcasm and ridicule," attacked newspapers, politicians, and vendors of patent medicine. An excellent example of his pungent comments appeared on 25 Nov. 1854 concerning Canadian newspapers: "The base banner under which they fight, bears the motto, 'Expediency is our God! Railroads are our politics!'" He also contributed articles on literary topics to the *Globe* and *Leader* (Toronto), and had several songs published, using music by James Paton Clarke*. He found time to edit an Anglican journal, the *Church* (after 5 Aug. 1852 the *Canadian Churchman*). In 1848 he printed "a little volume of poems by Canadian authors," *The Canadian Christian offering*, which contained five of his own poems; a volume of his writings, *Tales, sketches and lyrics*, appeared ten years later.

He was also involved in the *Anglo-American Magazine*. Founded in 1852 by Thomas Maclear* to counterbalance the flood of American journals entering Canada, the magazine was edited by Macgeorge in association with Gilbert Auchinleck. Appearing with literary, scientific, and news items, Macgeorge's contributions included "The chronicles of Dreepdaily," "The purser's cabin," "The editor's shanty," and a few poems. Despite Macgeorge's "abilities as a miscellaneous writer" the depressed economy signalled a brief life for the journal and in December 1855 it ceased publication, having had "many subscribers but few subscriptions."

Understandably this extensive literary involvement interfered with Macgeorge's parish work, and in 1858, when he was in Scotland, owing, it was said, to his wife's illness, a delegation from Streetsville complained to Strachan. On 26 December the bishop wrote to Macgeorge in Glasgow stating that his return to Streetsville would not be "profitable or satisfactory" to himself or his parishioners. Concluding his letter by saying that he was grievously disappointed in Macgeorge's career, Strachan offered him a country church where there would be much more to do. Macgeorge did not return to Canada. The next year he accepted appointment as incumbent of the newly formed congregation of St John the Evangelist, Oban, Scotland, where he served with great success. He was subsequently appointed synod clerk, dean of the united diocese of Argyll and The Isles (1876), and honorary canon of Cumbrae Cathedral. Failing health finally forced him to retire in 1880.

A man who came to Canada ostensibly as a rural clergyman and was felt to be a failure in this role became "a willing and liberal contributor to the pages of almost every literary periodical published in Upper Canada, during his sojourn in the country." He was described in 1862 by Henry James Morgan* thus: "Mr. Macgeorge is one of nature's own children; he is a man above the ordinary height; his locks quite silvery, his form erect. . . . [He] is a gentleman of true genius, and though his pen seems at times to rush, in spite of the hand that wields it and the soul that moves it[,] into the ludicrous, yet a more sober and pure-minded man than Mr Macgeorge, we venture to say is not to be found in Canada. Though a consistent, honest churchman, as some would think, a high churchman, yet a more amiable Christian and large-minded man we have seldom met. . . ."

James John Talman

Robert Jackson Macgeorge was the author of *The increase of Christ: a sermon preached before the diocesan synod of Argyll and the Isles, 16th September, 1868* (Glasgow, 1868); *The perfect law of liberty: a sermon, preached at Trinity Church, Streetsville, on Sunday, XIIth July, M. DCCC. XLVI* (Toronto, 1846); *The Son revealing the Father: funeral sermon of the Right Rev. A. Ewing . . .* (Glasgow, 1873); *Tales, sketches and lyrics* (Toronto, 1858); and the editor of *The Canadian Christian offering* (Toronto, 1848).

General Register Office (Edinburgh), Register of births and baptisms for the parish of Gorbals, December 1808 and January 1809; Register of marriages for the parish of Barony, 13 June 1841. *Church* (Toronto, Cobourg, [Ont.]), 26 March, 26 Aug. 1842; 13 Sept. 1844. Frederic Boase, *Modern English biography . . .* (6v., Truro, Eng., 1892–1921; repr. London, 1965). *Dominion annual register*, 1884. Morgan, *Bibliotheca Canadensis*; *Sketches of celebrated Canadians*. W. P. Bull, *From Strachan to Owen: how the Church of England was planted and tended in British North America* (Toronto, 1937). J. J. Talman, "Three Scottish-Canadian newspaper editor poets," *CHR*, 28 (1947): 166–77.

MACINTOSH. *See* MacKintosh

MACK, THEOPHILUS, physician, professor, and founder of a school of nursing; b. 22 April 1820 in

Dublin (Republic of Ireland), son of the Reverend Frederick Mack and Frances Lendrum; m. 10 July 1845 Catherine Jane Adams, daughter of Elias Smith Adams, the first mayor of St Catharines, Canada West; d. 24 Oct. 1881 in St Catharines.

Theophilus Mack arrived in Canada with his family in 1829 and was one of the first pupils enrolled in Upper Canada College. During the rebellion of 1837 he served for 18 months as a lieutenant in the navy. He then studied medicine under George Grassett in the military hospital at Amherstburg, Essex County, where his father was chaplain to the garrison. He graduated from Geneva College in New York State in 1843 with the degree of MD and was qualified for practice by the Medical Board of Canada West in April of that year.

Following graduation he settled in St Catharines where the many Irish labourers engaged in enlarging the Welland Canal promised a successful medical practice. In addition, he served as professor of materia medica for three sessions at the Buffalo Medical College but declined a permanent appointment because of the inconvenience of travelling from his residence in St Catharines. Augustus Jukes*, who went on to become inspector general of hospitals in Canada, was a student of Mack's from 1846 to 1849.

Mack claimed to be the first doctor in Canada West to specialize in the treatment of diseases of women. In order to do internal examinations he designed a speculum and had it made by a local tinsmith. An eminent American gynæcologist, Dr James Marion Sims, commented favourably on the design during a visit to Canada in 1852. Mack's interest in gynæcological conditions led to meetings with Sir James Young Simpson of Edinburgh and Sir James Paget of London. Mack also presented papers to the St Catharines Medical Society for Mutual Improvement dealing with gynæcological conditions including dilatation, incision, and division of the cervix uteri and excision of the neck of the uterus. In 1862 he reported performing 100 operations without complications.

In 1859 he had visited London where he was impressed by Florence Nightingale's nursing school. Following his return to Canada, he had made several attempts to establish a hospital for sailors and travellers to combat the great prejudice against publicly operated hospitals. However, he was not successful until 1865 when he founded the St Catharines General and Marine Hospital (after 1911 the St Catharines General Hospital) which contained 20 beds. Using his own funds Mack successfully overcame the prejudice against public hospitals by providing professional nurses. In 1873 he started the St Catharines Training School and Nurses Home (later the Mack Training School for Nurses) in association with the hospital, the first nursing school in Canada to operate under the Nightingale system. To further this enterprise he sent Miss Money, a nurse, to England, and the following year she returned with two trained nurses and five probationary nurses. The first class graduated in 1879 and the school has continued to this time.

In addition to his medical and teaching activities, Mack with the assistance of Eleazer Williams Stephenson* developed the potential of the mineral waters of St Catharines. During the War of 1812 a well had been dug to provide a local salt supply and Mack felt the saline water had medicinal qualities. In the 1850s he and Stephenson founded a thermal establishment, Springbank, in St Catharines, consisting of a hotel and sanitarium which attracted many patients.

At various times Mack served as president of the board and physician, as well as manager and consulting physician of the St Catharines General and Marine Hospital. He also served intermittently as coroner and water commissioner for St Catharines. Mack added to the knowledge of Ontario physicians concerning the treatment of obstetrical and gynæcological conditions, but his major contribution to Canadian medicine was the organization of a professional training school for nurses.

CHARLES M. GODFREY

Canada Lancet (Toronto), 14 (1881–82): 93, 96. *Canada directory*, 1857–58. *Canadian biog. dict.*, I: 218–21. *Illustrated historical atlas of the counties of Lincoln & Welland, Ont.* (Toronto , 1876; repr. Port Elgin, Ont., 1971). *Lovell's Canadian dominion directory*, 1871. *The Ontario medical register* . . . (Toronto), 1878. William Canniff, *The medical profession in Upper Canada, 1783–1850* . . . (Toronto, 1894). J. M. Gibbon and M. S. Mathewson, *Three centuries of Canadian nursing* (Toronto, 1947). M. A. Nutting and L. L. Dock, *A history of nursing* . . . (4v., New York and London, 1907–12). Ont., Dept. of Health, Hospitals Division, *The hospitals of Ontario: a short history*, comp. A. A. Allan (Toronto, 1934). J. L. Runnalls *et al.*, *A century with the St. Catharines General Hospital* (St Catharines, Ont., 1974). *St. Catharines centennial history*, [comp. V. C. Jones and Harold Meighan] (St Catharines, 1967).

MACKAY (MacKay, McKay), JOSEPH, businessman and philanthropist; b. 18 Sept. 1810 at Kildonan (Highland), Scotland, son of William McKay and Ann Matheson; d. 6 June 1881 in Montreal, Que.

Joseph Mackay was educated in Scotland. In 1832 he immigrated to Montreal where he established a wholesale dry goods business on Rue Saint-Paul. His brother Edward (b. 13 March 1813 in Kildonan) left Scotland in 1840, settled first in Kingston, Upper Canada, and then after six months moved to Montreal and became a clerk in Joseph's firm. He was made a partner in 1850. The same year their nephew Hugh (b. 1832 in Caithness) arrived from Scotland and entered the business; he was admitted to partnership in 1856. The business flourished and in 1860 Mackay Brothers moved into a large new building on McGill Street.

The Mackays were respected for their ability, integrity, and industry. Edward was prominent in the business community, serving as a director of the Bank of Montreal, the London and Lancashire Life and Fire Assurance Company, the Montreal Rolling Mills, and John Shedden*'s haulage firm, and as president of the Canada Cotton Manufacturing Company and the Colonial Building and Investment Association. In 1875 Joseph and Edward retired, leaving the Mackay Brothers business in the hands of Hugh who was assisted by his brothers Robert* and James. Hugh was a founding member (1880) and director of the Canadian Telephone Company, and a director of the Royal Canadian Insurance Company.

The family was well known in Liberal circles, and Edward was approached on several occasions to accept the Liberal nomination for the provincial riding of Montreal West. The offers were refused, but he was active on behalf of Liberal candidates in elections. Honoré Mercier* appointed Hugh Mackay to the Legislative Council on 4 June 1888. Mackay resigned nine days later because illness prevented him from taking his seat immediately and it was essential for Mercier to have as many of his supporters as possible present in the upper house: Mercier lacked a majority in the council, and every vote was important, particularly in view of the government's intention to introduce legislation to settle the contentious Jesuits' estates issue. Hugh remained in poor health and in 1890 left for Georgia for medical reasons; he died en route in St Louis, Mo., on 2 April.

The Mackays were Presbyterians. In 1864 Joseph had attended a meeting called to discuss the shortage of ministers for churches in the Eastern Townships and the Ottawa valley. As a result he became involved in the plans to establish the Presbyterian College of Montreal (opened in 1867). In addition to his original gift of $2,000, he made further liberal donations and was also active in soliciting subscriptions for the college. He served for a number of years on its board of managers. After his retirement from business in 1875, he became interested in the missionary work of the church, and whenever he travelled in Canada or overseas he made a point of visiting missionaries. In 1879 he was ordained an elder in the St Gabriel Street Church. Shortly before his death in 1881 he supported the establishment of a new mission in France. Visiting ministers and missionaries were often welcomed at Kildonan Hall, the residence of Joseph and Edward on Sherbrooke Street in Montreal. Joseph bequeathed $10,000 to the Presbyterian College, and Edward gave an additional sum of $40,000 at the time of Joseph's death to endow the Joseph Mackay Chair of Systematic Theology. Edward was also deeply interested in the church; he made bequests to religious and charitable institutions totalling over $70,000 of which some $44,000 went to different aspects of church work. Shortly after Edward's death on 6 May 1883, his heirs also donated $40,000 to endow the Edward Mackay Chair at the Presbyterian College.

The Mackays were best known for their support of work with handicapped children. A school, the Protestant Institution for Deaf-Mutes and for the Blind, was established in Montreal in 1869, but the Mackays were not involved in its earliest phases. Joseph began his participation in its affairs in 1874 when it was in financial difficulties, and he was elected a governor in that year. In 1876 larger premises were urgently needed; he gave property on Décarie Boulevard, and at his own expense erected a four-storey building. He assumed the presidency, and in 1878 the school was renamed in his honour, the Mackay Institution for Protestant Deaf Mutes. When Joseph died, the presidency passed first to Edward and then in 1883 to Hugh. Edward and Hugh contributed financially, but took less part in the daily activities of the school than Joseph, who had been a frequent and welcome visitor. The school continues today as the Mackay Centre for Deaf and Crippled Children.

The Mackays were successful businessmen and important members of the Scottish Presbyterian community in Montreal. They participated in the life of the city, and considered it their duty to devote substantial sums to charitable and religious ends. Over the years they amassed considerable wealth, and it was estimated that Joseph, Edward, and Hugh each left an estate of approximately a million dollars. They never married, and their estates passed in turn from Joseph to Edward to Hugh and finally to Hugh's surviving brother Robert.

D. Suzanne Cross

Arch. of the Presbyterian College (Montreal), N. A. Macleod, "A brief history of the Presbyterian College, Montreal, 1867–1917" (1917); Minute books of the board of management, I (1864–79); II (1880–95). Scottish Record Office (Edinburgh), Kildonan parish register, 1810. Mackay Institution for Protestant Deaf-Mutes and the Blind, *Annual report* (Montreal), 1871–1907. *La Minerve*, 4, 16 juin 1888. *Montreal Daily Witness*, 2, 21 June 1881; 1, 5 May 1883; 1, 16 April 1890. Borthwick, *Hist. and biog gazetteer*, 146. *Dominion annual register*, 1880–81; 1883. Campbell, *Hist. of Scotch Presbyterian Church*. L. H. Haworth, "A history of Mackay School for the deaf" (MA thesis, McGill Univ., Montreal, 1960).

McKAY, SMITH, merchant, sealing captain, mineralogist, and politician; b. in 1817 at Pictou, N.S.; m. 14 Oct. 1869 Susan Lock, and they had one son; d. 8 Dec. 1889 at St John's, Nfld.

Smith McKay arrived in St John's from Pictou in July 1844 and in 1850 was a partner of McKay and McKenzie, St John's general merchants and agents for the New York Mutual Life Assurance Company. In 1852 and 1853 McKay and McKenzie sent vessels to the seal-fishery and in the spring of the latter year Smith McKay acted as master of the sealing vessel *Clara*. In July 1853 he also is recorded as captain of the schooner *Snipe* which brought back several tons of oil after a successful hunt of humpback whales in St Mary's Bay, but the partnership of McKay and McKenzie dissolved in that year and Daniel J. Henderson became McKay's new partner. The firm was then known as McKay and Henderson. From February 1855 to July 1856 or later McKay was involved in salvage work around the Newfoundland coast and was authorized to recover the remains of the ship *City of Philadelphia*.

Probably through his friendship with Charles James Fox BENNETT, McKay became interested in mineral exploration. In 1857 he was conducting a survey on the northwest shore of Notre Dame Bay, an area which geologist John William Dawson* believed should yield abundant copper and other ores, and discovered copper at Tilt Cove, the first considerable discovery in Newfoundland. Lacking the financial resources to begin a venture by himself, he formed a partnership with Bennett under the name Union Copper Mine and the first mine was officially opened on 9 Aug. 1864 with McKay as manager. Experienced miners, recruited in Cornwall, England, by the firm, formed the major part of the work-force, and high-grade, hand-cobbed ore from beds or sheets between 3 and 40 feet thick was shipped to the United States and Europe. What had been a fishing settlement with 10 or 12 shacks had become in the depressed year of 1868 "the only flourishing settlement in the island" with 700 to 800 men employed at the site. The value of exports from the mine had reached £1,000,000 by 1879, and Newfoundland had become the sixth largest copper producer in the world by 1880.

Between the years 1859 and 1881 McKay was granted several licences "to work mines and minerals" in the northwest part of Newfoundland, especially in the White Bay area, but nothing is known of his fortune in these ventures. He was also involved in other mining companies as both partner and salaried manager.

By 1877 trouble began to develop between McKay and Bennett in connection with the operation of the mine at Tilt Cove. Bennett filed a bill in the Supreme Court of Newfoundland preferring several charges against McKay, claiming in effect that McKay owed him £19,000. McKay counter-claimed, but the court ruled in favour of Bennett and in July 1880 he bought McKay's interests in the mine for £45,000. Yet any wealth McKay accumulated through mining must have been quickly dissipated because in 1882 a certificate of insolvency and final discharge of his debts was granted by the Supreme Court of Newfoundland.

McKay and Bennett had also been partners in the political sphere. Supporting Bennett, McKay became one of the foremost figures in the vigorous anti-confederation election campaign of 1869. He ran successfully in Twillingate and Fogo where he had the definite advantage of being one of the major employers in the constituency. He was re-elected in 1873, 1882, and 1885.

In 1883 McKay was appointed to the politically sensitive position of chairman of the Board of Works by the prime minister, Sir William Vallance Whiteway*, and he held this position until his death. He had the delicate job of deciding on expenditures for local roads in the outports and in St John's. Moreover, he was chairman through the contentious period prior to the incorporation of the city of St John's in 1888 by colonial government edict; in this period the board was responsible for part of the city's government including sanitation and McKay's task was to prepare the city for the assumption of its own local administration. That McKay's handling of these matters was generally acceptable is attested to by tributes in several St John's newspapers at the time of his death.

CALVIN D. EVANS

Centre for Newfoundland Studies, Memorial Univ. of Newfoundland (St John's), H. F. Foss, "History of Tilt Cove in the olden days" (typescript, 1966). *Bennett* v. *McKay* (1874–84), 6 Nfld. R. 178, 241, 462. Joseph Hatton and Moses Harvey, *Newfoundland, the oldest British colony: its history, its present condition, and its prospects in the future* (London, 1883). *In re Smith McKay* (1884–96), 7 Nfld. R. 44. Smith McKay and C. [J.] F. Bennett, *Report no. 21, Union Mine, Tilt Cove . . .* (n.p., 1866). *Daily Colonist* (St John's), 10 Dec. 1889. *Evening Mercury*, 9 Dec. 1889. *Evening Telegram* (St John's), 4 Oct. 1883. *Patriot* (St John's), 10 Jan. 1872. *Public Ledger*, 26 July, 31 Dec. 1850; 4 March 1851; March 1852; 8 March 1853. *Royal Gazette* (St John's), 10 Dec. 1889. *Telegraph* (St John's), 22 Dec. 1869. *Times and General Commercial Gazette* (St John's), 30 Nov., 11 Dec. 1889. *When was that? A chronological dictionary of important events in Newfoundland down to and including the year 1922 . . .*, comp. H. M. Mosdell (St John's, 1923). *Who's who in and from Newfoundland . . .* (St John's, 1927), 39.

Melvin Baker, "Origins of St. John's municipal council, 1880–1888" (unpublished graduate paper, Memorial Univ. of Newfoundland, December 1974). Moses Harvey, "Copper, 1857," *Book of Nfld.* (Smallwood), II: 342. J. K. Hiller, "Confederation defeated: the Newfoundland election of 1869" (unpublished paper presented to the CHA, 1976); "The railway and local politics in Newfoundland, 1870–1901" (unpublished paper presented to the Atlantic Canada Studies Conference, 1974). *The old sealing days*, comp. James Murphy (St John's, 1971). T. [V.] Philbrook, *Fisherman, logger, merchant, miner: social change and industrialism in three Newfoundland communities* (St John's, 1966). Prowse, *Hist. of Nfld.* (1895). A. K. Snelgrove and D. M. Baird, *Mines and mineral resources of Newfoundland* (St John's, 1953). D. M. Baird, "Base metal deposits of the Buchans–Notre Dame Bay area, Newfoundland," Geological Assoc. of Can., *Proc.* (Toronto), 8 (1956–57), pt.1: 167–78. H. G. Donoghue *et al.*, "Tilt Cove copper operation of the Maritimes Mining Corporation, Limited," *Canadian Mining and Metallurgical Bull.* (Montreal), 52 (1959): 150–69. A. K. Snelgrove, "Geology and ore deposits of Betts Cove–Tilt Cove area, Notre Dame Bay, Newfoundland," *Canadian Mining and Metallurgical Bull.*, 24 (1931): 477–519.

McKEAND (Mackeand), ALFRED, soldier and businessman; b. 28 Sept. 1849 in the parish of Gorbals (now part of Glasgow), Scotland, son of James McKeand and Emma Kilnar; m. in 1879 a Miss Cochrane, and they had four children; d. 13 Feb. 1887 in Winnipeg, Man.

James McKeand was a partner in a wholesale dry goods firm in Glasgow which had a branch in Hamilton, Canada West. In 1854 he and his family settled in Hamilton, where he personally managed this branch. Alfred McKeand attended local schools until his early teens when he entered the employment of James and John Turner, wholesale grocers, as an office boy. He gradually worked his way up to bookkeeper and then confidential clerk of the establishment. In 1879 McKeand was accepted as a full partner, and with James Turner Jr, son of one of the owners, proceeded to Winnipeg to establish a western branch of Turner, McKeand and Company.

In Alfred's generation the McKeands became a decidedly military family. He had enlisted as a private in the 13th (Hamilton) Battalion of Infantry in 1869, joining three brothers. He progressed through several non-commissioned ranks before being promoted ensign on 28 May 1875 and lieutenant on 14 Jan. 1877. Once he was in Winnipeg, Lieutenant McKeand formally took leave of the 13th Battalion on 28 Jan. 1881, and on 13 May joined the Winnipeg Infantry Company. Two months later McKeand was promoted to captain and given the command of the company. He was instrumental in bringing the unit into the 90th Winnipeg Rifles upon the latter's formation in November 1883. As commanding officer of one of the battalion's founding units, Captain McKeand was appointed junior major on 26 March 1883.

When the North-West rebellion broke out in 1885 [*see* Louis RIEL], McKeand, then senior major, mobilized and led the 90th Battalion as its temporary commander in the absence of Lieutenant-Colonel William Nassau KENNEDY, who was in the Sudan with the Canadian voyageurs accompanying the Gordon relief expedition. The behaviour of some riflemen at Fish Creek (Sask.) in April betrayed the inexperience of the battalion which, however, went on to acquit itself fairly well in May in its support role at Batoche. He proved a competent and steadfast commander under fire; he received mention in the dispatches of Major-General Frederick Dobson Middleton*, who also recommended his promotion to brevet lieutenant-colonel. While the battalion was at Fish Creek, news had arrived of the death of Lieutenant-Colonel Kennedy in London, England, and Major McKeand had succeeded to the command of the 90th Winnipeg Rifles on 29 May 1885, a position he retained until his own death less than two years later.

McKeand was typical of the late-19th-century Ontario businessmen who recognized the economic link between the opening of the Canadian west and the expansion of the industrializing east. By extending his firm into the prairies he developed a personal stake in western Canada, and was also instrumental in maintaining those military corps considered necessary for the political security of the west; he did not hesitate to mobilize his battalion against an armed revolt which he believed threatened the future of the west in confederation.

J. A. RODGER LETOURNEAU

Canada, Dept. of Militia and Defence, *Report upon the suppression of the rebellion in the North-West Territories, and matters in connection therewith, in 1885* (Ottawa, 1886). *Daily Manitoban* (Winnipeg), 14 Feb. 1887. *Hamilton Spectator*, 6 Jan. 1894, 11 Oct. 1924, 26 June 1925. *Times* (Hamilton, Ont.), February 1887. E. J. Chambers, *The 90th Regiment: a regimental history of the 90th Regiment, Winnipeg Rifles* ([Winnipeg], 1906).

McKENNEY, HENRY, merchant and office-holder; b.*c.* 1826 in Amherstburg, Upper Canada, the second son of Henry McKenney, UEL, and Elizabeth Reily; m. 20 Aug. 1845 Lucy Stockwell, and they had two sons and two daughters; d. in late 1886 in Washington Territory.

Little is known about Henry McKenney's early life except that, when a small general store he operated in Amherstburg ran into financial difficulties, he resolved to start a new life in the west. On 10 June 1859, with his wife and eldest son, he arrived at Upper Fort Garry (Winnipeg) on the maiden voyage of the *Anson Northrup*, the first steamboat to ply the Red River. Shortly thereafter McKenney rented a building from Andrew McDERMOT and converted it into a hotel. The Royal, as McKenney called it, was the first hotel in Manitoba.

The firm of McKenney and Company was formed to trade in furs and operate a general store located in the hotel. McKenney's junior partner in this company was his half-brother, John Christian Schultz*. In 1862 McKenney sold his hotel to George Emmerling, and in June, with Schultz still as junior partner, he began to build a larger store at the intersection of the Portage la Prairie trail and the main road between Upper and Lower Fort Garry. Old settlers ridiculed the location as too isolated, but before long others built nearby. McKenney thus became the founder of Winnipeg; the store he built was located at what is today the corner of Portage and Main.

On 8 June 1861 McKenney had been chosen a petty magistrate, and on 25 Nov. 1862 Alexander Grant DALLAS, governor of Assiniboia, appointed him to succeed James Ross* as sheriff of Assiniboia and governor of the jail. McKenney himself was a compulsive litigant; between 1859 and 1869 he was involved in 30 personal lawsuits, most of them trivial, before the General Quarterly Court of Assiniboia.

McKenney and Schultz dissolved their partnership in August 1864, and McKenney decided to carry on the business alone. He obtained a court judgement ordering Schultz to pay his share of a £600 debt incurred by the company. When Schultz belligerently refused payment, McKenney, with the aid of two special constables, had him bound hand and foot and carted off to jail. Thereafter the half-brothers were bitter enemies.

In August 1861 McKenney had erected a sawmill on the Manigotagan River at the east side of Lake Winnipeg, and became the first to exploit the timber resources of this area. He had a three-masted schooner, the *Jessie McKenney*, built to haul the sawn lumber to the Red River Settlement. The Manigotagan River project was not a success, however, and he abandoned it in the fall of 1869, shipping the machinery back to Upper Fort Garry.

During his ten years in Red River, McKenney played a prominent role in the community and faithfully fulfilled his duties as magistrate, sheriff, and governor of the jail. But when Louis RIEL seized power in November 1869 and the future of Rupert's Land was in question, McKenney, in spite of his loyalist background, was one of the few native Canadians in the settlement who advocated annexation to the United States. He supported the election of Alfred Henry Scott*, a clerk in his store, as the Winnipeg delegate to the convention of January 1870. There was a rumour in Red River of a special reason for his attitude to Canada: on 21 March 1870 Alexander Begg* reported a story that McKenney "fears the coming of the Canadian Government to Red River on account of old debts he left behind him some years ago in Canada." McKenney's dislike of Canada may have been influenced by his animosity towards Schultz.

In May 1870 when the union with Canada appeared certain, McKenney rented out his store to a hardware firm, resigned his shrievalty, and moved to Pembina (N. Dak.) where he built a small store and set up a sawmill. He became sheriff of Pembina County on 9 June 1871, and thus had the distinction of having served as sheriff in both American and British jurisdictions. It was difficult to obtain timber for his sawmill, and so he shut it down and in 1874 returned to Winnipeg, where he acted as a manager and legal adviser for his sons who had taken over his store. He also dabbled in oil-painting and was active in municipal politics. In the Winnipeg civic election of January 1876 he ran for alderman but came last in the poll. In August 1876 McKenney sold his Winnipeg interests and was reputed to have moved to Oregon. He died in Washington Territory, late in 1886.

GEORGE F. REYNOLDS

PAM, MG 2, B4-1; MG 9, A46: 65; MG 12, E; Vert. files, John Christian Schultz. Begg, *Red River journal* (Morton). *Canadian North-West* (Oliver), I: 478, 515. J. J. Hargrave, *Red River* (Montreal, 1871). *Manitoba Daily Free Press*, 12 Feb., 10 March 1875; 3 Jan., 31 Aug. 1876. *New Nation* (Winnipeg), 28 April 1870. *Nor'Wester*, 2 Nov. 1864, 1 Dec. 1866, 25 Aug. 1868. William Douglas, "The forks becomes a city," HSSM *Papers*, [3rd ser., no.1] (1944–45): 51–80. G. F. Reynolds, "The man who created the corner of Portage and Main," HSSM *Papers*, 3rd ser., no.26 (1969–70): 5–40. "The sheriffs of Assiniboia, paper II," *Western Law Times* (Winnipeg), 2 (1891): 1–10, 181–86.

McKIERNAN, CHARLES, known as **Joe Beef**, soldier and innkeeper: b. *c.* 1835, probably at Virginia, County Cavan (Republic of Ireland); d. 15 Jan. 1889 in Montreal, Que.

Charles McKiernan is believed to have attended the artillery school at Woolwich (now part of London) as a boy, and to have been a quartermaster in the British army during the Crimean War (1854–56). Whenever his regiment was short of food, he had an unrivalled knack of somehow finding meat and provisions, hence his nickname Joe Beef. Although it has proved impossible to determine the date of his coming to America it seems to have been connected with the *Trent* affair [*see* Charles Hastings DOYLE]. He may have arrived at Halifax in 1861, or at Montreal in 1864; he is believed to have come with the 10th Brigade, Royal Artillery. Joe Beef was in charge of the military canteen on Île Sainte-Hélène in 1864. Four years later he obtained his discharge and opened in Montreal "Joe Beef's Canteen," an establishment soon known throughout North America.

Joe Beef chose his site wisely: on Rue Saint-Claude, in the heart of a district teeming with activity. Directly opposite was the Bonsecours market, and within a couple of hundred feet the port, where "carters of cord wood," bricks, and hay jostled with longshoremen and sailors. There were also factories nearby which employed a large number of workers. In 1875, when Rue Saint-Claude was widened, he was forced to move. But he refused to leave the port district and relocated further west, in a three-storey building on the corner of Rue de la Commune and Rue Callières. Thus he retained his clientele.

From the outset Joe Beef's inn was different. He did not set out to get rich but rather to make a reasonable profit while extending charity to the destitute. Consequently he always gave food and lodging to the down-and-out. "I never refuse a meal to a poor man," he told a journalist from *La Patrie*. "No matter who he is, whether English, French, Irish, Negro, Indian, or what religion he belongs to, he's sure to get a free meal at my place if he can't afford to pay for it." His generosity quickly assured him the friendship of the poor and every day between noon and one p.m. "about 300 longshoremen, beggars, odd-job men and outcasts from Montreal society" came into his premises.

Joe Beef's richest customers treated themselves to beef with onions, bread, butter, and tea with sugar, all for ten cents. The poorest received a bowl of soup and bread. The quality of the food served seems to have been excellent. According to one journalist, "assurances have been given that one of the largest firms supplying food and drink in the city considered [our] host one of its best clients, from the point of view of both the quality and the quantity of his purchases." Joe himself claimed that amongst his customers were the biggest eaters on the continent. He required 200 pounds of meat and 300 pounds of bread a day to satisfy this crowd. Some came in so ravenous that they threw themselves on the meat like wild animals and, from 1876 to 1884, there were seven recorded cases of asphyxia, three fatal, caused by eating far too quickly.

At Joe Beef's, one could also get a bed for the night. On the Rue de la Commune, in the ten second-floor rooms which served as a dormitory, there were more than 100 iron or wooden bunks. The inn closed at 11 p.m., at which time silence became compulsory. Those who chose to sleep there lined up at the bar to put down the ten cents for which they received a blanket. The shaggy ones were shaved by one of Joe's assistants who acted as "barber," and the filthiest had to take a bath. "After the bath, Joe sprinkled his boarder's body with an insecticide preparation, a yellow powder kept in a huge pepper pot." The clients had to sleep in the nude for "Joe claims it is better to burn more coal than to pay for washing the blankets."

In the evening an employee of the inn patrolled neighbouring streets looking for anyone in distress. "During the heavy winter storms, it often happens that drunks are found at night lying in a deep snow bank, where they would certainly die if they were not picked up by the night watchman and taken to the dormitory of the hotel. 'I would be the most unhappy of men,' Joe says, 'if the public learned one day that some poor wretch died of hunger or cold at my door.' In the morning the boarders are awakened at seven and for breakfast receive 'a Labrador chicken,' the owner's term for a herring and a large hunk of brown bread. The floors are swept, then covered with sawdust again, [and] sprinkled with chloride of lime. The windows are opened and 'the river breeze clears the air in the sleeping quarters.'" Joe did not stint on sanitary measures. In 1884 *La Patrie* noted that only once in eight years had the Montreal press recorded a death in his house, "whereas not a week passes without some deaths being reported in the almshouse on Dorchester Street, where the unfortunates sleep on the floor and have very meagre fare."

But how could such an establishment be run at a profit, when salaries had to be paid to some ten employees and board and lodging supplied free to many clients? Joe Beef seems in fact to have taken advantage of his lengthy service in the British army. Thus, as early as 1868 his status as an army veteran had exempted him from the heavy expense of obtaining an innkeeper's licence. In addition, he managed his business by insisting on the observance of regulations. A client who failed to conform was quickly called to order; if he repeated the offence he was thrown out. But such incidents were rare, for as *La Patrie* noted, "all the guests in this strange hostelry have the same respect for the owner as the English soldier has for his sergeant."

In the army Joe Beef had also learned to lay in plenty of stores. To serve 600 meals a day now was no particular problem for him. He had a farm at Longue-Pointe (now part of Montreal), where he raised animals for slaughter. Every day he bought all the bread not sold by Montreal bakers – 300 or 400 pounds – and when it got too stale he fed it to his animals. It was said that the scraps from the tables were devoured by the inhabitants of the strange menagerie (a buffalo, bears, wolves, foxes, and wild cats) he had bought from sailors and kept in the cellar of his inn.

But most of his income came from the sale of alcoholic beverages. In his establishment people drank a lot, but never without paying. According to *La Minerve* the 480 gallons of beer consumed each week would bring the innkeeper $360 and would represent only half of the drinks sold. When a customer was convicted of drunkenness, Joe often hastened to pay the fine, and temperance advocates were shocked by his conduct. In 1875 John DOUGALL, the owner of the *Montreal Daily Witness*, launched a campaign against the inn, denouncing it as "a den of perdition" and "a place of ill fame." For five years Joe let Dougall carry on, while making fun of him. Then on 20 April 1880 he brought a libel suit against him which made the whole town chuckle and earned Joe the apology he demanded.

The innkeeper was well regarded by the working class. Between 17 and 26 Dec. 1877 he gave the Lachine Canal labourers, who were on strike because of wage cut-backs, 3,000 loaves of bread and 500 gallons of soup. He paid the travel expenses of two delegations which went to Ottawa to present a defence of the workers' stand to the government. On 21 December 2,000 strikers gathered in front of his establishment to hear him speak. *La Minerve* the following day noted that he "delivered a facetious address in rhymed endings which was heartily applauded. The innkeeper aired grievances about the manner in which the 'bourgeois' treated their employees, and advised the strikers never to resort to violence to uphold their rights." A week later arbitrators named by both sides reached an agreement putting an end to the strike.

Less than three years later Joe similarly supported the strikers of the Hudon Cotton Mills Company, Hochelaga, giving them 600 loaves of bread on 26 April 1880. But these strikers were less successful than had been those at the Lachine Canal. They demanded a reduction in their workday from 12 to 10 hours, as well as a 15 per cent wage increase, and denounced the brutality of some of their foremen and irregularities in the payment of wages. However, they were forced to return to the job, having gained only a 30-minute reduction in their workday.

Joe also helped the Hôpital Notre-Dame and the Montreal General Hospital. Metal alms-boxes were prominently displayed on the ground floor of the inn asking visitors to make a contribution to support the two establishments. And as the account books show, the innkeeper regularly turned over to the hospitals the sums collected, even contributing to them himself. As well, he encouraged the work of the Salvation Army, which took up public subscriptions for the destitute. At his request, each Sunday members of this charitable organization stationed themselves in front of his inn and sang hymns, for which he gave them money. Moreover, at his death his establishment was taken over by them.

The innkeeper of the Rue de la Commune was a colourful figure with a satirical sense of humour. His business card introduced him as "the Son of the People," and stated: "He cares not for Pope, Priest, Parson or King William of the Boyne; all Joe wants is the Coin. He trusts in God in summer time to keep him from all harm; when he sees the first frost and snow poor old Joe trusts to the Almighty Dollar and good old maple wood to keep his belly warm, for [of] Churches, Chapels, Ranters, Preachers, Beechers and such stuff Montreal has already got enough." But he could be tolerant too. In April 1876 he declared to a French reporter: "A preacher can make as many converts as he likes in my canteen, for 10 cents a head. As for me, if I wanted to take the trouble, I could make them fall for any religion you like, just as I can make free thinkers of them. I propose to invite [Charles-Paschal-Télesphore Chiniquy*] to come and preach here when he gets back from the lower provinces." It is not known if the temperance orator was invited, but John Currie, the pastor of the American Presbyterian Church on nearby Rue Inspecteur, made an impression on Joe Beef; he was allowed to preach to Joe's clients for seven months before he set off for a tour of the United States. "He is a good man," the innkeeper had told his regulars, "and he can come and talk to you any time he likes."

Joe Beef was wed twice. About 1865 he had married Margaret McRae, who died on 26 Sept. 1871. For her funeral he harnessed the oddest animals of his menagerie to lead the procession to Mount Royal Cemetery. As he had retained the post of commissary in the militia, he was able to secure the services of a military brass band, which performed *en route* the funeral march from Handel's oratorio *Saul*. On the way back, at Joe's request, they played an old military ditty, "The girl I left behind me." A few months later, on 13 Feb. 1872, at Montreal, he married Mary McRae, his first wife's sister.

On 15 Jan. 1889 Joe Beef died suddenly of a heart attack, at the age of 54. The *Montreal Daily Witness* noted: "For twenty-five years he has enjoyed in his own way the reputation of being for Montreal what was in former days known under the pet sobriquet of the wickedest man. His saloon . . . was the resort of the most degraded men. It was the bottom of the pit, a sort of *cul de sac* where thieves could be corralled. The police declared it valuable to them as a place where these latter could be run down." But Joe was much more popular than the paper made him out to be. On 18 January his widow and six sons committed him to burial in what *La Minerve* termed the most impressive funeral held in Montreal since that of Thomas D'Arcy McGee* in 1868. Every office in the business district closed for the afternoon and 50 labour organizations sent representatives. The procession following the ornate hearse drawn by four horses "caparisoned in sombre-hued housings" was said to be several blocks long. "This crowd consisted of Knights of Labor, workers and manual labourers of all classes. All the luckless outcasts to whom the innkeeper-philanthropist had so often extended a helping hand had come forward, eager to pay a last tribute to his memory." At his death, *La Minerve* valued his assets at $80,000.

JEAN PROVENCHER

AC, Montréal, État civil, Anglicans, St Thomas (Montreal), 18 Jan. 1889. ANQ-M, État civil, Anglicans, St Thomas (Montreal), 28 Sept. 1871; Méthodistes, East End (Montreal), 13 Feb. 1872. *La Minerve*, 21, 22, 24 déc. 1877; 19, 20, 24, 26, 27 avril 1880; 16, 17, 19 janv. 1889. *La Patrie*, 24 mars 1882, 28–30 oct. 1884. *Gazette* (Montreal), 16 Jan. 1889. Rodolphe Fournier, *Lieux et monuments historiques de l'île de Montréal* (Saint-Jean [Saint-Jean-sur-Richelieu], Qué., 1974), 197. Jean Hamelin *et al.*, *Répertoire des grèves dans la province de Québec au XIXe siècle* (Montréal, 1970). *Montreal directory*, 1871–79. E. A. Collard, *Montreal yesterdays* (Toronto, 1962), 269–81. H. E. MacDermot, *A history of the Montreal General Hospital* (Montreal, 1950), 35. Rumilly, *Hist. de Montréal*, III: 24. Léon Trépanier, *On veut savoir* (4v., Montréal, 1960–62), IV: 197–98. Joseph Germano, "L'auberge de Joe Beef," *La Rev. nationale* (Montréal), 1 (1895): 634–38. É.-Z. Massicotte, "À Montréal, le long de l'ancien port," *BRH*, 43 (1937): 149–51.

MACKIESON, JOHN, physician and surgeon; b. 16 Oct. 1795 in the parish of Campsie (Strathclyde),

Scotland; m. 11 Feb. 1830 Matilda Brecken, and they had two sons and two daughters who lived to maturity; d. 27 Aug. 1885 in Charlottetown, P.E.I.

John Mackieson received a classical education in his native Scotland and studied medicine at the University of Glasgow, graduating in 1815. He practised in Liverpool before immigrating in 1821 to Prince Edward Island. Although Mackieson lived in Charlottetown, his practice extended throughout Queens County. His marriage in 1830 to a daughter of the merchant and assemblyman, Ralph Brecken*, connected him with a number of influential families, including the land-owning McDonalds of Glenaladale, the politically prominent Havilands, and the shipbuilding Peakes.

Mackieson was appointed to numerous official positions. In 1833 he became health officer for the port of Charlottetown, serving until 1851, and in 1848 was appointed surgeon general of the militia. He was also medical attendant to the jail. Other activities were as medical examining officer for the New York Life Insurance Company and elder of St James Presbyterian Church.

His most significant work, however, was as medical superintendent of the lunatic asylum opened in Charlottetown in 1848. For the next 26 years he worked zealously for the mentally ill, although he was paid little and his efforts were hampered by crowded conditions and limited resources. His humane and enlightened attitude toward the treatment of patients is shown by his providing them with facilities for physical exercise, setting up a small library, and allowing them "all liberty their condition will permit." Despite the lack of space, which he warned would cause the institution to become a place of detention rather than cure, Mackieson maintained that the proportion of recoveries he attained was greater than that of similar institutions in Britain and the United States.

Year after year he petitioned the legislature for additional space, adequate heating, and recreation yards. Although some of his requests were met, that for adequate accommodation was not, and as late as 1873 he deplored the fact that "a proportion of the patients are obliged to be entombed in the basement of the building." The following year a grand jury strongly criticized the asylum, citing cases of inmates confined in unsanitary underground cells, and Mackieson and the keeper, Richard M. Gidley, were indicted for misfeasance in the execution of their offices. Gidley was brought to trial, but a true bill was not found against Mackieson who nevertheless was forced to resign in July 1874. Although this event was unfortunate after Mackieson's years of devoted service, it was a key factor in getting action on the construction of a new asylum. Money for construction costs was approved by the legislature in 1876, and the new building was completed by 1880. Although no longer superintendent, Mackieson retained his interest in the institution, visiting it as late as 1884 when he was 89 years old.

Mackieson was also active in other areas of medicine. In 1856, for example, as chairman of the Prince Edward Island Medical Association, he unsuccessfully petitioned the assembly for an act that would set standards for the medical profession and prevent unqualified persons from practising. His awareness of proper medical procedures is best shown by the detailed records he kept, including his manuscript, "Sketches of medical and surgical cases," which described symptoms and methods of treatment. In 1878 he wrote a 488-page manuscript, "A formulary of medical and surgical prescriptions," which served as a prescription reference for practitioners and included quotations from leading medical authorities. Mackieson's two manuscripts portray a man of inquiring mind, both studious and precise. His diary, which he kept for almost 35 years, indicates that as well as being a skilled physician, he was a well-rounded man with kindly humour and a zest for life.

IRENE L. ROGERS

John Mackieson's "Sketches of medical and surgical cases, exhibiting a concise view of the character, causes, symptoms, morbid appearances, and method of treatment adopted in the more important cases, with notes and practical remarks; 1821 *et seq.*," and "A formulary of medical and surgical prescriptions, being a complete conspectus of recipes, compounds and pharmaceutical preparations, original and selected, by standard authorities, classified according to their medical virtues, and a copious index to the same, and of diseases in which they are administered, the whole forming a valuable daily reference of practitioners of medicine," are in the possession of R. G. Lea (Charlottetown).

PAPEI, John Mackieson, Diaries, 1852–85. P.E.I., House of Assembly, *Journal*, 1849–74. *Examiner* (Charlottetown), 1874–85. *Prince Edward Island Gazette* (Charlottetown), 1821. *Prince Edward Island Register* (Charlottetown), 1823–30. *Royal Gazette* (Charlottetown), 1830–52. *Past and present of P.E.I. . . .* (MacKinnon and Warburton).

MACKINTOSH (Macintosh), JOHN, farmer and politician; b. in December 1790 at Naufrage, Kings County, P.E.I.; m. in 1808 Margaret MacDonald, and they had eight daughters and three sons; d. 14 Dec. 1881 at Naufrage.

John MacKintosh, a Roman Catholic of Scottish descent, received no formal education in his native Kings County. Himself a freehold farmer in Lot 43, he was politicized against a background of suffering and injustice attributable to the proprietary system of land ownership established on the Island in 1767. Thus he became a radical Escheator and a staunch defender of the oppressed, often destitute, tenants of eastern Kings County.

MacKintosh was over 40 years of age and a leader

in his community when William Cooper* delivered his provocative address in the House of Assembly on 27 March 1832 urging that most of the land on the Island be escheated and regranted in small parcels to settlers. Tenant resistance to seizures by sheriffs for non-payment of rent became widespread, and at Naufrage in June 1834 a group of more than 100 armed tenants warned the sheriff and his deputies that they would "die to a man" before permitting the arrest of five persons charged with a previous assault on two constables. MacKintosh, who was recognized as having influence over his neighbours, acted as a moderating force on the occasion of the Naufrage riot. He had by then acquired a political profile and was clearly associated with Cooper and John LeLacheur* as an advocate of escheat. He declined to run for an assembly seat in the general election of November 1834, despite being nominated. However, he was returned unopposed at a by-election in the 1st District of Kings County on 16 Oct. 1835.

MacKintosh was not a gifted speaker, and the predominant feature of his early performance in the assembly was the consistent support he gave to Cooper and the escheat faction. This support naturally extended outside the house where MacKintosh, who spoke Gaelic fluently, performed a vital function in communicating the issues and aims of the movement to an often ill-informed tenantry. The level of public agitation increased in 1836 when a series of public meetings was held. At Hay River, Kings County, on 20 December, a meeting conducted by MacKintosh, Cooper, and LeLacheur unanimously approved a 34-point petition to King William IV requesting a court of escheat. Lieutenant Governor Sir John Harvey* quickly brought the petition to the attention of the assembly. The committee on privileges found the petition framed in "language calculated to excite the unwary inhabitants to disloyalty" and also found MacKintosh and his two fellow assemblymen "guilty of a false and scandalous libel on this House, and of a gross breach of its known privileges." An apology was drawn up, but all three refused to sign. The committee actually went part of the way in absolving MacKintosh by stating that he had "erred more through ignorance than design, in following the evil advice of the said William Cooper." MacKintosh was not, however, to be so easily separated from his two radical companions.

Re-elected in 1838, when the Escheat party won 18 of 24 seats, MacKintosh served without interruption until 1850. In the assembly he was dogmatic, truthful, and brief in his utterances. He exhibited a concern about financial outlays, a serious trait in a dour Scot, as he continually questioned expenditures and voted for their reduction. He also displayed an enlightened attitude towards the rights of the Island's Indian and Acadian minorities. In 1843, for example, he stated that the "Indians contribute towards the revenue, and they were as well entitled to the benefit of education as any other class of the community." In 1847 he refuted Edward PALMER's claim that the establishment of a commissioners' court for the Acadians of Tignish would only "introduce a spirit of litigation" among them, by arguing that such a court with a French-speaking commissioner was needed to give the Acadians "as fair a chance to obtain justice as was given to their fellow subjects." Most important, however, was his belief in the freedoms of the common man, in defence of which he was prepared to challenge not only the state but also the church.

In this latter regard, MacKintosh was charged with having interrupted divine service at St Margaret's Chapel on 7 Jan. 1844, and the case was tried at Georgetown the following summer. It is clear from the testimony that MacKintosh and the parish priest, John McDonald*, had been feuding previously and that the congregation was divided. The underlying cause of the feud was the land question, for Father McDonald was himself a proprietor in Queens County and many of his parishioners in eastern Kings County felt that the priest had been instrumental in persuading Lieutenant Governor Sir Henry Vere Huntley* to send troops to quell a disturbance on Samuel Cunard*'s estate at East Point in March 1843. McDonald did not deign to refute the charge and the breach with his parishioners grew wider. Bishop Bernard Donald MacDonald* subsequently asked the priest to leave the area, but he refused. On 1 Jan. 1844 MacKintosh proposed a meeting on short notice and he indicated that he wished to settle the differences between himself and the parish priest. McDonald could not attend the meeting, and the result was that a group sympathetic to MacKintosh elected new church elders who warned McDonald to leave the parish without delay. The following Sunday McDonald addressed the congregation at the close of mass, stating that he would not recognize the new elders because he had not appointed them. At this point MacKintosh rose and demanded to be heard, and was only silenced when the priest knelt in prayer at the altar. McDonald then instituted legal action against MacKintosh, but the latter was acquitted by a jury. His objective was realized when McDonald left the parish late in 1844 after being suspended from his duties by the bishop.

In the late 1840s MacKintosh supported the call for responsible government and continued as an advocate of escheat until his defeat at the polls in February 1850. Although George Coles* and the Liberals were in the ascendant and formed the first responsible government in April 1851, MacKintosh was unsuccessful in the elections of that year and of July 1853. Finally in June 1854 he was returned to the assembly. He quickly succeeded in embarrassing the Liberal government by supporting William Cooper's claim that, under the

Land Purchase Act of 1853, it was spending the people's money to purchase land to which the proprietors had no rightful claim or title. In addition, he felt that in certain cases the price paid was too high. Although his radicalism was now subdued, he continued to represent 1st Kings until he withdrew from politics in 1858 at age 67. He then lived in retirement until his death at age 90.

John MacKintosh displayed a tenacious concern for the plight of the tenants and played an important role not only in communicating the issues but also in maintaining a high level of unrest among them. He was a man of conviction, dedicated to the rights of the individual, with a capacity for independent action. As a man of the people committed to removing the curse of landlordism, he made a significant contribution to resolving the most contentious issue in 19th-century Island politics.

NICOLAS J. DE JONG

PAPEI, A. S. Burke, "History of the mission of St. Margaret's, Bear River"; RG 18, 1861 census. PRO, CO 226/52: 29 (copy at PAPEI). P.E.I., House of Assembly, *Debates and proc.*, 1855; *Journal*, 1837–38. *Examiner* (Charlottetown), 26 Nov. 1895. *Islander*, 27 Aug. 1844, 22 July 1853, 28 May 1858. *Patriot* (Charlottetown), 29 Dec. 1881, 21 Jan. 1884. *Royal Gazette* (Charlottetown), 3 April 1832; 17 June, 25 Nov. 1834; 13 Jan., 20 Oct. 1935; 31 Jan. 1837; 18 Feb. 1840; 2 March, 20 April 1841; 28 March, 4 April 1843; 27 Aug. 1844; 23 Feb., 23 March, 18 May 1847; 21 March 1849; 22 April 1851. *Canada's smallest prov.* (Bolger). J. C. Macmillan, *The history of the Catholic Church in Prince Edward Island from 1835 till 1891* (Quebec, 1913). A. B. Warburton, *A history of Prince Edward Island from its discovery in 1534 until the departure of Lieutenant-Governor Ready in A.D. 1831* (Saint John, N.B., 1923). David Weale and Harry Baglole, *The Island and confederation: the end of an era* (n.p., 1973).

McLEAN, ALLAN, horse-breaker and outlaw; b. in 1855 at Thompson's River Post (Kamloops, B.C.), seventh son of Donald McLean* and eldest son of Sophia Grant; d. 31 Jan. 1881, by hanging, in New Westminster, B.C.

Allan McLean's father, a Hudson's Bay Company chief trader, had taken charge of the company post at Thompson's River in 1855, the year after his marriage to Sophia Grant, a Colville Indian. Following Allan's birth, two daughters and two more sons, Charley and Archie, were born before Donald McLean died in the war against the Chilcotin Indians in 1864. The family was then ranching near the village of Cache Creek. For five years his widow received a small pension, but in 1867 she sold the ranch and later moved to Kamloops. Donald's sister refused to recognize his Indian marriage and claimed his estate, causing legal arguments to continue for years. Meanwhile the young family was thrown on its own resources, belonging to neither the white nor the Indian communities. The boys virtually grew up in the saddle, working at various ranches mainly as horse-breakers and jockeys.

In the depression of 1877 jobs were scarce in Kamloops; gold fever had abated and surveying for the Canadian Pacific Railway had ceased. The three boys ran wild, joined by Alex, half-breed son of Nicholas Hare, who was in trouble with the authorities for assault and cattle-rustling. Thefts of horses, ammunition, liquor, food, and clothing ensued in the district.

John Tannatt Ussher was a farmer who also served as gold commissioner, government agent, constable, and jailer; he had little time or incentive to chase wild horsemen who could easily break out of the pathetically insecure jail. With Allan in the lead, the boys' contempt for the law increased with more raids and threats to local dignitaries, including John Andrew Mara*, MLA and merchant, who, Charles Augustus Semlin* reported, had seduced their sister, Annie McLean, and fathered her child.

On 3 Dec. 1879 the outlaws stole a stallion from rancher William Palmer, who promptly reported its loss to Ussher. John Thomas Edwards, JP, issued a warrant for the arrest of the McLeans and Hare, and rewards were posted. With Amni Shumway as guide, Ussher, Palmer, and John McLeod set out to arrest them and surprised the boys drinking at their camp near Long Lake on 8 December. Ussher had not expected violence, but shots were fired and panic reigned. McLeod and Allan were wounded, and Ussher was killed. The McLeans fled to the Nicola Valley Indians, pausing at ranches to steal firearms. During their flight they killed another man, James Kelly. Allan, married to a daughter of Chief Chillihetza, probably hoped to instigate an Indian uprising, but gained no support. The McLeans and Hare then took refuge in a cabin near Douglas Lake.

The citizens of Kamloops, already fearing a general rebellion over Indian land grievances, felt decisive action was in order. Posses totalling some 70 men soon besieged the cabin and on 13 December, thirsty beyond endurance, the outlaws surrendered and were taken to Kamloops. There a preliminary hearing under Clement Francis Cornwall* committed them to New Westminster jail, charged with the murders of Ussher and Kelly.

The trial of Allan, Charley, and Archie McLean and of Alex Hare, opened on 13 March 1880 after arguments about venue and authority for this special assize. Judge Henry Pering Pellew Crease* stressed the plight of fatherless half-breeds as outcasts, but the guilty verdict was a foregone conclusion. On 20 March they were sentenced to hang. Yet the legal debate continued, since no proper commission had been issued for the special assize. Eventually the British Columbia Supreme Court decided unanimously on 26 June that the assizes were invalid. The boys endured a second trial on 10 November and were again sentenced to death. They were hanged on 31 Jan. 1881 at New Westminster, apparently repentant.

Allan left his widow and two children with the Nicola Valley Indians; his son George was decorated in 1917 for exceptional bravery at Vimy Ridge.

MARY BALF

Kamloops Museum (Kamloops, B.C.), HBC letters, 1879. *In the Supreme Court of British Columbia; the Queen vs. Allan McLean, Archibald McLean, Charles McLean, and Alexander Hare, indicted, found guilty, and sentenced to death for the murder of John Ussher . . .*, ed. H. P. P. Crease (Victoria, 1880). *Daily British Colonist* (Victoria), 11, 13, 14, 16, 18, 28 Dec. 1879; 1, 20 Jan., 15, 20 Feb., 11, 14, 16–20 March, 18 May, 1, 8, 9, 13, 27 June, 19 Nov. 1880; 23 Jan., 1 Feb. 1881. *Inland Sentinel* (Yale, B.C.), 25 Nov. 1880, 3 Feb. 1881. Mel Rothenburger, *"We've killed Johnny Ussher!": the story of the wild McLean boys and Alex Hare* (Vancouver, 1973). "German killer returns home; Kamloops crowd meets hero of Vimy Ridge who was awarded DCM," *Kamloops Telegram* (Kamloops, B.C.), 11 Oct. 1917.

McLEAN, JOHN, HBC fur-trader, explorer, public servant, and author; b. 24 July 1798 or 14 Dec. 1800 in Dervaig, Isle of Mull (Strathclyde), Scotland; m. first in 1837 Margaret Charles at Norway House (Man.), and they had one child; m. secondly in 1845 Clarissa, daughter of the Reverend James Evans*, at Rossville (Man.), and they had five children; d. 8 March 1890 in Victoria, B.C.

John McLean entered the service of the North West Company at Montreal in 1820, probably as an apprentice clerk, and continued with the Hudson's Bay Company when the two companies merged the following year. He served in the Ottawa River area until his transfer in 1833 to the Columbia or Western Department on the Pacific coast. At the end of the 1836–37 outfit McLean was sent to the Northern Department. When he reached Norway House in June the Council of the Northern Department, presided over by Governor George Simpson*, was holding its annual meeting to make arrangements for the forthcoming season's trade. McLean, with 16 years of service in the HBC, was eligible for promotion to chief trader, but much to his disappointment the governor and council of company officers promoted two more senior candidates. Although McLean interpreted this rejection to be a result of Governor Simpson's personal intervention, there does not seem to be any basis for such a charge. In his "Character book" Simpson acknowledged McLean's abilities as a fur-trader and believed that he was "likely to be promoted in due time."

McLean spent the next five years in charge of the Ungava District with headquarters at Fort Chimo (Que.), a post established in 1830, where he laboured relentlessly to develop an economic overland communication route between Fort Chimo and Fort Smith (now North West River, Labrador) on Hamilton Inlet. Believing that success in the area would result in his rapid promotion, McLean embarked on trips of exploration into the interior between 1838 and 1841. Setting out on 2 Jan. 1838, he and his companions followed a route previously explored in 1834 by his predecessor at Fort Chimo, Erland Erlandson*, and travelled about 533 miles in 47 days to Fort Smith at the mouth of the Naskaupi River. In June 1839, accompanied by a "strong crew" which included Erlandson, McLean went by canoe along the coast of Ungava Bay to George River which he ascended as far as it was navigable. Then, travelling overland, he reached Fort Nascopie, on Petitsikapau Lake (Labrador), before moving southeast on what is now known as the Churchill River, to become the first European to view the Grand (Churchill) Falls. At this point he was forced to turn back, and reached Fort Chimo on 20 September. The following year he canoed to Fort Smith by a different route from that taken two years earlier. In 1841, using information supplied by William Henry Allan Davies, the HBC officer in charge of the Esquimaux Bay District, who had ascended the Churchill River from its mouth to near the falls the previous year, McLean discovered a route around the falls and into the interior which the HBC immediately began using.

In spite of McLean's efforts, the profits of the area remained low and the expenses high, and in 1841 Governor Simpson ordered that communication with the district by sea be cut from once a year to once every two years. This directive intensified the feelings of isolation and abandonment which had developed during McLean's previous four years; even his promotion to chief trader in 1841 did little to reassure him. In 1842 McLean embarked on his first furlough in 22 years, and the unprofitable Ungava District was closed the following year.

He returned from the British Isles early in 1843, and in May led an HBC brigade from Lachine, Canada East, to Norway House. Accompanying him was Lieutenant John Henry LEFROY, an officer in the Royal Artillery, who was conducting a magnetic survey of British North America. Lefroy considered McLean to be "a person of intelligence and information beyond what one might expect from a man who has all his life been scraping beaver skins together at remote stations" and remarked on his ability to play the flute.

Poor health, however, prompted McLean to inform Simpson in June 1843 of his intention to retire should he be appointed to a "*second* Ungava." He attempted to secure adequate personal resources by offering the company the shares he owned as an officer, but it declined to buy them back and he was forced to remain in the service regardless of his posting. McLean was sent to Fort Simpson (N.W.T.) believing he would have charge of the Mackenzie River District. He did supervise the district operations for a year, but in June 1844 Simpson informed him that he had misinterpreted his instructions of the previous year and that Chief Trader Murdoch McPherson, an officer with more seniority, would be assuming command. For McLean this was the final indignity. Not content with venting his feelings on Simpson, he carried his demand for justice to the HBC governor and committee in London, who ruled that McLean had not suffered any more hardships than other company officers and fully supported Governor Simpson's actions. Completely disenchanted with the company, McLean retired on 1 June 1846.

He spent the next nine years in Guelph, Canada West, as a manager of the Bank of Montreal. In November 1855 a scandal involving the loss of £1,300 from his branch resulted in financial ruin for McLean and the end of his banking career when he took responsibility for the loss and turned over most of his savings as restitution. Although Erland Erlandson, whom McLean had hired to assist him at the bank, has since been suspected of the theft, largely because he left a large estate at his death in 1875, nothing has been proven, and McLean himself rejected this notion. By 1857 McLean had moved to Elora, Canada West, where he became the clerk of the division court, a position he held for more than 25 years.

McLean had remained actively interested in developments within the HBC, and in 1849 he published *Notes of a twenty-five years' service in the Hudson's Bay territory*, a work which remains one of the few firsthand accounts of the fur trade and the administration of Governor George Simpson. In 1869 he published several articles in the Elora *Lightning Express* describing his impressions of his 25 years in the west, with the purpose of encouraging the acquisition of the territory for Canada. In 1883 he left Elora for Victoria where several years later he died in the home of his daughter, having received during his lifetime little recognition for either his explorations or his publications. They are, however, now receiving attention in new studies of fur-trade history.

GARRON WELLS

John McLean published *Notes of a twenty-five years' service in the Hudson's Bay territory* (2v., London, 1849), repub. as *John McLean's notes of a twenty-five year's service in the Hudson's Bay territory*, ed. W. S. Wallace (Toronto, 1932); in 1869 he published a series of articles describing his impressions of his 25 years in the west in the *Lightning Express* (Elora, Ont.).

PAM, HBCA, A.6/25: ff. 118–118d; A.6/26: ff.145–145d; A.10/18: ff.490–93; B.134/c/1: f.422; B.134/c/15: f.180; B.134/g/2–8; B.154/z/1: f.421; B.188/d/15: ff.9d–10; B.223/b/10; B.239/g/12–14; B.239/g/16; B.239/k/2: ff.38, 70d, 124; D.4/23: ff.45, 136d; D.4/26: f.8; D.4/28: f.78; D.4/31: f.49d; D.4/32: f.97d; D.4/62: ff.55d–62; D.5/5: ff.164–164d; D.5/8: ff.311, 366; D.5/18: ff.52–53d; mfm. copy no.384. HBRS, XXX (Williams). J. H. Lefroy, *In search of the magnetic north: a soldier-surveyor's letters from the north-west, 1843–1844*, ed. G. F. G. Stanley (Toronto, 1955). Mactavish, *Letters of Letitia Hargrave* (MacLeod). *Daily Colonist* (Victoria), 9 March 1890. J. R. Connon, *"Elora"* (n.p., 1930; repub. as *The early history of Elora, Ontario, and vicinity*, intro. Gerald Noonan (Waterloo, Ont., 1974)). A. S. Morton, *Sir George Simpson, overseas governor of the Hudson's Bay Company: a pen picture of a man of action* (Toronto and Vancouver, 1944).

MCLEAN (MacLean), JOHN, Church of England bishop and educator; b. 17 Nov. 1828 at Portsoy (Grampian), Scotland, son of Charles McLean, a merchant, and Jannet Watson; m. in 1861 Kathleen Wilhelmina, daughter of the Reverend Richard Flood and Frances Mary Blake, at London, Canada West, and they had ten children; d. 7 Nov. 1886 at Prince Albert (Sask.).

Trained in science and classics, John McLean graduated with an MA from King's College (University of Aberdeen) in Scotland, in 1851. He then worked in London, England, for a manufacturing firm managed by an uncle and, having acquired some knowledge of French, German, and Spanish, was placed in charge of its foreign correspondence. Probably soon after arriving in London he became a member of the Church of England, and by 1858 he had also decided to seek ordination. In these decisions his continuing friendship with Robert Machray*, a fellow student at Aberdeen, played a part. Machray, who had been ordained in 1856 following a successful career at the University of Cambridge, became bishop of Rupert's Land in 1865. McLean, however, preceded him to British North America in 1858, after Isaac Hellmuth*, the secretary of the Colonial and Continental Church Society in British North America, persuaded him to emigrate to Canada West. There he was ordained deacon on 1 Aug. 1858 and priest on 15 December by Benjamin Cronyn*. Bishop Cronyn appointed him chaplain to the garrison and curate of St Paul's Cathedral in London, Canada West. There McLean remained until 1866 when he was summoned by Machray to Rupert's Land to assist in the revival of St John's College in Winnipeg as a theological seminary and higher school.

McLean and Machray, like John Strachan* earlier, may have had Episcopalian antecedents and connections, but it is more certain that, in the circumstances of the disruption of the Church of Scotland, they were drawn to the Church of England. Both were strongly evangelical, and, although staunch churchmen, neither had any sympathy with the Tractarian movement, particularly influential in the Church of Scotland. Yet both were inclined to take a conservative position on most issues, and felt a powerful attraction to the order and discipline of the Church of England. Nor, as young Scots of modest background and exceptional ability, do they seem to have been entirely oblivious to the greater opportunities offered by a career south of the Scottish border.

McLean's numerous activities in Rupert's Land after 1866 reflected not only Machray's plans for the extension of Anglican work in what was expected to be an era of development, but also his limited resources. At the end of December 1867, McLean began to hold services in a hall in the "rising little village of Winnipic," the beginning of the parish of Holy Trinity. Between 1866 and 1874 he taught at St John's College, of which he was warden and professor of divinity. He was also appointed examining chaplain to the bishop of Rupert's Land, archdeacon of Assiniboia, and, finally, rector of St John's Cathedral at Winnipeg.

During the Red River disturbance of 1869–70, McLean joined Machray in urging the Protestant inhabitants, the majority of whom were Anglican, towards a moderate course, and in advising them to send English-speaking delegates to the convention proposed by Louis RIEL for January 1870. At this same time, McLean attended Riel's prisoners, including Charles Arkoll Boulton*. Later he joined with the two ministers, John BLACK, Presbyterian, and George Young*, Methodist, to urge resistance to the Fenian raid of October 1871.

In 1873 the Church of England authorities were contemplating dividing the vast diocese of Rupert's Land. McLean went to Britain that year to raise funds for the proposed new diocese of Saskatchewan which would include much of the southern portions of the future provinces of Alberta and Saskatchewan. This was not McLean's first search for funds; in 1871, for St John's College, he had raised over $8,000 in Canada, where, as Machray often complained, support for northwestern missions was far from generous. On 3 May 1874 the archbishop of Canterbury consecrated McLean as the first bishop of Saskatchewan.

When he returned to the northwest, McLean went to the Prince Albert settlement, arriving there by dog-train in February 1875. He made arrangements for the building of the log church of St Mary (west of the present city), and there, on 9 Jan. 1876, he held his first ordination. In the winter of 1875–76 he also visited the established Stanley Mission (on the east shore of Mountain Lake, Sask.), where Holy Trinity Church had been built in 1859 by Indians under the direction of the Reverend Robert Hunt. The next winter he travelled to Fort Edmonton; here he helped William Newton, who had recently established the Anglican mission, arrange for the building of the forerunner of the present All Saints' Cathedral.

McLean describes his diocese at the time of its creation as "a vast area containing about 30,000 Indians, with a few small settlements of white people . . . no endowments, no missionaries, no churches." He had in fact an ordained missionary, a lay missionary, and a native deacon, but the challenge was indeed formidable. Despite the disappointingly slow development of the west in the next decade, McLean laid the foundations for the work of his church among white settlers and Indians. Although reduced in size in 1883 by the creation of the diocese of Qu'Appelle, McLean's diocese had 22 clergy and seven catechists by 1886. This reduction, which strained his friendship with Machray, McLean accepted with reluctance. In addition to building churches and mission stations and raising substantial endowments, McLean established Emmanuel College at Prince Albert, formally opened in 1879. Primarily conceived as a teaching centre for a native clergy, it also did the first work at the high school level in the North-West Territories, and McLean envisioned the college as the nucleus of a university. In May 1883 "an act to incorporate the University of Saskatchewan and to authorize the establishment of colleges within the limits of the diocese of Saskatchewan" received royal assent. McLean and Lawrence CLARKE were among those named to the university's first board.

In Prince Albert McLean was perhaps the leading figure, as the local newspaper and the journal of the HBC post show. The activities of his large family were followed with a similar interest, not unsurprising in an isolated community. Three of the five daughters were married in Prince Albert in the 1880s to clergymen, and the family was still in residence there in the 1890s. McLean seems to have had good relations with his laymen, but could be critical of clerical brethren such as the learned but eccentric Newton or the Reverend George McKay who, busy ministering from Fort Macleod (Alta) to Indians, mounted police, and ranchers, failed to keep in touch with his bishop. The church at large recognized McLean through honorary degrees in 1871 from Kenyon College, Ohio, Bishop's College, Lennoxville, Que., and Trinity College, Toronto, and in 1881 from St John's College, these having, it is worth noting, high church leanings.

Despite his difficulties McLean's accomplishments were substantial. He made valiant efforts to secure Anglican missionaries for the settlers attracted by the construction of the Canadian Pacific Railway, but his headquarters in Prince Albert was remote from the railway route chosen and he was preoccupied with the established work among the Indians and mixed-bloods. This work was not made easier by the strains that led to the North-West rebellion of 1885. Nevertheless, by the time of his death he had taken important steps towards the training of a native clergy, he had consolidated Anglican missionary work among the northern Crees, and had initiated it among the Blackfeet, Bloods, Piegans, and Sarcees of southern Alberta. McLean attributed to the work of the missionaries the comparative quietness, during the rising, among the Indians and mixed-bloods under Anglican influence.

In August 1886 after his last synod McLean visited his western missions, including Calgary and Edmonton. At the latter he was seriously injured when a runaway team caused him to be thrown from the "democrat" in which he was travelling. Already suffering from Bright's disease, and determined to reach his home in Prince Albert, the bishop, in a cold October, was floated down nearly 500 miles of the North Saskatchewan River in a small boat. He reached home but died on 7 November.

He was buried in St Mary's churchyard with all the pomp the Anglican Church and the town of Prince Albert could muster. The *Prince Albert Times and Saskatchewan Review* mourned him as the town's best friend, "the central figure of our community," and his old friend Machray praised his "great and varied gifts, readiness of utterance, and unceasing devotion."

LEWIS GWYNNE THOMAS

The most important sources for McLean's activities during his episcopate are the records of the Synod of the Diocese of Saskatchewan (Saskatoon) and the archives in London of the Society for the Propagation of the Gospel and of the Church Missionary Society.

PAM, HBCA, B.332/a/1; MG 2, C14; MG 3, D1; MG 12, B2. *Prince Albert Times and Saskatchewan Rev.* (Prince Albert, Sask.), 1882–86. Boon, *Anglican Church*. Robert Machray, *Life of Robert Machray, D.D., LL.D., D.C.L., archbishop of Rupert's Land, primate of all Canada, prelate of the Order of St. Michael and St. George* (Toronto, 1909). E. K. Matheson, "John McLean," *Leaders of the Canadian church*, ed. W. B. Heeney (2nd ser., Toronto, 1920), 225–52. William Newton, *Twenty years on the Saskatchewan, N.W. Canada* (London, 1897). W. F. Payton, *An historical sketch of the diocese of Saskatchewan of the Anglican Church of Canada* (n.p., [1973]).

McLELAN, ARCHIBALD WOODBURY, shipbuilder, shipowner, and politician; b. 20 Dec. 1824 at Londonderry, N.S., son of Gloud Wilson McLelan*, a member of the Nova Scotia House of Assembly, and Martha Spencer; m. in 1854 Caroline Metzler; d. 26 June 1890 at Halifax, N.S.

Archibald Woodbury McLelan was educated at Great Village, on the north shore of the Minas Basin, and then at Mount Allison Wesleyan Academy at Sackville, N.B. He acquired considerable experience at sea and was managing his father's shipping business and store in Great Village before the latter's death in 1858. That same year McLelan succeeded his father as representative in the assembly for Colchester County, and like him supported Joseph Howe* and the Reform party. McLelan was also a charter member of the local division of the Sons of Temperance organized in Great Village in 1850.

In partnership with his brother-in-law John M. Blaikie, McLelan began to build ships on the Great Village River. In 1863 they and two other partners constructed the 257-ton *Cleo*, and during the 1870s McLelan and Blaikie alone built the 750-ton *Wave King* (1872), the 900-ton *Wave Queen* (1873), and the 1,200-ton *Monarch* (1876). They continued to build ships into the early 1880s, using timber from the hardwood, spruce, and hackmatack forests of Colchester and Cumberland counties and framing timbers from the Acadian village of Memramcook, N.B., at the head of Cobequid Bay. McLelan's business prospered, and by 1867 it was generally understood that he was comfortably off.

With Howe, McLelan strongly opposed confederation through 1865, 1866, and after 1867. He believed the British North American provinces had disparate interests, and that the proposed financial terms were unjust to Nova Scotia. The debt allowance sounded fine in theory, and Alexander Tilloch Galt*'s idea for the equalization of debts was superficially persuasive. The debt allowance was, however, for McLelan, the wrong way round since the Canadian and Nova Scotian assets to be transferred to the new national government were not at all equal in quality. The Canadian assets of $62.5 million represented, to a considerable extent, uncollectable or bad debts while the Nova Scotian contribution of $8 million represented railways or other public works in reasonable condition that could be taken over as assets by the new dominion government. McLelan also opposed the way in which confederation had been achieved. After his election as member of parliament for Colchester in September 1867 he told the House of Commons when it met for the first time in Ottawa in November that the people of Nova Scotia had been insulted and betrayed. Although they had taken revenge at the polls by electing many anti-confederate members to the Commons, they were not yet satisfied and would try to get out of confederation altogether. While McLelan was impressed, as he himself admitted, with the power and the resources that he had now seen in Quebec and Ontario, he believed Nova Scotia could manage perfectly well on its own and that there was little or no commercial connection between Nova Scotia and central Canada. Nova Scotia probably had "more ships in the Port of Calcutta, in any day of the year, than . . . in all the ports of [the Province of] Canada."

McLelan, with Howe, looked to Great Britain for remedy, but early in 1868 Britain refused to accept Nova Scotia's appeal against confederation. The anti-confederates had then two choices: to continue to agitate, notwithstanding the British decision, or to make better terms with the new Dominion of Canada. McLelan and Howe took the latter course. Samuel Leonard Tilley* of New Brunswick urged the wisdom of concessions to Sir John A. Macdonald*, and so accommodation was gradually arrived at, though with great difficulty. Macdonald came to Halifax in August, and Howe and McLelan went to Portland, Maine, in January 1869 to meet with the minister of finance, Sir John Rose; "better terms" for Nova Scotia emerged. Howe took a seat in Macdonald's cabinet on 30 January but the bitter by-election he was forced to fight the following April in Hants permanently impaired his health. McLelan resigned as MP, accepted a seat in the Senate, and became one of three commissioners for overseeing the construction of the Intercolonial Railway at a salary of $3,000 a year. It was easy to allege that Howe and McLelan had been bought off, but probably not true. McLelan certainly was a man of principle, and, so far as the evidence allows, of probity; he now believed that there was nothing else, constitutionally, for Nova Scotia to do but to accept better terms and make the best of confederation.

During the 1870s McLelan's shipping business continued to prosper, and he also became involved in the Cobequid Marine Insurance Company. In 1875 he opposed George Brown*'s draft treaty with the United States that would allow Canadian ships to be registered in American ports since it would mean that Maritime shipyards would become shipbuilders for the Americans. It had once been the practice, notably in New Brunswick, to build ships for sale, especially to Great Britain, but, as McLelan told the Canadian Senate, "I scarcely know a man who followed that business but was ruined . . . our true policy is to build for ourselves, to build and sail our own ships." That same year, in the Senate, McLelan supported the National Policy, something he was always to believe in.

After the return of the Macdonald Conservative ministry in September 1878, McLelan was gradually drawn closer to the government. When James McDonald*, the minister of justice, retired in 1881 to the Supreme Court of Nova Scotia, McLelan joined the Macdonald government as president of the council, Howe's old portfolio. At the same time he gave up his Senate seat and was elected by his old constituents of Colchester County to the House of Commons. In July 1882, he became minister of marine and fisheries. He was an unusually good minister, being thoroughly familiar with the shipping business, and being by nature hard-working and judicious. Within a month of his appointment he had already visited Sable Island and all the lighthouses on the eastern coast of Nova Scotia, and was on his way up the St Lawrence to the Saguenay. Two years later, at the age of 59, he went to examine lighthouses on lakes Huron and Superior, in order, as he wrote Sir John A. Macdonald, "to deal more intelligently with the demands of MPs and others for lights, buoys, beacons." He was instrumental in organizing the meteorological bureau in the department, and in introducing a new system of gas buoys.

His tenure as minister of finance (December 1885 to January 1887) was not as successful; McLelan seems to have lacked the technical skill and probably accepted the position at Macdonald's insistence. When replaced by Sir Charles Tupper*, McLelan became postmaster general for a year and a half, and was responsible for introducing the parcel post system into Canada. By now, however, he wanted to be out of the cabinet, and on 10 July 1888 he accepted the position of lieutenant governor of Nova Scotia with a sigh of relief.

Nova Scotians had not altogether forgotten the persuasion exerted to get McLelan to accept confederation early in 1869, but his tenure at Government House, Halifax, was happier than Howe's had been 15 years before. His faintly bucolic style of living was more endearing than otherwise. His constituents from Colchester presented him with a fine Jersey cow, which was duly put to graze in a field at Government House and milked by the coachman; Mrs McLelan churned the butter herself since the cook refused. McLelan died rather unexpectedly in Halifax on 26 June 1890. He left a widow, three sons, a daughter, as well as at least one grandson, and, it was believed, a considerable estate.

McLelan was a man of judgement and good sense. He opposed confederation until impassable barriers has been reached, then made the best he could of it, and tried to persuade his fellow Nova Scotians to do the same. He also opposed further concessions to the Canadian Pacific Railway in 1885, along with his fellow Maritimer, the minister of finance, Leonard Tilley. He helped Macdonald strengthen the cabinet – it badly needed strengthening – in September 1885, when John Sparrow David Thompson* was brought from the Supreme Court bench in Halifax to become minister of justice. McLelan was fond of Macdonald and on 29 June 1889 wrote an appreciative letter to him: "Often when Council was perplexed and you had made things smooth and plain I have thought of the expression an old farmer made about my late father when he saw him accomplish something that had puzzled all the neighbours. 'There are wheels in that man that have never been moved yet' and so I have thought of my leader. . . ." He also enjoyed Macdonald's sense of humour, even at his own expense: when he and Thompson returned to Ottawa in June 1886, after a fruitless attempt to defeat William Stevens Fielding* in the 1886 provincial election, he came to cabinet newly barbered, with his hair slicked down, and Macdonald at once observed, "Why, McLelan, you look as if you had had a good licking!" McLelan was not a brilliant man, but, like Macdonald, he seemed to have forces and powers held in reserve.

P. B. WAITE

[No major collection of McLelan papers has so far turned up. Mount Allison University Library (Sackville, N.B.) has two groups of letters, under G. W. McLelan, the father, and A. W. McLelan, about 80 letters in all, mostly on family and business matters. The Dalhousie University Archives has some A. W. McLelan papers (MS 2–87). There are a few letters from A. W. McLelan in a file in PANS, under the name of G. W. McLelan. There are also letters from him to Sir John A. Macdonald in the Macdonald papers (PAC, MG 26, A, 232), in the Howe papers (PAC, MG 24, B29), and in the Thompson papers (PAC, MG 24, C4). McLelan's speech in the Nova Scotian assembly in 1865, opposing confederation, is printed as a separate pamphlet, *Speech on the union of the colonies . . .* (Halifax, 1865). Something of the background of McLelan's life is given in *Great Village history, commemorating the 40th anniversary of Great Village Women's Institute, 1920–1960 . . .* ([Great Village, N.S., 1960]). There are obituaries in the *Morning Chronicle* (Halifax), 27 June 1890, the *Morning Herald* (Halifax), 27 June 1890, and the *Eastern Chronicle* (New Glasgow, N.S.), 3 July 1890. P.B.W.]

MCMASTER, WILLIAM, businessman, politician, banker, and philanthropist; b. 24 Dec. 1811 in County Tyrone (Northern Ireland), son of William McMaster, a linen-draper; d. 22 Sept. 1887 in Toronto, Ont.

William McMaster was educated privately by a well-regarded local teacher, and when about ten he was converted and apparently joined the Baptist church in Omagh. After he had gained some experience as a clerk in an Irish mercantile house, he came to North America and, following a brief stay in New York City, moved to York (Toronto), Upper Canada, in August 1833. The popular version of McMaster's immigration holds that he arrived in York without friends or money, found employment as a clerk in Robert Cathcart's wholesale and retail dry goods firm, and owed his success to merit alone. Another account states that Cathcart, who had established his business in 1828 or 1829, later brought out his nephews from Ireland, one of whom was William McMaster. Both versions agree that McMaster rapidly became an asset to his employer. Within a year or two of his arrival he was a partner in the firm. In July 1844, when Cathcart retired, he took over the business.

McMaster's further success owed much to his skill in recognizing opportunities and to his ability to move in tune with important commercial trends. Decisions he made in 1844, to concentrate on wholesale dry goods and to move his company to Yonge Street, were shrewd ones. The dry goods trade, located at the southern end of Yonge Street, would prove to be one of Toronto's most profitable lines. An enterprise such as McMaster's fulfilled the requirements of a population clamouring for imported goods. In 1850 the business cleared $10,000, but apparently did not as yet rank among the largest general wholesalers in Toronto. The agents of R. G. Dun and Company reported McMaster's wealth to be in the $300,000–$400,000 range in 1853 and in the $600,000–$800,000 range in 1859. McMaster resisted the temptation to expand beyond his financial resources and his caution enabled him to emerge from the recession of 1857 with his business intact. Early in his career he had been described by Dun's agent as "probably the safest man in business in Toronto" and later reports repeated that his judgement could be relied upon for any credit he requested. By 1860, when the dry goods wholesalers had emerged as the wealthiest merchants in the city, McMaster's company was considered by R. G. Dun to be "the largest Dry Goods Concern in Western Canada."

Having no children, McMaster had taken two of his nephews from Ireland, Arthur Robinson McMaster and James Short McMaster, into the business as bookkeeper and English buyer respectively. They became his partners in the firm William McMaster and Nephews on 1 March 1859 and J. S. McMaster took up residence in Manchester to oversee the English interests of the company. Contemporaries described the family as "close people, their affairs known only to themselves."

William McMaster entered politics in 1862 when he was elected as a Liberal to represent the Midland division in the Legislative Council. His sympathies lay with men such as George Brown* and other Reformers concerned with the commercial expansion of Toronto and Canada West. He was drawn as well by their interest in measures to improve the position of evangelical Nonconformists, including his own Baptist co-religionists. In the spring of 1867 he served on the central executive committee of the newly revived Reform Association of Upper Canada and became a director of its Toronto branch. He received an appointment to the first dominion Senate and remained a member for the rest of his life. When he spoke in Senate debates, his comments were succinct and usually related to subjects that concerned him personally: banking and finance, bills affecting companies with which he was associated, and matters touching him as a Baptist.

By the early 1860s William McMaster and Nephews, originally an "active, pushing" business, had come to be regarded as an old firm dealing with an established clientele. This change may well have led McMaster, who had spoken of retiring as early as 1859, to expand his commercial interests. He relinquished the management of the company in 1863, though retaining a large financial interest, reputedly

$400,000, and the firm became known as A. R. McMaster and Brother. In the process of building up his business William McMaster had contributed markedly to Toronto's metropolitan development and to its attempt to wrest control of the central Canadian economy from Montreal. He was an active member of the Toronto Board of Trade, having been on its council eight times by 1861, after which he left the representation of the McMaster interest to other members of the family. During the late 1850s and the 1860s he was also a director of the Ontario Bank, the Wellington, Grey and Bruce Railway, the Canada Landed Credit Company, and the Toronto and Georgian Bay Canal Company (after 1865 the Huron and Ontario Ship Canal Company). He was a member of the first board of directors of the North-West Transportation, Navigation and Railway Company in 1858, which hoped to establish direct communication between Toronto and Rupert's Land so that the raw materials of the northwest might be exploited and its potential as a market tapped [*see* Allan MACDONELL].

The rivalry between Montreal and Toronto also played an important part in McMaster's decision to pursue a banking career in the 1860s. Even though he accepted an appointment as a Toronto director of the Bank of Montreal in 1864, McMaster was distressed by the ascendancy of the bank in Canada West. Under the leadership of its general manager, Edwin Henry King*, the bank was restricting the amount of credit available in Canada West by withdrawing capital to accommodate a constantly increasing business with the provincial government; in January 1864 the government transferred its account to the bank [*see* Robert CASSELS]. Two years later, the Bank of Montreal was the only bank to take advantage of new legislation enabling banks to surrender their notes in favour of those issued by the government; it thus became the sole agent for issuing the government notes. In the uncertain days which preceded the failure of the Bank of Upper Canada in 1866 and the Commercial Bank of Canada in 1867, McMaster and the Toronto business community moved to arrest the growing control of the Bank of Montreal in Canada West. McMaster and Archibald Greer, the Toronto manager for the Bank of Montreal, after remonstrating in vain with the bank against these policies of credit restriction, withdrew from it to establish a bank designed to meet the credit needs created by King's actions. The charter of the Bank of Canada, which had been inactive since 1858, was purchased from William CAYLEY and others, and in August 1866 amendments to this charter were obtained which changed the name to the Canadian Bank of Commerce and revised the required capital stock from $3,000,000 to $1,000,000. Unlike many of the banks proposed during the period, the Canadian Bank of Commerce had little difficulty in filling its initial subscription of shares. McMaster had brought to the new bank both the support of the Toronto business community and his own reputation as a shrewd businessman with private dealings on the New York and London money markets. His agents, Caldwell Ashworth in New York and J. S. McMaster, who moved his office to London's financial district, took on the international business of the bank.

On 18 April 1867 the shareholders of the bank had their first meeting. McMaster, who held 500 shares valued at $25,000, was elected president and Henry Stark Howland* vice-president. The directorate, drawn from the ranks of prominent Toronto businessmen and financiers, included such men as John Taylor* and John MACDONALD (who resigned within three weeks and was replaced by James Austin*). In June 1869 the bank increased its authorized capital stock to $2,000,000 and the following year parliament approved an increase to $4,000,000, as a result of the amalgamation with the Gore Bank. When in 1871 the directors increased the authorized capital to $6,000,000, matching that of the Bank of Montreal and the Merchants' Bank of Canada, the *Monetary Times* noted that theirs was a "bold, not to say ambitious policy." The amount was paid by 1874. Not all the directors shared McMaster's desire for growth at the expense of short-term profit. Austin left the board in 1870 and Howland resigned in 1874; both went to newer banks where a higher return might be expected from less capital.

McMaster had launched the Canadian Bank of Commerce amid great uncertainty about the future of Canadian banking. New legislation proposed in 1868 and introduced the following year by the federal minister of finance, John ROSE, was drawn up in consultation with King of the Bank of Montreal. The ability of chartered banks to issue notes of their own, the quantity of government securities which they might be required to hold, and the continuation of the existing system of branch banking were at stake. Under Rose's legislation Canadian banks would all have had to purchase government notes from the Bank of Montreal. Protests against Rose's proposals came from across the country but McMaster avoided leading the opposition of Ontario banks, leaving this role to George Hague*, cashier (general manager) of the Bank of Toronto. He also refused to chair the Senate committee on banking, commerce, and railways when the position was offered to him by Rose in April 1869. Although he declined in the fear that opposition by him to the legislation would endanger the bills he had before the house concerning the Canadian Bank of Commerce, he also felt that the banking community should use its influence to amend legislation that might seem to be inevitable rather than risk hardening the attitude of the government by open opposition. In the event, the government chose to withdraw the contentious legislation and Rose resigned.

The appointment of Francis HINCKS as minister of finance on 9 Oct. 1869 relieved McMaster of his awkward position. Hincks was sympathetic to the Ontario lobby and McMaster felt that he could accept Hincks's offer of the chairmanship of the Senate committee in 1870. McMaster gave Hincks steady support even in the face of opposition from his fellow Liberals, opposition he dismissed as opportunistic. He immersed himself in committee work which, despite weary moments, he seems to have enjoyed thoroughly, and he worked with Hincks to render the latter's banking legislation "as perfect as possible." In the end, the acts of 1870 and 1871 gave McMaster and other Ontario bankers the conditions they wanted to develop their institutions within the province.

By 1872 the Canadian Bank of Commerce had established a "large healthy business" and had built up a reserve fund of $1,000,000. In addition, it had absorbed the initial costs of opening new branches: 19 in Ontario, one in Montreal, and one in New York to facilitate "transactions in exchange." Two years later when the province slipped into a recession the growth of the bank slackened but McMaster and his fellow directors met the situation with confidence. They adopted a conservative policy aiming temporarily for "safety rather than large profits." The bank perhaps fared worse in the recession of 1882 because its management was growing old and less vigilant in assessing accounts. In the mid 1880s the liquidation of several large estates held by the bank revealed that their assets had been greatly overvalued. A historian of the bank describes the years 1884–87 as "possibly the most difficult" in its history.

In July 1886 McMaster stepped down as president of the Canadian Bank of Commerce at its annual meeting, citing as reasons his poor health and the need for new men. He remained a director, however, and proposed his successor, Henry W. Darling; a major reorganization of senior positions followed his resignation. By 1887 the bank had surpassed the Merchants' Bank of Canada in size and was now second only to the Bank of Montreal. McMaster's decision to place it in the first rank of competition among Canadian banks, a decision which had been contested by some members of his original board, was accepted by his successors as the determining factor in the policies they followed.

His success in business and finance attracted numerous directorships for McMaster. He was chairman of the Canadian board of directors of the Great Western Railway from at least 1867 until it was disbanded in 1874, and in the following year he was the only Canadian appointed to the English board when shareholders, disgruntled with the way in which the line had been operated in Canada, decided to reorganize the railway; he continued as a director of the English board until the railway was taken over by the Grand Trunk in 1882. He served the railway well in its financial negotiations with the Canadian government, in particular with regard to the arrangements made in 1869 for repayment of its government loans. McMaster was also president of the Freehold Loan and Savings Company, which under his direction became closely integrated with the Canadian Bank of Commerce, and he was 1st vice-president of the Confederation Life Association from its incorporation in 1871 until his death in 1887. He helped steer the association, with assets of over $100,000 in 1872, to its position as the second largest Canadian-based life insurance company in 1885. McMaster was one of the original directors of the Isolated Risk Fire Insurance Company (after 1873 the Isolated Risk and Farmers' Fire Insurance Company). He served for some time as a director of the London and Canadian Loan and Agency Company and of the Toronto General Trusts Company, a relatively new form of investment.

The triumphs McMaster engineered in business and finance were augmented by the work he undertook on behalf of the educational and religious needs of the Baptist constituency of central Canada. His contributions were influenced to some extent by the Reverend Robert Alexander Fyfe* of whose March Street Baptist Church (later Bond Street, and then Jarvis Street Baptist Church) McMaster was a member. As Daniel Edmund Thomson, a fellow Baptist and prominent Toronto lawyer, observed, McMaster was convinced that the Baptists were "a people of destiny" and he remained in that denomination even though his "business and social welfare would have been greatly promoted by his union with one of the larger and stronger bodies." There were, to be sure, some observers who wondered whether McMaster's reputed "love of aggrandizement" had too often choked his penchant for denominational philanthropy. Thomson pointed out on another occasion that the senator was "not naturally a generous man" and "graduated late as a philanthropist." Even when McMaster did earmark funds for charitable purposes his motives were sometimes questioned. Those few of his associates who had tried in vain to check the relentless expansion of McMaster's business might have sympathized with William Davies*, a Toronto meat-packer and fellow Baptist. Davies complained about the "hateful" spirit of "centralization" that had supposedly characterized McMaster's sizeable underwriting of the city's prestigious Jarvis Street Baptist Church in 1875.

Unquestionably McMaster placed a high premium on education. The senator generously aided the Toronto Mechanics' Institute. He served on the senate of the University of Toronto after 1873 and represented Baptist interests on the Council of Public Instruction from 1865 to 1875, roles which earned him commendations from Egerton RYERSON, superintendent of education. In addition, he served for many years as treasurer of the Upper Canada Bible Society, a non-sectarian organization.

It was in the professional and ministerial training of Baptists that McMaster was most actively involved. At one time he apparently had an affiliation with the Disciples of Christ but had given it up because they discountenanced an educated clergy. The pioneering Canada Baptist College in Montreal had been forced to close in 1849, and there is evidence that McMaster agreed to fund a successor, the proposed Maclay college. When this project failed, he assisted Fyfe in establishing a more substantial successor in Woodstock, Canada West. The Canadian Literary Institute (renamed Woodstock College in 1883), which opened in 1860, was designed as a co-educational facility offering instruction in arts and theology. When an opportunity presented itself in the late 1870s to move the institute's theological department from Woodstock to Toronto, McMaster was eager to seize it. His decision was inspired in part by his second wife, Susan Fraser, *née* Moulton, the widow of an American businessman, whom he had married in 1871, three years after the death of his first wife, Mary Henderson. Susan Moulton Fraser had long been impressed with the work of the Northern Baptist Convention in the United States and was anxious to see the Baptist constituency in Canada emulate its educational facilities. An even more important role in persuading McMaster to help was played by Mrs McMaster's American pastor, the Reverend John Harvard CASTLE, whom she had been instrumental in having called to the pulpit of Bond Street Baptist Church.

A special educational convention of Baptists in 1879 authorized the transfer of the theology department to Toronto and within a year McMaster had provided not only a site for it on Bloor Street but also an initial outlay of $100,000 and the pledge of an annual contribution of approximately $14,000. Although he was apparently reluctant to have his name associated with the building, his wishes were overborne in the naming of McMaster Hall. He insisted, however, on the school being known as a college rather than by the American term seminary. His British background and the hope that some arts subjects might ultimately supplement the theological curriculum may account for his insistence in this matter and explain why the school took the name Toronto Baptist College before it opened its doors to students in the fall of 1881.

For a time there was every prospect that this new denominational enterprise would federate with the University of Toronto, a relationship that many Baptists had encouraged in the belief that theological training should be the responsibility of each denomination and that a provincial university should instruct in the secular sphere. McMaster and others, however, eventually accepted the concept of an independent Baptist institution offering both theology and a more liberal and comprehensive arts programme at the collegiate level than was promised by the federation proposals of 1884–85. The leaders in this campaign for a separate institution included Castle, president of Toronto Baptist College, and two of his academic colleagues, Malcolm MacVicar*, a confidant of the senator's, and Theodore Harding Rand*, a prominent Maritime educator. It is possible that the senator's wife may have urged him to endorse this campaign; there is an even better possibility that McMaster had toyed with the idea independently.

The plans for the new institution were approved by the Baptist conventions and a bill was introduced in the Ontario Legislature in March 1887 providing for the union of Woodstock College and Toronto Baptist College under the name of McMaster University. The senator appeared before the legislature on its behalf. Even before the bill was assented to on 23 April, he had made out, on 7 April, a will leaving the bulk of his estate, some $900,000, as an endowment for the new university. Barely five months later, on 22 Sept. 1887, he was taken ill while attending a meeting about its affairs, and died later the same day. He was survived by his widow, a sister, and nephews. After her husband's death Susan Moulton McMaster donated the family's Bloor Street mansion to the university. It became Moulton College, a school for girls.

Throughout the proceedings of building up Woodstock College to university status, McMaster had apparently privately favoured Toronto, the home of the Baptist college, as the site. The university did indeed find its location in 1888 at McMaster Hall, Toronto; in 1930 it moved to Hamilton. Its subsequent growth into an important Canadian educational institution gives a special significance to McMaster's philanthropy, an activity he came to late in life after having achieved prominence as an influential banker and businessman.

IN COLLABORATION

We are grateful for the assistance of Charles M. Johnston and Wendy Cameron in the preparation of this biography.

Baker Library, R. G. Dun & Co. credit ledger, Canada, 26: 24, 183, 218, 237, 276; 27: 215, 294. Canadian Baptist Arch., Biog. files, J. H. Castle, William McMaster, Malcolm MacVicar, T. H. Rand; W. P. Cohoe, "The struggle for a sheepskin"; McMaster Univ., General corr., 1951–52 (H), 1957–59 (T); G. P. Gilmour corr., personal, 1962; Toronto Baptist College, Board of Trustees, Minute book, 12 April 1881 – 28 April 1887; Letters, 1880–86.

Can., Senate, *Debates*, 1867–84. *The Canadian Bank of Commerce: charter and annual reports, 1867–1907* (2v., Toronto, 1907), I. [William Davies], *Letters of William Davies, Toronto, 1854–61*, ed. W. S. Fox (Toronto, 1945). Toronto Board of Trade, *Annual report . . .* (Toronto), 1860–63; *Annual review of the commerce of Toronto . . .*, comp. W. S. Taylor (Toronto), 1867. *Globe*, 13, 16 Jan., 8

May 1860; 23 Sept. 1887. *Toronto Daily Mail*, 23, 26 Sept. 1887. *The Baptist year book . . .* (Toronto), 1882–86, especially the annual reports of the president of the Toronto Baptist College. *Cyclopædia of Canadian biog.* (Rose, 1888), 286–89. Dent, *Canadian portrait gallery*, III: 72–74. *Toronto directory*, 1834–85. Careless, *Brown*. Currie, *Grand Trunk Railway*. Denison, *Canada's first bank*. Robert Hamilton, "The founding of McMaster University" (BD thesis, McMaster Univ., Hamilton, Ont., 1938). *Hist. of Toronto and county of York*, II: 102–4. C. M. Johnston, *McMaster University* (2v., Toronto and Buffalo, N.Y., 1976–81). Douglas McCalla, "The Toronto wholesale trade in the 1850's: a study of commercial attitudes and practices" (unpublished paper, 1965). *McMaster University, 1890–1940 . . .* (Hamilton, 1940). Masters, *Rise of Toronto*. V. Ross and Trigge, *Hist. of Canadian Bank of Commerce*, II. C. B. Sissons, *Egerton Ryerson, his life and letters* (2v., Toronto and London, 1937–47). R. L. Kellock, "The Hon. William McMaster," *Canadian Baptist* (Midland, Ont.), 90 (1944), no.8: 1, 4. D. C. Masters, "Canadian bankers of the last century, I: William McMaster," *Canadian Banker*, 49 (1942): 389–96. D. E. Thomson, "William McMaster," *McMaster Univ. Monthly* (Toronto), 1 (1891–92): 97–103.

McMILLAN, JOHN, merchant, politician, and office-holder; b. 4 Aug. 1816 at Brodick, Island of Arran (Strathclyde), Scotland; m. in 1850 Mary Stewart McNutt, and they had five children; d. 12 Sept. 1886 at Saint John, N.B.

John McMillan came to northern New Brunswick in 1832 with his father, who settled at Campbellton. The younger McMillan was virtually self-educated and first worked in lumbering. He later became a successful merchant and with a partner, Jeremiah Travis, established the lumber firm of McMillan and Travis Company. The partners also had a general store in Campbellton. In addition to sending crews to cut timber on their own berths, they supplied goods on credit to other operators and purchased their timber when it came down the rivers. They shipped the product, chiefly in the form of deal, to Liverpool, England. Although they had competitors in nearby Dalhousie, N.B., McMillan claimed in 1858 that from Campbellton he and Travis controlled 80 per cent of the timber trade in Restigouche County.

McMillan was appointed a justice of the peace in 1845 and in 1857 was elected to the assembly for Restigouche County as a supporter of Charles Fisher* and Samuel Leonard Tilley*. He worked hard to build his support in the county and recommended to Tilley in 1858 that restraint be used in removing from minor government offices men who had engaged in political activities for the previous government of John Hamilton GRAY and Robert Duncan Wilmot*. When in November 1858 John Mercer Johnson* was forced to resign as postmaster general because of a scandal in his department, McMillan opposed the appointment of Charles Connell*, who subsequently embarrassed the government by issuing stamps bearing his own likeness rather than that of Queen Victoria. McMillan had suggested that Peter Mitchell*, the member for Northumberland, be appointed because he was better qualified and his selection would have pleased the northern part of the province.

Re-elected in 1861, McMillan became surveyor general in Tilley's administration on 26 July. McMillan's business partner, Jeremiah Travis, objected to his involvement in politics because it took too much of his time. Travis had been residing in Liverpool for several months each year to handle all the company's business outside the province, and he relied on McMillan to carry on the business in New Brunswick. This disagreement led to the breakup of their partnership in 1862 and was followed by charges from Travis that McMillan had hired men to cut timber illegally since he had become surveyor general. Travis asked Tilley to dismiss McMillan, but Tilley refused and McMillan continued in office till 1865. He improved the efficiency of his department by changing operating procedures and clarifying the duties of its employees, though opponents accused him of neglecting his duties in Fredericton to tend to his own business interests in the north of the province.

In March 1865 Tilley's government was defeated by Albert James SMITH and the opponents of New Brunswick's entry into confederation. One of only six pro-confederates elected in 1865 and the only member of Tilley's government to be re-elected, McMillan offered to resign his Restigouche seat and permit his defeated party leader to run in a by-election there. Tilley declined the offer. With Abner Reid McClelan, McMillan then led the small opposition in the assembly and defended confederation against its opponents in the Smith government.

The French-speaking Roman Catholic voters in Westmorland, Kent, and Gloucester counties had voted against confederation in the March 1865 election, and the following October McMillan encouraged Tilley to seek allies in Canada who might influence the French-speaking clergy in New Brunswick to support union. McMillan felt there was more hope of turning them from their opposition than there would be of changing the views of Irish Catholics, who had also opposed confederation in 1865. His analysis, however, proved faulty. Tilley was able to win over the Irish clergy, especially Bishop James Rogers* of Chatham, and in the election of May–June 1866 many Irish Catholics supported the pro-confederates. The Fenian raids and the resignation from the Smith government of the Irish Catholic spokesman, Timothy Warren Anglin*, also aided the Irish switch. French-speaking voters, however, maintained their opposition to confederation. In this 1866 election McMillan's immense popularity assured his personal success in Restigouche, which had a majority of English-speaking voters.

McMillan became postmaster general in the administration of Tilley and Peter Mitchell which succeeded Smith's government. Like many leading New Brunswick politicians, however, he withdrew from the provincial scene after 1 July 1867 and in September was chosen by acclamation as the first representative of Restigouche County in the House of Commons. His decision to run caused confusion because in August he had been appointed federal post office inspector of New Brunswick. Alexander Campbell*, the postmaster general in the government of Sir John A. Macdonald*, felt that he could not hold this office and simultaneously sit in parliament. McMillan therefore resigned the office, but after spending only one session as an MP he vacated his seat and in 1868 again took up the position of post office inspector, living in Saint John. Until his death in 1886 he supervised the operation of all post offices in the province, checked accounts, investigated complaints, and hired all employees.

John McMillan was described as a Liberal in politics. Although a firm supporter of Tilley and confederation, his career was not marked by any major achievement. A capable businessman, he served the province well as surveyor general and postmaster general and he appears to have been a competent administrator.

WILLIAM ARTHUR SPRAY

PAC, MG 27, I, D15, 3, McMillan to Tilley, 12 April 1858; 4, McMillan to Tilley, 6 Sept., 23 Oct. 1858, and Travis to Tilley, 23 Oct. 1858; 9, McMillan to Tilley, 16 Oct. 1860; 10, Travis to Tilley, 23 July 1861, and Tilley to Travis, 27 July 1861; 12, Watters to Tilley, 29 May 1862; 13, Travis to Tilley, 6, 18 Sept. 1862, and Tilley to Travis, 23 Sept. 1862; 20, Morrison to Tilley, 22 July 1867, and Campbell to Tilley, 7, 8 Aug. 1867. PANB, "N.B. political biog." (J. C. and H. B. Graves), II: 160. PRO, CO 188/145, Gordon to Cardwell, 17 April 1886. *Daily Sun* (Saint John, N.B.), 25 May, 13, 20 Sept. 1886. *Gleaner and Northumberland Schediasma* (Chatham, N.B.), 18 Nov. 1850. *New Brunswick Reporter and Fredericton Advertiser*, 2, 23 Aug. 1861; 13 Sept. 1867. *Royal Gazette* (Fredericton), 22 Oct. 1845. *Canadian directory of parl.* (J. K. Johnson). *Dominion annual register*, 1886. James Hannay, *Hist. of N.B.*; *Wilmot and Tilley* (Toronto, 1907). McNutt, *New Brunswick*.

McMILLAN (MacMillan), JOSEPH C., printer and trade union leader; b. in 1836 in Scotland; he and his wife Mary had at least three children; d. 9 Jan. 1889 at Toronto, Ont.

Journeyman printer Joseph C. McMillan arrived in Toronto in 1867 or 1868. In December 1868 he joined the Toronto Typographical Union, local no. 91 of the United States–based National Typographical Union (later the International Typographical Union), and he rose rapidly through its ranks to become vice-president of the local in December 1870. The following year, when he was acclaimed president, the membership of the local was 190. He was a prominent leader in the Toronto printers' strike of 1872, called when demands for an increased wage scale and a nine-hour day were vigorously opposed by the Master Printers Association led by George Brown*. McMillan and 12 other members of the TTU were arrested in May for seditious conspiracy. They were later released on bail and in November the charges against them were dropped after the Trade Unions Act was passed.

In September 1872 McMillan and two of his TTU colleagues, David Sleeth Jr and James S. Williams*, formed the printing firm of Williams, Sleeth and McMillan and bought the *Ontario Workman*, the first major Canadian labour newspaper, from the Toronto Cooperative Printing Company. This purchase was partly funded by a loan from Prime Minister Sir John A. Macdonald* who had earlier that year cemented his bonds with the fledgling Canadian trade union movement by passing the Trade Unions Act in response to George Brown's attack on the printers. The paper ceased publication in 1875 although there was a brief attempt to revive it in late 1877. The firm continued, however, as a job printing shop until 1882, and the partners lived as next-door neighbours on Ontario Street for some 10 years. From 1882 to 1884 McMillan ran a small book and stationery store, which was a centre for labour activity and served as an agency for the Toronto *Trades Union Advocate*. In 1884 McMillan returned to the printer's case with the *Grip* (Toronto) and later was employed by Warwick and Sons with whom he remained as foreman until his death.

McMillan had represented the TTU in the Toronto Trades Assembly from 1872 to 1878. He served the assembly as a trustee, responsible for its financial transactions, except from January to August 1875 when he was president. McMillan also represented the TTA at various Canadian Labor Union conventions. He became treasurer of this association in 1877 and was a member of its parliamentary committee in 1876 and 1877. In these various offices he was a key member of the Toronto "junta" which in the 1870s lobbied for the changes in federal legislation that firmly established the legal basis of trade unionism. These changes included the Trade Unions Act of 1872, amendments to the "violence, threats and molestation" provisions of the criminal law in 1875 and 1876, and the Breaches of Contract Act of 1877. The last three acts were especially important because they legalized strikes and ended the legal discrimination against workers previously entrenched in the old masters and servants acts. The new political responsiveness to workingmen clearly demonstrated the growing importance of the young labour movement.

In May 1881 McMillan and his close friend Williams were chosen by the TTU to start discussions aimed at founding a new central body in Toronto to replace the lapsed Toronto Trades Assembly. The initiative taken by the printers resulted in the formation of the Toronto Trades and Labor Council on which McMillan served one term as a representative in 1883. His career as an important Toronto labour leader, however, was coming to an end in 1881 because a new group of leaders with strategies alien to men such as McMillan rose to prominence through the Order of the Knights of Labor. This new leadership stood for the organization of all workers without regard for level of skill, sex, or race. In addition, some of them called for independent labour representation in all levels of government.

McMillan was in many ways typical of the artisans who provided leadership to the early labour movement in Canada. Like fellow printers Daniel John O'Donoghue*, John Armstrong, and Williams, he drew strength from the craft traditions of "the art preservative" with its requirements of literacy and pride in culture. He was able to pass his craft on to at least three of his sons, all of whom became printers in Toronto. In this he, and other printers of his generation, enjoyed a privilege that few of their fellow skilled workingmen were able to maintain against the incursion of machinery.

At his funeral on 12 Jan. 1889, friends, some 150 fellow craftsmen from the TTU, and lodge brothers from the Sons of Scotland, the Order of Chosen Friends, and the Iron Hall gathered to pay their last respects. The pallbearers included not only his old comrades Sleeth and Williams but another printer and co-conspirator of 1872, Edward Frederick Clarke*, who in the late 1880s became mayor of Toronto and a member of the provincial parliament; Clarke's prominence was a tribute to the battles men such as McMillan had waged throughout their adult years.

GREGORY S. KEALEY

CTA, Toronto assessment rolls, St David's Ward, Ontario Street, 1880. PAC, MG 26, A; MG 28, I44; I72; RG 31, A1, 1871, Toronto, St David's Ward. Canadian Labor Union, *Proceedings of the Canadian Labor Union congresses, 1873–77*, comp. L. E. Wismer (Ottawa, 1951). International Typographical Union, *Report of proc.* (New York, etc.), 1868–89. *Empire* (Toronto), 14 Jan. 1889. *Evening News* (Toronto), 14 Jan. 1889. *Globe*, 1868–89. *Ontario Workman* (Toronto), 1872–74. *Toronto Daily Mail*, 14 Jan. 1889. *Trades Union Advocate* (Toronto), 1882–83. *Toronto directory*, 1868–90.

G. S. Kealey, *Toronto workers respond to industrial capitalism, 1867–1892* (Toronto, 1980); "The working class response to industrial capitalism in Toronto, 1867–1892" (PHD thesis, Univ. of Rochester, N.Y., 1977). Wayne Roberts, "The last artisans: Toronto printers, 1896–1914," *Essays in Canadian working class history*, ed. G. S. Kealey and Peter Warrian (Toronto, 1976), 125–42. S. F. Zerker, "A history of the Toronto Typographical Union, 1832–1925" (PHD thesis, Univ. of Toronto, 1972). G. S. Kealey, "'The honest workingman' and workers' control: the experience of Toronto skilled workers, 1860–1892," *Labour* ([Halifax and Rimouski, Que.]), 1 (1976): 32–68. S. [F.] Zerker, "The development of collective bargaining in Toronto printing industry in the nineteenth century," *Industrial Relations* (Quebec), 30 (1975): 83–97; "George Brown and the printers' union," *Journal of Canadian Studies*, 10 (1975), no.1: 42–48.

McMURRAY, THOMAS, author, journalist, temperance worker, and settler; b. 7 May 1831 at Paisley, Scotland, the son of a weaver from County Armagh (Northern Ireland) and Jane Baxter from Alloa, Scotland; m. 10 June 1850 his second cousin, Elizabeth, and they had at least nine children; last known living in February 1884.

Thomas McMurray, following his father's occupation, began work as a draw-boy when he was seven and at 11 became a weaver. Not satisfied with this trade he served a three-year apprenticeship to a butter and egg merchant and obtained a limited education in night school. At 15 he determined to be a sailor, but on his first voyage he abandoned ship in New York, and worked for a time on the New York and Erie Railroad. After his return home in 1848 he was employed first as a salesman in Glasgow, then operated a business of his own in Paisley, and followed that with nine years in Belfast, for seven of which he was a commercial traveller. In May 1861 McMurray, hoping to provide better for his large family, immigrated with his wife and children to the Muskoka district of Canada West, where he became one of the first settlers in Draper Township (included at that time in Victoria County). He purchased and farmed 400 acres of land on the south branch of the Muskoka River, about two miles east of the village of Muskoka Falls, and on the incorporation of the united townships of Draper, Macaulay, Stephenson, and Ryde in 1867 became the first reeve.

In Parry Sound on 14 Sept. 1869 he began publication of the *Northern Advocate*, the first newspaper issued in the Muskoka–Parry Sound area. He moved the paper in September 1870 to Bracebridge where he also opened a general store and real estate business and built a large residence known as The Grove. Unfortunately, he overextended himself financially, and when the depression of 1873 in the United States spread to Canada he was forced into bankruptcy, in July 1874. He returned to Parry Sound where he founded another newspaper, the *North Star*, and on 17 Aug. 1875 he became crown lands agent for part of Parry Sound District, established in 1870. In March 1879 he sold the paper and later that year, on 30 June, he resigned his crown lands position and moved near Parkdale (now part of Toronto) to carry on temperance work.

McMurray was continuously active in public life.

He was a trustee of the Bracebridge Wesleyan Methodist Church, the first such church in Muskoka, and, for a time, was county master of the Orange order. Two objectives, however, dominated McMurray's life: the settlement of the Muskoka–Parry Sound area and the total suppression of the liquor traffic. In support of the former he published *The free grant lands of Canada* (1871), and of the latter *Temperance lectures* (1873). He extolled the advantages of the free grant area in speeches, correspondence, and newspaper articles; he also promoted the improvement of roads and bridges as well as the building of churches, schools, and, above all, a railway in the Muskoka–Parry Sound region. As were many others at the time, McMurray was greatly moved by the suffering of the poor in the British Isles as well as in Canadian towns and cities. He believed that the free grant lands (opened in 1868) offered fertile soil, a suitable climate for agriculture, and waiting markets; he did not observe that much of that fertile soil was but a thin cover over rock and would soon be exhausted when the protecting forests were removed, nor did he foresee the menace to the small farm arising both from mechanization and the settlement of the west.

McMurray had first become connected with the temperance movement in Paisley when, at 14, he joined a total abstinence society; he became identified with the Irish Temperance League in Belfast in 1858. In Muskoka and Parry Sound he worked actively for prohibition, which was becoming a leading issue in Canadian life. When he left Parry Sound in 1879 the Canada Temperance Act of 1878, commonly called the Scott Act, had just been passed, extending a form of local option to every province, and thus encouraging temperance societies and church groups to continue the fight for total prohibition. The Sons of Temperance, of which McMurray was a provincial deputy grand worthy patriarch, had taken a leading role in 1875 in establishing the Dominion Alliance for the Total Suppression of the Liquor Traffic, an organization formed to coordinate the efforts of the numerous existing societies. Under the auspices of the Sons of Temperance and the Dominion Alliance McMurray spent a number of years organizing new divisions and lecturing in Ontario centres such as Brighton, Brampton, Trenton, Kingston, and Perth. His words, both spoken and written, epitomized temperance thought of the time: "I believe in Prohibition, total Prohibition. Nothing less will do."

In February 1884 McMurray was working in the Eastern Townships under the Grand Division of Quebec of the Sons of Temperance. No further trace of him has been found, but he was only 52 at that time and may well have obtained other positions which demanded a man of his initiative and energy.

FLORENCE B. MURRAY

Thomas McMurray was the author of *The free grant lands of Canada, from practical experience of bush farming in the free grant districts of Muskoka and Parry Sound* (Bracebridge, Ont., 1871) and *Temperance lectures; with autobiography* (Toronto, 1873), reprinted under the title of *Temperance talks; with autobiography* (Toronto, 1887).

Muskoka and Haliburton, 1615–1875; a collection of documents, ed. F. B. Murray (Toronto, 1963). *Canada Citizen and Temperance Herald* (Toronto), 5, 19 Oct., 14 Dec. 1883. *Christian Guardian*, 24 Sept., 29 Oct. 1879; 4 April, 3 Oct. 1883; 27 Feb. 1884. *North Star* (Parry Sound, Ont.), 18 July 1879. [W. E. Hamilton], *Guide book & atlas of Muskoka and Parry Sound districts, 1879* (Toronto, 1879; repr. Port Elgin, Ont., 1971). Geraldine Coombe, *Muskoka past and present* (Toronto, 1976).

McMURRICH, JOHN, merchant, businessman, and politician; b. 3 Feb. 1804 near Paisley, Scotland; m. 4 Aug. 1841 Janet Dixon, and they had four sons; d. 13 Feb. 1883 at Toronto, Ont.

John McMurrich received his early commercial training in the Glasgow firm of Playfair, Bryce and Company. He was sent to Upper Canada in 1833 to work for the recently founded affiliate Bryce, Buchanan and Company at York (Toronto). From 1834 until 1837 he worked in the firm's Kingston branch, then returned to Toronto as a partner in the wholesale dry goods firm of Bryce, McMurrich and Company. He had full charge of its operations in Toronto; his partner, John D. Bryce, resided in Glasgow and managed the British side of the business. Within the next decade, the firm became one of Toronto's chief dry goods houses. By the 1860s, and perhaps earlier, it had come to specialize in staple British textiles, for which demand was sure and profit margins were modest.

McMurrich was a Presbyterian and in the disruption of the church in Canada in 1844 took the Free Church side. He helped found Knox Church in Toronto in 1844, served it for 32 years as an elder, and was among its most influential laymen until his death. He was also an active member of the City Mission Society, the Upper Canada Religious Tract and Book Society, and the Sabbath Observance Association, which he helped to organize in 1852. He was a generous contributor to charities, especially the Toronto Home for Incurables, founded in 1874.

A Reformer, McMurrich was an early political ally of George Brown*. In 1846, at a meeting of the St Andrew's Society where Brown was under heavy attack for remarks he had made about Judge Archibald McLean*, McMurrich, an older and more established figure in the community, spoke strongly in Brown's defence. On the formation of the Anti-Clergy Reserves Association in 1850, McMurrich became a member of the executive. When the Legislative Council became elective in 1856, he contested the Saugeen division, denouncing the government of Sir Allan Napier MacNab* and Étienne-Paschal Taché* as "the most corrupt Ministry that had cursed Canada at any period during the last twenty years." He lost, but captured the division in an 1862 by-election called when the sitting member, James Patton, joined the ministry. He held the seat until 1864. In the late 1850s he worked closely with Brown in his effort to draw together Upper Canadian Reformers. At confederation, he was elected to the first Ontario legislature as a Liberal, representing York North, but he was narrowly defeated by Alfred Boultbee in the 1871 election and did not again run for office.

Toronto City Council appointed McMurrich as the Free Church representative to the first Toronto Public School Board from 1847 to 1849. He was elected unopposed to the board in 1858 for a two-year term. He stressed particularly that local government, like the provincial government, was becoming too costly, a theme he pursued in 1860, when he was elected an alderman in the city council and became chairman of its finance committee for one year. He was re-elected to the Public School Board in 1862, served on it until 1870, and was its chairman from 1865 to 1867 and again in 1870.

A charter member of the Toronto Board of Trade, McMurrich was often elected to its council and continued to be an active member even in the 1870s when many of his surviving contemporaries had reduced their role in it. Like many other Toronto merchants, he also sought to develop and sustain local companies, but his was an extraordinary record of involvement, especially in the 1860s and 1870s when he was president or vice-president of at least six Toronto firms. For some years a director of Toronto's Western Assurance Company, incorporated in 1851, he became its president in the 1860s after it had suffered some "disastrous losses"; he retained the position until he died, seeing the company into much more prosperous times. He was founding vice-president in 1851, and later president, of the Commercial Building and Investment Society; he was also president for many years of a small allied company which when it was organized had links with early Reform politicians, the Home District Mutual Fire Insurance Company. In 1870 he helped reorganize the troubled Royal Canadian Bank and was a director from 1871 to 1875 and vice-president in 1872–73. He shrewdly sold his own shares in the company when it merged into the short-lived Consolidated Bank of Canada.

To a man as mindful of the metropolitan nature of Toronto business as McMurrich, transport and communications, after finance, were of prime importance. In 1852 when the Toronto and Guelph Railway was first organized, he unsuccessfully sought a seat on its board, but soon sold his shares to the Grand Trunk interests which were taking over the company. He was one of a group of Toronto businessmen who in 1857 organized the North-West Transportation, Navigation, and Railway Company. In 1859 he ran for its vice-presidency, was defeated by Lewis Moffatt, and withdrew from the company altogether the next year. He was director (1870–72) and vice-president (1871–72) of the Toronto, Grey and Bruce Railway, which was then under construction and already in financial difficulties. At about the same time he was involved in a takeover by Toronto businessmen of the fledging Dominion Telegraph Company; he became its president in 1870, held this post until 1876, and helped the company grow from a contractor's speculation into a genuine competitor of the much larger Montreal Telegraph Company.

Each of the companies of which he was president or vice-president had a full-time official in charge of most management functions, but, as the Toronto *Globe* noted in 1883, McMurrich's "incumbency of these offices was in no case a sinecure. It was foreign to his character to discharge any trust in a perfunctory manner. . . ." In taking on some of the positions he assumed, it is clear that he was not primarily seeking remuneration, and he was not, on the whole, a large shareholder in the companies that he headed; evidently he regarded such work to some extent as a public service.

McMurrich was an important figure in Toronto for over 40 years, especially in its rapidly expanding business world. By a "deliberate, conservative" strategy, he had avoided the perils of bankruptcy that ended the businesses of so many early merchants and had moved far beyond the wholesale trade. That he was able to do so suggests the importance to his later career of the two principal associates he drew into his Toronto firm, Samuel Gunn and J. S. Playfair. With his second son, George, they carried on the dry goods business for a few years after his death, but then wound it up. McMurrich lived to see his eldest son, William Barclay, a lawyer, elected mayor of Toronto in 1881 and 1882. Another son, James Playfair*, became a distinguished biologist.

Douglas McCalla

PAC, MG 24, D16, 23: 19782–85. Toronto Board of Education, Education Centre Library, Reference Services, Hist. Coll., Board of Trustees for Common Schools, Minutes, 20 Nov. 1847–29 Dec. 1849; Public School Board, Minutes, 18 Jan. 1854–4 Jan. 1861; 16 Jan. 1861–20 March 1878. *Globe*, 1850–60; 14, 16 Feb. 1883. *Monetary Times*, 1868–83. *Dominion annual register*, 1883: 320–21. *Toronto directory*, 1850–88. Wallace, *Macmillan dict.*, 483. Careless, *Brown*. *Centennial story: the Board of Education for the City of Toronto, 1850–1950*, ed. H. M. Cochrane (Toronto, 1950). *Robertson's landmarks of Toronto*, VI: 81.

McQUESTEN, CALVIN, physician, manufacturer, and capitalist; b. in 1801 in Bedford (Manchester), N.H., son of David McQuesten, a farmer, and Margaret Fisher; m. first Margarette Lerned (1801–41), secondly Esther Baldwin (1816–51), and lastly Elizabeth Fuller (d. 1897); he had three surviving sons; d. 20 Oct. 1885 at Hamilton, Ont.

Calvin McQuesten graduated with a teaching certificate from Bradford Academy, Bradford, Mass., in 1825 and taught school for two years, possibly at Bradford Academy and then in Washington, N.H. In 1827 he began studying medicine at Bowdoin College, Brunswick, Maine, graduating MD in 1829. He practised in Sandbornton Bridge, N.H., before moving in 1832 to Brockport, near Rochester, N.Y., where his practice seems to have prospered.

McQuesten's first business venture was the establishment of McQuesten and Budlong's drugstore in Brockport. In 1835 he became involved in another business endeavour. Earlier that year his cousin, John Fisher, arrived in Hamilton, Upper Canada, from New York State to attempt to set up a foundry. Unable to secure credit from local capitalists who viewed Hamilton as a commercial rather than an industrial centre, he sought the financial backing of McQuesten. On 1 Oct. 1835 the two cousins joined with Priam B. Hill of Brockport and Joseph S. Janes of Hamilton to form a general co-partnership to manufacture threshing machines and stoves. Fisher brought his inventions and technical knowledge to the partnership, McQuesten supplied $1,500, Hill provided additional capital, and Janes contributed the land on which the foundry was built.

The history of the company, variously known as McQuesten, Janes and Company, McQuesten and Fisher Company, and McQuesten and Company, provides an example of industrial organization prior to the widespread adoption of limited liability incorporation after the mid century. Partnership was a means of combining the talents and resources of several individuals; however, its inflexibility required the dissolution of the business when new talents were required or active partners wished to resign. In this company the durations of the partnerships were limited to specific periods of time after which outstanding accounts were settled and profits apportioned. In 1836, for instance, Priam Hill moved to Wisconsin Territory and sold out to McQuesten, giving the latter a controlling interest in the business. Partnerships were further dissolved, altered, and reconstituted in 1843, 1848, and 1853; in the last instance six skilled craftsmen employed by the firm were made partners, including three nephews of McQuesten, moulder Stephen Payson Sawyer, machinist Luther D. Sawyer, and tinsmith William W. McQuesten.

After 1835 McQuesten divided his time between his medical practice in Brockport, sales trips for the company, and the purchase of raw materials and equipment from American suppliers. In 1839 he ceased practising medicine and moved to Hamilton to devote his time to the management of the company. Fisher died in 1856 and the following year McQuesten retired, liquidating his holdings, reputedly valued at $500,000; Luther Sawyer then gained control of the foundry and later joined with Hart Almerrin Massey* to form the Sawyer and Massey Company.

McQuesten put his capital to work in both financial and industrial enterprises. In 1860 he held over $32,000 in Gore Bank stock, an interest which led to his election as a director in 1862 and vice-president in 1867. In the latter role he was critical of the direction given the Gore Bank, especially by the president, Thomas Clark Street*, and in 1868 he charged Street with obscuring the excessive indebtedness to the bank of the Hamilton firm of Buchanan, Hope and Company, which had failed the previous year [*see* Adam HOPE], and with over-investment in the Bank of Upper Canada and the Commercial Bank of the Midland District, both of which had failed. These poor investments had severely compromised the bank's capital. McQuesten had the support of the bank's shareholders and in 1868 was the only director re-elected. The following year he was a member of a committee, initiated by Æmilius Irving*, that negotiated the merger in 1870 of the Gore Bank with the Canadian Bank of Commerce [*see* William MCMASTER]. McQuesten converted his holdings in the Gore Bank into stock in the Canadian Bank of Commerce. He also held stock in other financial institutions such as the Victoria Mutual and Insurance Company and the Dominion Fire and Marine Insurance Company. Having made his money in industry, he reinvested some of his capital in other industrial enterprises including the Ontario Worsted Company, the Canadian Felt Hat Company, and the Hespeler Mills (textiles). He also held shares in the Dominion Salvage and Wrecking Company and the Hamilton Tribune Printing and Publishing Company. The largest portion of his fortune, however, was invested in real estate, principally in Hamilton but also in mortgages on Ontario farms.

McQuesten's upbringing had been profoundly religious. Most of his life in the United States had been spent in the northeast during a period of intense revivalism. McQuesten became a proponent of evangelical theology and, as an elder, tried to persuade the Presbyterian congregation of Brockport to adopt some of the methods of revivalism, thereby lessening its potentially disruptive power. In Hamilton McQuesten continued his religious activities, devoting his time and money to the encouragement of Presbyterianism. He was prominent in the establishment of the MacNab Street (1854) and St Paul's (1857) Presbyterian churches in Hamilton, and Knox Presbyterian Church (1874) in Dundas, Ont., and received appeals for aid from Presbyterians in other parts of North America. In his travels through Canada and the United States, he made notes on the architectural and acoustical design of many churches and his advice was heeded in the construction of Central Presbyterian Church (1857–58) in Hamilton. He was also active in the Hamilton branch of the Upper Canada Bible Society as treasurer from 1844 to 1849 and vice-president from 1849 until his death. McQuesten assisted Edward Jackson* with the establishment in 1861 of the Wesleyan Female College in Hamilton, a non-sectarian diploma and degree granting institution; from 1861 to 1872 he was vice-president of the college and then president until his death. After his retirement McQuesten also indulged in his favourite pastime, the study of evangelical Protestant theology, especially the work of Jonathan Edwards. In later years, probably because his efforts to inject American evangelicalism into Canadian Presbyterianism were rejected, he refused to belong to any congregation and built a small chapel on his estate for private use.

Calvin McQuesten, like many of the American immigrants after 1820 who brought either capital or expertise to Upper Canada, contributed to the development of Canadian industry while amassing a private fortune. After Calvin's death the McQuesten family continued its association with Hamilton. Calvin's son Isaac Baldwin lived in Whitehern, the house Calvin had bought in 1852, now an historic site. His grandson Thomas Baker McQuesten, a Hamilton philanthropist, became a minister in the provincial government of Mitchell Hepburn*.

DAVID G. BURLEY

AO, McQuesten papers. HPL, McQuesten papers. Whitehern Museum (Hamilton, Ont.), McQuesten papers. *Hamilton Spectator*, 21 Oct. 1885. *Monetary Times*, 6 Aug., 29 Oct., 12 Nov. 1868; 5 Aug. 1869. *Compliments of the Sawyer–Massey Co., Limited* (n.p., 1906).

McVICAR, KATE (Katie), shoe worker and union leader; b. *c.* 1856 at Hamilton, Canada West; d. there 18 June 1886.

Katie McVicar, daughter of a poor Scottish tinsmith and his English-born wife, joined two older sisters in the Hamilton labour force in the early 1870s. Like most women who went into factory work in the late 19th century, she began as a single woman, living at home, in order to augment her family's income. However, unlike most, she remained single and continued to live at home until her early death at the age of 30. Her comparative longevity as a factory operative accounts to some degree for her emergence as a prominent leader in the Knights of Labor.

The Knights, with their broad vision of unionizing all workers regardless of gender, race, or level of skill, were extremely active in organizing women throughout North America. The order's first local assemblies in Hamilton were created in April 1882, and by December it was actively trying to recruit women. The following year a series of letters appeared in the *Palladium of Labor*, the organ of the Knights of Labor in Hamilton, which spoke eloquently of the need to organize women in factories and domestic service, and described at the same time the sizeable problems involved in unionizing them. These letters were signed "A Canadian Girl," probably a pseudonym for Katie McVicar. The author argued that the techniques used in organizing men – holding mass meetings, mounting platforms, and making speeches – would never work for women. Instead she appealed for a few courageous women to come forward and meet with their brother Knights to secure aid.

This plea was answered in the *Palladium* by "A Knight of Labor" who suggested careful, secret discussion among female shop-mates, until ten who favoured forming an assembly had been identified. At that point they should contact him through the *Palladium*. He would then arrange a secret meeting to explain the Knights' principles to the women and to organize them formally into a local assembly. The order's operation as a secret society made it a particularly valuable vehicle for women, he argued, since it allowed them to avoid public notoriety and thus would protect their modesty.

Women, under the leadership of McVicar, must have followed this advice. In January 1884, local assembly 3040, which included female textile workers and shoe operatives, was formed in Hamilton. In April of that year, the female shoe operatives split and formed their own Excelsior Assembly (local assembly 3179), the first local in Canada comprised exclusively of women, with McVicar as directress. Although the number of women who belonged to the two assemblies actually declined from 221 in 1884 to 67 in 1885, the Knights organized at least eight other women's locals in Ontario in the 1880s and involved many other women workers in integrated locals. The first female representatives at the Trades and Labor Congress of Canada, beginning in 1886, were all Knights of Labor.

Katie McVicar's leadership of local assembly 3179 gave her an unusual prominence in the Hamilton labour force and it appears that after her death other members of Excelsior were not willing to replace her. Local assembly 3179 applied in 1887 and 1888 for special dispensation from the parent body to allow a brother Knight from local assembly 2132 (shoemakers) to function as their master workman. McVicar's death deprived the order in Ontario of one of the few capable female leaders who was willing to play a public role.

GREGORY S. KEALEY

Catholic Univ. of America Arch. (Washington), Terence V. Powderly papers (mfm. at PAC). York Univ. (Downsview, Ont.), York Social Hist. Project, Data file on Hamilton.

Knights of Labor, *Record of proc. of the General Assembly* (Philadelphia), 1883–86. Trade and Labor Congress of Canada, *Report of proc.* ([Ottawa]), 1886–91. *Hamilton Spectator*, 19 June 1886. *Journal of United Labor* (Philadelphia), 25 April 1886. *Labor Reformer* (Toronto), 26 June 1886. *Palladium of Labor* (Hamilton, Ont.), 29 Sept., 6, 13, 20 Oct., 3, 10 Nov. 1883. *Times* (Hamilton), 24 June 1886. J. E. Garlock, "A structural analysis of the Knights of Labor: a prolegomenon to the history of the producing classes" (PHD thesis, Univ. of Rochester, N.Y., 1974). G. S. Kealey, "The working class response to industrial capitalism in Toronto, 1867–1892" (PHD thesis, Univ. of Rochester, 1977). B. D. Palmer, "Most uncommon common men: craft, culture, and conflict in a Canadian community, 1860–1914" (PHD thesis, State Univ. of New York, Binghamton, 1977). Wayne Roberts, *Honest womanhood: feminism, femininity and class consciousness among Toronto working women, 1893 to 1914* (Toronto, 1976). G. [S.] Kealey, "Artisans respond to industrialism: shoemakers, shoe factories and the Knights of St. Crispin in Toronto," CHA *Hist. Papers*, 1973: 137–57.

MARCHAND, LOUIS (his original name was **Levi Koopman**), merchant, Patriote, public servant, businessman, and politician; b. 15 March 1800 at Amsterdam (Netherlands), son of Solomon Koopman, a jeweller, and Judith Diutz; d. 1 July 1881 in Montreal, Que.

Louis Marchand was a descendant of a Jewish family, originally from Prague (Czechoslovakia), that had settled in Amsterdam and had attained prominence in business and financial circles both in the Netherlands and in Paris. His father took the French name of Marchand in gratitude for the restoration of religious rights to the Jews in the Kingdom of Holland by Napoleon I. At the age of 18, Levi, who had received a good primary education in both Dutch and French, went to England to study English. While in that country he also became familiar with the history of British colonial acquisitions and inquired about the prospects for making a suitable living in North America. Soon after his return to the Netherlands he left for the United States where he worked for a short period. In 1823, receiving word that his father had died, he went back to his native land. There he took possession of his inheritance, only to lose everything on the stock market. It was at this point that he turned again to the United States in order to make his fortune anew.

A few months after his return Marchand went to Boston, where he heard talk of Lower Canada, and in particular of Montreal. Arriving in that city in 1826, he took lodgings in a boarding-house on Rue Saint-Gabriel which was frequented by rich merchants from the Chambly River region, including Eustache Soupras* of Saint-Mathias. Soupras was looking for a clerk for his firm and, impressed with the young Dutchman's knowledge of accounting, he immediately took him into his employ. Marchand soon left Montreal and went with Soupras to Saint-Mathias.

In the course of the next few years Marchand acquired a good name in Saint-Mathias and at Chambly, where he often had to go on business for Soupras. The inhabitants of both villages were most sympathetic and hospitable to the "young Frenchman," as they called him. In consequence, he decided to settle permanently in Lower Canada and to enter fully into French Canadian society. Thus he converted to the Roman Catholic faith, and on 4 June 1828 was baptized at Chambly by Bishop Jean-Jacques Lartigue*, at which time he changed his name from Levi to Louis. On 4 Oct. 1830, at Longueuil, he married Charlotte, daughter of François Céré, who was a prominent farmer there; they were to have five sons and five daughters. In the mean time, since the volume of his firm's transactions had increased substantially, Soupras had taken Marchand into partnership, and the two men set up Soupras et Marchand at Saint-Mathias, with a branch in Chambly. Marchand then began acquiring a wider circle of acquaintances in the Richelieu valley and before long throughout the district of Montreal. In 1832 he joined 74 other shareholders to found the Champlain and St Lawrence Railroad. He continued to engage in trade, enjoying success until 1837.

On the eve of the rebellion Marchand wholeheartedly supported the Patriotes. He participated in the assembly at Saint-Mathias, and then went as an official delegate of his village to the Assemblée des Six Comtés held at Saint-Charles-sur-Richelieu on 23 Oct. 1837. On 10 November he was one of a group of Patriotes under Pierre-Paul Démaray* and Joseph-François Davignon who attacked a cavalry troop returning from reconnoitring at Saint-Athanase (Iberville, Que.). Having implicated himself by participating in the popular unrest, Marchand fled to the United States on 17 November with Soupras and Timothée Franchère*. The next day he was in Highgate, Vt, where in December he expressed to Robert Nelson* a desire to join the liberation army which the latter was trying to organize. At the beginning of 1838, trusting the promises of immunity made by Captain Frederick Marryatt*, Marchand returned to Lower Canada, but he immediately had to surrender in Missisquoi County to Amable Loiselle, dispatched to arrest him. Incarcerated in the Montreal prison on 5 January on a charge of high treason, Marchand nearly died there. It was not until Lord Durham [Lambton*] issued his amnesty on 8 July that he was set free, on £1,000 bail. He returned to Saint-Mathias and found himself completely ruined because his property had been looted during his absence. Later in 1838 he was appointed a justice of the peace at Saint-Jean (Saint-Jean-sur-Richelieu), a post he held for four years, and in 1841 he acted as returning officer in Verchères County. Unable to find the means to resume his business, he decided to settle in Montreal in 1844.

That year Marchand entered into partnership with Narcisse-Birtz Desmarteau and began managing one of the two dry goods stores they jointly owned. In 1847 he held the office of assessor for the East Ward. At that time, sensing the potential of a steamship line to transport goods and passengers between Montreal and Quebec, he participated, with Jacques-Félix Sincennes*, Pierre-Édouard Leclère*, Desmarteau and others, in founding the Richelieu Company. He and Desmarteau jointly bought 12 shares in the steamer *Jacques Cartier*, and thus became major shareholders in the company. Marchand was active in the Association Saint-Jean-Baptiste de Montréal, serving as its vice-president in 1848 and again in 1849, when he and others sought a charter for the organization. The following year he became a director of the Richelieu Company, and he served as vice-president from 1852 to 1855 and again from 1860 to 1862. Also in 1850 he replaced Charles-Séraphin Rodier* on the Montreal Harbour Commission, sitting as a member until 1855. He and the two other commissioners, John Try* and John Young*, enlarged the port and deepened Lake Saint-Pierre, thereby making a substantial contribution to the improvement of navigation on the St Lawrence. In 1851 he terminated his partnership with Desmarteau and opened his own dry goods and wholesale grocery business.

Already a fairly prominent figure in Montreal, Marchand decided to enter municipal politics. He was elected a councillor for Saint-Louis Ward in 1852, and was re-elected the following year. During his second term he served on the fire committee and, despite the opposition of some members of council, he succeeded in pushing through several by-laws, including one forbidding the building of wooden houses, to guard against a recurrence of the great fire of 1852. These drastic measures were regarded with great hostility by some citizens. Probably as a result of this animosity Marchand did not seek re-election in 1854, despite the urgings of Wolfred Nelson*, who had been a companion in arms in 1837 and was now running for mayor. Soon after, Marchand returned to the Netherlands to be with his family.

Observing upon his return to Canada East that the political climate in Montreal had changed, he agreed to re-enter politics. He was elected councillor for the East Ward in 1856 and alderman in the same ward in 1857. In the latter year he served as acting mayor, replacing Henry Starnes* for six months. In this capacity he prevented a riotous conflict between Irish Catholics and Orangemen on 12 July by taking stern measures and making use of the influence he had with many of the city's Protestants. Re-elected alderman in 1858, 1859, and 1860, he served as chairman of the finance committee in the last two years. He resigned as alderman in 1860 and left politics.

As well as being active in politics, Marchand continued to manage his growing wholesale firm and engaged in various other business ventures. In 1852 he joined 64 of the most important Montreal capitalists in setting up the Montreal Exchange. Four years later he became president of the Montreal and Three Rivers Navigation Company, a position he held until 1858. In 1857 he formed a partnership with Louis Renaud* and Jean-Baptiste RENAUD to found the De Salaberry Navigation Company of Montreal. In 1858 he joined the council of the Montreal Board of Trade of which he remained an active member until 1861.

During the last 20 years of his life, Marchand pursued his career in business and held several important public offices. He closed his firm in 1861 and the following year began to act as a banker and stockbroker. Appointed to the census commission in 1861, he became master of Trinity House in Montreal the following year and retained this office until that body was abolished in 1873. For several years he also served as a justice of the peace in Montreal and was a member of the first magistrates' commission of the District of Montreal. Marchand is believed to have retired from business in 1878, the year his wife died. Several of their children were still alive at the time of his death, including the eldest son, Louis-François-Wilfrid*, who is known especially for his translation of the account Pehr Kalm* wrote of his travels in North America.

MICHEL DE LORIMIER

Louis Marchand left a diary but it has not been located.

AC, Montréal, État civil, Catholiques, Notre-Dame de Montréal, 4 juill. 1881. ANQ-M, État civil, Catholiques, Saint-Antoine (Longueuil), 4 oct. 1830; Saint-Joseph (Chambly), 4 juin 1828. ANQ-Q, QBC 25, Événements de 1837–1838, nos.47, 48, 308, 465, 1363. Arch. de l'Assoc. Saint-Jean-Baptiste de Montréal (Montréal), Procès-verbaux des assemblées générales, 1848–49. Canadian Jewish Congress Arch. (Montreal), "Notes sur Louis Marchand," David Rome, compil. (typescript). Montreal Board of Trade Arch. (Montreal), Minute books, 1858–61 (mfm. at ANQ-M). National Harbours Board (Montreal), Port of Montreal arch., Montreal Harbour Commission, Minute books, 1850–55.

Bas-Canada, *Statuts*, 1831–32, c.58. Can., Prov. du, *Statuts*, 1849, c.149; 1852–53, c.24, c.146; 1857, c.170, c.171. *Official documents and other information relating to the improvement of the ship channel between Montreal and Quebec* (Montreal, 1884), 197–98. *La Minerve*, 2 juill. 1881. *L'Opinion publique*, 22 mars 1877. *Le Populaire* (Montréal), 15 déc. 1837. *The Canadian album: men of Canada; or, success by example . . .* , ed. William Cochrane and J. C. Hopkins (5v., Brantford, Ont., 1891–96), II: 101. *Dominion annual register*, 1880–81: 418. Fauteux, *Patriotes*, 312–13. *Montreal directory*, 1842–81. *Quebec almanac*, 1838–41. *Souvenir Maisonneuve; esquisse historique de la ville de Montréal avec portraits et biographies . . .* (Montréal, [1894]), 111–12. Atherton, *Montreal*, II: 594. L.-É. Morin, *Histoire des travaux de la Commission du havre dans le port de Montréal* (Montréal, 1894), 4–5. Robert Rumilly, *Histoire de la Société Saint-Jean-Baptiste de Montréal: des Patriotes au fleurdelisé, 1834–1948* (Montréal, 1975), 59. Tulchinsky, *River barons*. Patricia Joseph, "Un Hollandais patriote de 1837," *La Presse* (Montréal), 5 juin 1937: 70. Léon Trépanier, "Saint-Mathias en 1837–38," Soc. hist. de la vallée du Richelieu, *Cahier* (s.l.), 5 (s.d.): 10–16; "Un Montréalais du siècle dernier: l'immigrant juif Louis Marchand," *Cahiers des Dix*, 30 (1965): 131–48 (this article was first published as "La vie extraordinaire d'un échevin de Montréal," *La Patrie*, 24, 31 juill., 7, 14 août 1955). Gerald Tulchinsky, "Une entreprise maritime canadienne-française: la Compagnie du Richelieu, 1845–1854," *RHAF*, 26 (1972–73): 559–82.

MARIE-ANNE, ESTHER (Christine) SUREAU, *dit* **BLONDIN**, named **Mother.** *See* SUREAU

MARIE DU SACRÉ-CŒUR. *See* FISBACH

MARLING, ALEXANDER, public servant and author: b. 11 April 1832 in Ebley (Gloucestershire), England, youngest son of John F. Marling, a cloth manufacturer, and his wife, the daughter of Malcolm McFarlane of Inverness, Scotland; m. in 1859 Julia Hewlett, and they had three children; d. 12 April 1890 in Toronto, Ont.

Alexander Marling immigrated to Canada with his parents in 1842 and entered Upper Canada College in Toronto that year. After graduation he remained in the city and spent five years in a mercantile house before being made a clerk in the department of education, under Egerton RYERSON, in 1854. Four years later he became chief clerk. According to his superior, Deputy Superintendent John George Hodgins*, Marling acquired a reputation for "thorough efficiency." On the appointment of Adam CROOKS as Ontario's first minister of education in 1876, Marling was made secretary of the department, a post he held until his elevation in January 1890 to the rank of deputy minister succeeding Hodgins.

While working in the department of education, Marling had studied law, graduating from the University of Toronto in 1862. Unfortunately his duties "did not allow his advance to the bar" but he was a member of the Law Society of Upper Canada. He also published two books on education. *The Canada educational directory, and year book for 1876*, dedicated to Ryerson, was a useful compilation of information on the public and private educational systems and personnel in each province of Canada at that time; the sections on Ontario and Quebec were particularly detailed. *A brief history of public and high school text-books authorized for the province of Ontario, 1846–1889*, commissioned by the education minister, George William Ross*, and published in 1890, drew comparisons with practices in several American states and provided a useful summary of the textbook question. It was apparently part of Ross's determined campaign to establish one authorized text in each subject.

Marling's main avocational interests were the church and the military. He was a "steadfast adherent" to the Church of England, an advocate of religious instruction "whether in private, public or Sunday schools," and a staunch supporter of Bishop Strachan School in Toronto, being a member of its council. He joined the volunteer force in 1862 at the time of the *Trent* affair [*see* Charles Hastings DOYLE] and for some years was a member of the 3rd Battalion, Victoria Rifles, and the 2nd Battalion, Queen's Own Rifles. After passing through the military school conducted by the 47th Foot he received a captain's certificate.

Just three months after becoming deputy minister of education, the office he had no doubt coveted most during his career, Marling died and was succeeded by John Millar*.

Marling seems to have been a typical public servant: efficient and well liked but not spectacular. Obituary notices described him as a "first-class officer, accurate, painstaking, kindly, courteous and honourable," and as "a Christian gentleman." He also received the ultimate tribute to a public servant: "never have we heard of his doing anything with which either Minister, teacher or publisher could justly be dissatisfied."

J. DONALD WILSON

Alexander Marling was the author of *A brief history of public and high school text-books authorized for the province of Ontario, 1846–1889, prepared by the Education Department* (Toronto, 1890) and the editor of *The Canada educational directory, and year book for 1876 . . .* (Toronto, 1876).

AO, RG 2, E-1, box 3: J. G. Hodgins to Egerton Ryerson, 29 Nov. 1872. *Canada Educational Monthly and School Magazine* (Toronto), 12 (1890): 187–88. *Educational Journal* (Toronto), 4 (1890–91): 25. *Cyclopædia of Canadian biog.* (Rose, 1886), 620.

MARTIN, FÉLIX (baptized **Félix-François-Marie**), Jesuit priest, teacher, architect, and author; b. 4 Oct. 1804 at Auray, France, son of Jacques-Augustin Martin, a merchant, and Anne-Armèle Lauzer; d. 25 Nov. 1886 in Paris, France.

After studying under the Jesuits at the Petit Séminaire de Sainte-Anne in Auray, Félix Martin, inspired by his teachers and his elder brother Arthur, entered the noviciate at Montrouge, near Paris, in 1823; he transferred to the Noviciat Saint-Louis at Avignon in the following year. He studied philosophy at the Petit Séminaire de L'Arc at Dole in 1825 and the next year became a teacher at the Collège Saint-Acheul, in Amiens. When the 1830 revolution brought about the temporary dispersal of the Jesuit community in France, Martin was forced to take refuge at Brigue,

Switzerland, where he finished his theological studies and was ordained priest in 1831. In the years from 1832 to 1839 he devoted himself particularly to teaching religion, mathematics, and drawing in Jesuit institutions and, when necessary, undertook parish and administrative duties. He spent this period in Spain, in France (at the residence in Vannes and the Collège Saint-Acheul), and then in Belgium (at the Collège de Brugelette). In 1839 he was in France, at Angers, where until 1842 he was engaged in preaching and in studying English.

On 31 May 1842 Martin arrived at Montreal with a group of Jesuits who had been invited by Bishop Ignace BOURGET to re-establish the Society of Jesus in the Province of Canada [*see* Jean-Pierre Chazelle*]. He lived for a brief period at the bishop's palace and then at La Prairie, Canada East, where he prepared a series of sermons and retreats; as a result, during the next six years he preached in several parishes and colleges in the Montreal region. In 1844 he was appointed superior of the Jesuits in Canada East, to replace Chazelle who was now directing the missions in Canada West [*see* Clément Boulanger*]. Armed with the pedagogical experience he had acquired in France, Martin founded the Collège Sainte-Marie at Montreal, himself assuming the duties of procurator, prefect of studies, and assistant master. The institution was temporarily set up in 1848 in confined quarters on Rue Saint-Alexandre and took in some 57 pupils during its first year. The Jesuits, who proposed to offer complete classical and commercial courses, had to have larger premises; Martin thus planned and began supervising the erection of a new edifice which housed the college from 1851. The first law school for French-speaking students in Canada East was inaugurated at the college that year, as a result of pressures exerted on Bourget and Martin by some influential Montreal lawyers [*see* François-Maximilien BIBAUD]. Martin took advantage of his position as rector from 1851 to 1857 to introduce into the institution the programmes and traditions of the Collège Saint-Acheul and of the Collège de Brugelette. Hence discipline and the performance of religious duties were key features in the education given to the pupils.

During the 1820s Martin had been introduced to draughting and the fundamentals of architecture by his brother Arthur, a Jesuit who specialized in restoring Gothic churches in France. Soon after his arrival in Lower Canada, Martin drew up the plans for a number of religious buildings. Thus in 1843, with the help of architect Pierre-Louis Morin, he designed the front of St Patrick's Church in Montreal. His name was also associated with the blueprints for the church of the Saint-François-Xavier mission at Caughnawaga; this church, begun in 1845, was remarkable for its projecting bell tower. From 1847 Martin supervised the construction of the new Collège Sainte-Marie according to his plans. This building, partially completed in 1851, was described as "solid but naïve" in conception; it had a complex system of sectional areas which could be adapted to the needs of a day-school, a residence for the Jesuit fathers, a noviciate, and a public chapel. The central portion of the Jesuit noviciate in the village of Sault-au-Récollet (North Montreal) was also erected under his supervision and according to his plans in 1852. Throughout this period Félix Martin was often consulted about the building and interior decoration of churches. In all probability he assisted architect Victor BOURGEAU in his work and he is thought also to have taught the architect's son.

Martin took a special interest in the religious history of New France. As soon as he arrived in Canada he began collecting the scattered documents connected with the Jesuit missions in the former French colony. With this task in mind, in 1844 he established the archives of the Collège Sainte-Marie, where he deposited the manuscripts and unpublished correspondence of the Society of Jesus unearthed by his persistent research throughout the religious communities of Quebec City. This development led him to take a closer interest in the *Relations des Jésuites*; after translating in 1852 the *Relation* by François-Joseph Bressani* that had been published in Italian 200 years earlier, Martin promoted a plan for the re-issue of the *Relations des Jésuites* covering the period 1611 to 1672, a venture completed at Quebec in 1858 under the direction of Georges-Barthélemi Faribault*, Édouard-Gabriel Plante, Jean-Baptiste-Antoine Ferland*, and Charles-Honoré Laverdière*. His most significant contribution was, however, the preparation with Fortuné Demontézon, of *Mission du Canada; relations inédites de la Nouvelle-France . . .*, which was brought out in two volumes in Paris in 1861. With an introduction and appendix drafted by Martin, this work included a collection of *Relations* for 1672 to 1679 which had not previously been published.

Recognized for his skill as a researcher, Martin received financial assistance from the government of the Province of Canada to carry out various projects. Thus in 1856 he was given the task of uncovering the traces of the old settlements of the Huron nation at Penetanguishene, Canada West, and he left an interesting manuscript on this subject. The following year he was commissioned to hunt through the archives kept in Paris and Rome for documents relating to Canadian history. On his return in 1858 he became a founding member of the Société Historique de Montréal. The next year was the centenary of the death of Louis-Joseph de Montcalm* and Martin embarked on a large-scale biographical study of him; it was not until 1867, however, that *Le Marquis de Montcalm et les dernières années de la colonie française au Canada (1756–1760)* appeared in Paris. His liking for biography prompted him subsequently to write a number of books about the principal martyrs of New France, published in various editions and translations.

Martin became superior of the Jesuits' residence at Quebec in 1859 but had to return to France two years later to get treatment for his eyes. In 1862, after a brief stay at the École Sainte-Geneviève in Paris as spiritual director, he became rector of the Collège Saint-François-Xavier, in the town of Vannes. He was transferred to the residence at Poitiers in 1865 and there he served as superior, at the same time continuing his work on the history of New France, as his correspondence and the visit of historian Abbé Henri-Raymond Casgrain* in the following year attest. From 1868 he stayed at the Collège de l'Immaculée-Conception in Paris, where he took charge of the library and later served as superior. A witness of the Prussian occupation in 1870 and the Paris Commune in 1871, he kept a private diary of his impressions of these events. In consequence of the 1880 decree ordering the dissolution of the teaching congregations in France, Martin retired with a group of Jesuits to a residence in Paris where he died six years later. He had never found a way of carrying out his plan to return to Canada.

GEORGES-ÉMILE GIGUÈRE

[As one of the scholars who undertook to reassess the historical role of the Canadian church, Félix Martin tried, through a great deal of research, to bring together the major documents relating to the Jesuit missions in New France. In this connection he was associated with the following publications: *Relation des jésuites sur les découvertes et les autres événements arrivés en Canada, au nord et à l'ouest des États-Unis (1611–1672)* . . . , E. B. O'Callaghan, édit., Félix Martin, trad. (Montréal, 1850); [F. J. Bressani], *Relation abrégée de quelques missions des pères de la Compagnie de Jésus dans la Nouvelle-France* . . . , Félix Martin, trad. (Montréal, 1852); Claude Dablon, *Relation de ce qui s'est passé de plus remarquable aux missions des pères de la Compagnie de Jésus en la Nouvelle-France les années 1673 à 1679* . . . , Félix Martin et J. G. Shea, édit. (Montréal et New York, 1860); and *Mission du Canada; relations inédites de la Nouvelle-France (1672–[1679]) pour faire suite aux anciennes relations (1615–1672)* . . . , Fortuné Demontézon et Félix Martin, édit. (2v., Paris, 1861).

Martin also wrote a number of historical works of which the most important are: *Le Marquis de Montcalm et les dernières années de la colonie française au Canada (1756–1760)* (Paris, 1867); *Le R. P. Isaac Jogues, de la Compagnie de Jésus, premier apôtre des Iroquois* (Paris, 1873); *Hurons et Iroquois; le P. Jean de Brébeuf, sa vie, ses travaux, son martyre* (Paris, 1877). To locate the articles by Martin on archæology and on the study of the Huron Indians see: *L'Album littéraire et musical et la rev. canadienne* (Montréal), 1848. His religious publications are listed in Augustin de Backer *et al.*, *Bibliothèque de la Compagnie de Jésus*, Carlos Sommervogel, édit. (3e éd., 9v., Bruxelles et Paris, 1890–1900). G.-É. G.]

Arch. de la Compagnie de Jésus, prov. du Canada français (Saint-Jérôme, Qué.), Fonds général, 1632–61. IBC, Centre de documentation, Fonds Morisset, 2, M379/F376. Firmin Vignon, *Le P. Martin* ([Montréal, 1886]). *DOLQ*, I: 170, 637–49. Paul Desjardins, *Le collège Sainte-Marie de Montréal* (2v., Montréal, 1940–[44]), I: 177–276. *Les établissements des jésuites en France depuis quatre siècles* . . . , Pierre Delattre, édit. (5v., Enghien et Wetteren, Belgique, 1949–57). Guy Frégault, "La recherche historique au temps de Garneau (la correspondance Viger-Faribault)," *Centenaire de l'Histoire du Canada de François-Xavier Garneau* . . . , [J.-J. Lefebvre, édit.] (Montréal, 1945), 371–90. Serge Gagnon, *Le Québec et ses historiens de 1840 à 1920: la Nouvelle-France de Garneau à Groulx* (Québec, 1978). G.-É. Giguère, "La restauration de la Compagnie de Jésus au Canada, 1839–1857" (2v. of manuscripts in the author's possession; copies are available at various Jesuit archival repositories, libraries, and houses). J.-C. Marsan, *Montréal en évolution: historique du développement de l'architecture et de l'environnement montréalais* (Montréal, 1974). Luc Noppen, *Les églises du Québec (1600–1850)* (s.l., 1977). Léon Pouliot, *Étude sur les relations des jésuites de la Nouvelle-France (1632–1673)* (Montréal et Paris, 1940).

MEE-MAY. *See* MĪMĪY

MERRILL, HORACE, contractor, engineer, civil servant, and manufacturer; b. 10 May 1809 at Enfield, N.H., son of Nathaniel Merrill and Sarah Huse; m. in 1842 Adaline Church, and they had nine children; d. 22 May 1883 in Ottawa, Ont.

Horace Merrill began training as a cabinet-maker at age 14. He later described himself as a civil engineer but he apparently did not receive any formal training as such. He came to the Ottawa valley in 1826 and worked as a millwright, first for George Hamilton* at Hawkesbury, Upper Canada, and later for Levi Bigelow at Buckingham, Lower Canada. Some time during the 1830s he became a contractor, probably building slides and booms for the square timber and lumbering industries of the Ottawa valley. Certainly his engineering abilities were sufficiently respected by 1840 for him to obtain the contract to build a substantial mill with 26 saws on the Gatineau River for Alonzo Wright*. By 1847, according to the eminent engineer Thomas Coltrin Keefer*, Merrill had "probably constructed more dams, slides and booms on the Ottawa than any other person now on it."

Merrill had joined the Board of Works, later the Department of Public Works, about 1846; for the first few years he supervised the construction of public improvements on the Madawaska River and advised the Madawaska River Improvement Company which had been established by local lumbermen to build works on the river's tributaries. He seems to have impressed his superiors in the department, particularly Keefer, and in January 1849 he was appointed superintendent of the Ottawa works, based in Bytown (Ottawa), a position he was to retain until his retirement in 1875. As superintendent he directed the construction, operation, and maintenance of all works on the Ottawa and its tributaries undertaken by the department for the descent of timber rafts and logs and for the transportation of supplies up-river to the shanties. Among his achievements was the Carillon Dam, completed in 1858, which improved navigation by raising the water level at the Long Sault Rapids. By 1870 he was responsible for slides, booms, dams, bridges, canals, piers, and buildings at 11 stations on the Ottawa, 15 on the Madawaska, 31 on the Petawawa, 11 on the Dumoine, and one each on the Gatineau, Coulonge, and Noire rivers.

Merrill's interest and influence were by no means confined to the Ottawa valley. As the acknowledged expert on river improvements within the department, he was consulted regarding the design and construction of works to open to lumbermen the virgin forests along the Saguenay, Saint-Maurice, Trent, and French rivers. In 1851 Merrill supervised the deepening of the 12-mile Chambly Canal and a decade later surveyed the 124-mile Rideau Canal for potential mill sites. He also designed the Saint-Maurice slides at Shawinigan and Grand-Mère, and the Saguenay slides in the 1860s. Throughout his long career as superintendent Merrill consistently and usually "in the strongest manner" campaigned for more government works on the Ottawa and other rivers to encourage the growth of the lumbering industry. In this effort he had considerable success and was, as a result, generally popular with the lumbering community. He also urged the department to prevent sawmill owners from dumping their waste into the river, a campaign which was less popular with lumbermen.

A man of considerable energy, Merrill engaged in other economic endeavours. About 1854 he supervised the construction of a large sawmill for John J. Harris and Henry Franklin BRONSON, two Americans who had obtained hydraulic lots which Merrill had set out on the islands near the Chaudière Rapids at Ottawa. His major business enterprises, however, were his foundries in Ottawa. Some time before 1864 Merrill and Joseph Merrill CURRIER of New Edinburgh (now part of Ottawa) purchased N. S. Blasdell and Company's Victoria Foundry, famous throughout Canada for its fine axes. Employing about 20 people in 1864, this substantial business manufactured steam engines, lathes, agricultural implements, grist- and sawmill machinery, and planing machines (for which the company had received a gold medal from the Prince of Wales in 1861), as well as smaller items such as axes and nails. By 1880 the Victoria Foundry supplied the Department of Public Works with nearly all the spikes for their Ottawa works, an activity which, given Merrill's connection with the Ottawa works until his retirement in 1875, seems more than coincidental. Indeed, the Victoria Foundry became so busy that by 1876 he and Currier had acquired a second foundry on Victoria Island and Merrill had set up Merrill and Company to operate a third foundry and machine shop at the Chaudière Falls. In the 1860s Merrill had been a director of the Ottawa Consumers Gas Company and the Ottawa City Passenger Railway Company.

Horace Merrill is chiefly known through his engineering and business activities. He was, however, also a master of the Dalhousie Masonic Lodge and a Presbyterian. Following his death on 22 May 1883, a few days after that of his wife, his businesses were carried on by his sons, Horace B. and Milton W. Merrill.

SANDRA GILLIS

PAC, MG 28, III46, 1: no.13; RG 11, ser.II, 11, 60, 65, 76, 269, 377–78; ser. III, 88–99; ser.IV, 177; ser.VI, 11–16; RG 31, A1, 1851, Bytown; 1861, Ottawa City, Ottawa Ward; 1871, Ottawa City. Can., Prov. of, Legislative Assembly, *App. to the journals*, 1851, II, app.G.G.; 1852–53, IX, app.M.M.M.M.; 1857, V, app.29, C. City of Ottawa, Assessment Dept., *Assessment roll* (Ottawa), 1876–77, 1879, 1883, 1886. *Ottawa Daily Citizen*, 23, 25 May 1883. *Canadian biog. dict.*, I: 77–78. *Ottawa directory*, 1863–84. J. W. Hughson and C. C. J. Bond, *Hurling down the pine: the story of the Wright, Gilmour and Hughson families, timber and lumber manufacturers in the Hull and Ottawa region and on the Gatineau River, 1800–1920* (Old Chelsea, Que., 1964). Charles Roger, *Ottawa past and present, or, a brief account of the first opening up of the Ottawa country . . .* (Ottawa, 1871). A. H. D. Ross, *Ottawa, past and present* (Toronto, 1927), 156–57. H. J. [W.] Walker, *The Ottawa story through 150 years* (Ottawa, 1953).

METCALF, WILLIAM GEORGE, physician; b. 4 July 1847 in Uxbridge, Canada West, son of George Metcalf and Jane Morphet, who had immigrated from England in 1845; m. first 31 May 1876 Alice Elizabeth Bustin of Uxbridge, and they had three children; m. secondly 21 June 1883 Emma Clarke of Elora, Ont., daughter of the Honourable Charles Clarke*; d. 16 Aug. 1885 in Kingston, Ont.

William George Metcalf received his elementary education in Uxbridge, except for five years when the family lived in Ashburn in Whitby Township. In 1870 he entered the Toronto School of Medicine which was affiliated with the University of Toronto. The university class and prize list for MB candidates in 1872 records that Metcalf stood first in surgery, second in medical jurisprudence, third in obstetrics, and fourth in medicine. He became a member of the College of Physicians and Surgeons of Ontario on 12 April 1872 and received his MD in 1874.

In 1870, as a medical student, Metcalf had served under Dr Joseph Workman*, superintendent of the Toronto Lunatic Asylum, and had become his clinical assistant on 7 Aug. 1871. After obtaining his MD, Metcalf practised medicine in Windsor, Ont., for a few months before returning to the Toronto asylum when Workman retired in July 1875. He remained there until June 1877, then transferred to the asylum at London as assistant medical superintendent to Dr Richard Maurice Bucke*. Less than a year later, on 4 April 1878, Metcalf was appointed acting superintendent of the Rockwood Asylum, Kingston, when illness incapacitated Dr John Robinson DICKSON. After Dickson's resignation Metcalf was appointed medical superintendent on 20 June 1879. John Woodburn Langmuir*, the inspector of asylums in Ontario, set his annual salary at $1,600.

The year before Metcalf arrived at Rockwood the control of the institution had been transferred from the federal to the provincial government. This transfer severed the asylum's connection with the federal penitentiary in Kingston and Metcalf was faced with the difficult task of transforming the institution from an asylum for criminal lunatics into a hospital for the mentally ill. He concentrated on developing the programme of increasingly humane treatment of patients which had begun under Dr John Palmer Litchfield* and continued under Dickson. He abolished physical restraint and instituted occupational and recreational activities ranging from tending the garden which supplied the kitchen to dances and concerts. His journal records his progress. On 25 Feb. 1880, he wrote, "Entertainment – The asylum dramatic club gave their first performance this evening, assisted by others from the city. 'The Stage-struck Clerk' was put on the boards and for the first attempt was very creditable."

In 1882 Metcalf persuaded his friend and future brother-in-law, Dr Charles Kirk Clarke*, to come to Kingston as assistant superintendent. Both had been pupils of Workman and their partnership provided a long-awaited opportunity to put the ideas they had discussed many years before into practice. Metcalf's annual reports after 1882 indicate their many innovations. From an essentially custodial institution, the asylum at Kingston became a model of its kind which attracted distinguished visitors. Among them was Daniel Hack Tuke, a celebrated English authority on mental hospitals, who in 1884 expressed himself as "well satisfied with the condition of things here."

In 1882 Bucke had initiated an "open door" policy at the London asylum to increase the patients' sense of freedom. The system, soon instituted at the Kingston asylum, was not without risk. It was, however, particularly tragic that Metcalf should become a fatal victim of his own reforms. On the morning of 13 Aug. 1885, while Metcalf and Clarke were making their rounds, Metcalf was stabbed in the abdomen by Patrick Maloney, a patient suffering from paranoia. Despite all efforts to save him Metcalf died on 16 Aug. 1885 and Maloney was charged with murder. At Metcalf's funeral the pallbearers included doctors Workman, Daniel Clark*, Bucke, Charles William Covernton*, William Osler*, and architect Kivas Tully*.

Because of his youth and inexperience Metcalf's appointment as medical superintendent had been criticized in the provincial legislature. Despite this inauspicious start he had soon proved himself to be an extremely competent and courageous administrator. In less than seven years he succeeded in overcoming the opposition of a staff whose attitude towards patients was extremely punitive. His achievement in transforming Rockwood from a custodial institution for insane criminals into a general asylum earned him the respect of his medical colleagues throughout Canada and the United States. His untimely death at the hands of a patient liberated by the "open door" policy had particular poignancy.

CYRIL GREENLAND

AO, RG 10, ser.20-F, Asylum for the Insane (Kingston, Ont.), Medical superintendent's journal, 1880–89. Asylum for the Insane, Kingston, *Annual report* (Kingston), 1878–79. *Dominion annual register*, 1885. *The Ontario medical register* . . . (Toronto), 1874. Cyril Greenland, *Charles Kirk Clarke: a pioneer of Canadian psychiatry* (Toronto, 1966). *The institutional care of the insane in the United States and Canada*, ed. H. M. Hurd (4v., Baltimore, Md., 1916–17; repr. New York, 1973), IV.

MEYERS. *See* MYERS

MICHEL, Sir JOHN, soldier; b. 1 Sept. 1804 in Dorset, England, son of Lieutenant-General John Michel and his second wife, Anne Fane; d. 23 May 1886 at the family seat, Dewlish House, Dorchester, Dorset.

John Michel was educated at Eton, and entered the army as an ensign in 1823. Most of his early service was in the 64th Foot. It is clear that his career was assisted by family connections and family wealth; but the fact that in 1832–33 he attended the senior department (later the staff college) of the Royal Military College, Sandhurst, suggests a serious interest in his profession. From 1835 to 1840 he was aide-de-camp to his uncle, General Sir Henry Fane, who was commander-in-chief in India. On 15 May 1838 Michel married Louise Anne, a daughter of Colonel Chatham Horace Churchill, quartermaster general in India; they were to have at least two sons and three daughters. In 1840 Michel purchased a majority in the 6th Foot, and two years later the lieutenant-colonelcy of that regiment. The 6th was sent to South Africa in August 1846, and Michel commanded it there in the Kaffir Wars of 1846–47 and 1851–53, sometimes serving as commander of independent columns. During this, his first active service, he showed himself an energetic leader. James McKay, a sergeant in the 74th Foot, who saw him at work (he calls him Mitchell), says he was "the beau ideal of an able campaigning commander" and "a father and friend" to his men. After a period of home service in the brevet rank of colonel, he took part in the Crimean War as chief of staff of the Turkish contingent that was taken into British pay, as a local major-general.

After a short period of service in the Cape Colony, Michel was ordered to China in 1857; but *en route* his ship was wrecked and he was subsequently diverted to India, where the mutiny had broken out. In the last stages of the mutiny in 1858–59 Michel, now a substantive major-general, successfully conducted the pursuit of Tantia Topi, defeating his forces in a series of engagements and reducing him to the status of a fugitive who was shortly caught and hanged. At the end of 1859 Michel was sent to command a division in the war with China. His division took part in successful actions in August 1860, and in October it fell to it to burn the Summer Palace at Peking in reprisal for the torture and murder of British prisoners. Having become a KCB for his work in the mutiny, Michel was now promoted to GCB.

In June 1865 he succeeded Lieutenant-General Sir William Fenwick WILLIAMS in the command of the forces in British North America (the appointment was officially styled lieutenant-general on the staff). He remained in this command until October 1867, and thus had to deal with the first and most serious phase of the Fenian troubles. Whenever the Fenian menace moved the government of the Province of Canada to call out units of the volunteer force for active duty, these were placed under Michel by order in council and he exercised command over regulars and volunteers alike. Nine companies of volunteers were so called out for frontier service in November 1865; at the same time Michel reinforced the regular garrison of London, Canada West, and took steps to improve the telegraph network in the eastern part of the upper province. In March 1866, 10,000 volunteers were called out (the actual number appearing for duty turned out to be 14,000), and in the crisis caused by the raids of June 1866 [*see* Alfred Booker*] the whole volunteer force of Canada, some 20,000 men, was called out and placed under Michel. He had asked for, and obtained, two more regular battalions from the United Kingdom in March 1866 and in August a panic caused in Canada West by renewed Fenian threats led Michel, in conjunction with Viscount Monck*, the governor general, to ask the British government for still larger reinforcements. These were sent, in numbers only slightly smaller than had been requested; and in the spring of 1867 there were over 15,000 regulars under Michel's command. Monck soon began to incline to the view that the force might be somewhat reduced but Michel opposed any reduction.

For two long periods, 30 Sept. 1865–12 Feb. 1866 and 10 Dec. 1866–25 June 1867, Michel was administrator of the government in Monck's absence, though he did not move from his headquarters at Montreal. Writing to John A. Macdonald* in February 1866 to say that he expected raids and would like to see more volunteer companies called out, he said whimsically, "In writing this note, I am consulting with my Minister of War, giving him the opinions of the Commander of the Forces, which, as Administrator I think it would be desirable to carry out." Generally speaking, Michel sought to prevail on the colonials to take on a larger share of the defence burden, while Canadian ministers, unwilling to incur expense, preferred to leave it with the regulars. Early in 1867 Alexander Campbell*, the acting minister of militia, wrote to Macdonald in England describing how Michel, on the basis of intelligence received, sent "of his own motion of course" Colonel Garnet Joseph Wolseley* to negotiate with General George Gordon Meade of the United States Army, and also asked Campbell to call out "the Volunteers." Campbell politely demurred. In consequence, he wrote, "Our Volunteers are still sleeping with their wives to the great comfort of both and with great prospective benefit to the country."

Michel was painfully aware of how inadequate and exposed were the country's military communications. In August and September 1865, soon after his arrival in Canada, he made a reconnaissance by canoe, in company with Admiral Sir James Hope, commanding the Royal Navy's American station, of the route between the St Lawrence and Lake Huron by the French River, Lake Nipissing, and the Mattawa and Ottawa rivers. He cautiously advised against either setting up a crown colony at Red River or uniting the Hudson's Bay Company's territories with Canada until "a safe communication for military purposes" was established with Upper Fort Garry (Winnipeg). In October 1865 he gave the engineer Casimir Stanislaus Gzowski* a letter to the colonial secretary explaining that he considered the Ottawa–French River navigation route, which Gzowski was promoting, vital to the country's security. In a valedictory message to the Canadian people he urged the importance of this project. During his last months in Canada he expressed the opinion that the Fenian movement was now "torpid," and also recorded an optimistic view of the prospects for Anglo-American peace. Michel's Canadian command was cut short by concern for his wife's health. When he left Montreal for England on 15 Oct. 1867, having been succeeded by Sir Charles Ash Windham*, he received addresses from the city corporation and the Montreal volunteers warmly praising his work as commander and administrator.

In 1873 Michel was placed in charge of the first "autumn manoeuvres" held in England, a development which can be traced to the influence of the Franco-Prussian War. From 1875 to 1880 he was commander-in-chief in Ireland, where his "social qualities and ample means" are said to have made him popular and where he became an Irish privy councillor (and thus Right Honourable). In March 1885, a little more than a year before his death, he was made a field-marshal.

Field-Marshal Sir Henry Evelyn Wood, who served under Michel in India as a subaltern, described him as "a clever, handsome, well-educated officer, a fine horseman, active and of great determination." He served in Canada at a difficult and critical period, and his work seems to have been competently done. Campbell's letter to Macdonald in 1867 suggests that the Canadian ministers tended to think him something of a fussbudget, but Macdonald wrote in 1866: "There is not a more active or zealous officer than Sir John Michel."

C. P. STACEY

PAC, MG 26, A, 57–59, 100; RG 7, G1, 163–65; G6, 16–17; G9, 44–47; G10, 1–2. Can., Parl., *Sessional papers*, 1867–68, VII, no.35. Can., Prov. of, Parl., *Sessional papers*, 1866, II, no.4. [J. A. Macdonald], *Correspondence of Sir John Macdonald . . .* , ed. Joseph Pope (Toronto, 1921). James McKay, *Reminiscences of the last Kafir war, illustrated with numerous anecdotes* (Grahamstown, South Africa, 1871; repr. Cape Town, 1970). G. J. Wolseley, *Narrative of the war with China in 1860 . . .* (London, 1862; repr. Wilmington, Del., 1972); *The South African diaries of Sir Garnet Wolseley, 1875*, ed. Adrian Preston (Cape Town, 1971). *Montreal Gazette*, 16 Oct. 1867. *Times* (London), 25 May 1886. *The annual register: a review of public events at home and abroad* (London), 1886. *DNB*. G.B., WO, *Army list*, 1824. *Hart's army list*, 1852; 1856; 1866; 1872. Notman and Taylor, *Portraits of British Americans*, II. Creighton, *Macdonald, young politician*. J. W. Fortescue, *A history of the British army* (13v. in 14 and 6v. maps, London, 1899–1930), XII–XIII. J. M. Hitsman, *Safeguarding Canada, 1763–1871* ([Toronto]), 1968). A. J. Smithers, *The Kaffir wars, 1779–1877* (London, 1973). C. P. Stacey, *Canada and the British army, 1846–1871: a study in the practice of responsible government* (London and Toronto, 1936; rev. ed., [Toronto], 1963). Evelyn Wood, *The revolt in Hindustan, 1857–59* (London, 1908).

MILLER, JAMES ANDREWS, lawyer, judge, and politician; b. 29 July 1839 in Galt (now part of Cambridge), Upper Canada, second son of John Miller, a lawyer; m. 8 June 1865 Henrietta Ranney of St Catharines, Canada West; d. 1 Nov. 1886 in Winnipeg, Man.

James Andrews Miller was educated in Galt, Simcoe, and Toronto, and in 1859 he received a BA with honours in classics and mathematics from Trinity College, Toronto. He articled with Richard Miller in St Catharines, where he practised law after being called to the bar of Upper Canada in 1863. Two years later Miller earned a BCL from Trinity College (which conferred a DCL on him in 1873). He served as president of the Lincoln County Conservative constituency association for many years, and in a federal by-election in Lincoln in 1877 was the unsuccessful Conservative candidate.

On 11 Oct. 1880 Miller was created a QC, and nine days later was appointed a puisne judge of the Court of Queen's Bench of Manitoba. He accepted this appointment with Sir John A. Macdonald*'s assurance that he intended to appoint Miller chief justice when the incumbent, Edmund Burke WOOD, who was in ill health, no longer held the position. In May 1882 Miller protested the low salaries paid to Manitoba judges and threatened to resign unless they were increased. He did not carry out this threat immediately, however. When the federal government appointed Lewis WALLBRIDGE chief justice later that year, Miller resigned from the bench, effective 31 Dec. 1882. The Law Society of Manitoba supported Miller, at least in the matter of salaries, and showed its high regard by presenting him with a silver tea-service.

Miller now resumed the practice of law. He was admitted to the Manitoba bar on 8 Feb. 1883, but refused to pay the usual admission fee on the ground that a former judge had a right to admission as a "visitor" of the law society. His name was struck from the rolls on 10 Oct. 1884, but he was reinstated in June 1885 after a court ruled in his favour.

At the request of Premier John NORQUAY, Miller had turned once again to politics, and on 23 Jan. 1883 he ran unsuccessfully as the Conservative candidate in the provincial constituency of Rockwood. However, after being appointed to replace Alexander Macbeth Sutherland as attorney general on 6 September, Miller was elected by a large majority in the constituency of Varennes on 28 Sept. 1883. Varennes was in an area over which both Manitoba and Ontario claimed jurisdiction, and in fact on the day Miller was elected the inhabitants had also voted in an Ontario provincial election as part of the Algoma riding. As Manitoba's attorney general, Miller met with the Ontario premier, Oliver Mowat*, and they agreed to submit the dispute to the Judicial Committee of the Privy Council, which ruled in Ontario's favour in July 1884. Miller thus lost his assembly seat and resigned from the government on 11 Dec. 1884.

When a new system of land registration was introduced in 1885, Miller was named the first registrar general. On 27 Oct. 1886 Miller slipped on the stairs of the McKenzie Hotel in Winnipeg, where he lived, and fell to a marble floor below. He was a very heavy man, and he sustained injuries which resulted in his death five days later.

LEE GIBSON

Arch. of Western Canadian Legal Hist., Faculty of Law, Univ. of Manitoba (Winnipeg), Docs. relating to the striking of the Honourable J. A. Miller's name from the roll of the law society. Law Soc. of Manitoba (Winnipeg), Minute books, 21 July 1881; 27, 29 May 1882. PAC, MG 26, A. *Daily*

Manitoban (Winnipeg), 1 Nov. 1886. *Daily Sun* (Winnipeg), 24 Dec. 1883. *Manitoba Daily Free Press*, 25, 29, 30 Oct., 6 Nov. 1880; 17 Oct., 3, 6 Nov., 19 Dec. 1882; 1, 3, 9, 16, 24 Jan., 5–7, 13, 28, 29 Sept. 1883; 6 March, 3, 11 Dec. 1884; 29, 30 Oct., 2–4 Nov. 1886. *St. Catharines Journal* (St Catharines, [Ont.]), 8 June 1865. R. D. and Lee Gibson, *Substantial justice: law and lawyers in Manitoba, 1670–1970* (Winnipeg, 1972), 136–38, 143–45, 156, 159–60.

MILLER, JOHN CLASSON (Clausin, Clauson), lumberman, politician, and office-holder; b. 16 Dec. 1836 in Yonge Township, Leeds County, Upper Canada, son of Samuel Miller and Melita Hayes; m. 2 Aug. 1859 Adelaide Augusta Chamberlain, and they had at least one child, John Bellamy; d. 2 April 1884 at Colton, Calif., and was buried at Parry Sound, Ont.

John Classon Miller was educated at local schools in Leeds County, and as a young man bought a mercantile business at Seeleys Bay from George Tennant. He was active in political affairs and was for a time deputy sheriff for the United Counties of Leeds and Grenville. When he moved to Toronto he was employed by the Ontario Crown Lands Department on 10 March 1868. Although classified initially as a clerk, later as chief clerk, Miller acted as superintendent of woods and forests until he was forced to resign on 31 Dec. 1871 because of a partial loss of sight. Under his supervision the sums paid by the lumbermen to the government for timber dues, ground rents, and bonuses had increased greatly. Miller then joined Anson Greene Phelps Dodge and other lumbermen in the purchase from H. B. Rathbun and Son of extensive timber limits and a sawmill in Parry Sound. The new firm was incorporated in 1872 as Parry Sound Lumber Company. In 1877 Miller took over Dodge's interests in the business, thereby becoming the owner and general manager of one of the most important companies in the Georgian Bay area. By 1878 the company was sawing 11 or 12 million feet of lumber annually, bringing in 4,000 barrels of flour a year, and operating a general store in Parry Sound. A second mill, also in Parry Sound, was purchased in 1880; over the years shipping facilities and docks were expanded and a shingle mill and box shook factory were added. After Miller's death his son served as president of the company, which survived until 1931.

In 1875 Miller was the Liberal candidate in the newly established provincial riding of Muskoka and Parry Sound. It was a difficult constituency to contest and to represent; large in area but sparsely populated, it was divided by the divergent interests of the two regions in such matters as transportation and tariffs on American goods, and also by conflicts between the settlers and the lumbermen concerning the ownership of the pine stands. Although Miller was elected with a majority, on 17 Sept. 1875 he was disqualified on petition with a variety of charges. The decision was reversed by the Court of Error and Appeal on 22 Jan. 1876, and Miller immediately took his seat in the legislature. From the beginning Miller was active in debates, especially those relating to railways, lumbering, and land settlement, and he was a strong supporter of government subsidies for roads and railways to open underpopulated areas of the province such as the one he represented. To encourage settlement he proposed an amendment to the Free Grants and Homestead Act of 1868 which would have permitted a settler who had occupied his holding for six months to sell his improvements under specified conditions. Although the amendment did not pass it won general approval in his riding.

Miller retained his seat in the provincial election of 1879 with a substantial majority, but resigned in 1882 to contest the riding in the federal election against Colonel William Edward O'Brien. Although the first count showed Miller leading, a recount indicated that O'Brien had won by three votes. By this time Miller's health was failing rapidly. He spent the winter of 1883 in Florida and the following winter in California where he died of tuberculosis.

FLORENCE B. MURRAY

Ont., Legislative Library, Newspaper Hansard, 1876–82 (mfm. at AO); Ministry of Consumer and Commercial Relations, Companies Branch (Toronto), Parry Sound Lumber Company file, no.13877in. Parry Sound Public Library (Parry Sound, Ont.), J. C. Miller news-cuttings scrapbook, 1875–80. Univ. of Toronto, Thomas Fisher Rare Book Library, Rare Books and Special Coll. Dept., Muskoka clipping coll., 1869–1944. Alexander Kirkwood and J. J. Murphy, *The undeveloped lands in northern & western Ontario; information regarding resources, products and suitability for settlement* . . . (Toronto, 1878), 78–79. Ont., Legislative Assembly, *Journals*, 1876–82; *Statutes*, 1872, c.98. *Globe*, 4 April 1884. *CPC*, 1875–83. *Dominion annual register*, 1879–82; 1884. [W. E. Hamilton], *Guide book & atlas of Muskoka and Parry Sound districts, 1879* (Toronto, 1879; repr. Port Elgin, Ont., 1971), 2, 15–17, 31. T. W. H. Leavitt, *History of Leeds and Grenville, Ontario, from 1749 to 1879* . . . (Brockville, Ont., 1879; repr. Belleville, Ont., 1972), 113–14, 174, 198. *A miscellany of notes and sketches on the history of Parry Sound*, comp. Sam Brunton (Parry Sound, 1969).

MILLIER, HILAIRE, Roman Catholic priest; b. 26 Feb. 1823 at Contrecœur, Lower Canada, son of Jean-Baptiste Millier, a farmer, and Thérèse Labossière; d. 13 Aug. 1889 at Saint-Hyacinthe, Que.

Hilaire Millier received a classical and theological education at the Séminaire de Saint-Hyacinthe, and after ordination to the priesthood on 9 Feb. 1851, taught philosophy there for more than four years. He then served in the parish ministry until his retirement in 1885. A missionary at Stanstead from September 1855 to September 1856, he was parish priest for four years at Saint-Hilaire, then from 1860 to 1861 at

Saint-Athanase in Iberville, and finally was appointed parish priest at Sorel on 11 Sept. 1861.

On his arrival at Sorel, Abbé Millier set out to finish the construction of a general hospital, begun by his predecessor Joseph-Magloire Limoges. When it opened on 22 Oct. 1862, the Sisters of Charity of the Hôtel-Dieu in Saint-Hyacinthe took over its management. He also endowed the Congregation of Notre-Dame with a magnificent convent. His major achievement, however, was the founding of the Petit Séminaire or classical college of Sorel. The idea of building the college was first advanced in 1853 by a lay committee. The bishop of Saint-Hyacinthe, Charles La Rocque*, at first had reservations about the project, thinking it would harm the colleges already in the diocese; he did not admit its importance until 1868 when he instructed Abbé Millier to proceed with it. The bishop, however, wanted to exclude laymen from the enterprise. "This undertaking," he wrote on 20 Feb. 1868, "must be supposed to be an entirely ecclesiastical endeavour, and must be the work of the priest and not of the citizens of Sorel, however worthy they may be." In addition to the classical programme, the college was to organize an industrial one for young people seeking a career in commerce or industry. The college would in the event be directed by school commissioners from its beginnings in September 1868 until 1870, when it came under the control of the Roman Catholic Episcopal Corporation of Saint-Hyacinthe.

When disputes arose between Bishop La Rocque and a group of liberals of Saint-Hyacinthe [*see* Charles La Rocque], Abbé Millier offered the former the hospitality of Sorel; he declared himself a determined adversary "of the irreligious and impious ideas" that seemed prevalent in the small episcopal town. "In these circumstances," he wrote on 6 Feb. 1868, "may I suggest Sorel to you, My Lord, as a place where Your Lordship will be more at ease, at least this is my hope, for you will breathe in a more Catholic atmosphere. I venture to say, My Lord, that there is no trace here of that Voltairian spirit on which the town of Saint-Hyacinthe seems to pride itself and which Christian faith and the episcopacy deplore."

In 1869 Millier asked his bishop to retire him, for reasons of health. A petition from the inhabitants of Sorel commending him, and the pleas of Bishop La Rocque, led him to reconsider his decision. In 1874 further disabilities forced him to ask for a less onerous charge. Finally, in 1875 he was given the quiet parish of Saint-Mathieu in Belœil, with a curate to relieve him of the heaviest tasks. He himself, however, had to convince his flock of the necessity of renovating the parish church. After a ministry of ten years at Saint-Mathieu, he retired to the convent of the Sisters of St Joseph at Saint-Hyacinthe, where he served as chaplain. He died there on 13 Aug. 1889.

Hilaire Millier, a man heedful of the views of his superiors, received from Bishop La Rocque the titles of diocesan adviser in 1866 and vicar general in 1868. In 1875 the new bishop of the diocese, Louis-Zéphirin Moreau*, maintained him in his offices and in 1877 made him canon of the cathedral. As a churchman he did not perhaps make a profound impression, but in the light of his achievements, the praise of Abbé Azarie Couillard-Després* for "his fine intelligence, his pastoral zeal . . . and his talent as an administrator," seems merited.

RÉAL BOUCHER

Arch. de la chancellerie de l'évêché de Saint-Hyacinthe (Saint-Hyacinthe, Qué.), XVII, C-54, 1884; C-66, 1868–69, 1874; Cahier hors série, Isidore Desnoyers, "Monographie de la paroisse Saint-Pierre-de-Sorel," 177ff.; "Notice biographique sur les missionnaires et les curés de Sorel," 33–34; Reg. des lettres des évêques, sér. I, 5: 380. AP, Sainte-Trinité (Contrecœur), Reg. des baptêmes, mariages et sépultures, 1823. *Le Courrier de Saint-Hyacinthe*, 15 août 1889. *Le Sorelois* (Sorel, Qué.), 16 août 1889. C.-P. Choquette, *Histoire du séminaire de Saint-Hyacinthe depuis sa fondation jusqu'à nos jours* (2v., Montréal, 1911–12), I. Azarie Couillard-Després, *Histoire de Sorel de ses origines à nos jours* (Montréal, 1926), 207–22.

MĪMĪY (Gabriel Coté, Mee-may, Pigeon), chief of a band of Saulteaux; b. probably near Swan Lake (Man.); d. 12 Dec. 1884 on the Cote Reserve (Sask.).

Gabriel Coté, son of a French-speaking mixed-blood father and a Saulteaux mother, was a hunter of note who by 1850 had gathered around him a small group of English-speaking mixed-bloods and Saulteaux Indians. Coté and his band lived near the Swan River and traded at the Hudson's Bay Company post of Fort Pelly on the upper Assiniboine River. Although principally woodland hunters, by the late 1860s Coté and his followers had begun to spend a part of every year on the plains.

Coté was recognized by the HBC as the principal chief of the Swan River area, and was reported as such to the government officials, Alexander MORRIS, David Laird*, and William Joseph Christie*, who came to Fort Qu'Appelle to make treaty with the Indians of the area in September 1874. The commissioners subsequently regarded Coté as the principal leader of all the Saulteaux; however, neither the Quill Lakes nor the Qu'Appelle River Saulteaux recognized him as their spokesman or leader, a point they made clear at the council. In fact, these groups distrusted Coté because of his relationship with the HBC and his willingness to cooperate with government officials. At the opening of the treaty negotiations the Qu'Appelle River Saulteaux allegedly threatened Coté's life and then confined him to his tent in order to make the government aware of their dissatisfaction over the sale in 1870 of Rupert's Land by the HBC to the Canadian government. They saw this land as belonging to the Indians, and one of their chiefs, PASKWĀW, demanded that the money paid to the HBC by the Canadian government be turned over to the Indians. The treaty commissioners explained that the Canadian government recognized the right of the Indians to the land and wanted to make a treaty that would deal justly with their claims. However, the commissioners further explained that the HBC also possessed rights to the land and that the government had to deal as justly with the company as it did with the Indians. The Saulteaux apparently found this answer satisfactory, and Coté was permitted to sign Treaty no. 4, but only on behalf of his own band.

Coté returned to the Swan River area and selected a site 20 miles below Fort Pelly for his reserve. The site did not please some of the woodland hunters and about one-third of the band joined the Saulteaux living on the Shoal River. With the remainder of the band (some 270), Coté stayed on the reserve he had chosen and farmed there until his death in 1884.

Gabriel Coté owes the regard accorded him by whites largely to his ability to work well with them. His relationship with the HBC explains why the treaty commissioners mistakenly regarded him as the principal Saulteaux chief, and his willingness to cooperate with both company and government officials brought the distrust of other Saulteaux leaders. Oral tradition among some Saulteaux bands to this day names Coté a "company chief," or one who owed his position to the HBC. His readiness to accept a new way of life led those who wanted to retain the old ways to reject his leadership.

JOHN L. TOBIAS

PAC, RG 10, B3, 3614, file 4063; 3625, file 5489; 3642, file 7581; 3654, file 8904; 3716, file 22541. Can., Parl., *Sessional papers*, 1883, IV, no.5. Morris, *Treaties of Canada with the Indians*. A. J. Ray, *Indians in the fur trade: their role as trappers, hunters, and middlemen in the lands southwest of Hudson Bay, 1660–1870* (Toronto and Buffalo, N.Y., 1974).

MINAHIKOSIS (Little Pine, literally little pine tree, known in French as **Petit Pin**), chief of a band of Plains Cree; b.*c.* 1830 probably in the vicinity of Fort Pitt (Sask.); d. in April 1885 on the Poundmaker Reserve (Sask.).

Little Pine, the son of a Blackfoot woman and a Plains Cree warrior, lived most of his life near Fort Pitt and Battleford (Sask.). In the 1860s he won a reputation as a warrior while participating in the armed migration of Plains Crees into Blackfoot territory which contained the last of the buffalo ranges. He was in the forefront of the Cree effort to wrest control of the Cypress Hills from the Blackfeet and was one of the leaders at the battle of Belly River (near Lethbridge, Alta) in 1870 where they checked the Cree migration. By the end of the decade, Little Pine led his own band of about 300 persons.

Determined to follow the life of the buffalo hunt and to preserve the culture based upon it, Little Pine refused to take treaty with the Canadian government in 1876 along with other Cree leaders of the Saskatchewan River district. He continued his resistance to Treaty no.6 in 1877 and 1878. Little Pine and Big Bear [MISTAHIMASKWA], who also refused to sign, found the treaty inadequate because it contained no guarantees against the imposition of an alien culture. They were especially concerned about the application of the white man's laws, a concern made more pressing by the recent arrival of the North-West Mounted Police. Not until July 1879 did Little Pine adhere to the treaty, and then only as a means of obtaining assistance for his people who faced starvation because of the disappearance of the buffalo from the Canadian ranges.

Even after taking treaty, Little Pine wanted to follow the life of the hunt and moved to the Cypress Hills area to be close to the last buffalo ranges in the United States. From 1879 to 1883 he made friends with the traditional enemy of the Crees, the Blackfeet, and especially with their leader Crowfoot [ISAPO-MUXIKA], who had also come to the Cypress Hills in search of buffalo. Along with other plains chiefs who were dissatisfied with the treaties, Little Pine began efforts to establish one huge reserve for all the Plains Indians. They asked the Canadian government to establish adjoining reserves for the various plains tribes and thereby create an Indian territory of almost 1,000 square miles. The government refused the request, accusing Little Pine of trying to establish an Indian confederacy. Instead, wishing to break up the concentration of Indians in the Cypress Hills, the government insisted that the bands disperse and return to the districts where they had lived before taking treaty; because all the bands were suffering from hunger, the government was able to force them to leave by refusing assistance until they complied.

In 1883 Little Pine and his band moved to the Battleford area and camped next to the reserve of Poundmaker [PĪTIKWAHANAPIWĪYIN]. With Poundmaker he organized a council of Cree chiefs of the Battleford and Fort Pitt area to be held in June 1884 near Battleford to discuss the idea of one large reserve for all Plains Crees. In the mean time, the government was pressing Little Pine to allow them to survey a small reserve for his band, but he declined.

At the Sun Dance (Thirst Dance) which preceded the council at Battleford, a NWMP unit under the command of Leif Newry Fitzroy Crozier* came into the camp to arrest an Indian for assaulting a government official. The Indians resented this intrusion, and a crisis developed that could have resulted in the annihilation of the police unit had Little Pine and Big Bear not prevented bloodshed by appealing for peace. To avert further trouble, the council was disbanded before the plan for the creation of one large reserve could be discussed. Nevertheless, Little Pine and Big Bear persisted in their efforts to create a large Indian territory. On two occasions between June and August 1884 they requested reserves adjacent to existing ones near Battleford, but were refused. Undaunted, Little Pine and Big Bear continued their efforts. At a council of the Plains Crees of the Saskatchewan River area, held at Duck Lake in August 1884, plans were made for a meeting during the summer of 1885 of all Plains Crees [*see* KAMĪYISTOWESIT]. In addition, Little Pine invited the Blackfeet to meet with him in the late spring of 1885 to enlist their support for the proposal.

Little Pine's activities in late 1884 and early 1885 were severely curtailed by eye problems and general ill health. Reports did, however, continue to reach government officials of Little Pine's leadership in the agitation and of his alleged call to arms if all else failed. By March 1885 Little Pine's followers were again suffering from hunger and he led them to Battleford to appeal for aid. When they found the town deserted they began to loot it for food, despite Little Pine's efforts to prevent this action. On 31 March he and his band went to the Poundmaker Reserve, and several days later Little Pine succumbed to his illnesses. Following Little Pine's death the band remained at the Poundmaker Reserve; they participated in the battle of Cut Knife Hill in May 1885, and as a group were regarded as rebels.

Little Pine's efforts on behalf of his people were an integral part of the unrest on the prairies in the two decades preceding the rebellion of 1885. He attempted to avert the calamity his people faced with the disappearance of the buffalo and to maintain their political and cultural integrity against the threat from alien values. That his efforts failed does not detract from his importance.

JOHN L. TOBIAS

PAC, RG 10, B3, 3576, file 309; 3582, file 949; 3604, file 2589; 3655, file 9000; 3668, file 10644; 3672, file 10853; 3697, file 15423; 3701, file 17169; 3703, file 17728; 3705, file 17936; 3745, file 29506/4. PAM, HBCA, B.60/a/34. H. A. Dempsey, *Crowfoot, chief of the Blackfeet* (Edmonton, 1972). W. B. Fraser, "Big Bear, Indian patriot," *Historical essays on the prairie provinces*, ed. Donald Swainson (Toronto, 1970), 71–88. Desmond Morton, *The last war drum: the North West campaign of 1885* (Toronto, 1972). F. G. Roe, *The North American buffalo: a critical study of the species in its wild state* (Toronto, 1951). Stanley, *Birth of western Canada*.

MISTAHIMASKWA (Big Bear, known in French as **Gros Ours)**, Plains Cree chief; b. *c.* 1825, probably near Fort Carlton (Sask.); d. 17 Jan. 1888 on the Poundmaker Reserve (Sask.). Over the course of his life he had several wives and at least four sons.

Big Bear's parents are unknown but may have been Saulteaux; he seems to have grown up with the Plains Cree bands that usually wintered along the North Saskatchewan River and hunted south every summer for buffalo. He received his power bundle, song, and probably his name as a result of a vision of the Bear Spirit, the most powerful spirit venerated by the Crees. The power bundle, never opened unless to be worn ritually in war or in dance, contained a skinned-out bear's paw, complete with claws, sewn on a scarlet flannel. At appropriate times, Big Bear wore the paw around his neck; he believed that when the weight of it rested against his soul, he was in a perfect power position and that nothing then could hurt him.

In November 1862 Big Bear was reported by Charles Alston Messiter to be "the head chief" of a "large camp of Crees" near Fort Carlton. However, Hudson's Bay Company trader John Sinclair later reported that about 1865 Big Bear "removed from Carlton to Pitt, and became the head man of a small band of his relatives who resided at Pitt, numbering about twelve tents, or perhaps twenty men." Sinclair knew him there as a "good Indian" but did not acknowledge Big Bear as a chief until much later, which implies less that Big Bear had little authority among his people than that he was too independent to suit either traders or missionaries.

The traditional activities of hunting and warfare occupied Big Bear until the 1870s brought the police, the treaties, and the end of the buffalo. He and his band are known to have taken part in the hostilities between the Plains Cree and the Blackfeet which culminated in the battle at Belly River (near Lethbridge, Alta) in October 1870. Jerry Potts* later reported that between 200 and 300 Crees and 40 Blackfeet were killed; if these estimates are correct, Belly River was the largest Indian battle known to have been fought on the Canadian plains. It was certainly the last.

As the number of whites on the plains increased, so Big Bear was confirmed in his independent spirit. In 1873 he clashed with Gabriel Dumont* when the Métis leader tried to dictate how the buffalo should be run on the summer hunt. In the summer of 1874 HBC trader William McKay was commissioned by the Canadian government to visit the Plains Indians with presents of tea and tobacco and to explain carefully why the North-West Mounted Police were coming. McKay reported that the Plains Cree "all received the presents in a friendly manner," but that "two families of Big Bear's band . . . objected to receive any, stating they were given them as a bribe to facilitate a future treaty." McKay also records that Big Bear's camp consisted of 65 lodges (about 520 people), while that of Sweet

Grass [Wikaskokiseyin*], who as early as 1871 had been named "The Chief of the Country" by the HBC and who had been baptized Abraham by Father Albert Lacombe*, had only 56.

Big Bear proved even more problematic to the Reverend George Millward McDougall*, commissioned in 1875 to "tranquillize" the Plains Indians regarding the treaty Canada planned for them. The Methodist missionary found most of the "principal men . . . moderate in their demands," but thought Big Bear a mischief-maker because he was "trying to take the lead in their council." Big Bear had declared: "when we set a fox-trap we scatter pieces of meat all round, but when the fox gets into the trap we knock him on the head; We want no bait; let your chiefs come like men and talk to us."

Lieutenant Governor Alexander MORRIS came "like a man" in August 1876 to negotiate Treaty no.6, which dealt with the rights to 120,000 square miles of land, and he found Big Bear something more than a mischief-maker. The chief did not come to Fort Carlton, and he only appeared at Fort Pitt on 13 September, the day after all official ceremonies were completed. Sweet Grass and the other Cree and Chipewyan chiefs urged him to sign, as they had, but Big Bear, who said he had been sent to speak for all Crees and Assiniboins still hunting on the plains, replied, "Stop, my friends. . . . I will request [the governor] to save me from what I most dread – hanging; it was not given to us to have the rope about our necks." Morris concluded that Big Bear was simply a coward; however, since the Crees believed their souls to reside along the nape of their necks, the statement might also be seen as a powerfully prophetic metaphor of what would happen within a decade to all the Plains Indians. In any case, Big Bear did not sign, the first major chief on the Canadian prairies not to do so.

Big Bear refused to take treaty for the next six years, which was as long as the buffalo lasted. His defiance drew more and more independent warriors to his camp. He met the new lieutenant governor of the North-West Territories, David Laird*, at Sounding Lake (Alta) in August 1878, but he would neither sign nor accept presents, and so there could be no question of his designating a reserve. In October the band led by Little Pine [MINAHIKOSIS] discovered surveyors near the present site of Medicine Hat (Alta); the chief claimed they had no right to survey and sent for Big Bear who was at the Red Deer Forks (Sask.), while the surveyors sent for the police at Fort Walsh (Sask.). Colonel Acheson Gosford Irvine* agreed with Big Bear that the surveyors should stop their work until the matter was settled between Big Bear and the lieutenant governor "when the leaves come out."

In the winter of 1878–79 Big Bear was at the height of his influence; the buffalo had not come north that winter (they never would again in numbers) and the plains people now understood that their tiny reserves and $5 annual payments would mean nothing if the hunting, which Morris had assured them would continue as before, were destroyed. In March 1879 Father Jean-Marie-Joseph Lestanc, who was wintering with the Métis at Red Deer Forks, reported: "All the tribes – that is the Sioux, Blackfoot, Bloods, Sarcees, Assiniboines, Stoneys, Crees and Saulteaux – now form but one party. . . . Big Bear, up to this time, cannot be accused of uttering a single objectionable word, but the fact of his being the head and soul of all our Canadian plains Indians leaves room for conjecture. . . . All are in great want. . . . [They] consider the treaties . . . are of no value. . . ." Superintendent Leif Newry Fitzroy Crozier* of the NWMP rode to the forks to investigate and reported that nothing had come of the gathering. However, several thousand Indians and Métis did spend a hard winter there and it is possible that Sitting Bull [TA-TANKA I-YOTANK], Crowfoot [ISAPO-MUXIKA], and perhaps even Gabriel Dumont consulted with Big Bear and the disillusioned warriors who were continually joining his band; if cooperation between these traditional enemies had resulted, it would have been an event unprecedented in western Indian history.

Edgar Dewdney*, Sir John A. Macdonald*'s new Indian commissioner, arrived at Fort Walsh in June 1879. Big Bear could not confront him with a united Indian front but did speak with him for several days about the vanishing buffalo and the inadequate treaties. Because of their destitution, however, Little Pine signed the treaty on behalf of 472 people on 2 July and was immediately paid treaty money and given rations; Big Bear still refused. He moved south into Montana where most of Canada's treaty Indians, with Dewdney's encouragement, soon joined him, and where along with the American Indians they hunted the last of the buffalo. By 1882 these too were gone and the treaty Indians began returning north to petition the government for food. Big Bear's band tried fishing at Cypress Lake (Sask.) and eating gophers, but it was hopeless. On 8 Dec. 1882 Big Bear signed Treaty no.6 at Fort Walsh so that the police would give his people food. His personal following then numbered 247.

Big Bear said his people wanted their reservation near Fort Pitt, and in July 1883 his band moved north at the government's expense. He spent that summer visiting his old friends on their small reserves along the North Saskatchewan. All were destitute: agriculture, their only activity, was either non-existent or pathetic. That fall Big Bear began to harass the government in a new way by changing his mind about where he wanted his reserve. A series of visits, by Indian Department officials Hayter Reed and Dewdney, and by the deputy superintendent general of Indian affairs, Lawrence Vankoughnet*, from Ottawa, simply confirmed him in his stubbornness, and when his rations were cut off because of it the band freighted for the HBC while he sent messages to all the Cree chiefs to join him in a united Indian council to work for one large Indian reserve on the North Saskatchewan. To accomplish this, the *Saskatchewan Herald* reported that Big Bear "has made up his mind to go to Ottawa . . . if there is a head to the [Indian] Department he is bound to find him, for he will deal with no one else." By April 1884 Big Bear and his band, swollen to about 500, began moving toward Battleford and by 16 June well over 2,000 Indians from the Saskatchewan reserves were gathered at the reserve of Poundmaker [PĪTIKWAHANAPIWĪYIN] for a Thirst Dance given by Big Bear; it was the largest united effort ever made by the Plains Cree.

Thirst Dances were expressly forbidden by the government; in any case the government did not allow rations to Indians off their reserves. However, Big Bear's dance proceeded and during the celebration Kāwīcitwemot, a young warrior, beat John Craig, the farm instructor of the Little Pine reserve, when the latter abused him and refused to give him food. Craig called the police and Crozier arrived from Battleford with about 90 men. Crozier was incensed at Craig's "indiscretion," but since the police had been called, it was necessary that they arrest the culprit. When the police and some 400 armed, furious warriors faced each other, a single shot would have plunged the northwest into an Indian war. The police managed to haul Kāwīcitwemot from among his fellows while Big Bear, Little Pine, and Poundmaker prevented violence by shouting, "Peace, Peace!"; later the police placated the warriors to an extent by handing out large food supplies. Face had been saved all around, but as Crozier reported to Dewdney, "it is yet incomprehensible to me how some one did not fire. . . ." Unless the department could "*keep* their confidence . . . there is only one other [policy] – and that is to fight them."

Big Bear did not want to fight Canada; he knew that in such a battle, as Crozier wrote with heavy irony, "the country no doubt would get rid of the Indians and all troublesome questions in connection with them in a comparatively short time. . . ." Big Bear's demands are clearly presented in the rough English notes made of two speeches he gave to chiefs at Duck Lake (Sask.) and at Carlton in August 1884. First, he argued that the treaty they signed had been changed by Ottawa: "half the sweet things were taken out and lots of sour things left in." A new treaty with a new reserve concept was necessary. Secondly, the Indians needed one representative from all the tribes to speak for them. "The choice of our representative ought to be given to us every four years." He concluded: "Crowfoot is working for the same thing as I am."

All summer Big Bear carried this message for a united stand against the government; on 17 August he met Louis RIEL in Prince Albert (Sask.). They had met in Montana earlier apparently without result, but this meeting disturbed Dewdney more than any gathering of Indians. Hayter Reed was ordered to investigate the Indian complaints and when his incredibly complacent report was at last forwarded to Vankoughnet in Ottawa the latter reminded Dewdney on 4 Feb. 1885 that the Indians "have really received very much more than the Govt. was under the Treaty bound to give them."

Such official complacency destroyed Big Bear's last attempts at negotiated change: during that winter, 1884–85, the warrior society – those men who retold their old *coup* stories every night but who had fought no enemy nor so much as run a buffalo in four years – gradually separated themselves from the old chief. The band was camped with the Wood Crees at Frog Lake (Alta), 50 miles north of Fort Pitt, when the news arrived that the Métis had routed Crozier at Duck Lake on 26 March. On 2 April Big Bear's men, led by his son Āyimisīs (Little Bad Man) and the war chief Wandering Spirit [KAPAPAMAHCHAKWEW] burst into the Maundy Thursday service in the Frog Lake Catholic church and forced all the unarmed whites of the settlement outside. Wandering Spirit began by shooting Indian agent Thomas Trueman Quinn; Big Bear rushed forward shouting, "Stop, stop!" But there was no stopping the men, warriors once again. Nine men, including the two Oblate priests [*see* Léon-Adélard FAFARD] were killed; only two white women and William Bleasdell Cameron*, the HBC clerk who was protected by the Cree wife of trader James Kay Simpson, escaped. When Simpson returned that evening from a trading trip to Pitt, he found the settlement destroyed and the warriors dancing the Scalp Dance. Later, at Big Bear's trial, Simpson reported the conversation he had had with his friend of 40 years: "now this affair . . . will be all on you, carried on your back." The old chief answered: "it is not my doings, and the young men won't listen, and I am very sorry for what has been done."

When news of Frog Lake spread, the name Big Bear became synonymous with "bloodthirsty killer," but in fact Āyimisīs and Wandering Spirit were now the band leaders. On 13 April they surrounded Fort Pitt with 250 warriors, and sent an ultimatum to NWMP Inspector Francis Jeffrey DICKENS that, unless the civilians surrendered and the police left, they would attack. Big Bear wrote a note to an old acquaintance, Sergeant J. A. Martin: "Try and get away before the afternoon, as the young men are all wild and hard to keep in hand." On 14 April, hopelessly outnumbered, Dickens and his 25 men retreated by river to Battleford while the 28 civilians led by HBC trader William John McLean* and his family surrendered to the Indians. The warriors then pillaged and burned the empty fort.

From testimony given by McLean at Big Bear's

trial, it is clear that the old chief did his best to protect the captives in camp but he was an outcast; later, when asked how Āyimisīs had treated Big Bear, McLean replied, "With utter contempt." Without him, however, the warriors demonstrated no wider strategy than simply local pillage; they made no attempt to join Poundmaker in his attack on Battleford or Riel at Batoche. Finally, Major-General Thomas Bland Strange* and his Canadian troops arrived at Fort Pitt and on 28 May they attacked Wandering Spirit's strong position on a hill north of Frenchman Butte. Strange was repulsed but the Indians retreated as well; during the battle Big Bear remained in the rear with the captives and women. However, a story current to this day on the Poundmaker Reserve recounts that when Samuel Benfield Steele*'s scouts attacked and routed Big Bear's followers at Loon Lake Narrows on 3 June, Big Bear walked between the attacking police and the fleeing Cree with his "bear's claw [that] rested in the hollow of his throat. As long as he wore that claw there, nothing could hurt him. . . . It was as if he placed an invisible wall between his people and the soldiers."

After Loon Lake the band further scattered before General Frederick Dobson Middleton*'s advancing soldiers, victorious over the Métis at Batoche on 12 May. Kāwīcitwemot had been killed at Frenchman Butte; Āyimisīs fled to Montana; Wandering Spirit surrendered and in November 1885 he and five others of Big Bear's band were hanged for their part in the Frog Lake killings. Big Bear slipped past all the soldiers looking for him and gave himself up to a startled policeman at Fort Carlton on 2 July 1885.

Big Bear and 14 of his band were transported to Regina, and his trial before Judge Hugh Richardson* and a jury of six on a charge of treason-felony began on 11 Sept. 1885. Poundmaker had already been convicted of the same charge – intending to levy war against the queen – and, though evidence was provided that the old chief had taken no part in the fighting and had tried to prevent bloodshed, Richardson made it clear to the jury that a claim for innocence could only be made if Big Bear had actually left his band when it "rose in insurrection." Since there was no question of that, within 15 minutes the jury brought in a sentence of "Guilty with a recommendation to mercy." On 25 September, Richardson sentenced him to three years in Stony Mountain Penitentiary. Just before the sentencing, Big Bear made one last speech for his people: "'Many of my band are hiding in the woods, paralyzed with terror. . . . I plead again,' he cried, stretching forth his hands, 'to you, the chiefs of the white men's laws, for pity and help to the outcasts of my band!'" The court record of the speech cannot be located; only Cameron, a witness at the trial, mentions it.

At Stony Mountain Big Bear was taught carpentry; in July 1886, perhaps because of Poundmaker's death at Blackfoot Crossing (Alta), he was baptized. Crowfoot and other chiefs not involved in the rebellion petitioned Dewdney several times for Big Bear's release, and in February 1887 the prison doctor reported that "Convict No. 103 [Big Bear] . . . is getting worse. He is weak and shows signs of great debility by fainting spells which are growing more frequent. . . ." As a result, on 4 March 1887, he was released. Those of his band still in Canada had been scattered among various reserves, and so he returned to the Poundmaker Reserve on 8 March. He died there on 17 Jan. 1888, perhaps from the final mortifying effects of prison and purposelessness. The Indian agent wrote of his death, "He has had domestic troubles lately, his wife preferring the society of other men. She would leave the Reserve and the old veteran would follow her for days, until he overdid himself." He was buried in the Roman Catholic cemetery on the Poundmaker Reserve, roughly on the site of his last Thirst Dance.

Big Bear was a traditional chief, chosen and followed by the Plains Cree because of his wisdom rather than because he was acknowledged by trader or missionary or government official for his cooperation. For him the land, the water, the air, and the buffalo were gifts from the Great Spirit to all mankind; everyone might use them, but in no sense could one person own them or forbid their use to others. He saw white civilization as humiliatingly destructive of Indian civilization, but he resisted whites with ideas, not useless guns. He was the last of the great chiefs to try to unite the North American peoples against European invasion, and to that end he wanted a new treaty: one huge reserve for all Plains Indians. If his young men had not followed Riel's example, perhaps he could have persuaded other Plains chiefs that his way was their only hope.

The penitentiary records list Big Bear as 5′ $5\frac{1}{4}$″ tall; photographs reveal him to be stocky, with a strong, craggy face. John George DONKIN in his book *Trooper and redskin* . . . described him as "a little shrivelled-up piece of humanity . . . his cunning face seamed and wrinkled like crumpled parchment." Yet Cameron, when referring to Big Bear, corroborated Dewdney's evaluation of his independent personality and wrote: "Big Bear had great natural gifts. . . . Had [he] been a white man and educated, he would have made a great lawyer or a great statesman. . . . [He was] imperious, outspoken, fearless." He was indeed a great statesman, but not in the white tradition.

RUDY WIEBE

PAC, RG 10, B3, 3576; 3692; 3697, file 15423; RG 13, B2, 804–25. PAM, MG 12, B1, Corr., nos.901, 1136. Can., Parl., *Sessional papers*, 1882, V, no.6; 1886, XIII, no.52. J. G. Donkin, *Trooper and redskin in the far north-west: recollections of life in the North-West Mounted Police, Cana-*

da, 1884–1888 (London, 1889; repr. Toronto, 1973). C. A. Messiter, *Sport and adventure among the North American Indians* (London, 1890). Morris, *Treaties of Canada with the Indians*. C. P. [Mulvany], *The history of the North-West rebellion of 1885 . . .* (Toronto, 1885; repr. 1971). *Settlers and rebels: being the official reports to parliament of the activities of the Royal North-West Mounted Police force from 1882–1885* (Toronto, 1973). *Edmonton Bulletin*, 2 May 1885. *Lethbridge Herald* (Lethbridge, Alta.), 7 Jan. 1909. *Lethbridge News* (Lethbridge), 30 April 1890. *Saskatchewan Herald* (Battleford, [Sask.]), 18 Nov. 1878, 24 March 1879, 8 March 1884, 15 June 1885.

W. B. Cameron, *Blood red the sun* (rev. ed., Calgary, 1950), 214–15. H. A. Dempsey, *Crowfoot, chief of the Blackfeet* (Edmonton, 1972); *Jerry Potts, plainsman* (Calgary, 1966). W. B. Fraser, "Big Bear, Indian patriot," *Historical essays on the prairie provinces*, ed. Donald Swainson (Toronto, 1970), 71–88. Constance Kerr Sissons, *John Kerr* (Toronto, 1946). Stanley, *Birth of western Canada*; *Louis Riel*. Rudy Wiebe, *The temptations of Big Bear* (Toronto, 1973). R. S. Allen, "Big Bear," *Saskatchewan Hist.* (Saskatoon), 25 (1972): 1–17. Maria Campbell, "She who knows the truth of Big Bear: history calls him traitor, but history sometimes lies," *Maclean's* (Toronto), 88 (1975), no.9: 46–50. D. G. Mandelbaum, "The Plains Cree," American Museum of Natural Hist., *Anthropological Papers* (New York), 37 (1941): 155–316. Rudy Wiebe, "All that's left of Big Bear: in a small bag, in a small room in New York City, the great spirit rests," *Maclean's*, 88 (1975), no.9: 52–55.

MONRO. *See* MUNRO

MONTGOMERY, DONALD, educator and politician; b. 3 May 1848 in Valleyfield, P.E.I., son of Malcolm Montgomery and Christine MacDonald; d. 14 May 1890 in Charlottetown, P.E.I.

The youngest child of a farmer who had emigrated from Scotland in 1840, Donald Montgomery received his early education in the predominantly Gaelic-speaking Scottish Presbyterian community of Valleyfield in Queens County. In 1865 and 1866 he taught in rural schools in southern Kings County before proceeding to Prince of Wales College in Charlottetown for at least one year of study, during which he won several prizes and came first in his class. At some point prior to mid 1868 he also attended the colony's Normal School, and by the early 1870s was master of the grammar school at Harrington, near Charlottetown.

On 25 Aug. 1874 Montgomery was appointed master of the Normal School and Model School, at an annual salary of $650. He soon began reorganizing the institution, which had degenerated into more or less a grammar school for Charlottetown students, and he attempted to make its focus once again the training of teachers. Montgomery had one assistant in the Normal School and at various times either one or two in the Model School department. The role of religion in the public educational system was a central issue in the political life of Prince Edward Island during these years, and in April 1876 he testified before a parliamentary committee investigating education that his institution was entirely secular in practice and was modelled after the Albany Normal School in New York State. The committee, whose establishment he had earlier recommended, reported that Montgomery's normal school, although an excellent secondary academy, was still not providing uniform professional training for Island teachers. However, the fault was not entirely the master's, because candidates for teaching licences were not required to attend the Normal School, and in fact under the provisions of the education act of 1868 were offered little incentive to do so. Montgomery's work had earlier been praised by the local press and by William McPhail*, the thorough school visitor for Queens County.

In September 1876 the government of Louis Henry Davies* came to power on a promise to establish a completely non-sectarian school system. Although Montgomery apparently agreed with the thrust of the new government's reforming Public Schools Act of 1877, he was dismissed in July of that year. The most probable explanation is that the government wished to make the Normal School into a more thoroughly professional institution and believed that Montgomery lacked the qualifications necessary for the position. Rumours circulated as to whether he was offered another post, but soon after his dismissal he left the Island to enrol in the law school attached to McGill College. He had never fully abandoned his studies, and indeed during his first year as master of the Normal School had taken classes in Latin and Greek at Prince of Wales College.

The Davies government, a coalition, rapidly disintegrated, and in September 1878 Montgomery, who had returned to the Island in the summer, won a by-election for the Belfast constituency, which included his native district. He was re-elected in the general election of 9 April 1879 and during the two assembly sessions of that year, although an Orangeman, he supported the Conservatives led by the Roman Catholic William Wilfred Sullivan*. Despite being "by nature, remarkably quiet, retiring and self-contained," he immediately established himself as a formidable debater. On 25 September the Sullivan government appointed him, at age 31, chief superintendent of education (at a salary of $1,200), which necessitated his resignation from the assembly. During the committee hearings of 1876 he had recommended the creation of such an office, which Davies had instituted in the following year. As chief superintendent he was to enforce the Public Schools Act of 1877, prepare annual reports, suggest improvements in the system, and, in general, supervise publicly funded education under the direction of the board of education, composed of the cabinet, the principal of Prince of Wales College, and himself.

It appears from all surviving evidence that Montgomery was an excellent choice as chief superintendent, despite predictable political criticism at the time of his appointment. He was a man of clear judgement, outstanding executive ability, and great energy. He at once set about classifying all Island schools into three groups, according to the level of work done in each. In the early 1880s he also introduced a uniform course of studies for each grade; on 24 Jan. 1883 he wrote, "I look upon the adoption of it as the most important step yet taken in the administration of our Public School system." As a man who had begun teaching with the lowest classification of licence and had experience at every level of education in the province, little escaped his notice. He encouraged the improvement of school accommodations, equipment, appearance, and surroundings and during his tenure the problem of vacant schools virtually disappeared. A constant goal was "to give the teacher a more ennobling view of his calling," and to this end he put the full weight of his office behind the establishment of the "Provincial Educational Institute," a sort of annual convention which teachers were given two days to attend each October. He was the institute's first president, and apparently it was he who arranged for papers to be delivered by professors from Prince of Wales and by leading teachers. The institute served as a voluntary association of teachers, and it appears that Montgomery had had such a body in mind for several years: in 1875 he and William McPhail had organized the short-lived Queens County Teachers Association. Yet he was not successful in all his endeavours: daily average school attendance, as a percentage of enrolment, remained, in his opinion, unsatisfactorily low (although certainly no worse than in most provinces); his proposal for the appointment of an Acadian professor at Prince of Wales to specialize in the training of French-speaking teachers was not acted upon by the government; and he appears to have been frustrated in his desire for a "more practical" curriculum.

Although not an extrovert, Montgomery took a personal and visible interest in the working and results of the educational system. He attempted to make rural students attending Prince of Wales College and Normal School (amalgamated in 1879) feel welcome in the capital, he personally sponsored a prize in French at the college, and he encouraged students and former teachers when they continued their studies elsewhere; one suspects that he took a particular interest in those of Scottish background from his own part of the Island. He inspected the advanced schools himself, although in later years he sometimes entrusted the task to young university graduates whom he knew well. In addition, he played a leading role in the intellectual life of Charlottetown, organizing the Natural History Society and actively participating in the Shakespeare Club.

Montgomery, whose heart had been weakened by vaccination against smallpox late in 1885, died in 1890 at age 42. He left a widow, Mary Isabella McPhail (daughter of the former school visitor), whom he had married on 10 Aug. 1887; they had no children. In an obituary the Charlottetown *Examiner* reported rumours "that he entertained doubts at one time concerning the Divinity of our Lord . . . doubts . . . long since removed." Montgomery's father-in-law, in a family letter, reported that "Mr. Montgomery was '*satisfied*' in departing this life. I say satisfied because that was the word he used."

Donald Montgomery, as master of the Normal School and especially as chief superintendent of education, was part of a Scottish Protestant hegemony in the educational system of Prince Edward Island, one of the first major figures in that tradition to be born in the New World. He played perhaps the most important single role in translating the sound school legislation of 1877 into sound practice. When he died the Island had an excellent educational system for a rural province of that era, a source of pride in the difficult years after confederation. His earlier political connections were clearly regarded as irrelevant and the press overflowed with the sentiment that, because of his exceptional administrative ability, he had been exactly the man for the job and had set a standard against which the performance of his successors would be measured.

IAN ROSS ROBERTSON

[Donald Montgomery's annual reports as chief superintendent of education are found in: P.E.I., Legislative Council, *Journal*, 1880, app.7; House of Assembly, *Journal*, 1881, app.C; 1882, app.D; 1883, app.B; 1884, app.B; 1885, app.F; 1886, app.A; 1887; app.A; 1888, app.A; 1889, app. A; 1890, app.C. His reports to the Board of Education as master of the Normal School were not published, but the following should be consulted: *Reports of the visitors of schools, for the three counties of Prince Edward Island* (Charlottetown), for 1874 (especially p.36) and 1875 (pp.6–7), as well as the *Report of the parliamentary committee appointed to investigate and report upon the manner in which the education law has been and is being carried on in the public educational establishments of this Island* (Charlottetown, [1876]), 4, 15, 19, 20, 22, also published in P.E.I., House of Assembly, *Journal*, 1876, app.AA. For his brief career as an assemblyman, *see* P.E.I., House of Assembly, *Debates and proc.*, 1879. I. R. R.]

The following items of interest for this biography were found in the Sir Andrew Macphail papers in the possession of Mrs Dorothy Lindsay (Montreal); J. H. Good to Macphail, 20 April 1884; Montgomery to Macphail, 3 Nov., 15 Dec. 1883; 5 March 1886; William McPhail to Andrew Macphail, 17 May 1890; "Music and drama" scrapbook; and a brief undated (1888?) article on Montgomery. The Lindsay-Macphail scrapbook I, also in the possession of Mrs Lindsay, includes the following useful item: Andrew Macphail to

Catherine McPhail, 29 Sept. 1884. PAPEI, Natural Hist. Soc. for P.E.I., Letters; Minute book: 1–19; RG 5, Minutes, 25 Aug. 1874; 30 Sept., 24 Nov., 22 Dec. 1876; 25 Sept. 1879; RG 16, Land registry records, Conveyance registers, liber 16: f.96; liber 26: f.784. Supreme Court of Prince Edward Island (Charlottetown), Estates division, liber 12: f.415 (will of Donald Montgomery, 10 May 1890) (mfm. at PAPEI).

Educational Rev. (Saint John, N.B.), 1 (1887–88). Grand Orange Lodge of Prince Edward Island, *Annual report*, 1879; 6, 17, 22 (copy in the possession of the Grand Orange Lodge of P.E.I., Charlottetown). P.E.I., House of Assembly, *Journal*, 1868, app.BB; 1875, app.CC; 1881, app.C: 34; 1891, app.A: xxii, 72; Legislative Council, *Journal*, 1866, app.13: 284; 1867, app.6a, warrant nos.481, 1802, app.7; 1880, app.7: 23. *Daily Patriot* (Charlottetown), 15 May 1890. *Examiner* (Charlottetown), 7 Dec. 1874; 28 June 1875; 24 April, 25 Dec. 1876; 30 June, 11 July, 17 Dec. 1877; 18 April, 1 May, 8 June, 25 July, 19, 20, 26 Sept. 1878; 29 Sept., 3 Oct. 1879; 10 Aug. 1887; 15, 16 May 1890. *Herald* (Charlottetown), 13 Feb., 11 Sept., 9 Oct. 1889. *Island Argus* (Charlottetown), 13 April, 28 Dec. 1875. *Island Farmer* (Summerside, P.E.I.), 8, 15, 22 May 1890. *Island Guardian and Christian Chronicle* (Charlottetown), 16 May 1890. *Patriot* (Charlottetown), 12 July 1877; 13, 19, 21, 28 Sept. 1878; 13, 27 Sept., 2 Oct. 1879. *Pioneer* (Alberton, P.E.I.; Montague, P.E.I.), 11 July 1877, 6 March 1878, 1 Oct. 1879, 5 March 1880. *Prince Edward Island Agriculturist* (Summerside), 19 May 1890. *Summerside Journal and Western Pioneer*, 22 May 1890. A. [J.] Leard, "The historical development of the Prince Edward Island Teachers' Federation to 1969" (M.Ed. thesis, Univ. of New Brunswick, Fredericton, 1971), 26–27. M. O. McKenna, "The impact of cultural forces on commitment to education in the province of Prince Edward Island" (PHD thesis, Boston College, Chestnut Hill, Mass., 1964), 171–72, 263. Robertson, "Religion, politics, and education in P.E.I.," chap.9–11; epilogue; "Sir Andrew Macphail as a social critic" (PHD thesis, Univ. of Toronto, 1974), 22, 29. S. N. Robertson, "The public school system," *Past and present of P.E.I.* (MacKinnon and Warburton), 381a–89a.

MOODIE, SUSANNA. *See* STRICKLAND

MOODY, RICHARD CLEMENT, soldier, colonial administrator, and public servant; b. 13 Feb. 1813 at St Ann's Garrison, Barbados, West Indies, second son of Thomas Moody, RE; m. in 1852 at Newcastle upon Tyne, England, Mary Susannah, daughter of Joseph Hawks, justice of the peace and banker, and they had 11 children; d. 31 March 1887 at Bournemouth, England.

Richard Clement Moody's father, who had been private secretary to several important officials in the West Indies, was seconded to the Colonial Office in 1824 because of his knowledge of the islands. Richard was educated in England by a tutor and at private schools. At the age of 14 he entered the Royal Military Academy at Woolwich (now part of London), leaving in December 1829 to obtain instruction in the Ordnance Survey of Great Britain. Gazetted 2nd lieutenant in the Corps of Royal Engineers on 5 Nov. 1830, he was posted to the Ordnance Survey of Ireland in 1832. The following year, he was posted to St Vincent, West Indies, and from July 1838 to October 1841 he was professor of fortifications at Woolwich. Between these postings he suffered two of the serious illnesses which were to mark his army life. On 23 Jan. 1835 he was promoted lst lieutenant.

In 1841 Moody was named lieutenant governor of the Falkland Islands, a region considered of some importance because of the interest in Antarctica. His report on the natural features of the islands won him commendation, and in 1843 he was appointed the first governor and commander-in-chief of the islands and their dependencies. The British government being unwilling to spend funds, Moody employed the small garrison force to erect buildings. He governed with the aid of an Executive and a Legislative Council. The colonists, though they liked him, did not credit him with doing much for development: no survey was made and no system of land tenure devised.

On his return to England, Moody was promoted lst captain in August 1849. He served briefly on special duty at the Colonial Office, and then rejoined the Royal Engineers in November. After being given command of Newcastle upon Tyne, he served in Malta, where he was promoted lieutenant-colonel in January 1855. He commanded the Royal Engineers at Edinburgh with some distinction and his ability as a draughtsman, evident in a plan for the restoration of Edinburgh Castle, attracted the attention of the secretary of war. On 28 April 1858 he was promoted brevet colonel.

A few months later, on 23 August, Colonel Moody accepted at a salary of £1,200 the appointment of chief commissioner of lands and works and lieutenant governor of British Columbia. The War Office also made him commander of the British Columbia Detachment, Royal Engineers, a corps to be sent to the new colony created by act of parliament on 2 August.

Sir Edward Bulwer-Lytton, secretary of state for the colonies, had selected the Corps of Royal Engineers because of its "superior discipline and intelligence." Alarmed by the threat of American control of the Fraser River gold-fields, and knowing the only protection on the coast was a small force of Royal Engineers surveying the land boundary line and of marines from HMS *Plumper* and HMS *Satellite* surveying the water boundary, Bulwer-Lytton anticipated the request for aid sent by Governor James Douglas* of Vancouver Island. The Colonial Office asked the War Office to recommend a field officer for a corps of 150 (later increased to 172) sappers and miners: "a man of good judgment possessing a knowledge of mankind." The War Office chose Moody; in his favour for a position that would combine military and civil duties were his good military record, his experience as colonial governor, and his father's reputation. Moody's appointment was for one year from his arrival in the colony, with an extension possible if he notified the British government it was necessary. Both Moody and Douglas, sworn in as governor of British Columbia in November 1858, were informed that the imperial government would pay only the governor's salary, that the colony was to be self-supporting, and that the cost of the Royal Engineers was to be defrayed from land sales.

The force Moody commanded included three captains (Robert Mann Parsons, John Marshall Grant, and Henry Reynolds Luard), two subalterns, and a surgeon. For a commissary officer Moody made use of Captain William Driscoll Gosset, a retired Royal Engineer, who had been given a civil appointment as treasurer. Gosset proved as incapable as Moody of keeping account of expenditures and created enormous difficulties for Douglas by his mismanagement of the Assay Office. The men in the British Columbia Detachment received colonial pay varying from one to five shillings a day, an amount higher than the three shillings paid to the Royal Marines who were to supplement Moody's labour force in 1859. The sappers and miners were also promised a grant of 30 acres of land after six years of continuous service. By 1862 the annual cost of maintaining the Royal Engineers in British Columbia had risen to £22,325.

So little was known in London about the distant colony that the duties assigned the force were legion. Moody, keeping military considerations in mind, was to select, with the governor's approval, a site for a capital city and a maritime town where customs duties could be collected. He was to choose town sites which had a military advantage. The Royal Engineers were to build public works – they were sent, Bulwer-Lytton said, for scientific and practical purposes, "not solely for military objects." They were to survey town sites and country lands, plan and engineer roads, and examine harbours. Moody was to report on the mineral wealth, the fisheries, and other resources. The principal obligation excluded from duty was police work – a matter in which Colonel Moody immediately involved himself.

At the Colonial Office there was some suspicion that Moody might not show proper respect for Douglas, the able governor of Vancouver Island, who had spent his life in the fur trade. Bulwer-Lytton met with Moody several times to emphasize Douglas' authority, and gave him detailed written instructions. Officials at the Colonial Office later admitted Moody's position had not been well defined. From his subsequent actions it is also evident that Moody read too much into a letter by Herman Merivale, under-secretary of state for the colonies, which referred to his position as "special" and promised that his duties would be free from interference "except under circumstances of the gravest necessity." Years later, Moody blamed his difficulties on the fact that he was put "in a false position, not of my own seeking, but at the earnest solicitation of the Secy of State."

Two groups of the Royal Engineers reached Victoria in October and November 1858. The main party reached the colony on 12 April 1859, two months after 139 Royal Marines had arrived from the China Station. Moody, his wife, and four children had departed from Liverpool on 30 Oct. 1858 to travel by the Panama route, and reached Victoria on 25 December. En route they met young men of their own class seeking employment or adventure in the gold-fields. They thus arrived with a circle of friends whose social ties set them apart from Douglas. Two days after his arrival Moody sent the first of his many private letters to the Colonial Office. He had entirely disarmed Douglas "of all jealousy," he reported. "I have assured him I understand my instructions to be that *I am entirely under his orders* and that he will find me support him loyally. . . ." Moody's penchant for writing private letters was criticized as "an objectionable and unfair practice" by officers of the Colonial Office who felt they "ought to take care that no man finds that he has gained an advantage over the Governor of a Colony."

On 4 Jan. 1859 Moody was sworn in at Victoria as chief commissioner of lands and works and lieutenant governor of British Columbia. Douglas intended to appoint him to the Executive Council which he planned for the colony, but in April he learned that Moody's commission as lieutenant governor was dormant, operative only "in the event of the death or absence of the Governor." Since his own commission gave him wide powers, Douglas decided to postpone setting up a council and to govern by proclamation. Moody resented his exclusion from the law-making process since he had the power to govern during the governor's frequent absences from the gold colony, but he deferred to him and abstained from assuming office on these occasions.

Before leaving England, Moody had decided from maps that the high north bank of the Fraser River had strategic importance and that military reserves should be established near the river's entrance. Douglas had told him of a site above Annacis Island that would probably be suitable for the seaport. As Moody journeyed up the Fraser early in January 1859, his attention was arrested by a location in this vicinity which seemed ideal for the site of the capital city. But on reaching Fort Langley on 6 January he learned that trouble had broken out among the miners at Hills Bar. With what Douglas called "admirable promptitude," Moody left at once for Yale, accompanied by Judge Matthew Baillie Begbie*, a lieutenant of the *Plumper*, and the 22 engineers of his advance party, already at Langley. At Yale, Moody went unarmed to the miners' camp and was saluted by them. Aware of Moody's military support, the notorious California outlaw Ned McGowan surrendered, to be tried by Judge Begbie and fined. Order was restored. "The glory being won – the bills now have to be paid, to the tune of 10,000 dollars," declared Amor De Cosmos* in the *British Colonist.* "British Columbia must feel pleased with her first war, – so cheap – all for nothing." The cost had been increased by Moody's ordering up from Langley to Hope 30 Royal Marines from the *Plumper* and two field pieces.

HMS *Plumper*, sent to Langley to provide aid, conveyed Moody on his further examination of the river sites. Douglas had had Joseph Despard Pemberton, the colonial surveyor of Vancouver Island, lay out a town site of 900 acres, called Derby, adjoining the Hudson's Bay Company's reserve at Langley, on the south bank of the Fraser. Lots had been sold at an auction in Victoria on 25 Nov. 1858, bringing in a revenue of £13,000. It was generally assumed that this site would be the capital of the colony. Moody saw at a glance that Derby was too close to the American border. Descending the river he decided the location he had noticed earlier on the north bank was a site "in which a Military Man wd delight" and suited to serve the double function of capital city and seaport. On 28 January, "in a spirit of entire deference to my chief," he recommended it to Douglas.

On 1 February the governor ordered immediate surveys; on 4 February he forwarded Moody's report to the Colonial Office, indicating his approval; the following day he requested Queen Victoria to choose a name for the site the Royal Engineers called Queenborough. On 14 February Douglas issued a proclamation stating that this was to be the site of the capital city, and notifying purchasers of Langley lots that these could be surrendered and the money used to pay for lots in the proposed city. On 17 February he approved the construction of a residence for the lieutenant governor, barracks, a small church, offices, and a customs house. In retrospect, he acted with dispatch, but the Moodys considered him a "dilly-dallier" for not issuing his proclamation earlier. In London, Merivale received with relief the news about the agreement over the location of the capital but from this time on relations between Douglas and Moody were seldom harmonious.

Moody's site was on a steep hillside, thickly covered with cedar, fir, spruce, and hemlock. The undergrowth was impenetrable. Pemberton thought the location too heavily timbered, too elevated, and too expensive to grade; its impregnability might be unquestionable, but "if . . . this quality renders it inaccessible to the merchantmen of the Pacific, and to the trade of the Puget Sound, what object could an enemy have in attacking it?" It was three months before the Royal Engineers, with assistance from Royal Marines and civilians, felled the trees and the hillside was turned into "the imperial stumpfield." The streets were not properly laid out when town lots to the value of £89,170 were sold. One mile distant, however, the Royal Engineers' camp at "Sapperton" was taking shape, with a barracks, a guardroom and cells, storehouses, and a powder magazine.

Moody had been instructed in England not to employ civilian surveyors, but did so until the governor, annoyed at the cost and the methods used, dismissed them on 27 June. In August, when Moody's requisitions rose to £25,000, the marines were withdrawn. "He has no power to employ anyone," Mrs Moody wrote her mother. "Indeed *now* he has *no* civilians under him & it only requires him to speak well of anyone to the Govr for *him* to determine not to do so for them!"

On 22 July 1859 Douglas proclaimed New Westminster, the choice of the queen, as the name of the city. He made it a port of entry and established customs duties. Merchants, who had already arrived, were as distressed as he about the slow progress with public works. "Hurried designs in so grave a matter as the grades for a Capital of a country, cannot be too strongly deprecated," Moody told the governor in December. "I would suggest to you that the *Colony* itself must first become great and flourishing before we can undertake works on a scale of magnificence," Douglas replied, "and that a Town just laid out and not yet disassociated from the primeval forest cannot be dealt with as a great City that has existed for Centuries."

During Moody's first year in the colony little advance was made on Douglas' priorities of road-building and the survey of country lands. Miners were flocking to the interior, and improved communication was imperative. In May and June 1859 the Royal Engineers had surveyed and improved the 123-mile Harrison-Lillooet trail which Douglas had opened with volunteer labour in the winter of 1858–59. But men had been diverted from converting the trail into a wagon road to resurvey Port Douglas (Douglas), Yale, and Hope. A six-mile trail, costing from £60 to £70 a mile, had been built for military purposes to connect New Westminster with Burrard Inlet (the North Road), and a route from Hope to Lytton had been explored. The London *Times* on 30 Jan. 1860 reported: "Soldiers cannot be expected to do this sort of work. The *impedimenta* they carry with them, the costliness of their provisions and of their transport, the loss of time in drilling and squaring and scrubbing and cleaning them, make them the most expensive of labourers." New Westminster's merchants found the lack of roads handicapped their opportunity to provision the mines. They demanded that public works proceed at a faster pace and that they be given a voice in government. On 16 July 1860 Douglas yielded partly by permitting local self-government through incorporation of the city, thereby shifting the cost of local improvements to the citizens. The higher level of taxation led to complaints that Douglas was shackling the development of the city as a commercial centre.

In the spring of 1861 a memorial was prepared by the residents of New Westminster for the Duke of Newcastle, now colonial secretary, complaining about money "most injudiciously squandered," contracts for roads awarded without public advertisement, faulty administration of public lands, and government reserves set aside for the benefit of government officers. Angered by these charges, Douglas demanded that Moody, the chief commissioner of lands and works, inform him about any government officer who had acquired land from the government except at a public auction or who had registered a pre-emption. The records did show purchases by Moody and his associates. The newspapers provided more information. The *British Colonist* had reported on 4 Oct. 1860 that Moody had stuck a paper on a tree at Red Earth Fork (Princeton) to pre-empt 200 acres, and in February 1861 the New Westminster *British Columbian* published a letter from "a farmer" alleging Moody was guilty of land-grabbing. Finally on 29 Aug. 1861 Moody announced his intention to sell his rural land to actual settlers, although he retained a large suburban lot near New Westminster bought with Douglas' permission in 1859 and then developed into his model farm, Mayfield. As late as 1873 he held 3,049 acres of land. In a June 1861 letter to Douglas he had tried to shift blame for any wrongful disposal of crown lands to the district magistrates, who were responsible for "all matters relating to unsurveyed Lands, viz – those open to preemption." To the charge that the Royal Engineers' surveys had been "desultory" he replied that this was the result of too frequent requests having been made for them to supply other services.

The governor believed that British Columbia could never become great or prosperous without a highway system, and that it was imperative the miners be supplied with food at less than famine prices. At his urging, the officers did concentrate most of their attention on the road system. Captain Grant completed the Douglas-Lillooet road in 1860, and the next year he built 25 miles of the wagon road from Hope to the gold mines on the Similkameen and at Rock Creek. The Yale to Lytton road following the Fraser River was surveyed in 1861, and in 1862 Douglas ordered construction to begin on his project, the 400-mile wagon road from Yale to the Cariboo. The "Great North Road" was Douglas' conception. Moody had been asked in October 1861 to produce a plan, but had declined because he was unfamiliar with the country. Douglas sent a stinging rebuke for failure to learn about the interior. In March 1862 Moody produced a plan for two roads in addition to the Fraser River highway, but the governor had "no desire to foster these undertakings" and, on his orders, Captain Grant commenced work on the Great North Road in May 1862 with 53 sappers. They built the first six miles north from Yale through the solid rock face. An equally difficult stretch of nine miles from Spence's Bridge along the Thompson River was also built. The greater part of the remainder of the road was let out on contract to civilians who received cash or bonds or the right to collect tolls. Three officers, captains Grant and Luard and Lieutenant Henry Spencer Palmer, gave invaluable service either in building a part of the road or in supervising the contractors. In October 1863 at Yale the Royal Engineers conducted the opening ceremony of the highway.

Moody's heart was in military projects, not roads. When the crisis over San Juan Island culminated in 1859 in joint British and American military occupation of the island, the defence of New Westminster, which had "great facilities for communication by water, as well as by future great trunk railways into the interior," was uppermost in his mind. The imperial government would not agree to a military frontier settlement on the south bank of the Fraser River across from New Westminster, but it did agree to the setting aside of naval reserves on Burrard Inlet. Moody had New Westminster connected by a road to Port Moody and to the Burrard Inlet, future site of Vancouver.

Under his direction, the Royal Engineers established at New Westminster the first observatory in the colony, printed both the *Government Gazette for the colonies of Vancouver Island and British Columbia* and maps based on reconnaissances and surveys, built the first churches, and designed the colony's first postage stamp and its coat of arms. Moody was civic-minded: he helped to found the hospital and the industrial exhibition at New Westminster, and his library became the foundation of the city's public library. Though he was not robust, and overwork caused him to look "so old & grey," the citizens of New Westminster knew him as a friendly, even jolly man – "cheerie like," his wife said. John Robson*, the fiery editor of the *British Columbian*, was under his spell and wanted him to be governor of British Columbia.

As early as January 1860 the Colonial Office felt that it had been a mistake to give Moody a civil appointment, and also to send the Royal Engineers: "The labor of the Engineers as surveyors is neither economical nor adapted to a country were rapidity of work is the chief requirement." The San Juan dispute saved them from withdrawal, and Newcastle postponed a decision until his return from accompanying the Prince of Wales to Canada. Evidence of Moody's unsuitability accumulated: his "imperfect method in conveying public lands," his penchant for writing letters, and his extravagance. In accord with his usual practice, Douglas minimized his difficulties. He informed the Colonial Office that he and Moody were "uniformly cordial, confidential and friendly," and he praised Moody for his "mild, conciliatory and gentlemanly bearing." By 1862, however, he realized that Moody was doing his own reputation harm, and his patience became exhausted. It had become necessary for him, he told Newcastle, to issue the most precise instructions in matters of finance and administration. When the imperial authorities demanded that the colony pay half of all the costs of the Royal Engineers, Douglas told the Colonial Office that they were "a costly ornament," who were to British Columbia what "the old man of the sea was to Sinbad."

In April 1863 Newcastle, realizing that Moody had not sought permission for a longer term, and that the colony could not afford the Royal Engineers, decided to withdraw the corps. With the Cariboo mining population swollen to 4,000 persons, it was a bad time to remove the chief commissioner of lands and works, but to leave Moody in British Columbia "with nothing but a subordinate Civil office" was not possible. Douglas hoped to retain Captain Luard's services, but Moody informed the Colonial Office that Luard was unfit to succeed him as commissioner. Chartres Brew* was given the appointment.

On 6 November the people of New Westminster gathered at a farewell dinner for Colonel Moody and his officers. The Moodys departed with their seven children, 22 officers and men, eight wives and 17 children, leaving behind 130 sappers and miners who had elected to remain.

Moody became a regimental colonel on 8 December and in March 1864 he was given command of the Royal Engineers in the Chatham District in England. On 25 Jan. 1866 he was promoted major-general and retired from the service on full pay. He lived quietly at Lyme Regis in Dorset, hoping always to return to British Columbia, until his death from apoplexy while he was on a visit to Bournemouth.

There was some truth in the *Daily British Colonist*'s statement of March 1863 that the Royal Engineers had been a clog on the executive. Had Moody been more willing to recognize Douglas' talents, experience, and knowledge of the country, the governor would have consulted him more frequently and acted less arbitrarily. Moody took an unfair advantage of Douglas in trading on his father's reputation at the Colonial Office, and in the end his constant complaints wore down Newcastle, who decided not only to disband the British Columbia Detachment but also to retire Douglas early from the governorship.

MARGARET A. ORMSBY

Richard Clement Moody's "First impressions: letter . . . to Arthur Blackwood, February 1, 1858," ed. W. E. Ireland, was published in *BCHQ*, 15 (1951): 85–107.

PABC, Add. MSS 60; B.C., Colonial secretary, Corr. outward, January 1859–September 1863 (letterbook); B.C., Dept. of Lands and Works, Corr., 1859–63; B.C., Royal Engineers, Corr. outward, 1859–63; Colonial corr., R. C. Moody corr.; Crease coll., Moody corr. PRO, CO 60/3–17. G.B., Parl., Command paper, 1859 (1st session), XVII, [2476], pp.15–108, *British Columbia: papers relative to the affairs of British Columbia, part I*; 1859 (2nd session), XXII, [2578], pp.297–408, *British Columbia: papers relative to the affairs of British Columbia, part II*. [M. S. Moody], "Mrs. Moody's first impressions of British Columbia," ed. Jacqueline Gresko, *British Columbia Hist. News* (Victoria), 11 (1977–78), nos.3–4: 6–9. *British Columbian*, 1861–63. *Daily British Colonist* (Victoria), 1858–63. *Times* (London), 6 April 1887. *Victoria Gazette*, 1859–60.

DNB. M. C. L. Cope, "Colonel Moody and the Royal Engineers in British Columbia" (MA thesis, Univ. of British Columbia, Vancouver, 1940). F. W. Howay, *The work of the Royal Engineers in British Columbia, 1858 to 1863 . . .* (Victoria, 1910). Dorothy Blakey Smith, "The first capital of British Columbia: Langley or New Westminster?" *BCHQ*, 21 (1957–58): 15–50. K. S. Weeks, "The Royal Engineers, Columbia detachment – their work in helping to establish British Columbia," *Canadian Geographical Journal* (Montreal), 27 (July–December 1943): 30–45. Madge Wolfenden, "Pathfinders and road-builders: Richard Clement Moody, R.E.," *British Columbia Public Works: Journal of the Department of Public Works* (Victoria), April 1938: 3–4. F. M. Woodward, "The influence of the Royal Engineers on the development of British Columbia," *BC Studies*, 24 (winter 1974–75): 3–51; "'Very dear soldiers' or 'very dear laborers': the Royal Engineers in British Columbia, April 1860," *British Columbia Hist. News*, 12 (1978–79), no.1: 8–15.

MOORE, DENNIS, manufacturer, capitalist, and philanthropist; b. 20 Aug. 1817 at Grimsby, Upper Canada; m. first 1 June 1842 Susan Tyson; m. secondly 1 Aug. 1854 Mary Hunt, and they had one son and four daughters; d. 20 Nov. 1887 at Hamilton, Ont.

In 1831 Dennis Moore moved to Hamilton from Grimsby where he had spent his boyhood. He entered an apprenticeship with Edward Jackson*, a tinsmith who had started business in 1830, and in 1833 Jackson took Moore and several other apprentices into the firm as partners. From then until Jackson's death in 1872, the business was conducted by changing and complicated partnerships, although for much of the time the firm operated under the name of D. Moore and Company.

The firm had begun by manufacturing tinware but, probably some time in the 1840s, added a foundry and diversified into the production of stoves and machine castings. Financial details of the company's operations are difficult to uncover: in 1862, 40 men were employed and $50,000 in raw materials used; three years later goods worth $125,000 were made; by 1869 the value of production had increased to $150,000 and 50 men were employed. Information is lacking but it is clear that Moore accumulated considerable wealth from the company's business. In 1848 he owned real estate in Hamilton worth between $10,000 and $15,000 and D. Moore and Company owned nine profitable stores. He also speculated in western Canadian real estate. In 1882 with Edward GURNEY, the Toronto and Hamilton stove manufacturer, and John Edward Rose and Alexander Sutherland of Toronto, he became associated with the promoters of the Saskatchewan Land and Homestead Company, one of the many firms incorporated in that year for the purpose of settling lands in Manitoba and the North-West Territories. Moore's investments in other manufacturing and financial institutions led to his election in the 1870s and 1880s as director of several companies, most located in Hamilton, including the Canada Life Assurance Company, the Bank of Hamilton, and the Hamilton Bridge and Tool Company.

This prominence was also reflected in Moore's public and political activities. In February 1851, for example, he had been one of the 24 leading Hamilton citizens – including Sir Allan Napier MacNab*, Edward Jackson, Robert William Harris*, partner in the largest wholesale importing firm in the Province of Canada, Robert Reid Smiley*, proprietor of the province's largest printing firm, and James Osborne, the city's leading grocer – who petitioned the federal government to send troops to put down a strike by workers on the Great Western Railway. Moore, who could not accept violent protest from a class to which he had belonged, believed that the government ought to "overawe the turbulent, afford protection to the peaceable and industrious, and in case of necessity, aid the civil power in enforcing the laws." In the federal election of 1882, when he ran as a Liberal candidate in the two-member riding of Hamilton, Moore was labelled as a defender of the manufacturing class by his Conservative opponents, though he spent much effort upon the labour vote, which was crucial. He shared Edward Blake*'s qualified acceptance of tariff protection for manufactured goods and low or no tariffs on raw materials, and was open to the Conservative charges that such a policy was clearly in his interest as a manufacturer. These charges probably helped to defeat both Moore and his fellow Liberal candidate in Hamilton.

A sincere Methodist, Moore was a benefactor of several Hamilton churches and of Methodist philanthropic activities. In 1851 he was a trustee of the MacNab Street Third Wesleyan Methodist Church, in 1856 a trustee of the First Wesleyan Methodist Church, and in 1866 a founder of Centenary Methodist Church, of which he was trustee and class leader until his death. Also in 1866 he was listed as a director of the Hamilton branch of the Upper Canada Bible Society. In 1861 he had been one of the several prominent Hamiltonians, including Edward Jackson and Calvin MCQUESTEN, who sought the incorporation of the Wesleyan Female College and in 1872 he became vice-president of the institution. For many years he contributed $1,600 annually to Victoria College in Cobourg for a chair in the sciences. He was also a regent of Victoria and on his death left $25,000 for the endowment of a professorship in chemistry and physics. His will provided $6,000 for the missionary society of the Methodist Church and smaller sums for several Hamilton benevolent institutions.

The career of Dennis Moore contains many of the elements of the myth of the mid-Victorian self-made man. By hard work and righteous living, he rose from humble origins to become a successful businessman who left an estate of about $200,000. The Reverend Hugh Johnston, a friend who had also been one of his pastors, said in a funeral oration that although "possessing no dazzling qualities, a man of straightforward common sense and few words, he made life a great success."

DAVID G. BURLEY

Christian Guardian, 30 Nov. 1887. *Globe*, 27 May 1882. *Hamilton Spectator*, 5, 12, 15 Feb. 1851; 26 June 1882; 21, 24 Nov. 1887. *Monetary Times*, 4 Feb. 1876. *Cyclopædia of Canadian biog.* (Rose, 1886). Wallace, *Macmillan dict.* Nathanael Burwash, *The history of Victoria College* (Toronto, 1927), 237; *Memorials of the life of Edward & Lydia Ann Jackson* (Toronto, 1876), 7–11. *The Centenary Church, the United Church of Canada, 24 Main Street West, Hamilton, Ontario, 1868–1968* ([Hamilton, Ont., 1968]), 5–6. *Hamilton, the Birmingham of Canada* (Hamilton, 1892). M. B. Katz, *The people of Hamilton, Canada West: family and class in a mid-nineteenth century city* (Cambridge, Mass., and London, 1975), 177, 179, 195. V. Ross and Trigge, *Hist. of Canadian Bank of Commerce*, III: 155. C. B. Sissons, *A history of Victoria University* (Toronto, 1952), 195.

MORRIS, ALEXANDER, lawyer, judge, businessman, politician, and public servant; b. 17 March 1826 in Perth, Upper Canada, eldest son of William Morris* and Elizabeth Cochran; m. in November 1851 Margaret Cline of Cornwall, Canada West, and they had 11 children; d. 28 Oct. 1889 in Toronto, Ont.

Alexander Morris was born to privilege, privilege which he used to expand the fortunes of his family and his country. He spent his childhood in the military settlement of Perth among the mercantile and political élite of which his father was a leading member. William Morris had served in the House of Assembly and the Legislative Council of Upper Canada and was appointed to the Legislative and Executive councils of the Province of Canada. He was active in the interests of Scottish colonists and the Church of Scotland, and in the founding of Queen's College at Kingston. His son inherited the legacy of a mid-Victorian sense of public duty and family place as well as a network of political friends. Educated initially at Perth Grammar School, Alexander was sent to Scotland in 1841 where he spent two years at Madras College, St Andrews, and at the University of Glasgow. He was employed for the next three years in Montreal by Thorne and Heward, commission merchants, acquiring skills which were to be of use to him throughout his career. In particular, his command of French was aided by a three-month sojourn with a French Canadian family at Belle-Rivière (Mirabel), Canada East.

In 1847 Morris moved to Kingston to study law as an articled clerk, along with Oliver Mowat*, under John A. Macdonald*. He was admitted into the second year at Queen's College. He "worked so hard his health gave way," and in 1848 he left Kingston and returned to Montreal. In January 1849 he matriculated into McGill College and later that year became the first person to graduate in arts. He later received a BCL (1850), an MA (1852), and a DCL (1862) from McGill. He completed his legal apprenticeship in the office of William BADGLEY and John Joseph Caldwell Abbott* in Montreal, and in 1851 was admitted to the bar in both Canada East and Canada West. For "family reasons," possibly his father's ill health, he set up practice in Montreal that year and, by the time he entered political life in 1861, he and his partner Frederick William Torrance had been able to build up a "large and lucrative practise" in commercial law in a city rapidly expanding its economy and becoming the focus of transportation networks. His marriage in 1851 to a niece of Philip VanKoughnet* undoubtedly further advanced his career.

Like other young men of his time in the Province of Canada, Morris was enraptured by dreams of imperial destiny. Business interests, family connections, and personal inclination led to him to argue that Canadians should elevate themselves above sectional squabbles and take their rightful place in the building of an empire. He did not hesitate to express his ideas publicly, and his essay, *Canada and her resources*, was awarded 2nd prize in 1855 by Governor General Sir Edmund Walker Head* and the Paris exhibition committee in Canada. A plodding, descriptive pamphlet, it predicts a glorious future for this "fertile British Province" where "political liberty . . . educational advantages and religious privileges" would surely "attract men of energy and industry." In 1849 Morris had become vice-president of the Mercantile Library Association in Montreal and lectured his fellow members on "The North American Indian, their origin, present conditions and oratory," an early indication of one of the consuming passions of his later life. To this same audience he delivered in 1858 his lecture, "Nova Britannia; or, British North America, its extent and future," which attracted some attention; when it was published as a pamphlet all 3,000 copies were sold in ten days. In it Morris predicted the federation of British American colonies and the construction of the Intercolonial and Canadian Pacific railways. He had been interested in these subjects since his youthful reading of the report by Lord Durham [Lambton*] and had actively identified himself with federal union, having been in 1849 one of the delegates at a meeting of the British American League in Kingston where this proposal was discussed. Foreshadowing Morris' role in the west, *Nova Britannia* also argued that Canada should display a "large-spirited and comprehensive appreciation of the requirements of the country, and a proper sense of the responsibilities to be assumed in regard to the well-being of the native and other inhabitants, and the due development of the resources of the territory." In this, his most important work of the period, he expressed ideas which were becoming both acceptable and exciting in the Canada of the 1850s. A lecture in 1858 to the Mercantile Library Association, and then to the mechanics' institute at Hemmingford, Canada East, on "The Hudson's Bay and Pacific territories" hammered home another theme of the day: opposition to the Hudson's Bay Company, and annexation by Canada of its territories. Morris saw Canada as the rightful owner of Rupert's Land, and felt that HBC activities must be curtailed if Canada's new empire was to flourish.

Yet Morris was never a one-dimensional political man. At 27 he had published an academic treatise on the railway consolidation acts of Canada, a work of some utility in the pre-confederation decades. Like his father Morris was also active in the affairs of the Church of Scotland. At first mainly interested in missionary and educational work, in 1856 he assisted in beginning and in editing a children's magazine, the *Juvenile Presbyterian.* A ruling elder of the synod of the Presbyterian Church in Canada and a trustee from 1858 of Queen's College at Kingston, Morris was named one of the delegates to go to Scotland in 1859 to find a new principal for the school. As a result of the work of this delegation, William Leitch*, an old acquaintance of Morris' father, was chosen. Morris himself had the opportunity to meet a number of the prominent leaders of the Scottish church and to take up friendships made by his father on earlier visits. In Glasgow he met for the first time George Monro Grant* who was to be principal of Queen's in the 1880s when Morris was chairman of the board. Morris had also been elected a fellow in arts of McGill College in 1854 and in 1857 was elected to the board of governors.

Morris was an attractive public figure by the 1860s. A successful lawyer with good family connections and interests in education and his church, he was an able public speaker in English who could also cope in French and whose style in English could encompass the heights and extravagances of the new imperialism of the St Lawrence. Morris had been considering political life for some time and had made inquiries about a suitable riding. In 1861 he was elected as a

Liberal-Conservative for Lanark South in Canada West; his father had represented Lanark in the Upper Canadian assembly for more than ten years. According to Morris, "the people brought me out without my knowledge and returned me by a majority of upwards of four hundred so that my sphere of influence is widening. I was very reluctant to accept but as it was my father's County . . . could not say no." He recognized his family obligations and, as a song composed to celebrate his victory suggests, his constituents also saw him primarily as a successor to his father: "With he has been an honest man,/In virtue he has shone,/ The Father's virtue we ha'e seen/Reflected in the Son."

By 1864 Morris had returned with his family to Perth to take up residence in his constituency and to open a law partnership. His business interests, like those of many of his class, were expanding on the eve of confederation. Investments in iron ore, plumbago, and canals led not unnaturally to an interest in railways and the advocacy of a railway from Montreal to Ottawa and thence to Perth and Parry Sound. By 1867 Morris had taken a leading role in founding the Bedford Navigation Company; he and Richard John Cartwright* were among the directors. He was also named to the board of the Commercial Bank of Canada in that year.

In parliament Morris spoke strongly for confederation, seeing there a solution to the difficulties of Upper Canadian farmers whose sons were leaving for Wisconsin and Minnesota. He returned to the themes of *Nova Britannia*, stating that Canadians either must rise in "strength and wealth and power by means of this union, under the sheltering protection of Britain, or . . . must be absorbed by the great power beside us." The solution for the problems of the Canadas was not representation by population but "the broader scheme of Confederation." Morris' role in parliament was minor but in June 1864, following the defeat of the government of Sir Étienne-Paschal Taché* and John A. Macdonald, Morris and John Henry POPE met with George Brown* and carried his offer of cooperation to Macdonald, thus helping to make possible the "Great Coalition" which brought about confederation three years later.

In the first federal election Morris was re-elected in Lanark South, ensuring, as Macdonald had anticipated, that he would now be able to "begin to play for taking a prominent part in the Conservative ranks." After some urging, Macdonald appointed Morris to the cabinet as minister of inland revenue on 16 Nov. 1869. Morris' cabinet position was confirmed by his return by acclamation in Lanark South in the necessary by-election.

Morris' ten years in parliament were useful if not outstanding. He clearly served his constituents to their satisfaction and provided consistent support to Macdonald. He introduced two liberal reforms, the abolition of public executions and the municipal registration of vital statistics, which found easy acceptance. He gave the impression of being less partisan than many of his colleagues and was thus able to be a conciliator at a crucial time in Canadian political history.

The difficulties of federal politics, medical advice to retire from politics, and financial troubles resulting from a dearth of legal business in Perth, led Morris to leave federal politics in July 1872. "If I must retire," Morris had written to Macdonald in May 1871, "I would like you to send me to Manitoba as Judge. The work would be light & though an exile, the country has a future & I could be of use, to [Lieutenant Governor Adams George Archibald*]."

From July to December of 1872 Morris served as the first chief justice of the Court of Queen's Bench of Manitoba, a task which would hardly seem suitable for a sick man. In addition, he acted as administrator of Manitoba and the North-West Territories after the departure of Lieutenant Governor Archibald in mid October. This latter role enabled him to continue his close political correspondence with Macdonald on a more official footing. His first task as chief justice was to travel throughout Red River to revise and confirm the federal electoral lists, and to make himself known in the new province. In September he was witness to riots during the federal election in Winnipeg and he recommended the formation of a dominion police force which would be paid and directed locally. His advice was not acted upon. Riots and other disturbances were not unusual in the aftermath of the Red River rebellion led by Louis RIEL, which had bequeathed a legacy of lawlessness and a disregard for constituted authority; skirmishes between the Métis and the settlers from Ontario were frequent. Morris' court was a "bear garden" where "I have had a conflict of authorities & practises – the old Assiniboia ideas – the Ontario & the Quebec, *en lutte*. Fortunately, the legislature here, adopted English practise & English law, and I . . . have quietly enforced both, and have carried *with me the French Bar*." His inclination was to look for a compromise, for "I determined from the hour I entered the province, to know no parties in it, & have steadily maintained that position."

Morris' goal was to see a peaceful, stable Manitoba based largely on the Ontario model, with an acquiescent and cooperative French population. To this end he pressed as interim administrator for a speedy settlement of Métis land claims to divert support from Riel in his bid for election in Provencher in September 1872 and to provide assistance for the substantial number of Métis he expected would desert Riel for the leadership of the more moderate Pascal Breland*. The settling of land claims was his first major crisis as administrator and he felt that he had survived it well, writing to Macdonald in November 1872 that "with firmness & temper I expect to pilot the ship of state through, all right." His health improved and such small and perhaps Pyrrhic victories persuaded Morris to reverse his earlier decision to refuse the lieutenant governorship of Manitoba. In October 1872 he had told Macdonald that he would appreciate the offer but would decline the appointment on grounds of health, yet on 2 December he was sworn in as lieutenant governor of Manitoba and of the North-West Territories. Gilbert McMicken*, who administered the oath of office, had perhaps voiced the doubts of others when on 13 October he advised Macdonald against the appointment of a man with a "sensitive and nervous temperament." Yet Morris soon surprised such observers with his abilities, particularly his tact in the handling of the disparate, strong-willed, and inexperienced groups of politicians and self-styled local leaders with whom he was faced. As lieutenant governor, Morris was responsible for the administration of federal moneys, Indian affairs, crown lands, and customs, and also served in a private capacity as Macdonald's own representative.

One of the more significant of Morris' accomplishments during his five-year term as lieutenant governor of Manitoba was the rapid introduction of responsible government in the new province. Although the impetus may well have come from his own fear of disharmony and awkward political situations, the result of forcing an early move to responsible government was probably beneficial, concentrating political attention as it did on present alliances and future policies rather than on recriminations over past defeats and hostility to the federal power. Whether as a result of his own weakness or as a crowning accomplishment of his political ideals, with the resignation of the Executive Council and its leading member, Henry Joseph CLARKE, in July 1874, Morris called on Marc-Amable Girard* to accept the premiership, and for the first time Manitoba's cabinet was chosen not by the lieutenant governor but by the premier. In Morris' push for responsible government one might also see the broader motive of the spread of familiar political traditions; such a concern had been reflected in Macdonald's instructions to him as chief justice to impose a municipal government system upon the existing parishes of Red River. Macdonald's purpose in this was clear: "The Emigrant from Ontario will understand its working and it will introduce a feeling of responsibility and self government among the people, of which they are, as yet, altogether ignorant. They have hitherto relied entirely on the Hudson's Bay Company and have never thought nor acted for themselves."

The achievement of responsible government by 1874 meant at least that Morris lightened the burden of "managing the animals composing his Ministry." He was a man of considerably greater political experience than most of Manitoba's politicians and complained wearily of the constant bickering among Clarke and Joseph Royal*, Stewart Mulvey, Francis Evans Cornish*, and representatives of other political factions. "I have to read every Bill and play law clerk," he told Macdonald, "but they make a sad mess with amendments in the Houses." As the political ambitions of the local legislature grew, Morris increasingly lost patience with petty rivalries, which rarely rose above the level of personal feuds.

Although his role in provincial politics thus declined, Morris retained influence in some areas which were to be of significance for Manitoba's development. For some time he continued to attend the meetings of the cabinet, although it is difficult to know how often he did so or what role he played in its proceedings. He was an active participant in dominion-provincial affairs relating to "better terms" for Manitoba, particularly in matters involving railways where he took part in some negotiations and in composing memoranda for submission to the federal government. Morris also had a keen interest in education. He set in motion some provisions for school laws, but his major achievement was the founding in 1877 of the University of Manitoba. G. M. Grant was to write: "In the founding of the University he had achieved a measure of co-operation among the different religious groups which had not been found possible in any other Province of Canada at that time." Morris' contribution was in the good working relationships he maintained with the three major churches in Manitoba: Church of England, Roman Catholic, and Presbyterian. His relationship with Alexandre-Antonin Taché*, the Roman Catholic archbishop of St Boniface, although uneasy because of the latter's concern for Riel and the Métis, was marked by formal politeness rather than open conflict. Thus when Robert Machray*, the Anglican archbishop of Rupert's Land, suggested the establishment of a non-denominational university with affiliated religious colleges, Morris, who was closely associated with both McGill and Queen's, was quick to respond. Making use of a suggestion by Taché that the model of the University of London be considered, he brought "the existing colleges together to form the working body of a university for Manitoba." In his speech from the throne in January 1877 Morris announced the proposed university bill, introducing "this measure as one of great importance and as an evidence of the rapid progress of the country, towards the possession of so many of the advantages which the older Provinces of the Dominion already enjoy."

Morris was lieutenant governor of the North-West Territories from 1872 to 1876 when the North-West Territories Act of 1875 established a government for the territories independent of that for Manitoba. He was faced with the task, as the *Manitoba Daily Free*

Press in Winnipeg said, "of bringing order out of chaos in a territory larger than half the continent of Europe." To assist him there was a motley Council of the North-West Territories, for which provision was first made in 1869 but which was not formally appointed by the federal government until December 1872. The council's senior member was Girard and only two of the original 11 members, Robert Hamilton and William Joseph Christie*, were residents of the territories. Always hampered by an apparent lack of both interest and funds on the part of the federal government, and by the requirement for legislation to be approved by Ottawa before coming into force, Morris was responsible for establishing a mail service (started in 1876), licensing stipendiary magistrates, and making provision for liquor regulations and, eventually, for making treaties with and assisting the Indians. He constantly advocated the establishment of a police force in the west. "The preservation of order in the North West," he told Macdonald, was "the most important matter of the future"; he was conscious of the presence of the Sioux [*see* TA-TANKA I-YOTANK], which might well provoke other Indian tribes, and also of the influence of the threats to survival caused by the dying out of the buffalo. The presence of "men in red coats" he saw as necessary to prevent outbreaks such as those in Minnesota in 1862. The Cypress Hills massacre in June 1873 pointed out the need for law forces on the prairies and Morris emphasized to Macdonald the importance of bringing to justice the whites responsible for the massacre.

It was in Indian affairs that Morris seemed to find the greatest satisfaction. Between 1873 and 1876 he involved himself personally as the queen's representative in bargaining and treaty-making with the Indians, signing on behalf of the crown treaties nos.3, 4, 5, and 6, which encompassed a large portion of the territory between Lake Superior and the Rocky Mountains, and revising treaties nos.1 and 2. Each of these treaties required considerable preparation, diplomatic skill, and quickness of mind during the negotiations as well as a willingness to follow up on the promises made. Morris attended to all these duties, and the peaceful settlement of the northwest owes something to him as well as to the weakened physical state of the Plains Indians.

After some difficulties and almost three years of protracted negotiations, the "North-West Angle Treaty," or Treaty no.3, was signed on 3 Oct. 1873. Morris headed a three-man mission whose other members were Joseph-Alfred-Norbert PROVENCHER and Simon James Dawson*. With the invaluable assistance of some Red River Métis, and by using a judicious balance of threats and cajolements, he succeeded in convincing the Ojibwas of the Lake of the Woods area, in what is now northwestern Ontario, of the government's determination finally to settle with them. Although two earlier treaties had been signed in 1871 by Lieutenant Governor Archibald with Indians in what is now southern Manitoba, Treaty no.3 was the prototype for those that followed. This time extensive negotiations took place and the adhesion of all the groups concerned was ensured. In addition, Treaty no.3 transferred large areas of land long before they were required by white settlers, and included provisions regarding the resources on the lands being transferred. The revisions later made to treaties nos.1 and 2 incorporated provisions regarding annuities and cash settlements similar to those in Treaty no.3.

Although he felt that no expense should be spared in making treaties, Morris was under constraints from Ottawa to offer only limited annuities and gifts in order not to raise the expectations of the Indians to the west. In response, he argued with Ottawa that if annuities were limited, there should be allowance for granting schools and other educational provisions for the Indians. He also successfully argued that they had always been led to expect their rights would be recognized before settlement took place, and therefore that treaties should be made well in advance of settlement to preserve peace and goodwill.

Following the practices confirmed in the Proclamation of 1763 and the treaties concluded by William Benjamin Robinson* in the 1840s and 1850s, Morris recognized the aboriginal rights of the Indians to their lands, accepted their relinquishment of these rights, and in return guaranteed to them what must have seemed a continuation of their way of life by permitting hunting and fishing on the unsettled lands in the territories they had ceded. The principle of allotting small reserves in scattered locations was not simply to avoid arousing the jealousy of white settlers or to diminish the military strength of the Indians. He wished to avoid the American system of "removal" and to cultivate a conservative "home feeling of attachment to the soil," which would be communally owned to maintain cohesion in the face of immigration.

Morris also believed that it was "of importance to strengthen the hands of the Chiefs and Councillors by a due recognition of their offices and respect being shewn them. They should be strongly impressed with the belief that they are officers of the Crown, and that it is their duty to see that the Indians of their tribes obey the provisions of the treaties." To this end, suits, medals, rifles, and larger annuities were to be given to chiefs and councillors and though Morris, like many whites, tended to overestimate the political power of the Indian chiefs, it is likely that this material assistance enabled them to maintain a stable leadership in their rapidly altered world.

All these methods were conservative but the goal was, from an Indian point of view, revolutionary: assimilation. Although in 1876, during negotiations at

Fort Carlton (Sask.) on Treaty no.6, Morris assured Big Bear [MISTAHIMASKWA] that the government did not intend to "interfere with the Indian's daily life" or "bind him," but "only help him to make a living on the reserves," it is true that anticipation of gradual social and economic change was an integral part of each treaty. Most western treaties made provision for education on the reserve, to, in Morris' words, "train the new generation in the arts of civilization," and "a very important feature" of all treaties was the supply of "agricultural implements, oxen, cattle (to form the nuclei of herds), and seed grain," the tools necessary to transform hunters into farmers. Like many Victorians, Morris saw the advantages of the proposed way of life not simply in terms of helping new wards to become self-supporting; by "elevating" the Indian population, "Canada will be enabled to feel, that in a truly patriotic spirit, our country has done its duty by the red men of the North-West, and thereby to herself." In a classic imperialist manner Morris considered the rewards of empire due only to those who recognized the responsibilities of their self-assumed burden and fulfilled their Christian duty.

Treaty-making had not been easy. The stakes were high, and the tact and stamina required were considerable. But for Morris the opportunity to play this role in the transformation of the west, of which he had dreamed so long ago, was an immensely satisfying experience. The symbolism of treaty-making, the language, and the ceremony also seem to have appealed to his sense of the dignity of his position, and he was to feel their loss keenly. After the Canadian parliament passed the North-West Territories Act in April 1875 Morris appeared dejected and suffered a loss of interest in his work. In November he wrote to Macdonald: "My sphere here, has lost its attraction, by the proposed cutting off, of the North West. I wish I had been left to complete my work there, during the remainder of my term of two years. However I have settled the Indian policy & the work will go on. Now that I am in health, I am weary of the loneliness & want of companionship here, & to my family, it is an exile." When the act was proclaimed on 7 Oct. 1876 David Laird* became lieutenant governor of the North-West Territories but Morris continued as lieutenant governor of Manitoba and assumed as well the lieutenant governorship of Keewatin District which was created at the same time to the north (as far as the Arctic Ocean) and east of Manitoba; he retained these posts until December 1877. Morris had not been consulted in the drafting of the 1875 act, and he would have preferred to see the administration of the territories conducted from Winnipeg (Fort Pelly was the proposed seat of government). When a reconstituted council was appointed for the territories with three members, all of them white government officials, he wrote that "it is a crying shame that the half breeds have been ignored. It will result in trouble and is most unjust."

As he prepared to end his exile and return to Ontario, Morris could take some pride in his achievements in Manitoba and the northwest. Apart from his work with the Indians, the introduction of responsible government in Manitoba, and the establishment of a university, he had brought a measure of peace to the relations between the old settlers of Red River, the Métis, and the new settlers from Ontario. He had fulfilled Macdonald's goal of making a new society in the west which was patterned on the institutions of Ontario but which retained the support of the French population.

The major weakness of his administration lay in the failure to preserve Métis lands in Manitoba. Although Morris had seen the necessity of an early settlement of the land allotment question to maintain peace in the province, he had been unable to prevent the speculation in scrip which led to the dispossession of the Métis. Morris always considered his sympathies to "have been strongly with the native raised population," but his admiration of the native people apparently did not extend to all Métis (there were significant exceptions) and he was much dismayed by their partisanship and factionalism. More important perhaps is the question of Morris' own interest in the Métis lands. During his time in Manitoba he purchased many sections of land in Winnipeg, including a portion close to Portage and Main streets where he later built the Morris Block. He bought land elsewhere in the province and invested financially in various land companies. It would have been almost uncharacteristic for a successful commercial lawyer like Morris not to have seized this "magnificent gift" to expand his family's fortunes as some Métis suspected he had done. But it would have been unforgivable for him as lieutenant governor had his land purchases been undertaken at the expense of the people whose rights he should have protected. He appeared to have no response to those half breeds who taunted him at election meetings with cries of "today we see Mr. McMicken and his friends all behind us on our children's lands."

Morris returned to a public welcome at Perth in 1878 but by late summer he was prepared to return to political life and was anxiously writing to Bishop Taché inquiring about his chances of being elected in the federal Manitoba riding of Marquette. Losing the Conservative nomination to Joseph O'Connell Ryan, Morris decided to stand for Selkirk, and on 7 Aug. 1878 was nominated by John NORQUAY. Although he found some support in Winnipeg, Morris' campaign raised little enthusiasm among either the Métis or the old settlers in the parishes around the city. The *Free Press*, which supported his opponent Donald Alexander Smith*, mocked Morris' love of pomp and circumstance as lieutenant governor and attacked him as avaricious, "first of all availing himself of Manitoba's climatic virtues as a sanatorium, and afterward fattening his estate in the green pastures of Government House." Questions were raised in the *Free Press* about his acquisition of Métis land, especially about the actions of Gilbert McMicken, the dominion lands agent and Morris' own agent, who was said to have used advance knowledge of what lands would be distributed. Even allowing for the bias in newspaper reporting, Morris seems to have defended himself unconvincingly; his oratory was weak, his manner evasive and self-important. He lost the election to Smith by 10 votes.

Shortly after, Matthew Crooks CAMERON resigned his Toronto East seat in the Ontario Legislative Assembly, and Morris ran in the by-election. He was elected on 21 Dec. 1878. His victory was confirmed in the general election in June of the following year when he defeated Oliver Mowat, the premier of Ontario and Liberal candidate in that riding, by 57 votes. His contributions to the Ontario legislature were not extensive; he seemed content to serve as the opposition house leader under William Ralph Meredith* and to receive his laurels. In 1880 he published *The treaties of Canada with the Indians of Manitoba and the North-West Territories*, a comprehensive history and discussion of the Indian treaties in the northwest from 1871 to 1876. He was appointed QC by Ontario in 1876 and by the dominion government in 1881. In 1886 he accepted a formal address from his fellow Conservatives on 25 years in public life. He championed the cause of federal rights against Mowat's Liberals and reputedly prevailed in 1881 on the *Toronto Daily Mail* to support the Conservative party, writing some of the editorials on the subject himself.

Morris, never strong physically, was beset by "hereditary rheumatism of the head" and other nervous disorders, and was not in good health in these years in spite of rest and treatment in England. On medical orders he declined to seek re-election in 1886. He was not idle, however. He was active in the Presbyterian Church and had continued his connection with Queen's College, serving as chairman of the board of trustees from 1883 to his death. Because of his financial and political connections across the dominion, he was in demand too for the boards of financial institutions and was associated with various companies including the North American Life Assurance Company and the Imperial Bank of Canada. During these last years he concerned himself with building his estate in the newly fashionable Muskoka. He also found pleasure in following the careers of his large and devoted family, all of whom had entered the professions. His youngest son, Edmund Montague*, was a preoccupation as Morris sought the best possible education for him in Europe and America in the fields of art and architecture.

At his death on 28 Oct. 1889 at the age of 63, Morris was eulogized as "a kindly man, a faithful public servant, a loyal elder of the church, working for his day and generation, and one whose public life was without a stain." From a more distant perspective he may be seen as a man of considerable ability with the advantage of being born into a well-connected political family in a small society in the mid 19th century. He shared the visions of young men of his class and through family and fortune was able to play a brief part in shaping the future of an expanding nation. He had the geniality of spirit and generous manner one might expect from a successful professional man who had suffered few setbacks in his career, and the concern for expanding the family's position that would not be uncommon in the first son of a Scots immigrant. An epitaph might be found in a note from his eldest son, Alexander Cline, to his youngest son, Edmund, in 1894: "Father never failed to make a friend of everyone he met, and his success in life was in no small measure due to this. You inherit a good name. Make the best of it."

JEAN FRIESEN

Alexander Morris was the author of: . . . *Canada and her resources: an essay, to which, upon a reference from the Paris exhibition committee of Canada, was awarded, by His Excellency Sir Edmund Walker Head, bart., governor general of British North America . . . , the second prize* (Montreal, 1855; 2nd ed., Montreal and London, 1855); *The Hudson's Bay and Pacific territories: a lecture* (Montreal, 1859); *Nova Britannia; or, British North America, its extent and future: a lecture* (Montreal, 1858); *Nova Britannia; or, our new Canadian dominion foreshadowed: being a series of lectures, speeches and addresses*, ed. [J. C. Dent] (Toronto, 1884); . . . *Speech delivered in the Legislative Assembly . . . during the debate on the subject of the confederation of the British North American provinces* (Quebec, 1865), and *The treaties of Canada with the Indians of Manitoba and the North-West Territories, including the negotiations on which they were based, and other information relating thereto* (Toronto, 1880; repr. [1885?]; repr. 1971). Under the anonym of "A Canadian loyalist," he wrote, with H. E. Montgomerie, *The question answered: "Did the ministry intend to pay rebels?" in a letter to His Excellency the Right Honourable the Earl of Elgin and Kincardine, K.T., governor general of British North America . . .* (Montreal, 1849). Morris also compiled *An analytical index to the act 20th Victoriæ, cap. XLIV., amending the judicature acts of Lower Canada* (Montreal, 1857) and *The railway clauses consolidation acts of Canada, 14 & 15 Victoriæ, chapter 51, and 16 Victoriæ, chapter 169, with an alphabetical and analytical index thereto* (Montreal, 1853).

AASB, T. AO, MU 2164–70. PAC, MG 26, A. PAM, MG 12, B. G. M. Grant, "Churches and schools in the north-west," John Macoun *et al.*, *Manitoba and the great north-west: the field for investment; the home of the emigrant, being a full and complete history of the country . . .* (Guelph, Ont., 1882), 523–39. [William Morris], "Twilight in Jamaica," *Douglas Library Notes* (Kingston, Ont.), 14 (1965), no.2. R. G. Babion, "Alexander Morris: his place in

Canadian history" (MA thesis, Queen's Univ., Kingston, 1945). F. A. Milligan, "The lieutenant-governorship in Manitoba, 1870–1882" (MA thesis, Univ. of Manitoba, Winnipeg, 1948). D. R. Owram, "The great north-west: the Canadian expansionist movement and the image of the west in the nineteenth century" (PHD thesis, Univ. of Toronto, 1976). J. T. Saywell, *The office of lieutenant-governor: a study in Canadian government and politics* (Toronto, 1957). L. H. Thomas, *The struggle for responsible government in the North-West Territories, 1870–97* (Toronto, 1956). L. F. Wilmot, "The Christian churches of the Red River Settlement and the foundation of the University of Manitoba: an historical analysis of the process of transition from frontier college to university" (MA thesis, Univ. of Manitoba, 1979). Lila Staples, "The Honourable Alexander Morris: the man; his work," CHA *Report*, 1928: 91–100.

MORRIS, EDWARD, businessman, politician, and office-holder; b. in 1813 in Waterford (Republic of Ireland), son of Simon Morris; m. in 1852 Katherine Howley of St John's, Nfld, and they had one daughter; d. 3 April 1887 at St John's.

Edward Morris was educated at St John's College, Waterford. In 1832 he came to Newfoundland to join the firm of his uncle, Patrick Morris*, which was engaged in passenger transport and the provision trade between St John's and Ireland. Edward looked after much of his uncle's business and made frequent trips to Europe on its behalf. Patrick Morris, however, was winding down his firm in the 1830s and liquidated it in 1839. Three years later, Edward Morris established himself as a commission agent and auctioneer in St John's, but he was apparently unsuccessful and gave up the businesses in the late 1840s. About 1842, through the patronage of his uncle who was then colonial treasurer, he had been employed by the Savings Bank, which at that time was part of the Treasurer's Department. In 1851 Morris' diary records him as living modestly with his father on a small farm near St John's. He became cashier, or general manager, of the bank in 1852 and retained that position until 1886.

After his arrival in St John's, Morris immediately became part of the Irish Catholic élite in the city and was soon prominent in the Benevolent Irish Society. He was also keenly interested in politics. His uncle had been a leader in the agitation which helped to gain representative institutions for Newfoundland in 1832 and he himself was a cousin of John Kent*, a prominent Liberal since 1833 and premier from 1858 to 1861. Edward would have liked to sit in the assembly of Newfoundland as both his father, who represented Placentia in the 1840s, and his uncle had done. Bishop John Thomas Mullock*, however, forbade him to run in the 1855 election, having already decided who was to represent the Liberals before Morris declared his candidacy. This was a severe disappointment to Morris but he accepted the decision with characteristic resignation, and his loyalty to his church and to the Liberal party was not shaken. His family connections and his long association with the Benevolent Irish Society brought him a reward in May 1855 when the new government of Philip Francis Little* appointed him assembly reporter. In 1858 he was named by Governor Sir Alexander Bannerman* to the Legislative Council and the same year was elected president of the Benevolent Irish Society.

He had now a position of minor eminence in St John's and moved to a good address. For 15 years he worked indefatigably for the charitable and social interests of the society, and managed the Savings Bank scrupulously and efficiently. In the Legislative Council, Morris was one of the few members to support confederation with the other British North American colonies during the late 1860s. He gradually gained seniority in the council and became president in 1870 despite objections from Governor Stephen John Hill*: the president of the council acted for the governor in the latter's absence and Hill considered Morris to be of an inferior social standing. Morris remained president for 16 years, however, and, although Hill secured the chief justice as administrator, he twice acted as chief administrator, in 1870 because the change had not yet been made and in 1883 because the chief justice was absent.

Morris' diary reveals him as an honest and kind man. Lacking ambition or great intelligence, he achieved his success through the efforts of friends and family connections. Always conscious of this help, and realizing that he could never penetrate the inner circle of St John's society, Morris was usually uncomfortable at formal occasions, and happiest when playing cards, talking and drinking whisky punch with friends. His was a quiet life of modest achievement.

JAMES K. HILLER

Arch. of the Archdiocese of St John's, Edward Morris diary (mfm. copy at Maritime Hist. Group Arch.). Maritime Hist. Group Arch., Morris name file. PRO, CO 194/179. *Newfoundlander*, April 1839, 22 Sept. 1842. *Times and General Commercial Gazette* (St John's), 6 April 1887.

MORRIS, MARY CHRISTIANNE. *See* PAUL

MORRISON, ANGUS, lawyer and politician; b. 20 Jan. 1822 in Edinburgh, Scotland, second son of Hugh Morrison and Mary Curran, and younger brother of Joseph Curran MORRISON; m. 5 Aug. 1846 Janet Anne Gilmor, and they had four sons and two daughters; d. 10 June 1882 in Toronto, Ont.

Angus Morrison was brought to Upper Canada by his father, a widower and a discharged sergeant in the 42nd Foot (Royal Highland Regiment). Hugh Morrison settled in Georgina Township in June 1830 with the apparent intention of farming. By January 1831 he had married Frances (Fanny), sister of John Montgomery*, moved to York (Toronto), and opened the Golden Ball Tavern. There is no record of Angus having attended Upper Canada College as is often reported; more likely, he attended a grammar school in Toronto, though after the death of his father in August 1834 and a rift in the family over the estate, he may have received much of his education from his brother. In 1839, when Joseph opened a law office with William Hume Blake*, Angus joined the firm as clerk. Called to the bar in 1845, the younger Morrison established his own practice on King Street, the financial and commercial heart of the city.

Morrison was an extremely popular and well-known young man in the city. Broad-chested, of average height, with thick curly hair and stylish mutton chop sideburns, he was considered a gentleman of fashion. Much of his public reputation, however, was based on his athletic achievements. He competed in the annual sculling races on Lake Ontario, being declared "Champion of Toronto Bay" in 1840 and 1841, and as an avid curler he took part in many of the all-day matches held on the bay. Morrison helped organize the Toronto Curling Club and the Toronto Rowing Club, serving as president of the latter for many years. Consistent with his Scottish background, he was also active in the St Andrew's Society. Predictably, Morrison parlayed his family relations, social connections, and public image into a substantial legal practice based on corporate affiliations rather than court appearances. He acted as solicitor for many institutions, including the Ontario Building Society, the University of Toronto, and, after it opened in 1867, the Canadian Bank of Commerce. Morrison's popularity also undoubtedly assisted his election as alderman for St James' Ward in 1853 and 1854.

In the summer of 1854, following the collapse of the ministry of Francis HINCKS and Augustin-Norbert Morin*, Morrison was chosen the Reform candidate for the newly created riding of Simcoe North at a convention held at Barrie. Winning the election in July, he soon proved a capable politician. Although Toronto-based, he maintained a high public profile in his riding and supported popular local issues. Perhaps more important, Morrison shrewdly played a strategic role in the distribution of local patronage whenever the opportunity arose.

Morrison's popularity in Simcoe North was, however, based on his involvement in, and promotion of, transportation schemes. In these years when both metropolis and hinterland eagerly supported the development of transportation networks, Morrison, as a representative of both Toronto and Simcoe North interests, quite naturally gained much support by encouraging railways, canals, navigation companies, and, of particular interest to his constituents, colonization roads. Not surprisingly, he was returned by acclamation in 1857. In the election of 1861, however, because the transportation developments had not paid the expected dividends, Morrison was forced into a vigorous campaign, and barely managed to retain his seat. By 1863 matters were worse; some of the developments, such as the Northern Railway, of which he had been a director, were deeply in debt, causing financial difficulties for the Simcoe County Council and providing ammunition for his opponents. The election, which Morrison lost, was a riotous one in which it was reported that "Whiskey was sent into the Townships in streams."

A coalition Reformer, Morrison was recruited by the Conservatives in Niagara for a by-election in September 1864; he won by a slim majority. In the elections of 1867, although unsuccessful in the provincial riding of Simcoe North, he retained Niagara in the federal parliament for the Conservatives and was re-elected in 1872. In the House of Commons he continued to be involved in transportation schemes and, presumably because of his experience, acted as one of the party whips. In 1874 Morrison took on the difficult task of trying to win the federal riding of Toronto Centre from the Liberal, Robert Wilkes*. He was unsuccessful, and although Wilkes's election was overturned a few months later, Morrison declined to run again.

In December 1874 Morrison allowed his name to be placed on the mayoralty ballot in Toronto, along with Francis Henry Medcalf* and Andrew Taylor McCORD, but withdrew from the contest before the poll. The following December, however, he actively pursued the nomination for mayor and after a strong campaign easily defeated the incumbent, Medcalf. The *Globe* reported that Morrison's "personal popularity" was the key to his victory; indeed, he lost only one of the nine wards, polling 4,425 votes to Medcalf's 2,673.

As mayor, Morrison characteristically maintained a high public profile. In 1876 he represented Toronto at the Philadelphia Centennial International Exhibition, where he purchased the prize-winning fountain and donated it to the citizens of Toronto; at the same exhibition, he watched Edward (Ned) Hanlan* win the sculling race and presented him with a gold watch. Easily re-elected in 1877 and 1878, Morrison proved to be a capable administrator. He oversaw a reorganization of the standing committees which included the creation of the executive committee. He also completed a long-overdue restructuring of the Water Works Commission, and in 1878 he concluded negotiations with the federal government which allowed the city to take over the exhibition grounds.

As was the case during his first experience on city council in the 1850s, Morrison again found that railways were an important issue for Toronto. Attempting to avoid the financial calamities of earlier promotions, and considering the depressed nature of the economy, men such as George LAIDLAW were promoting the construction of narrow gauge feeder lines. The Toronto City Council had supported these schemes, and between 1868 and 1876 had awarded $710,000 in bonuses to several projects, including $100,000 in 1873 to Laidlaw's Credit Valley Railway. By the beginning of Morrison's first term many lines were in financial difficulty, especially the Credit Valley. Laidlaw, unable to attract private capital, was energetically pursuing funds at all levels of government. As a director, shareholder, and solicitor of the Credit Valley, Morrison had been regarded by the promoters of the railway as a good choice for mayor, though some had expressed concern that he lacked the "vim" to push a second bonus through the council. Nevertheless, only a few weeks after Morrison's election in 1875, the city council received the required petitions asking for the granting of a bonus of $250,000. The issue was delayed pending a report by the city engineer, Francis SHANLY, and it was not until 7 March 1877, at a boisterous council meeting, replete with resignations of aldermen, that the by-law effecting a bonus was passed. According to provincial statute, by-laws for bonuses required the approval of the ratepayers and Morrison chaired a public meeting to promote the acceptance of this by-law. When the vote was taken on 3 April, it was approved.

Although nominated for a fourth term in December 1878, Morrison declined to stand, and after a half-hearted bid for the mayoralty in 1880 retired from public life. His law firm, by this time styled Morrison, Sampson and Gordon, had flourished and undoubtedly provided him with a more than adequate income. He had been made a QC in 1873. His death, on the night of 10 June 1882, was a shock to the entire community and his funeral, a municipal event, was reported to have consisted of more than 90 carriages.

VICTOR LORING RUSSELL

AO, MU 472, Thomas McCraken to Alexander Campbell, 26 Oct. 1876; MU 508, Alexander Campbell to R. J. Cartwright, 28 June 1873; MU 1376, J. A. Macdonald to Egerton Ryerson, 7 Feb. 1862; RG 1, C-IV, Georgina Township papers, Concession 7, Lot 3; RG 22, ser.6-2, York County, Will of Hugh Morrison, 11 June 1833; RG 49, I-7-B-3, box 8, Credit Valley Railway file. CTA, Angus Morrison information file; RG 1, A1, 1876; 12 June 1882; RG 2, B1, 1876; 1877; RG 5, H1. PAC, MG 24, B40, 5: 237–38.

Canadian North-West (Oliver), II: 875. Macdonald, *Letters* (J. K. Johnson and Stelmack), II: 160, 247. *Canadian Freeman* (Toronto), 15 June 1863; 8 Sept. 1864; 22, 29 Aug., 19 Sept. 1867. *Colonial Advocate* (Toronto), 12 Aug. 1834. *Examiner* (Toronto), 11 March 1840. *Globe*, December 1874, January 1876. *Northern Advance and County of Simcoe General Advertiser* (Barrie, [Ont.]), 12, 19, 26 July 1854; 5 Feb. 1857; 12 June 1861; 3, 24 June 1863; 8 Aug. 1867. *Canadian biog. dict.*, I: 419–20. *Dominion annual register*, 1882: 352. *Toronto directory*, 1833–34; 1846–47; 1850; 1856; 1871–80. A. F. Hunter, *A history of Simcoe County* (2v., Barrie, 1909; repr. 1948). Angus MacMurchy, *Sketch of the life and times of Joseph Curran Morrison and Angus Morrison* . . . (n.p., [1918]). V. Ross and Trigge, *Hist. of Canadian Bank of Commerce*, II: 10. D. G. G. Kerr, "The 1867 elections in Ontario: the rules of the game," *CHR*, 51 (1970): 369–85.

MORRISON, JOSEPH CURRAN, lawyer, politician, and judge; b. 20 Aug. 1816 in Ireland, eldest son of Hugh Morrison and his first wife, Mary Curran, and elder brother of Angus MORRISON; m. 23 July 1845 Elizabeth Bloor, and they had three sons and three daughters; d. 6 Dec. 1885 in Toronto, Ont.

The family background and early life of Joseph Curran Morrison remain obscure. Accounts of Morrison given by his contemporaries make passing references to his father's Scottish origins and his mother's supposed family connections. It is certain, however, that Morrison attended the Royal Belfast Academical Institution in 1826; in 1830 his family immigrated to Upper Canada. In 1831 his father became an innkeeper at York (Toronto) and Joseph was attending Upper Canada College. Hugh Morrison died in August 1834 and Joseph Curran became involved in a dispute with his father's second wife, Frances (Fanny), sister of John Montgomery*, over the division of the estate. As a result, the children of Mary Curran left their stepmother, and Joseph, at 18, became the head of a household consisting of four younger brothers and sisters. In 1834 he enrolled as a law student and entered the office of Simon Ebenezer Washburn*. One of his younger brothers, Angus, was to follow him into law and politics.

After Joseph's admission to the bar in 1839, he formed a partnership with another of Washburn's pupils, William Hume Blake*; in 1842 George Skeffington Connor* joined the firm. Morrison, who attended mainly to its commercial clients, prospered as a lawyer and he shared an interest in Reform politics with his partners. In 1841 he acted as campaign secretary for Isaac BUCHANAN. Two years later he was appointed clerk of the Executive Council and he served it for four years in its capacity as a Court of Appeal. During the 1840s Morrison established connections with several other Reformers: in 1844 he pledged funds to aid George Brown* in founding the *Globe* and he shared with Francis HINCKS an interest in establishing a public school system. Morrison was appointed to the Board of Education (which became the Council of Public Instruction in 1850) when it first met in 1843 and continued as a member for 30 years. Egerton RYERSON noted in 1857 that Morrison, after he had gained elective office, "devoted more time than any other political man in Canada" to serving as mediator or "connecting link" between Ryerson and the council on the one hand and the legislature on the other.

Morrison's political career had begun in 1848 when

he successfully contested the riding of York West. As a member of the assembly he supported the Reform administration of Louis-Hippolyte La Fontaine* and Robert Baldwin*. From 1852 until 1857 he represented Niagara, initially winning the riding in a by-election called when Hincks, who had been elected in two constituencies, vacated the seat. In June 1853 Morrison was appointed solicitor general in the government of Hincks and Augustin-Norbert Morin*, a post he held until the ministry was defeated in September 1854. While in the Hincks ministry, Morrison became increasingly Conservative in his politics. In 1856 he joined the ministry of Sir Allan Napier MacNab* and Étienne-Paschal Taché* shortly before its resignation on 23 May. On 24 May he was appointed receiver general in the newly formed government of John A. Macdonald* and Taché, as well as a member of the Board of Railway Commissioners. During 1856 he also acted as commissioner for consolidating the statutes of Upper Canada. In the elections of 1857 Morrison did not stand for the riding of Niagara and the *Globe* implied that this decision was made under pressure from his constituents. He was unsuccessful in these elections, losing first in Peel and then in a contest with Oliver Mowat* in Ontario South. Voters in Ontario South paid little attention to Morrison's measured defence of the government's record and his emphasis on accommodation with Canada East on such issues as representation by population and separate schools. With two other defeated ministers Morrison resigned from the cabinet in February 1858. One month later he lost another bid to sit in the assembly, this time in a by-election in Oxford North. In February 1860, after a year as registrar of the city of Toronto, Morrison was invited by Macdonald to enter the ministry as solicitor general, He accepted but again failed to secure a seat, losing a by-election in Grey in February 1861. Apparently at the urging of his colleagues, Morrison reversed his decision to resign his office and stayed on in the face of opposition censure until March 1862.

Morrison's career was modelled on that of Francis Hincks, closely combining political office with the promotion of railways. He wrote of his years in government that he had been "behind the scenes," a remark which can be taken as a warning of the difficulty in assessing the extent of his influence. Most closely identified with the Ontario, Simcoe and Huron railway (after 1858 the Northern Railway), he was one of its original directors and, from 1852 to 1862, its president. During this ten-year span the railway experienced a series of unsatisfactory attempts to establish boat services from the Collingwood terminus, bankruptcy in 1857, as well as the first years of Frederic William CUMBERLAND's successful reorganization in the 1860s. Although he was questioned during the 1853 court case about the "£10,000 job" in which Hincks and John George Bowes* were implicated, Morrison does not seem to have been involved with their sale of debentures of the Ontario, Simcoe and Huron Railroad Union Company.

Morrison had connections, both as a lawyer and as a politician, with railways other than the Northern through promoters such as Isaac Buchanan and Samuel Zimmerman*. Although Morrison was known as "the member for Zimmerman," these links were often limited to brief periods during which the promoters had particular need of Morrison's skills in law or as a mediator. In 1853 he was appointed parliamentary agent for the Great Western Railway. In the same year he chaired a shareholders' meeting which agreed to a merger of the proposed Toronto and Guelph Railway with the Grand Trunk. On another occasion the factions contending over the Woodstock and Lake Erie Railway and Harbour Company after the death in 1857 of Zimmerman, its promoter, proved too much even for Morrison's ability as a negotiator. Zimmerman's death had left his transportation schemes in disarray. The trustees of his estate made Morrison president of the railway in April 1857, but when mediation failed and a parliamentary inquiry was called, he resigned within the month. While working for the trustees, Morrison, as receiver general, was able to persuade Thomas Gibbs Ridout*, cashier of the Bank of Upper Canada, to have the bank assume Zimmerman's paper assets of £2,000,000, assets which, according to historian B. D. Dyster, were "fraudulently inflated" and "hung about with shadowy liabilities in transport and banking." In so doing, Morrison, according to Dyster, "covered up for a deeply implicated ministry," but heavily burdened the Bank of Upper Canada. His activities as a member of both the ministry and the business community demonstrated the conflict of interest which was increasingly discrediting Morrison and his fellow politicians.

On 18 March 1862 Morrison was appointed a puisne judge of the Court of Common Pleas. He was promoted to the Court of Queen's Bench in August 1863 and transferred to the Ontario Court of Appeal on 30 Nov. 1877. Despite poor health during his later years, he remained in office until 1885. As a lawyer Morrison had acted for the prosecution in several of the more notorious murder trials of his day, including that of James McDermott and Grace Marks in 1853 and, in 1860, that of James Brown for the murder of John Sheridan Hogan*. As a judge, he was again involved in several sensational trials, and he passed sentence on the last 11 Fenians to be tried in Toronto for their participation in the raids of 1866. His reputation as a judge rested on his knowledge of business law and on the intuition, understanding of human nature, and common sense he brought to his cases. Although an obituary in the *Canada Law Journal* expressed doubts whether the "reasons for his judgements were always sound," it did pay tribute to these qualities and conceded that Morrison was "singularly correct in the result."

Popular in private life, Morrison was remembered with affection by those who had worked with him in court. He was president of the Toronto St Andrew's Society from 1850 to 1852 and he served the University of Toronto as senator for 25 years and as its chancellor from 1863 to 1876. His interest in horticulture made his home, Woodlawn, purchased from William Hume Blake in 1844, something of a showplace for its gardens and conservatory as well as a centre for his noted hospitality. Blake might complain of Morrison's "utter want of reticence" but most contemporaries found it impossible to quarrel with his humour and good sense and he remained on friendly terms with men such as George Brown who eventually became a political opponent. In the politics of his day Morrison had played an important, if unobtrusive, role as a link betweeen the political leaders he served and the business community.

IN COLLABORATION

AO, MU 139, W. H. Blake to Edward Blake, 18 April 1868; Hardy (Arthur Sturgis) papers; RG 1, C-IV, Georgina Township papers, Concession 7, Lot 3; RG 22, ser.6-2, York County, will of Hugh Morrison, 11 June 1833. PAC, MG 24, B40, 5: 895; D16, 48; MG 26, A. York County Surrogate Court (Toronto), no.5844, will of J. C. Morrison, 5 July 1882 (mfm. at AO).

Canada Law Journal, new ser., 21 (1885): 425–26. Macdonald, *Letters* (J. K. Johnson and Stelmack), I-II. Northern Railway of Canada, *Report submitted by the board of directors . . .* (Toronto), 1860–63. Ontario, Simcoe and Huron Railroad Union Company, *Report by the chief engineer to the directors* (Toronto), 1852–53; *Report submitted by the board of directors . . .* (Toronto), 1854-55; 1857–58. *Globe*, 12 Jan., July 1854; January 1858; 26 June, 8–9 Oct. 1861; 7 Dec. 1885. *Mail* ([Niagara-on-the-Lake, Ont.]), July–November 1856; 13, 20 May, December 1857. *Whitby Chronicle* (Whitby, [Ont.]), 26 Nov. 1857–7 Jan. 1858. Dent, *Canadian portrait gallery*, IV: 48–49. *Dominion annual register*, 1885: 271–72. *Political appointments, 1841–65* (J.-O. Coté). Read, *Lives of judges*, 347–64. Careless, *Brown*. B. D. Dyster, "Toronto 1840–1860: making it in a British Protestant town" (1v. in 2, PHD thesis, Univ. of Toronto, 1970). Angus MacMurchy, *Sketch of the life and times of Joseph Curran Morrison and Angus Morrison . . .* (n.p., [1918]). Joseph Schull, *Edward Blake, the man of the other way (1833–1881)* (Toronto, 1975). C. B. Sissons, *Egerton Ryerson, his life and letters* (2v., Toronto and London, 1937–47). Shortt, "Hist. of Canadian currency, banking and exchange: the passing of the Upper Canada and Commercial banks," *Canadian Banker*, 12: 193–216.

MORRISON, THOMAS FLETCHER, master mariner, farmer, and politician; b. 22 Feb. 1808 at Londonderry, Colchester County, N.S., son of Joseph A. Morrison, farmer, and Isabella Fletcher; m. first in 1838, Hannah Faulkner; m. secondly in 1844, Margaret Brown Fletcher; d. 23 July 1886 at Folly Village, Colchester County, N.S.

Thomas Fletcher Morrison's family had immigrated to New England from Ireland about 1720, and in 1760 his grandfather, Captain John Morrison, moved from New Hampshire to the district of Cobequid (Colchester) where he farmed and served as a member of the assembly. Thomas himself received little formal education, but by private study he learned navigation and for more than 25 years engaged in the coasting trade as a master mariner. When he left the sea he took up farming as his principal vocation, although he also assumed minor offices such as immigration agent and surveyor of shipping, and busied himself in community work, especially in the local Presbyterian church.

Elected to the provincial assembly as a Liberal for Londonderry Township in 1855, and re-elected for the North Division of Colchester in May 1859, Morrison served until 1863. According to one observer, his first speech "threw the Commons all aghast"; many members thought that the English actor, David Garrick, "had risen from the dead and taken up his abode in Londonderry." The stentorian sounds, comic reminiscences, excited tone, and magnificent peroration set him apart. One listener thought he owed his style to the "eccentric pulpit oratory of 'Father Taylor,'" which he had heard in Boston, or perhaps to the "ranting and roaring, and oratory run mad" of the temperance quacks. Another attributed his quality of voice to its "long and constant use amid the roaring of the winds and the swelling of the waves." In any case, he quickly won the sobriquet of "Rolling Billows." A plain-spoken man, he would not let himself be humbugged by anyone. As a junior member he told the Conservative premier, James William Johnston*, that he would "as soon . . . expect to find the ferocious tiger converted into the gentleness of the lamb, by the moral suasion of an alligator . . . as to find [him] standing for the liberties . . . of the people."

Morrison did not run in 1863 and was not in the assembly when confederation was mooted, but he vigorously supported the anti-confederates in the press before being elected again to the assembly in September 1867. Because he held that the British North America Act was unconstitutional, he incurred in the assembly the gibes of Hiram Blanchard*, the leader of the pro-confederates, who invited the English law lords to attend Morrison's school and partake of his vast knowledge of constitutional law. But though he remained adamantly opposed to confederation, Morrison refused, good party man that he was, to join extreme anti-confederates such as Dr George MURRAY and William Kidston in accusing the provincial government of "accepting the situation." Sometimes Morrison suggested that confederation would collapse by itself because it was an unnatural creation; more often he urged that Joseph Howe*'s "better terms of 1869" be treated as a first instalment from the federal government due Nova Scotia, and that, after further instalments, the people be consulted. If they did not accept the situation, delegates should be sent to Britain to shout "repeal, repeal, repeal" forcefully enough to awaken even "the stupid, slumbering ministry . . . in Downing Street." Before the provincial election of 1871 Morrison pictured "poor old Nova Scotia, lying in the cold, icy, despotic embrace of Canada, lacerated, torn and bleeding at every pore," and vowed that not a single pro-confederate would be elected.

Though he was known primarily as a critic, Morrison sponsored the bill which in 1870 introduced the secret ballot in elections. Originally hostile to the measure, he now hoped the ballot would reduce the influence of the dominion confederates in provincial elections. He was disappointed, however, that the Legislative Council eliminated the coloured cards which permitted illiterates to vote without assistance. The first use of the ballot in an 1870 by-election not being to the anti-confederates' satisfaction, they voted in the assembly in 1871 and 1873, over Morrison's opposition, to abolish it, but the Legislative Council rejected the assembly's resolutions on both occasions. Morrison, however, defended an assembly prerogative when he bitterly denounced a Conservative proposal to transfer the trial of controverted elections from committees of the assembly to the courts, primarily because it gave discretionary power to pro-confederate judges. This debate produced the most celebrated of Morrison's perorations, in which he invoked the spirits of Reason, Liberty, and Patriotism to keep control of the provincial parliament out of the hands of irresponsible judges: "Spirit of Reason, where art thou? Hast thou fled from these benches, and allowed despotism and lunacy to reign in thy stead? Genius of Liberty, whither hast thou fled? Fleest thou to the dark recesses of the mountain's brow, there to hide thy head until this storm of despotism passes over . . . Spirit of Patriotism . . . come back to your post. . . ."

Re-elected in 1871, Morrison stood at the bottom of the poll in Colchester County in 1874. But the Liberal government of Philip Carteret Hill* in January 1876 appointed him a legislative councillor, and, according to one observer, "the record of his closing years is the record of the legislative council." This was especially true between 1879 and 1882, for although Arthur McNutt Cochran nominally led the Liberals in the upper house, Morrison provided the major criticism of the Conservative administrations of Simon Hugh Holmes* and John Sparrow David Thompson*, successfully assaulting government measures such as the debt-funding bill of 1879 and the bridge bills of 1881 and 1882. But not even he could get his fellow Liberals to defeat the government's chief proposal of 1882, the railway consolidation bill. Morrison interpreted the council's role of "calm, sober second thought" to go as far as exploring the government's innermost motives and supervising its financial policies and procedure in detail. He thus helped stamp upon the council a partisan image it never lost.

When the Liberals again took office in August 1883 Morrison became an executive councillor, and, on the death of Cochran a year later, government leader in the upper house as well. As leader he vigorously defended the administration's demands on Ottawa for better financial terms to a hard-pressed province, sometimes developing an argument, original with him, that the federal government owed Nova Scotia more than $800,000 on its debt allowance account. His exchanges on this matter with a second councillor from Colchester, Conservative Samuel Creelman*, enlivened the council's proceedings in his last years.

A self-made, self-educated man, Morrison became highly knowledgeable, if not expert, in many facets of public business. Although regarded as an "original," he was too much of a partisan to be genuinely innovative. But his style of oration undoubtedly made him unique in the annals of the Nova Scotia legislature.

J. MURRAY BECK

N.S., House of Assembly, *Debates and proc.*, 1856–63; 1868–74; Legislative Council, *Journal of proc.*, 1876–86. *Acadian Recorder*, 26 July 1856. *Morning Chronicle* (Halifax), 24 July 1886. *Canadian biog. dict.*, II: 495–96. [Benjamin] Russell, "Reminiscences of a legislature," *Dalhousie Rev.*, 3 (1923–24): 5–16.

MORTON, SILVANUS, merchant, shipowner, and politician; b. 13 April 1805 in Liverpool, N.S., probably the son of James Morton and Lucy Gorham; m. 9 Jan. 1833 Ezelia Ford, and they had six children; d. 8 Feb. 1887 at Milton, N.S.

Silvanus Morton shared his family's interest in the timber industry in southern Nova Scotia and by 1828 he had begun to acquire land in Liverpool Township. He also developed an interest in shipping; by 1840 he owned a 170-ton brig, the *Milton*. In his lifetime he owned, wholly or partly, about ten vessels and employed both these and others to ship lumber to the West Indies. On the local market he sold timber cut at his own three mills, foodstuffs brought from Halifax, from Canada, and from the United States, and sugar and molasses imported from the West Indies.

In 1856 Morton became a founding shareholder in the Milton Railroad Company. By then he was a prominent and wealthy resident of Queens County, and he held a number of minor offices in the county such as overseer of the poor for Milton. But Morton was not without detractors in the community; he and other members of a committee appointed to examine the public accounts of Queens County in 1856 were accused of incompetence in the performance of their task, a charge investigated and rejected by the county court. The *Liverpool Transcript* reported that a court case in which Morton sued a debtor "presented some extraordinary features on the part of the defence, and considerable hard swearing took place." The difficulties of the litigations in which Morton became involved may have been a result of a certain pomposity on Morton's part, revealed in October 1857 when he used the columns of the *Transcript* to lecture a young man he mistakenly believed to have stolen a few fish from him.

In 1859 Morton entered provincial politics, as a Reform candidate, by contesting the Queens County assembly seat held by John Campbell. Morton promised "to displace the most offensive appointments made by the late Government . . . to give every possible opposition to any Sectarian influence . . . to use every exertion towards economy in the expenditure of the Public Revenue." He lost by six votes, in a contest which produced "some little fighting and squabbling of a rather spirited turn," but he took the seat in 1860 after an inquiry into the election by a house committee.

In an assembly containing Joseph Howe*, Morton shared the fate of most back-benchers in his party. Records of debates do not indicate that Morton ever spoke, other than to present an occasional bill or petition on matters affecting Queens County. He did not, however, shirk his duties in the assembly; he attended its sessions, served on various committees, and was independent enough to be the only member to dissent from a report presented in 1863 on Indian affairs. In the same year Morton informed a gathering of constituents that he wanted to retire from public life, and he did not run again.

While Silvanus Morton sat in the assembly his sons Charles and John played an increasingly important role in the family's business affairs. Morton acquired additional property in the mid 1860s and transferred much of it to his sons. By 1869 he was a justice of the peace. He was also the fourth largest shareholder and president of the Bank of Liverpool, founded in 1871. Many shareholders suffered severe losses when the bank collapsed in 1873, the situation being made worse by the fact that shareholders were responsible for twice the value of their shares. Morton was dead when the Supreme Court of Nova Scotia rendered the final judgement against shareholders in 1888; his estate settled promptly, but, according to the *Liverpool Advance* of 9 Feb. 1887, Morton himself had been "obliged with many others ultimately to succumb" to the financial calamities which the bank failure had unleashed.

DONALD F. CHARD

R. J. Long, "The annals of Liverpool and Queens County, 1760–1867" (1926) is in the possession of Seth Bartling (Liverpool, N.S.) (typescript at Dalhousie Univ. Library, Halifax; mfm. at PANS). PANS, MS file, Banks, Bank of Liverpool, 1878–80. Queens County Court of Probate (Liverpool), Original estate papers, A, 1887–93 (mfm. at PANS). Queens County Registry of Deeds (Liverpool), 9, 1827–31; 13, 1843–46; 14, 1846–51; 19, 1864–65; 20, 1866 (mfm. at PANS). N.S., House of Assembly, *Debates and proc.*, 1861; *Journal and proc.*, 1860–63. *Liverpool Advance*, 9 Feb. 1887. *Liverpool Transcript*, 1854–63. *Directory of N.S. MLAs*, 258. *McAlpine's N.S. directory*, 1868–69: 683. Harry Eisenhauer, "The Bank of Liverpool (1871–1879)," *Canadian Paper Money Journal* (Toronto), 9 (1973): 6–8, 21.

MOSS, THOMAS, lawyer, politician, and judge; b. 20 Aug. 1836 in Cobourg, Upper Canada, eldest of the four children of John Moss and Ann Quigley; m. 28 July 1863 Amy (d. 1880), eldest daughter of Robert Baldwin Sullivan*, and they had two daughters and six sons (two sons died in infancy); d. 4 Jan. 1881 in Nice, France.

Soon after the birth of Thomas Moss, his family moved to Toronto where his father acquired and operated a brewery. Thomas was educated at Gale's Institute and then at Upper Canada College from 1850 to 1854 where in his final year he was head boy and won the governor general's prize. He continued his education at the University of Toronto, receiving its first scholarships in mathematics and classics and becoming prominent in the Literary and Debating Society before graduating in 1858 with a BA and three gold medals. In 1859 he received an MA and wrote the prize-winning thesis for that year. Moss maintained his connection with the university by filling the posts of registrar from 1861 to 1873, senator, and, from 1874 to his death, vice-chancellor. During these two decades when the university was suffering difficulties, Moss was one of its staunchest defenders. After his death the university named a building and established two scholarships in classics in his honour.

Moss began the study of law in 1858 in the Toronto office of Adam CROOKS and Hector Cameron and was called to the bar in 1861. He practised law first with Cameron, then with James Patton and Featherston Osler*. In 1871 he formed a successful partnership with his brother Charles*, later chief justice of Ontario, William Alexander FOSTER, a leader of the Canada First movement, and Osler; Robert Alexander Harrison* joined the firm in the following year. In 1871 Moss was appointed equity lecturer for the Law Society of Upper Canada and elected a bencher. When he was its chairman, the law society's committee on legal education prepared a report which led to the establishment of a law school in 1873. In 1872 he was appointed a member of the Law Reform Commission, and was named a QC. That same year he was offered the vice-chancellorship in the Court of Chancery by Sir John A. Macdonald*'s government but he declined because the salary was insufficient for the needs of a large family and his own style of living. Still in his mid 30s, Moss was now well established in his profession and was a member of the Toronto, National, and Rideau clubs. Although he had been a Roman Catholic, by the time of his marriage he had become a member of the Church of England and supported the low church group.

In 1873 Moss turned briefly to a new career. In December he allowed his name to be put forward as a Liberal candidate in a federal by-election in Toronto West. With support from members of the Toronto Trades Assembly and the Canada First movement, and with the Pacific Scandal in the air, Moss won election in the normally Conservative constituency. The victory provided the new government of Alexander Mackenzie* with an important impetus and confidence which it carried into the federal general election in January 1874. Re-elected, Moss was chosen, as one of the promising young Liberals, to move the address in reply to the speech from the throne. He was not, however, particularly active in parliament and only introduced two minor bills. He assisted the government in drawing up the new Insolvent Act of 1874 and spoke twice in favour of the Supreme Court Bill of 1875.

As a lawyer, Moss had had professional contact with and admiration for Edward Blake*; the two men were close friends and seat-mates in the House of Commons. Both supported some of the ideas of the Canada First movement, and although neither man belonged to it, they were willing to use it to their own political ends. Moss was therefore identified with the Blake wing of the Liberal party and, like Blake, opposed George Brown*'s dominance in the Ontario Liberal party. In January 1875 Moss joined in founding the Toronto *Liberal* as a "more progressive" Liberal organ than George Brown's *Globe*.

Moss nevertheless retained the respect and confidence of both Mackenzie and Brown, and was thus able to play an important role in the spring of 1875 when, as Blake's representative, he participated in the negotiations that led to Blake's return to the federal cabinet in the justice portfolio. In 1875 he was active in the provincial election campaign. That fall, however, he was offered a judgeship on the Court of Error and Appeal for Ontario. He was suffering from financial difficulties, his heavy investments in the *Liberal* having been lost when the newspaper failed in July 1875, and the judgeship would give him a large, constant income. After he was assured by Blake that his departure would not hurt his friend's position in the ongoing power struggle in the Liberal party, he accepted and was commissioned on 8 Oct. 1875. He was appointed chief justice of the Court of Appeal on 30 Nov. 1877 and a year later, at the age of 41, became chief justice of Ontario.

As a judge, Moss was known for the easy, graceful manner with which he conducted cases and for the untiring energy and thought which went into his judgements. He rarely wrote dissenting opinions, but he seemed to enjoy writing separate, often lengthy, concurring judgements. Moss rendered a number of important decisions, several being remarkable for their protection of the rights of individuals against the arbitrary use of power by governments or large corporations. In *Yeomans* v. *the Corporation of the County of Wellington* (1879), Moss, noting "that individual property rights shall not be sacrificed for the general good, and that the citizen shall not be required to relinquish his private property to the state without receiving a fair equivalent," found that an individual property owner was entitled to compensation because a county road had been constructed so as to injure his property. In *Fitzgerald et al.* v. *the Grand Trunk Railway Company* (1880) he denied that a large corporation could free itself from liability for negligence by the inclusion of a clause in contracts denying that it had any responsibility. This particularly influential decision was upheld in the Supreme Court of Canada and was relied upon in later cases.

In 1880 Moss was forced to cease attending the court because of ill health and was ordered to a warmer climate. He left with some of his family for the south of France but during the ocean voyage caught a severe cold from which he was unable to recover.

J. G. Snell

AO, MU 159–62. *Canada Law Journal*, new ser., 17 (1881): 55–60. *Reports of cases decided in the Court of Appeal* [of Ontario] . . . , comp. J. S. Tupper *et al.* (27v., Toronto, 1878–1901), I–V. *Globe*, 1863, 1873–74, 6 Jan. 1881. *Leader*, 1873. *Toronto Daily Mail*, 6–7 Jan. 1881. Dent, *Canadian portrait gallery*, I: 353–55. Read, *Lives of judges*, 387–403. N. F. Davin, *The Irishman in Canada* (London and Toronto, 1877), 608–9. D. W. Swainson, "Personnel of politics," 255–59. D. P. Gagan, "The relevance of 'Canada First,'" *Journal of Canadian Studies*, 5 (1970), no.4: 36–44. J. [G.] Snell, "The West Toronto by-election of 1873 and Thomas Moss," *OH*, 58 (1966): 236–56.

MOUSSEAU, JOSEPH-ALFRED, lawyer, journalist, writer, politician, and judge; b. 18 July 1838 at Berthier-en-Haut (Berthierville), Lower Canada, son of Louis Mousseau and Sophie Duteau, *dit* Grandpré; m. there on 20 Aug. 1862 Hersélie Desrosiers, and they had 11 children; d. 30 March 1886 in Montreal, Que.

Joseph-Alfred Mousseau's family must have immigrated to Canada by the 17th century, since Jacques Mousseaux, *dit* Laviolette, whose parents came from

Azay-le-Rideau, near Tours, France, married Marguerite Sauriot (or Sauviot) on 16 Sept. 1658, at Ville-Marie (Montreal). Joseph-Alfred attended the Académie de Berthier but, according to his contemporaries, he was largely self-educated. He came to Montreal to study law and worked there under Louis-Auguste Olivier, Thomas Kennedy RAMSAY, Lewis Thomas DRUMMOND, and Louis Bélanger. He was called to the bar in 1860 and appointed a QC in 1873. For 20 years he practised both civil and criminal law with the legal firm of Mousseau, Chapleau et Archambault, which became Mousseau et Archambault when Joseph-Adolphe Chapleau* left. Noting that he was a fiend for work, his friend Laurent-Olivier David* observed: "He had a good mind, possessing sound judgement, a splendid memory and a lively imagination. He was above all a worker, a plodder, who spent his nights studying, consulting sources, preparing his speeches or his writing. Often, after arguing in court all day, he would set to work again at eight o'clock in the evening, and continue until three or four in the morning. He kept himself awake by taking ten or more cups of coffee and frequently other stimulants. A disastrous habit."

While engaged in legal practice, Mousseau was also active as a journalist and writer. On 2 Jan. 1862 a new paper, *Le Colonisateur*, began publication in Montreal as the successor to *La Guêpe*, started by Cyrille Boucher* and Adolphe Ouimet*. The journal's goal was to assist settlement in the province. Mousseau was one of its proprietors, along with Ludger Labelle*, Chapleau, Louis-Wilfrid Sicotte, and David. In this group were adherents of both political parties. These young intellectuals set out to cut across party lines and to carry out the patriotic project of fostering settlement in the province. They wanted to provide the public with the information essential for the success of the colonizing venture. Because agriculture was closely linked to settlement, in the article of 2 Jan. 1862 outlining their intentions they also committed themselves to the improvement of "that art" on which "the prosperity of a country" depends. In order to survive *Le Colonisateur* had to attract as many readers as possible. It therefore opened its columns not only to subjects related to settlement, such as political economy, industry, and commerce, but also to literature and science. Mousseau's contributions were anonymous, like all the other articles, for the journal was put together on a committee basis. But it is known that he contributed for only a short period since the final issue of the paper was published on 27 June 1863 and by then David and André-Napoléon Montpetit* had been its sole editors for some months. It is easy to understand why such a specialized journal would not last long. During its run it gave extensive coverage to the report of Narcisse-Fortunat Belleau* on settlement, which had been published at the end of 1861, advocated bold measures such as the creation of a ministry of colonization and of an agricultural bank granting loans on landed property, called on the public to support the building of chapels in the "settlements" because the latter had always prospered "when they had missionaries in charge," publicized the places "most suitable for settlement" and the government policies favouring it, and stressed new measures relating to immigration, repatriation, and settlement. *Le Colonisateur*, in fact, virtually exhausted the topic. It was already at a low point when in December 1862 a rival, *Le Défricheur*, was launched at L'Avenir by Jean-Baptiste-Éric Dorion*, the former general manager of the paper *L'Avenir*, and it ground to a final halt on 27 June 1863.

Seven years later Mousseau embarked on another newspaper venture. In 1870, with David and George-Édouard Desbarats*, he founded *L'Opinion publique* at Montreal. This weekly had some novel features: a new engraving process, "leggotype" (a variation of lithography), was used to attain an unprecedented quality of reproduction; the articles were written carefully, indeed with some literary pretensions, and were all signed; the publication had no definite political orientation, which according to David "makes composing it stimulating and pleases both parties." *L'Opinion publique* was successful and profitable for a while. After two years the circulation reached the unusual figure of 12,000 to 13,000, but in 1873, at the time of the Pacific Scandal, the paper was undermined by internal divisions. Scanning it, one becomes aware that Mousseau contributed regularly for three years, signing the column on international politics. It is also evident that he had literary and scientific interests, and that he was becoming increasingly sensitive to domestic politics; indeed he took pleasure in pointing out that while *L'Opinion publique* had not made him rich it had given him access to Bagot County. It is to be noted that Mousseau was in tune with the spirit of the periodical and, contrary to the trend of 19th-century journalism, had nothing of the polemicist who wields the pen as if it were a sword.

Mousseau also wrote two literary pieces. The first was a *Lecture publique . . . sur Cardinal et Duquet, victimes de 1837–38, prononcée lors du 2e anniversaire de la fondation de l'Institut canadien-français, le 16 mai 1860.* In it he described the lives and characters of Joseph-Narcisse Cardinal* and Joseph Duquet*, who having refused to join the insurgents in 1837 took part in the rebellion of 1838 because they counted then on the general cooperation of the population, the forces in the two Canadas, and the help of the Americans. Beyond these two "martyrs of nationality and liberty," Mousseau wanted to extol all those "who have loved their country and their nationality." The list of those he admired included Elzéar Bédard*, Louis Bourdages*, and Joseph

Papineau*, but not the leader of the rebellion, Louis-Joseph Papineau*.

Mousseau's second work, *Contre-poison: la Confédération c'est le salut du Bas-Canada; il faut se défier des ennemis de la Confédération*, published on 25 July 1867, is better known. Writing with the interests of the Conservative party in view, the author replied to the pamphlet in which Dorion had declared himself, in the name of the Rouges, against confederation. A plea in support of the "great and splendid" confederation, "the worthy consummation of such a splendid past which definitively establishes the French-Canadian nationality, creates a great nation, and gives the country a solid and lasting foundation," Mousseau's pamphlet was also a condemnation of the party of "the ungodly, the annexationists and the ex-agents of the secret societies" who refused to accept confederation. *Le Courrier de Saint-Hyacinthe* summed up its significance in three concise statements: "It abounds in information; its style is extremely vigorous. All voters should have a copy."

Mousseau's zeal in defending Conservative interests at the time of confederation was an indication that he might enter politics, and that zeal would again be seen during the Pacific Scandal. In the federal election campaign of 1872 he, with Chapleau, Clément-Arthur Dansereau*, and others, had a great influence on the youth of Montreal, who were becoming completely unresponsive to the scheming, manipulative tactics to which Sir George-Étienne Cartier* and the old hands of the party still clung, failing to realize that the party was thereby slipping from their control. The progressive thinking of these young conservative lawyers might have set back the emerging nationalist party which brought together both Liberals and Conservatives. But Mousseau was not content to have only an ideological influence; clearly he wanted to jump into the political arena. In January 1874, when the abolition of the double mandate opened the way for newcomers, he ran in the federal election in Bagot where the seat had been left vacant when Pierre-Samuel GENDRON chose the provincial one. Since the Conservative party was in a shaky position as a result of the Pacific Scandal, Mousseau tried to secure the support of some of the moderate Liberals. He promised to give free play to Alexander Mackenzie*'s new ministry and to judge it solely on its political performance. Probably as a result of these tactics he beat his opponent Jean-Baptiste Bourgeois, the former "Danton" of the Parti National, by 43 votes.

During the first phase of his political career Mousseau sat with the opposition. He made a good impression, although his role was necessarily a minor one. When they had relinquished office, the Conservatives had left pending such important questions as the creation of the Supreme Court of Canada, a general amnesty in the northwest, and the New Brunswick separate schools. These issues prompted the French Canadians to adopt a nationalist standpoint. It was this stance that characterized Mousseau's political actions in the house, where it associated him with the Parti National group to which Louis-Amable Jetté*, David, and Honoré Mercier* belonged.

One of Mousseau's first moves in parliament was to support Liberal Henri-Thomas Taschereau's attempt to limit the jurisdiction of the Supreme Court of Canada to cases coming under federal law. Taschereau felt that it would be unjust for judges who were mostly strangers to the province of Quebec and its *Code civil* to be able to reverse decisions of Quebec judges; his amendment was rejected by 118 to 40. Mousseau expected to see the Quebec Liberals split with the government on this issue, but party discipline prevailed over his colleagues' nationalism.

On 12 Feb. 1875 Mousseau put forward an amendment to Mackenzie's resolution concerning a general amnesty for those involved in the 1869–70 disturbances in the northwest. He made a five-hour speech proposing that the three exceptions stated in the resolution be deleted and a full amnesty be granted covering Louis RIEL, Ambroise-Dydime Lépine*, and William Bernard O'Donoghue*, for whom the Mackenzie proposal envisaged banishment for five years. His amendment was supported by the Conservatives François-Louis-Georges Baby* and Louis-François-Roderick Masson*. In the vote only 23 Conservatives from Quebec supported it, although Mousseau had once more expected support from some of the Quebec Liberals.

On the New Brunswick schools issue Mousseau adopted virtually the same position as Masson. In 1873 he had already given vigorous support in *L'Opinion publique* to the cause of the New Brunswick Roman Catholics. He maintained this position, which was more nationalist than political, when John Costigan* reintroduced the question in parliament hoping to obtain an amendment to the British North America Act by which Catholics in New Brunswick would be accorded the same rights as the Catholic minority in Ontario and the Protestant minority in Quebec. This motion was rejected in the name of provincial autonomy. Once again Mousseau's nationalist ambitions were frustrated and this led him to deplore the political dissensions paralysing the life of French Canadians as a nation. Like Masson, Chapleau, Mercier, and even Joseph-Édouard CAUCHON, he began to wish that the Conservatives would unite with "the Liberals of the province, 90 per cent of whom share their Conservative principles and their national ideal." The most natural ally, however, would probably have been the Ontario Liberals. In order to survive, Mackenzie and his followers had once more had to join forces with the supporters of Antoine-Aimé Dorion* and Luther Hamilton Holton*. Gradually, however, they lost their Reform character and progressive look, and began to display conservative tendencies. Hence they may well have been ready to repudiate their alliance with the "old Rouges" of the province of Quebec for a better matched alliance with the promoters of the party of union. This would have meant the end of the party of Sir John A. Macdonald* and Cartier, and the Conservatives of long standing could not accept such an eventuality.

While some French Canadians dreamed of an alliance, the Mackenzie government was struggling with the economic crisis which had affected the western world since the end of 1873. The Liberal party's official policy was free trade, and it was with considerable reluctance that Mackenzie adopted certain protectionist measures. They provoked a wide-ranging debate in the house on economic policy during which, on 10 March 1876, Mousseau delivered a thoroughly documented speech, published first in *La Minerve* on 20 and 21 March and later as *Le tarif, protection et libre échange*. Mousseau advanced the tenets of Macdonald's National Policy, which would become fashionable during the 1878 election campaign.

Having been active in the opposition, Mousseau easily won Bagot County in the general elections of 17 Sept. 1878 and his name was immediately put forward for a ministerial post in the new government. But Mousseau was not so ambitious. In a letter to Macdonald he joked about the forming of the government: "I suppose that at this moment 'each one is showing his tricks,' that is to say every one wants to be a minister." He and his friends would be happy if one of the three portfolios intended for the province went to Chapleau. Mousseau was then very busy with the events following the *coup d'état* of the previous 2 March by which Luc LETELLIER de Saint-Just, lieutenant governor of Quebec, had dismissed the government of Charles-Eugène Boucher* de Boucherville. In *Le 38me fauteuil* Joseph Tassé* clearly explains the role Mousseau played in what the Conservatives of the day called "the downfall of M. Letellier." Mousseau was then being pressured to act on the federal level by the Quebec Conservatives, who had been frustrated in all the measures to which they had resorted since the *coup d'état*: a petition to the administrator of Canada and another to the federal government, collective action and individual pressure, polemics in the papers, and so on. On 11 March 1879 he made a motion of censure in the house against Letellier, thus forcing the government to act. After a protracted, stormy debate, parliament passed Mousseau's motion, the first in a long series of measures leading to the dismissal of the lieutenant governor of Quebec. But in the Letellier affair Mousseau was under the influence of Chapleau, then premier of Quebec. Mousseau's political life was thereafter strongly marked and directed by the ambitions and indeed the whims of Chapleau, who was emerging as the strongest and most exacting Quebec political figure of his day.

On 8 Nov. 1880 Mousseau was summoned into the federal government as president of the Executive Council. On 20 May 1881 he became secretary of state, although he promised Sir John he would accept a position on the bench as soon as Chapleau was ready to leave the Quebec government for Ottawa, where every 19th-century politician preferred to finish his career. But at Chapleau's suggestion Macdonald effected an exchange of posts in July 1882: Chapleau became a federal minister and Mousseau became premier of Quebec.

Because he lacked aggressiveness, the will to do battle, and the spur of strong ambitions, Mousseau was not, however, destined to play a pre-eminent political role. His appointment as a federal minister had come only with a particularly favourable combination of circumstances, and he had the reputation for not being "equal to" his portfolio and for appearing "more and more out of his depth among the other ministers." His unfailing cheerfulness, his cordiality, his sense of humour, and his high spirits cast him rather as the ideal mediator, even scapegoat. It is understandable that politicians born to the game did not fail to take advantage of this fact. Of all the "orthodox" Conservatives, Mousseau, whose kindliness might be thought to be matched by broadmindedness, was perhaps the one most readily accepted by both factions of the party, as Chapleau claimed. He was certainly the one who would best enable Macdonald and Chapleau to govern the province of Quebec through an intermediary.

It is obvious that in this political situation the province was sacrificed to Ottawa, just as Mousseau was sacrificed to Chapleau, to the unity of the party, and to the interests of Montreal, which was gambling for its prosperity on the federal level. Returned in Jacques-Cartier, Mousseau was condemned to become a second-rate premier, especially since the province he inherited on 31 July 1882 was divided. Chapleau's final political gesture had been the sale of the Quebec, Montreal, Ottawa and Occidental Railway, the western section at a low price to the federal government and the eastern section to a syndicate formed and run by Louis-Adélard SENÉCAL, the financial mainstay of the Quebec Conservative party. This sale had attracted criticism because it had stripped the province of its most valuable property for the benefit of Ottawa, Montreal (which would become a major terminus), and Senécal. As a result the "Castors," a group within the Quebec Conservative party opposed to the "Senécalistes," came into existence [*see* François-Xavier-Anselme TRUDEL]. Once Chapleau was in Ottawa Mousseau became the object of the Castors' attacks and his position quickly became untenable. In the autumn of 1883 he tried to win over the Castors by negotiating the entry of John Jones Ross* and Louis-Olivier Taillon* into his government. He also secured the collaboration of a number of English-speaking Conservatives. But the Ultramontanes, followers of Trudel, refused adamantly to be reconciled with the man they called "Chapleau's shadow." The by-election on 16 Nov. 1883, in which François-Xavier Lemieux*, a Liberal of the Rouge school, was elected in Lévis thanks to the Castors' support, showed the futility of Mousseau's efforts. According to Hector-Louis Langevin*, Sir John's lieutenant in Ottawa, Lemieux was elected "obviously out of hatred for Senécal, Mousseau, Chapleau and company." After this defeat, union of the two factions of the Conservative party was obviously necessary but Mousseau was incapable of bringing it about, having neither the prestige nor the skill to do so. He therefore resigned in January 1884, at the request of the federal leaders, leaving the task of uniting the Conservatives and attempting the reconstruction of the provincial government to Ross, a moderate Castor.

When on 22 Jan. 1884 Mousseau became a puisne judge of the Superior Court for the district of Rimouski, he bid farewell to public life. At a low ebb, he died on 30 March 1886 in Montreal as the result of a chill. If he was only 47, when he was said to be constituted to reach 80, it was perhaps because politics had not served him as well as he had served politics.

ANDRÉE DÉSILETS

[The career of Joseph-Alfred Mousseau cannot be studied without consulting most of the major archival collections of the political figures of his era and official publications of the federal and provincial governments. In addition to Mousseau's writings, various newspapers and other published works provide a wealth of information and deserve mention. A.D.]

J.-A. Mousseau was the author of: *Contre-poison: la Confédération c'est le salut du Bas-Canada; il faut se défier des ennemis de la Confédération* (Montréal, 1867); *Lecture publique . . . sur Cardinal et Duquet, victimes de 1837–38, prononcée lors du 2e anniversaire de la fondation de l'Institut canadien-français, le 16 mai 1860* (Montréal, 1860); and *Le tarif, protection et libre échange; discours prononcé . . . le 10 mars 1876* (Montréal, 1876). Charles Langelier, *Souvenirs politiques* [de 1878 à 1896] (2v., Québec, 1909–12). Joseph Tassé, *Le 38me fauteuil ou souvenirs parlementaires* (Montréal, 1891). *Le Canadien*, 1862–86, especially 27 juin 1882; 31 mars, 1er avril 1886. *Le Colonisateur* (Montréal), 2 janv. 1862–27 juin 1863. *Le Courrier de Saint-Hyacinthe*, 1862–86, especially 1er août 1867; janvier–février 1874; 30 mai 1882. *Le Journal de Québec*, 1862–86, especially 31 mars, 2 avril 1886. *La Minerve*, 1862–86, especially janvier–février 1874; septembre 1878; 9 nov. 1880; 17, 19, 23 mai 1881; mai–juin, 26, 28, 29 juill. 1882; 31 mars–2 avril 1886. *L'Opinion publique*, 1870–74. Borthwick, *Hist. and biog. gazetteer*. *Canadian biog. dict.*, II: 290–91. *CPC*, 1874–84. *Dominion annual register*, 1886. Le Jeune, *Dictionnaire*. P.-G. Roy, *Les juges de la prov. de Québec*. P.-B. Casgrain, *Étude historique: Letellier de Saint-Just et son temps* (Quebéc, 1885). L.-O. David, *Histoire du Canada depuis la Confédération* (Montréal, 1909); *Mélanges historiques et littéraires* (Montréal, 1917); *Souvenirs et biographies, 1870–1919* (Montréal, 1911). Désilets, *Hector-Louis Langevin*. Rumilly, *Hist. de la prov. de Québec*, I-IV.

MUIR, JOHN, coal-master, farmer, sawmill operator, and politician; b. 28 May 1799 in Ayrshire (now part of Strathclyde), Scotland; m. Annie Miller, and they had five children; d. 4 April 1883 at Sooke, B.C.

John Muir, an Ayrshire coal-master, was living in Manchester when he was recruited by the Hudson's Bay Company in November 1848 to work their coalfields on Vancouver Island. Surface coal deposits had been discovered in the region of Fort Rupert (near present day Port Hardy) in 1835, but little had been done to exploit them. By 1848, however, the Royal Navy and the Pacific Mail Steamship Company were negotiating with the HBC to purchase coal supplies for their steamers. As its local employees were unfamiliar with coal mining, the HBC had turned to Britain for recruits.

Within three weeks of signing a three-year contract as overman, Muir led a party including his wife, their four sons, their widowed daughter with her two infant children, and two nephews to Gravesend, England, where they boarded the barque *Harpooner*. Shrewdly, Muir had secured miners' contracts for his sons, one of whom was only nine years old, and for his nephews. The party arrived at Fort Victoria, Vancouver Island, in June 1849. After a short stay they boarded the HBC brig *Mary Dare* for Fort Rupert near their base of operations; they disembarked on 24 September.

Muir, after surveying the Suquash field, realized that the coal was located chiefly along the beach of Beaver Harbour, where a small reserve had been gathered by hand and piled near the water by local Indians. Muir knew, however, that such coal was salt-ridden and the limits to its supply were obvious; consequently he began digging inland. With only a handful of miners to assist him, and having no machinery, animals, or heavy equipment, he made slow progress. Construction of Fort Rupert was not yet complete and iron goods were in especially short supply. All work was therefore performed by hand with the result that the miners literally only scratched the surface. The primitive methods, coupled with the general worthlessness of the Suquash coal measures, were bound to result in ultimate failure. Still, on 26 Jan. 1850 Muir reported to Eden Colvile*, the governor of Rupert's Land, that despite reaching a depth of 41′ 6″ without signs of a good seam, he was optimistic that one would be found.

Up to this time, Muir had acted merely as the leader of his small group, maintaining tight control over both his family and his opinions. Although he had voiced some concern about the quality of the food and had asked Colvile for more fresh provisions, he made no recorded complaint about discipline at the fort, poor equipment, or Indian harassment, all of which were beginning to alarm his family. He was, moreover, constantly faced with the demands of his subordinates that they be freed from above-ground labouring duties. According to their own interpretation of their contracts, theirs was the demanding, skilled pit-work for which they had been trained, whereas surface work, such as draining, clearing, hauling, and reinforcing the pit head, was the company's responsibility – one it was obliged to fulfil but rarely did.

By early summer 1850, relations between the miners and the HBC employees at Fort Rupert had deteriorated sharply. A series of incidents culminated in the arrest and chaining of Muir's son Andrew* and his nephew John McGregor. These men had refused to work as labourers, a defiance that had led the fort's principal officer, George Blenkinsop, to take the action he did. He released the two miners after six days, hoping the confinement would restore a sense of discipline. It did not, for on 2 July Andrew Muir and John McGregor led all the miners, except John Muir, in a desertion to California. Both government and HBC officials investigated the situation, and Blenkinsop was criticized. In the meantime, Muir, his miners having departed, refused to work alone.

Leaving the company's employ when his contract expired late in 1851, Muir relocated at Sooke on farm land previously owned by Walter Colquhoun Grant*. In 1852, however, James Douglas*, HBC chief factor and governor of Vancouver Island, recalled Muir to be overman at the company's newly opened Nanaimo coalfield on the understanding that Muir would have complete control over all mining matters. Muir agreed, and signed a two-year contract which he dutifully fulfilled. Replaced in 1854 by Boyd Gilmour, another Ayrshire coal-master, Muir retired to his now extended land holdings at Sooke. Here he devoted his energies to Woodside Farm.

Muir was joined by his son Andrew and nephew Archibald, after they returned from San Francisco. The three men had become artisans skilled in several trades and they soon turned to cutting spars, squared timber, and piles. In 1855 they acquired the engines, boilers, and machinery from a wrecked steamship, thereby obtaining the means to erect the island's first steam sawmill. By 1859, Muir and Company of Sooke was exporting 40,000 board feet from its wharf and in 1860 it opened a lumberyard at Victoria. Distracted by a nearby gold-rush at Leech River, the Muirs sold their lumbering operations in 1864. Curiously, the Muir family sought coal and not gold deposits in the area, and, being unsuccessful, repurchased their original sawmill in 1867. With characteristic energy, the family increased both production and sales. The company continued operation until it was closed in 1892, nine years after Muir's death.

John Muir had proved in part the wisdom of employing experienced miners for the embryo coal industry. By developing the forests and fields of Sooke, he and his kinsmen settled a relatively isolated area; by opening foreign and local markets for their lumber, they added substantially to the local economy. Of significance, too, was their sense of public duty. Muir had accepted an appointment as justice of the peace in 1854 and was the elected member for the Sooke district to the first assembly of Vancouver Island, 1856–61. From 1862 to 1866 he served on the Legislative Council, though he found it difficult to attend meetings. His son Andrew was the first sheriff of Vancouver Island. Few pioneers contributed as much to the island as John Muir, and his close-knit extended family created one of the first successful family firms on Vancouver Island. They can be regarded as the prototype of what was to become common in the island's business community of the later 19th century.

DANIEL T. GALLACHER

PABC, Fort Nanaimo corr., August 1852–September 1853 (transcript); Andrew Muir, Diary, 9 Nov. 1848–5 Aug. 1850; Vert. file, Muir family; John Muir. HBRS, XIX (Rich and A. M. Johnson). *Daily British Colonist* (Victoria), 4 April 1883. B. M. Gough, *The Royal Navy and the northwest coast of North America, 1810–1914: a study of British maritime ascendancy* (Vancouver, 1971), 98–101. Rich, *Hist. of HBC*, II: 644. P. M. Johnson, "Fort Rupert," *Beaver*, outfit 302 (spring 1972): 4–15. J. H. Kemble, "Coal from the northwest coast, 1848–1850," *BCHQ*, 2 (1938): 123–30. W. K. Lamb, "Early lumbering on Vancouver Island, part II, 1856–66," *BCHQ*, 2 (1938): 95–121. B. A. McKelvie, "The founding of Nanaimo," *BCHQ*, 8 (1944): 169–88.

MULGRAVE, Marquess of NORMANBY, GEORGE AUGUSTUS CONSTANTINE PHIPPS, Earl of. *See* PHIPPS

MULVANY, CHARLES PELHAM, Church of England clergyman, teacher, and author; b. 20 May 1835 in Dublin (Republic of Ireland), son of Henry William Mulvany, a barrister-at-law; Elizabeth Mulvany who died in childbirth in July 1880 at Toronto, Ont., was probably his wife; d. 31 May 1885 at Toronto.

Charles Pelham Mulvany entered Trinity College, Dublin, in 1850 and was elected a scholar of the house in 1854 before receiving a BA with 1st class honours in classics in June 1856. In his college years Mulvany wrote verse for the *Nation*, and in 1856 edited Trinity's *College Magazine*; he later contributed to the

Irish Metropolitan Magazine (1857–58). Following graduation he joined the Royal Navy in which he apparently served as a surgical assistant. In later years Mulvany claimed to have been a naval surgeon with an MD degree, but this is improbable; certainly he never practised medicine in civilian life.

After a brief stint in the navy Mulvany immigrated to Canada about 1859. In 1866 he comes into view in Toronto when he joined the 2nd Battalion, Queen's Own Rifles, during the Fenian scare. However, before any Fenian raid took place Mulvany moved to Lennoxville, Canada East, where he enlisted in the militia in Sherbrooke, rising to the rank of lieutenant, and joined the faculty of Bishop's College as a lecturer in classics. On his arrival the college conferred an honorary MA degree on him in consideration of previous work on the classical forms of English verse and on medieval hymnology. In 1867 he helped establish a literary periodical entitled the *Students' Monthly*. He left Bishop's the same year to serve as principal of the Niagara High School in Ontario, but he retired from teaching altogether in 1868 to take up an entirely new career in the Church of England.

Ordained deacon by John Travers Lewis*, bishop of the diocese of Ontario, in 1868 and priest in 1872, he was licensed curate to All Saints Church, Kingston, in 1868, and later to various parishes in Lanark, Prince Edward, and Northumberland counties. Having grown weary of rural parish life, Mulvany retired from active clerical work in 1878 and moved to Toronto to take up a career as a writer.

At this juncture a veritable flood of material began to flow from his pen for Toronto's newspapers and periodicals, particularly *Rose-Belford's Canadian Monthly and National Review*. Mulvany's initial publication in book form was a collection of *Lyrics, songs and sonnets* (1880), prepared jointly with Amos Henry Chandler. In 1880 he found employment with W. J. Gage and Company; there he edited the firm's monthly *Canada School Journal* for two years and a Latin text by Julius Cæsar (1881). By this time Mulvany's interests had turned to Canadian history. He co-authored *The history of the county of Brant, Ontario* (1883) and wrote "A brief history of Canada and the Canadian people" which appeared in both the *History of the county of Peterborough, Ontario* (1884) and the *History of Toronto and the county of York, Ontario* (1885). This lengthy and error-ridden essay is an overview of Canadian political and constitutional developments written in the classic whig-liberal tradition, emphasizing the struggle for responsible government and confederation. At the time of his death, Mulvany was expanding this study into a full history of liberalism in Canada. His most important work, however, was *Toronto: past and present; a handbook of the city* (1884), written in the "booster" tradition to commemorate the city's semi-centennial. As a reference source on Toronto in the 1880s the work is indispensable, containing as it does a mine of information on the city's social, economic, and political institutions, as well as on many of its leading citizens, streets, and buildings. Mulvany's last major publication was *The history of the North-West rebellion of 1885* (1885), a hastily prepared book which appealed to the contemporary biases of most English-speaking Canadians. The author detailed the military exploits of those heroic "citizen-soldiers" who punished Louis RIEL and the "half-breeds" for attempting to establish "an island of mediaevalism and of alien race in the midst of the spread of English Canadian civilization."

GERALD KILLAN

C. P. Mulvany was the author of "A brief history of Canada and the Canadian people," published in *History of Toronto and county of York, Ontario* . . . (2v., Toronto, 1885), I, and also in *History of the county of Peterborough, Ontario* . . . (Toronto, 1884), 1–209. His article, "County and town of Peterborough, Ontario," also appears in *History of the county of Peterborough* . . . , 215–372. Mulvany contributed to *The history of the county of Brant, Ontario* . . . (Toronto, 1883) and his other historical writings include *The history of the North-West rebellion of 1885* . . . (Toronto, 1885; repr. 1971) and *Toronto: past and present; a handbook of the city* (Toronto, 1884; repr. 1970). His poetry is found in A. H. Chandler and C. P. Mulvany, *Lyrics, songs and sonnets* (Toronto, 1880), and in *A wreath of Canadian song; containing biographical sketches and numerous selections from deceased Canadian poets*, ed. Mrs C. M. Whyte-Edgar (Toronto, 1910), 143–46. He was also translator and editor of *Cæsar's "Bellum Britannicum"* . . . (Toronto, 1881).

Bishop's Univ. Arch. (Lennoxville, Que.), College Council, Record of meetings, 1861–76; Convocation register, 1854–85; Register, 1873–90. Church of England, Diocese of Ontario, Synod, *Journal* (Kingston, Ont.), 1868–85. *Globe*, 1 June 1885. *DNB*. *Dominion annual register*, 1885: 273. D. J. O'Donoghue, *The poets of Ireland: a biographical and bibliographical dictionary of Irish writers of English verse* (Dublin and London, 1912; repr. Detroit, 1968).

MUNRO (Monro), HECTOR, mason, building contractor, and real estate agent; b. 21 Jan. 1807 in Roxburghshire (now part of Borders), Scotland; m. in March 1832 at Edinburgh, Scotland, Jane Barnet, and they had three sons and three daughters; d. 5 Oct. 1888 in Montreal, Que.

Hector Munro received his training as a mason in Scotland under his father, who was a building contractor. He and his wife left Great Britain to settle in Montreal in 1832, but there is scant information about his activities during the years following his arrival. The earliest record of Hector Munro in Montreal is a notarial contract dated 1843 concerning the building of the Commercial Bank of the Midland District; on it he is described as a master builder. The Montreal directory of 1848 lists Munro as a contractor, a sure sign that in the years since his arrival he had acquired status in the construction field. Subsequently he built or repaired numerous buildings both in Montreal and elsewhere. The Bonsecours Market, constructed in the 1840s following the plans of architect William Footner at a cost of £70,000, was his most famous undertaking. This building, which was 500 feet long, served as both market and city hall.

Munro's principal clients were public institutions and large private companies. In the public sector he carried out a number of building contracts for the Protestant Board of School Commissioners for the City of Montreal and for Montreal itself; he also undertook canal construction for the provincial government. In the private sector his projects included participating in the construction, begun in 1854, of the section of the Grand Trunk linking Longueuil, Canada East, to the border of Canada West. Munro certainly benefited from the economic boom of the 1850s which fostered the growth of Montreal and was exemplified by the upsurge in railway construction. In 1852 he himself was one of the incorporators of companies in Canada West such as the London and Port Sarnia Railway Company, the Hamilton and Toronto Railway Company, and the Hamilton and Port Dover Railway Company.

During the 1860s Munro was more involved in real estate operations and management; thus in the Montreal directory for 1864–65 he listed himself as a "General Agent for the sale, lease and valuation of real estate, the preparation of plans, specifications and superintendence." Moreover he offered his services as an architect in 1874–75, according to the entry in the Montreal directory. At his death in 1888, the *Montreal Daily Witness* described him as a property owner, although the returns in the Montreal land register for that year show he owned only the land on which his residence in Saint-Antoine Ward stood.

Munro was also active in voluntary organizations. He was one of the pioneers of the Montreal Mechanics' Institute founded in 1840 and was its president from 1860 to 1862. In 1864 he was one of the founding members of the Seaman's Union Bethel, of Montreal. Evidently a staunch Presbyterian he was a deacon and an elder in the St Gabriel Street Church until 1870, and was an active member of the Montreal Auxiliary Bible Society. Finally, from 1865 to 1869, he was a member of the Protestant Board of School Commissioners for the City of Montreal.

Hector Munro was a figure of some significance in Montreal. By 1840 the city, in both its architecture and its town planning, was coming under the British influence later to be termed Victorian. This influence stemmed largely from the activity of individuals such as Munro; trained in Great Britain he pursued his career in Montreal at the time when that city was experiencing unprecedented growth and development. Hector Munro was one of those who shaped the physical environment of 19th-century Montreal.

JEAN-CLAUDE ROBERT

ANQ-M, État civil, Presbytériens, St Paul's Church (Montreal), 5 Oct. 1888; Minutiers, Théodore Doucet, 28 mai 1857; William Easton, 11 April 1844, 6 Jan. 1845; J. C. Griffin, 14 July 1847; J. H. Isaacson, 12 Aug. 1858; William Ross, 15 Sept. 1843, 23 May, 10 Sept. 1844. General Register Office (Edinburgh), Register of marriages for the parish of Edinburgh, March 1832. Can., Prov. du, *Statuts*, 1852–53, c.44, c.101, c.102; 1864, c.152. *Extracts of the books of reference of subdivisions of the city of Montreal*, ed. L.-W. Sicotte (Montreal, 1874). *Gazette* (Montreal), 8 Oct. 1888. *Montreal Daily Star*, 8 Oct. 1888. *Montreal Daily Witness*, 6 Oct. 1888. Borthwick, *Hist. and biog. gazetteer*, 185. *Montreal directory*, 1842–68; 1874. Campbell, *Hist. of Scotch Presbyterian Church*, 564, 605–6. [T. M. Gordon], *The Mechanics' Institute of Montreal, founded 1840; one hundredth anniversary, 1840–1940* ([Montreal, 1940]). J.-C. Marsan, *Montréal en évolution: historique du développement de l'architecture et de l'environnement montréalais* (Montréal, 1974).

MUNSON, Mrs LETITIA (Lecitia), herbalist, fortune-teller, and midwife; probably b. *c.* 1820 in North Carolina, although in 1882 she claimed to be 110; last known to be living in 1882.

Born a slave on a North Carolina plantation, Letitia was sent by her master "to learn the healing art, so as to be useful . . . among the hands." By her own account she spent five years with doctors and two with Indians, learning all she could of practical medicine and herbal remedies. After gaining her freedom she settled in Woodstock, Canada West, about 1861. She purchased two frame houses just outside the town and lived in one with her husband, a son, and a daughter. By the 1870s she had established herself as a herbalist and fortune-teller. She was also the confidante of women with unwanted pregnancies, whom she often advised to go the United States where they could have their children in the anonymity of poor houses. She also appears to have used her adjacent house to board pregnant women seeking privacy. It was in this house, on the morning of 16 Sept. 1882, that Ellen Weingardner was found dead on a blood-soaked mattress, the victim of an abortion in the eighth month of her pregnancy.

Ellen Weingardner had once been employed at a Woodstock hotel. About 1878 she became pregnant following an affair with one of the men working there. She took refuge at Mrs Munson's, where a girl was born to her in 1879. She then left Woodstock, only to return in April 1882 with her daughter and a man named John Camp, from Tilsonburg (Tillsonburg), Ont., who claimed to be her husband; she was again pregnant. Camp left in about a week, after making arrangements for Ellen's board with Mrs Munson. In early September Ellen moved to the adjacent house, where she was later found dead.

Evidence given at the inquest which followed the discovery of her body did not rule out the possibility of a self-inflicted abortion, but the doctors questioned were of the opinion that the pain entailed made such an action unlikely; there must have been an accomplice. The people of Woodstock had little doubt about the identity of the guilty party. It was reported at the time that "half remembered stories of alleged horrors connected with the Munson family were revived, and were one-half of what is said believed, this old negress must be the incarnation of untold villainy." There was, as well, a fair amount of circumstantial evidence against Mrs Munson. Her house, when searched, was found to contain objects which might be used in the performance of an abortion: a large quantity of clothes and bedding, several books and papers on medical subjects, various medicines and herbs, and several sharp instruments (one of which had been wrapped in cloth and hidden in a chest). The chief constable told the inquest that prostitutes had informed him "girls went . . . [to Mrs Munson] to get rid of their encumbrances." Finally, Mrs Munson herself had made contradictory statements concerning her knowledge of Miss Weingardner's condition. The inquest resulted in a charge against her of conducting or assisting in an abortion.

Mrs Munson was arraigned before the Oxford assizes in November. The evidence against her was presented once more. In defence, she replied that the instruments found in her home were used for lancing boils. She testified that she had counselled pregnant women to have their children in American poor houses and had once been offered a cow to kill a child born in her house, but she denied having ever performed an abortion. At the end of the trial the jury, although reported to be convinced of her "moral guilt," acquitted her of the charge.

The trial of Mrs Letitia Munson throws light on the lives of women who, because of their sex and poverty, would otherwise remain in shadow. As well, it gives an idea of the straits in which unmarried mothers found themselves during this period. Orphanages did not accept illegitimate offspring. Children might be abandoned to the streets of Toronto or boarded in its "baby farms," where they often died of neglect or overdoses of laudanum. In attempting to end a life that threatened her own Ellen Weingardner chose the most deperate of the grim options open to her.

GUS RICHARDSON

Infants' Home and Infirmary, *Annual report* (Toronto), 1878–80; 1884; 1886. *Globe*, 23, 26 Sept., 13, 17 Nov. 1882. *Sentinel-Review* (Woodstock, Ont.), 22 Sept., 24 Nov. 1882.

MURRAY, ALEXANDER, geologist, explorer, and first director of the Geological Survey of Newfoundland; b. 2 June 1810 in Dollerie House, Crieff, Scotland, second son of Anthony Murray, the 8th Laird of Dollerie, and Helen Fletcher Bower; d. 18 Dec. 1884 at Crieff.

The two prime virtues justly ascribed to Scotland's Highlanders are fidelity and courage, and these are indeed manifest in the life of Alexander Murray. His great-grandfather, a Jacobite, was believed to have been killed at Culloden (1746). His father served in the Royal Navy in the 1790s, commanded East Indiamen on voyages to the Far East between 1800 and 1810, and finally retired to the Perthshire countryside as laird of Dollerie. Alex's ingrained sense of duty was a consequence of the "lang pedigree" of the Murrays of Dollerie, but he was never known to play the patrician.

Alex was educated at home until 1819 when he was enrolled at the Royal High School in Edinburgh. He disliked *Auld Reekie*, did not get on at school, and was soon into every kind of mischief from rock fights to using vulgar language. His father, who favoured Alexander though the eldest son Anthony was the heir, took him back to Dollerie House and hired a tutor to prepare him for the Royal Navy on which Alex's heart was set.

Alex was enrolled at the Royal Naval College, Portsmouth, from 6 May 1824 to 24 Dec. 1825. Seamanship was emphasized at the college but the curriculum included mathematics, history, geography, drawing, fencing, French, and dancing. His first active service was on the *Tweed* as college midshipman, and his final charge was mate of the *Revenge*. He served on the Home, Mediterranean, and West Indies stations, and was wounded on the *Philomel* at the battle of Navarino, 20 Oct. 1827. He had passed his examinations for advancement to lieutenant by 1830 but in the peacetime navy there was little chance of promotion and on 5 March 1835 he was discharged at his own request. His shipboard years were reflected later in his rich late-Georgian naval vocabulary of swear-words, possession of which, it was then held, distinguished "the man of spirit" from "the man of worth." "Usually good natured and genial, Murray was, nevertheless, quick-tempered," and could be pugnacious when circumstances demanded action. Home on leave at Crieff in December 1832, during the Reform Bill crisis, he spurred his mare straight at a barricade set up to keep voters from supporting Tory Sir George Murray*, uncle of young Anthony Murray's wife, and scattered the mob guarding it.

In 1836 Alex purchased farmland a few miles north of Woodstock, Upper Canada, where a number of retired British army and naval officers had settled. The following spring he married Fanny Cooper Judkins in

Scotland and the young couple immigrated to Canada intending to support themselves by farming. Unfortunately their arrival coincided with a severe economic depression deepened by the bitter rebellion of 1837. Murray was temporarily attached to the naval brigade of Lieutenant Andrew Drew* which invaded United States territory when the steamer *Caroline* was intercepted and destroyed on 29 Dec. 1837. He later served in the Oxford County militia and was commissioned as a captain of the 3rd Regiment. After a reasonable trial period in the depression years Alex decided the farm would not provide a living and in 1841 the Murrays with their infant daughter and son returned to England. Murray, using the offices of Sir George Murray, applied unsuccessfully for re-appointment to the Royal Navy.

On 10 Sept. 1841 the Canadian parliament passed a bill to finance a geological survey of the united provinces and a principal aspirant to the directorship was William Edmond Logan* whose brother was associated with Alex's brother Anthony, now the laird of Dollerie, in a prominent Edinburgh legal firm. Sir George Murray, as master general of the Ordnance, was persuaded by Anthony to recommend Logan to Sir Charles Bagot*, governor general of Canada. Some time during the winter of 1841 Logan had become acquainted with Alex Murray and in January 1842, before his appointment to the directorship (April 1842), he agreed to favour Murray for employment provided he learned sufficient geology to be able to carry out independent mapping. Murray began by using Charles Lyell's *Elements of geology* (London, 1838) but soon confessed to Logan in dismay that "some of the *nouns* in the Chonchological series rather alarm me" and "although I can now form some idea of the Theory of the science, I am still quite ignorant of the manner in which it is turned into practice." Murray had received a thorough grounding in mathematics, nautical astronomy, and navigation from the Royal Naval College, and in the spring he taught himself surveying on Anthony's lands. In the summer he practised triangulation in the Grampian Mountains, assisted by Sir William Murray, Anthony's brother-in-law. Through the sponsorship of Sir George Murray and Logan, Alex was appointed to the Geological Survey of Great Britain as an assistant and by July was receiving practical instruction mostly in Wales from Logan and Henry Thomas De la Beche, director of the survey. The winter months were spent studying chemistry and drafting, as well as working with the survey staff at the Museum of Economic Geology in London.

In early spring 1843 Murray was deputized assistant provincial geologist of the Canadian survey, on 2 May he arrived back in Canada, and on 6 June he commenced geological mapping of the region from Toronto to beyond Lake Couchiching. On this excursion Murray identified the first metamorphosed rocks recognized in Canada, near the falls of the Severn River. His family was settled in Woodstock, but separation was typical of a geologist's life, and he concluded his annual diary in 1843: "I have been with my wife and . . . children under a month altogether. . . ."

The following two summers Murray assisted Logan in surveying the Gaspé peninsula, and explored the Bonaventure, Matane, Sainte-Anne, and Saint-Jean river valleys. Most of his later mapping was in Canada West, from the Ottawa River to Windsor, and northwest as far as Sault Ste Marie. Field studies in 1847 resulted in the establishment of the classical Huronian system, a belt of Precambrian sedimentary and volcanic rocks later found to extend in an arc sweeping from Sault Ste Marie to Noranda, Que. He discovered nickel and cobalt mineralization in the Wallace Mine – the first credited recognition for Canada – the succeeding summer. In 1856, following up a large magnetic anomaly near present-day Creighton (now part of Walden), Ont., Murray identified nickel and copper mineralization, and gave this first hint of the ore potential of the Sudbury basin in his published report. In June 1851 Murray was directed by Logan to examine asphaltic deposits in Enniskillen Township. In his report he noted their limited extent and, offhandedly, commented on associated seepages of petroleum, which at that time had little commercial value. Some seven years later, at another petroleum seepage located by Murray near Black Creek, James Miller WILLIAMS was producing oil.

Geologizing in Canada West ranged from country road rambles to cutting lines by axe through almost impenetrable wilderness forests with attendant hardships of work and travel, shortages of food, and at times unruly crews. Murray was not without unconventional traits when in the field; he was known to chase troublemakers at gunpoint and was addicted to morning dips, even in freezing weather, for "cleanliness was a sort of hobby with him."

In contrast to Logan, who was an independently wealthy bachelor, Murray depended either on the uncertain future of the survey, in doubt at least five times during his service, or on accepting an allowance, along with cautionary financial advice, from Anthony. Consequently he often suffered from anxiety and a sense of unimportance. On 17 Feb. 1850 he wrote to Logan: "I cannot help feeling strong misgivings . . . of my worthiness . . . but I can at the same time assure you that the fault is more attributable to want of head, than want of heart." Yet only the previous week, Logan had written to his own brother that "if I were deprived of Mr Murray whose duties are of a nature similar to my own & who is competent to explore separately, the Survey would take nearly twice the time without him than it would with him."

In midsummer of 1857 Murray was notified that his younger brother Willam had been amongst those massacred in the Indian Mutiny. Upon hearing that his only son was to embark for active service in India, Murray obtained passage for Glasgow, was shipwrecked near the Île de Mingan, but succeeded in reaching the old country in time to say goodby to his son. The death of his wife on 27 Feb. 1861 as the result of a sleighing accident in Woodstock devastated Murray emotionally. The field season of 1861 saw him afloat in an "*exceedingly crank*, and *anything* but *safe*" boat mapping sedimentary formations and collecting fossils from Owen Sound northwestward to Sault Ste Marie. In St Joseph Channel, off Campement d'Ours Island, a furious squall struck the boat pitching its four occupants into dangerously rough water. Luckily, their plight was seen by a young girl, Margaret Walker, who got a skiff out to their aid.

The years 1862–64 witnessed another of the financial crises so common during Logan's directorship of the survey. The first definitive report, commonly known as the *Geology of Canada*, was published in 1863. Politicians now could see no reason to continue supporting a geological survey and by January 1864 its funds were spent. It was not until 8 June that an appropriation was voted for the survey's continuance but by then Murray, at 54, was commencing a new career as first director of the Geological Survey of Newfoundland. Geological reconnaissances had been made of the island: in the interior by William Eppes Cormack* in 1822, along some coastal areas by Joseph Beete Jukes* in 1839–40, and in the northwest by James RICHARDSON in 1861–62. Murray's Newfoundland explorations turned out to be even more arduous than those of his Canadian years. In the summer of 1866 while mapping near Cape St George he either broke a fibula or separated an Achilles tendon, but instead of seeking medical attention remained in the field and completed the mapping programme he had set for himself. Although he was crippled for life as a result of the injury he continued to carry out field-work until 1880. In late 1867 Murray's son, on learning that the "*Gov*" was courting Elizabeth Cummins, aged about 29, wrote to Logan urging him to lure Murray to Canada until the following spring "when his work in the woods w[d] keep him away from the fascinating creature" because, if he should marry her, it would "make him miserable for the rest of his life – & probably send him to his grave a good many years before his time." On 28 Jan. 1868 the marriage took place, proved to be most happy, and added from time to time to the population of Newfoundland a total of six children.

Murray was responsible for the preparation of the first complete geological map of Newfoundland and when in 1873 the Newfoundland government declined to cover the cost of printing it Murray financed its publication out of his own pocket. In 1875 a further activity for him resulted from the ambitious continental transportation plans of Sandford Fleming* which included a railway link in Newfoundland; Murray was assigned the task of overseeing the logistics of a survey of the proposed trans-island route. Two years later Queen Victoria appointed Murray CMG for his scientific services in Canada and Newfoundland, and on 2 June 1877 he was presented with the decoration by Lady Glover, wife of Sir John Hawley GLOVER, lieutenant governor of Newfoundland.

Geological survey of Newfoundland, a 536-page compilation of reports by Murray and James Patrick Howley (his assistant whom he had trained) went on sale for $2.00 a copy in St John's in 1881. Except for a paper entitled "Glaciation of Newfoundland" presented the following year at the inaugural assembly of the Royal Society of Canada, this was Murray's last contribution to science. A special motion passed at the society's meeting admitted Murray, nominally a Newfoundlander, as an "additional member." Murray was not in attendance because of the ills of old age – with increased frequency the crippled limb and the anguishing pains of gout led to sleepless nights. By 1883 his health was so poor that his continued employment became impossible and he resigned from the survey to return to Scotland. On 18 Dec. 1884 he died in Belmont Cottage, Crieff.

In Canada, Murray was so overshadowed by Logan that his accomplishment of mapping the geology of Canada West almost single-handedly has never been given the recognition it deserves. In 1864 when Murray first arrived in Newfoundland it was almost *terra incognita* except for the coast. Within 20 years his survey led to the opening of the interior by showing that mineral, timber, and agricultural resources were present and that Newfoundlanders need no longer depend only on the fisheries.

RICHARD DAVID HUGHES

[Alexander Murray was the author of *The economic value of a geological survey, being a popular lecture before the Athenæum of St. John's, Newfoundland, delivered the 15th February, 1869* (Montreal, 1869); "Geography and resources of Newfoundland," Royal Geographical Soc., *Journal* (London), 47 (1877): 267–78; "Glaciation of Newfoundland," RSC *Trans.*, 1st ser., 1 (1883), sect. IV: 55–76; "Mineral resources of Newfoundland," *Nature* (London and New York), 23 (1880–81): 46–47; "Mining in Newfoundland," *Engineering and Mining Journal* (New York), 31 (January–June 1881): 430; and *Roads: a popular lecture delivered before the Athenaeum Institute, on March 26th, 1877* (St John's, 1877). With J. P. Howley he compiled the *Geological survey of Newfoundland* (London, 1881) and his later reports are included with Howley's in *Reports of Geological Survey of Newfoundland, from 1881 to 1909* (St John's, 1918). The most complete bibliography of Murray's writings is *Geologic literature on North America, 1785–1918*, comp.

J. M. Nickles (2v., Washington, 1923–24), I: 770–71. Alexander Murray diaries for 1843 and 1882, a Murray family pedigree (n.d., copy), "Reminiscences" of Helen Murray (*c.* 1891–92, typescript), and a "Personal paper: some memories of Alexander Murray" by Helen Murray (1892) are in the possession of R. D. Hughes (Kamloops, B.C.). R.D.H.]

McGill Univ. Arch., Sir William Logan papers. PAC, MG 29, B15, 40; D61, 14. Geological Survey of Canada, [*Report of progress for the year 1843*] (Montreal, 1845), 55–56; *Report of progress for the year 1848–49* (Toronto, 1850), 42–45; *Report of progress for the years 1853–54–55–56* (Toronto, 1857), 180; *Report of progress from its commencement to 1863* . . . (Montreal, 1863). B. J. Harrington, *Life of Sir William E. Logan, Kt., LL.D., F.R.S., F.G.S., &c., first director of the Geological Survey of Canada* . . . (Montreal, 1883). Nfld., Select Committee to Enquire into the Geological Survey of Newfoundland, *Report* . . . (St John's, 1869). Morgan, *Sketches of celebrated Canadians*, 753–54. Zaslow, *Reading the rocks*, 20–21, 43–44, 53, 68–70, 81, 96–97. Robert Bell, "Alexander Murray, F.G.S., F.R.S.C., C.M.G.," *Canadian Record of Science* (Montreal), 5 (1892–93): 77–96.

MURRAY, GEORGE, physician, surgeon, and politician; b. 2 Nov. 1825 at Barney's River, Pictou County, N.S., son of David Murray, farmer, and Margaret Huggan; m. in June 1854 Mary Ann Patterson; d. 12 Feb. 1888 at New Glasgow, N.S.

Grandson of Walter Murray, who migrated from Scotland on the *Hector*, George Murray received his high school education at Pictou Academy, and then taught for four years in Nova Scotia public schools. In 1846 he entered the Pennsylvania Medical College in Philadelphia, attracted there by the reputation of a fellow Nova Scotian, Dr William R. Grant, the first surgeon in the United States to remove an ovarian tumour. Murray studied in Grant's private office and won his praise. He then returned to Nova Scotia and in 1850 opened a practice at Barney's River; four years later he moved to New Glasgow, where he practised until his death. He attained such a position in his profession that the Medical Society of Nova Scotia elected him its representative to the 1876 international medical congress in Philadelphia.

Nothing during his life excited Murray more than the method of bringing Nova Scotia into confederation and the terms of union itself. He ran as an anti-confederate (Liberal) candidate in the 1867 provincial election, and led the poll in the three-member riding of Pictou. In the assembly none blasted more vigorously than he the "treachery most foul" which had tricked Nova Scotians out of their sovereign legislature. In 1868 he felt that the anti-confederate government was doing its utmost to have the union repealed, but not so in 1869. With William Kidston of Victoria and Robert Chambers of Colchester he led a group of seven assemblymen who accused the government of having "accepted the situation" and denounced Attorney General Martin Isaac WILKINS as a "trimmer" on repeal. The same year he presented a petition from Pictou that a delegation be sent to Washington to ascertain the terms for the admission of Nova Scotia into the American union, and later a resolution stating that, unless Nova Scotia was released from confederation, the queen should be asked to "absolve us from our allegiance to the British Crown." In the end he was forced to withdraw the "annexationist" petition, and Provincial Secretary William Berrian Vail* made use of a procedural device, amounting to a form of closure, to prevent debate on the "annexationist" resolution.

Throughout 1870 and 1871 Murray continued to harass the government on the repeal question, stamping himself as one of the most independent Nova Scotian assemblymen. During the 1871 provincial election, however, he denied the allegation that he had ever been an annexationist, and the *British Colonist* (Conservative) gloated that "he had devoured the 'leek' in the presence of the sturdy Scotsmen of Pictou"; all three Liberals lost to Conservatives (confederates). Disgustedly, the *Morning Chronicle* (Liberal) complained that Murray's violent opposition to the Liberal government had destroyed party unity in Pictou. In 1874 these divisions had not yet healed, and Conservatives won the Pictou seats by acclamation. Prevailed upon to run in 1878, Murray accepted or rejected elements of his party's platform as he pleased, leading the Pictou *Colonial Standard* (Conservative) to observe he was "a Government man to-day, an opposition man to-morrow, an Ishmaelite the day after, and the wandering Jew of politics the whole time." In the midst of recession both Murray and the Liberal government were defeated, but as usual Murray outpolled the other Liberals.

Fiery in politics, in ordinary life Murray was the moderate *par excellence*. As an elder of the Primitive and later the United (now Westminster) Presbyterian Church in New Glasgow, he was known as a peacemaker. During his 35 years of medical practice, he established a reputation for an even temperament and a gentle manner. Although a general practitioner, he fully used his surgical skills developed under Grant and performed operations, uncommon at that time, for cataract of the eye and harelip; he was perhaps the first Nova Scotian to operate successfully for cleft palate or staphylorrhaphy. Expecting no remuneration from the poor, he never acquired much more than a competence. Murray was probably the leading physician in eastern Nova Scotia, and was widely known throughout Pictou County.

J. MURRAY BECK

N.S., House of Assembly, *Debates and proc.*, 1868–71. *British Colonist* (Halifax), 1867–74. *Colonial Standard* (Pictou, N.S.), 10 Sept. 1878. *Eastern Chronicle* (New

Glasgow, N.S.), 16 Feb. 1888. *Morning Chronicle* (Halifax), 1867–74, 1878. *Canadian biog. dict.*, II: 482–83. *Directory of N.S. MLAs*, 264. Beck, *Government of N.S.*, 152–53. J. M. Cameron, *Political Pictonians: the men of the Legislative Council, Senate, House of Commons, House of Assembly, 1767–1967* (Ottawa, [1967]), 18.

MUSGRAVE, Sir ANTHONY, colonial administrator and author; b. 31 Aug. 1828 at St John's, Antigua, third of 11 children of Anthony Musgrave and Mary Harris Sheriff; m. 3 Aug. 1854 Christiana Elizabeth Byam (d. 1859), and they had two children; m. secondly in 1870 Jeanie Lucinda Field; d. 9 Oct. 1888 at Brisbane, Queensland.

Anthony Musgrave's family had established itself early in the 19th century in Antigua where both his grandfather and father held public office. Anthony received a "strictly orthodox" education at a grammar school in Antigua and what his father regarded as a better education in Great Britain. On his return to Antigua he was appointed, on 14 Sept. 1850, private secretary to Robert James Mackintosh, governor-in-chief of the Leeward Islands. In April 1851 he travelled to England and was admitted as a student to the Inner Temple. On 24 Jan. 1854 the Duke of Newcastle, secretary of state for the colonies, formally notified Musgrave that he had been selected for the position of colonial secretary of Antigua and Musgrave therefore abandoned his legal studies. He served as colonial secretary from 1854 to 1860 and as acting president of Nevis from 1860 to 1861 when he became temporary administrator of St Vincent. The Duke of Newcastle was impressed with Musgrave's "capacity and zeal" and commissioned him lieutenant governor of St Vincent in 1862.

Musgrave was notified of his appointment as governor of Newfoundland on 12 Sept. 1864 and arrived at St John's on 5 October. The extensive powers he had wielded in Nevis and St Vincent were in contrast to those he could exercise as governor of Newfoundland, a colony with a much larger population and full responsible government. Throughout his tenure Musgrave was to argue that the solution to Newfoundland's desperate economic condition, destitute population, and factious politics was the union of the British North American colonies. Confederation was supported by the new secretary of state for the colonies, Edward Cardwell, and from his first speech before a cautious and ambivalent legislature to the end of his governorship in 1869 Musgrave directed his energies to accomplishing that goal. He soon realized that Newfoundland would not be rushed into accepting the scheme and sought to build support for it. In 1865 a new Conservative premier, Frederic Bowker Terrington Carter*, a Protestant, replaced Hugh William HOYLES, and brought with him into the government as colonial secretary Ambrose Shea*, a Roman Catholic. Both Carter and Shea had been delegates to the Quebec conference and were strong supporters of confederation; Musgrave encouraged these changes and could well believe that this coalition forecast the acceptance of confederation after the elections expected in the fall of 1865.

Confederation was not, however, an issue in these elections as the ministry felt it prudent to allow more time to convince voters of the tangible benefits of union as a cure for Newfoundland's economic problems. In April 1866 Musgrave reported to Cardwell that the new House of Assembly favoured confederation but that all would depend on the terms of admission; he could not, however, persuade the government even to take up the question let alone discuss the possibility of sending delegates to London with those from Canada and the maritime colonies. Musgrave had suggested to Cardwell in February 1866 that he might "turn the screws" by threatening to reduce the naval garrison at St John's, but the Colonial Office wisely ignored his suggestion, recognizing that initiative for union had to come from the colony itself. Moreover, the French Shore question had caused renewed exasperation between English and French diplomats and Downing Street saw the prospective new negotiator, should Newfoundland join Canada, as an additional encumbrance in an already complicated problem.

Disheartened but still optimistic, Musgrave visited Ottawa in November 1867 to witness the opening of the first session of the new dominion parliament. In long hours of private discussions with Governor General Lord Monck* and Sir John A. Macdonald* he formulated terms of admission to confederation that he thought would be acceptable to his council and assembly. But, when another session of the legislature ended in May 1868, his efforts had still produced no results. The loss of his son in the early summer, together with the ambivalence of officials in the Colonial Office and of the Newfoundland government, left Musgrave disconsolate, and he took leave in England.

During his stay in London, Musgrave was consulted by the new secretary of state for the colonies, the Duke of Buckingham, about confederation and the French fishing treaties. On his return to Newfoundland in December 1868 he was confident that the legislature would agree to confederation and, believing it virtually accomplished, raised the matter of his future employment with Macdonald and the Colonial Office. He knew that Frederick Seymour*'s term as governor of British Columbia was due to expire and asked that he be considered as Seymour's successor. When Seymour died on 10 June 1869, Musgrave was immediately granted the post. His mandate from the Colonial Office was to unite the Pacific colony with Canada.

Musgrave met his successor in Newfoundland,

Stephen John Hill*, at Halifax, and confidently informed him that Newfoundland's entry into the dominion was inevitable. In the last session of the legislature a greater acceptance of confederation had been evinced and it was to be a major issue in the election in late 1869. Nevertheless the confederates in the event managed to win only nine seats, while the oppositionists captured 21. Many reasons for the collapse of the confederation movement were offered, such as the implacable opposition of most Roman Catholics, divisions among the merchants, and the highly emotional character of the anti-confederate campaign. The Colonial Office preferred to put the responsibility not on local isssues, Musgrave, or themselves, but on the Canadians, whom they judged to be precipitate in their haste to have Musgrave sent to British Columbia.

Musgrave arrived in British Columbia on 23 Aug. 1869, having travelled from Halifax to New York, then by rail to San Francisco, and steamer to Victoria. He was the first governor to have travelled to British Columbia by rail and, given his mandate to unite the colony with Canada, his trip west impressed upon him the value of a transcontinental railway in forging the link. The colony was as anxious to receive the governor as the secretary of state had been to send him, for Lord Granville had been reluctant to leave it in the hands of the temporary administrator, Philip James Hankin. There were many long standing grievances, and among government officials little initiative. Far from confident about its future, the colony looked for a bold leader and a decisive administrator.

Musgrave found that the pressing matters of administration confronting him were largely a consequence of Seymour's neglect of duty. Lord Granville had requested Musgrave's "serious attention" to Seymour's disregard for instructions in drawing up the estimates and revenues for 1869; two Supreme Court judges were independently deciding cases in one jurisdiction; crown agents complained that the colony's financial position was "imperfectly understood" by the colonists; there was no treasurer, the duties being carried out by a clerk "who has given no security for the safe custody of the Public Monies"; the vexed question of the governor's salary had never been settled; no reply had been made to inquiries from the secretary of state for the colonies respecting revised postal arrangements for the colony. Having been constrained by perfunctory administrative tasks as a governor in Newfoundland, Musgrave was anxious to display his capabilities and determined to direct events. He spent nearly six weeks after his arrival in the colony touring major mainland settlements and in his first six months corrected many of the outstanding problems. He could then devote all his energies to the union of the colony with Canada.

Once Musgrave was installed in British Columbia, Lord Granville's unqualified support for its inclusion in the dominion was made known. Musgrave himself did not need convincing on the desirability of federations in general, and his future in the colonial service would hinge largely on his success in British Columbia. Yet on his mainland tour he had observed less than unanimous sentiment about confederation; his government also had shown little enthusiasm for the project and in February 1869 the Legislative Council had voted against the measure. However, Musgrave was determined to make the issue a government-sponsored measure and to seize the initiative from individuals, including Amor De Cosmos*, who were campaigning for it and who were in communication with officials in Canada. Musgrave realized also that to overcome the opposition of prominent officials and members of the community such as Henry Pering Pellew Crease*, Joseph William Trutch*, and John Sebastian Helmcken* he would have to ensure adequate provision in the terms of union for government officials. Finally, he felt that if the dominion guaranteed the construction of a railway to British Columbia, the opposition and indifference of the general population to union would soon give way to enthusiasm.

Musgrave convened the Executive Council to discuss terms of entry almost every day from 31 Jan. 1870 through the first two weeks of February, despite being bedridden as a result of a severe leg injury. On 1 January he had appointed Helmcken and Robert William Weir Carrall* as unofficial members of the council, thereby permitting two legislative councillors to take part in the executive's deliberations. Once terms of union were drafted Musgrave commended them to the Legislative Council, which convened on 15 February; he was careful to emphasize that he had no wish to force confederation on British Columbia without a reference first to its British subjects. He announced his intention to modify the colony's constitution to institute representative government by providing for the election of a majority of the members of Legislative Council. He also declared himself opposed to any form of responsible government which he believed was too expensive for the colony, a position with which men such as Crease and Helmcken heartily concurred.

Musgrave knew that neither the Colonial Office's nor his own advocacy of the cause of confederation could ensure unfailing support of government officials in the Legislative Council and he set out to persuade Crease, Trutch, and the influential Dr Helmcken of the importance of their strong support. He took Trutch into his confidence; he knew that Helmcken would agree with the principle of confederation if the terms were attractive to British Columbia; and before the council met he was able to inform Crease of his efforts to secure a judgeship for him. The fact that Crease introduced confederation and presented the first arguments in its favour before the Legislative Council is eloquent testimony to Musgrave's influence over his officers. Confederation was now a legitimate measure of the government and the issue was successfully removed from the initiative of agitators outside it.

The debate on the proposed terms took place in the Legislative Council from 9 March to 6 April 1870. They were adopted with some modifications and then submitted to the Canadian parliament. In letters to the Colonial Office and to the governor general of Canada, Sir John Young*, Musgrave argued that adoption of the terms *in toto* as mutually agreed upon would be a certainty if Canada could guarantee construction of a railway. With agitation for confederation beginning to give way to demands for responsible government, Musgrave considered Canada's promise of a railway as essential if the growing movement for self-government was to be contained.

Musgrave could not travel to Ottawa for negotiations over terms because of his leg injury but he was confident that Trutch, Helmcken, and Carrall, his appointees as delegates, would serve the colony's best interests. Near the end of July news of the satisfactory conclusion of negotiations reached him and he was particularly gratified by the dominion's commitment to undertake construction of a transcontinental railway. When the Colonial Office's approval of his suggestions for altering the colony's constitution was received on 14 October, he immediately issued writs calling for the election of nine of the 15 members in the new Legislative Council which would be charged with accepting or rejecting the terms of confederation. Until its first meeting Musgrave was given broad powers to oversee the election, including those of determining the qualifications of electors and candidates and of establishing the electoral districts. The only qualification Musgrave imposed upon the male electors was the ability to read English and three months residence in their district.

The election of 1870 was fought more on the question of responsible government and when it should be introduced than on confederation. Therefore, in his speech opening the newly constituted Legislative Council on 5 Jan. 1871, Musgrave promised a bill to provide for its introduction if the council adopted the proposed terms of union. On 20 January the terms were accepted and Musgrave dispatched Trutch to Ottawa and then to London to complete the final arrangements for the colony's formal entry into the dominion. Relieved by the outcome, Musgrave predicted the result would expedite the entry of Newfoundland and Prince Edward Island.

With responsible government soon to be a certainty, Musgrave was anxious that his guarantees to his officials, whose support for confederation had been essential to the successful outcome, be placed in writing. He introduced a civil list bill to place the appointments of public officials on a legal foundation and to give them higher salaries in order to protect them from the "jobbing combinations" which he considered to be the more deleterious results of responsible government. The bill became law but both it and the governor were criticized by colonists and by officials at the Colonial Office who considered it a mistake for a "moribund legislature," comprised largely of appointed members, to increase salaries.

After his frustrations in Newfoundland at having to work within the constraints of responsible government and at his failure to get Newfoundland to accept confederation, it was a testimony to his administrative abilities that in less than two years British Columbia was prepared for admission as the sixth province of Canada. He was appointed CMG for his services on 12 April 1871 but he was now anxious to leave the colony. He was offered the first lieutenant governorship of the province but he regarded the cost of living as too high to enable him to stay on at the lower salary he would receive. Moreover, he continued to suffer from the effects of his leg injury and he wanted surgical advice from doctors in London. In addition, his wife Jeanie was pregnant and he wished to avoid crossing the Rockies and the Atlantic in winter. Thus on 25 July 1871 Musgrave left the colony before the return of Joseph Trutch, his successor and the first lieutenant governor of the province.

Musgrave went on to important posts as governor of Natal (1872–73), South Australia (1873–77), Jamaica (1877–83), and Queensland (1885–88) where he died, appropriately, in the midst of a constitutional furore over the principle of the supremacy of a responsible ministry. In South Australia and Queensland, colonies with full responsible government, he had had more time on his hands, and had published his views on a variety of economic questions in journals and pamphlets. Some of these were subsequently revised and published in one volume as *Studies in political economy*. He was made KCMG in 1875, a further recognition of a distinguished career in colonial service.

KENT M. HAWORTH

Anthony Musgrave was the author of *Studies in political economy* (London, 1875; repr. New York, 1968).

Duke Univ. Library (Durham, N.C.), Field–Musgrave family papers. National Library of Australia (Canberra), Anthony Musgrave papers. PABC, B.C., Governor (Musgrave), Despatches to London, 11 Jan. 1868–24 July 1871 (letterbook copies); Colonial corr., Anthony Musgrave corr.; Crease coll., Anthony Musgrave, corr. outward; Helmcken papers, Anthony Musgrave, corr. outward; O'Reilly coll., Anthony Musgrave, corr. outward. PAC, MG 26, A. PRO, CO 7/103: Newcastle to Musgrave, 24 Jan. 1854; CO 60; CO 194; CO 398. "The annexation petition of 1869," ed. W. E. Ireland, *BCHQ*, 4 (1940): 267–87. B.C., Legislative Council, *Journals*, 1869–71. [J. S. Helmcken], *The reminis-*

cences of Doctor John Sebastian Helmcken*, ed. Dorothy Blakey Smith ([Vancouver], 1975). *Cariboo Sentinel*, 1869–71. *Daily British Colonist and Victoria Chronicle*, 1869–71. *Government Gazette – British Columbia* (Victoria), 1869–71. *Victoria Daily Standard*, 1870–71. *ADB*. *The Colonial Office list* . . . (London), 1871. *DNB*.

British Columbia & confederation, ed. W. G. Shelton (Victoria, 1967). R. J. Cain, "The administrative career of Sir Anthony Musgrave" (MA thesis, Duke Univ., 1965). J. W. Cell, *British colonial administration in the mid-nineteenth century: the policy-making process* (New Haven, Conn., and London, 1970). Creighton, *Road to confederation*. C. D. W. Goodwin, *Economic enquiry in Australia* (Durham, 1966). K. M. Haworth, "Governor Anthony Musgrave, confederation, and the challenge of responsible government" (MA thesis, Univ. of Victoria, 1975). W. P. Morrell, *British colonial policy in the mid-Victorian age: South Africa, New Zealand, the West Indies* (Oxford, 1969). W. L. Morton, *The critical years: the union of British North America, 1857–1873* (Toronto, 1964). E. C. Moulton, "The political history of Newfoundland, 1861–1869" (MA thesis, Memorial Univ. of Newfoundland, St John's, 1960). V. L. Oliver, *The history of the island of Antigua, one of the Leeward Caribbees in the West Indies, from the first settlement in 1635 to the present time* (3v., London, 1894–99). Ormsby, *British Columbia*; "The relations between British Columbia and the dominion of Canada, 1871–1885" (PHD thesis, Bryn Mawr College, Bryn Mawr, Pa., [1937]). J. H. Parry and P. M. Sherlock, *A short history of the West Indies* (London and New York, 1956). Barry Scott, "The governorship of Sir Anthony Musgrave, 1883–1888" (BA honours thesis, Univ. of Queensland, St Lucia, Australia, 1955). Waite, *Life and times of confederation*. W. M. Whitelaw, *The Maritimes and Canada before confederation* (Toronto, 1934; repr. 1966). Isabel Bescoby, "A colonial adminstration; an analysis of administration in British Columbia, 1869–1871," *Canadian Public Administration* (Toronto), 10 (1967): 48–104. K. M. Haworth and C. R. Maier, "'Not a matter of regret': Granville's response to Seymour's death," *BC Studies*, 27 (autumn 1975): 62–66. F. W. Howay, "Governor Musgrave and confederation," RSC *Trans.*, 3rd ser., 15 (1921), sect.II: 15–31. K. A. Waites, "Responsible government and confederation: the popular movement for popular government," *BCHQ*, 6 (1942): 97–123. W. M. Whitelaw, "Responsible government and the irresponsible governor," *CHR*, 13 (1932): 364–86.

MYERS, SAMUEL H. (the name is sometimes written **Meyers** or **Myres**, but he signed Myers), miner and labour organizer; b. in 1838 in Ireland; d. unmarried 3 May 1887 at Nanaimo, B.C.

Samuel H. Myers immigrated to British Columbia from Ireland in 1858 to join the Fraser River gold-rush. During the 1860s and early 1870s he lived an itinerant life, following the gold-rushes and working at various jobs. In 1860–61 he was an expressman between Port Douglas (Douglas), at the head of Harrison Lake, and Lillooet on the Fraser River. From 1862 to 1867 he shared in various placer mining claims on Antler, Williams, and Grouse creeks in the Cariboo goldfields. In March 1865 at Victoria he was fined for drunken violence against an Indian woman. In 1869 he was at Lytton where he had earlier worked as a ferryman on the Thompson River, and two years later he joined the rush to the new gold discoveries at Omineca. By 1877 he had settled down as a miner in the coalfield around Nanaimo.

Production in the Nanaimo coalfield, first exploited by the Hudson's Bay Company in the 1850s, rose sharply following the discovery in 1869 by Robert DUNSMUIR of the Wellington seam. When Myers entered the industry as a miner in the mid 1870s the output was continuing to expand rapidly; in 1879 almost 250,000 tons were being mined, and by 1889 production had risen to over 500,000 tons. Employment in the fields grew accordingly: in 1869, 200 men worked in the single mine at Nanaimo, but ten years later 732 men were employed in the coal pits of Nanaimo and nearby Wellington, and by 1889, 1,927 men worked for three companies in ten pits. Although most of the actual face-workers were experienced miners, mainly from Great Britain, some, like Myers, turned to coal mining from other occupations. Among the labour force were an increasing number of Chinese and a diminishing group of native Indians. Eighty per cent of the coal was exported, mostly to California, where it had to compete in price with coal from the American northwest, Australia, and Great Britain.

The mining boom intensified clashes between the men and their employers. In the years 1877–83 there were four major strikes by face-workers, three of them ending in defeat, against the two companies that produced virtually all of the coal: in 1877 and 1883 against Robert Dunsmuir's Wellington collieries for increases in tonnage rates; in 1880 (successfully) against the Nanaimo operations of the British-owned Vancouver Coal Mining and Land Company to resist reductions in payment per ton; and in 1881 against the same company to protest extra loading not considered "customary." In both 1877 and 1883 the Wellington miners organized themselves into a "Miners Mutual Protective Association" despite Dunsmuir's threat to discharge any man openly joining a union. The two strikes against Dunsmuir were classic confrontations with the use of police (the militia was also called out in 1877), imported strike-breakers, evictions from company houses, as well as the arrest and trial of strikers. The 1883 strike ended with the strikers clamouring for Dunsmuir to discharge those Chinese he had begun to employ as face-workers rather than labourers. The striking miners did not object to Chinese working in the mines (some employed Asians to load for them), but wanted the Asians kept in the non-responsible positions called for in the Coal Mines Regulations Act of 1877.

In December 1883, following the failure of the Wellington strike in which he was involved, Myers organized the Calvin Ewing Local Assembly 3017 of the Knights of Labor in Nanaimo, the first unit of the Knights in British Columbia. Myers had first read about the Knights in a radical Irish nationalist newspaper, the New York *Irish World and American Industrial Liberator*, and then, earlier in 1883, he had spent eight weeks in San Francisco where he had been initiated into the secret work of the order by a California Knight, Calvin Ewing, and had obtained an organizer's commission.

Although the Miners Mutual Protective Association continued to exist after the 1883 strike, some time in the spring of 1884 local assembly 3017 seems to have become the focus of union activity in the Nanaimo area; allied with it was a cooperative society which operated a retail store. In Victoria, however, Reginald Nuttall had received an organizer's commission directly from Terence Vincent Powderly, the leader of the Knights in North America, on the recommendation of prominent Toronto Knight Daniel John O'Donoghue*, and in March 1884 Nuttall organized local assembly 3107. Myers, surprised at the overlapping jurisdictions, complained that Nuttall was a mere "real estate and stock broker" who "could not instruct in anything." In August and September 1884 Myers organized new assemblies for coal miners at Wellington (local assembly 3429) in British Columbia, and at Newcastle, Carbonado, and Osceola in Washington Territory (local assemblies 3395, 3418, and 3422); other Knights' assemblies emerged at New Westminster, Vancouver, and in construction camps along the Canadian Pacific Railway (local assemblies 5506, 5507, 5570, 8608, and 8707). In August 1887 six local assemblies combined to form district assembly 203 of the Knights of Labor, one of eight in Canada.

The entry of the Knights of Labor into British Columbia came during one of the peak periods of agitation against the Chinese population. Chinese imported as labourers for the Canadian Pacific Railway fuelled an already established prejudice. The Knights were initially most successful in organizing white urban workers and miners who felt threatened by the competition of the Chinese. Myers, for example, described himself as "combatting the Chinese curse" and Nuttall claimed to be the founder of the "Pacific Coast League Anti-Chinese Association." Yet, revealing a contradiction within the movement Myers commended Powderly for his courageous assault on racism in the United States, and Nuttall described himself proudly as "an Internationalist," "a Free Thinker," "a confirmed Republican," and "a Liberal of advanced views."

Although the Knights as a body did not directly enter electoral politics in British Columbia, their supporters were active in the 1886 provincial campaign. In the Nanaimo electoral district, Myers and fellow-miner James Lewis, running as "Workingmen's" candidates, opposed large land grants (such as that recently made to Robert Dunsmuir for the Esquimalt and Nanaimo Railway), Chinese labour, and the liquor traffic, and called for compulsory arbitration of industrial disputes; they promised to "promote the interest of Capital and Labor so that they may work harmoniously to develop the resources of the Province." The election results were disappointing: Myers was at the bottom of the poll with only 30 votes, and Lewis next to last with 78; winning candidates were William Raybould and Robert Dunsmuir, Dunsmuir heading the poll with 366 votes. In a by-election a few months later, Myers announced his candidacy but soon withdrew in favour of Lewis, who nevertheless finished at the bottom of the poll.

In addition to his union activities Myers was a prominent member of the Independent Order of Good Templars, serving as an officer in the Grand Lodge of British Columbia; temperance sentiment was strong among the Knights throughout North America. He was also a member of the Ancient Order of Foresters and the Ancient Order of United Workmen, each of which offered insurance benefits attractive to coal miners.

The Nanaimo coal pits in which Myers worked were dry, often dusty, and usually gassy, and were therefore prone to explosions. Between 1879 and 1888, four major and two minor explosions killed 262 men. On 3 May 1887 the worst of these killed 147 men at the Vancouver Coal Mining and Land Company's no.1 mine in Nanaimo. Samuel Myers was among the men trapped on no.5 level, Old Slope, who succumbed to after-damp. He died intestate and the pay due to him was used to erect a marker over his grave in St Peter's Roman Catholic cemetery in Nanaimo.

Although it was said that the affairs of the Nanaimo assembly of the Knights fell into confusion only after Myers' death, there is some evidence that it did not enrol even a majority of the miners when he was alive. Of the 97 white men killed in the explosion only 29 were associated with the Knights and just six of these were members in good standing. However, local assembly 3017 had grown from 17 charter members in 1883 to 241 in the following year before declining to 150 by 1885, the last year for which data are available.

Samuel Myers' working life in British Columbia spanned the transition from the loose partnerships of individual "free miners" washing out alluvial gold with minimal equipment to heavily capitalized limited companies operating extensive coal and hard rock mines in which the working miner was only a hired hand, unable as an individual to protect his interests. Myers, who justifiably described himself as "the father of the Knights of Labor in B.C.," is representative of those workingmen who turned to unions to redress the balance.

H. Keith Ralston and Gregory S. Kealey

Catholic Univ. of America Arch. (Washington), Terence V. Powderly papers (mfm. at PAC). PABC, GR 216; GR 431, B.C., Attorney General, Inquisitions, "Inquest into explosion in No.1 mine, Nanaimo, 3 May 1887"; Colonial corr., Lands and Works Dept. corr. St Peter's (Roman Catholic) Church (Nanaimo, B.C.), Cemetery records, 11 May 1887.

B.C., Legislative Assembly, *Sessional papers*, 1874–90 (annual reports of the minister of mines); 1878–86 (lists of persons entitled to vote in the electoral district of Nanaimo); 1889: 472. Knights of Labor, *Proc. of the General Assembly* ([Philadelphia]), 1887. *Daily British Colonist* (Victoria), 5, 12, 19 June, 10, 24 July 1860; 1 March, 9 Aug. 1861; 19 May 1862; 15 March 1865. *Free Press* (Nanaimo), 17 Dec. 1881; 16, 22, 25 Aug., 24 Oct., 3 Nov. 1883; 26 Jan., 9 Feb., 10 Sept., 22 Oct. 1884; 13, 20 Feb., 16 Oct., 17 Nov., 22, 25, 30 Dec. 1885; 11, 21 May, 1 June 1887. *Industrial News* (Victoria), 1885–86. *Journal of United Labor* (Philadelphia), 1887. *The British Columbia directory . . .* (Victoria), 1882–85; 1887. *CPC*, 1887. *First Victoria directory . . .* , comp. Edward Mallandaine (Victoria), 1871. J. N. G. Bartlett, "The 1877 Wellington miners' strike" (BA essay, Univ. of British Columbia, Vancouver, 1975). J. E. Garlock, "A structural analysis of the Knights of Labor: a prolegomenon to the history of the producing classes" (PHD thesis, Univ. of Rochester, N.Y., 1974). D. R. Kennedy, "The Knights of Labor in Canada" (MA thesis, Univ. of Western Ontario, London, 1945; also pub. under the same title, London, 1956). J. E. Muller and M. E. Atchison, *Geology, history and potential of Vancouver Island coal deposits* (Ottawa, 1971). P. A. Phillips, *No power greater: a century of labour in British Columbia* (Vancouver, 1967). M. L. Tweedy, "The 1880 and 1881 strikes by the miners of the Vancouver Coal Company" (BA essay, Univ. of British Columbia, 1978).

N

NATHAL, LOUIS. *See* FRASSE DE PLAINVAL, LOUIS

NELLES, ABRAM (Abraham), Church of England clergyman, missionary, and translator; b. 25 Dec. 1805 at Forty-Mile Creek (Grimsby), Upper Canada, third son of Robert Nelles* and Elizabeth Moore; m. first 3 May 1831 Hannah Macklem (d. 6 July 1863) of Chippawa (now part of Niagara Falls, Ont.), and they had two sons; m. secondly in 1866 Sarah Macklem, a cousin of his first wife, and they had a son and a daughter; d. 20 Dec. 1884 in Brantford, Ont.

Abram Nelles was descended from a Mohawk River valley family of German origin. The loyalist migrations of the late 18th century brought this family of prosperous farmers from New York into the Niagara peninsula where they were the pioneers of the village of Forty-Mile Creek, Grimsby Township, Upper Canada. The Nelles family appears to have been an early benefactor of the Church of England and Abram pursued studies towards a career in the ministry at York (Toronto) under the direction of John Strachan* and Alexander Neil Bethune*. Nelles' father and grandfather had both been involved in the conduct of Indian diplomacy and it may have been this influence that led him at the age of 21 to offer his services as a student missionary to the Six Nations at Grand River.

Few clergymen in the western part of the diocese of Quebec were attracted to the isolation, the linguistic and cultural differences, and the uncertain living conditions of the Indian missions. Financial constraints made it impossible for the church in Upper Canada to underwrite costs, and agencies such as the Society for the Propagation of the Gospel and the interdenominational New England Company financed the missions. Bishop Charles James Stewart* of Quebec was pleased by Nelles' sense of commitment and entertained great hopes for his future. He petitioned the SPG to provide funds for an extra studentship at the Grand River Reserve so that Nelles might attach himself to the mission that the Reverend Robert Lugger* maintained there. The society obliged by providing an extra £50 per year, enabling Nelles to study Iroquoian dialects during a two-year apprenticeship from 1827 to 1829.

Ordained deacon at York by Bishop Stewart on 14 June 1829 and priested the following year, Nelles soon transferred his services from the SPG, which was experiencing financial difficulty, to the New England Company, which supported Lugger. Nelles was stationed at Tuscarora for the next several years and on 30 Sept. 1837 became the senior missionary to the Grand River community, Lugger having died the previous March. He was succeeded at Tuscarora by Adam Elliot*.

Nelles' new post carried with it the rectorship of the Mohawk Church and the principalship of the Mohawk Institute, a day-school operated by the New England Company for Indian students. Under his administration for 35 years, the institute, teaching both academic and practical subjects, became a model for Indian schools which had assimilation of the Indians as their object. As early as 1844 Nelles transformed the institute into a boarding-school for 50 children. Many students' families were scattered about the reserve and "living in" was necessary for the school's success. His students included several who became prominent Indian leaders, for example, George Henry Martin JOHNSON.

The missionary's concern for the welfare of his parishioners earned him the respect of both Indians and whites in the surrounding community. He was given a Mohawk name, Shadekareenhes, meaning "two trees of equal height." Nelles used his knowledge of the Mohawk language to publish in 1839 a hymnal entitled *A collection of psalms and hymns, in the Mohawk language, for the use of the Six Nations Indians*, translated by catechist Henry Aaron Hill*, and in 1842 an edition in Mohawk of the Book of Common Prayer; both were published in Hamilton, Upper Canada. Active in the affairs of the Anglican diocese of Huron after its formation in 1857, he received several ecclesiastical distinctions including, in 1868, those of canon of St Paul's Cathedral in London and rural dean of Brant. In 1872 he retired from the Mohawk Institute although he retained the rectorship of the Mohawk Church. Six years later he was appointed archdeacon of Brant by Bishop Isaac Hellmuth* and held that position together with the rectorship until his death in 1884. He was buried in the churchyard of the Mohawk Church.

DOUGLAS LEIGHTON

The Archives of the Diocese of Huron of the Anglican Church of Canada, located at Huron College, London, Ont., provides important information on the career of Abram Nelles in its holdings of the records of the Church Society of the diocese, the parish of Six Nations and the Indian mission papers, and the Cronyn letterbook covering the period 1858–67.

AO, Strachan (John) papers. Eva Brook Donly Museum (Simcoe, Ont.), Norfolk Hist. Soc. coll., Walsh papers, T. W. Walsh papers, 4624–27 (mfm. at PAC). PAC, MG 24, I131; RG 10, A2, 12. *The valley of the Six Nations: a collection of documents on the Indian lands of the Grand River*, ed. C. M. Johnston (Toronto, 1964). *Daily Expositor* (Brantford, Ont.), 20, 23 Dec. 1884. *Globe*, 24 Dec. 1884. Chadwick, *Ontarian families*, II: 157. J. L. Duncan, "Church of England missions among the Indians in the diocese of Huron to 1850" (MA thesis, Univ. of Western Ontario, London, 1936). C. M. Johnston, *Brant County: a history, 1784–1945* (Toronto, 1967). J. D. Leighton, "The development of federal Indian policy in Canada, 1840–1890" (PHD thesis, Univ. of Western Ontario, 1975). A. J. Clark, "Two rare translations into the Mohawk language," *OH*, 29 (1933): 1–7.

NELLES, SAMUEL SOBIESKI, Methodist minister and educator; b. 17 Oct. 1823 at Mount Pleasant, Upper Canada, eldest son of William Nelles and Mary Hardy; m. 3 July 1851 Mary Bakewell, daughter of the Reverend Enoch WOOD, and they had six children; d. 17 Oct. 1887 at Cobourg, Ont.

Samuel Sobieski Nelles' parents immigrated to Upper Canada from New York State after the War of 1812. Samuel was educated in local schools before attending Lewiston and Frederica academies in New York State and the Genesee Wesleyan Seminary in Lima, N.Y. From 1842 to 1844 he was a member of the first undergraduate class at Victoria College in Cobourg, and he graduated from Wesleyan University, Middletown, Conn., in 1846. After a year as principal of the Newburgh Academy in Lennox County, Canada West, he entered the ministry, serving on probation at Port Hope and Toronto. Ordained a minister of the Wesleyan Methodist Church in Canada in 1850, he was appointed professor of classics and acting principal of Victoria College in the same year. In 1851 he became principal and in 1854, succeeding his mentor and friend Egerton RYERSON, he was appointed president. He continued as president until 1884 when the college was renamed Victoria University, and then served as its chancellor and president until 1887.

Nelles was consistently active as a Methodist minister but his most important contribution was made to Victoria College. His role as its second founder and as the principal architect of its formative period was played amidst discouraging and challenging circumstances. Victoria College had been founded in 1841 as an outgrowth of Upper Canada Academy, a Methodist preparatory school chartered in 1836. The objective of Victoria's founders, including Anson Green* as well as John* and William Ryerson*, was not to establish a theological seminary; rather they believed that the academy would benefit "were it invested with the style and privileges of a College, and endowed by the liberality of the Legislature." The Wesleyan Methodist Conference, however, was not fully committed to the support of higher education. Thus the determined efforts of the administration of Louis-Hippolyte La Fontaine* and Robert Baldwin* to consolidate and secularize the emerging university system in 1849–50, in combination with the modest circumstances of the Methodists, nourished a mood of acute uncertainty about Victoria.

Although under the direction of Nelles the college became well established, its financial position remained precarious, a circumstance in itself symbolic of the continuing, if intermittent, controversy between the advocates of one provincial university and the supporters of denominational institutions. In this conflict Methodists were often ranged against their own brethren as well as members of other churches. Nelles, like his contemporaries who headed the other denominational colleges in the province, fought an unending battle to secure government grants and to accumulate an endowment. The former were eliminated in 1868 and a campaign to raise funds was begun by William Morley PUNSHON; a decade later the amount lost had been replaced by investment income. In reality, however, only strict economy and the continuing use of inadequate facilities enabled Victoria to survive. Nelles and his contemporaries were also confronted with a more formidable issue, that of responding constructively to the intellectual revolution which was being shaped by the writings of Charles Darwin and by the renewal of biblical scholarship.

Nelles was a quiet and cautious man as well as a succinct speaker and writer whose beliefs and objectives must be distilled from his actions and occasional utterances. As a Methodist minister, he was committed to an evangelical Christianity which relied heavily on religious experience and accepted John Wesley's amalgam of conservative theology and zeal for holiness in this life. As a scholar, Nelles believed his primary function was to demonstrate that "a properly conducted inquiry into the world of nature, whether natural or human, would reveal the wondrous handiwork of God," and thereby preserve the moral tradition of Canadian culture from the corrosion of the critical intellect.

From the outset, however, the distinctive feature of his outlook as Christian and academic was his tolerance and his receptiveness to the changing climate of opinion. In 1853 he emphasized that "Christianity itself brings happiness to men only in so far as it rectifies their disordered natures and brings . . . light to the understanding." But the gospel could not be fully understood without intellectual preparation. He stressed that "we are not called to choose between study and prayer. Study without prayer is arrogance, prayer without study is fanaticism; and neither arrogance nor fanaticism will find true wisdom." In his last years he was to remark that the "picture of Greece with the New Testament in her hands, may be taken . . . as an appropriate symbol of a true University. Greece . . . in a word, all human culture on its secular side. The New Testament . . . human development and perfection on its spiritual or divine side." The sciences and history "throw floods of light, and sometimes very perplexing cross-lights, upon the works and ways of God; and they have become a necessary study."

Such convictions led Nelles to give the writings of the Scottish "common sense" philosophers a central place in Victoria's curriculum, to promote specialization in order that the students learn "some few things well," and to encourage the study of the sciences and theology. In 1877 Faraday Hall, the first science building in the province, was opened at Victoria, the pride of Dr Eugene Emil Felix Richard Haanel*, one of the first European scientists to teach in Canada. Cautiously, Nelles sought instructors for the college "who, while possessed of a true love of learning . . . still adhere to the faith of Christ. . . . Such men, too, are less likely to teach for science what is yet only in the region of conjecture." In 1873 he was instrumental in establishing a faculty of theology at Victoria, thus making formal provision for the education of Methodist ministers. Significantly, its first dean was Nelles' colleague, Nathanael Burwash*, who from the outset endeavoured to reconcile Christian theology and the advances of science and introduced his students to the new methods of biblical scholarship. Nelles' concern for the quality of education in Victoria was matched by his determination that the college should use its full powers as a university. Hence, in addition to faculties of arts and theology, Victoria established faculties of medicine [*see* John Rolph*] and law in 1854 and 1862 respectively. Although these had a rather peripheral relationship with the college, their numerous graduates were very influential in the professions.

In 1887 the university had 697 students; 180 were in arts with 32 graduating (in 1854 there had been only 2 graduates). Nelles and his colleagues always recognized, however, that Victoria's position was uncertain. Thus, from the outset he was receptive to proposals for the consolidation of the various denominational colleges with the University of Toronto into one provincial university. His mature views on this subject were enunciated in his 1885 convocation address. Recognizing that the growth of the sciences and other disciplines had created an entirely new context, he commented on the need for "a place where all sound means of discipline can be employed, and all forms of knowledge cultivated, with the best facilities of the age." Every sect could not have a "genuine University" and the government could not "recognize the claims of one sect over another." The solution was to establish one national university. "But such a University for a Christian people should somehow employ . . . the power of the Christian faith." Federation appeared to offer the opportunity to give "a more positive Christian character to our higher education." Nelles emphasized that it was painful for him to contemplate federation for an institution to which he had given his "life's best energies," but he would support a scheme which would lead to the "liberal and Christian reconstruction of our Provincial University."

The act of federation was passed in April 1887, six months before his death, although its implementation would be delayed until November 1890 [*see* William GOODERHAM Jr]. At the general conference of the Methodist Church in 1886 Nelles had voted against acceptance of the proposed agreement, not because he had altered his stand but because he believed the terms would not assure Victoria's continuance as an institution for the "work of liberal Christian training of both laity and ministers." It was largely his stubborn insistence on and careful advocacy of these principles which ensured for Victoria and other federating institutions a well-defined role in the university curriculum and the authority to control the life and conduct of their students. Above all, he recognized that Victoria needed additional endowment income to maintain the quality of its staff and its facilities, and sought valiantly but with little success to collect such funds. His intense anxiety to serve the ends of Victoria and the Methodist community, as well as his prophetic awareness of the dilemma posed by the prospect of decay at Coburg and of ultimate absorption in the University of Toronto undoubtedly contributed to his final illness.

The death of Nelles was marked by an immense

outpouring of grief and respect from the students, alumni, and faculty of Victoria University, as well as from the Methodist Church and the citizens of Ontario. He had been honoured with a DD by Queen's College in 1860 and an LLD by Victoria in 1873. Although he held no high office in the church, he had been a delegate to other conferences on numerous occasions. He also served as president of the Ontario Teachers' Association in 1869 and 1870. He left no body of scholarly work, other than occasional sermons, addresses at convocations, and letters. His legacy consisted in large part of the students in whom he had inspired "an honest love of the truth," a measure of tolerance, and a concern for continuity between old beliefs and new knowledge. Victoria University would bring into federation a small but well-qualified staff, a body of loyal graduates, and an intellectual outlook deeply suffused with the Christian tradition, receptive to the claims of the sciences and of critical scholarship, and anxious to relate higher education to the needs of society. As a minister, Nelles earned deep respect and affection not as an orator but as one who enabled others to discover new insights. As a man, he was thoughtful, witty, fatherly in his dealings with students, and devoted to his children. His last message to the undergraduates was "Give the boys my love. . . ." His conference would testify that "the entire Church mourns the loss of so faithful a servant, so gifted a preacher, and so eminent a teacher."

G. S. FRENCH

Victoria Univ. Arch. (Toronto), Board of Regents, Minutes, 1884–89; Victoria College Board, Minutes, 1857–84. Victoria Univ. Library (Toronto), Nathanael Burwash papers; Samuel S. Nelles papers. *Acta Victoriana* (Cobourg, Ont.), 1 (1878–79)–11 (1887–88). Methodist Church (Canada, Newfoundland, Bermuda), Bay of Quinte Conference, *Minutes* (Toronto), 1884; 1888. Wesleyan Methodist Church in Canada, *Minutes* (Toronto), 1850; 1851; 1855. *Christian Guardian*, 1850–87. *Canadian biog. dict.*, I: 85–87. Cornish, *Cyclopædia of Methodism*. *Cyclopædia of Canadian biog.* (Rose, 1888), 363–64. Dent, *Canadian portrait gallery*, III: 45–47. Nathanael Burwash, *The history of Victoria College* (Toronto, 1927). A. B. McKillop, "A disciplined intelligence: intellectual enquiry and the moral imperative in Anglo-Canadian thought, 1850–1890" (PHD thesis, Queen's Univ., Kingston, Ont., 1976); published under the title *A disciplined intelligence: critical inquiry and Canadian thought in the Victorian era* (Montreal, 1979). Hilda Neatby, *Queen's University: to strive, to seek, to find, and not to yield*, ed. F. W. Gibson and Roger Graham (1v. to date, Montreal, 1978–). C. B. Sissons, *A history of Victoria University* (Toronto, 1952). R. J. Taylor, "The Darwinian revolution: the responses of four Canadian scholars" (PHD thesis, McMaster Univ., Hamilton, Ont., 1976). [A. H.] Reynar, "Samuel Sobieski Nelles, D.D., LL.D.," *Canadian Methodist Magazine*, 27 (January–June 1888): 526–34.

NORMAN, NATHAN, sealing captain, planter, office-holder, and politician; b. 22 Sept. 1809 at Brigus, Nfld; m. 9 Feb. 1841 Elizabeth Munden, and they had six children; d. 3 Sept. 1883 at Brigus.

Nathan Norman was a member of a family of substantial Newfoundland planters. He was educated in Brigus and trained in navigation at a school conducted by a British naval officer, Captain Youden, at nearby Bull Cove. A capable and efficient seaman, Norman commanded the brig *Bickley* in the Brigus-Halifax trade at the age of 21. He became a famous sealing captain in the heyday of the sail-powered sealing fleet (*c.* 1845) when about 400 Newfoundland vessels participated in the hunt. He was also an important planter in Labrador and for a number of years owned the largest fishing establishment in Indian Harbour on Groswater Bay, a rich fishing area, eventually selling out his room to Job Brothers and Company of St John's. As a planter controlling a sizeable part of the fishing trade in that remote area Norman no doubt also acted as a seasonal merchant and supplier on the coast, probably with a line of credit from St John's merchants such as Job Brothers or Punton and Munn of Harbour Grace. He was also said to have been the first man to explore the northern coast of Labrador in search of new cod fishing grounds.

Norman was the first justice of the peace for the Newfoundland territory of Labrador and was a friend and correspondent of Donald Alexander Smith*, sometime chief factor in Labrador of the Hudson's Bay Company. He represented Port de Grave in the House of Assembly from 1878 to 1882 as a member of the first administration of William Vallance Whiteway* and was locally celebrated for the provision of a public grindstone in his native Brigus.

C. W. ANDREWS and G. M. STORY

Business and general directory of Nfld., 1877: 15. *Chafe's sealing book* (1923). Prowse, *Hist. of Nfld.* (1895), 665. Nicholas Smith, *Fifty-two years at the Labrador fishery* (London, 1936), 10. [H.] B. Willson, *The life of Lord Strathcona and Mount Royal, G.C.M.G., G.C.V.O.* (2v., Boston and New York, 1915), I: 137, 165–66, 227–28.

NORMANBY, GEORGE AUGUSTUS CONSTANTINE PHIPPS, Earl of MULGRAVE and Marquess of. *See* PHIPPS

NORQUAY, JOHN, politician; b. 8 May 1841 near St Andrews (Man.), the fifth of six children of John Norquay and Isabella Truthwaite; m. in June 1862 Elizabeth Setter at Parkdale (Man.), and they had three daughters and five sons; d. 5 July 1889 in Winnipeg, Man.

John Norquay was a descendant of Hudson's Bay

Company servants who had worked on the northern rivers and the shores of Hudson Bay during the 18th century. His maternal grandmother, Elizabeth Vincent, was the daughter of a "country marriage" between an Indian or Métis woman and an HBC officer. John's father, a reliable jack of all trades at Norway House (Man.) in the mid 1830s, moved to the Red River Settlement in 1838 where he acquired a small farm and a few head of livestock. John had an unsettled childhood. His mother died in 1843 when he was two and his father in 1849. He was then raised by his paternal grandmother, Mrs James Spence, and by his teachers at the Anglican St John's Collegiate School in Red River. An able student, he soon became the protégé of David ANDERSON, bishop of Rupert's Land, who provided him with odd jobs and, in 1854, with a scholarship which allowed him to remain at school.

After graduation from St John's Collegiate School, about 1857, Norquay taught in the settlement. In 1858, at age 17, he was master of St James' Church school, and the following year moved to Parkdale where he met Elizabeth Setter, who was also a mixed-blood; they married three years later. In the mid 1860s they went to High Bluff near Portage la Prairie where Norquay engaged in farming. During lean times he traded furs on Lake Manitoba; he never achieved prosperity. Elizabeth, who died in 1933, was to recall that during these years they lived close to the land, in a log house with a mud fireplace and chimney, and with furniture constructed in the settlement. Their clothes were made from homespun wool, their flour was ground from wheat grown on their own land, and their soups were made from barley hulled in a wooden bowl with a wooden mallet; a rich dessert cake made with dried raspberries, blueberries, and saskatoons added a touch of luxury.

Politics, including the troubles of 1869–70, did not affect the family directly, although Norquay attended several of the public meetings concerned with Louis RIEL's provisional government and the transfer of the northwest from the HBC to Canada. When his cousin, also John Norquay, was elected to the provisional government, Norquay signed his election certificate. But the citizens of the new High Bluff constituency, meeting on 27 Dec. 1870, elected Norquay by acclamation to serve in Manitoba's first Legislative Assembly.

From about 1874 to the early 1880s Norquay and his family were to live on a small farm north of Winnipeg in the St Andrews district where English-speaking mixed-bloods were numerous. His personal finances were, if not straitened, certainly limited, but his salary after he had become a minister of the government in 1871 was sufficient to maintain a comfortable household: his children attended the schools of St John's (Anglican) parish. Norquay's high standing in the Anglican community and among the English-speaking mixed-bloods undoubtedly played a part in his election as St Andrews' political representative in 1874; he retained the seat until his death. Beginning in 1875 he was elected annually to represent his church at the synod of the diocese of Rupert's Land, and was regularly named to its executive committee as well as to the boards of St John's Collegiate School and St John's Ladies' School. Norquay was regarded with respect by most of his fellow citizens but also with a measure of good-natured amusement. His great size – he was over six feet tall and weighed about 300 pounds – prompted *Quiz*, the Winnipeg satirical newspaper, to poke fun at the picture of Norquay crushing the dainty chairs in the civilized salon of Governor General Lord Lorne [Campbell*]. Although crude comments concerning his mixed-blood ancestry were inevitable (in 1875, for example, Donald Gunn*, a member of the Legislative Council of Manitoba, referred to him as "Greasy John"), the prevailing mood was one of tolerance. His ability, education, and personal warmth, and the sense of continuity in the small society in which he lived, ensured that in the 1870s he would be a valued public servant.

Norquay had assumed leadership of one faction of English-speaking mixed-bloods in the unstable political situation which followed the Manitoba Act of 1870 and the arrival in the new province of Lieutenant Governor Adams George Archibald* in the same year. His position at this time was comparable to that of Dr John Christian Schultz* among the new Canadian element or of Joseph Royal* among the French Canadians from Quebec. As a representative of one of the moderate elements he soon became a member of the Board of Education of Manitoba, a justice of the peace, and even a supervisor of a smallpox quarantine. His stock rose still higher in the fall of 1871. The Canadian "Loyalists" created a chaotic situation, which challenged the government's ability to enforce the law, by conducting a series of public protest meetings intended to get Schultz a place in the provincial cabinet. Archibald secured the resignation from the cabinet of Alfred Boyd*, an English Canadian member who could not stand up to Schultz at these stormy meetings, and replaced him as minister of public works and agriculture with Norquay, whom he described as "a halfbreed of fair education and good abilities." By so doing Archibald had met and removed the issue of English Protestant representation which the Orange extremists had been stressing. Norquay took the oath of office on 14 Dec. 1871 and under Archibald's tutelage helped provide the stability which enabled the government to survive.

Norquay administered a department which constructed and maintained roads, bridges, and public buildings. He did his job well, was liked, and was respected as an orator and a representative of the old order of Red River. In 1872 he ran for the federal parliament in Marquette but was defeated by Robert Cunningham* by a margin of three votes to one. In his first years Norquay often collaborated with his erratic cabinet colleague, Henry Joseph CLARKE, and resigned with the rest of the ministry in July 1874 after Clarke's scandalous domestic arrangements and failure to protect Riel against Ontario-inspired legal charges alienated a majority in the legislature and led to a defeat of the government over proposals for redistribution. Because of his support for Clarke, Norquay did not serve in the short-lived government of Marc-Amable Girard* and was not invited into the Executive Council by Premier Robert Atkinson Davis* following the general election of 1874. But the group of English-speaking members of the legislature to which Norquay belonged could not be ignored, and in March 1875 he returned to the cabinet on the strength of Davis' promise of an electoral redistribution to allow more adequate representation of the growing English-speaking community. A compromise revision of the electoral boundaries ensured eight seats for each of three groups: the French, largely Métis but with a growing number of French Canadians; the old settlers, largely English-speaking mixed-bloods but with many Selkirk settlers; and the new settlers, mainly English-speaking Ontarians. The new settlers were still under-represented but Norquay defended the special treatment of the Métis and mixed-bloods because of their contributions as pioneers in the west and their efforts to show consideration for newcomers.

By 1878 Norquay's ascendancy in the assembly was unquestioned and his moderate stance on public issues had made him a representative of not just the mixed-bloods but of all Manitoba. He had met with setbacks, for example during the recent changes in cabinet, and he had made some important enemies, chief among whom was Schultz. Nevertheless Norquay's appointment to succeed Davis as premier in November 1878 was both predictable and popular. In the general election that month his government was returned with a majority similar to that of his predecessor; he could rely on support from a united French bloc, led by Joseph Royal, and enough English-speaking members to give him between 14 and 17 supporters in the 24-seat legislature.

Norquay's political career spanned a period which saw dramatic changes in the province. The population of Manitoba, which grew from 12,000 to about 30,000 between 1870 and 1877, doubled in the next four years and had doubled again by the time Norquay left office in 1887. These years of rapid development meant constant demands for more schools, public works, and land drainage, and for better and cheaper transportation facilities. Government spending increased dramatically from about $90,000 in 1876 to about $700,000 in 1886. The Norquay administrations between 1878 and 1886 were reasonably successful. His forceful negotiations and urgent representations at Ottawa won larger subsidies and enlarged boundaries for Manitoba, and his cabinets were competent in the administration of justice, public works, and agriculture.

Nevertheless, there were problems in his government, and they lay in his relationship with his caucus and also with the eastern Canadian party system. A Conservative in federal politics from the mid 1870s, Norquay had resisted the introduction of federal party lines into the provincial sphere, in part because he felt that a non-partisan front would strengthen his hand in negotiations with Ottawa and in part because of local political troubles. These troubles became apparent when, in the spring of 1879, he was nearly the victim of a political *coup* launched by his cabinet colleague Joseph Royal, with the approval of a leading Conservative in the opposition, Thomas Scott. This incongruous alliance of a French Canadian Roman Catholic from Quebec and an English-speaking Orangeman from Ontario was intended to cause a shift in support from the English-speaking mixed-blood premier to Royal and a new coalition cabinet. Royal probably believed that he could control most easily the introduction of eastern party divisions into Manitoba politics, while Scott undoubtedly wished to see the Conservative party firmly established in the province. The *coup* was overcome by Norquay's swift manœuvring. At a hastily assembled caucus of all the English-speaking members of the legislature, Norquay condoned, if he did not actually initiate, a round of anti-French speeches, and then offered to lead an "English" ministry which would be committed to a curtailment of French language rights and political representation. The premier won majority support in the caucus and demanded Royal's resignation from the cabinet. The challenge to Manitoba's French population, however, was reduced to a minor electoral redistribution, in which French-speaking members were left in control of six or seven seats instead of eight or nine, and a bill to abolish the printing of some official documents in French, which was reserved by Lieutenant Governor Joseph-Édouard CAUCHON and allowed to die by the federal government; by November 1879 Norquay's compromise ministry included Girard. The premier had written to Sir John A. Macdonald* in June, "I regret very much that I had to adopt such extreme measures with Royal but his treachery left me no alternative." The crisis had given Norquay further reason to distrust the influence of eastern Canadian party loyalties. His government, which won a resounding vote of confidence in the general election of December 1879, was, however, built upon an uneasy alliance of federal Liberals and Conservatives and of early French and English settlers, a coalition certain to collapse.

The issue around which all of Norquay's political problems seemed to gather was that of railways. The construction of the transcontinental Canadian Pacific Railway, the availability of branch lines, the level of freight rates, and the need for competition were at the centre of Manitoba politics in the 1880s. When the speculative boom in Winnipeg collapsed late in 1882, the city's board of trade attacked the freight rates of the CPR and when early frosts and low grain prices affected Manitoba farmers in 1883–84, they too attacked the railway. At the heart of these complaints and the debates over railways was a clause in the 1880 federal contract with the CPR syndicate, inserted at the insistence of George Stephen*, which guaranteed the company a monopoly on western traffic for 20 years. The monopoly clause became the focus of Manitoba politics and of Norquay's own struggle for political survival.

The Manitobans' desire for branch lines, competitive freight rates, and, it should be noted, speculative profits, resulted in applications for railway charters from groups of local businessmen as well as from investors in eastern Canada and the United States. Norquay's government was bound to approve these charters. Members of the legislature assumed they could break the CPR monopoly by constructing branch lines within the province and by establishing alternate rail links to the east. Norquay believed that the construction of the former was legally within the province's jurisdiction although his cabinet in developing policy was not so clear about the legality of building lines which would connect with American lines at the border. Prime Minister Macdonald, however, concerned with the health of the CPR, Canada's reputation with international investors, and the interests of eastern Canadian commerce, was equally bound to disallow the Manitoba charters if they infringed upon the so-called "monopoly clause." Conflict was inevitable.

The first federal disallowance of Manitoba railway charters came in 1882. Within months Thomas Greenway*, a farmer and land speculator who had moved from Ontario four years earlier, formed a small "Provincial Rights" opposition in the Manitoba assembly which had connections with the eastern Canadian Liberal party. Greenway and his colleagues argued, probably correctly, that Norquay, an avowed supporter of Macdonald in federal politics, had acquiesced in the establishment of the CPR monopoly; certainly in 1879 and perhaps again in 1882 Norquay had agreed to respect federal rail policy in exchange for additional financial aid for Manitoba. Whether he liked it or not, Norquay was tied to the federal Conservative party by the railway politics of the 1880s. He realized the benefits of the association when better financial terms than those provided by the Manitoba Act were negotiated for the province, as they were almost annually between 1879 and 1885, and he realized the problems when popular demand for improved rail service threatened to defeat his government. Norquay was a Conservative premier because his opponents were Liberals, but he was not necessarily the Conservatives' choice for leader.

The premier, for example, had never been on good terms with Schultz and his "Loyalists," and had alienated Scott in the 1879 ministerial changes. Other Conservative Orangemen from Ontario, such as Stewart Mulvey and Gilbert McMicken*, disliked Norquay because he was indecisive in his support of Macdonald's railway policy. There were always a few, like William Wagner, who objected to him because of his mixed blood; "by N. the *moccasin* will show itself through the finest patent leather boot," he wrote in 1885. Only the strong hand of Macdonald could quell the annual revolts from among the Manitoba Conservatives; only a command from his office could call out the troops to support Norquay in election campaigns. In 1883 Macdonald prevented the distribution of 10,000 protest leaflets, sponsored by the Orange order, which might have overturned the government; apparently because of an oversight, Norquay's government had failed to pass a bill incorporating the order at the last sitting of the legislature. In 1885 a crucial ministerial by-election was saved by Macdonald's telegram to prominent local Tories. According to Manitoba's lieutenant governor, James Cox Aikins*, the public meetings held when Macdonald passed through Winnipeg in 1886 on his CPR junket rekindled local Tory enthusiasm and rescued Norquay from certain defeat in the general election. Nevertheless, Macdonald had reservations about the Manitoba government and, on occasion, wished that Norquay could be replaced. But he always concluded that the premier despite "many faults and weaknesses is loyal to the Dominion," if not entirely committed to the dominion government.

Norquay in the 1880s was a man of influence, travelling as an equal with leaders of society and with businessmen such as Alexander Walker Ogilvie* and William Bain Scarth. His tours opened his eyes to the potential for private gain that accompanied the western boom. Thus early in the decade he joined several small syndicates which underwrote a railway, a coal-mine, and two gold-mines, as well as engaging in land speculation. There was nothing unusual about his association with businessmen and their ventures because the contemporary code of ethics forbade only private gain at public expense, but these undertakings do illustrate Norquay's membership in that large group of 19th-century leaders who combined political and business interests to the advantage of both. He rode the wave of optimism as if "to the manner born." About 1884 he purchased a comfortable new house in Winnipeg, and during his trips on public business he spent lavishly. His style was that of a Canadian, rather than a Red River, politician; like the province which he led, he had made the transition from the fur trade to the world of industrial capitalism.

His personal finances received a setback, however, when the Saskatchewan Coal Mining and Transportation Company, of which he was president, ran into financial difficulties in 1886, and, despite his frantic manœuvring, he was left with a $1,500 personal debt to his own government. What was worse, the opposition learned some details of his financial activities and accused him of bilking the people of Manitoba through his connection with a plot of land on which the provincial asylum was being built. The so-called "coal steal and asylum business" was investigated in 1886 by a royal commission headed by Chief Justice Lewis WALLBRIDGE, which found the charges against Norquay to be groundless. Nevertheless, electors were not reassured. The government had failed to meet public requests for services and, through haste or carelessness, could no longer account properly for its expenditures. The popular vote in the 1886 election was divided almost equally between opposition and government. Norquay survived, but with a reduced majority. He owed his narrow victory to Macdonald, to a modest gerrymander, and to his promise that the CPR monopoly would be ended.

The railway problem finally brought about Norquay's humiliation in 1887. His cabinet, influenced by rural protests, the demands of Winnipeg businessmen, the calculation that the province had a constitutional right to charter branch lines, or the conviction that bluff and negotiation would achieve their goal, pressed the construction of the Red River Valley Railway from Winnipeg to the international boundary where it could connect with an American line. The first sod was turned in July 1887. Committed to a disallowance policy if it were necessary, Macdonald used every tactic possible to stop the railway. The CPR itself played a desperate game between the two governments, seeking not to preserve the monopoly, which the company's leaders now regarded as doomed, but to secure a high price for relinquishing it. Throughout the summer of 1887 officers of the CPR obstructed the Manitoba contractors, subsidized sympathetic local newspapers, encouraged the revelations of Corydon Partlow Brown, a former Norquay cabinet member who wanted to avenge his removal from office, and kept in close contact with Macdonald, Governor General Lord Lansdowne*, and federal cabinet members. It was Sir Donald Alexander Smith*, a leading member of the CPR syndicate, who warned Macdonald that the Manitoba government had gone to London, attempting to negotiate financial arrangements for the Red River Valley Railway. George Stephen, president of the CPR, informed Macdonald that the Merchants' Bank of Canada would seek a dominion guarantee on further loans to Manitoba: "It appears Norquay is in extremis and it will be good for him if he is made to feel the effect of his misdeeds." Just as Norquay had been kept in power by the prime minister, so he was removed from office by him. In September, Macdonald advised Lieutenant Governor Aikins that Norquay had misused government funds; a special land revenue account, moneys held in trust for Métis children, was said to have been used to pay ordinary government bills. Rumours of financial scandal floated about Winnipeg for some weeks and then were made public by a former Norquay supporter, Edward Philip Leacock. At this point the pressure upon Norquay and his cabinet colleagues was intense.

During these hectic months Norquay alternated between euphoria and bitter depression. He was the most popular man in the province in the summer, when the Red River Valley Railway was forging ahead, and an outcast in late autumn, when his failure was complete. He had travelled to Chicago, New York, Montreal, and Toronto in search of funds for the Red River road but everywhere Macdonald's agents had preceded him. The Winnipeg merchant princes would not help him with financing. It was said that he had broken down in New York and gone on a spree and that, when reproached for his ingratitude to Macdonald, he had wept with remorse. Whatever the truth of such rumours, he was a dispirited man when he visited his friends around St Andrews in November. He still fought gamely, standing his ground in the face of accusations of corruption until, once again, Macdonald intervened. The prime minister was undoubtedly angry with Norquay for attending the Interprovincial Conference called by Premier Honoré Mercier* at Quebec City in October; the only non-Liberal in attendance, Norquay made the conference appear both bi-partisan and respectable. It may have been for this reason that Macdonald decided to play a more active role in the resolution of events. The occasion was a grant by Manitoba of about $256,000 to an entrepreneur for the Hudson Bay Railway; Ottawa had been supposed to grant the province 256,000 acres of land in exchange, but Macdonald denied that he had approved such a transfer: "I had to tell [Provincial Treasurer Alphonse-Alfred-Clément La Rivière*] that he must have dreamt this story." He thus created a shortfall of $256,000 in the Manitoba public accounts. Norquay's cabinet colleagues deserted and the government fell on 23 Dec. 1887. Its weak successor, led by David Howard Harrison*, was replaced within a month by the Liberal administration of Thomas Greenway which governed Manitoba for the next decade. The fall of Norquay was thus the herald of a revolution in provincial educational and cultural policy to be brought about by Greenway, Joseph Martin*, and Clifford Sifton*.

Norquay did not despair as a result of this defeat. He continued to assert his innocence of wrongdoing. Because of his great abilities he won the title of opposition leader when Greenway took office. But the Conservative party loyalists no longer trusted him and during the 18 months between his defeat and his death they schemed to find a government appointment that would get him out of politics. Macdonald was, however, adamant about not giving a public service job to an enemy, so Norquay was forced to take a position as a law clerk. He narrowly survived the Greenway landslide in the general election of July 1888, and continued to lead a small opposition group, but he found no charity in the Conservative party. By early 1889 he was selling insurance to supplement his income as a member of the legislature. Despite his effective criticisms of the government he could find little public support. In early July 1889 he was struck by a sudden ailment, perhaps appendicitis, and because of the heat, the severity of the attack, and his own corpulence, quickly died.

A wave of public sympathy greeted the news of Norquay's death on 5 July and large numbers of Manitobans contributed a dollar each to erect a monument to his memory. Macdonald, stung by criticism of his treatment of his former ally, hastened to write a letter of sympathy to his widow, but he also complained that he could not understand "how our friends should feel annoyed at me in not going through the form of condolence" when Norquay had been such a traitor to the party. He insisted for the next month that he had done nothing to get Norquay out of the premier's office; that, he said, had been the work of the premier's cabinet colleagues in Manitoba – and, besides, "I always liked Norquay personally, and regret much his untimely death."

John Norquay was one of the dominant figures in Manitoba in an era marked by rapid population growth, extraordinary social change, and seemingly constant negotiations with the federal government over the terms and even the nature of confederation. Despite the turbulent atmosphere, Norquay ruled with ease and represented the interests of his community at Ottawa with distinction. In the end economic conditions and political manœuvering pushed him into a corner where he was obliged to fight both the federal government and the CPR over the issue of railway monopoly. He lost, of course, and went into political exile. But although he controlled neither property nor power at the time of his death – a premature death which prevented him from demonstrating that he belonged in the company of the nation's political leaders – he still possessed the affection of his contemporaries in Red River. As Bishop Robert Machray* said, "Always there stood out the kind heart and amiable disposition, that endeared him wherever he was known."

GERALD FRIESEN

Anglican Church of Canada, Diocese of Rupert's Land Arch. (Winnipeg), St Andrew's Anglican Church (St Andrews, Man.), Baptismal register, 1859–72, entries 271, 411, 473 (mfm. at PAM); St Mary's la Prairie Anglican Church (Portage la Prairie, Man.), Baptismal register, 1855–83, entry 299; Marriage register, 1856–83, entry 20 (mfm. at PAM). AO, Scarth (W. B.) papers (mfm. at PAC). PAC, MG 26, A; MG 27, I, I19. PAM, MG 2, C14, Anderson to James Ross, 4 Feb. 1854, October 1855; MG 3, B1, election returns, 1 March 1870; MG 7, A1, no.7953, "Reminiscences of the Rev. Benjamin McKenzie, Matlock, Manitoba," 10–11 (typescript); MG 12, A, G. Hill to John Norquay, 17, 19 May 1871; B2, Alexander Morris to Alexander Mackenzie, 8, 10 July 1874; E, Donald Gunn to J. C. Schultz, 5 March 1875; S. Mulvey to J. C. Schultz, 5 Feb. 1888; MG 13, C1-C4; HBCA, B.154/a/31: f.9d; B.239/u/1: f.250d; E.4/1a: f.173d; E.4/2: ff.25d, 131d, 133, 158; E.5/10: f.22; E.5/11: f.18; "Notes on ancestry of Hon. John Norquay" (typescript).

Church of England, Diocese of Rupert's Land, Synod, *Report* (Winnipeg), 1877–89. Man., Legislative Assembly, *Journals*, 1876, app.: 16; 1886: 5–9, 15–18, 189–95; 1888–89, sessional paper, no.1. *Manitoba Daily Free Press*, 1874–89. *Manitoban* (Winnipeg), 1 July, 18 Nov., 16, 30 Dec. 1871; 7 Dec. 1872. *Le Métis* (Saint-Boniface, Man.), 23, 30 nov. 1871; 11 janv. 1872; 11 juill. 1874; 6 mars 1875. *Quiz* (Winnipeg), 9 Nov. 1878; 3 Feb., 1 March 1879. *Winnipeg Daily Times*, 1879–85. *CPC*, 1874–89. J. A. Jackson, "The disallowance of Manitoba railway legislation in the 1880's: railway policy as a factor in the relations of Manitoba with the Dominion, 1878–1888" (MA thesis, Univ. of Manitoba, Winnipeg, 1945). W. K. Lamb, *History of the Canadian Pacific Railway* (New York and London, 1977). F. A. Milligan, "The lieutenant-governorship in Manitoba, 1870–1882" (MA thesis, Univ. of Manitoba, 1948). T. D. Regehr, "The national [railway] policy and Manitoba railway legislation, 1879–1888" (MA thesis, Carleton Univ., Ottawa, 1963). Ellen Cooke, "Norquays in the Red River disturbances," *Manitoba Pageant* (Winnipeg), 21 (1975–76), no.2: 6–7.

O

OAKLEY, ALFRED, stone-cutter and trade union leader; b. *c.* 1846, probably in Brighton, England; d. 30 Sept. 1883 at Toronto, Ont. He was survived by his wife Emily.

Alfred Oakley arrived in Toronto in 1872. He soon became a trade union activist and first came to prominence in labour's campaign for the repeal of the "violence, threats and molestation" provisions in an 1872 amendment to the criminal law. The campaign was reinforced when five Toronto stone-cutters were found guilty of coercion and sentenced to 15-day jail terms for refusing to work alongside a strike-breaker. At a protest meeting sponsored by the Toronto Trades Assembly, Oakley denounced Police Magistrate Alexander McNabb as an "imbecile" and the law as "a disgrace to the country." In July of that year the Journeyman Stonecutters Union elected Oakley as their representative to the TTA and one month later he became vice-president of that body. The assembly was the first central labour organization in any Canadian city, with an active life from 1871 to 1878.

Before the federal Toronto West by-election held in the fall of 1875 Oakley solicited the opinions of the various candidates on the amendments of that year to the criminal law which had been passed as a result of labour's agitation since 1872 but which did not satisfy labour leaders. He reported to the TTA that the Liberal candidate, Alderman John Turner, was favourable to the TTA's position.

In 1876 Oakley was his union's delegate to the annual convention at Toronto of the Canadian Labor Union, formerly the Canadian Labor Protective Movement and Mutual Improvement Association founded in 1872 after the Nine Hour movement. Oakley was active at the convention in endorsing universal manhood suffrage and in advocating an improved provincial Mechanics' Lien Act. The latter was of great concern to workers in the building trades because it would ensure that labourers would be paid if contractors went bankrupt. He also seconded a motion expressing support for a new amendment to the criminal law introduced by Edward Blake*. The Canadian Labor Union chose its first parliamentary committee that year and Oakley was among those named to it.

An "advanced Radical" in politics, Oakley was active in Liberal campaigns. As a result he was a controversial figure among trade union leaders in Toronto where, after 1872 and the Trade Unions Act, Toryism was the prevailing orthodoxy. In 1880 he actively opposed the "Beaverback" currency reform campaign which, following American "greenbackism," called for a looser monetary supply, and which was put forward by the independent Alexander Whyte Wright* in the Toronto West federal by-election. Oakley gave his support to the Liberal candidate.

The following year Oakley was involved in the founding of the Toronto Trades and Labor Council, a successor to the TTA, and, after being defeated for the office of financial secretary, was elected treasurer and appointed to the legislative committee. As a member of the committee he lobbied for a federal factory act and for further changes in the provincial Mechanics' Lien Act. Re-appointed to the committee in 1882, he led the council in its endorsement of Oliver Mowat*'s new Lien Act passed to placate labour. In the hard-fought federal election campaign of 1882 in Toronto the working-class vote was of considerable importance. Oakley's attack on Sir John A. Macdonald*'s Conservative government during the campaign and his attempt to lead the TTLC to support the Liberal party brought partisan politics to the council and almost destroyed it. That same summer John Armstrong, a printer and supporter of the Conservative party, defeated Oakley for the presidency of the TTLC in a bitterly contested election, the legality of which was disputed for nearly two months. Oakley paid another price for political partisan activity; he was fired from his job as a city sewer inspector.

Oakley was involved in yet another political wrangle in the winter of 1882 when he came to the defence of the Liberal mayoralty candidate, John Jacob Withrow*. A leader of the Master Carpenters' Association during a strike in the spring of 1882, Withrow was roundly condemned by the TTLC for his role in this strike and his actions ten years earlier when he opposed the Nine Hour movement. Oakley managed to gain an open meeting for his candidate so that he could respond to labour's charges. Withrow's spirited defence of his actions convinced none of the other labour leaders, and he was defeated in a close election. Following this successful intervention in city politics, the TTLC decided to run candidates in the provincial election of 1883. Oakley was mentioned as a possible independent labour candidate for Toronto West, but, partly because of bad health, he stepped aside for his close friend, carpenter Thomas Moor. When Moor lost the nomination by a single vote to painter John W. Carter, Oakley charged "outside interference." Procedural irregularities were cited and a second vote was taken. After Carter won decisively on the second ballot, Moor and Oakley moved to make the nomination unanimous. In this first campaign in Toronto by an independent labour candidate, Carter won 48 per cent of the vote, losing by only 200 ballots.

Oakley's health continued to deteriorate and he resigned from the TTLC in April 1883. He died a few months later, at 37, from consumption, the dread occupational disease of stone-cutters. Surviving him were his father and two brothers, all stone-cutters living on Alfred's Toronto street block, and his wife. The struggle Oakley had carried on in the TTLC in favour of the Liberals was continued after his death by Daniel John O'Donoghue* who enjoyed a far greater degree of success.

GREGORY S. KEALEY

CTA, Toronto assessment rolls, St Stephen's Ward, 1880. PAC, MG 28, I44. Canadian Labor Union, *Proceedings of the Canadian Labor Union congresses, 1873–77*, comp. L. E. Wismer (Ottawa, 1951). Toronto City Council, *Minutes of proc.* (Toronto), 1878–82. *Globe*, 1875–83. *Toronto*

Daily Mail, 1875–83. *Trades Union Advocate* (Toronto), 1882–83. *Toronto directory*, 1872–83. G. S. Kealey, "The working class response to industrial capitalism in Toronto, 1867–1892" (PHD thesis, Univ. of Rochester, N.Y., 1977); "The life of a Toronto artisan: Thomas William Dowson, stonecutter," Committee on Canadian Labour Hist., *Bull.* ([Halifax]), 1 (spring 1976): 10–[14]. Wayne Roberts, "Artisans, aristocrats and handymen: politics and trade unionism among Toronto's skilled building trade workers, 1896–1914," *Labour* ([Halifax, Rimouski, Que.]), 1 (1976): 92–121.

O'CONNOR, JOHN, lawyer, politician, and judge; b. 21 Jan. 1824 in Boston, Mass., son of John O'Connor and Mary O'Connor; m. in April 1849 Mary Barrett, and they had nine children; d. 3 Nov. 1887 at Cobourg, Ont.

John O'Connor's parents emigrated from Ireland to Boston in 1823 and he was born there the following year. In 1828 the family moved to Maidstone Township, a Roman Catholic settlement in Essex County, Upper Canada. O'Connor, unable to do farm work because he had lost a leg in an accident, took up law in 1848. After studying in Sandwich (Windsor) and in Toronto, he was admitted to the bar of Upper Canada in 1854. He also became a member of the bar in the state of Michigan, but never practised there. He worked in Windsor with Charles T. Baby and from 1863 to 1865 in Toronto with John Blevins. Although a successful lawyer, he was not a prominent member of the bar and was not made a QC until 18 Dec. 1872 after he had entered the federal cabinet.

As a young man, O'Connor had worked briefly as a newspaper editor and he also showed an interest in local politics. He served as reeve of Windsor and was an Essex County councillor in 1859–60 and 1862–63. He was warden of Essex three times during the 1860s and chairman of the board of education of Windsor for 12 years. In 1860 O'Connor hoped to obtain the Conservative candidacy for an elective Legislative Council seat made vacant when Colonel John Prince* accepted a judgeship, but he withdrew in favour of Sir Allan Napier MacNab*. The following year, in a bitter campaign in Essex for the Legislative Assembly, he was defeated by Arthur Rankin. Rankin's election was voided on 9 March 1863 and on 7 April O'Connor was elected. Later in the same year, however, Rankin again defeated O'Connor in the general election. O'Connor was successful in the 1867 dominion elections and retained the Essex seat until 1874.

O'Connor quickly became an important Irish Catholic leader in the new federal parliament. During the 1860s Ontario's Irish Catholics correctly argued that they had not received a fair proportion of patronage posts from the Conservatives; the Liberals encouraged their claims. In 1870, increasing Catholic agitation posed problems for the Conservatives when lay leaders, supported by senior clerics, began to organize politically in an attempt to extract concessions from either party. O'Connor, the only Ontario Irish Catholic member, defended Conservative interests and succeeded in obtaining some support from Archbishop John Joseph LYNCH for an alliance of Irish Catholics with the Conservatives. O'Connor maintained a high degree of political visibility: in 1870 he published *Letters of John O'Connor, esq., M.P., on Fenianism*, which presented an impressive attack on the Fenians and emphasized the loyalty of the Canadian Irish; he worked on behalf of the Conservatives in the 1871 provincial campaign; and he devoted a substantial amount of his time to issues of concern to Irish Catholics.

In 1871 O'Connor was offered a cabinet post in the government of Sir John A. Macdonald*. Because there had been no strong Irish Catholic leader in federal politics since the assassination of Thomas D'Arcy McGee* in 1868, pressure to appoint and promote Catholics had intensified. Financial problems and the risk of defeat in a by-election in Essex precluded O'Connor's immediate acceptance, but on 2 July 1872, a few weeks before the general election, he entered the ministry as president of the Privy Council. He subsequently served until the government fell in 1873 as minister of inland revenue from 4 March to 30 June and as postmaster general from 1 July to 6 November. O'Connor held these minor portfolios only briefly and was given no opportunity to display his abilities.

O'Connor's defeat in Essex in the federal election of 1874 and the decline of his legal practice influenced his decision to leave Windsor and establish a practice in Ottawa. He was elected in that year as president of the St Patrick's Society of Ottawa and in 1875 he acted as chairman of the Ottawa O'Connell Centennial Celebration. In the 1878 federal election, when the Irish Roman Catholic vote was again important, he had no obvious seat to contest. With the help of party leaders O'Connor obtained the nomination for Russell, a safe eastern Ontario riding, and was elected once more. Arguments used in 1872 to justify his promotion to the cabinet still applied. O'Connor was not, however, given any major responsibility; he was probably already suffering from the illness that would incapacitate him by the 1880s. Instead he held a succession of minor portfolios: president of the Privy Council (17 Oct. 1878–15 Jan. 1880), postmaster general (16 Jan.–7 Nov. 1880 and again 20 May 1881–22 May 1882), and secretary of state (8 Nov. 1880–19 May 1881). He often missed cabinet meetings because of illness and rarely participated in debates; he was left with constituency and patronage problems, and he agreed to accept a judgeship in Ontario at the prime minister's convenience.

In 1880 he was offered a judgeship but refused it

because it was in Manitoba. He realized, however, that he would have trouble obtaining the nomination as Conservative candidate for Russell in the next election and asked Macdonald for help. The prime minister replied by dismissing him from the cabinet. O'Connor, who claimed that he had no intimation of this fate, was badly shaken. Always in financial distress, he was desperately anxious to obtain an Ontario judgeship while Macdonald was in power and he harassed the prime minister for alternative employment until a vacancy occurred. His chief argument was that his cabinet service had ruined his law practice and that he merited compensation. O'Connor greatly exaggerated his sacrifices. Like many other 19th-century politicians he had become financially dependent on government appointments because they were easy to obtain and seemed safe. In addition, the legal profession of Ontario was convinced that he was not qualified for a judgeship. Matthew Crooks CAMERON, a judge on the provincial Court of Queen's Bench, condemned such an appointment for O'Connor as early as 1878 and Macdonald's own minister of justice, Sir Alexander Campbell*, was to observe in 1883 that O'Connor "has become so obscured by disease and infirmity and desuetude that his appointment would be viewed as discreditable."

Macdonald, stating that he had "never deserted a Colleague & don't mean to begin now," on 5 July 1882 appointed O'Connor to prepare a brief on the boundary dispute between Ontario and Manitoba. The following March, with the job completed, O'Connor was again in need. Campbell attempted to prevent a judicial appointment by offering him additional financial aid and a seat on the commission for the consolidation of statutes. O'Connor accepted, but continued to press for a judgeship in Ontario. Macdonald finally appointed him a judge of the Court of Queen's Bench for Ontario on 11 Sept. 1884.

The appointment was, predictably, unpopular among the members of the legal profession. O'Connor was a mediocre judge and an embarrassment to both the government and the bench. He complained that he had to "scratch along on a beggarly salary," expecting the government to supplement his income. After receiving $13,273 for legal work in 1882–84, he billed the government for an additional payment of $27,085. When Macdonald ignored O'Connor, the judge sued the government and the case was before the Exchequer Court of Canada when O'Connor died in November 1887; his family never obtained any of the money.

O'Connor's name is remembered because he was the first Irish Roman Catholic judge of the Supreme Court of Judicature for Ontario. He achieved this position not because of his professional, administrative, or political skills, but because he was available to fill the role of leader among the Ontario Irish Catholics when their votes mattered to the Conservatives.

DONALD SWAINSON

John O'Connor was the author of *Letters of John O'Connor, esq., M.P., on Fenianism . . .* (Toronto, 1870).

AO, MU 469–87. PAC, MG 26, A; MG 27, I, D13. Can., House of Commons, *Debates*, 1867–68; 1879–81; 1886. "Parl. debates" (CLA mfm. project of parl. debates, 1846–74), 1873. *Parliamentary debates, Dominion of Canada . . .* (3v., Ottawa, 1870–72). *Globe*, 1882, 16 Sept. 1884, 4 Nov. 1887. *Toronto Daily Mail*, 1882, 1884, 4 Nov. 1887. *Canadian biog. dict.*, I: 266–67. *Canadian directory of parl.* (J. K. Johnson), 447–48. *CPC*, 1872–73; 1875; 1879; 1883. *Cyclopædia of Canadian biog.* (Rose, 1888), 412–13. Dent, *Canadian portrait gallery*, IV: 164–65. *Political appointments and judicial bench* (N.-O. Coté). Read, *Lives of judges*, 425–34. M. K. Christie, "Sir Alexander Campbell" (MA thesis, Univ. of Toronto, 1950). M. J. Galvin, "Catholic-Protestant relations in Ontario, 1864–1875" (MA thesis, Univ. of Toronto, 1962). Swainson, "Personnel of politics."

OILLE (Oill), GEORGE NICHOLAS, machinist, manufacturer, and businessman; b. in March 1817 in Pelham Township, Upper Canada, eldest of eight children of George Nicholas Oille and Elizabeth Decker; d. 28 March 1883 at St Catharines, Ont.

Details concerning George Nicholas Oille's early life and education are few. He apparently had a "natural genius for mechanics" and was entirely self-taught, "never even having served a brief apprenticeship." He may have worked at the Niagara Harbour and Dock Company, a foundry for steamboats at Niagara (Niagara-on-the-Lake), before arriving in St Catharines some time in 1847. As a consequence of the concentration of industry encouraged by the opening of the Welland Canal, St Catharines had developed into the major centre for the flour-milling industry in the Niagara peninsula and was becoming a hub of shipping. By 1850 Oille had erected a "large and extensive Furnace and Machine Shop," known as George N. Oille's Machine Shop and Foundry, where he was employing 30 workers in June 1856. In that year he manufactured a wide range of goods including mowers, cream separators, two-horse rail power engines, railway car wheels, axle-trees, steam-engines, and boilers, and his sales were reported at approximately $15,000.

The nature of the industrial growth of the Niagara peninsula in the 1860s caused Oille to begin specializing in the construction of marine engines. In 1861 he agreed to supply Louis Shickluna*, St Catharines' major shipbuilder, with a boiler for a ship to serve on the passenger run between St Catharines and Toronto. By 1863 Oille's foundry employed ten men for work on the engines and boilers of a propeller – a sailing craft fitted with an engine – owned by James Norris and Sylvester Neelon, prominent St Catharines merchants, and named the *America.* Launched by Shickluna's shipyard in 1863, the *America*, like most of that yard's vessels, was designed to carry flour to Montreal. In April 1864 the *City of Toronto*, a 615-ton passenger ship, began operation at Niagara; Oille had not only provided the boiler but also the 365-horsepower engine. A month later, Shickluna launched a 137-foot tugboat, *Samson*, in which all the internal machinery and engines had been built by Oille from plans drawn by Cyrus Dean, locomotive superintendent of the Welland Railway Company.

Despite Oille's initial successes with marine engines, competition for contracts was strong. In 1863 and 1864 Shickluna launched at least four other propellers, but their engines had been supplied by either John Gartshore of Dundas or the Davidson and Doran firm of Kingston. By 1866, however, Shickluna was again using Oille's foundry. The propeller *City of London*, launched in April 1866, was designed to ply between Port Stanley and other Lake Erie towns. Oille produced a condensing type of steam-engine for the craft, experimented in load distribution by placing the machinery six feet farther forward than was usual, and connected to the boiler an apparatus for flooding any part of the vessel with steam and water in case of fire. The informal contracting arrangement between Oille and Shickluna carried on into the 1870s. Between 1868 and 1873 Oille supplied the engines and boilers for seven propellers built by Shickluna, most of which were used in the flour and wheat trade with Montreal.

Oille's ability in constructing machinery for propellers is again evident with the *Prussia*, another vessel constructed by Shickluna, put into service in June 1873. He not only manufactured its low pressure engines but also designed a special steam crane for the ship's deck. George and his brother, Lucius Sterne, a prominent physician in St Catharines, were among the shareholders who owned the ship, which was designed primarily to carry passengers.

Although Shickluna was his largest customer, Oille's reputation had secured him contracts with other local shipbuilders. In 1865 he installed a 60-horsepower oscillating engine in a passenger steamer constructed by Melancthon Simpson in St Catharines and he supplied the engines for the propeller *Alma Munro*, owned by the Elgin Transportation Company of Port Stanley and constructed by Andrews and Son of Port Dalhousie (now part of St Catharines).

The career of George Nicholas Oille is an excellent example of how after 1850 industrial development combined with local circumstances to create specialists in certain new urban areas. Oille's innovative mechanical ability contributed much to the development of the marine engine, so vital to the shipbuilding and shipping industries of the St Catharines area. A man with few close friends, he was totally dedicated to his business and widely respected for his accomplishments.

BRUCE A. PARKER

Rutherford B. Hayes Library (Fremont, Ohio), Great Lakes coll., Marine papers, F. E. Hamilton. St Catharines Public Library (St Catharines, Ont.), Louis Shickluna scrapbook; Vert. file, Niagara peninsula – Ships and shipping. *Globe*, 29 March 1883. *London Advertiser* (London, Ont.), 29 March 1883. *London Free Press*, 21 April 1870. *Mail* ([Niagara-on-the-Lake, Ont.]), 27 April 1864. *St. Catharines Constitutional* (St Catharines), 30 April, 12 Nov. 1863; 12 April 1866; 16 April 1868. *St. Catharines Evening Journal* (St Catharines), 28 June 1838; 26 June 1856; 25 July 1861; 17 May 1864; 11 May 1865; 1 May 1869; 10 March 1871; 25 April 1872; 28 April, 9 June 1873. H. G. J. Aitken, *The Welland Canal Company: a study in Canadian enterprise* (Cambridge, Mass., 1954). James Croil, *Steam navigation and its relation to the commerce of Canada and the United States* (Toronto and Montreal, 1898; repr. Toronto, 1973). [F.] B. Cumberland, *A century of sail and steam on the Niagara River* (Toronto, 1913). G. P. de T. Glazebrook, *A history of transportation in Canada* (Toronto, 1938; repr. 2v., 1964; New York, 1969). Harlan Hatcher, *Lake Erie* (Indianapolis, Ind., and New York, 1945). R. S. Taylor, "The historical development of the four Welland canals, 1824–1933" (MA thesis, Univ. of Western Ontario, London, 1950). G. N. Tucker, *The Canadian commercial revolution, 1845–1851* (New Haven, Conn., 1936; repub., ed. H. G. J. Aitken, Toronto, 1964). D. B. Tyler, *Steam conquers the Atlantic* (New York and London, 1939). E. A. Cruikshank, "Notes on the history of shipbuilding and navigation on Lake Ontario up to the time of the launching of the steamship *Frontenac*, at Ernesttown, Ontario, 7th September, 1816," *OH*, 23 (1926): 33–44. C. H. J. Snider, "Mighty Maltese of Shipman's Corner," *Inland Seas* (Cleveland, Ohio), 25 (1969): 323–25. J. W. Watson, "The changing industrial pattern of the Niagara peninsula," *OH*, 37 (1945): 49–58.

OLIVER, ADAM, businessman and politician; b. 11 Dec. 1823 in Queens County, N.B., fourth son of John Oliver and Jeanett Armstrong; m. first 5 Dec. 1846 Elizabeth Grieve (d. 5 June 1866), and they had six children; m. secondly 13 June 1868 Ellen Rintoul, and they had four children; d. 9 Oct. 1882 at Ingersoll, Ont.

Educated in rural New Brunswick, Adam Oliver left for Westminster Township, Upper Canada, in 1836 and learned the trade of carpenter in London before moving to Ingersoll in 1850. Ingersoll was incorporated as a village in 1852 and it soon became a centre for a hardwood lumber trade as well as for wheat, farm implements, and, in the 1860s, cheese. Oliver benefited from the village's early growth by establishing a building and contracting business. In 1853 he secured a $30,000 to $40,000 contract to build a depot at Niagara Falls for the Great Western Railway. Having acquired property in Ingersoll in the mid 1850s, Oliver proceeded to develop it, building a brick residence and a steam-powered planing mill, and setting up a lumber yard. By 1861 his various businesses employed 24 men.

Oliver was active in public affairs in Ingersoll from the time of its incorporation. He was elected to the first village school board in 1852 and to the village council in 1855, 1856, and from 1859 to 1863, serving as village reeve from 1859 to 1862; he was also warden of Oxford County in 1862. Following a bitter verbal attack by Oliver on Reeve John Galliford in 1856, village elections were contested by rival Oliver and Galliford slates. Oliver objected that Galliford's handling of village affairs was secretive; however, control of the council would no doubt help his construction business and allow him to encourage the village's development northwards towards the railway and his property. As reeve, Oliver argued against Ingersoll's incorporation as a town, ostensibly out of fear that higher government costs would result but probably also still mindful of his own political interests: a popularly elected town mayor would have less control over his council than a village reeve who was the choice of council. His opposition to town status led to the defeat of the Oliver slate in 1863 and Ingersoll became a town in January 1865. Ironically, Oliver was elected Ingersoll's first mayor in 1865 and 1866. While reeve and later as mayor, he also served Ingersoll as magistrate. In addition, Oliver was a member of the Independent Order of Odd Fellows from 1856 to 1865, captain of the volunteer Ingersoll Infantry Company from 1864 to 1866, and a liberal supporter of Erskine Presbyterian Church, although he was not a communicant until 1868.

In 1867 he formed the Adam Oliver Company in partnership with William Cairns Bell and Hugh MacKay Sutherland*, at which time extensive additions were made to Oliver's mill and machinery at Ingersoll. With Bell assuming the management of the company, Oliver was free to contest Oxford South for the Reformers in Ontario's first provincial election against James Noxon, a John Sandfield Macdonald* coalitionist. Successful in 1867, Oliver was re-elected in 1871, defeating the Conservative candidate Stephen Richards*, an outsider. Aside from sponsoring legislation in 1868 to set standards for the manufacture of cheese and butter, both important products in his area, he did little for his constituency and abandoned it almost entirely in 1872, when he became preoccupied with business concerns in northwestern Ontario though he continued to reside in Ingersoll.

In 1871 fire destroyed a planing mill and lumber yard which his company had established in Orillia three years earlier. Transferring his equity from this venture to the Thunder Bay district, in 1872 he formed Oliver, Davidson and Company in partnerhsip with Joseph Davidson, a Toronto lumberman and former Ingersoll resident, and Peter Johnston Brown and Thomas Wells, two Ingersoll lawyers. The company established the district's first sawmill and planing mill near Fort William (now part of Thunder Bay, Ont.) in 1873. By 1874 it reportedly had rights to 40,000 acres and a total investment of $100,000 in the area. In January 1875 the dominion government announced that the largely uninhabited Fort William town plot was to be the Lake Superior terminus for the Canadian Pacific Railway. Oliver, Davidson and Company, holding 136 acres near the town plot and 42 lots in the town plot itself, was able to reap $12,410 from land sales to the government. In February the company acquired a $243,000 government contract to build a telegraph line from Fort William to Winnipeg. A $3,500 contract to build an engine-house in Fort William followed in September. In June 1876 the company contracted to operate the government telegraph line between Fort William and Rat Portage (Kenora).

Distressed by the failure to obtain the railway terminus for their own community, the inhabitants of nearby Prince Arthur's Landing (later Port Arthur, now part of Thunder Bay) complained that the chief beneficiary of the dominion Liberal government's contracts, Adam Oliver, was a Liberal member of the Ontario legislature. The result of their outcry was a Senate investigation into the land transactions. Its 1878 report stated that land valuation procedures had favoured property owners and the government had paid grossly inflated prices for land. Though the investigators of the Conservative-dominated Senate were obviously partisan and the testimony biased, Oliver was unquestionably embarrassed by a revelation about the generous compensation paid to his company for a hotel which was on land designated for the railway but which had been built after the government's plans for the railway reserve had been announced. By 1879 Oliver's active involvement in the northwest was over, although he retained business investments there until his death. Oliver's reputation suffered again in 1882 when the report of the Royal Commission on the Canadian Pacific Railway presented circumstantial evidence indicating that his company's Fort William to Winnipeg telegraph contract had been acquired through his influence with the Department of Public Works and in particular with its minister, Alexander Mackenzie*.

Compounding Oliver's problems in the 1870s was the collapse of his political career. In 1874 he had resigned from the Ontario legislature because of a possible contravention of the "independence of parliament" act: Oliver, Davidson and Company had inadvertently sold timber to a buyer for the provincial government. Oliver was returned by acclamation in the by-election held later that year, perhaps because the opposition was content to forgo the by-election in anticipation of the forthcoming general election. He won only a bare plurality in the 1875 general election and was unseated after an investigation found bribery and corrupt practices among certain of his supporters. Retiring from provincial politics, and with his interest in Ingersoll reviving, Oliver ran in the municipal elections of 1877 for the post of first deputy reeve but was defeated by James Noxon. Elected to that position in 1880, he resigned 4 months later, after being stricken with paralysis, and died in 1882. After his death, his partnerships were dissolved and his properties converted into securities. Oliver's wife inherited most of the estate, valued at $70,070.

G. N. EMERY

Ingersoll Town Hall (Ingersoll, Ont.), Assessment rolls, 1880–82; Map of town of Ingersoll, 1905. Oxford County Surrogate Court (Woodstock, Ont.), no. 1252, will of Adam Oliver, 26 Dec. 1882 (mfm. at AO). PAC, RG 31, A1, 1851, 1861, 1871, Ingersoll; 1842, 1851, Westminster Township. Can., Canadian Pacific Railway Royal Commission, *Report* (3v., Ottawa, 1882). *Thunder Bay district, 1821–1892: a collection of documents*, ed. and intro. [M.] E. Arthur (Toronto, 1973). *Ingersoll Chronicle* (Ingersoll), 1854–82. *Oxford Herald* (Ingersoll), 12 Jan. 1860–29 May 1862. *Thunder Bay Sentinel* ([Thunder Bay, Ont.]), 1875–79. *Canadian biog. dict.*, I: 678–81. *County of Oxford, gazetteer and general business directory, for 1862–3 . . .*, comp. James Sutherland (Ingersoll, 1862). *Oxford and Norfolk gazetteer, and general and business directory . . .*, [comp. James Sutherland] (Woodstock), 1867. *The Oxford gazetteer; containing a complete history of the county of Oxford, from its first settlement; together, with a full abstract of each census . . .*, comp. T. S. Shenston (Hamilton, [Ont.], 1852). Pierre Berton, *The national dream: the great railway, 1871–1881* (Toronto and Montreal, 1970), 229–39. George Emery, "Adam Oliver, Ingersoll and Thunder Bay district, 1850–82," *OH*, 68 (1976): 25–43.

OLIVER JULIAN, NORBERT THIBAULT, named **Brother.** *See* THIBAULT

O'MEARA, FREDERICK AUGUSTUS, Church of England clergyman and translator; b. 7 Jan. 1814 at Wexford (Republic of Ireland), the son of Charles P. O'Meara, schoolmaster, and Sarah Murphy; m. in 1840 Margaret Johnston Dallas of Orillia, Upper Canada, and they had one daughter and four sons, all their sons, including Thomas Robert*, becoming clergymen; d. 17 Dec. 1888 at Port Hope, Ont.

Frederick Augustus O'Meara entered Trinity College, Dublin, on 23 Jan. 1832, and graduated BA in 1837. Through the Dublin University Association of the Church Missionary Society he was led to missionary work. Made deacon by the bishop of London in October 1837, O'Meara left England in December in the employ of the Upper Canada Clergy Society. After his arrival in Toronto on 29 March 1838 he began work as a travelling missionary in the Home District. On 9 September he was ordained priest by Bishop George Jehoshaphat Mountain* at St John's Church, Woodhouse Township, near Simcoe, and was licensed to the Indian mission at Sault Ste Marie as successor to William McMurray*. He had worked in Tecumseth Township of the Home District with Featherstone Lake Osler*, who, needing clerical assistance in his large mission, was disappointed to lose him. For the two years O'Meara lived at the Sault, he ministered not only to the Indians there but also to those living at Garden River, nine miles away. The latter had come to the Sault when Sir John Colborne* promised them a village in 1830 but it had not been built and they had returned to Garden River. O'Meara quickly became immersed in the study of Ojibwa and within a year had translated part of the Book of Common Prayer into that language. The young Irishman's journals written at this time indicate his intense interest in evangelization and education.

Following its decision in 1830 to settle Indians in villages, the British government had attempted in 1835 to concentrate Indians from a large area, mainly north of lakes Superior and Huron, on Manitoulin Island. In 1838 these attempts were resumed. O'Meara was sent as chaplain in 1841 to replace Charles Crosbie Brough who had removed to London, Canada West, in that year. For more than 18 years O'Meara laboured within the settlement at Manitowaning and also journeyed to Bruce Mines, Owen Sound, and more frequently to Sault Ste Marie and Garden River. Two of his reports, both under the title *A mission to the Ottahwahs and Ojibwas, on Lake Huron*, were published in 1846: one describes the foundation of the mission, with references to the pioneering visit of Captain Thomas Gummersall Anderson* and the Reverend Adam Elliot* in 1835, and the other tells of his own labours in 1845–46. In company with the Reverend Richard Flood of the Delaware Indian mission O'Meara sailed to the British Isles late in 1846 seeking money for church building. The money he collected later aided in building St Paul's Church, Manitowaning, a task completed in 1849. During his stay he enjoyed visiting his mother, sisters, and brother in Dublin and was honoured by his old university with an honorary LLD. He made another overseas journey in 1854–55 to gain further support for his mission.

An important result of O'Meara's years on Manitoulin was the production of a number of translations into Ojibwa: a devotional work, *The faith and duty of a Christian*, 1844; the Book of Common Prayer, 1846; the Four Gospels, 1850; the New Testament, 1854; and the Psalms, 1856. In 1856 O'Meara received an assistant when Bishop John Strachan* ordained Peter Jacobs, an Indian who was the son of Methodist missionary PAHTAHSEGA and had been educated under Bishop David ANDERSON of Rupert's Land; O'Meara and Jacobs together produced the Pentateuch, with Proverbs and Isaiah, as well as a hymn book in 1861. Some of these books were reprinted and were used in Indian missions in both the United States and Rupert's Land. O'Meara had a good grasp of grammar through his training in classical languages and he was a diligent student of Ojibwa. So certain was he of his philological proficiency that in a review of the first two volumes of *Information respecting the history, condi-*

tions and prospects of the Indian tribes of the United States . . . he accused the editor, Henry Rowe Schoolcraft, of making glaring errors. He also expressed the opinion that Indian words worked into Henry Wadsworth Longfellow's *The song of Hiawatha* might have been rendered more accurately if the poet had not made use of Schoolcraft's books as he apparently had.

By 1850 progress was being made at the mission. The church, now the oldest in the diocese of Algoma, had been built and a boys' school begun. The next year Miss Hannah Foulkes came from England to teach Indian girls and her work met with O'Meara's warm approval; she stayed until she went to Garden River on her marriage to James Chance, an Englishman instructed in Ojibwa by O'Meara and ordained by Bishop Strachan in 1857. But despite all efforts the Indian establishment failed and the mission linked with it was weakened. Unlike the older Roman Catholic settlement at nearby Wikwemikong, from its beginning largely composed of Christian Indians who already had some experience in cultivating the land and who had in their new home a good fishing ground, the Manitowaning establishment had less homogeneity and a less favourable location. Many Indians who were gathered there accepted Christian baptism but as they came directly from the ancient freedom of lake and forest they were not attracted by the settled way of life. Some left for their former homes or returned to wandering, while a few moved to nearby Sheguiandah where the Anglican mission was re-established in 1865. Six years earlier, however, when his government salary was cut off because of a change in policy, O'Meara, discouraged and with family responsibilities, had decided to leave and to accept the incumbency of Georgetown, Canada West. Peter Jacobs wrote sadly from Manitowaning on 30 September: "Dr. O'Meara and his family left this afternoon. . . . I had hoped that they would have stayed here another winter. The Doctor called the Indians together yesterday evening, and after singing and prayer, gave them his parting address. . . . The Doctor is a great loss to this place: I shall miss him very much."

For the next eight years, while serving as a parish priest, O'Meara continued his interest in education and was at one time inspector of public schools in Esquesing Township. On behalf of the New England Company, which supported the Garden River mission, he made a tour of inspection of the Company's Brantford station in 1860. When Peter Jacobs died in 1864, O'Meara taught Ojibwa to his successor at Manitowaning, Jabez W. Sims. The next year, on behalf of the Church Society of the Toronto diocese, he accompanied Alexander Neil Bethune* on a deputation to Manitowaning to advise the Indians about relocating, following the treaty in 1862 which opened the island to white settlement. In 1867 he went to Port Hope to assist the ailing Jonathan Shortt* and he became rector on Shortt's death in the same year. A large contribution during his 20-year ministry in that parish was the completion of the present church and related buildings. He died "in harness" in Port Hope on 17 Dec. 1888.

O'Meara's ministry coincided with the first half-century of the diocese of Toronto and he was closely linked with church affairs during that long period. When a diocese of St Mary's (later Algoma) had been contemplated in 1849 his name had been mentioned for bishop. In a letter to Ernest Hawkins*, secretary of the Society for the Propagation of the Gosepel, John Strachan made a shrewd assessment of O'Meara's character, admitting that he possessed zeal and the true missionary spirit but was also of a hasty disposition and often rash and precipitate in judgement. "These defects in the temper of his mind seem to disqualify him for the high duties of the Episcopate where correctness and precision of judgment and firmness of character are as essential as the higher qualifications of piety and learning." O'Meara was a strong evangelical, firm in his opinions and ready in his expression of them. He was one of the founders in 1877 of the Protestant Episcopal Divinity School, later Wycliffe College, in Toronto and was in disagreement on that score with Bishop Bethune. But all three bishops of Toronto respected him and the third, Arthur Sweatman*, told the synod in 1889: "The Church has lost in him a truly loyal, gifted and valuable servant; I have lost a faithful and highly honoured friend."

THOMAS R. MILLMAN

[Among Frederick Augustus O'Meara's works are: "Historical and statistical information respecting the history and prospects of the Indian tribes of the United States . . . [review]," *Canadian Journal*, new ser., 3 (1858): 437–51; *Report of a mission to the Ottahwahs and Ojibwas, on Lake Huron* (London, 1846); and *Second report of a mission to the Ottahwahs and Ojibwas, on Lake Huron* (London, 1846). Many of O'Meara's translations into Ojibwa are listed in J. C. Pilling, *Bibliography of the Algonquian languages* (Washington, 1891), 379–82. The General Synod Archives of the Anglican Church of Canada in Toronto has a good collection of these translations. T.R.M.]

Anglican Church of Canada, General Synod Arch. (Toronto), F. A. O'Meara, Scrapbook. AO, Strachan (John) papers. [C. C. Brough], "The Manitoulin letters of the Rev. Charles Crosbie Brough," ed. R. M. Lewis, *OH*, 48 (1956): 63–80. Can., Prov. of, Legislative Assembly, *App. to the journals*, 1847, I, app. T.; 1858, VI, app.21. [Mrs James Chance [Hannah Foulkes]], *Our work among the Indians* . . . (London, Ont., n. d.). Church of England, Church Soc. of the Diocese of Toronto, *Annual report* (Toronto), 1847–49. Colonial and Continental Church Soc., *Annual report* (London), 1861–62. Colonial Church and School Soc., *Annual report* (London), 1852–60. New England Company, *History of the New England Company, from its incorporation, in the seventeenth century, to the present time* . . . (London, 1871). Soc. for the Propagation of the Gospel in

Foreign Parts, *Report* (London), 1849. *Canadian Ecclesiastical Gazette* (Toronto), 1 Oct. 1854; December 1855; January 1856; July, November 1857; 15 June, 1 Dec. 1860; 15 May, 1 June, 15 Dec. 1861; 14 June, 15 July 1862. *Church* (Cobourg, [Ont.], Toronto), 5 Jan. 1839; 30 Oct., 20 Nov. 1846; 3 Sept. 1847; 9 July 1854. *Church Chronicle* (Toronto), September 1863; December 1865; August 1867. *Church of England Magazine* (London), 27 July 1839. *Evangelical Churchman* (Toronto), 27 Dec. 1888. *Canada and its prov.* (Shortt and Doughty), IV: 693–725; V: 329–62. [F. W. Colloton and C. W. Balfour], *A historical record of the planting of the church in Sault Ste. Marie, Ont. (Diocese of Algoma) and the history of the mother-parish of St. Luke's* (n.p., [1932?]). J. W. Grant, "Rendezvous at Manitowaning" (paper delivered to the World Methodist Hist. Assoc., Toronto, 1977). *St. Paul's Anglican Church, Manitowaning, Manitoulin Island, Ontario, Canada* (Little Current, Ont., 1950). Ruth Bleasdale, "Manitowaning: an experiment in Indian settlement," *OH*, 66 (1974): 147–57.

ONASAKENRAT (Onesakenarat), JOSEPH (also known as **Sosé, Joseph Akwirente, Chief Joseph,** and **Le Cygne**), Iroquois chief and Methodist missionary; b. 4 Sept. 1845 on the seigneury of Lac-des-Deux-Montagnes, Canada East, the son of Lazare Akwirente; d. 7 Feb. 1881 at Oka, Que.

Joseph Onasakenrat's parents were full-blooded Iroquois who lived on the Ottawa River near the mission of Lac-des-Deux-Montagnes (Oka) established by the Sulpicians. Since both his parents belonged to the Roman Catholic Church, Joseph – or Sosé as he was called in Iroquois – was raised in that faith by the missionaries.

In April 1718 King Louis XV had granted the Sulpicians a seigneury at Lac des Deux Montagnes, then a relatively isolated spot 30 miles west of Montreal, where they could settle with the Algonkian and Iroquoian converts in their care. Previous settlements at Montreal and Sault-au-Récollet (Montréal-Nord) had exposed the natives to liquor sellers, and intemperance had become a serious problem [*see* Maurice Quéré* de Tréguron]. But ownership of the land at Lac des Deux Montagnes, where the mission was established in 1721, was to become a source of conflict between the priests and the natives [*see* François-Auguste Magon* de Terlaye]. As early as 1787 Chief Aughneeta informed Sir John Johnson*, the superintendent general of Indian affairs, that his people had left Sault-au-Récollet for the seigneury of Lac-des-Deux-Montagnes only after being promised "a Deed from the King of France." The chief maintained that "the desire of having a fixed Property of our own" had induced them to move, but that the Sulpicians claimed exclusive ownership of the seigneury and insisted that the "Land did not belong to us, no, not as much as the smallest Shrub."

On seven occasions between 1787 and 1851 the Iroquois publicly protested the Sulpicians' claim to ownership of the seigneury. The most serious confrontation arose in 1851 when Joseph Onasakenrat was a small boy. In the summer of that year a native Methodist preacher, the Reverend Peter Jones [Kahkewaquonaby*], visited the mission, discovered the unrest, and came close to convincing a number of Indians to abandon "Popery" and become Methodists. For the moment the Sulpicians were able to maintain their control by having the bishop of Montreal excommunicate the 15 leading native dissidents.

The Sulpicians, badly in need of a native spokesman sympathetic to their cause, saw in Joseph Onasakenrat a future leader. A gifted pupil, he was sent at age 15 to the Sulpicians' Petit Séminaire de Montréal. He studied for three years at the college (where Louis RIEL was a classmate) and then returned to Oka to become secretary to the Sulpicians under Antoine Mercier*. On 25 July 1868 the Iroquois elected Onasakenrat, then only 22 years old, their principal chief. To the surprise of the Sulpicians, he quickly showed his independence from them by drafting a petition to the governor general protesting against the society's control of the settlement. The Indians, he pointed out, could not secure title to their lands from the priests or even cut firewood without their permission. He then charged that "these pretended successors of Saint Peter live in a sumptuous place and dress in purple and the finest fabrics"; the priests, he said, were directly responsible for the "poverty and misery" of the Indians.

A much more serious setback for the Sulpicians than Joseph's defection was yet to come. In the winter of 1868 the French Canadian apostate, Charles-Paschal-Télesphore Chiniquy* preached for three days at Oka. After he left, the Iroquois appealed to the Methodists, who had missionaries in the area, to send one to them. Xavier Rivet was appointed to Oka. The overwhelming majority of the Iroquois then renounced Catholicism and joined the Wesleyan Methodist Church in Canada. Chief Joseph now began to fight his opponents with a new vengeance. On 18 Feb. 1869, without first seeking the priests' permission, he cut down a huge elm tree, thereby challenging their privilege of granting wood-cutting rights. On 26 February he marched with 40 of his band to the Sulpicians' residence and there in blunt, forceful language warned them to leave Oka in eight days or their lives would be in danger. Assured of the faithful support of the Algonkians, who constituted about one-fifth of the total Indian population of 500, the priests quickly obtained a warrant for Joseph's arrest. On 4 March he and his two fellow chiefs were seized by Montreal police, but within weeks Joseph was out of jail and again leading the struggle. In late December 1869 he forwarded another petition to the governor general in which he summarized the Iroquois complaint: "From what our fathers have told us we always believed as they believed, that these lands were given in the first instance by the King of France to the Seminary for our use and interest; now however we are told that the lands belong to the Seminary, and that we live on them and use them only because they permit us to do so." Nevertheless from 1868 the federal government had refused to accept the Oka Indians' claim to ownership of the seigneury and affirmed the Sulpicians' claim to sole legal title.

Throughout the 1870s the strife continued at Oka. The police, summoned by the priests, frequently arrested Iroquois for cutting wood in the forests and for tearing down fences erected by the Sulpicians. In December 1875 the Sulpicians dismantled the Methodist church in the Indian village, claiming that the Iroquois had had no legal right to erect it. Then on 15 June 1877 the Sulpicians' church itself mysteriously burnt down. The priests accused a number of Iroquois, who in turn claimed that they had arrived only after the fire had begun. Warrants were issued for the arrest of Chief Joseph and his father (both seen by a Sulpician at the scene of the fire), as well as a dozen others. All were accused of arson. Wealthy English-speaking Protestants in Montreal came forward to help the accused, providing bail and legal aid. The case was finally dismissed in 1881 after four juries failed to reach a verdict.

Upon his release on bail Joseph returned to Oka where he acted as interpreter for the resident Methodist missionary. He began translating the Bible and by June 1880 had translated the four Gospels from French into Iroquois. In 1880 he was himself ordained a minister by the Montreal Conference of the Methodist Church of Canada and assigned as a missionary to the Iroquois settlements at Caughnawaga and Saint-Régis. His ministry proved a short one, however, because he died suddenly at Oka on 7 Feb. 1881 at age 35.

In the last year of his life Joseph had reversed his stand against the Sulpicians and had begun advocating a peaceful solution to the conflict. The charges of arson had not yet been finally disposed of, but Joseph's ordination as a Methodist minister seems to have pacified him. He urged his people to accept the priests' offer to buy land for them elsewhere and to move them there at the Sulpicians' own expense. But in advocating moderation, Joseph lost the support of his people, who would follow his counsel only as long as he championed what they felt were their basic rights. Six months after his death the majority of the Oka Iroquois dramatically voted against his "peace policy." In the fall of 1881, when the time came to move to the lands in the Muskoka region of Ontario purchased for them by the Sulpicians, only one-fifth of the Iroquois consented to move. The "Oka Question" continued unresolved for 30 years after Joseph Onasakenrat's death, before the Supreme Court of Canada finally upheld the Sulpicians' title in 1910.

DONALD B. SMITH

ASSM, 8, A. McGill Univ. Arch., Wesleyan Methodist Church in Canada, Montreal District, Minutes, 1870–73. McGill Univ. Libraries (Montreal), Dept. of Rare Books and Special Coll., MS coll., CH101.S119, CH119.S139. Methodist Church (Canada, Newfoundland, Bermuda), Montreal Conference, *Minutes* (Toronto), 1884–90. Methodist Church of Canada, Missionary Soc., *Annual report* (Toronto), 1874–81; Montreal Conference, *Minutes* (Toronto), 1874–81. Amand Parent, *The life of Rev. Amand Parent, the first French-Canadian ordained by the Methodist Church . . .* (Toronto, 1887). A. R. Hassard, *Famous Canadian trials* (Toronto, 1924), 106–23. A. L. Hatzan, *The true story of Hiawatha and history of the Six Nation Indians* (Toronto, 1925). Philip Laforce, *A history of Gibson Reserve* (Bracebridge, Ont., n.d.). John Maclean, *Vanguards of Canada* (Toronto, 1918), 167–79. Claude Pariseau, "Les troubles de 1860–1880 à Oka: choc de deux cultures" (thèse de MA, McGill Univ., 1974). J. K. Foran, "Chronique d'Oka," *Le Canada* (Ottawa), 2, 10, 19, 22 juill., 3, 12, 19, 30 août, 9, 13 sept. 1918. Olivier Maurault, "Les vicissitudes d'une mission sauvage," *Rev. trimestrielle canadienne* (Montréal), 16 (1930): 121–49.

ONE ARROW. *See* KĀPEYAKWĀSKONAM

ONWANONSYSHON. *See* JOHNSON, GEORGE HENRY MARTIN

O'SULLIVAN, DANIEL TIM-DANIEL. *See* SULLIVAN, DANIEL

P

PACAUD, ÉDOUARD-LOUIS (baptized **Louis-Édouard**), lawyer, public servant, businessman, and politician; b. 20 Jan. 1815 at Batiscan, Lower Canada, son of Joseph Pacaud, a carpenter, navigator, and merchant, and Angélique Brown; m. first 28 July 1841 Anne-Hermine Dumoulin at Yamachiche; m. secondly 2 July 1868, at Trois-Rivières, Françoise Dumoulin, in all likelihood his first wife's cousin; four daughters were born of these marriages; d. 18 Nov. 1889 at Arthabaskaville (Arthabaska), Que.

Like his six brothers and four sisters, Édouard-Louis Pacaud had the advantage of sound teaching; he undertook his classical studies at the Séminaire de Nicolet between 1826 and 1832, and on 25 May 1836, after studying law under Antoine POLETTE and Edward Barnard in Trois-Rivières, he was granted his commission as a lawyer. He was practising there when the troubles of 1837–38 broke out, but unlike his brothers, PHILIPPE-NAPOLÉON, Charles-Adrien, and Joseph-Narcisse, he took no active part in the conflict. However, in January 1838 he got Judge Joseph-Rémi Vallières* de Saint-Réal to release the brother of Louis-Joseph Papineau*, notary André-Augustin, a participant in the battle at Saint-Charles-sur-Richelieu. On 5 Jan. 1839 Pacaud also made a speech in defence of his friend and future brother-in-law Joseph-Guillaume Barthe*, who had been committed to prison and "sought the benefit of a writ of habeas corpus" [*see* Jean-Roch Rolland*]. But by February 1840 he was writing to Ludger Duvernay* that he had come round to the plan of the union of the two Canadas, thus accepting the ideas of Louis-Hippolyte La Fontaine*.

From 1840 to 1844 Pacaud continued to concentrate on his legal practice, gradually becoming one of the most respected lawyers in his region and an important figure in Trois-Rivières. In February 1844 he was appointed bankrupt commissioner for this district, and took up his duties on 20 April. However, this office proved troublesome. The duties of the commissioner were regulated by three laws which came into effect in December 1843. Under the terms of this legislation, the commissioner was to receive a fee commensurate with his services, but a lawyer holding this office lost the right to practise. He also had to preside at the quarter sessions, to serve as a justice of the peace, and discharge "all the duties of the resident [judge] of the district during the latter's absences at the court of appeal." The office suited Pacaud but he was by no means satisfied with the remuneration, since for all these services he received "only the emoluments deriving from bankrupt businesses." After numerous letters to the governor general and several petitions to the Legislative Assembly, Pacaud managed to obtain an annual salary of £200 for the period from August 1846 to January 1850, when he probably ceased to act as commissioner. He failed, however, to win fair payment for the period from 1844 to 1846. Being obstinate and determined, he even asked the assembly in June 1851 to pass an act authorizing him to institute proceedings against the government to obtain compensation for his past services.

During the years 1836 to 1850 Pacaud sat on several committees, including one seeking to incorporate the town of Trois-Rivières in 1845, and his home became a meeting-place for its prominent citizens. He was also interested in business. In addition to lending money, from 1839 he took advantage of the proclamation of Lord Durham [Lambton*], issued in September 1838, which decreed that land grants would again be made to those in the militia in 1812 as a reward for their services. Since many militiamen did not want or for various reasons could not take possession of the land to which they were entitled, Pacaud undertook to buy their "claims" at absurdly low prices. No exact estimate can be made of how much land he acquired in this way, but it is certain that by the end of the 1840s he owned several lots in Trois-Rivières itself; during this decade he also bought just over 3,200 acres in the counties of Drummond, Mégantic, and Nicolet, from which he received "income and rent."

On 1 May 1850 Pacaud ran in the by-election in Mégantic. He attributed his defeat by Dunbar Ross* to the intrigues of Charles-Félix CAZEAU, the secretary of the archdiocese of Quebec, who in his opinion had prompted the local clergy to intervene on behalf of the successful candidate. Embittered, Pacaud denounced this clerical interference in newspapers and drew a sharp reply from Cazeau. With the support of the editors of *Le Moniteur canadien* of Montreal, Pacaud stood as a Reformer in the December 1851 general elections in Nicolet. His 16-point political programme emphasized the abolition of the Legislative Council and of seigneurial tenure as well as the settlement of the Eastern Townships; some points showed a lawyer's concern for the codification of laws, the reform of the administration of justice, and compensation for jury duty. Dr Thomas Fortier won the election, however, and this second defeat put an end to Pacaud's attempts to enter the assembly.

Pacaud had settled at Montreal around mid May 1850 and opened a law office. He announced in at least two newspapers that he was buying "claims of militiamen, land in the Eastern Townships, [and] government debentures." He became a member of the Institut Canadien in Montreal, to which he donated more than 40 volumes in June 1850. According to Wilfrid Laurier*, with whom he formed a friendship towards the end of the 1860s, Pacaud had some success in business; apparently in the years 1850–53 he invested "his money in copper mining operations," only to find himself "ruined" after a staggering drop in prices. This reverse of fortune may explain why Pacaud returned to Trois-Rivières, probably in 1854, and organized "a grand lottery" of land "for building [projects] at Trois-Rivières." He put 10,280 tickets on sale "at two dollars apiece" for a draw on 28 Feb. 1855 for 150 lots which he owned. It is not known, however, whether this venture brought Pacaud the anticipated results. In any case he was not short of means. In the same period the Hôtel du Canada was opened in a building belonging to him, and at the end of 1858 he had the "huge" Hôtel Saint-Maurice built. In addition, in 1859 he was a partner with Louis-Adélard SENÉCAL and Sévère Dumoulin in the Compagnie de Navigation de Trois-Rivières.

In 1861 or 1862 Pacaud established himself in Arthabaskaville where he soon acquired an extensive legal practice. An eloquent counsel, possessing imagination and conviction, he sometimes found himself, in Laurier's words, supporting "heresies before the court." He enhanced his reputation by successfully acting for his brother Philippe-Napoléon in a sensational two-year lawsuit (1864–66) against the parish priest of Saint-Norbert in Norbertville, which earned him the accolade of "extraordinarily zealous" from his opponents. Punctilious, and a man of principle, Pacaud even sued the Montreal Telegraph Company for $16 because it had failed to transmit a message in December 1870. That year he was a contributor to *La Revue légale* in Montreal, in which a number of case reports appeared over his signature.

Remaining true to his habits, Pacaud in the end played an important part at Arthabaskaville in political, economic, and social affairs. At least twice, in 1871 and 1874, he was among those who urged Laurier to stand as a Liberal in Drummond and Arthabaska; on the first of these occasions he even took issue publicly with his parish priest. He participated in the movement to settle the region by lending money to settlers, as did his brother Georges-Jérémie. Moreover, Pacaud did not fail to invest in land; between 1871 and 1884 he acquired no less than 550 acres in the county. In 1880 he helped found and served as president of the Syndicat Agricole d'Arthabaskaville, its purpose being to develop production of beet sugar. He served as a town councillor for a period, and took part in most local activities. Pacaud was "reasonably well off," and his "hospitality [had] long since become proverbial"; the intellectuals of the region gathered at his home.

Made a QC on 31 May 1878, Pacaud was *bâtonnier* of the Arthabaska bar from July 1884 to May 1887, and also *bâtonnier général* of the province in 1885–86. One of the first legislative councillors appointed by the government of Honoré Mercier*, Pacaud served for the division of Kennebec from 24 Aug. 1887 until his death in November 1889. He may have been ruthless as a lawyer and uncompromising as a small businessman; he stood out particularly for his activities in local and regional affairs.

PIERRE DUFOUR and GÉRARD GOYER

AAQ, 1 CB, XVI: 33. AC, Arthabaska, État civil, Catholiques, Saint-Christophe (Arthabaska), 22 nov. 1889. ANQ-MBF, État civil, Catholiques, Immaculée-Conception (Trois-Rivières), 2 juill. 1868; Sainte-Anne (Yamachiche), 28 juill. 1841; Saint-François-Xavier (Batiscan), 22 janv. 1815; Minutiers, J.-M. Badeaux, 29 févr. 1836; 2 janv., 8 mars, 2 mai, 8 juin, 15 août 1837; 23 juill. 1838; 22, 23 mars, 2 (nos.2867–69), 23 avril, 14, 17 mai, 21 juin, 30 oct. 1839; 19 juin 1840; 25, 27 févr. 1841; 18 janv. 1842; 18 févr. (nos.3480–81), 19 oct. 1843; 26 juill. 1848. ANQ-Q, AP-G-68, nos.406, 418, 445; AP-G-239/79; QBC 9, 4: f.91; QBC 25, Événements de 1837–38, no.3257. ASN, AO, Séminaire, V: 81; Inscription des élèves. *Debates of the Legislative Assembly of United Canada* (Gibbs *et al.*), IV–X. *Examen de fait et de droit touchant la cause jugée en Cour du banc de la reine, sur appel, à Québec, entre Philippe N. Pacaud, Ecr., appelant, et le révérend Pierre Roy, prêtre, intimé, le 20 mars 1866* (Québec, 1867). *L'Avenir*, 11, 25 mai, 8 juin 1850. *Le Canadien*, 31 déc. 1847, 7 nov. 1851. *L'Électeur* (Québec), 11 oct. 1881, 19 nov. 1889. *L'Ère nouvelle* (Trois-Rivières), 1853–juillet 1855; janvier–juin 1859; janvier–février 1860; 7 janv.–11 févr. 1861. *La Minerve*, 28 mai 1846. *Le Moniteur canadien* (Montréal), mai 1850–octobre 1855. [Contrary to assertions in some obituaries published after Pacaud's death and later reiterated in various works, including *RPQ*, he was not editor of *Le Moniteur*. He published a number of letters and articles in it in the years from 1850 to 1854, in particular in 1850 and 1851. P. D. and G. G.]

L'Opinion publique, 4 oct. 1877, 1er janv. 1880. *Quebec Mercury*, 16 May 1850. *L'Union des Cantons de l'Est* (Arthabaskaville [Arthabaska], Qué.), 23 févr., 23 nov. 1889. Fauteux, *Patriotes*, 343–44. Langelier, *Liste des terrains concédés*, 1713–14, 1741, 1744. *Montreal directory*, 1850–53. P.-G. Roy, *Les avocats de la région de Québec*, 327–28. *RPQ*, 435, 606. G. Turcotte, *Le Conseil législatif de Québec*, 195–96. Bernard, *Les Rouges*, 98. Alcide Fleury, *Arthabaska, capitale de Bois-Francs* (Arthabaska, 1961), 15–16, 85, 87, 106, 114–15, 142–143, 166, 217, 229. A.-R. Lavergne, *Histoire de la famille Lavergne* (Montréal, s.d.), 23–24. C.-É. Mailhot, *Les Bois-Francs* (4v., Arthabaska, 1914–25), II: 156–57; III: 281–302. [In the last volume Mailhot's discussion on the community of Arthabaska was drawn virtually in its entirety from the text of a lecture given by Lawrence Arthur Dumoulin Cannon* at the Club de Réforme de Montréal, on 26 April 1919. Mailhot expressed his appreciation to Cannon for allowing him to consult the full text of his speech. *Le Canada* (Montréal) published an incomplete account of this lecture, under the title "Portraits de quelques amis de sir Wilfrid Laurier," 28 April 1919. An identical account came out the same day in *La Presse* under the title "Sir Wilfrid a commencé son œuvre à Arthabaska." P.D. and G.G.]

Robert Rumilly, *Honoré Mercier et son temps* (2v., Montréal, 1975), II: 67, 89. Joseph Schull, *Laurier*, H.-J. Gagnon, trad. ([Montréal], 1968), 60, 76–81. *Les ursulines des Trois-Rivières depuis leur établissement jusqu'à nos jours* (4v., Trois-Rivières, 1888–1911), II: 535; III: 422; IV: 75, 395. "La conférence de l'hon. Wilfrid Laurier: un grand avocat des Bois Francs," *La Presse*, 21 déc. 1897.

PACAUD, PHILIPPE-NAPOLÉON, notary and Patriote; b. 22 Jan. 1812 at Quebec City, son of Joseph Pacaud, a carpenter, navigator, and merchant, and Angélique Brown; m. first 9 Sept. 1834 Julie-Aurélie Boucher de La Bruère at Boucherville, Lower Canada; m. secondly 19 Jan. 1847 Clarice Duval at Trois-Rivières; d. 27 July 1884 at Saint-Norbert-d'Arthabaska (Norbertville), Que.

Philippe-Napoléon Pacaud studied at the Séminaire de Nicolet from 1821 to 1829. After serving as a clerk for Louis Panet at Quebec City, he received his commission as a notary on 23 Jan. 1833. The following year Pacaud settled at Saint-Hyacinthe where he went into practice as a notary and apparently opened a business which eventually flourished. When his brother Charles-Adrien and his brother-in-law Dr Pierre-Claude Boucher* de La Bruère founded the Banque Canadienne de Saint-Hyacinthe in 1836, Pacaud was one of its principal directors.

In April 1837, following the adoption by the British government of Lord John Russell's resolutions which frustrated hopes of government reform, Patriote leaders decided to organize protest meetings [*see* Denis-Benjamin Viger*]. A permanent central committee was soon set up and Pacaud and Louis-Antoine Dessaulles* were among the Patriotes of Saint-Hyacinthe who went frequently to Édouard-Raymond Fabre*'s Montreal bookstore where the committee met. That autumn Pacaud helped to form at Saint-Hyacinthe a section of the Fils de la Liberté, of which he was appointed captain. Soon after, he met the Patriote leaders at Saint-Denis, on the Richelieu River, and suggested that to finance their struggle they issue bank notes redeemable by the state after it gained independence. The plan was adopted and Pacaud, who was appointed commissary general of the Patriote armies, was made responsible for implementing it. But the British troops and the Patriotes clashed too soon for him to launch the first $300,000 issue of this currency.

In November 1837, after fighting at Saint-Denis and Saint-Charles, Pacaud tried to flee to the United States with his brother Charles-Adrien and his brother-in-law. When their route was cut off, they had to turn back to Saint-Hyacinthe. Pacaud, who was wanted by the authorities, resorted to ruse to evade his pursuers. He hid in the attic of his own house, and then, disguised as a priest, took refuge for a while in the Séminaire de Saint-Hyacinthe. He subsequently hid in various other places until the proclamation of amnesty on 28 June 1838 made it possible for him to return home with impunity.

When there was renewed unrest that autumn the authorities made a number of preventive arrests. On 2 December Pacaud was apprehended for having attended a meeting on 2 November which had been called by Édouard-Élisée Malhiot*, a Patriote leader who had returned from the United States to organize a new armed uprising. Pacaud was committed to jail in Montreal but was released on 22 Jan. 1839 without having to stand trial. No doubt influenced by the death of his wife and two of their three children soon after he left prison, Pacaud left Saint-Hyacinthe in the 1840s. He sought his fortune at Saint-Norbert-d'Arthabaska, in a region newly opened to settlement which in all likelihood offered more prospects than Saint-Hyacinthe where there were already several other notaries.

In September 1854 the Crown Lands Department put Pacaud in charge of constructing a colonization road through the townships of Chester, Ham, and Wolfestown. He stood as a candidate in the riding of Drummond and Arthabaska in the 1857–58 elections but withdrew in favour of his friend Jean-Baptiste-Éric Dorion*. At Saint-Norbert-d'Arthabaska in 1862 Pacaud simultaneously held the offices of justice of the peace, captain in the militia, postmaster, and clerk of the court of commissioners for the district of Arthabaska. In 1864, fortified by his status and probably inspired by the radical ideas he had harboured in the turmoil of 1837–38, Pacaud brought an action against the parish priest of Saint-Norbert, Pierre Roy, accusing him of having embezzled, as secretary treasurer of the "local school corporation," $111.30 intended for school funds. His claim was rejected by the circuit court of the district of Arthabaska on 7 March 1865, whereupon Pacaud launched an appeal. On 20 March 1866 the Court of Queen's Bench decided in his favour and fined the defendant $40. The trial, at which Pacaud's attorney, his brother ÉDOUARD-LOUIS, had demanded that the parish priest be jailed, was a *cause célèbre.*

Unlike his brothers Georges-Jérémie, Édouard-Louis, and Charles-Adrien, who were all to some extent active in business, Pacaud confined himself, from his earliest days in Arthabaska until 1883, to his notarial practice and to offices such as those he held in 1862. He seems to have been removed from these offices following the return to power of Sir John A. Macdonald* and the Conservatives in 1878, and thus to have been placed in a precarious financial position.

Pacaud, who died in 1884, had remained an unquestioning admirer of Louis-Joseph Papineau*; according to Pacaud's own statement – which was noted around 1878 by Louis-Honoré Fréchette*, a close family friend – on the eve of the battle at Saint-Denis he had ordered the Patriote leader not to expose his life needlessly and had forced him at gunpoint to leave the area. Two of the five children of Pacaud's second marriage played important roles on the political scene. Jean-Baptiste-Napoléon-Gaspard became the member for North Essex and speaker of the Ontario legislature. Philippe-Olivier-Ernest*, the founder of the Quebec City newspaper *L'Électeur*, which subsequently became *Le Soleil*, was the principal political organizer for Wilfrid Laurier* and Honoré Mercier*.

PIERRE DUFOUR and GÉRARD GOYER

Philippe-Napoléon Pacaud's minute book is deposited at AC, Arthabaska.

AC, Arthabaska, État civil, Catholiques, Saint-Norbert (Norbertville), 30 juill. 1884. ANQ-M, État civil, Catholiques, Sainte-Famille (Boucherville), 9 sept. 1834. ANQ-MBF, État civil, Catholiques, Immaculée-Conception (Trois-Rivières), 19 janv. 1847. ANQ-Q, AP-G-239/79; État civil, Catholiques, Notre-Dame de Québec, 23 janv. 1812; QBC 7, 7, Trois-Rivières; 17, Arthabaska; QBC 9, 7:

f.94; QBC 25, Événements de 1837–38, nos.1551, 1555–59, 1563, 3548. ASN, AO, Séminaire, Inscription des élèves; AP-G, M.-G. Proulx, V: 4. Can., prov. du, Assemblée législative, *App. des journaux*, 1854–55, XIII, app.N.N.N. *Examen de fait et de droit touchant la cause jugée en Cour du banc de la reine, sur appel, à Québec, entre Philippe N. Pacaud, Ecr., appelant, et le révérend Pierre Roy, prêtre, intimé, le 20 mars 1866* (Québec, 1867). *L'Électeur* (Québec), 30 juill. 1884. *L'Opinion publique*, 4 oct. 1877, 27 févr., 6, 13 mars 1879 (the author of the articles in the last three issues, Jules Airvaux [L.-H. Fréchette], brought them together in *Philippe-N. Pacaud: biographie* (s.l.n.d.)). Fauteux, *Patriotes*, 117, 340–42, 383. P.-G. Roy, *Fils de Québec* (4 sér., Lévis, Qué., 1933), III: 173–75. David, *Patriotes*, 111–30. Robert Rumilly, *Papineau et son temps* (2v., Montréal, 1977). F.-J. Audet, "Philippe-Napoléon Pacaud," *BRH*, 33 (1927): 554–55.

PAHTAHSEGA (Pautaussigae, literally he who comes shining, or one who makes the world brighter; also known as **Peter Jacobs**), Methodist missionary; b. *c.* 1807 near Rice Lake, Newcastle District, Upper Canada; m. first *c.* 1826 Mary (d. 1828), a member of the Credit band of Mississaugas, and they had one daughter; m. secondly in May 1831 Elizabeth Anderson, and they had five children; d. 4 Sept. 1890 at the Rama Indian Reserve, near Orillia, Ont.

Peter Jacobs, whose parents died when he was three years old, was an Ojibwa, probably of the Mississaugas, and he later became an adopted member of the Credit band. He was one of the early native converts of William Case*, having first heard the Methodist missionary speak in 1824. Soon afterwards he attended school in Belleville, at Grand River, and then in 1826 at the Credit River mission. A fluent orator with some knowledge of English, Jacobs acted as an interpreter and prayer leader, assisting both Case and Peter Jones [Kahkewaquonaby*] in their efforts to Christianize the Indians. Indeed, shortly after his conversion, he read from the New Testament in English and Ojibwa at a meeting in New York of the Missionary Society of the Methodist Episcopal Church. An observer noted that "his broken English, added to the obvious simplicity and sincerity of his narrative, combined to render the scene truly impressive." In 1829 Jacobs was one of four Indians being educated by the Dorcas Missionary Society.

Despite this auspicious beginning Jacobs did not become a missionary for some years, probably because Case was fearful of the amorous proclivities he displayed after the death of his first wife in 1828. During the early 1830s he kept a store and "made a comfortable living," but by 1836 he was preaching to Indians near St Marys River. Two years later he accompanied James Evans* on his first missionary tour of the Lake Superior region. He remained behind, probably near Lac La Pluie (Rainy Lake, Ont.), when Evans returned briefly to Upper Canada.

In 1840 the Wesleyan Methodist Missionary Society in Britain, inspired by Evans' description of the immense potential of the northwest and doubtless desiring to outflank the Canadian Methodists from whom their church would soon separate, decided to establish a mission in the Hudson's Bay Company territories, a decision endorsed by the company. The principal mission station was founded at Rossville near Norway House (Man.) in September 1840; there Jacobs helped Evans build several houses for the resident Indians and inaugurate a varied programme of religious and secular education. Jacobs remained at his own main station of Fort Alexander (Man.) until he departed for England in 1842 for his ordination. In London he lived with Robert Alder*, the Wesleyan missionary secretary for British North America, under whose parental care Jacobs became an ardent Anglophile and a devoted adherent of English Methodism.

Returning to British North America, Jacobs was stationed at Fort Frances on Lac La Pluie (Rainy Lake). His letters in the late 1840s unfold a rather pathetic account of an intelligent and lonely man concerned with his wife's failing health, the education of his growing family, and the hostile forces which surrounded him. The Indians of Lac La Pluie "are like the Jews of old. 'Behold this people is a stiffnecked people.' They are wholly given to idolatry." They were fearful of their own conjurers and were ready to become dependents of anyone who would convert them. The HBC, upon which the mission relied, resisted the moral pressure of the missionary; Jacobs deplored the "diabolical doings of this Fort." Deprived of the wise guidance of Evans, his "Saint Paul," Jacobs read the Anglican service and John Wesley's sermons to the whites and considered the merits of various new mission sites. He finally left Fort Frances without permission in 1850.

Nevertheless, after a respite in Canada and England, Jacobs returned to the northwest in 1852; the account of his journey from Rice Lake to York Factory and return, published in 1853, provides a valuable description of the mission field and the perils of the region. As he travelled along the fur-traders' route, he was pleased with the well-developed missions at Rossville and Oxford House, the latter directed by Henry Bird STEINHAUER, another Indian convert. At York Factory Jacobs was disappointed at not meeting Methodist missionary John Ryerson*, whom he had expected to be visiting the area. Leaving hastily to avoid the onset of winter, he almost drowned in Lake Winnipeg and fought through a blizzard near Fort William (now part of Thunder Bay, Ont.) before boarding a steamer for Rice Lake and home. In 1853–54 he was stationed at the Saugeen Reserve and in 1855–56 at the Rama Reserve. He received no station in 1857 and was expelled from the conference the following year. The *Christian Guardian* noted in 1858 that Jacobs was in the United States soliciting funds without the approval of the church. Evidently Jacobs settled at Rama where he acted as school teacher, merchant, and interpreter, and supplemented his income by fishing and guiding. Although he appears to have undergone a reconversion in 1867, he was constantly bedevilled by heavy drinking and sank into poverty and oblivion. At his death, his reputation as a lecturer was recalled by local newspapers. He was survived by three of his six children; one son was a missionary in the Church of England. Another son, also named Peter Jacobs, who had died in 1864, had been a Church of England missionary as well.

Peter Jacobs' career was ultimately rather tragic. Largely assimilated himself, he brought European customs to the tribes in Ontario and the northwest. In a limited sphere he showed his brethren a new system of values and a new manner of existence. But he was the representative of a church which lacked the resources or the knowledge to conduct a comprehensive and imaginative programme of assimilation and which was both unwilling and unable to revitalize the Indians' own culture, and he soon reached the limits of his own usefulness.

G. S. French

Pahtahsega was the author of *Journal of the Reverend Peter Jacobs, Indian Wesleyan missionary, from Rice Lake to the Hudson's Bay territory, and returning; commencing May, 1852: with a brief account of his life; and a short history of the Wesleyan mission to that country* (Toronto, 1853; 2nd ed., Boston, 1853; [3rd ed.], New York, 1858).

Methodist Missionary Soc. Arch. (London), Wesleyan Methodist Missionary Soc., Corr., Canada, 1844–52 (mfm. at UCA). Carroll, *Case and his cotemporaries*. [James Evans], "Letters of Rev. James Evans, Methodist missionary, written during his journey to and residence in the Lake Superior region, 1838–39," ed. Fred Landon, *OH*, 28 (1932): 47–70; "Selections from the papers of James Evans, missionary to the Indians," ed. Fred Landon, *OH*, 26 (1930): 474–91. [Kahkewaquonaby], *Life and journals of Kah-ke-wa-quo-nā-by (Rev. Peter Jones), Wesleyan missionary*, [ed. Elizabeth Field] (Toronto, 1860). *Methodist Magazine and Quarterly Rev.* (New York), 1824–28. G. F. Playter, *The history of Methodism in Canada: with an account of the rise and progress of the work of God among the Canadian Indian tribes, and occasional notices of the civil affairs of the province* (Toronto, 1862). Wesleyan Methodist Church in Canada, *Minutes* (Toronto), 1858. *Wesleyan-Methodist Magazine* (London), 1843. *Christian Guardian*, 4 Dec. 1839; 1 April 1840; 23 Nov. 1842; 12 July 1843; 2 Aug., 20 Sept. 1848; 30 Oct. 1850; 17 March 1858; 10, 21 Sept. 1859; 30 Aug., 16 Oct. 1867. *Daily Times* (Orillia, Ont.), 4 Sept. 1890.

Cornish, *Cyclopædia of Methodism*. G. G. Findlay and W. W. Holdsworth, *The history of the Wesleyan Methodist Missionary Society* (5v., London, 1921–24). John Maclean, *Vanguards of Canada* (Toronto, 1918). D. B. Smith, "The Mississauga, Peter Jones, and the white man: the Algonkians' adjustment to the Europeans on the north shore of Lake Ontario to 1860" (PHD thesis, Univ. of Toronto, 1975).

PALLISER, JOHN, landed gentleman, big game hunter, and explorer; b. 29 Jan. 1817 in Dublin (Republic of Ireland), eldest son of Colonel Wray Palliser and Anne Gledstanes; d. 18 Aug. 1887 at Com[e]ragh House, Kilmacthomas, County Waterford (Republic of Ireland).

John Palliser belonged to a distinguished Irish family founded by William Palliser, archbishop of Cashel, who had come to Ireland from Yorkshire, England, to enter Trinity College, Dublin, in 1660. The devoutly Protestant Pallisers combined social eminence and a lively social, artistic, and intellectual life with a tradition of public service and conservative politics. They travelled extensively, living not only in Ireland at Derryluskan House, County Tipperary, at Comragh House, and in Dublin, but also in London, Rome, Florence, Paris, and Heidelberg.

Palliser was largely educated abroad and spoke French, German, and Italian, though in English his spelling was erratic. He entered Trinity College, Dublin, in 1834, attended intermittently, and abandoned his studies in 1838 without taking a degree. Other interests and activities claimed him. His family's social position carried obligations and he served as high sheriff in 1844, and later as deputy lieutenant and justice of the peace. On 20 Sept. 1839 he had received an appointment as captain in his father's regiment, the Waterford Artillery Militia, but no record has been found of any active service until the regiment was embodied on 14 Jan. 1855. He was on duty most of that year, attending artillery drill at Woolwich (now part of London), England, from 6 February to 6 May and afterwards commanding a detachment at Duncannon Barracks in County Wexford. When the regiment was mustered in 1857 Palliser was in North America. He saw service again briefly in 1862, but was once more abroad when the regiment was mustered in 1863, and resigned his commission to take effect on 14 July 1864. Though he is usually referred to as Captain Palliser, he does not appear to have had any other military experience.

The ruling preoccupation of Palliser, and most of his brothers and friends, seems to have been travel "in search of adventure and heavy game." One of these friends, William Fairholme, who was to become his brother-in-law in 1853, went buffalo hunting in 1840 on the "Grand Prairies of the Missouri." In eager emulation, Palliser set off in early 1847 on a visit to the New World which was to include "the regions still inhabited by America's aboriginal people . . . that ocean of prairies extending to the foot of the great Rocky Mountains." He spent 11 months on the prairies hunting buffalo ("a noble sport"), elk, antelope, and grizzly bear, and observing the life of the Indians and fur-traders. He left the west in 1848 and visited New Orleans and Panama before returning home in 1849. Back in London, where he lived with his great friend William Sandys Wright Vaux of the British Museum, Palliser wrote a lively book about his North American adventures, *Solitary rambles and adventures of a hunter in the prairies*, published in London in 1853, and it went through a number of editions.

Anxious to return to the western plains, Palliser, elected a fellow of the Royal Geographical Society on 24 Nov. 1856, submitted to the society a plan for the exploration of the southern prairies of British North America and the adjacent passes through the Rocky Mountains. His proposal was for a personal journey, with local voyageurs and hunters, across the little known plains and mountains immediately north of the 49th parallel. Keenly aware of official American explorations underway since 1853 to discover railway routes to the Pacific, the society took immediate action. It decided to recommend a more ambitious enterprise which would include scientific assistants, and asked the Colonial Office for a grant of £5,000 to finance the project.

John Ball, under-secretary of state for the colonies and an old friend of Palliser's, strongly supported the project, but added a third facet to it by insisting that the old North West Company canoe route be examined to help the Colonial Office judge whether or not the western plains were accessible from Canada by a route entirely within British territory. Little dependable information was available about the geographic features of the plains, their geology, climate, flora, fauna, and resources. Moreover, their "capability for agriculture" and settlement was a matter of dispute between the Hudson's Bay Company and its critics. Palliser was one of the few men with experience of travel on the prairies who was detached from the growing controversy about the future of western British North America. Ball and the colonial secretary, Henry Labouchere, thought that he would be an impartial observer and provide the knowledge for which they had such an urgent need – a need emphasized by the contradictory testimony heard by the select committee of the House of Commons on the HBC which began its hearings on 18 Feb. 1857 and reported late in the summer. The government of Canada was equally concerned about the future of the west and in the same year organized its own exploring expedition, led by George Gladman* in 1857, and by Henry Youle Hind* and Simon James Dawson* in 1858.

Ball worked closely with Palliser on detailed plans, and they consulted the Royal Society and such eminent scientists as Major-General Edward SABINE, Sir William Jackson Hooker, Sir John Richardson*, and Sir Roderick Impey Murchison, president of the Royal Geographical Society. They also consulted the few travellers who had experience west of the Great Lakes, and, most important of all, Sir George Simpson*, governor of the HBC territories in America. The HBC still provided the only means of communication with, and sources of supplies in, Rupert's Land and the Indian territories beyond; Simpson's assistance would be vital to the success of the expedition.

The Treasury was at last induced, largely through Ball's efforts, to make the appropriation of £5,000, which had later to be increased, as the cost of the expedition in the end came to a total of some £13,000. A technical team was recruited consisting of Dr James Hector*, geologist, naturalist, and physician, Eugène Bourgeau*, botanical collector, Lieutenant Thomas Wright Blakiston, RA, magnetical observer, who also made ornithological observations as a matter of personal interest, and John William Sullivan, secretary and astronomer. Scientific instructions were formulated individually by the learned authorities concerned, but Palliser, under instructions from the secretary of state for the colonies, was accepted as leader of the expedition – a formidable assignment for a country gentleman without business experience or professional training, though he alone of the party had had any experience in the west.

Palliser sailed for New York on 16 May 1857 with Hector, Bourgeau, and Sullivan. At Sault Ste Marie they picked up two waiting canoes with their voyageur crews and proceeded by steamship across the ice-covered Lake Superior to Isle Royale, Mich. There, on 12 June, they embarked in the canoes and after a month's arduous paddling and portaging reached Lower Fort Garry (Man.) on the Red River. While organizing men, horses, carts, provisions, Indian presents, ammunition, and other supplies, for which Simpson and the HBC had made preparation, the explorers consulted knowledgeable local people and studied the Red River Settlement.

On 21 July the expedition started on its journey across the plains, heading south up Red River to the American boundary, where they made careful observations in conjunction with a chance-met American land surveyor, Charles W. Iddings. From Pembina (N. Dak.) the party travelled west via St Joseph's (Walhalla) and Turtle Mountain (Man.) to Fort Ellice where they were joined by James McKay*, a noted mixed-blood guide. They made a quick trip to the boundary at Roche Percée (Sask.) before setting off for the South Saskatchewan River. Near the Elbow they turned northeast to Carlton House (Sask.) on the North Saskatchewan River, which was to be their base for the winter. Palliser went off via St Paul (Minn.) to New York to make application to the Colonial Office for more time and more money. While waiting for a reply he revisited New Orleans, returning to Carlton House for an early start in the spring of 1858. Meanwhile, Blakiston had joined the party at Carlton House, having brought the delicate instruments needed for magnetical observations by way of Hudson Bay, and he carried on hourly observations. Hector had journeyed to Fort Edmonton to recruit men for the next season's work.

On Palliser's arrival, the explorers headed west between the two branches of the Saskatchewan River. Near modern Irricana (Alta) the party separated to probe into the mountains for feasible passes. Palliser and Sullivan made a dash to the American boundary before crossing the mountains by the North Kananaskis Pass. Returning by the North Kootenay Pass, they rejoined the rest of the party to winter at Edmonton.

Blakiston, who had traversed both Kootenay passes, now left the expedition because of a quarrel with Sullivan which had widened to include Palliser. Hector had crossed the mountains through Vermilion Pass and returned by the Kicking Horse Pass; he devoted the winter to further exploration. Palliser hunted and examined the country south and east of the fort and then, with two newly arrived friends, Captain Arthur Brisco and William Roland Mitchell, travelled to Rocky Mountain House (Alta) to get to know the Blackfoot and Piegan Indians who frequented it, as he planned to travel through their country the next season. At Fort Edmonton the whole party enjoyed the hospitality of Chief Factor William Joseph Christie* and the highly sociable Palliser, with the aid of Mrs Christie, gave a tremendous ball.

In its final season, 1859, the expedition travelled southeast to the forks of the Red Deer and South Saskatchewan rivers in an attempt to connect with their westernmost point in 1857, and then south to the Cypress Hills, where the party broke up. Brisco and Mitchell went to Fort Benton (Mont.) and down the Missouri. Hector travelled northwest to cross the Rockies by Howse Pass in a final but unsuccessful attempt to discover a way through to the Pacific coast. Palliser and Sullivan journeyed directly west, then north, to cross the mountains by the North Kootenay Pass and follow the Kootenay River down to the Paddler's Lakes (Bonners Ferry, Idaho). Sullivan took the horses overland to Fort Colvile (Colville, Wash.), while Palliser voyaged down the Kootenay River and Lake in an Indian canoe.

At Fort Colvile Palliser and Sullivan re-equipped themselves to cross the border again for a final attempt to complete exploration of a route through British territory. Palliser sent Sullivan eastward from Fort Shepherd (B.C.) on the Columbia River while he himself forced a way west through difficult country until, near modern Midway (B.C.), he fell in with an American party engaged on the Boundary Survey of 1857–62. He had already encountered Lieutenant Henry Spencer Palmer, RE, who had studied the HBC trail from Fort Langley on the lower Fraser to Lake Osoyoos and assured Palliser that it lay north of 49°. Palliser was thus satisfied that a route through British territory had been established. Back at Fort Colvile, Palliser and Sullivan were rejoined by Hector before beginning the difficult trip down the Columbia and on to Victoria, then home via San Francisco and Panama. Palliser detoured to Montreal to visit Simpson, and reached Liverpool on 16 June 1860.

Before the work of the expedition was finished a final report had to be written and its bills, which greatly exceeded the Treasury appropriations, verified and settled. Members of the party spoke at meetings of the British Association for the Advancement of Science, the Royal Geographical Society, the Geological Society of London, the Ethnological Society of London, and the Botanical Society of Edinburgh. The reports, which appeared in 1859, 1860, and 1863, and the great map (1865) provided the first comprehensive, careful, and impartial observations to be published about the southern prairies and Rocky Mountains in what is now Canada. An essential source of information for the precursors of settlement, such as the North-West Mounted Police, the boundary surveyors, railway planners (notably Sir Sandford Fleming*), and other travellers, they are still useful. They added considerably to geographical knowledge of the region, and established that an extensive "fertile belt," well suited for stock-raising and cultivation, bordered the semi-arid prairie land of the south which is today known as "Palliser's Triangle." They emphasized the difficulty and expense of any possible route from Fort William (Thunder Bay, Ont.) to Red River, the old NWC canoe route. Settlers with cattle would prefer the much easier route through the United States; only mineral discoveries would provide economic justification for a route north of the border. They concluded that, though a railway might be built through the Rockies by one or other of the passes examined by the expedition, the cost of pushing road or rail through to the Pacific by any route entirely within British territory would be prohibitive. They urged the importance of providing for the future of the Indian inhabitants of the west before the buffalo disappeared and settlers began to flood into the country. The expedition had itself managed to avoid any serious clash with the plains Indians, but foresaw danger when settlement began.

The detailed records and observations of the expedition are largely attributable to Palliser's colleagues, but the fact that there was an expedition at all – an expedition which demonstrated to American expansionists the interest of the imperial government in the west – was a result of his initiative, while the extraordinary extent of country covered in three seasons owes much to his skill and zest as a traveller. The expedition earned Palliser the gold medal of the Royal Geographical Society in 1859, and, in 1877, a CMG.

Palliser succeeded to the family estates on his father's death in November 1862. That same year he went off to the West Indies on a semi-official mission, the nature of which remains a mystery. However, it is known that from Nassau he ran the "Yankee" blockade to visit the Confederate states. In 1869 he undertook yet another notable voyage, this time with his brother Frederick Hugh, in his own specially reinforced craft, to Novaya Zemlya (U.S.S.R.) and the Kara Sea. Again, big game and exploration were twin objectives.

Such ventures were costly. Born to wealth, neither Palliser nor his brothers seem to have been able to adapt themselves to a serious decline in the family fortune. Frequent travel meant that Palliser was not often at home to look after the family estates. These estates were heavily mortgaged, and had to be rescued by Fairholme money. When Palliser died they passed to his eldest niece, Caroline Fairholme. She, with her mother and her sisters, as well as with Frederick's family, had found a home with her unmarried, dearly loved uncle at Comragh House. There John Palliser died. He lies in a grave in little Kilrossanty churchyard.

IRENE M. SPRY

[This biography is based essentially on the same scattered and fragmentary sources as were used and recorded in my editorial work on the Champlain Society's volume, *The papers of the Palliser expedition, 1857–1860* (Toronto, 1968). A few new fragments of information have come to light since that work was done, in private, personal papers in Denmark and Ireland. These are of marginal interest in relation to Palliser's career and do not alter the basic ideas and interpretations recorded and discussed in the introduction, notes on sources, and footnotes of *The Palliser papers*. They have, however, strengthened my impression of the importance of family ties and responsibilities in the explorer's life, as well as of the influence of a closely knit group of friends. See also my article, "The Pallisers' voyage to the Kara Sea, 1869," *Musk-Ox* (Saskatoon, Sask.), 26 (1980): 13–20. I.M.S.]

PALMER, EDWARD, lawyer, landed proprietor, land agent, politician, and judge; b. 1 Sept. 1809 in Charlottetown, P.E.I., third son among 12 children of James Bardin Palmer* of Dublin and Millicent Jones of London, England; d. 3 Nov. 1889 in Charlottetown.

Edward Palmer's father, an Irish attorney, came to Prince Edward Island in 1802 as land agent for an absentee proprietor. From 1806 to 1812 the senior Palmer played a pivotal role in Island affairs, as adviser to Lieutenant Governor Joseph Frederick Wallet DesBarres*. But in 1812 DesBarres was recalled in disgrace, and the Loyal Electors, the political society Palmer led, was stigmatized as disloyal. Palmer was dismissed from the public offices he held, and it appears that he went through difficult years when Edward was a young child. Yet between 1816 and 1820 he was named land agent to several important land claimants or proprietors. Thus, well before he died in 1833, the elder Palmer had been thoroughly integrated into the local élite. He left to his family a claim to Lot One, the 23,700-acre township at the northwestern extremity of the colony.

Edward Palmer completed his education at Alexander Brown's grammar school in Charlottetown, and studied law in his father's office. He was admitted to the bar on 1 Nov. 1830, the second of three brothers who became lawyers. Four years later, he successfully contested the Family Compact stronghold of Charlottetown and Royalty. Although he took pains to deny charges "that I come forward under the influence of persons in executive authority," there could be no doubt that he stood to the right of centre. The politics of the 1830s in Prince Edward Island revolved around the militant Escheat movement [*see* William Cooper*], which demanded forfeiture of proprietary titles because of non-fulfilment of the conditions of the original grants in 1767. Distraint for non-payment of rent was in these circumstances an extremely controversial procedure leading frequently to assaults upon sheriffs and constables. In his first session as an assemblyman Palmer earned a reputation as a defender of the rights of property by opposing an amendment to the law governing replevin, or regaining possession of distrained goods, which would have benefited tenants. He also displayed solicitude for the rights of creditors in dealing with debtors, and advocated narrowing the franchise in "town and royalty" constituencies. He became identified, as well, as a spokesman for the specific interests and viewpoints of Charlottetown, proposing, for example, increased representation for the capital.

By the end of the 1830s Palmer had established himself as the second most prominent Tory assemblyman, after Joseph Pope*. Indeed, he acted as leader of the minority when Pope missed much of the session of 1840 and all of that of 1841. It was in the latter year that the Palmer family finally arrived at an agreement with Edward Cunard, the rival claimant to Lot One, to divide the township equally, and thus became landlords of some 12,000 acres. But because of the isolation of the township and the lengthy dispute over ownership, the occupiers of the land had become accustomed to paying no rent. According to the testimony of Nicholas Conroy* before the land commission of 1860, Palmer and Solicitor General James Horsfield Peters*, the Cunard family's land agent, early in 1843 persuaded most occupiers of land on Lot One to acknowledge the Palmer and Cunard claims. The terms were 999-year leases, at an annual rent of 1*s*. per acre, calculated from 1841. In a colony where, as Palmer had stated in the assembly in 1840, "Many individuals are not possessed of a shilling between January and December," Lot One, largely populated by Acadians with a sprinkling of Roman Catholic Irish, was notoriously impoverished. Many of those who attorned were unable to meet the terms they had signed, and the result, in the first half of 1844, was organized physical resistance to rent collection and distraint proceedings. Contemporary accounts suggest that the region was in a state close to insurrection. Yet the government, which in the previous year had sent troops to the eastern extremity of the Island to support the Cunard interests there, did not over-react, and the resistance passed. In 1845 Palmer and Peters were apparently able to resume collection of rent, which was often paid in service or in kind.

Palmer had become an executive councillor in 1842, and in 1846 he supported Joseph Pope when the latter was suspended from the council by the impetuous lieutenant governor, Sir Henry Vere Huntley*. In the following year Palmer resigned from the council and with Pope was part of a three-man delegation to London whose purpose was to ensure the governor's recall. Although the decision to replace Huntley had already been made, Palmer claimed in a private letter that the delegation had accelerated the change-over. With the arrival in December 1847 of Sir Donald Campbell*, who was strongly opposed to responsible government, the Family Compact once again had a friend in Government House. Earlier in the same year, Palmer had explained his own position on responsible government, the central political issue of the late 1840s. The tenants, he said, constituted a clear majority of the electorate, and "Entertaining the ideas which I believe the majority of them do with respect to the land question, I cannot think that it would be prudent, or that the project ought to be entertained, of giving them almost the entire government into their hands." He added that experience had shown him "the danger of yielding to popular clamour, and introducing those measures which lead to constant changes." He associated responsible government with "the democratical mass," "the mob," and "Red Republicans." In December 1848 Palmer was re-appointed to the Executive Council, and in a dispatch the governor justified his choice by virtue of the need for "an Official organ in the House of Assembly." He had already named Palmer solicitor general in September, replacing Peters, who was elevated to the Supreme Court. Palmer earlier had been chairman of an assembly committee which advocated the appointment of a second judge to the court, thus creating a position for Peters and opening up a public office for himself.

When Joseph Pope crossed the floor in 1849 and for most purposes voted with the Reformers led by George Coles*, Palmer succeeded him as leader of the Tories in the assembly, a position he held over the next decade. In all but one year from 1850 through 1858 his party formed a minority. He opposed responsible government (conceded in 1851), and most of the leading Liberal measures in the ensuing years. "Free education," by which school districts were to be relieved of paying for teachers' salaries, and by which payment was to become sufficient to attract and retain capable teachers, was denounced as "quite preposterous" when outlined by Coles in the assembly a year before its enactment in 1852. Palmer dreaded universal suffrage and argued against the Franchise Bill of 1853 "on the ground that it will give a political ascendancy to men destitute of property over those who possessed it." With such views, it is little wonder that Edward Whelan*, the leading Liberal journalist, labelled him as forming, along with land agent William Douse* and proprietor James Yeo*, the "extreme proprietary party" in the assembly. Palmer himself stated openly that he "had always been an advocate for the rights of proprietors."

Personalities were an important ingredient of Island politics, and in these years Palmer quarrelled bitterly with both Coles and Whelan. In 1851, after the granting of responsible government, he and Coles fought a bloodless duel with pistols, the cause of which is no longer known. Less than a year after the duel, Palmer and Whelan became involved in an uncommonly heated exchange in the assembly which led to both men being ordered to apologize for their unparliamentary language. The bad feelings continued, and in 1855, according to the official reporter, Palmer complained in the assembly that "there was a faction banded together for the purpose of injuring his character and standing, not only in political matters, but also in his professional capacity. A very angry discussion ensued."

The 1850s must have been a frustrating period in Palmer's career, for it seemed as though the Tories were condemned to a long period in opposition. They were able to take advantage of a delay in the confirmation of the Franchise Bill and temporary public dissatisfaction over the cost of the Free Education Act, to win an election in the summer of 1853, although the new session was not called until February of the next year. The Tory government was led by John Myrie Holl*, a legislative councillor, with Palmer as attorney general. But later in 1854, after the imperial government had approved the Liberals' Franchise Bill, Lieutenant Governor Sir Alexander Bannerman* forced a new election in June upon the protesting Tories. Coles returned to office in July with an 18 to 6 majority in the assembly; even in Charlottetown the extension of the franchise had a dramatic impact upon the relative strength of the two parties, as the majorities of Palmer and his running-mate, Francis LONGWORTH, were greatly reduced. Clearly, a new strategy was called for. In the session of 1855 it became apparent that the Tories were attempting to drive a wedge in the ranks of the government by drawing to the attention of radicals within the Liberal caucus the limitations in legislation on the land question. The result was the strange spectacle of such veteran Escheators as John MacKintosh and William Cooper*, who disputed the proprietors' claims and objected to the expense of purchasing estates, aligning themselves with ultra-Tories like Palmer.

It was over the Bible question that Palmer achieved his greatest success in dividing the Liberals, and especially their supporters at the mass level. Palmer, an Anglican, wholeheartedly backed the Protestant clergy in their campaign to place the "open Bible," with as few restrictions as possible, in publicly funded educational institutions. During the session of 1857 he declared that "education to be useful and safe to the people, should be based on the christian religion." He accused the Coles government of desiring "the total exclusion of the Scriptures from the schools." In an election held in 1858, Protestant voters deserted the Liberals in large numbers and when deadlock in the assembly led to a subsequent election in 1859 the Tories won decisively, forming an all-Protestant government led by Palmer, amid allegations that they had pandered to the religious prejudices of the Protestant majority.

The Tories had strongly criticized the Liberal (and indeed conventional) version of responsible government in which legislators held such paid offices as those of colonial treasurer and registrar of deeds. In its stead, they offered a system they called "non-departmentalism," which excluded paid officials from the assembly and Legislative Council. This innovation, conceptually linked to American doctrines concerning the separation of powers (for which Palmer had once professed strong admiration), would supposedly protect the "independence of the Legislature." Although critics, including Lieutenant Governor Sir Dominick Daly*, pointed out that it also implied a diminution of the responsibility of public officials to the assembly, and a consequent undermining of the fundamental principles of responsible government, this objection sat lightly with Palmer, who as late as 1857 had declared publicly that "it would be much better if there was no Responsible Government." But the new system meant less spoils for elected politicians, and there is evidence that Palmer lacked the unqualified enthusiasm of some non-elected Tories for it. Apparently it was commonly believed in 1859 that for financial reasons he would soon retire as assemblyman and premier to become the paid attorney general. The Tory experiment with "non-departmental" government was quietly discarded late in January 1863.

The most stubborn problem facing any Island administration in the colonial era was the land question. In opposition, Palmer and the Tories had criticized the details and implementation of the Coles government's policy, but in deference to public opinion had usually not voted against Liberal legislation. Once in office, Tory leaders were confronted with an especially delicate situation since, while politically accountable to an electorate strongly committed to abolition of leasehold tenure, in their private capacities they were often, like Palmer himself, proprietors or land agents. Their response to this dilemma was to appoint in 1860 a three-man commission to investigate differences between landlord and tenant and to make recommendations for their resolution. In the course of extensive hearings throughout the Island, Palmer's own name came up several times as an example of a landlord or lawyer, usually in a context that was politically embarrassing. Consequently, when the premier appeared before the commission, he did so primarily in order to answer criticism of his behaviour as a private individual. His government did not advocate the cause of the tenantry before the commission, leaving that task to two lawyers it retained on the tenants' behalf. The commissioners unanimously reported in favour of giving tenants the right to purchase the lands they occupied, with the value to be established by arbitration, if necessary. At the urging of Sir Samuel Cunard* and other large proprietors, the imperial government in 1862 disallowed Island legislation attempting to implement the recommendations of the commissioners. Thus the land commission had come to naught.

The government was more successful in resolving the Bible question. In 1860 a moderate "Bible clause" was added to existing legislation, giving the Scriptures the statutory basis in the schools desired by most Protestants, yet protecting against the compulsion and controversial interpretations feared by the large Roman Catholic minority. The educational system was further modified in the same year by conversion of the Central Academy, a government-supported grammar school in Charlottetown, into Prince of Wales College. This proved to be the Palmer government's most enduring achievement: the college soon earned an enviable academic reputation and for more than a century served as the apex of the Island's public education system. In 1862 the Legislative Council was made elective, a reform Palmer had advocated when in opposition in the 1850s, though a £100 property qualification for voters was also instituted. He himself had moved to the Legislative Council in 1860 (after winning 11 consecutive elections), as part of a manœuvre to counteract Liberal strength there.

Despite the disappearance of the contentious Bible question, the Conservatives failed in several attempts to mend their political fences with the Roman Catholic Church. Indeed, these failures and the resulting recriminations, along with polemical battles in the press between William Henry Pope* and Father Angus

McDONALD, combined to embitter sectarian relations as never before. In January 1863 the Tories won the general election for the assembly exclusively on the basis of support in Protestant constituencies, while all Roman Catholic constituencies voted Liberal. Palmer was personally acclaimed for Charlottetown on 11 February, in the first elections for the Legislative Council. But in less than a week he was faced with a cabinet crisis, which began when Lieutenant-Colonel John Hamilton GRAY, leader of the government in the assembly since 1860, resigned from the Executive Council. By 2 March Gray had gathered sufficient support within the Conservative party to wrest the premiership from an indignant and humiliated Palmer. Personalities and matters of style appear to have been more important than policy differences in the intra-party struggle; the stiff, unbending Palmer represented the old Tory party, and did not mix easily with the aggressive "new men" of Island conservatism, such as the two sons of Joseph Pope, William Henry and JAMES COLLEDGE. Yet, as a veteran politician of considerable prestige, whom Edward Whelan had once described as having "keen perception – no small share of cunning – inexhaustible force of character," Palmer was allowed to retain the attorney generalship, which he had assumed in late January, and he remained within the cabinet. Whelan shrewdly predicted that there would be dissension on the Executive Council in the future. Perhaps it was partially a desire to keep Palmer out of trouble which led to his being sent, instead of Gray, with W. H. Pope, the colonial secretary, on a fruitless delegation to England concerning the land question in the autumn of 1863.

Differences between Gray and Palmer surfaced publicly in November 1864 over the question of union of the British North American colonies. Gray strongly advocated confederation, and it is as an anti-confederate, particularly as the most obstructive delegate at the Quebec conference, that Palmer is best known to Canadian historians. Palmer first put his views on the general question of union on record at the end of April 1864 when the Legislative Council debated a resolution to appoint delegates to the Charlottetown conference, called to discuss a union of the three Maritime colonies. He stated that while he could envisage benefits for the British government in Maritime union, he could see none for the Island. "We would submit our rights and our prosperity, in a measure, into the hands of the General Government, and our voice in the united Parliament would be very insignificant." Given the seasonal isolation of the Island, there would be difficulty in ensuring effective participation in a government located elsewhere, and he expected little sympathy for any proposal to make Charlottetown the seat of government. He also predicted that union would result in increased taxation, and a portion of the liability for any expensive public projects undertaken in the future, like railway building, regardless of their value to Islanders. In summation, Palmer argued that "unless we can see that our position will be improved or our prospects brightened by a union, we had better let well alone and remain as we are" – a cautious position not inconsistent with his general political principles.

Although Palmer's remarks referred specifically to Maritime union, they also represented well his objections to a general British North American federation, as they were to emerge. Palmer himself attended both the Charlottetown and the Quebec conferences. There is little precise information on what was said at the Charlottetown conference, but a few months later, in the midst of his public dispute with Gray, Palmer claimed to have spoken out then against the principle of union and particularly representation by population as the basis for allocation of seats in the federal lower chamber; Charles Tupper*'s recently discovered minutes appear to bear out this claim. For the Quebec conference in October 1864, documentation is ample, and it is clear that from start to finish Palmer was a thorn in the flesh of those committed to union. He opened by moving that each provincial delegation, including the Canadians, have only one vote, he generally presented dissenting views, and at the end he successfully insisted that Resolution 72 be reworded so as not to imply assent on the part of the delegates to "the principles of the Report."

As soon as the Island delegates returned home and declared themselves on the question of union, it became apparent that Gray and Palmer could not continue long in the same cabinet. On 20 December Gray presented his resignation to the Executive Council, accusing Palmer of undermining the government by inconsistency over confederation. Palmer had spoken favourably of it at a banquet in Toronto, but had subsequently excused his remarks because of the requirements of civility on a festive occasion. Certainly at no other time did he endorse the plan. But in refuting Gray's charge of deliberate duplicity, Palmer made counter-allegations containing mis-statements which W. H. Pope, the Island's most determined confederate, pounced upon to force his resignation from the cabinet. A new administration, led by James Pope, who had supported Gray in both February–March 1863 and December 1864, but whose own position on confederation was ambiguous, took office on 7 January 1865. Palmer remained attorney general, though neither he nor Gray was a member of the reconstituted Executive Council.

Palmer had the satisfaction of knowing that a divided Conservative party could not lead the colony into confederation, which was extremely unpopular on the Island in the mid 1860s. The Charlottetown *Monitor* (to which Palmer himself was reputedly an occasional editorial contributor) commented at the height of the cabinet crisis that he had never had more public support than over his opposition to confederation. Although the near-unanimity of public sentiment makes it questionable to assign responsibility to any individual, it is noteworthy that pro-confederate politicians on the Island tended to blame Palmer in particular for thwarting the union movement. Charles Tupper carried confederation in Nova Scotia in defiance of public opinion and perhaps the same might have been done in Prince Edward Island had not individuals, Palmer being crucial because of his place in the government, forced the issue. But the question of his motives is somewhat complicated. There is every likelihood that he welcomed the opportunity to confront and unseat Gray, who had recently usurped his position as premier; no doubt the public acclaim because of his anti-confederacy was gratifying to a man who had never before been a popular hero; but it is also likely that at the base of his opposition to confederation was the belief, shared by most Islanders, that the colony had nothing to gain from union in the 1860s.

The confederation issue dominated Palmer's career after 1864. He kept in touch with anti-confederates in Nova Scotia and New Brunswick until the cause was lost on the mainland, he favoured making a separate agreement for renewal of reciprocity with the United States, he criticized the British government for exerting pressure in favour of union, and he opposed the "better terms" of 1869. He rarely missed an opportunity to prod the Legislative Council into declaring itself on confederation, and he left few stones unturned in adducing reasons not to join. Indeed he appears to have become almost single-minded over the issue; in considering the results of the assembly election of 1867, his pleasure at the overwhelming rejection of confederation seems to have outweighed any concern over the defeat of the Tory government. The party remained divided in the late 1860s, and when Palmer was defeated (for the only time in his political career) in an attempt to re-enter the assembly for Charlottetown in July 1870, W. H. Pope openly rejoiced.

With the Conservative party firmly in the grip of the Popes after 1870, Palmer changed political allegiance. On 22 April 1872, less than two months after winning a by-election for a rural constituency in the Legislative Council, he joined the Liberal and anti-confederate government formed by Robert Poore Haythorne*, who had been attempting to recruit him since mid 1869. On 3 June he succeeded his younger brother Charles as attorney general, probably by prior arrangement. The new administration had been elected in the midst of public alarm over the financial and, ultimately, political implications of the railway building by James Pope's second government. The electorate probably believed that if anyone could stave off union with Canada, it was solid anti-confederates like Haythorne, Palmer, and David Laird*, another ex-Tory who had changed parties over the issue. But when the legislature met, it was discovered that in order to hold a majority in the assembly, Haythorne and Palmer would have to meet the demands of the northern and eastern sections of the Island for immediate commencement of railway branch lines. Their representatives held the balance of power, and if Haythorne and Palmer would not do their bidding, Pope would. As Palmer, who had opposed building a railway from the start, despairingly said, "there is, therefore, no alternative but to undertake those branches and add to the vast amount of debt which the country has already incurred." The Island's financial position steadily deteriorated, and in early 1873 the government, including Palmer, conceded defeat and sent Haythorne and Laird to Ottawa to negotiate terms. In April 1873 the Haythorne government was replaced by James Pope's Tories who promised to secure "better terms." Pope was successful and confederation became a reality for Prince Edward Island on 1 July 1873.

Confederation meant the end of one career for Palmer and the beginning of another. In the last session of the Island legislature preceding union, the Pope government created three county judgeships in the knowledge that Ottawa would be paying the salaries. On 20 June Palmer, a QC since 1856 and a strong supporter of the measure in the Legislative Council just eight days earlier, was named judge of the new Queens County Court. The following year he was named chief justice, a controversial appointment of Alexander Mackenzie*'s government by which two well-respected sitting justices, J. H. Peters and Joseph Hensley*, were passed over. As a jurist, Palmer proved competent, although not greatly concerned with questions of legal principle. His decisions are not notable for the logical development of arguments, but some display at least a broad acquaintance with the authorities. It was probably predictable that he would be highly conservative and respectful of the rights of property. He himself had remained a landed proprietor until 31 March 1870, when he and the other members of his father's family sold their interest in Lot One to the Liberal government for 12*s.* 6*d.* per acre; this was one of the highest rates of payment received in the colonial era, despite the mediocre quality of the land, which had led to the rent on much of the estate being reduced from 1*s.* to 8*d.* per acre. His remarks in the legislature over the years also make it clear that he took a rather severe view of "crime and punishment." Palmer was still chief justice when he died at age 80 in 1889, after several months as an invalid. He was survived by eight of nine children, and by his wife, Isabella Phoebe Tremain, whom he had married in Quebec on 22 Sept. 1846. She would live to see

Herbert James*, the elder of their two sons, become Liberal premier in 1911. The family was left a substantial estate, consisting largely of cash and urban real estate, but the amounts involved, and comments Palmer made over the years, do not suggest that at any time he could be described as wealthy.

Edward Palmer played a prominent role in the public life of Prince Edward Island for more than half a century. It is as a politician that he particularly deserves to be remembered, and as such he was, for most of his career, primarily a parliamentarian rather than a popular tribune. His strengths within the legislature were rooted in his legal training, experience, and knowledge. In debate he displayed considerable ability to find apparent inconsistencies in opponents' arguments, a forensic skill no doubt intimately related to his frequent litigation work. When he died, it was said that he had been involved, on one side or the other, in virtually every important case in the Supreme Court and Court of Chancery between the mid 1840s and his elevation to the bench in 1873. For most of his early years in the assembly he was the only member who was a lawyer, and his speeches reflect an awareness of colonial and imperial law and precedent, parliamentary usages, and the importance of due process, a consideration sometimes forgotten in the overheated political atmosphere of the Island. Yet his legalism, or emphasis on proper procedure and form, proved also to be his weakness as leader of the opposition in the 1850s; when he did not get his own way and the Coles government did not recognize the importance of his procedural points, he tended to sulk and withdraw from the debate.

Palmer's lack of spontaneity contributed to his image as a dogged, humourless defender of the *status quo*. A tall, gaunt, ungainly man not given to mirth and not gifted with easy eloquence, he was a natural target for Edward Whelan's satiric pen. "He has been in opposition," wrote Whelan in 1854, "to every free and enlightened opinion of the age. . . . His never-failing and never-forgotten objection to every innovation, (for every change with him is an innovation) is that the time is not yet arrived for entertaining the proposition. . . . We have never seen him in joyous, happy, rollicking spirits. . . . " Yet Whelan admitted in the same article that Palmer was endowed with uncommon energy, perception, and determination, and without Palmer, he wrote, after responsible government "the [Tory] party would . . . have completely tumbled to pieces." In the later 1850s Palmer did more than hold his party together: he redirected its rhetorical assaults from Reform legislation to those who, allegedly, would exclude the Bible from the schools, and he diluted its ideology to the extent that the Tories could present themselves as having something more positive to offer than a return to the days before responsible government. In short, Palmer displayed sufficient strategic and tactical flexibility to propel the Family Compact back into power.

For the years prior to 1864 and the emergence of the confederation issue, Palmer can be summarized as a faithful and consistent spokesman for his class, the local oligarchy which owned much of the land in the colony and acted as an intermediary between the absentee proprietors who owned most of the remainder, and the Island population. From 1835 until 1870 he continuously represented Charlottetown, the centre of Family Compact power, in one branch or the other of the legislature, and reflected accurately the capital's views and fears, particularly its fear, especially apparent from the 1830s until the late 1850s, of "the democratical mass" in the countryside. In keeping with the Compact's tradition of vindictiveness, he several times acted as a lawyer in quasi-political prosecutions of leading Reformers, particularly Whelan, whom the Compact evidently wished to silence. Yet after 1864 there is a new dimension to Palmer's career. For the first time he acquired an Island-wide constituency in a personal sense, and transcended the limits of his party, class, and town. The explanation for his position on confederation is probably quite straightforward – like most Islanders, he could see no advantage in it for his native colony. It is difficult to dismiss his unease as the product of blind parochialism. He was a son of a member of the Dublin bar, and had travelled to the United Kingdom at least twice; in George Brown*'s words, Palmer was "a person of good sense & ability who has seen much of the world." His pre-eminent position among Island anti-confederates can be attributed to his being a recent premier, and particularly to the catalytic role he played in thwarting the unionist plans of Gray and W. H. Pope in November–December 1864. Thus the two most striking achievements of Palmer's political career, his resuscitation of his party in the late 1850s and his prevention of its taking action on confederation in the mid 1860s, came before and after his premiership. By contrast, his years as premier were relatively barren, especially concerning the main problem in Island public life, the land question – a record of failure which can be traced to the commitments he shared with other members of his party and his class.

Although without brilliant abilities, Edward Palmer was a major force in Island politics during a generation in which there were such exceptionally talented figures as Coles, Whelan, and the Popes; his longevity and success are tributes to his perseverance and the good use he made of his talents and education.

IAN ROSS ROBERTSON

[Two collections of papers in the PAPEI contain significant material on Edward Palmer: the Edward Palmer papers which are chiefly of value for the delegation of 1847 and his ousting as premier in 1863; and the Palmer family papers which include commissions, correspondence from the 1830s to the 1870s, and a typescript genealogy. Unfortunately, a notation on the back of item 199 in the latter collection, initialled EP and dated March 1876 mentions "burning old useless Papers." Several of his written legal judgements as chief justice are included in *Reports of cases determined in the Supreme Court, Court of Chancery, and Vice Admiralty Court of Prince Edward Island . . .* , comp. F. L. Haszard and A. B. Warburton (2v., Charlottetown, 1885–86), II. The author is indebted to Mr Michael J. W. Finley for his commentary on the quality of Palmer's written legal judgements.

The best sources for Edward Palmer's views over the years are the reports of the proceedings of the legislature. For the House of Assembly debates, see *Royal Gazette* (Charlottetown), 1835–53; *Islander*, 1845, 1854; P.E.I., House of Assembly, *Debates and proc.*, 1858–59. For the debates in the Legislative Council, *see* P.E.I., Legislative Council, *Debates and proc.*, 1860–61; 1863–70; 1872–73; *Examiner* (Charlottetown), 1862. It was believed by many, including Edward Whelan, that Palmer contributed editorials to the *Monitor* (Charlottetown), published as a weekly from 1857 until 1865; a good collection for 1857–64 survives at the PAPEI.

Information on Palmer's career will be found in: *Examiner*, 14 Aug. 1847; 6, 13 March, 10, 17 April, 5, 26 June 1854; 23 Jan. 1860; 16, 23 Feb., 2, 9 March, 31 Aug. 1863; 9 May 1864; 27 Feb., 10 April 1865; 28 June 1869; 15 Jan., 26 Feb., 11, 25 March 1872; 3, 10 Aug. 1874; 4 Nov. 1889; *Herald* (Charlottetown), 24 July, 6 Nov., 11 Dec. 1889; *Island Argus* (Charlottetown), 20 Feb. 1872; 28 July 1874; *Island Farmer* (Summerside, P.E.I.), 9 May, 7 Nov. 1889 (available only at the office of the *Journal-Pioneer*, Summerside); *Island Guardian and Christian Chronicle* (Charlottetown), 7 Nov. 1889; *Islander*, 7 July 1843; 9, 16 Oct. 1846; 22 June 1853; 3, 10 March, 4 Aug. 1854; 20 Jan. 1860; 25 June, 2 July 1869; 22 July, 7 Oct. 1870; *Palladium* (Charlottetown), 29 March 1845; *Patriot* (Charlottetown), 26 June 1869; 14 July 1870; 9 March, 6, 13 April 1872; 4, 6 Nov. 1889; 19 May 1890; *Protestant and Evangelical Witness* (Charlottetown), 12 Nov., 24 Dec. 1864; *Royal Gazette*, 9 Nov. 1830; 5 March 1833; 21 Jan., 2, 16 Dec. 1834; 14 March 1837; 9, 16, 30 Oct., 6, 13 Nov. 1838; 24 March 1840; 11 June "Extra," 28 June, 12 July 1842; 4, 11, 25 June, 3 Sept. 1844; 11 Aug. 1846; 23 Nov. 1847; 10 Oct., 28 Nov., 5 Dec. 1848; 29 Jan. 1850; 5 March "Extra," 8, 15 March 1852; 14, 21 March "Extra," 20 June, 11 July 1853; 4 Dec. 1856; 11 June 1857; 31 Jan. 1860; 23 June "Extra" 1873; *Summerside Journal and Western Pioneer* (Summerside), 24 June 1869, 7 Nov. 1889; *Vindicator* (Charlottetown), 27 March 1863.

The following manuscript sources are of value in such areas as Palmer's legal career, his position as a landowner and land agent, his status as a member of the Family Compact: ANQ-Q, État civil, Anglicans, Cathedral of the Holy Trinity (Quebec), 22 Sept. 1846; N.B. Museum, Tilley family papers, box 5, packet 3, no.59; box 6, packet 2, nos.18, 20 (photocopies at PAPEI); PAPEI, John Mackieson, Diaries, 25 June 1851; "Scrapbook containing papers relating to Joseph Pope, W. H. Pope, and J. C. Pope," Joseph Pope to W. H. Pope, 10 Feb. 1842; RG 1, Commission books, I: 291; RG 5, Minutes, 4 Aug. 1842; 26 Dec. 1848; 24 April 1851; 17, 18 Feb. 1854; 3 June 1872; RG 6, Court of Chancery, Minutes, 27 May 1831; Supreme Court, Minutes, 1 Nov. 1830, 23 Feb. 1831; Minutes, Prince County, 2, 3 Oct. 1844; RG 15, Cunard estate rent book, Lot 1, 1841–66; Palmer estate rent books, 1862–69; RG 16, Land registry records, Conveyance registers, liber 24: f.859; liber 25: f.41; liber 27: f.70; liber 33: f.522; liber 45: f.123; liber 46: f.55; liber 49: ff.266, 352; liber 51: ff.183, 562; liber 67: f.244; liber 92: f.758; Land title docs., Lot 1, no.251–54, 1 July 1841. PRO, CO 226/63: 329–32; CO 226/69: 167, 172, 317–18, 320–21, 323–24; CO 226/71: 420–31; CO 226/72: 111–18, 131–33, 139–41, 143–48, 150; CO 226/74: 111–14, 117–18, 157–58; CO 226/80: 213–60, 620–23; CO 226/87: 321–23; CO 226/90: 94–104, 110–38, 157–60; CO 226/91: 309–14; CO 226/92: 29, 463–66; CO 226/98: 139, 150–52; CO 226/100: 468–69; CO 226/105: 399–400; CO 226/109: 144, 184; Supreme Court of Prince Edward Island, Estates Division, liber 4: f.16 (will of James Bardin Palmer, 2 Jan. 1830); liber 12: f.333 (will of Edward Palmer, 5 Feb. 1889) (mfm. at PAPEI); Westmorland Hist. Soc. (Dorchester, N.B.), Dorchester Penitentiary, Classification records (mfm. at PAPEI).

Printed primary sources useful for illuminating aspects of Palmer's life include the following: *Abstract of the proceedings before the Land Commissioners' Court, held during the summer of 1860, to inquire into the differences relative to the rights of landowners and tenants in Prince Edward Island*, reporters J. D. Gordon and David Laird (Charlottetown, 1862), 1, 39–40, 45, 47, 49–53, 67, 71, 74, 82, 104, 126, 152–53, 215, 229, 242–43, 247–48, 311; "Charles Tupper's minutes of the Charlottetown conference," ed. W. I. Smith, *CHR*, 48 (1967): 106, 112; P.E.I., House of Assembly, *Journal*, 1840, 130–31, app.P; 1841, 9; 1852, 87–89, 92–94, 98–104, app.R; 1862, app.B, warrant no.443; 1870, app.X; 1875, app.E; P.E.I., Legislative Council, *Journal*, 1860, 72–73; 1880, app.7, p.23; *Report of proceedings before the commissioners appointed under the provisions of "The Land Purchase Act, 1875,"* reporter P. S. MacGowan (Charlottetown, 1875), 126–28; *The union of the British provinces: a brief account of the several conferences held in the Maritime provinces and in Canada, in September and October, 1864, on the proposed confederation of the provinces . . .* , comp. Edward Whelan (Charlottetown, 1865; repr. Summerside, 1949), 181–83.

See also: F. W. P. Bolger, *Prince Edward Island and confederation, 1863–1873* (Charlottetown, 1964); MacKinnon, *Government of P.E.I.*; W. S. MacNutt, "Political advance and social reform, 1842–1861," *Canada's smallest prov.* (Bolger), 115–34; Robertson, "Religion, politics, and education in P.E.I."; David Weale and Harry Baglole, *The Island and confederation: the end of an era* (n.p., 1973); D. C. Harvey, "Dishing the Reformers," RSC *Trans.*, 3rd ser., 25 (1931), sect.II: 37–44; "The loyal electors," RSC *Trans.*, 3rd ser., 24 (1930), sect.II: 101–10; I. R. Robertson, "The Bible question in Prince Edward Island from 1856 to 1860," *Acadiensis*, 5 (1975–76), no.2: 3–25; "Party politics and religious controversialism in Prince Edward Island from 1860 to 1863," *Acadiensis*, 7 (1977–78), no.2: 29–59. I. R. R.]

PANNETON, CHARLES-MARIE (baptized **Charles-Marie-Xavier**), pianist and music teacher;

baptized 15 June 1845 at Montreal, Canada East, son of Charles-Heliodore Panneton, businessman, and Zoë Durondu; d. unmarried on 3 Jan. 1890 at Montreal.

Charles-Marie Panneton received his schooling at the Collège de Joliette, where his family had moved when he was a child. Showing musical talent, he was sent back to Montreal for private lessons with one of the city's leading music teachers, Paul Letondal. In 1864 his father sent him to Leipzig, Saxony, to study at the conservatory, but he turned back after only three days, bewildered by the strange language. This hasty retreat caused *Les Beaux-Arts* of Montreal to comment sarcastically: "If he will display as much zeal and energy as a pianist as he has shown in travelling to Leipzig and back, we may predict a brilliant destiny for him, an enormous reputation, and ability without equal in all the Americas." The following year Panneton left for Paris which he found more congenial than Leipzig. He stayed there until 1874, studying with Antoine-François Marmontel at the Conservatoire Royal de Musique et de Déclamation, with Camille Stamaty (whose pupils included Camille Saint-Saëns and Louis Gottschalk), and a teacher of theory. He frequented concert and opera performances and was a witness to the pro- and anti-Richard Wagner campaigns raging at the time, taking a moderately pro-Wagnerian position. He also gained access to the salons of Gioacchino Rossini, the composer, Charles Durand, *dit* Carolus-Duran, the painter, and L'Ancien, the violinist. At the time of the Franco-Prussian War, Panneton fled his home in suburban Chaville, Hauts-de-Seine, and went to La Ferté-Bernard, Sarthe. He contracted pleurisy and, on returning to Paris, found that during the siege his furniture and piano had been used as firewood.

Back in Montreal in 1874, Panneton taught music, but his precarious health made it necessary to avoid the Canadian winter and in the fall of 1877 he left for Denver, Colo. Active there as a pianist and teacher, he was for a few months in 1879 the organist at the Roman Catholic church. He returned to Montreal in the spring of 1881 and, because of his frailty, had to limit the number of his pupils; they included the pianist Jean-Baptiste Denys and Joseph Saucier*, who was to become an outstanding baritone. During his final illness he moved to the Hôpital Général in Montreal.

His musician friends – including Dominique Ducharme, Arthur Lavigne, and Romain-Octave Pelletier – admired Panneton for the broad education and the discerning taste he had acquired in Paris. He was well read in 17th-century and contemporary literature, he was a gifted amateur painter, and a witty raconteur with a weakness for puns and *bon mots*. He was too modest, and perhaps too frail, to give concerts. When he played for his friends occasionally, it was to express his admiration for a composition rather than to show off his virtuosity. His playing was praised for its clean touch and purity of style. Panneton is said to have composed ballads, mazurkas, and other piano pieces as well as a patriotic hymn "Rallions-nous" with lyrics by Benjamin Sulte* for the feast of Saint-Jean-Baptiste in 1874; but none of these appear to have been published.

HELMUT KALLMANN

Charles-Marie Panneton was the author of two articles published in the *Rev. canadienne*: "De la musique religieuse," 13 (1876): 812–21; 14 (1877): 407–14; "Le Colorado en 1880, suivi de quelques réflexions sur les États-Unis en général," 17 (1881): 344–54, 458–66, 522–31, 587–95.

ANQ-M, État civil, Catholiques, Notre-Dame de Montréal, 15 juin 1845. *Le Canada musical* (Montréal), 4 (1877): 109. P.-B. Migneault, "Feu Charles Marie Panneton," *Le Canada artistique* (Montréal), 1 (1890): 34–35. "Nouvelles artistiques canadiennes," *Le Canada musical*, 7 (1881): 181. "Originalité d'un futur artiste," *Les Beaux-Arts* (Montréal), 2 (1864): 70. *Le National* (Montréal), 18 janv. 1890. *La Presse*, 4 janv. 1890. *Rocky Mountain News* (Denver, Colo.), 6 April, 24 June, 3, 17, 31 Aug., 14 Dec. 1879. *Dictionnaire biographique des musiciens canadiens* (2e éd., Lachine, Qué., 1935). "Nos musiciens," *L'Art musical* (Montréal), 2 (1898): 271.

PAPAMAHCHAKWAYO. *See* KAPAPAMAHCHAKWEW

PARDEE, TIMOTHY BLAIR, lawyer and politician; b. 11 Dec. 1830 in Grenville County, Upper Canada, son of Aaron B. Pardee and Jane Elliott; m. Emma Kirby Forsyth of Lambton County, and they had six children; d. 21 July 1889 in Sarnia, Ont.

After leaving school Timothy Blair Pardee articled briefly in the Brockville law office of William Buell RICHARDS, later chief justice of Canada. But Pardee grew restless and abandoned law and the settled life of a small provincial town for the excitement of the California gold-rush in 1849. He passed two eventful but fruitless years in California before gold fever carried him, along with so many others, to Australia. After five years in the gold-fields there, he returned to Canada – without a fortune – to resume his studies in the office of Joshua Adams of Sarnia. He was called to the bar in 1861. Soon afterwards he was appointed crown attorney for Lambton County, a position he gave up in 1867 to run for political office. He was to be elected a bencher of the Law Society of Upper Canada in 1871 and named a QC in 1876.

A hearty, well-liked man about town, with a wealth of stories from his adventures, Pardee made an immediate success of politics. Running in the 1867 Ontario general election as a Reformer in Lambton he defeated the former warden of the county, Robert Rae, by a two-to-one margin. He was acclaimed in 1871 and again in the by-election of 1872 necessitated by his elevation to the cabinet. After redistribution in

1874 he held Lambton West for the Reform (or Liberal) party in four consecutive general elections, 1875, 1879, 1883, and 1886.

Premier Oliver Mowat* chose Pardee on 25 Oct. 1872 as provincial secretary in his first administration. A little more than a year later (4 Dec. 1873), upon the resignation and removal to Ottawa of Richard William Scott*, Pardee replaced him as commissioner of crown lands, a post he would hold for the next 16 years, longer than any other incumbent. The appointment of the popular but inexperienced western Ontario lawyer to a cabinet position usually reserved for an eastern Ontario lumberman surprised many people at the time. But Mowat, intent upon breaking up the cozy relationship that had developed between the department and the lumbermen, wanted someone with Pardee's ability and detachment to end the timber sale scandals and clean up the administrative chaos left behind by Scott. During his long term as commissioner Pardee did much, as did his long-time deputy, Thomas Hall Johnson (assistant commissioner of crown lands from 1869 to 1887), to regularize the administration of the province's natural resources and to restore the reputation of the department.

Crown lands was a demanding portfolio whose jurisdiction included surveys, colonization roads, mines, the administration of school lands, homesteads, and free grants. By far the most important function of the department, and its greatest revenue producer, was the regulation of logging in the provincial forests. The department held timber auctions whenever market conditions warranted, issued annual cutting licences, maintained a small field staff to oversee woods operations, and collected bonus, stumpage, and ground-rent payments from the lumbermen. Between 1867 and 1899 the woods and forests branch of the Crown Lands Department accounted for 28 per cent of the total provincial revenue, a proportion exceeded only by the federal subsidy.

After a providently timed sale of 5,031 square miles of timber by Scott just before the election in 1872 there was no need to put more timber on the market immediately, aside from small amounts of burnt timber and railway ties. Pardee, in fact, disposed of comparatively little timber during his long tenure of office, probably on account of the generally depressed condition of the trade. In 16 years he authorized only four auctions, in 1877, 1881, 1885, and 1887 for 375, 1,379, 1,012, and 459 square miles respectively – less than Scott had disposed of in 1872 alone. His last sale, for which timber dues were raised from 75¢ to $1 per 1,000 board foot of lumber and ground-rent was raised from $2 to $3 per square mile, occasioned a notable confrontation between the outraged lumbermen of the province and the government. On 14 Dec. 1887, the day before the auction, a deputation of lumbermen met with Pardee and Mowat in the parliamentary library. Mowat refused to back down on the new price schedules, and the lumbermen, thinking matters over later that evening, announced that they would not enter bids on the timber being offered for sale the next day. But come the time of the auction the natural avarice and mutual suspicions of the lumbermen undermined the boycott and the receipts from the auction were record bonus payments over and above ground-rent and dues to the provincial treasury.

Pardee was probably best known outside lumber circles as the minister responsible for Ontario's first forest protection legislation, an Act to Prevent the Forests from Destruction by Fire, passed in 1878. Though it relied upon the good will of lumbermen, this act focused public attention upon the menace of forest fire for the first time.

Pardee was a favourite in the legislature but, although he was a good stump orator, he seldom contributed to debates. He made his mark mainly in the lobbies and in the council chamber. It was said of him that he played the role of devil's advocate in the Mowat cabinet, exposing the weaknesses in potential appointments, policies, and government bills. In his last years his health deteriorated and he did not attend the legislature to defend his estimates during his last two sessions. When Mowat finally accepted his resignation on 25 Jan. 1889 expressions of regret came from both sides of the house. After his death Pardee was paid an immense tribute as well, in 1893, when his portrait was placed among those of seven other worthies of Ontario history on the western façade of the front portal of the new parliament buildings at Queen's Park.

H. V. Nelles

AO, Clarke (Charles) papers; MU 20–28; MU 1745, 14, 15 Dec. 1887; MU 2119, 1878; MU 2194; RG 1, especially A-I-8, 3; A-II-2, 6–8; A-VII, 19–22; E-6, 2–3; E-12, 5–6. PAC, MG 27, II, D14, 3–6; MG 28, III26, 704. Ont., Legislature, *Sessional papers*, 1871–90 (reports of the commissioners of crown lands). Aubrey White, *Forest fires and fire ranging: report . . . addressed to commissioner of crown lands* (Toronto, 1886). *Globe*, 31 Jan. 1878; 26 Jan., 22 July 1889. *Centennial edition of a history of the electoral districts, legislatures and ministries of the province of Ontario, 1867–1967*, comp. Roderick Lewis (Toronto, [1969]). *CPC*, 1889. *Cyclopædia of Canadian biog.* (Rose, 1886). Dent, *Canadian portrait gallery*, IV. *A statistical history of all the electoral districts of the province of Ontario since 1867*, comp. Roderick Lewis (Toronto, n.d.). C. R. W. Biggar, *Sir Oliver Mowat . . . a biographical sketch* (2v., Toronto, 1905). "A history of crown timber regulations from the date of the French occupation to the year 1899," Ont., Clerk of Forestry, *Annual report* (Toronto), 1899 (repr. 1907; 1957). R. S. Lambert and Paul Pross, *Renewing nature's wealth; a centennial history of the public management of lands, forests & wildlife in Ontario, 1763–1967* ([Toronto], 1967). H. V. Nelles, *The politics of development: forests, mines & hydro-electric power in Ontario, 1849–*

1941 (Toronto, 1974). Frank Yeigh, *Ontario's parliament buildings; or, a century of legislation, 1792–1892: a historical sketch* (Toronto, 1893).

PARSONS, ROBERT JOHN, journalist and politician; b.*c.* 1802 at Harbour Grace, Nfld; m. 5 Nov. 1835 Eliza Flood of St John's, Nfld, and they had at least one child, Robert John Parsons Jr; d. 20 June 1883 at St John's.

The early years of Robert John Parsons' life are obscure. He served an apprenticeship with the *Royal Gazette* in St John's and for six years was the foreman in charge of the printing office of Henry David Winton*, owner and editor of the *Public Ledger* (St John's). This association came to an end, however, in April 1833 when the two became embroiled in a fist-fight over a broken matrix. Parsons subsequently sued Winton and on 9 May 1833 was awarded £10 in damages for assault and battery. During the early 1830s Parsons' name had appeared as a member of the liberal group that was agitating for representative government, including such reformers as Dr William Carson*, Patrick Morris*, and John Kent*. After leaving the *Ledger* he became prominent in his own right as an associate of the Reform journalist John Valentine Nugent* and as managing editor of the *Newfoundland Patriot*, a weekly newspaper conceived by a group of the men who had "secured for the Colony a Parliamentary Government" and intended as the organ of the liberals in Newfoundland. Parsons became sole proprietor and editor of the *Patriot* in 1840.

In the columns of the paper, and later from his seat in the House of Assembly, Parsons was to display consummate skill in the art of political rhetoric. Fearless in his verbal assaults upon the bastions of privilege, untiring in his pursuit of legal and constitutional reform, and willing, on occasion, to castigate the excesses of his own party, Parsons was a power to be feared by all "despots who shall dare to subvert the charters of the land, and plant in their stead the unalloyed principles of arbitrary sway!" Chief Justice Henry John Boulton* was, in Parsons' view, one such despot, but the editor paid a price for the manner in which he made that opinion public. After a derisive editorial, commenting upon a charge by Boulton to a grand jury in May 1835, Parsons was cited for contempt of court by the chief justice. Assuming the roles of prosecutor, judge, and jury, Boulton convicted Parsons, fining him £50 and sentencing him to three months' imprisonment. The garrison was called out when Parsons' supporters threatened to tear down the court-house, a constitutional society was formed with the purpose of freeing the imprisoned journalist, and a petition with 5,000 signatures was dispatched to the Colonial Office. On instructions from London the sentence was remitted. Parsons was freed and his fine repaid. In the end his sufferings were, perhaps, well rewarded, for martyrdom is no bad foundation upon which to build a loyal following.

The acerbity of the editorials in the *Patriot* did not decrease. When in 1838, for example, the campaign to remove Boulton from office was successfully concluded, Parsons gleefully exhorted the "victims" of the chief justice to rejoice at the downfall of the tyrant. And when in 1839 Governor Henry Prescott* was resisting the authority of the assembly to appoint its own officers, Parsons referred to the governor as "a panderer and a partisan . . . one of the most unpopular governors that ever misruled our ill-used Country."

Parsons was bitterly opposed to the concept of the Amalgamated Legislature established in 1842, largely because it did not embody the principle of responsible government. As time passed he found other reasons to dislike the system, not the least in that through it the administration succeeded in transforming erstwhile "fiery democrats into staid admirers of fusty forms and ceremonies." The pointed reference in this particular case was to Kent and Morris, who had accepted appointments to the amalgamated house in 1842 and 1845 respectively and who supported Sir John Harvey*'s Militia Bill of 1846 which, in Parsons' opinion, "threatened a loss of constitutional liberty and an approach to despotic military government." It was the campaign led by the *Patriot* that ensured the defeat of the proposed legislation.

Parsons, a Presbyterian by birth and upbringing, though he eventually became an Anglican, had not found any significant conflict between his faith and his politics until 1840. In that year Bishop Michael Anthony Fleming* had used his personal influence and the full power of the Roman Catholic Church to secure the election of his candidate, Laurence O'Brien*, in a St John's by-election and to defeat the official Liberal candidate James Douglas*, a Protestant. After the election, the *Patriot* announced a new, "independent" brand of liberalism. Admitting that he had, heretofore, called upon religious prejudice to separate Roman Catholics from the Protestant merchants and thus to defeat "despotic Toryism," Parsons suggested that the results had been tragic and that Liberals should now set their faces against a resurrection of religious clamour and seek alliance with merchants who would support the "grand radical principle" of a "Responsible System of Government." Parsons' change of course was not entirely the result of his objections to clerical interference in politics. He was also becoming increasingly embittered by the continuing dominance of political, religious, and business leaders who were not natives of the colony. Thus within a month of the election of 1840 he had become a charter member of the Natives' Society with such men as Dr Edward Kielley*, Richard Barnes*, Philip Duggan, and John Ryan*. The society's aim was to strive to end the "usurpation of aliens" and to redress the "unpardonable error" of having counted "the unostentatious open-handed merchant as an enemy of popular rights or public improvements."

There is no implication here that Parsons had become a Conservative or that he had lost his popularity with the predominantly Roman Catholic population of St John's. In 1843, when a by-election was called for that riding after the death of Carson, he was elected to the Amalgamated Legislature, and in every successive election from that date until and including that of 1874 he was returned as a Liberal to represent the same constituency.

Throughout those years Parsons' trenchant pen and powerful voice were employed with great effect in promoting constitutional reform and natives' rights and in opposing confederation. During the struggle in the 1850s for responsible government, Parsons, allied with Kent, played a dominant role, and his personal campaigns conducted through the *Patriot* and from his seat in the legislature, epitomize the effective use of rhetoric. As a member of the committee including Hugh William HOYLES, Philip Francis Little*, Kent, Robert Prowse, and William Henry Ellis which was appointed by the house in 1857 to draft resolutions and addresses against the Fishery Convention of that year, Parsons played an important, although not preponderant, role; the exercise ultimately wrung from Great Britain the concession "that the consent of the community of Newfoundland is regarded by Her Majesty's Government as the essential preliminary to any modification of their territorial or maritime rights."

Parsons mellowed with time and was sufficiently removed from controversy in 1860 to be elected acting speaker of the House of Assembly in the absence of Speaker Ambrose Shea*. But until the year of his death he maintained unalloyed his commitment to his concept of patriotic duty. A controversialist, a violent partisan, and at times a political opportunist, Parsons stood out in the most turbulent years of Newfoundland's political history. From his entry into politics, he devoted all his talents to the goal of securing for Newfoundlanders the right to administer their own affairs freely. The "grand radical principle" of responsible government was his guiding star and the special status of the native Newfoundlander his secondary beacon. These alone determined his course. In so far as the Roman Catholic clergy supported the principle of responsible government, he supported them; in so far as they threatened the native Newfoundlanders, he opposed them. When the merchant class opposed responsible government, he opposed them; when they represented the native Newfoundlanders, he supported them.

Furthermore, and this was his great contribution, he produced an exciting newspaper that reflected the character of its editor. Parsons indeed lived up to the statement of the principles governing the policies of the paper that appeared beneath the masthead: "Here shall the press the people's rights maintain, unawed by influence and unbribed by gain, Here Patriot truth her glorious precepts draw, pledged to religion, liberty, and law."

LESLIE HARRIS

PANL, GN 5/2/A/1: 88–90. PRO, CO 194/85–206. Nfld., House of Assembly, *Journal*, 1833–83. *R.* v. *Parsons* (1829–45), 2 Nfld. R. 58. *Patriot* (St John's), 1833–83. *Public Ledger*, 1833–82. Gunn, *Political hist. of Nfld*. Leslie Harris, "The first nine years of representative government in Newfoundland" (MA thesis, Memorial Univ. of Newfoundland, St John's, 1959). Prowse, *Hist. of Nfld*. (1895). Wells, "Struggle for responsible government in Nfld."

PASKWĀW (Pasquah, Pisqua, The Plain, known in French as **Les Prairies**, literally it is a prairie), Plains Cree and chief of a band of Plains Saulteaux; b.*c*. 1828; d. 15 March 1889 on his reserve near Fort Qu'Appelle (Sask.).

Paskwāw was said to have been the son of Mahkesīs (Mahkaysis), a prominent chief of the Plains Cree who died in 1872. Prior to 1874, Paskwāw and his band lived near Leech Lake (Sask.) where they had a few houses, gardens, and a small herd of cattle. In spite of their unusual, if meagre, efforts at agriculture, the members of the band depended primarily on the buffalo hunt, small game, and fish for their livelihood.

Paskwāw attended the negotiation of Treaty no. 4 at Fort Qu'Appelle in September 1874, which brought together all the Plains Indians of what is now southern Saskatchewan. The terms of the treaty called for a cession of all Indian rights to the land in that area and a promise by the Indians to obey Canadian laws. In return, the Indians were offered a gratuity of $7 and an annuity of $5 for each band member, $15 for each headman, and $25 for each chief. They were promised a reserve of one square mile for every five Indians, the maintenance of a school on each reserve, certain farm implements, livestock, and other benefits. Each chief and headman was to receive a treaty medal and a suit of clothing every three years. Paskwāw's only recorded contribution to the discussion of these terms concerned the sale of Rupert's Land to Canada by the Hudson's Bay Company. He argued that the land belonged to the Indians and that the £300,000 paid to the HBC should have been given to them. In spite of the firm refusal of the Canadian representatives [*see* Alexander MORRIS] to consider this demand, Paskwāw signed the treaty.

The following year the Indian Department officials returned to Fort Qu'Appelle to pay the annuities and to distribute some of the articles due under the terms of the treaty. They found that Paskwāw's was the only band ready to receive its cattle and oxen. At this time he stated that he wished to have his reserve at Leech

Lake, where the band had been residing. Surveyor William Wagner was instructed to lay out the required amount of land, but Paskwāw began to vacillate. He remained near Fort Qu'Appelle and attempted to persuade other chiefs to join in refusing to have their reserves surveyed. Paskwāw apparently felt that if he allowed land to be surveyed for his band, he would be submitting to the domination of the whites. But in 1876 Indian agent Angus McKay was able to persuade the chief to permit Wagner to lay out a reserve of 57 square miles about five miles west of Fort Qu'Appelle.

Paskwāw and his band settled on this reserve, but his intrigues did not end. In the spring of 1878 he journeyed to Winnipeg for an interview with Lieutenant Governor Joseph-Édouard CAUCHON of Manitoba. The chief complained that food and building materials promised to him had not been delivered. He also declared that there was much unrest among the Plains Indians which could be alleviated if the government were to provide him with enough food and tobacco to hold a great feast for all these Indians, at which he would speak in favour of the Canadian government's policies. Indian Department officials interpreted this suggestion as a scheme by Paskwāw to increase his personal influence with other bands, and denied that food or building supplies had ever been promised him. In 1882 Paskwāw headed a movement of the Indians in the Fort Qu'Appelle area against the government's policy of paying annuities to each band on its own reserve, rather than at a mass gathering at Fort Qu'Appelle. The Indian Department officials alleged that the Indians wished to be paid their annuities at large assemblies in order to intimidate the small party of officials, forcing them to distribute more provisions and to make more promises than the government thought desirable. Paskwāw had initially declared that he would not take his money but quickly capitulated on discovering that his own band would not support him.

The return of Chief Piapot [Payipwat*] from the Cypress Hills in 1883 and his agitation for better terms for the Indians of Treaty no.4 brought renewed tension to the Qu'Appelle district. Paskwāw apparently supported Piapot's agitation but, entirely dependent upon the government for enough food to prevent starvation, he did not make this support explicit. In the spring of 1884 a false report of fighting between the North-West Mounted Police and a group of Piapot's followers startled the members of Paskwāw's band into hasty preparations for an armed clash with the authorities. Apart from this incident, Indian Department officials found little cause for concern with Paskwāw's band during the tense months preceding the North-West rebellion. When the uprising occurred in the spring of 1885 [*see* Louis RIEL], Paskwāw, together with Chief Maskawpistam (Muscowpetung) of the adjacent reserve, dispatched a telegram to Sir John A. Macdonald* proclaiming their loyalty and denouncing the insurrectionists to the north. The prime minister read the telegram in the House of Commons, and in reply to the chiefs promised that they would be well treated.

Paskwāw died of tuberculosis on 15 March 1889, after suffering from the disease for several years. Indian Agent John Bean Lash, who believed that the tribal system was a hindrance to Indian progress, successfully prevented the selection of a successor. In spite of the standing of Mahkesīs, his reputed father, Paskwāw had little influence beyond his own band. Well known for his intrigues, he succeeded only in annoying, not alarming, the Canadian government. In contrast to the actions of such other chiefs as Big Bear [MISTAHIMASKWA], his protests were short-sighted and his demands usually trivial.

KENNETH J. TYLER

PAC, RG 10, B3, 3582, file 889; 3584, file 1130/3A; 3602, file 1760; 3612, file 4012; 3613, file 4013; 3625, file 5489; 3632, file 6418; 3642, file 7581; 3654, file 8904; 3665, file 10094; 3672, file 10853/1; 3682, file 12667; 3686, file 13168; 3745, file 29506/4/1; 3761, file 32248; 3815, file 56405; 3875, file 90299. Can., House of Commons, *Debates*, 23 April 1885. Parl., *Sessional papers*, 1877, VII, no.11; 1884, III, no.4; 1885, III, no.3; 1890, X, no.12. [James Carnegie], Earl of Southesk, *Saskatchewan and the Rocky Mountains* . . . (Toronto and Edinburgh, 1875; repr. Edmonton, 1969).

PATERSON, PETER, merchant and capitalist; b. 13 Sept. 1807 at Blantyre Works (Blantyre), near Glasgow, Scotland, son of Peter Paterson and Jean Frazer; m. 9 Jan. 1837 Hannah Wilson (1815–92), and they had six sons and four daughters; d. 12 April 1883 at Toronto, Ont.

Peter Paterson Sr brought his family to York (Toronto) in 1819 and in 1821 established a hardware business. His sons David, John, and Peter were soon associated with him in a firm dealing in iron, Paterson and Sons. By the mid 1830s, however, Peter Jr had founded his own dry goods business in Toronto. The firm was so successful that its estimated worth was $50,000 in 1853 when he retired and turned it over to a nephew. In 1856 the business was taken over by Merrick Brothers who received financial backing from Paterson.

About 1858 Paterson purchased a 60-acre estate, which he named Blantyre Park, on Lake Ontario just east of Toronto, where he built a large residence. Although he maintained a home in Toronto, he spent a great deal of time at the estate during the remaining years of his life, developing improved crops and experimenting with new methods of farming. A member of the Church of England, he became one of the leading patrons of St John's Church, Norway (now part of Toronto), where he was rector's warden from 1857 to 1877; he frequently represented the parish at diocesan synod meetings.

Paterson's main contribution to Toronto was the role he played in the development of corporate institutions. Either he or his father (it is often difficult to determine which Peter Paterson – the subject, his father, or a nephew – is being referred to in sources) was an incorporator of the British America Fire and Life Assurance Company in 1834, and Peter Jr became a leading member of its board of trustees. In 1854 he and George Percival Ridout*, with whom he was frequently associated, toured cities in the northeastern United States to examine the possibility of extending the company's operations. Paterson later became deputy governor (vice-president) of the firm and then, succeeding Ridout, served as governor from June 1873 to 1882. In 1847 Peter and his brother David, along with Ezekiel Francis Whittemore and Charles Albert Berczy*, were among the founders of the Consumers' Gas Company of Toronto. Paterson was elected to the first board of directors in 1848 and remained a director until 1852; he again held office from 1854 to 1856. He was also active in the Farmers and Mechanics Building Society of Toronto, established in 1847 as a terminating (limited term) mortgage company. After the firm was successfully wound up in 1855, Joseph Davis RIDOUT, the president, Paterson, the vice-president, John Herbert Mason, the accountant, and several leading Toronto businessmen established a permanent institution, the Canada Permanent Building and Savings Society (which later became the Canada Permanent Mortgage Corporation). J. D. Ridout became president and Paterson vice-president, an office he retained until his death 28 years later. Paterson was elected a director of the Bank of Upper Canada in 1861 when Robert CASSELS was brought in to act as cashier (general manager) in an attempt to re-establish its strong financial position. Paterson remained a director until 1864, when he probably realized that the problems of the bank were insurmountable. Two years later the bank failed and he was elected one of the trustees to terminate its affairs.

Paterson took a particular interest in the development of institutions that would advance the commerce of Toronto. In 1845, along with Thomas Dennie Harris*, Whittemore, and G. P. Ridout, he helped establish the Toronto Board of Trade and was elected to its council. Five years later, when the Toronto Harbour Commission was formed, Paterson was one of the two commissioners appointed by the Board of Trade. He was also a founder of the Toronto Board of Fire Underwriters and served as president for several years before his death.

Paterson was a quiet, reserved man who played little part in the social institutions of the city, except as a member of the St Andrew's Society. He was a Conservative in his later years, although his background was Reform and he had supported Isaac BUCHANAN in the election of 1841. When he died Paterson left stocks, bonds, and personal property valued at $123,220 as well as extensive real estate holdings. His career illustrates how the influence of the early families of Toronto continued into the second generation and how what was, at least technically, a Reform family could become one of the pillars of the Toronto establishment.

FREDERICK H. ARMSTRONG

Baker Library, R. G. Dun & Co. credit ledger, Canada, 26: 24, 272, 351. Scottish Record Office (Edinburgh), Blantyre parish register, 13 Sept. 1807. York County Surrogate Court (Toronto), no.4780, will of Peter Paterson, 28 April 1883 (mfm. at AO). *Toronto Daily Mail*, 14, 16, 17 April 1883. *Standard dict. of Canadian biog*. (Roberts and Tunnell), II: 334–35. J. C. Hopkins, *Historical sketch of the British America Assurance Company . . .* (n.p., 1912), 4, 6–7. Middleton, *Municipality of Toronto*, I: 212, 230, 444, 504; III: 98–99. *75th birthday: 1848–1923, the Consumers' Gas Company of Toronto*, [comp. E. J. Tucker] (Toronto, 1923), 11, 14, 57. *The story of the Canada Permanent Mortgage Corporation, 1855–1925* (Toronto, 1925), 10, 13, 17, 25. "Paterson," *Ontarian Genealogist and Family Historian* (Toronto), 1 (1898–1901): 8–10.

PATRICK, WILLIAM, Methodist clergyman, businessman, and politician; b. 21 Feb. 1810 in Scarborough, Upper Canada, son of Asa Patrick and Belinda Gilbert; m. 31 May 1835 Abigail Ann, daughter of George Brouse*, and they had one child who died in infancy; d. 6 Aug. 1883 at Brockville, Ont.

William Patrick's father immigrated as a child to Upper Canada from Scotland and settled on a farm outside Newmarket. During the War of 1812 he was connected with the commissariat department in York (Toronto), and later followed commercial pursuits. He sent William first to a local common school and then to the Home District Grammar School run by John Strachan*. At an early age William showed a strong commitment to the Methodist faith, and in 1828 he studied at the Cazenovia Seminary in New York. (His strong Methodist convictions have led to confusion of his career with that of William Poyntz Patrick of Toronto, a prominent Methodist layman and later a member of the Catholic Apostolic Church who was a clerk in the office of the Upper Canadian House of Assembly and chief office clerk of the Legislative Assembly of the Province of Canada, and who died on 13 Oct. 1863.) From 1829 until early 1836 William Patrick devoted himself to the Methodist ministry in Upper Canada, having been ordained in 1833. During these years he served briefly on circuits and missions in Long Point in Leeds County, Belleville, Whitby, Perth, Prescott, and the Rideau area. "The extreme youth, pleasing manners, piety and pathetic manner in preaching, made young Patrick's ministrations exceedingly popular," but by 1835 his failing voice persuaded him to abandon the ministry and to become a merchant.

The next year Patrick and his wife opened a small store in Kemptville and three years later they moved to Prescott where he began a dry goods business. By 1851, at which time he went to England on an extensive buying trip, Patrick was a well-established, successful businessman and an agent for the Provincial Mutual and General Insurance Company. He later served as a director of the Ottawa and Prescott Railway. While in Prescott Patrick also acted as a Methodist lay preacher.

Politics beckoned, and in 1849, following the burning of the Parliament Buildings in Montreal, Patrick delivered an address of loyalty to the governor general, Lord Elgin [Bruce*], on behalf of the people of Grenville County. During his absence in England in 1851 he was nominated by the Reformers of Grenville to run in the election called for December of that year. Throughout the campaign he spoke in favour of reciprocity and the promotion of agriculture, lumbering, and trade with the northwest. He defeated Dr Hamilton Dribble Jessup, a veteran Conservative. Re-elected in 1854 for the riding, which had become Grenville South, Patrick was a follower of Francis Hincks and was one of the Hincksite Liberals backing the Conservative-dominated ministry of Sir Allan Napier MacNab* and Augustin-Norbert Morin*. As a member of the assembly, Patrick advocated increased government aid to the Methodist Victoria College at Cobourg.

In 1856 Patrick crossed the floor and joined the Reform opposition, but to many Grits he remained a "miserable toady" for his support of Hincks. Nevertheless he was elected as a moderate Reformer in both 1857 and 1861. As a Reformer he maintained an uneasy but continuous relationship with the rival leaders, George Brown* and John Sandfield Macdonald*, the member for Cornwall. Patrick was moving closer to Sandfield Macdonald's eastern Upper Canadian following. He supported the government of Sandfield Macdonald and Louis-Victor Sicotte formed in 1862, and unlike most Upper Canadian Reformers he remained with Macdonald during the crucial vote in March 1863 on the bill introduced by Richard William Scott* extending the rights of separate schools in Upper Canada. In the election of June 1863 Patrick was defeated by Conservative Walter Shanly*; ironically, despite his stand on separate schools, Patrick's disagreement with the endowment of certain religious institutions cost him the Catholic vote.

Patrick was a supporter of confederation and as the 1867 elections approached it was rumoured that John A. Macdonald* was negotiating with him about suitable coalition candidates for Grenville South, a rumour hotly denied by Shanly, the sitting Conservative member. When, however, the Reform convention met in June 1867, Brown, acting on the advice of Luther Hamilton Holton*, who was concerned to bring in Reformers with a broader basis of representation, engineered the selection of a surprised and somewhat bewildered Patrick as chairman. The convention denounced the coalition with John A. Macdonald's Conservatives and expelled William McDougall* from the party because of his support for coalition government. McDougall, the senior Reformer in John A. Macdonald's cabinet, nevertheless supported Patrick for the federal seat during the elections that summer, while John A. backed Shanly, who subsequently won.

In 1872 Patrick was elected mayor of Prescott and from 1873 to 1876 served as town treasurer. From May 1873 until his death he was sheriff of the united counties of Leeds and Grenville, a position which led him to move to Brockville in 1876. According to his obituary in the *Christian Guardian*, Patrick performed his duties as sheriff with a "keen sense of Christian duty"; "it was his custom to read the Scripture and pray with the criminals under his care." Patrick had maintained his involvement with the church both locally and nationally. In 1874, 1878, 1882, and 1883 he was an active delegate at the General Conference of the Methodist Church of Canada, and he was elected to its board of management. He left most of his estate for theological training at Victoria College and for the maintenance of missionaries abroad.

Bruce W. Hodgins

PAC, MG 24, B30; B40; MG 26, A. Surrogate Court of the United Counties of Leeds and Grenville (Brockville, Ont.), no.1092, will of William Patrick, 12 Oct. 1883 (mfm. at AO). Carroll, *Case and his cotemporaries*. *Brockville Recorder* (Brockville), 9 Aug. 1883. *Christian Guardian*, 1874, 19 March 1884. *Telegraph* (Prescott, [Ont.]), 1849, 1851, 1861, 1863, 1867. *Canadian biog. dict.*, I: 367–68. *CPC*, 1862. T. W. H. Leavitt, *History of Leeds and Grenville, Ontario, from 1749 to 1879 . . .* (Brockville, 1879; repr. Belleville, Ont., 1972).

PATTERSON, ROBERT J., slave and restaurant owner; b. in November 1809 in Richmond, Va; m. first Edith Bridges (d. 1881), and they had no children; m. secondly in 1882 Georgiana Sparrow; d. 2 Oct. 1884 in Saint John, N.B.

Robert J. Patterson was born a slave in Virginia and his first wife was also born in slavery. In 1842 he escaped to New York on a packet-boat and made his way to Boston where he remained for ten years. In the 1840s and 1850s, a number of escaped slaves came to Saint John and Patterson, hounded by fugitive slave hunters in Boston after the passing of the Fugitive

Slave Act of 1850, made his way there in 1852. He remained in Saint John for the rest of his life.

In 1856 Patterson and other former slaves organized the "Emancipation Ceremonies" which were held annually in Saint John for several years to commemorate the abolition of slavery in the British empire in 1833 and to urge the emancipation of slaves in the United States. Patterson and other former slaves gave speeches and sang anti-slavery songs at the celebrations which were attended by prominent whites and blacks.

About 1859 he opened an "oyster saloon" which developed into the "Empire Dining Saloon," the most popular establishment of its kind in Saint John. He soon had an extensive clientele and became a prosperous and respected member of the community. He was well known for his contributions to charity and for his assistance to the needy, both black and white. Patterson was a member of a small group of blacks who became successful businessmen in Saint John in the second half of the 19th century, and in 1860 he was made a free man of the city which allowed him to operate a business, a privilege accorded to few blacks in this period. He was involved with other blacks in the establishment of St Philip's Methodist Church, which opened in 1870, and he was one of the first trustees of the church. A popular man whose friendship was esteemed by many prominent citizens, Patterson was described at his death as "one of the most popular caterers in the Dominion of Canada."

WILLIAM ARTHUR SPRAY

Daily Sun (Saint John, N.B.), 3, 6 Oct. 1884. *Daily Telegraph* (Saint John), 3 Oct. 1884. *Morning News* (Saint John), 6, 11 Aug. 1856; 5 Aug. 1857; 6 Aug. 1858. *Saint John Globe*, 13 Dec. 1886. *Hutchinson's St. John directory* . . . (Saint John, N.B.), 1863–64. *McAlpine's St. John city directory* (Saint John), 1872–73, 1875–76, 1879–80.

PATTERSON, WILLIAM JEFFREY, printer, author, financial analyst, and secretary for business associations; b. in 1815 at Glasgow, Scotland; d. 12 June 1886 in Montreal, Que.

As a youth in Glasgow, William Jeffrey Patterson learned the printer's trade. After his apprenticeship he served as a journeyman and apparently turned quickly to proof-reading and type-setting. In 1847 he went to New York City, where he worked briefly as a printer before going west in the great gold-rush of 1848. He did not, however, reach California but made his home in Parkville, Mo., where he founded the *Parkville Luminary*. The resolutely anti-slavery bias of this paper roused a great deal of animosity and, after a riot in which he was hurt, he went to live for a while in Chicago and then moved to Canada. Around 1859 he settled at Montreal, where he worked for the printing firm of Owler and Stevenson and then for the *Montreal Witness* as commercial editor. At the end of April 1863 he became secretary to both the Montreal Board of Trade and the Montreal Corn Exchange Association. In this capacity he recorded the minutes of meetings, replied to correspondence, and furnished information to the business community.

Through his post as secretary, Patterson came to public attention. The knowledge he acquired about commercial transactions over the years made him a valuable man in the business world of Montreal, and even of Canada; hence in 1870 he was appointed secretary to the Dominion Board of Trade. As such, he organized the annual meeting of this body, which brought to Ottawa delegates of the boards of trade throughout the country, and he wrote the final report of the meeting.

By 1864 he had begun annual publication of the *Report on the trade and commerce of the city of Montreal*. This series, which soon made him famous in the Canadian business world, consolidated all the data pertaining to trade between Canada and other countries. It included lists of the wholesale prices of various foodstuffs and an analysis of the major sectors of manufacturing and trade. Particularly useful for the grain trade, the reports gave information on the shipment of grain, oats, and flour, both by rail and by canal. The scrupulous care which Patterson displayed made his work invaluable to his contemporaries, and it remains so for historians today. Because he wrote these reports for the Montreal Board of Trade and the Montreal Corn Exchange Association, he was provided with a subsidy; it was insufficient, and he had to find the additional funds for publication. In 1886 his successor as secretary to the two bodies, George Hadrill (who had been his assistant), published the last volume of the series. He adhered to the decision his predecessor had taken at the beginning of the year and refused to bear the publication costs. After 1886 the Montreal Board of Trade assumed responsibility for including in its annual reports the kind of data Patterson had collected.

In addition to the reports, Patterson published a number of more restricted studies relating to specific questions such as commercial relations with Great Britain, immigration, shipping in Canada, and the commercial and industrial potential of Newfoundland. Since his duties brought him into contact with federal officials, he was invited to compile statistical data for the Canadian government.

By his assessments of economic resources Patterson made an immense contribution to improving the efficiency of Montreal and Canadian business. His role as counsellor and representative of business circles kept him at the centre of the import-export activity of both Montreal and Canada for nearly a quarter of a century. He was well thought of and, when he died, the business associations he was connected with passed resolutions of condolence that were published in the newspapers, and the leaders of these associations, headed by their presidents, served as pallbearers at his funeral.

Patterson owned a residence in Saint-Antoine Ward in Montreal. One newspaper obituary stated that he was married and had a son, W. J. Ballantyne Patterson, who lived in San Antonio, Texas.

JEAN-CLAUDE ROBERT

[As secretary of the Montreal Board of Trade and of the Corn Exchange, Patterson compiled a series of statistics on trade and industry to be found in *Report on the trade and commerce of the city of Montreal . . .* (by 1867 it was being published under the title of *Statements relating to the home and foreign trade of the Dominion of Canada; also, annual report of the commerce of Montreal . . .*), issued annually from 1864 to 1878, and sporadically from 1878 to 1883. The information, accompanied by personal commentary, was drawn principally from official and brokers' circulars. A forerunner in the compilation of statistics on public finance and of an inventory of economic and human resources of British North America, Patterson wrote a number of works, the most important being *Some plain statements about immigration and its results* (Montreal, 1872); *Brief notes relating to the resources, industries, commerce and prospects of Newfoundland* (Montreal, 1876); *North-West Territory of Canada* (Montreal, 1881); and *The Dominion of Canada, with particulars as to its extent, climate, agricultural resources, fisheries, mines, manufacturing and other industries; also, details of home and foreign commerce including a summary of the census of 1881* (Montreal, 1883). J.-C. R.]

AC, Montréal, État civil, Presbytériens, American Presbyterian Church (Montreal), 17 June 1886. Montreal Board of Trade Arch. (Montreal), Minute books, 1881–88 (mfm. at PAC). *Extracts of the books of reference of the subdivisions of the city of Montreal*, ed. L.-W. Sicotte (Montreal, 1874). *Montreal Daily Star*, 14 June 1886. *Montreal Herald and Daily Commercial Gazette*, 14, 18 June 1886. *Montreal Witness*, 14 June 1886. *Dominion annual register*, 1886: 284. *Montreal directory*, 1858-86. J. I. Cooper, "The early editorial policy of the *Montreal Witness*," CHA *Report*, 1947: 53–62.

PAUL, MARY CHRISTIANNE (Christina, Christy Ann) (Morris), Micmac artist and artist's model; b.*c.* 1804 in Stewiacke, Colchester County, N.S., or Ship Harbour, Halifax County, N.S., daughter of Hobblewest Paul; d. 1886 in Halifax, N.S.

As a young girl, Mary Christianne Paul married Tom Morris, a Micmac of McNab Island, Halifax; he was considerably older than she, and an invalid for most of their married life. They had no children, but did adopt an orphaned niece, Charlotte, and a boy, Joe. Mrs Morris did exquisite work in the traditional Micmac crafts, supporting her family by the sale of quillwork and basketry. Her neeedlework, quillwork, splint basketry, and a full-sized canoe and paddles all won first prizes at various provincial exhibitions and she once sold two beaded costumes to Indian Commissioner William Chearnley for the impressive sum of $300. In 1854 she was living in Dartmouth, N.S., and a year later had moved across the harbour to the Northwest Arm, Halifax. There, "by her own industry," she built and furnished a green frame house and kept a few farm animals. When her niece married in 1857, Mrs Morris served wine and cake to a large crowd, and provided flute and violin music. Accounts of this ceremony describe her as "a lady well known and respected in this community," as indeed she was. Samuel and William Caldwell, mayors of Halifax, and Chearnley, the Indian agent, were her personal friends.

In 1860 a portrait of Mrs Morris by William Gush was presented to the Prince of Wales by the city of Halifax; it was a copy of one by the same artist which hung in her home. In it she is seated on the ground and wearing her self-made native costume which consisted of a beaded, peaked hat, a jacket, a woollen skirt appliquéd with ribbon, and beaded moccasins. She was evidently a favourite artist's model: known portraits include the two identical oils by Gush done in 1859, entitled "Christina Morris"; an undated watercolour, "Christy Ann," attributed to William Valentine*; and an undated drawing attributed to Rebecca Crane Starr, also entitled "Christy Ann." A pastel of a Micmac woman, done about 1850 by an unknown Nova Scotia artist, is of either Christianne or her niece Charlotte. Four Halifax photographers did studio portraits thought to be of Mrs Morris, in two of which she holds examples of her quillwork. Only two works of art by Mrs Morris herself have survived: a pair of snowshoes, woven in fine mesh for a mayor of Halifax, and her now-famous cradle panels done about 1868. The birch-bark panels are decorated with coloured porcupine quills in the Northern Lights, Starfish, and Fylfot motifs, on a white quill ground. Central designs are two moose, worked in black quills, a type of realistic motif rare in Micmac quillwork. The panels comprise the largest single piece of Micmac quillwork in existence, and show her to have been a master quiller.

Christianne Morris has been called "a pious woman of excellent character." By hard work and determination she took her family from life in a wigwam to a settled, middle-class existence. From the portraiture and works which survive her, she was also beautiful and gifted. One of Halifax's most interesting citizens in the 19th century, Christianne Morris is remembered not only as a model for the Nova Scotia painters who portrayed her but as a talented artist in her own right.

RUTH HOLMES WHITEHEAD

The Nova Scotia Museum (Halifax) possesses the snowshoes made by Mrs Morris and her quilled cradle panels are in the DesBrisay Museum (Bridgewater, N.S.).

Nova Scotia Museum, Accession books, 2, nos.4591, 4603; Harry Piers, "Uncatalogued notes on Micmac genealogies and biographical material"; "Uncatalogued notes on Morris porcupine quill cradle." PANS, MG 15, 6, no.1. Nova Scotia Industrial Exhibition, *Official report of the executive committee . . .* (Halifax), 1854. Provincial Agricultural and Industrial Exhibition of Nova Scotia, *Prize list and report of proc. . . .* (Halifax), 1868. *Evening Express* (Halifax), 4 July 1859. *Halifax Morning Sun*, 21 Aug. 1857, 4 July 1859. *Novascotian*, 24 Aug. 1857. R. H. Whitehead, "Christina Morris: Micmac artist and artist's model," *Material Hist. Bull.* (Ottawa), 3 (spring 1977): 1–14.

PAULET. *See* POLETTE

PAUTAUSSIGAE. *See* PAHTAHSEGA

PENNY, EDWARD GOFF, journalist, businessman, and politician; b. 15 May 1820 in Islington (now part of London), England, son of John Penny and Emmiley May; m. 13 Oct. 1857 at Montreal, Canada East, Eleanor Elizabeth Finley, *née* Smith, and they had one son, Edward Goff; d. 11 Oct. 1881 at Montreal.

Edward Goff Penny's father was a middle class London coal merchant of liberal views. Penny evidently received a practical education, perhaps in the working place as well as at institutions of formal learning, for along with a lively intelligence and writing ability he had a knowledge of shorthand. In 1844 he immigrated to Montreal, where his training earned him a position as cub reporter with the *Montreal Herald.* Since his employment was conditional upon learning French, Penny lived for six months with a family in Longueuil and acquired a reasonable facility in speaking the language. He served initially as a court reporter, to which practice he introduced shorthand techniques, and later became the *Herald*'s political correspondent while the legislature sat in Montreal from 1844 to 1849. At the same time he studied law and in 1850 was admitted to the Lower Canadian bar, though he never practised law as a profession.

Since the beginning of the 1840s the *Herald* had been widely accepted as Montreal's leading commercial newspaper, but its political reputation was less even. Memories of the rebellions of 1837–38, the debate over the act of union in 1841, and the violently Tory stance taken by the *Herald*'s previous editors, Adam THOM and James Moir Ferres*, were still vivid when Penny arrived in 1844. Robert Weir Jr, the paper's editor since 1838, had died in 1843 and David Kinnear* had taken over as editor-in-chief the following year. Under his direction the *Herald* began to acquire a reputation as a moderately conservative, though independent, journal. Penny later claimed that, as a newcomer untouched by existing national antipathies, he had had an influence in moderating the *Herald*'s stridently Tory tone. With Kinnear as the major shareholder, a group consisting of Penny, Andrew Wilson, the business manager, James Potts, the printer, and James Stewart, the commercial editor, in 1846 purchased the *Herald* from the heirs of Robert Weir Sr.

The new owners' claim to moderation was severely tested, however, during Montreal's convulsive reaction in 1849 to the Rebellion Losses Bill introduced by the Reform ministry of Louis-Hippolyte La Fontaine* and Robert Baldwin* and the consequent agitation for annexation. The *Herald* avoided the belligerent posturing and attacks on French Canada which marked most of Montreal's English language press over the period. By early July, however, the *Herald* was suggesting the peaceful annexation of Canada to the United States to offset the economic dislocation imposed by the advent of British free trade. Penny not only signed the Annexation Manifesto of October 1849, as did most of the *Herald*'s proprietors, but he was also the paid assistant secretary of the Montreal Annexation Association until its demise in 1850.

The *Herald* emerged from the crucible of 1849 an adherent of the Liberal or Rouge party forming in Canada East, a political position which Penny evidently found personally attractive. Easily the finest writer on the paper, he succeeded David Kinnear as editor-in-chief when the latter retired some time in the period 1856–57. By 7 Jan. 1863, a little over a month following Kinnear's death, Penny and Andrew Wilson had assumed control of the paper, and by March 1865 were its sole proprietors. While extending the *Herald*'s highly regarded coverage of Montreal's commercial affairs, Penny remained a firm supporter of the opposition Rouges and, in particular, the editorial champion of those English-speaking liberals clustered about Luther Hamilton Holton*, a political and personal friend. By the confederation era, Henry James Morgan* regarded Penny as "undoubtedly the ablest journalist connected with the Rouge, or Liberal, press."

Two events in particular served to set Penny apart from most of his fellow journalists: his attack upon the confederation scheme and his support of the Union during the American Civil War. Genuinely respecting American institutions, Penny dismissed the Southern cause as "vain and foolish" treason, and slavery as "the vilest, most gigantic, and once most widely spread crime of Christendom." He tried consistently to restrain Canadian anxieties over the potential Northern threat to Canada and viewed the more bombastic pro-Southern sentiments emanating from certain sections of the Conservative party as "insane." The "isolation and antagonism" he experienced as a result of his position surpassed the bitterness of any other political battle. Penny later recalled the Civil War years as "the winter of my career as a journalist."

From its beginnings in 1864, Penny considered the

confederation scheme as, at best, a "timid expedient." It avoided the central issue of proportional representation as demanded by Reformers in Canada West, and erected an expensive, vaguely defined federal system which potentially left Protestants in Canada East at the mercy of the far more populous French Canadians. He felt that "both English and French in Lower Canada . . . would be better off under the old union, with a fair addition to the Upper Canadian share of the representation." In a pamphlet published in January 1867, an uneven collection of arguments aimed directly at London, Penny claimed that the Colonial Office had already injured the principle of responsible government by its unconstitutional interference in favour of the confederation scheme. The imperial parliament should refuse to interfere further by rejecting the confederation legislation then before it. A subsequent anonymous pamphlet dismissed Penny as part of "a small rump of a quasi-annexation party in Canada," a charge echoed in the Montreal *Gazette.* Once the legislation had been passed, however, Penny requested *Herald* readers to give the new system a fair trial. Yet as late as 1873 Penny privately referred to George Brown*, the Reform leader and instigator of the confederation coalition, as a hypocritical opportunist who had "sold out to the enemy."

Although Penny at times was given to sulking, even threatening at the height of the Pacific Scandal in 1873 to take his journal out of the Liberal alliance after Brown's *Globe* had slighted him, he was highly regarded within Liberal party circles. Apart from his appointment in 1863 as a justice of the peace by the ministry of John Sandfield Macdonald* and Antoine-Aimé Dorion*, he received few public honours from the party. On 13 March 1874, however, after the victory of the Liberals under Alexander Mackenzie*, he was appointed to the Senate for the Alma division of Quebec and in May 1875 was chosen a Canadian commissioner to the Philadelphia Centennial International Exhibition of 1876.

Penny's *Herald* steadfastly supported Mackenzie's "sound and honest" government from 1874 through the election campaign of 1878. The *Herald* first greeted Sir John A. Macdonald*'s National Policy platform as a cynical bluff, but later as dangerous, "mischievous quackery." While attracted to free trade ideas, Penny recognized the problems that their implementation held for Canada beside an increasingly protectionist United States. Still he believed in a "natural current of affairs" in world trade and resisted government manipulation of the economy. He accepted the electoral verdict but believed that the protectionist policies would develop "like the fabled Dead Sea apples, which contained nothing but ashes within the beautiful rind."

Penny spoke not only as a newspaperman but also as a successful businessman. A director of the Montreal Telegraph Company, he was also, according to the Montreal *Gazette*, "a large shareholder and director of several leading public institutions." Penny had amassed by his death in 1881 a "fair fortune for a gentleman." In an obituary, the *Montreal Star*, reflecting the genuine regard in which other journalists held him, claimed that "as a political editor, Mr. Penny had no superior in the Dominion"; as if to prove this assertion, the prestigious *Montreal Herald* began to decline after his death.

LORNE STE. CROIX

Edward Goff Penny was the author of *The proposed British North American confederation; why it should not be imposed upon the colonies by imperial legislation* (Montreal, 1867). A reply to the pamphlet also appeared: *The proposed B.N.A. confederation; a reply to Mr. Penny's reasons why it should not be imposed upon the colonies by imperial legislation* (Montreal, 1867).

ANQ-Q, AP-G-203. AP, St Stephens Anglican Church (Montreal), Register of baptisms, marriages, and burials, 13 Oct. 1857. PAC, MG 24, B40, 8; MG 26, B; MG 27, I, E13. "The Annexation movement, 1849–50," ed. A. G. Penny, *CHR*, 5 (1924): 236–61. Can., Parl., *Sessional papers*, 1879, 10, no.152: 1–12. *Canada Gazette*, 1 Aug. 1863, 21 March 1874. *Elgin–Grey papers* (Doughty), I: 75–76; IV: 1492–94. *Gazette* (Montreal), 3 Feb. 1844, 9 March 1874, 12 Oct. 1881. *Globe*, 12, 14, 15 Oct. 1881. *Montreal Daily Witness*, 12 Oct. 1881. *Montreal Herald and Daily Commercial Gazette*, 7 Jan. 1863; 18 July, 17 Oct., 12 Nov. 1864; 25 Jan., 11, 25 March, 3, 17 April 1865; 19 Jan., 26 March 1867; 20 March 1874; 26 March, 19, 20, 23 Sept., 23 Oct. 1878; 12, 13 Oct. 1881. Beaulieu et J. Hamelin, *La presse québécoise*, I: 27–28. *Dominion annual register*, 1880–81. Wallace, *Macmillan dict.*, 589. H. C. Klassen, "L. H. Holton: Montreal businessman and politician, 1817–1867" (PHD thesis, Univ. of Toronto, 1970). Thomson, *Alexander Mackenzie.*

PERLEY, WILLIAM GOODHUE, lumber manufacturer, financier, and politician; b. 4 June 1820 at Enfield, N.H., son of John and Susanna Perley; m. first 14 Sept. 1846 Mabel E. Ticknor Stevens (she died in the early 1860s); m. secondly 20 June 1866 Georgianna M. Gale; d. 1 April 1890 at Ottawa, Ont.

William Goodhue Perley was educated at the common school in Enfield and probably entered the lumber trade during the late 1830s as a clerk. He then set up his own business at Lebanon, N.H., and established interests in northern New York State. He prospered by supplying lumber to the rapidly growing markets of Boston and New York City. By 1850, however, practically all the first class timber land in northern New York was depleted, and Perley (who maintained his home in Lebanon for some years) and his partner, Gordon B. Pattee, decided in 1852 to move their operation to the rich pine lands of the Ottawa valley. They purchased several hydraulic lots on Île de la Chaudière at the Chaudière Falls on the

Ottawa River and in 1853 started developing their mill site. By 1865 they were producing 16 million board feet of lumber per annum, mostly for the American market.

Pattee and Perley Company benefited from the Reciprocity Treaty of 1854 which allowed British North American timber into the United States duty-free. The firm leased large pine limits on the upper Madawaska River and in 1857 acquired additional hydraulic lots at the Chaudière Falls. In 1859, with the addition of John T. Brown, another Ottawa lumberman, the firm was reorganized as Perley, Pattee and Brown, Perley being the dominant figure. Despite the termination of the Reciprocity Treaty in 1866 and a series of severe trade depressions in the 1870s and 1880s, the firm continued to expand. In 1871 the mill was capitalized at $450,000 and employed 250 men for six months each year; by the time of Perley's death in 1890 production had risen to almost 70 million board feet of lumber per year. After his death the firm passed into the hands of his heirs, including his son George Halsey Perley*, before being dissolved in 1893.

Perhaps in response to the end of reciprocity Perley began to advocate measures to lower production costs, particularly improved transportation systems for the Ottawa valley. With Thomas Coltrin Keefer* and fellow lumbermen Joseph Merrill CURRIER, Joseph-Ignace Aumond*, and Robert Blackburn, he promoted the Ottawa City Passenger Railway Company, chartered in 1866. Its horse-drawn trams and sleighs not only provided Ottawa with its first urban transit system, but also gave the promoters a cheap and convenient system for moving lumber from mills at the Chaudière Falls and New Edinburgh (now part of Ottawa) to shipping points on the Rideau Canal and the Ottawa and Prescott Railway. In 1868 Perley joined Henry Franklin BRONSON and James SKEAD in setting up the Upper Ottawa Steamboat Company, a highly successful venture which reduced the cost of transporting supplies from Ottawa to up-river depots.

The need to cut production costs became more pressing after 1879 when Sir John A. Macdonald*'s Conservative government introduced its National Policy which raised tariff rates to protect and encourage Canadian industry. Many Ottawa valley lumbermen feared that the new rates would discriminate against their industry by failing to provide it with adequate protection from imports while making it vulnerable to a retaliatory tariff by the United States. Moreover, the quality of the products of the Canadian lumber industry had declined markedly since the early 1870s and Canadian exporters were already experiencing difficulties in overcoming American tariff walls. Perley, however, was a long-time protectionist and a confirmed Liberal-Conservative. He thought that all "young nations" needed a protective tariff to encourage economic development and was convinced that the forest industry was strong enough to bear "increased taxation on that account."

In response to the new Conservative policy Perley intensified his efforts to reduce and stabilize production costs. Along with fellow Ottawa lumberman John Rudolphus Booth*, and George C. Noble of St Albans, Vt, he purchased in 1879 several moribund railway charters in the Ottawa and Montreal areas and amalgamated the charters to form the Canada Atlantic Railway which would run from Ottawa to the American border by way of the port of Montreal. Perley, Booth, and Noble invested heavily in the project and construction started in 1880, but they also sought government aid. Perley reminded Macdonald that the National Policy greatly discriminated against the lumber trade, and that railways such as the Canada Atlantic which were designed to improve the industry's competitive position deserved special consideration. Though not enthusiastic for a railway which would invade the traffic area of the new Canadian Pacific Railway syndicate, Macdonald recognized the need to keep the support of Perley and his Tory friends, and provided a limited subsidy in 1885. By 1884 the Canada Atlantic had been completed as far as Coteau-Landing, Quebec, on the main line of the Grand Trunk, and in 1888 it reached Rouse's Point on the American border. From the beginning the line proved to be a success and its volume of traffic steadily increased.

Perley and his associates on the Canada Atlantic worked next to extend it up the Ottawa valley and across to Georgian Bay. Their objectives were, first, to transport supplies to the lumber camps more cheaply and enable the operators to move their mills closer to their timber limits, and second, to tap the grain traffic from the Canadian west by providing the shortest route to the mills and docks of Montreal. In 1888 they joined Tory lumberman Claude McLachlin of Arnprior in promoting the formation of two new railways, the Ottawa, Arnprior and Renfrew Railway Company and the Ottawa and Parry Sound Railway Company, to cover the distance between Ottawa and Parry Sound. Although this new initiative was vigorously opposed by both the Toronto Board of Trade, which contended that the wealth of Ontario's new northern frontier would be channelled to Ottawa instead of Toronto, and the CPR, it received the support of Oliver Mowat*'s Liberal government in Ontario and in 1896, six years after Perley's death, the Ottawa, Arnprior and Parry Sound Railway arrived at Depot Harbour on Georgian Bay.

Until relatively late in life William Perley remained very much a private man, more interested in business than in civic matters or politics. He took an interest in the affairs of Christ Church (Anglican) in Ottawa, was a regular contributor to philanthropic causes such as the Protestant Orphans' Home, and a director of the

Ottawa Ladies' College, but he did not take a conspicuous part in such affairs. Perley's concern for the financing of the Canada Atlantic, however, appears to have drawn him into public life. He campaigned for the Liberal-Conservative nomination in Ottawa in 1882 but placed third after Charles Herbert Mackintosh* and Joseph Tassé*. Feeling personal affront at his defeat by the much younger Mackintosh, and suspecting that Mackintosh was not a particularly ardent supporter of the Canada Atlantic, Perley resigned for a short time from the Liberal-Conservative party in anger. Nevertheless he and his associates did not give up. They worked assiduously to undermine Mackintosh's support after 1882. In 1887 Perley secured one of the Tory nominations for Ottawa City. He was elected but did not distinguish himself in the House of Commons. In April 1888, however, he made a major speech opposing Sir Richard John Cartwright*'s resolution for unrestricted reciprocity and defending the National Policy for its aid to the Canadian economy; he also called on the lumber community to develop its domestic market instead of depending on the American export trade. It was the only significant event of his parliamentary career and early in 1890 Perley became seriously ill. He died on the morning of 1 April 1890 at Ottawa.

ROBERT PETER GILLIS

PAC, MG 26, A,141: 54746; 142: 58155–73; 385: 180981–82, 181177–79; MG 27, II, D14, 5; F7, 1, file 3; MG 28, III26, 703; 706; RG 1, E1, 83: 627; RG 31, A1, 1871, schedule 6, industrial census, Ottawa, Victoria Ward. Can., House of Commons, *Debates*, 6 April 1888; *Statutes*, 1888, c.65; 1891, c.93. Can., Prov. of, *Statutes*, 1866, c.106. Ont., *Statutes*, 1888, c.71. *Ottawa Daily Citizen*, 20 May 1882, 3 April 1890. *Canadian directory of parl.* (J. K. Johnson). *Canadian men and women of the time* (Morgan, 1912), 704. *CPC*, 1887. *An encyclopædia of Canadian biography . . .* (3v., Montreal and Toronto, 1904–7), II. *Sutherland's city of Ottawa directory . . .* , comp. James Sutherland (Ottawa), 1869–70. Lucien Brault, *Ottawa: old & new* (Ottawa, 1946), 185–86, 194. A. R. M. Lower, *The North American assault on the Canadian forest: a history of the lumber trade between Canada and the United States . . .* (Toronto and New Haven, Conn., 1938; repr. New York, 1968), 123–47. A. H. D. Ross, *Ottawa, past and present* (Toronto, 1927), 157. G. R. Stevens, *Canadian National Railways* (2v., Toronto and Vancouver, 1960–62), II.

PERRÉ (Perri), HENRI, landscape painter and art teacher; b. probably in 1824 or 1825 in Strasbourg, France, of French and Prussian parents; d. unmarried 17 June 1890 in Toronto, Ont.

Henri Perré studied art in Dresden (German Democratic Republic) before being forced to flee to the United States after fighting in the 1849 uprisings in Saxony. References to his American career are primarily anecdotes of his friends who related that he had lived the life of a confirmed bachelor in the Carolinas, Cincinnati, Ohio, and Chicago before fighting in the Confederate army during the Civil War. He had made a brief visit to Toronto in 1854 and moved there in 1863. Perré, described by Canadian friends as eccentric but popular, lived in Toronto for much of the balance of his life, in the city's downtown district and for a time in the quarters of the Ontario Society of Artists.

Principally a landscape artist, he not only painted in the Don valley and the Toronto environs but also made numerous sketching trips by railway: to Ancaster, Dundas, and Preston, Ont., in 1874 and 1881; to Bic and Matapédia, Que., in 1882; as well as to Muskoka and Owen Sound, Ont. However, during 1877–78 he visited Philadelphia, with fellow artist John Wesley Bridgman*, and painted along the Schuylkill and Shenandoah rivers. Titles of his paintings indicate that in 1878 he visited Colorado and California at the time when Thomas Moran and other American artists were discovering the west, and several British Columbia views suggest that he went north from California to sketch there before that province had been linked to central Canada by rail. Perré's rural landscapes, primarily in oil and water-colour, are usually modest in size, with the exception of the large *Niagara Falls*. His realistic style is allied to that of the late Hudson River school of painters and other contemporary American landscapists. Despite his large output (approximately 150 works were exhibited at Ontario Society of Artists and Royal Canadian Academy exhibitions between 1874 and 1889), few are now in public collections. His academy diploma work, *Landscape* (in the National Gallery of Canada, Ottawa), and a water-colour, *Cliff and cove* (in the Art Gallery of Ontario, Toronto), are landscapes characterized by minute figures as central themes surrounded by trees, rocks, and water.

While teaching the antique, drawing from casts of classical sculpture, at the Ontario School of Art (now the Ontario College of Art), Toronto, from 1876 to 1882, Perré instructed the school's early students, including George Agnew Reid*. He probably also influenced the youthful Homer Ransford Watson*, whom he met at the Toronto photographic studio of William Notman*. They may have been sketching companions given the fact that Perré's *Dundas Road* and Watson's *The old Dundas Road* (National Gallery of Canada) both date from 1881. Perré was elected a member of the Ontario Society of Artists in 1874 and was a close associate of society members who proposed him as a charter member of the Royal Canadian Academy of Arts in 1880. He exhibited with both societies, as well as at the Art Association of Montreal and at the Toronto Industrial Exhibition. His paintings were displayed in the Canadian sections at the Philadelphia Centennial International Exhibition, 1876, and the Colonial and Indian Exhibition, London, 1886.

J. RUSSELL HARPER

Can., Dept. of Agriculture, *Colonial and Indian Exhibition of 1886: a revelation of Canada's progress and resources; extracts from British and colonial journals* (Ottawa, 1887). *Canadian Illustrated News* (Montreal), 10 June 1871, 29 June 1872. *Globe*, 19 June 1890. *L'Opinion publique*, 27 juin, 18 juill. 1872. Art Assoc. of Montreal, *Catalogue of the annual spring exhibition of works by Canadian artists* (Montreal), 1880–83. Harper, *Early painters and engravers*. National Gallery of Canada, *Catalogue of paintings and sculpture*, ed. R. H. Hubbard (3v., Ottawa and Toronto, 1957–60), III. Royal Canadian Academy of Arts, *Annual exhibition*, 1880–86. Toronto Industrial Exhibition, *Catalogue of the Art Department* (Toronto), 1881–90. W. [G.] Colgate, *Canadian art: its origin & development* (Toronto, 1943; repr. 1967). Harper, *Painting in Canada*. Newton MacTavish, *The fine arts in Canada* (Toronto, 1925). Edmund Morris, *Art in Canada: the early painters* ([Toronto, 1911?]). A. H. Robson, *Canadian landscape painters* (Toronto, 1932). J. W. L. Forster, "The early artists of Ontario," *Canadian Magazine*, 5 (May–October 1895): 17–22. "A guide to Canadian painters," comp. M. E. Hughes, *Ontario Library Rev.* (Toronto), 24 (1940): 187–209, 281–96.

PERREY, SYLVAIN-ÉPHREM (often written **Perry** or **Poirier**, but he always signed S. E. Perrey), Roman Catholic priest; b. 15 July 1800 or 1802 at Tignish, P.E.I., seventh of the nine children of Pierre Poirier and Marie Chiasson; d. 3 Aug. 1887 at Egmont Bay, P.E.I.

Sylvain-Éphrem Perrey was born some 50 years after the deportation of the Acadians of Île Saint-Jean (Prince Edward Island) in 1758, in circumstances that were difficult and uncertain. In 1799 his family was uprooted from its established home on the shores of Malpeque Bay and settled in the Tignish region. Perrey may have been baptized by Abbé Jacques-Ladislas de Calonne*, a missionary on the Island from 1799 to 1804. He went to school in Tignish, and then continued his studies at Rustico.

Perrey made up his mind at an early age to become a priest. In 1818 Abbé Joseph-Étienne Cécile, the parish priest of Rustico, recognized his talents and recommended him to Joseph-Octave Plessis*, the bishop of Quebec. Plessis got him accepted as a student at the Séminaire de Nicolet, and during the next eight years Perrey prepared for the priesthood. In his steady work at this institution he displayed the inexhaustible courage, determination, and perseverance that characterized all his life as a priest.

Returning to Prince Edward Island in 1826, Perrey finished his studies under the direction of Bishop Angus Bernard MacEachern*, and at the same time apparently became his secretary. On 28 July 1828 he was ordained priest in St Andrew's Church at St Andrews by the bishop. There were then only two other Catholic priests on the island, MacEachern and Bernard Donald MacDonald*; the latter looked after the Acadian missions from Rustico to Tignish. Upon ordination, Perrey was appointed parish priest at Tignish, and was given responsibility for the Acadian missions in Prince County.

In the period after the deportation Acadian settlers in the Maritimes had turned to their priests for guidance; thus the clergy had assumed a leadership role in the communities and their advice was constantly sought on both secular and religious matters. Because there were so few resident priests on Prince Edward Island, however, until the beginning of the 19th century the consolations of religion were brought to the Acadians and other Catholics by visiting missionaries and by laymen who had been granted certain special powers. Perrey, the first native-born priest on the Island, was destined to exercise great influence among the Acadians. For 15 years he worked with his flock, which was scattered between Tignish and Miscouche, a distance of more than 40 miles. "Sleeping on the snow in winter, on a damp bed under the trees in spring and autumn, navigating rivers by canoe or some other means in all seasons of the year and in all weathers," Perrey was "always cheerful, always content, always happy" as he carried on his ministry.

In 1844 Father Peter MacIntyre*, who had recently been ordained for the diocese of Charlottetown, was sent to Tignish; he served the western part of Prince County, while Perrey established his residence at Miscouche and ministered to the missions in the eastern section of the county. In 1860 failing eyesight obliged Perrey to take a well-earned rest. He retired to Tignish and went to live with his sister at Étang-des-Clous (Nail Pond), but in a few years had recovered sufficiently to take up his ministry again. In 1869 he was appointed first resident parish priest at Mount Carmel. A great celebration was held in Charlottetown in July 1878 to honour his golden jubilee in the priesthood. Finally, in 1879 he was forced to give up his ministry because he was almost totally blind.

Throughout his years as a priest Perrey participated in the progress of his diocese and took a keen interest in the needs of his people. When Bishop MacEachern founded St Andrew's College at St Andrews in 1830, Perrey was appointed a member of its board of trustees. Perrey also gave his support to St Dunstan's College in Charlottetown, which replaced St Andrew's College. In recognition of the help he had received to pursue his own studies, he endowed two scholarships, one at St Dunstan's College, the other at the Collège Saint-Joseph in Memramcook, N.B. Many young Island Acadians were to benefit from these scholarships. In 1841, when total abstinence societies were founded in the diocese, Perrey became president of the one established in Prince County. He was also a founding member of a mutual insurance society set up on 11 March 1846 on behalf of the diocesan clergy by Bishop Bernard Donald MacDonald, the second bishop of Charlottetown.

A competent administrator, Perrey built a presbytery at Tignish, completed the construction of churches at Tignish and Mount Carmel, and later enlarged the latter building to meet the needs of the increasing number of parishioners. According to those who knew him, "he was not . . . a good preacher, but was an excellent scolder." In the course of his studies at the Séminaire de Nicolet he had learned plainsong. He had a good voice and organized choirs in all his missions. His influence in this field was such that it continued to be felt in the parishes of Prince County almost until the liturgical renewal of the second Vatican Council.

Perrey spent his last days with his family at Egmont Bay. After his death in 1887, the parishioners of the communities to which he had ministered erected a monument to his memory in the cemetery at Egmont Bay.

FRANCIS-C. BLANCHARD

Le Moniteur acadien (Shédiac, N.-B.), 11 juill. 1878, 9 août 1887. Ivanhoë Caron, "Inventaire de la correspondance de Mgr Bernard-Claude Panet, archevêque de Québec," ANQ *Rapport*, 1933–34: 294, 312, 337, 344, 358. J.-H. Blanchard, *The Acadians of Prince Edward Island, 1720–1964* (Ottawa and Hull, Que., 1964); *Acadiens de l'Île-du Prince-Édouard* ([Charlottetown], 1956). *The Catholic Church in Prince Edward Island, 1720–1979*, ed. M. F. Hennessey (Charlottetown, 1979). [*L'Impartial illustré*], *numéro illustré: souvenir de la célébration du 100me anniversaire de la fondation de Tignish* (Tignish, Î.-P.-É., 1899). J. C. Macmillan, *The early history of the Catholic Church in Prince Edward Island* (Quebec, 1905); *The history of the Catholic Church in Prince Edward Island from 1835 till 1891* (Quebec, 1913). J.-W. Pineau, *Le clergé français dans l'Île du Prince-Édouard, 1721–1821* ([Québec, 1967]).

PERRY, GEORGE HUGO, civil engineer, publisher, editor, and author; b. 17 Dec. 1817 in County Wexford (Republic of Ireland); d. 25 March 1888 in Ottawa, Ont.

George Hugo Perry entered the Royal Navy as a midshipman and served seven years. He commenced the study of engineering in Wales and completed his studies under Sir John Benjamin MacNeill in Dublin. After some experience in railway and bridge construction in Ireland, Perry immigrated to Canada West in 1852, living in Wardsville and working for the Great Western Railway. From about 1853 until 1858 he was a member of the group that surveyed for the proposed Chats canal and also for possible canals on the Ottawa and French rivers. From 1859 to 1862 he was a civil engineer in partnership with George and William Austin in Ottawa. He surveyed and compiled a map of the Rideau Canal and its associated transportation routes in 1863.

In 1860 Perry had entered the newspaper business in partnership with Henry James Friel*, owner of the Ottawa *Union* since 1858. This Reform newspaper criticized the quality of municipal works in Ottawa and ran editorials on the local lumber trade; the impetus for both these interests probably came from Perry. From 1861 to 1865 he also published brochures containing transcripts of his speeches dealing with the Ottawa River as a transportation system and discussing the Ottawa valley's staple trade in timber. He was secretary of the Ottawa Association of Lumber Manufacturers. The rise of the city of Ottawa depended not only on the strength of the lumber industry but also, in Perry's view, on its choice as a permanent capital. The *Union*, which became the *Daily Union* in 1865, was a strong supporter of Ottawa as the capital of the Province of Canada but was against confederation, which, it felt, might lessen the power of Ottawa, balanced on the border of the united provinces. In 1866, when Ottawa's role was still being denigrated, Perry proposed an excursion for members from both houses of parliament up the Ottawa River, as far as the Rapides des Joachims, to convince them that the queen's choice of Ottawa was a good one.

In 1869 Perry succeeded John McTaggart as city engineer for Ottawa; he remained in the post until 7 April 1873. During his tenure a water supply and sewage system were planned for the capital; he also designed a bridge over the Rideau Canal. In 1870 Perry succeeded Carroll Ryan as editor of the *Volunteer Review and Military and Naval Gazette*, in which he published a series of articles on defence. The federal Department of Public Works chose him in 1874 to supervise the construction of the Culbute Canal and Dam on the north channel of the Ottawa around Allumette Island. He had proposed these works in a report in 1862 as a means of providing a 78-mile stretch of unobstructed steamboat navigation between Calumet Lake and the Rapides des Joachims. During construction, Perry lived in Chichester, Que. The importance of the canal at Culbute later gradually declined, as did the use of steamboats.

Perry returned to Ottawa when the canal was completed in 1887, the year in which he was given the honorary rank of lieutenant-colonel on the retired list.

COURTNEY C. J. BOND

G. H. Perry was the author of *Report on the supply of water, drainage and improvement of the city of Ottawa* (Ottawa, 1861); and *The staple trade of Canada: a lecture delivered in the Temperance Hall, Ottawa, on Tuesday, 18th March, 1862, before the mechanics' institute and Athenæum* (Ottawa, 1862). Other works by Perry are listed in Morgan, *Bibliotheca Canadensis*, 308.

PAC, MG 24, D8: 14237; I9: ff.5338–41; MG 26, A, 303: 174; 321: 50; RG 4, B29, 4. Can., Parl., *Sessional papers*, 1891, X, no.9, app.19: 32. *Free Press* (Ottawa), 26 March 1888. *Ottawa Daily Citizen*, 26 March 1888.

PETIT PIN. *See* MINAHIKOSIS

PHIPPS, GEORGE AUGUSTUS CONSTANTINE, 3rd **Earl of Mulgrave** and 2nd **Marquess of Normanby**, colonial administrator; b. 23 July 1819 at Whitby, England, only child of Constantine Henry Phipps, 1st Marquess of Normanby, a leading Whig politician, and Maria Liddell, eldest daughter of Thomas Henry, Lord Ravensworth; m. in 1844 Laura Russell, and they had seven children; d. 3 April 1890 at Brighton, England.

Lord Mulgrave's early years were spent in the army, serving in the Scots Fusilier Guards (1838–43) and the North Riding Yorkshire militia (1846–53), and in politics. He was Liberal member of parliament for Scarborough from 1847 to 1851 and again from 1852 to 1857, comptroller and later treasurer of the royal household (1851–58), and a party whip (1853–58).

In January 1858, in succession to John Gaspard Le Marchant*, Mulgrave was appointed lieutenant governor of Nova Scotia, at a time of constitutional uncertainty in that colony. The principle of responsible government had been formally adopted in the colony in 1848 but it was taking considerable time and controversy to establish its conventions and practices. Politicians wrangled over the exercise of the governor's diminishing prerogatives and readily exploited for partisan ends his anomalous position as both imperial agent and titular head of the local executive. Mulgrave's predicament was exacerbated by the difficulty of operating a sophisticated system of cabinet government in Nova Scotia where there existed neither disciplined parties nor the distinctive political principles or socio-economic antagonisms to create them. Since politics in Nova Scotia consisted of an internecine struggle to secure or retain office by all available means, political battles were fought with unrestrained ferocity and personal rancour.

Mulgrave became embroiled in these squabbles as a result of the election of May 1859 when the Conservative ministry of James William Johnston*, though defeated at the polls, refused to resign, as was later to become the accepted practice. In the absence of colonial precedents Mulgrave allowed the Conservatives to remain in office pending the next regular session of the legislature in January 1860, and rejected opposition demands for an early, special session to test the disposition of the lower house. When the assembly convened and the government was defeated in a vote of non-confidence early in February, he refused it a dissolution and William YOUNG then formed a Liberal administration. Further difficulties for Mulgrave arose from an exceptional flood of petitions which challenged the election of 20 of the 55 members on the ground that as holders of salaried public offices they were disqualified from sitting in the assembly under a provincial act of 1858. Liberal-dominated committees of the legislature proceeded to decide these controverted elections in favour of the Liberal candidates with such devious investigations and blatant bias that the Conservatives demanded a dissolution. When this was denied them by Mulgrave the Conservatives protested unavailingly to the colonial secretary, the Duke of Newcastle, when he was in the province in the summer of 1860, accompanying the Prince of Wales.

Mulgrave despaired of moderating the rabid factionalism of party contests with an infusion of the forbearance and courtesy he felt characterized British politics. During the early 1860s he saw no prospect that a federation of the British North American provinces would raise the level of political life and preferred the plan of maritime union as better suited to Nova Scotia's interests and less threatening to the imperial connection.

Mulgrave's interest was more congenially turned to a reorganization of the militia at a time when the outbreak of the American Civil War in 1861 focused attention on the state of defence in British North America. To remedy the unsatisfactory condition of the provincial militia, he encouraged the formation of volunteer rifle corps and persuaded the British authorities to supply modern weapons and instructors. By 1863 some 2,364 men had enrolled in 56 new volunteer companies formed by various ethnic groups and local communities; they provided their own equipment, accoutred themselves in exotic uniforms, and exhausted their martial ardour in rifle-shooting competitions. But Nova Scotian enthusiasm for the militia movement was a product of social fashion; after 1863 the craze passed and those volunteers who remained were gradually subsumed into the old battalions which sank back into their former state of inertia.

On the death of his father Mulgrave returned to England in July 1863 and spent the next seven years as lord-in-waiting to Queen Victoria and then captain of the corps of gentlemen-at-arms. In April 1871 he was appointed governor of Queensland, Australia. After an uneventful term he became in September 1874 governor of New Zealand where he clashed with the premier and refused a dissolution requested by him. In February 1879 Mulgrave was transferred to Victoria, Australia, where in 1881 he again fell into a similar dispute with the premier over a dissolution. Mulgrave left for England in August 1884 and retired from public life. He was created a privy councillor in 1851, KCMG in 1874, GCMG in 1877, and GCB in 1885.

Mulgrave was a colonial administrator of solid, business-like habits and considerable political sagacity who understood the complexities of constitutional practice and could manage men with a judicious blend of tact and firmness. But behind the conventional courtesy and preference for conciliation lay a strong, even stubborn, personality which was easily aroused when colonial politicians seemed to sacrifice public welfare for partisan purposes. Although he could be gracious and genial in conversation, he possessed a taciturn, somewhat humourless disposition. His undisguised indifference to popularity and dislike of vice-regal ostentation inhibited him from providing colonial society with the stylish, urbane leadership that was expected of a titled governor who no longer wielded effective political power.

PETER BURROUGHS

PANS, RG 2, sect.2, 1–2; RG 6, sect.2, 32. PRO, CO 217/221–32; CO 218/35–36. *Illustrated London News*, 20 Feb. 1858, 10 Feb. 1866, 19 April 1890. *Times* (London), 4 April 1890. *Whitby Gazette* (Whitby, Eng.), 11 April 1890. *DNB*. H. W. MacPhee, "The administration of the Earl of Mulgrave in Nova Scotia, 1858–1863" (MA thesis, Dalhousie Univ., Halifax, 1949). W. M. Whitelaw, *The Maritimes and Canada before confederation* (Toronto, 1934; repr. 1966). J. M. Beck, "The Nova Scotia 'disputed election' of 1859 and its aftermath," *CHR*, 36 (1955): 293–315.

PICKARD, HUMPHREY, Methodist minister, educator, and journalist; b. 10 June 1813 at Fredericton, N.B., son of Thomas Pickard and Mary Burpee; m. first 2 Oct. 1841 Hannah Maynard Thompson*, and they had two sons who died in early childhood; m. secondly 5 Sept. 1846 Mary Rowe Carr (d. 1887), and they had two daughters; d. 28 Feb. 1890 at Sackville, N.B.

Humphrey Pickard was the son of a Methodist businessman of New England descent. The religious influence of his home, and especially of his mother, was reinforced by his attendance from 1829 to 1831 at the Wesleyan Academy, Wilbraham, Mass., whose principal, Wilbur Fisk, was a leading figure in the Methodist Episcopal Church in the United States. In 1831 Pickard followed Fisk to the new Wesleyan University in Middletown, Conn. He returned to Fredericton to become a businessman after completing his first year of studies. Converted while a student and greatly influenced by Fisk's example, he decided in 1835 to become a Methodist minister and began by assisting Albert DesBrisay* in New Brunswick. After one year as a probationer, in Miramichi and in Fredericton, he returned to Wesleyan University in 1837, graduating in 1839.

Following his graduation, Pickard was stationed in the New Brunswick District of the British Wesleyan Conference, a missionary district administered by the Wesleyan Methodist Missionary Society. As an offshoot of the British conference, Methodism in the Maritime provinces was evangelical yet conservative, dominated by ministers sent from England, and dependent in its outlook. In 1841, after serving two years in Miramichi, Pickard was appointed to Saint John. He was ordained the following year and became editor of the *British North American Wesleyan Methodist Magazine*, the Methodist organ in the eastern colonies. The first years of his career coincided with the gradual emergence of a self-reliant attitude among his brethren, to which the parent conference would eventually respond. His first letter to the missionary society is characterized by an independent spirit, which in his case was nourished by the society's policy of according a lower status to ministers recruited in the colonies than to those secured in Britain.

Fortunately for Pickard, in January 1839 Charles Frederick Allison*, a prominent Methodist in Sackville, offered to build and endow a school in which "*Pure Religion* is not only taught, but *Constantly* brought before the youthful mind." This proposal was accepted eagerly by the missionaries who were determined to provide Methodist children with "an Education on Wesleyan Principles." In January 1843 the Mount Allison Wesleyan Academy, a preparatory school for boys, opened in Sackville, with Humphrey Pickard as its first principal. In his inaugural address of 29 June 1843 he defined education as "*that instruction and discipline which are necessary to prepare man for the duties and enjoyments of existence*"; in effect, it should raise man "from indulgence in gratification merely animal," and "lead him to seek acknowledged connexion and realized communion with God." To this end the curriculum would include classical literature, science, and philosophy. The Bible, however, he considered "our most valuable text book."

The academy, designed from the outset to diffuse knowledge and to form disciplined and moral characters in a Wesleyan atmosphere, proved to be highly successful and in 1848 the Methodists decided to establish a ladies' academy, which opened in 1854, also with Pickard as principal. The two academies provided instruction to the college matriculation level and a new institution, Mount Allison Wesleyan College (which later became Mount Allison University), opened its doors in 1862; Pickard was its president from 1862 to 1869.

In addition to his duties as founder and promoter of the principal Methodist educational institutions in the Maritimes, Pickard held numerous important posts. He was a major figure in the Wesleyan Methodist Conference of Eastern British America, an autonomous body established by the missionary society in 1855, and he served as its secretary from 1857 to

1860, its president in 1862 and 1870, and as a delegate to the British conference in 1857, 1862, and 1873. From 1869 to 1873 he was editor of the *Wesleyan* (Halifax), a Methodist newspaper, and book steward of the conference. Wesleyan University conferred a DD on him in 1857. When he retired from the active ministry in 1877 the conference in which he had served acknowledged his success in restoring several of its endeavours to sound financial positions.

After his death the *Wesleyan* commented that he had "an indomitable will and an immense capacity for work. . . . He was positive in speech and irresistible in debate; especially on all constitutional questions, and matters pertaining to the economy, discipline, or policy of the Church. For long years to come the presence of Dr. Humphrey Pickard will be missed from our council fires." An austere but sensitive man, he devoted himself with great tenacity and determination to the promotion of Methodism and higher education in a Christian context. His legacy was the academies and college in Sackville, and the great number of laymen and clergy whose minds were shaped by him as a teacher and minister.

G. S. FRENCH

Humphrey Pickard's "An inaugural address, delivered at the opening of the Wesleyan Academy, Mount Allison, Sackville, New Brunswick" was published in the *British North American Wesleyan Methodist Magazine* (Saint John, N.B., and Fredericton), 3 (1843): 281–92.

Methodist Missionary Soc. Arch. (London), Wesleyan Methodist Missionary Soc., Corr., Canada, 1837–47 (mfm. at UCA). United Church of Canada, Maritime Conference Arch. (Halifax), Joint meeting of Wesleyan Methodist missionaries from Nova Scotia, New Brunswick and Newfoundland districts, 12 July 1839; Wesleyan Methodist Church, New Brunswick District, Minutes, 1836, 2 Nov. 1842 (mfm. at UCA). Methodist Church (Canada, Newfoundland, Bermuda), New Brunswick and Prince Edward Island Conference, *Minutes* (Saint John), 1890. Methodist Church of Canada, New Brunswick and Prince Edward Island Conference, *Minutes* (Halifax), 1877. Edward Otheman, *Memoir and writings of Mrs. Hannah Maynard Pickard; late wife of Rev. Humphrey Pickard, A. M. . . .* (Boston, 1845). Wesleyan Methodist Church of Eastern British America, *Minutes* (Halifax), 1858; 1862; 1869–70. *Christian Guardian*, 19 March 1890. *Wesleyan* (Halifax), 1869–73, 1890.

Cornish, *Cyclopædia of Methodism*. *Cyclopædia of Canadian biog.* (Rose, 1888), 140–42. G. [S.] French, *Parsons & politics: the rôle of the Wesleyan Methodists in Upper Canada and the Maritimes from 1780 to 1855* (Toronto, 1962). D. W. Johnson, *History of Methodism in eastern British America, including Nova Scotia, New Brunswick, Prince Edward Island, Newfoundland and Bermuda . . .* ([Sackville, N.B.], n.d.). T. W. Smith, *History of the Methodist Church within the territories embraced in the late conference of eastern British America . . .* (2v., Halifax, 1877–90). David Allison, "Humphrey Pickard (1812–1890)," *Christian Guardian*, 9 March 1904.

PICKARD, JOHN, lumber merchant and politician; b. 27 April 1824 at Douglas, York County, N.B., son of David Pickard and Hephziba Burpee; m. in October 1851 Mary Yerxa; they had no children; d. 17 Dec. 1883 at Fredericton, N.B.

As a young man John Pickard worked with his father, a well-known mill-owner and merchant in Douglas. Pickard later established his own business as a general merchant in Fredericton and from the 1850s to the early 1880s was a prominent lumber merchant in York County. His partner for much of this period was Thomas Temple*, with whom he owned a large sawmill in Fredericton which in the 1850s produced an average of 25 million board feet of lumber yearly. Among other business ventures, Pickard was a founder and director with Temple, George Luther Hatheway*, Alexander Gibson*, and others of the People's Bank of New Brunswick, opened in Fredericton in 1864. He was also a director of the New Brunswick Railway Company which was incorporated in 1869, and one of the builders of the Fredericton branch of the railway completed in 1871. An active member in voluntary organizations, he was a master mason, grand master of the Orange order in New Brunswick from 1875 to 1878, and vice-president of the York County Agricultural Society in 1870, 1871, and 1878.

In 1865 Pickard became involved in politics when he and Charles Fisher* represented New Brunswick at a convention in Detroit at which a new reciprocal trade treaty between the British North American colonies and the United States was discussed. After the defeat of Samuel Leonard Tilley*'s government in the New Brunswick election in the spring of 1865, Pickard supported Albert James SMITH's administration in its opposition to New Brunswick's entry into a Canadian confederation. When John Campbell Allen*, Smith's attorney general, was appointed to the bench, Smith persuaded Pickard to oppose Charles Fisher in the York County by-election held in November 1865. Pickard was considered an ideal candidate because he was well known and liked in the county and it seemed that the pro-confederate Fisher stood little chance of success because he had been badly defeated in the earlier general election. However, on the hustings Fisher completely outclassed Pickard, who was not a good speaker. Pickard claimed that the majority opposed confederation, but he could not explain why, and Fisher resoundingly defeated him by more than 700 votes. The results of the closely watched battle gave new heart not only to the pro-confederates of New Brunswick but to their colleagues throughout British North America. Smith's government was forced out of office by Lieutenant Governor Arthur Hamilton Gordon* in April 1866 and on 1 July 1867 New Brunswick became one of the four provinces of Canada.

Pickard re-entered provincial politics in October 1867 by winning a by-election in York County called when Fisher switched to federal office. With Fisher appointed to the bench in October 1868, Pickard was elected by acclamation as member of parliament for York County; he was re-elected in 1872, 1874, 1878, and 1882. An independent Liberal, he supported Alexander Mackenzie*'s administration from 1874 to 1878 and frequently attacked Tilley, the leading New Brunswick Conservative. Pickard was especially bitter following the Liberals' defeat in 1878 when he accused Tilley of depriving him of the dispensation of patronage in York County because he opposed the new government. Although he vehemently attacked Sir John A. Macdonald*'s National Policy in 1882, Pickard's voice was seldom heard in parliament. He was described as a "practical legislator," and apparently had no special talent for politics. His repeated election by the voters of York County, however, testified to his reputation as an honest, friendly man who had earned people's respect as a merchant and public-spirited citizen.

William Arthur Spray

PANB, "N.B. political biog." (J. C. and H. B. Graves), II: 165. *Fredericton Evening Capital*, 18 Dec. 1883. *New Brunswick Reporter and Fredericton Advertiser*, 30 June, 27 Oct., 3, 10 Nov. 1865; 21 May, 6, 16 Oct. 1868; 9 July 1869; 14 Jan., 13 May 1870; 31 March 1871; 28 Jan. 1874; 16 Jan., 25 Sept. 1878; 2, 9, 16 July, 10 Dec. 1879; 19, 22 Dec. 1883. *Canadian biog. dict.*, II. *Canadian directory of parl.* (J. K. Johnson). *CPC*, 1883. *Dominion annual register*, 1883. Creighton, *Macdonald, young politician*; *Road to confederation*. *Fredericton's 100 years; then and now*, ed. Frank Baird (Fredericton, [1948]). Hannay, *Hist. of N.B.*; *Wilmot and Tilley* (Toronto, 1907). MacNutt, *New Brunswick*.

PIED DE CORBEAU. *See* Isapo-muxika

PIGEON. *See* Mīmīy

PILOTE, FRANÇOIS, Roman Catholic priest and educator; b. 4 Oct. 1811 at Saint-Antoine-de-Tilly, Lower Canada, son of Ambroise Pilote, a farmer, and Marguerite Coulombe; d. 5 April 1886 at Saint-Augustin-de-Desmaures, Que.

François Pilote studied at the Petit Séminaire de Québec from 1823 to 1832; he was a brilliant student. Ordained priest on 9 Aug. 1835, he lived for a while at the Séminaire de Nicolet, where he taught theology until 1836. That year he also became assistant to the director, Joseph-Onésime Leprohon*. At the end of 1836 he entered the Collège de Sainte-Anne-de-la-Pocatière (in what is now La Pocatière), where he was to spend 34 years, holding a series of offices: assistant director (1836–38), director (1838–47, 1851–57), bursar (1839–53, 1857–60, 1863–69), vice-superior (1852), and superior (1853–62, 1869–70). In 1870 he was appointed parish priest of Saint-Augustin, at Saint-Augustin-de-Desmaures, a post he retained for the rest of his life. His career as a parish priest seems uneventful in comparison with his years as an administrator in an educational institution. He is remembered because of his pronounced interest in the settlement of the Saguenay region, but more particularly for his efforts to promote scientific farming. On the other hand, running the Collège de Sainte-Anne-de-la-Pocatière really absorbed the better part of his energy.

Pilote's career perhaps illustrates the kind of problems that college administrators faced in the middle of the 19th century. Struggling with shortages of staff, men of his stamp were obliged to hold several posts simultaneously, even before they had gained experience in their working environment. In 1839 Abbé Pilote was director, bursar, and professor of theology. In 1842, when the college was enlarged in order to offer a commercial course, he was responsible for supervising construction work. In the absence of the superior, Alexis Mailloux*, Pilote had to assume authority. This overload of work meant that he was always exhausted. He was authoritarian, took decisions without consultation, and soon made enemies among his subordinates. To tame the opposition, he had no hesitation in interpreting rather freely the terms of appointment of the priests who were on the teaching staff under his direction. If a teacher attached to the institution showed signs of opposition, Pilote asked the bishop to summon the dissident staff member to parochial duties.

Pilote and his subordinates sometimes came into conflict over money matters. For example, during the school year 1853–54 a movement demanding revision of salaries developed among the clergy attached to the college as teachers. For some 10 years at least, the annual remuneration of the teachers had remained at £25. In December 1854 the staff asked for an increase of more than 30 per cent; after all the pupils' fees for board and lodging had just been raised. Pointing to the state of the college's finances, Pilote adamantly refused to grant any increase. Pierre-Flavien Turgeon*, the archbishop of Quebec, suggested granting wage parity with the teachers at the Séminaire de Québec. Hence in 1855 the remuneration of the priests engaged in teaching rose from £25 to £30. But eight years later the college's indebtedness forced the staff to accept a reduction in salary. Those who accused Pilote of squandering the financial resources of the college in the purchase of a property for the model farm and school of agriculture that he founded at Sainte-Anne-de-la-Pocatière in 1859, considered their criticisms even more justified. The salary reduction, which was decreed during the summer holidays of 1863, provided the resolution of the situation. Pilote judged it wise to resign, for the conflict had mobilized a number of the students and alarmed the public. But it was questionable whether the institution's prestige could be restored without the resumption of a position of authority by the person who had guided its material fortunes. After a trip to Europe "for his health," Pilote returned to undertake financial management of the college as bursar from 1863 to 1869. During this period he made repeated efforts to balance income and expenditures. It proved particularly difficult to obtain loans; creditors were becoming increasingly demanding. In 1867 the sale of some 2,000 acres of wooded land for $3,000 met only the pressing debts. Fees for the pupils' board and lodging increased substantially, reaching $90 annually, $20 and $10 more than those of the Collège de Rimouski and the Collège de Lévis respectively. Despite these extreme measures, the institution was faced with a debt of about $100,000 when Pilote left it in 1870. However, a subscription raised from the clergy of the whole province enabled it to stave off bankruptcy.

Pilote was widely remembered as a promoter of both settlement and agricultural education. "Our people, [who are] basically farmers and merchants, need to receive instruction in agriculture and trade," he wrote in 1855. He was of the opinion that the commercial course introduced at the Collège de Sainte-Anne-de-la-Pocatière in 1842 initiated the young in business procedures. Conscious that the liberal professions were overcrowded and that demographic pressures were particularly acute in the region of the south shore, he thought steps should be taken to ensure the expansion of the area under cultivation, and at the same time to improve farming practices. Consequently in 1848 he helped Abbé Nicolas-Tolentin HÉBERT to set up the Association des Comtés de L'Islet et de Kamouraska pour coloniser le Saguenay. Its corresponding secretary at the outset, he soon became its president. In 1850 he visited the Saguenay and Lac Saint-Jean region to make an inventory of its resources. On the basis of this exploratory trip he wrote a booklet entitled *Le Saguenay en 1851*, in which he recounted the history of the region and expressed the views of the clergy of his generation; according to him, settlement was a means of national survival, to the degree that it would check emigration to the United States. Closely involved in running the Association des Comtés de L'Islet et de Kamouraska, Pilote in 1850 warned the merchant and politician Jean-Charles CHAPAIS that public funds were being embezzled to the detriment of the settlers; a lumber company had in fact appropriated a sum intended for opening up settlement roads in order to build timber slides. In 1856 the association was dissolved; Pilote undertook in 1866 the liquidation of its affairs.

Pilote was also responsible for founding in 1859 the first agricultural school in Canada. At his suggestion, the Collège de Sainte-Anne-de-la-Pocatière gave permission for a model farm to be established on the property which he had largely assembled himself. Since the mid 1850s, the government of the Province of Canada had been planning to create institutions for training teachers. Despite the support of Chapais and Étienne Parent*, Pilote had not succeeded in persuading Pierre-Joseph-Olivier CHAUVEAU and George-Étienne Cartier* to establish a teachers' college at Sainte-Anne-de-la-Pocatière, to be integrated, he hoped, into his project of an agricultural school. In his view, teachers would have to receive their training in rural surroundings, to be made aware of the new importance of agriculture. Nevertheless, with the help of the influential Chapais, the school of agriculture was brought into existence. As a member of the legislature, Chapais first obtained special grants to enlarge the college. Then in 1858 he persuaded Cartier to withhold two and a half per cent of the subsidies to agricultural societies, in order to create a school for farmers. The school was opened in 1859, but in the succeeding 11 years only 94 students attended. This was a small number, considering the fact that the Board of Agriculture of Lower Canada offered $50 scholarships – 10 in 1863, 20 from 1864 on. In order to induce parents to enrol their children, Pilote vainly sought to secure payment of a scholarship higher than $50 per boarder. Instead of increasing, the number of students declined: seven in 1867, six in 1878, and three in 1869. It proved just as impossible as it was in France and the United States to attract large numbers to this kind of specialized institution. The government of Quebec, which had acquired jurisdiction over agricultural education in 1867, was concerned about the situation, especially since the two agricultural schools of the province, at Sainte-Anne-de-la-Pocatière and L'Assomption, received annual grants of $2,000, in addition to the amount expended on scholarships. A sub-committee of the Council of Agriculture of the province of Quebec launched an inquiry in the autumn of 1869. The commissioners concluded that young people were dissuaded from attending agricultural schools by the poverty of their parents, the unwillingness to lose free labour in a family operation, and the prejudice against science, combined with the attraction of classical education. The alternative proposed by Cléophe Cimon, a former MLA, and endorsed by the sub-committee, endangered the very existence of these institutions. Insisting on practical teaching, Cimon had been proposing the creation of one model farm per county since 1868. But Pilote thought it was necessary to combine theory and practice, and considered increasing the number of model farms to be a costly solution. In fact, he did not want farmers ever to associate their productivity with government subsidies. Pilote was so influential that Chauveau, the premier of the province of Quebec, had to abandon plans of reform, including his own idea of transferring agricultural education to the teachers' colleges in Quebec City or Montreal.

After leaving the Collège de Sainte-Anne-de-la Pocatière for the parish of Saint-Augustin in 1870, Pilote continued to take an interest in agricultural improvements. In Portneuf County, subscriptions to *La Gazette des campagnes* (Saint-Louis-de-Kamouraska and Sainte-Anne-de-la-Pocatière), a paper started in 1861 which was the organ of the school of agriculture, rose to 600, as a result of Pilote's efforts to circulate it. Practising what he preached, the parish priest even installed drain-pipes on the property owned by the parish council. The improved yield of the soil proved so persuasive to farmers that around 1886 a workshop for making drain-pipes was set up in the parish. On the provincial scene, Pilote remained until his death an active member of the Council of Agriculture, which had been instituted by the Quebec government after confederation. Little is known about the way in which Pilote discharged his duties as a parish priest, except that he contracted a personal debt of several thousand dollars in order to build a convent, which he made over to the Congregation of Notre-Dame in 1882.

SERGE GAGNON

Among François Pilote's writings are *Le Saguenay en 1851; histoire du passé, du présent et de l'avenir probable du Haut-Saguenay, au point de vue de la colonisation* (Québec, 1852); *Mémoire sur la paroisse, le village, le collège et l'école d'agriculture de Sainte-Anne devant accompagner divers objets envoyés par le collège Ste. Anne à l'Exposition universelle de Paris, en 1867* (Sainte-Anne-de-la-Pocatière [La Pocatière], Qué., 1867); and *Examen d'un plan de culture proposé par M. Cléophe Cimon, ci-devant député de Charlevoix . . .* (Sainte-Anne-de-la-Pocatière, 1868).

Arch. du collège de Sainte-Anne-de-la-Pocatière (La Pocatière), 13-31; 59-68. Julienne Barnard, *Mémoires Chapais; documentation, correspondance, souvenirs* (4v., Montréal et Paris, 1961–64), I–II. Auguste Béchard, *Galerie nationale: l'abbé François Pilote, curé de Saint-Augustin (Portneuf)* (Sainte-Anne-de-la-Pocatière, 1885). Adrien Bernier, *The contributions of the schools of Sainte-Anne-de-la-Pocatière to Catholic education in the province of Quebec* (Quebec, 1942). Serge Gagnon, "Le collège de Sainte-Anne au temps de l'abbé François Pilote: les conflits du personnel enseignant" (thèse de DES, univ. Laval, Québec, 1968). M. Hamelin, *Premières années du parlementarisme québécois*. Wilfrid Lebon, *Histoire du collège de Sainte-Anne-de-la-Pocatière* (2v., Québec, 1948–49). M.-A. Perron, *Un grand éducateur agricole: Édouard-A. Barnard, 1835–1898; essai historique sur l'agriculture de 1760 à 1900* ([Montréal], 1955). Normand Séguin, *La conquête du sol au 19e siècle* (s.l., [1977]). Serge Gagnon, "Le clergé, les notables et l'enseignement privé au Québec: le cas du collège de Sainte-Anne, 1840–1870," *SH*, no.5 (April 1970): 45–65.

PIM, BEDFORD CLAPPERTON TREVELYAN, naval officer and Arctic explorer; b. 12 June 1826 at Bideford, England, son of Edward Bedford Pim and Sophia Soltau Harrison; m. 3 Oct. 1861 Susanna Locock, and they had two sons; d. 30 Sept. 1886 at Deal, Kent, England.

Bedford Clapperton Trevelyan Pim was educated at the Royal Naval School, New Cross, and entered the Royal Navy in 1842. In 1845 he was appointed to the *Herald*, commanded by Captain Henry Kellett*, who had been commissioned to prepare Admiralty charts of the Pacific coast of Central America and Lower California. In the summer of 1849 the *Herald* was called to assist the *Plover* in the search of the seas north of the Bering Strait for the ships of Sir John Franklin* which had not been heard from since 1845. During the winter of 1849–50 Pim served under Captain Thomas Edward Laws Moore of the *Plover* which was based in Kotzebue Sound on the west coast of Alaska. From here Pim was ordered to make a journey to Mikhailovsk (Egg Island, Alaska), to question the Inuit of that area concerning Franklin's lost ships. This trip, although not successful in tracing Franklin, gave Pim valuable experience in travel by dog sledge in the Arctic. The *Herald* reached England in June 1851 and was paid off; Pim was promoted lieutenant on 6 September.

In the winter of 1851–52 Pim, with official British support, made a journey to St Petersburg (Leningrad, U.S.S.R.) in an unsuccessful endeavour to promote a search for the Franklin expedition on the north Siberian shore. After his return to England he sailed, in April 1852, on the *Resolute*, one of the five ships of the Franklin rescue squadron commanded by Sir Edward Belcher*. On entering Barrow Strait Belcher turned up Wellington Channel, ordering *Resolute* and *Intrepid*, the former commanded by Kellett and the latter by Francis Leopold McClintock*, to go west and search the Melville Island region. They were also told to keep a lookout for the rescue ship *Investigator*, commanded by Robert John LeMesurier McClure*, which had entered the Arctic by Bering Strait and had gone unreported for two years.

On 9 Sept. 1852 Kellett's party berthed near the Melville Island shore just east of Winter Harbour. Lieutenant George Frederick Mecham* visited the latter place and found a cached record of the *Investigator*. It stated that after discovering the last link in the northwest passage McClure had become ice-bound for months across Viscount Melville Sound on the north shore of Banks Island. It was too late for help to reach McClure that season, but as the starving crew was likely to desert their ship in early spring in a desperate attempt to reach the mainland, Pim was dispatched with two sledges. The larger man-hauled sledge broke down and Pim crossed the sound to Banks Island with two men, Robert Hoyle and Thomas Bidgood, in the bitter cold of March 1853 with a light dog sledge. It was a daring venture and was only warranted by extreme emergency. The inordinately long time spent on the journey, 28 days for 160 miles, may be explained by inexperience, foul weather, and the fact that McClure had been inexact in giving his position. Pim probably had to follow the shore of Banks Island to find the *Investigator*'s anchorage which was at Mercy Bay. He accomplished this on 6 April, just in time to avert the desertion of most of the ship's crew, an action which certainly would have been fatal to all who shared in it.

On their way home, carrying the 63 rescued men, Kellett's ship and its steam-tender were frozen in and spent the winter in the pack of Barrow Strait, and Belcher's ships were also ice-bound in Wellington Channel. In the spring of 1854 four ships were abandoned and the crews were taken to England on the *North Star* commanded by William John Samuel PULLEN and on two supply vessels; they arrived in England on 28 September. Kellett naturally expected that he and his men, who had rescued the discoverers of the northwest passage, would share in the £10,000 award granted for that achievement. McClure, by his impudent and somewhat unscrupulous assertion that he could have preserved the lives of his crew unaided, secured the entire reward for himself and his crew. This was particularly unjust to Pim whose exertions in saving the lives of the men and averting the scandal of a second Franklin disaster were rewarded by neither promotion nor any other public mark of distinction. However, he may have felt recompensed by the tribute from a gathering of the petty officers and men of the *Investigator* who, with more honesty than their captain, assured him that "Were it not for you, sir, many of us now present would never have seen old England again."

In January 1855 Pim was appointed to command the *Magpie* in the Baltic during the Crimean War, and in April 1857 to command the *Banterer* in Chinese waters, sustaining wounds on both services. In June 1859 he was promoted commander and assigned to the *Gorgon* on the West Indian station. While holding this commission he surveyed the proposed route for a canal to the Pacific across Nicaragua. He took a personal interest in this venture and when he became financially involved was censured by the Admiralty. He then served on the *Fury*, returned to England, and retired from active service in June 1861. In the course of seniority he became post captain in 1868 and rear-admiral in 1885.

As a civilian Pim made three more journeys to America in the interests of the Nicaraguan railway, a project abandoned in 1869. He then studied law and was admitted to the bar on 23 Jan. 1873, establishing a practice in which he dealt principally with Admiralty cases. He was elected MP for Gravesend, Kent, as a Conservative in 1874 and again in 1880. He had been elected a fellow of the Royal Geographical Society in 1854, and an associate of the Institute of Civil Engineers in April 1861. His services to seamen are commemorated by a memorial tablet and window in the church of the Seamen's Institute at Bristol. He was the best type of Victorian adventurer, "a true-hearted sailor of the old school, brave, generous and unselfish."

L. H. NEATBY

Bedford Clapperton Trevelyan Pim's works are listed in *National union catalog*. He is also the anonymous author of *Euryalus; tales of the sea, a few leaves from the diary of a midshipman* (London, 1860).

Baker Memorial Library, Dartmouth College (Hanover, N.H.), Stefansson coll., B. C. T. Pim, Notebook. Alexander Armstrong, *A personal narrative of the discovery of the north-west passage . . .* (London, 1857). [Edward Belcher], *The last of the Arctic voyages . . . in search of Sir John Franklin, during the years 1852–53–54 . . .* (2v., London, 1855). G. F. M'Dougall, *The eventful voyage of H.M. discovery ship "Resolute" to the Arctic regions . . .* (London, 1857). [J. A. Miertsching], *Frozen ships: the Arctic diary of Johann Miertsching, 1850–1854*, trans. and ed. L. H. Neatby (Toronto, 1967). B. [C.] Seeman, *Narrative of the voyage of H.M.S. Herald during the years 1845–51 . . .* (2v., London, 1853). *DNB*. L. H. Neatby, *The search for Franklin* (New York, 1970). Noel Wright, *Quest for Franklin* (London and Toronto, 1959).

PINSONEAULT, PIERRE-ADOLPHE (sometimes spelled **Pinsonnault** or **Pinsonault**, but he signed Pinsoneault), Roman Catholic priest, Sulpician, and bishop; b. 23 Nov. 1815 at Saint-Philippe-de-Laprairie, Lower Canada, son of Paul-Théophile Pinsoneault and Clotilde Raymond; d. 30 Jan. 1883 in Montreal, Que.

Pierre-Adolphe Pinsoneault belonged to a wealthy and influential family. His maternal grandfather, Jean-Baptiste Raymond*, was a prosperous businessman of La Tortue (Saint-Mathieu), and his father, who was a notary, was also involved in administering seigneuries and various other undertakings; two of his uncles, Jean-Moïse Raymond* and Joseph Masson*, held important positions in the business world. Pinsoneault studied at the Petit Séminaire de Montréal from 1824 to 1835. He was attracted to law but in the end chose an ecclesiastical career and entered the Grand Séminaire de Montréal. Continuing his studies at the Séminaire de Saint-Sulpice in Paris, he was ordained priest at Issy-les-Moulineaux, near Paris, on 19 Dec. 1840. He taught at the Petit Séminaire de Montréal from 1841 to 1843, and then from 1843 to 1849 ministered to the congregation of St Patrick's Church, which served the English-speaking Catholics of Montreal. In October 1848, although a Sulpician, he sided with the bishop of Montreal, Ignace BOURGET, in the controversy over the establishment of churches or chapels in the *faubourgs* of Montreal. The Sulpicians were opposed to a division of the parish of Notre-Dame, the only one in Montreal, which they administered. Pinsoneault declared to Bourget that he would never tolerate the kind of defiance of the Canadian episcopacy that the Society of Saint-Sulpice was showing. It may have been for this reason that he left the order in 1849, the year he was promoted canon of the cathedral in Montreal, a post he retained until 1856.

On 3 June 1854 the bishops of the ecclesiastical province of Quebec petitioned Pope Pius IX for the erection of two new dioceses in Canada West, at Hamilton and London. Within each diocese there would be a population of about 230,000, the majority, however, being Protestant. Through the good offices of the bishop of Toronto, Armand-François-Marie de Charbonnel*, whose secretariat he had temporarily been assigned to reorganize in 1850, Pinsoneault was able to write in August 1854 that he was preparing himself "more immediately for the awesome ministry to which divine Providence destined [him] in the very near future." Seven months later he confided to Bourget: "He [Charbonnel] writes to me often, and I can assure you that he is much more anxious that I am to see the matters now pending in Rome concluded." Pinsoneault was clearly Charbonnel's candidate for the bishopric of London, and this choice had the approval of Bourget. It was not, however, until 21 Feb. 1856 that Rome issued the decree for the erection of the diocese of London; its territory, carved from the diocese of Toronto, was to cover the counties of Middlesex, Lambton, Elgin, Kent, Essex, Huron, Perth, Oxford, and Norfolk. London became the episcopal see, and the incumbent, a suffragan to the archbishop of Quebec. On 18 May 1856 Pinsoneault was consecrated bishop by Charbonnel, who was assisted by two other bishops.

More than a month before Pinsoneault's consecration, a thorny problem had arisen. Father Thaddeus T. Kirwan, the parish priest of London, with the support of a number of his parishioners, objected to having a new French-speaking bishop come and take over his church as a cathedral, as well as to Pinsoneault's intention to replace the nuns of the Institute of the Blessed Virgin Mary with the Sisters of Charity of Providence of Montreal (Sisters of Providence). While vowing not to leave Montreal before the difficulty was settled, Pinsoneault stated that the London community "must submit like obedient children" under pain of being deprived of the services of the church. He even considered the possibility of "excommunicating" London. Despite the opposition, he took possession of his see on 29 June 1856. Following numerous threats from Pinsoneault, Father Kirwan was appointed parish priest of Port Sarnia (Sarnia) in the autumn of 1856, after receiving 1,800 *écus* from the bishop. According to Pinsoneault, Kirwan's grievances could be met by "buying him off," which was, in truth, the case. It is not possible to determine from available sources who was right in this conflict, but it can be said that Bishop Pinsoneault was very severe in his judgement of Kirwan; he even accused Kirwan of selling some land belonging to the London church without authorization from the bishop. Although Charbonnel had been in Europe since July 1856, Pinsoneault held him responsible for the Kirwan affair and accused him of having given insufficient attention to the matter of the new bishop's coming to London.

Pinsoneault was just as severe towards the priests of his diocese. Writing to Bishop Joseph La Rocque, the administrator of the diocese of Saint-Hyacinthe, in March 1857, he stressed that their "cupidity . . . is horrible," and declared that those who refused to submit to his new directives "will shear other sheep than mine." Disappointed in the quality of his clerics, Pinsoneault was determined never to allow them "the privilege of obtruding themselves or of trifling with me in the discharge of my official duties." He also had to deal with the complaints of the Irish Catholics, who regularly wrote to the newspapers denouncing "the French influence" and "the French-Canadian bishop of London."

At the beginning of January 1858 Pinsoneault left London; he established himself at Sandwich and on 25 January asked his ecclesiastical superiors in Quebec City to transfer the see there. The bishop justified his request by noting that London had no more than 800 communicants; there was not even enough work for one priest, the parish having celebrated only 20 marriages and 140 baptisms in 1857. Moreover, St Peter's Cathedral, a small London parish, had to find the $3,000 necessary to maintain the bishop but was already burdened with a debt of $10,000. Pinsoneault stated that the establishment of the episcopal see at London had been a mistake. Although Jean-Charles Prince*, the bishop of Saint-Hyacinthe, roundly denounced Pinsoneault's letter of 25 January, the latter, with the support of a substantial majority of the bishops, asked Rome during the summer of 1858 for an official transfer of the seat of the bishopric; Sandwich, he emphasized, had the finest church in the diocese, a sufficient number of clergy (attached to Assumption College) to provide the religious services worthy of a bishopric, and the largest concentration of worshippers. On 2 Feb. 1859 the prefect of the Sacred Congregation of Propaganda issued the decree transferring the episcopal see. Pinsoneault, who had gone to Rome to back his request, returned to Quebec on 30 May 1859 after an absence of more than seven months.

Pinsoneault's episcopal career was marred by another quarrel with a priest of his diocese, which contributed to the bishop's resignation in 1866. While he was in London, he had had differences with Jean Daudet, the parish priest of Amherstburg and a native of France. In 1862 Pinsoneault asked Daudet to resign because of his "physical and moral infirmities." He reproached him for no longer reading his breviary, for spending months on end without going to confession, for not saying mass during the week, for being drunk frequently, and also for having accused the bishop himself of illegal transfer of funds and of scandal-mongering. In September Pinsoneault stripped him of authority and replaced him with Joseph Zoëgal, who according to Daudet was the source of the accusations against him. A number of parishioners protested against the bishop's proceedings by invading the presbytery; returning to the charge, Pinsoneault had Daudet's sworn statement read from the pulpit, and denied the sacraments to the recalcitrant parishioners.

The exiled priest took up residence at St Michael's College in Toronto. Pinsoneault warned John Joseph LYNCH, the bishop of Toronto, that Daudet was "a spiteful, two-faced man," and received backing from his vicar general, Jean-Marie Bruyère. In December 1862, taking Bourget's advice, Daudet launched an appeal to his metropolitan, Charles-François Baillargeon*, archbishop of Quebec, against his bishop's decision; Baillargeon in turn decided to submit the case to Rome. The matter was a delicate one: Bourget stated to Cardinal Alessandro Barnabo that Daudet had given him complete satisfaction during his several years of ministry in Montreal, and the bishop-administrator of Detroit invited Daudet to come and live in his palace. Rome responded by appointing Baillargeon a commissioner of the Holy See for the purpose of settling the case. Baillargeon conducted an inquiry from April to October 1863, and, having heard both parties, gave a verdict in favour of Daudet on 28 Oct. 1863. Pinsoneault decided to appeal to Rome immediately. He suggested to the prefect of the Sacred Congregation of Propaganda that a commission of inquiry be set up, and he undertook to accept the commission's ruling as final. On 31 Jan. 1864 Pius IX issued a decree establishing a commission composed of Bourget of Montreal, Joseph-Bruno Guigues* of Ottawa, and Edward John Horan* of Kingston. The inquiry was held in Kingston on 14, 15, and 16 July 1864. After hearing various witnesses, the commissioners decided that the accusations against Daudet were unfounded, and that the expelled priest should be reinstated in his parish, although he must remain subject to the authority of his bishop. Yet the affair was not over. Daudet continued to complain about his bishop's attitude towards him. On 2 Nov. 1864 Pinsoneault appointed Daudet to Immaculée-Conception, a parish at Paincourt, relieving him of his duties at Amherstburg. The parish priest refused to hand over the presbytery, even when the bishop appointed a new incumbent on 3 December. Daudet appealed to the Holy See against his bishop's decision; he also wrote to all the bishops in Canada and obtained signatures for a petition against Pinsoneault's tyranny. Finally, in February 1865, Rome ordered Daudet to obey Pinsoneault or leave the diocese. Daudet chose to depart.

Daudet was not, however, the only one to complain about Pinsoneault. From December 1864 other priests followed his example and appealed to Rome for various reasons: Kirwan, who had been relieved of his office as parish priest of Port Sarnia in the summer of 1864 for having "broken away from any episcopal control"; the parish priest of Strathroy, who had been suspended and relieved of his duties in October of that year after having been denounced by several "respectable women" and having refused to discuss the matter with his bishop; and the parish priest of Irishtown (St Columban), who had likewise been suspended for dragging Pinsoneault into court over the bishop's refusal to repay a loan. The bishop had also come into conflict with several religious communities since his arrival at London. In 1859 the Jesuits had left Assumption College, which they had built at Sandwich, because of disagreements with Pinsoneault over administrative problems. Nor had their successors, the Benedictines of St Vincent's Abbey in the diocese of Pittsburgh, escaped the harassment of the bishop, who in 1862 had demanded the dismissal of the superior of the college. Unable "to obtain the English and French teachers indispensable for the educational needs of this diocese," the community left Sandwich in the summer of 1863. The Sisters of Charity of the Hôpital Général of Montreal (Grey Nuns), who had been established in the Essex peninsula since 1857, also had differences with Pinsoneault. In 1861 a quarrel broke out between the bishop and the mother house in Montreal. He wanted to have a say in the running of the local community, and he sought to make it into a house independent from the one in Montreal. The superior general in Montreal, whom Pinsoneault considered dictatorial and uncompromising, raised objections, and in the autumn of 1861 recalled the sisters to Montreal. The bishop complained about his reputation as a "destroyer of communities," but in truth those who managed to escape his condemnation were the exceptions. In time, Pinsoneault made enemies of a good many of the clergy. He despised Charbonnel and wrangled from time to time with various bishops in Canada East. Although he accused several of his priests of cupidity and laxity, he often treated himself to pleasure trips, spending winters in Cuba, Europe, and other places. He also misused his power of laying clerics, laymen, and parishes under interdict or excommunication.

When Bourget went to Rome in the winter of 1864–65, he was instructed by the Holy See to ask the bishop of London to tender his resignation. Bourget waited a year before carrying out this delicate task, and did not meet Pinsoneault until the summer of 1866. He advised him at that time to resign "in order to put an end to the discords prevailing in [his] diocese." Bourget repeated his advice on 17 August, warning Pinsoneault "that the continual accusations being taken to Rome against [his] administration" could only lead to a canonical inquiry, whose consequences might be disastrous for him in the event the charges proved justified. On 23 August Pinsoneault replied that he accepted, and on 9 Sept. 1866 he submitted a letter of resignation, advancing reasons of health (he was suffering from growing deafness) and the need for new blood in the diocese. In November 1867 John Walsh* was consecrated bishop of Sandwich.

During his ten years as bishop, at both London and Sandwich, Pinsoneault had brought a number of religious communities into his diocese, but had quarrelled with most of them. He had endeavoured to stabilize the finances of the diocese by instituting various taxes, rents, and diocesan collections. After his departure, however, the administrator of the diocese, Abbé Bruyère, could not avoid noting the deplorable state of diocesan finances, expenditures being four times the receipts. There is no doubt that this situation had also been a factor in Pinsoneault's dismissal.

Pinsoneault was transferred to the see of Birtha on 26 Nov. 1866, and lived in Albany, N.Y., until 1869, when he returned to Montreal. Under his ultramontane superior, Bourget, he carried out a number of responsibilities that required the presence of a bishop, presiding over ceremonies and performing the duties of an auxiliary. Pinsoneault took up the defence of ultramontane ideology in his publication *Le dernier chant du cygne sur le tumulus du gallicanisme; réponse à monseigneur Dupanloup* (Montreal, 1870). He struck down the advocates of liberalism in his *Lettres à un député* (1874), and helped edit ultramontane newspapers such as *Le Franc-Parleur.*

Bishop Pinsoneault died on 30 Jan. 1883 in Montreal, at the age of 67. His authoritarian behaviour and his lack of consideration for others had doomed his episcopacy to failure.

J. E. ROBERT CHOQUETTE

Pierre-Adolphe Pinsoneault was the author of *Le dernier chant du cygne sur le tumulus du gallicanisme; réponse à monseigneur Dupanloup* (Montréal, 1870) and *Lettres à un député* (Montréal, 1874).

ACAM, 255.113, 856–9, 858–2, 862–4, 864–25, –28, –31, –32, –33, –36, –39, –41; 465.101, 848–3, –4; 901.085, 850–1, 854–1, 855–1; RLB, 12: 658; 14: 491; 15: 229–31, 242, 256–58, 403–5. Arch. of the Diocese of London (London, Ont.), Letterbooks, 1–6 (1856–66); Register of official docs., 1856–59: 1–19. Allaire, *Dictionnaire*, I: 436. Beaulieu et J. Hamelin, *La presse québécoise*, I: 113. Gérard Brassard, *Armorial des évêques du Canada . . .* (Montréal, 1940). *Dominion annual register*, 1883. Cyprien Tanguay, *Répertoire général du clergé canadien par ordre chronologique depuis la fondation de la colonie jusqu'à nos jours* (Québec, 1868). *The city and diocese of London, Ontario, Canada: an historical sketch . . .*, comp. J. F. Coffey (London, 1885). N. F. Eid, *Le clergé et le pouvoir politique au Québec: une analyse de l'idéologie ultramontaine au milieu du XIXe siècle* (Montréal, 1978). J. K. A. Farrell [O'Farrell], "The history of the Roman Catholic Church in London, Ontario, 1826–1931" (MA thesis, Univ. of Western Ontario, London, 1949). *The township of Sandwich (past and present) . . .*, comp. Frederick Neal (Windsor, Ont., 1909).

PISQUA. *See* PASKWĀW

PĪTIKWAHANAPIWĪYIN (Poundmaker), Plains Cree chief; b.*c.* 1842 in what is now central Saskatchewan, the son of Sīkākwayān (Skunk Skin), a Stony Indian, and a mixed-blood mother; d. 4 July 1886 at Blackfoot Crossing (Alta).

Poundmaker was born into a prominent Plains Cree family from the House band, his maternal uncle being Mistawāsis (Big Child), a leading chief in the Eagle Hill (Alta) area. Although his mother was a descendant of a French Canadian, Poundmaker was entirely Plains Cree in culture and appearance. Robert Jefferson, the farm instructor on the Poundmaker Reserve, writing some years after Poundmaker's death, described him as "tall and good looking, slightly built and with an intelligent face, in which a large Roman nose was prominent; his bearing was so eminently dignified and his speech so well adapted to the occasion, as to impress every hearer with his earnestness and his views."

A trader who encountered Poundmaker in the late 1860s recalled that at that time "he was just an ordinary Indian, [an] ordinary man as other Indians." Poundmaker's life changed, however, after Crowfoot [ISAPO-MUXIKA], a head chief of the Blackfoot, lost a son in 1873 during a raid on a Cree camp. Not long after, when a short-lived peace treaty was made between the two tribes, one of Crowfoot's wives saw Poundmaker and was struck by his resemblance to her dead son. The Blackfoot chief immediately adopted the Cree and invited him to remain with the Blackfeet at Blackfoot Crossing, giving Poundmaker a Blackfoot name, Makoyi-koh-kin (Wolf Thin Legs).

When Poundmaker returned to the Crees, his influence with the Blackfeet as Crowfoot's son and the wealth in horses gained from his new family gave him increased status among his own people. By August 1876, when the Indians of central Saskatchewan came together at Fort Carlton to negotiate a treaty with the Canadian government, he was considered to be a councillor, or minor chief, under Pihew-kamihkosit (Red Pheasant) of the River People band. Unlike his uncle, Mistawāsis, Poundmaker questioned the intent of Treaty no.6 after the lieutenant governor of Manitoba and governor of the North-West Territories, Alexander MORRIS, outlined the terms. Poundmaker claimed that the government should be prepared to provide the Indians, including future generations, with instruction in farming and assistance after the buffalo had gone, in exchange for their lands. When the lieutenant governor demurred, Poundmaker said that he had no knowledge of building houses or farming, and added: "From what I can hear and see now, I cannot understand that I shall be able to clothe my children and feed them as long as the sun shines and water runs." In the end, however, Poundmaker accepted the terms of the treaty and signed on 23 Aug. 1876. Two years later, when Pihew-kamihkosit agreed to settle on a reserve, Poundmaker formed his own band which continued to hunt the diminishing herds of buffalo, but in 1879 he too accepted a reserve and settled at the confluence of Battle River and Cut Knife Creek, about 40 miles west of Battleford (Sask.); he continued to hunt whenever the opportunity arose.

In 1881, Poundmaker was chosen to accompany the Marquess of Lorne [Campbell*], governor general of Canada, on a tour from Battleford to Blackfoot Crossing. During this trip, Poundmaker impressed the viceregal party with his knowledge of Cree culture and his philosophy as a peacemaker. Poundmaker, too, was impressed with the information gained from the dignitaries and several months later, when providing a feast for his band, he urged his followers to remain peaceful; ". . . the whites will fill the country," he said, "and they will dictate to us as they please. It is useless to dream that we can frighten them, that time has passed. Our only resource is our work, our industry, our farms."

In 1883 as part of a government economy drive many Indian Department employees were dismissed and rations to the Indians reduced. Delays in delivering supplies caused rumours to spread that rations would be curtailed completely, and the Indians left to starve. Moreover, as complaints by the agents that the Indians were starving after the severe winter of 1883–84 went unheeded by officials in Ottawa, Poundmaker was unable to maintain peace among his followers, particularly the younger warriors. In June 1884, many Indians, including Big Bear [MISTAHIMASKWA] and his followers, assembled at Poundmaker's reserve to discuss the situation. In spite of the efforts of the North-West Mounted Police to disperse them, more than 1,000 Crees put on a Thirst Dance, their major religious celebration, in which the participants reaffirmed their faith in the sun spirit. During the ceremonies an Indian was accused of assaulting John Craig, the farm instructor on an adjacent reserve. Anticipating a possible outbreak of violence, the NWMP fortified the Battleford agency and sent a force of some 90 men to arrest the accused. However, Poundmaker and Big Bear refused to turn him over while the Thirst Dance was in progress, and Poundmaker offered himself as a hostage. Later, when the police threatened to arrest the wanted man forcibly, Poundmaker denounced their actions, angrily waving a four-bladed war club at them. But the fugitive was taken into custody and escorted to Battleford where he was sentenced to a week in jail.

The kind of discontent reflected in this altercation was rampant throughout much of the prairies, among Métis and Indians. It resulted in Métis spokesmen inviting Louis RIEL to return from Montana to seek a solution to Métis and Indian problems. Poundmaker played no part in sending for Riel; however, because of his leadership, especially of the young warrior element, at the outbreak of the rebellion in 1885 his camp grew in population to several times its normal size and included Cree, Stony, and even a number of Métis. After the Métis victory at Duck Lake in March and the killing of a farm instructor by Stony Indians, most of the white settlers abandoned their farms and fled to the barracks of the NWMP near Battleford, while a few others who had been taken prisoner by Poundmaker's followers found shelter in his lodge. The chief then travelled to the Battleford barracks located about a quarter of a mile from the village to see the Indian agent and to obtain overdue rations. When the agent refused to leave the protection of the NWMP, Poundmaker was unable to prevent the young warriors accompanying him from ransacking the village, which had also been abandoned for the barracks by its inhabitants.

After the Indians returned to Cut Knife Creek, Poundmaker remained their nominal leader with considerable influence, but a warrior's lodge erected in the camp became the real centre of authority. In particular, a number of Stonies who had been involved with the killing of the farm instructor actively supported a policy of open warfare against the whites. In the mean time, Lieutenant-Colonel William Dillon Otter*'s column arrived at Battleford. Deciding to "punish" Poundmaker for pillaging the village, Otter set off with 325 men, two cannons, and a Gatling gun to attack Poundmaker's camp near Cut Knife Hill. However, in the early morning of 2 May 1885 news of the advancing column was received, and a number of Cree and Stony warriors immediately set out to thwart the government attack. After seven hours' fighting, Otter's forces withdrew. Although Poundmaker had played no part in the battle he was able to prevent the warriors from pursuing the retreating forces. Otter's army was in sufficient disarray by this time that any Indian counterattack would have resulted in heavy losses.

After the attack, a number of Métis persuaded Poundmaker's camp to join Riel's forces at Batoche. Poundmaker himself made several attempts to travel instead to Devil's Lake, but the Stony warriors would not permit it. A short time later, when the Métis captured a wagon supply train, through the intervention of Poundmaker the prisoners were protected and well treated. When the camp learned that Riel's forces had been defeated at Batoche on 12 May, Poundmaker sent a priest, Father Louis Cochin, with a message to Major-General Frederick Dobson Middleton*, saying he was prepared to negotiate a peace settlement. The general rebuffed the appeal and demanded that Poundmaker surrender unconditionally at Battleford. On 26 May Poundmaker and his followers came into the fort, where they were immediately imprisoned.

Poundmaker was put on trial for treason at Regina in July 1885. "Everything I could do was done to stop bloodshed," Poundmaker protested in court. "Had I wanted war, I would not be here now. I should be on the prairie. You did not catch me. I gave myself up. You have got me because I wanted justice." He was found guilty and sentenced to three years in prison. After serving a year in Stony Mountain Penitentiary, Man., broken in spirit and health, he was released. Only four months later, while visiting his adopted father, Crowfoot, on the Blackfoot reserve, he suffered a lung haemorrhage and died. Not until the rebellion hysteria had passed was Poundmaker belatedly recognized as a man who had never abandoned the peacemaker's role and had fought only in defensive actions.

HUGH A. DEMPSEY

Can., Parl., *Sessional papers*, 1886, XIII, no.52. Louis Cochin, *Reminiscences . . . a veteran missionary of the Cree Indians and a prisoner in Poundmaker's camp in 1885 . . .* ([Battleford, Sask., 1927]). Robert Jefferson, *Fifty years on the Saskatchewan . . .* (Battleford, 1929). Morris, *Treaties of Canada with the Indians.* W. H. Williams, *Manitoba and the north-west: journal of a trip from Toronto to the Rocky Mountains . . .* (Toronto, 1882), 104–10. John Maclean, *Canadian savage folk: the native tribes of Canada* (Toronto, 1896). Norma Sluman, *Poundmaker* (Toronto, 1967). Stanley, *Birth of western Canada*; *Louis Riel.* Mary Weekes, *Great chiefs and mighty hunters of the western plains . . .* (Regina, [1947?]), 7–27. [Edward Ahenakew], "The story of the Ahenakews," ed. R. M. Buck, *Saskatchewan Hist.* (Saskatoon), 17 (1964): 12–23. J. W. Shera, "Poundmaker's capture of the wagon train in the Eagle Hills, 1885," *Alberta Hist. Rev.* (Edmonton), 1 (1953), no.1: 16–20.

PLAIN, THE. *See* PASKWĀW

PLAINVAL, LOUIS FRASSE DE. *See* FRASSE

PLUMB, JOSIAH BURR, businessman and politician; b. 25 March 1816 at East Haven, Conn., son of the Reverend Elijah Griswold Plumb and Grace Hubbard Burr; m. 30 May 1849 Elizabeth, the youngest daughter of Samuel Street* of Chippawa (now part of Niagara Falls), Canada West, and they had three sons and three daughters; d. 12 March 1888 at Niagara-on-the-Lake, Ont.

Before immigrating to Canada in 1865 Josiah Burr Plumb was manager of the State Bank of Albany, N.Y., and a director of several banks in Buffalo and Oswego. He had also been involved in the consolidation of several railway lines that eventually became the New York Central Railway. In early 1861, representing the Democratic party of New York State, he sat on a committee which conferred with representatives of the slave states in an attempt to prevent the impending conflict.

Immediately after the American Civil War Plumb retired from business and moved to the Niagara Falls area. He was soon associated with the Conservative party, doubtless through the influence of his brother-in-law, Thomas Clark Street*, one of the wealthiest men in Canada West. Plumb was brought to the attention of Sir John A. Macdonald* as early as 1872 by the editor of the Toronto *Mail*, Thomas Charles Patteson*, as a useful though at that time erratic acquisition for the party. Plumb entered politics in the general election of January 1874, partly out of chivalrous regard for Macdonald after the Pacific Scandal. He was elected for the county of Niagara but the election was voided. In a new election on 22 December Plumb was successful.

Plumb seems to have come to Ottawa as a widower, and he set out to enjoy himself. In 1875 he belonged to an Ottawa drinking circle called the Jim-Jam Club, with Joseph-Philippe-René-Adolphe Caron* and Senator Robert William Weir Carrall* of British Columbia. At the same time Plumb actively campaigned for Macdonald's National Policy in 1877 and 1878. He did not spare himself nor did he doubt success, and in the election of 1878 Macdonald and the Conservatives were swept back into power. Plumb was awarded a contested election and returned to the House of Commons on 20 March 1879.

An active parliamentarian, Plumb had something of the cockiness in the house that was characteristic of Sir Charles Tupper*. He was especially critical of Sir Richard John Cartwright* for his "vitriol-throwing." Liberal George William Ross* had already anticipated in the house that before long Plumb's "limping hexameters will be heard no more . . . and even the sublime effrontery with which he addresses the House must come to an end. The [political] grave, which I know he is not prepared to fill, is already dug for him." Ross was right. Plumb's 1879 majority in Niagara had been very narrow, and in 1882 Macdonald arranged to have the Niagara constituency disappear in a gerrymander. Plumb, probably by arrangement with Macdonald, contested Wellington North in the general election that year. He lost, and Macdonald appointed him to the Senate on 8 Feb. 1883.

Plumb was both active and popular in the Senate.

On the withdrawal of Sir Alexander Campbell* from the cabinet in January 1887, Plumb's experience, knowledge, and fluency made him the logical successor as government leader in the upper house. Then, on 4 April 1887, when William Miller* was forced out as Senate speaker owing to excessive drinking, Plumb replaced him, and remained in that position until his sudden death less than a year later.

Doubtless because of his American experience Plumb tried to lessen regional rivalries in Canadian politics. The great aim of parliament, he said in 1878, "should be to remove sectional jealousies, and to cement the Union into a whole. . . ." But he never rode his ideas too hard. With Plumb, as with Macdonald, politics was too important to be left dependent upon mere philosophical principles. In 1881 he quoted some lines that, he said, were favourites of Cartwright's, though Cartwright did not heed them as Plumb did. They can well serve as his epitaph:

> A genuine statesman must be on his guard
> If he must have beliefs, not believe them
> too hard.

P. B. Waite

AO, MU 2306–10; MU 2918–22. PAC, MG 26, A. Can., House of Commons, *Debates*, 1875–82. Can., Senate, *Debates*, 1883–88. *Toronto Daily Mail*, 13 March 1888. *Cyclopædia of Canadian biog.* (Rose, 1886), 367–69.

POIRIER. *See* Perrey

POLETTE (Paulet), ANTOINE, lawyer, judge, and politician; b. 24 Aug. 1807 at Pointe-aux-Trembles (Neuville), Lower Canada, son of Antoine Paulet, a farmer, and Marie-Josephe Bertrand; d. 6 Jan. 1887 at Trois-Rivières, Que.

The first Paulet to come to Canada from France was also named Antoine; born at Dieppe in 1626, he married at Quebec in 1655, and then settled at Saint-Pierre, on Île d'Orléans. Antoine Polette spent his childhood at Pointe-aux-Trembles. After attending the parish school, he studied for a year at the Petit Séminaire de Québec. At the age of 14 he became a clerk in the law office of Hilaire Miot-Girard at Quebec. He finished his legal training under Joseph Lagueux, was called to the bar in September 1828, and made his home at Trois-Rivières, where he practised from 1828 to 1860 and took an active part in the town's political life.

After representing Trois-Rivières on various commissions connected with the region's development (the commission for building a bridge over the Saint-Maurice in 1834, and the commission for incorporating the district's parishes in 1839), he became warden of the district in 1842 and mayor of Trois-Rivières in 1846. During his seven years as mayor he saw Trois-Rivières become the centre of a vast region newly opened to the lumber industry and to settlement. The town at this time acquired a telegraph office which linked it with Quebec and Montreal, gas lighting, a new market on Rue des Forges, and the first hall reserved for municipal council discussions.

Like most 19th-century politicians, Polette was not satisfied with working at the municipal level. In 1848 he became the member for the town of Trois-Rivières in the Legislative Assembly of the Province of Canada, and he continued to represent the riding until 1857. He sat in the assembly at a time when political parties were taking shape, and supported the governments of Louis-Hippolyte La Fontaine* and Robert Baldwin*, and of Francis Hincks and Augustin-Norbert Morin*. But in June 1854 he was one of seven members forming a group around Joseph-Édouard Cauchon and Louis-Victor Sicotte. These dissidents joined with the Rouges of Canada East and the opposition from Canada West to defeat Hincks, who refused to settle the serious issues of the abolition of seigneurial tenure and the clergy reserves. Their action explains why *L'Ère nouvelle* of Trois-Rivières hailed Polette's re-election in July 1854 as "a triumph of the opposition," although he is classed among the Bleus by modern historians. As an mla Polette served, in particular, on the committee on seigneurial tenure in 1851, the Select Committee to Enquire into the Causes Which Prevent or Retard the Settlement of the Eastern Townships, also in 1851, and the special committee on education in 1853 [*see* Louis Lacoste*].

Polette retired from politics in November 1857. In 1859 he was a member of the first Council of Public Instruction [*see* Pierre-Joseph-Olivier Chauveau], and the following year he was appointed a judge of the Superior Court. In this capacity, he served in 1873 on the royal commission of inquiry into the Pacific Scandal.

Polette was married three times: on 20 Feb. 1830, at Champlain, to his cousin Henriette, daughter of Jean-Baptiste Dubuc, a well-known merchant of Quebec and Batiscan; in 1834, at Quebec, to Anne, sister of the chief justice of the province, Jean-François-Joseph Duval; and in 1857 to Aurelia Sophia, daughter of Judge William King McCord*.

Louisette Pothier

AC, Trois-Rivières, État civil, Catholiques, Immaculée-Conception (Trois-Rivières), 1887. ANQ-Q, État civil, Catholiques, Saint-François-de-Sales (Neuville), 1807. Archives du séminaire de Trois-Rivières, D1, B17; E3, 46. ASQ, Fichier des anciens, 1817–18. PAC, MG 30, D1, 25: 17–30. *Le Courrier du Canada*, 10 janv. 1887. *L'Ère nouvelle* (Trois-Rivières), 1852–54. *Journal des Trois-Rivières*, 13 nov. 1847, 8 janv. 1848, 22 janv. 1853. *Le Journal des Trois-Rivières*, 10 janv. 1887, 22 nov. 1888. F.-J. Audet, *Les députés des Trois-Rivières*, 21. *Canadian biog. dict.*, I: 370–71. P.-G. Roy, *Les avocats de la région de Québec*, 358; *Les juges de la prov. de Québec*, 441.

Bernard, *Les Rouges*, 98, 118. Chapais, *Hist. du Canada*, VII: 71. Cornell, *Alignment of political groups*. Benjamin Sulte, *Mélanges historiques*, Gérard Malchelosse, édit. (21v., Montréal, 1918–34), III: 104–5. L.-P. Turcotte, *Le Canada sous l'Union*, II: 211–12. *Les ursulines des Trois-Rivières depuis leur établissement jusqu'à nos jours* (4v., Trois-Rivières, 1888–1911), III: 430. L.-P. Audet, "Urgel-Eugène Archambault instituteur (1851–1859)," *Cahiers des Dix*, 27 (1962): 135–76. Raphaël Bellemare, "L'auteur du 'Canadien émigrant,'" *BRH*, 3 (1897): 62–63. Albert Tessier, "Les voyages vers 1800," *Cahiers des Dix*, 6 (1941): 83–108.

POPE, JAMES COLLEDGE, entrepreneur, landed proprietor, land agent, and politician; b. 11 June 1826 in Bedeque, P.E.I., second son of Joseph Pope* and his first wife, Lucy Colledge; d. 18 May 1885 in Summerside, P.E.I.

James Colledge Pope's father, a native of Plymouth, England, immigrated in 1819 to Prince Edward Island. In the company of his older brothers Joseph became involved in the timber business at Bedeque, Prince County. By 1830 he was elected to the assembly, where he soon became the leading figure among those members opposed to a radical solution to the land question, serving as speaker from 1843 to 1849. The elder Pope earned a reputation for violence, even scurrility, in debate, and in the course of his most serious controversy, with Lieutenant Governor Sir Henry Vere Huntley* in 1846–47, he demonstrated a vindictiveness which he apparently transmitted to his sons, William Henry* and James. Joseph changed political allegiance in 1849, became a Reformer, and was appointed colonial treasurer when responsible government was conceded in 1851.

James received his early education on the Island, and about the age of 14 was sent to Saltash, near Plymouth, to attend school. Upon his return, he entered the family business at Bedeque. Although maturing in an intensely political environment, he does not appear to have been strongly attracted by politics until the late 1850s. He left Prince Edward Island to seek gold in California in 1849 as part of a group of 40 Island adventurers who purchased a brig, the *Fanny*, to make the trip. A vivid narrative account by a participant, Stephen MacCallum, describes Pope as "a stoutly built, light-haired young man" who greatly impressed his shipmates with his energy and daring. He was "strong and determined, with not a lazy bone in his body," and "not the man to abandon his purpose." The expedition made no one rich, and Pope contracted "camp fever," returning home to convalesce.

On the Island, James re-entered business with his father at Bedeque, and established his own store at nearby Summerside. He also engaged in such enterprises as running a packet boat between Bedeque and Shediac, N.B., a lucrative contract for which there was keen competition. No doubt with his father's support, he was appointed to several minor positions, including in 1851 that of collector of customs for the district of Bedeque (which included Summerside); he took as fees five per cent of the duties collected, which brought him approximately £100 to £120 per annum. In his own time, James was frequently referred to as a shipbuilder, but it would probably be more accurate to describe him as a contractor for ships; although he had worked in his father's shipyard at Bedeque in the 1840s and hence was familiar with the principles of shipbuilding, he does not appear to have been personally involved in the actual construction of vessels after the mid 1850s. Over the years he became increasingly distant from the process, and on 28 Jan. 1867 sold his shipyards at Bedeque and Summerside for £650 and £2,500, respectively, to members of the rising Holman family of Summerside. He owned shares in some 117 deep-sea and coastal vessels registered between 1853 and 1877, and was the sole owner of the vast majority of these although he rarely held them for a long period. James functioned primarily as a broker of ships, and his father, who lived from 1853 to 1868 in Liverpool, England, was instrumental in selling them there. For example, James registered 12 ships in his peak year (1864), ten of which he sold through Joseph in England. In both number of ships and total tonnage James Pope stood third among Island owners of the 19th century.

James's economic interests extended far beyond ship-brokerage, for he was involved in almost every type of activity where trade was possible and where money could be made: agriculture, fishing, real estate, the carrying trade, retailing, money-lending, and even ownership of the telegraphic link between Summerside and New Brunswick. To illustrate the diversity of his interests within agriculture alone: in 1856 he purchased for $10,000 "the Mann Estate," the northern moiety of Lot 27, for which his father had long been the agent; he served as land agent for other proprietors, including the controversial Father John McDonald*; he maintained a farm where he owned a large herd of cattle; and he speculated extensively in cargoes of produce. Virtually every Summerside merchant or entrepreneur of consequence was indebted to him at some point in the 1860s, and he claimed in 1871 that the annual value of his transactions with one Charlottetown merchant alone, Jedediah Slason Carvell, exceeded the entire colonial revenue. Particularly in the 1870s, he also had extensive interests in the area around Cascumpec Bay, some 40 miles west of Summerside. In 1876 a friendly newspaper stated that "He keeps hundreds of poor men constantly employed." He was one of the most prominent economic figures in the colony, a man whose power could also inspire fear.

On 1 June 1857 James Pope made a dramatic entry

into politics, winning a by-election for Prince County, 3rd District, his father's old riding, against William Warren LORD, a veteran Liberal executive councillor. The hard-fought contest was important because since February the Liberal government of George Coles* had come under intense criticism for allegedly attempting to exclude the Bible from publicly funded educational institutions. Although Pope's electoral card had not mentioned the Bible question, his success was interpreted as the first victory for the opposition. Once in the assembly, the blunt-spoken Pope immediately acquired a name for belligerence, making provocative accusations and engaging in heated personal recriminations with all the prominent Liberals. When the Tories formed a government led by Edward PALMER in 1859, and Pope was named to the Executive Council, Edward Whelan*, editor of the Charlottetown *Examiner*, commented that he had "a great deal of brass and perseverance, and no small share of talent." Yet until at least the mid 1860s James was overshadowed in Island politics by his brother, the intellectually gifted William Henry, one year his elder, who in 1859 became colonial secretary and editor of the leading Tory newspaper, the *Islander*. James impressed more by his forceful character than by skill or eloquence as a parliamentarian; on a later occasion, according to the official reporter, James stated that "he was a poor talker and when he did speak he did not always do so in the most satisfactory manner."

In April 1864, when union of the colonies was first seriously discussed in the assembly, a difference of opinion between the two brothers surfaced. William, who had been elected to the assembly in 1863, was an enthusiastic advocate first of Maritime union and then of a general British North American union. From the beginning, James expressed his doubts. Focussing on economic considerations, he could foresee no advantages for the Island. He was not a delegate to the Charlottetown and Quebec conferences, and was not involved in the bitter public controversies over confederation which erupted in November–December 1864 among the Island's leading executive councillors. Although in the ensuing cabinet crisis he backed the confederate premier, John Hamilton GRAY, against the anti-confederate attorney general, Edward Palmer, personal factors may have played a decisive role. William was in full agreement with Gray, and in February–March 1863 James had supported Gray's ousting of Palmer from premiership. The dispute late in 1864 led to the resignation of both Gray and Palmer from the Executive Council, and on 7 Jan. 1865 James Pope became premier.

It is questionable whether Pope wanted the premiership, for at this stage in his career he was primarily a businessman. There is no evidence that he actively sought the post, but Palmer had been discredited by losing a polemical battle with W. H. Pope, Gray did not wish to lead a government which could not carry the Quebec terms, and for a variety of reasons W. H. Pope was unacceptable to large segments of the Island population. At least in the House of Assembly, James behaved as a caretaker, particularly in the session of 1865. William strongly supported confederation in assembly debates, but James said that although "approving of the abstract principle of the proposed Union . . . the details, as adopted by the Quebec Conference, do not offer . . . fair terms to the people of the Island." In 1866 he presented to the assembly the famous "No terms Resolution," which stated that no satisfactory union "could ever be accomplished," and which led to William's resignation from the government. James was careful to say that his personal opinion on confederation was not so dogmatic as the resolution he sponsored: "Had he consulted his own individual views . . . he would have modified [the resolution] . . . he still thought that terms might be proposed which would be advantageous to this Island." But, he went on, since public opinion was so overwhelmingly opposed and since there were fears that union might be forced upon Islanders without their consent, he had decided to present a resolution which left no room for misunderstanding. Within months James demonstrated just how flexible his views were. He rejected Palmer's suggestion to send an anti-confederate delegate to London in 1866 to support Joseph Howe*, and when in London himself in August or September on private business, although apparently making no effort to meet Howe, he persuaded Nova Scotian and New Brunswick delegates to the impending final conference on confederation to pledge their support for an $800,000 grant from the federal treasury to buy up proprietary lands on the Island. On his way home at the end of September, he sent a letter to Samuel Leonard Tilley* suggesting that "a small Railway or Canal" might prove persuasive. But in Prince Edward Island the $800,000 proposal was widely interpreted as a last-minute attempt at bribery, and its major political results were to divide the Tories further and to undermine James Pope's credentials as an anti-confederate.

The Tories lost the election of 1867 decisively, and indeed the Popes and Gray did not contest their seats. Many, including Palmer, believed that the major reason for the rejection of the government was their summoning of troops from Halifax in mid 1865 to suppress the Tenant League, which was pledged to resist collection of rents. James Pope, himself a land agent and small proprietor, although not known for harshness in dealing with his own tenantry, was unequivocal in stating that the measure had been necessary to maintain law and order; in the following session he had declared that his government was "prepared to abide by the consequences." On 1 July 1866 the Pope government had, however, purchased the huge Cunard estate following the death of Sir Samuel Cunard* in April 1865, comprising more than 15 per cent of the Island's land mass, thus opening the way for approximately 1,000 tenants in 20 townships to become freeholders. In retrospect, this may have been the decisive turning-point in the struggle over the land question, for the terms of the debate were never quite the same again. The Island government was to make at least one significant land purchase in every succeeding year through 1871; in 1868 it purchased for £4,089 Pope's 7,413-acre estate, on which 124 tenants, mostly Irish Roman Catholics, were living. In virtually all cases their terms had been 999-year leases at an annual rental of 1*s*. per acre. Yet this major accomplishment of purchasing the Cunard estate had come too late to aid Pope's government in the election of February 1867, for it was identified with proprietary interests. In fact, among the general population the Tenant Leaguers received more credit for the purchase than did the government: their organized and calculated defiance had made rents difficult to collect, a factor in persuading the previously recalcitrant Cunard family to sell.

The confederate Tories, of whom James was generally considered to be one, were faced with a difficult task after the election. They were in eclipse within their own party, and following the death of Edward Whelan in December there was no prominent Liberal who advocated union of the colonies; hence there could be no hope of engineering a realignment of parties on the issue. Even those confederate politicians who survived the election, such as the new Tory leader in the assembly, Thomas Heath Haviland* Jr, did so only by pledging to take no action on confederation without first submitting proposals for union to the electorate. In this situation, confederate strategists began looking for another issue by which to return to office; they were to find it in the question of public support for denominational schools. In 1868 the Liberal government refused the demands of the ultramontane bishop of Charlottetown, Peter MacIntyre*, for public grants to Roman Catholic educational institutions. The Liberal party had always strongly defended the non-sectarian character of the educational system, although usually against ultra-Protestants. When the bishop and such Roman Catholic Liberals as Executive Councillor George William Howlan* made it clear that they were not satisfied, W. H. Pope's *Islander* endorsed a policy of limited concessions to MacIntyre. This was a particularly startling development because in the early 1860s William had been perhaps the colony's most outspoken critic of the doctrines, practices, and objectives of the Roman Catholic Church. J. H. Gray followed William's lead. When an assembly seat for Summerside (Prince County, 5th District) fell vacant in late 1868, James Pope announced his candidacy and published an electoral card promising aid to all "efficient schools" open to government inspection, regardless of who controlled them; in the same card he claimed to be "opposed to the endowment of any Sectarian institution." The active support of the *Islander*, Haviland, and the bishop was insufficient to prevent Pope's defeat; Angus MacMillan*, a political novice, received 58 per cent of the Roman Catholic and 59 per cent of the Protestant vote.

Although the time was not ripe for political realignment in November 1868, less than two years later James Pope became premier on the basis of an alliance between Conservative confederates and Roman Catholic Liberals. In the general election of 18 July 1870 the Liberals, led by Robert Poore Haythorne*, obtained a majority of the seats but, owing largely to Haythorne's unskilful leadership, they split over the school question a month later. On 10 September James Pope, who had resumed his party's leadership and successfully contested Prince County, 4th District, formed a coalition government in partnership with Howlan and a group of Roman Catholic members who had seceded from the Liberal caucus. Yet, in the Byzantine world of Island politics, the two factions were bound by a mutual self-denying pledge: there would be no action on confederation or the school question until the issues had been presented to the electorate. Thus Pope had returned to power on the basis of an expression of sympathy with the principle of aid to sectarian schools but without having to make an explicit commitment to do anything. At the same time, the anti-confederate group within the Tory party had been severely weakened by the defeat of its leading spokesmen, Palmer and David Laird*, at the general election. The Popes had constructed a new political juggernaut, one which would be out of power less than one year between 1870 and 1876.

In the words of Frank MacKinnon, describing the second Pope government, "Religion and union being barred, they made the railway their politics." Although the construction of a railway had not been seriously discussed at the election of 1870, there was a sudden upsurge of popular enthusiasm for the project in early 1871. W. H. Pope had long been an advocate of the iron horse, and James introduced railway legislation in the latter year. He spoke passionately and at length on the economic advantages of rail transportation, citing statistics and examples from New Brunswick to Mauritius, predicting indirect as well as obvious economic benefits, drawing upon personal knowledge of all sectors of the Island economy and his own experiences during his frequent business trips to England, and even forecasting a huge influx of American tourists. He was an aggressive mid-19th-century entrepreneur, and the railway clearly excited his imagination. In his opinion, "as business was then carried on in the commercial world, no country could possibly keep pace with the times, without her Railways." But the Prince Edward Island Railway rapidly proved to be a greater financial burden than the local treasury could bear, and by early 1873 virtually everyone had accepted union with Canada as the colony's only practicable alternative to bankruptcy. For Pope the immediate political consequences of the railway were disastrous. Even before the deadline for receipt of tenders, Island public opinion showed signs of alarm. On 5 July 1871 the anti-railway David Laird defeated James Duncan, the newly appointed chairman of the railway commission, in a by-election. By March 1872, when Pope again met the assembly, his majority had melted away, and his government was defeated. In a general election held on 4 April, the Liberals won an overwhelming victory; to retain a seat in the assembly, Pope was forced to retreat from strongly anti-confederate Bedeque to Tory Charlottetown, where he was virtually certain to be elected.

The campaign against Pope and the railway was led by two anti-confederate former Tories, Palmer and, particularly, Laird. Through his newspaper, the *Patriot*, and on the platform, Laird made two main allegations, aside from the undeniable fact that the question had never been submitted to the people at the polls: that the covert *raison d'être* of the railway was to bring the Island into confederation, and that its construction involved massive corruption and disregard for the public interest. The charges of a corrupt "railway ring" were never substantiated, and the claim that the contractors were guilty of bad judgement, if not incompetence and greed, which greatly increased the cost of the project, was investigated in mid 1872 by two American engineers appointed by the second Haythorne government. Despite the obvious desire of their employers to find evidence of malpractice, the investigators instead praised the conduct of Pope's contractors. The most serious criticisms which could be justly levelled against the former government appear to have been that they proceeded without an adequate survey and that their estimate of a 120-mile road between the termini of Georgetown and Alberton, which they made in assembly debates and in the contract, was 27 miles short of the road as actually constructed.

Perhaps more important in the long run is the suspicion Pope knew that the cost of the project, however reasonable in terms of the job to be done, would be the means of driving the Island into confederation. No decisive evidence has survived, although it is unlikely that Pope, an astute businessman, could have failed to recognize what rapidly became apparent to the confederate lieutenant governor, William Cleaver Francis Robinson*, and most anti-confederate politicians. It is certain that James's brother William was willing to contemplate any means short of military invasion to force the Island into confederation, and it is also certain that the family was closely united politically at this point, with William's *Islander* supporting James, and Joseph, a strong confederate, now colonial treasurer. But James was still first and foremost a commercial man, and it is entirely conceivable that his primary commitment was to the railway as a means of economic progress – a goal for which he was willing to contemplate confederation as an incidental result. Whether he would have advocated the railway without the certainty that Canada was eager to annex the Island (and thus would be available should the need for a financial rescue arise) is an interesting subject for speculation.

In any event, by February 1873 the Haythorne administration felt compelled to send a delegation to Ottawa to negotiate terms of entry into confederation. The dominion government gave the Island generous treatment, considering the circumstances: there would be "continuous communication" with the mainland, the railway was to be taken over, the land question settled, the colony's debts assumed, and the promised annual subsidy increased over the last previous offer. The Liberals decided to take these terms to the voters, and called a general election for 2 April. James Pope, who had been quietly attempting to lure dissident members of the Liberal caucus with concessions to the Roman Catholic Church over the school question, adapted his tactics brilliantly to the changed situation. He went on the offensive by declaring that the proposed terms were not good enough, and that the method of obtaining them was shoddy, and by accusing the Liberals of conspiring to manœuvre the people into confederation precipitately. He said that he would obtain much more for the Island, as he and his Conservative associates were personal friends and political brethren of Sir John A. Macdonald*. Pope won 20 of the 30 seats in the assembly, and after refusing to pledge to Governor Robinson that he would bring the Island into confederation regardless of the outcome of further negotiations, he proceeded to Ottawa with Haviland and Howlan. By persistence, they in fact won the promise of an increase of $25,500 in the annual subsidy to the Island.

Prince Edward Island entered the Dominion of Canada on 1 July 1873. James Pope was elected on 17 September for Prince in the House of Commons, and in Ottawa supported the crumbling Macdonald government. By this time, however, the unstable political alignments of the Island had been severely shaken by Bishop MacIntyre. There had been a general increase in tension over the school question during the first half of the year. Anticipating that MacIntyre would attempt to gain concessions, in the knowledge that anything established in law prior to union with Canada would, according to section 93 of the British North America Act, be under the protection of the federal government, in the April election the Protestant constituencies had extracted from their candidates pledges to maintain the *status quo*. None the less, Pope had the political advantage of having in the past publicly expressed sympathy with the Roman Catholic position on the school question. Thus all 12 Roman Catholic assemblymen elected in April gave him support that was decisive. For a time Pope was able to maintain Catholic backing without having to act, thanks to the pledge he had had to give to his constituents in Charlottetown. But there was soon friction with MacIntyre; after learning of an attempt by the bishop in mid May to persuade Roman Catholic members to block confederation in the legislature until the school question was settled to his satisfaction, Pope responded by rescinding an informal promise to allocate $10,000 to the bishop's schools (which he later said was to have been given "without any intention, whatever, of recognizing the principle of denominational schools"). MacIntyre then apparently raised such a furore behind closed doors that on 19 June the Pope–Howlan group made a private gift of $5,000 to the bishop. According to Pope and Howlan, this did not satisfy him, as a second $5,000 was not forthcoming. By August the bishop was denouncing his erstwhile political friends from the pulpits of his diocese. With his support, the Liberals won four of the six seats at stake in the 17 September by-elections. Pope declined to contest the federal general election of early 1874, in which the Liberals won all six Island seats, giving as his reason his belief that any Roman Catholic who supported him would incur "Episcopal censure" – and he had no desire to place his friends in such a position.

James Pope returned to the local House of Assembly on 5 April 1875 after being acclaimed a member for Summerside at a by-election. However, he did not enter the cabinet of his successor as premier, Lemuel Cambridge Owen*, and indeed maintained a position of relative independence. The major issue of the mid 1870s was the school question, and political alignments continued to shift. The Liberals had no intention of compromising on the principle of integrated, non-denominational schools, and, following their success in the federal election, had renounced their alliance of convenience with Bishop MacIntyre, having derived all the benefits they could without giving something in return. Over the life of the assembly, a consensus developed about the need for drastic reform of the educational system, which had been stagnating for several years; the difference of opinion centred on whether the imparting of religious instruction in the public schools was compatible with this goal.

The provincial election of August 1876 was fought solely on the school question, with Islanders dividing into "Free Schoolers" (predominantly Liberals) and "Denominationalists" (almost exclusively Tories). James Pope led the latter group, and faced a difficult situation, for his rank and file disagreed among themselves over the extent to which separate schools should be instituted. Pope's own position was that of his "Summerside card" of 1868, which he described as "accepting the assistance of the private schools" and "payment for results." Differences of opinion between his Roman Catholic and Protestant supporters soon appeared, and the Free Schoolers won a decisive victory. Pope and his principal lieutenant, Frederick de St Croix Brecken*, were personally defeated in Charlottetown by the Free Schoolers' leader, Louis Henry Davies*, and George Wastie DeBlois, a Tory. The reasons for the result, aside from Denominationalist divisions, were threefold: the brilliant platform abilities of the youthful Davies; the greater success of his party in making their campaign bi-partisan, by recruiting the aid of such long-time Tories as Haviland and DeBlois (both disillusioned supporters of Pope's Summerside card); and, perhaps most importantly, a general public sentiment that the time had come for resolution of the school question, and a consequent impatience with Pope's temporizing when compared with Davies' refusal to equivocate.

On 22 Nov. 1876, just over three months after his defeat in Charlottetown, Pope successfully contested a by-election for the federal constituency of Queens, in a campaign which provided the occasion for the Island's first experience with voting by ballot. In Ottawa he displayed the pugnacity which had marked his entrance into the local assembly, and his intemperate language appears to have startled leading members of the Liberal government and the speaker, as he vigorously advocated cabinet representation for the Island and improved winter communications with the mainland. Perhaps it was appropriate that when the Tories returned to power in 1878, Pope was named to the cabinet as minister of marine and fisheries, with, among other things, responsibility for reporting on the performance of the grossly inadequate steamer, the *Northern Light*, which he had already denounced in the strongest terms, and which the Macdonald government did not replace or even redesign during his tenure. As a cabinet minister, according to his nephew Joseph*, who was also his private secretary, "He was not an office man, nor given to the regular and methodical treatment of correspondence." Many of his surviving letters concern matters of patronage, including an attempt in 1879 to have his father appointed lieutenant governor of the Island. In the House of Commons, before and after coming to power, Pope defended the Conservative tariff policy as a means of applying pressure upon the United States in order to obtain reciprocal free trade, although admitting that it was unlikely the Americans would bend. He continued to describe himself as a free-trader by inclination and he warned Macdonald privately of the resentment among Islanders because of the unbalanced distribution of the costs and benefits of the National Policy.

The death of his brother William in October 1879 apparently combined with heavy losses at sea and by fire in the late 1870s to contribute to a deterioration in Pope's mental and physical health, perhaps a recurrence of a problem in the mid 1870s linked to business losses. After the session of 1881 he took a leave of absence from the cabinet; by this time, according to his eldest son Percy, his business affairs were "in a very hopeless state." Despite a rest in Prince Edward Island and the medical attention of, among others, Sir Charles Tupper*, he did not recover, although, out of concern for him, Macdonald and his colleagues agreed that he should remain in the cabinet. He did not contest the election of 1882, and indeed in the next year, at the request of Percy, was legally declared to be of unsound mind and incapable of managing his own affairs. He died in 1885, survived by his father, his wife, Eliza Pethick, whom he had married on 12 Oct. 1852, and five of their eight children. Although baptized a Methodist, James had been an Anglican for more than 30 years.

Despite his many shifts in position on the crucial political issues of his era in Prince Edward Island, James Pope was a relatively uncomplicated man. Chief Justice Sir Robert Hodgson* once provided Sir John A. Macdonald with an apt description of his attributes: "a man of good sound common sense, not very highly educated, of indomitable courage, perseverance and energy – proud and ambitious – what Dr Johnson terms 'a good hater' and of a very unforgiving disposition – a fair debater." Like his older brother William, he had an iron will; he did not have the cutting edge of William's intellect, but he was by far his superior in the handling of men and affairs. A highly successful entrepreneur known personally throughout a large part of the Island, he brought to politics the qualities which made him a force within the colony's economic life. His primary political asset appears to have been his ability as a leader of men, and particularly the impression of personal vigour which he conveyed to those around him. Not a polished man, Pope had little patience with those he could not bend to his will; on more than one occasion he and George Coles, another aggressive entrepreneur, nearly came to blows in the house, and in 1876 he and a Liberal assemblyman actually fought on the hustings.

In 1927 William Lawson Cotton*, a veteran Island journalist who had been close to James Pope in his heyday, wrote that, after Coles and Whelan, he "was the political leader who influenced most effectively the course of events in Prince Edward Island." Yet his political record was not one of uninterrupted success. The $800,000 proposal of 1866, the Summerside by-election two years later, and his campaign tactics in the provincial general election of 1876 may have constituted lapses in political judgement. However, it is arguable that at least the second of these was a calculated gamble which opened the way for future advances. In several local issues in which James Pope played a major part – the railway, denominational schools, confederation – his relationship with his brother was an important consideration and prompted much contemporary speculation. Unquestionably, the two brothers disagreed on some matters of consequence: James was careful not to associate himself with William's intemperate public attacks on Roman Catholic beliefs in the early 1860s, and he refused to follow his elder brother into the political wilderness over confederation after the Quebec conference. He was much less willing to close political doors behind him and make lasting enemies needlessly, which by the mid 1860s permitted him, rather than William, to play an active personal role in government. Although James entered politics in the late 1850s, he did not emerge as a Tory leader until 1865. After that, his enthusiasm for political life grew, and in the 1870s he was the dominant figure in Island politics. Together the two brothers rebuilt the Tory party, which had been shattered in 1864–65, and made it the vehicle for bringing the railway to the Island, and the Island itself into confederation; whoever was the mastermind, James, with his personal magnetism, played an indispensable part.

The sincerity and motives of the Popes were frequently under suspicion. Concerning the school question, to whose resolution his contribution was largely negative, James was extremely flexible, for adherence to a specific policy was entirely governed by time, circumstance, and political opportunities. For years, confederation was for him a question of extracting sufficiently favourable terms from Ottawa. If there was one idea to which James was strongly wedded, it was economic "progress." This is what various contemporary journalists meant when they wrote that he, a Tory, was "a man of liberal and progressive views." And a railway, with whatever consequences, was a necessary part of any progressive community in the latter part of the 19th century. More than anything else, James Pope was the embodiment of the vigorous entrepreneur, with "great push and energy" in both business and politics.

Ian Ross Robertson

[The author is indebted to Professor Lewis R. Fischer and Mr Marven Moore for information on James Pope's maritime business interests, to Mr Robert Allan Rankin for information on the history of Summerside, P.E.I., and to Mrs Irene L. Rogers who placed at his disposal the scrapbook of Bertie McCallum, which contains the account of the voyage of the brig *Fanny* to California in 1849; an abridged version of the account, edited by Mrs Rogers, has appeared in the *Island Magazine* (Charlottetown), no.4 (spring-summer 1978): 9–

14. The only known collection of J. C. Pope papers consists of seven letters exchanged between Pope and Lieutenant Governor William Robinson on 15 and 16 April 1873; copies are in PRO, CO 226/111: 90–98, and the letters were published in W. L. Cotton, *Chapters in our Island story* (Charlottetown, 1927), 66–71. *See also* PAPEI, "Scrapbook containing papers relating to Joseph Pope, W. H. Pope, and J. C. Pope."

Indications of Pope's views and debating style will be found in P.E.I., House of Assembly, *Debates and proc.*, 1858–66, 1871–73, 1875–76; Can., House of Commons, *Debates*, 1877–81. Information on his public career, family background, business activities, and personality will be found in the following: *Examiner* (Charlottetown), 20 Nov. 1854; 11 Feb. 1856; 18 May, 1, 8 June 1857; 7 March, 11 April 1859; 24, 31 March 1862; 6 Aug., 1 Oct., 31 Dec. 1866; 4 Feb. 1867; 2 Feb. 1874; 5, 19 April 1875; 31 July 1876; 17 April, 14, 19 Sept. 1878; 17 Sept. 1879; 18, 19, 21 May 1885; 30 April 1889; 3 Sept. 1895; *Herald* (Charlottetown), 20, 27 May, 17 June 1885; *Island Argus* (Charlottetown), 12 March, 16 April 1872; 11 March 1873; 4 July, 22 Aug. 1876; *Islander*, 15 Oct. 1852; 19 June 1857; 28 March 1862; 23 March, 3 Aug., 12 Oct. 1866; 25 Jan. 1867; 16 Oct., 27 Nov. 1868; 6 Aug. 1869; 8 July, 21 Oct. 1870; *Monitor* (Charlottetown), 3, 27 June 1857; *Patriot* (Charlottetown), 30 June, 18 Aug. 1876; 17 March 1877; 18 May 1885; 3 Sept. 1895; *Pioneer* (Alberton, P.E.I.), 29 Nov. 1876; *Pioneer* (Montague, P.E.I.), 1 May 1880; *Pioneer* (Summerside), 19, 26 May 1885; *Presbyterian and Evangelical Protestant Union* (Charlottetown), 21 May 1885; *Progress* (Summerside), 2, 9 Nov. 1868; *Protector and Christian Witness* (Charlottetown), 27 May 1857; *Summerside Journal and Western Pioneer* (Summerside), 21 May 1885; *Watchman* (Charlottetown), 5 Sept. 1895.

Material of relevance to Pope is scattered through the following collections of personal or family papers: the Tilley family papers at N.B. Museum (photocopies at PAPEI); the Sir John A. Macdonald papers at PAC (MG 26, A; mfm. at PAPEI); the Hunt coll., the Palmer family papers, and the Edward Palmer papers at PAPEI. Other manuscript sources of value include the following at the PAC: RG 42, ser. I, 150–71, 391–94, 462–63; at PAPEI: RG 1, Commission books, III: 1, 84–85; RG 6, Court of Chancery, Case papers, J. C. Pope, 1883; RG 9, Impost account, District of Bedeque, 1854; RG 15, Pope estate rent books, Lot 25, 1843–63; Lot 27, 1860–68; Lot 67, 1843–63; RG 16, Land registry records, Conveyance registers, liber 80: f.251; liber 82: ff.112, 556; liber 86: f.21; liber 87: ff.151, 231, 691; liber 89: f.904; liber 93: f.701; liber 97: f.846; Conveyance registers, Queen's County ser., liber 9: f.142; liber 14: f.821; Land title docs., Lot 27, Leases, doc. 314, 26 Jan. 1856; "List of rents due on township no.27" (1868); "List of tenants on half lot 27, with quantity of land held by each" (1868); at PRO, CO 226/88: 197–99; CO 226/104: 286–87, 312, 333–34. Relevant printed primary sources are as follows: *CPC*, 1876; P.E.I., House of Assembly, *Journal*, 1873, apps.A, EE; 1875, 29, app.E.; [Joseph Pope], *Public servant: the memoirs of Sir Joseph Pope*, ed. and comp. Maurice Pope (Toronto, 1960), 19–23, 27–34, 69.

The following are the most important secondary sources for this article: F. W. P. Bolger, *Prince Edward Island and confederation, 1863–1873* (Charlottetown, 1964); and Robertson, "Religion, politics, and education in P.E.I."; consult pp.225–26 of the latter for certain inadequacies, particularly on the question of Pope's relations with his Roman Catholic supporters, in the former's account of the interaction of the confederation issue with the school question in the crucial years 1872 and 1873. *See also*: W. L. Cotton, *Chapters in our Island story* (Charlottetown, 1927), 137–40. Creighton, *Road to confederation*, 222, 263, 307–8. E. D. Ives, *Lawrence Doyle: the farmer-poet of Prince Edward Island; a study in local songmaking* (Orono, Maine, 1971), 71–72, 81–84. G. A. Leard, *Historic Bedeque; the loyalists at work and worship in Prince Edward Island: a history of Bedeque United Church* (Bedeque, P.E.I., 1948), 20, 22, 40, 54–55, 61–62. MacKinnon, *Government of P.E.I.*, 87–88, 93, 127, 132–36, 307. W. E. MacKinnon, *The life of the party: a history of the Liberal party in Prince Edward Island* (Summerside, 1973), 42–43, 47–51, 53–55, 58–60. G. R. Montgomery, "Voyage of the brig 'Fanny'," *Past and present of P.E.I.* (MacKinnon and Warburton), 356a–59a. J. C. Macmillan, *The history of the Catholic Church in Prince Edward Island from 1835 till 1891* (Quebec, 1913), chap.23. "The Pope family," *Past and present of P.E.I.* (MacKinnon and Warburton), 397a–400a. Moncrieff Williamson, *Robert Harris, 1849–1919: an unconventional biography* (Toronto and Montreal, 1970), 29. L. R. Fischer, "The shipping industry of nineteenth century Prince Edward Island: a brief history," *Island Magazine*, no.4 (spring–summer 1978): 15–21. D. C. Harvey, "Confederation in Prince Edward Island," *CHR*, 14 (1933): 143–60. J. A. Maxwell, "Prince Edward Island and confederation," *Dalhousie Rev.*, 13 (1933–34): 53–60. I. R. Robertson, "The Bible question in Prince Edward Island from 1856 to 1860," *Acadiensis*, 5 (1975–76), no.2: 3–25; "Party politics and religious controversialism in Prince Edward Island from 1860 to 1863," *Acadiensis*, 7 (1977–78), no.2: 29–59. I.R.R.]

POPE, JOHN HENRY, farmer, lumberman, railway entrepreneur, and politician; b. 19 Dec. 1819 in Eaton Township, Lower Canada, son of John Pope and Sophia Laberee; m. 5 March 1845 Percis (Persis) Maria Bailey, and they had three children, two of whom survived infancy; d. 1 April 1889 in Ottawa, Ont.

John Henry Pope's paternal grandparents had moved as loyalists from Massachusetts to the Eastern Townships and his father had eventually settled on a farm in what is now the town of Cookshire. Pope went to local schools, but his education was unsystematic; his writing, doubtless like his speech, always retained a highly original syntax and force. His main ambition as a young man was to have the best farm in the district, and by the time of his marriage in 1845 he had probably taken over the main work on his father's farm. The family land was situated in a country of broad valleys and rolling uplands heavily forested in maple, birch, larch, pine, and cedar. Throughout his life, Pope continued to work on his farm and was noted for his improvement of cattle breeds through the importation of thoroughbred stock.

He took an active interest in local affairs, representing Eaton Township on the Sherbrooke County Council in the 1840s. During the rebellion of 1837–38 he had been a member of the Eaton Township militia and had done guard duty at the court-house in Sherbrooke. He continued his military interests by joining a cavalry company in the Eaton militia and under the Militia Act of 1855 was named captain of the Cookshire Troop of Volunteer Militia Cavalry. As an officer, he preferred good local men who knew the countryside and its ways rather than imported Britishers. At the time of the *Trent* crisis in 1861 [*see* Sir Charles Hastings DOYLE], Pope told Alexander Tilloch Galt* that he did not want to run the risk "of being thrown into the hands of some half-witted retired officer of the Army, or some pampered Frenchman, or some old fogy like Colonel — of this district."

Like his forebears, Pope was generally anti-American. In 1849 he took a firm stand against the strong annexationist movement in the Eastern Townships, a choice which put him in opposition to such regional notables as Galt, John Sewell Sanborn*, Hollis Smith*, and John Joseph Caldwell Abbott*. In July 1849 Pope attended the meeting in Kingston, Canada West, of the British American League, many of whose members favoured annexation to the United States. His purpose in attending was to attempt to keep the debate within constitutional limits, and there he first met John A. Macdonald*, who was to become his friend and political chief in the Liberal-Conservative party. In the general election of 1851 Pope unsuccessfully opposed Sanborn, who had been elected for Sherbrooke County in 1850 as an avowed annexationist; Pope again ran without success against Galt in an 1853 by-election in Sherbrooke Town and against Sanborn in the new riding of Compton County in the general election of 1854. Sanborn was not a candidate in Compton in 1857–58 general election, and Pope was elected by acclamation. He continued to represent the county without interruption in the assembly of the Province of Canada until confederation and in the House of Commons until his death in 1889. He frequently ran unopposed and, when he did face challengers, received at least two-thirds of the votes cast. In June 1864 he and Alexander MORRIS acted as intermediaries between George Brown* and John A. Macdonald in the initial discussions that led to the formation of the "Great Coalition."

Pope combined his duties as a politician with work on his farm and a wide variety of important business interests. With a partner, Cyrus S. Clarke of Portland, Maine, Pope owned the Brompton Mills Lumber Company which operated large sawmills at Brompton Falls (Bromptonville) in the eastern part of Compton County. One of his first acts as a legislator was to sponsor a bill to amend the charter issued in 1855 for the Eastern Townships Bank, so that it could begin operations. The Montreal banking community was unsympathetic to this Eastern Townships venture, but Pope and other promoters of the bank managed to subscribe almost half the capital locally and he remained a director of the successful bank until his death. Pope was an incorporator in 1866 with Andrew Paton of the Paton Manufacturing Company, a woollen mill in Sherbrooke. In 1868 George Stephen* joined them, thus beginning Pope's long acquaintance with Stephen and the leading capitalists of the Bank of Montreal. By 1872 the Sherbrooke mill employed 500 workers. Pope was a director, as well, of the Sherbrooke Water Power Company, the Sherbrooke Gas and Water Company, and the Compton Colonization Society, and the honorary president and a large stockholder in the Eastern Townships Agricultural Association.

Late in the 1850s Pope had become involved in exploiting copper mines in Ascot Township, Compton County, and in the 1860s acquired lands in Ditton Township, also in Compton, which yielded gold until they were virtually worked out in the early 1890s. In the 1870s it was charged that Pope had obtained 4,200 acres in Ditton Township by misrepresentation or even fraud. A provincial government investigation in 1877, however, cleared Pope by maintaining that he had bought the lands from a man who had acquired them without the usual settlement duties and the customary crown reservation of gold rights. There is evidence that the form of patent was varied to suit the circumstances, and that Pope had probably acquired the lands legally, but only just. In addition, the investigator named by the province was Richard William Heneken, a fellow director of Pope's in several Eastern Townships businesses. That Pope knew he had done well is probable. He always was to wear a massive gold chain and used to say, "I worked a good many years to get this chain – and got it at wholesale figures, too."

Perhaps the most significant of Pope's varied business dealings was the construction of railways. By the end of the 1860s short lines were frequently chartered in order to bring products to markets, but Pope had in mind a larger railway that would connect Sherbrooke, through Compton County, with Maine, and then continue to Saint John, N.B. The railway, of course, would serve his own constituency and his own lumber interests. The St Francis and Megantic International Railway was thus chartered federally in 1870 and the following year was given land and a construction subsidy by the government of Quebec. But competition from rival lines and difficulty in attracting capital impeded the railway's construction. Pope felt it essential that local governments participate and succeeded in having the Compton County Council subscribe over $225,000 to the project. The appropriation was annulled when it was put to the rate-payers, but a new by-law was passed by council and ratified by the rate-payers favouring the county's participation. This decision in turn was challenged in the courts and no railway bonds could be issued. Pope then put his own money into the company and 22 miles of track were laid by 1875. The project almost ruined Pope in health and purse, however, and in the same year the railway's land grant reverted to the province. In 1883 the railway received a federal subsidy and in 1887 became part of the Canadian Pacific Railway. George Stephen, Pope's business associate and the president of the CPR from 1881 to 1888, later said that the only reason the CPR took over the "Short Line" between Sherbrooke and Saint John was to relieve Pope of his personal commitments in the railway.

At the same time that he was heavily involved in business in the 1870s and 1880s, Pope was a leading cabinet minister in Sir John A. Macdonald's governments. He was first appointed minister of agriculture in October 1871 and retained the office until the government's resignation over the Pacific Scandal in November 1873. His view of Canada was not unlike Sir Charles Tupper*'s, that the country was a horizontal national market. Pope spoke frequently in parliament on the necessity of keeping a proper balance between expanding population and available markets and was opposed to accepting immigrants more quickly than they could be absorbed. In 1876 he endorsed Macdonald's and Tupper's views of what would become the National Policy: if the Americans were determined to keep Canadian products out of American markets, then Canada should restrict American access to Canadian markets.

Macdonald was to find Pope a valuable ally. Pope was impressive, tall, incisive, and commanding; but if he was at times terse, he was rarely hasty, and he was in general tolerant of opponents. Like the "practical lumberman" he once described himself as being, he gave a strong impression of powers held in reserve. A sure-footed and shrewd man of action, he had a tremendous capacity for work and little for leisure. His speeches in parliament called for fair play and no special favours. He disliked clerical interference in elections, even if eliminating it meant compromising a Conservative victory. In January 1875 he supported Alexander Mackenzie*'s proposal of amnesty for Louis RIEL and Ambroise-Dydime Lépine*, although he argued that even their five-year banishment was stupid. He wanted them granted "a full and complete pardon" because there was "no reason why they should be persecuted if the country would gain nothing thereby."

On Macdonald's return to power in 1878, Pope again became minister of agriculture, a portfolio that now included responsibility for the Library of Parliament, the infant public archives, and the census. His departmental work was done well, even if he frequently took on additional responsibilities as acting minister of railways and canals during the absence of Tupper. Pope became identified as one of the strongest supporters in the government of a railway to the Pacific. In 1879, when there was no one yet ready to undertake the project, he even thought of organizing a company to do it himself. After the fruitless attempts in 1879–80 of Macdonald, Tupper, and himself to find capitalists in London to build the railway, Pope suggested that George Stephen, Donald Smith*, and their partners in the St Paul, Minneapolis and Manitoba Railway be invited to build it. In 1878–79 the group had scored a financial coup in acquiring this railway, and Pope urged that their evident interest be encouraged before they invested their profits elsewhere. The move was successful, and on 21 Oct. 1880 the CPR construction contract was signed. As a friend and associate of Stephen, Pope was a strong advocate of the CPR throughout the five-year period of its construction and its financial difficulties. He did not hesitate, however, to criticize Stephen and his partners in 1882 for the steep freight rates they charged western farmers to transport grain over their Minnesota-Manitoba line. Yet it was largely owing to Pope that the CPR survived the major financial crisis of January 1884 when he persuaded a desperately reluctant Macdonald to brave the opposition of the Liberals, some cabinet ministers, and a large part of the Conservative caucus to aid the CPR with a $30 million loan. Stephen was grateful and on 4 Sept. 1884 wrote Macdonald in concern about Pope's health: "He is criminally careless of himself & unless you take him in hand . . . he will break down. His life & services to Canada at this moment can hardly be overestimated, second only to your own."

In September 1885, two months before the completion of the CPR, Pope was appointed minister of railways and canals. He took up the portfolio with his usual tenacity, but when Stephen resigned as CPR president in 1888 Pope was forced to deal with William Cornelius Van Horne*, an American. The two men were both fiercely determined and they quarrelled bitterly during the long arbitration over the British Columbia section of the transcontinental which had been built in the early 1880s by the government and which the CPR was to take over. Pope was also ill by this time. His family had been trying since 1887 to persuade him to retire, but he found that there was too much work to be done. In August 1888, holding the fort as he did so often while Macdonald was with his family at Rivière-du-Loup, Pope crawled to Montreal more dead than alive. There George Stephen saw him, looking "*shrunk* and *worn* beyond description." Pope none the less stuck to his office until two weeks before his death from cancer of the liver on 1 April 1889.

Pope left a substantial estate of $130,000 in cash, as well as lands, farm stock and buildings, and his home. The legatees were his wife, his son Rufus Henry*, who succeeded his father as MP for Compton, and his daughter Elizabeth, the wife of William Bullock Ives*, Conservative MP for Richmond and Wolfe since 1878. Elizabeth received the money "for her own use and absolutely free from the control of her husband." His three grandsons and the Church of England in Cookshire also received bequests.

John Henry Pope was a man of unusual capacity. His unprepossessing face concealed a mind of great penetration and judgement. His manner in the House of Commons, although not elegant, was very effective. Like Macdonald, he was no reformer, and he regarded men and situations as realities which must be bent to one's purpose. His arguments were telling, and few men had such enormous influence on Macdonald. During the CPR crisis in 1884, for instance, Pope was ruthless and unsentimental. "You will have to loan them the money," he told Macdonald, "because the day the CPR busts, the Conservative party busts the day after." It was perhaps the only argument that would have influenced Macdonald.

P. B. Waite

[Professor Andrée Désilets, Université de Sherbrooke, has made several useful suggestions in the preparation of this biography, and the bibliography she and her colleagues have compiled, *Bibliographie d'histoire des Cantons de l'Est* ([Sherbrooke, Qué.], 1975), is an essential beginning for any work on the history of the region.

There is no major collection of Pope papers. All the family papers seem to have disappeared, and this loss accounts in part for the dearth of information about Pope. The largest single source is Pope's correspondence with Sir John A. Macdonald in the Macdonald papers at PAC (MG 26, A). There is a limited but interesting collection of Pope letters in the Morris family papers at the McCord Museum, Montreal, mostly concerning the St Francis and Megantic International Railway, 1871–73. There are Pope letters in the Sir A. T. Galt papers at PAC (MG 27, I, D8) and in the Fonds Langevin at ANQ-Q (AP-G-134). Newspapers of the Eastern Townships report Pope's speeches: *Stanstead Journal* (Rock Island), *Sherbrooke Gazette and Eastern Townships Advertiser*, *Sherbrooke News*, and *Le Pionnier de Sherbrooke*. *Le Franc-Parleur* (Montréal), 2 févr. 1877, raises some questions about Pope's land transactions.

There is a considerable correspondence in the records of the Quebec Crown Lands Department (ANQ-Q, PQ, TF) on Pope's acquisition of land in Ditton Township alleged to be valuable for gold. The land records of Compton County, at the registry office in the county town of Cookshire (BE, Compton (Cookshire)), contain a wealth of references to Pope's purchases and sales of land and Pope's will.

There is an extended sketch of Pope by his friend Charles Herbert Mackintosh*, editor of the *Ottawa Daily Citizen* and later lieutenant governor of the North-West Territories, in L. S. Channell, *History of Compton County and sketches of the Eastern Townships, district of St. Francis, and Sherbrooke County* . . . (Cookshire, Que., 1896; repr. Belleville, Ont., 1975), 155–65, a work valuable as well for the farming and railway background of Pope and of his constituency. Mackintosh also gives an appreciation of Pope in an obituary in the *Ottawa Daily Citizen*, 2 April 1889. For Pope's marriage certificate, consult: AC, Saint-François (Sherbrooke), État civil, Épiscopaliens, Episcopal Church (Eaton), 5 March 1845. On Eaton Township, see: C. S. Lebourveau, *A history of Eaton; being an historical account of the first settlement of the township of Eaton* . . . (n.p., 1894; repr. Sherbrooke, 1965); for references to the Eastern Townships in general, *The Eastern Townships gazetteer and general business directory* . . . (St Johns [Saint-Jean-sur-Richelieu], Que., 1867; repr. Sherbrooke, 1967), is useful.

It is fair to say that Pope has been neglected in more recent times, though there are numerous references to him in Cornell, *Alignment of political groups*; Creighton, *Macdonald, old chieftain*; J. Hamelin et Roby, *Hist. économique*; M. Hamelin, *Premières années du parlementarisme québécois*; W. K. Lamb, *History of the Canadian Pacific Railway* (New York and London, 1977); Terrill, *Chronology of Montreal*; and Waite, *Canada, 1874–96*. The only modern work on Pope is W. S. Laberee, "Hon. John Henry Pope, Eastern Townships politician" (MA thesis, Bishop's Univ., Lennoxville, Que., 1966). P.B.W.]

POUNDMAKER. *See* PĪTIKWAHANAPIWĪYIN

POUTRÉ, FÉLIX, labourer, spy, and merchant; b. 3 Sept. 1814 at Sainte-Marguerite-de-Blairfindie (L'Acadie), Lower Canada, son of Pierre Poutré-Lavigne and Josephte Mercier; m. 28 Aug. 1837 Rose Bénac, at Saint-Jean (Saint-Jean-sur-Richelieu), Lower Canada, and they had five children; d. 22 Feb. 1885 in Montreal, Que.

Little is known about Félix Poutré's life, and no credence can be given to his autobiographical account, *Échappé de la potence: souvenirs d'un prisonnier d'État canadien en 1838*, for it is packed with trivia and falsehoods. A farm worker at Saint-Jean at the time of the 1837 rebellion, Poutré had to flee to the United States for unknown reasons after the battle at Saint-Charles-sur-Richelieu on 25 November. He returned the following summer and joined the Association des Frères-Chasseurs [*see* Robert Nelson*]. Arrested at the beginning of November 1838, he was incarcerated in Montreal on the 13th of that month and released by the attorney general 13 days later. In an affidavit dated 28 Nov. 1839 (but unknown to the public until 1913), sworn before Pierre-Édouard Leclère*, a justice of the peace and the superintendent of police, Poutré described the acts of espionage which he had undertaken since his release from prison. On behalf of the police authorities, he had kept a watch on Patriotes who had fled to the United States or lived in the Saint-Jean region. He then returned to rural life and is thought to have engaged unsuccessfully in trading in hay from 1840 to 1850. In 1872 he was living in Montreal and identified himself as a clerk; in 1880 he termed himself a merchant.

In his autobiography Poutré attempts to project a

very different image, that of a hero in the events of 1837–38 and a wily Patriote who managed to escape the death sentence. Bragging, he insinuates that he persuaded more than 3,000 persons to take the secret oath of the Association des Frères-Chasseurs, took part in the battle at Odelltown in November 1838, and surrendered to the authorities in face of the threat that his father's farm would be burned down. Supposedly he then spent several months in a prison cell, feigning madness to the point that his fellow prisoners and the prison officials believed he had really lost his mind.

A consummate rogue, Poutré succeeded in maintaining a false reputation as a hero thanks to Médéric Lanctot*, who helped him write his story for publication in 1862, and to Louis-Honoré Fréchette*, who adapted it for the stage that year under the title of *Félix Poutré ou l'échappé de la potence*. The public contributed in large measure to making him an almost legendary figure, for his autobiography ran to three editions during his lifetime (1862, 1869, 1884) and was also translated into English (1862), while Fréchette's drama was one of the plays most frequently performed throughout Quebec towards the end of the 19th century. Eager to turn his popularity to good account, Poutré gave lectures in the villages of Quebec and the towns of New England and lived for a time on the money brought in by his booklet.

It took the affirmation of Benjamin Sulte* in 1898 that Poutré had been an "employee of the government," and the disclosure by Gustave Lanctot* in 1913 of compromising documents, to unmask this bogus Patriote. Poutré was then relegated to the ranks of the traitors and spies in the story of the events of 1837 and 1838. What made him an extraordinary man, Ægidius Fauteux* wrote in 1950, "was not that he fooled his gaolers . . . , but that all his life he was able to cash in on his simulated patriotism without being denounced."

JEAN-PIERRE GAGNON and KENNETH LANDRY

[Félix Poutré was the author of *Échappé de la potence: souvenirs d'un prisonnier d'État canadien en 1838* (Montréal, 1862), translated as *Escaped from the gallows: souvenirs of a Canadian state prisoner in 1838* (Montreal, 1862). Louis-Honoré Fréchette dramatized the story in 1862, and published the play as *Félix Poutré: drame historique en quatre actes* (Montréal, [1871]). For more information on these two works see *DOLQ*, I: 204, 246–48. J.-P. G. and K.L.]

ANQ-Q, QBC 25, Événements de 1837–1838, nos.2812–15. *La Minerve*, 24 févr. 1885. *La Patrie*, 23 févr. 1885. *La Presse*, 23 févr. 1885. Fauteux, *Patriotes*, 354–56. Gustave Lanctot, *Faussaires et faussetés en histoire canadienne* (Montréal, 1948), 201–24. Lionel Audet-Lapointe, "Documents inédits sur Félix Poutré," *BRH*, 33 (1927): 753–59. Édouard Blondel, "Félix Poutré," *BRH*, 32 (1926): 419–21. "Les causes célèbres: Félix Poutré sous ses vrais couleurs," *La Patrie*, 27 oct. 1923: 23. Gustave Lanctot, "La fin d'une légende," *Rev. franco-américaine* (Montréal), 10 (1912–13): 282–91.

POWER, PATRICK, merchant and politician; b. 17 March 1815 at Kilmacthomas, County Waterford (Republic of Ireland), son of Lawrence and Katherine Power; m. in 1840 Ellen Gaul, and they had five sons and three daughters; d. 23 Feb. 1881 at Halifax, N.S.

Patrick Power immigrated to Nova Scotia with his parents in 1823 and received his early education in Halifax and Antigonish. In 1832 he began a retail business in Halifax with a brother-in-law. The partnership was soon dissolved and Power established his own dry goods firm, Patrick Power and Company, which eventually prospered. The firm owned a wharf in Halifax and had vessels of its own engaged in the coastal trade. He became a director of the People's Bank of Halifax and involved himself in the work of charitable organizations. Throughout the 1840s he supported Joseph Howe* and the Reformers in the struggle for responsible government and in 1848 was appointed a justice of the peace by the first Reform government led by James Boyle Uniacke*. In October 1851 Power was elected a Halifax alderman, an office he held until 1854. He was also a commissioner of the poor asylum from 1857 to 1874 and a prominent member in the Charitable Irish Society.

From 1860 to 1869 Power served as one of the three Roman Catholic members appointed to the Halifax Board of School Commissioners. With Michael HANNAN, he was involved in the delicate negotiations between Archbishop Thomas Louis Connolly* and the government of Charles Tupper* over the latter's 1865 legislation establishing a non-denominational public school system. Connolly feared political control of the schools and only reluctantly accepted the educational reforms in the face of Tupper's refusal to establish separate, Catholic schools. None the less, schools previously supported by church funds alone would now receive public funding under the jurisdiction of the Council of Public Instruction and an informal arrangement was reached whereby schools with exclusively Catholic teachers and students were allowed to exist throughout Nova Scotia.

As well as his close involvement in the controversial schools question, Power was in the midst of the fray over Nova Scotia's entry into confederation. As a prominent merchant he saw union with Canada sounding the death knell of Nova Scotia's important trade with the New England states which had grown under the Reciprocity Treaty of 1854. In confederation, he felt, this trade would be sacrificed to the protection of domestic markets for "Upper Canadian" goods. Despite his strong feelings on the subject, he was reluctant to accept a nomination as a candidate for the House of Commons. When, however, the Tupper government offered Power or his son a seat on the Legislative Council of Nova Scotia in return for his agreement not to run, Power was outraged enough to reconsider. He accordingly became a firm supporter of the anti-confederates led by Joseph Howe and William ANNAND, and was a candidate in Halifax in the federal election of September 1867. Power and his running mate, Alfred Gilpin Jones*, opposed the pro-confederates Stephen Tobin* and Steven Shannon, whom Archbishop Connolly had publicly proclaimed as the nominees of Halifax Roman Catholics. Voters in the city itself, more than half of whose population was Catholic, supported the pro-confederate candidates endorsed by the archbishop, but Power and Jones were elected on the basis of wide support in surrounding Halifax county.

For a time Power refused to take his seat in the House of Commons, but following the failure late in 1868 of Howe and Annand to have the British government repeal confederation, Power reluctantly allied himself with the Liberal opposition led by Alexander Mackenzie*. In 1870 Power broke with the Liberals and supported the Treaty of Washington in which Canada conceded access to its inshore fisheries to United States fishermen. Power, who would have preferred a treaty which approximated the expired Reciprocity Treaty of 1854, felt that the treaty as negotiated would at least reopen New England markets to Nova Scotia.

In the 1872 general election Power and Jones were defeated in Halifax by pro-confederate supporters of the government of Sir John A. Macdonald*. In 1874, however, following the resignation of Macdonald's government, Power and Jones were re-elected. Power's next four years in the Commons were uneventful; in 1876 he declined Alexander Mackenzie's offer to replace the ineffectual Thomas COFFIN in the cabinet. In 1878 Power was defeated in the Conservative sweep that returned Macdonald to office. Ill since 1877, he withdrew from politics entirely and died in 1881. Although he was at best a reluctant politician, the Halifax *Morning Chronicle* nevertheless claimed at his death that he had exercised "no small influence in the party councils." His infrequent participation in debates showed his continuing distrust of confederation, and he was described as "never what is known as a thick and thin supporter of his leaders."

Power was well respected in the community; his chief contribution to public life was through his active membership in numerous associations and his work on various boards and commissions dealing with education and the welfare of the poor and destitute. In recognition of his charities, Pope Pius IX had created him a knight of the Order of St Gregory the Great in 1870. In his will Power left money for the establishment of a Catholic orphanage and boys' home in Halifax. His son, Lawrence Geoffrey Power*, was a Liberal member of the Senate from 1877 to 1921.

DAVID B. FLEMMING

PAC, MG 26, A, 116; F, 3–4; RG 31, A1, 1871, Nova Scotia. PANS, RG 7, 66–69. *Parliamentary debates, Dominion of Canada* . . . (3v., Ottawa, 1870–72), III. *Evening Express* (Halifax), September 1867. *Morning Chronicle* (Halifax), February 1881. *Novascotian*, October 1851. *Canadian directory of parl.* (J. K. Johnson). *CPC*, 1876. *Cyclopædia of Canadian biog.* (Rose, 1886). *Dominion annual register*, 1880–81. *Standard dict. of Canadian biog.* (Roberts and Tunnell), II: 357–59. Wallace, *Macmillan dict.* Heritage Trust of Nova Scotia, *Seasoned timbers* (2v., Halifax, 1972–74), II. Sister Maura [Mary Power], *The Sisters of Charity, Halifax* (Toronto, 1956). Thomson, *Alexander Mackenzie.* Waite, *Life and times of confederation.* D. B. Flemming, "Archbishop Thomas L. Connolly, godfather of confederation," CCHA *Study Sessions*, 37 (1970): 67–84.

POZER, CHRISTIAN HENRY, lawyer and politician; b. 26 Dec. 1835 at the manor-house in the seigneury of Aubert-Gallion in Beauce, Lower Canada, son of William Pozer and Ann Milbourne; d. unmarried on 18 July 1884 at Saint-Georges, Que.

At the time of Christian Henry Pozer's birth the settlement of the upper Beauce region had just begun and, in a sense, it was the consolidation of properties in this region and its overall development, together with the prestige of his family, that accounted for the quite rapid advancement of his public career. His childhood was spent on the Aubert-Gallion seigneury, where his father had settled about 1830 in order to develop the fief that Christian's grandfather, George Pozer*, a Quebec merchant, had bought at the beginning of the century. At first life was rather arduous and lonely but, with the help of a grant from the Royal Institution for the Advancement of Learning, a tutor was engaged to teach the young Pozers. Nothing more definite is known about Christian Henry's education until he became a clerk in the law office of François-Xavier Lemieux* at Quebec. Called to the bar on 2 June 1860, he is thought to have practised for some time in Quebec City with Édouard Rémillard.

Meanwhile, his father's position in Beauce had stabilized. In 1852, after a hotly contested lawsuit concerning the estate of Christian's grandfather, William Pozer had secured confirmation of his titles to the seigneury and of his rights to the local fiefs of Saint-Étienne and Saint-Bernard. After his father's death in 1861, Christian Henry, who owned substantial grants of land in the townships of Shenley and Metgermette, began to draw his share of the income from the patrimonial estate jointly held by the nine children, the eldest of whom, William Milbourne Pozer, became the chief seigneur of Aubert-Gallion. Rents and other seigneurial dues, sales of land, as well as the operation of several flour-mills and sawmills, at a time when the population was increasing rapidly, guaranteed the family a sizeable income and enabled the young lawyer to pursue his political ambitions free from financial constraints.

Pozer had had his first taste of electoral skirmishing at the time of his legal training, and in 1863 he decided to enter the fray in Beauce, a large constituency with some ten polling stations located in the chief parishes. It required no small amount of boldness to oppose not only the Conservative party and its candidate, Henri-Elzéar Taschereau*, a member of the region's oldest seigneurial family which had had a decisive influence on local political opinion since the inception of the parliamentary régime, but also the clergy, who were hostile to this Protestant foreigner. Pozer's challenge unleashed a series of campaigns violent enough to occupy a prominent place in the annals of a period when elections were openly based on brutality, intimidation, and venality. Pozer lost in 1863, but by perfecting the methods that he denounced in his opponents he received twice as many votes as Taschereau in the election of 1867. He won a second victory in 1871 after an even more savage campaign; whisky and money flowed freely, and after each meeting a count was taken of the maimed. Pozer represented Beauce in both Quebec and Ottawa, but continued none the less to retain the good will of his constituents between elections. It is said that each year he visited all the parishes in the county, travelling with a trunk full of coins which he distributed at social gatherings in the evenings, and that his aloof manner, as well as his unusual height and corpulence, invested these proceedings with an air of great dignity.

Pozer's legislative career was less spectacular. As was the case for many of the opposition members elected to the first Quebec legislature, nothing separated him ideologically from the government party. His infrequent interventions were confined to issues affecting his county (often linked to his own interests) such as the creation of municipalities in various townships, and the defence of land-owners threatened by amendments to the gold-mines law. He played an active part in the government's promotion of roadbeds with wooden rails (later converted to railways), serving on the first boards of directors of the Levis and Kennebec Railway Company [*see* Louis-Napoléon LAROCHELLE] and of the Saint-François Valley and Kennebec Railway Company.

Apparently his conduct in the House of Commons was still more circumspect, even when, with the abolition of the double mandate by the provincial government in 1874, he followed to the federal capital some of the prominent figures of the Liberal party, which he had joined in 1863. His self-effacement should not result in his abilities as a loyal and vigilant politician and as an experienced organizer being forgotten. In 1876 the government of Alexander Mackenzie* summoned him to the Senate to represent the division of Lauzon. Pozer continued to live in Beauce with his mother and an unmarried sister, and saw to it that the county was kept within the sphere of influence of the Liberal party, as his correspondence with Wilfrid Laurier* attests.

From the time he took up a political career, he remained only marginally active as a lawyer; he gave up his position as a director of the Levis and Kennebec Railway Company after a few years, and family records suggest that his only other concerns related to the seigneurial rights of his family and to matters of interest to a few clients in the old seigneuries and surrounding townships. Only his real property, bequeathed to his five surviving brothers and sisters, was enumerated in the will that he dictated three years before his death, but there is every indication that this constituted the core of his fortune, and that, in short, behind the politician stood an important land-owner.

LOUISE DECHÊNE

McCord Museum (Montreal), Ross papers. Can., House of Commons, *Debates*, 1867–68. Can., Senate, *Debates*, 1876–77. Que., *Statuts*, 1869, c.54, c.58. Achintre, *Manuel électoral*. P.-G. Roy, *Les avocats de la région de Québec*. Wallace, *Macmillan dict*. Philippe Angers, *Les seigneurs et premiers censitaires de St-Georges-Beauce et la famille Pozer* (Beauceville, Qué., 1927). Philippe Angers et Robert Vézina, *Histoire de Saint-Georges de Beauce* (Saint-Georges, Qué., 1935). William Chapman, *Mines d'or de la Beauce; accompagné d'une carte topographique* (Lévis, Qué., 1881). Jean et Marcel Hamelin, *Les mœurs électorales dans le Québec de 1791 à nos jours* (Montréal, 1962). M. Hamelin, *Premières années du parlementarisme québécois*. Honorius Provost, *Chaudière Kennebec; grand chemin séculaire* (Québec, 1974); *Sainte-Marie de la Nouvelle-Beauce; histoire civile* (Québec, 1970); *La vallée de la Chaudière, géographie et histoire; notes d'enseignement* ([Québec], 1970). C. A. Scott, *The Levis and Kennebec Railway, and its difficulties: a brief history of Larochelle & Scott's connection with the line from its commencement to the present time* (Quebec, 1877).

PRAIRIES, LES. *See* PASKWĀW

PRATT, CHARLES, Church of England catechist, schoolmaster, and HBC fur-trader; b. *c.* 1816 into a tribe of Cree–Assiniboin known as the Young Dogs in the Little Lakes area of the Qu'Appelle valley (Sask.), probably the son of a Stony mother and a Cree or Métis father; d. in 1888 on the Gordon Indian Reserve (south of Wynyard, Sask.).

Charles Pratt was taken to the Red River Settlement (Man.) by the Reverend John West* and baptized into the Church of England on 8 June 1823. After receiving an education at the Red River Academy (West was one of his teachers), he drifted into the service of the Hudson's Bay Company in 1840. He was stationed at Fort Pelly (Sask.) where he remained until 1844. In 1848 he was back in Red River, studying with the Reverend William Cockran*. In the early 1850s Pratt returned to the Fort Pelly–Touchwood Hills–Qu'Appelle River area as a catechist and lay preacher to the Cree–Assiniboin Indians.

Although Pratt had to rely primarily on the buffalo hunt for his livelihood, he still preached the virtues of a sedentary Christian existence and attempted to encourage settlement at Fort Pelly and in the Touchwood Hills area. He also tried to set an example for the Indians, and in 1858 geologist and explorer Henry Youle Hind* found him well ensconced in a log house with a garden and six or seven cows. Unfortunately, Pratt's efforts met with little success even among the mixed-bloods. Preying Plains Indians, the vagaries of climate, and Pratt's lack of experience and equipment dictated failure of the agricultural settlement.

Pratt's status as a catechist among the Indians and mixed-bloods in the Qu'Appelle region was comparable to that of a medicine man, and he developed considerable influence among them. In 1873 he prevented an uprising among the Indians in the Touchwood Hills area and on 8 Sept. 1874 he acted as one of the interpreters at the Treaty no.4 negotiations at Fort Qu'Appelle, in which PASKWĀW and MĪMĪY participated.

Throughout his career Pratt was sponsored by the Church Missionary Society but despite his strong religious conviction he was unhappy with this connection. He complained frequently of insufficient financial support and considered his position little better than that of a slave. The poor funding and his lack of advancement were no doubt due in part to the racial discrimination which appeared within the society's operations, though he does not mention it directly. His disillusion reached a peak in 1874 when Joseph Reader, an Englishman, was appointed to head the Qu'Appelle missions in spite of the fact that he could neither speak Cree nor cope with the hardships of living on the prairies.

The church connection had had some social benefits for Pratt. In 1855 he had married Catherine Stevenson whose father was a farmer in the Red River Settlement. Their 11 children were to find modest positions in the church or in the HBC. There is some indication that Pratt may have married again in 1874 but the second marriage was considerably more unstable than the first; apparently his wife frequently abandoned him for lengthy stays with her parents. Always hard pressed to support his family by farming, fishing, or the hunt, with the disappearance of the buffalo he knew hunger and destitution. In 1876, ill and realizing that the west he loved was at an end, he settled on a reservation with the largely mixed-blood Gordon Indian band, where he remained as schoolmaster and catechist until his death in 1888. His last years were bitter for he knew only too well that the best days of the mixed-bloods had vanished.

FRITS PANNEKOEK

CMS Arch., C, C.1/0, Journals of Charles Pratt; Journals of Joseph Reader. PAC, RG 10, B3, 4073, file 438876. PAM, HBCA, A.32/49; B.159/a; E.4; E.5; E.6; MG 2, B3; MG 12, B. Saskatchewan Arch. Board (Regina), Arch. of the Anglican Diocese of Qu'Appelle. H. Y. Hind, *North-West Territory: reports of progress; together with a preliminary and general report on the Assiniboine and Saskatchewan exploring expedition* . . . (Toronto, 1859). Boon, *Anglican Church.*

PRICE, JAMES HERVEY, attorney and politician; b. in 1797 in Cumberland, England; m., probably before 1822, Elizabeth Anne Rubergall, and they had at least three sons and one daughter; d. 13 July 1882 in Shirley (Hampshire), England.

Little is known of James Hervey Price's life before he arrived in Upper Canada in 1828 with his wife and young son, except that he had studied law at Doctors' Commons in London. Two years after his arrival he acquired two tracts of land in York Township and built his home, Castlefield. Price continued his studies with George Rolph of Dundas, Upper Canada, and later with William Henry Draper* in York (Toronto). He was admitted to practise as an attorney in 1833 but never became a barrister. It was afterwards said of Price that he had earned the confidence of the farmers of York County by "the moderation of his charges as well as the benevolent disinterestedness of his advice."

The Price family had been accompanied to Canada by Mrs Price's sister, Mary Ann, who in 1830 became the second wife of Jesse Ketchum*. Between the Ketchum and Price families a close friendship developed. Influenced by Ketchum, a wealthy, prominent citizen and member of the House of Assembly for York from 1828 to 1834, Price quickly identified himself with the Reform cause. He was appointed city clerk on 3 April 1834 shortly after York was incorporated as the city of Toronto. He held the post during William Lyon Mackenzie*'s tenure as the first mayor and resigned on 26 Feb. 1835 following the Reformers' defeat in the elections for the city council of that year. The following year he was elected as one of the councillors for St David's Ward. With such leading Reformers as James LESSLIE, Dr John Rolph*, and Francis HINCKS, Price was a founder and director of the Bank of the People in 1835; he also served as its solicitor. Because he signed Mackenzie's notes to the bank to enable him to start his second newspaper, the *Constitution*, in 1836, Price was obliged to repay £100 with interest when Mackenzie fled to the United States two years later.

Regardless of his Reform interests, Price remained ambivalent towards party politics. A few days after Dr Charles Duncombe* had been sent to England in the summer of 1836 to protest the methods Lieutenant Governor Sir Francis Bond Head* had used in the elections of that year, Price was called upon to subscribe towards Duncombe's expenses. He did so, but some years later protested to Robert Baldwin* about the secret way in which Duncombe had been chosen and dispatched on this mission. It had been made to appear that Duncombe had been sent "by the Reformers as a body," when in fact a few of the leaders had taken this decision. "This I never forgot and from that time forward I determined never to become a party man and but for my confidence in you I never should have been one."

Price signed a declaration of the Toronto Reformers in 1837 but was not present at the secret meeting that autumn in John Doel*'s brewery during which Mackenzie proposed immediate resort to force, nor did he participate actively in the rebellion. Yet he must have been aware of what was afoot because it was at his house that Mackenzie and John Rolph met on the morning of 4 December to discuss the turn of events. That day some 300 men began to march down Yonge Street towards the city. Head hoped to persuade them to return home and felt his advice would be better heeded if conveyed by a prominent Reformer. The next day William Botsford Jarvis* asked Price to carry Head's message under a flag of truce but Price refused, saying that he would be suspected of going to join the rebels, and suggested Baldwin or Rolph in his stead. His refusal did not prevent him from falling under suspicion. He was arrested, jailed for 13 days, and his office was pilfered. Disappointed by the setback to reform in the aftermath of the rebellion, Price, with Lesslie, Hincks, and other Reformers, became a founder and director of the Mississippi Emigration Society, formed in March 1838 to secure a tract of land in Iowa for Reformers who wanted to leave Canada. However, the society's efforts failed.

In 1841, Price defeated John William Gamble* in the election in the 1st riding of York (York South after 1847) for the first parliament of the Province of Canada. During the first session he supported John Neilson* and Hincks in their criticisms of the act of union, consistently opposed the ministers chosen by Lord Sydenham [Thomson*], and denounced the Reformers whom the governor general had won over. Protesting the violence at the polls that had disgraced the recent elections and hampered Reform candidates, he demanded measures to ensure it would not occur in the future. Price nevertheless approved of Sydenham's plans to create elective district councils, but joined with Baldwin in an effort to remove from the proposed legislation clauses that would permit the governor general to appoint such officials as district wardens and municipal clerks.

When Sir Charles Bagot* reconstructed the ministry in September 1842, Price did not regard it as one he could support, and he had confidence only in its leaders, Louis-Hippolyte La Fontaine* and Baldwin. It had been rumoured that Price would become commissioner of crown lands but he was not offered the post. Although he subsequently declared that he would not have entered the government, he none the less felt he should not have been overlooked. On 19 October, shortly after the new ministers had taken office, Price announced his intention to resign his seat. Baldwin urged him to reconsider as did 900 freeholders of York County who signed a petition. Price yielded.

He became a determined opponent of Sir Charles Theophilus Metcalfe* and introduced a motion in the house on 1 Dec. 1843 regretting the resignation of the La Fontaine–Baldwin ministry, brought about by Metcalfe's policies on patronage. According to Price, if the governor general could dispense the crown's patronage without his ministers' advice, responsible government was only a "humbug." Price had by now modified his views of party politics and on this occasion declared himself as having always been a party man and stated that parties were necessary for constitutional government. His motion, which prompted an important debate on the issue of responsible government, carried.

Throughout the 1840s Price introduced or supported legislation in the interests of the farmers of the Home District, accusing the government of indifference to agricultural concerns. He tried to secure good roads at provincial rather than district expense, protested high official salaries when farmers were getting "only 3/ a bushel for wheat and 10/ a hundredweight for Pork," and wanted assessments reduced so as not to burden farmers. He also supported reforms later to be part of the Clear Grits' programme: vote by ballot, abolition of the laws of primogeniture, and measures to ensure the legislature's independence.

When the second La Fontaine–Baldwin ministry came to power, Price was made commissioner of crown lands, a post he held from 20 April 1848 to 27 Oct. 1851. In 1849, after a powerful speech in support of the ministry's Rebellion Losses Bill, his lodgings in Montreal were attacked during the riots that followed its passage.

A Congregationalist, a member of Zion Church, Toronto, and a staunch voluntaryist, Price favoured provincial support for common schools and a secular university. He was determined to bring about secularization of the clergy reserves and cancellation of the rectory patents set up by Lieutenant Governor Sir John Colborne* in 1836. For a while, he accepted Baldwin's cautious policy on these thorny issues, but in

September 1849, when his intention to resign from the cabinet became known, he was rumoured to be tired of Baldwin's temporizing. Price insisted he was simply weary of having to be absent from home for the parliamentary sessions, but Baldwin again persuaded him to change his mind. In the session of 1850 Price, speaking as a private member because of divisions within the ministry, introduced 32 resolutions dealing with the clergy reserves, which ended with a motion for an address to the crown asking for legislation to enable Canada to settle the problem itself. The motion was successful.

Price decided to contest York South again in the election of December 1851. He had tried to accelerate Baldwin's reforms but had stood by him during the session of 1851, supporting Hincks in asking for legal adjudication of the rectories question and helping to defeat reforms desired by some Clear Grits and William Lyon Mackenzie, now returned and elected in a by-election in Haldimand County the previous April. Mackenzie visited Price's riding in December, accused him of betraying his own constituents, and persuaded the Reform convention of York South to nominate David Gibson*. In the three-way contest that followed, both were defeated by John William Gamble, a Tory. (Price, unhappy at Mackenzie's interference in the election, then successfully sued Mackenzie for the remaining portion of unpaid pre-rebellion debts.) A letter Price wrote to Lesslie in 1864 shows that the bitterness of the electoral defeat was deep and long lasting. "I struggled with you [the Reformers] for twenty-five years, the very prime of my life, and was thrown aside, neglected, insulted and forgotten." Price took little part in politics thereafter.

Noted for his integrity, Price had neither speculated nor run into debt and had once boasted that he owed no bank a sixpence. When commissioner of crown lands he turned down offers from George Brown* and John Doel to buy land for him under their names. The Toronto *Globe* had commented in 1849 that "there is no man in Reform ranks who holds more thoroughly than Mr. Price the confidence of his party," and that there were "few men, if any, in whom the great mass of the liberal religious denominations of Canada place such perfect reliance."

Price had ceased to practise law by 1857 but was still resident in Toronto. By 1860 he had left Canada and was living near Bath, England, spending his time in "listless idleness." Nevertheless he continued to correspond with his Reform colleagues, advocating dissolution of the union and independence from the crown rather than representation by population as the solution for the troubles of Canada West. He enjoyed a long life in retirement, dying on 13 July 1882 at Shirley, near Southampton, England.

LILLIAN F. GATES

AO, MU 1805–949: MU 3278; MTL, Robert Baldwin papers. PAC, MG 24, B40. *Debates of the Legislative Assembly of United Canada* (Gibbs *et al.*), I–IX. *Examiner* (Toronto), 12 Sept. 1849, 17 Dec. 1851. *Globe*, 15 Sept., 4 Oct. 1849. *Dominion annual register*, 1882: 356. E. J. Hathaway, *Jesse Ketchum and his times: being a chronicle of the social life and public affairs of the province of Upper Canada during its first half century* (Toronto, 1929). Charles Lindsey, *The life and times of Wm. Lyon Mackenzie . . .* (2v., Toronto, 1862; repr. 1971).

PROULX, JEAN-BAPTISTE, Roman Catholic priest and missionary; b. 8 May 1808 in Lachine, Lower Canada, son of Louis-Basile Proulx, a farmer, and Marie-Thaïs Foisy; d. 25 March 1881 in Terrebonne, Que.

Little is known of Jean-Baptiste Proulx's early life. He entered the Séminaire de Saint-Hyacinthe in 1825, attended the Petit Séminaire de Montréal in 1829–30, and began his theological studies in 1831. Ordained priest on 26 July 1835 by Bishop Jean-Jacques Lartigue* and Bishop Rémi Gaulin* in Montreal, he was sent to La Prairie on 26 September. The following month, however, he was transferred to the diocese of Kingston in Upper Canada; its coadjustor bishop, Gaulin, intended to send him to Penetanguishene, which in the 17th century had been an area of Catholic missionary endeavour [*see* Jean de Brébeuf*].

Significant demographic and administrative changes were taking place in Upper Canada as Proulx began his mission at Penetaguishene in early November 1835. Immigration had greatly increased the Roman Catholic population of the province, necessitating expansion of the church's activities. As its strength grew, the church resumed its missionary work among the Indians and was eventually able to provide the Indians of the Coldwater-Penetanguishene area with the French-speaking priest they had requested in 1833. These ecclesiastical developments were paralleled by important changes in the policy and administration of the Indian Department. The reserve system which had emerged by the 1830s, based as it was on the goal of cultural assimilation, emphasized physical isolation, education, and religion in the "civilizing" of the Indians. This policy, and the wrong-headed enthusiasm of Lieutenant Governor Sir Francis Bond Head*, had resulted in the choice of Manitoulin Island as a reserve for the entire Indian population of Upper Canada. The island was ceded by treaty to the Indians in 1836 but the plan for the island would eventually prove unsuccessful [*see* Jean-Baptiste Assiginack*].

Proulx was to be affected still further by these changes for he was transferred to the mission station on the island in 1837. The following year the Church of England also established a mission there, manned at first by the Reverend Charles Crosbie Brough and after 1841 by Frederick Augustus O'MEARA. The relationship between the two missions exacerbated differences which already existed among the Indians of Manitoulin Island. Manitowaning, where the Indian Department established its headquarters in 1837–38 under the direction of experienced Superintendent Thomas Gummersall Anderson*, remained the centre of the Anglican-oriented "official" community: Roman Catholic and dissident Indians withdrew to the village of Wikwemikong where they formed a loose local "counter-culture." Proulx's mission became one of the focal points for this second community.

There was frequent wrangling between the communities of Wikwemikong and Manitowaning. The Indian Department wanted to create model agricultural communities; the Anglican mission acceded to these wishes, but enjoyed only a marginal existence. The Roman Catholic mission, however, encouraged a sense of independence from the government establishment and the Wikwemikong band combined limited cultivation with a traditional life based on hunting and fishing. The bitterness engendered in Manitowaning by Proulx's ignoring many of Superintendent Anderson's directives was increased by the growth and success of Wikwemikong. Relations between the Catholic missionary on the one side, and the Manitowaning office of the Indian Department and the Irish evangelical Anglican clergy on the other, varied from cool to hostile.

In addition to these political and administrative difficulties, Proulx faced the usual ones of severe winters and cultural barriers created by the variety of Indian dialects. He persisted despite these problems and seemed to enjoy greater success than his Church of England counterparts in winning the affection of his people. Even Brough acknowledged the zeal and energy of the "laborious enterprising Roman Catholic priest." Proulx was successful as a missionary for two reasons. The Roman Catholic Church was more flexible than the Church of England in its expectations about the way Christians should live, stressing participation in the visible life of the church rather than a complete change in life-style as the sign of conversion. Secondly, by establishing himself at Wikwemikong, Proulx demonstrated his independence of Manitowaning, and Indians with misgivings about the plans of that centre were drawn to the Catholic rather than the Anglican mission.

On 19 Dec. 1846 Michael Power*, Roman Catholic bishop of Toronto, in whose diocese Manitoulin Island was then situated, appointed the veteran missionary to Newmarket with responsibility for surrounding townships in York and Simcoe counties. In 1848 Proulx was transferred to Oshawa. Although he had expressed the desire to minister to the Indians of Red River (Man.), the shortage of priests in the diocese prevented his leaving; instead, Proulx found himself travelling through most of Ontario County for the next 12 years, meeting the needs of its pioneer Catholic community. He supervised the building and enlargement of churches in Highland Creek and Oshawa, established a separate school in the latter, and purchased land for presbyteries and other churches. In 1860 he was called to Toronto; after a brief stay at St Michael's Cathedral he was named chaplain to the garrison. He was appointed assistant to John Walsh* at St Mary's parish in 1862 and became its pastor in 1867. His effectiveness as a counsellor and an administrator was recognized in 1870 when Bishop John Joseph LYNCH made him dean of St Michael's. Proulx held this position until his death. In 1879 he was further honoured by being named a domestic prelate. Two years later he died unexpectedly while visiting his brother in Terrebonne.

Jean-Baptiste Proulx's career illustrates some important but often overlooked themes in Ontario's history. The difficulties of administering the Indian reserve policy are clearly seen in his Penetanguishene and Manitoulin years, and the impact of large numbers of immigrants upon religious structures can be observed through his work in the diocese of Toronto. Proulx's life spanned the period during which the pioneer community of Upper Canada became the settled province of Ontario, and a study of his career provides a helpful perspective on that development.

DOUGLAS LEIGHTON

Arch. of the Archdiocese of Toronto, Macdonell papers, AB31, no.11; AC07, no.5; Power letterbook, 1842–65. PAC, RG 10, A4; A5; CI, 3. [C. C. Brough], "The Manitoulin letters of the Rev. Charles Crosbie Brough," ed. R. M. Lewis, *OH*, 48 (1956): 63–80. *Globe*, 26 March 1881. *Montreal Daily Star*, 26 March 1881. Allaire, *Dictionnaire*, I. Ivanhoë Caron, "Inventaire de la correspondance de Mgr Bernard-Claude Panet, archevêque de Québec," ANQ *Rapport*, 1935–36: 234; "Inventaire de la correspondance de Monseigneur Joseph Signay, archevêque de Québec, 1825–1835," 1936–37: 154, 245, 302. L.-A. Desrosiers, "Correspondance de Mgr Ignace Bourget pour 1842 et 1843," ANQ *Rapport*, 1948–49: 426; "Correspondance de Mgr Jean-Jacques Lartigue de 1833 à 1836," 1943–44: 301, 306, 313, 314. *Dominion annual register*, 1880–81. Léon Pouliot, "Inventaire analytique de la correspondance de Mgr Ignace Bourget pour l'année 1845," ANQ *Rapport*, 1961–64: 39. Léon Pouliot et François Beaudin, "Inventaire analytique de la correspondance de Mgr Ignace Bourget pour les années 1849 et 1850," ANQ *Rapport*, 1969: 24. C.-P. Choquette, *Histoire du séminaire de Saint-Hyacinthe depuis sa fondation jusqu'à nos jours* (2v., Montréal, 1911–12). J. D. Leighton, "The development of federal Indian policy in Canada, 1840–1890" (PHD thesis, Univ. of Western Ontario, London, 1975). *The story of St. Paul's parish, Toronto . . .*, ed. Edward Kelly ([Toronto], 1922). Ruth Bleasdale, "Manitowaning: an experiment in Indian settlement," *OH*, 66 (1974): 147–57. [J.] D. Leighton, "The Manitoulin incident of 1863: an Indian-white confrontation in the province of Canada," *OH*, 69 (1977): 113–24. R. J.

Surtees, "The development of an Indian reserve policy in Canada," *OH*, 61 (1969): 87–98.

PROVENCHER (Villebrun, *dit* **Provencher), JOSEPH-ALFRED-NORBERT** (baptized **Joseph-Albert**), lawyer, journalist, and public servant; b. 6 Jan. 1843 at Baie-du-Febvre (Baieville), Canada East, son of Godfroi Villebrun, *dit* Provencher, a farmer, and Placide Lafrance; m. 24 May 1876 Louise Delagrave at Quebec City; d. 28 Oct. 1887 in Montreal, Que.

His father having died when he was very young, Joseph-Alfred-Norbert Provencher received his classical education at the Séminaire de Nicolet from 1851 to 1859 through the help of his uncle, Joseph-Norbert Provencher*, the bishop of St Boniface (Man.). When he left the college, he articled in Trois-Rivières in the law office of William McDougall. Around 1862, while engaged in his legal studies, Provencher founded the short-lived newspaper, *La Sentinelle* (Trois-Rivières). Called to the Montreal bar on 30 April 1864, he did not immediately go into practice, since a career as a journalist seemed more attractive, and he became night editor at *La Minerve* in Montreal. A contemporary journalist, Léon Ledieu, recounted that when Provencher arrived people wondered what "this tall, bulky fellow, with an odd-looking head, hands of a Hercules, sloppy garb, heavy gait, and enormous bushy mop of hair" could be doing in the editorial office of a newspaper. That year, with writers Napoléon Bourassa*, Joseph Royal*, and several others, he helped found *La Revue canadienne* (Montreal); in it he published several well-researched articles on such subjects as constitutional issues and political economy. For a time he was also secretary of the literary circle attached to the Cabinet de Lecture Paroissial.

In 1867 the Conservative party chose Provencher as candidate in the federal elections in Yamaska, a stronghold of the Liberal party; he was narrowly defeated by the Rouge candidate Moïse Fortier. He continued to hold the post of editor of *La Minerve*, which he had been given on the departure of Évariste Gélinas* in 1866. He left the paper in 1869 when he was appointed secretary to William McDougall*, the Ontario politician who was named the new lieutenant governor of the North-West Territories, the sale of which had just been negotiated in London. In October 1869 he went in this capacity to the Red River Settlement (Man.) in advance of McDougall, to assert the authority of the Canadian government in the territory, but on his arrival in St Norbert on 1 November was arrested and imprisoned. He explained to his captors, among them Louis RIEL, that the imperial parliament in London had authorized the annexation of the territories to Canada, and that the Canadian House of Commons, with the Hudson's Bay Company's agreement, had approved the terms of the transfer. Released after one day, he was escorted by Riel's troops to Pembina (West Lynne, Man.) and forced to seek refuge in American territory. There McDougall, who had unsuccessfully tried to enter the colony, ordered him to draft proclamations calling on the Métis to surrender their lands. It was later learned that McDougall did not have the authority to issue these proclamations and that they were not valid.

After McDougall's return to Ottawa and the re-establishment of order in the Red River region, Provencher presumably went back to central Canada. In October 1871 he was appointed immigration commissioner in Manitoba for the federal Department of Agriculture. In 1872 he was given the responsibility of representing the Canadian government in Paris, to encourage French immigration to Canada. He left Paris the following year to return to Manitoba as commissioner for the federal Department of Indian Affairs, a post he retained until 1876. His duties included negotiating treaties with a number of Indian nations to acquire their lands in return for compensation, including sums of money. Thus, with Simon James Dawson* he served on a commission led by Alexander MORRIS which in 1873 concluded Treaty no. 3 with the Ojibwa of the Lake of the Woods area, whereby the Ojibwa ceded all their lands to the Canadian government. After leaving the Department of Indian Affairs, Provencher practised law and worked as a notary in Winnipeg, in partnership with Michel Carey. In 1877 he represented the Collège de Saint-Boniface on the council of the University of Manitoba. Two years later he ran as a government candidate in the provincial elections in St Boniface, but received only 4 votes against 127 for his opponent, Alphonse-Alfred-Clément La Rivière*. As a result of this defeat, he decided to turn to writing again.

Back in Montreal in 1880, Provencher once more worked in the office of *La Minerve*, which was under the editorship of his friend Joseph Tassé*. For a short time he was editor of *Le Monde* (1883), and then of *La Presse* (1884–85). He also contributed to *Le Figaro* (Montreal) in 1883, to the *Nouvelles Soirées canadiennes* in 1884, and to *La Minerve* from 1885 to 1887. After a brief illness he died in Montreal in his 45th year, and was remembered as a journalist of superior talent and a conscientious and honest administrator. As journalist Léon Ledieu observed, "Provencher was the last of the Dansereau, Decelles and Dunn generation."

KENNETH LANDRY

[As a journalist Joseph-Alfred-Norbert Provencher wrote on a variety of subjects, including the British constitution, land credit, the agricultural census of Canada East, and the paper manufacturing industry. His articles can be found in a number of newspapers and journals including the *Rev. canadienne*, 1864–69, *La Minerve*, 1864–69, 1880–87, *Le Monde*, 1883, and *La Presse*, 1884–87. K. L.]

ANQ-Q, AP-G-134. Morris, *Treaties of Canada with the Indians*. *Le Canadien*, 2 nov. 1887. *L'Événement*, 22 avril 1870. *La Minerve*, 29 oct. 1887. *Le Monde*, 29 oct. 1887. *Le Monde illustré* (Montréal), 12 nov. 1887. *La Presse*, 29 oct. 1887. Beaulieu et J. Hamelin, *La presse québécoise*, II: 20; III: 51, 71. A.-G. Morice, *Dictionnaire historique des Canadiens et des Métis français de l'Ouest* (Québec et Montréal, 1908). J.-A.-I. Douville, *Histoire du collège-séminaire de Nicolet, 1803–1903, avec les listes complètes des directeurs, professeurs et élèves de l'institution* (2v., Montréal, 1903). Stanley, *Birth of western Canada*; *Louis Riel*. L. H. Thomas, *The struggle for responsible government in the North-West Territories, 1870–97* (Toronto, 1956). Donatien Frémont, "Alfred-Norbert Provencher, 1843–1887," RSC *Trans.*, 3rd ser., 51 (1957), sect.I: 29–41.

PRYOR, WILLIAM, merchant and banker; b. 16 March 1801 at Halifax, N.S., eldest son of William Pryor* and Mary Barbara Foss; m. in 1840 Johanna von Schwartz in Hamburg (German Federal Republic), and they had one son and four daughters; d. 8 June 1884 at Halifax.

The grandson of a New York loyalist of Anglican persuasion, William Pryor was born into a prominent Halifax merchant family. After receiving a rudimentary formal education, he entered the family business, serving his father first as a clerk and later as supercargo on vessels dispatched to foreign ports. In 1828 he became junior partner in the firm, which grew to include his two younger brothers as well as his brother-in-law. William Pryor and Sons pioneered in trade with Brazil and at its mid-Victorian height "carried on the largest mercantile business in Halifax." In 1862 its Lower Water Street premises were valued at £16,000 and the firm dealt primarily in the exchange of British American fish and timber for Caribbean sugar, rum, and molasses. Although once active in the international carrying trade, by 1866 the firm owned but 419 tons of shipping.

When his father died in 1859, William as his eldest son succeeded to control of the family enterprises, which included a directorship in the Halifax Banking Company. The younger Pryor's business career peaked in 1867 when he followed his father's example by becoming president of this, Halifax's oldest banking house. He had earlier succeeded his father as president of the Nova Scotia Marine Insurance Company and secured election to the presidency of the Halifax Chamber of Commerce. As befitted a man of property, William Pryor Jr also served in such fashionable philanthropic capacities as vice-president of the Nova Scotia Bible Society and as director of the Colonial and Continental Church Society and the St Paul's Alms House of Industry for Girls.

Despite a Tory political cast which expressed itself in his vigorous opposition to the coming of responsible government in the late 1840s, Pryor's enthusiasm for railways eventually carried him into an alliance with Nova Scotia's leading Reformer, Joseph Howe*. In 1854 the Liberal government of William YOUNG appointed Pryor to the board charged with supervising construction of the province's publicly financed railways. He retained the post until prompted to resign in 1858 in protest against the new Conservative administration's dismissal of James R. Forman, the chief engineer of the government railway system. Pryor's chairmanship of a Liberal nominating rally in Halifax a year later reiterated his lack of sympathy for Conservative politicians, and this alienation from Charles Tupper* may have contributed to Pryor's decision to oppose confederation. Probably more persuasive in shaping his views towards confederation was the fact that, being a traditionalist in business matters, Pryor had eschewed investment in mining and manufacturing, and accordingly, was indifferent to arguments that colonial union would industrialize Nova Scotia.

William Pryor was one of the first victims of the decay which afflicted the economy of the Maritime provinces late in the 19th century. Rendered complacent by years of prosperity in the commission import-export business, Pryor's firm found itself overextended in 1873 when an international business recession reduced consumer demand and froze commercial credit. By December Pryor was mortgaging his domestic real estate in an effort to secure additional working capital. The gambit failed, and in March 1875 William Pryor and Sons declared bankruptcy, with liabilities of $125,000 against assets of, at most, $70,000. Creditors were offered 40 cents on the dollar. A humiliated William Pryor resigned as president of the Halifax Banking Company and abandoned his prestigious Hollis Street residence. When he died intestate in 1884 he left an estate valued at $8,253.83, the bulk of which came from life insurance. His failure as a businessman, however, was not an isolated phenomenon, for he belonged to that host of Halifax merchants who could not cope with the passsing of Nova Scotia's "Golden Age."

DAVID A. SUTHERLAND

William Pryor was the author of *The Halifax & Quebec railway, considered with a view to its cost, as well as the prospective business of the road* (Halifax, 1851).

Halifax County Court of Probate (Halifax), no.3246 (mfm. at PANS). Halifax County Registry of Deeds (Halifax), Deeds, 143, 195, 197 (mfm. at PANS). PANS, RG 1, 453; RG 35A, 4. N.S., House of Assembly, *Debates and proc.*, 1855–58; *Journal and proc.*, 1859; *Statutes*, 1866, c.90. *Acadian Recorder*, 1875, 1884. *British Colonist* (Halifax), 1858. *Evening Express* (Halifax), 1858–59. *Halifax Morning Sun*, 1858, 1862. *Morning Chronicle* (Halifax), 1845–48, 1858–59. *Morning Herald* (Halifax), 1875, 1884. *Novascotian*, 1828, 1836, 1866–67, 1884. *Royal Gazette* (Halifax), 1875. *Belcher's farmer's almanack*, 1824–62. W. E. Boggs, *The genealogical record of the Boggs family, the descendants of Ezekiel Boggs* (Halifax, 1916).

McAlpine's Halifax city directory . . . (Halifax), 1869–85. *Nova Scotia registry of shipping: with standard rules for construction and classification*, comp. T. R. Dewolf (Halifax, 1866). J. W. Regan, *Sketches and traditions of the Northwest Arm (illustrated) and with panoramic folder of the Arm* (2nd ed., Halifax, 1909). V. Ross and Trigge, *Hist. of Canadian Bank of Commerce*, I.

PULLEN, WILLIAM JOHN SAMUEL, naval officer and Arctic explorer; b. 4 Dec. 1813 at Devonport, England, second child and eldest son of Lieutenant William Pullen and Amelia Mary Haswell; m. 25 Aug. 1845 Abigail Louisa Berton at Saint John, N.B., and they had four sons and one daughter; d. 11 Jan. 1887 at Torquay, England.

William John Samuel Pullen was educated at the Greenwich Hospital school and following family tradition entered the Royal Navy on 15 June 1828 as a 1st class volunteer. He served in the Mediterranean in the mid 1830s and in 1835 met Colonel William Light, surveyor general of South Australia, who persuaded Pullen to accompany him in 1836 to the new colony as an assistant surveyor. Pullen remained there until July 1841 surveying the mouth of the Murray River and the adjoining coast. He then returned to England and in May 1842 rejoined the navy as a mate. On 14 July 1842 he was appointed to HMS *Columbia* under the command of Captain William Fitz William Owen* and later of Lieutenant Peter Frederick SHORTLAND and was employed in surveying the Bay of Fundy and the Saint John River. Pullen was promoted lieutenant on 9 Nov. 1846 and remained on the *Columbia* until she was paid off in 1848.

As was the custom, Pullen, the junior lieutenant, was sent to the Admiralty to return the charts and chronometers. In London he accepted an appointment, 12 May 1848, as 1st lieutenant under Captain Thomas Edward Laws Moore in HMS *Plover*. The *Plover* was to sail for the Bering Strait as a base ship for an expedition in search of Sir John Franklin*. The expedition, which included Captain Henry Kellett* and HMS *Herald*, reached Chamisso Island in Kotzebue Sound, Alaska, on 15 July 1849 and Pullen was sent by Moore with two boats to search the coast near Cape Lisburne for a winter berth. He was unsuccessful and the ships proceeded to Wainwright Inlet.

On 27 July Moore ordered Pullen to set off with two officers and 22 men in four boats to search the north coast of the continent as far east as the Mackenzie River for signs of Franklin. At Point Barrow (Alaska), on 2 August, Pullen found the ice conditions so severe and the sea so shallow that two days later he sent the two largest boats back to Wainwright Inlet. With the Mackenzie River still some 500 miles to the east, Pullen and the remainder of the party continued along the shallow waters of the relatively unknown coast. Despite bad weather, and encounters with aggressive Inuit, Pullen reached the mouth of the Mackenzie on 2 September, and four days later he arrived at Fort McPherson (N.W.T.). The party was then dispersed to winter at the various Hudson's Bay Company posts in the area, such as Fort Franklin and Fort Simpson.

On 20 June 1850 Pullen and his men left Fort Simpson with Dr John Rae*, an HBC officer in the Mackenzie River District, bound for York Factory (Man.) and England. En route they received a dispatch from the Admiralty containing a commission dated 25 Jan. 1850 promoting Pullen commander and sanctioning the continuation of the search for Franklin, this time east of the Mackenzie "if Captain Pullen should consider it practicable." Pullen and his party returned to Fort Simpson where they were re-equipped and started down the Mackenzie on 11 July 1850 for the Beaufort Sea. They then travelled east, reaching Cape Bathurst by 8 August. However, beyond the cape the sea was a mass of broken jumbled ice making further progress impossible, and they travelled back up the Mackenzie to spend the winter of 1850–51 at Fort Simpson and at Big Island (N.W.T.). In the spring they left for York Factory with the annual HBC fur brigade and arrived back in London in October.

Pullen, in his two years in the Arctic, had commanded two expeditions, explored the coast from Point Barrow to the Mackenzie River, and ascertained that there were no signs of Franklin west of the Mackenzie. Almost immediately after his return to England he accepted another Arctic assignment on 20 Feb. 1852 when he was appointed to command HMS *North Star*, the store ship of Sir Edward Belcher*'s proposed Arctic expedition. In this ship Pullen spent the winters of 1852–53 and 1853–54 in Erebus and Terror bays, Beechey Island [*see* Robert MCCORMICK]. The *North Star* was the only ship of the five in the Belcher expedition to return to England in October 1854, the others being abandoned by order of Belcher when beset in the ice.

In 1855 Pullen assumed command of HMS *Falcon* in operations against the Russians in the Baltic and on 10 May 1856 he was promoted captain. In 1857–58 he was involved in operations in the Middle East which included the surveying of the route for the submarine telegraph cable from Suez to Aden. From 1859 to 1860 he was engaged in HMS *Cyclops* surveying the south and east coasts of Ceylon, and in 1863 in HMS *Terror*, taking charge of a survey of Bermuda. Pullen then served in coastguard ships from 1867 until he was placed on the retired list on 1 April 1870. He was promoted rear-admiral on 1 Feb. 1874 and vice-admiral on 1 Feb. 1879. Pullen was granted a Greenwich Hospital pension in February 1886 and died the following year.

HUGH FRANCIS PULLEN

W. J. S. Pullen was the author of "The Red Sea electric cable" and of "Voyage of H.M.S. 'Cyclops,' Captain W. J. S. Pullen, to the Red Sea, 1857–8," in *Nautical*

Magazine and Naval Chronicle (London), 27 (1858): 353–57 and 337–44 respectively. Pullen's account of his Arctic expedition is found in "Pullen in search of Franklin," *Beaver*, outfit 277 (March 1947): 40–43; outfit 278 (June 1947): 22–25.

State Library of South Australia, Arch. (Adelaide), "Biographical notes on Vice-Admiral William John Samuel Pullen"; "Manuscript narrative by Vice-Admiral W. J. S. Pullen. . . ." [Edward Belcher], *The last of the Arctic voyages . . . in search of Sir John Franklin, during the years 1852–53–54 . . .* (2v., London, 1855). J. W. Bull, *Early experiences of life in South Australia, and an extended colonial history* (Adelaide and London, 1884). G.B., Parl., Command paper, 1852, L, [1449], pp.695–735, *Arctic expedition: further correspondence and proceedings connected with the Arctic expedition*; 1854, XLII, [1725], pp.207–13, 235–40, 246–48, *Papers relative to the recent Arctic expeditions in search of Sir John Franklin and the crews of H.M.S. "Erebus" and "Terror."* W. H. Hooper, *Ten months among the tents of the Tuski, with incidents of an Arctic boat expedition in search of Sir John Franklin, as far as the Mackenzie River, and Cape Bathurst* (London, 1853). [John Rae], *John Rae's correspondence with the Hudson's Bay Company on Arctic exploration, 1844–1855*, ed. E. E. Rich and A. M. Johnson (London, 1953). *Russian war, 1855, Baltic: official correspondence*, ed. David Bonner-Smith (London, 1944). *DNB*. G.B., Adm., *Navy list*, 1846; 1847; 1849; 1852; 1855; 1857; 1864; 1868; 1870. W. L. Clowes *et al.*, *The Royal Navy; a history from the earliest times to the present* (7v., London, 1897–1903), VII.

PUNSHON, WILLIAM MORLEY, Methodist minister and author; b. 29 May 1824 at Doncaster, England, the only child of John Punshon and Elizabeth Morley; m. first 22 Aug. 1849 Maria Vickers (d. 1858), and they had at least four children; m. secondly 15 Aug. 1868 Fanny Vickers (d. 1870); m. thirdly 17 June 1873 Mary Foster; d. 14 April 1881 at Tranby Lodge, Brixton, Devon, England.

William Morley Punshon's father was a successful mercer who died in 1840. After a short business career Punshon was received on probation for the ministry in 1845 and ordained four years later. His rise in the church was rapid. He won early attention as a public speaker on religious themes, making an impressive debut at Exeter Hall, the evangelical centre in London, while still in his 20s. He was elected in 1859 to the "legal hundred," the body of preachers to whom John Wesley had assigned the legal conduct of the Methodist conference. In 1861 he helped to establish and edit the influential *Methodist Recorder* (London). And, in the early 1860s, Punshon waged a successful campaign to raise over £10,000 to build new churches in resort areas in order to carry the Methodist gospel to the watering-places in England.

Punshon came to Canada in 1868 at a time when the British conference exerted considerable legal authority over the colonial churches. After an initial inquiry by Egerton RYERSON and upon the formal suggestion of the Canadian church, the British conference appointed Punshon president of the conference of the Wesleyan Methodist Church in Canada. Living in Toronto, he held the position for five one-year terms from 1868 to 1872. In 1868 he was also appointed president of the Wesleyan Methodist Conference of Eastern British America (for one year) and the representative of the British conference to the Methodist Episcopal Church in the United States. The Canadian positions gave him power over the administrative and public life of his church (he described his office as "quasi-episcopal"), and his American position gave him the opportunity to tour extensively in the United States.

Coming to Canada also allowed Punshon to marry Fanny Vickers, the sister of his first wife. This type of marriage, still forbidden by English law, was generally accepted in Canada even though its legal status was not fully secure until 1882.

Punshon's reputation in England and his very visible presence in North America raised the respectability of Canadian Methodism. He took particular interest in missionary activity and in building new Wesleyan churches in the revived Gothic style. Their beauty, Punshon believed, not only spoke to the sacred reality of God on earth, but also to the high position that Methodism enjoyed in Canada where she was free from the shadow of an English establishment church. The greatest architectural monument to his work in Canada was the Metropolitan (Methodist) Church in Toronto.

Punshon used his lectures and sermons to raise funds for these new churches and other Methodist institutions. When Victoria College in Cobourg was faced with bankruptcy by the withdrawal of the government grant in 1868, he campaigned for a new endowment from pulpit and lectern and made a large personal contribution. His generous and conciliatory manner also helped to lay the foundation for the union of the Wesleyan Methodist Church in Canada, the Eastern British America conference, and the Methodist New Connexion Church in Canada. His last conference in 1872 did much of the preliminary work for the union, which would be completed in 1874 after Punshon had returned to England.

Punshon (who had received an LLD from Victoria College in 1872) went back to England in 1873 after declining a position teaching moral philosophy at the University of Toronto and offers of well-situated pulpits in the United States. He was elected president of the British Wesleyan conference for 1874 and then accepted the important office of missionary secretary the following year. Declining health limited his activities although he played an active role in support of lay representation in the annual Methodist conferences. A journey to the south of France and Italy failed to restore his strength, and he returned to England where he died in 1881.

William Morley Punshon was one of the most highly regarded English religious leaders to serve in Canada during the Victorian period. His public lectures and sermons during his long career achieved widespread popularity throughout the empire while his administrative ability, especially in support of conciliation, church expansion, and missions, served the British Wesleyan connection well for almost 40 years. Punshon also composed poetry of a meditative and devotional nature. All his writing tended to be parabolical in form and moral in intention; unfortunately, it has not aged well. He is now remembered in Canada primarily for his important contributions to the progress of Wesleyanism in the years immediately following confederation.

WILLIAM WESTFALL

William Morley Punshon was the author of "Broken cisterns," published in *The Canadian Methodist pulpit: a collection of original sermons, from living ministers of the Wesleyan Methodist Church in Canada*, ed. S. G. Phillips (Toronto and Montreal, 1875), 1–22; *Canada: its religious prospects; an address delivered before the English Wesleyan conference, at Manchester, July 26th, 1871* (Toronto, 1871); *Mutual obligation; or, the duties of the pulpit and the pew to each other, and of both to God: two addresses delivered in the Richmond Street Church, Toronto* (Toronto, [1869]), which was also published as *The pulpit and the pew: their duties to each other and to God . . .* (London, 1869); *The prodigal son: four discourses* (Toronto, 1868); *The Rev. W. M. Punshon, M.A.: a sketch of his life, with sermons recently delivered by him in London, and a variety of choice selections from his public addresses, discourses, and writings* (London, 1871); *Sabbath chimes; meditations in verse for the Sundays of a year* (London, 1868); *Select lectures and sermons* (Cincinnati, Ohio, 1860); *Sermons* (2v., London, 1882–84); and *Tabor; or, the class meeting: a plea and an appeal; addressed to hearers of the Wesleyan ministry . . .* (Toronto, 1855).

UCA, Biog. files, W. M. Punshon; Church hist. files, Ont., Toronto, Metropolitan Methodist Church; Wesleyan Methodist Church in Canada, Minutes, 1867–74. Joseph Dawson, *William Morley Punshon: the orator of Methodism* (London, [1906]). F. W. Macdonald, *The life of William Morley Punshon, LL.D.* (London, 1887; 2nd ed., 1887; 3rd ed., 1888). Alexander Sutherland, *Methodism in Canada; its work and its story: being the thirty-third Fernley lecture delivered in Penzance, 31st July 1903* (London, 1903; Toronto, 1904). M. A. Banks, "Marriage with a deceased wife's sister: law and practice in Upper Canada, with a summary of post-confederation changes," *Western Ontario Hist. Notes* (London), 25 (1969–70), no.2: 1–6. J. W. Caldwell, "The unification of Methodism in Canada, 1865–1884," United Church of Canada, Committee on Arch., *Bull.* (Toronto), 19 (1967).

R

RACINE, DOMINIQUE, Roman Catholic priest and bishop; b. 21 Jan. 1828 in the parish of Saint-Ambroise, Jeune-Lorette (Loretteville), Lower Canada, son of Michel Racine, a blacksmith, and Louise Pepin; d. 28 Jan. 1888 at Chicoutimi, Que.

Dominique Racine's father died at about the age of 40, leaving one daughter and six sons, the eldest of whom was 15. The family was brought up in very modest circumstances, verging on real poverty. From early childhood Dominique, the second youngest, was no doubt influenced by his brothers Michel and Antoine*, both of whom studied at the Seminaire de Québec. He himself studied there from 1840 to 1849, and then attended the Grand Séminaire until 1853 when he was ordained priest. The remainder of his life was extremely active. Until 1858 he was curate in the parish of Notre-Dame in Quebec, and a secretary in the office of the archdiocese. In 1859 he ministered to the parish of Saint-Basile. He was parish priest of Saint-Patrice at Rivière-du-Loup from 1859 to 1862, and first came into contact with the Saguenay region in 1862 when he was appointed vicar forane and parish priest of Chicoutimi.

Abbé Racine travelled all over this immense region with its rigorous climate for many years, building, preaching, and working unremittingly to organize the church in the Saguenay, and never failing to display the profound graciousness to which his contemporaries often testified. His efforts were crowned by the erection of the diocese of Chicoutimi (embracing the counties of Chicoutimi and Saguenay, Charlevoix, and Lac Saint-Jean), of which he became the first bishop on 4 Aug. 1878. Meanwhile he had established in the region both the first convent school, which in 1864 was entrusted to the Congregation of the Sisters, Servants of the Immaculate Heart of Mary, known as the Sisters of the Good Shepherd, and in 1873 a seminary which produced several generations of priests. Finally, in 1882 he founded the Hôtel-Dieu de Saint-Vallier at Chicoutimi, run by the Religieuses Hospitalières de la Miséricorde de Jésus (Augustinian Nuns), and a domestic training college at Roberval, for which the Ursulines of Quebec assumed responsibility. He was also active in public life, participating in the dispute over the railway from Quebec City to the Saguenay in which regional interests and those of Quebec financiers clashed, the controversies arising from the stagnant state of agriculture, and the latent conflict resulting from the iniquitous conditions imposed on lumbermen by the family of William Price*.

From 1871, as vicar general to Bishop Elzéar-Alexandre Taschereau*, Racine spoke out on current issues such as the controversy between the Université Laval and its Montreal branch [*see* Ignace BOURGET; Joseph DESAUTELS], the division of the diocese of Trois-Rivières [*see* Luc DESILETS], and the Jesuit estates question [*see* Antoine-Nicolas BRAUN]. In 1882 and 1885, in Rome, he served as the forceful spokesman for the archbishop of Quebec on the university question. His correspondence reveals his continuing attention to the affairs of Quebec as well as those of his diocese.

Racine thus made an important contribution to the creation and maintenance of the social power of the clergy in the Saguenay. This power was clearly demonstrated when the Hotel-Dieu de Saint-Vallier was founded. In January 1882 Bishop Racine had learned that the federal government had authorized the construction of a naval hospital in Chicoutimi. He wanted the hospital to be run by nuns, but the contract stipulated that a layman must manage it. Bishop Racine was opposed to a lay hospital and, as a friend of Sir Hector-Louis Langevin*, the minister of public works, he managed to overcome the opposition and to have the Religieuses Hospitalières de la Miséricorde de Jésus put in charge of the new institution. In so doing he was, however, able to win over all parties, and to form friendships among both the powerful and the humble. Proof of this came in the unusual activity following his death and the extraordinary manifestations of piety it called forth. The news of his death, which occurred in mid-winter, brought people of all ages and conditions from the diocese and beyond to Chicoutimi. Around his coffin, people fought for shreds of his clothing and stubs of candles; relics were made of his hair and his cassock; his heart was bequeathed to the seminary, his lungs to the nuns of the Hôtel-Dieu. One could cite many other facts attesting to the affection which this man had been able to command.

Reflecting on the socio-economic context and the cultural environment in which Bishop Racine lived, one can imagine the power he wielded. He was, it would seem, rightly credited with not abusing that power, and with managing his affairs with much wisdom. The spiritual orientation he sought to give his clergy, the simplicity and moderation he adopted in his public life, and the efforts he made to calm discord in the Saguenay, all substantiate this claim.

GÉRARD BOUCHER

ANQ-Q, État civil, Catholiques, Saint-Ambroise (Loretteville), 21 janv. 1828. ANQ-SLSJ, Coll. Victor Tremblay, Doc., 168–69. Arch. de l'évêché de Chicoutimi (Chicoutimi, Qué.), Reg. des lettres, I. *Mandements, lettres pastorales et circulaires des évêques de Chicoutimi, Monseigneur Dominique Racine, volume unique, 1878–1888* (Chicoutimi, 1903). *Le Canadien*, 30 janv. 1888. *Le Progrès du Saguenay* (Chicoutimi), 2 févr. 1888. Allaire, *Dictionnaire.* J.-C. Drolet, *Monseigneur Dominique Racine, bâtisseur de l'Église saguenéenne* ([Chicoutimi], 1968). F.-X.-E. Frenette, *Notices biographiques et notes historiques sur le diocèse de Chicoutimi* (Chicoutimi, 1945). *Histoire de l'Hôtel-Dieu Saint-Vallier de Chicoutimi, 1884–1934* (Chicoutimi, 1934). J.-H. Charland, "Mgr Dominique Racine, 1er évêque de Chicoutimi," *Rev. canadienne*, 3e sér., 1 (1888): 724–28. Raymond Vézina, "Théophile Hamel, premier peintre du Saguenay," *Saguenayensia* (Chicoutimi), 17 (1975): 10–16.

RAIMOND. *See* RAYMOND

RAMSAY, THOMAS KENNEDY, judge and author; b. 2 Sept. 1826 at Ayr, Scotland, son of David Ramsay, whose wife was a Miss Kennedy; d. unmarried 22 Dec. 1886 at Saint-Hugues, Que.

Thomas Kennedy Ramsay came from a family belonging to the landed gentry. After studying in his native town, he attended Madras College at St Andrews. In 1847 he emigrated to Canada with his parents, and they settled at Saint-Hugues. He articled in the Montreal office of William Collis Meredith, Strachan Bethune*, and Christopher DUNKIN, and was called to the bar of Lower Canada on 4 Oct. 1852. Two years later, while in practice, he founded the *Law Reporter*, with Louis-Siméon Morin*. In 1857 he was, according to the newspapers of the day, one of the founders of the *Lower Canada Jurist* (Montreal), to which he subsequently contributed on a number of occasions.

On 10 Feb. 1859 Ramsay accepted appointment as English-speaking secretary to the commission appointed to codify the civil laws of Canada East; Joseph-Ubalde Beaudry* was appointed the French-speaking secretary. René-Édouard Caron* chaired the three-man commission whose other members were Augustin-Norbert Morin* and Charles Dewey DAY. The 1857 statute creating this body provided for the appointment of two secretaries, one of whom was to have English as his native tongue but a thorough knowledge of French as well. Having lived in France for a few years, Ramsay had an excellent grasp of French. His task was to identify the articles of the Coutume de Paris that were still in force in Canada East. But on 25 Oct. 1862 Ramsay was removed from office; according to his successor, Thomas McCord, he had been dismissed "in consequence of a quarrel between him and the Ministry of the day, which had originated in political Causes."

After losing this post, Ramsay taught civil law for a brief period at Morrin College, founded in Quebec City in 1862 by Joseph Morrin*. He published at Montreal in 1863 a legal pamphlet entitled *Government commissions of inquiry*, in which he maintained that the government could grant to judges alone commissions to inquire into crimes and offences affecting the life or liberty of British subjects. "In politics he was a Conservative to the very core," said the *Montreal Daily Star* of Ramsay. A friend of George-Étienne Cartier*, Ramsay ran as a Conservative in Huntingdon in the 1863 elections for the assembly but was defeated by Robert Brown Somerville. In 1867 he stood in Châteauguay in the first federal elections but lost to Luther Hamilton Holton*.

From 1864 to 1868 Ramsay held the office of crown attorney at Montreal. In this capacity he appeared before Francis Godschall Johnson* in Sweetsburg (Cowansville) in 1866 to prosecute the Fenians charged with invading Canada East [*see* Charles-Joseph COURSOL]. According to the *Montreal Daily Star*, Ramsay "made out his cases in such an able manner that Hon. Justice Johnson sentenced the whole lot to be hanged," but the death sentences were subsequently commuted.

In 1867 Ramsay was made a QC. He became assistant judge of the Superior Court of the province of Quebec on 5 Sept. 1870, and was elevated to the Court of Queen's Bench on 30 Oct. 1873. He enjoyed an excellent professional reputation and in 1869 his compatriot Hector Fabre* remarked that "even at Westminster Mr. Ramsay would have attracted attention for the unshakeable firmness of his character and the loftiness of his views . . . , the rigour of his dialectic, [and] his profound erudition."

Ramsay, who owned part of the Ramezay seigneury, died suddenly at his residence in Saint-Hugues, while still serving on the bench. He was survived by one sister in Montreal and two brothers. His funeral was held in Christ Church Cathedral in Montreal on 24 Dec. 1886. The day before, the *Montreal Daily Star* had paid tribute to him: "By the sudden death of Mr Justice Ramsay the bench loses one of its ablest lawyers and its most irascible judge. Perhaps we could have better spared a more amiable man. His unfortunate habit of scolding lawyers, jurymen and newspaper men was so conspicuous as to rather obscure what was no less characteristic of the man, his rare legal talent. Judge Ramsay was a bundle of contradictions. A newspaper man himself, the press was his pet aversion. Professing the utmost admiration for the jury system, his presence on the bench added a new terror to jury service. Emphatically an upright judge, he never quite got rid of the prejudice of a Crown prosecutor. Fortunately he was endowed with a keen perception and with a great capacity for taking pains."

JEAN-CHARLES BONENFANT

[Thomas Kennedy Ramsay's work on the Commission appointed to codify the civil laws of Canada East led him to publish *Notes sur la Coutume de Paris indiquant les articles encore en force avec tout le texte de la coutume à l'exception des articles relatifs aux fiefs et censives, les titres du retrait lignager et de la garde noble et bourgeoise* (Montréal, 1863; 2e éd., 1864). In 1865 he published *A digested index to the reported cases in Lower Canada . . .* at Quebec. Later, in 1887, Charles Henry Stephens edited *Ramsay's appeal cases with notes and definitions of the civil and criminal law of the province of Quebec . . .* (Montreal), a digest of appellate decisions in the years from 1873 to 1886, prepared by Ramsay. A good deal of biographical information on Ramsay can be found in *Legal News* (Montreal), 10 (1887): 1–2, 15, 23, 31, 33, 89, 169, 330. J.-C. B.]

AC, Montréal, État civil, Anglicans, Christ Church Cathedral (Montreal), 23 Dec. 1886. *L'Événement*, 23 déc. 1886. *Gazette* (Montreal), 23 Dec. 1886. *La Minerve*, 23, 27 déc. 1886. *Montreal Daily Star*, 22–24, 27, 29 Dec. 1886. *Dominion annual register*, 1886. P.-G. Roy, *Les juges de la prov. de Québec*. Wallace, *Macmillan dict*. Laureau, *Hist. de la littérature canadienne*, 403. J. E. C. Brierley, "Quebec's civil law codification; viewed and reviewed," *McGill Law Journal* (Montreal), 14 (1968): 521–89.

RAND, SILAS TERTIUS, Baptist clergyman, missionary, philologist, and ethnologist; b. 18 May 1810 in Cornwallis, N.S., son of Silas Rand and his second wife, Deborah, sister of the Reverend Charles TUPPER; m. 10 May 1838 Jane Elizabeth McNutt of Liverpool, N.S., and they had 12 children; d. 4 Oct. 1889 at Hantsport, N.S.

Silas Tertius Rand was taught to read by his father and by a succession of country teachers. During his youth he worked as a farm labourer and at 18 embarked on his family's trade of bricklaying. He went back to school when he was about 22, mastered English grammar, and himself began teaching, alternating seasons of teaching and of bricklaying. At the same time, for short periods he began to attend Horton Academy at Wolfville, N.S., where he studied Latin and Greek. Over the years he also mastered French, Italian, German, Spanish, modern Greek, Micmac, Malecite, and Mohawk. In 1834 he was ordained a Baptist minister and undertook successive pastorates at Parrsboro, Horton (Hortonville), Liverpool, and Windsor in Nova Scotia, and then at Charlottetown, P.E.I. Like many other evangelical Nova Scotians of the day he was fired with the burgeoning overseas missionary spirit of the 1840s, and in 1847 toyed with the idea of serving in a foreign mission. His wife's opposition, however, and his own fascination with the Micmac language directed his attention instead to the neglected Indians of the Maritime colonies.

Acquainted with the wandering Micmac since childhood, Rand began his lifelong association with these Indians in 1846 when he undertook the study of their language. He found an able tutor in Joseph Brooks of Digby, a Frenchman with a Micmac wife. With the object of establishing a full-time Indian mission, but denied the sponsorship of the parsimonious Baptist Church, Rand enlisted the support of the crusading Protestant evangelicals of Halifax in 1849. They responded the following year with the formation of the Micmac Missionary Society, an overtly anti-Catholic organization designed to convert the Catholicized Indians.

Rand's missionary routine included summer visits to scattered Micmac bands, supervision of the mission community at Hantsport where he moved permanently from Charlottetown in 1853, and an interminable search for funds to keep the mission in operation. Although the Halifax-based missionary society helped to publicize and finance Rand's undertaking, the burden of fund-raising fell on Rand himself. He became increasingly disenchanted with denominationalism as he saw his enterprise suffer from Protestant pedantry and rivalries, and from the decline of vital religion. Two influences helped to sustain him in the 1860s. In 1864 he abandoned the practice of *colportage* or begging on which his mission had hitherto subsisted in favour of trusting in the Lord, the plan popularized by Georg Müller's successful reliance on unsolicited funds for his orphan houses in Bristol, England. Rand's refusal to ask Nova Scotians for donations to finance the mission led inexorably to his rejection of aid from the Micmac Missionary Society and its consequent dissolution in 1870. Meanwhile, in Halifax in 1869, during a religious revival led by a visitor from the Plymouth Brethren, Müller's own sect, Rand succumbed to the beliefs of this evangelical movement which embodied for him "the good old *Baptist doctrines* to which I have been accustomed from my childhood." He publicly denounced the Baptist denomination in 1872 and his Hantsport church replied with a formal excommunication as a member. Thereafter Rand remained a devotee of the "Plyms" and a fugitive from Nova Scotian denominationalism until the deeply divided Halifax Brethren expelled him in 1885 and he returned to the fold of the Baptist church.

These financial and religious vicissitudes in no way dampened his enthusiasm for the moral regeneration of the Indians. Rand considered himself to be first and foremost a missionary and the importance of his philological work should not be permitted to obscure the overwhelmingly religious motivations and aims of this intensely spiritual man who wished to raise the Indian through faith from the degradation caused by the white man. Motivated by guilt and pity, Rand believed that the Micmacs needed religion before civilization, and he threw himself into the study of the Micmac language as the most direct way of communicating the word of God to his charges. The prominence he gave to the preservation of the linguistic component of the Micmac culture represented an intermediate stage in his wider schema: anglicization and the other trappings of a civilized life formed the desired but more distant goal. He also considered his Bible translations a legacy to his missionary successors, though his only assistant, Benjamin Christmas, a Micmac, left the mission's service in 1860. Because the eccentric and erratic Rand was thrown on his own resources in the conduct of the mission and was primarily interested in evangelization, little was done to try to improve the material well-being of the Micmacs. The Catholic missionaries opposed his aims and would not join their efforts with his. The mission included a tract of land at Hantsport and a depot for the sale of Indian handicrafts, but Rand lacked the money to establish schools; he doled out in charity what little remained after mission expenses had been met.

Rand's study of Micmac customs and folklore also formed part of the evangelical design of the mission; by familiarizing himself with the language, he deepened his appreciation of the mental cast of the Indians, whose intelligence he highly esteemed. He did not believe that the Indians constituted a dying race: there was no dire foreboding of physical extinction in his poem, *The dying Indian's dream*.

Undeniably, Rand was more successful as a collector of the Indian heritage than as a Protestant evangelist. The former involved only cooperation on the part of the Micmacs, the latter threatened to overturn the delicate balance of their post-contact way of life, especially their Catholicism. Like most Protestant clergymen, Rand believed that the failure of the Indians to join the age of progress could be attributed to "the darkness, superstition and bigotry of Romanism." In the same way that the Catholicism of the Micmacs had attracted the attention of both Rand and his supporters in the first instance, so Catholicism defeated this experiment in Protestant evangelization. Rand had no choice but to accept his defeat. In 1873 he suggested that since the hold of the Catholic Church on the Micmacs could not apparently be broken, then "if the Lord will be pleased to regenerate and save them, He can do it where they are," in the Catholic Church. Rand, who could claim only one convert for 40 years of work, in 1874 rationalized his somewhat meagre missionary accomplishments thus: "My special work seems to be pretty clearly marked out. I must pioneer for others." Nevertheless he remained a pioneer without followers among Nova Scotian Protestants who variously applauded or criticized his solitary efforts from the sidelines while they totally ignored his eloquent plea for the white man's recognition of Indian rights and the white man's duty to improve the temporal and moral position of the Micmacs. As solace Rand devoted more and more time to his study of Micmac culture as the years passed, a study which won him recognition abroad and honorary degrees at home as he produced his scriptural translations in Micmac and Malecite, compiled his Micmac dictionary, and collected scores of legends including the time-honoured tales of Glooscap, the mythological hero of the Micmacs.

JUDITH FINGARD

Silas Tertius Rand's publications include *The jubilee historical sketch, of the Nova Scotia Baptist Association* . . . (Charlottetown, 1849); *A short statement of facts relating to the history, manners, customs, language, and literature of the Micmac tribe of Indians, in Nova-Scotia and P.E. Island* . . . (Halifax, 1850); *A short account of the Lord's work among the Micmac Indians . . . with some reasons for . . . seceding from the Baptist denomination* (Halifax, 1873); *A brief statement respecting the Micmac mission* (n.p., [1880]); *The dying Indian's dream, a poem* (3rd ed., Windsor, N.S., 1881); *The Micmac mission* (n.p., [1882]); *Dictionary of the language of the Micmac Indians* . . . (Halifax, 1888; repr. New York and London, 1972); *Legends of the Micmacs*, [ed. H. L. Webster] (New York and London, 1894; repr. 1971).

Atlantic Baptist Hist. coll., S. T. Rand papers. British and Foreign Bible Soc. Arch. (London), Foreign corr., letter of S. T. Rand, 6 Feb. 1856. National Museum of Man (Ottawa), "An annotated bibliography of the works of Silas Tertius Rand," comp. Sharon Blakeney (typescript) (1974). PANS, MS file, Silas Tertius Rand, Letters to Rev. George Patterson, 1874–85. Micmac Missionary Soc., *Annual report of the committee* (Halifax), 1850–63; 1866–67. Nova Scotia Bible Soc., *Report* (Halifax), 1885; 1888; 1889. *Christian Messenger* (Halifax), 1837–84. *Daily Sun* (Saint John, N.B.), 8 Oct. 1889. *Messenger and Visitor* (Saint John), 1885–89. *Morning Chronicle* (Halifax), 24 May 1872, 26 Jan. 1877. *Morning Herald* (Halifax), 30 Jan., 16 Feb. 1886. *Morning News* (Saint John), 15 June 1872. J. S. Clark, *Rand and the Micmacs* (Charlottetown, 1899). W. D. and R. S. Wallis, *The Micmac Indians of eastern Canada* (Minneapolis, Minn., 1955). L. F. S. Upton, "Colonists and Micmacs," *Journal of Canadian Studies*, 10 (1975), no.3: 44–56; "Indians and Islanders: the Micmacs in colonial Prince Edward Island," *Acadiensis*, 6 (1976–77), no.1: 21–42.

RATTRAY, WILLIAM JORDAN, journalist and author; b. in 1835 in London, England, the son of Alexander Rattray; d. 26 Sept. 1883 in Toronto, Ont.

William Jordan Rattray came to Canada West with his parents in about 1848, his father establishing himself in Toronto as a baker. William obtained his post-secondary education at the University of Toronto where he distinguished himself as a public speaker and debater. A well-rounded scholar, he received training in classical literature and biblical studies before graduating in 1858 with double firsts in natural sciences and mental and moral philosophy. Rather than enter the business world he devoted himself to journalism.

His first essays in the literary field were printed in the Toronto *Grumbler*; this witty and satirical paper, in which all articles appeared anonymously, began publication in the late 1850s and ceased in the early 1860s. Rattray's principal literary contributions were then made through the Toronto *Mail*, as an important member of its editorial staff. He wrote a column in the *Mail* every Saturday on ethical and religious topics, and contributed other items in which he attacked agnosticism and unbelief. A number of his articles also appeared in *Belford's Monthly Magazine* and *Rose-Belford's Canadian Monthly and National Review* during the late 1870s and early 1880s.

Rattray's wide-ranging interests, referred to in a number of his obituaries, are evident in his articles. They contain copious classical and biblical quotations, and suggest a wide reading in the science of the day. At the same time he was well acquainted with contemporary philosophical and religious thought, evident in his discussions of the then contentious matter of biological evolution. He also devoted considerable attention to Canadian politics and history.

Although Rattray published his articles in the company of such eminent figures as George Monro Grant* and John George Bourinot*, his most important work is the four-volume *The Scot in British North America*, published between 1880 and 1884. In preparing it Rattray was reflecting his father's origin, though he himself had never seen Scotland. The first volume, prefaced by a defence of Scots against the sneers and criticisms commonly levelled at them, provides a brief philosophical exposition of patriotism and nationalism, then a short history of Scotland, concluding with an account of the first Scottish arrivals in British North America. The Scot in public life is the subject of the second and third volumes; special attention is paid to the Maritimes in the third volume, which ends with an investigation of the Scot in professional life (education, law, and the church). In the fourth volume he deals with the Scottish involvement in the northwest; a final chapter discusses the Scot in journalism. Before the final volume was completed, Rattray died after a long, debilitating, and painful illness, so that "another hand" had to finish the work. Unfortunately neither the identity nor the contribution of this individual is known. The volumes may have been part of a series on ethnic groups projected by Toronto publisher Thomas Maclear*; *The Irishman in Canada* by Nicholas Flood Davin* had appeared in 1877 but no further volumes seem to have been produced after those by Rattray. Although not written in language that suits late-20th-century taste, Rattray's *magnum opus* deserves recognition as the first work published on Scots in Canada; it set an example and has had many successors.

Rattray's style appears heavy and ponderous to modern readers, especially because of his use of quotations, but in his day he was considered one of Canada's foremost writers. An obituary in the *Winnipeg Daily Times* stated that, after Goldwin Smith*, "he was the ablest writer in Canada," while the Toronto *Mail* declared: "He carries away with him a rare fund of scholarship and ability. He leaves behind him a name unstained by a dishonourable act or an untruthful word." An extremely retiring man with few close friends, he proves elusive in any search for information concerning his life and activities.

W. Stanford Reid

William Jordan Rattray was the author of *The Scot in British North America* (4v., Toronto, 1880–84) and a contributor to *Belford's Monthly Magazine: a Magazine of Literature and Art* (Toronto), 1 (December 1876–May 1877) – 3 (December 1877–May 1878), and to *Rose-Belford's Canadian Monthly and National Rev.* (Toronto), 1 (July–December 1878) – 8 (January–June 1882).

Toronto Daily Mail, 28 Sept. 1883. *Cyclopædia of Canadian biog.* (Rose, 1886). *Dominion annual register*, 1883. Wallace, *Macmillan dict.*

RAYMOND (Raimond), JOSEPH-SABIN, Roman Catholic priest, professor, vicar general, and author; b. 13 March 1810 at Saint-Hyacinthe, Lower Canada, son of Joseph Raimond, a merchant, and Louise Cartier; d. there 3 July 1887.

Joseph-Sabin Raymond studied at the Séminaire de Saint-Hyacinthe from 1817 to 1826; his teachers, who had been recruited by the founder, Antoine Girouard*, were former pupils of the Séminaire de Nicolet. After teaching for a year at the Collège de Chambly, he returned to the seminary, where he was to remain for the rest of his life. He taught in turn philosophy (1832–36) and theology (1852–62), as well as holding the posts of prefect of studies (1841–72, 1875–76) and superior (1847–53, 1859–83).

By the time he was ordained on 22 Sept. 1832, Raymond had become familiar with French Catholic writers; since the early 1830s he had been reading the works of Hugues-Félicité-Robert de La Mennais and of Charles Forbes, Comte de Montalembert, and had become interested in the Paris newspaper *L'Avenir*, the organ of the liberal Catholic writers. In 1833 he corresponded with La Mennais, and, from 1839 to 1852, with Montalembert, whose ideas he brought to Lower Canada; he met most of the great Catholic writers, including Prosper Guéranger, François-René de Chateaubriand, and Jean-Baptiste-Henri Lacordaire, on a trip to France and Italy in 1842 and 1843. These men were landmarks in Raymond's religious and intellectual pilgrimage, and they made him aware of "the necessity of religious studies."

His enthusiasm for the liberal Catholics and for La Mennais was fully shared by Jean-Jacques Lartigue*, the auxiliary to the bishop of Quebec at Montreal. However, the condemnation of La Mennais's philosophy in the 1834 encyclical *Singulari nos*, which described it as a "vain, futile [and] uncertain doctrine," left a deep impression on Raymond. For him, this meant a break with La Mennais, as he stressed in a long article in which he deferred to the instructions of the Vatican, but which Bishop Lartigue refused to have published. By this article Raymond made it clear that he conformed to orthodoxy in the teaching of philosophy at the Séminaire de Saint-Hyacinthe, and announced his acknowledgement of papal authority. Thus he followed the example of liberal Catholics such as Lacordaire and Montalembert who had dissociated themselves from the thinking of La Mennais.

Raymond nevertheless continued his work at the seminary during the 1830s. At the time of the 1837–38 rebellion, he did not stand aside from the vital issues under discussion, and he no doubt shared the belief that the bishops should petition the government for various democratic reforms. In any case, he used his influence in 1838 to obtain the release of Charles Vidal, a Patriote of Saint-Hyacinthe, thereby, reportedly, attracting the suspicions of Colonel Bartholomew Conrad Augustus Gugy*. Raymond travelled through Europe in 1842 and 1843, and made contact with the newspaper *L'Univers* and the journals *Annales de philosophie chrétienne* and *L'Université catholique* of Paris. He observed that the educational and research institutions in Paris and Rome were returning in their programmes to medieval conceptions widely held in the *ancien régime.* On his return to the seminary, Raymond became involved in extramural activities; from 1843 to 1852 he contributed articles on ancient and modern civilization, the Middle Ages, and religious studies to the *Mélanges religieux*, which was under the ægis of Ignace BOURGET, the bishop of Montreal. His principal concern, however, remained the direction of studies: to instruct "is our way of fighting," he wrote in 1844. Both orator and master of rhetoric at the seminary's annual graduation ceremony, the prefect addressed the students and their parents on topics such as religious studies, the papacy, the duties of the citizen, and the state of society. His speeches were published in *La Revue canadienne*.

The spirit of the seminary gradually began to permeate life in Saint-Hyacinthe. For example, at the Union catholique, a sort of college literary society founded around 1865, Raymond delivered public lectures on "moral strength," "the love of truth," "the intervention of the priest in the intellectual and social order," and "tolerance," thereby attacking the anticlericalism of the Institut Canadien of Saint-Hyacinthe and its spokesman, Louis-Antoine Dessaulles*. Dessaulles, in retort, publicly denounced the influence exerted by the seminary on *Le Courrier de Saint-Hyacinthe* since 1861; hence the town's two leading figures became embroiled in a long controversy lasting from January to July 1867. Central to the dispute were two of the major political and social questions of the 19th century: the relations between temporal and spiritual authorities, and the role of the clergy in secondary education. In connection with the matter of teaching, the sixth provincial council, held at Quebec in 1878, was to recommend that the colleges give their pupils a sound training in Christian philosophy.

The clergy had organized university teaching; it had also coordinated both the administration and the teaching of the classical colleges by affiliating them with the faculty of arts of the Université Laval. It was to further these efforts at standardization that Raymond and his colleague Abbé Isaac-Stanislas Lesieur-Désaulniers* collaborated in the 1870s in the "official restoration" of the medieval philosophy of the Dominican, Thomas Aquinas; Raymond's repeated requests to Lacordaire before the latter's death in 1861 were instrumental in persuading the community of the Dominicans to take up residence in Saint-Hyacinthe in 1873.

In his approval of Abbé Benjamin Pâquet*'s pamphlet, *Le Libéralisme*, published at Quebec in 1872, Raymond showed that he had understood, as did Archbishop Elzéar-Alexandre Taschereau*, the need to depolarize the dispute between liberalism and ultramontanism. Indeed, for Raymond, neither liberalism nor gallicanism, as Pius IX defined them, existed in Canada; at most there was a kind of Catholic liberalism which amounted to a conciliatory attitude to the civil authority and democratic liberties rather than a doctrine. This stand involved Raymond in a controversy with the newspaper *Le Nouveau Monde* and with Bishop Bourget at the beginning of 1873. Mgr Raymond, who had become a vicar general, continued to write apologetics during the last years of his life; unlike bishops Bourget and Louis-François Laflèche*, as an educator and writer he had neither a hard line to maintain nor pastoral instructions to have respected. Rather he adopted the oblique ways of the scholar who has learned the art and value of fine distinctions in controversy as in wider conflicts.

Raymond's activities well illustrate the social repercussions of clerical domination in education. As a teacher of philosophy and theology, he also represents the orthodox viewpoint. A scholar in the forefront of religious thinking, he did, however, dissociate himself from La Mennais to join hands with Rome. In the French Canadian kingdom of militant ultramontanism, Raymond was "accused" of "Catholic liberalism"; but his orthodoxy lost nothing by his search for new alliances and practical adjustments. After 1860 a new position of strength gave the clergy a different style of negotiation with political authority. Raymond had experienced this transition from the church "militant" to the church "triumphant," with all that the change implied in the manner and substance of its pronouncements and its works.

YVAN LAMONDE

[Among Joseph-Sabin Raymond's numerous works are: *De l'intervention du prêtre dans l'ordre intellectuel et social . . .* (Saint-Hyacinthe, Qué., 1877); *Devoir du citoyen . . .* ([Saint-Hyacinthe], 1875); *Devoirs envers le pape . . .* (Montréal, 1861); *Discours prononcé à la translation du corps de messire Girouard, au séminaire de St-Hyacinthe, le 17 juillet 1861* (Saint-Hyacinthe, 1861); *Discours sur la nécessité de la force morale adressé aux membres de l'Union catholique, le 29 janvier 1865* (Montréal, 1865); *Discours sur la tolérance prononcé devant l'Union catholique de Montréal, le 15 mars 1869* (Montréal, 1869); *Dissertation sur le pape* (Montréal, 1870); *Éloge de messire I.-S. Lesieur Desaulniers prononcé à la distribution des prix du séminaire de St. Hyacinthe, le 7 juillet 1868* (Saint-Hyacinthe, 1868); *Entretien sur les études classiques* (Montréal, 1872); *Entretien sur St. Thomas d'Aquin à l'occasion du sixième centenaire célébré en son honneur* (Saint-Hyacinthe, 1874); *Méditations sur la passion et le précieux sang de Notre-Seigneur Jésus-Christ* (Montréal, 1888); and *Nécessité de la religion dans l'éducation* (Saint-Hyacinthe, 1874).

Raymond also wrote numerous articles, sometimes under the pseudonyms "S," "Un Canadien catholique," and "Un catholique," in the following newspapers: *L'Abeille* (Québec), 22 nov., 13, 20 déc. 1849; *Le Courrier de Saint-Hyacinthe*, 15, 18, 22, 29 mars, 1er, 7, 12, 15, 19 avril 1853; 3 mai 1861; 13, 17 oct., 5, 15 déc. 1865; 12, 16 janv., 13 févr., 6 mars 1866; janvier-juillet 1867; *L'Écho du pays* (Saint-Charles[-sur-Richelieu], [Qué.]), 25 juill. 1833; 2 janv., 25 sept. 1834; *Mélanges religieux* (Montréal), 25 févr. 1842; 25 sept., 2, 12, 23 oct., 6, 9, 23, 27 nov. 1849; 15, 25 janv., 8, 12 févr., 3, 6, 10 sept. 1850; as well as in the following journals: *Le Foyer canadien* (Québec), 4 (1866): 95–120, 137–64; 6 (1868): 226–53; *Les Nouvelles Soirées canadiennes* (Québec), 6 (1887): 555–56; *Rev. canadienne*, 1 (1864): 104–11, 214–27, 347–64, 533–46, 673–85, 749–65; 3 (1866): 650–64, 752–65; 4 (1867): 79–97, 214–32; 8 (1871): 27–56; 11 (1874): 440–51, 843–49, 901–6; 13 (1876): 525–41, 575–87, 642–59: 15 (1878): 200–16; 16 (1879): 564–74; 20 (1884): 651–69; 21 (1885): 641–51.

Joseph-Sabin Raymond's papers and those of the Raymond family are held by the Arch. du séminaire de Saint-Hyacinthe (FG-3) and represent the most important source used in preparing this biography. There are also some items which relate to Raymond in the AAQ, the ACAM, the archives of the bishoprics of Saint-Hyacinthe and Trois-Rivières, and at the ASQ. Y. L.]

Binan [Alphonse Villeneuve], *Le grand-vicaire Raymond et le libéralisme catholique* (Montréal, 1872). *Le Nouveau Monde*, 8 janv. 1873. *Le Pays* (Montréal), février-juillet 1867. *Quebec Gazette*, 30 Nov. 1833; 24, 27 April 1835. Allaire, *Dictionnaire*, I: 465. C.-P. Choquette, *Histoire du séminaire de Saint-Hyacinthe depuis sa fondation jusqu'à nos jours* (2v., Montréal, 1911–12). Lareau, *Hist. de la littérature canadienne*, 453–54. A.-J. Plourde, *Dominicains au Canada* (3v. parus, Montréal, 1973–), I. Claude Galarneau, "L'abbé Joseph-Sabin Raymond et les grands romantiques français (1834–1857)," CHA *Report*, 1963: 81–88. Robert [Philippe] Sylvain, "Le premier disciple canadien de Montalembert: l'abbé Joseph-Sabin Raymond (avec une lettre inédite)," *RHAF*, 17 (1963–64): 93–103.

RECORD, CHARLES B., carriage maker, furniture dealer, and foundry owner; b. 21 Aug. 1817 at Hebron, Maine; m., probably in 1852, Charlotte Bennett, and they had a son and a daughter; d. 5 June 1890 in Moncton, N.B.

Charles B. Record learned the trade of house joiner and later that of carriage maker in Dover, Maine, where his parents had moved when he was a child. From 1836 to 1841 he practised his trades in Orono,

Maine, developing his mechanical skills and gaining valuable experience in business. By the latter year he was ready to move to a larger centre, and established himself in Saint John, N.B., where for the next three years he alternated between house building and carriage making. In 1844 he began working as a driver on Daniel Caldwell's mail coach line between Saint John and the Bend of Petitcodiac (Moncton). He later became Caldwell's partner in the business, but in 1851 sold his interest to establish Moncton's first company for the importation and sale of furniture. At his store he also introduced for sale Dr Abraham Gesner*'s recently developed discovery, kerosene or paraffin lamp oil. At a Saint John refinery the product was distilled from albertite, a mineral resembling coal which was mined in neighbouring Albert County.

During the 1850s Record witnessed rapid progress at the Bend, which was incorporated as the town of Moncton in April 1855. Joseph Salter* had established a thriving shipyard on the north bank of the Petitcodiac in 1847 and in September 1853 construction began on the European and North American Railway to link Saint John with Shediac by way of Moncton. Recognizing the business possibilities during a railway construction boom, Record in 1857 closed his furniture business and in March of the same year set up the Moncton Iron Foundry with George W. Scales as his partner. By late May they had completed their first casting for the European and North American Railway, and they soon branched out into the production of iron shapes to order and the manufacture of stoves and agricultural implements. Scales died in 1858, and Record then took sole direction of the business.

Record had a flair for invention, and his stoves and ploughs, of which there were 14 models, became acknowledged as high quality products in great demand. He worked long hours at his business, paid personal attention to improvements in patterns and to the welfare and safety of his employees, and even designed models of his products for sales purposes. In 1879 he turned over direction of the company to his son, Edwin Albert, who in association with Robert F. Boyer entered into some unwise contracts and within two years had brought the foundry to a halt. In 1882, when the business was sold at auction to satisfy creditors, Charles B. Record, Alfred Edward Peters, and others formed a joint-stock company to buy the physical plant. They soon re-established the foundry under the name of the Record Foundry and Machine Company and restored its reputation, its strongest market being in southern Quebec. By steadily expanding its facilities during the 1880s the firm came to occupy a 12-acre site. Its weekly payroll in 1889 was $500, and by 1900 it employed over 150 men.

During the 1870s Record had diversified his business activities by becoming involved in several significant Moncton concerns. He was president of the Moncton Tobacco Company which was founded in 1870 and employed 60 people until it was forced out of business by the recession in 1873. He was a charter stockholder in the Moncton Gas, Light and Water Company in 1877, and a director of both the Moncton Sugar Refinery incorporated in 1879 and the Moncton Cotton Manufacturing Company established in 1881. Record never sought public office because he retained his American citizenship, but as a Baptist who strongly supported free, non-sectarian schools he served as chairman of the Moncton school board from 1872, when the Common Schools Act came into effect, until 1874.

Record was known as a quiet, unassuming man, but the diversity of his career as tradesman, merchant, and manufacturer, and his rebuilding of his shattered business during the 1880s, attest that he was one of Moncton's strongest entrepreneurs in the 19th century.

C. ALEXANDER PINCOMBE

Westmorland County Registry Office (Dorchester, N.B.), libro KK: 443. *Moncton Times*, 11 Dec. 1889, 5 June 1890. *Morning News* (Saint John, N.B.), 20 July 1860. *New Brunswick Courier* (Saint John), 2 July 1836. *St. John Daily Telegraph and Morning Journal* (Saint John), 24 May 1871. *Westmorland Times* (Moncton, N.B.), 27 Sept. 1855. L. A. Machum, *A history of Moncton, town and city, 1855–1965* (Moncton, 1965). C. A. Pincombe, "The history of Monckton Township (ca. 1700–1875)" (MA thesis, Univ. of New Brunswick, Fredericton, 1969), 178, 184, 193, 194, 199, 200, 219, 230.

RENAUD, JEAN-BAPTISTE, merchant, businessman, and municipal councillor; b. 22 June 1816 at Lachine, Lower Canada, son of Jean-Baptiste Renaud, a voyageur, and Marie Gariépy; m. 18 Jan. 1841 Marie-Sophie Lefebvre at Montreal, and they had four children; d. 1 March 1884 in Quebec City.

Jean-Baptiste Renaud was of humble origin and soon gave up primary school to help his ailing father provide for the family. He started out as a carter in Montreal, where his brother Louis* soon joined him. The two were married on the same day in the parish of Notre-Dame in Montreal and the marriage certificates describe each as a "carter." About 1847, in Montreal, Louis Renaud began to trade in grain, flour, and perhaps also general foodstuffs. The following year he went into partnership with his brother to open a store on Rue Foundling. Louis, whose name appeared in the firm's designation of L. Renaud and Brother, seems to have been the leader in it.

Around 1850 Jean-Baptiste Renaud went to live in Quebec City, on Rue Sainte-Famille. The *Quebec directory* of 1850–51 mentions the firm of L. Renaud and Brother, produce merchants. The firm underwent changes towards the end of the 1850s, since the 1857–58 directory mentions only Jean-Baptiste Renaud, "provision merchant." At that time he was dealing in grain, flour, fish, and probably oils. During this period Renaud built the largest flour-mill in the Quebec region, at Beauport, as well as two smaller ones where "barley and split peas of superior quality" were processed. He also acquired a number of schooners for trade with the villages along the St Lawrence.

Operating at the heart of the region's commercial life, Renaud was aware that the prosperity of his business depended on the development of means of transport which would link Quebec to its hinterland. He believed that railways would provide the answer. His name was listed as a director of the North Shore Railway Company [*see* Guillaume-Eugène CHINIC] in 1857 and 1858. However, as the company became increasingly bogged down in interminable discussions and dubious political deals, Renaud, while not completely giving up his interest in railways, turned to shipping. Thus he took part in the incorporation of both the St Maurice Railway and Navigation Company and the Salaberry Navigation Company of Montreal in 1857, and the St Lawrence Navigation Company in 1861. His business and shipping interests naturally led him into other economic sectors. In 1862 he had a hand in the incorporation of the Quebec Marine Insurance Company. It is not known whether he was involved in the founding of the Union Bank of Lower Canada, incorporated with a capital of two million dollars in 1865 by a group of businessmen under the leadership of Charles E. Levey, but the Quebec City directory of 1871–72 lists him as one of its directors.

The 1860s were a period of social ascent for Renaud. He was a member of the Quebec Board of Trade in 1862 and sat on city council from 1862 to 1868 as representative for Saint-Pierre Ward. Far from giving up his interest in the development of means of communication, he was on the board of directors of the Quebec North Shore Turnpike Roads Company from 1866 to 1871. It is possible that the diversification of his portfolio led him in 1871 to reorganize his business interests. The Quebec directory of 1871–72 noted a new firm name, J.-B. Renaud and Company, and that of 1879–80 mentions his son Jean-Louis Renaud, Gaspard Le Moine, and Victor Chateauvert as among his partners. Shortly after, Le Moine and Chateauvert purchased the firm of J.-B. Renaud; it is not known, however, whether the new owners managed the Beauport mills. This reorganization of the company freed Renaud from a heavy burden and gave him time to concentrate even more on enterprises which he was already managing, as well as capital to embark on new ventures. At the beginning of the 1870s many Quebec businessmen were looking to the Lac Saint-Jean region as a promised land; among those interested were the directors of the Union Bank of Lower Canada and its vice-president Thomas McGreevy*, a railway contractor. Renaud also expressed enthusiasm for the development of this region and was eager for a railway to be built to link it with Quebec. In 1872–73 he was a member of the board of directors of the Quebec and Gosford Railway Company, which built an initial section from Quebec to Portneuf County, and he returned to the board in 1875 when the company became the Quebec and Lake St John Railway Company, retaining his directorship until 1877. Presumably, as a director of the Union Bank from 1871 to 1878, he represented its interests. While the railway to Lac Saint-Jean was still under construction, Quebec capitalists were already preparing to exploit this hinterland to the best advantage. In 1877, along with other businessmen, Renaud organized the Quebec and Lake St John Lumbering and Trading Company, of which he remained a director for the rest of his life.

In the absence of an analysis of his accounting records it is not known how Renaud weathered the severe economic depression that paralysed commerce from 1874 to 1878. On 12 June 1878 his warehouses are known to have been looted by strikers from the Quebec building yards, who unsuccessfully demanded higher wages; *Le Journal de Québec* on 13 June estimated that Renaud, who had not been afraid to harangue the strikers, had sustained losses of $2,000 (150 sacks of flour and 200 barrels). Ostensibly at least, he emerged from this crisis with undiminished energies. In 1878, perhaps taking advantage of the bankruptcies that had shaken business at Quebec, he opened an establishment specializing in "stoneware and earthenware" at 24 Rue Saint-Paul. This firm still exists under the name of "J.-B. Renaud & Cie" (Renaud's first milling business also continues, having moved its head office to Rivière-du-Loup in the 20th century). During the 1880s Renaud retained his interest in shipping. In 1882 he became a director of the Richelieu and Ontario Navigation Company [*see* Hugh ALLAN; Louis-Adélard SENÉCAL]. This appointment was not surprising since close ties were maintained between the Union Bank, the Richelieu and Ontario Navigation Company, and the St Lawrence Navigation Company.

Having a flair for speculation, Renaud took advantage of the urban development of Quebec City and the neighbouring towns to make profitable investments throughout his life. He gradually became an important landowner. In addition to his warehouses and docks in Quebec City and his 33-acre estate at Beauport, he owned 7 other properties in the city (one, in Saint-Saveur, was subdivided in 1884 into 233 lots) and 39 at Lévis and Lauzon; he also owned one building in Quebec City and one in Lévis, and held another at Rivière-du-Loup jointly with his partners Le Moine and Chateauvert.

At the beginning of the 1880s Renaud had become one of the principal French-speaking businessmen because of the volume of his investments and the diversity of his transactions. He maintained connections with English-speaking financial circles and with the world of politics, as is evidenced by his purchase of the Conservative paper *La Minerve*, with Joseph Tassé*, Alexandre Lacoste*, and Aimé Gélinas, on 30 Aug. 1880. But he always refused to run in provincial and federal elections on the pretext that he lacked the necessary education. While still fully active, he died suddenly, on 1 March 1884, without having carried out a project to which he was deeply attached: the building of a bridge between Cap-Rouge and Saint-Nicolas. As well as praising him for his honesty and drive, the obituary in *Le Courrier du Canada* stressed "his practical knowledge of men and of things, [and] the soundness of his judgement."

Renaud's death did not terminate his business, which continued to thrive under the skilful direction of his partners Le Moine and Chateauvert. In 1912 the firm of J.-B. Renaud had an annual volume of sales of $3,000,000, with 130 employees and 8 commercial travellers.

In collaboration with JEAN HAMELIN

ANQ-M, État civil, Catholiques, Notre-Dame de Montréal, 18 janv. 1841; Saints-Anges (Lachine), 23 juin 1816. ANQ-Q, Minutiers, Édouard Glackmeyer, 4 mai, 30 juill. 1875. AVQ, Rôles d'évaluation et d'imposition, 1871. BE, Québec, Reg. B, 145, no.69273. Musée d'Odanak (Odanak, Qué.), Fonds divers, Boîte 1, 30–39; Boîte 2, 32, 39–47; Boîte 7, 2. Can., Prov. du, *Statuts*, 1862, c.71. Qué., *Statuts*, 1884, c.91; 1886, c.92. *Le Courrier du Canada*, 3 mars 1884. *Le Journal de Québec*, 13 juin 1878. *Annuaire du commerce et de l'industrie de Québec*, J.-C. Langelier, compil. (Québec, 1873). Beaulieu et J. Hamelin, *La presse québécoise*, I: 57. *Quebec directory*, 1850–84. Rumilly, *Hist. de Montréal*, III: 102. B. J. Young, *Promoters and politicians: the North-Shore railways in the history of Quebec, 1854–85* (Toronto, 1978). É.-Z. Massicotte, "Deux grands négociants," *BRH*, 42 (1936): 339–40.

RICE, SAMUEL DWIGHT, Methodist minister and educator; b. 11 Sept. 1815 in Houlton, Maine, son of Samuel Rice, a physician, and Elizabeth Putnam; m. in 1843 Fanny Lavinia Starr of Halifax, N.S., and they had three daughters and five sons; d. 15 Dec. 1884 in Toronto, Ont.

Samuel Dwight Rice moved with his family in 1819 to Woodstock, N.B., where he received his early education. For two years he pursued a business career for which he had had some training, but the profound experience of his conversion to Methodism in 1834 eventually turned him from business to the Christian ministry. He was received on trial in the Wesleyan Methodist Church in 1837. His ordination four years later led to six years of pastorates in New Brunswick under Enoch WOOD, including a year spent collecting funds to establish a Wesleyan academy in Sackville (later Mount Allison University) [*see* Humphrey PICKARD]. In 1847 Rice accompanied Wood to Canada West, settling in a pastorate in Toronto where he was associated with Ephraim Evans*. He served in 1849 as the first governor at the Mount Elgin Industrial Institution, an industrial school for Indians at Muncey, before accepting a three-year pastorate in Kingston. He then moved to Victoria College, Cobourg, where he acted as treasurer in 1853 and as "moral and domestic governor" from 1854 to 1857. Serving next at Hamilton, he held various administrative posts from 1857 to 1862 before beginning his active involvement with the Hamilton Wesleyan Female College from 1863 to 1878. Following two years at St Marys he left Ontario and spent 1880–82 in Winnipeg. He returned to Toronto in 1883 as president of the General Conference of the Methodist Church of Canada and on 5 September was elected general superintendent of the Methodist Church, effective the following July when the four Methodist churches in Canada were officially united under the latter name. Rice favoured the union, believing it a means of forwarding the important doctrines and polity of Methodism, with greater opportunities for missionary work, for education, and for more general participation in the administration of the church's affairs.

Throughout his 47 years with the church Rice served as a pastor from Cape Breton Island to Winnipeg, held numerous administrative offices, acted as a delegate to many conferences, and displayed an on-going interest in education. Although he was a fine preacher his greatest gift was church administration and he held all but four of the major offices in the church. As Charles Bruce Sissons* noted, "he was the type of minister who built churches rather than filled them." Believing the church to be "responsible for the intellectual as well as the moral and religious culture of the people," he felt that education was the means by which Methodists could rise from the lower strata of society. While he was serving as governor at Victoria College his business experience eased the financial tensions somewhat but his strict discipline must have caused problems with President Samuel Sobieski NELLES and Rice "withdrew from the College in 1857." Two years before his departure a letter in the *Christian Guardian* had asked: "How Long Shall the Education of the Daughters of Canada Be Neglected?" Rice, who had been interested in the state of women's education at Victoria, answered this question by bringing to fruition a plan by which the Wesleyan college in Hamilton was established in 1861. After serving as its governor from 1863, Rice succeeded Mary Electa Adams* as principal in 1868, a post he held until 1878 when he was elected vice-president of the General Conference of the Methodist Church of Canada. During his tenure at the college he received an honorary DD from Victoria in 1867. Even in his last years his interest in education continued and he was a member of the board of education in Winnipeg in 1880–81.

Methodist journalist and author William Henry Withrow* likened Rice to Egerton RYERSON, and he was described as a "tall and commanding figure, with a strong and intellectual face." Withrow also spoke of Rice's "large-hearted catholicity of spirit" towards other Christian churches while still remaining "a true and progressive Methodist." Confident, assertive, and conservative, Rice was able to change his views in the interest of the church's well-being. His faith was characterized by conviction rather than emotion; his preaching was evangelical, but its substance was "the doctrine of the Gospel," at a time when doctrine was being diluted and preaching was becoming more and more anecdotal. To Rice's logical mind true faith enjoined conversion of the heart, but, going deeper, he referred to the one power that "can touch the human conscience . . . the Spirit of God." The basis of the church was holiness, the sense of God's reality and presence, not organization or political method. He believed "the doctrines and discipline of the Church" were essential and had built the Methodist Church to its strength and influence.

Without a doubt Rice saw the needs of Methodism more clearly than most of his contemporaries; in his view the church's life was in jeopardy. There was a subtle deterioration of both doctrine and polity, a certain carelessness in a time of expansion and progress, a loosening of the joints of Methodism. A champion of the purity of high Methodism, Rice became aware of the effects of the 1884 union of the four Methodist churches, at least two of which had no real doctrine of ordination and practised a charismatic worship amounting to little more than revival meetings. The church, the ministry, and the sacraments were theoretically accepted but they were overshadowed by a strong emphasis on personal salvation. Even conversion had become less exacting. Finally, a wave of liberal thought was to be followed by a tide of social emphasis, which a dozen Rices could not have stemmed.

ARTHUR G. REYNOLDS

Samuel Dwight Rice was the author of "The person and work of the Holy Spirit," *Canadian Methodist Magazine*, 7 (January–June 1878): 168–70.

Methodist Church (Canada, Newfoundland, Bermuda), Toronto Conference, *Minutes* (Toronto), 1885. *Canadian Methodist Magazine*, 21 (January–June 1885): 178–81; 24 (July–December 1886): 1–10. *Christian Guardian*, 17, 31 Oct. 1855; 17 June 1874; 18, 25 June, 2 July, 17, 24 Dec. 1884; 7 Jan. 1885; 10 Feb. 1904. *New Outlook* (Toronto), 17 Dec. 1930. Cornish, *Cyclopædia of Methodism*. *Dominion annual register*, 1885. *The Putnam lineage . . .*, comp. Eben Putnam (Salem, Mass., 1907). J. E. Sanderson, *The first century of Methodism in Canada* (2v., Toronto, 1908–10). C. B. Sissons, *A history of Victoria University* (Toronto, 1952).

RICHARDS, Sir WILLIAM BUELL, lawyer, politician, and judge; b. 2 May 1815 in Brockville, Upper Canada, the eldest son of Stephen Richards and Phoebe Buell, and brother of Stephen* and Albert Norton*; m. 19 Oct. 1846 Deborah Catherine Muirhead (d. 1869), and they had three sons and two daughters; d. 26 Jan. 1889 in Ottawa, Ont.

William Buell Richards was educated at the Johnstown District Grammar School in Brockville and the St Lawrence Academy in Potsdam, N.Y. After serving in the Brockville law offices of both his uncle, Andrew Norton Buell*, and George Malloch, he was called to the bar in 1837. He practised in partnership first with Malloch, and then after 1842 with Buell, thereby cementing the close relationship which already existed between the Buell and Richards families. In 1849 he became a bencher of the Law Society of Upper Canada and he was named a QC the following year.

As a young man Richards was active in a number of community organizations, including the Brockville Mechanics' Institute, a debating society, a lending library, the town council, agricultural societies, and numerous social clubs. Following the strong tradition of the Buells and the Richards, he was also an ardent Reformer. Throughout the 1840s he helped to revitalize the Reformers especially in the rural areas of Leeds where he became popular among older, established families and the recently arrived Irish Roman Catholics. In 1844 he was nominated to contest the constituency of Leeds in the general election, but he retired in favour of William Buell*, his uncle. Nominated again for the election of 1848, he defeated the arch-villain of Reformers in Leeds, Ogle Robert Gowan*; this victory was particularly satisfying because during the election campaign Gowan had questioned Richards' loyalty in the 1837–38 rebellion. Once elected, Richards became involved in the distribution of patronage to the long-ostracized Reformers of eastern Upper Canada, an activity he believed fully justifiable, even necessary.

A close friend of Robert Baldwin*, who was godfather to one of his children, Richards rose rapidly in the Reform administration. In 1851, after he again defeated Gowan, he was appointed attorney general in the administration of Francis HINCKS and Augustin-Norbert Morin*. In office, Richards displayed an interest in legal reform by promoting the reorganization of statute law and by helping to raise the requirements for admission to the bar. On 22 June 1853, amid considerable controversy because of what some claimed to have been a brief and undistinguished legal career, he was appointed a puisne judge of the Court of Common Pleas. Yet although political influence had helped Richards obtain the judgeship, he was, despite the protests, well qualified for the post. He became chief justice of that court on 22 July 1863.

As a judge Richards was widely acclaimed as "a man of large common sense" rather than as a brilliant jurist. He was also known for his wit, which he used especially to embarrass pompous lawyers. During the 1850s and 1860s Richards visited all regions of Canada West, holding spring and fall assizes in county towns. Because of his early experiences in Leeds County and his practical approach to the law, he became a popular judge whose decisions were seldom appealed. He heard a wide variety of cases involving boundary disputes, libel, testate questions, paternity suits, seduction charges, bad debts, and occasionally manslaughter and murder. Richards maintained detailed case-books that reported both on the evidence and on his own impressions of witnesses. No doubt this thoroughness was an important reason for his success as a judge and it helps to explain why he was appointed chief justice of Ontario's Court of Queen's Bench on 16 Nov. 1868.

Richards was involved in several well-known cases of the time. In 1858, along with William Henry Draper*, he had rendered a controversial decision in favour of the government of George-Étienne Cartier* and John A. Macdonald* over the "double shuffle" incident. He presided at the trial in 1868 of Patrick James Whelan*, charged with the assassination of Thomas D'Arcy McGee*, a trial marred by questionable procedure; Richards did not enhance his reputation when, after his appointment as chief justice, he sat in judgement on the appeal. In November 1874, trying a controverted election case in Kingston, he found Macdonald's campaign associates guilty of bribery, and the next month Macdonald was obliged to contest the seat in a by-election which he won by a narrow margin.

Richards also took part in early discussions concerning the creation of a supreme court for Canada, and in 1871 visited judges of the Supreme Court of the United States in Washington to evaluate the effectiveness of that court. When Alexander Mackenzie*'s government established the Supreme Court of Canada in 1875, Richards was a popular choice among Liberals and even among many Conservatives for the chief justiceship.

Richards' tenure as chief justice from 8 Oct. 1875 to 9 Jan. 1879 was characterized by controversy in parliament and in the press largely because of the contention surrounding the establishment of the court itself. Many Conservatives and a few Liberals who were strongly opposed to the Supreme Court objected to the high cost of the court and its isolation in Ottawa, as well as to its slowness in coming to decisions and to the poor reports that were made of the initial cases. They also pointed to the alleged nepotism of Justice Jean-Thomas Taschereau* and to the absenteeism of judges, including Richards himself who was often abroad studying court systems. These were politically inspired debates, and during the first years of the Supreme Court Richards and his fellow justices, especially William Alexander HENRY, were also confronted with the difficult task of establishing the court's role within the judicial system. A staunch defender of the court, he attempted to strengthen it while keeping it separate from the legislative arm of the federal government. As well as developing the court's early rules of order, he also dealt with questions concerning the right of appeal, the minimum worth of property cases heard before the court, and its relationship with the Judicial Committee of the Privy Council. He was particularly interested in the use of the court as an arbiter of dominion-provincial relations and his tours of Europe and the United States were to determine how other courts dealt with similar problems.

Late in his career Richards received several other appointments. From 1874 to 1876 he acted for Ontario on the arbitration committee established to settle the Ontario-Manitoba boundary dispute. He was created a knight bachelor in 1877 and was designated deputy governor general in the absence of Lord Dufferin [Blackwood*]. Despite a personal friendship with Sir John A. Macdonald which had begun in the 1860s, the prime minister and his associates pressed Richards to resign in January 1879, probably because of ill health. After his retirement he travelled widely, maintaining residences in France, Ottawa, and Toronto until he died of asthma in 1889.

IAN MACPHERSON

AO, MU 301–9. MTL, Robert Baldwin papers; William Warren Baldwin papers. PAC, MG 24, B75. *Canada Law Journal*, new ser., 25 (1889): 194–96. *Reports of the Supreme Court of Canada*, comp. George Duval *et al.* (64v., Ottawa, 1878–1923), I–II. *Brockville Recorder* (Brockville, [Ont.]), 1830–49. *Canadian biog. dict.*, I: 9–10. *CPC*, 1876. Dent, *Canadian portrait gallery*, I: 212–13. T. W. H. Leavitt, *History of Leeds and Grenville, Ontario, from 1749 to 1879 . . .* (Brockville, 1879; repr. Belleville, Ont., 1972). G. R. I. MacPherson, "The code of Brockville's Buells, 1830–1849" (MA thesis, Univ. of Western Ontario, London, 1966).

RICHARDSON, JAMES, farmer, schoolteacher, and geologist; b. 29 March 1810 in Perthshire, Scotland, the eldest of four children; m. Barbara McConnachay of Lachine, Lower Canada, and they had a son and a daughter; d. 18 Nov. 1883 at Matane, Que.

James Richardson immigrated to Canada in 1829 where he was employed as a farm labourer in Lachine and later as a teacher in Beauharnois County, near Montreal, before he was engaged by William Edmond Logan*, director of the newly established Geological

Survey of Canada, as an assistant on surveys of Lake Superior in 1846 and 1847. During succeeding summers, while living in Beauharnois, Canada East, Richardson served as assistant in a series of investigations by the Geological Survey which concentrated on interpreting the geology of the Eastern Townships of Canada East from the American border to the base of the Gaspé peninsula. These included work along the Chaudière River in 1850, near Beauharnois and Coteau-du-Lac in 1851, and from Montreal Island along the north shore of the St Lawrence to the Saint-Maurice River and Île d'Orléans in 1852.

Richardson played a major role in the collection of mineral specimens from the Ottawa and Quebec regions which were included in the Canadian exhibit at the universal exposition in Paris in 1855. This exhibit brought much needed recognition to the Geological Survey of Canada and personal honour to Logan.

A permanent appointment as an "explorer" with the Geological Survey was granted to Richardson in 1856. Although originally "hired to do camp work," he had shown "some native ability and no small amount of curiosity"; he had learned the fundamentals of geology and mapping through field experience and through association with Logan and other members of the survey staff. These skills were now applied in the direction of independent field operations. The first of Richardson's 14 reports on geological examinations in various parts of Canada, "On the geology and topography of the island of Anticosti and the Mingan islands," was published in 1857 as part of the survey's cumulative progress report for 1853–56. The Anticosti survey also added important new fossil specimens to the rapidly growing collections of the survey, collections which would later form a basis for the holdings of the National Museums of Canada.

Notable geological explorations along the Gaspé and the north shore of the St Lawrence River followed. In 1860 Richardson became the first to use photography in Canada to record geological features, in a traverse of the north shore and along the coast of Newfoundland. Further work on the northwestern coast of Newfoundland followed in 1861 and 1862, culminating in a large-scale map of the area. Unfortunately, his reports and map were never published, although, viewed later as classic work in the area, they were used by Alexander MURRAY, first director of the Geological Survey of Newfoundland.

Richardson investigated the Quebec region in detail, both north and south of the St Lawrence, during the years 1863–70. Logan was moved to comment in a report in 1863 that Richardson, though "a most valuable and indefatigable explorer," still required "aid in working up his materials into a report." This prolific period of field-work was interrupted in 1867 by several months with the Canadian exhibit at the universal exposition in Paris. His reports on his Canadian field investigations stressed deposits with mining potential, for instance the 1870 "Report of the country north of Lake St. John." This report had necessitated an arduous canoe trip north toward Lac Mistassini during which he first noted the copper-pyrite deposits at Lac Chibougamau.

The acquisition of the northwest by Canada and the entry of British Columbia into confederation in 1871 brought vast new challenges for the Geological Survey. Richardson accompanied Alfred Richard Cecil Selwyn*, the director of the survey since 1869, to British Columbia where he was to spend portions of the next nine years in lengthy field investigations, with emphasis upon coalfields and possible railway routes. This work again resulted in important fossil specimens being added to the national collection as well as the acquisition of an interesting photographic record of coastal British Columbia. Among the highlights of these years were a traverse of the Cariboo Road in 1871 and specialized studies of the coalfields on Vancouver Island including those at Nanaimo, Comox, and Cowichan, so important to the proposed transcontinental railway.

Richardson Inlet in the Queen Charlotte Islands was named in 1878 by George Mercer Dawson* in recognition of Richardson's contribution to the geological exploration of Canada. Unwilling retirement in 1880, under the recently acquired superannuation benefits of the Civil Service Act, was followed by temporary work collecting specimens for McGill College in Montreal. Richardson also served for a period as cabinet keeper for the Geological Survey, which in 1881 was integrated fully into the civil service when it moved from Montreal to Ottawa.

Geology developed in Canada during Richardson's career from being largely a self-taught discipline to one dominated by men of academic distinction with formal training. Richardson nevertheless made important contributions especially in his collection of mineral specimens and his innovation in the use of photographic records in geological survey work.

DAVID R. RICHESON

PAC, RG 45, 156, nos.2883–84; 169, nos.1476–79, 2609–12; 170, nos.1482–85, 1496–1509, 2613; 171, nos.1510–13, 1315–24. *Early Canada: a collection of historical photographs by officers of the Geological Survey of Canada*, comp. E. Hall (Ottawa, 1967), 6–11. Geological Survey of Canada, *Report of progress for the years 1853–54–55–56* (Toronto, 1857), 191–245; *Report of progress from its commencement to 1863 . . .* (Montreal, 1863), iv; *Report of progress for 1870–71* (Ottawa, 1872), 283–308; *Report of progress for 1871–72* (Montreal, 1872), 73–100. *Gazette* (Montreal), 22 Nov. 1888. *Dominion annual register*, 1883: 326–27. Wallace, *Macmillan dict.*, 627. F. J. Alcock, *A century in the history of the Geological Survey of Canada* (Ottawa, 1948). Zaslow, *Reading the rocks*.

RICHEY, MATTHEW, Wesleyan Methodist minister and educator; b. 25 May 1803 at Ramelton (Rathmelton), County Donegal (Republic of Ireland); m. in 1825 Louisa Matilda Nichols at Windsor, N.S., and they had five children; d. 30 Oct. 1883 at Halifax, N.S.

Matthew Richey's devout Presbyterian parents secured for him a solid classical education in the expectation that he would enter the ministry. Although not permitted to attend other churches, he managed to participate in Methodist prayer meetings and became convinced that "the Methodists are a *peculiar* people the people of God . . . with them I will by the grace of God, both *live* and *die*." Following his conversion, he accompanied his brother to Saint John, N.B., in 1819, and found work as a solicitor's clerk and later as a tutor in the local grammar school. He soon attracted the attention of the Reverend James Priestley, who persuaded him to become a candidate for the Methodist ministry. At the Nova Scotia District meeting in 1820, he was appointed assistant to the Reverend Duncan McColl* at St David, N.B., and in 1821 became a regular probationer in the Nova Scotia District of the British Wesleyan Conference, one part of the far-flung missionary enterprise supervised by the Wesleyan Methodist Missionary Society. He completed his probation in 1825 and was admitted to full connection.

Evangelical zeal and learning were nicely balanced in Richey's preaching. His first sermon before the district meeting was delivered "in a most pleasing, systematic and devout manner and without apparent effort." Within a decade he acquired a reputation as "a preacher never to be forgotten by any who listened to him." His published *Sermons delivered on various occasions* are scholarly, exegetical, and heavily laden with classical and historical allusions, but do not suggest the "gentle and persuasive eloquence" which was "equally admired by the most cultivated and intelligent, and by the simple and unlettered." Nor can one perceive in them the preacher who apparently moved easily from the most important Methodist pulpits in Halifax to the streets and squares where he spoke to the passing crowds. Clearly, however, he was most comfortable in an orderly and decorous atmosphere in which the sonorous periods of classical rhetoric could be delivered in the passionate tones that so impressed his listeners.

Richey served on several circuits in the Maritimes before being transferred in 1835 to Montreal in the Lower Canada District. In 1836 he was appointed the first principal of Upper Canada Academy in Cobourg, the Methodist coeducational preparatory school that became Victoria College in 1841. Richey was installed formally on 18 June 1836 and remained in office until 1840.

From 1836 to 1850, when he returned to Nova Scotia, Richey played an active part in the development of Methodism in the Canadas, a role that can be understood only in the context of the complex relationship between Canadian and British Methodism. Three years before Richey's arrival in Upper Canada, the British Wesleyans and the Canadian conference had entered into union. During Richey's principalship, relations between the two bodies deteriorated steadily, largely because the British Wesleyans insisted that the Canadian leaders were disloyal agitators whose campaign for civil and religious liberty would subvert the constitution, the British connection, and the principle of state support for religious institutions. The Canadian Methodists, led by Egerton RYERSON and his brothers, John* and William*, affirmed their loyalty and their determination to secure their rights as "Christians and as Canadian British subjects." They also refused to turn their journal, the *Christian Guardian* (Toronto), into a bland purveyor of religious news.

Richey, whose attitudes had been shaped by his northern Irish upbringing and the conservative outlook of the Wesleyans in Britain and Nova Scotia, was insistent that Methodism should be purified "from the pollution of politics" and stamped "with the resplendent signet of true British loyalty." In January 1840 he joined another Wesleyan minister, Joseph Stinson*, in assuring Governor General Charles Edward Poulett Thomson* that "the Church of England being in our estimation *The Established Church* of all the British Colonies, *we* entertain no objection to the distinct recognition of her as such," a principle that the Canadian Methodists would not accept. He strongly supported the unsuccessful efforts of his colleagues, Stinson and Robert Alder*, to bring the Canadian conference into line; their charges against Egerton Ryerson were put forward by Richey at the conference held in Belleville in June 1840. Soon afterward Stinson and Richey attended the fateful 1840 session of the conference of British Wesleyans in England at which the union of 1833 was dissolved.

On returning to Canada, Stinson and Richey organized a new Canada Western District under the supervision of the Wesleyan Methodist Missionary Society for those preachers and laity who were determined not to accept the jurisdiction and policies of the Canadian conference. Richey was secretary of this body in 1840 and 1841 and chairman from 1842 to 1845. Campaigning vigorously for the consolidation and extension of the Wesleyans' influence in Canada West, he bitterly resisted any suggestion that the two Methodist groups should reunite. He and his brethren asserted that it would be "a national calamity" to prevent the diffusion of British Methodism in Canada West, since through its scriptural influence the "triumph of democracy" might be "for ages, perhaps for ever averted" in the colony.

Nevertheless, threatened by dissension at home, the

rising costs of the missions in British North America, and the emergence of Anglo-Catholicism, the British conference moved toward reconciliation with the Canadians. Richey, transferred to Montreal in 1845 to become chairman of the Canada Eastern District, participated in the 1846 meeting of the British conference at which reunion between the British and Canadian conferences was accepted in principle. As the missionary society's representative at a special session of the Canada Western District meeting in February 1847, he sought to allay the fears of his brethren about the proposed union, even though he himself was still suspicious and critical of the Ryersons. Similarly, at a subsequent meeting between Robert Alder, the British conference representative, and the Wesleyan ministers, he emphasized that he had worked for reunion "at the sacrifice of the finest feelings of his heart." Characteristically, at the service which followed the passage of the terms of union by the Canadian conference in June 1847, Richey "imbued with the spirit of a seraph carried the audience with him in his feelings of charity and love while delivering his impromptu but unequalled address."

In 1847 and 1848 Richey was co-delegate or vice-president of the Canadian conference and in 1849 he became president. Moreover, although many Methodists, including Anson Green*, had criticized his record in managing the finances of Upper Canada Academy, he was offered the principalship of Victoria College. Unfortunately, in October 1849 he was severely injured in a carriage accident. This misfortune evidently strengthened his long-standing inclination to return to the Maritime provinces.

In 1850 Richey became involved in the anxious deliberations of the conference and the Victoria College board about the possibility of incorporating Victoria into the University of Toronto. It was suggested that Richey might be appointed supervisor of Methodist divinity students and professor of rhetoric and English in the university. He concluded, however, that this project was designed in someone else's interest and left abruptly for Nova Scotia. Later he commented that "the university is an anomalous semi-infidel affair in which religion, while ostensibly recognized, is virtually proscribed. Such an Institution is . . . no place for a Methodist Minister."

Following his return to Nova Scotia, Richey was appointed in 1852 chairman of the newly formed Western District, which had been created partly to provide a suitable place for him. As chairman, he was involved in the discussions which preceded the formation of the Conference of Eastern British America, a project that had been first considered in the early 1840s. Although he did not wish to take any step that would lead to independence from the British conference, Richey cooperated effectively with the missionary society in this matter. When the new conference was established in 1855, Richey became co-delegate, and from 1856 to 1861 and again in 1867–68 he served as president; during the years 1864–67 he was chairman of the Prince Edward Island District. His last official position before his retirement in 1870 was as chairman of the Saint John District.

Matthew Richey held the highest positions open to him in the Methodist community, but he does not seem to have been an aggressive ecclesiastical statesman in the mould of his colleagues, Robert Alder, Egerton Ryerson, or Enoch WOOD. Rather, he was an outwardly gentle and courteous man with a high estimate of his own importance and an intense commitment to Wesleyan Methodism, political conservatism, and the preservation of close religious and political links between Britain and British North America. In private he often enunciated his views in vitriolic and intemperate language, behaviour which may well have led his superiors to distrust his judgement. He was essentially a powerful evangelical preacher who, along with many others, appears not to have sensed the potential contradiction between the achievement of holiness in this world and acceptance of the existing political and social order. It would be easy simply to note with John Saltkill CARROLL that Richey had a "ready command of the most exuberant and elevated language, amounting almost to inflation of style," and to dismiss him as an overrated orator. In reality, however, he epitomized many of the characteristics of Wesleyan Methodism in his time. Besides supporting close links with the English Wesleyan tradition, he helped to foster in British North American Methodism concern for the institutional status of his church, political quietism, and hostility to cultural activities such as the theatre.

Richey's services to Methodism were recognized by Wesleyan University, Middletown, Conn., with the award of an MA in 1836 and a DD in 1847. He was described by John Fennings TAYLOR as "the most eloquent and accomplished speaker of all the Methodist connection in the Dominion of Canada." His friend and colleague, the Reverend John Lathern*, commented that Richey's biography of William Black*, the founder of Methodism in the Maritime provinces, was "a production of sterling excellence." He added: "The testimony of some who sat beneath his ministry is to the effect that the most heart-searching appeals they ever listened to from the pulpit were from his lips." "His memory," said Victoria's president Samuel Sobieski NELLES, "will be fondly cherished by all who knew him."

Matthew Richey died after a lengthy illness at Government House in Halifax, the official residence of his son, Lieutenant Governor Matthew Henry Richey*. No more appropriate place could have been found for one so closely identified with the history of Methodism in the North Atlantic world of the 19th century.

G. S. French

Matthew Richey was the author of *A funeral discourse, on occasion of the death of Mrs. J. A. Barry: delivered at the Methodist chapel, Halifax, on the evening of Sunday, 13th January, 1833* (Halifax, 1833); *The internal witness of the spirit, the common privilege of Christian believers: a discourse, preached at Halifax, before the Wesleyan ministers of the Nova-Scotia district, on the 24th of May, 1829* (Charlottetown, 1829); *A letter to the editor of The Church; in answer to his remarks on the Rev. Thomas Powell's essay on apostolical succession* (Kingston, Ont., 1843); *Life and immortality brought to light by the gospel: a sermon* (Halifax, 1832); *A memoir of the late Rev. William Black, Wesleyan minister, Halifax, N.S., including an account of the rise and progress of Methodism in Nova Scotia . . .* (Halifax, 1839); *The necessity and efficiency of the gospel: a sermon preached before the Branch Methodist Missionary Society of Halifax, Nova-Scotia, February 11th, 1827* (Halifax, 1827); *Persuasives to active benevolence: a sermon, preached at the Wesleyan chapel, Halifax, on Christmas evening, 1833, for the benefit of the poor* (Halifax, 1833); *A plea for the confederation of the colonies of British North America; addressed to the people and parliament of Prince Edward Island* (Charlottetown, 1867); *A sermon occasioned by the death of the Rev. William Croscombe, preached in Windsor, 30th October, and in Halifax, 6th November, 1859* (Halifax, 1859); *A sermon on the death of the Rev. William M'Donald, late Wesleyan missionary; preached at Liverpool, Wednesday, March 19, and in substance at Halifax, on Sunday, March 30, 1834* (Halifax, 1834); *A sermon preached at the dedication of the Wesleyan Methodist Church, Richmond Street, Toronto, on Sunday, June 29, 1845, and of the Wesleyan Methodist Church, Great St. James Street, Montreal, on Sunday, July 27, 1845* (London and Montreal, 1845); *Sermons delivered on various occasions* (Toronto, 1840); *A short and scriptural method with Antipedobaptists, containing strictures on the Rev. E. A. Crawley's treatise on baptism, in reply to the Rev. W. Elder's letters on that subject* (Halifax, 1835); *Two letters addressed to the editor of The Church, exposing the intolerant bigotry of that journal, and animadverting especially on the spirit and assumptions of an editorial article which appeared in its columns on the 7th April, 1843* (Toronto, 1843); and, with Joseph Stinson, of *A plain statement of facts, connected with the union and separation of the British and Canadian conferences* (Toronto, 1840). Also of interest is *Catalogue of books in theology & general literature, (from the library of the late Rev. Dr. Richey), among which are many rare & valuable works, now offered for sale by Messrs. MacGregor & Knight, stationers and booksellers, 125 Granville St., Halifax, N.S.* (Halifax, 1885).

Methodist Missionary Soc. Arch. (London), Wesleyan Methodist Missionary Soc., Corr., Canada (mfm. at UCA). UCA, Matthew Richey papers, 1841–54. United Church of Canada, Maritime Conference Arch. (Halifax), Matthew Richey papers, 1833–59 (mfm. at UCA). Carroll, *Case and his cotemporaries*. *Centenary of Methodism in Eastern British America, 1782–1882* (Halifax and Toronto, [1882]). John Lathern, "The Reverend Matthew Richey, D.D.," *Canadian Methodist Magazine*, 21 (January-June 1885): 259–68. Methodist Church (Canada, Newfoundland, Bermuda), Nova Scotia Conference, *Minutes* ([Halifax]), 1884. Wesleyan Methodist Church in Canada, *Minutes* (Toronto), 1824–45; 1847–50. Wesleyan Methodist Church of Eastern British America, *Minutes* (Halifax), 1855–74. *Christian Guardian*, 7 Nov. 1883. *Cyclopædia of Canadian biog.* (Rose, 1888). Notman and Taylor, *Portraits of British Americans*. G. E. Jaques, *Chronicles of the St. James St. Methodist Church, Montreal, from the first rise of Methodism in Montreal to the laying of the corner-stone of the new church on St. Catherine Street* (Toronto, 1888). D. W. Johnson, *History of Methodism in eastern British America, including Nova Scotia, New Brunswick, Prince Edward Island, Newfoundland and Bermuda . . .* ([Sackville, N.B.], n.d.). Sissons, *Egerton Ryerson*. T. W. Smith, *History of the Methodist Church within the territories embraced in the late conference of Eastern British America . . .* (2v., Halifax, 1877–90).

RIDOUT, JOSEPH DAVIS, merchant and businessman; b. 9 June 1809 at Bristol, England, son of George Ridout and Mary Ann Wright; m. first Julia Elizabeth Gould, *née* Bramley, and after her death in 1852, Caroline Cumberland; d. 4 June 1884 at Toronto, Ont., survived by his second wife and their two sons.

Joseph Davis Ridout's father emigrated from Bristol in 1820, going first to Philadelphia and then in 1826 to York (Toronto). Like his older brother George Percival*, however, Joseph remained in the United States, where he was employed, in New York and then in Boston, by Tarratt's, a firm of iron merchants based in Wolverhampton, England. In 1830 Joseph moved to York and, with the backing of Tarratt's, opened a retail iron and hardware store, Joseph D. Ridout and Company. His brother George Percival joined him in 1832, and their firm, Ridout Brothers and Company, entered the wholesale market as well. They soon built a substantial store, which would long be a Toronto landmark, at the northeast corner of King and Yonge streets.

Business success permitted and encouraged J. D. Ridout, like other Toronto wholesalers, to broaden his activities. In 1847 he helped found the Farmers and Mechanics Building Society, a mortgage company and the city's second such effort to supply construction capital for a growing population; he was its first vice-president and later became its president. The societies consisted of subscribers who paid set monthly subscriptions for a limited period of time in return for the right to borrow on mortgages to finance building projects. The societies were popular with businessmen, professionals, farmers, artisans, and clerks because they required little initial capital, met a clear and pressing need, and when wound up usually had surpluses which were distributed among the shareholders. Ridout was one of those who saw the advantages for investors and borrowers of developing permanent instead of terminating building societies. When the Farmers and Mechanics Building Society was dissolved in 1855, he and other members of the society and of the Toronto Building Society, established in 1846, joined to form the Canada Permanent Building and Savings Society (later the Canada Permanent Mortgage Corporation) [*see* Peter PATERSON]. Ridout was its first president and held the office for almost 30 years until forced by ill health to retire shortly before he died. Active day-to-day management of the company was in the hands of its capable secretary, John Herbert Mason, but Ridout was much more than a figure-head as president. Under their leadership, the company soon became much larger than any other of its kind in Canada.

Ridout's family and business lives were interconnected. From 1843 until it failed in 1866 he was a director of the Bank of Upper Canada, whose cashier (general manager) from 1821 to 1861, Thomas Gibbs Ridout*, was his cousin, and the husband of his first wife's sister. He was a member of the first board of the Toronto, Simcoe and Lake Huron Union Rail-road Company in 1849 and took a continuing interest in its affairs; about a decade later, when the company, by then the Northern Railway, was in financial difficulties, Ridout rejoined the board for several years. Frederic William CUMBERLAND, general manager of the Northern Railway from 1859 until his death in 1881, was married to a sister of Ridout's first wife and was the brother of his second wife. Ridout was active in the Toronto Board of Trade, particularly in its early years when his brother Percival was its president, and he was himself vice-president in 1854. With his brother he engaged in some land speculation in and around Toronto.

Ridout was Anglican in religion and Conservative in politics. He took no active part in political life except as a trustee of the first elected Toronto Public School Board in 1850. He joined the East York militia in 1833, saw action during the rebellion of 1837, and remained in the militia until 1867 when he retired with the rank of major. He helped to found Toronto's St George's Society in 1835 and was its president from 1851 to 1854. For some years a director of the Toronto Mechanics' Institute, he served as its president in 1860.

After his brother retired from the hardware business in 1866, Ridout took two long-time employees, James Aikenhead and Alexander Crombie, into the firm, changing its name to Ridout, Aikenhead, and Crombie. In 1876 he retired from the hardware business, leaving his partners to carry it on. The business still continues in the hands of the Aikenhead family, though it is now owned by Molson Companies Limited.

DOUGLAS MCCALLA

Christian Guardian, September–October 1830. *Globe*, 1850–60. *Monetary Times*, 1868–84. *Toronto Daily Mail*, 5, 9 June 1884. *Dominion annual register*, 1884; 242–43. *Toronto directory*, 1850–51; 1856; 1859–60; 1861; 1866; 1867–68. *Hist. of Toronto and county of York*, II: 137–39. *Robertson's landmarks of Toronto*, I: 329, 360a, 368–69; II: 759; III: 143, 208–9, 211, 246. *The story of the Canada Permanent Mortgage Corporation, 1855–1925* (Toronto, 1925). Michael Valpy, "Aikenhead's business was founded in 1830: notes for a store's history," *Globe and Mail* (Toronto), 7 June 1971.

RIEL, LOUIS, Métis spokesman, regarded as the founder of Manitoba, teacher, and leader of the North-West rebellion; b. 22 Oct. 1844 in the Red River Settlement (Man.), eldest child of Louis Riel* and Julie Lagimonière, daughter of Jean-Baptiste Lagimonière* and Marie-Anne Gaboury*; m. in 1881 Marguerite Monet, *dit* Bellehumeur, and they had three children, the youngest of whom died while Riel was awaiting execution; d. 16 Nov. 1885 by hanging at Regina (Sask.).

Louis Riel is one of the most controversial figures in Canadian history. To the Métis he is a hero, an eloquent spokesman for their aspirations. In the Canadian west in 1885 the majority of the settlers regarded him a villain; today he is seen there as the founder of those movements which have protested central Canadian political and economic power. French Canadians have always thought him a victim of Ontario religious and racial bigotry, and by no means deserving of the death penalty. Biographers and historians over the years since Riel's death have been influenced by one or other of these attitudes. He remains a mysterious figure in death as in life.

Riel was the eldest of 11 children in a close-knit, devoutly religious, and affectionate family. Both his parents were westerners, and he is said to have had one-eighth Indian blood, his paternal grandmother being a Franco-Chipewyan Métisse. Louis Sr, an educated man, had obtained land on the Red River where he gained a position of influence in the Métis community. In 1849 he organized the community to aid Pierre-Guillaume Sayer*, a Métis charged with violating the Hudson's Bay Company's trade monopoly. Sayer was released, an action which resulted in the end of that monopoly. As a child, young Louis would have heard much of his father's exploits.

While he was being educated in the Catholic schools in St Boniface, Riel attracted the attention of Bishop Alexandre-Antonin Taché*. Anxious to have bright Métis boys trained for the priesthood, Taché arranged in 1858 for Riel and three others, including

Louis Schmidt, to attend school in Canada. At the Petit Séminaire de Montréal Riel showed himself to be intelligent and studious, with a capacity for charming others, but he could also be moody, proud, and irritable.

The news of his father's death, which reached him in February 1864, was a traumatic shock for Riel. Always an introvert, subject to moods of depression, he seems to have lost confidence in his qualifications for the priesthood and withdrew from the college in March of the following year without graduating. Hoping to support his family in Red River, whom Riel Sr had left impoverished and in debt, Louis became a clerk in the Montreal law firm of Toussaint-Antoine-Rodolphe Laflamme*. But the subtleties of the law bored and annoyed Riel and he decided, in all likelihood in 1866, to return to Red River. He probably worked at odd jobs in Chicago and St Paul (Minn.) before arriving at St Boniface in July 1868.

The Red River that Riel had left ten years earlier was an isolated society of English-speaking mixed-bloods (the country-born), Scottish settlers, and the French-speaking, Roman Catholic Métis. During the early 19th century the Métis, the largest group, had developed a vigorous sense of nationality based on a distinctive culture which combined Indian and French Canadian elements. For the most part, the Métis were indifferent to farming, preferring the excitement of the buffalo hunt far out on the western plains. These annual hunts were superbly organized and disciplined affairs under the control of democratically elected leaders, and Métis adherence to the hunt was dramatically reflected in their quasi-military social organization. In contrast to the Métis, the country-born were predominantly Anglican, proud of their English culture, and settled on the land. The Scots settlers had adhered strictly to the Presbyterian church.

Riel found many changes on his return. Religious antipathies had become a notable feature of the settlement. At the same time the political climate was both uncertain and volatile. The settlement, part of the Rupert's Land held by the HBC, was still administered by a governor and the Council of Assiniboia, established by the HBC. The need for a new constitutional arrangement was acknowledged, but the issue was far from settled. Moreover, the old inhabitants now recognized that although their settlement was still isolated, it was the object of expansionist aspirations on the part of both the United States and Canada. Indeed, during Riel's absence the settlement had grown to almost 12,000 and the village of Winnipeg had emerged, largely populated by Canadians and a handful of Americans. In fact, what Riel found at Red River in July 1868 was an Anglo-Protestant Ontario community, hostile to Roman Catholicism and the social and economic values of the Métis.

The most influential and vociferous personality among the Canadians was Dr John Christian Schultz*, an Ontario-born physician, trader, and land speculator. For Schultz and his followers the future of the settlement was obvious – annexation to Canada. In the early 1850s the annexation of the northwest had become a popular political issue in Canada West as a consequence of the activities of George Brown* and William McDougall*, the leaders of the Clear Grits. In French Canada, land seekers had been encouraged to look north in their own province, but their political leaders, by entering the confederation coalition of 1864, had tacitly accepted the idea of acquiring the northwest. This bipartisan understanding was embodied in section 146 of the British North America Act of 1867 which provided for transcontinental expansion. Shortly after Riel's return to the west, it became known that Prime Minister Sir John A. Macdonald*, fearing the Minnesota annexationists, was again negotiating with the HBC for the transfer of Rupert's Land, ignoring the population at Red River and the Council of Assiniboia.

Meanwhile, a grasshopper plague in 1867–68 had caused much distress in the settlement. The Canadian government had proposed providing relief by financing the building of a road from Upper Fort Garry (Winnipeg) to Lake of the Woods; because the government anticipated that the country would soon be annexed it felt the road, named "the Dawson Road" after engineer Simon James Dawson*, would be essential. But the project was poorly administered, and the survey party assembled in the settlement by John Allan SNOW, head of the project, and Charles Mair*, its paymaster, who arrived together from Ontario in October 1868, included no French-speaking members. Mair, a poet and friend of McDougall, now the minister of public works, made himself thoroughly unpopular in the settlement by a series of articles in Ontario newspapers in January 1869 criticizing the Métis. He was opposed to the expedient biculturalism of the Red River Settlement, and, being an advocate of large-scale Ontario immigration to the northwest, was a natural ally of Dr Schultz, the road party's agent. Thomas Scott*, an Irishman and fervent Orangeman who was reckless, stubborn, and contemptuous of the Métis, joined the work crew in the summer of 1869.

At St Vital, an idle Riel had initially decided "to wait on events, quite determined just the same to take part in public affairs when the time should come." When the substance of Mair's articles became known to the settlement, Riel defended the Métis against this unjust criticism in a strong reply published in *Le Nouveau Monde* (Montreal) in February 1869. He attended and spoke at a meeting called on 19 July by well-established leaders of the Métis community, such as Pascal Breland* and William Dease, to discuss growing Métis fears about the course of events. Though the meeting underlined the need for concerted action, none was planned.

In July 1869 Métis suspicions had increased when McDougall ordered a survey of the settlement. The head of the survey party, Colonel John Stoughton DENNIS, was given specific instructions to respect the river lots of the settlers. Nevertheless, he received a cool reception in Upper Fort Garry and St Boniface after he arrived on 20 August, and his close association with Dr Schultz increased Métis fears. William Mactavish*, the governor of Assiniboia and of Rupert's Land, believed that "as soon as the survey commences the Half breeds and Indians will at once come forward and assert their right to the land and possibly stop the work till their claim is satisfied." He considered the survey premature and unwise, and he cautioned the Canadian government. Robert Machray*, the Anglican bishop of Rupert's Land, and Bishop Taché, who called at Ottawa on his way to Rome, also warned the government. But all representations were ignored by Macdonald. Indeed, in late September matters worsened when it was announced that McDougall, who with Sir George-Étienne Cartier* had concluded negotiations between the HBC and Canada in London, would be the first lieutenant governor of the territories. No poorer choice for the post could have been made, in view of the necessity for diplomatic caution in dealing with the officials of the HBC and with the lay and clerical spokesmen of the various groups at Red River. The transfer was to take place on 1 Dec. 1869.

As tensions mounted among the Métis it was clear that strong leadership was needed. Riel's experiences during the past ten years had produced a life-style very different from that of the buffalo-hunting Métis, but it was these people he now aspired to lead. The older, more established leaders had had little success and had shown little initiative. Riel – ambitious, well-educated, bilingual, young and energetic, eloquent, deeply religious, and the bearer of a famous name – was more than willing to provide what the times required.

Late in August 1869, from the steps of the St Boniface cathedral, Riel declared the survey a menace. On 11 October a group of Métis, including Riel, stopped the survey. A week later, the National Committee, with John Bruce as president and Riel as secretary, was formed in St Norbert with the support of the local priest, Joseph-Noël Ritchot*. This association of the clergy and the Métis is not surprising: a people surrounded or threatened by an alien culture frequently find in their church the chief sustainer of their traditions and aspirations. The able Bishop Taché had already put into print his understanding of and sympathy for the Métis as an integral, and now threatened, part of the settlement.

On 25 October Riel was summoned to appear before the Council of Assiniboia to explain his actions. He declared that the National Committee would prevent the entry of McDougall or any other governor unless the union with Canada was based on negotiations with the Métis and with the population in general. However, by 30 October McDougall had reached the border at the village of Pembina (N. Dak.) and, despite a written order from Riel, he proceeded to the HBC Pembina post (West Lynne, Man.). Here on 2 November McDougall was met by an armed Métis patrol, commanded by Ambroise-Dydime Lépine*, and ordered to return the next day to the United States. Also on the 2nd, Riel, with followers reported as numbering up to 400, who had been recruited from the fur-brigades recently returned to the settlement for the season, took possession of Upper Fort Garry without a struggle. It was a brilliant move on Riel's part – control of the fort symbolized control of all access to the settlement and the northwest.

The month of November 1869 was one of intense activity in the Red River Settlement, as Riel worked to unite its residents including established Métis such as Charles Nolin* and William Dease, who initially opposed him. On 6 November Riel issued an invitation to the English-speaking inhabitants to elect 12 representatives from their parishes to attend a convention with the Métis representatives. Somewhat reluctantly the country-born and the Selkirk settlers agreed with the proposal. At the first meeting of the convention little was accomplished and the English-speaking delegates, led by James Ross*, criticized the exclusion of McDougall from the settlement as smacking of rebellion. Riel angrily denied this allegation. Responding to another charge, he stated that he had no intention of invoking American intervention; throughout the resistance he insisted that the Métis were loyal subjects of the queen.

On 16 November Mactavish, as governor at Red River, issued a proclamation requiring the Métis to lay down their arms. In response Riel proposed a further step to the convention on 23 November: the formation of a provisional government to replace the Council of Assiniboia and to negotiate terms of union with Canada. He did not succeed in rallying the English-speaking parishes behind this move. Nor did they approve the "List of Rights" which Riel presented to the convention on 1 December after McDougall issued a proclamation stating that the northwest was part of Canada as of that day and that he was its lieutenant governor. The "List," probably composed by Riel, consisted of 14 items. It proposed representation in the Canadian parliament, guarantees of bilingualism in the legislature, a bilingual chief justice, and arrangements for free homesteads and Indian treaties. When the "List" was later printed and widely distributed many of the English-speaking population were converted to the view that the Métis demands were not unreasonable.

More serious opposition was mounted by Schultz, Dennis, and the Canadian element of the settlement. McDougall had requested Dennis to recruit a force to arrest the Métis occupying Upper Fort Garry, a threat Riel took seriously, but most of the English-speaking settlers refused to respond to Dennis' call to arms and he retired to Lower Fort Garry. Schultz, on the other hand, had fortified his house and store, and recruited about 50 followers as guards. He proposed to Dennis that he be allowed to attack Upper Fort Garry and capture Riel. Before this could happen Riel's soldiers surrounded Schultz's store and demanded his surrender. Realizing their position was hopeless, on 7 December the Canadians gave in and were imprisoned at Upper Fort Garry. The next day Riel established the provisional government, and Bruce was named president. On 18 December McDougall and Dennis left Pembina for Ontario, having been informed that the Canadian government had in fact postponed union until the British government or the HBC could guarantee a peaceable transfer.

Macdonald later admitted that under the circumstances the people of the community had had to form a government for the protection of life and property. Yet, in an alcoholic haze or because of urgent political problems in Canada, he did not, in fact, fully realize at the time the state of affairs in the settlement, and Canadians generally seemed unconcerned. On 6 December, nevertheless, Macdonald had sponsored a proclamation by the governor general of an amnesty to all in Red River who would lay down their arms. He also appointed a two-man goodwill mission consisting of Abbé Jean-Baptiste Thibault*, a priest who had been a missionary in the northwest for more than 35 years, and Colonel Charles-René-Léonidas d'IRUMBERRY de Salaberry. Thibault arrived in the settlement on Christmas Day, while de Salaberry remained in Pembina.

On 27 December, at the settlement, Riel took over from Bruce as president of the provisional government, and on the same day Donald Alexander Smith*, appointed by Macdonald's government as a special commissioner, arrived quietly with his brother-in-law Richard Charles HARDISTY, ostensibly on HBC business. When de Salaberry in his turn reached the settlement on 5 Jan. 1870 he and Thibault met with Riel and the Métis council. It was apparent then that they had no authority to negotiate terms of union; moreover, Thibault's discussions with the priests of the settlement converted him to the Métis viewpoint. Smith, a more formidable influence than the other two commissioners, had been charged by Macdonald to offer money or employment to any of the leaders in the settlement amenable to cooperation, and to present the Canadian government's plans. By distributing the government's money carefully he was able to attract several leading Métis but, after meeting with Riel on 6 January, he concluded that "no good could arise from entering into any negotiations with his Council." Smith decided to present his instructions at a public meeting. He had, however, left his official commission in Pembina to avoid its seizure by Riel who asked to see it. Now Smith was able, with the assistance of some of the Métis who were supporting him, to outmanœuvre the president and have Hardisty deliver the commission to him at Red River where he was under house arrest. Riel had to accede to Smith's desire for a mass meeting.

On 19 Jan. 1870 a large crowd assembled in the square at Fort Garry and, with Thomas Bunn* in the chair and Riel acting as interpreter, Smith made his case. Although it differed little from that of Thibault and de Salaberry, it was received calmly. Smith promised a liberal policy in confirming land titles to present occupants and representation on the proposed territorial council. The meeting was continued on the following day with an even larger crowd. The atmosphere of this session had changed and the listeners were now firmly behind Riel. Growing more confident and reaching the height of his influence, he realized that the meeting wanted something more than assurances of goodwill, and, taking the initiative, he proposed that a convention of 40 representatives, equally divided between the two language groups, meet the following week to consider Smith's instructions in detail. The proposal was approved. When the convention met on 26 January Riel was conciliatory, nominating Judge John Black* as chairman and agreeing that a new "List of Rights" should be prepared by a committee of six, three from each language group. A new, slightly modified "List" was presented on the 29th and the convention proceeded to debate it until 3 February when the last clause, no.19, was accepted. Riel then proposed that the convention demand the immediate grant of provincial status, presumably for the whole northwest. This would have meant control of crown lands and other natural resources, but the proposal was rejected, some considering it premature. He failed again on the 5th when he proposed that the convention repudiate the agreement between Canada and the HBC and that the negotiations be between Canada and the settlement.

On 7 February the convention discussed the new "List of Rights" first with Thibault and de Salaberry, and then with Smith, though Riel still contended that Smith could not provide any specific guarantees. Smith thereupon declared that he had been authorized to propose the sending of a delegation to Ottawa which would be given "a very cordial reception." The proposal, which would entail direct negotiations between Canada and the settlement, was what Riel had planned and advocated from the beginning of the resistance, and it was accepted with enthusiasm. Riel then suggested that since a government was needed until the parliament of Canada provided a constitution, both language groups should participate in the provisional government. The English-speaking representatives at the convention hesitated until a delegation sent on the 9th to consult with Governor Mactavish reported that although he refused to delegate his authority he agreed with the proposal. The country-born and the Scottish delegates were now satisfied that they should cooperate further with Riel.

The committee which had drafted the "List of Rights" in January was asked to submit a constitution for the provisional government. The committee's proposals, which were accepted on 10 February, established an assembly of 24 elected representatives drawn equally from the French-speaking and English-speaking parishes of the settlement. The General Quarterly Court of Assiniboia would continue to administer the law. Recognizing Riel's strong position, the committee also recommended that he be president. He then selected an executive of Thomas Bunn (secretary), William Bernard O'Donoghue* (treasurer), and James Ross (chief justice), and nominated a three-man delegation to proceed to Ottawa when required – Abbé Ritchot representing the Métis, Judge Black representing the English-speaking settlers, and Alfred Henry Scott* representing the Americans although he may have been a British subject. Riel had reached the pinnacle of his hopes and ambitions, and he could afford a gesture of generosity – he promised to release all the prisoners held at Upper Fort Garry.

It now appeared that a united front had been achieved in the settlement. The pro-American element, which in the persons of Enos Stutsman* and Oscar Malmros was intriguing in favour of annexation to the United States and promoting it through the *New Nation* begun in Winnipeg on 7 January, was seeing its limited influence on events diminishing. On the other hand the unscrupulous triumvirate of Schultz, Mair, and Thomas Scott was determined to foment civil war to eliminate Métis power. However, as outsiders they misjudged the willingness of the country-born and Scottish settlers to oppose the Métis. Unfortunately for all concerned the three men had escaped from Upper Fort Garry in January 1870. Schultz had made his way downstream to drum up support for an armed force in the English-speaking parishes and among the Indians. Mair and Scott had gone to Portage la Prairie, a Canadian settlement, where, to gain support, Scott retailed horror stories of his imprisonment. At Portage, Charles Arkoll Boulton*, captain of the 46th militia regiment and a member of Dennis' survey crew, was inveigled into assuming the leadership of a force which left Portage on 12 February with the objective of joining Schultz's party at Kildonan (now part of Winnipeg). The ostensible reason for action was to free the Canadian prisoners in Fort Garry. The last of them was released on 15 February, but this had no effect on Schultz, Mair, and Scott, and their real purpose – to overthrow the provisional government – was revealed. The Portage party, including Boulton, decided to return home but, contrary to Boulton's advice, marched as a body close to Fort Garry instead of dispersing to make their way west. News of the expedition had caused intense excitement in Fort Garry and every available man was called in to defend the fort. When the armed Portage party approached the fort on 17 February, a small force of some 50 men arrested the 48 Canadians, including Scott and Boulton, and took them to the recently vacated cells in Fort Garry. Schultz, realizing that he was a marked man, left for Ontario.

Riel correctly believed that it was the Canadians who were responsible for the turbulence in the settlement; they had twice resorted to force to overthrow him. One of them needed to be punished, and Boulton was condemned to death, a more severe sentence than any inflicted by a Métis leader on a disruptive member of a buffalo hunt. A number of people appealed for clemency, among them Donald Smith, but Riel only relented when he obtained from Smith a promise to persuade the English parishes to elect representatives. Thomas Scott, regarding the pardon as a sign of weakness, proceeded to insult his Métis guards who became so angry that they would have given him a severe beating had Riel not intervened. He warned Scott to behave. An ignorant and bigoted young man with a profound contempt for all mixed-bloods, Scott thought that the Métis were cowards. When he continued to make difficulties the guards insisted that he be tried by court martial and he was charged with insubordination; Scott was sentenced to death by a jury which was presided over by Ambroise-Dydime Lépine and which included Jean-Baptiste Lépine*, André Nault*, and Elzéar Goulet*. On this occasion the appeals of Smith and others were firmly rejected by Riel. Whether he was worried by the signs of insubordination among his followers, whether he persuaded himself that the settlement was in danger, or whether he thought it necessary to intimidate the Canadian conspirators and show Canada that the Métis and their government would have to be taken seriously, will always be debated. Professor G. F. G. Stanley believes the last consideration, Riel's own explanation, to be true. In the settlement the death of Scott on 4 March was soon forgotten but in Ontario the "murder" became a major issue. As people then and later have said, it was Riel's one great political blunder.

Bishop Taché arrived back in the settlement on 8 March 1870. He had been summoned from Rome, and as soon as he docked at Portland, Maine, in early February, he had a request from Cartier to come to Ottawa for discussions. Taché received a copy of the December proclamation of amnesty, which he was given to believe covered every action that had taken place or might take place before his return to the settlement, including any acts of violence. When he reached Red River he extended this assurance categorically to Riel and Ambroise-Dydime Lépine. On 15 March Taché met with the newly elected council and read a telegram from the secretary of state for the provinces, Joseph Howe*, which stated that the "List of Rights" was "in the main satisfactory" and that delegates should come to Ottawa to work out an agreement. Taché then requested that the prisoners be released. Riel agreed, and the jails were again emptied.

On 22 March Ritchot, Black, and A. H. Scott received yet another "List of Rights," this one prepared by the executive of the provisional government, which included the following provisions: that a province be established, not liable for any portion of the public debt of the dominion; that during a term of five years it not be subject to any direct taxation except for municipal purposes; that a sum equal to 80 cents per head be paid annually to the province by the Canadian government; that it have control of the public lands; that treaties with Indians accord with the wishes of the province; that uninterrupted steam communication from Upper Fort Garry to Lake Superior be provided and that all public buildings, bridges, roads, and other public works be paid for by the federal government; that the English and French languages be used in the provincial legislature and courts and in all public documents and acts; that the lieutenant governor and the judge of the superior court should be familiar with both the English and the French languages; that an amnesty be extended to all members of the provisional government and its servants; and that no further customs duties be imposed until there was uninterrupted railway communication between Winnipeg and St Paul. Before the delegates left, a fourth "List" was drawn up, doubtless with Riel's and Taché's blessing. This added a provision for separate schools according to the system existing in the province of Quebec, and outlined the structure for a provincial government. On 23 and 24 March 1870 the delegates set out for Ottawa.

When Schultz and Mair arrived in Toronto in early April they were secretly brought in touch with George Taylor Denison* III and other members of what became the Canada First group [*see* William Alexander FOSTER]. Ontarians had been up to now rather indifferent to the events in Red River, but news of Scott's execution made it possible to whip up a frenzy of hatred against Riel and the delegates. The Denison–Schultz activists secured the editorial support of most of the Toronto newspapers. They also planned meetings to be addressed by Schultz and Mair throughout the province. The appeal was anti-French, anti-Catholic, and to some extent anti-Macdonald for receiving a delegation representing the "murderers" of the "heroic" Thomas Scott. It was also arranged in Toronto that Ritchot and A. H. Scott would be arrested on a charge of abetting murder. They were indeed arrested soon after their arrival in Ottawa on 11 April, but were released because the judge decided that the Toronto warrant was not legal. They were then immediately re-arrested on a new warrant sworn in Ottawa. When the case was heard nine days later the crown prosecutor declined to proceed, and the delegates were finally free to pursue their mission.

On 22 April the delegates wrote to Howe requesting the opening of negotiations. Four days later Howe replied with a formal invitation to begin talks with Macdonald and Cartier. Ritchot was the real spokesman of the delegation, Black being inclined to compromise on the "List of Rights" and Scott being a silent supporter of Ritchot. Cartier and Macdonald rapidly discovered that the priest was a formidable negotiator, and that he was determined to extract concessions that would guarantee protection for the original inhabitants of Red River against the anticipated influx of Ontario land seekers and speculators. The results of the bargaining, embodied in the Manitoba Act of 1870, were a substantial achievement for Ritchot. Provincial status was granted to Manitoba (the name favoured by Riel), although Macdonald and Cartier succeeded in limiting the size of the province to about 1,000 square miles and not the entire northwest. Provincial control of natural resources, including all lands, was denied, but after hard bargaining 1,400,000 acres in the northwest were set aside for the Métis as a compromise. Bilingualism was recognized in the proceedings of the courts, the legislature, and in government publications. Historians have argued over whether the act was a genuine commitment to the extension of bilingualism to the west or, as some have suggested, merely a surrender to Riel's alleged dictatorship. A critical examination of the four lists of rights, which were the basis of the negotiations and the act, supports the former view. On one important point, however, Ritchot failed dismally – an updating of the amnesty of 6 December. Because of the political pressure of Ontario, being whipped up by Schultz and his associates, all that Ritchot could obtain was an oral assurance from Governor General Sir John Young* and Cartier that the British government was being asked to intervene; Ritchot noted in his journal: "His Excellency assured me that . . . Her Majesty was going to proclaim a general amnesty immediately, that we [the delegates] could set out for Manitoba, that the amnesty would arrive before us."

Somewhat isolated from the events in Ottawa, Riel had given his attention to the affairs of the settlement. As president of the provisional government, he had remained in Upper Fort Garry, though he returned control of the fort to the HBC to allow the resumption of trade. Perhaps more important, he worked assiduously to maintain the sometimes uneasy peace of the settlement. Nathaniel Pitt Langford, an American who visited it as an agent for the Northern Pacific, met Riel at this time and wrote: "Riel is about 28 years of age, has a fine physique, of active temperament, a great worker, and I think is able to endure a great deal. He is a large man . . . of very winning persuasive manners; and in his whole bearing, energy and ready decision are prominent characteristics; – and in this fact, lies his great powers – for I should not give him credit for great profundity, yet he is sagacious, and I think thoroughly patriotic and no less thoroughly incorruptible."

Ritchot arrived back in Red River on 17 June 1870 and met immediately with Riel who expressed satisfaction with the priest's account of events. A week later, when the assembly met in Upper Fort Garry, Ritchot outlined the reception given to the delegation in Ottawa, which he described as generally friendly. On the question of amnesty he forecast that since the Canadian government was unable or unwilling to issue it before union, it would be forthcoming from the queen. The assembly thereupon, on 24 June, unanimously approved the terms of the Manitoba Act. To Riel the prospects seemed bright. But Bishop Taché was worried because Ritchot had not brought back a written guarantee of amnesty. Fearing that he was vulnerable to charges of misrepresentation, Taché returned to Ottawa to see Cartier, but he received only the same sort of assurances as those given Ritchot.

A new concern had appeared in May 1870 when a military expedition had been dispatched to Red River under Colonel Garnet Joseph Wolseley* on an "errand of peace." The Canadian government had been considering such an expedition for some months, but Ontario's demand for action had much to do with its realization. Indeed, although Wolseley was a British officer, and the expedition had imperial troops as well as militia units, the latter were dominated by young Ontario Orangemen thirsting for Métis blood, Riel's in particular.

Throughout the negotiations, and in the early summer, Riel had grown uneasy about a deterioration of his support. Some Métis, mostly established farmers and traders, had never actually accepted his leadership and regarded him as an upstart. Another group, Professor William Lewis Morton* notes, "alternately supported and opposed him." This was a St Boniface élite whose members are to be distinguished from the hunters and unemployed tripmen among whom Riel drew his strongest support. At the same time, Riel was concerned about the weakening of the always fragile relations between the Métis and the English-speaking elements in the settlement. But perhaps most important, he was worried by reports of the attitude of the Ontario volunteers in the approaching Wolseley expedition. William Bernard O'Donoghue had been sowing seeds of mistrust of all Canadian politicians and seemed to be gaining influence, even though Taché on his arrival in St Boniface on 23 August assured Métis leaders that "there was not the slightest danger." But on the same day news arrived that the troops were nearing Red River; a governor had still not arrived to establish civil government, nor had word of the promised amnesty.

On 24 August Riel learned that the soldiers were planning to lynch him; he vacated Upper Fort Garry a few hours ahead of them. Accompanied by O'Donoghue and a few others, Riel crossed the Red River to Taché's palace in St Boniface. He told the bishop he had been deceived, but added: "No matter what happens now, the rights of the métis are assured by the Manitoba Bill; it is what I wanted – *My mission is finished*." Riel then proceeded to his home in nearby St Vital, where his mother lived; but growing more apprehensive about his safety he took refuge at St Joseph's mission, about ten miles south of the border in Dakota Territory.

The new lieutenant governor, named on 15 July 1870, was Adams George Archibald*, a father of confederation from Nova Scotia and a member of parliament. He arrived in the settlement on 2 September and was at once confronted with the problem of maintaining order. Winnipeg was a place of riotous turbulence. Two Métis were among those killed [*see* Elzéar Goulet] and sympathizers with the resistance were threatened or assaulted by the Ontario militia volunteers who seemed bent on nothing short of assassinating all the Métis. Faced with this difficult situation Archibald went about the business of establishing a civil administration. Fluent in French, he formed a first provincial cabinet which was strictly bi-racial in character and had no members from the Canadian party. Alfred Boyd* became provincial secretary and Marc-Amable Girard* provincial treasurer.

Riel was pleased with the results of the first provincial election, held in December 1870, in which a majority of the elected members seemed well disposed towards him. He must have been particularly pleased that Donald Smith defeated Schultz in Winnipeg, though Schultz was subsequently elected to the House of Commons, along with Smith and a Métis, Pierre Delorme. In February 1871, however, Riel became seriously ill, mentally overburdened with concern about his personal safety and with finding financial support for his family. It was not until May 1871 that he was strong enough to return home to St Vital.

Riel's old associate, O'Donoghue, had by this time rejected his former chief; the parting of ways had occurred on 17 Sept. 1870 when, at a meeting at St Norbert which Riel attended, the latter had opposed O'Donoghue's pleas to ask for the intervention of the United States in favour of the Métis. By October 1871 he had become the leader of a band of Fenians based across the international boundary. Having secured the support of John O'Neill* of Ridgeway fame, and counting on general support among the Métis, O'Donoghue planned to invade Manitoba. On 5 October he and some 35 followers crossed the border and captured the small HBC trading post of Pembina. But the Métis did not join them. Indeed, two Métis took O'Donoghue prisoner and turned him over to the American authorities. The invasion had lasted one day. However, the many rumours in Winnipeg concerning the seriousness of the Fenian threat had caused Archibald to issue a proclamation on the 4th calling on all loyal men "to rally round the flag." Several companies of armed horsemen were recruited, one of them under the command of Riel. Archibald went to St Boniface to review the volunteers, was given a cordial reception, and shook hands with their leaders, including Riel. Archibald's gesture was what Riel's lay and clerical friends had hoped for, because it implied that he would no longer be an object of persecution. There were few in the province who thought of hanging Riel.

But when news of Archibald's action reached Ontario there was an outburst of indignation. Mair was outraged and Denison led a campaign for his recall. Though both houses of the Manitoba legislature had enthusiastically endorsed Archibald's action, Riel became a political issue in Ontario. Premier Edward Blake*, in 1872, went as far as to offer a $5,000 reward to anyone who would bring about the arrest of Scott's "murderers." For Macdonald it was essential to avoid a Quebec-Ontario confrontation over the Riel question, or any other question, before the 1872 general election. Tension would subside, he believed, if Riel could be induced to stay out of Canada for a time. Taché was to be the agent of this manœuvre. Macdonald gave him $1,000 and when Taché returned to the northwest he persuaded Smith to add £600 to an expense fund for Riel's needs and the support of his family. Although he was bitter over his treatment, Riel accepted voluntary exile. He and Ambroise-Dydime Lépine made their way to St Paul, where they arrived on 2 March 1872. From St Paul Riel carried on an extensive correspondence with his friends in the settlement, particularly with Joseph Dubuc*, who had moved to St Boniface from Quebec in 1870 at the urging of Riel, Ritchot, Taché, and Cartier. But Riel felt increasingly insecure in St Paul, a centre swarming with Ontarians en route to Manitoba who could easily be induced by Schultz and the Ontario government's reward to effect his arrest. Believing he would be safer among his friends, Riel returned to Red River in late June.

Dubuc and others now urged Riel to be a candidate for the riding of Provencher in the September 1872 federal general election. He agreed, despite warnings that he would be murdered if he set foot in Ottawa. But there was a new turn of events: Cartier was defeated in Montreal East early in September and Macdonald turned to Manitoba to find a seat for his Quebec lieutenant. Riel agreed to withdraw his candidature, as did his opponent Henry Joseph CLARKE, in favour of Cartier, on condition that a settlement be reached on the guarantees made to the Métis regarding land. The question of amnesty he was prepared to leave to Cartier, whose sympathy on this point was a matter of record. On 14 September Cartier was elected by acclamation, but a mob of Canadians wrecked the offices of the two pro-Riel newspapers, the *Weekly Manitoban* (Winnipeg) and *Le Métis* (St Boniface). Even Smith was attacked by the Winnipeg rowdies.

For the next few months Riel was inactive. In Ottawa a renewed effort was made to secure the promised amnesty, but Macdonald was adamant; his political position was too weak after the election. The kaleidoscope of politics changed once again when Cartier died on 20 May 1873 in London. The champion of French rights in Manitoba, and the chief proponent in cabinet of an amnesty for Riel, was gone.

The death of Cartier meant a by-election would have to be held in Provencher, and Riel agreed to let his name stand, even though some of his friends predicted that he would never be allowed to take his seat and might well be killed; in fact, a warrant was issued at Winnipeg in September for Riel's arrest, as well as that of Ambroise-Dydime Lépine, for the "murder" of Scott. Lépine was arrested at St Vital, but Riel escaped after being warned by Andrew Graham Ballenden BANNATYNE. Riel was determined to plead his own case in parliament, where he knew he would have strong support among the French Canadian members. In the October by-election he was unopposed. Accompanied by Joseph Tassé*, Riel made his way to Montreal where Honoré Mercier* and two other friends conveyed him to Hull. At the last moment, however, Riel lost his courage and did not enter Ottawa, probably because he feared assassination or arrest on the murder charge. He returned to Montreal and in due course made his way to Plattsburg, N.Y., where he stayed with Oblate fathers. Here he was near Keeseville, a French Canadian lumber town, and, tired and depressed, he was often warmly received by the parish priest, Fabien Martin, *dit* Barnabé.

In November 1873 the Macdonald government resigned because of the Pacific Scandal; Alexander Mackenzie* became Liberal prime minister and called a general election for February 1874. In this election, which the Liberals won, Riel easily defeated Joseph Hamelin, the Liberal candidate in Provencher and a Métis who had not participated in the movement of 1869–70. Dubuc and Ritchot had campaigned actively on Riel's behalf. He travelled to Ottawa where he signed the oaths' book, but he was soon expelled from the house on the motion of Mackenzie Bowell*, seconded by Schultz. In September 1874, with the encouragement and support of Alphonse Desjardins*, Emmanuel-Persillier Lachapelle*, and the ultramontane Conservatives in Quebec, Riel was re-elected in the by-election in Provencher. He now saw his election as not only a victory for the Métis cause but also for the assertion of French and Catholic rights in Manitoba and the North-West Territories. However, he did not take his seat. Instead, he settled with Abbé Martin, Keeseville being close enough to Montreal to permit easy return to Canada. Here he learned that he had been expelled from the house for a second time.

On 13 October, in Winnipeg, Lépine's trial got under way after a year of delay, with Joseph Royal* and the prominent Quebec Conservative, Joseph-Adolphe Chapleau*, as defence counsel. In the first week of November Lépine was found guilty of Scott's murder and sentenced to death by Chief Justice Edmund Burke WOOD, despite the jury's recommendation for mercy. Quebec was outraged at the outcome of the trial and the newspapers demanded amnesty for Lépine and Riel. What saved Lépine and assisted Mackenzie in his dilemma, for he could not accede to Quebec without offending Ontario, was the intervention of the governor general, Lord Dufferin [Blackwood*]; on his own authority Dufferin in January 1875 commuted the death sentence to two years' imprisonment and the permanent forfeiture of political rights. Mackenzie, emboldened by the governor general's move, secured parliamentary approval in February of an amnesty for Riel and Lépine, conditional on their banishment for five years. As a member in the Ontario Legislative Assembly Mackenzie had been strongly anti-Riel. As a prime minister of Canada, however, he was forced to equivocate and compromise until Dufferin had provided a way out of the impasse. Ironically, perhaps, Mackenzie's actions resolved the prickly amnesty question.

Riel, exiled and with little apparent future, became more preoccupied with religious than political matters. During the strain of the previous five years he had suffered from bouts of nervous exhaustion, but now his mental and physical behaviour often revealed an obsession with the idea of a "mission": he saw himself at once as the guardian of the spiritual well-being of the Métis and as the prophet and priest of a new form of Christianity. He based much of this belief on a supportive letter he received from Bishop Ignace BOURGET of Montreal on 14 July 1875, in which the bishop stated: "I have the deep-seated conviction that you will receive in this life, and sooner than you think, the reward for all your mental sacrifices. . . . For He has given you a mission which you must fulfil in all respects." Riel already had experienced a mystical vision and an uncontrollable emotional seizure during a visit to Washington, D.C., in December 1874, and at Keeseville, Abbé Martin's household was being terrified by Riel's continuous shouting and crying. Unable to give him solace, the kindly priest appealed for help to Riel's uncle, John Lee, who lived near Montreal. Riel stayed with the Lees for several months, until his continued religious mania finally resulted in the interruption of a church service. The unbearable strain on his household induced Lee to consult Riel's political friend, Doctor Lachapelle, who arranged for Riel's admission to the asylum at Longue-Pointe (Hôpital Louis-H. LaFontaine, Montréal) on 6 March 1876, under the name Louis R. David.

The supervising doctor, Dr Henry HOWARD, agreed that confinement was the only course available to Riel's friends. However, Howard was much impressed by Riel's intelligence and knowledge of classical philosophy, the varieties of Christian belief, and Judaism. In commenting on Riel's peculiar theological ideas, he later wrote: "I never could satisfy myself thoroughly as to whether this sort of talk was not acting a part or an hallucination." During his brief stay at Longue-Pointe Riel continued to alternate between periods of lucidity and irrationality. The sisters in charge of the asylum feared that his political enemies would discover his presence and in May 1876 Lachapelle certified that Riel required constant attention and treatment which could only be provided in the Beauport asylum (Centre hospitalier Robert-Giffard) outside Quebec City. At Beauport Riel brooded on his mission and also occasionally became violent and excited. He wrote notes elaborating his theological principles, which were a fantastic *mélange* of Christian and Judaic ideas. But in time, although he could still be irrational on religious and political subjects, rest and calm had their effect. After a little more than a year and a half the medical superintendent of Beauport, Dr François-Elzéar Roy, discharged Riel with a warning to live a quiet life – if possible an outdoor life.

For the balance of 1877 and much of 1878 Riel was at Keeseville and other centres where he hoped to find work. Late in 1878 he went to St Paul. He discovered that many of the Métis in Manitoba had sold their land to Winnipeg land speculators, because they had no funds or skill to farm, and had moved to the valleys of the Saskatchewan and upper Missouri to hunt the now scarce buffalo. Riel travelled to the Canadian border, where he was visited by friends and members of his family; he learned that the Métis did not believe he had ever been insane, despite his sojourn in two Quebec asylums. He confided to a few friends that he had pretended to be mad.

With his exile still a year to run, Riel joined those Métis who, along with Indians of the Canadian plains, were wandering in the upper Missouri area of Montana territory, and he became a trader and interpreter. He found widespread economic hardship and demoralization among the Métis in this turbulent frontier area. At this time Riel, bearded and handsome, was in the prime of life. In 1881 he married a Métis girl, Marguerite Monet, *dit* Bellehumeur. He had had a passionate love affair with Évelina Martin, *dit* Barnabé, sister of the parish priest of Keeseville, but despite her desire to join him in Montana, Riel had broken the engagement, apparently because he could offer her no suitable home in the circumstances under which he was forced to live.

Riel soon involved himself in the turbulent politics of Montana, in spite of the warning that he should live a quiet life. He associated himself with the local Republican party because it seemed to be the best hope for procuring a reserve for the Métis and for curbing the whisky trade which was demoralizing his people. Appointed a deputy to fight this trade, Riel also participated in the 1882 congressional election. His involvement in the election subsequently produced a worrisome court case about vote manipulation, but in the end the charges against Riel were dismissed for insufficient evidence. In March 1883 he became an American citizen. That June he visited Winnipeg but returned to Montana determined to throw in his lot with his people there. In 1884 he accepted an invitation from the Jesuits to become the teacher at St Peter's mission on the Sun River, a tributary of the Missouri. He was a good teacher and conscientious, though as the months passed he became restless and bored by the routine.

But his people in the northwest did not forget him. It is not clear who in the District of Lorne was most influential in soliciting Riel's assistance with their grievances against the Canadian government. Gabriel Dumont*, the famous buffalo hunter, who had apparently met Riel at Red River in 1870, had been the recognized leader of the Métis community at Saint-Laurent (Saint-Laurent-Grandin, Sask.) since the early 1870s. His agreement with those who wished to solicit Riel's help, namely the Ontario settler William Henry Jackson* and English-speaking mixed-blood Andrew Spence of Prince Albert (Sask.), carried great weight, especially when he himself became one of the delegates who went to Montana to contact Riel in June 1884. The invitation to come to the South Saskatchewan offered Riel an opportunity to lead his people, a mission he had cherished for a decade. He agreed to assist in presenting the grievances of the district to the Canadian government and added that he would use this opportunity to pursue his personal claim for land in Manitoba. The delegation accepted these terms, and Riel left Montana confident that God would give him the success he longed for and that he would return home in September to continue his fight for the Métis there.

When Riel reached Batoche (Sask.) in the District of Lorne at the beginning of July 1884 he found an unhappy and angry population, white, Indian, and Métis. The relocation of the Canadian Pacific Railway's main line in the southern prairie region had produced a collapse of land values in nearby Prince Albert. Settlers did not hold clear title to their land despite the fact that many had lived for over three years in the district. For the more than 1,400 Métis in the area, the questions of unextinguished Indian rights to the land and the land surveys were the major issues. These Métis had been semi-nomadic hunters living far west of the Red River, who had not participated in the events of 1869–70. With the disappearance of the buffalo and with the encouragement of the missionaries, they were now beginning to settle into farming communities. Those who had settled first obtained the traditional and much preferred river lots; but after a federal survey in 1882 Métis settlers were forced to occupy square lots, and the federal government was refusing to re-survey the area.

Agitation for redress of grievances by white settlers had begun as early as 1883 with the formation of the Manitoba and North West Farmers' Co-operative and Protective Union to petition the federal government. That same year the Settlers' Union was formed by the Lorne radicals, and Jackson, its secretary, had been commissioned to contact the Métis of Saint-Laurent. Dumont had been cooperative, and in March 1884 had urged the preparation of a "list of rights," though some of the more militant Métis suggested action by force of arms. Yet in July, when Riel addressed meetings, first of Métis at Charles Nolin's house at Batoche, then of several hundred English-speaking settlers at Red Deer Hill, he impressed everyone with his moderation. About a week later he went to another meeting, where most of Prince Albert was in attendance, and again advocated a peaceful presentation of grievances and proposals. Riel's calmness and moderation gained him the support of most settlers, and put him in a position of some influence.

Meanwhile the Plains Cree leader, Big Bear [MISTAHIMASKWA], and his followers, assembled in June 1884 on the reserve of Poundmaker [PĪTIKWAHANAPIWĪYIN], were formulating demands to be made to the Indian Affairs branch of the federal government. Poundmaker and Big Bear were aware of the agitation in Lorne and held meetings with Riel soon after his arrival in the district. However, the native peoples' grievances had little in common with those Riel now represented, and these meetings did nothing to bring the two movements closer together.

The early favourable response to Riel among the white settlers yielded to growing opposition. The *Prince Albert Times and Saskatchewan Review* reversed its editorial policy, having been bribed by Edgar Dewdney*, the Indian commissioner and lieutenant governor of the territories. In addition, Riel did not have the support of the clergy. Father Alexis André* charged Riel with mixing religion and politics. On 1 Sept. 1884 Bishop Vital-Justin Grandin* of St Albert paid a conciliatory visit to Saint-Laurent accompanied by Amédée-Emmanuel Forget*, secretary to Dewdney; there is some evidence that Forget attempted, unsuccessfully, to "buy" Riel with a seat on the Council of the North-West Territories. Dumont calmed events somewhat by explaining: "We need him [Riel] here as our political leader. In other matters I am the chief here." Riel explained to Grandin what he wanted: "the inauguration of a responsible Government"; "the same privileges to the old settlers of the North-West Territories as those accorded to the old settlers of Manitoba"; the granting of "the lands, at present, in possession of the Halfbreeds" to them "in fee simple," and the issuing of patents to them "on application"; 240 acres for all mixed-bloods; the income from the sale of two million acres for the support of schools, hospitals, and orphanages and for the purchase of ploughs and of grain; and for all "works and contracts of the Government in the North-West Territories be given, as far as practicable to residents therein, in order to encourage them as they deserve and to increase circulation of cash in the Territories."

Riel and Jackson busied themselves at Prince Albert with the petition, and on 16 December it was sent to Ottawa, signed by Andrew Spence as chairman and Jackson as secretary of the joint English-Métis organization. The petition was a long one with 25 sections, land claims occupying a prominent place. The grievances of the Métis and Indians were recited and it was noted that while the territories had an population of 60,000, Manitoba had been granted provincial status with only 12,000. The petitioners thus included the suggestion that they "be allowed as in [1870], to send Delegates to Ottawa with their Bill of rights; whereby an understanding may be arrived at as to their entry into confederation, with the constitution of a free province." The petition was acknowledged by Chapleau, the secretary of state, and was referred to David Lewis Macpherson*, the minister of the interior, by Macdonald, the prime minister, who subesquently denied having received it. The acknowledgement by Chapleau was regarded by Jackson as a victory.

The question now arose for Riel as to whether or not to return to Montana as he had originally planned. At the same time he had not forgotten that his own land claims had not yet been settled by the federal government. Certainly he was a poor man who lived by charity and he had not hidden from the delegation the fact that he wished to press these claims: under the Manitoba Act, he pointed out, 240 acres were owing to him. He also had owned five lots which were of value for their hay, wood, and proximity to the Red River. He estimated that in all he was due a sum of $35,000. However, the federal government remained insensitive not only to Riel's claims but to the grievances of the petition.

By the end of February 1885 Riel had agreed to stay, claiming that "a vast multitude of nations" was waiting to support him. However, although the missionaries were sympathetic to the Métis cause they opposed any use of force or any encouragement of the Indians; by March Métis frustration had led to talk of resort to arms. Because of the opposition from the clergy and from some Métis, including Nolin, to violence, on 10 March the Métis decided to begin a novena, timed to end on the 19th, feast day of St Joseph, the patron saint of the Métis, to assist them in arriving at a decision. But, during a mass in the church at Saint-Laurent on 15 March, Riel remonstrated with the priest, Father Vital Fourmond, on his attitude to a Métis armed movement, in effect making a final break from the church. He was becoming more and more mystical and pietistic, and he spent much time in prayer. He deepened his rupture with the clergy by preaching his own theology to his followers; he renamed the days of the week, put the Lord's Day on Saturday as in Mosaic law, proposed that there be a new pope (Bourget, and later Taché), rejected the rule of Rome, and suggested that everyone would be priests in a new reformed Catholicism.

Frustrated by the lack of federal action, Riel was, in fact, having a renewed period of mental disturbance. But the appeal of his charismatic personality was strong, and by this time his more militant followers were seizing shotguns, rifles, and ammunition. On 18 March, hearing a rumour that 500 North-West Mounted Police were advancing towards them, Riel and approximately 60 supporters ransacked stores and seized a number of people, including Indian Agent John Bean Lash, near Batoche. Riel announced that "Rome has fallen" and that Bourget was the new pope. That evening at Saint-Laurent he signed his name Louis "David" Riel, and the next day he formed a provisional government, composed of 15 councillors, known as the "exovedate," which meant "those picked from the flock." Riel was not a member; to be one would not have fitted his role as a prophet by divine sanction.

Riel was nevertheless the undisputed leader of the movement, Dumont being the military head. Their intention was first to take Fort Carlton, and they tried without success to enlist the active support of the

English-speaking mixed-bloods. Needing supplies for his troops, Dumont ransacked a store at Duck Lake on 25 March. He then proceeded west and the next day encountered by chance a force commanded by NWMP Superintendent Leif Newry Fitzroy Crozier*. Despite the fact that the Métis were protected by natural cover and occupied high ground, Crozier, an impetuous and excitable officer, gave the order to fire. Of the government's 100 men, 12 were killed and 11 wounded. The Métis lost only five of about 300 men. If Riel, who had given the order to return the fire from the police, had not stopped the fighting, the government forces would have been annihilated. Riel and his followers spent the rest of the day in prayers for their dead, returning to Batoche on 31 March.

By early April Riel had given up hope of support from the English half-breeds and the whites, although he did still expect to be able to make alliances with the various Indian groups, who by this time had also taken up arms. At Battleford, Poundmaker's followers had broken into the buildings in the town, and the residents had been forced to take refuge in the NWMP barracks. At Eagle Hills the Stonies had killed a white farm instructor. On Big Bear's reserve the war chief, Wandering Spirit [KAPAPAMAHCHAKWEW] had displaced Big Bear and led the band in the violent attack on Frog Lake (Alta) on 2 April, where nine people were killed [*see* Léon-Adélard FAFARD]. Riel sent messages to the Indians to join the Métis movement, but chronic factionalism among the various Indian groups and a lack of understanding of Riel's goals produced only a few recruits. The Indian movement itself was never able to put up a united front, despite Big Bear's efforts in this direction, and lack of concerted action was a major cause of its collapse.

The events at Frog Lake, although the responsibility of the Indians and not the Métis, aroused horror and hatred of Riel throughout English Canada. That both Métis and Indians had legitimate grievances was ignored. Macdonald decided to crush the revolt, calling on Major-General Frederick Dobson Middleton*, then commanding the Canadian militia, to take the field. Middleton formulated a simple plan: he would march on Riel at Batoche from Fort Qu'Appelle (Sask.); at the same time Major-General Thomas Bland Strange* would march from Calgary to engage Big Bear, and proceed to join forces with Middleton; and Lieutenant-Colonel William Dillon Otter* was to relieve Battleford. Otter was successful, but suffered a serious setback at Cut Knife Hill (Sask.) at the hands of Poundmaker's warriors. Middleton was fired on by the Métis at Fish Creek (Sask.) on 24 April and was not able to continue his march to Batoche until 7 May.

The Métis were preparing their defences at Batoche, a series of pits skilfully hidden in the bush. Dumont, too realistic to believe that his forces could defeat the Canadians, had hoped that a well-conducted guerrilla campaign would force the government to negotiate. Riel had opposed these tactics and had decided upon concentrating their forces, about 175 or 200 men, at Batoche – in his mind the city of God. When Middleton's force of more than 800 men advanced on the village on 9 May, the result was a foregone conclusion despite what the English Canadian press later called the heroics of the militia led by Colonel Arthur Trefusis Heneage WILLIAMS. The battle, and the rebellion, was over on 12 May.

Dumont fled to the United States; on 15 May Riel, "cold and forlorn," chose to surrender to the scouts of the NWMP, who described him as "careworn and haggard; he has let his hair and beard grow long; He is dressed in a poorer fashion than most of the half breeds captured. While talking to Gen'l Middleton as could be seen from the outside of the tent, his eyes rolled from side to side with the look of a hunted man; He is evidently the most thoroughly frightened man in camp. . . ." On the following day the minister of militia, Joseph-Philippe-René-Adolphe Caron*, instructed Middleton to send Riel to Winnipeg under guard for trial, but Macdonald and his cabinet came to realize that if the trial was held in Winnipeg a unanimous verdict might not be secured, a distinctly unpleasant prospect for the government. When the party reached Moose Jaw (Sask.) on the CPR, it was redirected by Caron to Regina, where it arrived on 23 May 1885. In the territorial capital and its neighbourhood, hostility to the prisoner prevailed.

The difference in site also meant a different court procedure. Under Manitoba law a prisoner was entitled to a 12-man jury and half the jury might be French-speaking. On the other hand, the federal law governing court procedure in the territories called for only a six-man jury, with no assurance of bilingual rights. Moreover, at a trial held in one of the provinces the case would be heard by a superior court judge whose independence was guaranteeed by law and practice. Instead, Riel was tried in Regina by a stipendiary magistrate who held office at the pleasure of the federal government, and could be dismissed without cause at any time.

It was clear from the start that the trial would be a political one, and there is indisputable evidence that Macdonald's objective was to fix exclusive responsibility on Riel and to secure his conviction and execution as soon as possible. It was an understandable reaction to the inflamed opinion of Ontario, which cried for vengeance for the killing of Thomas Scott, the whites at Frog Lake, the men at Duck Lake, and the militiamen under Middleton's command. But Macdonald sadly misjudged the explosion of emotions in Quebec. In the event, the government's conduct of the case was to be a travesty of justice.

When Riel was brought to Regina he was imprisoned in the NWMP barracks in a $6\frac{1}{2}$ by $4\frac{1}{2}$ foot cell and shackled with ball and chain. All the defendants who were charged, including Jackson who had joined the Métis movement, were held incommunicado by the police until the chief prosecuting attorneys arrived on 1 July. In the interval, the government's lawyers were sifting the evidence against Riel and the others, and preparing the formal charges, utilizing the documents which had been retrieved from Riel's headquarters and on the battlefield.

The presiding magistrate was to be Hugh Richardson*, an Englishman who had been named a stipendiary magistrate by the Mackenzie administration in 1876 and who was a member of the Council of the North-West Territories and legal adviser to the lieutenant governor of the North-West Territories. He was not bilingual. The five prosecuting attorneys were the deputy minister of justice, George Wheelock Burbidge, as well as leading members of the bar of eastern Canada: Christopher Robinson*, Thomas-Chase Casgrain*, Britton Bath Osler*, and David Lynch Scott*. François-Xavier Lemieux*, a successful criminal lawyer, was one of those who agreed to defend Riel, along with Charles Fitzpatrick*, Thomas Cooke Johnstone, and James Naismith Greenshields, also leading members of the bar in the east.

In retrospect, the defence lawyers' handling of Riel's case left much to be desired. They did not ask for dismissal on grounds of insanity, despite the fact that Jackson had been so acquitted a few days before. They also denied Riel the right to cross-examine witnesses, even though (as Riel put it during the trial) "they lose more than three-quarters of the good opportunities of making good answers . . . ," because they did not know the witnesses and the local circumstances. All this was a serious invasion of the prisoner's rights by his counsel. Lemieux also declared that the defence counsel would not be responsible for anything the prisoner might say during his first address to the jury. It is curious that Riel's lawyers did not demand that he be tried under the Canadian statute of 1868 which would have allowed a charge of treason-felony with life imprisonment as the penalty. Of the 84 trials held in Battleford and Regina for participants in the rebellion, 71 were for treason-felony, 12 for murder, and only one, Riel's, for high treason. The charge against Riel was under the medieval English statute of 1352 which carried a mandatory death penalty.

The trial opened on 20 July with the reading of the indictment, followed by arguments by Riel's counsel challenging the jurisdiction of the court and the trial procedure. Richardson rejected the defence arguments. Riel pleaded not guilty. On the following day the defence counsel argued for a postponement of the trial, on the grounds that they would be unable to conduct a defence in the absence of certain witnesses, including a number of alienists in eastern Canada. Richardson granted postponement for one week. Riel had asked for three witnesses who had fled to Montana, Gabriel Dumont and two other Métis, Napoléon Nault and Michel Dumas. Father André and his associate Father Fourmond did appear as defence witnesses, but not Lawrence Vankoughnet*, the superintendent-general of Indian affairs, and Alexander Mackinnon Burgess*, deputy minister of the interior, who, Riel argued, were custodians of documents which detailed Métis grievances. The third day's proceedings began on 28 July with the empanelling of the jury. As a measure of the inevitability of the final outcome it should be noted that of the 36 persons summoned by Richardson for jury service only one was French-speaking, and he was prevented by an accident from appearing. The crown challenged one prospective juror, the only Roman Catholic on the list. Thus, despite the fact that French Canadian and Métis jurors could have been secured from among the population of the territories, Riel was tried by a jury comprised entirely of English-speaking Protestants.

A perusal of the evidence indicates clearly that the crown selected witnesses who would testify that the prisoner had used his great influence with the Métis to lead them to arm themselves, and subsequently had determined the strategy of the uprising. Dumont, the witnesses implied, had been responsible only for the tactics adopted in the engagements. The prosecution elicited opinions from its witnesses that Riel's deep religious fervour was calculated to impress a simple-minded folk who had become his dupes and it made much of Riel's negotiations with the Indians. It also represented the prisoner as a self-seeking villain who was prepared in return for $35,000 to abandon the cause of the Métis. The prosecution sought to discredit witnesses called by the defence, and objected to the admission of evidence on the failure of the federal government to deal with long-standing complaints. It may well have feared the effect of such evidence on the jurors because even at this early date most westerners felt alienated by policies made in Ottawa for the benefit of central Canada.

Both Father André and Father Fourmond, questioned on Riel's behaviour, politics, and religion, were unshakeable in their opinion that Riel was insane. Defence counsel's star witness was Dr François-Elzéar Roy, superintendent of the Beauport asylum, who stated that Riel suffered from megalomania (today often referred to as paranoia). Roy was subjected to a savage cross-examination by Osler, whose questions implied that Roy had a financial interest in keeping patients in his custody. Dr Daniel Clark*, superintendent of the lunatic asylum in Toronto, testified that Riel was insane, but admitted he would have to have him under observation for some months before he could be positive that he was not malingering. Clark was highly critical of the McNaghten rules; this legal precedent established that a defence of insanity could be accepted only if it could be proved that the accused did not know the difference between right and wrong. To combat the impressive evidence of Riel's insanity the crown counsel resorted to extraordinary measures. Dr James Wallace, medical superintendent of the insane asylum in Hamilton, Ont., testified that Riel was sane, on the basis of about half an hour's interview and listening to the trial proceedings. Not only was his examination superficial, but defence counsel Charles Fitzpatrick elicited that Wallace had never read the works of the leading French authorities on megalomania. Dr Augustus Jukes*, the NWMP surgeon, was forced to admit under defence questioning that one could converse with a man and not be aware of insanity. With its case in such a precarious state, the prosecution recalled General Middleton and four other laymen who had had brief contacts with Riel.

The defence counsel could have made better use of Dr Clark's evidence, though it may have been that they had little or no experience in dealing with cases of insanity, or they may have had too little time to prepare their defence or to consult alienists in advance. Yet another curious feature of the conduct of the case was that the defence did not attempt to subpoena the diary which Riel kept between March and May 1885 and which was picked up on the battlefield along with his other papers and shipped to the Department of Justice in Ottawa. The Toronto *Globe* had published most of this diary by the time the trial began in Regina. The diary displays a curious mixture of prayers and pious assertions with religious interpretations of the events of the rebellion.

Fitzpatrick summed up the case for acquittal in perhaps the most passionately eloquent address ever heard in a Canadian courtroom. The first part was devoted to an exposition of the historic role of the Métis in the northwest, and the disabilities under which they had suffered. The remainder dealt cogently with Riel's actions during the rebellion, which were held to be incompatible with those of a sane man. The address had a profound effect on those present in the court, including the jurors. The judge then called on Riel, asking him whether he had anything to say. Riel would have preferred to defer his remarks until after the crown counsel had made its summation, but the judge denied the request. Riel then proceeded to address the court. The intense religiosity of the prisoner, a notable feature of his personality, was evident from the beginning and throughout his remarks. He spoke in a clear, eloquent, and earnest manner and dealt particularly with the question of his insanity. The address was quite rational in its description of the undemocratic institutions which prevailed in the territories. Robinson's summation for the prosecution was relatively brief and unemotional, and was chiefly concerned with the defence that Riel was insane. "My learned friends," he sagely observed, "must make their choice between their defences. They cannot claim for their client what is called a niche in the temple of fame and at the same time assert that he is entitled to a place in a lunatic asylum." Riel, he continued, "is neither a patriot nor a lunatic." How could a man live for 18 months as the most prominent man in the district without his insanity being detected? Robinson could find no evidence that Riel controlled his mania and used it for his own purpose. Finally, Robinson was dissatisfied with the evidence that had been provided by the defence concerning the circumstances of his incarceration in the two asylums.

The judge's charge to the jury was clearly biased against Riel. Richardson reiterated his claim that the court had full jurisdiction. In dealing with the question of insanity he suggested that Riel's claim for $35,000, and the disappearance of his irritability when brought to Regina, were facts which demonstrated reasoning power. Richardson concluded by asking the jury to apply the McNaghten rules to the case. On 1 August the jury returned a verdict of guilty with a recommendation of mercy. Richardson passed the death sentence.

But before delivering the sentence Richardson asked Riel the customary question of whether he had anything to say to the court. Riel seized the opportunity to deliver a much longer speech than the one he had made the previous afternoon. It was an entirely secular argument, with the exception of three brief references to the Deity, to his prophetic mission, and to the spirit which had guided his activities. He began by expressing satisfaction that he had not been regarded as insane. He then turned to a recital of the Manitoba disturbances of 1869–70, two-thirds of his remarks being devoted to this theme. Turning to his ambitions for the northwest, he described the policy he would follow if he were federal minister of immigration and his programme for settling the prairies. In essence it was a not unreasonable programme for creating a multi-cultural society. At the same time the address has shrewd observations and moving passages which typify the rhetorical power that had given him such an influence in the Métis community.

The verdict was appealed to the Court of Queen's Bench of Manitoba (the appeal court for the territories), and subsequently to the Judicial Committee of the Privy Council, but the appeals were dismissed. Meanwhile, petitions for the commutation of the death sentence flooded into Ottawa from thousands of French Canadians in Quebec, Massachusetts, and Manitoba. A considerable number of counter-petitions were sent from Ontario. The commutation petitions were based on the argument that Riel was insane and hence not responsible for his actions during the rebellion, or that his crime was a political one for which civilized nations no longer exacted the death penalty. Riel's fate had become a national issue that threatened to divide the cabinet, indeed the country, and a vast amount of editorial commentary was produced on the subject. Ontario newspapers favoured the execution and at least one, the Toronto *News*, went as far as to begin advocating polarization of politics on racial lines. On the other hand, Quebec journalists were highly critical of Macdonald and his cabinet, especially his French Canadian colleagues. Despite the immense pressure from mass meetings in Quebec, Chapleau, Hector-Louis Langevin*, and Caron did not resign, perhaps saving the country from further racial and religious conflict.

As a result of the insistence of Macdonald's French Canadian cabinet colleagues, he nevertheless agreed to have Riel re-examined. On 31 Oct. 1885 three doctors were instructed to report to the government on whether the prisoner was a reasonable and accountable being who could properly be executed. They were Dr Jukes of Regina, Dr François-Xavier Valade, a well-known general practitioner of Ottawa, and Dr Michael Lavell*, a specialist in obstetrics and warden of the Kingston penitentiary. Lavell and Jukes reported that Riel was sane. Valade's conclusion was that Riel was not an accountable being, that he was unable to distinguish between right and wrong on political and religious subjects. The whole consultation was undertaken in the utmost secrecy. Valade's testimony was falsified by the ministry in the report submitted to parliament in 1886 to make it appear that he had in fact agreed with the other two.

In general, the treason charge was a legal rationalization. But even if treason had been a sound charge, there were grounds for commuting the sentence in view of the conflicting testimony on Riel's sanity, the dictates of mercy, and the political character of the prosecution. In its political calculation, the government sadly misjudged the situation. French Canadians understandably would be suspicious of court decisions which had acquitted the two white settlers, Jackson and Thomas Scott, both tried for treason-felony, while finding 20 Métis and numerous Indians guilty. Perhaps nothing else could have been expected from the 70-year-old Macdonald, bereft of an outstanding French Canadian colleague. On 16 November at the NWMP barracks in Regina, Riel was hanged, meeting his death with dignity, calmness, and courage.

Psychiatrists from 1885 to the present have generally agreed that Riel suffered from megalomania. The only dissenter has been Dr Henry Howard who did not regard Riel as insane in the legal sense of the term. Professor Thomas Flanagan argues that "a more satisfying explanation of this madness can be put forward than simple personal aberrancy." Riel, he maintains, "and the North-West Rebellion of 1885 should be set in the context of today's comparative knowledge about millenarian movements, particularly the nativistic cults which have been much studied by anthropologists. From this point of view, a great deal of the behaviour of Riel and his followers ceases to be eccentric and inexplicable because it becomes part of a pattern of events which has been repeated hundreds of times in similar situations in other parts of the world." Riel, Flanagan continues, "understandably . . . began to think of himself as persecuted. His moods vacillated from depression and listlessness to exaltation. Towards the end of 1874, he began to see visions and have revelations about his divine mission. . . . [He] felt himself charged to bring about the religious renovation of the New World. . . . The métis were God's chosen people with a mission to revive religion in America. . . . [The] papacy would move to St. Boniface so the pope would be among the 'sacerdotal people.' The métis would have a glorious future in the North-West, but they would not possess it alone and selfishly. The nations of Europe would undertake a vast migration. . . ."

Professor Flanagan's view that Riel's mysticism had produced a cult, and that he was seeking to maintain his credibility among his followers, is no doubt correct. But Riel saw himself primarily as the advocate of justice for the Métis. Only in the 20th century have some westerners seen in him the pioneer of western protest movements directed against the political and economic power of central Canada.

The execution of Riel caused not only an outcry in Quebec but a notable change in local and national politics. Shortly after, the Parti National was organized in Quebec, led by Honoré Mercier, a brilliant orator. This party won the provincial election of 1886. In the federal election of 1887 there was a significant loss of Conservative seats to the Liberals, setting a trend which culminated in Wilfrid Laurier's victory in 1896 and a fundamental realignment in Canadian national politics.

When the federal government arranged for the acquisition of Rupert's Land in 1870, it also procured, by an amendment of the British North America Act, full and unlimited power to create any form of local government that it chose, uninhibited by section 92 of the act. The boundaries given to Manitoba were deliberately restricted to limit the political power of the Métis. Similarly the administrative arrangements for acquiring public lands and responses to resolutions of the Council of the North-West Territories in 1884 provided for no democratic input. Riel's hopes for the "New Nation" with full and effective biculturalism were doomed from the start. His ambition blinded him to these facts.

Of the events of 1869–70 Riel could truly say during the trial of 1885 that "through the grace of God I am the founder of Manitoba." It was a voice from the past that no longer corresponded with reality either in Manitoba or in the territories. There most Métis were inexorably pushed into numerous obscure ghettos in the parklands and forest belts often on the edge of Indian reserves. This was the end of the "New Nation," and the ultimate tragedy of Louis Riel.

LEWIS H. THOMAS

[The most important primary material on Louis Riel is found in collections of Riel papers at the PAM (MG 3, D), the AASB in the Fonds Taché, and the PAC (MG 27, I, F3). Other collections at the PAC containing relevant materials are the Sir John A. Macdonald papers (MG 26, A), the Edgar Dewdney papers (MG 27, I, C4), and the records of the Dept. of Justice (RG 13, B2). These and other collections are described in T. [E.] Flanagan and C. M. Rocan, "A guide to the Louis Riel papers," *Archivaria* (Ottawa), no.11 (winter 1980–81): 135–69. Riel was the author of *L'amnistie: mémoire sur les causes des troubles du Nord-Ouest et sur les négociations qui ont amené leur règlement amiable* ([Montréal], 1874), which appeared under the same title in *Le Nouveau Monde*, 4 févr. 1874, and also under the title *L'amnistie aux Métis de Manitoba: mémoire sur les causes des troubles du Nord-Ouest et sur les négociations qui ont amené leur règlement amiable* (Ottawa, 1874). His *Poésies religieuses et politiques* were published in Montreal in 1886, and his diaries have been edited by T. [E.] Flanagan, *The diaries of Louis Riel* (Edmonton, 1976); his early poetry was brought together by Gilles Martel *et al.* in *Louis Riel: poésies de jeunesse* (Saint-Boniface, Man., 1977). In 1978 the Riel Project, headed by Professors G. F. G. Stanley, Glen Campbell, T. E. Flanagan, Raymond Huel, and Gilles Martel, was established at the University of Alberta in Edmonton with a grant from the Social Sciences and Humanities Research Council of Canada to publish a critical edition of all the writings of Louis Riel.

Much primary material on the disturbances of 1869–70 and the rebellion of 1885 appears in printed documents of the Canadian government. One of the most important sources is Can., House of Commons, Select Committee on the Causes of the Difficulties in the North-West Territory in 1869–70, *Report* (Ottawa, 1874) (also published in Can., House of Commons, *Journals*, 1874, app.6). Can., Parl., *Sessional papers*, 1870, V, no.12; 1871, V, nos.20, 44; VI, no.47; 1886, V, no.6a; XII, nos.43–43i, all relating to the troubles of 1869–70 and the rebellion of 1885, are of great value. The *Sessional papers* for 1886, no.43c (the jury list and trial records), has been reprinted with an introduction by Desmond Morton as *The Queen v Louis Riel* (Toronto and Buffalo, N.Y., 1974). *See also*: Can., House of Commons, *Debates*, 1875–86; Senate, *Debates*, 1871–86.

Primary materials on the disturbances of 1869–70 will also be found in Begg, *Red River journal* (Morton), and Georges Dugas, *Histoire véridique des faits qui ont preparé le mouvement des Métis à la Rivière-Rouge en 1869* (Montréal, 1905), and on the rebellion of 1885 in *Telegrams of the North-West campaign, 1885*, ed. Desmond Morton and R. H. Roy (Toronto, 1972). The execution of Riel produced a flood of controversial literature, including [C. A.] Boulton, *Reminiscences of the North-West rebellions, with a record of the raising of Her Majesty's 100th Regiment in Canada . . .* (Toronto, 1886); [J.-A. Chapleau], *La question Riel; lettre* ([Ottawa, 1885]); Adolphe Ouimet et B.-A. Testard de Montigny, *La vérité sur la question métisse au Nord-Ouest; biographie et récit de Gabriel Dumont sur les événements de 1885* (Montréal, 1889); and [Napoléon Thompson], *The gibbet of Regina; the truth about Riel: Sir John A. Macdonald and his cabinet before public opinion, by one who knows* (New York, 1886). Also useful are: "Documents of western history: Louis Riel's petition of rights, 1884," ed. L. H. Thomas, *Saskatchewan Hist.* (Saskatoon), 23 (1970): 16–26; M. V. Jordan, *To Louis from your sister who loves you, Sara Riel* (Toronto, 1974); *Louis Riel: rebel of the western frontier or victim of politics and prejudice?*, ed. Hartwell Bowsfield (Toronto, 1969); and George Young, *Manitoba memories; leaves from my life in the prairie province, 1868–1884* (Toronto, 1897).

Biographies of Riel are: Hartwell Bowsfield, *Louis Riel: the rebel and the hero* (Toronto, 1971); Peter Charlebois, *The life of Louis Riel* (Toronto, 1975); W. McC. Davidson, *Louis Riel, 1844–1885; a biography* (Calgary, 1955); T. [E.] Flanagan, *Louis "David" Riel: "prophet of the new world"* (Toronto, 1979); J. K. Howard, *Strange empire; a narrative of the Northwest* (New York, 1952); and Stanley, *Louis Riel*.

The standard work on the history of the Métis is Marcel Giraud's monumental work, *Le Métis canadien; son rôle dans l'histoire des provinces de l'Ouest* (Paris, 1945); parts 4 to 6 are especially important. A popular version of their history is D. B. Sealey and A. S. Lussier, *The Métis, Canada's forgotten people* (Winnipeg, 1975). Another standard work by G. F. G. Stanley is his *Birth of western Canada*, and he is also the author of *Manitoba, 1870: a Metis achievement* ([Winnipeg], 1972). Riel's military lieutenant is the subject of George Woodcock, *Gabriel Dumont: the Métis chief and his lost world* (Edmonton, 1975). The papers presented at a conference on Riel were published in *Riel and the Métis: Riel mini-conference papers*, ed. A. S. Lussier (Winnipeg, 1979). Studies of Indian chiefs who were involved in the rebellion of 1885 are Norma Sluman, *Poundmaker* (Toronto, 1967), and Rudy Wiebe, *The temptations of Big Bear* (Toronto, 1973).

Other valuable secondary sources are: T. [E.] Flanagan, "Louis Riel: insanity and prophecy," *The settlement of the west*, ed. Howard Palmer (Calgary, 1977), 15–36, and "A new view of Louis Riel," Canadian Political Science Assoc., *Papers presented at the forty-fifth annual meeting . . . August 18–19, 1973* (3v., Ottawa, 1973), I, no.9; E. A. Mitchener, "The North Saskatchewan River settlement claims, 1883–1884," *Essays on western history: in honour of Lewis Gwynne Thomas*, ed. L. H. Thomas (Edmonton, 1976), 127–43; Desmond Morton, *The last war drum: the North West campaign of 1885* (Toronto, 1972); *The Riel rebellions: a cartographic history*, comp. W. A. Oppen ([Toronto], 1979); and L. H. Thomas, "A judicial murder – the trial of Louis Riel," *The settlement of the west*, ed. Howard Palmer (Calgary, 1977), 37–59. The rebellion of 1885 and the Riel trial are discussed in the context of Quebec history by Rumilly, *Hist. de la prov. de Québec*, V. Useful bibliographies include *Western Canada since 1870: a select bibliography and guide*, comp. A. F. J. Artibise (Vancouver, 1978), and *Louis Riel: a bibliography*, [comp. V. P. Arora] (Regina, 1972).

Riel's mental condition is discussed in numerous periodical or newspaper articles published from 1885 to the present, written by various specialists in mental disorders. Among the studies are Daniel Clark, "A psycho-medical history of Louis Riel," *American Journal of Insanity* (Utica, N.Y.),

44 (1887–88): 33–51, and "Riel's mental state; opinions of Dr. Clark, of the Toronto Asylum," *Globe*, 18 Nov. 1885; C. K. Clarke, "A critical study of the case of Louis Riel," *Queen's Quarterly*, 12 (1904–5): 379–88; 13 (1905–6): 14–26; Édouard Desjardins et Charles Dumas, "Le complexe médical de Louis Riel," *L'Union médicale du Canada* (Montréal), 99 (1970): 1870–78; H. Gilson, "Étude sur l'état mental de Louis Riel," *L'Encéphale: journal des maladies mentales et nerveuses* (Paris), 6 (1886): 51–60; Henry Howard, "Histoire médicale de Louis David Riel," *L'Étendard*, 13 juill. 1886; and E. R. Markson *et al.*, "The life and death of Louis Riel; a study in forensic psychiatry," Canadian Psychiatric Assoc., *Journal* (Ottawa), 10 (1965): 246–64. L.H.T.]

RINE, DAVID ISAAC KIRWIN (Kirwan), Methodist minister and temperance lecturer; b. in 1835 in Pennsylvania; d. 1 July 1882 in Detroit, Mich.

David Isaac Kirwin Rine was educated in Pennsylvania and studied briefly at Madison College, Uniontown, Pa. He left to apprentice in the printing trade where he learned, as he said, "to imbibe the genial glass." By 1865 he had become a Methodist minister in the Pittsburgh Conference and from 1868 to 1871 he served as minister of Second Methodist Church, Allegheny (now part of Pittsburgh). In 1871 Rine was implicated in ecclesiastical charges brought against the Reverend John H. Gray, of Christ Methodist Church in Pittsburgh, of scandalous and immoral conduct with a woman of "doubtful reputation." Although two church investigations found Gray not guilty, both men withdrew from the conference following the widely publicized trial. During the next five years Rine was twice arrested for theft in connection with his alcoholism and on the second occasion he was sentenced to two years in prison. Following his release he started a "patent business" but squandered all his earnings on alcohol. Then, in December 1876, he was converted at a series of temperance meetings in Pittsburgh led by Francis Murphy, a reformed drunkard and founder of the Gospel Temperance Movement.

After 1846, with the passage of the first prohibitionist law in Maine, more and more of the temperance effort in North America had been diverted into political and educational activity in the hope of getting prohibitive legislation passed. By the 1870s temperance work in Canada reflected this preoccupation with prohibition. Murphy's Gospel Temperance Movement, like other moral suasionist groups which preceded it and unlike prohibitionist organizations, directed its attention specifically at the individual, attempting to win the drunkard from alcohol through the emotional appeals of an evangelical Christian gospel. In Murphy's view, formed from his own experience, no one was too degraded to be beyond hope. Resolutions of reform were made visible by pledge signing and ribbon wearing, and strengthened by public testimony. After a campaign clubs were formed to provide a form of continuing aftercare. Although the majority of pledge signers were not problem drinkers, the movement did have an amazing success in reaching hard drinkers, and even tavern keepers.

Shortly after his conversion, Rine joined the movement and was soon one of the leaders as it spread from Pittsburgh with the force of a revival. By March 1877 he claimed to have won 35,000 pledges in Erie County, Pa, alone. Rine was invited to St Catharines, Ont., by concerned citizens and following a highly successful campaign there he was invited to Toronto in May 1877 by a committee headed by George MacLean Rose*. Apparently motivated by the desire to create his own movement in Canada, Rine accepted invitations with no guarantee of remuneration, quite unlike many of his contemporaries. His campaign in Toronto took on the proportions of Murphy's in Pittsburgh, and over the next ten months he carried his message to all the major towns of Ontario, as well as to Montreal and Quebec City. On 15 March 1878, at the height of his success, Rine was arrested near Stratford, Ont., on a charge of indecently assaulting a 15-year-old serving girl. He admitted to "a little playfulness" but vehemently denied the charge. Although it was reduced to common assault and Rine was acquitted by jury, his moral culpability and the adverse publicity destroyed his effectiveness as a temperance leader. In October 1878, following the death of his wife, Rine left Toronto and commenced three years of wandering. Late in 1881 he tried to recapture his success as a temperance lecturer, but was ignored even in Toronto. After ten weeks, during which he exhibited signs of mental instability, he moved on to Detroit. He was picked up there in January 1882, "a raving maniac . . . possessed of the delusion that he owned all Detroit." He died six months later in the Wayne County Home for the Insane without having regained his sanity.

Rine had duplicated Murphy's methods of appealing to the true drunkard who was in these years largely ignored by other temperance groups in the political struggles for prohibition. His success was due mainly to "his supreme disregard of all conventional and formal methods." He couched his lectures in common language and spoke of his own struggles with which the most degraded could identify and which they could use as a source of hope.

A. J. BIRRELL

Daily British Whig, September 1877–May 1878. *Evening Telegram* (Toronto), May 1877–October 1878, October 1881–July 1882. *Free Press* (Ottawa), 20 Sept.–10 Oct. 1877, March–April 1878 *Globe*, May 1877–October 1878, October 1881–July 1882. *Leader*, May 1877–October 1878. *Montreal Daily Witness*, October 1877. *Stratford Beacon* (Stratford, Ont.), February–May 1878. *Stratford Times* (Stratford), February–May 1878. R. E. Spence, *Prohibition in Canada; a memorial to Francis Stephens Spence* (Toronto, 1919). A. J. Birrell, "D. I. K. Rine and the Gospel

Temperance Movement in Canada," *CHR*, 58 (1977): 23–42.

RIORDON (Riordan), JOHN, paper manufacturer and newspaper publisher; b. probably in 1834 in Limerick (Republic of Ireland), son of Dr Jeremiah Riordon and Amelia Ames; d. 21 Sept. 1884 at St Leonards (East Sussex), England.

John Riordon came to Canada West with his family in 1849 or 1850. After a somewhat chequered career as a dry goods merchant in Brantford and later in St Louis, Mo., he decided in 1862 that paper manufacturing was a more lucrative pursuit, and so began construction of a paper-mill near St Catharines on the east side of the old Welland Canal. Shortly after it began operation on 30 July 1863 Riordon asked his younger brother Charles*, who had settled in Rochester, N.Y., with the rest of the family, to take over the task of running the mill. Over the next ten years, the two men, Charles managing and John selling, built the fledgling enterprise into one of the largest paper-making establishments in the country.

Luck no doubt played a part in John Riordon's success, but he demonstrated an ability to exploit existing opportunities, the mark of the successful 19th-century entrepreneur. The location of his establishment was good. The old Welland Canal supplied the mill with water, a cheap source of power (a mere $400 a year in 1863), augmented later by extra leases of surplus water from the Canadian government. Better yet, Riordon was alert to the commercial significance of the technological innovations revolutionizing the industry. In 1866 Charles went to England to purchase the latest machinery (including a Fourdrinier) for a new mill at Merritton (now part of St Catharines) which was soon producing paper from rags and straw. Two years later the mill began to use wood pulp for its newsprint production, and in 1875 John ordered wood-grinding machinery for a new pulp-mill and a second Fourdrinier for a new paper-mill. This modernization made the Riordon Paper Mills a Canadian pioneer in the mass production of cheap paper. Equally important, John proved a superb salesman. Initially the company had specialized in wrapping paper, but he soon supplied a wider and wider range of customers with a variety of papers, including the choice grades. The staple of the company became newsprint (sold at one point for under seven cents a pound) for which the rapidly growing dailies of the new dominion were ever hungry. As early as 1869 John Riordon was the chief supplier of newsprint to the Toronto *Globe*, then the most widely circulated daily in Canada. After the mid 1870s he shipped paper to newspapers as far afield as Montreal, Quebec City, Saint John, N.B., and Halifax. Riordon's wealth, in fact, was a by-product of the rise of the mass newspaper after confederation.

Riordon's success in the newsprint trade involved him directly in the newspaper business. After the *Globe* his other great customer was the Toronto *Mail*, a daily launched in 1872 as standard-bearer of the Conservative party in Ontario. However, the *Mail*'s vigorous challenge to the *Globe*'s hegemony proved too expensive during the depression of the mid 1870s, and by 1877 the paper could no longer pay its bills, including $26,000 owing to the Riordon Paper Mills. As the largest creditor and a good Conservative, Riordon (likely with some associates) took over the ownership of the newspaper in lieu of payment, satisfied the other creditors, and set about revitalizing this essential party organ. At the same time he helped to save another languishing Conservative newspaper, the Hamilton *Spectator*, by purchasing a small number of shares when the paper was reorganized by William Carey and William Southam*. Newspaper publishing had now entered Riordon's blood. Hector Willoughby Charlesworth*, the gossip of the press scene in Toronto, later claimed Riordon had wished to emulate "the famous New York publishers of forty years ago" who had become the first masters of a cheap, popular, and supposedly influential daily press. Although Riordon did not change the tone or character of the *Mail*, he did sponsor in 1881 the Toronto *Evening News*, a one-cent daily which under the editorship of Edmund Ernest Sheppard* used much local news and various sensational stunts to capture a working-class audience. Publisher of the *Mail* and owner of the *News*, the first a leader in the ranks of the party press that still dominated Canadian journalism and the latter a lusty entry in the ranks of the "people's press" that was popularizing this form of journalism, Riordon might seem to have realized his ambition.

Riordon began a campaign for a seat in the Senate in early 1879 to complement his other achievements. Though his stature as a wealthy entrepreneur, a good Conservative, and the *Mail*'s publisher might have seemed sufficient to justify the honour, Prime Minister Sir John A. Macdonald* refused to heed Riordon's repeated entreaties. Further pressure might have persuaded Macdonald but in 1882 Riordon was incapacitated by a head injury as a result of a fall from a horse. In the autumn of that year he retired from active business, transferring control of his mills and newspapers to his brother Charles. He then travelled overseas with his wife and son John to the Near East and Europe in search of rest and enjoyment. Unfortunately in May 1883, while in Venice, his condition worsened unexpectedly. Riordon was moved to St Leonards where he stayed until his death a year later.

Riordon's estate was valued at roughly one million dollars, proof of his business acumen. He was a self-made millionaire in the two highly competitive pursuits of paper-making and newspaper publishing. Little wonder that the *Monetary Times* thought "his life presents an example of industry which young men would do well to copy."

PAUL RUTHERFORD

[The best source of information on John Riordon, especially on his career as a paper manufacturer, is George Carruthers, *Paper-making* (Toronto, 1947), 483–511. Another account, largely dependent upon Carruthers, is J. A. Blyth, "The development of the paper industry in old Ontario, 1824–1867," *OH*, 62 (1970), especially 131–32. See also the obituaries in the *Toronto Daily Mail*, 22 Sept. 1884; the *Daily News* (St Catharines, Ont.), 22 Sept. 1884; and the *Monetary Times*, 26 Sept. 1884. The *Thorold Post and Niagara District Intelligencer* (Thorold, Ont.), 14 Nov. 1884, contains an account of Riordon's estate and will. There is some assorted information in the John A. Macdonald papers, MG 26, A, at the PAC, on Riordon's desire for a Senate seat and his sudden illness in Venice. H. [W.] Charlesworth's comments on Riordon appear in *Candid chronicles; leaves from the note book of a Canadian journalist* (Toronto, 1925), 75. P.R.]

RITCHIE, JOHN WILLIAM, lawyer, legislator, and judge; b. 26 March 1808 at Annapolis Royal, N.S., the son of Thomas Ritchie*, a politician and judge, and Elizabeth Wildman Johnston; m. in 1836 Amelia Rebecca Almon, and they had 12 children; d. 13 Dec. 1890 at Halifax, N.S.

John William Ritchie's father represented Annapolis County in the Nova Scotia assembly for many years and was a prominent lawyer and judge. John William was probably educated at Ichabod Corbett's school in Annapolis Royal, and was later tutored at home rather than sent to college. In the mid 1820s he began studying law in Halifax with his uncle, James William Johnston*, an influential lawyer who was to lead the Conservative party for more than 20 years. Admitted to the bar as attorney in January 1831 and as barrister a year later, Ritchie had few clients in his first ten years of practice in Halifax and devoted himself to further legal studies. He was defeated in 1836 in a bid to represent Annapolis County in the assembly, a seat previously held by both his father and his uncle, John Johnston. In the same year he married Amelia Rebecca, the daughter of William Bruce Almon*, a doctor and legislative councillor, thereby continuing a tradition of intermarriage among the Ritchie, Johnston, and Almon families.

When the Nova Scotia Council was divided into separate executive and legislative bodies in 1837 Ritchie was appointed law clerk of the Legislative Council, of which J. W. Johnston and his father-in-law were members. He also began to broaden his practice and in the ensuing decade established a reputation as a gifted lawyer. In 1850 Ritchie was a member, with William YOUNG, Jonathan McCully*, and Joseph Whidden, of a commission to revise the statutes of Nova Scotia, work he found congenial and suited to his legal training. He was an incorporator in 1856 of the Union Bank of Halifax, of which he was a director until 1866, and in December 1858 was named a QC. In 1859 the Colonial Office appointed Ritchie a member of a three-man commission to investigate the land question in Prince Edward Island. Although he represented the interests of the absentee proprietors, Ritchie agreed with Joseph Howe*, representative of the Island tenants, and the chairman, John Hamilton GRAY of New Brunswick, that the tenants should have the right to buy the land on which they lived and that the imperial government should provide a £100,000 fund to facilitate land purchases. At the insistence of the proprietors, the Colonial Office rejected the commissioners' plan, and the land question continued to bedevil Island life. A further mark of recognition was Ritchie's appointment in 1863 to the board of governors of Dalhousie University, a post he held until his death. In 1863 and 1864 he represented St Paul's and St George's Anglican churches of Halifax before the legislature when they successfully opposed Bishop Hibbert BINNEY's plans to incorporate a diocesan synod and give the bishop a veto over its decisions.

Like many other leading Nova Scotians, Ritchie exhibited sympathy for the Southern cause in the American Civil War. In 1864 Southern agents seized the Northern ship *Chesapeake* off the coast of Maine and killed one of its crew. The ship was recaptured by Northern forces, but was then escorted into Halifax by the Royal Navy. Ritchie assisted in the defence of the three New Brunswick men tried at Saint John in connection with the affair. He also acted as attorney in Halifax for his brother-in-law, Dr William Johnston Almon*, when the latter was charged with aiding the escape of the only Southern agent captured. This case never came to trial, but a representative of the Confederate states presented Ritchie with a gift of silver in recognition of the services he had provided. In accepting the gift, Ritchie praised the "almost super-human exertions" of the Southerners in defence of their "inalienable rights of liberty and property."

In May 1864 the government of J. W. Johnston and Charles Tupper* appointed Ritchie to the Legislative Council, and he joined the cabinet as solicitor general. He soon replaced Robert Barry Dickey* as government leader in the upper house and thus directed the passage through the council of important legislation dealing with common schools and Nova Scotia's entry into confederation. Ritchie was not a delegate to either the Charlottetown or Quebec conferences of 1864 at which the form of union was decided, but in September 1865 he represented Nova Scotia at the Confederate Trade Council in Quebec where the British North American colonies considered the future of the Reciprocity Treaty with the United States and committed themselves to a common commercial policy. From the autumn of 1864 he replaced Dickey as a leading spokesman in presenting the confederation scheme to a reluctant Nova Scotia, and his contribution, according to a biographer, was "infinitely greater than anything done by Dickey who seems to have received more of the credit. . . . " Ritchie guided Tupper's vague resolution favouring union through the Legislative Council in April 1866 and maintained close contact with Lieutenant Governor Sir William Fenwick WILLIAMS, a fellow native of Annapolis Royal, in the pursuit of the government's unionist aims. With Tupper, Jonathan McCully, Adams George Archibald*, and William Alexander HENRY, Ritchie was a Nova Scotia delegate to the London conference in the winter of 1866–67, at which the terms of union were finalized. In May 1867 he was rewarded with a seat in the Senate, and in September 1870 realized his ambitions with an appointment as puisne judge of the Supreme Court of Nova Scotia. In July 1873 he became judge in equity, in succession to J. W. Johnston and Archibald.

As a judge, Ritchie had the demeanour and the learning to make a strong impression on his contemporaries. His dignified manner and "eagle-like face . . . so clean cut and distinguished," were coupled, in the opinion of John George Bourinot*, with "very extensive and sound" legal knowledge and "acuteness of intellect." Robert Laird Borden* described him as "one of the ablest judges then, or at any time, on the Nova Scotia Bench," and Wallace Graham* considered him superior in talent to his brother, Sir William Johnston Ritchie*, chief justice of Canada from 1879 to 1892. In July 1882 John William Ritchie retired from the Nova Scotia bench, having suffered ill health since 1879. He spent his retirement at Belmont, the estate he had bought in 1857 overlooking the Northwest Arm at Halifax, and died there in 1890.

NEIL J. MACKINNON

John William Ritchie's equity decisions were collected in *The equity decisions of the Hon. John W. Ritchie, judge in equity of the province of Nova Scotia, 1873–1882*, ed. Benjamin Russell (Halifax, 1883). As a member, with William Young, Jonathan McCully, and Joseph Whidden, of the Commission for Consolidating the Laws of the Province of Nova Scotia, Ritchie was responsible for the preparation of N.S., *The private and local acts of Nova-Scotia* (Halifax, 1851), and N.S., *The revised statutes of Nova-Scotia* (Halifax, 1851).

PANS, RG 1, 202. *Acadian Recorder*, 14 May 1864. *British Colonist* (Halifax), 3 Sept. 1864. *Evening Express* (Halifax), 20 July 1866. *Morning Herald* (Halifax), 15 Dec. 1890. J. G. Bourinot, *Builders of Nova Scotia* . . . (Toronto, 1900). L. G. Power, "Our first president, the Honorable John William Ritchie, 1808–1890," N.S. Hist. Soc., *Coll.*, 19 (1918): 1–15. C. St. C. Stayner, "John William Ritchie, one of the fathers of confederation," N.S. Hist. Soc., *Coll.*, 36 (1968): 183–277.

RIVARD, SÉVÈRE, lawyer, politician, and businessman; b. 7 Aug. 1834 at Yamachiche, Lower Canada, son of Augustin Rivard-Laglanderie and Marguerite Rivard-Dufresne; m. 1 Aug. 1863 Delphine Choquette in Montreal, Canada East; d. there 4 Feb. 1888.

A descendant of Nicolas Rivard, *dit* Lavigne, who had settled in the Batiscan region in the 17th century, Sévère Rivard belonged to one of the oldest families in the country. After attending the Séminaire de Nicolet from 1848 to 1856, he studied law in Montreal under Toussaint-Antoine-Rodolphe Laflamme* and Edmund Barnard. He was called to the bar of Lower Canada in 1859 and then went into partnership with his colleague Benjamin-Antoine Testard* de Montigny, opening a law office on Rue Saint-Vincent in Montreal.

Rivard began to make himself known in 1867, the year in which he became a secretary, along with Joseph Royal*, of a committee of ten citizens set up to collect the money needed for sending contingents of Canadian Zouaves to Rome to defend the papacy [*see* Ignace BOURGET]. For his efforts he was made a chevalier of Pius IX in 1874. He was a convinced Ultramontane like most of the Canadian Zouaves; moreover in 1871 he participated in one of the preparatory meetings to draft the *Programme catholique* [*see* François-Xavier-Anselme TRUDEL].

An increasingly influential member of the Montreal bourgeoisie, Rivard, in partnership with Ferdinand DAVID, Gustave-Adolphe Drolet*, and the architect Michel Laurent, made a large fortune for himself by buying land in the north part of the city at the beginning of the 1870s and reselling it as building lots. In June 1872, with the consent of his partners, he offered Bishop Bourget a gift of land for a church in the village of Saint-Jean-Baptiste (now part of Montreal). Among other ventures, he was involved in a woollen mill at Yamachiche in 1870 and an organ business at Montreal in 1878. In addition, he participated in at least three financial syndicates which attempted during the period from June 1877 to 1881 to obtain control of the Quebec, Montreal, Ottawa and Occidental Railway Company. He went to the universal exposition in Paris in 1878 with his friend Drolet, the Canadian delegate, and both studied ways to develop commercial relations between Canada and Europe. In 1883, with Andrew Allan*, Alexander Walker Ogilvie*, Louis-Adélard SENÉCAL, and Joseph-Rosaire Thibaudeau*, among others, Rivard took part in organizing the Citizens' Gas Company of Montreal, with a subscribed capital of $1,000,000.

Rivard entered municipal politics in Montreal in

1870 with his election as councillor for Saint-Jacques Ward. Having beaten William Crevier by more than 200 votes on that occasion, he was re-elected in 1873 with a majority of 770 over Auguste Robert. He took a particular interest in the problems of the lighting committee, serving as its chairman by 1871; he also supervised the building of a new city hall, as a member of a special committee created for this purpose. Throughout his term on the council he was an acknowledged adversary of the mayor, Jean-Louis BEAUDRY. Although Beaudry was regarded as invincible, Rivard ousted him from the mayoralty in the 1879 elections, beating him by 290 votes, thanks in particular to the massive support of Saint-Antoine and Sainte-Marie wards (the first with an English-speaking and the second with a French-speaking majority), and despite the weak support from his own ward, Saint-Jacques. In 1880 he was re-elected mayor by acclamation. His mayoralty was distinguished by sustained efforts to put municipal finances on a sound footing after a decade of large-scale projects such as a sewage system, the development of the park on Mount Royal, and the building of the city hall. While continuing work on waterworks and the sanitation system, he succeeded in reducing the municipal debt of $12,000,0000, largely by increasing revenues from $600,000 to $1,500,000. From 1879 to 1881, concurrently with his mayoral duties, Rivard served as a harbour commissioner.

Rivard was a member of the Roman Catholic Board of School Commissioners of the City of Montreal from 16 Aug. 1870 to 29 Nov. 1877, and on 11 Dec. 1881 became a churchwarden of the parish of Notre-Dame for a period of three years. From October 1886 he also represented the division of Alma on the Legislative Council, having succeeded his long-time adversary, Jean-Louis Beaudry, who had recently died. In 1887 he held the post of treasurer of the Conservative party for the Montreal region, a largely honorary office. After being stricken with paralysis, he died on 4 Feb. 1888 in Montreal where he was buried four days later. He left a sizeable fortune, including a house on the corner of Sherbrooke and Saint-Denis, for which the asking price then was $15,000.

MARCEL CAYA

AC, Montréal, État civil, Catholiques, Notre-Dame de Montréal, 8 févr. 1888. (It has not been possible to locate a baptismal record for Sévère Rivard.) ANQ-M, État civil, Catholiques, Notre-Dame de Montréal, 1er août 1863. ASN, AP-G, J.-A.-I. Douville, Succession, II: 31; AP-G, M.-G. Proulx, V: 20. AVM, Doc. administratifs, Procès-verbaux du conseil municipal, 1870–73. PAC, MG 30, D1, 26. *La Minerve*, 6 févr. 1888. *CPC*, 1887: 239. G. Turcotte, *Le Conseil législatif de Québec. Histoire de la corporation de la cité de Montréal depuis son origine jusqu'à nos jours . . .* , J.-C. Lamothe *et al.*, édit. (Montréal, 1903). Rumilly, *Hist. de Montréal*, III: 27, 41, 135–36. Ovila Lefebvre, "M. Sévère Rivard," *La Patrie*, 11 juin 1950: 75. Léon Trépanier, "Figures de maires," *Cahiers des Dix*, 21 (1956): 179–99.

ROBERTSON, ALEXANDER ROCKE, lawyer, judge, and politician; b. 12 May 1841 in Chatham, Canada West, second son of Alexander Rocke Robertson and Effie Eberts; m. in 1868 in Chatham his cousin Margaret Bruce Eberts, and they had seven sons; d. 1 Dec. 1881 in Victoria, B.C.

Alexander Rocke Robertson's grandfather, who served for 30 years with the East India Company in Bengal, and his father were both graduates of the Royal College of Surgeons of Edinburgh; probably in the 1830s, his father immigrated to Chatham. Robertson attended the Caradoc Academy in Middlesex County. A precocious student, at the age of 16 he entered the law offices of Alexander D. McLean in Chatham where he completed articling before he was of age to write his final examination. To fill out the time before he could take it he spent a term in the office of Albert Prince. Admitted to the bar in 1863, Robertson went into partnership with Samuel Smith Macdonell in Windsor.

Perhaps encouraged by his uncle, John Waddell, who had immigrated to British Columbia in 1862, Robertson left Canada West for Vancouver Island at the end of March 1864. Travelling the Panama route with his aunt and cousin, he arrived in Victoria on 14 May 1864. He found, however, that the bar of Vancouver Island was open only to lawyers of British training and therefore closed to Canadian barristers. For a short time Robertson worked as editor of one of Victoria's newspapers, the *Daily Chronicle*. Displaying a keen mind and a breadth of reading, he wrote a series of penetrating editorials critical of the insularity of the local legal fraternity. Meanwhile George Anthony Walkem*, another Canadian lawyer, managed to break the British monopoly in the mainland colony by petitioning Governor James Douglas* and the imperial authorities. When Island legislation to admit colonial lawyers on the same footing as those of British training stalled in Victoria, an impatient Robertson moved to New Westminster in November 1864, and was immediately admitted to the bar of British Columbia. The following February, after appropriate legislation had finally been enacted, he was also admitted to the bar of Vancouver Island.

Robertson rapidly established a reputation as an outstanding advocate. From 1865 to 1867 he acted regularly both for the crown and as a defence attorney at sessions of the assize court held at Barkerville, even though in 1866 he moved his residence to Victoria upon the union of the two colonies. After the young lawyer's first case in New Westminster, even the sceptical chief justice, Matthew Baillie Begbie*, complimented him on his able and successful defence of an Indian charged with murder. Robertson attended the founding meeting of the Law Society of British Columbia on 22 July 1869, and became one of the original, and more active, benchers of the society. Hard working and erudite, Robertson gained a public reputation through his early professional success. In 1867, at two meetings to discuss the moving of the capital to Victoria and the union of British Columbia with Canada, he had spoken impressively in favour of both proposals. Though the latter cause met pockets of stern resistance among the colonial élite, Robertson, with his Upper Canadian origins, continued to be a staunch supporter of the link with the new Canada.

Robertson began his political career in 1870 when he served one term as mayor of Victoria. After Governor Anthony MUSGRAVE steered the colony through the shoals of opposition to confederation, Robertson, the object of a virtual draft by his constituents, topped the poll in Esquimalt in the 1871 election of the first provincial Legislative Assembly. The premier, John Foster McCreight*, selected Robertson as provincial secretary. Though his cabinet post, like McCreight's administration, lasted only a year, Robertson produced one major legislative landmark. Working with John Jessop*, the first superintendent of schools, he drafted the Public Schools Act of 1872, which, drawing heavily on Ontario's experience and legislation, maintained the non-sectarian, public system established in British Columbia's colonial era. A great believer in extending public support to the high school level and beyond, Robertson, when in opposition during 1873 and 1874, presented two resolutions in the assembly proposing the establishment of a provincial university.

Robertson served only one term in the legislature. Even during his year as minister he had continued to practise law, and he declined to stand again in 1875 despite pressure. In 1876 he acted as law agent for the dominion government, and in March 1880, along with McCreight and Walkem, represented the crown in the celebrated trial of Allan MCLEAN, his brothers, and Alex Hare.

In November 1880 Robertson accepted appointment to the Supreme Court of British Columbia, and took up residence in Kamloops. However, during the summer of 1881, he injured his knee while swimming and remained lame throughout the autumn. In November four doctors in Victoria attended the amputation of his leg. Robertson never recovered from the operation.

Though his obituary referred to Robertson as a man of "quiet and retiring habits," perhaps in deference to his modest and serious approach to the rough and tumble of frontier politics, he was known by his friends and family for his liveliness and humour, and for the delight he took in singing and music. A man of many sides, who acted for years as superintendent of the Sunday School of the Anglican St John's Church in Victoria, Robertson won the respect of his professional peers and of the wider community. The son of a medical family, Robertson began another family tradition, for two sons and a grandson were to follow him on the bench in British Columbia.

T. M. EASTWOOD and PAUL WILLIAMSON

PABC, B.C., Colonial secretary, Corr. inward, ff.142f, 1816; H. B. Robertson, "Alexander Rocke Robertson." *Cariboo Sentinel*, 4 July 1867. *Daily British Colonist* (Victoria), 16 Feb. 1865; 8 Jan., 19 March 1867; 28 Oct. 1871; 1 Dec. 1880; 3 Nov., 2 Dec. 1881; 30 Dec. 1882. *Victoria Daily Chronicle*, 27 Aug. 1864. F. H. Johnson, *A history of public education in British Columbia* (Vancouver, 1964), 44, 74; *John Jessop: goldseeker and educator; founder of the British Columbia school system* (Vancouver, 1971), 77, 80, 168. Alfred Watts, "The Honourable Mr. Justice Alexander Rocke Robertson, Justice, Supreme Court of British Columbia, 1880–1881," *Advocate* (Vancouver), 25 (1967): 142–43.

ROBERTSON, ANDREW, businessman and public servant; b. 18 June 1827 at Paisley, Scotland, son of Alexander Robertson and Grant Stuart Macdonald; m. 19 April 1850 Agnes Bow in Glasgow, Scotland, and they had ten children; d. 29 March 1890 in Montreal, Quebec.

Andrew Robertson received a classical education at the Paisley Grammar School, and then was instructed in the practical trade of weaving. In 1840 he moved to Glasgow and served the next four years in a dry goods store. At this time he took a position in a manufacturing establishment and was so successful that he was made a partner in 1848. Following medical advice, he immigrated in 1853 with his wife and two children to Montreal where he worked for the dry goods firm of Brown and Swan for two years. In 1855 or 1856 he established Andrew Robertson and Company, which specialized in yard goods. In the early 1860s Robertson built the Auburn Woolen Mill at Peterborough, Canada West, to manufacture Canadian tweed, only to sell the mill in 1867 in order to buy George Stephen*'s wholesale dry goods business in Montreal. Stephen's youngest brother, Francis, joined Robertson in the firm of Robertson, Stephen and Company, and in 1874 Robert Linton also became a partner. Robertson retired from the business in 1885, and at his death five years later left an estate valued at between $350,000 and $400,000. In 1891 Linton acquired the interest held in the firm by Robertson's heirs.

Robertson was known as a progressive, public-spirited, and charitable man. Early in his Montreal days he purchased and donated the land on which Erskine Presbyterian Church was built, and he was a member of that congregation until his death. He served twice as president of the St Andrew's Society in the 1860s, and belonged to the St James Club. During the American Civil War he was active in the militia, and served as first lieutenant and quartermaster of the Montreal Light Infantry. He was appointed justice of the peace in 1884. In 1872 he became a governor of the Montreal General Hospital, and later served as its treasurer, vice-president, and president, finally bequeathing $5,000 to the institution. Robertson was also president of the Montreal Board of Trade in 1876 and 1877, and of the Dominion Board of Trade in 1876. He was the first president in 1874 of the Commercial Travellers' Association of Canada, president of the Royal Canadian Insurance Company from 1876 to 1890, and president of the Bell Telephone Company of Canada from its establishment in 1880 until his death. He was also closely associated with Andrew Allan* and Alexander Walker Ogilvie* in forming the Citizens' Gas Company which in the early 1880s attempted unsuccessfully to challenge the domination of the Montreal Gas Company. In 1881 he journeyed to British Columbia with Sir Charles Tupper*, who described Robertson as a "merchant prince," in order to report on the feasibility of the Canadian Pacific Railway building a line between Victoria and Nanaimo. Although Robertson recommended such a move, the CPR did not undertake the construction.

Sir John A. Macdonald* was returned to power in 1878, and the next year he appointed Robertson, a Conservative supporter, to replace Thomas CRAMP, a Liberal appointee, on the Montreal Harbour Commission. His fellow commissioners soon elected him chairman, a position he held until his death, when he was succeeded by Henry Bulmer. The commission, which came under federal jurisdiction, drew its revenues from charges on shipping. Throughout Robertson's chairmanship the board was deeply in debt for improvements made previously in the harbour and for the deepening of the ship channel between Quebec and Montreal. In 1887, for example, the interest payment on its debt was over $220,000, and from 1881 to 1887 (with the exception of 1882), it experienced annual deficits of between $14,000 and $60,000. Further necessary improvements suffered accordingly. Simultaneously, Robertson had to contend with pressures to preserve Montreal's competitive position with respect to American ports by further deepening the harbour and channel and by creating additional berths through the extension of wharves and the construction of new piers. Moreover, port users demanded reduced shipping dues, but since the necessary improvements could be financed only through the commission's revenues, Robertson could introduce only modest reductions. Finally in 1888, despite widespread opposition, especially in Quebec City, the federal government assumed the commission's debt for the channel and freed it to pursue improvements.

Of special concern to Robertson was the damage and suffering caused by the floods which inundated large parts of Montreal in 1885, 1886, and 1887. Floods had been a serious problem from the earliest days of the city, but by the mid 1880s it was generally agreed that they could be tolerated no longer. Robertson played an important part in the negotiations between the harbour commissioners, the federal government, the city of Montreal, the Grand Trunk and the Canadian Pacific railways, the Montreal Board of Trade, and some private parties, all of whose interests were involved in flood control. The final master plan called for the construction of a guard pier to protect the waterfront from ice, the raising of the wharves above high water level, and the general improvement of railway and harbour facilities. Agreement had been reached but work had not yet begun at the time of Robertson's death in 1890.

Andrew Robertson was a less colourful and controversial figure than John Young*, a fellow immigrant from Scotland and a well-known predecessor on the harbour commission. As a successful businessman who participated fully in the commercial and social life of the city, Robertson's achievements were substantial, but his most significant contribution was made in his capacity as chairman of the harbour commission. Undoubtedly his reputation for personal integrity and his wide contacts within the community were assets in the negotiations which resulted in the federal government assuming the channel debt, a necessary step enabling the harbour commission to undertake major works in flood control and to provide adequate facilities for the growing needs of the port of Montreal.

D. SUZANNE CROSS

Andrew Robertson was the author of *Montreal a free port* . . . ([Montreal], 1880) and of *Statement made by Mr. Andrew Robertson, chairman, harbour commissioners, Montreal, on the business of the port for the year 1886* . . . ([Montreal], 1887).

National Harbours Board (Montreal), Port of Montreal arch., Montreal Harbour Commission, Letterbooks, 1879–90; Minute books, 1879–90. Harbour Commissioners of Montreal, *Annual reports* (Montreal), 1879–90. Charles Tupper, *Recollections of sixty years* (Toronto, 1914). Borthwick, *Hist. and biog. gazetteer*. Terrill, *Chronology of Montreal*. Atherton, *Montreal*, II-III. Rumilly, *Hist. de Montréal*, III.

ROBERTSON-ROSS, PATRICK, soldier and adjutant-general of the militia; b. 19 May 1828 in Scotland, second son of Lord Patrick Robertson, judge and wit, and Mary Cameron Ross; m. in 1851 Amelia Ann Maynard, and they had at least one son; d. 23 July 1883 at Boulogne, France.

Patrick Robertson was educated in Edinburgh before enlisting as a corporal in the Capetown Rifles at 19; he was commissioned as an ensign on 7 April 1848. After seeing active service in the Kaffir wars, Robertson fought with distinction in the Crimean War where he was appointed aide-de-camp to Major-General Sir William Eyre. When Eyre came to Canada in 1856 to command the British forces, Robertson, now brevet major, again served as his ADC, from 29 July 1856 to 1 May 1858, although he was on half pay from 3 April 1857. He returned to Britain in 1858 but was back in Canada in 1864, as a brevet lieutenant-colonel, for duty against the Fenians. When his uncle, General Hugh Ross, died on 24 June 1864, Robertson inherited his uncle's property in Scotland and changed his name to Robertson-Ross. He purchased a lieutenant-colonelcy, on 6 May of the next year, and returned to duty with depot battalions in England.

Robertson-Ross's experience in training militia at depots in Britain and connections he had made in Canada may account for his half-pay appointment on 9 May 1869 as adjutant-general of the Canadian militia. Sir George-Étienne Cartier*, the first minister of militia and defence, facing the Fenian threat and the impending withdrawal of the imperial garrison, had introduced the Militia Act of 1868. The act authorized a *levée en masse*, a general levy in order to establish a reserve militia, which necessitated the registration of all able-bodied males between the ages of 18 and 60, as well as 8 to 16 days training annually for 40,000 volunteers in an active militia. If insufficient numbers came forward for the active militia the authorities could resort to the ballot to acquire the required strength. By the time Robertson-Ross arrived, a Canadian deputy adjutant-general, Lieutenant-Colonel Walker Powell*, had set up the active militia and had arranged for the selection of its officers in each regimental district (which coincided with electoral districts) as well as for the continuation of their training in schools of military instruction associated with the British garrison, as had been done in the Province of Canada.

In his first annual report Robertson-Ross compared the structure created by Canada's Militia Act with the systems that had produced victories for the North in the American Civil War and for Prussia in the Austro-Prussian War. Recalling his own experience in South Africa, he recommended that Canadian cavalry be trained as mounted infantry and he also warned against a reduction of the permanent-staff brigade-majors, the key officers in the militia system. The new system was tested early during Robertson-Ross's tenure when he armed some militia units and the gunboats on the Great Lakes because of threats of Fenian raids in October 1869 and the following April. That month he was also called upon to furnish 750 militia to accompany Colonel Garnet Joseph Wolseley* and British regulars sent to suppress the Red River rebellion [*see* Louis RIEL]. Lieutenant-General James Alexander Lindsay*, who had come to Canada to arrange the evacuation of the British garrison and who organized the expeditionary force, reported that if Robertson-Ross had been left to himself it would have been only "half equipped." The militia's role in the western campaign and its success in checking Fenian raids in 1870 without the aid of the British garrison, which was being concentrated in Quebec for the withdrawal, encouraged Robertson-Ross to assert that Canada had "solved the problem of how to create a reserve force." Since, he said, an adjutant-general was only a staff officer required to carry out details of drill, discipline, and command under a general officer commanding an army, and the militia was now Canada's army, he recommended that his appointment be upgraded to a major-general and a GOC. Although Cartier was apparently willing to promote him, Lindsay reported adversely on him to the War Office and the proposal was then dropped by Sir John A. Macdonald*. In 1871 Robertson-Ross established permanent artillery batteries at Kingston and Quebec which were intended to act as schools of gunnery for the militia. Further competence was demonstrated by the force in 1871 when a small contingent proceeded to Upper Fort Garry (Winnipeg) without British aid. Yet, with the Fenian threat reduced, one-quarter of the militia volunteers throughout the country failed to re-enlist.

Robertson-Ross's annual report for 1872 provides a detailed account of the state of the militia. It also includes a description of his overland journey to British Columbia, travelling on Canadian soil and accompanied only by his 16-year-old son and a few guides. At Fort Garry he arranged for the militia uniform to be changed from green to red as a reassurance to the Indians who had trusted the British regulars. He commented on the problems created by whisky smuggling and horse stealing among the Indians and recommended a force of 550 soldiers as well as a chain of military posts for the territories rather than just a civil police force. In British Columbia he made arrangements for the establishment of a militia. This report shows that despite his reassurances he was concerned with the response to the militia generally; in Quebec, for instance, some units did not drill in 1872 and though he praised the militia spirit of the French Canadians he admitted the ballot might be needed in some districts. He met with Macdonald in December to discuss his findings and in the spring of 1873, after his report was published, legislation was introduced providing for judicial institutions in the territories but also for an armed force which was to become the North-West Mounted Police.

When Robertson-Ross's patron, Cartier, died in 1873, the adjutant-general promptly applied for more "active service" and returned to depot duty in England and then in Scotland; in 1880 he retired as a major-general. A new governor general, Lord Dufferin [Blackwood*], had arrived in Canada almost a year before Robertson-Ross left; he at first reported on him favourably but then said he was inefficient. The governor noted gossip that Robertson-Ross had owed his position to Cartier's penchant for his attractive wife, and he told the colonial secretary that Robertson-Ross had had to be peremptorily ordered by Sir John Young* not to hang Fenians summarily. However, the artillery schools he had set up, his proposals for the expansion of training that foreshadowed the opening of the Royal Military College of Canada in Kingston in 1876, and his recommendation for the creation of a general-officer-commanding, a post held by his successor, Major-General Sir Edward Selby Smyth*, show that Robertson-Ross knew what was needed in Canada. But an officer who had risen as a result of early front-line leadership and later because of useful connections with powerful military and civilian leaders was not fitted to carry through major military reforms; yet his more senior successors, with higher status and rank, were little more successful.

RICHARD A. PRESTON

Patrick Robertson-Ross was the author of "Report of a reconnaissance of the north-west provinces and Indian territories of the Dominion of Canada . . . ," Royal United Service Institution, *Journal* (London), 17 (1873): 543–67.

Can., Dept. of Militia and Defence, *Report on the state of the militia* (Ottawa), 1868–75. *Gentleman's Magazine and Hist. Rev.* (London), 197 (January–June 1855): 194; 217 (July–December 1864): 392–93; 218 (January–June 1865): 632. *DNB* (entry for Patrick Robertson). *Hart's army list*, 1853–83. Desmond Morton, *Ministers and generals, politics and the Canadian militia, 1868–1904* (Toronto and Buffalo, N.Y., 1970).

ROBINSON, Sir BRYAN, lawyer, politician, office-holder, and judge; b. 14 Jan. 1808 in Dublin (Republic of Ireland), youngest son of the Reverend Christopher Robinson, rector of Granard, County Longford, and Elizabeth Langrishe, daughter of a prominent Irish politician; m. 20 Aug. 1834 in London, England, Selina Brooking, and they had at least four daughters and one son; d. 6 Dec. 1887 in Ealing (now part of Greater London).

Bryan Robinson attended school in Castleknock, County Dublin, and entered Trinity College, Dublin, in October 1824. He left in 1828 before graduating and joined the staff of Admiral Thomas John Cochrane*, governor of Newfoundland. He was soon appointed sheriff of the Labrador coast, where his brother Hercules had served as a naval officer. On 4 May 1831 in Halifax he was admitted to practise as a barrister and attorney and at 23 began a legal career in Newfoundland that would span half a century. By March 1834 Robinson had been appointed master in chancery to the Legislative Council at St John's. In this newly created post, he would serve as a link with the assembly, give legal advice, and draft bills until 1858, except from 1842 to 1848 during the life of the Amalgamated Legislature.

Robinson attained prominence in August 1838 as a result of an altercation between assemblyman John Kent* and surgeon Edward Kielley* outside the house. Brought before the assembly on a speaker's warrant for having allegedly committed a breach of its privileges, Kielley was arrested for contempt, and retained Robinson as counsel. Robinson believed the issue was whether there was "a body of men in this colony who are above the law" and contended that the power claimed by the six-year-old assembly was unwarranted, needless, and contrary to common law. When Judge George Lilly*, finding Robinson's arguments "learned and very able," discharged Kielley, the assembly took the unprecedented step of having both Lilly and the sheriff put under arrest. Robinson then, on behalf of Kielley, sued Speaker William Carson*, Kent, and other assemblymen for £3,000 for assault and false imprisonment. The judgement, delivered by the Supreme Court judges before a crowded court-room on 29 Dec. 1838, relied on the exercise of similar powers to commit for contempt by the other British North American assemblies and went against Kielley.

The case of *Kielley* v. *Carson* aroused wide concern. The largely Protestant mercantile community in St John's, mindful that the assembly had succeeded in having Chief Justice Henry John Boulton* removed from office in August of that year, was alarmed at the attack on Kielley and on the judiciary's independence; it was already extremely concerned at the influence exerted by the Roman Catholic clergy in political affairs [*see* Edward Troy*]. During the trial Robinson had claimed that if the assembly's position was upheld, its direct interference in the courts was clearly to be feared. The St John's Chamber of Commerce petitioned for government by governor and council; merchants in Liverpool, England, called for troops to be sent; and British newspapers joined those in Newfoundland in taking up the case. With the merchants' support, Robinson went to London to appeal to the Judicial Committee of the Privy Council. After two hearings the committee delivered on 11 Jan. 1843 a precedent-setting opinion in Robinson's favour, finding the assembly to be a local legislature with every needed power but lacking the exclusive privileges of the British parliament.

In the mean time, Robinson had won some important cases including in 1838 a libel action against Robert John PARSONS, publisher of the *Patriot*, which had hinged on Parsons' claim that his publication of an assembly report was privileged and not subject to the courts. In June 1840 Robinson had been appointed, with Hugh Alexander Emerson and Edward Mortimer ARCHIBALD, to a commission to study the application of English criminal law to Newfoundland. Its report, which Governor Sir John Harvey* commended for able exposition, was received by the Amalgamated Legislature in March 1843. By this time Robinson had become the member for Fortune Bay, having been successful in the December 1842 elections. Robinson soon roused controversy in the legislature; in 1843 his bill to establish a Protestant and a Roman Catholic college was denounced by non-Anglican Protestants as a Church of England measure and had quickly to be dropped. In addition, Harvey's proposal to appoint him to the Executive Council "on grounds of his talents, influence, and disposition to serve the government" met with the opposition of Chief Justice John Gervase Hutchinson Bourne*, with whom Robinson was involved in a personal conflict. Robinson had complained to the Colonial Office in February 1843 about Bourne's prejudiced conduct as a judge and about his ignorance of law. For his part, Bourne alleged that Robinson and James Crowdy* had assisted Harvey financially and in return had received improper financial reward. Robinson refuted the charge to the satisfaction of the Colonial Office and on 8 August entered the council, on which he was to serve for some five years. Bourne, on the other hand, was dismissed from office in May of the following year.

Robinson played an active role in many debates and committees of the legislature. He helped prepare and presented bills for improving the administration of justice and the St John's police. In 1844 he sought to protect the Newfoundland fisheries from French encroachment through measures severely restricting the export of bait and illicit trade in it. Hence, when the assembly sent a delegation to England in 1857 to have the Fishery Convention with France annulled, he was chosen as the Commercial Society's delegate and provided useful legal assistance; Britain dropped the convention and pledged herself to respect Newfoundland's views. Convinced that the colony was "the key to the western world," Robinson wanted Newfoundland to attain her rightful position among the commercial countries of the world. He took a keen interest in developing steam communications between Newfoundland, Great Britain, and the United States, and in promoting St John's as a port of call for steamers.

By nature a conservative, Robinson, in the legislature's debate of February 1846, denounced Kent's resolutions for responsible government as ambiguous and contradictory. He contended party government was unsuited to Newfoundland: it lacked an aristocracy, an influential press, and the means of communication to modify local forces and "blend the feeling of the country into one general sentiment." His amendments emphasized the governor's responsibility to the sovereign for the acts of his government, and the accountability of the executive councillors, as individuals, to the people. Kent's resolutions, however, carried by one vote.

During the 1840s and the 1850s Robinson also served on the Board of Commissioners of Roads for St John's (in 1843 and 1851), on the Board of Health for the city (in 1847 and 1849), and as a justice of the peace. Appointed a QC on 13 Dec. 1844 and treasurer of the law society for some years, he served as acting solicitor general in 1845, 1847, and 1849, and acting attorney general in 1854. Through his private practice he became the most prominent barrister in St John's and in 1849 won an important civil rights case, *Hanrahan* v. *Barron and Doody*, which established a fisherman's right to put a lien for wages on the proceeds of a voyage that had been transferred from the planter to the supplying merchant. This judgement was confirmed by the law officers of the crown in 1850. On 4 July 1858 he was appointed 2nd assistant judge of the Supreme Court of Newfoundland, where he would sit for nearly 20 years.

Robinson's judicial decisions on a wide variety of property and contract cases reveal his innate conservatism, an understanding of the mercantile community, and a belief in the importance of the rule of law to both persons and commerce. He emphasized the need for the courts to adhere to the principles and precedents of British law. If judges bent "the established rule of law" to meet a personal sense of the hardship of a given transaction, the uncertainty resulting would, he thought, be disastrous in a commercial community; they must "apply the law with a steady hand." While he denounced the local system of credit as hazardous to merchants, demoralizing to planters, and "pestilent" for the fishermen, he insisted creditors should be "enabled to put the law in force against their debtors where the debtor has property"; otherwise no merchant would be reckless enough to issue supplies. For the peace of society "the rules which govern the disposition of property should be settled, and not fluctuating." Outrages on property or peace must be firmly met, otherwise "capital and industry would speedily seek a more secure and congenial domicile"; hence he refused bail in the case of the *Queen* v. *Gorman et al.*, which arose from an electoral riot in Harbour Main in 1860.

As a judge Robinson showed an unquestioned ability to reason from general principles in a wide perspective, taking equity, common sense, and possible consequences into account. A man with a marked spirit of independence, he frequently gave dissenting judgements. His decisions show considerable understanding of people and realities, conciliatoriness, and compassion. He also believed that a judge should play an active role. Accused in 1869 by the attorney general of invading the jury's province in the trial of *Berney* v. *O'Brien and Company*, Robinson replied that one of a judge's most important functions was "to assist a jury in arriving at a correct conclusion by telling them plainly what are his views respecting the proper inferences to be drawn from given facts." In the spring of 1870 Frederic Bowker Terrington Carter* and Edward Evans sought court restraint of a house committee appointed to investigate their election. In a judgement with a curiously modern ring, Robinson, ruling against the committee, asserted that Supreme Court judges had a "sacred duty . . . to interpose the shield of the law between public bodies and private individuals whenever judicial power is illegally claimed by the strong over the weak"; he argued that such a tribunal exercising independent authority was essential to secure respect for persons and property and the benefits of British law.

Robinson was appointed in March 1874 chairman of a three-man royal commission of inquiry which had been established by the House of Assembly to investigate the administration of the public accounts in the previous eight years. The propriety of a judge's serving on such a body was challenged and the commission was denounced by Robert John Pinsent* as likely to be a "political engine." Its reports, based on broad investigations and carried in part in the *Royal Gazette*, revealed that certain checks on accounts had been removed and public moneys misappropriated under the previous government of Charles James Fox BENNETT. As a result, the government established tighter control of the Board of Works, and the findings were used to help Carter defeat Bennett in the November elections. The following year the assembly put pressure on Robinson to release his notes of the commission's work. He declined, insisting that evidence had been given neither under oath nor in the knowledge it could be made fully public; he asserted that if a royal commission retroactively assumed such power it could be an "engine of oppression" since it might place the reputations of individuals beyond the courts' protection. He also stated that the public trusted his impartiality. In November 1874 he had in fact been commended by the governor, Sir Stephen John Hill*, for his assiduity and ability in discharging his duties on the commission.

Robinson always had broad interests in the community and local organizations. He served on the executive of the Benevolent Irish Society several times in the early 1830s, was active for many years in the Newfoundland Church of England Asylum for Widows and Orphans, and took the lead in organizing relief and work for the poor in 1869 after the assembly had discontinued its assistance. A staunch Anglican and warden of the parish of St John's in 1843, he remained interested in the Newfoundland Church Society for almost 30 years, sometimes serving on its management committee; within it he assisted Bishop Edward Feild*, who became a close friend. He was named to the Protestant Board of Education in 1852, and as a director of the Church of England branch of the St John's Academy in 1855. Elected for the Cathedral of St John the Baptist, he was a valuable member of the first diocesan synod of Newfoundland in 1873 and was one of the five laymen appointed to the diocesan executive committee. Robinson also took a lively part in St John's social and intellectual life, sitting on committees to organize celebrations for the completion of the Atlantic cable in 1857 and the visit of the Prince of Wales in 1860. He also gave public lectures to local societies.

Seriously interested in his country's agricultural development, Robinson served in the Agricultural Society at St John's for many years and was either its president or vice-president for much of the 1850s, 1860s, and 1870s. He owned a farm and won prizes for his crops. Under his presidency the society issued in 1850 a pamphlet to promote agriculture in which Robinson expressed high hopes for Newfoundland; he felt that the island, geographically at the same latitude as Canada and France, could and should become self-sufficient in food production and hence he pressed for local agricultural societies and increased assembly grants, to provide good seed, implements, and advice. Late in 1877 Robinson retired to England. Knighted at Windsor Castle on 12 December, he went to live with his daughters at Ealing where he remained active in Anglican concerns, especially the Society for the Propagation of the Gospel.

Over the years he had received many tributes to his legal ability, impartiality, dedication to duty, and sound judgement. A handsome man with full beard and heavy brows, serious mien, and an air of distinction, Robinson was one of the most polished speakers of the time. Early in his career, he made his name through passionate defence of the liberty of the individual, and, imbued with a strong sense of the heritage of British laws and institutions, he continued to stand up for the civil rights of individuals against unwarranted intrusions by the assembly and bureaucratic bodies. Convinced the courts must protect property and commerce, he also showed special concern for the rights and needs of both the employed and the poor. Robinson devoted his life to fulfilling his vision of Newfoundland as a thriving society with British institutions and a self-reliant economy.

PHYLLIS CREIGHTON

The reports: decisions of the Supreme Court of Newfoundland (St John's), 2 (1829–45)–6 (1874–84). *Novascotian*, 5 May 1831. *Public Ledger*, 1828–77. *Royal Gazette* (St John's), 1828–77. *Times* (London), 13 Dec. 1877, 9 Jan. 1878. *Times and General Commercial Gazette* (St John's),

1838–17 Dec. 1877, 4 Jan. 1888. Frederic Boase, *Modern English biography* . . . (6v., Truro, Eng., 1892–1921; repr. London, 1965), III: 221. *DNB*. Gunn, *Political hist. of Nfld.* Prowse, *Hist. of Nfld.* (1895). Malcolm MacDonell, "The conflict between Sir John Harvey and Chief Justice John Gervase Hutchinson Bourne," CHA *Report*, 1956: 45–54.

ROCHELEAU, *dit* **Lespérance, PIERRE.** *See* LESPÉRANCE

RODIER, CHARLES-SÉRAPHIN (baptized **Séraphin**; he added Jr to his name to distinguish himself from his uncle, Charles-Séraphin Rodier*), industrialist, financier, landowner, and politician; b. 6 Oct. 1818 in Montreal, Lower Canada, son of Jean-Baptiste Rodier, a baker, and Marie-Desanges Sedillot, *dit* Montreuil; m. 18 Jan. 1848 Angélique Meunier, *dit* Lapierre, and they had 12 children; d. 26 Jan. 1890 in his native city.

Little is known about Charles-Séraphin Rodier's youth. At the age of 14 he was working as a carpenter, and four years later he had become a building contractor. It was probably not until 1859 that he set up his factory for making agricultural implements on Rue Saint-Martin in Montreal. He produced threshing-machines which he sold to local farmers, and he demanded mortgages on their lands as security. His undertaking appears to be representative of an early stage in industrial development, that of factory production: artisans were hired on contract and paid by the job, and there was little division of labour.

Holding mortgages on his debtors' lands and investing heavily in property, Rodier became the largest individual landowner in the Montreal region. In 1881 *Le Monde* declared: "He has more than half a million dollars' worth of real estate in the town, not to mention numerous properties in suburban municipalities and in the country."

The financial sector also interested him. In 1861, with Jean-Louis BEAUDRY, André Lapierre, Hubert Paré*, and Romuald TRUDEAU, he founded the Banque Jacques-Cartier, serving as a director until 1870, and then as vice-president from 1870 to 1876. He was its principal shareholder, and is said to have lost about $145,000 in 1876 when the bank encountered financial difficulties; after this unfortunate occurrence he resigned. Subsequently he sat on the boards of directors of the Scottish Commercial Life Insurance Company and the Mutual Life Insurance Company.

Rodier had a brief political career, as town councillor of Saint-Antoine Ward in Montreal from 1847 to 1850. He was a member of the Conservative party and "was the close friend and favourite adviser" of Sir George-Étienne Cartier*. In 1888 Conservative newspapers recalled that in 1885, at the time of the Louis RIEL affair, he had remained loyal to the Conservative cabinet, and had firmly opposed the meeting on the Champ-de-Mars in Montreal. On 1 Dec. 1888 he was appointed to the Senate as representative for the division of Mille-Isles, an honour he had allegedly declined on two or three previous occasions.

Like the majority of businessmen in that period, Rodier took an active part in various associations. He was a churchwarden, president of the Association Saint-Jean-Baptiste and the St Vincent de Paul Society of Montreal, and a supporter of temperance campaigns. In addition, his large fortune enabled him to be a philanthropist. In 1869 he formed the 64th militia battalion (Voltigeurs de Beauharnois), becoming its first lieutenant-colonel.

Of humble origins, Charles-Séraphin Rodier was highly successful in business and by the end of his life had become the richest French Canadian of his day. At his death, newspapers estimated his fortune at more than $2,000,000. In the eyes of his contemporaries he was a self-made man, an illustration of the success stories that filled North American newspapers. Rodier's career is significant on two counts. He was a representative of those French Canadians of the bourgeoisie who, from the mid 19th century, succeeded in playing an active role in the economic development of the province of Quebec. *La Presse* said: "He was one of those superior men who have proved the aptitude of our race for business, and who have given it its rightful place among our enterprising fellow-citizens of English origin." Active in industry, finance, and landownership, as well as participating in political life and in various associations, Rodier exemplified the diversity of interests that still characterized businessmen in the second half of the 19th century.

PAUL-ANDRÉ LINTEAU

[Charles-Séraphin Rodier is mentioned in the lists of shareholders of chartered banks published in Can., Parl., *Sessional papers*, for some of the years from 1868 to 1877. There are Rodier family papers in the possession of Mme François Hone (Montreal). P.-A.L.]

AP, Notre-Dame de Montréal, Reg. des baptêmes, mariages et sépultures, 1818, 1848, 1890. BNQ, MSS-100. *L'Étendard*, 5 déc. 1888, 27 janv. 1890. *Gazette* (Montréal), 27 janv. 1890. *La Minerve*, 28 nov., 4 déc. 1888; 28 janv. 1890. *Le Monde*, 7 déc. 1888. *Montreal Daily Witness*, 27 Jan. 1890. *La Patrie*, 27 janv. 1890. *La Presse*, 12 déc. 1888; 27, 28 janv. 1890. *CPC*, 1889. J. Desjardins, *Guide parl.*, 252. *Montreal directory*, 1853–60. Atherton, *Montreal*, III: 85–86. *Histoire de la corporation de la cité de Montréal depuis son origine jusqu'à nos jours . . .* , J.-C. Lamothe *et al.*, édit. (Montréal, 1903). Rumilly, *Hist. de Montréal*, III. É.-Z. Massicotte, "Deux Rodier," *BRH*, 44 (1938): 120–22.

ROGERS, ALBERT BOWMAN, civil engineer; b. 28 May 1829 at Orleans, Mass., son of Zoar Rogers and Phebe S. Kenrich; m. first in 1857 Sarah Lawton

(d. 1858) of New York; m. secondly Nellie Brush of Iowa; d. 4 May 1889 at Waterville, Minn.

As a young man, Albert Bowman Rogers was apprenticed to a ship's carpenter, but made one sea voyage only. He entered the engineering faculty at Brown University in 1851 and after transferring to Yale the next year obtained his bachelor's degree in 1853. Following graduation he was employed as an engineer on the Erie Canal, before moving to Iowa and then to Minnesota. In 1862 he was commissioned major in the United States cavalry by the governor of Minnesota, Alexander Ramsey, during the uprising of the Dakota Sioux. The year before, he had joined the engineering staff of the Chicago, Milwaukee and St Paul Railroad where he gained the name of the "The Railway Pathfinder" for his location work. This brought him to the attention of James Jerome Hill of St Paul, a member of the executive committee of the Canadian Pacific Railway. Hill hired him in late February 1881 to take charge of all mountain location work for the company.

Rogers' main task was to find and locate two passes, through the Rockies and the Selkirk Mountains, which would provide the CPR with a direct route to the Pacific. In April he dispatched survey parties to work their way up the Bow River from Fort Calgary and explore both the Howse and the Kicking Horse passes in the Rockies. Rogers intended to tackle the Selkirks himself, since it was generally held that no pass existed through those mountains. He had studied the report of Walter Moberly*, a British Columbia government engineer who, in 1866, had sent one of his men up the west slope of the mountains along the route of the Illecillewaet River in the hope of finding a pass. The trip proved abortive; Moberly did not believe a pass existed. But Rogers, together with his nephew Albert and a party of Kamloops Indians, followed the same route to the summit of what was later named Mount Sir Donald. From this vantage point, in late June 1881, Rogers thought he saw a way through the barrier. He could not be certain because he had run out of supplies and was not able to explore the intervening 18 miles. None the less, he reported, in his enthusiasm, that a practicable route existed.

Rogers was determined to find the pass, which Hill had promised to name after him. "His driving ambition was to have his name handed down in history," his friend, the packer Thomas Edmond Wilson*, said of him. "For that he faced unknown dangers and suffered privations." "To have the key-pass in the Selkirks bear his name was the ambition he fought to realize."

In the summer of 1881 Rogers located the line through the Kicking Horse Pass. The following May he again attacked the Selkirks, this time approaching from the east by way of the Beaver River at its junction with the Columbia. Again he ran out of supplies and was forced to turn back. On 17 July he tried again, following the Beaver and its tributary the Bear to reach, at last, the same mountain-ringed meadow he had observed from the slopes of Mount Sir Donald the previous June. Henceforth, this would be known as Rogers Pass. The date was 24 July 1882.

Rogers was a controversial figure, a tobacco-chewing, hard-swearing eccentric who made many enemies through his irascibility and his parsimonious method of feeding his men, and also through jealousy, especially among those Canadian engineers who were irritated by the presence of an American rival. Marcus Smith*, in charge of construction in British Columbia, thought Rogers "a thorough fraud"; Charles Æneas Shaw, another colleague, echoed that estimate. A. E. Tregent, who worked for him in the Rockies, called him "a queer man, lots of bluff and bluster." To John Frank Stevens, one of his assistants, he was "a monomaniac on the subject of food." On the other hand, George Monro Grant*, who with Sandford Fleming* was sent to oversee Rogers' work in the summer of 1883, was high in his praises. "Not one engineer in a hundred would have risked, again and again, health and life as he did," Grant wrote. His companion, Tom Wilson, felt that Rogers was much misunderstood: "He cultivated a gruff manner to conceal the emotions that he seemed ashamed to let anyone sense." William Cornelius Van Horne*, the CPR's general manager, while admitting that Rogers was "somewhat eccentric and given to 'burning brimstone,' " also felt that he was "a very good man on construction, honest and fair dealing."

Hill swore by Rogers and when the CPR was completed in 1885 (Rogers was present at the driving of the last spike at Craigellachie), Hill hired him as a locating engineer on his Great Northern Railroad. Rogers' career ended when, at work for Hill in the Cœur d'Alene Mountains of Idaho in 1887, he was badly injured falling from his horse. He died two years later at the home of his brother in Waterville, Minn., after a long and painful illness from cancer of the stomach.

PIERRE BERTON

Canadian Pacific Arch. (Montreal), Letters from A. B. Rogers. Glenbow-Alberta Institute, T. E. Wilson and W. E. Round, "The last of the pathfinders" (1929); pub. as *Trail blazer of the Canadian Rockies*, ed. H. A. Dempsey (Calgary, 1972). Minnesota Hist. Soc. (St Paul), Cannon River Improvement Company papers; Scrapbooks, 2. PABC, Add. MSS 767, Marcus Smith to Joseph Hunter, 23 Feb. 1885. PAC, MG 28, III20, 1, C. Van Horne letterbook, no.1: 234–40; 2, C. Van Horne letterbook, no.7: 483–85.

B.C., Lands and Works Dept., *Columbia River exploration, 1865–6: instructions, reports, & journals* . . . (2v. in 1, Victoria, 1866–69), II: 15. A. L. Rogers, "Major A. B. Rogers' first expedition up the Illecillewaet valley, in 1881, accompanied by his nephew, A. L. Rogers: an account of the trip," A. O. Wheeler, *The Selkirk range* (2v., Ottawa, 1905), I: 417–23. G. M. Grant, "The C.P.R. by the Kicking Horse Pass and the Selkirks – X: the Rogers' Pass," *Week* (Toronto), 1 May 1884. *Winnipeg Daily Times*, 23 Jan. 1882. *Obituary record of graduates of Yale University deceased from June, 1880, to June, 1890 . . .* (New Haven, Conn., 1890), 535–36. Pierre Berton, *The national dream: the great railway, 1871–1881* (Toronto and Montreal, 1970); *The last spike: the great railway, 1881–1885* (Toronto and Montreal, 1971). J. M. Gibbon, *Steel of empire: the romantic history of the Canadian Pacific, the northwest passage of today* (Toronto, 1935). J. H. E. Secretan, *Canada's great highway: from the first stake to the last spike* (London and Ottawa, 1924). J. F. Stevens, *An engineer's recollections* (New York, 1936); repr. from *Engineering News-Record* (New York), 114 (January–June 1935)–115 (July–December 1935). B. A. McKelvie, "They routed the Rockies! Railway pathfinders forged steel links from east with west," *Vancouver Daily Province*, 3 Feb. 1945, magazine section. C. Æ. Shaw, "A 'prairie gopher' makes reply," *Vancouver Daily Province*, 27 Oct. 1934, magazine section.

ROLLAND (Roland), JEAN-BAPTISTE, printer, bookseller, businessman, municipal councillor, and senator; b. 2 Jan. 1815 at Verchères, Lower Canada, son of Pierre Roland, a farmer, and Euphrasine Donay; m. 7 Oct. 1839 Esther Boin at Saint-Laurent, near Montreal, Lower Canada, and they had four daughters and four sons; d. 22 March 1888 in Montreal.

Jean-Baptiste Rolland began life in modest circumstances. About 1828 his family moved to Saint-Hyacinthe where he received the rudiments of his education. In 1832 he left Saint-Hyacinthe and, according to tradition, made his way on foot to Montreal, arriving there virtually penniless. He succeeded, however, in finding a position as an apprentice typographer at *La Minerve*. In 1836 he went to the *Morning Courier*, also of Montreal, where he worked for four years as a journeyman. He then decided to become a printer and with John Thompson founded the firm of Rolland and Thompson, but in 1843 he separated from his partner to concentrate on the book trade.

It was really as a bookseller that Rolland made his mark. He had opened his first shop, on Rue Saint-Vincent in Montreal, in 1842 and had built up a market selling books door-to-door in the countryside. Seeking to broaden his field of endeavour, he began to publish numerous works, in particular school texts and religious books. This activity led him to attach a printing and binding establishment to the bookshop. Among other things, he printed *L'Écho du Cabinet de lecture paroissial* (Montreal) from 1861 to 1864, and then from 1880 to 1884 the *Journal de l'Éducation* (Montreal), undertaken with a view to carrying on the work of the *Journal de l'Instruction publique* (Quebec and Montreal), the official organ of the provincial department of education which had ceased publication in 1879 [*see* Pierre-Joseph-Olivier CHAUVEAU]. Although Rolland benefited from an annual government subsidy of $500, he was forced to give up the journal when the income from the publication proved insufficient.

Moreover, by the mid 19th century a bookstore was not confined to selling books. Rolland developed an extensive business in paper and stationery items, some of which came from France. He also manufactured account books of all sizes, and he sold imported objects such as clocks, jewellery, and perfumes. At the beginning of the 1860s he described himself in directories as a "bookseller, printer, binder and importer of goods from France and Germany."

Thus during the 1850s Rolland became a prosperous businessman, with a good reputation. This period also marked an important stage in the expansion of his undertakings. Around 1855, finding his premises too cramped, he moved his bookshop into a much larger building on Rue Saint-Vincent. Four years later he formed a partnership with his eldest son, Jean-Damien, and the firm became known as J.-B. Rolland et Fils. Rolland brought his other sons successively into the partnership when they became old enough to join it. At the end of the 1850s he moved to a house he had built on Rue Saint-Denis, on Viger Square. At that time his assets, including his business and his properties, were appraised at $100,000.

His enterprises continued to develop during the next two decades. In order to ensure a better supply of paper, the Rollands decided in 1881 to manufacture it themselves. The family thus provides a good example of the businessman turning industrialist. They chose Saint-Jérôme as the site for their future mill and the town granted them an exemption from municipal taxes for a period of 25 years. Set up in 1881 as the Rolland Paper Company, the mill began the following year to produce fine quality paper which the family had previously had to import from Europe. This paper soon acquired an excellent reputation, and in 1885 the company won a silver medal at the international exposition in Anvers, Belgium. Rolland, who was already elderly when the firm was established, entrusted its management to two of his sons, Jean-Damien and especially Stanislas-Jean-Baptiste; the latter, who had settled at Saint-Jérôme, ran the factory.

In addition to his book and stationery business, and its extension, the manufacture of paper, Rolland took an active interest in land development and house building. He began to acquire holdings and to build dwellings on them in the 1850s and in time became increasingly interested in this kind of operation. He had rows of houses constructed on Saint-Denis and Berri, and helped make Viger Square a select place of residence for the French-speaking bourgeoisie around the middle of the century. He also owned other dwellings and some shops in the east end of Montreal. In addition, he made himself known as a real estate developer and builder in Hochelaga, a suburban Montreal municipality where his son Jean-Damien and his son-in-law Joseph-Raymond Fournier*, *dit* Préfontaine, in turn held the office of mayor from 1876, and then that of municipal councillor after the annexation of Hochelaga to Montreal in 1883. Nor did Rolland ignore the financial world. He was on the board of directors of the Citizens' Insurance and Investment Company, and during the 1870s was one of the shareholders of the Banque Jacques-Cartier.

Rolland's involvement in politics was mainly at the local level. For some ten years he sat on the municipal council of Montreal as representative for the East Ward. First elected in 1861, he retained his seat until 1867; four years later he returned to council in place of Jacques-Alexis Plinguet*, who had resigned, and he remained on it until 1875. In 1879, as a member of the Conservative party, he was given the responsibility of reorganizing the finances of *La Minerve*, the party's organ in Montreal. That year the federal government appointed him to the Montreal Harbour Commission, upon which he served for the rest of his life. The peak of his political career was his appointment to the Senate on 22 Oct. 1887. There he represented the division of Mille-Îles, succeeding Louis-Adélard SENÉCAL, who had died 11 days earlier. Rolland was an officer of the militia for a period, and among other responsibilities to which he devoted himself were those of churchwarden of the parish of Notre-Dame at Montreal, president of the Association Saint-Jean-Baptiste of Montreal in 1879, and member of the Council of Arts and Manufactures of the province of Quebec from 1880 to 1883.

Rolland, a self-made man, illustrates well a type of social ascent characteristic of the 19th century. He began as a merchant, and later gained distinction by investing in manufacturing and by ensuring the continuance of his interests through his sons' association in them.

PAUL-ANDRÉ LINTEAU

[The records of the Rolland Paper Company, held at the company's head office in Montreal, were being organized when this biography was being prepared. They will be opened to researchers in 1982 when the company will celebrate its centenary. P.-A. L.]

ANQ-M, État civil, Catholiques, Saint-François-Xavier (Verchères), 3 janv. 1815; Saint-Laurent, 7 oct. 1839. Baker Library, R. G. Dun & Co. credit ledger, Canada, 5: 3; 6: 244. Can., Parl., *Doc. de la session*, 1872–82 (reports from Canadian chartered banks). *La Minerve*, 23 mars 1888. *La Presse*, 22 oct. 1887, 22 mars 1888. Beaulieu et J. Hamelin, *La presse québécoise*, I: 57, 221. Borthwick, *Hist. and biog. gazetteer,* 441–42. *Canadian biog. dict.*, I: 100–2. *Dominion annual register*, 1879: 356; 1880–81: 373; 1885: 166. C. E. Goad, *Atlas of the city of Montreal from special survey and official plans showing all buildings & names of owners* (2nd ed., 2v., Montreal, 1890). *Montreal directory*, 1853–64; 1881–88. Germain Cornez, *Saint-Jérôme* (2v., Saint-Jérôme, Qué., 1973–77), II: 15–16, 38, 213. *Histoire de la corporation de la cité de Montréal depuis son origine jusqu'à nos jours* . . . , J.-C. Lamothe *et al.*, édit. (Montréal, 1903), 215–24, 757–59. André Labarrère-Paulé, *Les laïques et la presse pédagogique au Canada français au XIX*[e] *siècle* (Québec, 1963), 130–38, 144–47, 152–55. P.-A. Linteau, "Histoire de la ville de Maisonneuve, 1883–1918" (thèse de PHD, univ. de Montréal, 1975).

ROSE, Sir JOHN, lawyer, financier, politician, and diplomat; b. 2 Aug. 1820 in Turriff (Grampian), Scotland, the son of William Rose and Elizabeth Fyfe; d. 24 Aug. 1888 in Langwell Forest near Ord of Caithness (Highland), Scotland.

Little is known about his parents but young John Rose was given a solid education at Udny Academy, a grammar school outside Aberdeen, and at King's College, one of the founding institutions of the University of Aberdeen. Rose's entrance into university at 13 was not uncommon at the time; after one year of study in the arts course, however, he dropped out of King's College. In 1836 he immigrated to Lower Canada with his parents, settling at Huntingdon, where he was a teacher for a brief period, before acting as tutor for the family of Colonel John By*. During the rebellions of 1837–38 he served as a volunteer and is believed to have assisted in recording court martial proceedings against captured Patriotes. He studied law in Montreal under Adam THOM and then under Charles Dewey DAY, and was called to the bar in 1842.

Rose attached himself to the rising mercantile and banking interests of the city and soon built a thriving practice in commercial law. Among his partners were Samuel Cornwallis Monk, later a prominent jurist in Quebec, and Thomas Weston Ritchie. Rose served as legal adviser in Canada to Edward Ellice* and was closely identified with the operations of the Hudson's Bay Company. His business associates included other members of the board of the Bank of Montreal, with a number of whom he signed the Annexation Manifesto in 1849. This step cost him the QC he had been given the year before, but he soon regained a respected position in Montreal life and was reinstated QC in 1853. In addition to his directorship of the Bank of Montreal, he served on the boards of the City Bank, the Montreal Telegraph Company, the Grand Trunk Railway, the New City Gas Company of Montreal, and the North British and Mercantile Insurance Company. He participated actively in such community enterprises as the Royal Institution for the Advancement of Learning, the Montreal Protestant House of Industry and Refuge, and the Mercantile Library Association. Intelligent, energetic, and personable, Rose was reputed to possess the largest law practice in Montreal by the early 1850s, his clients including the leaders of the business community: Sir George Simpson*, Hugh ALLAN, George Stephen*, and others.

Some ten years before, he had made the acquaintance of John A. Macdonald* and the two developed a close, lifelong friendship, Macdonald being five years older. Macdonald told Lord Carnarvon years later that as young men he, Rose, and a third man had paid a carefree visit to the United States as strolling musicians. "Macdonald played some rude instrument, Rose enacted the part of a bear and danced. . . . To the great amusement of themselves and every one else, they collected pence by their performance in wayside taverns." Their first collaboration in public affairs occurred in the summer of 1857 when Macdonald, as joint head of the Liberal-Conservative administration, asked Rose to accompany him to London to assist in obtaining financial support for the Intercolonial Railway from the British government. The ministry of Lord Palmerston refused to grant aid and the mission was unsuccessful.

Nevertheless, Macdonald was sufficiently impressed with Rose's legal and personal capabilities that he persuaded the Montreal lawyer to enter his ministry; although Rose had been importuned to enter public life since the early 1850s, he had decided not to commence a political career until he had acquired independent means. On 26 Nov. 1857 he was appointed solicitor general of Canada East and won a seat in Montreal in the ensuing general election. In the contest for the three-member riding Rose was the only ministerial candidate elected, George-Étienne Cartier* and Henry Starnes* going down to defeat. Rose was never as committed to politics and parties as Macdonald but he saw in government office a means of accomplishing important economic and national projects; in fact Rose was continually regarded with suspicion by members from Canada West as an agent of the HBC. During the "double shuffle" [*see* Cartier] in August 1858 he was receiver general for a day before resuming his post of solicitor general. On 11 Jan. 1859 he was appointed chief commissioner of public works, a post which brought him to the centre of the controversy regarding the construction of the new Parliament Buildings in Ottawa. Begun in 1860, the project was soon troubled by large over-expenditures as well as a lack of cooperation between the architects and the political and administrative heads of the Department of Public Works. Inevitably Rose's role in the complicated dispute meant criticism for him and on 12 June 1861, worn out by ill health and by the heavy demands of his public duties and a large professional practice, he resigned office. He kept his seat, however, and was re-elected in 1861 and 1863 for Montreal Centre.

A more satisfying achievement for him as commissioner of public works was the management of arrangements for the tour of British North America by the 19-year-old Prince of Wales in the summer of 1860, the first visit to North America by a direct heir to the British throne. Rose was responsible for coordinating the myriad details of transportation, communication, and accommodation for the progress of the substantial party of some 250 to 300 people across the Province of Canada. The administrative ability he revealed, as well as his poise in meeting unexpected situations such as the threat of trouble in Kingston [*see* John Hillyard Cameron*], were widely remarked upon. They laid the basis for the "lasting intimacy" which, according to a biographer of the future King Edward, was to grow up between Rose and the prince. In Montreal, where the party arrived in late August, the prince stayed in Rose's large residence on Mount Royal, with its fine view of the city and river, before continuing on to the United States on 20 September.

Rose did not take a prominent part in the confederation movement, although he was an unofficial delegate from the Protestant minority of Canada East at the London conference in 1866–67. His major public activity during these years was diplomatic, assisting in the settlement of HBC claims for losses incurred by the cession of lands to the United States in the Oregon Territory. The HBC had tried vainly to sell properties which it or its subsidiary, the Puget's Sound Agricultural Company, had abandoned following the 1846 treaty. In 1857 the British government took up the company's case, instructing its minister in Washington to discuss with the United States procedures to assess claims for compensation for property and privileges surrendered. The two countries eventually agreed on a joint commission on the model of those previously used for disputes over boundary and commercial claims. A treaty to this effect was signed in Washington in 1863 and Rose, who as counsel to the HBC in Canada had been involved in the question for years, was appointed the British commissioner in April 1864.

The United States appointed Alexander Smith Johnson, a judge of the federal Court of Appeals, as commissioner, an office was established in Washington, and the laborious task of assembling claims and evidence, from Oregon to England, began. It dragged on for three years, until May 1868, when arguments were presented to the commissioners. During this last phase Rose was engaged in discussions with the HBC and the British government in order to settle on a sum the company would be prepared to accept for its holdings. It was not until 10 Sept. 1869 that he and Johnson were able to announce a mutually acceptable award granting $450,000 in gold to the HBC and $200,000 to its subsidiary. The Oregon claims settlement, although a minor contribution to Anglo-American accord, was an important experience for Rose. Through its proceedings he became acquainted with a number of American public men, most notably

Caleb Cushing, the American counsel to the commission and a long-time adviser to the Department of State. These links were to be valuable to him in his larger diplomatic undertakings after 1869.

Rose had stood for election to the first dominion parliament in 1867, winning a seat for Huntingdon as a Conservative. He was a candidate for speaker of the House of Commons but had to withdraw in favour of James COCKBURN when another Quebec representative, Joseph-Édouard CAUCHON, was chosen speaker of the Senate. Shortly afterwards he was unexpectedly brought into the Macdonald cabinet upon the resignation of Alexander Tilloch Galt* as minister of finance. Rose's banking associations made him a natural choice and he was sworn in on 18 Nov. 1867.

His two-year occupancy of the finance portfolio was dominated by a great struggle over the nature of the dominion's first banking system. At issue was whether the individual Canadian banks should continue to possess the right of free note issue, a profitable activity, or whether there should be a state currency backed by government securities. Rose, worried about recent bank failures in Ontario, favoured the latter plan. He adopted as a model the recent National Bank Act of the United States (1863) which had established a uniform note issue supported by government debentures. This plan was also advocated by the dynamic Edwin Henry King*, the cashier (general manager) of the Bank of Montreal. Much the largest bank in Canada and perhaps in North America, the Bank of Montreal already possessed dominion securities and notes issued under Finance Minister Galt which it could use to acquire federal notes. A state currency would oblige the smaller Ontario banks to commit their limited capital to the purchase of securities and they might even have to recall loans to do so. There was also the probability they would have to borrow from Montreal to meet the large cash requirements needed for "moving the crops" each autumn. Allied to Rose's preference for a bond-supported currency was the proposal that branch banking be discouraged, to be replaced by small independent country banks, leaving the financing of major commerce and foreign trade to the large banks. It was clear that the Bank of Montreal, the Bank of British North America, and some institutions in the Maritime provinces would be in a position to carry out the latter function. Thus the issue was joined. The Canadian Bank of Commerce [*see* William MCMASTER], the Bank of Toronto, and other Ontario banks, together with banks in Quebec and Halifax, opposed the Rose plan. Their connections with the Liberal party ensured strong political opposition to legislation which Rose might introduce.

The battle raged through two sets of parliamentary hearings, one conducted by the Senate committee on banking, commerce, and railways, the other by the corresponding commons committee, which was chaired by Rose. The unhappiness with Rose's scheme showed itself clearly in a meeting of Ontario bankers held in Ottawa in April 1868 and in the replies to a commons committee questionnaire which were largely hostile to state issue of notes. Nevertheless Rose embodied his plan in resolutions he presented to parliament on 14 May 1869; one day of debate, 1 June, confirmed the strength of the opposition. Macdonald's cabinet was itself divided on the issue and the prime minister wisely decided to withdraw the measure. The struggle has been interpreted as one between Montreal, seeking to maintain its position as the country's financial centre, and the rising commercial and financial aspirations of Toronto. Rose, always closely identified with Montreal's interests, felt discredited by the rebuff to his legislation. It led directly to his decision, effective in September, to resign his portfolio, leave Canada, and enter the world of international finance.

As finance minister Rose had to supervise the consolidation of the public accounts of the various jurisdictions comprising the new federation. He also undertook the task of assimilating the separate tariffs and revenue duties of the Province of Canada, New Brunswick, and Nova Scotia. His first major budget speech was delivered on 7 May 1869 and showed a conservative approach to the management of expenditures and the growth of the public debt. He established the rule, for instance, that unused appropriations lapsed at the end of each fiscal year. In July 1868 he journeyed to England to place a loan of £2,000,000 for the Intercolonial Railway (his temporary use of the proceeds of this loan, raised partly under an imperial guarantee, occasioned an important constitutional dispute with the British Treasury), and in January 1869 he carried out negotiations with Archibald Woodbury MCLELAN and Joseph Howe* for "better [financial] terms" for Nova Scotia.

Rose also entered into discussions with the United States concerning issues unsettled since the abrogation of the Reciprocity Treaty of 1854. His discussions with Hamilton Fish, President Ulysses S. Grant's secretary of state, held in Washington from 8 to 11 July 1869, covered the temporary use of Canadian inshore waters by American fishermen, the free navigation of the St Lawrence River, the enlargement of the Canadian canals, and the assimilation of customs and excise duties with the United States. Rose was also prepared to offer free trade in certain manufactured products, as well as in natural goods, to the United States. This concession was publicly denied after he had left office by his successor, Sir Francis HINCKS, and by Prime Minister Macdonald. Given the strong anti-British North American sentiment in Congress after the Civil War, Rose's *projet* of a treaty was abortive.

Rose's conversations with Fish also touched on this

larger problem of the unsatisfactory state of Anglo-American relations resulting from the unsettled issues of the American Civil War. Foremost among the differences was the American desire for compensation under the "*Alabama* claims," an issue which Senator Charles Sumner, in an electrifying speech in April 1869, had linked to the cession of Canada to the United States. Rose and Fish discussed the state of opinion about Sumner's demand and considered possible means of adjusting Anglo-American differences. Rose indicated that his impending departure for a private business career in England offered an opportunity for him to be of service in this area.

Although Rose took up residence in London in the autumn of 1869 the opportunity to assist in improving Anglo-American relations did not arise until November 1870, when the British government of William Ewart Gladstone accepted a Foreign Office plan to establish a joint high commission charged with devising a mechanism for settling outstanding issues between the countries. In a memorandum to the foreign secretary, Lord Granville, on 26 November, Rose proposed that the American government might be sounded out on the plan through "some intermediate agency in no way responsible or accredited, but yet possessing in sufficient measure the good-will of each." Shortly afterwards he was asked to undertake the "agency," in the capacity of "a private person engaged in commercial transactions" with the United States. Essentially his task was to question, listen, and report back to London. The importance of his mission was underlined by the fact that his instructions were "shown to the Queen, Mr. Gladstone and the cabinet" and the expenses of his trip were borne by the British government.

Rose arrived in Washington on 9 Jan. 1871. There he remained for the next three weeks, conducting conversations with Fish, other members of the Grant administration, and leading senators. Early on, Rose confirmed the assertion of the British minister in Washington, Sir Edward Thornton, that there could be no cession of Canada in compensation for the *Alabama* claims, nor would Britain admit unqualified liability for the actions of Confederate cruisers. Liability would have to be determined by arbitration on the basis of mutually acceptable rules for the conduct of a neutral state. The discussions, long and involved, were carried out against the knowledge that the formidable Senator Sumner might at any time play the role of "spoiler." When Rose met him at a dinner party on 20 January he was baited by the senator: "Haul down that flag and all will be right."

Giving substance to the exchanges was the reality of massive economic and financial benefits to be realized from an Anglo-American settlement. Business and transportation interests on both sides of the Atlantic were pressing for an accommodation while the United States' plan of re-funding the Civil War debt depended upon substantial European support for a new bond issue. Rose was only too well aware of these considerations through his association with European and American banking groups. Arrangements for the formation of a joint high commission to review Anglo-American differences, and their effects on Canada, were accepted by the time Rose left Washington for Ottawa on 2 February.

Rose's place in the negotiations was emphasized when Lord Granville proposed his appointment to the joint high commission. Both Sir Edward Thornton and Fish were favourable but the suggestion was not acceptable to the Canadian cabinet. Macdonald and his colleagues felt that since Rose had severed his formal ties with Canada and held a pecuniary interest in the prospect of transatlantic friendship, he would not be a suitable person to represent Canada's interests. Governor General Lisgar [Young*] distrusted Rose, believing, in spite of Thornton's denials, that Rose had been negotiating with the Americans over the fisheries without Ottawa's approval. The alternative Granville had proposed was Macdonald, who clearly stood in a better position to have an eventual treaty accepted in Canada. Rose accepted the decision with his customary urbanity and returned to London.

This informal mission in 1871 marked the high point in Rose's diplomatic career. His achievement had been grounded on the crucial fact that he was *persona grata* in influential circles on both sides of the Atlantic. But Rose's individual qualities also contributed to the success of his efforts. "A natural diplomat of a high order," Lord Granville called him; "a man of tact and discretion," "moderate and fair," observed Thornton. Yet if Rose's activity as an expediter must be praised, it should be noted that his discussions with Fish failed to clarify all the points of disagreement between the parties. For example he did not press Fish on whether the "indirect claims" resulting from the *Alabama* depredations would continue to be asserted by the United States in the future arbitration. When they were brought forward in further negotiations at Geneva in 1872 the action almost destroyed the arbitration and the entire settlement. Yet the stakes in the restoration of favourable Anglo-American relations were high and ambiguity is often the truest wisdom in diplomacy.

Rose had moved to London in the midst of the effort to meet the needs of North American economic development through the creation of transatlantic partnerships in banking and finance. The utility of these connections was readily apparent. There were American government securities to be sold in Europe, as well as innumerable exchange transactions arising from the revival of commerce with the United States following the Civil War and intensified by the post-war boom in railway building. Rose took over the

London office, established in 1863, of the American firm of Morton, Bliss and Company; this major American banking house, operated by Rose's personal friend Levi Parsons Morton and his partner George Bliss, was noted for its involvement in railway interests. Rose was able to assume the position when Walter Burns, the man in charge, was obliged to withdraw from the firm after marrying the daughter of a competitor, John Pierpont Morgan. Typically, the London firm, styled Morton, Rose and Company after the arrival of the new partner in 1869, was not a branch office but a partnership, a separate legal entity that secured its own business, maintained a separate capital account, and simply cooperated with the American firm. Rose managed the London operation until he stepped down in favour of his second son, Charles Day, in 1876. But the elder Rose remained an active figure on the London financial scene, continuing his influence with his old firm until his unexpected death in 1888. He was a member of the London committee of the Bank of Montreal, a director of the Bank of British Columbia, and the deputy governor of the HBC from 1880 to 1883, and also had associations with a number of British banks and insurance companies.

Morton, Rose and Company stood in a strategic position to facilitate the growing volume of public and private investments across the Atlantic. Through Levi Morton it acted as a fiscal agent for the United States government from 1873 to 1884 and participated in the European phase of the re-funding of the American national debt. Through John Rose the company shared many important financial transactions with the Canadian government's principal financial agents in London, Baring Brothers and Company and Glyn, Mills, Currie and Company. It also handled offerings for the province of Quebec and the city of Montreal. It derived the normal commissions from the flotation and renewal of these public borrowings and also profited from Canadian government purchasing in London. These operations were undoubtedly lucrative for Morton, Rose and Company and for Sir John.

The most active field for Morton, Rose and Company was in railway financing. Here Rose's association with the Macdonald government was of vital significance. As a personal friend of both Macdonald and George Stephen he assisted in the negotiations that led to the creation in Ottawa on 21 Oct. 1880 of the original Canadian Pacific Railway syndicate, which included his firm, Morton, Rose and Company; the latter was also represented on the CPR board. The syndicate, with Rose's help, succeeded in attracting Morton, Bliss and Company, as well as other American banks, to aid in the substantial task of raising funds for the transcontinental line. Rose vigorously defended the CPR in London against the attacks of its rival, the Grand Trunk, lobbied for a Pacific steamship service contract for the company, and sought to coordinate land sales between the railway and the HBC, of which he was deputy governor. In 1882 Rose, accompanied by Sir Robert George Wyndham Herbert, permanent undersecretary at the Colonial Office, paid a visit to the Canadian northwest to examine CPR construction and the progress of settlement. Although his personal loyalty to the CPR could not be questioned, that of Morton, Rose and Company was later to be. This occurred well after the management of the firm had passed to his son, whom George Stephen believed to be sympathetic to the Grand Trunk. Desiring more vigorous representation in London, Stephen persuaded Barings to take on a CPR mortgage bond issue in 1885. Thereafter the firm's relationship with the railway was not as intimate.

But Rose in London was always more than a financier. In a functional sense he acted as a quasi-official representative for Canada from 1869 until the office of high commissioner was established in 1880. When Rose left Canada an order in council of 2 Oct. 1869 stated that he was "accredited to Her Majesty's Government as a gentleman possessing the confidence of the Canadian Government with whom Her Majesty's Government may properly communicate on Canadian affairs." His expenses were underwritten by the dominion but he received no salary. He soon proved his usefulness in coping with the problems resulting from Canada's acquisition of the northwest. "It is impossible to have an abler or more pleasant man with whom to transact business," Granville reported to Macdonald in 1870. The connection with Ottawa was maintained by the Liberal prime minister, Alexander Mackenzie*, upon whose suggestion Rose became the "Financial Commissioner for the Dominion of Canada" by order in council of 5 March 1875. But the comfortable association between Rose's financial activities and the informal agency of Canada could not be maintained indefinitely. In the summer of 1879, after the return of the Conservatives to power, Macdonald decided that a full-time official representative was needed in London. In August, on a visit to England, he informed Rose that Sir Alexander Galt would be appointed to the new position. Rose accepted the decision with his usual aplomb, and continued to be consulted by the dominion on financial and other matters even after Galt had taken up his duties. In May 1888, for instance, Sir Richard John Cartwright* complained in the house that Rose had gained commissions on a loan transaction that should have been undertaken by the high commissioner's office. Sir Charles Tupper*, minister of finance and high commissioner, explained that Rose, as a trustee of Canada's sinking fund in London, was entitled to remuneration for services.

It is impossible to record fully the subjects with which Rose dealt as an unofficial agent for Canada.

Almost every item of substance in the bilateral relationship received his attention. Sometimes this attention was expressed in confidential advice to Macdonald, sometimes in negotiations with the relevant departments of the British government, sometimes in writing to the newspapers on Canadian affairs. In addition Rose was often consulted by the Colonial Office or by British politicians on colonial questions. Here he showed an awareness of the empire as a whole and of what he considered the beneficial and reinforcing relationships between its parts. Not surprisingly he defended the *status quo* in the constitutional position of the self-governing colonies and in the means of conducting imperial relations. Basically detached from British party politics, Rose carried out his representations "behind the scenes," skilfully drawing upon his wide circle of connections in government and business for his purposes.

Colonial affairs did not occupy all Rose's time in England. In 1883 his acquaintance with the Prince of Wales led to his appointment as receiver general for the duchy of Cornwall, a historic estate whose income was reserved for the benefit of the heir apparent to the throne. In this post Rose managed an income of about £60,000 a year from properties in Cornwall and others in Kensington and Lambeth (both now part of London). He thus made a contribution to the unprecedented circumstance of Edward VII's accession in 1901 entirely free from debt. His membership in the prince's circle also brought Rose service on commissions concerned with various colonial and Indian exhibitions, projects in which Edward took a keen interest. Rose served on two royal commissions, one on copyright in 1875, the other on extradition in the following year. His honours are impressive: KCMG in 1870, shortly after he removed to England; a baronetcy, Rose of Montreal, in 1872 for his role in arranging the Washington conference; promotion to GCMG in 1878; and membership in the imperial Privy Council in 1886 (his friend Macdonald had been the only Canadian to receive this honour before him).

Rose was married twice. His first wife, whom he married on 3 July 1843, was Charlotte Temple of Vermont, widow of Irish poet Robert Sweeney, who had been killed in a celebrated duel in Montreal in 1838; she and Sir John were to have three sons and two daughters. An English friend described Lady Rose thus: "I have in a long life met many women I thought clever, but never one so clever as she was, or with such a genius for society." She died on 3 Dec. 1883, and on 24 Jan. 1887 Rose married Julia Charlotte Sophia Mackenzie-Stewart, widow of the 9th Marquis of Tweeddale. Rose himself died unexpectedly on 24 August of the following year, while deer stalking on the estate of the Duke of Portland in Scotland. Afflicted with a weak heart, he died in the excitement of shooting a stag. He was buried in Guildford, England, near a country estate, Losely Park, which he had rented for some years.

Rose is the quintessential representative of the North Atlantic community of the middle and late 19th century. Born in one corner of the Atlantic "triangle," he made his name in another, was closely connected with the third, and returned to his birthplace to fulfil a second career. Much more a financier and diplomat than a politician, he recognized the importance of a favourable political climate for the growth of economic enterprise. Thus he turned his natural gifts to the maintenance of reinforcing relationships between the corners of the "triangle." He was immensely aided in this task by his orderly mind, his grasp of detail, his discretion, his ability to inspire trust, and his charm and urbanity. These personal qualities were combined with a shrewd appreciation of the possibilities for financial gain and Rose died a wealthy man; his estate was valued at over £300,000. The extent to which his diplomatic and administrative achievements assisted his position as a private financier is impossible to measure but the value of the link cannot be doubted. He possessed a host of acquaintances and some close relationships with men in high places. Of the latter his friendship with Macdonald is uppermost. "Of all Sir John Macdonald's political associates in his later years," wrote Sir Joseph Pope*, "I am disposed to consider that, personally, he was most attached to Sir John Rose. . . ." John Morley's appraisal fairly characterizes the man: "He was one of the many Scots who have carried the British flag . . . over the face of the globe; his qualities had raised him to great prominence in Canada; he had enjoyed good opportunities of measuring the American ground; he was shrewd, wise, well read in the ways of men and the book of the world, and he had besides the virtue of being pleasant."

DAVID M. L. FARR

[There is no biography of Rose, nor have his private papers been located. A large mass of Rose correspondence extending over many years is contained in the Macdonald papers (MG 26, A) in the PAC. Rose was Barings' agent in Canada and the Baring Brothers and Company papers (PAC, MG 24, D21) contain his reports to the firm. The Alexander Mackenzie papers (MG 26, B) in the PAC also include Rose correspondence. There are Rose papers for the years 1850 to 1867 in the McLennan Library, McGill University Libraries (Montreal). Rose material may also be obtained in the L. P. Morton papers in the New York Public Library. Letters and memoranda from Rose are to be found throughout Colonial Office (CO 42 and CO 43) and Foreign Office (FO 5, FO 362, and FO 414) records in the PRO and in the files of the Department of State (RG 59) in the National Archives of the United States (Washington). Original material arising from Rose's reciprocity discussions in 1869 is reproduced in two notes edited by A. H. U. Colquhoun, *CHR*, 1 (1920): 54–60, and 8 (1927): 233–42. Rose's activities touched so many branches of government that evidence concerning them is widely scattered. There is also the fact that the unofficial character of his duties after 1869 tended to reduce formal communications.

Biographical sketches of Rose may be found in *Canadian directory of parl.* (J. K. Johnson); *Cyclopædia of Canadian biog.* (Rose, 1886); Dent, *Canadian portrait gallery*, IV: 70–72; *DNB*; *Dominion annual register*, 1880–85; and Morgan, *Sketches of celebrated Canadians*, 637–39. Secondary material is also scattered through biographies and memoirs of Rose's friends and associates in three countries, notably Creighton, *Macdonald, young politican* and *Macdonald, old chieftain*, and Joseph Pope, *Memoirs of the Right Honourable Sir John Alexander Macdonald, G.C.B., first prime minister of the Dominion of Canada* (rev. ed., Toronto, 1930). There are also a few more specialized treatments of phases in his career. Rose's involvement in the controversy over the construction of the Parliament Buildings is touched on in Hodgetts, *Pioneer public service*, chap.12. There is a discussion of the genesis of the Oregon Treaty in J. S. Galbraith, *The Hudson's Bay Company as an imperial factor, 1821–1869* ([Toronto], 1957), chap.13. The struggle over the dominion's first banking legislation is discussed in D. C. Masters, "Toronto vs. Montreal: the struggle for financial hegemony, 1860–1875," *CHR*, 22 (1941): 133–46; Shortt, "Hist. of Canadian currency, banking and exchange: government versus bank circulation," *Canadian Banker*, 12: 14–35; and in Denison, *Canada's first bank*. Rose's financial activities are touched on in Heather Gilbert, *Awakening continent: the life of Lord Mount Stephen . . .* (Aberdeen, Scot., 1965) and in Dolores Greenberg, "Yankee financiers and the establishment of trans-Atlantic partnerships: a re-examination," *Business Hist.* (London), 16 (1974): 17–35, and "A study of capital alliances: the St Paul & Pacific," *CHR*, 57 (1976): 25–39. The fullest treatment of Rose as Canadian agent in Britain is M. H. Long, "Sir John Rose and the informal beginnings of the Canadian high commissionership," *CHR*, 12 (1931): 23–43. *See also* D. M. L. Farr, "Sir John Rose and imperial relations: an episode in Gladstone's first administration," *CHR*, 33 (1952): 19–38, and *The Colonial Office and Canada, 1867–1887* (Toronto, 1955). There is a chapter on Rose as unofficial agent in London in W. I. Smith, "The origins and early development of the office of high commissioner" (PHD thesis, Univ. of Minnesota, Minneapolis, 1968), and in W. B. Turner, "Colonial self-government and the colonial agency: changing concepts of permanent Canadian representation in London, 1848 to 1880" (PHD thesis, Duke Univ., Durham, N.C., 1970). Rose's Washington negotiations of 1871 are described in R. C. Clark, "The diplomatic mission of Sir John Rose, 1871," *Pacific Northwest Quarterly* (Seattle, Wash.), 27 (1936): 227–42; G. [A.] Smith, *The Treaty of Washington, 1871: a study in imperial history* (Ithaca, N.Y., 1941); and J. O. McCabe, *The San Juan water boundary question* (Toronto, 1964). D.M.L.F.]

ROSS. *See* ROBERTSON-ROSS

ROSS, JAMES, Presbyterian minister, editor, and educator; b. 28 July 1811 at West River, Pictou County, N.S., son of the Reverend Duncan Ross* and Isabella Creelman; m. 27 Sept. 1838 Isabella, daughter of William Matheson, and they had a number of children; d. 15 March 1886 at Dartmouth, N.S.

James Ross and his wife-to-be attended the same school on the lower end of the East River, in Pictou County. He graduated from Dr Thomas McCulloch*'s academy at Pictou, received a teaching licence on 12 Oct. 1831, and accepted a "lucrative" position at the Westmorland County Grammar School in Sackville, N.B. After his father's death, James responded to a call from his congregation and was ordained to the Presbyterian ministry at West River on 3 Nov. 1835. He was paid £150 a year in cash and produce, and his congregation numbered over 175 families. Ross also operated a large farm at West River, edited, probably in 1842–43, the *Presbyterian Banner* (which merged with the *Mechanic and Farmer* in 1843 to become the *Eastern Chronicle*), served as synod clerk from 30 July 1839 to 25 June 1847, and taught divinity classes in Princetown (Malpeque), P.E.I., in 1846.

With the Reverend William McCulloch, son of Thomas McCulloch, Ross laid the strategy which led to the founding of a Presbyterian theological seminary at West River for the training of a local ministry. On 22 July 1846, two years before the seminary was officially opened, Ross was elected professor of biblical literature, and in July 1848 he accepted the additional post of professor of philosophy. The seminary, under the auspices of the Synod of the Presbyterian Church of Nova Scotia and housed in the ill-ventilated Temperance Hall above the schoolhouse in West River, received its first 12 students on 9 Nov. 1848. Ross taught at the seminary until 1858 at a salary of £175 per year, part of which was paid by a bequest from his mother-in-law's estate. To lighten his burden, Ross's congregation in West River was halved in 1848, and he dissolved his pastoral connections in 1851. The inadequate quarters of the seminary led to a fierce battle over the choice of a new location until 1856 when Truro was selected as the site. This controversy and a bitter rupture within his former congregation contributed to a breakdown of Ross's health in 1857, but when the seminary opened in its incomplete building in Truro on 1 Sept. 1858 he was able to resume teaching.

The union in 1860 of the Presbyterian Church of Nova Scotia and the Free Church of Nova Scotia caused a renewal of discussions about resuscitating Dalhousie College in Halifax, which had operated from 1838 to 1845 but had since been dormant. Urged on by George Monro Grant*, one of the first graduates of the West River seminary, on 29 April 1863 Charles Tupper* and Joseph Howe* got a bill to reorganize and refinance Dalhousie passed in the assembly. Ross's seminary classes were transferred from Truro to Dalhousie's dilapidated building on the parade ground at Halifax, and on 19 Oct. 1863 Ross was named president of the revived college. When it opened on 10 Nov. 1863 the college had 60 students and six faculty: Ross and William McCulloch, whose salaries were paid by the Presbyterian Church, Charles Macdonald*, paid by the Free Church, and the Reverend William LYALL, George Lawson*, and John Johnson, paid by Dalhousie. Ross initially reported "violent opposition" to the college among Presbyterians, but this evaporated during 1864 in the face of attacks by the Baptist partisans of Acadia College in Wolfville, N.S. By a vote of 30 to 14 the Nova Scotia assembly rejected on 29 March 1864 a bill which would have killed Dalhousie. In April Ross received an honorary degree from Queen's, the Presbyterian college in Kingston, Canada West.

During Ross's 22-year presidency enrolment tripled, the faculty increased to 21, and medical and law schools were established. The first BA was awarded in 1866, MA in 1869, PHD in 1872, BSC in 1880, and LLB in 1885. But success had not come easily. Professors competed with the "noisome invisible" odours of janitorial cooking in the basement and the decomposing cadavers used by anatomy classes in the attic; the recess of the "rising savages of Halifax," as Ross characterized the students of the nearby National School, rendered lectures inaudible; and military bands even had the pernicious habit of practising under the classroom windows. Financially Dalhousie faced a constant struggle. The initial commitment of the Presbyterian Church of Nova Scotia to pay its appointees was no doubt partly met by a $35,000 bequest to the church from Ross's father-in-law. By 1871 the college's position was portrayed as "extraordinary and humiliating." On 9 Oct. 1878 the Reverend John Forrest*, brother-in-law of George Munro*, was named to the board of governors. Within a year Munro, a native of Pictou County and a New York publisher, began contributions to Dalhousie of a size unprecedented in British North America to that time. These grants, totalling some $350,000, assured the future of the university.

Students expressed mixed opinions of Ross as a teacher, and Sir William YOUNG, chairman of the board of governors, stated in 1878 when he tried unsuccessfully to arrange Ross's retirement that "the health and bodily strength of the Principal are so much shaken to incapacitate him from the efficient teaching of his classes." This illness might explain why many students felt Charles Macdonald was the *de facto* university principal. In fairness it should be remembered that Ross had lost his wife and a daughter between 1875 and 1878.

Ross resigned as president on 1 May 1885 and was succeeded by John Forrest. He retired to his Dartmouth home, Morven, where he died on 15 March 1886. At his burial at Camp Hill Cemetery, Halifax, almost the entire student body of the university was present.

ALLAN C. DUNLOP

Dalhousie Univ. Arch., MS 2–8, J. A. Bell, "Dalhousie College and University." PANS, Vert. file, Genealogy – Tattrie family, Gordon Haliburton, "The Tattrie family of River John (1752–1952) . . ." (typescript, 1953). E. A. Betts, *Pine Hill Divinity Hall, 1820–1970; a history* (Truro, N.S., 1970). D. C. Harvey, *An introduction to the history of Dalhousie University* (Halifax, 1938). G. [G.] Patterson, *Studies in Nova Scotian history* (Halifax, 1940), 100–6. William Verwolf, "The West River Presbyterian Seminary," *Addresses at the celebration of the one hundred and fiftieth anniversary of the arrival in Nova Scotia of Rev. James Drummond MacGregor, D.D. . . .*, ed. Frank Baird (Toronto, 1937), 249–59. *Dalhousie Gazette* (Halifax), 12 Jan. 1903.

ROSS, JAMES GIBB, merchant, capitalist, and senator; b. 18 April 1819 in Carluke (Strathclyde), Scotland; d. 1 Oct. 1888 in Quebec City.

The son of a merchant, James Gibb Ross came to Canada and settled in Quebec City at the age of 15. Entering the wholesale and retail grocery firm of his two uncles, James* and Thomas Gibb, Ross worked as a clerk without pay for the first year; for his second year of service he received a salary of $200, which was subsequently increased to $400. Under the name of James Gibb and Company, his two uncles, in partnership with Elisha Lane, were in business together until the end of 1843, when James Gibb retired from the firm to go in with John Ross, James Gibb Ross's elder brother. This new partnership, using the name of Gibb and Ross, conducted a similar wholesale-retail grocery trade, and James Gibb Ross was employed by the firm from its formation, becoming a partner by April 1858. Recognized as the most important importers of wine and groceries in the city of Quebec, Gibb and Ross did a large and profitable business.

Following the death of James Gibb in the fall of 1858 the two brothers John and James Gibb Ross formed a partnership under the style of Ross and Company and continued the business. Maintaining their position as the largest grocery importers in Quebec City, they soon sought out other avenues of investment for their growing capital, and by 1861 had begun trading in lumber. As commission and general merchants, the partnership continued until 1868 when John Ross retired to form another grocery firm, John Ross and Company, based in Montreal and Quebec. James Gibb Ross maintained Ross and Company on his own and carried on a rapidly diversifying business as a general and commission merchant dealing in iron, lumber, timber, and wholesale groceries, and as agent for various British and American steamship lines. During the 1870s and 1880s his trading activities took him into the commodity markets of New York, Chicago, and Milwaukee, Wis., where at times his investment in such goods as tea, sugar, and grain was reportedly in the millions of dollars. On one occasion a syndicate in which Ross was the principal investor apparently succeeded in cornering the market in pork at Milwaukee. His interest in the lumber and timber trade also expanded and he was soon recognized as a major owner of sawmills in Quebec and Ontario. One of his mills, located at Lakefield, Ont., which was destroyed by fire in 1880, was valued at $25,000. During the 1880s, with his partners Horace Jansen Beemer and Benjamin Alexander Scott, he operated extensive timber cutting and milling operations in the Lac Saint-Jean region under the style of Ross, Beemer and Company, and at the time of his death he was completing the construction of the largest mill in the region at Pointe Scott.

From the late 1850s Ross had taken an interest in shipbuilding. Beginning with advances to other shipbuilders, he soon turned to constructing his own vessels. As early as June 1859 his first ship, the 676-ton sailing vessel *Leveu*, left the dry docks at Quebec City and before the end of the year he had completed two more. In 1877 Ross and Company appeared in the city directories as shipbuilders, owners, and brokers, and at the peak of his shipping activities towards the end of the 1870s Ross was reported to have owned a worldwide fleet of 80 vessels.

As a capitalist Ross occupied an influential position in the business community of Quebec and his name was associated with those of many of Canada's leading businessmen. In 1861 he figured prominently with Isaac BUCHANAN, James Bell Forsyth*, and Jean-Baptiste RENAUD in the group which formed the St Lawrence Navigation Company. With many of the same associates he formed the Quebec Marine Insurance Company in 1862 and the Quebec Elevator Company in 1863. Ross also had considerable investments in the Banque Nationale (75 shares), the Union Bank of Lower Canada ($12,000), and the Quebec Bank ($26,000), as declared in a government list of shareholders in Canadian chartered banks for 1868. Particularly active in the administration of the Quebec Bank, he served as vice-president from 1866 to 1869 and as president from 1869 until his death.

Ross also took an interest in railway development and in March 1873 advanced a considerable sum of money to the Levis and Kennebec Railway Company, saving the project from financial disaster. The following year he was appointed one of the trustees to oversee the management of a fund of $74,385 set aside by the company to guarantee the interest payments on bonds to be sold in London, England. In 1873 Ross was an active member of the group of capitalists who took control of the ailing North Shore Railway Company from Joseph-Édouard CAUCHON. Elected a member of the board of directors on 20 May 1873, along with Jean-Baptiste Renaud, Élisée Beaudet, Andrew Thomson, Willis Russell, William Rhodes*, Thomas McGreevy*, and John Burstall*, Ross was subsequently elected president of the company by his fellow directors. Unfortunately, the efforts of the new board to obtain sound financing were in vain and in 1875 the Quebec provincial government took control of the railway to form the publicly owned Quebec, Montreal, Ottawa and Occidental Railway. Ross was none the less still attracted by the prospects of this road, and, when it was put up for sale in 1882, he participated with Louis-Adélard SENÉCAL, Thomas McGreevy, Mathew Hamilton GAULT, Jean-Baptiste Renaud, Charles William CARRIER, Victor Hudon*, and others in a syndicate which offered to lease the line with an option to purchase. After the government of Joseph-Adolphe Chapleau* sold the western section of the QMOO to the Canadian Pacific Railway, the syndicate revised its offer and, as the North Shore Railway Company, negotiated the purchase of the eastern section for $4 million; Ross sat as a founding member on the board of directors. In December 1882, however, control of the North Shore Railway was sold to the Grand Trunk Railway. During these years Ross also had a large investment in the Quebec and Lake St John Railway Company, serving as director in 1877 and then as president from 1878.

James Gibb Ross played an important role in many of Quebec City's commercial and social associations. Intermittently a member of the council of the board of trade from 1856 to 1871, he served as president in 1862–63, and in 1874 was appointed a member of the Quebec Harbour Commission. With a group of Quebec's most influential citizens, including ex-mayors Charles Joseph ALLEYN and Sir Narcisse-Fortunat Belleau*, Joseph-Édouard Cauchon, James Bell Forsyth, and David Edward Price, Ross was a founding director of the Stadacona Club in 1861. Located at the corner of Rue Sainte-Anne and Rue d'Auteuil, the Stadacona Club was popular for many years among Quebec merchants and the officers stationed at the Citadel. In 1864 Ross participated in the incorporation of the Humane Society of Canada with Pierre Garneau*, Thomas D'Arcy McGee*, Jean-Baptiste Renaud, Georges-Honoré Simard*, and Isidore Thibaudeau*. This association was formed to reward acts of personal bravery in attempts to preserve human life and to bring to punishment acts of cruelty to animals.

In the 1872 federal general election Ross was an independent Conservative candidate in the constituency of Quebec Centre, seeking to represent the British Protestant minority of Quebec City. His contest with Cauchon, who was also running as an independent, quickly degenerated into a bitter campaign centred around racial and religious differences. On 5 August, the day of the election, a riot broke out between the supporters of each candidate and before calm was restored one of the rioters had been shot and killed. The veteran Cauchon won the seat, beating Ross by 330 votes. Running in the election of 1878, Ross was once again unable to carry the riding and lost to the independent Jacques Malouin. On 11 Jan. 1884 the Conservative government of Sir John A. Macdonald* appointed Ross to succeed the deceased David Edward Price as senator for the Laurentides division. Not a particularly active senator, Ross sat as a member of the upper house until his death four years later.

James Gibb Ross, a bachelor, died at the home of his brother, Frank, on 1 Oct. 1888, leaving an estate variously estimated at between five and ten million dollars. In his will Ross bequeathed a total of $525,000 to a number of charities, for the most part connected with the English minority in Quebec, though a £10,000 trust was set aside for the relief of the Protestant poor in his native Carluke. On 4 October he was buried at Mount Hermon Cemetery in Sillery, near Quebec City.

In collaboration with KENNETH S. MACKENZIE

Baker Library, R. G. Dun & Co. credit ledger, Canada, 5: 53, 241. BE, Québec, Reg. B, 51, no.20612; 53, no.21540; 54, no.22086; C, A1, nos.35, 120, 248. PAC, RG 68, 240: 349. Can., Parl., *Sessional papers*, 1867–68, VI, no.12. Can., Prov. of, *Statutes*, 1861, c.99, c.121; 1862, c.71; February–May 1863, c.23; 1864, c.146. Que., *Statutes*, 1882, c.20. C. A. Scott, *The Levis and Kennebec Railway, and its difficulties: a brief history of Larochelle & Scott's connection with the line from its commencement to the present time* (Quebec, 1877). *Gazette* (Montreal), 21, 29 May 1873. *La Minerve*, 3 oct. 1888. *Quebec Daily Mercury*, 2 Oct. 1888. *Quebec Gazette*, 12 Jan., 24 April 1844. *Canada, an encyclopædia* (Hopkins), I: 450. *Canada directory*, 1857–58. *Canadian directory of parl.* (J. K. Johnson), 508. *Canadian men and women of the time* (Morgan, 1898), 62–63, 1009. *Canadian men and women of the time* (Morgan, 1912), 1001. *CPC*, 1873: 295; 1878: 198; 1879: 241. *Cyclopædia of Canadian biog.* (Rose, 1888): 648–49. *Dominion annual register*, 1879: 248; 1880–81: 249; 1883: 234; 1885: 354; 1886: 154. *Political appointments and judicial bench* (N.-O. Coté), 170. *Quebec directory*, 1862–89. *RPQ*, 25. Rodolphe Gagnon, "Le chemin de fer de Québec au lac Saint-Jean (1854–1900)" (thèse de DES, univ. Laval, Québec, 1967). Gervais, "L'expansion du réseau ferroviaire québécois." Rossel Vien, *Histöire de Roberval, cœur du Lac-Saint-Jean* ([Chicoutimi, Qué., 1955]). F. W. Wallace, *Wooden ships and iron men: the story of the square-rigged merchant marine of British North America, the ships, their builders and owners, and the men who sailed them* (New York, [1924]). "Les disparus," *BRH*, 33 (1927): 311.

ROSS, SALLY (Sarah), Okanagan Indian and housewife; b.*c.* 1798 in the Columbia River area, daughter of an Okanagan Indian chief; m.*c.* 1812 presumably by Indian rites to Alexander Ross*, and on 24 Dec. 1828 she was baptized and married to Ross "by Banns with mutual consent" in the Anglican Upper Church (later St John's Church), Red River Settlement (Man.); they had at least 12 children; d. 26 Feb. 1884 in Winnipeg, Man.

Sally Ross was born into a peaceful tribe of Okanagan hunters and fishermen. Her simple life within the tribe was profoundly affected by the impact of three fur-trading companies upon the area. Sally probably met her future husband, Alexander Ross, soon after his arrival in the Columbia region as a clerk with the Pacific Fur Company at Fort Okanagan (Wash.) in 1811. Two years later that company was bought out by the North West Company, which, in turn, amalgamated with the Hudson's Bay Company in 1821. Ross worked for each of these firms in succession until 1825 when, as one of several "expensive clerks with large families," he was transferred by Governor George Simpson* to Red River. Ross set off with his eldest son, leaving Sally to follow with the other four children. She left Spokane House (near Spokane, Wash.) with the HBC express on 19 Sept. 1825 and ascended the Columbia River via Boat Encampment (B.C.) to Jasper House (Alta) where she wintered with her children. In May she left with the brigade going east, riding where practicable with one child secured behind her, another on the front on her saddle, and the two others on a second horse. She reached the Red River Settlement in the summer of 1826, the year of a disastrous flood, and with the four children spent the winter at Pembina (N. Dak.) where Alexander had business interests. The following year she proceeded to the Red River Settlement where she was to live for the next 57 years.

Alexander was, in turn, a merchant, a substantial farmer, and, by 1836, a councillor and the sheriff of Assiniboia. The Ross home on the Red River, Colony Gardens, a white, roughcast, two-storey stone building, was noted for its hospitality; "constantly thronged by visitors," it was a landmark in the settlement. According to Robert Clouston, who visited the settlement in 1843, Sally seldom appeared in public except in church, but she was a central figure in her large bustling household, and in her later years was known to the whole Red River community as "Granny Ross."

In his great "wilderness trilogy" of histories of the west, published between 1849 and 1856, Alexander Ross stressed the dependence of the fur-trader upon his Indian wife, the "tenderness existing between them," the protection afforded by her "vigilance," and the charm which "her smiles" added to his existence. He wrote more personally of his own grief and anxiety when he was forced to leave his family for Red River in 1825. Illiterate herself, Sally may well have contributed much of the detailed information on Indian tribal life which was included in his first two books.

When Alexander died in October 1856, he left the substantial portion of his estate to his wife and commended the younger children to her care. Although Sally was "destitute in the accomplishments of etiquette," her affection and her tender-hearted anxiety for all the children's welfare were unfailing and they remained loyal to their Indian mother. James* became a lawyer, schoolmaster, journalist, and, in 1869–70, an associate of Louis RIEL; Henrietta married John BLACK, the prominent Manitoba Presbyterian minister. Only one of Sally's children survived her, a daughter Mary who married the Reverend George Flett.

Sally Ross carried much of her Indian culture with her to Red River; there her concern for family relationships harmonized with that of the numerous Scots. Like many other Indian women, only now being studied by historians, Sally was a link between Indian tribal life, the mixed-bloods, and the new white communities of traders. She became a devout Christian, the centre of a lively and intelligent household, and she was one of the women who contributed to the shaping of Manitoba society.

LAURENDA DANIELLS

PABC, Add. MSS 345. PAM, HBCA, A.36/11: ff.214–15, will of Alexander Ross, 25 June 1856; E.5/1–11; MG 2, C14; MG 7, B7. J. W. Bond, *Minnesota and its resources to which are appended camp-fire sketches or notes of a trip from St. Paul to Pembina and Selkirk settlement on the Red River of the north* (New York, 1853). *Canadian North-West* (Oliver). *Documents relating to the North West Company*, ed. W. S. Wallace (Toronto, 1934). A. [E. S.] Martin, *The Hudson's Bay Company's land tenures and the occupation of Assiniboia by Lord Selkirk's settlers, with a list of grantees under the Earl and the company* (London, 1898). Alexander Ross, *Adventures of the first settlers on the Oregon or Columbia River: being a narrative of the expedition fitted out by John Jacob Astor, to establish the "Pacific Fur Company"; with an account of some Indian tribes on the coast of the Pacific* (London, 1849; repr. Ann Arbor, Mich., 1966); *The fur hunters of the far west; a narrative of adventures in the Oregon and Rocky Mountains* (2v., London, 1855); "Letters of a pioneer," ed. George Bryce, HSSM *Trans.*, 63 (1903); *Red River Settlement.* Manitoba Daily Free Press, 1872–74, 27 Feb. 1884. *Nor'Wester*, 1859–69, especially 25 June 1862. W. J. Healy, *Women of Red River: being a book written from the recollections of women surviving from the Red River era* (Winnipeg, 1923). Sylvia Van Kirk, "'Women in between': Indian women in fur trade society in western Canada," CHA *Hist. papers*, 1977: 30–46.

ROUSSELOT, BENJAMIN-VICTOR, Roman Catholic priest and Sulpician; b. 17 Jan. 1823 at Cholet, France, son of Jean Rousselot and Marie Allion; d. 31 Aug. 1889 in Montreal, Que.

Benjamin-Victor Rousselot was the sixth child of a bourgeois family that engaged in manufacturing and banking. After classical studies at Angers and a year of philosophy with the Sulpicians in Nantes, he entered the Séminaire de Saint-Sulpice in Paris, at the same time as Ernest Renan who was beginning his theological studies. The seminary provided a solid grounding in both biblical exegesis and theology; open to the influence of the German Catholic school, it sought to integrate theology with day to day living and to develop the historical sense which the scholastic tradition lacked. The ultramontane thinking of Arthur Le Hir had a considerable influence on Rousselot. Unfortunately, he was unable to concentrate fully on his studies because of delicate health and failing eyesight. These handicaps meant that he had to look beyond the seminary at the time of his ordination on 19 Dec. 1846; as a result, he went to work as an assistant priest with the youth of his native village for a six-year period. In October 1853 he was finally admitted to the *solitude*, the Sulpician noviciate at Issy-les-Moulineaux, dept of Hauts-de-Seine, which was under the direction of Étienne-Michel Faillon*. Observing Rousselot's physical inability to undertake the intellectual tasks of the Society of Saint-Sulpice, Faillon guided him towards the pastoral ministry of the Montreal house, accompanying him there when he himself made a second trip to Canada in 1854.

From the time of his arrival Rousselot began to familiarize himself with the two fields in which he would labour in Montreal: the parish of Notre-Dame, which was in debt and overwhelmed by the responsibility of serving the whole city through a network of churches to which the parish denied legal authority; and the chaplaincy to the Sisters of Charity of the Hôpital Général of Montreal (Grey Nuns), in whose good works he was to share. In fact, after two years as confessor to the nuns, he began to develop plans for a crèche for children between two and seven years of age who were in disadvantaged circumstances. The Rousselot family in France protested, fearing that his inheritance would be consumed by the expenditures he was preparing to make. Nevertheless, on 26 July 1858 construction of the building for the Asile Saint-Joseph got under way on a Rue Saint-Bonaventure site donated by the Grey Nuns.

By June 1859, when Bishop Ignace BOURGET presided at the service to mark the opening of the Asile Saint-Joseph, Rousselot had enlisted financial support for it through private and public solicitation. This first shelter, which had been conceived on a French model, proved an immediate success, and Rousselot persuaded the Grey Nuns to undertake a second project. On 6 May 1860 work began on a Rue Sainte-Catherine site in Montreal which he had purchased with the intent of building the Asile Nazareth; it was finished in December 1861. The success of this nursery for "the class [that was] not in easy circumstances" was ensured by contributions from parents and benefactors, as well as by a monthly supplement of 25 cents per boarder provided from 1870 by the Legislative Assembly of the province of Quebec. From its inception the establishment received a certain number of blind children. In the spring of 1870 Rousselot created a specialized institution for blind children, connected to the building of the Asile Nazareth. This new endeavour, which had been inspired by innovative developments in this field in Paris, was an instant success because of the adoption of Louis Braille's system; in 1871 people were astonished to observe that the new pupils could already read, write, and perform musical pieces just like other children. In addition to this institution, which later became the Institut pour les Aveugles, Rousselot helped set up the Notre-Dame Hospital in Montreal in 1880, assisting Dr Emmanuel-Persillier Lachapelle* to rent the premises and furnish it appropriately by contributing personally and by standing surety.

On 7 April 1866 Rousselot had left his inconspicuous post as chaplain to take the highly controversial charge of parish priest of Notre-Dame in Montreal. A decree issued by the Sacred Congregation of Propaganda on 22 Dec. 1865 had set out the compromise agreed to by the Sulpicians and by Bishop Bourget which would open the way to the division of the single parish of Montreal [*see* Ignace Bourget; Joseph Desautels]. The decree in fact inaugurated ten years of crisis and quarrels among the Montreal clergy. The first nine months of Rousselot's service as parish priest gave rise to a canonical dispute between the superior of the Séminaire de Saint-Sulpice, Joseph-Alexandre Baile, and the bishop of Montreal. The bishop sought to have Baile put the decree into effect by presenting him with a plan of division which excluded Baile from chairing the parish council; Baile, alleging that certain difficulties had become insurmountable, refused to budge and stirred up public support for the Sulpicians. Caught in this power struggle, Rousselot began work on a project to restore and finish the interior of the church, completed in 1874.

Rousselot was often tempted to resign, since he personally favoured a policy of compromise and silence. His unobtrusive and discreet style, as well as his ultramontane concept of the role of the church, brought him closer in theory to Bourget, an affinity especially evident in 1869–70 in the period of the Vatican Council and the Guibord affair. In Rousselot's view, this council was the divinely inspired answer to the evils corrupting the age; the faithful should trust its conclusions and rely on prayer. He fully subscribed to the affirmation in dogma of papal infallibility: "Reassure yourselves, if the priest errs in his religious teachings, there is someone to straighten him out . . . , his bishop, whose principal duty is to keep watch over both the doctrines and the conduct of his clergy. . . . If the bishop makes a mistake detrimental to sound doctrine, there is someone in the church charged by its divine founder to straighten him out . . . , the Pope." Warned on 18 Nov. 1869 by the vicar general, Alexis-Frédéric Truteau*, that the late Joseph Guibord*, who had been a member of the Institut Canadien of Montreal, should not be buried in consecrated ground, Rousselot, as parish priest, complied. An ensuing civil suit ended in a judgement in favour of Guibord's widow, Henriette Brown, in 1874, decreeing that Guibord was to be buried in the Catholic cemetery of Côte-des-Neiges. Rousselot made a public pronouncement of the soundness of the church's position concerning those who had read works on the Index of Prohibited Books and its freedom with regard to the civil authority: "It is ridiculous for a layman to order a priest to sprinkle a corpse and to pray for its soul."

Rousselot's anti-liberalism and anti-gallicanism did not, however, prevent a resurgence of hostility between the bishop and representatives of the parish of Notre-Dame; indeed, the conflict over the division of the parish reached new heights in 1871, with Bourget proposing to obtain civil incorporation of the churches of Notre-Dame parish. In June 1872 Rousselot was obliged to go to Europe, leaving his post for the summer, because he was wretchedly overtired and plagued by violent headaches. In his absence Pius IX issued a decree, dated 30 July, officially recognizing Bourget's claims. When the statute on the parishes came into force on 23 Feb. 1875, Rousselot found that the territory for which he was responsible had suddenly shrunk with no alleviation of the burden of debt being shouldered by the parish council. He devoted his remaining years at Notre-Dame to new work improving the interior of the church, until on 2 Oct. 1882 he was appointed parish priest of Saint-Jacques in Montreal.

Rousselot took no further part in public issues, except for intervening in favour of the textbooks used by the Brothers of the Christian Schools (traditional protégés of the Sulpicians) during the quarrel in 1880 over the bill to secure uniformity in school texts. The wisdom he showed at the time of the Louis Riel affair was typical of the man: in the course of a service at Saint-Jacques in November 1885, he expressed a wish to see it divested of political overtones. He seems to have concentrated on his welfare activities; in a will made in May 1886 he bequeathed his entire estate to the Asile Nazareth, before he left for several months in France to take a cure necessitated by a spinal cord infection. Returning to his pastoral duties, he undertook that year to enlarge Saint-Jacques. He died on 31 Aug. 1889 of the illness with which he had been stricken three years earlier. His contemporaries especially remembered this modest parish priest's considerable efforts on behalf of the poor and the underprivileged. A French Sulpician, of bourgeois family, who had come to settle in Montreal, he had indeed made his most original contribution to its life by his social and educational innovations.

LOUIS ROUSSEAU

ACAM, 355.101; 588.201; 901.141; RLB, 15; 18. Arch. de la Compagnie de Saint-Sulpice (Paris), Dossier 121, no.31. Arch. départementales, Maine-et-Loire (Angers, France), État civil, Cholet, 17 janv. 1823. Arch. des Sœurs grises (Montréal), Ancien journal, I: 119-20; Dossier, Hospice Saint-Joseph, Chronique, I; Historique; Dossier, Nazareth, le fondateur, Testament de M. Rousselot, p.s.s.; Rousselot, Saint-Sulpice; "Salles d'asile tenues par les Sœurs de la charité de Montréal, dites vulgairement Sœurs grises dans la ville et le diocèse de Montréal" (Montréal, 1870). ASSM, 21, Lettres de B.-V. Rousselot; 49, Dossier 56. Ernest Renan, *Souvenirs d'enfance et de jeunesse* (Paris, 1883). *La Minerve*, 17, 21 mai 1866; 3 sept. 1889. Allaire, *Dictionnaire*, I: 482. Henri Gauthier, *Sulpitiana* ([2e éd.], Montréal, 1926). E.-P. Benoît, *Histoire de l'hôpital Notre-Dame, 1800–1923* (Montréal, 1923). Henri Gauthier, *La Compagnie de Saint-Sulpice au Canada* (Montréal, 1912). André Labarrère-Paulé, *Les instituteurs laïques au Canada français, 1836–1900* (Québec, 1965), 340. Olivier Maurault, *La paroisse: histoire de l'église Notre-Dame de Montréal* (2e éd., Montréal, 1957), 64–79. Estelle Mitchell, *Mère Jane Slocombe, neuvième supérieure générale des Sœurs grises de Montréal, 1819–1872* (Montréal et Paris, 1964). Léon Pouliot, "Il y a cent ans: le démembrement de la paroisse Notre-Dame," *RHAF*, 19 (1965–66): 350–83.

ROWSELL, HENRY, bookseller, stationer, and publisher; b. 21 Feb. 1807 in London, England, son of Samuel and Sarah Rowsell; m. 1 Aug. 1835 Elizabeth Lewis, and they had one son and two daughters; d. 28 July 1890 in Toronto, Ont.

Henry Rowsell learned the book business in his father's Cheapside bookshop, and in 1829 established his own business in London. In 1833 he immigrated to Canada with his brother William, and by 1835 had opened a book and stationery store in Toronto. From 1 July 1835 to 11 July 1836 he kept a diary which throws some light on polite society in the provincial capital. When the diary begins Rowsell is awaiting his English fiancée. She arrived on 19 July and they were married two weeks later in St James' (Anglican) Church, of which they became members. He indulged his fondness for sports, literature, and music, joining the Toronto Cricket Club, the Shakespeare Club (immediate forerunner of the Toronto Literary Club), and an amateur musical society. He went to the races, to an exhibition of the Toronto Horticultural Society, and to the Theatre Royal when it opened in 1836. Henry and William Rowsell were both founding members of the St George's Society in 1835 and Henry later held office as treasurer. Henry was also a charter member in 1844 of the Toronto Board of Trade, of which he became secretary, and of the Toronto Building Society. In 1848 he was treasurer of the Toronto Philharmonic Society, and in 1849 local secretary of the American Art Union. He also took an active interest in the House of Industry, serving for some time as secretary and treasurer.

In the politics of the pre-rebellion period Rowsell was a strong supporter of the Tory group in Upper Canada. In March 1836 he joined the executive committee of the British Constitutional Society, founded in 1832, and in the election called by Sir Francis Bond Head* for May 1836 canvassed on behalf of William Henry Draper* in Toronto. He also published in October *The speeches, messages, and replies of His Excellency Sir Francis Bond Head*, which he dedicated to the lieutenant governor. The pamphlet was printed at the press of the *Patriot*, but shortly thereafter, Henry and William opened a printing office, H. and W. Rowsell Company. They also inaugurated a lending library, containing, according to Anna Jameson [Murphy*], "two or three hundred common novels." Their own advertisement states that the library was "constantly supplied with all the new and interesting publications as soon as published." It was still in operation in 1849. A branch library and bookshop was established in Kingston probably in the late 1830s and it lasted until about 1842.

After William Rowsell returned to England in October 1846, Henry's partners were Samuel THOMPSON, 1846–59, William Ellis, 1859–72, and Henry Hutchison, 1872–80. Rowsell devoted his attention largely to bookselling while his partners managed the printing and publishing end of the business. By about 1850 the firm was for a short time the most important publishing house in Canada West. It published a constant flow of pamphlets, tracts, annual reports, almanacs, directories, music books, school and university texts, legal and medical works, and books of general interest. The most ambitious undertaking was the publication, under the editorship of John MCCAUL, of the *Maple-Leaf; or Canadian Annual, a Literary Souvenir* (1847–49), an illustrated Canadian annual, described by Samuel Thompson in 1884 as "not since . . . surpassed, if equalled . . . in combined beauty and literary merit by any work that has issued from the Canadian Press." In *Rowsell's city of Toronto and county of York directory, for 1850–1 . . .* , Rowsell and Thompson are listed as "publishers to the University [of Toronto] and booksellers to the University and Upper Canada College." They also published the *Church*, an Anglican newspaper (1846–55), the *Patriot* (1849–53), the *British Colonial Magazine* (1853), the *British Colonist* (1853–57), and the *Canadian Ecclesiastical Gazette* (1854–62). As Rowsell and Ellis, the firm, while continuing as publisher to the Toronto synod of the Church of England, specialized in legal publications, including the *Upper Canada law and equity reports*.

Publishing seems always, however, to have been a secondary interest for Henry Rowsell who was primarily a bookseller. He was intent on making his bookstore the best in Toronto, and it became the favourite rendezvous of writers, scholars, sportsmen, and professional men, who were attracted not only by the large and varied stock but also by the courteous manner, wide book knowledge, and public spirit of the proprietor. At this period a publisher could build up sufficient capital to extend his publishing activity either by entering the wholesale book and stationery distribution business or by obtaining lucrative government printing contracts. James Campbell and Son, Copp, Clark Publishing Company, W. J. Gage, and others chose the former; John Lovell and Company and Hunter, Rose and Company chose the latter. Rowsell elected to stay in the retail book business. In addition to books, he regularly sold lithographic maps, prints, and pictures, and occasionally held art exhibits in his store. Rowsell published at least seven catalogues of his bookstock, advertising a wide range of books both general and specialized from British, American, and Canadian publishers.

Henry Rowsell retired in 1880, and for the next decade lived in seclusion in Toronto. Increasing deafness and loss of eyesight prevented him from taking part in the social activities which, like his business concerns, had won him respect. He left an estate of close to $50,000 with legacies to five grandchildren and to the Church of England. From 1880 until his own death in 1909, Henry Hutchison carried on the retail store and publishing house as Rowsell and Hutchison.

H. Pearson Gundy

[Henry Rowsell issued sales catalogues including the following held by MTL: *Rowsells' catalogue of books, January 1st, 1846* (Toronto, 1846); *Rowsell's catalogue of books, March, 1848* (Toronto, 1848); *Catalogue of books, for sale by Henry Rowsell, King Street, Toronto* (Toronto, 1852); *Catalogue of books, for sale by Henry Rowsell, King Street, Toronto* (Toronto, 1856); *1872–73 price list of university books, for sale by Rowsell & Hutchison* . . . ([Toronto, 1872]); *1873–4: a select catalogue of books for the young, adapted for presents, and for Sunday school prizes; for sale by Rowsell & Hutchinson* . . . ([Toronto, 1873]); and *1873–74 price list of university books, for sale by Rowsell & Hutchison* . . . ([Toronto, 1873]).

A few of his letters, all of minor importance, are in CTA, Toronto City Council papers (mfm. at AO). His last will and testament, probated 7 Aug. 1890 (no.8022), may be found in the York County Surrogate Court records (mfm. at AO). The Anglican Church of Canada, General Synod Arch. (Toronto) holds a typewritten transcript of Henry Rowsell's diary for the period 1 July 1835 to 11 July 1836. Much of the diary was published in F. N. Walker, *Sketches of old Toronto* (Toronto, 1965). Another diary, concerning mainly a trip to England in 1882–83, is held by UWO.

Samuel Thompson, *Reminiscences of a Canadian pioneer for the last fifty years: an autobiography* (Toronto, 1884; repub. Toronto and Montreal, 1968), includes information on the Rowsell brothers, and there is a brief but inaccurate biographical sketch in *Landmarks of Canada; what art has done for Canadian history* . . . (2v., Toronto, 1917–21; repr. in lv., 1967), no.3709. Advertisements of the Rowsell firm under its successive partnerships may be found in *Toronto directory*, 1837–80, and in the *British Colonist*, the *Canadian Family Herald*, the *Church*, and the *Patriot* of Toronto; in the *Canada Bookseller; Miscellany and Advertiser* (Toronto), 1872; and in the Kingston *Chronicle & Gazette* and *Daily News*. Many Rowsell imprints can be found in *Biblio. of Canadiana* (Staton and Tremaine) and *Biblio. of Canadiana: first supp*. (Boyle and Colbeck).

William Rowsell's return to England and the dissolution of the partnership are referred to in the *Church*, 11 Sept. 1846, the *Globe*, 15 Aug. 1850, and in the obituary notices for Henry Rowsell in the *Globe*, 30 July 1890, and in the *Canadian Churchman* (Toronto), 14 Aug. 1890. H.P.G.]

ROY, MARIE. *See* Fisbach

RUSSELL, ANDREW, surveyor and public servant; b. 29 June 1804 in Glasgow, Scotland, son of Alexander Russell and Janet (Jeanette) Jamieson; m. 16 May 1834 Lucy Chandler Lord, and they had three sons, two of whom became surveyors, and four daughters; d. 24 Feb. 1888 in Toronto and was buried in Ottawa, Ont.

Andrew Russell received his education in Glasgow before coming to Canada with his parents, sister, and brother Alexander Jamieson Russell in May 1822. The family settled in Leeds Township, Mégantic County, Lower Canada. In June 1829 Andrew was appointed superintendent of roads and settlement on crown lands in the county. He received a commission as surveyor of lands in Lower Canada in August 1830, and on 14 May of the following year he was named census commissioner for Mégantic County; he conducted the census taken there that year.

In November 1839 Russell was hired as a draftsman in the surveyor general's office in Lower Canada. Following union of the Canadas in February 1841, he became a surveyor and draftsman in the surveyor general's department, and then in 1842 senior surveyor and draftsman in the Canada West division of the surveying branch of the Crown Lands Department. At this time large areas of Canada West were being opened for settlement, and the senior surveyor had an important position, being responsible for preparing maps of the province, organizing surveys of public lands, and instructing surveyors as well as examining and reporting on their work and preserving their plans and reports. As head of the surveying branch he also examined candidates for licences as surveyors.

Under Russell's direction improvements were made in the system of surveying in Canada West. Before the union, surveying was done by compass; he instituted a system based on astronomical observation and during his tenure of office the transit theodolite replaced the compass in determining angles. Experiments were made in the method of laying out townships; the areas along the north shore of Lake Huron were surveyed in a system employed in the United States, with townships six miles square divided into 36 sections of one square mile and these subdivided into quarter sections.

Russell became assistant commissioner of crown lands in July 1857. The department had several branches dealing with many things: surveying; land claims; Jesuits' estates, the crown domain, and the seigneury of Lauson in Canada East; accounts; woods and forests; fisheries; ordnance lands; colonization roads in Canada West; and Indian lands. Although Russell seems to have exercised direct control over only those areas of the department's business with which the commissioner chose not to concern himself, he was involved in a movement towards consolidation of authority in the central office, which was resisted by the local agents who foresaw a reduction in their numbers. In 1862 Russell testified before a royal commission investigating the workings of the department and reported a lack of "well-ordered distribution of labour and responsibility." A modern study has noted that "shortcomings continued to plague the unwieldy Department until 1867." After confederation, when the Crown Lands Department was reorganized and divided by province, Russell assumed the position of assistant commissioner for Ontario. Suddenly, on 20 Aug. 1869, he was asked to resign by the commissioner, Stephen Richards*. Richards immediately replaced Russell with one of his own friends, Thomas Hall Johnson, gave no explanation for the dismissal, and made no charges of wrong-doing or incompetence against Russell. Russell was appointed resident agent for the sale of public lands in Wellington County, a position which happened to be vacant at the time.

He moved immediately from Toronto to Elora, but it was not with the intention of staying. In September 1869 he applied for a position in the land department of the northwest. He did move to Ottawa in 1870 where he was "engaged in the topographical labour" connected with the Canadian census of 1871. In March 1874 he joined the new Department of the Interior as chief clerk in the Dominion Lands Branch. The next year a board of examiners, consisting of the surveyor general of Canada and eight others, was established in May to examine applications for commissions as deputy land surveyor of dominion lands; Russell was appointed to this board the same year and served on it until January 1885. He retired from the Department of the Interior on 31 Dec. 1883. On this occasion the deputy minister of the department declared that "to him perhaps more than to any other man, living or dead, we owe the perfection which has been attained in our system of public land surveys."

Russell had been a long-time member of the Canadian Institute, serving on its council in 1858–59 and 1867–68 and as first vice-president in 1869–70. He was named an honorary member of the Association of Dominion Land Surveyors at the time of its first meeting in February 1884. The following March a group of its leading members called upon him to present him with an illuminated address expressing the esteem in which he was held for his "high standard of public morality, integrity and faultless character" and his substantial contribution to the development of the profession of surveying. "Rightly may we style you the Father of Astronomic Surveying in Canada and proud are we of so worthy a progenitor."

MARGARET COLEMAN

PAC, RG 68, 107: f.315; 108: f.424. Can., Parl., *Sessional papers*, 1875–86, Annual reports of the Dept. of the Interior, 1874–85; Prov. of, Legislative Assembly, *App. to the journals*, 1846, III, app.E.E.; 1854–55, X, app.M.M.; 1857–59, Reports of the commissioner of crown lands, 1856–58; Parl., *Sessional papers*, 1860–66, Reports of the commissioner of crown lands, 1859–65; February–May 1863, IV, no.11. *Globe*, 21, 25, 31 Aug. 1869; 25 Feb. 1888. *Cyclopædia of Canadian biog.* (Rose, 1886). Hodgetts, *Pioneer public service*. R. S. Lambert and Paul Pross, *Renewing nature's wealth; a centennial history of the public management of lands, forests & wildlife in Ontario, 1763–1967* ([Toronto], 1967).

RYAN, THOMAS, businessman, politician, and office-holder; b. 21 Aug. 1804 at Ballinakill (County Laois, Republic of Ireland); m. and had one son who died in 1866; m. secondly 4 Sept. 1871 in Fribourg, Switzerland, Wilhelmine-Dudding Perrault de Linière, *née* Montenach, granddaughter of Marie-Charles-Joseph Le Moyne* de Longueuil; d. 25 May 1889 in Montreal, Que.

Thomas Ryan's family had sufficient means to send him and his two brothers, Edward and John B.*, to the Jesuit college of Clonglowes Wood in County Kildare. Thomas attended from 1815 to 1822, after which he emigrated to Canada to enter into business with his brother Edward. Initially, the brothers maintained commercial ties with the Liverpool office of Baring Brothers, the large London-based mercantile-banking firm, and it is likely that consignments were shipped to Ryan Brothers and Company at Quebec City in the late 1820s. By 1838 the firm was actively soliciting business from Barings; in that year Thomas went to Dublin to establish a branch to deal with the import-export business of the company and he offered to act for Barings in Ireland. This undertaking seems to have been short-lived: Barings pulled out of Ireland and Ryan returned to Canada in the mid 1840s.

In Canada Ryan became the chief commercial correspondent for the London office of Barings. He had maintained his connections with Canada while in Ireland and his Quebec City business had handled tea imports from the Orient through Barings' London office. Ryan functioned as an agent for Barings, communicating much-needed information regarding commodity prices, duties, and freight and exchange rates, and advising them on such financial matters as the Montreal and Quebec municipal debenture issues in 1852 and 1853. He provided Barings with confidential information on firms applying to them for credit or commercial accounts. He also introduced certain businessmen to them, including, in 1852, Peter McGill [McCutcheon*], president of the Bank of Montreal, and John Ross*, a particularly good friend of Ryan's, who late in that year travelled to England to arrange for the financing of the Grand Trunk Railway.

In 1859 Barings, which had a large financial interest in the Grand Trunk, intended to use Ryan's knowledge of the commodity trade in North America to test the feasibility of the transportation route from Chicago to Boston through Canada. Approximately 10,000 barrels of flour were purchased in Chicago and sent on the Grand Trunk to Montreal and from there to Boston. The experiment failed: Barings barely escaped a substantial loss and shipments of flour from the Midwest continued to be sent by the traditional all-American route. The failure of this venture seems to have ended Ryan's commercial connection with Barings.

Ryan's role as informant for and confidant of Barings must have enhanced his position in the Canadian commercial élite. Ties to large British firms formed a vital component of the British imperial economic system and Ryan was connected with one of the world's largest financial houses. Other businessmen, including Francis HINCKS, had sought the Barings' agency in Canada, but Ryan remained the unofficial commercial agent until the late 1850s.

Ryan's involvement in business activities was extensive. By the mid 1840s he was a partner with Henry Chapman in Ryan, Chapman and Company, general merchants, in both Montreal and Quebec. Until its dissolution in 1852 the firm also acted as representatives for the Globe Insurance Company and Lloyd's of London. The company's successor, styled Ryan Brothers and Company, was a successful mercantile firm and received good credit ratings. Thomas and Edward were described in 1858 by R. G. Dun and Company as being "always spoken of as Substantial & Respectable People. They watch their bus[iness] closely, are never in trouble very cautious, close & careful." They further noted in 1860 that the popular elder brother, Edward, managed the business in Quebec City, and that Thomas, who managed the firm in Montreal and directed from there the operations of both offices, was "unmarried, queer & somewhat peculiar & inclined in his bus[iness] intercourse to be opinionative & overbearing."

By 1849 Thomas Ryan was operating steamboats along the St Lawrence River and the lower Great Lakes, probably in conjunction with his brother, John B. In 1853 Thomas was one of the incorporators of the Canadian Steam Navigation Company, in competition with Hugh ALLAN to obtain government subsidies for the transatlantic service. After its establishment in 1875 Ryan was, however, on the board of directors of the Richelieu and Ontario Navigation Company, an enterprise which Allan made into the largest and most successful shipping firm on the St Lawrence; at one time Ryan's investment in the company amounted to $45,000. Ryan remained a director until 11 Feb. 1882 when Louis-Adélard SENÉCAL assumed the presidency.

In addition to his shipping interests, Ryan served as a director of the Bank of Montreal from 1847 to 1881 and as the bank's vice-president from 1860 to 1873. A director of the Dominion Type Foundry Company, the North British and Mercantile Insurance Company, and the Montreal and Western Land Company, he was also among the incorporators of the Montreal Exchange in 1852, the Montreal City Passenger Railway in 1861, and the Chaudière Valley Railway Company and the Kennebec Gold Mining Company in 1864. Ryan had become a prominent figure in Montreal early in his career as was demonstrated by his election as president of the Montreal Board of Trade for 1849–50. He was also appointed lieutenant-colonel in the local militia. Between 1855 and 1861 he served as consul in Montreal for France, Denmark, Lubeck, Bremen, and Hamburg.

In 1863 Ryan was elected for Victoria division in the Legislative Council of the Province of Canada to replace Luther Hamilton Holton* who had resigned to seek a seat in the assembly. As a legislative councillor, Ryan was interested in questions affecting Canada's trade and in 1865 served on the mission which visited Brazil, Mexico, and the British West Indies in an effort to improve commerce with those regions. In the same year he acted as chairman of the Canadian representatives at the reciprocity convention in Detroit. During the confederation debates he strongly supported an appointed upper house of the federal legislature on the grounds that such a house, composed of representatives of a social group differing from that in the assembly, would effectively check the latter body. In October 1867 he was appointed to the Senate, where he took an active interest in legislation affecting shipping, banking, railways, copyright, and commerce.

Ryan was active in the Montreal Irish Catholic

community which during the 19th century was tightly knit and sharply focused on the pugnacious defence of religious and ethnic institutions. When in 1860 Bishop Ignace BOURGET attempted to change St Patrick's Church, which had been serving all of Montreal's Irish Catholics since 1847, into a canonical parish church for both French- and English-speaking residents of a smaller portion of the city, the parishioners objected. The infuriated Irishmen dispatched Ryan and Thomas D'Arcy McGee* to appeal directly to Rome. Although they were successful it was not until 1873 that the matter was settled to the satisfaction of the congregation. Ryan continued to represent Irish Catholic interests in Montreal, acting as a member of the Catholic committee of the Council of Public Instruction for the province of Quebec from 1869. Unlike many of his fellow Irish Catholics, Ryan, by the time of his death in 1889, had acquired influence in the community and achieved commercial success.

GERALD J. J. TULCHINSKY and ALAN R. DEVER

AC, Montréal, État civil, Catholiques, Saint-Antoine (Longueuil), 25 mai 1889. AO, MU 469, Ryan to Alexander Campbell, 21 Dec. 1871; MU 471, 26 Sept. 1872; MU 472, 1 Dec. 1872; MU 475, 9 June 1883. Baker Library, R. G. Dun & Co. credit ledger, Canada, 5: 79. PAC, MG 24, D21; RG 4, C2. QUA, Canada Steamship Lines Ltd records, La Compagnie du Richelieu, Dividend book, 1867–87; Richelieu and Ontario Navigation Company, Records. Can., Senate, *Debates*, 1871–84. *The case of St. Patrick's congregation, as to the erection of the new canonical parish of St. Patrick's, Montreal* (Montreal, 1866). *Gazette* (Montreal), 28 July 1866, 25 May 1889. *La Minerve*, 27 mai 1889. *Montreal Courier*, 26 Nov. 1849. *Montreal Daily Star*, 25 May 1889. *Montreal Herald and Daily Commercial Gazette*, 27 May 1889. *Montreal Witness*, 29 May 1889. *La Patrie*, 25 mai 1889. *Canadian directory of parl.* (J. K. Johnson). *CPC*, 1877. *Cyclopædia of Canadian biog.* (Rose, 1886), 581. *Political appointments, 1841–65* (J.-O. Coté). G. Turcotte, *Le Conseil législatif de Québec*, 290–91. Denison, *Canada's first bank*, II. *Golden jubilee of St. Patrick's Orphan Asylum: the work of Fathers Dowd, O'Brien and Quinlivan, with biographies and illustrations*, ed. J. J. Curran (Montreal, 1902), 4, 22, 41. S. E. C. Hart, "The elective Legislative Council in Canada under the union: its role in the political scene" (MA thesis, Queen's Univ., Kingston, Ont., 1960). R. W. Hidy, *The house of Baring in American trade and finance: English merchant bankers at work, 1763–1861* (Cambridge, Mass., 1949). Gerald Berry, "A critical period in St. Patrick's parish, Montreal, 1866–74," CCHA *Report*, 11 (1943–44): 117–28. Alexandre Jodoin, "La famille de Montenach," *BRH*, 6 (1900): 365–72. "Prominent figures in the Board's early history," *Journal of Commerce of Canada* (Gardenvale, Que.), 55 (1927), no.4: 26–27.

RYERSE, AMELIA (Harris), author and diarist; b. in February 1798 at Port Ryerse, Upper Canada, the daughter of Samuel Ryerse*, UEL, and Sarah Underhill; d. 19 March 1882 in London, Ont.

Amelia Ryerse's parents immigrated to Canada from the United States shortly after the American revolution, initially going to New Brunswick but finally settling at Long Point, Norfolk County, Upper Canada, in 1794. Her formal education appears to have been limited to attendance for one or more years in a school at Niagara Falls prior to 1812. Amelia's father, who had commanded a company of New Jersey volunteers in the Revolutionary War, was placed in charge of the Norfolk County militia shortly after his arrival in Upper Canada, and subsequently was appointed lieutenant-colonel and lieutenant of the county. In 1810 he resigned these and his other offices because of illness; he died of tuberculosis in June 1812. In May 1814 American troops attacked the Ryerse farm and burned all the buildings except the main house.

On 28 June 1815 Amelia married John Harris, a master in the Royal Navy whom she had known less than six weeks. Tradition has it that she and another 17-year-old girl were among the settlers who had met a boat from a naval reconnaissance survey of the harbour between Long Point and Turkey Point, on which Harris was serving, and that, pointing to him, Amelia said, "There is the man I shall marry." A fortnight after the wedding Harris was advised by Sir Edward Campbell Rich Owen that he had been assigned to a hydrographic survey of the Great Lakes under Captain William Fitz William Owen*. Harris was based in Kingston and during the next two years, until he retired on half pay on 1 Sept. 1817, Amelia presided over domestic affairs at the headquarters of the survey, which served as the residence for the officers; she was also involved in the preparation of draft maps of the surveyed areas. In 1817 John, Amelia, and their first child took up residence near Port Ryerse, on land which Amelia acquired as the daughter of a loyalist. They remained there until 1834 when they moved to Eldon House in London. John had been treasurer of the London District since 1821 and, after district headquarters were moved from Vittoria to London in 1826, residence in London was more convenient for him than commuting.

After her husband's death in 1850 Amelia concentrated on her family. By 1859 it was established. Her three sons were lawyers. All of her seven surviving daughters were well married, six of them to Englishmen, including four officers in the British regiments which had been stationed in London, and this widespread family corresponded constantly in letters still preserved. In 1857 her eldest son, John, spent the summer in England and his mother wrote to him weekly. There is evidence that Amelia fell into the habit of making daily notes in the preparation of these letters and that this led to her commencing a diary on 12 Sept. 1857. She continued it for almost 25 years, to within weeks of her death, and entries are missing for only 325 of the almost 9,000 days covered. The most serious gap, for about four months during a serious illness in 1861, is compensated for by the fact that her daughter-in-law, Sophia Howard (the daughter of Egerton RYERSON), who was living in Eldon House during this period, also kept a diary from 1 Sept. 1860 to 31 Dec. 1861.

The chief value of Amelia's diary is literary rather than historical or sociological. Nevertheless, since Eldon House was a social centre a considerable number of the members of London's leading families appear in its pages, as well as prominent personages including Edward Blake*, George Brown*, John A. Macdonald*, and Egerton Ryerson. In conjunction with her letters, and those written by other members of the family, it provides a detailed portrait of a well-to-do 19th-century family. However, its real importance derives from its author's consistent point of view about the events she chronicles, the clarity and objectivity of her analysis of character, as well as the dramatic fashion in which she succeeds in presenting seemingly prosaic events; the resemblance to the work of Jane Austen is striking. Despite Amelia's sparse formal education she was extremely well read in English literature, history, and theology and had a first-rate mind. Her abilities are evident not only throughout her diary and letters but also in her other major literary project.

In 1861, at the request of her cousin Egerton Ryerson, she wrote "historical memoranda" describing her father's immigration and his subsequent activities until 1810. She extended the narrative in 1879 to cover the period to May 1814 and this account included reports on her birth and early life as well as the attack on the farm. The revised essay was included in Ryerson's *The loyalists of America*. In the view of Charles Bruce Sissons*, "these thirty pages serve to brighten the dutiful narrative of Ryerson's second volume and present as factual and interesting an account of the early settlement of Upper Canada as is anywhere to be found."

ROBIN S. HARRIS

Amelia Ryerse was the author of "Historical memoranda by Mrs. Amelia Harris, of Eldon House, London, Ontario . . . ," published in Egerton Ryerson, *The loyalists of America and their times: from 1620 to 1816* (2nd ed., 2v., Toronto and Montreal, 1880; repr. New York, 1970), II: 228–56; the memoranda were reprinted in *Loyalist narratives from Upper Canada*, ed. J. J. Talman (Toronto, 1946), 109–48. The diaries of Amelia Ryerse are held at UWO.

[Egerton Ryerson], *My dearest Sophie; letters from Egerton Ryerson to his daughter*, ed. C. B. Sissons (Toronto, 1955), xxxiii–xxxvi. R. [S.] Harris, "The beginnings of the hydrographic survey of the Great Lakes and the St. Lawrence River," *Historic Kingston*, no.14 (1965): 24–39. L. H. Tasker, "The United Empire Loyalist settlement at Long Point, Lake Erie," *OH*, 2 (1900).

RYERSON, EGERTON (his complete given name was **Adolphus Egerton** but he never used the first), Methodist minister, author, editor, and educational administrator; b. 24 March 1803 in Charlotteville Township, Norfolk County, Upper Canada, fifth son of Joseph Ryerson* and Mehetable Stickney; m. first 10 Sept. 1828 Hannah Aikman (d. 1832) at Hamilton, Upper Canada, and they had two children; m. secondly 8 Nov. 1833 Mary Armstrong at York (Toronto), Upper Canada, and they had two children; d. 19 Feb. 1882 at Toronto.

Two circumstances in Egerton Ryerson's early life exercised a lasting influence on his career. One was the loyalist environment in which he grew up. His father, Joseph, and his uncle Samuel Ryerse*, both American born, had served as loyalist officers in the American revolution and afterwards had fled north to New Brunswick before moving to Upper Canada in the 1790s. As a half-pay officer Joseph had received a substantial land grant and established his family on a farm near Vittoria, the first capital of the London District. Appointed to a series of important local offices, both Joseph and Samuel became part of the loyalist establishment in the district while members of their families married into other leading loyalist clans in the area. Joseph and his three eldest sons all served against the Americans in the War of 1812. Egerton, too young to be actively involved, saw a brother badly wounded and the destruction of lands and property belonging to friends and relatives. Among the Ryerson family, memories of pioneering a new land and defending it, of principles sustained and loyalty reaffirmed, would breed a deep and abiding attachment to both their native land and the maintenance of the British connection in North America.

The second great formative influence was evangelical Christianity. Like so many of his generation Ryerson was touched early in life by the wave of Protestant revivalism that swept North America in the late 18th and early 19th centuries. The Ryerson children were raised by a devout mother of Methodist sympathies who taught them a personal and vital form of Christian belief and her precepts were reinforced by the Methodist circuit-riders who criss-crossed Norfolk County during Egerton's childhood. Some time immediately after the War of 1812, according to his own account, Egerton, like three of his elder brothers, "became deeply religious. . . . My consciousness of guilt and sinfulness was humbling, oppressive and distressing; and my experience of relief, after lengthened fastings, watching and prayers, was clear, refreshing and joyous. In the end I simply trusted in Christ, and looked to Him for a present salvation. . . ." In 1816 his mother and two of his older brothers joined the Methodist Church. His Anglican father was "extremely opposed" to the Methodists and when at 18 Egerton applied for membership in the local Methodist society he was told "you must either leave them or leave my house." Egerton took the latter course. The rift lasted for two years and was repaired only when the father acquiesced in his son's convictions. The episode reveals something of the determination and impetuosity characteristic of Ryerson all his life. It also reveals the depth of his "conversion" experience. From the time he was a young man Ryerson's personal odyssey was defined by his determination "never to rest contented until he [Christ] becomes not only my wisdom, but my sanctification and my full redemption." Loyalism and Methodism would form the warp and woof of Ryerson's life and thought throughout his long career.

Ryerson's family was sufficiently well off to enable him to take advantage of the limited educational facilities available at the time. Most of his schooling took place under James Mitchell at the London District Grammar School in Vittoria. Between 1821 and 1823 he served as an assistant to his brother GEORGE, who was master in the school. During these years Ryerson absorbed the essentials of an English and classical education and was also introduced to two works that would become lasting influences – William Paley's *Principles of moral and political philosophy* and Sir William Blackstone's *Commentaries.* In August 1824, perhaps with the intention of becoming a lawyer, Ryerson went to Hamilton to study with John Law at the Gore District Grammar School.

After only a few months' study in Hamilton, Ryerson's formal education was ended by a prolonged illness in the winter of 1824–25. During his recovery he became convinced that he had been preserved from death to serve God's purpose as a Methodist minister. He irrevocably accepted God's call on 24 March 1825, his 22nd birthday, and preached his first sermon at Beamsville on Easter Sunday of that year. Thus Egerton became one of five Ryerson boys to enter the Methodist ministry: he followed in the footsteps of William* and John* as George, the eldest, and Edway (Edwy) Marcus, the youngest, would follow in his. Formally received on trial in September 1825 by the Canada Conference, the governing body of the Methodist Episcopal Church in Upper Canada, Egerton served his apprenticeship on the York and Yonge Street circuit and then as a missionary among the Indians at the Credit River. In September 1827 he was admitted to full connection and ordained. He spent the next two years assigned to the Cobourg and Ancaster circuits.

During these years the rigorous routine of a travelling preacher's life was interrupted by two diversions that would put Ryerson's name before a much wider audience than any Methodist circuit could offer. In 1826 a sermon, delivered the previous summer at the funeral of Bishop Jacob Mountain* by John Strachan*, appeared in print; in it Strachan, the leading Church of England clergyman in Upper Canada, traced the rise of the Anglican church in the colony, contending that it was the established church and attacking the Methodists as ignorant American enthusiasts, unsound in religion and disloyal in politics. None of the arguments were new, but on this occasion the Methodists in York chose not to remain silent and Ryerson, still a probationary preacher, was one of those invited to frame a reply. In a long letter printed in the *Colonial Advocate* (York) in May 1826 he challenged all of Strachan's assertions. No less than Strachan himself, Ryerson sought a society that was both Christian and British. But he denied that an established church was either scriptural or an essential part of the British constitution, and quoted authors ancient and modern to support his case. He rejected the charges of ignorance by citing the intellectual training required of all Methodist preachers and also challenged the contention that most of them were Americans. Ryerson's letter and the ensuing debate in the provincial press "thrilled the Methodist mind in the country," in the words of John Saltkill CARROLL, and called attention to Ryerson's remarkable abilities as a spokesman for the Methodist cause. In 1827 Strachan again put forward his claims in a series of letters written in England to garner support for both the Church of England and the colony's newly chartered university. In the public uproar that followed, Ryerson was only one critic among many, but in eight clearly reasoned and broad-ranging letters, published first in the *Upper Canada Herald* (Kingston) in June 1828 and later that year as a pamphlet, he again defended the character of Methodism, argued the case for religious equality, and broadened his attack to include the educational policies of what he claimed to be an Anglican-dominated executive.

His forays against Strachan brought Ryerson to the centre of Methodist affairs. In 1829 he was elected by conference as the first editor of the new Methodist newspaper, the *Christian Guardian.* Over the next decade he would be its dominant editorial voice, responsible for the paper from the first issue in November 1829 until August 1832, from October 1833 until June 1835, and again from June 1838 until June 1840. A large Methodist constituency and Ryerson's own editorial talents made the *Guardian* one of the most widely read and politically influential papers in the colony. From the beginning it reflected not only the temporal but also the spiritual concerns of Ryerson's own life. One subsidiary object of the paper, he wrote in 1830, was "to support and vindicate religious and civil rights"; but the paper's principal purpose was to promote " practical Christianity – to teach men how to live and how to die." Serving also as book steward for 1829–32 and 1833–35, Ryerson established a book room and helped lay the foundations of a flourishing publishing establishment which eventually became the Ryerson Press.

During the early 1830s Ryerson was involved in

another important aspect of the institutional development of his church. In 1832, at the invitation of the colonial administration, the politically conservative British Wesleyans decided to expand their own work into Upper Canada. Colonial Methodists were divided over the appropriate response. Although some objected to any cooperation at all, the majority of conference, led by John Ryerson, voted to support a union between the two churches in order to avoid wasteful duplication and open conflict and to disprove the continuing charges of American sympathies. Egerton vigorously supported this policy in the *Guardian* and within conference, and was selected to go to England to complete the negotiations with the English conference as well as to lay a variety of Methodist interests before the Colonial Office. He returned to Upper Canada in September 1833. Just 30 years of age, fresh from his first trip abroad and the successful representation of his church in Britain, and re-elected editor of the *Guardian*, Ryerson had begun to establish himself, in Carroll's words, as the Methodists' "leader in all public questions."

The style and character of the man had also begun to take permanent shape. Summarizing contemporary opinion, Charles Bruce Sissons* concludes that Ryerson was a competent rather than an outstanding preacher. The basis for his public reputation would lie in the written rather than the spoken word. At his best Ryerson could write prose laced with vigorous rhetoric, flashes of wit, and powerful imagery. He could also, particularly as he grew older, be long-winded and pontifical, his prose weighted down by endless quotations and irrelevant appeals to the history of any subject from time immemorial. His style was shaped by the Methodist homiletics of the day and encompassed the best and the worst of the genre.

To his many friends and admirers Ryerson was a generous, warm, kind, inspiring man, "trusting and trustworthy," endowed with "grand qualities of mind and heart." Others, particularly those who ran afoul of him in controversy, did not share this opinion. In his younger days Ryerson was generally careful to distinguish between the personalities and the arguments of his opponents. As editor of the *Guardian* he did not routinely indulge in the character assassination and innuendo typical of contemporary colonial journalism. Yet he was also acutely sensitive to slights or imputations about his own character and principles, and when provoked could descend into excesses of personal abuse unbecoming in a clergyman and public figure. These tendencies increased as he grew older so that even a sympathetic contemporary observer was led to remark that "both in writing and in debate he is not very choice of the means by which he abolishes an opponent, so long as it is done." His was not a singular failing in mid-19th-century Canada and in many instances Ryerson had a strong claim to just cause. None the less he himself recognized it as a flaw. "I have," he told his daughter, Mrs Sophia Howard Harris, in 1870, "written and printed many things that I afterwards very much regretted. For many years I have been accustomed to keep for a day or a week what I have written, before committing it to press."

When he believed it to be necessary Ryerson could rethink his positions and make tactical compromises but his reluctance to admit such shifts publicly left him open to recurring charges of disingenuousness and hypocrisy. Such assessments were also encouraged by a strain of self-righteousness in his personality. Though his diaries and private letters often reveal him struggling with self-doubt, his public demeanour bespoke great assurance that his designs and God's were one. Thomas Dalton* was one of the first of Ryerson's contemporaries who captured this trait when he wrote in 1834 that Ryerson "pretends to be Heaven's Lord Chancellor, and consequently the depository of all the secrets of that high court."

Throughout his life Ryerson was a relentless worker. He could call up enormous reserves of energy, endurance, and discipline – products of his early labours on his father's farm, the physical rigours of a circuit-rider's life, and above all, the conviction that he must be a worthy steward of the time God gave him. He was also a constant student. He was forever learning a new language: Ojibwa at the Credit River mission, Hebrew in his spare time in the early 1840s, French and German on his trips to the Continent. The core of his religious and social thought had been shaped by rigorous study of the scriptures and the great Methodist divines: Wesley himself, Adam Clarke, and Richard Watson. He was also an avid reader of the classics of British and European history and political thought, and the "serious" contemporary literature such as the great English quarterlies. On any subject he chose he could command a remarkable variety of sources and quotations. His persistent interest in secular knowledge and in contemporary cultural and political affairs tempered the asperities of a faith that in other men could breed a disdain for temporal things or even an outright anti-intellectualism. On the other hand his secular interests, reinforced and justified by his religious convictions, also drew him into the political conflicts that haunted the colony in the 1830s and 1840s to a degree that, amongst Upper Canadian clergymen, was matched only by his great antagonist, John Strachan.

As pamphleteer and editor between 1826 and 1832 Ryerson had gradually become associated in the public mind with those who identified themselves as political Reformers. It was a natural alliance at the time, for many of the issues that galvanized Reformers were also those of most concern to Methodist leaders: the disposition of the clergy reserves, the right to solemnize marriages, the control of many of the educational institutions by the Church of England, and a number of similar issues affecting denominational equality.

Ryerson's spirited editorial attacks on Anglican ascendancy, his leading role in organizing and drafting the petition of the Friends of Religious Liberty in December 1830 [*see* Jesse Ketchum*], and his denunciation in 1831 of the attack by Sir John Colborne* on the Methodists for political meddling, all seemed to identify him not just as a leading Methodist but as a leading Reformer as well. Thus it was not surprising that in 1832 a Tory mob in Peterborough, looking for symbols of reform on which to vent their anger, set fire to effigies of both William Lyon Mackenzie* and Ryerson.

When Ryerson returned from England in the autumn of 1833, however, he struck an unexpected theme. In the first of a series of "Impressions of England," published in the *Guardian*, he attacked as infidel, republican, and anti-Methodist, radical leaders such as Joseph Hume and John Arthur Roebuck* who were close allies of Canadian Reformers. At the same time he praised the English "moderate Tories" among whom were to be found "a considerable portion of the *evangelical clergy* and, we think, a majority of Wesleyan Methodists." Their political prudence, "genuine liberality and religious beneficence," he concluded, "claim respect and imitation." The "Impressions" caused a political uproar. To friends and enemies alike Ryerson appeared to reverse direction and commit himself to Toryism. The Reform press had a field-day at his expense, condemning him as an apostate and traitor, and many of his Methodist brethren concurred. To Ryerson himself, however, the change was one of emphasis, not principle. His passionate recitals of the grievances of Upper Canada had in fact masked an intellectual temper that was profoundly loyalist and conservative.

Two central convictions, shaped by his early life and by his reading of Blackstone, Paley, Wesley, Clarke, and Watson, formed the core of his political thought. First, he revered the body of constitutional theory and practice developed in Britain since 1688 and inherited, he believed, by Upper Canadians through the Constitutional Act of 1791. To Ryerson, civil institutions were among the means established by God to enable man to seek sanctification in this life and everlasting happiness with God in the next. No system of government designed by man was better suited to serve these purposes than the British constitution. By providing institutional bulwarks against arbitrary rule, it protected the civil and religious liberties of the subject and, through petitions to parliament and appeals to the crown, it furnished the means of seeking redress of grievances. Because of its mixed nature – its incorporation of king, lords, and commons (in the colony, governor, council, and assembly) – it provided the mechanism to balance and reconcile the different interests of society and thereby secure good government for the whole community. Wise policy, Ryerson would repeatedly say, not only arose from but also ensured "both the prerogatives and due influence of the Crown, and the constitutional rights of the people."

The second fundamental principle that shaped his political thought was the importance of the imperial tie. Given his warm attachment to British institutions, all proposals for outright independence were anathema. At the same time he believed that the imperial authority and its local representatives must be responsive to local interests and circumstances. Thus Ryerson, like so many others of his generation, had to come to grips with a proposition that, on the face of it, seemed absurd: Upper Canada could be both self-governing and a colony. If some believed that sentiment alone could keep separatist tendencies in check, many others, Ryerson included, did not. To him, the "responsible government" of Robert Baldwin* was but a first step to independence. Its logic was to destroy the mixed constitution by eliminating the independent prerogative of the crown, the most palpable link between colony and parent state. So long as the imperial government was broadly responsive to public opinion, preserved the right of appeal for redress, and followed existing constitutional usages in dealing with the colony, Ryerson would oppose any innovations that threatened to weaken the imperial tie or modify the constitution inherited by the colony.

From the late 1820s until the mid 1840s Ryerson would attempt to govern his political course in accordance with these two principles. It was not an easy task. It would lead him from one side of the political spectrum to the other and back again, and leave him open to charges of political opportunism that, in the eyes of many Upper Canadians though not in his own, were difficult to refute.

By late 1833, when he published "Impressions," Ryerson had become convinced that the main enemy was the Reform movement, not the administration. He did not dispute the fact that Upper Canadians still had justifiable complaints but, he argued, appeals to the crown and the imperial parliament were bringing redress. In particular, the royal dispatches of 1832 and 1833 had led Lieutenant Governor Colborne to modify many of the partisan policies of the previous decade. To Ryerson, in other words, the cause of Reform had been largely won. Of course Methodists had changed their tune, he would reply to his critics in 1835, "and for a simple and sufficient reason, the administration of government towards them has been essentially changed." The Reformers, on the other hand, were seeking no longer to remedy real grievances but to introduce organic changes in the constitution. Thus, with the same energy he had exerted on behalf of Reform in the early 1830s, by mid decade Ryerson had thrown himself into the defence of existing authority.

Ryerson was absent from Upper Canada from November 1835 to June 1837, having been sent by conference to England as part of an attempt to put the affairs of the Methodists' new academy at Cobourg in order. Begun with the greatest optimism in the early 1830s, Upper Canada Academy was in the most desperate financial straits by mid decade. It was Ryerson's job to obtain a royal charter for it and, more importantly, to travel throughout Britain soliciting money for its support. Both tasks proved difficult but the latter was the more painful: to be a stranger and to have to beg, he confided to his diary, was "the most disagreeable of all employments." He obtained the charter, none the less, and promises of financial support from British Wesleyans and the imperial government. Though away from home during these months, he continued to be a force in Upper Canadian politics, writing lengthy letters to the *Christian Guardian* and to English newspapers criticizing the Reformers and defending the policies of Lieutenant Governor Sir Francis Bond Head*.

Ryerson ended 1837 with a blistering sermon condemning those who had participated in the rebellion. He himself, however, was already beginning to have second thoughts about Head's administration. It was one thing to defend the existing constitution against "republican" or "democratic" radicalism but quite another to tolerate arbitrary rule. Despite the clearly expressed will of the crown and the assembly, the Legislative Council had refused to approve a loan to Upper Canada Academy in 1837 – a scandalous departure, Ryerson argued, from constitutional precedent. A Tory legislature appeared to be attempting once more to place the clergy reserves in Anglican hands. In the wake of the rebellion civil liberties were being trampled upon and early in 1838 the case of Marshall Spring Bidwell*, who had been forced into exile at the whim of the lieutenant governor, roused Ryerson to issue a ringing public denunciation of the authorities and a defence of the constitutional rights of the subject. In Ryerson's view Head's successor, Sir George Arthur*, brought no improvement; indeed Arthur seemed determined to sustain all of the most objectionable pretensions of traditional colonial Toryism. From June 1838, when Ryerson returned as editor of the *Guardian*, his energies were again directed towards attacking the policies of the local executive and its supporters inside and outside the legislature. Once more he had entered the camp of the anti-government alliance.

It was in these circumstances that Ryerson was temporarily converted to the constitutional proposals of Lord Durham [Lambton*]. To those who recalled with some glee his earlier opposition to colonial cabinet responsibility he replied in June 1839 that "the history of the last three years" had proved that no other means existed to ensure a just and equitable local administration. By the end of 1840, however, Ryerson had returned to more familiar ground. In Lord Sydenham [Thomson*], who was determined to form a broad party of moderate opinion, to treat all denominations equally, and to be responsive to public opinion while at the same time preserving the prerogatives of the crown, Ryerson believed he had found the patriot governor who could implement "truly liberal conservative policy" and thus sustain the mixed constitution in the colonial setting. When Sydenham died in 1841 Ryerson wrote an obituary that heaped encomium upon encomium. At its heart was an expression of his own most fervent wish for the province: "his Lordship has solved the difficult problem, that a people may be colonists and yet be free."

In June 1840 Ryerson ended his last stint as editor of the *Guardian* and was assigned to a pastorate in Toronto. He remained, however, a central figure in Methodist affairs. A number of issues had begun to divide Canadian and British Wesleyans in the late 1830s, raising doubts about the value of the union into which they had entered in 1833. One of these was the editorial policy of the *Guardian*, which members of the British conference felt Ryerson had made into "a political and party organ" of colonial radicalism. Though Ryerson was sustained by large majorities at conference, clashes over this and other matters of policy led to the dissolution of the union in 1840. Egerton and his brother William were appointed delegates to the British conference and spent the summer of 1840 in England negotiating the details of separation. In the following year Egerton was selected as the first principal of Victoria College, the successor to Upper Canada Academy, though he was not formally inducted into the post until June 1842. He remained principal until 1847 but his active role in the college was short-lived. In 1844 he took up a new post as a government administrator and, at the same time, became involved in one of the most celebrated political conflicts in Upper Canadian history.

In November 1843, because of a dispute over control of patronage, Governor Sir Charles Theophilus Metcalfe*'s Reform ministers had resigned from office. In the next few months Metcalfe and his new chief minister in Canada West, William Henry Draper*, began to search for a base of support in the leading moderates of both parties and all denominations. Among those consulted for general advice was Ryerson and, most probably in January 1844, consultation turned into a more positive offer of a place in the administration.

It is not difficult to see why Metcalfe wanted Ryerson. An appointment for Ryerson would disprove charges that he was too partial to Anglicans and high Tories and would favourably influence the large Methodist vote. Ryerson was on close terms with other political moderates and his accession might bring their support as well. A place on the council itself was, however, out of the question. Ryerson did not want an unequivocally political appointment and Draper discovered that it was not possible in any case. Thus Ryerson was offered the post of superintendent of schools for Canada West, which was not formally political; his acceptance would, however, signify his support for the ministry.

Why Ryerson himself was tempted by the offer is another question. Certainly he believed that at stake was a major constitutional issue upon which men must declare themselves. Moreover, he had always thought that an effective system of national education was one of the highest goals of practical, liberal policy and he was no doubt deeply attracted by the chance to play a role in promoting its development. But there may have been other reasons as well. On two previous occasions in the early 1840s he had expressed an interest in becoming involved in primarily secular projects and it may have been that Ryerson was somewhat restless in these years and eager to test his talents in a wider sphere than that afforded by Upper Canadian Methodism alone.

He may also have been tempted by the new political atmosphere of the years after 1840. The many leading politicians of the decade with whom he was on close personal terms accorded him a degree of respect he had not received from an earlier generation of Upper Canadian notables. Moreover, whatever their differences on particular issues, Ryerson's vision of the future development of Canadian society had much in common with that of such men as Draper and Francis HINCKS. They were ready to recognize the legitimate interests of Methodists and other dissenters within the body politic, they were men of the centre who rejected the extremes of either radicalism or Toryism, and their concern for economic development and the modernization of public services and institutions was as great as their commitment to the preservation of a distinct British-American society. In other words, Ryerson may have been attracted to the job because he believed that politics and policy were moving in more congenial and promising directions than in the conflict-ridden decade of the 1830s. In any case and for whatever reasons, Ryerson accepted Metcalfe's offer in early 1844, though his appointment was not formally announced until September.

Apparently Metcalfe and Draper had asked only that Ryerson agree to serve as superintendent of common schools. It seems to have been Ryerson himself who proposed that he also step into the public arena in defence of the governor. He did so in part because he thought that his appointment was at risk unless the ministry was sustained by the electorate. But his behaviour was also fully in character. For Ryerson it was never enough to stand up and be counted; he had to smite the enemy hip and thigh as well. Thus he set about writing *Sir Charles Metcalfe defended against the attacks of his late counsellors*, published first as a series of letters in the *British Colonist* (Toronto) in the late spring and early summer of 1844 and later that year as a pamphlet of some 165 pages.

Though the letters ranged widely over British and colonial constitutional and political history and included a variety of arguments favourable to Metcalfe's position, Ryerson focused on the patronage question. The Reform ministry, he argued, proposed to use patronage to strengthen the grip of extreme partyism on the country. This in itself was dangerous enough, for partyism prized partisanship and factionalism over independent judgement and the public interest, and rewarded loyalty rather than merit. In this respect the Reformers were reviving all the evils of Family Compact rule when patronage had been used for the benefit of a faction and a sect rather than the community as a whole. But more importantly, by attempting to control patronage, the Reform ministers were attacking the British connection itself: to put the control of patronage primarily in the hands of the council was to undermine the independent authority of the governor and thereby fatally weaken the link with the crown. To accede to such a principle would give Canada "Responsible Government in a sense that would make the Crown a 'tool' in the hands of a party; or in a sense, as the Imperial Government emphatically declare, would make '*Canada an independent republic.*' " Thus the duty of the people of Canada in the present crisis was clear: to sustain the kind of responsible government which had been established by Sydenham, which was approved by the imperial government, "*AND WHICH SIR CHARLES METCALFE HAS MOST EXPLICITLY AND FULLY AVOWED.*"

The Metcalfe ministry won the elections of 1844 for many reasons, though no doubt Ryerson's "Defence" and the loyalty cry he helped to raise played a part in influencing moderate opinion. His appointment to an important public position may also have influenced Methodist voters for it represented a long-delayed recognition of their importance and their claims to full membership in Upper Canadian society. The affair also won Ryerson the lasting enmity of some Reformers, George Brown* amongst them, and a recurring epithet, "Leonidas," for Ryerson's smug comparison of his own role in 1844 with that of the hero of Thermopylæ. Ryerson himself left Canada West in October 1844 for his first tour of educational establishments in Britain and on the Continent, and did not return until December 1845. In the following year, working closely with Draper, he began the task of reorganizing the structure of elementary education in the colony.

He could not, however, detach himself immediately from the political role he had played in 1844. He had publicly allied himself with Metcalfe and with

Draper's Conservative ministry. Upon the victory of the Reformers in the elections of 1847–48 it was commonly rumoured that Ryerson would be replaced as superintendent of schools. He survived for several reasons. Impressed by his competence, Lord Elgin [Bruce*] gave Ryerson his full support against those who wished to dismiss him for political reasons. Ryerson also had warm allies within the ministry, such as William Hamilton Merritt*, and influential admirers within the party. Above all, Francis Hincks, worried about the Methodist vote, was prepared to bury the political enmity of the mid 1840s. By late 1849 Ryerson had prevailed. His chief enemy in the ministry, Malcolm Cameron*, had resigned, new school legislation that undercut Ryerson's position had been set aside, and Ryerson had been invited to remain in office and to prepare a revised school bill incorporating the experience of his four years as superintendent. The way was now clear for him to begin the most significant phase of his life's work.

Ryerson's main preoccupation in the two decades after 1850 was to give form and substance to his vision of the appropriate system of education for Canada West. That vision had been taking shape for years, derived in equal parts from the lessons of scripture and Methodist theology, from his reading of the early 19th-century debates in Britain and America about the importance of popular education, from his participation in the editorial warfare over educational policy in Upper Canada, and from his study of other school systems during his tour of Europe in 1844–45. Though Ryerson wrote voluminously about education throughout his public life, his ideas were expressed most fully and systematically in his *Report on a system of public elementary instruction for Upper Canada*, written after his return from Europe.

At the heart of his educational ideas lay his Christian faith. Next to religion itself, he believed, education was the great agent of God's purpose for man. Carried out in a Christian context, education promoted virtue and usefulness in this world and union with God in the next. Because it made good and useful individuals it was also a key agent in supporting the good society, inasmuch as it helped to promote social harmony, self-discipline, and loyalty to properly constituted authority. To Ryerson it was the duty of education to develop "all the intellectual powers of man, teach him self-reliance as well as dependence on God, excite him in industry and enterprise, and instruct him in his rights as well as the duties of man."

From these principles Ryerson drew his particular goals. First and foremost, a system of education must be Christian: a secular education was a danger to the child and the society as well as a denial of God's message to mankind. Secondly, in order to have its intended effects on all children, schooling must be universal. A truly national system must also be "extensive" or "comprehensive": it must meet the needs of all ranks and vocations by providing both elementary and advanced institutions of education. As well the system must be both British and Canadian. The schools had a duty to uphold the British tie and respect for British constitutional government, and at the same time to foster local patriotism and serve the particular needs and circumstances of Upper Canada's social and economic life. Finally, the system must be the active concern of government. As an ordinance of God "designed by the Supreme Being 'to be a minister of God for good' to a whole people," government had a duty to sustain and encourage those institutions which promoted the temporal and eternal welfare of its citizens. These were the goals Ryerson would pursue in his remarkably long career as superintendent of education in the upper province.

When Ryerson first took office in 1844 there were already more than 2,500 elementary schools in Canada West: financed by a combination of government grants, property taxation, and tuition fees; run by locally elected boards of education; and supervised and coordinated, though in a somewhat ineffective way, by an established central Education Office. Ryerson, in other words, did not create a school system; he inherited one. Throughout his career, moreover, his success was in large part the product of a climate of opinion highly favourable to his aims. Politicians, editors, and other public figures of all religious and political persuasions were sympathetic to the expansion of schooling. School boards and taxpayers provided most of the financial and political support at the local level and imposed broad limits within which central policy could operate. Thus system-building was a cooperative venture rather than the sole achievement of any one individual. More than anyone else, however, it was Ryerson who gave the emerging system its particular shape and character. Between 1844 and 1876 he was involved in a multitude of projects, ranging from the drafting of his major school legislation of 1846, 1850, and 1871 to writing school textbooks, promoting school libraries, and creating a museum of art and science. But his four major achievements were the creation of conditions which made universal access to elementary education possible, the promotion of improvements in the quality of the school programme, changes in the function and character of the grammar schools, and the establishment of an effective administrative structure.

He sought universality and improved quality in several ways. In a period when much of the province was still being settled Ryerson provided the legislative and financial devices that enabled even new, small communities to provide schools for themselves. He also led the campaign, which culminated in the Schools Act of 1871, to make every elementary school tuition-free and to introduce Ontario's first tentative measure of compulsory attendance. For Ryerson, however, it was not enough to ensure that the rudiments alone were universally available. Through exhortation and regulation he tried to make certain that the programme of studies extended well beyond the "three Rs" so that the elementary schools not only began but completed all of the schooling most children and their parents would want or need. He tried to ensure that textbooks were pedagogically sound and reflected the political, social, and religious values he believed should underpin Upper Canadian society. Finally, he did what he could to promote improved teaching. In 1847 he established the first teacher-training institution and he constantly attempted to set progressively higher standards for the certification of elementary school teachers.

Ryerson's achievement with respect to the grammar schools was twofold. First, by persuading the politicians and the public to accept the principle that grammar schools should have access to local taxation, he put these institutions on a sound financial footing for the first time in their history and transformed them into unequivocally public institutions. Secondly, he attempted to turn the grammar schools into effective secondary schools. By the gradual introduction of an entrance examination and a prescribed curriculum that clearly delimited the functions of elementary and grammar schools, he linked these institutions hierarchically. At the same time, he attempted to ensure that the grammar schools would offer a high-quality, broadly based education, consisting of English, mathematics, and classical studies, to that minority of students continuing beyond the elementary level.

By creating an effective administrative system for his own department, Ryerson became a member of that small group of pioneer public servants who, in J. E. Hodgetts' words, made responsible government "a working reality." He established a strong central authority and a system of local inspection designed to ensure that provincial policy could be implemented and enforced. His own daily routine was dominated by an immense volume of correspondence generated by the problems of institution-building at the local level – correspondence that required him to write hundreds of letters a month in response to requests for guidance and advice. By careful attention to the detail of the organizational machinery at his command he secured both financial and administrative responsibility throughout the system. He reduced the routine work of administration as well as his relations with the local authorities to a body of systematic procedure that covered everything from the gathering of a multitude of statistics to the means by which local boards could function fairly and efficiently in the day-to-day running of the schools. An intensely methodical administrator, Ryerson created the first effective social service bureaucracy in the province's history.

He was, however, not only a school administrator but, in Alison Prentice's phrase, a "school promoter" as well. Through his speeches, his educational tours of the province, and the *Journal of Education for Upper Canada*, which he edited from 1848 to 1875, he reported the best ideas from home and abroad, exhorted local boards to introduce this or that new idea, and launched his own campaigns for such major innovations as free schools and compulsory education.

Part of his promotional task, perhaps the least welcome part, was to defend the place of grant-aided Roman Catholic separate schools within the system. Though these schools represented only a small proportion of the total number of schools in operation, they became the subject of prolonged political, religious, and sectional controversy in the mid 19th century. Though Ryerson had no a priori objections to denominational schools where a common faith was shared by the whole population, he did not approve of sectarian schools in a denominationally diverse society like Canada West. He thought such schools impractical in most parts of the country, divisive, and unnecessary on the grounds that all the essential, shared doctrines of Christianity could be taught in the elementary schools without reference to the peculiar doctrines of each sect. None the less he had inherited responsibility for the separate schools from the School Act of 1841 and could see no way of abolishing them, given the union of the Canadas which ensured the Catholic minority of Canada West the powerful support in the legislature of their Lower Canadian brethren. Thus Ryerson found himself repeatedly forced to defend the *status quo*, or to justify a succession of unpalatable political compromises on the issue, in an attempt to fend off both the abolitionists and those who sought the extension of the Catholic system. The additional rights won by Roman Catholics in 1853, 1855, and 1863 were modest compared to their demands; Ryerson was largely successful in preserving the unity of the school system. But his role made him appear to endorse the survival of the separate schools against the clearly expressed will of the majority of politicians and electors in Canada West, and kept him deeply embroiled in public debate from 1852 to 1865, when the issue was finally disposed of as part of the confederation settlement.

If Ryerson disliked the separate school controversy, however, it was because he believed the question to be insoluble and divisive, not because he thought it inappropriate for public servants to become involved in political questions. The modern conventions of civil service neutrality and anonymity were still in a formative stage in the period and Ryerson stands out as a Canadian example of that transitional group of mid-Victorian reformer-bureaucrats whom George Kitson Clark has labelled "statesmen in disguise." Because Ryerson believed that the disposition of educational issues should not be subject to politics or partyism, he had made the Education Office a semi-autonomous agency with no distinct ministerial head. Though formally responsible to the Executive Council, Ryerson himself assumed an almost ministerial role. He established policy, sought political support for it inside and outside parliament, and defended it in public. Moreover his notion of his public duty transcended responsibility to a particular ministry or even parliament. In effect he saw himself as the guardian of the public interest in all educational matters. Even in the late 1860s Ryerson did not think it anomalous, when his own views conflicted with those of a member of the cabinet, to confront the minister with the threat that he would take his side of the case directly to the public. Nor did he feel constrained to keep his activities within the formal jurisdiction of his office. While in England in 1851, for example, he acted as an emissary for the administration to the Colonial Office on the clergy reserves issue and published anonymous letters on the same subject in the *Times.* He regularly exchanged political gossip and advice with politicians to whom he was personally close, especially William Draper, Francis Hincks, and John A. Macdonald*, and on at least one occasion privately used his influence among Methodist leaders to sway their politics and their votes.

Throughout his superintendency, moreover, he remained an active participant in the affairs of Upper Canadian Methodism. With the exception of the year 1854–55, when a brief but tempestuous dispute over the rights of Methodist ministers to require attendance at class meetings led to Ryerson's temporary resignation from conference, he continued to serve on important conference committees, including the board of Victoria College. In the late 1860s and in the 1870s he was an active supporter at conference of the negotiations for Methodist union and was honoured in 1874 for his contributions to the institutional development of Canadian Methodism by his election as the first president of the Methodist Church of Canada. This continuing clerical role, however, involved him once again in a highly contentious political issue, the university question.

Ryerson always claimed that he was a warm supporter of a provincial university, and no doubt he was in the sense that he generally supported any measure that would sustain effective professional schools and provide common standards for examinations and degrees among the various colleges in the province. Indeed he himself had written the original draft of Hincks's University Act of 1853, which incorporated these ideas. But Ryerson was also a resolute defender of the denominational colleges as agencies for ensuring a Christian education and environment for young men who did not live at home. And he had an immense personal commitment to the survival of Victoria College, which he had done so much to foster in the 1830s and 1840s. For both reasons he was an energetic supporter of public aid to the denominational colleges throughout the 1850s and 1860s. He took a leading role between 1859 and 1863 in the concerted attempt by several denominations to force the government to give them access to the funds of the University of Toronto and in the abortive campaign in 1868 to prevent the new government of Ontario from abolishing the existing grants to the denominational colleges. In the controversy surrounding the question, Ryerson always attempted to claim the high ground as champion of the interests of Christianity and high standards in education. But to those who believed in the virtues of a civic university, free from sectarian control and large enough to offer a comprehensive liberal and professional education, he inevitably appeared as the partisan of denominational self-interest and sectarian political scheming.

The 1850s were for Ryerson among the most satisfying years of his life. He had experienced his share of personal tragedy in the two previous decades with the deaths of his first wife and both their children. By the 1850s, however, he and his second wife had settled in a comfortable house in Toronto, and had two growing children, Charles Egerton and Sophia. Though Charlie was a constant worry to his father because of his lack of earnestness and studiousness, he became a welcome sporting and sailing companion later in Ryerson's life. Sophie, as Ryerson's warm and often moving letters to his daughter reveal, was the love of his life, particularly since his relationship with his second wife was somewhat distant and at times strained. The 1850s were also among his most productive years as superintendent. In a sequence of major legislation between 1850 and 1855 he had put the common school system in order, begun the reform of the grammar schools, and played a role in reshaping the provincial university. He was on close terms with most of the influential politicians of the day, and received broad support from both parties and from the provincial press; even the *Globe* found good things to say about him for much of the decade. He basked in the accolades of Lord Elgin during ceremonies connected with the building of the Normal School in Toronto, and was invited in 1854 to serve as a member of a commission of inquiry into the state of King's College (University of New Brunswick) in Fredericton, N.B. Among other ornaments of public approbation he accumulated three honorary degrees: a DD from Wesleyan University, Middletown, Conn., in 1842; an MA from the University of Toronto in 1857; and an LLD from Victoria College in 1861. His reputation and his public role seemed permanently and securely established.

Towards the end of the decade, however, both his personal and his professional circumstances became more troubled. In the late 1850s his pride was badly wounded by a contretemps with John Langton*, the provincial auditor. Langton, the first to admit that Ryerson was a superb administrator, had written in 1856 that Ryerson had "the genius of order and system," and that "his accounts and vouchers are a model for all our public departments." But between 1855 and 1857 Langton also discovered and exposed the fact that Ryerson had personally collected the interest on public funds held in his name. It was not an illegal practice at the time, and Ryerson believed he had ministerial approval for it, but it was also ceasing to be acceptable conduct in the public mind. He promised to pay back the entire amount and a sympathetic government granted him virtually the equivalent sum in back salary. But he was stung by the accusations against his probity and shaken by the way in which those charges remained current long after the issue had been formally settled. Then, in 1862, approaching the age of 60, Ryerson suffered a prolonged and severe illness marked by the recurrence of headaches, dizziness, and coughing. His illness forced him to reduce his traditional schedule of work and as he recovered in the succeeding years he took his first real vacations and embarked on a regimen of vigorous exercise. Among other things he built a skiff, and over the next few years sailed and rowed nine times from Toronto to Long Point, five of these adventures, much to the consternation of friends and family, being undertaken alone. Though he would regain much of his strength by the mid 1860s, he would suffer relapses for the rest of his life and was never again able to carry the burden of work he had once borne.

From the late 1850s onwards, moreover, he discovered that there was a price to be paid for insulating the department from the political process, for he began to have difficulties persuading the politicians to interest themselves in his projects, carry forward his legislation, and defend him when he was under attack. These difficulties, perhaps more than anything else, convinced him by the late 1860s that a ministerial head was essential if the interests of the department and the school system were to be adequately protected. At the same time he began to accumulate a growing number of enemies. His public attack in 1858 on the educational policies of the short-lived coalition between George Brown and the Lower Canadian Reformers marked the reopening of hostilities between Ryerson and Brown which would last until the latter's death. Along with this incident his role in the university question and his close relations with John A. Macdonald alienated many leading Brownite Liberals. Nor did Ryerson learn prudence from the political controversies in which he found himself involved. When in 1867 the Reform party called for an end to coalitions and a return to party politics, Ryerson replied with a pamphlet entitled *The new Canadian dominion: dangers and duties of the people in regard to their government*, in which he returned to the themes of 1844, warning against the dangers of partyism – its "intolerance," its "excesses and oppressions," and the "unscrupulous partisanship" of "this hermaphrodite spawn of cast-off colonial despotism and selfishness." All of this controversy contributed to what Oliver Mowat* would describe, in a letter to Ryerson in 1873, as "the antagonism towards you which has so long prevailed in the Liberal party."

Illness and the frustrations of public life led Ryerson to talk sporadically about retirement throughout the 1860s. At the same time, however, he was anxious to complete his agenda for educational reform. In 1866–67 he made his last educational tour of Europe and America, out of which came two reports, written in 1868: one on the education of the deaf, dumb, and blind, and the other on the state of American and European education along with recommendations for the improvement of the Ontario system. Late in the same year he submitted draft legislation designed to improve the details of school law and to introduce universal free elementary education, compulsory attendance, and a new structure for secondary education.

His initial hopes for quick and easy passage of the school bill were soon dashed. In part this disappointment was due to the constant attacks mounted by the opposition Liberals, many of them directed at Ryerson personally. But it was also due to the emergence of real public debate about a wide variety of educational issues. Differences of opinion in the legislature and the press, along with opposition to parts of the bill from teachers' organizations and from local opinion expressed during Ryerson's tour of the province in 1869, led to the temporary withdrawal of the bill and to considerable modification of it. The new School Act, finally passed early in 1871, contained most of Ryerson's major recommendations in one form or another and remains as one of the great landmarks of his career. But it was passed amidst a degree of political debate and personal bitterness not experienced by Ryerson since the late 1840s.

Ryerson's last years in office were unhappy ones. Again some of this unhappiness was due to the political and personal antagonisms among Liberals over the previous 30 years–antagonisms that boiled over in 1872 in his bitter and sustained public conflict with Edward Blake*. But it was not merely a matter of personalities and political differences. From the administration of John Sandfield Macdonald* onwards, successive ministries were determined to regularize the procedures of the Education Office and, more importantly, to exercise a firm hand in educational policy-making. In Ryerson's view this effort was an invasion of his prerogatives as well as a denigration of his own role to that of "a clerk," and seemed motivated by the most base political partisanship. Each incursion – from the simple attempt by the provincial treasurer in 1868 to impose financial controls on the department to the suspension of his school regulations in 1872 and the plans to modify his book depository – was met with resistance and, too often, with a barrage of invective hurled at those he conceived to be his persecutors. In 1872 Blake seemed to invite conflict; Mowat was far more conciliatory. He sought Ryerson's advice, allowed him considerable latitude in the administration of the department, and applied liberal amounts of soft sawder when Ryerson's sensitivities were bruised. But he was no less determined than Blake to be his own master. As Mowat put it on one occasion when a quarrel threatened: "I would much rather co-operate with you . . . but if I must have a fight with the Chief Superintendent . . . instead of his co-operation, as in my position I ought to have, I must still do what I consider to be my duty."

The conflicts of the years 1872–75 invited either resignation or dismissal. Yet neither option could be exercised. Ryerson repeatedly expressed a wish to resign but he did not have the financial resources to sustain himself independently: for years he had given generously to help finance a variety of Methodist causes including Victoria College, he had a nephew to educate, and he may also have lived somewhat beyond his means. Thus he needed to assure himself of a government pension and could not afford to make any grand gestures over policies with which he disagreed. Either Blake or Mowat would probably have welcomed his resignation but there were political difficulties in providing him with a permanent pension and differences within the Liberal party itself over the kind of reorganization the Education Office should undergo. Dismissal, on the other hand, was out of the question. Ryerson's reputation remained high in many quarters and he was still, as even the Liberals recognized, a power among Methodist voters. It was not until late 1875 that Mowat finally took the matter in hand, and made the decision to create a ministry of education [*see* Adam CROOKS] and to provide a pension for Ryerson. He formally left office in February 1876, just over a month before his 73rd birthday.

Retirement, however, did not mean a life of leisure. Since the early 1860s Ryerson had devoted his spare moments to what he was convinced was his last "mission" in life – a history of the United Empire Loyalists. In 1876 the project became his full-time occupation and most of that year was spent in England where he put in long hours of research in the British Museum. Over the succeeding five years he finished the two large volumes that make up *The loyalists of America and their times.* Beyond that he completed a school textbook on political economy and a history of Canadian Methodism. He was working on his autobiography when, in the summer of 1881, his health began to fail. He died on 19 Feb. 1882. Following a large and impressive funeral service he was buried in Mount Pleasant Cemetery, Toronto.

Ryerson's life spans the growth of Upper Canada virtually from first settlement to the social and economic maturity of the 1870s. For most of those years he was a major figure in its history. Particularly before 1850 he played a central part in the institutional growth of Methodism, one of the province's largest denominations. As well, he helped to articulate and publicize "the grievances of Upper Canada," and contributed to the debate about the nature of colonial-imperial relations. If most historians now reject an older view that Ryerson determined single-handed the results of the elections of 1836 and 1844, still he remains an influential figure in these events and one of the leading spokesmen for that majority of Upper Canadians who sought some middle way to reconcile self-government and the imperial tie.

But it is his contribution to Canadian education that remains his greatest legacy. He was one of the founders of Victoria College, its first principal, and a generous benefactor through some of its most difficult years. He was a vigorous protagonist of the right of all the denominational colleges to survive and prosper in the province. And he attempted to make the grant-aided schools universal and comprehensive and to create an effective system of public administration at both the local and provincial levels.

Few of his educational ideas were original. John Strachan, for one, had anticipated many of them, while others were the common coinage of an era when school systems were being constructed in many different places. Nor was his vision without flaws. He had an unsure hand when it came to providing for the advanced education of young women. To some of his contemporaries his version of non-denominationalism in education appeared as little more than a disguised and proselytizing form of evangelical Protestantism. And his hopes for social improvement through education were vitiated by a belief, widely shared by his generation, that social and economic inequalities were the unchangeable realities of man's fallen estate. During his lifetime there were already divergent views about the merits of the school system, and since his death the assessments of his work have been diverse and conflicting. But on one point there has been consensus. More than any other person Ryerson gave the Ontario school system its particular character, one that, because of his enormous influence in his own generation, would become during the later 19th century a model for most of English-speaking Canada.

R. D. GIDNEY

[Egerton Ryerson's writings were extensive, both in manuscript and in print, and there is also a considerable body of historical work relating to his life. Aspects of his career, for example, are treated in all of the standard works on 19th-century Ontario and he plays a particularly important role in the histories of religion and education.

There are three major collections of Ryerson papers. Most of his personal correspondence is in the Egerton Ryerson papers at UCA but there is also a small, important collection of correspondence in the Hodgins (John George) papers (MU 1375–81) at AO. The immense files of the Education Department (RG 2) at AO also contain many series which are valuable for various aspects of Ryerson's work: the most important are C-1 and C-2, which consist of the letterbooks and drafts of outgoing correspondence, and C-6-C, the incoming correspondence. Though these files deal mainly with routine administrative matters, they also include important political correspondence and Ryerson's views on the widest variety of subjects. There are many other state and personal manuscript collections in various Ontario depositories that contain letters or statements by or about Ryerson. Perhaps the most valuable are the John A. Macdonald papers (MG 26, A) at PAC.

Ryerson used the press extensively to promote his views and reply to his critics. Thus such papers as the *Kingston Herald* (Kingston, [Ont.]) and Toronto's *British Colonist*, *Globe*, and *Leader* are valuable sources. By far the most important, however, is the *Christian Guardian*, and not only during his editorship, for he was a contributor all his life. As well there is the *Journal of Education for Upper Canada* (later the *Journal of Education for Ontario*) (Toronto), which he edited from 1848 to 1875. Aside from the routine administrative business of the Education Office the *Journal* contains important editorials by him and most of his major speeches on educational matters.

The annual reports of the Department of Public Instruction for Upper Canada and later Ontario, published between 1846 and 1875, were largely his work and contain important material on all aspects of the development of the school system. He also wrote a number of special reports on educational subjects, most of which are printed in the appendices to the *Journals* of the Legislative Assembly of the Province of Canada and the *Sessional papers* of the province of Ontario.

Over his lifetime he wrote a large number of pamphlets and books on a broad range of topics, including politics, religion, education, and history. Most of these are listed in *Bibliography of Canadiana* (Staton and Tremaine) or can be found in the pamphlet collection at AO. Some of his more important and representative works are: *Letters from the Reverend Egerton Ryerson to the Hon. and Reverend Doctor Strachan . . .* (Kingston, 1828); *The affairs of the Canadas, in a series of letters, by a Canadian* (London, 1837); *Sir F. B. Head and Mr. Bidwell; the cause and circumstances of Mr. Bidwell's banishment by Sir F. B. Head, correctly stated and proved, by a United Empire Loyalist* (Kingston, 1838); *The clergy reserve question; as a matter of history – a question of law – and a subject of legislation; in a series of letters to the Hon. W. H. Draper, M.P.P.* (Toronto, 1839); *Inaugural address on the nature and advantages of an English and liberal education, delivered . . . at the opening of Victoria College, June 21, 1842 . . .* (Toronto, 1842); *Sir Charles Metcalfe defended against the attacks of his late counsellors* (Toronto, 1844); *Report on a system of public elementary instruction for Upper Canada* (Montreal, 1847); *Dr. Ryerson's letters in reply to the attacks of foreign ecclesiastics against the schools and municipalities of Upper Canada . . .* (Toronto, 1857); *Dr. Ryerson's letters in reply to the attacks of the Hon. George Brown, M.P.P.* (Toronto, 1859); *University question: the Rev. Dr. Ryerson's defence of the Wesleyan petitions to the legislature, and of denominational colleges as part of our system of public instruction, in reply to Dr. Wilson and Mr. Langton . . .* (Quebec, 1860); *The new Canadian dominion: dangers and duties of the people in regard to their government* (Toronto, 1867); *A special report on the systems and state of popular education on the continent of Europe, in the British Isles, and the United States of America . . .* (Toronto, 1868); *First lessons on agriculture; for Canadian farmers and their families* (Toronto, 1870); *First lessons in Christian morals; for Canadian families and schools* (Toronto, 1871); *Elements of political economy; or, how individuals and a country become rich* (Toronto, 1877); *The loyalists of America and their times: from 1620 to 1816* (2v., Toronto and Montreal, 1880); *Canadian Methodism; its epochs and characteristics* (Toronto, 1882).

Many of Ryerson's more important letters and reports are published, sometimes in highly edited form, in *Documentary history of education in U.C.* (Hodgins). Though these volumes need to be used with care, they remain indispensable. An invaluable collection of personal correspondence is found in *My dearest Sophie; letters from Egerton Ryerson to his daughter*, ed. C. B. Sissons (Toronto, 1955). A formal record of Ryerson's role in Methodism can be found in the published and unpublished minutes of the conferences of the various Methodist churches in Canada from 1824 to 1874.

Ryerson's autobiography was incomplete at his death: it was edited by John George Hodgins* and published in 1883 as *The story of my life . . .* (Toronto). There are several other biographical studies. Nathanael Burwash* wrote *Egerton Ryerson* (Toronto, 1903; revised and enlarged by C. B. Sissons in 1927) before J. H. Putman produced *Egerton Ryerson and education in Upper Canada* (Toronto, 1912), and Clara Thomas has written a brief but vivid character study in her *Ryerson of Upper Canada* (Toronto, 1969). An excellent introduction for young people is Laura Damania's *Egerton Ryerson* (Don Mills, Ont., 1975), which was translated into French the next year by Richard Bergeron and published at Longueuil, Que. The definitive biography, however, is Sissons, *Egerton Ryerson*. Though now dated in some respects, this work is richly textured, lucid, and comprehensive. Much of Ryerson's important correspondence is reproduced in its two volumes.

Ryerson's role in the development of early Canadian Methodism is considered in G. [S.] French, *Parsons & politics: the rôle of the Wesleyan Methodists in Upper Canada and the Maritimes from 1780 to 1855* (Toronto, 1962) and a contemporary perspective is added by John Carroll in *Case and his cotemporaries*. His part in the university, separate schools, and clergy reserves questions is put in context in J. S. Moir, *Church and state in Canada West: three studies in the relation of denominationalism and nationalism, 1841–1867* (Toronto, 1959). On the separate school question see also F. A. Walker, *Catholic education and politics in Upper Canada: a study of the documentation relative to the origin of Catholic elementary schools in the Ontario school system* (Toronto and Vancouver, 1955; repub. Toronto, 1976). For the intellectual background of Ryerson's thought see McKillop, *Disciplined intelligence*.

There are few studies of 19th-century Ontario education in

which Ryerson does not play a significant part. Two of the more important recent contributions primarily concerned with him are A. F. Fiorino, "The philosophical roots of Egerton Ryerson's idea of education as elaborated in his writings preceding and including the report of 1846" (PHD thesis, Univ. of Toronto, 1975), and Alison Prentice, *The school promoters; education and social class in mid-nineteenth century Upper Canada* (Toronto, 1977). His contributions to Victoria College are considered in C. B. Sissons, *A history of Victoria University* (Toronto, 1952).

Several articles in two recent collections are also directly concerned with his views and his role in system-building: *Education and social change: themes from Ontario's past*, ed. M. B. Katz and P. H. Mattingly (New York, 1975); and *Egerton Ryerson and his times*, ed. Neil McDonald and Alf Chaiton (Toronto, 1978). There are two articles edited by Sissons containing material not incorporated into his biography: "Four early letters of Egerton Ryerson," *CHR*, 23 (1942): 58–64, and "Canadian Methodism in 1828: a note on an early Ryerson letter," *Douglas Library Notes* (Kingston), 12 (1963), no.3: 2–6. Other recent articles include: R. D. Gidney, "Centralization and education: the origins of an Ontario tradition," *Journal of Canadian Studies*, 7 (1972), no.4: 33–48; R. D. Gidney and D. A. Lawr, "Egerton Ryerson and the origins of the Ontario secondary school," *CHR*, 60 (1979): 442–65; R. S. Harris, "Egerton Ryerson," *Our living tradition, second and third series*, ed. R. L. McDougall (Toronto, 1959), 244–67; Alex McGregor, "Egerton Ryerson, Albert Carman and the founding of Albert College, Belleville," *OH*, 63 (1971): 205–16; David Onn, "Egerton Ryerson's philosophy of education: something borrowed or something new?" *OH*, 61 (1969): 77–86; M. V. Royce, "Arguments over the education of girls: their admission to grammar schools in this province," *OH*, 67 (1975): 1–13; J. D. Wilson, "The Ryerson years in Canada West," *Canadian education: a history*, ed. J. D. Wilson *et al.* (Scarborough, Ont., 1970), 214–40. R.D.G.]

RYERSON, GEORGE, militia officer, teacher, Methodist preacher, and Catholic Apostolic minister; b. probably in March 1791 in Sunbury County, N.B., eldest son of Joseph Ryerson* and Mehetable Stickney; m. first in 1820 or 1821 Sarah (d. 10 July 1829), sister of John Rolph*, and they had one son and one daughter; m. secondly 15 June 1836 Sophia Symes of London, England, and they had one daughter; m. thirdly in 1853 Isabella Dorcas, daughter of the American jurist and politician Ansel Sterling, and they had one son, George Ansel Sterling*; d. 19 Dec. 1882 in Toronto, Ont.

George Ryerson was about eight when his loyalist family left New Brunswick to settle in Norfolk County, Upper Canada, on a generous land grant on the shores of Lake Erie. George's father had come to rejoin his brother, Samuel, and the two families set about establishing themselves as part of the local gentry. Being the eldest son, George, with his bookish tastes, no doubt influenced his younger brothers, and Colonel Ryerson was anything but pleased that William*, John*, EGERTON, and Edway Marcus followed George's example rather than that of the second son, Samuel, the only one to whom farming appealed. Despite their father's objection to their devotion to reading, the boys attended the London District Grammar School near their farm. If relations between George and his father were strained, they improved quickly when, at the age of 21, George joined his father, and brothers William and John, to fight for their king.

In the tense months which preceded the declaration of war in June 1812, the militia in Norfolk under Colonel Joseph Ryerson was reorganized into two regiments, both of which established flank companies. The 1st Norfolk militia, with the elder Ryerson continuing in command, listed Lieutenant George Ryerson as second in command of their flank company. In August 1812 this company played a significant role under Major-General Isaac Brock* at the capture of Detroit; it was charged with constructing the masked batteries which fired the only shots of the engagement. Ryerson had scarcely had time to savour the victory when he was further honoured by being chosen to carry dispatches containing the news to Colonel Thomas Talbot*.

After being stationed at the Sugar Loaf, Ryerson and his company moved on in mid November to Fort Erie. They were placed in support of the batteries at Frenchman Creek, where they had their first taste of combat. On 28 November the Americans launched a fierce pre-dawn attack on the batteries; before being repulsed they inflicted heavy casualties, one of whom was Ryerson. A shot hit him in the face, entering his mouth, knocking out several teeth, and exiting through the right side of his badly fractured jaw. For days he could barely swallow, for months he could not speak, and it was not until several years later that the wound healed. Even then the bone in his jaw never set properly and the lasting effects of the wound "impaired his utterance, and spoiled the ease of his elocution." Determined to return to combat, in the spring of 1813 Ryerson had "enlisted men for a lieutenancy" in the Volunteer Incorporated Militia Battalion and by summer was back on active duty. He participated in the battles of Stoney Creek and Beaver Dams (1813) as well as Fort Erie and Lundy's Lane (1814) before being "seized with typhus fever, from which he almost died." This ended his active involvement in the war although he was listed as in service until the regiment disbanded in April 1816. He then received a land grant in Norfolk as well as an award of £56 9*s.* 9*d.* from the Loyal and Patriotic Society of Upper Canada; although he attempted to obtain a government pension, the Medical Board of Upper Canada, despite the severity of his injuries, found that he was "not labouring under any Disability."

It was probably during his convalescence that Ryerson, a member of the Church of England, decided to join its clergy. He was therefore not caught up in the tide of Methodism which, to the great distress of their father, swept away his brothers John and William, but rather proceeded to the United States to obtain a classical education. When he returned to Canada, expecting to be ordained, Ryerson found that his impaired speech coupled with an edict from England calling for restraint in increasing the clergy's numbers, had caused the deferment of his preliminary examination and effectively ruined his chances. Back in Norfolk he took possession of his land grant, became the teacher in the grammar school, and gave early "indications of taking a prominent part in the life of Upper Canada." On 31 July 1821 he was appointed a justice of the peace for the London District, and in the general election in 1824, no doubt proclaiming the Reform ideals which he was to hold throughout his life, he was an unsuccessful candidate in Norfolk for the House of Assembly. Late in 1827 he sailed for London to attempt to straighten out complications which had arisen in the settlement of the estate of his wife's mother. From the time of his rejection by the Church of England until his departure, two factors seem to have dominated his actions: his growing closeness to his brother Egerton and, more importantly, his search for a practical expression of his Christian energy.

Despite George's inability to provide much direction to his own affairs, he was influential in those of Egerton. He was probably the "kind friend" who supplied his teenage brother with books of a classical nature to memorize, and examined him on them afterwards. In 1821, when their father's opposition to active involvement in Methodism forced Egerton to leave home, George made him an assistant at the school for two years. Further "guided by his brother," Egerton entered the Gore District Grammar School to continue his classical studies in 1824. George seems to have played a paternalistic role in Egerton's development, and his counsel continued to be preeminent with Egerton until the elder Ryerson withdrew from public affairs.

Before George finally accepted his inability to penetrate the ranks of the Church of England clergy, he displayed an admirable degree of creativity in attempting entry. In 1816 he had founded the Vittoria Sunday School, one of the first such enterprises in the province, and by April 1826 was involved in the Sunday School Union Society, planned to encompass the entire province. He unsuccessfully applied to Sir Peregrine Maitland* for patronage of the project on 9 June of that year, doubtless with an eye to his own involvement in a vastly expanded network of Sunday schools. The previous year he had applied to John Strachan* for a missionary posting at the Grand River Reserve and, after Strachan's suggestion that immediate endeavour among these Indians might influence any decision, Ryerson began to visit the reserve. But Ryerson's further suggestion to Maitland that he be appointed permanent Anglican missionary at the reserve also fell upon deaf ears and it was probably at this time that George abandoned hope of a position in the established church and decided to follow a course he had no doubt been considering for some time; he would join his brothers in the Methodist Episcopal Church. By late 1826 he was questioning Egerton concerning the latter's work for the Methodists among the Indians, and in February 1827 George preached at the quarterly Methodist meeting at the Credit River Indian Reserve. This informal connection was interrupted later in 1827 when George set off on his first trip to Britain.

Shortly after his arrival early in 1828 George received a letter from a committee headed by Jesse Ketchum* asking him to act as the agent for a petition, signed by 8,000 Upper Canadians, presenting the arguments of non-Anglicans to counter those contained in Strachan's "Ecclesiastical Chart." A select committee of the British House of Commons had been formed to investigate the civil government in Canada, including the disposal of the clergy reserves and the charter for a university in Upper Canada; at issue was the number of practising members of each denomination in the province. Ryerson presented the petition to the house in May and gave testimony before the committee in June before returning home. The report which the committee issued later that year was favourable to the non-Anglicans and Charles Bruce Sissons* claimed that Ryerson "was the first of the Canadian reformers . . . to seek redress at the foot of the throne, and perhaps not the least effective."

His connection with the Methodists was formalized shortly after his return when, on 8 Oct. 1828, he was received on trial and stationed at the Credit River mission. In the light of future events it is ironic that on this occasion he was placed on a committee with William Case* and James Richardson* "to correspond with the British Conference, in order to establish a friendly relation and intercourse between the two connexions." Ryerson dedicated himself to his work among the Indians for slightly more than two years; he was transferred to the Grand River mission in 1830. During this period he continued to sit on the committee and was seriously considered for the position of editor of the *Christian Guardian* when it was founded in 1829. After much discussion Egerton was chosen as editor but at his request George contributed articles and advice over the next two years. Early in 1830 George used the pages of the *Guardian* to rebut an attack from "Calculator" which had appeared in the *Upper Canada Herald* (Kingston) on 13 January accusing him of giving evidence in Britain which exaggerated the number of non-Anglicans in the province. Ryerson's experience in Britain in 1828 and his position on the committee precipitated his being selected to accompany Peter Jones [Kahkewaquonaby*] to England in 1831 to raise money for the

Indian missions and to present further petitions to parliament on behalf of the non-Anglicans; he could also attend to the still unresolved matter of the Rolph estate.

The two men arrived in Liverpool on 30 April after spending some time in the United States, where Ryerson was impressed by the "Religious Liberty" evident in the republic. The British Wesleyans dispensed much hospitality, but more condescension, and Ryerson's correspondence indicates a growing distaste for his hosts and a firm opposition to union between the Canadian and British conferences. He suspected the British conference of seeking both power for its own sake and a dumping ground for its redundant preachers; he had only to remember his own treatment by the Church of England. Moreover, his words suggest an overriding, perhaps understandable, pessimism: his pious wife had died working among the Indians in 1829, his industrious brother Samuel the next year; the intrigues surrounding the settlement of the Rolph estate continued, reflecting distasteful self-interest; the worldly concerns of his British brethren were set against what he considered the appalling godlessness of London; and now cholera erupted in London and Paris, threatening an apocalyptic destruction of a decadent society. Unable to reconcile the tenets of Methodism with the reality surrounding him, Ryerson, when exposed to the community led by Edward Irving, converted once again. Irving's movement, which was to become the Catholic Apostolic Church, was based on a belief in the unity of all Christians adhering to the Apostles' Creed and it attempted to eliminate sectarian rivalries by emphasizing spiritual life and the importance of ritual worship. Believing that "God's answer was a restoration of the gifts of the Spirit," including prophecy and speaking in tongues, the community's members withdrew into their meetings, had their "prophets" select 12 "apostles," and awaited the second Advent. Almost immediately after joining, George "altogether retired from public life," as Egerton claimed in his reply to a scathing attack by William Lyon Mackenzie* who accused George of preaching "toryism in the *unknown tongues.*" Regardless of Mackenzie's vituperation or his brothers' sorrow, George Ryerson had finally found his ecclesiastical niche. Even as George tried to explain his withdrawal to Egerton, he remained concerned about his younger brother, who was obviously on the threshold of an influential career, and he warned Egerton to "avoid popular politics. There is a mystery of iniquity about the subject which you do not understand."

Early in 1833 the brothers were reunited when Egerton arrived in England to obtain the Methodist union favoured by himself and his brother John, who had become Egerton's principal adviser. During that summer George persuaded Egerton to accompany him to several Irvingite gatherings; while Egerton found Irving "the perfect gentleman" in private, he confessed that "his pulpit exercises made the most unfavourable impression." George may have returned to Canada briefly in 1834 or 1836 in the company of William R. Caird, an influential member of the movement, and aided him in obtaining entry to Methodist pulpits. George did not, however, finally settle in Toronto until 1836.

Ryerson was designated angel (bishop) in Toronto in 1837 and was "placed in charge of work in America, as apostles messenger." His was the second Catholic Apostolic congregation created in the province, Kingston having established one the previous year, and apart from some minor aggravation by Methodists concerning the loss of a few members to his church, he seems to have lived out his remaining years in tranquil obscurity. In 1843 Catholic Apostolic "services [were] temporarily discontinued & [the] flock put in care of the Bishop of the Ch. of England in Toronto"; Ryerson revived the congregation in the fall of 1848 in the building next to his home on Bay Street. A fire on 16 Aug. 1861 destroyed both buildings and the peripatetic congregation was then forced to accommodate itself in rented premises until 1878. Ryerson "gave up the Angelship" in 1872 but remained involved in the church until his death. Although he generally led a quiet life during his years in Toronto, he may have commanded an outpost east of the Don River during the rebellion of 1837 and he acted as secretary to the trustees of the Toronto General Hospital, at least in 1847. He proudly assembled with other veterans of the War of 1812 at Brock's Monument during the visit of the Prince of Wales in 1860 and in Toronto in 1861.

After his conversion George's relationships with his brothers are difficult to assess. He had always been closest to Egerton and, despite some bickering in the 1850s and 1860s about the settlement of their father's estate, in 1873 Egerton claimed "though he and I have since differed in religious opinions, no other than the most affectionate brotherly feelings has ever existed between us to this day." Viewing the loss of George with regret and sorrow, the brothers may have deflected their frustration and anger to the movement which had caused the separation. Egerton sarcastically noted that the Catholic Apostolic Church found its converts among "unsuspecting persons of strong imagination and ardent temperament, especially when in a low state of religious enjoyment." John had indicated an appreciably stronger resentment in 1838 when he suggested to Egerton that a £100 reward should be collected for "the Christian act of Col. Brown," who had kicked an Irvingite downstairs for telling an attempted suicide that he was possessed of the devil.

George was to outlive all his brothers, dying of "no particular cause, but . . . the result of the infirmities consequent upon his great age." By his later years he had become known as something of an eccentric, but mainly as the older brother of Egerton Ryerson. The final measure of the obscurity surrounding the man, who at one time seemed the Ryerson who would be remembered, can be seen in the heading of his lengthy obituary in the *Globe*, "The late Rev. Wm. Ryerson."

CHARLES DOUGALL

Methodist Missionary Soc. Arch. (London), Wesleyan Methodist Missionary Soc., Corr., Canada, "Resolutions on Mess' Ryerson and Jones' visit, 1831: extract from minutes of a meeting of the general committee held May 11, 1831" (mfm. at UCA). PAC, RG 8, I (C ser.), 703c: 15–16. UCA, Church hist. files, Ont., Toronto, Catholic Apostolic Church, "History of the congregation gathered in Toronto, Can., by restored Apostles – a Catholic Apostolic Church"; Egerton Ryerson papers. [William] Canniff, "Fragments of the War of 1812: the Rev. George Ryerson and his family," *Belford's Monthly Magazine: a Magazine of Literature and Art* (Toronto), 2 (1877): 299–308. Carroll, *Case and his cotemporaries.* J. G. Hodgins, *The Ryerson brothers* ([Toronto], n.d.) (copy at AO). Methodist Episcopal Church in Canada, *Minutes of the annual conference* ([Toronto]), 1828–32. Egerton Ryerson, *The story of my life . . .*, ed. J. G. Hodgins (Toronto, 1883). [George Ryerson], "George Ryerson to Sir Peregrine Maitland, 9 June 1826," ed. C. B. Sissons, *OH*, 44 (1952): 23–29. *Advocate* (Toronto), 29 May 1834. *Christian Guardian*, 21 Nov. 1829; 23 Jan., 6, 20 Feb. 1830; 5 March, 9, 16 April, 7 May, 25 June 1831; 25 Jan., 29 Feb., 18 April 1832; 6 Nov. 1833; 19 Nov. 1834. *Colonial Advocate* ([Toronto]), 5 July, 7 Aug. 1828; 26, 30 Oct., 7 Nov. 1833. *Globe*, 21, 22 Dec. 1882. *Toronto Daily Mail*, 20, 21 Dec. 1882. *Upper Canada Herald* (Kingston, [Ont.]), 13 Jan. 1830; also issued as [Calculator], *[Letter] to Mr. George Ryerson* (Hamilton, [Ont.], 1829?).

Cornish, *Cyclopædia of Methodism. Dominion annual register*, 1882. A. W. Ryerson, *The Ryerson genealogy: genealogy and history of the Knickerbocker families of Ryerson, Ryerse, Ryerss; also Adriance and Martense families; all descendants of Martin and Adriaen Reyersz (Reyerszen), of Amsterdam, Holland*, ed. A. L. Holman (Chicago, 1916). L. J. Ryerson, *The genealogy of the Ryerson family in America, 1646–1902* (New York, 1902). D. B. Read, *Life and times of Major-General Sir Isaac Brock, K.B.* (Toronto, 1894), 147–59. *Robertson's landmarks of Toronto*, II: 633–64; IV: 545–50; VI: 587. G. [A.] S. Ryerson, *Looking backward* (Toronto, 1924). P. E. Shaw, *The Catholic Apostolic Church, sometimes called Irvingite: a historical study* (New York, 1946). Sissons, *Egerton Ryerson.*

S

SABINE, Sir EDWARD, soldier and scientist; b. 14 Oct. 1788 in Dublin (Republic of Ireland), fifth son and ninth child of Joseph Sabine and Sarah Hunt; m. 1826 Elizabeth Juliana Leeves; d. 26 June 1883 in Richmond (now part of Greater London), England.

Edward Sabine went to school at Marlow, England, and in 1803 entered the Royal Military Academy at Woolwich (now part of London). He was commissioned 2nd lieutenant in December 1803, and promoted to 1st lieutenant in July 1804. After duty in Gibraltar, he was assigned to the Royal Horse Artillery and became a 2nd captain in 1813. In May of that year he set sail for Halifax, N.S., in the *Manchester*, which was attacked on 24 June by an American privateer, the *Yorktown.* After a brisk engagement, in which Sabine distinguished himself, the *Manchester* was captured. Sabine, released the following month, proceeded from Halifax to Quebec, which he disliked: "If the fortifications disappointed me, much more the town; a more wretched, narrow, filthy place I have rarely seen." He was placed in charge of a small outpost near Quebec and took part in resisting the American advance on Lower Canada in the winter of 1813–14. In August and September 1814 he served on the Niagara frontier of Upper Canada under George Gordon Drummond*. Sabine was in charge of the batteries at the siege of Fort Erie, and was twice mentioned in dispatches.

With the advent of peace in 1815, men of the British armed forces contributed increasingly to exploration and scientific work. Sabine returned to England in August 1816, and as a supernumerary was able to pursue his scientific interests, especially magnetism, astronomy, and ornithology. He was elected a fellow of the Royal Society of London in 1818 and, on the recommendation of the society's council, was appointed astronomer to the expedition of 1818 commanded by John Ross* in search of a northwest passage. Sabine performed experiments on the length of the seconds pendulum, noting variations in the period of the vibrations of the pendulum at different latitudes, and thus obtained information about the shape of the earth. He also carried out extensive magnetic measurements, assisted by James Clark Ross*, and made important ornithological observations. Though many of Sabine's scientific findings were claimed by Ross as his own upon the expedition's return, Sabine was later able to recover credit for them.

From May 1819 until November 1820 Sabine was assigned to the Arctic expedition of the *Hecla*, commanded by William Edward Parry*, who unlike John Ross warmly acknowledged Sabine's scientific contributions. His pendulum experiments on this voyage gained Sabine the Royal Society's Copley Medal in 1821. He had also alleviated the tedium of the Arctic winter by editing and writing much of the *North*

Georgia Gazette, and Winter Chronicle, published on board the *Hecla*, which ran to 21 numbers. Between 1821 and 1823 Sabine continued to travel extensively, conducting further pendulum experiments at many different latitudes. On 31 Dec. 1827 he was promoted 1st captain, and from 1827 to 1829 he was given leave from the artillery to act as one of the secretaries of the Royal Society. In 1828 he was appointed one of three scientific advisers to the Admiralty, following the abolition of the Board of Longitude.

Sabine long believed in Christopher Hansteen's theory that the earth had two magnetic poles in each hemisphere and that there was a correlation between magnetic and meteorological phenomena. Moreover, he believed that the soundness of these theories would be revealed by a systematic and world-wide survey of terrestrial magnetism. In 1830 Sabine was posted to Ireland with his company; he was, however, able to continue his scientific work, and in 1834 began work on what was to be the first complete magnetic survey of the British Isles. James Clark Ross and Humphrey Lloyd of Trinity College, Dublin, also took part in the project. Sabine and Lloyd visited Berlin in 1838 to consult with Alexander von Humboldt, who in 1836 had written to the president of the Royal Society urging the establishment of magnetic observatories throughout the British empire. The society responded favourably to von Humboldt's proposal, and, prompted by Sabine, advised the government to order long-term simultaneous observations from stations on land and at sea. The observations on land were to be undertaken by the Royal Artillery, initially at observatories at St Helena, the Cape of Good Hope, and Toronto, for a period of three years. The Toronto observatory was headed by Charles James Buchanan Riddell*; Sabine undertook the general superintendence of the enterprise.

Sabine was especially active in promoting magnetic observations in Canada. In July 1840 Riddell wrote to him that magnetic and meteorological observations at Toronto had been underway since May. John Henry LEFROY, who replaced Riddell at Toronto in 1842, was directed by Sabine and worked in communication with "the principal cultivators of magnetic science in the United States." In 1845 he wrote that he had formerly intended to carry out the work personally, a measure of how closely he had identified himself with the North American survey.

The survey was certainly comprehensive. Sabine ordered Lefroy to go north and west of Toronto on magnetic expeditions. He corresponded with Sir John Harvey*, governor of Newfoundland, about observations to be carried out there. He also wrote to Captain Henry Wolsey BAYFIELD, RE, about extending the survey to the northeast, and to Sir William MacBean George Colebrooke* about the possibility of an observatory at Fredericton, N.B. Sabine's enterprise and skill in organization were impressive – in the winter of 1848–49 he planned to coordinate observations at the Toronto observatory with those at Great Bear Lake (N.W.T.) under Sir John Richardson*, at Melville Island (N.W.T.) under James Clark Ross, and at Barrow Strait (N.W.T.) under Captain Edward Joseph Bird.

Sabine's representations to the Royal Society, supported by those of Professor Joseph Henry from the Smithsonian Institution in Washington, secured the continuation of the Toronto observatory under the British government until 1853. In 1852, in his presidential address to the British Association for the Advancement of Science, Sabine claimed that the magnetic surveys of North America, sponsored by the British government, had been completed, but this statement was premature and he remained involved in scientific endeavours in British North America. In 1857 he announced plans to extend the survey "between Canada on the East and the Rocky Mountains on the West." He made suggestions about magnetic observations "for the Expedition proceeding to mark the Boundary in the 49th parallel of latitude, west of the Rocky Mountains"[*see* Samuel ANDERSON], and from 1859 to 1861 he assisted Charles Smallwood* of McGill College in obtaining instruments and arranging magnetic and meteorological observations at Île-Jésus near Montreal.

Sabine was active in magnetic studies in British North America, but his scientific aims were nothing less than understanding "the cosmical features of terrestrial magnetism"; that is, he wanted to understand the pattern of terrestrial magnetism, its distribution and variation, and its possible correlation with other geophysical phenomena. Geophysical and other world-wide studies of natural phenomena had many advocates in the mid 19th century. Sabine, however, was one of the few successful promoters of such enterprises. His reputation scarcely suffered even from his advocacy of Hansteen's erroneous views about terrestrial magnetism or from his refusal to adopt the theory that limited the origins of magnetism to the interior of the earth. Sabine continued to see magnetism as essentially a part of meteorology, and his research programmes were based on the view that different geophysical phenomena were interrelated.

The nature of his scientific interest kept Sabine closely involved with numerous scientific organizations. Besides being president of the British Association for the Advancement of Science in 1852, he was foreign secretary of the Royal Society of London in 1845, vice-president and treasurer in 1850, and president from 1861 to 1871. He was also a fellow of the Linnean and Royal Astronomical societies. Terrestrial magnetism was the subject of 15 papers written for the journals of the Royal Society; indeed, Sabine was the author of more than 100 scholarly papers. He delivered the Reade Lecture at the University of Cambridge in 1862, and was awarded honorary degrees by Oxford (DCL) and Cambridge (LLD). Among the many foreign honours he received was the Lalande Medal of the Institut de France.

Although science was his occupation, the army remained Sabine's professional base and his promotions came steadily, from regimental colonel in November 1851 to general in February 1870. He was awarded a KCB in 1869. Sabine retired from the army in October 1877 on full pay and died at Richmond on 26 June 1883.

TREVOR H. LEVERE

[The principal collection of Sir Edward Sabine's papers, with much Canadian material, is at the PRO (Meteorological Office, BJ 3) (mfm. at PAC). The Royal Soc. Arch. (London) also has a substantial collection of Sabine papers, and there are a few important documents in the library of the Royal Artillery Institution (Woolwich, Eng.). Complementary collections include the papers of Humphrey Lloyd at the Royal Soc. Arch. and at the Royal Greenwich Observatory (Hailsham, Eng.) and of Sir J. F. W. Herschel at the Royal Soc. Arch.

Sabine's published scientific papers are listed in the Royal Soc. of London's *Catalogue of scientific papers* (19v., London, 1867–1925; repr. Metuchen, N.J., 1968), V: 351–54; VIII: 805–6; XI: 251. His works include: *An account of experiments to determine the figure of the earth, by means of the pendulum vibrating seconds in different latitudes . . .* (London, 1825); *On the cosmical features of terrestrial magnetism, being the Reade Lecture, delivered in the Senate House of the University of Cambridge, in May 1862* (London, 1862); *Remarks on the account of the late voyage of discovery to Baffin's Bay, published by Captain J. Ross, R.N.* (London, 1819); "Terrestrial magnetism," *A manual of scientific enquiry; prepared for the use of her majesty's navy: and adapted for travellers in general*, ed. J. F. W. Herschel (London, 1849), 14–53; and appendices in W. E. Parry, *Journal of a voyage for the discovery of a north-west passage from the Atlantic to the Pacific; performed in the years 1819–20, in his majesty's ships Hecla and Griper . . .* (London, 1821), and *A supplement to the appendix of Captain Parry's voyage for the discovery of a north-west passage, in the years 1819–20: containing an account of the subjects of natural history* (London, 1824). He edited *Observations on days of unusual magnetic disturbance, made at the British colonial magnetic observatories, under the departments of the Ordnance and Admiralty* (1v. in 2, London, 1843–51); and ten volumes of magnetic observations at observatories, including three for Toronto, *Observations made at the magnetical and meteorological observatory at Toronto in Canada* (3v., London, 1845–57). He also brought together the issues of the journal published on the *Hecla*: *The North Georgia Gazette, and Winter Chronicle* (London, 1821; 2nd ed., 1822). T.H.L.]

"Memoir of General Sir Edward Sabine, F.R.S., K.C.B.," Royal Artillery Institution, *Minutes of proc.* (Woolwich), 12 (1884): 381–96. *DNB*. *Dictionary of scientific biography*, ed. C. C. Gillispie (14v., New York, 1970–76), XII: 49–53. Johannes Georgi, "Edward Sabine, ein grosser Geophysiker des 19. Jahrhunderts," *Deutsche Hydrographische Zeitschrift* (Hamburg, Federal Republic of Germany), 11 (1958): 225–39. Royal Soc. of London, *Proc.* (London), 51 (1892): xliii–li.

SAINT-AUBIN, EMMANUEL-MARIE BLAIN DE. *See* BLAIN

SAINT-JUST, LUC LETELLIER DE. *See* LETELLIER

SAKAYENGWARATON. *See* JOHNSON, JOHN

SALABERRY, CHARLES-RENÉ-LÉONIDAS D'IRUMBERRY DE. *See* IRUMBERRY

SAMUEL, LEWIS, merchant and philanthropist; b. in 1827 at Kingston upon Hull, England; m. in 1850 Kate Seckelman, and they had eight children including Sigmund*, a prominent philanthropist and patron of the arts in Toronto, Ont.; d. 10 May 1887 at Victoria, B.C., and was buried 18 May 1887 at Toronto.

Lewis Samuel was born to a Jewish family which had lived in England since the time of Oliver Cromwell. When he was eight, his parents moved to the east end of London, where his mother ran a shop and his father, a pious scholar, spent his days immersed in holy books. At 16, Samuel decided to emigrate and hired on as a cabin boy aboard a freighter bound for New York City. Upon his arrival in 1844, he found employment with a tailor. Searching for better economic opportunity, he became an itinerant peddler in upper New York State and by 1848 had settled in Syracuse, where he opened a dry goods store. He was accepted into the local Jewish community and soon married Kate Seckelman, who had recently emigrated from Sulzbach (Federal Republic of Germany).

Samuel, however, was proud of his English origin and wanted to live once again under the British flag. His elder brother, Mark, who had immigrated to Montreal and was engaged in the fur business, had long been urging Lewis to join him. In 1855 Lewis agreed, but soon found his new environment unpleasant. He disliked the fur business and the French atmosphere of the city, and his discontent grew after two of his children died of cholera. Within a year he was on his way to Toronto, a city unquestionably English in tone and alive with the promise of commercial success.

Mark was persuaded to follow and in 1856 the two brothers rented space in the Coffin Block on Wellington Street, establishing a wholesale hardware trade under the name of M. and L. Samuel and Company. The firm grew into a wholesale metals business, a development made possible by the Samuel family's connections in England. By the early 1860s Mark had returned to England to open a branch office in Liverpool; Lewis remained in Toronto, exporting a variety of Canadian raw materials in exchange for gas chandeliers, metals, chemicals, glass, and marble. A small temporary branch was later opened in Montreal with Emmanuel Samuel, Mark's son, directing the operations. By 1879 the firm had become M. and L. Samuel, Benjamin and Company with the admission of an additional partner, Alfred David Benjamin. Frank D. Benjamin, Alfred's brother, was to join the firm in 1888.

Lewis Samuel was anxious to participate further in Canada's expanding economy and invested in such ventures as the Ontario Lead and Barbed-Wire Company, one of the earliest firms in the country to produce barbed wire and a supplier to the Canadian Pacific Railway. In addition, he was a director of the Electric Manufacturing Company and president of the Metallic Roofing Company, both pioneering firms in their fields.

Lewis Samuel was an orthodox Jew; indeed, his religious observance had prevented his engaging in the retail trade since he would have had to open his business on Saturday, the Jewish sabbath. Almost immediately upon his arrival in Toronto he sought to organize the local Jews into a formalized community. The city's first synagogue, the Toronto Hebrew Congregation (now Holy Blossom Temple), was established within months of his arrival in 1856 and he served almost continuously as its president from 1862 to 1880. It was Samuel who insisted that the congregation engage a reader and also a ritual slaughterer to supply kosher meat. Moreover, he was responsible for the purchase of the land on which the first synagogue was built in 1876, funds for which were raised principally through his efforts. During the remainder of his life he sought successfully to preserve the traditional practices in the synagogue, which were under attack from reformers of the German school. So serious a threat did he consider the new movement that he insisted the deed to the synagogue include a stipulation that if the congregation departed from orthodoxy it would forfeit its right to use the building.

Samuel did not confine his social activity to the Jewish community. He was a member of the Sons of England Benefit Society and the St George's Society; he was also one of the trustees of the Oddfellows and in 1877 was president of the mechanics' institute. According to the *Toronto Daily Mail*, he "enjoyed for many years a distinguished position in the city, and both in private and public life was very popular." Widespread acceptance by the community enabled him to defend Jews whenever they were vilified in the local press.

In 1887 Samuel visited a daughter in San Francisco, a vacation his doctors said would improve his failing health. Returning to Vancouver, he took ill aboard ship and was carried ashore to a hotel in Victoria, where he died on 10 May. His body was taken to Toronto and his funeral cortège, well over $1\frac{1}{2}$ miles in length, was said to have been one of the largest ever seen in Toronto.

STEPHEN A. SPEISMAN

Toronto Hebrew Congregation Holy Blossom (Toronto), Deed to the site of the Richmond Street Synagogue, 1875; Minutes, 1856–85. *Globe*, 11 May 1887. *Toronto Daily Mail*, 11, 19 May 1887. *The Jew in Canada: a complete record of Canadian Jewry from the days of the French régime to the present time*, ed. A. D. Hart (Toronto and Montreal, 1926). Abraham Rhinewine, [*Der Id in Kanada*] (2v., Toronto, 1925–27), I. Sack, *Hist. of the Jews in Canada*. [Sigmund Samuel], *In return: the autobiography of Sigmund Samuel* ([Toronto], 1963). S. A. Speisman, "The Jews of Toronto: a history to 1937" (PHD thesis, Univ. of Toronto, 1975); *The Jews of Toronto: a history to 1937* (Toronto, 1979). S. J. Birnbaum, "Pioneers of Toronto's Jewish community," *Jewish Standard* (Toronto), 1 June 1934.

SAVARY, CHARLES, journalist and public servant; b. 21 Sept. 1845 at Coutances, France, son of Pierre-François-Théodore Savary, *substitut du procureur général* in the royal court at Caen, and Charlotte-Éliane Quénault; d. 9 Sept. 1889 in Ottawa.

Descended from a family of magistrates and lawyers, Charles Savary attended the Lycée Bonaparte in Paris from 1860 to 1863, graduating as a *bachelier*; he then studied law in Paris, where he obtained a doctorate in 1866. Savary had early developed an interest in politics and had been elected to the Assemblée nationale, as deputy for La Manche, at the age of 25. He served until 1881, beginning as a moderate royalist and ending as a moderate republican; from 1877 to 1879 he held the post of undersecretary of state to the minister of justice. Savary next devoted his energies to business. He had already participated in a number of financial ventures and in January 1881 had founded the Banque de Lyon et de la Loire, which from its inception made rapid progress. However, as a result of some irregularities, risky credit policies, and a drop in the value of its stock on the Bourse de Lyon, the bank failed in April 1882. Although numerous factors had contributed to its collapse, the bank's directors were held responsible and were heavily fined in 1884. As president, Savary received a five-year prison sentence and took refuge in Canada, arriving in Quebec City towards the middle of 1884.

Soon after, Savary was given a post as an editor on the newspaper *Le Canadien*. He signed the articles he wrote with the pseudonym Charles Quénault, but his identity was quickly discovered, along with the vagaries of his career. As a Frenchman, Savary immediately found himself suspected of being, at the very least, a liberal Catholic, if not, indeed, a free thinker, and he came under attack from François-Xavier-Anselme TRUDEL's paper *L'Étendard*. In 1885 Savary moved to Montreal; after a year with *La Patrie*, he went to *La Presse*. The next year he became editor-in-chief of *Le Moniteur du commerce*; founded in 1881, this newspaper primarily sought "to inform its readers about economic affairs and to suggest to the government measures favouring trade." Journalism focused on the French-speaking business community was in its infancy. When Savary joined *Le Moniteur* it was the sole organ directed primarily to this community in Montreal. From the outset, such editors-in-chief as Clément-Arthur Dansereau*, Jules Helbronner*, and L. Dagron-Richer had attained a high standard of excellence; Savary's advent would help maintain its fine reputation. A shrewd analyst and competent critic, he was particularly interested in banking matters, with which he was thoroughly familiar, as well as in trade and industry. In the issue of 18 Nov. 1887 he criticized the Banque d'Hochelaga and the Banque Jacques-Cartier for having purchased notes of the Central Bank of Canada of Toronto, then in a precarious state, at a time when the other banks had refused them and for having "hastened to pass them on to the public through their branches." These allegations occasioned a libel action, but the Court of Queen's Bench exonerated *Le Moniteur*. In 1886, Savary was largely responsible for organizing the Chambre de Commerce du District de Montréal, which brought together the city's major French-speaking businessmen. Because *Le Moniteur* served as the association's official organ for almost twenty years, it was able to reach a large audience in French-speaking business circles.

In 1888, for unknown reasons, Savary left Montreal and moved to Ottawa; he began working there for the Conservative paper *Le Canada*. That year he was appointed to a post in the Department of Agriculture as a statistician; he retained this post for the remaining year of his life.

Talented and enterprising, Charles Savary made a significant contribution in the course of his brief years in Quebec. Under his impetus, French business journalism grew enormously in stature. Six years after his death a correspondent writing to *Le Réveil*, a radical liberal paper in Montreal, even went so far as to claim that in his four years in Quebec Savary had "done more for the younger generation than two centuries of Sulpicians and Jesuits."

IN COLLABORATION

This biography is an abridged version of a much fuller study of Charles Savary's career that is available in Yves Saint-Germain's "The genesis of the French-language business press and journalists in Quebec, 1871–1914" (PHD thesis, Univ. of Delaware, Newark, 1975), 114–15, 203–19, 233–40. This thesis has a detailed bibliography relating to Savary's activities in both France and Canada. The sources listed here are those that proved most useful for elucidating Savary's career in Canada.

Savary's own works were *Feuilles volantes: recueil d'études et d'articles de journaux* (Ottawa, 1890) and two articles, "Les idées de M. Savary" and "L'union commerciale," published in *Le Drapeau* (Montréal), 1 (1889–90), no.1: 45–47 and no.2: 63–71 respectively.

La Minerve, 11 sept. 1889. *Le Moniteur de commerce* (Montréal), 1886–88, 13 sept. 1889. Beaulieu et J. Hamelin, *La presse québécoise*, III. Canadien [ ], "Navrance," *Le Réveil* (Montréal), 3 (septembre 1895–février 1896): 114–15.

SAWYER, DAVID. *See* KEZHEGOWINNINNE

SAWYER, WILLIAM, portrait painter and photographer; b. 9 Nov. 1820 in Montreal, Lower Canada, son of John Sawyer and Agnes Brown; m. 18 Nov. 1851 Eliza Jane Baxter, and they had 10 children; d. 9 Dec. 1889 in Kingston, Ont.

After considering a law career William Sawyer set out to become an artist, a profession which in 19th-century Canada promised little security. He obtained his early art training in Montreal; his first works are genre and landscape subjects, similar to those of Cornelius Krieghoff* and his contemporaries, and also portraits. By the mid 1840s Sawyer had established himself in a studio in Montreal where he sought out portrait commissions from the leading citizens. Even though he kept his prices low because of his inexperience, there was not enough work in Montreal and he became an itinerant portrait painter. He travelled extensively along the north shore of Lake Ontario as far west as Toronto, stopping off in Morrisburg, Brockville, Kingston, Belleville, Bowmanville, and Port Hope in search of portrait commissions from businessmen and lawyers in these thriving shoreline service centres for the opening frontier of Canada West.

In 1851 Sawyer married and with his wife made a short trip to New York to study before returning to Kingston in May 1852. Sawyer and his wife relocated in Montreal where they remained until 1855 when they settled permanently in Kingston; throughout this time Sawyer continued to visit towns as widely separated as Ottawa, Watertown, N.Y., and Peterborough, Canada West. He was successful enough by 1862 to travel to Scotland, England, France, and Belgium to visit galleries where he could see works by the most eminent portrait painters. Upon his return he divided his time between Kingston and Montreal; in the latter city he operated an "Art and Photographic Studio" in partnership with Edwin R. Turner, acting as both a painter and a photographer. In this connection he became involved in the controversy surrounding the use of the photograph in portrait painting, which he supported as long as it was only employed as a sketch might be. In 1863 Sawyer's considerable reputation brought him a commission to paint a portrait of John A. Macdonald* for the city hall in Kingston, where several of his portraits of mayors were already hanging. His commissions extended to three speakers of the Senate, who engaged him to paint their portraits for the Library of Parliament, and to Sir William Edmond Logan*, William Molson*, Charles Tupper*, and William Workman*, as well as to senators Frank Smith* and Robert Duncan Wilmot*.

As was often the custom Sawyer found it necessary to supplement his income: he painted figures for Thomas Robinson, a well-established local ornamental painter, gave art lessons, took photographs, and sent his work to competitive exhibitions where he often won monetary prizes. From his earliest years he promoted his work vigorously through exhibitions, advertising, and articles in newspapers, especially in Montreal. He was also an early promoter of the establishment of a national portrait gallery. In 1847, in the company of Krieghoff and several other artists, Sawyer participated in an exhibition of the Montreal Society of Artists, in 1867 he exhibited with the Society of Canadian Artists in Montreal, and in 1872 he sent works to the first exhibition of the Ontario Society of Artists at Toronto.

Sawyer's portraits are competent but not outstanding, showing in their visual qualities the contemporary influence of the photograph. They are substantial and factual as required by his 19th-century Canadian subjects, who were concerned with the enhancement of their position in the community. Indeed, Sawyer saw himself in much the same way, a figure of substance and reputation, and his view was corroborated by the regard in which he was held by those among whom he lived and worked.

MICHAEL BELL

[Portraits by Sawyer are held in Kingston, Ont., at the city hall and at the Agnes Etherington Art Centre at Queen's University; in Ottawa in the National Gallery of Canada, the PAC, and the Parliament Buildings; in Hamilton, Ont., in the Art Gallery of Hamilton; in the Montreal Museum of Fine Arts; in the Winnipeg Art Gallery; and in private collections.

A collection of genealogical data and letters is in the possession of W. G. Schram, and Mrs J. C. Wallace of Kingston also possesses genealogical data as well as Sawyer's day-books, 1856–66, his diary of his trip to Europe in 1862, and his account books, 1882–89. M.B.]

PAC, MG 26, A, 358: 166186–89. *Daily British Whig*, 10 Dec. 1889. *Gazette* (Montreal), 24 Jan. 1872. Harper, *Early painters and engravers*; *Painting in Canada*.

SCRIVEN, JOSEPH MEDLICOTT, preacher and hymnist; b. 10 Sept. 1819 in Banbridge, County Down (Northern Ireland), son of James Scriven and Jane Medlicott; d. unmarried 10 Aug. 1886 near Bewdley on Rice Lake, Ont.

Joseph Scriven attended Addiscombe Military College near London, England, from 1837 to 1839, preparing for service in India. He withdrew for reasons of health, but in 1842 he received a BA from Trinity College, Dublin. About this time he adopted the faith of the Plymouth Brethren, to which his parents had earlier been converted: the group believed in the priesthood of all male believers and the sufficiency of grace for justification and redemption. In 1845 he joined Plymouth Brethren friends in Woodstock, Canada West. He taught there and later at Brantford, where for two or three years in the early 1850s he conducted a private school. He also held religious services and preached throughout the district, and evidently it was here that his famous hymn, "What a friend we have in Jesus," was first drafted.

From 1855 he lived in Huron County near what is now Clinton, going frequently to read the Bible to the men engaged in building the Grand Trunk Railway to Goderich, "getting small thanks for his pains." "A big man, of pleasant countenance," he was deeply respected locally for his charity, piety, lack of concern for his own needs, and adherence to truth. About 1857 he moved to Bewdley, near Port Hope, joining the household of a retired naval officer, Robert Lamport Pengelly, as tutor. He became engaged to Pengelly's niece, Eliza Catherine Roach, who became ill and died in August 1860.

Scriven gathered around himself a Plymouth Brethren congregation, making converts by his preaching and manner of life and "acting as a sort of spiritual adviser to numerous families." He distributed poems and tracts of his own in the neighbourhood, including his *Hymns*, printed for that purpose. In the late 1860s or early 1870s he left the Pengellys for a cottage in Port Hope, preaching in the streets and in the taverns where workmen lunched, dismissed by some as "only old Joe," but to many of the poor with whom he more and more spent his time known as "the good man" – a name still used for him 35 years after his death. His preaching style, with simple language and quiet, unassuming delivery, was remembered, and still more so his charities, though they were silently performed. For years he tended the cow of a Port Hope widow and carried the milk to her customers; he sawed wood for those who could not pay; he sold his watch, brought from Ireland, to replace someone's lost cow; and more than he could well spare he gave to the needy, while his family in Dublin, somehow informed, first changed their remittances into useful articles and then stopped them altogether. From facts such as these the legends grew.

His last days were clouded with ill-health and despondency. James Sackville, his friend and fellow-believer, found Scriven ill and brought him to his house. One hot night in 1886 Scriven left his bed without disturbing anyone, probably to drink at a nearby spring: some hours later, presumably having fainted or fallen, he was found dead in the spillway of Sackville's grist-mill, a few feet from the spring. He was buried in the Pengelly burial-ground in an unmarked grave between Eliza Roach and Commander Pengelly. In 1920, owing largely to the concern of his future biographer Lewis Frederick Clarry, a monument was erected over his grave, a mile south of Bewdley, under the patronage of Sir Robert Laird Borden*, Newton Wesley Rowell*, and William Lyon Mackenzie King*, and was unveiled by Ontario Premier Ernest Charles Drury*.

"What a friend" had appeared first, unsigned, in Horace Lorenzo Hastings' *Social hymns: original and selected* (1865), and with Charles Crozart Converse's tune was popularized by Ira David Sankey. It was first ascribed to its author in a further Hastings collection of 1886, the year of his death. In 1869 Scriven had published in Peterborough his *Hymns and other verses,* 115 in all, which did not include "What a friend." Seven of his texts, including four from *Hymns*, appear in *What a friend we have in Jesus and other hymns by Joseph Scriven, with a sketch of the author*, published by the Reverend James Cleland in 1895. In 1919 Edward Samuel Caswell* printed an early version of "What a friend" with the title "Pray without ceasing." Hymnbooks have followed the text taken by Cleland from a manuscript Scriven had given to Sackville, until the hymn book of the Anglican and United churches in Canada was published in 1971, in which the last stanza is somewhat altered.

Called by Caswell in 1919 "beyond question the best-known piece of Canadian literature," "What a friend" seems the only one of Scriven's hymns to have circulated widely – ironically, as almost all of his others are more firmly constructed, without emotional softness, and developed from biblical texts. They show him to have been a moderately capable writer in a fine tradition, though one that was dying in his day. He gave away at least three manuscript copies of "What a friend," but excluded it from the work he chose to publish: chance, by bringing the poem separately into print and then matching it with the tune titled from it "Friendship," has preserved for us an uncharacteristic representation of the work of this devoted and courageous man.

JAY MACPHERSON

Joseph Medlicott Scriven's hymns can be found in his *Hymns and other verses* (Peterborough, Ont., 1869) and his *What a friend we have in Jesus and other hymns by Joseph Scriven, with a sketch of the author*, ed. James Cleland (Port Hope, Ont., 1895), as well as in *Canadian singers and their songs: a collection of portraits, autograph poems and brief biographies*, comp. E. S. Caswell ([3rd ed.], Toronto, 1925), 12, 186–87, 262; H. L. Hastings, *Social hymns: original and selected* (Boston, 1865); and *The hymn book of the Anglican Church of Canada and the United Church of Canada* ([Toronto], 1971). For information on Scriven and "What a friend we have in Jesus" see Protestant Episcopal Church in the United States of America, Joint Commission on the Revision of the Hymnal, *The hymnal 1940 companion* (3rd ed., New York, [1956]), 266, 554–55.

MTL, Biog. scrapbooks, XII: 77, E. M. Lindsay, "Reminiscences of Joseph Scriven." UCA, L. F. Clarry, "Joseph Scriven" (typescript).

SEELY, ALEXANDER McLEOD, businessman and office-holder; b. 10 Feb. 1812 in Saint John, N.B., the son of Seth Seely Jr; m. first 29 June 1834 Sarah Morrell (d. 1848) of Saint John, and they had four children; m. secondly 10 Oct. 1850 Lillian Ann Hammond of Charlestown (now part of Boston), Mass., and they had four children; d. 10 July 1882 at Saint John.

Alexander McLeod Seely's grandfather, a loyalist from Stamford, Conn., was granted land in Saint John in 1783, but decided instead to farm up-river on Long Reach. Seely's father became a seaman and later a captain on many ships, including the privateer *Nancy* in 1812, the year Alexander was born. Educated in the public schools of Saint John, Alexander became a lumber surveyor and in 1834 entered the employ of Thomas McMackin of Indiantown (now part of Saint John) as a clerk. By 1838 Seely had established himself as an independent timber merchant in the Saint John suburb of Portland. There he acquired a sawmill and expanded his interests to include the transport and export of lumber. In the 1840s he had two or more ships built for him on the west bank of the Saint John River and joined the Portland and Lancaster Steam Ferry Company, which provided ferry service across the as yet unbridged mouth of the river. In 1849 he became president of the ferry company and in 1850 its sole owner.

Seely, who since 1838 had been a freeman of Saint John, had decided by 1850 to move into the city, and thus simultaneously embarked on his second marriage and an expanded business career. With extensive contacts in the lumber business, including after 1851 the acquisition of the South Bay Boom Company, Seely became involved in shipbuilding in the early 1850s, having Alexander Sime construct a number of ships with which to tap a profitable British market. The 1,345-ton *Bride of the Sea*, for example, was launched in December 1853 and sold to Millers and Thompson of Liverpool. Seely also retained ownership of some cargo vessels, such as the *Sarah M.* Success in these enterprises led to his appointment about 1855 as a director of the Commercial Bank of New Brunswick, of which he became president in 1866. He had also been president of the Saint John Fire Insurance Company since 1856 and had acquired land in Maine which he sold in 1866 for $6,000. He bought shares in a variety of companies such as the Peoples Street Railway Company of Saint John in

1868, the western extension of the European and North American Railway in 1870 and 1872, the Spring Hill and Parrsborough Coal and Railway Company in 1872, and the New Brunswick Paper Company in 1876. His total wealth cannot be determined exactly, though it was significant; about 1870 his valuable investments and property holdings were augmented by $48,771 which was owed to him personally.

Of central importance to Seely's life was his affiliation with the Baptist Church. As early as the 1830s he was secretary of the church-supported Portland Abstinence Society and he was for many years a trustee and treasurer of the Leinster Street Baptist Church in Saint John. His work on various missionary boards and the New Brunswick Baptist Education Society led to his becoming president of the New Brunswick Baptist Home Missionary Board, and in 1867 vice-president of the Maritime Baptist Convention. He had served in 1864 as president of the Saint John Religious Tract Society and was selected as the Baptist representative on the senate of the University of New Brunswick. Like that of the Reverend Charles TUPPER, Seely's involvement in the church reflected the Baptist preoccupation in mid century with missionary work and education.

In recognition of his prominence in business and in the Baptist Church, Seely was appointed to the New Brunswick Legislative Council early in 1854. He did not distinguish himself as a speaker nor did he appear to have much political influence, a point emphasized by his not being appointed to the Canadian Senate in 1867 when about half of his colleagues were so honoured. By the mid 1870s he had become a senior member of the council and had earned a reputation as a meticulous legislator with expertise in parliamentary procedure and practice. In 1879 he was chosen president of the Legislative Council.

After 1880 Seely's health began to deteriorate and a decided feebleness preceded his death on 10 July 1882. In an obituary the Saint John *Daily Evening News* commented that a "courteous manner, obliging disposition and gentlemanly bearing, coupled with a high sense of honor," had marked his career.

C. M. WALLACE

N.B. Museum, Alexander McLeod Seely papers. PANB, "N.B. political biog." (J. C. and H. B. Graves). *Daily Sun* (Saint John, N.B.), 11 July 1882. *Daily Telegraph* (Saint John), 12 July 1882. *Morning News* (Saint John), 11 July 1882. *New Brunswick Courier* (Saint John), 15 April 1837. *Canadian biog. dict.*, II. *CPC*, 1880. *Dominion annual register*, 1882. *New-Brunswick almanac*, 1851; 1856; 1864; 1866; 1867. Esther Clark Wright, *Saint John ships and their builders* (Wolfville, N.S., [1975]). C. M. Robinson, "The pioneers of King Street," N.B. Hist. Soc., *Coll.* (Saint John), no.14 (1955): 29–45.

SEGHERS, CHARLES JOHN (Charles-Jean, Karl Jan), Roman Catholic priest and bishop; b. 26 Dec. 1839 at Ghent, Belgium, youngest son of Charles-François Seghers and Paulina Seghers; d. 28 Nov. 1886 near Nulato, Alaska.

Charles John Seghers was raised in Ghent by relatives because of the early deaths of his parents. After completing his studies at a Jesuit college in Ghent, he entered the diocesan seminary there in 1856. He was ordained deacon on 9 Aug. 1862 and in that year transferred to the American College at Louvain, Belgium, which had been founded in 1857 by American bishops to supply North America with English-speaking missionary clergy. Although he was in poor health, Seghers hoped to work in missions in the Washington Territory. Instead he responded to an appeal by Bishop Modeste Demers* of the crown colony of Vancouver Island. Seghers was ordained priest on 30 May 1863, and left for Victoria on 14 September.

Seghers worked as a parish priest, mainly at Victoria, for the next ten years. Poor health continued to trouble him and he almost succumbed to consumption in 1868 and 1869. After Bishop Demers' death on 28 July 1871 Seghers became diocesan administrator, and on 21 March 1873 Pope Pius IX named him to succeed Demers as bishop of Vancouver Island.

Much of Seghers' time as bishop was taken up in missionary activities among the various Indian groups on the west coast of the island and in Alaska, at that time attached to the island diocese. He was also a frank and eloquent defender of Catholic interests on the island and opposed Premier Andrew Charles ELLIOTT's attempt to impose the general education tax on Catholics in April 1876. In 1877 he began a missionary tour along the Yukon River. The trip lasted 14 months during which he had contact with native groups along the Yukon and near the Bering Sea. After returning to Victoria via San Francisco, he was dismayed to learn that Pope Leo XIII had appointed him on 6 May 1878 coadjutor to the ailing François-Norbert Blanchet, archbishop of the diocese of Oregon City, Oreg. In December 1880 he was also appointed administrator of the vicariate of Idaho.

Seghers spent most of the period from 1878 to early 1885 at Oregon City; his time was divided between administrative duties and apostolic journeys among whites and Indians in northern Idaho and western Montana. In 1885 Jean-Baptiste Brondel, Seghers' successor on Vancouver Island, became apostolic administrator of the new vicariate of Montana, which had been created on 5 March 1883, and Jean-J. Jonckau declined to replace him on Vancouver Island. Seghers received approval from Leo XIII to return to Vancouver Island. On 10 Feb. 1885 he became bishop of the diocese with the personal title of archbishop-bishop.

Seghers was eager to go back to the diocese and especially anxious to resume his missionary efforts in the northern interior. Soon after returning to Victoria, he was looking for new missionaries to work in the Aleutian Islands and the Alaska interior. He encouraged Father Joseph Mary Cataldo, superior of the Jesuits in the Rocky Mountains, to visit Europe to recruit the much-needed missionaries. He also prevailed upon Cataldo to let two Jesuits accompany him on a tour he proposed to undertake of central Alaska, and Cataldo appointed fathers Louis-Aloysius Robaut and Pascal Tosi. Seghers added a layman, Frank Fuller, who had worked in various northwest Jesuit missions. Several colleagues, including Tosi, protested against Seghers' choice of Fuller, who had shown signs of mental instability, but Seghers remained firm in his decision.

The expedition left Esquimalt, travelled by boat to Juneau, Alaska, and headed inland towards the Yukon River through the Chilkoot Pass. After a hazardous and exhausting trip of almost two months, from 13 July to 7 Sept. 1886, they reached the confluence of the Yukon and Stewart rivers. The expedition then headed north down the Yukon and into central Alaska.

Seghers soon learned that he faced competition in the area and that Octavius Parker, an Episcopalian missionary, was, in fact, near Nulato, the spot Seghers had designated as his choice for the first Catholic mission on the Yukon. Leaving the rest of his party, Seghers took Fuller and headed for Nulato in an effort to forestall Parker. During the journey Seghers recorded in his diary evidence of Fuller's increasing insanity. Early in the morning of 28 Nov. 1886, just a few miles from Nulato, Fuller shot and killed the archbishop. Bizarre rumours spread about the murder and there were even attempts to make a martyr of Seghers. However, the murder was no more than the act of a paranoid schizophrenic who, unable to escape a hostile environment, had interpreted Seghers as his enemy.

Seghers' contribution continued even after his death. He had been responsible for Cataldo's search in Europe for additional missionaries and the Jesuits felt themselves obliged to follow up this activity. Among Seghers' practical achievements was the placing of resident missionaries on the west coast of Vancouver Island. He also played a large part in encouraging the Sisters of St Anne in Montreal to send some of their number to central Alaska. A forceful, impetuous, but kind man, Seghers provided the Roman Catholic Church with the necessary leadership to expand and consolidate its missionary efforts in the Pacific northwest.

GERARD G. STECKLER

American College Arch., Katholieke Universiteit te Leuven (Louvain, Belgium), Charles-Jean Seghers file. Arch. de la Propagation de la Foi (Paris), Vancouver, f.202, Seghers à Certes, pièce 12618 (30 déc. 1878), pièce 12655 (13 juill. 1886). Arch. of the Archdiocese of Portland in Oregon (Portland, Oreg.), Blanchet f.III, 270, Johannes Card. Simeoni F°N, Blanchet, 19 sept. 1876. Oregon Prov. Arch. of the Society of Jesus (Spokane, Wash.), Barnum to [Robaut], 10 May 1886; Tosi to Cataldo, 24 Nov. 1886; Robaut to Cataldo, 28 Nov. 1886; Robaut to Jonckau, 31 July 1887; Cataldo to Jetté, 13 Jan. 1925. Maurice De Baets, *Mgr Seghers, l'apôtre de l'Alaska* (Paris et Poitiers, France, 1896); translated by Sister Mary Mildred as *The apostle of Alaska: life of the Most Reverend Charles John Seghers* (Paterson, N.J., 1943). *Reminiscences of the west coast of Vancouver Island*, comp. Charles Moser (Victoria, 1926). G. G. Steckler, "Charles John Seghers, missionary bishop in the American northwest, 1839–1886" (PHD thesis, Univ. of Washington, Seattle, 1963). J. M. Hill, "Archbishop Seghers, Pacific coast missionary," CCHA *Report*, 18 (1951): 15–23. Pascal Tosi, "Alaska, le pays – un voyage de pénétration," *Études religieuses, philosophiques, hist. et littéraires* (Paris), 60 (septembre–décembre 1893): 95-116.

SENÉCAL, LOUIS-ADÉLARD (often written Sénécal, but he signed Senécal), merchant, shipowner, entrepreneur, and politician; b. 10 July 1829 at Varennes, Lower Canada, son of Ambroise Sénécal, a farmer and grain merchant, and Marie-Anne Brodeur; m. 15 Jan. 1850 at Verchères, Delphine, daughter of Lieutenant-Colonel Joseph Dansereau, a merchant; d. 11 Oct 1887 in Montreal.

The Sénécal family came from Rouen, France. Adrien, a tailor by trade, immigrated to New France in 1673. Settling first at Trois-Rivières, he moved a few years later to Boucherville where his descendants turned to farming, and increased rapidly in number. Little is known of Louis-Adélard's early years, although his father is believed to have moved the family to Verchères soon after his son's birth. It is thought that he went to the local parish school, that he spent about two years in Vermont, during which he attended the common school in Burlington for some months, and that he returned to Verchères at the end of the 1840s. His marriage contract reveals a businessman's prudence: the couple agreed to community of property but each retained certain objects and rights acquired before the marriage. One clause provided that the wife could "on giving up community [of property] take back what she had brought to it," and another stipulated that the husband was to keep a legacy from his mother, amounting to £6,500 (sterling), which he "had employed for the purchase of trade goods and other chattels."

For Senécal, the years following his marriage were formative. On 13 May 1850, with Michel Senécal of Saint-Marc, he set up a general store at Verchères under the name of L. A. et M. Senécal. The contract provided that each partner would invest £100 in the firm's capital stock. Michel was to manage the store and keep the books, to be closed annually on 1 May;

he was to receive a salary. The partnership was to run for three years, and provided that the parties "could not withdraw from the said company for any reason whatsoever." At the end of each year losses or profits were to be shared equally. It is to be noted that in this contract the role of Louis-Adélard was not specified, and it was Michel who took on the day-to-day management of the undertaking, leaving his partner the time to attend to other business. On 12 July 1851, L. A. et M. Senécal was prematurely dissolved by mutual agreement: Michel bought the business with all the buildings, stock, and accounts, in return for a number of promissory notes issued in favour of Louis-Adélard.

In the autumn of 1851 Ambroise Sénécal joined forces with his son, appointing Louis-Adélard special procurator and sole business agent for a grain business. Louis-Adélard was authorized to buy grain for his father, set the price, and collect arrears of payment. Responsible for storage and delivery as well as for the bookkeeping, he agreed not to trade in grain on his own account. His father advanced the working capital and paid him a commission, while retaining access to the account books at any time and his right of veto in important decisions.

At the beginning of 1852 Louis-Adélard Senécal was forced to announce his bankruptcy, as a result of losses incurred in earlier commercial transactions. On 15 January he came to an agreement with the 24 creditors, who for the most part were Montreal suppliers of earthenware, paint, hardware, and other articles. His debts amounted to £1,864, and he agreed to pay eight shillings on the pound, in five quarterly instalments without interest. Among his creditors were the Richelieu Company, of which he would one day be president, and Adolphe Roy, who later became one of his principal financial backers. Ostensibly at least, Senécal was ruined – a painful situation which allowed his family to display its solidarity. At the time of the agreement of January 1852 his father mortgaged three properties to reassure Louis-Adélard's creditors, and his wife gave up her rights to a lot which he sold on 25 June for £4,000. Back on his feet again, Senécal kept his eyes open for a profitable venture and on 2 March 1853, in partnership with his father and father-in-law, he bought the steamship *George Frederick* for $4,700 from Edwin C. French of Cornwall, Canada West. They renamed it *Verchères* and Louis-Adélard, who had somehow learned the art of navigation, became its captain. On 9 April, before all the ice had gone from the river, the *Verchères* made a memorable maiden voyage from Ogdensburg, N.Y., to Montreal and, with the establishment of regular service between Verchères and Montreal a few months later, "le capitaine Senécal" (as he was later dubbed by the people of the region), would unknowingly become a local legend.

In the mid 1850s shipping was a promising field of endeavour. Neither roads nor railways were as yet serious competitors. In the Richelieu region there were signs of a new vitality and settlers were filling in the back sections of the seigneuries, between the Yamaska and Saint-François rivers. With the progress of industrialization in the United States from the 1840s and the Reciprocity Treaty in 1854, a promising axis for trade between Montreal and New York was opening via the Richelieu River, an axis strengthened in the 1860s by the American Civil War. No doubt Senécal did not immediately see all these possibilities, but he became aware of them as time passed. Even more important, shipping brought him into contact with the Montreal business community as well as with local figures, thus opening horizons to challenge his imagination and daring. According to an article in *La Minerve* of Montreal in 1887, Senécal established links between William Henry (Sorel), Canada East, and Montreal with the *Verchères* soon after it commenced service in 1853, between Sainte-Anne-de-Sorel and Montreal with the *Yamaska* at the beginning of 1858, between the Saint-François River and William Henry with the *Cygne*, and between Quebec and Montreal with the *Ottawa* in 1860 – the last endeavour to compete with the Richelieu Company [*see* Jacques-Félix Sincennes*]. This simplified outline, emphasizing Senécal's personal accomplishments during these years, disguises a much more complex, collective activity. It seems that Senécal was always a co-owner of the vessels, and his role in the different companies that were involved varied considerably. The case of the *Verchères* is revealing. On 4 Aug. 1854 he joined with his father-in-law and his brother Adolphe (who had inherited his father's share of the original company) to form a new company, Senécal, Dansereau et Compagnie to use the *Verchères* on the St Lawrence. Ownership of the company was divided into three equal parts, and its assets would consist of the *Verchères* as well as any other barges or boats the partners might acquire. The partners undertook to give priority to the venture and not to carry on any independent shipping business. All three could, as individuals, enter into transactions on behalf of the company and had unrestricted access to the account books. The partnership agreement was renewed periodically, with changed terms and a succession of partners: on 25 April 1855 Joseph Dansereau acquired Adolphe Senécal's share; on 9 Feb. 1857 Louis-Adélard sold a third of his stock to Pierre-Édouard Malhiot; and on 28 July the firm became Dansereau et Compagnie. More important, from 1855 the terms were altered to allow the partners to work alone or in other shipping companies, a change probably made at the request of Louis-Adélard, who was seeking to diversify his investment portfolio.

Senécal's entrepreneurial spirit showed in his readiness to seize every opportunity for profitable shipping transactions. On 30 Nov. 1855 he acquired a share in the People's Line. On 28 Jan. 1858 he went into partnership with other businessmen in the Yamaska Navigation Company, capitalized at $12,200; he expected thereby to be able to engage in transportation on the Yamaska and Saint-François rivers, as well as on the St Lawrence between Saint-Hugues and Montreal. It was Senécal who built the *Yamaska* for this company – in less than two and a half months, according to his obituary – as well as the *Cygne*. In 1859 he went into partnership with Sévère Dumoulin and Édouard-Louis PACAUD to form the Compagnie de Navigation de Trois-Rivières. In the same year, he joined his brother Adolphe, as Senécal et Senécal, to buy grain on commission in the parishes along the St Lawrence, and transport it to Victor Hudon*'s mills in Montreal. The following year he managed an office at Sorel for the Yamaska Navigation Company. He continued to diversify his activities and on 5 Feb. 1862 undertook to build five barges at a cost of $7,500 for H. Robertson and Company of Montreal. In April 1869, with Pierreville merchant Henri Vassal, Montreal merchant Louis Tourville, Adolphe Roy, and others, he set up a dredging enterprise, the St Francis and Yamaska Rivers Improvement and Deepening Company, with a capital reserve of $100,000.

The increased demand for labour, grain, hay, and manufactured products engendered by the American Civil War stimulated intense economic activity in the region of Montreal and the Richelieu River in the early 1860s and provided speculators with numerous opportunities. Senécal, who had been in business for some ten years, was in a position to take full advantage of these circumstances. Hundreds of notarial documents relative to land purchases, the transport of goods, shipbuilding, and lumber production attest to his feverish and wide-ranging activity. In effect, trade between Montreal and New York State via the Richelieu region formed the backbone for all his projects during this period. He is reputed to have had an interest in a fleet of some 11 steamships and 89 barges, used to transport lumber and grain between Montreal, Sorel, and Whitehall, N.Y. These barges (some 100 to 125 feet long and 20 to 23 feet wide, with holds 4 to 7 feet deep) cost about $1,500 each and could carry 6,000 to 10,000 bushels of wheat. Shipping became the springboard for an extension of Senécal's business, and the region between the Yamaska and Saint-François rivers, which in addition to a number of seigneuries included the townships of Wickham, Grantham, and Upton, constituted the territorial base for his economic interests.

During this period Senécal plunged boldly into land speculation. In 1860 he bought from Jonathan Saxton Campbell Wurtele*, a merchant and seigneur of Rivière-David, about $1,500 in copyholders' arrears. This contract apparently enabled him to acquire certain lots belonging to copyholders unable to pay their debts. Senécal was to use this method many times. Even more important was the purchase, in February 1866, of all the properties of Charles James Irwin Grant, Baron de Longueuil, in the township of Upton, with the capital and arrears on the rents, a sizeable acquisition, including 300 claimable debts totalling £10,287. On the purchase price of $24,000, he was to pay $12,000 down, $7,000 on receipt of the titles, and $5,000 in the next 18 months. Isaac Coote, Grant's agent, entered the service of the purchaser and took charge of managing the estate. In March 1866 Senécal increased his holding by buying the entire estate of the late Ignace Gill*, including a magnificent property bordering on the Odanak Indian Reserve, a piece of land on Île Ronde, and some lots in Durham and Upton townships. On 6 April he delegated Henri Vassal to settle the debts and liabilities of the estate. Then on 15 Feb. 1867 he completed his holdings by acquiring for $3,000 a number of lots owned by Grant in the townships of Hereford and Barford as well as in New Hampshire. But he was not solely interested in purchasing large blocks of land; the minute-books of local notaries record numerous transactions in his name concerning the purchase or sale of small lots. For example, apparently through the good offices of a municipal secretary, he bought several small parcels in the parish of Saint-David, sold by the corporation of Yamaska County for tax arrears, including a group of nine lots acquired on 7 Jan. 1867 for $149.43.

This property speculation did not prevent Senécal from expanding his network of businesses. On 15 Dec. 1862 he went into partnership with Carlos Darius Meigs, a skilled workman of Saint-Guillaume, under the name of Senécal et Meigs. At first the firm confined itself to operating a sawmill on Rivière David. Senécal provided the working capital and had sole right to the profits. Meigs managed the mill, was responsible for maintaining the equipment, and guaranteed to process annually 30,000 pine logs into planks, laths, and shingles; he received a monthly salary of $100, as well as a commission on the sawn lumber. Subsequently the company expanded into buying and selling barges, speculating in land, and dealing in mortgages: it usually lent at between 8 and 20 per cent interest. On 12 Oct. 1866 Senécal, acting in both his own name and that of the company, appointed Edward Campbell Wurtele, a merchant of Saint-David, general and special agent to manage the affairs of the firm and to direct the commercial operations he himself had undertaken until then.

Relieved of various responsibilities, Senécal took advantage of the heavy demand for timber of all kinds to invest in other mills; he developed a plan to build a modern mill with a large productive capacity at Pierreville, and hence sought to tighten his hold on vast areas of forest. He next endeavoured to reconcile his interests in lumber manufacture and in landed property; thus he had land cleared to supply his sawmills, then sold the land to settlers, who undertook as partial payment to clear another lot for him, and so the cycle began again.

In the spring of 1866, therefore, Senécal undertook to set up the Pierreville Steam Mills Company. He went into partnership with Henri Vassal, Valentine Cooke (a merchant of Drummondville), Louis Tourville and Joseph-Guillaume Tranchemontagne (both merchants of Montreal), and also with his associate Meigs. The partnership agreement of 12 May provided for an authorized capital of $24,000, divided into shares of $1,000. The board of directors, consisting of a president (Senécal) and a secretary (Vassal), was to deal with current matters, and an annual meeting of the shareholders would determine the distribution of dividends, elect the directors, and examine the account books. On 15 Aug. 1866 the Legislative Assembly ratified this agreement, despite a petition signed by about 100 opponents who claimed the proposed company was likely to monopolize the processing of timber in the region. Work began in the autumn, at a tongue of land on the Île du Fort, in the lower part of the Tardif channel, a body of water 50 to 100 feet wide that provided a natural passage for the wood to the mill. Meigs obtained the $26,500 contract for the construction of the establishment, to consist of two buildings: a sawmill 75 by 55 feet, equipped to produce 50,000 to 60,000 feet of planks daily, with a circular saw, five frames holding 89 vertical saws, and modern devices for making laths and shingles; and a flour-mill 65 by 46 feet housing, in addition to the millstones, machinery for carding and fulling cloth. A complex assembly of boilers and steam-engines drove the machinery. The company facilities included breakwaters, a bridge linking the Île du Fort to the north shore of the channel, and a loading dock. Meigs was given the responsibility of running the establishment and maintaining the equipment for two years, in return for a commission based on production. The mill began operations in December 1866 and immediately became an important centre of local development: it even became fashionable to take a trip from Sorel to visit it. *La Gazette de Sorel* of 21 Aug. 1869 noted that the establishment – which then included three mills, a carding-mill apparently having been added – employed more than 120 men and produced 83,000 feet of lumber daily, and that since the spring 59 vessels had left Pierreville, mostly bound for the United States; furthermore, the company is reported to have bought from the government a 37,000-acre timber limit in the townships of Simpson, Grantham, and Wendover. Senécal was closely involved in the management of the company. His principal concerns were keeping the mill supplied with logs, selling and distributing planks, and maintaining the firm's working capital. Since the company's cash reserve was small, it was often short of funds and Senécal resorted to discounting notes receivable to obtain liquid assets. Much later, his partners publicly accused him of having used the company to obtain funds for himself, either by personally collecting the discount on notes endorsed by the company, or by demanding excessive advances for logs which were not always delivered. In this way he eventually incurred a $40,000 debt to the company.

Senécal needed liquidity because of the growing multiplicity of his business operations. On 28 Jan. 1867 he and Vassal formed Vassal et Compagnie, to trade (from 14 Jan. 1867 to 1 May 1870) in "dry [and perishable] goods, grain, and any other items." The partners invested the same amount and all profits and losses were shared equally. On 25 March 1867 Senécal formed a partnership for a period of five years with Edward Campbell Wurtele, under the name of Wurtele et Senécal, to trade in lumber and grain with the United States, using 15 barges valued at $15,000. Here again, the partners had equal shares in the firm's capital, divided profits and losses equally, and were each authorized to make transactions binding on the company, which had its headquarters at Sorel.

By the autumn of 1867 Senécal was therefore the central figure in a vast commercial network. He was 38, and his contemporaries estimated (though without proof) that his annual volume of business reached $3,000,000. After living in Verchères during the 1850s, and then at Saint-David or Saint-Guillaume during the 1860s, he settled his family in Montreal. But his roots were in the Sorel region and he liked to identify himself as a Pierreville merchant. His father and father-in-law having died, he seems to have remained close to only one of his brothers, Ambroise, with whom he carried on business. He had two daughters: Delphire, who married Charles-Ignace Gill on 1 Jan. 1870, and Octavie, later the wife of William Blumhart. His two sons-in-law became both the sons he did not have and his business partners. For the present, Senécal was powerful and his fame had already spread far and wide. Auguste ACHINTRE in his *Manuel électoral* describes him as "tall, thin, bony, with a long neck, long legs, a bare forehead, prominent cheekbones, a keen eye, [a man] of few words"; always on the move, "he does not walk, he runs: if he sometimes stops, it is in a vehicle, to gain time, to decipher twenty telegrams and to reply to them." The key to his success lay in an irrepressible imagination which allowed him to marshal scattered resources around projects swiftly conceived and swiftly executed, extraordinary physical endurance, boldness and sang-froid in both the conception and realization of projects, rather flexible business ethics, and ever-alert curiosity. These qualities enabled him to bring together in aid of any given project Montreal capitalists to whom he paid high rates of interest, regional agents whose participation he secured through commissions or profits, and cheap local manpower. He knew all the tricks to get working capital: discounting bills of exchange, overdrawing his account, mortgaging property, manipulating the funds of the businesses he managed, ignoring dates of payment, charging exorbitant interest, quick speculation, and so forth. But Senécal was a conductor with a weakness: he played without a score – he had no overall accounting system for his transactions – and without rehearsal; he liked to conceive and execute pieces but did not like to develop them in detail.

It is not surprising that Senécal decided in the autumn of 1867 to have a go at politics; the double mandate enabled him to run in both the provincial riding of Yamaska and the federal constituency of Drummond and Arthabaska. For this powerful man, politics was another way of doing business, one more trump card. This opportunistic attitude did not prevent him, in this period, from having a few political ideas. He was at first linked with the Rouges, as a result of a previous relationship with Jean-Baptiste-Éric Dorion*, whose newspaper *Le Défricheur* (L'Avenir) he had financed; this paper, at Senécal's request, had then passed into the hands of Wilfrid Laurier* [*see* Pierre-Joseph Guitté*]. Senécal stood in 1867 as a Liberal candidate; he sat in the Quebec Legislative Assembly until 1871 and in the House of Commons until 1872. He was a discreet member, more active and talkative in committees where he drew on his business experience than in the house where he expressed himself with difficulty. Plagued with financial problems, he was often absent from parliamentary sessions.

On 20 Nov. 1867 Senécal went bankrupt in his own name and in the name of Senécal et Meigs, and deposited "all his assets and personal effects, property, books, letters and documents" with the official assignee, Tancrède Sauvageau. The bankruptcy brought about the dissolution of the Wurtele et Senécal partnership, Senécal giving up his rights in the company. A provisional statement of the creditors – for, as Sauvageau noted, "M. Senécal in drawing up the said statement had recourse to his memory rather than to his account books, having not kept regular accounts" – evaluated the bankruptcy at about $410,000, without considering debts to at least 14 other creditors. The real reasons for this bankruptcy remain obscure. Contemporaries felt that the business crisis precipitated by the closing of the American market following the end of the Reciprocity Treaty in 1866 caught Senécal short: he had fixed assets and inventories but no liquid assets to meet his many obligations. He proposed a composition with his creditors by which he would reimburse fully the preferred creditors' debts, amounting to $17,480, and pay 50 cents on the dollar, in semi-annual payments of $30,000, for the rest. He also agreed to the nomination by the creditors of three trustees to administer his property, with management expenses up to $2,500 annually to be charged to the estate. In return, he requested that Meigs and Vassal be discharged from liability for the notes they had endorsed. These terms were accepted by the 51 creditors at meetings held on 7 Dec. 1867 and 22 Jan. 1868, and on the latter date the property was officially transferred from Tancrède Sauvageau to the trustees. An important clause in the deed of transfer, however, declared that Senécal was to be employed at an undisclosed salary to administer and realize the estate under the supervision of the trustees, and to proceed with the business he had previously conducted. Senécal therefore was again in charge of his property, but under the vigilant eye of three trustees. With Meigs and Vassal, he continued his operations in the Pierreville Steam Mills Company, which had not been directly affected by this bankruptcy.

Senécal was not at the end of his troubles. On 20 June 1868 the Pierreville mills burned down: he rebuilt them in 47 days, equipping them with 146 vertical saws. In August fire razed his factory " for the extraction of liquid from hemlock bark" at Saint-Guillaume. On 14 Jan. 1870 fire again devastated the mills at Pierreville, but he got them back in operation, reportedly in 30 days. These were indeed difficult years and when he signed the marriage contract of his daughter Delphire, on 31 Dec. 1869, he was only able to provide her with $6,000 to be paid in six instalments, or, in the event he had no cash, in land and real property. No doubt unable to meet the repayment obligations of his 1867 composition with his creditors, Senécal was again declared insolvent at the beginning of 1870 and control of his property reverted to the official assignee, Sauvageau. According to a statement of his creditors, his debts totalled $407,559.79, and involved major Montreal firms: Adolphe Roy et Compagnie ($71,939), the Merchants' Bank of Canada ($66,899), E. Hudon, Fils et Compagnie ($61,310), Louis Gauthier ($31,060), the Banque du Peuple ($30,055), Louis Tourville ($17,008), Thomas Wilson ($16,773), and P. Larose ($16,509). The Pierreville Steam Mills Company made a claim of $15,079. The creditors held an emergency meeting. There were differences of opinion and, it can be surmised, much activity behind the scenes. On 11 Feb. 1870 Vassal offered to buy the assets of the bankrupt estate, paying the creditors eight cents on each dollar owing, with notes falling due over a period of several months. The notes, curiously enough, were endorsed by Adolphe Roy and Thomas Wilson. The creditors accepted Vassal's offer on 18 February and he immediately became the owner of Senécal's property. Nevertheless he was not free to sell the assets without

Sauvageau's consent until the notes given as a guarantee had been paid. In this transaction, Vassal seems to have been in collusion with his partner and, four days later, "all the movables and intangible assets which have been sold and assigned to the said Henri Vassal" returned to Senécal for the sum of $35,000, which Vassal declared he had received. On 26 September Senécal also recovered from Vassal some 60 lots in Saint-Bonaventure and some 50 in Saint-Guillaume for $45,222, apparently paid in cash. He mortgaged these properties in December to borrow $44,000 from Adolphe Roy and Thomas Wilson, the Montreal financial backers who continued to give him credit and honour his notes, "in order to sustain his business and help him in his speculations." In October Senécal and Vassal had made an agreement terminating their commercial operations and settling the share due to each; considering the small proportion of assets allotted to Vassal, it is clear that in all these undertakings he was little more than Senécal's agent. At the end of 1870, therefore, Senécal was by no means ruined as a result of his bankruptcy: still alert and on the look-out, he was waiting for better times.

Railway construction, which in the 1870s became a large-scale endeavour in Quebec, provided Senécal with a field of activity that came to occupy almost all his time, as shipping and lumbering had done in the 1850s and 1860s. He did not, however, abandon his still considerable interests in the Sorel region, but increasingly relied on such agents as his brother Ambroise (appointed on 16 March 1870), Charles-Ignace Gill (9 Jan. 1871), Pierre-Nérée Dorion (3 March 1871), and Louis Caya (25 Nov. 1873). At the beginning of the 1870s Senécal worked principally on building the Richelieu, Drummond and Arthabaska Counties Railway, of which he progressively obtained control. In the autumn of 1871 he completed the 48-mile section connecting Sorel and L'Avenir via Drummondville. Opened in 1872, this line rapidly became unusable when the wooden rails did not stand up to the rigours of the Quebec climate. On 12 November Senécal therefore sold the line to the South-Eastern Counties Junction Railway Company for $100,000. Three years later, this company gave him the contract to rebuild the Sorel–Drummondville section with steel rails and extend it south to Acton (Acton-Vale). The construction of this track, which was completed in 1876, proved truly epic and put Senécal's talent, energy, and enthusiasm to the test. Working in difficult circumstances and beset with obstacles, he was at the mercy of governments for financing, local interests for the route, businessmen for working capital, and inexperienced workmen and rudimentary equipment for construction. In order to succeed, he needed allies in the various levels of government and straw men in the head offices of the companies he directed. For this purpose he intervened in elections, and to help candidates of his choice maintained good relations with papers such as *Le Pays* (Montreal). But by 1871 Georges-Isidore Barthe*, the mayor of Sorel, had denounced the advent of the "reign of shady speculation," the practice of purchasing "electors retail" and reselling them "wholesale later," and the existence of a local network of politicians in Senécal's pay: Charles-Ignace Gill (member for Yamaska in the Quebec Legislative Assembly, 1871–74), Joseph-Nestor Duguay (member for Yamaska in the House of Commons, 1872–74), Jean-Baptiste Guèvremont and a man named Marchessault, both active in municipal politics. With the aid of his newspaper *La Gazette de Sorel*, Barthe also stood up for the taxpayers' interests against Senécal's plan to get the municipalities to increase their railway subsidies and to pay them before the completion of work. The mayor was not anxious to finance an individual who provided no guarantee, manipulated head offices, determined the location of stations to suit his friends, and claimed $80,000 when he was owed barely $27,000. These two implacable enemies engaged in a fight to the finish. In 1872 Senécal forced Barthe to resign as mayor over an issue involving a conflict of interest. In the federal election in Richelieu that year, he helped ensure the victory of Michel Mathieu*, which entailed the defeat of the ex-mayor. Nevertheless, Barthe was re-elected mayor at Sorel in January 1873.

In the field of railway construction, Senécal used the procedures that had served him so well in the past. He obtained the necessary lumber from his own mills on the Yamaska River, in Kingsey Township, and elsewhere. Straw men collected the grants and were responsible for the expenditures, the exact amount of which is unknown. He also had well-known financial backers, including Valentine Cooke (manager of the South-Eastern Counties Junction Railway Company), Adolphe Roy (now the president of the Pierreville Steam Mills Company), and Louis-Hercule Lafleur (a Montreal merchant). To get money quickly, he used his favourite technique – land speculation. In the autumn of 1873 alone, he bought 1,775 acres of land in the district of Arthabaska, 1,300 acres in the township of Wickham, and 800 in the township of Kingsey, not to mention the 6,450 acres he acquired for the Pierreville Steam Mills Company. His insatiable need for liquid assets led him to make things difficult for his friends. Around 1873 he is thought to have swindled Adolphe Roy out of $17,000 by issuing notes without funds to cover them, and in 1878 he apparently conspired to put the Pierreville Steam Mills Company into bankruptcy.

His need of money may also explain why in 1874 he abandoned the provincial Liberal party, which had been relegated to the opposition. He had long known that political power and capital on a grand scale went hand in hand and that charters and grants were obtained if "one is on the right side." An anecdote illustrates the kind of motivation behind his political activity: having invited his principal organizer in Yamaska County, Antoine Laferté, to desert to the Conservative camp, he apparently said to him: "Toine, I have decided to change parties and to wear blue, . . . with the Bleus I am going to make a lot more money . . . and we are going to get rich." While he was associated with the Liberal party, Senécal had dreamed of a coalition of Bleus and Rouges in provincial politics, in order to facilitate his relations with the government. But Henri-Gustave Joly*, the leader of the Quebec Liberals, opposed such a coalition in December 1874 and, as a crowning ingratitude, the Liberal party, once in power in Ottawa, refused to appoint Senécal a senator. Consequently, he began to cast sidelong glances at the Bleus. He made the acquaintance of Joseph-Adolphe Chapleau* and Clément-Arthur Dansereau* of the Conservative leadership, and in the federal by-election in Drummond and Arthabaska in 1877 took a stand against Laurier, whose defeat he ensured. Ironically, thanks to Luc LETELLIER de Saint-Just's *coup d'état*, the Liberals came to power in Quebec in 1878 just when important decisions were about to be taken concerning the Quebec, Montreal, Ottawa and Occidental Railway. This railway, launched and owned by the government, was to go along the north shore of the St Lawrence. The ambitious Senécal, who scented a killing in this venture, as well as in railway politics as a whole, wanted to be in on the spoils. Far from meeting his expectations, the new government, on the initiative of the premier, Joly, even refused to pay him $15,000 as reimbursement for work already completed. Senécal therefore used every possible means to get the lieutenant governor, Letellier de Saint-Just, relieved of his post and the Joly government defeated in the Legislative Assembly. Despite financial difficulties which forced him to mortgage his insurance policies, he was instrumental in the ousting of the Liberals from power in 1879. Upon becoming premier, Chapleau was therefore in no position to ignore him, especially since Senécal expected some expression of gratitude.

The Conservatives' assumption of office marked the beginning of a form of secret government in which the dominant figures were Dansereau, the party's publicity man, and Senécal, its treasurer. In office until 1882, the Conservative party was none the less torn by disputes: the ideological factions of moderate "Chapleautistes" and ultramontane "Castors" [*see* François-Xavier-Anselme TRUDEL] competed for intellectual dominance while rival financial factions – in particular the Canadian Pacific Railway Company, the Grand Trunk Railway of Canada, Sir Hugh ALLAN and the Montreal Ocean Steamship Company, and the Bank of Montreal – each sought to get their hands on issues of government bonds, railway grants, and the ownership of the Quebec, Montreal, Ottawa and Occidental Railway. On 1 March 1880 Chapleau appointed Senécal superintendent of the last-named company; Senécal brought in his son-in-law William Blumhart as secretary and general supplier. Senécal's salary was to equal 2.5 per cent of the net profits from the operation of the railway. He was given an official mandate to manage in the best interests of Quebec a company that was a heavy burden for the government, and an unofficial mandate to exploit the railway as an instrument of power for the "Chapleautistes." He himself added a third mandate: to take care of his own interests. The challenge was worthy of the man. He carried out his responsibilities by completing the Quebec, Montreal, Ottawa and Occidental through the construction of branch lines feeding the main line, and then transforming the railway into an instrument for patronage and a major source of revenue for the party. This was indeed a dark period in the political history of Quebec, when the man responsible for a public company was also the chief treasurer of a political party, and Senécal earned a severe rebuke from Laurier in an article entitled "La Caverne des 40 voleurs" in *L'Électeur* of 20 April 1881. In this article Laurier labelled Senécal a swindler, claiming that he had stolen from many of his former associates and ruined them, and he accused him of seeking to do the same with the people of Quebec. This virulent attack provoked Senécal into suing Laurier for "a false, scandalous and defamatory libel." The trial opened in Montreal on 5 Oct. 1881 and Laurier's counsel presented a survey of Senécal's business career, going back as far as 1858 when he was found guilty of receiving $50 under false pretences – a decision later reversed by a higher court. Accusation followed accusation and during the whole of October the trial was the centre of attention across the province. When it finished on 2 November the jurors were irremediably split and the case closed without a verdict. None the less, the expression "Sénécaleux" from then on became synonymous in the public mind with cheat, thief, and pilferer of the public purse.

As superintendent of the Quebec, Montreal, Ottawa and Occidental, Senécal reconstructed on a grand scale the scenarios that had become his trademark. Thus he bought the St Lawrence and Industry Village Rail-road, repaired it with materials belonging to the Quebec, Montreal, Ottawa and Occidental, and then sold it at a high price to the government. His greatest success was the liquidation of the Quebec, Montreal, Ottawa and Occidental in 1882. In February, he managed to sell the western section (Montreal-Ottawa) and its branch lines to the CPR for $4,000,000, realizing a personal profit generally estimated at $100,000. During the negotiation of the sale of the eastern section (Montreal-Quebec), Senécal was involved as the unnamed principal behind the North Shore Railway financial syndicate, one of the two groups interested in the purchase. This syndicate included Thomas McGreevy*, Joseph-Aldéric Ouimet, and Alphonse Desjardins*. Senécal's participation was revealed at the beginning of March, soon after the provincial cabinet had accepted the North Shore Railway offer of $4,000,000, and, despite a heated debate over Senécal's activity as a government employee, the Legislative Assembly approved the transaction, which was officially sanctioned on 27 May. In December Senécal resold this section to the Grand Trunk. He thus made an immediate profit on the sale, receiving both cash and shares in the Grand Trunk as payment, and then later realized a second profit when the shares rose in value with the Grand Trunk's sale of the same section to the CPR in 1885.

This crucial episode in railway development may in the end have been to Quebec's advantage, but definitely proved beneficial for Senécal. Certainly he made many enemies who attacked him from all sides – for example, the Liberals in *L'Électeur* and the Ultramontanes in a pamphlet entitled *Le Pays, le Parti et le Grand Homme*, which was published at Montreal in 1882. Yet, on the other hand, he became one of the most influential men in Quebec at the beginning of the 1880s. In 1880 he had been practically insolvent, to judge from the 78 notices of protest served on him by creditors, but by 1882 he was on his feet again financially. Managing a government undertaking had also opened new horizons. In 1881 and 1882 he went to France, as superintendent of the Quebec, Montreal, Ottawa and Occidental Railway, to negotiate the issue of a public loan, and he made contact with some of the important international financiers. After Chapleau left for the federal scene in 1882, Senécal decided to carve a place for himself in the vast network of international capital. He was rich enough to afford newspapers that lavished praise on him, and he benefited from his relations with the high financial circles of Montreal, where he was feared for his low cunning and admired for his boldness and energy. Furthermore, he had some important leverage: he was president of the Richelieu and Ontario Navigation Company (1882–87), the North Shore Railway Company (1883–86), and the Montreal City Passenger Railway Company (1883–84). In 1883 he was given the cross of commander in the French Legion of Honour, which earned him a demonstration of friendship and testimony of admiration from the highest-ranking Montreal political and financial figures, both English and French. The celebration was no mere public event. In a sense it became an historic moment, establishing for succeeding generations the image of a mythical Senécal who, in the words of Jean-Baptiste ROLLAND, "personifies the commercial and industrial genius of the country," and who, according to Chapleau, was the living symbol of the economic awakening of French-speaking Canadians. Quoting the motto which had inspired him all his life – "where there's a will, there's a way" – Senécal affirmed his resolve to continue his labours on a national scale.

The issuing of public bonds in Paris and the establishment in Quebec of the Crédit Foncier Franco-Canadien in 1881 had aroused an infatuation for "*vieille* France" in political and financial circles. It was fashionable to trade with France, which might become an important partner in the economic recovery of French Canadians and the development of Quebec's resources. Rumour had it that Senécal had returned from France and England in 1882 full of fresh ideas. In fact he was nursing three large projects that involved millions of dollars and brought him the adulation of some Montreal financiers: a company to install a transatlantic cable from Halifax to the coast of England, thereby decreasing the cost of telegraphic communications; a shipping link between Rouen and Quebec, financed by capital from Rouen, Montreal, and governmental sources; and a colonization company, drawing on international capital, to develop Quebec's natural resources. These were ventures worthy of an American "tycoon." The third project, the General Colonization and Industrial Enterprise Company, was beyond a doubt the most ambitious ever conceived by Senécal. The company, with a capital of 6 to 10 million dollars, was to be based on the acquisition of the properties comprising the estate of the late George Benson Hall*, which included the famous mills at Montmorency (now part of Beauport), with their extensive timber limits in the Gatineau, Saint-Maurice, and Beauce regions, as well as the Radnor ironworks near Trois-Rivières and several townships, or parts thereof, in southern Quebec.

With Sir Charles Tupper* (the Canadian high commissioner in London) and other associates, Senécal concentrated particularly on this last project during 1883. On 29 January Hall's heirs signed a promise of sale to Senécal. The following month Senécal asked the Quebec Legislative Assembly to grant a charter to the company, which included 27 prominent financiers from various regions of Quebec, and five foreign investors: R. H. Kimball, a New York banker; J. Belloni, owner of collieries in the United States; René Manraize, a Paris merchant; Émile Bonemant, a French agronomist, and Bradley Barlow, a Vermont senator. At the end of February, fearing that lobbying by the ultramontane members might block the grant of the powers demanded by the company, Senécal bought from Sherbrooke businessman Charles King the charter of the Eastern Townships Land and Improvement Company, which conferred extensive powers and enabled him to conduct his operations more freely. On 7 June he acquired the Hall properties in his own name for $1,600,000: $250,000 was paid in cash and four payments, ending on 2 July 1884, were scheduled for the remainder. Although the stakes were high, Senécal realized a substantial profit when he resold these properties two months later to the General Colonization Company (which he had meanwhile incorporated) for "$2,500,000, with $1,000,000 immediately, in paid-up company stock, and the balance of a million and a half, also in paid-up stock, as soon as he has supplied the company with a full discharge of any mortgage on the said property."

Still in search of investors, Senécal went to Europe in the autumn of 1883. He had numerous discussions with Poursin-Escande (the Canadian government agent in Paris), Hector Fabre* (the Quebec representative there), Sir Charles Tupper, and one Fichet (a millionaire from Le Havre, France). Negotiations dragged on and, worse still, an article in the *Mail* of Toronto and the *Morning Chronicle* of Quebec attacking Senécal's credibility put investors on their guard. Back in Canada in December, Senécal launched a libel action for $200,000 (raised to $250,000 in November 1884) against the first newspaper and another against the second. It seems, on the evidence of a handwritten note in Senécal's papers, that in January 1884 "the insurers in Edinburgh reportedly received unfavourable information from Montreal and changed their minds." Was this to be the end of a splendid dream? On 29 Jan. 1884 the board of directors of the General Colonization Company – on which sat Senécal, John McDougall Jr, Charles Rudolph Hosmer*, Louis-Joseph Forget, Télesphore-Eusèbe Normand, Jean-Baptiste-Amédée Mongenais, Paul-Étienne Grandbois, and Jean-Baptiste RENAUD – for want of capital revoked the purchase of the Hall properties concluded with Senécal the preceding year. Through his attorney, Alexandre Louthood, Senécal followed suit with Hall's heirs, thus losing his first payment to them of $250,000 and the interest on a payment of $210,000 which he owed. But despite his disappointments he did not give up, and on 15 February negotiated the purchase of the Radnor ironworks from Hall's heirs for $150,000. On 3 June this contract was renewed until 1 September on other terms but finally expired when the first instalment of $25,000 was not met.

Senécal's three national ventures collapsed for reasons still unknown. In fact, both the transatlantic cable project and the proposed Rouen-Quebec shipping company met the same fate as the General Colonization Company: despite some support in both French and English political circles, Senécal was unable to attract the capital necessary for projects of this magnitude. For 18 months they had claimed much of his time and energy, but had not prevented him from investing in a great many undertakings, such as the Coleraine Mining Company on 11 Oct. 1882, the Magog Textile and Print Company ($10,000) on 2 May 1883, and the Compagnie d'Imprimerie of *La Minerve* the following year. At the time of his death he held securities in the Anglo-Canadian Asbestos Company ($12,738), the Beet Sugar Company of the Province of Quebec ($1,000), the Sovereign Fire Insurance Company of Canada ($1,000), the Canadian Electric Light Company ($40,000), the Grand Trunk Railway of Canada ($500), the Household Fire Extinguisher Company ($2,000), the Megantic Mining Company ($10,000), the Richelieu Paper Manufacturing Company ($5,000), and the Royal Electric Company ($2,000). Various speculations accompanied these investments. On 19 Nov. 1885 he even attempted to return to railway construction, going into partnership with Philippe-Élisée Panneton and Marie-Louise-Alphonsine Giroux, the wife of Télesphore-Eusèbe Normand of Trois-Rivières, in order to build the Saint Lawrence, Lower Laurentian and Saguenay Railway, which would link Saint-Jean-des-Piles to the Quebec and Lake Saint John Railway. Two years later only a 22½-mile section had been built.

Senécal's great interest henceforth was the Richelieu and Ontario Navigation Company. On 13 Feb. 1882 he had been elected president, ousting Hugh Allan, who since 1875 had managed the company with an iron hand and made it one of Canada's largest shipping firms. In 1882 the company, operating between Quebec City and the Great Lakes, had a paid-up capital of about $1,500,000 and 22 ships. None the less, its earning capacity was decreasing, net profits having dropped from $90,722 in 1880 to $32,682 in 1881. The shareholders' dissatisfaction had served the purpose of Senécal, who aspired to the presidency to realize an ambitious project: to amalgamate the eastern section of the Quebec, Montreal, Ottawa and Occidental Railway with the Richelieu and Ontario Navigation Company to secure a monopoly of transportation on the St Lawrence. He had acquired 559 shares in the company – playing the stock exchange on margin, wrote *La Minerve*, pilfering from the public treasury, said his enemies – had found allies among the groups opposed to Allan, and had succeeded in getting himself elected director and then president.

Senécal's immediate objective was to make the company show a profit. The new board of directors took an inventory of assets, examined the various departments, analysed the books, revised the charges, and signed agreements with rival companies. Thus on 11 March 1882 the Quebec, Montreal, Ottawa and Occidental, of which Senécal was still general superintendent, undertook to pay $2,000 annually to the Richelieu and Ontario Navigation Company, provided the latter agreed to cancel its services to Maskinongé, Louiseville, and Yamachiche. On 16 November a similar agreement, involving a one-week suspension of services to Quebec, was concluded, in return for a payment of $1,000, with the North Shore

Railway financial syndicate, which now owned the eastern section of the Quebec, Montreal, Ottawa and Occidental. It was at a meeting on 21 November that Senécal really showed his hand: he persuaded the directors to allow the North Shore Railway syndicate, of which he was also president, to lease the Richelieu and Ontario Navigation Company for 99 years at the rate of $80,000 annually. When the syndicate agreed in December to sell the eastern section of the Quebec, Montreal, Ottawa and Occidental to the Grand Trunk, Senécal abandoned his attempt to unite these two great companies and to monopolize maritime and rail transportation in the St Lawrence region.

The administrative reforms instituted by Senécal in the operations of the Richelieu and Ontario Navigation Company did, however, begin to bear fruit. To the great satisfaction of the shareholders, profits rose to $85,806 in 1882 and the board of directors succeeded in reducing the operating costs by $24,000. During 1883 the company continued its cost-cutting policy, reducing staff and salaries wherever possible. Sorel became the sole "depot of the fleet," where the ships were laid up in winter and repaired. Moreover, efforts were made to eliminate rivals, or at least to reduce their number. By managing to place three of its directors, including Senécal, in the head office of the rival Lake St Francis Railway and Navigation Company, the Richelieu and Ontario extended its control.

Absorbed by his great international projects, Senécal was often absent during 1883, missing 26 of the 54 meetings of the board of directors of the Richelieu and Ontario. Subsequently he attended with greater regularity and used his energy to thwart its numerous competitors. In February 1885, in order to consolidate the firm's position in the western section of its territory, he signed an agreement with the Rome, Waterton and Ogdensburg Railway Company, whose terminus was at Cape Vincent, N.Y. By its terms, the Richelieu and Ontario was to provide a marine link between this terminus and Montreal, Toronto, and even Niagara Falls, Ont., on an agreed timetable and rates. It thus effectively excluded its competitors from a large part of the traffic in goods originating in New York State.

In 1886 the Richelieu and Ontario became interested in the Longueuil Navigation Company and the Laprairie Navigation Company among others, and on 5 February the directors authorized Senécal to increase their company's capital by $200,000 in order to acquire these two transportation companies. During the same year the Saguenay River circuit, operated by the St Lawrence Steam Navigation Company, was made over to the Richelieu and Ontario for nearly $200,000, with the guarantee that no other link would be set up by the former in the same sector or in any other sector served by the purchaser.

Thus, thanks to Senécal's aggressive policy, the prestige, profitability, and ascendancy of the Richelieu and Ontario Navigation Company increased greatly. His activity with this company also brought him personal advantages. Through the support of a number of members appointed to the board by virtue of shares which he had assigned to them, Senécal had made sure he had control of the company. It is not altogether clear how he proposed to utilize this power, but the inventory of his assets at his death shows that he had begun to use the company's funds for his own purposes and owed it $17,115.

Senécal was, however, beginning to feel the wear and tear of the years and in the autumn of 1886 he was forced to stay away from the board meetings on his doctor's orders. His friend Chapleau insisted on his being appointed to the Senate, an honour which he had been denied in 1883. Sir John A. Macdonald* allowed himself to be persuaded this time and on 25 Jan. 1887 invited Senécal to take the place of Louis-François-Roderick Masson*. It was the last token of appreciation offered to him by the Conservative party he had served so well. Stricken with paralysis at the beginning of October, Senécal passed away on 11 Oct. 1887 at his mansion on Rue Dubord in Montreal. His estate was left in extreme confusion. The notaries valued his assets at approximately $514,280, not counting his share in the Saint Lawrence, Lower Laurentian and Saguenay Railway; his liabilities, amounting to $700,000, included a gift of $50,000 to each of his two daughters. The inventory also mentions other assets of $800,000 from legal actions still in process, such as his $250,000 suit against the *Mail* and another of $100,000 against Laurier.

To follow Senécal's career is to describe in detail the fluctuations in the state of Quebec's economy during the second half of the 19th century. In 1850, when he was about 20, he had already begun to speculate in grain and lumber, and then to trade in them; by the end of his life he had become the most important French Canadian capitalist of his time. In the mid 19th century, trade in merchandise was an important source of profit, a situation he was able to exploit to the full. From the outset he applied himself rigorously (even in a scandalous and dishonest fashion, his critics alleged) to the accumulation of capital, in order steadily to enlarge his participation in a given economic sector or to launch into other promising fields. With capital amassed as a local merchant, Senécal broke into shipping, thanks in particular to the purchase of boats, shipbuilding, the rental of barges, and dredging. Continuing to expand his interests, he turned to lumber manufacture and trade, as well as to land speculation, in the end becoming an important landowner.

Despite his three bankruptcies, a consequence of too rapid an economic ascent, Senécal displayed cleverness and foresight, temporarily slowing down his activity and then, at the beginning of the 1870s, venturing into railway construction, an expanding field of considerable promise. At that time, by coordinating his economic and political efforts, he made an important place for himself in this sector of activity. His administrative participation in the Quebec, Montreal, Ottawa and Occidental, as well as in the North Shore Railway Company, placed him at the nerve centre of Quebec's railway system, a position from which he was well able to derive personal profit. The projected monopoly in shipping through the Richelieu and Ontario Navigation Company, at the beginning of the 1880s, shows the extent to which he had succeeded in asserting himself. Moreover, it was in this period that he decided to try his luck in business on the international scene. The project of the General Colonization Company alone involved him in a $3,000,000 transaction, but it collapsed for want of investors, causing Senécal enormous losses. Having returned to the national scene, the "capitaine de Pierreville" devoted his attention to the Richelieu and Ontario Navigation Company during the last years of his life.

In a period marked by the extensive growth of trusts in the United States and of large companies like the CPR in Canada, Senécal throughout his career remained an individual capitalist and conducted his affairs in a distinctively personal manner. Disdaining any integrated system of accounting, resorting to innumerable agents, sometimes acting against his own partners, and using for his personal investments the funds of companies for which he was responsible, he managed to conceal his operations from his contemporaries, but nevertheless was unable to gain the confidence of large investors and bankers who were indispensable to the success and continuance of his projects. Because of his complex personality and the aggressive way in which he conducted his affairs, he acquired a controversial and contradictory public image; he was seen on the one hand as a political, monopolistic, and pilfering "boss," and on the other as a patriot incarnating the economic ascent of French Canadians.

Despite the disorganized state of his affairs at his death, Senécal had succeeded in following the changing economic currents of his day better than any of his French Canadian contemporaries. The diversity and significance of the economic activity in which he engaged placed him in the front ranks of Canadian capitalists in the 19th century. Yet, although he was a leading entrepreneur who put a great deal of money to work, Senécal lacked the perspicacity to enable the painstaking bringing to fruition of projects which might have remained important national institutions in the economic development of Quebec.

HÉLÈNE FILTEAU, JEAN HAMELIN, and JOHN KEYES

[There is as yet no adequate biography of Louis-Adélard Senécal. The handful of authors who have written about him have taken their material from the lengthy obituary published in *La Minerve* (Montreal) of 12 Oct. 1887, without further verification. Senécal's role as superintendent of the Quebec, Montreal, Ottawa and Occidental Railway, is examined in B. J. Young, *Promoters and politicians: the North-Shore railways in the history of Quebec, 1854–85* (Toronto, 1978), and in Gaétan Gervais, "L'expansion du réseau ferroviaire québécois."

The lack of serious works on Senécal can be attributed both to the breadth of his personality and accomplishments and to the absence of archival sources. Senécal did not keep his personal papers, with the exception of cheque stubs, receipts, and a few documents which he stored in his attic and which have largely been destroyed. Only the Musée d'Odanak (Odanak, Qué.) holds a small collection of Senécal papers, consisting of notarial acts, telegrams, scattered letters, and a ledger relating to the affairs of Upton Township from 1866 to 1882. This repository also holds the Fonds Charles-Ignace Gill which contains certain documents pertaining to Senécal.

To write a life of Senécal proved a difficult task; it was therefore necessary to turn to the minute books of notaries, the records of the Richelieu and Ontario Navigation Company, and the newspapers of the day. However, there remain other unexplored sources, such as the correspondence of politicians closely connected with Senécal's career, as well as the archives of banking institutions and brokerage houses. H.F., J.H., and J.K.]

AC, Montréal, Minutiers, Narcisse Pérodeau, 27 déc. 1887, 18 févr. 1888; AC, Québec, Minutiers, E. G. Meredith, 7 June 1883; 15 Feb., 8 Aug., 13 Dec. 1884. AC, Richelieu (Sorel), Minutiers, Étienne Boucher, 25 déc. 1865, 24 mars 1866; L.-D.-E. Carier, 31 mars 1873, 21 nov. 1874, 18 mai 1880; J.-B. Commeault, 18 août 1860, 8 sept. 1863, 25 mars 1867; Victor Gladu, 1867-75; G.-T. Peltier, 28 mars 1865, 12 avril 1866. ANQ-M, Minutiers, C.-E. Belle, 15 janv. 1852; Félix Geoffrion, 12 mai, 29 sept., 12 oct. 1866; 22 janv. 1868; 18 févr. 1870; J.-H. Jobin, 12 sept. 1851; 4 août 1854; 5 févr. 1862; 15 févr., 20 nov. 1867; Pierre Ménard, 15 janv. 1850, 13 nov. 1851, 25 juin 1852, 16 août 1853. Arch. de l'univ. Laval, 137/2/1. ASN, AP-G, Hector Laferté; AP-G, Henri Vassal. PAC, MG 24, B2, 4; L3, 24; MG 26, A, 17, 141, 414; MG 27, I, C3; II, D16, 3; RG 31, A1, 1831, 1851, 1861, 1871, 1881 censuses for Pierreville, Sorel, and Verchères; RG 42, ser.I, 175–79, 213–16, 321–23, 410–12, 473–77. QUA, Canada Steamship Lines Ltd. records, Richelieu and Ontario Navigation Company, Minutes, 1881–87. Can., Prov. du, *Statuts*, 1858, c.63; 1866, c.115. *Débats de l'Assemblée législative* (M. Hamelin) [I]: 2. Qué., *Statuts*, 1869, c.63; 1875, c.2; 1882, c.20. *Canadian Illustrated News* (Montreal), 14 Feb. 1880. *Le Courrier de Saint-Hyacinthe*, 11 août 1868. *Le Courrier du Canada*, 13 oct. 1887. *L'Électeur* (Québec), 1880–82. *L'Étendard*, 9 févr., 30, 31 mai 1883. *L'Événement*, 4, 13, 14 sept. 1867. *Gazette* (Montreal), 12 Oct. 1887. *La Gazette de Sorel* (Sorel, Qué.), 1859–73. *Le Journal de Québec*, 23 févr., 7 mars, 6 août 1883. *La Minerve*, 25 avril 1868; 1er juin 1880; janvier 1883–mars 1884, 12 oct. 1887. *Montreal Daily Star*, 4 Jan., 11, 12 Oct. 1887. *La Patrie*, 12 oct. 1887. *La Presse*, 12 oct. 1887. *Quebec Daily Mercury*, 12 Oct. 1887.

Achintre, *Manuel électoral. Canadian biog. dict.*, II. *CPC*, 1873–80; 1889. *Cyclopædia of Canadian biog.* (Rose, 1888). *Dominion annual register*, 1879–86. Langelier, *Liste des terrains concédés. Montreal directory*, 1870–87. *RPQ*. Azarie Couillard-Després, *Histoire de Sorel de ses origines à nos jours* (Montréal, 1926). F.-L. Desaulniers, *Notes historiques sur la paroisse de Saint-Guillaume d'Upton* (Montréal, 1905). Alain Gamelin, "La Compagnie des moulins à vapeur de Pierreville, 1866–1906" (thèse de MA, [univ. du Québec, Trois-Rivières], 1980). Charles Gill, *Notes historiques sur l'origine de la famille Gill de Saint-François du Lac et Saint-Thomas de Pierreville, et histoire de ma propre famille* (Montréal, 1887). P.-A. Linteau *et al.*, *Histoire du Québec contemporain: de la Confédération à la crise (1867–1929)* (Montréal, 1979). Gérard Parizeau, *La société canadienne-française au XIX*[e] *siècle: essais sur le milieu* (Montréal, [1975]). Rumilly, *Hist. de Montréal*, III. Joseph Schull, *Laurier*, H.-J. Gagnon, trad. ([Montréal], 1968). F.-A. Angers, "Naissance de la pensée économique au Canada français," *RHAF*, 15 (1961–62): 204–29. Gerald Tulchinsky, "Une entreprise maritime canadienne-française: la Compagnie du Richelieu, 1845–1854," *RHAF*, 26 (1972–73): 559–82.

SHAKOYEN'KWARÁHTON. *See* JOHNSON, JOHN

SHANLY, FRANCIS (Frank), civil engineer and railway contractor; b. 29 Oct. 1820 at Stradbally (County Laois, Republic of Ireland), the eighth child and seventh son of James Shanly, barrister and estate manager, and his first wife Frances Elizabeth Mulvany, who died bearing Francis; m. 28 Sept. 1853 to Louisa Saunders of Guelph, Canada West, daughter of Thomas Saunders, colonel of the militia and clerk of the peace for Wellington County, and they had ten children; d. 13 Sept. 1882 of a heart attack.

James Shanly, an MA from Trinity College, Dublin, who had been called to the bar in 1809, intended that his sons should become professional men like himself. All six of his surviving sons were privately tutored in classics, algebra, chemistry, French, and drawing by Dublin's best masters. One boy, who showed special promise and was sent off to apprentice under a noted Liverpool civil engineer, died of consumption at the age of 20. This tragedy, combined with other disappointments, prompted James to seek a better future in Canada for his family: four surviving sons from his first marriage, his second wife (his first wife's sister), and the three children of that marriage. In 1836 the Shanly entourage moved through New York City, Toronto, and Hamilton to some improved acreage on the Thames River near London, Upper Canada, which they named Thorndale.

Emigation proved costly and ultimately disillusioning for the family patriarch, as the name chosen for the homestead suggests. James and his boys failed as farmers in plain view of all those around them who were making a go of it but whom they considered their social inferiors. The boys at least regarded "competition with unlettered boors whose labour and sweat were certain of all the reward *they* aimed at – a hundred acres of clearing with the stumps out," as fundamentally "hopeless." Nor could they comprehend how human beings could bear such mind-numbing toil, much less thrive on it. Eventually James gave up farming and opened a distillery, but in time it too failed.

The Shanly boys yearned for a more rewarding, exciting, and intellectually challenging life than the narrow world of Thorndale and one by one in the 1840s they left home to find it. James Jr took up law in nearby London. Then Walter* went away to become an engineer. Through a stroke of good fortune one of the Shanlys' neighbours was an amiable and powerful fellow countryman, Hamilton Hartley Killaly*, who was commissioner of the Board of Works for the province. In 1840 Killaly accepted Walter as one of his engineering protégés in the department. Walter in turn secured a place for his older brother Charles Dawson* as a clerk. But by the time Frank could extricate himself from the slowly dying distillery in 1846, the politicians has stripped Killaly of much of his power and imposed strict economies upon the reorganized Department of Public Works. Throughout 1846 Walter looked in vain for an opening for Frank on the Welland Canal reconstruction, to which he had recently been assigned, and on other government works. Eventually that year Frank found temporary employment himself, surveying the right of way for the Great Western Railway under the supervision of Charles B. Stuart. When the surveys were completed, construction was postponed indefinitely while the promoters tried to raise the necessary capital. Frank rejoined Walter briefly, but there were still no prospects of permanent work in the Niagara peninsula.

Anxious to find a place, preferably building railways, Frank reluctantly turned to the United States where in 1848, through the good offices of Killaly's son Jack, he secured a job as an assistant engineer for the contractor who was building the eastern division of the Ogdensburg and Lake Champlain Railroad. "I was very glad that you have at length succeeded in obtaining something like a footing on any terms," wrote Walter, who was thinking about a change of scene himself. "Stick close to it, be it ever so trifling in emolument." Shortly afterward Walter did give up his appointment with the Department of Public Works to take a more senior post on the western division of the same railway. "The name of the thing would be of great use to me," Walter admitted, "besides letting me into all the mysteries of laying down rails and some other minor details that I am at present practically ignorant of." During 1849–50 the Shanly brothers gained invaluable experience and mastered the technique of railway construction on the Ogdensburg road. As it neared completion they ached to return to "show the Canada folk how quickly Railroads can be built when they get the *right man* at them." But Canada was not ready for railways just yet. So Walter stayed on with the Ogdensburg and Lake Champlain as resident engineer while Frank followed his employer to his next job, working on the Union Canal in Pennsylvania.

In 1851 Walter returned to Canada as chief engineer of the Bytown and Prescott Railway. With the affairs of that short line well in hand he accepted a second chief engineership with the Toronto and Guelph Railway late the same year. Walter then called his brother back from his canal-building exile in the United States to supervise construction of the Toronto and Guelph. When this railway became the western extension of the Grand Trunk in 1853 the whole character of the work and the importance of the Shanly brothers' positions changed. The road had to be built to higher standards: timber trestles were replaced by iron bridges on massive stone pillars, and the line was extended to Port Sarnia (Sarnia) and beyond. They were fast becoming the most experienced railway engineers in the country and their services were in great demand. When their section of the Grand Trunk neared completion in 1856 Frank scouted for new opportunities in the Maritime colonies and in the northwestern United States before deciding to build the Welland Railway, his first important contracting job. During the 1860s Frank served as a consulting engineer for numerous railways in Ontario and Michigan, rebuilt the Northern Railway to proper standards, and operated a profitable stone quarry and railway tie supply business in Georgetown, Ont.

The Shanly brothers were reunited again in 1868. From 1858 to 1862 Walter had been general manager of the Grand Trunk system, a post he resigned to become involved in the Canada Starch Works [*see* William Thomas BENSON] and Liberal-Conservative politics in Grenville County, Canada West. An invitation to tender on construction of a railway tunnel through the Hoosac Mountains in northwestern Massachusetts enticed him out of semi-retirement. Walter and Frank formed a partnership and won the bidding. For the next two years they commanded a small army of men, animals, and machinery against an obstacle that had already defeated other men, the longest tunnel project attempted in the United States to that time. Unpredictable underground rivers made boring through the five miles of solid rock hazardous in the extreme and progress was slow. Nevertheless, by 1870 they had mastered most of the technical challenges involved. At this point Frank left the partnership to take up a number of promising opportunities in Ontario which had suddenly materialized with the opening of another railway boom.

For the next four years Frank Shanly was at the height of his career. As a railway contractor he had more work than he could handle and he was in constant demand as either a consulting engineer or an arbitrator. During this time he did consulting work or contracted for the Brantford, Norfolk and Port Burwell, the Cobourg and Peterborough, the Credit Valley, the Georgian Bay and Wellington, the Grand Junction, the Grand Trunk, the Great Western, the Kingston and Pembroke, the London, Huron and Bruce, the Midland, the Port Dover and Lake Huron, the Toronto, Grey and Bruce, the Wellington, Grey and Bruce, and the Port Whitby and Port Perry railways among others. In a day when railways were people's politics, it was only natural that railway engineers frequently became politicians. Walter had been a member for Grenville South since 1863 and in 1872 Frank joined him in the political arena, having been persuaded to stand for the Liberal-Conservatives in Toronto Centre in the general election. Although Frank was not a good public speaker and was notably shy in public, the Tory organizers were convinced that his towering reputation and their smooth machine would carry the day. However, both Walter and Frank went down to defeat, to William Henry BROUSE and Robert Wilkes* respectively. To add to the disappointment, Frank was left to take care of most of the $8,000 in election expenses.

This political misadventure was a portent of even greater disaster ahead. Frank had taken payment for his contracts in railway bonds as was the custom. He either borrowed on these bonds or sold them to raise the necessary cash to pay his men and purchase equipment and materials. When several railways of which he held bonds defaulted and the market for these securities virtually dried up, Frank Shanly was wiped out. Late in 1874 with notes falling due and no solid collateral in hand upon which to renew or pay off these loans, he threw himself upon the mercy of his creditors. Walter rescued him by assuming the bulk of his obligations. In return, Frank took a job as city engineer for Toronto in 1875, assigning his entire salary to his brother. For the next five years, while he worked on the straightening of the Don River and the planning of a municipal sewer system, Frank did his best to keep his creditors at bay and still feed his family.

In the last years of his life Frank Shanly was a driven man, tormented by pride and debts, which were still more than $90,000 at his death. When the Conservatives returned to power in 1878 he begged Sir John A. Macdonald* to give him a post commensurate with his talent and former status. The party, it seems, seldom neglected its friends. In 1880 Frank became chief engineer of the Intercolonial Railway at an annual salary of $6,500. This was a handsome sum, but not enough to repay his brother and erase all his outstanding debts. So, while he commuted between Toronto and Ottawa to administer Intercolonial affairs, he kept an eye open for a main chance. He needed another successful contracting coup. In July of 1881, for example, he and George Alexander Keefer* tried to get the contract for the Port Moody, B.C., section of the Canadian Pacific Railway, only to have their financial backer pull out at the last minute. The chance never came.

Nor could he find consolation in a happy family life. By 1880 only six of his ten children were still alive. Then in 1882 his oldest boy contracted tuberculosis and died. This tragedy, Walter Shanly recalled, "seemed entirely to crush him. He never rallied from it. His work was done. His indomitable energy had resulted in disappointment and failure in all his undertakings, which were large outside of the strict professional line, and he died of a broken spirit." In fact, he died of a heart attack on the overnight train to Ottawa, on 13 Sept. 1882.

Frank Shanly was one of Canada's most skilful and experienced railway engineers. He had the misfortune to be drawn into contracting, where the rewards of success were phenomenally greater, but where failure could be sudden, ruthless, and irredeemable. Frank was "a naturally endowed engineer," his brother Walter recorded near the end of his own life, "making it all the more to be deplored that he ever stepped aside, or down, to undertake the part of Contractor for which he was not at all fitted."

H. V. NELLES

Some of Francis Shanly's letters have been published in *Daylight through the mountain: letters and labours of civil engineers Walter and Francis Shanly*, ed. F. N. Walker (Montreal, 1957).

AO, MU 469–87; MU 2664–776. PAC, MG 26, A. Currie, *Grand Trunk Railway*. Hodgetts, *Pioneer public service*. T. C. Keefer, *Philosophy of railroads and other essays*, ed. H. V. Nelles (Toronto and Buffalo, N.Y., 1972).

SHIBLEY, SCHUYLER, farmer, businessman, and politician; b. 19 March 1820 in Portland Township, Upper Canada, son of Henry Shibley; m. in 1854 Mary Ann Greer, and they had at least three children; d. 18 Dec. 1890 at Kingston, Ont.

Schuyler Shibley, of German and UEL origin and of the Methodist faith, attended the Waterloo Academy near Kingston, Upper Canada. After completing his education in 1851–52 with a European tour, from which he returned "one of the best informed farmers of the province," he settled at Murvale, Portland Township, combining farming with business. With David Roblin* he "speculated extensively in U.E.L. scrip, became possessed of very large tracts of real estate, good, bad and indifferent, and was at times reputed to be very wealthy." Some of his holdings were rented to tenant farmers.

Shibley, described by one observer as "a rather fast gent," had a "paramour," Kate Davis, "a rather good looking person," who lived in Brooke Township, Lambton County, where he owned 400 acres. The liaison resulted in a child. These details became public knowledge in early September 1866 when they were arrested and charged with murdering this child, Kate Shibley, then three years old. On the grounds that he had been absent when the child died, Shibley was released from prison without having to stand trial. Evidence at the coroner's inquest, and later at Kate Davis' trial, however, revealed his involvement in a sordid and vicious affair. According to a newspaper account, the mother testified that he "had been there some ten days before [the child's death] and had given the child a most unmerciful beating for not saying its prayers, and ordered her to do the same whenever it refused." When the child would not say her prayers on 3 September, she was, according to another account, "whipped . . . with rawhide." She died during the night. A friend of the mother also testified to Shibley's physical brutality towards the child, who had been neglected ("the entire absence of food had . . . something to do with the result"), and was reported to have suffered internal injuries. Kate Davis, tried for manslaughter, was acquitted. The presiding judge "could not refrain from giving strong expression to his surprise and disappointment at the verdict, as well as at the conduct of both the prisoner and her paramour." Sarnia, where Shibley had been imprisoned, was well known to John A. Macdonald*, attorney general for Canada West, who was kept informed of his situation by Thomas W. Johnston, the prison doctor; he passed along a piece of intelligence that Shibley "seems to have been infatuated with the girl Davis and actually had his wife write her a letter of Condolence. [His] eyes poor fellow are now open. [If] he tries another, it will not be Miss Davis."

The public revelation of Shibley's sordid private life had no appreciable effect on his public career. He had already served as reeve of Portland. In 1867 he ran in Addington for the House of Commons, polling 991 votes to 1,120 for James Noxon Lapum. In view of the fact that he ran as a Conservative factionalist against an official Conservative (there was no Liberal candidate), he did well. He began his political career in earnest in 1868 by winning the wardenship of Frontenac County; he won again in 1869 and 1872. In the general election of 1872 he contested Addington, still as an independent Conservative, against Lapum, the official candidate. This time Shibley won an easy victory, 1,495 to 849. Although he had defeated a ministerial incumbent, he described himself in the *Canadian parliamentary companion* in 1873 as "A Conservative." He was re-elected in 1874, but the election was voided because several of his supporters, including his 15-year-old son, had bribed voters. He won the subsequent by-election held in the same year.

During these years he had several business connections of importance: along with other civic and political leaders, such as Alexander Campbell*, Richard John Cartwright*, and Dileno Dexter CALVIN, he served during the 1870s as a director of the Kingston and Pembroke Railway as well as the Royal Mutual Life Assurance Company.

Shibley's political manœuvrings from 1872 to 1874 are interesting for their context. His chief concern was patronage. Prior to 1872 he had had no success in several attempts to influence appointments. After that date the Conservative leaders recognized his electoral victory, and he was given control over his riding's patronage. Shibley's factionalist background, however, made him a logical target for Liberal wooing during the political crisis occasioned by the Pacific Scandal. During 1873 Alexander Mackenzie*, Edward Blake*, and Cartwright made a concerted attempt to win him over to their side. At the same time the Conservative leaders worked in desperation to maintain the support of wavering members of parliament such as Shibley. Although he was not required to vote against Macdonald's party in the House of Commons, he did defect to the Liberals before the government fell on 5 Nov. 1873. He remained a supporter of the Liberals until he was defeated in the Conservative sweep of 1878. He was, however, one of the few Ontario Conservative members to desert during the crisis; in doing so, he was still concerned with patronage not principle. Shibley's six years in the Commons were undistinguished; his voice was raised only about problems that related directly to his riding.

The career of Shibley reveals something about the 19th-century Canadian public, rural in this case, and the leaders of both political parties; they could, apparently with ease, accommodate a man known to be personally debauched and a candidate possessed of only the loosest political principles.

DONALD SWAINSON

AO, MU 500–15. PAC, MG 24, B40, 8–9; MG 26, A. Can., House of Commons, *Debates*, 1875–78. "Parl. debates" (CLA mfm. project of parl. debates, 1846–74), 1873–74. *Daily News* (Kingston, [Ont.]), 1866. *Globe*, 1866, 1872, 1874, 1878, 1890. *Sarnia Observer, and Lambton Advertiser* (Sarnia, [Ont.]), 14 Sept. 1866. *CPC*, 1873–75; 1879. W. S. Herrington, *History of the county of Lennox and Addington* (Toronto, 1913; repr. Belleville, Ont., 1972). Donald Swainson, "Richard Cartwright joins the Liberal party," *Queen's Quarterly*, 75 (1968): 124–34; "Schuyler Shibley and the underside of Victorian Ontario," *OH*, 65 (1973): 51–60.

SHORTLAND, PETER FREDERICK, Royal Navy officer and marine surveyor; b. in 1815, probably in England, the son of Thomas George Shortland, a captain in the Royal Navy, and Elizabeth Tonkin; m. in 1848 Emily Jones, and they had several children; d. 18 Oct. 1888 at Plymouth, England.

Peter Frederick Shortland entered the Royal Navy in January 1827 and two years later graduated with distinction from the Royal Naval College at Portsmouth. In 1834 he was appointed sub-lieutenant and in 1836–37 he served as mate of the *Rattlesnake*, during which time he assisted in the settlement of Melbourne, Australia, by making a survey of Port Phillip Bay, his first such work. On his return to England in 1838 he received a leave of absence and entered Pembroke College, Cambridge, from which he graduated 1st class in mathematics in 1842. He then applied to join the *Excellent* and was promoted lieutenant. Shortly after, he was sent to join the *Columbia* under Captain William Fitz William Owen*, who was just starting an extensive trigonometrical survey of the Bay of Fundy. Detailed soundings were to be taken, surveys were to be made of all rivers and creeks as far inland as their first bridges or to the farthest navigable point, and the exact positions of all settlements, mills, and factories were to be determined. The work was later broadened to include the examination of possible sites for a canal to link the Bay of Fundy with Northumberland Strait and of harbours which might be developed on the coasts of New Brunswick and Nova Scotia.

Shortland was actively involved throughout this survey, which was begun in 1842 and not completed until 1865. Owen, a demanding superior, reported in 1843 that Shortland had completed a series of measurements on the ice of the Saint John River for a distance of 90 miles as part of the triangulation for the survey of the river. He continually praised Shortland as an "intelligent" officer who "understands the precise objects in view, and pursues them with a proper spirit, and with a tact seldom acquired without much more experience." In 1844 Shortland was entrusted with the supervision of the survey of Passamaquoddy Bay and given command of the *Columbia*.

Shortland was promoted commander in 1848. In the same year the Admiralty considered cancelling the Bay of Fundy survey because of its expense and Owen, by now a rear-admiral, was told that his rank precluded him from engaging in the work. The Admiralty was persuaded to reconsider and Owen recommended that Shortland replace him. The survey was resumed in 1849 with Shortland in charge. Promoted post-captain in 1858, he reported in 1861 that the survey of the last piece of the Fundy coastline and of the Petitcodiac and Memramcook rivers had been completed. He then surveyed the southeast coast of Nova Scotia and worked on his charts before submitting the completed survey in 1865. He received the thanks of the Admiralty for his excellent work.

After his return to England Shortland was placed in charge of the *Hydra* and accepted postings to survey the coast of Sicily and later to take ocean soundings between Aden and Bombay. He retired from the Royal Navy in November 1870, but then studied law at Cambridge and was called to the bar in January 1873. He was promoted rear-admiral in 1876 and vice-admiral in January 1881 before his death in 1888. Shortland was a dedicated and conscientious officer who spent most of his naval career in a branch of the service which rarely receives the attention it deserves. He gave 23 years to the Bay of Fundy survey and his competence is evident in the 15 major charts he completed of the coast of Nova Scotia and the shores of the Bay of Fundy. They form the basis for present-day charts of the region.

WILLIAM ARTHUR SPRAY

Peter Frederick Shortland was the author of *Bay of Fundy: remarks for sailing directions, etc.* (2v., London, 1856–57); *Sounding voyage of her majesty's ship Hydra, 1868 . . .* (London, 1869); *A short account of the laws which govern Her Britannic Majesty's navy* (London, 1887); and *Nautical surveying* (London and New York, 1890).

G.B., Ministry of Defence, Hydrographic Dept. (Taunton, Somerset), Surveyors' letter file, no.44 (mfm. at UNBL). *Royal Gazette* (Fredericton), 3 Dec. 1842. *Times* (London), 19 Oct. 1888. *DNB*. *Memoirs of hydrography, including brief biographies of the principal officers who have served in H.M. Naval Surveying Service between the years 1750 and 1885*, comp. L. S. Dawson (2v., Eastbourne, Eng., [1883]–85; repr. in lv., London, 1969).

SICOTTE (Cicot), LOUIS-VICTOR (baptized **Louis**), lawyer, politician, and judge; b. 6 Nov. 1812 at Boucherville, Lower Canada, son of Toussaint Cicot, a farmer, and Marguerite Gauthier, *dit* Saint-Germain; d. 5 Sept. 1889 at Saint-Hyacinthe, Que.

Louis-Victor's ancestor, Jean Chicot, who came to New France in 1651, gained some historical notice. Étienne-Michel Faillon* records that on 6 May 1651 at Ville-Marie "the cruel Iroquois removed [his] hair with a piece of the skull"; he survived this scalping and lived for another 14 years.

Louis-Victor Sicotte received his secondary education at the Séminaire de Saint-Hyacinthe from 1822 to 1829. Information on his activities during the next few years is incomplete. It is known that he spent a few years in Montreal, and that he was a clerk with Larocque, Bernard et Cie, a French Canadian firm established in 1832, while preparing for the bar. He is thought to have studied law with Dominique Mondelet*, Louis-Hippolyte La Fontaine*, and Norbert Dumas. On 28 Dec. 1828 he was called to the bar. It is also known that he belonged to the group of young Patriotes led by Ludger Duvernay*, that he frequently visited the Librairie Fabre, a hotbed of nationalism, and that he was the secretary-treasurer of Aide-toi, le Ciel t'aidera, (God helps those who help themselves), an organization founded in March 1834 on the model of a similarly named French society which played a part in the July Revolution. This society, whose focus was on politics, introduced the celebration of Saint-Jean-Baptiste Day as the national festival of French Canadians. If it can be accepted that there is an "indisputable relationship" between the festival of 24 June and the founding of the Association Saint-Jean-Baptiste de Montréal, then Sicotte, who stated that he was "the first" to have had "the idea of a national festival under the patronage of Saint-Jean-Baptiste," can be considered the co-founder of this society. It was indeed at a banquet in Saint-Hyacinthe to honour Sicotte that Duvernay proposed Saint-Jean-Baptiste Day as a national festival.

On 16 Feb. 1832 Sicotte had published in the correspondence column of *La Minerve* of Montreal a strongly partisan letter, signed S******, which sparked a three-year controversy between *La Minerve* and *L'Écho du pays* of Saint-Charles on the one hand and *L'Ami du peuple, de l'ordre et des lois* of Montreal on the other. This letter, which outlined the difficult situation of French Canadians, went so far as to advocate immediate separation from Britain, and, if necessary, revolution. "There is considerable belief," he said, "in the possibility of a revolution, but at a distant date; I myself think it is close at hand."

There is no doubt that Sicotte was an ardent Patriote, but also no documentary evidence that he took an active part in the 1837 rebellion. The most that can be said is that his name is found, along with those of Jacques Viger*, Édouard-Raymond Fabre*, Louis-Hippolyte La Fontaine, Charles-Ovide Perrault*, Côme-Séraphin CHERRIER, and George-Étienne Cartier*, at the head of a list of contributors to a fund to compensate Duvernay in 1836 for "the losses and sacrifices he suffered in the cause of Reform" when he was imprisoned in 1832 for libelling the Legislative Council. Furthermore, in 1838 Sicotte confided to Duvernay that he was not convinced rebellion would help to ensure the country's acquiring the democratic freedoms it needed. In his view the insurrection was doomed to failure. Hence he would criticize the Patriotes' frontier raids in 1838, fearing they might provoke official sanctions and lead only to the dreaded union being imposed on Upper and Lower Canada.

In 1838 Sicotte settled in Saint-Hyacinthe, opening a law office on Rue Saint-Antoine; he was made a QC in 1854. His firm grew and he acquired a number of law partners including, in 1863, Magloire Lanctôt*. According to *Le Courrier de Saint-Hyacinthe*, he had a large clientele and became "one of the most eminent members of the bar in the district of Montreal"; given 19th-century traditions his position was bound to lead him into politics. Meanwhile he joined the Société des Amis, a literary society formed in 1842 and considered the forerunner of the Institut Canadien of Montreal.

In January 1848 Sicotte stood as a Reform candidate in Saint-Hyacinthe but was defeated by Thomas Boutillier*, a doctor, who was also a Reformer. After this setback, Sicotte won the seat by a large majority in 1851. He identified himself at that period as one of the dissident Reformers, a group that stood somewhere between the supporters of La Fontaine and the Rouges. As soon as Sicotte entered parliament, Augustin-Norbert Morin* offered him the portfolio of the Crown Lands Department, but he declined because the government of Francis HINCKS and Morin had no plans for the abolition of seigneurial tenure and the secularization of clergy reserves.

On 22 Feb. 1853 the Legislative Assembly appointed him chairman of a select committee on education in Canada East which addressed a questionnaire to all parish priests and Protestant ministers, as well as to municipal secretary-treasurers [*see* Louis Lacoste*]. According to historian André Labarrère-Paulé, the Sicotte report, submitted on 7 June 1853, was "the harbinger of a new climate more favourable to reforms and radical changes in the educational field." But the government was in such a critical situation that the Sicotte inquiry had no immediate impact [*see* Jean-Baptiste Meilleur*].

At this juncture the growing number of factions in the legislature was paralysing the Hincks–Morin government. For his part, Sicotte made an alliance with Joseph-Édouard CAUCHON, although he himself claimed to be a democrat and closer to the Rouges – who, in his words, were no redder than he was. In 1854, by a skilful parliamentary manœuvre on the important issues of the reserves and seigneurial tenure, Sicotte and Cauchon brought about a coalition of all opposition groups in the house which defeated the government. In the subsequent general elections Sicotte was returned by acclamation for Saint-Hyacinthe. In September 1854 he was chosen as the Rouge candidate for the post of speaker of the house, and thanks to the support of the Reformers of both Canada East and Canada West he was elected by 76 to 41, after Cartier, the ministerial candidate, had failed in his bid for the office. This development reveals the weakness of the government, which was forced to make alliances in order to survive: hence the resignation of Hincks and the formation of the Liberal-Conservative coalition under Sir Allan Napier MacNab* and Morin, whose aim was to create a stable government and settle the two major issues before it.

As speaker of the house, Sicotte was confined to a neutrality which removed him from the limelight. He was not completely forgotten, however; *La Minerve* gives this caricature: "Sicotte, with his butter-coloured gloves, his wretched little hat perched on his head, his figure muffled in a large black cloak reminiscent of a domino without a hood, and holding in his right hand his little handbook on parliamentary procedure bound in red leather." But in November 1857 Sicotte, who had just been re-elected by acclamation, entered a new phase of his career, accepting the portfolio of the Crown Lands Department left vacant by the resignation of Étienne-Paschal Taché*. During his brief term as commissioner of crown lands, Sicotte sponsored an especially important bill for the preservation and operation of the fisheries. This bill received the support of all the French Canadian members, regardless of party, because it encouraged an industry previously neglected in Canada East.

Sicotte appeared, then, to have entered the ranks of the Liberal-Conservative party. In fact, in August 1858, he refused a ministerial post in the government of George Brown* and Antoine-Aimé Dorion*, finding himself quite unable to betray his principles in order to join Brown. Justifying his decision, he explained: "I will never have dealings with those who insult and cast aspersions on my religion and . . . I will never give power to those who have used . . . their fanaticism and bigotry as means of advancement." The Brown–Dorion government was defeated 48 hours after it had been sworn in, and Sicotte again found himself in a Liberal-Conservative government, this time as commissioner of public works under Cartier and John A. Macdonald*. Sicotte was not, however, a convert to the party. Hence there is a bitter tone in his letters to Hector-Louis Langevin* when he speaks of Cartier and his manner of exercising power. "Friend Georges," he wrote one day, "has the knack of stirring up a storm over everything, and to this he owes the formation of three or four governments since 1855," and again, "It is the policy of M. Cartier and M. Macdonald to keep ambitious men constantly barking." When the government faced the issue of the choice of a capital, and, despite the vote of the house, affirmed that it would defer to the queen's selection of Ottawa, Sicotte resigned his portfolio on 10 Jan. 1859. He became the leader of the opposition from Canada East, and in May 1862, when the Cartier–Macdonald government was overthrown on the Militia Act, Sicotte formed a ministry with John Sandfield Macdonald*. This government brought together the moderate Liberals of the two sections of Canada, Sandfield Macdonald now leading the Reformers from Canada West and Sicotte having gradually replaced Dorion in Canada East after the latter's defeat in the 1861 election. Sicotte succeeded in gaining the support of men of talent and experience such as Thomas-Jean-Jacques LORANGER, François-Xavier Lemieux*, Lewis Thomas DRUMMOND, and Thomas D'Arcy McGee*; he also brought Dorion back into the ministry.

The Sandfield Macdonald–Sicotte government had to face insurmountable financial difficulties, for the American Civil War had already adversely affected foreign trade. The preceding government had been defeated on a legislative measure judged too expensive; the new one signed its death warrant by defending the Intercolonial Railway Bill, which was also considered too costly. Dorion, the provincial secretary, resigned on this issue, and Loranger disengaged himself by accepting the post of judge at Trois-Rivières after refusing to assume Dorion's office.

The Sandfield Macdonald–Sicotte government was also a victim of the defects of the system itself. It resorted to compromises with the principle of "double majority," especially in regard to Richard William Scott*'s bill to grant separate schools to the Catholics of Canada West, which was adopted despite the opposition of a majority of the members from Canada West. The government also ran into trouble on the issue of the representation of the province's two sections in the house, a recurrent concern in the parliament of the Province of Canada. Summoned to guide the country in a period of economic depression and political deadlock, the government was defeated on a motion of non-confidence on 8 May 1863. After this setback, Macdonald passed under the wing of George Brown, who increasingly imposed his requirements on Macdonald, considering him narrow-minded and spineless. Asked to "radicalize" his government, Macdonald tried to bring back Dorion. The latter refused unless he would "be recognized as leader of the Lower Canadian section." For his part, Sicotte declined "to serve under Dorion," and, as Brown persisted in his demand, Sicotte and all the ministers from Canada East tendered their resignations. The moderate element of Canada West was treated in the same fashion, to the benefit of Brown's chief associates.

Once more leader of the Liberals from Canada East, Dorion offered a cabinet post to Sicotte, but the latter refused it with disdain, well aware that the reshaping of the government had been undertaken at the behest of and under pressure from Brown. In his manifesto to the electors, Sicotte specifically stated: "It was required that control be in the hands of a certain man, and not in my own. But the direction decided upon in this way constituted a distinct policy with new tendencies, under a new banner. It involved the whole federal issue; it meant government of Canada by Upper Canada; for if the demand that such and such a man and such and such a direction be imposed on us were accepted, all sectional difficulties would be settled from the exclusive point of view of Upper Canada and in its exclusive interest." Sicotte even signed a pact with the groups in opposition to overthrow the Sandfield Macdonald–Dorion government. He agreed to support any motion of censure on condition "that it contained no retrospective criticism of the government of which he himself had been part." When the house returned on 21 Aug. 1863, it was he who proposed the motion of non-confidence, alleging that the formation of the new government had been unconstitutional and that the principle of double majority had been violated by the ministry, thus imperilling Canada East. The motion was rejected by 63 to 60: Sicotte did not have the support of the moderate Liberals, who refused to make any alliance whatever with Cartier's Conservatives. It was with this setback that Sicotte ended his political career.

A few days later, on 5 September, Sicotte became a puisne judge of the Superior Court for Saint-Hyacinthe District. The appointment caused a great stir in political circles. The parliamentary opposition was indignant that the government was muzzling one of its most formidable adversaries in this fashion. A motion of censure followed in the assembly and was narrowly rejected by 63 to 61. Sicotte's supporters themselves found it hard to understand his withdrawal, and interpreted it as a complete about-face. The house was functioning at the time with no solid parliamentary majority and Sicotte's departure, which meant one vote less for the opposition, therefore strengthened the government. The most conciliatory of his friends saw a reason for his action, however: Sicotte was the father of 11 children, and politics had literally ruined him. "The only excuse," wrote Laurent-Olivier David*, "was his poverty. . . . Let us add that he was disappointed, disillusioned, [and] offended by the way the house and even his friends had treated him." In short, Sicotte was at a crossroads; he chose the safest and probably the wisest path.

Taking stock of Sicotte's career, one may question whether there was any place in Canada East at that time for a party which in ideology fitted between the Conservatives and the Rouges. It seemed that the inevitable alliance with the Upper Canadian wing of a party – a wing in the event dominated and made intolerant by George Brown – meant certain disaster for the political career of any moderate Liberal. It was Brown who moved the pawns around on the contemporary political chessboard. The "Great Coalition" of 1864 was only a more spectacular demonstration of his daily manœuvring. In this game Sicotte was probably the greatest loser during the period of the union.

Having given 12 years to politics, Sicotte devoted almost a quarter of a century to the administration of justice in Saint-Hyacinthe. He retired on 7 Nov. 1887 and died on 5 Sept. 1889 at Saint-Hyacinthe. On 7 Nov. 1837 he had married Marguerite-Émélie Starnes, sister of Henry Starnes*. Of their 11 children, the eldest, Victor-Benjamin, became a lawyer in Saint-Hyacinthe, and their second son, Eugène, was a notary in Montreal.

Andrée Désilets

ANQ-Q, AP-G-68; AP-G-134. PAC, MG 26, A. Can., prov. du, Assemblée législative, *Journaux*, 1852–63.

G.[-É.] Cartier, *Discours de sir George Cartier . . .*, ed. Joseph Tassé (Montréal, 1893). *L'Ami du peuple, de l'ordre et des lois* (Montréal), 1832–35. *L'Avenir*, 1848. *Le Courrier de Saint-Hyacinthe*, 1856–89. *L'Écho du pays* (Saint-Charles[-sur-Richelieu], [Qué.]), 1833–35. *Legal News* (Montreal), 7 Sept. 1889. *La Minerve*, 1832–35. *La Patrie*, 6 sept. 1889. Ivanhoë Caron, "Papiers Duvernay conservés aux archives de la province de Québec," ANQ *Rapport*, 1926–27: 146, 156, 170, 181–82, 213–14. J. Desjardins, *Guide parl. Dictionnaire national des Canadiens français (1608–1760)* (2e éd., 3v., Montréal, 1965), I; III. Le Jeune, *Dictionnaire*, II. P.-G. Roy, *Les juges de la prov. de Québec*. Cyprien Tanguay, *Dictionnaire généalogique des familles canadiennes depuis la fondation de la colonie jusqu'à nos jours* (7v., [Montréal], 1871–90; réimpr., New York, 1969). L.-P. Audet, *Hist. de l'enseignement*, II. Bernard, *Les Rouges*. John Boyd, *Sir George-Étienne Cartier, baronet; sa vie et son temps; histoire politique du Canada de 1814 à 1873*, trans. Sylva Clapin (Montréal, [1918]). Careless, *Brown*; *Union of the Canadas*. Chapais, *Hist. du Canada*, VII–VIII. C.-P. Choquette, *Histoire de la ville de Saint-Hyacinthe* (Saint-Hyacinthe, Qué., 1930); *Histoire du séminaire de Saint-Hyacinthe depuis sa fondation jusqu'à nos jours* (2v., Montréal, 1911–12), I. Cornell, *Alignment of political groups*. L.-O. David, *Patriotes*; *L'Union des deux Canadas, 1841–1867* (Montréal, 1898). Désilets, *Hector-Louis Langevin*. André Labarrère-Paulé, *Les instituteurs laïques au Canada français, 1836–1900* (Québec, 1965). Robert Rumilly, *Histoire de la Société Saint-Jean-Baptiste de Montréal: des Patriotes au fleurdelisé, 1834–1948* (Montréal, 1975). Thomson, *Alexander Mackenzie*. L.-P. Turcotte, *Le Canada sous l'Union*. E.-Z. Massicotte, "Les tribunaux de police de Montréal," *BRH*, 26 (1920): 183. Robert Rumilly, "Quand la Société Saint-Jean-Baptiste a-t-elle été fondée?," *RHAF*, 1 (1947–48): 237–42.

SIMON. *See* CIMON

SIMPSON, ISOBEL GRAHAM (Finlayson), diarist; b. 20 Jan. 1811 in London, England, eldest daughter of Geddes Mackenzie Simpson and Frances Hume Hawkins; m. 10 Nov. 1838 Duncan Finlayson* at Bromley-by-Bow (now part of Greater London); d. 22 Aug. 1890 in London.

Isobel Graham Simpson's family had close associations with the Hudson's Bay Company. Her father, a successful London merchant, had as a partner Andrew Wedderburn Colvile, who in 1839 became the deputy governor of the HBC; in 1830 her younger sister Frances married George Simpson*, a cousin, who was governor of the HBC. When Duncan Finlayson, a highly respected HBC chief factor, visited George Simpson's in-laws while on furlough in 1838, he was captivated by "the amiable & accomplished Miss Simpson," and the couple were married in November. However, Isobel's health was considered too delicate to allow her to accompany her husband in the spring of 1839 to Rupert's Land where he was to assume the governorship of Assiniboia.

Isobel was determined to join her husband the following year, though grieved to part from her family. It is her lively, sensitive account of the journey from England to Red River (Man.) in the summer of 1840 for which she is remembered, one of the few records of fur-trade travel left by a European woman. Isobel sailed for Hudson Bay in June with Chief Trader James Hargrave* and his bride Letitia [Mactavish*], who described Isobel as "little & lady like, has a beautiful complexion & is very pretty." Reunited at York Factory (Man.), the Finlaysons embarked by York boat for the Red River Settlement. Isobel bore the inevitable inconveniences of this exposed mode of travel with good humour, enjoyed the "romantic" scenery, and admired the skill of their spirited crew. Her "Note book," as the diary is called, contains seven attractive, if amateurish, pencil sketches of the native people she encountered.

Although the colony exceeded her expectations, Isobel did not adapt well to life in the Red River Settlement. She visited Norway House in 1842 where her husband presided over the Council of Assiniboia, but she was not unhappy to leave the west in 1844 when Finlayson was transferred to the company depot at Lachine (Que.) near Montreal. Here Isobel lived, except for extended trips to Britain, until her husband retired to London in 1859. When her sister Frances died at Lachine in 1853, Isobel, who had no children of her own, became a second mother to Governor Simpson's family. She survived her husband by almost 30 years, dying at her home in London in 1890.

SYLVIA M. VAN KIRK

Extracts from the diary of Isobel Simpson were published in two issues of the *Beaver*, outfit 282 (September 1951): 32–35, and (December 1951): 32–37, under the title "York boat journal." The original is in PAM, HBCA, E.12/5.

PAM, HBCA, D.5/7: ff.96d., 193; D.5/12: f.116d.; D.5/37: f.58d.; D.5/50: f.343d.; D.6/1: ff.31d., 32d.; E.12/1: f.51; E.12/4: f.31. Mactavish, *Letters of Letitia Hargrave* (MacLeod).

SIMPSON, JOHN, merchant, miller, banker, and politician; b. 12 May 1812 at Rothes (Grampian), Scotland, the son of John Simpson and Margaret Petrie; d. 21 March 1885 at Bowmanville, Ont.

John Simpson Jr came from a family in Scotland composed mostly of traders, builders, or physicians; James Simpson, the celebrated surgeon, was his second cousin. In 1815 John and his parents immigrated to Upper Canada, settling first on the Scotch Line, near Perth, and later in Brockville. There John received a common school education before being hired in 1825 at a clerk in Charles Bowman's general store and mill at Darlington (Bowmanville), Durham County. He remained connected with the interests of Bowman and his family for some 37 years.

Simpson's business talents developed rapidly under

Bowman's tutelage, and he soon became Bowman's partner. As a miller, Simpson had few peers. In 1838 he won the gold medal offered by Lord Durham [Lambton*] for the best flour produced in British North America and in 1851 he won the highest award available in competition for a sample of flour entered at the Great Exhibition in London, England. When Bowman died in 1848, Simpson was named manager of his estate, and with his brother-in-law, John Burke, continued the mercantile and flour business.

Because of his involvement in the produce, grain, and flour trade, Simpson took an active part in every attempt to improve transportation in Durham County. In 1839, the year in which the Port Darlington Harbour Company began to make improvements to the harbour some two miles from Bowmanville, Simpson was named president of the firm. In 1858 he was a leading proponent of a toll-road from Bowmanville to Carden Township, which would have entailed the construction of a bridge across Lake Scugog. Although the bridge and the northern section of the road were never built, the road did go as far as Caesarea, thus enhancing Bowmanville's economic control over the area.

Simpson's most important business undertaking, however, was the creation of the Ontario Bank in 1857. In 1848 the Bank of Montreal, as part of an attempt to dominate the financial life of Canada West, had established a branch in Bowmanville and named Simpson manager. Shortly after, his responsibilities were expanded to include management of the Whitby branch. Then in 1856 a group of financiers involved in the Montreal City and District Savings Bank, led by Henry Starnes*, decided to enter the rapidly developing banking business of Canada West. They chose the rich agricultural districts of Ontario and Durham counties as their base. When they had obtained a charter for the Ontario Bank, Simpson undertook to promote it locally; to ensure acceptance in the area the bank's Montreal connections were kept secret, Simpson was named its president in 1857, and the head office was set up in Bowmanville. The bank was an instant success and soon began to attract Toronto investors. In the ensuing struggle over control between the Montreal and Toronto shareholders, which was to last almost 20 years, Simpson joined those from Toronto to prevent a relocation of the head office in Montreal. The Toronto group eventually won, and in 1874 the head office was moved to that city. Simpson resigned the presidency in 1878, although he retained his shares, worth about $16,000.

Though he restricted his active involvement to his Bowmanville investments, Simpson nevertheless participated in the creation and direction of a number of other major enterprises. He was an incorporator of the Bank of Western Canada in 1859, the London and Canadian Loan and Agency Company in 1863, and the Ontario Central Railway Company in 1874, and he was also a shareholder and director of the Joseph Hall Manufacturing Company in Oshawa.

A lifelong Liberal, Simpson entered public life via the usual route of appointment to the magistracy and election to a variety of township offices. In 1848 he was elected to the Newcastle District Council and in 1850 served as Darlington Township councillor. In addition, he was appointed a commissioner of the lunatic asylum in Toronto by Robert Baldwin*.

In 1856, when the Legislative Council became elective, the division of Queen's was created from the ridings of Ontario North, Victoria, and Durham West. Simpson, nominated by the Reformers, won by acclamation after Henry Jones Ruttan, the Conservative candidate, withdrew. Simpson was returned unopposed in 1864 and at confederation was called to the Senate where he served until his death. His political and economic influence in Ontario County was credited with winning many close contests for other Liberal candidates. With his business associate and political arch-rival, Thomas Nicholson GIBBS, his struggles were particularly hot. As local leaders of the rival parties, Simpson and Gibbs were invariably called upon to debate the leading questions of the day in every election contest in the area. In parliament Simpson's few contributions to debate were on the practical aspects of banking and monetary policy or in favour of religious or charitable organizations. His most important work was done as chairman of the parliamentary committee on printing; at his death it was stated in the Senate that his activities on the committee, starting in 1857, had saved the government over $100,000. Its reports were a textbook of sound business practice.

Simpson had married in May 1844 Annie Burke, the daughter of a Baptist minister, and he joined that church after her death in 1846. On 2 Nov. 1847 he married her younger sister, Sarah, and they had nine children, eight of whom survived him. In later life he joined the Disciples of Christ and was an active evangelist and Sunday school teacher.

LEO A. JOHNSON

Can., Prov. of, *Statutes*, 1857, c.159; Senate, *Debates*, 1885: 427–28. Upper Canada, *Statutes*, 1840, c.37. *Canadian Statesman* (Bowmanville, Ont.), 6 June, 4 July 1872; 27 March, 3 April 1885. *Globe*, 4, 7 Sept. 1874. *Mail*, 2 Sept. 1874. *Monetary Times*, 12 Nov. 1869. *Oshawa Vindicator* (Oshawa, [Ont.]), 7 Oct. 1857, 23 June 1858. *Whitby Chronicle* (Whitby, Ont.), 13 May 1858, 18 June 1874. *Canada, an encyclopædia* (Hopkins), I: 439. *Canadian biog. dict.*, I: 485–86. *Canadian directory of parl.* (J. K. Johnson). *DNB* (entry for James Simpson). *Dominion annual register*, 1885: 278. *Illustrated historical atlas of the counties of Northumberland and Durham, Ont.*, comp. H. Belden (Toronto, 1878; repr. Belleville, Ont., 1972), iii-iv, 105. J. E. [C.] Farewell, *County of Ontario;*

short notes as to the early settlement and progress of the county... (Belleville, 1973); first pub. with Ontario County, *By-laws of the council*... (Whitby, 1907). [R. G. Hamlyn *et al.*], *Bowmanville; a retrospect* ([Bowmanville, 1958]), 6, 21–22. W. H. Higgins, *The life and times of Joseph Gould* ... (Toronto, 1887; repr. Belleville, 1972), 281–82. L. A. Johnson, *History of the county of Ontario, 1615–1875* (Whitby, 1973), 245, 248, 250. V. Ross and Trigge, *Hist. of Canadian Bank of Commerce*, III: 205–6, 297. John Squair, *The townships of Darlington and Clarke, including Bowmanville and Newcastle, province of Ontario, Canada* (Toronto, 1927), 53, 132, 141–42.

SITTING BULL. *See* TA-TANKA I-YOTANK

SKEAD, JAMES, contractor, lumberman, and politician; b. 31 Dec. 1817 at Calder Hall, Moresby (Cumbria), England, eldest son of William Skead and Mary Selkirk; m. in 1842 Rosena MacKey and they had six children; d. 5 July 1884 in Ottawa, Ont.

James Skead was educated at Moresby and came to Canada in 1832 with his widowed father and two brothers. The family first settled on a farm at Île Jésus, Lower Canada, at the mouth of the Ottawa River. Several years later the Skeads moved up-river to Bytown (Ottawa), Upper Canada, which was rapidly developing as the commercial centre of the Ottawa valley, where the bulk of British North America's new staple export, square timber, was produced. James Skead soon began lumbering operations and in 1842 invested in various improvements along the Madawaska River, including a depot farm. At first his production was small and in 1843 he took out only one raft containing 33,500 cubic feet of red pine from crown lands along the Madawaska. His business grew rapidly, however, and two years later he produced 88,000 cubic feet and an additional 200,000 cubic feet in partnership with William Rogerson.

To reduce operating expenses and expand production Skead and the major Bytown area lumberers formed in 1844 the Madawaska River Improvement Company, a cooperative venture to build dams, slides, booms, and other works on the turbulent river. Through this involvement and his relationship with a brother-in-law, William MacKey, who had built a timber slide at the Chaudière Falls in 1835, Skead became expert in the construction of river works. In 1845 he was persuaded by the provincial Board of Works (the Department of Public Works after 1846) to build the Victoria slide at Bytown. His innovative design for the slide combined inclines with deceleration flats, a vast improvement over the older and dangerous single-pitch slides. Skead was again retained by the government in 1846 to construct slides and other works at various points on the Madawaska River.

In the 1840s Skead continued to expand his timber business, especially on the Madawaska and Mississippi rivers in Canada West. By 1851 he employed about 100 men in his woods operations and had opened a supply store in Bytown. In 1861 his work force had increased to 150 men, and the firm's annual average production was 600,000 cubic feet of pine and 16,000 sawlogs; he also received occasional contracts from the Department of Public Works for the construction of river improvements.

About 1851 Skead appears to have built a sawmill on the Ottawa River several miles above Bytown. He probably hoped to ship sawn lumber to the developing market in the northeastern United States but the mill was destroyed by fire after only a few years. In 1871 he again attempted to diversify his operations by building a large steam sawmill which incorporated the latest equipment near the site of his first mill. It was valued at $42,500 and was capable of manufacturing 7 million board feet of lumber, 500,000 shingles, and 500,000 laths each year. The mill became the centre of the small community of Skead's Mills (later Britannia and now part of Ottawa). In 1876 Skead became a major promoter and first president of the Ottawa Iron and Steel Manufacturing Company, which made mill machinery and other iron products. He was convinced that secondary manufacturing industries provided the only means to develop the Canadian economy more fully. Unfortunately the international trade depression of 1873–78 severely affected Skead's business ventures. By 1878 he was $10,000 in arrears with the federal government for slidage fees alone and in the same year he was taken to court by the Union Bank of Lower Canada under the Insolvency Act. Skead's financial embarrassment, however, did not harm his status with the élite of the capital, though it did destroy his business empire.

Throughout his career Skead promoted improvements, both public and private, to encourage the forest industry, bring agricultural settlement to the Ottawa valley, and develop the Ottawa River as the chief commercial route from the upper Great Lakes to the ports of Montreal, Quebec City, and New York. During the 1860s and 1870s he advocated the canalization of the Mattawa–French River system and he became a director of the Caughnawaga Ship Canal Company and the Georgian Bay Ship Canal Company. As well, with William Goodhue PERLEY and Henry Franklin BRONSON, he promoted the Upper Ottawa Steamboat Company, of which he became president, in an effort to provide dependable inexpensive shipment of supplies to forest operations up-river from Ottawa. Skead was also convinced after 1860 of the advantages of rail transportation for the timber trade. He was vice-president of the Canada Central Railway and the Montreal and City of Ottawa Junction Railway, and invested in the Ottawa and Prescott Railway and the Ottawa, Waddington and New York Railway and

Bridge Company. These efforts were combined with another to organize the timber operators in Ottawa into an association to lobby government agencies and to facilitate the exchange of information between firms. Skead became a charter director of the Ottawa Association of Lumber Manufacturers, formed in 1862, and remained on its board until it dissolved in 1868. Meanwhile he became president of the Ottawa Board of Trade in 1865 and served every year as an officer of this organization until 1883. In 1871–72 and 1876 he was a member of the executive committee of the Dominion Board of Trade and its president in 1879–80 and 1884.

After 1860, as one of Ottawa's prominent citizens, he also promoted such diverse ventures as the Bytown Consumers Gas Company (which became the Ottawa Gas Company in 1865), the Ottawa Immigrant Aid Society, the Carleton County and the City of Ottawa agricultural societies, the Rideau Club, the Ottawa St George's Society, and the Ottawa Rifle Association. He took an interest in farming and raised prize Ayrshire and Durham cattle. He was also president of the Ottawa Agricultural Insurance Company, the Agricultural and Arts Association of Ontario, and the Ontario Fruit Growers' Association.

Skead was elected to Ottawa City Council in 1861 and, in the following year, was returned by acclamation as the Conservative member for the Rideau division in the Legislative Council. He remained in the Legislative Council until confederation, when he was called to the Senate. In 1867 he contested the Carleton County provincial seat for the Conservatives but was defeated by Robert Lyon. On account of his financial difficulties Skead resigned from the Senate in January 1881 but was reappointed by the government of Sir John A. Macdonald* in the same year.

The variety of Skead's interests betrays a restless and dynamic personality. His business failure in the late 1870s, however, deeply affected him. Then in 1882 his lungs were seriously injured when he was thrown from a moving carriage. He was forced to retire, and died from his lung ailment in July 1884.

SANDRA GILLIS and ROBERT PETER GILLIS

PAC, MG 26, A; RG 11, ser.II, 18, file 5405; 21, file 220; 23, file 6403; 27, file 8143; 28, file 8438; 88, files 55048, 78533; 177; RG 31, A1, 1851, Ottawa, East Ward, p.169; 1861, Ottawa, Victoria Ward, p.215; 1871, Nepean Township, 3rd division, schedule 6. Can., Prov. of, Legislative Asembly, *App. to the journals*, 1844–45, I, app.P.; 1846, III, app.C.C.; 1852–53, app.M.M.M.M.; Parl., *Sessional papers*, 1861, II, no.4, app.F. *Bytown Gazette* ([Ottawa]), 28 Sept. 1848. *Free Press*, 5 July 1884. *Boyd's combined business directory for 1875–6 . . . of Montreal, Toronto, Hamilton, Ottawa, London & Kingston* . . . (Montreal, n.d.). *Canadian biog. dict.*, I. *Canadian directory of parl.* (J. K. Johnson). *CPC*, 1862–63. *Cyclopædia of Canadian biog.* (Rose, 1886). *Ottawa directory*, 1863–84. *Westboro, Ottawa's Westmount*, comp. Bower Lyon (Ottawa, 1913). [Charlotte Whitton], *A hundred years a-fellin' . . . 1842–1942* (Ottawa, n.d.), 54.

SMITH, Sir ALBERT JAMES, lawyer and politician; b. 12 March 1822 in Shediac, N.B., son of Thomas Edward Smith and Rebecca Beckwith; m. 11 June 1868 Sarah Marie Young, and they had one son; d. 30 June 1883 at Dorchester, N.B.

Albert James Smith's grandfather, Bowen Smith, was a Massachusetts loyalist who settled in Kingston, N.B., after the American revolution and moved to Shediac in 1807. His eldest son, Thomas, married a woman also of loyalist stock, and they had seven children. Operating a retail outlet in Shediac, Thomas Smith proved to be a shrewd entrepreneur specializing in the timber trade and merchandising. By the late 1830s he was prosperous enough to erect an impressive Georgian mansion for his family. Reared in relative comfort, Albert James Smith attended the Madras School of the Church of England and continued his education at the new Westmorland County Grammar School. After working for a year or two with his father in the store, he articled in the Dorchester law offices of Edward Barron Chandler*. At that time Chandler was the leader of the provincial "compact" government which dominated New Brunswick politics until 1854. Smith thus received an inside view of the political system while learning his profession. On 6 Feb. 1845 he was admitted as an attorney and on 4 Feb. 1847 was called to the bar. Intelligent and possessing a rapier tongue, Smith, "a tall man with black hair and black eyes," had marked success with juries and soon had a lucrative practice, especially in the areas of commercial and marine law. Appointed district receiver of crown debts and a member of the provincial barristers society, he appeared to be headed for a distinguished and profitable legal career.

A vacancy for Westmorland County in the House of Assembly in 1852 changed his course. Ignoring the advice of relatives and friends by offering himself as an opponent to the Chandler "compact," Smith issued his "political creed" before the by-election, identifying himself as a liberal who advocated such reforms as voting by ballot, biennial elections, an elected legislative council, strictly limited public spending, a reduced salary for the lieutenant governor, and the removal of the provincial capital from Fredericton, which was dominated by an "oligarchy . . . a few families." Elected easily on 18 May, Smith attended the short fall session and supported the government-sponsored European and North American Railway to be built from Saint John to Shediac. Over the next couple of years Smith rose to the front rank of a growing opposition which condemned the government for wanting "to jog along as they were."

What set Smith apart in the assembly was his vendetta against the privileges of the establishment. King's College, Fredericton, an enclave for the "sons of the richest men in the Province," became his favourite target. A "deep rooted prejudice," Smith warned, "had taken possession of the minds of the people in the rural districts against this College which neither time nor exertion could overcome." When Professor Joseph Marshall* d'Avray called Smith "Erostratus" for wanting to "burn down Diana's temple," Smith observed that d'Avray, recently "imported from England at the public expense," might now, at public expense, be sent "to Russia, where he would find more congenial employment." The forays against the institution led by Smith, most of them unsuccessful, became so animated in discussion that on one occasion, in 1856, the former attorney general, John Ambrose Street*, physically assaulted him in the assembly. Smith did, however, gather enough supporters to force an official inquiry which ultimately led to the transformation of the college into the University of New Brunswick in 1859 and reform under President William Brydone JACK.

The election of June 1854 resulted in a victory for the Reformers, and in November Smith became a member without portfolio of Charles Fisher*'s Executive Council. Others in the council were Samuel Leonard Tilley*, John Mercer Johnson*, James Brown*, William Henry Steeves*, and William Johnstone Ritchie*. It was a talented cabinet, "liberal to the back bone," with Smith considered the radical demagogue of the group. He stood solidly with his colleagues by supporting such reforms as voting by ballot, an extended franchise, voter registration, the initiation of money grants by the Executive Council, the reorganization of government departments, and the diminution of the powers of the lieutenant governor; in addition, he backed the nationalization of the European and North American in 1856. Yet, though probably the most feared adversary in the assembly, Smith was primarily a lawyer-businessman who looked first to his practice and played a secondary role in government.

Smith's talents on the stump and his independence within the government were illustrated during the debate over Tilley's prohibitory liquor bill of 1855. He did not believe the bill could be enforced, but he was even more disturbed by "its arbitrary and coercive principle." The legislation "was wrong – it was cruel," and "he would rather see the whole Province sink in obscurity rather than oppose the power of liberty." As soon as the act came into effect on 1 Jan. 1856, it proved inoperative and eventually led to the dismissal of the government by Lieutenant Governor John Henry Thomas Manners-Sutton* on 21 May. The "compact" rump, led by John Hamilton GRAY, was invited by Manners-Sutton to form the government, an action which was supported in a June general election. Though Smith had opposed the act, he was even more incensed at what he considered the unconstitutional actions of the lieutenant governor and his compact. Smith relentlessly pounded Gray and his colleagues while they were in power and played an important role in their defeat in the election of 1857. According to the Saint John *Morning News*, Smith had been "at all times dignified, consistent, and straightforward . . . an unflinching advocate of popular rights." The political establishment in the province was less enthusiastic about the aggressive activities of "Bully Albert Smith."

The Fisher government was again in power, though Smith was still without portfolio, perhaps because he and Fisher were barely on speaking terms. Smith's advocacy of change often took the form of opposition to the imperial influence, the governor, King's College, or Fredericton as the capital; Fisher was both registrar of King's College and a Fredericton stalwart. It was probably because they represented the diversity of the council that Fisher and Smith were sent to London together in 1858 as representatives to the ill-fated intercolonial conference on railways and British North American union. Over the next couple of years a Fisher–Smith feud almost immobilized the government, though Tilley kept it together until 1861, when Fisher was caught in a crown lands scandal and forced out of office. Tilley became the new premier with Smith as his chief lieutenant and attorney general from 27 April. Smith's sharp tongue and equally sharp temper fuelled the high feelings in the assembly; on one occasion Lestock DesBrisay followed Smith into the speaker's chamber, told him to stop "bullying" his opponents, and then "deliberately wrung his nose." Smith went after DesBrisay with a fireplace iron but was restrained.

Such incidents did not hurt Smith or the government, for they were both returned in the election of June 1861 and appeared to have four years of tranquillity ahead of them, especially after Manners-Sutton's departure in October. The fact that his replacement, Arthur Hamilton Gordon*, was a high-strung young aristocrat was ominous, however, and the American Civil War threatened to disrupt affairs in New Brunswick, especially if it led to increased public expenditures on the militia and the Intercolonial Railway, both of which Smith opposed. When Tilley departed for London on 30 October to participate in railway discussions, Smith was left in charge. Unfortunately, Gordon, whose opinion of colonial politicians rarely rose above disdain, did not like Smith. "I have had a little *Brush* with him but no *blood spilt*," Smith informed Tilley after his first meeting with Gordon, but that was as friendly as the relationship ever became. Militia appointments led to an open split between the two. Gordon considered the appointments his prerogative, and he made them, according to Smith, "in violation to what we consider the rights of the people." Smith insisted to Tilley that decisive action must be taken to protect "the dignity of our own position." Gordon never appreciated this concern.

As attorney general, Smith was competent though he appeared to be uncomfortable in office. He preferred the privilege of decision-making rather than the responsibility. That his own legal practice also remained a first priority was revealed by the "Missaguash Affair," in which he appeared to use the office of attorney general to introduce legislation that favoured his clients, upstream proprietors on the Missaguash River. The owners downstream, who had constructed an aboiteau (dike) on the river, immediately forwarded a petition calling for disallowance of the act to Gordon, who accepted it and, without legal advice or discussion with his attorney general, castigated Smith in a cold, formal letter. Though the act was never disallowed, the Duke of Newcastle, the colonial secretary, deprecated Smith's actions in a style, according to the Saint John *Morning News*, "more arrogant and dictatorial [than Gordon's], and in a spirit of greater unfairness." Needless to say, Smith returned the favour in kind, on 9 Feb. 1863. "Your situation and mine are widely different," he wrote in a public letter, addressed to Newcastle. "While you occupy a high Imperial position, I but fill an humble place in a small Province, in a remote part of the Empire. – Your voice and influence are powerful; mine are weak. Nevertheless my character and reputation are as dear to me, as yours are to you." He then turned to the matter of responsibility. "I am responsible for my official conduct to the Legislature and people of the Province, and not to you. The correctness of this proposition you admit. . . . Why not leave me to deal with the parties to whom I am responsible, uninfluenced by the uncalled for expression of any opinion by you."

By that time Smith was no longer a member of the government, having resigned on 10 Oct. 1862 because he disagreed with Tilley and the other members of the Executive Council who supported a significant provincial involvement in the Intercolonial Railway. Railways, in particular, Smith thought should be built by private funds. The increased taxation would lay a "heavy charge" which "our population and resources will not justify."

He appears to have been relieved to be out of office. Created a QC in 1862, he was at the top of his profession. As a member of the assembly he remained on good terms with Tilley and did not gloat when the Canadians scuttled the Intercolonial in 1863. For Lieutenant Governor Gordon, however, there was nothing but contempt. In 1864 Smith learned that Gordon was demanding his salary in sterling rather than colonial pounds, which would have imposed an additional £600 levy on the provincial treasury. Tilley supported the governor's position in the debate in the assembly; Smith opposed them both and on 29 May carried a majority in the house. On a popular issue, Smith had shown that he could be master of the assembly and that Tilley might be vulnerable. In the summer of 1864 another far more critical issue began to excite New Brunswickers. It was confederation.

Negotiations among the British Americans had matured into a full-blown British North American federation movement in 1864, with Tilley its New Brunswick apostle. Gordon had wanted a Maritime union, with himself as governor, but had lost the initiative. Smith was infuriated by the developments, and it was with an eye on Smith that Tilley constructed a coalition to carry the confederation project. Tilley recruited such former opponents as Chandler and Gray as well as discarded colleagues such as Fisher. The exclusion of Smith has never been fully explained. Perhaps he would not have joined. It is more likely that he was not invited because he was so completely opposed to any union scheme as well as to the Intercolonial Railway, which Tilley saw as the prize of negotiations. At any rate, by the time Tilley had returned from the ambulatory conference that had taken him to Charlottetown, Halifax, Quebec, Montreal, Ottawa, Toronto, and Niagara (Niagara-on-the-Lake), he encountered a hostile New Brunswick being given direction by Albert Smith, "The Douglas of Dorchester . . . the Lion of Westmorland." Late in November 1864 Smith published a "Letter to the Electors of the County of Westmorland," which was to become the force behind the anti-confederation blast in New Brunswick. The delegates to the conference, with a mandate to discuss only Maritime union, had acted unconstitutionally, he declared, and had placed the interests of Canada ahead of those of New Brunswick. The dominant Canadians would impose prohibitive taxes on the colony to pay for their past extravagances such as canals and railways. There would also be the cost of two governments rather than one and representation by population would place New Brunswick permanently in a subordinate position. When Tilley called an election early in 1865, Smith was ready for him. He stumped the province with a devastating speech in which he said that confederation had been conjured up in the "oily brains of Canadian politicians" as a solution to their own problems and as a scheme to exploit others. He warned his listeners to examine the two states, "one [Canada] suffering from anarchy and disquiet . . . [the other] New Brunswick . . . enjoying all the blessings of this life." The spectre of direct taxation served as a backdrop to the designs of the Canadians, who would increase in dominance as their population and appetite grew, relegating New Brunswick to the status of a "mere municipality." As an alternative Smith offered both continued reciprocity with the United States and the Western Extension

Railway, part of the European and North American, from Saint John to the American border. But fear of Canada was the essential ingredient in his message. Smith presented his case with "great force and animation" and the anti-confederates in New Brunswick, with Smith the "heart and soul of the opposition," shattered the union movement by carrying 26 of the 41 seats in the assembly. Four independents and 11 unionists were also elected.

After the anti-confederate victory Gordon had the mortifying task of inviting the despised Smith to form the government, though he tempered the chore by asking both Smith and Robert Duncan Wilmot*, a Conservative who opposed the Quebec plan, to select the Executive Council. Together they wrestled with the problem of choosing a cabinet from men united only in their opposition to the Quebec Resolutions. Some of the members of the cabinet they chose actually supported a British North American union with either a stronger central government or stronger provincial governments. John Campbell Allen* of Fredericton, the attorney general, was a Conservative like Wilmot and like him favoured a legislative union. Smith and George Luther Hatheway*, the chief commissioner of public works, wanted greatly increased provincial rights if any union scheme went forward, while Arthur Hill Gillmor*, the provincial secretary, and Timothy Warren Anglin* were opposed to all union schemes. Anglin, the leader of the Saint John Catholics, was considered an Irish radical and rebel by some and was especially difficult to work with because he refused to make any concessions or compromises. Since the Roman Catholic vote had been decisive in many constituencies where Smith's supporters won, the Anglin and Catholic position could not be ignored. The general consensus on the cabinet was that it was a "queer admixture of Tories and Liberals" though Gordon admitted they were "men of undoubted honesty" and "an improvement on . . . the previous Council." Smith, the president of the council, he described as "a man of some ability & considerable obstinacy. His views are narrow & his temper violent but though very impatient of opposition or control I believe him to possess the merits of honesty of purpose & resolution. He belongs to the radical section of politicians, but, at the same time, is very hostile towards the U.S."

The mutual distrust that existed between Smith and Gordon was only one of a variety of problems. The members of the council disagreed on most issues and policies, from the militia and railways to external relations and the role of the lieutenant governor. A master manipulator might have manœuvered among them with dexterity; Smith seemed paralysed by the situation. Shortly after assuming office in March 1865, Smith was characterized by the Saint John *Morning Telegraph* as the "ablest and most eloquent apostle of the genus and generation stand-still," a view proved unfair when the government introduced a new militia bill and a Western Extension Railway bill in the spring session of that year.

The determination of the British government to reverse the New Brunswick decision on confederation was Smith's greatest concern, and for that reason he and Attorney General Allen left for London on 20 June 1865 to counteract imperial pressures. They also sought support for a renewed reciprocity treaty, for a railway link between New Brunswick and Nova Scotia, and for a loan of £25,000 sterling from Baring Brothers to meet provincial fiscal obligations. Though they were successful on the last three, Edward Cardwell, the colonial secretary, made it clear that he was committed to confederation. He may have offered Smith a position such as a colonial governorship to induce his support.

Smith returned to New Brunswick less confident than he had been on leaving it. His council was becoming restless and his policies were in jeopardy. The first sod was turned on the Western Extension Railway on 10 Nov. 1865 but because of financial difficulties construction never proceeded. Anglin, who was strongly committed to the railway, chose to resign from the cabinet. Vacancies on the bench led to the appointment of Allen to the Supreme Court and in a brutally fought by-election in York County Charles Fisher defeated Smith's candidate, John PICKARD. Another vacancy on the bench caused more dissension and the defection from the cabinet of Andrew Rainsford Wetmore*, whose claims had been ignored. The American rejection of reciprocity early in 1866 left Smith without a programme and prompted the resignation of Wilmot, who now openly supported confederation. In the mean time, Gordon, as a dutiful imperial servant under pressure, exerted all the force he dared to achieve a union policy. In February 1866 Smith was compelled to take a hard look at his position. His original council was fragmented beyond recognition and his promises of reciprocity and the Western Extension had proved empty. The independents in the assembly were drifting away and were joined by deserters such as Wilmot and Wetmore. Though Smith was convinced he still had the support of the assembly and the province, he was also aware of his mounting failures and the increase in the pro-union sentiment. Gordon continuously pressed Smith to pursue a union policy that would be acceptable to the imperial authorities, the Canadians, and the majority of New Brunswickers. From late 1865 Smith probably realized he would have to follow such a course, but he vacillated for weeks before deciding to include a vague paragraph in the speech from the throne on 8 March 1866 suggesting that his government would advocate some form of British North American union.

Whether Smith had a plan in mind is not known. It

may have been no more than a notion to pursue some form of union. Opponents both within and outside his party never let him work out his ideas. Internally, the Acadian and Roman Catholic members would not support any union legislation. Externally, Charles Fisher and the confederates were determined that Smith should not carry confederation and claim the anticipated rewards. To that end they fought him in the assembly with a debate on an amendment to the speech from the throne, accusing him of failing to take adequate steps to protect the province from the threatened Fenian invasion. For four long weeks the debate dragged on and the government was paralysed. Gordon, convinced that his future in the colonial service depended upon his colony pursuing a union path, became alarmed as Smith appeared to abandon any move towards confederation. By the beginning of April Gordon could no longer tolerate the situation. He decided to force Smith from office by accepting a strongly worded pro-confederation reply to the speech from the throne from the upper house, the Legislative Council. In a colony with responsible government this was a highly irregular procedure for a governor to follow. Smith correctly insisted that it was his right to be consulted and to recommend, but Gordon cared little about the rights and dignity of colonials. Smith resigned. It was his only course. It was also a constitutional crisis of the first order and one that Tilley considered unnecessary since he was convinced Smith would have had to capitulate within a few weeks. Still, the confederates took office when it was offered to them by Gordon and immediately went to the electorate for approval.

Smith could not carry New Brunswick in the elections of May and June 1866. Those ideas and proposals that served so well in 1865 had proved a sham. There was no Western Extension, no reciprocity, no good government. Smith's opposition to union was also questionable. He dwelt on the detestable lieutenant governor, but Gordon's term was up and few seemed to care. The confederation party, with imperial backing, Canadian money, and good luck, including a Fenian invasion during the election, was not to be denied. Even the Roman Catholic bishops supported it in 1866. New Brunswickers were promised sound government, lower taxes, greater wealth, and more control over the new government. The confederates succeeded in associating Smith with the anti-confederates, the annexationists, and the Fenians. They implied there was a French and Roman Catholic conspiracy against Protestantism and the empire, with Smith its unwitting tool. Smith faced this shameful assault valiantly. He "felt proud of the French population of this country; they would compare favourably in every respect with the English population; *they were incorruptible and could not be bought!!!*" When the election was over Smith and his group of 8 faced 33 pro-confederates in the assembly. A pattern had been set for New Brunswick politics which would persist, the mainly Roman Catholic and Acadian bloc on one side and the predominantly Protestant and English-speaking bloc on the other.

The assembly was called together in June 1866 to pass a confederation resolution and Smith tried for a final time to head off the Quebec scheme. He called for a public referendum on any act of confederation, equal representation for provinces in the upper house, a limited number of members of parliament, a guarantee of a cabinet minister for each Maritime province, the establishment of a court to settle federal-provincial disputes, and strict control over taxation. His motions were rejected 26 to 8 and the "Fathers" were soon off to London, England, and the British North America Act. It was a thoroughly chastened Smith who was elected to the House of Commons for Westmorland in August 1867.

Like Joseph Howe* of Nova Scotia, that other notable anti-confederate from the Maritimes, Smith was watched with apprehension at Ottawa. Unlike Howe, who demanded the repeal of the British North America Act, Smith assured the House of Commons that "he had fought against Confederation, was conquered and laid down his arms, and was anxious to assist in working out the measure." That certainly did not mean he would accept whatever the government of Sir John A. Macdonald* proposed. He remained a determined provincial rights man to the end. He never overcame his distrust of the Canadians, a suspicion confirmed by the actions of the House of Commons in its first months. The new tariff structure, with its levy on such items as flour, sugar, tea, and molasses, was exactly what he had predicted. On 31 Dec. 1867 he delivered a speech in Saint John to a packed hall in which he concluded sadly: "We are utterly powerless. We are under the controlling power of Messrs. McDonald and [George-Étienne Cartier*]. . . . though there should be a change of Government, it would be no better for the people of the Maritime Provinces. The interests of Ontario were entirely distinct and at variance with all the other provinces."

During those early years at Ottawa Smith served as a totally independent member, wary of the old Canadians in all they did but finding the Liberals even more Ontario-centred and provincial than the Liberal-Conservatives. The alienation of the Maritime members was fed by the tariff increases, the purchase of Rupert's Land, the delay in the construction of the Intercolonial Railway, and the overwhelming dominance of the central Canadians in both the cabinet and the federal civil service. To make matters worse, opposition in the traditional sense was drowned by cries from the government benches as well as from the opposition side. When Smith, for example, called in 1870 for the "British Government to confer on us the power of looking after our commercial interests," he was charged with disloyalty and his proposal was dismissed. By that year the dissatisfaction with Ottawas had become so widespread in New Brunswick that all candidates in the provincial election in July condemned federal policies. Had Smith chosen to, he might have led a strong repeal, independence, or annexationist movement, especially after the disaster of the Treaty of Washington in 1871 by which the inshore fisheries of the Maritime provinces were opened to American fishermen without a *quid pro quo* such as the reciprocity urgently sought by Maritimers. Smith refused to give encouragement to the discontents, however, and remarked that "there had scarcely ever been a treaty between England and the United States in which the latter had not the best of it." For lack of an alternative, he supported the treaty. Most New Brunswick members followed him.

By 1872 Smith was regarded as the unofficial leader of the New Brunswick contingent in the House of Commons, generally giving his support to the Liberal-Conservatives. Up to that time Tilley had proved ineffectual in the cabinet and he was treated with some hostility both in and out of parliament. Paradoxically, Smith had become his major ally in the commons in defence of the interests of their province. The assault in 1872 by John Costigan* and some Quebec members on the New Brunswick Common Schools Act of the previous year, which deprived the Catholic population of public funding for their separate schools, saw Smith and Tilley working together to defend the position of the New Brunswick government. In the election of that year Smith publicly announced his "dissolution of partnership with the Grits" and his support for Macdonald's Liberal-Conservatives, who swept the province. The next year Smith was offered the lieutenant governorship of New Brunswick by an appreciative Macdonald, but he preferred to stay in the House of Commons. He was, also, not prepared to give up his legal practice. Within two months, however, Smith stood against Macdonald and with the Liberals. On 13 Aug. 1873 Macdonald, faced with the Pacific Scandal, adjourned the House of Commons in "an act of tyranny" the purpose of which, according to Smith, was to deprive parliament of its rights. On 6 November Macdonald resigned as prime minister to be replaced by Alexander Mackenzie* and the Liberals.

That Smith would join Mackenzie's cabinet no one doubted. Six years after confederation his role as the archetypal anti-confederate was forgotten. The Saint John *Daily Telegraph* described him as an "able lawyer . . . shipowner and capitalist" who was "in every way a man of mark" and was "personally popular." He became minister of marine and fisheries and carried 12 New Brunswick Liberals back to Ottawa in the election of January 1874. Tilley had accepted the lieutenant governorship of New Brunswick in the last hours of the Macdonald government, leaving Smith the unchallenged New Brunswick champion in Ottawa. Smith, in fact, came to the defence of Tilley when some Liberals attempted to undo his last-minute appointment, and in January 1874 went out of his way to praise his former colleague in a public testimonial.

The next four years were to be among the most rewarding in Smith's life. He had ended his apparently frisky bachelorhood on 11 June 1868 when he married 21-year-old Sarah Marie, the daughter of John Wilson Young, a prosperous Halifax capitalist. He built a spacious red-brick mansion called Woodlands at Dorchester, where their son, John Wilson Young Smith, grew up. In Ottawa, Smith was at the centre of affairs, with Mackenzie relying on him as the Maritime expert and confiding in him on many matters. When the ministry of justice became vacant in 1874, it was offered to Smith, probably on Edward Blake*'s recommendation, but was not accepted. Smith had participated that year in the doomed negotiations with the United States over reciprocity. He was, however, most comfortable as minister of marine and fisheries, an office which was of central importance to New Brunswick, and to which he was well suited as one of the "ablest marine lawyers" in Canada. He knew the law of the sea, international shipping and insurance, marketing, and negotiating. The ministry was to give Smith his greatest single triumph. The Americans were required to pay a financial compensation for the right to the east coast fishery by the Treaty of Washington, the amount to be settled by arbitration. Halifax was selected as the location for the necessary meetings, which began on 15 June 1877. Sir Alexander Tilloch Galt*, a Canadian, was the British representative, Ensign H. Kellogg was the American, and Maurice Delfoss of Belgium was the neutral arbitrator. Smith and his staff had spent years on their brief and at Halifax convinced Galt and Delfoss of the justice of the Canadian claim. On 23 November of that year the commission decided by a vote of two to one that the value of the fisheries for a 12-year period, 1871–83, be set at $5,500,000. Canada received $4,500,000 of which $500,000 was used to cover costs. The interest on the $4,000,000 was eventually designated for needs of the east coast fishery. Newfoundland got the other $1,000,000. The Halifax award was a monumental victory for Canada, if only because the United States had not won. Smith, "the ruling spirit throughout," was lionized: the *Canadian Illustrated News* (Montreal) featured him on its cover; and the Halifax *Herald* commented that "his attention to the case, his labor in aiding its conduct, and his anxiety to bring about a favorable result for Canada, do him a credit which has hitherto been refused." The British authorities concurred and on 25 May 1878 he was created a KCMG. Only a dozen others had been so honoured since confederation and he was the first native-born New Brunswicker to be knighted. The irony of Smith's triumph was not lost on those who remembered his role in the struggle over confederation, especially Peter Mitchell*, who had replaced Smith as president of the New Brunswick Executive Council in 1866 and had been Canada's first federal minister of marine and fisheries. He denigrated Smith in that office throughout Smith's term and made boorish claims that the Halifax award was the result of his own efforts before Smith had taken over in 1873.

In the federal election of 1878 the Macdonald Conservatives were returned to power on the platform of the National Policy as a solution to the depression that had plagued the Liberals throughout their years in office. Across New Brunswick, however, Smith's popularity helped to take 11 of the 16 seats. "No man in the Province can beat AJ Smith," wrote an observer. "I consider it only folly for any one to try." The completion of the Intercolonial Railway in 1876, the reconstruction of Saint John after the fire of 1877, and the erection of such government works as the federal penitentiary at Dorchester had all helped to alleviate the gloom of the depression in New Brunswick.

Over the next four years Smith served adequately, leading the opposition attack on occasion, but the spunk that had vivified his earlier years was missing. He had recently become quite portly, and he became known to critics as "Sir Albert the Lazy." Mackenzie had complained of the general lack of vitality in his cabinet while in office, and had referred to Smith, who "could be an efficient Minister if he took the trouble," as "fat and easy" and "lazy." By the time the 1882 election arrived Smith was vulnerable for the first time in his career. The Conservatives nominated Josiah Wood*, a talented young lawyer from Sackville, to run against him. It was a hard campaign, with the *Moncton Times* providing a focus for the opposition. "VOTE against the sectional Ontario Party," it urged. "WESTMORLAND CANNOT LONGER AFFORD TO BE MISREPRESENTED BY SIR ALBERT SMITH." This cry rang true to many of the newcomers who had recently moved to the county and could not identify with the honourable elder statesman and his past. After 30 years in politics Smith was finally defeated. "The power of the One Man Party is broken," crowed the *Times*, "the dictation of the Dorchester Corner Clique is at an end."

Smith reacted to his defeat at first with bitterness and then with bewilderment. He had come to think of the seat as his by right. Cut off from political life he lost his bearings. Even his health, which had been good until the election, began to deteriorate. By the spring of 1883 he was wasting away and he died on 30 June, leaving an estate in excess of $100,000.

Smith was not a great leader, nor did he initiate any major changes. There was always something of the village conservative in him even when he expressed his liberal views. True, he was anti-establishment, but it was old establishment, not the new of which he was a member. He was honest, sincere, and more consistent than most politicians, for he did not use politics to accumulate judgeships or governorships, all of which he refused. Ultimately, his opposition to confederation was the major event of Smith's career, though the victory over the Americans at Halifax was no mean achievement. As fashions in history change and as the nature of confederation is critically re-examined, Smith the dissenter can no longer be disregarded as a negative, narrow-minded, Maritime parochialist. He was not a statesman, but he was a discerning politician.

C. M. WALLACE

[Smith's 30 years in politics had been exceptional, marked by both honours and controversy, yet he has been almost totally banished from the history books. He left no papers to guarantee a niche for himself (they were destroyed after his death), nor did his wife and son wish to have their privacy invaded by a biography. That still does not account for the lack of interest in Smith. Of course he was from a fringe region and opposed confederation, two contingencies that go far to explain the indifference among the centralist-oriented historians who have dominated the writing on Canada's past. His knighthood and his role at the fisheries commission ordinarily should have attracted some curiosity, but it is Galt who is remembered, with little apparent justice. Smith also had the misfortune to be a member of the Mackenzie cabinet, which was unable to cope with the enormity of the depression of the 1870s and has been tarred with ineptitude. In New Brunswick history, Smith fares just as poorly. The earlier historians such as James Hannay* were intolerant of the opponents of confederation. More recently, much of New Brunswick history has been written from the imperial perspective, as garnered from the papers in the Colonial Office and such lieutenant governors as Manners-Sutton and Gordon. Not surprisingly Smith and most other colonial politicians who lacked the proper deference come off badly and are relegated to minor roles in a story about imperial officials. The New Brunswick sources, however, suggest quite a different interpretation.

The first modern study was C. M. Wallace, "The life and times of Sir Albert James Smith" (MA thesis, Univ. of New Brunswick, Fredericton, 1960), which was reworked as "Albert Smith, confederation, and reaction in New Brunswick, 1852–1882," *CHR*, 44 (1963): 285–312. J. E. Belliveau, *The splendid life of Albert Smith and the women he left behind* (Windsor, N.S., 1976), and "Sir Albert Smith, the Acadians and New Brunswick politics, 1852–1883," Soc. hist. acadienne, *Cahiers* (Moncton, N.-B.), 8 (1977): 65–79, have appeared but are marked by faulty research.

Hannay, *Hist. of N.B.*, II, is still useful, but the pre-confederation section is inadequate. Of considerable use are the following: J. K. Chapman, *The career of Arthur Hamilton Gordon, first Lord Stanmore, 1829–1912* (Toronto, 1964); MacNutt, *New Brunswick*; Waite, *Canada, 1874–96*, and *Life and times of confederation*; C. M. Wallace, "Sir Leonard Tilley: a political biography" (PHD thesis, Univ. of

Alberta, Edmonton, 1972); A. G. Bailey, "The basis and persistence of opposition to confederation in New Brunswick," *CHR*, 23 (1942): 374–97; and T. A. Burke, "Mackenzie and his cabinet, 1873–1878," *CHR*, 41 (1960): 128–48. There is also useful material in the following primary sources and biographical works. C.M.W.]

N. B. Museum, James Brown, Journal, 1844–70; E. B. Chandler papers; Jarvis family papers; Tilley family papers; Webster coll. PAC, MG 24, B29; MG 26, A; B; MG 27, I, D15. PANB, RG 2, RS6, 1854–67; Arthur Hill Gillmor papers. PRO, CO 188; CO 189. UNBL, MG H12a. Can., House of Commons, *Debates*, 1867–70, 1875–82. N.B., House of Assembly, *Journal*, 1852–67; *Reports of the debates*, 1852–57. "Parl. debates" (CLA mfm. project of parl. debates, 1846–74), 1873–74. *Parliamentary debates, Dominion of Canada* . . . (3v., Ottawa, 1870–72). *Chignecto Post* (Sackville, N.B.), 1877. *Daily Telegraph* (Saint John, N.B.), 1869–83. *Moncton Times*, 1877–83. *Morning Freeman* (Saint John), 1860–72. *Morning News* (Saint John), 1852–84. *Morning Telegraph* (Saint John), 1864–69. *Saint John Globe*, 1858–73. *Canadian biog. dict.*, II. *CPC*, 1862–82. *Dominion annual register*, 1883. M. O. Hammond, *Confederation and its leaders* (Toronto, 1917).

SMITH, BENNETT, shipbuilder and shipowner; b. 29 Nov. 1808 at Windsor, N.S., son of John Smith and Ann Grant; m. 27 Dec. 1832 Rachel Harris of Horton (Hortonville), N.S., and they had eight children; d. 11 Jan. 1886 at Windsor.

Bennett Smith's family lived in the Newport–Windsor area, and in the early 1800s his father established himself at what became known locally as Smith's Island, near the junction of the Avon and St Croix rivers. With his older brothers John and William, Bennett apprenticed in his father's shipyard at Windsor and at the latter's death in 1832 inherited the Smith's Island property. In July 1833 the three brothers launched the *Agenoria*, a brigantine of 107 tons which they operated until 1837. The first vessel Bennett built was the *Matchless*, a brig of 163 tons launched at Windsor in 1839 and owned by the Smith brothers and other merchants of Windsor and Newport. In the following year Bennett built the 195-ton brig *Eclipse* for John Duncan of Newport.

After a lapse of six years, during which time he probably engaged in farming and lumbering, Bennett Smith began building ships again and continued at Windsor without interruption for over 30 years. After 1846 he built 25 vessels, nearly all barques and ships of 700 to 1,300 tons. One of his first large vessels was the *Siam*, a ship of 721 tons built in 1852 at a cost of £4,977. Between 1853 and 1863 he built the *Humber*, *Princess Royal*, *British Queen*, and *British Lion*, ships whose tonnage ranged from 841 to 1,279 tons and whose costs varied from £6,465 to £11,686. In 1864 Smith launched his largest vessel, the *Nile*, a ship of 1,336 tons built at a cost of £13,210. Two of his later vessels were the *Malta*, a ship of 1,228 tons built in 1873 at a cost of £13,653, and the 1,318-ton *Black Watch*, which was built in 1877 and cost £13,270. Smith was the designer, master builder, manager, and principal shareholder of all his vessels, with additional shares being held by his brothers and other local merchants. All of his large vessels were involved in foreign trade, carrying many types of cargo to ports around the world. Smith also had vessels built for him by John Stewart at Saint John, N.B., and Samuel Smith at Bedford, N.S. He owned shares in vessels built by John A. Harvie and James Mosher at Newport.

After the construction of the *Black Watch* in 1877, Smith had a disagreement with his employees over wages and declared that he would not build another vessel in Windsor. He then closed his shipyard. In the late 1870s and early 1880s he had five vessels built for him by William and Robert Wallace at Gardner Creek, St John County, N.B., Gaius Turner at Harvey, York County, N.B., and John Fraser at Saint John. In addition, Smith owned shares in two large schooners built at Windsor by Shubael Dimock.

During his years as a shipbuilder and shipowner, Smith built a total of 27 vessels, all but one of which he owned and operated. An additional nine vessels were built for him and he held shares in eight others. In 1867, his peak year of ownership, Smith's fleet totalled 12 vessels. After 1874 shipbuilding gradually diminished in all areas of the Maritime provinces, although there was no abrupt decline until the mid 1880s. At the time of Smith's death in 1886 he had two very large vessels under construction by the Fraser and Wallace firms. Smith's business was taken over by his sons John and Charles, and in 1889 the *Loodiana*, a ship of 1,820 tons, the largest of the Smith fleet, was built by J. B. North at Hantsport, N.S. In 1904 the vessels which still remained in the fleet were sold.

In addition to his shipping business, Smith was a director of Avon Marine and Shipowners Insurance Company, based in Windsor. He took little interest in politics or societies of any kind, but was a benefactor and trustee of the Methodist church at Windsor. In 1858, on the death of Ichabod Dimock, Smith was elected a Liberal member of the House of Assembly for Hants County, but when his term of office ended in 1859 he did not seek re-election.

Smith had moved from Smith's Island to a large house in Windsor in 1866. At the time of his death he was one of the largest shipowners and one of the wealthiest and best known men in the Maritime provinces, though he was apparently not popular in his own community. His estate was valued at $600,000.

CHARLES A. ARMOUR

PAC, RG 42, A1, 16–52, 55, 80–85, 257, 258, 307–12, 368. PANS, MS file, Bennett Smith, Biog.; Bennett Smith,

Descendants. *Morning Chronicle* (Halifax), 13 Jan. 1886. *Novascotian*, 16 Jan. 1886. *Canadian biog. dict.*, II. *Directory of N.S. MLAs*.

SMITH, HENRY WILLIAM, lawyer, judge, and politician; b. in 1826 in St Kitts, British West Indies, eldest son of James Royer Smith and Cordelia Wigley; m. in 1853 Mary E. A. Poyntz, and they had several children; d. 1 Feb. 1890 at Halifax, N.S.

Although born in St Kitts, Henry William Smith spent his childhood in Wales and, after 1833, in Halifax where his father practised law with the firm of Smith and Hartshorn. In 1840 the Smith family moved to Bridgetown, Annapolis County, N.S. After study in his father's law office Smith was admitted as an attorney on 24 July 1848 and, one year later, as a barrister of the bar of Nova Scotia. He first practised law in Bridgetown in partnership with his father, but by 1852 both father and son were working and living in Halifax.

By 1854 Henry William Smith had left Halifax and was practising law in Shelburne. In the autumn of 1857 he moved from Shelburne to Liverpool, Queens County, N.S., and in December he petitioned Lieutenant Governor Sir John Gaspard Le Marchant* for an appointment as "Notary and Tabillion Public." There is no record that his request was granted, but on 8 May 1858 Smith was appointed registrar of probate for Queens County, an office he held until 1867. In Liverpool his life was apparently fully occupied by his legal career, his family, social affairs, and public duty, including his positions as major in the 1st Regiment of the Queens County militia, and, from 1872 to 1876, as governor of King's College in Windsor.

Undoubtedly the most important occurrence in the career of Henry William Smith, and the event that brought him out of his obscurity as a small town lawyer, was the movement for the political union of British North America. The scheme of union introduced by the Province of Canada in September 1864 to a Charlottetown conference called to debate Maritime union, and discussed a month later at Quebec, was embraced by many political leaders in Nova Scotia, including the government of Charles Tupper*, but opposition appeared as early as November. In its 1865 legislative session, 183 anti-confederation petitions, bearing over 15,000 signatures, were presented to the Nova Scotia assembly. This opposition shattered existing political alliances in the province and the "Nova Scotia" or "Peoples' Party," under the leadership of Joseph Howe*, launched a determined bid to defeat the "Botheration Scheme." Smith was actively involved, and on 18 Sept. 1867 he was one of three anti-confederate candidates elected from Queens County to the House of Assembly. In total, Nova Scotians elected 36 anti-confederate members to the 38-seat provincial assembly. Of the 19 members of the House of Commons from Nova Scotia elected in that year, 18 were anti-confederates.

Following the 1867 elections, the Nova Scotia government of William ANNAND turned its attention toward the possible repeal of the British North America Act insofar as it related to Nova Scotia. To accomplish this, Joseph Howe went to London in February 1868 to present Nova Scotia's case to the imperial authorities. Some days later the Executive Council requested that Annand, Jared Chipman Troop, and Henry William Smith go to London to assist Howe in his endeavours; they arrived on 12 March 1868. Although sources suggest that Howe did most of the real work of the delegation, Smith did at least accompany him to interviews with the colonial secretary and other officials where taxation, trade, and fishing policies were discussed. Although the British authorities agreed to ask the dominion government to review the impact of confederation on Nova Scotia in these areas, the delegation's bid for repeal was unsuccessful. Its members returned to Nova Scotia to receive the official thanks of the House of Assembly, with the door to constitutional repeal firmly shut behind them.

Smith remained active in Nova Scotian politics; he was re-elected in 1871 and on 19 April of that year was made a member of the Executive Council and attorney general of Nova Scotia. He held the latter office until 4 Jan. 1875. During these years he attended to the regular business of the provincial government and to negotiations with the federal government, including those in 1874 dealing with the provinces' withdrawal from the previously concurrent jurisdictions over immigration. On 15 Jan. 1875 Smith was elevated to the bench as a puisne judge of the Supreme Court of Nova Scotia, "which high position he . . . worthily filled" until his death in 1890.

JOHN N. GRANT

PANS, MG 1, 828; RG 1, 200, 8 May 1858; 203; 204, 19 April 1871; RG 3, 3; RG 5, GP, 11; R, 98. Univ. of King's College Arch. (Halifax), Bylaws, calendars, reports, and other records for 1868–80. N.S., House of Assembly, *Journal and proc.*, 1868, 1871–75. *Acadian Recorder*, 3 Feb. 1890. *Liverpool Transcript* (Liverpool, N.S.), 1857–60. *Morning Chronicle* (Halifax), 3 Feb. 1890. *Belcher's farmer's almanack*, 1848–75. *Catlaogue of portraits of the judges of the Supreme Court of Nova Scotia and other portraits, law courts, Halifax, N.S.*, [comp. R. V. Harris] ([Halifax?, 1929?]). Dalhousie Univ., *Directory of graduates and former students of the university, corrected to September, 1937* ([Halifax, 1937?]). John Doull, *Sketches of attorney generals of Nova Scotia, 1750–1926* (Halifax, 1964). E. R. Coward, *Bridgetown, Nova Scotia; its history to 1900* ([Bridgetown, 1955]). K. G. Pryke, *Nova Scotia and confederation, 1864–74* (Toronto, 1979). R. H. Campbell, "The repeal agitation in Nova Scotia, 1867–69," N.S. Hist. Soc., *Coll.*, 25 (1942): 95–129.

SMITH, JAMES, teacher, farmer, and writer; b. 5 Sept. 1820 at Caraquet, N.B.; m. Flavie Fournier; d. 18 May 1888 at Matapédia, Que.

James Smith's life, about which few details are known, was quite eventful. After studying at the Collège de Sainte-Anne-de-la-Pocatière in Lower Canada, he is thought to have entered the Grand Séminaire de Québec, but he soon left to pursue a career in what became his principal occupation, teaching. He lets the character Pierre in his *Les Soirées de la Baie-des-Chaleurs*, published in 1883, speak for him: "The teacher named Pierre had long taught in the province of Quebec and in New Brunswick, where he founded a school in defiance of the atheistic [school] law. . . . He later went to the United States, worked there to found Catholic schools for Canadian [emigrants], and had the good fortune to see this venture grow, spread, and become the first and main concern of our exiled brothers today." In 1856 Smith was a professor of English and mathematics at the new industrial college in Rimouski, Canada East, and from 1862 to 1865 he taught agriculture at the new Collège de Rimouski.

James Smith was always a deeply religious man. As the father of François-Xavier-Louis-Théodule, the first priest ordained in the diocese of Rimouski, he was accorded consideration and favours by the diocesan authorities, towards whom he always showed the greatest deference. A particular incident in 1878 could have upset this attitude of submission and respect. Smith had picked out a settler's lot in the 1st concession of Causapscal Township, on the road to Matapédia, a road on which he had directed part of the construction. After he had presented the lot to the ecclesiastical authorities for a parish church, Bishop Jean Langevin* decided that it should be constructed in a location better suited to the geographical distribution of the township's growing population, and gave possession of this lot, no.29, to Ferdinand Hepel. Smith, however, wanted to reclaim the property, and the two farmers firmly asserted their claims before the diocesan authorities of Rimouski. In a letter to Vicar General Edmond LANGEVIN, Hepel painted this picture of Smith: "His whole life has been an unending succession of schemes which have produced nothing worthwhile. He has tried everything, teaching, mechanics, commerce, navigation and farming, and has never got anywhere, by adopting methods of husbandry contrary to the wisdom of successful farmers. Even with his children able to help him, he has never managed to live off his land, sowing out of season, and finishing his planting when ordinarily it is almost harvest time." No doubt Hepel's animosity towards Smith accounts for the exaggerations of this passage, which nevertheless is instructive testimony concerning Smith's numerous occupations.

However, it is as a writer that James Smith left the most explicit evidence of his personality and the values that motivated him. His occasional writings in *Le Canadien* and *La Vérité*, both of Quebec City, and *Le Moniteur acadien* of Shediac, N.B., took up and amplified the themes developed in his three other unpretentious publications. The last of these, *Les Soirées de la Baie-des-Chaleurs*, is something of a treatise on education, showing the influence of the ideas of Mgr Jean-Joseph Gaume who stated: "Education makes the man." Religious education in Smith's view was the only way to overcome the evils of an age imbued with a spirit of freemasonry and thus characterized by Catholic liberalism, irreligion, separation of church and state, and disrespect for the authority of which the priest was the principal guardian.

In another field, Smith was one of a large group of authors who in the period from 1830 to about 1870 wrote a great deal about agriculture. In his second work, a small treatise entitled *Les Éléments de l'agriculture*, which appeared in 1862, he sought to demonstrate that agriculture was "the first, the most useful and consequently the most noble of the arts. In its train follow the prosperity and wealth of nations." The diversity of his interests had also been revealed six years earlier in a modest publication, *Havre de refuge*, which discusses the problems of transportation on the lower St Lawrence River.

James Smith's writings, then, reveal a man who, belonging to the great conservative and ultramontane movement of the second half of the 19th century, worked with sincerity and zeal for the advancement of agriculture, education, and the Catholic faith.

NOËL BÉLANGER

James Smith was the author of *Havre de refuge; Rimouski vs. Bic et chemin de fer des Trois Pistoles* (Québec, 1856); *Les Éléments de l'agriculture à l'usage de la jeunesse canadienne* (Québec, 1862); and *Les Soirées de la Baie-des-Chaleurs, ou entretiens sur l'éducation de l'enfance* (Montréal, 1883).

AP, Saint-Laurent (Matapédia), Reg. des baptêmes, mariages et sépultures, 18 mai 1888. Arch. de l'archevêché de Rimouski (Rimouski, Qué.), 355.146. Wallace, *Macmillan dict.* Charles Guay, *Chronique de Rimouski* (2v., Québec, 1873–74), II: 274. Lareau, *Hist. de la littérature canadienne*, 362. "Les disparus," *BRH*, 34 (1928): 640.

SMITH, JOHN, merchant and politician; b.*c.* 1819 in the United States of America, of German parents; m., probably *c.* 1849, to Mary, and they had at least ten children; d. 29 Sept. 1881 at Toronto, Ont.

John Smith arrived in Toronto from the United States in 1841, reputedly without capital. Commencing business as a retail grocer, by the late 1850s he had become a wholesale grocer and commission merchant and had already amassed a considerable fortune. In 1860 he joined the new wholesale grocery firm of Alexander Mortimer Smith, in which he invested approximately $60,000. The A. M. Smith Company successfully carried on an extensive trade with Halifax and throughout Ontario. John and A. M. Smith were also connected with the prosperous Ontario lumber trade and probably cooperated with Alexander's brother, John B., who was actively involved with a sawmill and timber stands in Simcoe County and a planing mill and sash and door factory in Toronto. Although the details of the business success of the A. M. Smith Company remain unclear, it can be noted that in 1863 it was assessed by R. G. Dun and Company as "cautious, economical and reliable." In 1865, when Alexander Smith retired from business, John Smith purchased the company and gave it his name. He entered new partnerships in 1867 and 1868 before apparently leaving the grocery business entirely by the end of the decade.

In the early 1870s John Smith invested his capital in real estate and banking securities, and in Sessions, Turner and Cooper Wholesale Boot and Shoe Company, the city's largest shoe factory. Founded in the mid 1860s by J. D. Sessions, John Turner, and James Cooper, this company had expanded rapidly and it opened new factories with modern machinery in 1870 and 1872; capital for the second expansion came from Smith, who invested $50,000, and he placed his son, John C., in the firm as a partner. When Turner retired in 1874, the firm was renamed Sessions, Cooper and Smith. Employing over 500 men and women, the company did a massive business throughout the 1870s but found its profit margins shrinking in a highly competitive industry which was plagued by overproduction. Smith's capital was crucial to the firm, as the astute R. G. Dun and Company evaluation frequently noted during the depression of the 1870s. Stating that he was "in too deeply with them to get out easily," Smith loaned the company an additional sum in excess of $50,000 before the end of the decade.

In the 1850s Smith had purchased extensive property on Isabella Street, just south of Bloor Street and then far north of the city's major activities. He built a substantial three-storey brick house for himself and later developed the surrounding area as the city grew. By 1880 he owned eight other large houses on the same street. He had also joined the board of directors of the Imperial Bank, the British America Assurance Company, and the Freehold Loan and Savings Company. In 1877 Smith entered municipal politics and was elected alderman from St James' Ward for three terms; he did not seek re-election in 1880. A Reformer in politics, he was known at city hall for his caution and as "a voice for honesty and economy." He was also a freemason, especially active in the 1860s.

Smith met his death accidentally under the wheels of a Toronto Street Railway car. His estate was valued at almost $350,000. He had prospered as the city grew. In most ways he was a typical Toronto merchant, unusual only in his claim of rising from rags to riches and in his marriage to a Roman Catholic though himself a Presbyterian.

GREGORY S. KEALEY

Baker Library, R. G. Dun & Co. credit ledger, Canada, 26. CTA, Toronto assessment rolls, St James' Ward, Isabella Street, 1861, 1871. PAC, RG 31, A1, 1861 and 1871, Toronto, St James' Ward (mfm. at AO). York County Surrogate Court (Toronto), no.4374, will of John Smith, 12 Oct. 1881 (mfm. at AO). Toronto City Council, *Minutes of proc.* (Toronto), 1877–80. *Evening News* (Toronto), 30 Sept. 1881. *Evening Telegram* (Toronto), 30 Sept. 1881. *Globe*, 18 Nov. 1870, 30 Sept. 1881. *Toronto World*, 30 Sept., 1, 2, 4 Oct. 1881. *Toronto directory*, 1846–83. G. S. Kealey, "The working class reponse to industrial capitalism in Toronto, 1867–1892" (PHD thesis, Univ. of Rochester, N.Y., 1977); "Artisans respond to industrialism: shoemakers, shoe factories and the Knights of St. Crispin in Toronto," CHA *Hist. papers*, 1973: 137–57.

SMITH, SIDNEY, lawyer, politician, and office-holder; b. 16 Oct. 1823 at Port Hope, Upper Canada, son of John David and Augusta Louisa Smith; m. 21 Jan. 1845 Mary Ann Bennett of Cobourg, Canada West, and they had five sons and one daughter; d. 27 Sept. 1889 at Cobourg.

Sidney Smith was born of a UEL family; his paternal grandfather, Elias, a successful merchant and trader, left New York and settled in Upper Canada, where he was a founder in 1792 of what was to become Port Hope. Sidney's father, John David, a merchant and distiller, sat in the House of Assembly of Upper Canada for Durham from 1828 to 1830. Sidney was educated privately and in the grammar school at Port Hope. He then studied law in the office of his brother, John Shuter, with whom he was later a partner, and was admitted to the bar in 1844. He was to continue the practice of law throughout his life, practising first in Cobourg, where he also acted as solicitor for the Commercial Bank of the Midland District, the Bank of Montreal, the Midland Railway of Canada, and the town of Cobourg, and then in Peterborough. In 1853 he was elected a municipal councillor for both Cobourg and the township of Hamilton, and was the warden for Northumberland and Durham.

The following year Smith was elected as a Reformer to the Legislative Assembly for Northumberland West and he was re-elected in 1857. He supported the administration of Sir Allan Napier MacNab* and Augustin-Norbert Morin* in 1854 and 1855 before going over to the opposition in 1856. From 2 Feb. 1858 until the government's defeat on the Militia Bill in May 1862, Smith was postmaster general in the cabinet of John A. Macdonald* and George-Étienne Cartier* and also a member of the Board of Railway Commissioners, except for the period of the "double shuffle" in August 1858. In one of the moves of that shuffle he was for 24 hours president of the council and minister of agriculture. Following the "double shuffle," John A. Macdonald, Philip Michael Matthew Scott VanKoughnet*, and Smith were the objects of actions under the "independence of parliament" act, 1857, which provided that persons sitting and voting in the assembly while legally disqualified were subject to financial penalty. The actions were heard in November 1858, and the judgements given in December "uniformly exonerated the defendants . . . and declared that the letter of the law had not been violated."

In 1858 Smith introduced the Upper Canada Jurors' Act and carried it through the assembly; in 1860 he gained the abolition of Sunday labour in the post offices in Canada West. His most notable accomplishment while in office occurred in 1859 when he concluded arrangements with the United States, Britain, France, Belgium, and Prussia for mail service to Canada and the United States. Mail from overseas, which had first crossed the Atlantic Ocean on Canadian steamships, would then cross the country on the Grand Trunk Railway. As "one of the very best and most efficient members of government," wrote a contemporary observer, Henry James Morgan*, "he has . . . the character of uniformly acting in an open, candid, and straightforward manner."

In July 1859 a party of the ministry, including John A. Macdonald, was caught in the disabled vessel *Ploughboy* while travelling to Sault Ste Marie. Sidney Smith's "fearless behaviour and effective services, the admiration of all on board" were recorded by a fellow passenger as having helped save the ship "from wreck on the dangerous shores of Lake Huron."

In the general election of 1861, Smith, although a popular minister and a close friend of Macdonald, was defeated by James COCKBURN. The Toronto *Globe*, which sharply criticized Smith personally, was particularly opposed because he remained in the ministry although committed to representation by population. He was, however, elected on 28 September of that year to the Legislative Council for Trent and he retained his portfolio of postmaster general. In 1863 he resigned his seat in the upper house to seek election to the assembly for the constituency of Victoria, but was defeated and resigned from politics. Smith returned, insolvent, to the full-time practice of law in Peterborough, where he also served in the militia as captain of the Peterborough Infantry Company no. 2. In November 1866 he was appointed inspector of registry offices for Canada West and continued in that capacity for the province of Ontario after confederation. He had become a QC in 1862. At his death the bar of Northumberland and Durham passed resolutions of "respect and esteem" and attended his funeral in a body along with "a large number of the public men of the Province."

DENIS SMITH

PAC, MG 26, A. Trent Univ. Arch. (Peterborough, Ont.), Sidney Smith papers. *The Canadian album: men of Canada; or, success by example . . .* , ed. William Cochrane and J. C. Hopkins (5v., Brantford, Ont., 1891–96), IV: 513. *Cyclopædia of Canadian biog.* (Rose, 1886). Morgan, *Sketches of celebrated Canadians.* Dent, *Last forty years.*

SMITH, WILLIAM OSBORNE, soldier; b. apparently in 1833, eldest son of W. H. Smith of Hendreowen (West Glamorgan), Wales; d. 11 May 1887 at Swansea, Wales.

In 1855 William Osborne Smith was appointed ensign in the 39th Foot, and promoted lieutenant later in the same year. He presumably joined the regiment in the Crimea, where it was then taking part in the siege of Sevastopol. The 39th was one of the five regiments moved to Canada directly from the Crimea in 1856, as a result of the enlistment controversy with the United States [*see* Joseph Howe*]. In 1858 Lieutenant Smith married Janet Colquhoun of Montreal. The following year, when the regiment was about to be transferred to Bermuda, he sold his commission and entered "mercantile life" in Montreal.

The military excitement in Canada resulting from the outbreak of the American Civil War brought Smith into the volunteer force, first as commander of a new company formed apparently in September 1861 and subsequently officially recognized, and then as commander with the rank of lieutenant-colonel of a battalion formed unofficially in December 1861 during the *Trent* crisis and gazetted on 22 Jan. 1862 as the 3rd Battalion Volunteer Militia Rifles. The battalion was later allowed to assume officially the title Victoria Rifles, which it had used from the beginning. In December 1864, after the Confederate raid from Canada on St Albans, Vt [*see* David THURSTON], the Canadian government called out for frontier service 30 volunteer companies organized in three battalions. Smith was appointed to command the 1st (Western) Administrative Battalion, which did duty on the Detroit frontier until July 1865. In November 1865, when the first extensive military precautions were taken against the Fenian Brotherhood, Smith was appointed to the militia staff as assistant adjutant-general at Montreal. From this time until 1881 he was on full-time military duty.

In the worst crisis of the Fenian troubles, the raids of June 1866 [*see* Alfred Booker*], Smith was in command on the frontier south of Montreal. On 5 June he made an arduous march with the Victoria Rifles and other troops from Hemmingford to Huntingdon, over roads broken up by rain, which probably averted an attack by Fenians assembled at Malone, N.Y. Major-General James Alexander Lindsay*, the regular officer commanding in Canada East, described Smith in his report on the operations as "a most valuable officer, energetic and active." In the Fenian raid of May 1870 Smith was again in charge on the Quebec frontier. Before the engagement at Eccles Hill on 25 May he had posted the small force on the ground, though he was actually absent arranging reinforcements at the moment when would-be raiders led by John O'Neill* crossed the border and were driven back. For his services on this occasion Smith received the CMG.

O'Neill attempted another raid, this time against Manitoba, on 5 Oct. 1871. It was frustrated by the United States authorities, but it was clear to the dominion government that the military force in Manitoba, two companies, was inadequate. A reinforcement of 200 men under Lieutenant-Colonel Thomas Scott was hastily organized and dispatched by way of the difficult Dawson route. At the same time a new military district (no.10) was authorized with headquarters at Winnipeg, and Smith was sent west to take charge of it. Travelling by American railways, he reached Fort Garry on 27 October. Winter was already closing in. Smith collected a group of voyageurs and set out to assist Scott's force struggling through the half-frozen waterways. He met it at the mouth of the Rainy River, and the expedition marched across the Red River ice into Fort Garry on 18 November.

For the next few years a considerable permanent military force, originally 300 men including an artillery detachment, was maintained at Winnipeg under Smith's command. A new post was constructed there and named Fort Osborne, presumably after Smith. The garrison, although not mounted, made its influence felt over a wide area. In 1874 a column of over 100 men commanded by Smith marched to the Qu'Appelle lakes (The Fishing Lakes), 351 miles west of Winnipeg, to provide a guard for the commissioners negotiating Treaty no.4 with the Cree and Saulteaux Indians. That summer, however, the organization of the North-West Mounted Police provided a better means for carrying out such tasks, and the permanent garrison at Winnipeg was finally done away with in 1877. Smith remained in charge of Military District no.10 until 1881, when he retired from the militia staff, still a lieutenant-colonel and apparently without a pension.

In the North West Rebellion of 1885 Smith raised the Winnipeg Light Infantry Battalion. This unit was sent to Calgary to join the Alberta Field Force commanded by Major-General Thomas Bland Strange*. Smith signed some telegrams as "commanding infantry brigade," though this appointment does not seem to be referred to elsewhere. The Winnipeg Light Infantry under Smith's command took part in the operations of Strange's column, including the inconclusive engagement of Frenchman Butte, where, Strange records, Smith counselled him to break off the action and retire, which he did. At the end of the campaign Smith apparently suffered an injury from which he never fully recovered.

He was an unsuccessful candidate in the riding of Morris in the Manitoba general election of 1886; he had failed similarly in Winnipeg in the federal general election of 1882, being defeated by Thomas Scott. In the spring of 1887 he went on a visit to his native Wales, where he died; his wife had predeceased him. A son, Edward Osborne Smith, served as an officer in the British army. William Osborne Smith was clearly an officer of ability, and a figure of considerable importance in the early history of the professional military forces of Canada.

C. P. STACEY

PAC, RG 9, Militia general orders, 1862–81. Can., Parl., *Sessional papers*, 1867–78, Reports on the state of the militia; 1886, V, no.6a. Can., Prov. of, Parl., *Sessional papers*, 1866, II, no.4. Morris, *Treaties of Canada with the Indians*. *Telegrams of the North-West campaign, 1885*, ed. Desmond Morton and R. H. Roy (Toronto, 1972). *Manitoba Daily Free Press*, 16 May 1887. *Montreal Gazette*, 17, 18, 20 Dec. 1861; 14 Jan. 1862; 20–29 Dec. 1864; 3 Jan. 1865. *Times* (London), 20 May 1887. *The annual register: a review of public events at home and abroad* (London), 1887. *Dominion annual register*, 1886. *Hart's army list*, 1859. C. T. Atkinson, *The Dorsetshire regiment: the thirty-ninth and fifty-fourth Foot and the Dorset Militia and Volunteers* (2v., Oxford, 1947), I. Desmond Morton, *Ministers and generals: politics and the Canadian militia, 1868–1904* (Toronto and Buffalo, N.Y., 1970). T. B. Strange, *Gunner Jingo's jubilee: an autobiography* (3rd ed., London, 1896). C. P. Stacey, "The military aspect of Canada's winning of the west, 1870–1885," *CHR*, 21 (1940): 1–24; "The second Red River expedition, 1871," *Canadian Defence Quarterly* (Ottawa), 8 (1930–31): 199–208.

SMITHE (Smith, Smyth, Smythe), WILLIAM, farmer and politician; b. 30 June 1842 in Matfen, Northumberland, England; d. 28 March 1887 in Victoria, B.C.

William Smithe, of Northumbrian ancestry, was educated in local schools at Whittington. As a young man he worked in the merchant trade in Newcastle upon Tyne before coming to British Columbia in 1862. He established residence in the Cowichan district, Vancouver Island, near Somenos; there he made his home until his death, except for a short period in 1866 when he lived in San Francisco and several months in 1868 when he tried his hand at mining on Grouse Creek in the Cariboo. In 1865 Smithe was appointed road commissioner for Cowichan, his first public office.

In 1871 his growing reputation as a community leader in the burgeoning farming district around Somenos, the most promising agricultural area on Vancouver Island, won Smithe one of the two seats for Cowichan in the first assembly elected following British Columbia's entry into confederation with Canada. During his first term he maintained an independent stance, refusing to support John Foster McCreight*, the first premier, or his successors, Amor De Cosmos*, whom Smithe admired, and George Anthony

Walkem*. In the election of 1875, Smithe and his friend and neighbour, John Drinkwater, won the two Cowichan seats for the anti-government forces with a campaign that capitalized on the failure of the Walkem government to begin construction on a road from Victoria to Cowichan for which appropriation had been made. Over six feet tall, erect, and handsome in a full beard, Smithe struck a fine figure on the hustings. He became known as an incisive and witty debater, though halting of speech. His marriage in 1873 to Martha, daughter of Archibald Renfrew Kier, a well-known farmer and Methodist of Somenos, had further secured his attachment to, and prominence in, the Cowichan district.

When the session of 1876 opened, Smithe assumed leadership of the opposition to the Walkem administration which had been returned to office. But loosely knit factions then dominated politics. Apparent government supporters, sometimes even cabinet members, often broke ranks. In this fluid atmosphere the government's failure to make any attempt at negotiations with Ottawa for the commencement of the British Columbia section of the Canadian Pacific Railway, coupled with accusations of fiscal irresponsibility, forced the Cabinet's resignation on 25 January. In the political manœuvring that ensued, Smithe relinquished his leadership of the loosely formed opposition to Andrew Charles ELLIOTT, who became the fourth premier in five years. Smithe was not included in Elliott's first cabinet, but in July 1876, upon the dismissal of the erratic Thomas Basil HUMPHREYS, he joined the four-man administration as minister of finance and agriculture. Smithe did not especially distinguish himself in a cabinet that continued to suffer, as had its predecessor, the consequences of impoverished finances and rancorous and futile wrangling with Ottawa, but he did succeed in retaining his seat amid the general collapse of his associates at the polls in March 1878.

For a second time Smithe took on the leadership of the opposition to Walkem, a duty he carried out in a business-like and temperate manner rather rare in the boisterous and factionally divided assembly. Smithe assumed the premiership when Robert Beaven*, successor to Walkem, met the assembly in January 1883 with the support of no more than 8 of the 24 members elected the previous summer. In office with the largest majority since confederation, Smithe had the goodwill of an electorate utterly exasperated at their government's inability to settle with Ottawa over the building of the transcontinental railway, the graving dock at Esquimalt, and a railway connecting Victoria and Nanaimo on Vancouver Island.

The problems Smithe inherited were, however, as much the result of local politics as of a history of bad relations with the federal government. Islanders demanded their own railway and the graving dock to offset the expected boom on the mainland once the transcontinental railway was completed. Mainlanders, long jealous of the island's exaggerated strength in the assembly, objected to the expense of the graving dock, which, it was becoming clear, was beyond British Columbia's means, and they were the more sorely aggrieved at the slow pace on the railway and the interminable stalemate with Ottawa. Smithe moved swiftly to come to an agreement with his federal counterpart, Sir John A. Macdonald*, himself eager to remove old grievances. By the Settlement Act passed by the British Columbia legislature in December 1883 and accepted by the federal government the following March, the Macdonald ministry, in exchange for 3,500,000 acres in the Peace River district of British Columbia, agreed to open the railway lands in the south to settlement, assume construction of the graving dock, and advance $750,000, for the building of the island railway. A contract for the latter was undertaken by a consortium of local businessmen led by Robert DUNSMUIR and American railway financiers Collis Potter Huntington and Leland Stanford. The consortium was granted some 2,000,000 acres on Vancouver Island and Dunsmuir was also granted the coal mining rights on these lands.

In one stroke Smithe had fashioned a settlement acceptable to both islanders and mainlanders and had embarked on an expansionary economic policy funded not with capital but with land. Land grants were also used to encourage schemes such as one proposed by William Baillie-Grohman to reclaim and settle land at the south end of Kootenay Lake, and others for the building of wagon roads as well as railways in the interior. One such grant caused a great public furore and a full-scale investigation. In 1884 Smithe negotiated a grant of 6,000 acres with William Cornelius Van Horne* of the CPR, apparently dispossessing several squatters. In return the CPR agreed to extend the line from Port Moody to the present site of Vancouver, an extension it would have had to make anyway to protect its interests.

In response to strong pressure from the community, Smithe's government passed several acts regulating the Chinese population, including the imposition of an annual licence fee of $10 on all Chinese over 15 years of age, and an act preventing Chinese from acquiring crown lands. Another act stopping Chinese immigration was disallowed by the federal authorities. In 1885, in response to British Columbia's agitation, the federal government instituted a $50 head tax on all oriental immigrants. Smithe was as strong as his colleagues in support of discriminatory legislation and a policy of "white immigration . . . to abate the Chinese evil." Nor did Smithe differ in his Indian policy from the accepted wisdom of the community. Although he had once accused Walkem and Beaven of frustrating the settlement of the Indian land question "by shifting, twisting, artful dodging," he just as severely limited Indian lands when he was given the responsibility for approving the establishment of reserves, arguing that because Indians did not cultivate much land they did not need much.

Smithe's victory in the election of 1886 confirmed the public's acceptance of his policy of land grants, railways, roads, reclamation, and Chinese exclusion. The CPR had been completed the year before, and an expanding population looked forward to prosperity and stability, apparently unconcerned about long-term costs. Smithe had broken the juggernaut of federal-provincial disputes and presided over a period of expansion and prosperity. A quiet, unassuming man, he occasionally used his wit to advantage: when asked by American newspapermen visiting in 1883 if British Columbia might one day annex itself to the Union in response to natural trading interests, he replied that British Columbia might instead annex Washington and Oregon. Financial success apparently followed political success, for Smithe had constructed a large house in Victoria to which he was preparing to move his family early in 1887 when he fell ill. He died of nephritis before his 45th birthday. It would be difficult to disagree with his contemporary Peter O'Reilly*, who remarked just before his death that Smithe, "by far the best man in the government," would be "a very great loss."

T. M. EASTWOOD

PABC, O'Reilly coll., 21, 27 March 1887; Vancouver Island, Colonial secretary, Corr. outward, 20 Sept. 1864–11 Sept. 1865 (letterbook copies). B.C., Legislative Assembly, *Journals*, 1879–83; *Sessional papers*, 1883–84. Can., Parl., *Sessional papers*, 1884, IX, no.15: 7–15. *Cariboo Sentinel*, 6, 9, 16 July, 6 Sept. 1868. *Daily Colonist* (Victoria), 1879–83, 22 Jan. 1887. *Victoria Daily Standard*, 29 March 1887. *CPC*, 1885. R. E. Gosnell, *A history of British Columbia* (n.p., 1906). E. B. Mercer, "Political groups in British Columbia, 1883–1898" (MA thesis, Univ. of British Columbia, Vancouver, 1937). M. A. Ormsby, "The relations between British Columbia and the dominion of Canada, 1871–1885" (PHD thesis, Bryn Mawr College, Bryn Mawr, Pa., [1937]). E. O. S. Scholefield and F. W. Howay, *British Columbia from the earliest times to the present* (4v., Vancouver, 1914). R. E. Gosnell, "Prime ministers of British Columbia: William Smythe," *Vancouver Daily Province*, 29 March 1921.

SNOW, JOHN ALLAN, surveyor; b. 31 March 1824 in Hull Township, Lower Canada, son of John Snow, a wheelwright; m. in 1851 Emma Catherine Bradley, and they had at least four sons and three daughters; d. 13 April 1888 in Ottawa, Ont.

After completing his education at the St Lawrence Academy at Potsdam, N.Y., John Allan Snow returned to Canada where he trained as a surveyor under Lindsay Alexander Russell*. On 11 Sept. 1847 he was made a deputy provincial surveyor. Between 1847 and 1865 he laid out a number of township boundaries in the counties of Renfrew, Lanark, Carleton, Frontenac, and Hastings, and in the district of Muskoka. He also supervised the construction of colonization roads, including, in 1866, the Monck Road between Lake Couchiching and the Hastings Road. This experience may have played a part in his being chosen two years later by William McDougall*, the Canadian minister of public works, to superintend the construction of a road from the Lake of the Woods to Upper Fort Garry (Winnipeg) on the route recommended a decade earlier by Simon James Dawson*. The immediate purpose of this project was to provide employment "to the distressed population" of the Red River Settlement and to "alleviate their sufferings" brought on by an almost complete crop failure. The long-range goal was to satisfy the demands of Canadian expansionists for better communication with the west.

On 27 Oct. 1868 Snow and Charles Mair*, the paymaster of the project, arrived at Upper Fort Garry from Chicago and St Paul (Minn.) with 18 tons of provisions. In accordance with his instructions, Snow, accompanied by Mair and Dr John Christian Schultz*, called on Governor William Mactavish* of the Hudson's Bay Company, who assured them that there was not the least objection to work beginning on the road. Mactavish felt that the project would bring some relief to the indigent settlers, and in any case he had not received instructions from London. In London, however, the governor and committee of the HBC protested the work "being undertaken by the Canadian government as a matter of right, as though the territory through which it is to pass were Canadian." At the same time they stated that no impediment would be offered and claimed that they had already taken measures for the relief of the settlement before the grant for the road was made.

Snow was disappointed at the lack of response to his call for men and found that despite the scarcity of provisions in the Red River Settlement those engaged wanted their wages partly in cash or clothing rather than entirely in provisions. He did, however, hire 40 men and work began on 9 Nov. 1868. They had cleared 28 miles of track by 1 April 1869 when the project closed down for lack of funds; on 16 March Snow departed for Ottawa to consult with the Department of Public Works, leaving Mair at Red River. Snow returned on 6 July with funds to resume operations, but he found that labourers were "extremely scarce in the settlement, caused by the unusual demand, for agricultural purposes" and because men had already been employed by the HBC.

In August 1869 Snow reported "considerable dissatisfaction" among some of his workers over their wages of $20 a month. At the end of September the discontented men struck for higher pay ($25 a month), stopping all work for a day and a half. Snow refused to pay them for the time lost during the strike, and they dragged him to the Seine River threatening to drown him. He submitted to their demands but that evening "proceeded to Fort Garry and laid information against five of the leaders in this robbery." Of the four who were indicted for aggravated assault two were found guilty and fined £4 each; one of the two was Thomas Scott*, who became involved in the 1869 rebellion in Red River [*see* Louis RIEL] and on 4 March 1870 was executed. In a memoir written in January 1874 Riel claimed that Scott had put a pistol to Snow's head during the incident on the Seine and only the intervention of some Métis had saved him. Snow, however, had not mentioned any Métis as being involved in the disturbance; in February 1870 he had told McDougall that their conduct was "with very few exceptions respectful, and their labour honestly performed." The dissatisfaction, he said, "was almost entirely confined to Canadians, and deserters from the American army."

Work continued on the road in 1869, Snow having to hire a large number of men from the "Scotch settlement" in Red River; he found them "quiet and well disposed people." But in October he reported a great deal of excitement among "the Canadian half-breed population." He suggested that a force of two or three hundred men would be needed to preserve order in the settlement, and in December he urged the intervention of Bishop Alexandre-Antonin Taché* and Governor Mactavish "to effect an amicable arrangement between Canada and the disaffected people." On 7 Dec. 1869 William McDougall, now lieutenant governor designate of the North-West Territories, called a halt to all work on the road and Snow left the settlement on 6 Jan. 1870.

Snow is representative of that vanguard of Canadians who provoked resistance in the Red River Settlement to Canada's westward expansion. The presence of his road-building party and of the survey crews under John Stoughton DENNIS were, at the time and later, considered to be partly responsible for the Red River rebellion. A select committee of the House of Commons inquiring in 1874 into the causes of the difficulties heard testimony about the road-building party. It was stated that rumours of misconduct by Snow's party were widely circulated and pretty generally believed among the Métis; according to settler Thomas Bunn*, they "tended to promote a feeling of suspicion and dislike of Canadians." Alexander Begg* had noted in his diary in 1869, for example, that Snow was accused of taking advantage of the unfortunate settlers by paying them starvation wages. This charge was, however, exaggerated, for the average wages of these labourers were as high as, and in some cases higher than, those paid workers on the road being built by Simon James Dawson from Lake Superior to the Lake of the Woods. Witnesses called by the committee complained that workers were forced to purchase provisions at inflated prices at a store believed to belong to Schultz. It was also said that some of the men who came with Snow from Ontario displayed contempt for the HBC and the settlers. Mair's letters to his brother while on the road party, published in Ontario newspapers, were considered insulting to the mixed-bloods and Mair had indeed been physically attacked by Annie, wife of postmaster Andrew Graham Ballenden BANNATYNE. The committee was told that Indians were sold liquor illegally by Snow, and he had in fact been convicted on this charge and fined £10. More disturbing to the Métis was the fear of being dispossessed of their lands. Rumours persisted of road builders purchasing from Indians lands which the Métis thought were theirs. Abbé Georges Dugas*, for instance, had complained to Bishop Taché in August 1869 about "gangs of adventurers" who "spread disorder among our people and seemed to be busier picking out land than working on the road." There was some truth to this charge. John Stoughton Dennis testified to the committee that Snow and Schultz had staked out and bought lands from the Indians at Oak Point (Sainte-Anne, Man.); Dennis had subsequently told Schultz that the Canadian government would not recognize such purchases.

In December 1869, disturbed that some Canadian newspapers held him responsible for the conflict at Red River, Snow stated that he was "not aware of having made an enemy among the disaffected people" and that he was the only government official at liberty in Red River, which circumstance he attributed to "the good feeling existing among these people towards me."

On his return to Ontario, Snow worked for the Quebec, Montreal, Ottawa and Occidental Railway Company. In 1875 he was employed as the city engineer for Hull and he laid out the boundaries of the newly incorporated city. Two years later Snow returned to the west to survey subdivisions in the region south of Winnipeg and between 1880 and 1883 he surveyed various parts of the prairies and British Columbia. In 1886 he went back to general engineering and survey work. He died of pneumonia in Ottawa in 1888.

HARTWELL BOWSFIELD

PAC, RG 11, B1(a), 265, doc. 4698, 4707, 4792, 4811, 5294, 6026; B1(b), 652, subject 429, docs. 3189, 3231, 3233, 3234. Begg, *Red River journal* (Morton). Can., House of Commons, *Journals*, 1874, app.6; Parl., *Sessional papers*, 1869, V, no.25; 1870, V, no.12; 1895, IX, no.13, pt.VI. *Muskoka and Haliburton, 1615–1875; a collection of documents*, ed. F. B. Murray (Toronto, 1963). *Ottawa Daily Citizen*, 14 April 1888. *Ottawa Evening Journal*, 14 April

1888. R. St G. Stubbs, *Four recorders of Rupert's Land; a brief survey of the Hudson's Bay Company courts of Rupert's Land* (Winnipeg, 1967). D. W. Thomson, *Men and meridians; the history of surveying and mapping in Canada* (3v., Ottawa, 1966-69). "John Allan Snow," Assoc. of Ontario Land Surveyors, *Annual report* (Toronto), 34 (1919): 82–83.

SOLA, ALEXANDER ABRAHAM DE. *See* DE SOLA

SOMERSET, Lord FREDERICK A. *See* BIRCHALL, REGINALD

SOMERVILLE, ALEXANDER, soldier, journalist, and author; b. 15 March 1811 in Oldhamstocks (Lothian), Scotland, eleventh child of James Somerville and Mary Orkney; m. 10 Jan. 1841 Emma Binks, and they had six children; d. 17 June 1885 in Toronto, Ont.

Alexander Somerville recounts his early life as a schoolboy, ploughman, sawyer, labourer, drainer, and quarryman in his memorable *Autobiography of a working man* (London, 1848). In 1832, while serving in the 2nd Dragoons (Scots Greys), he received 100 lashes as punishment for publishing a letter revealing the Reformist sympathies of fellow soldiers and their unease at the measures being used to control demonstrators during the Reform Bill crisis. There was an outcry in the press and parliament; £300 was collected on his behalf and those responsible for his flogging were officially rebuked. After purchasing his discharge he was involved in Chartist and Owenite agitations in London before serving bravely in the auxiliary legion in Spain from 1835 to 1837; he later sold a *History of the British Legion and war in Spain* for £100.

Back in England and worried once more about confrontations between agitators and the military, he published *Warnings to the people on street warfare.* He became Richard Cobden's agricultural adviser and was also the general agent for placing items favourable to Cobdenism in Fleet Street; under the *nom de plume* of the "Whistler at the Plough" he reported for various newspapers on the sufferings of Irish tenantry as seen on frequent trips and wrote on economic questions.

Somerville expressed his disenchantment with Cobden's pacifism in 1854 in *Cobdenic policy the internal enemy of England.* This split, coupled with mismanagement or fraud by his literary agents and publishers, caused Somerville's financial ruin despite his attempts at recovery by the frantic writing of articles on trade unions, electromagnetism, witchcraft, and folk customs and by a brief return to Scotland to act as an editor in Edinburgh. In 1857 he finally collapsed in delusions of persecution and conspiracy; his *Workingman's witness against the London literary infidels* cried his distress. In May 1858 he sailed with his family for Canada, "driven to America against my desire."

After this melodramatic career in the United Kingdom his life in Canada has seemed to some observers a "long decline." In fact he contributed in several important ways to Canadian journalism. Despite the devastating loss of his wife soon after arriving in Quebec, he nevertheless published analyses of the Canadian administrations, comments on conservatism, and a rehash of the 1832 Reform Bill crisis in the local newspapers. Living in abject poverty, he wrote *Conservative science of nations . . . being the first complete narrative of Somerville's diligent life* dealing with free trade, strikes, banking, and military history as well as adding to his earlier *Autobiography* and giving a penetrating report on Irish affairs.

Somerville, with his six children, drifted into Canada West in 1860, travelling through Brockville to Perth and Arnprior. The next year he moved through Kingston to Windsor and Detroit, then back to Brantford. In later newspaper articles he reported on all these communities in detail. After arriving at Hamilton in 1862 he wrote *Canada, a battle ground*, on the growing hostility towards the United States and the possible routes of American invasion. The *Canadian Illustrated News*, founded in Hamilton in 1862 and edited by Somerville, offered commentaries on military and business history, Canadian scenery, photography, agriculture, and immigration. When the journal changed owners in 1864 and moved to Toronto, Somerville stayed in Hamilton. In 1866 he covered the Fenian disturbances on the Niagara and Lake Erie frontiers; his vivid and earthy *Narrative of the Fenian invasion, of Canada* was published that year. Its account of the battle at Ridgeway (now part of Fort Erie, Ont.) was extremely critical of Alfred Booker*; as Somerville later had to admit, it was commissioned by officers who were Booker's enemies and "blind to fair play." Much of his sympathy for the cause of reform in Ireland disappeared after the Fenian experience.

Intending to return to England, he left Hamilton in 1868 with testimonials from the mayor, local members of parliament, and prominent citizens. Unfortunately the trip was thwarted by the assassination of Thomas D'Arcy McGee*, who had promised Somerville money for an "emigrant's handbook." He then moved through Ottawa to Montreal, where a new version of the *Canadian Illustrated News* was launched by George-Édouard Desbarats* in 1869. Until 1872 Somerville lodged at St Andrew's Society Home writing articles and editorials for the *News*, but Desbarats's affairs became tangled and when the journal was sold Somerville returned to Hamilton. In 1873 he moved to Toronto as editor of the *Church Herald.* For two years this Anglican journal featured vigorous articles by Somerville on political and economic topics, including pieces on American imports and Louis RIEL. Financial problems forced amalgamation with an American church paper and Somerville's position dwindled into that of "Canadian Editorial Correspondent." He continued his duties, which included travelling to Nova Scotia to do articles, until June 1875 when the paper ceased publication. Somerville remained in Toronto as a literary correspondent to various English, Welsh, Irish, and Scottish publications, and also wrote immigration propaganda for the Department of Agriculture, which awarded him a pension in 1876. Dominion handbooks for 1877 and 1883 bear marks of his graphic style, particularly in the chapter entitled "Why emigrate?" By the 1870s Somerville was elderly, mountainous (he weighed 300 lbs), and eccentric. Books and clippings from the British newspapers to which he wrote weekly letters filled his rooms at the City Hotel and later at a York Street boarding-house. He moved finally into a woodshed, living on cold porridge flavoured with bits of raw onion; from 1880 to 1885 he apparently wrote 5,000 pages of memoirs which have never been found.

Diligent, articulate, obsessed with his own importance, Alexander Somerville kept a sense of his significance as a public figure "instrumental in securing the abolition of flogging in the British Army," as a maker of opinion on Ireland in his "Whistler at the Plough" articles, and as an exposer of the dangers of pacifism. He took pride also in his contribution "to the utilitarian literature of British North America" by his outspoken and realistic reporting. "My life has been a battle," he wrote in the *Narrative of the Fenian invasion*, "and my battle has been the rights of man."

ELIZABETH WATERSTON

Alexander Somerville's writings include: *The autobiography of a working man* (London, 1848; repub., ed. John Carswell, 1951; repr. 1967); *Canada, a battle ground; about a kingdom in America* (Hamilton, [Ont.], 1862); *Cobdenic policy the internal enemy of England; the Peace Society, its combativeness; Mr. Cobden, his secretiveness; also, a narrative of historical incidents . . .* (London, 1854); *Conservative science of nations, (preliminary instalment), being the first complete narrative of Somerville's diligent life in the service of public safety in Britain* (Montreal and Toronto, 1860), also published under the title: *Narrative of an eventful life: a contribution to the conservative science of nations* (Hamilton, 1863); *History of the British Legion and war in Spain, from personal observation and other authentic sources . . .* (London, 1839); *Narrative of the Fenian invasion, of Canada . . .* (Hamilton, 1866); *Warnings to the people on street warfare; a series of weekly letters . . .* (7 pts., London, 1839); *The whistler at the plough; containing travels, statistics, and descriptions of scenery & agricultural customs in most parts of England . . .* (3v., Manchester, 1852–53), of which vols. II and III are titled *Free trade and the League: a biographic history . . .* and *Workingman's witness against the London literary infidels* (n.p., 1857). Other works are listed in *British Museum general catalogue*.

Canadian Illustrated News (Hamilton), 1862–64. *Canadian Illustrated News* (Montreal), 1869–72. *Church Herald* (Toronto), 1873–75. *Morning Chronicle* (Quebec), June 1859. *Quebec Mercury*, 1859. *DNB*. *Dominion annual register*, 1885. Morgan, *Bibliotheca Canadensis*, 355. W. J. Rattray, *The Scot in British North America* (4v., Toronto, 1880–84). W. M. Sandison, "Alexander Somerville," *Border Magazine* (Edinburgh), 18 (1913): 49–55.

SOSÉ. *See* ONASAKENRAT, JOSEPH

SOWENGISIK. *See* STEINHAUER, HENRY BIRD

SPENCE, THOMAS, gold-miner, contractor, and public servant; b. *c.* 1826 in Dundee, Scotland; d. unmarried 7 June 1881 in Victoria, B. C.

Little is known of Thomas Spence's early life, but judging by his writing skills he received little formal education. Many of his early years were spent in travel. He lived for some time in London, England, and left in 1845 for the Cape of Good Hope where he stayed 18 months. In 1847 he went to the Sandwich (Hawaiian) Islands and worked in the government service for up to two years. Prospects of wealth and opportunity in California during the gold-rush brought Spence to San Francisco in 1849; there he was a merchant for four years until he, too, joined the search for gold.

It appears that Spence was quite successful in his quest for gold, but, like many other Californians, he was drawn north by news of the rich finds of the Fraser River gold-rush. Arriving in British Columbia in May 1858, he discovered a rich claim on Cameron Bar. However, Spence continued placer mining only long enough to accumulate the funds to finance construction of part of the Cariboo Road, and with Joseph William Trutch* and Gustavus Blinn Wright* he was one of the three main contractors of the road. Although the construction proved difficult and costly, and profits were low, Spence completed the 32-mile section from Boston Bar to Lytton by February 1862 and later, in partnership with Trutch, he built another section of 11 miles from Sailors Bar to Chapmans Bar near the site of the present Alexandra Bridge.

Bridge building was to become another of Spence's accomplishments. Spence's Bridge, which replaced Cook's Ferry in February 1865, was the first bridge to span the Thompson River. It was washed out soon after it was built and it was only through the use of a borrowed Admiralty diving suit that stable footings could be established.

By 1865 the Cariboo Road was complete from Yale to Barkerville. There were 377 miles of 18-foot-wide road traversing some of the most rugged terrain in North America, and the colonial government was slowly recognizing that the roads required more expert maintenance than originally estimated. An unsuccessful effort to have roads maintained by a contract system was abandoned and on 28 March 1865 Spence was hired by his friend Joseph Trutch, now chief commissioner of lands and works, to become the first civilian superintendent of public works. His duties were to include supervision of road maintenance and road construction in the Cariboo district.

Although most of Spence's time was spent maintaining the road from Yale to Barkerville, he made numerous side-trips. In July 1865 Henry Maynard Ball, gold commissioner, described the hard-working Spence as being "as usual full of business." During the summer of 1866 he inspected construction of the Cache Creek to Savona's Ferry (Savona) section for which Wright held the contract. Spring was usually spent repairing such thoroughfares as the Brighton and Douglas roads on the lower mainland. One winter job almost ended in disaster. As he was supervising the construction of a new bridge over James Bay at Victoria in January 1869, Spence was plunged into the waters below when a pile-driver collapsed the old bridge; he escaped with a few bruises. In 1874 he engineered the removal of one of the Sister Rocks which impeded stern-wheel navigation between Hope and Yale on the Fraser River. From 1875 until his death Spence was engaged in removing Beaver Rock from Victoria harbour.

Thomas Spence died on 7 June 1881 as a result of falling down the stairs of a hotel in Victoria. His obituary in the *Daily British Colonist* described him as "an amiable, kind-hearted man. . . . He had an active mind and constantly conceived great schemes and projects of a public nature; but in their execution in this country he was scarcely ever successful in a pecuniary sense."

JAMES R. WARDROP

Bancroft Library, Univ. of California (Berkeley), Thomas Spence, Dictation; A. W. Vowell, "Mining districts of British Columbia." PABC, Henry Maynard Ball, Journal, 15 July 1865; Colonial corr., Thomas Spence corr. *Daily British Colonist* (Victoria), 6 Dec. 1859; 6 Jan. 1869; 7, 8 June 1881.

SPRAGGE, JOHN GODFREY, lawyer and judge; b. 16 Sept. 1806 at New Cross, Lewisham (now part of London), England, eldest son of Joseph Spragge*; m. in 1831 Catherine Rosamund Thom, daughter of Dr Alexander Thom*, army surgeon, and they had two sons and two daughters; d. 20 April 1884 at Toronto, Ont.

John Godfrey Spragge was educated at home by his father who had come to Canada in 1820 as master of the Upper Canada Central School. Later John attended John Strachan*'s Home District Grammar School in York (Toronto). In 1823 he was articled as a law student first to James Buchanan Macaulay*, the eminent jurist, and later to Robert Baldwin*. On 14 Nov. 1828 Spragge was called to the bar of Upper Canada and immediately set up practice in York. His career in equity law, applicable for civil cases not covered by common law, was successful and his practice prospered. Shortly after John Hillyard Cameron* was called to the bar in 1838, the two men entered into partnership as Spragge and Cameron.

Spragge served as surrogate judge of the Home District from 1836 to 1841, but he had a longer judicial career in the Court of Chancery. The Court of Chancery, as it had evolved in Great Britain, and as it was to function in Upper Canada from its creation in 1837, had jurisdiction in cases involving property rights, estates, wills, inheritances, trusts, and mortgages; estates of children, lunatics, and others deemed incompetent to handle their affairs; cases concerning accidents, copartnerships, alimony, leases, or sales; as well as cases of misrepresentation. The court could compel fulfilment of legal agreements and could commit persons found to be insane. It also governed letters patent issued by the crown. Spragge was appointed the first master in chancery on 20 June 1837 and was responsible for establishing the new court and devising a set of rules for the transaction of its business. The duties of the master included attendance at the meetings of the Legislative Council. On 13 July 1844 Spragge became registrar of the court and on 27 Dec. 1850 its vice-chancellor. Finally, on 27 Dec. 1869, he was appointed to succeed the Honourable Philip Michael Matthew Scott VanKoughnet* as chancellor. The following year he undertook a reorganization of the court which made it both more efficient and less costly.

During these years, Spragge established his reputation as an expert equity draftsman and a conscientious judge. Though not a brilliant man, he possessed qualities which made for a good jurist. His judgements were based upon careful and lengthy analysis of the facts in each case and he possessed a keen discernment of human motives. The quality of his decisions won him the respect of his colleagues. He was also active in the affairs of the Law Society of Upper Canada and of the bench generally. In 1835 he was elected a bencher of the law society and became its treasurer in 1841. He served on several of its committees and secured approval for the law society to appoint a reporter for the Court of Chancery. The reports of the court were published as the *Upper Canada Jurist*.

On 2 June 1847 Spragge published a letter addressed to the attorney general which suggested the establishment of a new court of appeal in Canada West. In this closely reasoned pamphlet, Spragge argued that the existing Court of Appeal was neither strong enough nor in possession of any real appeal powers, and that a new court of appeal should be formed consisting of judges from the courts of Queen's Bench and Chancery. In the same letter, Spragge defended the Court of Chancery against those who wished to abolish it. He felt that the common law courts could not administer equity law, and that the abolition of the Court of Chancery would deform Upper Canada's legal system. Throughout his letter Spragge displayed a deep respect for the English judicial system and showed a concern for wider access to the courts.

His standing as a jurist and his long service on the bench made his appointment to succeed Thomas Moss as chief justice of the Court of Appeal a logical one. He was sworn in on 19 May 1881 and later that year, with the passage of the Ontario Judicature Act which created the Supreme Court of Judicature for Ontario, Spragge assumed the title of chief justice of Ontario. He held this post until his death, serving briefly as administrator from 7 July to 6 Sept. 1882 in the absence of the lieutenant governor.

Although he never entered politics, some of the cases and issues before Spragge touched upon the political life of his time. On 8 July 1881 Spragge rendered judgement in the case of *McLaren* v. *Caldwell*. Peter McLaren*, a lumber merchant, sought to prevent Boyd Caldwell, a rival timber merchant farther upstream, from floating his logs downstream over McLaren's slipways. Spragge held that Caldwell did have the right to float his logs downstream through McLaren's property. While the case was still before the courts the Ontario government under Oliver Mowat* passed the Rivers and Streams Act which also supported Caldwell's position. However, when the act was referred to the federal government for review Sir John A. Macdonald* disallowed it on the grounds that it infringed upon private property rights, which he felt were the responsibility of the federal government. This conflict added fuel to the ongoing quarrel between the federal and provincial governments; the bill was re-enacted and disallowed again in 1882 and 1883. During this time the Supreme Court of Canada reversed Spragge's decision, but after the Judicial Committee of the Privy Council upheld it the act was finally allowed to stand in 1884. This controversy illustrates the attempt by the courts to work out a new balance of powers under the British North America Act.

In 1883 Spragge heard the case of *Hodge* v. *the Queen*. Archibald Hodge, owner of a Toronto tavern, was appealing the right of the Ontario legislature to appoint liquor licence commissioners. These commissioners had revoked Hodge's licence because he had allowed a billiard table to be used in his tavern after 7:00 p.m. Spragge upheld the commissioners and his decision was again sustained by the JCPC. This case was also significant in the constitutional development of the division of powers between federal and provincial governments.

As chief justice, Spragge sought to raise the salaries of the judges of the Court of Appeal so that men of ability would be attracted to Ontario's highest court. He also thought that circuit duty for the judges should cease as it disrupted the court's work and caused unnecessary delays. Both changes were aimed at increasing efficiency and improving the court's position in the legal hierarchy of the province. Spragge won the support of Oliver Mowat, but encountered opposition from the federal minister of justice, Sir Alexander Campbell*, and from Sir John A. Macdonald. Although debated for several years, the issue was finally resolved in Spragge's favour.

At the time of his death Spragge's accomplishments as a lawyer and jurist were freely acknowledged. The law society summed up his career by lauding his zeal, uprightness, learning, and ability and said that he compared favourably with the greatest judges of any country. He was "the last of the old regime."

BRIAN H. MORRISON

J. G. Spragge was the author of *A letter on the subject of the courts of law, of Upper Canada, addressed to the attorney general and solicitor general* (Toronto, 1847).

AO, MU 301–9; MU 469–87. *Canada Law Journal*, new ser., 17 (1881): 199–201; new ser., 20 (1884): 160–61, 233–34. *Canadian Law Times* (Toronto), 4 (1884): 233. *Globe*, 21 April 1884. *Toronto Daily Mail*, 21 April 1884. *Dominion annual register*, 1884. Read, *Lives of judges*. W. R. Riddell, *The legal profession in Upper Canada in its early periods* (Toronto, 1916). Waite, *Canada, 1874–96*.

STARCHILD. *See* KUKATOSI-POKA

STARR, JOHN LEANDER, merchant, insurance broker, and politician; b. 25 Oct. 1802 in Halifax, N.S., the eldest son of John Starr and Desiah Gore; d. 16 Aug. 1885 in New York City.

J. Leander Starr's father came to Halifax from rural Nova Scotia as a blacksmith late in the 1790s. He prospered and at the end of the Napoleonic wars had risen to become a merchant and magistrate, with a seat on the chamber of commerce and command of a local militia regiment. Young Leander, after receiving a private education locally, entered the family import-export business in 1823 as junior partner, with a one-third share in the profits. That same year he married Maria Sophia Ratchford, daughter of a prominent Parrsboro merchant. She died in 1829 after the birth of three children. The following year Leander married Frances Throckmorton, daughter of a New York City notable. Similarly advantageous marriages by several of his brothers and sisters meant that, by the early

1830s, Leander Starr enjoyed close family ties with the colonial gentry of Charlottetown and Bermuda and with officers of admiralty rank in the Royal Navy. These connections both spurred and facilitated young Starr's pursuit of status and respectability.

Meanwhile, Starr was faced with increasing business responsibilities. In 1827, shortly after being elected to the provincial assembly for Kings County, John Starr Sr died. Leander continued the family business, bringing in his brother William Joseph as junior partner. J. Leander Starr and Company engaged in timber speculation, shipbuilding, and general trade on a scale such as to assure it middling prominence on the Halifax waterfront. The late 1820s saw Leander attaining more and more of the social prestige he sought. He succeeded his father as a member of the chamber of commerce, as town magistrate, and as lieutenant-colonel of the Halifax militia. He was also elected to executive office in the Halifax Poor Man's Friend Society, became vice-president of the Charitable Irish Society, and attained a leading position within Halifax's emerging temperance movement – all before he had reached the age of 30.

J. Leander Starr's budding career received a check in 1831 when an audit of the affairs of his father, who had died intestate, indicated debts exceeding assets by £1,282. The family firm was forced to disband and John Starr's commercial property was auctioned off to pay his debts. Leander dissolved the partnership with his brother and began a second business career as one of the new profession of specialist insurance brokers and commission agents then emerging within the Halifax business community. Starr was successful because he secured agency rights for the majority of American marine, fire, and life insurance companies which were moving into the Maritimes during the 1830s. Aided by the presence of a cousin and a brother on the directorate of the Halifax Marine Insurance Association, Leander also became broker for that company. Building on this foundation, Starr emerged at the end of the 1830s as a member of Halifax's entrepreneurial élite. In addition to being a director of the Bank of British North America, he was president of the Halifax Gas Light and Water Company, agent for a Halifax-to-New York packet service, a director of the Bay of Fundy Steam Navigation Company, and an executive of the Nova Scotia Whaling Company. He also owned shares in the Halifax and Dartmouth Steamboat Company, the Halifax Hotel Company, the Halifax Library, the Avon Bridge Company, the Western Stage Coach Company, and the Albion Fire Insurance Company of Halifax.

Ambition, as well as the stewardship obligations associated with genteel status, made Starr active in civic affairs through the 1830s. Besides serving as president of organizations such as the mechanics' institute and the Nova Scotia Philanthropic Society, he was on the executive of the diocesan Church Society of the Church of England, the Nova Scotia Temperance Society, and the Halifax Horticultural Society, and further rose to the rank of master within the masonic order. Most significant of all, perhaps, was the increasing tendency for Starr to be named to the committees set up to organize the various picnics, regattas, and balls frequented by the garrison set. Affluence, generosity, polite manners, a graceful tongue, and literary flair expressed through the authorship of "small volumes" earned for Starr acceptance into the inner circle of Halifax's social establishment. In the mid 1830s he was named aide-de-camp to Lieutenant Governor Sir Colin Campbell*, a post he retained under Campbell's successor, Lord Falkland [CARY]. About the same time, Starr travelled abroad, where he gained access to Queen Victoria's London court, dined with King Louis-Philippe of France, and had his portrait painted by a French artist.

As his status rose, Starr adopted the life-style of the Halifax oligarchy. He had replaced Methodism by membership in the Church of England and in 1840 he purchased a palatial residence in Halifax's south end, valued at more than £3,000. He proceeded to fill the house with mahogany and rosewood furniture, a pianoforte, a 430-volume library, Sèvres vases, French porcelain, oil paintings, silver flatware (including service for 26), along with other accoutrements of genteel living. Significantly, despite his advocacy of temperance, Starr maintained a wine cellar stocked with over 600 bottles of madeira, port, sherry, champagne, hock, burgundy, and other wines. Extravagance on this scale, while it jeopardized his solvency, assured Starr of the prominence in which he apparently delighted.

In politics, Starr cultivated a modest Whiggery, which distinguished him from the ultra tories such as Enos Collins*, Henry Hezekiah Cogswell*, and Samuel Cunard* who dominated the Halifax gentry. In the 1826 provincial election he backed the reform-tinged candidacy of Beamish Murdoch*, and four years later ran unsuccessfully as a candidate for Halifax County, using rhetoric critical of the existing provincial oligarchy. Running again in 1836, Starr made his reform values explicit to the point of denouncing the General Mining Association's monopoly control of the province's coal resources, demanding a separation of the Executive and Legislative councils, and urging the liberalization of Halifax's non-elective and merchant-dominated municipal administration. His credibility as a reformer drew strength from the fact that he had been one of those Halifax magistrates to cooperate with Joseph Howe* when court action ensued as a result of the latter's attempt in 1835 to bring certain local officials to account for alleged corruption and incompetence. In the heated political climate of the 1830s, however, genteel Whiggery inspired more scepticism than enthusiasm. Starr was accused of pursuing "personal aggrandizement," and William Gossip of the anti-Reform Halifax *Times* commented: "I should as soon suspect him of being a Radical as I would the Editor of the *Novascotian* [Howe] of being a Tory." Pressured into withdrawal of his candidacy in 1836, Starr nevertheless remained an attractive political commodity in the eyes of British officialdom. In 1840, as part of an effort to defeat responsible government through liberalization of the provincial oligarchy, Starr gained appointment to the Legislative Council. A year later, after provincial legislation established a democratic municipal government in Halifax, Starr was elected alderman and narrowly missed being selected as the city's first mayor.

Starr's career had reached its apex in 1841, but it now abruptly collapsed. Having accumulated large debts, most of them probably deriving from the pursuit of genteel living, Starr found himself hard pressed when a sharp commercial recession hit the Halifax economy that autumn. In October, shortly after the business failure of his brother William, Leander was obliged to assign all his property to local creditors. The absence of formal bankruptcy legislation in Nova Scotia created doubt as to whether Starr was legally obliged to resign his public offices, particularly his seat in the Legislative Council, but a letter from the colonial secretary, Lord Stanley, reinforced the pressure applied by his colleagues to overcome his hesitancy. By February 1842 he had relinquished all his honorific positions in the community. The deepest humiliation was the public auction of his recently acquired mansion and all its elegant furnishings.

Yet the crisis of 1841 did not impoverish Leander Starr, nor did it end his business career. Complicated legal manœuvres enabled him to transfer to relatives that portion of his father's estate which he had held in trust. Moreover, he managed to retain the bulk of his insurance agencies. His success in preserving a semblance of respectability is indicated by his being selected a masonic provincial grand master after 1841. Nevertheless, Starr's career was in eclipse at a time when the uncertainties of the provincial economy made it difficult to recoup one's losses. In 1844 restlessness, combined with his being dismissed as broker for the Halifax Marine Insurance Association after having contracted to serve as agent for a competing Boston company, prompted Starr to leave Nova Scotia. He moved to New York City, where he continued in business as an insurance broker for the next 20 years. In the United States Starr maintained his literary interests, and in 1864 translated Fernán Caballero's novel, *La gaviota* (*The sea gull*).

J. Leander Starr died in New York City in 1885. His meteoric career illustrates the risks run by a colonial in attempting to gain acceptance into the officer-dominated élite of garrison society in Halifax.

DAVID A. SUTHERLAND

Halifax County Court of Probate (Halifax), no.S140 (estate of John Starr) (mfm. at PANS). Halifax County Registry of Deeds (Halifax), Deeds, 69: ff.55–57; 70: ff.527–31 (mfm. at PANS). PANS, MG 9, no.225, sect.1, "The Halifax gas story, 1840–1953"; MG 20, 66–67; 180; MS file, Starr family; "Masonic grand masters of the jurisdiction of Nova Scotia, 1738–1965," comp. E. T. Bliss (typescript, 1965); RG 1, 116, no.110; 254, no.67; RG 35A, 3, no.12. St Paul's Anglican Church (Halifax), Registers of baptisms, burials, and marriages, 25 Nov. 1833 (mfm. at PANS). Nova Scotia Philanthropic Soc., *The constitution, fundamental rules and bye laws of the Nova Scotia Philanthropic Society, established at Halifax, Nova Scotia, April 7, 1834, revised October 2, 1837* (Halifax, 1843). *Acadian Recorder*, 18 July 1821; 1 Jan. 1823; 8 March, 5 April, 11 Oct. 1828; 30 May 1829; 18–30 Sept., 13 Oct. 1830; 7 April 1832; 19 March, 16–25 April 1835; 12 Aug. 1836; 28 March 1840; 30 Oct. 1841. *Halifax Journal*, 1828–41. *Novascotian*, 10 Feb., 19 May, 30 June 1831; 19 April 1832; 17 Jan., 10 Oct. 1833; 23 Jan., 23 Oct. 1834; 14 July, 11 Aug., 1 Dec. 1836; 11 Jan. 1838; 28 Oct., 18 Nov. 1841; 13 Jan., 10 Feb. 1842. *Times* (Halifax), 19 July 1836; 8 Aug. 1837; 24 Nov. 1840; 12 Oct., 9 Nov. 1841; 13 Feb. 1844. *Belcher's farmer's almanack*, 1824–45. *Catalogue of household furniture, plate, glassware, china, paintings, wines, books, carriages, &c. &c. at the late residence of Hon. J. Leander Starr . . .* (Halifax, 1841). A. W. H. Eaton, *The history of Kings County, Nova Scotia . . .* (Salem, Mass., 1910; repr. Belleville, Ont., 1972).

STEINHAUER, HENRY BIRD (probably also known as **Sowengisik**, and may originally have been baptized as **George Kachenooting**), Methodist missionary, school teacher, and translator; b. probably *c.* 1818 in Upper Canada near the present Rama Indian Reserve, eldest son of Bigwind and Mary Kachenooting; m. 5 Aug. 1846 Mamenawatum (Seeseeb, Jessie Joyful) at Norway House (Man.), and they had five daughters and five sons (a great-grandson, Ralph Steinhauer, was lieutenant governor of Alberta from 1974 to 1979); d. 29 Dec. 1884 at Whitefish Lake (Alta).

The Ojibwa who became Henry Bird Steinhauer in 1828 was probably originally named Sowengisik. He took the new name after Methodist missionary William Case* found an American benefactor who agreed to provide for the education of an Indian youth if that youth adopted his name. It is possible that Steinhauer was also the person baptized as George Kachenooting by Case earlier in 1828, on 17 June, at Holland Landing, Upper Canada. Steinhauer attended the Grape Island school at the south end of Lake Couchiching from 1829 to 1832, and the Cazenovia Seminary in Cazenovia, N.Y., from 1832 to 1835. He was appointed by the Wesleyan Methodist Church to teach at the Credit River mission on Lake Ontario in 1835, and the following year Egerton RYERSON enrolled him at the Upper Canada Academy in Cobourg. His studies at the academy were interrupted for the year 1837–38 by an appointment to teach at the Alderville mission school in Northumberland County, Upper Canada, to which he returned after he graduated in 1839, at the head of his class.

In 1840 Steinhauer was dispatched to Lac La Pluie (Rainy Lake, Ont.) where he assisted the Reverend William Mason* as translator, interpreter, and teacher. Two years later, at the request of missionary James Evans*, he was sent to Rossville mission near Norway House. Evans felt that Steinhauer would readily master Cree because he spoke Ojibwa, which belongs to the same language group, and would thus be able to assist him in translating the Bible and hymns into his system of Cree syllabics. Steinhauer was the chief translator at Norway House by 1846. In 1851 he was asked to establish a Methodist mission at Oxford House (Man.), 200 miles northeast of Norway House, and he built the mission 20 miles from the Hudson's Bay Company fort. In the fall of 1854 Steinhauer, who was then the only Methodist missionary west of Norway House, accompanied John Ryerson* to England to publicize the western missionary work, returning the following spring.

Steinhauer was ordained at the conference of the Wesleyan Methodist Church in Canada in London, Canada West, in June 1855, and on the 8th of that month received news of his posting to Lac La Biche (Alta). He was not overly pleased with the posting and thought he might wish to return to the east for his children's education. He travelled west with Thomas Woolsey*, who was posted to Pigeon Lake (Alta). Although they were at the time the only Methodist missionaries in the northwest, they found that they were "surrounded by Romanists" and felt that they were "very closely watched by their two priests." Lac La Biche was originally selected for Steinhauer "on account of its being out of reach of the enemy, the murderous Blackfoot," but because he considered the location so removed from HBC posts, he did not encourage the development of a settled mission community there. He preferred instead to travel extensively among the Cree to carry out missionary activities.

The intense rivalry with the Roman Catholic missionaries at Lac La Biche, and the post's isolation from the fur-bearing animals and the buffalo herds, led Steinhauer, during the early summer of 1858, to move his mission south to Whitefish Lake where there was a band of Cree. The location was ideal, with land suitable for agriculture and a lake abounding with fish. During the winter of 1859–60, when smallpox swept the prairies, Steinhauer temporarily moved the band as a quarantine measure, and no lives were lost. He further ensured the well-being of his mission by discouraging traders from establishing trading-posts in the area in order to reduce the influx of alcohol. In 1864 Steinhauer opened the first Protestant church in the region, at Whitefish Lake. Later that year his eldest daughter, Abigail, was married in the church to John Chantler McDougall*, whose father, the Reverend George Millward McDougall*, performed the ceremony. With George McDougall and Peter Erasmus*, Steinhauer visited the Mountain Stonies that fall in an attempt to expand missionary work among them. Abigail was one of 16 people who died at Whitefish Lake during the smallpox epidemic of 1870. Such epidemics as well as poverty, hunger, and alcohol were continual problems surrounding mission work.

Steinhauer was appointed to Woodville, on Pigeon Lake, southwest of Edmonton, for the 1873–74 season. The Whitefish Lake mission was to be tended in his absence by Benjamin Sinclair, a local leader, but when he returned Steinhauer found it a shambles. Many families had moved away, fields were untended, and church attendance was down.

In an unusually critical letter to the Missionary Society of the Wesleyan Methodist Church in Canada, published in 1875, Steinhauer wrote, "A foreigner either as a missionary or otherwise, will never take so well with the natives of this country . . . there is always a distrust on the part of a native to the foreigner, from the fact that the native has been so long down-trodden by the white man." He referred to the immigration of whites into the west as a "blighting and benighting" influence and also criticized the missionary society for not heeding his pleas for essential materials. This letter represents a turning-point in Steinhauer's appraisal of his role as a missionary to the Cree. Although he never ceased to maintain his religious convictions, he did become less of a traditional missionary by, in effect, severing his obligations to the missionary society and asserting his Indian identity.

Shortly after his return from a conference in Brandon, Man., in 1884, an influenza epidemic swept the North-West Territories and Steinhauer fell seriously ill. He died on 29 December.

KRYSTYNA Z. SIECIECHOWICZ

UCA, Biog. files, H. B. Steinhauer. Methodist Church of Canada, Missionary Soc., *Annual report* (Toronto), 1875–77. Wesleyan Methodist Church in Canada, Missionary Soc., *Annual report* (Toronto), 1856; 1872–74. *Christian Guardian*, 1833; 1854–55; 29 April 1864. Cornish, *Cyclopædia of Methodism*. J. [C.] McDougall, *Parsons on the plains*, ed. Thomas Bredin (Don Mills, Ont., 1971). John Maclean, *Henry B. Steinhauer, his work among the Cree Indians of the western plains of Canada* (Toronto, n.d.);

James Evans, inventor of the syllabic system of the Cree language (Toronto, [1890]); *Vanguards of Canada* (Toronto, 1918). J. H. Riddell, *Methodism in the middle west* (Toronto, [1946]). [A. D.] Stephenson, *One hundred years of Canadian Methodist missions, 1824–1924* (Toronto, 1925). Gerald Hutchinson, "Early Wesleyan missions," *Alberta Hist. Rev.* (Edmonton), 6 (1958), no.4: 1–6. M. E. Jordon, "Henry Bird Steinhauer and the Whitefish Lake mission," *Alberta Hist. Rev.*, 3 (1955), no.4: 11–12. Margaret Stewart, "Indian receives D.D. degree," *Onward: a Paper for Young Canadians* (Toronto), 10 Oct. 1937. J. A. Youmans, "Along the line; Manitoba conference; the late H. B. Steinhauer," *Missionary Outlook: a Monthly Advocate, Record, and Rev.* (Toronto), 5 (1885), no.2: 25, 28.

STEPHENS, HARRISON, merchant; b. 17 Oct. 1801 at Jamaica, Vt, son of Samuel Stephens and Beulah Howard; m. 22 Feb. 1824 or 1825 Sarah Jackson, and they had three sons and two daughters; d. 16 May 1881 at Montreal, Que.

Harrison Stephens was educated at the district school in Jamaica, Vt, and at the academy in Middlebury. As a young man he worked as a sub-contractor on the canal system near Whitehall, and as a bootmaker in a tannery in Hubbardton. He later owned a small shoe factory in Swanton before moving in 1825 to Missisquoi Bay, Lower Canada, where he operated a large tannery. Two years later he relocated in either Bedford or Stanbridge and opened a sizeable boot and shoe factory. By the early 1830s he had settled in Montreal, where he had begun a business importing rice and tobacco from New York State; in it he had had a brief partnership with a fellow American, Edward Kellogg. Stephens might also have owned a hotel when he arrived in the city.

Although no records of his various enterprises survive, Stephens is known to have prospered immensely. According to a colleague, Jedediah Hubbell DORWIN, he "made the most rapid fortune of any merchant in Canada." By 1830 he was wealthy enough to have a large deposit in the Bank of Montreal. In spite of the size of his account, it was said that the bank's president, Peter McGill [McCutcheon*], refused to discount his notes, probably because Stephens was an American. Undaunted, Stephens began to withdraw large amounts: one draft was over $150,000. He took the money to New York by sleigh and earned 2 per cent on the transaction. Stephens' sudden and drastic action prompted John Torrance*, a director of the bank, to negotiate with Stephens on behalf of the institution. Stephens agreed to stop withdrawing his money, probably as a personal favour to Torrance. His relationship with the bank steadily improved thereafter and in 1845 he was elected a director; he served in that capacity until 1857.

By the mid 1830s or early 1840s Stephens had formed a new partnership with his brother, Sheldon, and John Young*. Stephens, Young and Company dealt principally in staples. Stephens recalled that in one year alone he sold 5,000 to 6,000 hogsheads of rum, a "common drink of the country," and the firm also dealt in vast quantities of flour and pork, having on hand up to 50,000 barrels of each at a time. Indeed, Stephens and Young, acting in conjunction with the New York firm of Hubbard and Company, claimed to control the Canadian pork market for most of this period. After conducting an extremely successful trade, Stephens dissolved his partnership with Young in 1846 and not long afterwards retired from the import business. Young entered a new partnership with Benjamin Holmes*, former cashier (general manager) of the Bank of Montreal.

Stephens was never involved in politics at any level, but not for lack of interest. Towards the end of his life he revealed that the reason he did not join Louis-Joseph Papineau* in 1837 was that he felt vulnerable because of his American birth. He knew Papineau well, remembering him as "a very kind-hearted patriotic statesman" and recalling that "the people had very considerable reason [for] . . . the Revolution of '37." "In those days there was a great deal of misgovernment . . . [but I] positively refused to offer any assistance to Papineau . . . and supported the . . . Government as it stood, because if I did not, I felt it was no place for me here. . . ." Stephens did take an active part, however, in the protectionist–free trade controversy that rocked the Montreal business community during the late 1840s. Aggravated by the free trade views of Young and a small group of local merchants, the Montreal protectionists formed a branch of the British American League [*see* George Moffatt*], of which Stephens was one of the vice-presidents. He was also a member of the group that waited on Louis-Hippolyte La Fontaine* in 1850 to press for higher tariffs. Deeply moved by the plight of his native country at the outset of the American Civil War, Stephens offered to raise at his own expense a regiment of men at nearby Rouses Point, N.Y., to fight under the command of Montreal's Colonel Frederick William Ermatinger* for the government of the United States. For undetermined reasons the offer was declined by the secretary for war.

Although retired from commercial affairs after 1846, Stephens was involved in numerous other business ventures. He acquired vast real estate holdings in Montreal, especially in the business section around St James Street (Rue Saint-Jacques), and he was believed to be the largest property owner in the city; he paid approximately the same amount of property tax as the Grand Trunk Railway. Stephens was listed among the promoters of the St Lawrence and Atlantic Railroad, the Caughnawaga canal [*see* John Young], the Montreal Railway Terminus Company, and the Merchants' Bank (of which he was one of the provisional directors in 1861), but he seems to have remained at most a shareholder in each. In addition he was one of the incorporators of the Montreal Board of Trade in 1841 and the Montreal Protestant House of Industry and Refuge in 1863. He is also mentioned as having been involved in at least one construction project, a new business premises for Henry* and James Morgan in 1866.

Stephens lived with his wife and children in his elegant home on Dorchester Street surrounded by three acres of manicured lawns and shrubs overlooking the city. He was a Unitarian, as were several other prominent Montrealers, including Sir Francis HINCKS, Benjamin Holmes, Thomas WORKMAN, and John Young. A person who neither smoked nor drank, he was regarded as "a man of excellent moral character." In his will he left a generous endowment of $2,000 to both the Church of the Messiah and the Montreal General Hospital.

GERALD J. J. TULCHINSKY

A "Biography of the late Harrison Stephens" is in the possession of Murray Ballantyne, Westmount, Que.

AC, Montréal, État civil, Unitariens, Messiah Unitarian Church (Montreal), 19 May 1881. McCord Museum (Montreal), J. H. Dorwin, "Antiquarian autographs," 103, 393. *Canadian biog. dict.*, II: 347. *Dominion annual register*, 1880–81: 430. Terrill, *Chronology of Montreal*. Denison, *Canada's first bank*, II. Tulchinsky, *River barons*.

STERLING. *See* STIRLING

STEVENS, PAUL (baptized **Paul-Jules-Joseph**), teacher, man of letters, and tutor; b. 1 May 1830 in Brussels (Belgium), son of Jacques-Joseph Stevens, a public works contractor who later became department head in the ministry of war, and Adélaïde-Rose-Josephe Wautier; d. 29 Oct. 1881 at Coteau-du-Lac, Que.

After university studies in Brussels, Paul Stevens emigrated to Canada, likely before July 1854. He settled at Berthier-en-Haut (Berthierville), Canada East, where on 10 May 1855 he married Marie Valier, *dit* Léveillé; they were to have at least four sons. Stevens became a teacher in Berthier-en-Haut, and from there, in 1856, he submitted to such newspapers as *Le Pays*, *La Patrie*, and *L'Avenir* of Montreal and *Le National* of Quebec a number of apologues, most of which were republished the following year in his collection of *Fables*. In August and September 1856 he became involved in a controversy with the editor of *Le Journal de Québec*, who on 20 August, the 25th anniversary of King Leopold I's accession to the throne, had accused the Belgian people of having robbed and disparaged France for 26 years. With wounded pride, Stevens undertook in the pages of *Le Pays* a fierce denunciation of the "scribbler" of *Le Journal de Québec*, calling on him to retract. *Le National*, a Liberal paper, reprinted Stevens' letters, and itself launched a few barbs at its rival newspaper. The quarrel subsided on 26 September.

According to Édouard-Zotique Massicotte*, shortly after this controversy Paul Stevens was named a correspondent to *La Patrie*, a paper launched in Montreal on 26 Sept. 1854 by Alfred-Xavier Rambau*; it is, however, impossible to confirm this assertion. In the autumn of 1857 he became a teacher of French at the Collège de Chambly and, soon after, its principal. In July 1858 Stevens settled in Montreal, where he gave French and drawing lessons. At that time he participated more actively in the Cabinet de Lecture paroissial, which he had frequented since its opening; he delivered numerous lectures there, and these were printed for the most part in *L'Écho du Cabinet de lecture paroissial*. In May 1860, with Édouard Sempé and Charles Sabatier [Wugk*], he founded *L'Artiste* (Montreal), a "journal of religion, criticism, literature, industrial arts and music." But the newspaper, like many periodicals of this kind, ceased publication after two issues because of a lack of subscribers; thus its editors were not able "to show old Europe that [Canada] also has its writers, musicians, and poets."

After the fruitless venture of *L'Artiste*, Stevens again taught French, this time at William Doran's school in Montreal. Later, when he was private secretary to Abbé Étienne-Michel Faillon*, he published in *L'Écho du Cabinet de lecture paroissial*, under the title of "Esquisses nationales," a series of studies of important figures in Canadian history, such as Catherine Thierry (Primot), Jean de Lauson* (the younger), and Adam Dollard* Des Ormeaux, or events such as the battle of the Monongahela. He also wrote a long "Exposé des principaux événements arrivés en Canada depuis Jacques-Cartier jusqu'à la mort de Champlain," which came out in instalments from 11 June 1864 to 15 July 1865. His essay shows that in addition to Faillon's writings, he was familiar with the works of Gabriel Sagard*, François Dollier* de Casson, Pierre-François-Xavier de Charlevoix*, François-Xavier Garneau*, Jean-Baptiste-Antoine Ferland*, and a number of other historians. At the time his *Contes populaires* was published in Montreal in 1867, he was a private tutor to the Chaussegros de Léry and Saveuse de Beaujeu families at Coteau-du-Lac, where he died on 29 Oct. 1881.

Paul Stevens' literary output was extensive and varied. His collection of *Fables*, 64 apologues dedicated to Denis-Benjamin Viger*, is a work of imitation. As Jacques Blais notes: "The excerpts from predecessors (Simonides, Phædrus, Æsop), the references to the gods of mythology, the changes of metre, the representations of animals and human beings, numerous circumstances, even several verses, belong to the fabulist of the 17th century [Jean de La Fontaine]." But in more than one place he showed originality. For example, as Blais observes, in one of his fables Stevens informs us that "Death turns a deaf ear to the woodcutter's pleas," and Blais also notes that "the adventure of the hare and the tortoise inspires a new moral": "Talent is superfluous, if one does not know how to use it."

His *Contes populaires*, most of which appeared first in *L'Écho du Cabinet de lecture paroissial*, can be grouped into categories: stories developed around a maxim or proverb, for example, "Never put off till tomorrow what may be done today" ("La fortune et Sylvain"), "Gentleness achieves more than violence" ("Pierriche"), "Never judge from appearances" ("Les trois frères"), "None so old that he hopes not for a year of life" ("Télesphore le Bostonnais"); stories in verse, probably the least successful of the collection and borrowed from the great French story-tellers ("Les trois souhaits," "Jacquot le bûcheux," "José le brocanteur"); and finally tales of social customs, in which Stevens exploits in his own way a number of popular 19th-century themes, including alcoholism ("Pierre Cardon") and exile in the United States ("Pierre Souci dit Va-De-Boncœur").

A more skilful versifier than fabulist, Stevens was nevertheless a good story-teller. Although he lacked the sparkle of Louis-Honoré Fréchette*, particularly in his *Contes de Jos Violon*, the Belgian writer has left us stories generally better written and better constructed than those of Léon-Pamphile Le May* or Narcisse-Henri-Édouard Faucher* de Saint-Maurice. Yet he was not very popular with the reading public of Quebec, despite the quality of his writing, and he remains an intellectual story-teller shaped by the 17th-century tradition. He transmits an international repertory without trying to give it local colour in either language or description. But his *Contes populaires* is still worth studying and deserves republishing. The style is pleasing and the language polished.

AURÉLIEN BOIVIN

[Paul Stevens published in Montreal in 1857 his *Fables*, a collection of apologues which had appeared in various Montreal and Quebec newspapers in the preceding years. An analysis of this work by Jacques Blais in *DOLQ*, I: 241–42, includes a complete list of the moral fables in the book and of the newspapers in which they were published. From 1859 until about the middle of the 1860s, *L'Écho du Cabinet de lecture paroissial* (Montréal) carried most of the lectures given by Stevens to the Cabinet de lecture paroissial, as well as a series of studies which he wrote on various personalities and events in Canadian history. In the course of these same years, this periodical also published numerous stories that Stevens brought together in 1867 in a collection entitled *Contes populaires* (Ottawa). I have examined these stories in *DOLQ*, I: 151–53, and included several pages of comment on them in my *Le Conte littéraire québécois au XIX*[e] *siècle: essai de bibliographie critique et analytique* (Montréal, 1975), 337–44. Another useful article is: "Bibliographie: contes populaires par Paul Stevens," *L'Écho du Cabinet de lecture paroissial*, 9 (1867): 399–400. A. B.]

AP, Sainte-Geneviève-de-Berthier (Berthierville), Reg. des baptêmes, mariages et sépultures, 10 mai 1855; Saint-Ignace (Coteau-du-Lac), Reg. des baptêmes, mariages et sépultures, 31 oct. 1881. Arch. de la ville de Bruxelles, État civil, Reg. des naissances, 1830, no.1430. [Victor Hugo], "Deux lettres inédites de Victor Hugo," *La Presse*, 5 janv. 1907. "Nouvelles et faits divers," *JIP*, 1 (1857): 202. *La Minerve*, 23 avril, 31 oct. 1857; 17 juill. 1858. *L'Ordre* (Montréal), 3 sept. 1860. *La Patrie*, 3 nov. 1881. É.-Z. Massicotte, "Paul Stevens, fabuliste et conteur," *BRH*, 51 (1945): 373–74. Joseph Royal, "*Contes populaires*, par Paul Stevens," *Rev. canadienne*, 4 (1867): 396–98.

STEVENSON, JOHN, lumberman, businessman, and politician; b. 12 Aug. 1812 in Hunterdon County, N.J., eldest son of Edward Stevenson and Mary Large; m. in 1841 Phoebe Eliza Hall (d. 1882), of Albany, N.Y., and they had seven children; d. 1 April 1884 in Napanee, Ont.

Although John Stevenson was a Presbyterian, his parents were Quakers whose ancestors had immigrated to Pennsylvania from England; his branch of the family moved to New Jersey, then to New York State, and, when he was still a child, to Leeds County, Upper Canada. Stevenson received a brief formal education at Brockville and taught school there for one year. In 1831 he became a clerk in the general store of Henry Lasher in Bath, Addington County, and after a few years a partner in the business with Lasher's son, John. When the partnership was dissolved in 1848, Stevenson opened his own store at Newburgh and two years later moved to Napanee, where he lived until his death.

Stevenson enjoyed a prosperous and diversified business career. At various times he operated a flour-mill, a foundry and axe shop, a brush factory, all in Napanee, as well as the Kingston Piano Company; he was president of the Richmond Road Company, which managed a toll-road running from Napanee to Clareview. He also contracted with Kingston Penitentiary authorities to have convicts manufacture furniture. In 1854 he and David Roblin* secured the contract to build the Grand Trunk Railway bridge over the Napanee River. Throughout the 1850s and 1860s he also conducted a lucrative loan, mortgage, and real estate business in the Napanee area.

It was in lumbering enterprises, however, that Stevenson acquired most of his wealth. In the early 1850s he obtained extensive timber limits in Hinchinbrooke Township, Frontenac County, from the administration of Francis HINCKS and Augustin-Norbert Morin*, and erected sawmills at Petworth and Napanee. In 1853 he and such lumbermen as Hugo Burghardt Rathbun and Roblin formed the Napanee and Salmon River Navigation Company to build slides to facilitate floating lumber to the Bay of Quinte. In the 1850s and 1860s lumbermen might engage in the highly speculative square timber trade to Quebec or in the sawn lumber trade across Lake Ontario to New York State. Stevenson wisely avoided investment in the former and thus escaped the financial difficulties suffered by such contemporaries as Roblin and Malcolm Cameron* when the British timber market collapsed after the Crimean War. He concentrated on the American trade and, to help supply his New York agents during the buoyant period following the Reciprocity Treaty of 1854, he had logs from his and other limits sawn at mills owned by Rathbun, Roblin, and Richard John Cartwright*. He also acquired a fleet of four schooners to carry the lumber to his agents in Oswego, N.Y. During the sailing season of 1858, for example, his schooner *Richmond* made 24 trips to Oswego, carrying nearly 2,000,000 feet of lumber and 5,000 bushels of rye.

Politically, Stevenson was a moderate Reformer. Although he had been secretary of the Reform Association of the Midland District in 1838, he did not contest an election until he moved to Napanee. After serving in 1857 as a councillor in Richmond Township, he was reeve of Napanee from 1860 to 1865, and first warden of Lennox and Addington County from 1863 to 1865. Stevenson had backed David Roblin in the general election of 1854, and the latter's subsequent support of the Morin–Sir Allan Napier MacNab* coalition. The Conservative *Napanee Standard* said of Stevenson in 1884: "He was what is called a Baldwin Reformer in politics, and like a good many more of that school did not take very kindly to the spurious article of Reform which later politicians have brought into vogue." Stevenson, like his Reform friends Roblin, Lewis WALLBRIDGE, Angus MORRISON, and John Ross*, thus supported the Liberal-Conservative coalition of 1854 rather than the "spurious" Grittism of George Brown*. Roblin's election in that year and his support for the Hincks–Morin administration shattered Reform ranks in Lennox and Addington, which became virtually a Conservative constituency, strongly factional and local in its politics. The new situation, however, provided the Reformer Stevenson with considerable political power, for his support of one or other Conservative faction was often sufficient to tip the election scales. Stevenson broke with Roblin in 1857 over a business dispute and in 1861 he was able to swing county Reform support behind a Conservative "loose fish," Augustus Frederick Garland Hooper, and secure Roblin's defeat.

The 1863 election contest was undoubtedly the master-stroke of Stevenson's political manœuvring. He had become the champion of the campaign to separate Lennox and Addington from Frontenac County and make Napanee the county seat; Hooper, however, supported Newburgh's claim to the seat. Stevenson threw his support behind Hooper's opponent, the "independent" Richard John Cartwright, on the condition that the latter maintain his independent stance until the county town issue was settled. Billa Flint*'s note to Stevenson shortly after parliament met indicates the outcome: "Mr. Cartwright and myself called on Atty Gen [John Sandfield Macdonald*] this forenoon, and after a friendly conference, we got your matter of [the] County Town arranged." In the proclamation issued that day, Lennox and Addington was formally separated from Frontenac County, Napanee designated the county seat, and Stevenson named provisional warden.

In the first provincial and federal elections held in Ontario in August 1867, Stevenson and Cartwright, by prior arrangement, ran "in pairs," and pledged their support for the coalitions of John Sandfield Macdonald and Sir John A. Macdonald* respectively. Stevenson handily carried the provincial seat, and was unanimously elected first speaker of the Ontario assembly. The speakership was a particular source of pride for Stevenson, who as a youth had supported another Lennox Reformer, Marshall Spring Bidwell*, elected speaker of the Upper Canadian assembly in 1829.

Stevenson's term as speaker from 1867 to 1871 has been described as one of "fair and impartial rulings" in which no decision was reversed. His correspondence with Sandfield Macdonald was devoted largely to matters reflecting the premier's penchant for government economy, such as reducing the number of house messengers or replacing permanent clerks with temporary help. On Stevenson's defeat in 1871 by the independent Conservative John Thomas Grange, a Napanee druggist, Sandfield wrote: "you became the unanimous choice of the first body of Representatives under the Confederation Act, for Ontario, and you discharged your duties faithfully."

The speakership was to be Stevenson's last public office. At the urging of friends he agreed, reluctantly and at the last minute, to oppose Cartwright in the federal election of 1872. He ran as an independent and was defeated after a campaign in which he supported many administration policies and several Liberal proposals. Ironically enough, his last campaign was in 1878, when the ageing Reformer, who as a lumberman opposed the proposed National Policy, stumped Lennox in favour of the now Liberal Cartwright while the finance minister was touring the Maritimes. If Stevenson's political career lacked consistency, it was because factional local issues were often at odds with larger political loyalties; many county politicians could survive only through flexibility.

JAMES A. EADIE

Lennox and Addington County Museum (Napanee, Ont.), Lennox and Addington Hist. Soc. coll., Roblin family papers, A, David Roblin papers; John Stevenson papers (mfm. at PAC). United Counties of Frontenac, Lennox and Addington, *Minutes of the Municipal Council* (Kingston, [Ont.]), 1850–53, 1861–62. Lennox and Addington County, *Minutes of the Provisional Council* (Napanee), 1863–64; *Minutes of the Council* (Napanee), 1865–66. *Napanee Standard* (Napanee), 1854–84. *Canadian biog. dict.*, I: 211–12. J. A. Eadie, "Politics in Lennox and Addington County in the pre-confederation period, 1854–1867" (MA thesis, Queen's Univ., Kingston, 1967). W. S. Herrington, *History of the county of Lennox and Addington* (Toronto, 1913; repr. Belleville, Ont., 1972).

STEWART, JAMES GREEN, HBC fur-trader and Arctic explorer; b. 21 Sept. 1825 in Quebec City, the son of the Honourable John Stewart*, member of the Executive Council of Lower Canada, and Eliza Maria Green; m. in 1854 Margaret Mowat, and they had at least five sons; d. 1 Sept. 1881 near Edmonton (Alta).

James Green Stewart was appointed an apprentice clerk in the Hudson's Bay Company in 1844 because Sir George Simpson* thought it "highly desirable to have a few young gentlemen respectably connected in this country [Canada] in the concern." After a year near Lake Superior he was posted to the Mackenzie River District, first to Fort Liard and then to Frances Lake (Yukon). From 1848 to 1852 he was Robert Campbell*'s assistant in establishing and supplying Fort Selkirk at the junction of the Pelly and Yukon rivers. This post marked the limit of Simpson's policy of expansion; at best it took seven years to get a return on an investment because of the difficulty in reaching the fort. The hardy voyageurs in the Mackenzie District had, according to James Anderson*, an "intense horror" of the trip up the Liard River; then came the worst series of portages in North America, consisting of at least 60 miles on foot across mountains to the Pelly. Stewart cheerfully specialized in this route, quickly earning Campbell's gratitude: "I could not be more ably supported had I all Hudson's Bay to choose from. . . ." Campbell's confidence was justified. In 1849, when the vital annual supplies from Fort Simpson (N.W.T.) had failed to reach Frances Lake by 1 November, Stewart, who had gone to Frances Lake from Fort Selkirk to meet them, barely survived the return trip. Yet he volunteered, in April 1850, to travel the 1,100 miles to Fort Simpson for the much-needed supplies. En route he rescued the survivor of the Pelly River Post which had experienced fire and cannibalism. At Fort Simpson, John Rae* gave him a boat half laden with supplies to take up the Liard, a trip he made successfully. Simpson remarked that Stewart's "exertions in this emergency are beyond all praise. . . ." James Anderson, who in 1851 became manager of the Mackenzie River District, was impressed by Stewart's advice to shift Fort Selkirk farther down the Yukon, and said: "Stewart with equal hardihood and Enterprise has a better education and far clearer judgement [than Campbell]."

However, Stewart's career lost its early promise. In the summer of 1851 he stayed at Fort Selkirk, permitting Campbell to complete the exploration of the Yukon downriver to Fort Yukon (Alaska) at the mouth of the Porcupine. Their roles were reversed in 1852 when Stewart was sent downriver to Fort Yukon for a cow while Campbell remained at Fork Selkirk. During Stewart's absence the post was attacked by the Chilkat who feared that their middleman trading position was in jeopardy with the establishment of HBC posts in the area. The Chilkat overpowered Campbell and pillaged the post. After his return to Fort Selkirk, Stewart conveyed what could be salvaged to Fort Yukon while Campbell set off for Fort Simpson and then to Lachine, Canada East, to obtain approval for re-establishing the post. Because of high costs and slow profit returns Simpson turned down the proposal, thus negating nearly 20 years of effort on the upper Liard and Pelly rivers.

As a supernumerary, Stewart briefly and rather inadequately took over Fort McPherson (N.W.T.) in 1854. He annoyed Anderson by telling him that Frances Lake could be abandoned but telling Simpson the opposite. Also he disobeyed orders by visiting the Red River Settlement. Stewart was posted briefly to Fort Carlton (Sask.) before being ordered north again to Fort Resolution (N.W.T.). He was to be second in command to Anderson of an expedition which the British government had asked the HBC to send down Back River to the Arctic to verify reports Rae had received from the Inuit that some of Sir John Franklin*'s expedition had perished on the Montreal Islands. Anderson arrived at Fort Resolution on 22 June 1855, dismissed the guides Stewart had chosen, and selected a different route. He also complained that because of "unnecessary hurry" Stewart had used poor bark for the special shortened canoes recommended by Rae for travelling in this area. Lacking the promised interpreters, the expedition could not properly interrogate the Inuit they met. The search of the Montreal Islands turned up small scattered bits of Franklin's ships. However, the expedition stopped short of what was later known to be the site of the tragedy, Starvation Cove on the mainland, because their frail craft, two weakened canoes and an inflatable Halkett boat, could not stand the unseasonably severe ice conditions. Moreover, the canoes kept breaking on the return trip up the 84 rapids of the Back River. Discord between Anderson and Stewart continued during this part of the trip, and after the expedition Anderson complained that Stewart had shown no initiative. Anderson also made a formal protest to the Council of the Northern Department when Stewart delayed dispatches by diverting the express to Norway House to pick up his wife and gave a highly coloured version of the expedition to Montreal newspapers. Simpson replied to Anderson: "Stewart has unfortunate failings for which he received from myself, at the request of the Council, a severe reprimand this season. . . ."

Just prior to the Arctic expedition Stewart was promoted to chief trader, and afterwards the British government awarded him £280 for his services. His efforts on two far-flung but relatively unproductive HBC enterprises now behind him, he served at Cumberland House (Sask.) from 1856 to 1862, at Oxford House (Man.) from 1865 to 1867, and finally at Norway House from 1867 to 1871. He became chief factor on 1 June 1869 but was not included in the new deed poll of 1871 despite his request. After settling at Clover Bar near Edmonton in 1878, he acted as an Indian agent for a year. He died of heart disease on 1 Sept. 1881. His best efforts had been in the Yukon where Campbell had named the Stewart River after him.

C. S. MACKINNON

PABC, James Anderson papers. PAM, HBCA, A.12/2; D.4/76a: 831; D.5/25: 590. Provincial Arch. of Alberta (Edmonton), James Green Stewart papers. [James Anderson], "Chief Factor James Anderson's Back River journal of 1855," ed. C. H. D. Clarke, *Canadian Field-Naturalist* (Ottawa), 54 (1940): 63–67, 84–89, 107–9, 125–26, 134–36; 55 (1941): 9–11, 21–26, 38–44. Clifford Wilson, *Campbell of the Yukon* (Toronto, 1970). E. J. Holmgren, "The diary of J. G. Stewart, 1855, describing his overland journey in search of the Franklin expedition," *Beaver*, outfit 310 (spring 1980): 12–17.

STEWART, JOHN CUNNINGHAM, public servant; b. 6 Nov. 1839 in Belfast (Northern Ireland); m. Geraldine M. L., daughter of Edward Mulberry Hodder*, and they had one son and two daughters; d. 26 Dec. 1888 in Ottawa, Ont.

John Cunningham Stewart's Irish education was "further improved . . . by a brief term" under Dr William S. Smith, rector of the High School of Quebec, before he entered the civil service on 25 Jan. 1855 as a junior clerk in the headquarters of the Post Office Department in Quebec. The Canadian Post Office had only four years earlier "cast off the imperial yoke," when responsibility for the service passed from the British to the Canadian government [*see* Thomas Allen Stayner*]. For the next 33 years Stewart was a part of a postal service which, no longer fettered by the need to balance the ledger, yet operating with a budget as a government department, burgeoned in response to the needs of Canadians. He served a thorough apprenticeship within the department in Ottawa. On 12 June 1857 he was promoted 2nd class clerk and on 1 Aug. 1861 was raised to 1st class and employed at postal headquarters.

Between 1866 and 1868 Stewart organized the Post Office Savings Bank branch. He was appointed chief clerk and superintendent of the branch on 25 Jan. 1868, and two months later, on 1 April, 81 banking facilities were opened simultaneously, thus aiding remote areas in Ontario and Quebec unserviced by established banks. In 1881 when the savings branch (now with some 300 local branches) was amalgamated with the money order branch, established in 1855 to reduce the sending of loose money through the mail in the form of registered "money letters," Stewart was named first superintendent of the combined system on 13 December.

Thereafter he moved in rarefied circles. In August 1884, when the prestigious British Association for the Advancement of Science held its annual meeting in Montreal, Stewart was invited to address it on the topic of the savings banks. He used the occasion to attempt to assuage the mounting fears of the chartered banks that the government intended to usurp their business. His paper was well received, and he forwarded a copy to Sir John A. Macdonald* with an easy familiarity that bespoke previous social contact.

In mid 1887 Stewart was dispatched to Britain to conduct an "exhaustive examination of the British system of financial accounts" and to suggest possible improvements to the Canadian post office system, which was using antiquated accounting procedures established in 1851. Stewart's recommendations were accepted *in toto* and on 1 Feb. 1888 he was placed in charge of all the financial operations of the department, as financial comptroller, with the rank of deputy head in the civil service. With this promotion he became the second-ranking civil servant in the department. He acknowledged his appointment to the prime minister, and successfully campaigned for free franking of correspondence for his department. By an order in council he was allowed to authorize free postage without the correspondence being seen by the deputy postmaster general, and this removed him one step farther from the control of the deputy minister; perhaps not entirely by coincidence his confirmation carried the stipulation that he was to rank below the deputy, William Henry Griffin*, in departmental affairs.

Stewart died after only 11 months in the position he had earned through diligent application. An extraordinary tribute was paid to him in the annual report of the postmaster general, and his pallbearers, including three cabinet ministers and Sandford Fleming*, bore eloquent testimony to the stature he had attained. Stewart had helped to make life in frontier Canada more liveable, and he had been able to move with the times and lay the foundations for future postal services.

His personal records have been destroyed and little is known of his private life; the emphasis on Stewart's devotion to duty in the obituaries and in all else written about him then was a reflection on the times.

KENNETH S. MACKENZIE

National Postal Museum (Ottawa), Circulars, *c.* April 1888; Post Office Savings Bank, Scrapbook; J. C. Stewart, "Report to the Postmaster General" (1887). PAC, MG 26, A; RG 1, E7, 46. Can., Parl., *Sessional papers*, 1867–89, Reports of the postmaster general, 1866–88. Can., Prov. of, Legislative Assembly, *App. to the journals*, 1856–59, Reports of the postmaster general, 1855–58; Parl., *Sessional papers*, 1860–66, Reports of the postmaster general, 1859–65. *Gazette* (Montreal), 3, 5 Sept. 1884. *Ottawa Daily Citizen*, 27 Dec. 1888. *CPC*, 1881.

STIRLING (Sterling), DAVID, architect and entrepreneur; b. 6 Dec. 1822 at Galashiels (Borders), Scotland, son of James Stirling, stonemason, and Margaret Sanderson; m. first 8 April 1852 Jane Fullerton in Pictou, N.S.; m. secondly 1 Dec. 1869 Clara Richmond Lea in Charlottetown, P.E.I., and they had one son; d. 13 April 1887 at Charlottetown.

Trained in Scotland, David Stirling immigrated to British North America about 1847 and during a lengthy career there designed and supervised the construction of all types of buildings in diverse architectural styles. His early years in the new land were spent in pursuit of viable opportunity. Stirling located initially at St John's, Nfld, which was slowly rebuilding after the great fire of 1846, and there he designed a handsome building for the Bank of British North America. In April 1850 he moved to Halifax, where he soon prepared designs for another branch of the same bank, a market-house and stores on Hollis Street. Five years later Stirling was drawn to the Scots settlement at Pictou, N.S., to design the Pictou County Court House. In Toronto, his next location, he worked for the architectural firm of Cumberland and Storm [*see* Frederic William CUMBERLAND; William George Storm*] on the imposing centre portion of Osgoode Hall, executed between 1857 and 1860. Finding that architectural design and supervision could not provide an adequate livelihood, Stirling turned twice to industrial activity. In 1851 he joined George LANG, a stonemason, in opening the Albert Freestone Quarries in Albert County, N.B., and ten years later he became a partner in the Chatham Foundry at Chatham, Canada West.

Stirling's principal interest, however, was architecture. Following his unsuccessful application to become clerk-of-the-works for the Parliament Buildings in Ottawa, he returned in 1862 to Halifax, then experiencing a building boom. In partnership with William HAY, whom he had known as clerk-of-the-works for the Cathedral of St John the Baptist in St John's and as a prominent architect and a Masonic brother in Toronto, Stirling was well positioned to capitalize upon this boom. Hay and Stirling carried out at least ten commissions, which included commercial, institutional, residential, and public buildings. Among these, the Halifax Club (1862), the residence of Alexander Keith* (designed in 1863), and the new Provincial Building (1863) attest to the firm's skill in applying the then fashionable Italianate design idiom. Although Hay was nominally the senior partner, contemporary accounts frequently credited the firm's work, including its designs, to Stirling. In 1863 the Halifax *Evening Express* believed his "abilities as an architect are too well known to require any encomiums." After Hay's departure about 1865, Stirling maintained his own office and accepted commissions in Halifax such as the Poors' Asylum (1867), the School for the Blind (1868), Fort Massey Presbyterian Church (1870), the best known of his several local churches, and in Charlottetown the Bank of Prince Edward Island (1867) and the Post Office (1871).

By 1870 Stirling was firmly established in the architectural sphere of the Maritimes and had taken a Halifax draughtsman, Andrew Dewar, into partnership. In addition to further ecclesiastical and residential work, such prominent structures as the Young Men's Christian Association (1872) and the Masonic Hall (1875) led Dewar to claim extravagantly in 1877 that the firm had authored "all the principal buildings in Halifax." In 1872, on the recommendation of Charles Tupper*, the federal Department of Public Works appointed Stirling dominion architect responsible for federal works in Nova Scotia. Design commissions, including the Pictou Customs and Inland Revenue Building (1872), were accompanied by site assessments, supervision of repairs, and contract certification. By the mid 1870s, however, economic depression had sharply reduced the number of architectural commissions in Halifax, and in 1877 Stirling's partnership with Dewar was dissolved.

Although Stirling continued to receive federal patronage for architectural work in Nova Scotia, the depression and his success in the competition to design the lunatic asylum at Charlottetown induced him to move there early in 1877. He soon formed a partnership with William Critchlow Harris*, the talented young architect who had apprenticed in his Halifax office between 1870 and 1875. The firm's commissions included Hensley Chapel at King's College, Windsor, N.S. (1877), and, in Prince Edward Island, the Kirk of St James, Charlottetown (1877), and Tryon Methodist Church, Tryon (1880). In their role as dominion architects for Prince Edward Island from 1880 Stirling and Harris also supervised the construction of federally designed public buildings at Summerside, Charlottetown, and Montague. In 1880 Stirling was made an associate architect of the new Canadian Academy of Arts, but by the mid 1880s declining health led him to retire from that institution and to pass over increasing responsibility in the firm to his young partner.

As well as his æsthetic bequest to the changing townscapes of the Maritime provinces, Stirling contributed socially to the communities in which he lived; he was a Mason, a member of the charitable North British Society of Halifax, and an officer of the Caledonia Curling Club in Charlottetown. Although in 1875 Critchlow Harris, William's father, did not regard Stirling as a "first rate architect," an obituary in the Charlottetown *Daily Patriot* described him as "an architect of repute." Stirling's reputation rests primarily upon the fine buildings surviving from his work in Halifax in the 1860s, and upon his later churches designed in the Gothic Revival style.

SUSAN BUGGEY and GARRY D. SHUTLAK

The diary of William Critchlow Harris is in the possession of R. C. Tuck, Charlottetown (mfm. at PANS).

General Register Office (Edinburgh), Registers for the parish of Galashiels, 3 April 1815; 27 Sept. 1818; 6 Dec. 1822; 1 Sept. 1824; 5 April 1825. PAC, RG 11, B1(b), 683, 753(a); B2(b), 2118; D2, 3840–42, 3844, 3848, 3855. PANS, MG 1, 68, box 50; MG 20, 232. QUA, David Stirling, Notebook (copy at PANS). Can., Dept. of Public Works, *General report of the minister of public works from 30th June, 1867, to 1st July, 1882 . . .* (Ottawa, 1883), xvii-xix. *Acadian Recorder*, 15 July 1865, 16 March 1867, 4 Jan. 1868, 19 Jan. 1880. *British Colonist* (Halifax), 9 Nov. 1869. *Daily Telegraph* (Saint John, N.B.), 11 July 1877. *Evening Express* (Halifax), 12 May 1862; 30 Oct., 9 Nov., 28 Dec. 1863; 15 Jan., 17 Oct. 1864; 26 April 1865; 4 May 1868; 20 April 1870. *Examiner* (Charlottetown), 2, 8 June 1877; 13 April 1887. *Halifax Evening Reporter*, 31 Jan. 1863; 11 Feb. 1864; 19 March 1870; 13 Jan., 9, 15 Oct. 1872; 4 July 1873; 24 May 1875. *Novascotian*, 29 April, 9, 25 Nov. 1850; 13 Oct. 1851; 19 April 1852. *Patriot* (Charlottetown), 8 May 1869, 14 April 1887. *The Halifax, N.S. business directory . . .*, comp. Luke Hutchinson (Halifax), 1863. *Hutchinson's N.S. directory*, 1864–67. *Lovell's N.S. directory*, 1871. *McAlpine's Halifax city directory . . .* (Halifax), 1869–81. *McAlpine's N.S. directory*, 1868–69. *Toronto directory*, 1859–60. C. A. Hale, *The early court houses of Nova Scotia* (2v., Can., Parks Canada, *Manuscript Report Series*, no.293, Ottawa, 1977), I: 93–115. Irene Rogers, *Reports on selected buildings in Charlottetown, P.E.I.* (Can., Parks Canada, *Manuscript Report Series*, no.269, Ottawa, 1976), 93–100, 209–14. C. J. Taylor, *The early court houses of Prince Edward Island* (Can., Parks Canada, *Manuscript Report Series*, no.289, Ottawa, 1977), 64–65. R. C. Tuck, *Gothic dreams: the life and times of a Canadian architect, William Critchlow Harris, 1854–1913* (Toronto, 1978), 18, 20, 22–48, 66–68, 90, 231. Susan Buggey, "Building Halifax, 1841–1871," *Acadiensis*, 10 (1980–81), no.1: 90–112.

STRICKLAND, SUSANNA (Moodie), settler and author; b. 6 Dec. 1803 in Bungay, Suffolk, England, youngest daughter of Thomas Strickland and Elizabeth Homer; d. 8 April 1885 at Toronto, Ont.

Susanna Strickland was a member of a 19th-century English family which, like the Brontës, Edgeworths, and Trollopes, was remarkable for the volume of its literary production. Five of the six Strickland girls pursued literary careers and a brother, Samuel*, wrote an autobiographical work late in his life. One of Susanna's elder sisters, Agnes, was internationally famous for *Lives of the queens of England . . .* (1840–48), which she wrote with the eldest sister, Elizabeth, and together they produced several other series of biographies of royal and illustrious personages. Although the Strickland name was best known for historical biography, the amazing literary output of the family, spanning eight decades from 1818 to 1895, included works of fiction, poetry, natural history, and autobiography.

Undoubtedly a number of factors combined to bring about the family's high degree of literary involvement. Some time between the birth of Catharine Parr* in 1802 and Susanna in December 1803, Thomas Strickland moved with his family from London, where he had managed the Greenland Docks, to Suffolk. After living in Bungay for a number of years he bought a 17th-century Flemish-style mansion, Reydon Hall, near Southwold on the Suffolk coast, and moved there at the end of 1808. The location of the mansion in a fertile rural and seaside region was conducive to an interest in flora and fauna, which is revealed in many of the Stricklands' writings. Susanna, for example, later wrote fondly of the region in *Roughing it in the bush* as the source of her literary aspirations: "It was while reposing beneath those noble trees that I had first indulged in those delicious dreams which are a foretaste of the enjoyments of the spirit-land. In them the soul breathes forth its aspiration in a language unknown to common minds; and that language is *Poetry*. . . . Here I had discoursed sweet words to the tinkling brook, and learned from the melody of waters the music of natural sounds." The "Old Hall" itself, and its library containing major works of history as well as editions of well-known English and classical poets, sparked a fascination for history in members of the family and inspired the writing of poems based on 18th-century models as well as on the works of Scott and Byron. Biographical and autobiographical works by members of the family indicate that the library was well used, mainly because of the pedagogical interest of Thomas Strickland. He and his wife tutored the elder children in the study of history, literature, languages, and mathematics as well as in practical skills, and the older children in turn assumed tutorial responsibilities for the younger girls.

Thomas Strickland re-entered business, becoming a partner in a coach factory in Norwich. His business necessitated residence in that city for part of each year and various members of the family accompanied him during some of these periods. The children, therefore, acquired town as well as rural experience. The experience of the town is reflected in the first book published by a member of the Strickland family, Catharine Parr's *The blind Highland piper and other stories* (1818).

There is evidence that it was, curiously, the youngest daughters, Susanna and Catharine, who first entertained literary ambitions. Thomas Strickland's death in 1818, followed a few months later by the publication of Catharine's book, brought about both the need for and the possibility of literary careers. Although Thomas bequeathed Reydon Hall to his wife, he left little or no money, and the coach manufactory had failed in the spring of 1818. Circumstances, therefore, urged the Strickland women to supplement the family income by writing for the literary markets available to young ladies during the pre-Victorian period. There was always a demand for children's books and Susanna and her sisters wrote many such works after the publication of *The blind Highland piper*. They also contributed stories and poems to the flourishing gift-book and annual trade of the 1820s. But the most significant outlet was magazines for women. It was in such periodicals as the *Lady's Magazine and Museum* . . . (1831–37) and the *Court Magazine and Monthly Critic* (1838–47) that Agnes and Elizabeth first published biographical sketches of royal ladies, and in *La Belle Assemblée* (1827–28) that Susanna's sketches of Suffolk life in the manner of Mary Russell Mitford's *Our village* (1824–32) appeared. Such early rural pieces served as models for the later Canadian sketches which Susanna wrote for the *Literary Garland* of Montreal and for her book, *Roughing it in the bush*.

Another facet of Susanna's early career that deserves mention is her work for the Anti-Slavery Society. The secretary to the society in the late 1820s was a minor poet, Thomas Pringle, who had resided for a number of years in South Africa. Susanna wrote to Pringle in connection with items she submitted to *Friendship's offering*, a gift-book which he edited. Correspondence and friendship followed; indeed, it seems that Pringle became a surrogate father to Susanna. She visited his home in Hampstead (now part of London) in 1830 and in early 1831, and it was there that she met John Wedderburn Dunbar Moodie*, whom she was to marry on 4 April 1831. It was also at Pringle's that Susanna met former black slaves from the West Indies. The result of such meetings was her two anti-slavery tracts, *The history of Mary Prince, a West Indian slave* . . . (1831) and *Negro slavery described by a negro: being the narrative of* [Ashton Warner] . . . (1831). The two pieces, especially the introduction to *Negro slavery*, relate Susanna's humanitarian awakening and indicate the source of the Dickensian attention to social injustice to which she gives expression in poems as well as in longer prose works.

Early in 1831, following her visits with the Pringles, Susanna took quarters of her own at 21 Chandor Street, Middleton Square, in the St Pancras area of London, intending to pursue a literary career. There was a temporary break in her engagement to Moodie, her volume of poems was about to be published, and she was writing the anti-slavery pamphlets and book reviews for Pringle. Over the period of a few weeks she became acquainted with many literary and artistic persons in a circle frequented by the Pringles, Leitch Ritchie, and other contributors to the annuals of the day. Her poetic contributions to the annuals were frequent, especially to *Forget me not* and *Friendship's offering*, and she received modest remuneration from their publishers. By 1831 she had enough poems, most of them previously published, to form a volume of 214 duodecimo pages, entitled *Enthusiasm; and other poems*, in which the theme is the transience of all earthly things. It is a didactic volume which cautions the reader against the pursuit of fame and celebrates the lives of pious persons and their love of God. A significant item in the book is "An appeal to the free," another account of slavery. *Enthusiasm* reveals a meditative and emotional temperament, a trait which had been shown in her girlhood and had earlier led to her conversion at the Congregational chapel in Wrentham, Suffolk, a conversion which shocked other more orthodox members of the family.

Following their marriage in 1831, Susanna and her husband lived first in London then in Southwold for a year but poor economic prospects prompted a decision to emigrate to Canada. Undoubtedly Susanna had heard favourable reports of Canada from Samuel, as Catharine's book, *The young emigrants; or, pictures of Canada* . . . (1826), makes evident. In a letter to Mary Russell Mitford in 1829 Susanna wrote: "He [Samuel] gives me such superb descriptions of Canadian scenery that I often long to accept his invitation to join him, and to traverse the country with him in his journeys for Government." According to the novel *Flora Lyndsay*, Dunbar Moodie preferred to emigrate to South Africa but chose Canada to please his wife. Emotionally, Susanna was most reluctant to leave England; she considered the departure a "fearful abyss" as she recalled it in *Roughing it*, but the decision was one of "stern necessity." Not having sufficient wealth to ensure a secure future for their children in England, the Moodies pursued the promise of economic success and high social status in Canada. They sailed from Edinburgh in July 1832 with the first child of the six they were to have. Catharine and her husband had left for Canada earlier the same year. The arrival of the Moodies in the New World was characterized by a comminglement of excitement at the scenic splendour of Lower Canada and the St Lawrence River and apprehension over being "stranger[s] in a strange land."

The Moodies bought a cleared farm in Hamilton Township, near Cobourg, Upper Canada, and in so doing chose a different course of settlement from that of other well-known writing families, such as the Traills, Langtons, and Stewarts, all of whom settled, immediately following their arrival, on uncleared land in the Peterborough area. These families, therefore, did not encounter the "Yankee" neighbours who were the source of many frustrating experiences for the Moodies and who also provided the material for subjects in literary sketches. A poor financial investment followed by a decision to sell the farm in 1834 and move to Douro, a backwoods township north of Peterborough, together with the expenses of settling in the backwoods, severely strained the Moodies' financial resources. The move, however, did have the advantage of placing the family nearer to Samuel, the Traills, and friends. Over the next five years the Moodies again attempted to establish a farm, but were unsuccessful and abandoned farming in late 1839 when Dunbar received an appointment as sheriff of the Victoria District (after 1849 of Hastings County). The family moved to Belleville in January 1840 and it was probably there that Susanna wrote the sketches and stories of backwoods life which eventually appeared as *Roughing it in the bush*.

It seems likely that their failure as pioneers was as much a result of temperament and personality as of anything else. The difficulties of clearing land and coping with climate, of communications, of finding and keeping agreeable hired persons were as great for the other settlers as for the Moodies, yet the Langtons, Stewarts, Traills, and Stricklands were relatively successful as pioneers and the books written by members of those families evidence a more positive, optimistic, and accepting approach to the pioneering experience than does *Roughing it*. Susanna's book opens with a reference to "the Dreadful Cholera" and closes with a metaphor for the backwoods, "the prison-house." Between the two there is certainly much dwelling on sickness, death, danger, and near-disaster; in other words, the book presents a largely, though not exclusively, negative view of pioneering in Canada. Such an emphasis is, perhaps, more the result of Mrs Moodie's personality and imagination, of her idea of what had literary appeal, than of her desire to present an account of pioneer life for the information of British gentlemen considering emigration. Although early letters reveal that Susanna was particularly vivacious, she was, according to Catharine Parr Traill, impulsive, "often elated and often depressed." Catharine observed in her sketch of the early life of Susanna that her sister's imagination was "romantic, tinged with gloom and grandeur, rather than wit and humor." Susanna's book of poems supports that view; it is characterized by warnings against earthly indulgence and consists of largely sombre and ominous verses such as "The deluge," "The avenger of blood," and "The destruction of Babylon." Her fiction too reveals a dark and melodramatic emphasis on miserliness, illegitimacy, malice, murder, and suffering, although ultimately vice is always punished and virtue rewarded. Clearly, the negative incidents and tone of *Roughing it* are consistent with most of Susanna's literary production and the character of the book is largely determined by a particular way of seeing the world.

Even under the duress of pioneering Susanna had never entirely relinquished her literary interests. During her early years in Canada she sent poems home for publication in the *Lady's Magazine*, a journal with which her sisters were involved. In addition, she had prose and poetry published in the *Canadian Literary Magazine* (1833) and in the *New York Albion* (1835), which circulated in Upper Canada. Comments in *Roughing it* also indicate that some of the poems which appeared in that book were written during residence in the backwoods. Then, in 1838, she began contributing to the *Literary Garland* in Montreal at the request of its publisher John Lovell*; she became one of the leading contributors to that periodical until its demise in 1851.

It was, however, during the first 15 years of her residence in Belleville that Susanna Moodie was able to devote herself vigorously to her literary career. Undoubtedly the access to better communications and the improved financial circumstances of their life in Belleville gave her the opportunity to develop that career and to augment the family income. She expanded prose pieces which she had written in England and had them published in the *Garland* as serialized novels; thus "The miser and his son" became *Mark Hurdlestone* (1853), and "Jane Redgrave" and "The doctor distressed" both formed part of *Matrimonial speculations* (1854). She submitted poems from *Enthusiasm*, as well as new ones written in Canada, for publication in the *Garland*, but her most significant contributions to the periodical were the six Canadian sketches which formed the nucleus of *Roughing it*. For a period of one year, in 1847–48, she and her husband also edited and contributed the majority of material to the *Victoria Magazine*, a journal which was intended to perform an educative function for the rising class of mechanics and tradesmen in the colony. The journal had a subscription list of approximately 475 but that was apparently insufficient for Joseph Wilson, the publisher, to continue the enterprise.

In 1852 Susanna began a short but highly satisfactory business relationship with the publisher Richard Bentley of London, England. She contributed to *Bentley's Miscellany* from 1852 to 1854; *Roughing it* was published by his firm in 1852, *Life in the clearings* followed in 1853, and *Flora Lyndsay* appeared in 1854, the last work to deal with the Moodies' Canadian experience. The other works by Susanna published by Bentley, three novels and a volume of novellas, all have English settings and are chiefly expanded versions of previously published materials.

The connection with the Bentley firm was undoubtedly a good one for Susanna Moodie: she had six books published in only three years, in addition to short pieces in the *Miscellany*, and she received more than £300 for these works. The copyright of *Roughing it* she sold outright for £50, but she received a further £50 because of its success. The other works were published on agreement that the author would receive half-profits and, except for *Matrimonial speculations*, each brought her an advance of £50. In addition, she must have received money from New York publishers. Letters to Bentley indicate that she was dealing with G. P. Putnam as well as Dewitt and Davenport for American editions of *Roughing it* and other works. Between 1852 and 1887 a number of her works were published in the United States by several different publishers.

Her relatively good fortune did not last long. Perhaps Susanna had exhausted herself in the activity of the early 1850s, for there was a long hiatus in her literary career and in her relationship with the Bentley firm. She attempted to resume both in 1865 by again writing to Bentley and submitting work, but the only item to be published was *The world before them* (1868). The letters to Bentley reveal that this new activity was necessitated by financial exigencies. Dunbar had been forced to resign his shrievalty in 1863 and was unable to gain other employment. He transferred all his property to one of their sons in return for maintenance for himself and his wife for the rest of their lives. Unfortunately Susanna and Dunbar did not get along well with their daughter-in-law, and when the son and his wife emigrated to Delaware the elder Moodies refused to accompany them. They moved to a small cottage outside of Belleville and survived as best they could. Susanna turned again to writing and to another "long neglected art," the painting of pictures of flowers which she sold for from one to three dollars apiece. These were difficult years for the Moodies; both of them suffered ill health and their other children were either unable or unwilling to assist them. The Moodies lived near Belleville until Dunbar's death in 1869 after which Susanna lived chiefly with her son Robert in Seaforth and Toronto, although she also boarded with friends in Belleville from 1 Oct. 1870 through 1871. She died in Toronto in 1885 and was buried in Belleville beside her husband.

Susanna Moodie's three best literary works, *Roughing it in the bush*, *Life in the clearings*, and *Flora Lyndsay*, constitute a chronicle of immigrant and pioneer experience dealing with all phases of the process from the decision to leave England to establishment in a Canadian town. *Flora Lyndsay*, the first chronologically, was the last of the three to be published, and is the third in order of quality and interest. It deals, in the form of a loosely structured novel, with the initial discussions of emigration by a young married couple, and continues through the final decision and the crossing. In a letter to her son-in-law, written about the time of the publication of the Canadian edition of *Roughing it* in 1871, Mrs Moodie observes that *Flora* "is Canadian and the real commencement of Roughing It." Although the book conveys some sense of the vicissitudes of emigration as well as the perils and tedium of the crossing, it does not dwell on these things nor does it have a strong story line. It consists chiefly of sketches and anecdotes about a large gallery of characters, ranging from those based on Mrs Moodie's neighbours and advisers in Suffolk to her fellow passengers and the one-eyed, alcoholic captain of the brig *Anne* on which they sailed for Quebec. That Susanna delighted in the study of human beings and was able to get them to talk about themselves is clearly evident in *Flora Lyndsay* as well as in the other two books of the trilogy; she listened and observed carefully and was able to capture humour and pathos in her reproductions. Included in *Flora Lyndsay* is a long story, almost a novel within a novel, based on Suffolk people; this was written by Susanna on the *Anne* when it was becalmed for three weeks off Newfoundland, at which time food rations became low. Unfortunately, the plot and style of the story clash with the air of authenticity and simplicity of the character sketches, for it bears an excess of pretentiousness, sentimentality, and didacticism, being a story of greed, murder, and repentance.

Roughing it in the bush is superior to any of Susanna's other works and, indeed, its quality has ensured an enduring recognition of Susanna Moodie as an important figure in Canadian literary history. Much attention has been given to the book, and it has been published in numerous editions in Britain and the United States as well as in Canada. In the 19th century it was admired by reviewers in all three countries for the lively style and humour with which it depicted colonial characters, backwoods customs, domestic practices, and natural surroundings. In the 20th century it has functioned as a touchstone for Canadian literary critics, being variously referred to as a valuable historical document, an early example of local colour or realistic fiction, and an expression of the romantic sensibility in 19th-century Canada. In the latter half of the 20th century, as more thorough and serious examinations of Canadian literature are being made, analyses are revealing hitherto ignored complexities of structure and style, and the personality of its author, as reflected in the book, is being seen as representative of persistent and deeply rooted elements in the collective experience of Canadians.

Although it is unlikely that the same richness will be discovered in *Life in the clearings*, as yet it has been neglected by literary historians and critics. The circumstances of the latter book were different from *Roughing it*: a request by Bentley for an account of life in the towns and of a trip to Niagara Falls to be used as a motif around which to centre a series of sketches and essays on colonial society. As a result, it resembles the books produced by such visiting Englishwomen as Harriet Martineau and Frances Trollope, and like their books it presents observations of the institutions and customs which were both reflecting and helping to shape North American society and culture. Although it contains some of the character sketches meant for *Roughing it*, it concentrates on the characteristics of a province which has recently achieved responsible government. There is repeated notice of the people's sense of liberty, their industrious habits, and their mechanical genius. The frequency of patriotic and optimistic statements probably indicates an effort by the author to stress that she was not anti-Canadian, as many readers of *Roughing it* had thought because of her cautionary statements to British gentlemen about the hazards of emigration.

Roughing it, unlike the other books, was generated by the traumatic experiences of emigration and backwoods life, and manifests, in its complexity, the tensions in the intellectual, emotional, and imaginative life of its author. It seems likely that it will continue to challenge future critics to new interpretations.

CARL P. A. BALLSTADT

Susanna [Strickland] Moodie wrote *Enthusiasm; and other poems* (London, 1831); *Flora Lyndsay: or, passages in an eventful life* (2v., London, 1854); *Geoffrey Moncton: or, the faithless guardian* (New York, [1855]); *Hugh Latimer; or, the school-boys' friendship* (London, 1828); *Life in the clearings versus the bush* (London, 1853); *Mark Hurdlestone, the gold worshipper* (2v., London, 1853); *Matrimonial speculations* (London, 1854); *Roughing it in the bush; or, life in Canada* (2v., London, 1852); *The world before them: a novel* (3v., London, 1868). With her sister, Catharine Parr Traill, she wrote *The little prisoner; or, passion and patience: and Amendment; or, Charles Grant and his sister* (London, 1828). Items by Susanna Moodie appear in *Ackermann's juvenile forget me not: a Christmas, New Year's, and birth-day present, for the youth of both sexes, M.DCCC.XXXII*, ed. Frederic Shoberl (London, [1832]); *Forget me not; a Christmas, New Year's, and birth-day present for MDCCCXXXI*, ed. Frederic Shoberl (London, [1831]); *The juvenile forget me not: a Christmas and New Year's gift, or birthday present for the year 1831*, ed. [A. M.] Hall (London, [1831]); *Marshall's Christmas box, a juvenile annual* (London, 1832). For further editions and other publications by Susanna Moodie see C. P. A. Ballstadt, "The literary history of the Strickland family . . ." (PHD thesis, Univ. of London, 1965).

A manuscript of C. P. [Strickland] Traill, "A slight sketch of the early life of Mrs. Moodie," is held by T. R. McCloy in Calgary.

British Library (London), Add. MSS 46653: ff.260-63; 46654; 46676: f.11. M. A. Fitzgibbon, "Biographical sketch," C. P. Traill, *Pearls and pebbles; or, notes of an old naturalist* . . . (Toronto, 1894), x-xiii. J. M. Strickland, *Life of Agnes Strickland* (Edinburgh and London, 1887), 4–5. A. Y. Morris, *Gentle pioneers: five nineteenth-century Canadians* (Toronto and London, 1968). Clara Thomas, "The Strickland sisters: Susanna Moodie, 1803–1885, Catharine Parr Traill, 1802–1899," *The clear spirit: twenty Canadian women and their times*, ed. M. Q. Innis (Toronto, 1966), 42–73. W. D. Gairdner, "Traill and Moodie: the two realities," *Journal of Canadian Fiction* (Fredericton), 1 (1972), no.2: 35–42. R. D. MacDonald, "Design and purpose," *Canadian Literature* (Vancouver), 51 (winter 1972): 20–31. T. D. MacLulich, "Crusoe in the backwoods: a Canadian fable?," *Mosaic* (Winnipeg), 9 (1975–76), no.2: 115–26. W. H. Magee, "Local colour in Canadian fiction," *Univ. of Toronto Quarterly* (Toronto), 28 (1958–59): 176–89.

STUART, GEORGE OKILL (O'Kill), lawyer, politician, and judge; b. 12 Oct. 1807 at York (Toronto), Upper Canada, son of George Okill Stuart*, a Church of England priest, and Lucy Brooks; m. in 1883 Margaret Black Stacey (there were no children); d. 5 March 1884 at Quebec City.

George Okill Stuart, born into an influential and respected family, was educated in Kingston, Upper Canada, and in Quebec before beginning the study of law in the Quebec office of his uncle, James Stuart*, attorney general of Lower Canada. He was called to the bar in 1830 and four years later joined his uncle in a partnership, which was dissolved in 1838 when the latter was named chief justice of Lower Canada. George Okill Stuart was also active in municipal affairs. From 1841 to 1843 he served as a solicitor for the city of Quebec. He was elected councillor for Saint-Louis Ward in December 1843 and during the following year sat on the committees for public health, finance, and elections. Stuart enjoyed continued success in municipal elections and on 9 Feb. 1846 the city council unanimously elected him the first English-speaking mayor of Quebec, to succeed René-Édouard Caron*. Stuart held the position for the next four years, during which time the city made improvements in street lighting and began the construction of a water supply and sewage system.

Stuart was viewed throughout his political career as a person with support from both English- and French-speaking groups. Stating that he would follow a "steady, independent and impartial course," he secured one of the two Quebec City seats when he ran for the provincial assembly in 1851 as an independent Conservative. In July 1854, however, he suffered overwhelming defeat in the constituency, now a three-member riding, at the hands of Charles Joseph ALLEYN, Jean Blanchet*, and Jean Chabot*. Talk of "roguery and perjury" during this election was so pervasive that Stuart contested the results, without success. After Blanchet resigned in March 1857 because of ill health Stuart was prevailed upon to accept nomination. He won the by-election of 14 April but retired from politics the following November when the session ended.

Stuart returned to his legal practice. He had served as *bâtonnier* (president) of the bar of Lower Canada for the district of Quebec from 1 May 1851 to 1 May 1853 and was instrumental in obtaining increased salaries for assistant judges. Named QC in 1854, he received a temporary appointment in September 1855 as assistant judge of the Superior Court of Lower Canada, under the provisions of the Seigniorial Act of 1854. By 1861 he was practising law in partnership with John Murphy, the firm of Stuart and Murphy lasting at least 11 years.

In April 1873 Henry Black*, a judge of the Vice-Admiralty Court and an uncle of Stuart's wife, sought and obtained Stuart's services as an assistant. Four months later Black died. Stuart, who was nominated to replace him on 27 October, took the oath of office on 2 Jan. 1874. Stuart had been particularly interested in admiralty law and his legal practice had possessed a sizeable maritime clientele. In addition, he had compiled a volume of case reports of the courts of King's Bench, Appeals, and Vice-Admiralty in 1834, and edited a work dealing with cases of maritime law on the St Lawrence in 1858 (a second volume was published in 1875). A decision by Stuart in 1880 concerning the brigantine *Atalaya*, detained for contravention of the imperial Foreign Enlistment Act of 1870, attracted much attention. He ruled that because the charges were unsubstantiated, the vessel was to be released and its owners recompensed for the costs and damages of detention. Judges of the Vice-Admiralty Court were appointed by Great Britain and there is evidence that during his later years Stuart questioned the dominion and imperial governments' responsibilities for the court. In 1891 the court was abolished and its functions were assumed by the Exchequer Court of Canada.

Stuart and his wife were leading members of Quebec society. He was also active in several Quebec businesses, including the Canada Fire Assurance Company and the Quebec Bank, and served on the board of directors of the St Maurice Railway and Navigation Company in 1857. In 1863 he was a lay delegate to the Quebec diocesan synod of the Church of England and from 1873 to 1875 he was honorary counsel for the Church Society. When he died the *Morning Chronicle* observed that Stuart's memory would be cherished by those who knew "what simple tastes and what a warm, affectionate and generous nature were partly concealed under a somewhat formal and reserved manner."

KENNETH S. MACKENZIE

George Okill Stuart compiled *Reports of cases argued and determined in the courts of King's Bench and in the provincial Court of Appeals of Lower Canada, with a few of the more important cases in the Court of Vice Admiralty . . .* (Quebec, 1834) and edited *Cases selected from those heard and determined in the Vice-Admiralty Court at Quebec . . .* (2v., London, 1858–75).

AO, MU 2923. PAC, MG 27, I, I27; RG 1, E1, 98; RG 4, C1, 295, file 880; 383, file 3204; RG 13, A1, 447, files 630, 1459. *Canada Gazette*, 18 Dec. 1854. *Cases selected from those heard and determined in the Vice-Admiralty Court at Quebec . . .*, ed. William Cook (Montreal, 1885), 215–39. *Quebec Gazette*, 27 July 1854. *Quebec Morning Chronicle*, 11 Feb. 1846; 14 Oct., 5, 17 Nov., 16 Dec. 1851; 5 July 1854; 18 July 1872; 24 July 1880; 5 March 1884; 4 July 1893. *Canadian biog. dict.*, II. *Dominion annual register*, 1884: 246–47. *Quebec directory*, 1844–81. P.-G. Roy, *Les juges de la prov. de Québec*. F.-X. Chouinard et Antonio Drolet, *La ville de Québec, histoire municipale* (3v., Québec, 1963–67), III.

STUART, JOHN, merchant and office-holder; b. 26 Dec. 1813 in Greenock, Scotland, son of James Stuart and Wilhelmina Matilda Sinclair; m. 15 Feb. 1844 to Louisa Anna Bindon at St John's, Nfld; d. 19 Dec. 1882 at St John's.

John Stuart probably came to Newfoundland in the early 1830s to work as a clerk for his father, a partner in the Greenock-based firm of Rennie, Stuart and Company. This firm, which had been active in the Newfoundland fish trade since the 1790s, exported cod to Europe, imported provisions for sale to outport fishermen, and supplied vessels for the seal and whale fisheries. Stuart probably replaced his father as the company's resident manager in St John's when the latter retired to Scotland in the late 1830s.

Stuart was a prominent leader in the St John's commercial community during the 1840s. Between 1842 and 1848 he was a major shareholder in 15 vessels newly registered in Newfoundland. He was a member of the St John's Chamber of Commerce, a founder and director of the short-lived Newfoundland Bank in 1844, and a director of the St John's Gas Light Company, which was also formed in 1844. The next year he was one of several merchants appointed at a public meeting to inquire into the best method of supplying water to St John's. Stuart was also a spokesman for the small, but influential, Scottish community in St John's. He served as a trustee of the Presbyterian St Andrew's Church which opened 3 Dec. 1843, and he occupied several executive offices in the Newfoundland Scottish Society between 1839 and 1848. A Conservative in politics, Stuart was appointed to the Legislative Council in November 1845 by Governor Sir John Harvey* to placate the Scottish community, which wanted greater representation on the Executive and Legislative councils, and in the same year he was named by the government to the boards of directors of the St John's Hospital and the St John's Academy. Stuart was also a vice-president of the St John's Turf Club in 1845 and a trustee of the Botanic Gardens in 1848.

Rennie, Stuart and Company experienced financial difficulties after its premises were destroyed in the St John's fire on 9 June 1846. There followed the disastrous seal fishery of 1848, which affected all but the largest firms such as Bowring Brothers [*see* Charles R. BOWRING], and Stuart declared the company bankrupt in October 1848. A month later he was appointed clerk to the House of Assembly by the governor, John Gaspard Le Marchant*. Like many bankrupt merchants he was able, through business and family connections, to start a new career as a civil servant.

Despite his previous Conservative politics, Stuart was to be non-partisan and respected by all politicians. This respect was clearly demonstrated when the Liberal government of John Kent* made him secretary to the Board of Works on 2 July 1858, an important position because the board was responsible for the management of all public buildings and roads in the colony. Stuart proved to be a thorough and conscientious secretary, but his efficiency was handicapped in the 1870s by a sharply increasing volume of work and the government's tardiness in providing additional staff. Stuart remained secretary to the Board of Works and clerk to the House of Assembly until his death in 1882 following a long illness.

MELVIN BAKER

Cathedral of St John the Baptist (Anglican) (St John's), Marriage registers, 1835–91 (mfm. at PANL). Maritime Hist. Group Arch., Board of Trade ser. 107–8 (entries for John Stuart). Nfld., *Blue book*, 1845–82; House of Assembly, *Journal*, 1832–82. *Royal Gazette* (St John's), 1832–82. *Business and general directory of Nfld.*, 1877. *Lovell's province of Newfoundland directory . . .* (Montreal), 1871. *The Newfoundland almanack . . .*, comp. Philip Tocque (St John's), 1848. Garfield Fizzard, "The Amalgamated Assembly of Newfoundland, 1841–1847" (MA thesis, Memorial Univ. of Newfoundland, St. John's, 1963). Prowse, *Hist. of Nfld.* (1895).

SULLIVAN, DANIEL (also known as **Daniel Tim-Daniel O'Sullivan**), blacksmith, innkeeper, and farmer; b. *c.* 1808 in Ireland; d. on or about 5 Jan. 1887 at Norway (now part of Toronto), Ont.

Daniel Sullivan achieved notoriety in the mid 1830s as a storm-centre of Toronto "street politics." Between 1832 and 1837 he was prosecuted for at least 13 offences involving individual or collective violence (assault and battery, riot, and affray), and appeared as prosecutor in at least four cases of a similar nature. In nearly every instance, Sullivan's adversaries were Tory partisans or Orangemen and the violence was connected with parliamentary elections or Orange demonstrations.

Although the frequency of Sullivan's court appearances attest to his pre-eminence as a practitioner of partisan rowdyism, his brothers, Jeremiah and Patrick, and a brother-in-law, Patrick Cassady, were also no mean performers. The Toronto *Recorder and General Advertiser*, an Orange organ, complained in July 1835: "The character of the Sullivan's is well known in this city, and not a row of any consequence takes place but the name of Sullivan is connected with it. . . . This name carries terror along with it, to every peaceable and well-minded citizen." William Lyon Mackenzie*, however, in a slighting reference to Robert Baldwin Sullivan*'s political tergiversations and upward social striving, asked: "Has not this same Mr. Sullivan . . . a few relatives in town, known as 'the Sullivans,' who have neither turned their coats, SOLD THEIR RELIGION, nor got ashamed of the hammer and anvil by which they earn their bread?" On another occasion Mackenzie referred to Daniel as R. B. Sullivan's "Cousin Dan," but there is no other evidence that they were related.

The nature of Sullivan's relations with Mackenzie is obscure but interesting. One might expect the puritanical Scot to have disliked the riotous Irish blacksmith and his hard-drinking Catholic lower-class associates, but apparently their support in Toronto was vital to a politician as dependent on popular favour as Mackenzie. Two incidents which occurred during the provincial election of 1834 suggest this. One night in early October, after a brawl on the hustings in which Sullivan had figured prominently, a pro-Tory mob attacked his house, endangering those within. Mackenzie, as mayor of Toronto, later imposed on two participants in the riot sentences so severe that a petition signed by many leading citizens was mounted on behalf of one of the convicted men, while milder sentences awarded by Mackenzie to Sullivan at the same time provoked accusations of favouritism. The night after the attack on Sullivan's house, a party of constables led by Toronto's chief constable, or high bailiff, William Higgins, clashed with a gang of anti-Tory rioters, one of whom was Sullivan, and a rioter, Patrick Burns, was killed. Mackenzie, spurred by complaints from the victim's friends, held a police court investigation of the incident and committed Higgins to stand trial for murder at the next assizes. The grand jury exonerated Higgins in April 1835 and returned a bill for riot against Sullivan and other companions of the dead man. Tory newspapers accused Mackenzie of collusion with the witnesses to create the case against Higgins, and stressed his friendly relations with Sullivan.

Mackenzie was not, however, the only prominent Reformer with whom Sullivan's name is associated in contemporary records. In November 1834, Toronto's Constitutional Reform Society named him to the St George's Ward committee which was to prepare for the municipal elections of 1835; his fellow-members included Judge George Ridout* and two aldermen, Dr John E. Tims* and Edward Wright. What part Sullivan may have taken in other elections is unknown, but a newspaper account of a brawl during the provincial election of 1836 reported that he visited the home of the Reform candidate, James Edward Small*, and left in the company of Ridout and a prominent Toronto radical, Charles Baker. Two of Sullivan's petitions for remission of sentence, dating from 1837 and 1848 respectively, bear the supporting signatures of a number of leading Reformers (some of them Protestant), including several merchants, city councilmen, and justices of the peace. On the later petition, Charles Durand calls Sullivan "a good citizen and worthy man." These petitions also contain Tory signatures, such as that of the former MLA and ex-mayor of Toronto, George Monro*, and two city councilmen, James Trotter and James Browne.

Sullivan's brief career as *primus inter pares* of the lower-class, anti-Tory Catholics of Toronto seems virtually to have ended in November 1837, when he was sentenced to three years in the Kingston Penitentiary for assault with intent to kill. The details of this case are unknown. Sullivan fared well in prison, labouring at his trade and avoiding disciplinary sanctions, and was released in March 1839. For the next ten years his whereabouts is unknown, but by September 1848 he was living in York Township. Here, but for a spell across the township line in Scarborough, he spent the rest of his life.

That Sullivan had not entirely abandoned his old ways as late as 1848 is shown by his trial for riot after he, his brother Patrick, and a third man attacked 14 armed Orangemen in a tavern. But he was becoming, in a small way, a man of property. Even in 1837 he had been tilling a small plot and employing men in stone-hauling. He now became both innkeeper and farmer, producing chiefly hay, potatoes, apples, and wool. The 1871 census shows him owning 157 acres and occupying 249 in all, although he possessed less at his death. In the 1870s he began to adopt the style of "yeoman." City directories of 1884 and 1885 call him "labourer," but his will styled him: "Daniel Tim-Daniel O'Sullivan, gentleman."

Sullivan, a sort of petty tribal leader of the Irish Catholic labouring element, was an equivalent of such petty Orange chieftains of mid-19th-century Toronto as John "Tory" Earls, an innkeeper and carter, called "Prince of Loafers," and William Davis, an innkeeper, minor civic official, and city councilman. His will, with its pious bequests (he left $50 each to Archbishop John Joseph LYNCH, the Toronto House of Providence, and Father Michael McCartin O'Reilly of St Joseph's Parish, Leslieville) and ban against his two nephews selling the land he left them outside the family, evinces the traditionalism of his outlook. If Sullivan was Irish and Catholic first and foremost, he did not, however, adhere to Bishop Alexander McDonell*'s anti-Reform entente with the Orange order in 1836 or shrink from marrying an Anglican Irishwoman in 1870. Nor did he conform to the stereotype of the 19th-century Irish Catholic manual labourer. Even in the 1830s he had rented quite a substantial house and always had the money to pay his fines and court costs. At his death he had risen modestly but significantly in the social scale.

PAUL ROMNEY

AO, RG 22, ser.7, 18, 15 May 1832, 8 May 1833; 19, 21 Nov. 1833, 19 Feb. 1834, 6 July 1837; 23, 5 Jan. 1849 (transcript at MTL). CTA, RG 7, F, 1834–46. Kingston Penitentiary Arch. (Kingston, Ont.), Punishment book, 1835–53; Work book, August 1837–March 1840. Land Registry Office for the Division of Toronto, Abstract index, 544–1, lot 4, concession 1, York Township; Instruments, nos.8563–66, 52049, 69204. PAC, RG 5, C1, 7, file 803; 281, file 47; RG 31, A1, 1851, York (East) Township, District 2: 312–13; 1861, York Township, District 1: f.22; 1871, District 45 (East York), Subdistrict A (York Township), Division 1, Schedule 1: 7; Schedule 3: 2; Schedule 4: 2; Schedule 5: 2 (mfm. at AO). York County Surrogate Court (Toronto), no.6279, will of Daniel O'Sullivan, 25 Jan. 1887 (mfm. at AO). *Constitution* (Toronto), 27 July 1836, 22 Nov. 1837. *Correspondent and Advocate* (Toronto), 25 Nov., 11, 18 Dec. 1834; 14, 21 Sept. 1836. *Courier of Upper Canada* (Toronto), 21 April 1835. *Patriot* (Toronto), 24 July 1835, 21 Nov. 1837. *Recorder and General Advertiser* (Toronto), 10 Jan., 15, 18 July 1835.

SUREAU (Sureault), *dit* **Blondin, ESTHER (Christine)**, named **Mother Marie-Anne**, founder of the Sisters of St Anne; b. 18 April 1809 at Terrebonne, Lower Canada, third child of Jean-Baptiste Sureau, *dit* Blondin, a farmer, and Marie-Rose Limoges; d. 2 Jan. 1890 at Lachine, Que.

Esther Sureau, *dit* Blondin, did not attend school as a child; in 1831 she was a boarder with the recently established Congregation of Notre-Dame at Terrebonne. Admitted the following year as a postulant, she soon became a novice in this community in Montreal. She was to adopt the name of Christine in memory of her stay at the noviciate. Because of poor health Esther returned home, but when she had recovered she was able to satisfy her desire to teach and accepted a post as teacher at Vaudreuil in 1833. She rapidly acquired an enviable reputation, and became headmistress of the parish school, which was known locally as the Blondin academy.

She was disturbed by the ignorance of rural children, and with the encouragement of her parish priest, Vicar General Paul-Loup Archambault*, and the permission of the bishop of Montreal, Ignace BOURGET, Christine Blondin, as she was then called, decided in 1848 to lay the foundations of a new community devoted to education. In September 1850, along with four of her companions, she made her profession, under the name of Mother Marie-Anne. The community (known under various designations before it finally assumed the name of Sisters of St Anne) was so successful in its recruiting that in 1853 it had 34 members and was transferred from Vaudreuil to Saint-Jacques-de-l'Achigan (Saint-Jacques). In 1864 the mother-house was located permanently in Lachine.

Although Mother Marie-Anne's career spanned four decades of religious life, she was to direct her community for only four of these years. A kind of moral drama began for her as soon as she arrived at Saint-Jacques-de-l'Achigan, with the appointment of Abbé Louis-Adolphe Maréchal as chaplain of the institute. According to him, the five-year-old community of the Sisters of St Anne had a tough challenge to meet in replacing the highly respected Sisters of the Sacred Heart of Jesus as teachers. Mother Marie-Anne and her colleagues were pushed along at a brisk pace by this domineering man who, in the opinion of the superior, exceeded his authority by meddling with the rules of the community. Since it had become impossible to maintain good relations between the founder of the Sisters of St Anne and their chaplain, one or other of them had to be sacrificed, to avoid deep rifts within the community. In August 1854 Bishop Bourget decided to depose Mother Marie-Anne and to appoint a new council. She was made superior of the Couvent de Sainte-Geneviève at Pierrefonds, which she herself had founded in 1851, and she went there at the beginning of November. Henceforth Mother Marie-Anne was kept at arm's length from the direction of the community. In 1864 she followed the sisters to Lachine, where they took up residence in the new mother-house, but her appointments as local counsellor, local assistant, and general counsellor were purely nominal; the founder of the Sisters of St Anne was in fact restricted to the humblest tasks.

Esther Blondin showed strength of character in her exemplary docility towards her bishop, and in her unreserved forgiveness of Abbé Maréchal and of those of her daughters who seemed forgetful of the past. Others would later honour an unappreciated founder, but her reputation would be restored only slowly. Until she died at the age of 80 on 2 Jan. 1890, Mother Marie-Anne was a serene and silent observer of the progress of her work. In the year of her death several hundred of her daughters were active in 42 institutions throughout North America.

EUGÈNE NADEAU

É.-J.[-A.] Auclair, *Histoire des Sœurs de Sainte-Anne; les premiers cinquante ans, 1850–1900* (Montréal, 1922). Frédéric Langevin, *Mère Marie-Anne, fondatrice de l'Institut des Sœurs de Sainte-Anne, 1809–1890; esquisse biographique* (2e éd., Montréal. 1937). Sœur Marie-Jean de Pathmos [Laura Jean], *Les Sœurs de Sainte-Anne; un siècle d'histoire* (1v. to date, Lachine, Qué., 1950–). Eugène Nadeau, *Martyre du silence; mère Marie-Anne, fondatrice des Sœurs de Sainte-Anne (1809–1890)* (Montréal et Lachine, [1956]); trans. by Sister Mary Camilla as *The life of Mother Mary Ann (1809–1890), foundress of the Sisters of Saint Ann* (Lachine, 1965).

SWAN, ANNA HAINING (Bates), giantess; b. 7 Aug. 1846 at Mill Brook, N.S., one of 13 children of Alexander Swan and Ann Graham; m. 17 June 1871 Martin Van Buren Bates, known as the "Kentucky giant"; d. 5 Aug. 1888 at Seville, Ohio.

Anna Haining Swan's father had emigrated from Dumfries, Scotland, to Nova Scotia; her mother was a Nova Scotian whose ancestors came from the Orkneys. Anna's parents and the other children in the family were normal in size, as was Anna herself as a baby. When she was 5 years old, however, Anna, the "Infant Giantess," was 4 feet 8 inches tall and weighed over 100 pounds; at 22 she was 7 feet 6 inches tall and weighed 350 pounds.

In 1862, when the great American showman P. T. Barnum heard about the Nova Scotian giantess, he sent an agent to New Annan, where she was then living, to bring the 16-year-old girl and her mother to New York. Besides the opportunity to earn $1,000 a month being exhibited at the American Museum on Broadway, Anna, who wanted more education, was pleased by Barnum's offer to provide her with a private tutor for three hours daily for three years. She also studied voice and piano. Barnum advertised Anna Swan as the tallest girl in the world, 8 feet 1 inch, dressed her in a costume made from 100 yards of satin and 50 yards of lace, and contrasted her with Commodore George Washington Morrison Nutt, who was 29 inches tall and weighed 24 pounds. Anna was the only giantess in the world at that time, and she attracted large crowds to whom she enjoyed talking. Barnum wrote that she was "an intelligent and by no means ill-looking girl, and during the long period while she was in my employ she was visited by thousands of persons."

Anna was nearly burned to death when Barnum's museum was destroyed by fire on 13 July 1865. The stairs were in flames and she was too large to escape through a window, but employees of the museum found a loft derrick nearby, smashed the wall around a window on the third floor, and lowered the giantess by block and tackle with 18 men holding the end of the rope. She went home to New Annan to recuperate, but returned soon after to New York to work in Barnum's new museum, which also burned in March 1868. That summer Anna visited her family and gave exhibitions in Nova Scotia before going back to the United States where she went on tour.

In 1871, when Anna Swan was crossing the Atlantic for a tour of Europe, she met Martin Van Buren Bates, the Kentucky giant who was advertised as 7 feet 8 inches tall and weighing 470 pounds, although he was actually 7 feet 2½ inches. A shipboard romance blossomed and they announced their engagement. They were married on 17 June at the Church of St Martin-in-the-Fields, London. After a short honeymoon they returned to London where they gave command performances before Queen Victoria and the Prince of Wales. Martin and Anna were advertised as "the largest married couple in the world" and travelled together in Europe for 14 months. They brought home many valuable gifts including a gold watch presented to Anna by Queen Victoria.

Bates bought a farm near Seville, Ohio, which he stocked with percheron horses and shorthorn cattle. He built a house with 14-foot ceilings, and doors 8½ feet high, and had furniture made to suit the two giants' size. They travelled during the summer with the W. W. Cole Circus.

"The tallest couple on the globe" had two children. On 19 May 1872, in London, Anna Swan Bates had a daughter, who died at birth, said to have been 27 inches long and to have weighed about 18 pounds. On 18 Jan. 1879 she gave birth at her home in Seville to a son. He was 30 inches long and weighed 23 pounds 12 ounces; his chest measured 16 inches and his head 19 inches around, and each foot was 5½ inches long. Although two doctors were in attendance, the baby died after 11 hours.

When Anna Swan died of consumption in 1888 she left an estate valued at $40,000. Some of her clothing and jewels were distributed among her family, and descendants have allowed some articles to be displayed in the Sunrise Trail Museum at Tatamagouche, N.S., near her birthplace at Mill Brook.

PHYLLIS R. BLAKELEY

[Information concerning Anna Swan Bates has been provided by Leonard Swan and R. L. Carruthers of the Sunrise Trail Museum (Tatamagouche, N.S.). The Swan family Bible is in the possession of Seldon Swan (Middleton, N.S.). P.R.B.]

Medina County Probate Court (Medina, Ohio), Record of deaths, no.3644, 10 June 1889. *Halifax Herald*, 7 June 1894. *Illustrated London News*, 24 June 1871. *Novascotian*, 24 March, 14 July 1851; 13 July 1871; 18 Aug. 1888. *Presbyterian Witness* (Halifax), 22 Feb. 1879. P. T. Barnum, *Struggles and triumphs; or, forty years' recollections of P. T. Barnum* (New York, 1930), 414–15. P. R. Blakeley, *Nova Scotia's two remarkable giants* (Windsor, N.S., 1970), 7–22. Irving Wallace, *The fabulous showman; the life and times of P. T. Barnum* (New York, 1959), 115, 141, 230–31, 269. P. R. Blakeley, "Anna Swan: Nova Scotia's giantess," *Atlantic Advocate* (Fredericton), 47 (1956–57), no.10: 35–38. Mary Burrows, "Anna Swan: Nova Scotia's famed giantess," *Chatelaine* (Montreal), 39 (1966), no.12: 38–39, 91–95.

SYME, JAMES, artist, gold-seeker, salmon-canner, and architect; b. in 1832 in Edinburgh, Scotland; d. 18 April 1881 at Victoria, B.C., survived by his wife Janet.

James Syme received training in the applied arts and design, perhaps at the Trustees Academy (later the Edinburgh School of Design). By 1859 he was living in San Francisco, and in 1862 he joined the Cariboo gold-rush. That year he and three other "free miners" recorded a set of claims on Williams Creek as "Syme & Co." The original partners were out by 1864 when Syme sold half his interest for $600 and transferred the other half, but the claim was still known as "Simes Co." in 1866.

Syme had lived in New Westminster during the winter of 1863–64, and settled there in 1865. He supported himself, at least in part, as an artist and ornamental plasterer, using skills he may have learned at the Edinburgh school, which in 1855 had listed a course in moulding and casting in plaster. Two works extant from these years are a plaster medallion of Sir James Douglas*, which was presented to Lady Douglas when the governor retired in 1864, and the ornamental ceilings and cornices in the house built in 1865 for river captain William Irving*. None of Syme's oil paintings from this, or the later period when he lived in Victoria, is known to have survived; they were said to show "an innate vigor" but to be "somewhat lacking in softness and delicacy of touch." Syme was also active in community affairs and organizations including the St Andrew's Society, the New Westminster Dramatic Club, the New Westminster Volunteer Rifle Corps, and the volunteer firefighters of Hyack Fire Company no.1.

As the gold-fields declined, many erstwhile gold-seekers began to exploit other untapped resources of the colony. In 1867 Syme undertook the first substantial attempt at salmon-canning in British Columbia. Contrary to oft-repeated assertions, his effort was no mere "kitchen stove" experiment, but an operation on a commercial scale. The product, put up in one-, two-, and six-pound cans, was offered for sale "in lots to suit" by a local merchant. It won prizes at the New Westminster exhibition and a trial shipment to Australia was well received. For the seasons of 1867 and 1868, and possibly 1869 as well, Syme operated in a former saltery complex at the site of Annieville on the south bank of the Fraser River opposite New Westminster. By 1869, however, the colony was in the midst of a general depression after the end of the gold-rushes. Lacking sufficient capital, Syme was unable to maintain his business, and by September the establishment he had used was offered for rent. Syme returned to San Francisco, where he worked in the atelier of the highly successful and popular artist Samuel M. Brooks, and was a member of the city's Scottish fraternal organizations, the St Andrew's Society and the Caledonian Club.

In 1874 he went to Victoria, for his health it was said, and soon established himself there as an architect, presumably qualified by his Scottish training. He executed several major commissions, including the first building for St Joseph's Hospital in Victoria, opened in 1876 by the Sisters of St Anne, and St Peter's Roman Catholic Church in Nanaimo in 1877. He also designed and supervised the construction of a number of houses, ranging from modest cottages to elaborate mansions. After 1877 he seems not to have been as active, partly because of the depressed state of construction in Victoria but also possibly because of that "combination of diseases culminating in liver dropsy" which ended his life at the age of 49.

Syme's career in colonial and early provincial British Columbia was typical of many. Relatively unsuccessful as a gold-seeker, he was forced to turn to other specialized pursuits in which he was skilled. These the fledgling society could not support as could a large urban centre like San Francisco. On the other hand, institutional restrictions did not prevent, as they might have done in an older and more sophisticated community, his taking up other occupations. No government fishery regulations hampered his attempt at salmon-canning, and he deserves to be recognized as the founder of the salmon-canning industry in British Columbia. Nor did professional rules prevent him from setting up as an architect and making a substantial contribution there as well.

H. KEITH RALSTON

PABC, GR 216, 35, 56. Caledonian Club of San Francisco, *Constitution and by-laws of the Caledonian Club of San Francisco* . . . (San Francisco, 1878). St Andrew's Society of San Francisco, *Historical report of the St. Andrew's Society, of San Francisco, Cal.* . . . (San Francisco, 1871). *British Columbia Examiner* (Yale and New Westminster), 23 Nov. 1867. *British Columbian* (New Westminster), 2 Dec. 1863; 12 March, 13, 16 April, 4 May 1864; 25 April, 20 May, 1, 15 July, 7 Oct., 2 Dec. 1865; 16, 23, 30 June, 12 Sept., 17 Oct., 10, 17, 28 Nov., 5 Dec. 1866; 16 Jan., 27 April, 13 July, 16, 19 Oct. 1867; 9 May, 3 Oct. 1868. *Daily British Colonist* (Victoria), 19 May 1868; 15 Jan. 1869; 8 Sept., 11, 14 Oct. 1874; 11 July, 22 Aug. 1875; 12, 13, 18 April, 6, 25 June, 5, 14 July 1876; 30 May, 24 June, 4, 10 July 1877; 5 Jan. 1878; 21 April 1881; 29 June 1883. *Free Press* (Nanaimo, B.C.), 28 Nov., 27 Dec. 1877. *Mainland Guardian* (New Westminster), 15, 25 Sept. 1869; 9 Sept., 10 Oct. 1874. *Victoria Daily Standard*, 3 April, 3, 10 June 1875. *Guide to the province of British Columbia for 1877–8* . . . (Victoria, 1877). *The San Francisco directory for the year commencing March, 1872* . . . (San Francisco, 1872), 631. John Mason, "The Edinburgh School of Design," *The book of the Old Edinburgh Club* (Edinburgh), 27 (1949): 67–96. Madge Wolfenden, "The early architects of British Columbia . . . ," *Western Homes and Living* (Vancouver), September 1958: 17–19.

T

TABARET, JOSEPH-HENRI, Roman Catholic priest, Oblate of Mary Immaculate, and educator; b. 12 April 1828 at Saint-Marcellin, France, son of Antoine Tabaret, a locksmith, and Adélaïde Forêt; d. 28 Feb. 1886 at Ottawa, Ont.

Joseph-Henri Tabaret attended boarding-school in Bourg-de-Péage before entering the Oblate noviciate at Notre-Dame de l'Osier, Isère, on 13 Sept. 1845. He made his profession on 14 Sept. 1846 and then continued his studies for the priesthood at Marseilles, Notre-Dame de l'Osier, and Goult, dept of Vaucluse. In 1850, on medical advice, the seminarist moved to Canada West where he was ordained priest on 21 December at Bytown (Ottawa) by Bishop Joseph-Bruno Guigues*. Tabaret's ministry in the parish of L'Orignal, which at the time included numerous missions, such as Alfred, Vankleek Hill, and Hawkesbury in Canada West, and Grenville, Bonsecours (Montebello), and Sainte-Angélique (Papineauville) in Canada East, lasted from 1851 to 1853 and had a profound influence on him. A broad-minded man, Tabaret quickly adapted to his new environment, and his work among the Scots, the Irish, and the French led him to respect these people and prepared him for the role of educator which he had long wanted to play. In the course of his college years he had in fact told a fellow-student: "I have but one desire: that is, to find a place where I may give myself to the education of youth."

His desire was realized in 1853 when he was appointed principal of the College of Bytown (which became the College of Ottawa in 1861 and received its charter as a university in 1866). The institution, which had been founded in 1848 by Guigues to "ensure ecclesiastical vocations, and to give society and religion men able to understand and defend the interests [of both]," was still in a formative stage. Although there were few students and great financial problems, Tabaret refused to be discouraged. Indeed it seems that the principal thought solely of the future, and that the obstacles strengthened his resolve. In a report to the Legislative Assembly of the Province of Canada in 1861, Tabaret estimated the value of the college buildings and land to be $70,000. The institution offered three programmes: preparatory, classical, and theological; some 100 students were enrolled in the first two and 15 in the third. There were 12 professors assisted by two discipline masters.

The principal had definite ideas about education. Convinced of the importance of bilingualism, Tabaret insisted on the necessity of teaching both French and English; the difficulties this might present were not in his opinion insurmountable. He considered such a measure imperative in that part of the country, for study of the two languages would "lessen those grievous prejudices that separate these two peoples who are so well calculated to have a high regard for one another." Thus he gained the respect of both Protestant and Catholic French Canadians and Irish. In addition to performing the duties of principal and teacher at the college, Tabaret, as the trusted friend of Guigues, held the office of vicar general of the diocese of Ottawa during the bishop's absence in 1862. From 1864 to 1867 he resided at Montreal as the provincial of the Oblates in Canada; in this capacity he took an interest in the Indian missions and in the recruiting of priests, particularly English-speaking ones, and strengthened existing endeavours.

Tabaret then returned to Ottawa, where he was rector of the new university from 1867 to 1874 and 1877 to 1886, and director of students from 1874 to 1877. He played an important part in the development of the university's curriculum, initiating its reorganization in 1874. Under the new programme the sciences and mathematics were given a significant place, commercial studies became part of the curriculum, and sporting activities were encouraged as a means of character formation. Tabaret improved pedagogical methods and gradually managed to increase the number of specialists among the teachers. Although Tabaret remained convinced of the importance of bilingual education, practical difficulties inherent in teaching in two languages led to the adoption of English as the language of instruction in almost all the courses in the new programme. (The university resumed bilingual instruction in 1901.) Among other things, the master plan also called for the creation of a school of civil engineering and an industrial school. The former was established in 1874, to Tabaret's delight. However, he died before he could set up the industrial school which he had dreamed of providing for Ottawa.

In 1879 Pope Leo XIII conferred a doctorate in theology on the rector. Tabaret, who had enjoyed the esteem of his former pupils and of two bishops, Guigues and Joseph-Thomas Duhamel*, can rightly be considered the man who built the University of Ottawa.

GASTON CARRIÈRE

Arch. départementales, Isère (Grenoble, France), État civil, Saint-Marcellin, 14 avril 1828. Can., Prov. of, Parl., *Sessional papers*, 1862, III, no.14. [Joseph Fillâtre], *A brief sketch of the life of the Rev. Father Joseph Henry Tabaret . . .* (Ottawa, 1886), also published as *Notice nécrologique du R. P. Joseph Henri Tabaret . . .* (Ottawa, 1886); "Le collège d'Ottawa," *Missions de la Congrégation des Missionnaires Oblats de Marie Immaculée* (Paris), 21 (1883): 105–18. Allaire, *Dictionnaire*, I: 505. *Canadian biog. dict.*, I: 628–29. Gaston Carrière, *Histoire documentaire de la Congrégation des Missionnaires Oblats de Marie-Immaculée dans l'Est du Canada* (12v., Ottawa, 1957–75), II: 21–61; VI: 183–329; *L'université d'Ottawa, 1848–1861* (Ottawa, 1960). Georges Simard, *Un centenaire; le père Tabaret, O.M.I., et son œuvre d'éducation* (Ottawa, 1928).

TASSIE, WILLIAM, teacher and headmaster; b. 10 May 1815 in Dublin (Republic of Ireland), third of the eight children of James Tassie and Mary Stewart; m. in 1834 in Dublin Sarah Morgan, and they had no children; d. 21 Nov. 1886 at Peterborough, Ont.

William Tassie immigrated to Nelson Township in Upper Canada in 1834 with his wife, parents, brothers, and sisters. He taught briefly in Nelson Township before accepting a position at the first common school in Oakville. In 1839 Tassie went to the Gore District Grammar School at Hamilton as assistant master under John Rae*. In 1853 he moved to Galt (now part of Cambridge) where, as headmaster of the newly established Galt Grammar School, he built a national reputation for both himself and the school.

Under Tassie the enrolment in the school grew from 12 in 1853 to between 250 and 300 at the height of its fame in the 1860s. Four out of five boys who attended came from homes outside Galt: from across Canada, from the United States, and even from the West Indies. Tassie's role was similar to that of John Strachan* during his teaching career at Cornwall and York (Toronto) earlier in the century; the alumni of their schools later formed a large percentage of the élite in Upper Canada. Families such as the Tuppers, Blakes, Mowats, Oslers, Codys, Keefers, Cronyns, Becks, Carlings, Boultons, Cayleys, and Galts sent their sons to "Tassie's School."

Tassie was an "old school" educator who opposed coeducation, favoured a curriculum centred on the classics, was a strict disciplinarian, and preferred residential schooling where the boys could be under constant supervision (at times over 40 boys stayed in his own home). According to a former pupil, the headmaster had "the bearing and dignity of a field-marshal and the walk and tread of an emperor." Yet he was a dedicated, high-principled teacher who drove himself as well as others. Tassie's aloofness was balanced by his sincerity and the warmth of his wife's character. Left in a difficult financial situation after his death, she received a life annuity of $340 from the school's old boys.

By the 1870s educational reform in Upper Canada had led to a stress on practical rather than classical education. In 1871 the Galt Grammar School was the first school in the province to be named a collegiate institute, but the introduction of provincial examinations, especially the intermediate examination begun in June 1876, and a system of grants paid according to the results of these examinations, precipitated the decline of the school. Students, especially those who had to pass the intermediate examination to become teachers, began to turn elsewhere and by 1881 the annual enrolment at the school had fallen to 50 boys. Tassie, however, held that education was largely for the building of character and remained a firm believer in education for its own sake, in clear defiance of the mounting preference for more scientific and practical training. But when many of his students were unsuccessful in provincial examinations his entire system came under criticism and pressure mounted on him to change his methods or leave. Unwilling to abandon his principles, he chose the latter course and resigned in the spring of 1881 under a cloud of controversy. He was succeeded by John E. Bryant, principal of Pickering College.

That fall Tassie opened a private boarding-school in Yorkville (now part of Toronto) where he again emphasized the classics. In 1884, still refusing to adapt his ideas to the changing conditions, he returned to the public system by accepting an appointment as headmaster of the Peterborough Collegiate Institute where his talents were sought, according to Henry John Cody*,"to improve its discipline." Indeed enrolment did increase and one year later students and teachers were reported to be working harmoniously.

While an active teacher, Tassie had advanced his own educational qualifications. He had received a BA from the University of Toronto in 1856 and an MA two years later. In 1871 he was awarded an honorary LLD from Queen's College in Kingston. Tassie had also served as president of the Ontario Grammar School Teachers' Association in 1869 and 1870 as well as in 1871 when it became the Ontario Grammar School Masters' Association.

On 21 Nov. 1886 Tassie suffered a fatal stroke. Tributes poured in but perhaps the most appropriate summary of his later years came from the *Educational Weekly*: "Doctor Tassie . . . belonged to a school of educators whose opinions and methods have had to succumb to newer educational ideals." By the last quarter of the century Tassie's educational methods were clearly outmoded.

J. DONALD WILSON

"The late Dr. Tassie," *Educational Weekly* (Toronto), 4 (July–December 1886): 728–29. *Galt Reporter* (Galt, Ont.), 20 June 1871; 21 May 1875; 9 Dec. 1879; 6, 13, 20 May, 3, 24 June, 16 Sept. 1881; 3 Feb., 3 March 1882; 11 Dec. 1885; 26 Nov., 24 Dec. 1886; 7, 21 Jan. 1887. *The Canadian almanac and repository of useful knowledge . . .* (Toronto), 1869–71. *Canadian biog. dict.*, I: 478–81. *Encyclopedia Canadiana*. H. J. Cody, "Dr. William Tassie (1815–1886)," *Canadian portraits: C.B.C. broadcasts*, ed. R. G. Riddell (Toronto, 1940), 107–16. *Picturesque and industrial Galt* (Galt, 1902), 39. Thomas Carscadden, "History of the Galt Collegiate Institute, 1881–1914," Waterloo Hist. Soc., *Annual report* (n.p.), 13 (1925): 134–38. H. J. Cody, "Dr. William Tassie," *School . . . Secondary Edition* (Toronto), 26 (1937–38): 565–72, 652.

TA-TANKA I-YOTANK (Ta-tanka Yotanka, Sitting Bull), chief of the Hunkapapa Sioux; b. *c.* 1836, probably in the Dakota Territory; d. 15 Dec. 1890 at Standing Rock (N. Dak.).

While still young, Sitting Bull gained a reputation as a warrior, and at the age of 16 he suffered a wound in battle which left him permanently lame. He became a medicine man and rapidly rose to be an influential leader among the Sioux. Although not directly involved in the "Minnesota Massacre" of 1862 [*see* Tatanka-najin*], Sitting Bull was one of the leaders, under Red Cloud, who resisted penetration by the United States Army into Sioux territory from 1865 to 1868. In the latter year, a treaty granted the Black Hills of Dakota to the Sioux. Within a few years, however, railway surveyors and settlers began appearing in the area and in 1874 reports of gold in the Black Hills attracted hundreds of prospectors and fortune-hunters. The Sioux prepared for war.

On 25 June 1876 the climax of these years of hostility between the whites and the Sioux came when Lieutenant-Colonel George Armstrong Custer, over-confident and eager to restore his eroded military prestige, led the 7th Cavalry against a large body of Sioux in the valley of the Little Bighorn River (Mont.). In the brief engagement, one of the bloodiest days of the American Indian wars, Custer and about 240 men were killed. Sitting Bull, the acknowledged leader in the Sioux victory, knew that now the full weight of the U.S. Army would be brought against him and he sought to avoid disaster. On 21 October he met with Colonel Nelson Appleton Miles, who was leading a campaign against the Sioux, to discuss the possibility of peace. Miles insisted that the Indians surrender their guns and horses and retire to reservations. Sitting Bull refused and fighting continued.

In November exhausted Sioux began to cross the

border into Canada, making camp in the Wood Mountain area in what is now southern Saskatchewan. In May, Sitting Bull followed. Inspector James Morrow Walsh* of the North-West Mounted Police, riding with half a dozen men into the camp which now contained 5,000 Sioux, met with Sitting Bull, as he had with the earlier arrivals, and assured him of protection from pursuit by the U.S. Army if the Sioux obeyed the laws of Canada and did not conduct raids across the border. Sitting Bull agreed to these terms, denouncing the Americans and claiming to be a "British Indian."

The summer of 1877 was filled with tension as minor incidents and disagreements threatened to erupt into war. Three American emissaries who attempted to convince Sitting Bull to return to the United States were imprisoned by the Sioux and were saved only by the intervention of Walsh and Acheson Gosford Irvine*, the assistant commissioner of the NWMP. On another occasion Walsh arrested three Indians for horse-stealing in the middle of the Sioux camp. Critical questions continued to worry those in positions of authority on the prairies. Would Sitting Bull, despite his promise, launch forays across the boundary, perhaps goading the U.S. Army into pursuing him onto Canadian soil? Would the presence of the Sioux on Blackfoot hunting-grounds provoke a war between the two fierce prairie tribes? Would Sitting Bull try to unite the western tribes against the whites in order to recover the buffalo country? Were rumours in 1878 of an alliance between Sitting Bull and Louis RIEL, then in Montana, accurate?

The United States government wanted Sitting Bull and his Sioux either to return to American territory, where it could exercise control over them, or to settle permanently in Canada. Canadian officials, who had no desire to adopt the Sioux, also wanted them to recross the border but did not dare risk war with the Indians by using force. At the suggestion of James Farquharson Macleod*, commissioner of the NWMP, the Canadian government arranged a meeting between General Alfred Howe Terry of the U.S. Army and Sitting Bull on 17 Oct. 1877 at Fort Walsh (Sask.). Distrusting the Americans and their promises of a pardon and just treatment, the chief refused to return to the United States and the meeting broke up. Nevertheless Macleod and Walsh continued to urge Sitting Bull to surrender, saying he would never be recognized as a British Indian or granted a reservation in Canada and warning him that the buffalo would disappear within a few years. The latter prediction came true all too quickly. In 1879 American traders and hunters set fires along the border to keep the buffalo south, and the end of the hunt on the Canadian prairies was in sight.

The friendship that developed between Walsh and Sitting Bull may have been the major reason for the lack of serious troubles involving the Sioux in western Canada. Walsh was, however, criticized for becoming too friendly with Sitting Bull and for failing to persuade him to return to the United States. This reaction probably explains Walsh's transfer to Fort Qu'Appelle in the summer of 1880; his replacement at Fort Walsh, Leif Newry Fitzroy Crozier*, was not able to maintain good relations with Sitting Bull. That summer the lack of buffalo and the refusal of the Canadian government to give the Sioux either a reservation or food led many to go back to the United States which had promised provisions.

During the winter of 1880–81 Sitting Bull, considering his own return, made inquiries about the reception of those who had surrendered. In the spring he met in Qu'Appelle with Colonel Samuel Benfield Steele* and Edgar Dewdney*, the commissioner of Indian affairs, who urged him to cross the border. Walsh wired from the east where he was on leave that it was safe for him to go back. Finally, in July, Jean-Louis Légaré, a local trader, led Sitting Bull and his remaining followers back to the United States, where they surrendered at Fort Buford (Buford, N. Dak.) on 19 July 1881.

Sitting Bull was allowed to settle on the Standing Rock Agency, where he remained. He toured briefly with Buffalo Bill's Wild West Show, visiting Toronto in August 1885. In the late 1880s a movement which prophesied the return of a Messiah who would exterminate the whites and return the buffalo swept the American west. This new religion and its Ghost Dance were outlawed. Sitting Bull, seeing a chance to recover his lost prestige and power, became a leader of the Messiah "craze." The authorities were still fearful of Sitting Bull's possible influence and issued a warrant for his arrest in December 1890. The Indian police who attempted to enforce the warrant at the reserve provoked Sitting Bull's followers, and in the exchange of gunfire Sitting Bull was one of those killed.

The greatest Indian enigma of his time, perhaps of all time, Sitting Bull was considered a hero by some and a savage murderer by others. Major Walsh, on hearing of his friend's death, said: "He was not the bloodthirsty man reports from the prairies made him out to be. He asked for nothing but justice. . . . he was not a cruel man, he was kind of heart; he was not dishonest, he was truthful."

J. W. GRANT MACEWAN

Glenbow-Alberta Institute, James Macleod papers. PAM, MG 6, A1, 24 April, 9 Nov. 1878; 24 March 1879; 22 May 1890. Can., House of Commons, *Debates*, 1878–82; Parl., *Sessional papers*, 1877, VII, no.9, app. D: 21; 1878, V, no.4, app. E: 34–35, 39–42, 47–49; 1880–81, III, no.3: 27–29; VIII, no.14: 93–101. *Fort Benton Record* (Fort Benton, [Mont.]), 1875–81. *Globe*, 8 April, 22, 24 Aug. 1885. *Manitoba Daily Free Press*, 1874–76. *Saskatchewan*

Herald (Battleford), 1878–80. *DAB*. A. B. Adams, *Sitting Bull: an epic of the plains* (New York, 1973). J. W. G. MacEwan, *Portraits from the plains* (Toronto, 1971), 128–40; *Sitting Bull: the years in Canada* (Edmonton, 1973). C. F. Turner, *Across the medicine line* (Toronto, 1973). J. P. Turner, *The North-West Mounted Police, 1873-1893 . . .* (2v., Ottawa, 1950). Stanley Vestal, *Sitting Bull, champion of the Sioux; a biography* (new ed., Norman, Okla., 1957). Gary Pennanen, "Sitting Bull: Indian without a country," *CHR*, 51 (1970): 123–40.

TAYLOR, JOHN FENNINGS, author and public servant; b. 14 March 1817 in London, England, the third son of George Taylor of Camberwell (now part of London); m. first 5 Dec. 1838 in Toronto, Upper Canada, his second cousin, Mary Elizabeth (d. 1851), second daughter of Colonel George Taylor Denison I, and they had one son and two daughters; m. secondly Georgina Rosalie Nanton of London, England, and they had five sons and one daughter; d. 4 May 1882 at Old Point Comfort, Va.

Upon completion of his formal education at Radley, Oxfordshire, England, John Fennings Taylor immigrated to Upper Canada in 1836, settling in Toronto. Through the influence of his uncle, also John Fennings Taylor (1801–76), the deputy clerk of the Legislative Council of Upper Canada, Fennings Taylor, as the younger man was known to avoid confusion, was appointed 1st office clerk of the council on 4 Dec. 1836. In 1841, following the union of the Canadas, he was transferred to the office of the Legislative Council of the united province, and the next year became its 1st office clerk. He was appointed additional clerk assistant in 1846, was promoted deputy clerk and clerk assistant in 1855, and in 1856 became, in addition, master in chancery. Following confederation in 1867 he was transferred to the office of the Senate of Canada as deputy clerk, and he served there conscientiously until his death, becoming 1st clerk assistant in 1868 and later master in chancery. In addition Taylor held a ceremonial commission as lieutenant-colonel in the militia, and was, *ex officio*, a commissioner for administering the oath of allegiance and declaration of qualification to senators and a commissioner of the Court of Queen's Bench in Ontario for taking affidavits. Like a growing number of Canadians in the mid 19th century, he had pursued a lifetime career as a public servant, and as such had gradually risen to a prominent position.

Fennings Taylor was best known, however, for his contributions to Canadian historical literature, predominantly as a biographer. His first and most noteworthy work was his collaboration as writer with Montreal photographer William Notman* in *Portraits of British Americans*. The work followed a "plan which has found favour in England" and was originally issued in monthly instalments before its publication as a three-volume work (1865–68). The writing of the 84 brief biographies of leading Canadian statesmen, divines, jurists, merchants, and, in particular, fathers of confederation, was a task for which Taylor was eminently qualified. He was in the enviable position of having both ready access to the parliamentary library and a close personal acquaintance on a non-partisan basis with many of his subjects. And, like Henry James Morgan* and Sir John George Bourinot*, his prominent position in the public service provided him with the financial means and the time to exercise his literary inclinations.

Taylor's biographies for *Portraits* were strongly influenced by the nascent romantic nationalism of the confederation era, the fervent assurance that Canada was on the threshold of national greatness. The sketches, a deft blend of presentism and patriotism, were pervaded by an exuberant sense of momentous achievement, stemming from Taylor's conviction that "events of great national importance [were] hourly passing into history." His patriotic grandiloquence had been manifested earlier in such spirited compositions as his proposed national anthem "God bless our new-born nation." But in his *magnum opus* it was tempered by judicious assessments of his subjects which reflected his belief that the sketches should be written "fairly and impartially, free alike from extravagant eulogy . . . or cynical ill-nature." Although the collection avoided lavish sycophancy, the biographies were for the most part strongly sympathetic; in the introduction Taylor lamented the tendency among Canadians to "disparage the position . . . of our public men; . . . to discredit generally the presence of high principle, and challenge particularly any claim to patriotic motives." He went to extraordinary lengths to maintain a balanced, if sometimes overly generous, impartiality. In discussing the chequered career of Sir Francis HINCKS, for instance, he observed that Hincks was a "statesman who had the courage to utilize to patriotic ends qualities that were base as well as . . . noble, and regardless alike of covert suspicion or open censure dared to fuse good with ill for the permanent advantage of Canada." The sketches, in general, were painstakingly researched and gracefully written in a dignified style. They revealed both a high-minded integrity and the zeal of the amateur historian.

In 1868, following the assassination of Thomas D'Arcy McGee*, Taylor expanded his biographical sketch of McGee in *Portraits* into a eulogistic pamphlet, *The Hon. Thos. D'Arcy McGee: a sketch of his life and death*. Displaying a strong empathy with McGee's romantic prophecies of a great dominion of the north and the creation of a new nationality, Taylor approvingly incorporated lengthy quotations from McGee's impassioned speeches on confederation. In this eloquent panegyric, McGee was portrayed as a courageous visionary whose genius for oratory had been a sacred trust bestowed by divine providence to help achieve confederation. The following year Taylor drew further from *Portraits*, expanding his accounts of Francis Fulford*, George Jehoshaphat Mountain*, and John Strachan* into *The last three bishops, appointed by the crown, for the Anglican Church of Canada*. With unrestrained admiration, at times bordering on hagiography, Taylor traced the lives and careers of the three Canadian bishops. He concentrated on their unswerving labours to consolidate the Church of England in Canada, which did much to remove religious matters from the control of parliament.

A decade later Taylor resumed his historical writing, exhibiting his accumulated parliamentary expertise in *Are legislatures parliaments? A study and review*. In this thoroughly researched study, rigorously documented with British and Canadian precedents, he sought to differentiate the terms "parliament" and "legislature." Far from engaging in etymological sophistry, this work reflects the strict constructionist approach Taylor adopted in his convincing plea for semantic exactitude. The book represented a fitting summation of Taylor's literary career, drawing upon both his vast parliamentary knowledge and his historical talents. It was largely responsible for the publication in 1880 of *The powers of Canadian parliaments* in which Samuel James WATSON stressed the evolving, rather than the strictly constructionist, development of Canadian parliaments and legislatures.

Fennings Taylor died on 4 May 1882 in Virginia where he had gone to recover his failing health. As the Montreal *Gazette* observed, "his urbanity of manner, his geniality and many sterling qualities endeared him to those with whom he came into contact, and his well-stored mind and keen and humorous perception of events made him an entertaining and instructive conversationalist." A memorial window was placed in the Church of St Alban the Martyr in Ottawa, of which he had been a devout member. He was also active in wider Anglican church matters, having been chosen frequently as a lay delegate to the diocesan and provincial synods. Both his public career and his historical interests reflect significantly much of Canada's literary, intellectual, and historical concerns and development during the confederation era.

MURRAY BARKLEY

John Fennings Taylor collaborated with William Notman to produce *Portraits of British Americans, with biographical sketches* (3v., Montreal, 1865–68), and was the author of *Thos. D'Arcy McGee: sketch of his life and death* (Montreal, 1868); new ed. pub. under title: *The Hon. Thos. D'Arcy McGee: a sketch of his life and death* (Montreal, 1868); of *The last three bishops, appointed by the crown, for the Anglican Church of Canada* (Montreal, 1869); and of *Are legislatures parliaments? A study and review* (Montreal, 1879).

PAC, MG 24, I56; RG 14, E2, 1835. *Gazette* (Montreal), 9 May 1882. *CPC*, 1881: 89. R. L. Denison, *The Canadian pioneer Denison family of county York, England and county York, Ontario: a history, genealogy and biography* (4v., Toronto, 1951–52). *Dominion annual register*, 1882: 362. Morgan, *Bibliotheca Canadensis*, 367–68. Watters, *Checklist*, 585. W. S. Wallace, "The two John Fennings Taylors," *CHR*, 28 (1947): 459.

TELARI-O-LIN. *See* VINCENT, ZACHARIE

TERESA, ELLEN DEASE, named **Mother.** *See* DEASE

TERESA, MARGARET BRENNAN, named **Sister.** *See* BRENNAN

THIBAULT (Thibeault), NORBERT, called **Brother Oliver Julian**, teacher, literary critic, and teaching brother; b. 11 July 1840 at Saint-Urbain-de-Charlevoix, Lower Canada, son of Olivier Thibeault, a farmer, and Carmelle Tremblay; d. there on 10 Aug. 1881.

Norbert Thibault entered the École Normale Laval in Quebec City when it opened in May 1857. A brilliant student, on 14 June 1859 he obtained a diploma permitting him to teach in model schools. After winning first prize for "rhetoric, Latin, Greek, and correctness of language," he received a diploma on 2 July 1860 enabling him to teach in academies. In September he was appointed an assistant master at the school and was to have a considerable influence upon his colleagues. Acting as an adviser to the Association des Instituteurs de la Circonscription de l'École Normale Laval from August 1860, he served as its secretary from 1861 to 1863, vice-president in 1863, and became president in August 1864. He delivered a number of lectures to its members. In 1864, when he was 24, he was being listened to "in scrupulous silence," and praised for his talents as an orator.

In January 1864, Thibault, Joseph Létourneau, and Charles-Joseph Lévesque, *dit* Lafrance, established *La Semaine* (Quebec), a "religious, pedagogical, literary and scientific review" that was the first in French Canada produced for and by teachers. The editors, while reiterating their respect for religious and political authorities, maintained that the teachers themselves must resolve pedagogical problems, as well as difficulties arising from their material or social circumstances. They must break out of their isolation and make teaching a more respected and remunerative occupation with fewer burdens. The man of letters in the editorial group, Thibault also took up the cudgels for the teaching profession, in order that a true "teaching class" might develop, for teachers had both aspirations and interests in common and a social role to play. The journal ceased publication in 1865 because of lack of money, the collective inertia of the teachers, and the absence of support from the government.

In February 1866, drawing on his experience with *La Semaine*, and convinced that "French literature was constantly and significantly developing in this country," Thibault became literary critic of *Le Courrier du Canada* of Quebec City. Introduced to the readers as "a talented young man, with sound judgement, a great love of work, and a ready pen," he proposed "to set up a kind of tribunal to examine and assess, with justice and moderation, if not with skill, the works of our writers" which he had reread "for perhaps the fifth time." Faithful to his motto, *Sponte favos, ægre spicula* (give honey willingly, sting with regret), he analysed numerous works of Canadian writers, including the poetry of Octave Crémazie*, whose *Promenade de trois morts* he cut to shreds. Taking no offence, the exiled poet had only admiration for the young teacher who "is truly opening the way for literary criticism." In a letter to Abbé Henri-Raymond Casgrain*, Crémazie recognized the talent of Thibault, champion of the classics and foe of the romantics, and acknowledged that through him "Canadian criticism will soon extricate itself from the ridiculous course it has followed up to now." Despite this commendation, Thibault gave up his vast project and contented himself with an occasional brief report for *Le Courrier du Canada* on pedagogical texts.

Norbert Thibault was a director of the Société de colonisation de Québec in 1865 and 1866. A member of the Institut Canadien of Quebec by January 1864, he served as its temporary secretary and assistant registrar that year, before becoming a director in 1865 and corresponding secretary in 1869. He was a captain-lieutenant in company no.7 of the 9th Battalion Voltigeurs de Québec (1864–67). He was also assistant secretary for the national subscription fund to commemorate François-Xavier Garneau* in February 1866. In 1871 he published a treatise entitled *De l'agriculture et du rôle des instituteurs, dans l'enseignement agricole*, which had first appeared in instalments in *Le Courrier du Canada* in 1870, under the pseudonym of Agricola. He may also have published a *Petite Histoire du Canada à l'usage des écoles élémentaires*, as a notice in *Le Courrier du Canada* of 23 Dec. 1870 indicates. However, no trace has been found of the *Traité d'éducation* which Ernest Gagnon* claimed he published in 1876.

Despite all this activity, Thibault was not happy; deprived of the joys of family life and contact with society, he felt he was on the wrong track, as he confessed to Ernest Gagnon in September 1871. He resigned his teaching post in October. It may have been because he had not been chosen as a candidate for Charlevoix in the June 1871 elections (as *Le Journal de Québec* of 11 March 1871 indicated in a paragraph which was reprinted in *Le Courrier du Canada* two days later), or because he was showing his irritation at not being re-elected to the management committee of the school that October. In the event, he was immediately approached to teach the workers of the Saint-Jean and Saint-Roch districts at Quebec, but he evidently preferred to give private lessons at his boarding-house, to judge from an announcement printed in *Le Courrier du Canada* from 25 Oct. to 15 Nov. 1871.

In April 1872 a notice in *L'Événement* of Quebec City intimated that Thibault had accepted the position of editor of *Le Courrier de Rimouski*, but four days later he entered the noviciate of the Brothers of the Christian Schools at Montreal. He took the habit on 25 May under the name of Brother Oliver Julian and was officially assigned on 3 August to Saint-Jean (Saint-Jean-sur-Richelieu). He was then appointed successively to Saint-Laurent near Montreal on 3 April 1873, to the parish of Saint-Jacques in Montreal on 1 Aug. 1873, to Saint John, N.B., on 5 June 1875, to Laval, Que., on 28 March 1876, again to Saint John on 9 Aug. 1876, and finally to Chambly, Que., on 18 April 1877. In the summer of 1877 he became deranged and was sent back to his family in August. The priest of his village, Ambroise Fafard, wrote on 25 Sept. 1878 requesting the bishop of Chicoutimi, Dominique RACINE, to intervene and force Thibault's religious community to help his family financially. He died at his home on 10 Aug. 1881.

If this tragic end, recounted by Ernest Gagnon in *Nouvelles pages choisies*, reveals Thibault's sensitivity, it still "must not," as André Labarrère-Paulé wrote, "make us forget the journalist of *La Semaine*." As Charles-Joseph Magnan* noted, he was "a serious writer, a man of letters endowed with considerable taste. His lively, deft pen has left pages that do honour to Canadian literature." He was also a *littérateur* who championed the cause of teachers.

AURÉLIEN BOIVIN

Norbert Thibault was the author of *De l'agriculture et du rôle des instituteurs, dans l'enseignement agricole* (Québec, 1871).

AP, Saint-Urbain (Saint-Urbain-de-Charlevoix), Reg. des baptêmes, mariages et sépultures, 11 juill. 1840, 12 août 1881. Arch. des Frères des écoles chrétiennes, District de Montréal (Laval, Qué.), Papiers divers sur Norbert Thibault, dit frère Oliver Julian. Octave Crémazie, *Œuvres complètes de Octave Crémazie publiées sous le patronage de l'Institut canadien de Québec*, H.-R. Casgrain et H.-J.-J.-B. Chouinard, édit. (Montréal, [1882]). *Le Courrier du Canada*, 16 févr., 22 juin 1866. *La Semaine* (Québec), 1864. Réal Bertrand, *L'École normale Laval; un siècle d'histoire (1857–1957)* (Québec, 1957). Aurélien Boivin, "Norbert Thibault, l'homme et l'œuvre" (Mémoire de licence, univ. Laval, Québec, 1968). Ernest Gagnon, *Nouvelles pages choisies* (Québec, 1925). André Labarrère-Paulé, *Les laï-*

ques et la presse pédagogique au Canada français au XIXe *siècle* (Québec, 1963). Guy Savoie, "Bio-bibliographie de Norbert Thibault" (Mémoire de licence, univ. Laval, 1968). C.-J. Magnan, "Éducateurs d'autrefois – anciens professeurs à l'École normal Laval – M. Norbert Thibault," *BRH*, 48 (1942): 172–78.

THOM, ADAM, teacher, journalist, lawyer, and public servant; b. 30 Aug. 1802 at Brechin (Tayside), Scotland, son of Andrew Thom, merchant, and Elizabeth Bisset; m. first a Miss Bisset; m. secondly Anne Blachford, and they had one son and one daughter; d. 21 Feb. 1890 in London, England.

Adam Thom studied at King's College (University of Aberdeen) from 1819 until 1823, receiving the degree of MA on 31 Aug. 1824; in 1840 he was awarded an LLD by the same institution. After graduating, he taught briefly at Udny Academy in Aberdeenshire before moving to Woolwich (now part of London) where he continued teaching. During this period he prepared a Latin grammar, *The complete gradus.*

In late 1832 Thom immigrated to Montreal. Here he began articling in the law office of James Charles Grant*, and on 1 Jan. 1833 he became editor of the *Settler, or British, Irish and Canadian Gazette* (Montreal). Originally intended to inform new immigrants of the problems they would face in British North America, the paper became a vehicle for Thom's antagonism to French Canadian views. His stated aim was to make Lower Canada a British province in fact as well as in name, an objective he felt was thwarted by anti-commercial and pro-democratic tendencies of the French Canadians. The response of the French Canadian press to the *Settler* and its editor was predictable, and the *Vindicator and Canadian Advertiser* (Montreal) [*see* Edmund Bailey O'Callaghan*] dubbed them the *"Slop-Pail"* and "Dr. Slop" respectively.

Publication of the *Settler* ceased on 31 Dec. 1833. Thom then turned to teaching classics, mathematics, and science at the Montreal Academical Institution while writing a pamphlet entitled *Letter to the Right Hon. E. G. Stanley, . . . secretary of state for the colonies*, published in 1834 under the pseudonym "An emigrant." On 1 Jan. 1835 Thom assumed editorship of the *Montreal Herald* and continued his journalistic assault on the French Canadians, at the same time intensifying his attacks on the British government's policy of "conciliation."

His editorial stance was buttressed by three series of letters, written by Thom but published in the *Herald* under different pseudonyms. Beginning on 20 April 1835, "Remarks on the petition of the convention, and on the petition of the constitutionalists by Anti-Bureaucrat" illustrated for all loyal Britons the groundless nature of the French Canadian grievances contained in the 92 Resolutions. A series "On the Canada Committee of 1828," commencing 30 July 1835, attacked the findings of the select committee of the House of Commons on the civil government of Canada, chaired by Thomas Frankland Lewis. The members of the committee had "strongly express[ed] their opinion, that the Canadians of French extraction should in no degree be disturbed in the peaceful enjoyment of their religion, laws and privileges. . . . " Thom saw here the origin of what he considered the imperial government's foolish policy of conciliation toward the French Canadians, a policy responsible for the exacerbation of the political and economic problems of the British in the province. The "Anti-Gallic letters" addressed to Governor General Lord Gosford [Acheson*] by Camillus, begun on 1 Oct. 1835, were prompted as much by Thom's fears of Gosford's pro-French-Canadian sentiments as by Thom's desire to inform the British public once again of the lamentable state of affairs in Lower Canada.

In 1836 the letters of Anti-Bureaucrat and of Camillus were published under the title *Canadian politics.* In the preface Thom publicly admitted his authorship and acknowledged as supporters of his views George Moffatt*, Peter McGill [McCutcheon*], and James Charles Grant, three powerful members of the Montreal English community. Thom had established himself with the English business élite in Montreal soon after his arrival in Lower Canada, and as early as November 1833 had been named secretary of the Beef-Steak Club, an association of some 30 leading merchants of the city.

The rebellion of 1837–38 reinforced Thom's arguments against French Canadians, for in his view the outbreak of violence proved their disloyalty beyond all doubt. He was pleased by the resultant recall of Lord Gosford and the appointment of Lord Durham [Lambton*], however, and while not totally enthusiastic about Durham's reputation as a liberal he did feel that the new governor general would take the time necessary to assess the Lower Canadian situation intelligently. Thom, who had been admitted to the bar in 1837, lost no time in offering his assistance to Durham, and on 25 Aug. 1838 was named an assistant-commissioner of the municipal commission, under Charles Buller*. The reaction of the French Canadian press to the appointment of "this irreconcilable enemy of the Canadiens . . . this hateful fanatic" was understandably hostile, but Buller received assurances from Stewart Derbishire*, another member of Durham's staff, that Thom was unaware that his manner of expression was offensive. On his part, Buller felt that "it was a great thing to show the violent parties in Canada that their denunciations should not succeed as heretofore in excluding men of ability from the public service."

Thom worked with fellow assistant commissioner William Kennedy to produce a paper that was incorporated into Lord Durham's *Report*; it reiterated, albeit more diplomatically, Thom's concern over the lack of internal improvements in Lower Canada and advocated control of municipal government by the "educated" and "propertied" men of the province. Thom became a spokesman for Durham and in December 1838 returned to England to help prepare the final draft of the report. He was credited by some with authorship of this document, but this rumour probably stemmed from Lord Brougham's campaign to discredit Durham.

Meanwhile a letter from Governor George Simpson* of the Hudson's Bay Company, dated 5 Jan. 1838, had informally offered Thom the newly created judicial post of recorder of Rupert's Land. The governor and committee of the company, despite being warned about Thom's francophobia, subsequently confirmed the offer, and Thom accepted the appointment and its salary of £500 sterling plus a living allowance of £200 per annum. In 1839 Thom journeyed to Red River (Man.) and commenced the second phase of his British North American career.

Prior to Thom's appearance, the administration of justice in the settlement had been informal and marked, according to Sheriff Alexander Ross*, by a "simple honesty." The HBC, however, in the course of a general administrative reorganization of the territory, decided "to establish as early as convenient a more regular and effectual administration of Justice." The recorder, functioning as legal organizer, adviser, magistrate, and councillor, was to be responsible for this rationalization and formalization of the judicial system.

Thom's reorganization was completed on 4 July 1839 and greatly pleased the governor and committee of the company. He also prepared a code of laws for the Council of Assiniboia in 1841 which was to prove of lasting value in that it formed the basis of a more comprehensive code written in 1862. Despite these efforts, however, the citizens of Red River were suspicious of their new judge. They were familiar with his Lower Canadian reputation, and their anxiety about his racial attitudes was compounded by their fears that as a salaried employee of the HBC Thom would not be objective in his judicial capacity. He did nothing to allay these fears. Apart from his pedantry and his refusal to speak French (knowledge of which was a prerequisite for the post) his actions in the court served to alienate the Métis population of the settlement. In 1842 he entered into a controversy with John Smithurst* over the authority of the Anglican bishop of Montreal in Rupert's Land. His "rediscovery" of the charter of 1670 and his insistence, enunciated in *A charge delivered to the grand jury of Assiniboia, 20th February, 1845*, that the chartered privileges of the company equalled the law of the land marked the beginning of an attack, on behalf of the company, on free trade in the settlement, and he believed that Alexander Ross was involved in the trade. In the same year he exceeded the limits of his legal authority, which stipulated that all capital cases were to be tried in Upper Canada, by sentencing a Saulteaux Indian, Capineseweet, to death, and further antagonized the settlement by attempting to increase the duty on American imports.

Armed with his interpretation of the charter, Thom encouraged the governor of Assiniboia, Alexander Christie*, to attack the illicit trade in furs that was common in the settlement. The assault began with the proclamation of a series of repressive measures, formulated by Thom, that included mail inspection and required the declaration by all importers that they were not involved in free trade [*see* Andrew McDermot]. This battle continued until the trial of Pierre-Guillaume Sayer* on 17 May 1849, in which Thom and Christie's successor, Major William Bletterman Caldwell, sought to make an example of some Métis who possessed a few illicit furs. The hearing was complicated by the fact that the courthouse was surrounded by hostile Métis threatening violence against Thom. Although a verdict of guilty was brought in, the company did not sentence Sayer; he was not only unconditionally released but was allowed to keep the furs. The crowd, led by Louis Riel* Sr, assumed that trade was therefore free and Thom, while legally vindicated, was practically defeated. It was at this point that Thom became a focal point for Métis discontent.

When Simpson arrived in the settlement shortly after the trial of Sayer the Métis presented him with a petition expressing their grievances against Thom and calling for his dismissal. A compromise was reached at a special meeting of the Council of Assiniboia on 31 May 1849 when Thom agreed to use French in his official duties. Simpson also persuaded Thom voluntarily to abstain from acting as recorder. But Thom refused to be intimidated by Métis threats and insisted on appearing in two court cases in 1850, which further damaged his reputation. In February he appeared as the defendant in *Matheson* v. *Thom*, a minor civil suit, in which he demanded an entirely English-speaking jury. He was overruled, but before leaving the room in a rage had insulted Cuthbert Grant*, the presiding official. Then in the *Foss* v. *Pelly* libel suit, resulting from Augustus Edward Pelly's accusation that Christopher Foss had committed adultery with Sarah McLeod*, the wife of Chief Factor John Ballenden*, Thom played a dominant role. He advised Foss, chief witness against Pelly, and Mrs Ballenden before the trial. When he was called into court to assist Governor Caldwell, the president of the court, he did everything in his power to obtain Pelly's conviction, including testifying on behalf of Foss. Pelly was ordered to pay Foss £300 in damages, but Foss and Mrs Ballenden took up residence together soon after and made ridiculous Thom's defence of them in court.

By this time Thom had lost much of his support within the company as well as in the Red River community. Simpson wrote of his "unfortunate temper [and] . . . overbearing manner" while the new governor of Rupert's Land, Eden Colvile*, noted that "the people like honesty and common sense quite as well as all Thom's long dissertations on General Principles." When Louis Riel, again acting as a spokesman for the Métis, announced in the fall of 1850 that his people would no longer tolerate Thom's presence in the court, the governor and committee decided to revoke his appointment as recorder. Thom was served notice of this decision on 10 April 1851, but was retained by the company as clerk of the Court of Assiniboia at his former salary of £700.

During his years in Red River Thom had spent his leisure time writing *The claims to the Oregon Territory considered* (1844), a precise argument against American demands for control of the west coast, and *Chronology of prophecy* (1848), a treatise on the Bible which marked a new outlet for his literary and critical abilities. Also, as clerk of the court, he co-operated with John Bunn* and Louis-François Laflèche* to write a report that called for an updating of the legal system of the colony.

In 1854 Thom left Red River and returned to Edinburgh where he lived until 1865. He then moved to London, and in 1885 published another religious work, *Emmanuel: both the germ and the outcome of the Scriptural alphabets, . . . a pentaglot miniature.* He died in 1890 and his will left an estate of £5,310 to his only surviving son, Adam Bisset Thom.

Adam Thom represented a unique link between Lower Canada and Rupert's Land in that his unyielding racial attitudes earned him the enmity of French Canadians and Métis alike. Thom's unsympathetic response to the Métis, combined with his advocacy of the assimilation of the French Canadians, reinforced the Métis' determination to survive as a culture. This determination, first manifested against Thom during the Sayer trial of 1849, found its ultimate expression in the violent response of the Métis to central Canadian imperialism in 1869–70.

KATHRYN M. BINDON

[Adam Thom published, under the pseudonym "An emigrant," *Letter to the Right Hon. E. G. Stanley, his majesty's principal secretary of state for the colonies* (Montreal, 1834). Letters which he signed "Anti-Bureaucrat" and "Camillus," first published in the *Montreal Herald* in 1835, were published as *Remarks on the petition of the convention, and on the petition of the constitutionalists* (Montreal, 1835) and *Anti-Gallic letters; addressed to his Excellency, the Earl of Gosford, governor-in-chief of the Canadas* (Montreal, 1836), before being issued together in 1836 as *Canadian politics* (Montreal). As "Ararat," he published *Cubbeer burr, or the tree of many trunks* (Montreal, 1841), and as "Septuagenarian Tory," *Queen alone, in every heart . . .* (London, 1876). He wrote the following under his own name: *The complete gradus; comprising the rules of prosody, succinctly expressed and rationally explained, on a new plan; and a comprehensive view of middle syllables* (London, 1832); *Review of the report made in 1828 by the Canada Committee of the House of Commons* (Montreal, 1835); *The claims to the Oregon Territory considered* (London, 1844); *A charge delivered to the grand jury of Assiniboia, 20th February, 1845* (London, 1848); *Chronology of prophecy: tracing the various courses of Divine Providence from the flood to the end of time; in the light as well of national annals as of Scriptural predictions* (London, 1848); *A few remarks on a pamphlet, entitled "A few words on the Hudson's Bay Company"; in a letter to Alexander Christie . . .* (London, 1848); *Barrow in furnace; no.I: a letter to the subscribers to the Common Law Fund in Overend, Gurney & Co., Limited (no.II: a letter to the hero of the story)* (London, 1869); *Overend and Gurney prosecution; in its relation to the public as distinguished from the defendants* (London, 1869); *The prosecutor's protest against judicial despotism and forensic monopoly: addressed to the lord chief justice of England* (London, 1869); *Bane and antidote together . . . , a letter from an octogenarian advocate of inspiration* (London, 1884); *Emmanuel alone, for His own sake through time and space alike* (London, 1885); and *Emmanuel: both the germ and the outcome of the Scriptural alphabets, and the metallic image; with an appendix of individual analogues: a pentaglot miniature* (London, 1885), a work translated into several languages. K.M.B.]

General Register Office (Edinburgh), Register of births for the parish of Brechin, September 1802. General Register Office (London), Death certificate, Adam Thom, 22 Feb. 1890. PAC, MG 24, A27, ser.2, 25–32, 50. PAM, HBCA, A.6/25, 4 March 1840; A.11/95, 31 Dec. 1844; A.12/3, 28 Oct. 1847; A.12/4; D.4/23, 5 Jan., 24 April 1838; D.4/25, 4 July 1838; D.4/44, 10 Dec. 1851 (mfm. at PAC). Begg, *Red River journal* (Morton), 1–148. Charles Buller, "Sketch of Lord Durham's mission to Canada in 1838," PAC *Report*, 1923, app.B: 341–69. *Canadian North-West* (Oliver). Donald Gunn and C. R. Tuttle, *History of Manitoba from the earliest settlement to 1835 . . . and from 1835 to the admission of the province into the dominion . . .* (Ottawa, 1880). J. J. Hargrave, *Red River* (Montreal, 1871). *HBRS*, XIX (Rich and A. M. Johnson). [J. G. Lambton], *Lord Durham's report on the affairs of British North America*, ed. C. P. Lucas (3v., Oxford, 1912; repr. New York, 1970), III. Mactavish, *Letters of Letitia Hargrave* (MacLeod). "Recorder Adam Thom," *Western Law Times* (Winnipeg), 1 (1890–91): 43–47; 2 (1891): 71–72. A. Ross, *Red River Settlement*. *Canadian Courant* (Montreal), 1832–34. *La Minerve*, 1832–38. *Montreal Gazette*, 1832–38. *Montreal Herald for the Country*, 1832–38. *Settler, or British, Irish and Canadian Gazette* (Montreal), 1833. *Vindicator and Canadian Advertiser* (Montreal), 1832–37. *Roll of alumni in arts of the University and King's College of Aberdeen, 1596–1860*, ed. P. J. Anderson (Aberdeen, Scot., 1900), 130. Wallace, *Macmillan dict.* K. M. Bindon, "Journalist and judge: Adam Thom's British North American career, 1833–1854" (MA thesis, Queen's Univ., Kingston, Ont., 1972). George Bryce, *A history of Manitoba; its resources and people*

(Toronto and Montreal, 1906). A. W. P. Buchanan, *The bench and bar of Lower Canada down to 1850* (Montreal, 1925). *Essays in the history of Canadian law*, ed. D. H. Flaherty (1v. to date, Toronto, 1981–). [R.] D. and Lee Gibson, *Substantial justice: law and lawyers in Manitoba* (Winnipeg, 1972). Marcel Giraud, *Le Métis canadien, son rôle dans l'histoire des provinces de l'Ouest* (Paris, 1945). R. St G. Stubbs, *Four recorders of Rupert's Land; a brief survey of the Hudson's Bay Company courts of Rupert's Land* (Winnipeg, 1967). E. M. Wrong, *Charles Buller and responsible government* (Oxford, 1926). F.-J. Audet, "Adam Thom (1802–1890)," RSC *Trans.*, 3rd ser., 35 (1941), sect.I: 1–12.

THOMPSON, SAMUEL, printer, editor, politician, and businessman; b. 27 Aug. 1810 in London, England, youngest of 11 children of William Thompson and Anna Hawkins; m. first in 1863 Elizabeth Cooper (d. 1868); m. secondly in 1871 Mary S. Thomson, and they had one son; d. 8 July 1886 in Toronto, Ont.

Samuel Thompson's father died in the year Samuel was born and his mother used part of a substantial inheritance to obtain a good education for her son in a day-school and then in a commercial academy. When he was 13, however, she lost most of the money in poor investments and Samuel was apprenticed to a printer. Having completed his apprenticeship he entered the timber trade under an older brother, but when two of his brothers decided to emigrate to Canada in expectation of quick wealth from farming, Samuel went along.

Arriving in York (Toronto) in September 1833, the three brothers lived successively in St Vincent, Sunnidale, and Nottawasaga townships in Upper Canada. They bought land in the first but farmed and worked on government road contracts in the latter two. When the brothers finally settled near Bradford in 1837, after two of their sisters had joined them, Samuel left the farm and sought a job in Toronto. Although he had had Reform sympathies since his apprenticeship days and many of his acquaintances in Toronto were Reformers, at the outbreak of rebellion, shortly after his arrival in Toronto, Thompson saw the issue as one of republicanism against monarchy and turned out to defend his sovereign.

Four months' enrolment in the city guards followed the suppression of the uprising, and then Thompson began a long career in the newspaper and printing business. For a few months in 1838 he was the manager of the *Palladium of British America and Upper Canada Mercantile Advertiser* for Charles Fothergill*. When this ceased publication in 1839 he bought a share in the Toronto *Commercial Herald*, but soon sold out, probably because of the strong Orange bias of the paper. At the same time as the sale, he entered into partnership with booksellers William and HENRY Rowsell to manage their printing business, which included the production of the *Church* as well as the *Maple-Leaf; or Canadian Annual, a Literary Souvenir*, to which Thompson submitted prose and verse. Thompson remained in partnership with Henry Rowsell until 1859.

In 1848 Thompson became editor of the *Toronto Patriot* under Edward George O'Brien*. The next year Ogle Robert Gowan* and Thompson took over the paper and they added the semi-weekly *United Empire* in 1852 before dissolving the partnership in 1853 by judicial arbitration. Thompson then bought the *British Colonist*, with two partners, from the widow of Hugh Scobie* and became editor. With the subscription list from the *Patriot* and $5,000 a year from John Hillyard Cameron* to keep the paper independent, the *Colonist* did well; by 1857 it printed four editions including the *News of the Week, or Weekly Colonist*, and had a total weekly circulation of 30,000. The financial panic of that year, however, severely damaged Cameron who ceased his subsidy. Because Thompson had maintained a moderate and independent editorial stand, he was offered support from both political factions. George Brown* and the Grits offered funds to keep the *Colonist* independent but Thompson, a moderate Conservative since the rebellion, turned to John A. Macdonald*. The money Macdonald offered was declined with gratitude, however, when George William Allan* offered support, his only stipulation being that the newspaper had to be a Conservative, but not necessarily a ministry, organ.

Thompson did support the government of Macdonald and George-Étienne Cartier* in spite of this freedom and the move cost him subscribers. In early 1858 the *Colonist* was sold to Daniel Morrison* and George Sheppard*, and in July Thompson was involved in setting up the *Atlas* in Toronto to compete with the *Colonist*. Later in the year he bought back the *Colonist* and merged the two newspapers. In 1858 he also secured the government printing contract and followed the government to Quebec the next year. In 1859–60 he published a cheap newspaper, the *Quebec Weekly Advertiser*, and his job-printing firm operated in Toronto and Quebec. In 1860 he also published *Thompson's Mirror of Parliament*, a forerunner of Hansard. In spite of all this activity the years in Quebec were difficult ones. The legislature reduced the amount of its printing and stiff competition hurt his other business. His creditors kept him going for a year but he finally became insolvent and his firm went under.

His employees were faithful after this set-back and several of them bought most of the firm's assets. Thompson was soon back in business in Quebec with four new partners including Robert Hunter and George MacLean Rose*, who would later form Hunter, Rose and Company. This respite was a short one, however, as Thompson was accused by French MLAS, including Cartier, of having slandered French Canadians in his paper. He lost the support of the government and switched his political allegiance to the alliance which was forming between John Sandfield Macdonald* and Louis-Victor SICOTTE. But he was soon threatened with arson and sold his business in Quebec. Declining a government job, he instead moved back to Toronto in 1860.

Upon his return, Thompson, no stranger to other parts of the business world – he had served as secretary-treasurer of the Toronto and Guelph Railway from 1852 to 1855 – became managing director of the Beaver Mutual Fire Insurance Association. The company, formed a year or two before, was not in a healthy state but Thompson was persuaded to take up the post by his old friend and former partner Henry Rowsell. Until 1876, when legislation compelling insurance companies to deposit a substantial sum of money with the government as security forced the company (after 1869 the Beaver and Toronto Mutual Fire Insurance Company) out of business, Thompson oversaw an expansion from 200 to 74,000 policies. He must have had a good deal of his own money invested in the company because its closing forced him to sell his household furnishings.

There were not many opportunities for Thompson at age 66. The publishing field was closed to him, although he did some writing and his autobiography was partially serialized in *Rose-Belford's Canadian Monthly and National Review* in 1881. His former public service career was long behind him; he had served first as a councillor and then as an alderman for St George's Ward from 1849 to 1854, and was active on various standing committees of the city council including the important finance and assessment committee at a time of substantial growth in the city. In the 1850s he had been vice-president of both the board of trade and the St George's Society.

For a time he contemplated a return to a much earlier career. When he was 71, his second wife, who was from well-connected loyalist stock, purchased land near Saskatoon (Sask.) from a colonization company so Thompson could take up farming. The company failed, however, and he turned to another aspect of his long career, that of bringing knowledge to the people of Toronto. In 1847, as secretary of the Commercial News Room, Thompson had arranged for its union with a new literary society, the Toronto Athenæum, in order to set up a library for the people of the city. In 1855 the Athenæum united with the Canadian Institute, of which Thompson was a member, and provided a free library. When the Toronto Public Library was set up in 1883 Thompson, who had recently lost a chance to become librarian at the University of Toronto because of a change of presidents, applied for the job of interim chief librarian. In his application he pointed out his service in setting up Toronto's first free library and suggested that the libraries of the Canadian and mechanics' institutes be joined with the new one. Though much in need of the money, Thompson was denied the post because of his age and instead was made the manager of one of the library's branches.

On the salary from this position he, his wife, and their young son lived in reduced circumstances but, having survived several personal catastrophes, Thompson did not despair. He communicated with the newspapers on political and national questions, was active in the York Pioneer Society, wrote poetry, and discharged his duties at the library. No doubt the warm reception accorded his memoirs, *Reminiscences of a Canadian pioneer for the last fifty years*, published in 1884, confirmed his belief that the many vicissitudes of his career had not been without value.

RONALD J. STAGG

Samuel Thompson was the author of *Reminiscences of a Canadian pioneer for the last fifty years: an autobiography* (Toronto, 1884; repub. Toronto and Montreal, 1968), the publisher of *Thompson's Mirror of Parliament* (Quebec), 1860, and a contributor to *Maple-Leaf; or Canadian Annual, a Literary Souvenir* (Toronto), 1847–49, and *Rose-Belford's Canadian Monthly and National Rev.* (Toronto), 7 (July–December 1881).

PAC, MG 24, I140. *Mackenzie's Weekly Message* (Toronto), 1 Dec. 1853, 28 Dec. 1855. *Dominion annual register*, 1886. *Early Toronto newspapers* (Firth).

THOMSON, JOHN, physician; b. in 1808, probably in Perthshire, Scotland, son of the Reverend James Thomson and Catherine McKay; m. 17 Feb. 1835 Mary Ann Abrams, and they had nine sons and a daughter who survived infancy; d. 13 Feb. 1884 at Chatham, N.B.

John Thomson's parents brought him as a child to the Miramichi River area of New Brunswick in September 1816. His father, a Secessionist Presbyterian minister in Perthshire, had decided to join the widespread emigration and had accepted a charge in the Newcastle–Chatham area. His son John went back to Scotland to study medicine, and in the early 1830s he received a certificate to practise from the University of Edinburgh. He then returned to the Miramichi and established himself at Chatham. Shortly after his arrival he was appointed medical superintendent of the Seaman's Hospital in Douglastown, a position he would fill for more than 50 years. In 1832 he was put in charge of the quarantine station for immigrants on Sheldrake Island in Miramichi Bay, and again in 1847 headed the station, then located on Middle Island in the same area. In June of that year an immigrant ship arrived from Liverpool; of its 467 passengers, 117 had died in passage and another 100 were incapacitated by typhus when they landed in New Brunswick. The epidemic, which was also carried by other ships, claimed the lives not only of passengers but also of medical workers who met them, including that of Thomson's colleague, Dr John Vondy*.

In his various assignments Thomson lacked the necessary facilities to house or cure the great numbers of diseased immigrants, and his work was also frustrated by impatient shipowners and by the lack of public health regulations in New Brunswick. In July 1848, for example, as health officer for the port of Miramichi, he recommended the quarantine of a vessel because it contained "two cases of typhus fever on board of the worst kind." Quarantine would have delayed the delivery of goods on board and idled the vessel during the height of the shipping season. On the appeal of the shipowners, a magistrate modified Thomson's quarantine order by allowing all the passengers to disembark at Chatham, arguing that "the interest of the Ship owners should suffer as little as possible from detention by the performance of Quarantine." Although boards of health existed in many counties of New Brunswick, they were often inactive and responded to crisis situations without the benefit of established procedures or adequate funding. Only towards the end of Thomson's medical career did the government begin to address itself seriously to the control of communicable disease. In the late 1870s an act was passed establishing county boards of health and providing for the sharing of their costs between the county and provincial governments. Finally in 1887 a provincial board of health was established and the province was divided into health districts.

Ironically, the growing sensitivity with which public health was beginning to be viewed may have prompted the spirited exchange between Thomson and the editor of the *Miramichi Advance* (Chatham) in 1879. The editor criticized Thomson's hospital in Douglastown (the Seaman's Hospital had been renamed Marine Hospital when it had come under the federal Department of Marine and Fisheries at confederation). Thomson's public defence of his work led to a one-third increase in the hospital's budget the following year, funds which permitted renovations to the institution and the reduction of disorderly and unsanitary conditions.

John Thomson's prominence on the Miramichi was a result of many years in practice and of his deep involvement in various community services and societies. Beginning in 1840, he served for more than 20 years as surgeon to the 2nd Battalion of Northumberland militia and in the 1870s and 1880s was a county coroner. He also lectured to the Douglastown Mechanics' Institute and served on the executive of the local Young Men's Christian Association which he helped organize. Throughout his life Thomson played an active role in the Presbyterian St John's Church in Chatham, a Secessionist congregation founded in 1832 by his brother-in-law, the Reverend John McCurdy.

ELIZABETH W. MCGAHAN

PANB, Northumberland County papers, Coroners lists and appointments; file 11/2/8 (papers respecting the establishment of a quarantine hospital on Sheldrake Island, 1832–49). St Andrew's United Church (Chatham, N.B.), Birth records (mfm. at PANB). St James and St John United Church (Newcastle, N.B.), Burial records (mfm. at PANB). Can., Parl., *Sessional papers*, 1877, IV, no.5; 1878, I, no.1; 1879, III, no.3; 1880–81, VI, no.11. *Gleaner and Northumberland Schediasma* (Chatham), 1835. *Miramichi Advance* (Chatham), 1879, 1884. *Union Advocate* (Chatham), 1884. *World* (Chatham), 1884. *Genealogical record & biographical sketches of the McCurdys of Nova Scotia*, comp. H. P. Blanchard (London, 1930). *New-Brunswick almanac*, 1835, 1843, 1865, 1868–84. F. E. Archibald, "Contribution of the Scottish church to New Brunswick Presbyterianism from its earliest beginnings until the time of the disruption, and afterwards, 1784–1852" (PHD thesis, Univ. of Edinburgh, 1933). Esther Clark Wright, *The Miramichi: a study of the New Brunswick river and of the people who settled along it* (Sackville, N.B., 1944). J. A. Fraser, *By favourable winds: a history of Chatham, New Brunswick* ([Chatham], 1975); *Gretna Green: a history of Douglastown, New Brunswick, Canada, 1783–1900* ([Chatham], 1969). W. B. Stewart, *Medicine in New Brunswick . . .* (Moncton, N.B., 1974).

THURSTON, DAVID, lumber dealer and consul; b. in 1818 or 1819 in Massachusetts; m. and had at least three children; last known to be living in 1889 in Toronto, Ont.

In the 1850s David Thurston immigrated to Montreal. Although he stayed there only a short time he did found the New England Society, dedicated to encouraging harmony between Canada and the United States. This aim of amity would become more important in later years as Thurston sought to deal with the international friction of the 1860s. After his brief sojourn in Montreal, Thurston moved on to Toronto where he established himself as a lumber dealer. His success must have been limited because he found it desirable to secure additional income. Thus he was employed by Erastus Wiman* who operated news depots and in 1859 he unsuccessfully petitioned to become a city assessor. In 1861 Thurston gained a new role of minor importance in Toronto.

In the 1860s the United States Department of State began a considerable expansion of its consular service in British North America. A consular agency was opened in Toronto in 1861 and Thurston, still an American citizen, was appointed consular agent. This post, which ranked below that of consul or consul general, required only limited work but Thurston showed an ability to fulfil his duties and, particularly, to attract the attention and approval of people of importance in the community.

At the time he began his service as an American official, relations between the provinces and the United States were subject to considerable friction. On the outbreak of the American Civil War he started to report to the government in Washington on the activities of "disloyal Americans" in the Toronto area. In 1864 his knowledge of Canadian affairs and the reputation he had built up as a "trouble-shooting consul" for the secretary of state, William Henry Seward, were recognized by his appointment as vice-consul at Quebec and vice-consul general at Montreal, in addition to his Toronto assignment. From May to July of that year he was in Montreal acting for the consul general. In October, in the absence of the consul at Quebec, Charles S. Ogden of Pennsylvania, Thurston was in Quebec City busily reporting to Seward not only on the activities of Southern agents in the area but also on the Quebec conference. Later that month he was transferred back to Montreal and he remained there until early January 1865. Thus he was in Montreal on 19 October when a group of Confederates crossed from Canada East into St Albans, Vt, robbed the banks, killing a citizen, and returned across the border. The subsequent capture and release of the raiders [*see* Charles-Joseph COURSOL] resulted in considerable international tension and Thurston was active in consulting with and advising alarmed Canadian officials, who called up 2,000 militia volunteers to police the border.

When the decision was made by Washington in 1864 to open a consulate in Toronto, Thurston's successful application for the post was supported by an impressive group including some American officials, George-Étienne Cartier* and John Hillyard Cameron*, as well as leaders of the Toronto community such as Bishop John Joseph LYNCH and a number of important businessmen. In 1865 an official of the State Department's consular bureau reported that Thurston was "well and favourably" known in the department and that he was a "true, earnest and energetic officer." His annual salary of $1,500 was sufficient to allow him to cease his activities as a lumber merchant. Once again near the scene of action, he had arrived back in Toronto in time to report on the Fenian raid at Ridgeway in June 1866 and on the resultant arrest, detention, and trial in Toronto of a number of American citizens.

In 1869 a new American administration removed Thurston from his post. He retained his American citizenship but decided to remain in Toronto and joined the Beaver and Toronto Mutual Fire Insurance Company, under the managing directorship of Samuel THOMPSON. Thurston was a director in 1869–70 and was a vice-president from 1870 to 1873. By 1876, when the insurance company failed, Thurston had returned to the lumber business, but again he did poorly and within a year he was forced to give up his offices and work from his home.

In 1878, after the American administration had again changed hands, Thurston was appointed vice-consul in Toronto under consul William C. Howells, and this was his major occupation for the next four years. Severe illness forced him to retire from this post as well as his lumber business in 1882. He moved in with his son, a Toronto lawyer, in 1889 and there is no evidence to indicate how long he lived beyond that date.

J. G. SNELL

CTA, Toronto assessment rolls, St James Ward, 1870, p. 52, no.1072. National Arch. (Washington), RG 59, Despatches from the United States consuls in Toronto, 1864–82; Letters of application, 1861–69, D. Thurston file; Miscellaneous letters of the Dept. of State, Telegram, David Thurston to W. H. Seward, 20 Oct. 1864; Telegram, Thurston to Seward, 13 Dec. 1864; Letter, W. M. Jones to Seward, 3 Nov. 1865; RG 84, Instructions to United States consuls in Toronto, 1864–71. *Toronto directory*, 1859–61; 1870–74; 1889. R. W. Winks, *Canada and the United States: the Civil War years* (rev. ed., Montreal, 1971).

TOBIN, JAMES WILLIAM, merchant, politician, and office-holder; baptized 11 May 1808 at Halifax, N.S., the second son of James Tobin* and Eleanor Lanigan; m. 11 Feb. 1834 Emily Cecilia, younger daughter of William Bullen, MD, at Cork (Republic of Ireland), and they had four children; d. 24 July 1881 in London, England.

James William Tobin first appears in Newfoundland in 1828, where his father, a Halifax merchant and a member of the Legislative Council, apparently had business interests. In January 1831 Tobin entered into partnership with John Bayley Bland of St John's to form Bland and Tobin. The firm was involved in the general trade of Newfoundland with Halifax as well as with the West Indies, Madeira, Liverpool, and Quebec. It operated a sailing packet service between Halifax and St John's until the arrival of a steam service in 1844. After his father's death in 1838, Tobin began making frequent trips to Ireland. The partnership between Bland and Tobin was dissolved on 31 Dec. 1839 and Tobin carried on the business with James B. Hutton as James Tobin and Company.

In February 1841 Tobin was appointed to the Executive Council by Governor Henry Prescott*, and he took his seat in April. When the Amalgamated Legislature was inaugurated the following year he was appointed a member. Tobin was not an active participant, however, being absent from St John's for much of the 1840s. During these years the firm of James Tobin and Company (apparently under the management of Hutton, agent at St John's) became heavily involved in the seal-fishery; from a single vessel in 1838 its ships numbered 15 in 1845, the largest fleet at St John's. After 1846, however, the size of the St John's fleet declined, and Tobin was particularly hard hit. In 1847 Laurence O'Brien*'s firm was the largest in the St John's fleet, and by 1850 Tobin was no longer sending vessels to this fishery.

Paralleling the trend in the seal-fishery, the firm's financial position was slipping in the 1840s. The 1846 fire in St John's destroyed Tobin's premises on Water Street. The next year fire again struck the firm and it lost its entire establishment on the south side of the harbour, valued at £3,000 to £4,000. This fire may have been the crippling blow, since it is possible that the Phoenix Assurance Company refused to honour the insurance policy on the buildings. In December 1849 the firm's last outport establishment, fishing premises at Seldom-Come-By on Fogo Island, was sold.

His declining fortunes brought Tobin back to Newfoundland. In 1848 he returned also to the Executive Council when the system of government again became bicameral. The legislature opened its session on 19 Dec. 1848 in a new building owned by Tobin on Water Street which it continued to occupy until 1850. In March 1849 Tobin was being considered for the post of collector of customs and later in that year he was appointed a special stipendiary magistrate and collector of customs for St George's on the French shore at an annual salary of £300. These lucrative appointments were ascribed to Tobin's assistance in the successful election of the British under-secretary of state for the colonies, Sir Benjamin Hawes, in the Irish seat of Kinsale. Tobin's appointment was not popular, however, since he was viewed in both St John's and St George's as an interloper. His independent methods aroused the English Protestant settlers on the coast: there were riots, legal actions (for example, Tobin was fined £150 in December 1852 for acting beyond his authority in arresting a planter who protested the imposition by Tobin of an unauthorized tax), and on one occasion Tobin was stoned. In July 1851 Robert John Pinsent* and Captain George Ramsay had been appointed justices of the peace and sent to St George's by the government to investigate the dissatisfaction of the inhabitants. They recommended to Governor John Gaspard Le Marchant* that the Catholic Tobin be replaced by a Protestant who would be better able to control the situation. Le Marchant feared that such a move would probably be interpreted as sectarian interference, and it was not until 1853 that Governor Ker BAILLIE Hamilton abolished Tobin's offices.

In April 1855 James Tobin presented himself as a candidate for election to the assembly for the district of Placentia–St Mary's. He withdrew, however, when he was appointed to the Legislative Council. In August he became financial secretary in the Liberal administration of Philip Francis Little*, the first after the introduction of responsible government.

In March 1857 Tobin went to London with a joint Conservative-Liberal delegation, having O'Brien, Little, and Hugh William HOYLES also among its members, to protest against the draft fishery convention which had been signed by the British and French governments in January 1857 but which the Newfoundland legislature had refused to ratify. The convention had been designed to alleviate the difficulties arising between French and English fishermen, and eventually Little's party concluded reluctantly that its terms would have to be accepted. But even this reluctant acceptance led Tobin to defect to the Conservatives. He was also thought to be the author of letters which appeared in the London *Globe* implying that the Liberal party was playing into the hands of the French by its interpretation of French rights under existing treaties and that the Roman Catholic bishop, John Thomas Mullock*, being an Irish Franciscan, also sided with the French. Governor Sir Alexander Bannerman* suspended Tobin from his posts in December 1858 after protests in the Executive Council and at public meetings in St John's. Tobin tried in vain for a year to have himself reinstated but he seems to have retired to the British Isles shortly afterwards.

James Tobin became involved in the affairs of Newfoundland for the last time during the pre-emption scandal of 1873. Speculators in London hoped to profit by manipulating the price of shares of the New York, Newfoundland and London Telegraph Company and, through publicity and lobbying, they attempted to pressure the Newfoundland administration of Charles James Fox BENNETT into exercising its right to pre-empt the company. The affair quite quickly turned into a fiasco of political intrigues and accusations between the parties led by Bennett and Frederic Bowker Terrington Carter*. Tobin's role was essentially that of a propagandist, an agent for the speculators.

Tobin returned to England after this final incursion into Newfoundland life and remained there until his death.

DAVID J. DAVIS

PANL, GN 1/3A, 1850–57, file 3, 7 Aug. 1855; GN 1/3A, 1858–59, file 1, 22 Dec. 1858. PRO, CO 194/150; 194/155; 194/167; 197/4. Nfld., *Blue book*, 1850. *Evening Telegram* (St John's), 1881. *Harbour Grace Standard* (Harbour Grace, Nfld.), 1881. *Newfoundlander*, 1831, 1849, 1851. *Public Ledger*, 1851, 1855, 1858. *Royal Gazette* (St John's), 1836–37, 1840–41, 1845, 1847. T. M. Punch, "Tobin genealogy," *Nova Scotia Hist. Quarterly* (Halifax), 5 (1975): 71–81. Prowse, *Hist. of Nfld.* (1972).

TOD, JOHN, HBC chief trader; b. in October 1794 in the Loch Lomond area of Dunbartonshire, Scotland; d. 31 Aug. 1882 at Victoria, B.C.

John Tod was the son of a clerk in the cotton-printing industry, and after a village school education he worked in a cotton warehouse in Glasgow. In 1811 he joined the Hudson's Bay Company and sailed with other apprentices from Stornoway to York Factory

(Man.) in the chartered ship *Edward and Ann.* From 1811 to 1817 Tod was stationed in the Severn District in the vicinity of Hudson Bay. He was at Trout Lake (N.W.T.) in 1814 when he was promoted clerk; the following year he was placed in charge of Severn House. In 1818 he was posted to the Island Lake District (Man.), remaining there until the end of outfit 1822–23.

Tod was posted to the New Caledonia District in 1823 and made the long overland journey from York Factory to McLeod Lake on the west side of the Rockies that same year. With Chief Factor John Stuart* in charge, the party included Tod's fellow officers Donald McKenzie* Jr and Samuel Black*, as well as the usual complement of oarsmen and other servants. The crossing was made by way of Île-à-la-Crosse (Sask.) and the Athabasca and Peace rivers; McLeod Lake was reached after three months' travel.

Tod joined James Murray Yale* at Fort George (Prince George, B.C.) on the Fraser River, spending a year with him before settling at Fort McLeod. (James Douglas* served with him there for the winter and spring of 1825–26.) During the nine years at Fort McLeod, Tod found time to read the many good books he discovered there. He also enjoyed the companionship of "the singing girl," "without whom life in such a wretched place . . . would be altogether insupportable."

Having "experienced much privation in New Caledonia which . . . injured his health," Tod was recalled to Nelson River in the York Factory District where in 1834 he received his commission as chief trader and was granted a year's leave of absence. He sailed for England from Hudson Bay in the company's vessel *Prince Rupert* and on the voyage he met Miss Eliza Waugh, a governess from the Red River District. Shortly after reaching England they were married.

Returning to Rupert's Land by way of New York and Canada early in 1835, the Tods apparently spent the 1835–36 season in the Red River District awaiting a posting. They then moved to Island Lake where Tod took charge of the post in 1836–37. By 1837 Eliza had suffered a mental breakdown and Tod was obliged to take her to relatives in Wales. When he returned to North America he was again posted to New Caledonia and travelled to Fort Vancouver (Vancouver, Wash.) in the autumn of 1838 in charge of the annual brigade. Crossing the mountains by a more southerly route than that taken in 1823, Tod and the brigade started from Norway House (Man.) and travelled by way of the Saskatchewan and Athabasca rivers to Jasper House (Alta). They reached the Big Bend of the Columbia River on horseback, and then travelled by boat to forts Colvile (Colville, Wash.) and Vancouver. Before proceeding to Fort Alexandria (Alexandria, B.C.) on the Fraser River on the border of the Cariboo country, Tod spent a profitable time at the company's farm in the fertile Cowlitz valley.

From 1839 to 1842 Tod served at Fort Alexandria, moving temporarily to Thompson's River Post (Kamloops) after the murder of Samuel Black in 1841. In August 1842 Tod took formal charge of that post. Under his supervision new buildings on the west bank of the Thompson River were completed and old fort was abandoned.

In 1849 Tod obtained a leave of absence on account of ill health and moved to Fort Nisqually on Puget Sound; while there he substituted for Chief Trader William Fraser TOLMIE. Later that same year he crossed Juan de Fuca Strait to Fort Victoria and selected 100 acres of land at Oak Bay for a farm. On furlough from 1850 to 1852, Tod officially retired from the company on 1 June 1852 and settled at Oak Bay. On 27 Aug. 1851 Governor Richard Blanshard* had nominated James Douglas, James Cooper*, and John Tod to the Legislative Council of Vancouver Island. All three took the oath of allegiance and their seats at its first session three days later. Tod served until his resignation in October 1858.

Although Tod's immediate superiors considered him "an excellent Trader" and "a very highly meritorious Officer," he did not progress in his HBC career beyond the rank of chief trader, possibly because he did not find favour with Governor Sir George Simpson*. Simpson admitted that Tod had "claims to promotion" because he was "a good Trader and expresses himself well by Letter." In addition, early in his career, he had established good relations with the Indians. However, Simpson felt that Tod was "not generally liked." Tod's dismissal of postmaster Andrew Wilson in 1833 on a charge of drunkenness that was later proved unfounded may have caused resentment.

In character Tod was a rough diamond, unconventional and radical. Thomas Simpson described him as a man "of excellent principle, but vulgar manners." Yet he was well read and able to play the flute as well as the fiddle. His appreciation of nature and his powers of observation are demonstrated in his letters as well as in his "Career of a Scotch boy," where he reveals himself as a good raconteur. In his correspondence with his friend Edward Ermatinger*, Tod unfolds his love of family, his hopes, his disappointments, and his moral and religious convictions. Towards the end of a long life he became a spiritualist.

Tod's family life was possibly more unconventional than that of most fur-traders. His first country wife was Catherine Birstone in the York Factory area and they had a son James about 1818, and there was "the girl who used to sing at McLeod's Lake" who bore him at least one daughter. Emmeline, who became the wife of William Henry Newton, was the only child of his marriage to Eliza Waugh. He and Sophia Lolo of Thompson's River Post, thought to be the daughter of Jean-Baptiste Lolo*, had seven children. John and Sophia were not formally married until 1863, news of

Eliza's death in 1857 having been much delayed in reaching Victoria.

The house that Tod built in 1851 on his farm at Oak Bay has been designated a heritage house. A creek, a rock, an inlet, and a mountain all commemorate his name.

MADGE WOLFENDEN

John Tod's reminiscences were published as "Career of a Scotch boy," ed. Madge Wolfenden, *BCHQ*, 18 (1954): 133–238.

Anglican Church of Canada, Diocese of British Columbia Arch. (Victoria), Christ Church Cathedral (Victoria), Parish registers, Baptisms, 1836–86; Marriages, 1837–72 (mfm. at PABC). Bancroft Library, Univ. of California (Berkeley), John Tod, "History of New Caledonia and the northwest coast" (transcript at PABC). PABC, Fort Kamloops journal, August 1841–December 1843; J. S. Helmcken, "Reminiscences" (5v., typescript, 1892); Malcolm McLeod coll., R. S. Miles to John McLeod, 2 Oct. 1837; John Tod, "Reminiscences of 1821" (copy); Vancouver Island, Colonial Secretary, Marriage licenses, 1 June 1859–22 Jan. 1867. PAC, MG 19, A2, ser.2, 5 (copy at PABC). PAM, HBCA, A.1/6; A.1/60; A.6/23; A.10/60; A.34/2; B.239/a/6; C.1/285; C.1/915; C.1/925; E.4/1a (transcripts at PABC). *The Hargrave correspondence, 1821–1843*, ed. G. P. de T. Glazebrook (Toronto, 1938). [John McLoughlin], *The letters of John McLoughlin from Fort Vancouver to the governor and committee, [1825–46]*, ed. E. E. Rich and intro. W. K. Lamb (3v., London, 1941–44), I–II. *Minutes of Council, Northern Department of Rupert Land, 1821–31*, ed. R. H. Fleming (Toronto, 1940). "The Nisqually journal," ed. V. J. Farrar, *Washington Hist. Quarterly* (Seattle), 10 (1919): 205–30; 11 (1920): 59–65, 136–49, 218–29, 294–302. Alexander Simpson, *The life and travels of Thomas Simpson, the Arctic discoverer* (London, 1845). Vancouver Island, Council, *Minutes . . . commencing August 30th, 1851, and terminating with the prorogation of the House of Assembly, February 6th, 1861* (Victoria, 1918). *Daily British Colonist* (Victoria), 1 Sept. 1882. *Victoria Daily Standard*, 2, 5 Sept. 1882. H. H. Bancroft, *Literary industries* (San Francisco, 1890). A.-G. Morice, *The history of the northern interior of British Columbia, formerly New Caledonia, 1660 to 1880* (Toronto, 1904).

TODD, ALPHEUS, librarian and author; b. 30 July 1821 in London, England, son of author Henry Cooke Todd; m. in 1845 Sarah Anne St John, and they had four sons and a daughter; d. 22 Jan. 1884 at Ottawa, Ont.

Alpheus Todd came to York (Toronto), Upper Canada, with his parents in 1833. When York was incorporated as Toronto in the following year, Todd, although barely in his teens, produced an engraved plan of the city. His efforts impressed Robert Baldwin Sullivan*, a prominent lawyer, who helped him obtain an appointment to the library of the House of Assembly of Upper Canada in 1835; Todd became assistant librarian the next year. Self-educated, he showed a keen interest in the study of British parliamentary practice and in its application to Canadian and other colonial situations. Five years after his first appointment he published *The practice and privileges of the two houses of parliament*. With the union of Upper and Lower Canada in 1841, Todd became assistant librarian of the Legislative Assembly on 19 September and his book, the only work of its kind, was officially adopted by the assembly for the use of its members.

Early in the summer of 1854 Todd wrote an important paper for the speaker of the assembly, John Sandfield Macdonald*, agreeing with the speaker's controversial objection to the dissolution of parliament by Governor General Lord Elgin [Bruce*] on the advice of the premier, Francis HINCKS. The house had been dissolved before the new session had conducted a single item of business, indeed before it had even finished the debate on the address in reply to the speech from the throne. In his cold, concise prose, Todd cited numerous precedents in British parliamentary tradition from as far back as the Elizabethan era and "amply vindicated" Macdonald's behaviour. Furthermore, the brief by Todd became the model for dozens more that he would write for members from both sides of the house during the ensuing years. The research undertaken for these briefs became an integral part of his monumental writings on British constitutional practice.

On 31 March 1856, Todd succeeded Dr W. Winder as chief librarian of the assembly and Antoine GÉRIN-LAJOIE was appointed his assistant. Todd had recently returned from an eight-month trip to Europe where he had been sent by the legislature to acquire books for the library which had suffered in two disastrous fires. The burning of the Parliament Buildings in Montreal during the riots of 1849 had destroyed all but 200 of the library's 14,000 volumes. Then, early in 1854, when parliament was temporarily located in Quebec City, its buildings were severely gutted. Although close to 9,000 of the 17,000 volumes in the library were saved and moved to the Séminaire de Québec, Todd had to cover the losses and expand the collection. During his trip he secured several hundred volumes as gifts from the British parliament and government, and bought thousands on the market. In France he acquired hundreds more. He returned to Quebec with over 17,000 volumes, having kept well within his relatively meagre budget. Thus Todd had formed the nucleus of a quality collection which by 1865 he had judiciously increased to 55,000 volumes. Late that year Todd took charge of the move to the new, permanent library in Ottawa, employing river barges for transportation. On 1 July 1867, he became librarian of the dominion parliamentary library, a post he held until his death. In 1866 he had published his *Brief suggestions in regard to the formation of local governments for Upper and Lower Canada*, a small work which considerably influenced the constitutions of Ontario and Quebec incorporated into the British North America Act.

Todd's most significant work was undoubtedly *On parliamentary government in England*, published in two volumes in 1867–69. These massive volumes were well received and made him an eminent authority throughout the empire. Indeed the *Edinburgh Review* declared that it was "a remarkable circumstance that we should be indebted to a resident in a distant colony . . . for one of the most useful and complete books which has ever appeared on the practical operation of the British Constitution." The *Westminster Review* called it "the most complete treatise" on royal prerogative and on parliamentary privilege. In his preface Todd indicated that he had misgivings about the increasing "democratic element" in Canada and that "considerable modifications" in British practice would be needed to enable colonial governments "to resist the encroachments of the tide of democratic ascendancy, which is everywhere uprising, and threatening to overwhelm 'the powers that be.' " His treatise thus emphasized the history of executive authority in the British system and "sought to vindicate for the monarchical element its appropriate sphere." The second volume was dedicated to Sir John A. Macdonald* and to the late Thomas D'Arcy McGee*, by whose "lamented and untimely decease" the author had lost a devoted friend. The work was translated into French, German, Spanish, and Italian, and was used extensively in the development of parliamentary institutions in late-19th-century Japan. In 1887–89 a new enlarged edition was published by Todd's son Arthur Hamlyn Todd and in 1892 Spencer Walpole edited an abridged edition.

In 1873 Todd played a major role as special adviser to Governor General Lord Dufferin [Blackwoood*] during the constitutional intricacies relating to the Pacific Scandal and the subsequent fall of the John A. Macdonald government. His second major work, *Parliamentary government in the British colonies* (1880), was dedicated to Lord Dufferin. In it Todd extended his study of responsible parliamentary government from Great Britain to British North America and, in lesser detail, to Australasia and South Africa, and he stressed the continuing constitutional role of the crown and its representative, the governor general. In his lengthy analysis of Canadian federalism he described the provinces as definitely subordinate but clearly recognized the importance of their local autonomy. He was extremely critical in his book of the way in which Macdonald, both before and after returning to office in 1878, had handled the question of the dismissal of Luc LETELLIER de Saint-Just, the lieutenant governor of Quebec. Macdonald, he said, had used "rash and ill considered" parliamentary resolutions, "subversive of kingly authority," as grounds for advising the governor general to dismiss Letellier, when the grave decision should have been that of the governor general in council and should have been accompanied by an explanation of the reasons for dismissal. In 1889 William McDougall*, veteran lawyer and politician, calling *Parliamentary government* "the only book of the kind as yet available to the political student," referred to its author as an industrious man of "gentle, unassuming, patient manner towards those who approached him. French or English, Grit or Tory, Government or Opposition were alike to him when in the quest of information." Todd's son edited an expanded second edition of this work in 1894.

The Marquess of Lorne [Campbell*] wrote in 1887 that he would never forget Todd's "anxious, patriotic and conscientious caution in talking over constitutional questions" with him during his period of office as governor general of Canada, and that Todd was a man of "utter disinterestedness, with clear and impartial and yet deeply held convictions." In 1881 Lorne had personally and successfully recommended him for a CMG. The historian William Kingsford* alleged that it was Macdonald's pique over Todd's "unimpeachable" opinion in the Letellier case that prevented him from receiving a knighthood or a Canadian honour. In the same year, however, Todd received an LLD from Queen's College at Kingston, and he was a founding member of the Royal Society of Canada in 1882. He also had a strong interest in theological studies. He was a minister of the Catholic Apostolic Church, to which he was deeply dedicated. At one point he had two congregations in his charge, one in Ottawa, the other in the United States.

As an authority on the operation of the British parliament, Todd's only contemporary rival was the British writer, Sir Thomas Erskine May. The importance to Canada of his work on the British colonies, however, was soon to be overshadowed by the constitutional writings of Sir John George Bourinot*. Nevertheless, when Sir John Forrest, a senior minister in the Australian government, met Arthur Hamlyn Todd in Ottawa in 1902, he commented to his host, Governor General Lord Minto [Elliot*], that "wherever the British flag flies, every Governor; every Premier; and every Minister is under the deepest obligation to [Alpheus] Todd."

BRUCE W. HODGINS

Alpheus Todd was the author of *The practice and privileges of the two houses of parliament: with an appendix of forms* (Toronto, 1840); *Brief suggestions in regard to the formation of local governments for Upper and Lower Canada, in connection with a federal union of the British North American provinces* (Ottawa, 1866), translated as *Quelques considérations sur la formation des gouvernements locaux du Haut et du Bas-Canada, dans l'union fédérale des provinces de l'Amérique britannique du Nord* (Ottawa, 1866); *On parliamentary government in England: its origin, development, and practical operation* (2v., London, 1867–69), a new edition of which, published in London in 1892 as *Parliamentary government . . .* , was translated as *Le gouvernement parlementaire en Angleterre . . .* (Paris, 1900); *On the position of a constitutional governor under responsible government* (Ottawa, 1878); *Parliamentary government in the British colonies* (London, 1880), a second edition of which was edited by his son A. H. Todd in 1894, and of the article "Is Canadian loyalty a sentiment or a principle?" in *Rose-Belford's Canadian Monthly and National Rev.* (Toronto), 7 (July-December 1881): 523–30.

PAC, MG 24, B30; I140. Univ. of Saskatchewan Library (Saskatoon), Special Coll., A. S. Morton coll., A. H. Todd, "Alpheus Todd, 1821–1884" (typescript, 1923). *Edinburgh Rev.* (London and Edinburgh), 125 (January–April 1867): 578–96. *Westminster Rev.* (London), new ser., 31 (January–April 1867): 527. *DNB*. *Dominion annual register,* 1884: 247–48. William Kingsford, *The early bibliography of the province of Ontario . . .* (Toronto and Montreal, 1892). Morgan, *Bibliotheca Canadensis*, 373–75. E. R. Cameron, "Alpheus Todd," *Canadian Bar Rev.* (Toronto), 3 (1925): 440–47. N.-E. Dionne, "Histoire de la bibliothèque du parlement à Québec, 1792–1892," RSC *Trans.*, 2nd ser., 8 (1902), sect.I: 3–15.

TOLMIE, WILLIAM FRASER, surgeon, HBC officer, and politician; b. 3 Feb. 1812 at Inverness, Scotland, elder son of Alexander Tolmie and Marjory Fraser; m. in February 1850 Jane, daughter of Chief Factor John Work*, and they had five daughters and seven sons, including Simon Fraser Tolmie*, premier of British Columbia; d. 8 Dec. 1886 near Victoria, B.C.

William Fraser Tolmie's mother died when he was three and he spent some years under the "irksome and capricious authority" of an aunt. He was educated at Inverness Academy and Perth Grammar School. An uncle encouraged his interest in medicine and is said to have financed his studies at the medical school of the University of Glasgow for two years, 1829–31. Although almost invariably referred to as Dr Tolmie, he was not an MD: during these two years he worked for credits toward a diploma as licentiate of the Faculty of Physicians and Surgeons of Glasgow, a body independent of the university. Tolmie did well in his studies, won prizes in chemistry and French, and received his diploma in the spring of 1831. He had hoped to study in Paris, but a near-fatal illness prevented him. When he recovered, he served from February to May 1832 as clerk in an emergency cholera hospital organized in Glasgow to cope with the epidemic then raging.

As a youth Tolmie had become greatly interested in botany, a study then closely associated with medicine. This brought him in contact with the famed botanist, William Jackson Hooker, then professor of botany at the University of Glasgow, and with Dr John Scouler, who had made a voyage to Fort Vancouver (Vancouver, Wash.) in a Hudson's Bay Company supply ship in 1825. In the summer of 1832 the HBC was looking for two medical officers for the Columbia District, and through Dr John Richardson*, the Arctic explorer, they consulted Hooker, who recommended Tolmie and Dr Meredith Gairdner*. Tolmie signed in London that September a five-year contract to serve in the dual capacity of clerk and surgeon. As a clerk he would receive an annual salary rising from £20 to £50, and as a surgeon £100 per annum.

Tolmie and Gairdner sailed in the HBC supply ship *Ganymede* on 15 Sept. 1832. The long, tedious, and uncomfortable voyage by way of Cape Horn was to last more than eight months. Tolmie, however, characteristically looked upon the voyage as "an admirable opportunity for self improvement," and undertook a methodical programme of reading that he pursued month after month. In addition to medicine, surgery, and natural history, he studied mathematics, geography, history, literature, and French. Whenever opportunity offered he collected bird and fish specimens, described them meticulously, dissected some, and preserved the skins of others. When the ship called at the Sandwich (Hawaiian) Islands he was able to add botanical notes and specimens to his collection. His voluminous diary of the voyage tells us much also about its author. He was a serious-minded youth, puritanical, and extremely conservative in political and religious opinions. He seems to have totally lacked a sense of humour. All his life he was a tireless worker. At one point in the voyage he found himself dropping into the habit of taking a siesta after dinner and of falling into "an indolent musing mood." "This habit . . . ," he noted in his diary, "has rather been gaining ground on me, and its pernicious effects are perceptible in my studies – it is a very insidious enemy and must be crushed in the bud."

Tolmie arrived at Fort Vancouver in May 1833. There he met Dr John McLoughlin*, chief factor in charge of the Columbia District, and was soon informed that he was to be sent to the northwest coast. He went first to Fort Nisqually (Wash.), then under construction at the south end of Puget Sound, where he expected to take ship for the north, but he remained for six months to tend an injured man. He was soon trading furs with the Indians and showed a marked aptitude for dealing with them. Late in the year he was able at last to leave and he arrived at Fort McLoughlin (Bella Bella, B.C.), a new post on Milbanke Sound, on 23 Dec. 1833. In June 1834 he joined the expedition led by Peter Skene Ogden* that intended to establish a trading post up the Stikine River, beyond the limits of Russian territory. Seeing this move as prejudicial to their trade, the Russians had built a fort at the mouth of the Stikine and refused to allow the expedition's ship to enter. Although the fort, in Tolmie's words, was only a "shapeless mass of logs and planks," Ogden decided not to attempt to force the issue. Later in the summer Ogden moved Fort Simpson from its original location on the Nass River to McLoughlin's Harbour (McLoughlin Bay at Port Simpson, B.C.) and Tolmie's diary vividly recounts the pillaging of the old fort by the Indians. In 1835, while at Fort McLoughlin, Tolmie learned from Indians that coal deposits existed at Beaver Harbour, on Vancouver Island. They were found later to be of poor quality, but it was the first discovery of coal on the island.

Tolmie returned to Fort Vancouver in the spring of 1836 and served as surgeon and manager of the Indian trade there until the spring of 1840. Then for a year he was the HBC travelling agent. Tolmie's contract had expired in 1837 and he had asked for a furlough, but difficulty in securing a replacement caused a delay of almost four years. When notification arrived in 1840 that the furlough would be granted, James Douglas*, deputizing for McLoughlin, informed the governor and committee that he would much regret Tolmie's departure "as in justice to him, I beg to assure you I have had none here who discharged the laborious duties of his two stations of Surgeon and Trader of this place with such zeal and attention."

The delay in the furlough had important consequences. Tolmie was of a deeply religious nature; he had conducted a well-attended Sunday school for Indians at Fort Vancouver and had thought seriously of becoming a missionary. But between 1837 and 1841 American missionaries had arrived, and "considerable revolution took place in my ideas. I saw that Missionary labor amongst the Indians was impracticable and fruitless of good results either to the teachers, or taught. . . ." If he were to become a missionary, "it would be among the poor of some of the large cities at home."

During his eight years in the Columbia District Tolmie developed a keen interest in natural history and the Indians. He sent at least two collections of birds, animals, and Indian artifacts to Scotland, one to the museum at Inverness and the other to Dr Scouler. He was especially interested in native languages and, beginning with the Chinook jargon, "the gibberish by which we communicate with the Indians . . . a vile compound of English, French, American & the Chenooke dialect," had compiled native vocabularies as his travels and transfers brought him into contact with different tribes; in 1839 he sent 17 of these to Scouler, who published them the following year.

Free at last to take his furlough, Tolmie left Fort Vancouver on 22 March 1841. He travelled overland to Upper Fort Garry (Winnipeg) where he had a friendly meeting with George Simpson* and discussed native languages with James Evans*, inventor of the Cree syllabic alphabet. Arriving at York Factory on 4 July, he was promptly put to work preparing furs for shipment to England. Letitia Hargrave [Mactavish*] wrote that "nothing cd exceed his devotion to duties."

Tolmie sailed from York Factory early in September and was in London by mid October. His leave gave him finally the opportunity to spend some time in Paris, in May and June 1842. He studied and observed in hospitals and other institutions, and engaged in many discussions of phrenology, which was then attracting both public and medical attention and in which he had considerable faith. His religious and political convictions were changing; he became somewhat of a universalist or unitarian, and leaned toward Owenite and radical views in politics. His diary, resumed in Paris after lapsing in 1835, shows him as having discussions with Louis-Joseph Papineau*.

Tolmie decided to continue in the HBC service and sailed from London in the *Columbia* on 10 Sept. 1842. While in England he had studied Spanish in the expectation that he would be sent to the company's post at Yerba Buena, on San Francisco Bay, but soon after his arrival at Fort Vancouver in May 1843 letters directed McLoughlin to send him to Fort Nisqually instead. The committee explained that while Tolmie was in London "we had much conversation with him on the subject of farming, to which he seems to have given a good deal of attention." As this letter suggests, Fort Nisqually had changed greatly since Tolmie had known it in 1833. Originally it was intended to be a trading post for the Puget Sound area and a safer navigational base for the company's ships in the coastal trade than the mouth of the Columbia. To these functions others had been added. In 1838, when the HBC licence for exclusive British trade west of the Rockies was due for renewal, the governor and committee had decided that they must strengthen British claims to the territory between the Columbia River and the 49th parallel. One step taken was the organization of a satellite concern, the Puget's Sound Agricultural Company, to conduct farming operations at Fort Nisqually and the Cowlitz River portage. Experience showed that good field crops could be raised at Cowlitz but that the Nisqually area was only suitable for grazing. Livestock could, however, be raised there on a substantial scale. In 1846 there would be 3,180 cattle, 8,312 sheep, and almost 300 horses at Nisqually, and these figures were exceeded in later years.

A second step was the encouragement of immigration to give the disputed area a British population. Immigrants were recruited in the Red River Settlement, and in 1841 a party consisting of 21 families totalling 116 persons set out for the Columbia. Of these, 14 families (77 persons) took up land in the vicinity of Fort Nisqually. But the experiment was a failure. The HBC had no legal title to the land and could only offer a settlement plan that amounted to operating the farms on shares; more fertile and attractive lands were available in the Willamette River valley, south of the Columbia. Tolmie took charge of Fort Nisqually just as the last of the Red River immigrants were departing for the Willamette, and when it had become evident that the influx of American immigrants would soon be so great that it was hopeless to compete with it.

Tolmie had gone to Nisqually in a three-fold capacity: medical officer, Indian trader, and manager of the agricultural operations of the Puget's Sound Company. However, his position was soon complicated by political considerations. A provisional government had been set up in 1843–44 for the Columbia, and American claims to the whole coastal region north to Alaska were being pressed in a militant fashion. The HBC came to terms with the provisional government, and Tolmie was chosen in 1846 to represent the company's settlers and interests in the Puget Sound region. The same year, under the provisions of the Oregon Treaty, the 49th parallel became the international boundary. Oregon was created an American territory in 1848, and its first governor arrived in March 1849.

Tolmie found himself in a position of increasing difficulty. Although the treaty professed to guarantee that "the farms, lands, and other property of every description belonging to the Puget's Sound Agricultural Company" were to be "confirmed," it soon became evident that the local population, viewing the company as a foreign monopoly, was not prepared to honour this provision. The most that the company could hope for was compensation for the properties it would be forced to abandon. Squatters were soon encroaching on the HBC holdings at Nisqually, and Tolmie was subject to harassment of various sorts which continued year after year until compensation was finally paid in 1869. In 1855 the situation was further complicated by the outbreak of an Indian war in Washington Territory (created in 1853) when the governor rashly pressed the cause of settlement. Tolmie was called upon to use his considerable influence with the Indians to protect both the company and the settlers. Yet his very success aroused suspicion; some wondered if the relative immunity of the HBC had not been due to connivance between the British and the Indians.

In 1843, when the governor and committee had directed McLoughlin to place Tolmie in charge at Nisqually, they had also instructed McLoughlin to organize the Puget's Sound Agricultural Company as an establishment distinct from the HBC proper. Tolmie believed that this arrangement stood in the way of his advancement in the HBC and that promotions would most likely go to those serving the parent company. On 31 March 1847 he was promoted chief trader, an appointment he felt was long overdue. Eight years later, on 26 Nov. 1855, he became a chief factor, for which Simpson's personal intervention was largely responsible. In 1857 Tolmie returned to the HBC service when he became a member of the board of management of the Oregon Department. But the company's active days in American territory were obviously numbered if not ended, and in 1859 Tolmie moved to Victoria. In 1861 he was named to the board of management of the Western Department, and from November 1863 he ranked as its senior member. The official date of his retirement from the HBC service was 31 May 1871, but he had been on furlough since 1 June 1870.

Soon after he moved to Victoria the HBC asked Tolmie to stand for the House of Assembly of Vancouver Island. He was elected in January 1860, re-elected in 1863, and was a member until the island colony joined British Columbia in 1866. He was a member of the first board of education, 1865–69, and of the first provincial board of education, 1872–79. He had been a strong supporter of confederation; in 1874 he was elected in a by-election to the provincial legislature, was re-elected in the general election of 1875, but when defeated in 1878 withdrew from public life. Throughout his life he was a temperance advocate, and at a time when such a stand was unusual he favoured extending the franchise to women.

In 1852, two years after his marriage, Tolmie had acquired some acreage on Vancouver Island, and after his move to Victoria with his family in 1859, Cloverdale Farm became the site of his large stone house, the first such private dwelling in British Columbia. On its eventual 1,100 acres he took a keen interest in farming and imported pure-bred stock. His children followed his own energetic and serious routine: his son Simon recalled lessons at 5:20 a.m. with his father, an hour's walk into Victoria, and then a regular day in school. After the death of his wife in 1880, Tolmie became somewhat of a recluse. Except on Christmas Day he took all his meals alone in his library.

Throughout his later years Tolmie's interest in botany and Indian vocabularies continued unabated. At least eight plants of which he collected the type specimen are named after him, and more would have been so named had it not been for the custom of honouring the classifier rather than the discoverer. In 1884, in collaboration with Dr George Mercer Dawson* of the Geological Survey of Canada, he published a collection of Indian vocabularies, aimed at nothing less than the tabulation of "about 211 words of one or more of the dialects of every Indian language spoken on the Pacific slope from the Columbia River north to the Tshilkat [Chilkat] River, and beyond, in Alaska; and from the outermost sea-board to the main continental divide in the Rocky Mountains."

Hubert Howe Bancroft* described Tolmie in 1878 as "rather below medium height, broad-shouldered and stout . . . high forehead, coarse features, round deep-set eyes glittering from under shaggy brows, large round ruby nose." J. S. Galbraith, while placing him below McLoughlin and Douglas, pays tribute to his "amazing capacity to endure irritations with calmness and courage, which won him the reluctant admiration of his most hostile critics." It has been aptly remarked that he was "a solemn man who could turn almost anything into hard work for his conscience." But he was an industrious and completely reliable servant of the companies which engaged him, and an outstanding citizen.

W. KAYE LAMB

[William Fraser Tolmie's papers are in the PABC, Add. MSS 557. They include diaries, which have been published as *The journals of William Fraser Tolmie, physician and fur trader* (Vancouver, 1963), and, in the form of a transcript, "History of Puget Sound and the northwest coast," autobiographical notes written in answer to specific questions from H. H. Bancroft, the original of which is held in Bancroft Library, Univ. of California (Berkeley). Tolmie's writings include: *Canadian Pacific Railway routes; the Bute Inlet and Esquimalt route no.6, and the Fraser valley and Burrard Inlet route no.2, compared as to the advantages afforded by each to the dominion and to the empire* (Victoria, 1877); *On utilization of the Indians of British Columbia* (Victoria, 1885); and *Comparative vocabularies of the Indian tribes of British Columbia with a map illustrating distribution* (Montreal, 1884), which he wrote with G. M. Dawson. Tolmie also contributed vocabularies to John Scouler, "Observations on the indigenous tribes of the N.W. coast of America," Royal Geographical Soc. of London, *Journal* (London), 11 (1841): 215–51. A letter from Tolmie defending the Hudson's Bay Company is in Oregon Pioneer Assoc., *Trans. of the annual re-union* (Salem), 12 (1884): 25–37. The records of the Puget's Sound Agricultural Company are in PAM, HBCA, F.8/1–F.26/1. See also: *Testimonials; Dr W. F. Tolmie* ([Victoria], 1871); S. F. Tolmie, "My father: William Fraser Tolmie, 1812–1886," *BCHQ*, 1 (1937): 227–40; [George Simpson], "Simpson to Tolmie," *BCHQ*, 1 (1937): 241–42; W. H. Stuart, "Some aspects of the life of William Fraser Tolmie" (MA thesis, Univ. of British Columbia, Vancouver, 1948); J. S. Galbraith, "Conflict on Puget Sound," *Beaver*, outfit 281 (March 1951): 18–22, and his *The Hudson's Bay Company as an imperial factor, 1821–1869* ([Toronto], 1957). W.K.L.]

TROOP, JACOB VALENTINE, businessman, shipowner, and politician; b. 28 July 1809 in Granville Ferry, N.S., second son of Valentine Troop and Tamar Bath; m. 11 July 1838 Catherine Fellows, and they had two sons and three daughters; d. 3 Oct. 1881 at Saint John, N.B.

In the late 1830s Jacob Valentine Troop, a merchant in Upper Granville, N.S., moved with his wife and young son to Saint John where he opened a general store on North Market Wharf. Located in a prosperous shipping centre, Troop soon realized that greater profits could be made by acquiring a vessel to transport fish and lumber to the West Indies and to return with sugar and molasses for his store. In 1847 he purchased a half-interest in the 60-ton schooner *Kate*. Later in the same year he acquired the first of several small vessels constructed in Granville Township, mainly by Abraham Young, for trade with the West Indies. Although by 1851 Troop was concentrating on shipping, he had also invested in real estate and was probably involved in some shipbuilding. The agents of R. G. Dun and Company noted in 1854 that he was expanding his business "cautiously and successfully."

From 1847 to 1879 Troop held shares in at least 61 vessels. He owned many of these in partnership with his eldest son Howard Douglas who in 1864 was taken into the firm (known thereafter as Troop and Son): the younger son, Jacob V. Jr., seems to have joined the company only after 1880. In 1864 Troop began a long and profitable association with shipbuilder John Stewart Parker of Tynemouth Creek, Saint John County, when he contracted to have the 669-ton *Bessie Parker* built. In the late 1860s, as trade with the West Indies became less profitable, the firm started acquiring larger vessels for the transoceanic trade and the Troop fleet was soon found in the four corners of the world. Among the vessels Parker built for the Troop fleet in the 1860s and 1870s were the 1,232-ton *Jacob V. Troop*, the 1,544-ton *Howard D. Troop*, and the 1,295-ton *J. V. Troop*. Another prominent New Brunswick shipbuilder, David Lynch*, built numerous vessels for the Troops throughout the 1870s and 1880s, including barques, such as the 1,699-ton *Cedar Croft*, and the ship *Rock Terrace*, the largest of Troop's Canadian-built vessels at 1,769 tons. Troop and Son also acted as commission merchants and ship-brokers. In 1872 R. G. Dun's agents reported that profits for the previous year were "in the neighborhood of $100,000." Troop, they further noted, "is a keen able manager & his son is a hard working shrewd man." Although later reports indicated that the firm had lost several vessels with little or no insurance, they still recorded substantial profits for it throughout the 1870s.

Troop's involvement in other areas was usually limited to pursuits associated with his business and financial concerns. From 1859 to 1871 he served on the managing and arbitration committees of the local chamber of commerce and he acted as port warden in 1862. Fearing that the legislative union of the British North American colonies would hurt the economy of New Brunswick, he decided to enter politics in 1865 to oppose confederation. On 4 March he and Andrew Rainsford Wetmore* were elected to represent the city of Saint John, defeating Samuel Leonard Tilley* and Charles Watters*, and Wetmore served briefly in the cabinet of Albert James SMITH. In the electoral contest of the following year, however, Wetmore joined forces with the pro-confederate Tilley. They defeated Troop and Samuel Robert Thomson*, New Brunswick entered confederation, and Troop never returned to politics. He became involved, to a limited extent, in the financial community of Saint John. A member of the board of directors of the Commercial Bank of New Brunswick in 1865, he was still a small shareholder in 1868, the year the bank failed. He was also one of the first directors of the Maritime Bank of the Dominion of Canada, formed at Saint John in 1872. Perhaps anticipating the problems the bank would encounter before its failure in 1887, Troop remained a director only until 1875.

In 1873 Troop became ill but continued to attend to his business affairs, including the inspection of every vessel before it left port. His death on 3 Oct. 1881 was precipitated by injuries sustained a few weeks earlier when he had fallen into the hold of one of his vessels. He left an estate valued at $110,000.

Estimates of the size of the entire fleet which the Troops had owned in whole or in part since 1847 vary from 84 to 96 vessels and may be incomplete. In addition, Troop and Son had also acted as agents for several shipping lines, including the Cunard Line, the White Star Line, and the Beaver Line. Howard Douglas continued to expand the Troop fleet after his father's death, adding in later years iron and steel vessels built in England and Scotland. In addition he acquired two steamships, also built in Great Britain. The firm, however, began to sustain heavy losses and at the time of Howard Douglas's death in 1912, the only vessel flying the Troop flag, the familiar red "T" in a white diamond on a blue background, was the magnificent four-masted 2,180-ton steel barque, *Howard D. Troop*. It was sold in that year and the era of the Troop fleet was over.

VALERIE SIMPSON

[The early business papers of Troop and Son, Saint John, N.B., were destroyed in the fire of 1877 and no records from the later period have been located. V.S.]

Baker Library, R. G. Dun & Co. credit ledger, Canada, 9: 70, 557k. Maritime Hist. Group Arch., Troop name file. N.B. Museum, G. H. Markham, "Digby biographical notes," 163; Millidge family papers; Parker family, account-books, 1823–86; Troop family file; W. W. White coll. PAC, RG 42, ser. I, 143–46 (mfm. at N.B. Museum). PANB, RG 7, RS71, J. V. Troop, 1881. UNBL, [Raymond Foster], "History of the shipbuilding industry in New Brunswick" (typescript, 1933). *Daily Sun* (Saint John), 3 Oct. 1881. *Saint John Globe*, 3 Oct. 1881. *Pedigree of Troop (Troup), Canada*, comp. J. D. E. Troop ([Sutton West, Ont.], 1974). *The Troop fleet in the days of sail: exhibition arranged by the Department of Canadian History, the New Brunswick Museum, 1960* ([Saint John, 1960]).

Esther Clark Wright, *Saint John ships and their builders* (Wolfville, N.S., [1975]). S. T. Spicer, *Masters of sail: the era of square-rigged vessels in the Maritime provinces* (Toronto, 1968). F. W. Wallace, *In the wake of the wind-ships: notes, records and biographies pertaining to the square-rigged merchant marine of British North America* (Toronto, 1927); *Wooden ships and iron men: the story of the square-rigged merchant marine of British North America, the ships, their builders and owners, and the men who sailed them* (Boston, 1937; repr. Belleville, Ont., 1973). G. B. Kaye, "Saint John heritage; the Troop house; days of sail," *Evening Times-Globe* (Saint John), 10 Nov. 1973. J. R. H. Wilbur, "The stormy history of the Maritime Bank (1872) to 1886," N.B. Hist. Soc., *Coll.* (Saint John), no.19 (1966): 69–76.

TRUDEAU, ROMUALD (he was baptized **Denys-Romuald**), pharmacist, merchant, author, and politician; b. 7 Feb. 1802 at Montreal, Lower Canada, son of François Trudeau and Marguerite Weilbrenner; m. 21 May 1833 Aurélie Paul, a schoolteacher, at Montreal; d. there 14 Jan. 1888.

Romuald Trudeau belonged to a family of the petty bourgeoisie which was hard-working yet impecunious and whose members were generally considered above urban artisans and farmers because of their outlook and education. Trudeau's father had a small retail dry goods and furs business in Montreal; having started without capital, he fell gradually into debt and was forced to liquidate early in 1824.

Little is known about Romuald's childhood. His later writings contain no significant recollections of his district, his family, or his friends. But one thing is certain: he was raised in a nationalistic environment. His family frequently visited that of Louis-Joseph Papineau* and on a few occasions his father even made a public show of sympathy for the Parti Canadien. The nationalistic mood of his family was certainly unlikely to encourage the boy to feelings of loyalty to the British government. It is known that he attended the preparatory classes at the Petit Séminaire de Montréal where in 1812 he began classical studies. A conscientious student, in his final year (Rhetoric) he won the general proficiency prize and the award for French composition. From the Gallican milieu in which he was educated he almost certainly drew a number of ideas that later proved formative.

When his studies were completed in 1820, Trudeau faced a relatively limited choice of careers: the priesthood, the retail business like his father, or the liberal professions. He decided on medicine and for two years trained under René-Joseph Kimber*, who was well known for his nationalistic ideas. While a student in a doctor's office, Trudeau witnessed some of the conflicts and partisan struggles in the colony. The autocratic spirit of the governor, Lord Dalhousie [Ramsay*], and his councils, the House of Assembly's numerous battles concerning expenditures, the question of the division of customs revenues between Upper and Lower Canada, the bitter and difficult dispute over the erection of the diocese of Montreal, were all hotly debated in the city. In 1822, the year in which Trudeau completed his medical studies, the

British merchants' demand for a union of the two Canadas increased the tension and raised a storm of outrage and protest throughout Lower Canada. Undoubtedly affected by these events, Trudeau undertook to keep a personal diary, called "Mes tablettes," whose entries date from 1820 and continue until 1845. This diary, which primarily reports the political context of the rebellions of 1837 and 1838, and occasionally records current economic and scientific developments, takes us to the heart of a tumultuous period.

A career as a pharmacist looked promising and Trudeau decided on it; a few days after his examination on 5 Nov. 1823 he received his licence to practise from the governor. On 21 November he bought "the whole dispensary . . . of Doctor R. J. Kimber for £900," and the following month he was able to open a small shop in Montreal in a rented house near Custom House Square where his father had his business. On 23 Jan. 1824, in the course of a chemical experiment, he suffered a terrible accident, his face being burned and his eyes quite seriously injured. He dictated his first will from his bed; all he had to bequeath was a bundle of old clothes to his brother Eugène. Upon recovery, he continued his work as a pharmacist. Seeing that tourists were coming to Montreal he hastened to organize a small department in his shop for American Indian arts and crafts. He put an advertisement in *La Minerve*, extolling the efficacy of his medicines and the originality of his handicrafts.

A member of the petty bourgeoisie by origin, profession, and marriage, Trudeau identified himself with a social milieu sensitive to French Canadian struggles. Moreover, the agricultural crisis, the inaccessibility of land in the countryside, the dramatic retreat of French-speaking people from the towns and their replacement by the British, and the cholera epidemic from 1832 to 1834, exacerbated hostile national feeling among French Canadians and encouraged popular political agitation. After the British government rejected the 92 Resolutions in 1834, Trudeau lost confidence in Great Britain and turned increasingly to independence as an objective. However, during the Patriote insurrections of 1837–38 he confined himself to a modest, unobtrusive role. Not much involved in any revolutionary organization, he did give material aid to a number of rebels. No doubt he was afraid at that time of upsetting his pregnant wife, who had suffered two miscarriages and who in 1838 gave birth to Lactance, their only child to survive.

After the suppression of the Patriote movement and the abdication of its principal leaders, Trudeau fell in line with the trend of political events. Initially opposed to the union of Upper and Lower Canada, he subsequently rallied to the Reform policies of Louis-Hippolyte La Fontaine* and to the clergy's assertion of ideological hegemony. In 1845 Trudeau bought a three-storey stone house on the corner of Saint-Paul and Saint-Jean-Baptiste streets, in which he set up shop. His patience and thrift during 20 years behind a druggist's counter had finally borne fruit. He then began purchasing land and lending money at eight per cent. The amount he invested was, however, relatively small, barely £500. He also further enlarged his business by adding a small line of religious objects and vestments. By 1850 Trudeau was a prominent druggist in easy circumstances and was thus able to find a place for himself in the Montreal bourgeoisie. He was elected a municipal councillor in 1852 and an alderman from 1853 to 1856. In 1861 he climbed another rung by becoming the president of the Association Saint-Jean-Baptiste de Montréal. Meanwhile he sat on numerous political committees and signed several petitions which brought him to public notice. In 1864, with some Liberals and discontented Conservatives, he formed a committee to oppose confederation. Anxious to have French Canadian institutions functioning in the economy, he participated in founding the Banque du Peuple in 1843, the St Maurice Railway and Navigation Company in 1857, and the Société de Colonisation du Bas-Canada and the Banque Jacques-Cartier in 1861; he was president of the last firm from 1869 to 1875. All this brought him some standing and prestige.

Trudeau's ambitions did not stop there. By establishing closer ties with religious communities and the clergy, he found another way up the social ladder. He had already won the good will of the Sisters of Charity of Providence (Sisters of Providence) in 1843 by supplying them with free medicine. Through his business in vestments and religious objects, he also maintained close relations with the Sulpicians and secured their good will. The minutes of the churchwardens' meetings for the parish of Notre-Dame in Montreal reveal on numerous occasions how this *petit bourgeois* had won their confidence. He served as churchwarden of the parish from 1848 to 1851 and in 1852 was commissioned to render the accounts for the preceding year. By virtue of having been a churchwarden, he was given several other administrative responsibilities within the parish. His open opposition to the Rouges earned him the confidence of Ignace BOURGET, the bishop of Montreal, who in 1858 appointed him treasurer of the Institut Canadien-Français of Montreal. Only his wife's death on 27 March 1866 cast a shadow on his life.

After 1870 the momentum of his progress was halted by the rapid industrialization and urbanization of Montreal, which produced stiff competition among small businessmen and prompted many of those prominent in the old town to move to the fashionable Sainte-Catherine and Sherbrooke streets. Trudeau should probably have relocated on Rue Notre-Dame, where commercial activity was increasingly concentrating, but he was attached to his surroundings and, having prospered in "old Montreal," preferred to remain loyal to his district even though his clientele was steadily dwindling. The financial crisis of 1873 further undermined his prospects and those of his son Lactance, who had recently gone into business. To cover him, Trudeau was obliged to mortgage his house for $4,800 to the Banque Jacques-Cartier. Even so, in 1878 Lactance was bankrupt and had then to resign himself to salaried employment. His death on 24 Jan. 1882 further saddened Trudeau's final years. Forsaken by his daughter-in-law and almost blind, he managed with great difficulty to provide for himself. He died in poverty on 14 Jan. 1888. His last will, drawn up on 18 Oct. 1886, reflected his destitution. The value of his house had been eroded by the $4,800 mortgage and ten years of unpaid interest, and he left liabilities of $1,207.40. In these circumstances his heirs renounced all rights to the estate. His grandson fared little better: starting out as a clerk to a minor retail merchant, he ended up as a commercial traveller.

RICHARD CHABOT

[Romuald Trudeau's diary, "Mes tablettes," at the ANQ-M (M-72-141), records various events of Montreal life from 1820 to 1848; typed copies are also available at the ANQ-Q and the Bibliothèque de la ville de Montréal. R.C.]

AC, Montréal, État civil, Catholiques, Notre-Dame de Montréal, 24 janv. 1882; Minutiers, J.-L. Coutlée, 31 déc. 1888; J.-A.-O. Labadie, 18 oct. 1886, 29 mars 1888; Valmore Lamarche, 17 oct. 1888, 20 févr. 1889. ANQ-M, État civil, Catholiques, Notre-Dame de Montréal, 7 févr. 1802, 21 mai 1833, 19 sept. 1838; Minutiers, Thomas Bédouin, 25 janv., 13 févr. 1824; Joseph Belle, 27 sept. 1845, 8 juin 1848; Narcisse Bourbonnière-Gaudry, 8 mars 1858, 26 oct. 1860; Théodore Doucet, 8 janv. 1870, 28 janv. 1876; Z.-J. Truteau, 19 mai 1833. AP, Notre-Dame de Montréal, Reg. des délibérations du conseil de la fabrique, 1834–77. AVM, Doc. administratifs, Rôles d'évaluation, 1847–88. PAC, MG 24, B2; B22; L3. *La Minerve*, 8 oct. 1829; 4, 7 janv. 1830; 6 juin 1861. *Montreal directory*, 1843–88. Rumilly, *Hist. de Montréal*, II. F.-J. Audet, "1842," *Cahiers des Dix*, 7 (1942): 215–54; "Toussaint Trudeau, 1826–1893," *BRH*, 47 (1941): 182–86. L.-P. Desrosiers, "Mes tablettes," *Cahiers de Dix*, 12 (1947): 75–92.

TRUDEL, FRANÇOIS-XAVIER-ANSELME (baptized **François-Anselme**), lawyer, journalist, and politician; b. 28 April 1838 at Sainte-Anne-de-la-Pérade (La Pérade), Lower Canada, son of François-Xavier Trudel and Julie Langevin; d. 17 Jan. 1890 in Montreal, Que.

The Trudel family emigrated from France in the 17th century and settled at L'Ange-Gardien near Quebec. François-Xavier-Anselme Trudel's father was a prosperous farmer in Sainte-Anne-de-la-Pérade, and his grandfather, Olivier Trudel, represented the county of Champlain in the Lower Canadian assembly from 1830 to 1838.

François-Xavier-Anselme Trudel entered the Séminaire de Nicolet in 1852. During his student years he seems to have shown interest in literature and in the various oratorical exercises then part of the classical programme. If a former classmate is to be believed, Trudel did not wait until he had finished his studies to make his début in journalism; he and some comrades became involved in a controversy with *Le Pays*, the main Liberal newspaper in Montreal. Young Trudel used this opportunity to defend zealously the religious principles instilled in him at the seminary, and to proclaim his unshakeable attachment to the Roman Catholic Church and its clergy. Although he abandoned the idea of joining clerical ranks, he remained committed to militant Catholic action throughout his life.

On completing his classical education in 1859, Trudel commenced studies at François-Maximilien BIBAUD's law school, articling with the firm of Charles-André Leblanc* and Francis Cassidy*, and then with Moreau, Ouimet et Morin. In December 1861 he was licensed to practise and embarked on what was to be a lengthy legal career. Originally in partnership with Paul Denis, an MLA, he later worked with Napoléon Charbonneau and Gustave Lamothe. While carrying on his profession he engaged in other pursuits, particularly journalism and politics. He was also active in literary societies, and wrote a number of essays.

Trudel's involvement in a wide variety of fields did not, however, result in intellectual and ideological fragmentation. On the contrary, his thinking and action reflected certain fundamental values which seem to have varied little in the course of his career as a writer, journalist, lawyer, and politician. These values, which other contemporary intellectuals shared, in their turn fitted into the conceptual framework known as ultramontane ideology. As a school of thought, ultramontanism, in the 19th century, denoted the tenets of the declared supporters of papal supremacy, and therefore of clerical supremacy in every sphere, whether religious, political, or social. Formulated in Europe by laymen such as Joseph de Maistre and priests such as Hugues-Félicité-Robert de La Mennais, and publicized by Louis Veuillot's newspaper *L'Univers* (Paris), this ideology was adopted and disseminated in Quebec in the mid 19th century by an influential group of clerics whose activity was supported by a no less influential group of French Canadian laymen including Cléophas Beausoleil*, Siméon Pagnuelo*, and Alphonse Desjardins*. This group, recruited primarily from the professional bourgeoisie, consisted of journalists, writers, and lawyers, who were also politicians, as was often the case in that period. Flaunting staunchly conservative political and social views, these intellectuals waged a bitter struggle, alongside such ultramontane clerical leaders as Ignace BOURGET and Louis-François Laflèche*, to ensure the victory of the fundamental principles underlying the political-religious ideology they were defending.

The body of ultramontane doctrine that inspired Trudel's thought and action had both political and religious dimensions whose main lines are easy to define. The political doctrine – which is central to the ultramontane frame of mind – is based on a number of assumptions about the respective attributes and powers of church and state. The church is an institution of divine origin which holds its powers from God, and thereby partakes of the very nature of its founder; the state is a human institution whose relationship with God is only indirect, hence it is subject to the limits and weaknesses inherent in human nature. The church, a perfect society, is infallible in all things (and Ultramontanes such as Trudel were quick to extend its infallibility beyond religious questions to political and social ones). The state, an imperfect society, is fallible. Finally, the church works on the supernatural plane and seeks an eternal good, the salvation of man. The state operates only on the natural plane, and seeks material, therefore precarious and perishable, goods.

According to this political creed, the state is perceived as distinctly inferior to the church in its nature and attributes, and in the objectives it pursues, hence the necessity for it to submit to the orders of the church, and to respect the integrity of the church's rights, in return for the latter's guarantee to recognize the legitimacy of the role of the state and of the power it exercises over those it governs. This interpretation of the church-state relationship is central to the ideological confrontations and struggles that marked Trudel's eventful career as a militant Ultramontane.

In his college years young Trudel had already pitted himself against the editors of the paper *Le Pays* in defence of his religious convictions. Even before he had finished articling, he had a further opportunity to demonstrate his ability as a journalist in articles he wrote for *La Minerve* of Montreal in 1859. During the following year he held the position of editorialist for about six months. Subsequently, he seems to have contributed, albeit sporadically, to Montreal papers of ultramontane leanings such as *Le Nouveau Monde* and *Le Franc-Parleur*. It is, however, difficult to assess the true extent of his association with these papers.

In fact, although a number of articles published in the ultramontane press apparently drew inspiration from Trudel's thinking, and included, sometimes in full, passages from pamphlets he had written, the contemporary custom of leaving articles unsigned makes it impossible to identify the author with certainty. On the other hand, it is easier to determine what Trudel contributed to literary journals which none the less had a religious character, such as the *Revue canadienne* of Montreal; a founder and co-owner of this periodical, he published several articles concerning the respective powers of church and state in 1870 and 1871. He also contributed occasionally to *L'Écho du Cabinet de lecture paroissial* (Montreal), a bulletin launched in 1858 under the patronage of the Sulpicians to further the work of their Cabinet de Lecture Paroissial, which had been founded the year before with the object of countering the influence of liberal literature considered anti-Christian and harmful to young people.

Trudel's literary and journalistic activity was therefore wide-ranging, although it did not go outside his usual ideological framework. At the beginning of the 1860s he wrote three essays on diverse topics for *L'Écho du Cabinet de lecture paroissial*. In 1861 he published "Les Destinées du peuple canadien," in which he broadly sketched the historical evolution of the country through an analysis based principally on moral and spiritual criteria. In 1862 Trudel completed a moral essay entitled "La Tempérance au point de vue social," and, a year later, a study on "Frédéric Ozanam et son œuvre," in which he paid tribute to one of the pioneers of Catholic social action in France. During the 1860s, Trudel was also particularly active in organizations and literary circles founded out of a sense of commitment to Catholicism and militant action. Hence from 1860 to 1869 he served as president of the literary circle attached to the Sulpicians' Cabinet de Lecture Paroissial, and also in this period of the Union Catholique de Montréal, a literary organization founded by the Jesuits in 1854 to counter the liberal influence of the Institut Canadien of Montreal. It was at this time that Trudel, seeking more effective action, conceived the idea of gathering various literary circles with similar commitments under one banner. With this in mind, in 1869 he drafted a *Mémoire sur la question de fusion des sociétés littéraires . . .* , in which he made a proposal to bring literary and professional associations together into one large body to be presided over jointly by clergy and laity. This plan does not, however, seem to have been implemented.

Two years earlier, in 1867, this lawyer and man of letters had spent several months in Europe, visiting England, France, and Italy. He may have taken this trip for cultural reasons or simply for relaxation. In any case, he seems to have taken advantage of his stay in each of these countries to establish contacts with Catholic leaders and writers whose political and religious convictions resembled his own. On his return to Canada that year, Trudel had another opportunity to give practical expression to his values and principles. He served on the committee created by Bishop Bourget to recruit the rudiments of an army of young volunteers willing to defend the papal states against the Italian nationalist armies under Giuseppe Garibaldi. The recruiting of the Papal Zouaves was the first of a series of undertakings in which ultramontane church authorities, beginning with Bishop Bourget and Bishop Laflèche, would call on Trudel for assistance.

In 1870, the Guibord affair gave Trudel the chance to place his talents as a lawyer at the service of his ultramontane ideal. The death of printer Joseph Guibord*, a friend of well-known Liberals and a member of the Institut Canadien, was the signal for another major confrontation between the ultramontane group and its opponents, the Rouges, whose radicalism it regarded as an imminent threat to Catholicism in Quebec. During the famous lawsuit to which the burial of Guibord gave rise in 1870, Trudel agreed to represent the parish council of Notre-Dame, in association with Louis-Amable Jetté* and Francis Cassidy. The pleadings of the ultramontane lawyers essentially defended the right of the parish council to refuse to bury Guibord's remains in a Catholic cemetery. However, the arguments, in particular those advanced by Trudel, rapidly transcended the case and attacked fundamental problems, especially relations between church and state. The ideas expounded on this subject supplied material for an essay he published a year later in the *Revue canadienne* entitled "Quelques réflexions sur les rapports de l'Église et de l'État." In it Trudel ransacked biblical and profane history to illustrate the doctrinal bases of the supremacy of church over state. Thus, in all cases of joint jurisdiction where the limits of civil and ecclesiastical authority were inadequately defined – a category in which the Guibord affair could be classified – it was necessary, Trudel stated, to distrust the pretensions of the state, which was "constantly tempted to claim [such cases] as belonging to its exclusive jurisdiction." His solution was never to lose sight of the fact that "there exists in all truth a Catholic and therefore Christian maxim [which affirms] the primacy or rather the *supremacy of the church over the state*. . . ."

It was this doctrine which in 1871 inspired the *Programme catholique* which Trudel helped to draft. Published in *Le Journal des Trois-Rivières*, on 20 April 1871, the programme constituted a manifesto for the provincial elections already set for the summer; it required future candidates to promise formally to "change and modify [the laws] as our lord bishops of the province might request, in order to bring them into harmony with the doctrines of the Roman Catholic Church." Trudel had not developed the programme by himself; some of the best known Ultramontanes of the time, such as Pagnuelo, Beausoleil, Desjardins, Magloire McLeod, Adolphe-Basile Routhier*, and Benjamin-Antoine Testard* de Montigny, had had a hand in drawing it up. There is every indication, however, that he took a leading role, since not only did the *Programme catholique* give concrete form to the arguments he publicly defended during the Guibord affair and in the *Revue canadienne*, but it was to Trudel especially that bishops Bourget and Laflèche gave official encouragement, as an electoral candidate, to persevere in the course laid down in the programme. This course proved to be especially difficult because those candidates known as the "Programmistes" had managed to alienate even the Conservatives, who were worried about the negative electoral effects of what they interpreted as an instrument of blackmail against their party. In the event, the Conservative vote was apparently not unduly affected by the ultramontane propaganda, since the government of Pierre-Joseph-Olivier CHAUVEAU was returned to office and Trudel was the only one of the programme's candidates elected. He represented his native county of Champlain in the Legislative Assembly until June 1875.

The provincial elections of 1871 were the prelude to a political career for Trudel extending over about two decades, during which time he performed various duties. In 1875, while he was still serving as an MLA, he was appointed queen's counsel in the province of Quebec, and five years later was given the same appointment by the federal government. At the end of October 1873 he had become senator for the division of Salaberry when his father-in-law, Louis Renaud*, gave up this seat; Trudel retained it for the rest of his life. During his tenure he paid particular attention to defending and justifying the existence of the Senate, which some groups sought to modify and others to abolish. To that end he published a report in 1880 entitled *Nos chambres hautes: Sénat et Conseil législatif* in which he warned abolitionists of the danger in removing an institution which he saw as an effective bulwark against the rising tide of liberalism.

The struggle against liberalism was not, however, enough to cement a durable alliance between Trudel and the Conservative party, led since 1878 on the provincial level by Joseph-Adolphe Chapleau*. The intractable ultramontanism of a Trudel could not accommodate itself to certain compromises to which the exercise of power sometimes led the Conservatives, who were often accused of being spineless in their responses to Liberal offensives, and even of betraying the Conservative cause itself. This disagreement on principles became conspicuous again during the quarrel between Montreal and Quebec over the university question [*see* Bourget; Joseph DESAUTELS]. As in the Guibord affair, Trudel was to be a central figure in the stormy debate which surrounded this issue. Indeed he and Pagnuelo, another well-known ultramontane lawyer, were chosen by the Montreal School of Medicine and Surgery, which was ultramontane in its allegiance, to defend the cause of its autonomy before the provincial private bills committee in May 1881. This committee had to determine the validity of a draft bill respecting the Université Laval "for the purpose of increasing the number of its chairs of Arts and other Faculties, within the limits of the province of Quebec." With the manifest support of some of the bishops, and in particular of Bourget and Laflèche, Trudel vigorously denounced the monopoly that he thought Laval was demanding to the detriment of the freedom of education sought by Montreal. Besides, would not centralization and standardization of teaching likely prepare the way for the eventual interference of the state in a sphere where, as in Europe, it was seeking to usurp the rights of the clergy? Trudel's speech appeared in a publication entitled *Projet de loi de l'université Laval devant le comité des bills privés*. The addresses by the counsel for the Montreal School of Medicine and Surgery failed to get the Laval bill thrown out. Nevertheless, Trudel refused to admit defeat, and after the bill was passed he set off for Rome in 1881, in an unsuccessful last attempt to block the hotly contested law. Three years later he became a member of a committee of citizens organized to fight the Laval bill, albeit with little success.

During the 1880s the gulf between the Ultramontanes and the Conservative party continued to widen. Although he was an uncompromising ultramontane leader, Trudel did make one last attempt at *rapprochement* before the final rupture. This, at any rate, is a possible interpretation of his article entitled "La Conciliation" in the *Revue canadienne* in 1881. In it, Trudel made a vigorous plea for conservatism, at all levels, whether in relations between church and state, in education, or in the programmes of politicial parties. As far as political parties were concerned, he stated, their differences were based on points of view that were divergent but not irreconcilable as long as they all wanted to secure the triumph of the fundamental principles of justice, peace, and charity.

But this policy of the outstretched hand does not seem to have yielded the anticipated results. A year later the ultramontane wing of the Conservative party published, under the pseudonym Castor, a pamphlet entitled *Le Pays, le Parti, et le Grand Homme*, which was a catalogue of the numerous grievances of the Ultramontanes against the Conservative party, and in particular their leader in Quebec, Premier Chapleau. He was taken to task fór, among other things, his many concessions to the Liberals, his political opportunism, and especially the improper dealings of the "clique" of politicians and businessmen which he had gathered around him. Although they were unable to confirm it – since the author had taken cover in anonymity – some contemporaries suspected two or three of the ultramontane leaders of being behind the pamphlet. Naturally, among those whose names were put forward was Trudel. Had not this "grand vicar," this "lay monk," as his enemies took ironic pleasure in dubbing him, already taken up his pen for the ultramontane cause on many occasions? The anonymity was well guarded, for although they suspected him his opponents were unable to find certain proof of their suspicions.

A year later, in 1883, Trudel made another gesture that might suggest he was the undisputed lay leader of the "Castor" wing, which the Conservative party increasingly considered as dangerous as the Liberal opposition. His gesture of defiance was the launching at Montreal of a newspaper, which, at least at its inception, was primarily intended to speak for Catholics. Initially called *L'Étoile du matin*, it was finally named *L'Étendard*. There had been some initial difficulties in getting Trudel's paper published; indeed, suspecting a hostile manœuvre against them, the Conservatives had managed to mobilize a number of ecclesiastical leaders to oppose its creation. These clerics, and in particular the bishop of Montreal, Édouard-Charles Fabre*, had tried in vain to persuade Trudel to give up his project. Co-owner of the paper with Testard de Montigny, a former Zouave, Trudel was also both its manager and editor.

By plunging immediately into the fray concerning the problems that mattered most to the Ultramontanes, *L'Étendard* amply justified the fears that Chapleau's party had had about it. Whether it was dealing with the Montreal School of Medicine and Surgery, impending elections, or the government's financial transactions, the "Castor" paper never hesitated to criticize, and made denunciations right and left. But it was principally with *Le Monde*, also in Montreal, that *L'Étendard* became involved in the most violent controversies. One of these led Trudel to institute a lawsuit in 1889 that created a great stir. The pleadings of counsel, published under the title of *Questions de libelle*, present Trudel's accusations, as plaintiff, that *Le Monde* had sought to destroy the personal reputation of himself and his ultramontane colleagues.

L'Étendard was the result of a prolonged disagreement between Trudel and the Conservatives. A final break did not occur, however, until 1886, when Trudel supported the Parti National of Honoré Mercier*. The Riel affair appears to have been the last of a long succession of ultramontane grievances against the Conservatives: judging their stance too cautious, Trudel and the "Castors" broke away from them to align themselves with the Liberals (moderate Liberals, to be precise) that Mercier's party brought together under the banner of nationalism.

On 17 Jan. 1890 the life of one of the men most deeply engrossed in the political and religious problems of his age came to an end. Conservatism, whether ideological, political, or social, was certainly a constant thread throughout the militant existence of Trudel, who died abruptly at the age of 51. On 27 April 1864 in Montreal he had married Zoé-Aimée, the only daughter of Louis Renaud, the marriage being solemnized by Bishop Ignace Bourget. At his death, he left four children (three others had died during his lifetime). The eldest, Henri-Louis-François-Xavier-Édouard, became editor of *L'Étendard* when his father passed away. His wife, with whom he had had differences in public, outlived him by 25 years, dying on 24 April 1915.

NADIA F. EID

François-Xavier-Anselme Trudel was the author of: *Mémoire sur la question de fusion des sociétés littéraires et scientifiques de Montréal* (Montréal, 1869); "Quelques réflexions sur les rapports de l'Église et de l'État," *Rev. canadienne*, 8 (1871): 202–20, 252–72, 359–74; *Nos chambres hautes: Sénat et Conseil législatif* (Montréal, 1880); *Projet de loi de l'université Laval devant le comité des bills privés, 20 mai 1881* (n.p., [1881?]); "La Conciliation," *Rev. canadienne*, 17 (1881): 77–85, 147–58; *Le Pays, le Parti et le Grand Homme* (Montréal, 1882); and *Questions de libelle* (Montréal, 1889).

Cour supérieure, Montréal; plaidoiries des avocats: in re *Henriette Brown* vs. *la fabrique de Montréal; refus de sépulture* (Montréal, 1870). Charles Langelier, *Souvenirs politiques [de 1878 à 1896]* (2v., Québec, 1909–12), [II]: 21–22. *L'Opinion publique*, 13 janv. 1881. *Rev. canadienne*, 3e sér., 3 (1890): 126. F.-J. Audet, *Les députés de Saint-Maurice et de Champlain*, 69–70. Beaulieu et J. Hamelin, *Journaux du Québec*; *La presse québécoise*, I: 56, 221. [F.-]M. Bibaud, *Le panthéon canadien; choix de biographies*, Adèle et Victoria Bibaud, édit. (2e éd., Montréal, 1891). Borthwick, *Hist. and biog. gazetteer*, 337–38. *Canadian biog. dict.*, II: 125–26. J. Desjardins, *Guide parl.*, 187, 253. Terrill, *Chronology of Montreal*. L.-O. David, *Mélanges historiques et littéraires* (Montréal, 1917), 61–63. "Les disparus," *BRH*, 34 (1928): 711. Grégoire Le Solitaire [ ], "Hon. F. X. A. Trudel," *Le Monde illustré* (Montréal), 16 févr. 1901: 700–1. É.-Z. Massicotte, "La famille du sénateur F.-X.-A. Trudel," *BRH*, 41 (1935): 615–23.

TUPPER, CHARLES, Baptist minister, educator, and author; b. 6 Aug. 1794 in Cornwallis Township, Kings County, N.S., son of Charles Tupper, a farmer, and Elizabeth West; m. first in 1818 Miriam Low, *née* Lockhart, and they had five children; m. secondly in 1852 Mary Miller; m. thirdly in 1868 Betsy Knowles, *née* Dimock; d. 19 Jan. 1881 at Tremont, Kings County, N.S.

Charles Tupper's parents had immigrated to Nova Scotia from Connecticut in the early 1760s. After farming for a short time, Tupper in 1813 began teaching in Cornwallis, although his own formal education was limited. The Tupper family had been Presbyterian but came increasingly under the influence of the Reverend Edward Manning*, the Baptist minister at Cornwallis. Following a period of great doubt and uncertainty, Tupper went through a conversion experience in February 1815 and was baptized by immersion on 14 May of that year. His conversion profoundly changed his life as he felt an almost immedate call to the ministry. He began preaching in 1816, since at that time there were no formal qualifications for the Baptist ministry in the Maritimes, and on 17 July 1817 was ordained by a council composed of laymen of the Horton and Cornwallis churches and the ministers Edward Manning and Theodore Seth Harding.

Tupper's active ministry lasted for 55 years, during which time he held pastorates in Nova Scotia, New Brunswick, and Prince Edward Island. He remained only a short time at most of these places and frequently returned to the Amherst, N.S., region where after 1821 he maintained a home and small farm. While serving on these pastorates, he often taught school to augment his meagre and uncertain minister's salary. A meticulous man, Tupper kept careful account of his activities and at the end of his career was able to record that in his ministry he had preached 8,191 sermons, attended 7,482 church-related meetings, and made 16,585 visits to church families.

Tupper's chief importance to the Baptist denomination, however, lay less in his pastoral work than in his other church-related activities. In 1824 he began to advocate total abstinence, a view that would not be popular in the Maritimes for a number of years. He established some of the first temperance societies in Nova Scotia and New Brunswick in 1829–30, and remained a devoted advocate of the principle for the rest of his life. In 1825 Tupper had begun his writing career, an activity that would occupy increasingly large amounts of his time. Realizing the growing importance of the press, he was foremost among those who advocated the establishment of a denominational paper to present the Baptist viewpoint and to act as a link for the scattered Baptist communities. When in 1826 the Baptist associations of Nova Scotia and New Brunswick agreed jointly to sponsor such a publication, Tupper was appointed first editor of the *Baptist Missionary Magazine of Nova-Scotia and New-Brunswick* (Saint John, N.B.), a post he held from 1827 to 1833. For the rest of his life he regularly contributed articles on temperance, education, missions, and Baptist history to church newspapers in the Maritimes, becoming one of the major apologists of the faith. He was also a leading advocate of Baptist union and was instrumental in the formation in 1846 of the Baptist Convention of Nova Scotia, New Brunswick, and Prince Edward Island.

Tupper seemed happiest during his frequent tours through the Maritimes, when he preached and collected subscriptions for the magazine or funds for the Nova Scotia Baptist Education Society. In June 1825 he became the first ordained Baptist minister from Nova Scotia to visit Prince Edward Island. He made another tour of the Island in 1827 and in 1833–34 served as pastor of churches in Bedeque and Tryon.

He was also deeply interested in education. Possessed of a fine mind, he virtually educated himself; by 1859 he had developed a reading knowledge of ten languages. As early as 1824 Tupper had urged the establishment of an institution of learning for Nova Scotia Baptists who were at the time excluded from Anglican King's College in Windsor. As first vice-president of the Baptist Education Society, he was a key figure in the establishment in 1828 of Horton Academy in Wolfville, N.S. When ten years later the academy was expanded to become Queen's (Acadia) College, Tupper worked with Edmund Albern CRAWLEY and others to support its growth. In addition, in 1838–39 and again in 1842 he served as interim principal of the Fredericton Seminary, the co-educational school of New Brunswick Baptists. In 1857 Acadia College awarded him the honorary degree of DD.

Tupper was one of the earliest advocates of an active role for Maritime Baptists in the foreign mission field, especially in Asia, and for many years he served on the Baptist convention's Board of Foreign Missions. Among Tupper's writings were books and pamphlets, including *Baptist principles vindicated: in reply to the Revd. J. W. D. Gray's work on baptism* (1844), a militant defence of his church's mode of baptism, and *Prohibition and anti-prohibition: being a series of letters . . . in favor of prohibition, and replies to the same, by John Bent* (1856), which illustrated the Baptist view of temperance as a religious issue. He sometimes became embroiled also in political controversies, and in 1837 was accused of "vasalating hypocritical" conduct because he had spoken his mind freely concerning the candidates and issues in a Cumberland County election. His son, Charles*, was to become a leading Conservative in Nova Scotia and Canada.

Tupper saw the Baptist denomination in the Maritimes grow from 12 ministers, 26 churches, and 1,207 members in 1815 (the year of his conversion) to 195 ministers, 348 churches, and almost 39,000 members in 1880 (the year before his death). He himself was one of the most important Baptist figures in the 19th-century Maritimes, and his preoccupations with education, the training of the ministry, religious and secular journalism, temperance, and missionary work closely reflected the concerns of the broader Baptist community. An obituary lamented that "A great man and a standard bearer in Israel has fallen. . . ."

BARRY M. MOODY

Charles Tupper was the author of *Baptist principles vindicated: in reply to the Revd. J. W. D. Gray's work on baptism* (Halifax, 1844) and *Prohibition and anti-prohibition: being a series of letters . . . in favor of prohibition, and replies to the same, by John Bent* (Saint John, N.B., 1856). Further works by Tupper are listed in "Manual of Baptist authors," comp. W. E. McIntyre (5v., typescript, 1905) at Acadia Univ. Arch., Atlantic Baptist Hist. coll.

Atlantic Baptist Hist. coll., Edward Manning corr., 1778–1859. PANS, MS file, "Cumberland squabbles" (letter from A. S. Blenkhorn, Minudie, to the Reverend Charles Tupper re voting, 25 June 1837). *Christian Messenger* (Halifax), 1863–81. *The Acadia record, 1838–1953*, comp. Watson Kirkconnell (4th ed., Wolfville, N.S., 1953). Eleanor Tupper, *Tupper genealogy, 1578–1971* (Beverly, Mass., 1972). I. E. Bill, *Fifty years with the Baptist ministers and churches of the Maritime provinces of Canada* (Saint John, 1880). T. D. Denham *et al.*, *The history of Germain Street Baptist Church, Saint John, N.B., for its first one hundred years, 1810–1910* (Saint John, 1910). A. W. H. Eaton, *The history of Kings County, Nova Scotia* . . . (Salem, Mass., 1910; repr. Belleville, Ont., 1972). M. A. Gibson, *Along the King's highway* (Lunenburg, N.S., 1964). G. E. Levy, *The Baptists of the Maritime provinces, 1753–1946* (Saint John, 1946). R. S. Longley, *Acadia University, 1838–1938* (Wolfville, 1939). *Memorials of Acadia College and Horton Academy for the half-century, 1828–1878* (Montreal, 1881). E. M. Saunders, *History of the Baptists of the Maritime provinces* (Halifax, 1902).

U

UNE FLÈCHE. *See* KĀPEYAKWĀSKONAM

V

VAIL, EDWIN ARNOLD, physician and politician; b. 19 Aug. 1817 at Sussex Vale (Sussex Corner), N.B., son of John Cougle Vail and Charlotte Hannah Arnold; m. first in 1842 Frances Charlotte Cougle, and they had two sons and two daughters; m. secondly in 1873 Harriet Courtland Murphy, and they had two daughters; d. 31 July 1885 at Sussex, N.B.

Edwin Arnold Vail was a member of a prominent loyalist family. His maternal grandfather, the Reverend Oliver Arnold*, had been the first Church of

England rector of Sussex Vale, and his father represented Kings County in the New Brunswick assembly for some 16 years and later served as county registrar. Educated in the local public school, in the early 1830s Vail went to Edinburgh and Glasgow to study medicine and in 1837 was granted an MD degree by the University of Glasgow. He returned to his home town and engaged in a successful general practice as a physician in Kings County and in parts of the adjoining counties of Queens, Albert, and Westmorland. From 1838 to 1869 he served as surgeon to the 2nd Battalion of Kings County militia and from 1870 until his death as surgeon to the 74th Battalion of Infantry. He was president of the New Brunswick Medical Society for one year in 1883–84. He was also a charter member of the Medical Council of the College of Physicians and Surgeons of New Brunswick, created in 1881, and served on that body until his death. Vail's professional skills and his willingness to employ them in the service of the poor as well as the affluent were admired by his contemporaries.

Vail's long career in New Brunswick politics began in 1857 when he was elected to the assembly for Kings County as a supporter of John Hamilton GRAY and the "compact" or Conservative minority in the house. Re-elected in 1861, Vail bitterly opposed the plan of the Liberal leader, Samuel Leonard Tilley*, to bring New Brunswick into confederation. A determined anti-confederate, Vail was re-elected in 1865 when the voters rejected Tilley's plans for union. Vail was speaker of the assembly under the government of Albert James SMITH until in April 1866 Lieutenant Governor Arthur Hamilton Gordon* forced the anti-confederates from office. In the ensuing general election and again in a by-election held the following year, Vail was defeated.

In 1870, still an unrepentant anti-confederate, Vail ran again for the assembly, and on the hustings "manifested great delight in showing that Confederation had proved as bad as he had predicted." Re-elected, he was again selected speaker when in February 1871 George Luther Hatheway* and George Edwin King* formed a non-party government specifically to pass a law establishing a non-denominational school system supported by direct taxation. Vail did not support the school legislation, but his appointment as speaker limited his participation in the debate. He was defeated in the election of late June 1874, only weeks after the suicide in Sussex of his 26-year-old son, William, also a physician. In the 1878 and 1882 general elections Vail was a successful candidate, and from March 1883 to March 1885 he was a member without portfolio in the Executive Council of the Liberal premier Andrew George Blair*. Following the reappearance after 1878 of more distinct Liberal and Conservative party labels, Vail had allied himself with the Liberal group. On 1 April 1885, just four months before his death, he was appointed to the Legislative Council.

Vail's public career was not as outstanding as that of his brother, William Berrian Vail*, a prominent Nova Scotia politician and federal minister of militia and defence in Alexander Mackenzie*'s government from 1874 to 1878. While serving in the assembly, however, E. A. Vail, known for his strong opposition to confederation, was also responsible for the passage of legislation which shortened the study of law from five to four years and which provided for all elections to the New Brunswick assembly to be held on the same day. He was also convinced that the Common Schools Act of 1871 which he had criticized did not produce an educational system worthy of the financial burden it placed on his constituents. At his death, Vail was described as a man of "generous impulses and strict integrity" whose "strongest hold on the people of Kings County was rather by reason of his private virtues than his political acts."

J. M. WHALEN

N.B. Museum, Observer [E. S. Carter], "Linking the past with the present" (clippings); G. H. Markham, "Kings County genealogical notes." PAC, RG 9, II, B4, 4: 346. PANB, "N.B. political biog." (J. C. and H. B. Graves). PRO, CO 193/4–48 (blue books, 1821–67) (copies at PAC). N.B., House of Assembly, *Journal*, 1879; *Reports of the debates*, 1865–66; Legislative Council, *Journal*, 1885. *Daily News* (Saint John, N.B.), 5, 6 June 1874. *Daily Sun* (Saint John), 1, 2 April, 1 Aug. 1885. *Daily Telegraph* (Saint John), 29 June 1870, 17 Feb. 1871, 5 March 1883, 1 Aug. 1885. *Morning Freeman* (Saint John), 18 Feb. 1871, 18 June 1874. *Morning News* (Saint John), 25 July 1842.

Canadian biog. dict., II. *CPC*, 1885. *Dominion annual register*, 1878–85. *The merchants' & farmers' almanack . . .* (Saint John), 1840–41; 1843–46; 1852–53; 1855–63. *New-Brunswick almanac*, 1825–36; 1838–39; 1842; 1846–54; 1864–69; 1882–85. Wallace, *Macmillan dict.* Hannay, *Hist. of N.B.* W. B. Stewart, *Medicine in New Brunswick . . .* (Moncton, N.B., 1974), 45–46, 52–53.

VAN NORMAN, JOSEPH, iron-founder and entrepreneur; b. 12 May 1796 at Sussex, N.J., son of John Van Norman and Sarah De Pue; m. 25 Aug. 1817 at Pembroke, Genesee County, N.Y., Roxilana Robinson, and they had at least seven children; d. 14 June 1888 in Tillsonburg, Ont.

Shortly after his birth, Joseph Van Norman's family moved to Canandaigua, N.Y. He developed an interest in iron manufacturing and this led to his building a small furnace which he operated for two or three years before moving to Manchester (now part of Niagara Falls, N.Y.) as a foreman in a foundry. In 1821 he immigrated to Charlotteville Township, Upper Canada, where four years earlier, John Mason, an English ironmaster, had established a primitive ironworks. Mason, attracted to the area by the availability of good iron ore and water-power, had built the ironworks at the site of the present town of Normandale, Ont. The furnace went into operation briefly, but only a few tons of iron were produced before Mason's death.

On 22 Aug. 1821 Van Norman agreed to purchase the site from Mason's widow, Elizabeth, for £25 cash on possession. Future payments were contingent on the success of the enterprise, which was a risky one on the frontier, requiring specialized equipment and skilled workmen. Mrs Mason would receive at the maximum an additional £125 currency and £150 to £225 in kind. Van Norman was joined in the purchase by various partners who, by early 1823, included Hiram Capron and George Tillson*. The partners spent between $6,000 and $8,000 to rebuild the furnace, and, employing 20 men, were soon producing iron. In 1824 or 1825 George Tillson sold his share to Capron and moved to present-day Tillsonburg, where he set up the Dereham Forge. On 7 May 1828 Joseph Van Norman and his brother Benjamin bought out Capron, and in about 1829 Elijah Leonard* joined the firm in charge of the furnace. Joseph became sole owner on 1 Jan. 1836.

He was also active in several other iron ventures: in 1823 or 1824, in partnership with a Mr Lamont, he founded at Port Dover, Upper Canada, the Dover Forge which he owned by 1827. In the late 1820s and early 1830s Joseph and Benjamin Van Norman were among the owners, who included Frederick R. Dutcher, of a foundry in York (Toronto). But the furnace at Normandale, or Long Point as it was often called, was Van Norman's main venture. At its peak, in about 1840, annual production was roughly 750 tons of cast and wrought iron products for domestic, agricultural, and industrial use. Its stoves, probably the first manufactured in Ontario, were certainly the first produced in quantity. As well, the need for locally dug iron ore, and for over 4,000 cords of wood per year for charcoal, provided an important economic stimulus to the region.

By 1847 Van Norman found that nearby ore and fuel supplies had dwindled so low that he had to move. For $21,000 he purchased the ironworks at Marmora, in Hastings County, from Peter McGill [McCutcheon*], but like his predecessors, Uriah Seymour and John G. Pendergast, failed to make it succeed. The Marmora ore, because of its high sulphur content, was more difficult to reduce than that of Normandale, and although Van Norman made the ironworks a technical success, he found himself unable to compete with imported British iron, the price of which had been lowered by the improvement of navigation on the St Lawrence.

Returning to Norfolk County, Van Norman won a contract with the Great Western Railway to provide iron for railway car wheels, and built a blast furnace in Houghton Township in 1854. When the iron proved to be of the wrong type to harden as was required for railway use, Van Norman lost the contract. This loss, coupled with the economic depression of the period, led to the closure of the foundry. Van Norman's career as an iron-founder ended, but he continued to engage in business. Since the late 1820s, in conjunction with his iron-making, he had been active as a contractor. His projects had included the construction of the Long Point lighthouse in 1830, the first Long Point cut in 1834, and plank roads connecting Port Dover with Hamilton and Otterville from 1840 to 1848. Following the closure of the Houghton furnace, Van Norman moved to Tillsonburg, probably in 1863, where he manufactured bricks, lime, and shingles. Here he spent the latter part of his life, living with his daughter, Mary Ann, who had married a son of his old business partner, George Tillson.

Joseph Van Norman's death in 1888 attracted little notice; he had not been active in iron manufacturing for nearly four decades. Yet he must be regarded as one of the most important 19th-century pioneers of the industry in Ontario and the men he trained in his shops made good use of their skills in other ventures.

NORMAN R. BALL

UWO, J. A. Bannister papers; James Hamilton papers, Hamilton and Warren papers. F. H. Baddeley, "An essay on the localities of metallic minerals in the Canadas, with some notices of their geological associations and situation, &c.," Literary and Hist. Soc. of Quebec, *Trans.*, 2 (1830–31): 424. Ont., Royal Commission on the Mineral Resources of Ontario and Measures for their Development, *Report* (Toronto, 1890), 320–26. *Observer* (Tillsonburg, Ont.), 22 June 1888. *Canadian biog. dict.*, I: 182–83. J. A. Bannister, "Long Point and its lighthouses," *Western Ontario Hist. Nuggets* (London), 5 (1944). G. C. Mackenzie, "The iron and steel industry of Ontario," Ont., Bureau of Mines, *Annual report* (Toronto), 1908: 190–94. W. J. Patterson, "The Long Point furnace," *Canadian Mining Journal* (Gardenvale, Que.), 60 (1939): 544–49. Thomas Ritchie, "Joseph Van Norman, ironmaster of Upper Canada," *Canadian Geographical Journal* (Montreal), 77 (July–December 1968): 46–51.

VENNOR, HENRY GEORGE, geologist, ornithologist, and weather prophet; b. 30 Dec. 1840 in Montreal, Lower Canada, son of Henry Vennor, a hardware merchant, and Marion Paterson; d. 8 June 1884 at Montreal.

Henry George Vennor received his early education at Philips School and the High School of Montreal, where he developed a keen interest in natural sciences. While still a schoolboy he assembled a collection, preserved in alcohol, of local snakes and other reptiles, which gained him honourable mention at a provincial exhibition. In the late 1850s he began attending McGill College, where he studied geology, mineralogy, zoology, and civil engineering under such prominent scientists as John William Dawson* and Thomas Sterry Hunt*. Before he graduated with honours in 1860, Vennor made a large collection of the fossils of Montreal Island, wrote several papers on local bird life for the *Canadian Naturalist and Geologist* of Montreal, and commenced a review of eastern Canadian song birds which was published in the *British American Magazine* of Toronto in 1864. After graduation he spent five years with the Montreal mercantile firm of John Frothingham* and William Workman*, and continued to collect fossils and birds. In 1865 Vennor accepted an apprenticeship under Sir William Edmond Logan*, head of the Geological Survey of Canada, whom he aided in a survey of Manitoulin Island, Canada West. The following year he was appointed a full member of the survey, and for the next 15 years worked in the region of southeastern Ontario and Pontiac County, Que., establishing basic distributions of various rock types and describing in detail their ecomomic mineral and metal deposits. To complete these tasks satisfactorily, Vennor had first to prepare adequate topographic base maps, an onerous job which he executed with patience and skill.

During 1866 Vennor was closely associated with the first recorded identification of gold in the Precambrian rocks of Ontario, at a small metals mine in Madoc Township, Hastings County. To his credit, Vennor played down the discovery's importance and foretold a quick collapse of the resulting gold-rush – a prediction borne out the following year. He remained a keen student of mining and mineral deposits, and did much to promote the interests of local operators. In 1872, for instance, he directed attention to the phosphate deposits of Ottawa County, Que., where a number of mines were subsequently worked at considerable profit during the phosphate boom of the 1880s.

In 1867 Vennor had published a paper on the vital question of the stratigraphy of the Precambrian Shield in the Hastings County area in the *Quarterly Journal* of the Geological Society of London, to which prestigious body he was elected in 1870. Apart from a few short papers, however, he wrote no more for scientific journals, his major contibutions appearing instead in seven reports of the Geological Survey of Canada. In 1876 he also published *Our birds of prey*, a volume profusely illustrated with William Notman*'s pasted-in photographic plates of stuffed raptors. The venture proved a commercial failure and Vennor was to complain that the book was "too expensive for Canada."

In 1881 Vennor resigned from the Geological Survey because his dealings in phosphate mining lands would create a conflict of interest which parliament was shortly to deny to officers of the survey. Vennor apparently also had serious disputes with Alfred Richard Cecil Selwyn*, Logan's successor at the survey, over working conditions and his reports (the results of Vennor's last five years of survey work were never published). Probably the advancement of better-trained younger men, such as George Mercer Dawson*, rankled, as it did with some of his colleagues. Vennor had done well with his broad natural sciences training in a region of exceedingly complex geology (still challenging today's earth scientists) and he had paid close attention to a main survey objective – economic development through mining. He maintained his interest by opening a consulting office in Montreal at this time.

Vennor's work led him outdoors most of the year, and not surprisingly he was a keen student of the weather and the problems of its prediction. In the fall of 1875, from a "feeling in his bones," he correctly predicted in local newspapers a green Christmas and a muddy New Year's Day for Montreal. The prediction aroused great public interest and led him to publish in 1877 the first *Vennor's almanac*. By gathering data on weather patterns in previous years and comparing the weather of the existing year against past activity, Vennor claimed to have discovered a "law of recurrences" which enabled him accurately to predict what weather would occur. The almanacs, issued annually, were widely read and acclaimed throughout eastern North America and grew so successful that in 1881 a separate American edition was issued, supplemented in 1882 and part of 1883 by the monthly *Vennor's weather bulletin*.

Vennor continued to work on his almanac until his death in June 1884, at which time Walter H. Smith took it up, supplementing Vennor's theories with his own system of "astrometeorology." In the 1885 edition of the almanac Smith claimed that Vennor was survived by a wife and three children, although other obituaries make no mention of his family. Indeed, his death was not noted in print by the scientfic world. Vennor received front page tributes from the *New York Times* and the Montreal *Gazette*, however, the latter referring to him as "a thoughtful student of science, whose work will live after him," a fitting tribute to this enigmatic man of science.

P. R. Eakins

Henry George Vennor was the author of "On the feathered songsters of the island of Montreal," *British American Magazine* (Toronto), 2 (1864): 606–10. He published in the *Canadian Naturalist and Geologist* "Notes on birds wintering in and around Montreal; from observations taken during the winters of 1856–57–58–59–60," 5 (1860): 425–30; "A short review of the sylviadæ or wood-warblers found in the vicinity of Montreal," 6 (1861): 349–62; "Cave in limestone near Montreal," new ser., 1 (1864): 14–16; "Ascending section of Laurentian rocks in the county of Hastings, Canada West," new ser., 3 (1868): 310–11, reprinted from Geological Soc. of London, *Quarterly Journal* (London), 23 (1867), pt.i, 256–57; and "Notes on some of the galena or sulphuret of lead deposits connected with the Laurentian rocks of Ontario," new ser., 7 (1875): 455–62. Vennor published "Report on the geology and economic minerals of parts of Hastings, Addington, and Peterborough counties" in the Geological Survey of Canada, *Report of progress for 1866–69* (Montreal, 1870), 143–71; "Abstract of a report on the geology of parts of the counties of Frontenac, Leeds, and Lanark, Ont.," *Report . . . for 1870–71* (Ottawa, 1872), 309–15; "Progress report of explorations and surveys in the counties of Leeds, Frontenac, and Lanark, with notes on the gold of Marmora, with assays by B. J. Harrington," *Report . . . for 1871–72* (Montreal, 1872), 120–41; "Report of explorations and surveys in the counties of Addington, Frontenac, Leeds, and Lanark (Ontario)," *Report . . . for 1872–73* (Montreal, 1873), 136–79; "Report of explorations and surveys in Frontenac, Leeds, and Lanark counties, with notes on the plumbago of Buckingham, and apatite of Templeton and Portland townships, Ottawa Co.," *Report . . . for 1873–74* (Montreal, 1874), 103–46; "Progress report of explorations and surveys in the rear portions of Frontenac and Lanark counties, together with notes of some of the economic minerals of Ontario," *Report . . . for 1874–75* ([Montreal], 1876), 105–65; and "Progress report of explorations and surveys made during the years 1875 and 1876 in the counties of Renfrew, Pontiac, and Ottawa, together with additional notes on the iron ores, apatite, and plumbago deposits of Ottawa County," *Report . . . for 1876–77* ([Montreal], 1878), 244–320. In American journals he published "Archæan of Canada," *American Journal of Science and Arts* (New Haven, Conn.), 3rd ser., 14 (July–December 1877): 313–16, and "Phosphates in Canada," *Engineering and Mining Journal* (New York), 33 (January–June 1882): 69. Vennor's other works are *Our birds of prey, or the eagles, hawks and owls of Canada* (Montreal, 1876), *Vennor's almanac* (Montreal), 1877–85, and *Vennor's weather bulletin* (Montreal), 1882–83.

AC, État civil, Congrégationalistes, Emmanuel Church (Montreal), 10 June 1884. ANQ-M, État civil, Congrégationalistes, Zion Church (Montreal), 20 May 1841. McGill Univ. Libraries (Montreal), Blacker Wood Library, H. G. Vennor papers. *Examiner* (Charlottetown), 14 June 1884. *Gazette* (Montreal), 9 June 1884. *New York Times*, 9 June 1884. *Appleton's cyclopædia of American biography*, ed. J. G. Wilson and John Fiske (7v., New York, 1887–1900), VI: 276–77. *Dominion annual register*, 1879–84. Zaslow, *Reading the rocks*.

VEREY, GEORGE, physician, teacher, and office-holder; b. probably in the 1830s in England; m. 31 Oct. 1876 Sarah Ann Coulson, and they had two sons and twin daughters; d. 19 Nov. 1881 at Edmonton (Alta).

George Verey was educated in London and studied medicine under Dr John Whaley at St Bartholomew's Hospital. He became a member of the Royal College of Surgeons of England on 31 May 1861 and for a time resided in Kilburn (now part of Greater London). By 1863 Verey had travelled to Australia where he practised medicine briefly; he had returned to England by 1866 and joined the British army as a surgeon in the Far East. Following his discharge from the army, his wandering and intemperate spirit led him to Montana where he served for a time as a medical officer in the United States Army.

Verey was in the Canadian west by 1871 when he travelled with George Millward McDougall* to Fort Edmonton; there he worked as a clerk for the Hudson's Bay Company. In the spring of 1874 he opened a school; it operated until the spring of 1875, when he departed for the Red River Settlement with a letter of introduction from Chief Factor Richard Charles HARDISTY. On his return to Edmonton that summer, he was engaged to teach school and tend to the medical needs of the Stony Indians at the Methodist mission at Morley (Alta) under the Reverend John Chantler McDougall*.

While Verey was at Morley in the winter of 1875–76, his former benefactor, Richard Hardisty, fell seriously ill with rheumatic fever and sent for him by dog team. After tending Hardisty successfully, Verey returned in the summer to Edmonton where he taught school, rather unhappily, over the next winter. In the spring of 1877 he went to Red River. There he entered into a partnership with James Stewart*, a Winnipeg druggist, and also practised medicine after being licensed by the College of Physicians and Surgeons of Manitoba. But, dependent on credit from Hardisty, he set out once again for Edmonton in the summer of 1878.

From 1878 to 1881 Verey's family grew to four children, and he built a house and operated a farm at Edmonton near the HBC's property. Because the community was still too small to support a doctor, he also ran a school for a year. In August 1879 he was appointed a justice of the peace for the North-West Territories and was active, along with Hardisty, also a justice of the peace, in prosecuting offenders in the district. Verey expanded his farm and became secretary of the local agricultural society, which disseminated practical scientific information on farming. In 1881 he was made clerk of the Edmonton sitting of the Saskatchewan District Court. At the same time his medical practice improved, but it was necessary for the district, which now had a population of almost 2,000, to provide a bonus of $130 for the purchase of an adequate stock of medicines.

Edward G. Verey, the doctor's brother, arrived late in 1881 to assist on the farm, but he departed suddenly and Dr Verey was apparently left depressed. After a week's illness Verey died unexpectedly from an accidental overdose of self-prescribed chloral (an admixture of alcohol and opium) on 19 Nov. 1881. He left no will, and his family appears to have been provided for by relatives in England, with Hardisty attending to their welfare. A considerable stock of medicines and a substantial clientele were taken over by Verey's successor, Dr Laurence John Munro from Winnipeg.

Verey is an example of the restless individual occasionally attracted to frontier societies. But unlike some, he had medical credentials which were certainly authentic, and the services he performed in the northwest were important in its early development. His experience and diverse interests were, in fact, well adapted to a pioneer society.

ANTHONY W. RASPORICH and IAN A. L. GETTY

Glenbow-Alberta Institute, Richard Hardisty papers, 1861–94. PAM, MG 10, A15. Provincial Arch. of Alberta (Edmonton), Dr George Verey family papers. Saskatchewan Arch. Board (Saskatoon), North-West Territories, Proclamations and orders of the lieutenant governor, 1876–79 (mfm. at Glenbow-Alberta Institute). Supreme Court of Alberta (Edmonton), Probate Section, Papers relating to the estate of George Verey, 1890–94. J. [C.] McDougall, *Opening the great west: experiences of a missionary in 1875–76*, intro. J. E. Nix (Calgary, 1970), 36. *Edmonton Bulletin*, 1880–82, in particular 26 Nov. 1881. *Henderson's directory of the city of Winnipeg . . .* (Winnipeg), 1880. *Manitoba directory . . .* (Winnipeg), 1877–79. H. C. Jamieson, *Early medicine in Alberta: the first seventy-five years* (Edmonton, 1947), 15–16, 36, 38, 112.

VÉZINA, FRANÇOIS, financier; b. 13 Aug. 1818 at Quebec City, son of François Vézina, a baker, and Claire Moisan; m. 11 June 1844 Éléonore Rinfret, *dit* Malouin, third daughter of Rémi Rinfret, *dit* Malouin, a master mason; d. 25 Jan. 1882 at Quebec, and was buried three days later in the Belmont cemetery at Sainte-Foy, Que.

François Vézina, the eldest child in a family of modest means, received his secondary education at the Petit Séminaire de Québec from 1829 to 1840. At the conclusion of his studies a natural aptitude for business led him to accept a position as clerk with the firm of Babineau et Gaudry, merchants and suppliers to the navy. During his 18 months in this position, he demonstrated by his industriousness and by his precise, cautious, and practical mind, that he had a real capacity for business. Louis-Joseph Massue* and notary Charles-Maxime Defoy were impressed by his abilities, and recommended him to Daniel McCallum, manager of the Canada Fire Insurance Company, who hired him. The great fires that ravaged the city of Quebec in 1845 struck the company hard and it went bankrupt, leaving its employees out of work. But Vézina, who already had a reputation and some friends, had little difficulty finding employment; John Sharples*, the supervisor of cullers, hired him to work for his office. In the space of six years Vézina had thus made contact with the principal business circles in Quebec City; meanwhile he had used his leisure to read works on political economy.

In 1848 the Quebec Building Society lost its secretary, who died leaving the accounts in an indescribable mess. The worried shareholders demanded drastic action. The French-speaking directors, including Guillaume-Eugène CHINIC and Dr Olivier Robitaille, suggested securing the services of Vézina, to the displeasure of many English-speaking shareholders. However, Sharples apparently managed to allay their fears and gain their support for Vézina. They had no reason to regret their choice; in January 1849 Vézina presented a clear, precise balance sheet, which earned the shareholders' admiration and secured his reputation as "a man [who handled] figures and financial matters with outstanding ability." Businessmen began to seek his advice, and investors regained confidence in the Quebec Building Society. Like all groups incorporated under the statutory regulations for building societies, the Quebec institution raised its capital by issuing shares on which members undertook to make periodic payments, and in turn lent the money as mortgages to them when they wanted to construct buildings or acquire real estate. Vézina did not agree with the society's rules and some features of its constitution. He studied similar societies, and even went to Toronto to familiarize himself with the way in which the building society in that city operated. In 1856, armed with this experience, he made a proposal to the shareholders to wind up the existing society and create the Quebec Permanent Building Society, for which he had worked out a structure, rules, and mode of operation. The new society would differ from the old by being more liberal in its loan policy and by not requiring all borrowers to be jointly responsible for its losses or profits. The shareholders accepted Vézina's proposal and appointed him secretary-treasurer of the new company, with power to liquidate the old one. The society prospered, and paid an average dividend of 10 per cent to its shareholders. In 1863 Vézina became president, a post he retained until his death.

It was also in 1848 that the members of the Society of St Vincent de Paul of Quebec, which had been founded by François Soulard in 1844, asked Vézina to help set up a savings bank for the less favoured class. Such banks, which had been in existence for some time in Europe and the United States, attempted to stimulate "habits of orderliness, economy and morality," and to "provide the worker with a way to build up capital for himself in the course of time." Often established and managed by philanthropists, at least in the earliest examples, these banks never discounted notes "without having provincial bonds as collateral security"; they invested savings in readily convertible debentures of public corporations, guaranteed a modest but stable rate of interest, and used a portion of their profits to support charitable institutions. On 11 May 1848, a 13-member committee of the Society of St Vincent de Paul, including Vézina who acted as secretary, met to lay the foundations of the Caisse d'Épargnes de Notre-Dame de Québec, which at its incorporation in 1855 became the Caisse d'Économie de Notre-Dame de Québec. The constitution and rules, based on those of the St Roch's Savings Bank, Quebec, were adopted on 28 May and the bank opened on 18 June. It accepted deposits ranging from 1*s.* 3*d.* to 500 louis, required ten days' notice for any withdrawal of ten louis or more, and guaranteed an interest rate of four and a half per cent. From the outset Vézina had played a major role; as the committee's secretary, he had a hand in the preparation of the rules and "the setting up of the books and forms" necessary for keeping accounts, and he was appropriately elected secretary of the first board of directors. Combining the posts of secretary and treasurer from 2 March 1851, he became the guiding spirit of the bank. It encountered difficulties initially because the workers were mistrustful but, thanks to the influence of the clergy and to prudent investments, the clientele increased to such an extent that in December 1851 the directors had to rent larger premises at 19 Rue Saint-Jean. From May 1852 the bank was open three times a week and during the financial year of 1853–54 it registered 308 new deposits. Resistance had been overcome and the enterprise launched.

It now had to be consolidated. Vézina devoted all his energies to this task. He was the bank's secretary-treasurer until April 1863, its cashier (general manager) from 1 May 1863 to May 1872, and then its manager until his death. Under the wise direction of Vézina and Olivier Robitaille, its president from 1849 to 1870, the Caisse d'Économie survived the recurrent crises that periodically disrupted the banking system, in particular that of 1856–57 which resulted in the bankruptcy of the St Roch's Savings Bank. On 27 Dec. 1871 the Caisse d'Économie de Notre-Dame de Québec applied for a charter authorizing it to continue with a capital of $1,000,000 provided by 2,500 shares of $400 each, with the privilege of increasing the capital to $2,000,000. This reorganization influenced the development of the Caisse d'Économie, which gradually came to act like a chartered bank. Early in the 20th century Alphonse Desjardins* in setting up the Caisse Populaire de Lévis reverted to the original spirit of the founders of the Caisse d'Économie.

The posts held by Vézina in the Quebec Permanent Building Society and in the Caisse d'Économie had placed him at the centre of French-speaking business circles. The members of these circles, as Vézina observed, often had landed property but did not always "possess the ready capital to give the necessary impetus to their businesses." The Caisse d'Économie served as a channel for the savings of the poor, but because it did not discount commercial notes it cut itself off from the business world. The founders of the Caisse d'Économie increasingly felt the need to establish a bank to serve merchants and industrialists. The 1856–57 crisis delayed the project until 1858. On 20 December of that year a group of businessmen including Ulric-Joseph Tessier*, Guillaume-Eugène Chinic, Isidore Thibaudeau*, Olivier Robitaille, Cirice Têtu, Abraham Hamel, Octave Crémazie*, and Vézina held a preliminary meeting. Two days later, 51 citizens, under the chairmanship of Mayor Hector-Louis Langevin*, decided to found the Banque Nationale, whose capital of $1,000,000 would be subscribed in $50 shares. The name of the bank was in itself a manifesto. Naturally, the Banque Nationale would be open to all those in business, whatever their ethnic group, but it reflected the desire of French-speaking businessmen to have a network of credit that they would control and could utilize as an instrument to forge a place for themselves in the world of commerce. And time was to prove them right. Vézina noted a few years later: "The success of the Banque Nationale has led our fellow citizens to have more confidence in themselves and not to leave to others sources of revenue which can be as usefully and easily exploited by themselves . . . , and has greatly increased and facilitated modes of investment and saving which have long been limited to the acquisition of landed property."

Here again, Vézina was the architect of a new institution. A founding member, he assumed the office of treasurer and prepared the charter, regulations, prospectus, and account books. He contacted subscribers during the summer of 1859, and on 26 December he was appointed cashier. On 28 April 1860 the bank began operations. It was not until June 1866 that the subscribed capital was paid up in full. The Banque Nationale, which from 1860 to 1875 had transactions of the order of $22,000,000 annually, had an immense influence in the Quebec region, but this has never been adequately studied. For its part, *Le Canadien* claimed in 1882 that the leather industry owed its prosperity to this institution. In 1924 the bank merged with the Banque d'Hochelaga to become the Banque Canadienne Nationale.

The founding of the Banque Nationale marked the peak of Vézina's career. Its success firmly established his reputation. Public corporations and business establishments such as the council of the parish of Notre-Dame de Québec, the De Léry Gold Mining Company, of which he was treasurer from 1870, the Quebec Harbour Commission, of which he was vice-president from 1870 to 1874, the firm of Hamel et Frères, and many others used his services. An uncompromising defender of private enterprise and a believer in the Scottish banking system, Vézina acted on several occasions as the spokesman for Quebec businessmen in their dealings with the government. Thus in March 1860 he publicly opposed the plan of Alexander Tilloch Galt* to create a treasury department to act as a state bank which would have a monopoly in the circulation of notes.

His many occupations did not prevent Vézina from taking a close interest in his family. He and his wife had ten children, seven of whom reached adulthood, and he was concerned to see that they got a good start in life. His son Adolphe succeeded him as secretary-treasurer of the Caisse d'Économie, and another son, Ludger, was an accountant in this bank. He gave the same careful attention to the future of French-speaking young men who were anxious to launch themselves into business. A score or more of those he trained held high office in branches of the Banque Nationale or found employment in the Canadian banking system. Despite his wife's death in 1880, Vézina did not slacken the pace of his activities, but he was to die suddenly in 1882, at the age of 63, from the after-effects of pneumonia.

In collaboration with JEAN HAMELIN

[François Vézina's first biographer, Jean-Chrysostome Langelier*, published his *Biographie de Frs. Vézina, caissier de la Banque Nationale* (Québec, 1876) during Vézina's lifetime. Written at the request of the staff of the Banque Nationale, the book, which in places verges on hagiography, is still basic for an understanding of both the man and the impressions his contemporaries had of him. Auguste Béchard* took much of his material from it, often simply copying passages, for the study of Vézina which he published in *Le Nouvelliste* (Québec) from 10 to 22 Dec. 1877, and subsequently brought out as a pamphlet entitled *Biographie de M. François Vézina, caissier de la Banque Nationale* . . . (Québec, 1878). Written with the education of a young audience in mind, Béchard's biography reflects the nationalist views current in certain professional circles in Quebec City. The articles by Pierre-Georges Roy* in *Fils de Québec* (4 sér., Lévis, Qué., 1933), IV: 28–30, and by Francis-Joseph Audet*, "François Vézina," *BRH*, 39 (1933): 117–20, are summaries of Langelier's study, as is the article on Vézina in the *Canadian biog. dict.*, I: 144–46. The *Dominion annual register*, 1882, provides no additional information on Vézina.

There are two reliable sources for the organizations founded by Vézina. The first, again by Auguste Béchard, is *Histoire de la Banque Nationale* . . . (Québec, 1878). Written on the basis of reports and financial statements of the Banque Nationale, this study has a supplement with articles published by Vézina between 1858 and 1860 in the Quebec City newspapers, *Le Canadien*, *Le Courrier du Canada*, and the *Morning Chronicle*. The second, *Récit historique de la progression financière de la Caisse d'Économie de Notre-Dame de Québec* (Québec, 1878), is a compilation by Vézina of reports and financial statements, and constitutes an excellent source for the history of the Caisse d'Économie.

Other sources useful for various aspects of Vézina's career include: Can., Prov. of, *Statutes*, 1858, c.131; 1859, c.103; 1866, c.140; Can., *Statutes*, 1871, c.7; *Quebec directory*, 1847–83. Finally, the dates for Vézina's birth and marriage are to be found in ANQ-Q, État civil, Catholiques, Notre-Dame de Québec, 13 août 1818, 11 juin 1844. His death date is given in *Le Canadien*, 25 janv. 1882, and *L'Opinion Publique*, 23 févr. 1882. J.H.]

VILLEBRUN, *dit* **Provencher, JOSEPH-ALFRED-NORBERT.** *See* PROVENCHER

VINCENT, CHARLES (baptized **Auguste-Victor-Charles**), Basilian priest and educator; b. 30 June 1828 at Vallon (Vallon-Pont-D'Arc), France, son of Joseph-Victor Vincent and Marie-Thérèse-Augustine Charrière; d. 1 Nov. 1890 at Toronto, Ont.

Charles Vincent was educated at Aubenas before entering the Basilian noviciate at Vernoux-en-Vivarais, Ardèche, France, in 1848. He continued his theological studies at the Basilian Collège d'Annonay before being received as a member of the Basilian community on 18 Sept. 1851. At that time the Basilians were considering a foundation in Toronto following an invitation from Bishop Armand-François-Marie de Charbonnel*, who had studied at Annonay. In 1852 Vincent joined one other unordained member and two priests as the first group of Basilians to travel to Toronto in order to establish a school. The decision to volunteer must have been especially difficult for Vincent because of close family ties; fearing opposition from his parents, he felt it necessary to leave without informing them even though his father was seriously ill. His mother's pleas for his return caused him anguish until he was able to visit France again five years later.

In Toronto the Basilians established St Mary's Lesser Seminary where classes began on 15 Sept. 1852. Early the next year the school was merged with the Christian Brothers' St Michael's College; Jean-Mathieu Soulerin*, who had arrived with Vincent, became superior. Vincent's classes went along without too much difficulty, despite the fact that he had never studied English; by the time he was ordained by Charbonnel on 22 May 1853 he was confident in the language.

St Michael's College was located in the bishop's palace before a permanent home was found for both it and the parish church of St Basil's on the estate of John Elmsley*. Soulerin, as superior of the college and pastor of the parish, came to count more and more on Vincent as "of all his confrères the one who has the best spirit, best minds his own business, delights in and gets along with the students, and has kept [his] initial piety." From 1857 Vincent held the office of treasurer of the college and was clearly second to Soulerin at St Michael's. He himself, however, was far from sharing the confidence his superior had in him. In 1856 he had written to the superior general of the Basilian fathers accusing himself of negligence, tepidity, lack of respect for authority, and a tendency to oversleep in the morning. "I lack," he wrote, "that energy that saints need." He hesitated to take formal religious vows, which were introduced in the community in 1852, until his visit to France in 1857.

The test of his energy and maturity came after 1865,

when Soulerin was elected superior general of the Basilians and returned to Annonay. Vincent was left as superior of St Michael's College, pastor of St Basil's parish, and effective head of the Basilians in America. His next years were to be made especially difficult because of a rift with Bishop John Joseph LYNCH, the successor to Charbonnel in 1860.

Lynch, who had founded Our Lady of Angels Seminary (later Niagara University) in New York State in 1856, was critical and suspicious of the Basilian work in Toronto. The chief factor in these difficulties was probably the bishop's scrupulosity about his responsibilities especially those affecting his rights and duties of supervision over Basilians in his diocese; the Basilians had not yet received papal approval as a full religious community and their legal position was therefore ambiguous. In the 1860s the bishop complained about the discipline and the quality of education in the college as well as about the mingling of students and parishioners at high mass. He also refused to ordain young Basilians unless they vowed obedience to him and swore to remain in his diocese. Soulerin found the bishop's attitude puzzling and disturbing. Vincent, younger and more deferential than Soulerin, was more successful in his relationship with Lynch, but in 1872 the troubles showed themselves in sharper form in a dispute over the activities of one of the Basilians. In 1874 Lynch, now an archbishop, demanded that Vincent be removed from office. Soulerin not only refused, but proceeded to name Vincent provincial to strengthen his position. Lynch petitioned Rome to intervene but the Holy See took a placatory approach, Vincent remained in office, and the affair gradually quietened down.

Vincent had become a capable administrator. In 1871–72 he extended the college building; the addition was paid for by 1876 despite the fact that the annual government grant of $3,000 had been discontinued in 1869. Then, to satisfy the archbishop, he worked out a structural change in the church, extending the sanctuary so that students could be placed on either side of the altar without having to mix with the congregation. In 1881 a more significant change came when St Michael's was affiliated with the University of Toronto. This affiliation was largely the work of Father John Reed Teefy*, but Vincent gave his younger colleague the support he needed. The archbishop seems to have been pleased, and his concerns from that time were mainly that Roman Catholic students should take advantage of what St Michael's offered. In any case, his reconciliation with Vincent had been formally expressed in 1878 when Vincent, on the 25th anniversary of his ordination, had been named vicar general of Toronto.

As superior of St Michael's, even before he was named provincial in 1874, Vincent had been exercising a supervisory role. The community's only other house in 1865 was in Owen Sound, in the diocese of Hamilton. In 1867 Vincent opened the first Basilian school in the United States, a minor seminary in Louisville, Ohio; it, however, had failed by 1873. In 1870 he sent Father Denis O'Connor* to Sandwich (Windsor), in the diocese of London, to head the group of Basilians taking over Assumption College (now part of University of Windsor) and parish. Four years later Bishop John Walsh* of London, in testimony of his confidence in the Basilians during their trouble with Bishop Lynch, invited them to take over a parish in Chatham, which was to be exchanged in 1878 for that of St John the Baptist in Amherstburg. The last of Vincent's foundations was St Anne's parish in Detroit, taken over in 1886, the first permanent Basilian establishment in the United States.

As the jubilee volume of the archdiocese of Toronto noted in 1892 Vincent, as superior, pastor, and provincial, always showed quick practical judgement and insight into character. He had a good sense of humour and remarkable simplicity. Other Basilians, it is recorded, found him a kind and gentle man, easy to approach and more to be loved than feared. With growing responsibilities as provincial and increasing troubles with his health, he gave up the office of pastor of St Basil's in 1880, and that of superior of St Michael's six years later. Finally, in 1890, diabetes forced him to resign as provincial a few months before his death.

JAMES HANRAHAN

R. J. Scollard of Toronto is in possession of 61 typescript volumes entitled "Notes on the history of the Congregation of the Priests of Saint Basil," which he has compiled since 1928. Volumes 1, 6–9, 12, 14, 23, and 34 were used in the preparation of this biography.

Basilian Arch. (Toronto), A.313, 1852, .51–53 (St Michael's College, Letters, 1852–90). Univ. of St Michael's College Arch. (Toronto), Charles Vincent, Letters. R. J. Scollard, *Dictionary of Basilian biography: lives of members of the Congregation of Priests of Saint Basil from its beginnings in 1822 to 1968* (Toronto, 1969). F. J. Boland, "An analysis of the problems and difficulties of the Basilian fathers in Toronto, 1850–1860" (PHD thesis, Univ. of Ottawa, 1955). James Hanrahan, *The Basilian fathers (1822–1972): a documentary study of one hundred and fifty years of the history of the Congregation of Priests of St. Basil* (Toronto, 1973). Mary Hoskin, *History of St. Basil's parish, St. Joseph Street* (Toronto, 1912). *Jubilee volume, 1842–1892: the archdiocese of Toronto and Archbishop Walsh*, [ed. J. R. Teefy] (Toronto, 1892). Charles Roume, *Origines et formation de la communauté des prêtres de Saint-Basile: contribution à l'histoire religieuse du Vivarais* (Privas, France, 1965). L. K. Shook, *Catholic post-secondary education in English-speaking Canada: a history* (Toronto and Buffalo, N.Y., 1971). "Laudemus viros gloriosos: Charles Vincent, C.S.B., 1828–1890," *Basilian Teacher* (Toronto), 4 (1959–60): 145–47. L. K. Shook, "St. Michael's College: the formative years, 1850–1853," CCHA *Report*, 17 (1950): 37–52.

VINCENT, ZACHARIE (Telari-o-lin), painter and sketcher; b. 28 Jan. 1815 at the Village-des-Hurons, Lower Canada, son of Gabriel Vincent and Marie Otis (Otisse, Hôtesse); m. 14 Aug. 1848 Marie Falardeau, the Iroquois widow of Édouard-Sébastien Falardeau, and they had three sons and one daughter; d. 9 Oct. 1886 at Quebec City.

Zacharie Vincent's Huron name, Telari-o-lin (which translates as "not divided" or "unmixed"), was not a hereditary one: the chieftains' council granted each child of a certain age an epithet corresponding to "his particular aptitudes . . . , his qualities, and his occupation." The Indian name he received suggests that Vincent was a pure-blooded Huron. However, a newspaper of the period claimed that his father, whose Indian name was Ouenouadahronhé, was the last such Huron: "He was the sole Indian of the village who was of unmixed blood and directly descended from the original tribe inhabiting the shores of Lake Huron. He was also the only one who had retained his forefathers' customs, and reared his family in [their] language, the younger inhabitants of the village at this time speaking only the French language and not knowing their own." But the fact that the paternal side of the family included the name of Bergevin and the maternal that of Otis, both European names, suggests that neither Gabriel Vincent nor his son were pure-blooded Hurons. Whatever the case, Zacharie inherited Huron features, and they, together with his determination to maintain the traditional way of life, helped to reinforce the notion that he was the last of the Hurons. A painting by Henry Daniel Thielcke, done in 1838 and now in the Château Ramezay Museum in Montreal, shows Vincent sporting "headgear of his own manufacture," while the other important figures of Huronia are wearing the tall beaver-skin hats of the white man. This distinction was a sign of "the historical memory of the race," according to Abbé Lionel-Saint-Georges Lindsay.

During the same period, Antoine Plamondon*, who came from Ancienne-Lorette (Que.), painted a full-length portrait of Vincent which won him a medal from the Literary and Historical Society of Quebec in 1838. The painting, acquired by Lord Durham [Lambton*] and sent to London in 1840, has been lost, but it inspired François-Xavier Garneau*'s poem "Le Dernier Huron": "Triumph, destiny/Your hour at last is come,/O nation, thou shalt be no more. . . ." The poet found in the portrait "the expression of thoughtful resignation." The interest aroused by the impending destruction of Huron culture was not unrelated to that aroused by the expectation at this time that the French-speaking people would disappear in North America. "May we erect a few monuments of ourselves before being drowned in the flood of immigration," exclaimed a journalist upon seeing Plamondon's portrait.

Influenced by Plamondon's canvas, Vincent began to paint self-portraits, in a desire to record his own image and thereby to keep alive the remembrance of Huronia. According to historiographical tradition, the Huron artist's training was confined to a little artistic advice from Plamondon. Vincent's work falls into three main groups: portraits of himself in traditional costume, sketches depicting traditional activities of his people, and landscape paintings of Ancienne-Lorette. Some of his canvases are in the Musée du Québec, and others in the Musée du Château Ramezay and the Musée d'Odanak. According to an author of the day, Vincent produced more than 600 drawings and paintings, many of which were bought by governors general such as Lord Durham, Lord Elgin [Bruce*], and Lord Monck*, as well as by Princess Louise, Marchioness of Lorne, and others. Legend also attributes to Vincent some small carved objects for the church of Notre-Dame-de-Lorette in the Village-des-Hurons, which are said to have been destroyed in the fire that devastated the church in 1959. However, there is no documentary evidence to substantiate these claims.

Although Vincent wanted to capture the traditional image of the Hurons, elements borrowed from European civilization can be seen in some of his paintings and sketches, which thus reveal the assimilation to which his people were already subject. Undeniably naïve, his work possesses enduring interest because of its intensity and sincerity. It reflected Vincent's desire to capture the spirit of a Huron America forever lost.

DAVID KAREL, MARIE-DOMINIC LABELLE,
and SYLVIE THIVIERGE

[We have been unable to identify any of Zacharie Vincent's sculptures. A few of his paintings – self-portraits, landscapes, and scenes of Huron life – are on display at the Château Ramezay Museum in Montreal and the Musée du Québec in Quebec City. D.K., M.-D.L., and S.T.]

AC, Québec, État civil, Catholiques, Saint-Roch (Québec), 14 oct. 1886. AP, Saint-Ambroise (Loretteville), Reg. des baptêmes, mariages et sépultures, 15 févr. 1808, 28 janv. 1815, 23 nov. 1848, 20 juill. 1850, 3 juin 1852, 1er mai 1854. IBC, Centre de documentation, Fonds Morisset, 2, V775.5/Z16. F.-X. Garneau, "Le dernier Huron," *Le répertoire national ou recueil de littérature canadienne*, James Huston, compil. (4v., Montréal, 1848–50), IV: 172–75. *Le Canadien*, 12 août 1840. *Le Journal de Québec*, 21 déc. 1878. *Le Populaire* (Montréal), 14 mai 1838. *Star and Commercial Advertiser* (Quebec), 8 April 1829. *Mariages de Loretteville (St-Ambroise-de-la-Jeune-Lorette), 1761–1969, Village des Hurons (Notre-Dame-de-Lorette), 1904–1969*, G.-E. Provencher, compil. (Québec, 1970). Harper, *La peinture au Canada*. L.-S.-G. Lindsay, *Notre-Dame de la Jeune-Lorette en la Nouvelle-France, étude historique* (Montréal, 1900). Gérard Morisset, *La peinture traditionnelle au Canada français* (Ottawa, 1960). Monique Duval, "Petit musée de la Huronnie à Loretteville," *Le Soleil* (Québec), 23 août 1972: 20.

VOSSNACK, EMIL (Emile), engineer, teacher, and artist; b. 11 Aug. 1839 at Remscheid (Federal Republic of Germany); m. *c.* 1865 in New York City, Ida Cassoni, and they had four children; d. 6 Sept. 1885 at Halifax, N.S.

Emil Vossnack received professional education at the Trade School and the Polytechnic School in Karlsruhe (Federal Republic of Germany). He practised as an engineer and taught mechanical engineering for a short time in Germany before emigrating to the United States. By 1860 Vossnack was living in Chicago where he was employed at the Illinois Central Railroad shops. During his two and a half years in Chicago he closely studied the first grain elevators being built in that city and assisted in designing one of them. Vossnack also lived in Paterson, N.J., and New York City. In the latter he instructed classes in mechanical engineering at the Cooper Union and the mechanics' institute, and was associated with Danforth and Cook's Locomotive Shop.

In 1870 Vossnack moved to Halifax. He was employed at the Nova Scotia Iron Works where he built the first locomotives manufactured in the province. Three of these were completed in 1872, and two more in 1873, but in that same year the company went into liquidation and his contract was terminated. Subsequently Vossnack was engaged at the Starr Manufacturing Works in Dartmouth. He built both iron pipe and small rope transmissions for this company and for the mills of the Summerside and Hebb companies in Bridgewater, while at the same time superintending a large machine shop in Halifax.

In June 1876 William and Alexander Moir consulted Vossnack regarding plans to build a water-power works, flour-mill, box mill, and grain elevator on the Nine Mile River at Bedford. They engaged him to prepare plans for the buildings, to design the machinery, and to superintend the whole works after completion. Vossnack finished this extensive enterprise entirely to their satisfaction, and was thus responsible for building the first grain elevator in the Maritime provinces.

In the 1870s there was much concern regarding the need for technical education to train men for the various industries necessary to exploit the vast natural resources of Nova Scotia. When the Technological Institute of Halifax was established for this purpose late in 1877, Vossnack was appointed lecturer in mechanical engineering, naval architecture, and instrumental drawing. Despite the lack of apparatus for effective instruction, his efforts were so successful that his students presented him with a purse and an address in token of their appreciation. In October 1878 he visited several technological schools in the United States where he collected a series of models, apparatus, and designs for use in teaching. At the request of his students Vossnack wrote a letter to the Nova Scotia Council of Public Instruction and to the Halifax school commissioners recommending the introduction of instrumental and free-hand drawing into the Nova Scotia school course as preparation for technical education. However, the Technological Institute of Halifax lasted only two years, and in March 1879 Vossnack was advertising for a position as a consulting engineer.

During the 1880s he became interested in the sulphite process of making wood-pulp for paper. In March 1883 he visited England and the Continent to study the method's advantages. The next spring he printed a pamphlet, *About sulphite wood fibre: a new substitute for rags in paper making, equal in strength, if not superior to rag pulp*. In 1884 he succeeded in starting a wood-pulp company at Granville Ferry, a pioneering enterprise in the use of the sulphite process in Nova Scotia. He then became involved in promoting wood-pulp mills at Ellerhouse, in Hants County, and at Milton, in Queens County.

Vossnack had become a naturalized Canadian in January 1878. As well as being a skilled and enterprising engineer and a devoted teacher, he was a talented amateur artist. His water-colour, "Regatta, 1879," was exhibited in 1949 at the "200 Years of Art in Halifax" exhibition. After a short but severe illness involving congestion of the brain, he died in 1885, at age 46.

ALICE HOSKINS

Emil Vossnack was the author of *About sulphite wood fibre: a new substitute for rags in paper making, equal in strength, if not superior to rag pulp* (Halifax, 1884) and *Drawing in public, high & normal schools: a letter . . . to the Council of Public Instruction for the province of Nova Scotia, and the school commissioners of the city of Halifax* (Halifax, 1879).

PANS, MS file, Emile Vossnack, Biog.; RG 18, A, 1 (Emil Vossnack, 28 Jan. 1878). N.S., Provincial Museum and Science Library, *Report* (Halifax), 1931–32. *Acadian Recorder*, 6 June 1878, 27 March 1879, 5 March 1883, 7 Sept. 1885. *Morning Chronicle* (Halifax) 21, 31 Dec. 1877; 16 Oct. 1878; 7 Sept. 1885; 31 Dec. 1887.

W

WALLACE, WILLIAM, journalist and politician; b. 4 Feb. 1820 near Galston (Strathclyde), Scotland, son of John Wallace and Anne (Ann) Spiers; m. in 1852 Mary Ann (Anne) Kent of Simcoe, Canada West; d. 28 Aug. 1887 at Simcoe.

William Wallace, a member of the Church of England, received a parish school education at Whithorn (Dumfries and Galloway) before immigrating to Canada in 1840 or 1842. He settled at Simcoe, where on 16 Jan. 1861 he founded the *British Canadian*, a paper he owned and edited until his death, when he was succeeded by his son. Conservative in politics, the newspaper reprinted quantities of fiction and was concerned with local affairs, monetary reform, and agriculture. As was common in the 19th century, Wallace ran a printing business in conjunction with his paper and in 1879 he opened a retail bookstore. He also obtained public employment: he was paymaster of the Intercolonial Railway in 1869–70, assistant secretary to the Intercolonial Railway commissioners in 1870–71, and commissariat officer of the eastern division of the Canadian Pacific Railway survey in 1871–72.

An eager politician, Wallace served on the Simcoe school board for 40 years and was chairman when he died. He was reeve (1858) and mayor (1884) of Simcoe and a member of the Norfolk County Council. By 1872 he was so anxious to sit in the House of Commons that he contested Norfolk South as a Conservative against both Henry John Killmaster, a Liberal, and the incumbent Conservative, Peter Lawson. Lawson appealed to Sir John A. Macdonald* to secure Wallace's withdrawal, and the prime minister leaned heavily on Wallace, both by personal letter and through the agency of Aquila WALSH, the member for Norfolk North, but Wallace and his supporters "would consent to no compromise." Lawson finally withdrew, and Wallace won the riding by a handy 110 votes. He did not stand in 1874, when Lawson was defeated, but after John Stuart, the Liberal victor, was unseated, Wallace easily won the ensuing by-election on 16 Dec. 1874. Narrowly elected in 1878, he was defeated in 1882 and did not contest the seat in the next general election in February 1887.

Wallace was an interesting, but not an important federal politician. Although possessing an independent turn of mind, he was a loyal Conservative and in his second parliamentary session defended the government during the Pacific Scandal. He was also an ardent supporter of imperial federation and strongly anti-American. In favour of compulsory voting, he was nevertheless opposed to the ballot on the ground that "every man had a right to know how his neighbour voted." Railways were one of his *bêtes noires*; in 1882 he doubted "exceedingly whether Canada has ever derived any benefit from railway companies." In his opinion, as he wrote strongly to Macdonald, the transcontinental railway and the accompanying land grants should under no circumstances be given to speculators, especially if they were foreign. He wanted public ownership of all railway and telegraph systems.

In 1874 Wallace was accused of improper behaviour while a member of the house. In November, during the by-election in Norfolk South, Prime Minister Alexander Mackenzie* told John Stuart, the Liberal candidate, that between 1869 and 1872 Wallace had as a railway employee received more in federal funds than he had filed vouchers for; moreover, he had remained on the federal pay-roll after his election though no longer employed by the railway, and up to June 1873 again received more federal funds than he had accounted for. The totals showed a difference of $60,000. Mackenzie made no direct accusation in public, but his implicit suggestion was damaging, especially when coupled with a blunt statement to Stuart that Wallace had overpaid himself by about $1,770 in salary. Other Liberals were less prudent: Joseph Rymal, the member for Wentworth South, for example, accused Wallace of dishonesty and said "it was not at all improbable that a portion of that $60,000 was expended by Mr. WALLACE in 1872 in corrupting the electors of Norfolk." Wallace won the by-election in 1874. As the story later unfolded in the House of Commons, it became clear that he was a careless accountant, not a dishonest official. It also became evident, however, that he had indeed committed the major indiscretion of remaining on the public pay-roll after his election in 1872. He was thereafter careful to see that his name was not associated with dubious practices, even though he was always a dedicated constituency man, assiduous in his use of patronage.

Wallace's major claim to fame was his advocacy of currency reform. He belonged to the 19th-century tradition of agitators for irredeemable paper money and government notes. Variants of the proposal were advocated by men as influential as Isaac BUCHANAN and William Alexander Thomson*. Depression tended to precipitate these campaigns, and the slump of the 1870s occasioned lengthy discussions on monetary policy. Wallace argued that the depression was simply a product of mismanagement, and was "due to the system of credit, a necessity under our policy. It is false and vicious, impoverishing the many and enriching the few, destroying industry and degrading the people. . . . They had idolised gold, placed it on a throne, made it master of the world, and, to day, it was crushing the life out of capital and destroying labour." He felt that inflation too was a result of the "same abominable system of credit." Many observers attributed the economic ills of the 1870s to overproduction. Wallace dismissed this argument with contempt, stating that "over-production is of itself an impossibility – that the wants of men are as illimitable as human thought – and man is able to consume all that he can produce." The monetary system even generated the "conflict between capital and labour all over the world." The solution to these problems, of course, was irredeemable paper currency. "It was plain that money of this kind which would buy all a man wanted and pay all his debts was good enough." He revealed the crudeness of his approach when he exclaimed: "The hon. Minister of Finance thinks it best to borrow money. I think it better to make it."

These views were presented to the House of Commons over a ten-year period in long and repetitive speeches. Wallace often met with heavy heckling, but in spite of boring and irritating his colleagues, he retained considerable popularity. In 1885, 34 government members of parliament petitioned Macdonald on Wallace's behalf, asking that he be appointed dominion land commissioner at Winnipeg. Macdonald declined to make the appointment, however. The Simcoe *Norfolk Reformer* was obviously correct when it commented in Wallace's obituary: "No doubt he would have risen much higher in the Dominion's service but for his unfortunate connection with the Paper Money party, of which he was looked upon as the leader."

DONALD SWAINSON

PAC, MG 26, A. Can., House of Commons, *Debates*, 1875–82. *British Canadian* (Simcoe, Ont.), 1861–87. *Globe*, 1874. *Norfolk Reformer* (Simcoe), 1 Sept. 1887. *Canadian directory of parl.* (J. K. Johnson). *CPC*, 1873; 1875; 1879; 1883; 1889. *Illustrated historical atlas of the county of Norfolk, Ont.*, comp. H. R. Page (Toronto, 1877; repr. Belleville, Ont., 1972). Lewis Brown, *A history of Simcoe, 1829–1929 . . .* (Simcoe, 1929). C. D. W. Goodwin, *Canadian economic thought: the political economy of a developing nation, 1814–1914* (Durham, N.C., and London, 1961). *Simcoe and Norfolk County: in commemoration of the Simcoe reunion of Norfolk County old boys, August 2nd to 7th, 1924* (Simcoe, 1924). Swainson, "Personnel of politics."

WALLBRIDGE, LEWIS, lawyer, politician, and judge; b. 27 Nov. 1816 at Belleville, Upper Canada, son of William Wallbridge and Mary Everett; d. unmarried 20 Oct. 1887 at Winnipeg, Man.

Lewis Wallbridge's paternal great-uncle and grandfather had settled in the Bay of Quinte area in Upper Canada around the turn of the century and considered themselves New England loyalists. His father was a farmer, trader, and lumber merchant in Belleville. Lewis first attended Dr Benjamin Workman's school in Montreal for two years and from 1831 and 1833 studied at Upper Canada College in York (Toronto). He articled briefly in Belleville and then in the Toronto office of Robert Baldwin*. Called to the bar in 1839, he began to practise law in Belleville, taking mainly land, chancery, and criminal cases. In 1855 he became an elected member of the Law Society of Upper Canada and the next year a QC.

After running unsuccessfully for Hastings South in the election of 1854, as a moderate Reformer against Clear Grit Billa Flint*, Wallbridge won the seat in 1857 against a Conservative candidate. In the second campaign he advocated representation by population, national education, and the promotion of free enterprise by curtailing aid to the Grand Trunk Railway and by opening the northwest to competitive commerce; the Toronto *Globe* was pleased with his win. Wallbridge used his influence to secure moderate delegates from the Belleville area for the Reform convention of 1859, which he himself did not attend. Particularly dedicated to the issues of rep by pop and retrenchment rather than the more radical aspects of the Reform programme, he was not unfriendly towards John A. Macdonald* personally; many of his colleagues in the assembly he regarded as "babblers" given to long-winded theoretical speeches. He was reluctant to run again in 1861 and only did so, it was alleged, to keep the seat out of the hands of a government not dedicated to rep by pop.

Like George Brown*, he was ambivalent towards John Sandfield Macdonald*'s first Reform ministry in May 1862, which supported the double majority principle, and in 1863 he absented himself from the vote on the government-sponsored bill introduced by Richard William Scott* extending separate schools. However, in May 1863 he joined other moderate Reformers in the reconstructed ministry of Sandfield Macdonald and Antoine-Aimé Dorion*, becoming solicitor general for Canada West. He was re-elected in August 1863 with a stress in his campaign once more on retrenchment and liberal capitalism and on prohibition and sabbatarian regulations. When the house met, the premier enthusiastically proposed him as speaker. Immediately the former speaker, Joseph-Édouard Turcotte*, led a noisy outburst accusing Wallbridge of being anti-Catholic and anti-French. The majority of Lower Canadians opposed the nomination but it was successful thanks to support from the Upper Canadian Reformers. Although John A. Macdonald and most Conservatives had voted against him, the Conservative *Daily British Whig* of Kingston described the new speaker as a "sensible, intelligent man . . . perhaps the best man the Grit party could have chosen," one who was really "a Conservative at heart." He was retained as speaker during the administration of Sir Étienne-Paschal Taché* and John A. Macdonald, formed in 1864, and during the "Great Coalition" later that year.

Wallbridge was the last speaker for the Province of Canada, presiding with tact, skill, and firmness over the stormy debates in 1865 leading to confederation. During the time of coalition, although still a Reformer, he increased his ties with John A. Macdonald, and he carried considerable influence with Macdonald in local patronage. In June 1867 Wallbridge made it clear that, with rep by pop now secured, he would not follow Brown into Reform opposition but would support the continuing coalition led by Macdonald. He did not run in the 1867 elections, a decision influenced by his desire to avoid confrontation with his anti-confederate and dedicated Grit brother, Thomas Campbell Wallbridge, member for Hastings North from 1863 to 1867. Ten years later, in 1877, he announced his candidacy as a Conservative in Hastings West for the federal contest of 1878. He believed his election would be a mere formality, but the Catholic vote was against him and many old Conservatives viewed with bitterness his earlier Reform connections. Although he helped successful candidates in neighbouring ridings, he himself was defeated. Afterwards he often wrote to Macdonald, passing on "what the country folk think."

His private life prospered. He had served as a director of the Bank of Upper Canada from 1862 until 1865, and had the largest and most respected legal practice in the Belleville area. By 1880 he was being described as "one of the oldest and most prominent barristers . . . in the province of Ontario." Now a noted gentleman farmer, he was elected that year as 2nd vice-president of the newly formed Beekeepers' Association. Wallbridge was an active member of the Church of England, but he served on the senate of the Episcopal Methodists' Albert College, where in 1869 his brother had established the professorship of mining and agriculture.

In December 1882 Wallbridge was named chief justice of Manitoba by the John A. Macdonald government although he had never held a judicial appointment. Justice Minister Sir Alexander Campbell* defended this action on the grounds of Wallbridge's familiarity with Manitoba lawyers, many of whom had come from Ontario, and of his extensive knowledge of legal matters relating to land which were important in Manitoba. Mackenzie Bowell*, who had been defeated by Thomas Campbell Wallbridge in Hastings North in 1863 and then defeated him in 1867, was far from convinced and wrote bitterly to Macdonald, referring to Lewis' "extreme egotism." However, Wallbridge left Belleville with glowing testimonials, including some from local French Canadians to whom he emphasized that he would uphold everyone's "perfect equality" before the law.

In Manitoba, Wallbridge quickly secured the respect of the legal profession. He continued to act as a local informant for Sir John A. Macdonald and tried to calm the sometimes stormy relations between Conservative premier John NORQUAY and the prime minister. In 1886 he served, with some initial reluctance, as the royal commissioner investigating charges of corruption against the Manitoba premier; in his report he exonerated Norquay of any personal wrongdoing. Wallbridge died the following year and was buried in Belleville.

BRUCE W. HODGINS

AO, Wallbridge family papers. PAC, MG 26, A. *Canada Law Journal*, new ser., 18 (1882): 429; 23 (1887): 361–62. Man., Legislative Assembly, *Journals*, 1886: 189–95. *Daily British Whig*, 14 Aug. 1863. *Globe*, 1882, 1887. *Hastings Chronicle* (Belleville, Ont.), 1857, 1861, 1867. *Intelligencer* (Belleville), 1880, 1887. *Canadian biog. dict.*, I: 185–86. *Cyclopædia of Canadian biog.* (Rose, 1888), 374. *Illustrated historical atlas of the counties of Hastings and Prince Edward, Ont.* (Toronto, 1878; repr. Belleville, 1972). G. E. Boyce, *Historic Hastings* (Belleville, 1967).

WALSH, AQUILA, civil engineer, politician, and civil servant; b. 15 May 1823 in Charlotteville Township, Upper Canada, second son of Francis Leigh (Legh) Walsh; m. 21 Nov. 1850 Jane Wilson Adams, and they had a son and four daughters; d. 6 March 1885 at Winnipeg, Man.

Aquila Walsh's grandfather, Thomas Leigh (Legh) Walsh, UEL, came in 1793 to Upper Canada where he was a provincial land surveyor, and from 1796 to 1810 the registrar of deeds for Norfolk County. Aquila's father, Francis Leigh Walsh, fought in the War of 1812, served as registrar of Norfolk County from 1810 until his death in 1884, and represented Norfolk in the House of Assembly of Upper Canada between 1824 and 1828 and in 1835–36.

Following his education at the London District Grammar School, Aquila Walsh became a civil engineer at Simcoe and a partner in the firm of Walsh and Mercer, provincial land surveyors and civil engineers. In 1848 he became deputy registrar of Norfolk County and retained that position until 1861 when he was elected to represent the county in the Legislative Assembly of the Province of Canada. He was re-elected in 1863.

A staunch supporter of the Conservative party throughout his life, Walsh persistently sought political rewards for his loyalty and was resentful and bitter when ignored. He was elected to the House of Commons in 1867 and hoped to become its first speaker. "Few of your supporters," he wrote to Sir John A. Macdonald* in October 1867, "have entered or remained in public life at a greater inconvenience or sacrifice than myself and none have received less in the way of consideration or promotion." In 1868 he was appointed chairman of the Intercolonial Railway Commission, a post he held until 1874. He sought to be a cabinet minister, superintendent of government railways, chairman of a commission on the Pacific railway in 1879, a senator, and lieutenant governor of Manitoba. When others were given recognition he protested, for example in 1879 when he again pointed to what he claimed to be extraordinary sacrifices in time, money, and business for the party.

Walsh was unsuccessful in Norfolk North in the elections of 1872 and 1878; he did not run in 1874, and his support for the Conservative candidate in the riding was not effective. He had ceased to control his constituency; his political usefulness was over.

However, his protests and "naggings" about his services continued. In 1882, shortly after he became mayor of Simcoe, he finally received a response.

Macdonald, as minister of the interior, noted in October 1881 that when this department was organized in 1873 the settlement of the west had barely begun. The construction of the Canadian Pacific Railway had provided an impetus to settlement, and the resulting increase in the volume of business connected with the administration of lands made it "absolutely necessary" to have an officer stationed in Winnipeg. Walsh was appointed commissioner of crown lands on 4 Feb. 1882, to take charge of the land-granting, timber, and mining business of the department in Manitoba and the North-West Territories.

Walsh was a conscientious, popular, and able officer. Yet he had personal reservations about the position. He complained that, having previously neglected his business for politics, he could not now "do credit" to his social position on his salary. He resented the fine home which the Hudson's Bay Company provided for its land agent, Charles John BRYDGES, and Brydges' "impertinence" in writing his long-time confidant Macdonald about land matters. Walsh was also annoyed that local patronage was controlled by the department in Ottawa. Having served as commissioner for just three years, Walsh died in March 1885.

HARTWELL BOWSFIELD

Eva Brook Donly Museum (Simcoe, Ont.), Norfolk Hist. Soc. coll., Walsh papers (mfm. at PAC). PAC, MG 26, A; RG 15, DII, 1, v.266, file 38372. *British Canadian* (Simcoe), 11 March 1885. *Manitoba Daily Free Press*, 9 March 1885. *Canadian directory of parl.* (J. K. Johnson). "Thomas William Walsh," Assoc. of Ontario Land Surveyors, *Annual report* (Toronto), 34 (1919): 86–87.

WANDERING SPIRIT. *See* KAPAPAMAHCHAKWEW

WARREN, JOHN HENRY, merchant and politician; b. *c.* 1812 in Devon, England, one of five children of William Warren, sailing captain and supply merchant based at St John's, Nfld; d. 28 April 1885 at Belgrave Terrace, Torquay, England, survived by two sons and three daughters.

Little is known of John Henry Warren's early life. In the late 1830s he was in partnership with William Wheatley in the fish and wholesale-retail trade in St John's. The firm became insolvent in 1840, and the following year Warren established his own business, a medium-sized operation exporting fish to Europe and providing supplies for vessels in the seal-fishery. For the latter trade Warren bought his manufactured goods through an agent in Britain, and he generally sold them at lower prices than most other merchants in the city. Of the vessels newly registered in Newfoundland between 1841 and 1853, 11 were owned by Warren. Although he lost his premises in the fire which largely destroyed St John's in 1846, Warren quickly rebuilt and continued in business until April 1851 when he declared bankruptcy and apparently leased his property to local merchants for an annual rental of £265. A year later he began his long career in Newfoundland politics.

A Conservative, Warren ran successfully in seven out of the nine elections held from 1852 to 1878. Except in 1873, he stood for the district of Bonavista Bay. In the 1850s this district was generally regarded as a Tory rotten borough. Its reputation reflected the great political influence Conservative politicians could exert in the predominantly Protestant area through their mercantile connections in St John's, such as J. and W. Stewart and Company, Baine, Johnston and Company, and Brooking and Company, all of which had branches in the Bonavista Bay district. In addition, the Protestant Conservatives could use sectarian arguments against their Catholic Liberal opponents as they did in the election of 1855. In that year a Central Protestant Committee was established at St John's to coordinate the campaign, but the Liberals, led by Philip Francis Little*, nevertheless won the election. Finally, Warren, although a St John's resident, appealed to the Bonavista Bay voters because his family, like most of those in the area, was from Devon, and such an association was an important asset in Newfoundland politics.

In 1861, after Governor Sir Alexander Bannerman* dismissed the Liberal ministry led by John Kent* and appointed a Conservative government under Hugh William HOYLES, Warren was named surveyor general and chairman of the Board of Works. The latter position, which he held until 1865, entailed responsibility for all public buildings, institutions, and roads in the colony. It was also the main vehicle for the distribution of public funds and hence gave control of patronage. By supporting union with Canada, the pro-confederation Conservatives were defeated in the general election of 1869 by an alliance of Roman Catholics and Water Street merchants led by Charles James Fox BENNETT, and Warren was himself unsuccessful in Bonavista Bay. Disavowing any further sympathy for confederation, the Conservatives, under the leadership of Frederic Bowker Terrington Carter*, had regrouped by 1873 and based their political appeal in the election of that year upon sectarianism. Warren and William Vallance Whiteway* successfully exploited the organization of the Orange lodges and were elected for the Protestant district of Trinity along with J. Steer. Although Bennett's party was returned to office it was soon forced to resign. New elections were held in 1874 and Carter obtained a large majority. Warren was re-elected for his old constituency of

Bonavista Bay with the help of the influential Orange lodges in the district, and once again was appointed surveyor general. He was defeated in the next election held in 1878 and was named to the Legislative Council on 13 Jan. 1879 by Premier Whiteway. He remained a member until his death.

Warren was perhaps typical of the St John's merchant who became a politician. He adroitly exploited the sectarian animosities of outport voters for political gain. Moreover, through his son-in-law, Charles R. BOWRING, a leading merchant, he had influence in the political and economic life of St John's and he was a strong supporter and protector of the interests of the mercantile community for many years both in the House of Assembly and later in the Legislative Council.

MELVIN BAKER

Maritime Hist. Group Arch., Board of Trade ser. 107–8 (entries for John Henry Warren); Warren name file. Supreme Court of Newfoundland (St John's), Registry, will of John Henry Warren, 7 Oct. 1885. Nfld., *Blue book*, 1852–85; House of Assembly, *Journal*, 1852–86. *Royal Gazette* (St John's), 1843–82. Devine, *Ye olde St. John's*. Gunn, *Political hist. of Nfld.* J. K. Hiller, "Confederation defeated: the Newfoundland election of 1869" (unpublished paper presented to the CHA, 1976). Prowse, *Hist. of Nfld.* (1895). Elinor Senior, "The origin and political activities of the Orange Order in Newfoundland, 1863–1890" (MA thesis, Memorial Univ. of Newfoundland, St John's, 1959).

WATSON, SAMUEL JAMES, journalist, poet, author, dramatist, and librarian; b.*c.* 1842 near Belfast (Northern Ireland); m. Margaret Janet; d. 30 Oct. 1881 in Toronto Ont.

Available details of Samuel James Watson's life are surprisingly few considering that he was librarian of the Legislative Library of Ontario for nine years. He had at least one brother in Canada, referred to as "J. M.," possibly the John M. Watson appointed assistant librarian after Samuel's death. There is mention of another brother, Isaac, who may also have worked at the legislature.

Samuel Watson was educated at the Royal Belfast Academical Institution before coming to Montreal about 1857 where at one time he worked as a journalist on the staff of the *Herald*. His knowledge of shorthand allowed him to act as a recorder, transcribing parliamentary proceedings, and in this capacity he reported the confederation debates of 1865. By 1871 he was in Toronto working as a reporter for the *Globe*; he was also employed as a sessional writer for the Ontario Legislative Assembly transcribing at various meetings. In February 1872 he was hired by the assembly at $20 per hour to record committee hearings of the "Proton Outrage" investigation [*see* Abram William LAUDER]. On 1 July 1872 he became librarian of the Legislative Library of Ontario. During the union period there had been a library that followed the peripatetic assembly; at confederation it was located permanently in Ottawa [*see* Alpheus TODD]. Watson's chief responsibility was to build up a new collection in Toronto. He increased the meagre 1,395 volumes held in 1872 to well over 10,000 by 1881, and prepared a catalogue of the holdings. He also began an interlibrary loan service with the Université Laval in Quebec City and the Quebec legislature. The value of his work may be reflected in his annual salary which climbed from $800 to $1,400 in 1881. In 1878 his health failed and the legislature granted him funds to visit Hot Springs, Ark. He recovered somewhat and continued as librarian, but was in poor health until he died.

In addition to writing for daily newspapers, Watson had published a variety of works. In 1870 a serial historical romance, "The peace-killer; or, the massacre of Lachine," appeared in the *Canadian Illustrated News*. With the late-17th-century French-Iroquois wars for a background, the tale, resembling mid-19th-century popular fiction, relates the enmity between an evil Abenaki and a noble Huron chief whose sister loves a courageous French solider. In 1874 Watson published the first volume of *The constitutional history of Canada* (a second volume was unfinished at his death), a study of Canada and its basis in the British constitution. *Ravlan*, a poetic drama set in Celtic England, appeared next, in 1876, with a long poem, "The legend of the roses." Inspired by the medieval *Voiage and travayle of John Maundeville, Kt.*, the "Legend" tells of a Christian maid saved from burning at the stake by Christ who changed the fire into red and white roses. The verse is workmanlike but suffers from too much philosophical rambling about weighty concerns. *Ravlan*, an inferior work in many ways, provides a typical example of literary poetic drama of the time in Canada with its pseudo-Shakespearian diction and verse, prolix sententious style, conventional melodramatic plot set in the distant past, and tragic ending. Finally, in 1880, Watson published *The powers of Canadian parliaments*, an examination of the Ontario government in relation to the federal one, the governor general, and the British parliament. It is surprisingly detailed for the work of a man neither a constitutional lawyer nor a scholar. In part it was a response to *Are legislatures parliaments? A study and review*, by John Fennings TAYLOR, which had appeared the previous year.

Watson is rarely spoken of now and is probably remembered only as the author of *Ravlan*. But the details of his life reveal a man of broader scope and accomplishment than *Ravlan* would suggest. He is a good example of those peripheral figures who have quietly sown the seeds of our present learning and literature in Canada.

RICHARD PLANT

Samuel James Watson was the author of *The constitutional history of Canada* (Toronto, 1874); *The legend of the roses: a poem; Ravlan: a drama* (Toronto, 1876). A shorter form of the poem, "The legend of the roses," was first published in *Canadian Illustrated News* (Montreal), 24 Dec. 1870. He also wrote "The peace-killer; or, the massacre of Lachine," which was published in weekly instalments in the *Canadian Illustrated News*, 2 July–27 Aug. 1870. This historical novel was translated, probably by Emmanuel-Marie BLAIN de Saint-Aubin, and published as "Le Brandon de discorde, ou le massacre de Lachine," in *L'Opinion publique*, 10 févr.–13 avril 1876. His last work was *The powers of Canadian parliaments* (Toronto, 1880).

CTA, Toronto assessment rolls, St Andrew's Ward, 1873, 1878; St George's Ward, 1881. PAC, MG 27, I, J13. Ont., Legislative Assembly, *Journals*, 1873: 12–14; 1874 (2nd session): 4–5; Legislature, *Sessional papers*, 1873, III, no.41; 1875–76, III, no.10; 1877, II, no.6; 1878, I, no.3; 1879, IV, no.12; 1880, III, no.12; 1881, III, no.12; 1882, VI, no.59. *Globe*, 31 Oct.–2 Nov. 1881. *Irish Canadian* (Toronto), 3 Nov. 1881. *Toronto World*, 31 Oct. 1881. *Dominion annual register*, 1880–81. *Toronto directory*, 1867–89. O. A. Cudney, *A chronological history of the Legislative Library of Ontario* (Ottawa, 1969). M. D. Edwards, *A stage in our past, English-language theatre in eastern Canada from the 1790s to 1914* ([Toronto], 1968), 95–96. É.-Z. Massicotte, "Samuel-James Watson," *BRH*, 24 (1918): 76.

WEBB, WILLIAM HOSTE, lawyer and politician; b. 24 Nov. 1820 in Hampshire, England, son of Edward Webb and Sarah Ann Whitcomb; m. in 1846 Isabella, daughter of Lieutenant-Colonel William Morris, and they had seven children; d. 19 Dec. 1890 at Sherbrooke, Que.

William Hoste Webb's father, a commander in the Royal Navy, emigrated to Canada with his family in 1836. At that time, immigration from Britain was increasing through the work of the British American Land Company, a colonizing venture formed in London to organize British settlement in the Eastern Townships, and the company had opened an office at Sherbrooke in 1835. Edward Webb settled in Brompton Township, on the Rivière Saint-François, and called the land he undertook to develop Hoste Farm in honour of Sir William Hoste, a famous officer under whom he had served during the Napoleonic Wars. Webb was a member of the British élite that dominated the political and economic life of the Eastern Townships in the 19th century. However, he died prematurely on 22 Nov. 1839, and it was through his son William Hoste that the Webb family exercised an influence in the region.

William Hoste had studied at the Royal Naval School in London. From 1841 to 1843, not many years after his arrival in Canada, he served as secretary to the council of the district of Brompton and to the school board, and in 1845 he was a representative in the newly established Brompton Township Council. It was not, however, until the 1850s that he became seriously involved in public life. In 1850, after articling in the law office of Mack and Muir in Montreal, Webb was called to the bar of Canada East, and from 1855 to 1857 and again from 1879 to 1883 he held the office of warden of Melbourne and Richmond townships. Following the elections of 1857–58, he entered the Legislative Assembly of the Province of Canada as representative for the new constituency of Richmond and Wolfe. In 1853 Sherbrooke had been subdivided into the two constituencies of Compton and of Sherbrooke and Wolfe. Some historians hold that the electoral map was redrawn specifically to increase Anglophone representation in the house. The "quiet invasion" of the Eastern Townships by French Canadians in the mid 19th century gives much substance to this hypothesis. In any case, the amalgamation of Richmond County (as the constituency of Sherbrooke County was renamed in 1855) with Wolfe County sharply affected Webb's political career, for although the former, according to the 1861 census, was 85 per cent English-speaking, the latter was 82 per cent French-speaking. Webb had no French-speaking opponent when he was elected in 1857 as a government candidate, but he was defeated in 1861 by Charles de Cazes*, the first French-speaking MLA from the Eastern Townships. However, the English-speaking voters in Richmond got their own back in 1863 when Webb was returned to parliament, where he strongly supported confederation. In the 1867 elections he allied himself with a French Canadian candidate, notary Jacques Picard of Wotton. Webb was to support Picard at the provincial level and Picard to support Webb at the federal. Picard would actually have preferred a seat in the House of Commons because he was convinced that French Canadians had "need of more members of their own extraction at Ottawa than in the parliament of Quebec." However, there were more English-speaking voters in the county, and he accepted the provincial nomination rather than risk losing "the member to whom the French Canadians are entitled." In return, he insisted on the alliance which guaranteed the Conservative party's double victory and the division of political power between the English- and French-speaking people in the riding. This type of alliance was increasingly common in the Eastern Townships until the end of the 19th century. It even proved to be the most reliable guarantee of good understanding between the two ethnic groups.

Webb was defeated in the 1874 elections that followed the Pacific Scandal, but the Conservative party rewarded him for 15 years of service by appointing him to the Legislative Council of Quebec for the division of Wellington. He held this seat from 1875 to 1887; the government of Honoré Mercier* then appointed him sheriff of the judicial district of Saint-

François, following an arrangement whereby Webb resigned from the council in favour of Liberal Francis Edward Gilman. It was while Webb was carrying out his duties as sheriff that his life ended in a dramatic fashion. He was stricken with an apoplectic fit on 19 Dec. 1890, minutes before an execution in the Sherbrooke prison.

ANDRÉE DÉSILETS

AC, Saint-François (Sherbrooke), Minutiers, William Ritchie, 23 Sept. 1846. PAC, RG 31, A1, 1851, 1861, Compton, Richmond-Wolfe, and Sherbrooke counties. Can., Prov. du, Assemblée législative, *Journaux*, 1846; 1854–55; *Statuts*, 1854–55, c.55; 1860, c.135. *Le Courrier de Saint-Hyacinthe*, 23 déc. 1890. *La Minerve*, 4 avril 1873; 13, 20, 23 déc. 1890. *Le Pionnier de Sherbrooke* (Sherbrooke, Qué.), 10 nov. 1866; 9 mars, 10 avril, 4 mai, 28 juin, juillet-octobre 1867; 27 nov. 1868; 27 mai 1869; 29 déc. 1876; 17 mars 1887; 19, 26 déc. 1890. *Sherbrooke Gazette and Eastern Townships Advertiser* (Sherbrooke), 15 Jan., 16 Aug. 1858; 29 Jan., 4 May 1859; 8 Aug. 1863; 28 Jan. 1865. *Stanstead Journal* (Rock Island, Que.), March 1887, 25 Dec. 1890. *Canadian biog. dict*, I: 27–28. *CPC*, 1869; 1872. J. Desjardins, *Guide parl.* G. Turcotte, *Le Conseil législatif de Québec*, 298–99. L. S. Channell, *History of Compton County, and sketches of the Eastern Townships, district of St. Francis, and Sherbrooke County . . .* (Cookshire, Que., 1896; repr. Belleville, Ont., 1975). Rumilly, *Hist. de la prov. de Québec*, II–III.

WEBER, ANNA (sometimes called **Nancy**), needleworker and fraktur artist; b. 3 June 1814 in Earl Township, Lancaster County, Penn., the fifth of ten children of John Weber and Catherine Gehman; d. 12 Oct. 1888 in Woolwich Township, Waterloo County, Ont.

Anna Weber, daughter of a Mennonite minister and farmer, immigrated to Upper Canada from Pennsylvania with a party of 13 in April 1825. Her family settled on a farm one mile south of Conestogo in a predominantly Pennsylvania-German Mennonite community. She lived with her parents, and, after the death of her father on 21 Jan. 1854, with her mother, who died on 2 June 1864. For the remainder of her life Anna was moved from household to household within the Mennonite community. She lived at the fringe, and largely at the expense, of her social group until her death, apparently from an accidental overdose of medicine.

After 1835, the year in which Anna had first made a sampler to demonstrate her skill at needlework, she did much stitchery. She made show towels – finely embroidered linen strips decorated with traditional motifs and designs for the hope chests of neighbourhood girls – stuffed animals, including horses and squirrels as toys for children, and hooked mats of hand-dyed woollen materials which depicted stylized scenes.

About 1855 Anna began the painting of distinctive pen and wash fraktur art, which she continued until her death. This form of art had originated in Germany more than two centuries previously but was highly developed by the Pennsylvania-Germans. It is a purely decorative art, often used to illustrate manuscripts, book-plates, and such family records as birth and baptismal certificates. There is a definite lack of perspective in these pieces and scale is ignored. Recurring motifs – hearts, tulips, paired birds, and the tree of life – appear in balanced, usually symmetrical, form. Anna inherited and developed these traditional designs but her actual subjects were usually taken from nature. Instead of the traditional unicorn, for example, Anna would portray a stylized horse.

Practically all of Anna Weber's fraktur works are signed and precisely dated, with the lettering forming an integral part of the painted frame around each design. Her paintings, which resemble art nouveau stained glass or tiles, display a good sense of composition and colours which are soft and yet definite. The whole effect is one of assurance, and presumably pleasure, in these sprightly finished products which were often made as gifts for children.

The majority of fraktur artists, including Mr Altsdorf who probably taught Anna in Pennsylvania, were schoolmasters. A female fraktur artist was an anomaly but Anna was the most original and prolific of Ontario's fraktur artists. Although afflicted with dropsy, arthritis, and the ailments of age, her concentrated efforts produced many fraktur paintings, of which about 60 are extant. Anna Weber was said to have been of "unbrilliant mind," but because of her individualistic temperament she was allowed to sign her paintings – a "sinful" practice in the self-denying Mennonite community. Like much folk art in Canada, Anna's is dominated by nature and her fraktur paintings also reflect her strong ethnic heritage.

E. REGINALD GOOD

M. S. Bird, *Ontario fraktur: a Pennsylvania-German folk tradition in early Canada* (Toronto, 1977). E. R. Good, *Anna's art: the fraktur art of Anna Weber, a Waterloo County Mennonite artist, 1814–1888* (Kitchener, Ont., 1976). J. R. Harper, *A people's art: primitive, naïve, provincial, and folk painting in Canada* (Toronto and Buffalo, N.Y., 1974). D. A. Shelley, *The fraktur-writings or illuminated manuscripts of the Pennsylvania Germans* (Allentown, Pa., 1961). J. J. Stoudt, *Early Pennsylvania arts and crafts* (New York and London, 1964). M. [S.] Bird, "Ontario fraktur art: a decorative tradition in three Germanic settlements," *OH*, 68 (1976): 247–72. Nancy-Lou Patterson, "Anna Weber hat das gemacht: Anna Weber (1814–1888) – a fraktur painter of Waterloo County, Ontario," *Mennonite Life* (North Newton, Kans.), 30 (1975), no.4: 15–19.

WELLS, WILLIAM BENJAMIN, lawyer, journalist, politician, author, and judge; b. 3 Oct. 1809 in

Augusta Township, Upper Canada, second son of William Wells and Sarah Clough; m. 23 Feb. 1843 Mary Julia Hogan, and they had four sons and five daughters; d. 8 April 1881 at Toronto, Ont.

William Benjamin Wells was the son of a loyalist who immigrated to Canada from New Hampshire in 1787. He was educated at the Augusta Grammar School under John Bethune*, as well as in the United States and Lower Canada, before studying law in the office of Marshall Spring Bidwell* in Kingston, Upper Canada. Wells was called to the bar in 1833 and began practising law in Prescott, in partnership with Read Burritt. At the same time he began a career as a Reform journalist and author. He operated the Prescott *Vanguard* for a short period prior to the rebellion of 1837 and contributed political articles to other papers in Upper Canada and in Montreal and New York. His father's affluence, as he wrote in 1837, permitted him to be independent of political influence. In 1834 and again in 1836 he was elected to represent Grenville in the House of Assembly of Upper Canada. He took an active part in the proceedings of the assembly and his political position, at first quite moderate, became increasingly radical after the election of 1836.

As a protest against the conduct of Sir Francis Bond Head* in that election Wells refused to take his seat and travelled to England in November for a meeting with the colonial secretary, Baron Glenelg, to object to the actions of Head and explain the demands of the Reformers. He planned to join Robert Baldwin* and Dr Charles Duncombe* who had both preceded him but found upon his arrival that they had already left England. Wells, however, stayed for nearly a year during which time he wrote and published *Canadiana: containing sketches of Upper Canada, and the crisis in its political affairs*. Though the book contained inaccuracies and was extreme in its treatment of Head and prominent Tories such as John Strachan*, it was a clear and well-argued presentation of the radical Reform programme of the time. It advocated such measures as responsible government, an elected legislative council, control of provincial revenue by the assembly, abolition of the clergy reserves, separation of church and state, annulment of the charter of the Canada Company, revision of the charter of King's College (Toronto), abolition of primogeniture, adoption of the secret ballot, reform of the land granting system, and a more equitable distribution of public offices. Wells ended with a threat of armed rebellion and the "forced separation" of the British North American colonies, should all other means of reform fail. His book does not appear to have had any great impact in Upper Canada but it did receive some attention from journalists and politicians in England.

After returning to Canada Wells took no part in the planning or execution of the rebellion of 1837. When word of the Toronto rising on 5–7 December reached him he was in Bytown (Ottawa) on business. He returned to Prescott, but believing that a warrant had been issued for his arrest he crossed the river to Ogdensburg, N.Y., on 16 Dec. 1837 with his older brother, Horace Clough Wells. In early 1838 he was in touch with other refugees in New York State including William Lyon Mackenzie* and David Gibson* and for a short time was a supporter of the Patriot movement to liberate Upper Canada by armed invasion. He was with the Patriots during the raid on Hickory Island, 22 Feb. 1838, but there are conflicting reports of his role in that event. A witness claimed that Wells had been among the attackers and had been seen in the company of the leader of the raid, Rensselaer Van Rensselaer, "lying in bed drunk with his clothes and boots on." Wells himself wrote to the *Brockville Recorder* in March 1838 declaring this account to be a lie and later produced affidavits, by two men who had been present at the raid, to show that his purpose at Hickory Island had been to dissuade the Patriots from attacking Upper Canada. In any case suspicion regarding his actions lead to his expulsion from the assembly on 27 Feb. 1838 by a vote of 30 to one.

Wells remained in Ogdensburg in the belief that he would be arrested if he returned to Upper Canada but in fact no official charge was ever laid against him. When, in reply to his personal petitions, this fact was made known to him by the Executive Council Office in November 1838, he returned to Prescott and resumed his law practice. Wells never again held elective office and in an attempt to re-enter public life in 1847 he was not even able to secure the Reform nomination for Grenville; it went to his former law partner Read Burritt, who was the member from 1847 to 1851. In the 1840s, however, Wells acted as a political confidant and adviser on patronage matters to Robert Baldwin in Grenville County. He was rewarded by being appointed by the Reform administration of Baldwin and Louis-Hippolyte La Fontaine* to be the first county court judge for Kent on 11 Jan. 1851. He immediately moved with his family to the county town, Chatham, where he continued to live until his retirement from the bench in 1878. His judicial career, while uneventful, was marked by a reputation for sound judgement. In a letter to William Lyon Mackenzie in 1859 Wells claimed to have handled 30,000 cases and travelled 15,000 miles in the performance of his duties. He never lost his early interest in literature and journalism and continued to contribute articles on law and sport to Canadian and American periodicals. He received a provincial pension from the date of his retirement, 2 Oct. 1878, until his death in 1881.

J. K. Johnson

William Benjamin Wells was the author of *Canadiana: containing sketches of Upper Canada, and the crisis in its political affairs* (London, 1837). An unpublished manuscript, "A short sketch of the history of Wm. Wells and his family" (1875), by I. B. Wells, is in the possession of Ruth McKenzie (Ottawa). See Morgan, *Bibliotheca Canadensis*, for a discussion on Wells's other writings.

AO, MU 1806, Wells to W. L. Mackenzie, 30 Jan. 1838; MU 1813, 20 March, 13, 30 July 1850; 22 Nov. 1851; MU 1814, 4 Jan. 1852; MU 1815, 12 Dec. 1859. MTL, Robert Baldwin papers. PAC, MG 24, C10; MG 26, A, 508; 510; 514; MG 29, D61, 18; RG 1, E3, 97; RG 68, General index, 1841–67: 135. Upper Canada, House of Assembly, *Journal*, 1835–38. *Brockville Recorder* (Brockville, [Ont.]), 1 Feb., 8, 22 March, 5 April 1838. Armstrong, *Handbook of Upper Canadian chronology*. *Dominion annual register*, 1880–81. W. S. Wallace, "The periodical literature of Upper Canada," *CHR*, 12 (1931): 4–22.

WHALE, ROBERT (Robert Reginald), painter; baptized 25 March 1805 at Altarnun, Cornwall, England, the son of Christopher and Grace Whale; m. in 1837 Ellen Heard, and they had five children including painters John Claude and Robert Heard; d. 2 July 1887 at Brantford, Ont.

Robert Whale demonstrated artistic talents, especially for portraiture, at an early age. The collections of local country gentlemen provided him with access to works by famous artists and he may have enjoyed the patronage of these gentlemen in the form of portrait commissions. Virtually self-taught, he reportedly copied many paintings at the National Gallery, London, and admiration for Sir Joshua Reynolds is evident in his work.

In 1852 Whale immigrated to Canada West with his wife and children; they settled in Burford, a village near Brantford. He did not lose any time in re-establishing himself as a painter, winning prizes for four paintings in the "Professional Category" in the Upper Canada Provincial Exhibition in the year of his arrival. He was a frequent exhibitor and prize-winner in these exhibitions until 1867, entering mainly landscapes, portraits, and animal subjects as well as some still-life, historical, marine, and non-Canadian studies. Whale did not sever his ties with England completely; he won a silver medal for a landscape sent to the international exhibition in London in 1862. His "A portrait of a lady" won 1st prize at the 1873 exhibition of the Ontario Society of Artists; three of his works appeared in the 1881 exhibition. That same year "A portrait of a lady" was presented at the second annual exhibition of the Royal Canadian Academy of Arts in Halifax, N.S. The following year Whale was listed as an associate of the academy at their showing and two of his portraits were displayed; works by him again appeared at their exhibitions in 1883 and 1886.

During his many years of painting, Whale, devoting himself totally to his art, travelled throughout western Ontario painting portraits and landscapes in Brantford, Hamilton, St Catharines, and at the Niagara Falls; he also made at least one trip to the White Mountains in New Hampshire. He completed numerous views of the Grand River area of Brant County as well as portraits of many of Brantford's distinguished citizens, and he painted portraits of Sir Allan Napier MacNab*, Adam Brown*, Sir George William Burton*, and Charles John BRYDGES. Depending on his income from painting to support his large family, Whale sometimes had difficulty making ends meet. To augment his funds he created a panorama of the Indian Mutiny of 1857, complete with colourful narrative, which was exhibited across the province. J. Russell Harper describes it as "combined horror movie, television thriller, and news documentary." Touring the county fairs, often in the company of his nephew and son-in-law, John Hicks Whale, who was an amateur artist, Whale participated in art competitions offering monetary prizes; apparently "the Whales monopolized all awards."

In the summer of 1870 Robert paid a short visit to England with John Hicks Whale who reported to his wife Mary that "Artist" wore himself out painting portraits of friends, even to the point of neglecting to visit his sisters. Robert's wife, ill during his absence, died in 1871 soon after his return to Canada. He went again to England shortly after, stayed until September 1876, and then lived with Mary in Brantford. There he continued to paint with his customary zeal.

Whale's paintings, almost exclusively in oils, vary greatly in quality, largely because so many were executed quickly to raise money; a number were painted as favours for friends and many are unsigned. The same compositional devices recur and he repeatedly copied his most popular canvasses. Whale was reported to have done the first nude studies in the province but it is doubtful that they were ever exhibited. At his best Whale was a competent and sensitive portraitist, expecially when the sitters were women and children. He was capable of the careful and skilful enrichment of facial features and adornments such as jewellery and lace. His career, however, illustrates the diverted ambition of many portrait painters in this period who were forced to produce marketable canvasses. Nevertheless, Whale's views of southern Ontario and portraits of its inhabitants present an important historical record despite the uneven quality of the paintings themselves.

LINDA BELSHAW BEATTY

National Gallery of Canada Library (Ottawa), Documentation and biblio. file, Robert Whale. PAC, MG 28, I126. *Weekly Expositor* (Brantford, Ont.), 15 Sept. 1876, 8 July 1887. Harper, *Early painters and engravers*. R. H. Hubbard, *Canadian landscape painting, 1670–1930; the artist and the land . . .* (Madison, Wis., 1973). *Robert Whale of Brant: a preliminary survey; Glenhyrst Arts Council, the Art Gallery of Brantford*, [comp. Mario Polidori] ([Brantford?, 1969?]). "Robert R. Whale, A.R.A., well-known artist," *Semi-centennial, 1877–1927; incorporation of the city of Brantford: the Brantford Expositor anniversary number* (Brantford, 1927), 129. A. H. Robson, *Canadian landscape painters* (Toronto, 1932).

WHITAKER, GEORGE, Church of England clergyman and educator; b. 9 Oct. 1811 at Bratton, Wiltshire, England, eighth child of Philip Whitaker, a farmer, and Anne Andrews; m. 22 Oct. 1844 Arundel Charlotte Burton, and they had at least eight children; d. 27 Aug. 1882 at Salisbury, England.

George Whitaker, whose parents were Baptists, was educated at Frome Grammar School and Charterhouse School. In 1829 he was admitted to Queens' College, Cambridge (BA 1833, MA 1836), becoming in 1834 fellow and in 1835 lecturer in classics. He had become an adherent of the Church of England and was ordained deacon on 4 June 1837 and priest on 27 May the following year. He left Queens' in the autumn of 1840 upon his appointment to the college living of Oakington, Cambridgeshire.

In 1851 Whitaker became the first provost and professor of divinity of the University of Trinity College, which was being built at that time in Toronto. He was chosen by a committee of four prominent clergymen in England who were requested by Bishop John Strachan* in February 1851 to find candidates for the provostship and two professorships: they should "belong to neither extreme of the Church, but . . . they should be true sons of the Church of England, not low, or what is called Evangelical, but equally distant from Romanism on the one hand and Dissent on the other." Early in November 1851 Whitaker arrived in Toronto, and his appointment was confirmed on 8 December; on this date the Reverend Edward St John Parry was named professor of classics and the Reverend George Clerk Irving professor of mathematics.

When Trinity College opened its doors to 30 students on 15 Jan. 1852, Whitaker faced immediate difficulties. Only half of the building had been completed and even by May his house, attached to it at one end, possessed neither bedrooms nor a bathroom. Whitaker decided that strict discipline was required in the college since he considered the divinity students transferring from the now closed Diocesan Theological Institution in the small town of Cobourg to be conceited. He laid down precise rules for chapel and meals; and students who ventured off the grounds were required to wear academic cap and gown and be back before evening chapel when doors were locked. Students found Whitaker dry, distant, reserved, and endowed with a "somewhat irascible temperament which, however, he usually kept under, or brought under, the control of a christian spirit and a sound judgment." In 1858 Whitaker, overcome by rage, expelled from the college George Taylor Denison* III, who had scribbled upon his notepaper while being lectured on the 30th Article. Yet his pupils came to respect him and perceive that he was a shy man whose intelligent face could light up "very pleasantly in animated conversation or in the telling or hearing of some good story." Whitaker was a solid if rather dull scholar who was faced with the difficult task of teaching in his daily morning lectures such varied theological subjects as Old Testament Hebrew, New Testament Greek, Christian doctrine, and pastoral theology. "His great forte was a painstaking, conscientious accuracy, which could not be satisfied without a minute and thorough investigation of every subject."

This conscientiousness and solidity served Whitaker well in the formative years of Trinity College. A competent administrator of a small institution, he dealt with scholarship requirements, the amending of college statutes, and discipline. He generally left financial matters to the bursar, Charles Magrath, but was closely involved in the attempts of the college council to control the Trinity College medical faculty and its dean, James Bovell*, which led to the resignation of the entire faculty on 2 July 1856.

In his capacity as the head of a Church of England college, Whitaker was also drawn into the wider controversies between the high and low church factions that had continued spasmodically since the writings of the Oxford Movement became known in Canada in the late 1830s. Benjamin Cronyn*, the evangelical bishop of Huron, was strongly offended by a motion introduced in his diocesan synod in June 1860 asking that Trinity College be more strongly supported. Subsequently Cronyn sent letters to Whitaker in which he attacked his theological teachings as being popish and subjected them to a Calvinistic critique. Whitaker made a vigorous defence, asserting that he had often said Mariolatry constituted an impassable gulf between Romanism and Anglicanism. He was opposed to prayers for the dead and thought the invocation of saints presumptuous. He used the term "sacrament" of baptism and communion only, "and I should reprove any young man under my care for applying it to any other rite." Cronyn referred to a manuscript known as "The Provost's Catechism" which, he alleged, was handed to divinity students on entering the college and contained a series of Whitaker's unorthodox doctrinal statements to be learned by them. Whitaker explained that his lectures had been copied by his pupils and handed on to others.

During this controversy Whitaker received the support of many clergy, including Edward Henry Dewar* who pointed out that neither Whitaker nor his pupils remotely approached the extremes of many Tractarians in England. Strachan's confidence in Whitaker never wavered and he rebuffed Cronyn's suggestions to the corporation of Trinity College in September 1862 that the provost be made head of the classical department and that a theology professor "acceptable to all parties" be appointed.

By September 1863 four of the five bishops of the

ecclesiastical province of Canada (Cronyn was the exception) had come out in support of Whitaker, and when the corporation of Trinity College voted in the provost's favour Cronyn and his diocesan representatives withdrew from that body. But the college became the *bête noire* for low churchmen and the anti-Trinity feeling was central to the disputes in the diocese of Toronto during the 1860s and 1870s. Yet Whitaker, an old-fashioned high churchman, criticized ritualists such as William Stewart Darling who introduced processional hymns and shortened services at Holy Trinity Church, Toronto, and in an 1866 sermon he warned of "a violent Puritan reaction." Active in synod debates, Whitaker became a candidate in September 1866 for coadjutor bishop to Strachan. He had not sought the post and withdrew when he saw that a majority of the lay vote was going to Thomas Brock FULLER; he thus enabled high churchman Alexander Neil Bethune* to be elected.

The following years underlined Whitaker's quiet, practical, and determined approach to personal, college, or diocesan matters. Because the financial position of Trinity College remained grim after the cessation of government grants to colleges in Canada West in 1862, he helped appoint a committee in 1869 to look into affiliation with the University of Toronto. He was also instrumental in the revival of a medical faculty at Trinity College, which was re-established with Edward Mulberry Hodder* as dean in March 1871. Although Whitaker sought to give Bethune support in the violent factional battles swirling around him in the diocese of Toronto, he himself tried to avoid controversy as much as possible. In April 1873 he told his friend, the Reverend Henry Roe of Bishop's College in Lennoxville, Que.: "I confess to an uneasy dislike to argue about the Eucharist. *All* language seems to break down in reasoning on that subject." Yet Whitaker was still being forced to defend himself and the college against charges of ritualism in divine service.

On 1 Oct. 1875 Whitaker, while remaining provost, was appointed by Bethune archdeacon of Toronto, despite the hostility shown him primarily by the laity. Evangelicals unsuccessfully opposed in February 1878 the holding of an election for a coadjutor to the ailing Bethune, due in England that summer for the Lambeth conference, because they feared Whitaker's probable victory. On the fifth ballot Whitaker was declared the winner, but an intervention by an evangelical layman, James Kirkpatrick Kerr*, forced a new ballot on procedural grounds. When the results of the sixth ballot, in which evangelical Robert Machray* came second to Whitaker, were again considered invalid, Bethune called off the election. Whitaker described this action as "a great relief to me personally" since his position as coadjutor would have been "most embarrassing and burdensome." In the following February, after Bethune's death, Whitaker was again brought forward by his anti-evangelical supporters, this time against the Reverend Edward Sullivan*. Nineteen ballots failed to elect a candidate, with Whitaker never getting a majority from the laity. Finally, a compromise candidate, Arthur Sweatman*, a moderate evangelical, was elected bishop of Toronto on the 24th ballot.

After this third electoral rejection Whitaker concluded that his continuing presence in the diocese could not fail to bring discord to the church, and he prepared to leave Toronto for England. Unfortunately it was hard to find a successor for the college, owing to the controversy surrounding Trinity and the presence of the evangelical college, later Wycliffe College, established in Toronto in 1877. After Joseph Albert LOBLEY and others had declined the provostship, an Englishman, the Reverend Charles William Edmund Body, was appointed early in June 1881. Whitaker then took up a country living at Newton Toney, near Salisbury, England. He died in Salisbury on 27 Aug. 1882, a little over a year after his return to England, and was buried at Newton Toney. An obituary by Henry Roe presented Whitaker as "a man acknowledged to be for learning, eloquence, devotion, and all good gifts, the *first* clergyman in the ecclesiastical province."

CHRISTOPHER FERGUS HEADON

George Whitaker was the author of: "The duty of mutual toleration by parties within the church," *Dominion Churchman* (Toronto), 11, 25 July, 22 Aug., 19 Sept., 17 Oct., 5 Dec. 1878; *The office of ritual in Christian worship: a sermon preached at St. George's Church, St. Catharines, on Wednesday, April 4, 1866* . . . (Toronto, 1866); *St. John the Baptist an exemplar to Christian ministers: a sermon preached in the chapel of Trinity College, Toronto, on Sunday, June 24, 1860* (Toronto, 1860); *A sermon: preached in the chapel of Trinity College, Toronto, on Sunday, June 27, 1852* . . . (Toronto, 1852); *Sermons preached in Toronto; for the most part in the chapel of Trinity College* (London and Toronto, 1882); *Soberness of mind; a sermon: preached in the chapel of Trinity College, Toronto, on Sunday, June 25, 1865* (Toronto, 1865); *Two letters to the lord bishop of Toronto, in reply to charges brought by the lord bishop of Huron against the theological teaching of Trinity College, Toronto* . . . (Toronto, 1860).

Anglican Church of Canada, General Synod Arch. (Toronto), J. W. Knight, "High church – low church controversy in the Anglican Church in the diocese of Toronto with emphasis on the episcopacy of Alexander Bethune, second bishop of Toronto" (typescript, 1971). AO, Strachan (John) papers, Letterbooks, 1839–66, 16 Feb. 1851; 1854–62, 29 Sept. 1862. Trinity College Arch. (Toronto), Beverley Jones papers; Henry Roe papers; Trinity College records, A/II/a, A/II/4. Church of England, Diocese of Toronto, Synod, *Proc.* (Toronto), 1861–64; *Journal* (Toronto), 1865–71. [Benjamin Cronyn], *The bishop of Huron's objections to the theological teaching of Trinity College, with the provost's reply* (Toronto, 1862). E. H. Dewar, *Plain words for plain people: an appeal to the laymen of Canada, in behalf of common sense and common honesty, being a review of the 'Strictures' on the two letters of Provost Whitaker* (Toronto, 1861). *The judgments of the Canadian bishops, on the documents submitted to them by the corporation of Trinity College, in relation to the theological teaching of the college* (Toronto, 1863). *The protest of the minority of the corporation of Trinity College, against the resolution approving of the theological teaching of that institution . . .* (London, [Ont.], 1864). [John Strachan], *An address delivered to the clergy and lay delegates of the diocese of Toronto, on Tuesday, June 25, 1861, by John, lord bishop of Toronto, in justification of Trinity College from recent attacks made upon that institution* (Toronto, 1861). C. E. Thomson, "The provost," *Rouge et Noir* (Toronto), 2 (1881), no.3: 4–5. Adam Townley, *A letter to the lord bishop of Huron: in personal vindication: and on the inexpediency of a new diocesan college* (Brantford, [Ont.], 1862). *Trinity College conducted as a mere boys' school, not as a college,* [ed. G. T. Denison] (Toronto, 1858). *Guardian* (London), 27 Dec. 1860; 3 Feb. 1864; 17 Jan., 24 Oct. 1866; 29 Jan. 1873; 26 Feb., 2 April 1879; 30 Aug. 1882. *Toronto Daily Mail*, 29 Aug. 1882. C. F. Headon, "The influence of the Oxford movement upon the Church of England in eastern and central Canada, 1840–1900" (PHD thesis, McGill Univ., Montreal, 1974). *A history of the University of Trinity College, Toronto, 1852–1952*, ed. T. A. Reed ([Toronto], 1952). H. E. Turner, "The evangelical movement in the Church of England in the diocese of Toronto, 1839–1879" (MA thesis, Univ. of Toronto, 1959). M. E. Reeves, "George Whitaker (1811–1882): a forgotten native of Bratton," *Wiltshire Archaeological Magazine* (Devizes, Eng.), 72–73 (1980): 135–39. C. E. Thomson, "The Reverend Geo. Whitaker, M.A., first provost, 1852–1881," *Trinity Univ. Rev.* (Toronto), 15 (1902): 100–1.

WHITE, EDWARD, sealing captain, shipbuilder, Methodist lay leader, and politician; b. 9 Oct. 1811 at Tickle Cove, Bonavista Bay, Nfld, the eldest of four children of William and Mary White; m. in 1835 Anne Weir of St John's, Nfld, and they had eight children; d. 1 June 1886 at St John's.

Edward White came from a family of fishermen of West Country origin who had lived in Newfoundland for three generations. From the age of eight he sailed the northern Newfoundland and Labrador waters with his father. Self-educated, White went to St John's as a young man and built up a small fleet of coastal schooners with which he engaged in the Labrador, Canadian, and Brazilian trade. In 1850, because he had an accident-free record, White was called to give evidence at Quebec to an inquiry by the Canadian assembly on navigation of the wreck-prone Strait of Belle Isle and provided the Canadian authorities with his own charts of the area.

White is remembered principally as a sealing-master. He made his first voyage to the ice in 1838 and for the next 45 years he engaged in the hunt in his own vessels or in ships owned jointly with Job Brothers and Company of St John's and Liverpool. A pioneer in the introduction of large wooden steamers, White supervised the building of the *Nimrod* (used by Ernest Henry Shackleton in his 1907–9 Antarctic expedition), the *Hector*, and the *Neptune* at Dundee, Scotland, and commanded them at the seal-hunt. Between 1866 and 1882 he landed nearly 300,000 seals worth close to $1 million. As a sealing-master he was characterized, by contemporaries and in traditional sealers' ballads, as having great skill, experience gained during a career which reached back to the early days of the hunt, impetuous energy, and Spartan discipline.

A leading Methodist lay figure at St John's, White was appointed to the Legislative Council in 1861 by Hugh William HOYLES; in 1882 Sir William Vallance Whiteway* named him to the Executive Council where he represented the Methodists in Whiteway's administration as minister without portfolio. During the 1860s White had been a strong advocate of confederation with the other British North American colonies and campaigned for this cause in 1867. He introduced the first sealing regulations in 1870, arguing for a fixed opening date for the hunt to ensure that the pups were mature enough to kill, and throughout this period he also supported the stipulation against Sunday killing. A strong advocate of measures to open the interior of the island to development through railway construction and mineral exploration, he took out exploration rights himself in many parts of the island and brought several properties into production. White was also involved in experimental farming; on his 50-acre farm west of St John's (now part of Bowring Park) he attempted to raise celery, tomatoes, corn, strawberries, and other "exotics."

C. W. ANDREWS and G. M. STORY

Edward White family papers are in the possession of G. M. Story (St John's).

Can., Prov. of, Legislative Assembly, *App. to the journals*, 1851, I, app.T. *Colonist* (St John's), 12 Sept. 1888. *Evening Mercury*, 12, 13 Jan. 1883, 1 June 1886. *Terra Nova Advocate and Political Observer* (St John's), 2 June 1886. *Chafe's sealing book* (1923), 23, 31, 36, 41–42, 48–56, 95, 97, 100, 102. G. M. Story, *George Street Church, 1873–1973* (St John's, 1973), 18, 23, 50–51, 53; "Hon. Edward White: a great sealing captain," *Newfoundland Record* (St John's), 1 (1962), no.3: 21–22.

WHITE, GEORGE HARLOW, painter; b.*c.* 1817 in London, England, the son of Elizabeth Harlow, an older sister of artist George Henry Harlow; nothing is definitely known about his father; d. unmarried 18 Dec. 1887 at the Charterhouse, London.

George Harlow White entered the Royal Academy schools, London, on 2 Jan. 1836; his address was given as the Charterhouse, where his mother was under-housekeeper, and he was recommended by Henry Sass at whose school, considered a preparatory school for the academy, he probably studied. Unfortunately there are no records of students' progress at the academy school. Early works exhibited in England included portrait studies, and there is some evidence that he worked as an illustrator. His main interest, however, in true Victorian fashion, developed towards picturesque landscapes and in this tradition he worked in Scotland, Ireland, Wales, and the Home Counties between 1839 and 1871.

On 17 Sept. 1871 the *Prussian* arrived in Quebec from Liverpool, carrying a "Geo H White, male, single, age 50, occupation labourer." The record of his six years in Canada is based almost entirely on hundreds of small pencil drawings and some water-colours, most of them meticulously dated, titled, and signed in his own hand. It has been stated that he bought a bush farm in Oro Township, Ont., but there is no documentary evidence to support the statement, although his sketches indicate that his home base was there, and that Shanty Bay was his earliest address in Canada. He probably lived with George Street, a freeholder in Oro from 1871 with a residence in Barrie from 1875. White's drawings and water-colours reveal a concentration of work in Simcoe County (Oro and Vespra townships and Barrie) in 1873 and 1874, with visits in the summer to the Muskoka region. In 1874 and 1875 he visited the Owen Sound area and returned to the Muskoka region where he produced about 70 sketches in the Huntsville area. In 1876 his travels extended to Ottawa, Quebec, and the St Lawrence–Lake Ontario region, and then, apparently, to the west of Canada. His western sketches, about 20 in all, are, unlike his other work, not dated and inscribed by the artist. They are catalogued, in the John Ross Robertson Collection at the Metropolitan Toronto Library, with place names such as Peace River and Fort Dunvegan (Dunvegan, Alta), and Yellowhead, Robson Peak, Savona's Ferry (Savona), Kamloops, Lytton, Salmon Cove, and Skeena River, B.C. Although they are all listed as October 1876 it is highly unlikely that White was able to visit and sketch all these places in one month. Studies of forests, lakes, trees, and pioneer life in the bush, as well as street and waterfront scenes of topographical and historical interest, comprise his modest contribution to the visual record of 19th-century Canada.

White was elected a member of the Ontario Society of Artists in March 1873 and continued to exhibit with the society until 1886. The majority of works he submitted were water-colours of British subject matter and in this respect he was no exception: Victorian taste, as manifested in Canada, found its standards in Britain, and picturesque landscape with romantic overtones dominated Canadian exhibitions. White was also a prolific exhibitor with the Art Association of Montreal (later Montreal Museum of Fine Arts) and with the Royal Canadian Academy, even after his return to England some time in 1877 (on 18 Sept. 1877 he was appointed a "poor brother" at the Charterhouse in London on the recommendation of Lord Chelmsford). In 1880, at the first annual meeting of the Canadian Academy of Arts (after 19 Aug. 1880 the Royal Canadian Academy of Arts), White was elected an honorary non-resident academician and Lucius Richard O'Brien* of Shanty Bay the first president.

Harlow White brought with him the English tradition of drawing and painting as an observant lover of nature. His experience in Canada made no marked change in his style and his major paintings continued to be of British landscapes, including even his Royal Canadian Academy diploma painting, *The River Conway, North Wales*, dated 1885. John William Harrell Watts*, first curator of the National Gallery of Canada, made this observation about him: "met him at time of the Colonial Exhibition [in London in 1886] and found him to be a fine genial old gentleman. . . ."

FRANCES K. SMITH

[A list of institutions which hold works by George Harlow White is contained in Harper, *Early painters and engravers*. Other works by White are held in the PAC, in the Art Gallery of Hamilton (Hamilton, Ont.), and in various private collections. F.K.S.]

Agnes Etherington Art Centre, Queen's Univ. (Kingston, Ont.), G. Harlow White corr. and catalogue raisonné records. Montreal Museum of Fine Arts, Reference Library, MS Watts. *Art Gallery of Ontario: the Canadian collection* (Toronto, 1970). *George Harlow White, RCA, 1817–1887 . . .*, comp. F. K. Smith ([Kingston, 1975]). *Landmarks of Canada; what art has done for Canadian history . . .* (2v., Toronto, 1917–21; repr. in 1v., 1967), I. National Gallery of Canada, *Catalogue of paintings and sculpture*, ed. R. H. Hubbard (3v., Ottawa and Toronto, 1957–60), III. A. H. Robson, *Canadian landscape painters* (Toronto, 1932). F. K. Smith, "A Victorian artist in Canada: George Harlow White, RCA, 1817–1887," *Canadian Collector* (Toronto), 12 (1977), no.2: 40–43.

WHITE, THOMAS, journalist and politician; b. 7 Aug. 1830 at Montreal, Lower Canada, elder son of Thomas White, originally from Westmeath County (Republic of Ireland), and Dorothea Smeaton; m. in 1853 Esther Vine of Quebec City, and they had seven daughters and three sons, among them Robert Smeaton*; d. 21 April 1888 at Ottawa, Ont.

Thomas White was educated at the High School of Montreal before following his father in the leather trade. In 1846 he began a three-year apprenticeship in the Montreal grocery firm of T. C. Panton. After his contract expired in May 1849, White worked as a clerk at Brantford and Peterborough in Canada West before settling in Toronto in 1850 where he learned the printing trade in the office of the queen's printer. He moved to Quebec City when the office followed the government there the following year.

As a consequence of a temperance address White gave in Quebec City, in 1852 he was invited by the queen's printer, Stewart Derbishire*, to join the editorial staff of the *Canada Gazette*. The next year White returned to Peterborough with his brother-in-law, Robert Romain, where they founded the *Peterborough Review* as a semi-weekly (later weekly). In 1855 his brother Richard joined him in Peterborough. Thomas was soon active in civic politics: he was elected reeve and then served on the Peterborough school board. In 1860 he decided to undertake the study of law and for the next four years worked in the law office of Sidney SMITH. He seems to have preferred journalism to law, however, and in 1864, with the help and connivance of John A. Macdonald*, moved to Hamilton with his brother to take over the *Daily Spectator and Journal of Commerce*; an important Conservative daily, it had been founded 18 years earlier by Robert Reid Smiley*. Thomas White was to serve on the grammar school board while he lived in Hamilton.

White was an able journalist. He was unusually well informed, and blessed with a cool, transparent style devoid of affectation but lively and humorous. On the issue of confederation the *Spectator* was as close to Macdonald's sentiments as any Conservative paper. It reflected his view that the principle of federation was a necessary but nevertheless dangerous American import; "it is some satisfaction to know that there were not wanting men in the [Quebec] Conference strongly wedded to the idea of simple legislative Union, and thoroughly alive to the dangers of the federal system. . . . The local Parliaments exercising these [local] functions by virtue of the privileges delegated to them, present a vastly different thing from the State Legislatures of the American Union."

White ran in the Ontario provincial election of 1867 for Wentworth South and lost by three votes. When Thomas Sutherland Parker, MP for Wellington Centre, died on 24 Oct. 1868, there was talk that White might run in that constituency, but Macdonald and White himself thought it an unwise risk; when White ran again he must run to win. As it turned out, that was easier said than done.

In 1868 Macdonald planned to strengthen the Conservative organ in Toronto, the *Leader*, which was creaking along under James Beaty*, its founding editor, and Sir John A. considered replacing Beaty with White, but the project did not go through. No change was made until 1872, when a new paper, the *Mail*, was started in Toronto under Charles Belford*. In 1869 John Sandfield Macdonald*, the premier of Ontario, asked White to go to England as immigration agent for the province. White's work in England seems to have met with considerable success. But he was soon needed again in Canada. Brown Chamberlin*, the editor of the Montreal *Gazette*, the leading English-language Conservative paper, wanted out. Macdonald arranged that Chamberlin would become queen's printer in Ottawa and Thomas and Richard White would then buy control of the Gazette Printing Company. They did so in 1870 and met with considerable success. During the 1870s Thomas White was a prominent member of the Montreal Board of Trade, serving on its executive committee for three years and representing it on the Dominion Board of Trade for a number of years.

The *Gazette* became a base for White's growing importance in the Conservative ranks in Quebec. Although Sir George-Étienne Cartier* clearly did not take kindly to suggestions from White about Montreal patronage, Cartier's reign was nearing an end. He was defeated in Montreal East in 1872 and died in May 1873, just as the Pacific Scandal was becoming an issue. At a meeting held on the Champ de Mars in Montreal on 5 August White tried to defend the Conservative government from attacks precipitated by the scandal, but found the going anything but easy. "How much did you get?" the crowd yelled at him. White probably had not got anything. He continued to try for a seat in the House of Commons. In the federal election of January 1874 he contested the riding of Prescott in Ontario but lost by six votes. On 19 Dec. 1874 he lost a by-election in Montreal West by seven votes, and when he contested the riding again on 30 Oct. 1875, he lost to Thomas WORKMAN by 50 votes. It was a remarkable run of bad luck. The following December he refused to run in a by-election in Argenteuil, Que., considering the possibility of winning hopeless.

Nevertheless White was by this time an important figure in the Conservative party of Quebec. The premier, Charles-Eugène Boucher* de Boucherville, and his treasurer, Levi Ruggles Church*, found their government in financial trouble; in 1876 the province's deficit amounted to approximately $600,000, most of which could be attributed to shaky railway financing. Unable to agree about how to proceed, they turned to a high-powered committee of Conservatives to arrange a way out: White was one of the group, with Macdonald, Narcisse-Fortunat Belleau*, Sir Hector-Louis Langevin*, and Louis-François-Roderick Masson*, and he worked closely with the treasurer.

The *Gazette* had always been a power within, and even outside, the party and was now more than ever before becoming the principal Conservative organ in the country. By the 1880s it was considered by no less an authority than Charles Herbert Mackintosh*, editor of the *Ottawa Daily Citizen*, to be second to none in Canada. White regularly wrote the paper's parliamentary reports from Ottawa during the 1870s with his usual mixture of suavity and authority. But, although he strongly supported the National Policy, he was never a rabid partisan. The *Gazette*'s editorial on Edward Blake*'s Aurora speech of 3 Oct. 1874 is a good example of White's judiciousness. It concluded: "We prefer to regard the speech as another added to the many evidences which surround us of the advancement and prosperity of this country. . . . There is leisure for speculative politicians to air their doctrines, and there is fortunately culture enough to appreciate and weigh their value." White could also be amusing about Blake: shortly before Blake became leader of the Liberal party in April 1880, White wrote, "In fact, Mr. Blake differs with everybody but Mr. Blake and he does not always agree with him. . . ."

White was now in parliament. He had been elected to the House of Commons in the general election of October 1878 for the Ontario riding of Cardwell; well might his triumphant return to Montreal be celebrated with a torchlight parade from Bonaventure Station. He was soon to become an important figure on the Conservative benches. A graceful, polished, indeed telling speaker, he gave the impression, usually a correct one, that he was master of his subject. White was certainly cabinet timber; he was, however, a Montrealer sitting for an Ontario riding and this complication undoubtedly delayed his appointment. It was characteristic of his range of talent that in the summer of 1885 he was appointed minister of the interior, a portfolio dealing almost exclusively with the west. White was the right man in the right place, and it was a pity he had not been appointed two years earlier, instead of having to pick up the pieces after the North-West rebellion. He had a tremendous capacity for work, a great span of knowledge, and a thick seam of common sense. Practically the first thing he did was to go to the North-West Territories in September and investigate for himself. A series of recommendations followed, including the suggestions that the preemption payments, due in 1885 to the federal government by the Métis for land, should be postponed for a year at least, and that William Pearce*, who had earned good opinions in Prince Albert (Sask.), should be sent to Batoche to seek out and settle the claims of the Métis there. The following summer White was on the Pacific coast, preceding Macdonald's visit there by a month. In 1887 a series of legislative measures began when the North-West Territories were given representation in parliament and Banff National Park was established. White was almost too successful a minister, for in October 1887 he was given the additional portfolio of superintendent general of Indian Affairs which Macdonald had held since 1878.

White was a remarkably painstaking and conscientious minister of the interior. He worked like a Trojan to understand the west, to master its problems. One MP from the northwest said all that needed to be said: "We trusted him, for he had no purpose to serve save that of the country." By 1888 White was already being considered as the man to succeed Sir Charles Tupper* in the finance portfolio; there was even talk that in time he might just be the successor to Macdonald himself. About 15 April 1888, however, White was taken ill with a bad cold, and, perhaps exhausted from overwork, he developed pneumonia. Even then, on 18 April he insisted on discussing Indian affairs with Edgar Dewdney*, the lieutenant governor of the North-West Territories, who was in Ottawa. White's pneumonia grew worse and he died on 21 April.

White's death stunned Macdonald. They had always been close, and White was one of the few men whom Macdonald addressed by his first name. When parliament resumed on 23 April the old man struggled manfully to his feet, determined to master his emotions and move the adjournment of the house himself. His efforts in vain, he collapsed at his desk in tears. Langevin had to move the adjournment and Wilfrid Laurier* seconded it. Laurier and White had found much to admire in each other, and Laurier's graceful speech that day was long remembered. The serious nature of White's loss to public service was revealed in the emptiness of speculation about a successor in office. And, as Sara Jeannette Duncan* concluded in her tribute to White in the *Week*, "on the streets and the corners of the streets, where the winter drifts still baffle the chilly sunshine and a few blades of green are dishearteningly looking for spring, men stand in transient groups of twos and threes and turn over the memories of his kindly deeds, his painstaking service, his upright behaviour. . . ." There are good men in politics.

P. B. WAITE

[There is no known collection of Thomas White papers. The Macdonald papers at the PAC (MG 26, A, 296) contain his letters to Macdonald from the 1860s through to 1888, and some of his letters turn up in other ministerial collections of the time. His ideas and his writing are seen in the *Gazette* (Montreal), the *Hamilton Spectator*, and the *Peterborough Rev.* (Peterborough, Ont.), and he was the author of *An exhibit of the progress, position and resources, of the County of Peterboro', Canada West, based upon the census of 1861 . . .* (Peterborough, [1861?]) and of *Our great west: a lecture delivered under the auspices of the Young Men's Christian Association of Christ Church Cathedral, on the evening of the 27th February, 1873* (Montreal, 1873). Lengthy obituaries appeared on 23 April 1888 in the *Daily Sun* (Saint John, N.B.), the *Gazette* (Montreal), the *Morning Herald* (Halifax), the *Toronto Daily Mail*, and several other papers, and there are biographical sketches in *Cyclopædia of Canadian biog.* (Rose, 1886), the *Canadian biog. dict.*, II: 36–38, and the *DNB*. There is an appreciation of White by Sara Jeannette Duncan in her column "Ottawa letter," in the *Week* (Toronto), 26 April 1888, and there are numerous references to him in Creighton, *Macdonald, old chieftain* and in Rumilly, *Hist. de la prov. de Québec*, I–V. A full appreciation of White's work and career still remains to be done. P.B.W.]

WIGHTMAN, JOSEPH, farmer, shipbuilder, merchant, office-holder, and politician; b. in 1806 in Dumfriesshire, Scotland, son of John Wightman and Margaret Ray Armstrong; m. 16 Jan. 1838 Margaret McDonald (Macdonald), and they had six sons and three daughters; d. 6 Feb. 1887 at Lower Montague, P.E.I.

Joseph Wightman attended school in Dumfries, receiving a university-level education at its Lockerby Academy. In 1823 he immigrated with his parents and sister to Prince Edward Island where they settled at St Andrew Point (Wightmans Point) in Lot 59, Kings County. They leased 179 acres of land from Sir James Montgomery, a major land-owner on the Island. In 1857 they purchased the property freehold, and later that year added an adjoining six acres. By the time of his death Wightman owned 34 properties.

One of the main crops grown successfully by Wightman was black oats; in fact he was so successful that on 4 March 1848 he won the premium for that grain at the Eastern Agricultural Society Grain Show held in Georgetown, P.E.I. The oats were shipped to England, a profitable venture, especially during the Crimean War. He also sold produce to American fishing vessels which came to the Island for supplies. On the executive council of the Royal Agricultural Society, Wightman, while in the legislature, was instrumental in having generous grants passed in 1856, 1857, and 1858 for the establishment of a model farm by the society to upgrade the quality of livestock and to experiment with seed grains. According to the 1861 census, Wightman produced the most grain, cheese, butter, lime, fish oil, and cloth in Lot 59, and owned numerous horses, cattle, and sheep.

In 1824 the family also reopened the fishing station established over 50 years earlier by David Higgins*, the original proprietor in the area. Wightman became active in fishing and its related industries, shipbuilding and merchandising. Vessels built in his own yard during the 1830s to 1860s were used to transport white pine and juniper to Great Britain. He was, as well, involved in the coastal trade. During the 1830s Wightman opened a general store near his homestead, St Andrew Point, and he and his father ran a tavern. He also operated two other stores: the first established in the 1840s at Georgetown and the second during the 1860s at Montague Bridge (Montague).

By the 1830s Wightman had also begun to participate in the community affairs of his area. In 1832 he was one of five commissioners appointed to oversee the planning and erection of a new building in Georgetown to house both a court-house and jail. The following year he was one of three commissioners nominated to the local board of health and he was promoted to the rank of captain in the militia, eventually retiring as a lieutenant-colonel. Wightman also served as a justice of the peace in the district and in 1849 he was high sheriff of Kings County.

An eloquent orator, Wightman possessed a reputation for honesty, diligence, and business acumen. This repute served him in good stead in 1838 when he was first elected to the House of Assembly for Kings, 2nd District. In 1842 he was elected in Kings, 3rd District, and held the seat until the summer of 1858 when he was elected in the newly created 4th District. Wightman did not sit in the house from 1862 to 1866, perhaps because two of his sons were killed in action in the American Civil War, but in 1867 he was elected for Kings, 3rd District, and in 1870 and 1873 for Kings, 4th District. Wightman was a supporter of the Liberal party throughout his political career.

Soon after entering the assembly, Wightman introduced a bill to improve the Island's electoral laws. He chaired several committees in the house, including one for the establishment of Prince of Wales College, and occasionally prepared addresses to the lieutenant governor from the assembly. During the 1854–59 Liberal government of George Coles*, Wightman was a member of the Executive Council, apparently without portfolio. In 1860 a land commission was appointed to settle the question of tenure [*see* Edward Palmer]. Wightman led a delegation from lots 59, 61, 63, and 64 in Kings County to the hearings. He informed the members that the people had a "bitter antipathy towards the rent-paying system" and "would dispose of almost the last article they possess to become freeholders."

Speaker of the House of Assembly from 1867 to 1870 and in 1872, Wightman was also commissioner of crown lands in 1872 and 1873. He entered the Legislative Council the following year, winning a by-election in Kings, 2nd District, and kept the seat in the general election in October of 1874. In 1876 and 1877 Wightman served as president, or speaker, of the council. While still a member of the Legislative Council, he re-entered the Executive Council in March 1879, this time in the coalition government of the Liberal-Conservative William Wilfred Sullivan*. He served on the executive until 1882 but because of illness did not choose to run in the general election held in that year.

Wightman possessed a shrewd business mind and an extraordinary ability to communicate. For more than 40 years he was a leading legislator on the Island. He lived in a time of adverse conditions yet he continually demonstrated perseverance and courage in dealing with problems and trials.

Marjorie L. Hyndman Coffin

P.E.I., Registry Office (Charlottetown), Township ledgers, liber 21: f.30 (mfm. at PAPEI). PAPEI, Prince Edward

Island shipping registers, 1787–1824 (mfm.); RG 5, Minutes, 1854–59; RG 16, Land registry records, Conveyance registers, liber 43: f.535; liber 45: f.16; Land title docs., Lot 53, leases. *Abstract of the proceedings before the Land Commissioners' Court, held during the summer of 1860, to inquire into the differences relative to the rights of landowners and tenants in Prince Edward Island*, reporters J. D. Gordon and David Laird (Charlottetown, 1862). Duncan Campbell, *History of Prince Edward Island* (Charlottetown, 1875; repr. Belleville, Ont., 1972). *Journeys to the Island of St. John or Prince Edward Island, 1775–1832*, ed. D. C. Harvey (Toronto, 1955). *Map of Prince Edward Island, in the Gulf of St. Lawrence, comprising the latest topographical information afforded by the Surveyor Generals Office and other authentic sources . . .*, comp. George Wright and H. J. Cundall (Charlottetown, 1859). P.E.I., House of Assembly, *Journal*, 1839–72; Legislative Council, *Journal*, 1872–82. *A plan of the Island of St. John in the province of Nova Scotia . . .*, comp. Samuel Holland (n.p., 1765). *A plan of the Island of St. John with the divisions of the counties, parishes & the lots as granted by government . . .*, comp. Samuel Holland (London, 1775). George Sutherland, *A manual of the geography and natural and civil history of Prince Edward Island . . .* (Charlottetown, 1861). *Haszard's Gazette* (Charlottetown), 1852. *Patriot* (Charlottetown), 1876. *Royal Gazette* (Charlottetown), 1827, 1832–34, 1841, 1855, 1861. *Weekly Recorder of Prince Edward Island* (Charlottetown), 1810–12. *Canadian biog. dict.*, II: 750. *CPC*, 1880. *Illustrated historical atlas of the province of Prince Edward Island . . .*, comp. J. H. Meacham (Philadelphia and Charlottetown, 1880; repr. Belleville, 1972). *Place-names of Prince Edward Island with meanings*, comp. Robert Douglas (Ottawa, 1925). MacKinnon, *Government of P.E.I.*, 212.

WILKES, HENRY, businessman, educator, and Congregational minister; b. 21 June 1805 at Birmingham, England, son of John Aston Wilkes and Susanna Philips; m. 5 June 1832 Lucy Hedge, in Montreal, Lower Canada; m. secondly in September 1839 Susan Holmes, widow of John McDonell; d. 17 Nov. 1886 in Montreal.

Henry Wilkes, the son of a Congregationalist who was a manufacturer, grew up in a region where manual labour was quickly giving way to machines, and at a time when English capitalism, in accordance with the theories of Scottish economist Adam Smith, was gaining impetus. At 14, having already received a sound business training, he began to sell the products of his father's factory. In 1820 the Wilkes joined the many English and Scottish Congregationalists then trying their luck overseas and immigrated to Upper Canada. They took up residence in York (Toronto) and then moved to Brantford, but Henry remained there for only a short time. By 1822 he was in Montreal, where he obtained employment as clerk in the towing company of John Torrance*; this company, which faced close competition from the Molsons' shipping firm, used steam tugboats to haul sailing ships from Quebec to the port of Montreal. In 1827 Henry Wilkes became a partner of David Torrance*; his earnings enabled him to undertake theological studies which he was eager to begin in order to become a Congregational minister.

After visiting his parents in Brantford, where in June 1828 he set up the first Congregational Sunday school, he went to Scotland, arriving in Glasgow in October 1829. Under the direction of the Reverend Adam Lillie* he prepared for admission to the Congregationalists' Theological Academy, and in 1832 he was ordained minister. Soon afterwards he returned to Canada, but he went back to Scotland almost immediately to take his MA. On 18 April 1833 he began his ministry in Edinburgh, taking advantage of his stay in Scotland to recruit Congregational ministers for Canada. This task had been delegated to him by the Canada Educational and Home Missionary Society, a body formed in Montreal in 1827 of which he had been both a director and the secretary. One of the first of these recruits was his former teacher, Adam Lillie, who had become a friend.

In June 1836 Wilkes himself came back to Canada as a delegate of the Congregational Union of England and Wales, a branch of the London Missionary Society, which had been founded in 1831 to promote Congregationalism in the British Isles; the Colonial Missionary Society, whose object was to establish Congregational churches in the English colonies, had joined the Congregational Union in 1836. Hence it was under these auspices that in October Henry Wilkes began to serve as minister of the First Congregational Church (Zion Church) in Montreal.

A Puritan sect which had evolved from the Church of England around 1590, Congregationalism was a logical extension of the Protestant concept that the faithful have a direct and exclusive relationship with Christ. Thus, properly speaking, there is no institutional church, rather local gatherings (congregations) of believers and an ideal, invisible church composed of the communities which, recognizing Christ as their Lord, are linked to him and cooperate fraternally. The first American Congregationalists were the Pilgrim Fathers of Plymouth (Massachusetts) who founded Harvard College in 1636. Indeed, there were Harvard graduates among the pastors ministering to the Congregationalists in Nova Scotia, just after the founding of the naval base at Halifax. But many of those who came to the Maritimes around the time of the American revolution were Baptists and this denomination began to experience renewal with the preaching of such men as Henry Alline*; even more important, Congregational circles were sympathetic to the Thirteen Colonies and as a result, by about 1800, Congregational churches in the Maritimes had virtually disappeared.

They began to appear, however, in Upper Canada, for instance at Frome (southeast of London) in 1819, under Joseph Silcox, and in Brantford where Adam Lillie had joined the Wilkes family. In Lower Canada, Richard Miles established the First Congregational Church on Rue Saint-Maurice, Montreal, in 1832. Montreal became the stronghold of Canadian Congregationalism when Henry Wilkes succeeded Miles in 1836; in 1842, with the collaboration of J. J. Carruthers, he founded the Congregational Theological Institute to train pastors, although in 1846 the lack of students obliged him to amalgamate his institute with the one in Toronto of which Adam Lillie was president.

A zealous proselytizer, Wilkes was an excellent speaker; backed by generous grants from the London Missionary Society and the Colonial Missionary Society, he made numerous tours through the Canadas, New Brunswick, and Nova Scotia to reorganize or found Congregational churches. Although he had only limited success in the Maritimes, he had better results in western Upper Canada, where the urban middle class had a natural affinity for Congregationalism.

It was, however, in Montreal that Wilkes was able to give free rein to his abundant energies. In November 1846 a new Zion Church was opened on Rue Sainte-Radegonde to accommodate the growing number of believers. In addition to official duties as administrator and Congregational minister, he served as president of the board of examiners for Protestant schools for 12 years. He contributed effectively to the development of commercial libraries and mechanics' institutes by attending meetings of their members, and by giving free informal lectures reflecting his early business experience. He also became involved in religious journalism, and in January 1842, with his friend Carruthers, started the *Harbinger* (Montreal), a successful newspaper which continued to publish until Carruthers left for Portland, Maine, in 1844. After an attempt at a weekly, the *Observer* of Montreal, which lasted only a year, he established the more successful *Canadian Independent* in Toronto, a periodical that was to continue under different titles from 1875 to 1925.

A devout Protestant, Wilkes early took an interest in the spiritual lot of French-speaking Catholics. When, on 13 Feb. 1839, the Reverend James Thompson, representative of the British and Foreign Bible Society in Montreal, appealed to ten or so of his compatriots to found the French Canadian Missionary Society, Wilkes made it his business to establish close ties between the Protestant body in Montreal and the powerful American and Foreign Christian Union; Robert Baird, its secretary, was interested in the progress of the evangelical mission at Grande-Ligne, Lower Canada, being run by two French-speaking Swiss Protestants, Louis Roussy* and Henriette Feller [Odin*]. At the meeting of the American and Foreign Christian Union on 11 May 1852, Wilkes declared that it was the duty of English and American Christians to enlighten French Canadians. The following year, on 6 Jan. 1853, he was able to write to Baird that between 636 and 681 French Canadians had been converted to the pure gospel. Six months later, on 9 June 1853, ex-Barnabite Alessandro Gavazzi delivered a violently anti-Catholic speech in Zion Church, where Wilkes ministered. A struggle ensued which brought military intervention. The result was half a dozen people killed and some 50 wounded. A moderate man, Wilkes had certainly not foreseen this outburst of popular passion.

The remainder of his career unfolded peacefully. In 1850 he had received the degree of THD from the University of Vermont, which had a strong Congregational tradition. McGill College in its turn conferred an LLD on him. For several years in succession the Congregational Union of Canada chose him as its chairman, and at its request Wilkes wrote a book on Congregationalism entitled *Internal administration of the churches*, which was published in 1859.

The 1851 census listed 11,674 Canadian Congregationalists, an advance largely attributable to Wilkes's efforts, and their numbers continued to increase in the decade following. With more pastors needed, it was decided in 1864 to transfer the Congregational Theological Institute from Toronto to Montreal. Wilkes was asked by the principal, his friend Lillie, to teach the courses in moral theology and homiletics. When Lillie died in October 1869, Wilkes resigned as pastor to succeed him as principal.

Age brought physical disabilities. He was racked with rheumatism, from which hydrotherapy in England and the United States gave him scant relief. He died in Montreal, in his sleep, on 17 Nov. 1886.

PHILIPPE SYLVAIN

Published sermons and speeches by Henry Wilkes are listed in Morgan, *Bibliotheca Canadensis*, 391–92.

AC, Montréal, État civil, Congregationalistes, Zion Church (Montreal), 20 Nov. 1886. Notman and Taylor, *Portraits of British Americans*. Wallace, *Macmillan dict.* D. [G.] Creighton, *The empire of the St. Lawrence* (Toronto, 1956), 213, 260. E. B. Eddy, "The beginnings of Congregationalism in the early Canadas" (THD thesis, Emmanuel College, Toronto, 1957). J. S. Moir, *The church in the British era, from the British conquest to confederation* (Toronto and Montreal, 1972) 152–53, 166. Robert [Philippe] Sylvain, *Clerc, garibaldien, prédicant des deux mondes: Alessandro Gavazzi (1809–1889)* (2v., Québec, 1962), II: 307–8, 395, 398. H. H. Walsh, *The Christian Church in Canada* (Toronto, 1956), 220. John Wood, *Memoir of Henry Wilkes, D.D., LL.D., his life and times* (Montreal and London, 1887).

WILKINS, HARRIETT (Harriet) ANNIE, teacher and poet; b. in 1829 in Bath, England, daughter of the Reverend John Wilkins, a Congregationalist minister; d. 7 Jan. 1888 in Hamilton, Ont.

Harriett Annie Wilkins arrived in Hamilton with her family in about 1846. Her father, who had come to act as an interim pastor at the First Congregational Church, Hamilton, died a year or so after his arrival. The poor health of her mother combined with the marriage of her older sister forced Harriett to care for those who remained at home. Her classical and musical knowledge enabled her to conduct a seminary for young ladies and teach music in the family home. She augmented her income by writing poetry. Soon after her arrival in Hamilton she began an association with the *Spectator and Journal of Commerce* which was to last 30 years: she regularly submitted poems to the "Poet's Corner" and all but one of her five books of poetry (issued as by "Harriett Annie") were printed in the *Spectator* office. *The holly branch* (1851), *The acacia* (1860 and 1863), *Autumn leaves* (1869), and *Victor Roy; a masonic poem* (1882) were published in Hamilton; *Wayside flowers* (1876), a collection of her poems, was published in Toronto. Her poems also appeared in the *Canadian Illustrated News* (Hamilton).

The poetry seems to have had a fairly wide circulation and *Wayside flowers* was reviewed as far away as Chicago. In the preface, the Reverend William Stephenson of Hamilton, who knew the author well, praised her Christian virtues and expressed hope that her "natural, hearty, and pure" poetry would be well received by a generous public. Copies of her volumes continue to be found in widely dispersed places, indicating its contemporary appeal. But it is now read more for the reflection it presents of the times than for its intrinsic merit. The subject matter, often of particular interest to local historians, includes nature, history, mythology, legend, events of the day at home and abroad, and milestones in the lives of all sorts and conditions of men. The treatment is usually strongly religious. Harriett Annie joined the Church of England after her arrival in Hamilton and a number of her poems suggest that she was an ardent admirer of freemasonry.

The *Spectator* gave Harriett Annie a laudatory obituary that was unusually long for an impoverished schoolmistress. It and reminiscences of those who knew her portray a Victorian lady who ministered faithfully to the sick, the unfortunate, the neglected, and the forgotten, including prisoners in the jail; they also describe a good teacher and a well-educated woman of considerable literary ability.

KATHARINE GREENFIELD

Harriett Annie Wilkins was the author of *The acacia* (Hamilton, [Ont.], 1860; [2nd ed.], 1863); *Autumn leaves* (Hamilton, 1869); *The holly branch* (Hamilton, 1851); *Victor Roy; a masonic poem* (Hamilton, 1882); and *Wayside flowers* (Toronto, 1876).

HPL, Scrapbook of clippings of Harriett Annie Wilkins. *Canadian Illustrated News* (Hamilton), 1862–64. *Hamilton Herald* (Hamilton), 14 Dec. 1901; 22 Oct. 1910; 7 June, 30 Aug. 1912. *Hamilton Spectator*, 9 Jan. 1888, 15 April 1916, 26 July 1924. *Hamilton directory*, 1853–90.

WILKINS, LEWIS MORRIS, lawyer, politician, and judge; b. 24 May 1801 in Halifax, N.S., son of Lewis Morris Wilkins* and Sarah Creighton; d. 15 March 1885 at Windsor, N.S.

Born into an influential loyalist and Church of England family, Lewis Morris Wilkins was educated in Windsor at King's Collegiate School and at King's College, graduating BA in 1819. He was noted for his quick temper, and once attacked his college roommate, Thomas Chandler Haliburton*, with a poker. After graduating, he read law with William Fraser of Windsor, was admitted to the bar in 1823, and practised in that community until 1856. On 30 Jan. 1828 Wilkins married Sarah Rachel Thomas, reputedly the most beautiful young lady in the province at that time; their three children all predeceased him.

In 1833 Wilkins stood as the Tory candidate for Windsor Township; the outcome of the election was disputed, but a legislative committee speedily awarded him the seat. A staunch Tory, Wilkins became one of Joseph Howe*'s most eloquent foes after the latter's entry into the assembly in 1837. Their verbal antipathy entertained the legislature for years, as Howe taunted "the stately bird of Hants" who was over six feet tall. On 25 Jan. 1838 Wilkins was appointed a member of the Legislative Council. The following year, with Alexander Stewart*, he represented the council in London during negotiations over responsible government. Unlike the assembly delegates, Herbert Huntington* and William YOUNG, Wilkins and Stewart were supported by both Lieutenant Governor Sir Colin Campbell* and the Tory party. In London Wilkins argued forcibly for a strong, independent Legislative Council, while denouncing the federal union proposed by Lord Durham [Lambton*].

Wilkins made little political progress during the following years because the centre of political action was clearly becoming the elective assembly; in 1843 he resigned from the council to run for an assembly seat for Hants County as a reformer who supported Howe. Once elected, however, he reverted to his former conservatism, denouncing the movement towards responsible government and labelling Howe "essentially a low blackguard." On 19 June 1846 Wilkins became a minister without portfolio in the Conservative government of James William Johnston* but lost the 1847 election in Hants and entered a political decline. He expected to inherit his father's seat on the Supreme Court in 1848, but despite his being a QC and having Lieutenant Governor Sir John Harvey*'s recommendation that he possessed "natural talent, professional knowledge . . . eloquence, high principle and a remarkably calm . . . temper," the vacancy went to Edmund Murray Dodd*.

In 1852 Wilkins, whose brother MARTIN ISAAC was also an MLA, was re-elected as the Tory member for Windsor Township, subsequently becoming one of the leading Conservatives in opposition to the Liberal government of Howe and James Boyle Uniacke*. Although his party supported a policy of privately financed railway construction, Wilkins no doubt saw the political and economic expediency of supporting Howe's proposal to build a publicly financed line from Halifax to Windsor. In early 1854 his sudden reversal to support Howe shocked the Tories, and his appointment as provincial secretary in the Liberal cabinet on 4 April was denounced as payment for services rendered to the Liberal cause. On 14 Aug. 1856 he replaced T. C. Haliburton as a puisne judge of the Supreme Court, and his vacant assembly seat went by acclamation to the recently defeated Howe. The *Acadian Recorder*, in a scathing editorial, denounced Wilkins' political opportunism, stating that his "long, long struggle over a foul, dark and crooked way . . . [had] only sufficed to make [him] an assistant judge of the Supreme Court in a third rate British colony."

Wilkins weathered these attacks and continued as a judge until he retired in 1876. He was reputed to be the last member of the provincial bench to quote Latin orators in his decisions, but although capable, he was not brilliant. It was generally conceded that he lacked correctness in his legal procedures and that he had "really a genius for words, or he never could utter so many to express so little."

Wilkins repeatedly proclaimed himself a dedicated Tory, but his political vacillation and undisguised quest for high office remained permanent stains on an otherwise blameless, but dull, career. Few honours were accorded him in later life other than a DCL from King's College in 1874. After retiring, he wrote and published three religious treatises. Although Wilkins and his wife had a reputation for lavish entertaining and he carried himself with a dignity bordering on pomposity, his career had brought him little financial gain, since his estate yielded only $31,000.

LOIS K. KERNAGHAN

Lewis Morris Wilkins was the author of *An aspect of the facts, which presents a harmony of the narratives of the Synoptists, who relate Our Lord's miracle of giving sight to the blind, on the occasion of His passing through Jericho* (n.p., n.d.); *Is there sufficient evidence to show, that St. John designed to declare or to intimate, in his gospel, that the Synoptists were mistaken when they related that Jesus at the last supper kept the Jewish Passover?* (n.p., [1880]); and *The "Lord's Supper" as He instituted it* (Halifax, 1881).

PANS, MS file, Wilkins family, Geneal.; RG 5, R, 18. Howe, *Speeches and letters* (Chisholm). *Acadian Recorder*, 26 April, 6 Sept. 1856. *Directory of N.S. MLAs*. Beck, *Government of N.S.* W. R. Livingston, *Responsible government in Nova Scotia: a study of the constitutional beginnings of the British Commonwealth* (Iowa City, 1930). F. W. Vroom, *King's College: a chronicle, 1789–1939; collections and recollections* (Halifax, 1941).

WILKINS, MARTIN ISAAC, lawyer and politician; b. 14 Sept. 1804 in Halifax, N.S., son of Lewis Morris Wilkins* and Sarah Creighton; m., probably in 1828, Jane Mortimer, *née* Wallace; d. 16 Aug. 1881 in Halifax.

Martin Isaac Wilkins and his brother LEWIS MORRIS were the grandsons of Isaac Wilkins, a politically active New York loyalist who had settled in Nova Scotia in 1784, and the sons of the veteran member of the assembly for Lunenburg and puisne judge of the Supreme Court of Nova Scotia. Martin Isaac was educated at the Anglican King's College in Windsor, N.S., and was graduated BA from that institution in 1824. Admitted to the Nova Scotia bar in 1828, Wilkins became a successful lawyer in Pictou, settling there perhaps because his father owned property in the district.

From the 1820s to the time of confederation, the people of Pictou County were divided into two camps, one of which was Church of Scotland (Kirk), Tory in politics, and largely of Highland extraction; the other, the majority group, was Anti-Burgher (secessionist), Reform in politics, and mainly of Scottish Lowland origin. Wilkins, one of the few Anglicans in Pictou, threw his support behind the minority Kirk–Tory faction. He became a strong opponent of Dr Thomas McCulloch*, founder of Pictou Academy and a leading Reformer, and in 1843 contributed to and edited the *Pictou Observer*, the voice of the Kirk and its supporters. Prior to the gaining of responsible government in Nova Scotia in 1848, many Tories considered Pictou a hotbed of radicalism. Perhaps for this reason Wilkins was defeated as a Tory candidate in Pictou during the elections of 1840 and 1843. He tried again, however, and was elected in 1851 for the township of Pictou and re-elected in 1855 to represent the county. In February 1857 he accepted the position of solicitor general in the Conservative government of James William Johnston*, but he resigned in protest two years later when Robert Barry Dickey* of Cumberland County was appointed to the Legislative Council to fill the vacancy left by David Creighton, a Pictonian. Wilkins also objected to a three-man delegation being sent to England to discuss the proposed Intercolonial Railway without specific approval by the legislature.

Estranged from his colleagues, he returned to the practice of law.

Wilkins re-entered the assembly in 1867 after successfully running as an anti-confederate in a bitter campaign in Pictou. At the same time he published a pamphlet, *Confederation examined in the light of reason and common sense*, which argued that the inclusion of Nova Scotia in confederation through the British North America Act was unconstitutional because the province's entry had not been sanctioned by provincial statute. Some of Wilkins' arguments were used by the Nova Scotia delegation which sought repeal of the act in London in 1868, but the British authorities dismissed his legal objections. He continued to oppose confederation, however, and during his tenure as the attorney general in William ANNAND's anti-confederate government from 1867 to 1871, his views continued to receive support. In August 1868 he made a speech in the assembly which contained a thinly disguised threat that annexation to the United States would be preferable to confederation. When called before Lieutenant Governor Charles Hastings DOYLE to explain his strong rhetoric, Wilkins denied having threatened an appeal to another country and asserted his loyalty to the British crown. The incident cost him respect, seriously weakened his position as an anti-confederate, and led his political friends as well as his enemies to doubt his sincerity. Following negotiations by Joseph Howe* and Archibald Woodbury MCLELAN with Sir John ROSE for "better terms" for Nova Scotia, Wilkins, sensing that the tide was running against him, in January 1869 moved the acceptance of the new agreement in the assembly. When he resigned from the Executive Council two years later, after unsuccessfully soliciting a judgeship from Sir John A. Macdonald*, he accepted the post of protonotary of the Supreme Court in Halifax and remained in that position until his death.

Wilkins is remembered as a rather pathetic figure in his last years; weighing over 300 pounds, his political and legal ideas discredited, and disappointed with his court posting, he spent some of his time writing a book in which he attempted to prove there was no hell. Although Joseph Howe denigrated him as "a poltroon and a braggart" who pocketed his salary for merely proposing "a string of buncombe resolutions which everybody laughed at and nobody remembers," others described him as the "most interesting character" and the "best speaker" in the assembly, and as a "clever though eccentric" man.

R. A. MACLEAN

Martin Isaac Wilkins was the author of *Confederation examined in the light of reason and common sense: and the British N.A. Act shewn to be unconstitutional* (Halifax, 1867) and *Speeches delivered . . . in the House of Assembly of Nova Scotia, session 1868, on resolutions relative to repeal of the "British North America act, 1867"* (Halifax, 1868).

PANS, MG 1, 963A; MG 3, 272–75; RG 7, 50; MS file, Harry Piers, Notes; MS file, Wilkins family, Geneal. Howe, *Speeches and letters* (Chisholm), II. *Acadian Recorder*, 3 May 1856, 16 Aug. 1881. *Halifax Herald*, 19 Aug. 1902. *Pictou Bee* (Pictou, N.S.), 1 Feb. 1837. *Directory of N.S. MLAs*. *Dominion annual register*, 1880–81. *Encyclopedia Canadiana*. J. M. Cameron, *Political Pictonians: the men of the Legislative Council, Senate, House of Commons, House of Assembly, 1767–1967* (Ottawa, [1967]), 18. G. [G.] Patterson, *Studies in Nova Scotian history* (Halifax, 1940). John Doull, "Four attorney-generals," N.S. Hist. Soc., *Coll.*, 27 (1947): 5–10. Harry Moody, "Political experiences in Nova Scotia," *Dalhousie Rev.*, 14 (1934–35): 65–76. [Benjamin] Russell, "Reminiscences of a legislature," *Dalhousie Rev.*, 3 (1923–24): 5–16. H. L. Scammell, "Martin Isaac Wilkins, opponent of confederation in Canada," N.S. Hist. Soc., *Coll.*, 36 (1968): 303–25.

WILLAN, JOHN HENRY, journalist and lawyer; b. 17 March 1826 in Quebec City, son of Thomas William Willan, lawyer, and Julia Gugy, sister of Bartholomew Conrad Augustus Gugy*; d. 22 May 1888 in Quebec City.

John Henry Willan's Canadian birth made him a rarity among 19th-century English-speaking journalists. He was, however, educated in England and Normandy. While in England he published two letters in *Fraser's Magazine for Town and Country* (London) describing life in Quebec to British readers. In 1844 he returned to Quebec City and studied law with Andrew Stuart*. At the same time Willan began what was to be a lifelong career in journalism, editing in 1845 the *Quebec Times*, a conservative journal, and in 1846–47 the *Freeman's Journal and Commercial Advertiser* (Quebec), which he turned into the "fiercest of the Canadian Tory magazines."

In 1846 he published a monograph entitled *To whom are we to belong?* in which he made an eloquent plea for emigration from Britain. He wrote a spate of letters on this subject both to London papers such as the *Times*, the *Herald*, the *Standard*, the *Post*, and *John Bull*, and to such Quebec papers as the long-established *Quebec Gazette*, the Liberal *Quebec Spectator*, the newly founded *Morning Chronicle*, and the *Emigrant*. Willan also acted as parliamentary reporter for the *Montreal Gazette* in 1847, reporting from memory the critical debates involving William Henry Draper*, Henry Sherwood*, Louis-Hippolyte La Fontaine*, Robert Baldwin*, and Francis HINCKS as they vied for control of the government.

In 1848 Willan became editor of the *Emigrant*, a Tory newspaper that opposed the Rebellion Losses Bill in 1849 and reproached England for bidding adieu to the colonies. He moved to the *Quebec Mercury* in 1850 as political editor and law reporter. During the annexationist crisis, the *Mercury*, while not actively urging that Canada join the United States, did support the right of annexationists to express their views, and Willan protested against the La Fontaine–Baldwin government's dismissal of Montreal annexationists from their positions. He also supported Joseph Légaré*, an annexationist candidate in Quebec County in the by-election of Janurary 1850, and waged a running journalistic war against *Le Canadien* which was anti-annexationist. Willan added a literary magazine to his responsibilities in 1852, assisting on the short-lived *Our Journal* (Quebec). The *Mercury* continued under Willan's editorship till 1862 when Josiah BLACKBURN leased the paper from its owners, the Cary family, to support Reformer John Sandfield Macdonald*. As opposition, Willan founded the ultra-Tory *Exponent*. It ran for six months in 1863 under his editorship, but in March 1864, when the Tories under John A. Macdonald* returned to power, Willan was invited by owner George Thomas Cary to return to the *Mercury*. Willan redirected the *Mercury* into support of confederation, and settled down to bickering with the *Quebec Gazette* over local issues.

Willan's legal career had been maintained over the years. He had been admitted to the bar in 1857 and was known for his eloquence in expounding the law as a criminal lawyer. In 1861 he published *A manual of the criminal law of Canada* and in 1867 he turned his legal perceptions toward constitutional theory, publishing *Some loose suggestions for the improvement of the criminal law in its present state of transition*.

His death on 22 May 1888 ended a double career which had established him as a pioneer in the theory of Canadian criminal law and as "one of the well-known figures in Lower Canadian journalism."

ELIZABETH WATERSTON

John Henry Willan was the author of: *A manual of the criminal law of Canada* (Quebec, 1861); *Some loose suggestions for the improvement of the criminal law in its present state of transition* (Quebec, 1867); *Thoughts on the position of the British inhabitants composing the minority in Lower Canada, brought about by the maladministration of justice, and the tyranny of the majority in that province, and the remedy therefor* (Quebec, 1859); and *To whom are we to belong? Dedicated to her majesty's principal secretary of state for the colonies* (Quebec, 1846).

PAC, MG 30, D1, 30: 717–21. Thomas White, *Newspapers, their development in the province of Quebec: a lecture delivered . . . under the auspices of the Young Men's Christian Association of Montreal, on the 5th November, 1883* ([Montreal, 1883]). *Emigrant* (Quebec), 1848–49. *Exponent* (Quebec), 1863. *Freeman's Journal and Commercial Advertiser* (Quebec), 1846–47. *Our Journal* (Quebec), 1853. *Quebec Daily Mercury*, 1850–62, 1864–67. *Quebec Times*, 1845. Beaulieu et J. Hamelin, *La presse québécoise*, I. *Canada, an encyclopædia* (Hopkins), V. Morgan, *Bibliotheca Canadensis. A history of Canadian journalism . . .* (2v., Toronto, 1908–59; v.2 by W. A. Craick). W. H. Kesterton, *A history of journalism in Canada* (Toronto, 1967). S. M. E. Read, "An account of English journalism in Canada from the middle of the eighteenth-century to the beginning of the twentieth, with special emphasis being given to the periods prior to confederation" (MA thesis, McGill Univ., Montreal, 1925).

WILLIAMS, ARTHUR TREFUSIS HENEAGE, militia officer, businessman, and politician; b. 13 June 1837 at Port Hope, Upper Canada, eldest son of John Tucker Williams, MHA for Durham and first mayor of Port Hope, and Sarah Ward, daughter of Thomas Ward, judge and registrar of Durham County; m. in 1859 Emily W. Seymour, daughter of Benjamin Seymour, later a senator, and they had five children including Lieutenant-Colonel Victor Arthur Seymour; d. 4 July 1885 aboard the steamer *Northwest* on the North Saskatchewan River, near Fort Pitt (Sask.).

Arthur Williams grew up at Penryn Park, his father's estate at Port Hope, attended Upper Canada College as a contemporary of Edward Blake*, and inherited major holdings when his father died in 1854. After a year in the law office of James Scott and Nesbitt Kirchhoffer in Port Hope, he finished his education at the University of Edinburgh and travelled extensively in Europe. Although he enrolled with the Law Society of Upper Canada in 1859, he was not called to the bar. Instead, he "delighted to call himself a farmer," managed his property, and participated in Port Hope's mushroom expansion in the 1860s.

In 1867, Williams was elected to the provincial legislature as a Conservative member for East Durham. He was returned by acclamation in 1871. Handsome, popular, and unassuming, he was by that time a justice of the peace, a real estate agent, a director of the Midland Railway of Canada, and chairman of the Port Hope harbour commission. In 1873 he launched the Midland Loan and Savings Company and served as its president. To his constituents, a major achievement was negotiating a reduction of Hope Township's notorious indebtedness to the municipal loan fund from $115,207 to only $34,949. He accomplished this by persuading the province to assume much of the liability. In 1875 he did not stand for re-election to the provincial legislature but in 1878 he defeated a Liberal to win the seat in the House of Commons for East Durham, to which he was re-elected in 1882.

In the federal house Williams spoke rarely but worked for his East Durham constituents in the small change of political patronage and public works. Experience and loyalty brought prompt appointment as party whip in 1878. Political influence was also a useful adjunct for Williams' chief hobby, the militia.

From his father, who had led the local militia in 1837, Williams inherited enthusiasm for the military and a sense that leadership was a social obligation. On 17 Oct. 1862 he had been appointed captain of one of Port Hope's three volunteer militia companies. In

1865–66 he spent the winter with his company on the St Clair frontier, watching for Fenian attacks. In 1866 he commanded a provisional militia battalion at Kingston. Later that year, on 16 November, when rural militia companies were formed into battalions, he took command of the 46th East Durham Battalion, a post he held for almost 19 years until his death.

As a "parliamentary colonel," he secured such favours as the command of the Canadian rifle team which competed at Wimbledon (now part of Greater London), England, in 1880. By speaking on behalf of the rural militia in the house Williams upheld it against the more efficient city corps. In 1883, rebuked by Major-General Richard George Amherst Luard* for insubordination during a discussion concerning parliamentary control of the militia, Williams used his political influence to help ensure the general's prompt removal. In 1885, as the British empire thrilled to the attempted rescue of General Charles George Gordon at Khartoum and drifted close to war with Russia, Williams was one of several Canadian militia colonels who offered to raise battalions for imperial service. His prominence even encouraged rumours that he might be the next lieutenant governor of Ontario.

In fact, Williams' search for a military career was not attributable, as Sir John A. Macdonald* suggested, to his being "anxious for excitement or notoriety" as much as it was to the temporary disorder of his financial affairs. Particularly, he had invested $50,000 in grazing land in the northwest, without apparent return. Ironically, it was there that he would find his military opportunity. When rebellion broke out at the end of March 1885 [*see* Louis RIEL], Williams was given command of the Midland Battalion, a collection of rural companies from eastern Ontario. Sending a regular stream of advice and criticism to the prime minister and other officials, Williams set off for the front on 6 April 1885. After having travelled along the uncompleted route of the Canadian Pacific Railway north of Lake Superior, he arrived on the *Northcote* by the South Saskatchewan River with two companies in time to join Major-General Frederick Dobson Middleton*'s column before the battle at Batoche (Sask.). On the fourth day of the battle he precipitated the pell-mell rush of militiamen that cost the Canadians 30 casualties, five dead and 25 wounded, but ended the Métis resistance. To militia officers chafing at Middleton's leadership, Williams became the hero of the campaign. Heroism was enhanced by martyrdom. Hardship, exertion, bad food, and sleeping on muskeg were all blamed when Williams collapsed on 1 July. He was carried to the captain's cabin of the steamer *Northwest*. "Well, it would be hard lines if I should be bowled over now," he allegedly remarked. On the morning of 4 July, after three days of fever and delirium, he was dead.

Colonel Williams was the only nationally known figure to die in the northwest campaign and his body was brought home in state. A huge funeral was held in Port Hope where citizens erected a statue in his honour. Parliament voted his orphaned children a special pension. Then, like most heroes, he was gradually forgotten. To Charles Arkoll Boulton*, a contemporary, Williams "represented what might be termed Young Canada"; to posterity, he reflects a model of the patriotic landed gentleman, using his wealth and position for dignified public service, accepting payment in the currency of honour and prestige. In short, Arthur Williams was an anachronism.

DESMOND MORTON

A. T. H. Williams papers are in the possession of Mr Michael Wladyka, Port Hope, Ont.

PAC, MG 26, A; MG 27, I, D3. [C. A.] Boulton, *Reminiscences of the North-West rebellions, with a record of the raising of Her Majesty's 100th Regiment in Canada . . .* (Toronto, 1886). Can. House of Commons, *Debates*, 13 April 1880. *Telegrams of the North-West campaign, 1885*, ed. Desmond Morton and R. H. Roy (Toronto, 1972). *Globe*, 16 July 1885. *Canadian biog. dict.*, I. *Cyclopædia of Canadian biog.* (Rose, 1886). Wallace, *Macmillan dict.* G. T. Denison, *Soldiering in Canada: recollections and experiences* (Toronto, 1900). Desmond Morton, *The last war drum: the North West campaign of 1885* (Toronto, 1972); *Ministers and generals: politics and the Canadian militia, 1868–1904* (Toronto and Buffalo, N.Y., 1970).

WILLIAMS, JAMES MILLER, carriage maker, manufacturer, entrepreneur, and politician; b. 14 Sept. 1818 at Camden, N.J.; m. in 1842 M. C. Jackson of London, Canada West, and they had three sons and a daughter; d. 25 Nov. 1890 in Hamilton, Ont.

James Miller Williams apprenticed as a carriage maker in his birthplace before immigrating with his family to London, Upper Canada, in 1840. There he plied his trade, and within two years entered into partnership with Marcus Holmes to manufacture carriages. He soon bought out his partner and ran the business alone until he moved to Hamilton. By 1851 he was operating the Hamilton Coach and Carriage Factory which employed 70 men and produced ten vehicles per week, many of them for public transit. The increasing number of fare-paying passengers on both urban and interurban lines was shifting the carriage industry away from concentration on vehicles for individual use. Williams also contracted to manufacture cars for the Great Western Railway. Some time before 1857 he and his partner, H. G. Cooper, established the firm of Williams and Cooper, carriage manufacturers. Cooper bought him out in 1859.

In the 1850s Williams became interested in petroleum. Few at the time knew much about petroleum, although James Young in Scotland and Abraham Gesner* in Nova Scotia sparked some interest in it. Questions of supply and demand and of uses, as well as technical problems of recovery, refining, and transportation, were still unanswered, and it was not certain whether petroleum could become the foundation for a viable industry. For many years the existence of petroleum in southwestern Ontario had been known, and the Geological Survey of Canada had drawn attention to the deposits, but commercial possibilities had not been explored. However, about 1850 two brothers from Woodstock, Henry and Charles Nelson Tripp, became interested in the possibilities of producing asphalt from the "gum beds" of Enniskillen Township in Lambton County. They acquired land on Black Creek, began producing asphalt, and in 1854 incorporated the International Mining and Manufacturing Company. The following year their asphalt received an honourable mention at the universal exhibition in Paris. However, the Tripps were unsuccessful financially and the company passed to Williams. By 1857 J. M. Williams and Company was refining petroleum, albeit crudely, at Oil Springs, Lambton County, and by 1860 Williams had set up a refinery in Hamilton; the next year he and his associates, working as the Canadian Oil Company, had reportedly invested over $42,000 in the venture.

Much fruitless debate has taken place over whether Williams was the first man in North America to drill successfully for oil. A claim has been made for Edwin Laurentine Drake of Pennsylvania. Williams was working finds before Drake, but because he left no record of his work, and his early ventures were of little interest to contemporary journalists, there is no way of knowing whether his early wells were drilled or dug and cribbed. The significant fact is that he was the first entrepreneur with sufficient capital, business acumen, technical understanding, and tenacity to tackle the petroleum of Lambton County. Spurred by the sudden growth in the use of petroleum-based lubricants and illuminants, he succeeded in his enterprise, thereby demonstrating the viability of an Ontario petroleum industry.

Like many of his contemporaries, Williams was an entrepreneur of diverse interests. His investment in oil through such companies as J. M. Williams and Company and the Canadian Oil Company was only part of his career. He gradually passed control of the oil interests to his son, Charles Joseph Williams, and in 1879 sold the Canadian Oil Company to him. His success in oil led him into the financial and investment field. He was actively involved in the Hamilton Provident and Loan Society, the Mutual Life Association of Canada, the Victoria Mutual Fire Insurance Company of Canada, the Bank of Hamilton (founded in 1872), the Hamilton and Lake Erie Railway, the Hamilton and North Western Railway, and the Wellington, Grey and Bruce Railway. By 1871 Williams had established J. M. Williams and Company, manufacturers of wholesale tin ware, a firm he sold to his son in 1876.

Financially successful and secure, Williams turned to politics. First elected an alderman in Hamilton, he was returned to the Ontario legislature as the Liberal member for Hamilton in 1867, 1871, and 1875. Upon his retirement from politics in 1879, he was appointed registrar of Wentworth County, a position he held until his death in November 1890.

NORMAN R. BALL and EDWARD PHELPS

Baker Library, R. G. Dun & Co. credit ledger, Canada, 25: 107, 147, 166, 208, 213, 287. Robert Bell, "The petroleum field of Ontario," RSC *Trans.*, 1st ser., 5 (1887), sect. IV: 101–13. *Hamilton and its industries: being a historical and descriptive sketch of the city of Hamilton and its public and private institutions, manufacturing and industrial interests, public citizens, etc.*, comp. E. P. Morgan and F. L. Harvey (Hamilton, Ont., 1884; 2nd ed., 1884). T. S. Hunt, "Notes on the history of petroleum or rock oil," *Canadian Naturalist and Geologist*, 6 (1861): 241–55. Charles Robb, "On the petroleum springs of western Canada," *Canadian Journal*, new ser., 6 (1861): 313–23. [J. F. Tyrrell], *The oil districts of Canada; compiled from official and other reliable sources* (New York, 1865). *Hamilton Spectator*, 30 Aug. 1851. *Times* (Hamilton), 26 Nov. 1890. *Canada directory*, 1851; 1857–58. Fergus Cronin, "North America's father of oil," *Imperial Oil Rev.* (Toronto), 39 (1955), no.2: 16–20; repub. in *Imperial Oil Rev.*, 42 (1958), no.3: 22–25. "The driller that history forgot: unsung and unpraised, Dr. H. C. Tweedel drilled New Brunswick's first oil well and beat 'Col.' Drake as the first American oil driller," *Imperial Oil Rev.*, 39 (1955), no.1: 21.

WILLIAMS, JOHN ÆTHURULD, Methodist clergyman; b. 19 Dec. 1817 at Carmarthen (Dyfed), Wales, son of John David Williams and Elizabeth Rhodes; m. first in December 1839 Catharine Robinson (d. 1856) of Prescott, Upper Canada, and they had five children; m. secondly in August 1857 Rebecca Clarke of Ernestown, Canada West, and they had six children, three of whom survived infancy; d. 16 Dec. 1889 at Toronto, Ont.

John Æthuruld Williams, orphaned at 12, was raised by relatives in London, England, where he attended Hoxton Academy and was employed in a newspaper office. In 1834 he immigrated to Prescott, and there went into business. On 21 Feb. 1836, at a Wesleyan Methodist prayer meeting, he was converted, joined the church, and commenced reading voraciously the great writings of Methodism. Feeling a call to the ministry, he became a local preacher in 1846, was ordained in 1850, and over the next four decades served in 18 communities throughout Ontario. From 1859 to 1861 he was chairman of his church's Owen Sound District, and after 1870 he was invariably chairman of the district in which his charge was located.

After the Wesleyan Methodist Church in Canada and the Methodist New Connexion Church in Canada united in 1874 to form the Methodist Church of Canada, Williams was a delegate to each quadrennial general conference of the new church. While serving in Simcoe, Ont., in 1874 he was elected president of the London conference, a post he held for two years. In 1878 he was awarded an honorary DD from Victoria College at Cobourg, "a spontaneous tribute to his character and attainments." In 1882 he was elected vice-president of the general conference, his church's second highest, but largely honorary, position.

In September 1883 the four principal Canadian Methodist churches met in Belleville at the general conference of united Methodist bodies to work out an amalgamation. Williams, then a minister in St Catharines, represented the Methodist Church of Canada at this conference, and on a resolution by Albert Carman*, president of the General Conference of the Methodist Episcopal Church in Canada, he was unanimously elected president of the united general conference. Williams won widespread praise for his capable and impartial administration of the proceedings which resulted in the four churches uniting in 1884 to form the Methodist Church. That year he was elected president of the new church's London conference and went as a Canadian delegate to the centennial conference of American Methodism at Baltimore, Md.

Following the death, in 1884, of the Reverend Samuel Dwight RICE, one of the two Methodist general superintendents, the General Conference of the Methodist Church selected Williams as a temporary replacement. The following year he and Albert Carman were made general superintendents for terms of four and eight years respectively. The most senior of the church's permanent officials, the general superintendents were responsible for the national affairs of the church during the four-year interval between general conferences, and they served as visible symbols of Methodist unity. Williams' death in 1889, after a year of serious illness, prevented him from serving his full term.

Although not a decisive influence in the development of Canadian Methodism, Williams was closely identified with the major concerns of his church. He was "a temperance preacher by example as well as voice." He was also strong in his denunciation of Roman Catholicism: in an 1888 address printed in *Vital questions* he described "Romish Dogma" as "a source of religious, social and national peril" which interfered with Christ's authority and the free exercise of the mind, and was a threat to Protestant religious liberty. Williams was reported to be an effective preacher when aroused, though he sometimes spoke over the heads of his audience, and he contributed to Methodist hymnology by publishing verses of, and articles on, early Methodist poets.

Williams' rise to high office is best attributed to his administrative capacity and personal character, and perhaps as well to his identification with Methodist evangelical traditions. Intelligent and well read, despite a limited formal education, he forcefully defended those traditions against German religious materialism and other influences. Though an 1874 description presented him as a vigorous debater and a combative, outspoken, and highly independent person, the responsibilities of high office mellowed his abrasive qualities and in any case his honesty and sensitivity had never permitted lasting hostility. With his death, his church lost a valued link with the piety and service which were identified with Canadian Methodism in its heroic phase, a half century earlier.

G. N. EMERY

The published minutes of the annual conferences of the Methodist Church of Canada for 1874–83, and of the Methodist Church (Canada, Newfoundland, Bermuda), General Conference, *Journal of proc.*, 1883, and of its Niagara Conference, *Minutes*, for 1890, are available at UCA.

J. A. Williams was the author of *Certainties in religion . . .* (Toronto, 1882), 1–27, in *Lectures and sermons delivered before the Theological Union of the University of Victoria College* (2v., Toronto, 1888), I; "Chairman's address," *Vital questions: the discussions of the General Christian Conference held in Montreal, Que., Canada, October 22nd to 25th, 1888, under the auspices and direction of the Montreal branch of the Evangelical Alliance* (Montreal, 1889), 188–89; "The less known poets of Methodism," *Canadian Methodist Magazine*, 26 (July–December 1887): 545–48; "The minor poets of Methodism," *Canadian Methodist Magazine*, 25 (January–June 1887): 146–56, 242–51, 431–40.

Carroll, *Case and his cotemporaries*, IV: 483. "Memorials of the Rev. John A. Williams, D.D.," *Methodist Magazine*, 31 (January–June 1890): 289–96. *Christian Guardian*, 11 June 1873; 24 Dec. 1884; 8, 22 Sept. 1886; 18, 25 Dec. 1889; 24 Feb. 1904. *Globe*, 17, 20 Dec. 1889. *Canadian biog. dict.*, I: 73–75. Cornish, *Cyclopædia of Methodism*, I: 151, 657; II: 302. *Cyclopædia of Canadian biog.* (Rose, 1888), 294–95. J. W. Caldwell, "The unification of Methodism in Canada, 1865–1884," United Church of Canada, Committee on Arch., *Bull.* (Toronto), 19 (1967).

WILLIAMS, Sir WILLIAM FENWICK, soldier and military and colonial administrator; b. 4 Dec. 1800 in Annapolis Royal, N.S., son of Maria Walker and possibly Thomas Williams; d. unmarried on 26 July 1883 in London, England.

It was widely believed at the time of his birth and throughout his career that William Fenwick Williams' father was Edward Augustus*, Duke of Kent and Strathearn, who had been living in Halifax and who left for England, with Thérèse-Bernardine de Saint-

Laurent*, in August 1800. Williams himself made no effort to discredit this possibility, which would have meant he was Queen Victoria's half-brother. Williams' putative father, however, was the commissary general and barrack master of the British garrison at Halifax. William, like his elder brother Thomas, was destined for a military career and in May 1815 he entered the Royal Military Academy at Woolwich (London) England. Following his graduation he spent some years travelling and, owing to the slowness of all military appointments in the decade after Waterloo, was commissioned 2nd lieutenant in the Royal Artillery only in July 1825. He served on army stations in Gibraltar, Ceylon (Sri Lanka), and England, and was promoted 2nd captain in 1840, 1st captain in 1846, and brevet colonel in 1854. In 1841 he went to Constantinople (Istanbul) with Captain Collingwood Dickson to reform the Turkish arsenal. In 1843 he was appointed British commissioner in charge of defining the Turkish-Persian border, a task that took nine years and for which he was awarded a CB in 1852.

When the Crimean War broke out in 1854, Williams was appointed British commissioner to the Turkish army in Anatolia, to help reorganize it after the Turks had been badly defeated by the Russians in the opening months of the war. He reached Kars, in the far northeast of Turkey, in September 1854 but returned shortly to Erzurum to persuade Turkish authorities to reinforce Kars. Receiving news in May 1855 of a Russian plan to take Kars, he went back there on 7 June. A Russian army of 25,000 attacked a week later. It was repulsed with heavy losses, but Kars was invested and another Russian attack was launched on 7 August. The Russian general, Murav'ev, attacked again on 29 September, and failed, losing 6,000 men. By now, however, hunger, cold, and cholera were beginning to take effect on the population of Kars, and early in November, when news came that there would be no reinforcements, Williams decided to negotiate a surrender. He told Murav'ev that if unconditional surrender were insisted upon, they would spike every gun, burn every flag, and then let him work his will on the town's survivors. Murav'ev was generous to such a spirited enemy; the garrison marched out with their flags and with their swords. Williams was given a comfortable imprisonment at Ryazan, and when the Crimean War ended a few months later he was presented to Czar Alexander II before returning to London in March 1856.

There he was lionized. His defence of Kars had been one of the great achievements of the British army in a war in which achievements had been few. Williams was made a KCB and given an Oxford DCL; France gave him the Grand Cross of the Legion of Honour; and the British parliament voted him an annual pension of £1,000 for life. He was made a major-general, given command of the Woolwich garrison, and elected to parliament for Calne in July 1856, a seat he held until April 1859.

He then accepted appointment as commander-in-chief of the British forces in British North America, and was thus in a position to organize the defences of the Province of Canada when the American Civil War broke out in April 1861. Williams believed Southern independence was permanent, and that in consequence the North would seek in British North America, especially Canada West, "a balance for lost theatres of ambition." As he wrote to the Duke of Cambridge, "our danger begins when their war ends. . . ." Three additional British regiments were sent to Canada at Williams' request and, in December 1861, at the time of the *Trent* crisis, a further 15,000 troops followed. Williams ordered heavy batteries set up at Toronto and Kingston. In fact, Governor General Lord Monck* had trouble holding Williams in and convincing the old warhorse that Britain was not yet actually at war with the United States. Williams' energy was not matched, however, by Canada's provincial legislature; in May 1862, when the crisis was to all appearances over, it threw out the militia bill by which the government of George-Étienne Cartier* and John A. Macdonald* proposed to raise an active militia force of 50,000 men at an annual cost of $1,110,000. The succeeding moderate Reform government strenuously opposed any significant Canadian defence measures. Hence Colonial Secretary Edward Cardwell insisted in 1864 on the concentration of British forces in the valley of the St Lawrence, rather than having them strung out in small units from Quebec to London, Canada West, without any substantial support from a militia in the event of American military action. Cardwell's insistence drew no immediate objection from Williams, who believed that neither the government nor the people of Canada had lived up to the promises of military support made during the *Trent* crisis and felt that the withdrawal of troops from much of western Upper Canada might force them to make adequate defensive preparations. Williams complained to London on 13 June 1864 of Canada's "fruitless party politics," but he wrote when they were at a particularly unproductive stage, on the day before the fall of the Étienne-Paschal Taché*–Macdonald ministry. A week later, however, the Taché–Macdonald–George Brown* coalition was formed; it was committed to the federation of all the British North American provinces and, imperial authorities hoped, the creation of a Canadian defence force.

Williams' next tour of duty was to be in his native province. The lieutenant governor of Nova Scotia, Sir Richard Graves MACDONNELL, had been frequently critical of moves toward confederation, which the British government, by the end of 1864, firmly supported. The difficulties of persuading Nova Scotia to adopt confederation were substantial, but Cardwell decided the chances would be much improved by a positive and likeable lieutenant governor. Sir Richard went to Hong Kong, and Sir William Fenwick Williams arrived in Nova Scotia in November 1865.

Williams was a soldier, told to do what he could. His good temper and military fame had made him popular in his native province even before he arrived, but Nova Scotians who opposed confederation could be under no illusions. When chided by Lord Monck for having encouraged the anti-confederate government of Albert James SMITH in New Brunswick by not mentioning confederation in his speech from the throne in February 1866 – an omission both deliberate and regarded by Nova Scotia Premier Charles Tupper* as essential – Williams admitted to Arthur Hamilton Gordon*, lieutenant governor of New Brunswick, that the omission had deceived few people. "My total abandonment of Confederation [in the throne speech] is too much like Punch even for their sincere belief. They know what I was sent here for." With confederation in mind, in March Williams invited William ANNAND, leader of the anti-confederates in the Nova Scotia assembly, to suggest a new confederation conference. Annand refused but another opposition member, William Miller*, agreed. This move was received most favourably by Tupper, as well it might be; but it did not break the log jam, for that depended on a clear-cut commitment by the Smith government in New Brunswick either for or against confederation. Once the Smith government was forced out of power there, as it was on 10 April, then Tupper could, and did that same day, move the resolution for confederation in the Nova Scotia assembly. A week later, on 17 April, while British troops were being sent from Halifax by ship to meet the Fenian threat in the St Croix estuary, the Nova Scotia assembly passed the confederation resolution by a vote of 31 to 19. When Cardwell retired as colonial secretary in July 1866, he warmly congratulated Williams. "Let us rejoice together," he wrote, "in the success which has attended your Mission, & in the now, I trust, secure & certain union of the B.N.A. Provinces."

Sir William Fenwick Williams continued as lieutenant governor of Nova Scotia until October 1867, when he was replaced by Charles Hastings DOYLE. Williams was a free man for the next three years and spent some time in Sussex, N.B., where he had relatives, and also travelled to England. In September 1870 he was made governor and commander-in-chief of Gibraltar, and stayed there until 1876. His last official appointment was as constable of the Tower of London, in May 1881. Williams died at his hotel in Pall Mall and was buried in Brompton cemetery.

Williams was an interesting example of a colonial-born son of a British military family. He had been a good soldier, with something of a colonial's self-reliance and willingness to take on responsibility. He was firm as a rock when it came to duty, but he was never a slave-driver. However, one must not assume that, in the conventional phrase of the time, he lived and died "a gallant old soldier." Edward William Watkin* described him in 1861 as "a worn out old roué who *might* get the 10,000 men the Iron Duke spoke of *into* Hyde Park, but who never could get them out again." By 1861 this was an all too general opinion. The young, eager British colonels who came out to Canada in December 1861, Garnet Joseph Wolseley* for example, believed that if war with the United States really came, Williams would have to be replaced. When in 1870 it was suggested to the British government that Williams might be given charge of the Red River expedition, Edward Cardwell, then secretary for war, agreed with Colonial Secretary Lord Granville that Williams would be hopeless. Useful enough for military command in time of peace, and in carrying confederation in Nova Scotia, Williams was now, in Cardwell's mind, impossible for "a post of great difficulty or requiring great power of discretion." The comment about difficulty is understandable – Williams was now nearing 70 – but the reference to discretion is biting. Williams may indeed have had, as a friend said, "the kindliest, gentlest heart that ever beat"; that was not inconsistent with his having become, at the end of his career, as many others doubtless do, something of a Colonel Blimp.

P. B. WAITE

[There are obituaries of Sir William Fenwick Williams in the *Montreal Herald and Daily Commercial Gazette*, the *Morning Chronicle* (Halifax), and the *Times* (London), all for 28 July 1883, and in the *Illustrated London News*, 4 Aug. 1883. There is a small but useful collection of Williams papers in the N.B. Museum consisting mainly of letters he received. During the period of his North American command from 1859 to 1865 Williams wrote some 300 letters to the Duke of Cambridge, commander-in-chief of the British Army. These are in the Royal Arch., Windsor, Eng. There are letters from Williams in the Cardwell papers and in the Carnarvon papers at the PRO (PRO 30/48 and PRO 30/6 respectively), and in the Stanmore (Arthur Hamilton Gordon) papers at the UNBL (MG H 12a). More official sources are his dispatches to the secretary of state for war, PRO, WO 1; his dispatches from Nova Scotia, PRO, CO 217; and his very interesting telegram book, PANS, RG 2, sect.2, 5–6.

For an eye-witness account of the siege of Kars see Humphry Sandwith, *A narrative of the siege of Kars* . . . (3rd ed., London, 1856). The most useful secondary source for his British North American career is Adrian Preston, "General Sir William Fenwick Williams, the American Civil War and the defence of Canada, 1859–65: observations on his military correspondence to the Duke of Cambridge, commander-in-chief at the Horse Guards," *Dalhousie Rev.*, 56 (1976–77): 605–29. *See also* Elisabeth Batt, *Monck, governor general, 1861–1868* (Toronto, 1976); Creighton, *Road to confederation*; K. G. Pryke, *Nova Scotia and con-*

federation, 1864–74 (Toronto, 1979); C. P. Stacey, *Canada and the British army, 1846–1871: a study in the practice of responsible government* (rev. ed., [Toronto], 1963); and Waite, *Life and times of confederation*; as well as Dent, *Canadian portrait gallery*, IV: 5–9, and Notman and Taylor, *Portraits of British Americans*, I: 51–66. There is a good article on Williams in the *DNB*, but it omits his North American career. P.B.W.]

WOOD, EDMUND BURKE, lawyer, politician, and judge; b. probably 13 Feb. 1820 at or near Fort Erie, Upper Canada, the fourth son of Samuel and Charlotte Wood; m. in April 1855 Jane Augusta Marter of Brantford, Canada West; d. 7 Oct. 1882 at Winnipeg, Man.

Edmund Burke Wood was the son of an Irish-American farmer who had immigrated to the Niagara District shortly after the War of 1812. He was educated in local schools at Fort Erie and, after the loss of an arm had apparently ruled out remaining on the farm, became a teacher in Wentworth County. Wood found teaching both unrewarding and unpromising, however, and entered Oberlin College, Ohio, from which he graduated with a BA in 1848. The following year he enrolled as a student with the Law Society of Upper Canada, articling first with the firm of Samuel Black Freeman and Stephen James Jones in Hamilton, and later with Archibald Gilkison of Brantford. Through the influence of Jones, he was appointed clerk of the county court and deputy clerk of the crown in Brant County in 1853, thereby becoming widely known in local legal circles. He resigned both offices after being called to the bar in 1854 and subsequently established a profitable legal partnership in Brantford with Peter Ball Long. Industrious, thorough, and knowledgeable, Wood soon emerged as one of Brantford's most prominent lawyers, and during his 20-year career in the county courts handled celebrated cases in criminal, common, and equity law. An abrasive and difficult colleague, he practised alone after the dissolution of his partnership in 1860.

Wood's business and political careers were inextricably linked. In the mid 1850s he became the solicitor and one of the principal promoters of the Buffalo and Lake Huron Railway, a line which promised to open profitable trading opportunities for Brantford in New York State. In 1863, partially to extend his personal influence and partially to promote the railway, he first ran for public office, winning the West Brant seat in the Legislative Assembly as a moderate Reformer. After the Buffalo and Lake Huron line was taken over by the Grand Trunk Railway the following year, Wood came increasingly under the influence of Charles John BRYDGES of the Grand Trunk and his friends in the Conservative party. As Brydges wrote to John A. Macdonald* in 1864, Wood was "quite ready to take the shilling if you were in a position to offer it to him." Although a nominal Liberal throughout his career, Wood disregarded George Brown*'s call to retreat from the "Great Coalition" in 1866, evidently because of Grand Trunk influence. To the disappointment of the supporters of Brown, in 1867 Wood accepted the office of treasurer of Ontario in John Sandfield Macdonald*'s "Patent Combination" coalition ministry. The leading Reformer in the Ontario cabinet, he was elected as a coalitionist to both the Ontario legislature and the House of Commons in 1867, despite his repudiation by the Liberal riding association in South Brant.

Wood remained treasurer of Ontario for more than four years despite frequent quarrels with Sandfield Macdonald and open disagreements with the federal wing of the coalition. Leading a group of ministerial mavericks at Ottawa he opposed the grant of "better terms" to Nova Scotia, and refused to support Sandfield's defence of the federal government in 1869. As treasurer he zealously guarded the financial interests of Ontario. Echoing the sectionalist rhetoric of pre-confederation Reformers, he assumed a firm stance during the financial arbitration between Ontario and Quebec. He was equally influential in guarding his own interests. Once called "an active paid agent of the Grand Trunk" by the Toronto *Globe*, Wood, unlike most of his party, opposed the construction of narrow gauge railways in the province.

In 1871, following a provincial election which left control of the legislature in doubt and which demonstrated Wood's inability to secure Liberal support for the coalition, he resigned his post dramatically as the "Patent Combination" struggled vainly for survival. After the ministry's collapse, he rejoined the Liberal party and supported the new provincial Reform government of Edward Blake*. But his career in provincial politics had been ruined by his association with the Conservatives, and he was not asked to join the cabinet by either Blake or Oliver Mowat*. Gradually his interest shifted to federal politics. Although he did not contest his seat in the federal election of 1872, he resigned from the Ontario legislature upon the passing of the "dual representation" act and returned to the commons in 1873 in a by-election in West Durham, a safe Liberal riding opened by Blake's decision to sit for South Bruce. The booming voice which had earned him the sobriquet "Big Thunder" was effective artillery against the Conservatives during the Pacific Scandal of 1873. But, despite his experience and ability, Wood was not selected to join Alexander Mackenzie*'s Liberal cabinet, formed in November 1873.

In financial difficulty as a result of his luxurious style of living and sometimes dissolute behaviour, Wood accepted in March 1874 the office of chief justice of Manitoba, which carried a stipend of almost $5,000 per annum. For the next eight years Wood was a controversial figure on the Manitoba bench. From his first trial, that of Ambroise-Dydime Lépine*, Louis RIEL's lieutenant in the resistance of 1869–70, he sought to reassert the authority of the bench and the supremacy of British institutions in the province. After an impressive début, however, his stature quickly diminished as he became embroiled in local political disputes, federal-provincial railway controversies, and potential conflicts of interest with John Christian Schultz*, from whom he had borrowed money for his palatial residence in Winnipeg. "He is beyond question the making of an excellent Judge," wrote Lieutenant Governor Alexander MORRIS, "if he would only put on the dignity & impartiality of the Judge, and confine himself to his own sphere." Wood failed, however, to adjust his temperament to the neutrality demanded of the bench. Even polished, learned, and well-reasoned judgements in a series of important cases could not restore a reputation tarnished by fits of temper and the occasional bout of intemperance.

In March 1881 Wood's enemies among the local lawyers and politicians, including Joseph Royal* and Henry Joseph CLARKE, petitioned the federal government for his removal on the grounds of partiality, dishonesty, and insobriety. He was now a pathetic figure, partially paralysed by a series of strokes, with poor hearing and barely coherent speech. On 7 Oct. 1882, before the charges levied against him could be fully investigated, Wood collapsed on the bench and died later that evening. He was survived by his wife, four sons, and two daughters, whom he left in the precarious financial circumstances to which he had been accustomed for most of his life.

Wood was a man of great intellect and learning, and his abilities were rarely questioned. In his native province he became a QC and bencher of the Law Society of Upper Canada, and in Manitoba he was named to the presidency of the Historical and Scientific Society of Manitoba. Yet he was headstrong and impatient, and earned a reputation for opportunism and venality that belied the evangelical Christianity to which he adhered as a low churchman of the Church of England. Few of his accomplishments were truly enduring, and the praise heard after his death was spare and restrained. "For those who were disposed to criticise adversely the judicial career of Chief Justice Wood," read an obituary, "it will be well to remember that it fell to his lot to do the chopping, slashing and clearing, so to speak, of a new country. And if the work was not ornamental or artistic, it was at least useful."

J. DANIEL LIVERMORE

Edmund Burke Wood was the author of *Arguments of Hon. E. B. Wood, before the arbitrators, under the British North America Act of 1867 . . .* (Toronto, 1870); *Mr. Wood's argument before the provincial arbitrators on the modes proposed for the apportionment of the excess of debt and division of assets between Ontario and Quebec* (Toronto, 1870); *Petitions and reply to the charges preferred against the Hon. E. B. Wood, C. J., Province of Manitoba* (Ottawa, 1882); *Speech . . . delivered on the 15th December, 1868, in the Legislative Assembly of Ontario . . .* (Toronto, 1869); and *Speech . . . delivered on the 10th December, 1869, in the Legislative Assembly of Ontario . . .* (Toronto, 1869). Some of his legal decisions as chief justice of Manitoba are found in *Judgments in the Queen's Bench, Manitoba,* comp. Daniel Carey (Winnipeg, 1875; repr. Calgary and New York, 1918), and *Reports of cases argued and determined in the Court of Queen's Bench in Manitoba both at law and in equity . . . during the time of Chief Justice Wood, from 1875 to 1883 . .*, ed. E. D. Armour (Toronto and Edinburgh, 1884).

AO, MU 136–273. PAC, MG 24, B40; MG 26, A. PAM, MG 12, B; E. QUA, Alexander Mackenzie papers. *Canadian Law Times* (Toronto), (1882): 529–30. *The Canadian legal directory: a guide to the bench and bar of the dominion of Canada,* ed. H. J. Morgan (Toronto, 1878). Dent, *Canadian portrait gallery*, I. [R.] D. and Lee Gibson, *Substantial justice: law and lawyers in Manitoba, 1670–1970* (Winnipeg, 1972). R. St G. Stubbs, "Hon. Edmund Burke Wood," HSSM *Papers*, 3rd ser., no.13 (1958): 27–47.

WOOD, ENOCH, Methodist minister, administrator, and mission superintendent; baptized 13 Feb. 1802 near Gainsborough, England, son of William and Sarah Wood; d. 31 Jan. 1888 at Toronto, Ont.

Enoch Wood was educated in Gainsborough, where at the age of 16 he helped his friend Thomas Cooper, the future Chartist, organize a school for the poor. Although baptized an Anglican, he converted to Methodism and served as a local lay preacher on the Gainsborough Wesleyan circuit. The loss of five Wesleyan missionaries in the British West Indies by drowning early in 1826 led to Wood's reception on trial for the ministry and his ordination for missionary service in London on 28 May 1826. He served in Montserrat and St Christopher until July 1829 when he was transferred to Saint John, N.B. His ministry in New Brunswick was outstanding; he served in Saint John, 1829–31 and 1836–46; Miramichi, 1831–33; and Fredericton, 1833–36 and 1846–47. In 1830 he was received into full connection with the British Wesleyan conference. He was chairman of the New Brunswick District from 1843 to 1847. During his ministry, Wesleyan Methodism was greatly extended in New Brunswick and large churches were erected at Chatham and Saint John.

In 1847 Wood accompanied the Reverend Dr Robert Alder*, representative of the British conference, to the meeting in Toronto, Canada West, at which the difficult question of reunion of the Canadian and British Wesleyans was discussed. Wood's wise counsel helped to re-establish the union. That same year he was appointed superintendent of missions of the Wesleyan Methodist Church in Canada and he moved to Toronto. He was president of the church from 1851 to 1857 and from 1862 to 1863. He continued as superintendent of missions until 1874 when the Methodist Church of Canada was formed through the union of the two Wesleyan conferences of British North America and the Methodist New Connexion Church of Canada. Wood was a delegate to its first general conference in September 1874 and was appointed its general secretary of missions. He was elected president of the newly formed Toronto Conference of the Methodist Church in 1874 and again the following year. On his retirement from his office as general secretary in 1878 he was named honorary secretary of missions. Wood had also been involved in the support of Victoria College, Cobourg, and in 1860 he had received the degree of doctor of divinity from that institution.

A man of broad vision, Wood made a tour of the Indian missions of the Canada conference and in 1848 drew up plans for an industrial school for Indians at Muncey, Canada West. The British Wesleyans placed their Indian missions in the Hudson's Bay Company territories under his superintendency in 1851 in preparation for their final transfer to the Canadian conference in 1854. That year the Wesleyan congregations in Canada East also joined the conference, and two years later mission work was commenced among the French Canadians; in 1858 a mission to British Columbia was started and four ministers were dispatched. The Reverend George Young* was appointed the first Methodist missionary to the white settlers of the Canadian west in 1868. Shortly after, plans were started for the establishment of the Canadian mission to Japan and in 1873 the first two missionaries were sent.

Wood's first wife, a native of England, died in 1828 at St Christopher. In late 1829 he married Caroline Matilda Merritt (Merrett) of Saint John, and they had five sons and six daughters. Two sons, Robert A. and John O., who became Toronto businessmen, and one daughter, Mary Bakewell, wife of the Reverend Samuel Sobieski NELLES, reached adulthood. Wood died at his home in Toronto on 31 Jan. 1888 after many years of illness; his wife survived him by only eight months. An obituary in the *Christian Guardian* described Wood as a kind but firm man of considerable administrative ability and an excellent preacher warmly attached to Wesleyan Methodism.

CALVIN GLENN LUCAS

Methodist Missionary Soc. Arch. (London), Wesleyan Methodist Missionary Soc., Corr., Canada, 1829–83 (mfm. at UCA). UCA, Biog. files, Enoch Wood; Methodist Church of Canada, Missionary Soc., Minutes, 1874–83; Toronto Conference, Minutes, 1874–75; Wesleyan Methodist Church in Canada, Missionary Soc., Board of Management, Minutes, 1851–74. *British North American Wesleyan Methodist Magazine* (Saint John, N.B., and Fredericton), 1 (1840–41)–5 (1846–47). Methodist Church of Canada, General Conference, *Journal of the proc.* (Toronto), 1874. *Methodist Magazine*, 1 (January–June 1875)–32 (July–December 1890). *Methodist Magazine* (London), 1815–21. *Nova-Scotia and New-Brunswick Wesleyan Methodist Magazine* (Halifax), 1 (1832). *Wesleyan* (Halifax), 1838–40. Wesleyan Methodist Church, *Minutes of the conferences* (London), 6 (1825–30): 140, 248, 369, 482, 550; 11 (1848–51): 620; 12 (1852–54): 146–49, 454, 501, 521; Missionary Soc., *Missionary Notices* (London), 5 (1826–28): 73–76, 388; 6 (1829–31): 74. Wesleyan Methodist Church in Canada, *Minutes* (Toronto), 1847–74; Missionary Soc., *Annual report* (Toronto), 1847–74. *Wesleyan-Methodist Magazine* (London), 1822–55. *Wesleyan Repository and Literary Record* (Toronto), 1 (1860–61): 51–54. *Christian Guardian*, 1847–88.

Commemorative biog. record, county York, 51. Cornish, *Cyclopædia of Methodism*. *Cyclopædia of Canadian biog.* (Rose, 1888), 585. Nathanael Burwash, *The history of Victoria College* (Toronto, 1927). *Early Saint John Methodism and history of Centenary Methodist Church, Saint John, N.B.; a jubilee souvenir*, ed. G. A. Henderson (Saint John, 1890).

WORKMAN, THOMAS, businessman and politician; b. 17 June 1813 at Ballymacash, near Lisburn (Northern Ireland), seventh son of Joseph Workman and Catherine Goudie; m. in 1845 Annie, daughter of John Eadie (there were no children); d. 9 Oct. 1889 in Montreal, Que.

Thomas Workman immigrated to Canada in May 1827, joining his brothers in Montreal. He continued his education at the Union School, established by his brother Benjamin in 1819, where he was given a thorough mercantile training as well as instruction in English grammar, classics, and mathematics. After working in the office of the *Canadian Courant*, which Benjamin Workman had acquired from Nahum Mower* in 1829, Thomas was employed by John White and Company, Montreal merchants. About 1834 he became a clerk in the wholesale iron and hardware firm of John Frothingham* and his own brother William*. Thomas became a partner in 1843 and following the retirement in 1859 of William and of Frothingham, he assumed control of the business which, under his direction, continued its growth as the largest wholesale hardware house in Canada. As well as importing goods from Britain and the United States, after 1853 it had begun manufacturing hardware at its own plant in Montreal's new industrial quarter along the Lachine Canal.

With the success of the firm, Workman moved aggressively into other ventures such as banking, becoming a director and later vice-president and president of the Molson's Bank, established in 1855. As well, Workman became involved as a director, along with Mathew Hamilton GAULT, in the commencement of operations in 1871 by the Sun Mutual Life Insurance Company of Montreal (later the Sun Life Assurance Company of Canada). Workman served as its first president from 1871 until his death in 1889. His other business interests included the Citizens' Insurance Company of Canada, the City and District Savings Bank, the Stadacona Fire and Life Insurance Company, and the Canada Shipping Company; he was also a director of the Montreal Merchants' Exchange and Reading Room from 1863 to 1882, and invested heavily in Montreal real estate. From 1866 to 1887 he was a justice of the peace.

Like a number of other young Irish Protestant immigrants to Lower Canada, Workman joined the Doric Club, founded in Montreal in 1836 to preserve the "British connection." The group's 150 members assisted the authorities on a number of occasions. Workman, as a volunteer, participated in the defeat of the rebels at the bloody battle of Saint-Eustache and at Saint-Benoît, in the latter stages of the rebellion of 1837–38. Although these volunteers earned a lasting reputation for unbridled burning, looting, and murder, Workman was proud of his membership in this organization and later fondly remembered their exploits.

In 1867 Workman was elected as a Liberal to the Canadian parliament from Montreal Centre, but did not seek re-election in 1872 or 1874. In October 1875 he was returned to the House of Commons from Montreal West, defeating Thomas WHITE in a sharply fought by-election, made necessary by the removal of the incumbent, Frederick McKenzie. In the commons Workman defended the interests of Montreal banking, manufacturing, and shipping firms. He did not run in 1878, and the seat passed to Gault, his business associate and a Conservative.

Workman supported a number of institutions in Montreal, including the Irish Protestant Benevolent Society, of which he was president for two years, the Fraser Institute, the Mackay Institution for Protestant Deaf Mutes, and McGill College. A Presbyterian until 1840 and member of the St Gabriel Street Church, he converted to Unitarianism under the influence of the Reverend John Cordner*, and was one of the founders of Montreal's Church of the Messiah. On his death from diabetes, following the death of his wife by a few months, Workman bequeathed large sums from his estate, valued at one million dollars, to McGill College and local charities.

GERALD J. J. TULCHINSKY

AC, Montréal, État civil, Unitariens, Messiah Unitarian Church (Montreal), 11 Oct. 1889. PAC, MG 30, D1, 31: 24. Sun Life Assurance Company of Canada Arch. (Montreal), Card index to minutes, 1870–1931. Can., House of Commons, *Debates*, 1867–70, 1875–78; Parl., *Sessional papers*, 1880–81, VII, no.13. *Parliamentary debates, Dominion of Canada* . . . (3v., Ottawa, 1870–72), II–III. *Gazette* (Montreal), 10 Oct. 1889. *La Minerve*, 10 oct. 1889. *Montreal Daily Star*, 10 Oct. 1889. *CPC*, 1877. *Cyclopædia of Canadian biog.* (Rose, 1886), 778. *Montreal directory*, 1863–87. Campbell, *Hist. of Scotch Presbyterian Church.* G. H. Harris, *The president's book; the story of the Sun Life Assurance Company of Canada* (Montreal, 1928). Phillip Hewett, *Unitarians in Canada* (Toronto, 1978). "The company's first president," *Sunshine* (Montreal), January 1896: 4.

WORTS, JAMES GOODERHAM, distiller, businessman, and banker; b. 4 June 1818 at Great Yarmouth, Norfolk, England, eldest son of James Worts and Elizabeth Gooderham; m. 1 Oct. 1840 Sarah Bright, and they had three sons and six daughters; d. 20 June 1882 at Toronto, Ont.

James Gooderham Worts's father, a mill-owner from 1813 to 1831 in Lowestoft and in Bungay, Suffolk, made the decision to immigrate to Upper Canada, perhaps in the hope of improving his family's economic prospects. James Worts and his eldest son left Great Yarmouth in May 1831 and eventually settled in York (Toronto) where James established a milling business. He chose a site southeast of York at the mouth of the Don River and began construction of a stone windmill. In June 1832 the remaining members of the Worts family, accompanied by some members of the Gooderham family, to whom they were related by marriage, arrived in York. James Worts then formed the partnership of Worts and Gooderham with his brother-in-law, William GOODERHAM Sr. A trial run of the windmill from October to December 1832 proved the need for an auxiliary steam-engine which was added the next spring.

It is possible that James Gooderham Worts attended school in Montreal until the fall of 1831. He was orphaned early in 1834: his mother died in childbirth and two weeks later his father drowned himself in the mill's well. William Gooderham, who took complete charge of the business, also assumed responsibility for his nephew and began to groom him for a partnership in the firm, to which a distillery was added in 1837. In 1845 Worts became a partner in his uncle's firm, which was renamed Gooderham and Worts.

Although he achieved substantial wealth and a reputation in his own right, James Gooderham Worts's career was so closely linked to the business interests of his uncle that he was somewhat overshadowed and their joint achievements cannot easily be separated. Worts devoted most of his time to managing the distillery which experienced remarkable growth. After both Worts and Gooderham began to diversify their business interests in the 1850s, Worts soon played the more prominent public role. He invested heavily in the Bank of Toronto, incorporated in 1855, and, by 1863, he was the second largest stockholder with shares to the value of $27,000. He was vice-president of the bank from 1858 until 1881 when he succeeded his partner in the presidency for the few months he outlived him. By 1856 Worts had also become a director of the Ontario, Simcoe and Huron Railroad Union (its name was changed in 1858 to the Northern Railway Company of Canada), although he withdrew in 1858 after suffering substantial financial losses. These losses may have been a factor in turning the partners' attention to narrow gauge lines which could be constructed more cheaply, thereby giving a larger return on their investments. Between 1870 and 1872 Worts was an important shareholder and a director of the Toronto and Nipissing Railway, incorporated in 1868, in which the firm of Gooderham and Worts was in 1871 the largest shareholder. Gooderham and Worts, and J. G. Worts himself, were again important shareholders in the Toronto, Grey and Bruce Railway, also incorporated in 1868. Worts held meetings and sponsored excursions to promote these railways and gain the support and financial involvement of municipalities through which the railways might pass. He was nevertheless not interested only in narrow gauge lines: in 1871 he joined David Lewis Macpherson* and Toronto backers in proposing the Interoceanic Railway, to link central Canada with the Pacific Ocean, a venture in which Gooderham did not take part.

Worts represented the firm of Gooderham and Worts at the first meeting of the Canadian Ship Owners' Association held in June 1857; he sat on the board of the Toronto Harbour Commission from 1856 to 1863 and was chairman from 1865 to 1882. He also served as vice-president and president of the Toronto Board of Trade from 1865 to 1869.

Wort's only foray into politics occurred in 1867. A delegation of about 200 businessmen in the federal riding of Toronto East asked him on 22 August to run after the withdrawal from the contest of their previous candidate, Alexander Mortimer Smith, a Toronto entrepreneur and municipal politician. Worts agreed, but attacks mounted by opposing candidates and the shouts of hecklers at his nomination meeting revealed strong resentment of the economic power Gooderham and Worts wielded within the city. This reaction demonstrated to Worts that he had little support outside the commercial sector of the constituency, and he too removed himself from the contest on 24 August. Worts's public defence of his business practices, in particular his conviction that dissatisfied customers need not return, showed his lack of tact and tended to confirm the *Globe*'s judgement that he would "never reach even a middling position as a politician."

Like Gooderham, Worts lived near the distillery, on an estate he built himself called Lindenwold. He focused his life on business, family, and the Church of England, being vestry clerk at Little Trinity Church for over 30 years and a warden from 1874 to 1882. With his cousin, George Gooderham*, he alternated as master of the Toronto Hunt Club between 1870 and 1881; he was also a supporter of the Toronto Mechanics' Institute as his father had been. With William Gooderham and William Cawthra*, Worts was a major contributor to the building fund organized to add a wing to the Toronto General Hospital for the treatment of infectious diseases.

When Worts died of malaria in 1882, he left an estate valued at over $1,500,000. His confidence in his influence led him to direct in his will that his son-in-law, William Henry Beatty, be elected a director of the Bank of Toronto, and that his second son, Thomas Frederick, replace him as a director of the Canada Permanent Loan and Savings Company, a position Worts had held since 1859. His eldest living son, James Gooderham Worts Jr, was already secretary of the distillery. Worts was remembered as being deliberate in reaching decisions and iron-willed in carrying them out, a description fitting his position at the centre of enterprises employing several hundred men. He was also described as a willing source of advice to those with serious projects to launch. This concern for the expanding business life of the community increased the influence which Gooderham and Worts might have exercised solely on the basis of their own large holdings.

DIANNE NEWELL

AO, RG 22, ser.6–2, York County, Will of James Worts, 11 May 1831. MTL, Biog. scrapbooks, VII: 481; XXIX: 25. York County Surrogate Court (Toronto), no.4605, will of J. G. Worts, 3 July 1882 (mfm. at AO). Bank of Toronto, *List of stockholders as on the 30 June 1863* (Toronto, 1863). *Canadian Merchants' Magazine and Commercial Rev.* (Toronto), 1 (April–September 1857): 148, 327; 2 (October 1857–March 1858): 391. "Canadian railways, no.XXV: Toronto and Nipissing Railway," *Engineering: an Illustrated Weekly Journal* (London), 17 Oct. 1879. Ont., Legislature, *Sessional papers*, 1871–72, II, nos.29, 35. Ontario, Simcoe and Huron Railroad Union Company, *Report submitted by the board of directors . . .* (Toronto), 1854–55; 1857–58. Toronto Board of Trade, *Annual report . . .* (Toronto), 1860–63; *Annual review of the commerce of Toronto . . .*, comp. W. S. Taylor (Toronto), 1867; 1870; *Annual statement of the trade of Toronto . . .*, comp. J. M. Trout (Toronto), 1865. *Globe*, 7 Feb. 1862, 22 Aug. 1881, 21 June 1882, 6 March 1885. *Leader*, 23–26 Aug. 1867. *Monetary Times*, 1869–83. *Toronto Daily Mail*, 21 June 1882. *Canadian biog. dict.*, I: 62–70. Chadwick, *Ontarian families*, I: 158. *Dominion annual register*, 1882. Masters, *Rise of Toronto*. Middleton, *Municipality of Toronto*. *Robertson's landmarks of Toronto*. Joseph Schull, *100 years of banking in Canada: a history of the Toronto-Dominion Bank* (Toronto, 1958). E. B. Shuttleworth, *The windmill and its times: a series of articles dealing with the early days of the windmill* (Toronto, 1924).

WRIGHT, AMOS, politician and public servant; b. 24 Nov. 1809 in Leeds County, Upper Canada, near the present village of Mallorytown, son of Abraham Wright, UEL; m. in 1833 Maria Raymond, and they had at least three children; d. 31 May 1886 at Port Arthur (now part of Thunder Bay), Ont.

As a child Amos Wright moved with his family to Richmond Hill in York County and his education does not seem to have continued after the move. It was in Richmond Hill that he became established as a farmer and mill-owner, and he was elected reeve of Markham Township in 1850. One year later he was elected to the assembly from the riding of York East, defeating Edward William Thomson*. At first he supported the Reform ministry of Francis HINCKS and Augustin-Norbert Morin*. Like Joseph Hartman* of York North and David Christie* of Wentworth, he moved into a more radical position than the ministry; this trend is discernible in the journals of the fourth parliament although his voting record was by no means consistent. The voters of York East returned him in the election of 1854, against a moderate Reform opponent, John Sheridan Hogan*, but the ambiguity of his stand on crucial issues brought denunciation from both the Clear Grit and the Conservative press. The *Toronto Daily Patriot and Express* declared that he "was so flattered and fondled by great men in high offices that he looked as bewildered with unexpected honors as an interesting widow giving herself away in matrimony for the fourth time."

For the decade following 1854, Wright was a consistent supporter of George Brown* and the Clear Grit party on issues of wide significance such as representation by population. However, his rare interventions in debate and the few resolutions he supported reveal the narrowness of interest in a rural constituency of his time. As a supporter of confederation, he followed Brown into the coalition of 1864, but he did not rejoin the opposition when Brown resigned from the ministry in the following year. The ferment among Upper Canadian Reform groups in 1866 temporarily recreated some of the pressures that Wright had successfully weathered a decade earlier and, in selecting a candidate for the first dominion parliament, the Reformers of York East chose a different standard-bearer, James Metcalfe.

Wright's absence from parliament proved to be a brief one. A vacancy was created in York West by the resignation of William Pearce Howland*, the newly appointed lieutenant governor of Ontario, and Wright successfully contested the federal by-election of 1868. He chose to retire from politics before the election in 1872. In 1875 with Liberal governments in Toronto and Ottawa he received appointments from both: in April he became the federal Indian agent and in May the province's crown land agent for the Thunder Bay area.

With the Conservatives in power federally after 1878, criticism of Wright's work increased, but the dispute which brought about his dismissal arose from more than political differences. Simon James Dawson*, the local MP, had strong views on local patronage and on northern development. As a Catholic he urged the appointment of Catholic Indian agents to please Bishop Jean-François JAMOT, in whose diocese northwestern Ontario lay, whereas Wright, a Methodist, praised Methodist missionary efforts among the Indians. The political and religious tensions were brought to a head by a case involving a conflict of interest. Wright purchased, from Binessie (Pinessie), the chief of the Fort William Indian band, part of the property the band had recently acquired from the Ontario Crown Lands Department. The chief later complained to the federal authorities that Wright had brought undue pressure to bear upon him and that the price he had agreed to accept was well below current land values. Although the transaction was allowed to stand, the federal government was provided with an opportunity to change personnel without changing policy. It was argued that "Mr. Wright's conduct in this matter has to say the least materially impaired his usefulness" and, over some protest from local Liberals, a new Indian agent was appointed in 1883.

Wright continued in his provincial appointment until his death three years later. The preponderance of free grant applications from Markham Township may reflect the land agent's continuing link with the area in which his family still resided. Wright also held several other posts during his life. He was a member of the senate of Victoria College in Cobourg, an associate judge for York County, chairman of the board of the grammar school commissioners in Richmond Hill, and president of both the mechanics' institute and the agricultural society in Thunder Bay.

Despite his record of "usefulness and social popularity," Amos Wright remained a minor actor in the political drama in Canada in the mid 19th century. His career reveals both the predicament of the so-called "loose fish" in an era when party organization was strengthening, and the powerful but limited interests of the loyalist, Methodist, and rural society he represented for so long; it also throws light upon the political reward system of the 1870s when a young and developing north was considered an appropriate area for the appointment of ageing party men for whom no Senate seat was contemplated.

ELIZABETH ARTHUR

AO, MU 3154. PAC, MG 26, A, 289; 293; RG 10, B2, 1081; 1083; 1090. Can., Prov. of, Legislative Assembly, *Journals*, 1852–66. *Globe*, 12, 22 March 1853. *Toronto Daily Patriot and Express*, 23 Feb., 18 March 1853. *CPC*, 1862–72. Cornell, *Alignment of political groups*.

WRIGHT, GEORGE, surveyor and office-holder; b. 21 Dec. 1810 in Charlottetown Royalty, P.E.I., son of George Wright* and Phoebe Cambridge; m. in

1839 Sarah Matilda Goff, and they had seven children; d. 17 Dec. 1887 in Charlottetown Royalty.

George Wright was descended from a family of surveyors. His grandfather, Thomas Wright*, his uncle Charles*, and his father all held the office of surveyor general of Prince Edward Island. Wright evidently studied under the direction of his father and by 1829 was working in the office of the surveyor general. In 1835 his father was appointed administrator of the government after the death of Lieutenant Governor Sir Aretas William Young*, and Wright was appointed acting surveyor general to replace his father. He received the same post in 1837 and in 1841 when George Sr was again appointed administrator. Throughout this period, documents refer to the younger Wright as assistant or deputy in the department, although no official appointment had been made. After the death of his father on 17 March 1842 Wright was provisionally appointed surveyor general until instructions arrived from England. The Colonial Office queried the appointment, which was chiefly supported by a letter of recommendation from George Wright Sr, indicating that they were not in favour of the post remaining in the same family for three generations. However, Lieutenant Governor Sir Henry Vere Huntley* gave assurances that no one else in the colony possessed the necessary qualifications and Wright's appointment was officially confirmed.

As surveyor general, Wright was responsible for the laying out of roads, township and county boundaries, and the supervision and surveying of crown lands. When the colony attained responsible government in 1851 many of the duties which the surveyor general had performed were transferred to the office of registrar of deeds and keeper of plans. This new post, held by Reformer William Swabey*, was included in the civil list, the costs of which the Reformers under George Coles* had agreed to assume in return for responsible government. Wright's office was not included in the civil list, and although he remained surveyor general until 1854 he received no salary. Legislative grants were still made, however, for specific cartographic and surveying work he carried out.

Wright had never taken an active political role but his appointment as registrar of deeds and keeper of plans in the short-lived John Myrie Holl* administration in 1854 clearly identified him as a Conservative. When the Liberals returned to office the same year Wright was quickly replaced as registrar by Swabey and Joseph Ball was made surveyor general. With the election of Edward PALMER's Conservative administration in 1859 Wright became colonial treasurer and held this office for eight years. Upon a change of government in 1867 Wright retired from his post and returned to private land surveying. He did not hold office again with the exception of the largely honorary post of usher of the black rod in 1877 and 1878.

Successor to a position which had been in the family since 1773, George Wright failed to achieve the political power associated with the post in the earlier years of the colony. His greatest contribution, cartographic rather than political, was perhaps more in keeping with the post. Maps he drew while in the surveyor general's office are exact in detail and record the growth of the colony. His 1852 map of Prince Edward Island was the basic cartographic source for over 70 years.

H. T. HOLMAN

George Wright was the compiler of *Map of Prince Edward Island, in the Gulf of St. Lawrence, comprising the latest topographical information afforded by the Surveyor Generals Office and other authentic sources* . . . (Charlottetown, 1852).

PAPEI, RG 1, Commission books, I: 272, 293; II: 21, 156, 177, 211, 224; III: 204, 247, 250; IV: 263, 299, 309. PRO, CO 226/63: 72–92; 226/64: 40–47, 95, 162. P.E.I., *Acts*, 1851, c.3; c.31; House of Assembly, *Journal*, 1836–45; 1878–79. *Examiner* (Charlottetown), 19 Dec. 1887. *Haszard's Gazette* (Charlottetown), 23 Nov. 1852. *Royal Gazette* (Charlottetown), 22 Dec. 1835; 29 March, 8 Nov. 1842; 15 Nov. 1852; 19 April 1859; 20 March 1867. *Summerside Journal and Western Pioneer* (Summerside, P.E.I.), 22 Dec. 1887.

Y

YATES, HORATIO, physician, educator, and administrator; b. 11 Feb. 1821 in Otsego County, N.Y., elder son of Hannah Palmer and Dr William Yates; m. 8 Sept. 1846 at Kingston, Canada West, Jane Bower, and they had three daughters; d. 11 March 1882 at Kingston.

At age 12 Horatio Yates was sent from his parents' farm in Otsego County to live with his uncle Noble Palmer, a chemist in Kingston. In 1838 he was articled to Dr James Sampson* of Kingston as a medical student, then attended the University of Pennsylvania where he was granted an MD in 1842. He passed the examination of the Medical Board in Canada West in July 1842 and spent the next year in England at St George's Hospital, London. In 1843 he returned and settled in Kingston.

When the Female Benevolent Society [*see* Harriet DOBBS] opened its charity hospital in 1845 in the building vacated by the parliament of the Province of Canada, Yates offered his services. His association with the hospital (later the Kingston General Hospital), which provided patient care and trained medical students, became his main interest. In the succeeding years the hospital suffered from financial and management problems, and late in 1853 Yates decided to seek election as alderman so he could serve on the hospital board and attempt to effect badly needed improvements in both facilities and management. Yates and a colleague, Dr John Robinson DICKSON, were elected as aldermen and joined the board in 1854.

In January of that year Yates was elected chairman of the board of health. He instituted a comprehensive programme which minimized the severity of the cholera epidemic that summer and he published articles to inform the public about primary preventive measures. He advised a general clean-up, improved drainage, and proper personal care, and recommended that people sleep on second or third floors "to avoid noxious gases."

Yates's main preoccupation remained the hospital and he assumed control of its improvement and reorganization. After reviewing the situation in 1854 he persuaded the non-medical members of the hospital board not to close the institution because of the heavy debt; he agreed to take personal responsibility for its operation. By hiring a new steward, a matron, and two orderlies as well as by inviting local doctors to assist at the hospital and control the admitting and discharging of patients, Yates helped improve both patient care and medical training. Essential repairs were made to the building and he managed a reduction in the debt by coupling rigid economy with successful appeals for larger grants. In 1856 an amendment to the act of incorporation created a close association between Queen's College and the hospital, and placed control of the hospital with a separate, more responsible board. Yates continued on the new board and was elected its chairman in 1866.

Yates had also been a founder of the medical faculty of Queen's College in 1854 and was its professor of the principles and practice of medicine. He arranged for senior medical students, under the supervision of their teachers, to take over the duties of the house surgeon at the hospital, thus saving the hospital £100 a year. Yates attempted to mediate a conflict which arose in 1864 in the medical faculty between several doctors, led by Dickson, and the trustees of the college. Following Dickson's resignation as dean of the faculty, Yates held the post for two years. He refused to join the dissident members of the faculty who resigned and set up the Royal College of Physicians and Surgeons of Kingston in 1866, with Dickson as president. Instead he devoted himself to the hospital where he continued to lecture in clinical medicine. In July 1870, however, he did accept an appointment to the staff of the college.

Because of the change of governments at confederation the province made no grants to hospitals in 1867. Kingston General Hospital managed to stay open on credit extended by the Commercial Bank of the Midland District but the hospital was threatened with closure when the bank suspended payment on 22 October. Yates's vigorous and effective search for funds kept the hospital open. He negotiated a 15-year grant from the federal government for the hospital as one serving "the mariners on the Lakes." He also secured increased grants from the province and campaigned annually for small grants from Frontenac County and nearby villages.

Yates's interests were not confined to medicine. He became chairman of the parks committee for Kingston in 1855 and chairman of the Kingston Horticultural Society in 1857. During his tenures the two groups cooperated in landscaping the city park. He was also a member of the small group that purchased a telescope and established an observatory in the park in 1856. Yates was appointed surgeon to "A" battery of the Royal Canadian Horse Artillery in 1873 and surgeon to the new Royal Military College of Canada in 1876. In 1880 illness forced him to give up teaching and most of his private practice. He did, however, continue as chairman of the hospital board until his death in 1882.

MARGARET SHARP ANGUS

Kingston General Hospital Arch. (Kingston, Ont.), Papers and records, 1854–82. QUA, Corporation of City of Kingston, City records, 181; Queen's Univ. medical faculty records, X, box 8, vol.1; XI, box 11, vol.1. *Chronicle and News*, 9 Jan. 1857. *Daily British Whig*, 11 March 1882. *Daily News* (Kingston), 2–26 Jan. 1854. *Canadian biog. dict.*, I. Margaret Angus, *Kingston General Hospital, 1832–1972: a social and institutional history* (Montreal and London, Ont., 1973). M. I. Campbell, *100 years: Orphans Home and Widows Friend Society, 1857*–1957 ([Kingston, 1957?]).

YOUNG, DAVID, merchant, railway promoter, and civic official; b. 14 Jan. 1848 near Glasgow, Scotland, son of David Young; m. 31 July 1875 Lydia Marion Brown, and they had two children; d. 5 Aug. 1887 in Saratoga Springs, N.Y.

David Young was an orphan when he came to Canada at the age of ten to live with his uncle, Robert Young, in Georgetown, Canada West. In his early teens he ran away from home and over the next six years was successively an errand boy in a grocery store in Toronto, a sailor out of Oakville (Ont.), and a soldier in the United States army in which he became a quartermaster sergeant. After three years of army life, he obtained his discharge and entered the dry goods business as a clerk, initially in Georgetown and subsequently at St Louis, Mo., Natchez, Miss., Mobile, Ala, and New Orleans, La.

Returning to Canada in 1870, Young joined the Ontario Rifles and that autumn arrived in Winnipeg with the 3rd company as a part of the Red River expedition. He took his discharge in June 1871 and joined John Higgins' Winnipeg dry goods firm as a clerk. By "tact, perseverance and energy" Young helped to build the firm into one of the largest and most prosperous in the city. On 1 Feb. 1875 Higgins admitted him as a partner, and in 1880, when the two men retired from active business, they were each worth close to a quarter of a million dollars.

During the 1870s Young was a leading figure in Winnipeg sporting, cultural, and political life. He was a founder, and for many years president, of the Dufferin Park Association, formed by the leading athletic clubs in the city to build an athletic facility for field sports; he was also a member of the Garry Lacrosse Club, the Manitoba Turf Club, the Winnipeg Amateur Literary and Dramatic Association, the Ariel Club, and the Assemblies Club.

From its inception, Young took an active interest in the Winnipeg Board of Trade and in February 1879 was elected to its council. There was considerable anxiety in Winnipeg in the late 1870s over the proposed route of the Canadian Pacific Railway. Initial plans called for it to pass through Selkirk to the north of Winnipeg. Young associated himself with the various efforts of the Winnipeg business community to attract the main line of the CPR to Winnipeg and to build a line from Winnipeg to the southwestern portion of the province. He was one of the original promoters of the Manitoba South-Western Colonization Railway Company, incorporated in May 1879, and later served as its secretary-treasurer. A major point of conflict between this railway company and the city of Winnipeg was the construction of a bridge over the Red River in the area of Point Douglas (now part of Winnipeg). Young won a seat on the city council in the election of January 1879, and for the year that he sat on council he remained a director of the railway, an apparent conflict of interest which was questioned by other council members.

Young was equally active in provincial and federal politics. An ardent Conservative, he supported Alexander MORRIS against Donald Alexander Smith* in the Selkirk constituency during the federal election of 1878. When Morris was narrowly defeated, Young and Archibald Wright immediately launched a suit protesting Smith's election on the grounds of corrupt practices. The petitioners were initially unsuccessful but their appeal to the Supreme Court of Canada was upheld and Smith was unseated. By then Young had broken with the Conservatives in the province, and did not aid Thomas Scott in his successful campaign against Smith in a by-election in September 1880.

In 1881, because of ill health, Young began spending considerable time in Florida where he established a nursery and an orange grove. After the loss of his wife in 1884, his health deteriorated. A popular man in Winnipeg, Young left the city permanently in November 1885, and died in Saratoga Springs in 1887. He was buried in Winnipeg.

JOHN E. KENDLE

PAM, MG 7, B7, Marriages, no.124; MG 12, A; B2. Alexander Begg and W. R. Nursey, *Ten years in Winnipeg: a narration of the principal events in the history of the city of Winnipeg from the year A.D. 1870, to the year A.D. 1879, inclusive* (Winnipeg, 1879). Can., House of Commons, *Debates*, 1880-81; *Journals*, 1880-81; Parl., *Sessional papers*, 1880-81, IX, no.46. Can., *Statutes*, 1879, c.66. *Manitoba Daily Free Press*, 1878-80, 1887. A. F. J. Artibise, *Winnipeg; a social history of urban growth, 1874-1914* (Montreal and London, 1975). W. T. R. Preston, *The life and times of Lord Strathcona* (London, 1914). [H.] B. Willson, *The life of Lord Strathcona & Mount Royal, G.C.M.G., G.C.V.O. (1820-1914)* (London and Toronto, 1915).

YOUNG, GEORGE PAXTON, clergyman, professor, school inspector, and author; b. 9 Nov. 1818 at Berwick upon Tweed, England; d. unmarried 26 Feb. 1889 in Toronto, Ont.

George Paxton Young was born into the family of a Church of Scotland clergyman and received his early education in Berwick upon Tweed. He then attended the celebrated Royal High School in Edinburgh and the University of Edinburgh, where he graduated with an MA. In 1843, after a brief period teaching mathematics at the Dollar Academy, he entered the newly founded Theological Hall of the Free Church in Edinburgh. On completion of his divinity course he was admitted as a licentiate of the Free Church and took up his first charge at Martyrs' Church, Paisley. In 1847 or 1848 he immigrated to Canada and on 22 Nov. 1850 was inducted as minister of Knox Church, Hamilton, Canada West. He served as moderator of the Hamilton presbytery for the year 1851–52. In 1853 he resigned his pastoral charge and was appointed to the faculty of Knox College, Toronto.

Young taught in both the divinity and the preparatory departments at the college for the next decade. Then in 1864 he resigned his professorship and accepted Egerton RYERSON's invitation to become the first full-time grammar school inspector for Canada West. In 1865 he was also appointed inspector of Roman Catholic separate schools by Ryerson. In 1868 Young returned to Knox College to conduct the preparatory department and in 1870 was appointed professor of mental and moral philosophy. The next year, after declining an invitation to become professor of mathematics at Victoria College in Cobourg, he succeeded James Beaven* in the chair of metaphysics and ethics at University College, Toronto, a post he held for the rest of his life.

Young was sometimes described by contemporaries as a shy, retiring man who lived a quiet bachelor's life and preferred above all the seclusion of his study. This judgement was perhaps based more on his demeanour than on the actual record of his life, for

Young was always involved in public affairs and in the currents of contemporary scholarship. Throughout his life he was active in the Canadian (later Royal Canadian) Institute, presenting many papers before that body and holding several offices between 1856 and 1871. He was an active supporter of church union among Presbyterians, urging it upon his congregation as early as 1853, contributing favourable articles to the *Globe*, and sponsoring motions to this effect at synod. As grammar school inspector between 1864 and 1867, Young repeatedly toured Canada West, visiting each school and examining the ability of the teachers and the progress of the pupils. On the basis of his accumulating knowledge, he wrote a series of perceptive and highly critical reports on the inadequacies of the grammar schools and delineated changes he considered necessary. His analysis of the problems provided Ryerson with both ammunition and ideas for reform, and many of Young's suggestions were incorporated into the school act of 1871 that replaced grammar schools with high schools which would provide general education and with collegiate institutes which would prepare students for entrance to university. Young's resignation as school inspector in 1867 did not break his ties with the provincial school system. He served as president of the Ontario Teachers' Association in 1871, and was a member of the Council of Public Instruction in 1871–72. As a member of the Committee of Examiners after 1871 he continued to play an important role in educational policy-making in Ontario until the last few months before his death.

Young's scholarly activities and interests were wide and varied. His earliest publication was a collection of sermons, *Miscellaneous discourses and expositions of Scripture*, a volume which reveals wide reading, a talent for exegesis, and a felicitous prose style. Throughout his life he pursued an early interest in mathematics, publishing in Canadian, American, and English journals a number of papers on the theory of equations which drew high praise from eminent mathematicians of the time. In philosophy, the subject he taught most of his life, he published relatively little; yet it was perhaps here that his impact on Canadian thought was greatest. Though initiated as a student at Edinburgh into Scottish "common sense" philosophy, he became critical of it early in his teaching career at Knox and by 1862 had largely rejected it. In its place he turned, like many others of his generation, to Kant and then to the British Idealism of Edward Caird and Thomas Hill Green. Through Young, a generation of students at the University of Toronto were introduced to the political and ethical theories of men attempting to preserve Christian beliefs and at the same time come to terms with modernity.

Young's own theological views were also affected by his philosophical shift. He never became a sceptic, for British Idealism provided him with new philosophical underpinnings for his faith. But it did apparently lead him to dissent from some aspects of Presbyterian doctrine, or at least to question the traditional justifications for those doctrines. His resignation from Knox College in 1864 may have been prompted by his doubts. He was never to teach theology again, and in later life he refused even to act as elder or Sunday School teacher in the church to which he belonged, St Andrew's, Toronto. On the other hand he remained, till the end of his life, not only in his own mind but in the view of both his students and his church, a convinced and practising Christian.

Young was above all a teacher. The memoirs left by his students, many of whom had no special interest in or aptitude for philosophy, conjure up a charismatic figure who could light fires of enthusiasm for difficult ideas, illuminate even the most complex philosophical passages, and bring a warmth and humanity to the classroom that few students could resist. Young left a considerable record of scholarship behind him, especially in mathematics. He left his mark on Ontario's school system. But it was his ability as a teacher that made him a legend in his time and gave him his influence over the intellectual development of a generation of University of Toronto students.

R. D. Gidney

George Paxton Young was the author of *The ethics of freedom: notes selected, translated and arranged by his pupil James Gibson Hume* (Toronto, 1911); *Freedom and necessity: a lecture, delivered in Knox' College on the 6th April, 1870, at the close of the college session* (Toronto, 1870); "Lecture on the philosophical principles of natural religion," *Home and Foreign Record of the Canada Presbyterian Church* (Toronto), 2 (1862–63): 29–38; *Miscellaneous discourses and expositions of Scripture* (Edinburgh and Hamilton, [Ont.], 1854).

AO, MU 134, G. P. Young; RG 2, C-2, box 16, no.1316; C-6-C, Young to Egerton Ryerson, 12 April 1864. PAC, MG 24, B40, pp.199–201. UTA, A73-0026, Office of Statistics and Records, Dept. of Graduate Records, G. P. Young file. H. Calderwood, "Professor George Paxton Young, LL.D.," *Knox College Monthly and Presbyterian Magazine* (Toronto), 10 (May–October 1889): 1–4. William Caven, "Professor Young," *Knox College Monthly and Presbyterian Magazine*, 9 (November 1888–April 1889): 265–68. *Doc. hist. of education in U.C.* (Hodgins). *Varsity* (Toronto), 1 Dec. 1888, 2 March 1889. *Weekly Globe*, 25 Aug. 1876. Dent, *Canadian portrait gallery*, III. *Canadian education: a history*, ed. J. D. Wilson *et al.* (Scarborough, Ont., 1970). McKillop, *Disciplined intelligence. The University of Toronto and its colleges, 1827–1906*, [ed. W. J. Alexander] (Toronto, 1906), 353–54. J. A. Irving, "The development of philosophy in central Canada from 1850 to 1900," *CHR*, 31 (1950): 252–87.

YOUNG, Sir WILLIAM, lawyer, politician, judge, and philanthropist; b. 8 Sept. 1799 in Falkirk, Scotland, son of John Young* and Agnes Renny; d. 8 May 1887 at Halifax, N.S.

Although William Young and his younger brother George Renny* cherished the affection of their mother, it was their father, the well-known "Agricola," who was altogether predominant in the formation of their characters. William, having by his own account received an honours degree from the University of Glasgow by the age of 14, arrived in Halifax with his family in April 1814. Ambitious for fame and riches, he readily accepted his father's "idea of accumulating a fortune as quickly as possible, under any flag, and . . . the idea that it was not impossible to be a literary man and a merchant." When British troops occupied Castine, Maine, in September 1814, John Young was among the Halifax merchants who stationed themselves there and, with a large stock of dry goods brought from Britain, he conducted a thriving trade, both legally and illegally, until the following April. His agent in Halifax was 15-year-old William, who carried out almost faultlessly his father's meticulous instructions. Between June and October 1815 William acted as the agent of John Young and Company in New York, this time receiving instructions from his father in Halifax, who reported so favourably on his performance that his uncle William Renny in Edinburgh concluded he was "a very extraordinary young man."

If his father's instructions taught him anything, it was to be hard-hearted and ruthless, even to border on the unscrupulous, in order to maximize profits. But William and George were "blind to [their father's] faults" and "united to the world against any criticism of his methods or character"; they were, said D. C. Harvey*, "a compact family in search of fortune." Late in 1815 William entered into a partnership with James Cogswell in an auction and commission business in Halifax, and he apparently continued commercial pursuits until 1820. By this time he had developed strong opinions of his own; thus he was so certain Pictou Academy was not a proper place for his brother George to attend that he caused Principal Thomas McCulloch* to say "young men . . . do not always consider . . . what injury they may do to persons whose labours deserve well of the community."

William's subnormal height – he was so short that he never lost the nickname "little Billy Young" – may have led to his assertiveness. His self-assurance appears in 1820 when, in seeking an indenture of apprenticeship in the legal firm of the brothers Charles Rufus* and Samuel Prescott FAIRBANKS, he asked that any payment to him should depend on the value of his services. Not expecting to pay him anything, the Fairbanks agreed reluctantly to allow him £30 the first year in preference to "any arrangement which would leave any thing in our discretion." The apprenticeship ended on a sour note in 1823. In that year John Young, having secured wide recognition through his *Letters of Agricola* . . . (1822), contested a by-election against C. R. Fairbanks in the township of Halifax. William not only worked strenuously for his father, but allegedly communicated the "secrets" of Fairbanks' campaign to him, and Fairbanks thereafter would have nothing to do with his apprentice. This was only one of a number of incidents which prevented the Youngs from gaining the respect they wanted; "Timothy Touchstone" in the Pictou *Colonial Patriot* suggested that John Young was dishonourable in pursuit of his ambitions, and his sons may have learned their father's lesson all too well.

John Young lost to Fairbanks in 1823, but he was elected for Sydney County in 1824 with William acting as his campaign manager. In his turn John Young secured William's release from his indenture to an irritated Fairbanks by invoking the assistance of Chief Justice Sampson Salter Blowers* and two other judges of the Supreme Court. Finally admitted as attorney in 1825 and barrister the following year, William began the practice of law in Halifax. By 1830 he had established himself sufficiently to marry Anne Tobin, the daughter of Michael Tobin Sr, in a Church of England ceremony. The staunch Presbyterian groom and devout Roman Catholic bride lived in complete harmony, perhaps helped by the fact that they had no children.

In 1834 William formed a legal partnership and insurance business with his brother George that would last until the 1850s. During the early 1830s William was earning about $8,000 a year, a large sum, and his day books and ledgers are so thorough that household expenses are calculated to the last penny. While not highly learned in the law, he was "an excellent tactician [who] impressed himself strongly on courts and juries," and as a result he participated in the great majority of appeal cases. Already he had begun his life-long clashes with James William Johnston*, a prominent lawyer and future leader of the Conservative party. Early in 1832 a veritable "explosion" occurred in the Court of Chancery when Johnston stated he would treat Young's opinions with contempt.

Because an aspiring lawyer needed to get into politics, in 1832 Young contested a vacant seat in Cape Breton County, then encompassing the whole island, against Richard Smith*, manager of the General Mining Association at Sydney. Young had already won the gratitude of newly arrived Highland Scotsmen by helping them to find lands, and over the next two decades he would assist his compatriots in other ways. The result at the first three polling places was a tie, but when voting began at the fourth and last, Chéticamp, 150 Scotsmen, armed with clubs, expelled Smith's friends from the hustings in a celebrated riot and secured Young's election. Later, however, a committee of the assembly found that George Young was a leading perpetrator of the outrage, and that he had acted "with the concurrence and sanction of . . . William Young" whose election was accordingly invalidated.

In the general election of 1836 Young easily won in the newly created Cape Breton county of Juste-au-Corps, which, largely through him, had its name changed to Inverness in 1837. For two decades he was re-elected with the support of its merchants and, more especially, its Catholic laymen and clergy, who constituted a majority of the population. Like his father, William attached himself to the popular cause which, thanks to Joseph Howe*, had now gained majority support in the assembly. But the Youngs failed to get the recognition they hoped for in the political sphere because of a common belief that they carefully calculated their political course of action in terms of their personal interests. Both were highly annoyed in 1837 when Howe moved to replace John Young's moderate resolutions with his own twelve resolutions, a tough statement of the Reformers' grievances and demands which blasted the unrepresentativeness of the Council of Twelve and urged that greater responsibility to the electors be introduced into the political system, especially through an elective legislative council.

That autumn William experienced a traumatic shock in the death of his father who had been his "guide," "friend," and "companion." His sorrow did not deter him from advancing to British officials the claims of himself and George, then in England. Because the Colonial Office was preparing to replace the Nova Scotia Council with executive and legislative councils, he warned his brother to make good use of his presence in England, "a chance wch is not likely ever to recur." That either could have believed the young and inexperienced George would receive preferment seems preposterous, and he got nothing. But neither did William, and for a time he and the lieutenant governor, Sir Colin Campbell*, were not on good terms. William continued to ponder whether he should remain an assemblyman and hope for an executive councillorship, or go to the Legislative Council and let George take his seat in Inverness.

Nothing during the session of 1838 made him want to stay in the assembly. Plaintively he noted that leading Reformers showed greater respect for the unofficial Tory leader, James Boyle Uniacke*, than for himself: "Uniacke & I had a set-to and are on terms of open hostility – Howe and [Laurence O'Connor Doyle*] cultivate his good graces rather than mine." He felt somewhat better in September when he was the only Reformer in a delegation of four which went to Quebec City for constitutional discussions with Lord Durham [Lambton*] and Charles Buller*. Like so many others, he became an immediate convert to Durham's "extraordinary talents . . . irresistible force of reasoning . . . vigorous yet easy flow of ornamental eloquence," and he was highly indignant when the actions of "the pusillanimous Whigs" in Britain led to Durham's resignation as governor general.

In 1839, when Colonial Secretary Lord Glenelg seemed to backtrack on his earlier promises of instituting genuinely representative executive and legislative councils and of surrendering the casual and territorial revenues of the crown for a modest civil list, the assembly sent Young and Herbert Huntington* to press its case in London. The ever provident Young was appalled at the expense: "Ordered a suit of clothes & frock coat on Bond Street – The price extravagant, but it is necessary that I sh$^{d.}$ be fashionably drest." Occasionally, during that summer in England, Young became optimistic, especially over the Colonial Office's promise to open five free ports in Nova Scotia, thereby permitting foreign trade to be carried on more expeditiously. "Here is another great point secured & wch would never have been effected without the delegation." But Young's impression that the new colonial secretary, Lord Normanby, was ignorant of Nova Scotia affairs and would rely on advice from the official faction, was altogether accurate. A dispatch about which Lord Normanby talked to him would, Young knew, be unsatisfactory to Nova Scotia Reformers on both the civil list question and the composition of the councils.

By 1840 the Reformers had concluded that Lieutenant Governor Campbell was deliberately frustrating their endeavours, and Young was active in securing a resolution for his recall. That action brought the new governor general, Charles Edward Poulett Thomson*, to Halifax where he arranged for a coalition executive council of the species that became his trademark. After Young saw Thomson, he understood that Howe, Huntington, and himself would represent the Reformers in the council, but only Howe received an appointment in the council formed by Campbell's successor, Lord Falkland [Cary]. Huntington would have to wait until it was decided whether he was "an animal that will run in harness"; meanwhile, Young's claims would remain in abeyance. Believing that Howe had put his own interests first, Young complained that he had been given no reason for his exclusion. Not until January 1842, after Huntington had resisted all overtures, did Young finally become a councillor and cease his opposition to the coalition of Howe and J. W. Johnston. That year, too, Young, always a friend of Roman Catholic causes, joined Howe in securing the incorporation of St Mary's College in Halifax, and also in denying to the Baptists a grant towards the capital cost of a building for Acadia College in Wolfville. Thus Young played a part in the alienation of the Baptists from the Reformers which would markedly affect Nova Scotia politics in the years to come.

Because he had accepted the post of collector of excise at Halifax, Howe relinquished the speakership of the assembly in 1843 to be succeeded by Young. But, showing its very different attitudes towards Howe and Young, the assembly required the latter to resign from the council even though it had permitted Howe to be both speaker and councillor simultaneously. As speaker, Young could support the Reformers' cause only in committee and in the newspapers. But he and his brother may have contributed most to the popular cause in defending Reform newspapermen in a series of libel suits, which were really political trials intended by the Tories to destroy some of their chief critics. Since Young invariably opposed Johnston in these cases, the antipathy between the two men became even more marked; once Chief Justice Brenton Halliburton* threatened to bar them both from his court unless they behaved with propriety. Young went so far as to allege in the assembly that the judges were antagonistic towards the Reform party and Reform lawyers because they sought to remove abuses in which the judges had a vested interest: a special meeting of the bar society, seemingly attended only by Tories, repudiated these sentiments.

Young's involvement in the partisan warfare reached its zenith in 1846 in a personal clash with Lieutenant Governor Falkland over Young's association with the provisional committee of the Halifax and Quebec Railway, and the naming of himself and his brother George as the railway's colonial solicitors. Falkland, who seemed to lose all objectivity after the Reformers' withdrawal from the coalition in December 1843, ordered the tabling in the assembly of a letter that accused the Youngs of associating with dubious English speculators and of naming "some of the most respectable Gentlemen" in railway prospectuses without their authorization. Thoroughly outraged, Howe blurted out that more of such conduct would force some colonist to "hire a black man, to horsewhip a Lieutenant Governor in the Streets," and even the colonial secretary suggested to Falkland that the publication of the letter must have been an "inadvertence." But an unrepentant Falkland replied that if the facts hurt the Youngs' reputation, "the fault is theirs not mine." Admittedly he had denied William Young the civilities usually accorded the speaker, but he was not called upon to explain his distaste for the Youngs' society. Nevertheless, it would seem that the Youngs' impropriety at worst was grossly exaggerated, and that Falkland's intervention was that of a partisan participant in all-out warfare.

Young campaigned actively in the crucial and, for the Reformers, successful election of 5 Aug. 1847. Early in 1848 he was again elected speaker despite Johnston's charge that he abused the office by his partisanship. He had no desire to be in the new Reform administration unless it was as attorney general and leader of the first ministry under responsible government. These positions went to J. B. Uniacke, once a Tory but since 1844 the acknowledged leader of the Reformers. The shrewdly calculating Young let his brother George accept an executive councillorship, while he retained the more prestigious speakership and the opportunity to augment his personal fortunes in the practice of law and in business pursuits. He was also in a position to accept favours from the government; thus he was one of four commissioners who in 1851 produced the first series of revised statutes. In one instance, however, his actions were meddling; during a visit to Washington in 1850 he gathered information about the terms on which Nova Scotia might secure a reciprocal trade agreement with the United States. The Nova Scotia Executive Council disliked the terms and disliked more the impropriety of Young's intervention.

George Young died in 1853, but despite their close relationship, William experienced a sense of relief, for his brother had been having bouts of insanity since 1851. Henceforth, the whirligig of fortune turned strongly in Young's favour. In April 1854, when J. B. Uniacke was "fairly used up and wholly unfit for public business," and Howe was about to become chief railway commissioner, Young assumed almost by default the leadership of the government and the attorney generalship. Within days he was finding that "my new job is no sinecure. Every day & almost every night has brought its own occupation."

While Young's professed philosophy was to "do what one believes to be right and to leave the result to a Providence wiser than ourselves," he seemed more likely to follow the line of least resistance. Pressed incessantly for offices by his supporters, he gave way where Howe had not, and patronage in its most blatant form may thus be said to have begun under the Young administration. His desire to avoid the onus of decision making led him to see a coup when in 1854 J. W. Johnston agreed to become the second Nova Scotia delegate to a convention in Washington on reciprocity and the fisheries. Francis Hincks of Canada thought it "absurd" to include the leader of the opposition, but Young considered it a "good move" because it "relieves the government of some part of the responsibility." When specific instructions to the Nova Scotia delegates did not arrive from the Colonial Office, Young and Johnston remained in Halifax. Again Young was not disappointed. "Now we are free as a Government from the responsibility of the Treaty which is highly unacceptable to a large body of our people and will be resisted I believe *à l'outrance* by Johnston." Young carefully concealed his personal opinion of the treaty's merits, but he was certain that the assembly would accept it.

Young did not let his premiership interfere with a trip to Europe planned for late June 1854; accompanied by his wife and two Scottish nephews, he had "a delightful tour" as far as Vienna, seeing "many curious things." Late in the same year he called the assembly into session to deal with the Reciprocity Treaty. Although Johnston and Howe both protested that Nova Scotia was being asked to give up the sole use of its fisheries without equivalent concessions and, more especially, without consultation with its government or legislature, Young was a good prophet and the assembly accepted the treaty by a substantial majority. In the same session of 1854–55 Young brought to fruition an objective he had pursued for some time, the abolition of the Court of Chancery. Acting partly on rational grounds, Young was also moved by a burning desire to remove from office an old *bête noire*, Alexander Stewart*, the master of the rolls. Young's critics were right that he had "not grasped the basis on which the fusion of law and equity could be brought about," and the result was a muddle in the administration of justice.

In the election of May 1855 Young and the Liberals improved their standing in the assembly by two or three seats, but it was only a numerical gain, since the election brought from Cumberland County the Conservative Dr Charles Tupper*, a rough-and-tumble fighter for whom Young was no match in the legislature. More than once during 1856 the government was in a state of confusion and even collapse. First, it was during a lengthy debate on patronage in which Young would neither announce nor denounce the principle that "to the victors belong the spoils," although he denied it had been introduced. Later, it was on a bill to support education by compulsory assessment, to which provisions for separate schools were to be added in committee. Young had spent a vast amount of time on the bill, but it was too much to expect that a measure introducing two highly controversial sets of principles would pass easily. Forced to defer it, he was not in a position to re-introduce it in 1857. Meanwhile, intrigues were going on, allegedly to induce some freshmen Liberal members to bring down the government and establish a no-party or third-party administration. An attempt was then to be made to get Brenton Halliburton to resign and install J. W. Johnston as chief justice. "We have had," wrote Young, "a series of most unscrupulous & singular intrigues . . . [but] the plot has failed & a good majority . . . [was] secured."

Something else perturbed him even more. During the session his two Catholic colleagues on the Executive Council, James W. McLeod and Michael Tobin, his wife's cousin, resigned because they felt the government's bestowal of preferment on themselves and their co-religionists was not adequate. Although Young got a Catholic to fill one vacancy, Lieutenant Governor Sir John Gaspard Le Marchant* told him he had not "by any means brought [his] ship into smooth water." Meanwhile, Young could only sit by and wonder if Joseph Howe's "violent rupture" with Irish Roman Catholics over his American recruitment campaign for the British forces in the Crimean War "may operate however unjustly against the Government." Unfortunately for Young, his worst fears were realized when Howe alienated the French and Scottish Catholics as well. As a result, on 18 Feb. 1857, ten Catholic and two Protestant Liberals helped to vote out the Liberals and usher in a Johnston government without an election.

Following his ouster, Young visited northern Europe and confessed that "our party fights shrank into small dimensions." He yearned for the office of chief justice, but when the aged Brenton Halliburton seemed determined to follow the usual course of his predecessors and cling to office until death, Young's interest in politics revived. In 1858 he strongly opposed the agreement that Johnston and the Liberal, Adams George Archibald*, had made for the return to Nova Scotia of ownership of its mines and minerals which had been conferred on the Duke of York in 1826 and later fell into the hands of the General Mining Association. For years Young had fought for a similar agreement, but he could not now bear to have the question settled by his chief opponent. The mining areas retained by the GMA he thought too extensive and the GMA's rental and royalty payments inadequate to serve the best interests of Nova Scotia.

The late 1850s were years of political rancour when, to use the parties' names for each other, anti-Roman Catholic Liberal "proscriptionists" opposed a "Romo-Johnstonite" administration. Although the Catholic historian, Nicholas Meagher*, holds Howe mainly responsible for the religious warfare, he insists that "Young lent himself to Howe's proscription creed in all its fulness and harshness." Understandably, then, religion dominated the election of 12 May 1859. Young deserted Catholic Inverness to run in Protestant Cumberland and out-polled Charles Tupper in that three-member riding. The closeness of the results, 29 Liberals to 26 Conservatives, and the near-certainty that the party controlling the government would name the next chief justice meant that the violent political struggle would continue unabated. When Young approached Lieutenant Governor Lord Mulgrave [PHIPPS] and the colonial secretary for an immediate summoning of the legislature, he was told that Johnston might follow the normal practice and wait until early the next year to convene. The Johnston government maintained that some Liberals elected were disqualified from sitting in the assembly because they held paid offices in the colony, but those whose eligibility was disputed joined the other Liberals in voting out Johnston and installing Young as premier on 10 Feb. 1860. To avoid having to run in a by-election in Cumberland, Young assumed an office hitherto unknown in Nova Scotia, the unpaid presidency of the council.

With the new government installed, the assembly could establish committees to determine whether the supposedly disqualified members had been validly elected. Not surprisingly, a committee over which Young presided confirmed the Liberal Lewis Smith in his seat because he had not been appointed to his paid office according to the prescribed forms. The overall result of the committees' work was to give the Liberals an additional seat. Furious, the opposition assumed the title "Constitutionalists," and labelled the Liberals "Usurpers" and Young "the first law-breaker." Despite the fulminations of Johnston and Tupper, Mulgrave and the colonial secretary replied that the assembly was the sole determinant of its own elections, and any appeal must be to public opinion within the colony itself.

Chief Justice Halliburton died on 16 July 1860, and within days the Tories were insisting that his successor not be Young, whom they charged with shamelessly outraging all the proprieties of public life. The lieutenant governor having approved Young's nomination, the *Acadian Recorder* of 28 July came out in mourning, even though the Prince of Wales arrived in Halifax that day to begin his North American tour. Despite all sorts of appeals to London, the appointment stood and Young had attained his highest ambition.

During his 21 years as chief justice, Young was known less for the quality of his decisions than for the "curious chirography" of his written judgements and his vanity – because he could not bear to be at a lower level than his associates on the bench, "his chair was always piled up with a mountain of cushions." His judgements, like his legal knowledge, lacked profundity and tended to be "showy rather than substantial." As with all his formal speeches, he normally delivered them in a highly dramatic manner. In his first years on the bench he could not escape the controversy that had always seemed to envelop him. After a long imbroglio with Thomas J. Wallace, Young suspended him from practice for contempt, only to have the Judicial Committee of the Privy Council declare that he had used a sanction beyond his powers. It took a strong protest from John Sparrow David Thompson* before Young abandoned the practice of letting a client with a grievance against his solicitor express his complaint in open court without sworn testimony or without moving for process to start legal proceedings on the grievance.

Like his fellow judges, Young was accused of haranguing grand juries on the benefits of Nova Scotia's entry into confederation, and even as he denied it, he admitted that he had never concealed his own opinions. Early in 1867 he acted as the unofficial emissary of Lieutenant Governor Sir William Fenwick WILLIAMS to explain to the colonial secretary the state of affairs in Nova Scotia. Young's services on behalf of confederation may have largely contributed to his being made a KB in 1869.

As late as 1879 Young incurred the wrath of the *Morning Chronicle* as "an imprudent judge" who criticized juries for not convicting the accused when he thought the evidence was ample. Generally, however, in his later years he basked in the respect flowing from his office. In turn, he engaged in all sorts of good works, and although critics might allege their principal purpose was to ensure widespread credit for the donor, many have had beneficial effects to the present day. The Citizens' Free Library began when Young purchased the Halifax Mechanics' Institute library and presented it to the city council; he also gave substantial gifts of books and money throughout the years. He was largely responsible for obtaining the present Point Pleasant Park from the imperial authorities, and having the grant run for 999, rather than 99 years; its handsome gates were his gift in 1886. Next to George Munro*, Young was Dalhousie University's greatest benefactor in the 19th century. As governor for 42 years and chairman of the board for 36, he strove to make Dalhousie the provincial university, and he contributed generously to its library, scientific apparatus, scholarships, and endowment funds. On 27 April 1887 on the South Common he laid the cornerstone of a university building (now the Forrest Building), made possible through his gift of $20,000, which was the beginning of a new Dalhousie campus. It was his last public act, for he died on 8 May. In his later years, especially after his retirement from the bench in 1881, he had received numerous honours, including an honorary degree from Queen's College at Kingston, Ont.

Young's will continued his benefactions to the extent of almost $200,000, out of a total estate of about $350,000. He had probably inherited money from his wife and father, his law practice and business pursuits had been lucrative, and he had been a shrewd moneylender. His will directed that statuary from his extensive gardens be placed in the Public Gardens in Halifax and provided $8,000 to complete and ornament the new road, which was named Young Avenue, from Inglis St to Point Pleasant Park. The will also established Sir William Young's Benevolent and Charitable Fund, with an endowment of $100,000, the interest from which was to go to ten societies or organizations in which he had interested himself. At Dalhousie he endowed further academic awards and to it went half the residue of his estate. Certainly he had made sure that his name would live on in Nova Scotia.

Through sheer persistence Young had, in the end, secured the public attention and exercised the power he had always craved. His success had come through politics even though the journalist Charles Rohan was partly right that by nature he was "an austere, ungenial being [with hardly] a warm corner in his heart for any other one of God's creatures." Undoubtedly his financial resources helped him; his personal outlay in his first ill-fated election in 1832 was about £1,000, and his agents may have spent even more in providing refreshments at the public houses of Cumberland in 1859. To many acquaintances he always remained "little Billy Young," who, one said, "never failed to keep [an eye] unblinkingly fixed on his own interest," and who, according to another, was so "tricky a character that he probably never ate his dinner without a stratagem." Though articulate and eloquent, he had his failings as a public speaker. He was poor at enunciation and his utterances were like "the popping of water from a jug"; he expectorated them "in knots, inextricably tangled and running into each other." Some, like J. W. Johnston, criticized his exaggerated "manner of seeking notice and applause"; certainly his speeches, especially his public lecture on Robert Burns in 1859, were "generously overdone." But despite his lack of the usual attributes of the successful politician, cool calculation, moderate, though not outstanding ability, and more than a little luck had carried him to both his main goals, the premiership and the chief justiceship.

J. MURRAY BECK

William Young's journal for 1839 was published in PANS *Report* (Halifax), 1973, app.B: 22–74.

PAC, MG 24, B29, especially vol.6. PANS, MG 1, 554, 793; MG 2, 719–82; MG 20, 674, no.9; 675, no.1; MS file, Rev. Thomas McCulloch, Corr., 1816–26. Howe, *Speeches and letters* (Chisholm). N. S., House of Assembly, *Debates and proc.*, 1855–60; *Journal and proc.*, 1833–60. *Acadian Recorder*, 1833–60. *British Colonist* (Halifax), 1848–60. *Colonial Patriot* (Pictou, N.S.), 1827–34. *Morning Chronicle* (Halifax), 1844–60. *Morning Herald* (Halifax), 1887. *Novascotian*, 1833–60. *Times* (Halifax), 1834–48. *Cyclopædia of Canadian biog.* (Rose, 1888), 398–400. Dent, *Canadian portrait gallery*, IV: 43–47. Beck, *Government of N.S.* D. C. Harvey, *An introduction to the history of Dalhousie University* (Halifax, 1938). J. L. MacDougall, *History of Inverness County, Nova Scotia* ([Truro, N.S., 1922]; repr. Belleville, Ont., 1976). E. M. Saunders, *Three premiers of Nova Scotia: the Hon. J. W. Johnstone, the Hon. Joseph Howe, the Hon. Charles Tupper, M.D., C.B.* (Toronto, 1909). J. M. Beck, "The Nova Scotian 'disputed election' of 1859 and its aftermath," *CHR*, 36 (1955): 293–315. D. C. Harvey, "Pre-Agricola John Young, or a compact family in search of fortune," N.S. Hist. Soc., *Coll.*, 32 (1959): 125–59. Benjamin Russell, "Reminiscences of the Nova Scotia judiciary," *Dalhousie Rev.*, 5 (1925–26): 499–512.

YOUNG, Sir WILLIAM ALEXANDER GEORGE, naval officer and colonial administrator; b. *c.* 1827, son of Captain William Young, RN; m. 20 March 1858 Cecilia Eliza Cowan Cameron, stepdaughter of Chief Justice David Cameron* and niece of Governor James Douglas*, and they had three sons and three daughters; d. 25 April 1885 in Accra, Gold Coast (Ghana).

In 1841 William Alexander George Young followed in his father's footsteps by enlisting in the Royal Navy. Evidently a precocious lad, he was promoted clerk in 1845, and then served as paymaster, purser, and secretary to two commodores in the succeeding decade. Appointed captain in February 1855 and decorated for his services in the Baltic during the Crimean War, Young was highly praised by his commander. The endorsement was undoubtedly largely responsible for his appointment by the Foreign Office as secretary of the British Boundary Commission in New Caledonia.

In that capacity Young arrived in Victoria in June 1857, and he soon became involved in its social life. He got along splendidly with Governor James Douglas and by the summer of 1858 was informally assisting Douglas, whose niece he had just married, with the mushrooming clerical duties brought on by the influx of people in the Fraser River gold-rush. When in November Douglas assumed the governorship of British Columbia, in addition to that of Vancouver Island, he needed help with the press of business. In the emergency, he seconded Young's services from the boundary commission and temporarily named him colonial secretary for British Columbia, the appointment being approved by the Colonial Office on 3 March 1859. Young at first declined the position, declaring the £500 annual salary insufficient, but Douglas prevailed upon him to accept, promising future salary increases. For some time following this appointment, Young continued to draw salaries from both the navy and the boundary commission. In addition, he acted as auditor of British Columbia and began to assume the duties of colonial secretary of Vancouver Island until by September 1859 he was writing officially in Governor Douglas' absence from the island.

The dual role as colonial secretary of British Columbia and acting colonial secretary of Vancouver Island placed Young in a position of considerable authority. Although not vested with direct executive authority, the colonial secretary was the ranking member of the civil service, being the official adviser to the governor and his channel of communication with the public. Young discharged his responsibilities so efficiently that he quickly earned the complete confidence of Douglas, who relied heavily on him for advice. In a confidential assessment to the secretary of state for the colonies, the Duke of Newcastle, in February 1863, Douglas praised Young's "decided business talents," responsible manner, and untiring application; "his services have been invaluable and to me indispensable, and no other person is so extensively acquainted with the business of the two Colonies or so capable of carrying out the general line of policy and the system of Government so successfully inaugurated in each."

By 1863 Young had built a large house not far from Douglas' in James Bay near the new legislative buildings in Victoria. When in 1861 the Colonial Office, heeding complaints by mainlanders, had ordered officials for British Columbia to reside in that colony, Young was the only one allowed to remain in Victoria with Douglas. Among his land holdings were 25 town lots in Victoria, one in Nanaimo, and 247 acres in Esquimalt, and he invested heavily in businesses on the island. Young, like Douglas, consequently became increasingly identified with the interests of Victoria, and a prominent member of what Amor De Cosmos* labelled Vancouver Island's "Family-Company Compact."

Early in 1863 the Duke of Newcastle decided to separate the two colonies completely by replacing Douglas with a governor for each colony and by giving each its own executive and legislative councils. Young was forced to choose. He decided to remain in Victoria and on 20 Aug. 1863 gave up the colonial secretaryship of the mainland and its salary of £800. In his letter of resignation he asked to be confirmed as the colonial secretary of Vancouver Island; this request was never granted and he remained in an acting capacity. As acting colonial secretary he was the ranking member of both the Executive and the Legislative councils of Vancouver Island but instead of taking his seat in the latter, he sought, possibly at Douglas' urging, election to the assembly for the four-member riding of Victoria. If successful, he would be able to act as a spokesman for the government in the assembly, a role previously undertaken by Attorney General George Hunter Cary*. During the campaign Young opposed responsible government, advocated improvements to Victoria's inner harbour, and defended maintaining it as a free port (all policies Douglas supported). Amor De Cosmos, running in the same riding, attacked Young in the press, claiming that he had been "requisitioned" to stand by an "irresponsible" and "obstructionist" administration. Nevertheless, endorsed by prominent members of Victoria's commercial establishment, Young topped the poll, besting De Cosmos by a narrow margin.

Young's tenure in the assembly was not a happy one because after Douglas' retirement, announced on 14 March 1864, the mainlanders were free to retaliate against Victoria and pursue their own economic policies. The day Douglas announced his retirement from office, Young applied for a year's leave of absence from the Executive Council of Vancouver Island on the grounds of overwork and impaired health. Two months later Young and his family left for England with Douglas. While Douglas visited relatives in Scotland and toured the continent, Young took charge of Douglas' personal affairs, looking after his investments and his son's education. They corresponded weekly and returned together to Victoria in June 1865.

During Young's absence both colonies had experienced a major recession, and once he resumed his seats in the Executive and Legislative councils, Governor Arthur Edward KENNEDY of Vancouver Island appointed him to a board of inquiry investigating the island's rapidly deteriorating financial situation. The board's report called for retrenchment in public works rather than in the civil establishment, and recommended additional borrowing to cover the growing deficit. The report was not well received by the government's critics who now supported the union of the two colonies in order to reduce the need to maintain two expensive civil establishments. Young also alienated the reform element when he suggested that income and property qualifications for membership in the assembly should be raised to $2,500 and $3,000, respectively.

As the depression deepened, the assembly voted to accept union on any terms "Her Majesty's Government may be pleased to grant." Then on 6 Aug. 1866, to the profound dismay of all islanders, the imperial parliament terminated the government of Vancouver Island and extended the jurisdication of the mainland to the island. Governor Kennedy left Victoria on 23 October, and Young remained as administrator until Governor Frederick Seymour* of British Columbia proclaimed the new legislation on 19 November.

To Young, union meant the loss of a job and the choice of remaining in Victoria or seeking a posting elsewhere. Although Seymour recognized Young's experience and ability, he did not trust him because of his Victoria connections. Nevertheless, following the dismissal of Treasurer Charles William Franks in January 1867, he temporarily appointed Young to take his place, and in July made him acting colonial secretary. Almost a year later he requested that the Colonial Office not confirm Young in the latter office because he was "so mixed up in the affairs of Victoria that I cannot give him the entire confidence which a governor should repose in his Colonial Secretary." But when the Colonial Office appointed Philip James Hankin instead, Seymour abruptly protested that he had "never made a complaint" against Young, whom he characterized as an "excellent painstaking Public Officer." In an astounding display of independence, Seymour then delayed installing Hankin for more than three months, until the end of the Legislative Council session over which Young was presiding. But the damage had been done. On 4 May 1869 Young applied to the Executive Council for 12 months' leave at half pay and passage for himself and his family back to England. The leave was refused. After auctioning most of their household possessions, Young and his family reluctantly left the colony on 1 June 1869. Nine days later, Seymour unexpectedly died.

Young never did receive compensation for loss of office caused by Seymour's negligence, although the Colonial Office later became aware of the injustice he had suffered. Young was appointed financial secretary of Jamaica at the same salary he had received in British Columbia, and in 1872 was invalided back to England after an attack of yellow fever. Five years later he was named a CMG and appointed governor of the Gold Coast in Africa. He died there on 25 April 1885.

Next to Douglas and Sir Matthew Baillie Begbie*, Young was perhaps the most able of the colonial officials to serve in Vancouver Island and British Columbia. His intimate association with Douglas was a political asset but also contributed to his downfall. But for the Hankin affair, Young almost certainly would have remained in Victoria and might well have left his imprint on events that led to confederation and subsequent provincial affairs.

JAMES E. HENDRICKSON

There is much important material on William Alexander George Young in the PRO, CO 60, CO 305, and CO 398 (mfm. at PABC).

Anglican Church of Canada, Diocese of British Columbia Arch. (Victoria), Christ Church Cathedral (Victoria), Parish registers, Baptisms, 1836–86; Marriages, 1837–72 (mfm. at PABC). PABC, James Douglas, Corr. outward, 22 March 1867–11 Oct. 1870, James Douglas to Jane Dallas, 2 Dec. 1868; Governor (Douglas), Corr. outward, 22 June 1850 – 5 March 1859, James Douglas to J. C. Prevost, 29 Dec. 1858; 27 May 1859 – 9 Jan. 1864, James Douglas to M. B. Begbie, 28 Oct. 1863; Vancouver Island, Colonial secretary, Corr. outward, 1859–60 (letterbook copies); Executive Council, Minutes, October 1863, March 1864. B.C., Legislative Council, *Journals*, 29 April 1868. *Daily British Colonist and Victoria Chronicle*, 1858–70. *Times* (London), 27 May 1885. W. K. Lamb, "Sir James goes abroad," *BCHQ*, 3 (1939): 283–92; "Some notes on the Douglas family," *BCHQ*, 17 (1953): 41–51. J. W. Long, "The origin and development of the San Juan Island water boundary controversy," *Pacific Northwest Quarterly* (Seattle, Wash.), 43 (1952): 187–213. R. L. Smith, "The Hankin appointment, 1868," *BC Studies*, 22 (summer 1974): 26–39.

GENERAL BIBLIOGRAPHY AND LIST OF ABBREVIATIONS

List of Abbreviations

AAQ Archives de l'archidiocèse de Québec
AASB Archives de l'archevêché de Saint-Boniface
AC Archives civiles
ACAM Archives de la chancellerie de l'archevêché de Montréal
ADB *Australian dictionary of biography*
ANQ Archives nationales du Québec
ANQ-M Archives nationales du Québec, centre régional de Montréal
ANQ-MBF Archives nationales du Québec, centre régional de la Mauricie/Bois-Francs
ANQ-Q Archives nationales du Québec, centre d'archives de la Capitale
ANQ-SLSJ Archives nationales du Québec, centre régional du Saguenay/Lac-Saint-Jean
AO Archives of Ontario
AP Archives paroissiales
ASN Archives du séminaire de Nicolet
ASQ Archives du séminaire de Québec
ASSM Archives du séminaire de Saint-Sulpice, Montréal
AUM Archives de l'université de Montréal
AVM Archives de la ville de Montréal
AVQ Archives de la ville de Québec
BCHQ *British Columbia Historical Quarterly*
BE Bureau d'enregistrement
BNQ Bibliothèque nationale du Québec
BRH *Le Bulletin des recherches historiques*
CCHA Canadian Catholic Historical Association
CHA Canadian Historical Association
CHR *Canadian Historical Review*
CMS Church Missionary Society
CPC *Canadian parliamentary companion*
CTA City of Toronto Archives
DAB *Dictionary of American biography*
DCB *Dictionary of Canadian biography*
DNB *Dictionary of national biography*
DOLQ *Dictionnaire des œuvres littéraires du Québec*
HBC Hudson's Bay Company
HBCA Hudson's Bay Company Archives
HBRS Hudson's Bay Record Society
HPL Hamilton Public Library
HSSM Historical and Scientific Society of Manitoba
IBC Inventaire des biens culturels
JIP *Journal de l'Instruction publique*
MTL Metropolitan Toronto Library
NWMP North-West Mounted Police
OH *Ontario History*
PABC Provincial Archives of British Columbia
PAC Public Archives of Canada
PAM Provincial Archives of Manitoba
PANB Provincial Archives of New Brunswick
PANL Provincial Archives of Newfoundland and Labrador
PANS Public Archives of Nova Scotia
PAPEI Public Archives of Prince Edward Island
PRO Public Record Office
QUA Queen's University Archives
RHAF *Revue d'histoire de l'Amérique française*
RPQ *Répertoire des parlementaires québécois*
RSC Royal Society of Canada
SCHÉC Société canadienne d'histoire de l'Église catholique
SH *Social History*
UCA United Church Archives
UNBL University of New Brunswick Library
USPG United Society for the Propagation of the Gospel
UTA University of Toronto Archives
UWO University of Western Ontario Library

General Bibliography

The General Bibliography is based on the sources most frequently cited in the individual bibliographies of volume XI. It should not be regarded as providing a complete list of background materials for the history of Canada in the 19th century.

Section I describes the principal archival sources and is arranged by country. Section II is divided into two parts: part A contains printed primary sources including documents published by the various colonial, provincial, and federal governments; part B provides a listing of the contemporary newspapers most frequently cited by contributors to the volume. Section III includes dictionaries, indexes, inventories, almanacs, and directories. Section IV contains secondary works of the 19th and 20th centuries, including a number of general histories and theses. Section V describes the principal journals and the publications of various societies consulted.

I: ARCHIVAL SOURCES

CANADA

ARCHIVES CIVILES. *See* Québec, ministère de la Justice

ARCHIVES DE LA CHANCELLERIE DE L'ARCHEVÊCHÉ DE MONTRÉAL. A detailed inventory of many of the registers and files of this repository can be found in *RHAF*, 19 (1965–66): 652–64; 20 (1966–67): 146–66, 324–41, 669–700; 24 (1970–71): 111–42.

The following were used in the preparation of volume XI:

Dossiers
- 255: Diocèses du Canada
  - .113: London
- 295: Diocèses du Québec
  - .098–101: Québec
  - .104: Trois-Rivières
- 350: Paroisses
  - 355.101: Notre-Dame
- 420: Clergé
  - .041: Blanchet, Augustin-Magloire
  - .080: Manseau, Antoine
- 465: Religieux, pères
  - .101: Compagnie de Saint-Sulpice
  - .105: Clercs de Saint-Viateur
- 468: Sulpiciens décédés entre 1877–96
  - .103: Baile, Joseph-Alexandre
- 588: Laïcs, "R"
  - .201: Riel, Louis
- 752: Gouvernements
  - .704: Code civil; bill des registres
- 778: Association et divers
  - .867: Hôpital Saint-Jean-de-Dieu
- 901: Fonds Lartigue-Bourget
  - .055: Mgr Bourget; lettres personnelles et voyages à Rome (1846–47; 1854–56)
  - .085: Lettres de Adolphe Pinsonneault, p.s.s.; Étienne Hicks; Michael Power, v.g.
  - .086: Mgr Desautels; mission à Rome
  - .133: Institut canadien; imprimés
  - .134: Institut canadien; catalogue de la bibliothèque
  - .135: Institut canadien; correspondance
  - .136: Notre-Dame
  - .141: Notre-Dame; division
- 990: Autres fonds
  - .027: Chanoine Hyacinthe Hudon; correspondance

RCD: Registres et cahiers divers
- 41–44: Mission de Mgr Desautels à Rome

RL: Registres de lettres
- RLB: Registres des lettres de Mgr Bourget. An analytical inventory of the correspondence of Mgr Ignace BOURGET from 1837 to 1850 was published in ANQ *Rapport*, 1945–46: 137–224; 1946–47: 81–175; 1948–49: 343–477; 1955–57: 177–221; 1961–64: 9–68; 1965: 87–132; 1966: 191–252; 1967: 123–70; 1969: 3–146.
- RLL: Registres des lettres de Mgr Lartigue. The correspondence of Mgr Jean-Jacques Lartigue* from 1819 to 1840 is inventoried in ANQ *Rapport*, 1941–42: 345–496; 1942–43: 1–174; 1943–44: 207–334; 1944–45: 173–266; 1945–46: 39–134.

ARCHIVES DE L'ARCHEVÊCHÉ DE SAINT-BONIFACE, St Boniface, Man.

The following collections were cited in volume XI:

F: Fonds Fisher-D'Eschambault
P: Fonds Provencher
T: Fonds Taché; lettres reçues
Ta: Fonds Taché; lettres envoyées

ARCHIVES DE L'ARCHIDIOCÈSE DE QUÉBEC. A guide to the collection is available in SCHÉC *Rapport*, 2 (1934–35): 65–73.

Series cited in volume XI:

A: Évêques et archevêques de Québec
12 A: Registres des insinuations ecclésiastiques
20 A: Lettres manuscrites des évêques de Québec
210 A: Registres des lettres expédiées. Inventories of the correspondence of a number of the bishops and archbishops of Quebec are available in ANQ *Rapport* including the following: correspondence of Mgr Bernard-Claude Panet* for the years 1806 to 1833 in *Rapport*, 1933–34: 233–421; 1934–35: 319–420; 1935–36: 155–272; correspondence of Mgr Joseph Signay* for the years 1825 to 1839, in *Rapport*, 1936–37: 123–330; 1937–38: 21–146 (which includes also the correspondence of Mgr Pierre-Flavien Turgeon* as coadjutor); 1938– 39: 180–357.
211 A: Registres des requêtes
C: Secrétairerie et chancellerie
CB: Structures de direction
1 CB: Vicaires généraux
CD: Discipline diocésaine
511 CD: Collège de Lévis
515 CD: Séminaire de Nicolet
61 CD: Paroisses
Diocèse de Québec (in process of reclassification)
CF: Rapports avec les organismes de pastorale
53 CF: Action catholique générale
CG: Relations interconfessionnelles et civiles
20 CG: Ville de Québec
CN: Église canadienne
321 CN: Diocèse d'Ottawa
60 CN: Gouvernement du Canada
CP: Église du Québec
26 CP: Diocèse de Montréal
CR: Province ecclésiastique de Québec
33 CR: Diocèse de Trois-Rivières

ARCHIVES DE LA VILLE DE MONTRÉAL.

The following were used in the preparation of volume XI:

Documentation
Biographies des conseillers
Membres des conseils municipaux
Documents administratifs
Procès-verbaux et dossiers du conseil municipal, des comités et commissions
Rôles d'évaluation

ARCHIVES DE LA VILLE DE QUÉBEC. A useful publication of this repository is *État sommaire des Archives de la ville de Québec* (Québec, 1977), edited by Murielle Doyle-Frenière.

The following series were consulted in volume XI:

Procès-verbaux du conseil
Rôles d'évaluation et d'imposition

ARCHIVES DE L'UNIVERSITÉ DE MONTRÉAL. The Service des archives of the Université de Montréal has prepared and published an important series relating to the collections in its custody; a list of these can be found in *Bibliographie des publications du Service des archives* (3e éd., Montréal, 1980), compiled by Jacques Ducharme and Denis Plante.

The following are cited in volume XI:

P 58: Collection Baby. The researcher may usefully consult the *Catalogue de la collection François-Louis-Georges Baby*, compiled by Camille Bertrand, with preface by Paul Baby and introduction by Lucien Campeau (2v., Montréal, 1971). Manuscript copies of the bulk of the collection Baby, being classified at present, are located at the PAC.
H: Affaires religieuses et communautés
H3: Paroisse Notre-Dame de Montréal
I: Éducation
I2: Université de Montréal
M: Mémoires et relations de voyages
Q1: Documents hors séries
U: Correspondance générale

ARCHIVES DU SÉMINAIRE DE NICOLET, Nicolet, Qué. This repository, which is at present classifying its materials, has a catalogue index and both nominal and thematic card indexes.

In volume XI the following were used:

AO: Archives officielles
Séminaire
AP: Archives privées
G: Grandes collections
L.-É. Bois
J.-A.-I. Douville
Hector Laferté
J.-C.-C. Marquis
M.-G. Proulx
Henri Vassal

ARCHIVES DU SÉMINAIRE DE QUÉBEC. Analytical and chronological card indexes as well as numerous inventories are at the disposal of researchers.

The following were cited in volume XI:

C: Livres de comptes du séminaire
C 43: 1844–49
Fichier des anciens
Fonds C.-H. Laverdière, Notes et correspondance
Fonds Viger-Verreau
Cartons: Papiers de H.-A.-J.-B. Verreau; Jacques Viger
Série O: Cahiers manuscrits
095–125; 0139–52: Jacques Viger, "Ma Saberdache." *See* Fernand Ouellet, "Inventaire de la Saberdache de Jacques Viger," ANQ *Rapport*, 1955–57: 31–176.
0165–71: Journal personnel de Jacques Viger, 1835–51
Lettres
N: 1659–1887
MSS: Cahiers manuscrits divers
12: Grand livre du séminaire de 1733 à 1856
13: Plumitif du Conseil du séminaire commencé en 1678
34: E.-A. Taschereau, Journal du séminaire commencé en 1849
433: A.-E. Gosselin, Officiers et professeurs du séminaire de Québec, 1663–1860
634–36: T.-É. Hamel, Notes sur sa correspondance, 1866–75
678: C.-É. Légaré, Journal du 17 avril 1873 au 24 sept. 1876
MSS-M: Cahiers de cours manuscrits
183: A.-H. Gosselin, Cours de philosophie par l'abbé T.-A. Chandonnet, 1861–62
220: Cyrias Pelletier, Cours de philosophie par l'abbé T.-A. Chandonnet, 1861
222: L.-N. Bégin, Cours de philosophie par l'abbé T.-A. Chandonnet, 1860–61
230: Antoine Lapommerai, Cours de philosophie par l'abbé T.-A. Chandonnet, 1860–65
474–77: Ovide Brunet, Cours et notes de botanique, et herbier, 1861–62
479: Arthur Maheux, Cours de botanique par l'abbé Ovide Brunet, 1860–76
484: Louis Beaudet, Journal de voyage, notes de botanique et herbier par l'abbé Ovide Brunet, 1866
586: J.-C.-K. Laflamme, Cours de philosophie par l'abbé T.-A. Chandonnet, 1866–68
775: Adrien Papineau, Divers cours par l'abbé T.-A. Chandonnet, 1864–65
1112: L.-O. Gauthier, Répertoire historique par l'abbé T.-A. Chandonnet, 1865
Polygraphie: Affaires surtout extérieures
Séminaire: Affaires diverses
Université
Cartons: Administration et correspondance
Série U: Administration et sociétés

ARCHIVES DU SÉMINAIRE DE SAINT-SULPICE, Montréal.
The following series were cited in volume XI:
Section 8: Seigneuries, fiefs, arrière-fiefs et domaines
A: Seigneurie du Lac-des-Deux-Montagnes
Section 21: Correspondance générale
Section 24: Histoire et géographie, biographie, divers
Dossier 2: Biographies
Section 27: Séminaire, évêchés et paroisses
Section 49: Prédication
Dossier 56: Rousselot, Benjamin-Victor

ARCHIVES JUDICIAIRES. *See* Québec, ministère de la Justice

ARCHIVES NATIONALES DU QUÉBEC. In 1980 the archives undertook to establish a new uniform classification system for all its regional centres. Because work on volume XI was well advanced we have continued to use the old classification system. Tables are available at the ANQ enabling researchers to go from one system to the other.

ANQ–MAURICIE/BOIS-FRANCS, Trois-Rivières
The following are cited in volume XI:
État civil
Minutiers

ANQ–MONTRÉAL
For more information concerning the documents held in this regional centre, consult "État sommaire des Archives nationales du Québec à Montréal," ANQ *Rapport*, 1972: 1–29.
The following are cited in volume XI:
Archives privées
M-72-41: Bibaud, Maximilien
M-72-141: Trudeau, Romuald
M-72-148: Cherrier, C.-S.
État civil
Minutiers
Testaments

ANQ–QUÉBEC
For more information concerning the documents held in this centre, consult *État général des archives publiques et privées* (Québec, 1968).
The following are cited in volume XI:
AP: Archives privées
G: Grandes collections
16: Brousseau, Léger
36: Chapais, Thomas
41: Chauveau, P.-J.-O.
43: Cherrier, C.-S.
68: Duvernay, Ludger
134: Langevin, famille
149: Lesage, Siméon
184: Meilleur, J.-B. et Alphonse
203: Penny, E. G.
239: Roy, P.-G.

242: Taché, famille
417: Papineau, famille
P: Petites collections
344: Cauchon, Joseph
Cartothèque
Plans
État civil
Minutiers
PQ: Province de Québec
É: Éducation
TF: Terres et forêts
TP: Travaux publics
QBC: Québec et Bas-Canada
6: Secrétaire provincial
7: Nominations de juges de paix
9: Licences
25: Procureur général
27: Instruction publique

ANQ–SAGUENAY/LAC-SAINT-JEAN, Chicoutimi. The following are cited in volume XI:
Archives privées
Collection Victor Tremblay

ARCHIVES OF ONTARIO, Toronto. Unpublished inventories, calendars, catalogue entries, guides, and other finding aids are available in the archives, which is also making available finding aids on microfiche.
Materials used in volume XI include:
MU 20–28: Bailey (John C.) papers
132–34: Biographical sketches collection
136–273: Blake (Edward) papers
301–9: Buell (Andrew Norton) papers
469–87: Campbell (Sir Alexander) papers
500–15: Cartwright family papers
535–50: Church records collection
1058: Foster (William Alexander) papers
1143: Gilkison (William and Jasper T.) papers
1197–284: Hamilton Brothers records and Hawkesbury Lumber Company records
1375–81: Hodgins (John George) papers
1720: Lesslie family papers
1745: Lumberman's Association of Ontario papers
1805–949: Mackenzie–Lindsey papers
2017–22: Mechanics' Institute collection
2164–70: Morris (Alexander) papers
2194: Niagara Falls Park papers
2306–10: Patteson (Thomas Charles) papers
2390–98: Ridout papers
2399: Roaf (James R.) papers
2664–776: Shanly (Francis) papers
2918–22: Street (Samuel) papers
2923: Stuart family papers
3154: Wright (Amos) papers
3278: Price (James Hervey) papers
RG 1: Records of the Ministry of Natural Resources
A: Offices of surveyor general and commissioner of crown lands
I: Correspondence
2: Surveyor general's letterbooks
4: Commissioner's letterbook
6: Letters received, surveyor general and commissioner
8: Assistant commissioner's letterbooks
II: Reports and statements
2: Commissioner's reports
6: Statements
VII: Miscellaneous records
C: Lands Branch
IV: Township papers
E: Woods and Forests Branch
6: Reports and memoranda
12: Miscellaneous records
RG 2: Records of the Ministry of Education
B: General Board of Education (second) and Council of Public Instruction
3: Minutes, Council of Public Instruction
C: Department of Public Instruction
1: Outgoing general correspondence
2: Drafts of outgoing general correspondence
6: Incoming general correspondence
C: Incoming general correspondence, 1841–76
D: Department of Education, office of the minister
1: Outgoing general correspondence
2: Drafts of outgoing correspondence
3: Incoming general correspondence
4: Interdepartmental correspondence
E: Office of the deputy minister and historiographer
1: Documentary history manuscripts
RG 8: Records of the Department of the Provincial Secretary
I-6: Office of the registrar general
B: County marriage registers, 1841–1934
RG 10: Records of the Ministry of Health
ser.20: Psychiatric Hospitals Branch
F: Kingston Psychiatric Hospital
RG 22: Court records
ser.6-2: Records of the Surrogate Court of Ontario
York County records
ser.7: Courts of General Quarter Sessions of the Peace
14–33: Home District, Minutes
RG 31: Ministry of Consumer and Commercial Relations

RG 49: Offices of the Legislative Assembly
I: Divisions/Branches of Department of Provincial Secretary
7: Office of the clerk of the Legislature
B: Sessional papers
3: Railway sessional papers

ARCHIVES PAROISSIALES. Specific holdings in Quebec parish archives include the registers of baptisms, marriages, and burials, with copies at the Archives civiles of the judicial district in which the parish is located. Parish archives usually contain many other documents, including parish account books, vestry records, and registers of parish confraternities.

ATLANTIC BAPTIST HISTORICAL COLLECTION, Acadia University, Wolfville, N.S. Information on this collection may be found in *A catalogue of the Maritime Baptist Historical Collection in the library of Acadia University* (Kentville, N.S., 1955).

The materials used in volume XI include:
"Manual of Baptist authors." Compiled by W. E. McIntyre. 5 vols., typescript, 1905.
Edward Manning correspondence
S. T. Rand papers

BIBLIOTHÈQUE NATIONALE DU QUÉBEC, DÉPARTEMENT DES MANUSCRITS, Montréal. A description of the collections held in this department is found in *Catalogue des manuscrits* (Montréal), the latest edition of which was published in 1978.

The following were cited in volume XI:
Manuscrits
MSS-30: Cherrier, Côme-Séraphin
MSS-100: Rodier, succession
MSS-101: Société historique de Montréal
Collection La Fontaine. For a complete inventory of this collection see *Inventaire de la collection Lafontaine*, Elizabeth Nish, compil. (Montréal, 1967).

BUREAU D'ENREGISTREMENT. *See* Québec, ministère de la Justice

CANADIAN BAPTIST ARCHIVES, McMaster Divinity College, Hamilton, Ont.

The following material was used in volume XI:
Biographical files
Toronto Baptist College records
Board of Trustees
Minute books
Correspondence
Executive Committee
Minute books

CITY OF TORONTO ARCHIVES.

Materials used in the preparation of volume XI include:
RG 1: City Council
A: Minutes
B: Papers
RG 2: Finance Committee
B1: Communications
RG 5: City Clerk's Department
F: Assessment rolls
H: Elections
1: Nominations books
RG 7: Mayor's office
F: Mayor's court

DALHOUSIE UNIVERSITY ARCHIVES, Halifax.

The following materials were consulted in the preparation of volume XI:
MS 1: Dalhousie University records
1: Board of Governors
A: Minutes
MS 2: Private manuscripts
87: A. W. McLelan papers
MS 4: Business records
1: Campbell papers
63: James Dickie & Co. papers

GLENBOW-ALBERTA INSTITUTE ARCHIVES, Calgary.

Materials used in the preparation of volume XI include:
Canada North West Land Company papers
CPR town site sales books
City of Calgary papers
Minutes
Richard Hardisty papers
James F. Macleod papers

HAMILTON PUBLIC LIBRARY, Special Collections Department, Hamilton, Ont.

The following were used in the preparation of volume XI:
Hamilton biography
Buchanans
Adam Hope
Hope family
McQuesten papers
Scrapbooks

HUDSON'S BAY COMPANY ARCHIVES. *See* Provincial Archives of Manitoba

INVENTAIRE DES BIENS CULTURELS. *See* Québec, ministère des Affaires culturelles

MCGILL UNIVERSITY ARCHIVES, Montreal. A complete inventory of the collections held by this repository is in preparation.

The following were cited in volume XI:
Board of Governors records
Abraham de Sola papers

Sir William Logan papers
McGill High School archives
McGill Normal School archives
Montreal General Hospital records
Wesleyan Methodist Church in Canada, Montreal District, Minutes

MARITIME HISTORY GROUP ARCHIVES, Memorial University of Newfoundland, St John's. For information on the collection of research studies prepared by Memorial University students which is held by the archives see *Check list of research studies pertaining to the history of Newfoundland in the Archives of the Maritime History Group* (4th ed., [St John's], 1981).

Materials used in the preparation of volume XI include:
Board of Trade series 107–8
Name file collection. This consists of some 8,000 files, arranged by surname, concerning anyone connected in any way with the Newfoundland trade or fisheries, 1640–1850. The files are compiled from a wide range of sources, and each entry includes a reference to the original source.

METROPOLITAN TORONTO LIBRARY. For information on the library's manuscript holdings, see *Guide to the manuscript collection in the Toronto Public Libraries* (Toronto, 1954).

The following were consulted for volume XI:
Robert Baldwin papers
William Warren Baldwin papers
Biographical scrapbooks
John George Howard papers
Humber Valley archives
T. A. Reed scrapbooks
Toronto scrapbooks

NEW BRUNSWICK MUSEUM, Saint John, N.B. For a description of its holdings *see* New Brunswick Museum, Archives Division, *Inventory of manuscripts, 1967* ([Saint John, 1967]).

Materials used in volume XI include:
Marianne Grey Otty collections
  Earle family papers, Genealogy
  Otty family papers
Tilley family papers

PROVINCIAL ARCHIVES OF BRITISH COLUMBIA, Victoria. Manuscript collections are being listed in PABC, *Manuscript inventory*, ed. Frances Gundry (3v. to date, [Victoria], 1976–).

The following were found useful in the preparation of volume XI:
Add. MSS 60: Mary Susannah (Hawks) Moody papers
315: Robert Stevenson, Diary and memo book
345: G. A. Rhodes, Red River Settlement papers
412: O'Reilly family papers
436: A. F. Buckham papers
A: Canadian Collieries (Dunsmuir) Limited papers
523: C. F. Houghton letterbook
525: John Robson papers
527: Barnard family papers
557: W. F. Tolmie papers
767: Joseph Hunter papers
810: A. T. Bushby, "Journal of a trip to Wild Horse Creek and back," 1864
British Columbia, Colonial secretary, Correspondence outward
British Columbia, Department of Lands and Works
  Coal prospecting licenses, register and index
  Correspondence
  Mining licenses
Colonial correspondence. An artificial series created from the letters inward to the departments of the colonial governments of British Columbia and Vancouver Island from both individuals and other government departments. The letters are filed under the names of the senders.
Crease collection
GR 184: British Columbia, Department of Mines, Inspector of mines, Correspondence outward
216: British Columbia, Government agent records, Cariboo
224: British Columbia, Government agent records, Lillooet
495: Canada, Commission on Indian Reserves of British Columbia, 1876, Correspondence
O'Reilly collection
Vancouver Island, Colonial Secretary, Correspondence outward
Vancouver Island, Executive Council, Minutes
Vancouver Island, Governor (Douglas), Correspondence outward

PROVINCIAL ARCHIVES OF MANITOBA, Winnipeg. This repository puts at the disposal of researchers a central card index and unpublished preliminary inventories and finding aids.

Materials consulted in preparing volume XI include the following:
MG 1: Indians, exploration and fur trade
  D: Fur trade, individuals
    2: Mactavish, William
MG 2: Red River Settlement
  A: Selkirk period
    6: Red River Settlement papers
  B: Council of Assiniboia
    1: Minutes of Council of Assiniboia
    3: Census
    4-1: Minutes of General Quarterly Court

C: Individuals and settlement
- 1: Kennedy, William
- 4: Isbister, Alexander Kennedy
- 6: Bannatyne, Andrew Graham Ballenden
- 8: McDermot, Andrew
- 14: Ross, Alexander, family
- 40: McBeath, Robert, Sr

MG 3: Red River disturbance, Northwest rebellion, and related papers
B: Individuals *re* Red River disturbance and Red River expedition
- 1: Bunn, Thomas
- 5: Taché, Alexandre-Antonin
- 11: Woodington, Henry
- 16-2: Laurie, Patrick Gammie

D: Louis Riel

MG 6: Military records and law enforcement
A: North West Mounted Police
- 1: Walsh, James Morrow

MG 7: Church records and religious figures
A: Rupert's Land
- 1: Ecclesiastical province of Rupert's Land

B: Church of England
- 4: St Andrew's Church
- 7: St John's Cathedral, 1813–1901

C: Presbyterian
- 12: Black, John

D: Roman Catholic
- 8: St Boniface

MG 8: Immigration, settlement, and local histories
B: Individuals
- 52: McEwen, Mrs A. E.
- 61: Reid, Alexander

MG 9: Literary manuscripts and theses
A: Manuscripts and related papers
- 46: Lee, Charles H.

MG 10: Associations and institutions
A: Professional groups and trade unions
- 15: College of Physicians and Surgeons of Manitoba

F: Historical societies and museums
- 2: Historical and Scientific Society of Manitoba

MG 12: Lieutenant governors
A: Archibald, Adams George
B: Morris, Alexander
- 1: Lieutenant governor's collection
- 2: Ketcheson collection

C: Cauchon, Joseph-Édouard
E: Schultz, John Christian

MG 13: Premiers
C: Norquay, John

MG 14: Public life
B: Political and judicial figures
- 26: Dubuc, Joseph
- 59: Kennedy, William Nassau

C: Individuals
- 20: McArthur, Alexander
- 54: Gordon, Gordon "Lord"
- 66: Barber, Edmund Lorenzo

RG 2: Manitoba Executive Council
A: Orders in council
- 1: 1870–85

HBCA: Hudson's Bay Company Archives. The Hudson's Bay Record Society has published numerous series of documents held by the HBCA, now located at PAM, since 1938 [*see* section II]. The PRO and the PAC hold microfilm copies of the records for the years 1670 to 1870. For more information concerning copies held at the PAC and the finding aids that are available see: *General inventory, manuscripts, 3.* The articles by R. H. G. Leveson-Gower, "The archives of the Hudson's Bay Company," *Beaver*, outfit 264 (December 1933): 40–42, 64, and by Joan Craig, "Three hundred years of records," *Beaver*, outfit 301 (autumn 1970): 65–70, provide useful information to researchers.

The following were cited in volume XI:

Section A: London office records
- A.1/: London minute books
- A.6/: London correspondence outwards – official
- A.7/: London locked private letterbooks
- A.10/: London inward correspondence – general
- A.11/: London inward correspondence from HBC posts
- A.12/: London inward correspondence from governors of HBC territories
- A.16/: Officers' and servants' ledgers and account books
- A.31/: Lists of commissioned officers
- A.32/: Servants' contracts
- A.34/: Servants' characters and staff records
- A.36/: Officers' and servants' wills
- A.44/: Register books of wills and administrations of proprietors, etc.
- A.64/: Miscellaneous books

Section B: North America trading post records
- B.17/a: Bersimis journals
- B.27/a: Carlton House (Sask.) journals
- B.38/a: Fort Chimo journals
- B.60/a: Edmonton House journals
- B.60/b: Edmonton House correspondence books
- B.60/c: Edmonton House correspondence inward
- B.77/a: Fort George (Big River) journals
- B.80/a: Fort Good Hope journals
- B.85/a: Fort Halkett journals
- B.123/a: Martin Fall journals
- B.133/a: Mistassini journals
- B.134/c: Montreal correspondence inward
- B.134/g: Montreal abstracts of servants' accounts
- B.135/a: Moose journals

B.135/c: Moose correspondence inward
B.135/g: Moose abstracts of servants' accounts
B.135/z: Moose miscellaneous items
B.154/a: Norway House journals
B.154/z: Norway House miscellaneous items
B.159/a: Fort Pelly journals
B.186/a: Rupert House journals
B.186/b: Rupert House correspondence books
B.188/d: Fort St James account books
B.200/b: Fort Simpson (Mackenzie River) correspondence books
B.200/c: Fort Simpson (Mackenzie River) correspondence inward
B.214/c: Tadoussac correspondence inward
B.223/b: Fort Vancouver (Columbia District) correspondence books
B.234/a: Winisk River journal
B.235/b: Winnipeg correspondence books
B.239/a: York Factory journals
B.239/g: York Factory abstracts of servants' accounts, Northern Department
B.239/k: York Factory minutes of Council, Northern Department
B.239/u: York Factory servants' engagement registers, Northern Department
B.332/a: Prince Albert journals
B.373/a: Little Whale River journals
B.373/c: Little Whale River correspondence inward
Section C: Records of ships owned or chartered by the HBC
C.1/: Ships' logs
Section D: Governors' papers
D.4/: George Simpson correspondence outward
D.5/: George Simpson correspondence inward
D.6/: George Simpson minutes and correspondence concerning will
D.7/: Eden Colvile correspondence inward
D.8/: Alexander Grant Dallas correspondence
D.9/: William Mactavish correspondence outward
D.13/: Commissioner's outward letterbooks to London
D.14/: Commissioner's outward letterbooks to HBC officials
D.20/: Commissioner's correspondence inward
Section E: Miscellaneous records
E.4/: Red River Settlement church registers
E.5/: Red River Settlement census returns
E.6/: Red River Settlement land registers and records
E.12/1–4: Duncan Finlayson private papers
E.12/5: Isobel Finlayson private journal
Section F: Records of allied and subsidiary companies
F.8/–F.26/: Puget's Sound Agricultural Company papers

PROVINCIAL ARCHIVES OF NEW BRUNSWICK, Fredericton. For information on its manuscript holdings see *A guide to the manuscript collections in the Provincial Archives of New Brunswick*, comp. A. B. Rigby (Fredericton, 1977).

Materials used in the preparation of volume XI include:

"New Brunswick political biography." Compiled by J. C. and H. B. Graves. 11 vols., typescript.

RG 2: Records of the central executive
RS6: Minutes and orders-in-council of the Executive Council
RG 7: Records of the Probate Courts
RS71: Saint John County Probate Court records
RG 11: Records of the Department of Education
RS115: Licensing and appointment records
7: Inspection of schools, Monthly reports
RS117: Teachers' Training School and Teachers' College records
1: Official registers
2: General record books

PROVINCIAL ARCHIVES OF NEWFOUNDLAND AND LABRADOR, St John's. For information on the collection see *Preliminary inventory of the holdings . . .* and *Supplement . . .* (2 nos., St John's, 1970–74).

The following materials were cited in volume XI:

Government records – Newfoundland
GN 1: Governor's office
3A: Incoming correspondence
3B: Letterbooks, outgoing correspondence
GN 2: Department of the colonial secretary
1: Letterbooks, outgoing correspondence
2: Incoming correspondence
GN 3: Registry of Grants
2: Register of crown land sales

PUBLIC ARCHIVES OF CANADA, Ottawa. The PAC has published a *Guide to the manuscript groups and record groups of the Manuscript Division*, compiled by Grace Maurice Hyam (1978), and a guide to the Federal Archives Division, compiled by Terry Cook and G. T. Wright and entitled *Historical records of the government of Canada* ([2nd ed.], 1981). Collections at the PAC are listed in the *Union list of manuscripts* which it publishes, and it has also issued a provisional edition of a *Guide to Canadian photographic archives* (1979). Addenda to published inventories, unpublished inventories of manuscript and record groups at the PAC, and finding aids to individual collections are available at the PAC, which also makes available a large number of finding aids on microfiche.

The following inventories to materials in the

Manuscript and the Federal Archives divisions which were used in the preparation of volume XI have been published:

Catalogue of census returns on microfilm, 1666–1881 (1981).

General inventory, manuscripts, volume 1, MG 1–MG 10 (1971).

General inventory, manuscripts, volume 2, MG 11–MG 16 (1976).

General inventory, manuscripts, volume 3, MG 17–MG 21 (1974).

General inventory, manuscripts, volume 4, MG 22–MG 25 (1972).

General inventory, manuscripts, volume 5, MG 26–MG 27 (1972).

General inventory, manuscripts, volume 7, MG 29 (1975).

General inventory, manuscripts, volume 8, MG 30 (1977).

General inventory series, no.1: records relating to Indian affairs (RG 10) (1975).

General inventory series, no.2: records of the R.C.M.P. (RG 18) (1975).

General inventory series, no.4: records of the Privy Council (RG 2) (1977).

General inventory series, no.6: records of Statistics Canada (RG 31) (1977).

General inventory series, no.8: records of the Department of Public Works (RG 11) (1977).

General inventory series: records of the Surveys and Mapping Branch (RG 88) (1979).

An older series of inventories has been largely superseded by unpublished inventories available at the PAC, but the following are still useful:

Record Group 1, Executive Council, Canada, 1764–1867 (1953).

Record Group 4, civil and provincial secretaries' offices, Canada East, 1760–1867; Record Group 5, civil and provincial secretaries' offices, Canada West, 1788–1867 (1953).

Record Group 7, Governor general's office (1953).

Record Group 8, British military and naval records (1954).

Record Group 9, Department of Militia and Defence, 1776–1922 ([1957]).

The following were cited in volume XI:

MG 8: Documents relatifs à la Nouvelle-France et au Québec (XVIIe–XXe siècles)
- F: Documents relatifs aux seigneuries et autres lieux
  - 77: Saint-Jean

MG 18: Pre-conquest papers
- H: New France
  - 6: Collection Taché
  - 25: Collection Peter Robinson

MG 19: Fur trade and Indians
- A: Fur trade, general
  - 2: Ermatinger estate
  - 21: Hargrave family
  - 29: Anderson, James
- D: Fur trade, post records, and journals
  - 12: Peel's River House (Fort McPherson)
- E: Red River Settlement
  - 9: Rice, F. W.

MG 23: Late eighteenth-century papers
- D: New Brunswick
  - 1: Chipman, Ward, Sr and Jr

MG 24: Nineteenth-century pre-confederation papers
- A: British officials and political figures
  - 27: Durham, John George Lambton, 1st Earl of
  - 33: Metcalfe, Charles Theophilus Metcalfe, Baron
- B: North American political figures and events
  - 2: Papiers Papineau
  - 25: Bellingham, Sydney Robert
  - 29: Howe, Joseph
  - 30: Macdonald, John Sandfield
  - 40: Brown, George
  - 46: Cherrier, Côme-Séraphin
  - 51: Little, Philip Francis
  - 54: Chauveau, Pierre-Joseph-Olivier
  - 59: Dessaulles, Louis-Antoine
  - 60: Daly, Thomas Mayne, Sr
  - 68: Hincks, Sir Francis
  - 75: Buell, William
  - 125: Coursol, Charles-Joseph
- C: Correspondents of political figures
  - 4: Thompson, Sir John Sparrow
  - 10: Graham, Christopher H.
- D: Industry, commerce, and finance
  - 7: Hamilton, George
  - 8: Wright family
  - 12: Dorwin, Jedediah Hubbell
  - 16: Buchanan, Isaac, and family
  - 21: Baring Brothers and Company
  - 24: Bethune, Donald
  - 36: Glyn Mills and Company
  - 63: Gray family
  - 79: Young, John
- E: Transportation
  - 1: Merritt, William Hamilton, and family
  - 17: Watkin, Sir Edward William
- F: Military and naval figures
  - 28: Bayfield, Henry Wolsey
- G: Militia
  - 45: Salaberry, famille de
- H: Exploration, travel, and surveys
  - 25: Lefroy, Sir John Henry
- I: Immigration, land, and settlement
  - 3: McGillivray family of Glengarry
  - 8: Macdonell of Collachie

9: Hill collection
26: Hamilton, Alexander
56: Taylor, John F.
61: Joseph, Abraham
63: Gosse, P. H.
81: Association des comtés de L'Islet et de Kamouraska pour coloniser le Saguenay
94: Glackmeyer, Louis-Édouard
106: Keefer collection
131: Nelles, Robert
140: Thompson, Samuel, and family
K: Education and cultural development
3: Painchaud, Abbé Charles-François
L: Miscellaneous
3: Collection Baby
MG 26: Papers of the prime ministers
A: Macdonald, Sir John Alexander
B: Mackenzie, Alexander
D: Thompson, Sir John Sparrow David
E: Bowell, Sir Mackenzie
F: Tupper, Sir Charles
MG 27: Political figures, 1867–1950
I: 1867–96
B: Governors general
3: Dufferin and Ava, Frederick Temple Blackwood, 1st Marquess of
C: Lieutenant governors
3: Chapleau, Sir Joseph-Adolphe
4: Dewdney, Edgar
6: McDougall, William
8: Morris, Alexander
D: Cabinet ministers
3: Caron, Sir Adolphe-Philippe
4: Cartier, Sir George-Étienne
8: Galt, Sir Alexander Tilloch
11: Langevin, Sir Hector
13: O'Connor, John
15: Tilley, Sir Samuel Leonard
E: Members of the House of Commons and the Senate
13: Penny, Edward Goff
F: Provincial political figures
3: Riel, Louis
8: Ouimet, Gédéon
I: Correspondents of political figures
19: Smith, Henry Hall
27: Stuart, George O'Kill
J: Related political papers
13: Watson, Samuel James
II: 1896–1921
D: Cabinet ministers
14: Scott, Richard William
16: Tarte, Joseph-Israël
F: Provincial political figures
7: Latchford, Francis Robert
MG 28: Records of post-confederation corporate bodies
I: Societies and associations
37: Ottawa Protestant Orphan's Home
44: Labour Council of Metropolitan Toronto
72: International Typographical Union
126: Royal Canadian Academy of Arts
II: Financial institutions
3: Merchants' Bank of Canada
III: Business establishments
20: Canadian Pacific Railway
26: Bronsons and Weston Lumber Company
46: Hill and Hill
MG 29: Nineteenth-century post-confederation manuscripts
A: Economic
2: Keefer, Samuel
B: Scientific
1: Fleming, Sandford
6: Smith, Marcus
15: Bell, Robert
C: Social
10: Ferrier, A. D.
34: Dougall, John, and family
37: Allan, Hugh
D: Cultural
29: Bibaud, Maximilien
40: Fréchette, Louis-Honoré
60: Dent, John Charles
61: Morgan, Henry James
E: Professional and public life
24: Higginson, William
29: Denison, George Taylor, III
74: Campbell, John Colin Armour
MG 30: Manuscripts of the first half of the twentieth century
C: Social
97: Kelso, John Joseph
D: Cultural
1: Audet, Francis-Joseph
37: Griffin, Martin Joseph
MG 40: Records and manuscripts from British repositories
I: Admiralty Hydrographic Department
2: Bayfield, Henry Wolsey
RG 1: Executive Council, Canada, 1764–1867
E: State records
1: Minute books (state matters)
3: Upper Canada state papers
7: Submissions to council
L: Land records
3: Upper Canada and Canada, petitions
RG 2: Privy Council Office
1: Minutes and orders in council
RG 4: Civil and provincial secretaries' offices, Quebec, Lower Canada, and Canada East
B: Office records

28: Bonds, licenses, and certificates
29: Militia records
C: Provincial secretary's correspondence
1: Numbered correspondence files
2: Letterbooks, Quebec, Lower Canada
RG 5: Civil and provincial secretaries' offices, Upper Canada and Canada West
A: Civil secretary's office
1: Upper Canada sundries
B: Miscellaneous records
11: Miscellaneous records relating to education
C: Provincial secretary's correspondence
1: Numbered correspondence files
RG 7: Governor general's office
G1: Dispatches from the Colonial Office
G6: Dispatches from the British minister at Washington
G9: Drafts of dispatches to the Colonial Office
G10: Drafts of secret and confidential dispatches to the Colonial Office
RG 8: British military and naval records
I: C series (British military records)
RG 9: Department of Militia and Defence
I: Pre-confederation records
C: Adjutant-general's office, United Canada
4: General orders
5: Pensions and land grants
6: Register of officers
7: Officers' commissions
8: Subject files
II: Post-confederation records
A: Deputy minister's office
1: Correspondence
B: Adjutant-general's office and headquarters
4: Registers and lists of officers and men
RG 10: Indian affairs
A: Administrative records of the imperial government
1: Records of the governor general and the lieutenant governors
1–7: Upper Canada, civil control
2: Records of the superintendent's office
8–21: Superintendent general's office
4: Records of the chief superintendent's office, Upper Canada
498–509, 749: Letterbooks
5: Records of the civil secretary's office
142–262, 752–60: Correspondence
510–20: Letterbooks
622–23: Drafts
6: General office files
116–18: Departmental organization
1011: Paudash papers
B: Ministerial administration records
2: Deputy superintendent general's office
521–27, 1078–133: Letterbooks
3: Central registry system
1855–3554: Red (Eastern) series
3555–4375: Black (Western) series
7555–919: Central registry files
8: General headquarters administration records
766–68A: G. M. Matheson, Notes and indices
C: Field office records
I: Superintendency records
3: Northern (Manitowaning) superintendency
6: Six Nations (Grand River) superintendency
803–93: Correspondence
II: Agency records
Duck Lake agency, Saskatchewan
1591–92: Correspondence
1593–601, 9112–17: General administration files
RG 11: Department of Public Works
A: Board of Works records
1: Official correspondence
1–39: Registered correspondence
B: Department of Public Works
1: Registry records
a: Official correspondence
149–597, 3974: Registered correspondence
b: Registers and indexes
615–708: Subject registers
752–54: Staff registers
d: Railway Branch records
828–36: Records of the Intercolonial Railway
e: 837–43: Commission of inquiry into matters relating to the construction of the Parliament Buildings
2: Registry records
b: Registers and indexes
2117–20: General indexes
D: Chief architect's office
2: Letterbooks
RG 13: Department of Justice
A: Central registry files
1: Indexes and registers
B: Special records
2: Records relating to Louis Riel and the North-West uprising
C: Branch records
1: Legal Branch
1393–854: Capital case files
RG 14: Records of parliament
E: Senate
2: Letterbooks
RG 15: Department of the Interior
D: Dominion lands administration

II: Dominion Lands Branch
1: Correspondance, headquarters
RG 16: Department of National Revenue
A: Customs
2: Correspondence and returns, Province of Canada
RG 18: Royal Canadian Mounted Police
A: Comptroller's office
1: Official correspondence series
1–606: Subject files
B: Commissioner's office
7: Personnel records
RG 19: Department of Finance
C: Agencies and acts administered by the Department of Finance
1: Bank of Upper Canada
RG 30: Canadian National Railways
120–32: Hamilton and North Western Railway
167–96: Northern Railway
197–216: Northern and North Western Railway
326–31: Galt and Guelph Railway
361–63: Hamilton and Toronto Railway
1414: Toronto, Simcoe and Huron Union Railroad
1596–98, 2028–29: Ontario, Simcoe and Huron Union Railroad
10484–90: Montreal Telegraph Company
RG 31: Statistics Canada
A: Census Division
1: Census records
RG 42: Department of Marine
I: Shipping registers
RG 43: Department of Railways and Canals
B: Canal Branch
4: Field office records
b: Ottawa–St Lawrence canals
RG 45: Geological Survey of Canada
123–77: Field notebooks
RG 48: Dominion Astronomical Observatories
29–32: Records of Boundary Commissioner Captain D. R. Cameron
RG 68: Department of the Registrar General
1: Registration of proclamations, commissions, letters patent, warrants, and other instruments issued under the great seal of Canada
RG 93: Atmospheric Environment Service
A: Registers and indexes
2: Registers of correspondence received and sent

PUBLIC ARCHIVES OF NOVA SCOTIA, Halifax. For a description of the collections see *Inventory of manuscripts in the Public Archives of Nova Scotia* (Halifax, 1976).

Materials used in the preparation of volume XI include:
MG 1: Papers of families and individuals
160A: William Marsters Brown, Genealogy
277–311: Arthur W. H. Eaton, Documents
550–58: Thomas McCulloch, Documents
793: Simon B. Robie, Documents
817–63: Thomas B. Smith, Genealogy
963A: Martin Isaac Wilkins, Documents
MG 2: Political papers
719–25: George Renny Young papers
726–30: John Young papers
731–82: Sir William Young papers
MG 3: Business papers
272–75: Martin Isaac Wilkins, Pictou, N.S.
MG 4: Churches and communities
37: Guysborough, History
48: St Matthew's Church, Halifax
122: Onslow Township, Township book
MG 5: Cemeteries
MG 9: Scrapbooks
MG 15: Ethnic collections
6: Indians
MG 20: Societies and special collections
61–70: Charitable Irish Society, Halifax, collection
180: Halifax Poor Man's Friend Society collection
230–73, 471, 475: North British Society collection
670–707: Nova Scotia Historical Society, unpublished papers
674, no.9: A. H. McKinnon, "William Young: member of the legislature for Inverness"
675, no.1: N. H. Meagher, "Sir William Young"
MS file, Wilkins family, Genealogy
RG 1: Bound volumes of Nova Scotia records for the period 1624–1867
60–110: Dispatches from the secretary of state to the governors of Nova Scotia
111–28: Dispatches from the governors of Nova Scotia to the secretary of state
186–214½ H: Council, Minutes
224–65: Miscellaneous documents
341–96c: Special subjects
361½: Onslow, Town records
443–54: Census and poll tax
448–50: Nova Scotia census, 1838
453: Halifax County census, 1851
RG 2: Records of the governors' and lieutenant-governors' offices
Sect.2: Correspondence
RG 3: Records of the Executive Council of Nova Scotia
3: Memorandum book, 1872–75

RG 5: Records of the Legislative Assembly of Nova Scotia
E: Election writs
16: Polling lists, Antigonish County; Election returns, Antigonish and Guysborough counties
GP: Governor's petitions
2: Miscellaneous, 1850–54
11: Requests for appointment as notary public
P: Petitions
41–50: Miscellaneous "B"; Petitions requesting a grant of money
R: Reports and resolutions
RG 6: Secretary of state's office
Sect.2: Letters from secretary of state for Canada to lieutenant governors of Nova Scotia
32: Confidential letterbook
RG 7: Records of the provincial secretary of Nova Scotia
1–142: Letters received
RG 14: Education
70: Provincial secretary of Nova Scotia, Correspondence
RG 18: Immigration and ship passenger lists
Ser.A: Naturalization of aliens and oaths of allegiance
RG 32: Vital statistics
132–69: Marriage bonds
RG 35A: Halifax city and county assessments
1–4: Halifax city assessments
RG 39: Supreme Court
C: Civil and criminal cases

PUBLIC ARCHIVES OF PRINCE EDWARD ISLAND, Charlottetown.

Materials used in the preparation of volume XI include:

Bank of Prince Edward Island, Minute book
John Mackieson, Diaries
Natural History Society for Prince Edward Island
Letters
Minute book
Edward Palmer papers
Palmer family papers
"Scrapbook containing papers relating to Joseph Pope, W. H. Pope, and J. C. Pope"
RG 1: Lieutenant Governor, Commission books
RG 5: Executive Council, Minutes
RG 6: Court records
Supreme Court records
Minutes
Court of Chancery records
Case papers
Minutes
RG 15: Rent books
RG 16: Registry Office, Land registry records
Conveyance registers
Land title documents
RG 18: Census records, 1841, 1861

QUÉBEC, MINISTÈRE DE LA JUSTICE. The Archives civiles and the Archives judiciaires du Québec are now separate repositories under the jurisdiction of the Ministère de la Justice as a result of reclassification of the former Archives judiciaires. They are deposited at the court-houses in the administrative centres of the provincial judicial districts.

ARCHIVES CIVILES. These archives hold documents for the past 100 years, including the registers of births, marriages, and deaths, notaries' *minutiers* (minute books), and records of surveyors active in the district; earlier documents are at the ANQ.

ARCHIVES JUDICIAIRES. The new Archives judiciaires contain the records of the various courts of justice; current documents, from about the past five years, are at the court-houses, while documents from the previous 25 years will be in one of the 13 record centres being organized by the Ministère de la Justice, and documents more than 30 years old will be in the regional centres of the ANQ.

BUREAU D'ENREGISTREMENT. The registry offices hold all property titles and contracts affecting real estate: sales, marriages, wills and estates, mortgages, conveyances, assignments, gifts, guardian- and trusteeships. At present there are 82 registry offices in the province. A list of the judicial districts and registry offices can be found in *The Quebec legal telephone directory*, ed. Andrée Frenette-Lecoq (Montreal, 1980).

QUÉBEC, MINISTÈRE DES AFFAIRES CULTURELLES, Centre de documentation, Québec. The Ministère des Affaires culturelles has consolidated the collection of all previously existing centres into one documentation centre, including that of the Inventaire des Biens culturels.

The following were cited in volume XI:

Fonds Morisset
1: Architecture et œuvres d'art par localité
15868–84: Yamachiche, église
2: Artistes et artisans
A517/L382: Amiot, Laurent
B772.5/V64/1: Bourgeau, Victor
F177/A634.7: Falardeau, Antoine-Sébastien
G492.5/C997.5: Gingras, Cyrille
L169.5/A495.1: Lafrance, Ambroise-Adhémar
L445.2/A23.8/1–4: Leblanc, Augustin
L673/P622: Lespérance, Pierre
M379/F316: Martin, Félix
085.3/J65.5: Ostell, John
V775.5/Z16: Vincent, Zacharie

QUEEN'S UNIVERSITY ARCHIVES, Kingston, Ont. For information on the collection see *A guide to the holdings of Queen's University Archives* (Kingston, 1978). The Lorne and Edith Pierce collection is described in detail in *A catalogue of Canadian manuscripts collected by Lorne Pierce and presented to Queen's University* (Toronto, 1946).

Collections consulted in the preparation of volume XI include:

Calvin Company records
Canada Steamship Lines Ltd. records
  La Compagnie du Richelieu
    Procès-verbaux
  Richelieu and Ontario Navigation Company
    Minutes
Corporation of the City of Kingston
  City records
  Minutes of council
  Reports of committees
House of Industry records
Alexander Mackenzie papers
M. L. Magill papers
Charles Mair papers
Lorne and Edith Pierce collection of Canadian manuscripts
  Isabella Valancy Crawford, manuscripts
Queen's University records
  Queen's University letters
  Queen's University medical faculty records
David Stirling, Notebook

UNITED CHURCH ARCHIVES, CENTRAL ARCHIVES OF THE UNITED CHURCH OF CANADA, Toronto. The present-day United Church Archives is a descendant of 19th- and 20th-century archival collections of various Canadian Methodist, Presbyterian, Congregationalist, and Evangelical/United Brethren in Christ bodies. The collection is housed in the Central Archives of the United Church of Canada at Victoria University, Toronto. The Central Archives collection is national in scope. Material of local interest, including the official records of the conferences concerned, is housed in regional conference archives.

Materials used in volume XI include:

Biography files
John Black, Correspondence
Church history files
Methodist Church of Canada records
  Missionary Society
    Minutes
  Toronto conference
    Minutes
Matthew Richey papers
Egerton Ryerson papers
Wesleyan Methodist Church in Canada records

UNIVERSITY OF NEW BRUNSWICK LIBRARY, Archives and Special Collections Department, Fredericton.

Materials used in volume XI include:

MG H: Historical
  H12a: Gordon, Sir Arthur Hamilton, 1st Baron Stanmore, Papers
UA: University archives
RG 109: University manuscripts

UNIVERSITY OF TORONTO ARCHIVES, Toronto. Finding aids are available within the archives for its major collections.

Materials used in the preparation of volume XI include:

Daniel Wilson, Journal excerpts
  A70–0005: Senate, Minutes, 1850–73
A73–0015/001: Upper Canada, General Board of Education, Minutes, 14 June 1823–11 March 1833
  A73–0026: Department of Graduate Records files
  A74–0018: Upper Canada College records

UNIVERSITY OF WESTERN ONTARIO, D. B. Weldon Library, London, Ont. A description of the municipal record and personal manuscript collections is available on microfiche in *Regional collection: the D. B. Weldon Library catalogue*, ed. S. L. Sykes (4 fiches, London, 1977).

The following material was used in the preparation of volume XI:

H. C. R. Becher papers
Fred Landon papers
Amelia Ryerse (Harris) papers
Thomas Swinyard papers

GREAT BRITAIN

CHURCH MISSIONARY SOCIETY ARCHIVES, London. For copies of materials in the PAC see *General inventory, manuscripts, 3: MG 17–MG 21* (Ottawa, 1974).

The following were consulted for volume XI:

C: Committee of Correspondence (pre-1880)
  C.1: North West America mission, Rupert's Land
    I: Letterbooks, individual correspondence, outgoing, 1852–87
    L: Letterbooks, despatches, outgoing, 1821–82
    M: Mission books, incoming letters, 1822–76
    O: Original letters, journals and papers, incoming, 1822–80
G 1: East Asia (Group 1) Committee (post-1880)
  C.1: North West America mission, Rupert's Land
    P: Précis of letters, incoming, 1881–1924

PUBLIC RECORD OFFICE, London. For an introduction to the holdings and arrangement of this archives see

Guide to the contents of the Public Record Office (3v., London, 1963–68). For copies of PRO documents available at the PAC see *General inventory, manuscripts, 2*.

Materials cited in volume XI include:

Admiralty
- Admiralty and Secretariat
  - ADM 1: Papers
  - ADM 9: Returns of officers' services
  - ADM 11: Indexes and compilations, series II
  - ADM 196: Records of officers' services
- Navy Board
  - ADM 107: Passing certificates

Colonial Office. [*See* R. B. Pugh, *The records of the Colonial and Dominions offices* (London, 1964).]
- Antigua and Monserrat
  - CO 7: Original correspondence
- British Columbia
  - CO 60: Original correspondence
  - CO 398: Entry books
- Canada
  - CO 42: Original correspondence
  - CO 43: Entry books
- New Brunswick
  - CO 188: Original correspondence
  - CO 189: Entry books
  - CO 193: Miscellanea
- Newfoundland
  - CO 194: Original correspondence
  - CO 195: Entry books
  - CO 197: Sessional papers
- Nova Scotia and Cape Breton
  - CO 217: Original correspondence
  - CO 218: Entry books
- Prince Edward Island
  - CO 226: Original correspondence
- Vancouver Island
  - CO 305: Original correspondence

Foreign Office. [See *Records of the Foreign Office, 1782–1939* (London, 1969).]
- General Correspondence
  - FO 5: America, United States of, series II
- Confidential print
  - FO 414: America, North
- Private collections
  - FO 362: Granville papers
- Maps and plans
  - FO 925: Maps and plans

Public Record Office
- Documents acquired by gift, deposit, or purchase
  - PRO 30/6: Carnarvon papers
  - PRO 30/48: Cardwell papers

War Office
- Correspondence
  - WO 1: In-letters
- Returns
  - WO 25: Registers, various
- Ordnance office
  - WO 49: Accounts, various

UNITED SOCIETY FOR THE PROPAGATION OF THE GOSPEL, London. The archives is in the process of reorganizing and reclassifying some material. Thus classifications used by Canadian archives holding USPG microfilm do not always correspond to those of the archives itself. Indexes are available at USPG, however, and most dated references are easily transferred. For copies of USPG archives documents in the PAC see *General inventory, manuscripts, 3*.

The following were consulted:

C/CAN: Unbound letters from Canada. A nominal card index is available at USPG.
- Tor: Toronto

D: Original letters received from 1850, bound in volumes. Handlist of writers and places, not alphabetical, available at USPG.

E: Reports from SPG missionaries from 1856, bound in volumes. Handlist available at USPG.

UNITED STATES

BAKER LIBRARY, Harvard University, Graduate School of Business Administration, Boston.

The following material was consulted in the preparation of volume XI:

R. G. Dun collection
- Manuscript credit ledgers

II: PRINTED PRIMARY SOURCES

A: OFFICIAL PUBLICATIONS AND CONTEMPORARY WORKS

ARCHIVES NATIONALES DU QUÉBEC, Québec. *Rapport*. 54 vols. 1920/21–77. There is an index to the contents of the first 42 volumes: *Tables des matières des rapports des Archives du Québec, tomes 1 à 42 (1920–1964)* ([Québec], 1965).

[BEGG, ALEXANDER.] *Alexander Begg's Red River journal and other papers relative to the Red River resistance of 1869–1870*. Edited with an introduction by William Lewis Morton. (Champlain Society publications, XXXIV.) Toronto, 1956; reprinted New York 1969.

BRITISH COLUMBIA

LEGISLATIVE ASSEMBLY

Journals, used for 1872–90.

Sessional papers, used for 1872–90. The

sessional papers for 1872–75 are included in its *Journals.*

LEGISLATIVE COUNCIL

Journals, 1864–71.

PUBLICATIONS

For a bibliography of the publications of the government of British Columbia, *see* M. C. Holmes, *Publications of the government of British Columbia, 1871–1947* . . . (Victoria, 1950).

CANADA

HOUSE OF COMMONS/CHAMBRE DES COMMUNES

Debates/Débats, used for 1867–90. Official publication of the House of Commons debates began in 1875. The debates for 1867– are being edited by Peter Busby Waite and those for 1867–70 have been published, 1967–79. [*See also*: "Parliamentary debates."]

Journals/Journaux, used for 1867–90.

PARLIAMENT/PARLEMENT

Sessional papers/Documents de la session, used for 1867–95.

SENATE/SÉNAT

Debates/Débats, used for 1867–90. Official publication of the Senate debates began in English in 1871 and in French in 1896. The volumes for 1867–70 have been edited by Peter Busby Waite and were published in 1968–77. The debates after 1871 are being republished with parallel English and French versions, edited by A. Pamela Hardisty, 1980– .

Statutes of Canada/Statuts du Canada, used for 1871–91. In 1873 the title became *Acts of the parliament of the dominion of Canada/Actes du parlement de la puissance du Canada*.

PUBLICATIONS

For useful guides to the publications of the government of Canada, *see* O. B. Bishop, *Canadian official publications* (Oxford and Toronto, 1981), and M. V. Higgins, *Canadian government publications: a manual for librarians* (Chicago, 1935).

CANADA, PROVINCE OF

LEGISLATIVE ASSEMBLY/ASSEMBLÉE LÉGISLATIVE

Appendix to the . . . journals of the Legislative Assembly of the Province of Canada/Appendice . . . des journaux de la province du Canada, 1841–59. Continued by Canada, Province of, Parliament/Parlement, *Sessional papers/Documents de la session*.

Journals of the Legislative Assembly of the Province of Canada/Journaux de l'Assemblée legislative de la province du Canada, 1841–66.

PARLIAMENT/PARLEMENT

Parliamentary debates on the subject of the confederation of the British North American provinces, 3rd session, 8th provincial parliament of Canada/Débats parlementaires sur la question de la confédération des provinces de l'Amérique britannique du Nord, 3e session, 8e parlement provincial du Canada. Quebec, 1865; the *Parliamentary debates* were reprinted at Ottawa in 1951.

Sessional papers . . . of the Province of Canada/Documents de la session . . . de la province du Canada, 1860–66. Supersedes Canada, Province of, Legislative Assembly/Assemblée législative, *Appendix to the . . . journals/Appendice . . . des journaux*.

Statutes of the Province of Canada . . . /Statuts de la province du Canada . . ., 1841–66. The statutes were published under the title *Provincial statutes of Canada/Les statuts provinciaux du Canada* from 1841 to 1851.

PUBLICATIONS

For a critical bibliography of the English-language publications of the Province of Canada, *see* O. B. Bishop, *Publications of the government of the Province of Canada, 1841–1867* (Ottawa, 1963). See also *The Legislative Assembly of the Province of Canada: an index to journal appendices and sessional papers, 1841–1866*, comp. P. A. Damphouse (London, Ont., 1974).

The Canadian North-West, its early development and legislative records; minutes of the councils of the Red River colony and the Northern Department of Rupert's Land. Edited by Edmund Henry Oliver. (PAC publications, 9.) 2 vols. Ottawa, 1914–15.

CARROLL, JOHN [SALTKILL]. *Case and his cotemporaries; or, the Canadian itinerants' memorial: constituting a biographical history of Methodism in Canada, from its introduction into the province, till the death of the Rev. William Case in 1855*. 5 vols. Toronto, 1867–77.

CHAMPLAIN SOCIETY, Toronto

PUBLICATIONS

50 vols. to date, exclusive of the Hudson's Bay Company series [*see* HBRS], the Ontario series, and the unnumbered series. Issued only to elected members of the society who are limited in numbers.

XXVIII: Mactavish, *Letters of Letitia Hargrave* (MacLeod).

XXXIV: Begg, *Red River journal* (Morton).

Debates of the Legislative Assembly of United Canada, 1841–1867. General editor, Elizabeth [Nish] Gibbs. 11 vols. in 18 to date. Montreal, 1970– .

Débats de la législature provinciale de la province de Québec. 15 vols. Québec, 1879–95. Title varies: [I]–[II], *Débats de la législature provinciale de la province de Québec*; [III]–[XIII], *Débats de la législature de la province de Québec*; XIV–XV, *Débats de l'Assemblée législative de la province de Québec*. Editors: [I]–[III], G.-Alphonse Desjardins; [IV]–[XI], Alphonse Desjardins; [XII]–[XIII], N. Malenfant; XIV–XV, Louis-Georges Desjardins.

Débats de l'Assemblée législative. Marcel Hamelin, édit. 4 vols. parus. Québec, 1974– .
[I]: *[1re législature, 1867–1870]*.
[II]: *2e législature, 1871–1875.*
[III]: *3e législature, 1875–1878.*
[IV]: *8e législature, 1893–1897.*

Documentary history of education in Upper Canada from the passing of the Constitutional Act of 1791 to the close of Rev. Dr. Ryerson's administration of the Education Department in 1876. Edited by John George Hodgins. 28 vols. Toronto, 1894–1910.

The Elgin–Grey papers, 1846–1852. Edited with notes and appendices by Arthur George Doughty. (PAC publication.) 4 vols. Ottawa, 1937.

GREAT BRITAIN, PARLIAMENT, HOUSE OF COMMONS PAPER, 1857 (session II), XV, 224, 260 (whole volume). *Report from the select committee on the Hudson's Bay Company; together with the proceedings of the committee, minutes of evidence, appendix and index.*

HARGRAVE, LETITIA. *See* MACTAVISH

[HOWE, JOSEPH.] *The speeches and public letters of Joseph Howe (based upon Mr. Annand's edition of 1858).* Revised and edited by Joseph Andrew Chisholm. 2 vols. Halifax, 1909.

HUDSON'S BAY RECORD SOCIETY, Winnipeg
PUBLICATIONS
31 vols. to date. General editor for vols.I–XXII, Edwin Ernest Rich; vols.XXIII–XXV, Kenneth Gordon Davies; vols.XXVI–XXX, Glyndwr Williams; vols.XXXI– , Hartwell Bowsfield. Vols.I–XII were issued in association with the Champlain Society [*q.v.*] and reprinted in 1968 in Nendeln, Liechtenstein.
XIX: [Colvile, Eden.] *London correspondence inward from Eden Colvile, 1849–1852.* Edited by Edwin Ernest Rich, assisted by Alice Margaret Johnson, with an introduction by William Lewis Morton. London, 1956.
XXI, XXII: Rich, *Hist. of HBC* [*see* section IV].
XXX: *Hudson's Bay miscellany, 1670–1870.* Edited with introductions by Glyndwr Williams. Winnipeg, 1975.

Journal de l'instruction publique/Journal of Education for Lower Canada. Quebec and Montreal. 1 (1857)–23 (1879). Official publications of the Department of Public Instruction, published variously at Quebec and Montreal. The two editions were completely independent, and neither was a translation of the other.

[MACDONALD, JOHN ALEXANDER.] *The letters of Sir John A. Macdonald.* (PAC publications, The papers of the prime ministers series, I–II.) 2 vols. Ottawa, 1968–69. I: *1836–1857.* Edited by James Keith Johnson. II: *1858–1861.* Edited by James Keith Johnson and Carole B. Stelmack.

[MACTAVISH, LETITIA.] *The letters of Letitia Hargrave.* Edited with introduction and notes by Margaret Arnett MacLeod. (Champlain Society publications, XXVIII.) Toronto, 1947.

MANITOBA
LEGISLATIVE ASSEMBLY
Journals, used for 1876–90.

MORRIS, ALEXANDER. *The treaties of Canada with the Indians of Manitoba and the North-West Territories, including the negotiations on which they were based, and other information relating thereto.* Toronto, 1880; reprinted [1885?]; reprinted 1971.

NEW BRUNSWICK
HOUSE OF ASSEMBLY
Journal, used for 1852–79.
Reports of the debates, used for 1850–80. From 1874 the debates have the title *Synoptic report of the proceedings*.
LEGISLATIVE COUNCIL
Journal, used for 1870–85.
PUBLICATIONS
For a bibliography of the publications of the government of New Brunswick, *see* O. B. Bishop, *Publications of the governments of Nova Scotia, Prince Edward Island, New Brunswick, 1758–1952* (Ottawa, 1957).

NEWFOUNDLAND
Blue book, used for 1832–90.
HOUSE OF ASSEMBLY
Journal, used for 1832–89.

NOVA SCOTIA
HOUSE OF ASSEMBLY
Journal and proceedings, used for 1833–90.
Debates and proceedings, used for 1855–75.
LEGISLATIVE COUNCIL
Debates and proceedings, used for 1858–75.
Journal of the proceedings, used for 1854–86.
PUBLICATIONS
For a bibliography of the publications of the government of Nova Scotia, *see* O. B. Bishop, *Publications of the governments of Nova Scotia, Prince Edward Island, New Brunswick, 1758–1852* (Ottawa, 1957).

ONTARIO
LEGISLATIVE ASSEMBLY
Journals, used for 1867–90.
LEGISLATURE
Sessional papers, used for 1870–90.
PUBLICATIONS
For a bibliography of the publications of the government of Ontario during the period

covered by this volume, *see* O. B. Bishop, *Publications of the government of Ontario, 1867–1900* (Toronto, 1976).

"Parliamentary debates." Canadian Library Association project to microfilm the debates of the legislature of the Province of Canada and the parliament of Canada for the period 1846–74.

PRINCE EDWARD ISLAND

HOUSE OF ASSEMBLY

Debates and proceedings, used for 1855–90. The title was *The parliamentary reporter; or, debates and proceedings* up to 1886.

Journal, used for 1835–91.

LEGISLATIVE COUNCIL

Debates and proceedings, used for 1860–73.

Journal, used for 1860–82.

PUBLICATIONS

For a bibliography of the publications of the government of Prince Edward Island, *see* O. B. Bishop, *Publications of the governments of Nova Scotia, Prince Edward Island, New Brunswick, 1758–1952* (Ottawa, 1957).

PUBLIC ARCHIVES OF CANADA, Ottawa. *Report*; *Rapport*. Begun in 1881. Annually until 1952; irregularly thereafter.

QUEBEC

LEGISLATIVE ASSEMBLY/ASSEMBLÉE LÉGISLATIVE

Journals/Journaux, used for 1867–68 to 1880.

PARLIAMENT/PARLEMENT

Sessional papers/Documents de la session, used for 1869 to 1886.

Statutes of the province of Quebec/Statuts de la province de Québec, used for 1869 to 1886.

PUBLICATIONS

For a bibliography of the publications of the government of Quebec, see *Répertoire des publications gouvernementales du Québec de 1867 à 1964*. André Beaulieu *et al.*, comp. (Québec, 1968).

ROSS, ALEXANDER. *The Red River settlement: its rise, progress, and present state; with some account of the native races and its general history to the present day.* London, 1856; reprinted Minneapolis, Minn., 1957, and Edmonton, 1972.

B: NEWSPAPERS

Numerous sources have been used to determine the various titles of newspapers and their dates of publication. The printed sources include, for all areas of the country: Canadian Library Assoc., *Canadian newspapers on microfilm, catalogue* (2pts. in 3, Ottawa, 1959–69), and *Union list of Canadian newspapers held by Canadian libraries/Liste collective des journaux canadiens disponibles dans les bibliothèques canadiennes* (Ottawa, 1977); for British Columbia: Madge Wolfenden, "The early government gazettes," *BCHQ*, 7 (1943): 171–90; for Manitoba: J. W. Dafoe, "Early Winnipeg newspapers," HSSM *Papers*, 3rd ser., no.3 (1947): 14–24, and D. M. Loveridge, *A historical directory of Manitoba newspapers, 1859–1978* (Winnipeg, 1980); for New Brunswick: Harper, *Hist. directory* [*see* section III]; for Newfoundland: "Chronological list of Newfoundland newspapers in the public collections at the Gosling Memorial Library and Provincial Archives," comp. Ian McDonald (copy deposited in the Reference Library, Arts and Culture Centre, St John's); for Nova Scotia: D. C. Harvey, "Newspapers of Nova Scotia, 1840–1867," *CHR*, 26 (1945): 279–301, and G. E. N. Tratt, *A survey and listing of Nova Scotia newspapers, 1752–1957, with particular reference to the period before 1867* (Halifax, 1979); for Ontario: *Catalogue of Canadian newspapers in the Douglas Library, Queen's University*, [comp. L. C. Ellison *et al.*] (Kingston, 1969), *Early Toronto newspapers* (Firth) [*see* section III], and W. S. Wallace, "The periodical literature of Upper Canada," *CHR*, 12 (1931): 4–22; for Prince Edward Island: W. L. Cotton, "The press in Prince Edward Island," *Past and present of P.E.I.* (MacKinnon and Warburton), 112–21 [*see* section IV], and R. L. Cotton, "Early press," *Historic highlights of Prince Edward Island*, ed. M. C. Brehaut (Charlottetown, 1955), 40–45; and for Quebec: Beaulieu et J. Hamelin, *La presse québécoise* [*see* section III].

Acadian Recorder, Halifax. Began publication 16 Jan. 1813 as a weekly. A tri-weekly was also published from 5 Sept. 1863, and a daily from 1868. It ceased publication on 10 May 1930.

L'Avenir, Montréal. Published from 24 June 1847 to 22 Dec. 1857.

British Colonist, Halifax. Its full title initially was *British Colonist: a Literary, Political and Commercial Journal.* Published from 25 July 1848 until 31 Dec. 1874 as a tri-weekly; a weekly was added in January 1849 and a daily edition on 13 Dec. 1869. From 11 Sept. 1851 until 20 Jan. 1855, the title was *British Colonist, and North American Railway Journal.*

British Colonist, Toronto. Began as a weekly on 1 February 1838 and became a semi-weekly in August 1843. A daily edition, the *Daily Colonist*, began in November 1851 and a weekly, the *News of the Week, or Weekly Colonist*, in August 1852. In September 1860 the daily and semi-weekly editions were dropped, but the *News of the Week* continued until December 1861.

British Colonist, Victoria. See *Daily Colonist*

British Columbian, New Westminster, B.C. Published under a variety of titles from 13 Feb. 1861 to 25 July 1869 and from December 1881 to July

1950. Its frequency varied between weekly and semi-weekly, except from 16 March to 25 July 1869 when it was published as a daily in Victoria. In 1886 it became the weekly edition of the *Columbian.*

British Whig, Kingston, Ont. See *Daily British Whig*

Canadian Illustrated News, Montreal. Published from 30 Oct. 1869 to 22 Dec. 1883.

Canadian Monetary Times and Insurance Chronicle, Toronto. See *Monetary Times*

Le Canadien, Québec. Published from 22 Nov. 1806 to 11 Feb. 1893.

Cariboo Sentinel, Barkerville, B.C. Published from 6 June 1865 to 30 Oct. 1875 although publication was suspended for several short periods. The paper was published at various times as a weekly, a semi-weekly, and a semi-monthly.

Christian Guardian, Toronto. Published as a weekly at York (Toronto) from 21 Nov. 1829 until 10 June 1925 when it was superseded by the *New Outlook*, which was in turn succeeded by the *United Church Observer* on 1 March 1939. A general index of the *Christian Guardian* for the years 1829–67 is available at the UCA. A selective index for church news and general historical information is in preparation for the period after 1867.

Chronicle & Gazette, Kingston, Ont. See *Daily News*

Chronicle and News, Kingston, Ont. See *Daily News*

Le Courrier de Saint-Hyacinthe, Saint-Hyacinthe, Qué. Began publication on 24 Feb. 1853.

Le Courrier du Canada, Québec. Published from 2 Feb. 1857 to 11 April 1901.

Daily British Colonist, Victoria. See *Daily Colonist*

Daily British Colonist and Victoria Chronicle. See *Daily Colonist*

Daily British Whig, Kingston, Ont. Began publication as the semi-weekly *British Whig* in February 1834. The paper also appeared under the titles *British Whig and General Advertiser for the Midland District* and *British Whig and General Advertiser for Canada West*. On 1 Jan. 1849 it became the *Daily British Whig*, and the *Weekly British Whig* was also published. On 1 Dec. 1926 the paper merged with the *Daily Standard* to became the *Whig-Standard*.

Daily Colonist, Victoria. Published under various titles from 11 Dec. 1858 to the present. Until 28 July 1860 the full name was the *British Colonist*; from 31 July 1860 to 23 June 1866, it was the *Daily British Colonist.* On 25 June 1866 it absorbed the *Victoria Daily Chronicle* (1862–66) and from then to 6 Aug. 1872 was known as the *Daily British Colonist and Victoria Chronicle*; from 7 Aug. 1872 to 31 Dec. 1886 the name was the *Daily British Colonist*, and from 1 Jan. 1887 to the present, the *Daily Colonist.* The paper began as a weekly, then on 16 May 1859 a tri-weekly issue was added (the weekly continuing as the *Weekly British Colonist*). The paper published five issues per week beginning on 31 July 1860, and after 4 Feb. 1861 became a full-scale daily.

Daily Evening Mercury, Quebec. See *Quebec Daily Mercury*

Daily Free Press, Winnipeg. See *Manitoba Free Press*

Daily Mail and Empire, Toronto. See *Mail*

Daily News, Kingston, Ont. Published from 7 Oct. 1851 to 1908, it was sometimes issued as the *Kingston Daily News*, the *Kingston News*, and the *News and Times.* In April 1908 it became the *Daily Standard* and on 1 Dec. 1926 merged with the *Daily British Whig* to form the *Whig-Standard.* From 1847 to about 1899 a weekly edition, the *Chronicle and News*, was published. The predecessors of the latter were the *Kingston Gazette* (1810–18), the *Kingston Chronicle* (1819–33), and the semi-weekly *Chronicle & Gazette* (29 June 1833–1847), which had as its full title *Chronicle & Gazette and Kingston Commercial Advertiser* until 1840 when the sub-title was dropped.

Daily Standard, Kingston, Ont. See *Daily News*

Daily Sun, Saint John, N.B. Published from 29 July 1878 as the *Daily Sun*, from 2 June 1887 as the *St. John Daily Sun*, and from 5 May 1906 as the *Sun.* On 14 March 1910 it merged with the *Daily Telegraph* to become the *Daily Telegraph and the Sun* (later the *Telegraph-Journal*).

Daily Telegraph, Saint John, N.B. See *Telegraph*

Daily Witness, Montreal. See *Montreal Daily Witness*

L'Étendard, Montréal. Published from 1 May 1883 to 20 March 1893.

L'Événement, Québec. Published from 13 May 1867 to 3 March 1967.

Evening Express, Halifax. Published as a tri-weekly from 4 Jan. 1858 to 30 Dec. 1872 as the *Evening Express and Commercial Record*, in 1873 it became a daily as the *Evening Express, Daily Edition.* On 16 July 1874 it became the *Evening Express* and apparently ceased publishing on 31 Dec. 1874.

Evening Mercury, St John's. Published as a daily from 1882 to 31 Dec. 1889 when it was superseded by the *Evening Herald* which was published until about 1920.

Evening Star, Montreal. See *Montreal Star*

Evening Telegram, St John's. Published as a daily from 3 April 1879 to the present.

Evening Telegram, Toronto. Published daily from 18 April 1876 to 30 Oct. 1971, first as the *Evening Telegram*, and then as the *Telegram.* After 25 Feb. 1949 it was called the *Toronto Telegram.*

Examiner, Charlottetown. Published under a variety of titles from 7 Aug. 1847 until 1922; the *Examiner* began as a weekly which lasted until at least the end of December 1876. For a brief period from 23

Feb. 1850 to 7 April 1851 it published as a semi-weekly under the title *Examiner and Semi-Weekly Intelligencer.* A daily edition was published from 17 May 1877 until June 1922, and a *Weekly Examiner* was issued from 30 Nov. 1877 until about 1906.

Examiner, Toronto. Published as a weekly from 3 July 1838 until 29 Aug. 1855 when it merged with the *Globe.*

Free Press, Ottawa. Published as a daily from December 1869, it became the *Ottawa Free Press* on 13 Aug. 1888.

Gazette, Montreal. Began publication on 3 June 1778.

La Gazette de Montréal. See *Gazette*

La Gazette du commerce et littéraire, pour la ville et district de Montréal. See *Gazette*

La Gazette littéraire pour la ville et district de Montréal. See *Gazette*

Globe, Toronto. Began as a weekly on 5 March 1844, became a semi-weekly 4 Nov. 1846, a tri-weekly 3 July 1849, and a daily 3 Oct. 1853. A second weekly series began 6 July 1849 and continued to 28 Jan. 1914. On 5 Jan. 1877 it amalgamated with the *Canada Farmer*, and its title changed to *Weekly Globe and Canada Farmer.* A second semi-weekly series was published from 19 Oct. 1853 to 2 July 1855 when it became a tri-weekly which lasted until 1864. There was a second daily, the *Evening Globe*, from 19 Dec. 1861 to 20 July 1908. The *Western Globe*, published weekly in Toronto but issued from London, Canada West, lasted from 16 Oct. 1845 until at least 1851. The title became the *Globe and Mail* when it merged with the *Daily Mail and Empire* on 23 Nov. 1936 and publication continues under this title to the present.

Halifax Herald. Published from 14 Jan. 1875 until it merged with the *Halifax Chronicle* to form the *Halifax Chronicle-Herald* on 1 Jan. 1949. Until 31 Dec. 1891 its title was the *Morning Herald*; thereafter it was called the *Halifax Herald*.

Hamilton Spectator, Hamilton, Ont. Published from 15 July 1846 to the present, first as a semi-weekly, the *Spectator and Journal of Commerce*, then on 10 May 1852 as the *Daily Spectator and Journal of Commerce*. On 31 March 1865 it became the *Spectator*, on 12 Aug. 1867 the *Daily Spectator*, and in 1876–77 the *Spectator* again. By 30 April 1883 it was known as the *Hamilton Daily Spectator*, the name it retained until 21 March 1890 when the format changed and the title became the *Hamilton Spectator*.

Herald, Montreal. Published from 19 Oct. 1811 to 18 Oct. 1957. This paper published, at least from 1867 to 1913, a weekly edition under the title *Montreal Weekly Herald.*

Islander, Charlottetown. Published as a weekly from 2 Dec. 1842 until June 1874. Its full title was the *Islander, or Prince Edward Weekly Intelligencer and Advertiser* until 21 Jan. 1853 when it became the *Islander, or Prince Edward Island Weekly Intelligencer and Advertiser*, and in December 1872 the *Prince Edward Islander: a Weekly Newspaper of General Intelligence*. It was absorbed by the *Weekly Patriot* in July 1874.

Le Journal de Québec, Québec. Published from 1 Dec. 1842 to 1 Oct. 1889.

Le Journal des Trois-Rivières. Published from 19 May 1865 to 19 March 1891. A *Journal des Trois-Rivières* was also published from 29 Aug. 1847 to 31 Dec. 1853.

Kingston Chronicle, Kingston, Ont. See *Daily News*

Leader, Toronto. A semi-weekly edition began on 1 July 1852 and a weekly edition on 7 July 1852. A daily edition was added on 11 July 1853. The semi-weekly ceased publication in 1864, but the daily and weekly editions continued until 1878.

Mail, Toronto. Began publication as a daily on 30 March 1872. Its name was changed to the *Toronto Daily Mail* on 2 Aug. 1880. The paper merged with the *Empire* (Toronto) to become the *Daily Mail and Empire* on 7 Feb. 1895. The *Daily Mail and Empire* merged with the *Globe* to become the *Globe and Mail* on 23 Nov. 1936.

Manitoba Daily Free Press, Winnipeg. See *Manitoba Free Press*

Manitoba Free Press, Winnipeg. Founded on 30 Nov. 1872 as a weekly, it became the *Daily Free Press* on 6 July 1874 and the *Manitoba Daily Free Press* on 8 April 1876. Its title was changed to the *Manitoba Morning Free Press* on 5 June 1894 and the *Manitoba Free Press* on 27 Jan. 1915. It became the *Winnipeg Free Press* on 2 Dec. 1931 and publication has continued under this title to the present.

La Minerve, Montréal. Published from 9 Nov. 1826 to 27 May 1899.

Moncton Times, Moncton, N.B. Began publication on 10 Dec. 1868 as a weekly. A daily edition was added on 11 Aug. 1877 and is still being published. There have been several slight variations in the title.

Le Monde, Montréal. See *Le Monde canadien*

Le Monde canadien, Montréal. Published from 19 Sept. 1867 to 5 July 1900.

Monetary Times, Toronto. Published from 15 Aug. 1867 as the weekly *Canadian Monetary Times and Insurance Chronicle*, it became the *Monetary and Commercial Times, Insurance Chronicle* on 25 March 1870 and the *Monetary Times and Trade Review, Insurance Chronicle* on 8 July 1871. After some further name changes it became the *Monetary Times* in June 1931. It was issued as a monthly from 1943 until it was absorbed in September 1970 by the *Executive*.

Montreal Daily Herald. See *Herald*

Montreal Daily Star. See *Montreal Star*

Montreal Daily Witness. Published from 13 Aug. 1860 to 11 July 1913. The weekly edition, *Montreal Witness*, appeared from 5 Jan. 1846 to May 1938.

Montreal Gazette. See *Gazette*

Montreal Gazette and Commercial Advertiser. See *Gazette*

Montreal Herald. See *Herald*

Montreal Herald and Daily Commercial Gazette. See *Herald*

Montreal Herald for the Country. See *Herald*

Montreal Star. Published from 16 Jan. 1869 to 25 Sept. 1979.

Montreal Weekly Herald. See *Herald*

Montreal Witness. See *Montreal Daily Witness*

Morning Chronicle, Halifax. Published under various titles from 24 Jan. 1844 to the present. It began as a tri-weekly which lasted until 1877; a daily was added on 3 Aug. 1864, and a weekly was also printed from 1844 until 1912. The paper became the *Halifax Chronicle* on 22 Jan. 1927, and on 1 Jan. 1949 it merged with the *Herald* to become the *Halifax Chronicle-Herald*, and the *Chronicle-Herald* after 26 Dec. 1959.

Morning Chronicle, Quebec. See *Quebec Chronicle-Telegraph*

Morning Herald, Halifax. See *Halifax Herald*

Morning News, Saint John, N.B. Published from 16 Sept. 1839 until 8 April 1884 under a variety of titles. It began as a tri-weekly, and became a daily on 2 Jan. 1869.

Morning Telegraph, Saint John, N.B. See *Telegraph*

New Brunswick Courier, Saint John, N.B. A weekly, it began publication on 2 May 1811 and continued to 1865.

New Brunswick Reporter and Fredericton Advertiser. Published from 23 Nov. 1844 to December 1902. It was a weekly, except from May 1882 to March 1888, when it was issued semi-weekly. On 6 Oct. 1888 the title changed to *Reporter and Fredericton Advertiser.*

Newfoundlander, St John's. Published from 1806 until 1884 although issues are only available from 1827. The paper was a weekly until 3 May 1852 when it became a semi-weekly.

New Outlook, Toronto. See *Christian Guardian*

Nor'Wester, Winnipeg. The first newspaper published in the Red River Settlement, it appeared from 28 Dec. 1859 to 24 Nov. 1869.

Le Nouveau Monde, Montréal. See *Le Monde canadien*

Novascotian, Halifax. Published under various titles from 1824 to 25 Dec. 1925. Its full title initially was the *Novascotian or Colonial Herald*, but on 2 Jan. 1840 it became just the *Novascotian.* It was called the *Nova Scotian and Weekly Chronicle* from 1892 until 13 Oct. 1922. At that time the format changed and it was published as the *Nova Scotian: Nova Scotia's Farm and Home Journal* until it ceased publication.

L'Opinion publique, Montréal. Published from 1 Jan. 1870 to 27 Dec. 1883.

Ottawa Citizen. Began in 1844 as the *Packet*, a weekly, but became the *Ottawa Citizen* on 22 Feb. 1851. A semi-weekly edition was added on 4 Oct. 1859 which by 15 May 1865 had become a daily. From 18 Aug. 1871 to 25 June 1890 it was called the *Ottawa Daily Citizen*, and between 26 June 1890 and 13 May 1892 it was the *Daily Citizen.* Thereafter it was known as the *Ottawa Citizen*, under which title it is still published.

Ottawa Free Press. See *Free Press*

La Patrie, Montréal. Published from 24 Feb. 1879 to 9 Jan. 1978. This paper became a weekly from 15 Nov. 1957.

Patriot, Charlottetown. Began as a weekly on 8 July 1865, becoming a semi-weekly in 1867 and absorbing the *Islander* in June 1874. The *Weekly Patriot* was added in July 1874, and on 4 April 1881 the semi-weekly edition became the *Daily Patriot*; it continues as the *Evening Patriot.* The paper is sometimes said to have begun publication on 5 July 1859 because it was numbered consecutively from the *Protestant and Evangelical Witness*, but for various reasons, including religious affiliation and financial support, it is not strictly correct to assume that the *Patriot* was a continuation of the *Protestant.*

Patriot, Kingston, Ont., and Toronto. Began publication as a weekly in Kingston in 1828 as the *Patriot and Farmer's Monitor.* Moved to York (Toronto) on 7 Dec. 1832. A semi-weekly edition began in November 1833 and continued to April 1852; in March 1834 the title was changed to the *Patriot*, and in 1839 to the *Toronto Patriot.* In April 1850 a daily edition was added, entitled the *Toronto Daily Patriot and Express*; it continued to 1855 and was absorbed, for a time, by the *Leader* (Toronto). The weekly ceased publication in 1878.

Patriot, St John's. Published as a weekly from 1833 to June 1890. In 1842 the name was changed from the *Newfoundland Patriot* to the *Patriot & Terra Nova Herald.* In 1877 it became the *Patriot and Catholic Herald* for four issues only. In 1878 it was the *Patriot and Terra Nova Advocate.*

La Presse, Montréal. Began publication on 20 Oct. 1884.

Public Ledger, St John's. Published from about 1820 to 1882 as a semi-weekly, then as a tri-weekly, and finally, in 1859, as a daily. Its full title was the *Public Ledger and Newfoundland General Advertiser* until 3 Feb. 1875 when it became the *Public Ledger.*

Quebec Chronicle. See *Quebec Chronicle-Telegraph*

Quebec Chronicle-Telegraph. Began publication on 18 May 1847.

Quebec Daily Evening Mercury. See *Quebec Daily Mercury*

Quebec Daily Mercury. Published from 5 Jan. 1805 to 17 Oct. 1903.

Quebec Mercury. See *Quebec Daily Mercury*

Quebec Morning Chronicle. See *Quebec Chronicle-Telegraph*

Royal Gazette, Charlottetown. Published from 1791 to the present. This paper began as a semi-monthly entitled *Royal Gazette, and Miscellany of the Island of Saint John* published by the king's or queen's printer. Subsequently it became a weekly.

Royal Gazette, St John's. Published from 27 Aug. 1807 as a weekly. Its full title was the *Royal Gazette and Newfoundland Advertiser*. In October 1924 the paper became the *Newfoundland Gazette*.

St. John Daily Sun. See *Daily Sun*

St. John Daily Telegraph and Morning Journal. See *Telegraph*

Saint John Globe, Saint John, N.B. Began publication in 1858 as the *Daily Evening Globe*; on 26 Sept. 1866 it became the *Saint John Globe*. It merged with the *Evening Times-Star* in January 1927 to form the *Evening Times-Globe* which is still published.

Le Sauvage, Montréal. See *L'Avenir*

Telegraph, Saint John, N.B. Begun as a tri-weekly, the *Morning Telegraph*, on 20 Sept. 1862, this paper became the *Weekly Telegraph* one week later, and a daily, the *St. John Daily Telegraph and Morning Journal*, on 1 July 1869. Its title was changed to the *Daily Telegraph* on 8 Sept. 1873 and after absorbing the Saint John *Sun* to the *Daily Telegraph and the Sun* from 14 March 1910 to 14 July 1923. On 16 July 1923 the paper merged with the *Daily Journal* and became the *Telegraph-Journal*, which is still published. This paper appeared under many variant titles. The titles appearing in this volume include the *Daily Telegraph*, *Morning Telegraph*, *St. John Daily Telegraph and Morning Journal*, and *Weekly Telegraph*.

Times and General Commercial Gazette, St John's. Published from 15 Aug. 1832 until 23 March 1895. It was a weekly until 25 Dec. 1844, and thereafter a semi-weekly.

Toronto Daily Mail. See *Mail*

Toronto Daily Patriot and Express. See *Patriot*

Toronto Patriot. See *Patriot*

Toronto World. Published as a daily from August 1880 until 9 April 1921 when it was absorbed by the *Daily Mail and Empire*. From 24 May 1891 it published a weekly, the *Sunday World*, which the *Daily Mail and Empire* continued to publish until 8 Nov. 1924.

Victoria Daily Standard. Published as a daily from 20 June 1870 to 31 Aug. 1889. The title was *Evening Standard* after 4 Aug. 1888.

Weekly British Whig, Kingston, Ont. See *Daily British Whig*

Weekly Globe, Toronto. See *Globe*

Weekly Telegraph, Saint John, N.B. See *Telegraph*

III: REFERENCE WORKS

ACHINTRE, AUGUSTE. *Manuel électoral; portraits et dossiers parlementaires du premier parlement de Québec*. Montréal, 1871; réimprimé 1871.

AKRIGG, GEORGE PHILLIP VERNON, and HELEN B. AKRIGG. *1001 British Columbia place names*. Vancouver, 1969. 2nd edition, 1970. 3rd edition, 1973.

ALLAIRE, JEAN-BAPTISTE-ARTHUR. *Dictionnaire biographique du clergé canadien-français*. 6 vols. Montréal et Saint-Hyacinthe, Qué., 1908–34.

[I]: *Les anciens*. Montréal, 1910.

[II]: *Les contemporains*. Saint-Hyacinthe, 1908.

[III]: [*Suppléments*.] 6 parts in 1 vol. Montréal, 1910–19.

[IV]: *Le clergé canadien-français: revue mensuelle* ([Montréal]), 1 (1919–20). Only one volume of this journal was published.

[V]: *Compléments*. 6 parts in 1 vol. Montréal, 1928–32.

[VI]: Untitled. Saint-Hyacinthe, 1934.

ALMANACS. The almanacs have been listed under this heading to facilitate their identification. Because titles within series vary and publishers or editors often change, the almanacs have in the main been listed under a general title, with the specifics found on title-pages following. The information in square brackets is given as a guide and may not be completely accurate.

Belcher's farmer's almanack, [published in Halifax from 1824 to 1930]. Edited by Clement Horton Belcher from 1824 to 1870 when its publication was taken over by the firm of McAlpine and Barnes, later the McAlpine Publishing Company. From 1824 to 1831 its title was *The farmer's almanack . . .* ; in 1832 it became *Belcher's farmer's almanack . . .* , a title it retained with minor variations until its disappearance.

Montreal pocket almanack, [from 1842 to 1891]. Published by Jos. Starke and Company, 1842–79; J. Theo. Robinson, 1880–91. From 1842 to 1854 and in 1856, the title was *The Montreal pocket almanack, and general register* . . . ; in 1855, 1857, and 1859, *The Montreal pocket almanack* . . . ; in 1858, 1860, and 1861, from 1864 to 1872, and from 1880 to 1891, *Starke's pocket almanac and general register* . . . ; in 1862 and 1863, *Starke's pocket almanack* . . . ; from 1873 to 1879, *Starke's pocket almanac, advertiser and general register*. . . .

New-Brunswick almanac, [published in Saint John, N.B., from at least 1825 to 1885 (last issue used in vol. XI)]. In 1828 its title was *An almanack* . . . , but by 1832 it had become *The New-Brunswick almanack*. . . . In 1849 it became *The New-Brunswick almanac, and register . . . prepared by the Fredericton Athenæum*.

Quebec almanac/Almanach de Québec, [published from 1780 to 1841, except for 1781, 1790, and 1793]. Publishers: William Brown, 1788; Samuel Neilson, 1791; John Neilson, 1794–1823; Neilson and Cowan, 1824–36; S. Neilson, 1837; W. Neilson, 1838–41. From 1780 to 1791, its title was *Almanach de Québec* . . . ; from 1794 to 1796, *Almanac de Québec* . . . ; in 1797 and 1798, *Almanac de Québec . . . /The Quebec almanac* . . . ; from 1803 to 1812, *Almanach de Québec; et état civil et militaire de l'Amérique-britannique . . . /The Quebec almanac; and British American royal kalendar* . . . ; from 1813 to 1841, *The Quebec almanac; and British American royal kalendar*. . . .

Armstrong, Frederick Henry. *Handbook of Upper Canadian chronology and territorial legislation*. London, Ont., 1967.

Audet, Francis-Joseph. *Les députés de Montréal (ville et comtés), 1792–1867*. Montréal, 1943.

——— *Les députés de Saint-Maurice (1808–1838) et de Champlain (1830–1838)*. (Pages trifluviennes, sér. A, 12.) Trois-Rivières, 1934.

——— *Les députés des Trois-Rivières (1808–1838)*. (Pages trifluviennes, sér. A, 11.) Trois-Rivières, 1934.

Australian dictionary of biography. 7 vols. to date. Melbourne, 1966– . General editor for vols. I–V, Douglas Pike; vol. VI, Bede Nairn; vols. VII– , Bede Nairn and Geoffrey Serle.

Beaulieu, André, et Jean Hamelin. *La presse québécoise des origines à nos jours*. [2e éd.] 4 vols. parus. Québec, 1973– .

Belcher's farmer's almanack. See Almanacs

A bibliography of Canadiana, being items in the Public Library of Toronto, Canada, relating to the early history and development of Canada. Edited by Frances Maria Staton and Marie Tremaine. Toronto, 1934; reprinted 1965.

A bibliography of Canadiana: first supplement. . . . Edited by Gertrude Mabel Boyle with Marjorie Colbeck. Toronto, 1959; reprinted 1969.

A bibliography of the Prairie provinces to 1953 with biographical index. Compiled by Bruce Braden Peel. 2nd edition. Toronto and Buffalo, N.Y., 1973.

Bishop, Olga Bernice *et al*. *Bibliography of Ontario history, 1867–1976: cultural, economic, political, social*. (Ontario historical studies series.) 2 vols. Toronto, 1980.

Borthwick, John Douglas. *History and biographical gazetteer of Montreal to the year 1892*. Montreal, 1892.

——— *Montreal, its history, to which is added biographical sketches, with photographs, of many of its principal citizens*. Montreal, 1875.

British Museum general catalogue of printed books. Photolithographic edition to 1955. 263 vols. London, 1959–66. A new catalogue, *The British Library catalogue of printed books to 1975*, began publication in 1980.

Business and general directory of Newfoundland. See Directories

Canada, an encyclopædia of the country: the Canadian dominion considered in its historic relations, its natural resources, its material progress, and its national development. Edited by John Castell Hopkins. 6 vols. and index. Toronto, 1898–1900.

Canada directory. See Directories

The Canadian biographical dictionary and portrait gallery of eminent and self-made men. 2 vols. Toronto, 1880–81.

The Canadian directory of parliament, 1867–1967. Edited by James Keith Johnson. (PAC publication.) Ottawa, 1968.

The Canadian men and women of the time: a handbook of Canadian biography. Edited by Henry James Morgan. 1st edition. Toronto, 1898. 2nd edition. 1912.

The Canadian parliamentary companion. Published in Quebec in 1862 and 1863, in Montreal from 1864 to 1874, and in Ottawa from 1875 to date. Appeared irregularly from 1862, then usually annually from 1871. The 1898–99 edition has the title *The parliamentary guide* . . . and the volumes from 1901 to date *The Canadian parliamentary guide*. . . . Editors: Henry James Morgan from 1862 to 1864, in 1869 and from 1871 to 1874; Charles Herbert Mackintosh from 1877 to 1881; John Alexander Gemmill from 1883 to 1897.

Canadian Religious Conference. *Abridged guide to the archives of religious communities in Canada/Guide sommaire des archives des communautés au Canada*. Ottawa, 1974.

Canadiana, 1867–1900: monographs; Canada's national bibliography/Canadiana, 1867–1900: monographies; la bibliographie nationale du Canada. Microfiche edition. Ottawa, 1980– .

Catalogue of pamphlets in the Public Archives of Canada/Catalogue des brochures aux Archives publiques du Canada. [1493–1931.] Compiled by Magdalen Casey. (PAC publications, 13.) 2 vols. Ottawa, 1931–32.

CENTRE D'ÉTUDES ACADIENNES, UNIVERSITÉ DE MONCTON. *Inventaire général des sources documentaires sur les Acadiens.* 3 vols. Moncton, N.-B., 1975–77.

CHADWICK, EDWARD MARION. *Ontarian families; genealogies of United-Empire-Loyalist and other pioneer families of Upper Canada.* 2 vols. Toronto, 1894–98; reprinted 2 vols. in 1, Lambertville, N.J., 1970. Vol. 1 reprinted with an introduction by William Felix Edmund Morley, Belleville, Ont., 1972.

CHAFE, LEVI G. *Chafe's sealing book: a history of the Newfoundland sealfishery from the earliest available records down to and including the voyage of 1923.* Edited by Harris Munden Mosdell. 3rd edition. St John's, 1923. The first two editions were published as *Report of the Newfoundland seal-fishery, from 1863, "the first year of the steamers," to 1894*, in 1894, and *Report of the Newfoundland seal fishery from 1863 (the first year of the steamers) to 1905*, in 1905.

Commemorative biographical record of the county of York, Ontario; containing biographical sketches of prominent and representative citizens and many of the early settled families. Toronto, 1907.

COOKE, ALAN, and CLIVE HOLLAND. *The exploration of northern Canada, 500 to 1920: a chronology.* Toronto, 1978.

CORNISH, GEORGE HENRY. *Cyclopædia of Methodism in Canada, containing historical, educational, and statistical information. . . .* 2 vols. Toronto and Halifax, 1881–1903.

A cyclopædia of Canadian biography, being chiefly men of the time. . . . Edited by George MacLean Rose. (Rose's national biographical series, I–II.) 2 vols. Toronto, 1886–88.

DENT, JOHN CHARLES. *The Canadian portrait gallery.* 4 vols. Toronto, 1880–81.

DESJARDINS, JOSEPH. *Guide parlementaire historique de la province de Québec, 1792 à 1902.* Québec, 1902.

Dictionary of American biography. Edited by Allen Johnson *et al.* 20 vols., index, and 2 supplements [to 1940]. New York, 1928–58; reprinted 22 vols. in 11 and index, [1946?–58]. 4 additional supplements [to 1960]. Edited by Edward Topping James *et al.* [1973–80.] *Concise DAB.* [1964.] 2nd edition. 1977. 3rd edition. 1980.

Dictionary of national biography. Edited by Leslie Stephen and Sidney Lee. 63 vols., 3 supplements, and index and epitome [to 1900]. London, 1885–1903. 6 additional supplements [to 1960]. Edited by Sidney Lee *et al.* 1912–71. *Concise DNB.* 2 vols. [1953]–61. *Corrections and additions to the "Dictionary of national biography."* Boston, 1966.

Dictionnaire des œuvres littéraires du Québec. Maurice Lemire *et al.*, éditeurs. 2 vols. parus [à 1939]. Montréal, 1978– .

DIRECTORIES. Issued initially as single works, these frequently became regular, usually annual, publications in the 19th century. Because titles within series varied greatly and editors or compilers frequently changed, the directories most often used in the preparation of volume XI have been listed below by region and under a general title, with the dates of the relevant years following. Details of various titles and publishers given on title pages, as well as of the places of publication of these directories, can be found in Ryder, *Checklist of Canadian directories.*

Canada directory, [1851–66]. Used in volume XI were *The Canada directory . . .*, ed. R. W. S. Mackay (Montreal, 1851); *The Canada directory for 1857–58 . . .* (Montreal, [1857]); *Mitchell & Co.'s Canada classified directory for 1865–66* (Toronto, [1865]); *Lovell's Canadian dominion directory for 1871 . . .* (Montreal, [1871]).

Halifax directory. Used in vol. XI were *Nugent's business directory of the city of Halifax for 1858–9* (Halifax, 1858); *The Halifax, N.S. business directory, for 1863 . . .*, comp. Luke Hutchinson (Halifax, 1863); *McAlpine's Halifax city directory . . .*, for 1869–70 to 1886–87.

Hamilton directory. Used in volume XI were *City of Hamilton directory . . .* (Hamilton, 1853; 1856; 1858); *Hutchinson's Hamilton directory for 1862–63 . . .* (Hamilton, 1862); *Sutherland & Co.'s Hamilton city directory for 1866* (Ingersoll, Ont., 1866); *Sutherland's city of Hamilton and county of Wentworth directory . . .* (Hamilton, 1867–68; 1868–69); *Sutherland's city of Hamilton directory . . .* (Hamilton, 1869; 1870); *City of Hamilton directory for 1871–2 . . .* (Hamilton, 1871); *Cherrier & Kirwin's Hamilton directory for 1872–73 . . .* (Montreal, [1872]); *McAlpine's Hamilton city and county of Wentworth directory, 1875 . . .* (Montreal, [1875]); *City of Hamilton annual alphabetical, general, street, miscellaneous and subscribers' classified business directory . . .* (Hamilton), from 1874 to 1889–90.

Montreal directory, [1842–43 to 1893–94]. Montreal. Edited by Robert Walter Stuart Mackay, 1842–54; Mrs R. W. S. Mackay, 1855–63; John Lovell, 1853–[93]. Title varies: *The Montreal directory . . .*, 1842–43 to 1855; *Mackay's Montreal directory . . .*, 1856–57 to

1867–68; *Montreal directory . . .* , 1868–69 to 1874–75; *Lovell's Montreal directory . . .* , 1875–76 to 1893–94.

Newfoundland directory. Used in volume XI were *Lovell's province of Newfoundland directory for 1871 . . .* (Montreal, 1871); *Business and general directory of Newfoundland, 1877 . . .* , compiled by John A. Rochfort (Montreal, 1877).

Nova Scotia directory. Used in Volume XI were *Hutchinson's Nova Scotia directory for 1864–65 . . .* (Halifax, [1864]); *Hutchinson's Nova Scotia directory for 1866–67 . . .* (Montreal, [1866]); *McAlpine's Nova Scotia directory for 1868–69 . . .* (Halifax, [1868]); *McAlpine's Nova Scotia directory for 1890–1897 . . .* (Halifax, [1890]); *Province of Nova Scotia directory for 1871 . . .* , comp. John Lovell (Montreal, [1871]).

Ottawa directory. Used in vol. XI were *"The Ottawa Citizen" directory of Ottawa, 1863 . . .* (Ottawa, 1863); *Ottawa city and counties of Carleton and Russell directory, 1866–67*, comp. James Sutherland (Ottawa, 1866); *Sutherland's city of Ottawa directory . . .* (Ottawa, 1868; 1869–70); *Hunter, Rose and Co.'s city of Ottawa directory . . . for 1870–71 . . .* , comp. W. H. Irwin (Ottawa, 1870); *Cherrier & Kirwin's Ottawa directory for 1872–73 . . .* (Montreal, 1872); *City of Ottawa alphabetical, general, miscellaneous and subscribers' classified business directory, August 1873 to August 1874 . . .* (Ottawa, 1873); *Ottawa directory for 1874–75 . . .* (Ottawa, 1874): *Ottawa directory, 1875, and dominion guide . . .* (Ottawa, 1875); *City of Ottawa and central Canada directory . . .* (Ottawa, 1876); *City of Ottawa . . . directory and dominion guide . . .* (Ottawa), from 1875 to 1884.

Quebec directory. Some of the directories used in vol. XI were *Quebec directory and strangers' guide to the city and environs, 1844–45*, comp. Alfred Hawkins (Quebec, 1844); *The Quebec directory, and city and commercial register, 1847–48*, comp. Alfred Hawkins (Montreal, 1847); *Mackay's Quebec directory for 1848–49 . . .* (Quebec, 1848; 1850; 1852); *Quebec business directory, compiled in June and July, 1854 . . .* , comp. Samuel McLaughlin (Quebec, 1854); *McLaughlin's Quebec directory . . .* (Quebec, 1855; 1857); *The Quebec directory for 1858–59 . . .* , comp. G. H. Cherrier and P. M. Hamelin (Quebec, 1858); *The Quebec directory . . .* (Quebec), for 1860–61 to 1889–90, first published by Georges-Hippolyte Cherrier* and then by A.-Benjamin Cherrier, with slightly varying titles.

Saint John directory. Used in vol. XI were *Hutchinson's St. John directory for 1863–64 . . .* (Saint John, N.B., 1863); *McAlpine's St. John directory . . .* (Saint John), for 1872–73 to 1887–88.

Toronto directory. Toronto. Used in vol. XI were *York commercial directory, street guide, and register, 1833–4 . . .* , comp. George Walton ([1833]); *The city of Toronto and the Home District commercial directory and register with almanack and calendar for 1837 . . .* , comp. George Walton ([1837]); *The Toronto directory, and street guide, for 1843–4*, comp. Francis Lewis (1843); *Brown's Toronto City and Home District directory, 1846–7 . . .* (1846); *Rowsell's city of Toronto and county of York directory, for 1850–1 . . .* , ed. J. Armstrong (1850); *Brown's Toronto general directory, 1856 . . .* ([1856]), also issued for 1861; *Caverhill's Toronto city directory, for 1859–60 . . .* , comp. W. C. F. Caverhill ([1859]); *Hutchinson's Toronto directory, 1862–63 . . .* , comp. Thomas Hutchinson ([1862]); *Mitchell's Toronto directory, for 1864–5 . . .* (1864); *City of Toronto illustrated business directory for 1865 . . .* (1865); *Mitchell & Co.'s general directory for the city of Toronto, and gazetteer of the counties of York and Peel, for 1866* (1866); *City of Toronto directory, for 1867–8 . . .* , comp. James Sutherland (1867); *W. C. Chewett & Co's Toronto city directory, 1868–9 . . .* (1868); *Robertson & Cook's Toronto city directory for 1870 . . .* , comp. W. H. Irwin and E. F. Owen (1870; 1871); *Toronto city directory, May, 1873 to May, 1874 . . .* , comp. W. H. Irwin (1873); *Fisher & Taylor's Toronto directory, for the year 1874 . . .* ([1874]); *Toronto directory . . .* , 1875 to 1882; *Toronto city directory . . .* , 1883 to 1890.

A directory of the members of the Legislative Assembly of Nova Scotia, 1758–1958. Introduction by Charles Bruce Fergusson. (PANS publications, Nova Scotia series, II.) Halifax, 1958.

The dominion annual register and review . . . [1878–86]. Edited by Henry James Morgan *et al.* 8 vols. Montreal, Ottawa, and Toronto, 1879–87.

Early Toronto newspapers, 1793–1867: a catalogue of newspapers published in the town of York and the city of Toronto from the beginning to confederation. Edited by Edith Grace Firth, with an introduction by Henry Cummings Campbell. Toronto, 1961.

Encyclopedia Canadiana. Edited by John Everett Robbins *et al.* 10 vols. Ottawa, [1957–58]. [Revised edition.] Edited by Kenneth H. Pearson *et al.* Toronto, [1975].

FAUTEUX, ÆGIDIUS. *Patriotes de 1837–1838*. Montréal, 1950.

GREAT BRITAIN, ADMIRALTY. *The navy list. . . .* London, 1846–86.

——— WAR OFFICE. *A list of the general and field officers as they rank in the army. . . .* [London, 1754–1868.]

——— *A list of the officers of the army and of the Corps of Royal Marines on full, retired, and half pay. . . .* London, 1849–64.

——— *The monthly army list.* London, 1798–1940. *See also* HART, HENRY GEORGE. *The new annual army list. . . .*

Guide des sources d'archives sur le Canada français, au Canada. (PAC publication.) Ottawa, 1975.

Guide to the reports of the Public Archives of Canada, 1872–1972. Compiled by Françoise Caron-Houle. (PAC publication.) Ottawa, 1975.

The Halifax, N.S. business directory. See DIRECTORIES

Hamilton directory. See DIRECTORIES

Handbook of North American Indians. General editor: William C. Sturtevant. 3 vols. to date. Washington, 1978– .

HARPER, JOHN RUSSELL. *Early painters and engravers in Canada.* [Toronto], 1970.

——— *Historical directory of New Brunswick newspapers and periodicals.* Fredericton, 1961.

HART, HENRY GEORGE. *The new annual army list. . . .* London, 1839–1916. The cover-title is *Hart's army list.*

Hutchinson's Nova Scotia directory. See DIRECTORIES

Hutchinson's St. John directory. See DIRECTORIES

[LANGELIER, JEAN-CHRYSOSTOME.] *List of lands granted by the crown in the province of Quebec from 1763 to 31st December 1890.* Quebec, 1891. Published in French as *Liste des terrains concédés par la couronne dans la province de Québec de 1763 au 31 décembre 1890.* 1891.

LE JEUNE, LOUIS[-MARIE]. *Dictionnaire général de biographie, histoire, littérature, agriculture, commerce, industrie et des arts, sciences, mœurs, coutumes, institutions politiques et religieuses du Canada.* 2 vols. Ottawa, [1931].

Lovell's Canadian dominion directory. See DIRECTORIES

Lovell's province of Newfoundland directory. See DIRECTORIES

LOWTHER, BARBARA JOAN [SONIA HORSFIELD], and MURIEL LAING. *A bibliography of British Columbia: laying the foundations, 1849–1899.* Victoria, 1968.

McAlpine's Halifax city directory. See DIRECTORIES

McAlpine's Nova Scotia directory. See DIRECTORIES

McAlpine's St. John city directory. See DIRECTORIES

MANITOBA LIBRARY ASSOCIATION. *Pioneers and early citizens of Manitoba: a dictionary of Manitoba biography from the earliest times to 1920.* [Compiled by Marjorie Morley *et al.*] Winnipeg, [1971].

Mitchell & Co.'s Canada classified directory. See DIRECTORIES

Montreal directory. See DIRECTORIES

Montreal pocket almanack. See ALMANACS

MORGAN, HENRY JAMES. *Bibliotheca Canadensis: or, a manual of Canadian literature.* Ottawa, 1867; reprinted Detroit, 1968.

——— *Sketches of celebrated Canadians, and persons connected with Canada, from the earliest period in the history of the province down to the present time.* Quebec and London, 1862; reprinted Montreal, 1865.

The national union catalog, pre-1956 imprints. . . . 710 vols. to date. London and Chicago, 1968– .

New-Brunswick almanac. See ALMANACS

New Brunswick history: a checklist of secondary sources/Guide en histoire du Noveau-Brunswick: une liste de contrôle des sources secondaires. Compiled by Hugh A. Taylor. (Publication of PANB.) Fredericton, 1971. *. . . first supplement.* Compiled by Eric L. Swanick. (N.B., Legislative Library publication.) Fredericton, 1974.

The new encyclopædia Britannica. Edited by Warren E. Preece *et al.* 15th edition. 30 vols. Chicago and Toronto, 1979.

Newfoundland directory. See DIRECTORIES

NOTMAN, WILLIAM, and [JOHN] FENNINGS TAYLOR. *Portraits of British Americans, with biographical sketches.* 3 vols. Montreal, 1865–68.

Nova Scotia directory. See DIRECTORIES

Nugent's business directory of the city of Halifax. See DIRECTORIES

Ottawa directory. See DIRECTORIES

Place-names and places of Nova Scotia. Introduction by Charles Bruce Fergusson. (PANS publications, Nova Scotia series, III.) Halifax, 1967; reprinted Belleville, Ont., 1976.

Political appointments and elections in the Province of Canada from 1841 to 1860. Compiled by Joseph-Olivier Coté. Quebec, 1860. *. . . from 1841 to 1865.* 2nd edition. Ottawa, 1866. *. . . and appendix from 1st January, 1866, to 30th June, 1867, and index,* edited by Narcisse-Omer Coté, Ottawa, 1918.

Political appointments, parliaments and the judicial bench in the dominion of Canada, 1867 to 1895. Edited by Narcisse-Omer Coté. Ottawa, 1896.

Quebec almanac. See ALMANACS

Quebec directory. See DIRECTORIES

READ, DAVID BREAKENRIDGE. *The lives of the judges of Upper Canada and Ontario, from 1791 to the present time.* Toronto, 1888.

Répertoire des parlementaires québécois, 1867–1978. André Lavoie *et al.*, compilateurs. Québec, 1980.

Roy, Pierre-Georges. *Les avocats de la région de Québec*. Lévis, Qué., 1936.

——— *Les juges de la province de Québec*. (ANQ publication.) Québec, 1933.

Ryder, Dorothy E. *Checklist of Canadian directories, 1790–1950/Répertoire des annuaires canadiens*. Ottawa, 1979.

Saint John directory. See Directories

A standard dictionary of Canadian biography: the Canadian who was who. Editors: Charles George Douglas Roberts and Arthur Leonard Tunnell. 2 vols. Toronto, 1934–38.

A statutory history of the steam and electric railways of Canada, 1836–1937, with other data relevant to operation of Department of Transport. Compiled by Robert Dorman. Ottawa, 1938.

Story, Norah. *The Oxford companion to Canadian history and literature*. Toronto, 1967. *Supplement*. . . . General editor: William Toye. Toronto, 1973.

Terrill, Frederick William. *A chronology of Montreal and of Canada from A.D. 1752 to A.D. 1893, including commercial statistics, historic sketches of commercial corporations and firms and advertisements, arranged to show in what year the several houses and corporate bodies originated; together with calendars of every year from A.D. 1752 to A.D. 1925*. Montreal, 1893.

Thériault, Michel. *The institutes of consecrated life in Canada from the beginning of New France up to the present: historical notes and references/Les instituts de vie consacrée au Canada depuis les débuts de la Nouvelle-France jusqu'à aujourd'hui: notes historiques et références*. Ottawa, 1980.

Toronto directory. See Directories

Turcotte, Gustave. *Le conseil législatif de Québec, 1774–1933*. Beauceville, Qué., 1933.

Union list of manuscripts in Canadian repositories/Catalogue collectif des manuscrits des archives canadiennes. Edited by Robert Stanyslaw Gordon *et al.* (PAC publication.) Ottawa, 1968. Revised edition. Edited by E. Grace Maurice Hyam. 2 vols. and 2 supplements. 1975–79.

Walbran, John Thomas. *British Columbia coast names, 1592–1906, to which are added a few names in adjacent United States territory: their origin and history*. . . . Ottawa, 1909; reprinted Vancouver, 1971; reprinted Seattle, Wash., and London, 1972.

Wallace, William Stewart. *The Macmillan dictionary of Canadian biography*. 4th edition. Edited by William Angus McKay. Toronto, [1978].

Watters, Reginald Eyre. *A checklist of Canadian literature and background materials, 1628–1960* . . . . 2nd edition. Toronto and Buffalo, N.Y., [1972].

IV: STUDIES (books and theses)

Abbott, Maude Elizabeth [Seymour]. *History of medicine in the province of Quebec*. Toronto, 1931; Montreal, 1931.

Atherton, William Henry. *Montreal, 1535–1914*. 3 vols. Montreal, 1914.

Audet, Louis-Philippe. *Histoire de l'enseignement au Québec*. . . . [1608–1971.] 2 vols. Montréal et Toronto, 1971.

——— *Le système scolaire de la province de Québec*. 6 vols. Québec, 1950–56.

Beck, James Murray. *The government of Nova Scotia*. (Canadian government series, 8.) Toronto, 1957.

Belisle, Alexandre. *Histoire de la presse franco-américaine; comprenant l'historique de l'émigration des Canadiens-français aux États-Unis, leur développement, et leurs progrès*. Worcester, Mass., 1911.

Bernard, Jean-Paul. *Les Rouges: libéralisme, nationalisme et anticléricalisme au milieu du XIXe siècle*. Montréal, 1971.

The book of Newfoundland. Edited by Joseph Roberts Smallwood. 6 vols. St John's, 1937–75.

Boon, Thomas Charles Boucher. *The Anglican Church from the Bay to the Rockies: a history of the ecclesiastical province of Rupert's Land and its dioceses from 1820 to 1950*. Toronto, 1962.

Campbell, Robert. *A history of the Scotch Presbyterian Church, St. Gabriel Street, Montreal*. Montreal, 1887.

Canada and its provinces: a history of the Canadian people and their institutions. Edited by Adam Shortt and Arthur George Doughty. 23 vols. Toronto, 1913–17.

Canada's smallest province: a history of P.E.I. Edited by Francis William Pius Bolger. [Charlottetown], 1973.

Careless, James Maurice Stockford. *Brown of "The Globe."* 2 vols. Toronto, 1959–63; reprinted 1972.

——— *The union of the Canadas: the growth of Canadian institutions, 1841–1857*. (Canadian centenary series, 10.) Toronto, 1967.

Chapais, Thomas. *Cours d'histoire du Canada*. 8 vols. Québec, 1919–34; Montréal, 1919–34; réimprimé Trois-Rivières, 1972.

Cornell, Paul Grant. *The alignment of political groups in Canada, 1841–1867*. (Canadian studies in history and government, 3.) Toronto, 1962.

Creighton, Donald [Grant]. *John A. Macdonald,*

the young politician. Toronto, 1952; reprinted 1965.

——— *John A. Macdonald, the old chieftain*. Toronto, 1955; reprinted 1965.

——— *The road to confederation; the emergence of Canada: 1863–1867*. Toronto, 1964.

CURRIE, ARCHIBALD WILLIAM. *The Grand Trunk Railway of Canada*. Toronto, 1957.

DAVID, LAURENT-OLIVIER. *Les Patriotes de 1837–1838*. Montréal, [1884]; réimprimé, [1937].

DENISON, MERRILL. *Canada's first bank: a history of the Bank of Montreal*. 2 vols. Toronto and Montreal, 1966–67. Translated into French by Paul A. Horguelin and Jean-Paul Vinay as *La première banque au Canada: histoire de la Banque de Montréal*. 2 vols. Toronto and Montreal, 1966–67.

DENT, JOHN CHARLES. *The last forty years: Canada since the union of 1841*. 2 vols. Toronto, 1881. An abridged edition, edited by Donald [Wayne] Swainson, was published at Toronto in 1972 as *The last forty years: the union of 1841 to confederation* (Carleton library, 62).

DÉSILETS, ANDRÉE. *Hector-Louis Langevin: un Père de la Confédération canadienne (1826–1906)*. (Université Laval, Institut d'histoire, Cahiers, 14.) Québec, 1969.

DEVINE, PATRICK K. *Ye olde St. John's, 1750–1936*. [St John's, 1936]; republished as *Ye olde St. John's, 1750–1939*. [St John's, 1939.]

GERVAIS, GAÉTAN. "L'expansion du réseau ferroviaire québécois (1875–1895)." Thèse de PHD, université d'Ottawa, 1978.

GUNN, GERTRUDE E. *The political history of Newfoundland, 1832–1864*. (Canadian studies in history and government, 7.) Toronto, 1966.

HAMELIN, JEAN, et YVES ROBY. *Histoire économique du Québec, 1851–1896*. (Histoire économique et sociale du Canada français.) Montréal, 1971.

HAMELIN, MARCEL. *Les premières années du parlementarisme québécois (1867–1878)*. (Université Laval, Institut d'histoire, Cahiers, 19.) Québec, 1974.

HANNAY, JAMES. *History of New Brunswick*. 2 vols. Saint John, N.B., 1909.

HARPER, JOHN RUSSELL. *Painting in Canada: a history*. [Toronto], 1966. 2nd edition. Toronto and Buffalo, N.Y., 1977. Translated as *La peinture au Canada des origines à nos jours*. [Québec], 1966.

HEAGERTY, JOHN JOSEPH. *Four centuries of medical history in Canada and a sketch of the medical history of Newfoundland*. 2 vols. Toronto, 1928.

History of Toronto and county of York, Ontario; containing an outline of the history of the dominion of Canada; a history of the city of Toronto and the county of York, with the townships, towns, villages, churches, schools; general and local statistics; biographical sketches, etc., etc. 2 vols. Toronto, 1885.

HODGETTS, JOHN EDWIN. *Pioneer public service: an administrative history of the united Canadas, 1841–1867*. (Canadian government series, 7.) Toronto, 1955.

LAREAU, EDMOND. *Histoire de la littérature canadienne*. Montréal, 1874.

MCKILLOP, ALEXANDER BRIAN. *A disciplined intelligence: critical inquiry and Canadian thought in the Victorian era*. Montreal, 1979.

MACKINNON, FRANK [FRANCIS PERLEY TAYLOR]. *The government of Prince Edward Island*. (Canadian government series, 5.) Toronto, 1951; reprinted 1974.

MACNUTT, WILLIAM STEWART. *New Brunswick, a history: 1784–1867*. Toronto, 1963.

MASTERS, DONALD CAMPBELL. *The rise of Toronto, 1850–1890*. Toronto, 1947.

MIDDLETON, JESSE EDGAR. *The municipality of Toronto: a history*. 3 vols. Toronto and New York, 1923.

MONET, JACQUES. *The last cannon shot: a study of French-Canadian nationalism, 1837–1850*. Toronto, 1969; reprinted Toronto and Buffalo, N.Y., 1976.

MONIÈRE, DENIS. *Le développement des idéologies au Québec: des origines à nos jours*. Montréal, 1977. Translated into English by Richard Howard as *Ideologies in Quebec: the historical development*. Toronto, 1981.

MORTON, WILLIAM LEWIS. *Manitoba: a history*. Toronto, 1957. 2nd edition. 1967.

ORMSBY, MARGARET ANCHORETTA. *British Columbia: a history*. [Toronto], 1958. [Revised edition.] 1971.

OUELLET, FERNAND. *Histoire économique et sociale du Québec, 1760–1850: structures et conjoncture*. (Histoire économique et sociale du Canada français.) Montréal et Paris, 1966; réimprimé en 2 vols. Montréal, 1971. Translated as *Economic and social history of Quebec, 1760–1850: "structures" and "conjonctures."* [Toronto], 1980.

Past and present of Prince Edward Island; embracing a concise review of its early settlement, development and present conditions, written by the most gifted authors of the province; to which is appended a compendium of life sketches of representative men and families of the island. Advisory editors, Donald Alexander MacKinnon and Alexander Bannerman Warburton. Charlottetown, [1906].

PROWSE, DANIEL WOODLEY. *A history of Newfoundland from the English, colonial, and foreign records*. London and New York, 1895. 2nd edition. London, 1896. 3rd edition. Edited by James Raymond Thoms and Frank Burnham Gill. St

John's, 1971. Reprint of 1895 edition. Belleville, Ont., 1972.

RICH, EDWIN ERNEST. *The history of the Hudson's Bay Company, 1670–1870.* (HBRS publications, XXI, XXII.) 2 vols. London, 1958–59. Another edition. 3 vols. Toronto, 1960. A copy of this work available at PAC contains notes and bibliographical material omitted from the printed version.

ROBERTSON, IAN ROSS. "Religion, politics and education in Prince Edward Island from 1856 to 1877." Unpublished MA thesis, McGill University, Montreal, 1968.

Robertson's landmarks of Toronto: a collection of historical sketches of the old town of York from 1792 until 1833, and of Toronto from 1834 to [1914]. Edited by John Ross Robertson. 6 series [6 vols.]. Toronto, 1894–1914; vols. I and III reprinted Belleville, Ont., 1976, 1974 respectively.

ROSS, VICTOR, and ARTHUR ST L. TRIGGE. *A history of the Canadian Bank of Commerce, with an account of the other banks which now form part of its organization.* 3 vols. Toronto, 1920–34.

ROY, JOSEPH-EDMOND. *Histoire du notariat au Canada depuis la fondation de la colonie jusqu'à nos jours.* 4 vols. Lévis, Qué., 1899–1902.

RUMILLY, ROBERT. *Histoire de la province de Québec.* 41 vols. parus. Montréal, [1940]– . 2e édition pour les vol. I à IX, s.d.; 3e édition pour les vol. I à VI, s.d.; réimpression en cours de la 1re édition, 13 vols. parus, Montréal, 1971– .

——— *Histoire de Montréal.* 5 vols. Montréal, 1970–74.

SACK, BENJAMIN G. *History of the Jews in Canada from the earliest beginnings to the present day.* [Translated by Ralph Novek.] Montreal, 1945. Only one volume published. [2nd edition] with title *History of the Jews in Canada.* [Edited by Maynard Gertler.] 1965.

SISSONS, CHARLES BRUCE. *Egerton Ryerson, his life and letters.* 2 vols. Toronto, 1937–47.

STANLEY, GEORGE FRANCIS GILMAN. *The birth of western Canada: a history of the Riel rebellions.* London and Toronto, 1936. [2nd edition.] [Toronto], 1960.

——— *Louis Riel.* Toronto, 1963.

SWAINSON, DONALD [WAYNE]. "The personnel of politics: a study of the Ontario members of the second federal parliament." Unpublished PHD thesis, University of Toronto, 1968.

SYLVAIN, PHILIPPE. "Libéralisme et ultramontanisme au Canada français: affrontement idéologique et doctrinal (1840–1865)," *The shield of Achilles: aspects of Canada in the Victorian age.* Edited by William Lewis Morton. Toronto and Montreal, 1968, 111–38, 220–55.

THOMSON, DALE C. *Alexander Mackenzie, Clear Grit.* Toronto, 1960.

Les travailleurs québécois, 1851–1896. Jean Hamelin, éditeur. (Collection Histoire des travailleurs québécois, 2.) Montréal, 1973. 2e édition. 1975.

TULCHINSKY, GERALD J. J. *The river barons: Montreal businessmen and the growth of industry and transportation, 1837–53.* Toronto and Buffalo, N.Y., 1977.

TURCOTTE, LOUIS-PHILIPPE. *Le Canada sous l'Union, 1841–1867.* 2 vols. Québec, 1871–72. 2e édition. 1882.

WAITE, PETER BUSBY. *Canada, 1874–1896: arduous destiny.* (Canadian centenary series, 13.) Toronto and Montreal, 1971.

——— *The life and times of confederation, 1864–1867: politics, newspapers, and the union of British North America.* [Toronto], 1962. 2nd edition, with corrections. 1962.

WALLACE, WILLIAM STEWART. *A history of the University of Toronto, 1827–1927.* Toronto, 1927.

WELLS, ELIZABETH A. "The struggle for responsible government in Newfoundland, 1846–1855." Unpublished MA thesis, Memorial University of Newfoundland, St John's, 1966.

ZASLOW, MORRIS. *Reading the rocks: the story of the Geological Survey of Canada, 1842–1972.* Toronto and Ottawa, 1975.

V: JOURNALS AND STUDIES (ARTICLES)

Acadiensis: Journal of the History of the Atlantic Region/Revue de l'histoire de la région atlantique. Fredericton. Published by the Department of History of the University of New Brunswick. 1 (1971–72)– .

BC Studies. Vancouver. 1 (winter 1968–69)– .

Beaver: a Magazine of the North. Winnipeg. Published by the HBC. 1 (1920–21)– . *Index*: 1 (1920–21)–outfit 284 (June 1952–March 1954).

British Columbia Historical Quarterly. Victoria. Published by the PABC in cooperation with the British Columbia Historical Association. 1 (1937)–21 (1957–58).

Le Bulletin des recherches historiques. Published usually in Lévis, Que. Originally the organ of the Société des études historiques, it became in March 1923 the journal of the Archives de la province de Québec (now the ANQ). 1 (1895)–70 (1968).

Index: 1 (1895)–31 (1925) (4v., Beauceville, Qué., 1925–26). For subsequent years there is an index on microfiche at the ANQ-Q.

Les Cahiers des Dix. Montréal et Québec. Published by "Les Dix." 1 (1936)– .

Canada Law Journal. Toronto. 1 (1855)–10 (1864); new series, 1 (1865)–58 (1922). Title varies: 1 (1855)–new series, 3 (1876), have the title *Upper Canada Law Journal*.

Canadian Banker. Toronto and Montreal. 1 (1893–94)– . Title varies: *Journal of the Canadian Bankers' Association*, 1 (1893–94)–43 (1935–36); *Canadian Banker*, 44 (1936–37)–80 (1973); *Canadian Banker & ICB Review*, 81 (1974)– . *Index*: 1 (1893–94)–30 (1922–23); 31 (1923–24)–71 (1964); 72 (1965)–78 (1971).

CANADIAN CATHOLIC HISTORICAL ASSOCIATION/SOCIÉTÉ CANADIENNE D'HISTOIRE DE L'ÉGLISE CATHOLIQUE, Ottawa. Publishes simultaneously a *Report* in English and a *Rapport* in French, of which the contents are entirely different. 1 (1933–34)– . *Index*: 1 (1933–34)–25 (1958). Title varies: *Study Sessions/Sessions d'étude* from 1966.

CANADIAN HISTORICAL ASSOCIATION/SOCIÉTÉ HISTORIQUE DU CANADA, Ottawa. *Annual Report*. 1922– . *Index*: 1922–51; 1952–68. Title varies: *Historical Papers/Communications historiques* from 1966.

Canadian Historical Review. Toronto. 1 (1920)– . *Index*: 1 (1920)–10 (1929); 11 (1930)–20 (1939); 21 (1940)–30 (1949); 31 (1950)–51 (1970). The Université Laval has also published an index: *Canadian Historical Review, 1950–1964: index des articles et des comptes rendus de volumes*, René Hardy, compil. (Québec, 1969). A continuation of the *Review of Historical Publications relating to Canada*: 1 (1895–96)–22 (1917–18); *Index*: 1 (1895–96)–10 (1905); 11 (1906)–20 (1915).

Canadian Journal. Toronto. Publication of the Canadian Institute which became the Royal Canadian Institute in 1914. Began as the *Canadian Journal: a Repertory of Industry, Science and Art; and a Record of the Proceedings of the Canadian Institute*, 1 (1852–53)–3 (1854–55). Title was modified to the *Canadian Journal of Industry, Science and Art*, new series, 1 (1856)–11 (1866–67), and to the *Canadian Journal of Science, Literature and History*, new series, 12 (1868–70)–15 (1876–78). Superseded by the *Proceedings of the Canadian Institute, Toronto, being a Continuation of "The Canadian Journal of Science, Literature and History*," third series, 1 (1879–83)–7 (1888–89). Merged for a few years with the Canadian Institute, *Transactions*, then published irregularly for a time as Canadian Institute, *Proceedings*, new series, 1 (1895–98). Published as Royal Canadian Institute, *Proceedings*, third series or series IIIa, 1 (1935–36)–

Canadian Methodist Magazine. Toronto and Halifax. 1 (January–June 1875)–64 (July–December 1906). Title varies: 1 (January–June 1875)–28 (July–December 1888), *Canadian Methodist Magazine*; 29 (January–June 1889)–42 (July–December 1895), *Methodist Magazine*; 43 (January–June 1896)–64 (July–December 1906), *Methodist Magazine and Review*.

Canadian Naturalist and Geologist. Montreal. See *Canadian Naturalist and Quarterly Journal of Science*

Canadian Naturalist and Quarterly Journal of Science. Montreal. 1 (1856–57)–8 (1863); new series, 1 (1864)–10 (1883). Vols. 1 (1856–57)–new series, 3 (1866–68), have the title *Canadian Naturalist and Geologist*. Continued by *Canadian Record of Science*.

Dalhousie Review. Halifax. Published by Dalhousie University. 1 (1921–22)– .

Historic Kingston. Kingston, Ont. Published by the Kingston Historical Society. 1 (1952)– .

HISTORICAL AND SCIENTIFIC SOCIETY OF MANITOBA, Winnipeg. This society has had numerous publications. These include *Report*, 1 (1880)–27 (1906); several series known as *Transactions*, 1 (October 1882)–72 (November 1906); new series, 1 (November 1924)–5 (July 1930); 3rd series, 1 (1944–45)–35 (1978–79) (the title of these transactions varies: *Publication*, 1–2, 4–6; *Transactions*, 3, 7–72; new series; *Papers*, 3rd series); *Manitoba History*, 1 (1946–49); *Manitoba Pageant*, 1 (1956)–24 (1978–79); and *Manitoba History*, 1 (1980)– .

Journal of Canadian Studies/Revue d'études canadiennes. Peterborough, Ont. Published by Trent University. 1 (1966)– .

Literary and Historical Society of Quebec/Société littéraire et historique de Québec, Québec. *Transactions*. [1st series], 1 (1824–29)–5 (1861–62); new series, 1 (1862–63)–30 (1924).

Methodist Magazine. Toronto. See *Canadian Methodist Magazine*

NOVA SCOTIA HISTORICAL SOCIETY, Halifax. *Collections*. 1 (1878)– . An index for 1 (1878)–32 (1959) is in 33 (1961).

Ontario History. Toronto. Published by the Ontario Historical Society. 1 (1899)– . An index to volumes 1 (1899) to 64 (1972) appears in *Index to the publications of the Ontario Historical Society, 1899–1972* (1974). Title varies: *Papers and Records* to 1946.

Queen's Quarterly. Kingston, Ont. Published by Queen's University. 1 (1893–94)– . *Index*: 1 (1893–94)–60 (1953); 61 (1954)–75 (1968).

Revue canadienne. Montréal. 1 (1864)–53 (1907);

nouvelle série, 1 (1908)–27 (1922). Volumes 17 (1881)–23 (1887) are also called nouvelle série, v.1–7; vols.24 (1888)–28 (1892) also called 3e série, v.1–[5]. *Index*: 1 (1864)–53 (1907).

Revue d'histoire de l'Amérique française. Montréal. Published by the Institut d'histoire de l'Amérique française. 1 (1947–48)– . Index: 1 (1947–48)–10 (1956–57); 11 (1957–58)–20 (1966–67); 21 (1967–68)–30 (1976–77).

ROYAL SOCIETY OF CANADA/SOCIÉTÉ ROYALE DU CANADA, Ottawa. *Proceedings and Transactions/Mémoires et comptes rendus*. 1st series, 1 (1882–83)–12 (1894); 2nd series, 1 (1895)–12 (1906); 3rd series, 1 (1907)–56 (1962); 4th series, 1 (1963)– . *General index*: 1st series-2nd series; *Subject index*: 3rd series, 1 (1907)–31 (1937); *Author index*: 3rd series, 1 (1907)–35 (1941); *Index*: 1st series –3rd series, 37 (1943).

SHORTT, ADAM. "The history of Canadian currency, banking and exchange," Canadian Bankers' Association, *Journal*, 7 (1899–1900): 209–26, 311–32; 8 (1900–1): 1–15, 145–64, 227–43, 305–26; 9 (1901–2): 1–21, 101–21, 183–202, 271–89; 10 (1902–3), no.1: 21–40; no.2: 25–45, no.3: 11–28; no.4: 12–29; 11 (1903–4): 13–20, 106–23, 199–218, 308–27; 12 (1904–5): 14–35, 193–216, 265–82; 13 (1905–6): 11–28, 95–115, 184–208, 272–88; 14 (1906–7): 7–27.

Social History, a Canadian Review/Histoire sociale, revue canadienne. Ottawa. 1 (April 1968)– .

CONTRIBUTORS

Contributors

ALLODI, MARY. Assistant curator, Canadiana Department, Royal Ontario Museum, Toronto, Ontario.
Adolphus Bourne.

ANDREAE, CHRISTOPHER. Historian, Parkhill, Ontario.
Walter M. Buck.

ANDREWS, C. W. Professor of biology, Memorial University of Newfoundland, St John's, Newfoundland.
Nathan Norman. Edward White. [Biographies written in collaboration with G. M. Story.]

ANGUS, MARGARET SHARP. Writer, Kingston, Ontario.
John Robinson Dickson. Harriet Dobbs (Cartwright). Horatio Yates.

ARMOUR, CHARLES A. University archivist, Dalhousie University, Halifax, Nova Scotia.
Colin Campbell. William Dawson Lawrence. Bennett Smith.

ARMSTRONG, FREDERICK H. Associate professor of history, University of Western Ontario, London, Ontario.
Joseph-Olivier Coté. Thomas Cramp. Frederic William Cumberland [in collaboration with P. Baskerville]. *James Dougall. Edward Gurney. Alexander Harvey. William Hay. Peter Paterson*.

ARTHUR, ELIZABETH. Professor of history, Lakehead University, Thunder Bay, Ontario.
Amos Wright.

†AUDET, LOUIS-PHILIPPE. Professeur à la retraite, Sillery, Québec.
Louis Giard.

BAILEY, ALFRED G. Professor emeritus of history, University of New Brunswick, Fredericton, New Brunswick.
John Babbitt.

BAKER, MELVIN. Graduate student in history, University of Western Ontario, London, Ontario.
Robert Alexander. Thomas Howley. John Stuart. John Henry Warren.

BAKER, WILLIAM M. Associate professor of history, University of Lethbridge, Alberta.
Isaac Burpee.

BALF, MARY. Formerly curator and archivist, Kamloops Museum, British Columbia.
Allan McLean.

BALL, NORMAN R. Archivist, Public Archives of Canada, Ottawa, Ontario.
Joseph Van Norman. James Miller Williams [in collaboration with E. Phelps].

BALLSTADT, CARL P. A. Associate professor of English, McMaster University, Hamilton, Ontario.
Susanna Strickland (Moodie).

BARKLEY, MURRAY. Research associate, Massey Project, Avonmore, Ontario.
William Richard Mulharen Burtis. William Elder. John Fennings Taylor.

BASKERVILLE, PETER. Assistant professor of history, University of Victoria, British Columbia.
Frederick Chase Capreol. Robert Cassels. Frederic William Cumberland [in collaboration with F. H. Armstrong]. *John Hamilton*.

BEATTY, LINDA BELSHAW. Art consultant, Royal Bank Plaza, Toronto, Ontario.
Robert Whale.

BECK, J. MURRAY. Formerly professor of political science, Dalhousie University, Halifax, Nova Scotia.
Thomas Fletcher Morrison. George Murray. Sir William Young.

BÉLANGER, NOËL. Professeur d'histoire, Université du Québec à Rimouski, Québec.
James Smith.

BELL, MICHAEL. Assistant director, National Gallery of Canada, Ottawa, Ontario.
William Sawyer.

BELLAVANCE, MARCEL. Chef adjoint, Histoire et Archéologie, Parcs Canada, Québec, Québec.
Charles-Félix Cazeau [in collaboration with P. Dufour].

BENSLEY, EDWARD HORTON. Honorary lecturer in the history of medicine; honorary Osler librarian, McGill University, Montreal, Quebec.
Robert Palmer Howard.

BERNARD, JEAN-PAUL. Professeur d'histoire, Université du Québec à Montréal, Québec.
Maurice Laframboise.

BERNIER, JACQUES. Professeur assistant d'histoire, Université Laval, Québec, Québec.
Pierre Beaubien.

BERTON, PIERRE. Writer, Kleinburg, Ontario.
Albert Bowman Rogers.

BILAS, IRENE. Library assistant, University of Calgary Library, Alberta.
Pierre-Étienne Fortin.

BINDON, KATHRYN M. Assistant professor of history, Concordia University, Montreal, Quebec.
Adam Thom.

BIRRELL, A. J. Chief, Acquisition and Research Section, National Photography Collection, Public Archives of Canada, Ottawa, Ontario.
David Isaac Kirwin Rine.

BLAKELEY, PHYLLIS R. Associate provincial archivist, Public Archives of Nova Scotia, Halifax, Nova Scotia.
William Alexander Henry. Anna Haining Swan (Bates).

BLAKEY SMITH, DOROTHY. Formerly archivist, Provincial Archives of British Columbia, Victoria, British Columbia.
Thomas Elwyn.

BLANCHARD, FRANCIS-C. Coordonnateur de français, Charlottetown, Île-du-Prince-Édouard.
Sylvain-Éphrem Perrey.

BLISS, MICHAEL. Professor of history, University of Toronto, Ontario.
John Harris. John Macdonald.

BOIVIN, AURÉLIEN. Professionnel de recherche, *Dictionnaire des œuvres littéraires du Québec*, Université Laval, Québec, Québec.
Paul Stevens. Norbert Thibault, called *Brother Oliver Julian*.

BOND, COURTNEY C. J. Ottawa, Ontario.
George Hugo Perry.

†BONENFANT, JEAN-CHARLES. Professeur de droit, Université Laval, Québec, Québec.
Thomas-Jean-Jacques Loranger. Thomas Kennedy Ramsay.

BOUCHARD, ANTOINE. Professeur de musique, Université Laval, Québec, Québec.
Célestin Lavigueur.

BOUCHARD, GÉRARD. Professeur, Département des sciences humaines, Université du Québec à Chicoutimi, Québec.
Dominique Racine.

BOUCHER, RÉAL. Enseignant, Centre d'études universitaires dans l'Ouest québécois, Rouyn, Québec.
Hilaire Millier.

BOUFFARD, LUCIE. Service des relations publiques, Université Laval, Québec, Québec.
Joseph Laurin [in collaboration with R. Tremblay].

BOVEY, JOHN A. Provincial archivist, Provincial Archives of British Columbia, Victoria, British Columbia.
Louis Frasse de Plainval.

BOWSFIELD, HARTWELL. Associate professor of history, York University, Downsview, Ontario.
John Black. John Allan Snow. Aquila Walsh.

†BREDIN, THOMAS F. Vice-principal, St John's–Ravenscourt School, Winnipeg, Manitoba.
Henry Septimus Beddome.

BROCK, DANIEL JAMES. Teacher of history, London and Middlesex County Roman Catholic Separate School Board, London, Ontario.
Alexander Henderson. Lawrence Lawrason.

†BRODIE, ALEXANDER H. Professor of English, University of Guelph, Ontario.
George Frederick Cameron.

BROWN, JENNIFER S. H. Adjunct assistant professor of anthropology, Northern Illinois University, DeKalb, Illinois, U.S.A.
George Barnston [in collaboration with S. M. Van Kirk]. *William Lucas Hardisty*.

BUGGEY, SUSAN. Head, Construction History, Research Division, Parks Canada, Ottawa, Ontario.
Henry George Hill. George Lang. David Stirling [in collaboration with G. D. Shutlak].

BURLEY, DAVID G. Graduate student in history, McMaster University, Hamilton, Ontario.
John Gordon. Calvin McQuesten. Dennis Moore.

BURNSIDE, ALBERT. United Church senior minister, Edith Rankin Memorial Church, Kingston, Ontario.
John Hicks Eynon.

BURROUGHS, PETER. Professor of history, Dalhousie University, Halifax, Nova Scotia.
Lucius Bentinck Cary. Sir Richard Graves MacDonnell. George Augustus Constantine Phipps.

CAISSIE, FRANCES. Agent de recherche, Assemblée nationale du Québec, Québec.
Joseph-Godric Blanchet.

CALNAN, DAVID M. Assistant to the clerk, Regional Municipality of York, Newmarket, Ontario.
Henry Corby.

CARELESS, J. M. S. Professor of history, University of Toronto, Ontario.
James Lesslie.

CARRIÈRE, GASTON, O.M.I. Archiviste, Archives historiques oblates, Ottawa, Ontario.
Pierre Aubert. Jean-François-Régis Déléage. Joseph-Henri Tabaret.

CAYA, MARCEL. Directeur, Service des archives, McGill University, Montréal, Québec.
Sévère Rivard.

CHABOT, RICHARD. Assistant-professeur d'histoire, Université du Québec à Montréal, Québec.
Romuald Trudeau.

CHARD, DONALD F. Historic park planner, Parks Canada, Dartmouth, Nova Scotia.
Silvanus Morton.

CHOQUETTE, J. E. ROBERT. Professeur agrégé de sciences religieuses, Université d'Ottawa, Ontario.
Pierre-Adolphe Pinsoneault.

CLARK, LOVELL C. Professor of history, University of Manitoba, Winnipeg, Manitoba.
Henry Joseph Clarke.

COFFIN, MARJORIE L. HYNDMAN. Teacher, Charlottetown, Prince Edward Island.
Joseph Wightman.

COLEMAN, MARGARET. Ottawa, Ontario.
Andrew Russell.

COLLARD, EDGAR ANDREW. Editor emeritus of the Montreal *Gazette*, Ottawa, Ontario.
William Turnbull Leach.

COLLARD, ELIZABETH. Writer and museum consultant, Ottawa, Ontario.
George Armstrong. Allan Aaron Edson. George Whitefield Farrar. Azarie Lavigne. Edward C. Macdonald.

COMEAU, LOUIS R. Ex-recteur, Université Sainte-Anne, Church Point, Nouvelle-Écosse.
Simon d'Entremont.

CORBEIL, PIERRE. Professeur d'histoire, Collège de Drummondville, Québec.
Christopher Dunkin.

CORNELL, PAUL G. Professor of history, University of Waterloo, Ontario.
William Cayley.

CRAIG, G. M. Professor of history, University of Toronto, Ontario.
Michael Barrett. Henry Holmes Croft. John McCaul.

CREIGHTON, PHYLLIS. Translations editor, *Dictionary of Canadian biography/Dictionnaire biographique du Canada*, University of Toronto Press, Ontario.
Sir Bryan Robinson.

CROSS, D. SUZANNE. Teacher, Vanier College, Montreal, Quebec.
Joseph Mackay. Andrew Robertson.

DANIELLS, LAURENDA. University archivist, University of British Columbia, Vancouver, British Columbia.
Sally Ross.

DAVIS, DAVID J. Provincial archivist, Provincial Archives of Newfoundland and Labrador, St John's, Newfoundland.
James William Tobin.

DECHÊNE, LOUISE. Professeur d'histoire, McGill University, Montréal, Québec.
Christian Henry Pozer.

DE JONG, NICOLAS J. Provincial archivist, Public Archives of Prince Edward Island, Charlottetown, Prince Edward Island.
John MacKintosh.

DEMPSEY, HUGH A. Chief curator, Glenbow-Alberta Institute, Calgary, Alberta.
Isapo-muxika. Pītikwahanapiwīyin.

DEROME, ROBERT. Professeur d'histoire de l'art, Université du Québec à Montréal, Québec.
Pierre Lespérance [in collaboration with S. Normand].

DÉSILETS, ANDRÉE. Professeur d'histoire, Université de Sherbrooke, Québec.
Auguste Achintre. Joseph-Édouard Cauchon. Jean-Charles Chapais. Marie Fisbach, named *Marie du Sacré-Cœur (Roy). Joseph-Alfred Mousseau. Louis-Victor Sicotte. William Hoste Webb.*

DESJARDINS, ÉDOUARD, M.D. Rédacteur émérite, *L'Union médicale du Canada,* Montréal, Québec.
Joseph Emery-Coderre.

DEVER, ALAN R. Graduate student in history, McGill University, Montréal, Québec.
Thomas Ryan [in collaboration with G. J. J. Tulchinsky].

DOUGALL, CHARLES. Supervisory editor, *Dictionary of Canadian biography/Dictionnaire biographique du Canada,* University of Toronto Press, Ontario.
George Ryerson.

DOYON, CHARLES. Graduate student in history, York University, Downsview, Ontario.
Dugald Lorn MacDougall.

DROUIN, E. O., O.M.I. Archiviste, Archives oblates, Edmonton, Alberta.
Léon-Adélard Fafard. Henri Faraud.

DUCHESNE, RAYMOND. Étudiant gradué, Institut d'histoire et de sociopolitique des sciences, Université de Montréal, Québec.
François-Xavier Bélanger. George John Bowles.

DUFOUR, PIERRE. Historien, Parcs Canada, Québec, Québec.
Charles-Félix Cazeau [in collaboration with M. Bellavance]. *Édouard-Louis Pacaud. Philippe-Napoléon Pacaud.* [Biographies written in collaboration with G. Goyer.]

DUNLOP, ALLAN C. Senior research assistant, Public Archives of Nova Scotia, Halifax, Nova Scotia.
John Barnhill Dickie. James Ross.

DYSTER, BARRIE. Lecturer in history, University of New South Wales, Kensington, New South Wales, Australia.
Robert Dick.

EADIE, JAMES A. Head, Department of History, Napanee District Secondary School, Napanee, Ontario.
Edmund John Glyn Hooper. John Stevenson.

EAGAN, WILLIAM E. Associate professor of history, Moorhead State University, Minnesota, U.S.A.
Robert Barlow.

EAKINS, P. R. Associate professor of geological sciences, McGill University, Montréal, Québec.
Henry George Vennor.

EASTWOOD, T. M. Archivist, Provincial Archives of British Columbia, Victoria, British Columbia.
Alexander Rocke Robertson [in collaboration with P. Williamson]. *William Smithe.*

EDDY, BARBARA J. Education librarian, Memorial University of Newfoundland, St John's, Newfoundland.
Michael John Kelly.

EDWARDS, MURRAY D. Adjunct professor of theatre; coordinator of extension programmes in fine arts, University of Victoria, British Columbia.
Sarah Holman (Dalton) [in collaboration with F. R. Hines].

EID, NADIA F. Professeur d'histoire, Université du Québec à Montréal, Québec.
François-Xavier-Anselme Trudel.

ELLIOTT, SHIRLEY B. Legislative librarian, Legislative Library, Halifax, Nova Scotia.
Duncan Campbell. Angus Morrison Gidney.

EMERY, G. N. Associate professor of history, University of Western Ontario, London, Ontario.
Adam Oliver. John Æthuruld Williams.

EVANS, A. MARGARET. Formerly professor and chairman, Department of History, University of Guelph, Ontario.
Sir Matthew Crooks Cameron. Peter Gow.

EVANS, CALVIN D. Assistant librarian, University of Alberta, Edmonton, Alberta.
Charles R. Bowring. Smith McKay.

FALARDEAU, JEAN-CHARLES. Professeur titulaire de sociologie, Université Laval, Québec, Québec.
Antoine Gérin-Lajoie.

FARR, DAVID M. L. Professor of history; director of the Paterson Centre for International Programs, Carleton University, Ottawa, Ontario.
Sir John Rose.

†FERGUSSON, CHARLES BRUCE. Archivist, Public Archives of Nova Scotia, Halifax, Nova Scotia; associate professor of history, Dalhousie University, Halifax, Nova Scotia.
Thomas Dickson Archibald.

FERRON, MADELEINE. Écrivain, Outremont, Québec.
Henri-Jules Juchereau Duchesnay.

FILTEAU, HÉLÈNE. Auxiliaire de recherche, *Dictionnaire biographique du Canada/Dictionary of Canadian biography,* Les Presses de l'université Laval, Québec, Québec.
Louis-Adélard Senécal [in collaboration with J. Hamelin and J. Keyes].

FILTEAU, HUGUETTE. Codirectrice de la rédaction, *Dictionnaire biographique du Canada/Dictionary of Canadian biography,* Les Presses de l'université Laval, Québec, Québec.
Guillaume-Eugène Chinic [in collaboration with J. Hamelin]. *Félix-Emmanuel Juneau.*

FINGARD, JUDITH. Professor of history, Dalhousie University, Halifax, Nova Scotia.
Silas Tertius Rand.

FIRTH, EDITH G. Head, Canadian History Department, Metropolitan Toronto Library, Ontario.
John George Howard.

FLEMMING, DAVID B. Project historian, Parks Canada, Halifax, Nova Scotia.
Michael Hannan. Patrick Power.

FRENCH, G. S. President, Victoria University, Toronto, Ontario.
Samuel Sobieski Nelles. Pahtahsega. Humphrey Pickard. Matthew Richey.

FRIESEN, GERALD. Associate professor of history, University of Manitoba, Winnipeg, Manitoba.
John Norquay.

FRIESEN, JEAN. Associate professor of history, University of Manitoba, Winnipeg, Manitoba.
Alexander Morris.

GAGAN, DAVID. Professor of history, McMaster University, Hamilton, Ontario.
William Alexander Foster.

GAGNON, JEAN-PIERRE. Historien, Service historique, Ministère de la Défense nationale, Ottawa, Ontario.
Félix Poutré [in collaboration with K. Landry].

GAGNON, SERGE. Professeur d'histoire, Université du Québec à Trois-Rivières, Québec.
Napoléon Aubin. Edmond Lareau. Nazaire Leclerc. François Pilote.

GALARNEAU, CLAUDE. Professeur titulaire d'histoire, Université Laval, Québec, Québec.
Angus McDonald.

GALLACHER, DANIEL T. Curator of modern history, British Columbia Provincial Museum, Victoria, British Columbia.
Robert Dunsmuir. John Muir.

GARON, GÉRALD. Professeur d'histoire, Collège d'enseignement général et professionnel de Rimouski, Québec.
Edmond Langevin.

GATES, LILLIAN F. Ithaca, New York, U.S.A.
James Hervey Price.

GERVAIS, GAÉTAN. Professeur adjoint d'histoire, Université Laurentienne, Sudbury, Ontario.
Ashley Hibbard. Louis-Napoléon Larochelle.

GETTY, IAN A. L. Executive director, Nakota Institute, Stoney Indian Tribe, Morley, Alberta.
George Verey [in collaboration with A. W. Rasporich].

GIBBS, ELIZABETH. Teacher of history, Dawson College, Westmount, Quebec.
William Badgley.

GIBSON, LEE. Free-lance researcher, Winnipeg, Manitoba.
James Andrews Miller.

GIDNEY, R. D. Associate professor of history and comparative education, University of Western Ontario, London, Ontario.
Egerton Ryerson. George Paxton Young.

GIGUÈRE, GEORGES-ÉMILE. Historien, Montréal, Québec.
Félix Martin.

GILLETT, MARGARET. Professor of education, McGill University, Montreal, Quebec.
William Lunn.

GILLIS, ROBERT PETER. Chief, Manpower and social development records, Federal Archives Division, Public Archives of Canada, Ottawa, Ontario.
Henry Franklin Bronson. John Hamilton. James Little. William Goodhue Perley. James Skead [in collaboration with S. Gillis].

GILLIS, SANDRA. Senior planner, Cultural Resources, Agreements for Recreation and Conservation Branch, Parks Canada, Ottawa, Ontario.
Horace Merrill. James Skead [in collaboration with R. P. Gillis].

GODFREY, CHARLES M. Professor of rehabilitative medicine, University of Toronto, Ontario.
Theophilus Mack.

GOOD, E. REGINALD. Student in history and German, University of Waterloo, Ontario.
Anna Weber.

GORDON, STANLEY. Doctoral candidate in history, University of Alberta, Edmonton, Alberta.
Lawrence Clarke.

GOYER, GÉRARD. Rédacteur-historien principal, *Dictionnaire biographique du Canada/Dictionary of Canadian biography*, Les Presses de l'université Laval, Québec, Québec.
Édouard-Louis Pacaud. Philippe-Napoléon Pacaud. [Biographies written in collaboration with P. Dufour.]

GRANT, JOHN N. Research associate, Atlantic Institute of Education, Halifax, Nova Scotia.
Henry William Smith.

GRANT, JOHN WEBSTER. Professor of church history, Victoria University, Toronto, Ontario.
John Saltkill Carroll.

GREENFIELD, KATHARINE. Head, Special Collections, Hamilton Public Library, Ontario.
Harriett Annie Wilkins.

GREENLAND, CYRIL. Professor of social work and associate professor of psychiatry, McMaster University, Hamilton, Ontario.
William George Metcalf.

GRESKO, JACQUELINE. Instructor in history, Douglas College, New Westminster, British Columbia.
Louis-Joseph d'Herbomez.

GUNDY, H. PEARSON. Professor emeritus of English language and literature, Queen's University, Kingston, Ontario.
John Creighton. Henry Rowsell.

HALLERAN, MICHAEL F. H. Archival consultant, Victoria, British Columbia.
Thomas Basil Humphreys.

HAMELIN, JEAN. Directeur général adjoint, *Dictionnaire biographique du Canada/Dictionary of Canadian biography*, Les Presses de l'université Laval; professeur d'histoire, Université Laval, Québec, Québec.
Pierre-Joseph-Olivier Chauveau [in collaboration with P. Poulin]. *Guillaume-Eugène Chinic* [in collaboration with Huguette Filteau]. *Jean-Baptiste Renaud* [in collaboration]. *Louis-Adélard Senécal* [in collaboration with Hélène Filteau and J. Keyes]. *François Vézina* [in collaboration].

HAMILTON, WILLIAM B. Director, Atlantic Institute of Education, Halifax, Nova Scotia.
William Lyall.

HANN, RUSSELL G. Graduate student in history, Toronto, Ontario.
James A. Fahey.

HANRAHAN, JAMES, C.S.B. Superior general, Basilian fathers, Toronto, Ontario.
Charles Vincent.

HARDY, RENÉ. Professeur d'histoire, Université du Québec à Trois-Rivières, Québec.
Joseph Auclair. Gualbert Gervais. Pierre-Auguste Leroy.

HARPER, J. RUSSELL. Formerly professor of fine arts, Concordia University, Montreal, Quebec.
William George Richardson Hind. Henri Perré.

HARRIS, LESLIE. Vice-president (academic), Memorial University of Newfoundland, St John's, Newfoundland.
Sir Edward Mortimer Archibald. Robert John Parsons.

HARRIS, ROBIN S. Professor of higher education, University of Toronto, Ontario.
Amelia Ryerse (Harris).

HARVEY, FERNAND. Chercheur, Institut québécois de recherche sur la culture, Québec, Québec.
James Sherrard Armstrong.

HAWORTH, KENT M. Archivist, Provincial Archives of British Columbia, Victoria, British Columbia.
Sir Anthony Musgrave.

HAYNE, DAVID M. Professor of French, University of Toronto, Ontario.
Frédéric Houde.

HEADON, CHRISTOPHER FERGUS. Historian, Toronto, Ontario.
George Whitaker.

HENDRICKSON, JAMES E. Associate professor of history, University of Victoria, British Columbia.
Sir William Alexander George Young.

HILLER, JAMES K. Associate professor of history, Memorial University of Newfoundland, St John's, Newfoundland.
Charles James Fox Bennett. John Joseph Dearin. Thomas Glen. Walter Grieve. Edward Morris.

HINES, FRANCES R. Voice instructor, University of Western Ontario, London, Ontario.
Sarah Holman (Dalton) [in collaboration with M. D. Edwards].

HODGETTS, J. E. Professor of political economy, University of Toronto, Ontario.
Alfred Brunel.

HODGINS, BRUCE W. Professor of history, Trent University, Peterborough, Ontario.
William Patrick. Alpheus Todd. Lewis Wallbridge.

HOLLAND, CLIVE A. Curator and assistant librarian, Scott Polar Research Institute, Cambridge, England.
Sir Richard Collinson. Hans Hendrik.

HOLMAN, H. T. Law student, Charlottetown, Prince Edward Island.
George Wright.

HORRALL, S. W. Head, Historical Section, Royal Canadian Mounted Police Headquarters, Ottawa, Ontario.
John George Donkin. Kukatosi-poka.

HOSKINS, ALICE. Education officer, Art Gallery of Nova Scotia, Halifax, Nova Scotia.
Emil Vossnack.

HOTCHKISS, R. A. Teacher of history, Bay Ridge Secondary School, Kingston, Ontario.
Charles John Brydges [in collaboration with A. Wilson].

HOUSTON, SUSAN E. Chairman and associate professor, Department of History, York University, Downsview, Ontario.
Andrew Taylor McCord.

HUGHES, RICHARD DAVID. Public services librarian, Cariboo College, Kamloops, British Columbia.
Alexander Murray.

HUMPHRIES, CHARLES W. Associate professor of history, University of British Columbia, Vancouver, British Columbia.
John Joseph Lynch.

HYMAN, BARRY E. Assistant provincial archivist, Provincial Archives of Manitoba, Winnipeg, Manitoba.
Robert McBeath. Andrew McDermot.

INGRAM, JOHN D. Department head and teacher of history, Sisler High School, Winnipeg, Manitoba.
Alexander McArthur.

JAMESON, SHEILAGH S. Formerly chief archivist, Glenbow-Alberta Institute, Calgary, Alberta.
John Glenn.

JARRELL, RICHARD A. Associate professor of natural science, York University, Downsview, Ontario.
Sir John Henry Lefroy [in collaboration with C. M. Whitfield].

JENNINGS, JOHN N. Professor of history, Trent University, Peterborough, Ontario.
John French.

JOHNSON, J. K. Professor of history, Carleton University, Ottawa, Ontario.
William Benjamin Wells.

JOHNSON, LEO A. Associate professor of history, University of Waterloo, Ontario.
Abram Farewell. Thomas Nicholson Gibbs. William Gooderham. John Simpson.

JOHNSON, ROBERT E. Professor emeritus of biology, Knox College, Galesburg, Illinois, U.S.A.
Isaac Israel Hayes. Robert McCormick.

JOHNSTON, CHARLES M. Professor of history, McMaster University, Hamilton, Ontario.
John Harvard Castle.

JONES, ELWOOD H. Master, Otonabee College; associate professor of history, Trent University, Peterborough, Ontario.
Henry Corry Rowley Becher. Josiah Blackburn.

JONES, FREDERICK. Senior lecturer in history, Dorset Institute of Higher Education, England.
Ker Baillie Hamilton. Sir Hugh William Hoyles.

JUDD, CAROL M. Research consultant, Heritage Enterprises, Ottawa, Ontario.
Alexis Bonami, dit *Lespérance.*

KALLMANN, HELMUT. Chief, Music Division, National Library of Canada, Ottawa, Ontario.
Charles-Marie Panneton.

KAREL, DAVID. Professeur agrégé d'histoire, Université Laval, Québec, Québec.
Zacharie Vincent [in collaboration with M.-D. Labelle and S. Thivierge].

KEALEY, GREGORY S. Associate professor of history, Dalhousie University, Halifax, Nova Scotia.
Joseph C. McMillan. Kate McVicar. Samuel H. Myers [in collaboration with H. K. Ralston]. *Alfred Oakley. John Smith.*

KENDLE, JOHN E. Professor of history, University of Manitoba, Winnipeg, Manitoba.
David Young.

KENNEDY, J. E. Assistant dean, College of Arts and Science; professor of physics, University of Saskatchewan, Saskatoon, Saskatchewan.
William Brydone Jack.

KENT, V. GLEN. Rector, St Paul's Parish, Port Morien, Nova Scotia.
Hibbert Binney.

KERNAGHAN, LOIS K. Historical researcher, Public Archives of Nova Scotia, Halifax, Nova Scotia.
Michael Septimus Brown. Mary Jane Katzmann (Lawson). Lewis Morris Wilkins.

KEYES, JOHN. Rédacteur-historien, *Dictionnaire biographique du Canada/Dictionary of Canadian biography*, Les Presses de l'université Laval, Québec, Québec.
Louis-Adélard Senécal [in collaboration with Hélène Filteau and J. Hamelin].

KILLAN, GERALD. Associate professor of history, King's College, London, Ontario.

Charles Pelham Mulvany.

KLASSEN, HENRY C. Associate professor of history, University of Calgary, Alberta.
Simon Jackson Hogg. Norman Wolfred Kittson.

LABELLE, MARIE-DOMINIC. Étudiante en histoire de l'art, Université Laval, Québec, Québec.
Zacharie Vincent [in collaboration with D. Karel and S. Thivierge].

LABRÈQUE, MARIE-PAULE R. Directrice, Bibliothèque municipale, Acton-Vale, Québec.
Pierre-Samuel Gendron.

LAMB, W. KAYE. Formerly dominion archivist, Vancouver, British Columbia.
Alexander Caulfield Anderson. Alexander Grant Dallas. William Fraser Tolmie.

LAMONDE, YVAN. Professeur d'histoire, Centre d'études canadiennes-françaises, McGill University, Montréal, Québec.
François-Maximilien Bibaud [in collaboration with A. Morel]. *Thomas-Aimé Chandonnet. Joseph-Sabin Raymond.*

LANDRY, KENNETH. Professionnel de recherche, *Dictionnaire des œuvres littéraires du Québec*, Université Laval, Québec, Québec.
Félix Poutré [in collaboration with J.-P. Gagnon]. *Joseph-Alfred-Norbert Provencher.*

LAPLANTE, CORINNE. Directrice, Accueil Sainte-Famille, Tracadie, Nouveau-Brunswick.
François-Xavier Babineau.

LAVOIE, ELZÉAR. Professeur d'histoire, Université Laval, Québec, Québec.
Léger Brousseau.

†LAWR, DOUGLAS A. Professor of history of education, University of Western Ontario, London, Ontario.
John Lynch.

LEBLOND, SYLVIO. Professeur émérite, Université Laval, Québec, Québec.
James Douglas.

LEEFE, JOHN G. Teacher; member of the Legislative Assembly, Liverpool, Nova Scotia.
Samuel Prescott Fairbanks.

LEIGHTON, DOUGLAS. Assistant professor of history, University of Western Ontario, London, Ontario.
Sir James Macaulay Higginson. George Henry Martin Johnson. John Johnson. Abram Nelles. Jean-Baptiste Proulx.

LE MOIGNAN, MICHEL. Gaspé, Québec.
William Hyman [in collaboration with R. Samson].

LETOURNEAU, J. A. RODGER. Managing director, Canadian Railway Museum, Saint-Constant, Québec.
William Nassau Kennedy. Alfred McKeand.

LEVERE, TREVOR H. Associate professor, Institute for the History and Philosophy of Science and Technology, University of Toronto, Ontario.
Sir Edward Sabine.

LÉVESQUE, BENOÎT. Professeur de sociologie, Université du Québec à Rimouski, Québec.
Étienne Champagneur.

LEWIS, ZANE H. Curator of social history, British Columbia Provincial Museum, Victoria, British Columbia.
Alexander Edmund Batson Davie.

LINTEAU, PAUL-ANDRÉ. Professeur d'histoire, Université du Québec à Montréal, Québec.
Charles-Séraphin Rodier. Jean-Baptiste Rolland.

LITTLE, J. I. Assistant professor of history, Simon Fraser University, Burnaby, British Columbia.
Lewis Thomas Drummond. Lucius Seth Huntington.

LIVERMORE, J. DANIEL. Foreign service officer, Department of External Affairs, Ottawa, Ontario.
Catherine Honoria Hume (Blake). Edmund Burke Wood.

LIVESAY, DOROTHY. Lecturer in creative writing, Simon Fraser University, Burnaby, British Columbia.
Isabella Valancy Crawford.

LORIMIER, MICHEL DE. Rédacteur-historien, *Dictionnaire biographique du Canada/Dictionary of Canadian biography*, Les Presses de l'université Laval, Québec, Québec.
Louis Marchand.

LORTIE, LÉON. Professeur à la retraite, Montréal, Québec.
Joseph-Alexandre Crevier. François-Alexandre-Hubert La Rue.

LUCAS, CALVIN GLENN. Archivist-historian, United Church Archives, Victoria University, Toronto, Ontario.
Enoch Wood.

MCCALLA, DOUGLAS. Associate professor of history, Trent University, Peterborough, Ontario.
Isaac Buchanan. Adam Hope. John McMurrich. Joseph Davis Ridout.

MCDONALD, RONALD H. Historian, Parks Canada, Halifax, Nova Scotia.
Sir Charles Hastings Doyle.

MCDOUGALL, ELIZABETH ANN KERR. Historian, Montreal, Quebec.
Alexander Ferrie Kemp.

MACEWAN, J. W. GRANT. Formerly lieutenant governor of Alberta, Calgary, Alberta.
Ta-tanka I-yotank.

MCGAHAN, ELIZABETH W. Instructor in history, University of New Brunswick, Fredericton, New Brunswick.
Sylvester Zobieski Earle. John Thomson.

MACGILLIVRAY, ROYCE. Associate professor of history, University of Waterloo, Ontario.
John Cameron.

MCGOVERN, KATHLEEN. Archivist, Loretto Abbey, Toronto, Ontario.
Ellen Dease, named *Mother Teresa.*

MCILWRAITH, THOMAS F. Associate professor of geography, University of Toronto, Ontario.
George Laidlaw.

MACKAY, JEAN LAYTON. Meadow Bank, Prince Edward Island.
James Barrett Cooper. William Warren Lord.

MACKENZIE, A. A. Associate professor of history, St Francis Xavier University, Antigonish, Nova Scotia.
John Bourinot.

MACKENZIE, ANN. Instructor in history, University of Western Ontario, London, Ontario.
George Buckland.

MACKENZIE, KENNETH S. Acting head of research, National Postal Museum, Ottawa, Ontario.
Charles William Carrier. Henry Dinning [in collaboration]. *James Gibb Ross* [in collaboration]. *John Cunningham Stewart. George Okill Stuart.*

MCKENZIE, RUTH. Writer, Ottawa, Ontario.
Henry Wolsey Bayfield. William Thomas Benson.

MACKINNON, C. S. Associate professor of history, University of Alberta, Edmonton, Alberta.
James Green Stewart.

MacKinnon, Neil J. Associate professor of history, St Francis Xavier University, Antigonish, Nova Scotia.
John William Ritchie.

MacLean, R. A. Chairman, Department of History, St Francis Xavier University, Antigonish, Nova Scotia.
Stewart Campbell. Hubert Girroir. Martin Isaac Wilkins.

Macleod, Roderick Charles. Associate professor of history, University of Alberta, Edmonton, Alberta.
Francis Jeffrey Dickens.

MacMillan, David S. Professor of history, Trent University, Peterborough, Ontario.
Allan Gilmour.

McNally, Larry S. Archivist, Public Archives of Canada, Ottawa, Ontario.
Charles Legge.

MacPherson, Ian. Associate professor of history, University of Victoria, British Columbia.
Sir William Buell Richards.

Macpherson, Jay. Professor of English, Victoria University, Toronto, Ontario.
Joseph Medlicott Scriven.

Mainer, George Graham. Teacher, Sutton District High School, Ontario.
James Good.

Miller, Carman. Chairman and associate professor, Department of History, McGill University, Montreal, Quebec.
Charles Dewey Day. Alexander Abraham de Sola. Theodore Hart.

Millman, Thomas R. Formerly archivist, Anglican Church of Canada, Toronto, Ontario.
Joseph Albert Lobley. Frederick Augustus O'Meara.

Moody, Barry M. Assistant professor of history, Acadia University, Wolfville, Nova Scotia.
John Mockett Cramp. Edmund Albern Crawley. Avard Longley. Charles Tupper.

Morel, André. Professeur titulaire de droit, Université de Montréal, Québec.
François-Maximilien Bibaud [in collaboration with Y. Lamonde].

Morrison, Brian H. Librarian, Ministry of Labour, Toronto, Ontario.
John Godfrey Spragge.

Morton, Desmond. Professor of history, University of Toronto, Ontario.
William Smith Durie. Arthur Trefusis Heneage Williams.

†Morton, W. L. Professor of history, University of Manitoba, Winnipeg, Manitoba.
William Bletterman Caldwell. Charles-René-Léonidas d'Irumberry de Salaberry.

Murray, Florence Beatrice. Professor emeritus of library science, University of Toronto, Ontario.
Thomas McMurray. John Classon Miller.

†Nadeau, Eugène, o.m.i. Ottawa, Ontario.
Esther Sureau, dit *Blondin*, named *Mother Marie-Anne.*

Naftel, William D. Senior historian, Atlantic region, Parks Canada, Halifax, Nova Scotia.
David Honeyman.

Neatby, L. H. Formerly professor of classics, University of Saskatchewan, Saskatoon, Saskatchewan.
Bedford Clapperton Trevelyan Pim.

Nelles, H. V. Professor of history, York University, Downsview, Ontario.
Samuel Keefer. Timothy Blair Pardee. Francis Shanly.

Neufeld, Peter L. Historian-journalist, Minnedosa, Manitoba.
Éphrem-A. Brisebois.

Newell, Dianne. Assistant professor of history, University of British Columbia, Vancouver, British Columbia.
William Gooderham. James Gooderham Worts.

Nichol, James W. Playwright, Toronto, Ontario.
Reginald Birchall.

Noppen, Luc. Professeur agrégé d'histoire de l'art, Université Laval, Québec, Québec.
Victor Bourgeau. Pierre Gauvreau [in collaboration with A. J. H. Richardson]. *Augustin Leblanc.*

Normand, Sylvio. Étudiant gradué en histoire, Université Laval, Québec, Québec.
Pierre Lespérance [in collaboration with R. Derome].

Ormsby, Margaret A. Professor emerita of history, University of British Columbia, Vancouver, British Columbia.
Francis Jones Barnard. Andrew Charles Elliott. John Carmichael Haynes. Richard Clement Moody.

Ormsby, William G. Provincial archivist, Archives of Ontario, Toronto, Ontario.
Sir Francis Hincks.

Ouellet, Fernand. Professeur d'histoire, Université d'Ottawa, Ontario.
Thomas Storrow Brown.

†Pacey, Desmond. Vice-president, University of New Brunswick, Fredericton, New Brunswick.
Juliana Horatia Gatty (Ewing) [with additions by J. St. John].

†Painchaud, Robert. Professor of history, University of Winnipeg, Manitoba.
Théogène Fafard.

Pannekoek, Frits. Director, Historic Sites Service, Edmonton, Alberta.
David Anderson. Charles Pratt.

Paradis, Rodolphe O. Chercheur scientifique, Ministère de l'Agriculture du Canada, Saint-Jean-sur-Richelieu, Québec.
William Couper.

Parker, Bruce A. Port Hope, Ontario.
George Nicholas Oille.

Patterson, G. H. Associate professor of history, University of Toronto, Ontario.
John Charles Dent.

Peake, F. A. Professor of history, Laurentian University, Sudbury, Ontario.
Abraham Cowley. Frederick Dawson Fauquier.

Pease, Jane H. Professor of history, University of Maine, Orono, Maine, U.S.A.
Josiah Henson [in collaboration with W. H. Pease].

Pease, William H. Professor of history, University of Maine, Orono, Maine, U.S.A.
Josiah Henson [in collaboration with J. H. Pease].

Peel, Bruce. Librarian, University of Alberta, Edmonton, Alberta.
James Hunter.

Perin, Roberto. Professeur adjoint d'histoire et directeur du programme d'études canadiennes, York University, Downsview, Ontario.
Joseph-Alexandre Baile. Joseph Desautels.

Phelps, Edward. Regional history librarian, D. B. Weldon Library, University of Western Ontario, London, Ontario.

James Miller Williams [in collaboration with N. R. Ball].

PINCOMBE, C. ALEXANDER. Formerly director and archivist, Moncton Museum, New Brunswick.
Bliss Botsford. James MacGregor McCurdy. Charles B. Record.

PLANT, RICHARD. Assistant professor of drama, Queen's University, Kingston, Ontario.
Samuel James Watson.

PLOUFFE, MARCEL. Conseiller en audiovisuel, Université Laval, Québec, Québec.
Charles Joseph Alleyn.

POLLACK, GLADYS BARBARA. Graduate student in history, McGill University, Montreal, Quebec.
William Darling. Mathew Hamilton Gault [in collaboration with G. J. J. Tulchinsky].

POLLIN, STANLEY. Foreign service officer, Canadian High Commission, Jamaica.
Robert Hay. John Jacques.

POTHIER, LOUISETTE. Professeur d'histoire, Séminaire de Sherbrooke, Québec.
Simon-Xavier Cimon. Joseph Gaudet. Antoine Polette.

POULIN, PIERRE. Assistant de recherche, Département d'histoire, Université Laval, Québec, Québec.
Pierre-Joseph-Olivier Chauveau [in collaboration with J. Hamelin].

†POULIOT, LÉON, S. J. Assistant-archiviste de la Compagnie de Jésus, Saint-Jérôme, Québec.
Antoine-Nicolas Braun.

PRESTON, RICHARD A. W. K. Boyd professor of history; director of Canadian studies, Duke University, Durham, North Carolina, U.S.A.
Patrick Robertson-Ross.

PROULX, GEORGES-ÉTIENNE. Secrétaire général, Collège de Lévis, Québec.
Joseph-David Déziel.

PROVENCHER, JEAN. Chercheur autonome, Québec, Québec.
Charles McKiernan, known as *Joe Beef.*

PROVOST, GUY. Professeur agrégé de français, Collège militaire royal de Saint-Jean, Saint-Jean-sur-Richelieu, Québec.
Oscar Dunn.

PROVOST, HONORIUS, PTRE. Archiviste, Séminaire de Québec, Québec.
Michel Forgues.

PRYKE, KENNETH G. Professor of history, University of Windsor, Ontario.
Thomas Coffin.

PULLEN, HUGH FRANCIS. Rear admiral (retired), Chester Basin, Nova Scotia.
William John Samuel Pullen.

PURDY, J. D. Associate professor of history and comparative education, University of Western Ontario, London, Ontario.
Joseph Hemington Harris.

RALSTON, H. KEITH. Assistant professor of history, University of British Columbia, Vancouver, British Columbia.
Samuel H. Myers [in collaboration with G. S. Kealey]. *James Syme.*

RASPORICH, ANTHONY W. Professor of history; associate dean of the Faculty of Social Sciences, University of Calgary, Alberta.
John Jeremiah Bigsby. George Verey [in collaboration with I. A. L. Getty].

REA, J. E. Professor of history, University of Manitoba, Winnipeg, Manitoba.
Andrew Graham Ballenden Bannatyne.

READ, COLIN FREDERICK. Assistant professor of history, Huron College, London, Ontario.
John Stoughton Dennis.

REID, W. STANFORD. Professor emeritus of history, University of Guelph, Ontario.
William Jordan Rattray.

REYNOLDS, ARTHUR G. Toronto, Ontario.
Samuel Dwight Rice.

REYNOLDS, GEORGE F. Winnipeg, Manitoba.
Henry McKenney.

RICHARDSON, A. J. H. Formerly chief of research, Parks Canada, Ottawa, Ontario.
Pierre Gauvreau [in collaboration with L. Noppen].

RICHARDSON, GUS. Law student, Toronto, Ontario.
Mrs Letitia Munson.

RICHESON, DAVID R. Historian, National Museum of Man, Ottawa, Ontario.
James Richardson.

ROBERT, JEAN-CLAUDE. Professeur d'histoire, Université du Québec à Montréal, Québec.
Côme-Séraphin Cherrier. Ferdinand David. Hector Munro. William Jeffrey Patterson.

ROBERTSON, IAN ROSS. Associate professor of history, University of Toronto, Ontario.
Angus McDonald. Donald Montgomery. Edward Palmer. James Colledge Pope.

ROBY, YVES. Vice-doyen aux études avancées et à la recherche, Faculté des lettres, Université Laval, Québec, Québec.
Ferdinand Gagnon.

ROGERS, IRENE L. Historian, Prince Edward Island Heritage Foundation, Charlottetown, Prince Edward Island.
Mark Butcher. John Mackieson.

ROLAND, CHARLES G. Jason A. Hannah professor of the history of medicine, McMaster University, Hamilton, Ontario.
George William Campbell. John Fulton.

ROMNEY, PAUL. Graduate student in history, University of Toronto, Ontario.
Daniel Sullivan.

ROPER, GORDON. Professor emeritus of history, Trent University, Peterborough, Ontario.
John Herbert Caddy.

ROSS, ALEXANDER M. Formerly professor of English language and literature, University of Guelph, Ontario.
William Johnston.

ROUSSEAU, LOUIS. Professeur de sciences religieuses, Université du Québec à Montréal, Québec.
Benjamin-Victor Rousselot.

ROY, JEAN-LOUIS. Directeur du journal *Le Devoir*, Montréal, Québec.
Charles-Odilon Beauchemin.

RUGGLE, RICHARD E. Rector, St Paul's Anglican Church, Norval, Ontario.
James Black. Thomas Brock Fuller.

RUMILLY, ROBERT. Écrivain, Montréal, Québec.
Luc Letellier de Saint-Just.

RUSSELL, VICTOR LORING. Archivist, City of Toronto Archives, Toronto, Ontario.
Angus Morrison.

RUTHERFORD, PAUL. Associate professor of history, University of Toronto, Ontario.
John Riordon.

STE. CROIX, LORNE. Historical projects officer, Heritage Conservation Division, Ministry of Culture and Recreation, Toronto, Ontario.
Jean-Louis Beaudry. Charles-Joseph Coursol. Edward Goff Penny.

ST. JOHN, JUDITH. Formerly head, Osborne Collection of Early Children's Books, Toronto Public Library, Toronto, Ontario.
Juliana Horatia Gatty (Ewing) [additions made to biography by D. Pacey].

SAINT-PIERRE, JOCELYN. Historien, Responsable de la reconstitution des débats, Bibliothèque de la législature, Assemblée nationale, Québec, Québec.
Daniel Carey.

SAMSON, ROCH. Ethnologue, Parcs Canada, Québec, Québec.
William Hyman [in collaboration with M. Le Moignan].

SAMUEL, RODRIGUE. Professeur d'histoire, Collège des Jésuites, Québec, Québec.
Henry Howard.

SAVARD, PIERRE. Professeur titulaire d'histoire; directeur, Centre de recherches canadiennes-françaises, Université d'Ottawa, Ontario.
George Couture.

SÉGUIN, NORMAND. Professeur d'histoire, Université du Québec à Trois-Rivières, Québec.
Nicolas-Tolentin Hébert.

SENIOR, ELINOR KYTE. Historian, Montreal, Quebec.
Eleazar David David.

†SHAW, EDWARD CHARLES. Formerly owner and curator, Red River House Museum, St Andrews, Manitoba.
William Kennedy.

SHUTLAK, GARRY D. Archivist, Public Archives of Nova Scotia, Halifax, Nova Scotia.
David Stirling [in collaboration with S. Buggey].

SIECIECHOWICZ, KRYSTYNA Z. Sessional lecturer in anthropology, University of Toronto, Ontario.
Henry Bird Steinhauer.

SIMPSON, VALERIE. Curator, New Brunswick Museum, Saint John, New Brunswick.
Jacob Valentine Troop.

SMITH, DENIS. Professor of political studies, Trent University, Peterborough, Ontario.
Sidney Smith.

SMITH, DONALD B. Associate professor of history, University of Calgary, Alberta.
Elizabeth Field (Jones; Carey). Kezhegowinninne. Joseph Onasakenrat.

SMITH, FRANCES K. Curator emeritus, Agnes Etherington Art Centre, Queen's University, Kingston, Ontario.
George Harlow White.

SMITH, ROBERT L. Instructor in history, Fraser Valley College, Chilliwack, British Columbia.
Sir Arthur Edward Kennedy.

SMITH, SHIRLEE ANNE. Archivist, Hudson's Bay Company Archives, Provincial Archives of Manitoba, Winnipeg, Manitoba.
James Laurence Cotter. Richard Charles Hardisty.

SNELL, J. G. Associate professor of history, University of Guelph, Ontario.
John Dougall. Thomas Moss. David Thurston.

SPEISMAN, STEPHEN A. Director, Ontario Region Archives, Canadian Jewish Congress, Toronto, Ontario.
Lewis Samuel.

SPRAY, WILLIAM ARTHUR. Professor of history, St Thomas University, Fredericton, New Brunswick.
John McMillan. Robert J. Patterson. John Pickard. Peter Frederick Shortland.

SPRY, IRENE M. Professor emeritus of economics, University of Ottawa, Ontario.
Samuel Anderson. John Palliser.

†SPURR, JOHN W. Chief librarian emeritus, Royal Military College of Canada, Kingston, Ontario.
Edward John Barker.

STACEY, C. P. University professor emeritus, University of Toronto, Ontario.
Sir John Michel. William Osborne Smith.

STAGG, RONALD J. Professor of history, Ryerson Polytechnical Institute, Toronto, Ontario.
Joseph Gould. Samuel Thompson.

STAMP, ROBERT M. Co-ordinator, Canadian Studies Program, University of Calgary, Alberta.
Adam Crooks.

STANLEY, DELLA M. M. Lecturer in history, Queen's University, Kingston, Ontario.
Gilbert-Anselme Girouard.

STECKLER, GERARD G. Associate professor of history, Gannon University, Erie, Pennsylvania, U.S.A.
Charles John Seghers.

STEWART, IAN M. Graduate student in history, University of Toronto, Ontario.
John Delaney.

STEWART, J. DOUGLAS. Professor of art history, Queen's University, Kingston, Ontario.
George Browne.

STILLAR, ALAN. Ex-rédacteur-historien, *Dictionnaire biographique du Canada/Dictionary of Canadian biography*, Les Presses de l'université Laval, Québec, Québec.
Jean-François Jamot.

STORY, G. M. Professor of English, Memorial University of Newfoundland, St John's, Newfoundland.
Edwin Duder. Nathan Norman [in collaboration with C. W. Andrews]. *Edward White* [in collaboration with C. W. Andrews].

†STORY, NORAH. Free-lance writer and consultant, Scarborough, Ontario.
William Gamble.

SUTHERLAND, DAVID A. Associate professor of history, Dalhousie University, Halifax, Nova Scotia.
William Annand. William Pryor. John Leander Starr.

SWAINSON, DONALD. Professor of history, Queen's University, Kingston, Ontario.
William Henry Brouse. Dileno Dexter Calvin. James Cockburn. Joseph Merrill Currier. Thomas Mayne Daly. Allan Macdonell. John O'Connor. Schuyler Shibley. William Wallace.

SYLVAIN, PHILIPPE. Professeur titulaire d'histoire; directeur, Laboratoire d'histoire religieuse, Université Laval, Québec, Québec.

Emmanuel-Marie Blain de Saint-Aubin. Ignace Bourget. Joseph Doutre. Elzéar Gérin. Jean-Étienne Landry. Joseph La Rocque. Henry Wilkes.

TALMAN, JAMES JOHN. Professor of history, University of Western Ontario, London, Ontario.
Michael Boomer. Robert Jackson Macgeorge.

TAYLOR, M. BROOK. Graduate student in history, University of Toronto, Ontario.
Francis Longworth. John Longworth.

TEECE, WENDY K. Victoria, British Columbia.
John Ash.

THIVIERGE, SYLVIE. Étudiante en histoire de l'art, Université Laval, Québec, Québec.
Zacharie Vincent [in collaboration with D. Karel and M.-D. Labelle].

THOMAS, LEWIS GWYNNE. Professor emeritus of history, University of Alberta, Edmonton, Alberta.
John McLean.

THOMAS, LEWIS H. Professor of history, University of Alberta, Edmonton, Alberta.
Louis Riel.

THOMAS, MORLEY K. Director general, Canadian Climate Centre, Downsview, Ontario.
George Templeman Kingston.

THOMPSON, FREDERIC FRASER. Professor and head, Department of History, Royal Military College of Canada, Kingston, Ontario.
Sir John Hawley Glover. William Howorth.

TOBIAS, JOHN L. Instructor in history, Red Deer College, Alberta.
Kamīyistowesit. Mīmīy. Minahikosis.

TODD, PATRICIA A. Lecturer, Faculty of Fine Arts, Concordia University, Montreal, Quebec.
James D. Duncan.

TRATT, GERTRUDE E. N. Teacher, Halifax, Nova Scotia.
William Gossip.

TREMBLAY, ROBERT. Rédacteur-historien, *Dictionnaire biographique du Canada/Dictionary of Canadian biography*, Les Presses de l'université Laval, Québec, Québec.
Joseph Laurin [in collaboration with L. Bouffard]. *Richard Henry Leahey* [in collaboration with C. A. Waite].

TRÉPANIER, LISE. Moncton, Nouveau-Brunswick.
Louis Archambeault [in collaboration with P. Trépanier].

TRÉPANIER, PIERRE. Professeur d'histoire, Université de Montréal, Québec.
Louis Archambeault [in collaboration with L. Trépanier].

TROFIMENKOFF, SUSAN MANN. Professeur agrégé d'histoire, Université d'Ottawa, Ontario.
Eliza Lanesford Foster (Cushing).

TULCHINSKY, GERALD J. J. Associate professor of history, Queen's University, Kingston, Ontario.
Sir Hugh Allan [in collaboration with B. J. Young]. *George Brush. Jedediah Hubbell Dorwin* [in collaboration]. *James Ferrier. Mathew Hamilton Gault* [in collaboration with G. B. Pollack]. *Thomas Ryan* [in collaboration with A. R. Dever]. *Harrison Stephens. Thomas Workman.*

TURNER, H. E. Associate professor of history, McMaster University, Hamilton, Ontario.
Henry James Grasett.

TYLER, KENNETH J. Research consultant, Ottawa, Ontario.
Kāpeyakwāskonam. Kiwisānce. Paskwāw.

VACHON, CLAUDE. Analyste en procédés administratifs, Ministère du Revenu du Québec, Québec.
Louis-Édouard Glackmeyer.

VAN KIRK, SYLVIA M. Associate professor of history, University of Toronto, Ontario.
George Barnston [in collaboration with J. S. H. Brown]. *Alexander Kennedy Isbister. Kapapamahchakwew. Isobel Graham Simpson (Finlayson).*

VASS, ELINOR BERNICE. Library technician, Charlottetown, Prince Edward Island.
George Wastie DeBlois.

VÉZINA, RAYMOND. Conservateur, Section d'art documentaire, Archives publiques du Canada, Ottawa, Ontario.
Antoine-Sébastien Falardeau.

VINCENT, THOMAS B. Associate professor of English, Royal Military College of Canada, Kingston, Ontario.
John LePage. Elizabeth Newell Lockerby (Bacon).

VOISINE, NIVE. Professeur d'histoire, Université Laval, Québec, Québec.
Augustin-Magloire Blanchet. Louis-Édouard Bois. Luc Desilets.

WAITE, CATHERINE A. Manuscript editor, *Dictionary of Canadian biography/Dictionnaire biographique du Canada*, University of Toronto Press, Ontario.
Richard Henry Leahey [in collaboration with R. Tremblay].

WAITE, P. B. Professor of history, Dalhousie University, Halifax, Nova Scotia.
Archibald Woodbury McLelan. Josiah Burr Plumb. John Henry Pope. Thomas White. Sir William Fenwick Williams.

WALLACE, C. M. Associate professor of history, Laurentian University, Sudbury, Ontario.
John Waterbury Cudlip. John Hamilton Gray. Alexander McLeod Seely. Sir Albert James Smith.

WARDROP, JAMES R. Associate curator of modern history, Modern History Division, British Columbia Provincial Museum, Victoria, British Columbia.
Thomas Spence.

WATERSTON, ELIZABETH. Professor of English, University of Guelph, Ontario.
Alexander Somerville. John Henry Willan.

WEALE, DAVID E. Assistant professor of history, University of Prince Edward Island, Charlottetown, Prince Edward Island.
John Hamilton Gray.

WELLS, GARRON. Assistant archivist, Hudson's Bay Company Archives, Provincial Archives of Manitoba, Winnipeg, Manitoba.
John McLean.

WERTHEIMER, DOUGLAS. Newspaper publisher, Calgary, Alberta.
Philip Henry Gosse.

WESTFALL, WILLIAM. Associate professor and coordinator of Canadian studies, York University, Downsview, Ontario.
William Morley Punshon.

WHALEN, J. M. Archivist, Public Archives of Canada, Ottawa, Ontario.
Edwin Arnold Vail.

WHITEHEAD, RUTH HOLMES. Curatorial assistant in history, Nova Scotia Museum, Halifax, Nova Scotia.
Mary Christianne Paul (Morris).

WHITFIELD, CAROL M. Chief research, Halifax Defence Complex Restoration Project, Parks Canada, Halifax, Nova Scotia.
Sir John Henry Lefroy [in collaboration with R. A. Jarrell].

WHITTAKER, D. RIK. Conservator, New Brunswick Museum, Saint John, New Brunswick.
James Stanley Harris.

WIEBE, RUDY. Professor of English, University of Alberta, Edmonton, Alberta.
Mistahimaskwa.

WILBUR, RICHARD. Educational and media consultant, Montreal, Quebec.
William Moore Kelly.

WILLIAMSON, PAUL. Lawyer, Vancouver, British Columbia.
Alexander Rocke Robertson [in collaboration with T. M. Eastwood].

WILSON, ALAN. Professor of history, Trent University, Peterborough, Ontario.
Charles John Brydges [in collaboration with R. A. Hotchkiss].

WILSON, J. DONALD. Professor of history of education, University of British Columbia, Vancouver, British Columbia.
Alexander Marling. *William Tassie*.

WILSON, KEITH. Professor of educational administration and foundations, University of Manitoba, Winnipeg, Manitoba.
John ffolliott Crofton.

WINEARLS, JOAN. Map librarian, University of Toronto Library, Ontario.
Thomas Devine.

WOLFENDEN, MADGE. Formerly assistant provincial archivist, Provincial Archives of British Columbia, Vancouver, British Columbia.
John Tod.

WOLFF, ANNETTE R. Writer, Montreal, Quebec.
Abraham Joseph.

YOUNG, BRIAN J. Associate professor of history, McGill University, Montreal, Quebec.
Sir Hugh Allan [in collaboration with G. J. J. Tulchinsky].

YOUNG, MARY BERNITA. Archivist for the Sisters of St Joseph of Toronto, Willowdale, Ontario.
Margaret Brennan, named *Sister Teresa*.

ZERKER, SALLY F. Associate professor of social science, York University, Downsview, Ontario.
Abram William Lauder.

INDEX OF IDENTIFICATIONS

CATEGORIES

Agriculture

Architects

Armed forces

Artisans

Arts

Authors

Blacks

Business

Educators

Engineers

Explorers

Fur trade

Journalists

Labour organizers

Legal and judicial

Mariners

Medicine

Native peoples

Office-holders

Politicians

Religious

Scientists

Surveyors

Women

Index of Identifications

Like the network of cross-references within biographies, this index is designed to assist readers in following their interests through the volume. Most of the groupings are for occupations carried out within Canada (occupations carried out in other countries are noted only when carried out by persons who had earlier settled in Canada). Some groupings, however, were established to help readers approach the past from other perspectives. Women appear in a separate grouping, as do blacks, a reflection of the interest in their history, but they may also be found under the occupations in which they engaged. Native peoples are given by tribe.

Some of the categories require explanation. Under "agriculture" is to be found a variety of persons known to have been actively engaged in the development of land. Those who speculated in land will be found under "business," but "improvers" includes land agents, gentlemen farmers, and colonizers, and under "settlers" are brought together those who were small landowners. Surveyors, hydrographers, and cartographers have been grouped under "surveyors." The distinction between fine arts and "artisans" was difficult to make in some instances; silversmiths, for example, appear under "arts," and potters under "artisans." Governors and lieutenant governors are brought together under the heading "colonial administrators." Only persons who saw active service are included in the "militia" sub-group of the "armed forces." The latter incorporates naval officers, but civilian captains and pilots are placed under "mariners." Fur-traders, although they might have appeared under "business," are given a separate listing since they are so numerous.

The DCB/DBC attempts by its assignments to encourage research in new areas as well as in familiar ones, but its selection of individuals to receive biographies reflects the survival of documentation and the areas historians have chosen to investigate. This index should not, therefore, be used for quantitative judgements about the centuries covered; it is merely a guide to what is contained in volume XI.

AGRICULTURE

ARCHITECTS

ARMED FORCES

American

British

Army

Navy

Canadian

Irregulars

Militia

Papal States

ARTISANS

ARTS

AUTHORS

BLACKS

BUSINESS

INDEX OF IDENTIFICATIONS

EDUCATORS

ENGINEERS

EXPLORERS

FUR TRADE

JOURNALISTS

LABOUR ORGANIZERS

LEGAL AND JUDICIAL

Judges

Lawyers

Notaries

MARINERS

MEDICINE

NATIVE PEOPLES

Blackfoot

Bloods

Crees

Hurons

Inuit

Iroquois

Micmacs

Mohawks

Ojibwas

Okanagans

Saulteaux

Sioux

OFFICE-HOLDERS

Colonial administrators

Officials, appointed

POLITICIANS

Federal

Municipal and local

Provincial and territorial

RELIGIOUS

Baptists

Bible Christians

Catholic Apostolics

Church of England

Congregationalists

Disciples of Christ

Jews

WOMEN

GEOGRAPHICAL INDEX

CANADA

Alberta

British Columbia
Mainland
Vancouver Island

Manitoba

New Brunswick

Newfoundland and Labrador
Labrador
Newfoundland

Northwest Territories

Nova Scotia
Cape Breton Island
Mainland

Ontario
Centre
East
Niagara
North
Southwest

Prince Edward Island

Quebec
Bas-Saint-Laurent–Gaspésie/
Côte-Nord
Montréal/Outaouais
Nord-Ouest/Saguenay–Lac-Saint-Jean/
Nouveau-Québec
Québec
Trois-Rivières/Cantons-de-l'Est

Saskatchewan

Yukon

OTHER COUNTRIES

Belize
Bermuda
Egypt
France
Gibraltar
Great Britain
Guyana
India
Ireland
Italy
Republic of South Africa
Sri Lanka
Turkey
United States of America
West Indies

ONTARIO

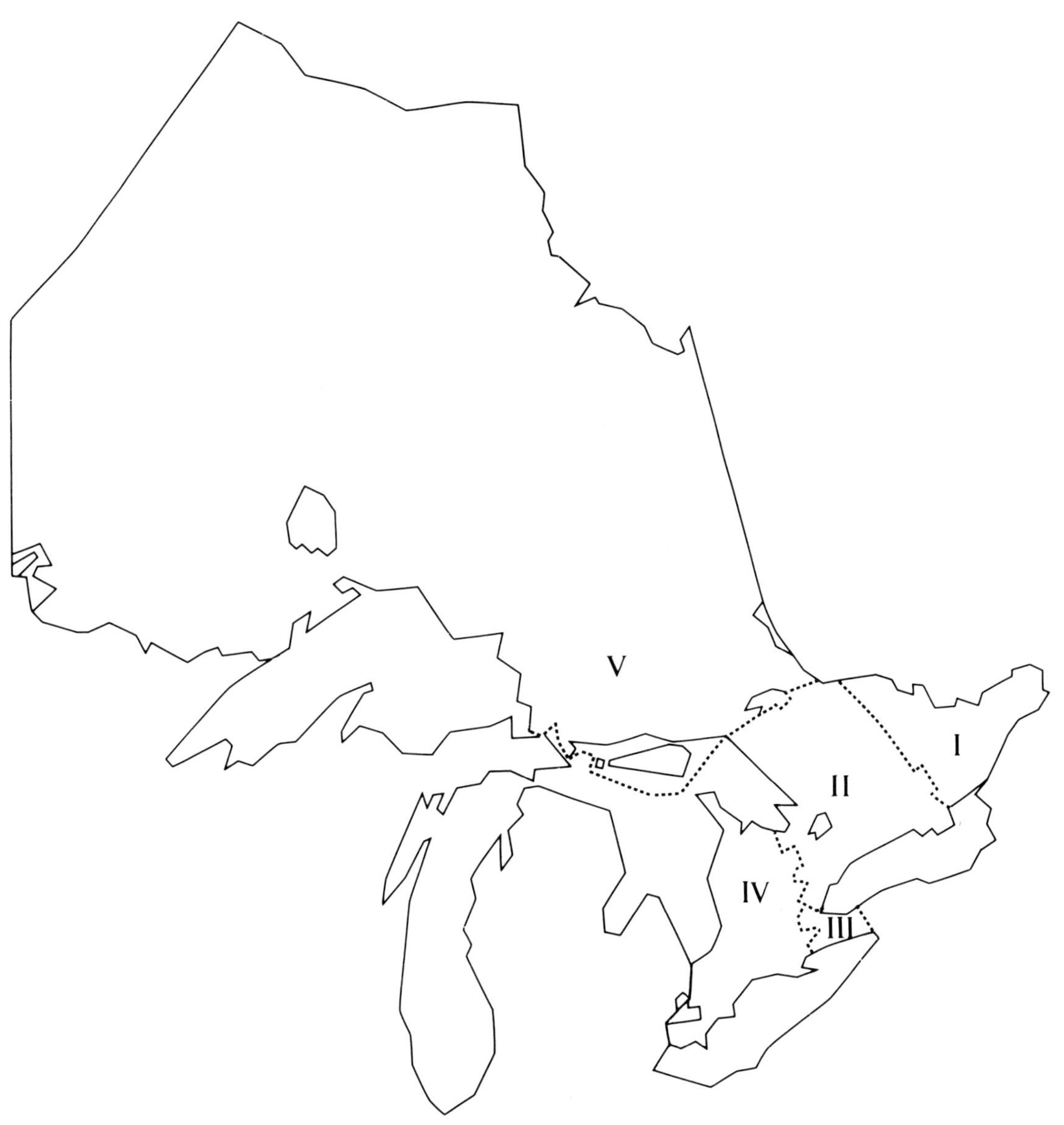

I—East
II—Centre
III—Niagara
IV—Southwest
V—North

QUEBEC

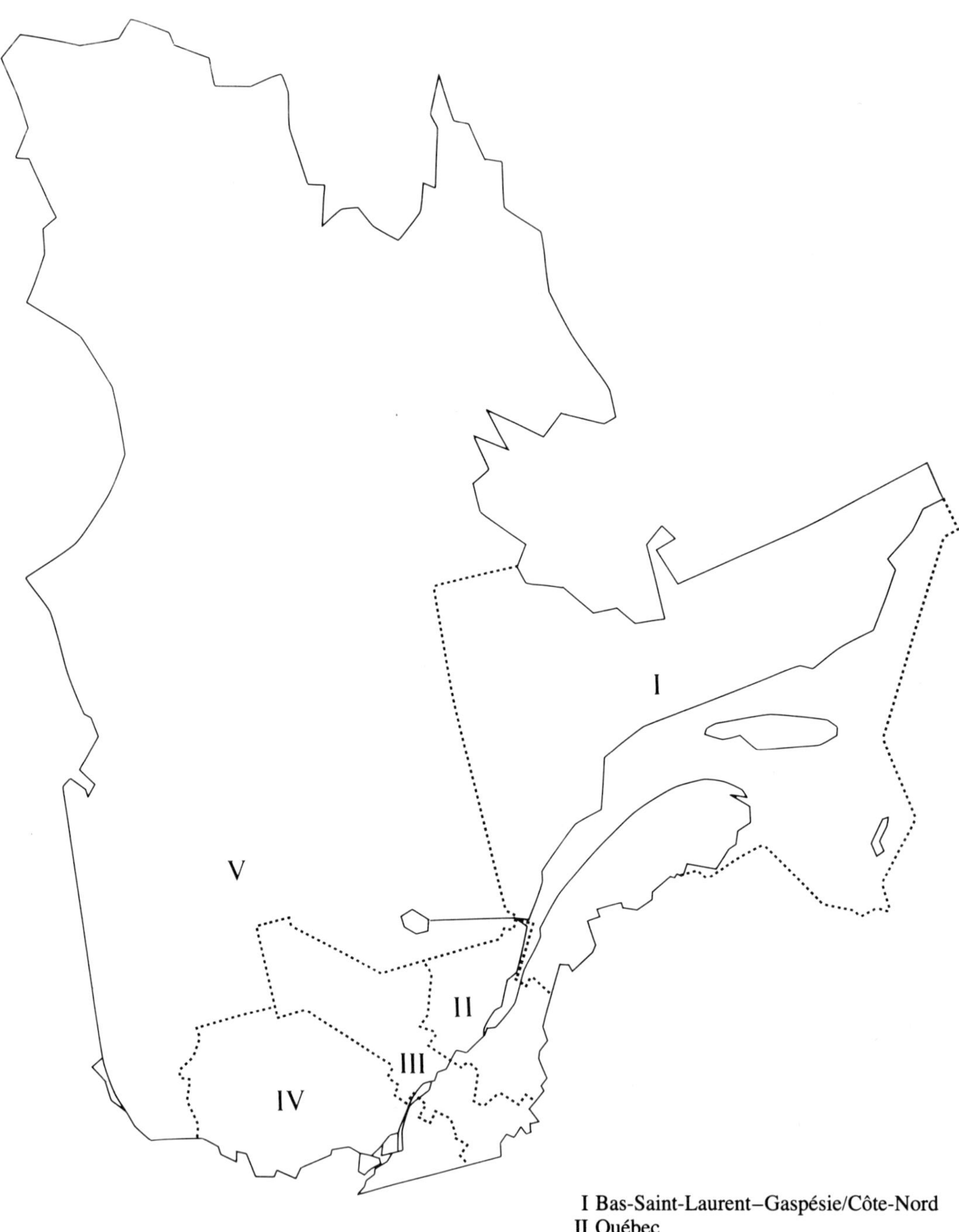
I
II
III
IV
V
I Bas-Saint-Laurent–Gaspésie/Côte-Nord
II Québec
III Trois-Rivières/Cantons-de-l'Est
IV Montréal/Outaouais
V Nord-Ouest/Saguenay–Lac-Saint-Jean/
Nouveau-Québec

Geographical Index

The Geographical Index is divided into two sections: Canada, including the biographies of persons whose careers were centred in one or more particular areas of this country, and Other Countries, including biographies of those who were born in Canada or who settled in Canada but made an impact elsewhere.

For the purposes of this index, Canada is divided according to the present provinces and territories, listed alphabetically, with five provinces being further subdivided. British Columbia, Newfoundland and Labrador, and Nova Scotia each have two subdivisions. Ontario and Quebec appear in five subdivisions as shown in the maps; those for Quebec are based on the administrative regions defined by the Direction générale du domaine territorial of the Ministère des Terres et Forêts.

A biography is found in a division according to the locale of the activity of the subject as an adult. Places of birth, education, retirement, and death have not been considered. Persons whose functions may have spanned several regions, such as a bishop or a governor, have been listed according to the seat of their office. Merchants are listed in the area of the primary location of their business.

Only persons who were born in, or who settled in, the territory of present-day Canada are listed in the second section. They are given under the country or countries in which they had a career or in which they were active. In this second section modern political divisons are used except for those in the West Indies, which is listed as a separate unit. Present-day dependencies of Great Britain are listed separately, again with the exception of those in the West Indies.

CANADA

ALBERTA

BRITISH COLUMBIA

Mainland

Vancouver Island

MANITOBA

NEW BRUNSWICK

NEWFOUNDLAND AND LABRADOR

Labrador

Newfoundland

NORTHWEST TERRITORIES

NOVA SCOTIA

Cape Breton

Mainland

ONTARIO

Centre

East

Niagara

North

Southwest

PRINCE EDWARD ISLAND

QUEBEC

Bas-Saint-Laurent–Gaspésie/Côte-Nord

Montréal/Outaouais

Nord-Ouest/Saguenay–Lac-Saint-Jean/Nouveau-Québec

Québec

Trois-Rivières/Cantons-de-l'Est

SASKATCHEWAN

YUKON

OTHER COUNTRIES

NOMINAL INDEX

Nominal Index

Included in this index are the names of persons mentioned in volume XI. They are listed by their family names, with titles and first names following. Wives are entered under their maiden names with their married names in parentheses. Persons who appear in incomplete citations in the text are fully identified when possible. An asterisk indicates that the person has received a biography in a volume already published, or will probably receive one in a subsequent volume. A death date or last floruit date refers the reader to the volume in which the biography will be found. Numerals in bold face indicate the pages on which a biography appears. Titles, nicknames, variant spellings, married and religious names are fully cross-referenced.